Contents in Brief

Contents

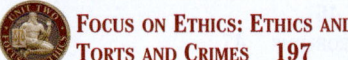

Unit 3 Contracts and E-Contracts 201

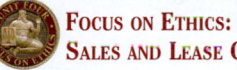

Unit 8 Business Organizations 671

CONCEPT SUMMARIES

EXHIBITS

INSIGHT INTO THE GLOBAL ENVIRONMENT

INSIGHT INTO E-COMMERCE

INSIGHT INTO ETHICS

EMERGING TRENDS IN BUSINESS LAW

CONTEMPORARY LEGAL DEBATES

BUSINESS APPLICATIONS

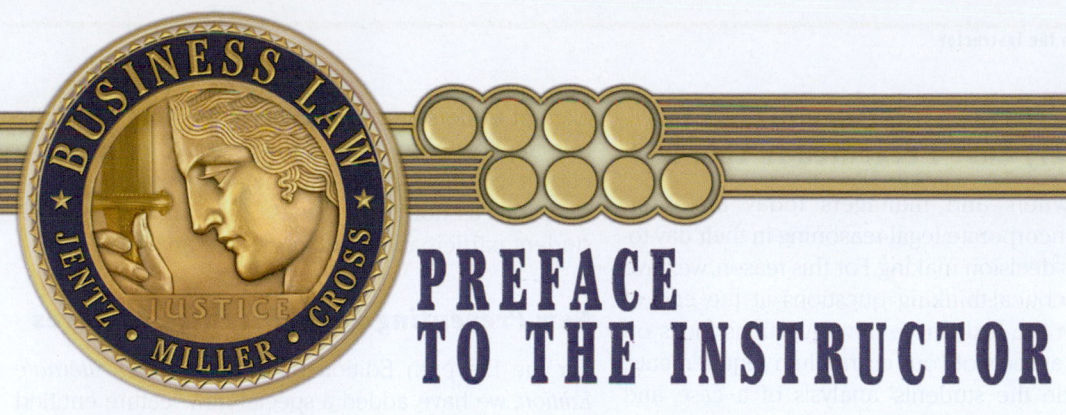

PREFACE TO THE INSTRUCTOR

The study of business law and, more generally, the legal environment of business has universal applicability. A student entering virtually any field of business must have at least a passing understanding of business law in order to function in the real world. Additionally, students preparing for a career in accounting, government and political science, economics, and even medicine can use much of the information they learn in a business law and legal environment course. In fact, every individual throughout his or her lifetime can benefit from a knowledge of contracts, real property law, landlord-tenant relationships, and other topics. Consequently, we have fashioned this text as a useful "tool for living" for all of your students (including those taking the CPA exam).

For the Eleventh Edition of *Business Law: Alternate Edition,* we have spent a great deal of effort making this book more contemporary, exciting, and visually appealing than ever before to encourage your students to learn the law. We have also designed many new features and special pedagogical devices that focus on the legal, ethical, global, and e-commerce environments, while addressing core curriculum requirements.

What Is New in the Eleventh Edition

Instructors have come to rely on the coverage, accuracy, and applicability of *Business Law: Alternate Edition*. To make sure that our text engages your students' interests, solidifies their understanding of the legal concepts presented, and provides the best teaching tools available, we now offer the following items either in the text or in conjunction with the text.

New *Insight* Features

For the Eleventh Edition, we have created **three special new *Insight* features—*Insight into E-Commerce,* *Insight into Ethics,* and *Insight into the Global Environment.*** These features, which appear in selected chapters, provide valuable insights into how the courts and the law are dealing with specific contemporary issues. Each of these features ends with a critical-thinking question that explores some cultural, environmental, political, social, or technological aspect of the issue.

1. ***Insight into E-Commerce***—When the topic involves some new technology or how the Internet is affecting a particular area of law, we include an *Insight into E-Commerce* feature. For example, Chapter 1 contains an *Insight into E-Commerce* feature on *How the Internet Is Expanding Precedent;* Chapter 8 has a feature on *Search Engines versus Copyrights;* and Chapter 41 includes a feature on *Moving Company Information to the Internet.*
2. ***Insight into Ethics***—When the topic has ethical implications, we include an *Insight into Ethics* feature. For example, Chapter 2's *Insight into Ethics* feature is entitled *Implications of an Increasingly Private Justice System;* Chapter 14's feature addresses *Internet Click Fraud;* and Chapter 51's feature covers *An Auditor's Duty to Correct Certified Opinions.*
3. ***Insight into the Global Environment***—Because business transactions today are increasingly global, we have also included a feature that discusses global implications or explains how foreign nations deal with a particular topic. For example, there is an *Insight into the Global Environment* feature in Chapter 5 titled *Breach of Trust Issues Hit Major German Corporations,* one in Chapter 19 on *International Use and Regulation of the Internet,* and one in Chapter 42 on *Moving Your Small Business Online: Seller Beware.*

New Critical-Thinking Questions at the End of *Every* Case Presented in This Text

Business owners and managers today are often required to incorporate legal reasoning in their day-to-day business decision making. For this reason, we have added two critical-thinking questions at the end of each case in the text. These new questions focus on meeting the aspects of your curriculum requirements, helping guide the students' analysis of a case, and strengthening their legal-reasoning skills. The following set of *Dimension* questions will challenge your students' understanding of the case materials beyond simple retention:

- *The Ethical Dimension.*
- *The E-Commerce Dimension.*
- *The Global Dimension.*
- *The Legal Environment Dimension.*

These new case-ending questions are in addition to the *What If the Facts Were Different?* questions and *Impact of This Case on Today's Law* sections that appeared in the Tenth Edition.

Suggested answers to all questions following cases can be found in both the *Instructor's Manual* and the *Answers Manual* that accompany this text. (The full title of this manual is *Answers to Questions and Case Problems and Alternate Problem Sets with Answers.*)

New *Special Case Analysis* Questions

Instructors have frequently requested that we teach their business law students how to analyze case law. We discuss the fundamental topic of how to read and understand case law in Chapter 1 and cover How to Brief Cases and Analyze Case Problems in Appendix A. For this edition, we have gone one step further: the instructor's side of this text's companion Web site now provides a *Special Case Analysis* question that is based on an extended excerpt of a case. Instructors can download the questions, as well as the extended case versions of these selected cases, by accessing their side of this text's Web site. Answers to these questions are also available to instructors online. Instructors can use these *Special Case Analysis* questions to test students' ability to perform IRAC (Issue, Rule, Application, and Conclusion) case analysis. Students must identify the legal issue presented in the case's extended excerpt, understand the rule of law, determine how the rule applies to the facts of the case, and describe the court's conclusion. An instructor can assign these questions as homework or use them in class to elicit student participation and teach case analysis.

New *Preventing Legal Disputes* Features

For the Eleventh Edition of *Business Law: Alternate Edition,* we have added a special new feature entitled *Preventing Legal Disputes.* These brief features offer practical guidance on steps that businesspersons can take in their daily transactions to avoid legal disputes and litigation. These features are integrated throughout the text as appropriate to the topics being discussed. Nearly every chapter in this edition has one *Preventing Legal Disputes* feature.

Reviewing Features in Every Chapter

For the Eleventh Edition of *Business Law: Alternate Edition,* we have included a new and improved feature at the end of every chapter that helps solidify students' understanding of the chapter materials. The feature appears just before the *Terms and Concepts* and is entitled *Reviewing [chapter topic].* Each of these *Reviewing* features presents a hypothetical scenario and then asks a series of questions that require students to identify the issues and apply the legal concepts discussed in the chapter. These features are designed to help students review the chapter topics in a simple and interesting way and see how the legal principles discussed in the chapter affect the world in which they live. An instructor can use these features as the basis for in-class discussion or encourage students to use them for self-study prior to completing homework assignments. **Suggested answers to the questions posed in the *Reviewing* features can be found in both the *Instructor's Manual* and the *Answers Manual* that accompany this text.**

The *Reviewing* features are also tied to a new set of questions for each chapter in the Web-based CengageNOW system, to be discussed next. Students can read through the scenario in the text and then answer the four Applications and Analysis questions online. **By using the CengageNOW system, students will receive instant feedback on their answers to these questions, and instructors will obtain automatically graded assignments that enable them to assess students' understanding of the materials.**

Improved Content and Features on CengageNOW for *Business Law: Alternate Edition* Interactive Assignment System

For those instructors who want their students to learn how to identify and apply the legal principles they study in this text, we have created new content and improved the features of our Web-based product for this edition. The system provides interactive, automatically graded assignments for every chapter and unit in this text. For each of the fifty-two chapters, we have devised different categories of multiple-choice questions that stress different aspects of learning the chapter materials. By using the optional **CengageNOW** system, students can complete the assignments from any location via the Internet and can receive instant feedback on why their answers to questions were incorrect or correct (if the instructor wishes to allow feedback). Instructors can customize the system to meet their own specifications and can track students' progress.

1. **Chapter Review Questions**—The first set of ten to fifteen questions reviews the basic concepts and principles discussed in the chapter. These questions often include questions based on the cases presented in the text.
2. **Brief Hypotheticals**—The next group of seven to ten questions emphasizes spotting the issue and identifying the rule of law that applies in the context of a short factual scenario.
3. **Legal Reasoning**—The third category includes five questions that require students to analyze the factual situation provided and apply the rules of law discussed in the chapter to arrive at an answer.
4. **Application and Analysis**—The final set of four questions for each chapter is new and is linked to the *Reviewing* features (discussed previously) that appear in every chapter of the text. The student is required to read through the hypothetical scenario, analyze the facts presented, identify the issues in dispute, and apply the rules discussed in the chapter to answer the questions.
5. **Essay Questions**—In addition to the multiple-choice questions available on CengageNOW, we now also provide essay questions that allow students to compose and submit essays online. Students' essays are automatically recorded to the gradebook, which permits instructors to quickly and easily evaluate the essays and record grades.
6. **Video Questions**—CengageNOW also now includes links to the Digital Video Library for *Business Law: Alternate Edition* so that students can access and view the video clips and answer questions related to the topics in the chapter.
7. **Cumulative Questions for Each Unit**—In addition to the questions relating to each chapter, the CengageNOW system provides a set of cumulative questions, entitled "Synthesizing Legal Concepts," for each of the eleven units in the text.
8. **Additional Advantages of CengageNOW**—Instructors can utilize the system to upload their course syllabi, create and customize homework assignments, keep track of their students' progress, communicate with their students about assignments and due dates, and create reports summarizing the data for an individual student or for the whole class.

Expanded Ethics Coverage and New Questions of Ethics in Every Chapter

For the Eleventh Edition of *Business Law: Alternate Edition,* we have significantly revised and updated the chapter on ethics and business decision making (Chapter 5). The chapter now presents a more practical, realistic, case-study approach to business ethics and the dilemmas facing businesspersons today. The emphasis on ethics is reiterated in materials throughout the text, particularly the *Focus on Ethics* features that conclude every unit, the *Insight into Ethics* features, and the pedagogy that accompanies selected cases and features. We also discuss **corporate governance issues** as appropriate within the ethics chapter, the corporations chapters, and the *Focus on Ethics* feature that concludes Unit Eight on business organizations.

For this edition, we have also added ***A Question of Ethics* based on a case from 2006 or 2007 to every chapter of the text.** These problems provide modern-day examples of the kinds of ethical issues faced by businesspersons and the ways courts typically resolve them.

More on the Sarbanes-Oxley Act of 2002

In a number of places in this text, we discuss the Sarbanes-Oxley Act of 2002 and the corporate scandals that led to the passage of that legislation. For example, Chapter 5 contains a section examining the requirements of the Sarbanes-Oxley Act relating to confidential reporting systems. In Chapter 41, we discuss this act in the context of securities law and present an exhibit (Exhibit 41–4) containing some of the key provisions of the act relating to corporate accountability with respect to securities transactions. Finally, in Chapter 51, we again look at provisions of the Sarbanes-Oxley Act as they relate to public accounting firms and accounting practices.

Because the act is a topic of significant concern in today's business climate, we also include excerpts and explanatory comments on the Sarbanes-Oxley Act of 2002 as Appendix H. Students and instructors alike will find it useful to have the provisions of the act immediately available for reference.

Business Law: Alternate Edition on the Web

For the Eleventh Edition of *Business Law: Alternate Edition,* we have redesigned and streamlined the text's Web site so that users can easily locate the resources they seek. When you visit our Web site at **www.cengage.com/blaw/jentz**, you will find a broad array of teaching/learning resources, including the following:

- ***Relevant Web sites*** for all of the *Emerging Trends* features that are presented in this text.
- ***Sample answers*** to the *Case Problem with Sample Answer,* which appears in the *Questions and Case Problems* at the end of every chapter. This problem/answer set is designed to help your students learn how to answer case problems by acquainting them with model answers to selected problems. In addition, we offer the answers to the hypothetical *Questions with Sample Answers* on the Web site as well as in the text (Appendix I).
- ***Videos*** referenced in the new *Video Questions* (discussed shortly) that appear in selected chapters of this edition of *Business Law: Alternate Edition.*
- ***Internet exercises*** for every chapter in the text (at least two per chapter). These exercises have been refocused to provide more practical information to business law students on topics covered in the chapters and to acquaint students with the legal resources that are available online.
- ***Interactive quizzes*** for every chapter in this text.
- ***Special Case Analysis questions*** that are based on the extended excerpts of selected chapter cases challenge students to strengthen their analytical skills using the IRAC (Issue, Rule, Application, and Conclusion) method, as discussed earlier. The questions, extended case excerpts, and answers are available only to instructors online.
- ***Glossary terms*** for every chapter in the text.
- ***Flashcards*** that provide students with an optional study tool to review the key terms in every chapter.
- ***PowerPoint slides*** that have been revised for this edition.
- ***Legal reference materials*** including a "Statutes" page that offers links to the full text of selected statutes referenced in the text, a Spanish glossary, and links to other important legal resources available for free on the Web.
- ***Law on the Web features*** that provide links to the URLs that appear at the end of every chapter in the text.
- ***Link to CengageNOW for* Business Law: Alternate Edition *Interactive Assignment System*** with different types of questions related to every chapter in the text and one set of cumulative questions for each unit in the text.
- ***Link to our Digital Video Library*** that offers a compendium of more than sixty-five video scenarios and explanations.
- ***Online Legal Research Guide*** that offers complete yet brief guidance to using the Internet and evaluating information obtained from the Internet. As an online resource, it now includes hyperlinks to the Web sites discussed for click-through convenience.
- ***Court case updates*** that present summaries of new cases from various West legal publications, are continually updated, and are specifically keyed to chapters in this text.

A Comprehensive Digital Video Library

For this edition of *Business Law: Alternate Edition,* we have included special *Video Questions* at the end of selected chapters. Each of these questions directs students to the text's Web site (at **www.cengage.com/blaw/jentz**) to view a video relevant to a topic covered in the chapter. This is followed by a series of questions based on the video. The questions are again repeated on the Web site, when the student accesses the video. An access code for the videos can be packaged with each new copy of this textbook for no additional charge. If Digital Video Library access did not come packaged with the textbook, students can purchase it online at **www.cengage.com/blaw/dvl**.

These videos can be used for homework assignments, discussion starters, or classroom demonstrations and are useful for generating student interest. Some of the videos are clips from actual movies, such as *The Jerk* and *Bowfinger.* By watching a video and answering the questions, students will gain an understanding of how the legal concepts they have studied in the chapter apply to the real-life situation portrayed in the video. **Suggested answers for all of the *Video Questions* are given in both the *Instructor's Manual* and the *Answers Manual* that accompany this text.** The videos are part of our Digital Video Library, a compendium of more than sixty-five video scenarios and explanations.

Additional Special Features of This Text

We have included in *Business Law: Alternate Edition,* Eleventh Edition, a number of pedagogical devices and special features, including those discussed here.

Emerging Trends

Presented throughout this text are a number of features titled *Emerging Trends.* These features examine new developments in business law and the legal environment and their potential effect on businesspersons. Here are some examples of these features:

- *E-Discovery and Cost-Shifting* (Chapter 3).
- *Stand-Your-Ground Laws* (Chapter 9).
- *Removing Class-Action Lawsuits to the Federal Courts* (Chapter 23).
- *New Issues in Online Privacy and Employment Discrimination* (Chapter 34).

Contemporary Legal Debates

Contemporary Legal Debates features are also interspersed throughout the Eleventh Edition. These features introduce the student to a controversial issue that is now being debated within the legal community. A *Where Do You Stand?* section concluding each feature asks the student to identify her or his position on the issue. Some examples of these features are:

- *Tort Reform* (Chapter 6).
- *Are Online Fantasy Sports Gambling?* (Chapter 13).
- *A Shareholder Access Rule* (Chapter 39).
- *Should the EPA Take the Threat of Global Warming into Account?* (Chapter 45).

Business Applications

Today's students of business law and the legal environment will likely become tomorrow's business owners and managers. As such, they will need to know about some of the more practical aspects of the legal environment. To this end, we have prepared eight boxed-in *Business Application* features that outline some of the legal pitfalls encountered in business relationships. Each feature identifies a legal issue of particular significance to businesspersons, explains how the courts have ruled on that issue, and then provides practical guidelines and advice for persons confronted with such issues. All of these features are new or have been substantially revised or rewritten for this edition. The following are some of the topics covered in the *Business Application* features:

- *Protecting Trade Secrets* (Chapter 8)
- *Independent-Contractor Negligence* (Chapter 31)
- *Restricting Union Communications via Corporate E-Mail Systems* (Chapter 33)
- *Dealing with the Fair Debt Collection Practices Act's Requirements* (Chapter 44)

Preventing Legal Disputes

As already discussed, these features provide practical information to future business owners and managers on how to avoid legal problems. Nearly every chapter includes one *Preventing Legal Disputes* feature, integrated as appropriate with the topics being discussed.

Concept Summaries

Whenever key areas of the law need additional emphasis, we provide a *Concept Summary.* These summaries have always been a popular pedagogical tool in this text. There are now more than fifty of these summaries, many of which have been modified to achieve greater clarity.

Exhibits

When appropriate, we also illustrate important aspects of the law in graphic form in exhibits. In all, more than one hundred exhibits are featured in the text. For this edition, we have added eight new exhibits, and we have modified existing exhibits to achieve better clarity. Some examples of the new exhibits are:

- Exhibit 2–3, Basic Differences in the Traditional Forms of ADR.
- Exhibit 8–2, Existing Generic Top Level Domain Names.
- Exhibit 26–2, Defenses against Liability on Negotiable Instruments.
- Exhibit 38–1, Offshore Low-Tax Jurisdictions.
- Exhibit 39–1, Directors' Management Responsibilities.
- Exhibit 41–1, Basic Functions of the Securities and Exchange Commission.

An Effective Case Format

For this edition, we have carefully selected recent cases that not only provide on-point illustrations of the legal principles discussed in the chapter but also are of high interest to students. In all, more than 70 percent of the cases in the Eleventh Edition are from 2006 or 2007, and more than a dozen are from 2008.

Each case in *Business Law: Alternate Edition,* Eleventh Edition, is presented in the following basic format:

- ***Case Title and Full Case Citation*** The case title and full case citation (including all parallel citations) are presented at the beginning of each case. When available, a URL is provided for finding the case online.
- ***Background and Facts*** This section contains a summary, in the authors' own words, of the events leading up to the lawsuit.
- ***Decision and Rationale*** In this section, we summarize, in our own words, the outcome of the case. Additionally, when appropriate, the exact words of the court are quoted.

As discussed earlier, each summarized case in this edition now concludes with two case-ending questions. These questions are listed below in addition to a few other sections you will see in selected cases throughout the text.

- ***Company Profiles***—Certain cases include a profile describing the history of the company involved to give students an awareness of the context of the case before the court. Some profiles include the URL for the company's Web site.
- ***What If the Facts Were Different?***—Many cases conclude with this unique section. The student is asked to decide whether a specified change in the facts of the case would alter its outcome. **Suggested answers to these questions are included in both the *Instructor's Manual* and the *Answers Manual* that accompany this text.**
- ***The Ethical [E-Commerce, Global, or Legal Environment] Dimension***—These special new questions ask students to explore different aspects of the issues of the case and help instructors meet core curriculum requirements for business law. **Suggested answers to these questions are included in both the *Instructor's Manual* and the *Answers Manual* that accompany this text.**
- ***Impact of This Case on Today's Law***—Because many students are unclear about how some of the older cases presented in this text affect today's court rulings, we include a section at the end of the classic cases to clarify the relevance of the particular case to modern law.

Two Test Banks Available

To provide instructors with even greater flexibility in teaching, we offer two separate *Test Banks,* each with a complete set of questions for every chapter of *Business Law: Alternate Edition,* Eleventh Edition. These two *Test Banks* have been significantly revised and many new questions added. Those instructors who would like to alternate the tests they give their students each semester can now do so without having to create additional testing materials. In addition, instructors who would like to pick and choose from the questions offered have twice as many options for questions in each category (true/false, multiple choice, essay).

Questions and Case Problems with Sample Answers

In response to those instructors who would like students to have sample answers available for some of the *Questions and Case Problems,* we have included two questions with sample answers in each chapter. The *Question with Sample Answer* is a hypothetical question for which students can access a sample answer in Appendix I at the end of the text. Every chapter also has one *Case Problem with Sample Answer* that is based on an actual case and answered on the text's Web site (located at **www.cengage.com/blaw/jentz**). Students can compare the answers provided to their own answers to determine whether they have done a good job of responding to the question and to learn what should be included when answering the end-of-chapter *Questions and Case Problems.*

The Most Complete Supplements Package Available Today

This edition of *Business Law: Alternate Edition* is accompanied by a vast number of teaching and learning supplements. We have already mentioned the CengageNOW for *Business Law: Alternate Edition* Interactive Assignment System and the supplemental resources available on the text's Web site. In addition, there are numerous other supplements, including those listed below, that make up the complete teaching/learning package for the Eleventh Edition. For further information on the *Business Law: Alternate Edition* teaching/learning package, contact your local sales representative or visit the text's Web site at **www.cengage.com/blaw/jentz**.

Printed Supplements

- ***Instructor's Manual***—Includes case synopses, additional cases addressing the issue for selected cases, background information, teaching suggestions, and lecture enhancements, as well as suggested answers to all the case-ending and feature-ending questions, the questions in the *Reviewing* features at the end of each chapter, and additional materials on the *Focus on Ethics* sections at the end of each unit. (Also available on the *Instructor's Resource CD-ROM*, or IRCD.)
- ***Study Guide***—Includes essay questions and sample CPA exam questions.
- **Two Comprehensive *Test Banks***—*Test Bank 1* and *Test Bank 2* each contain approximately 1,040 multiple-choice questions with answers, more than 1,040 true/false questions with answers, and two short essay questions per chapter (104 in each *Test Bank*). Additionally, there is one question for every *Emerging Trends* and *Contemporary Legal Debates* feature, and two multiple-choice questions for each *Focus on Ethics* section. (Also available on the IRCD.)
- ***Answers to Questions and Case Problems and Alternate Problem Sets with Answers***—Provides answers to all the questions and case problems presented in the text, including *A Question of Ethics* and *Video Questions*, as well as suggested answers to all the case-ending questions, feature-ending questions, and the questions in the *Reviewing* features at the end of each chapter. (Also available on the IRCD.)

Software, Video, and Multimedia Supplements

- ***Instructor's Resource CD-ROM (IRCD)***—The IRCD includes the following supplements: *Instructor's Manual, Answers Manual, Test Bank 1* and *Test Bank 2*, Case-Problem Cases, Case Printouts, Lecture Outline System, PowerPoint slides, ExamView, *Instructor's Manual* for the *Drama of the Law* video series, *Handbook of Landmark Cases and Statutes in Business Law and the Legal Environment, Handbook on Critical Thinking and Writing in Business Law and the Legal Environment*, and *A Guide to Personal Law*.
- **ExamView Testing Software** (also available on the IRCD).
- **Lecture Outline System** (also available on the IRCD).
- **PowerPoint slides** (also available on the IRCD).
- **WebTutor**—Features discussion groups, testing, student progress tracking, and business law course materials.
- **Case-Problem Cases** (available only on the IRCD).
- **Transparencies** (available only on the IRCD).
- **Westlaw®**—Ten free hours for qualified adopters.
- **Digital Video Library**—Provides access to more than sixty-five videos, including the *Drama of the Law* videos and video clips from actual Hollywood movies. Access to our Digital Video Library is available in an optional package with each new text at no additional cost. If the Digital Video Library access did not come packaged with the textbook, your students can purchase it online at **www.cengage.com/blaw/dvl**.

For Users of the Tenth Edition

First of all, we want to thank you for helping make *Business Law: Alternate Edition*, one of the best-selling business law texts in America today. Second, we want to make you aware of the numerous additions and changes that we have made in this edition—many in response to comments from reviewers. For example, we have added more examples and incorporated the latest United States Supreme Court decisions throughout the text as appropriate. We have substantially revised and reorganized the business organizations unit (Unit Eight), particularly the chapters on corporations (Chapter 38 through 40), which have been changed to be more in line with the reality of modern corporate law. We have simplified and streamlined the chapter on securities law (Chapter 41), and we have revised and reorganized the property chapters (Chapters 47 and 48).

Significantly Revised Chapters

Every chapter of the Eleventh Edition has been revised as necessary to incorporate new developments in the law or to streamline the presentations. A number of new trends in business law are also addressed in the cases and special features of the Eleventh Edition. Other major changes and additions made for this edition include the following:

- Chapter 2 (Courts and Alternative Dispute Resolution)—To provide greater clarity on important foundational issues, many parts of this chapter were reworked, including the discussions of personal jurisdiction, Internet jurisdiction, standing to sue, and appellate review. A chart was added to illustrate the differences among various methods of alternative dispute resolution, and we present a 2006 United States Supreme Court decision on arbitration clauses. In addition, the discussion of electronic filing systems and online dispute resolution was updated. An *Insight into Ethics* feature was added to discuss how the use of private judges is affecting the justice system.
- Chapter 3 (Court Procedures)—The section on electronic evidence and discovery issues has been updated to include the federal rules that took effect in 2006.
- Chapter 4 (Constitutional Authority to Regulate Business)—The chapter has been thoroughly revised and updated to incorporate recent court decisions, such as a 2008 case on search warrants and business premises. New examples have been added throughout, and the materials reworked to focus on business context. The chapter includes discussions of the USA Patriot Act's effect on constitutional rights and recent decisions on preemption, unprotected speech, freedom of religion, and privacy rights. A *Contemporary Legal Debates* feature addresses whether *State Regulation of Internet Prescription Transactions Violates the Dormant Commerce Clause.*
- Chapter 5 (Ethics and Business Decision Making)—This chapter has been significantly revised and now includes a new section that provides step-by-step guidance on making ethical business decisions. All new cases were added, including a 2008 case on the behavior of business managers and owners. An *Insight into the Global Environment* feature addresses ethical issues faced by German corporations.
- Chapter 6 (Intentional Torts)—A discussion of the compensatory and punitive damages available in tort actions was added, and a *Contemporary Legal Debates* feature addresses *Tort Reform.* Two cases from 2007 are included, one on the scope of an Internet service provider's immunity for online defamation and the other on invasion of privacy. New subsections discuss trends in appropriation (right of publicity) claims and abusive or frivolous litigation.
- Chapter 8 (Intellectual Property and Internet Law)—The materials on intellectual property rights have been thoroughly revised and updated to reflect the most current laws and trends. Several recent United States Supreme Court cases are presented (specifically, the 2007 patent decision in *KSR International Co. v. Teleflex, Inc.*, and the 2006 trademark decision in *Menashe v. V Secret Catalogue, Inc.*). A subsection on counterfeit goods and a 2006 law addressing counterfeit goods has been added to the trademark section. The materials on domain names, cybersquatting, and licensing have been revamped. The section on patents was expanded and new examples were added. The discussion of file-sharing was updated. The chapter also includes updated information on international treaties protecting intellectual property and an *Insight into E-Commerce* feature on *Search Engines versus Copyright Owners.*
- Chapter 9 (Criminal Law and Cyber Crime)—New materials on identity theft and criminal spamming laws were added, and the existing materials were streamlined to focus more on corporate criminal liability. A 2008 case on embezzlement by a business owner is presented. An updated discussion of sentencing guidelines is included, and the discussion of defenses to criminal charges was revised. An *Emerging Trends* feature covers *Stand-Your-Ground Laws* (state laws allowing the use of deadly force in homes and vehicles to thwart violent crimes such as robbery, carjacking, and sexual assault).
- Chapters 10 through 19 (the Contracts unit)—Throughout this unit, we have added more examples to clarify and enhance our already impressive contract law coverage. We have also included

more up-to-date information and new features on topics likely to generate student interest, such as the *Contemporary Legal Debates* feature entitled *Are Online Fantasy Sports Gambling?* (in Chapter 13) and the feature on *Internet Click Fraud* (in Chapter 14). We have changed the titles of Chapters 14 and 15 to clearly describe the contents of each chapter in plain English (for example, the title "Mistakes, Fraud, and Voluntary Consent" replaces the former title "Genuineness of Assent"). We have chosen cases, problems, and examples for this unit that garner student interest, such as the Mike Tyson example in Chapter 16, and have revised the text to improve clarity and reduce legalese.

- Chapters 20 through 23 (the unit on Domestic and International Sales and Lease Contracts)—We have streamlined and simplified our coverage of the Uniform Commercial Code. We have added numerous new examples throughout the unit to increase student comprehension. Because no state has adopted the 2003 amendments to Articles 2 and 2A, we eliminated references to these amendments throughout the chapters.
- Chapters 24 through 27 (the unit on Negotiable Instruments)—We have updated this unit throughout to accommodate the reality of digital banking and funds transfers. In Chapter 24, we added an *Insight into the Global Environment* feature exploring the negotiability of checks in other nations. We added a new *Concept Summary* in Chapter 25 and replaced the *Concept Summary* on defenses in Chapter 26 with a more visually appealing exhibit on the same topic. In Chapter 27, we revised the materials to incorporate the Check-Clearing in the 21st Century Act (Check 21 Act) and included an *Emerging Trends* feature discussing how *Using Digital Cash Facilitates Money Laundering.*
- Chapters 28 through 30 (the unit on Creditors' Rights and Bankruptcy)—This unit has been revised to be more up to date and comprehensible. Chapter 29 (Secured Transactions) was substantially reorganized to clarify the general rules of priority and the exceptions to those rules. The bankruptcy law chapter (Chapter 30) is based on law after the 2005 Reform Act and includes updated dollar amounts of various provisions of the Bankruptcy Code.
- Chapter 33 (Employment and Labor Law) and Chapter 34 (Employment Discrimination)—These two chapters covering employment law have been thoroughly updated to include discussions of legal issues facing employers today. Chapter 33 includes updated minimum wage figures and Social Security and Medicare percentages. It also discusses overtime rules and provides the most current information on unionization, strikes, and employment monitoring.

  Chapter 34 now includes the latest developments and United States Supreme Court decisions, such as a decision that applied Title VII of the Civil Rights Act of 1964 to an employer with fewer than fifteen employees and another that set the standard of proof for retaliation claims. The text discussion of burden of proof in unintentional discrimination cases has been revised and clarified. An *Emerging Trends* feature examines *New Issues in Online Privacy and Employment Discrimination,* and a new *Business Application* feature discusses *Interviewing Job Applicants with Disabilities.*
- Chapters 35 through 42 (the Business Organizations unit)—This unit has been substantially reorganized and updated to improve the flow and clarity, and provide more practical information and recent examples. In Chapter 35 (Sole Proprietorships and Franchises), we added a section on the Franchise Rule that includes the 2007 amendments to the rule. In Chapter 36 (Partnerships and Limited Liability Partnerships), we added several examples, reworked the section on fiduciary duties, and clarified the materials on dissociation.

  The most significant changes to the unit were made in the corporations chapters (Chapters 38 through 40). Chapter 38 now includes a more updated discussion of promotional activities, and the materials on incorporation procedures were completely revised to reflect current state laws. New sections were added on offshore low-tax jurisdictions, venture capital, and private equity financing. In Chapter 39, we added coverage of the landmark case *Guth v. Loft* (on the duty of loyalty), a new exhibit, and updated materials on Sarbanes-Oxley. We also added discussions of various committees of the board of directors, corporate sentencing guidelines, and proxies, including new e-proxy rules. The topic of shareholder voting concerning executive pay is discussed, and a *Contemporary Legal Debates* feature explores the possibility of *A Shareholder Access Rule.* Chapter 40 has been revised to include share exchanges, clarify successor liability, improve coverage of appraisal rights, and rework the material on tender offers. We include discussion of takeover defenses and directors' fiduciary duties.

The chapter on securities law (Chapter 41) was revamped to make this difficult topic more understandable to students. The chapter now includes a new exhibit and overview of the functions of the Securities and Exchange Commission and a practical explanation of the *Howey* test. We also provide a simplified list of contents of a registration statement and an updated discussion of the registration process that clarifies current rules on a free-writing prospectus.

The final chapter in this unit (Chapter 42 on Law for Small Businesses) has also been considerably revised to address practical considerations, such as choosing to do business as a limited liability company, protecting trademarks, and avoiding liability. It also includes a feature on what businesspersons should consider before moving their small business online.

- Chapter 43 (Administrative Law)—This chapter has been reworked to focus on the practical significance of administrative law for businesspersons. A new section was added on the Administrative Procedure Act, and another section addresses how the courts give *Chevron* deference to agency rules. We include a 2008 case on how courts give *Chevron* deference to agency interpretation. Informal agency actions are covered, and a new subsection discusses the exhaustion doctrine.
- Chapter 45 (Environmental Law)—The materials on air pollution and the subsection on wetlands have been updated. Two of the cases in the chapter are from 2008, and a *Contemporary Legal Debates* feature discusses the 2007 Supreme Court decision in *Massachusetts v. Environmental Protection Agency* relating to global warming.
- Chapter 46 (Antitrust Law)—We added new examples and coverage of leading cases throughout the chapter, particularly in the discussions of price fixing, relevant product market, and relevant geographic market.
- Chapters 47 and 48 (the Property unit)—We reorganized and reworked the materials in the two property chapters as reviewers requested. Chapter 47 now begins with a section discussing the differences between personal and real property, and why the law makes this distinction. The materials on forms of property ownership (such as fee simple and joint tenancy) were moved from the personal property chapter (Chapter 47) to the real property chapter (48). The coverage of bailments was updated and simplified. Chapter 48 also includes more information on real estate sales contracts, including listing agreements, escrow agreements, marketable title, title searches, and title insurance.

Acknowledgments for Previous Editions

Since we began this project many years ago, a sizable number of business law professors and others have helped us in various phases of the undertaking. The following reviewers offered numerous constructive criticisms, comments, and suggestions during the preparation of all previous editions.

Jeffrey E. Allen
University of Miami

Judith Anshin
Sacramento City College

Thomas M. Apke
California State University, Fullerton

Raymond August
Washington State University

William Auslen
San Francisco City College

Mary B. Bader
Moorhead State University

Frank Bagan
County College of Morris

John J. Balek
Morton College, Illinois

Michael G. Barth
University of Phoenix

David L. Baumer
North Carolina State University

Barbara E. Behr
Bloomsburg University of Pennsylvania

Robert B. Bennett, Jr.
Butler University

Heidi Boerstler
University of Colorado at Denver

Lawrence J. Bradley
University of Notre Dame

Doug Brown
Montana State University

Kristi K. Brown
University of Texas at Austin

William J. Burke
University of Massachusetts, Lowell

Kenneth Burns
University of Miami

Daniel R. Cahoy
Pennsylvania State University

Jeanne A. Calderon
New York University

Joseph E. Cantrell
DeAnza College, California

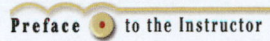

Donald Cantwell
University of Texas at Arlington

Robert Chatov
State University of New York, Buffalo

Robert J. Cox
Salt Lake Community College

Thomas Crane
University of Miami

Kenneth S. Culott
University of Texas at Austin

Larry R. Curtis
Iowa State University

Richard Dalebout
Brigham Young University

William H. Daughtrey, Jr.
Virginia Commonwealth University

Michele A. Dunkerley
University of Texas at Austin

O. E. Elmore
Texas A&M University

Robert J. Enders
California State Polytechnic University, Pomona

Michael Engber
Ball State University

David A. Escamilla
University of Texas at Austin

Frank S. Forbes
University of Nebraska at Omaha

Joe W. Fowler
Oklahoma State University

Stanley G. Freeman
University of South Carolina

Christ Gaetanos
State University of New York, Fredonia

Chester S. Galloway
Auburn University

Bob Garrett
American River College, California

Gary L. Giese
University of Colorado at Denver

Thomas Gossman
Western Michigan University

Patrick O. Gudridge
University of Miami School of Law

James M. Haine
University of Wisconsin, Stevens Point

Gerard Halpern
University of Arkansas

Christopher L. Hamilton
Golden West College, California

JoAnn W. Hammer
University of Texas at Austin

Charles Hartman
Wright State University, Ohio

Richard A. Hausler
University of Miami School of Law

Harry E. Hicks
Butler University, Indianapolis

Janine S. Hiller
Virginia Polytechnic Institute and State University

Rebecca L. Hillyer
Chemeketa Community College

E. Clayton Hipp, Jr.
Clemson University

Anthony H. Holliday, Jr.
Howard University

Telford Hollman
University of Northern Iowa

June A. Horrigan
California State University, Sacramento

John P. Huggard
North Carolina State University

Terry Hutchins
Pembroke State University, North Carolina

Robert Jesperson
University of Houston

Bryce J. Jones
Northeast Missouri State University

Margaret Jones
Southwest Missouri State College

Peter A. Karl III
SUNY Institute of Technology at Utica

Jack E. Karns
East Carolina University

Tamra Kempf
University of Miami

Judith Kenney
University of Miami

Barbara Kincaid
Southern Methodist University

Carey Kirk
University of Northern Iowa

Nancy P. Klintworth
University of Central Florida

Kurtis P. Klumb
University of Wisconsin at Milwaukee

Kathleen M. Knutson
College of St. Catherine, St. Paul, Minnesota

M. Alan Lawson
Mt. San Antonio College

Susan Liebeler
Loyola University

Thomas E. Maher
California State University, Fullerton

Sal Marchionna
Triton College, Illinois

Gene A. Marsh
University of Alabama

Karen Kay Matson
University of Texas at Austin

Woodrow J. Maxwell
Hudson Valley Community College, New York

Bruce E. May
University of South Dakota

Gail McCracken
University of Michigan, Dearborn

John W. McGee
Southwest Texas State University

Cotton Meagher
University of Nevada at Las Vegas

Roger E. Meiners
University of Texas at Arlington

Gerald S. Meisel
Bergen Community College, New Jersey

Richard Mills
Cypress College

David Minars
City University of New York, Brooklyn

Leo Moersen
The George Washington University

Alan Moggio
Illinois Central College

Violet E. Molnar
Riverside City College

James E. Moon
Meyer, Johnson & Moon, Minneapolis

Melinda Ann Mora
University of Texas at Austin

Bob Morgan
Eastern Michigan University

Joan Ann Mrava
Los Angeles Southwest College

Dwight D. Murphey
Wichita State University

Daniel E. Murray
University of Miami School of Law

Paula C. Murray
University of Texas

Gregory J. Naples
Marquette University

George A. Nation III
Lehigh University

Caleb L. Nichols
Western Connecticut State University

John M. Norwood
University of Arkansas

Michael J. O'Hara
University of Nebraska at Omaha

Rick F. Orsinger
College of DuPage, Illinois

Daniel J. O'Shea
Hillsborough Community College

Thomas L. Palmer
Northern Arizona University

Charles M. Patten
University of Wisconsin, Oshkosh

Patricia Pattison
Texas State University, San Marcos

Peyton J. Paxson
University of Texas at Austin

Ralph L. Quinones
University of Wisconsin, Oshkosh

Carol D. Rasnic
Virginia Commonwealth University

Marvin H. Robertson
Harding University

Gary K. Sambol
Rutgers State University

Rudy Sandoval
University of Texas, San Antonio

Sidney S. Sappington
York College of Pennsylvania

Martha Sartoris
North Hennepin Community College

Barbara P. Scheller
Temple University

S. Alan Schlact
Kennesaw State University, Georgia

Lorne H. Seidman
University of Nevada at Las Vegas

Roscoe B. Shain
Austin Peay University

Bennett D. Shulman
Lansing Community College, Michigan

S. Jay Sklar
Temple University

Dana Blair Smith
University of Texas at Austin

Michael Smydra
Oakland Community College–Royal Oak

Arthur Southwick
University of Michigan

Sylvia A. Spade
University of Texas at Austin

John A. Sparks
Grove City College, Pennsylvania

Brenda Steuer
North Harris College, Houston

Craig Stilwell
Michigan State University

Irwin Stotsky
University of Miami School of Law

Larry Strate
University of Nevada at Las Vegas

Raymond Mason Taylor
North Carolina State University

H. Allan Tolbert
Central Texas College

Jesse C. Trentadue
University of North Dakota

Edwin Tucker
University of Connecticut

Gary Victor
Eastern Michigan University

William H. Volz
Wayne State University

David Vyncke
Scott Community College, Iowa

William H. Walker
Indiana University–Purdue University, Fort Wayne

Diana Walsh
County College of Morris

Robert J. Walter
University of Texas at El Paso

Gary Watson
California State University, Los Angeles

John L. Weimer
Nicholls State University, Louisiana

Marshall Wilkerson
University of Texas at Austin

Arthur D. Wolfe
Michigan State University

Elizabeth A. Wolfe
University of Texas at Austin

Daniel R. Wrentmore
Santa Barbara City College

Norman Gregory Young
California State Polytechnic University, Pomona

Ronald C. Young
Kalamazoo Valley Community College, Michigan

We would also like to give credit to the following reviewers for their useful input during development of the CengageNOW for *Business Law: Alternate Edition* Interactive Assignment System.

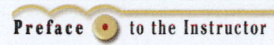

Nena Ellison
Florida Atlantic University

Jacqueline Hagerott
Franklin University

Melanie Morris
Raritan Valley Community College

William H. Volz
Wayne State University

Acknowledgments for the Eleventh Edition

In preparing the Eleventh Edition of *Business Law: Alternate Edition*, we worked closely with the following reviewers, each of whom offered us valuable suggestions for how to improve the text:

Maria Kathleen Boss
California State University, Los Angeles

Rita Cain
University of Missouri–Kansas City

Jeanne A. Calderon
New York University

Nanette C. Clinch
San Jose State University

Larry R. Curtis
Iowa State University

Leslie E. Lenn
St. Edwards University

Barry S. Morinaka
Baker College–Michigan

S. Alan Schlact
Kennesaw State University, Georgia

Elisabeth Sperow
California Polytechnic University, San Luis Obispo

Charles R. B. Stowe
Sam Houston State University

Melanie Stallings Williams
California State University–Northridge

As in all past editions, we owe a debt of extreme gratitude to the numerous individuals who worked directly with us or at Cengage Learning. In particular, we wish to thank Rob Dewey for his helpful advice and guidance during all of the stages of this new edition, and Vicky True for her expertise as acquisitions editor. We extend our thanks to Jan Lamar, our longtime developmental editor, for her many useful suggestions and for her efforts in coordinating reviews and ensuring the timely and accurate publication of all supplemental materials. We are also indebted to Lisa Lysne for her support and excellent marketing advice, and to Brian Courter and Kristen Meere for their skills in managing the Web site.

Our production manager and designer, Bill Stryker, made sure that we came out with an error-free, visually attractive Eleventh Edition. We appreciate his efforts more than he can ever imagine. We are also indebted to the staff at Parkwood Composition, our compositor. Their ability to generate the pages for this text quickly and accurately made it possible for us to meet our ambitious printing schedule.

We especially wish to thank Katherine Marie Silsbee for her management of the entire project, as well as for the application of her superb research and editorial skills. We also wish to thank Lavina Leed Miller for her significant contributions to this project, and William Eric Hollowell, who co-authored the *Instructor's Manual*, the *Study Guide*, and the two *Test Banks*, for his excellent research efforts. We were fortunate enough to have the proofreading services of Pat Lewis and Kristi Wiswell. We also thank Vickie Reierson and Roxanna Lee for their proofreading and other assistance, which helped to ensure an error-free text. Finally, we thank Suzanne Jasin of K & M Consulting for her many special efforts on this project.

In addition, we would like to give special thanks to all of the individuals who were instrumental in developing and implementing the new CengageNOW for *Business Law: Alternate Edition* Interactive Assignment System. These include Rob Dewey, Jan Lamar, Lisa Lysne, and Vicky True at Cengage, and Katherine Marie Silsbee, Roger Meiners, Lavina Leed Miller, William Eric Hollowell, and Kimberly Wallan, who helped develop the content for this unique Web-based product.

Through the years, we have enjoyed an ongoing correspondence with many of you who have found points on which you wish to comment. We continue to welcome all comments and promise to respond promptly. By incorporating your ideas, we can continue to write a business law text that is best for you and best for your students.

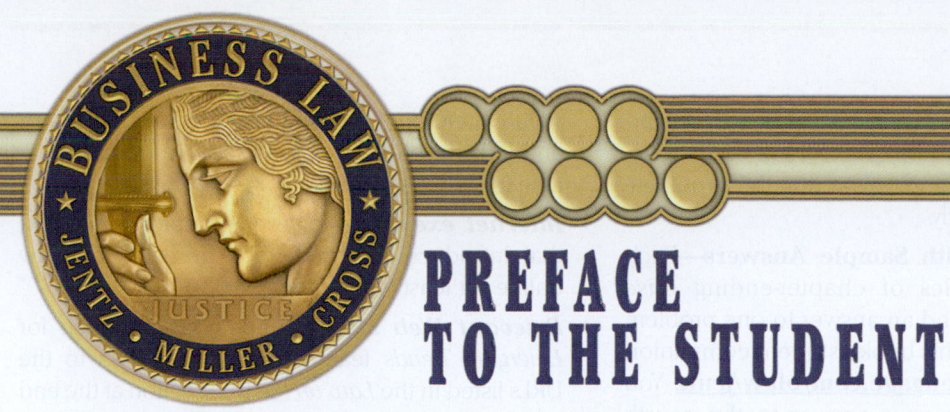

PREFACE TO THE STUDENT

Welcome to the world of business law and the legal environment. You are about to embark on the study of one of the most important topics you should master in today's changing world. A solid understanding of business law can, of course, help you if you are going into the world of business. If you decide on a career in accounting, economics, finance, political science, or history, understanding how the legal environment works is crucial. Moreover, in your role as a consumer, you will be faced with some legal issues throughout your lifetime—renting an apartment, buying a house, obtaining a mortgage, and leasing a car, to mention only a few. In your role as an employee (if you don't go into business for yourself), you will need to know what rights you have and what rights you don't have. Even when you contemplate marriage, you will be faced with legal issues.

What You Will Find in This Text

As you will see as you thumb through the pages in this text, we have tried to make your study of business law and the legal environment as efficient and enjoyable as possible. To this end, you will find the following aids:

1. **Mastering Terminology—**through *Key Terms* that are boldfaced, listed at the end of each chapter, and explained fully in the *Glossary* at the end of the book.
2. **Understanding Concepts—**through numerous *Concept Summaries* and *Exhibits*.
3. **Observing the Law in the Context of the Real World—**through a *Reviewing* feature at the end of every chapter.
4. **Seeing How Legal Issues Can Arise—**through *Video Questions* based on Web-available short videos, many from actual Hollywood movies.
5. **Figuring Out How the Law Is Evolving—**through a feature called *Emerging Trends*.
6. **Determining Today's Legal Controversies—**through a feature called *Contemporary Legal Debates*.
7. **Gaining Insights into How the Law Affects or Is Affected by Other Issues—**through three new *Insight* features called *Insight into E-Commerce*, *Insight into Ethics*, and *Insight into the Global Environment*.

The above list, of course, is representative only. You will understand much more of what the law is about as you read through the *court cases* presented in this book.

Improving Your Ability to Perform Legal Reasoning and Analysis

Although business law may seem to be a mass of facts, your goal in taking this course should also be an increased ability to use legal reasoning and analysis to figure out how legal situations will be resolved. To this end, you will find the following key learning features to assist you in mastering legal reasoning and analysis:

- **Finding and Analyzing Case Law—**In Chapter 1, you will find a section with this title that explains:
  1. Legal citations.
  2. The standard elements of a case.
  3. The different types of opinions a court can issue.
  4. How to read and understand cases.
- **Briefing a Case—**In Appendix A, you will see how to brief and analyze case problems. This explanation teaches you how to break down the elements of a case and will improve your ability to answer the *Case Problems* in each chapter.
- **Questions with Sample Answers—**At the end of each chapter, there is one hypothetical factual scenario that presents a legal question for which you

can access a *sample answer* in Appendix I (and also on the text's Web site). This allows you to practice and to see if you are answering the hypothetical problems correctly.

- **Case Problems with Sample Answers**—Each chapter has a series of chapter-ending *Case Problems.* You can find an answer to one problem in each chapter on this book's student companion Web site at **www.cengage.com/blaw/jentz**. You can easily compare your answer to the court's answer in the actual case.
- **Impact of This Case on Today's Law**—Each classic case concludes with a short section that explains the relevance of older case law to the way courts reason today.
- **What If the Facts Were Different?**—This section, found at the end of selected cases, encourages you to think about how the outcome of a case might be different if the facts were altered.
- **The Ethical [E-Commerce, Global, or Legal Environment] Dimension**—Every case in this text concludes with two critical-thinking questions, which may include *What If the Facts Were Different?* questions, as discussed above. For this edition, we've included several new possibilities—*(The Ethical Dimension, The E-Commerce Dimension, The Global Dimension,* and *The Legal Environment Dimension).* These questions ask you to explore the law in a variety of contexts to help you meet the specific curriculum requirements for business law students.

The Companion Student Web Site

As already mentioned, the companion student Web site at **www.cengage.com/blaw/jentz** provides you with short videos on various legal topics and with sample answers to one case problem per chapter. In addition, you will find the following:

- ***Interactive quizzes*** for every chapter.
- A ***glossary*** of terms for every chapter in the text.
- ***Flashcards*** that provide an optional study tool for reviewing the key terms in every chapter.
- ***Appendix A: How to Brief and Analyze Case Problems*** that will help you analyze cases. This useful appendix for the book is also provided on the Web site and can be downloaded.
- ***Legal reference materials*** including a "Statutes" page that offers links to the full text of selected statutes referenced in the text, a Spanish glossary, and links to other important legal resources available for free on the Web.
- ***Internet exercises*** for every chapter in the text that introduce you to how to research the law online (at least two per chapter).
- ***Relevant Web sites*** for additional research for *Emerging Trends* features, as well as links to the URLs listed in the *Law on the Web* section at the end of each chapter.
- ***Online Legal Research Guide*** that offers complete yet brief guidance to using the Internet and evaluating information obtained from the Internet. As an online resource, it now includes hyperlinks to the Web sites discussed for click-through convenience.
- ***Court case updates*** for follow-up research on topics covered in the text.
- ***Link to CengageNOW for* Business Law: Alternate Edition *Interactive Assignment System*** with different types of questions related to every chapter in the text and one set of cumulative questions for each unit in the text. (Available on an instructor's request, see below.)

Interactive Assignments on the Web

Some of you may have instructors who provide assignments using our world-class interactive Web-based system, called **CengageNOW for *Business Law: Alternate Edition* Interactive Assignment System.**

CengageNOW for *Business Law: Alternate Edition* Interactive Assignment System allows you to improve your mastery of legal concepts and terminology, legal reasoning and analysis, and much more. Your instructor will give you further information if she or he decides to use this Web-based system.

Of course, whether or not you are using the CengageNOW system, you will wish to consider purchasing the *Study Guide,* which can help you get a better grade in your course (see the inside cover for details).

The law is all around you—and will be for the rest of your life. We hope that you begin your first course in business law and the legal environment with the same high degree of excitement that we, the authors, always have when we work on improving this text, now in its Eleventh Edition. *Business Law: Alternate Edition* has withstood the test of time—several million students before you have already used and benefited from it.

Dedication

To Alicia and Etienne,

Keep your buoyant spirits always.
Keep your laughter always.
Keep your friends forever.

Your Friend,
R.L.M.

To my wife, JoAnn; my children, Kathy, Gary, Lori, and Rory; and my grandchildren, Erin, Megan, Eric, Emily, Michelle, Javier, Carmen, and Steve.

G.A.J.

To my parents and sisters.

F.B.C.

UNIT ONE

The Legal Environment of Business

CONTENTS

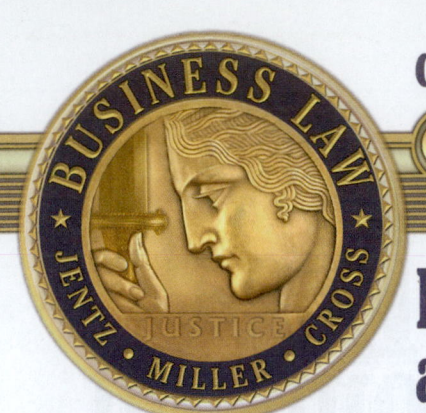

CHAPTER 1

Introduction to Law and Legal Reasoning

One of the important functions of law in any society is to provide stability, predictability, and continuity so that people can be sure of how to order their affairs. If any society is to survive, its citizens must be able to determine what is legally right and legally wrong. They must know what sanctions will be imposed on them if they commit wrongful acts. If they suffer harm as a result of others' wrongful acts, they must know how they can seek redress. By setting forth the rights, obligations, and privileges of citizens, the law enables individuals to go about their business with confidence and a certain degree of predictability. The stability and predictability created by the law provide an essential framework for all civilized activities, including business activities.

What do we mean when we speak of "the law"? Although this term has had, and will continue to have, different definitions, they are all based on a general observation: at a minimum, **law** consists of *enforceable rules governing relationships among individuals and between individuals and their society.* These "enforceable rules" may consist of unwritten principles of behavior established by a nomadic tribe. They may be set forth in a law code, such as the Code of Hammurabi in ancient Babylon (c. 1780 B.C.E.) or the law code of one of today's European nations. They may consist of written laws and court decisions created by modern legislative and judicial bodies, as in the United States. Regardless of how such rules are created, they all have one thing in common: they establish rights, duties, and privileges that are consistent with the values and beliefs of their society or its ruling group.

Those who embark on a study of law will find that these broad statements leave unanswered some important questions concerning the nature of law. Part of the study of law, often referred to as **jurisprudence,** involves learning about different schools of jurisprudential thought and discovering how the approaches to law characteristic of each school can affect judicial decision making.

We open this introductory chapter with an examination of that topic. We then look at an important question for any student reading this text: How does the legal environment affect business decision making? We next describe the basic sources of American law, the common law tradition, and some general classifications of law. We conclude the chapter with sections offering practical guidance on several topics, including how to find the sources of law discussed in this chapter (and referred to throughout the text) and how to read and understand court opinions.

SECTION 1 Schools of Jurisprudential Thought

You may think that legal philosophy is far removed from the practical study of business law and the legal environment. In fact, it is not. As you will learn in the chapters of this text, how judges apply the law to specific disputes, including disputes relating to the business world, depends in part on their philosophical approaches to law.

Clearly, judges are not free to decide cases solely on the basis of their personal philosophical views or on their opinions about the issues before the court. A judge's function is not to *make* the laws—that is the function of the legislative branch of government—but to interpret and apply them. From a practical point of view, however, the courts play a significant role in defining what the law is. This is because laws enacted by legislative bodies tend to be expressed in general terms. Judges thus have some flexibility in interpreting and applying the law. It is because of this flexibility that different courts can, and often do, arrive at different conclusions in cases that involve nearly identical issues, facts, and applicable laws. This flexibility also means that each judge's unique personality, legal philosophy, set of values, and intellectual attributes necessarily frame the judicial decision-making process to some extent.

Over time several significant schools of legal, or jurisprudential, thought have evolved. We now look at some of them.

The Natural Law School

An age-old question about the nature of law has to do with the finality of a nation's laws, such as the laws of the United States at the present time. For example, what if a particular law is deemed to be a "bad" law by a substantial number of that nation's citizens? Must a citizen obey the law if it goes against his or her conscience to do so? Is there a higher or universal law to which individuals can appeal? One who adheres to the natural law tradition would answer these questions in the affirmative. **Natural law** denotes a system of moral and ethical principles that are inherent in human nature and that people can discover through the use of their natural intelligence, or reason.

The natural law tradition is one of the oldest and most significant schools of jurisprudence. It dates back to the days of the Greek philosopher Aristotle (384–322 B.C.E.), who distinguished between natural law and the laws governing a particular nation. According to Aristotle, natural law applies universally to all humankind.

The notion that people have "natural rights" stems from the natural law tradition. Those who claim that a specific foreign government is depriving certain citizens of their human rights implicitly are appealing to a higher law that has universal applicability. The question of the universality of basic human rights also comes into play in the context of international business operations. Should rights extended to workers in the United States, such as the right to be free of discrimination in the workplace, be extended to workers employed by a U.S. firm doing business in another country that does not provide for such rights? This question is rooted implicitly in a concept of universal rights that has its origins in the natural law tradition.

The Positivist School

In contrast, **positive law,** or national law (the written law of a given society at a particular point in time), applies only to the citizens of that nation or society. Those who adhere to the **positivist school** believe that there can be no higher law than a nation's positive law. According to the positivist school, there is no such thing as "natural rights." Rather, human rights exist solely because of laws. If the laws are not enforced, anarchy will result. Thus, whether a law is "bad" or "good" is irrelevant. The law is the law and must be obeyed until it is changed—in an orderly manner through a legitimate lawmaking process. A judge with positivist leanings probably would be more inclined to defer to an existing law than would a judge who adheres to the natural law tradition.

The Historical School

The **historical school** of legal thought emphasizes the evolutionary process of law by concentrating on the origin and history of the legal system. Thus, this school looks to the past to discover what the principles of contemporary law should be. The legal doctrines that have withstood the passage of time—those that have worked in the past—are deemed best suited for shaping present laws. Hence, law derives its legitimacy and authority from adhering to the standards that historical development has shown to be workable. Adherents of the historical school are more likely than those of other schools to strictly follow decisions made in past cases.

Legal Realism

In the 1920s and 1930s, a number of jurists and scholars, known as legal realists, rebelled against the historical approach to law. **Legal realism** is based on the idea that law is just one of many institutions in society and that it is shaped by social forces and needs. The law is a human enterprise, and judges should take social and economic realities into account when deciding cases. Legal realists also believe that the law can never be applied with total uniformity. Given that judges are human beings with unique personalities, value systems, and intellects, different judges will obviously bring different reasoning processes to the same case.

Legal realism strongly influenced the growth of what is sometimes called the **sociological school** of jurisprudence. This school views law as a tool for promoting justice in society. In the 1960s, for example, the justices of the United States Supreme Court played a leading role in the civil rights movement by upholding long-neglected laws calling for equal treatment for all Americans, including African Americans and other minorities. Generally, jurists who adhere to this philosophy of law are more likely to depart from past decisions than are those jurists who adhere to the other schools of legal thought. *Concept Summary 1.1* reviews the schools of jurisprudential thought.

SECTION 2

Business Activities and the Legal Environment

As those entering the world of business will learn, laws and government regulations affect virtually all business activities—from hiring and firing decisions to workplace safety, the manufacturing and marketing of products, business financing, and more. To make good business decisions, a basic knowledge of the laws and regulations governing these activities is beneficial—if not essential. Realize also that in today's world a knowledge of "black-letter" law is not enough. Businesspersons are also pressured to make ethical decisions. Thus, the study of business law necessarily involves an ethical dimension.

Many Different Laws May Affect a Single Business Transaction

As you will note, each chapter in this text covers a specific area of the law and shows how the legal rules in that area affect business activities. Though compartmentalizing the law in this fashion promotes conceptual clarity, it does not indicate the extent to which a number of different laws may apply to just one transaction.

Consider an example. Suppose that you are the president of NetSys, Inc., a company that creates and maintains computer network systems for its clients, including business firms. NetSys also markets software for customers who require an internal computer network. One day, Hernandez, an operations officer for Southwest Distribution Corporation (SDC), contacts you by e-mail about a possible contract concerning SDC's computer network. In deciding whether to enter

CONCEPT SUMMARY 1.1
Schools of Jurisprudential Thought

School of Thought	Description
THE NATURAL LAW SCHOOL	One of the oldest and most significant schools of legal thought. Those who believe in natural law hold that there is a universal law applicable to all human beings. This law is discoverable through reason and is of a higher order than positive (national) law.
THE POSITIVIST SCHOOL	A school of legal thought centered on the assumption that there is no law higher than the laws created by the government. Laws must be obeyed, even if they are unjust, to prevent anarchy.
THE HISTORICAL SCHOOL	A school of legal thought that stresses the evolutionary nature of law and that looks to doctrines that have withstood the passage of time for guidance in shaping present laws.
LEGAL REALISM	A school of legal thought, popular during the 1920s and 1930s, that left a lasting imprint on American jurisprudence. Legal realists generally advocated a less abstract and more realistic and pragmatic approach to the law, an approach that would take into account customary practices and the circumstances in which transactions take place. Legal realism strongly influenced the growth of the *sociological school* of jurisprudence, which views law as a tool for promoting social justice.

into a contract with SDC, you should consider, among other things, the legal requirements for an enforceable contract. Are there different requirements for a contract for services and a contract for products? What are your options if SDC **breaches** (breaks, or fails to perform) the contract? The answers to these questions are part of contract law and sales law.

Other questions might concern payment under the contract. How can you guarantee that NetSys will be paid? For example, if payment is made with a check that is returned for insufficient funds, what are your options? Answers to these questions can be found in the laws that relate to negotiable instruments (such as checks) and creditors' rights. Also, a dispute may occur over the rights to NetSys's software, or there may be a question of liability if the software is defective. Questions may even be raised as to whether you and Hernandez had the authority to make the deal in the first place. A disagreement may arise from other circumstances, such as an accountant's evaluation of the contract. Resolutions of these questions may be found in areas of the law that relate to intellectual property, e-commerce, torts, product liability, agency, business organizations, or professional liability.

Finally, if any dispute cannot be resolved amicably, then the laws and the rules concerning courts and court procedures spell out the steps of a lawsuit. Exhibit 1–1 illustrates the various areas of law that may influence business decision making.

To prevent potential legal disputes, businesspersons need to be aware of the many different laws that may apply to a single business transaction. It is equally important for businesspersons to understand enough about the law to know when to turn to an attorney for advice.

Ethics and Business Decision Making

Merely knowing the areas of law that may affect a business decision is not sufficient in today's business world. Businesspersons must also take ethics into account. As you will learn in Chapter 5, *ethics* is generally defined as the study of what constitutes right or wrong behavior. Today, business decision makers

EXHIBIT 1–1 • Areas of the Law That May Affect Business Decision Making

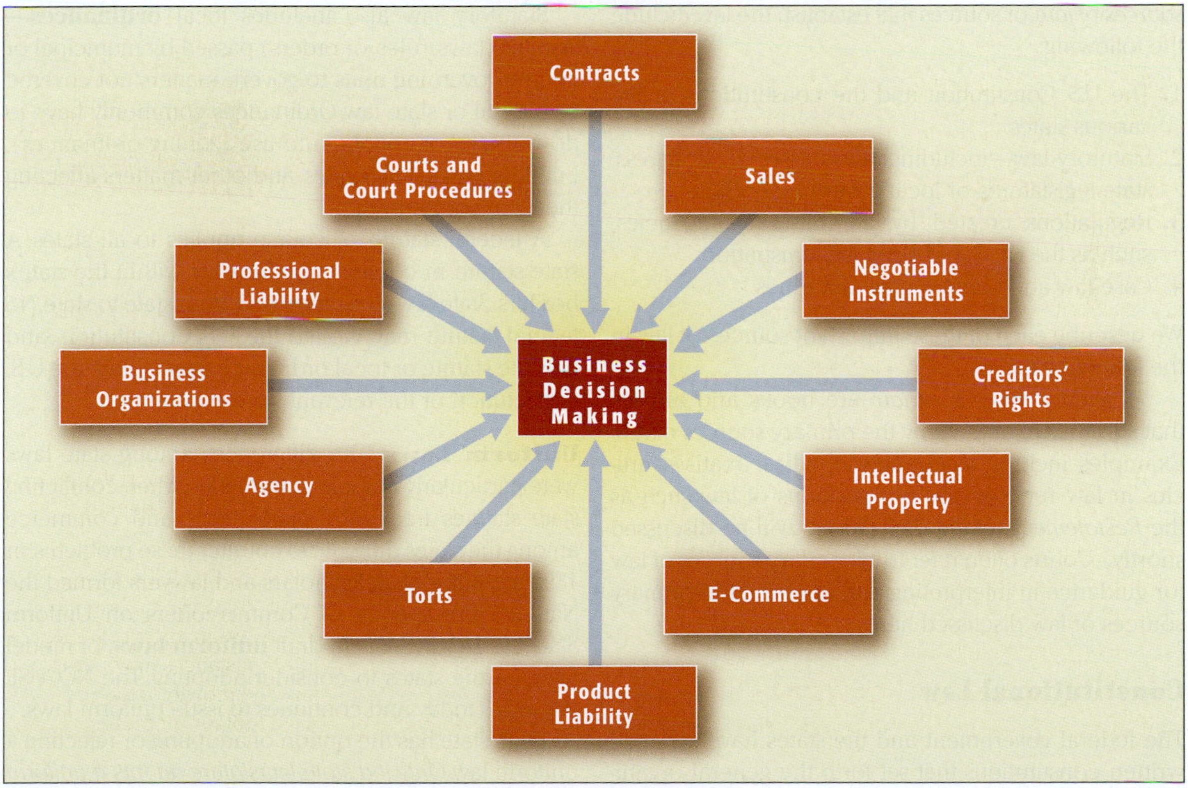

need to consider not just whether a decision is legal, but also whether it is ethical.

Throughout this text, you will learn about the relationship between the law and ethics, as well as about some of the types of ethical questions that often arise in the business context. For example, the unit-ending *Focus on Ethics* features in this text are devoted solely to the exploration of ethical questions pertaining to selected topics treated within the unit. We have also added several new features for this edition that stress the importance of ethical considerations in today's business climate. These include the new *Ethical Dimension* questions that conclude many of the cases presented in this text and the *Insight into Ethics* features that appear in selected chapters. We have also included *A Question of Ethics* case problems at the ends of the chapters to introduce you to the ethical aspects of specific cases involving real-life situations. Additionally, Chapter 5 offers a detailed look at the importance of ethical considerations in business decision making.

SECTION 3

Sources of American Law

There are numerous sources of American law. *Primary sources of law*, or sources that establish the law, include the following:

1. The U.S. Constitution and the constitutions of the various states.
2. Statutory law—including laws passed by Congress, state legislatures, or local governing bodies.
3. Regulations created by administrative agencies, such as the Food and Drug Administration.
4. Case law and common law doctrines.

We describe each of these important sources of law in the following pages.

Secondary sources of law are books and articles that summarize and clarify the primary sources of law. Examples include legal encyclopedias, treatises, articles in law reviews, and compilations of law, such as the *Restatements of the Law* (which will be discussed shortly). Courts often refer to secondary sources of law for guidance in interpreting and applying the primary sources of law discussed here.

Constitutional Law

The federal government and the states have separate written constitutions that set forth the general organization, powers, and limits of their respective governments. **Constitutional law** is the law as expressed in these constitutions.

According to Article VI of the U.S. Constitution, the Constitution is the supreme law of the land. As such, it is the basis of all law in the United States. A law in violation of the Constitution, if challenged, will be declared unconstitutional and will not be enforced, no matter what its source. Because of its importance in the American legal system, we present the complete text of the U.S. Constitution in Appendix B.

The Tenth Amendment to the U.S. Constitution reserves to the states all powers not granted to the federal government. Each state in the union has its own constitution. Unless it conflicts with the U.S. Constitution or a federal law, a state constitution is supreme within the state's borders.

Statutory Law

Laws enacted by legislative bodies at any level of government, such as the statutes passed by Congress or by state legislatures, make up the body of law generally referred to as **statutory law.** When a legislature passes a statute, that statute ultimately is included in the federal code of laws or the relevant state code of laws (these codes are discussed later in this chapter).

Statutory law also includes local **ordinances**—statutes (laws, rules, or orders) passed by municipal or county governing units to govern matters not covered by federal or state law. Ordinances commonly have to do with city or county land use (zoning ordinances), building and safety codes, and other matters affecting the local community.

A federal statute, of course, applies to all states. A state statute, in contrast, applies only within the state's borders. State laws thus may vary from state to state. No federal statute may violate the U.S. Constitution, and no state statute or local ordinance may violate the U.S. Constitution or the relevant state constitution.

Uniform Laws The differences among state laws were particularly notable in the 1800s, when conflicting state statutes frequently made trade and commerce among the states difficult. To counter these problems, in 1892 a group of legal scholars and lawyers formed the National Conference of Commissioners on Uniform State Laws (NCCUSL) to draft **uniform laws,** or model laws, for the states to consider adopting. The NCCUSL still exists today and continues to issue uniform laws.

Each state has the option of adopting or rejecting a uniform law. *Only if a state legislature adopts a uniform law does that law become part of the statutory law of that state.* Note that a state legislature may adopt all or part of a uniform law as it is written, or the legislature may rewrite the law however the legislature wishes. Hence, even though many states may have adopted a uniform law, those states' laws may not be entirely "uniform."

The earliest uniform law, the Uniform Negotiable Instruments Law, was completed by 1896 and adopted in every state by the early 1920s (although not all states used exactly the same wording). Over the following decades, other acts were drawn up in a similar manner. In all, more than two hundred uniform acts have been issued by the NCCUSL since its inception. The most ambitious uniform act of all, however, was the Uniform Commercial Code.

The Uniform Commercial Code The Uniform Commercial Code (UCC), which was created through the joint efforts of the NCCUSL and the American Law Institute,[1] was first issued in 1952. All fifty states,[2] the District of Columbia, and the Virgin Islands have adopted the UCC. It facilitates commerce among the states by providing a uniform, yet flexible, set of rules governing commercial transactions. The UCC assures businesspersons that their contracts, if validly entered into, normally will be enforced. Because of its importance in the area of commercial law, we cite the UCC frequently in this text. We also present the full text of the UCC in Appendix C.

Administrative Law

Another important source of American law is **administrative law,** which consists of the rules, orders, and decisions of administrative agencies. An **administrative agency** is a federal, state, or local government agency established to perform a specific function. Administrative law and procedures, which will be examined in detail in Chapter 43, constitute a dominant element in the regulatory environment of business. Rules issued by various administrative agencies now affect virtually every aspect of a business's operations, including its capital structure and financing, its hiring and firing procedures, its relations with employees and unions, and the way it manufactures and markets its products.

1. This institute was formed in the 1920s and consists of practicing attorneys, legal scholars, and judges.

2. Louisiana has not adopted Articles 2 and 2A (covering contracts for the sale and lease of goods), however.

Federal Agencies At the national level, numerous **executive agencies** exist within the cabinet departments of the executive branch. The U.S. Food and Drug Administration, for example, is an agency within the U.S. Department of Health and Human Services. Executive agencies are subject to the authority of the president, who has the power to appoint and remove officers of federal agencies. There are also major **independent regulatory agencies** at the federal level, such as the Federal Trade Commission, the Securities and Exchange Commission, and the Federal Communications Commission. The president's power is less pronounced in regard to independent agencies, whose officers serve for fixed terms and cannot be removed without just cause.

State and Local Agencies There are administrative agencies at the state and local levels as well. Commonly, a state agency (such as a state pollution-control agency) is created as a parallel to a federal agency (such as the U.S. Environmental Protection Agency). Just as federal statutes take precedence over conflicting state statutes, so federal agency regulations take precedence over conflicting state regulations.

Case Law and Common Law Doctrines

The rules of law announced in court decisions constitute another basic source of American law. These rules of law include interpretations of constitutional provisions, of statutes enacted by legislatures, and of regulations created by administrative agencies. Today, this body of judge-made law is referred to as **case law.** Case law—the doctrines and principles announced in cases—governs all areas not covered by statutory law or administrative law and is part of our common law tradition. We look at the origins and characteristics of the common law tradition in some detail in the pages that follow. See *Concept Summary 1.2* on the next page for a review of the sources of American law.

SECTION 4

The Common Law Tradition

Because of our colonial heritage, much of American law is based on the English legal system, which originated in medieval England and continued to evolve in the following centuries. Knowledge of this system is necessary to understanding the American legal system today.

CONCEPT SUMMARY 1.2
Sources of American Law

Source	Description
CONSTITUTIONAL LAW	The law as expressed in the U.S. Constitution and the state constitutions. The U.S. Constitution is the supreme law of the land. State constitutions are supreme within state borders to the extent that they do not violate a clause of the U.S. Constitution or a federal law.
STATUTORY LAW	Laws (statutes and ordinances) created by federal, state, and local legislatures and governing bodies. None of these laws may violate the U.S. Constitution or the relevant state constitution. Uniform statutes, when adopted by a state, become statutory law in that state.
ADMINISTRATIVE LAW	The rules, orders, and decisions of federal, state, or local government administrative agencies.
CASE LAW AND COMMON LAW DOCTRINES	Judge-made law, including interpretations of constitutional provisions, of statutes enacted by legislatures, and of regulations created by administrative agencies.

Early English Courts

The origins of the English legal system—and thus the U.S. legal system as well—date back to 1066, when the Normans conquered England. William the Conqueror and his successors began the process of unifying the country under their rule. One of the means they used to do this was the establishment of the king's courts, or *curiae regis*. Before the Norman Conquest, disputes had been settled according to the local legal customs and traditions in various regions of the country. The king's courts sought to establish a uniform set of customs for the country as a whole. What evolved in these courts was the beginning of the **common law**—a body of general rules that applied throughout the entire English realm. Eventually, the common law tradition became part of the heritage of all nations that were once British colonies, including the United States.

Courts of Law and Remedies at Law The early English king's courts could grant only very limited kinds of **remedies** (the legal means to enforce a right or redress a wrong). If one person wronged another in some way, the king's courts could award as compensation one or more of the following: (1) land, (2) items of value, or (3) money. The courts that awarded this compensation became known as **courts of law,** and the three remedies were called **remedies at law.** (Today, the remedy at law normally takes the form of monetary **damages**—an amount given to a party whose legal interests have been injured.) Even though the system introduced uniformity in the settling of disputes, when a complaining party wanted a remedy other than economic compensation, the courts of law could do nothing, so "no remedy, no right."

Courts of Equity and Remedies in Equity

Equity is a branch of law, founded on what might be described as notions of justice and fair dealing, that seeks to supply a remedy when no adequate remedy at law is available. When individuals could not obtain an adequate remedy in a court of law, they petitioned the king for relief. Most of these petitions were decided by an adviser to the king, called a **chancellor,** who had the power to grant new and unique remedies. Eventually, formal chancery courts, or **courts of equity,** were established.

The remedies granted by the equity courts became known as **remedies in equity,** or equitable remedies. These remedies include *specific performance* (ordering a party to perform an agreement as promised), an *injunction* (ordering a party to cease engaging in a specific activity or to undo some wrong or injury), and *rescission* (the cancellation of a contractual obligation). We discuss these and other equitable remedies in more detail at appropriate points in the chapters that follow, particularly in Chapter 18.

As a general rule, today's courts, like the early English courts, will not grant equitable remedies unless the remedy at law—monetary damages—is inadequate. For example, suppose that you form a contract (a legally binding agreement—see Chapter 10) to purchase a parcel of land that you think will be just perfect for your future home. Further suppose that the seller breaches this agreement. You could sue the seller for the return of any deposits or down payment you might have made on the land, but this is not the remedy you really seek. What you want is to have the court order the seller to go through with the contract. In other words, you want the court to grant the equitable remedy of specific performance because monetary damages are inadequate in this situation.

Equitable Maxims In fashioning appropriate remedies, judges often were (and continue to be) guided by so-called **equitable maxims**—propositions or general statements of equitable rules. Exhibit 1–2 lists some important equitable maxims. The last maxim listed in that exhibit—"Equity aids the vigilant, not those who rest on their rights"—merits special attention. It has become known as the equitable doctrine of **laches** (a term derived from the Latin *laxus*, meaning "lax" or "negligent"), and it can be used as a defense. A **defense** is an argument raised by the **defendant** (the party being sued) indicating why the **plaintiff** (the suing party) should not obtain the remedy sought. (Note that in equity proceedings, the party bringing a lawsuit is called the **petitioner,** and the party being sued is referred to as the **respondent.**)

The doctrine of laches arose to encourage people to bring lawsuits while the evidence was fresh. What constitutes a reasonable time, of course, varies according to the circumstances of the case. Time periods for different types of cases are now usually fixed by **statutes of limitations.** After the time allowed under a statute of limitations has expired, no action (lawsuit) can be brought, no matter how strong the case was originally.

Legal and Equitable Remedies Today

The establishment of courts of equity in medieval England resulted in two distinct court systems: courts of law and courts of equity. The systems had different sets of judges and granted different types of remedies. During the nineteenth century, however, most states in the United States adopted rules of procedure that resulted in the combining of courts of law and equity. A party now may request both legal and equitable remedies in the same action, and the trial court judge may grant either or both forms of relief.

The distinction between legal and equitable remedies remains relevant to students of business law, however, because these remedies differ. To seek the proper remedy for a wrong, one must know what remedies are available. Additionally, certain vestiges of the procedures used when there were separate courts of law and equity still exist. For example, a party has the right to demand a jury trial in an action at law, but not in an action in equity. Exhibit 1–3 on page 10 summarizes the procedural differences (applicable in most states) between an action at law and an action in equity.

The Doctrine of *Stare Decisis*

One of the unique features of the common law is that it is *judge-made* law. The body of principles and doctrines that form the common law emerged over time as judges decided legal controversies.

EXHIBIT 1–2 • Equitable Maxims

1. *Whoever seeks equity must do equity.* (Anyone who wishes to be treated fairly must treat others fairly.)
2. *Where there is equal equity, the law must prevail.* (The law will determine the outcome of a controversy in which the merits of both sides are equal.)
3. *One seeking the aid of an equity court must come to the court with clean hands.* (Plaintiffs must have acted fairly and honestly.)
4. *Equity will not suffer a wrong to be without a remedy.* (Equitable relief will be awarded when there is a right to relief and there is no adequate remedy at law.)
5. *Equity regards substance rather than form.* (Equity is more concerned with fairness and justice than with legal technicalities.)
6. *Equity aids the vigilant, not those who rest on their rights.* (Equity will not help those who neglect their rights for an unreasonable period of time.)

EXHIBIT 1–3 • Procedural Differences between an Action at Law and an Action in Equity

Procedure	Action at Law	Action in Equity
Initiation of lawsuit	By filing a complaint	By filing a petition
Parties	Plaintiff and defendant	Petitioner and respondent
Decision	By jury or judge	By judge (no jury)
Result	Judgment	Decree
Remedy	Monetary damages	Injunction, specific performance, or rescission

Case Precedents and Case Reporters When possible, judges attempted to be consistent and to base their decisions on the principles suggested by earlier cases. They sought to decide similar cases in a similar way and considered new cases with care because they knew that their decisions would make new law. Each interpretation became part of the law on the subject and served as a legal **precedent**—that is, a decision that furnished an example or authority for deciding subsequent cases involving similar legal principles or facts.

In the early years of the common law, there was no single place or publication where court opinions, or written decisions, could be found. By the early fourteenth century, portions of the most important decisions of each year were being gathered together and recorded in *Year Books,* which became useful references for lawyers and judges. In the sixteenth century, the *Year Books* were discontinued, and other forms of case publication became available. Today, cases are published, or "reported," in volumes called **reporters,** or *reports.* We describe today's case reporting system in detail later in this chapter.

Stare Decisis* and the Common Law Tradition** The practice of deciding new cases with reference to former decisions, or precedents, became a cornerstone of the English and American judicial systems. The practice formed a doctrine known as ***stare decisis[3] (a Latin phrase meaning "to stand on decided cases").

Under this doctrine, judges are obligated to follow the precedents established within their jurisdictions. The term *jurisdiction* refers to an area in which a court or courts have the power to apply the law—see Chapter 2. Once a court has set forth a principle of law as being applicable to a certain set of facts, that court and courts of lower rank (within the same jurisdiction) must adhere to that principle and apply it in future cases involving similar fact patterns. Thus, *stare decisis* has two aspects: first, that decisions made by a higher court are binding on lower courts; and second, that a court should not overturn its own precedents unless there is a compelling reason to do so.

The doctrine of *stare decisis* helps the courts to be more efficient because if other courts have carefully analyzed a similar case, their legal reasoning and opinions can serve as guides. *Stare decisis* also makes the law more stable and predictable. If the law on a given subject is well settled, someone bringing a case to court can usually rely on the court to make a decision based on what the law has been in the past.

A Typical Scenario To illustrate how the doctrine of *stare decisis* works, consider an example. Suppose that the lower state courts in Georgia have reached conflicting conclusions on whether drivers are liable for accidents they cause while merging into freeway traffic. Some courts have held drivers liable even though the drivers looked and did not see any oncoming traffic and even though witnesses (passengers in their cars) testified to that effect. To settle the law on this issue, the Georgia Supreme Court decides to review a case involving this fact pattern. The court rules that, in such a situation, the driver who is merging into traffic is liable for any accidents caused by that driver's failure to yield to freeway traffic—even if that driver looked carefully and did not see an approaching vehicle.

The Georgia Supreme Court's decision on this matter is a **binding authority**—a case precedent, statute, or other source of law that a court must follow when

3. Pronounced *ster*-ay dih-*si*-ses.

deciding a case. In other words, the Georgia Supreme Court's decision will influence the outcome of all future cases on this issue brought before the Georgia state courts. Similarly, a decision on a given question by the United States Supreme Court (the nation's highest court), no matter how old, is binding on all courts.

Departures from Precedent Although courts are obligated to follow precedents, sometimes a court will depart from the rule of precedent if it decides that the precedent should no longer be followed. If a court decides that a ruling precedent is simply incorrect or that technological or social changes have rendered the precedent inapplicable, the court might rule contrary to the precedent. Cases that overturn precedent often receive a great deal of publicity.

Note that judges do have some flexibility in applying precedents. For example, a lower court may avoid applying a precedent set by a higher court in its jurisdiction by distinguishing the two cases based on their facts. When this happens, the lower court's ruling stands unless it is appealed to a higher court and that court overturns the decision.

When There Is No Precedent Occasionally, the courts must decide cases for which no precedents exist, called *cases of first impression.* For example, as you will read throughout this text, the extensive use of the Internet has presented many new and challenging issues for the courts to decide. In deciding cases of first impression, courts often look at *persuasive authorities* (precedents from other jurisdictions) for guidance. A court may also consider a number of factors, including legal principles and policies underlying previous court decisions or existing statutes, fairness, social values and customs, **public policy** (governmental policy based on widely held societal values), and data and concepts drawn from the social sciences. Which of these sources is chosen or receives the greatest emphasis depends on the nature of the case being considered and the particular judge or judges hearing the case.

Stare Decisis and Legal Reasoning

Legal reasoning is the reasoning process used by judges in deciding what law applies to a given dispute and then applying that law to the specific facts or circumstances of the case. Through the use of legal reasoning, judges harmonize their decisions with those that have been made before, as the doctrine of *stare decisis* requires.

Students of business law and the legal environment also engage in legal reasoning. For example, you may be asked to provide answers for some of the case problems that appear at the end of every chapter in this text. Each problem describes the facts of a particular dispute and the legal question at issue. If you are assigned a case problem, you will be asked to determine how a court would answer that question, and why. In other words, you will need to give legal reasons for whatever conclusion you reach.[4] We look here at the basic steps involved in legal reasoning and then describe some forms of reasoning commonly used by the courts in making their decisions.

Basic Steps in Legal Reasoning At times, the legal arguments set forth in court opinions are relatively simple and brief. At other times, the arguments are complex and lengthy. Regardless of the length of a legal argument, however, the basic steps of the legal reasoning process remain the same. These steps, which you also can follow when analyzing cases and case problems, form what is commonly referred to as the *IRAC method* of legal reasoning. IRAC is an acronym formed from the first letters of the following words: Issue, Rule, Application, and Conclusion. To apply the IRAC method, you would ask the following questions:

1. *What are the key facts and issues?* For example, a plaintiff comes before the court claiming *assault* (a wrongful and intentional action in which one person makes another fearful of immediate physical harm—part of a class of actions called *torts*). The plaintiff claims that the defendant threatened her while she was sleeping. Although the plaintiff was unaware that she was being threatened, her roommate heard the defendant make the threat. The legal issue, or question, raised by these facts is whether the defendant's actions constitute the tort of assault, given that the plaintiff was not aware of those actions at the time they occurred.
2. *What rules of law apply to the case?* A rule of law may be a rule stated by the courts in previous decisions, a state or federal statute, or a state or federal administrative agency regulation. In our hypothetical case, the plaintiff **alleges** (claims) that the defendant committed a tort. Therefore, the applicable law is the common law of torts—specifically, tort law governing assault (see Chapter 6 for more

4. See Appendix A for further instructions on how to analyze case problems.

detail on intentional torts). Case precedents involving similar facts and issues thus would be relevant. Often, more than one rule of law will be applicable to a case.

3. *How do the rules of law apply to the particular facts and circumstances of this case?* This step is often the most difficult because each case presents a unique set of facts, circumstances, and parties. Although cases may be similar, no two cases are ever identical in all respects. Normally, judges (and lawyers and law students) try to find **cases on point**—previously decided cases that are as similar as possible to the one under consideration. (Because of the difficulty—and importance—of this step in the legal reasoning process, we discuss it in more detail in the next subsection.)
4. *What conclusion should be drawn?* This step normally presents few problems. Usually, the conclusion is evident if the previous three steps have been followed carefully.

Forms of Legal Reasoning Judges use many types of reasoning when following the third step of the legal reasoning process—applying the law to the facts of a particular case. Three common forms of reasoning are deductive reasoning, linear reasoning, and reasoning by analogy.

Deductive Reasoning. Deductive reasoning is sometimes called *syllogistic reasoning* because it employs a **syllogism**—a logical relationship involving a major premise, a minor premise, and a conclusion. Consider the hypothetical case presented earlier, in which the plaintiff alleged that the defendant committed assault by threatening her while she was sleeping. The judge might point out that "under the common law of torts, an individual must be *aware* of a threat of danger for the threat to constitute assault" (major premise); "the plaintiff in this case was unaware of the threat at the time it occurred" (minor premise); and "therefore, the circumstances do not amount to an assault" (conclusion).

Linear Reasoning. A second important form of legal reasoning that is commonly employed might be thought of as "linear" reasoning because it proceeds from one point to another, with the final point being the conclusion. A comparison will help make this form of reasoning clear. Imagine a knotted rope, with each knot tying together separate pieces of rope to form a tightly knotted length. As a whole, the rope represents a linear progression of thought logically connecting various points, with the last point, or knot, representing the conclusion. Suppose that a tenant in an apartment building sues the landlord for damages for an injury resulting from an allegedly inadequately lit stairway. The court may engage in a reasoning process involving the following "pieces of rope":

1. The landlord, who was on the premises the evening the injury occurred, testifies that none of the other nine tenants who used the stairway that night complained about the lights.
2. The fact that none of the tenants complained is the same as if they had said the lighting was sufficient.
3. That there were no complaints does not prove that the lighting was sufficient but does prove that the landlord had no reason to believe that it was not.
4. The landlord's belief was reasonable because no one complained.
5. Therefore, the landlord acted reasonably and was not negligent with respect to the lighting in the stairway.

From this reasoning, the court concludes that the tenant is not entitled to compensation on the basis of the stairway's allegedly insufficient lighting.

Reasoning by Analogy. Another important type of reasoning that judges use in deciding cases is reasoning by *analogy*. To reason by **analogy** is to compare the facts in the case at hand to the facts in other cases and, to the extent that the patterns are similar, to apply the same rule of law to the present case. To the extent that the facts are unique, or "distinguishable," different rules may apply. For example, in case A, the court held that a driver who crossed a highway's center line was negligent. Case B involves a driver who crosses the line to avoid hitting a child. In determining whether case A's rule applies in case B, a judge would consider what the reasons were for the decision in A and whether B is sufficiently similar for those reasons to apply. If the judge holds that B's driver is not liable, that judge must indicate why case A's rule is not relevant to the facts presented in case B.

There Is No One "Right" Answer

Many persons believe that there is one "right" answer to every legal question. In most situations involving a legal controversy, however, there is no single correct result. Good arguments can often be made to support either side of a legal controversy. Quite often, a case does not involve a "good" person suing a "bad" person. In many cases, both parties have acted in good faith in some measure or in bad faith to some degree.

Additionally, each judge has her or his own personal beliefs and philosophy, which shape, at least to some extent, the process of legal reasoning. This means that the outcome of a particular lawsuit before a court cannot be predicted with absolute certainty. In fact, in some cases, even though the weight of the law would seem to favor one party's position, judges, through creative legal reasoning, have found ways to rule in favor of the other party in the interests of preventing injustice. Legal reasoning and other aspects of the common law tradition are reviewed in *Concept Summary 1.3*.

SECTION 5 The Common Law Today

Today, the common law derived from judicial decisions continues to be applied throughout the United States. Common law doctrines and principles govern all areas *not* covered by statutory or administrative law. In a dispute concerning a particular employment practice, for example, if a statute regulates that practice, the statute will apply rather than the common law doctrine that applied prior to the enactment of the statute.

The Continuing Importance of the Common Law

Because the body of statutory law has expanded greatly since the beginning of this nation, thus narrowing the applicability of common law doctrines, it might seem that the common law has dwindled in importance. This is not true, however. Even in areas governed by statutory law, there is a significant interplay between statutory law and the common law. For example, many statutes essentially codify existing common law rules, and regulations issued by various administrative agencies usually are based, at least in part, on common law principles. Additionally, the courts, in interpreting statutory law, often rely on the

CONCEPT SUMMARY 1.3
The Common Law Tradition

Aspect	Description
Origins of the Common Law	The American legal system is based on the common law tradition, which originated in medieval England. Following the conquest of England in 1066 by William the Conqueror, king's courts were established throughout England, and the common law was developed in these courts.
Legal and Equitable Remedies	The distinction between remedies at law (money or items of value, such as land) and remedies in equity (including specific performance, injunction, and rescission of a contractual obligation) originated in the early English courts of law and courts of equity, respectively.
Case Precedents and the Doctrine of *Stare Decisis*	In the king's courts, judges attempted to make their decisions consistent with previous decisions, called precedents. This practice gave rise to the doctrine of *stare decisis*. This doctrine, which became a cornerstone of the common law tradition, obligates judges to abide by precedents established in their jurisdictions.
Stare Decisis and Legal Reasoning	Legal reasoning refers to the reasoning process used by judges in applying the law to the facts and issues of specific cases. Legal reasoning involves becoming familiar with the key facts of a case, identifying the relevant legal rules, applying those rules to the facts, and drawing a conclusion. In applying the legal rules to the facts of a case, judges may use deductive reasoning, linear reasoning, or reasoning by analogy.

common law as a guide to what the legislators intended.

Furthermore, how the courts interpret a particular statute determines how that statute will be applied. If you wanted to learn about the coverage and applicability of a particular statute, for example, you would necessarily have to locate the statute and study it. You would also need to see how the courts in your jurisdiction have interpreted and applied the statute. In other words, you would have to learn what precedents have been established in your jurisdiction with respect to that statute. Often, the applicability of a newly enacted statute does not become clear until a body of case law develops to clarify how, when, and to whom the statute applies.

Restatements of the Law

The American Law Institute (ALI) has drafted and published compilations of the common law called *Restatements of the Law*, which generally summarize the common law rules followed by most states. There are *Restatements of the Law* in the areas of contracts, torts, agency, trusts, property, restitution, security, judgments, and conflict of laws. The *Restatements*, like other secondary sources of law, do not in themselves have the force of law, but they are an important source of legal analysis and opinion on which judges often rely in making their decisions.

Many of the *Restatements* are now in their second, third, or fourth editions. We refer to the *Restatements* frequently in subsequent chapters of this text, indicating in parentheses the edition to which we are referring. For example, we refer to the second edition of the *Restatement of the Law of Contracts* as simply the *Restatement (Second) of Contracts*.

SECTION 6 Classifications of Law

The substantial body of the law may be broken down according to several classification systems. For example, one classification system divides law into substantive law and procedural law. **Substantive law** consists of all laws that define, describe, regulate, and create legal rights and obligations. **Procedural law** consists of all laws that delineate the methods of enforcing the rights established by substantive law. Other classification systems divide law into federal law and state law, private law (dealing with relationships between private entities) and public law (addressing the relationship between persons and their governments), and national law and international law. Here we look at still another classification system, which divides law into civil law and criminal law, as well as at what is meant by the term *cyberlaw*.

Civil Law and Criminal Law

Civil law spells out the rights and duties that exist between persons and between persons and their governments, as well as the relief available when a person's rights are violated. Typically, in a civil case, a private party sues another private party (although the government can also sue a party for a civil law violation) to make that other party comply with a duty or pay for the damage caused by failure to comply with a duty. Much of the law that we discuss in this text is civil law. Contract law, for example, covered in Chapters 10 through 19, is civil law. The whole body of tort law (see Chapters 6 and 7) is also civil law.

Criminal law, in contrast, is concerned with wrongs committed *against the public as a whole.* Criminal acts are defined and prohibited by local, state, or federal government statutes. Criminal defendants are thus prosecuted by public officials, such as a district attorney (D.A.), on behalf of the state, not by their victims or other private parties. (See Chapter 9 for a further discussion of the distinction between civil law and criminal law.)

Cyberlaw

As mentioned, the use of the Internet to conduct business transactions has led to new types of legal issues. In response, courts have had to adapt traditional laws to situations that are unique to our age. Additionally, legislatures have created laws to deal specifically with such issues. Frequently, people use the term **cyberlaw** to refer to the emerging body of law that governs transactions conducted via the Internet. Cyberlaw is not really a classification of law, nor is it a new *type* of law. Rather, it is an informal term used to describe traditional legal principles that have been modified and adapted to fit situations that are unique to the online world. Of course, in some areas new statutes have been enacted, at both the federal and the state levels, to cover specific types of problems stemming from online communications. Throughout this book, you will read how the law in a given area is evolving to govern specific legal issues that arise in the online context.

SECTION 7

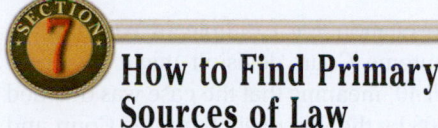

How to Find Primary Sources of Law

This text includes numerous citations to primary sources of law—federal and state statutes, the U.S. Constitution and state constitutions, regulations issued by administrative agencies, and court cases. (A **citation** is a reference to a publication in which a legal authority—such as a statute or a court decision or other source—can be found.) In this section, we explain how you can use citations to find primary sources of law. Note that in addition to the primary sources being published in sets of books as described next, most federal and state laws and case decisions are also available online.

Finding Statutory and Administrative Law

When Congress passes laws, they are collected in a publication titled *United States Statutes at Large*. When state legislatures pass laws, they are collected in similar state publications. Most frequently, however, laws are referred to in their codified form—that is, the form in which they appear in the federal and state codes. In these codes, laws are compiled by subject.

United States Code The *United States Code* (U.S.C.) arranges all existing federal laws by broad subject. Each of the fifty subjects is given a title and a title number. For example, laws relating to commerce and trade are collected in Title 15, "Commerce and Trade." Titles are subdivided by sections. A citation to the U.S.C. includes both title and section numbers. Thus, a reference to "15 U.S.C. Section 1" means that the statute can be found in Section 1 of Title 15. ("Section" may also be designated by the symbol §, and "Sections," by §§.) In addition to the print publication of the U.S.C., the federal government also provides a searchable online database of the *United States Code* at **www.gpoaccess.gov/uscode/index.html**.

Commercial publications of federal laws and regulations are also available. For example, West Group publishes the *United States Code Annotated* (U.S.C.A.). The U.S.C.A. contains the official text of the U.S.C., plus notes (annotations) on court decisions that interpret and apply specific sections of the statutes. The U.S.C.A. also includes additional research aids, such as cross-references to related statutes, historical notes, and library references. A citation to the U.S.C.A. is similar to a citation to the U.S.C.: "15 U.S.C.A. Section 1."

State Codes State codes follow the U.S.C. pattern of arranging law by subject. They may be called codes, revisions, compilations, consolidations, general statutes, or statutes, depending on the preferences of the states. In some codes, subjects are designated by number. In others, they are designated by name. For example, "13 Pennsylvania Consolidated Statutes Section 1101" means that the statute can be found in Title 13, Section 1101, of the Pennsylvania code. "California Commercial Code Section 1101" means that the statute can be found under the subject heading "Commercial Code" of the California code in Section 1101. Abbreviations are often used. For example, "13 Pennsylvania Consolidated Statutes Section 1101" is abbreviated "13 Pa. C.S. § 1101," and "California Commercial Code Section 1101" is abbreviated "Cal. Com. Code § 1101."

Administrative Rules Rules and regulations adopted by federal administrative agencies are initially published in the *Federal Register*, a daily publication of the U.S. government. Later, they are incorporated into the *Code of Federal Regulations* (C.F.R.). Like the U.S.C., the C.F.R. is divided into fifty titles. Rules within each title are assigned section numbers. A full citation to the C.F.R. includes title and section numbers. For example, a reference to "17 C.F.R. Section 230.504" means that the rule can be found in Section 230.504 of Title 17.

Finding Case Law

Before discussing the case reporting system, we need to look briefly at the court system (which will be discussed in detail in Chapter 2). There are two types of courts in the United States, federal courts and state courts. Both the federal and the state court systems consist of several levels, or tiers, of courts. *Trial courts*, in which evidence is presented and testimony given, are on the bottom tier (which also includes lower courts that handle specialized issues). Decisions from a trial court can be appealed to a higher court, which commonly is an intermediate *court of appeals*, or an *appellate court*. Decisions from these intermediate courts of appeals may be appealed to an even higher court, such as a state supreme court or the United States Supreme Court.

State Court Decisions Most state trial court decisions are not published in books (except in New

York and a few other states, which publish selected trial court opinions). Decisions from state trial courts are typically filed in the office of the clerk of the court, where the decisions are available for public inspection. Written decisions of the appellate, or reviewing, courts, however, are published and distributed (both in print and via the Internet). As you will note, most of the state court cases presented in this book are from state appellate courts. The reported appellate decisions are published in volumes called *reports* or *reporters*, which are numbered consecutively. State appellate court decisions are found in the state reporters of that particular state. Official reports are volumes that are published by the state, whereas unofficial reports are privately published.

Regional Reporters. State court opinions appear in regional units of the National Reporter System, published by West Group. Most lawyers and libraries have the West reporters because they report cases more quickly, and are distributed more widely, than the state-published reporters. In fact, many states have eliminated their own reporters in favor of West's National Reporter System. The National Reporter System divides the states into the following geographic areas: *Atlantic* (A. or A.2d), *North Eastern* (N.E. or N.E.2d), *North Western* (N.W. or N.W.2d), *Pacific* (P., P.2d, or P.3d), *South Eastern* (S.E. or S.E.2d), *South Western* (S.W., S.W.2d, or S.W.3d), and *Southern* (So. or So.2d). (The *2d* and *3d* in the preceding abbreviations refer to *Second Series* and *Third Series*, respectively.) The states included in each of these regional divisions are indicated in Exhibit 1–4, which illustrates West's National Reporter System.

Case Citations. After appellate decisions have been published, they are normally referred to (cited) by the name of the case; the volume, name, and page number of the state's official reporter (if different from West's National Reporter System); the volume, name, and page number of the National Reporter; and the volume, name, and page number of any other selected reporter. (Citing a reporter by volume number, name, and page number, in that order, is common to all citations; often, as in this book, the year the decision was issued will be included in parentheses, just after the citations to reporters.) When more than one reporter is cited for the same case, each reference is called a *parallel citation.*

Note that some states have adopted a "public domain citation system" that uses a somewhat different format for the citation. For example, in Wisconsin, a Wisconsin Supreme Court decision might be designated "2008 WI 40," meaning that the case was decided in the year 2008 by the Wisconsin Supreme Court and was the fortieth decision issued by that court during that year. Parallel citations to the *Wisconsin Reports* and West's *North Western Reporter* are still included after the public domain citation.

Consider the following case citation: *Ramirez v. Health Net of Northeast, Inc.*, 285 Conn. 1, 938 A.2d 576 (2008). We see that the opinion in this case can be found in Volume 285 of the official *Connecticut Reports,* which reports only the decisions of the Supreme Court of Connecticut, on page 1. The parallel citation is to Volume 938 of the *Atlantic Reporter, Second Series,* page 576. In presenting opinions in this text, in addition to the reporter, we give the name of the court hearing the case and the year of the court's decision. Sample citations to state court decisions are explained in Exhibit 1–5 on pages 18–20.

Federal Court Decisions Federal district (trial) court decisions are published unofficially in West's *Federal Supplement* (F.Supp. or F.Supp.2d), and opinions from the circuit courts of appeals (reviewing courts) are reported unofficially in West's *Federal Reporter* (F., F.2d, or F.3d). Cases concerning federal bankruptcy law are published unofficially in West's *Bankruptcy Reporter* (Bankr. or B.R.).

The official edition of the United States Supreme Court decisions is the *United States Reports* (U.S.), which is published by the federal government. Unofficial editions of Supreme Court cases include West's *Supreme Court Reporter* (S.Ct.) and the *Lawyers' Edition of the Supreme Court Reports* (L.Ed. or L.Ed.2d). Sample citations for federal court decisions are also listed and explained in Exhibit 1–5.

Unpublished Opinions Many court opinions that are not yet published or that are not intended for publication can be accessed through Westlaw® (abbreviated in citations as "WL"), an online legal database maintained by West Group. When no citation to a published reporter is available for cases cited in this text, we give the WL citation (see Exhibit 1–5 for an example). Can a court consider unpublished decisions as persuasive precedent? See this chapter's *Insight into E-Commerce* feature on pages 22 and 23 for a discussion of this issue.

EXHIBIT 1–4 • West's National Reporter System—Regional/Federal

Regional Reporters	Coverage Beginning	Coverage
Atlantic Reporter (A. or A.2d)	1885	Connecticut, Delaware, District of Columbia, Maine, Maryland, New Hampshire, New Jersey, Pennsylvania, Rhode Island, and Vermont.
North Eastern Reporter (N.E. or N.E.2d)	1885	Illinois, Indiana, Massachusetts, New York, and Ohio.
North Western Reporter (N.W. or N.W.2d)	1879	Iowa, Michigan, Minnesota, Nebraska, North Dakota, South Dakota, and Wisconsin.
Pacific Reporter (P., P.2d, or P.3d)	1883	Alaska, Arizona, California, Colorado, Hawaii, Idaho, Kansas, Montana, Nevada, New Mexico, Oklahoma, Oregon, Utah, Washington, and Wyoming.
South Eastern Reporter (S.E. or S.E.2d)	1887	Georgia, North Carolina, South Carolina, Virginia, and West Virginia.
South Western Reporter (S.W., S.W.2d, or S.W.3d)	1886	Arkansas, Kentucky, Missouri, Tennessee, and Texas.
Southern Reporter (So. or So.2d)	1887	Alabama, Florida, Louisiana, and Mississippi.
Federal Reporters		
Federal Reporter (F., F.2d, or F.3d)	1880	U.S. Circuit Courts from 1880 to 1912; U.S. Commerce Court from 1911 to 1913; U.S. District Courts from 1880 to 1932; U.S. Court of Claims (now called U.S. Court of Federal Claims) from 1929 to 1932 and since 1960; U.S. Courts of Appeals since 1891; U.S. Court of Customs and Patent Appeals since 1929; U.S. Emergency Court of Appeals since 1943.
Federal Supplement (F.Supp. or F.Supp.2d)	1932	U.S. Court of Claims from 1932 to 1960; U.S. District Courts since 1932; U.S. Customs Court since 1956.
Federal Rules Decisions (F.R.D.)	1939	U.S. District Courts involving the Federal Rules of Civil Procedure since 1939 and Federal Rules of Criminal Procedure since 1946.
Supreme Court Reporter (S.Ct.)	1882	United States Supreme Court since the October term of 1882.
Bankruptcy Reporter (Bankr.)	1980	Bankruptcy decisions of U.S. Bankruptcy Courts, U.S. District Courts, U.S. Courts of Appeals, and the United States Supreme Court.
Military Justice Reporter (M.J.)	1978	U.S. Court of Military Appeals and Courts of Military Review for the Army, Navy, Air Force, and Coast Guard.

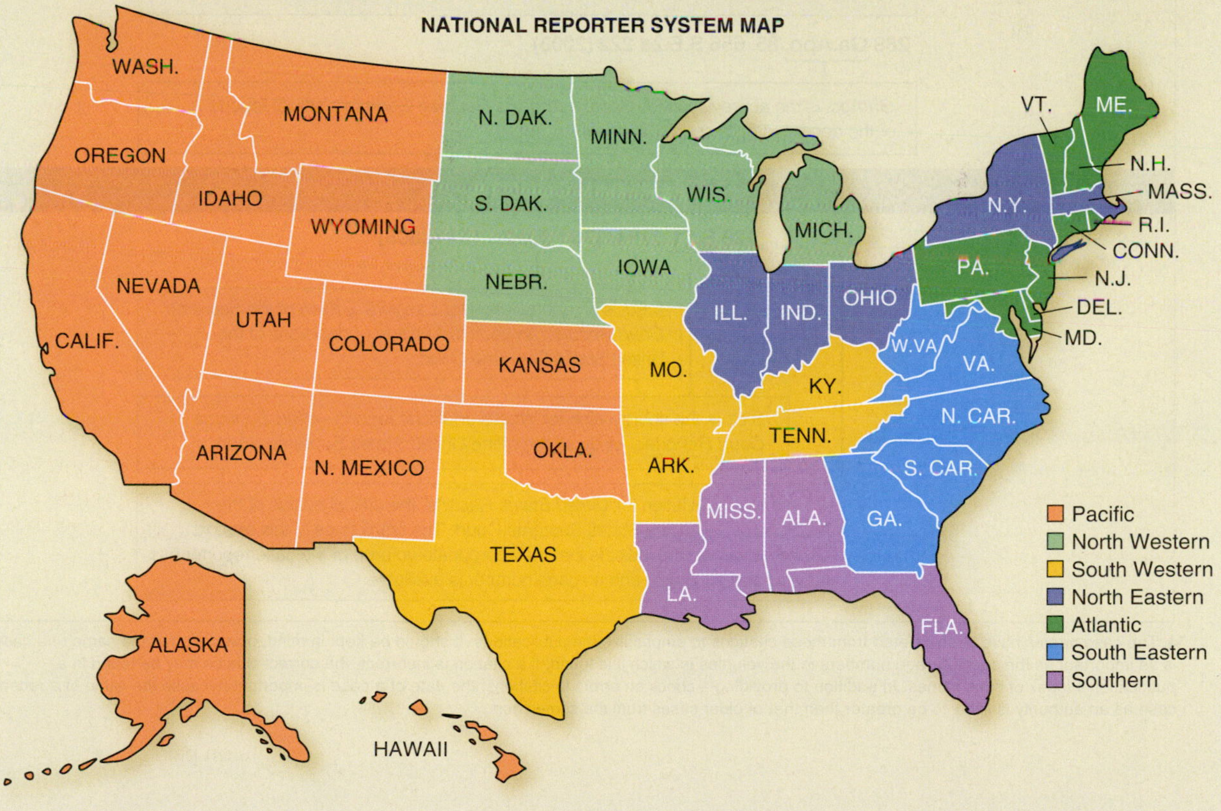

EXHIBIT 1–5 • How to Read Citations

STATE COURTS

274 Neb. 796, 743 N.W.2d 632 (2008)[a]

N.W. is the abbreviation for West's publication of state court decisions rendered in the *North Western Reporter* of the National Reporter System. *2d* indicates that this case was included in the *Second Series* of that reporter. The number 743 refers to the volume number of the reporter; the number 632 refers to the page in that volume on which this case begins.

Neb. is an abbreviation for *Nebraska Reports,* Nebraska's official reports of the decisions of its highest court, the Nebraska Supreme Court.

159 Cal.App.4th 1114, 72 Cal.Rptr.3d 81 (2008)

Cal.Rptr. is the abbreviation for West's unofficial reports—titled *California Reporter*—of the decisions of California courts.

8 N.Y.3d 422, 867 N.E.2d 381, 835 N.Y.S.2d 530 (2007)

N.Y.S. is the abbreviation for West's unofficial reports—titled *New York Supplement*—of the decisions of New York courts.

N.Y. is the abbreviation for *New York Reports,* New York's official reports of the decisions of its court of appeals. The New York Court of Appeals is the state's highest court, analogous to other states' supreme courts. In New York, a supreme court is a trial court.

289 Ga.App. 85, 656 S.E.2d 222 (2008)

Ga.App. is the abbreviation for *Georgia Appeals Reports,* Georgia's official reports of the decisions of its court of appeals.

FEDERAL COURTS

___ U.S. ___, 128 S.Ct. 1184, 170 L.Ed.2d 151 (2008)

L.Ed. is an abbreviation for *Lawyers' Edition of the Supreme Court Reports,* an unofficial edition of decisions of the United States Supreme Court.

S.Ct. is the abbreviation for West's unofficial reports—titled *Supreme Court Reporter*—of decisions of the United States Supreme Court.

U.S. is the abbreviation for *United States Reports,* the official edition of the decisions of the United States Supreme Court. The blank lines in this citation (or any other citation) indicate that the appropriate volume of the case reporter has not yet been published and no page number is available.

a. The case names have been deleted from these citations to emphasize the publications. It should be kept in mind, however, that the name of a case is as important as the specific page numbers in the volumes in which it is found. If a citation is incorrect, the correct citation may be found in a publication's index of case names. In addition to providing a check on errors in citations, the date of a case is important because the value of a recent case as an authority is likely to be greater than that of older cases from the same court.

EXHIBIT 1–5 • How to Read Citations—Continued

FEDERAL COURTS (Continued)

512 F.3d 582 (9th Cir. 2008)

9th Cir. is an abbreviation denoting that this case was decided in the U.S. Court of Appeals for the Ninth Circuit.

533 F.Supp.2d 740 (W.D.Mich. 2008)

W.D.Mich. is an abbreviation indicating that the U.S. District Court for the Western District of Michigan decided this case.

ENGLISH COURTS

9 Exch. 341, 156 Eng.Rep. 145 (1854)

Eng.Rep. is an abbreviation for *English Reports, Full Reprint*, a series of reports containing selected decisions made in English courts between 1378 and 1865.

Exch. is an abbreviation for *English Exchequer Reports*, which includes the original reports of cases decided in England's Court of Exchequer.

STATUTORY AND OTHER CITATIONS

18 U.S.C. Section 1961(1)(A)

U.S.C. denotes *United States Code*, the codification of *United States Statutes at Large*. The number 18 refers to the statute's U.S.C. title number and 1961 to its section number within that title. The number 1 in parentheses refers to a subsection within the section, and the letter A in parentheses to a subdivision within the subsection.

UCC 2–206(1)(b)

UCC is an abbreviation for *Uniform Commercial Code*. The first number 2 is a reference to an article of the UCC, and 206 to a section within that article. The number 1 in parentheses refers to a subsection within the section, and the letter b in parentheses to a subdivision within the subsection.

***Restatement (Second) of Torts*, Section 568**

Restatement (Second) of Torts refers to the second edition of the American Law Institute's *Restatement of the Law of Torts*. The number 568 refers to a specific section.

17 C.F.R. Section 230.505

C.F.R. is an abbreviation for *Code of Federal Regulations*, a compilation of federal administrative regulations. The number 17 designates the regulation's title number, and 230.505 designates a specific section within that title.

EXHIBIT CONTINUES

EXHIBIT 1–5 • How to Read Citations—Continued

WESTLAW® CITATIONS[b]

2008 WL 427478

WL is an abbreviation for Westlaw. The number 2008 is the year of the document that can be found with this citation in the Westlaw database. The number 427478 is a number assigned to a specific document. A higher number indicates that a document was added to the Westlaw database later in the year.

UNIFORM RESOURCE LOCATORS (URLs)

http://www.westlaw.com[c]

The suffix *com* is the top level domain (TLD) for this Web site. The TLD *com* is an abbreviation for "commercial," which usually means that a for-profit entity hosts (maintains or supports) this Web site.

westlaw is the host name—the part of the domain name selected by the organization that registered the name. In this case, West Group registered the name. This Internet site is the Westlaw database on the Web.

www is an abbreviation for "World Wide Web." The Web is a system of Internet servers that support documents formatted in *HTML* (hypertext markup language). HTML supports links to text, graphics, and audio and video files.

http://www.uscourts.gov

This is "The Federal Judiciary Home Page." The host is the Administrative Office of the U.S. Courts. The TLD *gov* is an abbreviation for "government." This Web site includes information and links from, and about, the federal courts.

http://www.law.cornell.edu/index.html

This part of a URL points to a Web page or file at a specific location within the host's domain. This page is a menu with links to documents within the domain and to other Internet resources.

This is the host name for a Web site that contains the Internet publications of the Legal Information Institute (LII), which is a part of Cornell Law School. The LII site includes a variety of legal materials and links to other legal resources on the Internet. The TLD *edu* is an abbreviation for "educational institution" (a school or a university).

http://www.ipl.org/div/news

This part of the Web site points to a static *news* page at this Web site, which provides links to online newspapers from around the world.

div is an abbreviation for "division," which is the way that the Internet Public Library tags the content on its Web site as relating to a specific topic.

ipl is an abbreviation for "Internet Public Library," which is an online service that provides reference resources and links to other information services on the Web. The IPL is supported chiefly by the School of Information at the University of Michigan. The TLD *org* is an abbreviation for "organization" (normally nonprofit).

b. Many court decisions that are not yet published or that are not intended for publication can be accessed through Westlaw, an online legal database.

c. The basic form for a URL is "service://hostname/path." The Internet service for all of the URLs in this text is *http* (hypertext transfer protocol). Because most Web browsers add this prefix automatically when a user enters a host name or a hostname/path, we have omitted the http:// from the URLs listed in this text.

Old Case Law On a few occasions, this text cites opinions from old, classic cases dating to the nineteenth century or earlier; some of these are from the English courts. The citations to these cases may not conform to the descriptions given above because the reporters in which they were published were often known by the names of the persons who compiled the reporters and have since been replaced.

SECTION 8

How to Read and Understand Case Law

The decisions made by the courts establish the boundaries of the law as it applies to virtually all business relationships. It thus is essential that businesspersons know how to read and understand case law. The cases that we present in this text have been condensed from the full text of the courts' opinions and are presented in a special format. In each case, we have summarized the background and facts, as well as the court's decision and rationale, in our own words and have included only selected portions of the court's opinion. For those who wish to review court cases as part of research projects or to gain additional legal information, the following sections will provide useful insights into how to read and understand case law.

Case Titles

The title of a case, such as *Adams v. Jones,* indicates the names of the parties to the lawsuit. The *v.* in the case title stands for *versus,* which means "against." In the trial court, Adams was the plaintiff—the person who filed the suit. Jones was the defendant. If the case is appealed, however, the appellate court will sometimes place the name of the party appealing the decision first, so the case may be called *Jones v. Adams* if Jones is appealing. Because some appellate courts retain the trial court order of names, it is often impossible to distinguish the plaintiff from the defendant in the title of a reported appellate court decision. You must carefully read the facts of each case to identify the parties. Otherwise, the discussion by the appellate court may be difficult to understand.

Terminology

The following terms, phrases, and abbreviations are frequently encountered in court opinions and legal publications. Because it is important to understand what is meant by these terms, phrases, and abbreviations, we define and discuss them here.

Parties to Lawsuits As mentioned previously, the party initiating a lawsuit is referred to as the *plaintiff* or *petitioner,* depending on the nature of the action, and the party against whom a lawsuit is brought is the *defendant* or *respondent*. Lawsuits frequently involve more than one plaintiff and/or defendant. When a case is appealed from the original court or jurisdiction to another court or jurisdiction, the party appealing the case is called the **appellant.** The **appellee** is the party against whom the appeal is taken. (In some appellate courts, the party appealing a case is referred to as the *petitioner,* and the party against whom the suit is brought or appealed is called the *respondent.*)

Judges and Justices The terms *judge* and *justice* are usually synonymous and represent two designations given to judges in various courts. All members of the United States Supreme Court, for example, are referred to as justices, and justice is the formal title often given to judges of appellate courts, although this is not always the case. In New York, a *justice* is a judge of the trial court (which is called the Supreme Court), and a member of the Court of Appeals (the state's highest court) is called a *judge*. The term *justice* is commonly abbreviated to J., and *justices,* to JJ. A Supreme Court case might refer to Justice Alito as Alito, J., or to Chief Justice Roberts as Roberts, C.J.

Decisions and Opinions Most decisions reached by reviewing, or appellate, courts are explained in written **opinions.** The opinion contains the court's reasons for its decision, the rules of law that apply, and the judgment.

Unanimous, Concurring, and Dissenting Opinions. When all judges or justices unanimously agree on an opinion, the opinion is written for the entire court and can be deemed a *unanimous opinion.* When there is not a unanimous opinion, a *majority opinion* is written; the majority opinion outlines the

INSIGHT INTO E-COMMERCE
How the Internet Is Expanding Precedent

The notion that courts should rely on precedents to decide the outcome of similar cases has long been a cornerstone of U.S. law. Nevertheless, the availability of "unpublished opinions" over the Internet is changing what the law considers to be precedent. An *unpublished opinion* is a decision made by an appellate court that is not intended for publication in a reporter (the bound books that contain court opinions).[a] Courts traditionally have not considered unpublished opinions to be "precedent," binding or persuasive, and attorneys were often not allowed to refer to these decisions in their arguments.

An Increasing Number of Decisions Are Not Published in Case Reporters but Are Available Online

The number of court decisions not published in printed books has risen dramatically in recent years. By some estimates, nearly 80 percent of the decisions of the federal appellate courts are unpublished. The number is equally high in some state court systems. California's intermediate appellate courts, for example, publish only about 7 percent of their decisions.

Even though certain decisions are not intended for publication, they are posted ("published") almost immediately on online legal databases, such as Westlaw and Lexis. With the proliferation of free legal databases and court Web sites, the general public also has almost instant access to the unpublished decisions of most courts. This situation has caused a substantial amount of debate over whether unpublished opinions should be given the same precedential effect as published opinions.

Should Unpublished Decisions Establish Precedent?

Prior to the Internet, one might have been able to justify not considering unpublished decisions to be precedent on the grounds of fairness. How could courts and lawyers be expected to consider the reasoning in unpublished decisions if they were not printed in the case reporters? Now that opinions are so readily available on the Web, however, this justification is no longer valid. Moreover, it now seems unfair not to consider these decisions as

a. Recently decided cases that are not yet published are also sometimes called *unpublished opinions,* but because these decisions will eventually be printed in reporters, we do not include them here.

view supported by the majority of the judges or justices deciding the case. If a judge agrees, or concurs, with the majority's decision, but for different reasons, that judge may write a *concurring opinion.* A *dissenting opinion* presents the views of one or more judges who disagree with the majority's decision. The dissenting opinion is important because it may form the basis of the arguments used years later in overruling the precedential majority opinion.

Other Types of Opinions. Occasionally, a court issues a *per curiam* opinion. *Per curiam* is a Latin phrase meaning "of the court." In *per curiam* opinions, there is no indication as to which judge or justice authored the opinion. This term may also be used for an announcement of a court's disposition of a case that is not accompanied by a written opinion. Some of the cases presented in this text are *en banc* decisions. When an appellate court reviews a case *en banc,* which is a French term (derived from a Latin term) for "in the bench," generally all of the judges "sitting on the bench" of that court review the case.

A Sample Court Case

Knowing how to read and understand court opinions and the legal reasoning used by the courts is an essential step in undertaking accurate legal research. A further step is "briefing," or summarizing, the case. Legal researchers routinely brief cases by reducing the texts of the opinions to their essential elements. Instructions on how to brief a case are given in Appendix A.

The cases within the chapters in this text have already been analyzed and briefed by the authors, and the essential aspects of each case are presented precedent to some extent because they are so publicly accessible.

Another argument against allowing unpublished decisions to be precedent concerns the quality of the legal reasoning set forth in these decisions. Staff attorneys and law clerks frequently write unpublished opinions so that judges can spend more time on the opinions intended for publication. Consequently, some claim that allowing unpublished decisions to establish precedent could result in bad precedents because the reasoning may not be up to par. If the decision is regarded merely as persuasive precedent, however, then judges who disagree with the reasoning are free to reject the conclusion.

The United States Supreme Court Changes Federal Rules on Unpublished Opinions after 2007

In spite of objections from several hundred judges and lawyers, the United States Supreme Court made history in 2006 when it announced that it would allow lawyers to refer to (cite) unpublished decisions in all federal courts. The new rule, Rule 32.1 of the Federal Rules of Appellate Procedure, states that federal courts may not prohibit or restrict the citation of federal judicial opinions that have been designated as "not for publication," "non-precedential," or "not precedent." The rule applies only to federal courts and only to unpublished opinions issued after January 1, 2007. It does not specify the effect that a court must give to one of its unpublished opinions or to an unpublished opinion from another court. Basically, the rule simply makes all the federal courts follow a uniform rule that allows attorneys to cite—and judges to consider as persuasive precedent—unpublished decisions beginning in 2007.

The impact of this new rule remains to be seen. At present, the majority of states do not allow their state courts to consider the rulings in unpublished cases as persuasive precedent, and this rule does not affect the states. The Supreme Court's decision, however, provides an example of how technology—the availability of unpublished opinions over the Internet—has affected the law.

CRITICAL THINKING

INSIGHT INTO THE SOCIAL ENVIRONMENT

Now that the Supreme Court is allowing unpublished decisions to form persuasive precedent in federal courts, should state courts follow? Why or why not?

in a convenient format consisting of two sections: *Background and Facts* and *Decision and Rationale.* This format is illustrated in the sample court case in Exhibit 1–6 on pages 24 and 25, which has been annotated to explain the kind of information that is contained in each section. In the remaining chapters of this book, the basic format is often expanded to include special introductory sections, or special comments or considerations following the cases.

The case we present and annotate in Exhibit 1–6 is an actual case that the U.S. Court of Appeals for the Ninth Circuit decided in 2008. The Seattle Center is an entertainment "zone" near downtown Seattle, Washington, that attracts almost ten million tourists every year. The center encompasses theaters, arenas, museums, exhibition halls, conference rooms, outdoor stadiums, and restaurants. Street performers add to the festive atmosphere. Under the authority of the city, the center's director issued rules to address safety concerns and other matters. Staff at the Seattle Center cited one of the street performers, a balloon artist, for several rule violations. The artist filed a suit in a federal district court against the city and others, alleging that the rules violated his rights under the U.S. Constitution. The court issued a judgment in the plaintiff's favor. The city appealed to the U.S. Court of Appeals for the Ninth Circuit.

EXHIBIT 1–6 • A Sample Court Case

This section contains the citation—the name of the case, the name of the court that heard the case, the year of the decision, and the reporter in which the court's opinion can be found.

BERGER v. CITY OF SEATTLE

U.S. Court of Appeals,

Ninth Circuit, 2008.

512 F.3d 582.

This section identifies the parties and describes the events leading up to the trial and its appeal. The decision of the lower court is included, as well as the issue to be decided by the U.S. Court of Appeals for the Ninth Circuit.

A document that, when filed with a court, initiates a lawsuit.

A court decree ordering a person to do or refrain from doing a certain act.

The First Amendment to the Constitution guarantees, among other freedoms, the right of free speech—to express one's views without governmental restrictions.

A judgment that a court enters without beginning or continuing a trial. It can be entered only if no facts are in dispute and the only question is how the law applies.

Background and Facts In the heart of the city of Seattle, Washington, is the Seattle Center, an entertainment zone covering eighty acres of land. Within this area, the city requires that all street performers follow the so-called Campus Rules. One such rule, Rule F.1, requires a permit for street performers and requires badges to be worn during street performances. Michael Berger, a street performer, has been performing there since the 1980s. After the Campus Rules were enacted in 2002, Berger obtained a permit. Thereafter, Seattle Center authorities received numerous publicly filed complaints alleging that Berger had exhibited threatening behavior. Also, the Seattle Center staff reported several rule violations. In 2003, Berger filed a **complaint** seeking damages and an **injunctive relief**, alleging that the Campus Rules violated the **First Amendment** to the U.S. Constitution. In 2005, a federal district court granted **summary judgment** to Berger. The city appealed the district court's order of summary judgment to the U.S. Court of Appeals for the Ninth Circuit and sought to reverse with instructions to enter summary judgment in its favor.

This section contains the court's decision and reasoning on the issue before it. An appellate court's decision is often phrased with reference to the decision of the lower court from which the case was appealed. For example, an appellate court may "affirm" or "reverse" a lower court's ruling. A court's rationale indicates the relevant laws and legal principles, and the court's reasoning that led to its conclusion.

Sent back.

A federal court that hears appeals from the federal district courts located within its geographical boundaries.

Decision and Rationale The U.S. Court of Appeals for the Ninth Circuit reversed the summary judgment to Berger and **remanded** the case to the district court for further proceedings consistent with the appellate court's opinion. The **appellate court** stated that restrictions on oral or written speech "must be justified without reference to the content of the regulated speech, [and] they must be narrowly tailored to serve a significant government interest. * * * " If a licensing statute affects only certain messages, it would lack neutrality. Seattle's licensing requirement for the Seattle Center did not, according to the court, discriminate based on content. Further, the court stated

EXHIBIT 1–6 • A Sample Court Case—Continued

that "The Seattle Center authorities enacted the permit requirement after encountering 'chronic' territorial disputes between performers and threats to public citizens by street performers." The court was convinced that street performers did pose a threat to the city's interest in maintaining order in the Seattle Center. It stated that the Seattle Center rules satisfied "requirements for valid restrictions on expression under the First Amendment."

REVIEWING Introduction to Law and Legal Reasoning

Suppose that the California legislature passes a law that severely restricts carbon dioxide emissions from automobiles in that state. A group of automobile manufacturers files a suit against the state of California to prevent the enforcement of the law. The automakers claim that a federal law already sets fuel economy standards nationwide and that fuel economy standards are essentially the same as carbon dioxide emission standards. According to the automobile manufacturers, it is unfair to allow California to impose more stringent regulations than those set by the federal law. Using the information presented in the chapter, answer the following questions.

1. Who are the parties (the plaintiffs and the defendant) in this lawsuit?
2. Are the plaintiffs seeking a legal remedy or an equitable remedy? Why?
3. What is the primary source of the law that is at issue here?
4. Where would you look to find the relevant California and federal laws?

TERMS AND CONCEPTS

administrative agency 7
administrative law 7
allege 11
analogy 12
appellant 21
appellee 21
binding authority 10
breach 5
case law 7
case on point 12
chancellor 8
citation 15
civil law 14
common law 8
constitutional law 6
court of equity 8
court of law 8
criminal law 14
cyberlaw 14
damages 8
defendant 9
defense 9
equitable maxims 9
executive agency 7
historical school 3
independent regulatory agency 7

jurisprudence 2
laches 9
law 2
legal realism 3
legal reasoning 11
natural law 3
opinion 21
ordinance 6
petitioner 9
plaintiff 9
positive law 3
positivist school 3
precedent 10
procedural law 14
public policy 11
remedy 8
remedy at law 8
remedy in equity 8
reporter 10
respondent 9
sociological school 4
***stare decisis* 10**
statute of limitations 9
statutory law 6
substantive law 14
syllogism 12
uniform law 6

QUESTIONS AND CASE PROBLEMS

1–1. How does statutory law come into existence? How does it differ from the common law? If statutory law conflicts with the common law, which law will govern?

1–2. QUESTION WITH SAMPLE ANSWER

After World War II, which ended in 1945, an international tribunal of judges convened at Nuremberg, Germany. The judges convicted several Nazis of "crimes against humanity." Assuming that the Nazi war criminals who were convicted had not disobeyed any law of their country and had merely been following their government's (Hitler's) orders, what law had they violated? Explain.

- **For a sample answer to Question 1–2, go to Appendix I at the end of this text.**

1–3. Assume that you want to read the entire court opinion in the case of *Menashe v. V Secret Catalogue, Inc.*, 409 F.Supp.2d 412 (S.D.N.Y. 2006). The case focuses on whether "SEXY LITTLE THINGS" is a suggestive or descriptive trademark and on which of the parties to the suit used the mark first in commerce. (Note that this case is presented in Chapter 8 of this text as Case 8.2.) Refer to the subsection entitled "Finding Case Law" in this chapter, and then explain specifically where you would find the court's opinion.

1–4. This chapter discussed a number of sources of American law. Which source of law takes priority in the following situations, and why?

(a) A federal statute conflicts with the U.S. Constitution.
(b) A federal statute conflicts with a state constitutional provision.
(c) A state statute conflicts with the common law of that state.
(d) A state constitutional amendment conflicts with the U.S. Constitution.

1–5. In the text of this chapter, we stated that the doctrine of *stare decisis* "became a cornerstone of the English and American judicial systems." What does *stare decisis* mean, and why has this doctrine been so fundamental to the development of our legal tradition?

1–6. What is the difference between a concurring opinion and a majority opinion? Between a concurring opinion and a dissenting opinion? Why do judges and justices write concurring and dissenting opinions, given that these opinions will not affect the outcome of the case at hand, which has already been decided by majority vote?

1–7. Courts can overturn precedents and thus change the common law. Should judges have the same authority to overrule statutory law? Explain.

1–8. "The judge's role is not to make the law but to uphold and apply the law." Do you agree or disagree with this statement? Discuss fully the reasons for your answer.

1–9. Assume that Arthur Rabe is suing Xavier Sanchez for breaching a contract in which Sanchez promised to sell Rabe a Van Gogh painting for $3 million.

(a) In this lawsuit, who is the plaintiff and who is the defendant?
(b) Suppose that Rabe wants Sanchez to perform the contract as promised. What remedy would Rabe seek from the court?
(c) Now suppose that Rabe wants to cancel the contract because Sanchez fraudulently misrepresented the painting as an original Van Gogh when in fact it is a copy. What remedy would Rabe seek?
(d) Will the remedy Rabe seeks in either situation be a remedy at law or a remedy in equity? What is the difference between legal and equitable remedies?
(e) Suppose that the trial court finds in Rabe's favor and grants one of these remedies. Sanchez then appeals the decision to a higher court. On appeal, which party will be the appellant (or petitioner), and which party will be the appellee (or respondent)?

1–10. A QUESTION OF ETHICS

*On July 5, 1884, Dudley, Stephens, and Brooks—"all able-bodied English seamen"—and a teenage English boy were cast adrift in a lifeboat following a storm at sea. They had no water with them in the boat, and all they had for sustenance were two one-pound tins of turnips. On July 24, Dudley proposed that one of the four in the lifeboat be sacrificed to save the others. Stephens agreed with Dudley, but Brooks refused to consent—and the boy was never asked for his opinion. On July 25, Dudley killed the boy, and the three men then fed on the boy's body and blood. Four days later, a passing vessel rescued the men. They were taken to England and tried for the murder of the boy. If the men had not fed on the boy's body, they would probably have died of starvation within the four-day period. The boy, who was in a much weaker condition, would likely have died before the rest. [*Regina v. Dudley and Stephens, *14 Q.B.D. (Queen's Bench Division, England) 273 (1884)]*

(a) The basic question in this case is whether the survivors should be subject to penalties under English criminal law, given the men's unusual circumstances. Were the defendants' actions necessary but unethical? Explain your reasoning. What ethical issues might be involved here?

(b) Should judges ever have the power to look beyond the written "letter of the law" in making their decisions? Why or why not?

LAW ON THE WEB

Today, business law and legal environment professors and students can go online to access information on almost every topic covered in this text. A good point of departure for online legal research is the Web site for *Business Law: Alternate Edition*, Eleventh Edition, which can be found at **www.cengage.com/blaw/jentz**. There you will find numerous materials relevant to this text and to business law generally, including links to various legal resources on the Web. Additionally, every chapter in this text ends with a *Law on the Web* feature that contains selected Web addresses.

You can access many of the sources of law discussed in Chapter 1 at the FindLaw Web site, which is probably the most comprehensive source of free legal information on the Internet. Go to

www.findlaw.com

The Legal Information Institute (LII) at Cornell Law School, which offers extensive information about U.S. law, is also a good starting point for legal research. The URL for this site is

www.law.cornell.edu

The Library of Congress offers extensive links to state and federal government resources at

www.loc.gov

Legal Research Exercises on the Web

Go to **www.cengage.com/blaw/jentz**, the Web site that accompanies this text. Select "Chapter 1" and click on "Internet Exercises." There you will find the following Internet research exercises that you can perform to learn more about some of the important sources of law discussed in Chapter 1 and other useful legal sites on the Web.

Internet Exercise 1–1: Legal Perspective
Internet Sources of Law

Internet Exercise 1–2: Management Perspective
Online Assistance from Government Agencies

Internet Exercise 1–3: Social Perspective
The Case of the Speluncean Explorers

CHAPTER 2

Courts and Alternative Dispute Resolution

Today in the United States there are fifty-two court systems—one for each of the fifty states, one for the District of Columbia, and a federal system. Keep in mind that the federal courts are not superior to the state courts; they are simply an independent system of courts, which derives its authority from Article III, Section 2, of the U.S. Constitution. By the power given to it under Article I of the U.S. Constitution, Congress has extended the federal court system beyond the boundaries of the United States to U.S. territories such as Guam, Puerto Rico, and the Virgin Islands.[1] As we shall see, the United States Supreme Court is the final controlling voice over all of these fifty-two systems, at least when questions of federal law are involved.

Every businessperson will likely face a lawsuit at some time in his or her career. Thus, anyone involved in business needs to have an understanding of the American court systems, as well as the various methods of dispute resolution that can be pursued outside the courts. In this chapter, after examining the judiciary's role in the American governmental system, we discuss some basic requirements that must be met before a party may bring a lawsuit in front of a particular court. We then look at the court systems of the United States in some detail. We conclude the chapter with an overview of some alternative methods of settling disputes, including online dispute resolution.

1. In Guam and the Virgin Islands, territorial courts serve as both federal courts and state courts; in Puerto Rico, they serve only as federal courts.

SECTION 1 The Judiciary's Role in American Government

As you learned in Chapter 1, the body of American law includes the federal and state constitutions, statutes passed by legislative bodies, administrative law, and the case decisions and legal principles that form the common law. These laws would be meaningless, however, without the courts to interpret and apply them. This is the essential role of the judiciary—the courts—in the American governmental system: to interpret the laws and apply them to specific situations.

As the branch of government entrusted with interpreting the laws, the judiciary can decide, among other things, whether the laws or actions of the other two branches are constitutional. The process for making such a determination is known as **judicial review.** The power of judicial review enables the judicial branch to act as a check on the other two branches of government, in line with the system of checks and balances established by the U.S. Constitution.[2]

The power of judicial review is not mentioned in the Constitution (although many constitutional scholars conclude that the founders intended the judiciary to have this power). Rather, this power was explicitly established by the United States Supreme Court in 1803 by its decision in *Marbury v. Madison,*[3] in which the Supreme Court stated, "It is emphatically the province and duty of the Judicial Department to say

2. In a broad sense, judicial review occurs whenever a court "reviews" a case or legal proceeding—as when an appellate court reviews a lower court's decision. When referring to the judiciary's role in American government, however, the term *judicial review* is used to indicate the power of the judiciary to decide whether the actions of the other two branches of government do or do not violate the U.S. Constitution.

3. 5 U.S. (1 Cranch) 137, 2 L.Ed. 60 (1803).

what the law is. . . . If two laws conflict with each other, the courts must decide on the operation of each. . . . So if the law be in opposition to the Constitution . . . [t]he Court must determine which of these conflicting rules governs the case. This is the very essence of judicial duty." Since the *Marbury v. Madison* decision, the power of judicial review has remained unchallenged. Today, this power is exercised by both federal and state courts.

SECTION 2 Basic Judicial Requirements

Before a lawsuit can be brought before a court, certain requirements must be met. These requirements relate to jurisdiction, venue, and standing to sue. We examine each of these important concepts here.

Jurisdiction

In Latin, *juris* means "law," and *diction* means "to speak." Thus, "the power to speak the law" is the literal meaning of the term **jurisdiction.** Before any court can hear a case, it must have jurisdiction over the person (or company) against whom the suit is brought (the defendant) or over the property involved in the suit. The court must also have jurisdiction over the subject matter of the dispute.

Jurisdiction over Persons or Property Generally, a particular court can exercise ***in personam* jurisdiction** (personal jurisdiction) over any person or business that resides in a certain geographic area. A state trial court, for example, normally has jurisdictional authority over residents (including businesses) of a particular area of the state, such as a county or district. A state's highest court (often called the state supreme court)[4] has jurisdictional authority over all residents within the state.

A court can also exercise jurisdiction over property that is located within its boundaries. This kind of jurisdiction is known as ***in rem* jurisdiction,** or "jurisdiction over the thing." Suppose that a dispute arises over the ownership of a boat in dry dock in Fort Lauderdale, Florida. The boat is owned by an Ohio resident, over whom a Florida court normally cannot exercise personal jurisdiction. The other party to the dispute is a resident of Nebraska. In this situation, a lawsuit concerning the boat could be brought in a Florida state court on the basis of the court's *in rem* jurisdiction.

Long Arm Statutes. Under the authority of a state **long arm statute,** a court can exercise personal jurisdiction over certain out-of-state defendants based on activities that took place within the state. Before a court can exercise jurisdiction over an out-of-state defendant under a long arm statute, though, it must be demonstrated that the defendant had sufficient contacts, or *minimum contacts,* with the state to justify the jurisdiction.[5] Generally, this means that the defendant must have enough of a connection to the state for the judge to conclude that it is fair for the state to exercise power over the defendant. For example, if an out-of-state defendant caused an automobile accident or sold defective goods within the state, a court will usually find that minimum contacts exist to exercise jurisdiction over that defendant. Similarly, a state may exercise personal jurisdiction over a nonresident defendant who is sued for breaching a contract that was formed within the state.

Corporate Contacts. Because corporations are considered legal persons, courts use the same principles to determine whether it is fair to exercise jurisdiction over a corporation.[6] A corporation normally is subject to personal jurisdiction in the state in which it is incorporated, has its principal office, and is doing business. Courts apply the minimum-contacts test to determine if they can exercise jurisdiction over out-of-state corporations.

The minimum-contacts requirement is usually met if the corporation advertises or sells its products within the state, or places its goods into the "stream of commerce" with the intent that the goods be sold in the state. Suppose that a business is incorporated under the laws of Maine but has a branch office and manufacturing plant in Georgia. The corporation also advertises and sells its products in Georgia. These activities would likely constitute sufficient contacts with the state of Georgia to allow a Georgia court to exercise jurisdiction over the corporation.

4. As will be discussed shortly, a state's highest court is often referred to as the state supreme court, but there are exceptions. For example, the court that is labeled the Supreme Court in New York is actually a trial court.

5. The minimum-contacts standard was first established in *International Shoe Co. v. State of Washington,* 326 U.S. 310, 66 S.Ct. 154, 90 L.Ed. 95 (1945).

6. In the eyes of the law, corporations are "legal persons"—entities that can sue and be sued. See Chapter 38.

Some corporations, however, do not sell or advertise products or place any goods in the stream of commerce. Determining what constitutes minimum contacts in these situations can be more difficult, as the following case—involving a resort hotel in Mexico and a hotel guest from New Jersey—illustrates.

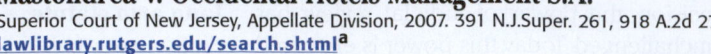

CASE 2.1 Mastondrea v. Occidental Hotels Management S.A.

Superior Court of New Jersey, Appellate Division, 2007. 391 N.J.Super. 261, 918 A.2d 27.
lawlibrary.rutgers.edu/search.shtml[a]

• **Background and Facts** Libgo Travel, Inc., in Ramsey, New Jersey, with Allegro Resorts Management Corporation (ARMC), a marketing agency in Miami, Florida, placed an ad in the *Newark Star Ledger,* a newspaper in Newark, New Jersey, to tout vacation packages for accommodations at the Royal Hideaway Playacar, an all-inclusive resort hotel in Quintana Roo, Mexico. ARMC is part of Occidental Hotels Management, B.V., a Netherlands corporation that owns the hotel with Occidental Hoteles Management S.A., a Spanish company. In response to the ad, Amanda Mastondrea, a New Jersey resident, bought one of the packages through Liberty Travel, a chain of travel agencies in the eastern United States that Libgo owns and operates. On June 16, 2003, at the resort, Mastondrea slipped and fell on a wet staircase, breaking her ankle. She filed a suit in a New Jersey state court against the hotel, its owners, and others, alleging negligence. The defendants asked the court to dismiss the suit on the ground that it did not have personal jurisdiction over them. The court ruled in part that it had jurisdiction over the hotel. The hotel appealed this ruling to a state intermediate appellate court.

• **Decision and Rationale** The state intermediate appellate court affirmed the lower court's ruling. "This evidence was sufficient to support the assertion of * * * personal jurisdiction over the Hotel in this State." The appellate court noted that the hotel's operations were located entirely in Mexico and that the hotel was not registered, licensed, or otherwise authorized to do business in New Jersey. In spite of this lack of business presence in that state, the reviewing court looked at the "Tour Operators Agreements" in effect between the hotel and Libgo Travel. A specific number of rooms were allotted to clients of Libgo at agreed-upon rates. Libgo was required to provide the hotel with weekly sales reports. Libgo had to confirm all reservations in writing. Moreover, the hotel "purposely and successfully" sought vacationers from New Jersey, and it derived a profit from them. Finally, the owners of the hotel entered into cooperative marketing agreements with Libgo Travel.

• **What If the Facts Were Different?** *If Mastondrea had not seen Libgo and Allegro's ad, but had bought a Royal Hideaway vacation package on the recommendation of a Liberty Travel agent, is it likely that the result in this case would have been different? Why or why not?*

• **The Global Dimension** *What do the circumstances and the holding in this case suggest to a business firm that actively attempts to attract customers in a variety of jurisdictions?*

a. In the "SEARCH THE N.J. COURTS DECISIONS" section, type "Mastondrea" in the box, and click on "Search!" In the result, click on the case name to access the opinion. Rutgers University Law School in Camden, New Jersey, maintains this Web site.

Jurisdiction over Subject Matter Subject-matter jurisdiction refers to the limitations on the types of cases a court can hear. Certain courts are empowered to hear certain kinds of disputes.

General and Limited Jurisdiction. In both the federal and the state court systems, there are courts of *general* (unlimited) *jurisdiction* and courts of *limited jurisdiction.* A court of general jurisdiction can decide cases involving a broad array of issues. An example of a court of general jurisdiction is a state trial court or a federal district court. An example of a state court of limited jurisdiction is a probate court. **Probate courts** are state courts that handle only matters relating to the transfer of a person's assets and obligations after that person's death, including issues relating to the custody and guardianship of children. An example of a federal court of limited subject-matter jurisdiction is a bankruptcy court. **Bankruptcy courts** handle only bankruptcy proceedings, which are governed by federal bankruptcy law (discussed in Chapter 30).

A court's jurisdiction over subject matter is usually defined in the statute or constitution creating the court. In both the federal and the state court systems, a court's subject-matter jurisdiction can be limited not only by the subject of the lawsuit but also by the sum in controversy, whether the case is a felony (a more serious type of crime) or a misdemeanor (a less serious type of crime), or whether the proceeding is a trial or an appeal.

Original and Appellate Jurisdiction. A court's subject-matter jurisdiction is also frequently limited to hearing cases at a particular stage of the dispute. Courts in which lawsuits begin, trials take place, and evidence is presented are referred to as *courts of original jurisdiction.* Courts having original jurisdiction are courts of the first instance, or trial courts. In the federal court system, the *district courts* are trial courts. In the various state court systems, the trial courts are known by different names, as will be discussed shortly.

Courts having appellate jurisdiction act as reviewing courts, or appellate courts. In general, cases can be brought before appellate courts only on appeal from an order or a judgment of a trial court or other lower court. In other words, the distinction between courts of original jurisdiction and courts of appellate jurisdiction normally lies in whether the case is being heard for the first time.

Jurisdiction of the Federal Courts

Because the federal government is a government of limited powers, the jurisdiction of the federal courts is limited. Federal courts have subject-matter jurisdiction in two situations.

Federal Questions. Article III of the U.S. Constitution establishes the boundaries of federal judicial power. Section 2 of Article III states that "[t]he judicial Power shall extend to all Cases, in Law and Equity, arising under this Constitution, the Laws of the United States, and Treaties made, or which shall be made, under their Authority." In effect, this clause means that whenever a plaintiff's cause of action is based, at least in part, on the U.S. Constitution, a treaty, or a federal law, a **federal question** arises. Any lawsuit involving a federal question comes under the judicial authority of the federal courts and can originate in a federal court. People who claim that their constitutional rights have been violated, for example, can begin their suits in a federal court. Note that in a case based on a federal question, a federal court will apply federal law.

Diversity of Citizenship. Federal district courts can also exercise original jurisdiction over cases involving **diversity of citizenship.** This term applies whenever a federal court has jurisdiction over a case that does not involve a question of federal law. The most common type of diversity jurisdiction has two requirements:[7] (1) the plaintiff and defendant must be residents of different states, and (2) the dollar amount in controversy must exceed $75,000. For purposes of diversity jurisdiction, a corporation is a citizen of both the state in which it is incorporated and the state in which its principal place of business is located. A case involving diversity of citizenship can be filed in the appropriate federal district court. If the case starts in a state court, it can sometimes be transferred, or "removed," to a federal court. A large percentage of the cases filed in federal courts each year are based on diversity of citizenship.

As noted, a federal court will apply federal law in cases involving federal questions. In a case based on diversity of citizenship, in contrast, a federal court will apply the relevant state law (which is often the law of the state in which the court sits).

Exclusive versus Concurrent Jurisdiction

When both federal and state courts have the power to hear a case, as is true in suits involving diversity of citizenship, **concurrent jurisdiction** exists. When cases can be tried only in federal courts or only in state courts, **exclusive jurisdiction** exists. Federal courts have exclusive jurisdiction in cases involving federal crimes, bankruptcy, and most patent and copyright claims; in suits against the United States; and in some areas of admiralty law (law governing transportation on ocean waters). State courts also have exclusive jurisdiction over certain subjects—for example, divorce and adoption. When concurrent jurisdiction exists, a party may choose to bring a suit in either a federal court or a state court.

7. Diversity jurisdiction also exists in cases between (1) a foreign country and citizens of a state or of different states and (2) citizens of a state and citizens or subjects of a foreign country. These bases for diversity jurisdiction are less commonly used.

Jurisdiction in Cyberspace

The Internet's capacity to bypass political and geographic boundaries undercuts the traditional basis on which courts assert personal jurisdiction. This basis includes a party's contacts with a court's geographic jurisdiction. As already discussed, for a court to compel a defendant to come before it, there must be at least minimum contacts—the presence of a salesperson within the state, for example. Are there sufficient minimum contacts if the only connection to a jurisdiction is an ad on a Web site originating from a remote location?

The "Sliding-Scale" Standard Gradually, the courts are developing a standard—called a "sliding-scale" standard—for determining when the exercise of personal jurisdiction over an out-of-state Internet-based defendant is proper. In developing this standard, the courts have identified three types of Internet business contacts: (1) substantial business conducted over the Internet (with contracts and sales, for example); (2) some interactivity through a Web site; and (3) passive advertising. Jurisdiction is proper for the first category, is improper for the third, and may or may not be appropriate for the second.[8] An Internet communication is typically considered passive if people have to voluntarily access it to read the message and active if it is sent to specific individuals.

In certain situations, even a single contact can satisfy the minimum-contacts requirement. A Louisiana man, Daniel Crummey, purchased a used recreational vehicle (RV) from sellers in Texas after viewing numerous photos of the RV on eBay. The sellers' statements on eBay stated that "everything works great on this RV and will provide comfort and dependability for years to come. This RV will go to Alaska and back without problems!" Crummey picked up the RV in Texas but on the drive back to Louisiana, the RV quit working. He filed a lawsuit in Louisiana against the sellers alleging that the vehicle was defective. The sellers claimed that the Louisiana court lacked jurisdiction, but the court held that because the sellers had used eBay to market and sell the RV to a Louisiana buyer, jurisdiction was proper.[9]

8. For a leading case on this issue, see *Zippo Manufacturing Co. v. Zippo Dot Com, Inc.*, 952 F.Supp. 1119 (W.D.Pa. 1997).

9. *Crummey v. Morgan*, 965 So.2d 497 (La.App. 1st Cir. 2007).

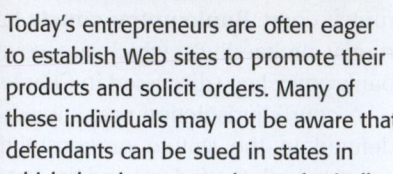

Today's entrepreneurs are often eager to establish Web sites to promote their products and solicit orders. Many of these individuals may not be aware that defendants can be sued in states in which they have never been physically present, provided they have had sufficient contacts with that state's residents over the Internet. Businesspersons who contemplate making their Web sites the least bit interactive should consult an attorney to find out whether by doing so they will be subjecting themselves to jurisdiction in every state. Becoming informed about the extent of potential exposure to lawsuits in various locations is an important part of preventing litigation.

International Jurisdictional Issues Because the Internet is international in scope, international jurisdictional issues have understandingly come to the fore. The world's courts seem to be developing a standard that echoes the requirement of "minimum contacts" applied by the U.S. courts. Most courts are indicating that minimum contacts—doing business within the jurisdiction, for example—are enough to exercise jurisdiction over a defendant. The effect of this standard is that a business firm may have to comply with the laws in any jurisdiction in which it actively targets customers for its products.

To understand some of the problems created by Internet commerce, consider a French court's judgment against the U.S.-based Internet company Yahoo!, Inc. Yahoo operates an online auction site on which Nazi memorabilia have been offered for sale. In France, the display of any objects depicting symbols of Nazi ideology is illegal and leads to both criminal and civil liability. The International League against Racism and Anti-Semitism filed a suit in Paris against Yahoo for displaying Nazi memorabilia and offering them for sale via its Web site.

The French court asserted jurisdiction over Yahoo on the ground that the materials on the company's U.S.-based servers could be viewed on a Web site accessible in France. The French court ordered Yahoo to eliminate all Internet access in France to the Nazi memorabilia offered for sale through its online auctions. Yahoo then took the case to a federal district court in the United States, claiming that the French court's order violated the First Amendment to the U.S. Constitution. Although the federal district court ruled in favor of Yahoo, the U.S. Court of Appeals for the

CONCEPT SUMMARY 2.1
Jurisdiction

Type of Jurisdiction	Description
PERSONAL	Exists when a defendant is located within the territorial boundaries within which a court has the right and power to decide cases. Jurisdiction may be exercised over out-of-state defendants under state long arm statutes. Courts have jurisdiction over corporate defendants that do business within the state, as well as corporations that advertise, sell, or place goods into the stream of commerce in the state.
PROPERTY	Exists when the property that is subject to a lawsuit is located within the territorial boundaries within which a court has the right and power to decide cases.
SUBJECT MATTER	Limits the court's jurisdictional authority to particular types of cases. 1. *Limited jurisdiction*—Exists when a court is limited to a specific subject matter, such as probate or divorce. 2. *General jurisdiction*—Exists when a court can hear cases involving a broad array of issues.
ORIGINAL	Exists with courts that have the authority to hear a case for the first time (trial courts).
APPELLATE	Exists with courts of appeal and review. Generally, appellate courts do not have original jurisdiction.
FEDERAL	1. *Federal questions*—When the plaintiff's cause of action is based at least in part on the U.S. Constitution, a treaty, or a federal law, a federal court can exercise jurisdiction. 2. *Diversity of citizenship*—In cases between citizens of different states when the amount in controversy exceeds $75,000 (or in cases between a foreign country and citizens of a state or of different states and in cases between citizens of a state and citizens or subjects of a foreign country), a federal court can exercise jurisdiction.
CONCURRENT	Exists when both federal and state courts have authority to hear the same case.
EXCLUSIVE	Exists when only state courts or only federal courts have authority to hear a case.
JURISDICTION IN CYBERSPACE	Because the Internet does not have physical boundaries, traditional jurisdictional concepts have been difficult to apply in cases involving activities conducted via the Web. Gradually, the courts are developing standards to use in determining when jurisdiction over a Web site owner or operator in another state is proper. A significant legal challenge with respect to cyberspace transactions has to do with resolving jurisdictional disputes in the international context.

Ninth Circuit reversed. According to the appellate court, U.S. courts lacked personal jurisdiction over the French groups involved.[10] The *Yahoo* case represents the first time a U.S. court was asked to decide whether to honor a foreign judgment involving business conducted over the Internet. The federal appeals court's ruling leaves open the possibility that Yahoo, and anyone else who posts anything on the Internet, could be held answerable to the laws of any country in which the message might be received. *Concept Summary 2.1* reviews the various types of jurisdiction, including jurisdiction in cyberspace.

10. *Yahoo! Inc. v. La Ligue Contre le Racisme et l'Antisemitisme*, 379 F.3d 1120 (9th Cir. 2004), *cert.* denied, __ U.S. __, 126 S.Ct. 2332, 164 L.Ed.2d 841 (2006).

Venue

Jurisdiction has to do with whether a court has authority to hear a case involving specific persons, property, or subject matter. **Venue**[11] is concerned with the most appropriate location for a trial. For example, two state courts (or two federal courts) may have the authority to exercise jurisdiction over a case, but it may be more appropriate or convenient to hear the case in one court than in the other.

Basically, the concept of venue reflects the policy that a court trying a suit should be in the geographic neighborhood (usually the county) where the incident leading to the lawsuit occurred or where the parties involved in the lawsuit reside. Venue in a civil case typically is where the defendant resides, whereas venue in a criminal case is normally where the crime occurred. Pretrial publicity or other factors, though, may require a change of venue to another community, especially in criminal cases in which the defendant's right to a fair and impartial jury has been impaired.

Standing to Sue

In order to bring a lawsuit before a court, a party must have **standing to sue,** or a sufficient "stake" in a matter to justify seeking relief through the court system. In other words, to have standing, a party must have a legally protected and tangible interest at stake in the litigation. The party bringing the lawsuit must have suffered a harm or been threatened with a harm by the action about which she or he has complained. At times, a person can have standing to sue on behalf of another person. For example, suppose that a child suffers serious injuries as a result of a defectively manufactured toy. Because the child is a minor, another person, such as a parent or a legal guardian, can bring a lawsuit on the child's behalf.

Standing to sue also requires that the controversy at issue be a **justiciable**[12] **controversy**—a controversy that is real and substantial, as opposed to hypothetical or academic. For example, to entice DaimlerChrysler Corporation to build a $1.2 billion Jeep assembly plant in the area, the city of Toledo, Ohio, gave the company a ten-year local property tax exemption as well as a state franchise tax credit. Toledo taxpayers filed a lawsuit in state court, claiming that the tax breaks violated the commerce clause in the U.S. Constitution. The taxpayers alleged that the tax exemption and credit injured them because they would have to pay higher taxes to cover the shortfall in tax revenues. In 2006, the United States Supreme Court ruled that the taxpayers lacked standing to sue over the incentive program because their alleged injury was "conjectural or hypothetical"—that is, there was no justiciable controversy.[13]

SECTION 3 The State and Federal Court Systems

As mentioned earlier in this chapter, each state has its own court system. Additionally, there is a system of federal courts. Although no two state court systems are exactly the same, the right-hand side of Exhibit 2–1 illustrates the basic organizational framework characteristic of the court systems in many states. The exhibit also shows how the federal court system is structured. We turn now to an examination of these court systems, beginning with the state courts. (See this chapter's *Insight into Ethics* feature on pages 36–37 for a discussion of the impact that the use of private judges and out-of-court settlements is having on the nation's court systems and our notions of justice.)

State Court Systems

Typically, a state court system includes several levels, or tiers, of courts. As indicated in Exhibit 2–1, state courts may include (1) local trial courts of limited jurisdiction, (2) state trial courts of general jurisdiction, (3) state courts of appeals (intermediate appellate courts), and (4) the state's highest court (often called the state supreme court). Generally, any person who is a party to a lawsuit has the opportunity to plead the case before a trial court and then, if he or she loses, before at least one level of appellate court. Finally, if the case involves a federal statute or federal constitutional issue, the decision of a state supreme court on that issue may be further appealed to the United States Supreme Court.

The states use various methods to select judges for their courts. Usually, voters elect judges, but in some states judges are appointed. For example, in Iowa, the

11. Pronounced *ven*-yoo.
12. Pronounced jus-*tish*-a-bul.
13. *DaimlerChrysler v. Cuno,* 547 U.S. 332, 126 S.Ct. 1854, 164 L.Ed.2d 589 (2006).

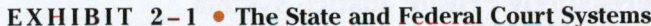

EXHIBIT 2–1 • The State and Federal Court Systems

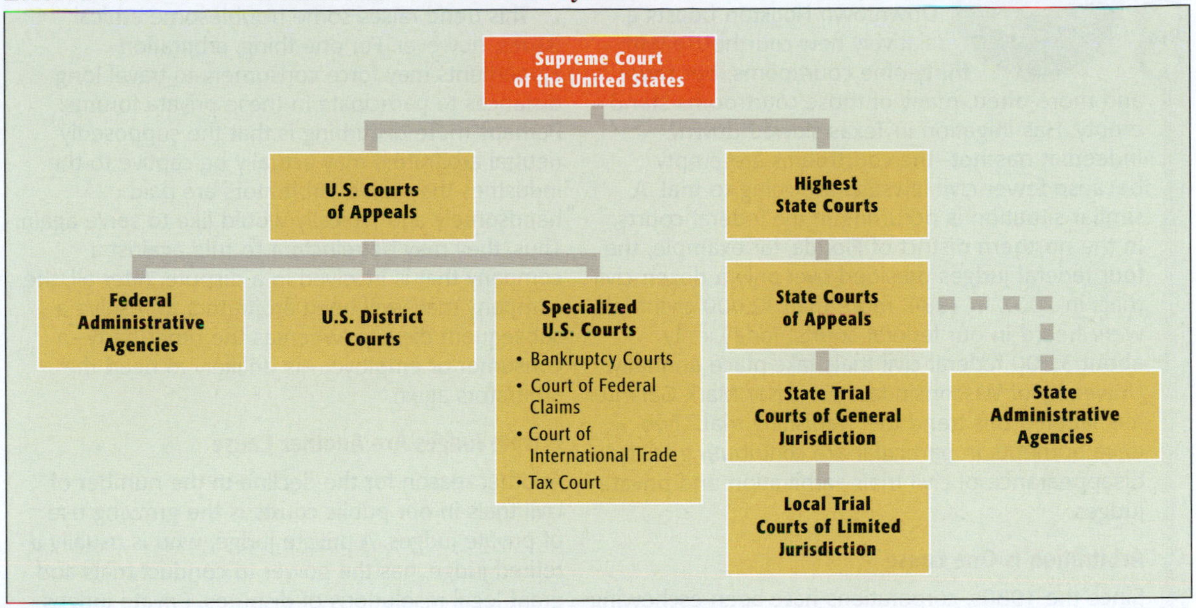

governor appoints judges, and then the general population decides whether to confirm their appointment in the next general election. The states usually specify the number of years that judges will serve. In contrast, as you will read shortly, judges in the federal court system are appointed by the president of the United States and, if they are confirmed by the Senate, hold office for life—unless they engage in blatantly illegal conduct.

Trial Courts Trial courts are exactly what their name implies—courts in which trials are held and testimony is taken. State trial courts have either general or limited jurisdiction. Trial courts that have general jurisdiction as to subject matter may be called county, district, superior, or circuit courts.[14] State trial courts of general jurisdiction have jurisdiction over a wide variety of subjects, including both civil disputes and criminal prosecutions. In some states, trial courts of general jurisdiction may hear appeals from courts of limited jurisdiction.

Courts of limited jurisdiction as to subject matter are often called special inferior trial courts or minor judiciary courts. **Small claims courts** are inferior trial courts that hear only civil cases involving claims of less than a certain amount, such as $5,000 (the amount varies from state to state). Suits brought in small claims courts are generally conducted informally, and lawyers are not required (in a few states, lawyers are not even allowed). Decisions of small claims courts and municipal courts may sometimes be appealed to a state trial court of general jurisdiction.

Other courts of limited jurisdiction include domestic relations courts, which handle primarily divorce actions and child-custody disputes; local municipal courts, which mainly deal with traffic cases; and probate courts, as mentioned earlier.

Appellate, or Reviewing, Courts Every state has at least one court of appeals (appellate court, or reviewing court), which may be an intermediate appellate court or the state's highest court. About three-fourths of the states have intermediate appellate courts. Generally, courts of appeals do not conduct new trials, in which evidence is submitted to the court and witnesses are examined. Rather, an appellate court panel of three or more judges reviews the record of the case on appeal, which includes a transcript of the trial proceedings, and then determines whether the trial court committed an error.

Usually, appellate courts focus on questions of law, not questions of fact. A **question of fact** deals with what really happened in regard to the dispute being tried—

14. The name in Ohio and Pennsylvania is Court of Common Pleas; the name in New York is Supreme Court, Trial Division.

INSIGHT INTO ETHICS

Implications of an Increasingly Private Justice System

Downtown Houston boasts a relatively new courthouse with thirty-nine courtrooms, but more and more often, many of those courtrooms stand empty. Has litigation in Texas slowed down? Indeed, it has not—the courtrooms are empty because fewer civil lawsuits are going to trial. A similar situation is occurring in the federal courts. In the northern district of Florida, for example, the four federal judges presided over only a dozen civil trials in 2007. In 1984, more than 12,000 civil trials were heard in our federal courts. Today, only about 3,500 federal civil trials take place annually. University of Wisconsin law professor Mark Galanter has labeled this trend the "vanishing trial." Two developments in particular are contributing to the disappearance of civil trials—arbitration and private judges.

Arbitration Is One Cause

Since the 1980s, corporations have been eschewing the public court system and taking cases to arbitration instead. Every day millions of Americans sign arbitration agreements, often unknowingly committing themselves to allow private arbitrators to solve their disputes with employers and the corporations with which they do business, such as cell phone service providers.

This trend raises some troublesome ethical issues, however. For one thing, arbitration agreements may force consumers to travel long distances to participate in these private forums. Perhaps more disturbing is that the supposedly neutral arbitrators may actually be captive to the industries they serve. Arbitrators are paid handsomely and typically would like to serve again. Thus, they may be reluctant to rule against a company that is involved in a dispute. After all, the company may well need arbitrators to resolve a subsequent dispute, whereas the other party—a consumer or employee—is unlikely to need the arbitrators again.

Private Judges Are Another Cause

Another reason for the decline in the number of civil trials in our public courts is the growing use of private judges. A private judge, who is usually a retired judge, has the power to conduct trials and grant legal resolutions of disputes. Private judges increasingly are being used to resolve commercial disputes, as well as divorces and custody battles, for two reasons. One reason is that a case can be heard by a private judge much sooner than it would be heard in a public court. The other reason is that proceedings before a private judge can be kept secret.

such as whether a party actually burned a flag. A **question of law** concerns the application or interpretation of the law—such as whether flag-burning is a form of speech protected by the First Amendment to the Constitution. Only a judge, not a jury, can rule on questions of law. Appellate courts normally defer to the trial court's findings on questions of fact because the trial court judge and jury were in a better position to evaluate testimony—by directly observing witnesses' gestures, demeanor, and other nonverbal behavior during the trial. At the appellate level, the judges review the written transcript of the trial, which does not include these nonverbal elements. Thus, an appellate court will not tamper with a trial court's finding of fact unless it is clearly erroneous (contrary to the evidence presented at trial) or when there is no evidence to support the finding.

Highest State Courts The highest appellate court in a state is usually called the supreme court but may be designated by some other name. For example, in both New York and Maryland, the highest state court is called the Court of Appeals. In Maine and Massachusetts, the highest court is labeled the Supreme Judicial Court. In West Virginia, the highest state court is the Supreme Court of Appeals.

The decisions of each state's highest court on all questions of state law are final. Only when issues of federal law are involved can the United States Supreme Court overrule a decision made by a state's highest court. Suppose that a city ordinance prohibits citizens from engaging in door-to-door advocacy without first registering with the mayor's office and receiving a permit. Further suppose that a religious group sues the city, arguing that the law violates the freedoms of speech and religion guaranteed by the First Amendment. If the state supreme court upholds the law, the group could appeal the decision to the United States Supreme Court—because a constitutional (federal) issue is involved.

The Federal Court System

The federal court system is basically a three-tiered model consisting of (1) U.S. district courts (trial courts of

In Ohio, for example, a state statute allows the parties to any civil action to have their dispute tried by a retired judge of their choosing who will make a decision in the matter.[a] Recently, though, private judging came under criticism in that state because private judges were conducting jury trials in county courtrooms at taxpayers' expense. A public judge, Nancy Margaret Russo, refused to give up jurisdiction over one case on the ground that private judges are not authorized to conduct jury trials. The Ohio Supreme Court agreed. As the state's highest court noted, private judging raises significant public-policy issues that the legislature needs to consider.[b]

One issue is that private judges charge relatively large fees. This means that litigants who are willing and able to pay the extra cost can have their case heard by a private judge long before they would be able to set a trial date in a regular court. Is it fair that those who cannot afford private judges should have to wait longer for justice? Similarly, is it ethical to allow parties to pay extra for secret proceedings before a private judge and thereby avoid the public scrutiny of a regular trial? Some even suggest that the use of private judges is leading to two different systems of justice.

a. See Ohio Revised Code Section 2701.10.

b. *State ex rel. Russo v. McDonnell,* 110 Ohio St.3d 144, 852 N.E.2d 145 (2006). (The term *ex rel.* is Latin for *ex relatione.* This phrase refers to an action brought on behalf of the state, by the attorney general, at the instigation of an individual who has a private interest in the matter.)

A Threat to the Common Law System?

The decline in the number of civil trials may also be leading to the erosion of this country's common law system. As discussed in Chapter 1, courts are obligated to consider precedents—the decisions rendered in previous cases with similar facts and issues—when deciding the outcome of a dispute. If fewer disputes go to trial because they are arbitrated or heard by a private judge, then they will never become part of the body of cases and appeals that form the case law on that subject. With fewer precedents on which to draw, individuals and businesses will have less information about what constitutes appropriate business behavior in today's world. Furthermore, private dispute resolution does not allow our case law to keep up with new issues related to areas such as biotechnology and the online world. Thus, the long-term effects of the decline of public justice could be a weakening of the common law itself.

CRITICAL THINKING

INSIGHT INTO THE SOCIAL ENVIRONMENT

If wealthier individuals increasingly use private judges, how will our justice system be affected in the long run?

general jurisdiction) and various courts of limited jurisdiction, (2) U.S. courts of appeals (intermediate courts of appeals), and (3) the United States Supreme Court.

Unlike state court judges, who are usually elected, federal court judges—including the justices of the Supreme Court—are appointed by the president of the United States, subject to confirmation by the U.S. Senate. Article III of the Constitution states that federal judges "hold their offices during good Behaviour." In effect, this means that federal judges have lifetime appointments. Although they can be impeached (removed from office) for misconduct, this is rarely done. In the entire history of the United States, only seven federal judges have been removed from office through impeachment proceedings.

U.S. District Courts At the federal level, the equivalent of a state trial court of general jurisdiction is the district court. U.S. district courts have original jurisdiction in federal matters, and federal cases typically originate in district courts. There are other federal courts with original, but special (or limited), jurisdiction, such as the federal bankruptcy courts and others shown earlier in Exhibit 2–1 on page 35.

There is at least one federal district court in every state. The number of judicial districts can vary over time, primarily owing to population changes and corresponding changes in caseloads. Currently, there are ninety-four federal judicial districts. Exhibit 2–2 on the next page shows the boundaries of the U.S. district courts, as well as the U.S. courts of appeals.

U.S. Courts of Appeals In the federal court system, there are thirteen U.S. courts of appeals—referred to as U.S. circuit courts of appeals. Twelve of the federal courts of appeals (including the Court of Appeals for the D.C. Circuit) hear appeals from the federal district courts located within their respective judicial circuits, or geographic boundaries (shown in Exhibit 2–2).[15] The Court of Appeals for the Thirteenth Circuit, called

15. Historically, judges were required to "ride the circuit" and hear appeals in different courts around the country, which is at the origin of the name "circuit court."

EXHIBIT 2–2 • **Geographic Boundaries of the U.S. Courts of Appeals and U.S. District Courts**

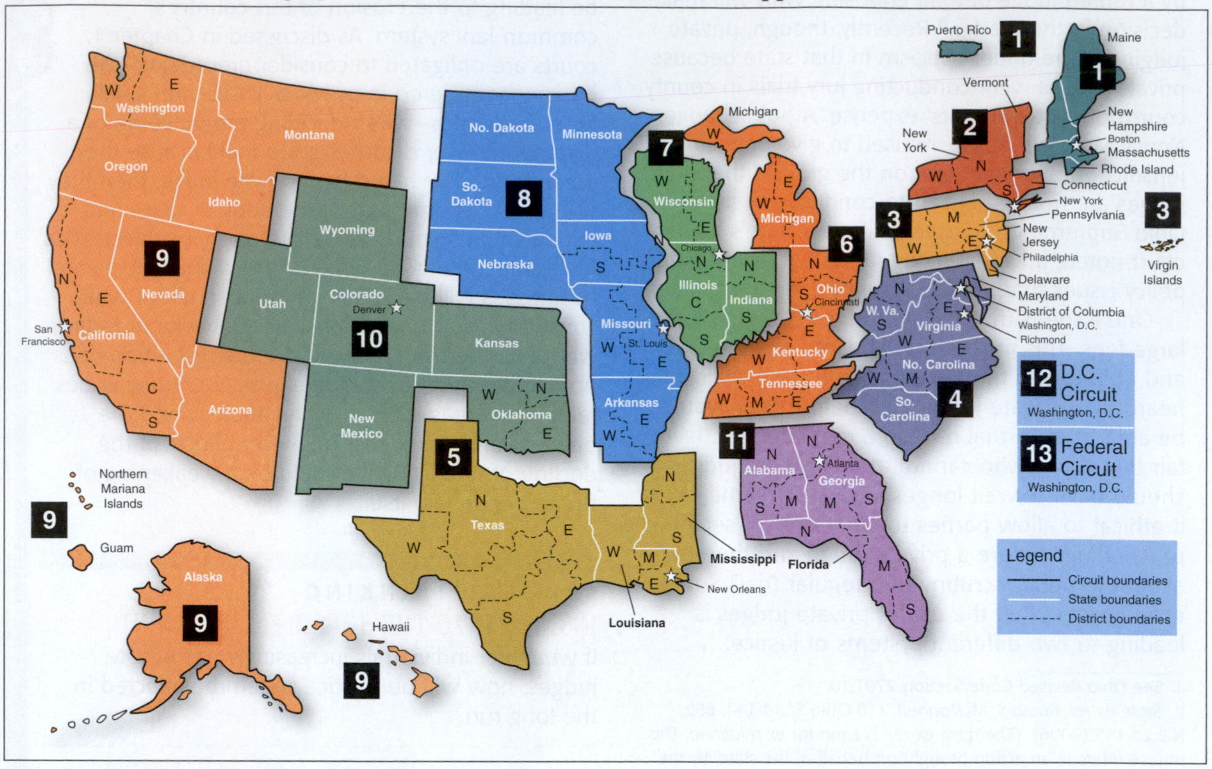

Source: Administrative Office of the United States Courts.

the Federal Circuit, has national appellate jurisdiction over certain types of cases, such as those involving patent law and those in which the U.S. government is a defendant. The decisions of a circuit court of appeals are binding on all courts within the circuit court's jurisdiction and are final in most cases, but appeal to the United States Supreme Court is possible.

United States Supreme Court At the highest level in the three-tiered federal court system is the United States Supreme Court. According to the language of Article III of the U.S. Constitution, there is only one national Supreme Court. All other courts in the federal system are considered "inferior." Congress is empowered to create other inferior courts as it deems necessary. The inferior courts that Congress has created include the second tier in our model—the U.S. circuit courts of appeals—as well as the district courts and the various federal courts of limited, or specialized, jurisdiction.

The United States Supreme Court consists of nine justices. Although the Supreme Court has original, or trial, jurisdiction in rare instances (set forth in Article III, Sections 1 and 2), most of its work is as an appeals court. The Supreme Court can review any case decided by any of the federal courts of appeals, and it also has appellate authority over cases involving federal questions that have been decided in the state courts. The Supreme Court is the final arbiter of the Constitution and federal law.

Appeals to the Supreme Court. To bring a case before the Supreme Court, a party requests the Court to issue a writ of *certiorari*.[16] A **writ of *certiorari*** is an order issued by the Supreme Court to a lower court requiring the latter to send it the record of the case for review. The Court will not issue a writ unless at least four of the nine justices approve of it. This is called the **rule of four.** Whether the Court will issue a writ of *certiorari* is entirely within its discretion, and most petitions for writs are denied. (Thousands of cases are filed with the Supreme Court each year, yet it hears, on average, fewer than one hundred of these cases.[17]) A denial is not a decision on the merits of a case, nor does it indicate agreement with the lower court's opin-

16. Pronounced sur-shee-uh-*rah*-ree.

17. From the mid-1950s through the early 1990s, the Supreme Court reviewed more cases per year than it has since then. In the Court's 1982–1983 term, for example, the Court issued written opinions in 151 cases. In contrast, during the Court's 2007–2008 term, the Court issued written opinions in only 72 cases.

CONCEPT SUMMARY 2.2
Types of Courts

Court	Description
TRIAL COURTS	Trial courts are courts of original jurisdiction in which actions are initiated. 1. *State courts*—Courts of general jurisdiction can hear any case that has not been specifically designated for another court; courts of limited jurisdiction include, among others, domestic relations courts, probate courts, municipal courts, and small claims courts. 2. *Federal courts*—The federal district court is the equivalent of the state trial court. Federal courts of limited jurisdiction include the bankruptcy courts and others shown in Exhibit 2–1 on page 35.
INTERMEDIATE APPELLATE COURTS	Courts of appeals are reviewing courts; generally, appellate courts do not have original jurisdiction. About three-fourths of the states have intermediate appellate courts; in the federal court system, the U.S. circuit courts of appeals are the intermediate appellate courts.
SUPREME COURT	The highest state court is that state's supreme court, although it may be called by some other name. Appeal from state supreme courts to the United States Supreme Court is possible only if a federal question is involved. The United States Supreme Court is the highest court in the federal court system and the final arbiter of the Constitution and federal law.

ion. Also, denial of the writ has no value as a precedent. Denial simply means that the lower court's decision remains the law in that jurisdiction.

Petitions Granted by the Court. Typically, the Court grants petitions in cases that raise important constitutional questions or when the lower courts have issued conflicting decisions on a significant issue. The justices, however, never explain their reasons for hearing certain cases and not others, so it is difficult to predict which type of case the Court might select. (See *Concept Summary 2.2* to review the various types of courts in the federal and state court systems.)

SECTION 4 Alternative Dispute Resolution

Litigation—the process of resolving a dispute through the court system—is expensive and time consuming. Litigating even the simplest complaint is costly, and because of the backlog of cases pending in many courts, several years may pass before a case is actually tried. For these and other reasons, more and more businesspersons are turning to **alternative dispute resolution (ADR)** as a means of settling their disputes.

The great advantage of ADR is its flexibility. Methods of ADR range from the parties sitting down together and attempting to work out their differences to multinational corporations agreeing to resolve a dispute through a formal hearing before a panel of experts. Normally, the parties themselves can control how the dispute will be settled, what procedures will be used, whether a neutral third party will be present or make a decision, and whether that decision will be legally binding or nonbinding. ADR also offers more privacy than court proceedings and allows disputes to be resolved relatively quickly.

Today, more than 90 percent of civil lawsuits are settled before trial using some form of ADR. Indeed, most states either require or encourage parties to undertake ADR prior to trial. Many federal courts have instituted ADR programs as well. In the following pages, we examine the basic forms of ADR.

Negotiation

The simplest form of ADR is **negotiation,** a process in which the parties attempt to settle their dispute informally, with or without attorneys to represent them. Attorneys frequently advise their clients to negotiate a settlement voluntarily before they proceed to trial. In some courts, pretrial negotiation is mandatory before parties can proceed to trial. Parties may even try to negotiate a settlement during a trial or after the trial but before an appeal. Negotiation traditionally involves just the parties themselves and (typically) their attorneys. The attorneys, though, are advocates—they are obligated to put their clients' interests first.

Mediation

In **mediation,** a neutral third party acts as a mediator and works with both sides in the dispute to facilitate a resolution. The mediator normally talks with the parties separately as well as jointly, emphasizes points of agreement, and helps the parties to evaluate their options. Although the mediator may propose a solution (called a mediator's proposal), he or she does not make a decision resolving the matter. The mediator, who need not be a lawyer, usually charges a fee for his or her services (which can be split between the parties). States that require parties to undergo ADR before trial often offer mediation as one of the ADR options or (as in Florida) the only option.

One of the biggest advantages of mediation is that it is not as adversarial in nature as litigation. In mediation, the mediator takes an active role and attempts to bring the parties together so that they can come to a mutually satisfactory resolution. The mediation process tends to reduce the antagonism between the disputants, allowing them to resume their former relationship while minimizing hostility. For this reason, mediation is often the preferred form of ADR for disputes involving business partners, employers and employees, or other parties involved in long-term relationships.

Today, characteristics of mediation are being combined with those of arbitration (to be discussed next). In *binding mediation,* for example, the parties agree that if they cannot resolve the dispute, the mediator can make a legally binding decision on the issue. In *mediation-arbitration,* or "med-arb," the parties first attempt to settle their dispute through mediation. If no settlement is reached, the dispute will be arbitrated.

Arbitration

A more formal method of ADR is **arbitration,** in which an arbitrator (a neutral third party or a panel of experts) hears a dispute and imposes a resolution on the parties. Arbitration differs from other forms of ADR in that the third party hearing the dispute makes a decision for the parties. Exhibit 2–3 outlines the basic differences among the three traditional forms of ADR. Usually, the parties in arbitration agree that the third party's decision will be *legally binding,* although the parties can also agree to *nonbinding* arbitration. (Additionally, arbitration that is mandated by the courts often is not binding on the parties.) In nonbinding arbitration, the parties can go forward with a lawsuit if they do not agree with the arbitrator's decision.

The Arbitration Process In some respects, formal arbitration resembles a trial, although usually the procedural rules are much less restrictive than those governing litigation. In a typical arbitration, the par-

EXHIBIT 2–3 • Basic Differences in the Traditional Forms of ADR

Type of ADR	Description	Neutral Third Party Present	Who Decides the Resolution
Negotiation	Parties meet informally with or without their attorneys and attempt to agree on a resolution.	No.	The parties themselves reach a resolution.
Mediation	A neutral third party meets with the parties and emphasizes points of agreement to bring them toward resolution of their dispute.	Yes.	The parties, but the mediator may suggest or propose a resolution.
Arbitration	The parties present their arguments and evidence before an arbitrator at a hearing, and the arbitrator renders a decision resolving the parties' dispute.	Yes.	The arbitrator imposes a resolution on the parties that may be either binding or nonbinding.

ties present opening arguments and ask for specific remedies. Evidence is then presented, and witnesses may be called and examined by both sides. The arbitrator then renders a decision, called an **award.**

An arbitrator's award is usually the final word on the matter. Although the parties may appeal an arbitrator's decision, a court's review of the decision will be much more restricted in scope than an appellate court's review of a trial court's decision. The general view is that because the parties were free to frame the issues and set the powers of the arbitrator at the outset, they cannot complain about the results. The award will be set aside only if the arbitrator's conduct or "bad faith" substantially prejudiced the rights of one of the parties, if the award violates an established public policy, or if the arbitrator exceeded her or his powers (by arbitrating issues that the parties did not agree to submit to arbitration).

Arbitration Clauses and Statutes Virtually any commercial matter can be submitted to arbitration. Frequently, parties include an **arbitration clause** in a contract (a written agreement—see Chapter 10) specifying that any dispute arising under the contract will be resolved through arbitration rather than through the court system. Parties can also agree to arbitrate a dispute after it arises.

Most states have statutes (often based in part on the Uniform Arbitration Act of 1955) under which arbitration clauses will be enforced, and some state statutes compel arbitration of certain types of disputes, such as those involving public employees. At the federal level, the Federal Arbitration Act (FAA), enacted in 1925, enforces arbitration clauses in contracts involving maritime activity and interstate commerce. Because of the breadth of the commerce clause (see Chapter 4), arbitration agreements involving transactions only slightly connected to the flow of interstate commerce may fall under the FAA.

The question in the following case was whether a court or an arbitrator should consider a claim that an entire contract, including its arbitration clause, is rendered void by the alleged illegality of a separate provision in the contract.

CASE 2.2 Buckeye Check Cashing, Inc. v. Cardegna

Supreme Court of the United States, 2006. 546 U.S. 440, 126 S.Ct. 1204, 163 L.Ed.2d 1038.
www.law.cornell.edu/supct/index.html[a]

• **Background and Facts** Buckeye Check Cashing, Inc., cashes personal checks for consumers in Florida. Buckeye agrees to delay submitting a check for payment in exchange for a consumer's payment of a "finance charge." For each transaction, the consumer signs a "Deferred Deposit and Disclosure Agreement," which states, "By signing this Agreement, you agree that i[f] a dispute of any kind arises out of this Agreement * * * th[e]n either you or we or third-parties involved can choose to have that dispute resolved by binding arbitration." John Cardegna and others filed a suit in a Florida state court against Buckeye, alleging that the "finance charge" represented an illegally high interest rate in violation of Florida state laws, rendering the agreement "criminal on its face." Buckeye filed a motion to compel arbitration. The court denied the motion. On Buckeye's appeal, a state intermediate appellate court reversed this denial, but on the plaintiffs' appeal, the Florida Supreme Court reversed the lower appellate court's decision. Buckeye appealed to the United States Supreme Court.

• **Decision and Rationale** The United States Supreme Court reversed the judgment of the Florida Supreme Court and remanded the case for further proceedings. The Court ruled that a challenge to the validity of a contract as a whole, and not specifically to an arbitration clause contained in the contract, must be resolved by an arbitrator. The Court set out three propositions. "First, as a matter of substantive federal arbitration law, an arbitration provision is severable [capable of being legally separated] from the remainder of the contract. Second, unless the challenge is to the arbitration clause itself, the issue of the contract's validity is considered by the arbitrator in the first instance. Third, this arbitration law applies in state as well as federal courts." The Court concluded that here, because the plaintiffs challenged the contract's "finance charge," but not its arbitration provisions, those provisions were enforceable apart from the remainder of the contract. "The

a. In the "Supreme Court Collection" menu at the top of the page, click on "Search." When that page opens, in the "Search for:" box, type "Buckeye Check," choose "All decisions" in the accompanying list, and click on "Search." In the result, scroll to the name of the case and click on the appropriate link to access the opinion.

CASE CONTINUES

CASE 2.2 CONTINUED challenge should therefore be considered by an arbitrator, not a court." The plaintiffs also argued that the only arbitration agreements to which the Federal Arbitration Act (FAA) applies are those involving contracts and that the Buckeye agreement was not a contract because it was "void *ab initio*" (from the beginning). The FAA allows a challenge to an arbitration provision "upon such grounds as exist at law or in equity for the revocation [cancellation] of any contract." The Court reasoned that this includes contracts that later prove to be void. "Otherwise, the grounds for revocation would be limited to those that rendered a contract voidable—which would mean (implausibly) that an arbitration agreement could be challenged as voidable but not as void."

- **The Ethical Dimension** *Does the holding in this case permit a court to enforce an arbitration agreement in a contract that the arbitrator later finds to be void? Is this fair? Why or why not?*

- **The Legal Environment Dimension** *As indicated in the parties' arguments and the Court's reasoning in this case, into what categories can contracts be classified with respect to their enforceability?*

Arbitrability When a dispute arises as to whether the parties to a contract with an arbitration clause have agreed to submit a particular matter to arbitration, one party may file suit to compel arbitration. The court before which the suit is brought will not decide the basic controversy but must decide the issue of *arbitrability*—that is, whether the matter is one that must be resolved through arbitration. If the court finds that the subject matter in controversy is covered by the agreement to arbitrate, then a party may be compelled to arbitrate the dispute. Even when a claim involves a violation of a statute passed to protect a certain class of people, a court may determine that the parties must nonetheless abide by their agreement to arbitrate the dispute. Usually, a court will allow the claim to be arbitrated if the court, in interpreting the statute, can find no legislative intent to the contrary.

No party, however, will be ordered to submit a particular dispute to arbitration unless the court is convinced that the party has consented to do so.[18] Additionally, the courts will not compel arbitration if it is clear that the prescribed arbitration rules and procedures are inherently unfair to one of the parties.[19]

The terms of an arbitration agreement can limit the types of disputes that the parties agree to arbitrate. When the parties do not specify limits, however, disputes can arise as to whether the particular matter is covered by the arbitration agreement, and it is up to the court to resolve the issue of arbitrability. In the following case, the parties had previously agreed to arbitrate disputes involving their contract to develop software, but the dispute involved claims of copyright infringement (see Chapter 8). The question was whether the copyright infringement claims were beyond the scope of the arbitration clause.

18. See, for example, *Wright v. Universal Maritime Service Corp.*, 525 U.S. 70, 119 S.Ct. 391, 142 L.Ed.2d 361 (1998).

19. *Hooters of America, Inc. v. Phillips*, 173 F.3d 933 (4th Cir. 1999).

CASE 2.3 NCR Corp. v. Korala Associates, Ltd.

United States Court of Appeals, Sixth Circuit, 2008. 512 F.3d 807.
www.ca6.uscourts.gov[a]

- **Background and Facts** In response to a need to upgrade the security of its automated teller machines (ATMs), NCR Corporation developed a software solution to install in all of its machines. At the same time, Korala Associates, Ltd. (KAL), claimed to have developed a similar security upgrade for NCR's ATMs. Indeed, KAL had entered into a contract with NCR in 1998 (the "1998 Agreement") to develop such software. To enable KAL to do so, NCR loaned to KAL a proprietary ATM that contained copyrighted software called APTRA XFS. NCR alleged that KAL "obtained access to, made unauthorized use of, and engaged in unauthorized copying of the APTRA XFS software." By so doing, KAL

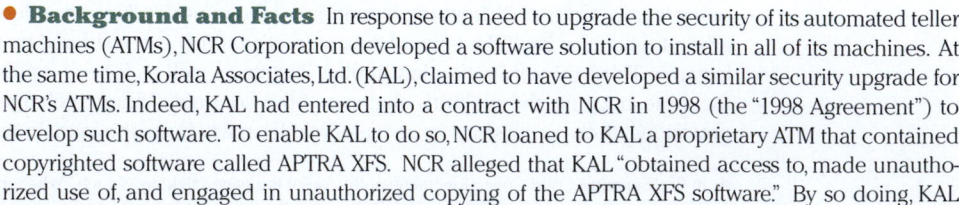

a. Click on "Opinions Search" and then on "Short Title;" and type "NCR." Click on "Submit Query." Next, click on the opinion link in the first column of the row corresponding to the name of this case.

CASE 2.3 CONTINUED developed its own version of a security upgrade for NCR's ATMs. When NCR brought a suit against KAL, the latter moved to compel arbitration under the terms of the 1998 Agreement between the two companies. At trial, KAL prevailed. NCR appealed the order compelling arbitration to the U.S. Court of Appeals for the Sixth Circuit.

- **Decision and Rationale** The U.S. Court of Appeals for the Sixth Circuit affirmed the judgment compelling arbitration as to NCR's claims relating to direct copyright infringement of certain software. The court pointed out that the 1998 Agreement clearly provided for arbitration. The court still faced the issue of determining whether NCR's claims fell within the substantive scope of the Agreement. "As a matter of Federal law, any doubts concerning the scope of arbitrable issues should be resolved in favor of arbitration." Because the arbitration clause in the 1998 Agreement was so broad, the appellate court reasoned that a trial court should follow the "presumption of arbitration and resolve doubts in favor of arbitration." Consequently, the court found that the copyright infringement claim that NCR alleged fell within the scope of the arbitration agreement.

- **The Ethical Dimension** *Could NCR have a claim that KAL had engaged in unfair competition because KAL had engaged in unethical business practices? (Hint: Unfair competition may occur when one party deceives the public into believing that his or her goods are the goods of another.) Why or why not?*

- **The Legal Environment Dimension** *Why do you think that NCR did not want its alleged claims decided by arbitration?*

Mandatory Arbitration in the Employment Context A significant question in the last several years has concerned mandatory arbitration clauses in employment contracts. Many claim that employees' rights are not sufficiently protected when they are forced, as a condition of being hired, to agree to arbitrate all disputes and thus waive their rights under statutes specifically designed to protect employees. The United States Supreme Court, however, has held that mandatory arbitration clauses in employment contracts are generally enforceable.[20] (Recently, however, some courts have been striking arbitration clauses because they shocked the conscience of the courts. See the *Business Application* feature on the following page.)

The United States Supreme Court has made it clear that arbitration clauses in employment contracts are enforceable under the FAA. Nevertheless, to prevent future disputes, business owners and managers would be wise to exercise caution when drafting such clauses and requiring employees to sign them. It is especially important to make certain that the terms of the agreement (including how the parties will split the costs of the arbitration procedure, for example) are not so one sided and unfair that a court could declare the entire agreement unenforceable.

Other Types of ADR

The three forms of ADR just discussed are the oldest and traditionally the most commonly used forms. As mentioned earlier, a variety of new types of ADR have emerged in recent years, including those described here.

1. In **early neutral case evaluation,** the parties select a neutral third party (generally an expert in the subject matter of the dispute) to evaluate their respective positions. The parties explain their positions to the case evaluator, and the case evaluator assesses the strengths and weaknesses of each party's claims.
2. In a **mini-trial,** each party's attorney briefly argues the party's case before the other and a panel of representatives from each side who have the authority to settle the dispute. Typically, a neutral third party (usually an expert in the area being disputed) acts as an adviser. If the parties fail to reach an agreement, the adviser renders an opinion as to how a court would likely decide the issue.
3. Numerous federal courts now hold **summary jury trials (SJTs),** in which the parties present their arguments and evidence and the jury renders a verdict.

20. For a landmark decision on this issue, see *Gilmer v. Interstate/Johnson Lane Corp.*, 500 U.S. 20, 111 S.Ct. 1647, 114 L.Ed.2d 26 (1991).

BUSINESS APPLICATION
Arbitration Clauses in Employment Contracts

MANAGEMENT FACES A LEGAL ISSUE

Arbitration is normally simpler, speedier, and less costly than litigation. For that reason, business owners and managers today often include arbitration clauses in their contracts, including employment contracts. What happens, though, if a job candidate whom you wish to hire (or an existing employee whose contract is being renewed) objects to one or more of the provisions in an arbitration clause? If you insist that signing the agreement to arbitrate future disputes is a mandatory condition of employment, will such a clause be enforceable? Put another way, in which situations might a court invalidate an arbitration agreement because it is considered *unconscionable* (morally unacceptable—shocks the conscience)?

WHAT THE COURTS SAY

The United States Supreme Court has consistently taken the position that because the Federal Arbitration Act (FAA) favors the arbitration of disputes, arbitration clauses in employment contracts should generally be enforced. Nonetheless, some courts have held that arbitration clauses in employment contracts should not be enforced if they are too one sided and unfair to the employee. In one case, for example, the U.S. Court of Appeals for the Ninth Circuit refused to enforce an arbitration clause on the ground that the agreement was unconscionable—so one sided and unfair as to be unenforceable under "ordinary principles of state contract law." The agreement was a standard-form contract drafted by the employer (the party with superior bargaining power), and the employee had to sign it without any modification as a prerequisite to employment. Moreover, only the employees were required to arbitrate their disputes, while the employer remained free to litigate any claims it had against its employees in court. Among other things, the contract also severely limited the relief that was available to employees. For these reasons, the court held the entire arbitration agreement unenforceable.[a] Other courts have cited similar reasons for deciding not to enforce one-sided arbitration clauses.[b]

In a more recent case, employees of a large California law firm were given copies of that firm's new dispute-resolution program. The program culminated in final binding arbitration for most employment-related claims by and against the firm's employees. The new program became effective three months after it was distributed. After leaving employment at the law firm, an employee filed a lawsuit alleging failure to pay overtime wages. She also claimed that her former employer's dispute-resolution program was unconscionable. The reviewing court found that the dispute-resolution program was presented to the employees on a take-it-or-leave-it basis and was therefore procedurally unconscionable. The court also found that the program was substantively unconscionable because it required employees to waive claims if those employees failed to give the firm notice and demand for mediation within one year from the time when the claim was known.[c]

IMPLICATIONS FOR MANAGERS

Although the United States Supreme Court has made it clear that arbitration clauses in employment contracts are enforceable under the FAA, managers should be careful when drafting such clauses. It is especially important to make sure that the terms of the agreement are not so one sided that a court could declare the entire agreement unconscionable.

Managers should also be aware that the proposed Arbitration Fairness Act might eventually become law. This planned "consumer protection" bill would render unenforceable all predispute mandatory arbitration provisions in consumer, employment, and franchise contracts. It would amend the FAA and seriously restrict the ability of firms to require arbitration.

a. *Circuit City Stores, Inc. v. Adams,* 279 F.3d 889 (9th Cir. 2002). (This was the Ninth Circuit's decision, on remand, after the United States Supreme Court reviewed the case.)

b. See, for example, *Hooters of America, Inc. v. Phillips,* 173 F.3d 933 (4th Cir. 1999); and *Hardwick v. Sherwin Williams Co.,* 2002 WL 31992364 (Ohio App. 8 Dist. 2003).

c. *Davis v. O'Melveny & Myers, LLC,* 485 F.3d 1066 (9th Cir. 2007).

The jury's verdict is not binding, but it does act as a guide to both sides in reaching an agreement during the mandatory negotiations that immediately follow the trial.

4. Other alternatives being employed by the courts include summary procedures for commercial litigation and the appointment of special masters to assist judges in deciding complex issues.

Providers of ADR Services

Both government agencies and private organizations provide ADR services. A major provider of ADR services is the **American Arbitration Association (AAA),** which was founded in 1926 and now handles more than two hundred thousand claims each year in its numerous offices around the country. Cases brought before the AAA are heard by an expert or a panel of experts in the area relating to the dispute and are usually settled quickly. Generally, about half of the panel members are lawyers. To cover its costs, the AAA charges a fee, paid by the party filing the claim. In addition, each party to the dispute pays a specified amount for each hearing day, as well as a special additional fee in cases involving personal injuries or property loss.

Hundreds of for-profit firms around the country also provide dispute-resolution services. Typically, these firms hire retired judges to conduct arbitration hearings or otherwise assist parties in settling their disputes. The judges follow procedures similar to those of the federal courts and use similar rules. Usually, each party to the dispute pays a filing fee and a designated fee for a hearing session or conference.

Online Dispute Resolution

An increasing number of companies and organizations are offering dispute-resolution services using the Internet. The settlement of disputes in these online forums is known as **online dispute resolution (ODR).** The disputes resolved in these forums have most commonly involved disagreements over the rights to domain names (Web site addresses—see Chapter 8) or the quality of goods sold via the Internet, including goods sold through Internet auction sites.

At this time, ODR may be best for resolving small- to medium-sized business liability claims, which may not be worth the expense of litigation or traditional ADR methods. Rules being developed in online forums, however, may ultimately become a code of conduct for everyone who does business in cyberspace. Most online forums do not automatically apply the law of any specific jurisdiction. Instead, results are often based on general, more universal legal principles. As with offline methods of dispute resolution, any party may appeal to a court at any time.

SECTION 5 International Dispute Resolution

Businesspersons who engage in international business transactions normally take special precautions to protect themselves in the event that a party with whom they are dealing in another country breaches an agreement. Often, parties to international contracts include special clauses in their contracts providing for how disputes arising under the contracts will be resolved.

Forum-Selection and Choice-of-Law Clauses

As you will read in Chapter 20, parties to international transactions often include forum-selection and choice-of-law clauses in their contracts. These clauses designate the jurisdiction (court or country) where any dispute arising under the contract will be litigated and the nation's law that will be applied. When an international contract does not include such clauses, any legal proceedings arising under the contract will be more complex and attended by much more uncertainty. For example, litigation may take place in two or more countries, with each country applying its own national law to the particular transactions.

Furthermore, even if a plaintiff wins a favorable judgment in a lawsuit litigated in the plaintiff's country, the defendant's country could refuse to enforce the court's judgment. As will be discussed in Chapter 52, for reasons of courtesy, the judgment may be enforced in the defendant's country, particularly if the defendant's country is the United States and the foreign court's decision is consistent with U.S. national law and policy. Other nations, however, may not be as accommodating as the United States, and the plaintiff may be left empty-handed.

Arbitration Clauses

Parties to international contracts also often include arbitration clauses in their contracts that require a neutral third party to decide any contract disputes. In international arbitration proceedings, the third party may be a neutral entity (such as the International Chamber of Commerce), a panel of individuals representing both parties' interests, or some other group or organization. The United Nations Convention on the Recognition and Enforcement of Foreign Arbitral Awards[21]—which has been implemented in more than fifty countries, including the United States—assists in the enforcement of arbitration clauses, as do provisions in specific treaties among nations. The American Arbitration Association provides arbitration services for international as well as domestic disputes.

21. June 10, 1958, 21 U.S.T. 2517, T.I.A.S. No. 6997 (the "New York Convention").

REVIEWING Courts and Alternative Dispute Resolution

Stan Garner resides in Illinois and promotes boxing matches for SuperSports, Inc., an Illinois corporation. Garner created the concept of "Ages" promotion–a three-fight series of boxing matches pitting an older fighter (George Foreman) against a younger fighter, such as John Ruiz or Riddick Bowe. The concept included titles for each of the three fights ("Challenge of the Ages," "Battle of the Ages," and "Fight of the Ages"), as well as promotional epithets to characterize the two fighters ("the Foreman Factor"). Garner contacted George Foreman and his manager, who both reside in Texas, to sell the idea, and they arranged a meeting at Caesar's Palace in Las Vegas, Nevada. At some point in the negotiations, Foreman's manager signed a nondisclosure agreement prohibiting him from disclosing Garner's promotional concepts unless the parties signed a contract. Nevertheless, after negotiations between Garner and Foreman fell through, Foreman used Garner's "Battle of the Ages" concept to promote a subsequent fight. Garner filed a suit against Foreman and his manager in a federal district court located in Illinois, alleging breach of contract. Using the information presented in the chapter, answer the following questions.

1. On what basis might the federal district court in Illinois exercise jurisdiction in this case?
2. Does the federal district court have original or appellate jurisdiction?
3. Suppose that Garner had filed his action in an Illinois state court. Could an Illinois state court exercise personal jurisdiction over Foreman or his manager? Why or why not?
4. Assume that Garner had filed his action in a Nevada state court. Would that court have personal jurisdiction over Foreman or his manager? Explain.

TERMS AND CONCEPTS

alternative dispute resolution (ADR) 39
American Arbitration Association (AAA) 45
arbitration 40
arbitration clause 41
award 41
bankruptcy court 31
concurrent jurisdiction 31
diversity of citizenship 31
early neutral case evaluation 43
exclusive jurisdiction 31
federal question 31
***in personam* jurisdiction 29**
***in rem* jurisdiction 29**
judicial review 28
jurisdiction 29
justiciable controversy 34
litigation 39
long arm statute 29
mediation 40
mini-trial 43
negotiation 39
online dispute resolution (ODR) 45
probate court 30
question of fact 35
question of law 36
rule of four 38
small claims court 35
standing to sue 34
summary jury trial (SJT) 43
venue 34
writ of *certiorari* 38

QUESTIONS AND CASE PROBLEMS

2-1. In an arbitration proceeding, the arbitrator need not be a judge or even a lawyer. How, then, can the arbitrator's decision have the force of law and be binding on the parties involved?

2-2. QUESTION WITH SAMPLE ANSWER

The defendant in a lawsuit is appealing the trial court's decision in favor of the plaintiff. On appeal, the defendant claims that the evidence presented at trial to support the plaintiff's claim was so scanty that no reasonable jury could have found for the plaintiff. Therefore, argues the defendant, the appellate court should reverse the trial court's decision. Will an appellate court ever reverse a trial court's findings with respect to questions of fact? Discuss fully.

- **For a sample answer to Question 2-2, go to Appendix I at the end of this text.**

2-3. Appellate courts normally see only written transcripts of trial proceedings when they are reviewing cases. Today, in some states, videotapes are being used as the official trial reports. If the use of videotapes as official reports continues, will this alter the appellate process? Should it? Discuss fully.

2-4. Marya Callais, a citizen of Florida, was walking along a busy street in Tallahassee, Florida, when a large crate flew off a passing truck and hit her, causing numerous injuries. She experienced a great deal of pain and suffering, incurred significant medical expenses, and could not work for six months. She wants to sue the trucking firm for $300,000 in damages. The firm's headquarters are in Georgia, although the company does business in Florida. In what court might Callais bring suit—a Florida state court, a Georgia state court, or a federal court? What factors might influence her decision?

2-5. E-Jurisdiction. American Business Financial Services, Inc. (ABFI), a Pennsylvania firm, sells and services loans to businesses and consumers. First Union National Bank, with its principal place of business in North Carolina, provides banking services. Alan Boyer, an employee of First Union, lives in North Carolina and has never been to Pennsylvania. In the course of his employment, Boyer learned that the bank was going to extend a $150 million line of credit to ABFI. Boyer then attempted to manipulate the price of ABFI's stock for personal gain by sending disparaging e-mails to ABFI's independent auditors in Pennsylvania. Boyer also posted negative statements about ABFI and its management on a Yahoo bulletin board. ABFI filed a suit in a Pennsylvania state court against Boyer, First Union, and others, alleging wrongful interference with a contractual relationship, among other things. Boyer filed a motion to dismiss the complaint for lack of personal jurisdiction. Could the court exercise jurisdiction over Boyer? Explain. [*American Business Financial Services, Inc. v. First Union National Bank*, __ A.2d __ (Pa.Comm.Pl. 2002)]

2-6. Arbitration. Alexander Little worked for Auto Stiegler, Inc., an automobile dealership in Los Angeles County, California, eventually becoming the service manager. While employed, Little signed an arbitration agreement that required the submission of all employment-related disputes to arbitration. The agreement also provided that any award over $50,000 could be appealed to a second arbitrator. Little was later demoted and terminated. Alleging that these actions were in retaliation for investigating and reporting warranty fraud and thus were in violation of public policy, Little filed a suit in a California state court against Auto Stiegler. The defendant filed a motion with the court to compel arbitration. Little responded that the arbitration agreement should not be enforced because, among other things, the appeal provision was unfairly one sided. Is this provision enforceable? Should the court grant Auto Stiegler's motion? Why or why not? [*Little v. Auto Stiegler, Inc.*, 29 Cal.4th 1064, 63 P.3d 979, 130 Cal.Rptr.2d 892 (2003)]

2-7. Jurisdiction. KaZaA BV was a company formed under the laws of the Netherlands. KaZaA distributed KaZaA Media Desktop (KMD) software, which enabled users to exchange digital media, including movies and music, via a peer-to-peer transfer network. KaZaA also operated the KaZaA.com Web site, through which it distributed the KMD software to millions of California residents and other users. Metro-Goldwyn-Mayer Studios, Inc., and other parties in the entertainment industries based in California filed a suit in a federal district court against KaZaA and others, alleging copyright infringement. KaZaA filed a counterclaim, but while legal action was pending, the firm passed its assets and its Web site to Sharman Networks, Ltd., a company organized under the laws of Vanuatu (an island republic east of Australia) and doing business principally in Australia. Sharman explicitly disclaimed the assumption of any of KaZaA's liabilities. When the plaintiffs added Sharman as a defendant, Sharman filed a motion to dismiss on the ground that the court did not have jurisdiction. Would it be fair to subject Sharman to suit in this case? Explain. [*Metro-Goldwyn-Mayer Studios, Inc. v. Grokster, Ltd.*, 243 F.Supp.2d 1073 (C.D.Cal. 2003)]

2-8. CASE PROBLEM WITH SAMPLE ANSWER

Michael and Karla Covington live in Jefferson County, Idaho. When they bought their home, a gravel pit was across the street. In 1995, the county converted the pit to a landfill. Under the county's operation, the landfill accepted major appliances, household garbage, spilled grain, grass clippings, straw, manure, animal carcasses, containers with hazardous content warnings, leaking car batteries, and waste oil, among other things. The deposits were often left uncovered, attracting insects and other scavengers and contaminating the groundwater. Fires broke out, including at least one started by an intruder who entered the property through an unlocked gate. The Covingtons complained to the state, which inspected the landfill, but no changes were made to address their concerns. Finally, the Covingtons filed a suit in a federal district court against the county and the state, charging violations of federal environmental laws. Those laws were designed to minimize the risks of injuries from fires, scavengers, groundwater contamination, and other pollution dangers. Did the Covingtons have standing to sue? What principles apply? Explain. [*Covington v. Jefferson County,* 358 F.3d 626 (9th Cir. 2004)]

- **To view a sample answer for Problem 2–8, go to this book's Web site at www.cengage.com/blaw/jentz, select "Chapter 2," and click on "Case Problem with Sample Answer."**

2–9. E-Jurisdiction. Xcentric Ventures, LLC, is an Arizona firm that operates the Web sites RipOffReport.com and BadBusinessBureau.com. Visitors to the sites can buy a copy of a book titled *Do-It-Yourself Guide: How to Get Rip-Off Revenge.* The price ($21.95) includes shipping to anywhere in the United States, including Illinois, to which thirteen copies have been shipped. The sites accept donations and feature postings by individuals who claim to have been "ripped off." Some visitors posted comments about George S. May International Co., a management consulting firm. The postings alleged fraud, larceny, possession of child pornography, and possession of controlled substances (illegal drugs). May filed a suit in a federal district court in Illinois against Xcentric and others, charging, among other things, "false descriptions and representations." The defendants filed a motion to dismiss for lack of jurisdiction. What is the standard for exercising jurisdiction over a party whose only connection to a jurisdiction is over the Web? How would that standard apply in this case? Explain. [*George S. May International Co. v. Xcentric Ventures, LLC,* 409 F.Supp.2d 1052 (N.D.Ill. 2006)]

2–10. Jurisdiction. In 2001, Raul Leal, the owner and operator of Texas Labor Contractors in East Texas, contacted Poverty Point Produce, Inc., which operates a sweet potato farm in West Carroll Parish, Louisiana, and offered to provide field workers. Poverty Point accepted the offer. Jeffrey Brown, an owner of, and field manager for, the farm, told Leal the number of workers needed and gave him forms for them to fill out and sign. Leal placed an ad in a newspaper in Brownsville, Texas. Job applicants were directed to Leal's car dealership in Weslaco, Texas, where they were told the details of the work. Leal recruited, among others, Elias Moreno, who lives in the Rio Grande Valley in Texas, and transported Moreno and the others to Poverty Point's farm. At the farm, Leal's brother Jesse oversaw the work with instructions from Brown, lived with the workers in the on-site housing, and gave them their paychecks. When the job was done, the workers were returned to Texas. Moreno and others filed a suit in a federal district court against Poverty Point and others, alleging, in part, violations of Texas state law related to the work. Poverty Point filed a motion to dismiss the suit on the ground that the court did not have personal jurisdiction. All of the meetings between Poverty Point and the Leals occurred in Louisiana. All of the farmwork was done in Louisiana. Poverty Point has no offices, bank accounts, or phone listings in Texas. It does not advertise or solicit business in Texas. Despite these facts, can the court exercise personal jurisdiction? Explain. [*Moreno v. Poverty Point Produce, Inc.,* 243 F.R.D. 275 (S.D.Tex. 2007)]

2–11. A QUESTION OF ETHICS

Linden Research, Inc., operates a multiplayer role-playing game in the virtual world known as "Second Life" at **secondlife.com**. *Participants create avatars to represent themselves on the site. In 2003, Second Life became the only virtual world to recognize participants' rights to buy, own, and sell digital content—virtual property, including "land." Linden's chief executive officer, Philip Rosedale, joined efforts to publicize this recognition and these rights in the real-world media. Rosedale also created an avatar to tout the rights in Second Life town meetings. March Bragg, an experienced Pennsylvania attorney, was a Second Life participant whose avatar attended the meetings, after which Bragg began to invest in Second Life's virtual property. In April 2006, Bragg bought "Taessot," a parcel of virtual land. Linden decided that the purchase was improper, however, and took Taessot from Bragg. Linden also froze Bragg's account, effectively confiscating all of his virtual property and currency. Bragg filed a suit against Linden and Rosedale, claiming that the defendants acted unlawfully. [*Bragg v. Linden Research, Inc., *487 F.Supp.2d 593 (E.D.Pa. 2007)]*

(a) In the federal district court in Pennsylvania that was hearing the suit, Rosedale, who lives in California, filed a motion to dismiss the claim against him for lack of personal jurisdiction. On what basis could the court deny this motion and assert jurisdiction? Is it fair to require Rosedale to appear in a court in a distant location? Explain.

(b) To access Second Life, a participant must accept its "Terms of Service" (TOS) by clicking an "accept" button. Under the TOS, Linden has the right "at any time for any reason or no reason to suspend or terminate your Account," to refuse to return a participant's money, and to amend the terms at its discretion. The terms also stipulate that any dispute be resolved by binding arbitration in California. Is there anything unfair about the TOS? Should the court compel Bragg to arbitrate this dispute? Discuss.

2–12. VIDEO QUESTION

Go to this text's Web site at **www.cengage.com/blaw/jentz** and select "Chapter 2." Click on "Video Questions" and view the video titled *Jurisdiction in Cyberspace.* Then answer the following questions.

(a) What standard would a court apply to determine whether it has jurisdiction over the out-of-state computer firm in the video?

(b) What factors is a court likely to consider in assessing whether sufficient contacts existed when the only connection to the jurisdiction is through a Web site?

(c) How do you think the court would resolve the issue in this case?

LAW ON THE WEB

For updated links to resources available on the Web, as well as a variety of other materials, visit this text's Web site at

www.cengage.com/blaw/jentz

For the decisions of the United States Supreme Court, as well as information about the Supreme Court and its justices, go to either

www.supremecourtus.gov

or

www.oyez.org

The Web site for the federal courts offers information on the federal court system and links to all federal courts at

www.uscourts.gov

The National Center for State Courts (NCSC) offers links to the Web pages of all state courts. Go to

www.ncsconline.org

For information on alternative dispute resolution, go to the American Arbitration Association's Web site at

www.adr.org

Legal Research Exercises on the Web

Go to **www.cengage.com/blaw/jentz**, the Web site that accompanies this text. Select "Chapter 2" and click on "Internet Exercises." There you will find the following Internet research exercises that you can perform to learn more about the topics covered in this chapter.

Internet Exercise 2–1: Legal Perspective
Alternative Dispute Resolution

Internet Exercise 2–2: Management Perspective
Resolve a Dispute Online

Internet Exercise 2–3: Historical Perspective
The Judiciary's Role in American Government

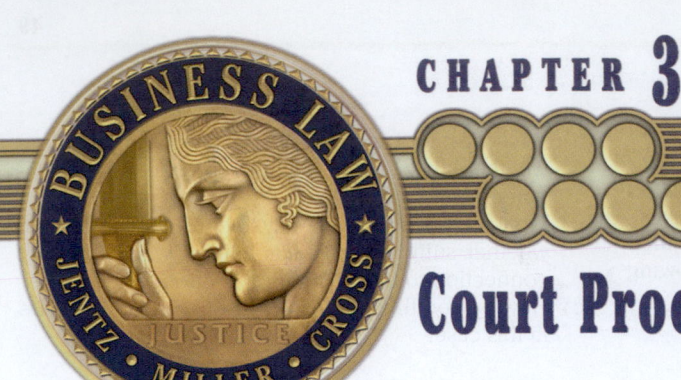

CHAPTER 3

Court Procedures

American and English courts follow the *adversarial system of justice.* Although clients are allowed to represent themselves in court (called *pro se* representation),[1] most parties to lawsuits hire attorneys to represent them. Each lawyer acts as his or her client's advocate, presenting the client's version of the facts in such a way as to convince the judge (or the judge and jury, in a jury trial) that this version is correct.

Most of the judicial procedures that you will read about in the following pages are rooted in the adversarial framework of the American legal system. In this chapter, after a brief overview of judicial procedures, we illustrate the steps involved in a lawsuit with a hypothetical civil case (criminal procedures will be discussed in Chapter 9).

1. This right was definitively established in *Faretta v. California,* 422 U.S. 806, 95 S.Ct. 2525, 45 L.Ed.2d 562 (1975).

SECTION 1

Procedural Rules

The parties to a lawsuit must comply with the procedural rules of the court in which the lawsuit is filed. Although most people, when considering the outcome of a case, think of matters of substantive law, procedural law can have a significant impact on one's ability to assert a legal claim. Procedural rules provide a framework for every dispute and specify what must be done at each stage of the litigation process. All civil trials held in federal district courts are governed by the **Federal Rules of Civil Procedure (FRCP).**[2] Each state also has rules of civil procedure that apply to all courts within that state. In addition, each court has its own local rules of procedure that supplement the federal or state rules.

Stages of Litigation

Broadly speaking, the litigation process has three phases: pretrial, trial, and posttrial. Each phase involves specific procedures, as discussed throughout this chapter. Although civil lawsuits may vary greatly in terms of complexity, cost, and detail, they typically progress through the specific stages charted in Exhibit 3–1.

To illustrate the procedures involved in a civil lawsuit, we will use a simple hypothetical case. The case arose from an automobile accident, which occurred when a car driven by Antonio Carvello, a resident of New Jersey, collided with a car driven by Jill Kirby, a resident of New York. The accident took place at an intersection in New York City. Kirby suffered personal injuries, which caused her to incur medical and hospital expenses as well as lost wages for four months. In all, she calculated that the cost to her of the accident was $100,000.[3] Carvello and Kirby have been unable to agree on a settlement, and Kirby now must decide whether to sue Carvello for the $100,000 compensation she feels she deserves.

2. The United States Supreme Court has authority to set forth these rules, as spelled out in 28 U.S.C. Sections 2071–2077. Generally, though, the federal judiciary appoints committees that make recommendations to the Supreme Court. The Court then publishes any proposed changes in the rules and allows for public comment before finalizing the rules.

3. In this example, we are ignoring damages for pain and suffering or for permanent disabilities. Often, plaintiffs in personal-injury cases seek such damages.

EXHIBIT 3–1 • Stages in a Typical Lawsuit

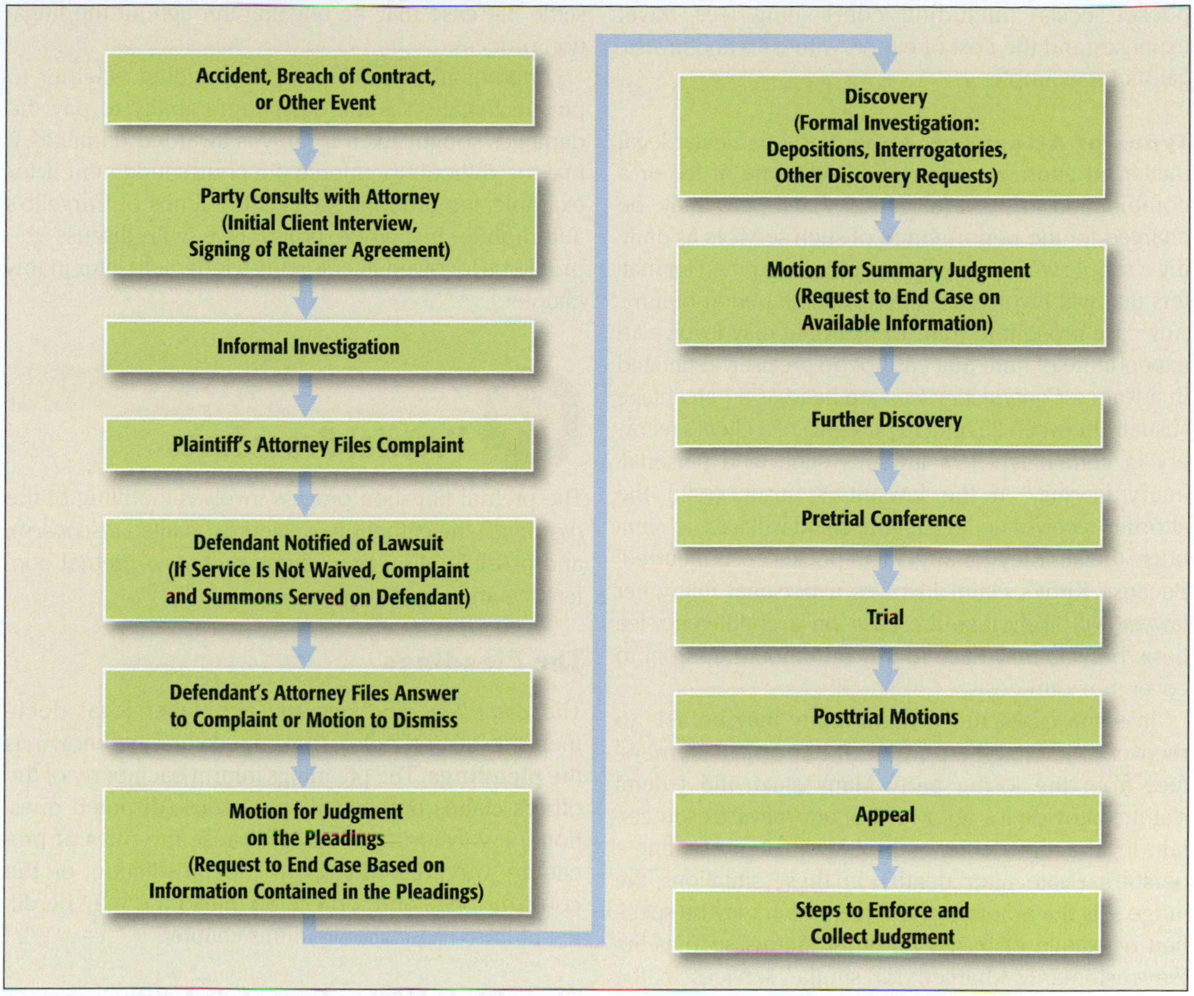

The First Step: Consulting with an Attorney

As mentioned, rules of procedure often affect the outcome of a dispute—a fact that highlights the importance of obtaining the advice of counsel. The first step taken by virtually anyone contemplating a lawsuit is to seek the guidance of a qualified attorney.[4] In the hypothetical Kirby-Carvello case, assume that Kirby consults with a lawyer. The attorney will advise her regarding what she can expect in a lawsuit, her probability of success at trial, and the procedures that will be involved. If more than one court would have jurisdiction over the matter, the attorney will also discuss the advantages and disadvantages of filing in a particular court. Depending on the court hearing the case, the attorney will give Kirby an idea of how much time it will take to resolve the dispute through litigation and provide an estimate of the costs involved.

The attorney will also inform Kirby of the legal fees that she will have to pay in an attempt to collect damages from the defendant, Carvello. Attorneys base their fees on such factors as the difficulty of a matter, the amount of time involved, the experience and skill of the attorney in the particular area of the law, and the cost of doing business. In the United States, legal fees range from $125 to $600 per hour or even higher (the average fee per hour is between $175 and $300). In addition, the client is also responsible for paying

4. See Chapter 42 for a discussion of the importance of obtaining legal counsel and for guidelines on how to locate attorneys and retain their services.

various expenses related to the case (called "out-of-pocket" costs), including court filing fees, travel expenses, and the cost of expert witnesses and investigators, for example.

Types of Attorneys' Fees For a particular legal matter, an attorney may charge one type of fee or a combination of several types. *Fixed fees* may be charged for the performance of such services as drafting a simple will. *Hourly fees* may be computed for matters that will involve an indeterminate period of time. Any case brought to trial, for example, may involve an expenditure of time that cannot be precisely estimated in advance. *Contingency fees* are fixed as a percentage (usually between 25 and 40 percent) of a client's recovery in certain types of lawsuits, such as a personal-injury lawsuit.[5] If the lawsuit is unsuccessful, the attorney receives no fee, but the client will have to reimburse the attorney for any out-of-pocket costs incurred. Because Kirby's claim involves a personal injury, her lawyer will likely take the case on a contingency-fee basis, but she may have to pay an amount up front to cover the court costs.

In some cases, the winning party may be able to recover at least some portion of her or his attorneys' fees from the losing party. Many state and federal statutes provide for an award of attorneys' fees in certain legal actions, such as probate matters (settling a person's estate after death). In these situations, the judge sets the amount of the fee, which may be specified by statute or based on other factors, such as the fee customarily charged for similar services in the area. An attorney will advise the client as to whether she or he would be entitled to recover some or all of the attorneys' fees in a case.

Settlement Considerations Once an attorney has been retained, the attorney is required to pursue a resolution of the matter on the client's behalf. Nevertheless, the amount of energy an attorney will spend on a given case is also determined by how much time and funds the client wishes to devote to the process. If the client is willing to pay for a lengthy trial and one or more appeals, the attorney may pursue those actions. Often, however, once a client learns the substantial costs involved in litigation, he or she may decide to pursue a settlement of the claim. Attempts to settle the case may be ongoing throughout the litigation process.

Another important factor in deciding whether to pursue litigation is the defendant's ability to pay the damages sought. Even if Kirby is awarded damages, it may be difficult to enforce the court's judgment if, for example, the amount exceeds the limits of Carvello's automobile insurance policy. (We will discuss the problems involved in enforcing a judgment later in this chapter.)

SECTION 2 Pretrial Procedures

The pretrial litigation process involves the filing of the *pleadings,* the gathering of evidence (called *discovery*), and possibly other procedures, such as a pretrial conference and jury selection.

The Pleadings

The *complaint* and *answer* (and other legal documents discussed below), taken together, are known as the **pleadings.** The pleadings inform each party of the other's claims and specify the issues (disputed questions) involved in the case. Because the rules of procedure vary depending on the jurisdiction of the court, the style and form of the pleadings may be different from those shown in this chapter.

The Plaintiff's Complaint Kirby's action against Carvello commences when her lawyer files a **complaint**[6] with the clerk of the appropriate court. The complaint contains a statement alleging (1) the facts showing that the court has jurisdiction, (2) the facts establishing the plaintiff's basis for relief, and (3) the remedy the plaintiff is seeking. Complaints can be lengthy or brief, depending on the complexity of the case and the rules of the jurisdiction.

Exhibit 3–2 illustrates how a complaint in the Kirby-Carvello case might appear. The complaint asserts facts indicating that the federal district court has jurisdiction because of diversity of citizenship. It then gives a brief statement of the facts of the accident and alleges that Carvello negligently drove his vehicle through a red light, striking Kirby's car and causing

5. Note that attorneys may charge a contingency fee in only certain types of cases and are typically prohibited from entering into this type of fee arrangement in criminal cases, divorce cases, and cases involving the distribution of assets after death.

6. Sometimes, the document filed with the court is called a *petition* or a *declaration* instead of a complaint.

EXHIBIT 3–2 • A Typical Complaint

IN THE UNITED STATES DISTRICT COURT
FOR THE SOUTHERN DISTRICT OF NEW YORK

JILL KIRBY Plaintiff, v. ANTONIO CARVELLO Defendant.	CIVIL NO. 09-1047 COMPLAINT

The plaintiff brings this cause of action against the defendant, alleging as follows:

1. This action is between the plaintiff, who is a resident of the State of New York, and the defendant, who is a resident of the State of New Jersey. There is diversity of citizenship between the parties.
2. The amount in controversy, exclusive of interest and costs, exceeds the sum of $75,000.
3. On September 10th, 2008, the plaintiff, Jill Kirby, was exercising good driving habits and reasonable care in driving her car through the intersection of Boardwalk and Pennsylvania Avenue, New York City, New York, when the defendant, Antonio Carvello, negligently drove his vehicle through a red light at the intersection and collided with the plaintiff's vehicle.
4. As a result of the collision, the plaintiff suffered severe physical injury, which prevented her from working, and property damage to her car.

WHEREFORE, the plaintiff demands judgment against the defendant for the sum of $100,000 plus interest at the maximum legal rate and the costs of this action.

By Joseph Roe

Joseph Roe
Attorney for Plaintiff
100 Main Street
New York, New York

1/2/09

serious personal injury and property damage. The complaint goes on to state that Kirby is seeking $100,000 in damages, although in some state civil actions the plaintiff need not specify the amount of damages sought.

Service of Process. Before the court can exercise jurisdiction over the defendant (Carvello)—in effect, before the lawsuit can begin—the court must have proof that the defendant was notified of the lawsuit. Formally notifying the defendant of a lawsuit is called **service of process.** The plaintiff must deliver, or serve, a copy of the complaint and a **summons** (a notice requiring the defendant to appear in court and answer the complaint) to the defendant. The summons notifies Carvello that he must file an answer to the complaint within a specified time period (twenty days in the federal courts) or suffer a default judgment against him. A **default judgment** in Kirby's favor would mean that she would be awarded the damages alleged in her

EXHIBIT 3–3 • A Typical Summons

UNITED STATES DISTRICT COURT
FOR THE SOUTHERN DISTRICT OF NEW YORK

CIVIL ACTION, FILE NO. 09-1047

JILL KIRBY

Plaintiff,

v.

SUMMONS

ANTONIO CARVELLO

Defendant.

To the above-named Defendant:

You are hereby summoned and required to serve upon Joseph Roe, plaintiff's attorney, whose address is 100 Main Street, New York, NY, an answer to the complaint which is herewith served upon you, within 20 days after service of this summons upon you, exclusive of the day of service. If you fail to do so, judgment by default will be taken against you for the relief demanded in the complaint.

C. H. Hynek
CLERK

January 2, 2009
DATE

John Dolan
BY DEPUTY CLERK

complaint because Carvello failed to respond to the allegations. A typical summons is shown in Exhibit 3–3.

Method of Service. How service of process occurs depends on the rules of the court or jurisdiction in which the lawsuit is brought. Under the Federal Rules of Civil Procedure, anyone who is at least eighteen years of age and is not a party to the lawsuit can serve process in federal court cases. In state courts, the process server is often a county sheriff or an employee of an independent company that provides process service in the local area. Usually, the server hands the summons and complaint to the defendant personally or leaves it at the defendant's residence or place of business. In some states, process can be served by mail if the defendant consents (accepts service). When the defendant cannot be reached, special rules provide for alternative means of service, such as publishing a notice in the local newspaper. In some situations, such as when the parties are in other countries or no other alternative is available, courts have even allowed service of process via e-mail, provided that it is reasonably calculated to provide notice and an opportunity to respond.[7]

In cases involving corporate defendants, the summons and complaint may be served on an officer or on a *registered agent* (representative) of the corporation. The name of a corporation's registered agent can usually be obtained from the secretary of state's office in the state where the company incorporated its business (and, frequently, from the secretary of state's office in any state where the corporation does business).

Did the plaintiff in the following case effect proper service of the summons and the complaint on an out-of-state corporation?

7. See, for example, *Rio Properties, Inc. v. Rio International Interlink,* 284 F.3d 1007 (9th Cir. 2002).

CASE 3.1 Cruz v. Fagor America, Inc.

California Court of Appeal, Fourth District, Division 1, 2007.
52 Cal.Rptr.3d 862, 146 Cal.App.4th 488.

• **Background and Facts** At the San Diego County Fair in California in the summer of 2001, Alan Cruz's parents bought a pressure cooker distributed by Fagor America, Inc. On September 10, sixteen-year-old Cruz tried to take the lid off of the pressure cooker and was burned on the left side of his torso and thigh. Cruz's parents e-mailed Fagor to alert the company to what had happened. Fagor denied liability. Cruz filed a suit in a California state court against Fagor, alleging negligence and product liability (see Chapters 7 and 23). Cruz mailed a summons and a copy of the complaint to Fagor by certified mail, return receipt requested. The envelope was addressed to "Patricio Barriga, Chairman of the Board, FAGOR AMERICA, INC., A Delaware Corporation, 1099 Wall Street, Lyndhurst, NJ 07071-3678." The receipt was returned with the signature of "Tina Hayes." When Fagor did not file an answer to Cruz's complaint, Cruz obtained a default judgment and was awarded damages of $259,114.50. More than nine months later, Barriga claimed that he had not been notified of the suit, and Fagor filed a motion to set aside the judgment. The court granted the motion, in part, on the ground that Cruz's service of process had not been effective. Cruz appealed to a state intermediate appellate court.

• **Decision and Rationale** The state intermediate appellate court reversed the decision of the lower court, ruling that it erred in concluding that the judgment against Fagor was void for the lack of a valid service of process. The appellate court concluded that Cruz met all of the requirements for serving an out-of-state corporation. In compliance with a California state statute, Cruz sent the summons and a copy of the complaint via first-class mail, return receipt requested. Significantly, Cruz addressed the service to Barriga, Fagor's president, not to the corporation itself. Barriga did not sign the receipt, but Hayes did. Under a state statute, service is proper when the summons and a copy of the complaint are delivered to "a person authorized by the corporation to receive service." According to a representative of the U.S. Postal Service, Hayes was a Fagor employee who regularly received mail on her employer's behalf. "The only reasonable inference from the evidence in the record is that Hayes was authorized to accept mail on behalf of Fagor's president at the time she signed the return receipt for the summons and complaint." Furthermore, reasoned the court, "By virtue of her authority to accept mail on Fagor's behalf, Hayes's notice of the action is imputed to Fagor and its officers. * * * To hold otherwise would be to ignore the realities of corporate life, in which the duty to sign for mail received often resides with a designated mailroom employee, a receptionist, a secretary, or an assistant."

• **What If the Facts Were Different?** *Suppose that Cruz had misaddressed the envelope but the summons had still reached Hayes, and Cruz could prove it. Would this have been sufficient to establish valid service? Explain.*

• **The Ethical Dimension** *Should a plaintiff be required to serve a defendant with a summons and a copy of a complaint more than once? Why or why not?*

Waiver of Formal Service of Process. In many instances, the defendant is already aware that a lawsuit is being filed and is willing to waive (give up) her or his right to be served personally. The Federal Rules of Civil Procedure (FRCP) and many states' rules allow defendants to waive formal service of process, provided that certain procedures are followed. Kirby's attorney, for example, could mail to defendant Carvello a copy of the complaint, along with "Waiver of Service of Summons" forms for Carvello to sign. If Carvello signs and returns the forms within thirty days, formal service of process is waived. Moreover, under the FRCP, defendants who agree to waive formal service of process receive additional time to respond to the complaint (sixty days, instead of twenty days). Some states provide similar incentives to encourage defendants to waive formal service of process and thereby reduce associated costs and foster cooperation between the parties.

The Defendant's Response Typically, the defendant's response to the complaint takes the form of an **answer.** In an answer, the defendant either admits or denies each of the allegations in the plaintiff's complaint and may also set forth defenses to those allegations. Under the federal rules, any allegations that are not denied by the defendant will be deemed by the court to have been admitted. If Carvello admits to all of Kirby's allegations in his answer, a judgment will be entered for Kirby. If Carvello denies Kirby's allegations, the matter will proceed further.

Affirmative Defenses. Carvello can also admit the truth of Kirby's complaint but raise new facts to show that he should not be held liable for Kirby's damages. This is called raising an **affirmative defense.** As will be discussed in subsequent chapters, defendants in both civil and criminal cases can raise affirmative defenses. For example, Carvello could assert Kirby's own negligence as a defense by alleging that Kirby was driving negligently at the time of the accident. In some states, a plaintiff's contributory negligence operates as a complete defense. In most states, however, the plaintiff's own negligence constitutes only a partial defense (see Chapter 7).

Counterclaims. Carvello could also deny Kirby's allegations and set forth his own claim that the accident occurred as a result of Kirby's negligence and that therefore she owes Carvello for damage to his car. This is appropriately called a **counterclaim.** If Carvello files a counterclaim, Kirby will have to submit an answer to the counterclaim.

Dismissals and Judgments before Trial

Many actions for which pleadings have been filed never come to trial. The parties may, for example, negotiate a settlement of the dispute at any stage of the litigation process. There are also numerous procedural avenues for disposing of a case without a trial. Many of them involve one or the other party's attempts to get the case dismissed through the use of various motions.

A **motion** is a procedural request submitted to the court by an attorney on behalf of her or his client. When one party files a motion with the court, that party must also send to, or serve on, the opposing party a *notice of motion.* The notice of motion informs the opposing party that the motion has been filed. **Pretrial motions** include the motion to dismiss, the motion for judgment on the pleadings, and the motion for summary judgment, as well as the other motions listed in Exhibit 3–4.

Motion to Dismiss Either party can file a **motion to dismiss** requesting the court to dismiss the case for the reasons stated in the motion, although normally it is the defendant who requests dismissal. A defendant could file a motion to dismiss if the plaintiff's complaint fails to state a claim for which relief (a remedy) can be granted. Such a motion asserts that even if the facts alleged in the complaint are true, they do not give rise to any legal claim against the defendant. For example, if the allegations in Kirby's complaint do not constitute negligence on Carvello's part, Carvello could move to dismiss the case for failure to state a claim. Defendant Carvello could also file a motion to dismiss on the grounds that he was not properly served, that the court lacked jurisdiction, or that the venue was improper.

If the judge grants the motion to dismiss, the plaintiff generally is given time to file an amended complaint. If the judge denies the motion, the suit will go forward, and the defendant must then file an answer. Note that if Carvello wishes to discontinue the suit because, for example, an out-of-court settlement has been reached, he can likewise move for dismissal. The court can also dismiss a case on its own motion.

Motion for Judgment on the Pleadings At the close of the pleadings, either party may make a **motion for judgment on the pleadings,** which asks the court to decide the issue solely on the pleadings without proceeding to trial. The judge will grant the motion only when there is no dispute over the facts of the case and the sole issue to be resolved is a question of law. For example, in the Kirby-Carvello case, if Carvello had admitted to all of Kirby's allegations in his answer and had raised no affirmative defenses, Kirby could file a motion for judgment on the pleadings.

In deciding a motion for judgment on the pleadings, the judge may consider only the evidence contained in the pleadings. In contrast, in a motion for summary judgment, discussed next, the court may consider evidence outside the pleadings, such as sworn statements and other materials that would be admissible as evidence at trial.

Motion for Summary Judgment Either party can file a **motion for summary judgment,** which asks the court to grant a judgment in that party's favor without a trial. As with a motion for judgment on the pleadings, a court will grant a motion for summary judgment only if it determines that no facts are in dis-

EXHIBIT 3–4 • Pretrial Motions

MOTION TO DISMISS

A motion normally filed by the defendant in which the defendant asks the court to dismiss the case for a specified reason, such as improper service, lack of personal jurisdiction, or the plaintiff's failure to state a claim for which relief can be granted.

MOTION TO STRIKE

A motion filed by the defendant in which the defendant asks the court to strike (delete) from the complaint certain paragraphs contained in the complaint. Motions to strike help to clarify the underlying issues that form the basis for the complaint by removing paragraphs that are redundant or irrelevant to the action.

MOTION TO MAKE MORE DEFINITE AND CERTAIN

A motion filed by the defendant to compel the plaintiff to clarify the basis of the plaintiff's cause of action. The motion is filed when the defendant believes that the complaint is too vague or ambiguous for the defendant to respond to it in a meaningful way.

MOTION FOR JUDGMENT ON THE PLEADINGS

A motion that may be filed by either party in which the party asks the court to enter a judgment in his or her favor based on information contained in the pleadings. A judgment on the pleadings will be made only if there are no facts in dispute and the only question is how the law applies to a set of undisputed facts.

MOTION TO COMPEL DISCOVERY

A motion that may be filed by either party in which the party asks the court to compel the other party to comply with a discovery request. If a party refuses to allow the opponent to inspect and copy certain documents, for example, the party requesting the documents may make a motion to compel production of those documents.

MOTION FOR SUMMARY JUDGMENT

A motion that may be filed by either party in which the party asks the court to enter judgment in his or her favor without a trial. Unlike a motion for judgment on the pleadings, a motion for summary judgment can be supported by evidence outside the pleadings, such as witnesses' affidavits, answers to interrogatories, and other evidence obtained prior to or during discovery.

pute and the only question is how the law applies to the facts. A motion for summary judgment can be made before or during a trial, but it will be granted only if, when the evidence is viewed in the light most favorable to the other party, there clearly are no factual disputes in contention.

To support a motion for summary judgment, one party can submit evidence obtained at any point prior to trial that refutes the other party's factual claim. The evidence may consist of **affidavits** (sworn statements by parties or witnesses) or documents, such as a contract. Of course, the evidence must be *admissible* evidence—that is, evidence that the court would allow to be presented during the trial. As mentioned, the use of additional evidence is one feature that distinguishes the motion for summary judgment from the motion to dismiss and the motion for judgment on the pleadings.

Discovery

Before a trial begins, the parties can use a number of procedural devices to obtain information and gather evidence about the case. Kirby, for example, will want to know how fast Carvello was driving, whether he had been drinking or was under the influence of any medication, and whether he was wearing corrective lenses if he was required by law to do so while driving. The process of obtaining information from the opposing party or from witnesses prior to trial is known as **discovery.** Discovery includes gaining access to witnesses, documents, records, and other types of evidence. In federal courts, the parties are required to make initial disclosures of relevant evidence to the opposing party.

The Federal Rules of Civil Procedures and similar state rules set forth the guidelines for discovery activity. Generally, discovery is allowed regarding any matter that is relevant to the claim or defense of any party. Discovery rules also attempt to protect witnesses and parties from undue harassment, and to safeguard privileged or confidential material from being disclosed. Only information that is relevant to the case at hand—or likely to lead to the discovery of relevant information—is discoverable. If a discovery request involves privileged or confidential business information, a court can deny the request and can limit the scope of discovery in a number of ways. For example, a court can require the party to submit the materials to the judge in a sealed envelope so that the judge can decide if they should be disclosed to the opposing party.

Discovery prevents surprises at trial by giving both parties access to evidence that might otherwise be hidden. This allows the litigants to learn as much as they can about what to expect at a trial before they reach the courtroom. Discovery also serves to narrow the issues so that trial time is spent on the main questions in the case.

Depositions and Interrogatories Discovery can involve the use of depositions or interrogatories, or both. A **deposition** is sworn testimony by a party to the lawsuit or by any witness, recorded by an authorized court official. The person deposed gives testimony and answers questions asked by the attorneys from both sides. The questions and answers are recorded, sworn to, and signed. These answers, of course, will help the attorneys prepare their cases. Depositions also give attorneys the opportunity to evaluate how their witnesses will conduct themselves at trial. In addition, depositions can be employed in court to *impeach* (challenge the credibility of) a party or a witness who changes testimony at the trial. A deposition can also be used as testimony if the witness is not available at trial.

Interrogatories are written questions for which written answers are prepared and then signed under oath. The main difference between interrogatories and written depositions is that interrogatories are directed to a party to the lawsuit (the plaintiff or the defendant), not to a witness, and the party can prepare answers with the aid of an attorney. Whereas depositions are useful for eliciting candid responses from a party and answers not prepared in advance, interrogatories are designed to obtain accurate information about specific topics, such as, for example, how many contracts were signed and when. The scope of interrogatories is also broader because parties are obligated to answer questions, even if that means disclosing information from their records and files.

Requests for Admissions One party can serve the other party with a written request for an admission of the truth of matters relating to the trial. Any fact admitted under such a request is conclusively established as true for the trial. For example, Kirby can ask Carvello to admit that his driver's license was suspended at the time of the accident. A request for admission shortens the trial because the parties will not have to spend time proving facts on which they already agree.

Requests for Documents, Objects, and Entry upon Land A party can gain access to documents and other items not in her or his possession in order to inspect and examine them. Carvello, for example, can gain permission to inspect and copy Kirby's car repair bills. Likewise, a party can gain "entry upon land" to inspect the premises.

Request for Examinations When the physical or mental condition of one party is in question, the opposing party can ask the court to order a physical or mental examination by an independent examiner. If the court agrees to make the order, the opposing party can obtain the results of the examination. Note that the court will make such an order only when the need for the information outweighs the right to privacy of the person to be examined.

Electronic Discovery Any relevant material, including information stored electronically, can be the object of a discovery request. The federal rules and most state rules (as well as court decisions) now specifically allow individuals to obtain discovery of electronic "data compilations." Electronic evidence, or **e-evidence,** consists of all computer-generated or electronically recorded information, such as e-mail, voice mail, spreadsheets, word-processing documents, and other data. E-evidence can reveal significant facts that are not discoverable by other means. For example, computers automatically record certain information about files—such as who created the file and when, and who accessed, modified, or transmitted it—on their hard drives. This information can only be obtained from the file in its electronic format—not from printed-out versions.

Amendments to the Federal Rules of Civil Procedure that took effect in December 2006 deal specifically with the preservation, retrieval, and production of electronic data. Although traditional means, such as interrogatories and depositions, are still used to find out whether e-evidence exists, a party must usually hire an expert to retrieve the evidence in its electronic format. The expert uses software to reconstruct e-mail exchanges to establish who knew what and when they knew it. The expert can even recover files from a computer that the user thought had been deleted. Reviewing back-up copies of documents and e-mail can provide useful—and often quite damaging—information about how a particular matter progressed over several weeks or months.

Electronic discovery has significant advantages over paper discovery, but it is also time consuming and expensive. These costs are amplified when the parties involved in the lawsuit are large corporations with many offices and employees. Who should pay the costs associated with electronic discovery? For a discussion of how the courts are handling this issue, see this chapter's *Emerging Trends* feature on pages 62 and 63.

Pretrial Conference

After discovery has taken place and before the trial begins, the attorneys may meet with the trial judge in a **pretrial conference,** or hearing. Usually, the hearing consists of an informal discussion between the judge and the opposing attorneys after discovery has taken place. The purpose of the hearing is to explore the possibility of a settlement without trial and, if this is not possible, to identify the matters that are in dispute and to plan the course of the trial. In particular, the parties may attempt to establish ground rules to restrict the number of expert witnesses or discuss the admissibility or costs of certain types of evidence.

The Right to a Jury Trial

The Seventh Amendment to the U.S. Constitution guarantees the right to a jury trial for cases at law in *federal* courts when the amount in controversy exceeds $20. Most states have similar guarantees in their own constitutions (although the threshold dollar amount is higher than $20). The right to a trial by jury need not be exercised, and many cases are tried without a jury. In most states and in federal courts, one of the parties must request a jury, or the judge presumes the parties waive this right. If there is no jury, the judge determines the truth of the facts alleged in the case.

Jury Selection

Before a jury trial commences, a panel of jurors must be selected. Although some types of trials require twelve-person juries, most civil matters can be heard by six-person juries. The jury selection process is known as ***voir dire.***[8] During *voir dire* in most jurisdictions, attorneys for the plaintiff and the defendant ask prospective jurors oral questions to determine whether a potential jury member is biased or has any connection with a party to the action or with a prospective witness. In some jurisdictions, the judge may do all or part of the questioning based on written questions submitted by counsel for the parties.

During *voir dire,* a party may challenge a certain number of prospective jurors *peremptorily*—that is, ask that an individual not be sworn in as a juror without providing any reason. Alternatively, a party may challenge a prospective juror *for cause*—that is, provide a reason why an individual should not be sworn in as a juror. If the judge grants the challenge, the individual is asked to step down. A prospective juror, however, may not be excluded by the use of discriminatory challenges, such as those based on racial criteria or gender. (See *Concept Summary 3.1* on the following page for a review of pretrial procedures.)

SECTION 3 The Trial

Various rules and procedures govern the trial phase of the litigation process. There are rules governing what kind of evidence will or will not be admitted during the trial, as well as specific procedures that the participants in the lawsuit must follow.

Opening Statements

At the beginning of the trial, both attorneys are allowed to make **opening statements** setting forth the facts that they expect to prove during the trial. The opening statement provides an opportunity for each lawyer to give a brief version of the facts and the supporting evidence that will be used during the trial. Then the plaintiff's case is presented. In our hypothetical case, Kirby's lawyer would introduce evidence (relevant documents, exhibits, and the testimony of witnesses) to support Kirby's position.

8. Pronounced *vwahr deehr.* These old French verbs mean "to speak the truth." In legal language, the phrase refers to the process of questioning jurors to learn about their backgrounds, attitudes, and similar attributes.

Rules of Evidence

Whether evidence will be admitted in court is determined by the **rules of evidence**—a series of rules that have been created by the courts to ensure that any evidence presented during a trial is fair and reliable. The Federal Rules of Evidence govern the admissibility of evidence in federal courts.

Evidence Must Be Relevant to the Issues

Evidence will not be admitted in court unless it is relevant to the matter in question. **Relevant evidence** is evidence that tends to prove or disprove a fact in question or to establish the degree of probability of a fact or action. For example, evidence that a suspect's gun was in the home of another person when a victim was shot would be relevant—because it would tend to prove that the suspect did not shoot the victim.

Even relevant evidence may not be admitted in court if its reliability is questionable or if its probative (proving) value is substantially outweighed by other important considerations of the court. For example, a

CONCEPT SUMMARY 3.1
Pretrial Procedures

Procedure	Description
PLEADINGS	1. *The plaintiff's complaint*—The plaintiff's statement of the cause of action and the parties involved, filed with the court by the plaintiff's attorney. After the filing, the defendant is notified of the suit through service of process. 2. *The defendant's response*—The defendant's response to the plaintiff's complaint may take the form of an answer, in which the defendant admits or denies the plaintiff's allegations. The defendant may raise an affirmative defense and/or assert a counterclaim.
PRETRIAL MOTIONS	1. *Motion to dismiss*—A motion requesting the judge to dismiss the case for reasons that are provided in the motion (such as failure to state a claim for which relief can be granted). 2. *Motion for judgment on the pleadings*—May be made by either party; will be granted only if no facts are in dispute and only questions of law are at issue. 3. *Motion for summary judgment*—May be made by either party; will be granted only if no facts are in dispute and only questions of law are at issue. Unlike the motion for judgment on the pleadings, the motion for summary judgment may be supported by evidence outside the pleadings, such as testimony and other evidence obtained during the discovery phase of litigation.
DISCOVERY	The process of gathering evidence concerning the case; involves (1) *depositions* (sworn testimony by either party or any witness); (2) *interrogatories* (in which parties to the action write answers to questions with the aid of their attorneys); and (3) requests for admissions, documents, examinations, or other information relating to the case. Discovery may also involve electronically recorded information, such as e-mail, voice mail, and other data.
PRETRIAL CONFERENCE	A pretrial hearing, at the request of either party or the court, to identify the matters in dispute after discovery has taken place and to explore the possibility of settling the dispute without a trial. If no settlement is possible, the parties plan the course of the trial.
JURY SELECTION	In a jury trial, the selection of members of the jury from a pool of prospective jurors. During a process known as *voir dire,* the attorneys for both sides may challenge prospective jurors either for cause or peremptorily (for no cause).

video or a photograph that shows in detail the severity of a victim's injuries would be relevant evidence, but the court might exclude this evidence on the ground that it would emotionally inflame the jurors.

Hearsay Evidence Not Admissible Generally, hearsay is not admissible as evidence. **Hearsay** is defined as any testimony given in court about a statement made by someone else who was not under oath at the time of the statement. Literally, it is what someone heard someone else say. For example, if a witness in the Kirby-Carvello case testified in court concerning what he or she heard another observer say about the accident, that testimony would be hearsay, or secondhand knowledge. Admitting hearsay into evidence carries many risks because, even though it may be relevant, there is no way to test its reliability.

In the following case, the plaintiff's evidence consisted in part of printouts of Web pages purporting to indicate how the pages appeared at a prior point in time. The defendant challenged this evidence as hearsay.

CASE 3.2 Novak v. Tucows, Inc.

United States District Court, Eastern District of New York, 2007. __ F.Supp.2d __.

Background and Facts In 1997, Robert Novak registered the domain name **petswarehouse.com** and began selling pet supplies and livestock online. Within two years, the site had become one of the most popular sites for pet supplies in the United States. Novak obtained a trademark for the **petswarehouse.com** name and transferred its registration to Nitin Networks, Inc., which was owned by Tucows, Inc., a Canadian firm. In an unrelated matter, John Benn obtained a judgment against Novak in an Alabama state court. Tucows transferred the name to the court on its order on May 1, 2003. After a state intermediate appellate court reversed the judgment, the name was returned to Novak on October 1, 2004. Novak filed a suit in a federal district court against Tucows and Nitin, arguing that the transfer of the name out of his control for seventeen months destroyed his pet-supply business. Novak alleged several violations of federal and state law, including trademark infringement and conversion. Tucows responded with, among other things, a motion to strike some of Novak's exhibits.

Decision and Rationale The court granted Tucows's motion to strike Novak's exhibits. The defendants had contended that Novak's exhibits were printouts of Internet pages and that as such they constituted inadmissible hearsay. Further, one of the exhibits was a printout from **RegisterSite.com** as it purportedly appeared in 2003. Novak had obtained this printout through a Web site called Internet Archive, which provides access to a digital library of Internet sites. The court concluded that "where postings from Internet Web sites are not statements made by declarants testifying at trial and are offered to prove the truth of the matter asserted, such postings generally constitute hearsay under [the Federal Rules of Evidence]. Furthermore, such documents have not been properly authenticated pursuant to [the Federal Rules of Evidence]. Therefore, in the absence of any authentication of plaintiff's Internet printouts, combined with lack of any assertion that such printouts fall under a viable exception to the hearsay rule, defendant's motion to strike [certain exhibits] is granted."

The Ethical Dimension *Hearsay is literally what a witness says he or she heard another person say. What makes the admissibility of such evidence potentially unethical?*

The E-Commerce Dimension *In this case, the plaintiff offered as evidence the printouts of Web pages that he claimed once appeared on others' Web sites. What makes such evidence questionable until proved accurate?*

EMERGING TRENDS IN BUSINESS LAW
E-Discovery and Cost-Shifting

Before the computer age, discovery involved searching through paper records—physical evidence. Today, less than 0.5 percent of new information is created on paper. Instead of sending letters and memos, for example, people send e-mails—almost 600 billion of them annually in the United States. The all-inclusive nature of electronic information means that electronic discovery (e-discovery) now plays an important role in almost every business lawsuit.

Changes in the Federal Rules of Civil Procedure

As e-discovery has become ubiquitous, the Federal Rules of Civil Procedure (FRCP) have changed to encompass it. Amended Section 26(f) of the FRCP, for example, requires that the parties confer about "preserving discoverable information" and discuss "any issues relating to . . . discovery of electronically stored information, including the electronic forms in which it should be produced."

The most recent amendment to Section 34(a) of the FRCP expressly permits one party to a lawsuit to request that the other produce "electronically stored information—including . . . data compilation stored in any medium from which information can be obtained." The new rule has put in place a two-tiered process for discovery of electronically stored information. Relevant and nonprivileged information that is reasonably accessible is discoverable as a matter of right. Discovery of less accessible—and therefore more costly to obtain—electronic data may or may not be allowed by the court. The problem of the costs of e-discovery is discussed further below.

The *Ameriwood* Three-Step Process

The new federal rules were applied in *Ameriwood Industries, Inc. v. Liberman,* a major case involving e-discovery in which the court developed a three-step procedure for obtaining electronic data.[a] In the first step, *imaging,* mirror images of a party's hard drives can be required. The second step involves *recovering* available word-processing documents, e-mails, PowerPoint presentations, spreadsheets, and other files. The final step is *full disclosure* in which a party sends the other party all responsive and nonprivileged documents and information obtained in the previous two steps.

Limitations on E-Discovery and Cost-Shifting

Complying with requests for electronically discoverable information can cost hundreds of thousands, if not millions, of dollars, especially if a party is a large corporation with thousands of employees creating millions of electronic documents. Consequently, there is a trend toward limiting e-discovery. Under the FRCP, a court can limit electronic discovery (1) when it would be unreasonably cumulative or duplicative, (2) when the requesting party has already had ample opportunity during discovery to obtain the information, or (3) when the burden or expense outweighs the likely benefit.

a. 2007 WL 685623 (E.D.Mo. 2007).

Examination of Witnesses

Because Kirby is the plaintiff, she has the burden of proving that her allegations are true. Her attorney begins the presentation of Kirby's case by calling the first witness for the plaintiff and examining, or questioning, the witness. (For both attorneys, the types of questions and the manner of asking them are governed by the rules of evidence.) This questioning is called **direct examination.** After Kirby's attorney is finished, the witness is subject to **cross-examination** by Carvello's attorney. Then Kirby's attorney has another opportunity to question the witness in *redirect examination,* and Carvello's attorney may follow the redirect examination with a *recross-examination.* When both attorneys have finished with the first witness, Kirby's attorney calls the succeeding witnesses in the plaintiff's case, each of whom is subject to examination by the attorneys in the manner just described.

Potential Motion and Judgment At the conclusion of the plaintiff's case, the defendant's attorney has the opportunity to ask the judge to direct a verdict for the defendant on the ground that the plaintiff has presented no evidence to support her or his claim. This is called a **motion for a judgment as a matter of law** (or a **motion for a directed verdict** in state courts). In considering the motion, the judge looks at the evidence in the light most favorable to the plaintiff and grants the motion only if there is insufficient

Many courts are allowing responding parties to object to e-discovery requests on the ground that complying with the request would cause an undue financial burden. In a suit between E*Trade and Deutsche Bank, for example, the court denied E*Trade's request that the defendant produce its hard drives because doing so would create an undue burden.[b]

In addition, sometimes when a court finds that producing the requested information would create an undue financial burden, the court orders the party to comply but shifts the cost to the requesting party (usually the plaintiff). A major case in this area involved Rowe Entertainment and the William Morris Agency. When the e-discovery costs were estimated to be as high as $9 million, the court determined that cost-shifting was warranted.[c] In deciding whether to order cost-shifting, courts increasingly take into account the amount in controversy and each party's ability to pay. Sometimes, a court may require the responding party to restore and produce representative documents from a small sample of the requested medium to verify the relevance of the data before the party incurs significant expenses.[d]

IMPLICATIONS FOR THE BUSINESSPERSON

1. Whenever there is a "reasonable anticipation of litigation," all the relevant documents must be preserved. Preserving data can be a challenge, particularly for large corporations that have electronic data scattered across multiple networks, servers, desktops, laptops, handheld devices, and even home computers.
2. Even though an e-mail is deleted, it is not necessarily eliminated from one's hard drive, unless it is completely overwritten by new data. Thus, businesspersons should be aware that their hard drives can contain information they presumed no longer existed.

FOR CRITICAL ANALYSIS

1. How might a large corporation protect itself from allegations that it intentionally failed to preserve electronic data?
2. Given the significant and often burdensome costs associated with electronic discovery, should courts consider cost-shifting in every case involving electronic discovery? Why or why not?

RELEVANT WEB SITES

To locate information on the Web concerning the issues discussed in this feature, go to this text's Web site at www.cengage.com/blaw/jentz, select "Chapter 3," and click on "Emerging Trends."

b. *E*Trade Securities, LLC v. Deutsche Bank A.G.*, 230 F.R.D. 582 (D.Minn. 2005). This is a *Federal Rules Decision* not designated for publication in the *Federal Supplement*, citing *Zubulake v. UBS Warburg, LLC*, 2003 WL 21087884 (S.D.N.Y. 2003).

c. *Rowe Entertainment, Inc., v. William Morris Agency, Inc.*, 2002 WL 975713 (S.D.N.Y. 2002).

d. See, for example, *Quinby v. WestLB AG*, 2006 WL 2597900 (S.D.N.Y. 2006).

evidence to raise an issue of fact. (Motions for directed verdicts at this stage of a trial are seldom granted.)

Defendant's Evidence The defendant's attorney then presents the evidence and witnesses for the defendant's case. Witnesses are called and examined by the defendant's attorney. The plaintiff's attorney has the right to cross-examine them, and there may be a redirect examination and possibly a recross-examination. At the end of the defendant's case, either attorney can move for a directed verdict, and the test again is whether the jury can, through any reasonable interpretation of the evidence, find for the party against whom the motion has been made. After the defendant's attorney has finished introducing evidence, the plaintiff's attorney can present a **rebuttal,** which includes additional evidence to refute the defendant's case. The defendant's attorney can, in turn, refute that evidence in a **rejoinder.**

Closing Arguments, Jury Instructions, and Verdict

After both sides have rested their cases, each attorney presents a closing argument. In the **closing argument,** each attorney summarizes the facts and evidence presented during the trial and indicates why the facts and evidence support his or her client's claim. In addition to generally urging a verdict in favor of the client, the closing arguments typically reveal the shortcomings of the points made by the opposing party during the trial.

Attorneys generally present closing arguments whether or not the trial was heard by a jury. If it was a jury trial, the judge then instructs the jury in the law that applies to the case (these instructions are often called *charges*), and the jury retires to the jury room to deliberate a verdict. In most civil cases, the standard of proof is a *preponderance of the evidence.*[9] In other words, the plaintiff (Kirby in our hypothetical case) need only show that her factual claim is more likely to be true than the defendant's. (As you will read in Chapter 9, in a criminal trial the prosecution has a higher standard of proof to meet—it must prove its case *beyond a reasonable doubt.*)

Once the jury has reached a decision, it issues a **verdict** in favor of one party; the verdict specifies the jury's factual findings. In some cases, the jury also decides on the amount of the *award* (the compensation to be paid to the prevailing party). After the announcement of the verdict, which marks the end of the trial itself, the jurors are dismissed. (See *Concept Summary 3.2* for a review of trial procedures.)

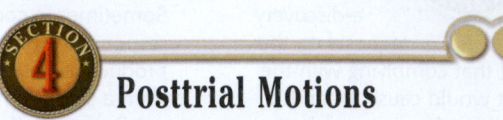

9. Note that some civil claims must be proved by "clear and convincing evidence," meaning that the evidence must show that the truth of the party's claim is highly probable. This standard is often applied in situations that present a particular danger of deception, such as allegations of fraud.

SECTION 4

Posttrial Motions

After the jury has rendered its verdict, either party may make a posttrial motion. The prevailing party usually requests that the court enter a judgment in accordance with the verdict. The nonprevailing party frequently files one of the motions discussed next.

Motion for a New Trial

At the end of the trial, a motion can be made to set aside an adverse verdict and any judgment and to hold a new trial. The **motion for a new trial** will be granted only if the judge is convinced, after looking at all the evidence, that the jury was in error, but does not feel it

CONCEPT SUMMARY 3.2
Trial Procedures

Procedure	Description
OPENING STATEMENTS	Each party's attorney is allowed to present an opening statement indicating what the attorney will attempt to prove during the course of the trial.
EXAMINATION OF WITNESSES	1. Plaintiff's introduction and direct examination of witnesses, cross-examination by defendant's attorney, possible redirect examination by plaintiff's attorney, and possible recross-examination by defendant's attorney. 2. At the close of the plaintiff's case, the defendant may make a motion for a directed verdict (or judgment as a matter of law), which, if granted by the court, will end the trial before the defendant presents witnesses. 3. Defendant's introduction and direct examination of witnesses, cross-examination by plaintiff's attorney, possible redirect examination by defendant's attorney, and possible recross-examination by plaintiff's attorney. 4. Possible rebuttal of defendant's argument by plaintiff's attorney, who presents more evidence. 5. Possible rejoinder by defendant's attorney to meet that evidence.
CLOSING ARGUMENTS, JURY INSTRUCTIONS, AND VERDICT	Each party's attorney argues in favor of a verdict for his or her client. The judge instructs (or charges) the jury as to how the law applies to the issue, and the jury retires to deliberate. When the jury renders its verdict, this brings the trial to an end.

is appropriate to grant judgment for the other side. This will usually occur when the jury verdict is obviously the result of a misapplication of the law or a misunderstanding of the evidence presented at trial. A new trial can also be granted on the grounds of newly discovered evidence, misconduct by the participants during the trial (such as when an attorney has made prejudicial and inflammatory remarks), or error by the judge.

Motion for Judgment *N.O.V.*

If Kirby wins, and if Carvello's attorney has previously moved for a directed verdict, then Carvello's attorney can now make a **motion for judgment *n.o.v.***—from the Latin *non obstante veredicto,* meaning "notwithstanding the verdict." (Federal courts use the term *judgment as a matter of law* instead of *judgment n.o.v.*) Such a motion will be granted only if the jury's verdict was unreasonable and erroneous. If the judge grants the motion, then the jury's verdict will be set aside, and a judgment will be entered in favor of the opposing party (Carvello). If the motion is denied, Carvello may then appeal the case. (Kirby may also appeal the case, even though she won at trial. She might appeal, for example, if she received a smaller monetary award than she had sought.)

SECTION 5 The Appeal

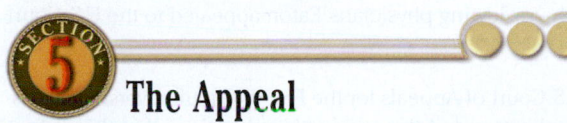

Either party may appeal not only the jury's verdict but also the judge's ruling on any pretrial or posttrial motion. Many of the appellate court cases that appear in this text involve appeals of motions for summary judgment or other motions that were denied by trial court judges. Note that a party must have legitimate grounds to file an appeal (some legal error) and that few trial court decisions are reversed on appeal. Moreover, the expenses associated with an appeal can be considerable.[10]

Filing the Appeal

If Carvello decides to appeal the verdict in Kirby's favor, then his attorney must file a *notice of appeal* with the clerk of the trial court within a prescribed period of time. Carvello then becomes the *appellant* or *petitioner.* The clerk of the trial court sends to the reviewing court (usually an intermediate court of appeals) the *record on appeal.* The record contains all the pleadings, motions, and other documents filed with the court and a complete written transcript of the proceedings, including testimony, arguments, jury instructions, and judicial rulings.

Carvello's attorney will file an appellate *brief* with the reviewing court. The **brief** is a formal legal document outlining the facts and issues of the case, the judge's rulings or jury's findings that should be reversed or modified, the applicable law, and arguments on Carvello's behalf (citing applicable statutes and relevant cases as precedents). The attorney for the *appellee* (Kirby, in our hypothetical case) usually files an answering brief. Carvello's attorney can file a reply, although it is not required. The reviewing court then considers the case.

Appellate Review

As mentioned in Chapter 2, a court of appeals does not hear any evidence. Rather, it reviews the record for errors of law. Its decision concerning a case is based on the record on appeal and the briefs and arguments. The attorneys present oral arguments, after which the case is taken under advisement. The court then issues a written opinion. In general, appellate courts do not reverse findings of fact unless the findings are unsupported or contradicted by the evidence.

An appellate court has the following options after reviewing a case:

1. The court can *affirm* the trial court's decision.
2. The court can *reverse* the trial court's judgment if it concludes that the trial court erred or that the jury did not receive proper instructions.
3. The appellate court can *remand* (send back) the case to the trial court for further proceedings consistent with its opinion on the matter.
4. The court might also affirm or reverse a decision *in part.* For example, the court might affirm the jury's finding that Carvello was negligent but remand the case for further proceedings on another issue (such as the extent of Kirby's damages).
5. An appellate court can also *modify* a lower court's decision. If the appellate court decides that the jury awarded an excessive amount in damages, for example, the court might reduce the award to a more appropriate, or fairer, amount.

10. See, for example, *Phansalkar v. Andersen Weinroth & Co.,* 356 F.3d 188 (2d Cir. 2004).

Appellate courts apply different standards of review depending on the type of issue involved and the lower courts' rulings. Generally, these standards require the reviewing court to give a certain amount of deference, or weight, to the findings of lower courts on specific issues. The following case illustrates the importance of standards of review as a means of exercising judicial restraint.

CASE 3.3 Evans v. Eaton Corp. Long Term Disability Plan

United States Court of Appeals, Fourth Circuit, 2008. 514 F.3d 315.

• **Background and Facts** Eaton Corporation is a multinational manufacturing company that funds and administers a long-term disability benefits plan for its employees. Brenda Evans was an employee at Eaton. In 1998, due to severe rheumatoid arthritis, Evans quit her job at Eaton and filed for disability benefits. Eaton paid disability benefits to Evans without controversy prior to 2003, but that year, Evans's disability status became questionable. Her physician had prescribed a new medication that had dramatically improved Evans's arthritis. In addition, Evans had injured her spine in a car accident in 2002 and was claiming to be disabled by continuing back problems as well as arthritis. But diagnostic exams during that period indicated that the injuries to Evans's back were not severe, and she could cook, shop, do laundry, wash dishes, and drive about seven miles a day. By 2004, several physicians who reviewed Evans's file had determined that she could work and was no longer totally disabled, and Eaton terminated Evans's disability benefits. Evans filed a complaint in the U.S. District Court for South Carolina alleging violations of the Employee Retirement Income Security Act of 1974 (ERISA, which is a federal law regulating pension plans, will be discussed in Chapter 33). The district court examined the evidence in great detail and concluded that Eaton's termination of Evans's benefits was an abuse of discretion because the physicians who testified in Evans's favor were more believable than the reviewing physicians. Eaton appealed to the U.S. Court of Appeals for the Fourth Circuit.

• **Decision and Rationale** The U.S. Court of Appeals for the Fourth Circuit reversed the district court's award of benefits to Evans and remanded the case with instructions that the district court enter a judgment in favor of Eaton. The appellate court pointed out that Eaton had numerous years of experience in administering its long-term disability benefits plan. The plan clearly gave the company discretionary authority to determine eligibility for benefits in addition to the power and discretion to determine all questions of fact arising with the plan's administration, interpretation, and application. Courts "when faced with discretionary language like that in the planned instrument in this case" can never forget their duty of deference and their secondary "rather than primary role in determining a claimant's right to benefits." Eaton's discretionary standards protect important values such as the enhanced prospects of achieving consistent application of the plan's provisions. Had the appellate court allowed the trial court's decision to stand, it would not have preserved the "plan's decision makers' functions against judicial intrusion."

• **What If the Facts Were Different?** *Suppose that the district court had concluded that Eaton Corporation's termination of Evans's benefits was not an abuse of discretion, and Evans had appealed. In that situation, would Evans have had any grounds for appealing the district court's decision? Explain.*

• **The Ethical Dimension** *The appellate court noted in this case that the district court's decision—which granted benefits to Evans—may arguably have been a better decision under these facts. If the appellate court believed that the district court's conclusion was right, then why did it reverse the decision? What does this tell you about the standards for review that judges use?*

Higher Appellate Courts

If the reviewing court is an intermediate appellate court, the losing party may decide to appeal the decision to the state's highest court, usually called its supreme court. Although the losing party has a right to ask (petition) a higher court to review the case, the party does not have a right to have the case heard by the higher appellate court. Appellate courts normally have discretionary power and can accept or reject an appeal. As with the United States Supreme Court, getting a case heard in most state supreme courts is unlikely. If the petition is granted, new briefs must be filed before the state supreme court, and the attorneys may be allowed or requested to present oral arguments. Like the intermediate appellate courts, the supreme court can reverse or affirm the lower appellate court's decision or remand the case. At this point, the case typically has reached its end (unless a federal question is at issue and one of the parties has legitimate grounds to seek review by a federal appellate court). *Concept Summary 3.3* reviews the options that the parties may pursue after the trial.

SECTION 6

Enforcing the Judgment

The uncertainties of the litigation process are compounded by the lack of guarantees that any judgment will be enforceable. Even if the jury awards Kirby the full amount of damages requested ($100,000), for example, Carvello's auto insurance coverage might have lapsed, in which event the company would not pay any of the damages. Alternatively, Carvello's insurance policy might be limited to $50,000, meaning that Carvello personally would have to pay the remaining $50,000.

CONCEPT SUMMARY 3.3
Posttrial Options

Procedure	Description
POSTTRIAL MOTIONS	1. *Motion for a new trial*—If the judge believes that the jury was in error but is not convinced that the losing party should have won, the motion normally will be granted. It can also be granted on the basis of newly discovered evidence, misconduct by the participants during the trial, or error by the judge. 2. *Motion for judgment n.o.v. ("notwithstanding the verdict")*—The party making the motion must have filed a motion for a directed verdict at the close of the presentation of evidence during the trial; the motion will be granted if the judge is convinced that the jury was in error.
APPEAL	Either party can appeal the trial court's judgment to an appropriate court of appeals. 1. *Filing the appeal*—The appealing party must file a notice of appeal with the clerk of the trial court, who forwards the record on appeal to the appellate court. Attorneys file appellate briefs. 2. *Appellate review*—The appellate court does not hear evidence but bases its opinion, which it issues in writing, on the record on appeal and the attorneys' briefs and oral arguments. The court may affirm or reverse all (or part) of the trial court's judgment and/or remand the case for further proceedings consistent with its opinion. Most decisions are affirmed on appeal. 3. *Further review*—In some cases, further review may be sought from a higher appellate court, such as a state supreme court. If a federal question is involved, the case may ultimately be appealed to the United States Supreme Court.

Requesting Court Assistance in Collecting the Judgment

If the defendant does not have the funds available to pay the judgment, the plaintiff can go back to the court and request that the court issue a *writ of execution.* A **writ of execution** is an order directing the sheriff to seize and sell the defendant's nonexempt assets, or property (certain assets are exempted by law from creditors' actions). The proceeds of the sale would then be used to pay the damages owed, and any excess proceeds would be returned to the defendant. Alternatively, the nonexempt property itself could be transferred to the plaintiff in lieu of an outright payment. (Creditors' remedies, including those of judgment creditors, as well as exempt and nonexempt property, will be discussed in more detail in Chapter 28.)

Availability of Assets

The problem of collecting a judgment is less pronounced, of course, when a party is seeking to satisfy a judgment against a defendant with substantial assets that can be easily located, such as a major corporation. Usually, one of the factors considered by the plaintiff and his or her attorney before a lawsuit is initiated is whether the defendant has sufficient assets to cover the amount of damages sought. In addition, during the discovery process, attorneys routinely seek information about the location of the defendant's assets that might potentially be used to satisfy a judgment.

REVIEWING Court Procedures

Ronald Metzgar placed his fifteen-month-old son, Matthew, awake and healthy, in his playpen. Ronald left the room for five minutes and on his return found Matthew lifeless. A toy block had lodged in the boy's throat, causing him to choke to death. Ronald called 911, but efforts to revive Matthew were to no avail. There was no warning of a choking hazard on the box containing the block. Matthew's parents hired an attorney and sued Playskool, Inc., the manufacturer of the block, alleging that the manufacturer had been negligent in failing to warn of the block's hazard. Playskool filed a motion for summary judgment, arguing that the danger of a young child choking on a small block was obvious. Using the information presented in the chapter, answer the following questions.

1. Suppose that the attorney the Metzgars hired agreed to represent them on a contingency-fee basis. What does that mean?
2. How would the Metzgars' attorney likely have served process (the summons and complaint) on Playskool, Inc.?
3. Should Playskool's request for summary judgment be granted? Why or why not?
4. Suppose that the judge denied Playskool's motion and the case proceeded to trial. After hearing all the evidence, the jury found in favor of the defendant. What options do the plaintiffs have at this point if they are not satisfied with the verdict?

TERMS AND CONCEPTS

affidavit 57
affirmative defense 56
answer 56
brief 65
closing argument 63
complaint 52
counterclaim 56
cross-examination 62
default judgment 53
deposition 58
direct examination 62
discovery 57

e-evidence 58
Federal Rules of Civil Procedure (FRCP) 50
hearsay 61
interrogatories 58
motion 56
motion for a directed verdict 62
motion for a judgment as a matter of law 62
motion for a new trial 64
motion for judgment *n.o.v.* 65
motion for judgment on the pleadings 56
motion for summary judgment 56
motion to dismiss 56
opening statement 59
pleadings 52
pretrial conference 59
pretrial motion 56
rebuttal 63
rejoinder 63
relevant evidence 60
rules of evidence 60
service of process 53
summons 53
verdict 64
***voir dire* 59**
writ of execution 68

QUESTIONS AND CASE PROBLEMS

3–1. Attorneys in personal-injury and other tort lawsuits (see Chapters 6 and 7) frequently charge clients on a contingency-fee basis; that is, a lawyer will agree to take on a client's case in return for, say, 30 percent of whatever damages are recovered. What are some of the social benefits and costs of the contingency-fee system? In your opinion, do the benefits of this system outweigh the costs?

3–2. QUESTION WITH SAMPLE ANSWER

When and for what purpose is each of the following motions made? Which of them would be appropriate if a defendant claimed that the only issue between the parties was a question of law and that the law was favorable to the defendant's position?

(a) A motion for judgment on the pleadings.
(b) A motion for a directed verdict.
(c) A motion for summary judgment.
(d) A motion for judgment *n.o.v.*

- **For a sample answer to Question 3–2, go to Appendix I at the end of this text.**

3–3. In the past, the rules of discovery were very restrictive, and trials often turned on elements of surprise. For example, a plaintiff would not necessarily know until the trial what the defendant's defense was going to be. In the last several decades, however, new rules of discovery have substantially changed this situation. Now each attorney can access practically all of the evidence that the other side intends to present at trial, with the exception of certain information—namely, the opposing attorney's work product. Work product is not a clear concept. Basically, it includes all of the attorney's thoughts on the case. Can you see any reason why such information should not be made available to the opposing attorney? Discuss fully.

3–4. Washoe Medical Center, Inc., admitted Shirley Swisher for the treatment of a fractured pelvis. During her stay, Swisher suffered a fatal fall from her hospital bed. Gerald Parodi, the administrator of her estate, and others filed an action against Washoe seeking damages for the alleged lack of care in treating Swisher. During *voir dire,* when the plaintiffs' attorney returned a few minutes late from a break, the trial judge led the prospective jurors in a standing ovation. The judge joked with one of the prospective jurors, whom he had known in college, about his fitness to serve as a judge and personally endorsed another prospective juror's business. After the trial, the jury returned a verdict in favor of Washoe. The plaintiffs moved for a new trial, but the judge denied the motion. The plaintiffs then appealed, arguing that the tone set by the judge during *voir dire* prejudiced their right to a fair trial. Should the appellate court agree? Why or why not?

3–5. Advance Technology Consultants, Inc. (ATC), contracted with RoadTrac, L.L.C., to provide software and client software systems for the products of global positioning satellite (GPS) technology being developed by RoadTrac. RoadTrac agreed to provide ATC with hardware with which ATC's software would interface. Problems soon arose, however. ATC claimed that RoadTrac's hardware was defective, making it difficult to develop the software. RoadTrac contended that its hardware was fully functional and that ATC had simply failed to provide supporting software. ATC told RoadTrac that it considered their contract terminated. RoadTrac filed a suit in a Georgia state court against ATC alleging breach of contract. During discovery, RoadTrac requested ATC's customer lists and marketing procedures. ATC objected to providing this information because RoadTrac and ATC had become competitors in the GPS industry. Should a party to a lawsuit have to hand over its confidential business secrets as part of a discovery request? Why or why not? What limitations might a court consider imposing before requiring ATC to produce this material?

3–6. Jury Selection. Ms. Thompson filed a suit in a federal district court against her employer, Altheimer & Gray, seeking damages for alleged racial discrimination in violation of federal law. During *voir dire,* the judge asked the prospective jurors whether "there is something about this kind of lawsuit for money damages that would start any of you leaning for or against a particular party?" Ms. Leiter, one of the prospective jurors, raised her hand and explained that she had "been an owner of a couple of businesses and am currently an owner of a business, and I feel that as an employer and owner of a business that will definitely sway my judgment in this case." She explained, "I am constantly faced with people that want various benefits or different positions in the company or better contacts or, you know, a myriad of issues that employers face on a regular basis, and I have to decide whether or not that person should get them." Asked by Thompson's lawyer whether "you believe that people file lawsuits just because they don't get something they want," Leiter answered, "I believe there are some people that do." In answer to another question, she said, "I think I bring a lot of background to this case, and I can't say that it's not going to cloud my judgment. I can try to be as fair as I can, as I do every day." Explain the purpose of *voir dire* and how Leiter's response should be treated in light of that purpose. [*Thompson v. Altheimer & Gray,* 248 F.3d 621 (7th Cir. 2001)]

3–7. CASE PROBLEM WITH SAMPLE ANSWER

To establish a Web site, a person must have an Internet service provider or hosting company, register a domain name, and acquire domain name servicing. Pfizer, Inc., Pfizer Ireland Pharmaceuticals, and Warner-Lambert Co. (collectively, Pfizer) filed a suit in a federal district court against Domains By Proxy, Inc., and other persons alleged to be behind two Web sites—genericlipitors.com and econopetcare.com. Among the defendants were an individual and a company that, according to Pfizer, were located in a foreign country. Without investigating other means of serving these two defendants, Pfizer asked the court for permission to accomplish service of process via e-mail. Under what circumstances is service via e-mail proper? Would it be appropriate in this case? Explain. [*Pfizer, Inc. v. Domains By Proxy,* ___ F.Supp.2d ___ (D.Conn. 2004)]

- **To view a sample answer for Problem 3–7, go to this book's Web site at www.cengage.com/blaw/jentz, select "Chapter 3," and click on "Case Problem with Sample Answer."**

3–8. Motion for Judgment *n.o.v.* Gerald Adams worked as a cook for Uno Restaurants, Inc., at Warwick Pizzeria Uno Restaurant & Bar in Warwick, Rhode Island. One night, shortly after Adams's shift began, he noticed that the kitchen floor was saturated with a foul-smelling liquid coming from the drains and backing up water onto the floor. He complained of illness and went home, where he contacted the state health department. A department representative visited the restaurant and closed it for the night, leaving instructions to sanitize the kitchen and clear the drains. Two days later, in the restaurant, David Badot, the manager, shouted at Adams in the presence of other employees. When Adams shouted back, Badot fired Adams and had him arrested. Adams filed a suit in a Rhode Island state court against Uno, alleging that he had been unlawfully terminated for contacting the health department. A jury found in favor of Adams. Arguing that Adams had been fired for threatening Badot, Uno filed a motion for judgment *n.o.v.* (also known as a motion for judgment as a matter of law). What does a court weigh in considering whether to grant such a motion? Should the court grant the motion in this case? Why or why not? [*Adams v. Uno Restaurants, Inc.,* 794 A.2d 489 (R.I. 2002)]

3–9. A QUESTION OF ETHICS

*Narnia Investments, Ltd., filed a suit in a Texas state court against several defendants, including Harvestons Securities, Inc., a securities dealer. (Securities are documents evidencing the ownership of a corporation, in the form of stock, or debts owed by it, in the form of bonds.) Harvestons is registered with the state of Texas and thus may be served with a summons and a copy of a complaint by serving the Texas Securities Commissioner. In this case, the return of service indicated that process was served on the commissioner "by delivering to JoAnn Kocerek defendant, in person, a true copy of this [summons] together with the accompanying copy(ies) of the [complaint]." Harvestons did not file an answer, and Narnia obtained a default judgment against the defendant for $365,000, plus attorneys' fees and interest. Five months after this judgment, Harvestons filed a motion for a new trial, which the court denied. Harvestons appealed to a state intermediate appellate court, claiming that it had not been served in strict compliance with the rules governing service of process. [*Harvestons Securities, Inc. v. Narnia Investments, Ltd.,* *218 S.W.3d 126 (Tex.App.—Houston [14 Dist.] 2007)]*

(a) Harvestons asserted that Narnia's service was invalid in part because "the return of service states that process was delivered to 'JoAnn Kocerek'" and did not show that she "had the authority to accept process on behalf of Harvestons or the Texas Securities Commissioner." Should such a detail, if it is required, be strictly construed and applied? Should it apply in this case? Explain.

(b) Whose responsibility is it to see that service of process is accomplished properly? Was it accomplished properly in this case? Why or why not?

LAW ON THE WEB

For updated links to resources available on the Web, as well as a variety of other materials, visit this text's Web site at

www.cengage.com/blaw/jentz

If you are interested in learning more about the Federal Rules of Civil Procedure (FRCP) and the Federal Rules of Evidence (FRE), you can access them via the Internet at the following Web site:

www.law.cornell.edu

Procedural rules for several of the state courts are also online and can be accessed via the courts' Web pages. You can find links to the Web pages for state courts at the Web site of the National Center for State Courts. Go to

www.ncsconline.org

The American Bar Association maintains a gateway to information on legal topics, including the court systems and court procedures, at

www.abalawinfo.org

Legal Research Exercises on the Web

Go to **www.cengage/com/blaw/jentz**, the Web site that accompanies this text. Select "Chapter 3" and click on "Internet Exercises." There you will find the following Internet research exercises that you can perform to learn more about the topics covered in this chapter.

Internet Exercise 3–1: Legal Perspective
Civil Procedure

Internet Exercise 3–2: Management Perspective
Small Claims Courts

Internet Exercise 3–3: Technological Perspective
Virtual Courtrooms

CHAPTER 4

Constitutional Authority to Regulate Business

The U.S. Constitution is the supreme law in this country.[1] As mentioned in Chapter 1, neither Congress nor any state may pass a law that conflicts with the U.S. Constitution. Laws that govern business have their origin in the lawmaking authority granted by this document.

In this chapter, we examine some basic constitutional concepts and clauses and their significance for businesspersons. We then look at certain freedoms guaranteed by the first ten amendments to the U.S. Constitution—the Bill of Rights—and discuss how these freedoms affect business activities.

1. See Appendix B for the full text of the U.S. Constitution.

SECTION 1

The Constitutional Powers of Government

Following the Revolutionary War (1775–1783), the states—through the Articles of Confederation—created a *confederal form of government* in which the states had the authority to govern themselves and the national government could exercise only limited powers. When problems arose because the nation was facing an economic crisis and state laws interfered with the free flow of commerce, a national convention was called, and the delegates drafted the U.S. Constitution. This document, after its ratification by the states in 1789, became the basis for an entirely new form of government.

A Federal Form of Government

The new government created by the Constitution reflected a series of compromises made by the convention delegates on various issues. Some delegates wanted sovereign power to remain with the states; others wanted the national government alone to exercise sovereign power. The end result was a compromise—a **federal form of government** in which the national government and the states *share* sovereign power.

The Constitution sets forth specific powers that can be exercised by the national government and provides that the national government has the implied power to undertake actions necessary to carry out its expressly designated powers (or *enumerated powers*). All other powers are expressly "reserved" to the states under the Tenth Amendment to the Constitution.

The Regulatory Powers of the States As part of their inherent sovereignty, state governments have the authority to regulate affairs within their borders. As mentioned, this authority stems, in part, from the Tenth Amendment to the Constitution, which reserves all powers not delegated to the national government to the states or to the people. State regulatory powers are often referred to as **police powers.** The term does not relate solely to criminal law enforcement but rather refers to the broad right of state governments to regulate private activities to protect or promote the public order, health, safety, morals, and general welfare. Fire and building codes, antidiscrimination laws, parking regulations, zoning restrictions, licensing requirements, and thousands of other state statutes covering virtually every aspect of life have been enacted pursuant to states' police powers. Local governments, including cities, also exercise police powers.[2] Generally, state laws enacted pursuant to a state's police powers carry a strong presumption of validity.

Delineating State and National Powers

The broad language of the Constitution has left much room for debate over the specific nature and scope of the respective powers of the states and the national government. Generally, it has been the task of the courts to determine where the boundary line between state and national powers should lie—and that line shifts over time, moving first one way and then the other like a pendulum. During certain periods, the national government has met with little resistance from the courts when extending its regulatory authority over broad areas of social and economic life. During other periods, in contrast, the courts, and particularly the United States Supreme Court, have tended to interpret the Constitution in such a way as to curb the national government's regulatory powers.

Relations among the States

The Constitution also includes provisions concerning relations among the states in our federal system. Particularly important are the privileges and immunities clause and the full faith and credit clause.

The Privileges and Immunities Clause

Article IV, Section 2, of the U.S. Constitution provides that the "Citizens of each State shall be entitled to all Privileges and Immunities of Citizens in the several States." This clause is often referred to as the interstate **privileges and immunities clause.**[3] It prevents a state from imposing unreasonable burdens on citizens of another state—particularly with regard to means of livelihood or doing business. When a citizen of one state engages in basic and essential activities in another state (the "foreign state"), the foreign state must have a *substantial reason* for treating the nonresident differently from its own residents. Basic activities include transferring property, seeking employment, or accessing the court system. The foreign state must also establish that its reason for the discrimination is *substantially related* to the state's ultimate purpose in adopting the legislation or activity.[4]

In general, the idea is to prevent any state (including municipalities within the state) from discriminating against citizens of other states in favor of its own. The clause does not prohibit all discrimination. It applies only to discrimination for which the state cannot demonstrate a substantial reason significantly related to its objective. For example, giving hiring preferences to state or city residents has been found to violate the privileges and immunities clause.[5] In contrast, requiring nonresidents to pay more for hunting licenses or tuition at state universities has been found *not* to violate the clause because the state articulated a substantial reason for the difference.[6]

The Full Faith and Credit Clause

Article IV, Section 1, of the U.S. Constitution provides that "Full Faith and Credit shall be given in each State to the public Acts, Records, and judicial Proceedings of every other State." This clause, which is referred to as the **full faith and credit clause,** applies only to civil matters. It ensures that rights established under deeds, wills, contracts, and similar instruments in one state will be honored by other states. It also ensures that any judicial decision with respect to such property rights will be honored and enforced in all states.

The full faith and credit clause was originally included in the Articles of Confederation to promote mutual friendship among the people of the various states. In fact, it has contributed to the unity of American citizens because it protects their legal rights as they move about from state to state. It also protects the rights of those to whom they owe obligations, such as a person who is awarded monetary damages by a court. The ability to enforce such rights is extremely important for the conduct of business in a country with a very mobile citizenry.

2. Local governments derive their authority to regulate their communities from the state because they are creatures of the state. In other words, they cannot come into existence unless authorized by the state to do so.

3. Interpretations of this clause commonly use the terms *privilege* and *immunity* synonymously. Generally, the terms refer to certain rights, benefits, or advantages enjoyed by individuals.

4. This test was first announced in *Supreme Court of New Hampshire v. Piper,* 470 U.S. 274, 105 S.Ct. 1272, 84 L.Ed.2d 205 (1985). For another example, see *Lee v. Miner,* 369 F.Supp.2d 527 (D.Del. 2005).

5. *United Building and Construction Trades Council of Camden County and Vicinity v. Mayor and Council of City of Camden,* 465 U.S. 208, 104 S.Ct. 1020, 79 L.Ed.2d 249 (1984). See also *Council of Insurance Agents + Brokers v. Viken,* 408 F.Supp.2d 836 (D.S.Dak. 2005).

6. *Baldwin v. Fish and Game Commission of Montana,* 436 U.S. 371, 98 S.Ct. 1852, 56 L.Ed.2d 354 (1978); and *Saenz v. Roe,* 526 U.S. 489, 119 S.Ct. 1518, 143 L.Ed.2d 689 (1999).

The Separation of the National Government's Powers

To prevent the possibility that the national government might use its power arbitrarily, the Constitution provided for three branches of government. The legislative branch makes the laws, the executive branch enforces the laws, and the judicial branch interprets the laws. Each branch performs a separate function, and no branch may exercise the authority of another branch.

Additionally, a system of **checks and balances** allows each branch to limit the actions of the other two branches, thus preventing any one branch from exercising too much power. Some examples of these checks and balances include the following:

1. The legislative branch (Congress) can enact a law, but the executive branch (the president) has the constitutional authority to veto that law.
2. The executive branch is responsible for foreign affairs, but treaties with foreign governments require the advice and consent of the Senate.
3. Congress determines the jurisdiction of the federal courts and the president appoints federal judges, with the advice and consent of the Senate, but the judicial branch has the power to hold actions of the other two branches unconstitutional.[7]

The Commerce Clause

To prevent states from establishing laws and regulations that would interfere with trade and commerce among the states, the Constitution expressly delegated to the national government the power to regulate interstate commerce. Article I, Section 8, of the Constitution explicitly permits Congress "[t]o regulate Commerce with foreign Nations, and among the several States, and with the Indian Tribes." This clause, referred to as the **commerce clause,** has had a greater impact on business than any other provision in the Constitution. The commerce clause provides the basis for the national government's extensive regulation of state and even local affairs.

One of the early questions raised by the commerce clause was whether the word *among* in the phrase "among the several States" meant *between* the states or *between and within* the states. For some time, the courts interpreted the commerce clause to apply only to commerce between the states (*interstate* commerce) and not commerce within the states (*intrastate* commerce). In 1824, however, the United States Supreme Court decided the landmark case of *Gibbons v. Ogden.*[8] The Court ruled that commerce within the states could also be regulated by the national government as long as the commerce *substantially affected* commerce involving more than one state.

The Expansion of National Powers under the Commerce Clause In *Gibbons v. Ogden,* the Supreme Court expanded the commerce clause to cover activities that "substantially affect interstate commerce." As the nation grew and faced new kinds of problems, the commerce clause became a vehicle for the additional expansion of the national government's regulatory powers. Even activities that seemed purely local in nature came under the regulatory reach of the national government if those activities were deemed to substantially affect interstate commerce.

In 1942, for example, the Supreme Court held that wheat production by an individual farmer intended wholly for consumption on his own farm was subject to federal regulation.[9] In *Heart of Atlanta Motel v. United States,*[10] a landmark case decided in 1964, the Supreme Court upheld the federal government's authority to prohibit racial discrimination nationwide in public facilities, including local motels, based on its powers under the commerce clause. The Court noted that "if it is interstate commerce that feels the pinch, it does not matter how local the operation that applies the squeeze."

The Commerce Power Today Today, the national government continues to rely on the commerce clause for its constitutional authority to regulate business activities in the United States. The breadth of the commerce clause permits the national government to legislate in areas in which Congress has not explicitly been granted power. In the last fifteen years, however, the Supreme Court has begun to curb somewhat the national government's regulatory authority under the commerce clause. In 1995, the Court held—for the first time in sixty years—that Congress had exceeded its regulatory authority under the commerce clause. The Court struck down an act that banned the possession of guns within one thousand feet of any school because the act attempted to regu-

7. As discussed in Chapter 2, the power of judicial review was established by the United States Supreme Court in *Marbury v. Madison,* 5 U.S. (1 Cranch) 137, 2 L.Ed. 60 (1803).

8. 22 U.S. (9 Wheat.) 1, 6 L.Ed. 23 (1824).

9. *Wickard v. Filburn,* 317 U.S. 111, 63 S.Ct. 82, 87 L.Ed. 122 (1942).

10. 379 U.S. 241, 85 S.Ct. 348, 13 L.Ed.2d 258 (1964).

late an area that had "nothing to do with commerce."[11] Subsequently, the Court invalidated key portions of two other federal acts on the ground that they exceeded Congress's commerce clause authority.[12]

Medical Marijuana and the Commerce Clause In one notable case, however, the Supreme Court did allow the federal government to regulate noncommercial activities taking place wholly within a state's borders. Eleven states, including California, have adopted "medical marijuana" laws, which legalize marijuana for medical purposes. Marijuana possession, however, is illegal under the federal Controlled Substances Act (CSA).[13] After the federal government seized the marijuana that two seriously ill California women were using on the advice of their physicians, the women filed a lawsuit. They argued that it was unconstitutional for the federal statute to prohibit them from using marijuana for medical purposes that were legal within the state. In 2003, the U.S. Court of Appeals for the Ninth Circuit agreed, reasoning that the marijuana in this situation would never enter the stream of commerce. In 2005, however, the United States Supreme Court held that Congress has the authority to prohibit the *intra*state possession and noncommercial cultivation of marijuana as part of a larger regulatory scheme (the CSA).[14] In other words, state laws that allow the use of medical marijuana do not insulate the users from federal prosecution.

State Actions and the "Dormant" Commerce Clause The United States Supreme Court has interpreted the commerce clause to mean that the national government has the *exclusive* authority to regulate commerce that substantially affects trade and commerce among the states. This express grant of authority to the national government, which is often referred to as the "positive" aspect of the commerce clause, implies a negative aspect—that the states do *not* have the authority to regulate interstate commerce. This negative aspect of the commerce clause is often referred to as the "dormant" (implied) commerce clause.

The dormant commerce clause comes into play when state regulations impinge on interstate commerce. In this situation, the courts weigh the state's interest in regulating a certain matter against the burden that the state's regulation places on interstate commerce. For example, the Supreme Court invalidated state regulations that, in the interest of promoting traffic safety, limited the length of trucks traveling on the state's highways. The Court concluded that the regulations imposed a "substantial burden on interstate commerce" yet failed to "make more than the most speculative contribution to highway safety."[15] Because courts balance the interests involved, it is difficult to predict the outcome in a particular case. For a discussion of how state regulations pertaining to Internet prescriptions might violate the dormant commerce clause, see this chapter's *Contemporary Legal Debates* feature on pages 76 and 77.

The Supremacy Clause and Federal Preemption

Article VI of the U.S. Constitution, commonly referred to as the **supremacy clause,** provides that the Constitution, laws, and treaties of the United States are "the supreme Law of the Land." When there is a direct conflict between a federal law and a state law, the state law is rendered invalid. Because some powers are *concurrent* (shared by the federal government and the states), however, it is necessary to determine which law governs in a particular circumstance.

Preemption of State Laws **Preemption** occurs when Congress chooses to act exclusively in an area in which the federal government and the states have concurrent powers. A valid federal statute or regulation will take precedence over a conflicting state or local law or regulation on the same general subject. Often, it is not clear whether Congress, in passing a law, intended to preempt an entire subject area against state regulation, and it is left to the courts to determine whether Congress intended to exercise exclusive power over a given area. No single factor is decisive as to whether a court will find preemption.

Generally, congressional intent to preempt will be found if a federal law regulating an activity is so pervasive, comprehensive, or detailed that the states have no room to regulate in that area. Also, when a federal statute creates an agency to enforce the law, matters

11. The Court held the Gun-Free School Zones Act of 1990 to be unconstitutional in *United States v. Lopez,* 514 U.S. 549, 115 S.Ct. 1624, 131 L.Ed.2d 626 (1995).

12. *Printz v. United States,* 521 U.S. 898, 117 S.Ct. 2365, 138 L.Ed.2d 914 (1997), involving the Brady Handgun Violence Prevention Act of 1993; and *United States v. Morrison,* 529 U.S. 598, 120 S.Ct. 1740, 146 L.Ed.2d 658 (2000), concerning the federal Violence Against Women Act of 1994.

13. 21 U.S.C. Sections 801 *et seq.*

14. *Gonzales v. Raich,* 545 U.S. 1, 125 S.Ct. 2195, 162 L.Ed.2d 1 (2005).

15. *Raymond Motor Transportation, Inc. v. Rice,* 434 U.S. 429, 98 S.Ct. 787, 54 L.Ed.2d 664 (1978).

CONTEMPORARY LEGAL DEBATES

Does State Regulation of Internet Prescription Transactions Violate the Dormant Commerce Clause?

Every year, about 30 percent of American households purchase some prescription drugs online. As such transactions become more common, questions are being raised about who has the authority to regulate them. As explained in the text, under the Tenth Amendment to the U.S. Constitution, the states have the authority to regulate activities affecting the safety and welfare of their citizens. In the late 1800s, the states used this authority to begin regulating the dispensing of prescription medicines—physicians were granted the exclusive right to prescribe drugs, and pharmacists were given the exclusive right to dispense them. The courts routinely upheld these state laws.[a] All states have continued to use their police powers to regulate the licensing of pharmacists and physicians, as well as the prescribing and dispensing of drugs. But does this authority extend to out-of-state physicians and pharmacists who prescribe drugs and fill prescriptions via the Internet?

The States Attempt to Regulate Internet Prescriptions

About 40 percent of the states have attempted to regulate Internet prescription transactions by changing their licensing laws to require a "safe" consulting relationship between the prescribing physician and the pharmacist who dispenses the prescription drugs. Some states, for example, require an electronic diagnosis before a prescription can be filled—the patient completes an online questionnaire that is "approved" by a physician who then transmits the prescription to a pharmacist. Other states, however, specifically prohibit a physician from creating a prescription unless he or she has physical contact with the patient. Another approach is to try to regulate Internet pharmacies. In Nevada, for example, residents cannot obtain a prescription from an Internet pharmacy unless it is licensed and certified under the laws of that state.

Recently, the New York State Bureau of Narcotic Enforcement took an additional regulatory step and began investigating all companies in New Jersey and Mississippi that had supplied prescription medicines to New York residents via Internet transactions. None of the companies under investigation has offices in New York State. Furthermore, the authority to enforce regulations involving prescription drugs and their distributors generally belongs to the federal Food and Drug Administration.

Are the States Violating the Dormant Commerce Clause?

As explained in the text, the courts have held that the dormant commerce clause prohibits the states from regulating interstate commerce. Hence, the states may not institute regulations that impose an undue burden on interstate commerce. In the past, the courts have used the dormant commerce clause in

a. See, for example, *Dent v. West Virginia,* 129 U.S. 114, 9 S.Ct. 231, 32 L.Ed. 623 (1889).

that may come within the agency's jurisdiction will likely preempt state laws. For example, in 2008, the United States Supreme Court ruled that the federal regulation of medical devices preempted state common law claims for negligence, strict liability, and implied warranty. The case involved a man who alleged that he was injured by a faulty medical device (a balloon catheter that had been inserted into his artery following a heart attack). The Court reasoned that the Medical Device Amendments of 1976 had included a preemption clause and that the device had passed the U.S. Food and Drug Administration's rigorous premarket approval process. Therefore, the man's claims that the device was unsafe were preempted.[16]

Preemption and State Regulation Aimed at Global Warming A question of preemption was raised in 2006, when California governor Arnold Schwarzenegger signed into law the first state statute attempting to limit the amount of greenhouse-gas emissions from automobiles within the state.[17] Under federal law, the Environmental Protection Agency (EPA) is the agency that regulates and sets standards for air pollution and tailpipe emissions across the country (see Chapter 45). Normally, because EPA regulations are comprehensive and detailed, they preempt state statutes attempting to regulate the same topic. California is in a different position from other states, though, because it has been given special permission

16. *Riegel v. Medtronic, Inc.,* ___ U.S. ___, 128 S.Ct. 999, 169 L.Ed.2d 892 (2008).

17. The law amends California Health and Safety Code Section 43018.5.

evaluating state regulations that affected out-of-state pharmacies involved in activities such as mail-order prescriptions.[b]

Today, the question is whether state laws that attempt to regulate Internet prescription transactions, such as those described above, violate the dormant commerce clause. To date, no court has ruled directly on this issue, but there have been cases involving similar state efforts to regulate other out-of-state Internet activities. A number of courts have accepted the argument that under the dormant commerce clause, the federal government can assume full regulatory power over any firms conducting business over the Internet because they are engaged in interstate commerce.[c]

Other courts, however, have taken the opposing view and found that state regulation of Internet activities does *not* always violate the dormant commerce clause. In one case, a court upheld a New York law that banned the sale of cigarettes to New York residents over the Internet on the ground that the state had an interest in protecting the health of its citizens.[d] In another case, a Texas statute that prohibited automobile manufacturers from selling vehicles on their Web sites was upheld on similar grounds.[e]

Whether the reasoning in these cases will be extended to cases involving Internet prescriptions remains to be seen. Some laws seem likely to be upheld. The Nevada law mentioned earlier that requires Internet pharmacies to be licensed in the state is an example. Because this law applies equally to in-state pharmacies and out-of-state Internet pharmacies, it is nondiscriminatory. In addition, the requirement that an Internet pharmacy obtain a license before doing business in the state would probably *not* be considered an undue burden on interstate commerce.

WHERE DO YOU STAND?

Clearly, there are two sides to this debate. Many states contend that they must regulate the provision of prescription drugs via the Internet in order to ensure the safety and well-being of their citizens. In some instances, however, the states may be imposing such regulations at the behest of traditional pharmacies, which do not like online competition.

What is your stand on whether state regulation of Internet prescription drug transactions violates the dormant commerce clause of the Constitution? Realize that if you agree that it does, then you probably favor less state regulation. If you believe that it does not, then you probably favor more state regulation.

b. See, for example, *Pharmaceutical Manufacturers' Association v. New Mexico Board of Pharmacy*, 86 N.M. 571, 525 P.2d 931 (N.M.App. 1974); and *State v. Rasmussen*, 213 N.W.2d 661 (Iowa 1973).

c. See, for example, *American Libraries Association v. Pataki*, 969 F.Supp. 160 (S.D.N.Y. 1997).

d. *Brown & Williamson Tobacco Corp. v. Pataki*, 320 F.3d 200 (2d Cir. 2003).

e. *Ford Motor Co. v. Texas Department of Transportation*, 264 F.3d 493 (5th Cir. 2001).

to regulate air pollution in the past. Nevertheless, the Bush administration and the EPA opposed this new legislation and claimed that it was preempted by the federal standards. Although Californians clearly have an interest in more stringent emissions standards due to the number of vehicles operating within that state, the validity of the California legislation remained uncertain throughout 2007. In 2008, the EPA ruled against giving California a preemption waiver to regulate emissions. Instead, the EPA began soliciting public comments in preparation for enacting more sweeping federal regulation of all carbon dioxide emissions rather than just vehicle emissions. If the EPA moves forward with enacting more stringent regulations on a federal level, a court would likely find that California's statute was preempted. (We will discuss an important 2007 ruling from the United States Supreme Court on the topic of global warming in Chapter 45.)

The Taxing and Spending Powers

Article I, Section 8, provides that Congress has the "Power to lay and collect Taxes, Duties, Imposts, and Excises." Section 8 further requires uniformity in taxation among the states, and thus Congress may not tax some states while exempting others. Traditionally, if Congress attempted to regulate indirectly, by taxation, an area over which it had no authority, the courts would invalidate the tax. Today, however, if a tax measure is reasonable, it is generally held to be within the national taxing power. Moreover, the expansive interpretation of the commerce clause almost always provides a basis for sustaining a federal tax.

Article I, Section 8, also gives Congress its spending power—the power "to pay the Debts and provide for the common Defence and general Welfare of the United States." Congress can spend revenues not only to carry out its expressed powers but also to promote any objective it deems worthwhile, so long as it does not violate the Bill of Rights. The spending power necessarily involves policy choices, with which taxpayers may disagree.

SECTION 2

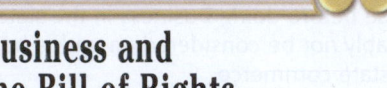

Business and the Bill of Rights

The importance of a written declaration of the rights of individuals eventually caused the first Congress of the United States to submit twelve amendments to the U.S. Constitution to the states for approval. The first ten of these amendments, commonly known as the **Bill of Rights,** were adopted in 1791 and embody a series of protections for the individual against various types of interference by the federal government.[18] The protections guaranteed by these ten amendments are summarized in Exhibit 4–1.[19] Some of these constitutional protections apply to business entities as well. For example, corporations exist as separate legal entities, or *legal persons,* and enjoy many of the same rights and privileges as *natural persons* do.

Limits on Both Federal and State Governmental Actions

As originally intended, the Bill of Rights limited only the powers of the national government. Over time, however, the United States Supreme Court "incorporated" most of these rights into the protections against state actions afforded by the Fourteenth Amendment to the Constitution. That amendment, passed in 1868 after the Civil War, provides in part that "[n]o State shall . . . deprive any person of life, liberty, or property, without due process of law." Starting in 1925, the Supreme Court began to define various rights and liberties guaranteed in the U.S. Constitution as constituting "due process of law," which was required of state governments under the Fourteenth Amendment. Today, most of the rights and liberties set forth in the Bill of Rights apply to state governments as well as the national government. In other words, neither the fed-

18. Another of these proposed amendments was ratified more than two hundred years later (in 1992) and became the Twenty-seventh Amendment to the U.S. Constitution. See Appendix B.

19. See the U.S. Constitution in Appendix B for the complete text of each amendment.

EXHIBIT 4–1 • Protections Guaranteed by the Bill of Rights

First Amendment: Guarantees the freedoms of religion, speech, and the press and the rights to assemble peaceably and to petition the government.

Second Amendment: States that the right of the people to keep and bear arms shall not be infringed.

Third Amendment: Prohibits, in peacetime, the lodging of soldiers in any house without the owner's consent.

Fourth Amendment: Prohibits unreasonable searches and seizures of persons or property.

Fifth Amendment: Guarantees the rights to indictment by grand jury, to due process of law, and to fair payment when private property is taken for public use; prohibits compulsory self-incrimination and double jeopardy (being tried again for an alleged crime for which one has already stood trial).

Sixth Amendment: Guarantees the accused in a criminal case the right to a speedy and public trial by an impartial jury and with counsel. The accused has the right to cross-examine witnesses against him or her and to solicit testimony from witnesses in his or her favor.

Seventh Amendment: Guarantees the right to a trial by jury in a civil case involving at least twenty dollars.[a]

Eighth Amendment: Prohibits excessive bail and fines, as well as cruel and unusual punishment.

Ninth Amendment: Establishes that the people have rights in addition to those specified in the Constitution.

Tenth Amendment: Establishes that those powers neither delegated to the federal government nor denied to the states are reserved to the states and to the people.

a. Twenty dollars was forty days' pay for the average person when the Bill of Rights was written.

eral government nor state governments can deprive persons of those rights and liberties.

The rights secured by the Bill of Rights are not absolute. As you can see in Exhibit 4–1, many of the rights guaranteed by the first ten amendments are described in very general terms. For example, the Fourth Amendment prohibits *unreasonable* searches and seizures, but it does not define what constitutes an unreasonable search or seizure. Similarly, the Eighth Amendment prohibits excessive bail or fines, but no definition of *excessive* is contained in that amendment. Ultimately, it is the United States Supreme Court, as the final interpreter of the Constitution, that defines our rights and determines their boundaries.

Freedom of Speech

A democratic form of government cannot survive unless people can freely voice their political opinions and criticize government actions or policies. Freedom of speech, particularly political speech, is thus a prized right, and traditionally the courts have protected this right to the fullest extent possible.

Symbolic speech—gestures, movements, articles of clothing, and other forms of expressive conduct—is also given substantial protection by the courts. For example, in 1989 the United States Supreme Court ruled that the burning of the American flag as part of a peaceful protest is a constitutionally protected form of expression.[20] Similarly, participating in a hunger strike, holding signs at an antiwar protest, or wearing a black armband would be protected as symbolic speech.

Reasonable Restrictions Expression—oral, written, or symbolized by conduct—is subject to reasonable restrictions. A balance must be struck between a government's obligation to protect its citizens and those citizens' exercise of their rights. Reasonableness is analyzed on a case-by-case basis. If a restriction imposed by the government is content neutral, then a court may allow it. To be content neutral, the restriction must be aimed at combating some societal problem, such as crime, and not be aimed at suppressing the expressive conduct or its message. For example, courts have often protected nude dancing as a form of symbolic expression but have also allowed content-neutral laws that ban all public nudity, not just erotic dancing.[21]

20. *Texas v. Johnson,* 491 U.S. 397, 109 S.Ct. 2533, 105 L.Ed.2d 342 (1989).

21. See, for example, *Rameses, Inc. v. County of Orange,* 481 F.Supp.2d 1305 (M.D.Fla. 2007) and *City of Erie v. Pap's A.M.,* 529 U.S. 277, 120 S.Ct. 1382, 146 L.Ed.2d 265 (2000).

The United States Supreme Court has also held that schools may restrict students' free speech rights at school events. In 2007, for example, the Court heard a case involving a high school student who had held up a banner saying "Bong Hits 4 Jesus" at an off-campus but school-sanctioned event. In a split decision, the majority of the Court ruled that school officials did not violate the student's free speech rights when they confiscated the banner and suspended the student for ten days. Because the banner could reasonably be interpreted as promoting the use of marijuana, and because the school had a written policy against illegal drugs, the majority concluded that the school's actions were justified. Several justices disagreed, however, noting that the majority's holding creates a special exception that will allow schools to censor any student speech that mentions drugs.[22]

Corporate Political Speech Political speech by corporations also falls within the protection of the First Amendment. For example, many years ago the United States Supreme Court ruled that a Massachusetts statute, which prohibited corporations from making political contributions or expenditures that individuals were permitted to make, was unconstitutional.[23] Similarly, the Court has held that a law forbidding a corporation from placing inserts in its billing to express its views on controversial issues violates the First Amendment.[24] Although the Supreme Court has reversed this trend somewhat,[25] corporate political speech continues to be given significant protection under the First Amendment. For example, in 2003 and again in 2007 the Supreme Court struck down some portions of bipartisan campaign-finance reform laws as unconstitutional restraints on corporate political speech.[26]

Commercial Speech The courts also give substantial protection to *commercial speech,* which consists

22. *Morse v. Frederick,* ___ U.S. ___, 127 S.Ct. 2618, 168 L.Ed.2d 290 (2007).

23. *First National Bank of Boston v. Bellotti,* 435 U.S. 765, 98 S.Ct. 1407, 55 L.Ed.2d 707 (1978).

24. *Consolidated Edison Co. v. Public Service Commission,* 447 U.S. 530, 100 S.Ct. 2326, 65 L.Ed.2d 319 (1980).

25. See *Austin v. Michigan Chamber of Commerce,* 494 U.S. 652, 110 S.Ct. 1391, 108 L.Ed.2d 652 (1990), in which the Supreme Court upheld a state law prohibiting corporations from using general corporate funds for independent expenditures in state political campaigns.

26. *McConnell v. Federal Election Commission,* 540 U.S. 93, 124 S.Ct. 619, 157 L.Ed.2d 491 (2003); and *Federal Election Commission v. Wisconsin Right to Life, Inc.,* ___U.S.___, 127 S.Ct. 2652, 168 L.Ed.2d 329 (2007).

of communications—primarily advertising and marketing—made by business firms that involve only their commercial interests. The protection given to commercial speech under the First Amendment is not as extensive as that afforded to noncommercial speech, however. A state may restrict certain kinds of advertising, for example, in the interest of preventing consumers from being misled by the advertising practices. States also have a legitimate interest in the beautification of roadsides, and this interest allows states to place restraints on billboard advertising. For example, in one Florida case, the court found that a law preventing a nude dancing establishment from billboard advertising was constitutionally permissible because it directly advanced a substantial government interest in highway beautification and safety.[27]

Generally, a restriction on commercial speech will be considered valid as long as it meets three criteria: (1) it must seek to implement a substantial government interest, (2) it must directly advance that interest, and (3) it must go no further than necessary to accomplish its objective. At issue in the following case was whether a government agency had unconstitutionally restricted commercial speech when it prohibited the inclusion of a certain illustration on beer labels.

27. *Café Erotica v. Florida Department of Transportation,* 830 So.2d 181 (Fla.App. 1 Dist. 2002); review denied by *Café Erotica/We Dare to Bare v. Florida Department of Transportation,* 845 So.2d 888 (Fla. 2003).

CASE 4.1 Bad Frog Brewery, Inc. v. New York State Liquor Authority

United States Court of Appeals, Second Circuit, 1998. 134 F.3d 87.
www.findlaw.com/casecode/index.html[a]

Background and Facts Bad Frog Brewery, Inc., makes and sells alcoholic beverages. Some of the beverages feature labels that display a drawing of a frog making the gesture generally known as "giving the finger." Bad Frog's authorized New York distributor, Renaissance Beer Company, applied to the New York State Liquor Authority (NYSLA) for brand label approval, as required by state law before the beer could be sold in New York. The NYSLA denied the application, in part, because "the label could appear in grocery and convenience stores, with obvious exposure on the shelf to children of tender age." Bad Frog filed a suit in a federal district court against the NYSLA, asking for, among other things, an injunction against the denial of the application. The court granted summary judgment in favor of the NYSLA. Bad Frog appealed to the U.S. Court of Appeals for the Second Circuit.

Decision and Rationale The U.S. Court of Appeals for the Second Circuit reversed the judgment of the district court and remanded the case for judgment to be entered in favor of Bad Frog. The appellate court held that the NYSLA's denial of Bad Frog's application violated the First Amendment. The ban on the use of the labels lacked a "reasonable fit" with the state's interest in shielding minors from vulgarity, and the NYSLA did not adequately consider alternatives to the ban. The court acknowledged that the NYSLA's interest "in protecting children from vulgar and profane advertising" was "substantial." The question was whether banning Bad Frog's labels "directly advanced" that interest. "In view of the wide currency of vulgar displays throughout contemporary society, including comic books targeted directly at children, barring such displays from labels for alcoholic beverages cannot realistically be expected to reduce children's exposure to such displays to any significant degree." The court concluded that a "commercial speech limitation" must be "part of a substantial effort to advance a valid state interest, not merely the removal of a few grains of offensive sand from a beach of vulgarity." Finally, as to whether the ban on the labels was more extensive than necessary to serve this interest, the court pointed out that there were "numerous less intrusive alternatives." For example, the NYSLA's "concern could be less intrusively dealt with by placing restrictions on the permissible locations where the appellant's products may be displayed within * * * stores."

What If the Facts Were Different? *If Bad Frog had sought to use the offensive label to market toys instead of beer, would the court's ruling likely have been the same? Explain your answer.*

The Legal Environment Dimension *Whose interests are advanced by the banning of certain types of advertising?*

a. Under the heading "US Court of Appeals," click on "2nd." Enter "Bad Frog Brewery" in the "Party Name Search" box and click on "search." On the resulting page, click on the case name to access the opinion.

Unprotected Speech The United States Supreme Court has made it clear that certain types of speech will not be protected under the First Amendment. Speech that violates criminal laws (threatening speech and pornography, for example) is not constitutionally protected. Other unprotected speech includes "fighting words" (speech that is likely to incite others to respond violently).

Speech that harms the good reputation of another, or defamatory speech (see Chapter 6), also is not protected under the First Amendment. To constitute defamation and thus have no First Amendment protection, the speech in question must be an assertion of fact and not merely an opinion. Unlike an opinion, a statement of purported fact can be verified and may require proof in a lawsuit claiming that the statement is defamatory. In the following case, the issue was whether a certain statement was an unprotected factual assertion.

CASE 4.2 Lott v. Levitt

United States District Court, Northern District of Illinois, Eastern Division, 2007.
469 F.Supp.2d 575.

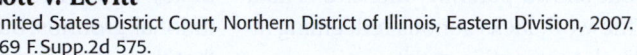

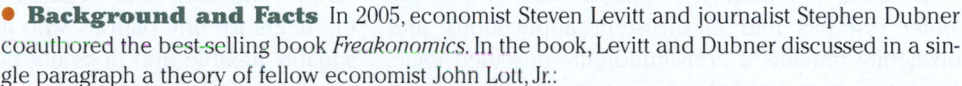

- **Background and Facts** In 2005, economist Steven Levitt and journalist Stephen Dubner coauthored the best-selling book *Freakonomics*. In the book, Levitt and Dubner discussed in a single paragraph a theory of fellow economist John Lott, Jr.:

> * * * There is an * * * argument that we need more guns on the street, but in the hands of the right people * * *. The economist John R. Lott, Jr., is the main champion of this idea. His calling card is the book *More Guns, Less Crime,* in which he argues that violent crime has decreased in areas where law-abiding citizens are allowed to carry concealed weapons. His theory might be surprising, but it is sensible. If a criminal thinks his potential victim may be armed, he may be deterred from committing the crime. Handgun opponents call Lott a pro-gun ideologue * * *. There was the troubling allegation that Lott actually invented some of the survey data that support his more-guns/less-crime theory. Regardless of whether the data were faked, Lott's admittedly intriguing hypothesis doesn't seem to be true. When other scholars have tried to replicate his results, they found that right-to-carry laws simply don't bring down crime.

Economist John McCall sent Levitt an e-mail regarding this paragraph. McCall cited an issue of *The Journal of Law and Economics,* in which other scholars claimed to "replicate" Lott's research. Levitt responded, "It was not a peer refereed edition of the *Journal.* For $15,000, he was able to buy an issue and put in only work that supported him. My best friend was the editor and was outraged the press let Lott do this." Based in part on this e-mail, Lott filed a suit in a federal district court against Levitt and others, claiming, among other things, defamation. Levitt filed a motion to dismiss this claim.

- **Decision and Rationale** The federal district court denied the motion to dismiss Lott's complaint. The court explained that the test to determine if a statement is factual is "whether the statement is precise, readily understood, and susceptible of being verified as true or false." Language that is "loose, figurative, or hyperbolic" most likely expresses an opinion. Statements that are subjective, theoretical, or conjectural likewise comprise opinions. Expressions of opinion are protected under the First Amendment. But the statement of a speaker or writer who claims to possess "objectively verifiable facts" may be actionable. Levitt's e-mail was "a string of defamatory assertions * * * that—no matter how rash or short-sighted Levitt was when he made them—cannot be reasonably interpreted as innocent or mere opinion." Therefore, Levitt's e-mail met the test. "First, it would be unreasonable to interpret Levitt's unqualified statement that the journal edition was not 'peer refereed' as Levitt merely giving his opinion on the 'peers' * * *. Second, a reasonable reader would not interpret Levitt's assertion that 'For $15,000, he was able to buy an issue and put in only work that supported him' as simply a statement of Levitt's opinion." Finally, the assertion that the editor of the *Journal* was "outraged" could be verified by the editor, who might also be able to attest to the truth or falsity of the other statements. The court encouraged the parties to attempt to settle their dispute before proceeding to trial.

- **The Legal Environment Dimension** *Did the statements about Lott in* Freakonomics *constitute unprotected speech? Explain.*

- **The Ethical Dimension** *Should the First Amendment protect all speech? Why or why not?*

Obscene Speech. The Supreme Court has also held that the First Amendment does not protect obscene speech. Establishing an objective definition of obscene speech has proved difficult, however, and the Court has grappled from time to time with this problem. In a 1973 case, *Miller v. California,*[28] the Supreme Court created a test for legal obscenity, including a set of requirements that must be met for material to be legally obscene. Under this test, material is obscene if (1) the average person finds that it violates contemporary community standards; (2) the work taken as a whole appeals to a prurient (arousing or obsessive) interest in sex; (3) the work shows patently offensive sexual conduct; and (4) the work lacks serious redeeming literary, artistic, political, or scientific merit.

Because community standards vary widely, the *Miller* test has had inconsistent applications, and obscenity remains a constitutionally unsettled issue. Numerous state and federal statutes make it a crime to disseminate obscene materials, and the Supreme Court has often upheld such laws, including laws prohibiting the sale and possession of child pornography.[29]

Online Obscenity. A significant problem facing the courts and lawmakers today is how to control the dissemination of obscenity and child pornography via the Internet. Congress first attempted to protect minors from pornographic materials on the Internet by passing the Communications Decency Act (CDA) of 1996. The CDA declared it a crime to make available to minors online any "obscene or indecent" message that "depicts or describes, in terms patently offensive as measured by contemporary community standards, sexual or excretory activities or organs."[30] Civil rights groups challenged the act, and ultimately the Supreme Court ruled that portions of the act were unconstitutional. The Court held that the terms *indecent* and *patently offensive* covered large amounts of nonpornographic material with serious educational or other value.[31]

Subsequent Attempts to Regulate Online Obscenity. Congress's second attempt to protect children from online obscenity, the Child Online Protection Act (COPA) of 1998,[32] met with a similar fate. Although the COPA was more narrowly tailored than its predecessor, the CDA, it still used "contemporary community standards" to define which material was obscene and harmful to minors. Ultimately, in 2004 the Supreme Court concluded that it was likely that the COPA did violate the right to free speech and prevented enforcement of the act.[33]

In 2000, Congress enacted the Children's Internet Protection Act (CIPA),[34] which requires public schools and libraries to install **filtering software** to keep children from accessing adult content. Such software is designed to prevent persons from viewing certain Web sites based on a site's Internet address or its **meta tags,** or key words. The CIPA was also challenged on constitutional grounds, but in 2003 the Supreme Court held that the act does not violate the First Amendment. The Court concluded that because libraries can disable the filters for any patrons who ask, the system is reasonably flexible and does not burden free speech to an unconstitutional extent.[35]

Because of the difficulties of policing the Internet as well as the constitutional complexities of prohibiting online obscenity through legislation, it remains a continuing problem in the United States (and worldwide).

Freedom of Religion

The First Amendment states that the government may neither establish any religion nor prohibit the free exercise of religious practices. The first part of this constitutional provision, which is referred to as the **establishment clause,** has to do with the separation of church and state. The second part of the provision is known as the **free exercise clause.**

The Establishment Clause The establishment clause prohibits the government from establishing a state-sponsored religion, as well as from passing laws that promote (aid or endorse) religion or that show a preference for one religion over another. Establishment clause issues often involve such matters as the legality of allowing or requiring school prayers, using state-issued school vouchers to pay for tuition at religious schools, teaching evolutionary versus creationist theory, and giving state and local government aid to religious organizations and schools.

28. 413 U.S. 15, 93 S.Ct. 2607, 37 L.Ed.2d 419 (1973).
29. For example, see *Osborne v. Ohio,* 495 U.S. 103, 110 S.Ct. 1691, 109 L.Ed.2d 98 (1990).
30. 47 U.S.C. Section 223(a)(1)(B)(ii).
31. *Reno v. American Civil Liberties Union,* 521 U.S. 844, 117 S.Ct. 2329, 138 L.Ed.2d 874 (1997).
32. 47 U.S.C. Section 231.
33. *American Civil Liberties Union v. Ashcroft,* 542 U.S. 646, 124 S.Ct. 2783, 159 L.Ed.2d 690 (2004). See also *Ashcroft v. American Civil Liberties Union,* 535 U.S. 564, 122 S.Ct. 1700, 152 L.Ed.2d 771 (2002); and *American Civil Liberties Union v. Ashcroft,* 322 F.3d 240 (3d Cir. 2003).
34. 17 U.S.C. Sections 1701–1741.
35. *United States v. American Library Association,* 539 U.S. 194, 123 S.Ct. 2297, 156 L.Ed.2d 221 (2003).

Federal or state laws that do not promote or place a significant burden on religion are constitutional even if they have some impact on religion. "Sunday closing laws," for example, make the performance of some commercial activities on Sunday illegal. These statutes, also known as "blue laws" (from the color of the paper on which an early Sunday law was written), have been upheld on the ground that it is a legitimate function of government to provide a day of rest to promote the health and welfare of workers. Even though closing laws admittedly make it easier for Christians to attend religious services, the courts have viewed this effect as an incidental, not a primary, purpose of Sunday closing laws.

The Free Exercise Clause The free exercise clause guarantees that no person can be compelled to do something that is contrary to his or her religious beliefs. For this reason, if a law or policy is contrary to a person's religious beliefs, exemptions are often made to accommodate those beliefs.

When religious practices work against public policy and the public welfare, though, the government can act. For example, regardless of a child's or parent's religious beliefs, the government can require certain types of vaccinations in the interest of public welfare. The government's interest must be sufficiently compelling, however. The United States Supreme Court ruled in 2006 that the government had failed to demonstrate a sufficiently compelling interest in barring a church from the sacramental use of an illegal controlled substance. (The church members used hoasca tea, which is brewed from plants native to the Amazon rain forest and contains a hallucinogenic drug, in the practice of a sincerely held religious belief.)[36]

For business firms, an important issue involves the accommodation that businesses must make for the religious beliefs of their employees. Generally, if an employee's religion prohibits her or him from working on a certain day of the week or at a certain type of job, the employer must make a reasonable attempt to accommodate these religious requirements. The only requirement is that the belief be religious in nature and sincerely held by the employee.[37] (See Chapter 34 for a further discussion of religious freedom in the employment context.)

36. *Gonzales v. O Centro Espirita Beneficiente Uniao Do Vegtal,* 546 U.S. 418, 126 S.Ct. 1211, 163 L.Ed.2d 1017 (2006).

37. *Frazee v. Illinois Department of Employment Security,* 489 U.S. 829, 109 S.Ct. 1514, 103 L.Ed.2d 914 (1989).

Searches and Seizures

The Fourth Amendment protects the "right of the people to be secure in their persons, houses, papers, and effects." Before searching or seizing private property, law enforcement officers must usually obtain a **search warrant**—an order from a judge or other public official authorizing the search or seizure.

Search Warrants and Probable Cause To obtain a search warrant, law enforcement officers must convince a judge that they have reasonable grounds, or probable cause, to believe a search will reveal evidence of a specific illegality. To establish **probable cause,** the officers must have trustworthy evidence that would convince a reasonable person that the proposed search or seizure is more likely justified than not. Furthermore, the Fourth Amendment prohibits *general* warrants. It requires a particular description of whatever is to be searched or seized. General searches through a person's belongings are impermissible. The search cannot extend beyond what is described in the warrant.

The requirement for a search warrant has several exceptions. One exception applies when the items sought are likely to be removed before a warrant can be obtained. For example, if a police officer has probable cause to believe that an automobile contains evidence of a crime and that the vehicle will likely be unavailable by the time a warrant is obtained, the officer can search the vehicle without a warrant.

Searches and Seizures in the Business Context Constitutional protection against unreasonable searches and seizures is important to businesses and professionals. Equally important is the government's interest in ensuring compliance with federal and state regulations, especially rules meant to protect the safety of employees and the public.

Because of the strong governmental interest in protecting the public, a warrant usually is not required for the seizure of spoiled or contaminated food. In addition, warrants are not required for searches of businesses in such highly regulated industries as liquor, guns, and strip mining. General manufacturing is not considered to be one of these highly regulated industries, however.

Normally, government inspectors do not have the right to search business premises without a warrant, although the standard of probable cause is not the same as that required in nonbusiness contexts. The existence of a general and neutral enforcement plan often will justify issuance of the warrant. Lawyers and accountants frequently possess the business records of their clients, and inspecting these documents while they are out of the hands of their true owners also requires a warrant.

In the following case, after receiving a report of suspected health-care fraud, state officials entered and searched the office of a licensed physician without obtaining a warrant. The physician claimed that the search was unreasonable and improper.

CASE 4.3 United States v. Moon

United States Court of Appeals, Sixth Circuit, 2008. 513 F.3d 527.

www.ca6.uscourts.gov[a]

Background and Facts Young Moon was a licensed physician, specializing in oncology and hematology. Moon operated a medical practice in Crossville, Tennessee. As part of her practice, Moon contracted with the state of Tennessee to provide medical treatment to patients pursuant to a state and federally funded health benefit program for the uninsured known as "TennCare." Moon routinely utilized chemotherapy medications in her treatment of cancer patients insured under the program. In March 2001, the Tennessee Bureau of Investigation (TBI) received a complaint from one of Moon's employees alleging that she had administered partial doses of chemotherapy medication while billing the insurance program for full doses. In January 2002, investigating agents conducted an on-site review at Moon's office. The agents identified themselves, informed Moon of a general complaint against her, and requested permission to "scan" particular patient records. Moon agreed. She also provided agents with a location where they could scan the requested files. Later, Moon attempted to suppress the evidence arguing that it was obtained without a search warrant. The federal district court sentenced Moon to 188 months in prison, followed by two years of supervised release. She was also ordered to pay restitution of $432,000. She appealed her conviction and sentence to the U.S. Court of Appeals for the Sixth Circuit.

Decision and Rationale The U.S. Court of Appeals for the Sixth Circuit affirmed the district court's decision. The appellate court pointed out that although the Fourth Amendment prohibits the government from conducting unreasonable searches and seizures, there is an exception. "The well-delineated exception at issue here is consent. If an officer obtains consent to search, a warrantless search does not offend the Constitution." Further, "consent is voluntary when it is unequivocal, specific, and intelligently given, uncontaminated by duress or coercion." Moon clearly stated that it would be acceptable for agents to access requested files and that they could "scan whatever they needed to." Thus, a search warrant was not necessary.

What If the Facts Were Different? *Assume that Dr. Moon had proven that using partial doses of the chemotherapy drugs did not affect the "cure" rate for her cancer patients. Would the court have ruled differently? Why or why not?*

The Legal Environment Dimension *Does the length of Dr. Moon's prison sentence seem appropriate? Why or why not?*

a. Click on "Opinions Search," and in the "Short Title contains" box, type in "Moon." Click on "Submit Query." Under "Published Opinions," select the link to "08a0031p.06" to access the opinion.

Border Searches of Computers Warrantless border searches have long been upheld by the courts as a means to prevent persons from physically bringing drugs, contraband, and illegal aliens into the United States. In recent years, the courts have also started allowing border guards to search through the temporary files stored on laptop computers and to use the history of Web pages viewed as criminal evidence.

Consider, for example, a 2006 case involving Stuart Romm, a suspended lawyer from Massachusetts who traveled to British Columbia on business. A border agent asked to see Romm's laptop computer and briefly examined the Internet cache, or temporary folder showing the history of Web sites that Romm had visited. The border guards discovered that Romm had looked at some child pornography Web sites and detained him while a forensic computer specialist analyzed the hard drive. Analysis confirmed that Romm had viewed ten images of child pornography and then deleted (or at least attempted to delete) the images from his computer. Romm was convicted and sentenced to serve ten to fifteen years in prison. A federal appellate court upheld his conviction.[38] The holding in this case could be applied to any type of illegal material found on a laptop computer during a border search, including unauthorized images of copyrighted materials or confidential business data (see Chapter 8).

Self-Incrimination

The Fifth Amendment guarantees that no person "shall be compelled in any criminal case to be a witness against himself." Thus, in any federal or state (because the due process clause extends the protection to state courts) proceeding, an accused person cannot be forced to give testimony that might subject him or her to any criminal prosecution.

The Fifth Amendment's guarantee against self-incrimination extends only to natural persons. Therefore, neither corporations nor partnerships receive Fifth Amendment protection. When a partnership is required to produce business records, it must do so even if the information provided incriminates the individual partners of the firm. In contrast, sole proprietors and sole practitioners (those who fully own their businesses) cannot be compelled to produce their business records. These individuals have full protection against self-incrimination because they function in only one capacity; there is no separate business entity.

SECTION 3

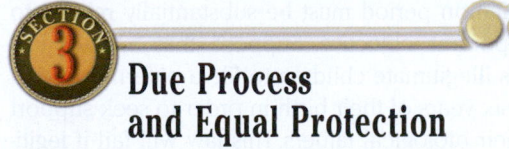

Due Process and Equal Protection

Other constitutional guarantees of great significance to Americans are mandated by the *due process clauses* of the Fifth and Fourteenth Amendments and the *equal protection clause* of the Fourteenth Amendment.

Due Process

Both the Fifth and Fourteenth Amendments provide that no person shall be deprived "of life, liberty, or property, without due process of law." The **due process clause** of these constitutional amendments has two aspects—procedural and substantive. Note that the due process clause applies to "legal persons" (that is, corporations), as well as to individuals.

Procedural Due Process *Procedural* due process requires that any government decision to take life, liberty, or property must be made equitably; that is, the government must give a person proper notice and an opportunity to be heard. Fair procedures must be used in determining whether a person will be subjected to punishment or have some burden imposed on her or him. Fair procedure has been interpreted as requiring that the person have at least an opportunity to object to a proposed action before an impartial, neutral decision maker (which need not be a judge). Thus, for example, if a driver's license is construed as a property interest, the state must provide some sort of opportunity for the driver to object before suspending or terminating the license.

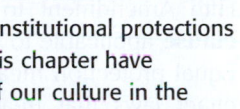

Many of the constitutional protections discussed in this chapter have become part of our culture in the United States. Due process, especially procedural due process, has become synonymous with what Americans consider "fair." For this reason, businesspersons seeking to avoid legal disputes should consider giving due process to anyone who might object to some business decision or action, whether that person is an employee, a partner, an affiliate, or a customer. For instance, giving ample notice of new policies to all affected persons is a prudent move, as is giving them at least an opportunity to express their opinions on the matter. Providing an opportunity to be heard is often the ideal way to make people feel that they are being treated fairly. If people believe that a businessperson or firm is fair and listens to both sides of an issue, they are less likely to sue that businessperson or firm.

Substantive Due Process Substantive due process protects an individual's life, liberty, or property against certain government actions regardless of the

38. *United States v. Romm*, 455 F.3d 990 (9th Cir. 2006).

fairness of the procedures used to implement them. Substantive due process limits what the government may do in its legislative and executive capacities. Legislation must be fair and reasonable in content and must further a legitimate governmental objective. Only when state conduct is arbitrary, or shocks the conscience, however, will it rise to the level of violating substantive due process.

If a law or other governmental action limits a fundamental right, the state must have a legitimate and compelling interest to justify its action. Fundamental rights include interstate travel, privacy, voting, marriage and family, and all First Amendment rights. Thus, a state must have substantial reason for taking any action that infringes on a person's free speech rights. In situations not involving fundamental rights, a law or action does not violate substantive due process if it rationally relates to any legitimate government purpose. Under this test, virtually any business regulation will be upheld as reasonable.

Equal Protection

Under the Fourteenth Amendment, a state may not "deny to any person within its jurisdiction the equal protection of the laws." The United States Supreme Court has interpreted the due process clause of the Fifth Amendment to make the **equal protection clause** applicable to the federal government as well. Equal protection means that the government cannot enact laws that treat similarly situated individuals differently.

Both substantive due process and equal protection require review of the substance of the law or other governmental action rather than review of the procedures used. When a law or action limits the liberty of all persons to do something, it may violate substantive due process; when a law or action limits the liberty of some persons but not others, it may violate the equal protection clause. Thus, for example, if a law prohibits all advertising on the sides of trucks, it raises a substantive due process question; if it makes an exception to allow truck owners to advertise their own businesses, it raises an equal protection issue.

In an equal protection inquiry, when a law or action distinguishes between or among individuals, the basis for the distinction, or classification, is examined. Depending on the classification, the courts apply different levels of scrutiny, or "tests," to determine whether the law or action violates the equal protection clause. The courts use one of three standards: strict scrutiny, intermediate scrutiny, or the "rational basis" test.

Strict Scrutiny The most difficult standard to meet is that of *strict scrutiny.* Under strict scrutiny, the classification must be necessary to promote a *compelling state interest.* Generally, few laws or actions survive strict-scrutiny analysis by the courts.

Strict scrutiny is applied when a law or action prohibits some persons from exercising a fundamental right or classifies individuals based on a *suspect trait*—such as race, national origin, or citizenship status. For example, to prevent violence caused by racial gangs in prisons, corrections officials in California segregated prisoners by race for up to sixty days after they entered (or were transferred to) a correctional facility. A prisoner challenged that policy. Ultimately, the United States Supreme Court held that all racial classifications, because they are based on a suspect trait, must be analyzed under strict scrutiny.[39]

Intermediate Scrutiny Another standard, that of *intermediate scrutiny,* is applied in cases involving discrimination based on gender or legitimacy. Laws using these classifications must be *substantially related to important government objectives.* For example, an important government objective is preventing illegitimate teenage pregnancies. Therefore, because males and females are not similarly situated in this regard—only females can become pregnant—a law that punishes men but not women for statutory rape will be upheld, even though it treats men and women unequally.

The state also has an important objective in establishing time limits (called *statutes of limitation*) for how long after an event a particular type of action can be brought. Such limits prevent persons from bringing fraudulent and stale (outdated) claims. Nevertheless, the limitation period must be substantially related to the important objective. Suppose that a state law requires illegitimate children to file a paternity action within six years of their birth in order to seek support from their biological fathers. This law will fail if legitimate children can seek support from their fathers at any time because distinguishing between support claims on the basis of legitimacy has no relation to the objective of preventing fraudulent or stale claims.

39. *Johnson v. California,* 543 U.S. 499, 125 S.Ct. 1141, 160 L.Ed.2d 949 (2005).

The "Rational Basis" Test In matters of economic or social welfare, a classification will be considered valid if there is any conceivable *rational basis* on which the classification might relate to a legitimate government interest. It is almost impossible for a law or action to fail the rational basis test. Thus, for example, a city ordinance that in effect prohibits all pushcart vendors, except a specific few, from operating in a particular area of the city will be upheld if the city provides a rational basis—such as reducing the traffic in the particular area—for the ordinance. In contrast, a law that provides unemployment benefits only to people over six feet tall would clearly fail the rational basis test because it could not further any legitimate government objective.

SECTION 4 Privacy Rights

The U.S. Constitution does not explicitly mention a general right to privacy. In a 1928 Supreme Court case, *Olmstead v. United States*,[40] Justice Louis Brandeis stated in his dissent that the right to privacy is "the most comprehensive of rights and the right most valued by civilized men." The majority of the justices at that time did not agree, and it was not until the 1960s that a majority on the Supreme Court endorsed the view that the Constitution protects individual privacy rights. In a landmark 1965 case, *Griswold v. Connecticut*,[41] the Supreme Court held that a constitutional right to privacy was implied by the First, Third, Fourth, Fifth, and Ninth Amendments.

Federal Statutes Affecting Privacy Rights

In the last several decades, Congress has enacted a number of statutes that protect the privacy of individuals in various areas of concern. In the 1960s, Americans were sufficiently alarmed by the accumulation of personal information in government files that they pressured Congress to pass laws permitting individuals to access their files. Congress responded in 1966 with the Freedom of Information Act, which allows any person to request copies of any information on her or him contained in federal government files. In 1974, Congress passed the Privacy Act, which also gives persons the right to access such information. Since then, Congress has passed numerous other laws protecting individuals' privacy rights with respect to financial transactions, electronic communications, and other activities in which personal information may be gathered and stored by organizations.

40. 277 U.S. 438, 48 S.Ct. 564, 72 L.Ed. 944 (1928).

41. 381 U.S. 479, 85 S.Ct. 1678, 14 L.Ed.2d 510 (1965).

Medical Information Responding to the growing need to protect the privacy of individuals' health records—particularly computerized records—Congress passed the Health Insurance Portability and Accountability Act (HIPAA) of 1996.[42] This act, which took effect on April 14, 2003, defines and limits the circumstances in which an individual's "protected health information" may be used or disclosed.

The HIPAA requires health-care providers and health-care plans, including certain employers who sponsor health plans, to inform patients of their privacy rights and of how their personal medical information may be used. The act also states that a person's medical records generally may not be used for purposes unrelated to health care—such as marketing, for example—or disclosed to others without the individual's permission. Covered entities must formulate written privacy policies, designate privacy officials, limit access to computerized health data, physically secure medical records with lock and key, train employees and volunteers on their privacy policies, and sanction those who violate the policies. These protections are intended to assure individuals that their health information, including genetic information, will be properly protected and not used for purposes that the patient did not know about or authorize.

The Patriot Act In the wake of the terrorist attacks of September 11, 2001, Congress passed legislation often referred to as the USA Patriot Act.[43] The Patriot Act has given government officials increased authority to monitor Internet activities (such as e-mail and Web site visits) and to gain access to personal financial information and student information. Law enforcement officials can now track a person's telephone and

42. The HIPAA was enacted as Pub. L. No. 104-191 (1996) and is codified in 29 U.S.C.A. Sections 1181 *et seq.*

43. The Uniting and Strengthening America by Providing Appropriate Tools Required to Intercept and Obstruct Terrorism Act of 2001, also known as the USA Patriot Act, was enacted as Pub. L. No. 107-56 (2001) and extended in early 2006 by Pub. L. No. 109-173 (2006).

e-mail communications to find out the identity of the other party or parties. The government must certify that the information likely to be obtained by such monitoring is relevant to an ongoing criminal investigation but does not need to provide proof of any wrongdoing to gain access to this information.[44] Privacy advocates argue that this law adversely affects the constitutional rights of all Americans, and it has been widely criticized in the media, fueling a public debate over how to secure privacy rights in an electronic age.

44. See, for example, a case in which a federal appeals court upheld the government's warrantless monitoring of electronic communications. *American Civil Liberties Union v. National Security Agency*, 493 F.3d 644 (6th Cir. 2007).

Other Laws Affecting Privacy

State constitutions and statutes also protect individuals' privacy rights, often to a significant degree. Privacy rights are also protected under tort law (see Chapter 6). Additionally, the Federal Trade Commission has played an active role in protecting the privacy rights of online consumers (see Chapter 44). The protection of employees' privacy rights, particularly with respect to electronic monitoring practices, is an area of growing concern (see Chapter 33).

REVIEWING Constitutional Authority to Regulate Business

A state legislature enacted a statute that required any motorcycle operator or passenger on the state's highways to wear a protective helmet. Jim Alderman, a licensed motorcycle operator, sued the state to block enforcement of the law. Alderman asserted that the statute violated the equal protection clause because it placed requirements on motorcyclists that were not imposed on other motorists. Using the information presented in the chapter, answer the following questions.

1. Why does this statute raise equal protection issues instead of substantive due process concerns?
2. What are the three levels of scrutiny that the courts use in determining whether a law violates the equal protection clause?
3. Which standard of scrutiny, or test, would apply to this situation? Why?
4. Applying this standard, or test, is the helmet statute constitutional? Why or why not?

TERMS AND CONCEPTS

Bill of Rights 78
checks and balances 74
commerce clause 74
due process clause 85
equal protection clause 86
establishment clause 82
federal form of government 72
filtering software 82
free exercise clause 82
full faith and credit clause 73
meta tags 82
police powers 72
preemption 75
privileges and immunities clause 73
probable cause 83
search warrant 83
supremacy clause 75
symbolic speech 79

QUESTIONS AND CASE PROBLEMS

4–1. A Georgia state law requires the use of contoured rear-fender mudguards on trucks and trailers operating within Georgia state lines. The statute further makes it illegal for trucks and trailers to use straight mudguards. In approximately thirty-five other states, straight mudguards are legal. Moreover, in Florida, straight mudguards are explicitly required by law. There is some evidence suggesting that contoured mudguards might be a little safer than straight mudguards. Discuss whether this Georgia statute violates any constitutional provisions.

4–2. QUESTION WITH SAMPLE ANSWER

Thomas worked in the nonmilitary operations of a large firm that produced both military and nonmilitary goods. When the company discontinued the production of nonmilitary goods, Thomas was transferred to a plant producing military equipment. Thomas left his job, claiming that it violated his religious principles to participate in the manufacture of goods to be used in destroying life. In effect, he argued, the transfer to the military equipment plant forced him to quit his job. He was denied unemployment compensation by the state because he had not been effectively "discharged" by the employer but had voluntarily terminated his employment. Did the state's denial of unemployment benefits to Thomas violate the free exercise clause of the First Amendment? Explain.

- **For a sample answer to Question 4–2, go to Appendix I at the end of this text.**

4–3. A business has a backlog of orders, and to meet its deadlines, management decides to run the firm seven days a week, eight hours a day. One of the employees, Abe Placer, refuses to work on Saturday on religious grounds. His refusal to work means that the firm may not meet its production deadlines and may therefore suffer a loss of future business. The firm fires Placer and replaces him with an employee who is willing to work seven days a week. Placer claims that by terminating his employment, his employer has violated his constitutional right to the free exercise of his religion. Do you agree? Why or why not?

4–4. The framers of the U.S. Constitution feared the twin evils of tyranny and anarchy. Discuss how specific provisions of the Constitution and the Bill of Rights reflect these fears and protect against both of these extremes.

4–5. Freedom of Speech. Henry Mishkoff is a Web designer whose firm does business as "Webfeats." When Taubman Co. began building a mall called "The Shops at Willow Bend" near Mishkoff's home, Mishkoff registered the domain name "shopsatwillowbend.com" and created a Web site with that address. The site featured information about the mall, a disclaimer indicating that Mishkoff's site was unofficial, and a link to the mall's official site. Taubman discovered Mishkoff's site and filed a suit in a federal district court against him. Mishkoff then registered other various names, including "taubmansucks.com," with links to a site documenting his battle with Taubman. (A Web name with a "sucks.com" moniker attached to it is known as a *complaint name,* and the process of registering and using such names is known as *cybergriping*.) Taubman asked the court to order Mishkoff to stop using all of these names. Should the court grant Taubman's request? On what basis might the court protect Mishkoff's use of the names? [*Taubman Co. v. Webfeats,* 319 F.3d 770 (6th Cir. 2003)]

4–6. CASE PROBLEM WITH SAMPLE ANSWER

To protect the privacy of individuals identified in information systems maintained by federal agencies, the Privacy Act of 1974 regulates the use of the information. The statute provides for a minimum award of $1,000 for "actual damages sustained" caused by "intentional or willful actions" to the "person entitled to recovery." Buck Doe filed for certain disability benefits with an office of the U.S. Department of Labor (DOL). The application form asked for Doe's Social Security number, which the DOL used to identify his claim on documents sent to groups of claimants, their employers, and the lawyers involved in their cases. This disclosed Doe's Social Security number beyond the limits set by the Privacy Act. Doe filed a suit in a federal district court against the DOL, alleging that he was "torn . . . all to pieces" and "greatly concerned and worried" because of the disclosure of his Social Security number and its potentially "devastating" consequences. He did not offer any proof of actual injury, however. Should damages be awarded in such circumstances solely on the basis of the agency's conduct, or should proof of some actual injury be required? Why? [*Doe v. Chao,* 540 U.S. 614, 124 S.Ct. 1204, 157 L.Ed.2d 1122 (2004)]

- **To view a sample answer for Problem 4–6, go to this book's Web site at www.cengage.com/blaw/jentz, select "Chapter 4," and click on "Case Problem with Sample Answer."**

4–7. Due Process. In 1994, the Board of County Commissioners of Yellowstone County, Montana, created Zoning District 17 in a rural area of the county and a planning and zoning commission for the district. The commission adopted zoning regulations, which provided, among other things, that "dwelling units" could be built only through "on-site construction." Later, county officials were unable to identify any health or safety concerns that were addressed by requiring on-site construction. There was no evidence that homes built off-site would negatively affect property values or cause harm to any other general welfare interest of the community. In December 1999, Francis and Anita Yurczyk bought two forty-acre tracts in District 17. The Yurczyks also bought a modular home and moved it onto the property the following spring. Within days, the county advised the Yurczyks that the home violated the on-site construction regulation and would have to be removed. The Yurczyks filed a suit in a Montana state court against the county, alleging, among other things, that the zoning regulation violated their due process rights. Does the Yurczyks' claim relate to procedural or substantive due process rights? What standard would the court apply to determine whether the regulation is constitutional? How should the court rule? Explain. [*Yurczyk v. Yellowstone County*, 2004 MT 3, 319 Mont. 169, 83 P.3d 266 (2004)]

4–8. Supremacy Clause. The Federal Communications Act of 1934 grants the right to govern all *interstate* telecommunications to the Federal Communications Commission (FCC) and the right to regulate all *intrastate* telecommunications to the states. The federal Telephone Consumer Protection Act of 1991, the Junk Fax Protection Act of 2005, and FCC rules permit a party to send unsolicited fax ads to recipients with whom the party has an "established business relationship" if those ads include an "opt-out" alternative. Section 17538.43 of California's Business and Professions Code (known as "SB 833") was enacted in 2005 to provide the citizens of California with greater protection than that afforded under federal law. SB 833 omits the "established business relationship" exception and requires a sender to obtain a recipient's express consent (an "opt-in" provision) before faxing an ad to that party into or out of California. The Chamber of Commerce of the United States filed a suit against Bill Lockyer, California's state attorney general, seeking to block the enforcement of SB 833. What principles support the plaintiff's position? How should the court resolve the issue? Explain. [*Chamber of Commerce of the United States v. Lockyer*, 463 F.3d 1076 (E.D.Cal. 2006)]

4–9. Freedom of Speech. For decades, New York City has had to deal with the vandalism and defacement of public property caused by unauthorized graffiti. Among other attempts to stop the damage, in December 2005 the city banned the sale of aerosol spray-paint cans and broad-tipped indelible markers to persons under twenty-one years of age and prohibited them from possessing such items on property other than their own. By May 1, 2006, five people—all under age twenty-one—had been cited for violations of these regulations, while 871 individuals had been arrested for actually making graffiti. Artists who wished to create graffiti on legal surfaces, such as canvas, wood, and clothing, included college student Lindsey Vincenty, who was studying visual arts. Unable to buy her supplies in the city or to carry them in the city if she bought them elsewhere, Vincenty and others filed a suit in a federal district court on behalf of themselves and other young artists against Michael Bloomberg, the city's mayor, and others. The plaintiffs claimed that, among other things, the new rules violated their right to freedom of speech. They asked the court to enjoin the enforcement of the rules. Should the court grant this request? Why or why not? [*Vincenty v. Bloomberg*, 476 F.3d 74 (2d Cir. 2007)]

4–10. A QUESTION OF ETHICS

Aric Toll owns and manages the Balboa Island Village Inn, a restaurant and bar in Newport Beach, California. Anne Lemen owns the "Island Cottage," a residence across an alley from the Inn. Lemen often complained to the authorities about excessive noise and the behavior of the Inn's customers, whom she called "drunks" and "whores." Lemen referred to Theresa Toll, Aric's wife, as "Madam Whore." Lemen told the Inn's bartender Ewa Cook that Cook "worked for Satan," was "Satan's wife," and was "going to have Satan's children." She told the Inn's neighbors that it was "a whorehouse" with "prostitution going on inside" and that it sold illegal drugs, sold alcohol to minors, made "sex videos," was involved in child pornography, had "Mafia connections," encouraged "lesbian activity," and stayed open until 6:00 A.M. *Lemen also voiced her complaints to potential customers, and the Inn's sales dropped more than 20 percent. The Inn filed a suit in a California state court against Lemen, asserting defamation and other claims.* [Balboa Island Village Inn, Inc. v. Lemen, *40 Cal.4th 1141, 156 P.3d 339 (2007)*]

(a) Are Lemen's statements about the Inn's owners, customers, and activities protected by the U.S. Constitution? Should such statements be protected? In whose favor should the court rule? Why?

(b) Did Lemen behave unethically in the circumstances of this case? Explain.

LAW ON THE WEB

For updated links to resources available on the Web, as well as a variety of other materials, visit this text's Web site at

www.cengage.com/blaw/jentz

For an online version of the Constitution that provides hypertext links to amendments and other changes, as well as the history of the document, go to

www.constitutioncenter.org

For discussions of current issues involving the rights and liberties contained in the Bill of Rights, go to the Web site of the American Civil Liberties Union at

www.aclu.org

For a menu of selected constitutional law decisions by the United States Supreme Court, go to the Web site of Cornell Law School's Legal Information Institute at

www.law.cornell.edu/supct/cases/conlaw.htm

Legal Research Exercises on the Web

Go to **www.cengage.com/blaw/jentz**, the Web site that accompanies this text. Select "Chapter 4" and click on "Internet Exercises." There you will find the following Internet research exercises that you can perform to learn more about the topics covered in this chapter.

Internet Exercise 4–1: Legal Perspective
Commercial Speech

Internet Exercise 4–2: Management Perspective
Privacy Rights in Cyberspace

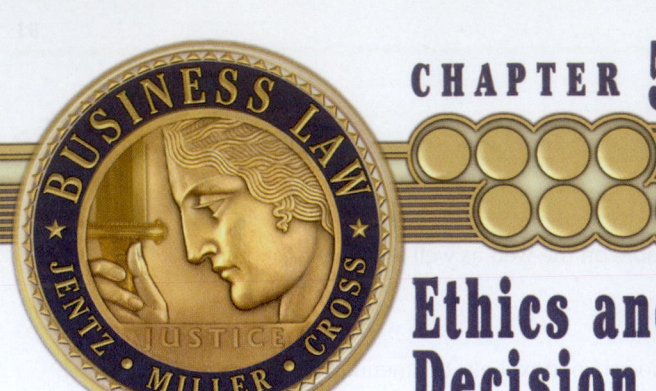

CHAPTER 5

Ethics and Business Decision Making

All of the following businesspersons have been in the news recently:

- Dennis Kozlowski (former chairman and chief executive officer of Tyco International).
- Mark H. Swartz (former chief financial officer of Tyco International).
- Jeffrey Skilling (former chief executive officer of Enron Corporation).
- Bernard Ebbers (former chief executive officer of WorldCom).

What do these individuals have in common? They are all in prison, and some may stay there until they die. They were all convicted of various crimes ranging from overseeing revenue exaggeration in order to increase stock prices to personal use of millions of dollars of public company funds. Not only did they break the law, but they also clearly violated even the minimum ethical principles that a civil society expects to be followed. Other officers and directors of the companies mentioned in the preceding list cost shareholders billions of dollars. In the case of those companies that had to enter bankruptcy, such as Enron Corporation, tens of thousands of employees lost their jobs.

Acting ethically in a business context is not child's play; it can mean billions of dollars—up or down—for corporations, shareholders, and employees. In the wake of the recent scandals, Congress attempted to prevent similar unethical business behavior in the future by passing stricter legislation in the form of the Sarbanes-Oxley Act of 2002, which will be explained in detail in Chapters 41 and 51. This act generally imposed more reporting requirements on corporations in an effort to deter unethical behavior and encourage accountability.

SECTION 1 Business Ethics

As you might imagine, business ethics is derived from the concept of ethics. **Ethics** can be defined as the study of what constitutes right or wrong behavior. It is a branch of philosophy focusing on morality and the way moral principles are derived. Ethics has to do with the fairness, justness, rightness, or wrongness of an action.

What Is Business Ethics?

Business ethics focuses on what is right and wrong behavior in the business world. It has to do with how businesses apply moral and ethical principles to situations that arise in the workplace. Because business decision makers must often address more complex ethical issues in the workplace than they face in their personal lives, business ethics is more complicated than personal ethics.

Why Is Business Ethics Important?

For an answer to the question of why business ethics is so important, reread the list at the beginning of this chapter. All of the individuals who are sitting behind bars could have avoided their fates. Had they engaged in ethical decision making throughout their business careers, they would never have followed their different paths to criminal behavior. The corporations, shareholders, and employees who suffered because of those individuals' unethical and criminal behavior certainly paid a high price. Thus, an in-depth understanding of business ethics is important to the long-run viability of any corporation today. It is also important to the well-being of individual officers and directors and to the firm's employees. Finally, unethical corporate decision making can negatively affect suppliers, consumers, the community, and society as a whole.

At the end of every unit in this book, you will be exposed to a series of ethical issues in features called *Focus on Ethics.* In each of these unit-ending features, we expand on the concepts of business ethics that we present in this chapter.

Common Reasons Why Ethical Problems Occur

Not that many years ago, the popular painkiller Vioxx was recalled because its long-term use increased the risk of heart attack and stroke. Little by little, evidence surfaced that the drug's maker, Merck & Company, knew about these dangers yet allowed Vioxx to remain on the market. Merck's failure to recall the drug earlier could potentially have adversely affected the health of thousands of patients. In addition, Merck has undergone investigations by both Congress and the U.S. Department of Justice. Merck was facing thousands of lawsuits, years of litigation, and millions of dollars in attorneys' fees and settlements when it agreed, in November 2007, to settle all outstanding cases concerning Vioxx for $4.85 billion. How did a major corporation manage to make so many missteps? The answer is simply that certain officers and employees of Merck felt that it was not necessary to reveal the results of studies that might have decreased sales of Vioxx.

In other words, the common thread among the ethical problems that occur in business is the desire to increase sales (or not lose them), thereby increasing profits and, for the corporation, increasing market value. In most situations, though, ethically wrong behavior by a corporation turns out to be costly to everyone concerned. Just ask the shareholders of Merck (and, of course, Enron, WorldCom, and Tyco).

Short-Run Profit Maximization Some people argue that a corporation's only goal should be profit maximization, which will be reflected in a higher market value. When all firms strictly adhere to the goal of profit maximization, resources tend to flow to where they are most highly valued by society. Ultimately, profit maximization, in theory, leads to the most efficient allocation of scarce resources.

Corporate executives and employees have to distinguish, though, between *short-run* and *long-run* profit maximization. In the short run, the employees of Merck & Company may have increased profits because of the continuing sales of Vioxx. In the long run, though, because of lawsuits, large settlements, and bad publicity, profits have suffered. Thus, business ethics is consistent only with long-run profit maximization.

Determining Society's Rules—The Role of Corporate Influence Another possible cause of bad business ethics has to do with corporations' role in influencing the law. Corporations may use lobbyists to persuade government agencies not to institute new regulations that would increase the corporations' costs and reduce their profits. Once regulatory rules are promulgated, corporations may undertake actions to reduce their impact. One way to do this is to make it known that members of regulatory agencies will always have jobs waiting for them when they leave the agencies. This revolving door, as it is commonly called, has existed as long as there have been regulatory agencies at the state and federal levels of government.

The Importance of Ethical Leadership

Talking about ethical business decision making is meaningless if management does not set standards. Furthermore, managers must apply the same standards to themselves as they do to the employees of the company.

Attitude of Top Management One of the most important ways to create and maintain an ethical workplace is for top management to demonstrate its commitment to ethical decision making. A manager who is not totally committed to an ethical workplace rarely succeeds in creating one. Management's behavior, more than anything else, sets the ethical tone of a firm. Employees take their cues from management. For example, an employee who observes a manager cheating on her expense account quickly learns that such behavior is acceptable.

Managers who set unrealistic production or sales goals increase the probability that employees will act unethically. If a sales quota can be met only through high-pressure, unethical sales tactics, employees will try to act "in the best interest of the company" and will continue to behave unethically.

A manager who looks the other way when she or he knows about an employee's unethical behavior also sets an example—one indicating that ethical transgressions will be accepted. Managers have found that discharging even one employee for ethical reasons has a tremendous impact as a deterrent to unethical behavior in the workplace.

Behavior of Owners and Managers Business owners and managers sometimes take more active roles in fostering unethical and illegal conduct. This may indicate to their co-owners, co-managers, employees, and others that unethical business behavior will be tolerated. The following case illustrates how business owners' misbehavior can have negative consequences for themselves and their business. Not only can a court sanction the business owners and managers, but it can also issue an injunction that prevents them from engaging in similar patterns of conduct in the future.

CASE 5.1 Baum v. Blue Moon Ventures, LLC

United States Court of Appeals, Fifth Circuit, 2008. 513 F.3d 181.

- **Background and Facts** Douglas Baum runs an asset recovery business, along with his brother, Brian Baum, and his father, Sheldon Baum (the Baums). The Baums research various unclaimed funds, try to locate the rightful owner, and receive either a finder's fee or the right to some or all of the funds recovered. In 2002, the Baums became involved in a federal district court case by recruiting investors—through misrepresentation—to file a lawsuit against a receiver (a court-appointed person who oversees a business firm's affairs), among others. The district court in that case determined that the Baums' legal allegations were without merit and that their conduct was a malicious attempt to extort funds. The court sanctioned the Baums for interfering in the case, wrongfully holding themselves out to be attorneys licensed to practice in Texas, lying to the parties and the court, and generally abusing the judicial system.

The district court also issued a permanent injunction against all three Baums to prohibit them from filing claims related to the same case in Texas state courts without the express permission of Judge Lynn Hughes (the district court judge). In June 2005, the Baums entered an appearance in the bankruptcy proceeding (bankruptcy will be discussed in Chapter 30) involving Danny Hilal and Blue Moon Ventures, LLC. Blue Moon's primary business was purchasing real property at foreclosure sales and leasing those properties to residential tenants. Sheldon Baum claimed to be a creditor in the bankruptcy, but he would not identify his claim. Brian Baum misled the parties and the court about being a licensed attorney in Texas. Douglas Baum participated by posting a fake notice stating that the Internal Revenue Service might foreclose on some property to collect unpaid taxes. The bankruptcy court concluded that this was a continuation of a pattern of malicious conduct and forwarded a memo on the case to the district court that had imposed the sanctions on the Baums. The district court, after conducting two hearings and listening to testimony from all of the Baums, also found that the Baums had continued in their abusive practices. The district court therefore modified and expanded its injunction to include the filing of any claim in any federal or state court or agency in Texas. Douglas Baum filed an appeal, claiming that the court had exceeded its power and arguing that the injunction would impede his business.

- **Decision and Rationale** The U.S. Court of Appeals for the Fifth Circuit upheld the modified prefiling injunction as it applied to all filings in Texas state courts, in lower federal courts located in Texas, and in administrative agencies in Texas. In contrast, the court struck down those portions of the injunction that required the Baums to obtain Judge Hughes's permission prior to filing a claim in any court or agency located outside the state of Texas, or prior to filing in any federal appellate court. The appellate court accepted that a district court has jurisdiction to impose prefiling injunctions to deter abusive and harassing litigation. "Federal courts have both the inherent power and the Constitutional obligation to protect their jurisdiction from conduct [that] impairs their ability to carry out [their] functions." It further stated that federal courts have the power to prevent plaintiffs from future filings when those plaintiffs consistently abuse the court system and harass their opponents. Nevertheless, the district court "had abused its discretion" with its

CASE 5.1 CONTINUED broad extension of the prefiling injunction, and therefore, those requirements were not upheld. Furthermore, the appellate court noted that "those [other] courts or agencies are capable of taking appropriate action on their own."

- **The Legal Environment Dimension** *What might the Baums have done to avoid the sanctions that were imposed on them in this case?*

- **The Ethical Dimension** *Are there situations in which a business owner's conduct would be more reprehensible than the Baums' behavior in this case? Explain.*

SECTION 2 Approaches to Ethical Reasoning

Each individual, when faced with a particular ethical dilemma, engages in **ethical reasoning**—that is, a reasoning process in which the individual examines the situation at hand in light of his or her moral convictions or ethical standards. Businesspersons do likewise when making decisions with ethical implications.

How do business decision makers decide whether a given action is the "right" one for their firms? What ethical standards should be applied? Broadly speaking, ethical reasoning relating to business traditionally has been characterized by two fundamental approaches. One approach defines ethical behavior in terms of duty, which also implies certain rights. The other approach determines what is ethical in terms of the consequences, or outcome, of any given action. We examine each of these approaches here.

In addition to the two basic ethical approaches, a few theories have been developed that specifically address the social responsibility of corporations. Because these theories also influence today's business decision makers, we conclude this section with a short discussion of the different views of corporate social responsibility.

Duty-Based Ethics

Duty-based ethical standards often are derived from revealed truths, such as religious precepts. They can also be derived through philosophical reasoning.

Religious Ethical Standards In the Judeo-Christian tradition, which is the dominant religious tradition in the United States, the Ten Commandments of the Old Testament establish fundamental rules for moral action. Other religions have their own sources of revealed truth. Religious rules generally are absolute with respect to the behavior of their adherents. For example, the commandment "Thou shalt not steal" is an absolute mandate for a person who believes that the Ten Commandments reflect revealed truth. Even a benevolent motive for stealing (such as Robin Hood's) cannot justify the act because the act itself is inherently immoral and thus wrong.

Kantian Ethics Duty-based ethical standards may also be derived solely from philosophical reasoning. The German philosopher Immanuel Kant (1724–1804), for example, identified some general guiding principles for moral behavior based on what he believed to be the fundamental nature of human beings. Kant believed that human beings are qualitatively different from other physical objects and are endowed with moral integrity and the capacity to reason and conduct their affairs rationally. Therefore, a person's thoughts and actions should be respected. When human beings are treated merely as a means to an end, they are being treated as the equivalent of objects and are being denied their basic humanity.

A central theme in Kantian ethics is that individuals should evaluate their actions in light of the consequences that would follow if *everyone* in society acted in the same way. This **categorical imperative** can be applied to any action. For example, suppose that you are deciding whether to cheat on an examination. If you have adopted Kant's categorical imperative, you will decide *not* to cheat because if everyone cheated, the examination (and the entire education system) would be meaningless.

The Principle of Rights Because a duty cannot exist without a corresponding right, duty-based ethical standards imply that human beings have basic rights. The principle that human beings have certain fundamental rights (to life, freedom, and the pursuit of happiness, for example) is deeply embedded in Western culture. As discussed in Chapter 1, the natural law tradition embraces the concept that certain actions (such as killing another person) are morally wrong because they are contrary to nature (the natural desire to continue living). Those who adhere to this **principle of rights,** or "rights theory," believe that a key factor in determining whether a business decision is ethical is how that decision affects the rights of others. These others include the firm's owners, its employees, the consumers of its products or services, its suppliers, the community in which it does business, and society as a whole.

A potential dilemma for those who support rights theory, however, is that they may disagree on which rights are most important. When considering all those affected by a business decision, for example, how much weight should be given to employees relative to shareholders, customers relative to the community, or employees relative to society as a whole?

In general, rights theorists believe that whichever right is stronger in a particular circumstance takes precedence. Suppose that a firm can either keep a plant open, saving the jobs of twelve workers, or shut the plant down and avoid contaminating a river with pollutants that would endanger the health of thousands of people. In this situation, a rights theorist can easily choose which group to favor. (Not all choices are so clear-cut, however.)

Outcome-Based Ethics: Utilitarianism

"The greatest good for the greatest number" is a paraphrase of the major premise of the utilitarian approach to ethics. **Utilitarianism** is a philosophical theory developed by Jeremy Bentham (1748–1832) and modified by John Stuart Mill (1806–1873)—both British philosophers. In contrast to duty-based ethics, utilitarianism is outcome oriented. It focuses on the consequences of an action, not on the nature of the action itself or on any set of preestablished moral values or religious beliefs.

Under a utilitarian model of ethics, an action is morally correct, or "right," when, among the people it affects, it produces the greatest amount of good for the greatest number. When an action affects the majority adversely, it is morally wrong. Applying the utilitarian theory thus requires (1) a determination of which individuals will be affected by the action in question; (2) a **cost-benefit analysis,** which involves an assessment of the negative and positive effects of alternative actions on these individuals; and (3) a choice among alternative actions that will produce maximum societal utility (the greatest positive net benefits for the greatest number of individuals).

Corporate Social Responsibility

For many years, groups concerned with civil rights, employee safety and welfare, consumer protection, environmental preservation, and other causes have pressured corporate America to behave in a responsible manner with respect to these causes. Thus was born the concept of **corporate social responsibility**—the idea that those who run corporations can and should act ethically and be accountable to society for their actions. Just what constitutes corporate social responsibility has been debated for some time, however, and there are a number of different theories today.

Stakeholder Approach One view of corporate social responsibility stresses that corporations have a duty not just to shareholders, but also to other groups affected by corporate decisions (stakeholders). Under this approach, a corporation would consider the impact of its decision on the firm's employees, customers, creditors, suppliers, and the community in which the corporation operates. The reasoning behind this "stakeholder view" is that in some circumstances, one or more of these other groups may have a greater stake in company decisions than the shareholders do. Although this may be true, it is often difficult to decide which group's interests should receive greater weight if the interests conflict (see the earlier discussion of conflicting rights).

Corporate Citizenship Another theory of social responsibility argues that corporations should behave as good citizens by promoting goals that society deems worthwhile and taking positive steps toward solving social problems. The idea is that because business controls so much of the wealth and power of this country, business in turn has a responsibility to society to use that wealth and power in socially beneficial ways. Under a corporate citizenship view, companies are judged on how much they donate to social causes, as well as how they conduct their operations with respect to employment discrimination, human rights, environmental concerns, and similar issues.

In the following case, a corporation's board of directors did not seem to doubt the priority of the firm's responsibilities. Focused solely on the profits delivered into the hands of the shareholders, the board failed to check the actions of the firm's chief executive officer (CEO) and, in fact, appeared to condone the CEO's misconduct. If the board had applied a different set of priorities, the shareholders might have been in a better financial position, however. A regulatory agency soon found the situation "troubling" and imposed a restriction on the firm. The board protested. The protest reminded the court of "the old saw about the child who murders his parents and then asks for mercy because he is an orphan."

CASE 5.2 Fog Cutter Capital Group, Inc. v. Securities and Exchange Commission

United States Court of Appeals, District of Columbia Circuit, 2007. 474 F.3d 822.

• **Background and Facts** The National Association of Securities Dealers (NASD) operates the Nasdaq, an electronic securities exchange, on which Fog Cutter Capital Group was listed.[a] Andrew Wiederhorn had founded Fog Cutter in 1997 to manage a restaurant chain and make other investments. With family members, Wiederhorn controlled more than 50 percent of Fog Cutter's stock. The firm agreed that if Wiederhorn was terminated "for cause," he was entitled only to his salary through the date of termination. If terminated "without cause," he would be owed three times his $350,000 annual salary, three times his largest annual bonus from the previous three years, and any unpaid salary and bonus. "Cause" included the conviction of a felony. In 2001, Wiederhorn became the target of an investigation into the collapse of Capital Consultants, LLC. Fog Cutter then redefined "cause" in his termination agreement to cover only a felony involving Fog Cutter. In June 2004, Wiederhorn agreed to plead guilty to two felonies, serve eighteen months in prison, pay a $25,000 fine, and pay $2 million to Capital Consultants. The day before he entered his plea, Fog Cutter agreed that while he was in prison, he would keep his title, responsibilities, salary, bonuses, and other benefits. It also agreed to a $2 million "leave of absence payment." In July, the NASD delisted Fog Cutter from the Nasdaq. Fog Cutter appealed this decision to the Securities and Exchange Commission (SEC), which dismissed the appeal. Fog Cutter petitioned the U.S. Court of Appeals for the District of Columbia Circuit for review.

• **Decision and Rationale** The U.S. Court of Appeals for the District of Columbia Circuit denied Fog Cutter's petition for review of the SEC's decision. The NASD was concerned with the integrity and the public's perception of the Nasdaq exchange in light of Wiederhorn's legal troubles and the Fog Cutter board's acceptance of his demands. The appellate court was unconvinced by Fog Cutter's complaint that the SEC had failed to take into account the company's sound business reasons for acting as it did. The court looked at the deal that Fog Cutter made with Wiederhorn that cost the company almost $5 million during a year in which it reported a $4 million loss. In short, "the decision was in accordance with NASD rules giving the organization broad discretion to determine whether the public interest requires delisting securities in light of events at a company. The rule is obviously consistent with [the law], and NASD's decision did not burden competition."

• **The Ethical Dimension** *Should the court have given more consideration to the fact that Fog Cutter was not convicted of a violation of the law? Why or why not?*

• **The Global Dimension** *What does the decision in this case suggest to foreign investors who may be considering investments in securities listed on U.S. exchanges?*

a. Securities (stocks and bonds) can be bought and sold through national exchanges. Whether a security is listed on an exchange is subject to the discretion of the organization that operates it. The Securities and Exchange Commission oversees the securities exchanges (see Chapter 41).

Creating Ethical Codes of Conduct

One of the most effective ways to set a tone of ethical behavior within an organization is to create an ethical code of conduct. A well-written code of ethics explicitly states a company's ethical priorities and demonstrates the company's commitment to ethical behavior.

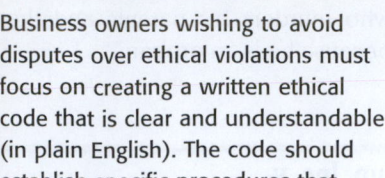

Business owners wishing to avoid disputes over ethical violations must focus on creating a written ethical code that is clear and understandable (in plain English). The code should establish specific procedures that employees can follow if they have questions or complaints. It should assure employees that their jobs will be secure and that they will not face reprisals if they do file a complaint. Business owners should also explain to employees why these ethics policies are important to the company. A well-written code might include examples to clarify what the company considers to be acceptable and unacceptable conduct.

Providing Ethics Training to Employees For an ethical code to be effective, its provisions must be clearly communicated to employees. Most large companies have implemented ethics training programs in which management discusses with employees on a face-to-face basis the firm's policies and the importance of ethical conduct. Some firms hold periodic ethics seminars during which employees can openly discuss any ethical problems that they may be experiencing and learn how the firm's ethical policies apply to those specific problems. Smaller firms should also offer some form of ethics training to employees, because this is one factor that courts will consider if the firm is later accused of an ethics violation.

The Sarbanes-Oxley Act and Web-Based Reporting Systems The Sarbanes-Oxley Act of 2002[1] requires that companies set up confidential systems so that employees and others can "raise red flags" about suspected illegal or unethical auditing and accounting practices.

Some companies have created online reporting systems to accomplish this goal. In one such system, employees can click on an icon on their computers that anonymously links them with Ethicspoint, an organization based in Portland, Oregon. Through Ethicspoint, employees can report suspicious accounting practices, sexual harassment, and other possibly unethical behavior. Ethicspoint, in turn, alerts management personnel or the audit committee at the designated company to the potential problem. Those who have used the system say that it is less inhibiting than calling a company's toll-free number.

SECTION 3 How the Law Influences Business Ethics

Although business ethics and the law are closely related, they are not always identical. Here, we examine some situations in which what is legal and what is ethical may not be the same.

The Moral Minimum

Compliance with the law is normally regarded as the **moral minimum**—the minimum acceptable standard for ethical business behavior. In many corporate scandals, had most of the businesspersons involved simply followed the law, they would not have gotten into trouble. Note, though, that in the interest of preserving personal freedom, as well as for practical reasons, the law does not—and cannot—codify all ethical requirements. As they make business decisions, businesspersons must remember that just because an action is legal does not necessarily make it ethical. Look at Exhibit 5–1. Here, you see that there is an intersection between what is ethical and what is legal. Businesspersons should attempt to operate in the area where what is legal and what is ethical intersect.

EXHIBIT 5–1 • The Intersection of What Is Legal and What Is Ethical

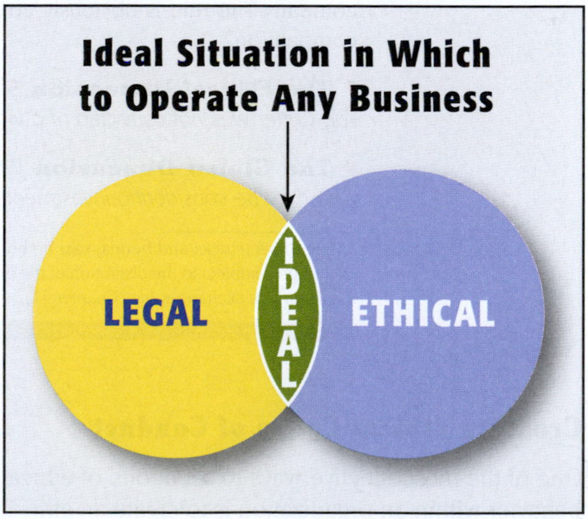

1. 15 U.S.C. Sections 7201 *et seq.* This act will be discussed in Chapters 41 and 51.

Excessive Executive Pay As just mentioned, business behavior that is legal may still be unethical. Consider executive pay. There is no law that specifies what public corporations can pay their officers. Consequently, "executive-pay scandals" do not have to do with executives breaking the law. Rather, such scandals have to do with the ethical underpinnings of executive-pay scales that can exceed millions of dollars. Such high pay for executives may appear unethical when their companies are not making very high profits (or are even suffering losses) and their share prices are falling.

Even this subject, though, does not lend itself to a black-and-white ethical analysis. As with many other things, there is a market for executives that operates according to supply and demand. Sometimes, corporate boards decide to offer executives very large compensation packages in order either to entice them to come to work for the company or to keep them from leaving for another corporation. There is no simple formula for determining the ethical level of compensation for a given executive in a given company. If a law were passed that limited executive compensation to, say, twenty times the salary of the lowest-paid worker in the company, there would be fewer individuals willing to undergo the stress and long hours associated with running major companies.

Determining the Legality of a Given Action It may seem that determining the legality of a given action should be simple. Either something is legal or it is not. In fact, one of the major challenges businesspersons face is that the legality of a particular action is not always clear. In part, this is because there are so many laws regulating business that it is increasingly possible to violate one of them without realizing it. The law also contains numerous "gray areas," making it difficult to predict with certainty how a court will apply a given law to a particular action.

Determining whether a planned action is legal thus requires that decision makers keep abreast of the law. Normally, large business firms have attorneys on their staffs to assist them in making key decisions. Small firms must also seek legal advice before making important business decisions because the consequences of just one violation of a regulatory rule may be costly.

Ignorance of the law will not excuse a business owner or manager from liability for violating a statute or regulation. In one case, Riverdale Mills Corporation was held liable when an employee attempted to board a plane with two cans of flammable hazardous material from Riverdale in his luggage. The court found that even though the employer was unaware of the employee's actions—and the employee was ignorant of the illegality of his actions—Riverdale had violated Federal Aviation Administration (FAA) regulations.[2]

The Law Cannot Control All Business Behavior

Congress, the regulatory agencies, and state and local governments do not have perfect knowledge. Often they only discover the negative impact of corporate activities after the fact. The same can be true of corporate executives. They do not always know the full impact of their actions. When asbestos was used for insulation, for example, the corporations that supplied it did not know that it was capable of causing a rare type of cancer.

At other times, though, the law is not ambiguous. Nevertheless, it may still be unable to control business behavior—at least initially.

Breaking the Law—Backdating Stock Options Stock options are a device that potentially rewards hard work. Publicly held corporations offer stock options to employees at the current price of the company's stock on the day that the options are granted. If at a later time the market price of the stock has gone up, an employee can exercise the stock options and reap the difference between the price of the options and the current market price.

In 2006 and 2007, it was revealed that a number of large corporations had backdated stock options. If stock options are granted and the price of the company's stock subsequently falls or does not rise very much, the value of the stock options is essentially zero. One way around this problem is to go back and change the date on which the stock options were granted to the employee. In other words, the date of the stock options is simply moved back to a day when the stock had a lower price than it has currently, thereby making the options valuable again.

Backdating is illegal if companies do not follow proper accounting procedures and the disclosure rules of the Securities and Exchange Commission (SEC). It is also illegal if the company misrepresents the authorization for, or falsifies records relating to, the

2. *Riverdale Mills Corp. v. FAA*, 417 F.Supp.2d 167 (D.Mass. 2006).

backdating. For example, in February 2007, the former chief executive officer of Brocade Communications Systems, Inc., Gregory L. Reyes, Jr., was sentenced to twenty-one months in prison, plus a $15 million fine for "tampering" with records of stock option grants. At least a dozen other business executives face similar charges.

The backdating scandal is another example of unethical behavior resulting in long-run profit reduction. As of 2008, at least 250 public companies had disclosed that they had undertaken internal investigations to discover if backdating had occurred without following proper procedures. The companies involved faced more than 125 shareholder lawsuits and as many SEC investigations, plus fifty-eight U.S. Department of Justice investigations and even six criminal cases.

Misleading Regulators—The Case of OxyContin In 1996, the pharmaceutical company Purdue Pharma, LP, started marketing a "wonder" narcotic painkiller called OxyContin. This powerful, long-lasting drug provides pain relief for twelve hours. Just a few years after its introduction, Purdue Pharma's annual sales of the drug reached $1 billion.

The company's executives initially contended that OxyContin, because of its time-release formulation, posed no risk for serious abuse or addiction. Quickly, though, experienced drug abusers and even teenagers discovered that chewing on an OxyContin tablet or crushing one and snorting the powder produced a powerful high, comparable to that of heroin. By 2000, large parts of the United States were experiencing increases in addiction and crime related to OxyContin.

In reality, the company and three of its executives had fraudulently marketed OxyContin for over six years as a drug unlikely to lead to abuse. Internal company documents showed that even before OxyContin was marketed, executives recognized that if physicians knew that the drug could be abused and become addictive, they would be less likely to prescribe it. Consequently, the company simply kept the information secret.

On May 10, 2007, Purdue Pharma and three former executives pleaded guilty to criminal charges that they had misled regulators, patients, and physicians about OxyContin's risks of addiction. Purdue Pharma agreed to pay $600 million in fines and other payments. The three ex-executives agreed to pay $34.5 million in fines. Once again, company executives engaged in unethical reasoning because they wanted to maximize profits in the short run, rather than engaging in behavior that would lead to profit maximization in the long run.

"Gray Areas" in the Law

In many situations, business firms can predict with a fair amount of certainty whether a given action is legal. For instance, firing an employee solely because of that person's race or gender clearly violates federal laws prohibiting employment discrimination. In some situations, though, the legality of a particular action may be less clear.

Suppose that a firm decides to launch a new advertising campaign. How far can the firm go in making claims for its products or services? Federal and state laws prohibit firms from engaging in "deceptive advertising." At the federal level, the test for deceptive advertising normally used by the Federal Trade Commission is whether an advertising claim would deceive a "reasonable consumer."[3] At what point, though, would a reasonable consumer be deceived by a particular ad?

In addition, many rules of law require a court to determine what is "foreseeable" or "reasonable" in a particular situation. Because a business has no way of predicting how a specific court will decide these issues, decision makers need to proceed with caution and evaluate an action and its consequences from an ethical perspective. The same problem often occurs in cases involving the Internet because it is often unclear how a court will apply existing laws in the context of cyberspace. Generally, if a company can demonstrate that it acted in good faith and responsibly in the circumstances, it has a better chance of successfully defending its action in court or before an administrative law judge.

The following case shows that businesses and their customers have different expectations with respect to the standard of care regarding the handling of personal information. The case also illustrates that the legal standards in this area may be inconsistent and vague.

3. See Chapter 44 for a discussion of the Federal Trade Commission's role in regulating deceptive trade practices, including misleading advertising.

CASE 5.3 Guin v. Brazos Higher Education Service Corp.

United States District Court, District of Minnesota, 2006. __ F.Supp.2d __.

● **Background and Facts** Brazos Higher Education Service Corporation, which is based in Waco, Texas, makes and services student loans. Brazos issued a laptop computer to its employee John Wright, who worked from an office in his home in Silver Spring, Maryland, analyzing loan information. Wright used the laptop to store borrowers' personal information. In September 2004, Wright's home was burglarized and the laptop was stolen. Based on Federal Trade Commission (FTC) guidelines and California state law (which requires notice to all resident borrowers), Brazos sent a letter to all of its 550,000 customers. The letter stated that "some personal information associated with your student loan, including your name, address, Social Security number and loan balance, may have been inappropriately accessed by [a] third party." The letter urged borrowers to place "a free 90-day security alert" on their credit bureau files and review FTC consumer assistance materials. Brazos set up a call center to answer further questions and track any reports of identity theft. Stacy Guin, a Brazos customer, filed a suit in a federal district court against Brazos, alleging negligence. Brazos filed a motion for summary judgment.

● **Decision and Rationale** The court granted the defendant's motion for summary judgment and dismissed the case. Brazos may have owed Guin a duty of care, but neither Brazos nor Wright breached that duty. Wright had followed Brazos's written security procedures, which was all that the law requires. The court acknowledged that Brazos had a duty to protect the security and confidentiality of its customers' personal information. Under the Gramm-Leach-Bliley (GLB) Act, a financial institution must "develop, implement, and maintain a comprehensive written information security program that * * * contains administrative, technical, and physical safeguards that are appropriate to * * * the sensitivity of any customer information." Guin argued that Brazos breached this duty by (1) "providing Wright with [personal information] that he did not need for the task at hand," (2) "permitting Wright to continue keeping [personal information] in an unattended, insecure personal residence," and (3) "allowing Wright to keep [personal information] on his laptop unencrypted." The court disagreed. Brazos had established written security policies and other mandated safeguards for its customers' personal information. Brazos gave Wright access to the information because Wright needed it to analyze loan portfolios. Besides, the GLB Act does not prohibit someone from working with sensitive data on a laptop computer in a home office or require that the data be encrypted.

● **What If the Facts Were Different?** *Suppose that Wright had not been a financial analyst and his duties for Brazos had not included reviewing confidential loan data. How might the opinion of the court have been different?*

● **The Ethical Dimension** *Do businesses have an ethical duty to use enhanced security measures to protect confidential customer information? Why or why not? Does the fact that Brazos allowed its employees to store customers' unencrypted personal information on a laptop outside the office violate any ethical duty?*

SECTION 4

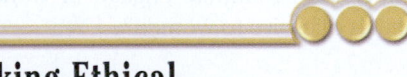

Making Ethical Business Decisions

As Dean Krehmeyer, executive director of the Business Roundtable's Institute for Corporate Ethics, once said, "Evidence strongly suggests being ethical—doing the right thing—pays." Instilling ethical business decision making into the fabric of a business organization is no small task, even if ethics "pays." The job is to get people to understand that they have to think more broadly about how their decisions will affect employees, shareholders, customers, and even the community. Great companies, such as Enron and the accounting firm

Arthur Andersen, were brought down by the unethical behavior of a few. A two-hundred-year-old British investment banking firm, Barings Bank, was destroyed by the actions of one employee and a few of his friends. Clearly, ensuring that all employees get on the ethical business decision-making "bandwagon" is crucial in today's fast-paced world.

The George S. May International Company has provided six basic guidelines to help corporate employees judge their actions. Each employee—no matter what his or her level in the organization—should evaluate his or her actions using the following six guidelines:

1. *The law.* Is the action you are considering legal? If you do not know the laws governing the action, then find out. Ignorance of the law is no excuse.
2. *Rules and procedures.* Are you following the internal rules and procedures that have already been laid out by your company? They have been developed to avoid problems. Is what you are planning to do consistent with your company's policies and procedures? If not, stop.
3. *Values.* Laws and internal company policies reinforce society's values. You might wish to ask yourself whether you are attempting to find a loophole in the law or in your company's policies. Next, you have to ask yourself whether you are following the "spirit" of the law as well as the letter of the law or the internal policy.
4. *Conscience.* If you have any feeling of guilt, let your conscience be your guide. Alternatively, ask yourself whether you would be happy to be interviewed by a national news magazine about the actions you are going to take.
5. *Promises.* Every business organization is based on trust. Your customers believe that your company will do what it is supposed to do. The same is true for your suppliers and employees. Will your actions live up to the commitments you have made to others, both inside the business and outside?
6. *Heroes.* We all have heroes who are role models for us. Is what you are planning on doing an action that your hero would take? If not, how would your hero act? That is how you should be acting.

SECTION 5

Business Ethics on a Global Level

Given the various cultures and religions throughout the world, conflicts in ethics frequently arise between foreign and U.S. businesspersons. For example, in certain countries the consumption of alcohol and specific foods is forbidden for religious reasons. Under such circumstances, it would be thoughtless and imprudent for a U.S. businessperson to invite a local business contact out for a drink.

The role played by women in other countries may also present some difficult ethical problems for firms doing business internationally. Equal employment opportunity is a fundamental public policy in the United States, and Title VII of the Civil Rights Act of 1964 prohibits discrimination against women in the employment context (see Chapter 34). Some other countries, however, offer little protection for women against gender discrimination in the workplace, including sexual harassment.

We look here at how the employment practices that affect workers in other countries, particularly developing countries, have created some especially difficult ethical problems for U.S. sellers of goods manufactured in foreign nations. We also examine some of the ethical ramifications of laws prohibiting bribery and the expansion of ethics programs in the global community.

Monitoring the Employment Practices of Foreign Suppliers

Many U.S. businesses now contract with companies in developing nations to produce goods, such as shoes and clothing, because the wage rates in those nations are significantly lower than those in the United States. Yet what if a foreign company hires women and children at below-minimum-wage rates, for example, or requires its employees to work long hours in a workplace full of health hazards? What if the company's supervisors routinely engage in workplace conduct that is offensive to women?

Given today's global communications network, few companies can assume that their actions in other nations will go unnoticed by "corporate watch" groups that discover and publicize unethical corporate behavior. As a result, U.S. businesses today usually take steps to avoid such adverse publicity—either by refusing to deal with certain suppliers or by arranging to monitor their suppliers' workplaces to make sure that the employees are not being mistreated.

The Foreign Corrupt Practices Act

Another ethical problem in international business dealings has to do with the legitimacy of certain side payments to government officials. In the United States, the majority of contracts are formed within the private sector. In many foreign countries, however, government officials make the decisions on most major construction and manufacturing contracts because of extensive government regulation and control over trade and industry. Side payments to government officials in exchange for favorable business contracts are not unusual in such countries, nor are they considered to be unethical. In the past, U.S. corporations doing business in these nations largely followed the dictum, "When in Rome, do as the Romans do."

In the 1970s, however, the U.S. press uncovered a number of business scandals involving large side payments by U.S. corporations to foreign representatives for the purpose of securing advantageous international trade contracts. In response to this unethical behavior, in 1977 Congress passed the Foreign Corrupt Practices Act (FCPA), which prohibits U.S. businesspersons from bribing foreign officials to secure beneficial contracts. (For a discussion of how a German corporation ran afoul of Germany's anti-bribery laws, see this chapter's *Insight into the Global Environment* feature on the following page.)

Prohibition against the Bribery of Foreign Officials The first part of the FCPA applies to all U.S. companies and their directors, officers, shareholders, employees, and agents. This part prohibits the bribery of most officials of foreign governments if the purpose of the payment is to get the official to act in his or her official capacity to provide business opportunities.

The FCPA does not prohibit payment of substantial sums to minor officials whose duties are ministerial. These payments are often referred to as "grease," or facilitating payments. They are meant to accelerate the performance of administrative services that might otherwise be carried out at a slow pace. Thus, for example, if a firm makes a payment to a minor official to speed up an import licensing process, the firm has not violated the FCPA. Generally, the act, as amended, permits payments to foreign officials if such payments are lawful within the foreign country. The act also does not prohibit payments to private foreign companies or other third parties unless the U.S. firm knows that the payments will be passed on to a foreign government in violation of the FCPA.

Accounting Requirements In the past, bribes were often concealed in corporate financial records. Thus, the second part of the FCPA is directed toward accountants. All companies must keep detailed records that "accurately and fairly" reflect their financial activities. In addition, all companies must have accounting systems that provide "reasonable assurance" that all transactions entered into by the companies are accounted for and legal. These requirements assist in detecting illegal bribes. The FCPA further prohibits any person from making false statements to accountants or false entries in any record or account.

Penalties for Violations In 1988, the FCPA was amended to provide that business firms that violate the act may be fined up to $2 million. Individual officers or directors who violate the FCPA may be fined up to $100,000 (the fine cannot be paid by the company) and may be imprisoned for up to five years.

INSIGHT INTO THE GLOBAL ENVIRONMENT
Breach of Trust Issues Hit Major German Corporations

Whether you call it immoral, unethical, illegal, or a breach of trust, bribery by any name is wrong. In recent years, officers and managing directors at several major German corporations have been investigated, arrested, and fined for bribery. One German firm that has faced numerous charges is Siemens, a venerable corporation that was founded in 1847. Siemens built the first long-distance telegraph line in Europe from Berlin to Frankfurt in 1849. Today, the company, which its almost 500,000 workers like to call the House of Siemens, has operations in communications, radar, traffic control, and cell phones.

Corruption Charges Are Not New

When global competition intensified in the 1980s and 1990s, Siemens began to face fierce competition from multinational giants such as General Electric. To maintain the company's cash flow and sales dominance, some of Siemens's managers started bribing potential clients—usually government agencies—to generate new business. In the early 1990s, the German government investigated Siemens's activities and convicted nine of the company's managers on bribery charges. The judge in the case wondered why the managers kept referring to the company as the "House of Siemens"—a name that, in the judge's view, implies "that the firm rises above the muck of ordinary business; it conveys a sense of moral exemption and entitlement." Of course, part of Siemens's problem may have been the somewhat ambiguous approach to bribery taken by German law. Bribes paid to foreign officials were tax deductible in Germany until 1999.

Unethical Actions Continue

Apparently, Siemens did not learn its lesson, for complaints about its behavior continued. In the early 2000s, Swiss authorities began an investigation that continued for a year and a half. The allegations of corruption did not trouble Heinrich von Pierer, Siemens's chair, however, or spur him to look into his managers' behavior. Instead, he stated simply, "I'm aware that our organization is hard to understand for outsiders. The job of board members is primarily strategic. Going over the books is the responsibility of others."

Several years later, the company finally disclosed that about $600 million in "suspicious transactions" (read "bribes") had been discovered. By 2007, von Pierer had resigned, and the chief executive officer decided not to ask for a new contract. In the meantime, a German court had convicted two former Siemens executives of bribery and fined the company about $50 million.

Once again, ambiguities in German law entered the case. One former Siemens executive told the court that he did indeed authorize millions of dollars of bribes to win contracts from an Italian electric company. He insisted, though, that he did not break any laws and that the payments were not illegal because German law only forbids payments to "civil servants." The executive contended that the payments he made to the Italian company's managers were made to representatives of a private-sector company, not to "civil servants." German prosecutors had to admit that the legal definition of what constitutes a civil servant allows room for interpretation.

Bribing the Union

Siemens executives may not have restricted their activities to bribing "civil servants" or private-sector managers. One Siemens executive, Johannes Feldmayer, has been arrested on a special type of bribery charge. He has been accused of bribing the head of a workers' organization, a type of independent labor union. Apparently, Siemens wanted a counterweight to IG Metall, the most powerful German union, and Feldmayer allegedly oversaw the transfer of some $45 million to the independent union to facilitate this. Earlier, another major German corporation, Volkswagen (VW), faced similar charges of making illegal payments to the head of its workers' council. Peter Harz, formerly VW's head of labor relations, pleaded guilty to the charges and paid a fine of about $750,000.

CRITICAL THINKING

INSIGHT INTO POLITICS

Clearly, the corporate culture at Siemens, at least in the last few decades, did not distinguish among actions that were both ethical and legal, actions that were unethical but perhaps legal, and actions that were both unethical and illegal. What could top management at that company have done to instill a different corporate culture that would have resulted in a different outcome?

REVIEWING Ethics and Business Decision Making

Isabel Arnett was promoted to chief executive officer (CEO) of Tamik, Inc., a pharmaceutical company that manufactures a vaccine called Kafluk, which supposedly provides some defense against bird flu. The company began marketing Kafluk throughout Asia. After numerous media reports that bird flu could soon become a worldwide epidemic, the demand for Kafluk increased, sales soared, and Tamik earned record profits. Tamik's CEO, Arnett, then began receiving disturbing reports from Southeast Asia that in some patients, Kafluk had caused psychiatric disturbances, including severe hallucinations, and heart and lung problems. Arnett was informed that six children in Japan had committed suicide by jumping out of windows after receiving the vaccine. To cover up the story and prevent negative publicity, Arnett instructed Tamik's partners in Asia to offer cash to the Japanese families whose children had died in exchange for their silence. Arnett also refused to authorize additional research within the company to study the potential side effects of Kafluk. Using the information presented in the chapter, answer the following questions.

1. This scenario illustrates one of the main reasons why ethical problems occur in business. What is that reason?
2. Would a person who adheres to the principle of rights consider it ethical for Arnett not to disclose potential safety concerns and to refuse to perform additional research on Kafluk? Why or why not?
3. If Kafluk prevented fifty Asian people who were infected with bird flu from dying, would Arnett's conduct in this situation be ethical under a utilitarian model of ethics? Why or why not?
4. Did Tamik or Arnett violate the Foreign Corrupt Practices Act in this scenario? Why or why not?

TERMS AND CONCEPTS

business ethics 92
categorical imperative 95
corporate social responsibility 96
cost-benefit analysis 96
ethical reasoning 95
ethics 92
moral minimum 98
principle of rights 96
utilitarianism 96

QUESTIONS AND CASE PROBLEMS

5–1. Some business ethicists maintain that whereas personal ethics has to do with "right" or "wrong" behavior, business ethics is concerned with "appropriate" behavior. In other words, ethical behavior in business has less to do with moral principles than with what society deems to be appropriate behavior in the business context. Do you agree with this distinction? Do personal and business ethics ever overlap? Should personal ethics play any role in business ethical decision making?

5–2. QUESTION WITH SAMPLE ANSWER

If a firm engages in "ethical" behavior solely for the purpose of gaining profits from the goodwill it generates, the "ethical" behavior is essentially a means toward a self-serving end (profits and the accumulation of wealth). In this situation, is the firm acting unethically in any way? Should motive or conduct carry greater weight on the ethical scales in this situation?

- **For a sample answer to Question 5–2, go to Appendix I at the end of this text.**

5–3. Susan Whitehead serves on the city planning commission. The city is planning to build a new subway system, and Susan's brother-in-law, Jerry, who owns the Custom Transportation Co., has submitted the lowest bid for the system. Susan knows that Jerry could complete the job for the estimated amount, but she also knows that once Jerry finishes this job, he will probably sell his company and retire. Susan is concerned that Custom Transportation's subsequent management might not be as easy to work with if revisions need to be made on the subway system after its completion. She is torn as to whether she should tell the city about the potential changes in Custom Transportation's management. If the city knew about the instability of Custom Transportation, it might prefer to give the contract to one of Jerry's competitors, whose bid was only slightly higher than Jerry's. Does Susan have an ethical obligation to disclose the information about Jerry to the city planning commission? How would you apply duty-based ethical standards to this question? What might be the outcome of a utilitarian analysis? Discuss fully.

5–4. Assume that you are a high-level manager for a shoe manufacturer. You know that your firm could increase its profit margin by producing shoes in Indonesia, where you could hire women for $40 a month to assemble them. You also know, however, that human rights advocates recently accused a competing shoe manufacturer of engaging in exploitative labor practices because the manufacturer sold shoes made by Indonesian women working for similarly low wages. You personally do not believe that paying $40 a month to Indonesian women is unethical because you know that in their impoverished country, $40 a month is a better-than-average wage rate. Assuming that the decision is yours to make, should you have the shoes manufactured in Indonesia and make higher profits for your company? Or should you avoid the risk of negative publicity and the consequences of that publicity for the firm's reputation and subsequent profits? Are there other alternatives? Discuss fully.

5–5. Shokun Steel Co. owns many steel plants. One of its plants is much older than the others. Equipment at the old plant is outdated and inefficient, and the costs of production at that plant are now twice as high as at any of Shokun's other plants. Shokun cannot increase the price of its steel because of competition, both domestic and international. The plant employs more than a thousand workers; it is located in Twin Firs, Pennsylvania, which has a population of about forty-five thousand. Shokun is contemplating whether to close the plant. What factors should the firm consider in making its decision? Will the firm violate any ethical duties if it closes the plant? Analyze these questions from the two basic perspectives on ethical reasoning discussed in this chapter.

5–6. CASE PROBLEM WITH SAMPLE ANSWER

Eden Electrical, Ltd., owned twenty-five appliance stores throughout Israel, at least some of which sold refrigerators made by Amana Co. Eden bought the appliances from Amana's Israeli distributor, Pan El A/Yesh Shem, which approached Eden about taking over the distributorship. Eden representatives met with Amana executives. The executives made assurances about Amana's good faith, its hope of having a long-term business relationship with Eden, and its willingness to have Eden become its exclusive distributor in Israel. Eden signed a distributorship agreement and paid Amana $2.4 million. Amana failed to deliver this amount in inventory to Eden, continued selling refrigerators to other entities for the Israeli market, and represented to others that it was still looking for a long-term distributor. Less than three months after signing the agreement with Eden, Amana terminated it, without explanation. Eden filed a suit in a federal district court against Amana, alleging fraud. The court awarded Eden $12.1 million in damages. Is this amount warranted? Why or why not? How does this case illustrate why business ethics is important? [*Eden Electrical, Ltd. v. Amana Co.,* 370 F.3d 824 (8th Cir. 2004)]

- **To view a sample answer for Problem 5–6, go to this book's Web site at www.cengage.com/blaw/jentz, select "Chapter 5," and click on "Case Problem with Sample Answer."**

5–7. Ethical Conduct. Richard Fraser was an "exclusive career insurance agent" under a contract with Nationwide Mutual Insurance Co. Fraser leased computer hardware and software from Nationwide for his business. During a dispute between Nationwide and the Nationwide Insurance Independent Contractors Association, an organization representing Fraser and other exclusive career agents, Fraser prepared a letter to Nationwide's competitors asking whether they were interested in acquiring the represented agents' policyholders. Nationwide obtained a copy of the letter and searched its electronic file server for e-mail indicating that the letter had been sent. It found a stored e-mail that Fraser had sent to a co-worker indicating that the letter had been sent to at least one competitor. The e-mail was retrieved from the co-worker's file of already received and discarded messages stored on the server. When Nationwide canceled its contract with Fraser, he filed a suit in a federal district court against the firm, alleging, among other things, violations of various federal laws that prohibit the interception of electronic communications during transmission. In whose favor should the court rule, and why? Did Nationwide act ethically in retrieving the e-mail? Explain. [*Fraser v. Nationwide Mutual Insurance Co.*, 352 F.3d 107 (3d Cir. 2004)]

5–8. Ethical Conduct. Unable to pay more than $1.2 billion in debt, Big Rivers Electric Corp. filed a petition to declare bankruptcy in a federal bankruptcy court in September 1996. Big Rivers' creditors included Bank of New York (BONY), Chase Manhattan Bank, Mapco Equities, and others. The court appointed J. Baxter Schilling to work as a "disinterested" (neutral) party with Big Rivers and the creditors to resolve their disputes and set an hourly fee as Schilling's compensation. Schilling told Chase, BONY, and Mapco that he wanted them to pay him an additional percentage fee based on the "success" he attained in finding "new value" to pay Big Rivers' debts. Without such a deal, he told them, he would not perform his mediation duties. Chase agreed; the others disputed the deal, but no one told the court. In October 1998, Schilling asked the court for nearly $4.5 million in compensation, including the hourly fees, which totaled about $531,000, and the percentage fees. Big Rivers and others asked the court to deny Schilling any fees on the basis that he had improperly negotiated "secret side agreements." How did Schilling violate his duties as a "disinterested" party? Should he be denied compensation? Why or why not? [*In re Big Rivers Electric Corp.*, 355 F.3d 415 (6th Cir. 2004)]

5–9. Ethical Conduct. Ernest Price suffered from sickle-cell anemia. In 1997, Price asked Dr. Ann Houston, his physician, to prescribe OxyContin, a strong narcotic, for the pain. Over the next several years, Price saw at least ten different physicians at ten different clinics in two cities, and used seven pharmacies in three cities, to obtain and fill simultaneous prescriptions for OxyContin. In March 2001, when Houston learned of these activities, she refused to write more prescriptions for Price. As other physicians became aware of Price's actions, they also stopped writing his prescriptions. Price filed a suit in a Mississippi state court against Purdue Pharma Co. and other producers and distributors of OxyContin, as well as his physicians and the pharmacies that had filled the prescriptions. Price alleged negligence, among other things, claiming that OxyContin's addictive nature caused him injury and that this was the defendants' fault. The defendants argued that Price's claim should be dismissed because it arose from his own wrongdoing. Who should be held *legally* liable? Should any of the parties be considered *ethically* responsible? Why or why not? [*Price v. Purdue Pharma Co.*, 920 So.2d 479 (Miss. 2006)]

5–10. Ethical Leadership. In 1999, Andrew Fastow, chief financial officer of Enron Corp., asked Merrill Lynch, an investment firm, to participate in a bogus sale of three barges so that Enron could record earnings of $12.5 million from the sale. Through a third entity, Fastow bought the barges back within six months and paid Merrill for its participation. Five Merrill employees were convicted of conspiracy to commit wire fraud, in part, on an "honest services" theory. Under this theory, an employee deprives his or her employer of "honest services" when the employee promotes his or her own interests, rather than the interests of the employer. Four of the employees appealed to the U.S. Court of Appeals for the Fifth Circuit, arguing that this charge did not apply to the conduct in which they engaged. The court agreed, reasoning that the barge deal was conducted to benefit Enron, not to enrich the Merrill employees at Enron's expense. Meanwhile, Kevin Howard, chief financial officer of Enron Broadband Services (EBS), engaged in "Project Braveheart," which enabled EBS to show earnings of $111 million in 2000 and 2001. Braveheart involved the sale of an interest in the future revenue of a video-on-demand venture to nCube, a small technology firm, which was paid for its help when EBS bought the interest back. Howard was convicted of wire fraud, in part, on the "honest services" theory. He filed a motion to vacate his conviction on the same basis that the Merrill employees had argued. Did Howard act unethically? Explain. Should the court grant his motion? Discuss. [*United States v. Howard*, 471 F.Supp.2d 772 (S.D.Tex. 2007)]

5–11. A QUESTION OF ETHICS

Steven Soderbergh is the Academy Award–winning director of Erin Brockovich, Traffic, *and many other films. CleanFlicks, LLC, filed a suit in a federal district court against Soderbergh, fifteen other directors, and the Directors Guild of America. The plaintiff asked the court to rule that it had the right to sell DVDs of the defendants' films altered without the defendants' consent to delete scenes of "sex, nudity, profanity and gory violence." CleanFlicks sold or rented the edited DVDs under the slogan "It's About Choice" to consumers, sometimes indirectly through retailers. It would not sell to retailers that made unauthorized copies of the edited films. The defendants, with DreamWorks, LLC, and seven other movie studios that own the copyrights to the films, filed a counterclaim against CleanFlicks and others engaged in the same business, alleging copyright infringement. Those filing the counterclaim asked the court to enjoin (prevent) CleanFlicks and the others from making and marketing altered versions of the films. [*CleanFlicks of Colorado, LLC v. Soderbergh, *433 F.Supp.2d 1236 (D.Colo. 2006)]*

(a) Movie studios often edit their films to conform to content and other standards and sell the edited versions to network television and other commercial buyers. In this case, however, the studios objected when CleanFlicks edited the films and sold the altered versions directly to consumers. Similarly, CleanFlicks made unauthorized copies of the studios' DVDs to edit the films, but objected to others' making unauthorized copies of the altered versions. Is there anything unethical about these apparently contradictory positions? Why or why not?

(b) CleanFlicks and its competitors asserted, among other things, that they were making "fair use" of the studios' copyrighted works. They argued that by their actions "they are criticizing the objectionable content commonly found in current movies and that they are providing more socially acceptable alternatives to enable families to view the films together, without exposing children to the presumed harmful effects emanating from the objectionable content." If you were the judge, how would you view this argument? Is a court the appropriate forum for making determinations of public or social policy? Explain.

5–12. VIDEO QUESTION

Go to this text's Web site at **www.cengage.com/blaw/jentz** and select "Chapter 5." Click on "Video Questions" and view the video titled *Ethics: Business Ethics an Oxymoron?* Then answer the following questions.

(a) According to the instructor in the video, what is the primary reason that businesses act ethically?
(b) Which of the two approaches to ethical reasoning that were discussed in the chapter seems to have had more influence on the instructor in the discussion of how business activities are related to societies? Explain your answer.
(c) The instructor asserts that "in the end, it is the unethical behavior that becomes costly, and conversely ethical behavior creates its own competitive advantage." Do you agree with this statement? Why or why not?

LAW ON THE WEB

For updated links to resources available on the Web, as well as a variety of other materials, visit this text's Web site at

www.cengage.com/blaw/jentz

You can find articles on issues relating to shareholders and corporate accountability at the Corporate Governance Web site. Go to

www.corpgov.net

For an example of an online group that focuses on corporate activities from the perspective of corporate social responsibility, go to

www.corpwatch.org

Global Exchange offers information on global business activities, including some of the ethical issues stemming from those activities, at

www.globalexchange.org

Legal Research Exercises on the Web

Go to **www.cengage.com/blaw/jentz**, the Web site that accompanies this text. Select "Chapter 5" and click on "Internet Exercises." There you will find the following Internet research exercises that you can perform to learn more about the topics covered in this chapter.

Internet Exercise 5–1: Legal Perspective
Ethics in Business

Internet Exercise 5–2: Management Perspective
Environmental Self-Audits

UNIT ONE · FOCUS ON ETHICS

Ethics and the Legal Environment of Business

In Chapter 5, we examined the importance of ethical standards in the business context. We also offered suggestions on how business decision makers can create an ethical workplace. Certainly, it is not wrong for a businessperson to try to increase his or her firm's profits. But there are limits, both ethical and legal, to how far businesspersons can go. In preparing for a career in business, you will find that a background in business ethics and a commitment to ethical behavior are just as important as a knowledge of the specific laws that are covered in this text. Of course, no textbook can give an answer to each and every ethical question that arises in the business environment. Nor can it anticipate the types of ethical questions that will arise in the future, as technology and globalization continue to transform the workplace and business relationships.

The most we can do is examine the types of ethical issues that businesspersons have faced in the past and that they are facing today. In the *Focus on Ethics* sections in this book, we provide examples of specific ethical issues that have arisen in various areas of business activity.

In this initial *Focus on Ethics* feature, we look first at the relationship between business ethics and business law. We then examine various obstacles to ethical behavior in the business context. We conclude the feature by exploring the parameters of corporate social responsibility through a discussion of whether corporations have an ethical duty to the community or society at large.

Business Ethics and Business Law

Business ethics and business law are closely intertwined because ultimately the law rests on social beliefs about right and wrong behavior in the business world. Thus, businesspersons, by complying with the law, are acting ethically. Mere legal compliance (the "moral minimum" in terms of business ethics), however, is often not enough. This is because the law does not—and cannot—provide the answers for all ethical questions.

In the business world, numerous actions may be unethical but not necessarily illegal. Consider an example. Suppose that a pharmaceutical company is banned from marketing a particular drug in the United States because of the drug's possible adverse side effects. Yet no law prohibits the company from selling the drug in foreign markets—even though some consumers in those markets may suffer serious health problems as a result of using the drug. At issue here is not whether it would be legal to market the drug in other countries but whether it would be *ethical* to do so. In other words, the law has its limits—it cannot make all ethical decisions for us. Rather, the law assumes that those in business will behave ethically in their day-to-day dealings. If they do not, the courts will not come to their assistance.

Obstacles to Ethical Business Behavior

People sometimes behave unethically in the business context, just as they do in their private lives. Some businesspersons knowingly engage in unethical behavior because they think that they can "get away with it"—that no one will ever learn of their unethical actions. Examples of this kind of unethical behavior include padding expense accounts, casting doubts on the integrity of a rival co-worker to gain a job promotion, and stealing company supplies or equipment. Obviously, these acts are unethical, and some of them are illegal as well. In some situations, however, businesspersons who would choose to act ethically may be deterred from doing so because of situational circumstances or external pressures.

Ethics and the Corporate Environment Individuals in their personal lives normally are free to decide ethical issues as they wish and to follow through on those decisions. In the business world, and particularly in the corporate environment, rarely is such a decision made by *one* person. If you are an officer or a manager of a large company, for example, you will find that the decision as to what is right or wrong for the company is not totally yours to make. Your input may weigh in the decision, but ultimately a corporate decision is a collective undertaking.

Additionally, collective decision making, because it places emphasis on consensus and unity of opinion, tends to hinder individual ethical assertiveness. Suppose that a director has ethical concerns about a planned corporate venture that promises to be highly profitable. If the other directors have no such misgivings, the director who does may be swayed by the others' enthusiasm for the project and downplay her or his own criticisms.

Furthermore, just as no one person makes a collective decision, so no one person (normally) is held accountable for the decision. The corporate

(Continued)

enterprise thus tends to shield corporate personnel from both individual exposure to the consequences of their decisions (such as direct experience with someone who suffers harm from a corporate product) and personal accountability for those decisions.

Ethics and Management Much unethical business behavior occurs simply because management does not always make clear what ethical standards and behaviors are expected of the firm's employees. Although most firms now issue ethical policies or codes of conduct, these policies and codes are not always effective in creating an ethical workplace. At times, this is because the firm's ethical policies are not communicated clearly to employees or do not bear on the real ethical issues confronting decision makers. Additionally, particularly in a large corporation, unethical behavior in one corporate department may simply escape the attention of the officers in control of the corporation or those responsible for implementing and monitoring the company's ethics program.

Unethical behavior may also occur when corporate management, by its own conduct, indicates that ethical considerations take a back seat. If management makes no attempt to deter unethical behavior—through reprimands or employment terminations, for example—it will be obvious to employees that management is not all that serious about ethics. Likewise, if a company gives promotions or salary increases to those who clearly use unethical tactics to increase the firm's profits, then employees who do not resort to such tactics will be at a disadvantage. An employee in this situation may decide that because "everyone else does it," he or she might as well do it, too.

Of course, an even stronger encouragement to unethical behavior occurs when employers engage in blatantly unethical or illegal conduct and expect their employees to do so as well. An employee in this situation faces two options, neither of which is satisfactory: participate in the conduct or "blow the whistle" on (inform authorities of) the employer's actions—and, of course, risk being fired. (See Chapter 33 for a more detailed discussion of this ethical dilemma and its consequences for employees.)

Corporate Social Responsibility

As discussed in Chapter 5, just what constitutes corporate social responsibility has been debated for some time. In particular, questions arise concerning a corporation's ethical obligations to its community and to society as a whole.

A Corporation's Duty to the Community In some circumstances, the community in which a business enterprise is located is greatly affected by corporate decisions and therefore may be considered a stakeholder. Assume, for example, that a company employs two thousand workers at one of its plants. If the company decides that it would be profitable to close the plant, the employees—and the community—would suffer as a result. To be considered ethical in that situation (and, in some circumstances, to comply with laws governing plant shutdowns), a corporation must take both employees' needs and community needs into consideration when making such a decision.

Another ethical question sometimes arises when a firm moves into a community. Does the company have an obligation to evaluate first how its presence will affect that community (even though the community is not a stakeholder yet)? This question has surfaced in regard to the expansion of Wal-Mart Stores, Inc., into smaller communities. Generally, most people in such communities welcome the lower prices and wider array of goods that Wal-Mart offers relative to other, smaller stores in the area. A vocal minority of people in some communities, however, claim that smaller stores often find it impossible to compete with Wal-Mart's prices and thus are forced to go out of business. Many of these smaller stores have existed for years and, according to Wal-Mart's critics, enhance the quality of community life. These critics claim that it is unethical of Wal-Mart to disregard a town's interest in the quality and character of its community life.

In addition to expanding, Wal-Mart has been consolidating some of its smaller stores into large "superstores." As it consolidates, Wal-Mart is closing stores in some of the very towns in which it drove its smaller competitors out of business. This development raises yet another ethical question: Does a store such as Wal-Mart have an obligation to continue operations in a community once it has driven its competitors out of business?

A Corporation's Duty to Society Perhaps the most disputed area of corporate social responsibility is the nature of a corporation's duty to society at large. Those who contend that corporations should first and foremost attend to the goal of profit maximization would argue that it is by generating profits that a firm can best contribute to society.

Focus on Ethics

Society benefits by profit-making activities because profits can only be realized when a firm markets products or services that are desired by society. These products and services enhance the standard of living, and the profits accumulated by successful business firms generate national wealth. Our laws and court decisions promoting trade and commerce reflect the public policy that the fruits of commerce (wealth) are desirable and good. Because our society values wealth as an ethical goal, corporations, by contributing to that wealth, automatically are acting ethically.

Those arguing for profit maximization as a corporate goal also point out that it would be inappropriate to use the power of the corporate business world to further society's goals by promoting social causes. Determinations as to what exactly is in society's best interest involve questions that are essentially political, and therefore the public, through the political process, should have a say in making those determinations. Thus, the legislature—not the corporate boardroom—is the appropriate forum for such decisions.

Critics of the profit-maximization view believe that corporations should become actively engaged in seeking and furthering solutions to social problems. Because so much of the wealth and power of this country is controlled by business, business in turn has a responsibility to society to use that wealth and power in socially beneficial ways. Corporations should therefore promote human rights, strive for equal treatment of minorities and women in the workplace, take steps to preserve the environment, and generally not profit from activities that society has deemed unethical. The critics also point out that it is ethically irresponsible to leave decisions concerning social welfare up to the government, because many social needs are not being met sufficiently through the political process.

It Pays to Be Ethical

Most corporations today have learned that it pays to be ethically responsible—even if this means less profit in the short run (and it often does). Today's corporations are subject to more intensive scrutiny—by both government agencies and the public—than corporations of the past. "Corporate watch" groups monitor the activities of U.S. corporations, including activities conducted in foreign countries. Through the Internet, complaints about a corporation's practices can easily be disseminated to a worldwide audience. Similarly, dissatisfied customers and employees can voice their complaints about corporate policies, products, or services in Internet chat rooms and other online forums. Thus, if a corporation fails to conduct its operations ethically or to respond quickly to an ethical crisis, its goodwill and reputation (and future profits) will likely suffer as a result.

There are other reasons as well for a corporation to behave ethically. For example, companies that demonstrate a commitment to ethical behavior—by implementing ethical programs, complying with environmental regulations, and promptly investigating product complaints, for example—often receive more lenient treatment from government agencies and the courts. Additionally, investors may shy away from a corporation's stock if the corporation is perceived to be socially irresponsible. Finally, unethical (and/or illegal) corporate behavior may result in government action, such as new laws imposing further requirements on corporate entities.

DISCUSSION QUESTIONS

1. What might be some other deterrents to ethical behavior in the business context, besides those discussed in this *Focus on Ethics* feature?
2. Can you think of a situation in which a business firm may be acting ethically but not in a socially responsible manner? Explain.
3. Why are consumers and the public generally more concerned with ethical and socially responsible business behavior today than they were, say, fifty years ago?
4. Suppose that an automobile manufacturing company has to choose between two alternatives: contributing $1 million annually to the United Way or reinvesting the $1 million in the company. In terms of ethics and social responsibility, which is the "better" choice?
5. Have Internet chat rooms and online forums affected corporate decision makers' willingness to consider the community and public interest when making choices? Are corporate decision makers more apt to make ethical choices in the cyber age? Explain.

UNIT TWO

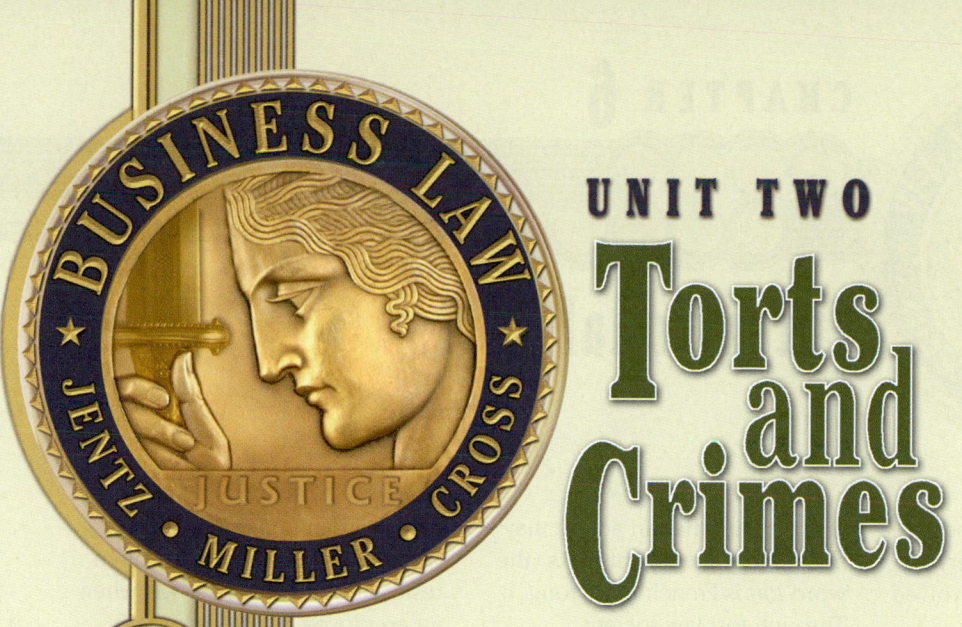

Torts and Crimes

CONTENTS

CHAPTER 6

Intentional Torts

Part of doing business today—and, indeed, part of everyday life—is the risk of being involved in a lawsuit. The list of circumstances in which businesspersons can be sued is long and varied. A customer who is injured by a security guard at a business establishment, for example, may attempt to sue the business owner, claiming that the security guard's conduct was wrongful. Any time that one party's allegedly wrongful conduct causes injury to another, an action may arise under the law of **torts** (the word *tort* is French for "wrong"). Through tort law, society compensates those who have suffered injuries as a result of the wrongful conduct of others.

Many of the lawsuits brought by or against business firms are based on the tort theories discussed in this chapter, which covers intentional torts, and the next chapter, which discusses unintentional torts. *Intentional torts* arise from intentional acts, whereas *unintentional torts* often result from carelessness (as when an employee at a store knocks over a display case, injuring a customer). In addition, this chapter discusses how tort law applies to wrongful actions in the online environment. Tort theories also come into play in the context of product liability (liability for defective products), which will be discussed in detail in Chapter 23.

SECTION 1 The Basis of Tort Law

Two notions serve as the basis of all torts: wrongs and compensation. Tort law is designed to compensate those who have suffered a loss or injury due to another person's wrongful act. In a tort action, one person or group brings a lawsuit against another person or group to obtain compensation (monetary damages) or other relief for the harm suffered.

The Purpose of Tort Law

The basic purpose of tort law is to provide remedies for the invasion of various *protected interests*. Society recognizes an interest in personal physical safety, and tort law provides remedies for acts that cause physical injury or that interfere with physical security and freedom of movement. Society recognizes an interest in protecting property, and tort law provides remedies for acts that cause destruction or damage to property. Society also recognizes an interest in protecting certain intangible interests, such as personal privacy, family relations, reputation, and dignity, and tort law provides remedies for violation of these interests.

Damages Available in Tort Actions

Because the purpose of tort law is to compensate the injured party for the damage suffered, you need to have an understanding of the types of damages that plaintiffs seek in tort actions. The high cost to society of sizable damages awards in tort cases has fueled the tort reform movement, which is discussed in this chapter's *Contemporary Legal Debates* feature on pages 118 and 119.

Compensatory Damages **Compensatory damages** are intended to compensate or reimburse a plaintiff for actual losses—to make the plaintiff whole and put her or him in the same position that she or he would have been had the tort not occurred. Compensatory damages awards are often broken down into special damages and general damages. *Special damages* compensate the plaintiff for quantifiable monetary losses, such as medical expenses, lost wages and benefits (now and in the future), extra costs, the loss of irreplaceable items, and the costs of repairing or replacing damaged property. *General damages* compensate individuals (not companies) for the nonmonetary aspects of the harm suffered, such as pain and suffering. A court might award general damages for physical or emotional pain and suffering, loss of companionship, loss of consortium (losing the emotional and physical benefits of a spousal relationship), disfigurement, loss of reputation, or loss or impairment of mental or physical capacity.

Punitive Damages Occasionally, the courts may also award **punitive damages** in tort cases to punish the wrongdoer and deter others from similar wrongdoing. Punitive damages are appropriate only when the defendant's conduct was particularly egregious or reprehensible. Usually, this means that punitive damages are available mainly in intentional tort actions and only rarely in negligence lawsuits (*negligence* actions will be discussed in Chapter 7). They may be awarded, however, in suits involving *gross negligence*, which can be defined as an intentional failure to perform a manifest duty in reckless disregard of the consequences of such a failure for the life or property of another.

Courts exercise great restraint in granting punitive damages to plaintiffs in tort actions because punitive damages are subject to the limitations imposed by the due process clause of the U.S. Constitution (discussed in Chapter 2). In *State Farm Mutual Automobile Insurance Co. v. Campbell*,[1] the United States Supreme Court held that to the extent an award of punitive damages is grossly excessive, it furthers no legitimate purpose and violates due process requirements. Although this case dealt with intentional torts (fraud and intentional infliction of emotional distress), the Court's holding applies equally to punitive damages awards in gross negligence cases (as well as to product liability cases).

Although the following case involved a product liability claim (which will be discussed in Chapter 23), the decision illustrates how courts analyze whether punitive damages awards are excessive.

1. 538 U.S. 408, 123 S.Ct. 1513, 155 L.Ed.2d 585 (2003).

CASE 6.1 Buell-Wilson v. Ford Motor Co.

Court of Appeal, Fourth District, Division 1, California, 2008.
160 Cal.App.4th 1107, 73 Cal.Rptr.3d 277.

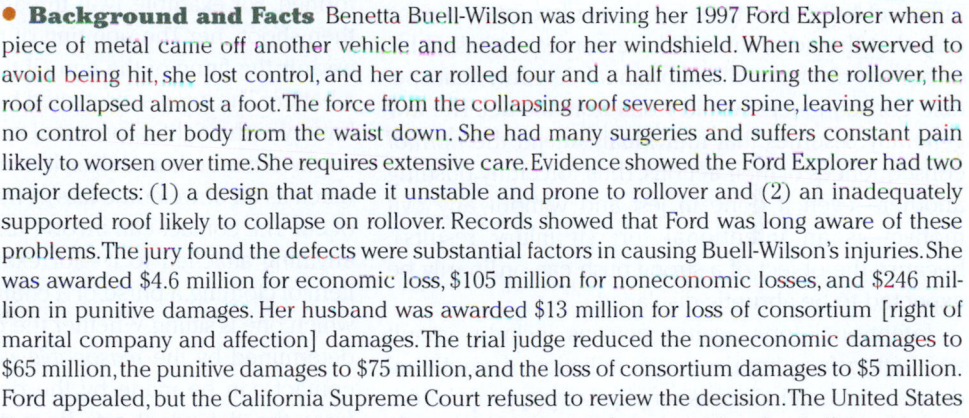

Background and Facts Benetta Buell-Wilson was driving her 1997 Ford Explorer when a piece of metal came off another vehicle and headed for her windshield. When she swerved to avoid being hit, she lost control, and her car rolled four and a half times. During the rollover, the roof collapsed almost a foot. The force from the collapsing roof severed her spine, leaving her with no control of her body from the waist down. She had many surgeries and suffers constant pain likely to worsen over time. She requires extensive care. Evidence showed the Ford Explorer had two major defects: (1) a design that made it unstable and prone to rollover and (2) an inadequately supported roof likely to collapse on rollover. Records showed that Ford was long aware of these problems. The jury found the defects were substantial factors in causing Buell-Wilson's injuries. She was awarded \$4.6 million for economic loss, \$105 million for noneconomic losses, and \$246 million in punitive damages. Her husband was awarded \$13 million for loss of consortium [right of marital company and affection] damages. The trial judge reduced the noneconomic damages to \$65 million, the punitive damages to \$75 million, and the loss of consortium damages to \$5 million. Ford appealed, but the California Supreme Court refused to review the decision. The United States Supreme Court vacated the judgment and remanded the case for reconsideration in light of recent decisions by the Court concerning excessive damage awards.

Decision and Rationale The California Court of Appeal considered the amount of damages on remand. The court held that the \$65 million in noneconomic damages awarded to a forty-six-year-old plaintiff who had been healthy prior to the accident was excessive and would be reduced to \$18 million. That amount is one that "a reasonable person would estimate as fair compensation" in this case. The large award was granted by a jury that acted out of "passion and prejudice." Ford also contended that the punitive damages award "is excessive under the federal due

CASE CONTINUES

CASE 6.1 CONTINUED process clause of the 14th Amendment to the United States Constitution." The court concluded that "after reducing the noneconomic damage award to Mrs. Wilson to $18 million, the award of punitive damages is excessive and is, therefore, reduced to $55 million, an approximate two-to-one ratio of the total compensatory damage award ($4.6 million in economic damages + $18 million in noneconomic damages + $5 million in loss of consortium damages = $27.6 million × 2 = $55.2 million)." This is more in line with the guidelines set by the United States Supreme Court regarding punitive damages.[a]

- **The Ethical Dimension** *The court stated that punitive damages are designed to punish the defendant for reprehensible behavior. If so, should the punitive damages go to one plaintiff or be shared by all buyers of Ford products or by the general public? Why or why not?*
- **The Legal Environment Dimension** *Why did the appellate court indicate that the plaintiff had been "healthy prior to the accident"?*

a. The Supreme Court of California granted review of this case and had not yet issued a decision at the time this book went to press [187 P.3d 887, 80 Cal.Rptr.3d 27 (2008)].

SECTION 2 Intentional Torts against Persons

An **intentional tort,** as the term implies, requires intent. The **tortfeasor** (the one committing the tort) must intend to commit an act, the consequences of which interfere with the personal or business interests of another in a way not permitted by law. An evil or harmful motive is not required—in fact, the actor may even have a beneficial motive for committing what turns out to be a tortious act. In tort law, *intent* means only that the actor intended the consequences of his or her act or knew with substantial certainty that specific consequences would result from the act. The law generally assumes that individuals intend the *normal* consequences of their actions. Thus, forcefully pushing another—even if done in jest and without any evil motive—is an intentional tort (if injury results), because the object of a strong push can ordinarily be expected to be abruptly displaced.

Intentional torts against persons include assault and battery, false imprisonment, infliction of emotional distress, defamation, invasion of privacy, appropriation, fraudulent misrepresentation, and torts related to misuse of litigation. We discuss these torts in the following subsections.

Assault and Battery

Any intentional, unexcused act that creates in another person a reasonable apprehension of immediate harmful or offensive contact is an **assault.** Note that apprehension is not the same as fear. If a contact is such that a reasonable person would want to avoid it, and if there is a reasonable basis for believing that the contact will occur, then the plaintiff suffers apprehension whether or not she or he is afraid. The interest protected by tort law concerning assault is the freedom from having to expect harmful or offensive contact. The arousal of apprehension is enough to justify compensation.

The *completion* of the act that caused the apprehension, if it results in harm to the plaintiff, is a **battery,** which is defined as an unexcused and harmful or offensive physical contact *intentionally* performed. For example, Ivan threatens Jean with a gun, then shoots her. The pointing of the gun at Jean is an assault; the firing of the gun (if the bullet hits Jean) is a battery. The interest protected by tort law concerning battery is the right to personal security and safety. The contact can be harmful, or it can be merely offensive (such as an unwelcome kiss). Physical injury need not occur. The contact can involve any part of the body or anything attached to it—for example, a hat or other item of clothing, a purse, or a chair or an automobile in which one is sitting. Whether the contact is offensive is determined by the *reasonable person standard.*[2] The contact can be made by the defendant or by some force the defendant sets in motion—for example, a rock thrown, food poisoned, or a stick swung.

Compensation If the plaintiff shows that there was contact, and the jury (or judge, if there is no jury) agrees that the contact was offensive, then the plaintiff

2. The *reasonable person standard* is an "objective" test of how a reasonable person would have acted under the same circumstances. See the subsection entitled "The Duty of Care and Its Breach" in Chapter 7.

has a right to compensation. There is no need to establish that the defendant acted out of malice. The underlying motive does not matter, only the intent to bring about the harmful or offensive contact to the plaintiff. In fact, proving a motive is never necessary. A plaintiff may be compensated for the emotional harm or loss of reputation resulting from a battery, as well as for physical harm.

Defenses to Assault and Battery A defendant who is sued for assault, battery, or both can raise any of the following legally recognized defenses:

1. *Consent.* When a person consents to the act that is allegedly tortious, there may be a complete or partial defense to liability.
2. *Self-defense.* An individual who is defending her or his life or physical well-being can claim self-defense. In a situation of either *real* or *apparent* danger, a person may normally use whatever force is *reasonably* necessary to prevent harmful contact (see Chapter 9 for a more detailed discussion of self-defense).
3. *Defense of others.* An individual can act in a reasonable manner to protect others who are in real or apparent danger.
4. *Defense of property.* Reasonable force may be used in attempting to remove intruders from one's home, although force that is likely to cause death or great bodily injury normally cannot be used just to protect property.

False Imprisonment

False imprisonment is defined as the intentional confinement or restraint of another person's activities without justification. It involves interference with the freedom to move without restriction. The confinement can be accomplished through the use of physical barriers, physical restraint, or threats of physical force. Moral pressure does not constitute false imprisonment. Furthermore, it is essential that the person being restrained not agree to the restraint.

Businesspersons often face suits for false imprisonment after they have attempted to confine a suspected shoplifter for questioning. Under the laws of most states, merchants may detain persons suspected of shoplifting and hold them for the police. Although laws vary from state to state, normally only a merchant's security personnel—not salesclerks or other employees—have the right to detain suspects. Reasonable or probable cause must exist to believe that the person being detained has committed a theft. Additionally, most states require that any detention be conducted in a *reasonable* manner and for only a *reasonable* length of time. Tackling a customer suspected of theft in the parking lot would be considered unreasonable in many jurisdictions.

Businesspersons who operate retail establishments need to make sure that their employees are aware of the limitations on the privilege to detain. Even if someone is suspected of shoplifting, businesspersons (and employees) must have probable cause to stop and question the person and must behave reasonably and detain the person for only a sensible amount of time. Undue force or unreasonable detention can lead to liability for the business.

Intentional Infliction of Emotional Distress

The tort of *intentional infliction of emotional distress* can be defined as an intentional act that amounts to extreme and outrageous conduct resulting in severe emotional distress to another. To be **actionable** (capable of serving as the ground for a lawsuit), the act must be extreme and outrageous to the point that it exceeds the bounds of decency accepted by society. For example, a prankster telephones a pregnant woman and says that her husband and two sons have just been killed in a horrible accident (although they have not). As a result, the woman suffers intense mental pain and has a miscarriage. In that situation, the woman would be able to sue for intentional infliction of emotional distress.

Courts in most jurisdictions are wary of emotional distress claims and confine them to situations involving truly outrageous behavior. Acts that cause indignity or annoyance alone usually are not sufficient. Many times, however, repeated annoyances (such as those experienced by a person who is being stalked), coupled with threats, are enough.

Note that when the outrageous conduct consists of speech about a public figure, the First Amendment's guarantee of freedom of speech also limits emotional distress claims. For example, *Hustler* magazine once printed a fake advertisement that showed a picture of Reverend Jerry Falwell and described him as having lost his virginity to his mother in an outhouse while he was drunk. Falwell sued the magazine for intentional

CONTEMPORARY LEGAL DEBATES

Tort Reform

The question of whether our tort law system is in need of reform has aroused heated debate. While some argue that the current system imposes excessive costs on society, others contend that the system protects consumers from unsafe products and practices.

"End the Tort Tax and Frivolous Lawsuits," Say the Critics

Critics of the current tort law system contend that it encourages too many frivolous lawsuits, which clog the courts, and is unnecessarily costly. In particular, they say, damages awards are often excessive and bear little relationship to the actual damage suffered. Such large awards encourage plaintiffs to bring frivolous suits, hoping that they will "hit the jackpot." Trial lawyers, in turn, are eager to bring the suits because they are paid on a contingency-fee basis, meaning that they receive a percentage of the damages awarded.

The result, in the critics' view, is a system that disproportionately rewards a few lucky plaintiffs while imposing enormous costs on business and society as a whole. They refer to the economic burden that the tort system imposes on society as the "tort tax." According to one recent study, more than $300 billion per year is expended on tort litigation, including plaintiffs' and defendants' attorneys' fees, damages awards, and other costs. Most of the costs are from class-action lawsuits involving product liability or medical malpractice.[a] (A *class action* is a lawsuit in which a single person or a small group of people represents the interests of a larger group.) Although even the critics would not contend that the tort tax encompasses the entire $300 billion, they believe that it includes a sizable portion of that amount. Furthermore, they say, the tax appears in other ways. Because physicians, hospitals, and pharmaceutical companies are worried about medical malpractice suits, they have changed their behavior. Physicians, for example, engage in defensive medicine by ordering more tests than necessary. PricewaterhouseCoopers has calculated that the practice of defensive medicine increases health-care costs by more than $100 billion per year.

To solve the problems they perceive, critics want to reduce both the number of tort cases brought each year and the amount of damages awards. They advocate the following tort reform measures: (1) limit the amount of punitive damages that can be awarded; (2) limit the amount of general noneconomic damages that can be awarded (for example, for pain and suffering); (3) limit the amount that attorneys can collect in contingency fees; and (4) to discourage the filing of meritless suits, require the losing party to pay both the plaintiff's and the defendant's expenses.

"The Current System Promotes Fairness and Safefy," Say Their Opponents

Others are not so sure that the current system needs such drastic reform. They say that the prospect of tort lawsuits encourages companies to produce safer products and deters them from putting dangerous products on the market. In the health-care industry,

a. Lawrence J. McQuillan, Hovannes Abramyan, and Anthony P. Archie, *Jackpot Justice: The True Cost of America's Tort System* (San Francisco: Pacific Research Institute, 2007).

infliction of emotional distress and won, but the United States Supreme Court overturned the decision. The Court held that creators of parodies of public figures are protected under the First Amendment from intentional infliction of emotional distress claims. (The Court used the same standards that apply to public figures in defamation lawsuits, discussed next.)[3]

3. *Hustler Magazine, Inc. v. Falwell*, 485 U.S. 46, 108 S.Ct. 876, 99 L.Ed.2d 41 (1988). For another example of how the courts protect parody, see *Busch v. Viacom International, Inc.*, 477 F.Supp.2d 764 (N.D.Tex. 2007), involving a fake endorsement of televangelist Pat Robertson's diet shake.

Defamation

As discussed in Chapter 4, the freedom of speech guaranteed by the First Amendment is not absolute. In interpreting the First Amendment, the courts must balance the vital guarantee of free speech against other pervasive and strong social interests, including society's interest in preventing and redressing attacks on reputation.

Defamation of character involves wrongfully hurting a person's good reputation. The law imposes a general duty on all persons to refrain from making false, defamatory *statements of fact* about others. Breaching the potential for medical malpractice suits has led to safer and more effective medical practices.

Imposing limits on the amount of punitive and general noneconomic damages would be unfair, say the system's defenders, and would reduce efficiency in our legal and economic system. After all, corporations conduct cost-benefit analyses when they decide how much safety to build into their products. Any limitation on potential damages would mean that corporations would have less incentive to build safer products. Indeed, Professor Stephen Teret of the Johns Hopkins University School of Public Health says that tort litigation is an important tool for preventing injuries because it forces manufacturers to opt for more safety in their products rather than less.[b] Limiting contingency fees would also be unfair, say those in favor of the current system, because low-income consumers who have been injured could not afford to pay an attorney to take a case on an hourly fee basis—and an attorney would not expend the time needed to pursue a case without the prospect of a large reward in the form of a contingency fee.

Tort Reform in Reality

While the debate continues, the federal government and a number of states have begun to take some steps toward tort reform. At the federal level, the Class Action Fairness Act (CAFA) of 2005[c] shifted jurisdiction over large interstate tort and product liability class-action lawsuits from the state courts to the federal courts. The intent was to prevent plaintiffs' attorneys from shopping around for a state court that might be predisposed to be sympathetic to their clients' cause and to award large damages in class-action suits.

At the state level, more than twenty states have placed caps ranging from $250,000 to $750,000 on noneconomic damages, especially in medical malpractice suits. More than thirty states have limited punitive damages, with some imposing outright bans.

WHERE DO YOU STAND?

Large damages awards in tort litigation have to be paid by someone. If the defendant is insured, then insurance companies foot the bill. Ultimately, though, high insurance rates are passed on to consumers of goods and services in the United States. Consequently, tort reform that reduces the size and number of damages awards ultimately will mean lower costs of goods and services to consumers. The downside of these lower costs, though, might be higher risks of medical malpractice and dangerous products. Do you believe that this trade-off is real? Why or why not?

b. "Litigation Is an Important Tool for Injury and Gun Violence Prevention," Johns Hopkins University Center for Gun Policy and Research, July 15, 2006.

c. 28 U.S.C.A. Sections 1711–1715, 1453.

this duty in writing or other permanent form (such as an electronic recording) involves the tort of **libel.** Breaching this duty orally involves the tort of **slander.** The tort of defamation also arises when a false statement of fact is made about a person's product, business, or legal ownership rights.

Note that generally only false statements that represent something as a fact (such as "Vladik cheats on his taxes") constitute defamation. Expressions of personal opinion (such as "Vladik is a jerk") are protected by the First Amendment and normally cannot lead to tort liability.

The Publication Requirement The basis of the tort of defamation is the publication of a statement or statements that hold an individual up to contempt, ridicule, or hatred. *Publication* here means that the defamatory statements are communicated (either intentionally or accidentally) to persons other than the defamed party. If Thompson writes Andrews a private letter falsely accusing him of embezzling funds, the action does not constitute libel. If Peters falsely states that Gordon is dishonest and incompetent when no one else is around, the action does not constitute slander. In neither case was the message communicated to a third party.

The courts have generally held that even dictating a letter to a secretary constitutes publication, although the publication may be privileged (a concept that will be explained shortly). Moreover, if a third party merely overhears defamatory statements by chance, the courts usually hold that this also constitutes publication. Defamatory statements made via the Internet are actionable as well. Note also that any individual who repeats or republishes defamatory statements normally is liable even if that person reveals the source of the statements.

Damages for Libel Once a defendant's liability for libel is established, *general damages* are presumed as a matter of law. General damages are designed to compensate the plaintiff for nonspecific harms such as disgrace or dishonor in the eyes of the community, humiliation, injured reputation, and emotional distress—harms that are difficult to measure. In other words, to recover damages in a libel case, the plaintiff need not prove that he or she was actually injured in any way as a result of the libelous statement.

Damages for Slander In contrast to cases alleging libel, in a case alleging slander, the plaintiff must prove *special damages* to establish the defendant's liability. The plaintiff must show that the slanderous statement caused her or him to suffer actual economic or monetary losses. Unless this initial hurdle of proving special damages is overcome, a plaintiff alleging slander normally cannot go forward with the suit and recover any damages. This requirement is imposed in slander cases because oral statements have a temporary quality. In contrast, a libelous (written) statement has the quality of permanence, can be circulated widely, and usually results from some degree of deliberation on the part of the author.

Exceptions to the burden of proving special damages in cases alleging slander are made for certain types of slanderous statements. If a false statement constitutes "slander *per se*," no proof of special damages is required for it to be actionable. In most states, the following four types of utterances are considered to be slander *per se:*

1. A statement that another has a loathsome disease (historically, leprosy and sexually transmitted diseases, but now also including allegations of mental illness).
2. A statement that another has committed improprieties while engaging in a profession or trade.
3. A statement that another has committed or has been imprisoned for a serious crime.
4. A statement that a person (usually only an unmarried person and sometimes only a woman) is unchaste or has engaged in serious sexual misconduct.

Defenses to Defamation Truth is normally an absolute defense against a defamation charge. In other words, if a defendant in a defamation case can prove that the allegedly defamatory statements of fact were true, normally no tort has been committed. Other defenses to defamation may exist if the speech is *privileged* or concerns a public figure. Note that the majority of defamation actions are filed in state courts, and state laws differ somewhat in the defenses they allow, such as privilege (discussed next).

Privileged Speech. In some circumstances, a person will not be liable for defamatory statements because she or he enjoys a **privilege,** or immunity. With respect to defamation, privileged communications are of two types: absolute and qualified.[4] Only in judicial proceedings and certain government proceedings is an *absolute privilege* granted. For example, statements made by attorneys and judges in the courtroom during a trial are absolutely privileged. So are statements made by government officials during legislative debate, even if the legislators make such statements maliciously—that is, knowing them to be untrue. An absolute privilege is granted in these situations because judicial and government personnel deal with matters that are so much in the public interest that the parties involved should be able to speak out fully and freely and without restriction.

In other situations, a person will not be liable for defamatory statements because he or she has a *qualified,* or *conditional, privilege.* An employer's statements in written evaluations of employees are an example of a qualified privilege. Generally, if the statements are made in good faith and the publication is limited to those who have a legitimate interest in the communication, the statements fall within the area of qualified privilege. The concept of conditional privilege rests on the common law assumption that in some situations, the right to know or speak is equal in importance to the right not to be defamed. If a communication is conditionally privileged, to recover damages, the plaintiff must show that the privilege was abused.

4. Note that the term *privileged communication* in this context is not the same as privileged communication between a professional, such as an attorney, and his or her client. The latter type of privilege will be discussed in Chapter 51, in the context of the liability of professionals.

Public Figures. Public officials who exercise substantial governmental power and any persons in the public limelight are considered *public figures.* In general, public figures are considered "fair game," and false and defamatory statements about them that are published in the press will not constitute defamation unless the statements are made with **actual malice.** To be made with actual malice, a statement must be made *with either knowledge of its falsity or a reckless disregard of the truth.*[5]

Statements made about public figures, especially when they are communicated via a public medium, are usually related to matters of general public interest; they refer to people who substantially affect all of us. Furthermore, public figures generally have some access to a public medium for answering disparaging falsehoods about themselves; private individuals do not. For these reasons, public figures have a greater burden of proof in defamation cases (they must prove actual malice) than do private individuals.

Invasion of Privacy

A person has a right to solitude and freedom from prying public eyes—in other words, to privacy. As mentioned in Chapter 4, the courts have held that certain amendments to the U.S. Constitution imply a right to privacy. Some state constitutions explicitly provide for privacy rights, as do a number of federal and state statutes. Tort law also safeguards these rights through the tort of *invasion of privacy.* Four acts qualify as invasions of privacy:

1. *Appropriation of identity.* Under the common law, using a person's name, picture, or other likeness for commercial purposes without permission is a tortious invasion of privacy. Most states today have also enacted statutes prohibiting *appropriation* (discussed further in the next subsection).
2. *Intrusion into an individual's affairs or seclusion.* For example, invading someone's home or searching someone's personal computer without authorization is an invasion of privacy. This tort has been held to extend to eavesdropping by wiretap, unauthorized scanning of a bank account, compulsory blood testing, and window peeping.
3. *False light.* The publication of information that places a person in a false light is another category of invasion of privacy. This could be a story attributing to someone ideas not held or actions not taken by that person. (The publication of such a story could involve the tort of defamation as well.)
4. *Public disclosure of private facts.* This type of invasion of privacy occurs when a person publicly discloses private facts about an individual that an ordinary person would find objectionable or embarrassing. A newspaper account of a private citizen's sex life or financial affairs could be an actionable invasion of privacy, even if the information revealed is true, because it is not of public concern.

The following case included an allegation of an intrusion into an individual's affairs or seclusion.

5. *New York Times Co. v. Sullivan,* 376 U.S. 254, 84 S.Ct. 710, 11 L.Ed.2d 686 (1964). As mentioned earlier, the First Amendment protects the creator of a parody from liability for defamation of a public figure.

CASE 6.2 Anderson v. Mergenhagen

Court of Appeals of Georgia, 2007. 283 Ga.App. 546, 642 S.E.2d 105.

• **Background and Facts** After Dick and Karyn Anderson's marriage collapsed and they divorced, Karyn harassed Dick's new wife, Maureen, until Maureen obtained a warrant for Karyn's arrest. According to Maureen, Karyn's new boyfriend, Paul Mergenhagen, then began following Maureen. On more than a dozen occasions between mid-2003 and mid-2005, Paul took photos of, and made obscene gestures to, Maureen as she was driving in her car or walking with her children. Frightened and upset, Maureen called the police several times. Paul admitted that he had followed Maureen at least four times and had taken at least forty photos of her car. The security guard at the entrance to the Andersons' subdivision corroborated Maureen's account that Paul often lay in wait for her and that she was "visibly shaken and upset, almost to the point of tears," at least once. Maureen filed a suit in a Georgia state court against Paul, alleging, among other things, invasion of privacy. The court issued a summary judgment in Paul's favor on this charge. Maureen appealed to a state intermediate appellate court.

CASE CONTINUES

CASE 6.2 CONTINUED

- **Decision and Rationale** The state intermediate appellate court reversed the grant of summary judgment to Paul on Maureen's invasion of privacy claim. The court remanded the case for trial on the issue of whether Maureen was followed and photographed so frequently as to amount to an intrusion into her privacy. As the appellate court stated, "The right of privacy is embraced within the absolute rights of personal security and personal liberty * * *." The court stated that this was indeed a situation of intrusion upon seclusion or solitude. Unreasonable intrusion involves a prying or intrusion that would be offensive or objectionable to a reasonable person. Having one's photograph taken changes from a relatively harmless activity to a tortious one when there is repetition. Repeatedly following a pregnant woman and photographing her at least forty times "creates a jury question as to whether the defendant's actions amounted to a course of hounding the plaintiff that intruded upon her privacy."

- **What If the Facts Were Different?** *Suppose that Dick and Karyn had two children and Dick had been awarded custody of them. If Paul had been watching Maureen to determine her fitness to care for the children, would the result in this case have been different? Explain.*

- **The Legal Environment Dimension** *To succeed on a claim of intrusion into an individual's affairs or seclusion, should a plaintiff have to prove a physical intrusion? Why or why not?*

Appropriation

The use of another person's name, likeness, or other identifying characteristic, without permission and for the benefit of the user, constitutes the tort of **appropriation** (sometimes referred to as the *right of publicity*). Under the law, normally an individual's right to privacy includes the right to the exclusive use of his or her identity. For example, in one early case, Vanna White, the hostess of the popular *Wheel of Fortune* game show, brought a case against Samsung Electronics America, Inc. Without permission, Samsung had included in an advertisement a robotic image dressed in a wig, gown, and jewelry, in a setting that resembled the *Wheel of Fortune* set, in a stance for which White is famous. The court ruled in White's favor, holding that the tort of appropriation does not require the use of a celebrity's name or actual likeness. The court stated that Samsung's robot ad left "little doubt" as to the identity of the celebrity that the ad was meant to depict.[6]

Degree of Likeness In recent cases, courts have reached different conclusions as to the degree of likeness that is required to impose liability for the tort of appropriation. In one case, a former professional hockey player, Anthony "Tony" Twist, who had a reputation for fighting, sued the publishers of the comic book *Spawn*, which included an evil character named Anthony Tony Twist Twistelli. The Missouri Supreme Court held that the use of Tony Twist's name alone was sufficient proof of likeness to support a misappropriation claim.[7] Ultimately, the hockey player was awarded $15 million in damages.[8]

In California, in contrast, Keirin Kirby, the lead singer in a 1990s funk band called Deee-Lite, lost her appropriation claim against the makers of the video game *Space Channel 5*. Although the video game's character "Ulala" had some of Kirby's distinctive traits—hot pink hair, short skirt, platform shoes, and dance moves—there were not enough similarities, according to the state appellate court, to constitute misappropriation.[9]

Right of Publicity as a Property Right As mentioned, the common law tort of appropriation in many states has become known as the right of publicity.[10] Rather than being aimed at protecting a person's right to be left alone (privacy), this right aims to protect an individual's pecuniary (financial) interest in the commercial exploitation of his or her identity. In other words, it gives public figures, celebrities, and entertainers a right to sue anyone who uses their images for commercial benefit without their permission. Cases involving the right of publicity generally turn on whether the use was commercial. For instance, if a tel-

6. *White v. Samsung Electronics America, Inc.*, 971 F.2d 1395 (9th Cir. 1992).

7. *Doe v. TCI Cablevision*, 110 S.W.3d 363 (Mo. 2003).

8. The amount of damages was appealed and subsequently affirmed. See *Doe v. McFarlane*, 207 S.W.3d 52 (Mo.App. 2006).

9. *Kirby v. Sega of America, Inc.*, 144 Cal.App.4th 47, 50 Cal.Rptr.3d 607 (2006).

10. See, for example, California Civil Code Sections 3344 and 3344.1.

evision news program reports on a celebrity and shows an image of the person, the use likely would not be classified as commercial; in contrast, including the celebrity's image on a poster without his or her permission would be a commercial use.

Because the right of publicity is similar to a property right, most states have concluded that the right is inheritable and survives the death of the person who held the right. Normally, though, the person must provide for the passage of the right to another in her or his will. In 2007, for example, a court held that because Marilyn Monroe's will did not specifically state a desire to pass the right to publicity to her heirs, the beneficiaries under her will did not have a right to prevent a company from marketing T-shirts and other merchandise using Monroe's name, picture, and likeness.[11]

Fraudulent Misrepresentation

A misrepresentation leads another to believe in a condition that is different from the condition that actually exists. This is often accomplished through a false or an incorrect statement. Although persons sometimes make misrepresentations accidentally because they are unaware of the existing facts, the tort of **fraudulent misrepresentation,** or *fraud,* involves *intentional* deceit for personal gain. The tort includes several elements:

1. A misrepresentation of material facts or conditions with knowledge that they are false or with reckless disregard for the truth.
2. An intent to induce another party to rely on the misrepresentation.
3. A justifiable reliance on the misrepresentation by the deceived party.
4. Damages suffered as a result of that reliance.
5. A causal connection between the misrepresentation and the injury suffered.

For fraud to occur, more than mere **puffery,** or *seller's talk,* must be involved. Fraud exists only when a person represents as a fact something he or she knows is untrue. For example, it is fraud to claim that the roof of a building does not leak when one knows that it does. Facts are objectively ascertainable, whereas seller's talk—such as "I am the best accountant in town"—is not, because the speaker is representing a subjective view.

Normally, the tort of fraudulent misrepresentation occurs only when there is reliance on a *statement of fact.* Sometimes, however, reliance on a *statement of opinion* may involve the tort of fraudulent misrepresentation if the individual making the statement of opinion has superior knowledge of the subject matter. For example, when a lawyer makes a statement of opinion about the law in a state in which the lawyer is licensed to practice, a court would construe reliance on such a statement to be equivalent to reliance on a statement of fact.

Abusive or Frivolous Litigation

Persons or businesses generally have a right to sue when they have been injured. In recent years, however, an increasing number of meritless lawsuits have been filed—sometimes simply to harass the defendant. Defending oneself in any legal proceeding can be costly, time consuming, and emotionally draining. Tort law recognizes that people have a right not to be sued without a legally just and proper reason. It therefore protects individuals from the misuse of litigation. Torts related to abusive litigation include malicious prosecution and abuse of process.

If the party that initiated a lawsuit did so out of malice and without probable cause (a legitimate legal reason), and ended up losing that suit, the party can be sued for *malicious prosecution.* In some states, the plaintiff (who was the defendant in the first proceeding) must also prove injury other than the normal costs of litigation, such as lost profits. *Abuse of process* can apply to any person using a legal process against another in an improper manner or to accomplish a purpose for which the process was not designed. The key difference between the torts of abuse of process and malicious prosecution is the level of proof. Abuse of process does not require the plaintiff to prove malice or show that the defendant (who was previously the plaintiff) lost in a prior legal proceeding.[12] Abuse of process is also not limited to prior litigation. It can be based on the wrongful use of subpoenas, court orders to attach or seize real property, or other types of formal legal process. *Concept Summary 6.1* on the following page reviews intentional torts against persons.

11. *Shaw Family Archives, Ltd. v. CMG Worldwide, Inc.,* 486 F.Supp.2d 309 (S.D.N.Y. 2007), presented as Case 50.1.

12. *Bernhard-Thomas Building Systems, LLC v. Duncan,* 918 A.2d 889 (Conn.App. 2007); and *Hewitt v. Rice,* 154 P.3d 408 (Colo. 2007).

CONCEPT SUMMARY 6.1
Intentional Torts against Persons

Name of Tort	Description
Assault and Battery	Any unexcused and intentional act that causes another person to be apprehensive of immediate harm is an assault. An assault resulting in physical contact is battery.
False Imprisonment	An intentional confinement or restraint of another person's movement without justification.
Intentional Infliction of Emotional Distress	An intentional act that amounts to extreme and outrageous conduct resulting in severe emotional distress to another.
Defamation (Libel or Slander)	A false statement of fact, not made under privilege, that is communicated to a third person and that causes damage to a person's reputation. For public figures, the plaintiff must also prove that the statement was made with actual malice.
Invasion of Privacy	Publishing or otherwise making known or using information relating to a person's private life and affairs, with which the public has no legitimate concern, without that person's permission or approval.
Appropriation	The use of another person's name, likeness, or other identifying characteristic without permission and for the benefit of the user.
Fraudulent Misrepresentation (Fraud)	A false representation made by one party, through misstatement of facts or through conduct, with the intention of deceiving another and on which the other reasonably relies to his or her detriment.
Abusive Litigation	The filing of a lawsuit without legitimate grounds and with malice or the use of a legal process in an improper manner.

SECTION 3 Business Torts

Most torts can occur in any context, but a few torts, referred to as **business torts,** apply only to wrongful interferences with the business rights of others. Business torts generally fall into two categories—interference with a contractual relationship and interference with a business relationship.

Wrongful Interference with a Contractual Relationship

The body of tort law relating to *wrongful interference with a contractual relationship* has increased greatly in recent years. A landmark case in this area involved an opera singer, Joanna Wagner, who was under contract to sing for a man named Lumley for a specified period of years. A man named Gye, who knew of this contract, nonetheless "enticed" Wagner to refuse to carry out the agreement, and Wagner began to sing for Gye. Gye's action constituted a tort because it interfered with the contractual relationship between Wagner and Lumley. (Of course, Wagner's refusal to carry out the agreement also entitled Lumley to sue Wagner for breach of contract.)[13]

Three elements are necessary for wrongful interference with a contractual relationship to occur:

1. A valid, enforceable contract must exist between two parties.
2. A third party must know that this contract exists.
3. This third party must *intentionally induce* a party to the contract to breach the contract.

In principle, any lawful contract can be the basis for an action of this type. The contract could be between a firm and its employees or a firm and its customers. Sometimes, a competitor of a firm draws away one of the firm's key employees. Only if the original employer can show that the competitor knew of the contract's existence, and intentionally induced the breach, can damages be recovered from the competitor.

13. *Lumley v. Gye*, 118 Eng.Rep. 749 (1853).

Wrongful Interference with a Business Relationship

Businesspersons devise countless schemes to attract customers, but they are prohibited from unreasonably interfering with another's business in their attempts to gain a greater share of the market. There is a difference between *competitive practices* and *predatory behavior*—actions undertaken with the intention of unlawfully driving competitors completely out of the market.

Attempting to attract customers in general is a legitimate business practice, whereas specifically targeting the customers of a competitor is more likely to be predatory. For example, the mall contains two athletic shoe stores: Joe's and Sprint. Joe's cannot station an employee at the entrance of Sprint to divert customers to Joe's and tell them that Joe's will beat Sprint's prices. Doing this would constitute the tort of wrongful interference with a business relationship because it would interfere with a prospective (economic) advantage; such behavior is commonly considered to be an unfair trade practice. If this type of activity were permitted, Joe's would reap the benefits of Sprint's advertising.

Although state laws vary on wrongful interference with a business relationship, generally a plaintiff must prove that the defendant used predatory methods to intentionally harm an established business relationship or prospective economic advantage. The plaintiff must also prove that the defendant's interference caused the plaintiff to suffer economic harm.

Defenses to Wrongful Interference

A person will not be liable for the tort of wrongful interference with a contractual or business relationship if it can be shown that the interference was justified, or permissible. Bona fide competitive behavior is a permissible interference even if it results in the breaking of a contract.

For example, if Jerrod's Meats advertises so effectively that it induces Sam's Restaurant to break its contract with Burke's Meat Company, Burke's Meat Company will be unable to recover against Jerrod's Meats on a wrongful interference theory. After all, the public policy that favors free competition through advertising outweighs any possible instability that such competitive activity might cause in contractual relations. Although luring customers away from a competitor through aggressive marketing and advertising strategies obviously interferes with the competitor's relationship with its customers, courts typically allow such activities in the spirit of competition.

SECTION 4 Intentional Torts against Property

Intentional torts against property include trespass to land, trespass to personal property, conversion, and disparagement of property. These torts are wrongful actions that interfere with individuals' legally recognized rights with regard to their land or personal property. The law distinguishes real property from personal property (see Chapter 47). *Real property* is land and things permanently attached to the land. *Personal property* consists of all other items, which are basically movable. Thus, a house and lot are real property, whereas the furniture inside a house is personal property. Cash and securities are also personal property.

Trespass to Land

The tort of **trespass to land** occurs any time a person, without permission, enters onto, above, or below the surface of land that is owned by another; causes anything to enter onto the land; or remains on the land or permits anything to remain on it. Actual harm to the land is not an essential element of this tort because the tort is designed to protect the right of an owner to exclusive possession. Common types of trespass to land include walking or driving on another's land; shooting a gun over another's land; throwing rocks at or spraying water on a building that belongs to someone else; building a dam across a river, thereby causing water to back up on someone else's land; and constructing one's building so that it extends onto an adjoining landowner's property.

Trespass Criteria, Rights, and Duties

Before a person can be a trespasser, the real property owner (or other person in actual and exclusive possession of the property, such as a person who is leasing the property) must establish that person as a trespasser. For example, "posted" trespass signs expressly establish as a trespasser a person who ignores these signs and enters onto the property. Any person who enters onto another's property to commit an illegal act (such as a thief entering a lumberyard at night to steal lumber) is established impliedly as a trespasser, without posted signs.

At common law, a trespasser is liable for damages caused to the property and generally cannot hold the owner liable for injuries that the trespasser sustains on the premises. This common law rule is being abandoned in many jurisdictions, however, in favor of a "reasonable duty" rule that varies depending on the status of the parties. For example, a landowner may have a duty to post a notice that the property is patrolled by guard dogs. Also, under the "attractive nuisance" doctrine, a landowner may be held liable for injuries sustained by young children on the landowner's property if the children were attracted to the premises by some object, such as a swimming pool or an abandoned building. Finally, an owner can remove a trespasser from the premises—or detain a trespasser on the premises for a reasonable time—through the use of reasonable force without being liable for assault, battery, or false imprisonment.

Defenses against Trespass to Land

Trespass to land involves wrongful interference with another person's real property rights. If it can be shown that the trespass was warranted, however, as when a trespasser enters to assist someone in danger, a defense exists. Another defense exists when the trespasser can show that he or she had a license to come onto the land. A *licensee* is one who is invited (or allowed to enter) onto the property of another for the licensee's benefit. A person who enters another's property to read an electric meter, for example, is a licensee. When you purchase a ticket to attend a movie or sporting event, you are licensed to go onto the property of another to view that movie or event. Note that licenses to enter onto another's property are *revocable* by the property owner. If a property owner asks a meter reader to leave and the meter reader refuses to do so, the meter reader at that point becomes a trespasser.

Trespass to Personal Property

Whenever any individual, without consent, takes or harms the personal property of another or otherwise interferes with the lawful owner's possession and enjoyment of personal property, **trespass to personal property** occurs. This tort may also be called *trespass to chattels* or *trespass to personalty.* In this context, harm means not only destruction of the property, but also anything that diminishes its value, condition, or quality. Trespass to personal property involves intentional meddling with a possessory interest (an interest arising from possession), including barring an owner's access to personal property. If Kelly takes Ryan's business law book as a practical joke and hides it so that Ryan is unable to find it for several days prior to the final examination, Kelly has engaged in a trespass to personal property.

If it can be shown that trespass to personal property was warranted, then a complete defense exists. Most states, for example, allow automobile repair shops to hold a customer's car (under what is called an *artisan's lien,* discussed in Chapter 28) when the customer refuses to pay for repairs already completed.

Conversion

Whenever a person wrongfully possesses or uses the personal property of another as if the property belonged to her or him, the tort of **conversion** occurs. Any act that deprives an owner of personal property or of the use of that property without that owner's permission and without just cause can be conversion. Often, when conversion occurs, a trespass to personal property also occurs because the original taking of the personal property from the owner was a trespass, and wrongfully retaining it is conversion. Conversion requires a more serious interference with the personal property than trespass, in terms of the duration and extensiveness of use.

Conversion is the civil side of crimes related to theft, but it is not limited to theft. Even when the rightful owner consented to the initial taking of the property so there was no theft or trespass, a failure to return the personal property may still be conversion. For example, Chen borrows Marik's iPod to use while traveling home from school for the holidays. When Chen returns to school, Marik asks for his iPod back, but Chen says that he gave it to his little brother for Christmas. In this situation, Marik can sue Chen for conversion, and Chen will have to either return the iPod or pay damages equal to its value.

Similarly, even if a person mistakenly believed that she or he was entitled to the goods, a tort of conversion may still have occurred. In other words, good intentions are not a defense against conversion; in fact, conversion can be an entirely innocent act. Someone who buys stolen goods, for example, has committed the tort of conversion even if he or she did not know the goods were stolen. Note that even the taking of electronic records and data may form the basis of a common law conversion claim.[14] So can the wrongful taking of a

14. See *Thyroff v. Nationwide Mutual Insurance Co.,* 8 N.Y.3d 283, 864 N.E.2d 1272 (2007).

domain name.[15] Thus, the personal property need not be tangible (physical) property.

Disparagement of Property

Disparagement of property occurs when economically injurious falsehoods are made about another's product or property rather than about another's reputation (as in the tort of defamation). *Disparagement of property* is a general term for torts that can be more specifically referred to as *slander of quality* or *slander of title*.

Slander of Quality Publishing false information about another's product, alleging it is not what its seller claims, constitutes the tort of **slander of quality,** or **trade libel.** The plaintiff must prove that actual damages proximately resulted from the slander of quality. In other words, the plaintiff must show not only that a third person refrained from dealing with the plaintiff because of the improper publication but also that the plaintiff suffered damages because the third person refrained from dealing with him or her. The economic calculation of such damages—they are, after all, conjectural—is often extremely difficult.

An improper publication may be both a slander of quality and a defamation of character. For example, a statement that disparages the quality of a product may also, by implication, disparage the character of a person who would sell such a product.

15. See *Kremen v. Cohen,* 325 F.3d 1035 (9th Cir. 2003).

Slander of Title When a publication falsely denies or casts doubt on another's legal ownership of property, resulting in financial loss to the property's owner, the tort of **slander of title** occurs. Usually, this is an intentional tort in which someone knowingly publishes an untrue statement about another's ownership of certain property with the intent of discouraging a third person from dealing with the person slandered. For example, it would be difficult for a car dealer to attract customers after competitors published a notice that the dealer's stock consisted of stolen autos. See Concept Summary 6.2 for a review of intentional torts against property.

SECTION 5

Cyber Torts

Torts can also be committed in the online environment. Torts committed via the Internet are often called **cyber torts.** Over the years, the courts have had to decide how to apply traditional tort law to torts committed in cyberspace. Consider, for example, issues of proof. How can it be proved that an online defamatory remark was "published" (which requires that a third party see or hear it)? How can the identity of the person who made the remark be discovered? Can an Internet service provider (ISP), such as America Online, Inc. (AOL), be forced to reveal the source of an anonymous comment? We explore some of these questions in this section, as well as some legal issues that have arisen with respect to bulk e-mail advertising.

CONCEPT SUMMARY 6.2
Intentional Torts against Property

Name of Tort	Description
TRESPASS TO LAND	The invasion of another's real property without consent or privilege. Once a person is expressly or impliedly established as a trespasser, the property owner has specific rights, which may include the right to detain or remove the trespasser.
TRESPASS TO PERSONAL PROPERTY	The intentional interference with an owner's right to use, possess, or enjoy his or her personal property without the owner's consent.
CONVERSION	The wrongful possession or use of another person's personal property without just cause.
DISPARAGEMENT OF PROPERTY	Any economically injurious falsehood that is made about another's product or property; an inclusive term for the torts of *slander of quality* and *slander of title.*

Defamation Online

Recall from the discussion of defamation earlier in this chapter that one who repeats or otherwise republishes a defamatory statement is subject to liability as if he or she had originally published it. Thus, publishers generally can be held liable for defamatory contents in the books and periodicals that they publish. Now consider online message forums. These forums allow anyone—customers, employees, or crackpots—to complain about a business firm's personnel, policies, practices, or products. Regardless of whether the complaint is justified and whether it is true, it might have an impact on the firm's business. One of the early questions in the online legal arena was whether the providers of such forums could be held liable, as publishers, for defamatory statements made in those forums.

Immunity of Internet Service Providers

Newspapers, magazines, and television and radio stations may be held liable for defamatory remarks that they disseminate, even if those remarks are prepared or created by others. Prior to the passage of the Communications Decency Act (CDA) of 1996, the courts grappled on several occasions with the question of whether ISPs should be regarded as publishers and thus be held liable for defamatory messages made by users of their services. The CDA resolved the issue by stating that "[n]o provider or user of an interactive computer service shall be treated as the publisher or speaker of any information provided by another information content provider."[16] In other words, Internet publishers are treated differently from publishers in print, television, and radio, and are not liable for publishing defamatory statements, provided that the material came from a third party.

In a leading case on this issue, decided the year after the CDA was enacted, America Online, Inc. (AOL, now part of Time Warner, Inc.), was not held liable even though it failed to promptly remove defamatory messages of which it had been made aware. In upholding a district court's ruling in AOL's favor, a federal appellate court stated that the CDA "plainly immunizes computer service providers like AOL from liability for information that originates with third parties." The court explained that the purpose of the statute is "to maintain the robust nature of Internet communication and, accordingly, to keep government interference in the medium to a minimum."[17] The courts have reached similar conclusions in subsequent cases, extending the CDA's immunity to Web message boards, online auction houses, Internet dating services, and any business that provides e-mail and Web browsing services.[18]

In the following case, the court considered the scope of immunity that could be accorded to an online roommate-matching service under the CDA.

16. 47 U.S.C. Section 230.

17. *Zeran v. America Online, Inc.*, 129 F.3d 327 (4th Cir. 1997); *cert.* denied, 524 U.S. 937, 118 S.Ct. 2341, 141 L.Ed.2d 712 (1998).

18. See *Universal Communications Systems, Inc. v. Lycos, Inc.*, 478 F.3d 413 (1st Cir. 2007); *Barrett v. Rosenthal*, 40 Cal.4th 33, 51 Cal.Rptr.3d 55 (2006); *Delfino v. Agilent Technologies, Inc.*, 145 Cal.App. 4th 790, 52 Cal.Rptr.3d 376 (2006); *Noah v. AOL Time Warner, Inc.*, 261 F.Supp.2d 532 (E.D.Va. 2003); and *Carafano v. Metrosplash.com, Inc.*, 339 F.3d 1119 (9th Cir. 2003).

CASE 6.3 Fair Housing Council of San Fernando Valley v. Roommate.com, LLC

United States Court of Appeals, Ninth Circuit, 2008. 521 F.3d 1157.

• **Background and Facts** Roommate.com, LLC (Roommate), operates an online roommate-matching Web site at **www.roommates.com**. The site helps individuals find roommates based on their descriptions of themselves and their roommate preferences. Roommate has approximately 150,000 active listings and receives about a million user views per day. To become members of Roommate, users respond to a series of online questions, choosing from answers in drop-down and select-a-box menus. Users disclose information about themselves and their roommate preferences based on age, gender, and other characteristics, as well as on whether children will live in the household. Members can create personal profiles, search lists of compatible roommates, and send "roommail" messages to other members. Roommate also e-mails newsletters to members seeking housing, listing compatible members who have places to rent. The Fair Housing Councils of San Fernando Valley and San Diego, California, filed a suit in a federal district court against Roommate, claiming that the defendant violated the Fair Housing Act (FHA) by asking for and distributing the information in its member profiles. The court held that the Communications Decency Act (CDA) barred this claim and dismissed it. The councils appealed to the U.S. Court of Appeals for the Ninth Circuit.

CASE 6.3 CONTINUED • **Decision and Rationale** The U.S. Court of Appeals for the Ninth Circuit concluded that the CDA does not provide immunity to Roommate for all of the content of its Web site and e-mail newsletters. "Roommate[s] created the questions and choice of answers, and designed its Web site registration process around them." Therefore, Roommate is "the 'information content provider' as to the questions and can claim no immunity for posting them on its Web site, or for forcing subscribers to answer them as a condition of using its services." Because Roommate forced subscribers to answer questions in which they divulged protected characteristics, it was responsible, at least in part, for the development of the content and could be held liable for any unlawful content. The court noted that asking questions "certainly can violate the Fair Housing Act and analogous laws in the physical world" and reasoned that illegal questions "don't magically become lawful when asked electronically online." The appellate court reversed the lower court's dismissal and remanded the case to the lower court to determine "whether the alleged actions for which Roommate is not immune violated the Fair Housing Act."

• **The Ethical Dimension** *Do Internet service providers have an ethical duty to advise their users if the information that the users provide for distribution through the Internet service providers might violate the law? Explain.*

• **The E-Commerce Dimension** *Should the courts continue to regard the CDA's grant of immunity to Internet service providers as vigorously as in the past? Why or why not?*

Piercing the Veil of Anonymity A threshold barrier to anyone who seeks to bring an action for online defamation is discovering the identity of the person who posted the defamatory message online. ISPs can disclose personal information about their customers only when ordered to do so by a court. Consequently, businesses and individuals often resort to filing lawsuits against "John Does" (John Doe is a fictitious name that is used when the name of the particular person is not known). Then, using the authority of the courts, they attempt to obtain from the ISPs the identities of the persons responsible for the messages. This strategy has worked in some cases,[19] but not in others.[20] Courts typically are reluctant to deter those who would potentially post messages on the Internet from exercising their First Amendment right to speak anonymously. After all, speaking anonymously is part of the nature of the Internet and helps to make it a useful forum for public discussion.

Spam

Bulk, unsolicited e-mail ("junk" e-mail) sent to all of the users on a particular e-mailing list or all of the members of a newsgroup is often called **spam.**[21] Typically, spam consists of product ads. Spam can waste user time and network bandwidth (the amount of data that can be transmitted within a certain time). It also imposes a burden on an ISP's equipment as well as on an e-mail recipient's computer system.[22] Because of the problems associated with spam, the majority of states now have laws regulating its transmission. In 2003, the U.S. Congress also enacted a law to regulate the use of spam, although the volume of spam has actually increased since the law was enacted.

Statutory Regulation of Spam In an attempt to combat spam, thirty-six states have enacted laws that prohibit or regulate its use. Many state laws regulating spam require the senders of e-mail ads to instruct the recipients on how they can "opt out" of further e-mail ads from the same sources. For instance, in some states an unsolicited e-mail ad must include a toll-free phone number or return e-mail address through which the recipient can contact the sender to request that no more ads be e-mailed. The most stringent state law is California's antispam law, which went into effect on January 1, 2004. That law follows the "opt-in" model favored by consumer groups and antispam advocates. In other words, the law prohibits any person or business from sending e-mail ads to or from any e-mail address in California unless the recipient has

19. *Does v. Hvide,* 770 So.2d 1237 (Fla.App.3d 2000).

20. See, for example, *Doe v. Cahill,* 884 A.2d 451 (Del.Supr. 2005); and *Dendrite International, Inc. v. Doe No. 3,* 342 N.J.Super. 134, 775 A.2d 756 (2001).

21. The term *spam* is said to come from a Monty Python song with the lyrics, "Spam spam spam spam, spam spam spam spam, lovely spam, wonderful spam." Like these lyrics, spam online is often considered to be a repetition of worthless text.

22. For an early case in which a court found that spam constituted a trespass to personal property because of the burden on the ISP's equipment, see *CompuServe, Inc. v. Cyber Promotions, Inc.,* 962 F.Supp. 1015 (S.D. Ohio 1997).

expressly agreed to receive e-mails from the sender. An exemption is made for e-mail sent to consumers with whom the advertiser has a "preexisting or current business relationship."

The Federal CAN-SPAM Act In 2003, Congress enacted the Controlling the Assault of Non-Solicited Pornography and Marketing (CAN-SPAM) Act, which took effect on January 1, 2004. The legislation applies to any "commercial electronic mail messages" that are sent to promote a commercial product or service. Significantly, the statute preempts state antispam laws except for those provisions in state laws that prohibit false and deceptive e-mailing practices.

Generally, the act permits the use of unsolicited commercial e-mail but prohibits certain types of spamming activities, including the use of a false return address and the use of false, misleading, or deceptive information when sending e-mail. The statute also prohibits the use of "dictionary attacks"—sending messages to randomly generated e-mail addresses—and the "harvesting" of e-mail addresses from Web sites through the use of specialized software. Notwithstanding the requirements of the federal act, the reality is that the problem of spam is difficult to address because much of it is funneled through foreign servers.

REVIEWING Intentional Torts

Two sisters, Darla and Irene, are partners in an import business located in a small town in Rhode Island. Irene is married to a well-known real estate developer and is campaigning to be the mayor of their town. Darla is in her mid-thirties and has never been married. Both sisters travel to other countries to purchase the goods they sell at their retail store. Irene buys Indonesian goods, and Darla buys goods from Africa. After a tsunami (tidal wave) destroys many of the cities in Indonesia to which Irene usually travels, she phones one of her contacts there and asks him to procure some items and ship them to her. He informs her that it will be impossible to buy these items now because the townspeople are being evacuated due to a water shortage. Irene is angry and tells the man that if he cannot purchase the goods, he should just take them without paying for them after the town has been evacuated. Darla overhears her sister's instructions and is outraged. They have a falling-out, and Darla decides that she no longer wishes to be in business with her sister. Using the information presented in the chapter, answer the following questions.

1. Suppose that Darla tells several of her friends about Irene's instructing the man to take goods without paying for them after the tsunami disaster. Under which intentional tort theory discussed in this chapter might Irene attempt to sue Darla? Would Irene's suit be successful? Why or why not?
2. Now suppose that Irene wins the election and becomes the city's mayor. Darla then writes a letter to the editor of the local newspaper disclosing Irene's misconduct. What intentional tort might Irene accuse Darla of committing? What defenses could Darla assert?
3. If Irene accepts goods shipped from Indonesia that were wrongfully obtained, has she committed an intentional tort against property? Explain.
4. Suppose now that Irene, who is angry with her sister for disclosing her business improprieties, writes a letter to the editor falsely accusing Darla of having sexual relations with her neighbor's thirteen-year-old son. For what intentional tort or torts could Darla sue Irene in this situation?

TERMS AND CONCEPTS

QUESTIONS AND CASE PROBLEMS

6–1. Richard is an employee of the Dun Construction Corp. While delivering materials to a construction site, he carelessly backs Dun's truck into a passenger vehicle driven by Green. This is Richard's second accident in six months. When the company owner, Dun, learns of this latest accident, a heated discussion ensues, and Dun fires Richard. Dun is so angry that he immediately writes a letter to the union of which Richard is a member and to all other construction companies in the community, stating that Richard is the "worst driver in the city" and that "anyone who hires him is asking for legal liability." Richard files a suit against Dun, alleging libel on the basis of the statements made in the letters. Discuss the results.

6–2. QUESTION WITH SAMPLE ANSWER

Lothar owns a bakery. He has been trying to obtain a long-term contract with the owner of Martha's Tea Salons for some time. Lothar starts a local advertising campaign on radio and television and in the newspaper. This advertising campaign is so persuasive that Martha decides to break the contract she has had with Harley's Bakery so that she can patronize Lothar's bakery. Is Lothar liable to Harley's Bakery for the tort of wrongful interference with a contractual relationship? Is Martha liable for this tort?

- **For a sample answer to Question 6–2, go to Appendix I at the end of this text.**

6–3. Gerrit is a former employee of ABC Auto Repair Co. He enters ABC's repair shop, claiming that the company owes him $800 in back wages. Gerrit argues with ABC's general manager, Steward, and Steward orders him off the property. Gerrit refuses to leave, and Steward tells two mechanics to throw him off the property. Gerrit runs to his truck, but on the way, he grabs some tools valued at $800; then he drives away. Gerrit refuses to return the tools.

(a) Discuss whether Gerrit has committed any torts.
(b) If the mechanics had thrown Gerrit off the property, would ABC be guilty of assault and battery? Explain.

6–4. Bombardier Capital, Inc., provides financing to boat and recreational vehicle dealers. Bombardier's credit policy requires dealers to forward immediately to Bombardier the proceeds of boat sales. When Howard Mulcahey, Bombardier's vice president of sales and marketing, learned that dealers were not complying with this policy, he told Frank Chandler, Bombardier's credit director, of his concern. Before Chandler could obtain the proceeds, Mulcahey falsely told Jacques Gingras, Bombardier's president, that Chandler was, among other things, trying to hide the problem. On the basis of Mulcahey's statements, Gingras fired Chandler and put Mulcahey in charge of the credit department. Under what business tort theory discussed in this chapter might Chandler recover damages from Mulcahey? Explain.

6–5. Trespass to Property. America Online, Inc. (AOL), provides services to its customers or members, including the transmission of e-mail to and from other members and across the Internet. To become a member, a person must agree not to use AOL's computers to send bulk, unsolicited, commercial e-mail (spam). AOL uses filters to block spam, but bulk e-mailers sometimes use other software to thwart the filters. National Health Care Discount, Inc. (NHCD), sells discount optical and dental service plans. To generate leads for NHCD's products, sales representatives, who included AOL members, sent more than 300 million pieces of spam through AOL's computer system. Each item cost AOL an estimated $0.00078 in equipment expenses. Some of the spam used false headers and other methods to hide the source. After receiving more than 150,000 complaints from its members, AOL asked NHCD to stop. When the spam continued, AOL filed a suit in a federal district court against NHCD, alleging, in part, trespass to chattels—an unlawful interference with another's rights to possess personal property. AOL asked the court for a summary judgment on this claim. Did the spamming constitute trespass to chattels? Explain. [*America Online, Inc. v. National Health Care Discount, Inc.*, 121 F.Supp.2d 1255 (N.D. Iowa 2000)]

6–6. Intentional Torts against Property. In 1994, Gary Kremen registered the domain name "sex.com" with Network Solutions, Inc., to the name of Kremen's business, Online Classifieds. Later, Stephen Cohen sent Network Solutions a letter that he claimed to have received from Online Classifieds. It stated that "we have no objections to your use of the domain name sex.com and this letter shall serve as our authorization to the Internet registrar to transfer sex.com to your corporation." Without contacting Kremen, Network Solutions transferred the name to Cohen, who subsequently turned sex.com into a lucrative business. Kremen filed a suit in a federal district court against Cohen and others, seeking the name and Cohen's profits. The court ordered Cohen to return the name to Kremen and pay $65 million in damages. Cohen ignored the order and disappeared. Against what other parties might Kremen attempt to obtain relief? Under which theory of intentional torts against property might Kremen be able to file an action? What is the likely result, and why? [*Kremen v. Cohen*, 337 F.3d 1024 (9th Cir. 2003)]

6–7. Invasion of Privacy. During the spring and summer of 1999, Edward and Geneva Irvine received numerous "hang-up" phone calls, including three calls in the middle of the night. With the help of their local phone company, the Irvines learned that many of the calls were from the telemarketing department of the *Akron Beacon Journal* in Akron, Ohio. The *Beacon*'s sales force was equipped with an automatic dialing machine. During business hours, the dialer was used to maximize productivity by calling multiple phone numbers at once and connecting a call to a sales representative only after it was answered. After business hours, the *Beacon* programmed its dialer to dial a list of disconnected numbers to determine whether they had been reconnected. If the dialer detected a ring, it recorded the information and dropped the call. If the automated dialing system crashed, which it did frequently, it redialed the entire list. The Irvines filed a suit in an Ohio state court against the *Beacon* and others, alleging, among other things, an invasion of privacy. In whose favor should the court rule, and why? [*Irvine v. Akron Beacon Journal*, 147 Ohio App.3d 428, 770 N.E.2d 1105 (9 Dist. 2002)]

6–8. Defamation. Lydia Hagberg went to her bank, California Federal Bank, FSB, to cash a check made out to her by Smith Barney (SB), an investment services firm. Nolene Showalter, a bank employee, suspected that the check was counterfeit. Showalter called SB and was told that the check was not valid. As she phoned the police, Gary Wood, a bank security officer, contacted SB again and was informed that its earlier statement was "erroneous" and that the check was valid. Meanwhile, a police officer arrived, drew Hagberg away from the teller's window, spread her legs, patted her down, and handcuffed her. The officer searched her purse, asked her whether she had any weapons or stolen property and whether she was driving a stolen vehicle, and arrested her. Hagberg filed a suit in a California state court against the bank and others, alleging, among other things, slander. Should the absolute privilege for communications made in judicial or other official proceedings apply to statements made when a citizen contacts the police to report suspected criminal activity? Why or why not? [*Hagberg v. California Federal Bank*, FSB, 32 Cal.4th 350, 81 P.3d 244, 7 Cal.Rptr.3d 803 (2004)]

6–9. CASE PROBLEM WITH SAMPLE ANSWER

Between 1996 and 1998, Donna Swanson received several anonymous, handwritten letters that, among other things, accused her husband, Alan, of infidelity. In 1998, John Grisham, Jr., the author of *The Firm* and many other best-selling novels, received an anonymous letter that appeared to have been written by the same person. Grisham and the Swansons suspected Katherine Almy, who soon filed a suit in a Virginia state court against them, alleging, among other things, intentional infliction of emotional distress. According to Almy, Grisham intended to have her "really, really, suffer" for writing the letters, and the three devised a scheme to falsely accuse her. They gave David Liebman, a handwriting analyst, samples of Almy's handwriting. These included copies of confidential documents from her children's files at St. Anne's–Belfield School in Charlottesville, Virginia, where Alan taught and Grisham served on the board of directors. In Almy's view, Grisham influenced Liebman to report that Almy might have written the letters and misrepresented this report as conclusive, which led the police to confront Almy. She claimed that she then suffered severe emotional distress and depression, causing "a complete disintegration of virtually every aspect of her life" and requiring her "to undergo extensive therapy." In response, the defendants asked the court to dismiss the complaint for failure to state a claim. Should the court grant this request? Explain. [*Almy v. Grisham*, 273 Va. 68, 639 S.E.2d 182 (2007)]

- **To view a sample answer for Problem 6–9,**

go to this book's Web site at www.cengage.com/blaw/jentz, select "Chapter 6," and click on "Case Problem with Sample Answer."

6-10. A QUESTION OF ETHICS

*White Plains Coat & Apron Co. is a New York–based linen rental business. Cintas Corp. is a nationwide business that rents similar products. White Plains had five-year exclusive contracts with some of its customers. As a result of Cintas's soliciting of business, dozens of White Plains' customers breached their contracts and entered into rental agreements with Cintas. White Plains demanded that Cintas stop its solicitation of White Plains' customers. Cintas refused. White Plains filed a suit in a federal district court against Cintas, alleging wrongful interference with existing contracts. Cintas argued that it had no knowledge of any contracts with White Plains and had not induced any breach. The court dismissed the suit, ruling that Cintas had a legitimate interest as a competitor to solicit business and make a profit. White Plains appealed to the U.S. Court of Appeals for the Second Circuit. [*White Plains Coat & Apron Co. v. Cintas Corp.*, 8 N.Y.3d 422, 867 N.E.2d 381 (2007)]*

(a) What are the two important policy interests at odds in wrongful interference cases? When there is an existing contract, which of these interests should be accorded priority?

(b) The U.S. Court of Appeals for the Second Circuit asked the New York Court of Appeals to answer a question: Is a general interest in soliciting business for profit a sufficient defense to a claim of wrongful interference with a contractual relationship? What do you think? Why?

LAW ON THE WEB

For updated links to resources available on the Web, as well as a variety of other materials, visit this text's Web site at

www.cengage.com/blaw/jentz

You can find cases and articles on torts, including business torts, in the tort law library at the Internet Law Library's Web site. Go to

www.lawguru.com/ilawlib

Legal Research Exercises on the Web

Go to **www.cengage.com/blaw/jentz**, the Web site that accompanies this text. Select "Chapter 6" and click on "Internet Exercises." There you will find the following Internet research exercises that you can perform to learn more about the topics covered in this chapter.

Internet Exercise 6–1: Legal Perspective
Online Defamation

Internet Exercise 6–2: Management Perspective
Legal and Illegal Uses of Spam

CHAPTER 7

Negligence and Strict Liability

The intentional torts discussed in Chapter 6 all involve acts that the tortfeasor (the one committing the tort) intended to commit. In this chapter, we examine the tort of negligence, which involves acts that depart from a reasonable standard of care and therefore create an unreasonable risk of harm to others. Negligence suits are probably the most prevalent type of lawsuits brought against businesses today. It is therefore essential that businesspersons understand their potential liability for negligent acts. In the concluding pages of this chapter, we also look at another basis for liability in tort—*strict liability*. Under this tort doctrine, liability does not depend on the actor's negligence or intent to harm, but on the breach of an absolute duty to make something safe.

SECTION 1 Negligence

In contrast to intentional torts, in torts involving **negligence,** the tortfeasor neither wishes to bring about the consequences of the act nor believes that they will occur. The actor's conduct merely creates a risk of such consequences. If no risk is created, there is no negligence. Moreover, the risk must be foreseeable; that is, it must be such that a reasonable person engaging in the same activity would anticipate the risk and guard against it. In determining what is reasonable conduct, courts consider the nature of the possible harm. Creating a very slight risk of a dangerous explosion might be unreasonable, whereas creating a distinct possibility of someone's burning his or her fingers on a stove might be reasonable.

Many of the actions discussed in the chapter on intentional torts constitute negligence if the element of intent is missing (or cannot be proved). Suppose that Juarez walks up to Natsuyo and intentionally shoves her. Natsuyo falls and breaks her arm as a result. In this situation, Juarez has committed an intentional tort (battery). If Juarez carelessly bumps into Natsuyo, however, and she falls and breaks her arm as a result, Juarez's action constitutes negligence. In either situation, Juarez has committed a tort.

To succeed in a negligence action, the plaintiff must prove each of the following:

1. That the defendant owed a duty of care to the plaintiff.
2. That the defendant breached that duty.
3. That the plaintiff suffered a legally recognizable injury.
4. That the defendant's breach caused the plaintiff's injury.

We discuss here each of these four elements of negligence.

The Duty of Care and Its Breach

Central to the tort of negligence is the concept of a **duty of care.** This concept arises from the notion that if we are to live in society with other people, some actions can be tolerated and some cannot, and some actions are reasonable and some are not. The basic principle underlying the duty of care is that people are free to act as they please so long as their actions do not infringe on the interests of others.

When someone fails to comply with the duty to exercise reasonable care, a potentially tortious act may have been committed. Failure to live up to a standard of care may be an act (setting fire to a building) or an omission (neglecting to put out a campfire). It may be a careless act or a carefully performed but nevertheless dangerous act that results in injury. Courts consider the nature of the act (whether it is outrageous or commonplace), the manner in which the act is performed (heedlessly versus cautiously), and the nature of the injury (whether it is serious or slight) in determining whether the duty of care has been breached.

The Reasonable Person Standard Tort law measures duty by the **reasonable person standard.** In determining whether a duty of care has been breached, for example, the courts ask how a reasonable person would have acted in the same circumstances. The reasonable person standard is said to be (though in an absolute sense it cannot be) objective. It is not necessarily how a particular person *would* act. It is society's judgment of how an ordinarily prudent person *should* act. If the so-called reasonable person existed, he or she would be careful, conscientious, even tempered, and honest. That individuals are required to exercise a reasonable standard of care in their activities is a pervasive concept in business law, and many of the issues discussed in subsequent chapters of this text have to do with this duty.

In negligence cases, the degree of care to be exercised varies, depending on the defendant's occupation or profession, her or his relationship with the plaintiff, and other factors. Generally, whether an action constitutes a breach of the duty of care is determined on a case-by-case basis. The outcome depends on how the judge (or jury, if it is a jury trial) decides a reasonable person in the position of the defendant would act in the particular circumstances of the case. In the following subsections, we examine the degree of care typically expected of landowners and professionals.

The Duty of Landowners Landowners are expected to exercise reasonable care to protect individuals coming onto their property from harm. In some jurisdictions, landowners may even have a duty to protect trespassers against certain risks. Landowners who rent or lease premises to tenants are expected to exercise reasonable care to ensure that the tenants and their guests are not harmed in common areas, such as stairways, entryways, and laundry rooms (see Chapter 48).

Duty to Warn Business Invitees of Risks. Retailers and other firms that explicitly or implicitly invite persons to come onto their premises are usually charged with a duty to exercise reasonable care to protect these **business invitees.** For example, if you entered a supermarket, slipped on a wet floor, and sustained injuries as a result, the owner of the supermarket would be liable for damages if, when you slipped, there was no sign warning that the floor was wet. A court would hold that the business owner was negligent because the owner failed to exercise a reasonable degree of care in protecting the store's customers against foreseeable risks about which the owner knew or *should have known.* That a patron might slip on the wet floor and be injured as a result was a foreseeable risk, and the owner should have taken care to avoid this risk or warn the customer of it.[1]

Obvious Risks Provide an Exception. Some risks, of course, are so obvious that an owner need not warn of them. For example, a business owner does not need to warn customers to open a door before attempting to walk through it. Other risks, however, even though they may seem obvious to a business owner, may not be so in the eyes of another, such as a child. For example, a hardware store owner may not think it is necessary to warn customers that, if climbed, a stepladder leaning against the back wall of the store could fall down and harm them. It is possible, though, that a child could tip the ladder over while climbing it and be hurt as a result.

The issue in the following case was whether the obviousness of the existence of wet napkins on the floor of a nightclub obviated the owner's duty to its customers to maintain the premises in a safe condition.

1. A business owner can warn of a risk in a number of ways; for example, to warn of a hole in the business's parking lot, the owner could place a sign, traffic cone, sawhorse, board, or the like near the hole.

CASE 7.1 Izquierdo v. Gyroscope, Inc.

District Court of Appeal of Florida, Fourth District, 2007. 946 So.2d 115.

Background and Facts Giorgio's Grill in Hollywood, Florida, is a restaurant that becomes a nightclub after hours. At those times, traditionally, as Giorgio's manager knew, the wait staff and

CASE CONTINUES

CASE 7.1 CONTINUED customers threw paper napkins into the air as the music played. The napkins landed on the floor, but no one picked them up. If they became too deep, customers pushed them to the side. Because drinks were occasionally spilled, sometimes the napkins were wet. One night, Jane Izquierdo went to Giorgio's to meet a friend. She had been to the club five or six times and knew of the napkin-throwing tradition. She had one drink and went to the restroom. On her return, she slipped and fell, breaking her leg. After surgery, she relied on a wheelchair for three months and continued to suffer pain. She filed a suit in a Florida state court against Gyroscope, Inc., the owner of Giorgio's, alleging negligence. A jury returned a verdict in favor of the defendant, and Izquierdo filed a motion for a new trial, which the court denied. She appealed to a state intermediate appellate court.

• **Decision and Rationale** The state intermediate appellate court reversed the lower court's decision, concluding that "the trial court abused its discretion" in denying Izquierdo's motion. The appellate court remanded the case for a new trial. The court reasoned that "the uncontroverted evidence shows at least some negligence on the part of the restaurant." The court emphasized, "[I]mportantly, the manager of the restaurant admitted that permitting the wet napkins to remain on the floor was a hazardous condition." Izquierdo testified that she slipped, fell down on a wet floor, and found napkins on her shoes. "The inference that the wet napkins on the floor caused her fall clearly was the only reasonable inference which could be drawn from the facts." Izquierdo knew of the napkin-throwing tradition, and the existence of napkins on the floor was obvious, but these circumstances "merely discharge[d] the landowner's duty to warn. It does not discharge the landowner's duty to maintain the premises in a reasonably safe condition."

• **What If the Facts Were Different?** *Should the result in this case have been different if, in all the years that the napkin-throwing tradition existed, no one had ever fallen on the napkins before Izquierdo? Why or why not?*

• **The Legal Environment Dimension** *Does a plaintiff's knowledge of a dangerous condition erase a defendant's potential liability for negligently permitting the dangerous condition to exist? Explain.*

It can sometimes be difficult for business owners to determine whether risks are obvious. Because the law imposes liability on business owners who fail to discover hidden dangers on the premises and protect patrons from being injured, it is advisable to post warnings of any potential risks on the property. Businesspersons should train their employees to be on the lookout for possibly dangerous conditions on the premises at all times and to notify a superior immediately if they notice something unsafe. Making the business premises as safe as possible for all persons who might be there, including children, elderly persons, and individuals with disabilities, is one of the best ways to prevent potential legal disputes.

The Duty of Professionals If an individual has knowledge or skill superior to that of an ordinary person, the individual's conduct must be consistent with that status. Professionals—including physicians, dentists, architects, engineers, accountants, and lawyers, among others—are required to have a standard minimum level of special knowledge and ability. Therefore, in determining what constitutes reasonable care in the case of professionals, the court takes their training and expertise into account. In other words, an accountant cannot defend against a lawsuit for negligence by stating, "But I was not familiar with that general principle of accounting."

If a professional violates his or her duty of care toward a client, the client may bring a suit against the professional, alleging **malpractice,** which is essentially professional negligence. For example, a patient might sue a physician for *medical malpractice.* A client might sue an attorney for *legal malpractice.* The liability of professionals will be examined in further detail in Chapter 51.

No Duty to Rescue Although the law requires individuals to act reasonably and responsibly in their relations with one another, if a person fails to come to the aid of a stranger in peril, that person will not be considered negligent under tort law. Assume that you are walking down a city street and see a pedestrian about to step directly in front of an oncoming bus. You realize that the person has not seen the bus and is unaware of the danger. Do you have a legal duty to warn that individual? No. Although most people would probably concede that, in this situation, the observer has an *ethical* duty to warn the other, tort law does not impose a general duty to rescue others in peril. Duties may be imposed in regard to certain types of peril, however. For example, most states require a motorist involved in an automobile accident to stop and render aid. Failure to do so is both a tort and a crime.

The Injury Requirement and Damages

To recover damages (receive compensation), the plaintiff in a tort lawsuit must prove that she or he suffered a *legally recognizable* injury. In other words, the plaintiff must have suffered some loss, harm, wrong, or invasion of a protected interest. This is true in lawsuits for intentional torts as well as lawsuits for negligence. Essentially, the purpose of tort law is to compensate for legally recognized harms and injuries resulting from wrongful acts. If no harm or injury results from a given negligent action, there is nothing to compensate—and no tort exists.

For example, if you carelessly bump into a passerby, who stumbles and falls as a result, you may be liable in tort if the passerby is injured in the fall. If the person is unharmed, however, there normally can be no suit for damages because no injury was suffered. Although the passerby might be angry and suffer emotional distress, few courts recognize negligently inflicted emotional distress as a tort unless it results in some physical disturbance or dysfunction.

Compensatory damages are the norm in negligence cases. Occasionally, though, a court will award punitive damages if the defendant's conduct was grossly negligent, meaning that the defendant intentionally failed to perform a duty with reckless disregard of the consequences to others.

Causation

Another element necessary to the tort of negligence—and intentional torts as well—is *causation.* If a person breaches a duty of care and someone suffers injury, the wrongful activity must have caused the harm for a tort to have been committed.

Causation in Fact and Proximate Cause

In deciding whether the requirement of causation is met, the court must address two questions:

1. *Is there causation in fact?* Did the injury occur because of the defendant's act, or would it have occurred anyway? If an injury would not have occurred without the defendant's act, then there is causation in fact. **Causation in fact** can usually be determined by use of the *but for* test: "but for" the wrongful act, the injury would not have occurred. This test determines whether there was an actual cause-and-effect relationship between the act and the injury suffered. In theory, causation in fact is limitless. One could claim, for example, that "but for" the creation of the world, a particular injury would not have occurred. Thus, as a practical matter, the law has to establish limits, and it does so through the concept of proximate cause.
2. *Was the act the proximate, or legal, cause of the injury?* **Proximate cause,** or *legal cause,* exists when the connection between an act and an injury is strong enough to justify imposing liability. Consider an example. Ackerman carelessly leaves a campfire burning. The fire not only burns down the forest but also sets off an explosion in a nearby chemical plant that spills chemicals into a river, killing all the fish for a hundred miles downstream and ruining the economy of a tourist resort. Should Ackerman be liable to the resort owners? To the tourists whose vacations were ruined? These are questions of proximate cause that a court must decide.

Both questions must be answered in the affirmative for liability in tort to arise. If a defendant's action constitutes causation in fact but a court decides that the action is not the proximate cause of the plaintiff's injury, the causation requirement has not been met—and the defendant normally will not be liable to the plaintiff.

Foreseeability Questions of proximate cause are linked to the concept of foreseeability because it would be unfair to impose liability on a defendant unless the defendant's actions created a foreseeable risk of injury. Probably the most cited case on the concept of foreseeability and proximate cause is the *Palsgraf* case. The question before the court was as follows: Does the defendant's duty of care extend only to those who may be injured as a result of a foreseeable risk, or does it extend also to persons whose injuries could not reasonably be foreseen?

CASE 7.2 Palsgraf v. Long Island Railroad Co.

Court of Appeals of New York, 1928. 248 N.Y. 339, 162 N.E. 99.

• **Background and Facts** The plaintiff, Helen Palsgraf, was waiting for a train on a station platform. A man carrying a package was rushing to catch a train that was moving away from a platform across the tracks from Palsgraf. As the man attempted to jump aboard the moving train, he seemed unsteady and about to fall. A railroad guard on the car reached forward to grab him, and another guard on the platform pushed him from behind to help him board the train. In the process, the man's package, which (unknown to the railroad guards) contained fireworks, fell on the railroad tracks and exploded. There was nothing about the package to indicate its contents. The repercussions of the explosion caused scales at the other end of the train platform to fall on Palsgraf, causing injuries for which she sued the railroad company. At the trial, the jury found that the railroad guards had been negligent in their conduct. The railroad company appealed. The appellate court affirmed the trial court's judgment, and the railroad company appealed to New York's highest state court.

• **Decision and Rationale** The New York Court of Appeals dismissed Palsgraf's complaint. The conduct of the railroad employees may have been negligent toward the man with the package, but it was not negligent in relation to Palsgraf, who was standing far away. The railroad was not negligent toward her because her injury had not been foreseeable. "Nothing in the situation gave notice * * * of peril to persons thus removed. * * * [No] hazard was apparent to the eye of ordinary vigilance * * * with reference to her." The court stated the principle as "the risk reasonably to be perceived defines the duty to be obeyed." To rule otherwise "would entail liability for any and all consequences, however novel or extraordinary."

• **Impact of This Case on Today's Law** *The* Palsgraf *case established foreseeability as the test for proximate cause. Today, the courts continue to apply this test in determining proximate cause—and thus tort liability for injuries. Generally, if the victim of a harm or the consequences of a harm done are unforeseeable, there is no proximate cause.*

• **The Global Dimension** *What would be the advantages and disadvantages of a universal principle of proximate cause applied everywhere by all courts in all relevant cases? Discuss.*

SECTION 2 Defenses to Negligence

The basic defenses to liability in negligence cases are (1) assumption of risk, (2) superseding cause, and (3) contributory and comparative negligence. Additionally, defendants often defend against negligence claims by asserting that the plaintiffs failed to prove the existence of one or more of the required elements for negligence.

Assumption of Risk

A plaintiff who voluntarily enters into a risky situation, knowing the risk involved, will not be allowed to recover. This is the defense of **assumption of risk.** The requirements of this defense are (1) knowledge of the risk and (2) voluntary assumption of the risk. This defense is frequently asserted when the plaintiff is injured during recreational activities that involve known risk, such as skiing and parachuting.

The risk can be assumed by express agreement, or the assumption of risk can be implied by the plaintiff's knowledge of the risk and subsequent conduct. For example, a driver entering an automobile race knows there is a risk of being injured or killed in a crash. The driver has assumed the risk of injury. Of course, the plaintiff does not assume a risk different from or greater than the risk normally carried by the activity. In our example, the race driver assumes the risk of being injured in the race but not the risk that the banking in the curves of the racetrack will give way during the race because of a construction defect.

Risks are not deemed to be assumed in situations involving emergencies. Neither are they assumed when a statute protects a class of people from harm and a member of the class is injured by the harm. For example, courts have generally held that an employee cannot assume the risk of an employer's violation of safety statutes passed for the benefit of employees.

In the following case, a ball kicked by a player practicing on a nearby field injured a man who was attending his son's soccer tournament. The question before the court was whether a bystander who was not watching a soccer match at the time of injury had nevertheless assumed the risk of being struck by a wayward ball.

CASE 7.3 Sutton v. Eastern New York Youth Soccer Association, Inc.

New York Supreme Court, Appellate Division, Third Department, 2004.
8 A.D.3d 855, 779 N.Y.S.2d 149.

Background and Facts On May 30, 1999, James Sutton's son, a member of the Latham Circle Soccer Club, was participating in a Highland Soccer Club Tournament at Maalyck Park in Glenville, New York. Sutton attended as a spectator. After watching his son's second game from the sidelines, Sutton walked to the end of the field to a tent that his son's team had put up thirty to forty yards behind the goal line to provide shade for the players when they were not engaged on the field. Half a dozen players from the Guilderland Soccer Club were on the field warming up for the next game. In the tent, while taking a sandwich from a cooler, Sutton was struck in the chest and knocked off his feet by a ball kicked from the field by a Guilderland player, Ian Goss. Sutton filed a suit in a New York state court against the Eastern New York Soccer Association and others sponsoring or participating in the tournament, as well as Goss, seeking to recover damages for knee injuries he sustained as a result of the accident. The court found that Sutton had assumed the risk of being struck by a soccer ball, issued a summary judgment in favor of all of the defendants, and dismissed the complaint. Sutton appealed this order to a state intermediate appellate court.

Decision and Rationale The state intermediate appellate court affirmed the order of the lower court. "The doctrine of assumption of risk can apply not only to participants of sporting events, but to spectators and bystanders who are not actively engaged in watching the event at the time of their injury. Indeed, the spectator at a sporting event, no less than the participant, accepts the dangers that [are inherent] in it so far as they are obvious and necessary." This "tournament involved hundreds of players with teams playing at various times on at least five fields and plaintiff had been at the tournament all morning, surrounded by this activity." Sutton argued that the "defendants unreasonably enhanced the risk of injury * * * by essentially inviting him to stand at the end of the field through their placement of the team tent." The court reasoned, however, that "just as the owner of a baseball park is not responsible for the spectator who leaves his or her seat and walks through a potentially more hazardous zone to reach a bathroom or concession stand, thereby assuming the open and obvious risk of being hit by a ball, defendants here cannot be held responsible for the risk assumed by plaintiff when he, aware that players were active on the field, left the sidelines and stood in the tent positioned in the arguably more dangerous zone behind the goal line." Also, Sutton "was familiar with the game of soccer, having admittedly been a frequent spectator of the game for over 14 years."

The Legal Environment Dimension *What is the basis underlying the defense of assumption of risk, and how does that basis support the court's decision in the Sutton case?*

What If the Facts Were Different? *Had the plaintiffs prevailed, how might the sites for soccer matches be different today?*

Superseding Cause

An unforeseeable intervening event may break the causal connection between a wrongful act and an injury to another. If so, the intervening event acts as a *superseding cause*—that is, it relieves a defendant of liability for injuries caused by the intervening event. For example, Derrick, while riding his bicycle, negligently hits Julie, who is walking on the sidewalk. As a result of the impact, Julie falls and fractures her hip. While she is waiting for help to arrive, a small aircraft crashes nearby and explodes, and some of the fiery debris hits her, causing her to sustain severe burns. Derrick will be liable for the damages caused by Julie's fractured hip, but normally he will not be liable for the injuries caused by the plane crash—because the risk of a plane crashing nearby and injuring Julie was not foreseeable.

Contributory and Comparative Negligence

All individuals are expected to exercise a reasonable degree of care in looking out for themselves. In the past, under the common law doctrine of **contributory negligence,** a plaintiff who was also negligent (failed to exercise a reasonable degree of care) could not recover anything from the defendant. Under this rule, no matter how insignificant the plaintiff's negligence was relative to the defendant's negligence, the plaintiff would be precluded from recovering any damages. Today, only a few jurisdictions still hold to this doctrine.

In the majority of states, the doctrine of contributory negligence has been replaced by a **comparative negligence** standard. The comparative negligence standard enables both the plaintiff's and the defendant's negligence to be computed and the liability for damages distributed accordingly. Some jurisdictions have adopted a "pure" form of comparative negligence that allows the plaintiff to recover damages even if her or his fault is greater than that of the defendant. Many states' comparative negligence statutes, however, contain a "50 percent" rule, under which the plaintiff recovers nothing if she or he was more than 50 percent at fault. Under this rule, a plaintiff who is 35 percent at fault could recover 65 percent of his or her damages, but a plaintiff who is 65 percent (over 50 percent) at fault could recover nothing.

SECTION 3

Special Negligence Doctrines and Statutes

A number of special doctrines and statutes relating to negligence are also important. We examine a few of them here.

Res Ipsa Loquitur

Generally, in lawsuits involving negligence, the plaintiff has the burden of proving that the defendant was negligent. In certain situations, however, the courts may presume that negligence has occurred, in which case the burden of proof rests on the defendant—that is, the defendant must prove that he or she was *not* negligent. The presumption of the defendant's negligence is known as the doctrine of ***res ipsa loquitur,***[2] which translates as "the facts speak for themselves."

This doctrine is applied only when the event creating the damage or injury is one that ordinarily does not occur in the absence of negligence. Suppose that a person undergoes abdominal surgery and following the surgery has nerve damage in her spine near the area of the operation. In this situation, the person can sue the surgeon under a theory of *res ipsa loquitur,* because the injury would not have occurred in the absence of the surgeon's negligence.[3] For the doctrine of *res ipsa loquitur* to apply, the event must have been within the defendant's power to control, and it must not have been due to any voluntary action or contribution on the part of the plaintiff.

Negligence *Per Se*

Certain conduct, whether it consists of an action or a failure to act, may be treated as **negligence *per se*** ("in or of itself"). Negligence *per se* may occur if an individual violates a statute or an ordinance providing for a criminal penalty and that violation causes another to be injured. The injured person must prove (1) that the statute clearly sets out what standard of conduct is expected, when and where it is expected, and of whom it is expected; (2) that he or she is in the class intended to be protected by the statute; and (3) that the statute was designed to prevent the type of injury that he or she suffered. The standard of conduct required by the statute is the duty that the defendant owes to the plaintiff, and a violation of the statute is the breach of that duty.

For example, a statute provides that anyone who operates a motor vehicle on a public highway and fails to give full time and attention to the operation of that vehicle is guilty of inattentive driving. After an accident involving two motor vehicles, one of the drivers is cited for and later found guilty of violating the inattentive driver statute. If the other driver was injured and subsequently files a lawsuit, a court could consider the violation of the statute to constitute negligence *per se.* The statute sets forth a standard of attentive driving specifically to protect the safety of the traveling public.[4]

2. Pronounced *rihz ihp*-suh *low*-kwuh-duhr.
3. See, for example, *Gubbins v. Hurson,* 885 A.2d 269 (D.C. 2005).
4. See, for example, *Wright v. Moore,* 931 A.2d 405 (Del.Supr. 2007).

"Danger Invites Rescue" Doctrine

Under the "danger invites rescue" doctrine, a person who is injured while going to someone else's rescue can sue the person who caused the dangerous situation. The original wrongdoer is liable not only for the injuries to the person who was placed in danger, but also for injuries to an individual attempting a rescue. The idea is that the rescuer should not be held liable for any damages because he or she did not cause the danger and because danger invites rescue. For example, Ludlam, while driving down a street, fails to see a stop sign because he is trying to end a squabble between his two young children in the car's backseat. Salter, on the curb near the stop sign, realizes that Ludlam is about to hit a pedestrian walking across the street at the intersection. Salter runs into the street to push the pedestrian out of the way, and Ludlam's vehicle hits Salter instead. Ludlam will be liable for Salter's injury as the rescuer, as well as for any injuries the other pedestrian (or any bystanders) may have sustained.

Special Negligence Statutes

A number of states have enacted statutes prescribing duties and responsibilities in certain circumstances. For example, most states now have what are called **Good Samaritan statutes.**[5] Under these statutes, persons who are aided voluntarily by others cannot turn around and sue the "Good Samaritans" for negligence. These laws were passed largely to protect physicians and other medical personnel who volunteer their services for free in emergency situations to those in need, such as individuals hurt in car accidents.[6]

Many states have also passed **dram shop acts,**[7] under which a tavern owner or bartender may be held liable for injuries caused by a person who became intoxicated while drinking at the bar or who was already intoxicated when served by the bartender. Some states' statutes also impose liability on *social hosts* (persons hosting parties) for injuries caused by guests who became intoxicated at the hosts' homes. Under these statutes, it is unnecessary to prove that the tavern owner, bartender, or social host was negligent. Sometimes, the definition of a "social host" is broadly fashioned. For example, in a New York case, the court held that the father of a minor who hosted a "bring-your-own-keg" party could be held liable for injuries caused by an intoxicated guest.[8]

5. These laws derive their name from the Good Samaritan story in the Bible. In the story, a traveler who had been robbed and beaten lay along the roadside, ignored by those passing by. Eventually, a man from the region of Samaria (the "Good Samaritan") stopped to render assistance to the injured person.

6. See, for example, the discussions of various state statutes in *Chamley v. Khokha,* 730 N.W.2d 864 (N.D. 2007); and *Mueller v. McMillian Warner Insurance Co.,* 2006 WI 54, 290 Wis.2d 571, 714 N.W.2d 183 (2006).

7. Historically, a dram was a small unit of liquid, and spirits were sold in drams. Thus, a dram shop was a place where liquor was sold in drams.

SECTION 4 Strict Liability

Another category of torts is called **strict liability,** or *liability without fault.* Intentional torts and torts of negligence involve acts that depart from a reasonable standard of care and cause injuries. Under the doctrine of strict liability, a person who engages in certain activities can be held responsible for any harm that results to others even if the person used the utmost care.

Development of Strict Liability

The modern concept of strict liability traces its origins, in part, to the 1868 English case of *Rylands v. Fletcher.*[9] In the coal-mining area of Lancashire, England, the Rylands, who were mill owners, had constructed a reservoir on their land. Water from the reservoir broke through a filled-in shaft of an abandoned coal mine nearby and flooded the connecting passageways in an active coal mine owned by Fletcher. Fletcher sued the Rylands, and the court held that the defendants (the Rylands) were liable, even though the circumstances did not fit within existing tort liability theories. The court held that a "person who for his own purposes brings on his land and collects and keeps there anything likely to do mischief if it escapes . . . is *prima facie* [on initial examination] answerable for all the damage which is the natural consequence of its escape."

British courts liberally applied the doctrine that emerged from the *Rylands v. Fletcher* case. Initially, few U.S. courts accepted this doctrine, presumably because the courts were worried about its effect on the expansion of American business. Today, however, the doctrine of strict liability is the norm rather than the exception.

8. *Rust v. Reyer,* 91 N.Y.2d 355, 693 N.E.2d 1074, 670 N.Y.S.2d 822 (1998).

9. 3 L.R.–E & I App. [Law Reports, English & Irish Appeal Cases] (H.L. [House of Lords] 1868).

Abnormally Dangerous Activities

Strict liability for damages proximately caused by an abnormally dangerous, or ultrahazardous, activity is one application of strict liability. Courts apply the doctrine of strict liability in these situations because of the extreme risk of the activity. Abnormally dangerous activities are those that involve a high risk of serious harm to persons or property that cannot be completely guarded against by the exercise of reasonable care—activities such as blasting or storing explosives. Even if blasting with dynamite is performed with all reasonable care, there is still a risk of injury. Balancing that risk against the potential for harm, it seems reasonable to ask the person engaged in the activity to pay for injuries caused by that activity. Although there is no fault, there is still responsibility because of the dangerous nature of the undertaking.

Other Applications of Strict Liability

Persons who keep wild animals are strictly liable for any harm inflicted by the animals. The basis for applying strict liability is that wild animals, should they escape from confinement, pose a serious risk of harm to persons in the vicinity. An owner of domestic animals (such as dogs, cats, cows, or sheep) may be strictly liable for harm caused by those animals if the owner knew, or should have known, that the animals were dangerous or had a propensity to harm others.

A significant application of strict liability is in the area of product liability—liability of manufacturers and sellers for harmful or defective products. Liability here is a matter of social policy and is based on two factors: (1) the manufacturing company can better bear the cost of injury because it can spread the cost throughout society by increasing prices of goods, and (2) the manufacturing company is making a profit from its activities and therefore should bear the cost of injury as an operating expense. We will discuss product liability in greater detail in Chapter 23. Strict liability is also applied in certain types of *bailments* (a bailment exists when goods are transferred temporarily into the care of another—see Chapter 47).

REVIEWING Negligence and Strict Liability

Alaina Sweeney went to Ragged Mountain Ski Resort in New Hampshire with a friend. Alaina went snow tubing down a snow-tube run designed exclusively for snow tubers. There were no Ragged Mountain employees present in the snow-tube area to instruct Alaina on the proper use of a snow tube. On her fourth run down the trail, Alaina crossed over the center line between snow-tube lanes, collided with another snow tuber, and was injured. Alaina filed a negligence action against Ragged Mountain seeking compensation for the injuries that she sustained. Two years earlier, the New Hampshire state legislature had enacted a statute that prohibited a person who participates in the sport of skiing from suing a ski-area operator for injuries caused by the risks inherent in skiing. Using the information presented in the chapter, answer the following questions.

1. What defense will Ragged Mountain probably assert?
2. The central question in this case is whether the state statute establishing that skiers assume the risks inherent in the sport bars Alaina's suit. What would your decision be on this issue? Why?
3. Suppose that the court concludes that the statute applies only to skiing and does not apply to snow tubing. Will Alaina's lawsuit be successful? Explain.
4. Now suppose that the jury concludes that Alaina was partly at fault for the accident. Under what theory might her damages be reduced in proportion to the degree to which her actions contributed to the accident and her resulting injuries?

TERMS AND CONCEPTS

assumption of risk 138
business invitee 135
causation in fact 137
comparative negligence 140
contributory negligence 140
dram shop act 141
duty of care 134
Good Samaritan statute 141
malpractice 136
negligence 134
negligence *per se* 140
proximate cause 137
reasonable person standard 135
***res ipsa loquitur* 140**
strict liability 141

QUESTIONS AND CASE PROBLEMS

7–1. Shannon's physician gives her some medication and tells her not to drive after she takes it, as the medication induces drowsiness. In spite of the doctor's warning, Shannon decides to drive while medicated. Owing to her lack of alertness, she fails to stop at a traffic light and crashes into another vehicle, causing a passenger to be injured. Is Shannon liable for the tort of negligence? Explain.

7–2. QUESTION WITH SAMPLE ANSWER

Ruth carelessly parks her car on a steep hill, leaving the car in neutral and failing to engage the parking brake. The car rolls down the hill and knocks down an electric line. The sparks from the broken line ignite a grass fire. The fire spreads until it reaches a barn one mile away. The barn houses dynamite, and the burning barn explodes, causing part of the roof to fall on and injure Jim, a passing motorist. Which element of negligence is of the greatest concern here? What legal doctrine resolves this issue? Will Jim be able to recover damages from Ruth?

- **For a sample answer to Question 7–2, go to Appendix I at the end of this text.**

7–3. Danny and Marion Klein were injured when part of a fireworks display went astray and exploded near them. They sued Pyrodyne Corp., the pyrotechnic company that was hired to set up and discharge the fireworks, alleging, among other things, that the company should be strictly liable for damages caused by the fireworks display. Will the court agree with the Kleins? What factors will the court consider in making its decision? Discuss fully.

7–4. CASE PROBLEM WITH SAMPLE ANSWER

New Hampshire International Speedway, Inc., owned the New Hampshire International Speedway, a racetrack next to Route 106 in Loudon, New Hampshire. In August 1998, on the weekend before the Winston Cup race, Speedway opened part of its parking facility to recreational vehicles (RVs). Speedway voluntarily positioned its employee Frederick Neergaard at the entrance to the parking area as a security guard and to direct traffic. Leslie Wheeler, who was planning to attend the race, drove an RV south on Route 106 toward Speedway. Meanwhile, Dennis Carignan was also driving south on Route 106 on a motorcycle, on which Mary Carignan was a passenger. As Wheeler approached the parking area, he saw Neergaard signaling him to turn left, which he began to do. At the same time, Carignan attempted to pass the RV on its left side, and the two vehicles collided. Mary sustained an injury to her right knee, lacerations on her ankle, and a broken hip. She sued Speedway and others for negligence. Which element of negligence is at the center of this dispute? How is a court likely to rule in this case, and why? [*Carignan v. New Hampshire International Speedway, Inc.*, 858 A.2d 536 (N.H. 2004)]

- **To view a sample answer for Problem 7–4, go to this book's Web site at www.cengage.com/blaw/jentz, select "Chapter 7," and click on "Case Problem with Sample Answer."**

7–5. Negligence. In July 2004, Emellie Anderson hired Kenneth Whitten, a licensed building contractor, to construct a two-story addition to her home. The bottom floor was to be a garage and the second floor a home office. In August, the parties signed a second contract under which Whitten agreed to rebuild a deck and railing attached to the house and to further improve the office. A later inspection revealed gaps in the siding on the new garage, nails protruding from incomplete framing, improper support for a stairway to the office, and gaps in its plywood flooring. One post supporting the deck was cracked; another was too short. Concrete had not been poured underneath the old posts. A section of railing was missing, and what was installed was warped, with gaps at the joints. Anderson filed a suit in a Connecticut state court against Whitten, alleging that his work was "substandard, not to code, unsafe and not done in a [workmanlike] manner." Anderson claimed that she would have to pay someone else to repair all of the work. Does Whitten's "work" satisfy the requirements for a claim grounded in negligence? Should Anderson's complaint be dismissed, or should she be awarded damages? Explain. [*Anderson v. Whitten*, 100 Conn.App. 730, 918 A.2d 1056 (2007)]

7–6. Defenses to Negligence. Neal Peterson's entire family skied, and Peterson started skiing at the age of two. In 2000, at the age of eleven, Peterson was in his fourth year as a member of a ski race team. One morning in February, Peterson was practicing his skills and was coming down a slope so fast that his skis were not touching the ground. At that point, Peterson collided with David Donahue. Donahue, a forty-three-year-old advanced skier, was skating (skiing slowly) across the slope toward the parking lot. Peterson and Donahue knew that falls or collisions and accidents and injuries were possible with skiing. Donahue saw Peterson "split seconds" before the impact, which knocked Donahue out of his skis and down the slope ten or twelve feet. When Donahue saw Peterson lying motionless nearby, he immediately sought help. To recover for his injuries, Peterson filed a suit in a Minnesota state court against Donahue, alleging negligence. Based on these facts, which defense to a claim of negligence is Donahue most likely to assert? How is the court likely to apply that defense and rule on Peterson's claim? Why? [*Peterson* ex rel. *Peterson v. Donahue,* 733 N.W.2d 790 (Minn.App. 2007)]

7–7. A QUESTION OF ETHICS

*Donald and Gloria Bowden hosted a late afternoon cookout at their home in South Carolina, inviting mostly business acquaintances. Justin Parks, who was nineteen years old, attended the party. Alcoholic beverages were available to all of the guests, even those who, like Parks, were not minors but were underage. Parks consumed alcohol at the party and left with other guests. One of these guests detained Parks at the guest's home to give Parks time to "sober up." Parks then drove himself from this guest's home and was killed in a one-car accident. At the time of his death, he had a blood alcohol content of 0.291 percent, which exceeded the state's limit for driving a motor vehicle. Linda Marcum, Parks's mother, filed a suit in a South Carolina state court against the Bowdens and others, alleging that they were negligent. [*Marcum v. Bowden, *372 S.C. 452, 643 S.E.2d 85 (2007)]*

(a) Considering the principles discussed in this chapter, what are arguments in favor of, and opposed to, holding social hosts liable in this situation? Explain.

(b) The states vary widely in assessing liability and imposing sanctions in the circumstances described in this problem. Broadly, in other words, justice is not equal for parents and other social hosts who serve alcoholic beverages to underage individuals. Why?

7–8. VIDEO QUESTION

Go to this text's Web site at **www.cengage.com/blaw/jentz**, and select "Chapter 7." Click on "Video Questions" and view the video titled *Jaws.* Then answer the following questions.

(a) In the video, the mayor (Murray Hamilton) and a few other men try to persuade Chief Brody (Roy Scheider) not to close the town's beaches. If Brody keeps the beaches open and a swimmer is injured or killed because he failed to warn swimmers about the potential shark danger, has Brody committed the tort of negligence? Explain.

(b) Can Chief Brody be held liable for any injuries or deaths to swimmers under the doctrine of strict liability? Why or why not?

(c) Suppose that Chief Brody goes against the mayor's instructions and warns townspeople to stay off the beach. Nevertheless, several swimmers do not heed his warning and are injured as a result. What defense or defenses could Brody raise under these circumstances if he is sued for negligence?

LAW ON THE WEB

For updated links to resources available on the Web, as well as a variety of other materials, visit this text's Web site at

www.cengage.com/blaw/jentz

You can find cases and articles on torts, including business torts, in the tort law library at the Internet Law Library's Web site. Go to

www.lawguru.com/ilawlib

Legal Research Exercises on the Web

Go to **www.cengage.com/blaw/jentz**, the Web site that accompanies this text. Select "Chapter 7" and click on "Internet Exercises." There you will find the following Internet research exercises that you can perform to learn more about the topics covered in this chapter.

Internet Exercise 7–1: Legal Perspective
Negligence and the *Titanic*

Internet Exercise 7–2: Management Perspective
The Duty to Warn

CHAPTER 8

Intellectual Property and Internet Law

Most people think of wealth in terms of houses, land, cars, stocks, and bonds. Wealth, however, also includes **intellectual property,** which consists of the products that result from intellectual, creative processes. Although it is an abstract term for an abstract concept, intellectual property is nonetheless wholly familiar to virtually everyone. *Trademarks, service marks, copyrights,* and *patents* are all forms of intellectual property. The book you are reading is copyrighted. The software you use, the movies you see, and the music you listen to are all forms of intellectual property. We provide a comprehensive synopsis of these forms of intellectual property, as well as intellectual property that consists of *trade secrets*, in *Concept Summary 8.1* on page 165. In this chapter, we examine each of these forms in some detail.

Intellectual property has taken on increasing significance globally as well as in the United States. Today, the value of the world's intellectual property probably exceeds the value of physical property, such as machines and houses. For many U.S. companies, ownership rights in intangible intellectual property are more important to their prosperity than are their tangible assets. As you will read in this chapter, a pressing issue for businesspersons today is how to protect these valuable rights in the online world.

The need to protect creative works was voiced by the framers of the U.S. Constitution over two hundred years ago: Article I, Section 8, of the U.S. Constitution authorized Congress "[t]o promote the Progress of Science and useful Arts, by securing for limited Times to Authors and Inventors the exclusive Right to their respective Writings and Discoveries." Laws protecting patents, trademarks, and copyrights are explicitly designed to protect and reward inventive and artistic creativity. Although intellectual property law limits the economic freedom of some individuals, it does so to protect the freedom of others to enjoy the fruits of their labors—in the form of profits.

SECTION 1 Trademarks and Related Property

A **trademark** is a distinctive mark, motto, device, or implement that a manufacturer stamps, prints, or otherwise affixes to the goods it produces so that they can be identified on the market and their origins made known. In other words, a trademark is a source indicator. At common law, the person who used a symbol or mark to identify a business or product was protected in the use of that trademark. Clearly, by using another's trademark, a business could lead consumers to believe that its goods were made by the other business. The law seeks to avoid this kind of confusion. In this section, we examine various aspects of the law governing trademarks.

In the following classic case concerning Coca-Cola, the defendants argued that the Coca-Cola trademark was entitled to no protection under the law because the term did not accurately represent the product.

CASE 8.1 The Coca-Cola Co. v. The Koke Co. of America

Supreme Court of the United States, 1920. 254 U.S. 143, 41 S.Ct. 113, 65 L.Ed. 189.
www.findlaw.com/casecode/supreme.html[a]

• **Company Profile** John Pemberton, an Atlanta pharmacist, invented a caramel-colored, carbonated soft drink in 1886. His bookkeeper, Frank Robinson, named the beverage Coca-Cola after two of the ingredients, coca leaves and kola nuts. Asa Candler bought the Coca-Cola Company (**www.cocacolacompany.com**) in 1891, and within seven years, he made the soft drink available in all of the United States, as well as in parts of Canada and Mexico. Candler continued to sell Coke aggressively and to open up new markets, reaching Europe before 1910. In doing so, however, he attracted numerous competitors, some of which tried to capitalize directly on the Coke name.

• **Background and Facts** The Coca-Cola Company sought to enjoin (prevent) the Koke Company of America and other beverage companies from, among other things, using the word *Koke* for their products. The Koke Company of America and other beverage companies contended that the Coca-Cola trademark was a fraudulent representation and that Coca-Cola was therefore not entitled to any help from the courts. The Koke Company and the other defendants alleged that the Coca-Cola Company, by its use of the Coca-Cola name, represented that the beverage contained cocaine (from coca leaves), which it no longer did. The trial court granted the injunction against the Koke Company, but the appellate court reversed the lower court's ruling. Coca-Cola then appealed to the United States Supreme Court.

• **Decision and Rationale** The United States Supreme Court upheld the district court's decision. The Court acknowledged that before 1900 Coca-Cola's goodwill was enhanced by the presence of a small amount of cocaine, but that the cocaine had long been eliminated from the drink.[b] The Court underscored that Coca-Cola was not "a medicine" and that its attraction did not lie in producing "a toxic effect." Since 1900 sales had greatly increased. The name had come to characterize a well-known beverage to be had almost anywhere "rather than a compound of particular substances." The Court noted that before this suit was brought Coca-Cola had advertised that the public would not find cocaine in Coca-Cola. "It would be going too far to deny the plaintiff relief against a palpable fraud because possibly here and there an ignorant person might call for the drink with the hope for incipient cocaine intoxication."

• **Impact of This Case on Today's Law** *In this early case, the United States Supreme Court made it clear that trademarks and trade names (and nicknames for those marks and names, such as the nickname "Coke" for "Coca-Cola") that are in common use receive protection under the common law. This holding is significant historically because it is the predecessor to the federal statute later passed to protect trademark rights—the Lanham Act of 1946, to be discussed next. In many ways, this act represented a codification of common law principles governing trademarks.*

• **What If the Facts Were Different?** *Suppose that Coca-Cola had been trying to make the public believe that its product contained cocaine. Would the result in this case likely have been different? Why or why not?*

---

a. This is the "U.S. Supreme Court Opinions" page within the Web site of the "FindLaw Internet Legal Resources" database. This page provides several options for accessing an opinion. Because you know the citation for this case, you can go to the "Citation Search" box, type in the appropriate volume and page numbers for the *United States Reports* ("254" and "143," respectively, for the *Coca-Cola* case), and click on "get it."

b. In reality, until 1903 the amount of active cocaine in each bottle of Coke was equivalent to one "line" of cocaine.

Statutory Protection of Trademarks

Statutory protection of trademarks and related property is provided at the federal level by the Lanham Act of 1946.[1] The Lanham Act was enacted, in part, to protect manufacturers from losing business to rival companies that used confusingly similar trademarks. The Lanham Act incorporates the common law of trademarks and provides remedies for owners of trademarks who wish to enforce their claims in federal court. Many states also have trademark statutes.

Trademark Dilution In 1995, Congress amended the Lanham Act by passing the Federal Trademark Dilution Act,[2] which extended the protection available to trademark owners by allowing them to bring a suit in federal court for trademark **dilution.** Until the passage of this amendment, federal trademark law prohibited only the unauthorized use of the same mark on competing—or on noncompeting but "related"—goods or services when such use would likely confuse consumers as to the origin of those goods and services. Trademark dilution laws protect "distinctive" or "famous" trademarks (such as Jergens, McDonald's, Dell, and Apple) from certain unauthorized uses even when the use is on noncompeting goods or is unlikely to confuse. More than half of the states have also enacted trademark dilution laws.

Use of a Similar Mark May Constitute Trademark Dilution A famous mark may be diluted not only by the use of an *identical* mark but also by the use of a *similar* mark. In 2003, however, the United States Supreme Court ruled that to constitute dilution, the similar mark must reduce the value of the famous mark or lessen its ability to identify goods and services. Therefore, lingerie maker Victoria's Secret could not establish a dilution claim against a small adult store named "Victor's Little Secret" because there was not enough evidence that Victoria's Secret's mark would be diminished in value.[3]

A similar mark is more likely to lessen the value of a famous mark when the companies using the marks provide related goods or compete against each other in the same market. For example, a woman was operating a coffee shop under the name "Sambuck's Coffeehouse" in Astoria, Oregon, even though she knew that "Starbucks" is one of the largest coffee chains in the nation. When Starbucks Corporation filed a dilution lawsuit, the federal court ruled that use of the "Sambuck's" mark constituted trademark dilution because it created confusion for consumers. Not only was there a "high degree" of similarity between the marks, but also both companies provided coffee-related services and marketed their services through "stand-alone" retail stores. Therefore, the use of the similar mark (Sambuck's) reduced the value of the famous mark (Starbucks).[4]

Trademark Registration

Trademarks may be registered with the state or with the federal government. To register for protection under federal trademark law, a person must file an application with the U.S. Patent and Trademark Office in Washington, D.C. Under current law, a mark can be registered (1) if it is currently in commerce or (2) if the applicant intends to put it into commerce within six months.

In special circumstances, the six-month period can be extended by thirty months, giving the applicant a total of three years from the date of notice of trademark approval to make use of the mark and file the required use statement. Registration is postponed until the mark is actually used. Nonetheless, during this waiting period, any applicant can legally protect his or her trademark against a third party who previously has neither used the mark nor filed an application for it. Registration is renewable between the fifth and sixth years after the initial registration and every ten years thereafter (every twenty years for those trademarks registered before 1990).

Trademark Infringement

Registration of a trademark with the U.S. Patent and Trademark Office gives notice on a nationwide basis that the trademark belongs exclusively to the registrant. The registrant is also allowed to use the symbol ® to indicate that the mark has been registered. Whenever that trademark is copied to a substantial degree or used in its entirety by another, intentionally or unintentionally, the trademark has been *infringed* (used without authorization). To sue for trademark infringement, a person need not have registered the

1. 15 U.S.C. Sections 1051–1128.
2. 15 U.S.C. Section 1125.
3. *Moseley v. V Secret Catalogue, Inc.*, 537 U.S. 418, 123 S.Ct. 1115, 155 L.Ed.2d 1 (2003). (A different case involving Victoria's Secret's trademark is presented as Case 8.2 on the following two pages.)
4. *Starbucks Corp. v. Lundberg*, 2005 WL 3183858 (D.Or. 2005).

trademark, but registration does furnish proof of the date of inception of the trademark's use.

When a trademark has been infringed, the owner has a cause of action against the infringer. Under the Lanham Act, a trademark owner that successfully proves infringement can recover actual damages, plus the profits that the infringer wrongfully received from the unauthorized use of the mark. In addition, the court may grant an *injunction* to prevent further infringement and has the authority to order that any goods bearing the unauthorized trademark be destroyed.

A central objective of the Lanham Act is to reduce the likelihood that consumers will be confused by similar marks. For that reason, only those trademarks that are deemed sufficiently distinctive from all competing trademarks will be protected.

Distinctiveness of Mark

A trademark must be sufficiently distinct to enable consumers to identify the manufacturer of the goods easily and to distinguish between those goods and competing products.

Strong Marks Fanciful, arbitrary, or suggestive trademarks are generally considered to be the most distinctive (strongest) trademarks. Marks that are fanciful, arbitrary, or suggestive are protected as inherently distinctive without demonstrating secondary meaning. These marks receive automatic protection because they serve to identify a particular product's source, as opposed to describing the product itself.

Fanciful trademarks include invented words, such as "Xerox" for one manufacturer's copiers and "Kodak" for another company's photographic products. Arbitrary trademarks are those that use common words in an uncommon way that is nondescriptive, such as "English Leather" used as a name for an aftershave lotion (and not for leather processed in England). Suggestive trademarks imply something about a product without describing the product directly. For example, the trademark "Dairy Queen" suggests an association between the products and milk, but it does not directly describe ice cream.

Secondary Meaning Descriptive terms, geographic terms, and personal names are not inherently distinctive and do not receive protection under the law until they acquire a secondary meaning. A secondary meaning may arise when customers begin to associate a specific term or phrase (such as London Fog) with specific trademarked items (coats with "London Fog" labels). Whether a secondary meaning becomes attached to a term or name usually depends on how extensively the product is advertised, the market for the product, the number of sales, and other factors.

Once a secondary meaning is attached to a term or name, a trademark is considered distinctive and is protected. The United States Supreme Court has held that even a color can qualify for trademark protection, once customers associate that color with the product.[5] In 2006, a federal court held that trademark law protects the particular color schemes used by the sports teams of four state universities, including Ohio State University and Louisiana State University.[6]

At issue in the following case was whether a certain mark was suggestive or descriptive.

5. *Qualitex Co. v. Jacobson Products Co.*, 514 U.S. 159, 115 S.Ct. 1300, 131 L.Ed.2d 248 (1995).

6. *Board of Supervisors of Louisiana State University v. Smack Apparel Co.*, 438 F.Supp.2d 653 (E.D.La. 2006).

CASE 8.2 Menashe v. V Secret Catalogue, Inc.

United States District Court, Southern District of New York, 2006. 409 F.Supp.2d 412.

• **Background and Facts** In autumn 2002, Victoria's Secret Stores, Inc., and its affiliated companies, including V Secret Catalogue, Inc., began to develop a panty collection to be named "SEXY LITTLE THINGS." In spring 2004, Ronit Menashe, a publicist, and Audrey Quock, a fashion model and actress, began to plan a line of women's underwear also called "SEXY LITTLE THINGS." Menashe and Quock designed their line, negotiated for its manufacture, registered the domain name **www.sexylittlethings.com**, and filed an intent-to-use (ITU) application with the U.S. Patent and Trademark Office (USPTO). In July, Victoria's Secret's collection appeared in its stores in Ohio, Michigan, and California, and, in less than three months, was prominently displayed in all its stores, in its catalogues, and on its Web site. By mid-November, more than 13 million units of the line had

CASE 8.2 CONTINUED been sold, accounting for 4 percent of the company's sales for the year. When the firm applied to register "SEXY LITTLE THINGS" with the USPTO, it learned of Menashe and Quock's ITU application. The firm warned the pair that their use of the phrase constituted trademark infringement. Menashe and Quock filed a suit in a federal district court against V Secret Catalogue and others, asking the court to, among other things, declare "noninfringement of the trademark."

● **Decision and Rationale** The court concluded that "SEXY LITTLE THINGS" was a suggestive mark that Victoria's Secret used in commerce prior to the time the plaintiffs filed their ITU application. For this reason, Victoria's Secret had "priority in the Mark," and Menashe and Quock were not entitled to a judgment of "noninfringement." The court explained that "to merit trademark protection, a mark must be capable of distinguishing the products it marks from those of others." A descriptive term conveys an immediate idea of the ingredients, qualities, or characteristics of the goods. In contrast, a suggestive term requires imagination, thought, and perception to reach a conclusion as to the nature of the goods. Suggestive marks are automatically protected because they are inherently distinctive; that is, their intrinsic nature serves to identify a particular source of a product. Descriptive marks are not inherently distinctive and may only be protected on a showing of secondary meaning—that is, that the purchasing public associates the mark with a particular source. In this case, the court held that the mark "SEXY LITTLE THINGS" was suggestive because it calls to mind the phrase "sexy little things" popularly used to refer to attractive young women. The court observed that because of this suggestive nature, the mark prompts the purchaser to mentally associate the lingerie with its targeted twenty- to thirty-year-old consumers. Courts have classified marks that both describe the product and evoke other associations as inherently distinctive. In addition, the court reasoned that Victoria's Secret's use of the mark does not deprive competitors of ways to describe their lingerie products. "Indeed, Victoria's Secret's own descriptions of its lingerie in its catalogues and Web site illustrate that there are numerous ways to describe provocative underwear."

● **The E-Commerce Dimension** *If Victoria's Secret had just used the label "Sexy Little Things" on its Web site for online-only sales of this line of underwear, would the outcome of this case have been any different? Why or why not?*

● **The Legal Environment Dimension** *Why is it important to allow those who have applied for trademark protection–in this case, ITU applicants Menashe and Quock–to defend preemptively against the use of the mark by another party? (Hint: Why were Menashe and Quock seeking a court declaration of "noninfringement of a trademark"?)*

Generic Terms Generic terms that refer to an entire class of products, such as *bicycle* and *computer,* receive no protection, even if they acquire secondary meanings. A particularly thorny problem arises when a trademark acquires generic use. For example, *aspirin* and *thermos* were originally the names of trademarked products, but today the words are used generically. Other examples are *escalator, trampoline, raisin bran, dry ice, lanolin, linoleum, nylon,* and *corn flakes.*

Sometimes, a company's use of a particular generic phrase or mark becomes so closely associated with that company that the firm claims it should be protected under trademark law. In one case, for example, America Online, Inc. (AOL), sued AT&T Corporation, claiming that AT&T's use of "You Have Mail" on its WorldNet Service infringed AOL's trademark rights in the same phrase. The court ruled, however, that because each of the three words in the phrase was a generic term, the phrase as a whole was generic. Although the phrase had become widely associated with AOL's e-mail notification service, and thus might have acquired a secondary meaning, this issue was of no significance in the case. The court stated that it would not consider whether the mark had acquired any secondary meaning because "generic marks with secondary meaning are still not entitled to protection."[7]

Trade Dress

The term **trade dress** refers to the image and overall appearance of a product. Trade dress is a broad concept and can include either all or part of the total

7. *America Online, Inc. v. AT&T Corp.,* 243 F.3d 812 (4th Cir. 2001).

image or overall impression created by a product or its packaging. For example, the distinctive decor, menu, layout, and style of service of a particular restaurant may be regarded as trade dress. Trade dress can also include the layout and appearance of a catalogue, the use of a lighthouse as part of the design of a golf hole, the fish shape of a cracker, or the G-shaped design of a Gucci watch.

Basically, trade dress is subject to the same protection as trademarks. In cases involving trade dress infringement, as in trademark infringement cases, a major consideration is whether consumers are likely to be confused by the allegedly infringing use.

Service, Certification, and Collective Marks

A **service mark** is essentially a trademark that is used to distinguish the *services* (rather than the products) of one person or company from those of another. For example, each airline has a particular mark or symbol associated with its name. Titles and character names used in radio and television are frequently registered as service marks.

Other marks protected by law include certification marks and collective marks. A **certification mark** is used by one or more persons, other than the owner, to certify the region, materials, mode of manufacture, quality, or other characteristic of specific goods or services. When used by members of a cooperative, association, or other organization, it is referred to as a **collective mark.** Examples of certification marks are the phrases "Good Housekeeping Seal of Approval" and "UL Tested." Collective marks appear at the ends of motion picture credits to indicate the various associations and organizations that participated in the making of the films. The union marks found on the tags of certain products are also collective marks.

Counterfeit Goods

Counterfeit goods copy or otherwise imitate trademarked goods but are not genuine. The importation of goods that bear a counterfeit (fake) trademark poses a growing problem for U.S. businesses, consumers, and law enforcement. In addition to having negative financial effects on legitimate businesses, sales of certain counterfeit goods, such as pharmaceuticals and nutritional supplements, can present serious public health risks. It is estimated that nearly 7 percent of the goods imported into the United States from abroad are counterfeit.

Stop Counterfeiting in Manufactured Goods Act In 2006, Congress enacted the Stop Counterfeiting in Manufactured Goods Act[8] (SCMGA) to combat the growing problem of counterfeit goods. The act makes it a crime to intentionally traffic in or attempt to traffic in counterfeit goods or services, or to knowingly use a counterfeit mark on or in connection with goods or services. Prior to this act, the law did not prohibit the creation or shipment of counterfeit labels that were not attached to any product.[9] Therefore, counterfeiters would make labels and packaging bearing another's trademark, ship the labels to another location, and then affix them to an inferior product to deceive buyers. The SCMGA has closed this loophole by making it a crime to knowingly traffic in or attempt to traffic in counterfeit labels, stickers, packaging, and the like, regardless of whether the item is attached to any goods.

Penalties for Counterfeiting Persons found guilty of violating the SCMGA may be fined up to $2 million or imprisoned for up to ten years (or more if they are repeat offenders). If a court finds that the statute was violated, it must order the defendant to forfeit the counterfeit products (which are then destroyed), as well as any property used in the commission of the crime. The defendant must also pay restitution to the trademark holder or victim in an amount equal to the victim's actual loss. For example, in one case the defendant pleaded guilty to conspiring with others to import cigarette-rolling papers from Mexico that were falsely marked as "Zig-Zags" and sell them in the United States. The court sentenced the defendant to prison and ordered him to pay $566,267 in restitution. On appeal, the court affirmed the prison sentence but reversed the restitution because the amount exceeded the amount of actual loss suffered by the legitimate sellers of Zig-Zag rolling papers.[10]

Trade Names

Trademarks apply to *products*. The term **trade name** is used to indicate part or all of a business's name, whether the business is a sole proprietorship, a partner-

8. Pub. L. No. 109-181 (2006), which amended 18 U.S.C. Sections 2318–2320.

9. See, for example, *United States v. Giles*, 213 F.3d 1247 (10th Cir. 2000).

10. For a case discussing the appropriate measure of restitution, see *United States v. Beydoun*, 469 F.3d 102 (5th Cir. 2006).

ship, or a corporation. Generally, a trade name is directly related to a business and its goodwill. A trade name may be protected as a trademark if the trade name is also the name of the company's trademarked product—for example, Coca-Cola. Unless also used as a trademark or service mark, a trade name cannot be registered with the federal government. Trade names are protected under the common law, but only if they are unusual or fancifully used. The word *Safeway*, for example, was sufficiently fanciful to obtain protection as a trade name for a grocery chain.[11]

SECTION 2 Cyber Marks

In cyberspace, trademarks are sometimes referred to as **cyber marks.** We turn now to a discussion of various trademark issues that are unique to cyberspace, such as domain names and cybersquatting, and how new laws and the courts are addressing these issues.

Domain Names

Conflicts over rights to domain names first emerged as e-commerce expanded on a worldwide scale and have reemerged in the last ten years. By using the same, or a similar, domain name, parties have attempted to profit from the goodwill of a competitor, sell pornography, offer for sale another party's domain name, and otherwise infringe on others' trademarks. A **domain name** is the core part of an Internet address—for example, "westlaw.com." It includes at least two parts. Every domain name ends with a generic top level domain (TLD), which is the part of the name to the right of the period. The TLD typically indicates the type of entity that operates the site. For example, *com* is an abbreviation for *commercial,* and *edu* is short for *education.* Although originally there were only six possible TLDs, several more generic TLDs are now available, some of which are not restricted to a particular type of entity (see Exhibit 8–1 on the following page for a list of generic TLDs and their uses).

The second level domain (SLD), which is the part of the name to the left of the period, is chosen by the business entity or individual registering the domain name. Competition among firms with similar names and products for SLDs has caused numerous disputes over domain name rights. The Internet Corporation for Assigned Names and Numbers (ICANN), a nonprofit corporation, oversees the distribution of domain names. ICANN also facilitates the settlement of domain name disputes and operates an online arbitration system. In recent years, however, ICANN has been criticized for failing to keep up with the sheer volume of complaints involving domain names and accusations of cybersquatting. **Cybersquatting** occurs when a person registers a domain name that is the same as, or confusingly similar to, the trademark of another and then offers to sell the domain name back to the trademark owner.

Anticybersquatting Legislation

During the 1990s, cybersquatting led to so much litigation that Congress passed the Anticybersquatting Consumer Protection Act of 1999[12] (ACPA), which amended the Lanham Act—the federal law protecting trademarks discussed earlier. The ACPA makes it illegal for a person to "register, traffic in, or use" a domain name (1) if the name is identical or confusingly similar to the trademark of another and (2) if the one registering, trafficking in, or using the domain name has a "bad faith intent" to profit from that trademark.

The act does not define what constitutes bad faith. Instead, it lists several factors that courts can consider in deciding whether bad faith exists. For example, courts focus on the trademark rights of the other person and whether the alleged cybersquatter intended to divert consumers in a way that could harm the goodwill represented by the trademark. Courts also consider whether the alleged cybersquatter offered to transfer or sell the domain name to the trademark owner, or intended to use the domain name to offer goods and services.

The Ongoing Problem of Cybersquatting

The ACPA was intended to stamp out cybersquatting, but it continues to present a problem for businesses today, largely because, as mentioned, more TLDs are available and many more companies are registering domain names. Indeed, domain name registrars have proliferated. These companies charge a fee to businesses and individuals to register new names and to renew annual registrations (often through automated software). Many of these companies also buy and sell

11. *Safeway Stores v. Suburban Foods,* 130 F.Supp. 249 (E.D.Va. 1955).

12. 15 U.S.C. Section 1129.

EXHIBIT 8–1 • Existing Generic Top Level Domain Names

.aero	Reserved for members of the air-transportation industry.
.asia	Restricted to the Pan-Asia and Asia Pacific community.
.biz	For businesses.
.cat	Reserved for the Catalan linguistic and cultural community.
.com	Originally intended for commercial organizations, but is now unrestricted in the United States.
.coop	Restricted to cooperative associations.
.edu	For postsecondary educational establishments.
.gov	Reserved for government agencies in the United States.
.info	For informational sites, but is unrestricted.
.int	Reserved for international organizations established by treaty.
.jobs	Reserved for human resource managers.
.mil	For the U.S. military.
.mobi	Reserved for consumers and providers of mobile products and services.
.museum	Reserved for museums.
.name	Reserved for individuals and families.
.net	Originally intended for network infrastructures, but is now unrestricted.
.org	Originally intended for noncommercial organizations, but is now unrestricted.
.pro	Restricted to certain credentialed professionals.
.tel	For business services involving connections between a telephone network and the Internet.
.travel	Reserved for the travel industry.

expired domain names. Although all domain name registrars are supposed to relay information about these transactions to ICANN and the other companies that keep a master list of domain names, this does not always occur. The speed at which domain names change hands and the difficulty in tracking mass automated registrations have created an environment in which cybersquatting can flourish.

Cybersquatters have also developed new tactics, such as typosquatting, or registering a name that is a misspelling of a popular brand, such as hotmai.com or myspac.com. Because many Internet users are not perfect typists, Web pages using these misspelled names get a lot of traffic. More traffic generally means increased profit (advertisers often pay Web sites based on the number of unique visits, or hits), which in turn provides incentive for more cybersquatters. Also, if the misspelling is significant, the trademark owner may have difficulty proving that the name is identical or confusingly similar to the trademark of another, as the ACPA requires.

Cybersquatting is costly for businesses, which must attempt to register all variations of a name to protect their domain name rights from would-be cybersquatters. Large corporations may have to register thousands of domain names across the globe just to protect their basic brands and trademarks.

Applicability of the ACPA and Sanctions under the Act The ACPA applies to all domain name registrations. Successful plaintiffs in suits brought under the act can collect actual damages and profits, or they can elect to receive statutory damages ranging from $1,000 to $100,000.

Although some companies have been successful suing under the ACPA, there are roadblocks to succeeding in such lawsuits. Some domain name registrars offer privacy services that hide the true owners of Web sites, making it difficult for trademark owners to identify cybersquatters. Thus, before a trademark owner can bring a suit, he or she has to ask the court for a subpoena to discover the identity of the owner of the infringing Web site. Because of the high costs of court proceedings, discovery, and even arbitration, many disputes over cybersquatting are settled out of court. Some companies have found that simply purchasing the domain name from the cybersquatter is the least expensive solution.

Meta Tags

Search engines compile their results by looking through a Web site's key-word field. **Meta tags,** or key words, may be inserted into this field to increase the likelihood that a site will be included in search engine results, even though the site may have nothing to do with the inserted words. Using this same technique, one site may appropriate the key words of other sites with more frequent hits so that the appropriating site will appear in the same search engine results as the more popular sites. Using another's trademark in a meta tag without the owner's permission, however, normally constitutes trademark infringement.

Some uses of another's trademark as a meta tag may be permissible if the use is reasonably necessary and does not suggest that the owner authorized or sponsored the use. For example, Terri Welles, a former model who had been "Playmate of the Year" in *Playboy* magazine, established a Web site that used the terms *Playboy* and *Playmate* as meta tags. Playboy Enterprises, Inc. (PEI), which publishes *Playboy,* filed a suit seeking to prevent Welles from using these meta tags. The court determined that Welles's use of PEI's meta tags to direct users to her Web site was permissible because it did not suggest sponsorship and there were no descriptive substitutes for the terms *Playboy* and *Playmate.*[13]

Dilution in the Online World

As discussed earlier, trademark *dilution* occurs when a trademark is used, without authorization, in a way that diminishes the distinctive quality of the mark. Unlike trademark infringement, a claim of dilution does not require proof that consumers are likely to be confused by a connection between the unauthorized use and the mark. For this reason, the products involved need not be similar. In the first case alleging dilution on the Web, a court precluded the use of "candyland.com" as the URL for an adult site. The successful lawsuit was brought by the company that manufactures the "Candyland" children's game and owns the "Candyland" mark.[14]

Licensing

One way to make use of another's trademark or other form of intellectual property, while avoiding litigation, is to obtain a license to do so. A license in this context is essentially an agreement, or contract, permitting the use of a trademark, copyright, patent, or trade secret for certain purposes. The party that owns the intellectual property rights and issues the license is the *licensor,* and the party obtaining the license is the *licensee.* A licensor might, for example, allow the licensee to use the trademark as part of its company name, or as part of its domain name, but not otherwise use the mark on any products or services. Often, selling a license to an infringer is an inexpensive solution to the problem, at least when compared with the costs associated with litigation.

Note, however, that under modern law a licensor of trademarks has a duty to maintain some form of control over the nature and quality of goods or services sold under the mark. If the license does not include any provisions to protect the quality of goods or services provided under the trademark, then the courts may conclude that the licensor has abandoned the trademark and lost her or his trademark rights.[15] To avoid such problems, licensing agreements normally include detailed provisions that protect the trademark owners' rights.

To avoid litigation, anyone signing a licensing contract should consult with an attorney to make sure that the specific wording in the contract is very clear as to what rights are or are not being conveyed. Moreover, to prevent misunderstandings over the scope of the rights being acquired, the licensee should determine whether any other parties hold licenses to use that particular intellectual property and the extent of those rights.

SECTION 3 Patents

A **patent** is a grant from the government that gives an inventor the right to exclude others from making, using, and selling an invention for a period of twenty years from the date of filing the application for a patent. Patents for designs, as opposed to inventions, are given for a fourteen-year period. The applicant must demonstrate to the satisfaction of the U.S. Patent and Trademark Office that the invention, discovery,

13. *Playboy Enterprises, Inc. v. Welles,* 279 F.3d 796 (9th Cir. 2002). See also *Rhino Sports, Inc. v. Sport Court, Inc.,* ___ F.Supp.2d ___ (D.Ariz. 2007).

14. *Hasbro, Inc. v. Internet Entertainment Group, Ltd.,* 1996 WL 84853 (W.D.Wash. 1996).

15. This is referred to as a *naked license,* and a trademark owner who fails to exercise adequate control over the mark is estopped, or prevented, from asserting his or her rights. See, for example, *Barcamerica International USA Trust v. Tyfield Importers, Inc.,* 289 F.3d 589 (9th Cir. 2002); and *Exxon Corp. v. Oxxford Clothes, Inc.,* 109 F.3d 1070 (5th Cir. 1997).

process, or design is novel, useful, and not obvious in light of current technology.

In contrast to patent law in many other countries, in the United States the first person to invent a product or process gets the patent rights rather than the first person to file for a patent on that product or process. Because it can be difficult to prove who invented an item first, however, the first person to file an application is often deemed the first to invent (unless the inventor has detailed prior research notes or other evidence). An inventor can publish the invention or offer it for sale prior to filing a patent application but must apply for a patent within one year of doing so or forfeit the patent rights. The period of patent protection begins on the date the patent application is filed, rather than when the patent is issued, which may sometimes be years later. After the patent period ends (either fourteen or twenty years later), the product or process enters the public domain, and anyone can make, sell, or use the invention without paying the patent holder.

Searchable Patent Databases

A significant development relating to patents is the availability online of the world's patent databases. The Web site of the U.S. Patent and Trademark Office (see the *Law on the Web* section at the end of this chapter for its URL) provides searchable databases covering U.S. patents granted since 1976. The Web site of the European Patent Office (its URL is also in the *Law on the Web* section) provides online access to 50 million patent documents in more than seventy nations through a searchable network of databases. Businesses use these searchable databases in many ways. Because patents are valuable assets, businesses may need to perform patent searches to list or inventory their assets. Patent searches may also be conducted to study trends and patterns in a specific technology or to gather information about competitors in the industry. In addition, a business might search patent databases to develop a business strategy in a particular market or to evaluate a job applicant's contributions to a technology. Although online databases are accessible to anyone, businesspersons might consider hiring a specialist to perform advanced patent searches.

What Is Patentable?

Under federal law, "[w]hoever invents or discovers any new and useful process, machine, manufacture, or composition of matter, or any new and useful improvement thereof, may obtain a patent therefor, subject to the conditions and requirements of this title."[16] Thus, to be patentable, the item must be novel and not obvious.

In sum, almost anything is patentable, except (1) the laws of nature,[17] (2) natural phenomena, and (3) abstract ideas (including algorithms[18]). Even artistic methods, certain works of art, and the structure of storylines are patentable, provided that they are novel and not obvious. Plants that are reproduced asexually (by means other than from seed), such as hybrid or genetically engineered plants, are patentable in the United States, as are genetically engineered (or cloned) microorganisms and animals.

In the following case, the focus was on the application of the test for proving whether a patent claim is "obvious."

16. 35 U.S.C. 101.

17. Note that in 2006, several justices of the United States Supreme Court indicated that they believed a process to diagnose vitamin deficiencies should not be patentable, because allowing a patent would improperly give a monopoly over a scientific relationship, or law of nature. Nevertheless, the majority of the Supreme Court allowed the patent to stand. *Laboratory Corporation of America Holdings v. Metabolite Laboratories, Inc.*, 548 U.S. 124, 126 S.Ct. 2921, 165 L.Ed.2d 399 (2006).

18. An *algorithm* is a step-by-step procedure, formula, or set of instructions for accomplishing a specific task—such as the set of rules used by a search engine to rank the listings contained within its index in response to a particular query.

CASE 8.3 KSR International Co. v. Teleflex, Inc.

Supreme Court of the United States, 2007. __ U.S. __, 127 S.Ct. 1727, 167 L.Ed.2d 705.

Background and Facts Teleflex, Inc., sued KSR International Company for patent infringement. Teleflex holds the exclusive license to a patent for a device developed by Steven J. Engelgau. The patent issued is entitled "Adjustable Pedal with Electronic Throttle Control." In brief, the Engelgau patent combines an electronic sensor with an adjustable automobile pedal so that the pedal's position can be transmitted to a computer that controls the throttle in the vehicle's engine. KSR contended that the patent in question could not create a claim because the subject matter was obvious. During the trial, the district court found that several existing patents involving electronic pedal sensors for computer-

CASE 8.3 CONTINUED controlled throttles basically covered all of the important aspects of the Engelgau patent. On appeal, the U.S. Court of Appeals for the Federal Circuit reversed the district court ruling. KSR appealed to the United States Supreme Court.

- **Decision and Rationale** The United States Supreme Court reversed the judgment of the court of appeals and remanded the case. The Court pointed out that in many previous decisions it had held "that a patent for a combination which only unites old elements with no change in their respective functions * * * obviously withdraws what is already known into the field of its monopoly and diminishes the resources available to skillful [persons]. * * * If a technique has been used to improve one device, and a person of ordinary skill in the art would recognize that it would improve similar devices in the same way, using the technique is obvious unless its actual application is beyond his or her skill." In essence, the Court saw little difference between what existed in the "teachings" of previously filed patents and the adjustable electronic pedal disclosed in the Engelgau patent.

- **The Legal Environment Dimension** *If a person of ordinary skill can implement a predictable variation of another's patented invention, does the Court's opinion indicate that the item is likely not to be patentable? Explain.*

- **The Ethical Dimension** *Based on the Court's reasoning, what other factors should be considered when determining the obviousness of a patent?*

Patents for Software At one time, it was difficult for developers and manufacturers of software to obtain patent protection because many software products simply automate procedures that can be performed manually. In other words, it was thought that computer programs did not meet the "novel" and "not obvious" requirements previously mentioned. Also, the basis for software is often a mathematical equation or formula, which is not patentable. In 1981, however, the United States Supreme Court held that it is possible to obtain a patent for a *process* that incorporates a computer program—providing, of course, that the process itself is patentable.[19] Subsequently, many patents have been issued for software-related inventions.

Patents for Business Processes In 1998, in a landmark case, *State Street Bank & Trust Co. v. Signature Financial Group, Inc.*,[20] the U.S. Court of Appeals for the Federal Circuit ruled that business processes were patentable. After this decision, numerous technology firms applied for business process patents. Walker Digital applied for a business process patent for its "Dutch auction" system, which allowed consumers to make offers for airline tickets on the Internet and led to the creation of Priceline.com. Amazon.com obtained a business process patent for its "one-click" ordering system, a method of processing credit-card orders securely. Indeed, after the *State Street* decision, the number of Internet-related patents issued by the U.S. Patent and Trademark Office increased dramatically.

Patent Infringement

If a firm makes, uses, or sells another's patented design, product, or process without the patent owner's permission, the tort of patent infringement occurs. Patent infringement may arise even though the patent owner has not put the patented product into commerce. Patent infringement may also occur even though not all features or parts of a product are identical to those used in the patented invention, provided that the features are equivalent. (With respect to a patented process, however, all steps or their equivalent must be copied for infringement to exist.)

Note that, as a general rule, under U.S. law no patent infringement occurs when a patented product is made and sold in another country. In 2007, this issue came before the United States Supreme Court in a patent infringement case that AT&T Corporation had brought against Microsoft Corporation. AT&T holds a patent on a device used to digitally encode, compress, and process recorded speech. Microsoft's Windows operating system, as Microsoft admitted, incorporated software code that infringed on AT&T's patent. The only question

19. *Diamond v. Diehr*, 450 U.S. 175, 101 S.Ct. 1048, 67 L.Ed.2d 155 (1981).
20. 149 F.3d 1368 (Fed.Cir. 1998).

before the Supreme Court was whether Microsoft's liability extended to computers made in another country. The Court held that it did not. Microsoft was liable only for infringement in the United States and not for the Windows-based computers sold in foreign locations. The Court reasoned that Microsoft had not "supplied" the software for the computers but had only electronically transmitted a master copy, which the foreign manufacturers then copied and loaded onto the computers.[21]

Remedies for Patent Infringement

If a patent is infringed, the patent holder may sue for relief in federal court. The patent holder can seek an injunction against the infringer and can also request damages for royalties and lost profits. In some cases, the court may grant the winning party reimbursement for attorneys' fees and costs. If the court determines that the infringement was willful, the court can triple the amount of damages awarded (treble damages).

In the past, permanent injunctions were routinely granted to prevent future infringement. In 2006, however, the United States Supreme Court ruled that patent holders are not automatically entitled to a permanent injunction against future infringing activities—the courts have discretion to decide whether equity requires it. According to the Supreme Court, a patent holder must prove that it has suffered irreparable injury and that the public interest would not be disserved by a permanent injunction.[22]

This decision gives courts discretion to decide what is equitable in the circumstances and allows them to consider what is in the public interest rather than just the interests of the parties. For example, in the first case applying this rule, a court found that although Microsoft had infringed on the patent of a small software company, the latter was not entitled to an injunction. According to the court, the small company was not irreparably harmed and could be adequately compensated by damages. Also, the public might suffer negative effects from an injunction because the infringement involved part of Microsoft's widely used Office suite software.[23]

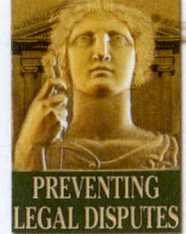

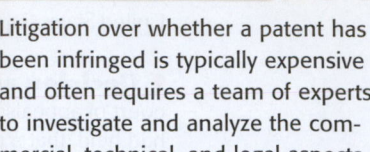

PREVENTING LEGAL DISPUTES

Litigation over whether a patent has been infringed is typically expensive and often requires a team of experts to investigate and analyze the commercial, technical, and legal aspects of the case. Because of these costs, a businessperson facing patent infringement litigation—either as the patent holder or as the alleged infringer—should carefully evaluate the evidence as well as the various settlement options. If both sides appear to have good arguments as to whether the patent was infringed or whether it was valid, it may be in a firm's best interest to settle the case. This is particularly true if the firm is not certain that the court would grant an injunction.

Similarly, if the patented technology is not commercially significant to one's business, it might be best to consider a nonexclusive license as a means of resolving the dispute. This option is more important for patent holders now that injunctions may be harder to obtain. Settlement may be as simple as an agreement that one party will stop making, using, or selling the patented product or process, or it may involve monetary compensation for past activities and/or licensing for future activities.

SECTION 4 Copyrights

A **copyright** is an intangible property right granted by federal statute to the author or originator of a literary or artistic production of a specified type. Today, copyrights are governed by the Copyright Act of 1976,[24] as amended. Works created after January 1, 1978, are automatically given statutory copyright protection for the life of the author plus 70 years. For copyrights owned by publishing houses, the copyright expires 95 years from the date of publication or 120 years from the date of creation, whichever is first. For works by more than one author, the copyright expires 70 years after the death of the last surviving author.

These time periods reflect the extensions of the length of copyright protection enacted by Congress in the Copyright Term Extension Act of 1998.[25] Critics challenged this act as overstepping the bounds of Congress's power and violating the constitutional

21. *Microsoft Corp. v. AT&T Corp.*, ___ U.S. ___, 127 S.Ct. 1746, 167 L.Ed.2d 737 (2007).
22. *eBay, Inc. v. MercExchange, LLC*, 547 U.S. 388, 126 S.Ct. 1837, 164 L.Ed.2d 641 (2006).
23. *Z4 Technologies, Inc. v. Microsoft Corp.*, 434 F.Supp.2d 437 (E.D.Tex. 2006).
24. 17 U.S.C. Sections 101 *et seq.*
25. 17 U.S.C. Section 302.

requirement that copyrights endure for only a limited time. In 2003, however, the United States Supreme Court upheld the act in *Eldred v. Ashcroft.*[26] This holding obviously favored copyright holders by preventing copyrighted works from the 1920s and 1930s from losing protection and falling into the public domain for an additional two decades.

Copyrights can be registered with the U.S. Copyright Office in Washington, D.C. A copyright owner no longer needs to place the symbol © or the term *Copr.* or *Copyright* on the work to have the work protected against infringement. Chances are that if somebody created it, somebody owns it.

What Is Protected Expression?

Works that are copyrightable include books, records, films, artworks, architectural plans, menus, music videos, product packaging, and computer software. To be protected, a work must be "fixed in a durable medium" from which it can be perceived, reproduced, or communicated. Protection is automatic. Registration is not required.

To obtain protection under the Copyright Act, a work must be original and fall into one of the following categories:

1. Literary works (including newspaper and magazine articles, computer and training manuals, catalogues, brochures, and print advertisements).
2. Musical works and accompanying words (including advertising jingles).
3. Dramatic works and accompanying music.
4. Pantomimes and choreographic works (including ballets and other forms of dance).
5. Pictorial, graphic, and sculptural works (including cartoons, maps, posters, statues, and even stuffed animals).
6. Motion pictures and other audiovisual works (including multimedia works).
7. Sound recordings.
8. Architectural works.

Section 102 Exclusions Section 102 of the Copyright Act specifically excludes copyright protection for any "idea, procedure, process, system, method of operation, concept, principle, or discovery, regardless of the form in which it is described, explained, illustrated, or embodied." Note that it is not possible to copyright an *idea*. The underlying ideas embodied in a work may be freely used by others. What is copyrightable is the particular way in which an idea is expressed. Whenever an idea and an expression are inseparable, the expression cannot be copyrighted. Generally, anything that is not an original expression will not qualify for copyright protection. Facts widely known to the public are not copyrightable. Page numbers are not copyrightable because they follow a sequence known to everyone. Mathematical calculations are not copyrightable.

Compilations of Facts Unlike ideas, *compilations* of facts are copyrightable. Under Section 103 of the Copyright Act a compilation is "a work formed by the collection and assembling of preexisting materials or data that are selected, coordinated, or arranged in such a way that the resulting work as a whole constitutes an original work of authorship." The key requirement in the copyrightability of a compilation is originality. If the facts are selected, coordinated, or arranged in an original way, they can qualify for copyright protection. Therefore, the white pages of a telephone directory do not qualify for copyright protection because the facts (names, addresses, and telephone numbers) are listed in alphabetical order rather than being selected, coordinated, or arranged in an original way.[27] The Yellow Pages of a telephone directory, in contrast, can qualify for copyright protection.[28] Similarly, a compilation of information about yachts listed for sale may qualify for copyright protection.[29]

Copyright Infringement

Whenever the form or expression of an idea is copied, an infringement of copyright has occurred. The reproduction does not have to be exactly the same as the original, nor does it have to reproduce the original in its entirety. If a substantial part of the original is reproduced, the copyright has been infringed.

Damages for Copyright Infringement Those who infringe copyrights may be liable for damages or criminal penalties. These range from actual damages or statutory damages, imposed at the court's discretion, to criminal proceedings for willful violations. Actual damages are based on the harm caused to the copyright holder by the infringement, while

26. 537 U.S. 186, 123 S.Ct. 769, 154 L.Ed.2d 683 (2003).

27. *Feist Publications, Inc. v. Rural Telephone Service Co.,* 499 U.S. 340, 111 S.Ct. 1282, 113 L.Ed.2d 358 (1991).

28. *Bellsouth Advertising & Publishing Corp. v. Donnelley Information Publishing, Inc.,* 999 F.2d 1436 (11th Cir. 1993).

29. *BUC International Corp. v. International Yacht Council, Ltd.,* 489 F.3d 1129 (11th Cir. 2007).

statutory damages, not to exceed $150,000, are provided for under the Copyright Act. Criminal proceedings may result in fines and/or imprisonment.

The "Fair Use" Exception An exception to liability for copyright infringement is made under the "fair use" doctrine. In certain circumstances, a person or organization can reproduce copyrighted material without paying royalties (fees paid to the copyright holder for the privilege of reproducing the copyrighted material). Section 107 of the Copyright Act provides as follows:

> [T]he fair use of a copyrighted work, including such use by reproduction in copies or phonorecords or by any other means specified by [Section 106 of the Copyright Act], for purposes such as criticism, comment, news reporting, teaching (including multiple copies for classroom use), scholarship, or research, is not an infringement of copyright. In determining whether the use made of a work in any particular case is a fair use the factors to be considered shall include–
>
> (1) the purpose and character of the use, including whether such use is of a commercial nature or is for nonprofit educational purposes;
>
> (2) the nature of the copyrighted work;
>
> (3) the amount and substantiality of the portion used in relation to the copyrighted work as a whole; and
>
> (4) the effect of the use upon the potential market for or value of the copyrighted work.

Because these guidelines are very broad, the courts determine whether a particular use is fair on a case-by-case basis. Thus, anyone reproducing copyrighted material may still be committing a violation. In determining whether a use is fair, courts have often considered the fourth factor to be the most important.

In the following case, the owner of copyrighted music had issued a license to the manufacturer of karaoke devices to reproduce the sound recordings, but had not given its permission to reprint the song lyrics. The issue was whether the manufacturer should pay additional fees to display the lyrics at the same time as the music was playing. The manufacturer claimed, in part, that its use of the lyrics was educational and therefore did not constitute copyright infringement under the fair use exception.

CASE 8.4 Leadsinger, Inc. v. BMG Music Publishing

United States Court of Appeals, Ninth Circuit, 2008. 512 F.3d 522.
www.ca9.uscourts.gov[a]

Background and Facts Leadsinger, Inc., manufactures and sells karaoke devices. Specifically, it sells a microphone that has a chip inside with embedded songs and lyrics that appear at the bottom of a TV screen. This device is similar to those in which compact discs and DVDs are inserted to display lyrics on a TV monitor. All karaoke devices necessarily involve copyrighted works. BMG Music Publishing owns and administers copyrights for such music. BMG had issued to Leadsinger the appropriate licenses to copyrighted musical compositions under Section 115 of the Copyright Act. Leadsinger sought a declaration that it was entitled to print or display song lyrics in real time with song recordings without paying any additional fees. In contrast, BMG demanded that Leadsinger and other karaoke companies pay a "lyric reprint" fee and a "synchronization" fee. Leadsinger refused to pay, filing for a declaratory judgment to resolve whether it had the right to display song lyrics in real time with sound recordings without paying any additional fees. The district court concluded that a Section 115 license did not grant Leadsinger the right to display visual images *and* lyrics in real time with music. Leadsinger appealed to the U.S. Court of Appeals for the Ninth Circuit.

Decision and Rationale The U.S. Court of Appeals for the Ninth Circuit affirmed the district court's decision to dismiss Leadsinger's complaint without the possibility of amending it. The court pointed out that a copyright holder has a right to control "the synchronization of musical compositions with the content of audiovisual works." Consequently, courts have required parties to obtain synchronization licenses from copyright holders. Moreover, "lyrics are copyrightable as a literary work and, therefore, enjoy separate protection under the Copyright Act." Leadsinger's microchip that stores visual images and visual representations of lyrics falls within the definition

a. Click on "Opinions." When that page opens, click on "2008" and then on "January." Scroll down to "01/02/08." Find the case name and click on it to access the opinion.

CASE 8.4 CONTINUED

of an audiovisual work. Leadsinger could not avail itself of the fair use doctrine simply by arguing that karaoke devices help teach singing.

- **The Global Dimension** *Could Leadsinger have attempted to show that its karaoke programs were used extensively abroad to help others learn English? If successful in this line of reasoning, might Leadsinger have prevailed on appeal? Explain your answer.*

- **The Legal Environment Dimension** *What was the underlying basis of Leadsinger's attempt to avoid paying additional licensing fees to BMG?*

Copyright Protection for Software

In 1980, Congress passed the Computer Software Copyright Act, which amended the Copyright Act of 1976 to include computer programs in the list of creative works protected by federal copyright law.[30] The 1980 statute, which classifies computer programs as "literary works," defines a computer program as a "set of statements or instructions to be used directly or indirectly in a computer in order to bring about a certain result."

The unique nature of computer programs, however, has created problems for the courts in applying and interpreting the 1980 act. Generally, the courts have held that copyright protection extends not only to those parts of a computer program that can be read by humans, such as the "high-level" language of a source code, but also to the binary-language object code, which is readable only by the computer.[31] Additionally, such elements as the overall structure, sequence, and organization of a program have been deemed copyrightable, but generally not the "look and feel" of computer programs.[32] The "look and feel" of computer programs refers to their general appearance, command structure, video images, menus, windows, and other screen displays.

SECTION 5 Copyrights in Digital Information

Copyright law is probably the most important form of intellectual property protection on the Internet. This is because much of the material on the Internet consists of works of authorship (including multimedia presentations, software, and database information), which are the traditional focus of copyright law. Copyright law is also important because the nature of the Internet requires that data be "copied" to be transferred online. Traditionally, many of the controversies arising in this area of the law have involved copies.

The Copyright Act of 1976

When Congress drafted the principal U.S. law governing copyrights, the Copyright Act of 1976, cyberspace did not exist for most of us. At that time, the primary threat to copyright owners was from persons making unauthorized *tangible* copies of works. Because of the nature of cyberspace, however, one of the early controversies was determining at what point an intangible, electronic "copy" of a work has been made. The courts have held that loading a file or program into a computer's random access memory, or RAM, constitutes the making of a "copy" for purposes of copyright law.[33] RAM is a portion of a computer's memory into which a file, for example, is loaded so that it can be accessed. Thus, a copyright is infringed when a party downloads software into RAM without owning the software or otherwise having a right to download it.[34] Today, technology has vastly increased the potential for copyright infringement. For a discussion of whether search engines that use thumbnail images of copyrighted materials are liable for infringement, see this chapter's *Insight into E-Commerce* feature on pages 160 and 161.

Further Developments in Copyright Law

In the last fifteen years, Congress has enacted legislation designed specifically to protect copyright holders in a digital age. Particularly significant are the No

30. Pub. L. No. 96-517 (1980), amending 17 U.S.C. Sections 101, 117.

31. See *Stern Electronics, Inc. v. Kaufman*, 669 F.2d 852 (2d Cir. 1982); and *Apple Computer, Inc. v. Franklin Computer Corp.*, 714 F.2d 1240 (3d Cir. 1983).

32. *Whelan Associates, Inc. v. Jaslow Dental Laboratory, Inc.*, 797 F.2d 1222 (3d Cir. 1986).

33. *MAI Systems Corp. v. Peak Computer, Inc.*, 991 F.2d 511 (9th Cir. 1993).

34. *DSC Communications Corp. v. Pulse Communications, Inc.*, 170 F.3d 1354 (Fed. Cir. 1999).

INSIGHT INTO E-COMMERCE
Search Engines versus Copyright Owners

Since their humble beginnings more than a decade ago, search engines have become ubiquitous in the e-commerce world. Every day, millions of consumers use search engines to locate various products on the Web. A major legal question arises, however, when the results of a search include copyrighted intellectual property, such as books, downloadable software, movies and other videos, and images. Can the owner of the search engine that returned these results be held liable for copyright infringement?

The Betamax Doctrine

The basic rule that has governed issues relating to the application of new technology for uses that might include copyright infringement was set out more than two decades ago by the United States Supreme Court in the landmark case *Sony Corporation of America v. Universal City Studios.*[a] The case involved the then new technology of the videocassette recorder (VCR), which was available in two formats—VHS and Betamax. Owners of copyrighted television programs, concerned that VCR owners were using the equipment to copy TV programs, brought a suit against a VCR manufacturer, claiming that it was liable for its customers' copyright infringement. The Supreme Court, however, in what became known as the *Betamax doctrine,* held that the manufacturer was not liable for creating a technology that certain customers might use for copyright infringing purposes, as long as that technology was capable of substantial noninfringing uses. Legal scholars believe that the Betamax doctrine has allowed for the development of many other technologies that are capable of both infringing and noninfringing uses—including CD-ROM burners, DVRs, TiVo, Apple's iPod, and even the personal computer.

As discussed later in the text, twenty years after the *Sony* case, organizations and companies in the music and film industries brought a copyright infringement suit against Grokster, Morpheus, and KaZaA, the makers of file-sharing software that allowed millions of individuals to copy copyrighted music. In that case, the Supreme Court did find that there was ample evidence that the software makers had taken steps to promote copyright infringement, but significantly the Court did not overturn the Betamax doctrine. The Court did not specify what steps are necessary to impose liability on the provider of a technology, however.[b]

Does Providing Thumbnail Images Violate Copyright Law?

Just as VCRs and file-sharing technology raised new issues of copyright infringement, so does today's search engine technology. In response to a search

a. 464 U.S. 417, 104 S.Ct. 774, 78 L.Ed.2d 574 (1984).

b. *Metro-Goldwyn-Mayer Studios, Inc. v. Grokster, Ltd.,* 545 U.S. 913, 125 S.Ct. 2764, 162 L.Ed.2d 781 (2005).

Electronic Theft Act of 1997[35] and the Digital Millennium Copyright Act of 1998.[36]

The No Electronic Theft Act Prior to 1997, criminal penalties could be imposed under copyright law only if unauthorized copies were exchanged for financial gain. Yet much piracy of copyrighted materials was "altruistic" in nature; that is, unauthorized copies were made and distributed not for financial gain but simply for reasons of generosity—to share the copies with others. To combat altruistic piracy and for other reasons, Congress passed the No Electronic Theft (NET) Act of 1997.

NET extended criminal liability for the piracy of copyrighted materials to persons who exchange unauthorized copies of copyrighted works, such as software, even though they realize no profit from the exchange. The act also altered the traditional "fair use" doctrine by imposing penalties on those who make unauthorized electronic copies of books, magazines, movies, or music for *personal* use. The criminal penalties for violating the act are relatively severe; they include fines as high as $250,000 and incarceration for up to five years.

The Digital Millennium Copyright Act of 1998 The passage of the Digital Millennium Copyright Act (DMCA) of 1998 gave significant protection to owners of copyrights in digital information.[37]

35. Pub. L. No. 105-147 (1997). Codified at 17 U.S.C. Sections 101, 506; 18 U.S.C. Sections 2311, 2319, 2319A, 2320; and 28 U.S.C. Sections 994 and 1498.

36. 17 U.S.C. Sections 512, 1201–1205, 1301–1332; and 28 U.S.C. Section 4001.

37. This act implemented the World Intellectual Property Organization Copyright Treaty of 1996, which will be discussed later in this chapter.

request, numerous search engines show thumbnail images of books, album covers, and copyrighted photographs. Arriba Soft Corporation (now ditto.com), for example, operated a search engine that displayed its results in the form of thumbnail pictures. It obtained its database of photographs by copying images from other Web sites. When professional photographer Leslie Kelly discovered that his copyrighted photographs were part of Arriba's database, he brought a suit for copyright infringement. Arriba prevailed, as the Ninth Circuit Court of Appeals ruled that its thumbnails were a fair use under the Copyright Act.[c]

A recent innovation enables search engines to search specifically for images. Google Image Search, for example, stores thumbnail images of its search results on Google's servers. The thumbnail images are reduced, lower-resolution versions of full-size images stored on third party computers. In 2005, *Perfect 10,* a men's magazine that features high-resolution photographs of topless and nude women, brought a suit to enjoin Google from caching and displaying its photographs as thumbnails. *Perfect 10* argued that because Google "created the audience" for its sites and indexes, Google should be liable for whatever infringements occurred on those sites. The magazine also contended that Google had directly infringed *Perfect 10*'s copyrights by in-line linking and framing images published on other sites. (The case was combined with a similar suit brought against Amazon.com for its A9 search engine.) Once again, however, as in its *Arriba* decision, the Ninth Circuit Court of Appeals held that the thumbnails constituted a fair use. Pointing out the public benefit that search engines provide, the court said that until *Perfect 10* gave Google specific URLs for infringing images, Google had no duty to act and could not be held liable. The court further held that Google could not "supervise or control" the third party Web sites linked to its search results.[d] In sum, the court refused to hold the creators of image search technology liable for users' infringement because the technology is capable of both infringing and noninfringing uses—just as the Betamax doctrine protected VCR manufacturers from liability for users' infringement.

CRITICAL THINKING

INSIGHT INTO TECHNOLOGY

What has changed in the world of technology since the Betamax doctrine was enunciated? Does the fact that more and more intellectual property is being digitized and made available online alter the reasoning underlying the Betamax doctrine?

c. *Kelly v. Arriba Soft Corporation,* 336 F.3d 811 (9th Cir. 2003).

d. *Perfect 10, Inc. v. Amazon.com, Inc.,* 487 F.3d 701 (9th Cir. 2007).

Among other things, the act established civil and criminal penalties for anyone who circumvents (bypasses, or gets around—by using a special decryption program, for example) encryption software or other technological antipiracy protection. Also prohibited are the manufacture, import, sale, and distribution of devices or services for circumvention.

The DMCA provides for exceptions to fit the needs of libraries, scientists, universities, and others. In general, the law does not restrict the "fair use" of circumvention methods for educational and other noncommercial purposes. For example, circumvention is allowed to test computer security, to conduct encryption research, to protect personal privacy, and to enable parents to monitor their children's use of the Internet. The exceptions are to be reconsidered every three years.

The DMCA also limits the liability of Internet service providers (ISPs). Under the act, an ISP is not liable for any copyright infringement by its customer *unless* the ISP is aware of the subscriber's violation. An ISP may be held liable only if it fails to take action to shut the subscriber down after learning of the violation. A copyright holder must act promptly, however, by pursuing a claim in court, or the subscriber has the right to be restored to online access.

MP3 and File-Sharing Technology

Soon after the Internet became popular, a few enterprising programmers created software to compress large data files, particularly those associated with music. The reduced file sizes make transmitting music over the Internet feasible. The most widely known compression and decompression system is MP3, which enables music fans to download songs or entire CDs onto their computers or onto portable listening devices, such as Rio or iPod. The MP3 system also made it possible for music fans to access other music fans' files by engaging in file-sharing via the Internet.

Peer-to-Peer (P2P) Networking File-sharing via the Internet is accomplished through what is called **peer-to-peer (P2P) networking.** The concept is simple. Rather than going through a central Web server, P2P uses numerous personal computers (PCs) that are connected to the Internet. Files stored on one PC can be accessed by others who are members of the same network. Sometimes this is called a **distributed network** because parts of the network are distributed all over the country or the world. File-sharing offers an unlimited number of uses for distributed networks. For example, thousands of researchers allow their home computers' computing power to be simultaneously accessed through file-sharing software so that very large mathematical problems can be solved quickly. Additionally, persons scattered throughout the country or the world can work together on the same project by using file-sharing programs.

Sharing Stored Music Files When file-sharing is used to download others' stored music files, copyright issues arise. Recording artists and their labels stand to lose large amounts of royalties and revenues if relatively few CDs are purchased and then made available on distributed networks, from which everyone can get them for free. The issue of file-sharing infringement has been the subject of an ongoing debate for some time.

For example, in the highly publicized case of *A&M Records, Inc. v. Napster, Inc.*,[38] several firms in the recording industry sued Napster, Inc., the owner of the then popular Napster Web site. The Napster site provided registered users with free software that enabled them to transfer exact copies of the contents of MP3 files from one computer to another via the Internet. Napster also maintained centralized search indices so that users could locate specific titles or artists' recordings on the computers of other members. The firms argued that Napster should be liable for contributory and vicarious[39] (indirect) copyright infringement because it assisted others in obtaining copies of copyrighted music without the copyright owners' permission. The federal district court agreed, and the U.S. Court of Appeals for the Ninth Circuit affirmed, holding Napster liable for violating copyright laws. The court reasoned that Napster was liable for its users' infringement because the technology that Napster had used was centralized and gave it "the ability to locate infringing material listed on its search indices and the right to terminate users' access to the system."

After the *Napster* decision, the recording industry filed and won numerous lawsuits against companies that distribute online file-sharing software. The courts held these companies liable based on two theories: contributory infringement, which applies if the company had reason to know about a user's infringement and failed to stop it, and vicarious liability, which exists if the company was able to control the users' activities and stood to benefit financially from their infringement.

The Evolution of File-Sharing Technologies In the wake of the *Napster* decision, other companies developed new technologies that allow P2P network users to share stored music files, without paying a fee, more quickly and efficiently than ever. Software such as Morpheus, KaZaA, and LimeWire, for example, provides users with an interface that is similar to a Web browser.[40] Companies need not locate songs for users on other members' computers. Instead, the software automatically annotates files with descriptive information so that the music can easily be categorized and cross-referenced (by artist and title, for instance). When a user performs a search, the software is able to locate a list of peers that have the file available for downloading. Also, to expedite the P2P transfer, the software distributes the download task over the entire list of peers simultaneously. By downloading even one file, the user becomes a point of distribution for that file, which is then automatically shared with others on the network.

Because the file-sharing software was decentralized and did not use search indices that would enable the companies to locate infringing material, they had

38. 239 F.3d 1004 (9th Cir. 2001).

39. *Vicarious (indirect) liability* exists when one person is subject to liability for another's actions. A common example occurs in the employment context, when an employer is held vicariously liable by third parties for torts committed by employees in the course of their employment.

40. Note that in 2005, KaZaA entered into a settlement agreement with four major music companies that had alleged copyright infringement. KaZaA agreed to offer only legitimate, fee-based music downloads in the future.

no ability to supervise or control which music (or other media files) their users exchanged. In addition, it was difficult for courts to apply the traditional doctrines of contributory and vicarious liability to these new technologies.

The Supreme Court's *Grokster* Decision

In 2005, the United States Supreme Court expanded the liability of file-sharing companies in its decision in *Metro-Goldwyn-Mayer Studios, Inc. v. Grokster, Ltd.*[41] In that case, organizations in the music and film industry (the plaintiffs) sued several companies that distribute file-sharing software used in P2P networks, including Grokster, Ltd., and StreamCast Networks, Inc. (the defendants). The plaintiffs claimed that the defendants were contributorily and vicariously liable for the infringement of their end users. The Supreme Court held that "one who distributes a device [software] with the object of promoting its use to infringe the copyright, as shown by clear expression or other affirmative steps taken to foster infringement, is liable for the resulting acts of infringement by third parties."

Although the Supreme Court did not specify what kind of affirmative steps are necessary to establish liability, it did note that there was ample evidence that the defendants had acted with the intent to cause copyright violations. (Grokster, Ltd., later settled this dispute out of court and stopped distributing its software.) Essentially, this means that file-sharing companies that have taken affirmative steps to promote copyright infringement can be held secondarily liable for millions of infringing acts that their users commit daily. Because the Court did not define exactly what is necessary to impose liability, however, a substantial amount of legal uncertainty remains concerning this issue. Although some file-sharing companies have been shut down, illegal file-sharing—and lawsuits against file-sharing companies and the individuals who use them—has continued in the years since this decision.

SECTION 6 Trade Secrets

The law of trade secrets protects some business processes and information that are not, or cannot be, patented, copyrighted, or trademarked against appropriation by competitors. **Trade secrets** include customer lists, plans, research and development, pricing information, marketing methods, production techniques, and generally anything that makes an individual company unique and that would have value to a competitor.

Unlike copyright and trademark protection, protection of trade secrets extends both to ideas and to their expression. (For this reason, and because a trade secret involves no registration or filing requirements, trade secret protection may be well suited for software.) Of course, the secret formula, method, or other information must be disclosed to some persons, particularly to key employees. Businesses generally attempt to protect their trade secrets by having all employees who use the process or information agree in their contracts, or in confidentiality agreements, never to divulge it. (See the *Business Application* feature on the next page.)

State and Federal Law on Trade Secrets

Under Section 757 of the *Restatement of Torts*, "One who discloses or uses another's trade secret, without a privilege to do so, is liable to the other if (1) he [or she] discovered the secret by improper means, or (2) his [or her] disclosure or use constitutes a breach of confidence reposed in him [or her] by the other in disclosing the secret to him [or her]." The theft of confidential business data by industrial espionage, as when a business taps into a competitor's computer, is a theft of trade secrets without any contractual violation and is actionable in itself.

Until thirty years ago, virtually all law with respect to trade secrets was common law. In an effort to reduce the unpredictability of the common law in this area, a model act, the Uniform Trade Secrets Act, was presented to the states for adoption in 1979. Parts of the act have been adopted in more than thirty states. Typically, a state that has adopted parts of the act has adopted only those parts that encompass its own existing common law. Additionally, in 1996 Congress passed the Economic Espionage Act,[42] which made the theft of trade secrets a federal crime. We will examine the provisions and significance of this act in Chapter 9, in the context of crimes related to business.

Trade Secrets in Cyberspace

New computer technology is undercutting a business firm's ability to protect its confidential information, including trade secrets.[43] For example, a dishonest

41. 545 U.S. 913, 125 S.Ct. 2764, 162 L.Ed.2d 781 (2005).

42. 18 U.S.C. Sections 1831–1839.

43. Note that in at least one case, a court has held that customers' e-mail addresses may constitute trade secrets. See *T-N-T Motorsports, Inc. v. Hennessey Motorsports, Inc.*, 965 S.W.2d 18 (Tex.App.—Houston [1 Dist.] 1998); rehearing overruled (1998); petition dismissed (1998).

BUSINESS APPLICATION
Protecting Trade Secrets

MANAGEMENT FACES A LEGAL ISSUE

Most successful businesses have trade secrets. The law protects trade secrets indefinitely provided that the information is not generally known, is kept secret, and has commercial value. Sometimes, of course, a business needs to disclose secret information to a party in the course of conducting business. For example, a company may need to engage a consultant to revamp a computer system or hire a marketing firm to implement a sales program. In addition, the company may also wish to expand its operations and will need a foreign agent or distributor. All of these individuals or firms may need access to some of the company's trade secrets. One way to protect against the unauthorized disclosure of such information is through *confidentiality agreements.* In such an agreement, one party promises not to divulge information about the other party's activities to anyone else and not to use the other party's confidential information for his or her own benefit. Most confidentiality agreements are included in licensing and employment contracts. The legal question is whether the courts will uphold such an agreement if a business claims it has been violated.

WHAT THE COURTS SAY

The courts are divided on the validity of confidentiality agreements, particularly in employment contracts. At issue is often whether the trade secrets described in the confidentiality agreement are truly "secrets." If they are generally known outside the employer's business, the courts normally will not enforce the agreement. When a clear argument can be made that such secrets are truly secret, a court normally will enforce a confidentiality agreement. For example, consider an insurance company. An employee signed both a confidentiality agreement and a *noncompete clause* (see Chapter 13). Just before quitting, that employee copied her employer's proprietary sales, marketing, and product information sheets. She then used them while working for her new employer. She also solicited former clients to move their business to her new employer's firm. An appellate court upheld an injunction preventing this employee from using, divulging, disclosing, or communicating trade secrets and confidential information derived from her former employer.[a]

In the technology sector, confidentiality agreements are widespread for obvious reasons. One case involved a complicated system for testing flash memory cards, like those used in digital cameras and MP3 music players. An employee copied project documents he had authored and transmitted them to a third party for the purpose of using those documents to launch his own independent business. This employee had signed an explicit confidentiality agreement. At trial, one of his defenses was that his former employer had not used reasonable efforts to maintain secrecy because some employees were uncertain how to apply the company's procedures for handling confidential and trade secret documents. The court was unimpressed. The former employee was prevented from using those trade secrets.[b]

Employers often attempt to protect trade secrets by requiring potential employees to sign noncompete agreements. If the employer would suffer irreparable harm from the former employee's accepting employment with a competitor, the court will often uphold such agreements.[c]

IMPLICATIONS FOR MANAGERS

Most companies should require their employees to sign a confidentiality agreement to protect trade secrets. That is not enough, though. A company should have formal written procedures that apply to the selection and retention of documents relating to valuable trade secrets. If these documents exist only on hard drives, the firm should put an encryption system in place and limit access to the files that contain trade secrets.

a. *Freeman v. Brown Hiller, Inc.,* ___ S.W.3d ___, 2008 WL 868252. (Ark.App. 2008).

b. *Verigy US, Inc. v. Mayder,* ___ F.Supp.2d ___, 2008 WL 564634 (N.D.Cal. 2008).

c. *Gleeson v. Preferred Sourcing, LLC,* 883 N.E.2d 164 (Ind.App. 2008).

CONCEPT SUMMARY 8.1
Forms of Intellectual Property

	Definition	How Acquired	Duration	Remedy for Infringement
PATENT	A grant from the government that gives an inventor exclusive rights to an invention.	By filing a patent application with the U.S. Patent and Trademark Office and receiving its approval.	Twenty years from the date of the application; for design patents, fourteen years.	Monetary damages, including royalties and lost profits, *plus* attorneys' fees. Damages may be tripled for intentional infringements.
COPYRIGHT	The right of an author or originator of a literary or artistic work, or other production that falls within a specified category, to have the exclusive use of that work for a given period of time.	Automatic (once the work or creation is fixed in a durable medium). Only the *expression* of an idea (and not the idea itself) can be protected by copyright.	For authors: the life of the author plus 70 years. For publishers: 95 years after the date of publication or 120 years after creation.	Actual damages plus profits received by the party who infringed or statutory damages under the Copyright Act, *plus* costs and attorneys' fees in either situation.
TRADEMARK (SERVICE MARK AND TRADE DRESS)	Any distinctive word, name, symbol, or device (image or appearance), or combination thereof, that an entity uses to distinguish its goods or services from those of others. The owner has the exclusive right to use that mark or trade dress.	1. At common law, ownership created by use of the mark. 2. Registration with the appropriate federal or state office gives notice and is permitted if the mark is currently in use or will be within the next six months.	Unlimited, as long as it is in use. To continue notice by registration, the owner must renew by filing between the fifth and sixth years, and thereafter, every ten years.	1. Injunction prohibiting the future use of the mark. 2. Actual damages plus profits received by the party who infringed (can be increased under the Lanham Act). 3. Destruction of articles that infringed. 4. *Plus* costs and attorneys' fees.
TRADE SECRET	Any information that a business possesses and that gives the business an advantage over competitors (including formulas, lists, patterns, plans, processes, and programs).	Through the originality and development of the information and processes that constitute the business secret and are unknown to others.	Unlimited, so long as not revealed to others. Once revealed to others, it is no longer a trade secret.	Monetary damages for misappropriation (the Uniform Trade Secrets Act also permits punitive damages if willful), *plus* costs and attorneys' fees.

employee could e-mail trade secrets in a company's computer to a competitor or a future employer. If e-mail is not an option, the employee might walk out with the information on a flash pen drive.

SECTION 7 International Protection for Intellectual Property

For many years, the United States has been a party to various international agreements relating to intellectual property rights. For example, the Paris Convention of 1883, to which about 170 countries are signatory, allows parties in one country to file for patent and trademark protection in any of the other member countries. Other international agreements in this area include the Berne Convention, the TRIPS agreement, and the Madrid Protocol.

The Berne Convention

Under the Berne Convention (an international copyright agreement) of 1886, as amended, if an American writes a book, every country that has signed the convention must recognize the American author's copyright in the book. Also, if a citizen of a country that has not signed the convention first publishes a book in one of the 170 countries that have signed, all other countries that have signed the convention must recognize that author's copyright. Copyright notice is not needed to gain protection under the Berne Convention for works published after March 1, 1989.

The laws of many countries, as well as international laws, are being updated to reflect changes in technology and the expansion of the Internet. Copyright holders and other owners of intellectual property generally agree that changes in the law are needed to stop the increasing international piracy of their property. The World Intellectual Property Organization (WIPO) Copyright Treaty of 1996, a special agreement under the Berne Convention, attempts to update international law governing copyright protection to include more safeguards against copyright infringement via the Internet. The United States signed the WIPO treaty in 1996 and implemented its terms in the Digital Millennium Copyright Act of 1998, which was discussed earlier in this chapter.

The Berne Convention and other international agreements have given some protection to intellectual property on a global level. Another significant worldwide agreement to increase such protection is the Trade-Related Aspects of Intellectual Property Rights agreement—or, more simply, the TRIPS agreement.

The TRIPS Agreement

Representatives from more than one hundred nations signed the TRIPS agreement in 1994. It was one of several documents that were annexed to the agreement that created the World Trade Organization, or WTO, in 1995. The TRIPS agreement established, for the first time, standards for the international protection of intellectual property rights, including patents, trademarks, and copyrights for movies, computer programs, books, and music. The TRIPS agreement provides that each member country must include in its domestic laws broad intellectual property rights and effective remedies (including civil and criminal penalties) for violations of those rights.

Members Cannot Discriminate against Foreign Intellectual Property Owners

Generally, the TRIPS agreement forbids member nations from discriminating against foreign owners of intellectual property rights (in the administration, regulation, or adjudication of such rights). In other words, a member nation cannot give its own nationals (citizens) favorable treatment without offering the same treatment to nationals of all member countries. For instance, if a U.S. software manufacturer brings a suit for the infringement of intellectual property rights under a member nation's national laws, the U.S. manufacturer is entitled to receive the same treatment as a domestic manufacturer. Each member nation must also ensure that legal procedures are available for parties who wish to bring actions for infringement of intellectual property rights. Additionally, a related document established a mechanism for settling disputes among member nations.

Covers All Types of Intellectual Property

Particular provisions of the TRIPS agreement relate to patent, trademark, and copyright protection for intellectual property. The agreement specifically provides copyright protection for computer programs by stating that compilations of data, databases, and other materials are "intellectual creations" and are to be protected as copyrightable works. Other provisions relate to trade secrets and the rental of computer programs and cinematographic works.

The Madrid Protocol

In the past, one of the difficulties in protecting U.S. trademarks internationally was the time and expense involved in applying for trademark registration in foreign countries. The filing fees and procedures for trademark registration vary significantly among individual countries. The Madrid Protocol, which President George W. Bush signed into law in 2003, may help to resolve these problems. The Madrid Protocol is an international treaty that has been signed by seventy-three countries. Under its provisions, a U.S. company wishing to register its trademark abroad can submit a single application and designate other member countries in which the U.S. company would like to register its mark. The treaty is designed to reduce the costs of international trademark protection by more than 60 percent, according to proponents.

Although the Madrid Protocol may simplify and reduce the cost of trademark registration in foreign countries, it remains to be seen whether it will provide significant benefits to trademark owners. Even assuming that the registration process will be easier, there is still the issue of whether member countries will enforce the law and protect the mark.

REVIEWING Intellectual Property and Internet Law

Two computer science majors, Trent and Xavier, have an idea for a new video game, which they propose to call "Hallowed." They form a business and begin developing their idea. Several months later, Trent and Xavier run into a problem with their design and consult with a friend, Brad, who is an expert in designing computer source codes. After the software is completed but before Hallowed is marketed, a video game called "Halo 2" is released for both the Xbox and Game Cube systems. Halo 2 uses source codes similar to those of Hallowed and imitates Hallowed's overall look and feel, although not all the features are alike. Using the information presented in the chapter, answer the following questions.

1. Would the name "Hallowed" receive protection as a trademark or as trade dress?
2. If Trent and Xavier had obtained a business process patent on Hallowed, would the release of Halo 2 infringe on their patent? Why or why not?
3. Based only on the facts described above, could Trent and Xavier sue the makers of Halo 2 for copyright infringement? Why or why not?
4. Suppose that Trent and Xavier discover that Brad took the idea of Hallowed and sold it to the company that produced Halo 2. Which type of intellectual property issue does this raise?

TERMS AND CONCEPTS

certification mark 150
collective mark 150
copyright 156
cyber mark 151
cybersquatting 151
dilution 147
distributed network 162
domain name 151
intellectual property 145
meta tag 152
patent 153
peer-to-peer (P2P) networking 162
service mark 150
trade dress 149
trade name 150
trade secret 163
trademark 145

QUESTIONS AND CASE PROBLEMS

8–1. Professor Wise is teaching a summer seminar in business torts at State University. Several times during the course, he makes copies of relevant sections from business law texts and distributes them to his students. Wise does not realize that the daughter of one of the textbook authors is a member of his seminar. She tells her father about Wise's copying activities, which have taken place without her father's or his publisher's permission. Her father sues Wise for copyright infringement. Wise claims protection under the fair use doctrine. Who will prevail? Explain.

8–2. QUESTION WITH SAMPLE ANSWER

In which of the following situations would a court likely hold Ursula liable for copyright infringement?

(a) Ursula goes to the library and photocopies ten pages from a scholarly journal relating to a topic on which she is writing a term paper.
(b) Ursula makes blouses, dresses, and other clothes and sells them in her small shop. She advertises some of the outfits as Guest items, hoping that customers might mistakenly assume that they were made by Guess, the well-known clothing manufacturer.
(c) Ursula teaches Latin American history at a small university. She has a VCR and frequently tapes television programs relating to Latin America. She then takes the videos to her classroom so that her students can watch them.

- **For a sample answer to Question 8–2, go to Appendix I at the end of this text.**

8–3. Domain Name Disputes. In 1999, Steve and Pierce Thumann and their father, Fred, created Spider Webs, Ltd., a partnership, to, according to Steve, "develop Internet address names." Spider Webs registered nearly two thousand Internet domain names at an average cost of $70 each, including the names of cities, the names of buildings, names related to a business or trade (such as air-conditioning or plumbing), and the names of famous companies. It offered many of the names for sale on its Web site and through eBay.com. Spider Webs registered the domain name "ERNESTANDJULIOGALLO.COM" in Spider Webs' name. E. & J. Gallo Winery filed a suit against Spider Webs, alleging, in part, violations of the Anticybersquatting Consumer Protection Act (ACPA). Gallo asked the court for, among other things, statutory damages. Gallo also sought to have the domain name at issue transferred to Gallo. During the suit, Spider Webs published anticorporate articles and negative opinions about Gallo, as well as discussions of the suit and of the risks associated with alcohol use, at the URL ERNESTANDJULIOGALLO.COM. Should the court rule in Gallo's favor? Why or why not? [*E. & J. Gallo Winery v. Spider Webs, Ltd.*, 129 F.Supp.2d 1033 (S.D.Tex. 2001)]

8–4. CASE PROBLEM WITH SAMPLE ANSWER

Gateway, Inc., sells computers, computer products, computer peripherals, and computer accessories throughout the world. By 1988, Gateway had begun its first national advertising campaign using black-and-white cows and black-and-white cow spots. By 1991, black-and-white cows and spots had become Gateway's symbol. The next year, Gateway registered a black-and-white cow-spots design in association with computers and computer peripherals as its trademark. Companion Products, Inc. (CPI), sells stuffed animals trademarked as "Stretch Pets." Stretch Pets have an animal's head and an elastic body that can wrap around the edges of computer monitors, computer cases, or televisions. CPI produces sixteen Stretch Pets, including a polar bear, a moose, several dogs, and a penguin. One of CPI's top-selling products is a black-and-white cow that CPI identifies as "Cody Cow," which was first sold in 1999. Gateway filed a suit in a federal district court against CPI, alleging trade dress infringement and related claims. What is trade dress? What is the major factor in cases involving trade dress infringement? Does that factor exist in this case? Explain. [*Gateway, Inc. v. Companion Products, Inc.*, 384 F.3d 503 (8th Cir. 2004)]

- **To view a sample answer for Problem 8–4, go to this book's Web site at www.cengage.com/blaw/jentz, select "Chapter 8," and click on "Case Problem with Sample Answer."**

8–5. Patent Infringement. As a cattle rancher in Nebraska, Gerald Gohl used handheld searchlights to find and help calving animals (animals giving birth) in harsh blizzard conditions. Gohl thought that it would be more helpful to have a portable searchlight mounted on the outside of a vehicle and remotely controlled. He and Al Gebhardt developed and patented practical applications of this idea—the Golight and the wireless, remote-controlled Radio Ray, which could rotate 360 degrees—and formed Golight, Inc., to make and market these products. In 1997, Wal-Mart Stores, Inc., began selling a portable, wireless, remote-controlled searchlight that was identical to the Radio Ray except for a stop piece that prevented the light from rotating more than 351 degrees. Golight sent Wal-Mart a letter claiming that its device infringed Golight's patent. Wal-Mart sold its remaining inventory of the devices and stopped carrying the product. Golight filed a suit in a federal district court against Wal-Mart, alleging patent infringement. How should the court rule? Explain. [*Golight, Inc. v. Wal-Mart Stores, Inc.*, 355 F.3d 1327 (Fed.Cir. 2004)]

8–6. Copyright Infringement. Bridgeport Music, Inc., is in the business of publishing music and exploiting musical composition copyrights. Westbound Records, Inc., is in the business of recording and distributing sound recordings. Bridgeport and Westbound own the composition and recording copyrights to "Get Off Your Ass and Jam" by George Clinton, Jr., and the Funkadelics. The recording "Get Off" opens with a three-note solo guitar riff that lasts four seconds. The rap song "100 Miles and Runnin" contains a two-second sample from the guitar solo, at a lower pitch, looped and extended to sixteen beats, in five places in the song, with each looped segment lasting about seven seconds. "100 Miles" was included in the sound track of the movie *I Got the Hook Up,* which was distributed by No Limit Films. Bridgeport, Westbound, and others filed a suit in a federal district court against No Limit and others, alleging copyright infringement. Does a musician commit copyright infringement when he or she copies any part—even as little as two seconds—of a copyrighted sound recording without the permission of the copyright's owner? If so, how can an artist legally incorporate a riff from another's work in his or her own recording? Discuss. [*Bridgeport Music, Inc. v. Dimension Films,* 410 F.3d 792 (6th Cir. 2005)]

8–7. Trade Secrets. Briefing.com offers Internet-based analyses of investment opportunities to investors. Richard Green is the company's president. One of Briefing.com's competitors is StreetAccount, LLC (limited liability company), whose owners include Gregory Jones and Cynthia Dietzmann. Jones worked for Briefing.com for six years until he quit in March 2003 and was a member of its board of directors until April 2003. Dietzmann worked for Briefing.com for seven years until she quit in March 2003. As Briefing.com employees, Jones and Dietzmann had access to confidential business data. For instance, Dietzmann developed a list of contacts through which Briefing.com obtained market information to display online. When Dietzmann quit, however, she did not return all of the contact information to the company. Briefing.com and Green filed a suit in a federal district court against Jones, Dietzmann, and StreetAccount, alleging that they appropriated these data and other "trade secrets" to form a competing business. What are trade secrets? Why are they protected? Under what circumstances is a party liable at common law for their appropriation? How should these principles apply in this case? [*Briefing.com v. Jones,* 2006 WY 16, 126 P.3d 928 (2006)]

8–8. Trademarks. In 1969, Jack Masquelier, a professor of pharmacology, discovered a chemical antioxidant made from the bark of a French pine tree. The substance supposedly assists in nutritional distribution and blood circulation. Horphag Research, Ltd., began to sell the product under the name Pycnogenol, which Horphag registered as a trademark in 1993. Pycnogenol became one of the fifteen best-selling herbal supplements in the United States. In 1999, through the Web site **healthierlife.com**, Larry Garcia began to sell Masquelier's Original OPCs, a supplement derived from grape pits. Claiming that this product was the "true Pycnogenol," Garcia used the mark as a meta tag and a generic term, attributing the results of research on Horphag's product to Masquelier's and altering quotations from scientific literature to substitute the name of Masquelier's product for Horphag's. Customers who purchased Garcia's product contacted Horphag about it, only to learn that they had not bought Horphag's product. Others called Horphag to ask whether Garcia "was selling . . . real Pycnogenol." Horphag filed a suit in a federal district court against Garcia, alleging, among other things, that he was diluting Horphag's mark. What is trademark dilution? Did it occur here? Explain. [*Horphag Research, Ltd. v. Garcia,* 475 F.3d 1029 (9th Cir. 2007)]

8–9. A QUESTION OF ETHICS

*Custom Copies, Inc., in Gainesville, Florida, is a copy shop that, on request, reproduces and distributes, for profit, material published and owned by others. One of the copy shop's primary activities is the preparation and sale of coursepacks, which contain compilations of readings for college courses. For a particular coursepack, a teacher selects the readings and delivers a syllabus to the copy shop, which obtains the materials from a library, copies them, and then binds and sells the copies. Blackwell Publishing, Inc., in Malden, Massachusetts, publishes books and journals in medicine and other fields and owns the copyrights to these publications. Blackwell and others filed a suit in a federal district court against Custom Copies, alleging copyright infringement for its "routine and systematic reproduction of materials from plaintiffs' publications, without seeking permission," to compile coursepacks for classes at the University of Florida. The plaintiffs asked the court to issue an injunction and award them damages, as well the profit from the infringement. The defendant filed a motion to dismiss the complaint. [*Blackwell Publishing, Inc. v. Custom Copies, Inc., ___ *F.Supp.2d* ___ (N.D.Fla. 2006)]*

(a) Custom Copies argued in part that it did not "distribute" the coursepacks. Does a copy shop violate copyright law if it only copies materials for coursepacks? Does the copying fall under the "fair use" exception? Should the court grant the defendant's motion? Why or why not?

(b) What is the potential impact of creating and selling copies of a book or journal without the permission of, and the payment of royalties or a fee to, the copyright owner? Explain.

8-10. VIDEO QUESTION

Go to this text's Web site at **www.cengage.com/blaw/jentz** and select "Chapter 8." Click on "Video Questions" and view the video titled *The Jerk*. Then answer the following questions.

(a) In the video, Navin (Steve Martin) creates a special handle for Mr. Fox's (Bill Macy's) glasses. Can Navin obtain a patent or a copyright protecting his invention? Explain your answer.

(b) Suppose that after Navin legally protects his idea, Fox steals it and decides to develop it for himself, without Navin's permission. Has Fox committed infringement? If so, what kind—trademark, patent, or copyright?

(c) Suppose that after Navin legally protects his idea, he realizes he doesn't have the funds to mass-produce the glasses' special handle. Navin therefore agrees to allow Fox to manufacture the product. Has Navin granted Fox a license? Explain.

(d) Assume that Navin is able to manufacture his invention. What might Navin do to ensure that his product is identifiable and can be distinguished from other products on the market?

LAW ON THE WEB

For updated links to resources available on the Web, as well as a variety of other materials, visit this text's Web site at

www.cengage.com/blaw/jentz

An excellent overview of the laws governing various forms of intellectual property is available at FindLaw's Web site. Go to

profs.lp.findlaw.com

You can find answers to frequently asked questions (FAQs) about patents, trademarks, and copyrights—and links to registration forms, statutes, international patent and trademark offices, and numerous other resources—at the Web site of the U.S. Patent and Trademark Office. Go to

www.uspto.gov

To perform patent searches and to access information on the patenting process, go to

www.bustpatents.com

You can also access the European Patent Office's Web site at

www.epo.org

For information on copyrights, go to the U.S. Copyright Office at

www.copyright/gov

You can find extensive information on copyright law—including United States Supreme Court decisions in this area and the texts of the Berne Convention and other international treaties on copyright issues—at the Web site of the Legal Information Institute at Cornell University's School of Law. Go to

www.law.cornell.edu/wex/index.php/Copyright

Legal Research Exercises on the Web

Go to **www.cengage.com/blaw/jentz**, the Web site that accompanies this text. Select "Chapter 8" and click on "Internet Exercises." There you will find the following Internet research exercises that you can perform to learn more about the topics covered in this chapter.

Internet Exercise 8–1: Legal Perspective
Unwarranted Legal Threats

Internet Exercise 8–2: Management Perspective
Protecting Intellectual Property across Borders

Internet Exercise 8–3: Technological Perspective
File-Sharing

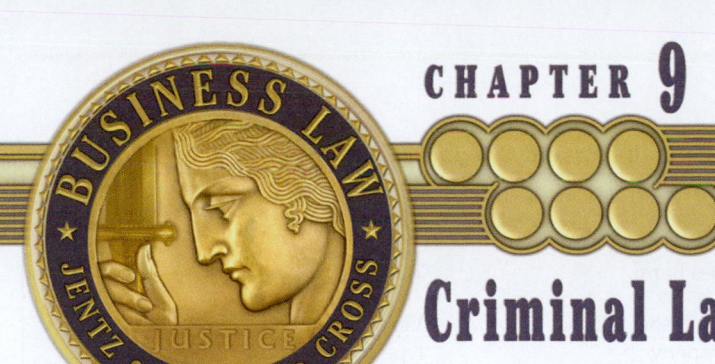

CHAPTER 9

Criminal Law and Cyber Crime

The law imposes various sanctions in attempting to ensure that individuals engaging in business in our society can compete and flourish. These sanctions include those imposed by civil law, such as damages for various types of tortious conduct (discussed in Chapters 6 and 7); damages for breach of contract (to be discussed in Chapter 18); and the equitable remedies discussed in Chapters 1 and 18. Additional sanctions are imposed under criminal law. Indeed, many statutes regulating business provide for criminal as well as civil penalties. Therefore, criminal law joins civil law as an important element in the legal environment of business.

In this chapter, after explaining some essential differences between criminal law and civil law, we look at how crimes are classified and at the elements that must be present for criminal liability to exist. We then examine the various categories of crimes, the defenses that can be raised to avoid criminal liability, and the rules of criminal procedure. We conclude the chapter with a discussion of crimes that occur in cyberspace, which are often referred to as *cyber crime.* Generally, cyber crime refers more to the way in which particular crimes are committed than to a new category of crimes.

SECTION 1

Civil Law and Criminal Law

Recall from Chapter 1 that *civil law* pertains to the duties that exist between persons or between persons and their governments. Criminal law, in contrast, has to do with crime. A **crime** can be defined as a wrong against society proclaimed in a statute and punishable by a fine and/or imprisonment—or, in some cases, death. As mentioned in Chapter 1, because crimes are *offenses against society as a whole,* they are prosecuted by a public official, such as a district attorney (D.A.) or an attorney general (A.G.), not by the victims. Once a crime has been reported, the D.A. typically has the discretion to decide whether to file criminal charges and also determines to what extent to pursue the prosecution or carry out additional investigation.

Major Differences between Civil Law and Criminal Law

Because the state has extensive resources at its disposal when prosecuting criminal cases, there are numerous procedural safeguards to protect the rights of defendants. We look here at one of these safeguards—the higher burden of proof that applies in a criminal case—as well as the harsher sanctions for criminal acts compared with civil wrongs. Exhibit 9–1 on the following page summarizes these and other key differences between civil law and criminal law.

Burden of Proof In a civil case, the plaintiff usually must prove his or her case by a *preponderance of the evidence.* Under this standard, the plaintiff must convince the court that based on the evidence presented by both parties, it is more likely than not that the plaintiff's allegation is true.

In a criminal case, in contrast, the state must prove its case **beyond a reasonable doubt.** If the jury views the evidence in the case as reasonably permitting either a guilty or a not guilty verdict, then the jury's verdict must be not guilty. In other words, the government (prosecutor) must prove beyond a reasonable doubt that the defendant has committed every essential element of the offense with which she or he is charged. If the jurors are not convinced of the defendant's guilt beyond a reasonable doubt, they must find the defendant not guilty. Note also that in a criminal

EXHIBIT 9–1 • Key Differences between Civil Law and Criminal Law

Issue	Civil Law	Criminal Law
Party who brings suit	Person who suffered harm.	The state.
Wrongful act	Causing harm to a person or to a person's property.	Violating a statute that prohibits some type of activity.
Burden of proof	Preponderance of the evidence.	Beyond a reasonable doubt.
Verdict	Three-fourths majority (typically).	Unanimous.
Remedy	Damages to compensate for the harm or a decree to achieve an equitable result.	Punishment (fine, imprisonment, or death).

case, the jury's verdict normally must be unanimous—agreed to by all members of the jury—to convict the defendant. (In a civil trial by jury, in contrast, typically only three-fourths of the jurors need to agree.)

Criminal Sanctions The sanctions imposed on criminal wrongdoers are also harsher than those that are applied in civil cases. Remember from Chapters 6 and 7 that the purpose of tort law is to enable a person harmed by the wrongful act of another to obtain compensation from the wrongdoer, rather than to punish the wrongdoer. In contrast, criminal sanctions are designed to punish those who commit crimes and to deter others from committing similar acts in the future. Criminal sanctions include fines as well as the much harsher penalty of the loss of one's liberty by incarceration in a jail or prison. Most criminal sanctions also involve probation and sometimes require performance of community service, completion of an educational or treatment program, or payment of restitution. The harshest criminal sanction is, of course, the death penalty.

Civil Liability for Criminal Acts

Some torts, such as assault and battery, provide a basis for a criminal prosecution as well as a civil action in tort. Suppose that Jonas is walking down the street, minding his own business, when a person attacks him. In the ensuing struggle, the attacker stabs Jonas several times, seriously injuring him. A police officer restrains and arrests the wrongdoer. In this situation, the attacker may be subject both to criminal prosecution by the state and to a tort lawsuit brought by Jonas to obtain compensation for his injuries. Exhibit 9–2 illustrates how the same wrongful act can result in both a civil (tort) action and a criminal action against the wrongdoer.

SECTION 2 Classification of Crimes

Depending on their degree of seriousness, crimes are classified as felonies or misdemeanors.

Felonies

Felonies are serious crimes punishable by death or by imprisonment in a federal or state penitentiary for one year or longer.[1] The Model Penal Code[2] provides for four degrees of felony:

1. Capital offenses, for which the maximum penalty is death.
2. First degree felonies, punishable by a maximum penalty of life imprisonment.
3. Second degree felonies, punishable by a maximum of ten years' imprisonment.
4. Third degree felonies, punishable by up to five years' imprisonment.

Although criminal laws vary from state to state, some general rules apply when grading crimes by

1. Some states, such as North Carolina, consider felonies to be punishable by incarceration for at least two years.

2. The American Law Institute issued the Official Draft of the Model Penal Code in 1962. The Model Penal Code contains four parts: (1) general provisions, (2) definitions of special crimes, (3) provisions concerning treatment and corrections, and (4) provisions on the organization of corrections. The Model Penal Code is not a uniform code, however. Because of our federal structure of government, each state has developed its own set of laws governing criminal acts. Thus, types of crimes and prescribed punishments may differ from one jurisdiction to another.

EXHIBIT 9–2 • Civil (Tort) Lawsuit and Criminal Prosecution for the Same Act

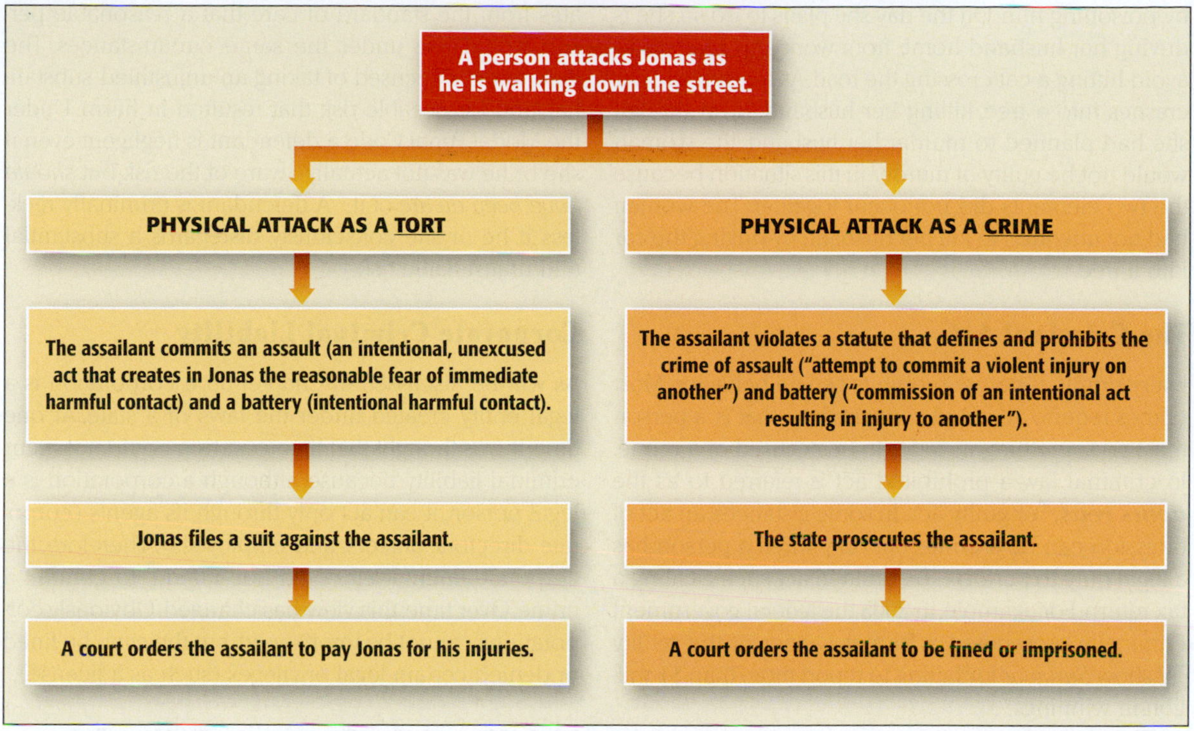

degree. For example, most jurisdictions punish a burglary that involves a forced entry into a home at night more harshly than a burglary that takes place during the day and involves a nonresidential building or structure. A homicide—the taking of another's life—is classified according to the degree of intent involved.

For example, first degree murder requires that the homicide be premeditated and deliberate, as opposed to a spontaneous act of violence. When no premeditation or deliberation is present but the offender acts with *malice aforethought* (that is, with wanton disregard for the consequences of his or her actions for the victim), the homicide is classified as second degree murder. A homicide that is committed without malice toward the victim is known as *manslaughter. Voluntary manslaughter* occurs when the intent to kill may be present, as in a crime committed in the heat of passion, but malice is lacking. A homicide is classified as *involuntary manslaughter* when it results from an act of negligence (such as when a drunk driver causes the death of another person) and there is no intent to kill.

Misdemeanors and Petty Offenses

Under federal law as well as under the law of most states, any crime that is not a felony is considered a **misdemeanor.** Misdemeanors are less serious crimes punishable by a fine or by incarceration for up to one year. Disorderly conduct and trespass are common misdemeanors. In most jurisdictions, **petty offenses** are considered to be a subset of misdemeanors. Petty offenses are minor violations, such as disturbing the peace and violating building codes. Even for petty offenses, however, a guilty party can be put in jail for a few days, fined, or both, depending on state law.

Whether a crime is a felony or a misdemeanor can determine in which court the case is tried and, in some states, whether the defendant has a right to a jury trial. Many states have several classes of misdemeanors. For example, in Illinois, misdemeanors are either Class A (confinement for up to a year), Class B (not more than six months), or Class C (not more than thirty days).

SECTION 3 Criminal Liability

Two elements must exist for a person to be convicted of a crime: (1) the performance of a prohibited act and (2) a specified state of mind, or intent, on the part of the actor. Additionally, to establish criminal liability, there must be a *concurrence* between the act and the intent. In other words, these two elements must occur together.

For example, a woman intends to kill her husband by poisoning him. On the day she plans to do so, she is driving her husband home from work and swerves to avoid hitting a cat crossing the road. As a result, the car crashes into a tree, killing her husband. Even though she had planned to murder her husband, the woman would not be guilty of murder in this situation because the two elements did not occur together. The woman had not intended to kill her husband by driving the car into a tree.

The Criminal Act

Every criminal statute prohibits certain behavior. Most crimes require an act of *commission*—that is, a person must *do* something in order to be accused of a crime. In criminal law, a prohibited act is referred to as the ***actus reus,***[3] or guilty act. In some instances, an act of omission can be a crime, but only when a person has a legal duty to perform the omitted act, such as filing a tax return. For example, in 2005 the federal government criminally prosecuted a former winner of the reality TV show *Survivor* for failing to report more than $1 million in winnings.

The *guilty act* requirement is based on one of the premises of criminal law—that a person should be punished for harm done to society. For a crime to exist, the guilty act must cause some harm to a person or to property. Thinking about killing someone or about stealing a car may be morally wrong, but the thoughts do no harm until they are translated into action. Of course, a person can be punished for *attempting* murder or robbery, but normally only if substantial steps toward the criminal objective have been taken.

State of Mind

A wrongful mental state (***mens rea***)[4] is also typically required to establish criminal liability. The required mental state, or intent, is indicated in the applicable statute or law. Murder, for example, involves the guilty act of killing another human being, and the guilty mental state is the desire, or intent, to take another's life. For theft, the guilty act is the taking of another person's property, and the mental state involves both the awareness that the property belongs to another and the desire to deprive the owner of it.

A guilty mental state can be attributed to acts of negligence or recklessness as well. *Criminal negligence* involves the mental state in which the defendant deviates from the standard of care that a reasonable person would use under the same circumstances. The defendant is accused of taking an unjustified, substantial, and foreseeable risk that resulted in harm. Under the Model Penal Code, a defendant is negligent even if she or he was not actually aware of the risk but *should have been aware* of it.[5] A defendant is criminally reckless if he or she consciously disregards a substantial and unjustifiable risk.

3. Pronounced *ak*-tuhs *ray*-uhs.
4. Pronounced *mehns ray*-uh.

Corporate Criminal Liability

As will be discussed in Chapter 38, a corporation is a legal entity created under the laws of a state. At one time, it was thought that a corporation could not incur criminal liability because, although a corporation is a legal person, it can act only through its agents (corporate directors, officers, and employees). Therefore, the corporate entity itself could not "intend" to commit a crime. Over time, this view has changed. Obviously, corporations cannot be imprisoned, but they can be fined or denied certain legal privileges (such as a license).

Liability of the Corporate Entity Today, corporations are normally liable for the crimes committed by their agents and employees within the course and scope of their employment.[6] For such criminal liability to be imposed, the prosecutor normally must show that the corporation could have prevented the act or that there was authorized consent to, or knowledge of, the act by persons in supervisory positions within the corporation. In addition, corporations can be criminally liable for failing to perform specific duties imposed by law (such as duties under environmental laws or securities laws).

Liability of Corporate Officers and Directors Corporate directors and officers are personally liable for the crimes they commit, regardless of whether the crimes were committed for their private benefit or on the corporation's behalf. Additionally, corporate directors and officers may be held liable for the actions of employees under their supervision. Under the *responsible corporate officer* doctrine, a court may impose criminal liability on a corporate officer regardless of whether he or she participated in, directed, or even knew about a given criminal violation.

5. Model Penal Code Section 2.02(2)(d).
6. See Model Penal Code Section 2.07.

PREVENTING LEGAL DISPUTES

Because corporate officers and directors can be held liable for the crimes of their subordinates, the former should always be aware of any criminal statutes relevant to their particular industry or trade. In addition, firms would be wise to train their employees in how to comply with the multitude of applicable laws, particularly environmental laws and health and safety regulations, which frequently involve criminal sanctions.

SECTION 4

Types of Crimes

Numerous actions are designated as criminal. Federal, state, and local laws provide for the classification and punishment of hundreds of thousands of different criminal acts. Generally, though, criminal acts can be grouped into five broad categories: violent crime (crimes against persons), property crime, public order crime, white-collar crime, and organized crime. Cyber crime—which consists of crimes committed in cyberspace with the use of computers—is, as mentioned earlier in this chapter, less a category of crime than a new way to commit crime. We will examine cyber crime later in this chapter.

Violent Crime

Certain crimes are called *violent crimes*, or crimes against persons, because they cause others to suffer harm or death. Murder is a violent crime. So is sexual assault, or rape. Assault and battery, which were discussed in Chapter 6 in the context of tort law, are also classified as violent crimes. **Robbery**—defined as the taking of money, personal property, or any other article of value from a person by means of force or fear—is also a violent crime. Typically, states have more severe penalties for *aggravated robbery*—robbery with the use of a deadly weapon.

Each of these violent crimes is further classified by degree, depending on the circumstances surrounding the criminal act. These circumstances include the intent of the person committing the crime, whether a weapon was used, and (for crimes other than murder) the level of pain and suffering experienced by the victim.

Property Crime

The most common type of criminal activity is property crime, or those crimes in which the goal of the offender is some form of economic gain or the damaging of property. Robbery is a form of property crime, as well as a violent crime, because the offender seeks to gain the property of another. We look here at a number of other crimes that fall within the general category of property crime.

Burglary Traditionally, **burglary** was defined as breaking and entering the dwelling of another at night with the intent to commit a felony. Originally, the definition was aimed at protecting an individual's home and its occupants. Most state statutes have eliminated some of the requirements found in the common law definition. The time of day at which the breaking and entering occurs, for example, is usually immaterial. State statutes frequently omit the element of breaking, and some states do not require that the building be a dwelling. When a deadly weapon is used in a burglary, the perpetrator can be charged with *aggravated burglary* and punished more severely.

Larceny Under the common law, the crime of **larceny** involved the unlawful taking and carrying away of someone else's personal property with the intent to permanently deprive the owner of possession. Put simply, larceny is stealing or theft. Whereas robbery involves force or fear, larceny does not. Therefore, picking pockets is larceny, not robbery. Similarly, taking company products and supplies home for personal use, if one is not authorized to do so, is larceny. (Note that a person who commits larceny generally can also be sued under tort law because the act of taking possession of another's property involves a trespass to personal property.)

Most states have expanded the definition of property that is subject to larceny statutes. Stealing computer programs may constitute larceny even though the "property" consists of magnetic impulses. Stealing computer time may also be considered larceny. So, too, may the theft of natural gas or Internet and television cable service. Trade secrets can be subject to larceny statutes.

The common law distinguishes between grand and petit larceny depending on the value of the property taken. Many states have abolished this distinction, but in those that have not, grand larceny (or theft of an item worth above a certain amount) is a felony and petit larceny is a misdemeanor.

Arson The willful and malicious burning of a building (and, in some states, personal property) owned by another is the crime of **arson.** At common law, arson applied only to burning down another person's house. The law was designed to protect human life. Today, arson statutes have been extended to cover the destruction of any building, regardless of ownership, by fire or explosion.

Every state has a special statute that covers the act of burning a building for the purpose of collecting insurance. If Shaw owns an insured apartment building that is falling apart and sets fire to it himself or pays someone else to do so, he is guilty not only of arson but also of defrauding the insurer, which is an attempted larceny. Of course, the insurer need not pay the claim when insurance fraud is proved.

Receiving Stolen Goods It is a crime to receive stolen goods. The recipient of such goods need not know the true identity of the owner or the thief. All that is necessary is that the recipient knows or should know that the goods are stolen, which implies an intent to deprive the owner of those goods.

Forgery The fraudulent making or altering of any writing (including electronic records) in a way that changes the legal rights and liabilities of another is **forgery.** If, without authorization, Severson signs Bennett's name to the back of a check made out to Bennett, Severson is committing forgery. Forgery also includes changing trademarks, falsifying public records, counterfeiting, and altering a legal document.

Obtaining Goods by False Pretenses It is a criminal act to obtain goods by false pretenses, such as buying groceries with a check knowing that one has insufficient funds to cover it. Using another's credit-card number to obtain goods is an additional example of obtaining goods by false pretenses. Statutes dealing with such illegal activities vary widely from state to state.

Public Order Crime

Historically, societies have always outlawed activities that are considered contrary to public values and morals. Today, the most common public order crimes include public drunkenness, prostitution, gambling, and illegal drug use. These crimes are sometimes referred to as *victimless crimes* because they normally harm only the offender. From a broader perspective, however, they are deemed detrimental to society as a whole because they may create an environment that gives rise to property and violent crimes.

White-Collar Crime

Crimes occurring in the business context are popularly referred to as white-collar crimes. Although there is no official definition of **white-collar crime,** the term is commonly used to mean an illegal act or series of acts committed by an individual or business entity using some nonviolent means to obtain a personal or business advantage. Usually, this kind of crime takes place in the course of a legitimate business occupation. Corporate crimes fall into this category. Certain property crimes, such as larceny and forgery, may also be white-collar crimes if they occur within the business context. The crimes discussed next normally occur only in the business environment.

Embezzlement When a person entrusted with another person's property or funds fraudulently appropriates that property or those funds, **embezzlement** occurs. Typically, embezzlement is carried out by an employee who steals funds. Banks are particularly prone to this problem, but embezzlement can occur in any firm. In a number of businesses, corporate officers or accountants have fraudulently converted funds for their own benefit and then "jimmied" the books to cover up their crime. Embezzlement is not larceny because the wrongdoer does not *physically* take the property from the possession of another, and it is not robbery because no force or fear is used.

It does not matter whether the accused takes the funds from the victim or from a third person. If the financial officer of a large corporation pockets a certain number of checks from third parties that were given to her to deposit into the corporate account, she is embezzling. Frequently, an embezzler takes a relatively small amount at one time but does so repeatedly over a long period. This might be done by underreporting income or deposits and embezzling the remaining amount, for example, or by creating fictitious persons or accounts and writing checks to them from the corporate account.

Practically speaking, an embezzler who returns what has been taken may not be prosecuted because the owner is unwilling to take the time to make a complaint, cooperate with the state's investigative efforts, and appear in court. Also, the owner may not want the crime to become public knowledge. Nevertheless, the intent to return the embezzled property is not a defense to the crime of embezzlement.

When an employer collects withholding taxes from his or her employees yet fails to remit these funds to the state, does such an action constitute a form of embezzlement? This was the primary issue in the following case.

CASE 9.1 George v. Commonwealth of Virginia

Court of Appeals of Virginia, 2008. 51 Va.App. 137, 655 S.E.2d 43.
www.courts.state.va.us/wpcap.htm[a]

Background and Facts Dr. Francis H. George owned and operated a medical practice in Luray, Virginia. From 2001 to 2004, George employed numerous individuals, including nursing assistants, nurse practitioners, and a pediatrician. George withheld funds from his employees' salaries, funds that represented state income taxes owed to the commonwealth[b] of Virginia. George placed these funds in the same banking account that he used to pay his personal and business expenses. During this period, George failed to file withholding tax returns required by state law. Moreover, he did not remit the withheld funds to the state. At trial, a jury convicted George on four counts of embezzlement. George appealed to the state intermediate appellate court claiming, among other things, that the evidence was insufficient to sustain the convictions because the state did not prove that he was entrusted with the property of another.

Decision and Rationale The Court of Appeals of Virginia denied George's appeal to set aside his conviction. The evidence clearly established that George used for his own benefit funds that he held in trust for the state. Thus, he was guilty of embezzlement. "To sustain a conviction of embezzlement, the Commonwealth must prove that the accused wrongfully appropriated to his or her own benefit property entrusted or delivered to the accused with the intent to deprive the owner thereof." George contended that the withheld funds amounted to nothing more than a debt he owed the Commonwealth; therefore, he did not commit embezzlement. The appellate court pointed out that the withholding taxes that George had collected and maintained in his possession were in fact in trust for the Commonwealth. George "neither remitted the withheld funds to the Commonwealth nor maintained them for its benefit. In fact, [George] continued to use the money as though it were his own."

What If the Facts Were Different? *Assume that George had actually kept a separate account for taxes withheld from his employees' salaries, but he simply failed to remit them to the state. Would the court have ruled differently? If so, in what way?*

The Ethical Dimension *Does an employer ever have a valid reason for failing to remit withholding taxes to the state? Why or why not?*

a. Scroll down and click on case "0332064" for January 15, 2008, to access this opinion.

b. In addition to Virginia, three other states designate themselves as commonwealths—Kentucky, Massachusetts, and Pennsylvania. The term *commonwealth* dates to the fifteenth century when it meant "common well-being."

Mail and Wire Fraud One of the most potent weapons against white-collar criminals is the Mail Fraud Act of 1990.[7] Under this act, it is a federal crime to use the mails to defraud the public. Illegal use of the mails must involve (1) mailing or causing someone else to mail a writing—something written, printed, or photocopied—for the purpose of executing a scheme to defraud and (2) contemplating or organizing a scheme to defraud by false pretenses. If, for example, Johnson advertises by mail the sale of a cure for cancer that he knows to be fraudulent because it has no medical validity, he can be prosecuted for fraudulent use of the mails.

Federal law also makes it a crime (wire fraud) to use wire, radio, or television transmissions to defraud.[8]

7. 18 U.S.C. Sections 1341–1342.

8. 18 U.S.C. Section 1343.

Violators may be fined up to $1,000, imprisoned for up to twenty years, or both. If the violation affects a financial institution, the violator may be fined up to $1 million, imprisoned for up to thirty years, or both.

The following case involved charges of mail fraud stemming from the use of telemarketing to solicit funds that were misrepresented as going to support charities. The question for the court was whether the prosecution could offer proof of the telemarketers' commission rate when no one had lied about it.

CASE 9.2 United States v. Lyons

United States Court of Appeals, Ninth Circuit, 2007. 472 F.3d 1055.

• **Background and Facts** In 1994, in California, Gabriel Sanchez formed the First Church of Life (FCL), which had no congregation, services, or place of worship. Timothy Lyons, Sanchez's friend, formed a fund-raising company called North American Acquisitions (NAA). Through FCL, Sanchez and Lyons set up six charities—AIDS Research Association, Children's Assistance Foundation, Cops and Sheriffs of America, Handicapped Youth Services, U.S. Firefighters, and U.S. Veterans League. NAA hired telemarketers to solicit donations on the charities' behalf. Over time, more than $6 million was raised, of which less than $5,000 was actually spent on charitable causes. The telemarketers kept 80 percent of the donated funds as commissions, and NAA took 10 percent. Most of the rest of the funds went to Sanchez, who spent it on himself. In 2002, Lyons and Sanchez were charged in a federal district court with mail fraud and other crimes. Throughout the trial, the prosecution referred to the high commissions paid to the telemarketers. The defendants were convicted, and each was sentenced to fifteen years in prison. They asked the U.S. Court of Appeals for the Ninth Circuit to overturn their convictions, asserting that the prosecution had used the high cost of fund-raising as evidence of fraud even though the defendants had not lied about the cost.

• **Decision and Rationale** The U.S. Court of Appeals for the Ninth Circuit upheld the convictions. The defendants' "undoing was not that the commissions were large but that their charitable web was a scam. Donors were told their contributions went to specific charitable activities when, in reality, almost no money did." The court acknowledged that a failure to reveal the high cost of fund-raising to potential donors does not establish fraud. "The mere fact that a telemarketer keeps [80 percent] of contributions it solicits cannot be the basis of a fraud conviction, and neither can the fact that a telemarketer fails to volunteer this information to would-be donors." But when "nondisclosure is accompanied by intentionally misleading statements designed to deceive the listener," the high cost of fund-raising may be introduced as evidence of fraud. "The State may vigorously enforce its antifraud laws to prohibit professional fundraisers from obtaining money on false pretenses or by making false statements." Here, in addition to the proof of the telemarketers' commissions, the prosecution offered evidence of Lyons and Sanchez's specific misrepresentations and omissions regarding the defendants' use of the donated funds. All of this "evidence underscored the fact that virtually none of the money that ended up in the bank accounts of the six FCL charities went to any charitable activities at all, let alone the specific charitable activities mentioned in the telemarketers' calls. * * * Admission of evidence regarding the fundraising costs was essential to understanding the overall scheme and the shell game of the multiple charities."

• **The Ethical Dimension** *It may have been legal in this case, but was it ethical for the prosecution to repeatedly emphasize the size of the telemarketers' commissions? Why or why not?*

• **The Legal Environment Dimension** *In what circumstance would the prosecution be prevented from introducing evidence of high fund-raising costs? Explain.*

Bribery The crime of bribery involves offering to give something of value to a person in an attempt to influence that person, who is usually, but not always, a public official, to act in a way that serves a private interest. Three types of bribery are considered crimes: bribery of public officials, commercial bribery, and bribery of foreign officials. As an element of the crime of bribery, intent must be present and proved. The bribe itself can be anything the recipient considers to be valuable. Realize that the *crime of bribery occurs when the bribe is offered*—it is not required that the bribe be accepted. *Accepting a bribe* is a separate crime.

Commercial bribery involves corrupt dealings between private persons or businesses. Typically, people make commercial bribes to obtain proprietary information, cover up an inferior product, or secure new business. Industrial espionage sometimes involves commercial bribes. For example, a person in one firm may offer an employee in a competing firm some type of payoff in exchange for trade secrets or pricing schedules. So-called kickbacks, or payoffs for special favors or services, are a form of commercial bribery in some situations.

Bribing foreign officials to obtain favorable business contracts is a crime. This crime was discussed in detail in Chapter 5, along with the Foreign Corrupt Practices Act of 1977, which was passed to curb the use of bribery by U.S. businesspersons in securing foreign contracts.

Bankruptcy Fraud Federal bankruptcy law (see Chapter 30) allows individuals and businesses to be relieved of oppressive debt through bankruptcy proceedings. Numerous white-collar crimes may be committed during the many phases of a bankruptcy action. A creditor, for example, may file a false claim against the debtor, which is a crime. Also, a debtor may fraudulently transfer assets to favored parties before or after the petition for bankruptcy is filed. For instance, a company-owned automobile may be "sold" at a bargain price to a trusted friend or relative. Closely related to the crime of fraudulent transfer of property is the crime of fraudulent concealment of property, such as the hiding of gold coins.

Insider Trading An individual who obtains "inside information" about the plans of a publicly listed corporation can often make stock-trading profits by purchasing or selling corporate securities based on this information. *Insider trading* is a violation of securities law and will be considered more fully in Chapter 41. Basically, securities law prohibits a person who possesses inside information and has a duty not to disclose it to outsiders from trading on that information. He or she may not profit from the purchase or sale of securities based on inside information until the information is made available to the public.

The Theft of Trade Secrets As discussed in Chapter 8, trade secrets constitute a form of intellectual property that for many businesses can be extremely valuable. The Economic Espionage Act of 1996[9] makes the theft of trade secrets a federal crime. The act also makes it a federal crime to buy or possess another person's trade secrets, knowing that the trade secrets were stolen or otherwise acquired without the owner's authorization.

Violations of the act can result in steep penalties. The act provides that an individual who violates the act can be imprisoned for up to ten years and fined up to $500,000. If a corporation or other organization violates the act, it can be fined up to $5 million. Additionally, the law provides that any property acquired as a result of the violation, such as airplanes and automobiles, and any property used in the commission of the violation, such as computers and other electronic devices, is subject to criminal forfeiture—meaning that the government can take the property. A theft of trade secrets conducted via the Internet, for example, could result in the forfeiture of every computer or other device used to commit or facilitate the violation as well as any assets gained.

Organized Crime

White-collar crime takes place within the confines of the legitimate business world. Organized crime, in contrast, operates *illegitimately* by, among other things, providing illegal goods and services. Traditionally, the preferred markets for organized crime have been gambling, prostitution, illegal narcotics, and loan sharking (lending funds at higher-than-legal interest rates), along with more recent ventures into counterfeiting and credit-card scams.

Money Laundering The profits from organized crime and illegal activities amount to billions of dollars a year, particularly the profits from illegal drug transactions and, to a lesser extent, from racketeering, prostitution, and gambling. Under federal law, banks,

9. 18 U.S.C. Sections 1831–1839.

savings and loan associations, and other financial institutions are required to report currency transactions involving more than $10,000. Consequently, those who engage in illegal activities face difficulties in depositing their cash profits from illegal transactions.

As an alternative to storing cash from illegal transactions in a safe-deposit box, wrongdoers and racketeers have invented ways to launder "dirty" money to make it "clean." This **money laundering** is done through legitimate businesses. Assume that Harris, a successful drug dealer, becomes a partner with a restaurateur. Little by little, the restaurant shows increasing profits. As a partner in the restaurant, Harris is able to report the "profits" of the restaurant as legitimate income on which he pays federal and state taxes. He can then spend those funds without worrying that his lifestyle may exceed the level possible with his reported income.

RICO In 1970, in an effort to curb the entry of organized crime into the legitimate business world, Congress passed the Racketeer Influenced and Corrupt Organizations Act (RICO) as part of the Organized Crime Control Act.[10] The statute makes it a federal crime to (1) use income obtained from racketeering activity to purchase any interest in an enterprise, (2) acquire or maintain an interest in an enterprise through racketeering activity, (3) conduct or participate in the affairs of an enterprise through racketeering activity, or (4) conspire to do any of the preceding activities.

The broad language of RICO has allowed it to be applied in cases that have little or nothing to do with organized crime. In fact, today the statute is used to attack white-collar crimes more often than organized crime. In addition, RICO creates civil as well as criminal liability.

Criminal Provisions RICO incorporates by reference twenty-six separate types of federal crimes and nine types of state felonies—including many business-related crimes, such as bribery, embezzlement, forgery, mail and wire fraud, and securities fraud.[11] For purposes of RICO, a "pattern of racketeering activity" requires a person to commit at least two of these offenses. Any individual who is found guilty is subject to a fine of up to $25,000 per violation, imprisonment for up to twenty years, or both. Additionally, the statute provides that those who violate RICO may be required to forfeit (give up) any assets, in the form of property or cash, that were acquired as a result of the illegal activity or that were "involved in" or an "instrumentality of" the activity.

Civil Liability In the event of a RICO violation, the government can seek civil penalties, including the divestiture of a defendant's interest in a business (called forfeiture) or the dissolution of the business. Moreover, in some cases, the statute allows private individuals to sue violators and potentially recover three times their actual losses (treble damages), plus attorneys' fees, for business injuries caused by a violation of the statute. This is perhaps the most controversial aspect of RICO and one that continues to cause debate in the nation's federal courts.

The prospect of receiving treble damages in civil RICO lawsuits has given plaintiffs financial incentive to pursue businesses and employers for violations. For example, Mohawk Industries, Inc., one of the largest carpeting manufacturers in the United States, was sued by a group of its employees for RICO violations. The employees claimed Mohawk conspired with recruiting agencies to hire and harbor illegal immigrants in an effort to keep labor costs low. The employees argued that Mohawk's pattern of illegal hiring expanded Mohawk's hourly workforce and resulted in lower wages for the plaintiffs. Mohawk filed a motion to dismiss, arguing that its conduct had not violated RICO. In 2006, however, a federal appellate court ruled that the plaintiffs had presented sufficient evidence of racketeering activity and remanded the case for a trial.[12] (See *Concept Summary 9.1* for a review of the different types of crimes.)

SECTION 5 Defenses to Criminal Liability

In certain circumstances, the law may allow a person to be excused from criminal liability because she or he lacks the required mental state. Criminal defen-

10. 18 U.S.C. Sections 1961–1968.

11. See 18 U.S.C. Section 1961(1)(A). The crimes listed in this section include murder, kidnapping, gambling, arson, robbery, bribery, extortion, money laundering, securities fraud, counterfeiting, dealing in obscene matter, dealing in controlled substances (illegal drugs), and a number of others.

12. *Williams v. Mohawk Industries, Inc.*, 465 F.3d 1277 (11th Cir. 2006); *cert.* denied, ___ U.S. ___, 127 S.Ct. 1381, 167 L.Ed.2d 174 (2007). For another example, see *Trollinger v. Tyson Foods, Inc.*, 2007 WL 1574275 (E.D.Tenn. 2007).

CONCEPT SUMMARY 9.1
Types of Crimes

Crime Category	Definition and Examples
VIOLENT CRIME	*Definition*: Crime that causes others to suffer harm or death. *Examples*: Murder, assault and battery, sexual assault (rape), and robbery.
PROPERTY CRIME	*Definition*: Crime in which the goal of the offender is some form of economic gain or the damaging of property; the most common form of crime. *Examples*: Burglary, larceny, arson, receiving stolen goods, forgery, and obtaining goods by false pretenses.
PUBLIC ORDER CRIME	*Definition*: Crime that is contrary to public values and morals. *Examples*: Public drunkenness, prostitution, gambling, and illegal drug use.
WHITE-COLLAR CRIME	*Definition*: An illegal act or series of acts committed by an individual or business entity using some nonviolent means to obtain a personal or business advantage; usually committed in the course of a legitimate occupation. *Examples*: Embezzlement, mail and wire fraud, bribery, bankruptcy fraud, insider trading, and the theft of trade secrets.
ORGANIZED CRIME	*Definition*: A form of crime conducted by groups operating illegitimately to satisfy the public's demand for illegal goods and services (such as gambling and illegal narcotics). *Examples*: 1. *Money laundering*—The establishment of legitimate enterprises through which "dirty" money (obtained through criminal activities, such as illegal drug trafficking) can be "laundered" (made to appear to be legitimate income). 2. *RICO*—The Racketeer Influenced and Corrupt Organizations Act (RICO) of 1970 makes it a federal crime to (a) use income obtained from racketeering activity to purchase any interest in an enterprise, (b) acquire or maintain an interest in an enterprise through racketeering activity, (c) conduct or participate in the affairs of an enterprise through racketeering activity, or (d) conspire to do any of the preceding activities. RICO provides for both civil and criminal liability.

dants may also be relieved of criminal liability if they can show that their criminal actions were justified, given the circumstances. Among the most important defenses to criminal liability are infancy, intoxication, insanity, mistake, consent, duress, justifiable use of force, necessity, entrapment, and the statute of limitations. Additionally, in some cases defendants are given *immunity* from prosecution and thus are relieved, at least in part, of criminal liability for their actions. We look next at each of these defenses.

Note that procedural violations (such as obtaining evidence without a valid search warrant) may also operate as defenses. Evidence obtained in violation of a defendant's constitutional rights may not be admitted in court. If the evidence is suppressed, then there may be no basis for prosecuting the defendant.

Infancy

The term *infant,* as used in the law, refers to any person who has not yet reached the age of majority (see Chapter 13). At common law, children under the age of seven could not commit a crime, and it was presumed that children between the ages of seven and fourteen were incapable of committing crimes because of their incapacity to appreciate right and wrong. Today, most state courts no longer presume that children are incapable of criminal conduct, but may evaluate the particular child's state of mind. In all states, certain courts handle cases involving children who allegedly have violated the law. Courts that handle juvenile cases may also have jurisdiction over additional matters. In most states, a child may be treated as an adult and tried in a regular court if she or he is above a certain age (usually fourteen) and is charged with a felony, such as rape or murder.

Intoxication

The law recognizes two types of intoxication, whether from drugs or from alcohol: involuntary and voluntary. *Involuntary intoxication* occurs when a person either is physically forced to ingest or inject an intoxicating substance or is unaware that such a substance contains drugs or alcohol. Involuntary intoxication is a defense to a crime if its effect was to make a person incapable of understanding that the act committed was wrong or incapable of obeying the law. Voluntary intoxication is rarely a defense, but it may be effective in cases in which the defendant was so *extremely* intoxicated as to negate the state of mind that a crime requires.

Insanity

Just as a child may be incapable of the state of mind required to commit a crime, so also may a person who suffers from a mental illness. Thus, insanity may be a defense to a criminal charge. The courts have had difficulty deciding what the test for legal insanity should be, however, and psychiatrists as well as lawyers are critical of the tests used. Almost all federal courts and some states use the relatively liberal standard set forth in the Model Penal Code:

> A person is not responsible for criminal conduct if at the time of such conduct as a result of mental disease or defect he or she lacks substantial capacity either to appreciate the wrongfulness of his [or her] conduct or to conform his [or her] conduct to the requirements of the law.

Some states use the *M'Naghten* test,[13] under which a criminal defendant is not responsible if, at the time of the offense, he or she did not know the nature and quality of the act or did not know that the act was wrong. Other states use the irresistible-impulse test. A person operating under an irresistible impulse may know an act is wrong but cannot refrain from doing it. Under any of these tests, proving insanity is extremely difficult. For this reason, the insanity defense is rarely used and usually is not successful.

Mistake

Everyone has heard the saying "Ignorance of the law is no excuse." Ordinarily, ignorance of the law or a mistaken idea about what the law requires is not a valid defense. In some states, however, that rule has been modified. People who claim that they honestly did not know that they were breaking a law may have a valid defense if (1) the law was not published or reasonably made known to the public or (2) the people relied on an official statement of the law that was erroneous.

A *mistake of fact*, as opposed to a *mistake of law*, operates as a defense if it negates the mental state necessary to commit a crime. If, for example, Oliver Wheaton mistakenly walks off with Julie Tyson's briefcase because he thinks it is his, there is no theft. Theft requires knowledge that the property belongs to another. (If Wheaton's act causes Tyson to incur damages, however, Wheaton may be subject to liability for trespass to personal property or conversion, torts that were discussed in Chapter 6.)

Consent

What if a victim consents to a crime or even encourages the person intending a criminal act to commit it? **Consent** is not a defense to most crimes. The law forbids murder, prostitution, and drug use whether the victim consents or not. Consent may serve as a defense, however, in certain situations when it negates an element of the alleged criminal offense. Because crimes against property, such as burglary and larceny, usually require that the defendant intended to take someone else's property, the fact that the owner gave the defendant permission to take it will operate as a defense. Consent or forgiveness given after a crime has been committed is never a defense, although it can affect the likelihood of prosecution.

Duress

Duress exists when the *wrongful threat* of one person induces another person to perform an act that he or she would not otherwise have performed. In such a situation, duress is said to negate the mental state necessary to commit a crime because the defendant was forced or compelled to commit the act. Duress can be used as a defense to most crimes except murder.

13. A rule derived from *M'Naghten's* Case, 8 Eng.Rep. 718 (1843).

Duress excuses a crime only when another's unlawful threat of serious bodily injury or death reasonably causes the defendant to do a criminal act. In addition, there must have been no opportunity for the defendant to escape or avoid the threatened danger.[14] Essentially, to successfully assert duress as a defense, the defendant must reasonably believe in the immediate danger, and the jury (or judge) must conclude that the defendant's belief was reasonable.

Justifiable Use of Force

Probably the best-known defense to criminal liability is **self-defense.** Other situations, however, also justify the use of force: the defense of one's dwelling, the defense of other property, and the prevention of a crime. In all of these situations, it is important to distinguish between deadly and nondeadly force. *Deadly force* is likely to result in death or serious bodily harm. *Nondeadly force* is force that reasonably appears necessary to prevent the imminent use of criminal force.

Generally speaking, people can use the amount of nondeadly force that seems necessary to protect themselves, their dwellings, or other property, or to prevent the commission of a crime. Deadly force can be used in self-defense only when the defender *reasonably believes* that imminent death or grievous bodily harm will otherwise result and has no other means of escaping or avoiding the situation. Deadly force normally can be used to defend a dwelling only if the unlawful entry is violent and the person believes deadly force is necessary to prevent imminent death or great bodily harm. In some jurisdictions, however, deadly force can also be used if the person believes it is necessary to prevent the commission of a felony in the dwelling. Many states are expanding the situations in which the use of deadly force can be justified—see this chapter's *Emerging Trends* feature on pages 184 and 185.

Necessity

Sometimes, criminal defendants can be relieved of liability by showing that a criminal act was necessary to prevent an even greater harm. According to the Model Penal Code, the defense of **necessity** is justifiable if "the harm or evil sought to be avoided by such conduct is greater than that sought to be prevented by the law defining the offense charged."[15] For example, in one case a convicted felon was threatened by an acquaintance with a gun. The felon grabbed the gun and fled the scene, but subsequently he was arrested under a statute that prohibits convicted felons from possessing firearms. In this situation, the necessity defense succeeded because the defendant's crime avoided a "greater evil."[16]

Entrapment

Entrapment is a defense designed to prevent police officers or other government agents from enticing persons to commit crimes in order to later prosecute them for criminal acts. In the typical entrapment case, an undercover agent *suggests* that a crime be committed and somehow pressures or induces an individual to commit it. The agent then arrests the individual for the crime. For entrapment to be considered a defense, both the suggestion and the inducement must take place. The defense is not intended to prevent law enforcement agents from setting a trap for an unwary criminal; rather, the intent is to prevent them from pushing the individual into it. The crucial issue is whether the person who committed a crime was predisposed to commit the illegal act or did so because the agent induced it.

Statute of Limitations

With some exceptions, such as the crime of murder, statutes of limitations apply to crimes just as they do to civil wrongs. In other words, the state must initiate criminal prosecution within a certain number of years. If a criminal action is brought after the statutory time period has expired, the accused person can raise the statute of limitations as a defense. The running of the time period in a statute of limitations may be tolled—that is, suspended or stopped temporarily—if the defendant is a minor or is not in the jurisdiction. When the defendant reaches the age of majority or returns to the jurisdiction, the statute revives—that is, its time period begins to run or to run again.

Immunity

At times, the state may wish to obtain information from a person accused of a crime. Accused persons are understandably reluctant to give information if it will be used to prosecute them, and they cannot be forced to do so. The privilege against self-incrimination is

14. See, for example, *State v. Heinemann,* 282 Conn. 281, 920 A.2d 278 (2007).

15. Model Penal Code Section 3.02.

16. *United States v. Paolello,* 951 F.2d 537 (3d Cir. 1991).

EMERGING TRENDS IN BUSINESS LAW

Stand-Your-Ground Laws

Traditionally, the justifiable use of force, or self-defense, doctrine required prosecutors to distinguish between deadly and nondeadly force. In general, state laws have allowed individuals to use the amount of nondeadly force that is necessary to protect themselves, their dwellings, or other property, or to prevent the commission of a crime.

The Duty-to-Retreat Doctrine

In the past, most states allowed deadly force to be used in self-defense only if the individual reasonably believed that imminent death or bodily harm would otherwise result. Additionally, the attacker had to be using unlawful force, and the defender had to have no other possible response or alternative way out of the life-threatening situation.[a] Today, many states, particularly in the Northeast, still have "duty-to-retreat" laws on their statute books. Under these laws, when a person's home is invaded or an assailant approaches, the person is required to retreat unless her or his life is in danger. Juries have sometimes been reluctant to apply the duty-to-retreat doctrine, however. In a famous case in the 1980s, Bernard Goetz shot and injured four young men who asked him for money while he was riding the subway in New York City. The jury found that Goetz had reasonably believed that he was in danger of being physically attacked.[b]

Stand-Your-Ground Legislation on the Increase

Whereas the duty-to-retreat doctrine attempts to reduce the likelihood that deadly—or even nondeadly—force will be used in defense of one's person or home, today several states are taking a very different approach and expanding the occasions when deadly force can be used in self-defense. Because such laws allow or even encourage the defender to stay and use force, they are known as "stand-your-ground" laws.

On October 1, 2005, for example, Florida enacted a statute that allows the use of deadly force to prevent the commission of a "forcible felony," including not only murder but also such crimes as robbery, carjacking, and sexual battery.[c] The law applies to both homes and vehicles. Under this statute, Floridians may use deadly force without having to prove that they feared for their safety. In other words, a Florida resident now has the right to shoot an intruder in his or her home or a would-be carjacker even if there is no physical threat to the owner's safety. The law prohibits the arrest, detention, or prosecution of individuals covered by the law and also prohibits civil suits against them.

Since the Florida statute was enacted, Alabama, Alaska, Arizona, Georgia, Indiana, Kentucky, Louisiana,

a. *State v. Sandoval,* 342 Or. 506, 156 P.3d 60 (2007).

b. *People v. Goetz,* 506 N.Y.S.2d 18, 497 N.E.2d 41 (1986). See also *People v. Douglas,* 29 A.D.3d 47, 809 N.Y.S.2d 36 (2006); and *State v. Augustin,* 101 Haw. 127, 63 P.3d 1097 (2002).

c. Florida Statutes Section 776.012.

guaranteed by the Fifth Amendment to the U.S. Constitution, which reads, in part, "nor shall [any person] be compelled in any criminal case to be a witness against himself." In cases in which the state wishes to obtain information from a person accused of a crime, the state can grant *immunity* from prosecution or agree to prosecute for a less serious offense in exchange for the information. Once immunity is given, the person now has an absolute privilege against self-incrimination and therefore can no longer refuse to testify on Fifth Amendment grounds.

Often, a grant of immunity from prosecution for a serious crime is part of the **plea bargaining** between the defending and prosecuting attorneys. The defendant may be convicted of a lesser offense, while the state uses the defendant's testimony to prosecute accomplices for serious crimes carrying heavy penalties.

SECTION 6 Criminal Procedures

Criminal law brings the force of the state, with all of its resources, to bear against the individual. Criminal procedures are designed to protect the constitutional rights of individuals and to prevent the arbitrary use of power on the part of the government.

The U.S. Constitution provides specific safeguards for those accused of crimes. The United States Supreme Court has ruled that most of these safeguards apply not only in federal court but also in state courts by virtue of the due process clause of the Fourteenth Amendment. These protections include the following:

1. The Fourth Amendment protection from unreasonable searches and seizures.

Michigan, Mississippi, Missouri, Montana, Oklahoma, Pennsylvania, South Dakota, Washington, and Wyoming have passed or are considering passing similar laws. Utah already had a "stand-your-ground" law.[d] Louisiana's statute, which mimics the Florida statute, was passed after Hurricane Katrina devastated New Orleans. In Louisiana, there is now a presumption of innocence for anyone who uses deadly force when threatened with violence in his or her home, car, or place of business.

North Carolina's stand-your-ground statute is typical. It states that "(a) A lawful occupant within a home or other place of residence is justified in using any degree of force that the occupant reasonably believes is necessary, including deadly force, against an intruder to prevent a forcible entry into the home or residence or to terminate the intruder's unlawful entry (i) if the occupant reasonably apprehends that the intruder may kill or inflict serious bodily harm to the occupant or others in the home or residence, or (ii) if the occupant reasonably believes that the intruder intends to commit a felony in the home or residence. (b) A lawful occupant within a home or other place of residence does not have a duty to retreat from an intruder in the circumstances described in this section."[e]

Although the media sometimes describe stand-your-ground laws as "new," these statutes are actually based on a centuries-old precedent. The laws are a throwback to the "castle" doctrine, which was derived from English common law in the 1700s, when a person's home was considered to be his or her castle.[f]

IMPLICATIONS FOR THE BUSINESSPERSON

1. States that have enacted stand-your-ground laws often include places of business as well as homes and vehicles. Consequently, businesspersons in those states can be less concerned about the duty-to-retreat doctrine.
2. Presumably, business liability insurance will eventually be less costly in stand-your-ground states.

FOR CRITICAL ANALYSIS

1. Those who oppose stand-your-ground laws argue that they encourage vigilantism and preemptive shootings. Do you agree? Explain.
2. "A person's home is his or her castle." Does this traditional saying justify the use of deadly force against an intruder under all circumstances? Why or why not?

RELEVANT WEB SITES

To locate information on the Web concerning the issues discussed in this feature, go to this text's Web site at **www.cengage.com/blaw/jentz**, select "Chapter 9," and click on "Emerging Trends."

d. Utah Code Ann. 76-2-402 and 76-2-407.

e. North Carolina General Statutes Ann. 14–51.1.

f. One reference to the castle doctrine can be found in William Blackstone, *Commentaries on the Laws of England*, Book 4, Chapter 16.

2. The Fourth Amendment requirement that no warrant for a search or an arrest be issued without probable cause.
3. The Fifth Amendment requirement that no one be deprived of "life, liberty, or property without due process of law."
4. The Fifth Amendment prohibition against **double jeopardy** (trying someone twice for the same criminal offense).[17]
5. The Fifth Amendment requirement that no person be required to be a witness against (incriminate) himself or herself.
6. The Sixth Amendment guarantees of a speedy trial, a trial by jury, a public trial, the right to confront witnesses, and the right to a lawyer at various stages in some proceedings.
7. The Eighth Amendment prohibitions against excessive bail and fines and cruel and unusual punishment.

17. The prohibition against double jeopardy means that once a criminal defendant is found not guilty of a particular crime, the government may not reindict the person and retry him or her for the same crime. The prohibition does not preclude a *civil* lawsuit against the same person by the crime victim to recover damages. For example, a person found not guilty of assault and battery in a criminal case may be sued by the victim in a civil tort case for damages. Additionally, a state's prosecution of a crime will not prevent a separate federal prosecution of the same crime, and vice versa. For example, a defendant found not guilty of violating a state law can be tried in federal court for the same act, if the act is also defined as a crime under federal law.

The Exclusionary Rule

Under what is known as the **exclusionary rule,** all evidence obtained in violation of the constitutional rights spelled out in the Fourth, Fifth, and Sixth Amendments generally is not admissible at trial. All evidence derived from the illegally obtained evidence is known as the "fruit of the poisonous tree," and such evidence normally must also be excluded from the trial proceedings. For example, if a confession is obtained after an illegal arrest, the arrest is the "poisonous tree," and the confession, if "tainted" by the arrest, is the "fruit."

As you will read shortly, under the *Miranda* rule, suspects must be advised of certain constitutional rights when they are arrested. For example, the Sixth Amendment right to counsel is one of the rights of which a suspect must be advised when she or he is arrested. In many cases, a statement that a criminal suspect makes in the absence of counsel is not admissible at trial unless the suspect has knowingly and voluntarily waived this right.

Purpose of the Exclusionary Rule The purpose of the exclusionary rule is to deter police from conducting warrantless searches and from engaging in other misconduct. The rule is sometimes criticized because it can lead to injustice. Many a defendant has "gotten off on a technicality" because law enforcement personnel failed to observe procedural requirements based on the above-mentioned constitutional amendments. Even though a defendant may be obviously guilty, if the evidence of that guilt was obtained improperly (without a valid search warrant, for example), it cannot be used against the defendant in court.

Exceptions to the Exclusionary Rule Over the last several decades, the United States Supreme Court has diminished the scope of the exclusionary rule by creating some exceptions to its applicability. For example, if illegally obtained evidence would have been discovered "inevitably" and obtained by the police using lawful means, the evidence will be admissible at trial.[18] The Court has also created a "good faith" exception to the exclusionary rule.[19] Under this exception, if the police officer who used a technically incorrect search warrant form to obtain evidence was acting in good faith, the evidence will be admissible. Additionally, the courts can exercise a certain amount of discretion in determining whether evidence has been obtained improperly—a possibility that somewhat balances the scales.

The *Miranda* Rule

In regard to criminal procedure, one of the questions many courts faced in the 1950s and 1960s was not whether suspects had constitutional rights—that was not in doubt—but how and when those rights could be exercised. Could the right to be silent (under the Fifth Amendment's prohibition against self-incrimination) be exercised during pretrial interrogation proceedings or only during the trial? Were confessions obtained from suspects admissible in court if the suspects had not been advised of their right to remain silent and other constitutional rights?

To clarify these issues, the United States Supreme Court issued a landmark decision in 1966 in *Miranda v. Arizona,* which we present here. Today, the procedural rights required by the Court in this case are familiar to virtually every American.

18. *Nix v. Williams,* 467 U.S. 431, 104 S.Ct. 2501, 81 L.Ed.2d 377 (1984).
19. *Massachusetts v. Sheppard,* 468 U.S. 981, 104 S.Ct. 3424, 82 L.Ed.2d 737 (1984).

CASE 9.3 Miranda v. Arizona

Supreme Court of the United States, 1966. 384 U.S. 436, 86 S.Ct. 1602, 16 L.Ed.2d 694.

• **Background and Facts** On March 13, 1963, Ernesto Miranda was arrested at his home for the kidnapping and rape of an eighteen-year-old woman. Miranda was taken to a Phoenix, Arizona, police station and questioned by two officers. Two hours later, the officers emerged from the interrogation room with a written confession signed by Miranda. A paragraph at the top of the confession stated that the confession had been made voluntarily, without threats or promises of immunity, and "with full knowledge of my legal rights, understanding any statement I make may be used against me." Miranda was at no time advised that he had a right to remain silent and a right to have a lawyer present. The confession was admitted into evidence at the trial, and Miranda was convicted and sentenced to prison for twenty to thirty years. Miranda appealed the decision, claiming that he had not been informed of his constitutional rights. The Supreme Court of Arizona held that Miranda's constitutional rights had not been violated and affirmed his conviction. The *Miranda* case was subsequently reviewed by the United States Supreme Court.

CASE 9.3 CONTINUED

• **Decision and Rationale** The United States Supreme Court reversed Miranda's conviction, holding that he could not be convicted of the crime on the basis of his confession because his confession was inadmissible as evidence. The Court ruled that for any statement made by a defendant to be admissible, the defendant must be informed of certain constitutional rights before a police interrogation. These are (1) that he or she has a right to remain silent; (2) that anything said can and will be used against the individual in court (to warn a person in custody of "the consequences of forgoing" the right to remain silent); (3) that he or she has the right to have an attorney present during questioning; and (4) that if the individual cannot afford an attorney, one will be appointed. If the accused waives his or her rights to remain silent and to have counsel present, the government must be able to demonstrate that the waiver was made knowingly and intelligently.

• **Impact of This Case on Today's Law** *Police officers routinely advise suspects of their "*Miranda *rights" on arrest. When Ernesto Miranda himself was later murdered, the suspected murderer was "read his* Miranda *rights." Despite significant criticisms and later attempts to overrule the* Miranda *decision through legislation, the requirements stated in this case continue to provide the benchmark by which criminal procedures are judged today.*

• **The Legal Environment Dimension** *The goal of the* Miranda *decision was to prevent the police from using "grilling" tactics to elicit "forced" confessions. Today, camcorders are so small and cheap that all interrogations, even at the scene of a crime, can be digitally recorded. Does this mean that the* Miranda *rights are less important? Why or why not?*

Exceptions to the *Miranda* Rule As part of a continuing attempt to balance the rights of accused persons against the rights of society, the Supreme Court has made a number of exceptions to the *Miranda* ruling. For example, the Court has recognized a "public safety" exception, holding that certain statements—such as statements concerning the location of a weapon—are admissible even if the defendant was not given *Miranda* warnings.[20] The Court has also clarified that, in certain circumstances, a defendant's confession need not be excluded as evidence even if the police failed to inform the defendant of his or her *Miranda* rights.[21] If other, legally obtained evidence admitted at trial is strong enough to justify the conviction without the confession, then the fact that the confession was obtained illegally can, in effect, be ignored.[22]

The Supreme Court has also ruled that a suspect must unequivocally and assertively request to exercise her or his right to counsel in order to stop police questioning. Saying, "Maybe I should talk to a lawyer" during an interrogation after being taken into custody is not enough. The Court held that police officers are not required to decipher the suspect's intentions in such situations.[23]

Criminal Process

As mentioned earlier in this chapter, a criminal prosecution differs significantly from a civil case in several respects. These differences reflect the desire to safeguard the rights of the individual against the state. Exhibit 9–3 on the next page summarizes the major steps in processing a criminal case. We now discuss three phases of the criminal process—arrest, indictment or information, and trial—in more detail.

Arrest Before a warrant for arrest can be issued, there must be probable cause for believing that the individual in question has committed a crime. As discussed in Chapter 4, *probable cause* can be defined as a substantial likelihood that the person has committed or is about to commit a crime. Note that probable cause involves a likelihood, not just a possibility. Arrests can be made without a warrant if there is no time to get one, but the action of the arresting officer is still judged by the standard of probable cause.

20. *New York v. Quarles,* 467 U.S. 649, 104 S.Ct. 2626, 81 L.Ed.2d 550 (1984).

21. *Moran v. Burbine,* 475 U.S. 412, 106 S.Ct. 1135, 89 L.Ed.2d 410 (1986).

22. *Arizona v. Fulminante,* 499 U.S. 279, 111 S.Ct. 1246, 113 L.Ed.2d 302 (1991).

23. *Davis v. United States,* 512 U.S. 452, 114 S.Ct. 2350, 129 L.Ed.2d 362 (1994).

EXHIBIT 9–3 • Major Procedural Steps in a Criminal Case

ARREST
Police officer takes suspect into custody. Most arrests are made without a warrant. After the arrest, the officer searches the suspect, who is then taken to the police station.

BOOKING
At the police station, the suspect is searched again, photographed, fingerprinted, and allowed at least one telephone call. After the booking, charges are reviewed, and if they are not dropped, a complaint is filed, and a magistrate (judge) reviews the case for probable cause.

INITIAL APPEARANCE
The defendant appears before the judge, who informs the defendant of the charges and of his or her rights. If the defendant requests a lawyer and cannot afford one, a lawyer is appointed. The judge sets bail (conditions under which a suspect can obtain release pending disposition of the case).

GRAND JURY
A grand jury determines if there is probable cause to believe that the defendant committed the crime. The federal government and about half of the states require grand jury indictments for at least some felonies.

PRELIMINARY HEARING
In a court proceeding, a prosecutor presents evidence, and the judge determines if there is probable cause to hold the defendant over for trial.

INDICTMENT
An *indictment* is a written document issued by the grand jury to formally charge the defendant with a crime.

INFORMATION
An *information* is a formal criminal charge, or criminal complaint, made by the prosecutor.

ARRAIGNMENT
The defendant is brought before the court, informed of the charges, and asked to enter a plea.

PLEA BARGAIN
A *plea bargain* is a prosecutor's promise to make concessions (or promise to seek concessions) in return for a defendant's guilty plea. Concessions may include a reduced charge or a lesser sentence.

GUILTY PLEA
In many jurisdictions, most cases that reach the arraignment stage do not go to trial but are resolved by a guilty plea, often as a result of a plea bargain. The judge sets the case for sentencing.

TRIAL
Trials can be either jury trials or bench trials. (In a bench trial, there is no jury, and the judge decides questions of fact as well as questions of law.) If the verdict is "guilty," the judge sets a date for the sentencing. Everyone convicted of a crime has the right to an appeal.

Indictment or Information Individuals must be formally charged with having committed specific crimes before they can be brought to trial. If issued by a grand jury, such a charge is called an **indictment.**[24] A **grand jury** does not determine the guilt or innocence of an accused party; rather, its function is to hear the state's evidence and to determine whether a reasonable basis (probable cause) exists for believing that a crime has been committed and that a trial ought to be held.

Usually, grand juries are called in cases involving serious crimes, such as murder. For lesser crimes, an individual may be formally charged with a crime by an **information,** or criminal complaint. An information will be issued by a government prosecutor if the prosecutor determines that there is sufficient evidence to justify bringing the individual to trial.

Trial At a criminal trial, the accused person does not have to prove anything; the entire burden of proof is on the prosecutor (the state). As discussed at the beginning of this chapter, the burden of proof is higher in a criminal case than in a civil case. The prosecution must show that, based on all the evidence, the defendant's guilt is established *beyond a reasonable doubt.* If there is reasonable doubt as to whether a criminal defendant did, in fact, commit the crime with which she or he has been charged, then the verdict must be "not guilty." Note that giving a verdict of "not guilty" is not the same as stating that the defendant is innocent; it merely means that not enough evidence was properly presented to the court to prove guilt beyond a reasonable doubt.

Courts have complex rules about what types of evidence may be presented and how the evidence may be brought out in criminal cases, especially in jury trials. These rules are designed to ensure that evidence presented at trials is relevant, reliable, and not prejudicial toward the defendant.

Federal Sentencing Guidelines

In 1984, Congress passed the Sentencing Reform Act. This act created the U.S. Sentencing Commission, which was charged with the task of standardizing sentences for *federal* crimes. The commission's guidelines, which became effective in 1987, established a range of possible penalties for each federal crime and required the judge to select a sentence from within that range. In other words, the guidelines originally established a mandatory system because judges were not allowed to deviate from the specified sentencing range. Some federal judges felt uneasy about imposing the long prison sentences required by the guidelines on certain criminal defendants, particularly first-time offenders and those convicted in illegal substances cases involving small quantities of drugs.[25]

Shift Away from Mandatory Sentencing In 2005, the Supreme Court held that certain provisions of the federal sentencing guidelines were unconstitutional.[26] The case involved Freddie Booker, who was arrested with 92.5 grams of crack cocaine in his possession. Booker admitted to police that he had sold an additional 566 grams of crack cocaine, but he was never charged with, or tried for, possessing this additional quantity. Nevertheless, under the federal sentencing guidelines the judge was required to sentence Booker to twenty-two years in prison. Ultimately, the Supreme Court ruled that this sentence was unconstitutional because a jury did not find beyond a reasonable doubt that Booker had possessed the additional 566 grams of crack.

Essentially, the Supreme Court's ruling changed the federal sentencing guidelines from mandatory to advisory. Depending on the circumstances of the case, a federal trial judge may now depart from the guidelines if she or he believes that it is reasonable to do so.

Increased Penalties for Certain Criminal Violations It is important for businesspersons to understand that the sentencing guidelines still exist and provide for enhanced punishment for certain types of crimes. The U.S. Sentencing Commission recommends stiff sentences for many white-collar crimes, including mail and wire fraud, commercial bribery and kickbacks, and money laundering. Enhanced penalties are also suggested for violations of the Sarbanes-Oxley Act (discussed in Chapter 5).[27]

24. Pronounced in-*dyte*-ment.

25. See, for example, *United States v. Angelos,* 347 F.Supp.2d 1227 (D.Utah 2004).

26. *United States v. Booker,* 543 U.S. 220, 125 S.Ct. 738, 160 L.Ed.2d 621 (2005).

27. As required by the Sarbanes-Oxley Act of 2002, the U.S. Sentencing Commission revised its guidelines in 2003 to impose stiffer penalties for corporate securities fraud—see Chapter 41.

In addition, the commission recommends increased penalties for criminal violations of employment laws (see Chapters 33 and 34), securities laws (see Chapter 41), and antitrust laws (see Chapter 46). The guidelines set forth a number of factors that judges should take into consideration when imposing a sentence for a specified crime. These factors include the defendant company's history of past violations, management's cooperation with federal investigators, and the extent to which the firm has undertaken specific programs and procedures to prevent criminal activities by its employees.

SECTION 7

Cyber Crime

Some years ago, the American Bar Association defined **computer crime** as any act that is directed against computers and computer parts, that uses computers as instruments of crime, or that involves computers and constitutes abuse. Today, because much of the crime committed with the use of computers occurs in cyberspace, many computer crimes fall under the broad label of **cyber crime.** Here we look at several types of activity that constitute cyber crimes against persons or property. Other cyber crimes will be discussed in later chapters as they relate to particular topics, such as banking or consumer law.

Cyber Theft

In cyberspace, thieves are not subject to the physical limitations of the "real" world. A thief can steal data stored in a networked computer with Internet access from anywhere on the globe. Only the speed of the connection and the thief's computer equipment limit the quantity of data that can be stolen.

Financial Crimes Computer networks also provide opportunities for employees to commit crimes that can involve serious economic losses. For example, employees of a company's accounting department can transfer funds among accounts with little effort and often with less risk than would be involved in transactions evidenced by paperwork.

Generally, the dependence of businesses on computer operations has left firms vulnerable to sabotage, fraud, embezzlement, and the theft of proprietary data, such as trade secrets or other intellectual property. As noted in Chapter 8, the piracy of intellectual property via the Internet is one of the most serious legal challenges facing lawmakers and the courts today.

Identity Theft A form of cyber theft that has become particularly troublesome in recent years is **identity theft.** Identity theft occurs when the wrongdoer steals a form of identification—such as a name, date of birth, or Social Security number—and uses the information to access the victim's financial resources. This crime existed to a certain extent before the widespread use of the Internet. Thieves would "steal" calling-card numbers by watching people using public telephones, or they would rifle through garbage to find bank account or credit-card numbers. The identity thieves would then use the calling-card or credit-card numbers or would withdraw funds from the victims' accounts. The Internet, however, has turned identity theft into perhaps the fastest-growing financial crime in the United States. The Internet provides those who steal information offline with an easy medium for using items such as stolen credit-card numbers while remaining protected by anonymity.

Three federal statutes deal specifically with identity theft. The Identity Theft and Assumption Deterrence Act of 1998[28] made identity theft a federal crime and directed the U.S. Sentencing Commission to incorporate the crime into its sentencing guidelines. The Fair and Accurate Credit Transactions Act of 2003[29] gives victims of identity theft certain rights in working with creditors and credit bureaus to remove negative information from their credit reports. This act will be discussed in detail in Chapter 44 in the context of consumer law. The Identity Theft Penalty Enhancement Act of 2004[30] authorized more severe penalties in aggravated cases in which the identity theft was committed in connection with the thief's employment or with other serious crimes (such as terrorism or firearms or immigration offenses).

Hacking

Persons who use one computer to break into another are sometimes referred to as **hackers.** Hackers who break into computers without authorization often commit cyber theft. Sometimes, however, their principal aim is to prove how smart they are by gaining access to others' password-protected computers and

28. 18 U.S.C. Section 1028.
29. 15 U.S.C. Sections 1681 *et seq.*
30. 18 U.S.C. Section 1028A.

causing random data errors or making toll telephone calls for free.[31]

Cyberterrorism Hackers who, rather than trying to gain attention, strive to remain undetected so that they can exploit computers for a serious impact are called **cyberterrorists.** Just as "real" terrorists destroyed the World Trade Center towers and a portion of the Pentagon on September 11, 2001, cyberterrorists might explode "logic bombs" to shut down central computers. Such activities obviously can pose a danger to national security.

The Threat to Business Activities Any business may be targeted by cyberterrorists as well as hackers. The goals of a hacking operation might include a wholesale theft of data, such as a merchant's customer files, or the monitoring of a computer to discover a business firm's plans and transactions. A cyberterrorist might also want to insert false codes or data. For example, the processing control system of a food manufacturer could be changed to alter the levels of ingredients so that consumers of the food would become ill.

A cyberterrorist attack on a major financial institution, such as the New York Stock Exchange or a large bank, could leave securities or money markets in flux and seriously affect the daily lives of millions of citizens. Similarly, any prolonged disruption of computer, cable, satellite, or telecommunications systems due to the actions of expert hackers would have serious repercussions on business operations—and national security—on a global level. Computer viruses are another tool that can be used by cyberterrorists to cripple communications networks.

Spam

As discussed in Chapter 6, spamming (sending bulk unsolicited e-mail) has become a major problem for businesses. A few states, such as Maryland and Virginia, have passed laws that make spamming a crime.[32] Under the Virginia statute, it is a crime against property to use a computer or computer network "with the intent to falsify or forge electronic mail transmission information or other routing information in any manner." Attempting to send spam to more than 2,500 recipients in a twenty-four-hour period is a felony. The Virginia law also includes provisions authorizing the forfeiture of assets obtained through an illegal spamming operation. The Maryland law is similar in that it prohibits spamming that falsely identifies the sender, the routing information, or the subject. Under the Maryland law, however, the number of spam messages required to convict a person of the offense is much lower. Sending only ten illegal messages in twenty-four hours violates the statute, and the more spam sent, the more severe the punishment will be, up to a maximum of ten years in prison and a $25,000 fine.

In 2006, a Virginia appellate court upheld the first felony conviction for criminal spamming in the United States against Jeremy Jaynes, who until his arrest was the eighth most prolific spammer in the world. Jaynes, a resident of North Carolina, had sent more than ten thousand junk messages a day using sixteen Internet connections and a number of aliases (such as Gaven Stubberfield). Because he had sent some of the messages through servers in Virginia, the court found that Virginia had jurisdiction over Jaynes. He was convicted of three counts of felony spamming and sentenced to nine years in prison.

Prosecuting Cyber Crime

The "location" of cyber crime (cyberspace) has raised new issues in the investigation of crimes and the prosecution of offenders. A threshold issue is, of course, jurisdiction. A person who commits an act against a business in California, where the act is a cyber crime, might never have set foot in California but might instead reside in New York, or even in Canada, where the act may not be a crime. If the crime was committed via e-mail, the question arises as to whether the e-mail would constitute sufficient "minimum contacts" (see Chapter 2) for the victim's state to exercise jurisdiction over the perpetrator.

Identifying the wrongdoer can also be difficult. Cyber criminals do not leave physical traces, such as fingerprints or DNA samples, as evidence of their crimes. Even electronic "footprints" can be hard to find and follow. For example, e-mail may be sent through a remailer, an online service that guarantees that a message cannot be traced to its source.

For these reasons, laws written to protect physical property often are difficult to apply in cyberspace. Nonetheless, governments at both the state and the federal level have taken significant steps toward

31. The total cost of crime on the Internet is estimated to be several billion dollars annually, but two-thirds of that total is said to consist of unpaid-for long-distance calls.

32. See, for example, Maryland Code, Criminal Law, Section 3-805.1, and Virginia Code Ann. Sections 18.2–152.3:1.

controlling cyber crime, both by applying existing criminal statutes and by enacting new laws that specifically address wrongs committed in cyberspace.

The Computer Fraud and Abuse Act

Perhaps the most significant federal statute specifically addressing cyber crime is the Counterfeit Access Device and Computer Fraud and Abuse Act of 1984 (commonly known as the Computer Fraud and Abuse Act, or CFAA).[33] Among other things, this act provides that a person who accesses a computer online, without authority, to obtain classified, restricted, or protected data (or attempts to do so) is subject to criminal prosecution. Such data could include financial and credit records, medical records, legal files, military and national security files, and other confidential information in government or private computers. The crime has two elements: accessing a computer without authority and taking the data.

This theft is a felony if it is committed for a commercial purpose or for private financial gain, or if the value of the stolen data (or computer time) exceeds $5,000. Penalties include fines and imprisonment for up to twenty years. A victim of computer theft can also bring a civil suit against the violator to obtain damages, an injunction, and other relief.

33. 18 U.S.C. Section 1030.

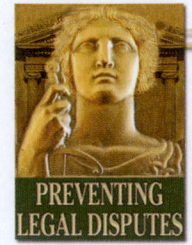

PREVENTING LEGAL DISPUTES

Although outside hackers are a threat to businesses, employees, former employees, and other "insiders" are responsible for most computer abuse, including breaches of information security. Therefore, businesspersons need to be cautious about which employees have access to computer data and to give employees access only to information that they need to know. Another important preventive measure is to have employees agree, in a written contract, not to disclose confidential information during or after employment without the employer's consent. Business owners should also make sure that they use the latest methods available to secure their computer systems, including firewalls and encryption techniques, for example.

REVIEWING Criminal Law and Cyber Crime

Edward Hanousek worked for Pacific & Arctic Railway and Navigation Company (P&A) as a roadmaster of the White Pass & Yukon Railroad in Alaska. Hanousek was responsible "for every detail of the safe and efficient maintenance and construction of track, structures and marine facilities of the entire railroad," including special projects. One project was a rock quarry, known as "6-mile," above the Skagway River. Next to the quarry, and just beneath the surface, ran a high-pressure oil pipeline owned by Pacific & Arctic Pipeline, Inc., P&A's sister company. When the quarry's backhoe operator punctured the pipeline, an estimated 1,000 to 5,000 gallons of oil were discharged into the river. Hanousek was charged with negligently discharging a harmful quantity of oil into a navigable water of the United States in violation of the criminal provisions of the Clean Water Act (CWA). Using the information presented in the chapter, answer the following questions.

1. Did Hanousek have the required mental state (*mens rea*) to be convicted of a crime? Why or why not?
2. Which theory discussed in the chapter would enable a court to hold Hanousek criminally liable for violating the statute regardless of whether he participated in, directed, or even knew about the specific violation?
3. Could the quarry's backhoe operator who punctured the pipeline also be charged with a crime in this situation? Explain.
4. Suppose that at trial, Hanousek argued that he could not be convicted because he was not aware of the requirements of the CWA. Would this defense be successful? Why or why not?

TERMS AND CONCEPTS

actus reus 174
arson 176
beyond a reasonable doubt 171
burglary 175
computer crime 190
consent 182
crime 171
cyber crime 190
cyberterrorist 191
double jeopardy 185
duress 182
embezzlement 176
entrapment 183
exclusionary rule 185
felony 172
forgery 176
grand jury 189
hacker 190
identity theft 190
indictment 189
information 189
larceny 175
mens rea 174
misdemeanor 173
money laundering 180
necessity 183
petty offense 173
plea bargaining 184
robbery 175
self-defense 183
white-collar crime 176

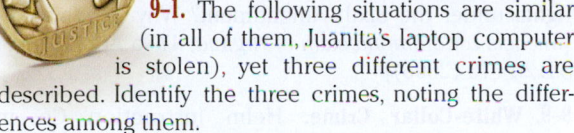

QUESTIONS AND CASE PROBLEMS

9–1. The following situations are similar (in all of them, Juanita's laptop computer is stolen), yet three different crimes are described. Identify the three crimes, noting the differences among them.

(a) While passing Juanita's house one night, Sarah sees a laptop computer left unattended on Juanita's lawn. Sarah takes the laptop, carries it home, and tells everyone she owns it.
(b) While passing Juanita's house one night, Sarah sees Juanita outside with a laptop computer. Holding Juanita at gunpoint, Sarah forces her to give up the computer. Then Sarah runs away with it.
(c) While passing Juanita's house one night, Sarah sees a laptop computer on a desk inside. Sarah breaks the front-door lock, enters, and leaves with the computer.

9–2. Which, if any, of the following crimes necessarily involves illegal activity on the part of more than one person?

(a) Bribery.
(b) Forgery.
(c) Embezzlement.
(d) Larceny.
(e) Receiving stolen property.

9–3. QUESTION WITH SAMPLE ANSWER

Armington, while robbing a drugstore, shot and seriously injured a drugstore clerk, Jennings. Subsequently, in a criminal trial, Armington was convicted of armed robbery and assault and battery. Jennings later brought a civil tort suit against Armington for damages. Armington contended that he could not be tried again for the same crime, as that would constitute double jeopardy, which is prohibited by the Fifth Amendment to the Constitution. Is Armington correct? Explain.

- **For a sample answer to Question 9–3, go to Appendix I at the end of this text.**

9–4. Rafael stops Laura on a busy street and offers to sell her an expensive wristwatch for a fraction of its value. After some questioning by Laura, Rafael admits that the watch is stolen property, although he says he was not the thief. Laura pays for and receives the wristwatch. Has Laura committed any crime? Has Rafael? Explain.

9–5. Theft of Trade Secrets. Four Pillars Enterprise Co. is a Taiwanese company owned by Pin Yen Yang. Avery Dennison, Inc., a U.S. corporation, is one of Four Pillars' chief competitors in the manufacture of adhesives. In 1989, Victor Lee, an Avery employee, met Yang and Yang's daughter Hwei Chen. They agreed to pay Lee $25,000 a year to serve as a consultant to Four Pillars. Over the next eight years, Lee supplied the Yangs with confidential Avery reports, including information that Four Pillars used to make a new adhesive that had been developed by Avery. The Federal Bureau of Investigation (FBI) confronted Lee, and he agreed to cooperate in an operation to catch the Yangs. When Lee next met the Yangs, he showed them documents provided by the FBI. The documents bore "confidential" stamps, and Lee said that they were Avery's confidential property. The FBI arrested the Yangs with the documents in their possession. The Yangs and Four Pillars were charged with, among other crimes, the attempted theft of trade secrets. The defendants argued in part that it was impossible for them to have committed this crime because the documents were not actually trade secrets. Should the court acquit them? Why or why not? [*United States v. Yang,* 281 F.3d 534 (6th Cir. 2002)]

9–6. CASE PROBLEM WITH SAMPLE ANSWER

The Sixth Amendment secures to a defendant who faces possible imprisonment the right to counsel at all critical stages of the criminal process, including the arraignment and the trial. In 1996, Felipe Tovar, a twenty-one-year-old college student, was arrested in Ames, Iowa, for operating a motor vehicle while under the influence of alcohol (OWI). Tovar was informed of his right to apply for court-appointed counsel and waived it. At his arraignment, he pleaded guilty. Six weeks later, he appeared for sentencing, again waived his right to counsel, and was sentenced to two days' imprisonment. In 1998, Tovar was convicted of OWI again, and in 2000, he was charged with OWI for a third time. In Iowa, a third OWI offense is a felony. Tovar asked the court not to use his first OWI conviction to enhance the third OWI charge. He argued that his 1996 waiver of counsel was not "intelligent" because the court did not make him aware of "the dangers and disadvantages of self-representation." What determines whether a person's choice in any situation is "intelligent"? What should determine whether a defendant's waiver of counsel is "intelligent" at critical stages of a criminal proceeding? [*Iowa v. Tovar,* 541 U.S. 77, 124 S.Ct. 1379, 158 L.Ed.2d 209 (2004)]

- **To view a sample answer for Problem 9–6, go to this book's Web site at www.cengage.com/blaw/jentz, select "Chapter 9," and click on "Case Problem with Sample Answer."**

9–7. Larceny. In February 2001, a homeowner hired Jimmy Smith, a contractor claiming to employ a crew of thirty workers, to build a garage. The homeowner paid Smith $7,950 and agreed to make additional payments as needed to complete the project, up to $15,900. Smith promised to start the next day and finish within eight weeks. Nearly a month passed with no work, while Smith lied to the homeowner that materials were on "back order." During a second month, footings were created for the foundation, and a subcontractor poured the concrete slab, but Smith did not return the homeowner's phone calls. After eight weeks, the homeowner confronted Smith, who promised to complete the job, worked on the site that day until lunch, and never returned. Three months later, the homeowner again confronted Smith, who promised to "pay [him] off" later that day but did not do so. In March 2002, the state of Georgia filed criminal charges against Smith. While his trial was pending, he promised to pay the homeowner "next week" but again failed to refund any of the funds paid. The value of the labor performed before Smith abandoned the project was between $800 and $1,000, the value of the materials was $367, and the subcontractor was paid $2,270. Did Smith commit larceny? Explain. [*Smith v. State of Georgia,* 592 S.E.2d 871 (Ga.App. 2004)]

9–8. Trial. Robert Michels met Allison Formal through an online dating Web site in 2002. Michels represented himself as the retired chief executive officer of a large company that he had sold for millions of dollars. In January 2003, Michels proposed that he and Formal create a *limited liability company* (a special form of business organization discussed in Chapter 37)—Formal Properties Trust, LLC—to "channel their investments in real estate." Formal agreed to contribute $100,000 to the company and wrote two $50,000 checks to "Michels and Associates, LLC." Six months later, Michels told Formal that their LLC had been formed in Delaware. Later, Formal asked Michels about her investments. He responded evasively, and she demanded that an independent accountant review the firm's records. Michels refused. Formal contacted the police. Michels was charged in a Virginia state court with obtaining funds by false pretenses. The Delaware secretary of state verified, in two certified documents, that "Formal Properties Trust, L.L.C." and "Michels and Associates, L.L.C." did not exist in Delaware. Did the admission of the Delaware secretary of state's certified documents at Michels's trial violate his rights under the Sixth Amendment? Why or why not? [*Michels v. Commonwealth of Virginia,* 47 Va.App. 461, 624 S.E.2d 675 (2006)]

9–9. White-Collar Crime. Helm Instruction Co. in Maumee, Ohio, makes custom electrical control systems. Helm hired Patrick Walsh in September 1998 to work as comptroller. Walsh soon developed a close relationship with Richard Wilhelm, Helm's president, who granted Walsh's request to hire Shari Price as Walsh's assistant. Wilhelm was not aware that Walsh and Price were engaged in an extramarital affair. Over the next five years, Walsh and Price spent more than $200,000 of Helm's money on themselves. Among other things, Walsh drew unauthorized checks on Helm's accounts to pay his personal credit-card bills and issued to Price and himself unauthorized salary increases, overtime payments, and tuition reimbursement payments, altering Helm's records to hide the payments. After an investigation, Helm officials confronted Walsh. He denied the affair with Price, claimed that his unauthorized use of Helm's funds was an "interest-free loan," and argued that it was less of a burden on the company to pay his credit-card bills than to give him the salary increases to which he felt he was entitled. Did Walsh commit a crime? If so, what crime did he commit? Discuss. [*State v. Walsh,* 113 Ohio App.3d 1515, 866 N.E.2d 513 (6 Dist. 2007)]

9–10. A QUESTION OF ETHICS

A troublesome issue concerning the constitutional privilege against self-incrimination is the extent to which law enforcement officers may use trickery *during an interrogation to induce a suspect to incriminate himself or herself. For example, in one case two officers questioned Charles McFarland, who was incarcerated in a state prison, about his connection to a handgun that had been used to shoot two other officers. McFarland was advised of his rights but was not asked whether he was willing to waive those rights. Instead, to induce McFarland to speak, the officers deceived him into believing that "[n]obody is going to give you charges." McFarland made incriminating admissions and was indicted for possessing a handgun as a convicted felon. [*United States v. McFarland*, 424 F.Supp.2d 427 (N.D.N.Y. 2006)]*

(a) Review Case 9.3, *Miranda v. Arizona,* on pages 186 and 187 in this chapter. Should McFarland's statements be suppressed—that is, not be treated as admissible evidence at trial—because he was not asked whether he was willing to waive his rights prior to making his self-incriminating statements? Does the *Miranda* rule apply to McFarland's situation?

(b) Do you think that it is fair for the police to resort to trickery and deception to bring those who have committed crimes to justice? Why or why not? What rights or public policies must be balanced in deciding this issue?

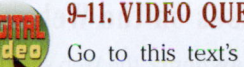

9-11. VIDEO QUESTION

Go to this text's Web site at **www.cengage.com/blaw/jentz** and select "Chapter 9." Click on "Video Questions" and view the video titled *Casino.* Then answer the following questions.

(a) In the video, a casino manager, Ace (Robert DeNiro), discusses how politicians "won their 'comp life' when they got elected." "Comps" are the free gifts that casinos give to high-stakes gamblers to keep their business. If an elected official accepts comps, is he or she committing a crime? If so, what type of crime? Explain your answers.

(b) Assume that Ace committed a crime by giving politicians comps. Can the casino, Tangiers Corp., be held liable for that crime? Why or why not? How could a court punish the corporation?

(c) Suppose that the Federal Bureau of Investigation wants to search the premises of Tangiers for evidence of criminal activity. If casino management refuses to consent to the search, what constitutional safeguards and criminal procedures, if any, protect Tangiers?

LAW ON THE WEB

For updated links to resources available on the Web, as well as a variety of other materials, visit this text's Web site at

www.cengage.com/blaw/jentz

The Bureau of Justice Statistics in the U.S. Department of Justice offers an impressive collection of statistics on crime at the following Web site:

ojp.usdoj.gov/bjs

For summaries of famous criminal cases and documents relating to these trials, go to the Web site of truTV (formerly Court TV) at

www.trutv.com/sitemap/index.html

Many state criminal codes are now online. To find your state's code, go to the following home page and select "States" under the link to "Cases & Codes":

www.findlaw.com

You can learn about some of the constitutional questions raised by various criminal laws and procedures by going to the Web site of the American Civil Liberties Union at

www.aclu.org

The following Web site, which is maintained by the U.S. Department of Justice, offers information ranging from the various types of cyber crime to a description of how they are being prosecuted:

www.cybercrime.gov

Legal Research Exercises on the Web

Go to **www.cengage.com/blaw/jentz**, the Web site that accompanies this text. Select "Chapter 9" and click on "Internet Exercises." There you will find the following Internet research exercises that you can perform to learn more about the topics covered in this chapter.

Internet Exercise 9–1: Legal Perspective
Revisiting *Miranda*

Internet Exercise 9–2: Management Perspective
Hackers

Internet Exercise 9–3: International Perspective
Fighting Cyber Crime Worldwide

Ethics and Torts and Crimes

UNIT TWO · FOCUS ON ETHICS

Ethical and legal concepts are often closely intertwined. This is because the common law, as it evolved in England and then in America, reflects society's values and customs. This connection between law and ethics is clearly evident in the area of tort law, which provides remedies for harms caused by actions that society has deemed wrongful. Criminal law is also rooted in common law concepts of right and wrong behavior, although common law concepts governing criminal acts are now expressed in, or replaced by, federal, state, and local criminal statutes. The number of torts and crimes has continued to expand as new ways to commit wrongs have been discovered.

The laws governing torts, crimes, and intellectual property—the areas of law covered in this unit—constitute an important part of the legal environment of business. In each of these areas, new legal (and ethical) challenges have emerged as a result of developments in technology. Today, we are witnessing some of the challenges posed by the use of new communications networks, particularly the Internet. In this *Focus on Ethics* feature, we look at the ethical dimensions of selected topics discussed in the preceding chapters, including some issues that are unique to the cyber age.

Privacy Rights in an Online World

Privacy rights are protected under constitutional law, tort law, and various federal and state statutes. How to protect privacy rights in the online world, though, has been a recurring problem over the past ten years. One difficulty is that individuals today often are not even aware that information about their personal lives and preferences is being collected by Internet companies and other online users. Nor do they know how that information will be used. "Cookies" installed in computers may allow users' Web movements to be tracked. Google now offers a Gmail service that automatically scans and saves information about its users. Persons who purchase goods from online merchants or auctions inevitably must reveal some personal information, often including their credit-card numbers.

The Increased Value of Personal Information

One of the major concerns of consumers in recent years has been the increasing value of personal information for online marketers, who are willing to pay a high price to those who collect and sell them such information. Because of these concerns—and the possibility of lawsuits based on privacy laws—businesses marketing goods online need to exercise care. Today, many online businesses create and post on their Web sites a privacy policy disclosing how any information obtained from their customers will be used.

The Duty of Care and Personal Information

Selling data can bolster a company's profits, which may satisfy the firm's duty to its owners, but when the information is personal, its sale may violate an ethical or legal duty. In what circumstances might a party who sells information about someone else have a duty to that other party with respect to the sale of the information?

The courts have found that private investigators owe a duty not to disclose private information about a person without a legitimate reason. In one case, for example, a man contacted an Internet-based investigation and information service and requested information about Amy Boyer. The man provided his name, address, and phone number and paid the fee online using his credit card. In return, the company provided him with Boyer's home address, birth date, Social Security number, and work address. The man then drove to Boyer's workplace and fatally shot her. The police subsequently discovered that the man maintained a Web site where he referred to stalking and killing Boyer. Boyer's mother filed a suit against the online information service for disclosing her daughter's private information without investigating the reason for the request. The state supreme court found that because the threats of stalking and identity theft were sufficiently foreseeable, the company had a duty to exercise reasonable care in disclosing a third person's personal information to a client.[1]

In another case, a man hired a licensed private investigator to follow his ex-girlfriend. The woman complained to the police that the investigator was stalking her, and criminal charges were filed against the investigator. The court concluded that the private detective had a duty to exercise reasonable care in disclosing the woman's personal information to the client (her former boyfriend). Because the private detective refused to testify as

1. *Remsburg v. Docusearch, Inc.,* 149 N.H. 148, 816 A.2d 1001 (2003).

(Continued)

to why he was hired to follow the woman, the court found that the investigator's conduct was not for a legitimate purpose.[2]

Privacy Rights in the Workplace

Another area of concern today is the extent to which employees' privacy rights should be protected in the workplace. Traditionally, employees have been afforded a certain "zone of privacy" in the workplace. For example, the courts have concluded that employees have a reasonable expectation of privacy with respect to personal items contained in their desks or in their lockers. Should this zone of privacy extend to personal e-mail sent via the employer's computer system? This question and others relating to employee privacy rights in today's cyber age will be discussed in greater detail in Chapter 33, in the context of employment law.

Should Civil Liberties Be Sacrificed to Control Crime and Terrorist Activities in the Cyber Age?

In an era when criminal conspirators and terrorists use the Internet to communicate and even to recruit new members, an issue that has come to the forefront is whether it is possible to control many types of crime and terrorist activities without sacrificing some civil liberties. Governments in certain countries, such as Russia, have succeeded in controlling online criminal communications to some extent by monitoring the e-mail and other electronic transmissions of users of specific Internet service providers. In the United States, however, any government attempt to monitor Internet use to detect criminal conspiracies or terrorist activities does not sit well with the American people. The traditional attitude has been that civil liberties must be safeguarded to the greatest extent feasible.

After the terrorist attacks in September 2001, Congress enacted legislation—including the USA Patriot Act mentioned in Chapter 4—that gave law enforcement personnel more authority to conduct electronic surveillance, such as monitoring Web sites and e-mail exchanges. For a time, it seemed that the terrorist attacks might have made Americans more willing to trade off some of their civil liberties for greater national security. Today, though, many complain that this legislation has gone too far in curbing traditional civil liberties guaranteed by the U.S. Constitution. As terrorists find more ways of using the Internet for their purposes, determining the degree to which individuals should sacrifice personal freedoms in exchange for greater protection will likely become even more difficult.

Global Companies and Censorship Issues—Google China

Doing business on a global level can sometimes involve serious ethical challenges. Consider the ethical firestorm that erupted when Google, Inc., decided to market "Google China." This version of Google's widely used search engine was especially tailored to the Chinese government's censorship requirements. To date, the Chinese government has maintained strict control over the flow of information in that country. The government's goal is to stop the flow of what it considers to be "harmful information." Web sites that offer pornography, criticism of the government, or information on sensitive topics, such as the Tiananmen Square massacre in 1989, are censored—that is, they cannot be accessed by Web users. Government agencies enforce the censorship and encourage citizens to inform on one another. Thousands of Web sites are shut down each year, and the sites' operators are subject to potential imprisonment.

Google's code of conduct opens with the company's informal motto: "Don't be evil." Yet critics question whether Google is following this motto. Human rights groups have come out strongly against Google's decision, maintaining that the company is seeking profits in a lucrative marketplace at the expense of assisting the Chinese Communist Party in suppressing free speech. In February 2006, Tom Lantos, who was the only Holocaust survivor serving in Congress until his death in 2008, stated that the "sickening collaboration" of Google and three other Web companies (Cisco Systems, Microsoft Corporation, and Yahoo!, Inc.) with the Chinese government was "decapitating the voice of dissidents" in that nation.[3]

Google's Response

Google defends its actions by pointing out that its Chinese search engine at least lets users know which sites are being censored. Google China

2. *Miller v. Blackden,* 154 N.H. 448, 913 A.2d 742 (2006).

3. As quoted in Tom Ziller, Jr., "Web Firms Questioned on Dealings in China," *The New York Times,* February 16, 2006.

includes the links to censored sites, but when a user tries to access a link, the program states that it is not accessible. Google claims that its approach is essentially the "lesser of two evils": if U.S. companies did not cooperate with the Chinese government, Chinese residents would have less user-friendly Internet access. Moreover, Google asserts that providing Internet access, even if censored, is a step toward more open access in the future because technology is, in itself, a revolutionary force.

The Chinese Government's Defense

The Chinese government insists that in restricting access to certain Web sites, it is merely following the lead of other national governments, which also impose controls on information access. As an example, it cites France, which bans access to any Web sites selling or portraying Nazi paraphernalia. The United States itself prohibits the dissemination of certain types of materials, such as child pornography, over the Internet. Furthermore, the U.S. government monitors Web sites and e-mail communications to protect against terrorist threats. How, ask Chinese officials, can other nations point their fingers at China for engaging in a common international practice?

Do Gun Makers Have a Duty to Warn?

One of the issues facing today's courts is how tort law principles apply to harms caused by guns. Across the nation, many plaintiffs have filed negligence actions against gun manufacturers, claiming that gun makers have a duty to warn users of their products of the dangers associated with gun use. Would it be fair to impose such a requirement on gun manufacturers? Some say no, because such dangers are "open and obvious." (Recall from Chapter 7 that, generally, there is no duty to warn of open and obvious dangers.) Others contend that warnings could prevent numerous gun accidents.

State courts addressing this issue have generally ruled that manufacturers have no duty to warn users of the obvious risks associated with gun use. For example, New York's highest court has held that a gun manufacturer's duty of care does not extend to those who are injured by the illegal use of handguns.[4]

4. *Hamilton v. Beretta U.S.A. Corp.,* 96 N.Y.2d 222, 750 N.E.2d 1055, 727 N.Y.S.2d 7 (2001).

Trademark Protection versus Free Speech Rights

Another legal issue involving questions of fairness pits the rights of trademark owners against the right to free speech. The issue—so-called cybergriping—is unique to the cyber age. Cybergripers are individuals who complain in cyberspace about corporate products, services, or activities. For a trademark owner, the issue becomes particularly thorny when cybergriping sites add the word *sucks* or *stinks* or some other disparaging term to the trademark owner's domain name. These sites, sometimes referred to collectively as "sucks" sites, are established solely for the purpose of criticizing the products or services sold by the trademark owner.

A number of companies have sued the owners of such sites for trademark infringement in the hope that a court or an arbitrating panel will order the site owner to cease using the domain name. To date, however, companies have had little success pursuing this alternative. In one case, for example, Bally Total Fitness Holding Corporation sued Andrew Faber, who had established a "Bally sucks" site for the purpose of criticizing Bally's health clubs and business practices. Bally claimed that Faber had infringed on its trademark. The court did not agree, holding that the "speech"—consumer commentary—on Faber's Web site was protected by the First Amendment. In short, Bally could not look to trademark law for a remedy against cyber critics.[5]

The courts have been reluctant to hold that the use of a business's domain name in a "sucks" site infringes on the trademark owner's rights. After all, one of the primary reasons trademarks are protected under U.S. law is to prevent customers from becoming confused about the origin of the goods for sale—and a cybergriping site certainly does not create such confusion. Furthermore, U.S. courts give extensive protection to free speech rights, including the right to express opinions about companies and their products.[6] Nevertheless, when a site's domain name is confusingly similar to a competitor's trade name and the site is used to

5. *Bally Total Fitness Holding Corp. v. Faber,* 29 F.Supp.2d 1161 (C.D.Cal. 1998).

6. Many businesses have concluded that although they cannot control what people say about them, they can make it more difficult for it to be said. Today, businesses commonly register such insulting domain names before the cybergripers themselves can register them.

disparage that competitor, a court may allow a lawsuit for infringement or for cybersquatting.[7]

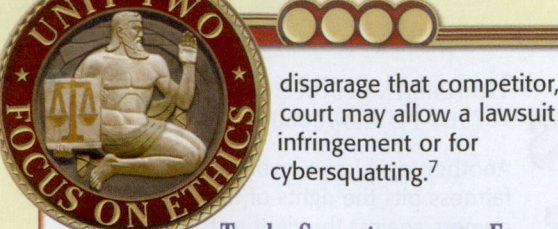

Trade Secrets versus Free Speech Rights

Another ongoing issue with ethical dimensions is the point at which free speech rights come into conflict with the right of copyright holders to protect their property by using encryption technology. This issue came before the California Supreme Court in the case of *DVD Copy Control Association v. Bunner.*[8] Trade associations in the movie industry (the plaintiffs) sued an Internet Web site operator (the defendant) who had posted the code of a computer program that cracked technology used to encrypt DVDs. This posed a significant threat to the plaintiffs because, by using the code-cracking software, users would be able to duplicate the copyrighted movies stored on the DVDs.

In their suit, the plaintiffs claimed that the defendant had misappropriated trade secrets. The defendant argued that software programs designed to break encryption programs were a form of constitutionally protected speech. When the case reached the California Supreme Court, the court held that although the First Amendment applies to computer code, computer code is not a form of "pure speech" and the courts can therefore protect it to a lesser extent. The court reinstated the trial court's order that enjoined (prevented) the defendant from continuing to post the code.

DISCUSSION QUESTIONS

1. Some observers maintain that privacy rights are quickly becoming a thing of the past. In your opinion, is it possible to protect privacy rights in today's online world?
2. Many argue that the federal government should not be allowed to monitor the Internet activities and e-mail exchanges of its citizens without obtaining a warrant. Yet others maintain that in some situations, when time is of the essence, such monitoring may be necessary to keep Americans safe from terrorism. Where should the line be drawn between justifiable and unjustifiable governmental interference with American citizens' civil liberties?
3. Do companies, such as Google, that do business on a global level have an ethical duty to foreign citizens not to suppress free speech, or is it acceptable to censor the information that they provide in other nations at the request of a foreign government?
4. In your opinion, should gun manufacturers have a duty to warn gun users of the dangers of using guns? Would such a warning be effective in preventing gun-related accidents?
5. Generally, do you believe that the law has struck a fair balance between the rights of intellectual property owners and the rights of the public?

---

7. See, for example, *Sunlight Saunas, Inc. v. Sundance Sauna, Inc.,* 427 F.Supp.2d 1032 (D.Kan. 2006).

8. 31 Cal.4th 864, 75 P.3d 1, 4 Cal.Rptr.3d 69 (2003). But see also *O'Grady v. Superior Court,* 139 Cal.App.4th 1423, 44 Cal.Rptr.3d 72 (2006), in which a state appellate court distinguished the situation from the *Bunner* case and held that Apple, Inc., could prevent an online publisher from disclosing confidential information about the company's impending product.

UNIT THREE

Contracts and E-Contracts

CONTENTS

CHAPTER 10

Nature and Terminology

The noted legal scholar Roscoe Pound once said that "[t]he social order rests upon the stability and predictability of conduct, of which keeping promises is a large item."[1] Contract law deals with, among other things, the formation and keeping of promises. A **promise** is a person's assurance that the person will or will not do something.

Like other types of law, contract law reflects our social values, interests, and expectations at a given point in time. It shows, for example, to what extent our society allows people to make promises or commitments that are legally binding. It distinguishes between promises that create only *moral* obligations (such as a promise to take a friend to lunch) and promises that are legally binding (such as a promise to pay for merchandise purchased). Contract law also demonstrates which excuses our society accepts for breaking certain types of promises. In addition, it indicates which promises are considered to be contrary to public policy—against the interests of society as a whole—and therefore legally invalid. When the person making a promise is a child or is mentally incompetent, for example, a question will arise as to whether the promise should be enforced. Resolving such questions is the essence of contract law.

1. R. Pound, *Jurisprudence*, Vol. 3 (St. Paul, Minn.: West Publishing Co., 1959), p. 162.

SECTION 1 An Overview of Contract Law

Before we look at the numerous rules that courts use to determine whether a particular promise will be enforced, it is necessary to understand some fundamental concepts of contract law. In this section, we describe the sources and general function of contract law. We also provide the definition of a contract and introduce the objective theory of contracts.

Sources of Contract Law

The common law governs all contracts except when it has been modified or replaced by statutory law, such as the Uniform Commercial Code (UCC),[2] or by administrative agency regulations. Contracts relating to services, real estate, employment, and insurance, for example, generally are governed by the common law of contracts.

Contracts for the sale and lease of goods, however, are governed by the UCC—to the extent that the UCC has modified general contract law. The relationship between general contract law and the law governing sales and leases of goods will be explored in detail in Chapter 20. In the discussion of general contract law that follows, we indicate in footnotes the areas in which the UCC has significantly altered common law contract principles.

2. See Chapters 1 and 20 for further discussions of the significance and coverage of the UCC. The UCC is presented in Appendix C at the end of this book.

The Function of Contract Law

The law encourages competent parties to form contracts for lawful objectives. Indeed, no aspect of modern life is entirely free of contractual relationships. Even ordinary consumers in their daily activities acquire rights and obligations based on contract law. You acquire rights and obligations, for example, when you purchase an iPod or when you borrow funds to buy a house. Contract law is designed to provide stability and predictability, as well as certainty, for both buyers and sellers in the marketplace.

Contract law deals with, among other things, the formation and enforcement of agreements between parties (in Latin, *pacta sunt servanda*—"agreements shall be kept"). By supplying procedures for enforcing private contractual agreements, contract law provides an essential condition for the existence of a market economy. Without a legal framework of reasonably assured expectations within which to make long-run plans, businesspersons would be able to rely only on the good faith of others. Duty and good faith are usually sufficient to obtain compliance with a promise, but when price changes or adverse economic factors make compliance costly, these elements may not be enough. Contract law is necessary to ensure compliance with a promise or to entitle the innocent party to some form of relief.

Definition of a Contract

A **contract** is "a promise or a set of promises for the breach of which the law gives a remedy, or the performance of which the law in some way recognizes as a duty."[3] Put simply, a contract is a legally binding agreement between two or more parties who agree to perform or to refrain from performing some act now or in the future. Generally, contract disputes arise when there is a promise of future performance. If the contractual promise is not fulfilled, the party who made it is subject to the sanctions of a court (see Chapter 18). That party may be required to pay damages for failing to perform the contractual promise; in limited instances, the party may be required to perform the promised act.

The Objective Theory of Contracts

In determining whether a contract has been formed, the element of intent is of prime importance. In contract law, intent is determined by what is called the **objective theory of contracts,** not by the personal or subjective intent, or belief, of a party. The theory is that a party's intention to enter into a legally binding agreement, or contract, is judged by outward, objective facts as interpreted by a *reasonable* person, rather than by the party's own secret, subjective intentions. Objective facts include (1) what the party said when entering into the contract, (2) how the party acted or appeared (intent may be manifested by conduct as well as by oral or written words), and (3) the circumstances surrounding the transaction. We will look further at the objective theory of contracts in Chapter 11, in the context of contract formation.

3. *Restatement (Second) of Contracts,* Section 1. The *Restatement of the Law of Contracts* is a nonstatutory, authoritative exposition of the common law of contracts compiled by the American Law Institute in 1932. The *Restatement,* which is now in its second edition (a third edition is being drafted), will be referred to throughout the following chapters on contract law.

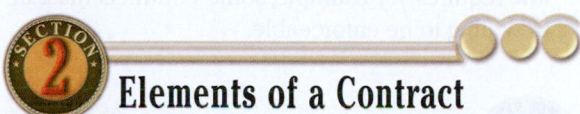

SECTION 2 Elements of a Contract

The many topics that will be discussed in the following chapters on contract law require an understanding of the basic elements of a valid contract and the way in which a contract is created. The topics to be covered in this unit on contracts also require an understanding of the types of circumstances in which even legally valid contracts will not be enforced.

Requirements of a Valid Contract

The following list briefly describes the four requirements that must be met before a valid contract exists. If any of these elements is lacking, no contract will have been formed. (Each requirement will be explained more fully in subsequent chapters.)

1. *Agreement.* An agreement to form a contract includes an *offer* and an *acceptance.* One party must offer to enter into a legal agreement, and another party must accept the terms of the offer.
2. *Consideration.* Any promises made by the parties to the contract must be supported by legally sufficient and bargained-for *consideration* (something of value received or promised, such as money, to convince a person to make a deal).
3. *Contractual capacity.* Both parties entering into the contract must have the contractual *capacity* to do so; the law must recognize them as possessing characteristics that qualify them as competent parties.
4. *Legality.* The contract's purpose must be to accomplish some goal that is legal and not against public policy.

Defenses to the Enforceability of a Contract

Even if all of the above-listed requirements are satisfied, a contract may be unenforceable if the following requirements are not met. These requirements typically are raised as *defenses* to the enforceability of an otherwise valid contract.

1. *Genuineness of assent, or voluntary consent.* The apparent consent of both parties must be genuine, or voluntary. For example, if a contract was formed as a result of fraud, undue influence, mistake, or duress, the contract may not be enforceable.
2. *Form.* The contract must be in whatever form the law requires; for example, some contracts must be in writing to be enforceable.

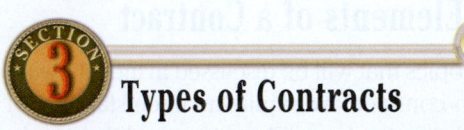

SECTION 3 Types of Contracts

There are many types of contracts. In this section, you will learn that contracts can be categorized based on legal distinctions as to formation, performance, and enforceability.

Contract Formation

As you can see in Exhibit 10–1, three classifications, or categories, of contracts are based on how and when a contract is formed. We explain each of these types of contracts in the following subsections.

Bilateral versus Unilateral Contracts

Every contract involves at least two parties. The **offeror** is the party making the offer. The **offeree** is the party to whom the offer is made. Whether the contract is classified as *bilateral* or *unilateral* depends on what the offeree must do to accept the offer and bind the offeror to a contract.

Bilateral Contracts. If the offeree can accept simply by promising to perform, the contract is a **bilateral contract.** Hence, a bilateral contract is a "promise for a promise." No performance, such as payment of funds or delivery of goods, need take place for a bilateral contract to be formed. The contract comes into existence at the moment the promises are exchanged.

For example, Javier offers to buy Ann's digital camcorder for $200. Javier tells Ann that he will give her the funds for the camcorder next Friday when he gets paid. Ann accepts Javier's offer and promises to give him the camcorder when he pays her on Friday. Javier and Ann have formed a bilateral contract.

Unilateral Contracts. If the offer is phrased so that the offeree can accept the offer only by completing the contract performance, the contract is a **unilateral contract.** Hence, a unilateral contract is a "promise for an act."[4] In other words, the time of contract formation in a unilateral contract is not the moment when promises are exchanged but the moment when the contract is *performed.* A classic example of a unilateral contract is as follows: O'Malley says to Parker, "If you carry this package across the Brooklyn Bridge, I'll give you $20."

4. Clearly, a contract cannot be "one sided," because, by definition, an agreement implies the existence of two or more parties. Therefore, the phrase *unilateral contract,* if read literally, is a contradiction in terms. As traditionally used in contract law, however, the phrase refers to the kind of contract that results when only one promise is being made (the promise made by the offeror in return for the offeree's performance).

EXHIBIT 10–1 • Classifications Based on Contract Formation

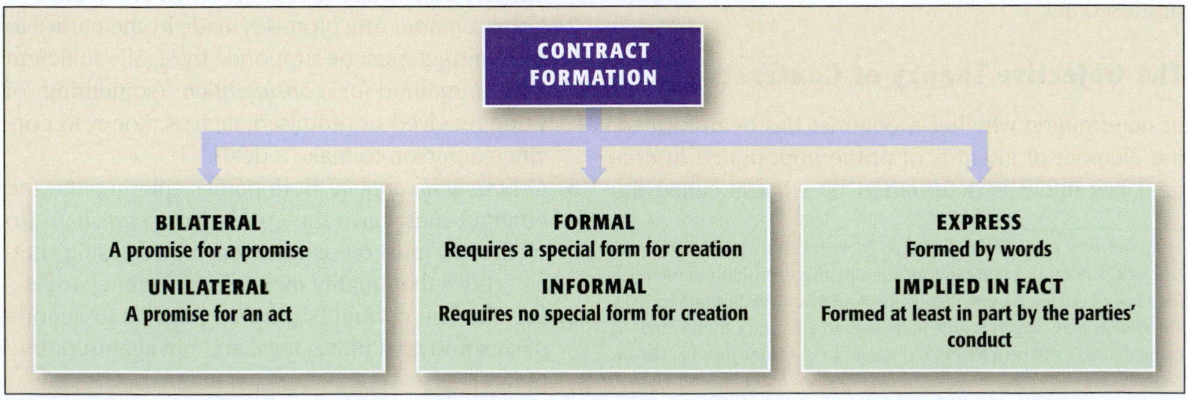

Only on Parker's complete crossing with the package does she fully accept O'Malley's offer to pay $20. If she chooses not to undertake the walk, there are no legal consequences.

Contests, lotteries, and other competitions involving prizes are examples of offers to form unilateral contracts. If a person complies with the rules of the contest—such as by submitting the right lottery number at the right place and time—a unilateral contract is formed, binding the organization offering the prize to a contract to perform as promised in the offer.

Can a school's, or an employer's, letter of tentative acceptance to a prospective student, or a possible employee, qualify as a unilateral contract? That was the issue in the following case.

CASE 10.1 Ardito v. City of Providence

United States District Court, District of Rhode Island, 2003. 263 F.Supp.2d 358.

Background and Facts In 2001, the city of Providence, Rhode Island, decided to begin hiring police officers to fill vacancies in its police department. Because only individuals who had graduated from the Providence Police Academy were eligible, the city also decided to conduct two training sessions, the "60th and 61st Police Academies." To be admitted, an applicant had to pass a series of tests and be deemed qualified by members of the department after an interview. The applicants judged most qualified were sent a letter informing them that they had been selected to attend the academy if they successfully completed a medical checkup and a psychological examination. The letter for the applicants to the 61st Academy, dated October 15, stated that it was "a conditional offer of employment." Meanwhile, a new chief of police, Dean Esserman, decided to revise the selection process, which caused some of those who had received the letter to be rejected. Derek Ardito and thirteen other newly rejected applicants—who had all completed the examinations—filed a suit in a federal district court against the city, seeking a halt to the 61st Academy unless they were allowed to attend. They alleged that, among other things, the city was in breach of contract.

Decision and Rationale The court held that the October 15 letter was a unilateral offer that the plaintiffs had accepted, and issued an injunction to prohibit the city from conducting the 61st Police Academy unless the plaintiffs were included. The court found the October 15 letter to be "a classic example of an offer to enter into a unilateral contract. The October 15 letter expressly stated that it was a 'conditional offer of employment' and the message that it conveyed was that the recipient would be admitted into the 61st Academy if he or she successfully completed the medical and psychological examinations." The court contrasted the letter with "notices sent to applicants by the City at earlier stages of the selection process. Those notices merely informed applicants that they had completed a step in the process and remained eligible to be considered for admission into the Academy. Unlike the October 15 letter, the prior notices did not purport to extend a 'conditional offer' of admission." The court concluded that "the plaintiffs accepted the City's offer of admission into the Academy by satisfying the specified conditions. Each of the plaintiffs submitted to and passed lengthy and intrusive medical and psychological examinations."

What If the Facts Were Different? *Suppose that the October 15 letter had used the phrase "potential offer of employment" instead of using the word "conditional." Would the court in this case still have considered the letter to be a unilateral contract? Why or why not?*

The Legal Environment Dimension *Why did the court order the city to stop the 61st Police Academy unless the plaintiffs were included?*

A Problem with Unilateral Contracts. A problem arises in unilateral contracts when the **promisor** (the one making the promise) attempts to *revoke* (cancel) the offer after the **promisee** (the one to whom the promise was made) has begun performance but before the act has been completed. The promisee can accept the offer only on full performance, and under traditional contract principles, an offer may be revoked at any time before the offer is accepted. The present-day view, however, is that an offer to form a unilateral contract becomes irrevocable—cannot be revoked—once performance has begun. Thus, even though the offer has not yet been accepted, the offeror is prohibited from revoking it for a reasonable time period.

For instance, in the earlier example involving the Brooklyn Bridge, suppose that Parker is walking across the bridge and has only three yards to go when O'Malley calls out to her, "I revoke my offer." Under traditional contract law, O'Malley's revocation would terminate the offer. Under the modern view of unilateral contracts, however, O'Malley will not be able to revoke his offer because Parker has undertaken performance and walked all but three yards of the bridge. In these circumstances, Parker can finish crossing the bridge and bind O'Malley to the contract.

Formal versus Informal Contracts Another classification system divides contracts into formal contracts and informal contracts. **Formal contracts** are contracts that require a special form or method of creation (formation) to be enforceable. *Contracts under seal* are a type of formal contract that involves a formalized writing with a special seal attached.[5] In the past, the seals were often made of wax and impressed on the paper document. Today, the significance of the seal in contract law has lessened, though standard-form contracts still sometimes include a place for a seal next to the signature lines. *Letters of credit,* which are frequently used in international sales contracts, are another type of formal contract. As will be discussed in Chapter 22, letters of credit are agreements to pay contingent on the purchaser's receipt of invoices and bills of lading (documents evidencing receipt of, and title to, goods shipped).

5. The contract under seal has been almost entirely abolished under such provisions as UCC 2–203 (Section 2–203 of the Uniform Commercial Code). In sales of real estate, however, it is still common to use a seal (or an acceptable substitute).

Informal contracts (also called *simple contracts*) include all other contracts. No special form is required (except for certain types of contracts that must be in writing), as the contracts are usually based on their substance rather than their form. Typically, businesspersons put their contracts in writing to ensure that there is some proof of a contract's existence should problems arise.

Express versus Implied-in-Fact Contracts Contracts may also be categorized as *express* or *implied* by the conduct of the parties. We look here at the differences between these two types of contracts.

Express Contracts. In an **express contract,** the terms of the agreement are fully and explicitly stated in words, oral or written. A signed lease for an apartment or a house is an express written contract. If a classmate calls you on the phone and agrees to buy your textbook from last semester for $45, an express oral contract has been made.

Implied-in-Fact Contracts. A contract that is implied from the conduct of the parties is called an **implied-in-fact contract** or an *implied contract.* This type of contract differs from an express contract in that the *conduct* of the parties, rather than their words, creates and defines the terms of the contract. (Note that a contract may be a mixture of an express contract and an implied-in-fact contract. In other words, a contract may contain some express terms, while others are implied.)

Requirements for Implied-in-Fact Contracts. For an implied-in-fact contract to arise, certain requirements must be met. Normally, if the following conditions exist, a court will hold that an implied contract was formed:

1. The plaintiff furnished some service or property.
2. The plaintiff expected to be paid for that service or property, and the defendant knew or should have known that payment was expected.
3. The defendant had a chance to reject the services or property and did not.

For example, you need an accountant to complete your tax return this year. You look through the Yellow Pages and find an accountant with an office in your neighborhood. You drop by the firm's office, explain your problem to an accountant, and learn what fees will be charged. The next day you return and give her administrative assistant all the necessary information and documents, such as canceled checks and W-2 forms. You then walk out the door without saying anything expressly to the accountant. In this situation, you have entered into an implied-in-fact contract to pay the accountant the usual and reasonable fees for her services. The contract is implied by your conduct and by hers. She expects to be paid for completing your tax return, and by bringing in the records she will need to do the work, you have implied an intent to pay her.

During the construction of a home, the homeowner often requests that the builder make changes in the original specifications. When do these changes form part of an implied-in-fact contract for which the homeowner is liable to the builder for any extra expenses? That was the issue in the following case.

CASE 10.2 Uhrhahn Construction & Design, Inc. v. Hopkins

Court of Appeals of Utah, 2008. 179 P.3d 808.

• **Background and Facts** Uhrhahn Construction & Design, Inc., was hired by Lamar and Joan Hopkins for several projects in the building of their home. Each project was based on a cost estimate and specifications. The proposals accepted by the Hopkinses each said that any changes in the signed contracts would be done only "upon written orders." When work was in progress, the Hopkinses made several requests for changes. There was no written record of these changes, but the work was performed and paid for by the Hopkinses. This dispute arose from the couple's request that Uhrhahn use Durisol blocks rather than cinder blocks in some construction. The original proposal specified cinder blocks, but the Hopkinses told Uhrhahn that the change should be made as Durisol blocks were "easier to install than traditional cinder block and would take half the time." The homeowners said the total cost would be the same. Uhrhahn orally agreed to the change but then discovered that Durisol blocks were more complicated to use than cinder blocks, and Uhrhahn demanded extra payment. The Hopkinses refused to pay, claiming the cost should be the same. Uhrhahn sued. The trial court held for Uhrhahn, finding that the Durisol blocks were more costly to install. The Hopkinses appealed.

• **Decision and Rationale** The Utah appeals court affirmed the decision of the trial court, finding that there was a valid contract between the parties and that both parties had agreed to oral changes in the contract. All of the elements of a contract existed: offer and acceptance, competent parties, and consideration. The terms were clearly specified in the proposals accepted by the Hopkinses. Uhrhahn promised to perform work in exchange for payment. While the contract stated that any changes would be in writing, both parties waived that term in the contract when they agreed to some changes in the work performed. As often happens in construction, changes were requested that were outside the contract. The builder did the work, and the buyer accepted the work and paid for it. Such oral modification of the original contract creates an enforceable contract, and payment is due for the extra work. This is an implied-in-fact contract. The Hopkinses requested Uhrhahn to perform certain work. Uhrhahn expected to be compensated for the work, and the Hopkinses knew, or should have known, that Uhrhahn would be paid for this work that was outside the specifications of the original contract.

• **What If the Facts Were Different?** *Suppose that the Hopkinses and Uhrhahn had not agreed to deviate from the contract on previous occasions, and that the Hopkinses had not paid for any additional work performed by Uhrhahn. How might this have changed the court's ruling in this case?*

• **The E-Commerce Dimension** *Would the outcome have been different if the parties had communicated by e-mail for all details regarding changes in the work performed? Explain.*

Contract Performance

Contracts are also classified according to the degree to which they have been performed. A contract that has been fully performed on both sides is called an **executed contract.** A contract that has not been fully performed by the parties is called an **executory contract.** If one party has fully performed but the other has not, the contract is said to be executed on the one side and executory on the other, but the contract is still classified as executory.

Assume that you agree to buy ten tons of coal from the Northern Coal Company. Further assume that Northern has delivered the coal to your steel mill, where it is now being burned. At this point, the contract is executed on the part of Northern and executory on your part. After you pay Northern for the coal, the contract will be executed on both sides.

Contract Enforceability

A **valid contract** has the elements necessary to entitle at least one of the parties to enforce it in court. Those elements, as mentioned earlier, consist of (1) an agreement consisting of an offer and an acceptance of that offer, (2) supported by legally sufficient consideration, (3) made by parties who have the legal capacity to enter into the contract, and (4) made for a legal purpose. As you can see in Exhibit 10–2, valid contracts may be enforceable, voidable, or unenforceable. Additionally, a contract may be referred to as a *void contract.* We look next at the meaning of the terms *voidable, unenforceable,* and *void* in relation to contract enforceability.

Voidable Contracts A **voidable contract** is a valid contract but one that can be avoided at the option of one or both of the parties. The party having the option can elect either to avoid any duty to perform or to *ratify* (make valid) the contract. If the contract is avoided, both parties are released from it. If it is ratified, both parties must fully perform their respective legal obligations.

As you will read in Chapter 13, contracts made by minors, insane persons, and intoxicated persons may be voidable. For example, contracts made by minors generally are voidable at the option of the minor (with certain exceptions). Additionally, contracts entered into under fraudulent conditions are voidable at the option of the defrauded party. Contracts entered into under legally defined duress or undue influence are also voidable (see Chapter 14).

Unenforceable Contracts An **unenforceable contract** is one that cannot be enforced because of certain legal defenses against it. It is not unenforceable because a party failed to satisfy a legal requirement of the contract; rather, it is a valid contract rendered unenforceable by some statute or law. For example, certain contracts must be in writing (see Chapter 15), and if they are not, they will not be enforceable except in certain exceptional circumstances.

Void Contracts A **void contract** is no contract at all. The terms *void* and *contract* are contradictory. A void contract produces no legal obligations on any of the parties. For example, a contract can be void because one of the parties was adjudged by a court to

EXHIBIT 10–2 • Enforceable, Voidable, Unenforceable, and Void Contracts

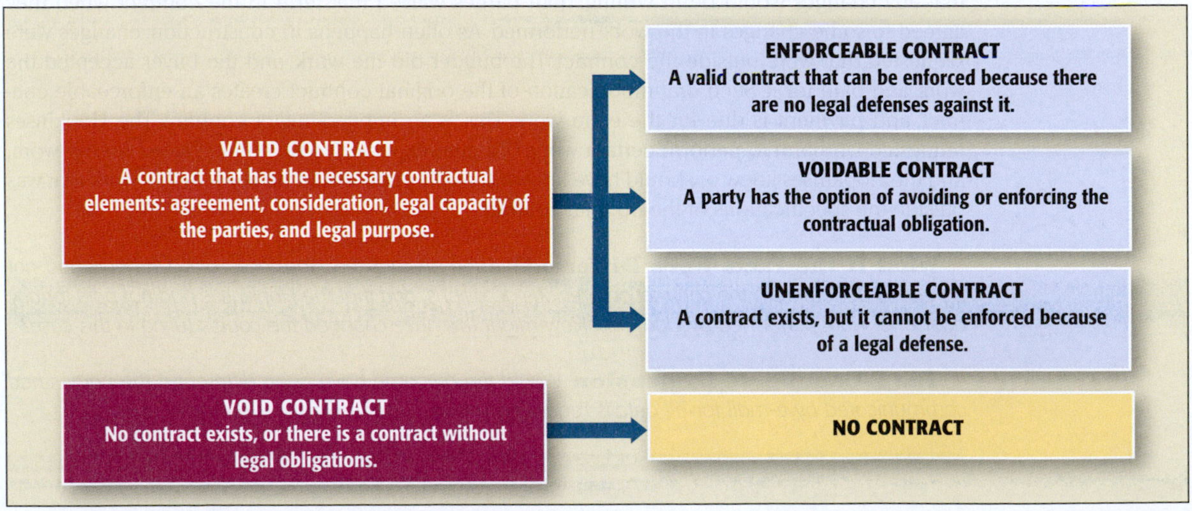

be legally insane (and thus lacked the legal capacity to enter into a contract—see Chapter 13) or because the purpose of the contract was illegal. To review the various types of contracts, see *Concept Summary 10.1.*

SECTION 4

Quasi Contracts

Quasi contracts, or contracts *implied in law,* are not actual contracts. Express contracts and implied-in-fact contracts are actual contracts formed by the words or actions of the parties. Quasi contracts, in contrast, are fictional contracts created by courts and imposed on parties in the interests of fairness and justice. Quasi contracts are therefore equitable, rather than contractual, in nature.

Usually, quasi contracts are imposed to avoid the *unjust enrichment* of one party at the expense of another. The doctrine of unjust enrichment is based on the theory that individuals should not be allowed to profit or enrich themselves inequitably at the expense of others. When the court imposes a quasi contract, a plaintiff may recover in ***quantum meruit,***[6] a Latin phrase meaning "as much as he or she deserves." *Quantum meruit* essentially describes the extent of compensation owed under a contract implied in law.

Suppose that a vacationing physician is driving down the highway and finds Potter lying unconscious on the side of the road. The physician renders medical aid that saves Potter's life. Although the injured, unconscious Potter did not solicit the medical aid and was not aware that the aid had been rendered, Potter received a valuable benefit, and the requirements for a quasi contract were fulfilled. In such a situation, the law will impose a quasi contract, and Potter normally will have to pay the physician for the reasonable value of the medical services rendered.

Limitations on Quasi-Contractual Recovery

Although quasi contracts exist to prevent unjust enrichment, the party obtaining the enrichment is not held liable for the fair value in some situations.

6. Pronounced *kwahn*-tuhm *mehr*-oo-wit.

CONCEPT SUMMARY

CONCEPT SUMMARY 10.1
Types of Contracts

Aspect	Definition
FORMATION	1. *Bilateral*—A promise for a promise.
	2. *Unilateral*—A promise for an act (acceptance is the completed performance of the act).
	3. *Formal*—Requires a special form for creation.
	4. *Informal*—Requires no special form for creation.
	5. *Express*—Formed by words (oral, written, or a combination).
	6. *Implied in fact*—Formed by the conduct of the parties.
PERFORMANCE	1. *Executed*—A fully performed contract.
	2. *Executory*—A contract not fully performed.
ENFORCEABILITY	1. *Valid*—The contract has the necessary contractual elements: agreement (offer and acceptance), consideration, legal capacity of the parties, and legal purpose.
	2. *Voidable*—One party has the option of avoiding or enforcing the contractual obligation.
	3. *Unenforceable*—A contract exists, but it cannot be enforced because of a legal defense.
	4. *Void*—No contract exists, or there is a contract without legal obligations.

Basically, a party who has conferred a benefit on someone else unnecessarily or as a result of misconduct or negligence cannot invoke the principle of quasi contract. The enrichment in those situations will not be considered "unjust."

For example, you take your car to the local car wash and ask to have it run through the washer and to have the gas tank filled. While it is being washed, you go to a nearby shopping center for two hours. In the meantime, one of the workers at the car wash has mistaken your car for the one that he is supposed to hand wax. When you come back, you are presented with a bill for a full tank of gas, a wash job, and a hand wax. Clearly, a benefit has been conferred on you. But this benefit has been conferred because of a mistake by the car wash employee. You have not been *unjustly* enriched under these circumstances. People normally cannot be forced to pay for benefits "thrust" on them.

When an Actual Contract Exists

The doctrine of quasi contract generally cannot be used when there is an *actual contract* that covers the matter in controversy. For example, Bateman contracts with Cameron to deliver a furnace to a building owned by Jones. Bateman delivers the furnace, but Cameron never pays Bateman. Jones has been unjustly enriched in this situation, to be sure. Bateman, however, cannot recover from Jones in quasi contract because Bateman had an actual contract with Cameron. Bateman already has a remedy—he can sue for breach of contract to recover the price of the furnace from Cameron. The court does not need to impose a quasi contract in this situation to achieve justice.

SECTION 5 Interpretation of Contracts

Sometimes, parties agree that a contract has been formed but disagree on its meaning or legal effect. One reason this may happen is that one of the parties is not familiar with the legal terminology used in the contract. To an extent, *plain language* laws (enacted by the federal government and a majority of the states) have helped to avoid this difficulty. Sometimes, though, a dispute may arise over the meaning of a contract simply because the rights or obligations under the contract are not expressed clearly—no matter how "plain" the language used.

In this section, we look at some common law rules of contract interpretation. These rules, which have evolved over time, provide the courts with guidelines for deciding disputes over how contract terms or provisions should be interpreted. Exhibit 10–3 provides a brief graphic summary of how these rules are applied.

To avoid disputes over contract interpretation, business managers should make sure that their intentions are clearly expressed in their contracts. Careful drafting of contracts not only helps prevent potential disputes over the meaning of certain terms but may also be crucial if the firm brings or needs to defend against a lawsuit for breach of contract. By using simple, clear language and avoiding legalese, managers take a major step toward avoiding contract disputes.

EXHIBIT 10–3 • Rules of Contract Interpretation

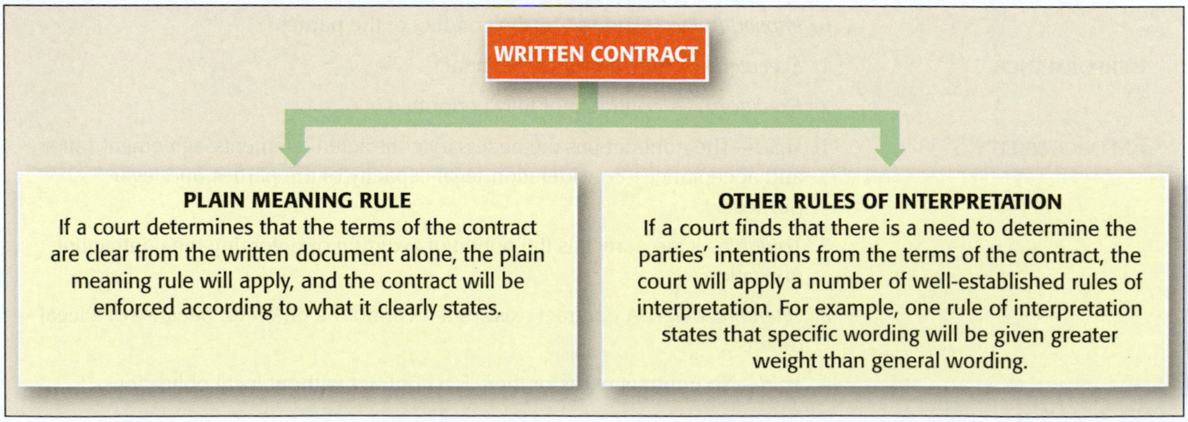

WRITTEN CONTRACT
PLAIN MEANING RULE
If a court determines that the terms of the contract are clear from the written document alone, the plain meaning rule will apply, and the contract will be enforced according to what it clearly states.
OTHER RULES OF INTERPRETATION
If a court finds that there is a need to determine the parties' intentions from the terms of the contract, the court will apply a number of well-established rules of interpretation. For example, one rule of interpretation states that specific wording will be given greater weight than general wording.

The Plain Meaning Rule

When a contract's writing is clear and unequivocal, a court will enforce it according to its obvious terms. The meaning of the terms must be determined from *the face of the instrument*—from the written document alone. This is sometimes referred to as the *plain meaning rule.*

Under this rule, if a contract's words appear to be clear and unambiguous, a court cannot consider *extrinsic evidence*—that is, any evidence not contained in the document itself. If a contract's terms are unclear or ambiguous, however, extrinsic evidence may be admissible to clarify the meaning of the contract. The admissibility of such evidence can significantly affect the court's interpretation of ambiguous contractual provisions and thus the outcome of litigation. The following case illustrates these points.

CASE 10.3 Wagner v. Columbia Pictures Industries, Inc.

California Court of Appeal, Second District, Division 7, 2007.
146 Cal.App.4th 586, 52 Cal.Rptr.3d 898.

Background and Facts Actor Robert Wagner entered into an agreement with Spelling-Goldberg Productions (SGP) "relating to Charlie's Angels (herein called the 'series')." The contract entitled Wagner to 50 percent of the net profits that SGP received "for the right to exhibit photoplays of the series and from the exploitation of all ancillary, music and subsidiary rights in connection therewith." SGP hired Ivan Goff and Ben Roberts to write the series, under a contract subject to the Writers Guild of America Minimum Basic Agreement (MBA).[a] The MBA stipulates that the writer of a television show retains the right to make and market films based on the material, subject to the producer's right to buy this right if the writer decides to sell it within five years. The first "Charlie's Angels" episode aired in 1976. In 1982, SGP sold its rights to the series to Columbia Pictures Industries, Inc. Years later, Columbia bought the movie rights to the material from Goff's and Roberts's heirs. In 2000 and 2003, Columbia produced and distributed two "Charlie's Angels" films. Wagner filed a suit in a California state court against Columbia, claiming a share of the profits from the films. The court granted Columbia's motion for summary judgment. Wagner appealed to a state intermediate appellate court.

Decision and Rationale The state intermediate appellate court affirmed the lower court's judgment. The contract "unambiguously" stated the conditions under which the parties were to share the films' profits, and those conditions had not occurred. Wagner offered evidence to show that a previous contract with SGP had been intended to give him half of the net profits from a property titled "Love Song" received from all sources without limitation as to source or time. Wagner argued that the "Charlie's Angels" agreement used identical language in its profits provision, which thus should be interpreted to give him the same share. The court stated that an "agreement is the writing itself." Extrinsic evidence is not admissible "to show intention independent of an unambiguous written instrument." In this case, even if the parties intended Wagner to share in the profits from all sources, "they did not say so in their contract." Under the language of the contract, Wagner was entitled to share in the profits from the exercise of the movie rights to "Charlie's Angels" if those rights were exploited as "ancillary" or "subsidiary" to the primary "right to exhibit photoplays of the series" but not if those rights were acquired separately. SGP's contract with Goff and Roberts was subject to the MBA, under which the writers kept the movie rights, which the producer could buy if the writers opted to sell them within five years. SGP did not acquire the movie rights to "Charlie's Angels" by exercising this right within the five-year period. Columbia obtained those rights independently more than five years later.

What If the Facts Were Different? *How might the result in this case have been different if the court had admitted Wagner's evidence of the "Love Song" contract?*

The Legal Environment Dimension *Under what circumstance would Wagner's evidence of the "Love Song" contract have been irrelevant and yet he would still have been entitled to a share of the profits from the "Charlie's Angels" movies?*

a. The Writers Guild of America is an association of screen and television writers that negotiates industrywide agreements with motion picture and television producers.

Other Rules of Interpretation

Generally, a court will interpret the language to give effect to the parties' intent as *expressed in their contract.* This is the primary purpose of the rules of interpretation—to determine the parties' intent from the language used in their agreement and to give effect to that intent. A court normally will not make or remake a contract, nor will it interpret the language according to what the parties *claim* their intent was when they made it. The courts use the following rules in interpreting contractual terms:

1. Insofar as possible, a reasonable, lawful, and effective meaning will be given to all of a contract's terms.
2. A contract will be interpreted as a whole; individual, specific clauses will be considered subordinate to the contract's general intent. All writings that are a part of the same transaction will be interpreted together.
3. Terms that were the subject of separate negotiation will be given greater consideration than standardized terms and terms that were not negotiated separately.
4. A word will be given its ordinary, commonly accepted meaning, and a technical word or term will be given its technical meaning, unless the parties clearly intended something else.[7]
5. Specific and exact wording will be given greater consideration than general language.
6. Written or typewritten terms will prevail over preprinted ones.
7. Because a contract should be drafted in clear and unambiguous language, a party who uses ambiguous expressions is held to be responsible for the ambiguities. Thus, when the language has more than one meaning, it will be interpreted against the party who drafted the contract.
8. Evidence of trade usage, prior dealing, and course of performance may be admitted to clarify the meaning of an ambiguously worded contract (these terms will be defined and discussed in Chapter 20). When considering custom and usage, a court will look at what is common to the particular business or industry and to the locale where the contract was made or is to be performed.

7. See, for example, *Citizens Communications Co. v. Trustmark Insurance*, 303 F.Supp.2d 197 (2004).

REVIEWING Nature and Terminology

Grant Borman, who was engaged in a construction project, leased a crane from Allied Equipment and hired Crosstown Trucking Company to deliver the crane to the construction site. Crosstown, while the crane was in its possession and without permission from either Borman or Allied Equipment, used the crane to install a transformer for a utility company, which paid Crosstown for the job. Crosstown then delivered the crane to Borman's construction site at the appointed time of delivery. When Allied Equipment learned of the unauthorized use of the crane by Crosstown, it sued Crosstown for damages, seeking to recover the rental value of Crosstown's use of the crane. Using the information presented in the chapter, answer the following questions.

1. What are the four requirements of a valid contract?
2. Did Crosstown have a valid contract with Borman concerning the use of the crane? If so, was it a bilateral or a unilateral contract? Explain.
3. What are the requirements of an implied-in-fact contract? Can Allied Equipment obtain damages from Crosstown based on an implied-in-fact contract? Why or why not?
4. Should a court impose a quasi contract on the parties in this situation to allow Allied to recover damages from Crosstown? Why or why not?

TERMS AND CONCEPTS

bilateral contract 204
contract 203
executed contract 208
executory contract 208
express contract 206
formal contract 206
implied-in-fact contract 206
informal contract 206
objective theory of contracts 203
offeree 204
offeror 204
promise 202
promisee 206
promisor 206
***quantum meruit* 209**
quasi contract 209
unenforceable contract 208
unilateral contract 204
valid contract 208
void contract 208
voidable contract 208

QUESTIONS AND CASE PROBLEMS

10–1. Suppose that Everett McCleskey, a local businessperson, is a good friend of Al Miller, the owner of a local candy store. Every day on his lunch hour, McCleskey goes into Miller's candy store and spends about five minutes looking at the candy. After examining Miller's candy and talking with Miller, McCleskey usually buys one or two candy bars. One afternoon, McCleskey goes into Miller's candy shop, looks at the candy, and picks up a $1 candy bar. Seeing that Miller is very busy, he waves the candy bar at Miller without saying a word and walks out. Is there a contract? If so, classify it within the categories presented in this chapter.

10–2. QUESTION WITH SAMPLE ANSWER

Janine was hospitalized with severe abdominal pain and placed in an intensive care unit. Her doctor told the hospital personnel to order around-the-clock nursing care for Janine. At the hospital's request, a nursing services firm, Nursing Services Unlimited, provided two weeks of in-hospital care and, after Janine was sent home, an additional two weeks of at-home care. During the at-home period of care, Janine was fully aware that she was receiving the benefit of the nursing services. Nursing Services later billed Janine $4,000 for the nursing care, but Janine refused to pay on the ground that she had never contracted for the services, either orally or in writing. In view of the fact that no express contract was ever formed, can Nursing Services recover the $4,000 from Janine? If so, under what legal theory? Discuss.

- **For a sample answer to Question 10–2, go to Appendix I at the end of this text.**

10–3. Burger Baby restaurants engaged Air Advertising to fly an advertisement above the Connecticut beaches. The advertisement offered $1,000 to any person who could swim from the Connecticut beaches to Long Island across Long Island Sound in less than a day. At 10:00 A.M. on Saturday, October 10, Air Advertising's pilot flew a sign above the Connecticut beaches that read, "Swim across the Sound and Burger Baby pays $1,000." On seeing the sign, Davison dived in. About four hours later, when he was about halfway across the Sound, Air Advertising flew another sign over the Sound that read, "Burger Baby revokes." Davison completed the swim in another six hours. Is there a contract between Davison and Burger Baby? Can Davison recover anything?

10–4. Bilateral versus Unilateral Contracts. D.L. Peoples Group (D.L.) placed an ad in a Missouri newspaper to recruit admissions representatives, who were hired to recruit Missouri residents to attend D.L.'s college in Florida. Donald Hawley responded to the ad, his interviewer recommended him for the job, and he signed, in Missouri, an "Admissions Representative Agreement," which was mailed to D.L.'s president, who signed it in his office in Florida. The agreement provided, in part, that Hawley would devote exclusive time and effort to the business in his assigned territory in Missouri and that D.L. would pay Hawley a commission if he successfully recruited students for the school. While attempting to make one of his first calls on his new job, Hawley was accidentally shot and killed. On the basis of his death, a claim was filed in Florida for workers' compensation. (Under Florida law, when an accident occurs outside Florida, workers' compensation benefits are payable only if the employment contract was made in Florida.) Was this admissions representative agreement a bilateral or a unilateral contract? What are the consequences of the distinction in this case? Explain. [*D.L. Peoples Group, Inc. v. Hawley*, 804 So.2d 561 (Fla.App. 1 Dist. 2002)]

10–5. Interpretation of Contracts. East Mill Associates (EMA) was developing residential "units" in East

Brunswick, New Jersey, within the service area of the East Brunswick Sewerage Authority (EBSA). The sewer system required an upgrade to the Ryder's Lane Pumping Station to accommodate the new units. EMA agreed to pay "fifty-five percent (55%) of the total cost" of the upgrade. At the time, the estimated cost to EMA was $150,000 to $200,000. Impediments to the project arose, however, substantially increasing the cost. Among other things, the pumping station had to be moved to accommodate a widened road nearby. The upgrade was delayed for almost three years. When it was completed, EBSA asked EMA for $340,022.12, which represented 55 percent of the total cost. EMA did not pay. EBSA filed a suit in a New Jersey state court against EMA for breach of contract. What rule should the court apply to interpret the parties' contract? How should that rule be applied? Why? [*East Brunswick Sewerage Authority v. East Mill Associates, Inc.*, 365 N.J.Super. 120, 838 A.2d 494 (A.D. 2004)]

10–6. CASE PROBLEM WITH SAMPLE ANSWER

In December 2000, Nextel South Corp., a communications firm, contacted R.A. Clark Consulting, Ltd., an executive search company, about finding an employment manager for Nextel's call center in Atlanta, Georgia. Over the next six months, Clark screened, evaluated, and interviewed more than three hundred candidates. Clark provided Nextel with more than fifteen candidate summaries, including one for Dan Sax. Nextel hired Sax for the position at an annual salary of $75,000. Sax started work on June 25, 2001, took two weeks' vacation, and quit on July 31 in the middle of a project. Clark spent the next six weeks looking for a replacement, until Nextel asked Clark to stop. Clark billed Nextel for its services, but Nextel refused to pay, asserting, among other things, that the parties had not signed an agreement. Nextel's typical agreement specified payment to an employment agency of 20 percent of an employee's annual salary. Clark filed a suit in a Georgia state court against Nextel to recover in *quantum meruit.* What is *quantum meruit?* What should Clark have to show to recover on this basis? Should the court rule in Clark's favor? Explain. [*Nextel South Corp. v. R.A. Clark Consulting, Ltd.*, 266 Ga.App. 85, 596 S.E.2d 416 (2004)]

- **To view a sample answer for Problem 10–6, go to this book's Web site at www.cengage.com/blaw/jentz, select "Chapter 10," and click on "Case Problem with Sample Answer."**

10–7. Contract Enforceability. California's Subdivision Map Act (SMA) prohibits the sale of real property until a map of its subdivision is filed with, and approved by, the appropriate state agency. In November 2004, Black Hills Investments, Inc., entered into two contracts with Albertson's, Inc., to buy two parcels of property in a shopping center development. Each contract required that "all governmental approvals relating to any lot split [or] subdivision" be obtained before the sale but permitted Albertson's to waive this condition. Black Hills made a $133,000 deposit on the purchase. A few weeks later, before the sales were complete, Albertson's filed with a local state agency a map that subdivided the shopping center into four parcels, including the two that Black Hills had agreed to buy. In January 2005, Black Hills objected to concessions that Albertson's had made to a buyer of one of the other parcels, told Albertson's that it was terminating its deal, and asked for a return of its deposit. Albertson's refused. Black Hills filed a suit in a California state court against Albertson's, arguing that the contracts were void. Are these contracts valid, voidable, unenforceable, or void? Explain. [*Black Hills Investments, Inc. v. Albertson's, Inc.*, 146 Cal.App.4th 883, 53 Cal.Rptr.3d 263 (4 Dist. 2007)]

10–8. A QUESTION OF ETHICS

*International Business Machines Corp. (IBM) hired Niels Jensen in 2000 as a software sales representative. In 2001, IBM presented a new "Software Sales Incentive Plan" (SIP) at a conference for its sales employees. A brochure given to the attendees stated, "[T]here are no caps to your earnings; the more you sell, * * * the more earnings for you." The brochure outlined how the plan worked and referred the employees to the "Sales Incentives" section of IBM's corporate intranet for more details. Jensen was given a "quota letter" that said he would be paid $75,000 as a base salary and, if he attained his quota, an additional $75,000 as incentive pay. In September, Jensen closed a deal with the U.S. Department of the Treasury's Internal Revenue Service that was worth over $24 million to IBM. Relying on the SIP brochure, Jensen estimated his commission to be $2.6 million. IBM paid him less than $500,000, however. Jensen filed a suit in a federal district court against IBM, contending that the SIP brochure and quota letter constituted a unilateral offer that became a binding contract when Jensen closed the sale. In view of these facts, consider the following questions. [*Jensen v. International Business Machines Corp., *454 F.3d 382 (4th Cir. 2006)]*

(a) Would it be fair to the employer in this case to hold that the SIP brochure and the quota letter created a unilateral contract if IBM did not intend to create such a contract? Would it be fair to the employee to hold that no contract was created? Explain.

(b) The "Sales Incentives" section of IBM's intranet included a clause providing that "[m]anagement will decide if an adjustment to the payment is appropriate" when an employee closes a large transaction. Jensen's quota letter stated, "[The SIP] program does not constitute a promise by IBM to make any distributions under it. IBM reserves the right to adjust the program terms or to cancel or otherwise modify the program at any time." How do these statements affect your answers to the above questions? From an ethical perspective, would it be fair to hold that a contract exists despite these statements?

10-9. VIDEO QUESTION

Go to this text's Web site at **www.cengage.com/blaw/jentz** and select "Chapter 10." Click on "Video Questions" and view the video titled *Bowfinger.* Then answer the following questions.

(a) In the video, Renfro (Robert Downey, Jr.) says to Bowfinger (Steve Martin), "You bring me this script and Kit Ramsey and you've got yourself a 'go' picture." Assume for the purposes of this question that their agreement is a contract. Is the contract bilateral or unilateral? Is it express or implied? Is it formal or informal? Is it executed or executory? Explain your answers.

(b) What criteria would a court rely on to interpret the terms of the contract?

(c) Recall from the video that the contract between Bowfinger and the producer was oral. Suppose that a statute requires contracts of this type to be in writing. In that situation, would the contract be void, voidable, or unenforceable? Explain.

LAW ON THE WEB

For updated links to resources available on the Web, as well as a variety of other materials, visit this text's Web site at

www.cengage.com/blaw/jentz

The 'Lectric Law Library provides information about contract law, including a definition of a contract and the elements required for a contract. Go to

www.lectlaw.com/def/c123.htm

You can keep abreast of recent and planned revisions of the *Restatements of the Law*, including the *Restatement (Second) of Contracts,* by accessing the American Law Institute's Web site at

www.ali.org

Legal Research Exercises on the Web

Go to **www.cengage.com/blaw/jentz**, the Web site that accompanies this text. Select "Chapter 10" and click on "Internet Exercises." There you will find the following Internet research exercises that you can perform to learn more about the topics covered in this chapter.

Internet Exercise 10–1: Legal Perspective
Contracts and Contract Provisions

Internet Exercise 10–2: Management Perspective
Implied Employment Contracts

Internet Exercise 10–3: Historical Perspective
Contracts in Ancient Mesopotamia

CHAPTER 11

Agreement

An essential element for contract formation is **agreement**—the parties must agree on the terms of the contract and manifest to each other their **mutual assent** (agreement) to the same bargain. Ordinarily, agreement is evidenced by two events: an *offer* and an *acceptance*. One party offers a certain bargain to another party, who then accepts that bargain. The agreement does not necessarily have to be in writing. Both parties, however, must manifest their assent to the same bargain. Once an agreement is reached, if the other elements of a contract are present (consideration, capacity, and legality—discussed in subsequent chapters), a valid contract is formed, generally creating enforceable rights and duties between the parties.

Note that not all agreements are contracts. John and Kevin may agree to play golf on a certain day, but a court would not hold that their agreement is an enforceable contract. A *contractual* agreement arises only when the terms of the agreement impose legally enforceable obligations on the parties.

In today's world, contracts are frequently formed via the Internet. For a discussion of online offers and acceptances, see Chapter 19, which is devoted entirely to the subject of electronic contracts, or e-contracts.

SECTION 1 Requirements of the Offer

As mentioned in Chapter 10, the parties to a contract are the *offeror,* the one who makes an offer or proposal to another party, and the *offeree,* the one to whom the offer or proposal is made. An **offer** is a promise or commitment to do or refrain from doing some specified thing in the future. Under the common law, three elements are necessary for an offer to be effective:

1. The offeror must have a serious intention to become bound by the offer.
2. The terms of the offer must be reasonably certain, or definite, so that the parties and the court can ascertain the terms of the contract.
3. The offer must be communicated to the offeree.

Once an effective offer has been made, the offeree has the power to accept the offer. If the offeree accepts, an agreement is formed (and thus a contract arises, if other essential elements are present). The requirements for traditional offers apply to online offers as well, as you will read in Chapter 19.

Intention

The first requirement for an effective offer is a serious intent on the part of the offeror. Serious intent is not determined by the *subjective* intentions, beliefs, and assumptions of the offeror. As discussed in Chapter 10, courts generally adhere to the *objective theory of contracts* in determining whether a contract has been formed. Under this theory, a party's words and conduct are held to mean whatever a reasonable person in the offeree's position would think they meant. The court will give words their usual meanings even if "it were proved by twenty bishops that [the] party . . . intended something else."[1]

1. Judge Learned Hand in *Hotchkiss v. National City Bank of New York,* 200 F. 287 (2d Cir. 1911), aff'd 231 U.S. 50, 34 S.Ct. 20, 58 L.Ed. 115 (1913).

Offers made in obvious anger, jest, or undue excitement do not meet the intent test because a reasonable person would realize that a serious offer was not being made. Because these offers are not effective, an offeree's acceptance does not create an agreement. Suppose that you and three classmates ride to school each day in Davina's new automobile, which has a market value of $20,000. One cold morning, the four of you get into the car, but Davina cannot get the car started. She yells in anger, "I'll sell this car to anyone for $500!" You drop $500 in her lap. Given these facts, a reasonable person, taking into consideration Davina's frustration and the obvious difference in worth between the market value of the car and the proposed purchase price, would declare that her offer was not made with serious intent and that you did not have an agreement.

The concept of intention can be further clarified through an examination of the types of expressions and statements that are *not* offers. We look at these expressions and statements in the subsections that follow. In the classic case of *Lucy v. Zehmer,* presented here, the court considered whether an offer made "after a few drinks" met the serious-intent requirement.

CASE 11.1 Lucy v. Zehmer

Supreme Court of Appeals of Virginia, 1954. 196 Va. 493, 84 S.E.2d 516.

Background and Facts W. O. Lucy and J. C. Lucy, the plaintiffs, filed a suit against A. H. Zehmer and Ida Zehmer, the defendants, to compel the Zehmers to transfer title of their property, known as the Ferguson Farm, to the Lucys for $50,000, as the Zehmers had allegedly agreed to do. Lucy had known Zehmer for fifteen or twenty years and for the last eight years or so had been anxious to buy the Ferguson Farm from Zehmer. One night, Lucy stopped in to visit the Zehmers in the combination restaurant, filling station, and motor court they operated. While there, Lucy tried to buy the Ferguson Farm once again. This time he tried a new approach. According to the trial court transcript, Lucy said to Zehmer, "I bet you wouldn't take $50,000 for that place." Zehmer replied, "Yes, I would too; you wouldn't give fifty." Throughout the evening, the conversation returned to the sale of the Ferguson Farm for $50,000. At the same time, the parties continued to drink whiskey and engage in light conversation. Eventually, Lucy enticed Zehmer to write up an agreement to the effect that the Zehmers would sell the Ferguson Farm to Lucy for $50,000 complete. Later, Lucy sued Zehmer to compel him to go through with the sale. Zehmer argued that he had been drunk and that the offer had been made in jest and hence was unenforceable. The trial court agreed with Zehmer, and Lucy appealed.

Decision and Rationale The Supreme Court of Appeals of Virginia reversed the ruling of the lower court. The state supreme court ordered the Zehmers to carry through with the sale. The court noted that Lucy attempted to testify in detail as to what was said and done the night of the transaction. "Zehmer was not intoxicated to the extent of being unable to comprehend the nature and consequences of the instrument he executed, and hence that instrument is not to be invalidated on that ground." The court found that the execution of the agreement was a serious business transaction, as evidenced by a number of circumstances. These included the discussion of the contract for forty minutes or more before it was signed, its rewriting to reflect Mrs. Zehmer's interest, the discussion of what was to be included in the sale, the provision for an examination of the title, the completeness of the instrument, and Lucy's taking possession of the agreement without Zehmer's request that he give it back. As the court explained, "We must look to the outward expression of a person as manifesting his intention rather than to his secret and unexpressed intention."

Impact of This Case on Today's Law *This is a classic case in contract law because it illustrates so clearly the objective theory of contracts with respect to determining whether a serious offer was intended. Today, the courts continue to apply the objective theory of contracts and routinely cite* Lucy v. Zehmer *as a significant precedent in this area.*

CASE CONTINUES

CASE 11.1 CONTINUED • **What If the Facts Were Different?** *Suppose that the day after Lucy signed the purchase agreement for the farm, he decided that he didn't want it after all, and Zehmer sued Lucy to perform the contract. Would this change in the facts alter the court's decision that Lucy and Zehmer had created an enforceable contract? Why or why not?*

Expressions of Opinion An expression of opinion is not an offer. It does not indicate an intention to enter into a binding agreement. Consider an example. Hawkins took his son to McGee, a physician, and asked McGee to operate on the son's hand. McGee said that the boy would be in the hospital three or four days and that the hand would *probably* heal a few days later. The son's hand did not heal for a month, but the father did not win a suit for breach of contract. The court held that McGee had not made an offer to heal the son's hand in a few days. He had merely expressed an opinion as to when the hand would heal.[2]

Statements of Future Intent A statement of an *intention* to do something in the future is not an offer. If Arif says, "I *plan* to sell my stock in Novation, Inc., for $150 per share," a contract is not created if John "accepts" and tenders the $150 per share for the stock. Arif has merely expressed his intention to enter into a future contract for the sale of the stock. If John accepts and tenders the $150 per share, no contract is formed because a reasonable person would conclude that Arif was only *thinking about* selling his stock, not *promising* to sell it.

Preliminary Negotiations A request or invitation to negotiate is not an offer. It only expresses a willingness to discuss the possibility of entering into a contract. Statements such as "Will you sell Blythe Estate?" or "I wouldn't sell my car for less than $5,000" are examples. A reasonable person in the offeree's position would not conclude that these statements indicated an intention to enter into a binding obligation. Likewise, when the government or private firms require construction work, they invite contractors to submit bids. The *invitation* to submit bids is not an offer, and a contractor does not bind the government or private firm by submitting a bid. (The bids that the contractors submit are offers, however, and the government or private firm can bind the contractor by accepting the bid.)

2. *Hawkins v. McGee,* 84 N.H. 114, 146 A. 641 (1929).

Agreements to Agree Traditionally, agreements to agree—that is, agreements to agree to the material terms of a contract at some future date—were not considered to be binding contracts. The modern view, however, is that agreements to agree may be enforceable agreements (contracts) if it is clear that the parties intended to be bound by the agreements. In other words, under the modern view the emphasis is on the parties' intent rather than on form.

For example, after a person was injured and nearly drowned on a water ride at Six Flags Amusement Park, Six Flags, Inc., filed a lawsuit against the manufacturer that designed the particular ride. The defendant manufacturer claimed that there was no binding contract between the parties, only preliminary negotiations that were never formalized into a construction contract. The court, however, held that a faxed document specifying the details of the water ride, along with the parties' subsequent actions (beginning construction and handwriting notes on the fax), was sufficient to show an intent to be bound. Because of the court's finding, the manufacturer was required to provide insurance for the water ride at Six Flags, and its insurer was required to defend Six Flags in the personal-injury lawsuit that arose out of the incident.[3]

Increasingly, the courts are holding that a preliminary agreement constitutes a binding contract if the parties have agreed on all essential terms and no disputed issues remain to be resolved.[4] In contrast, if the parties agree on certain major terms but leave other terms open for further negotiation, a preliminary agreement is binding only in the sense that the parties have committed themselves to negotiate the unde-

3. *Six Flags, Inc. v. Steadfast Insurance Co.,* 474 F.Supp.2d 201 (D.Mass. 2007).

4. See, for example, *Tractebel Energy Marketing, Inc. v. AEP Power Marketing, Inc.,* 487 F.3d 89 (2d Cir. 2007); and *Florine On Call, Ltd. v. Fluorogas Limited,* No. 01-CV-186 (W.D.Tex. 2002), contract issue affirmed on appeal at 380 F.3d 849 (5th Cir. 2004). A significant precedent in this area is *Texaco, Inc. v. Pennzoil Co.,* 729 S.W.2d 768 (Tex.App.—Houston [1st Dist.] 1987, writ ref'd n.r.e.). (Generally, a complete Texas Court of Appeals citation includes the writ-of-error history showing the Texas Supreme Court's disposition of the case. In this case, *writ ref'd n.r.e.* is an abbreviation for "writ refused, no reversible error," which means that Texas's highest court refused to grant the appellant's request to review the case, because the court did not think there was any reversible error.)

cided terms in good faith in an effort to reach a final agreement.[5]

In the following case, the dispute was over an agreement to settle a case during a trial. One party claimed that the agreement formed via e-mail was binding, and the other party claimed it was merely an agreement to agree, or an agreement to work out the terms of a settlement in the future. Can an exchange of e-mails create a complete and unambiguous agreement? That was the question the court had to address in this case.

5. See, for example, *MBH, Inc. v. John Otte Oil & Propane, Inc.*, 727 N.W.2d 238 (Neb.App. 2007); and *Barrand v. Whataburger, Inc.*, 214 S.W.3d 122 (Tex.App.—Corpus Christi 2006).

CASE 11.2 Basis Technology Corp. v. Amazon.com, Inc.

Appeals Court of Massachusetts, 2008. 71 Mass.App.Ct. 29, 878 N.E.2d 952.
www.malawyersweekly.com/macoa.cfm[a]

• **Background and Facts** Basis Technology Corporation created software and provided technical services for Amazon.com, Inc.'s, Japanese-language Web site. The agreement between the two companies allowed for separately negotiated contracts for additional services that Basis might provide to Amazon. At the end of 1999, Basis and Amazon entered into stock-purchase agreements. Later, Amazon objected to certain actions related to the securities that Basis sold. Basis sued Amazon for various claims involving these securities and for nonpayment of services performed by Basis that were not included in the original agreement. During the trial, the two parties appeared to reach an agreement to settle out of court via a series of e-mail exchanges outlining the settlement. When Amazon reneged, Basis served a motion to enforce the proposed settlement. The trial judge entered judgment against Amazon, which appealed.

• **Decision and Rationale** The Appeals Court of Massachusetts affirmed the trial court's finding that Amazon intended to be bound by the terms of the March 23 e-mail. The court examined the evidence consisting of e-mails between the two parties. It pointed out that in open court and on the record, counsel "reported the result of the settlement without specification of the terms." Amazon claimed that the e-mail terms were not complete and definite enough to form an agreement. The court noted, nonetheless, that "provisions are not ambiguous simply because the parties have developed different interpretations of them." In the exchange of e-mails, the essential business terms were indeed resolved. Afterwards, the parties were simply proceeding to record the settlement terms, not to create them. The e-mails constituted a complete and unambiguous statement of the parties' desire to be bound by the settlement terms.

• **What If the Facts Were Different?** *Assume that the attorneys for both sides had simply had a phone conversation that included all of the terms to which they actually agreed in their e-mail exchanges. Would the court have ruled differently? Why or why not?*

• **The Ethical Dimension** *Under what circumstances could Amazon justify its "about-face" after having agreed in an e-mail to the settlement terms?*

a. In the search box on the right, enter "71 Mass.App.Ct. 29" and click on "Search." On the resulting page, click on the case name to access the court's opinion.

To avoid potential legal disputes, businesspersons should be cautious when drafting a memorandum outlining a preliminary agreement or understanding with another party. If all the major terms are included, a court might hold that the agreement is binding even though it was intended to be only a tentative agreement. One approach to avoid being bound to the terms of a preliminary agreement is to include in the writing not only the points on which the parties agree, but also the points of disagreement. Alternatively, a person might add a disclaimer to the memorandum stating that, although the parties anticipate entering into a contract in the future, neither party intends to be legally bound to the terms that were discussed. That way, the other party cannot claim that an agreement on all the essential terms has already been reached.

Advertisements In general, advertisements—including representations made in mail-order catalogues, price lists, and circulars—are treated not as offers to contract but as invitations to negotiate. Suppose that Loeser advertises a used paving machine. The ad is mailed to hundreds of firms and reads, "Used Loeser Construction Co. paving machine. Builds curbs and finishes cement work all in one process. Price: $42,350." If Star Paving calls Loeser and says, "We accept your offer," no contract is formed. Any reasonable person would conclude that Loeser was not promising to sell the paving machine but rather was soliciting offers to buy it. If such an ad were held to constitute a legal offer, and fifty people accepted the offer, there would be no way for Loeser to perform all fifty of the resulting contracts. He would have to breach forty-nine contracts. Obviously, the law seeks to avoid such unfairness.

Price lists are another form of invitation to negotiate or trade. A seller's price list is not an offer to sell at that price; it merely invites the buyer to offer to buy at that price. In fact, the seller usually puts "prices subject to change" on the price list. Only in rare circumstances will a price quotation be construed as an offer.[6]

Although most advertisements and the like are treated as invitations to negotiate, this does not mean that an advertisement can never be an offer. On some occasions, courts have construed advertisements to be offers because the ads contained definite terms that invited acceptance (such as an ad offering a reward for the return of a lost dog).[7]

The plaintiff in the following case argued that an ad on a Web site constituted an offer, which he accepted.

6. See, for example, *Nordyne, Inc. v. International Controls & Measurements Corp.*, 262 F.3d 843 (8th Cir. 2001).

7. The classic example is *Lefkowitz v. Great Minneapolis Surplus Store, Inc.*, 251 Minn. 188, 86 N.W.2d 689 (1957).

CASE 11.3 Trell v. American Association for the Advancement of Science

United States District Court, Western District of New York, 2007. __ F.Supp.2d __.

Background and Facts The American Association for the Advancement of Science (AAAS) maintains Science NOW, a daily Internet news service, and publishes *Science,* a scholarly journal. An ad on the Science NOW Web site asks for "news tips" and states that each tip will be investigated for its suitability as an item for Science NOW or an article for *Science.* In response to the ad, Erik Trell, a professor and physician, submitted a manuscript in which he claimed to have solved a famous mathematical problem, popularly known as Beal's Conjecture. AAAS decided that Trell's manuscript contained neither news nor a solution to Beal's Conjecture and declined to publish it. Trell filed a suit in a federal district court against AAAS and others, alleging, among other things, breach of contract. Trell asserted, in part, that the Science NOW ad was an offer, which he accepted with his submission of a manuscript. The defendants filed a motion to dismiss this claim.

Decision and Rationale The court granted the defendants' motion and dismissed the plaintiff's complaint. The appellate court found that the advertisement for "news tips" on the Science NOW Web site could not be construed as an offer. Rather, "statements that urge the general public to take some action in response thereto" are commonly characterized as advertisements: "Advertisements are not offers—they invite offers. Likewise, responses to advertisements are not acceptances—they are offers." Just because the advertisement was soliciting ideas (news tips) rather than goods makes little difference. The use of the Internet to advertise the offer also does not change the outcome. Science NOW's ad for news tips was not an offer but an invitation for offers.

The Ethical Dimension *Besides breach of contract, Trell charged the defendants with fraud, misappropriation of property, breach of fiduciary duty, unfair competition, conversion, and conspiracy with intent to defraud. What might have been Trell's motivation for all of these charges? Is this a reasonable basis for a lawsuit? Discuss.*

The E-Commerce Dimension *Should the court have made an exception to the rule applied in this case because the ad was posted on the Internet? Why or why not?*

Auctions In an auction, a seller "offers" goods for sale through an auctioneer, but this is not an offer to form a contract. Rather, it is an invitation asking bidders to submit offers. In the context of an auction, a bidder is the offeror, and the auctioneer is the offeree. The offer is accepted when the auctioneer strikes the hammer. Before the fall of the hammer, a bidder may revoke (take back) her or his bid, or the auctioneer may reject that bid or all bids. Typically, an auctioneer will reject a bid that is below the price the seller is willing to accept.

When the auctioneer accepts a higher bid, he or she rejects all previous bids. Because rejection terminates an offer (as will be discussed later), those bids represent offers that have been terminated. Thus, if the highest bidder withdraws his or her bid before the hammer falls, none of the previous bids is reinstated. If the bid is not withdrawn or rejected, the contract is formed when the auctioneer announces, "Going once, going twice, sold!" (or something similar) and lets the hammer fall.

Traditionally, auctions have been referred to as either "with reserve" or "without reserve." In an auction with reserve, the seller (through the auctioneer) may withdraw the goods at any time before the auctioneer closes the sale by announcement or by the fall of the hammer. All auctions are assumed to be auctions with reserve unless the terms of the auction are explicitly stated to be *without reserve*. In an auction without reserve, the goods cannot be withdrawn by the seller and must be sold to the highest bidder. In auctions with reserve, the seller may reserve the right to confirm or reject the sale even after "the hammer has fallen." In this situation, the seller is obligated to notify those attending the auction that sales of goods made during the auction are not final until confirmed by the seller.[8]

Definiteness of Terms

The second requirement for an effective offer involves the definiteness of its terms. An offer must have terms that are reasonably definite so that, if it is accepted and a contract formed, a court can determine if a breach has occurred and can provide an appropriate remedy. The specific terms required depend, of course, on the type of contract. Generally, a contract must include the following terms, either expressed in the contract or capable of being reasonably inferred from it:

1. The identification of the parties.
2. The identification of the object or subject matter of the contract (also the quantity, when appropriate), including the work to be performed, with specific identification of such items as goods, services, and land.
3. The consideration to be paid.
4. The time of payment, delivery, or performance.

An offer may invite an acceptance to be worded in such specific terms that the contract is made definite. Suppose that Marcus Business Machines contacts your corporation and offers to sell "from one to ten MacCool copying machines for $1,600 each; state number desired in acceptance." Your corporation agrees to buy two copiers. Because the quantity is specified in the acceptance, the terms are definite, and the contract is enforceable.

Courts sometimes are willing to supply a missing term in a contract when the parties have clearly manifested an intent to form a contract. If, in contrast, the parties have attempted to deal with a particular term of the contract but their expression of intent is too vague or uncertain to be given any precise meaning, the court will not supply a "reasonable" term because to do so might conflict with the intent of the parties. In other words, the court will not rewrite the contract.[9]

Communication

A third requirement for an effective offer is communication—the offer must be communicated to the offeree. Ordinarily, one cannot agree to a bargain without knowing that it exists. Suppose that Estrich advertises a reward for the return of his lost dog. Hoban, not knowing of the reward, finds the dog and returns it to Estrich. Hoban cannot recover the reward because she did not know it had been offered.[10]

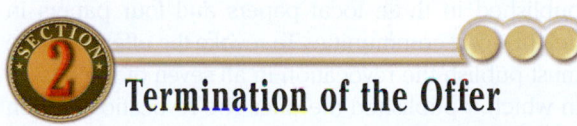

SECTION 2 Termination of the Offer

The communication of an effective offer to an offeree gives the offeree the power to transform the offer into a binding, legal obligation (a contract) by an acceptance. This power of acceptance, however, does not

8. These rules apply under both the common law of contracts and the Uniform Commercial Code (UCC)—see UCC 2–328.

9. See Chapter 20 and UCC 2–204. Article 2 of the UCC specifies different rules relating to the definiteness of terms used in a contract for the sale of goods. In essence, Article 2 modifies general contract law by requiring less specificity.

10. A few states allow recovery of the reward, but not on contract principles. Because Estrich wanted his dog to be returned and Hoban returned it, these few states would allow Hoban to recover on the basis that it would be unfair to deny her the reward just because she did not know it had been offered.

continue forever. It can be terminated either by action of the parties or by operation of law.

Termination by Action of the Parties

An offer can be terminated by action of the parties in any of three ways: by revocation, by rejection, or by counteroffer.

Revocation of the Offer by the Offeror

The offeror's act of withdrawing (revoking) an offer is known as **revocation.** Unless an offer is irrevocable (discussed shortly), the offeror usually can revoke the offer (even if he or she has promised to keep it open) as long as the revocation is communicated to the offeree before the offeree accepts. Revocation may be accomplished by express repudiation of the offer (for example, with a statement such as "I withdraw my previous offer of October 17") or by performance of acts that are inconsistent with the existence of the offer and are made known to the offeree (for example, selling the offered property to another person in the presence of the offeree).

In most states, a revocation becomes effective when the offeree or the offeree's agent (a person acting on behalf of the offeree) actually receives it. Therefore, if a letter revoking an offer is mailed on April 1 and arrives on April 3, the revocation becomes effective on April 3.

An offer made to the general public can be revoked in the same manner that the offer was originally communicated. Suppose that a department store offers a $10,000 reward to anyone providing information leading to the apprehension of the persons who burglarized the store's downtown branch. The offer is published in three local papers and four papers in neighboring communities. To revoke the offer, the store must publish the revocation in all seven of the papers in which it published the offer. The revocation is then accessible to the general public, even if some particular offeree does not know about it.

Irrevocable Offers

Although most offers are revocable, some can be made irrevocable—that is, they cannot be revoked, or canceled. An option contract involves one type of irrevocable offer. Increasingly, courts also refuse to allow an offeror to revoke an offer when the offeree has changed position because of justifiable reliance on the offer. (In some circumstances, "firm offers" made by merchants may also be considered irrevocable—see the discussion of the "merchant's firm offer" in Chapter 20.)

Option Contract. An **option contract** is created when an offeror promises to hold an offer open for a specified period of time in return for a payment (consideration) given by the offeree. An option contract takes away the offeror's power to revoke the offer for the period of time specified in the option. If no time is specified, then a reasonable period of time is implied. Suppose that you are in the business of writing movie scripts. Your agent contacts the head of development at New Line Cinema and offers to sell New Line your latest movie script. New Line likes your script and agrees to pay you $25,000 for a six-month option. In this situation, you (through your agent) are the offeror, and New Line is the offeree. You cannot revoke your offer to sell New Line your script for the next six months. If after six months no contract has been formed, however, New Line loses the $25,000, and you are free to sell the script to another movie studio.

Real Estate Option Contracts. Option contracts are also frequently used in conjunction with the sale or lease of real estate. For example, you might agree with a landowner to lease a home and include in the lease contract a clause stating that you will pay $9,000 for an option to purchase the home within a specified period of time. If you decide not to purchase the home after the specified period has lapsed, you forfeit the $9,000, and the landlord is free to sell the property to another buyer.

Additionally, contracts to lease business premises often include options to renew the leases at certain intervals, such as after five years. Typically, a lease contract containing a renewal option requires notification—that is, the person leasing the premises must notify the property owner of his or her intention to exercise the renewal option within a certain number of days or months before the current lease expires.

Detrimental Reliance and Promissory Estoppel. When the offeree justifiably relies on an offer to her or his detriment, the court may hold that this *detrimental reliance* makes the offer irrevocable. For example, Sue Fox has rented commercial property from Luis Rivera for the past thirty-three years under a series of five-year leases. As their seventh lease nears its end, Fox tells Rivera that she is going to look at other, less expensive properties as possible sites for her business. Wanting Fox to remain a tenant, Rivera promises to reduce the rent in their next lease. In reliance on the promise, Fox continues to occupy and do business on Rivera's property and does not look at other sites. When they sit down to negotiate a new lease, however, Rivera says he has changed his mind and will increase the rent. Can he effectively revoke his promise?

Normally, he cannot, because Fox has been relying on his promise to reduce the rent. Had the promise not been made, she would have relocated her business. This is a case of detrimental reliance on a promise, which therefore cannot be revoked. In this situation, the doctrine of **promissory estoppel** comes into play. To **estop** means to bar, impede, or preclude someone from doing something. Thus, promissory estoppel means that the promisor (the offeror) is barred from revoking the offer, in this situation because the offeree has already changed her actions in reliance on the offer. We look again at the doctrine of promissory estoppel in Chapter 12 in the context of consideration.

Detrimental Reliance and Partial Performance. Detrimental reliance can also occur when an offeree partially performs in response to an offer to form a unilateral contract. As discussed in Chapter 10, an offer to form a unilateral contract invites acceptance only by full performance; merely promising to perform does not constitute acceptance. Injustice can result if an offeree expends time and funds in partial performance, only to have the offeror revoke the offer before performance can be completed. Many courts will not allow the offeror to revoke the offer after the offeree has performed some substantial part of his or her duties.[11] In effect, partial performance renders the offer irrevocable, giving the original offeree reasonable time to complete performance. Of course, once the performance is complete, a unilateral contract exists.

Rejection of the Offer by the Offeree If the offeree rejects the offer, the offer is terminated. Any subsequent attempt by the offeree to accept will be construed as a new offer, giving the original offeror (now the offeree) the power of acceptance. A rejection is ordinarily accomplished by words or conduct indicating an intent not to accept the offer. As with a revocation, a rejection of an offer is effective only when it is actually received by the offeror or the offeror's agent.

Note that merely inquiring about an offer does not constitute rejection. Suppose that a friend offers to buy your PlayStation 3 for $300, and you respond, "Is that your best offer?" or "Will you pay me $375 for it?" A reasonable person would conclude that you did not reject the offer but merely made an inquiry for further consideration of the offer. You can still accept and bind your friend to the $300 purchase price. When the offeree merely inquires as to the firmness of the offer, there is no reason to presume that he or she intends to reject it.

Counteroffer by the Offeree A **counteroffer** is a rejection of the original offer and the simultaneous making of a new offer. Suppose that Burke offers to sell his home to Lang for $270,000. Lang responds, "Your price is too high. I'll offer to purchase your house for $250,000." Lang's response is called a counteroffer because it rejects Burke's offer to sell at $270,000 and creates a new offer by Lang to purchase the home at a price of $250,000.

At common law, the **mirror image rule** requires the offeree's acceptance to match the offeror's offer exactly—to mirror the offer. Any change in, or addition to, the terms of the original offer automatically terminates that offer and substitutes the counteroffer. The counteroffer, of course, need not be accepted; but if the original offeror does accept the terms of the counteroffer, a valid contract is created.[12]

Termination by Operation of Law

The power of the offeree to transform the offer into a binding, legal obligation can be terminated by operation of law through the occurrence of any of the following events:

1. Lapse of time.
2. Destruction of the specific subject matter of the offer.
3. Death or incompetence of the offeror or the offeree.
4. Supervening illegality of the proposed contract.

Lapse of Time An offer terminates automatically by law when the period of time *specified in the offer* has passed. For example, Alejandro offers to sell his camper to Kelly if she accepts within twenty days. Kelly must accept within the twenty-day period or the offer will lapse (terminate). The time period specified in an offer normally begins to run when the offer is actually received by the offeree, not when it is formed or sent. If the offer states that it will be left open until a particular date, then the offer will terminate at midnight on that day. When the offer is delayed (through the

11. *Restatement (Second) of Contracts,* Section 45.

12. The mirror image rule has been greatly modified in regard to sales contracts. Section 2–207 of the UCC provides that a contract is formed if the offeree makes a definite expression of acceptance (such as signing the form in the appropriate location), even though the terms of the acceptance modify or add to the terms of the original offer (see Chapter 20).

misdelivery of mail, for example), the period begins to run from the date the offeree would have received the offer, but only if the offeree knows or should know that the offer is delayed.[13]

If the offer does not specify a time for acceptance, the offer terminates at the end of a *reasonable* period of time. What constitutes a reasonable period of time depends on the subject matter of the contract, business and market conditions, and other relevant circumstances. An offer to sell farm produce, for example, will terminate sooner than an offer to sell farm equipment because farm produce is perishable and subject to greater fluctuations in market value.

Destruction of the Subject Matter An offer is automatically terminated if the specific subject matter of the offer is destroyed before the offer is accepted.[14] If Johnson offers to sell his prize greyhound to Rizzo, for example, but the dog dies before Rizzo can accept, the offer is automatically terminated. Johnson does not have to tell Rizzo that the animal has died for the offer to terminate.

Death or Incompetence of the Offeror or Offeree An offeree's power of acceptance is terminated when the offeror or offeree dies or is deprived of legal capacity to enter into the proposed contract. A revocable offer is personal to both parties and cannot pass to the heirs, guardian, or estate of either. Furthermore, this rule applies whether or not the other party had notice of the death or incompetence. If the offer is irrevocable, however, the death of the offeror or offeree does not terminate the offer.[15]

Supervening Illegality of the Proposed Contract A statute or court decision that makes an offer illegal automatically terminates the offer.[16] For example, Lee offers to lend Kim $10,000 at an annual interest rate of 12 percent. Before Kim can accept the offer, a law is enacted that prohibits interest rates higher than 10 percent. Lee's offer is automatically terminated. (If the statute is enacted after Kim accepts the offer, a valid contract is formed, but the contract may still be unenforceable—see Chapter 13.) *Concept Summary 11.1* provides a review of the ways in which an offer can be terminated.

SECTION 3 Acceptance

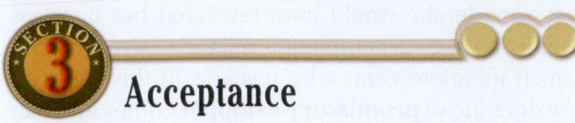

Acceptance is a voluntary act by the offeree that shows assent (agreement) to the terms of an offer. The offeree's act may consist of words or conduct. The acceptance must be unequivocal and must be communicated to the offeror.

Unequivocal Acceptance

To exercise the power of acceptance effectively, the offeree must accept unequivocally. This is the *mirror image rule* previously discussed. If the acceptance is subject to new conditions or if the terms of the acceptance change the original offer, the acceptance may be deemed a counteroffer that implicitly rejects the original offer.

An acceptance may be unequivocal even though the offeree expresses dissatisfaction with the contract. For example, "I accept the offer, but I wish I could have gotten a better price" is an effective acceptance. So, too, is "I accept, but can you shave the price?" In contrast, the statement "I accept the offer but only if I can pay on ninety days' credit" is not an unequivocal acceptance and operates as a counteroffer, rejecting the original offer.

Certain terms, when added to an acceptance, will not qualify the acceptance sufficiently to constitute rejection of the offer. Suppose that in response to an offer to sell a piano, the offeree replies, "I accept; please send a written contract." The offeree is requesting a written contract but is not making it a condition for acceptance. Therefore, the acceptance is effective without the written contract. If the offeree replies, "I accept if you send a written contract," however, the acceptance is expressly conditioned on the request for a writing, and the statement is not an acceptance but a counteroffer. (Notice how important each word is!)[17]

13. *Restatement (Second) of Contracts,* Section 49.
14. *Restatement (Second) of Contracts,* Section 36.
15. *Restatement (Second) of Contracts,* Section 48. If the offer is such that it can be accepted by the performance of a series of acts, and those acts began before the offeror died, the offeree's power of acceptance is not terminated.
16. *Restatement (Second) of Contracts,* Section 36.

17. As noted in footnote 12, in regard to sales contracts, the UCC provides that an acceptance may still be valid even if some terms are added. The new terms are simply treated as proposed additions to the contract.

CONCEPT SUMMARY 11.1
Methods by Which an Offer Can Be Terminated

By Action of the Parties	1. *Revocation*—Unless the offer is irrevocable, it can be revoked at any time before acceptance without liability. Revocation is not effective until received by the offeree or the offeree's agent. Some offers, such as a merchant's firm offer and option contracts, are irrevocable. Also, in some situations, an offeree's detrimental reliance and/or partial performance will cause a court to rule that the offeror cannot revoke the offer. 2. *Rejection*—Accomplished by words or actions that demonstrate a clear intent not to accept the offer; not effective until received by the offeror or the offeror's agent. 3. *Counteroffer*—A rejection of the original offer and the making of a new offer.
By Operation of Law	1. *Lapse of time*—The offer terminates (a) at the end of the time period specified in the offer or (b) if no time period is stated in the offer, at the end of a reasonable time period. 2. *Destruction of the subject matter*—When the specific subject matter of the offer is destroyed before the offer is accepted, the offer automatically terminates. 3. *Death or incompetence of the offeror or offeree*—If the offeror or offeree dies or becomes incompetent, this terminates the offer (unless the offer is irrevocable). 4. *Supervening illegality*—When a statute or court decision makes the proposed contract illegal, the offer automatically terminates.

Silence as Acceptance

Ordinarily, silence cannot constitute acceptance, even if the offeror states, "By your silence and inaction, you will be deemed to have accepted this offer." This general rule applies because an offeree should not be obligated to act affirmatively to reject an offer when no consideration has passed to the offeree to impose such a duty.

In some instances, however, the offeree does have a duty to speak. In these situations, her or his silence or inaction will operate as an acceptance. For example, silence may be an acceptance when an offeree takes the benefit of offered services even though he or she had an opportunity to reject them and knew that they were offered with the expectation of compensation. Suppose that Sayre watches while a stranger rakes his leaves, even though the stranger has not been asked to rake the yard. Sayre knows the stranger expects to be paid and does nothing to stop her. Here, his silence constitutes an acceptance, and an implied-in-fact contract is created (see Chapter 10). He is bound to pay a reasonable value for the stranger's work.

Silence can also operate as acceptance when the offeree has had prior dealings with the offeror. Suppose that a business routinely receives shipments from a certain supplier and always notifies that supplier when defective goods are rejected. In this situation, silence regarding a shipment will constitute acceptance.

Communication of Acceptance

Whether the offeror must be notified of the acceptance depends on the nature of the contract. In a bilateral contract, communication of acceptance is necessary because acceptance is in the form of a promise (not performance) and the contract is formed when the promise is made (rather than when the act is performed). The offeree must communicate the acceptance to the offeror. Communication of acceptance is not necessary, however, if the offer dispenses with the requirement. Additionally, if the offer can be accepted by silence, no communication is necessary.

Because a unilateral contract calls for the full performance of some act, acceptance is usually evident, and notification is therefore unnecessary. Nevertheless, exceptions do exist, such as when the offeror requests notice of acceptance or has no way of determining whether the requested act has been performed. In addition, sometimes the law requires notice of acceptance, and thus notice is necessary.[18]

Mode and Timeliness of Acceptance

Acceptance in bilateral contracts must be timely. The general rule is that acceptance in a bilateral contract is timely if it is made before the offer is terminated. Problems may arise, though, when the parties involved are not dealing face to face. In such situations, the offeree should use an authorized mode of communication.

Acceptance takes effect, thus completing formation of the contract, at the time the offeree sends or delivers the communication via the mode expressly or impliedly authorized by the offeror. This is the so-called **mailbox rule,** which the majority of courts follow. Under this rule, if the authorized mode of communication is the mail, then an acceptance becomes valid when it is dispatched (placed in the control of the U.S. Postal Service)—*not* when it is received by the offeror.

The mailbox rule was created to prevent the confusion that arises when an offeror sends a letter of revocation but, before it arrives, the offeree sends a letter of acceptance. Thus, whereas a revocation becomes effective only when it is *received* by the offeree, an acceptance becomes effective on *dispatch* (when sent, even if it is never received), provided that an *authorized* means of communication is used.

The mailbox rule does not apply to instantaneous forms of communication, such as when the parties are dealing face to face, by telephone, or by fax. There is still some uncertainty in the courts as to whether e-mail should be considered an instantaneous form of communication to which the mailbox rule does not apply. If the parties have agreed to conduct transactions electronically and if the Uniform Electronic Transactions Act (to be discussed in Chapter 19) applies, then e-mail is considered sent when it either leaves control of the sender or is received by the recipient. This rule takes the place of the mailbox rule when the Uniform Electronic Transactions Act applies but essentially allows an e-mail acceptance to become effective when sent (as it would if sent by U.S. mail).

Authorized Means of Acceptance A means of communicating acceptance can be expressly authorized—that is, expressly stipulated in the offer—or impliedly authorized by the facts and circumstances surrounding the situation or by law.[19] An acceptance sent by means not expressly or impliedly authorized normally is not effective until it is received by the offeror.

When an offeror specifies how acceptance should be made (for example, by overnight delivery), *express authorization* is said to exist, and the contract is not formed unless the offeree uses that specified mode of acceptance. Moreover, both offeror and offeree are bound in contract the moment this means of acceptance is employed. For example, Shaylee & Perkins, a Massachusetts firm, offers to sell a container of antique furniture to Leaham's Antiques in Colorado. The offer states that Leaham's must accept the offer via FedEx overnight delivery. The acceptance is effective (and a binding contract is formed) the moment that Leaham's gives the overnight envelope containing the acceptance to the FedEx driver.

When the Preferred Means of Acceptance Is Not Indicated. Most offerors do not expressly specify the means by which the offeree is to accept. When the offeror does not specify expressly that the offeree is to accept by a certain means, or that the acceptance will be effective only when received, acceptance of an offer may be made by any medium that is *reasonable under the circumstances.*[20]

Whether a mode of acceptance is reasonable depends on what would reasonably be expected by parties in the position of the contracting parties. Courts look at prevailing business usages and other surrounding circumstances such as the method of communica-

18. Under UCC 2–206(1)(b), an order or other offer to buy goods for prompt shipment may be treated as an offer contemplating either a bilateral or a unilateral contract and may be accepted by either a promise to ship (bilateral contract) or actual shipment (unilateral contract). If the offer is accepted by actual shipment of the goods, the buyer must be notified of the acceptance within a reasonable period of time, or the buyer may treat the offer as having lapsed before acceptance [UCC 2–206(2)]. See also Chapter 20.

19. *Restatement (Second) of Contracts,* Section 30, provides that an offer invites acceptance "by any medium reasonable in the circumstances," unless the offer is specific about the means of acceptance. Under Section 65, a medium is reasonable if it is one used by the offeror or one customary in similar transactions, unless the offeree knows of circumstances that would argue against the reasonableness of a particular medium (the need for speed because of rapid price changes, for example).

20. *Restatement (Second) of Contracts,* Section 30. This is also the rule under UCC 2–206(1)(a).

tion the parties have used in the past and the means that were used to convey the offer. The offeror's choice of a particular means in making the offer implies that the offeree is authorized to use the same *or a faster* means for acceptance. Suppose that two parties have been negotiating a deal via fax and then the offeror sends a formal contract offer by priority mail without specifying the means of acceptance. In that situation, the offeree's acceptance by priority mail or by fax is impliedly authorized.

When the Authorized Means of Acceptance Is Not Used. An acceptance sent by means not expressly or impliedly authorized normally is not effective *until it is received by the offeror.* Suppose that Frank Cochran is interested in buying a house from Ray Nunez. Cochran faxes an offer to Nunez that clearly specifies acceptance by fax. Nunez has to be out of town for a few days, however, and doesn't have access to a fax machine. Therefore, Nunez sends his acceptance to Cochran via FedEx instead of by fax. In this situation, the acceptance is not effective (and no contract is formed) until Cochran receives the FedEx delivery. The use of an alternative method does not render the acceptance ineffective if the substituted method performs the same function or serves the same purpose as the authorized method.[21]

Exceptions The following are three basic exceptions to the rule that a contract is formed when an acceptance is sent by authorized means:

1. If the offeree's acceptance is not properly dispatched, in most states it will not be effective until it is received by the offeror. For example, if an offeree types in the recipient's e-mail address incorrectly when accepting an offer via e-mail, or if the offeree faxes an acceptance to the wrong telephone number, it will not be effective until received by the offeror. If U.S. mail is the authorized means for acceptance, the offeree's letter must be properly addressed and have the correct postage. Nonetheless, if the acceptance is timely sent and timely received, despite the offeree's carelessness in sending it, it may still be considered to have been effective on dispatch.[22]
2. If the offer stipulates when acceptance will be effective, then the offer will not be effective until the time specified. The offeror has the power to control the offer and can stipulate both the means by which the offer is accepted and the precise time that an acceptance will be effective. For example, an offer might state that acceptance will not be effective until it is received by the offeror, or it might make acceptance effective twenty-four hours after being shipped via DHL delivery.
3. Sometimes, an offeree sends a rejection first, then later changes his or her mind and sends an acceptance. Obviously, this chain of events could cause confusion and even detriment to the offeror, depending on whether the rejection or the acceptance arrived first. In such situations, the law cancels the rule of acceptance on dispatch, and the first communication received by the offeror determines whether a contract is formed. If the rejection arrives first, there is no contract.[23]

For a review of the effective time of acceptance, see *Concept Summary 11.2* on the next page.

SECTION 4

Technology and Acceptance Rules

Clearly, some of the traditional rules governing acceptance do not seem to apply to an age in which acceptances are commonly delivered via e-mail, fax, or other delivery system, such as FedEx or DHL. For example, when accepting an online offer, the mailbox rule does not apply to online acceptances, which typically are communicated instantaneously to the offeror. Nonetheless, the traditional rules—and the principles that underlie those rules—provide a basis for understanding what constitutes a valid acceptance in today's online environment. This is because, as in other areas of the law, much of the law governing online offers and acceptances has been adapted from traditional law to a new context.

Although online offers are not significantly different from traditional offers contained in paper documents, online acceptances have posed some unusual problems for the court. These problems, as well as other aspects of e-contracting, will be discussed in detail in Chapter 19.

21. See, for example, *Osprey, L.L.C. v. Kelly Moore Paint Co.,* 984 P.2d 194 (Okla. 1999).

22. *Restatement (Second) of Contracts,* Section 67.

23. *Restatement (Second) of Contracts,* Section 40.

CONCEPT SUMMARY 11.2
Effective Time of Acceptance

Acceptance	Time Effective
By Authorized Means of Communication	Effective at the time communication is sent (deposited in a mailbox or delivered to a courier service) via the mode expressly or impliedly authorized by the offeror (mailbox rule). *Exceptions:* 1. If the acceptance is not properly dispatched, it will not be effective until received by the offeror. 2. If the offeror specifically conditioned the offer on receipt of acceptance, it will not be effective until received by the offeror. 3. If acceptance is sent after rejection, whichever is received first is given effect.
By Unauthorized Means of Communication	Effective on receipt of acceptance by the offeror (if timely received, it is considered to have been effective on dispatch).

REVIEWING Agreement

Shane Durbin wanted to have a recording studio custom-built in his home. He sent invitations to a number of local contractors to submit bids on the project. Rory Amstel submitted the lowest bid, which was $20,000 less than any of the other bids Durbin received. Durbin called Amstel to ascertain the type and quality of the materials that were included in the bid and to find out if he could substitute a superior brand of acoustic tiles for the same bid price. Amstel said he would have to check into the price difference. The parties also discussed a possible start date for construction. Two weeks later, Durbin changed his mind and decided not to go forward with his plan to build a recording studio. Amstel filed a suit against Durbin for breach of contract. Using the information presented in the chapter, answer the following questions.

1. Did Amstel's bid meet the requirements of an offer? Explain.
2. Was there an acceptance of the offer? Why or why not?
3. Suppose that the court determines that the parties did not reach an agreement. Further suppose that Amstel, in anticipation of building Durbin's studio, had purchased materials and refused other jobs so that he would have time in his schedule for Durbin's project. Under what theory discussed in the chapter might Amstel attempt to recover these costs?
4. How is an offer terminated? Assuming that Durbin did not inform Amstel that he was rejecting the offer, was the offer terminated at any time described here? Explain.

TERMS AND CONCEPTS

acceptance 224
agreement 216
counteroffer 223
estop 223
mailbox rule 226
mirror image rule 223
mutual assent 216
offer 216
option contract 222
promissory estoppel 223
revocation 222

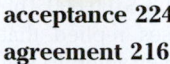

QUESTIONS AND CASE PROBLEMS

11-1. Ball writes to Sullivan and inquires how much Sullivan is asking for a specific forty-acre tract of land Sullivan owns. In a letter received by Ball, Sullivan states, "I will not take less than $60,000 for the forty-acre tract as specified." Ball immediately sends Sullivan a telegram stating, "I accept your offer for $60,000 for the forty-acre tract as specified." Discuss whether Ball can hold Sullivan to a contract for the sale of the land.

11-2. QUESTION WITH SAMPLE ANSWER

Schmidt, operating a sole proprietorship, has a large piece of used farm equipment for sale. He offers to sell the equipment to Barry for $10,000. Discuss the legal effects of the following events on the offer:

(a) Schmidt dies prior to Barry's acceptance, and at the time he accepts, Barry is unaware of Schmidt's death.
(b) The night before Barry accepts, fire destroys the equipment.
(c) Barry pays $100 for a thirty-day option to purchase the equipment. During this period, Schmidt dies, and later Barry accepts the offer, knowing of Schmidt's death.
(d) Barry pays $100 for a thirty-day option to purchase the equipment. During this period, Barry dies, and Barry's estate accepts Schmidt's offer within the stipulated time period.

- **For a sample answer to Question 11-2, go to Appendix I at the end of this text.**

11-3. Perez sees an advertisement in the newspaper indicating that the ABC Corp. is offering for sale a two-volume set of books, *How to Make Repairs around the House,* for $39.95. All Perez has to do is send in a card requesting delivery of the books for a thirty-day trial period. If he does not ship the books back within thirty days of delivery, ABC will bill him for $39.95. Discuss whether Perez and ABC have a contract under either of the following circumstances:

(a) Perez sends in the card and receives the books in the U.S. mail. He uses the books to make repairs and fails to return them within thirty days.
(b) Perez does not send in the card, but ABC sends him the books anyway through the U.S. mail. Perez uses the books and fails to return them within thirty days.

11-4. On Thursday, Dennis mailed a letter to Tanya's office offering to sell his car to her for $3,000. On Saturday, having changed his mind, Dennis sent a fax to Tanya's office revoking his offer. Tanya did not go to her office over the weekend and thus did not learn about the revocation until Monday morning, just a few minutes after she had mailed a letter of acceptance to Dennis. When Tanya demanded that Dennis sell his car to her as promised, Dennis claimed that no contract existed because he had revoked his offer prior to Tanya's acceptance. Is Dennis correct? Explain.

11-5. Definiteness of Terms. Southwick Homes, Ltd., develops and markets residential subdivisions. William McLinden and Ronald Coco are the primary owners of Southwick Homes. Coco is also the president of Mutual Development Co. Whiteco Industries, Inc., wanted to develop lots and sell homes in Schulien Woods, a subdivision in Crown Point, Indiana. In September 1996, Whiteco sent McLinden a letter enlisting Southwick Homes to be the project manager for developing and marketing the finished lots (lots where roads had been built and on which utility installation and connections to water and sewer lines were complete); the letter set out the roles and expectations of each of the parties, including the terms of payment. In October 1997, Whiteco sent Coco a letter naming Mutual Development the developer and general contractor for the houses to be built on the finished lots. A few months later, Coco told McLinden that he would not share in the profits from the construction of the houses. McLinden and others filed a suit in an Indiana state court against Coco and others, claiming, in part, a breach of fiduciary duty. The defendants responded that the letter to McLinden lacked such essential terms as to render it unenforceable. What terms must an agreement include to be an enforceable contract? Did the letter sent to McLinden include these terms? In whose favor should the court rule? Explain. [*McLinden v. Coco,* 765 N.E.2d 606 (Ind.App. 2002)]

11-6. CASE PROBLEM WITH SAMPLE ANSWER

The Pittsburgh Board of Public Education in Pittsburgh, Pennsylvania, as required by state law, keeps lists of eligible teachers in order of their rank or standing. According to an "Eligibility List" form made available to applicants, no one may be hired to teach whose name is not within the top 10 percent of the names on the list. In 1996, Anna Reed was in the top 10 percent. She was not hired that year, although four other applicants who placed lower on the list—and not within the top 10 percent—were hired. In 1997 and 1998, Reed was again in the top 10 percent, but she was not hired until 1999. Reed filed a suit in a federal district court against the board and others. She argued, in part, that the state's requirement that the board keep a list constituted an offer, which she accepted by participating in the process to be placed on that list. She claimed that the board breached this contract by hiring applicants who ranked lower than she did. The case was transferred to a Pennsylvania state court. What are the requirements of an offer? Do the circumstances in this case meet those requirements? Why or why not? [*Reed v. Pittsburgh Board of Public Education,* 862 A.2d 131 (Pa.Cmwlth. 2004)]

- **To view a sample answer for Problem 11-6, go to this book's Web site at www.cengage.com/blaw/jentz, select "Chapter 11," and click on "Case Problem with Sample Answer."**

11-7. Intention. Music that is distributed on compact discs and similar media generates income in the form of "mechanical" royalties. Music that is publicly performed, such as when a song is played on a radio, included in a movie or commercial, or sampled in another song, produces "performance" royalties. Each of these types of royalties is divided between the songwriter and the song's publisher. Vincent Cusano is a musician and songwriter who performed under the name "Vinnie Vincent" as a guitarist with the group KISS in the early 1980s. Cusano co-wrote three songs entitled "Killer," "I Love It Loud," and "I Still Love You" that KISS recorded and released in 1982 on an album titled *Creatures of the Night.* Cusano left KISS in 1984. Eight years later, Cusano sold to Horipro Entertainment Group "one hundred (100%) percent undivided interest" of his rights in the songs "other than Songwriter's share of performance income." Later, Cusano filed a suit in a federal district court against Horipro, claiming, among other things, that he never intended to sell the writer's share of the mechanical royalties. Horipro filed a motion for summary judgment. Should the court grant the motion? Explain. [*Cusano v. Horipro Entertainment Group,* 301 F.Supp.2d 272 (S.D.N.Y. 2004)]

11-8. Agreement. In 2000, David and Sandra Harless leased 2.3 acres of real property at 2801 River Road S.E. in Winnabow, North Carolina, to their son-in-law and daughter, Tony and Jeanie Connor. The Connors planned to operate a "general store/variety store" on the premises. They agreed to lease the property for sixty months with an option to renew for an additional sixty months. The lease included an option to buy the property for "fair market value at the time of such purchase (based on at least two appraisals)." In March 2003, Tony told David that the Connors wanted to buy the property. In May, Tony gave David an appraisal that estimated the property's value at $140,000. In July, the Connors presented a second appraisal that determined the value to be $160,000. The Connors offered $150,000. The Harlesses replied that "under no circumstances would they ever agree to sell their old store building and approximately 2.5 acres to their daughter . . . and their son-in-law." The Connors filed a suit in a North Carolina state court against the Harlesses, alleging breach of contract. Did these parties have a contract to sell the property? If so, what were its terms? If not, why not? [*Connor v. Harless,* 176 N.C.App. 402, 626 S.E.2d 755 (2006)]

11-9. Offer. In August 2000, in California, Terry Reigelsperger sought treatment for pain in his lower back from chiropractor James Siller. Reigelsperger felt better after the treatment and did not intend to return for more, although he did not mention this to Siller. Before leaving the office, Reigelsperger signed an "informed consent" form that read, in part, "I intend this consent form to cover the entire course of treatment for my present condition and for any future condition(s) for which I seek treatment." He also signed an agreement that required the parties to submit to arbitration "any dispute as to medical malpractice. . . . This agreement is intended to bind the patient and the health care provider . . . who now or in the future treat[s] the patient." Two years later, Reigelsperger sought treatment from Siller for a different condition relating to his cervical spine and shoulder. Claiming malpractice with respect to the second treatment, Reigelsperger filed a suit in a California state court against Siller. Siller asked the court to order the dispute to be submitted to arbitration. Did Reigelsperger's lack of intent to return to Siller after his first treatment affect the enforceability of the arbitration agreement and consent form? Why or why not? [*Reigelsperger v. Siller,* 40 Cal.4th 574, 150 P.3d 764, 53 Cal.Rptr.3d 887 (2007)]

11-10. A QUESTION OF ETHICS

In 1980, Kenneth McMillan and his associate in a dental practice obtained life insurance policies that designated each the beneficiary of the other. They set up automatic withdrawals from their bank accounts to pay the premiums. Later, Laurence Hibbard joined the practice, which was renamed Bentley, McMillan and Hibbard, P.C. (professional corporation), or BMH. When the three terminated their business relationship in 2003, McMillan sold his BMH stock to Hibbard. But Hibbard did not pay, and McMillan obtained a judgment against him for $52,972.74. When Hibbard still did not pay, McMillan offered him a choice. In lieu of paying the judgment, Hibbard could take over the premiums on Bentley's insurance policy or "cash" it in. Either way, the policy's proceeds *would be used to pay off loans against the policy—which McMillan had arranged—and Hibbard would accept responsibility for any unpaid amount. Hibbard signed the agreement but did not make a choice between the two options. McMillan filed a suit in a Georgia state court against Hibbard, seeking reimbursement for the premiums paid since their agreement. [*Hibbard v. McMillan*, 284 Ga.App. 753, 645 S.E.2d 356 (2007)]*

(a) McMillan asked the court to award him attorneys' fees because Hibbard had been "stubbornly litigious," forcing McMillan to litigate to enforce their agreement. Should the court grant this request? Are there any circumstances in which Hibbard's failure to choose between McMillan's options would be justified? Explain.

(b) Generally, parties are entitled to contract on their own terms without the courts' intervention. Under the principles discussed in this chapter, what are some of the limits to this freedom? Do any of these limits apply to the agreement between McMillan and Hibbard? Why or why not?

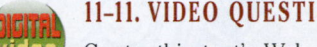

11-11. VIDEO QUESTION

Go to this text's Web site at **www.cengage.com/blaw/jentz** and select "Chapter 11." Click on "Video Questions" and view the video titled *Offer and Acceptance.* Then answer the following questions.

(a) On the video, Vinny indicates that he can't sell his car to Oscar for four thousand dollars and then says, "maybe five . . . ." Discuss whether Vinny has made an offer or a counteroffer.

(b) Oscar then says to Vinny, "Okay, I'll take it. But you gotta let me pay you four thousand now and the other thousand in two weeks." According to the chapter, do Oscar and Vinny have an agreement? Why or why not?

(c) When Maria later says to Vinny, "I'll take it," has she accepted an offer? Why or why not?

LAW ON THE WEB

For updated links to resources available on the Web, as well as a variety of other materials, visit this text's Web site at

www.cengage.com/blaw/jentz

To learn what kinds of clauses are included in typical contracts for certain goods and services, you can explore the collection of contract forms made available by FindLaw at

forms.lp.findlaw.com

Legal Research Exercises on the Web

Go to **www.cengage.com/blaw/jentz**, the Web site that accompanies this text. Select "Chapter 11" and click on "Internet Exercises." There you will find the following Internet research exercises that you can perform to learn more about the topics covered in this chapter.

Internet Exercise 11–1: Legal Perspective
Contract Terms

Internet Exercise 11–2: Management Perspective
Sample Contracts

Internet Exercise 11–3: Ethical Perspective
Offers and Advertisements

CHAPTER 12

Consideration

The fact that a promise has been made does not mean the promise can or will be enforced. Under Roman law, a promise was not enforceable without some sort of *causa*—that is, a reason for making the promise that was also deemed to be a sufficient reason for enforcing it. Under the common law, a primary basis for the enforcement of promises is consideration. **Consideration** is usually defined as the value (such as cash) given in return for a promise (such as the promise to sell a stamp collection on receipt of payment) or in return for a performance.

SECTION 1 Elements of Consideration

Often, consideration is broken down into two parts: (1) something of *legally sufficient value* must be given in exchange for the promise; and (2) usually, there must be a *bargained-for* exchange.

Legal Value

The "something of legally sufficient value" may consist of (1) a promise to do something that one has no prior legal duty to do, (2) the performance of an action that one is otherwise not obligated to undertake, or (3) the refraining from an action that one has a legal right to undertake (called a **forbearance**). Consideration in bilateral contracts normally consists of a promise in return for a promise, as explained in Chapter 10. For example, suppose that in a contract for the sale of goods, the seller promises to ship specific goods to the buyer, and the buyer promises to pay for those goods when they are received. Each of these promises constitutes consideration for the contract.

In contrast, unilateral contracts involve a promise in return for a performance. Suppose that Anita says to her neighbor, "When you finish painting the garage, I will pay you $100." Anita's neighbor paints the garage. The act of painting the garage is the consideration that creates Anita's contractual obligation to pay her neighbor $100.

What if, in return for a promise to pay, a person refrains from pursuing harmful habits (a forbearance), such as the use of tobacco and alcohol? Does such forbearance constitute legally sufficient consideration? This was the issue before the court in the following case, which is one of the classics in contract law with respect to consideration.

CASE 12.1 Hamer v. Sidway

Court of Appeals of New York, Second Division, 1891. 124 N.Y. 538, 27 N.E. 256.

• **Background and Facts** William E. Story, Sr., was the uncle of William E. Story II. In the presence of family members and guests invited to a family gathering, the elder Story promised to pay his nephew $5,000 ($72,000 in today's dollars) if he would refrain from drinking, using tobacco, swearing, and playing cards or billiards for money until he reached the age of twenty-one. (Note that in 1869, when this contract was formed, it was legal in New York to drink and play cards for money prior to the

CASE 12.1 CONTINUED age of twenty-one.) The nephew agreed and fully performed his part of the bargain. When he reached the age of twenty-one, he wrote and told his uncle that he had kept his part of the agreement and was therefore entitled to $5,000. The uncle replied that he was pleased with his nephew's performance, writing, "I have no doubt but you have, for which you shall have five thousand dollars, as I promised you. I had the money in the bank the day you was twenty-one years old that I intend for you, and you shall have the money certain. . . . P. S. You can consider this money on interest." The nephew received his uncle's letter and thereafter consented that the money should remain with his uncle according to the terms and conditions of the letter. The uncle died about twelve years later without having paid his nephew any part of the $5,000 and interest. The executor of the uncle's estate (Franklin Sidway, the defendant in this action) claimed that there had been no valid consideration for the promise and therefore refused to pay the $5,000 (plus interest) to Louisa Hamer, a third party to whom the nephew had transferred his rights in the note. The court reviewed the case to determine whether the nephew had given valid consideration under the law.

- **Decision and Rationale** The Court of Appeals of New York disagreed with Sidway. The court ruled that the nephew had provided legally sufficient consideration by giving up smoking, drinking alcohol, swearing, and playing cards or billiards for money until he became twenty-one and was therefore entitled to the money. Sidway argued that the nephew had suffered no detriment, because what he had done was in his own best interest. The court pointed out that "in general a waiver of any legal right at the request of another party is a sufficient consideration for a promise." In this case, the court noted that "the promisee used tobacco, occasionally drank liquor, and he had a legal right to do so. That right he abandoned for a period of years upon the strength of the promise of [his uncle] that for such forbearance he would give him $5,000. * * * It is of no moment whether such performance actually proved a benefit to the promisor."

- **Impact of This Case on Today's Law** *Although this case was decided more than a century ago, the principles enunciated in the case remain applicable to contracts formed today, including online contracts. For a contract to be valid and binding, consideration must be given, and that consideration must be something of legally sufficient value.*

- **What If the Facts Were Different?** *If the nephew had not had a legal right to engage in the behavior that he agreed to forgo, would the result in this case have been different? Explain.*

Bargained-for Exchange

The second element of consideration is that it must provide the basis for the bargain struck between the contracting parties. The promise given by the promisor (offeror) must induce the promisee (offeree) to offer a return promise, a performance, or a forbearance, and the promisee's promise, performance, or forbearance must induce the promisor to make the promise.

This element of bargained-for exchange distinguishes contracts from gifts. Suppose that Paloma says to her son, "In consideration of the fact that you are not as wealthy as your brothers, I will pay you $5,000." The fact that the word *consideration* is used does not, by itself, mean that consideration has been given. Indeed, this is not an enforceable promise because the son does not have to do anything in order to receive the promised $5,000.[1] The son need not give Paloma something of legal value in return for her promise, and the promised $5,000 does not involve a bargained-for exchange. Rather, Paloma has simply stated her motive for giving her son a gift.

Does asking a bank for change for a $50 or $100 bill initiate a bargained-for exchange? The bank in the following case argued that obtaining change is not a contractual transaction because there is no consideration.

1. See *Fink v. Cox*, 18 Johns. 145, 9 Am.Dec. 191 (N.Y. 1820).

CASE 12.2 Barfield v. Commerce Bank, N.A.[a]

United States Court of Appeals, Tenth Circuit, 2007. 484 F.3d 1276.
www.kscourts.org/ca10[b]

• **Background and Facts** Chris Barfield, an African American man, entered a branch of Commerce Bank, N.A., in Wichita, Kansas, and requested change for a $50 bill. He was refused change on the ground that he did not have an account with the bank. The next day, Chris Barfield's father, James Barfield, asked a white friend, John Polson, to make the same request at the bank. The teller gave Polson change without asking whether he had an account. A few minutes later, James Barfield entered the bank, asked for change for a $100 bill, and was told that he could not be given change unless he was an account holder. The Barfields filed a suit in a federal district court against Commerce Bank, alleging discrimination on the basis of race in the impairment of their ability to contract. The court granted the bank's motion to dismiss the suit for failure to state a claim. The Barfields appealed this ruling to the U.S. Court of Appeals for the Tenth Circuit.

• **Decision and Rationale** The reviewing court reversed the lower court's dismissal of the plaintiffs' complaint and remanded the case "for further proceedings in accordance with this opinion." The court pointed out that whenever a merchant denies service or refuses to engage in business with a customer attempting to contract with that merchant, there is a violation of federal law. In any event, every contract must be supported by consideration to be enforceable. "Consideration is defined as some right, interest, profit, or benefit accruing to one party, or some forbearance, detriment, loss, or responsibility, given, suffered, or undertaken by the other." In the transaction proposed by the Barfields, "they would give up something of value (a large-denomination bill) in exchange for something they valued more (smaller-denomination bills). It is hard to see why this is not a contract. * * * Consideration does not need to have quantifiable financial value * * * ." The consideration that the bank would have obtained through this exchange would have been increased goodwill and perhaps a future client. There is consideration in an exchange of paper money as there can be in any other bargained-for exchange.

• **The Ethical Dimension** *In most circumstances, parties are free to make whatever promises they wish, but only those promises made with consideration will be enforced as contracts. What is the purpose of this requirement?*

• **The Legal Environment Dimension** *The courts generally do not weigh the sufficiency of consideration according to the comparative economic value of what is exchanged. Should they? Why or why not?*

---

a. *N.A.* is an abbreviation for National Association.

b. In the first paragraph, click on "plaintiff/defendant case name." In the result, scroll through the list to the name of the case and click on it to access the opinion. Washburn University School of Law Library in Topeka, Kansas, maintains this Web site.

SECTION 2

Adequacy of Consideration

Legal sufficiency of consideration involves the requirement that consideration be something of legally sufficient value in the eyes of the law. Adequacy of consideration involves "how much" consideration is given. Essentially, adequacy of consideration concerns the fairness of the bargain.

Courts Typically Will Not Consider Adequacy

On the surface, when the items exchanged are of unequal value, fairness would appear to be an issue. In general, however, a court will not question the adequacy of consideration based solely on the comparative value of the things exchanged. In other words, the determination of whether consideration exists does not depend on a comparison of the values of the things exchanged. Something need not be of direct economic or financial value to be considered legally sufficient consideration. In many situations, the exchange of promises and potential benefits is deemed sufficient as consideration.

Under the doctrine of freedom of contract, courts leave it up to the parties to decide what something is worth, and the parties are normally free to make bad bargains. If people could sue merely because they had entered into an unwise contract, the courts would be overloaded with frivolous suits.

Evidence of Grossly Inadequate Consideration

When there is a gross disparity in the amount or value of the consideration exchanged, the inadequate consideration may raise a red flag for a court to look more closely at the bargain. This is because shockingly inadequate consideration can indicate that fraud, duress, or undue influence was involved or that the element of bargained-for exchange was lacking.

Judges are uneasy about enforcing unequal bargains, and it is the courts' task to police contracts and make sure that there was not some defect in a contract's formation that negates mutual assent. If an elderly person sells her Mercedes-Benz convertible to her neighbor for $5,000 even though it is worth well over $50,000, the disparity in value may indicate that the sale involved undue influence or fraud. When the consideration is grossly inadequate, a court may also declare the contract unenforceable because it is unconscionable,[2] which generally means that the contract is so one sided under the circumstances as to be clearly unfair.[3] (*Unconscionability* will be discussed further in Chapter 13.)

SECTION 3 Agreements That Lack Consideration

Sometimes, one of the parties (or both parties) to an agreement may think that consideration has been exchanged when in fact it has not. Here, we look at some situations in which the parties' promises or actions do not qualify as contractual consideration.

Preexisting Duty

Under most circumstances, a promise to do what one already has a legal duty to do does not constitute legally sufficient consideration.[4] The preexisting legal duty may be imposed by law or may arise out of a previous contract. A sheriff, for example, cannot collect a reward for providing information leading to the capture of a criminal if the sheriff already has a legal duty to capture the criminal.

Likewise, if a party is already bound by contract to perform a certain duty, that duty cannot serve as consideration for a second contract.[5] For example, Bauman-Bache, Inc., begins construction on a seven-story office building and after three months demands an extra $75,000 on its contract. If the extra $75,000 is not paid, the contractor will stop working. The owner of the land, finding no one else to complete the construction, agrees to pay the extra $75,000. The agreement is unenforceable because it is not supported by legally sufficient consideration; Bauman-Bache was bound by a preexisting contract to complete the building.

Unforeseen Difficulties The rule regarding preexisting duty is meant to prevent extortion and the so-called holdup game. What happens, though, when an honest contractor who has contracted with a landowner to construct a building runs into extraordinary difficulties that were totally unforeseen at the time the contract was formed? In the interests of fairness and equity, the courts sometimes allow exceptions to the preexisting duty rule. In the example just mentioned, if the landowner agrees to pay extra compensation to the contractor for overcoming unforeseen difficulties, the court may refrain from applying the preexisting duty rule and enforce the agreement. When the "unforeseen difficulties" that give rise to a contract modification involve the types of risks ordinarily assumed in business, however, the courts will usually assert the preexisting duty rule.[6]

2. Pronounced un-*kon*-shun-uh-bul.

3. See, for example, *Rissett v. W. B. Doner & Co.*, 293 F.3d 164 (4th Cir. 2002).

4. See *Foakes v. Beer*, 9 App.Cas. 605 (1884); and *Cobern v. Whatmusic Holdings, Ltd.*, 2003 WL 22073940 (Chan.Div. 2003).

5. See, for example, *Braude & Margulies, P.C. v. Fireman's Fund Insurance Co.*, 468 F.Supp.2d 190 (D.D.C. 2007).

6. Note that under Article 2 of the Uniform Commercial Code (UCC), an agreement modifying a contract needs no consideration to be binding. See UCC 2–209(1).

Rescission and New Contract The law recognizes that two parties can mutually agree to rescind, or cancel, their contract, at least to the extent that it is executory (still to be carried out). **Rescission**[7] is the unmaking of a contract so as to return the parties to the positions they occupied before the contract was made. Sometimes, parties rescind a contract and make a new contract at the same time. When this occurs, it is often difficult to determine whether there was consideration for the new contract, or whether the parties had a preexisting duty under the previous contract. If a court finds there was a preexisting duty, then the new contract will be invalid because there was no consideration.

Past Consideration

Promises made in return for actions or events that have already taken place are unenforceable. These promises lack consideration in that the element of bargained-for exchange is missing. In short, you can bargain for something to take place now or in the future but not for something that has already taken place. **Past consideration** is no consideration.

Suppose that Elsie, a real estate agent, does her friend Judy a favor by selling Judy's house and not charging any commission. Later, Judy says to Elsie, "In return for your generous act, I will pay you $3,000." This promise is made in return for past consideration and is thus unenforceable; in effect, Judy is stating her intention to give Elsie a gift.

Does prior employment constitute valid consideration for a *covenant not to compete* clause (or a *noncompete agreement*—see Chapter 13)? That was the issue in the following case.

7. Pronounced reh-*sih*-zhen.

CASE 12.3 Access Organics, Inc. v. Hernandez

Supreme Court of Montana, 2008. 341 Mont. 73, 175 P.3d 899.

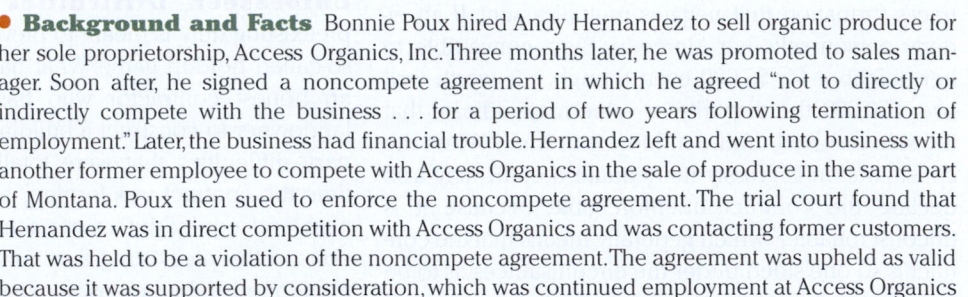

• **Background and Facts** Bonnie Poux hired Andy Hernandez to sell organic produce for her sole proprietorship, Access Organics, Inc. Three months later, he was promoted to sales manager. Soon after, he signed a noncompete agreement in which he agreed "not to directly or indirectly compete with the business . . . for a period of two years following termination of employment." Later, the business had financial trouble. Hernandez left and went into business with another former employee to compete with Access Organics in the sale of produce in the same part of Montana. Poux then sued to enforce the noncompete agreement. The trial court found that Hernandez was in direct competition with Access Organics and was contacting former customers. That was held to be a violation of the noncompete agreement. The agreement was upheld as valid because it was supported by consideration, which was continued employment at Access Organics at the time the agreement was signed. The court ordered Hernandez not to compete directly with Access Organics for the two-year period called for in the agreement. Hernandez appealed.

• **Decision and Rationale** The Montana Supreme Court reversed the decision, holding that agreements not to compete are restraints of trade that are not favored unless certain conditions are met. The court stated that although noncompete contracts are upheld in some circumstances, the agreement in this case failed for lack of consideration. If the noncompete agreement had been a part of the original employment bargain, then there might have been a bargained-for exchange. Here, Hernandez was simply told to sign the agreement when he was already working for Access Organics. His prior employment would not be consideration, because past consideration is not sufficient to support a promise. This was an "afterthought agreement" that could have been valid had it been supported by a pay increase or some other new benefit, but it was not. Hernandez received no new benefit from the agreement. Because the agreement was unsupported by consideration, it did not create an enforceable contract.

• **The Ethical Dimension** *Unless employees have access to trade secrets or other proprietary information, is it ethical to require them to sign noncompete agreements as a condition of employment? Explain your answer.*

CASE 12.3 CONTINUED • **The Legal Environment Dimension** *How could Access Organics have obtained a non-compete agreement from Hernandez that would have been enforceable?*

Illusory Promises

If the terms of the contract express such uncertainty of performance that the promisor has not definitely promised to do anything, the promise is said to be *illusory*—without consideration and unenforceable. A promise is illusory when it fails to bind the promisor. For example, a corporate president says to her employees, "All of you have worked hard, and if profits continue to remain high, a 10 percent bonus at the end of the year will be given—if management thinks it is warranted." The employees continue to work hard, and profits remain high, but no bonus is given. This is an *illusory promise,* or no promise at all, because performance depends solely on the discretion of the president (the management). There is no bargained-for consideration, only a declaration that management may or may not do something in the future. The president is not obligated (incurs no detriment) now or later.

Option-to-Cancel Clauses Option-to-cancel clauses in term contracts sometimes present problems in regard to consideration. When the promisor has the option to cancel the contract before performance has begun, then the promise is illusory. Suppose that Abe contracts to hire Chris for one year at $5,000 per month, reserving the right to cancel the contract at any time. On close examination of these words, you can see that Abe has not actually agreed to hire Chris, as Abe could cancel without liability before Chris started performance. This contract is therefore illusory. But if Abe had instead reserved the right to cancel the contract at any time *after* Chris has begun performance by giving Chris *thirty days' notice,* the promise would not be illusory. Abe, by saying that he will give Chris thirty days' notice, is relinquishing the opportunity (legal right) to hire someone else instead of Chris for a thirty-day period. If Chris works for one month, at the end of which Abe gives him thirty days' notice, Chris has an enforceable claim for $10,000 in salary.[8]

Requirements Contracts and Output Contracts Problems with consideration may also arise in other types of contracts because of uncertainty of performance.[9] Uncertain performance is characteristic of requirements and output contracts, for example. In a *requirements contract,* a buyer and a seller agree that the buyer will purchase from the seller all of the goods of a designated type that the buyer needs, or requires. In an *output contract,* the buyer and seller agree that the buyer will purchase from the seller all of what the seller produces, or the seller's output. These types of contracts will be discussed further in Chapter 20. *Concept Summary 12.1* on the next page provides a convenient summary of the main aspects of consideration.

SECTION 4

Settlement of Claims

Businesspersons or others can settle legal claims in several ways, and it is important to understand the nature of consideration given in these kinds of settlement agreements, or contracts. In an *accord and satisfaction,* which is a common means of settling a claim, a debtor offers to pay a lesser amount than the creditor purports to be owed. Other common methods used to settle claims include a *release* and a *covenant not to sue.*

Accord and Satisfaction

The concept of **accord and satisfaction** involves a debtor's offer of payment and a creditor's acceptance of a lesser amount than the creditor originally claimed was owed. The *accord* is the agreement under which one of the parties undertakes to give or perform—and the other to accept, in satisfaction of a claim—something other than that on which the parties originally agreed. *Satisfaction* takes place when the accord is executed. A basic rule is that there can be no satisfaction unless there is first an accord. For accord and satisfaction to occur, the amount of the debt *must be in dispute.*

8. For another example, see *Vanegas v. American Energy Services,* 224 S.W.3d 544 (Tex.App.—Eastland 2007).

9. See, for example, *Johnson Controls, Inc. v. TRW Vehicle Safety Systems,* 491 F.Supp.2d 707 (E.D.Mich. 2007).

CONCEPT SUMMARY 12.1
Consideration

Elements of Consideration	Consideration is the value given in exchange for a promise. A contract cannot be formed without sufficient consideration. Consideration is often broken down into two elements: 1. *Legal value*—Something of legally sufficient value must be given in exchange for a promise. This may consist of a promise, a performance, or a forbearance. 2. *Bargained-for exchange*—There must be a bargained-for exchange.
Adequacy of Consideration	Adequacy of consideration relates to how much consideration is given and whether a fair bargain was reached. Courts will inquire into the adequacy of consideration (if the consideration is legally sufficient) only when fraud, undue influence, duress, or the lack of a bargained-for exchange may be involved.
Agreements That Lack Consideration	Consideration is lacking in the following situations: 1. *Preexisting duty*—Consideration is not legally sufficient if one is either by law or by contract under a *preexisting duty* to perform the action being offered as consideration for a new contract. 2. *Past consideration*—Actions or events that have already taken place do not constitute legally sufficient consideration. 3. *Illusory promises*—When the nature or extent of performance is too uncertain, the promise is rendered illusory and unenforceable.

Liquidated Debts If a debt is *liquidated,* accord and satisfaction cannot take place. A liquidated debt is one whose amount has been ascertained, fixed, agreed on, settled, or exactly determined. For example, if Kwan signs an installment loan contract with her banker in which she agrees to pay a specified rate of interest on a specified amount of borrowed funds at monthly intervals for two years, that is a liquidated debt. The total obligation is precisely known to both parties, and reasonable persons cannot dispute the amount owed.

Suppose that Kwan has missed her last two payments on the loan and the creditor demands that she pay the overdue debt. Kwan makes a partial payment and states that she believes this payment is all she should have to pay and that the debt will be satisfied if the creditor accepts the payment. In the majority of states, acceptance of a lesser sum than the entire amount of a liquidated debt is *not* satisfaction, and the balance of the debt is still legally owed. The rationale for this rule is that the debtor has not given any consideration to satisfy the obligation of paying the balance to the creditor—because the debtor has a preexisting legal obligation to pay the entire debt.

Unliquidated Debts An *unliquidated debt* is the opposite of a liquidated debt. Here, reasonable persons may differ over the amount owed. It is not settled, fixed, agreed on, ascertained, or determined, and thus acceptance of the payment of a lesser amount operates as satisfaction, or discharge, of the debt. For example, Devereaux goes to the dentist's office and the dentist tells him that he needs three special types of gold inlays. The price is not discussed, and there is no standard fee for this type of procedure. Devereaux has the work done and leaves the office. At the end of the month, the dentist sends him a bill for $3,000.

Devereaux, believing that this amount grossly exceeds what a reasonable person would believe the debt owed should be, sends a check for $2,000. On the back of the check he writes, "payment in full for three gold inlays." The dentist cashes the check. Because the situation involves an unliquidated debt—the amount has not been agreed on—the payment accepted by the dentist normally will eradicate the debt. One argument to support this rule is that the parties give up a legal right to contest the amount in dispute, and thus consideration is given.

Release

A **release** is a contract in which one party forfeits the right to pursue a legal claim against the other party. It bars any further recovery beyond the terms stated in the release. For example, your car is damaged in an automobile accident caused by Donovan's negligence. Donovan offers to give you $1,000 if you will release him from further liability resulting from the accident. You believe that this amount will cover your damages, so you agree and sign the release. Later, you discover that it will cost $1,500 to repair your car. Can you collect the balance from Donovan?

The answer is normally no; you are limited to the $1,000 specified in the release because the release represents a valid contract. You and Donovan both agreed to the bargain, and sufficient consideration was present. The consideration was the legal detriment you suffered (by releasing Donovan from liability, you forfeited your right to sue to recover damages in exchange for $1,000).

Clearly, you are better off if you know the extent of your injuries or damages before signing a release. Releases will generally be binding if they are (1) given in good faith, (2) stated in a signed writing (which is required in many states), and (3) accompanied by consideration.[10]

Covenant Not to Sue

A **covenant not to sue** is an agreement to substitute a contractual obligation for some other type of legal action based on a valid claim. Unlike a release, a covenant not to sue does not always bar further recovery. Suppose (continuing the earlier example) that you agree with Donovan not to sue for damages in a tort action if he will pay for the damage to your car. If Donovan fails to pay, you can bring an action against him for breach of contract.

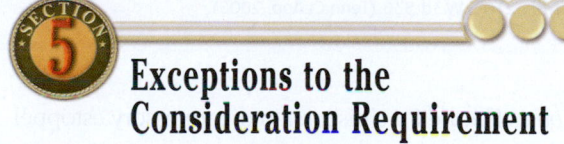

SECTION 5 Exceptions to the Consideration Requirement

There are some exceptions to the rule that only promises supported by consideration are enforceable. The following types of promises may be enforced despite the lack of consideration:

1. Promises that induce detrimental reliance, under the doctrine of promissory estoppel.
2. Promises to pay debts that are barred by a statute of limitations.
3. Promises to make charitable contributions.

10. Under the UCC, a written, signed waiver or renunciation by an aggrieved party discharges any further liability for a breach, even without consideration.

Promissory Estoppel

As discussed in Chapter 11, under the doctrine of *promissory estoppel* (also called *detrimental reliance*), a person who has reasonably and substantially relied on the promise of another may be able to obtain some measure of recovery. This doctrine is applied in a wide variety of contexts in which a promise is otherwise unenforceable, such as when a promise is not supported by consideration. Under this doctrine, a court may enforce an otherwise unenforceable promise to avoid the injustice that would otherwise result.

Requirements to State a Claim for Promissory Estoppel For the doctrine to be applied, the following elements are required:

1. There must be a clear and definite promise.
2. The promisor should have expected that the promisee would rely on the promise.
3. The promisee reasonably relied on the promise by acting or refraining from some act.
4. The promisee's reliance was definite and resulted in substantial detriment.
5. Enforcement of the promise is necessary to avoid injustice.

If these requirements are met, a promise may be enforced even though it is not supported by consideration.[11] In essence, the promisor will be *estopped* (prevented) from asserting the lack of consideration as a defense.

Application of the Doctrine Promissory estoppel was originally applied to situations involving gifts (I promise to pay you $350 a week so that you will not have to work) and donations to charities (I promise to contribute $50,000 a year toward the orphanage). Later, courts began to apply the doctrine to avoid inequity or hardship in other situations, including business transactions.

For example, the Air Force has opened the bidding process for construction of a new building at Elmendorf Air Force Base in Anchorage, Alaska. A general contractor, Vern Hickel, anxious to get the job, contacts eight different subcontractors to find the lowest price on electrical work. Bussell, an electrical subcontractor, tells Hickel that he will do the electrical portion of the project for $477,498. Hickel reasonably relies on this amount when he submits his primary bid for the entire project to the Air Force and wins the contract. After the bidding is over, Bussell realizes that he made

11. *Restatement (Second) of Contracts,* Section 90.

CONTEMPORARY LEGAL DEBATES

Promissory Estoppel and Employment Contracts

Today, approximately 85 percent of American workers have the legal status of "employees at will." Under this common law employment doctrine, which applies in all states except Montana, an employer may fire an employee for any reason or no reason. The at-will doctrine, however, does not apply to any employee who has an employment contract or who falls under the protection of a state or federal statute—which is, of course, a large number of employees. Even when an employee is subject to the employment-at-will doctrine, the courts sometimes make exceptions to the doctrine based on tort theory or contract principles or on the ground that a termination violates an established public policy (see Chapter 33).

These exceptions to the at-will doctrine, however, apply only when a current employee's employment is *terminated.* Should they also apply when a company fails to *hire* a job candidate after promising to do so? For example, a job candidate, relying on a company's offer of employment, quits his or her existing job, moves to another city, and rents or buys housing in the new location. Then the company decides not to hire the candidate after all. Given the candidate's detrimental reliance on the company's job offer, should the company be prevented from revoking its offer under the doctrine of promissory estoppel? This question has come before a number of courts. As yet, however, the courts have not reached a consensus on the issue. Some jurisdictions allow the doctrine of promissory estoppel to be applied, but others do not.

Promissory Estoppel Should Not Be Applied

Many jurisdictions believe that reliance on a prospective employer's promise of at-will employment is unreasonable as a matter of law. Courts in these jurisdictions reason that a job applicant should know that, even if she or he is hired, the employer could terminate the employment at any time for any reason without liability. According to these courts, it would be contrary to reason to allow someone who has not yet begun work to recover damages under a theory of promissory estoppel, given that the same person's job could be terminated without liability one day after beginning work.

Consider a case example. Arlie Thompson had worked for nine years at a hospital as a technician assistant when she was laid off. A year later, the same hospital offered her a clerical position, which she accepted. She was measured for a new uniform, given a security badge, and provided with the password for the computer system. Thompson, who was then working at another job, quit the other position in reliance on the hospital's job offer. Shortly thereafter, the hospital asked her to take a test. When she failed the test, the hospital refused to hire her. Thompson filed a suit claiming that the doctrine of promissory estoppel should prevent the hospital from revoking its offer. The court, however, held that the hospital's promise of employment was not sufficiently "clear and definite" for that doctrine to be applied.[a]

a. *Thompson v. Bridgeport Hospital,* 2001 WL 823130 (Conn.Super. 2001). See also *Lower v. Electronic Data Systems Corp.,* 494 F.Supp.2d 770 (S.D. Ohio 2007); and *Rice v. NN, Inc., Ball & Roller Division,* 210 S.W.3d 536 (Tenn.Ct.App. 2006).

a mistake and refuses to perform the electrical work for Hickel for $477,498. Hickel has to hire another subcontractor at a substantially higher cost to complete the electrical work.

Under the doctrine of promissory estoppel, Hickel can sue Bussell for the cost difference because he detrimentally relied on Bussell's bid even though there was no consideration for Bussell's promise to do the work for $477,498.[12] (See this chapter's *Contemporary Legal Debates* feature for a discussion of promissory estoppel and promises of employment.)

Promises to Pay Debts Barred by a Statute of Limitations

Statutes of limitations in all states require a creditor to sue within a specified period to recover a debt. If the creditor fails to sue in time, recovery of the debt is barred by the statute of limitations. A debtor who promises to pay a previous debt even though recovery is barred by the statute of limitations makes an enforceable promise. *The promise needs no consideration.* (Some states, however, require that it be in writing.) In effect, the promise extends the limitations period, and

12. See *Alaska Bussell Electric Co. v. Vern Hickel Construction Co.,* 688 P.2d 576 (1984); also see *Commerce Bancorp, Inc. v. BK International Insurance Brokers, Ltd.,* 490 F.Supp.2d 556 (D.N.J. 2007).

Promissory Estoppel Should Be Applied

A number of other jurisdictions, however, have held that a person can recover damages incurred as a result of resigning from a former job in reliance on an offer of at-will employment. These jurisdictions have determined that when a prospective employer knows or should know that a promise of employment will induce the future employee to leave his or her current job, the employer should be responsible for the prospective employee's damages. After all, without the offer from the prospective employer, the prospective employee would have continued to work in his or her prior position.

This approach is reflected in a case from 2007 involving Thomas Frey. In 1999, Frey was working for a firm at which he had substantial benefits and would have been entitled to stock options. Then Andrew Taitz of Workhorse Custom Chassis, LLC, offered Frey a position, promising him a large bonus if the company's earnings exceeded $39.1 million by the end of 2002. In reliance on that promise, Frey left his job and took the position at Workhorse.

By the end of 2002, projections indicated that Workhorse's earnings would exceed the required level. Frey therefore believed that he was entitled to the bonus when he left the company in January 2003. In the spring of 2003, Frey asked for his bonus, but Taitz responded that because Frey no longer worked for the company, he was not entitled to the bonus. Frey filed a lawsuit against Workhorse, claiming, among other things, that he was entitled to damages under the doctrine of promissory estoppel because he had left a lucrative and secure position to take the job at Workhorse.

Although Workhorse claimed at the trial that its 2002 earnings were only around $37.6 million, the audited financial statements it presented had been completed ten months late and were subject to a 5 percent margin of error. Workhorse also admitted that many employees would have received substantial bonuses if the earnings had exceeded $39.1 million. A jury found Frey's argument convincing and awarded him $648,220. Workhorse moved for a judgment as a matter of law and for a new trial, but the court ruled that Frey had presented enough evidence to support the jury's verdict.[b]

WHERE DO YOU STAND?

Some jurisdictions maintain that it is irrational to apply the doctrine of promissory estoppel to a promise of at-will employment, given that the employee could be fired after working for only one day on the job. Other jurisdictions conclude that the doctrine should apply because the employer should reasonably expect a job candidate in this situation to act in reliance on the promise. Does one of these two arguments have greater merit than the other? What is your position on this issue?

b. *Frey v. Workhorse Custom Chassis, LLC*, ___ F.Supp.2d ___ (S.D.Ind. 2007). For a case allowing a job candidate to recover damages from a prospective employer, see *Goff-Hamel v. Obstetricians & Gynecologists, P.C.*, 256 Neb. 19, 588 N.W.2d 798 (1999).

the creditor can sue to recover the entire debt or at least the amount promised. The promise can be implied if the debtor acknowledges the barred debt by making a partial payment.

Charitable Subscriptions

Subscriptions to religious, educational, and charitable institutions are promises to make gifts. Traditionally, these promises were unenforceable because they are not supported by legally sufficient consideration. A gift, after all, is the opposite of bargained-for consideration. The modern view, however, is to make exceptions to the general rule by applying the doctrine of promissory estoppel.

Suppose that a church solicits and receives pledges (commitments to contribute funds) from church members to erect a new church building. On the basis of these pledges, the church purchases land, hires architects, and makes other contracts that change its position. Because of the church's detrimental reliance, a court may enforce the pledges under the theory of promissory estoppel. Alternatively, a court may find consideration in the fact that each promise was made in reliance on the other promises of support or that the trustees, by accepting the subscriptions, impliedly promised to complete the proposed undertaking.

REVIEWING Consideration

John operates a motorcycle repair shop from his home but finds that his business is limited by the small size of his garage. Driving by a neighbor's property, he notices a for-sale sign on a large, metal-sided garage. John contacts the neighbor and offers to buy the building, hoping that it can be dismantled and moved to his own property. The neighbor accepts John's payment and makes a generous offer in return: if John will help him dismantle the garage, which will take a substantial amount of time, he will help John reassemble it after it has been transported to John's property. They agree to have the entire job completed within two weeks. John spends every day for a week working with his neighbor to disassemble the building. In his rush to acquire a larger workspace, he turns down several lucrative repair jobs. Once the disassembled building has been moved to John's property, however, the neighbor refuses to help John reassemble it as he originally promised. Using the information presented in the chapter, answer the following questions.

1. Are the basic elements of consideration present in the neighbor's promise to help John reassemble the garage? Why or why not?
2. Suppose that the neighbor starts to help John but then realizes that, because of the layout of John's property, putting the building back together will take much more work than dismantling it took. Under which principle discussed in the chapter might the neighbor be allowed to ask for additional compensation?
3. What if John's neighbor made his promise to help reassemble the garage at the time he and John were moving it to John's property, saying, "Since you helped me take it down, I will help you put it back up." Would John be able to enforce this promise? Why or why not?
4. Under what doctrine discussed in the chapter might John seek to recover the profits he lost when he declined to do repair work for one week?

TERMS AND CONCEPTS

accord and satisfaction 237
consideration 232
covenant not to sue 239
forbearance 232
past consideration 236
release 238
rescission 236

QUESTIONS AND CASE PROBLEMS

12–1. Tabor is a buyer of file cabinets manufactured by Martin. Martin's contract with Tabor calls for delivery of fifty file cabinets at $40 per cabinet in five equal installments. After delivery of two installments (twenty cabinets), Martin informs Tabor that because of inflation, Martin is losing money and will promise to deliver the remaining thirty cabinets only if Tabor will pay $50 per cabinet. Tabor agrees in writing to do so. Discuss whether Martin can legally collect the additional $100 on delivery to Tabor of the next installment of ten cabinets.

12–2. QUESTION WITH SAMPLE ANSWER

Bernstein owns a lot and wants to build a house according to a particular set of plans and specifications. She solicits bids from building contractors and receives three bids: one from Carlton for $160,000, one from Friend for $158,000, and one from Shade for $153,000. She accepts Shade's bid. One month after beginning construction of the house, Shade contacts Bernstein and informs her that because of inflation and a recent price hike for materials, he will not finish the house unless Bernstein agrees to pay an extra $13,000. Bernstein reluctantly agrees to pay the additional sum. After the house is finished, however, Bernstein refuses to pay the extra $13,000. Discuss whether Bernstein is legally required to pay this additional amount.

- **For a sample answer to Question 12–2, go to Appendix I at the end of this text.**

12–3. Daniel, a recent college graduate, is on his way home for the Christmas holidays from his new job. He gets caught in a snowstorm and is taken in by an elderly couple, who provide him with food and shelter. After the snowplows have cleared the road, Daniel proceeds home. Daniel's father, Fred, is most appreciative of the elderly couple's action and in a letter promises to pay them $500. The elderly couple, in need of funds, accept Fred's offer. Then, because of a dispute between Daniel and Fred, Fred refuses to pay the elderly couple the $500. Discuss whether the couple can hold Fred liable in contract for the services rendered to Daniel.

12–4. Costello hired Sagan to drive his racing car in a race. Sagan's friend Gideon promised to pay Sagan $3,000 if she won the race. Sagan won the race, but Gideon refused to pay the $3,000. Gideon contended that no legally binding contract had been formed because he had received no consideration from Sagan in exchange for his promise to pay the $3,000. Sagan sued Gideon for breach of contract, arguing that winning the race was the consideration given in exchange for Gideon's promise to pay the $3,000. What rule of law discussed in this chapter supports Gideon's claim?

12–5. Accord and Satisfaction. E. S. Herrick Co. grows and sells blueberries. Maine Wild Blueberry Co. agreed to buy all of Herrick's 1990 crop under a contract that left the price unliquidated. Herrick delivered the berries, but a dispute arose over the price. Maine Wild sent Herrick a check with a letter stating that the check was the "final settlement." Herrick cashed the check but filed a suit in a Maine state court against Maine Wild, on the ground of breach of contract, alleging that the buyer owed more. What will the court likely decide in this case? Why? [*E. S. Herrick Co. v. Maine Wild Blueberry Co.,* 670 A.2d 944 (Me. 1996)]

12–6. CASE PROBLEM WITH SAMPLE ANSWER

As a child, Martha Carr once visited her mother's 108-acre tract of unimproved land in Richland County, South Carolina. In 1968, Betty and Raymond Campbell leased the land. Carr, a resident of New York, was diagnosed as having schizophrenia and depression in 1986, was hospitalized five or six times, and subsequently took prescription drugs for the illnesses. In 1996, Carr inherited the Richland property and, two years later, contacted the Campbells about selling the land. Carr asked Betty about the value of the land, and Betty said that the county tax assessor had determined that the land's *agricultural value* was $54,000. The Campbells knew at the time that the county had assessed the total property value at $103,700 for tax purposes. A real estate appraiser found that the *real market value* of the property was $162,000. On August 6, Carr signed a contract to sell the land to the Campbells for $54,000. Believing the price to be unfair, however, Carr did not deliver the deed. The Campbells filed a suit in a South Carolina state court against Carr, seeking specific performance of the contract. At trial, an expert real estate appraiser testified that the real market value of the property was $162,000 at the time of the contract. Under what circumstances will a court examine the adequacy of consideration? Are those circumstances present in this case? Should the court enforce the contract between Carr and the Campbells? Explain. [*Campbell v. Carr,* 361 S.C. 258, 603 S.E.2d 625 (S.C. App. 2004)]

- **To view a sample answer for Problem 12–6, go to this book's Web site at www.cengage.com/blaw/jentz, select "Chapter 12," and click on "Case Problem with Sample Answer."**

12–7. Preexisting Duty. New England Rock Services, Inc., agreed to work as a subcontractor on a sewer project on which Empire Paving, Inc., was the general contractor. For drilling and blasting a certain amount of rock, Rock Services was to be paid $29 per cubic yard or on a time-and-materials basis, whichever was less. From the beginning, Rock Services encountered problems. The primary obstacle was a heavy concentration of water, which, according to the custom in the industry, Empire should have controlled but did not. Rock Services was compelled to use more costly and time-consuming methods than anticipated, and it was unable to complete the work on time. The subcontractor asked Empire to pay for the rest of the project on a time-and-materials basis. Empire signed a modification of the original agreement. On completion of the work, Empire refused to pay Rock Services the balance due under the modification. Rock Services filed a suit in a Connecticut state court against Empire. Empire claimed that the modification lacked consideration and was thus not valid and enforceable. Is Empire right? Why or why not? [*New England Rock Services, Inc. v. Empire Paving, Inc.,* 53 Conn. App. 771, 731 A.2d 784 (1999)]

12–8. Consideration. In 1995, Helikon Furniture Co. appointed Tom Gaede as an independent sales agent for the sale of its products in parts of Texas. The parties signed a one-year contract that specified, among other things, the commissions that Gaede would receive. Over a year later, although the parties had not signed a new contract, Gaede was still representing Helikon when it was acquired by a third party. Helikon's new management allowed Gaede to continue to perform for the same commissions and sent him a letter stating that it would make no changes in its sales representatives "for at least the next year." Three months later, in December 1997, the new managers sent Gaede a letter proposing new terms for a contract. Gaede continued to sell Helikon products until May 1997, when he received a letter effectively reducing the amount of his commissions. Gaede filed a suit in a Texas state court against Helikon, alleging breach of contract. Helikon argued, in part, that there was no contract because there was no consideration. In whose favor should the court rule, and why? [*Gaede v. SK Investments, Inc.*, 38 S.W.3d 753 (Tex.App.—Houston [14 Dist.] 2001)]

12–9. Settlement of Claims. In Gulf Shores, Alabama, Shoreline Towers Condominium Owners Association authorized Resort Development, Inc. (RDI), to manage Shoreline's property. On Shoreline's behalf, RDI obtained a property insurance policy from Zurich American Insurance Co. In October 1995, Hurricane Opal struck Gulf Shores. RDI filed claims with Zurich regarding damage to Shoreline's property. Zurich determined that the cost of the damage was $334,901. Zurich then subtracted an applicable $40,000 deductible and sent checks to RDI totaling $294,901. RDI disputed the amount. Zurich eventually agreed to issue a check for an additional $86,000 in return for RDI's signing a "Release of All Claims." Later, contending that the deductible had been incorrectly applied and that this was a breach of contract, among other things, Shoreline filed a suit against Zurich in a federal district court. How, if at all, should the agreement reached by RDI and Zurich affect Shoreline's claim? Explain. [*Shoreline Towers Condominium Owners Association, Inc. v. Zurich American Insurance Co.*, 196 F.Supp.2d 1210 (S.D.Ala. 2002)]

12–10. A QUESTION OF ETHICS

*John Sasson and Emily Springer met in January 2002. John worked for the U.S. Army as an engineer. Emily was an attorney with a law firm. Six months later, John bought a townhouse in Randolph, New Jersey, and asked Emily to live with him. She agreed but retained the ownership of her home in Monmouth Beach. John paid the mortgage and the other expenses on the townhouse. He urged Emily to quit her job and work from "our house." In May 2003, Emily took John's advice and started her own law practice. In December, John made her the beneficiary of his $150,000 individual retirement account (IRA) and said that he would give her his 2002 BMW M3 car before the end of the next year. He proposed to her in September 2004, giving her a diamond engagement ring and promising to "take care of her" for the rest of her life. Less than a month later, John was critically injured by an accidental blow to his head during a basketball game and died. On behalf of John's estate, which was valued at $1.1 million, his brother Steven filed a complaint in a New Jersey state court to have Emily evicted from the townhouse. Given these facts, consider the following questions. [*In re Estate of Sasson, *387 N.J.Super. 459, 904 A.2d 769 (App.Div. 2006)]*

(a) Based on John's promise to "take care of her" for the rest of her life, Emily claimed that she was entitled to the townhouse, the BMW, and an additional portion of John's estate. Under what circumstances would such a promise constitute a valid, enforceable contract? Does John's promise meet these requirements? Why or why not?

(b) Whether or not John's promise is legally binding, is there an ethical basis on which it should be enforced? Is there an ethical basis for not enforcing it? Are there any circumstances under which a promise of support should be—or should not be—enforced? Discuss.

LAW ON THE WEB

For updated links to resources available on the Web, as well as a variety of other materials, visit this text's Web site at

www.cengage.com/blaw/jentz

To find recent cases on contract law, access Cornell University's School of Law site at

www.law.cornell.edu/wex/index.php/Contracts

Legal Research Exercises on the Web

Go to **www.cengage.com/blaw/jentz**, the Web site that accompanies this text. Select "Chapter 12" and click on "Internet Exercises." There you will find the following Internet research exercises that you can perform to learn more about the topics covered in this chapter.

Internet Exercise 12–1: Legal Perspective
Legal Value of Consideration

Internet Exercise 12–2: Management Perspective
Promissory Estoppel

Internet Exercise 12–3: International Perspective
Contract Consideration in Canada

CHAPTER 13

Capacity and Legality

In addition to agreement and consideration, for a contract to be deemed valid the parties to the contract must have **contractual capacity—**the legal ability to enter into a contractual relationship. Courts generally presume the existence of contractual capacity, but in some situations, such as those involving mentally incompetent persons or minors, capacity is lacking or may be questionable. Similarly, contracts calling for the performance of an illegal act are illegal and thus void—they are not contracts at all. In this chapter, we examine contractual capacity and some aspects of illegal bargains.

Realize that capacity and legality are not inherently related other than that they are both contract requirements. We treat these topics in one chapter merely for convenience and reasons of space.

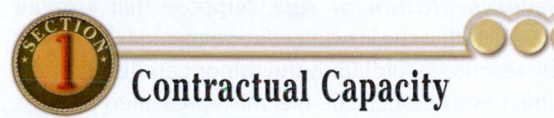

SECTION 1 Contractual Capacity

Historically, the law has given special protection to those who bargain with the inexperience of youth or those who lack the degree of mental competence required by law. A person who has been determined by a court to be mentally incompetent, for example, cannot form a legally binding contract with another party. In other situations, a party may have the capacity to enter into a valid contract but also have the right to avoid liability under it. For example, minors—or *infants,* as they are commonly referred to in legal terminology—usually are not legally bound by contracts. In this section, we look at the effect of youth, intoxication, and mental incompetence on contractual capacity.

Minors

Today, in virtually all states, the **age of majority** (when a person is no longer a minor) for contractual purposes is eighteen years.[1] In addition, some states provide for the termination of minority on marriage. Minority status may also be terminated by a minor's **emancipation,** which occurs when a child's parent or legal guardian relinquishes the legal right to exercise control over the child. Normally, minors who leave home to support themselves are considered emancipated. Several jurisdictions permit minors to petition a court for emancipation themselves. For business purposes, a minor may petition a court to be treated as an adult.

The general rule is that a minor can enter into any contract that an adult can, provided that the contract is not one prohibited by law for minors (for example, the sale of tobacco or alcoholic beverages). A contract entered into by a minor, however, is voidable at the option of that minor, subject to certain exceptions. To exercise the option to avoid a contract, a minor need only manifest an intention not to be bound by it. The minor "avoids" the contract by disaffirming it.

A Minor's Right to Disaffirm The legal avoidance, or setting aside, of a contractual obligation is referred to as **disaffirmance.** To disaffirm, a minor must express his or her intent, through words or conduct, not to be bound to the contract. The minor must disaffirm the entire contract, not merely a portion of it.

1. The age of majority may still be twenty-one for other purposes, such as the purchase and consumption of alcohol.

For example, the minor cannot decide to keep part of the goods purchased under a contract and return the remaining goods.

A contract can ordinarily be disaffirmed at any time during minority[2] or for a reasonable period after reaching majority. What constitutes a "reasonable" time may vary. Two months would probably be considered reasonable, but except in unusual circumstances, a court may not find it reasonable to wait a year or more after coming of age to disaffirm. If an individual fails to disaffirm an executed contract within a reasonable time after reaching the age of majority, a court will likely hold that the contract has been ratified (*ratification* will be discussed shortly).

Note that an adult who enters into a contract with a minor cannot avoid his or her contractual duties on the ground that the minor can do so. Unless the minor exercises the option to disaffirm the contract, the adult party normally is bound by it.

A Minor's Obligations on Disaffirmance

Although all states' laws permit minors to disaffirm contracts (with certain exceptions), states differ on the extent of a minor's obligations on disaffirmance.

Majority Rule. Courts in a majority of states hold that the minor need only return the goods (or other consideration) subject to the contract, provided the goods are in the minor's possession or control. Suppose that Jim Garrison, a seventeen-year-old, purchases a computer from Radio Shack. While transporting the computer to his home, Garrison negligently drops it, breaking the plastic casing. The next day, he returns the computer to Radio Shack and disaffirms the contract. Under the majority view, this return fulfills Garrison's duty even though the computer is now damaged. Garrison is entitled to receive a refund of the purchase price (if paid in cash) or to be relieved of any further obligations under a credit agreement.

Minority Rule. An increasing number of states, either by statute or by court decision, place an additional duty on the minor—the duty to restore the adult party to the position that she or he held before the contract was made. Consider an example. Sixteen-year-old Joseph Dodson bought a pickup truck for $4,900 from a used-car dealer. Although the truck developed mechanical problems nine months later, Dodson continued to drive it until the engine blew up and the truck stopped running. Then Dodson disaffirmed the contract and attempted to return the truck to the dealer for a full refund of the purchase price. When the dealer refused to accept the pickup or refund the money, Dodson filed a lawsuit. Ultimately, the Tennessee Supreme Court allowed Dodson to disaffirm the contract but required him to compensate the seller for the depreciated value—not the purchase price—of the pickup.[3] This case illustrates the trend among today's courts to hold a minor responsible for damage, ordinary wear and tear, and depreciation of goods that the minor used prior to disaffirmance.

Exceptions to a Minor's Right to Disaffirm State courts and legislatures have carved out several exceptions to the minor's right to disaffirm. Some contracts cannot be avoided simply as a matter of law, on the ground of public policy. For example, marriage contracts and contracts to enlist in the armed services fall into this category. Other contracts may not be disaffirmed for other reasons, including those discussed here.

Misrepresentation of Age. Suppose that a minor tells a seller that she is twenty-one years old when she is really seventeen. Ordinarily, the minor can disaffirm the contract even though she has misrepresented her age. In many jurisdictions, however, a minor who has misrepresented his or her age can be bound by a contract, at least under certain circumstances. First, several states have enacted statutes for precisely this purpose. In these states, misrepresentation of age is enough to prohibit disaffirmance. Other statutes prohibit disaffirmance by a minor who has engaged in business as an adult. Second, some courts refuse to allow minors to disaffirm executed (fully performed) contracts unless they can return the consideration received. The combination of the minors' misrepresentation and their unjust enrichment has persuaded these courts to *estop* (prevent) minors from asserting contractual incapacity.

Contracts for Necessaries. A minor who enters into a contract for necessaries may disaffirm the contract but remains liable for the reasonable value of the goods. **Necessaries** are items that fulfill basic needs, such as food, clothing, shelter, and medical services, at a level of value required to maintain the minor's stan-

2. In some states, however, a minor who enters into a contract for the sale of land cannot disaffirm the contract until she or he reaches the age of majority.

3. *Dodson v. Shrader,* 824 S.W.2d 545 (Tenn.Sup.Ct. 1992) is a seminal case on this subject. See also *Restatement (Third) of Restitution,* Sections 16 and 33 (2004).

dard of living or financial and social status. Thus, what will be considered a necessary for one person may be a luxury for another. Additionally, what is considered a necessary depends on whether the minor is under the care or control of his or her parents, who are required by law to provide necessaries for the minor. If a minor's parents provide him or her with shelter, for example, then a contract to lease shelter (such as an apartment) normally will not be classified as a contract for necessaries.

Generally, then, for a contract to qualify as a contract for necessaries, (1) the item contracted for must be necessary for the minor's subsistence, (2) the value of the necessary item must be up to a level required to maintain the minor's standard of living or financial and social status, and (3) the minor must not be under the care of a parent or guardian who is required to supply this item. Unless these three criteria are met, the minor can disaffirm the contract *without* being liable for the reasonable value of the goods used.

The issue in the following case was whether, under the doctrine of necessaries, a medical service provider could collect from a minor the cost of emergency services rendered to the minor when his mother did not pay.

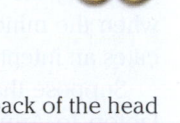

CASE 13.1 Yale Diagnostic Radiology v. Estate of Harun Fountain

Supreme Court of Connecticut, 2004. 267 Conn. 351, 838 A.2d 179.

- **Background and Facts** In March 1996, Harun Fountain was shot in the back of the head at point-blank range by a playmate. Fountain required extensive lifesaving medical services from a variety of providers, including Yale Diagnostic Radiology. Yale billed Fountain's mother, Vernetta Turner-Tucker, for the cost of its services ($17,694), but she did not pay. Instead, in January 2001, Turner-Tucker filed for bankruptcy (see Chapter 30), and all of her debts, including the amount owed to Yale, were discharged. Meanwhile, she filed a suit in a Connecticut state court against the boy who shot Fountain and obtained funds for Fountain's medical care. These funds were deposited in an account, which is sometimes referred to as an "estate," established on Fountain's behalf. Yale filed a suit against Fountain's estate, asking the court to order the estate to pay Yale's bill, but the court ruled against Yale. Yale appealed to a state intermediate appellate court, which reversed this ruling and ordered the payment. The estate appealed to the state supreme court.

- **Decision and Rationale** The Connecticut Supreme Court affirmed the judgment of the lower court. Yale could collect from Fountain's estate for the cost of its services under the doctrine of necessaries. The state supreme court explained that "Connecticut has long recognized the common-law rule that a minor child's contracts are voidable" but "a minor may not avoid a contract for goods or services necessary for his health." The court reasoned that this principle is based on the theory of quasi contract. "Thus, when a medical service provider renders necessary medical care to an injured minor, two contracts arise: the primary contract between the provider and the minor's parents; and an implied-in-law contract between the provider and the minor himself. The primary contract between the provider and the parents is based on the parents' duty to pay for their children's necessary expenses * * * . The secondary implied-in-law contract between the medical services provider and the minor arises from equitable considerations, including the law's disfavor of unjust enrichment. Therefore, where necessary medical services are rendered to a minor whose parents do not pay for them, equity and justice demand that a secondary implied-in-law contract arise between the medical services provider and the minor who has received the benefits of those services."

- **What If the Facts Were Different?** *What might have happened in future cases if the court had held that there was no implied-in-law contract between Fountain and Yale Diagnostic Radiology?*

- **The Ethical Dimension** *How does the result in this case encourage payment on contracts for necessaries?*

Insurance and Loans. Traditionally, insurance has not been viewed as a necessary, so minors can ordinarily disaffirm their insurance contracts and recover all premiums paid. Some jurisdictions, though, prohibit the right to disaffirm insurance contracts—for example, when minors contract for life insurance on their own lives. Financial loans are seldom considered to be necessaries.

Ratification In contract law, **ratification** is the act of accepting and giving legal force to an obligation that previously was not enforceable. A minor who has reached the age of majority can ratify a contract expressly or impliedly. *Express* ratification takes place when the individual, on reaching the age of majority, states orally or in writing that he or she intends to be bound by the contract. *Implied* ratification takes place when the minor, on reaching the age of majority, indicates an intent to abide by the contract.

Suppose that Lin enters into a contract to sell her laptop to Arturo, a minor. If, on reaching the age of majority, Arturo writes a letter to Lin stating that he still agrees to buy the laptop, he has *expressly* ratified the contract. If, instead, Arturo takes possession of the laptop as a minor and continues to use it well after reaching the age of majority, he has *impliedly* ratified the contract.

If a minor fails to disaffirm a contract within a reasonable time after reaching the age of majority, then the court must determine whether the conduct constitutes ratification or disaffirmance. Generally, a contract that is *executed* (fully performed by both parties) is presumed to be ratified. A contract that is still *executory* (not yet fully performed by both parties) normally is considered to be disaffirmed.

Parents' Liability As a general rule, parents are not liable for contracts made by minor children acting on their own. This is why businesses ordinarily require parents to cosign any contract made with a minor. The parents then become personally obligated under the contract even if their child avoids liability.

Normally, minors are personally liable for their own torts. The parents of the minor can *also* be held liable in certain situations. In some states, parents may be liable if they failed to exercise proper parental control over the minor child when they knew or should have known that this lack of control posed an unreasonable risk of harm to others. Suppose that parents allow their eleven-year-old child to drive a car on public roads. If the child drives negligently and causes someone else to be injured, the parents may be held liable for the minor's tort (negligence). Other states have enacted statutes that impose liability on parents for certain tortious acts, such as those that are willful or grossly negligent, that their children commit. *Concept Summary 13.1* reviews the rules relating to contracts by minors.

Intoxication

Intoxication is a condition in which a person's normal capacity to act or think is inhibited by alcohol or some other drug.[4] A contract entered into by an intoxicated person can be either voidable or valid (and thus

4. Note that if an alcoholic makes a contract while sober, there is no lack of capacity. See *Wright v. Fisher,* 32 N.W. 605 (Mich. 1887).

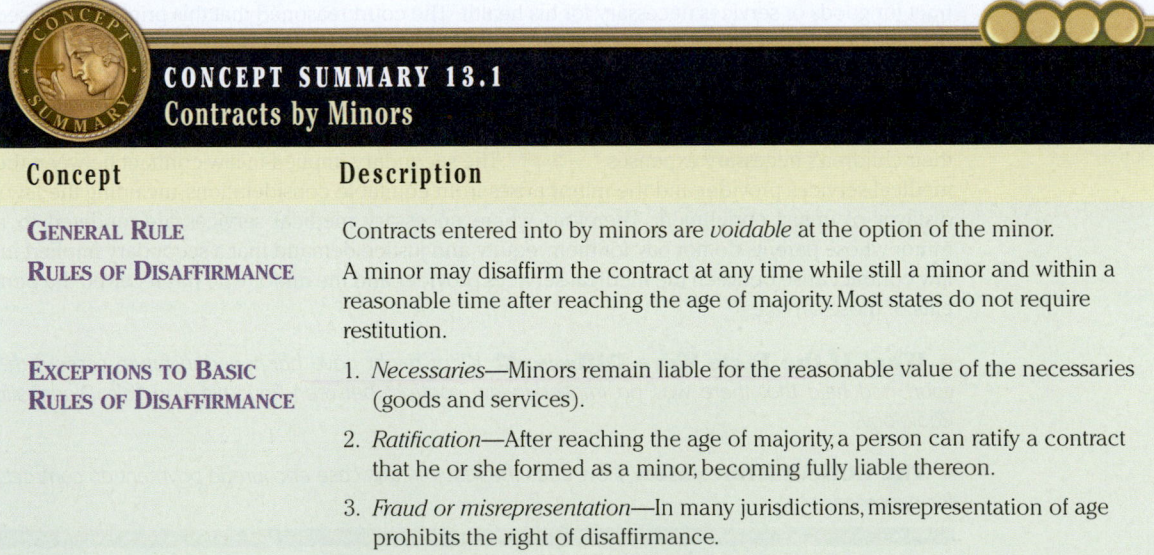

CONCEPT SUMMARY 13.1
Contracts by Minors

Concept	Description
GENERAL RULE	Contracts entered into by minors are *voidable* at the option of the minor.
RULES OF DISAFFIRMANCE	A minor may disaffirm the contract at any time while still a minor and within a reasonable time after reaching the age of majority. Most states do not require restitution.
EXCEPTIONS TO BASIC RULES OF DISAFFIRMANCE	1. *Necessaries*—Minors remain liable for the reasonable value of the necessaries (goods and services). 2. *Ratification*—After reaching the age of majority, a person can ratify a contract that he or she formed as a minor, becoming fully liable thereon. 3. *Fraud or misrepresentation*—In many jurisdictions, misrepresentation of age prohibits the right of disaffirmance.

enforceable). If the person was sufficiently intoxicated to lack mental capacity, then the contract may be voidable even if the intoxication was purely voluntary. For the contract to be voidable, however, the person must prove that the intoxication impaired her or his reason and judgment so severely that she or he did not comprehend the legal consequences of entering into the contract.

If, despite intoxication, the person understood the legal consequences of the agreement, the contract will be enforceable. The fact that the terms of the contract are foolish or obviously favor the other party does not make the contract voidable (unless the other party *fraudulently* induced the person to become intoxicated).

As a practical matter, courts rarely permit contracts to be avoided on the ground of intoxication because it is difficult to determine whether a party was sufficiently intoxicated to lack contractual capacity. Many courts prefer to look at objective indications of agreement when dealing with intoxicated parties.[5]

Disaffirmance If a contract is voidable because of a person's intoxication, that person has the option of disaffirming it while intoxicated and for a reasonable time after becoming sober—the same option available to a minor. To avoid the contract in most states, the person claiming intoxication must be able to return all consideration received—except in contracts involving necessaries. Contracts for necessaries are voidable, but the intoxicated person is liable in quasi contract for the reasonable value of the consideration received.

Ratification An intoxicated person, after becoming sober, may ratify a contract expressly or impliedly, just as a minor may do on reaching majority. Implied ratification occurs when a person enters into a contract while intoxicated and fails to disaffirm the contract within a *reasonable* time after becoming sober. Acts or conduct inconsistent with an intent to disaffirm—such as the continued use of property purchased under a voidable contract—will also ratify the contract. See *Concept Summary 13.2* for a review of the rules relating to contracts by intoxicated persons.

Mental Incompetence

Contracts made by mentally incompetent persons can be void, voidable, or valid. We look here at the circumstances that determine which of these classifications apply.

When the Contract Will Be Void If a court has previously determined that a person is mentally incompetent and has appointed a guardian to represent the individual, any contract made by the mentally incompetent person is *void*—no contract exists. Only the guardian can enter into binding legal obligations on the incompetent person's behalf.

When the Contract Will Be Voidable If a court has not previously judged a person to be mentally incompetent but in fact the person was

5. See, for example, Case 11.1 *(Lucy v. Zehmer)* in Chapter 11.

CONCEPT SUMMARY 13.2
Contracts by Intoxicated Persons

Concept	Description
GENERAL RULES	If a person was sufficiently intoxicated to lack the mental capacity to comprehend the legal consequences of entering into the contract, the contract may be *voidable* at the option of the intoxicated person. If, despite intoxication, the person understood these legal consequences, the contract will be enforceable.
DISAFFIRMANCE	An intoxicated person may disaffirm the contract at any time while intoxicated and for a reasonable time after becoming sober but must make full restitution. Contracts for necessaries are voidable, but the intoxicated person is liable for the reasonable value of the goods or services.
RATIFICATION	After becoming sober, a person can ratify a contract that she or he formed while intoxicated, becoming fully liable thereon.

incompetent at the time the contract was formed, the contract may be voidable. A contract is *voidable* if the person did not know he or she was entering into the contract or lacked the mental capacity to comprehend its nature, purpose, and consequences. Only the mentally incompetent person has the option to avoid the contract, not the other party. The contract may then be disaffirmed or ratified (if the person regains mental competence). Like intoxicated persons, mentally incompetent persons must return any consideration and pay for the reasonable value of any necessaries they receive.

For example, Milo, who had not been previously declared incompetent by a judge, agrees to sell twenty lots in a prime residential neighborhood to Anastof. At the time of entering the contract, Milo is mentally incompetent and is confused over which lots he is selling and how much they are worth. As a result, he contracts to sell the properties for substantially less than their market value. If the court finds that Milo was unable to understand the nature and consequences of the contract, Milo can avoid the sale, provided that he returns any consideration he received.

When the Contract Will Be Valid A contract entered into by a mentally incompetent person (whom a court has not previously declared incompetent) may also be *valid* if the person had capacity *at the time the contract was formed.* A person may be able to understand the nature and effect of entering into a certain contract yet simultaneously lack capacity to engage in other activities. If so, the contract will be valid because the person does not lack contractual capacity.[6] Similarly, an otherwise mentally incompetent person may have a *lucid interval*—a temporary restoration of sufficient intelligence, judgment, and will—during which she or he will be considered to have full legal capacity. See *Concept Summary 13.3* for a review of the rules relating to contracts entered into by mentally incompetent persons.

SECTION 2 Legality

For a contract to be valid and enforceable, it must be formed for a legal purpose. A contract to do something that is prohibited by federal or state statutory law is illegal and, as such, void from the outset and thus unenforceable. Also, a contract that calls for a tortious act or an action contrary to public policy is illegal and unenforceable. It is important to note that a contract or a clause in a contract may be illegal even in the absence of a specific statute prohibiting the action promised by the contract.

Contracts Contrary to Statute

Statutes often prescribe the terms of contracts. We now examine several ways in which contracts may be contrary to statute and thus illegal.

6. Modern courts no longer require a person to be completely irrational to disaffirm contracts on the basis of mental incompetence. A contract may be voidable if, by reason of a mental illness or defect, an individual was unable to act reasonably with respect to the transaction and the other party had reason to know of the condition.

CONCEPT SUMMARY 13.3
Contracts by Mentally Incompetent Persons

VOID	If a court has declared a person to be mentally incompetent and appointed a legal guardian, any contract made by that person is void from the outset.
VOIDABLE	If a court has *not* declared a person mentally incompetent, but that person lacked the capacity to comprehend the subject matter, nature, and consequences of the agreement, then the contract is voidable at that person's option.
VALID	If a court has *not* declared a person mentally incompetent and that person was able to understand the nature and effect of the contract at the time it was formed, then the contract is valid and enforceable.

Contracts to Commit a Crime Any contract to commit a crime is a contract in violation of a statute. Thus, a contract to sell an illegal drug (the sale of which is prohibited by statute) is not enforceable, and a contract to provide inside information regarding the sale of securities is unenforceable (violations of securities laws will be discussed in Chapter 41). Should the object or performance of the contract be rendered illegal by statute *after* the contract has been entered into, the contract is considered to be discharged by law. (See the discussion of impossibility or impracticability of performance in Chapter 17.)

Usury Virtually every state has a statute that sets the maximum rate of interest that can be charged for different types of transactions, including ordinary loans. A lender who makes a loan at an interest rate above the lawful maximum commits **usury.** The maximum rate of interest varies from state to state, as do the consequences for lenders who make usurious loans. Some states allow the lender to recover only the principal of a loan along with interest up to the legal maximum. In effect, the lender is denied recovery of the excess interest. In other states, the lender can recover the principal amount of the loan but no interest.

Although usury statutes place a ceiling on allowable rates of interest, exceptions have been made to facilitate business transactions. For example, many states exempt corporate loans from the usury laws, and nearly all states allow higher-interest-rate loans for borrowers who could not otherwise obtain funds.

Gambling All states have statutes that regulate gambling—defined as any scheme that involves a distribution of property by chance among persons who have paid a valuable consideration for the opportunity (chance) to receive the property. Gambling is the creation of risk for the purpose of assuming it. Traditionally, state statutes have deemed gambling contracts to be illegal and thus void.

In several states, however, including Louisiana, Michigan, Nevada, and New Jersey, casino gambling is lawful. In other states, certain forms of gambling are legal. California, for example, has not defined draw poker as a crime, although criminal statutes prohibit numerous other types of gambling games. A number of states allow gambling at horse races, and the majority of the states have legalized state-operated lotteries, as well as lotteries (such as bingo) conducted for charitable purposes. Many states also allow gambling on Indian reservations.

Sometimes, it is difficult to distinguish a gambling contract from the risk sharing inherent in almost all contracts. In one case, five co-workers each received a free lottery ticket from a customer and agreed to split the winnings if one of the tickets turned out to be the winning one. At first glance, this may seem entirely legal. The court, however, noted that the oral contract in this case "was an exchange of promises to share winnings from the parties' individually owned lottery tickets upon the happening of the uncertain event" that one of the tickets would win. Consequently, concluded the court, the agreement at issue was "founded on a gambling consideration" and therefore was void.[7]

Online Gambling A significant issue today is how gambling laws can be applied in the Internet context. Because state laws pertaining to gambling differ, online gambling raises a number of unique issues. For example, if a state does not allow casino gambling or offtrack betting, what can the state government do if its residents place bets online? Also, where does the actual act of gambling occur? Suppose that a resident of New York places bets via the Internet at a gambling site located in Antigua. Is the actual act of "gambling" taking place in New York or in Antigua? According to a New York court in one case, "if the person engaged in gambling is located in New York, then New York is the location where the gambling occurred."[8] Other states' courts may take a different view, however.

Another issue is whether entering into contracts that involve gambling on sports teams that do not really exist—fantasy sports—is a form of gambling. For a discussion of this issue, see this chapter's *Contemporary Legal Debates* feature on pages 252 and 253.

Sabbath (Sunday) Laws Statutes referred to as Sabbath (Sunday) laws prohibit the formation or performance of certain contracts on a Sunday. These statutes, which date back to colonial times, are often called blue laws. **Blue laws** get their name from the blue paper on which New Haven, Connecticut, printed its town ordinance in 1781 that prohibited work and required businesses to close on Sunday. According to a few state and local laws, all contracts entered into on a Sunday are illegal. Laws in other states or municipalities prohibit only the sale of certain types of merchandise, such as alcoholic beverages, on a Sunday.

7. *Dickerson v. Deno*, 770 So.2d 63 (Ala. 2000).
8. *United States v. Cohen*, 260 F.3d 68 (2d Cir. 2001).

CONTEMPORARY LEGAL DEBATES

Are Online Fantasy Sports Gambling?

As many as 20 million adults in the United States play some form of fantasy sports via the Internet. A fantasy sport is a game in which participants, often called owners, build teams composed of real-life players from different real-life teams. A fantasy team then competes against the fantasy teams belonging to other "owners." At the end of each week, the statistical performances of all the real-life players are translated into points, and the points of all the players on an owner's fantasy team are totaled. Although a wide variety of fantasy games are available, most participants play fantasy football. On many fantasy sports sites, participants pay a fee in order to play and use the site's facilities, such as statistical tracking and message boards; at the end of the season, prizes ranging from T-shirts to flat-screen televisions are awarded to the winners.

In other instances, the participants in fantasy sports gamble directly on the outcome. In a fantasy football league, for example, each participant-owner adds a given amount to the pot and then "drafts" his or her fantasy team from actual National Football League players. At the end of the football season, each owner's points are totaled, and the owner with the most points wins the pot.

Congress Weighs In

As online gambling has expanded, Congress has attempted to regulate it. In late 2006, a federal law went into effect that makes it illegal for credit-card companies and banks to engage in transactions with Internet gambling companies.[a] Although the law does not prohibit individuals from placing online bets, in effect it makes it almost impossible for them to do so by preventing them from obtaining financing for online gambling. At first glance, the legislation appears comprehensive, but it specifically exempts Internet wagers on horse racing, state lotteries, and fantasy sports. Hence, one could argue that Congress has determined that fantasy sports do not constitute a prohibited Internet gambling activity.

Testing the Gambling Aspect in Court

Thus far, the courts have had the opportunity to rule only on whether the pay-to-play fantasy sports sites that charge an entrance fee and offer prizes to the winners are running gambling operations. Charles Humphrey brought a lawsuit against Viacom, ESPN, *The Sporting News,* and other hosts of such fantasy sports sites under a New Jersey statute that allows the recovery of gambling losses. Humphrey claimed that the fantasy sports leagues were games of chance, not games of skill, because events beyond the participants' control could determine the

a. Security and Accountability for Every Port Act, Public L. No. 109-347, Sections 5361–5367, 120 Stat. 1884 (2006). (A version of the Unlawful Internet Gambling Enforcement Act of 2006 was incorporated into this statute as Title VIII.)

In most states with such statutes, contracts that were entered into on a Sunday can be ratified during a weekday. Also, if a contract that was entered into on a Sunday has been fully performed (executed), normally it cannot be rescinded (canceled). When the date of performance of a contract ends on Sunday, the general view is that the contract is performable on the next business day, and therefore it is not illegal. Many states do not enforce Sunday laws, and some state courts have held these laws to be unconstitutional because they interfere with the freedom of religion.

Licensing Statutes All states require that members of certain professions or occupations obtain licenses allowing them to practice. Physicians, lawyers, real estate brokers, architects, electricians, and stockbrokers are but a few of the people who must be licensed. Some licenses are obtained only after extensive schooling and examinations, which indicate to the public that a special skill has been acquired. Others require only that the particular person be of good moral character and pay a fee.

Generally, business licenses provide a means of regulating and taxing certain enterprises and protecting the public against actions that could threaten the general welfare. For example, in nearly all states, a stockbroker must be licensed and must file a bond with the state to protect the public from fraudulent stock transactions. Similarly, a plumber must be licensed and bonded to protect the public against incompetent plumbers and to protect the public health. Only per-

outcome—for example, a star quarterback might be injured. He also pointed out that in the offline world, federal law prohibits any games of chance, such as sweepstakes or drawings, that require entrants to submit consideration in order to play. *Consideration* has been defined as the purchase of a product or the payment of money. For these reasons, he argued, the entrance fees constituted gambling losses that could be recovered.

The federal district court that heard the case ruled against Humphrey, mostly on procedural grounds, but the court did conclude that as a matter of law the entrance fees did not constitute "bets" or "wagers" because the fees are paid unconditionally, the prizes offered are for a fixed amount and certain to be awarded, and the defendants do not compete for the prizes.[b] The court also observed that if a combination of entrance fees and prizes constituted gambling, a host of contests ranging from golf tournaments to track meets to spelling bees and beauty contests would be gambling operations—a conclusion that the court deemed "patently absurd."[c] Note, however, that the case involved only pay-to-play sites. The court did not have to address the question of whether fantasy sports sites that enable participants to contibute to a pot in the hopes of winning it at the end of the season constitute gambling sites.

WHERE DO YOU STAND?

Determining what is and what is not gambling does not always lend itself to an easy answer. If you buy a mutual fund that consists of a broad array of stocks and your purpose is to enhance your standard of living during your retirement, no one considers that gambling. In contrast, if you are a day trader—buying and selling stocks during a one-day period—you are clearly "betting" that the stocks you buy in the morning and then sell in the evening will have gone up in value. Should day trading be deemed gambling and therefore illegal? Where do you draw the line between what is and what is not gambling in our society?

b. *Humphrey v. Viacom, Inc.*, ___ F.Supp.2d ___ , 2007 WL1797648 (D.N.J. 2007).

c. In reaching this conclusion, the federal district court cited portions of an Arizona Supreme Court ruling, *State v. American Holiday Association, Inc.*, 151 Ariz. 312, 727 P.2d 807 (1986).

sons or businesses possessing the qualifications and complying with the conditions required by statute are entitled to licenses.

When a person enters into a contract with an unlicensed individual, the contract may still be enforceable, depending on the nature of the licensing statute. Some states expressly provide that the lack of a license in certain occupations bars the enforcement of work-related contracts. If the statute does not expressly declare this, one must look to the underlying purpose of the licensing requirements for a particular occupation. If the purpose is to protect the public from unauthorized practitioners, a contract involving an unlicensed individual normally is illegal and unenforceable. If the underlying purpose of the statute is to raise government revenues, however, a contract entered into with an unlicensed practitioner generally is enforceable—although the unlicensed person is usually fined.

Contracts Contrary to Public Policy

Although contracts involve private parties, some are not enforceable because of the negative impact they would have on society. Examples include a contract to commit an immoral act, such as selling a child, and a contract that prohibits marriage. We look here at certain types of business contracts that are often said to be *contrary to public policy.*

Contracts in Restraint of Trade Contracts in restraint of trade (anticompetitive agreements) usually adversely affect the public policy that favors competition in the economy. Typically, such contracts also violate one or more federal or state statutes.[9] An exception is recognized when the restraint is reasonable and is contained in an ancillary (secondary, or subordinate) clause in a contract. Many such exceptions involve a type of restraint called a **covenant not to compete,** or a *restrictive covenant.*

Covenants Not to Compete and the Sale of an Ongoing Business. Covenants (promises) not to compete are often contained as ancillary clauses in contracts concerning the sale of an ongoing business. A covenant not to compete is created when a seller agrees not to open a new store in a certain geographic area surrounding the existing store. Such agreements enable the seller to sell, and the purchaser to buy, the goodwill and reputation of an ongoing business. If, for example, a well-known merchant sells her store and opens a competing business a block away, many customers will likely do business at the merchant's new store. This, in turn, renders less valuable the good name and reputation purchased for a price by the new owner of the old store. If a covenant not to compete is not ancillary to a sales agreement, however, it is void, because it unreasonably restrains trade and is contrary to public policy.

9. Federal statutes include the Sherman Antitrust Act, the Clayton Act, and the Federal Trade Commission Act (see Chapter 46).

Covenants Not to Compete in Employment Contracts. Agreements not to compete (sometimes referred to as *noncompete agreements*) can also be contained in employment contracts. People in middle- or upper-level management positions commonly agree not to work for competitors or not to start competing businesses for a specified period of time after termination of employment. Such agreements are legal in most states so long as the specified period of time (of restraint) is not excessive in duration and the geographic restriction is reasonable. What constitutes a reasonable time period may be shorter in the online environment than in conventional employment contracts because the restrictions apply worldwide. (For a further discussion of this issue, see this chapter's *Business Application* feature on page 256.)

To be reasonable, a restriction on competition must protect a legitimate business interest and must not be any greater than necessary to protect that interest.[10] In the following case, the court had to decide whether it was reasonable for an employer's noncompete agreement to restrict a former employee from competing "in any area of business" in which the employer was engaged.

10. See, for example, *Gould & Lamb, LLC v. D'Alusio,* 949 So.2d 1212 (Fla.App. 2007). See also *Moore v. Midwest Distribution, Inc.,* 76 Ark.App. 397, 65 S.W.3d 490 (2002).

CASE 13.2 Stultz v. Safety and Compliance Management, Inc.

Court of Appeals of Georgia, 2007. 285 Ga.App. 799, 648 S.E.2d 129.

• **Background and Facts** Safety and Compliance Management, Inc. (S&C), in Rossville, Georgia, provides alcohol- and drug-testing services in multiple states. In February 2002, S&C hired Angela Burgess. Her job duties included providing customer service, ensuring that specimens were properly retrieved from clients and transported to the testing lab, contacting clients, and managing the office. Burgess signed a covenant not to compete "in any area of business conducted by Safety and Compliance Management . . . for a two-year period . . . beginning at the termination of employment." In May 2004, Burgess quit her job to work at Rossville Medical Center (RMC) as a medical assistant. RMC provides medical services, including occupational medicine, medical physicals, and workers' compensation injury treatment. RMC also offers alcohol- and drug-testing services. Burgess's duties included setting patient appointments, taking patient medical histories, checking vital signs, performing urinalysis testing, administering injections, conducting alcohol-breath tests, and collecting specimens for drug testing. S&C filed a suit in a Georgia state court against Burgess and others (including a defendant named Stultz), alleging, among other things, that she had violated the noncompete agreement. The court issued a summary judgment in S&C's favor. Burgess appealed to a state intermediate appellate court.

• **Decision and Rationale** The appellate court reversed the judgment of the lower court. The reviewing court pointed out that noncompete clauses in employment contracts cannot

CASE 13.2 CONTINUED impose an unreasonable restraint of trade. "A three-element test of duration, territorial coverage, and scope of activity has evolved as a helpful tool in examining the reasonableness of the particular factual setting to which it is applied." The noncompete clause in Burgess's employment contract stated that she would "not compete in any area of business conducted by [her employer]." This agreement, concluded the court, was intended to prevent any type of competing activity whatsoever. The covenant not to compete was "overly broad and indefinite." Therefore, it was unenforceable.

- **The Ethical Dimension** *To determine the enforceability of a covenant not to compete, the courts balance the rights of an employer against those of a former employee. What are these rights? How did S&C's covenant not to compete tip the balance in the employer's favor?*
- **The Global Dimension** *Should an employer be permitted to restrict a former employee from engaging in a competing business on a global level? Why or why not?*

Enforcement Problems. The laws governing the enforceability of covenants not to compete vary significantly from state to state. In some states, such as Texas, such a covenant will not be enforced unless the employee has received some benefit in return for signing the noncompete agreement. This is true even if the covenant is reasonable as to time and area. If the employee receives no benefit, the covenant will be deemed void. California prohibits the enforcement of covenants not to compete altogether.

If a covenant is found to be unreasonable in time or geographic area, courts in some jurisdictions may convert the terms into reasonable ones and then enforce the reformed covenant. A court normally will engage in this kind of rewriting of the terms only in rare situations, however, when it is necessary to prevent undue burdens or hardships.

Unconscionable Contracts or Clauses

Ordinarily, a court does not look at the fairness or equity of a contract. For example, the courts generally do not inquire into the adequacy of consideration (as discussed in Chapter 12). Persons are assumed to be reasonably intelligent, and the courts will not come to their aid just because they have made an unwise or foolish bargain. In certain circumstances, however, bargains are so oppressive that the courts relieve innocent parties of part or all of their duties. Such bargains are deemed **unconscionable** because they are so unscrupulous or grossly unfair as to be "void of conscience."[11] A contract can be unconscionable on either procedural or substantive grounds, as discussed in the following subsections and illustrated graphically in Exhibit 13–1 on page 257.

Procedural Unconscionability. *Procedural* unconscionability has to do with how a term becomes part of a contract and involves factors that make it difficult for a party to know or understand the contract terms—for example, inconspicuous print, unintelligible language ("legalese"), or the lack of an opportunity to read the contract or to ask questions about its meaning. Procedural unconscionability may also occur when there is such disparity in bargaining power between the two parties that the weaker party's consent is not voluntary. Contracts entered into because of one party's vastly superior bargaining power may be deemed unconscionable. These situations often involve an **adhesion contract,** which is a contract written exclusively by one party (the dominant party, usually the seller or creditor) and presented to the other (the adhering party, usually the buyer or borrower) on a take-it-or-leave-it basis.[12] In other words, the adhering party has no opportunity to negotiate the terms of the contract. Standard-form contracts are often adhesion contracts.

Substantive Unconscionability. *Substantive* unconscionability characterizes those contracts, or portions of contracts, that are oppressive or overly harsh. Courts generally focus on provisions that deprive one party of the benefits of the agreement or leave that party without a remedy for nonperformance by the other. For example, a person with little income and with only a

11. The Uniform Commercial Code incorporated the concept of unconscionability in Sections 2–302 and 2A–108. These provisions, which apply to contracts for the sale or lease of goods, will be discussed in Chapter 20.

12. For a classic case involving an adhesion contract, see *Henningsen v. Bloomfield Motors, Inc.,* 32 N.J. 358, 161 A.2d 69 (1960).

BUSINESS APPLICATION
Covenants Not to Compete in the Internet Context

MANAGEMENT FACES A LEGAL ISSUE

For some companies today, particularly those in high-tech industries, trade secrets are their most valuable assets. Often, to prevent departing employees from disclosing trade secrets to competing employers, business owners and managers have their key employees sign covenants not to compete. In such a covenant, the employee typically agrees not to set up a competing business or work for a competitor in a specified geographic area for a certain period of time. Generally, the time and geographic restrictions must be reasonable. A serious issue facing management today is whether time and space restrictions that have been deemed reasonable in the past serve as a guide to what might constitute reasonable restrictions in today's changing legal landscape, which includes the Internet environment.

WHAT THE COURTS SAY

There is little case law to guide management on this issue. One case involved Mark Schlack, who worked as a Web site manager for EarthWeb, Inc., in New York. Schlack signed a covenant stating that, on termination of his employment, he would not work for any competing company for one year. When he resigned and accepted an offer from a company in Massachusetts to design a Web site, EarthWeb sued to enforce the covenant not to compete. The court refused to enforce the covenant, in part because there was no evidence that Schlack had misappropriated any of EarthWeb's trade secrets or clients. The court also stated that because the Internet lacks physical borders, a covenant prohibiting an employee from working for a competitor anywhere in the world for one year is excessive in duration.[a]

In a later case, a federal district court enforced a one-year noncompete agreement against the founder of a law-related Web site business even though no geographic restriction was included in the agreement. According to the court, "Although there is no geographic limitation on the provision, this is nonetheless reasonable in light of the national, and indeed international, nature of Internet business."[b]

The sale of an Internet-only business involves literally the full worldwide scope of the Internet itself. In a relatively recent case, a company selling vitamins over the Internet was sold for more than $2 million. The purchase agreement contained a noncompete clause. For four years after the sale, the seller was prohibited from engaging in the sale of nutritional and health products via the Internet. The court pointed out that the seller was still able to engage in his former business by other means using non-Internet markets. The seller also remained free to sell other types of products on the Internet. Notwithstanding the noncompete agreement, the seller created at least two other Internet sites from which he sold health products and vitamins. The court held for the buyer of the Internet-only business and enjoined (prevented) the seller from violating the noncompete agreement.[c]

IMPLICATIONS FOR MANAGERS

Management in high-tech companies should avoid overreaching in terms of time and geographic restrictions in noncompete agreements. Additionally, when considering the reasonability of time and place restrictions, the courts tend to balance time restrictions against other factors, such as geographic restrictions. Because for Web-based work the geographic restriction can be worldwide in scope, the time restriction should be narrowed considerably to compensate for the extensive geographic restriction.

a. *EarthWeb, Inc. v. Schlack,* 71 F.Supp.2d 299 (S.D.N.Y. 1999).

b. *West Publishing Corp. v. Stanley,* 2004 WL 73590 (D.N.D. 2004).

c. *MyVitaNet.com v. Kowalski,* __ F.Supp.2d __, 2008 WL 203008 (S.D. Ohio 2008).

fourth-grade education agrees to purchase a refrigerator for $4,000 and signs a two-year installment contract. The same type of refrigerator usually sells for $900 on the market. Some courts have held this type of contract to be unconscionable because the contract terms are so oppressive as to "shock the conscience" of the court.[13]

Substantive unconscionability can arise in a wide variety of business contexts. For example, a contract clause that gives the business entity free access to the courts but requires the other party to arbitrate any dispute with the firm may be unconscionable.[14] Similarly, an arbitration clause in a credit-card agreement that prevents credit cardholders from obtaining relief for abusive

13. See, for example, *Jones v. Star Credit Corp.*, 59 Misc.2d 189, 298 N.Y.S.2d 264 (1969). This case will be presented in Chapter 20 as Case 20.3.

14. See, for example, *Wisconsin Auto Loans, Inc. v. Jones,* 290 Wis.2d 514, 714 N.W.2d 155 (2006).

EXHIBIT 13–1 • Unconscionability

UNCONSCIONABLE CONTRACT OR CLAUSE

This is a contract or clause that is void for reasons of public policy.

PROCEDURAL UNCONSCIONABILITY

This occurs if a contract is entered into, or a term becomes part of, the contract because of a party's lack of knowledge or understanding of the contract or the term.

FACTORS THAT COURTS CONSIDER

- Is the print inconspicuous?
- Is the language unintelligible?
- Did one party lack an opportunity to ask questions about the contract?
- Was there a disparity of bargaining power between the parties?

SUBSTANTIVE UNCONSCIONABILITY

This exists when a contract, or one of its terms, is oppressive or overly harsh.

FACTORS THAT COURTS CONSIDER

- Does a provision deprive one party of the benefits of the agreement?
- Does a provision leave one party without a remedy for nonperformance by the other?

debt-collection practices under consumer law may be unconscionable.[15] Contracts drafted by insurance companies and cell phone providers have been struck down as substantively unconscionable when they included provisions that were overly harsh or one sided.[16]

Exculpatory Clauses Closely related to the concept of unconscionability are **exculpatory clauses**—clauses that release a party from liability in the event of monetary or physical injury *no matter who is at fault.* Indeed, courts sometimes refuse to enforce such clauses on the ground that they are unconscionable. For example, an employer requires its employees to sign a contract containing a provision that shields the employer from liability for any injuries to those employees. In that situation, a court would usually hold the exculpatory clause to be contrary to public policy.[17]

Exculpatory clauses found in rental agreements for commercial property are frequently held to be contrary to public policy, and such clauses are almost always unenforceable in residential property leases.

Although courts view exculpatory clauses with disfavor, they do enforce such clauses when they do not contravene public policy, are not ambiguous, and do not claim to protect parties from liability for intentional misconduct. Businesses such as health clubs, racetracks, amusement parks, skiing facilities, horse-rental operations, golf-cart concessions, and skydiving organizations frequently use exculpatory clauses to limit their liability for patrons' injuries. Because these services are not essential, the firms offering them are sometimes considered to have no relative advantage in bargaining strength, and anyone contracting for their services is considered to do so voluntarily.

Sometimes, a company includes an indemnification provision in its contracts with *independent contractors* (see Chapter 31). Such a provision, or clause, removes any responsibility on the company's part for accidents that happen to the independent contractor while working for the company. When is such a provision against public policy? This was the main question in the following case.

15. See, for example, *Coady v. Cross County Bank*, 2007 WI App 26, 299 Wis.2d 420, 729 N.W.2d 732 (2007).

16. See, for example, *Gatton v. T-Mobile USA, Inc.*, 152 Cal.App.4th 571, 61 Cal.Rptr.3d 344 (2007); *Kinkel v. Cingular Wireless, LLC*, 223 Ill.2d 1, 857 N.E.2d 250, 306 Ill.Dec. 157 (2006); and *Aul v. Golden Rule Insurance Co.*, 2007 WI App 165, 737 N.W.2d 24 (2007).

17. For a case with similar facts, see *Little Rock & Fort Smith Railway Co. v. Eubanks*, 48 Ark. 460, 3 S.W. 808 (1887). Today, this type of exculpatory clause may also be illegal on the basis of a violation of a state workers' compensation law.

CASE 13.3 Speedway SuperAmerica, LLC v. Erwin

Court of Appeals of Kentucky, 2008. 250 S.W.3d 339.

• **Background and Facts** Speedway SuperAmerica, LLC, hired Sebert Erwin to provide "General Contracting" for five years, but reserved the right to end the contract at any time. The contract contained an *indemnification* clause. Under that clause, Erwin promised to "hold harmless" Speedway for anything that happened to him while working for the company. One day, Erwin was told to report to a Speedway gas station in another city and help remove a walk-in freezer. When he was helping load it on a truck, he fell and was injured. Erwin sued Speedway for damages resulting from the injury he suffered. Speedway counterclaimed, seeking enforcement of the contract's indemnification clause. Erwin moved to dismiss the counterclaim on the grounds that the indemnification clause was invalid and unenforceable because it was against public policy. The trial court held for Erwin. Speedway appealed.

• **Decision and Rationale** The appeals court affirmed the trial court's ruling, holding that the indemnification clause was contrary to public policy and could not be enforced. The contract was one sided because it was between a chain of convenience stores and a single worker. While such contracts are not always against public policy, they are when there is no bargaining between parties of similar strength. Here, the situation involved one worker with an eighth-grade education contracting with a large company; the bargaining powers were clearly unequal. Erwin was called an independent contractor despite not having control over his work. The contract stated that he agreed to defend the owner and hold it harmless in the event of any negligence. As an independent contractor rather than an employee, Erwin had no right to workers' compensation or other benefits that an employee normally would be due (see Chapter 31 for a full discussion of the distinction between employees and independent contractors). The contract was the equivalent of an exculpatory clause, releasing the employer from any liability regardless of fault. It could not be enforced.

• **What If the Facts Were Different?** *Suppose that Erwin worked for another company as a mover and his employer had sent him to help Speedway move the freezer. Suppose further that the indemnification clause was in a contract signed between Speedway and Erwin's employer. Would that clause be valid? Explain your answer.*

• **The Ethical Dimension** *What benefit was there for Speedway to impose such a clause on Erwin?*

Discriminatory Contracts Contracts in which a party promises to discriminate on the basis of race, color, national origin, religion, gender, age, or disability are contrary to both statute and public policy. They are also unenforceable.[18] For example, if a property owner promises in a contract not to sell the property to a member of a particular race, the contract is unenforceable. The public policy underlying these prohibitions is very strong, and the courts are quick to invalidate discriminatory contracts. Exhibit 13–2 illustrates the types of contracts that may be illegal because they are contrary to statute or public policy.

18. The major federal statute prohibiting discrimination is the Civil Rights Act of 1964, 42 U.S.C. Sections 2000e–2000e-17. For a discussion of this act and other acts prohibiting discrimination in the employment context, see Chapter 34.

Effect of Illegality

In general, an illegal contract is void—that is, the contract is deemed never to have existed, and the courts will not aid either party. In most illegal contracts, both parties are considered to be ***in pari delicto***[19] (equally at fault). In such cases, the contract is void. If the contract is executory, neither party can enforce it. If it has been executed, there can be neither contractual nor quasi-contractual recovery.

That one wrongdoer who is a party to an illegal contract is unjustly enriched at the expense of the other is of no concern to the law—except under certain special circumstances that will be discussed below. The major justification for this hands-off atti-

19. Pronounced in *pah*-ree deh-*lick*-tow.

EXHIBIT 13–2 • Contract Legality

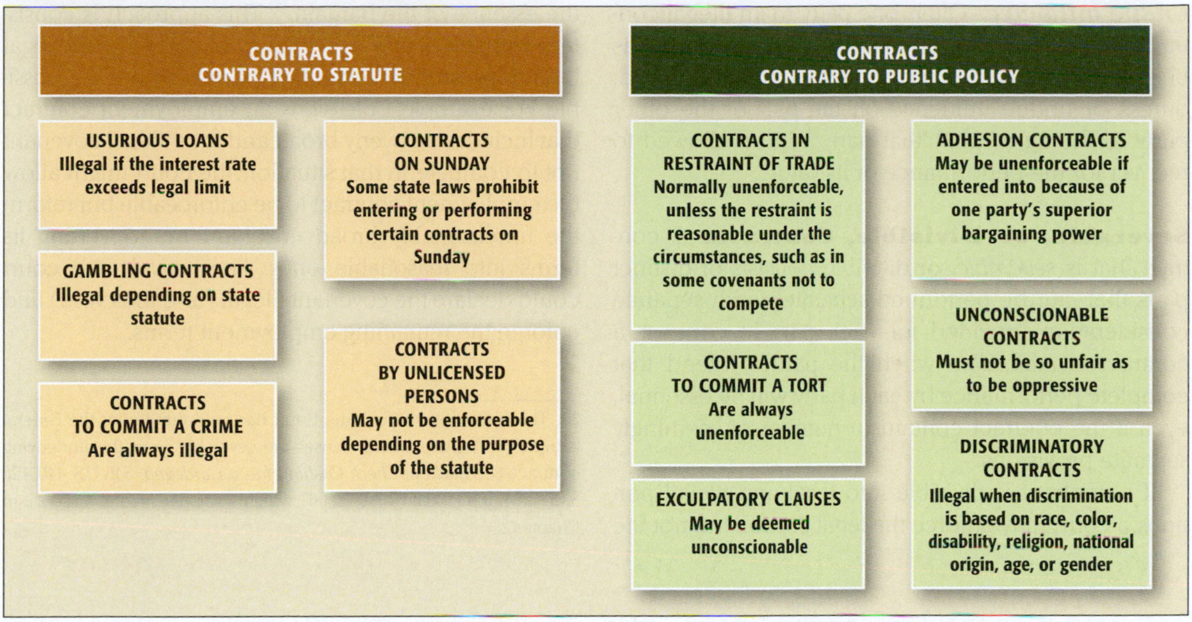

tude is that it is improper to place the machinery of justice at the disposal of a plaintiff who has broken the law by entering into an illegal bargain. Another justification is the hoped-for deterrent effect of this general hands-off rule. A plaintiff who suffers loss because of an illegal bargain should presumably be deterred from entering into similar illegal bargains.

Exceptions to the General Rule There are some exceptions to the general rule that neither party to an illegal bargain can sue for breach and that neither party can recover for performance rendered.

Justifiable Ignorance of the Facts. When one of the parties is relatively innocent, that party can often recover any benefits conferred in a partially executed contract. In this situation, the courts will not enforce the contract but will allow the parties to return to their original positions. An innocent party who has fully performed under the contract may sometimes enforce the contract against the guilty party. For example, a trucking company contracts with Gillespie to carry goods to a specific destination for a normal fee of $5,000. The trucker delivers the goods and later finds out that the contents of the shipped crates were illegal. Although the law specifies that the shipment, use, and sale of the goods were illegal, the trucker, being an innocent party, can still legally collect the $5,000 from Gillespie.

Members of Protected Classes. When a statute is clearly designed to protect a certain class of people, a member of that class can enforce a contract in violation of the statute even though the other party cannot. For example, flight attendants and pilots are subject to a federal statute that prohibits them from flying more than a certain number of hours every month. If an attendant or a pilot exceeds the maximum, the airline must nonetheless pay for those extra hours of service.

State statutes often regulate the sale of insurance. If an insurance company violates a statute when selling insurance, the purchaser can nevertheless enforce the policy and recover from the insurer.

Withdrawal from an Illegal Agreement. If an agreement has been only partly carried out and the illegal portion of the bargain has not yet been performed, the party rendering performance can withdraw from the contract and recover the performance or its value. For example, Sam and Jim decide to wager (illegally) on the outcome of a boxing match. Each deposits money with a stakeholder, who agrees to pay the winner of the bet. At this point, each party has performed part of the agreement, but the illegal element of the agreement will not occur until the funds are paid to the winner. Before such payment occurs, either party is entitled to withdraw from the bargain by giving notice of repudiation to the stakeholder.

Contract Illegal through Fraud, Duress, or Undue Influence. Often, one party to an illegal contract is more at fault than the other. When a party has been induced to enter into an illegal bargain by fraud, duress, or undue influence on the part of the other party to the agreement, that party will be allowed to recover for the performance or its value.

Severable, or Divisible, Contracts A contract that is *severable,* or divisible, consists of distinct parts that can be performed separately, with separate consideration provided for each part. In contrast, a contract is *indivisible* when the parties intend that complete performance by each party will be essential, even if the contract contains a number of seemingly separate provisions.

If a contract is divisible into legal and illegal portions, a court may enforce the legal portion but not the illegal one, so long as the illegal portion does not affect the essence of the bargain.[20] This approach is consistent with the courts' basic policy of enforcing the legal intentions of the contracting parties whenever possible. For example, Cole signs an employment contract that includes an overly broad and thus illegal covenant not to compete. In that situation, the court might allow the employment contract to be enforceable but reform the unreasonably broad covenant by converting its terms into reasonable ones. Alternatively, the court could declare the covenant illegal (and thus void) and enforce the remaining employment terms.

20. The United States Supreme Court has held that under the Federal Arbitration Act, arbitration clauses are severable from the underlying contract. See *Buckeye Check Cashing, Inc. v. Cardegna,* 546 U.S. 440, 126 S.Ct. 1204, 163 L.Ed.2d 1038 (2006), which was presented as Case 2.2 in Chapter 2.

REVIEWING Capacity and Legality

Renee Beaver started racing go-karts competitively in 1997, when she was fourteen. Many of the races required her to sign an exculpatory clause to participate, which she or her parents regularly signed. In 2000, she participated in the annual Elkhart Grand Prix, a series of races in Elkhart, Indiana. During the event in which she drove, a piece of foam padding used as a course barrier was torn from its base and ended up on the track. A portion of the padding struck Beaver in the head, and another portion was thrown into oncoming traffic, causing a multikart collision during which she sustained severe injuries. Beaver filed an action against the race organizers for negligence. The organizers could not locate the exculpatory clause that Beaver was supposed to have signed. Race organizers argued that she must have signed one to enter the race, but even if she had not signed one, her actions showed her intent to be bound by its terms. Using the information presented in the chapter, answer the following questions.

1. Did Beaver have the contractual capacity to enter a contract with an exculpatory clause? Why or why not?
2. Assuming that Beaver did, in fact, sign the exculpatory clause, did she later disaffirm or ratify the contract? Explain.
3. Now assume that Beaver had stated that she was eighteen years old at the time that she signed the exculpatory clause. How might this affect Beaver's ability to disaffirm or ratify the contract?
4. If Beaver did not actually sign the exculpatory clause, could a court conclude that she impliedly accepted its terms by participating in the race? Why or why not?

TERMS AND CONCEPTS

adhesion contract 255
age of majority 245
blue laws 251
contractual capacity 245
covenant not to compete 254
disaffirmance 245
emancipation 245
exculpatory clause 257
in pari delicto 258
necessaries 246
ratification 248
unconscionable 255
usury 251

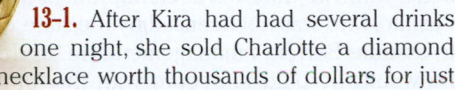

QUESTIONS AND CASE PROBLEMS

13–1. After Kira had had several drinks one night, she sold Charlotte a diamond necklace worth thousands of dollars for just $100. The next day, Kira offered the $100 to Charlotte and requested the return of her necklace. Charlotte refused to accept the $100 or return the necklace, claiming that there was a valid contract of sale. Kira explained that she had been intoxicated at the time the bargain was made and thus the contract was voidable at her option. Was Kira correct? Explain.

13–2. QUESTION WITH SAMPLE ANSWER

A famous New York City hotel, Hotel Lux, is noted for its food as well as its luxury accommodations. Hotel Lux contracts with a famous chef, Chef Perlee, to become its head chef at $6,000 per month. The contract states that should Perlee leave the employment of Hotel Lux for any reason, he will not work as a chef for any hotel or restaurant in New York, New Jersey, or Pennsylvania for a period of one year. During the first six months of the contract, Hotel Lux heavily advertises Perlee as its head chef, and business at the hotel is excellent. Then a dispute arises between the hotel management and Perlee, and Perlee terminates his employment. One month later, he is hired by a famous New Jersey restaurant just across the New York state line. Hotel Lux learns of Perlee's employment through a large advertisement in a New York City newspaper. It seeks to enjoin (prevent) Perlee from working in that restaurant as a chef for one year. Discuss how successful Hotel Lux will be in its action.

- **For a sample answer to Question 13–2, go to Appendix I at the end of this text.**

13–3. Joanne is a seventy-five-year-old widow who survives on her husband's small pension. Joanne has become increasingly forgetful, and her family worries that she may have Alzheimer's disease (a brain disorder that seriously affects a person's ability to carry out daily activities). No physician has diagnosed her, however, and no court has ruled on Joanne's legal competence. One day while she is out shopping, Joanne stops by a store that is having a sale on pianos and enters into a fifteen-year installment contract to buy a grand piano. When the piano arrives the next day, Joanne seems confused and repeatedly asks the deliveryperson why a piano is being delivered. Joanne claims that she does not recall buying a piano. Explain whether this contract is void, voidable, or valid. Can Joanne avoid her contractual obligation to buy the piano? If so, how?

13–4. Covenants Not to Compete. In 1993, Mutual Service Casualty Insurance Co. and its affiliates (collectively, MSI) hired Thomas Brass as an insurance agent. Three years later, Brass entered into a career agent's contract with MSI. This contract contained provisions regarding Brass's activities after termination. These provisions stated that, for a period of not less than one year, Brass could not solicit any MSI customers to "lapse, cancel, or replace" any insurance contract in force with MSI in an effort to take that business to a competitor. If he did, MSI could at any time refuse to pay the commissions that it otherwise owed him. The contract also restricted Brass from working for American National Insurance Co. for three years after termination. In 1998, Brass quit MSI and immediately went to work for American National, soliciting MSI customers. MSI filed a suit in a Wisconsin state court against Brass, claiming that he had violated the noncompete terms of his MSI contract. Should the court enforce the covenant not to compete? Why or why not? [*Mutual Service Casualty Insurance Co. v. Brass,* 2001 WI App 92, 242 Wis.2d 733, 625 N.W.2d 648 (2001)]

13–5. Unconscionability. Frank Rodziewicz was driving a Volvo tractor-trailer on Interstate 90 in Lake County, Indiana, when he struck a concrete barrier. His tractor-trailer became stuck on the barrier, and the Indiana State Police contacted Waffco Heavy Duty Towing, Inc., to assist in the recovery of the truck. Before beginning work,

Waffco told Rodziewicz that it would cost $275 to tow the truck. There was no discussion of labor or any other costs. Rodziewicz told Waffco to take the truck to a local Volvo dealership. Within a few minutes, Waffco pulled the truck off the barrier and towed it to Waffco's nearby towing yard. Rodziewicz was soon notified that, in addition to the $275 towing fee, he would have to pay $4,070 in labor costs and that Waffco would not release the truck until payment was made. Rodziewicz paid the total amount. Disputing the labor charge, however, he filed a suit in an Indiana state court against Waffco, alleging, in part, breach of contract. Was the towing contract unconscionable? Would it make a difference if the parties had discussed the labor charge before the tow? Explain. [*Rodziewicz v. Waffco Heavy Duty Towing, Inc.*, 763 N.E.2d 491 (Ind.App. 2002)]

13–6. CASE PROBLEM WITH SAMPLE ANSWER Millennium Club, Inc., operates a tavern in South Bend, Indiana. In January 2003, Pamela Avila and other minors gained admission by misrepresenting themselves to be at least twenty-one years old. According to the club's representatives, the minors used false driver's licenses, "fraudulent transfer of a stamp used to gain admission by another patron or other means of false identification." To gain access, the minors also signed affidavits falsely attesting to the fact that they were aged twenty-one or older. When the state filed criminal charges against the club, the club filed a suit in an Indiana state court against Avila and more than two hundred others, charging that they had misrepresented their ages and seeking damages of $3,000 each. The minors filed a motion to dismiss the complaint. Should the court grant the motion? What are the competing policy interests in this case? If the club was not careful in checking minors' identification, should it be allowed to recover? If the club reasonably relied on the minors' representations, should the minors be allowed to avoid liability? Discuss. [*Millennium Club, Inc. v. Avila*, 809 N.E.2d 906 (Ind.App. 2004)]

- **To view a sample answer for Problem 13–6, go to this book's Web site at www.cengage.com/blaw/jentz, select "Chapter 13," and click on "Case Problem with Sample Answer."**

13–7. Covenant Not to Compete. Gary Forsee was an executive officer with responsibility for the U.S. operations of BellSouth Corp., a company providing global telecommunications services. Under a covenant not to compete, Forsee agreed that for a period of eighteen months after termination from employment, he would not "provide services . . . in competition with [BellSouth] . . . to any person or entity which provides products or services identical or similar to products and services provided by [BellSouth] . . . within the territory." *Territory* was defined to include the geographic area in which Forsee provided services to BellSouth. The *services* included "management, strategic planning, business planning, administration, or other participation in or providing advice with respect to the communications services business." Forsee announced his intent to resign and accept a position as chief executive officer of Sprint Corp., a competitor of BellSouth. BellSouth filed a suit in a Georgia state court against Forsee, claiming, in part, that his acceptance of employment with Sprint would violate the covenant not to compete. Is the covenant legal? Should it be enforced? Why or why not? [*BellSouth Corp. v. Forsee*, 265 Ga.App. 589, 595 S.E.2d 99 (2004)]

13–8. Licensing Statutes. Under California law, a contract to manage a professional boxer must be in writing, and the manager must be licensed by the State Athletic Commission. Marco Antonio Barrera is a professional boxer and two-time world champion. In May 2003, José Castillo, who was not licensed by the state, orally agreed to assume Barrera's management. He "understood" that he would be paid in accord with the "practice in the professional boxing industry, but in no case less than ten percent (10%) of the gross revenue" that Barrera generated as a boxer and through endorsements. Among other accomplishments, Castillo negotiated an exclusive promotion contract for Barrera with Golden Boy Promotions, Inc., which is owned and operated by Oscar De La Hoya. Castillo also helped Barrera settle three lawsuits and resolve unrelated tax problems so that Barrera could continue boxing. Castillo did not train Barrera, pick his opponents, or arrange his fights, however. When Barrera abruptly stopped communicating with Castillo, Castillo filed a suit in a California state court against Barrera and others, alleging breach of contract. Under what circumstances is a contract with an unlicensed practitioner enforceable? Is the alleged contract in this case enforceable? Why or why not? [*Castillo v. Barrera*, 146 Cal.App.4th 1317, 53 Cal.Rptr.3d 494 (2 Dist. 2007)]

13–9. A QUESTION OF ETHICS

Dow AgroSciences, LLC (DAS), makes and sells agricultural seed products. In 2000, Timothy Glenn, a DAS sales manager, signed a covenant not to compete. He agreed that for two years from the date of his termination, he would not "engage in or contribute my knowledge to any work or activity involving an area of technology or business that is then competitive with a technology or business with respect to which I had access to Confidential Information during the five years immediately prior to such termination." Working with DAS business, operations, and research and development personnel, and being a member of high-level teams, Glenn had access to confidential DAS information, including agreements with DAS's business partners, marketing plans, litigation details, product secrets, new product development, future plans, and pricing strategies. In 2006, Glenn resigned to work for Pioneer Hi-Bred International, Inc., a DAS competitor. DAS filed a suit in an Indiana state court against Glenn, asking that he be enjoined from accepting any "position that would call on him to use confidential DAS information." [Glenn v. Dow AgroSciences, LLC, *861 N.E.2d 1 (Ind.App. 2007)*]

(a) Generally, what interests are served by enforcing covenants not to compete? What interests are served by refusing to enforce them?
(b) What argument could be made in support of reforming (and then enforcing) illegal covenants not to compete? What argument could be made against this practice?
(c) How should the court rule in this case? Why?

13–10. VIDEO QUESTION

Go to this text's Web site at **www.cengage.com/blaw/jentz** and select "Chapter 13." Click on "Video Questions" and view the video titled *The Money Pit*. Then answer the following questions.

(a) Assume that a valid contract exists between Walter (Tom Hanks) and the plumber. Recall from the video that the plumber had at least two drinks before agreeing to take on the plumbing job. If the plumber was intoxicated, is the contract voidable? Why or why not?
(b) Suppose that state law requires plumbers in Walter's state to have a plumber's license and that this plumber does not have a license. Would the contract be enforceable? Why or why not?
(c) In the video, the plumber suggests that Walter has been "turned down by every other plumber in the valley." Although the plumber does not even look at the house's plumbing, he agrees to do the repairs if Walter gives him a check for $5,000 right away "before he changes his mind." If Walter later seeks to void the contract because it is contrary to public policy, what should he argue?

LAW ON THE WEB

For updated links to resources available on the Web, as well as a variety of other materials, visit this text's Web site at

www.cengage.com/blaw/jentz

For a table that includes links to every state's statutory provisions governing the emancipation of minors, go to

topics.law.cornell.edu/wex/table_emancipation

For more information on restrictive covenants in employment contracts, you can access an article written by attorneys at Loose Brown & Associates, P.C., at

www.loosebrown.com/articles/art009.pdf

Legal Research Exercises on the Web

Go to **www.cengage.com/blaw/jentz**, the Web site that accompanies this text. Select "Chapter 13" and click on "Internet Exercises." There you will find the following Internet research exercises that you can perform to learn more about the topics covered in this chapter.

Internet Exercise 13–1: Legal Perspective
Covenants Not to Compete

Internet Exercise 13–2: Management Perspective
Minors and the Law

Internet Exercise 13–3: Social Perspective
Online Gambling

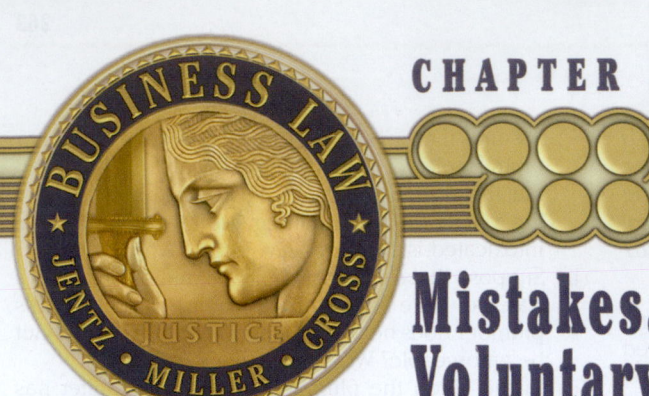

CHAPTER 14

Mistakes, Fraud, and Voluntary Consent

An otherwise valid contract may still be unenforceable if the parties have not genuinely agreed to its terms. As mentioned in Chapter 10, lack of genuineness of assent, or voluntary consent, can be used as a defense to the contract's enforceability. Voluntary consent may be lacking because of a mistake, misrepresentation, undue influence, or duress—in other words, because there is no true "meeting of the minds." Generally, a party who demonstrates that he or she did not truly agree to the terms of a contract can choose either to carry out the contract or to rescind (cancel) it and thus avoid the entire transaction. In this chapter, we examine the kinds of factors that may indicate a lack of voluntary consent.

SECTION 1 Mistakes

We all make mistakes, so it is not surprising that mistakes are made when contracts are formed. In certain circumstances, contract law allows a contract to be avoided on the basis of mistake. It is important to distinguish between *mistakes of fact* and *mistakes of value or quality*. Only a mistake of fact makes a contract voidable.

Mistakes of Fact

Mistakes of fact occur in two forms—*bilateral* and *unilateral*. A bilateral, or mutual, mistake is made by *both* of the contracting parties. A unilateral mistake is made by only *one* of the parties. We look next at these two types of mistakes and illustrate them graphically in Exhibit 14–1.

Bilateral (Mutual) Mistakes of Fact A bilateral, or mutual, mistake occurs when both parties are mistaken as to an existing *material fact*—that is, a fact important to the subject matter of the contract. It is a "mutual misunderstanding concerning a basic assumption on which the contract was made."[1] When a bilateral mistake occurs, normally the contract is voidable by the adversely affected party and can be rescinded, or canceled. For example, Gilbert contracts to sell Magellan three tracts of undeveloped land for $6 million on the basis of a surveyor's report showing the layout and acreage. After agreeing to the price, the parties discover that the surveyor made an error and that the tracts actually contain 10 percent more acreage than reported. In this situation, Gilbert can seek rescission (cancellation) of the contract based on mutual mistake. The same result—rescission—would occur if both parties had mistakenly believed that the tracts of land were adjoining but they were not.[2]

A word or term in a contract may be subject to more than one reasonable interpretation. If the parties to the contract attach materially different meanings to the term, a court may allow the contract to be rescinded because there has been no true "meeting of the minds."[3] The classic example is *Raffles v. Wichelhaus*,[4] a case decided by an English court in 1864. Wichelhaus agreed to buy a shipment of Surat

1. *Restatement (Second) of Contracts*, Section 152.

2. See, for example, *Rawson v. UMLIC VP, LLC*, 933 So.2d 1206 (Fla.App. 2006).

3. The only way for a court to find out the meaning that each party attached to the contract term is to allow the parties to introduce *parol evidence*, which is basically oral testimony about the terms of their agreement. Parol evidence will be discussed in Chapter 15.

4. 159 Eng.Rep. 375 (1864).

EXHIBIT 14–1 • Mistakes of Fact

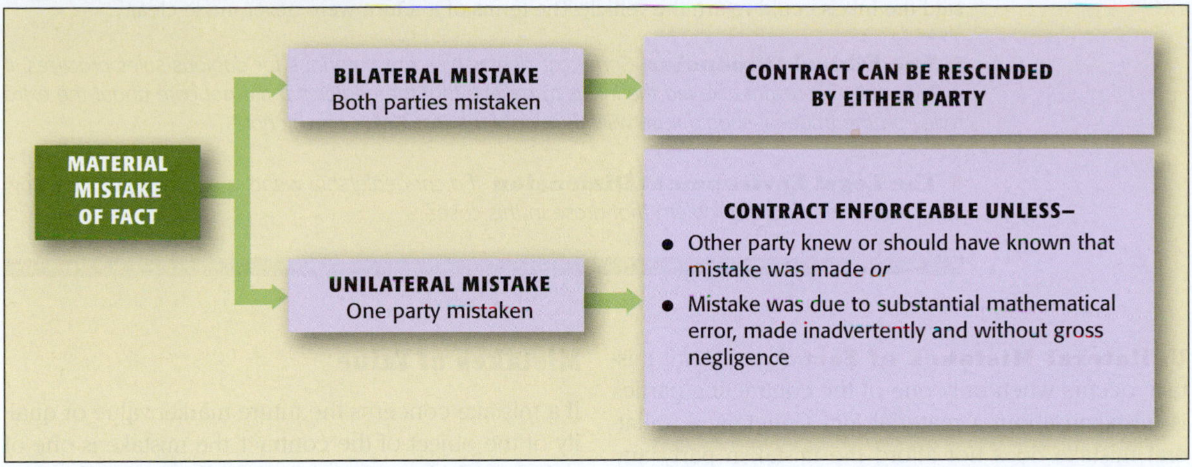

cotton from Raffles, "to arrive 'Peerless' from Bombay." There were two ships named *Peerless* sailing from Bombay, India, however. Wichelhaus was referring to the *Peerless* that sailed in October; Raffles meant a different *Peerless* that sailed in December. When Raffles tried to deliver the goods in December, Wichelhaus refused to accept them, and a lawsuit followed. The court held in favor of Wichelhaus, concluding that a mutual mistake had been made because the parties had attached materially different meanings to an essential term of the contract.

In the following case, the court had to grapple with a question of mutual mistake that was perhaps not what it seemed to be.

CASE 14.1 Inkel v. Pride Chevrolet-Pontiac, Inc.

Supreme Court of Vermont, 2008. 945 A.2d 855.

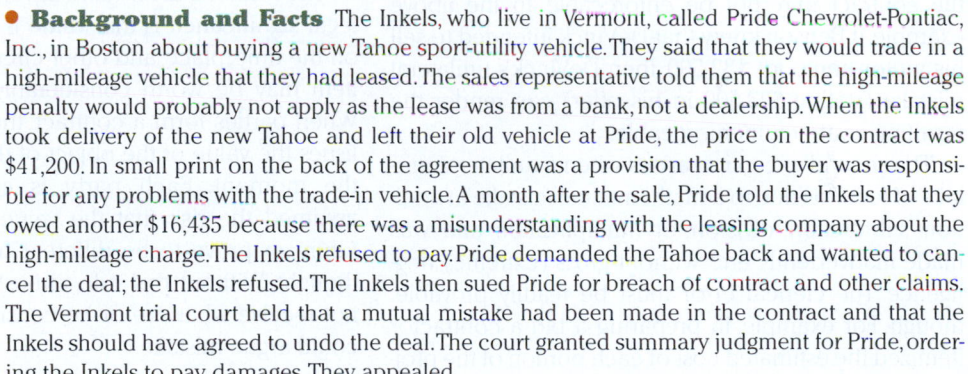

• **Background and Facts** The Inkels, who live in Vermont, called Pride Chevrolet-Pontiac, Inc., in Boston about buying a new Tahoe sport-utility vehicle. They said that they would trade in a high-mileage vehicle that they had leased. The sales representative told them that the high-mileage penalty would probably not apply as the lease was from a bank, not a dealership. When the Inkels took delivery of the new Tahoe and left their old vehicle at Pride, the price on the contract was $41,200. In small print on the back of the agreement was a provision that the buyer was responsible for any problems with the trade-in vehicle. A month after the sale, Pride told the Inkels that they owed another $16,435 because there was a misunderstanding with the leasing company about the high-mileage charge. The Inkels refused to pay. Pride demanded the Tahoe back and wanted to cancel the deal; the Inkels refused. The Inkels then sued Pride for breach of contract and other claims. The Vermont trial court held that a mutual mistake had been made in the contract and that the Inkels should have agreed to undo the deal. The court granted summary judgment for Pride, ordering the Inkels to pay damages. They appealed.

• **Decision and Rationale** The Supreme Court of Vermont reversed in favor of the Inkels, holding that it was not clear that there was a mutual mistake and that Pride may have engaged in consumer fraud. A mutual mistake means both parties were ignorant of the same facts. Pride knew the terms of its contract, and the Inkels knew their vehicle was high mileage. It appears that either Pride was hiding the truth about what would happen due to the high mileage on the trade-in vehicle, or the Inkels were trying to take advantage of Pride's ignorance about the extra payoff needed to their bank for their high-mileage vehicle. Even if there was a mutual mistake, which

CASE CONTINUES

CASE 14.1 CONTINUED should be determined at trial, it was not clear that Pride offered to rescind the contract when it said the Inkels could return the vehicle. The terms of a return were never made clear.

- **The Ethical Dimension** *Some car dealerships are notorious for dubious sales practices. If a Pride sales representative led the Inkels to believe that the dealership did not care about the extra miles on the trade-in, should it be willing to incur the loss? Why or why not?*

- **The Legal Environment Dimension** *If a car dealership wants a quality reputation, how can it avoid the kind of problem that arose in this case?*

Unilateral Mistakes of Fact A unilateral mistake occurs when only one of the contracting parties is mistaken about a material fact. Generally, a unilateral mistake does not afford the mistaken party any right to relief from the contract. Normally, the contract is enforceable. For example, DeVinck intends to sell his motor home for $32,500. When he learns that Benson is interested in buying a used motor home, DeVinck faxes Benson an offer to sell the vehicle to him. When typing the fax, however, DeVinck mistakenly keys in the price of $23,500. Benson immediately sends DeVinck a fax accepting DeVinck's offer. Even though DeVinck intended to sell his motor home for $32,500, his unilateral mistake falls on him. He is bound in contract to sell the motor home to Benson for $23,500.

There are at least two exceptions to this general rule.[5] First, if the *other* party to the contract knows or should have known that a mistake of fact was made, the contract may not be enforceable. In the above example, if Benson knew that DeVinck intended to sell his motor home for $32,500, then DeVinck's unilateral mistake (stating $23,500 in his offer) can render the resulting contract unenforceable.

The second exception arises when a unilateral mistake of fact was due to a mathematical mistake in addition, subtraction, division, or multiplication and was made inadvertently and without gross (extreme) negligence. The clerical error must be readily provable, though. For example, in preparing a bid a contractor itemized the estimated cost of each portion of the project, but made a mistake in addition when totaling the estimated costs, resulting in a total significantly lower than the correct total. Because the clerical error can be easily ascertained, a court may allow any contract resulting from the bid to be rescinded. Alternatively, a court may reform the contract to reflect the accurate total.

5. The *Restatement (Second) of Contracts,* Section 153, liberalizes the general rule to take into account the modern trend of allowing avoidance even though only one party has been mistaken.

Mistakes of Value

If a mistake concerns the future market value or quality of the object of the contract, the mistake is one of *value,* and the contract normally is enforceable. Mistakes of value can be bilateral or unilateral; but either way, they do not serve as a basis for avoiding a contract. Suppose that Hari buys a violin from Bev for $250. Although the violin is very old, neither party believes that it is extremely valuable. Later, however, an antiques dealer informs the parties that the violin is rare and worth thousands of dollars. Although both parties were mistaken, the mistake is not a mistake of *fact* that warrants contract rescission. This would be true even if, at the time of contracting, only Bev believed the violin was not particularly valuable (a unilateral mistake) and Hari thought it was rare and worth more than $250.

The reason that mistakes of value or quality have no legal significance is that value is variable. Depending on the time, place, and other circumstances, the same item may be worth considerably different amounts. When parties form a contract, their agreement establishes the value of the object of their transaction—for the moment. Each party is considered to have assumed the risk that the value will change in the future or prove to be different from what he or she thought. Without this rule, almost any party who did not receive what she or he considered a fair bargain could argue mistake.

SECTION 2

Fraudulent Misrepresentation

Although fraud is a tort (see Chapter 6), it also affects the authenticity of the innocent party's consent to the contract. When an innocent party is fraudulently induced to enter into a contract, the contract normally can be avoided because that party has not *voluntarily* consented to its terms.[6] Ordinarily, the innocent party can either rescind (cancel) the contract and be restored to her or his original position or enforce the contract and seek damages for any injuries resulting from the fraud.

Generally, fraudulent misrepresentation refers only to misrepresentation that is consciously false and is intended to mislead another. The person making the fraudulent misrepresentation knows or believes that the assertion is false or knows that she or he does not have a basis (stated or implied) for the assertion.[7] Typically, fraudulent misrepresentation consists of the following elements:

1. A misrepresentation of a material fact must occur.
2. There must be an intent to deceive.
3. The innocent party must justifiably rely on the misrepresentation.

With its anonymity and rapidly changing technology, the online world is a hospitable environment for fraudulent misrepresentation. In 2006, for example, users of an online dating service sued Yahoo!, Inc., for fraudulent misrepresentation in connection with personal ads posted online. The plaintiffs claimed that Yahoo was deliberately creating false profiles and sending them to subscribers as "potential new matches." Although Yahoo insisted that it was immune from such suits under the Communications Decency Act of 1996 (see the in-depth discussion in Chapter 6), the court held that the company was not entitled to immunity because Yahoo itself had provided the content.[8] Another source of fraudulent misrepresentation on the Web is "click fraud," the topic of this chapter's *Insight into Ethics* feature on pages 270 and 271.

Misrepresentation Has Occurred

The first element of proving fraud is to show that misrepresentation of a material fact has occurred. This misrepresentation can occur by words or actions. For example, the statement "This sculpture was created by Michelangelo" is a misrepresentation of fact if another artist sculpted the statue. Similarly, suppose that Swan tells the owner of an art gallery that she is interested in buying only paintings by a particular artist. The owner immediately leads Swan over to six individual paintings. Here, the gallery owner, without saying a word, has represented by his conduct that the six paintings are works of that artist. If Swan buys one of the paintings and it turns out to have been painted by another artist, she can sue the gallery owner for fraud. The identity of the artist would be a material fact in the formation of either contract.

Statements of opinion and representations of future facts (predictions) are generally not subject to claims of fraud. Every person is expected to exercise care and judgment when entering into contracts, and the law will not come to the aid of one who simply makes an unwise bargain. Statements such as "This land will be worth twice as much next year" or "This car will last for years and years" are statements of opinion, not fact. Contracting parties should recognize them as such and not rely on them. An opinion is usually subject to contrary or conflicting views; a fact is objective and verifiable. Thus, a seller of goods is allowed to use *puffery* to sell his or her wares without liability for fraud.

In certain cases, however, particularly when a naïve purchaser relies on a so-called expert's opinion, the innocent party may be entitled to rescission or reformation. (*Reformation* is an equitable remedy granted by a court in which the terms of a contract are altered to reflect the true intentions of the parties—see Chapter 18.) The issue in the following case was whether the statements made by instructors at a dance school to one of the school's students qualified as statements of opinion or statements of fact.

6. *Restatement (Second) of Contracts,* Sections 163 and 164.
7. *Restatement (Second) of Contracts,* Section 162.
8. *Anthony v. Yahoo!, Inc.,* 421 F.Supp.2d 1257 (N.D.Cal. 2006).

CASE 14.2 Vokes v. Arthur Murray, Inc.

District Court of Appeal of Florida, Second District, 1968. 212 So.2d 906.

• **Company Profile** Arthur Murray, founder of Arthur Murray, Inc. (**www.arthurmurray.com**), began teaching people how to dance in 1919. At the time, social dancing was becoming increasingly popular among young people, in part because so many adults were shocked by the new "jazz dancing." Across America, young people wanted to learn the new steps—the turkey trot, the fox-trot,

CASE CONTINUES

CASE 14.2 CONTINUED the kangaroo dip, the chicken scratch, the bunny hug, the grizzly bear, and others. By the 1930s, Murray's instructors were giving lessons on cruise ships, in tourist hotels, and to the employees of New York stores during the employees' lunch breaks. In 1937, Murray founded the Arthur Murray Studios, a chain of franchised dance schools. During the 1950s, Murray sponsored a television show—*The Arthur Murray Party*—to attract students to the schools. Murray retired in 1964, estimating that he had taught more than 20 million people how to dance.

Background and Facts Audrey E. Vokes, a widow without family, wished to become "an accomplished dancer" and to find "a new interest in life." In 1961, she was invited to attend a "dance party" at J.P. Davenport's "School of Dancing," an Arthur Murray, Inc., franchise. Vokes went to the school and received elaborate praise from her instructor for her grace, poise, and potential as "an excellent dancer." The instructor sold her eight half-hour dance lessons for $14.50 each, to be utilized within one calendar month. Subsequently, over a period of less than sixteen months, Vokes bought a total of fourteen dance courses, which amounted to 2,302 hours of dancing lessons at Davenport's school, for a total cash outlay of $31,090.45 (in 2008, this would amount to nearly $140,000). When it became clear to Vokes that she did not, in fact, have the potential to be an excellent dancer, she filed a suit against the school, alleging fraudulent misrepresentation. When the trial court dismissed her complaint, she appealed.

Decision and Rationale The state intermediate appellate court reinstated the complaint and remanded the case to the trial court to allow Vokes to prove her case. The appellate court held that Vokes could avoid the contract because it was procured by false representations that she had a promising career in dancing. The court acknowledged that ordinarily, to be grounds for rescission, a misrepresentation must be one of fact rather than of opinion. "A statement of a party having * * * superior knowledge may be regarded as a statement of fact although it would be considered as opinion if the parties were dealing on equal terms. It could be reasonably supposed here that defendants had 'superior knowledge' as to whether plaintiff had 'dance potential.'"

Impact of This Case on Today's Law *This case has become a classic in contract law because it clearly illustrates an important principle. The general rule—that a misrepresentation must be one of fact rather than of opinion to be actionable—does not apply in certain situations, such as when one party misrepresents something about which he or she possesses superior knowledge (Vokes's dancing ability, in this case).*

The Ethical Dimension *If one of Vokes's fellow students, rather than her instructor, had praised her ability and encouraged her to buy more lessons, should the result in this case have been different? Explain.*

Misrepresentation by Concealment Misrepresentation can also take place when a party takes specific action to conceal a fact that is material to the contract.[9] Suppose that Rakas contracts to buy a new car from Bustamonte, a dealer in new automobiles. The car has been used as a demonstration model for prospective customers to test-drive, but Bustamonte has turned back the odometer. Rakas cannot tell from the odometer reading that the car has been driven nearly one thousand miles, and Bustamonte does not tell Rakas the distance the car has actually been driven. Bustamonte's concealment constitutes misrepresentation by conduct.

As another example, suppose that Cummings contracts to purchase a racehorse from Garner. The horse is blind in one eye, but when Garner shows the horse, he skillfully conceals this fact by keeping the horse's head turned so that Cummings does not see the defect. The concealment constitutes fraud.

Misrepresentation of Law Misrepresentation of law *ordinarily* does not entitle a party to relief from a contract. For example, Camara has a parcel of property that she is trying to sell to Pye. Camara knows that a local ordinance prohibits building anything higher

9. *Restatement (Second) of Contracts*, Section 160.

than three stories on the property. Nonetheless, she tells Pye, "You can build a condominium fifty stories high if you want to." Pye buys the land and later discovers that Camara's statement was false. Normally, Pye cannot avoid the contract because at common law people are assumed to know state and local ordinances. Additionally, a layperson should not rely on a statement made by a nonlawyer about a point of law.

Exceptions to this rule occur, however, when the misrepresenting party is in a profession that is known to require greater knowledge of the law than the average citizen possesses. The courts are recognizing an increasing number of such professions. For example, the courts recognize that clients expect their real estate brokers to know the law governing real estate sales and land use. If Camara, in the preceding example, had been a lawyer or a real estate broker, her misrepresentation of the area's zoning status would probably have constituted fraud.

Misrepresentation by Silence Ordinarily, neither party to a contract has a duty to come forward and disclose facts. Therefore, a contract cannot be set aside because certain pertinent information is not volunteered. Suppose that you are selling a car that has been in an accident and has been repaired. You do not need to volunteer this information to a potential buyer. If, however, the purchaser asks you if the car has had extensive bodywork and you lie, you have committed a fraudulent misrepresentation.

Exceptions. Exceptions to the general rule do exist. Generally, if the seller knows of a serious potential problem that could not reasonably be suspected by the buyer, the seller may have a duty to speak. For example, if a city fails to disclose to bidders subsoil conditions that will cause great expense in constructing a sewer system, the city is guilty of fraud. Normally, the seller must disclose only "latent" defects—that is, defects that could not readily be discovered. Thus, termites in a house may not be a latent defect because a buyer could normally discover their presence through a termite inspection.

When the parties are in a *fiduciary relationship* (one of trust, such as the relationship between business partners or between attorneys and their clients—see Chapter 31), there is a duty to disclose material facts; failure to do so may constitute fraud.[10] Statutes provide still other exceptions to the general rule of nondisclosure. The Truth-in-Lending Act, for example, requires disclosure of certain facts in financial transactions (see Chapter 44).

Duty to Prospective Employees. A duty to disclose information may also arise in an employment context when the employer either misrepresents or conceals information from a prospective employee during the hiring process. Courts have held employers liable for fraudulent misrepresentation about a company's financial health during hiring interviews. In one case, for example, applicants for jobs at the El-Jay Division asked about El-Jay's future. The employer represented during interviews that business was growing, that sales were up, and that the future looked promising. In reality, company management had already planned to close the El-Jay facility. In the subsequent trial, the court stated that the employer could be held liable for either failing to disclose material facts or making representations that were misleading because they were in the nature of "half-truth."[11]

In another case, the employer was found liable for fraud because it failed to disclose a potential takeover of the company. Representatives from a brokerage firm approached Philip McConkey, a former New York Giants professional football player, and offered him a position with their company. Because McConkey had heard rumors that the firm was going to be acquired by another firm, he asked about a possible takeover. He was assured on several occasions that the company was absolutely not going to be sold to another firm. When it was sold a few months later, McConkey was fired. He filed a lawsuit and won a substantial damages award based on the company's fraudulent misrepresentation.[12]

Intent to Deceive

The second element of fraud is knowledge on the part of the misrepresenting party that facts have been falsely represented. This element, normally called ***scienter,***[13] or "guilty knowledge," signifies that there was an *intent to deceive*. *Scienter* clearly exists if a party knows a fact is not as stated. *Scienter* also exists if a

10. *Restatement (Second) of Contracts,* Sections 161 and 173.

11. *Meade v. Cedarapids, Inc.,* 164 F.3d 1218 (9th Cir. 1999).

12. *McConkey v. Aon Corp.,* 354 N.J.Super. 25, 804 A.2d 572 (2002). Note that a number of subsequent cases have disputed this court's calculation of damages in situations involving fraudulent misresprentation. See, for example, *Goldstein v. Miles,* 859 A.2d 313 (Md.App. 2004); and *Horton v. Ross University School of Medicine,* 2006 WL 1128705 (D.N.J. 2006).

13. Pronounced *sy-en-ter*.

INSIGHT INTO ETHICS
Internet Click Fraud

For many of the Internet's best-known companies, including Google and Yahoo, advertising is the main source of their revenues. Every user of the Internet encounters a multitude of advertisements that invite the user to "click" on the ad to get further information about the product or service. What every user may not know, however, is that the companies selling such ads charge fees based on the number of clicks. Thus, the more clicks, the higher the advertising revenues of the company selling the advertising space. Meanwhile, Web advertisers, who buy space for their ads on sites such as those run by Google and Yahoo, want to pay only for valid clicks—those done by humans with a real interest in the product.

Enter Click Fraud

This system of charging for advertising based on the number of clicks has given rise to many allegations of click fraud, which occurs "when someone clicks on a search advertisement with an ill intent and with no intention of doing business with the advertiser. [Click fraud involves] purposeful clicks on an advertisement for some kind of improper purpose."[a] The exact dimensions of click fraud are unknown, but some commentators think it could amount to as much as $1 billion per year. Fraud-detection specialist Fair Isaac Corporation believes that 10 to 15 percent of advertising traffic on the Internet is "pathological," indicating a high probability of click fraud.

There are several different types of click fraud. For example, suppose that Company A and Company B are direct competitors. Company A directs its employees to click repetitively on Company B's online ads in an attempt to run up the advertising fees that Company B will have to pay. In another type of click fraud, the owners of the sites running the ads simply use Internet robots to click on the ads so as to increase the revenues that they receive from running the advertising. Of course, Company A, in the previous example, could also use robots to click on Company B's ads.

Whether it is generated by humans or robots, click fraud is unethical and, at a mimimum, violates

a. *Click Defense, Inc. v. Google, Inc.,* No. 5:05-CV-02579-RMW (N.D.Cal. complaint filed June 24, 2005). This case was subsequently settled.

party makes a statement that he or she believes is not true or makes a statement recklessly, without regard to whether it is true or false. Finally, this element is met if a party says or implies that a statement is made on some basis, such as personal knowledge or personal investigation, when it is not.

Assume that Meese, a securities broker, offers to sell BIM stock to Packer. Meese assures Packer that BIM shares are blue-chip securities—that is, they are stable, entail limited risk, and yield a good return on investment over time. In fact, Meese knows nothing about the quality of BIM stock and does not believe that what he is saying is true. Meese's statement is thus a misrepresentation. If Packer is induced by Meese's intentional misrepresentation of a material fact to enter into a contract to buy the stock, normally he can avoid his obligations under the contract.

Innocent Misrepresentation If a person makes a statement that she or he believes to be true but that actually misrepresents material facts, the person is guilty only of an **innocent misrepresentation,** not of fraud. When an innocent misrepresentation occurs, the aggrieved party can rescind the contract but usually cannot seek damages. For example, Parris tells Roberta that a tract of land contains 250 acres. Parris is mistaken—the tract contains only 215 acres—but Parris had no knowledge of the mistake. Roberta relies on the statement and contracts to buy the land. Even though the misrepresentation is innocent, Roberta can avoid the contract if the misrepresentation is material.

Negligent Misrepresentation Sometimes, a party will make a misrepresentation through carelessness, believing the statement is true. If a person fails to exercise reasonable care in uncovering or disclosing the facts or does not use the skill and competence that her or his business or profession requires, it could constitute **negligent misrepresentation.** For example, an operator of a weight scale certifies the weight of Sneed's commodity, even though the scale's accuracy has not been checked in more than a year.

In virtually all states, such negligent misrepresentation is equal to *scienter,* or knowingly making a misrepresentation. In effect, negligent misrepresentation is treated as fraudulent misrepresentation, even though the implied covenant of good faith and fair dealing, which requires honesty and the observance of reasonable standards of fair dealing between contracting parties (see Chapter 22). Additionally, when Web site owners purposefully inflate the number of clicks so that they can charge more for advertising, they can be sued for, among other things, unjust enrichment.

Indeed, in the past few years, both Google and Yahoo have been the defendants in click fraud suits, several of which have been settled for amounts reaching tens of millions of dollars.[b] Google now uses filtering software so that it does not count repetitive clicks that presumably come from Internet robots.

Click Fraud's Close Cousin—Lead Fraud

Closely related to click fraud is lead fraud. "Leads" in this context are simply the names of individuals who have expressed an interest in purchasing a certain product, such as insurance. NetQuote, for example, is a lead-generating site for insurance companies. Users can submit requests on NetQuote's Web page, and NetQuote then sells these "qualified" leads to insurance companies. NetQuote now has brought a fraud claim against MostChoice, a competitor, charging that MostChoice had an employee submit hundreds of fraudulent requests through the NetQuote system.[c] NetQuote maintains that when it submitted these leads to its insurance company clients, the conversion rate—the percentage of leads that actually purchase insurance—dropped dramatically, thereby reducing the value of the leads to the insurance companies.

b. See, for example, *Checkmate Strategic Group, Inc. v. Yahoo!, Inc.*, No. 2:05-CV-04588-CAS-FMO (C.D.Cal. preliminary settlement approved June 28, 2006); *Bradley v. Google, Inc.*, 2006 WL3798134 (N.D.Cal. 2006, voluntarily dismissed after a settlement in 2007); and *Lane's Gifts and Collectibles, LLC v. Yahoo! Inc.*, No. CV-2005-52-1 (Ark.Cir.Ct. complaint filed February 17, 2005).

CRITICAL THINKING

INSIGHT INTO TECHNOLOGY

"As long as each click on an ad link on the Web triggers a commission that has to be paid, we will be facing a financial formula that gives rise to unethical behavior." Do you think that technology will some day be able to distinguish between bona fide clicks by truly interested parties and bogus clicks? Why or why not?

c. *NetQuote, Inc. v. Byrd*, 504 F.Supp.2d 1126 (D.Colo. 2007). This case has not yet been fully resolved.

the misrepresentation was not purposeful. In negligent misrepresentation, culpable ignorance of the truth supplies the intention to mislead, even if the defendant can claim, "I didn't know."

Reliance on the Misrepresentation

The third element of fraud is reasonably *justifiable reliance* on the misrepresentation of fact. The deceived party must have a justifiable reason for relying on the misrepresentation, and the misrepresentation must be an important factor (but not necessarily the sole factor) in inducing that party to enter into the contract. Suppose that to rent a car, an eighteen-year-old misrepresents his age and presents a false driver's license listing his age as twenty-two. In that situation, the car-rental agency would be justified in relying on this misrepresentation (provided that the proof of identity was not clearly false).[14]

Reliance is not justified if the innocent party knows the true facts or relies on obviously extravagant statements. If a used-car dealer tells you, "This old Cadillac will get fifty miles to the gallon," you normally will not be justified in relying on the statement. Or suppose that Kovich, a bank director, induces Mallory, a co-director, to sign a guaranty that the bank's assets will satisfy its liabilities, stating, "We have plenty of assets to satisfy our creditors." If Mallory knows the true facts, he will not be justified in relying on Kovich's statement. If, however, Mallory does not know the true facts *and has no way of discovering them,* he may be justified in relying on Kovich's statement.

The same rule applies to defects in property sold. If the defects are of the kind that would be obvious on inspection, the buyer cannot justifiably rely on the seller's representations. If the defects are hidden or latent (that is, not apparent on the surface), the buyer is justified in relying on the seller's statements.

Injury to the Innocent Party

Most courts do not require a showing of injury when the action is to rescind (cancel) the contract. These courts hold that because rescission returns the parties to the positions they held before the contract was

14. See, for example, *Fogel v. Enterprise Leasing Co. of Chicago*, 353 Ill.App.3d 165, 817 N.E.2d 1135, 288 Ill.Dec. 485 (2004).

made, a showing of injury to the innocent party is unnecessary.

For a person to recover damages caused by fraud, proof of an injury is universally required. The measure of damages is ordinarily equal to the property's value had it been delivered as represented, less the actual price paid for the property. Additionally, because fraud actions necessarily involve wrongful conduct, courts may also award *punitive damages*, or *exemplary damages*.[15] As discussed in Chapter 6, punitive damages are damages intended to punish the defendant and are granted to a plaintiff over and above the proved, actual compensation for the loss. Because of the potential for punitive damages, which normally are not available in contract actions, plaintiffs prefer to include a claim for fraudulent misrepresentation in their contract disputes.

PREVENTING LEGAL DISPUTES

To avoid making comments that might later be construed as a misrepresentation of material fact, business owners and managers should be careful what they say to clients and customers. Those in the business of selling products or services should assume that all customers are naïve and are relying on the seller's representations. Instruct employees to phrase their comments so that customers understand that any statements that are not factual are the employee's opinion. If someone asks a question that is beyond the employee's knowledge, it is better to say that he or she does not know than to guess and have the customer rely on a representation that turns out to be false. This can be particularly important when the questions concern topics such as compatibility or speed of electronic and digital goods, software, or related services.

Businesspersons should also be prudent about what they say when interviewing potential employees. They should not speculate on the financial health of the firm or exaggerate the company's future prospects. Exercising caution in one's statements to others in a business context is the best way to avoid potential legal actions for fraudulent misrepresentation.

15. See, for example, *McIver v. Bondy's Ford, Inc.*, 963 So.2d 136 (Ala.App. 2007); and *Alexander v. Meduna*, 47 P.3d 206 (Wyo. 2002).

SECTION 3 Undue Influence

Undue influence arises from special kinds of relationships in which one party can greatly influence another party, thus overcoming that party's free will. A contract entered into under excessive or undue influence lacks voluntary consent and is therefore voidable.[16]

How Undue Influence May Occur

As mentioned, undue influence arises from relationships in which one party may dominate another party, thus unfairly influencing him or her. Minors and elderly people, for example, are often under the influence of guardians (persons who are legally responsible for another). If a guardian induces a young or elderly ward (the person whom the guardian looks after) to enter into a contract that benefits the guardian, undue influence may have been exerted. Undue influence can arise from a number of confidential or fiduciary relationships: attorney-client, physician-patient, guardian-ward, parent-child, husband-wife, or trustee-beneficiary.

The essential feature of undue influence is that the party being taken advantage of does not, in reality, exercise free will in entering into a contract. Just because a person is elderly or suffers from some physical or mental impairment, however, does not mean that she or he was the victim of undue influence—there must be clear and convincing evidence that the person did not act out of her or his free will.[17] Similarly, the existence of a confidential relationship alone is insufficient to prove undue influence.[18]

To determine whether undue influence has been exerted, a court must ask, "To what extent was the transaction induced by domination of the mind or emotions of the person in question?" It follows, then, that the mental state of the person in question will often demonstrate to what extent the persuasion from the outside influence was "unfair."

The Presumption of Undue Influence

When the principal in a confidential relationship benefits from that relationship, a presumption of undue influence arises. In a relationship of trust and confidence,

16. *Restatement (Second) of Contracts,* Section 177.

17. See, for example, *Bailey v. Turnbow,* 273 Va. 262, 639 S.E.2d 291 (2007); and *Hooten v. Jensen,* 94 Ark.App. 130, 227 S.W.3d 431 (2006).

18. See, for example, *Landers v. Sgouros,* 224 S.W.3d 651 (Mo.App. 2007); and *Ware v. Ware,* 161 P.3d 1188 (Alaska 2007).

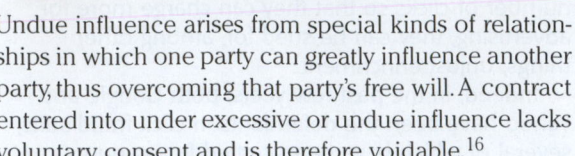

such as that between an attorney and a client, the dominant party (the attorney) must exercise the utmost good faith in dealing with the other party. When a contract enriches the dominant party, the court will often *presume* that the contract was made under undue influence. For example, if a guardian enters into a contract on behalf of the ward that financially benefits the guardian and the ward challenges the contract, a presumption arises that the guardian has taken advantage of the ward. To rebut (refute) this presumption successfully, the guardian has to show that full disclosure was made to the ward, that consideration was adequate, and that the ward received, if available, independent and competent advice before completing the transaction. Unless the presumption can be rebutted, the contract will be rescinded (canceled).

SECTION 4 Duress

Consent to the terms of a contract is not voluntary if one of the parties is *forced* into the agreement. Recall from Chapter 9 that forcing a party to do something, including entering into a contract, through fear created by threats is legally defined as *duress*. In addition, blackmail or extortion to induce consent to a contract constitutes duress. Duress is both a defense to the enforcement of a contract and a ground for the rescission of a contract.

The Threatened Act Must Be Wrongful or Illegal

To establish duress, there must be proof of a threat to do something that the threatening party has no right to do. The threatened act must be legally or morally wrongful and must render the person incapable of exercising free will. Suppose that Joan accidentally crashes into Olin's car, which is stopped at a red traffic light. Joan has no automobile insurance, but she has substantial assets. At the scene of the accident, Olin claims to have suffered whiplash and tells Joan he will agree not to file a lawsuit against her if she pays him $5,000. Joan initially refuses, but after an argument, Olin says, "If you don't pay me $5,000 immediately, I'm going to sue you for $25,000." Joan then gives Olin a check for $5,000 to avoid the lawsuit. The next day, Joan stops payment on the check. When Olin later sues to enforce their oral settlement agreement for $5,000, Joan claims duress as a defense to its enforcement. In this situation, because Olin had a right to sue Joan, threatening to sue her will not constitute duress. A court would not consider the threat of a civil suit to constitute duress.

Economic Duress

Economic need generally is not sufficient to constitute duress, even when one party exacts a very high price for an item that the other party needs. If the party exacting the price also creates the need, however, *economic duress* may be found.

For example, the Internal Revenue Service (IRS) assesses a large tax and penalty against Weller. Weller retains Eyman, the accountant who prepared the tax returns on which the assessment was based, to challenge the assessment. Two days before the deadline for filing a reply with the IRS, Eyman declines to represent Weller unless he signs a very high contingency-fee agreement for the services. This agreement would be unenforceable. Although Eyman has threatened only to withdraw his services, something that he is legally entitled to do, he is responsible for delaying the withdrawal until the last days before the deadline. Because it would be impossible at that late date to obtain adequate representation elsewhere, Weller would be forced either to sign the contract or to lose his right to challenge the IRS assessment.

SECTION 5 Adhesion Contracts and Unconscionability

Questions concerning genuineness of assent may arise when the terms of a contract are dictated by a party with overwhelming bargaining power and the signer must agree to those terms or go without the commodity or service in question. As explained in Chapter 13, such contracts, which are written *exclusively* by one party and presented to the other party on a take-it-or-leave-it basis, are often referred to as *adhesion contracts*. These contracts often use standard forms, which give the adhering party no opportunity to negotiate the contract terms.

Standard-Form Contracts

Standard-form contracts often contain fine-print provisions that shift a risk naturally borne by one party to the other. A variety of businesses use such contracts. Life insurance policies, residential leases, loan agreements, and employment agency contracts are often standard-form contracts. To avoid enforcement of the contract or of a particular clause, the aggrieved party must show that the parties had substantially unequal bargaining positions and that enforcement would be manifestly unfair or oppressive. If the required showing is made, the contract or particular term is deemed *unconscionable* and is not enforced.

Adhesion contracts are standard in the retail automobile industry. The following case arose out of an arbitration clause in such a contract between an auto dealership and its customer.

CASE 14.3 Simpson v. MSA of Myrtle Beach, Inc.

Supreme Court of South Carolina, 2007. 373 S.C. 14, 644 S.E.2d 663.
www.findlaw.com/11stategov/sc/scca.html[a]

• **Background and Facts** MSA of Myrtle Beach, Inc., in South Carolina does business as Addy's Harbor Dodge (Addy), a car dealership. Sherry Simpson signed a contract with Addy to trade in her 2001 Toyota 4Runner for a new 2004 Dodge Caravan. Directly above the signature line on the first page of the contract, a signee was instructed in bold type to "SEE ADDITIONAL TERMS AND CONDITIONS ON OPPOSITE PAGE." The additional terms and conditions contained an arbitration clause, which provided, among other things, that "in no event shall the arbitrator be authorized to award punitive, exemplary, double, or treble damages (or any other damages which are punitive in nature or effect) against either party." Six months later, Simpson filed a suit in a South Carolina state court against Addy, claiming that the dealer had misrepresented the trade-in value of her vehicle, artificially increased the purchase price, and failed to provide all rebates promised, in violation of state statutes. Addy filed a motion to compel arbitration. Simpson responded that the arbitration clause was unconscionable and unenforceable. The court denied Addy's motion. Addy appealed to the South Carolina Supreme Court.

• **Decision and Rationale** The state supreme court affirmed the lower court's denial of Addy's motion to compel arbitration. The reviewing court pointed out that unconscionability involves the absence of meaningful choice due to one-sided contract provisions. The "absence of meaningful choice on the part of one party generally speaks to the fundamental fairness of the bargaining process in the contract at issue." The court further pointed out that the arbitration clause was printed in very small type and embedded in one paragraph out of the sixteen included on a single page. Thus, the arbitration clause was inconspicuous. "The general rule is that courts will not enforce a contract which is violative of public policy, statutory law, or provisions of the Constitution." The state supreme court found that the arbitration clause was both unconscionable and unenforceable. The terms limiting Simpson's remedies were oppressive and one sided.

• **The Ethical Dimension** *Could the court have severed the unconscionable portions of the arbitration clause and otherwise allowed arbitration to proceed? Why or why not?*

• **The Legal Environment Dimension** *The dealer's contract also provided that Addy did not have to submit to arbitration any claims it might have against Simpson for "monies owed" and that these claims "shall not be stayed pending the outcome of arbitration." Is this provision unconscionable? Discuss.*

a. In the "2007" section, click on "March." In the result, click on the number next to the name of the case to access the opinion.

Unconscionability and the Courts

Technically, unconscionability under Section 2–302 of the Uniform Commercial Code (UCC) applies only to contracts for the sale of goods. Many courts, however, have broadened the concept and applied it in other situations.

Although unconscionability was discussed in Chapter 13, it is important to note here that the UCC gives courts a great degree of discretion to invalidate or strike down a contract or clause as being unconscionable. As a result, some states have not adopted Section 2–302 of the UCC. In those states, the legislature and the courts prefer to rely on traditional notions of fraud, undue influence, and duress. (See *Concept Summary 14.1* for a review of all of the factors that may indicate a lack of voluntary consent.)

CONCEPT SUMMARY 14.1
Voluntary Consent

Problems of Assent	Rule
Mistakes	1. *Unilateral*—Generally, the mistaken party is bound by the contract, unless the other party knows or should have known of the mistake, or in some states, the mistake is an inadvertent mathematical error in addition, subtraction, and the like that is committed without gross negligence. 2. *Bilateral (mutual)*—If both parties are mistaken about a material fact, such as the identity of the subject matter, either party can avoid the contract. If the mistake relates to the value or quality of the subject matter, either party can enforce the contract.
Fraudulent Misrepresentation	Three elements are necessary to establish fraudulent misrepresentation: 1. A misrepresentation of a material fact has occurred. 2. There has been an intent to deceive. 3. The innocent party has justifiably relied on the misrepresentation.
Undue Influence/Duress	1. *Undue influence*—Arises from special relationships, such as fiduciary relationships, in which one party's free will has been overcome by the undue influence of another. Usually, the contract is voidable. 2. *Duress*—Defined as forcing a party to enter into a contract under fear of threat—for example, the threat of violence or economic pressure. The party forced to enter into the contract can rescind the contract.
Adhesion Contracts and Unconscionability	Concerns one-sided bargains in which one party has substantially superior bargaining power and can dictate the terms of a contract. Unconscionability typically occurs as a result of the following: 1. Standard-form contracts in which a fine-print provision purports to shift a risk normally borne by one party to the other (for example, a liability disclaimer). 2. Take-it-or-leave-it adhesion contracts in which the buyer has no choice but to agree to the seller's dictated terms if the buyer is to procure certain goods or services.

REVIEWING Mistakes, Fraud, and Voluntary Consent

Chelene had been a caregiver for Marta's eighty-year-old mother, Janis, for nine years. Shortly before Janis passed away, Chelene convinced her to buy Chelene's house for Marta. The elderly woman died before the papers were signed, however. Four months later, Marta used her inheritance to buy Chelene's house without having it inspected. The house was built in the 1950s, and Chelene said it was in "perfect condition." Nevertheless, one year after the purchase, the basement started leaking. Marta had the paneling removed from the basement walls and discovered that the walls were bowed inward and cracked. Marta then had a civil engineer inspect the basement walls, and he found that the cracks had been caulked and painted over before the paneling was installed. He

REVIEWING CONTINUES

REVIEWING Mistakes, Fraud, and Voluntary Consent, Continued

concluded that the "wall failure" had existed "for at least thirty years" and that the basement walls were "structurally unsound." Using the information presented in the chapter, answer the following questions.

1. Can Marta obtain rescission of the contract based on undue influence? If the sale to Janis had been completed before her death, could Janis have obtained rescission based on undue influence? Explain.
2. Can Marta sue Chelene for fraudulent misrepresentation? Why or why not? What element(s) might be lacking?
3. Now assume that Chelene knew that the basement walls were cracked and bowed and that she had hired someone to install paneling prior to offering to sell the house. Did she have a duty to disclose this defect to Marta? Could a court find that Chelene's silence in this situation constituted misrepresentation? Explain.
4. If Chelene knew about the problem with the walls but did not know that the house was structurally unsound, could she be liable for negligent misrepresentation? Why or why not?
5. Can Marta avoid the contract on the ground that both parties made a mistake about the condition of the house? Explain.

TERMS AND CONCEPTS

innocent misrepresentation 270
negligent misrepresentation 270
***scienter* 269**

QUESTIONS AND CASE PROBLEMS

14–1. Juan is an elderly man who lives with his nephew, Samuel. Juan is totally dependent on Samuel's support. Samuel tells Juan that unless he transfers a tract of land he owns to Samuel for a price 35 percent below its market value, Samuel will no longer support and take care of him. Juan enters into the contract. Discuss fully whether Juan can set aside this contract.

14–2. QUESTION WITH SAMPLE ANSWER

Grano owns a forty-room motel on Highway 100. Tanner is interested in purchasing the motel. During the course of negotiations, Grano tells Tanner that the motel netted $30,000 during the previous year and that it will net at least $45,000 the next year. The motel books, which Grano turns over to Tanner before the purchase, clearly show that Grano's motel netted only $15,000 the previous year. Also, Grano fails to tell Tanner that a bypass to Highway 100 is being planned that will redirect most traffic away from the front of the motel. Tanner purchases the motel. During the first year under Tanner's operation, the motel nets only $18,000. At this time, Tanner learns of the previous low profitability of the motel and the planned bypass. Tanner wants his money back from Grano. Discuss fully Tanner's probable success in getting his money back.

• **For a sample answer to Question 14–2, go to Appendix I at the end of this text.**

14–3. Discuss whether either of the following contracts will be unenforceable on the ground that voluntary consent is lacking:

(a) Simmons finds a stone in his pasture that he believes to be quartz. Jenson, who also believes that the stone is quartz, contracts to purchase it for $10. Just before delivery, the stone is discovered to be a diamond worth $1,000.

(b) Jacoby's barn is burned to the ground. He accuses Goldman's son of arson and threatens to have the prosecutor bring a criminal action unless Goldman agrees to pay him $5,000. Goldman agrees to pay.

14-4. Lund offered to sell Steck his car and told Steck that the car had been driven only 25,000 miles and had never been in an accident. Steck hired Carvallo, a mechanic, to appraise the condition of the car, and Carvallo said that the car probably had at least 50,000 miles on it and most likely had been in an accident. In spite of this information, Steck still thought the car would be a good buy for the price, so he purchased it. Later, when the car developed numerous mechanical problems, Steck sought to rescind the contract on the basis of Lund's fraudulent misrepresentation of the auto's condition. Will Steck be able to rescind his contract? Explain.

14-5. Fraudulent Misrepresentation. In 1987, United Parcel Service Co. and United Parcel Service of America, Inc. (together known as UPS), decided to change the parcel delivery business from relying on contract carriers to establishing its own airline. During the transition, which took sixteen months, UPS hired 811 pilots. At the time, UPS expressed a desire to hire pilots who remained throughout that period with its contract carriers, which included Orion Air. A UPS representative met with more than fifty Orion pilots and made promises of future employment. John Rickert, a captain with Orion, was one of the pilots. Orion ceased operation after the UPS transition, and UPS did not hire Rickert, who obtained employment about six months later as a second officer with American Airlines, but at a lower salary. Rickert filed a suit in a Kentucky state court against UPS, claiming, in part, fraud based on the promises made by the UPS representative. UPS filed a motion for a directed verdict. What are the elements for a cause of action based on fraudulent misrepresentation? In whose favor should the court rule in this case, and why? [*United Parcel Service, Inc. v. Rickert,* 996 S.W.2d 464 (Ky. 1999)]

14-6. Negligent Misrepresentation. Cleveland Chiropractic College (CCC) promised prospective students that CCC would provide clinical training and experience—a critical part of a chiropractic education and a requirement for graduation and obtaining a license to practice. Specifically, CCC expressly promised that it would provide an ample variety of patients. CCC knew, however, that it did not have the ability to provide sufficient patients, as evidenced by its report to the Council on Chiropractic Education, an accreditation body through which chiropractic colleges monitor and certify themselves. In that report, CCC said that patient recruitment was the "joint responsibility" of the college and the student. During the 1990s, most of the "patients" that students saw were healthy persons whom the students recruited to be stand-in patients. After graduating and obtaining licenses to practice, Michael Troknya and nineteen others filed a suit in a federal district court against CCC, alleging, among other things, negligent misrepresentation. What are the elements of this cause of action? Are they satisfied in this case? Why or why not? [*Troknya v. Cleveland Chiropractic Clinic,* 280 F.3d 1200 (8th Cir. 2002)]

14-7. CASE PROBLEM WITH SAMPLE ANSWER

The law firm of Traystman, Coric and Keramidas represented Andrew Daigle in a divorce in Norwich, Connecticut. Scott McGowan, an attorney with the firm, handled the two-day trial. After the first day of the trial, McGowan told Daigle to sign a promissory note in the amount of $26,973, which represented the amount that Daigle then owed to the firm, or McGowan would withdraw from the case, and Daigle would be forced to get another attorney or to continue the trial by himself. Daigle said that he wanted another attorney, Martin Rutchik, to see the note. McGowan urged Daigle to sign it and assured him that a copy would be sent to Rutchik. Feeling that he had no other choice, Daigle signed the note. When he did not pay, the law firm filed a suit in a Connecticut state court against him. Daigle asserted that the note was unenforceable because he had signed it under duress. What are the requirements for the use of duress as a defense to a contract? Are the requirements met here? What might the law firm argue in response to Daigle's assertion? Explain. [*Traystman, Coric and Keramidas v. Daigle,* 84 Conn.App. 843, 855 A.2d 996 (2004)]

- **To view a sample answer for Problem 14-7, go to this book's Web site at www.cengage.com/blaw/jentz, select "Chapter 14," and click on "Case Problem with Sample Answer."**

14-8. Fraudulent Misrepresentation. According to the student handbook at Cleveland Chiropractic College (CCC) in Missouri, *academic misconduct* includes "selling . . . any copy of any material intended to be used as an instrument of academic evaluation in advance of its initial administration." Leonard Verni was enrolled at CCC in Dr. Aleksandr Makarov's dermatology class. Before the first examination, Verni was reported to be selling copies of the test. CCC investigated and concluded that Verni had committed academic misconduct. He was dismissed from CCC, which informed him of his right to an appeal. According to the handbook, at the hearing on appeal a student could have an attorney or other adviser, present witnesses' testimony and other evidence, and "question any testimony . . . against him/her." At his hearing, however, Verni did not bring his attorney, present evidence on his behalf, or question any adverse witnesses. When the dismissal was upheld, Verni filed a suit in a Missouri state court against CCC and others, claiming, in part, fraudulent misrepresentation. Verni argued that because he "relied" on the handbook's "representation" that CCC would follow its appeal procedure, he was unable to properly refute the charges against him. Can Verni succeed with this argument? Explain. [*Verni v. Cleveland Chiropractic College*, 212 S.W.3d 150 (Mo. 2007)]

14–9. A QUESTION OF ETHICS

*On behalf of BRJM, LLC, Nicolas Kepple offered Howard Engelsen $210,000 for a parcel of land known as lot five on the north side of Barnes Road in Stonington, Connecticut. Engelsen's company, Output Systems, Inc., owned the land. Engelsen had the lot surveyed and obtained an appraisal. The appraiser valued the property at $277,000, after determining that it was 3.0 acres and thus could not be subdivided because it did not meet the town's minimum legal requirement of 3.7 acres for subdivision. Engelsen responded to Kepple's offer with a counteroffer of $230,000, which Kepple accepted. On May 3, 2002, the parties signed a contract. When Engelsen refused to go through with the deal, BRJM filed a suit in a Connecticut state court against Output, seeking specific performance and other relief. The defendant asserted the defense of mutual mistake on at least two grounds. [*BRJM, LLC v. Output Systems, Inc.*, *100 Conn.App. 143, 917 A.2d 605 (2007)]*

(a) In the counteroffer, Engelsen asked Kepple to remove from their contract a clause requiring written confirmation of the availability of a "free split," which meant that the property could be subdivided without the town's prior approval. Kepple agreed. After signing the contract, Kepple learned that the property was not entitled to a free split. Would this circumstance qualify as a mistake on which the defendant could avoid the contract? Why or why not?

(b) After signing the contract, Engelsen obtained a second appraisal that established the size of lot five as 3.71 acres, which meant that it could be subdivided, and valued the property at $490,000. Can the defendant avoid the contract on the basis of a mistake in the first appraisal? Explain.

14–10. VIDEO QUESTION

Go to this text's Web site at **www.cengage.com/blaw/jentz** and select "Chapter 14." Click on "Video Questions" and view the video titled *Mistake*. Then answer the following questions.

(a) What kind of mistake is involved in the dispute shown in the video (mutual or unilateral, mistake of fact or mistake of value)?

(b) According to the chapter, in what two situations would the supermarket be able to rescind a contract to sell peppers to Melnick at the incorrectly advertised price?

(c) Does it matter if the price that was advertised was a reasonable price for the peppers? Why or why not?

LAW ON THE WEB

For updated links to resources available on the Web, as well as a variety of other materials, visit this text's Web site at

www.cengage.com/blaw/jentz

For a discussion of fraudulent misrepresentation, go to the Web site of attorney Owen Katz at

www.katzlawoffice.com/misrep.html

For a collection of leading cases on contract law, including cases involving topics covered in this chapter, go to

www.lectlaw.com/files/lws49.htm

Legal Research Exercises on the Web

Go to **www.cengage.com/blaw/jentz**, the Web site that accompanies this text. Select "Chapter 14" and click on "Internet Exercises." There you will find the following Internet research exercises that you can perform to learn more about the topics covered in this chapter.

Internet Exercise 14–1: Legal Perspective
Negligent Misrepresentation and *Scienter*

Internet Exercise 14–2: Management Perspective
Fraudulent Misrepresentation

Internet Exercise 14–3: Economic Perspective
Economic Duress

CHAPTER 15

The Statute of Frauds—Writing Requirement

As discussed in Chapter 14, a contract that is otherwise valid may still be unenforceable if the parties have not voluntarily consented to its terms. An otherwise valid contract may also be unenforceable for another reason—because it is not in the proper form. For example, certain types of contracts are required to be in writing or evidenced by a memorandum, note, or electronic record. The writing requirement does not mean that an agreement must be a formal written contract. All that is necessary is some written proof that a contract exists, such as an e-mail exchange evidencing the agreement. Under what is called the **Statute of Frauds,** certain agreements are required by law to be in writing. If there is no written evidence of the contract, it may not be enforceable.

In this chapter, we examine the kinds of contracts that require a writing under the Statute of Frauds and some exceptions to the writing requirement. We also discuss the *parol evidence rule,* which courts follow when determining whether evidence that is extraneous, or external, to written contracts may be admissible at trial. Though not inherently related to the Statute of Frauds, the parol evidence rule has general application in contract law. We cover these topics within one chapter primarily for reasons of convenience and space.

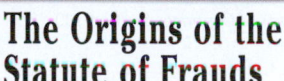

SECTION 1 The Origins of the Statute of Frauds

At early common law, parties to a contract were not allowed to testify. This led to the practice of hiring third party witnesses. As early as the seventeenth century, the English recognized the many problems presented by this practice and enacted a statute to help deal with it. The statute, passed by the English Parliament in 1677, was known as "An Act for the Prevention of Frauds and Perjuries." The act established that certain types of contracts, to be enforceable, had to be evidenced by a writing and signed by the party against whom enforcement was sought.

Today, every state has a statute, modeled after the English act, that stipulates what types of contracts must be in writing or evidenced by a writing. Although the statutes vary slightly from state to state, all states require certain types of contracts to be in writing or evidenced by a written (or electronic) memorandum signed by the party against whom enforcement is sought, unless certain exceptions apply. (These exceptions will be discussed later in this chapter.) In this text, we refer to these statutes collectively as the Statute of Frauds. The actual name of the Statute of Frauds is misleading because it neither applies to fraud nor invalidates any type of contract. Rather, it denies *enforceability* to certain contracts that do not comply with its requirements.

SECTION 2 Contracts That Fall within the Statute of Frauds

The following types of contracts are said to fall "within" or "under" the Statute of Frauds and therefore are required to be in writing or evidenced by a written memorandum or record:

1. Contracts involving interests in land.
2. Contracts that cannot by their terms be performed within one year from the day after the date of formation.

3. Collateral, or secondary, contracts, such as promises to answer for the debt or duty of another and promises by the administrator or executor of an estate to pay a debt of the estate personally—that is, out of her or his own pocket.
4. Promises made in consideration of marriage.
5. Under the Uniform Commercial Code (UCC), contracts for the sale of goods priced at $500 or more.[1]

Contracts Involving Interests in Land

A contract calling for the sale of land is not enforceable unless it is in writing or evidenced by a written memorandum. Land is *real property* and includes all physical objects that are permanently attached to the soil, such as buildings, fences, trees, and the soil itself (see Chapter 47). The Statute of Frauds operates as a *defense* to the enforcement of an oral contract for the sale of land. For example, if Sam contracts orally to sell Blackacre to Betty but later decides not to sell, under most circumstances Betty cannot enforce the contract.

The Statute of Frauds also requires written evidence of contracts for the transfer of other interests in land. For example, mortgage agreements and leases (see Chapter 48) normally must be written, although most state laws provide for the enforcement of short-term oral leases. Similarly, an agreement that includes an option to purchase real property must be in writing for the option to be enforced.[2]

The One-Year Rule

A contract that cannot, *by its own terms,* be performed within one year *from the day after* the contract is formed must be in writing to be enforceable.[3] Suppose that Superior University forms a contract with Kimi San stating that San will teach three courses in history during the coming academic year (September 15 through June 15). If the contract is formed in March, it must be in writing to be enforceable—because it cannot be performed within one year. If the contract is not formed until July, however, it will not have to be in writing to be enforceable—because it can be performed within one year.

The test for determining whether an oral contract is enforceable under the one-year rule of the Statute of Frauds is whether performance is *possible* within one year from the day after the date of contract formation—not whether the agreement is *likely* to be performed within one year. When performance of a contract is objectively impossible during the one-year period, the oral contract will be unenforceable. Exhibit 15–1 illustrates graphically the application of the one-year rule.

1. Although in 2003 it was proposed that this amount be changed from $500 to $5,000, no state has yet adopted this higher dollar threshold (see Chapter 20).

2. See, for example, *Michel v. Bush,* 146 Ohio App.3d 208, 765 N.E.2d 911 (2001); and *Stickney v. Tullis-Vermillion,* 165 Ohio App.3d 480, 847 N.E.2d 29 (2006).

3. *Restatement (Second) of Contracts,* Section 130.

EXHIBIT 15–1 • The One-Year Rule

Under the Statute of Frauds, contracts that by their terms are impossible to perform within one year from the day after the date of contract formation must be in writing to be enforceable. Put another way, if it is at all possible to perform an oral contract within one year from the day after the contract is made, the contract will fall outside the Statute of Frauds and be enforceable.

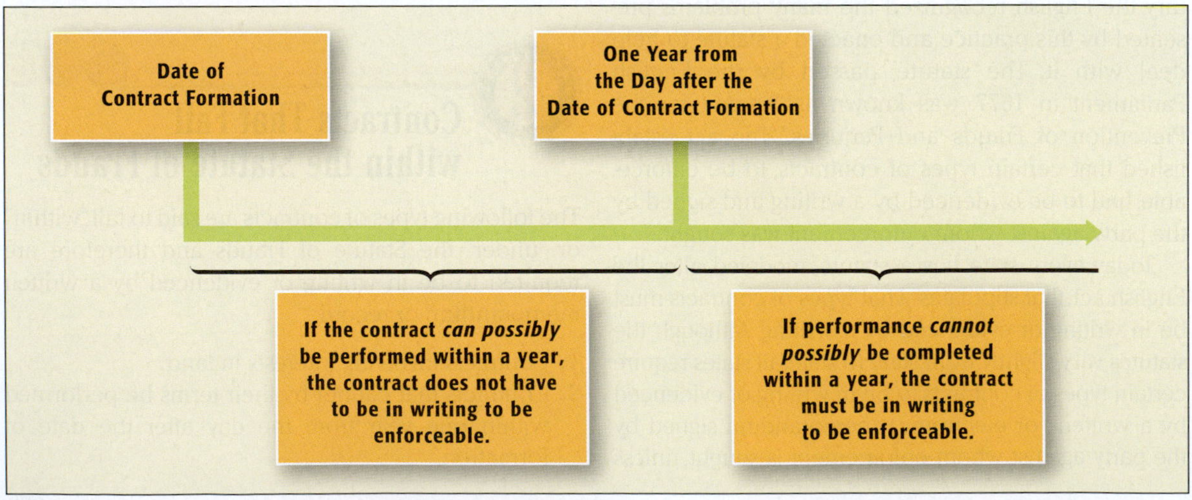

Suppose that Bankers Life orally contracts to lend $40,000 to Janet Lawrence "as long as Lawrence and Associates operates its financial consulting firm in Omaha, Nebraska." The contract does not fall within the Statute of Frauds—no writing is required—because Lawrence and Associates could go out of business in one year or less. In this event, the contract would be fully performed within one year.[4] Similarly, an oral contract for lifetime employment does not fall within the Statute of Frauds. Because an employee who is hired "for life" can die within a year, the courts reason that the contract can be performed within one year.[5]

In the following case, an employee argued that her employer's oral promise to pay her a certain amount as a bonus in installments over 107 months was removed from the Statute of Frauds because the total sum could have been paid within one year.

4. See *Warner v. Texas & Pacific Railroad Co.*, 164 U.S. 418, 17 S.Ct. 147, 41 L.Ed. 495 (1896).

5. See, for example, *Gavengno v. TLT Construction Corp.*, 67 Mass.App.Ct. 1102, 851 N.E.2d 1133 (2006); *Czapla v. Commerz Futures, LLC*, 114 F.Supp.2d 715 (N.D.Ill. 2000); and *Doherty v. Doherty Insurance Agency, Inc.*, 878 F.2d 546 (1st Cir. 1989).

CASE 15.1 Sawyer v. Mills

Court of Appeals of Kentucky, 2007. __ S.W.3d __.

• **Background and Facts** Barbara Sawyer was a paralegal in Melbourne Mills's law firm. Mills had promised Sawyer that he would reward her for assisting in instituting class-action lawsuits. The parties, however, never specified the amount of the bonus nor when it would be paid to Sawyer. After Mills's firm received a substantial settlement in a class-action suit, Sawyer and her husband met with Mills. Sawyer's husband secretly recorded the conversation. The tape recording confirmed that Mills agreed to pay Sawyer a bonus of $1 million, plus the cost of a luxury car. The total amount was to be paid in monthly installments of $10,000. Mills agreed to sign a writing verifying the terms, but he never did. Sawyer received a total of $165,000, and then the payments stopped. Sawyer sued. Mills filed a motion for summary judgment prior to trial, arguing that Sawyer's claims were barred by the Statute of Frauds. The trial proceeded, nonetheless, and the jury returned a verdict in favor of Sawyer for $900,000. Mills filed a motion for a judgment notwithstanding the verdict, again arguing that the agreement between him and Sawyer was barred by the Statute of Frauds. The trial court agreed and granted the motion.

• **Decision and Rationale** The appellate court affirmed the lower court's judgment notwithstanding the verdict. The reviewing court pointed out that Sawyer claimed the Statute of Frauds was not applicable "because the agreement was capable of being performed within one year." But the oral agreement would have taken over one hundred months to be completed. Sawyer countered with the argument that, in spite of the parties not contemplating performance in less than one year, the agreement *could* have been performed in less than one year. The court pointed out that the secret tape recording "clearly shows that Mills never intended to pay Sawyer the bonus as a lump sum and Sawyer is recorded agreeing to the monthly payments. The parties never contemplated that the bonus would be paid within one year." The Statute of Frauds barred Sawyer's claim against Mills because she produced no writing.

• **What If the Facts Were Different?** *Would an oral agreement between Sawyer and Mills to begin the bonus's installment payments on a certain date—July 1, 2008, for example—and complete them no later than fifteen months from that date have been outside the one-year rule of the Statute of Frauds? Explain.*

• **The Legal Environment Dimension** *Sawyer contended that the writing requirement of the Statute of Frauds was met through the combination of the recording of the parties' conversation and the checks Mills signed to Sawyer totaling $165,000. Obviously, the court did not agree. Why not?*

Collateral Promises

A **collateral promise,** or secondary promise, is one that is ancillary (subsidiary) to a principal transaction or primary contractual relationship. In other words, a collateral promise is one made by a third party to assume the debts or obligations of a primary party to a contract if that party does not perform. Any collateral promise of this nature falls under the Statute of Frauds and therefore must be in writing to be enforceable. To understand this concept, it is important to distinguish between primary and secondary promises and obligations.

Primary versus Secondary Obligations

As a general rule, a contract in which a party assumes a primary obligation does not need to be in writing to be enforceable. Suppose that Bancroft forms an oral contract with Harmony's Floral Boutique to send his mother a dozen roses for Mother's Day. Bancroft's oral contract with Harmony's provides that he will pay for the roses when he receives the bill for the flowers. Bancroft is a direct party to this contract and has incurred a *primary* obligation under the contract. Because he is a party to the contract and has a primary obligation to Harmony's, this contract does not fall under the Statute of Frauds and does not have to be in writing to be enforceable. If Bancroft fails to pay the florist and the florist sues him for payment, Bancroft cannot raise the Statute of Frauds as a defense.

In contrast, a contract in which a party assumes a secondary obligation does have to be in writing to be enforceable. Now suppose that Bancroft's mother borrows $10,000 from the International Trust Company on a promissory note payable six months later. Bancroft promises the bank officer handling the loan that he will pay the $10,000 *only if his mother does not pay the loan on time.* Bancroft, in this situation, becomes what is known as a *guarantor* on the loan—that is, he is guaranteeing to the bank that he will pay back the loan if his mother fails to do so—and has incurred a *secondary* obligation. This kind of collateral promise, in which the guarantor states that he or she will become responsible only if the primary party does not perform, must be in writing to be enforceable. Exhibit 15–2 illustrates the concept of a collateral promise. (We will return to the concept of guaranty and the distinction between primary and secondary obligations in Chapter 28, in the context of creditors' rights.)

An Exception—The "Main Purpose" Rule

An oral promise to answer for the debt of another is covered by the Statute of Frauds *unless* the guarantor's main purpose in incurring a secondary obligation is to secure a personal benefit. This type of contract need not be in writing.[6] The assumption is that a court can infer from the circumstances of a particular case whether the "leading objective" of the promisor was to secure a personal benefit and thus, in effect, to answer for her or his own debt.

Consider an example. Braswell contracts with Custom Manufacturing Company to have some machines custom-made for Braswell's factory. She promises Newform Supply, Custom's supplier, that if Newform continues to deliver the materials to Custom for the production of the custom-made machines, she will guarantee payment. This promise need not be in writing, even though the effect may be to pay the debt

6. *Restatement (Second) of Contracts,* Section 116.

EXHIBIT 15–2 • Collateral Promises

A collateral (secondary) promise is one made by a third party (C, in this exhibit) to a creditor (B, in this exhibit) to pay the debt of another (A, in this exhibit), who is primarily obligated to pay the debt. Under the Statute of Frauds, collateral promises must be in writing to be enforceable.

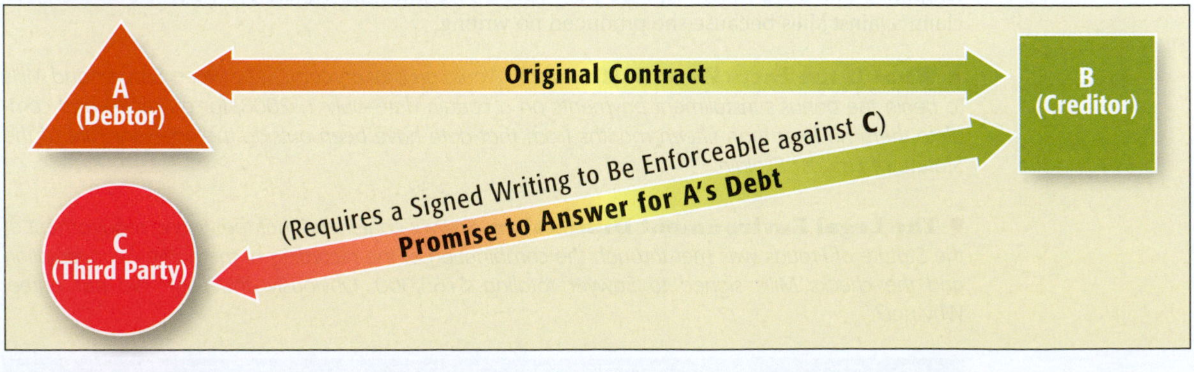

of another. This is because Braswell's main purpose in forming the contract is to secure a benefit for herself.

Another typical application of the main purpose rule occurs when one creditor guarantees a debtor's debt to another creditor to prevent litigation. This allows the debtor to remain in business long enough to generate profits sufficient to pay both creditors.

Promises Made in Consideration of Marriage

A unilateral promise to make a monetary payment or to give property in consideration of a promise to marry must be in writing. If Baumann promises to pay Villard $10,000 if Villard promises to marry Baumann's daughter, the promise must be in writing. The same rule applies to **prenuptial agreements**—agreements made before marriage that define each partner's ownership rights in the other partner's property. A couple might make such an agreement if, for example, a prospective wife wishes to limit the amount her prospective husband can obtain if the marriage ends in divorce. Prenuptial agreements must be in writing to be enforceable.[7]

Consideration Generally Required Generally, courts tend to give more credence to prenuptial agreements that are accompanied by consideration. For example, Maureen, who has few assets, and Kaiser, who has a net worth of $300 million, plan to marry. Kaiser has several children, and he wants them to receive most of his wealth on his death. The couple form a prenuptial agreement in which Kaiser promises to give Maureen $100,000 a year for the rest of her life should they divorce. Kaiser offers to give Maureen $500,000 if she consents to the agreement. If Maureen consents to the agreement and accepts the $500,000, very likely a court will hold this to be a valid prenuptial agreement should it ever be contested.

Courts have used the same reasoning to require adequate consideration in *postnuptial agreements* (agreements entered into after the marriage that define each spouse's rights). Suppose that one year after a couple married, they entered into an agreement concerning the division of marital assets in the event of divorce. The husband, a medical student, agreed to give the wife one-half of his future earnings if he instigated a divorce. The wife, in turn, promised not to return to her dental career, which she had given up when they married, and not to leave the marriage. Is the agreement enforceable? According to many states' courts, the answer is no. Because the wife in this situation had already given up her career to stay at home and tend to the household, this promise was based on past consideration, which is no consideration. Also, because the parties were not having marital difficulties at the time, she was not giving up anything by promising to stay in the marriage.[8]

Must Be Voluntarily Entered In some circumstances, a prenuptial agreement will not be enforceable even if it is in writing. For example, an agreement is not enforceable if the party against whom enforcement is sought proves that he or she did not sign the agreement voluntarily. (For a further discussion of this topic, see this chapter's *Contemporary Legal Debates* feature on pages 284 and 285.)

Contracts for the Sale of Goods

The Uniform Commercial Code (UCC) includes Statute of Frauds provisions that require written evidence of a contract for the sale of goods priced at $500 or more (see Chapter 20). A writing that will satisfy the UCC requirement need only state the quantity term; other terms agreed on can be omitted or even stated imprecisely in the writing, as long as they adequately reflect both parties' intentions. A written memorandum or series of communications evidencing a contract will suffice. The contract will not be enforceable, however, for any quantity greater than that set forth in the writing. In addition, the writing must have been signed by the person to be charged—that is, by the person who refuses to perform or the one being sued. Beyond these two requirements, the writing normally need not designate the buyer or the seller, the terms of payment, or the price. Requirements of the Statute of Frauds under the UCC will be discussed in more detail in Chapter 20.

Exceptions to the Applicability of the Statute of Frauds

Exceptions to the applicability of the Statute of Frauds are made in certain circumstances. We look here at these exceptions.

7. To add certainty to the enforceability of prenuptial agreements, the National Conference of Commissioners on Uniform State Laws issued the Uniform Prenuptial Agreements Act (UPAA) in 1983. The act provides that a prenuptial agreement must be in writing to be enforceable and that the agreement becomes effective when the parties marry.

8. See, for example, *Bratton v. Bratton*, 136 S.W.3d 595 (Tenn. 2004).

CONTEMPORARY LEGAL DEBATES

Prenuptial Agreements and Advice of Counsel

The drafting and signing of prenuptial agreements are often at odds with the very concept of marriage. After all, the parties purport to be in love with each other and desirous of sharing all aspects of their lives. Under these circumstances, the thought of involving lawyers in the negotiation of a prenuptial agreement seems inappropriate. Nonetheless, prenuptial agreements are drafted and entered into every day. Cases occasionally come before the courts in which a party to a prenuptial agreement claims that the agreement should not be enforced because he or she was not advised to consult his or her own attorney before signing the agreement.

Some Jurisdictions Require Independent Counsel

In a growing number of jurisdictions, courts regard the advice of independent counsel as a significant factor in determining whether a party signed a prenuptial agreement voluntarily. In other words, if a prospective spouse did not have the advice of her or his own attorney before signing the agreement, that could indicate that the agreement was not signed voluntarily. In one case, for example, a woman challenged the enforceability of a prenuptial agreement on the ground that her husband's lawyer, who was hired to draft the agreement, did not advise her to have it reviewed by her own attorney. The Supreme Court of North Dakota held that the agreement could in fact be unenforceable for this reason.[a] In a subsequent case involving similar facts, the Supreme Court of North Dakota reiterated that "adequate legal representation will often be the best evidence that a spouse signed the agreement knowledgeably and voluntarily."[b]

Many courts have been particularly suspicious of prenuptial agreements involving a waiver by the future wife of all spousal support in the event of marriage and divorce. The reasoning has been that any prenuptial support waiver might undermine the permanency of the marital relationship, which would be contrary to public policy.

Other Jurisdictions Do Not Require Independent Counsel

Other jurisdictions take a different approach. For example, in a highly publicized case involving baseball player Barry Bonds, the California Supreme Court held that a prenuptial agreement was enforceable even though Bonds's wife was not advised to obtain independent counsel before signing it. The wife, who was Swedish and had little knowledge of English, later stated that she had not understood that by signing the agreement, she would forfeit any right to the earnings and property

a. *Estate of Lutz*, 563 N.W.2d 90 (N.Dak. 1997).
b. See *Binek v. Binek*, 673 N.W.2d 594 (N.Dak. 2004).

Partial Performance In cases involving contracts relating to the transfer of interests in land, a court may grant *specific performance* (performance of the contract according to its precise terms) of an oral contract that has been partially performed. For instance, when the purchaser has paid part of the price, taken possession of the property, and made permanent improvements to it, the parties clearly cannot be returned to the positions they occupied before the contract was formed. Whether a court will enforce an oral contract pertaining to land due to partial performance is usually determined by the degree of injury that would otherwise result. The party seeking performance must have reasonably relied on the contract (and on the other party's continuing agreement) and so changed her or his position that injustice can be avoided only by specific enforcement.[9]

Under the UCC, an oral contract for the sale of goods is enforceable to the extent that a seller accepts payment or a buyer accepts delivery of the goods (see Chapter 20 for a fuller discussion of this exception).[10] The existence and extent of a contract to supply computer kiosks for use in school cafeterias were in dispute in the following case.

9. *Restatement (Second) of Contracts,* Section 129.
10. UCC 2–201(3)(c).

acquisitions of the parties during their marriage. The court, however, held that the agreement was enforceable. The court concluded that the evidence indicated that the wife had consented to the terms of the agreement.[c]

In another case, just days before the wedding, a man drove his future wife to his attorney's office and asked her to sign a prenuptial agreement as a precondition of their marriage. The agreement provided that each spouse waived his or her rights to the other spouse's property. The attorney advised the woman to obtain independent counsel and gave her an opportunity to review the document before signing it, but she did neither. After her husband's death, she claimed that the agreement was invalid because she had not signed it voluntarily. She stated that she had been very embarrassed by the scene in the attorney's office when she signed the agreement and had just wanted to "get it over with." Nonetheless, the court held that the agreement was valid. The court declared that while the husband's actions were "certainly not laudatory" and could be "fairly characterized as surprise tactics," they did not negate the "voluntary nature of the execution."[d]

In a more recent case, the Connecticut Supreme Court rejected a trial court's conclusion that the ex-wife had had insufficient time to digest and understand the disclosure on the day she signed the agreement. The appellate court ruled that "it is the party's responsibility to delay the signing of an agreement that is not understood."[e]

WHERE DO YOU STAND?

Some observers argue that enforcing prenuptial agreements when both parties did not have the advice of independent counsel unduly burdens the financially weaker party to the marriage, customarily the woman. Others contend that allowing financially successful future spouses to protect their assets encourages more marriages to take place.

Clearly, the courts are divided on the issue of whether prenuptial agreements should be upheld despite the lack of independent counsel by both parties. Should the advice of independent counsel be a requirement for a valid prenuptial agreement? What is your position on this issue?

c. *In re Marriage of Bonds*, 24 Cal.4th 1, 5 P.3d 815, 99 Cal.Rptr.2d 252 (2000).

d. *In re Estate of Ingmand*, 2001 WL 855406 (Iowa App. 2001).

e. *Friezo v. Friezo*, 281 Conn. 166, 914 A.2d 533 (2007).

CASE 15.2 School-Link Technologies, Inc. v. Applied Resources, Inc.

United States District Court, District of Kansas, 2007. 471 F.Supp.2d 1101.

Background and Facts Applied Resources, Inc. (ARI), makes computer hardware for point-of-sale systems—kiosks consisting of computers encased in chassis on which card readers or other payment devices are mounted. School-Link Technologies, Inc. (SLT), sells food-service technology to schools. In August 2003, the New York City Department of Education (NYCDOE) asked SLT to propose a cafeteria payment system that included kiosks. SLT asked ARI to participate in a pilot project, orally promising ARI that it would be the exclusive supplier of as many as 1,500 kiosks if the NYCDOE awarded the contract to SLT. ARI agreed. SLT intended to cut ARI out of the deal, however, and told the NYCDOE that SLT would be making its own kiosks. Meanwhile, SLT paid ARI in advance for a certain number of goods but insisted on onerous terms for a written contract to which ARI would not agree. ARI suspended production of the prepaid items and refused to

CASE CONTINUES

CASE 15.2 CONTINUED refund more than $55,000 that SLT had paid. SLT filed a suit in a federal district court against ARI. ARI responded with, among other things, a counterclaim for breach of contract, asserting that SLT failed to use ARI as an exclusive supplier as promised. ARI sought the expenses it incurred for the pilot project and the amount of profit that it would have realized on the entire deal. SLT filed a motion for summary judgment on this claim.

- **Decision and Rationale** The district court denied SLT's motion for summary judgment on ARI's counterclaim for breach of contract "with respect to goods which SLT already received and accepted, [that is], the goods for the pilot program with the NYCDOE." The court acknowledged that, according to the Uniform Commercial Code, a contract for a sale of goods for a price of $500 or more generally must be in writing and must be signed by the party against whom enforcement is sought. The court reasoned that "because the NYCDOE contract undisputedly involved the sale of goods in excess of $500, the parties' oral contract that ARI would be the exclusive supplier of kiosks for the project is not enforceable in the absence of an applicable exception to this general rule." Under the partial performance exception to the rule, an oral contract for a sale of goods for more than $500 that would otherwise be unenforceable for the lack of a writing is enforceable to the extent that the seller delivers the goods and the buyer accepts them. In that situation, the performance serves as a substitute for the required writing. Thus, in this case, the court concluded that the alleged oral contract between SLT and ARI, to the effect that ARI would be the exclusive supplier of kiosks for SLT's contract with NYCDOE, was enforceable to the extent that ARI had delivered the kiosks for the pilot project and SLT had accepted them. The court added, however, that "the remaining aspect of that claim is barred by the Statute of Frauds."

- **The Ethical Dimension** *Are there additional theories on which ARI's request for relief could be based in this case? What common thread underlies these theories?*

- **The Legal Environment Dimension** *Could ARI have successfully asserted a claim against SLT based on fraudulent misrepresentation? Explain.*

Admissions In some states, if a party against whom enforcement of an oral contract is sought "admits" in pleadings, testimony, or otherwise in court that a contract for sale was made, the contract will be enforceable.[11] A contract subject to the UCC will be enforceable, but only to the extent of the quantity admitted.[12] Thus, if the president of Ashley Corporation admits under oath that an oral agreement was made with Com Best to buy certain business equipment for $10,000, the agreement will be enforceable, but only to the extent it is admitted.

Promissory Estoppel In some states, an oral contract that would otherwise be unenforceable under the Statute of Frauds may be enforced under the doctrine of promissory estoppel, based on detrimental reliance. Recall from Chapter 12 that if a promisor makes a promise on which the promisee justifiably relies to his or her detriment, a court may *estop* (prevent) the promisor from denying that a contract exists. Section 139 of the *Restatement (Second) of Contracts* provides that in these circumstances, an oral promise can be enforceable notwithstanding the Statute of Frauds if the reliance was foreseeable to the person making the promise and if injustice can be avoided only by enforcing the promise. (Note the similarities between this exception and the doctrine of partial performance discussed above: both require reasonable reliance and operate to estop a party from claiming that no contract exists.)

Special Exceptions under the UCC Special exceptions to the applicability of the Statute of Frauds apply to sales contracts. Oral contracts for customized goods may be enforced in certain circumstances. Another exception has to do with oral contracts *between merchants* that have been confirmed in a written memorandum. These exceptions and those mentioned above will be examined in greater detail in Chapter 20, when we discuss the UCC provisions regarding the Statute of Frauds. Exhibit 15–3 graphically summarizes the types of contracts that fall under the Statute of Frauds and the various exceptions that apply.

11. *Restatement (Second) of Contracts,* Section 133.
12. UCC 2–201(3)(b).

EXHIBIT 15–3 • Contracts Subject to the Statute of Frauds

a. Under a 2003 amendment to the UCC that has not been adopted by any state, a contract for a sale of goods must involve goods priced at $5,000 or more (this dollar threshold may increase in the future) to be subject to the writing requirement of the Statute of Frauds. This amendment also exempts contracts for the sale of goods from the one-year rule.

b. Some states follow Section 133 (on admissions) and Section 139 (on promissory estoppel) of the *Restatement (Second) of Contracts*.

SECTION 3

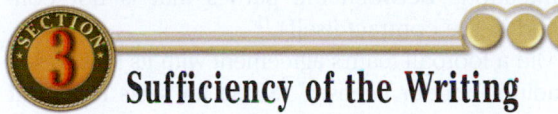

Sufficiency of the Writing

The Statute of Frauds and the UCC require either a written contract or a memorandum (written evidence of the oral contract) signed by the party against whom enforcement is sought, unless there is a legally recognized exception. The signature need not be placed at the end of the document but can be anywhere in the writing. It can be an initial rather than the full name. Indeed, it can even be some form of electronic signature, such as a person's name keyed in at the bottom of an e-mail message.[13] (For a discussion of electronic signatures, see Chapter 19.)

What Constitutes a Writing?

A writing can consist of any order confirmation, invoice, sales slip, check, fax, or e-mail—or such items in combination. The written contract need not consist of a single document to constitute an enforceable contract. One document may incorporate another document by expressly referring to it. Several documents may form a single contract if they are physically attached, such as by staple, paper clip, or glue. Several documents may form a single contract even if they are only placed in the same envelope.

Suppose that Simpson orally agrees to sell some land next to a shopping mall to Terro Properties. Simpson gives Terro an unsigned memo that contains a legal description of the property, and Terro gives Simpson an unsigned first draft of their contract. Simpson sends Terro a signed letter that refers to the memo and to the first and final drafts of the contract. Terro sends Simpson an unsigned copy of the final draft of the contract with a signed check stapled to it. Together, the documents can constitute a writing sufficient to satisfy the Statute of Frauds and bind both parties to the terms of the contract as evidenced by the writings.

What Must Be Contained in the Writing?

A memorandum or note evidencing the oral contract need only contain the essential terms of the contract, not every term. There must, of course, also be some indication that the parties voluntarily agreed to the terms. A faxed memo of the terms of an agreement could be sufficient if it shows that there was a meeting of the minds and that the faxed terms were not just part of the preliminary negotiations.[14]

As mentioned earlier, under the UCC, a writing evidencing a contract for the sale of goods need only state the quantity and be signed by the party to be

13. See, for example, *Rosenfeld v. Zerneck*, 4 Misc.3d 193, 776 N.Y.S.2d 458 (N.Y.Sup. 2004); and *Lamle v. Mattel, Inc.*, 394 F.3d 1355 (Fed.Cir. 2005).

14. See, for example, *Coca-Cola Co. v. Babyback's International, Inc.*, 841 N.E.2d 557 (Ind.App. 2006).

charged. Under most state Statute of Frauds provisions, the writing must also name the parties and identify the subject matter, the consideration, and the essential terms with reasonable certainty. In addition, contracts for the sale of land often are required to state the price and describe the property with sufficient clarity to allow them to be determined without reference to outside sources.

Note that because only the party against whom enforcement is sought must have signed the writing, a contract may be enforceable by one of its parties but not by the other. For example, Rock orally agrees to buy Betty Devlin's lake house and lot for $150,000. Devlin writes Rock a letter confirming the sale by identifying the parties and the essential terms of the sales contract—price, method of payment, and legal address—and signs the letter. Devlin has made a written memorandum of the oral land contract. Because she signed the letter, she normally can be held to the oral contract by Rock. Devlin cannot enforce the contract against Rock, however, because he has not signed or entered into a written contract or memorandum and can assert the Statute of Frauds as a defense.

SECTION 4 The Parol Evidence Rule

Sometimes, a written contract does not include—or contradicts—an oral understanding reached by the parties before or at the time of contracting. For example, Laura is about to lease an apartment. As she is signing the lease, she asks the landlord whether cats are allowed in the building. The landlord says that they are and that Laura can keep her cat in the apartment. The lease that Laura actually signs, however, contains a provision prohibiting pets. Later, a dispute arises between Laura and the landlord over whether the landlord agreed that Laura could have a cat in the apartment. Will Laura be able to introduce evidence at trial to show that, at the time the written contract was formed, the landlord orally agreed that she could have a cat, or will the written contract absolutely control?

In determining the outcome of contract disputes such as the one between Laura and her landlord, the courts look to a common law rule governing the admissibility in court of oral evidence, or *parol evidence*. Under the **parol evidence rule,** if a court finds that the parties intended their written contract to be a complete and final statement of their agreement, then it will not allow either party to present parol evidence (testimony or other evidence of communications between the parties that is not contained in the contract itself).[15]

Did a football team's agreement with its fans to sell "stadium builder licenses" (SBLs) for seats represent the parties' entire contract, or could an SBL brochure vary the agreement? That was the question in the following case.

15. *Restatement (Second) of Contracts,* Section 213.

CASE 15.3 Yocca v. Pittsburgh Steelers Sports, Inc.

Supreme Court of Pennsylvania, 2004. 578 Pa. 479, 854 A.2d 425.

• **Company Profile** Pittsburgh Steelers Sports, Inc., is the operating company for the National Football League's (NFL's) Pittsburgh Steelers (**www.steelers.com**). Art Rooney founded the company, which his family still owns. The team began in 1933 as the Pittsburgh Pirates, named after the baseball team. One of the star players in the early years was Byron "Whizzer" White, who led the NFL in rushing in 1938. White became a justice of the United States Supreme Court in 1962. Renamed in a contest sponsored by the *Pittsburgh Post-Gazette* in 1940, the Steelers had winning seasons only eight times in their first forty years. In the 1970s and 1980, the Steelers won the Super Bowl four times, adding a fifth title in 2006. Groundbreaking for a new stadium took place in 1999.

• **Background and Facts** In October 1998, Pittsburgh Steelers Sports, Inc., and others (collectively, the Steelers) sent Ronald Yocca a brochure that advertised a new stadium to be built for the Pittsburgh Steelers football team. The brochure publicized the opportunity to buy stadium builder licenses (SBLs), which grant the right to buy annual season tickets to the games. Prices varied depending on the seats' locations, which were indicated by small diagrams. Yocca applied for an SBL, listing his seating preferences. The Steelers sent him a letter notifying him of the section in which his seat was located. A diagram included with the letter detailed the parameters of the sec-

CASE 15.3 CONTINUED tion, but it differed from the brochure's diagrams. The Steelers also sent Yocca documents setting out the terms of the SBL and requiring his signature. These documents included an integration clause[a] that read, "This Agreement contains the entire agreement of the parties." Yocca signed the documents, and the Steelers told him the specific location of his seat. When he arrived at the stadium, however, the seat was not where he expected it to be. Yocca and other SBL buyers filed a suit in a Pennsylvania state court against the Steelers, alleging, among other things, breach of contract. The court ordered the dismissal of the complaint. The plaintiffs appealed to a state intermediate appellate court, which reversed this order. The defendants appealed to the state supreme court.

● **Decision and Rationale** The Pennsylvania Supreme Court reversed the lower court's judgment. The state supreme court held that the SBL documents constituted the parties' entire contract and under the parol evidence rule could not be supplemented by previous negotiations or agreements. Because the plaintiffs based their complaint on the claim that the defendants violated the terms of the brochure, and the brochure was not part of the contract, the complaint was properly dismissed. The court explained, "The SBL Brochure did not represent a promise by the Steelers to sell SBLs to Appellees. Rather, the Brochure was merely an offer by the Steelers to sell Appellees the right to be assigned an unspecified seat in an unspecified section of the new stadium and the right to receive a contract to buy an SBL for that later-assigned seat. * * * The SBL Agreement clearly represented the parties' contract concerning the sale of SBLs. Unlike the SBL Brochure, the SBL Agreement reflected a promise by the Steelers to actually sell Appellees a specific number of SBL seats in a specified section. Furthermore, the SBL Agreement * * * explicitly stated that it represented the parties' entire contract regarding the sale of SBLs."

● **What If the Facts Were Different?** *Suppose that the Steelers had not sent Yocca a diagram with the letter notifying him of his seat's section and that the SBL documents had not included an integration clause. Would the result have been different?*

● **The Legal Environment Dimension** *Could Yocca and the other plaintiffs have plausibly argued that the terms of the SBL brochure must have been integrated within the SBL agreement because those terms were needed to define and describe the section assignments to which the agreement referred? Explain.*

a. An *integration clause* is a provision stating that all of the terms of the parties' agreement are included in the written contract. Integrated contracts will be discussed later in this chapter.

Exceptions to the Parol Evidence Rule

Because of the rigidity of the parol evidence rule, the courts have created the following exceptions:

1. *Contracts subsequently modified.* Evidence of any *subsequent modification* (oral or written) of a written contract can be introduced into court. Keep in mind that the oral modifications may not be enforceable if they come under the Statute of Frauds—for example, if they increase the price of the goods for sale to $500 or more or increase the term for performance to more than one year. Also, oral modifications will not be enforceable if the original contract provides that any modification must be in writing.[16]
2. *Voidable or void contracts.* Oral evidence can be introduced in all cases to show that the contract was voidable or void (for example, induced by mistake, fraud, or misrepresentation). The reason is simple: if deception led one of the parties to agree to the terms of a written contract, oral evidence attesting to the fraud should not be excluded. Courts frown on bad faith and are quick to allow such evidence when it establishes fraud.
3. *Contracts containing ambiguous terms.* When the terms of a written contract are ambiguous and require interpretation, evidence is admissible to show the meaning of the terms.
4. *Incomplete contracts.* When the written contract is incomplete in that it lacks one or more of the essential terms, the courts allow evidence to "fill in the gaps."

16. UCC 2–209(2), (3).

5. *Prior dealing, course of performance, or usage of trade.* Under the UCC, evidence can be introduced to explain or supplement a written contract by showing a prior dealing, course of performance, or usage of trade.[17] These terms will be discussed in further detail in Chapter 20, in the context of sales contracts. Here, it is sufficient to say that when buyers and sellers deal with each other over extended periods of time, certain customary practices develop. These practices are often overlooked in the writing of the contract, so courts allow the introduction of evidence to show how the parties have acted in the past. Usage of trade—practices and customs generally followed in a particular industry—can also shed light on the meaning of certain contract provisions, and thus evidence of trade usage may be admissible.
6. *Contracts subject to an orally agreed-on condition precedent.* As you will read in Chapter 17, sometimes the parties agree that a condition must be fulfilled before a party is required to perform the contract. This is called a *condition precedent.* If the parties have orally agreed on a condition precedent and the condition does not conflict with the terms of a written agreement, then a court may allow parol evidence to prove the oral condition. The parol evidence rule does not apply here because the existence of the entire written contract is subject to an orally agreed-on condition. Proof of the condition does not alter or modify the written terms but affects the *enforceability* of the written contract.

   For example, a city leases property for an airport from a helicopter business and the lease is renewable every five years. During the second five-year lease, a dispute arises, and the parties go to mediation. They enter into a settlement memorandum under which they agree to amend the lease agreement subject to the approval of the city council. The city amends the lease, but the business refuses to sign it, contending that the council has not given its approval. In this situation, the council's approval is a condition precedent to the formation of the settlement memorandum contract. Therefore, the parol evidence rule does not apply, and oral evidence is admissible to show that no agreement exists as to the terms of the settlement.[18]

7. *Contracts with an obvious or gross clerical (or typographic) error that clearly would not represent the agreement of the parties.* Parol evidence is admissible to correct an obvious typographic error. Suppose that Bazza agrees to lease 1,000 square feet of office space from Stone Enterprises at the current monthly rate of $3 per square foot. The signed written lease provides for a monthly lease payment of $300 rather than the $3,000 agreed to by the parties. Because the error is obvious, Stone Enterprises would be allowed to admit parol evidence to correct the mistake.

Integrated Contracts

The key in determining whether evidence will be allowed basically depends on whether the written contract is intended to be a complete and final statement of the terms of the agreement. If it is so intended, it is referred to as an **integrated contract,** and extraneous evidence (evidence derived from sources outside the contract itself) is excluded.

An integrated contract can be either completely or partially integrated. If it contains all of the terms of the parties' agreement, then it is completely integrated. If it contains only some of the terms that the parties agreed on and not others, it is partially integrated. If the contract is only partially integrated, evidence of consistent additional terms is admissible to supplement the written agreement.[19] Note that for both complete and partially integrated contracts, courts exclude any evidence that *contradicts* the writing and allow parol evidence only to add to the terms of a partially integrated contract. Exhibit 15–4 illustrates the relationship between integrated contracts and the parol evidence rule.

SECTION 5 The Statute of Frauds in the International Context

As you will read in Chapter 20, the Convention on Contracts for the International Sale of Goods (CISG) provides rules that govern international sales contracts between citizens of countries that have ratified the convention (agreement). Article 11 of the CISG does not incorporate any Statute of Frauds provisions. Rather, it states that a "contract for sale need not be

17. UCC 1–205, 2–202.

18. *Castroville Airport, Inc. v. City of Castroville,* 974 S.W.2d 207 (Tex.App.—San Antonio 1998).

19. *Restatement (Second) of Contracts,* Section 216; and UCC 2–202.

EXHIBIT 15–4 • Parol Evidence Rule

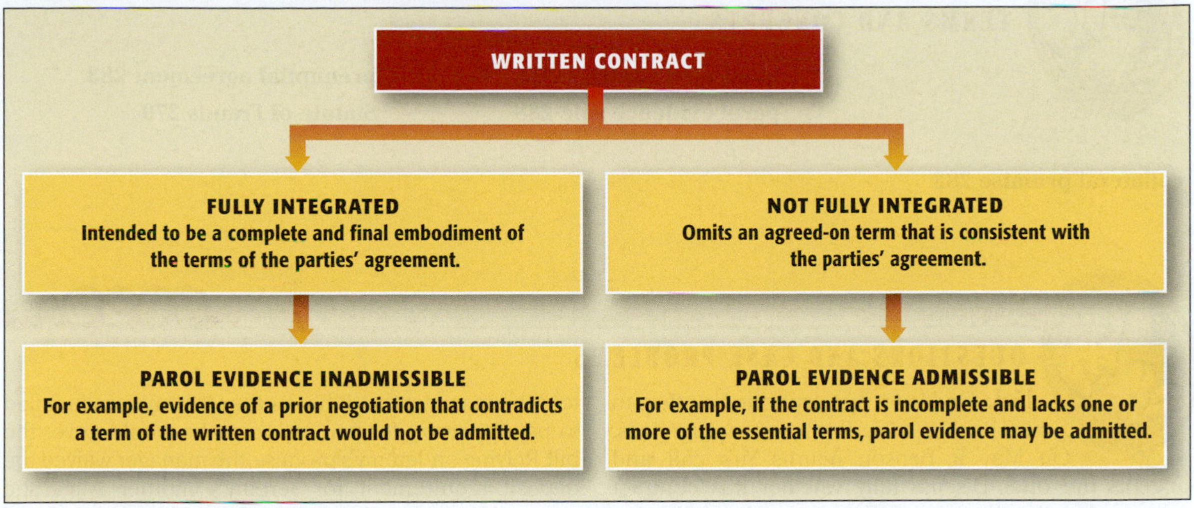

concluded in or evidenced by writing and is not subject to any other requirements as to form."

Article 11 accords with the legal customs of most nations, which no longer require contracts to meet certain formal or writing requirements to be enforceable. Ironically, even England, the nation that created the original Statute of Frauds in 1677, has repealed all of it except the provisions relating to collateral promises and to transfers of interests in land. Many other countries that once had such statutes have also repealed all or parts of them. Some countries, such as France, have never required certain types of contracts to be in writing.

REVIEWING The Statute of Frauds—Writing Requirement

Charter Golf, Inc., manufactures and sells golf apparel and supplies. Ken Odin had worked as a Charter sales representative for six months when he was offered a position with a competing firm. Charter's president, Jerry Montieth, offered Odin a 10 percent commission "for the rest of his life" if Ken would turn down the offer and stay on with Charter. He also promised that Odin would not be fired unless he was dishonest. Odin turned down the competitor's offer and stayed with Charter. Three years later, Charter fired Odin for no reason. Odin sued, alleging breach of contract. Using the information presented in the chapter, answer the following questions.

1. Would a court likely decide that Odin's employment contract falls within the Statute of Frauds? Why or why not?
2. Assume that the court does find that the contract falls within the Statute of Frauds and that the state in which the court sits recognizes every exception to the Statute of Frauds discussed in the chapter. What exception provides Odin with the best chance of enforcing the oral contract in this situation?
3. Now suppose that Montieth had taken out a pencil, written "10 percent for life" on the back of a register receipt, and handed it to Odin. Would this satisfy the Statute of Frauds? Why or why not?
4. Assume that Odin had signed a written employment contract at the time he was hired to work for Charter, but it was not completely integrated. Would a court allow Odin to present parol evidence of Montieth's subsequent promises?

TERMS AND CONCEPTS

collateral promise 282

integrated contract 290

parol evidence rule 288

prenuptial agreement 283

Statute of Frauds 279

QUESTIONS AND CASE PROBLEMS

15-1. On May 1, by telephone, Yu offers to hire Benson to perform personal services. On May 5, Benson returns Yu's call and accepts the offer. Discuss fully whether this contract falls under the Statute of Frauds in the following circumstances:

(a) The contract calls for Benson to be employed for one year, with the right to begin performance immediately.

(b) The contract calls for Benson to be employed for nine months, with performance of services to begin on September 1.

(c) The contract calls for Benson to submit a written research report, with a deadline of two years for submission.

15-2. QUESTION WITH SAMPLE ANSWER

Mallory promises a local hardware store that she will pay for a lawn mower that her brother is purchasing on credit if the brother fails to pay the debt. Must this promise be in writing to be enforceable? Why or why not?

- **For a sample answer to Question 15-2, go to Appendix I at the end of this text.**

15-3. On January 1, Damon, for consideration, orally promised to pay Gary $300 a month for as long as Gary lived, with the payments to be made on the first day of every month. Damon made the payments regularly for nine months and then made no further payments. Gary claimed that Damon had breached the oral contract and sued Damon for damages. Damon contended that the contract was unenforceable because, under the Statute of Frauds, contracts that cannot be performed within one year must be in writing. Discuss whether Damon will succeed in this defense.

15-4. Jeremy took his mother on a special holiday to Mountain Air Resort. Jeremy was a frequent patron of the resort and was well known by its manager. The resort required each of its patrons to make a large deposit to ensure payment of the room rental. Jeremy asked the manager to waive the requirement for his mother and told the manager that if his mother for any reason failed to pay the resort for her stay there, he would cover the bill. Relying on Jeremy's promise, the manager waived the deposit requirement for Jeremy's mother. After she returned home from her holiday, Jeremy's mother refused to pay the resort bill. The resort manager tried to collect the sum from Jeremy, but Jeremy also refused to pay, stating that his promise was not enforceable under the Statute of Frauds. Is Jeremy correct? Explain.

15-5. Oral Contracts. Robert Pinto, doing business as Pinto Associates, hired Richard MacDonald as an independent contractor in March 1992. The parties orally agreed on the terms of employment, including payment to MacDonald of a share of the company's income, but they did not put anything in writing. In March 1995, MacDonald quit. Pinto then told MacDonald that he was entitled to $9,602.17—25 percent of the difference between the accounts receivable and the accounts payable as of MacDonald's last day. MacDonald disagreed and demanded more than $83,500—25 percent of the revenue from all invoices, less the cost of materials and outside processing, for each of the years that he worked for Pinto. Pinto refused. MacDonald filed a suit in a Connecticut state court against Pinto, alleging breach of contract. In Pinto's response and at the trial, he testified that the parties had an oral contract under which MacDonald was entitled to 25 percent of the difference between accounts receivable and payable as of the date of MacDonald's termination. Did the parties have an enforceable contract? What should the court rule, and why? [*MacDonald v. Pinto*, 62 Conn.App. 317, 771 A.2d 156 (2001)]

15-6. Interests in Land. Sierra Bravo, Inc., and Shelby's, Inc., entered into a written "Waste Disposal Agreement" under which Shelby's allowed Sierra to deposit on Shelby's land waste products, deleterious (harmful) materials, and debris removed by Sierra in the construction of a highway. Later, Shelby's asked Sierra why it had not constructed a waterway and a building pad suitable for a commercial building on the property, as they had orally agreed. Sierra denied any such agreement. Shelby's filed a suit in a Missouri state court against Sierra, alleging breach of contract. Sierra contended that any oral agreement was unenforceable under the Statute of Frauds. Sierra argued that because the right to *remove* minerals from land is considered a contract for the sale of an interest in land to which the Statute of Frauds applies, the Statute of Frauds should apply to the right to *deposit* soil on another person's property. How should the court rule, and why? [*Shelby's, Inc. v. Sierra Bravo, Inc.*, 68 S.W.3d 604 (Mo.App. S.D. 2002)]

15–7. CASE PROBLEM WITH SAMPLE ANSWER

Novell, Inc., owned the source code for DR DOS, a computer operating system that Microsoft Corp. targeted with allegedly anticompetitive practices in the early 1990s. Novell worried that if it filed a suit, Microsoft would retaliate with further alleged unfair practices. Consequently, Novell sold DR DOS to Canopy Group, Inc., a Utah corporation. The purposes of the sale were to obligate Canopy to bring an action against Microsoft and to allow Novell to share in the recovery without revealing its role. Novell and Canopy signed two documents—a contract of sale, obligating Canopy to pay $400,000 for rights to the source code, and a temporary license, obligating Canopy to pay at least $600,000 in royalties, which included a percentage of any recovery from the suit. Canopy settled the dispute with Microsoft, deducted its expenses, and paid Novell the remainder of what was due. Novell filed a suit in a Utah state court against Canopy, alleging breach of contract for Canopy's deduction of expenses. Canopy responded that it could show that the parties had an oral agreement on this point. On what basis might the court refuse to consider this evidence? Is that the appropriate course in this case? Explain. [*Novell, Inc. v. Canopy Group, Inc.*, 2004 UT App 162, 92 P.3d 768 (2004)]

- **To view a sample answer for Problem 15–7, go to this book's Web site at www.cengage.com/blaw/jentz, select "Chapter 15," and click on "Case Problem with Sample Answer."**

15–8. The Parol Evidence Rule. Carlin Krieg owned a dairy farm in St. Joe, Indiana, that was appraised at $154,000 in December 1997. In August 1999, Krieg told Donald Hieber that he intended to sell the farm for $106,000. Hieber offered to buy it. Krieg also told Hieber that he wanted to retain a "right of residency" for life in the farm. In October, Krieg and Hieber executed a purchase agreement that provided Krieg "shall transfer full and complete possession" of the farm "subject to [his] right of residency." The agreement also contained an integration clause that stated "there are no conditions, representations, warranties or agreements not stated in this instrument." In November 2000, the house was burned in a fire, rendering it uninhabitable. Hieber filed an insurance claim for the damage and received the proceeds, but he did not fix the house. Krieg filed a suit in an Indiana state court against Hieber, alleging breach of contract. Is there any basis on which the court can consider evidence regarding the parties' negotiations prior to their agreement for the sale of the farm? Explain. [*Krieg v. Hieber*, 802 N.E.2d 938 (Ind.App. 2004)]

15–9. Contract for a Sale of Goods. Milton Blankenship agreed in writing to buy 15 acres of Ella Mae Henry's junkyard property for $15,000 per acre with a ten-year option to buy the remaining 28.32 acres. Blankenship orally agreed to (1) begin operating a car skeleton processing plant within six to fifteen months; (2) buy as many car skeletons generated by the yard as Clifford Henry wanted to sell him, at a certain premium over the market price; and (3) allow all junk vehicles on the property to remain until they were processed at the new plant. Blankenship never operated such a plant, never bought any vehicles from the yard, and demanded that all vehicles be removed from the property. To obtain the remaining 28.32 acres, Blankenship filed a suit in a Georgia state court against Henry, who responded with a counterclaim for breach of contract. Under oath during discovery, Henry testified that their oral agreement allowed him to sell "as many of the car skeletons generated by the Henry junkyard" as he wished, and Blankenship testified that he had agreed to buy as many skeletons as Henry was willing to sell. Does the Statute of Frauds undercut or support Henry's counterclaim? Explain. [*Henry v. Blankenship*, 284 Ga.App. 578, 644 S.E.2d 419 (2007)]

15–10. A QUESTION OF ETHICS

*William Williams is an attorney in Birmingham, Alabama. In 1997, Robert Shelborne asked Williams to represent him in a deal in London, England, from which Shelborne expected to receive $31 million. Shelborne agreed to pay Williams a fee of $1 million. Their overseas contact was Robert Tundy, who said that he was with the "Presidency" in London. Tundy said that a tax of $100,010 would have to be paid for Shelborne to receive the $31 million. Shelborne asked James Parker, a former co-worker, to lend him $50,000. Shelborne signed a note agreeing to pay Parker $100,000 within seventy-two hours. Parker, Shelborne, and Williams wired the $50,000 to an account at Chase Manhattan Bank. They never heard from Tundy again. No $31 million was transferred to Shelborne, who soon disappeared. Williams then learned that no "Presidency" existed in London. Whenever Parker asked Williams about the note, Williams assured him that he would be paid. On Parker's behalf, Williams filed a suit in an Alabama state court against Shelborne, seeking the amount due on the note and damages. The court entered a judgment against the defendant for $200,000, but there were no assets from which to collect it. [*Parker v. Williams*, *977 So.2d 476 (Ala. 2007)]*

(a) Parker filed a suit in an Alabama state court against Williams, alleging, among other things, breach of contract. Parker offered as evidence a tape recording of a phone conversation in which Williams guaranteed Shelborne's loan. Is the court likely to rule in Parker's favor on the contract claim? Why or why not?

(b) In response to Parker's suit, Williams filed a counterclaim, seeking unpaid attorneys' fees relating to the suit that Williams filed against Shelborne on Parker's behalf. The court ruled against Williams on this claim. He appealed to the Alabama Supreme Court but failed to supply a transcript of the trial on his counterclaim, as it was his duty to do. Is the appellate court likely to rule in his favor? Why or why not?

(c) The sham deal at the center of this case is known to law enforcement authorities as advance fee fraud, commonly referred to as a "419 scam." Induced by a promise of a transfer of funds from an overpaid contract or some other suspect source, a victim may be asked to pay a tax or other fee first. Among the parties attracted by the 419 scam in this case, who, if anyone, behaved ethically? Discuss.

LAW ON THE WEB

For updated links to resources available on the Web, as well as a variety of other materials, visit this text's Web site at

www.cengage.com/blaw/jentz

The online version of UCC Section 2–201 on the Statute of Frauds includes links to definitions of certain terms used in the section. To access this site, go to

www.law.cornell.edu/ucc/2/2-201.html

To read a summary of cases concerning whether the exchange of e-mails satisfies the writing requirements of the Statute of Frauds, go to

www.internetlibrary.com/topics/statute_frauds.cfm

Wikipedia provides an interesting discussion of the history and current applicability of the Statute of Frauds, both internationally and in the United States, at

en.wikipedia.org/wiki/Statute_of_frauds

Legal Research Exercises on the Web

Go to **www.cengage.com/blaw/jentz**, the Web site that accompanies this text. Select "Chapter 15" and click on "Internet Exercises." There you will find the following Internet research exercises that you can perform to learn more about the topics covered in this chapter.

Internet Exercise 15–1: Legal Perspective
Promissory Estoppel and the Statute of Frauds

Internet Exercise 15–2: Management Perspective
"Get It in Writing"

Internet Exercise 15–3: Historical Perspective
The English Act for the Prevention of Frauds and Perjuries

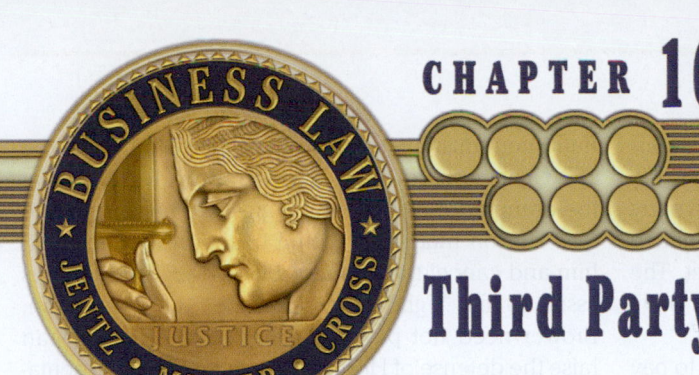

CHAPTER 16

Third Party Rights

Once it has been determined that a valid and legally enforceable contract exists, attention can turn to the rights and duties of the parties to the contract. A contract is a private agreement between the parties who have entered into it, and traditionally these parties alone have rights and liabilities under the contract. This principle is referred to as **privity of contract.**

A *third party*—one who is not a direct party to a particular contract—normally does not have rights under that contract.

There are exceptions to the rule of privity of contract. For example, privity of contract between a seller and a buyer is no longer a requirement to recover damages under product liability laws (see Chapter 23). In this chapter, we look at two other exceptions. One exception allows a party to a contract to transfer the rights or duties arising from the contract to another person through an *assignment* (of rights) or a *delegation* (of duties). The other exception involves a *third party beneficiary contract*—a contract in which the parties to the contract intend that the contract benefit a third party.

SECTION 1 Assignments and Delegations

In a bilateral contract, the two parties have corresponding rights and duties. One party has a *right* to require the other to perform some task, and the other has a *duty* to perform it. The transfer of contractual *rights* to a third party is known as an **assignment.** The transfer of contractual *duties* to a third party is known as a **delegation.** An assignment or a delegation occurs *after* the original contract was made.

Assignments

Assignments are important because they are involved in many types of business financing. Banks, for example, frequently assign their rights to receive payments under their loan contracts to other firms, which pay for those rights. If you obtain a loan from your local bank to purchase a car, you may later receive in the mail a notice from your bank stating that it has transferred (assigned) its rights to receive payments on the loan to another firm and that, when the time comes to repay your loan, you must make the payments to that other firm.

Financial institutions that make *mortgage loans* (loans to enable prospective home buyers to purchase land or a home) often assign their rights to collect the mortgage payments to a third party, such as GMAC Mortgage Corporation. Following the assignment, the home buyers are notified that they must make future payments *not* to the bank that loaned them the funds but to the third party. Millions of dollars change hands daily in the business world in the form of assignments of rights in contracts. If it were not possible to transfer (assign) contractual rights, many businesses could not continue to operate.

Terminology In an assignment, the party assigning the rights to a third party is known as the **assignor,** and the party receiving the rights is the **assignee.** Other traditional terms used to describe the parties in assignment relationships are **obligee** (the person to whom a duty, or obligation, is owed) and **obligor** (the person who is obligated to perform the duty).

The Effect of an Assignment When rights under a contract are assigned unconditionally, the rights of the assignor are extinguished.[1] The third party (the assignee) has a right to demand performance from the other original party to the contract. The assignee takes only those rights that the assignor originally had, however.

For example, Brower is obligated by contract to pay Horton $1,000. In this situation, Brower is the obligor because she owes an obligation, or duty, to Horton. Horton is the obligee, the one to whom the obligation, or duty, is owed. Now suppose that Horton assigns his right to receive the $1,000 to Kuhn. Horton is the assignor, and Kuhn is the assignee. Kuhn now becomes the obligee because Brower owes Kuhn the $1,000. Here, a valid assignment of a debt exists. Kuhn (the assignee-obligee) is entitled to enforce payment in court if Brower (the obligor) does not pay him the $1,000. These concepts are illustrated in Exhibit 16–1.

Rights Assigned Are Subject to the Same Defenses The assignee's rights are subject to the defenses that the obligor has against the assignor. Assume that in the preceding scenario, Brower owed Horton the $1,000 under a contract in which Brower agreed to buy Horton's MacBook laptop. Brower, in deciding to purchase the laptop, relied on Horton's fraudulent misrepresentation that the computer had a 160 gigabyte hard drive. When Brower discovers that the computer has only an 80 gigabyte hard drive, she tells Horton that she is going to return the laptop to him and cancel the contract. Even though Horton has assigned his "right" to receive the $1,000 to Kuhn, Brower need not pay Kuhn the $1,000—Brower can raise the defense of Horton's fraudulent misrepresentation to avoid payment.

Form of the Assignment In general, an assignment can take any form, oral or written. Naturally, it is more difficult to prove that an oral assignment occurred, so it is practical to put all assignments in writing. Of course, assignments covered by the Statute of Frauds must be in writing to be enforceable. For example, an assignment of an interest in land must be in writing to be enforceable. In addition, most states require contracts for the assignment of wages to be in writing.[2]

The circumstances in the following case illustrate some of the problems that can arise with oral assignments. The case also stands for the principle that an assignment, like any contract, must have consideration—in this case, a dance center's assumption of a choreographer's legal and financial duties associated with her choreography.

1. *Restatement (Second) of Contracts,* Section 317.

2. See, for example, California Labor Code Section 300. There are other assignments that must be in writing as well.

EXHIBIT 16–1 • Assignment Relationships

In the assignment relationship illustrated here, Horton assigns his *rights* under a contract that he made with Brower to a third party, Kuhn. Horton thus becomes the *assignor* and Kuhn the *assignee* of the contractual rights. Brower, the *obligor* (the party owing performance under the contract), now owes performance to Kuhn instead of Horton. Horton's original contract rights are extinguished after assignment.

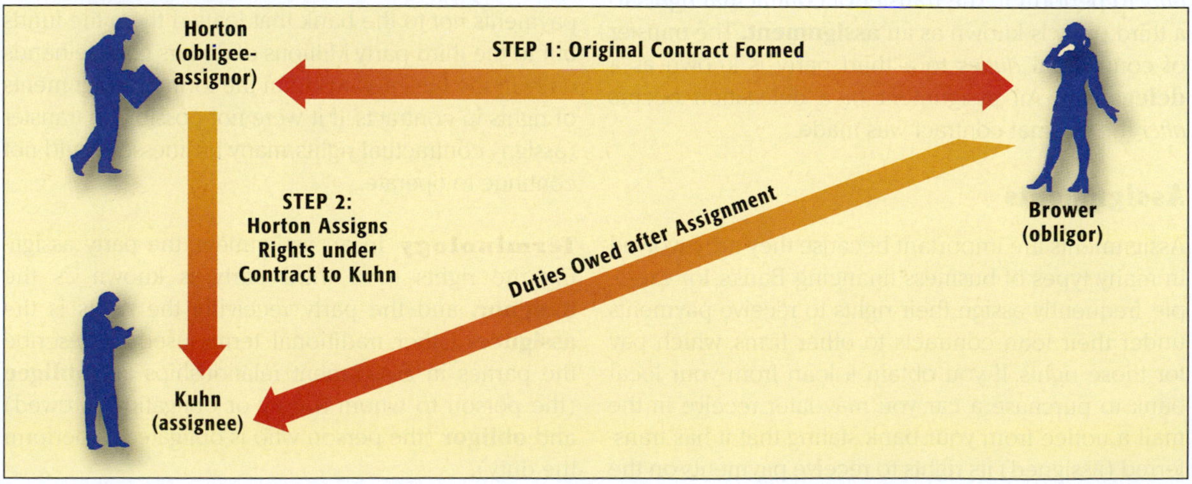

CASE 16.1 Martha Graham School and Dance Foundation, Inc. v. Martha Graham Center of Contemporary Dance, Inc.

United States Court of Appeals, Second Circuit, 2004. 380 F.3d 624.

• **Background and Facts** Martha Graham's career as a dancer, dance instructor, and choreographer began in the first third of the twentieth century. In the 1920s, she started a dance company and a dance school and choreographed works on commission. In the 1940s, she funded the Martha Graham Center of Contemporary Dance, Inc. (the Center). She sold her school to the Martha Graham School of Contemporary Dance, Inc. (the School), in 1956. By 1980, the Center encompassed the School. In 1989, two years before her death, Graham executed a will in which she gave Ronald Protas, the Center's general director, "any rights or interests" in "dance works, musical scores [and] scenery sets." After her death, Protas asserted ownership of all of Graham's dances and related property. In 1999, the Center's board removed Protas and, due to financial problems, suspended operations. Meanwhile, Protas founded the Martha Graham School and Dance Foundation, Inc., and began licensing Graham's dances. When the School reopened in 2001, Protas and his foundation filed a suit in a federal district court against the Center and others to enjoin their use of, among other things, seventy of the dances. The Center responded, in part, that Graham had assigned the dances to it. The court ruled that twenty-one of the dances had been assigned to the Center. The plaintiffs appealed to the U.S. Court of Appeals for the Second Circuit.

• **Decision and Rationale** The U.S. Court of Appeals for the Second Circuit affirmed the lower court's judgment on this issue, "commend[ing] the District Court for its careful rulings on the many issues in this complicated case." The appellate court held that Graham had received consideration for her assignment of certain dances (she benefited by being relieved of various administrative duties), and although the assignment had been oral, it had been reliably proved by written testimony. Evidence that Graham had assigned all of her pre-1956 dances to the Center were two letters from Lee Leatherman, the Center's executive administrator at the time. The letters, written in 1968 and 1971, indicated that "recently Miss Graham assigned performing rights to all of her works to the Martha Graham Center of Contemporary Dance, Inc.," and that "Martha has assigned all rights to all of her works to the Martha Graham Center, Inc." In addition, Jeannette Roosevelt, former president of the Center's board of directors, testified that Graham had given the dances to the Center prior to 1965 or 1966, when she joined the board. There was additional evidence that the Center had acted as the owner of the dances by entering into contracts with other parties, and that Graham was aware of this and did not object. Other evidence showed that the Center received royalties for the dances and treated them as its assets.

• **What If the Facts Were Different?** *Suppose that Graham had not benefited from the Center's assumption of the duties associated with her choreography. Would the alleged assignment have been valid? Why or why not?*

• **The E-Commerce Dimension** *If Graham's dances had existed as part of a database available only over the Internet, would the principles applied in this case, and the way in which they were applied, have been different? Why or why not?*

Rights That Cannot Be Assigned

As a general rule, all rights can be assigned. Exceptions are made, however, under certain circumstances. Some of these exceptions are described next.

When a Statute Expressly Prohibits Assignment. When a statute expressly prohibits assignment of a particular right, that right cannot be assigned. For example, Quincy is an employee of Specialty Computer, Inc. Specialty Computer is an employer under workers' compensation statutes in this state, and thus Quincy is a covered employee. Quincy is injured on the job and begins to collect monthly workers' compensation checks (see Chapter 33 for a discussion of workers' compensation laws). In need of a loan, Quincy borrows from Draper, assigning to Draper all of her future workers' compensation benefits. A state statute prohibits the assignment of future workers' compensation benefits, however, and thus such rights cannot be assigned.

When a Contract Is Personal in Nature. When a contract is for personal services, the rights under the contract normally cannot be assigned unless all that remains is a monetary payment.[3] Suppose that Brower signs a contract to be a tutor for Horton's children. Horton then attempts to assign to Kuhn his right to Brower's services. Kuhn cannot enforce the contract against Brower. Kuhn's children may be more difficult to tutor than Horton's; thus, if Horton could assign his rights to Brower's services to Kuhn, it would change the nature of Brower's obligation. Because personal services are unique to the person rendering them, rights to receive personal services are likewise unique and cannot be assigned.

When an Assignment Will Significantly Change the Risk or Duties of the Obligor. A right cannot be assigned if the assignment will significantly increase or alter the risks to or the duties of the obligor (the party owing performance under the contract).[4] Assume that Horton has a hotel, and to insure it, he takes out a policy with Southeast Insurance. The policy insures against fire, theft, floods, and vandalism. Horton attempts to assign the insurance policy to Kuhn, who also owns a hotel. The assignment is ineffective because it substantially alters Southeast Insurance's *duty of performance.* An insurance company evaluates the particular risk of a certain party and tailors its policy to fit that risk. If the policy is assigned to a third party, the insurance risk is materially altered because the insurance company may have no information on the third party. Therefore, the assignment will not operate to give Kuhn any rights against Southeast Insurance.

When the Contract Prohibits Assignment. When a contract specifically stipulates that a right cannot be assigned, then *ordinarily* the right cannot be assigned. Whether an antiassignment clause is effective depends, in part, on how it is phrased. A contract that states that any assignment is void effectively prohibits any assignment. Note that restraints on the power to assign operate only against the parties themselves. They do not prohibit an assignment by operation of law, such as an assignment pursuant to bankruptcy or death.

The general rule that a contract can prohibit assignment has several exceptions.

1. A contract cannot prevent an assignment of the right to receive monetary payments. This exception exists to encourage the free flow of funds and credit in modern business settings.
2. The assignment of rights in real estate often cannot be prohibited because such a prohibition is contrary to public policy in most states. Prohibitions of this kind are called restraints against **alienation** (transfer of land ownership).
3. The assignment of *negotiable instruments* (see Chapter 24) cannot be prohibited.
4. In a contract for the sale of goods, the right to receive damages for breach of contract or payment of an account owed may be assigned even though the sales contract prohibits such an assignment.[5]

Notice of Assignment Once a valid assignment of rights has been made, the assignee (the third party to whom the rights have been assigned) should notify the obligor (the one owing performance) of the assignment. For instance, in the previously discussed example, when Horton assigns to Kuhn his right to receive the $1,000 from Brower, Kuhn should notify Brower, the obligor, of the assignment. Giving notice is not legally necessary to establish the validity of the assignment: an assignment is effective immediately, whether or not notice is given. Two major problems arise, however, when notice of the assignment is not given to the obligor.

1. If the assignor assigns the same right to two different persons, the question arises as to which one has priority—that is, which one has the right to the performance by the obligor. Although the rule most often observed in the United States is that the first assignment in time is the first in right, some states follow the English rule, which basically gives priority to the first assignee who gives notice.
2. Until the obligor has notice of an assignment, the obligor can discharge his or her obligation by performance to the assignor (the obligee), and performance by the obligor to the assignor (obligee) constitutes a discharge to the assignee. Once the obligor receives proper notice, however, only performance to the assignee can discharge the

3. *Restatement (Second) of Contracts,* Sections 317 and 318.
4. Section 2–210(2) of the Uniform Commercial Code (UCC).
5. UCC 2–210(2).

obligor's obligations. In the Horton-Brower-Kuhn example, assume that Brower, the obligor, is not notified of Horton's assignment of his rights to Kuhn. Brower subsequently pays Horton the $1,000. Although the assignment was valid, Brower's payment to Horton discharges the debt. Kuhn's failure to give notice to Brower of the assignment has caused Kuhn to lose the right to collect the cash from Brower. If, however, Kuhn had given Brower notice of the assignment, Brower's payment to Horton would not have discharged the debt, and Kuhn would have had a legal right to require payment from Brower.

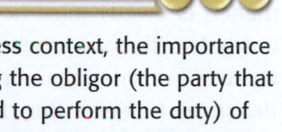

In a business context, the importance of notifying the obligor (the party that is obligated to perform the duty) of an assignment cannot be overemphasized. Providing notice of assignment, though not legally required, is one of the best ways to avoid potential legal disputes over assignments. Whether the businessperson is the assignee or the assignor, she or he should inform the obligor of the assignment. As already described, an assignee who does not give notice may lose the right to performance, but failure to notify the obligor may have repercussions for the assignor as well.

Consider what would happen if no notice is given by either the assignor or the assignee, and the obligor performs the duty for the assignor. In this situation, the assignee, to whom the right to receive performance was assigned, can sue the assignor for breach of contract. The assignor will also likely be involved in litigation if he or she has assigned a right to two different parties, which can happen when assigning rights that overlap somewhat (such as rights to receive profits from a given enterprise). Assignments of rights are extremely useful in business, but to prevent legal problems, businesspersons should be careful to assign the same rights only once and should always give the obligor notice of the assignment.

Delegations

Just as a party can transfer rights through an assignment, a party can also transfer duties. Duties are not assigned, however; they are *delegated.* Normally, a delegation of duties does not relieve the party making the delegation (the **delegator**) of the obligation to perform in the event that the party to whom the duty has been delegated (the **delegatee**) fails to perform. No special form is required to create a valid delegation of duties. As long as the delegator expresses an intention to make the delegation, it is effective; the delegator need not even use the word *delegate.* Exhibit 16–2 illustrates delegation relationships.

EXHIBIT 16–2 • Delegation Relationships

In the delegation relationship illustrated here, Brower delegates her *duties* under a contract that she made with Horton to a third party, Kuhn. Brower thus becomes the *delegator* and Kuhn the *delegatee* of the contractual duties. Kuhn now owes performance of the contractual duties to Horton. Note that a delegation of duties normally does not relieve the delegator (Brower) of liability if the delegatee (Kuhn) fails to perform the contractual duties.

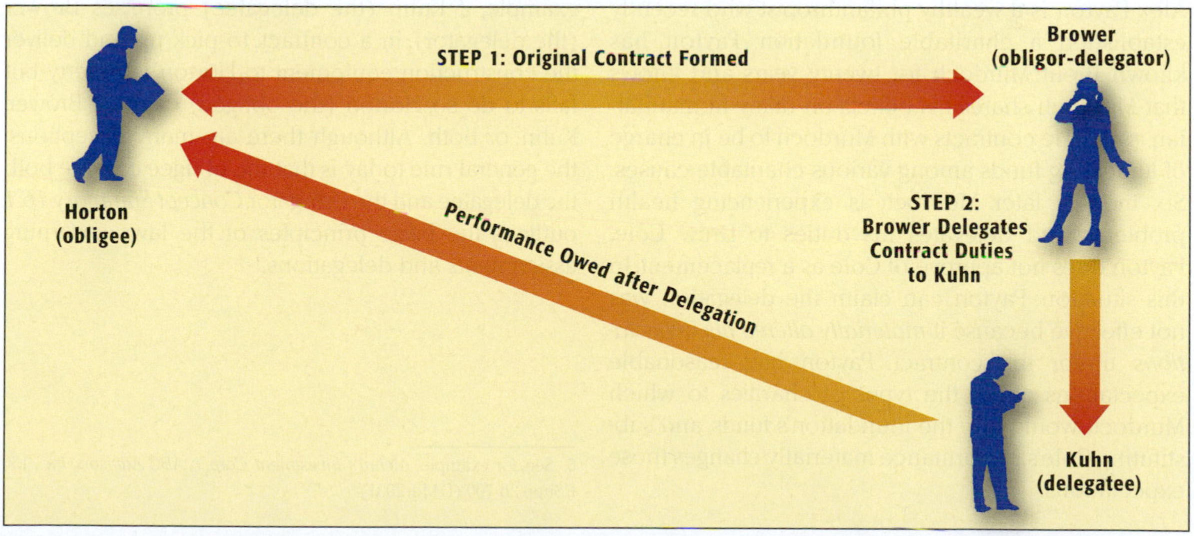

Duties That Cannot Be Delegated As a general rule, any duty can be delegated. There are, however, some exceptions to this rule. Delegation is prohibited in the circumstances discussed next.

When the Duties Are Personal in Nature. When special trust has been placed in the obligor or when performance depends on the personal skill or talents of the *obligor* (the person contractually obligated to perform), contractual duties cannot be delegated. For example, Horton, who is impressed with Brower's ability to perform veterinary surgery, contracts with Brower to have Brower perform surgery on Horton's prize-winning stallion in July. Brower later decides that she would rather spend the summer at the beach, so she delegates her duties under the contract to Kuhn, who is also a competent veterinary surgeon. The delegation is not effective without Horton's consent, no matter how competent Kuhn is, because the contract is for *personal* performance.

In contrast, nonpersonal duties may be delegated. Assume that Brower contracts with Horton to pick up and deliver heavy construction machinery to Horton's property. Brower delegates this duty to Kuhn, who is in the business of delivering heavy machinery. This delegation is effective because the performance required is of a *routine* and *nonpersonal* nature.

When Performance by a Third Party Will Vary Materially from That Expected by the Obligee. When performance by a third party will vary materially from that expected by the obligee (the one to whom performance is owed) under the contract, contractual duties cannot be delegated. Suppose that Alex Payton is a wealthy philanthropist who recently established a charitable foundation. Payton has known Brent Murdoch for twenty years and knows that Murdoch shares his beliefs on many humanitarian issues. He contracts with Murdoch to be in charge of allocating funds among various charitable causes. Six months later, Murdoch is experiencing health problems and delegates his duties to Drew Cole. Payton does not approve of Cole as a replacement. In this situation, Payton can claim the delegation was not effective because it *materially altered his expectations* under the contract. Payton had reasonable expectations about the types of charities to which Murdoch would give the foundation's funds, and substituting Cole's performance materially changes those expectations.

When the Contract Prohibits Delegation. When the contract expressly prohibits delegation by including an *antidelegation clause,* the duties cannot be delegated. For example, R.W. Stern Company contracts with Jan Pearson, a certified public accountant, to perform its annual audits for the next five years. If the contract prohibits delegation, then Pearson cannot delegate her duty to perform the audit to another accountant at the same firm. In some situations, however, when the duties are completely impersonal in nature, courts have held that the duties can be delegated notwithstanding an antidelegation clause.

Effect of a Delegation If a delegation of duties is enforceable, the obligee (the one to whom performance is owed) must accept performance from the delegatee (the one to whom the duties have been delegated). Consider again the example in which Brower delegates to Kuhn the duty to pick up and deliver heavy construction machinery to Horton's property. In that situation, Horton (the obligee) must accept performance from Kuhn (the delegatee) because the delegation was effective. The obligee can legally refuse performance from the delegatee only if the duty is one that cannot be delegated.

As noted, a valid delegation of duties does not relieve the delegator of obligations under the contract.[6] Thus, in the above example, if Kuhn (the delegatee) fails to perform, Brower (the delegator) is still liable to Horton (the obligee). The obligee can also hold the delegatee liable if the delegatee made a promise of performance that will directly benefit the obligee. In this situation, there is an "assumption of duty" on the part of the delegatee, and breach of this duty makes the delegatee liable to the obligee. For example, if Kuhn (the delegatee) promises Brower (the delegator), in a contract, to pick up and deliver the construction equipment to Horton's property but fails to do so, Horton (the obligee) can sue Brower, Kuhn, or both. Although there are many exceptions, the general rule today is that the obligee can sue both the delegatee and the delegator. *Concept Summary 16.1* outlines the basic principles of the laws governing assignments and delegations.

6. See, for example, *Mehul's Investment Corp. v. ABC Advisors, Inc.*, 130 F.Supp.2d 700 (D.Md. 2001).

CONCEPT SUMMARY 16.1
Assignments and Delegations

Which Rights Can Be Assigned, and Which Duties Can Be Delegated?	All rights can be assigned *unless:* 1. A statute expressly prohibits assignment. 2. The contract is for personal services. 3. The assignment will materially alter the obligor's risk or duties. 4. The contract prohibits assignment.	All duties can be delegated *unless:* 1. Performance depends on the obligor's personal skills or talents. 2. Special trust has been placed in the obligor. 3. Performance by a third party will materially vary from that expected by the obligee. 4. The contract prohibits delegation.
What If the Contract Prohibits Assignment or Delegation?	No rights can be assigned *except:* 1. Rights to receive funds. 2. Ownership rights in real estate. 3. Rights to negotiable instruments. 4. Rights to sales contract payments or damages for breach of a sales contract.	Generally, no duties can be delegated.
What Is the Effect on the Original Party's Rights?	On a valid assignment, effective immediately, the original party (assignor) no longer has any rights under the contract.	On a valid delegation, if the delegatee fails to perform, the original party (delegator) is liable to the obligee (who may also hold the delegatee liable).

Assignment of "All Rights"

When a contract provides for an "assignment of all rights," this wording may create both an assignment of rights and a delegation of duties.[7] Therefore, when general words are used (for example, "I assign the contract" or "I assign all my rights under the contract"), the contract normally is construed as implying both an assignment of the assignor's rights and a delegation of any duties of performance owed by the assignor under the contract being assigned. Thus, the assignor remains liable if the assignee fails to perform the contractual obligations.

SECTION 2 Third Party Beneficiaries

Another exception to the doctrine of privity of contract arises when the original parties to the contract intend at the time of contracting that the contract performance directly benefit a third person. In this situation, the third person becomes a **third party beneficiary** of the contract. As an **intended beneficiary** of the contract, the third party has legal rights and can sue the promisor directly for breach of the contract.

Who, though, is the promisor? In a bilateral contract, both parties to the contract are promisors because they both make promises that can be enforced. To determine the identity of the promisor in a third party beneficiary contract, the court will ask which party made the promise that benefits the third party—that person is the promisor. Allowing a third party to sue the promisor directly in effect circumvents the "middle person" (the promisee) and thus reduces the burden on the courts. Otherwise, the third party would sue the promisee, who would then sue the promisor.

Types of Intended Beneficiaries

At one time, third party beneficiaries had no legal rights in contracts. Over time, however, the concept developed that a third party for whose benefit a contract was formed (an intended beneficiary) could sue

7. *Restatement (Second) of Contracts,* Section 328; UCC 2–210(3), (4).

the promisor to have the contract enforced. In a classic case decided in 1859, *Lawrence v. Fox*,[8] the court permitted a third party beneficiary to bring suit directly against a promisor. This case established the rule that a *creditor beneficiary* can sue the promisor directly. A creditor beneficiary is one who benefits from a contract in which one party (the promisor) promises another party (the promisee) to pay a debt that the promisee owes to a third party (the creditor beneficiary). As an intended beneficiary, the creditor beneficiary can sue the promisor directly to enforce the contract and obtain payment on the debt.

Another type of intended beneficiary is a *donee beneficiary*. When a contract is made for the express purpose of giving a *gift* to a third party, the third party (the donee beneficiary) can sue the promisor directly to enforce the promise.[9] The most common donee beneficiary contract is a life insurance contract. For example, Akins (the promisee) pays premiums to Standard Life, a life insurance company, and Standard Life (the promisor) promises to pay a certain amount on Akins's death to anyone Akins designates as a beneficiary. The designated beneficiary is a donee beneficiary under the life insurance policy and can enforce the promise made by the insurance company to pay her or him on Akins's death.

As the law concerning third party beneficiaries evolved, numerous cases arose in which the third party beneficiary did not fit readily into either the creditor beneficiary or the donee beneficiary category. Thus, the modern view, and the one adopted by the *Restatement (Second) of Contracts*, does not draw such clear lines between the types of intended beneficiaries. Today, courts frequently distinguish only between *intended beneficiaries* (who can sue to enforce contracts made for their benefit) and *incidental beneficiaries* (who cannot sue, as will be discussed shortly).

The Vesting of an Intended Beneficiary's Rights

An intended third party beneficiary cannot enforce a contract against the original parties until the rights of the third party have *vested*, which means the rights have taken effect and cannot be taken away. Until these rights have vested, the original parties to the contract—the promisor and the promisee—can modify or rescind the contract without the consent of the third party.

8. 20 N.Y. 268 (1859).

9. *Seaver v. Ransom*, 224 N.Y. 233, 120 N.E. 639 (1918).

When do the rights of third parties vest? The majority of courts hold that the rights vest when any of the following occurs:

1. The third party materially changes his or her position in justifiable reliance on the promise.
2. The third party brings a lawsuit on the promise.
3. The third party demonstrates her or his consent to the promise at the request of the promisor or promisee.[10]

If the contract expressly reserves to the contracting parties the right to cancel, rescind, or modify the contract, the rights of the third party beneficiary are subject to any changes that result. If the original contract reserves the right to revoke the promise or change the beneficiary, the vesting of the third party's rights does not terminate that power.[11] For example, in most life insurance contracts, the policyholder reserves the right to change the designated beneficiary.

Intended versus Incidental Beneficiaries

The benefit that an **incidental beneficiary** receives from a contract between two parties is unintentional. Because the benefit is *unintentional*, an incidental beneficiary cannot sue to enforce the contract.

Determining Whether a Third Party Is an Intended or an Incidental Beneficiary In determining whether a third party beneficiary is an intended or an incidental beneficiary, the courts focus on the intent, as expressed in the contract language and implied by the surrounding circumstances. No single test is available to embrace all possible situations in which a third party is an intended beneficiary. One factor that courts consider is whether a reasonable person in the position of the beneficiary would believe that the promisee intended to confer on the beneficiary the right to enforce the contract. The courts also look at other factors. For example, if performance is to be rendered directly to the third party or the contract expressly designates the third party as a beneficiary, this strongly indicates that the third party is an *intended* beneficiary. Exhibit 16–3 graphically illustrates the distinction between intended beneficiaries and incidental beneficiaries.

10. *Restatement (Second) of Contracts,* Section 311.

11. Defenses against third party beneficiaries are given in the *Restatement (Second) of Contracts,* Section 309.

EXHIBIT 16–3 • Third Party Beneficiaries

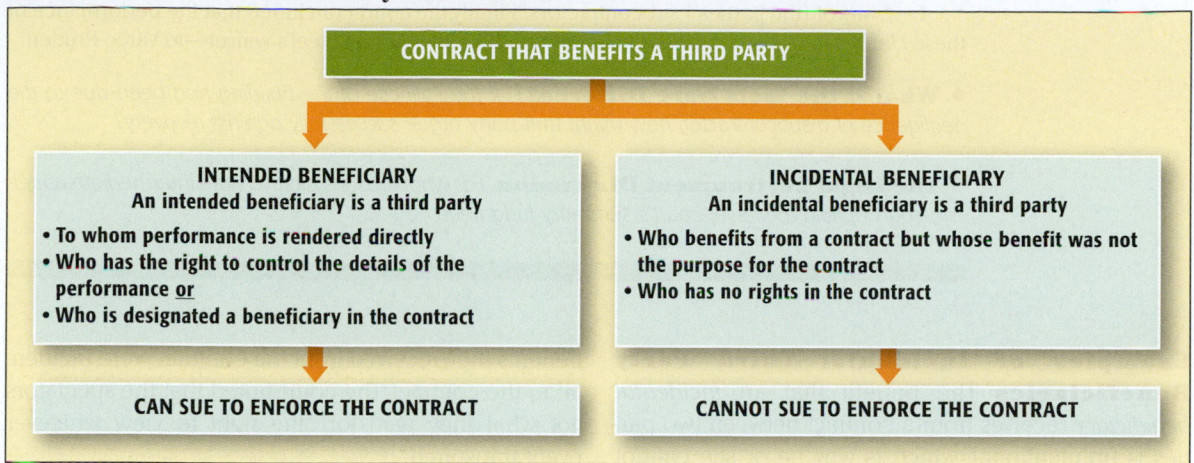

CONTRACT THAT BENEFITS A THIRD PARTY

INTENDED BENEFICIARY
An intended beneficiary is a third party
- To whom performance is rendered directly
- Who has the right to control the details of the performance or
- Who is designated a beneficiary in the contract

CAN SUE TO ENFORCE THE CONTRACT

INCIDENTAL BENEFICIARY
An incidental beneficiary is a third party
- Who benefits from a contract but whose benefit was not the purpose for the contract
- Who has no rights in the contract

CANNOT SUE TO ENFORCE THE CONTRACT

In the following case, a subcontractor claimed to be an intended beneficiary of the general contractor's contractual promise to obtain property insurance after the construction of an addition to a building was completed. The case illustrates how resolving the issue of whether a beneficiary is intended or incidental can have serious consequences for the beneficiary's liability.

CASE 16.2 Midwestern Indemnity Co. v. Systems Builders, Inc.

Court of Appeals of Indiana, 2004. 801 N.E.2d 661.

• Background and Facts Action Steel, Inc., entered into a contract with Systems Builders, Inc., a general contractor, to construct an addition to a commercial building in Indianapolis, Indiana. The contract provided that Action Steel would obtain, after the addition's completion, insurance which "shall include the interest of . . . subcontractors." The parties would then "waive all rights against . . . any of their subcontractors." Varco-Pruden Building, a subcontractor, designed the addition, which was completed in the summer of 1995. Action Steel obtained an insurance policy from Midwestern Indemnity Co. In January 1996, a snowstorm hit the Indianapolis area and the new addition collapsed. Midwestern paid more than $1.3 million to Action Steel for the loss. Because Midwestern paid for the loss, it stood in Action Steel's place in a suit filed in an Indiana state court against Varco-Pruden and others to recover this amount. Varco-Pruden filed a motion for summary judgment, arguing, in part, that it was a third party beneficiary of the waiver clause in the contract between Action Steel and Systems Builders. The court issued a summary judgment in favor of Varco-Pruden on this point. Midwestern appealed to a state intermediate appellate court, arguing that Varco-Pruden was not a third party beneficiary of the contract.

• Decision and Rationale The state intermediate appellate court affirmed the lower court's judgment. One who is not a party to a contract can enforce the contract as a third party beneficiary if (1) the contracting parties intended to benefit the third party; (2) the contract imposed a duty on one of the parties in favor of the third party; and (3) the performance of the terms of the contract rendered a direct benefit to the third party. According to the appellate court, a "plain reading" of the construction contract indicated that Action Steel intended to benefit Varco-Pruden. Under the contract's terms, when Action Steel bought property insurance after the project was complete, Action Steel intended that subcontractors, such as Varco-Pruden, would benefit from the waiver clause. The contract provided that the insurance "shall include the interest of * * * subcontractors." Furthermore, the contract imposed a duty on Action Steel, providing that

CASE CONTINUES

CASE 16.2 CONTINUED if it acquired insurance after the completion of the project, it "shall * * * waive all rights against * * * any of [the parties'] subcontractors." Finally, the court concluded that the performance of these clauses in the contract rendered a direct benefit—Action Steel's waiver—to Varco-Pruden.

- **What If the Facts Were Different?** *If the collapse of the building had been due to the negligence of a subcontractor, how might that party argue successfully against recovery?*

- **The Legal Environment Dimension** *For what reasons did the state intermediate appellate court uphold the lower court's summary judgment?*

Examples of Incidental Third Party Beneficiaries The benefit that an *incidental beneficiary* receives from a contract between two parties is unintentional, which is why he or she cannot enforce a contract. Any beneficiary who is not deemed an intended beneficiary is considered incidental.

For example, in one case, spectators at a Mike Tyson boxing match in which Tyson was disqualified for biting his opponent's ear sued Tyson and the fight's promoters for a refund on the basis of breach of contract. The spectators claimed that they had standing to sue the defendants as third party beneficiaries of the contract between Tyson and the fight's promoters. The court, however, held that the spectators did not have standing to sue because they were not in contractual privity with any of the defendants. Furthermore, any benefits they received from the contract were incidental to the contract. The court noted that the spectators got what they paid for: "the right to view whatever event transpired."[12]

In the following case, a national beauty pageant organization and one of its state affiliates agreed that the national organization would accept the winner of the state contest as a competitor in the national pageant. When the state winner was asked to resign her title, she filed a suit to enforce the agreement to have herself declared a contestant in the national pageant. The national organization argued that she was an incidental, not an intended, beneficiary of the agreement.

12. *Castillo v. Tyson,* 268 A.D.2d 336, 701 N.Y.S.2d 423 (Sup.Ct.App.Div. 2000). See also *Bowers v. Federation Internationale de l'Automobile,* 489 F.3d 316 (7th Cir. 2007).

CASE 16.3 Revels v. Miss America Organization

Court of Appeals of North Carolina, 2007. 182 N.C.App. 334, 641 S.E.2d 721.
www.aoc.state.nc.us/www/public/html/opinions.htm[a]

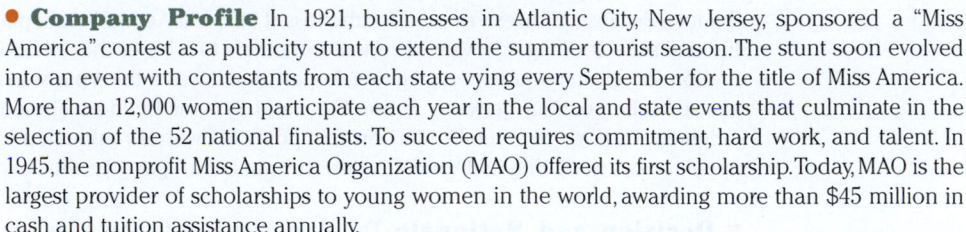

- **Company Profile** In 1921, businesses in Atlantic City, New Jersey, sponsored a "Miss America" contest as a publicity stunt to extend the summer tourist season. The stunt soon evolved into an event with contestants from each state vying every September for the title of Miss America. More than 12,000 women participate each year in the local and state events that culminate in the selection of the 52 national finalists. To succeed requires commitment, hard work, and talent. In 1945, the nonprofit Miss America Organization (MAO) offered its first scholarship. Today, MAO is the largest provider of scholarships to young women in the world, awarding more than $45 million in cash and tuition assistance annually.

- **Background and Facts** Miss North Carolina Pageant Organization, Inc. (MNCPO), is a franchisee of Miss America Organization (MAO). Under the "Miss America Organization Official Franchise Agreement," MNCPO conducts a public contest (the "State Finals") to select Miss North Carolina and to prepare Miss North Carolina for participation in the Miss America pageant (the "National Finals").[b] In return, MAO "accept[s] the winner of the State Finals . . . as a contestant in the National Finals." On June 22, 2002, MNCPO designated Rebekah Revels "Miss North Carolina 2002." On July 19, MAO received an anonymous e-mail (which was later determined to have been

a. In the "Court of Appeals Opinions" section, click on "2007." In the result, scroll to the "20 March 2007" section and click on the name of the case to access the opinion. The North Carolina Administrative Office of the Courts maintains this Web site.
b. A *franchise* is an arrangement by which the owner of a trademark, or other intellectual property, licenses the use of the mark to another party under specific conditions.

CASE 16.3 CONTINUED sent by Revels's ex-boyfriend), implying that she had formerly cohabited with a "male non-relative" and that nude photos of her existed. Revels confirmed the existence of the photos. On July 22, MAO and MNCPO asked Revels to resign as Miss North Carolina and told her that if she refused, she would be excluded from competing in the National Finals. On July 23, she resigned. She then filed a suit in a North Carolina state court against MAO, MNCPO, and others, asserting, among other things, breach of contract. The court issued a summary judgment in MAO's favor. Revels appealed this judgment to a state intermediate appellate court.

• **Decision and Rationale** The appellate court affirmed the lower court's judgment in favor of MAO. Revels contended that there was sufficient evidence that she was a third party beneficiary under the franchise agreement between MAO and MNCPO. The reviewing court held that "in order to establish a claim as a third-party beneficiary, plaintiff must show (1) that a contract exists between two persons or entities; (2) that the contract is valid and enforceable; and (3) that the contract was executed for the direct, and not intentional, benefit of the third party." But, the court pointed out, Revels was an incidental beneficiary of the agreement between MAO and MNCPO. Although the agreement provided that MAO would accept the winner of the State Finals as a contestant in the National Finals, this did not establish that the two organizations intended to make the winner a direct beneficiary of the agreement. Thus, Revels was an incidental beneficiary and could not maintain an action against MAO based on the agreement.

• **The Global Dimension** *If the agreement between MAO and MNCPO had involved a third party—an international pageant organization—would this have been a basis for concluding that Revels was a third party intended beneficiary? Why or why not?*

• **The E-Commerce Dimension** *How might Revels's third party status with respect to the agreement between MAO and MNCPO have been affected if the contracting parties had conducted their business online? Explain.*

REVIEWING Third Party Rights

Myrtle Jackson owns several commercial buildings that she leases to businesses, one of which is a restaurant. The lease states that tenants are responsible for securing all necessary insurance policies but the landlord is obligated to keep the buildings in good repair. The owner of the restaurant, Joe McCall, tells his restaurant manager to purchase insurance, but the manager never does so. Jackson tells her son-in-law, Rob Dunn, to perform any necessary maintenance for the buildings. Dunn knows that the ceiling in the restaurant needs repair but fails to do anything about it. One day a customer, Ian Faught, is dining in the restaurant when a chunk of the ceiling falls on his head and fractures his skull. Faught files suit against the restaurant and discovers that there is no insurance policy in effect. Faught then files suit against Jackson, arguing that he is an intended third party beneficiary of the lease provision requiring insurance and thus can sue Jackson for failing to enforce the lease (which requires the restaurant to carry insurance). Using the information presented in the chapter, answer the following questions.

1. Can Jackson delegate her duty to maintain the buildings to Dunn? Why or why not?
2. Who can be held liable for Dunn's failure to fix the ceiling, Jackson or Dunn?
3. Was Faught an intended third party beneficiary of the lease between Jackson and McCall? Why or why not?
4. Suppose that Jackson tells Dan Stryker, a local builder to whom she owes $50,000, that he can collect the rents from the buildings' tenants until the debt is satisfied. Is this a valid assignment? Why or why not?

TERMS AND CONCEPTS

alienation 298
assignee 295
assignment 295
assignor 295
delegatee 299
delegation 295
delegator 299
incidental beneficiary 302
intended beneficiary 301
obligee 295
obligor 295
privity of contract 295
third party beneficiary 301

QUESTIONS AND CASE PROBLEMS

16–1. Alexander has been accepted as a freshman at a college two hundred miles from his home for the fall semester. Alexander's wealthy uncle, Michael, decides to give Alexander a car for Christmas. In November, Michael makes a contract with Jackson Auto Sales to purchase a new car for $18,000 to be delivered to Alexander just before the Christmas holidays, in mid-December. The title to the car is to be in Alexander's name. Michael pays the full purchase price, calls Alexander and tells him about the gift, and takes off for a six-month vacation in Europe. Is Alexander an intended third party beneficiary of the contract between Michael and Jackson Auto Sales? Suppose that Jackson Auto Sales never delivers the car to Alexander. Does Alexander have the right to sue Jackson Auto Sales for breaching its contract with Michael? Explain.

16–2. QUESTION WITH SAMPLE ANSWER

Five years ago, Hensley purchased a house. At that time, being unable to pay the full purchase price, she borrowed funds from Thrift Savings and Loan, which in turn took a mortgage at 6.5 interest on the house. The mortgage contract did not prohibit the assignment of the mortgage. Then Hensley secured a new job in another city and sold the house to Sylvia. The purchase price included payment to Hensley of the value of her equity and the assumption of the mortgage debt still owed to Thrift. At the time the contract between Hensley and Sylvia was made, Thrift did not know about or consent to the sale. On the basis of these facts, if Sylvia defaults in making the house payments to Thrift, what are Thrift's rights? Discuss.

• **For a sample answer to Question 16–2, go to Appendix I at the end of this text.**

16–3. Marsala, a college student, signs a one-year lease agreement that runs from September 1 to August 31. The lease agreement specifies that the lease cannot be assigned without the landlord's consent. In late May, Marsala decides not to go to summer school and assigns the balance of the lease (three months) to a close friend, Fred. The landlord objects to the assignment and denies Fred access to the apartment. Marsala claims that Fred is financially sound and should be allowed the full rights and privileges of an assignee. Discuss fully who is correct, the landlord or Marsala.

16–4. Inez has a specific set of plans to build a sailboat. The plans are detailed, and any boatbuilder can construct the boat. Inez secures bids, and the low bid is made by the Whale of a Boat Corp. Inez contracts with Whale to build the boat for $4,000. Whale then receives unexpected business from elsewhere. To meet the delivery date in the contract with Inez, Whale delegates its obligation to build the boat, without Inez's consent, to Quick Brothers, a reputable boatbuilder. When the boat is ready for delivery, Inez learns of the delegation and refuses to accept delivery, even though the boat is built to her specifications. Discuss fully whether Inez is obligated to accept and pay for the boat. Would your answer be any different if Inez had not had a specific set of plans but had instead contracted with Whale to design and build a sailboat for $4,000? Explain.

16–5. Notice of Assignment. As the building services manager for Fulton County, Georgia, Steve Fullard oversaw custodial services. Fullard determined which services to contract for, received the bids, and recommended the selection of a vendor. After the selection of Total Quality Maintenance of Georgia (TQM) on a particular contract, Fullard supervised TQM's performance and received and processed its invoices. Later, TQM assigned its unpaid invoices to American Factors of Nashville, Inc., which forwarded copies to Fullard with a statement rubber-stamped on each invoice. The statement began with the word "NOTICE" and the name, address, and phone number of American Factors. It also said, "Remittance to other than American Factors of Nashville, Inc., does not constitute payment of this Invoice." Included with each invoice was a certification by TQM's president that the invoice had been assigned to American Factors. Nevertheless, the county paid TQM on these invoices, and American

Factors filed a suit in a Georgia state court against the county, claiming that it still owed American Factors. Did the county have sufficient notice of TQM's assignment? Can the county be required to pay the same invoice twice? Why or why not? [*Fulton County v. American Factors of Nashville, Inc.*, 551 S.E.2d 781 (Ga.App. 2001)]

16–6. Third Party Beneficiary. Acciai Speciali Terni USA, Inc. (AST), hired a carrier to ship steel sheets and coils from Italy to the United States on the *M/V Berane.* The ship's receipt for the goods included a forum-selection clause, which stated that any dispute would be "decided in the country where the carrier has his principal place of business." The receipt also contained a "Himalaya" clause, which extended "every right, exemption from liability, defense and immunity" that the carrier enjoyed to those acting on the carrier's behalf. Transcom Terminals, Ltd., was the U.S. stevedore—that is, Transcom off-loaded the vessel and stored the cargo for eventual delivery to AST. Finding the cargo damaged, AST filed a suit in a federal district court against Transcom and others, charging, among other things, negligence in the off-loading. Transcom filed a motion to dismiss on the basis of the forum-selection clause. Transcom argued that it was an intended third party beneficiary of this provision through the Himalaya clause. Is Transcom correct? What should the court rule? Explain. [*Acciai Speciali Terni USA, Inc. v. M/V Berane,* 181 F.Supp.2d 458 (D.Md. 2002)]

16–7. CASE PROBLEM WITH SAMPLE ANSWER

The National Collegiate Athletic Association (NCAA) regulates intercollegiate amateur athletics among the more than 1,200 colleges and universities with whom it contracts. Among other things, the NCAA maintains rules of eligibility for student participation in intercollegiate athletic events. Jeremy Bloom, a high school football and track star, was recruited to play football at the University of Colorado (CU). Before enrolling, he competed in Olympic and professional World Cup skiing events, becoming the World Cup champion in freestyle moguls. During the Olympics, Bloom appeared on MTV and was offered other paid entertainment opportunities, including a chance to host a show on Nickelodeon. Bloom was also paid to endorse certain ski equipment and contracted to model clothing for Tommy Hilfiger. On Bloom's behalf, CU asked the NCAA to waive its rules restricting student-athlete endorsement and media activities. The NCAA refused, and Bloom quit the activities to play football for CU. He filed a suit in a Colorado state court against the NCAA, however, asserting breach of contract on the ground that its rules permitted these activities if they were needed to support a professional athletic career. The NCAA responded that Bloom did not have standing to pursue this claim. What contract has allegedly been breached in this case? Is Bloom a party to this contract? If not, is he a third party beneficiary of it, and if so, is his status intended or incidental? Explain. [*Bloom v. National Collegiate Athletic Association,* 93 P.3d 621 (Colo.App. 2004)]

- **To view a sample answer for Problem 16–7, go to this book's Web site at www.cengage.com/blaw/jentz, select "Chapter 16," and click on "Case Problem with Sample Answer."**

16–8. Third Party Beneficiary. National Association for Stock Car Auto Racing, Inc. (NASCAR), sanctions stock car races. NASCAR and Sprint Nextel Corp. agreed that Sprint would become the Official Series Sponsor of the NASCAR Nextel Cup Series in 2004. The agreement granted sponsorship exclusivity to Sprint and contained a list of "Competitors" who were barred from sponsoring Series events. Excepted were existing sponsorships: in "Driver and Car Owner Agreements" between NASCAR and the cars' owners, NASCAR promised to "preserve and protect" those sponsorships, which could continue and be renewed at the owner's option despite Sprint's exclusivity. RCR Team #31, LLC, owns the #31 Car in the Series. Cingular Wireless, LLC (a Sprint competitor), had been #31 Car's primary sponsor since 2001. In 2007, Cingular changed its name to AT&T Mobility, LLC, and proposed a new paint scheme for the #31 Car that called for the Cingular logo to remain on the hood while the AT&T logo would be added on the rear quarter panel. NASCAR rejected the proposal. AT&T filed a suit in a federal district court against NASCAR, claiming, in part, that NASCAR was in breach of its "Driver and Car Owner Agreement" with RCR. Can AT&T maintain an action against NASCAR based on this agreement? Explain. [*AT&T Mobility, LLC v. National Association for Stock Car Auto Racing, Inc.,* 494 F.3d 1356 (11th Cir. 2007)]

16–9. A QUESTION OF ETHICS

*In 1984, James Grigg's mother was killed in a car accident. Royal Insurance Co. of America agreed to pay Grigg a number of monthly payments and two lump-sum payments of $50,000 due May 1, 1995, and May 1, 2005. Royal contracted with Safeco Life Insurance Co. to make the payments. In 1997, Grigg assigned the 2005 payment of $50,000 to Howard Foley for $10,000. Neither Grigg nor Foley notified Safeco or Royal. Four years later, Grigg offered to sell Settlement Capital Corp. (SCC) his interest in the 2005 payment. On SCC's request, an Idaho state court approved the transfer. Foley later notified Safeco of his interest in the payment, and in 2005, the court approved an arrangement by which Foley and SCC would share the $50,000. Shortly before the 2005 payment was made, however, it was revealed that Grigg had also tried to sell his interest to Canco Credit Union, whose manager, Timothy Johnson, paid Grigg for it. Later, Johnson assigned the interest to Robert Chris, who used it as collateral for a loan from Canco. Foley filed a suit in an Idaho state court against Grigg, asking the court to determine who, among these parties, was entitled to the 2005 payment. [*Foley v. Grigg, *144 Idaho 530, 164 P.3d 180 (2007)]*

(a) If the court applies the rule most often observed in the United States, who is likely to be awarded the $50,000? If the court applies the English rule, who will have priority to the payment?

(b) Regardless of the legal principles to be applied, is there a violation of ethics in these circumstances? Explain.

16-10. VIDEO QUESTION

Go to this text's Web site at **www.cengage.com/blaw/jentz** and select "Chapter 16." Click on "Video Questions" and view the video titled *Third Party Beneficiaries*. Then answer the following questions.

(a) Discuss whether a valid contract was formed when Oscar and Vinny bet on the outcome of a football game. Would Vinny be able to enforce the contract in court?

(b) Is the Fresh Air Fund an incidental or intended beneficiary? Why?

(c) Can Maria sue to enforce Vinny's promise to donate Oscar's winnings to the Fresh Air Fund?

LAW ON THE WEB

For updated links to resources available on the Web, as well as a variety of other materials, visit this text's Web site at

www.cengage.com/blaw/jentz

You can find a summary of the law governing assignments, as well as "SmartAgreement" forms that you can use for various types of contracts, including assignments, at

www.smartagreements.com

Legal Research Exercises on the Web

Go to **www.cengage.com/blaw/jentz**, the Web site that accompanies this text. Select "Chapter 16" and click on "Internet Exercises." There you will find the following Internet research exercises that you can perform to learn more about the topics covered in this chapter.

Internet Exercise 16–1: Legal Perspective
New York's Leading Decisions

Internet Exercise 16–2: Management Perspective
Professional Liability to Third Parties

CHAPTER 17

Performance and Discharge

Just as rules are necessary to determine when a legally enforceable contract exists, so also are they required to determine when one of the parties can justifiably say, "I have fully performed, so I am now discharged from my obligations under this contract." The legal environment of business requires the identification of some point at which the parties can reasonably know that their duties are at an end.

The most common way to **discharge,** or terminate, one's contractual duties is by the **performance** of those duties. For example, a buyer and seller have a contract for the sale of a 2010 Lexus for $39,000. This contract will be discharged by performance when the buyer pays $39,000 to the seller and the seller transfers possession of the Lexus to the buyer.

The duty to perform under a contract may be *conditioned* on the occurrence or nonoccurrence of a certain event, or the duty may be *absolute.* In the first part of this chapter, we look at conditions of performance and the degree of performance required. We then examine some other ways in which a contract can be discharged, including discharge by agreement of the parties and discharge by operation of law.

SECTION 1 Conditions

In most contracts, promises of performance are not expressly conditioned or qualified. Instead, they are *absolute promises.* They must be performed, or the parties promising the acts will be in breach of contract. In some situations, however, performance is contingent on the occurrence or nonoccurrence of a certain event. A **condition** is a possible future event, the occurrence or nonoccurrence of which will trigger the performance of a legal obligation or terminate an existing obligation under a contract.[1] If this condition is not satisfied, the obligations of the parties are discharged. Suppose that Alfonso offers to purchase a painting from Jerome only if an independent appraisal indicates that it is worth at least $10,000. Jerome accepts Alfonso's offer. Their obligations (promises) are conditioned on the outcome of the appraisal. Should the condition not be satisfied (for example, if the appraiser deems the value of the painting to be only $5,000), the parties' obligations to each other are discharged and cannot be enforced.

Three types of conditions can be present in contracts: conditions *precedent,* conditions *subsequent,* and *concurrent* conditions. Conditions are also classified as *express* or *implied.*

Conditions Precedent

A condition that must be fulfilled before a party's performance can be required is called a **condition precedent.** The condition precedes the absolute duty to perform, as in the Jerome-Alfonso example just discussed. Real estate contracts frequently are conditioned on the buyer's ability to obtain financing. For example, Fisher promises to buy Calvin's house if Salvation Bank approves Fisher's mortgage application.

1. The *Restatement (Second) of Contracts,* Section 224, defines a condition as "an event, not certain to occur, which must occur, unless its nonoccurrence is excused, before performance under a contract becomes due."

The Fisher-Calvin contract is therefore subject to a condition precedent—the bank's approval of Fisher's mortgage application. If the bank does not approve the application, the contract will fail because the condition precedent was not met. Insurance contracts frequently specify that certain conditions, such as passing a physical examination, must be met before the insurance company will be obligated to perform under the contract.

Conditions Subsequent

When a condition operates to terminate a party's absolute promise to perform, it is called a **condition subsequent.** The condition follows, or is subsequent to, the arising of an absolute duty to perform. If the condition occurs, the party's duty to perform is discharged. For example, imagine that a law firm hires Koker, a recent law school graduate and newly licensed attorney. Their contract provides that the firm's obligation to continue employing Koker is discharged if Koker fails to maintain her license to practice law. This is a condition subsequent because a failure to maintain the license would discharge a duty that has already arisen.

Generally, conditions precedent are common; conditions subsequent are rare. The *Restatement (Second) of Contracts* does not use the terms *condition subsequent* and *condition precedent* but refers to both simply as conditions.[2]

Concurrent Conditions

When each party's performance is conditioned on the other party's performance or tender of performance (offer to perform), there are **concurrent conditions.** Concurrent conditions occur only when the contract calls for the parties to perform their respective duties *simultaneously*. For example, if a buyer promises to pay for goods when the seller delivers them, each party's promise to perform is mutually dependent. The buyer's duty to pay for the goods does not become absolute until the seller either delivers or tenders the goods. Likewise, the seller's duty to deliver the goods does not become absolute until the buyer tenders or actually makes payment. Therefore, neither can recover from the other for breach without first tendering performance.

2. *Restatement (Second) of Contracts,* Section 224.

Express and Implied-in-Fact Conditions

Conditions can also be classified as express or implied in fact. *Express conditions* are provided for by the parties' agreement. Although no particular words are necessary, express conditions are normally prefaced by the words *if, provided, after,* or *when.*

Conditions *implied in fact* are similar to express conditions in that they are understood to be part of the agreement, but they are not found in the express language of the agreement. Courts may imply conditions from the purpose of the contract or from the intent of the parties. Conditions are often implied when they are necessarily inherent in the actual performance of the contract.

Suppose that a clause in an automobile insurance policy states that, if involved in an accident, the insured must cooperate with the insurance company in the investigation, settlement, or defense of any claim or lawsuit. Alejandro Alvarado signs the contract and is later involved in an accident from which a negligence lawsuit against him arises. Alvarado knows that the insurance company is representing him in the suit; yet he fails to cooperate in his defense and does not appear in court on the date of the trial. The court enters a judgment against him, which prejudices the rights of the insurance company. In this situation, a court could find that the cooperation clause is a condition precedent to coverage under the policy because it was inherent in the actual performance of the contract. If so, because Alvarado did not cooperate with the insurer, he will not be covered under the policy, and the insurance company will not be liable for the damages awarded.[3]

SECTION 2 Discharge by Performance

The great majority of contracts are discharged by performance. The contract comes to an end when both parties fulfill their respective duties by performing the acts they have promised. Performance can also be accomplished by *tender.* **Tender** is an unconditional offer to perform by a person who is ready, willing, and able to do so. Therefore, a seller who places goods at the disposal of a buyer has tendered delivery and can demand payment. A buyer who offers to pay for goods

3. *Progressive County Mutual Insurance Co. v. Trevino,* 202 S.W.3d 811 (Tex.App.—San Antonio 2006).

has tendered payment and can demand delivery of the goods. Once performance has been tendered, the party making the tender has done everything possible to carry out the terms of the contract. If the other party then refuses to perform, the party making the tender can sue for breach of contract.

Types of Performance

There are two basic types of performance—*complete performance* and *substantial performance.* A contract may stipulate that performance must meet the personal satisfaction of either the contracting party or a third party. Such a provision must be considered in determining whether the performance rendered satisfies the contract.

Complete Performance When a party performs exactly as agreed, there is no question as to whether the contract has been performed. When a party's performance is perfect, it is said to be complete.

Normally, conditions expressly stated in a contract must be fully satisfied for complete performance to take place. For example, most construction contracts require the builder to meet certain specifications. If the specifications are conditions, complete performance is required to avoid material breach (*material breach* will be discussed shortly). If the conditions are met, the other party to the contract must then fulfill her or his obligation to pay the builder. If the specifications are not conditions and if the builder, without the other party's permission, fails to comply with the specifications, performance is not complete. What effect does such a failure have on the other party's obligation to pay? The answer is part of the doctrine of *substantial performance.*

Substantial Performance A party who in good faith performs substantially all of the terms of a contract can enforce the contract against the other party under the doctrine of substantial performance. Note that good faith is required. Intentionally failing to comply with the terms is a breach of the contract.

Confers Most of the Benefits Promised. Generally, to qualify as substantial, the performance must not vary greatly from the performance promised in the contract, and it must create substantially the same benefits as those promised in the contract. If the omission, variance, or defect in performance is unimportant and can easily be compensated for by awarding damages, a court is likely to hold that the contract has been substantially performed.

Courts decide whether the performance was substantial on a case-by-case basis, examining all of the facts of the particular situation. For example, in a construction contract, a court would look at the intended purpose of the structure and the expense required to bring the structure into complete compliance with the contract. Thus, the exact point at which performance is considered substantial varies.

Entitles the Other Party to Damages. Because substantial performance is not perfect, the other party is entitled to damages to compensate for the failure to comply with the contract. The measure of the damages is the cost to bring the object of the contract into compliance with its terms, if that cost is reasonable under the circumstances. If the cost is unreasonable, the measure of damages is the difference in value between the performance that was rendered and the performance that would have been rendered if the contract had been performed completely.

The following classic case emphasizes that there is no exact formula for deciding when a contract has been substantially performed.

CASE 17.1 Jacob & Youngs v. Kent

Court of Appeals of New York, 1921. 230 N.Y. 239, 129 N.E. 889.

Background and Facts The plaintiff, Jacob & Youngs, was a builder that had contracted with the defendant, George Kent, to construct a country residence for the defendant. A specification in the building contract required that "all wrought-iron pipe must be well galvanized, lap welded pipe of the grade known as 'standard pipe' of Reading manufacture." The plaintiff installed substantially similar pipe that was not of Reading manufacture. When the defendant became aware of the difference, he ordered the plaintiff to remove all of the plumbing and replace it with

CASE CONTINUES

CASE 17.1 CONTINUED the Reading type. To do so would have required removing finished walls that encased the plumbing—an expensive and difficult task. The plaintiff explained that the plumbing was of the same quality, appearance, value, and cost as Reading pipe. When the defendant refused to pay the plaintiff the $3,483.46 still owed for the work, the plaintiff sued to compel payment. The trial court ruled in favor of the defendant. The plaintiff appealed, and the appellate court reversed the trial court's decision. The defendant then appealed to the Court of Appeals of New York, the state's highest court.

● **Decision and Rationale** The Court of Appeals of New York held that the plaintiff had substantially performed the contract and affirmed the state intermediate appellate court's decision. The state's highest court explained, "The courts never say that one who makes a contract fills the measure of his duty by less than full performance. They do say, however, that an omission, both trivial and innocent, will sometimes be atoned for by allowance of the resulting damage, and will not always be the breach of a condition. * * * The question is one of degree * * * . We must weigh the purpose to be served, the desire to be gratified, the excuse for deviation from the letter, [and] the cruelty of enforced adherence." As for adjusting the contract price, "the measure of the allowance is not the cost of replacement, * * * but the difference in value" (the cost to complete). The builder was entitled to the amount owed to it, less the difference in value between the specified and substituted pipe (which the court stated would be "nominal or nothing").

● **Impact of This Case on Today's Law** *At the time of the* Jacob & Youngs *case, some courts did not apply the doctrine of substantial performance to disputes involving breaches of contract. This landmark decision contributed to a developing trend toward equity and fairness in those circumstances. Today, an unintentional and trivial omission or deviation from the terms of a contract will not prevent its enforcement but will permit an adjustment in the value of its performance.*

● **The Legal Environment Dimension** *A requirement of substantial performance is good faith. Do you think that Jacob & Youngs substantially performed all of the terms of the contract in good faith? Why or why not?*

Performance to the Satisfaction of Another Contracts often state that completed work must personally satisfy one of the parties or a third person. The question then is whether this satisfaction becomes a condition precedent, requiring actual personal satisfaction or approval for discharge, or whether the test of satisfaction is an absolute promise requiring such performance as would satisfy a *reasonable person* (substantial performance).

When the subject matter of the contract is *personal,* a contract to be performed to the satisfaction of one of the parties is conditioned, and performance must actually satisfy that party. For example, contracts for portraits, works of art, and tailoring are considered personal. Therefore, only the personal satisfaction of the party fulfills the condition—unless a court finds the party is expressing dissatisfaction only to avoid payment or otherwise is not acting in good faith.

Most other contracts need to be performed only to the satisfaction of a reasonable person unless they *expressly state otherwise.* When such contracts require performance to the satisfaction of a third party (for example, "to the satisfaction of Robert Ames, the supervising engineer"), the courts are divided. A majority of courts require the work to be satisfactory to a reasonable person, but some courts hold that the personal satisfaction of the third party designated in the contract (Robert Ames, in this example) must be met. Again, the personal judgment must be made honestly, or the condition will be excused.

Material Breach of Contract

A **breach of contract** is the nonperformance of a contractual duty. The breach is *material* when performance is not at least substantial.[4] If there is a material

4. *Restatement (Second) of Contracts,* Section 241.

breach, then the nonbreaching party is excused from the performance of contractual duties and can sue for damages resulting from the breach. If the breach is *minor* (not material), the nonbreaching party's duty to perform can sometimes be suspended until the breach has been remedied, but the duty to perform is not entirely excused. Once the minor breach has been cured, the nonbreaching party must resume performance of the contractual obligations undertaken.

Any breach entitles the nonbreaching party to sue for damages, but only a material breach discharges the nonbreaching party from the contract. The policy underlying these rules allows contracts to go forward when only minor problems occur but allows them to be terminated if major difficulties arise.

Under what circumstances is an employer excused from further performance under a contract with an employee? That was the question in the following case.

CASE 17.2 Shah v. Cover-It, Inc.

Appellate Court of Connecticut, 2004. 86 Conn.App. 71, 859 A.2d 959.

• **Background and Facts** In November 1997, Cover-It, Inc., hired Khalid Shah to work as its structural engineering manager. Shah agreed to work a flexible schedule of thirty-five hours per week. In exchange, he would receive an annual salary of $70,000 for five years, a 2 percent commission on the sales of products that he designed, three weeks of paid vacation after one year, a company car, time off to attend to prior professional obligations, and certain other benefits. Either party could terminate the contract with ninety days' written notice, but if Cover-It terminated it, Shah would receive monthly payments for the rest of the five-year term.[a] In June 1998, Shah went on vacation and did not return until September. In mid-October, Brian Goldwitz, Cover-It's owner and president, terminated Shah's contract. Shah filed a suit in a Connecticut state court against Cover-It and others. The court determined that Shah had breached the contract and rendered a judgment in the defendants' favor. Shah appealed to a state intermediate appellate court.

• **Decision and Rationale** The state intermediate appellate court affirmed the judgment of the lower court. The appellate court held that Shah had materially breached his contract with Cover-It and that this breach excused Cover-It from further performance of its contractual duties, specifically the payment to Shah of ninety days' salary and other amounts according to the contract's schedule. The court said, "The standards of materiality are to be applied in the light of the facts of each case in such a way as to further the purpose of securing for each party his expectation of an exchange of performances." In this case, among other things, Shah "took a ten-week vacation, which exceeded the time authorized." He then reported for work only two or three days per week and spent long periods of time surfing the Internet and reviewing Web sites that were unrelated to his professional duties. After the company asked Shah to document his attendance by using a time clock, he simply marked his time sheets with a "P" rather than actually clocking in. Finally, when Goldwitz asked about the completion time for certain projects, Shah responded that he was not sure but that he would take his time in completing them.

• **What If the Facts Were Different?** *Suppose that during his ten-week absence Shah was fulfilling prior professional obligations and that on his return he met Cover-It's hours and timekeeping requirements. Further suppose that Shah responded to Goldwitz's questions about his projects with reasonable estimates. Would the outcome of the case have been different? Why or why not?*

• **The E-Commerce Dimension** *If Shah had worked for Cover-It from his home by telecommuting over the Internet and other employees were therefore not aware of his conduct, would he have been in breach of his contract? Explain.*

a. The contract provided that for up to two years of service, Shah would be paid $20,000 per year; for three years of service, $30,000 per year; and for four years of service, $40,000 per year.

Anticipatory Repudiation

Before either party to a contract has a duty to perform, one of the parties may refuse to carry out his or her contractual obligations. This is called **anticipatory repudiation**[5] of the contract. When anticipatory repudiation occurs, it is treated as a material breach of contract, and the nonbreaching party is permitted to bring an action for damages immediately, even though the scheduled time for performance under the contract may still be in the future. Until the nonbreaching party treats an early repudiation as a breach, however, the repudiating party can retract her or his anticipatory repudiation by proper notice and restore the parties to their original obligations.[6]

Rationale for Treating Repudiation as Breach An anticipatory repudiation is treated as a present, material breach for two reasons. First, the nonbreaching party should not be required to remain ready and willing to perform when the other party has already repudiated the contract. Second, the nonbreaching party should have the opportunity to seek a similar contract elsewhere and may have a duty to do so to minimize his or her loss.[7]

Anticipatory Repudiation and Market Prices Quite often, anticipatory repudiation occurs when performance of the contract would be extremely unfavorable to one of the parties because of a sharp fluctuation in market prices. For example, Martin Corporation contracts to manufacture and sell ten thousand personal computers to ComAge, a retailer of computer equipment that has five hundred outlet stores. Delivery is to be made six months from the date of the contract. The contract price is based on Martin's present costs of purchasing inventory parts from others. One month later, three inventory suppliers raise their prices to Martin.

Based on these higher prices, Martin stands to lose $500,000 if it sells the computers to ComAge at the contract price. Martin immediately writes to ComAge, stating that it cannot deliver the ten thousand computers at the contract price. Martin's letter is an anticipatory repudiation of the contract. ComAge has the option of treating the repudiation as a material breach of contract and proceeding immediately to pursue remedies, even though the actual contract delivery date is still five months away.

Time for Performance

If no time for performance is stated in the contract, a *reasonable time* is implied.[8] If a specific time is stated, the parties must usually perform by that time. Unless time is expressly stated to be vital, however, a delay in performance will not destroy the performing party's right to payment.[9] When time is expressly stated to be "of the essence" or vital, the parties normally must perform within the stated time period because the time element becomes a condition.

SECTION 3

Discharge by Agreement

Any contract can be discharged by agreement of the parties. The agreement can be contained in the original contract, or the parties can form a new contract for the express purpose of discharging the original contract.

Discharge by Rescission

As mentioned in previous chapters, *rescission* is the process by which a contract is canceled or terminated and the parties are returned to the positions they occupied prior to forming it. For **mutual rescission** to take place, the parties must make another agreement that also satisfies the legal requirements for a contract. There must be an *offer,* an *acceptance,* and *consideration.* Ordinarily, if the parties agree to rescind the original contract, their promises not to perform the acts stipulated in the original contract will be legal consideration for the second contract (the rescission).

Agreements to rescind most executory contracts (in which neither party has performed) are enforceable, even if the agreement is made orally and even if the original agreement was in writing. Agreements to rescind contracts involving transfers of realty, however, must be evidenced by a writing. An exception applies under the Uniform Commercial Code (UCC) to agreements rescinding a contract for the sale of goods,

5. *Restatement (Second) of Contracts,* Section 253; Section 2–610 of the Uniform Commercial Code (UCC).
6. See UCC 2–611.
7. The doctrine of anticipatory repudiation first arose in the landmark case of *Hochster v. De La Tour,* 2 Ellis and Blackburn Reports 678 (1853), when an English court recognized the delay and expense inherent in a rule requiring a nonbreaching party to wait until the time of performance before suing on an anticipatory repudiation.
8. See UCC 2–204.
9. See, for example, *Manganaro Corp. v. Hitt Contracting, Inc.,* 193 F.Supp.2d 88 (D.D.C. 2002).

regardless of price, when the contract requires a written rescission.[10]

When one party has fully performed, an agreement to cancel the original contract normally will not be enforceable. Because the performing party has received no consideration for the promise to call off the original bargain, additional consideration is necessary to support a rescission contract.

Discharge by Novation

A contractual obligation may also be discharged through novation. A **novation** occurs when both of the parties to a contract agree to substitute a third party for one of the original parties. The requirements of a novation are as follows:

1. A previous valid obligation.
2. An agreement by all the parties to a new contract.
3. The extinguishing of the old obligation (discharge of the prior party).
4. A new contract that is valid.

For example, Union Corporation contracts to sell its pharmaceutical division to British Pharmaceuticals, Ltd. Before the transfer is completed, Union, British Pharmaceuticals, and a third company, Otis Chemicals, execute a new agreement to transfer all of British Pharmaceuticals' rights and duties in the transaction to Otis Chemicals. As long as the new contract is supported by consideration, the novation will discharge the original contract (between Union and British Pharmaceuticals) and replace it with the new contract (between Union and Otis Chemicals).

A novation expressly or impliedly revokes and discharges a prior contract.[11] The parties involved may expressly state in the new contract that the old contract is now discharged. If the parties do not expressly discharge the old contract, it will be impliedly discharged if the new contract's terms are inconsistent with the old contract's terms.

Discharge by Substituted Agreement

A *compromise*, or settlement agreement, that arises out of a genuine dispute over the obligations under an existing contract will be recognized at law. Such an agreement will be substituted as a new contract, and it will either expressly or impliedly revoke and discharge the obligations under any prior contract. In contrast to a novation, a substituted agreement does not involve a third party. Rather, the two original parties to the contract form a different agreement to substitute for the original one.

Discharge by Accord and Satisfaction

For a contract to be discharged by accord and satisfaction, the parties must agree to accept performance that is different from the performance originally promised. As discussed in Chapter 12, an *accord* is a contract to perform some act to satisfy an existing contractual duty that is not yet discharged.[12] A *satisfaction* is the performance of the accord agreement. An accord and its satisfaction discharge the original contractual obligation.

Once the accord has been made, the original obligation is merely suspended. The obligor (the one owing the obligation) can discharge the obligation by performing either the obligation agreed to in the accord or the original obligation. If the obligor refuses to perform the accord, the obligee (the one to whom performance is owed) can bring an action on the original obligation or seek a decree compelling specific performance on the accord.

Suppose that Frazer has a judgment against Ling for $8,000. Later, both parties agree that the judgment can be satisfied by Ling's transfer of his automobile to Frazer. This agreement to accept the auto in lieu of $8,000 in cash is the accord. If Ling transfers the car to Frazer, the accord is fully performed, and the debt is discharged. If Ling refuses to transfer the car, the accord is breached. Because the original obligation is merely suspended, Frazer can sue Ling to enforce the original judgment for $8,000 in cash or bring an action for breach of the accord.

SECTION 4

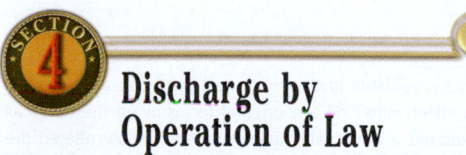

Discharge by Operation of Law

Under certain circumstances, contractual duties may be discharged by operation of law. These circumstances include material alteration of the contract, the running of the statute of limitations, bankruptcy, and the impossibility or impracticability of performance.

10. UCC 2–209(2), (4).

11. It is this immediate discharge of the prior contract that distinguishes a novation from both an accord and satisfaction, discussed in a later subsection, and an assignment of all rights, discussed in Chapter 16. In an *assignment of all rights,* the original party to the contract (the assignor) remains liable under the original contract if the assignee fails to perform the contractual obligations. In contrast, in a novation, the original party's obligations are completely discharged.

12. *Restatement (Second) of Contracts,* Section 281.

Alteration of the Contract

To discourage parties from altering written contracts, the law operates to allow an innocent party to be discharged when the other party has materially altered a written contract without consent. For example, contract terms such as quantity or price might be changed without the knowledge or consent of all parties. If so, the party who was not involved in the alteration can treat the contract as discharged or terminated.[13]

Statutes of Limitations

As mentioned earlier in this text, statutes of limitations restrict the period during which a party can sue on a particular cause of action. After the applicable limitations period has passed, a suit can no longer be brought. For example, the limitations period for bringing suits for breach of oral contracts is usually two to three years; for written contracts, four to five years; and for recovery of amounts awarded in judgments, ten to twenty years, depending on state law. Lawsuits for breach of a contract for the sale of goods generally must be brought within four years after the breach occurs.[14] By their original agreement, the parties can reduce this four-year period to not less than one year, but they cannot agree to extend it.

Bankruptcy

A proceeding in bankruptcy attempts to allocate the assets the debtor owns to the creditors in a fair and equitable fashion. Once the assets have been allocated, the debtor receives a **discharge in bankruptcy.** A discharge in bankruptcy will ordinarily bar enforcement of most of the debtor's contracts by the creditors. Partial payment of a debt *after* discharge in bankruptcy will not revive the debt. (Bankruptcy will be discussed in detail in Chapter 30.)

Impossibility or Impracticability of Performance

After a contract has been made, supervening events (such as a fire) may make performance impossible in an objective sense. This is known as **impossibility of performance** and can discharge a contract.[15] Performance may also become so difficult or costly due to some unforeseen event that a court will consider it commercially unfeasible, or impracticable.

Objective Impossibility of Performance

Objective impossibility ("It can't be done") must be distinguished from *subjective impossibility* ("I'm sorry, I simply can't do it"). For example, subjective impossibility occurs when a party cannot deliver goods on time because of freight car shortages or cannot make payment on time because the bank is closed. In effect, in each of these situations the party is saying, "It is impossible for *me* to perform," not "It is impossible for *anyone* to perform." Accordingly, such excuses do not discharge a contract, and the nonperforming party is normally held in breach of contract.

Note that to justify not performing the contract, the supervening event must have been unforeseeable at the time of the contract. Parties are supposed to consider foreseeable events, such as floods in a flood zone, at the time of contracting and allocate those risks accordingly through insurance and other means. Three basic types of situations, however, may qualify as grounds for the discharge of contractual obligations based on impossibility of performance:[16]

1. *When one of the parties to a personal contract dies or becomes incapacitated prior to performance.* For example, Fred, a famous dancer, contracts with Ethereal Dancing Guild to play a leading role in its new ballet. Before the ballet can be performed, Fred becomes ill and dies. His personal performance was essential to the completion of the contract. Thus, his death discharges the contract and his estate's liability for his nonperformance.
2. *When the specific subject matter of the contract is destroyed.* For example, A-1 Farm Equipment agrees to sell Gudgel the green tractor on its lot and promises to have it ready for Gudgel to pick up on

13. The contract is voidable, and the innocent party can also treat the contract as in effect, either on the original terms or on the terms as altered. For example, a buyer who discovers that a seller altered the quantity of goods in a sales contract from 100 to 1,000 by secretly inserting a zero can purchase either 100 or 1,000 of the items.

14. Section 2–725 of the UCC contains this four-year limitation period. A cause of action in sales contracts generally accrues when the breach occurs, regardless of the aggrieved party's lack of knowledge of the breach. For example, a breach of warranty normally occurs when the seller delivers the goods to the buyer.

15. *Restatement (Second) of Contracts,* Section 261.

16. *Restatement (Second) of Contracts,* Sections 262–266; UCC 2–615.

Saturday. On Friday night, however, a truck veers off the nearby highway and smashes into the tractor, destroying it beyond repair. Because the contract was for this specific tractor, A-1's performance is rendered impossible owing to the accident.

3. *When a change in law renders performance illegal.* For example, a contract to build an apartment building becomes impossible to perform when the zoning laws are changed to prohibit the construction of residential rental property at the planned location. A contract to paint a bridge using lead paint becomes impossible when the government passes new regulations forbidding the use of lead paint on bridges.[17]

Temporary Impossibility An occurrence or event that makes performance temporarily impossible operates to suspend performance until the impossibility ceases. Then, ordinarily, the parties must perform the contract as originally planned. If, however, the lapse of time and the change in circumstances surrounding the contract make it substantially more burdensome for the parties to perform the promised acts, the contract is discharged.

The leading case on the subject, *Autry v. Republic Productions,*[18] involved an actor (Gene Autry) who was drafted into the army in 1942. Being drafted rendered the actor's contract temporarily impossible to perform, and it was suspended until the end of the war. When the actor got out of the army, the purchasing power of the dollar had so diminished that performance of the contract would have been substantially burdensome to him. Therefore, the contract was discharged.

A more recent example involves a contract entered into shortly before Hurricane Katrina hit Louisiana. On August 22, 2005, Keefe Hurwitz contracted to sell his home in Madisonville, Louisiana, to Wesley and Gwendolyn Payne for a price of $241,500. On August 26—just four days after the parties signed the contract—Hurricane Katrina made landfall and caused extensive property damage to the house. The cost of repairs was estimated at $60,000, and Hurwitz would have to make the repairs before the *closing date* (see Chapter 48). Hurwitz did not have the funds and refused to pay $60,000 for the repairs only to sell the property to the Paynes for the previously agreed-on price of $241,500. The Paynes filed a lawsuit to enforce the contract. Hurwitz claimed that Hurricane Katrina had made it impossible for him to perform and had discharged his duties under the contract. The court, however, ruled that Hurricane Katrina had only caused a temporary impossibility. Hurwitz was required to pay for the necessary repairs and to perform the contract as written. In other words, he could not obtain a higher purchase price to offset the cost of the repairs.[19]

Commercial Impracticability When a supervening event does not render performance objectively impossible, but does make it much more difficult or expensive to perform, the courts may excuse the parties' obligations under the contract. For someone to invoke the doctrine of **commercial impracticability** successfully, however, the anticipated performance must become significantly more difficult or costly than originally contemplated at the time the contract was formed.[20]

The added burden of performing not only must be extreme but also *must not have been known by the parties when the contract was made.* In one case, for example, the court allowed a party to rescind a contract for the sale of land because of a potential problem with contaminated groundwater under the land. The court found that "the potential for substantial and unbargained-for" liability made contract performance economically impracticable. Interestingly, the court in that case also noted that the possibility of "environmental degradation with consequences extending well beyond the parties' land sale" was just as important to its decision as the economic considerations.[21]

The contract dispute in the following case arose out of the cancellation of a wedding reception due to a power failure. Is a power failure sufficient to invoke the doctrine of commercial impracticability?

17. *M. J. Paquet, Inc. v. New Jersey Department of Transportation,* 171 N.J. 378, 794 A.2d 141 (2002).
18. 30 Cal.2d 144, 180 P.2d 888 (1947).
19. *Payne v. Hurwitz,* 978 So.2d 1000 (La.App. 2008).
20. *Restatement (Second) of Contracts,* Section 264.
21. *Cape-France Enterprises v. Estate of Peed,* 305 Mont. 513, 29 P.3d 1011 (2001).

CASE 17.3 Facto v. Pantagis

Superior Court of New Jersey, Appellate Division, 2007. 390 N.J.Super. 227, 915 A.2d 59.
lawlibrary.rutgers.edu/search.shtml[a]

• **Background and Facts** Leo and Elizabeth Facto contracted with Snuffy Pantagis Enterprises, Inc., for the use of Pantagis Renaissance, a banquet hall in Scotch Plains, New Jersey, for a wedding reception in August 2002. The Factos paid the $10,578 price in advance. The contract excused Pantagis from performance "if it is prevented from doing so by an act of God (for example, flood, power failure, etc.), or other unforeseen events or circumstances." Soon after the reception began, there was a power failure. The lights and the air-conditioning shut off. The band hired for the reception refused to play without electricity to power their instruments, and the lack of lighting prevented the photographer and videographer from taking pictures. The temperature was in the 90s, the humidity was high, and the guests quickly became uncomfortable. Three hours later, after a fight between a guest and a Pantagis employee, the emergency lights began to fade, and the police evacuated the hall. The Factos filed a suit in a New Jersey state court against Pantagis, alleging breach of contract, among other things. The Factos sought to recover their prepayment, plus amounts paid to the band, the photographer, and the videographer. The court concluded that Pantagis did not breach the contract and dismissed the complaint. The Factos appealed to a state intermediate appellate court.

• **Decision and Rationale** The state intermediate appellate court agreed that the power failure relieved Pantagis of its contractual obligation, but held that Pantagis's inability to perform also relieved the Factos of their obligation. The court reversed the dismissal and remanded the case for an award to the Factos of the amount of their prepayment less the value of the services they received. The appellate court did not attribute any significance to the contract's reference to a power failure as "an act of God." The court reasoned that "even if a power failure caused by circumstances other than a natural event [was] not considered to be 'an act of God,' it still would constitute an unforeseen event or circumstance that would excuse performance." Of course, a power failure is not absolutely unforeseeable during hot summer months. But "absolute unforeseeability of a condition is not a prerequisite to the defense of impracticability." It is "the destruction or * * * deterioration of a specific thing necessary for the performance of the contract [that] makes performance impracticable." In this case, the power failure was area-wide and beyond the control of Pantagis, which was prevented from performing its contract. Because Pantagis was not in breach, however, did not mean that the Factos could not recover the amount they prepaid for the reception. When "one party to a contract is excused from performance as a result of an unforeseen event that makes performance impracticable, the other party is also generally excused from performance." Therefore, the power failure that relieved Pantagis of its obligation to the Factos also relieved the Factos of their obligation to Pantagis.

• **The Ethical Dimension** *Should Pantagis have offered to reschedule the reception? Would this have absolved Pantagis of the obligation to refund the Factos' prepayment? Explain.*

• **The Legal Environment Dimension** *Does a power failure always constitute the kind of unexpected occurrence that relieves a party of the duty to perform a contract? In what circumstances might a power failure have no effect on a contract? (Hint: Is electricity always necessary for the performance of a contract?)*

a. In the "Search by party name" section, select the "Appellate Division," type "Pantagis" in the "First Name:" box, and click on "Submit Form." In the result, click on the "click here to get this case" link to access the opinion. The Rutgers University School of Law in Camden, New Jersey, maintains this Web site.

Frustration of Purpose A theory closely allied with the doctrine of commercial impracticability is the doctrine of **frustration of purpose.** In principle, a contract will be discharged if supervening circumstances make it impossible to attain the purpose both parties had in mind when making the contract. As with commercial impracticability and impossibility, the supervening event must not have been reasonably

EXHIBIT 17–1 • Contract Discharge

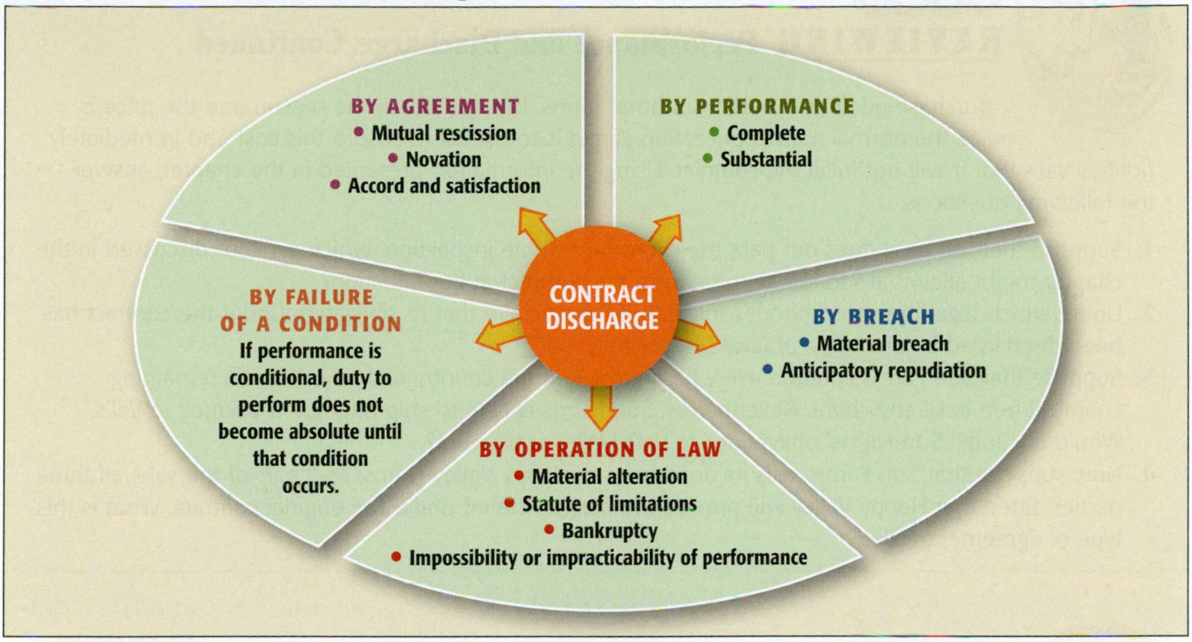

foreseeable at the time of the contracting. In contrast to impracticability, which usually involves an event that increases the cost or difficulty of performance, frustration of purpose typically involves an event that decreases the value of what a party receives under the contract.

Because many problems are foreseeable by contracting parties and value is subjective, courts rarely excuse contract performance on this basis. For example, in one case, New Beginnings was searching for a new location for its drug rehabilitation center. After receiving preliminary approval for the use of a particular building from the city zoning official, New Beginnings signed a three-year lease on the property. Then opposition from the community developed, and the city denied New Beginnings a permit to use the property for a rehab center. New Beginnings appealed the decision and eventually received a permit from the city, but by then the state was threatening to rescind all state contracts with New Beginnings if it moved into that location. Because New Beginnings would lose its funding if it actually moved onto the property, the value of the leased building was practically worthless. Nevertheless, the court refused to excuse New Beginnings from the lease contract on the ground of frustration of purpose because the situation was reasonably foreseeable.[22]

See Exhibit 17–1 for a summary of the ways in which a contract may be discharged.

22. *Adbar, L.C. v. New Beginnings C-Star,* 103 S.W.3d 799 (Mo.App. 2003).

REVIEWING Performance and Discharge

Val's Foods signs a contract to buy 1,500 pounds of basil from Sun Farms, a small organic herb grower, as long as an independent organization inspects the crop and certifies that it contains no pesticide or herbicide residue. Val's has a contract with several restaurant chains to supply pesto and intends to use Sun Farms' basil in the pesto to fulfill these contracts. While Sun Farms is preparing to harvest the basil, an unexpected hailstorm destroys half the crop. Sun Farms attempts to

REVIEWING CONTINUES

REVIEWING Performance and Discharge, Continued

purchase additional basil from other farms, but it is late in the season and the price is twice the normal market price. Sun Farms is too small to absorb this cost and immediately notifies Val's that it will not fulfill the contract. Using the information presented in the chapter, answer the following questions.

1. Suppose that the basil does not pass the chemical-residue inspection. Which concept discussed in the chapter might allow Val's to refuse to perform the contract in this situation?
2. Under which legal theory or theories might Sun Farms claim that its obligation under the contract has been discharged by operation of law? Discuss fully.
3. Suppose that Sun Farms contacts every basil grower in the country and buys the last remaining chemical-free basil anywhere. Nevertheless, Sun Farms is able to ship only 1,475 pounds to Val's. Would this fulfill Sun Farms' obligations to Val's? Why or why not?
4. Now suppose that Sun Farms sells its operations to Happy Valley Farms. As a part of the sale, all three parties agree that Happy Valley will provide the basil as stated under the original contract. What is this type of agreement called?

TERMS AND CONCEPTS

anticipatory repudiation 314
breach of contract 312
commercial impracticability 317
concurrent conditions 310
condition 309
condition precedent 309
condition subsequent 310
discharge 309
discharge in bankruptcy 316
frustration of purpose 318
impossibility of performance 316
mutual rescission 314
novation 315
performance 309
tender 310

QUESTIONS AND CASE PROBLEMS

17–1. The Caplans own a real estate lot, and they contract with Faithful Construction, Inc., to build a house on it for $360,000. The specifications list "all plumbing bowls and fixtures . . . to be Crane brand." The Caplans leave on vacation, and during their absence Faithful is unable to buy and install Crane plumbing fixtures. Instead, Faithful installs Kohler brand fixtures, an equivalent in the industry. On completion of the building contract, the Caplans inspect the work, discover the substitution, and refuse to accept the house, claiming Faithful has breached the conditions set forth in the specifications. Discuss fully the Caplans' claim.

17–2. QUESTION WITH SAMPLE ANSWER

Junior owes creditor Iba $1,000, which is due and payable on June 1. Junior has been in a car accident, has missed a great deal of work, and consequently will not have the funds on June 1. Junior's father, Fred, offers to pay Iba $1,100 in four equal installments if Iba will discharge Junior from any further liability on the debt. Iba accepts. Is this transaction a novation or an accord and satisfaction? Explain.

• **For a sample answer to Question 17–2, go to Appendix I at the end of this text.**

17–3. ABC Clothiers, Inc., has a contract with Taylor & Sons, a retailer, to deliver one thousand summer suits to Taylor's place of business on or before May 1. On April 1, Taylor senior receives a letter from ABC informing him that ABC will not be able to make the delivery as scheduled. Taylor is very upset, as he had planned a big ad campaign. He wants to file a suit against ABC immediately (on April 2). Taylor's son Tom tells his father that filing a lawsuit is not proper until ABC actually fails to deliver the suits on May 1. Discuss fully who is correct, Taylor or Tom.

17-4. In the following situations, certain events take place after the contracts are formed. Discuss which of these contracts are discharged because the events render the contracts impossible to perform.

(a) Jimenez, a famous singer, contracts to perform in your nightclub. He dies prior to performance.
(b) Raglione contracts to sell you her land. Just before title is to be transferred, she dies.
(c) Oppenheim contracts to sell you one thousand bushels of apples from her orchard in the state of Washington. Because of a severe frost, she is unable to deliver the apples.
(d) Maxwell contracts to lease a service station for ten years. His principal income is from the sale of gasoline. Because of an oil embargo by foreign oil-producing nations, gasoline is rationed, cutting sharply into Maxwell's gasoline sales. He cannot make his lease payments.

17-5. Heublein, Inc., makes wines and distilled spirits. Tarrant Distributors, Inc., agreed to distribute Heublein brands. When problems arose, the parties entered mediation. Under a settlement agreement, Heublein agreed to pay Tarrant the amount of its "net loss" as determined by Coopers & Lybrand, an accounting firm, according to a specified formula. The parties agreed that Coopers & Lybrand's calculation would be "final and binding." Heublein disagreed with Coopers & Lybrand's calculation, however, and refused to pay. The parties asked a court to rule on the dispute. Heublein argued that the settlement agreement included an implied condition precedent that Coopers & Lybrand would correctly apply the specified formula before Heublein would be obligated to pay. Tarrant pointed to the clause stating that the calculation would be "final and binding." With whom will the court agree, and why?

17-6. Performance. In May 1996, O'Brien-Shiepe Funeral Home, Inc., in Hempstead, New York, hired Teramo & Co. to build an addition to O'Brien's funeral home. The parties' contract did not specify a date for the completion of the work. The city of Hempstead issued a building permit for the project on June 14, and Teramo began work about two weeks later. There was some delay in construction because O'Brien asked that no construction be done during funeral services, but by the end of March 1997, the work was substantially complete. The city of Hempstead issued a "Certificate of Completion" on April 15. During the construction, O'Brien made periodic payments to Teramo, but there was a balance due of $17,950, which O'Brien did not pay. To recover this amount, Teramo filed a suit in a New York state court against O'Brien. O'Brien filed a counterclaim to recover lost profits for business allegedly lost due to the time Teramo took to build the addition and for $6,180 spent to correct problems caused by poor craftsmanship. Which, if any, party is entitled to an award in this case? Explain. [*Teramo & Co. v. O'Brien-Shiepe Funeral Home, Inc.*, 725 N.Y.S.2d 87 (A.D. 2 Dept. 2001)]

17-7. Substantial Performance. Adolf and Ida Krueger contracted with Pisani Construction, Inc., to erect a metal building as an addition to an existing structure. The two structures were to share a common wall, and the frames and panel heights of the new building were to match those of the existing structure. Shortly before completion of the project, however, it was apparent that the roofline of the new building was approximately three inches higher than that of the existing structure. Pisani modified the ridge caps of the buildings to blend the rooflines. The discrepancy had other consequences, however, including misalignment of the gutters and windows of the two buildings, which resulted in an icing problem in the winter. The Kruegers occupied the new structure but refused to make the last payment under the contract. Pisani filed a suit in a Connecticut state court to collect. Did Pisani substantially perform its obligations? Should the Kruegers be ordered to pay? Why or why not? [*Pisani Construction, Inc. v. Krueger,* 68 Conn.App. 361, 791 A.2d 634 (2002)]

17-8. CASE PROBLEM WITH SAMPLE ANSWER

Train operators and other railroad personnel use signaling systems to ensure safe train travel. Reading Blue Mountain & Northern Railroad Co. (RBMN) and Norfolk Southern Railway Co. entered into a contract for the maintenance of a signaling system that serviced a stretch of track near Jim Thorpe, Pennsylvania. The system included a series of poles, similar to telephone poles, suspending wires above the tracks. The contract provided that "the intent of the parties is to maintain the existing . . . facilities" and split the cost equally. In December 2002, a severe storm severed the wires and destroyed most of the poles. RBMN and Norfolk discussed replacing the old system, which they agreed was antiquated, inefficient, dangerous to rebuild, and expensive, but they could not agree on an alternative. Norfolk installed an entirely new system and filed a suit in a federal district court against RBMN to recover half of the cost. RBMN filed a motion for summary judgment, asserting, in part, the doctrine of frustration of purpose. What is this doctrine? Does it apply in this case? How should the court rule on RBMN's motion? Explain. [*Norfolk Southern Railway Co. v. Reading Blue Mountain & Northern Railroad Co.,* 346 F.Supp.2d 720 (M.D.Pa. 2004)]

- **To view a sample answer for Problem 17-8, go to this book's Web site at www.cengage.com/blaw/jentz, select "Chapter 17," and click on "Case Problem with Sample Answer."**

17-9. Material Breach. Kermit Johnson formed FB&I Building Products, Inc., in Watertown, South Dakota, to sell building materials. In December 1998, FB&I contracted with Superior Truss & Components in Minneota, Minnesota, "to exclusively sell Superior's open-faced wall panels, floor panels, roof trusses and other miscellaneous products." In March 2000, FB&I agreed to exclusively sell Component Manufacturing Co.'s building products in Colorado. Two months later, Superior learned of FB&I's deal with Component and terminated its contract with FB&I. That contract provided that on cancellation, "FB&I

will be entitled to retain the customers that they continue to sell and service with Superior products." Superior refused to honor this provision. Between the cancellation of FB&I's contract and 2004, Superior made $2,327,528 in sales to FB&I customers without paying a commission. FB&I filed a suit in a South Dakota state court against Superior, alleging, in part, breach of contract and seeking the unpaid commissions. Superior insisted that FB&I had materially breached their contract, excusing Superior from performing. In whose favor should the court rule and why? [*FB&I Building Products, Inc. v. Superior Truss & Components, a Division of Banks Lumber, Inc.*, 2007 SD 13, 727 N.W.2d 474 (2007)]

17-10. A QUESTION OF ETHICS

*King County, Washington, hired Frank Coluccio Construction Co. (FCCC) to act as general contractor for a public works project involving the construction of a small utility tunnel under the Duwamish Waterway. FCCC hired Donald B. Murphy Contractors, Inc. (DBM), as a subcontractor. DBM was responsible for constructing an access shaft at the eastern end of the tunnel. Problems arose during construction, including a "blow-in" of the access shaft that caused it to fill with water, soil, and debris. FCCC and DBM incurred substantial expenses from the repairs and delays. Under the project contract, King County was supposed to buy an insurance policy to "insure against physical loss or damage by perils included under an 'All-Risk' Builder's Risk policy." Any claim under this policy was to be filed through the insured. King County, which had general property damage insurance, did not obtain an all-risk builder's risk policy. For the losses attributable to the blow-in, FCCC and DBM submitted builder's risk claims, which the county denied. FCCC filed a suit in a Washington state court against King County, alleging, among other claims, breach of contract. [*Frank Coluccio Construction Co. v. King County, *136 Wash.App. 751, 150 P.3d 1147 (Div. 1 2007)]*

(a) King County's property damage policy specifically excluded, at the county's request, coverage of tunnels. The county drafted its contract with FCCC to require the all-risk builder's risk policy and authorize itself to "sponsor" claims. When FCCC and DBM filed their claims, the county secretly colluded with its property damage insurer to deny payment. What do these facts indicate about the county's ethics and legal liability in this situation?

(b) Could DBM, as a third party to the contract between King County and FCCC, maintain an action on the contract against King County? Discuss.

(c) All-risk insurance is a promise to pay on the "fortuitous" happening of a loss or damage from any cause except those that are specifically excluded. Payment usually is not made on a loss that, at the time the insurance was obtained, the claimant subjectively knew would occur. If a loss results from faulty workmanship on the part of a contractor, should the obligation to pay under an all-risk policy be discharged? Explain.

LAW ON THE WEB

For updated links to resources available on the Web, as well as a variety of other materials, visit this text's Web site at

www.cengage.com/blaw/jentz

For a summary of how contracts may be discharged and other principles of contract law, go to

www.rnoon.com/law_for_laymen/contracts/performance.html

Legal Research Exercises on the Web

Go to **www.cengage.com/blaw/jentz**, the Web site that accompanies this text. Select "Chapter 17" and click on "Internet Exercises." There you will find the following Internet research exercises that you can perform to learn more about the topics covered in this chapter.

Internet Exercise 17–1: Legal Perspective
Anticipatory Repudiation

Internet Exercise 17–2: Management Perspective
Commercial Impracticability

CHAPTER 18

Breach of Contract and Remedies

When one party breaches a contract, the other party—the nonbreaching party—can choose one or more of several remedies. A *remedy* is the relief provided for an innocent party when the other party has breached the contract. It is the means employed to enforce a right or to redress an injury.

The most common remedies available to a nonbreaching party include damages, rescission and restitution, specific performance, and reformation. As discussed in Chapter 1, a distinction is made between *remedies at law* and *remedies in equity.* Today, the remedy at law is normally monetary damages, which are discussed in the first part of this chapter. Equitable remedies include rescission and restitution, specific performance, and reformation, all of which will be examined later in the chapter. Usually, a court will not award an equitable remedy unless the remedy at law is inadequate. Special legal doctrines and concepts relating to remedies will be discussed in the final pages of this chapter.

SECTION 1 Damages

A breach of contract entitles the nonbreaching party to sue for monetary damages. As discussed in Chapter 6, damages are designed to compensate a party for harm suffered as a result of another's wrongful act. In the context of contract law, damages compensate the nonbreaching party for the loss of the bargain. Often, courts say that innocent parties are to be placed in the position they would have occupied had the contract been fully performed.[1]

Realize at the outset, though, that collecting damages through a court judgment requires litigation, which can be expensive and time consuming. Also keep in mind that court judgments are often difficult to enforce, particularly if the breaching party does not have sufficient assets to pay the damages awarded (as discussed in Chapter 3). For these reasons, the majority of actions for damages (or other remedies) are settled by the parties before trial.

1. *Restatement (Second) of Contracts,* Section 347; Section 1–106(1) of the Uniform Commercial Code (UCC).

Types of Damages

There are basically four broad categories of damages:

1. Compensatory (to cover direct losses and costs).
2. Consequential (to cover indirect and foreseeable losses).
3. Punitive (to punish and deter wrongdoing).
4. Nominal (to recognize wrongdoing when no monetary loss is shown).

Compensatory and punitive damages were discussed in Chapter 6 in the context of tort law. Here, we look at these types of damages, as well as consequential and nominal damages, in the context of contract law.

Compensatory Damages Damages compensating the nonbreaching party for the *loss of the bargain* are known as *compensatory damages.* These damages compensate the injured party only for damages actually sustained and proved to have arisen directly from the loss of the bargain caused by the breach of contract. They simply replace what was lost because of the wrong or damage and, for this reason, are often said to "make the person whole."

The standard measure of compensatory damages is the difference between the value of the breaching party's promised performance under the contract and the value of her or his actual performance. This amount is reduced by any loss that the injured party has avoided, however.

To illustrate: Wilcox contracts to perform certain services exclusively for Hernandez during the month of March for $4,000. Hernandez cancels the contract and is in breach. Wilcox is able to find another job during the month of March but can earn only $3,000. He can sue Hernandez for breach and recover $1,000 as compensatory damages. Wilcox can also recover from Hernandez the amount that he spent to find the other job. Expenses that are caused directly by a breach of contract—such as those incurred to obtain performance from another source—are known as **incidental damages.**

The measurement of compensatory damages varies by type of contract. Certain types of contracts deserve special mention. They are contracts for the sale of goods and for the sale of land.

Sale of Goods. In a contract for the sale of goods, the usual measure of compensatory damages is an amount equal to the difference between the contract price and the market price.[2] Suppose that Chrylon Corporation contracts to buy ten model UTS network servers from an XEXO Corporation dealer for $8,000 each. The dealer, however, fails to deliver the ten servers to Chrylon. The market price of the servers at the time the buyer learns of the breach is $8,150. Therefore, Chrylon's measure of damages is $1,500 ($10 \times \$150$) plus any incidental damages (expenses) caused by the breach. In a situation in which the buyer breaches and the seller has not yet produced the goods, compensatory damages normally equal lost profits on the sale, not the difference between the contract price and the market price.

2. In other words, the amount is the difference between the contract price and the market price at the time and place at which the goods were to be delivered or tendered. See UCC 2–708 and 2–713.

Sale of Land. Ordinarily, because each parcel of land is unique, the remedy for a seller's breach of a contract for a sale of real estate is specific performance—that is, the buyer is awarded the parcel of property for which she or he bargained (*specific performance* is discussed more fully later in this chapter). When this remedy is unavailable (for example, when the seller has sold the property to someone else), or when the buyer has breached, the measure of damages is ordinarily the same as in contracts for the sale of goods—that is, the difference between the contract price and the market price of the land. The majority of states follow this rule.

A minority of states follow a different rule when the seller breaches the contract and the breach is not deliberate.[3] When the breach was not willful, these states limit the prospective buyer's damages to a refund of any down payment made plus any expenses incurred (such as fees for title searches, attorneys, and escrows). This rule effectively returns purchasers to the positions they occupied prior to the sale, rather than giving them the benefit of the bargain.

Construction Contracts. The measure of damages in a building or construction contract varies depending on which party breaches and when the breach occurs. The owner can breach at three different stages of the construction:

1. Before performance has begun.
2. During performance.
3. After performance has been completed.

If the owner breaches *before performance has begun,* the contractor can recover only the profits that would have been made on the contract (that is, the total contract price less the cost of materials and labor). If the owner breaches *during performance,* the contractor can recover the profits plus the costs incurred in partially constructing the building. If the owner breaches *after the construction has been completed,* the contractor can recover the entire contract price, plus interest.

When the construction contractor breaches the contract either by failing to undertake construction or by stopping work partway through the project, the mea-

3. "Deliberate" breaches include the seller's failure to convey the land because the market price has gone up. "Nondeliberate" breaches include the seller's failure to convey the land because of a problem with the title, such as the discovery of an unknown *easement* that gives another a right of use over the property (see Chapter 48).

EXHIBIT 18–1 • Measurement of Damages—Breach of Construction Contracts

Party in Breach	Time of Breach	Measurement of Damage
Owner	Before construction has begun.	Profits (contract price less cost of materials and labor).
Owner	During construction.	Profits, plus costs incurred up to time of breach.
Owner	After construction is completed.	Contract price, plus interest.
Contractor	Before construction has begun.	Cost above contract price to complete work.
Contractor	Before construction is completed.	Generally, all costs incurred by owner to complete work.

sure of damages is the cost of completion, which includes reasonable compensation for any delay in performance. If the contractor finishes late, the measure of damages is the loss of use. These rules concerning the measurement of damages in breached construction contracts are summarized in Exhibit 18–1.

Construction Contracts and Economic Waste. If the contractor substantially performs, a court may use the cost-of-completion formula, but only if requiring completion will not entail unreasonable economic waste. *Economic waste* occurs when the cost of repairing or completing the performance as required by the contract greatly outweighs the benefit to the owner. For example, a contractor discovers that it will cost $20,000 to move a large coral rock eleven inches as specified in the contract. Because changing the rock's position will alter the appearance of the project only a trifle, a court would likely conclude that full completion would involve economic waste. Thus, the contractor will not be required to pay the full $20,000 to complete performance.

Consequential Damages

Foreseeable damages that result from a party's breach of contract are called **consequential damages,** or *special damages.* They differ from compensatory damages in that they are caused by special circumstances beyond the contract itself. They flow from the consequences, or results, of a breach.

For example, when a seller fails to deliver goods, knowing that the buyer is planning to use or resell those goods immediately, consequential damages are awarded for the loss of profits from the planned resale. (The buyer will also recover compensatory damages for the difference between the contract price and the market price of the goods.)

To recover consequential damages, the breaching party must know (or have reason to know) that special circumstances will cause the nonbreaching party to suffer an additional loss. This rule was enunciated in the classic case of *Hadley v. Baxendale,* which is presented next. In reading this decision, it is helpful to understand that in the mid-1800s in England large flour mills customarily kept more than one crankshaft on hand in the event that the main crankshaft broke and had to be repaired. It is against this background that the parties in the case presented here argued their respective positions on whether the damages resulting from the loss of profits while the crankshaft was repaired were reasonably foreseeable.

CASE 18.1 Hadley v. Baxendale

Court of Exchequer, 1854. 156 Eng.Rep. 145.

• **Background and Facts** The Hadleys (the plaintiffs) ran a flour mill in Gloucester. The crankshaft attached to the steam engine in the mill broke, causing the mill to shut down. The shaft had to be sent to a foundry located in Greenwich so that the new shaft could be made to fit the other parts of the engine. Baxendale, the defendant, was a common carrier that transported the

CASE CONTINUES

CASE 18.1 CONTINUED

shaft from Gloucester to Greenwich. The freight charges were collected in advance, and Baxendale promised to deliver the shaft the following day. It was not delivered for a number of days, however. As a consequence, the mill was closed for several days. The Hadleys sued to recover the profits lost during that time. Baxendale contended that the loss of profits was "too remote" to be recoverable. The court held for the plaintiffs, and the jury was allowed to take into consideration the lost profits. The defendant appealed.

• **Decision and Rationale** The Court of Exchequer ordered a new trial. The court explained that if an injury is outside the usual course of events, it must be shown that the breaching party had reason to foresee the injury. According to the court, to collect consequential damages the plaintiffs in this case would have to have given express notice of the special circumstances that caused the loss of profits. The court reasoned that "special circumstances were here never communicated by the plaintiffs to the defendants. It follows, therefore, that the loss of profits here cannot reasonably be considered such a consequence of the breach of contract as could have been fairly and reasonably contemplated by both the parties when they made this contract."

• **Impact of This Case on Today's Law** *This case established the rule that when damages are awarded, compensation is given only for those injuries that the defendant could reasonably have foreseen as a probable result of the usual course of events following a breach. Today, the rule enunciated by the court in this case still applies. To recover consequential damages, the plaintiff must show that the defendant had reason to know or foresee that a particular loss or injury would occur.*

• **The E-Commerce Dimension** *If a Web merchant loses business due to a computer system's failure that can be attributed to malfunctioning software, can the merchant recover the lost profits from the software maker? Explain.*

Business owners and managers should realize that it is sometimes impossible to prevent contract disputes. They should also understand that collecting damages through a court judgment requires litigation, which can be expensive and time consuming. Furthermore, court judgments are often difficult to enforce, particularly if the breaching party does not have sufficient assets to pay the damages awarded.[4]

For these reasons, parties generally choose to settle their contract disputes before trial rather than litigate in hopes of being awarded—and being able to collect—damages (or other remedies). In sum, there is wisdom in the old saying, "a bird in the hand is worth two in the bush."

Punitive Damages Punitive, or exemplary, damages generally are not recoverable in contract law, even for an intentional breach of contract. Because punitive damages are designed to punish a wrongdoer and set an example to deter similar conduct in the future, they have no legitimate place in contract law. A contract is simply a civil relationship between the parties, so breaching a contract is not a crime; nor does it necessarily harm society (as torts do). Thus, a court will not award punitive damages but will compensate one party for the loss of the bargain—no more and no less.

In a few situations, however, when a person's actions constitute both a breach of contract and a tort, punitive damages may be available. For example, some parties, such as an engineer and her client, may establish by contract a certain reasonable standard or duty of care. Failure to live up to that standard is a breach of contract, and the act itself may constitute negligence. Similarly, some intentional torts, such as fraud, may be tied to a breach of the terms of a contract and enable the injured party to seek punitive damages. Additionally, when an insurance company exhibits bad faith in failing to settle a claim on behalf of the insured party, courts may award punitive damages. Overall, though, punitive damages are almost never available in contract disputes.

4. Courts dispose of cases, after trials, by entering judgments. A judgment may order the losing party to pay monetary damages to the winning party. Collecting a judgment, however, can pose problems. For example, the judgment debtor may be insolvent (unable to pay his or her bills when they come due) or have only a small net worth, or exemption laws may prevent a creditor from seizing the debtor's assets to satisfy a debt (see Chapter 30).

Nominal Damages When no actual damage or financial loss results from a breach of contract and only a technical injury is involved, the court may award **nominal damages** to the innocent party. Awards of nominal damages are often small, such as one dollar, but they do establish that the defendant acted wrongfully. Most lawsuits for nominal damages are brought as a matter of principle under the theory that a breach has occurred and some damages must be imposed regardless of actual loss.

Suppose that Jackson contracts to buy potatoes from Stanley at fifty cents a pound. Stanley breaches the contract and does not deliver the potatoes. In the meantime, the price of potatoes has fallen. Jackson is able to buy them in the open market at half the price he contracted for with Stanley. He is clearly better off because of Stanley's breach. Thus, because Jackson sustained only a technical injury and suffered no monetary loss, he is likely to be awarded only nominal damages if he brings a suit for breach of contract.

Mitigation of Damages

In most situations, when a breach of contract occurs, the innocent injured party is held to a duty to mitigate, or reduce, the damages that he or she suffers. Under this doctrine of **mitigation of damages,** the duty owed depends on the nature of the contract.

For example, some states require a landlord to use reasonable means to find a new tenant if a tenant abandons the premises and fails to pay rent. If an acceptable tenant is found, the landlord is required to lease the premises to this tenant to mitigate the damages recoverable from the former tenant. The former tenant is still liable for the difference between the amount of the rent under the original lease and the rent received from the new tenant. If the landlord has not taken the reasonable steps necessary to find a new tenant, a court will likely reduce any award made by the amount of rent the landlord could have received had such reasonable means been used.

In the majority of states, a person whose employment has been wrongfully terminated owes a duty to mitigate the damages suffered because of the employer's breach of the employment contract. In other words, a wrongfully terminated employee has a duty to take a similar job if one is available. If the employee fails to do this, the damages awarded will be equivalent to the person's salary less the income he or she would have received in a similar job obtained by reasonable means. The employer has the burden of proving that such a job existed and that the employee could have been hired. Normally, the employee is under no duty to take a job of a different type and rank, however.

Whether a tenant farmer acceptably attempted to mitigate his damages on his landlord's breach of their lease was at issue in the following case.

CASE 18.2 Hanson v. Boeder

Supreme Court of North Dakota, 2007. 2007 ND 20, 727 N.W.2d 280.
www.ndcourts.com/court/opinions.htm[a]

Background and Facts In 1998, Paul Hanson signed a five-year lease to farm 1,350 acres of Donald Boeder's land in Steele County, North Dakota, for $50 per acre beginning with the 1999 crop year. Under the lease, Hanson could use grain bins with a capacity of 93,000 bushels and two machine sheds on the property. The rent was $67,515 per year, with half due on April 1 and the balance due on November 1. In 2003, Boeder and Hanson renewed the lease for a second five-year period. During both terms, Boeder and Hanson disagreed about Hanson's farming practices, but during the second term, their disagreement escalated. In August 2005, Boeder told Hanson that their lease was over. Boeder also told Hanson not to till the land in the fall because it had been leased to a new tenant who wanted to do it himself. Hanson continued to work Boeder's land, however, while running ads in the local newspapers for other farmland to rent. Unable to find other land, Hanson filed a suit in a North Dakota state court against Boeder for breach of contract, asking the court to assess damages. The court awarded Hanson $315,194.26 to cover his lost profits,

a. Click on the "By ND citation" link. In the result, click on "2007" and then the name of the case to access the opinion. The North Dakota Supreme Court maintains this Web site.

CASE CONTINUES

CASE 18.2 CONTINUED the lost use of the bins and sheds, and the value of the fall tillage. Boeder appealed to the North Dakota Supreme Court, arguing, in part, that Hanson failed to mitigate his damages.

• **Decision and Rationale** The Supreme Court of North Dakota affirmed the lower court's award of damages to Hanson. The state supreme court explained that normally, "for the breach of an obligation arising from contract, the measure of damages * * * is the amount which will compensate the party aggrieved for all the detriment proximately caused thereby or which in the ordinary course of things would be likely to result therefrom." The court recognized that "a person injured by the wrongful acts of another has a duty to mitigate or minimize the damages and must protect himself if he can do so with reasonable exertion or at trifling expense, and can recover from the delinquent party only such damages as he could not, with reasonable effort, have avoided." In this case, Hanson had not been aware of any farmland available for lease, and he had run ads in the local newspapers seeking other farmland to rent. That Hanson was unsuccessful affected the amount of his recovery, but it did not point to a failure to mitigate his damages.

• **The Ethical Dimension** *During the trial, Boeder tried to retract his repudiation of the lease to allow Hanson to continue farming for the rest of the lease term. Should the court have considered this an acceptable substitute to mitigate Hanson's damages? Why or why not?*

• **The Legal Environment Dimension** *Hanson initially asked the lower court to enforce the contract and requested damages only "in the alternative"—that is, only if specific performance was not available (pleading in the alternative is discussed later in this chapter). Could the court have awarded Hanson specific performance of the lease in this case? Should that relief have been granted? Explain.*

Liquidated Damages Provisions

A **liquidated damages** provision in a contract specifies that a certain dollar amount is to be paid in the event of a *future* default or breach of contract. (*Liquidated* means determined, settled, or fixed.) For example, a provision requiring a construction contractor to pay $300 for every day he or she is late in completing the project is a liquidated damages provision. Liquidated damages provisions are frequently used in construction contracts because it is difficult to estimate the amount of damages that would be caused by a delay in completion. They are also common in contracts for the sale of goods.[5]

Liquidated damages differ from penalties. A **penalty** specifies a certain amount to be paid in the event of a default or breach of contract and is designed to penalize the breaching party. Liquidated damages provisions normally are enforceable. In contrast, if a court finds that a provision calls for a penalty, the agreement as to the amount will not be enforced, and recovery will be limited to actual damages. To determine if a particular provision is for liquidated damages or for a penalty, the court asks two questions:

1. When the contract was entered into, was it apparent that damages would be difficult to estimate in the event of a breach?
2. Was the amount set as damages a reasonable estimate and not excessive?[6]

If the answers to both questions are yes, the provision normally will be enforced. If either answer is no, the provision normally will not be enforced. For example, in a case involving a sophisticated business contract to lease computer equipment, the court held that a liquidated damages provision that valued the computer equipment at more than four times its market value was a reasonable estimate. According to the court, the amount of actual damages was difficult to ascertain at the time the contract was formed because of the "speculative nature of the value of computers at termination of lease schedules."[7]

5. Section 2–718(1) of the UCC specifically authorizes the use of liquidated damages provisions.

6. *Restatement (Second) of Contracts,* Section 356(1).

7. *Winthrop Resources Corp. v. Eaton Hydraulics, Inc.,* 361 F.3d 465 (8th Cir. 2004).

SECTION 2

Rescission and Restitution

As discussed in Chapter 17, *rescission* is essentially an action to undo, or terminate, a contract—to return the contracting parties to the positions they occupied prior to the transaction.[8] When fraud, a mistake, duress, undue influence, misrepresentation, or lack of capacity to contract is present, unilateral rescission is available. Rescission may also be available by statute.[9] The failure of one party to perform entitles the other party to rescind the contract. The rescinding party must give prompt notice to the breaching party.

Restitution

Generally, to rescind a contract, both parties must make **restitution** to each other by returning goods, property, or funds previously conveyed.[10] If the physical property or goods can be returned, they must be. If the goods or property have been consumed, restitution must be made in an equivalent dollar amount.

Essentially, restitution involves the plaintiff's recapture of a benefit conferred on the defendant through which the defendant has been unjustly enriched. For example, Katie pays $10,000 to Bob in return for Bob's promise to design a house for her. The next day, Bob calls Katie and tells her that he has taken a position with a large architectural firm in another state and cannot design the house. Katie decides to hire another architect that afternoon. Katie can obtain restitution of the $10,000.

Restitution Is Not Limited to Rescission Cases

Restitution may be appropriate when a contract is rescinded, but the right to restitution is not limited to rescission cases. Because an award of restitution basically gives back or returns something to its rightful owner, this remedy may be sought in actions for breach of contract, tort actions, and other types of actions. For example, restitution can be obtained when funds or property has been transferred by mistake or because of fraud or incapacity. Restitution may also be available in situations involving embezzlement, conversion, theft, copyright infringement, or misconduct by a party in a confidential or other special relationship.

SECTION 3

Specific Performance

The equitable remedy of **specific performance** calls for the performance of the act promised in the contract. This remedy is often attractive to a nonbreaching party because it provides the exact bargain promised in the contract. It also avoids some of the problems inherent in a suit for damages. First, the nonbreaching party need not worry about collecting the judgment (see Chapter 3 for a discussion of the difficulties of enforcing court judgments). Second, the nonbreaching party need not look around for another contract. Third, the actual performance may be more valuable than the monetary damages.

Normally, however, specific performance will not be granted unless the party's legal remedy (monetary damages) is inadequate.[11] For this reason, contracts for the sale of goods rarely qualify for specific performance. The legal remedy—monetary damages—is ordinarily adequate in such situations because substantially identical goods can be bought or sold in the market. Only if the goods are unique will a court grant specific performance. For example, paintings, sculptures, or rare books or coins are so unique that monetary damages will not enable a buyer to obtain substantially identical substitutes in the market.

Sale of Land

A court may grant specific performance to a buyer in an action for a breach of contract involving the sale of land. In this situation, the legal remedy of monetary damages may not compensate the buyer adequately because every parcel of land is unique: the same land in the same location obviously cannot be obtained elsewhere. Only when specific performance is unavailable (for example, when the seller has sold the property to someone else) will monetary damages be awarded instead.

Is specific performance warranted when one of the parties has substantially—but not *fully*—performed under the contract? That was the question in the following case.

8. The rescission discussed here is *unilateral* rescission, in which only one party wants to undo the contract. In mutual rescission, both parties agree to undo the contract (see Chapter 17). Mutual rescission discharges the contract; unilateral rescission is generally available as a remedy for breach of contract.

9. The Federal Trade Commission and many states have rules or statutes allowing consumers to unilaterally rescind contracts made at home with door-to-door salespersons. Rescission is allowed within three days for any reason or for no reason at all. See, for example, California Civil Code Section 1689.5.

10. *Restatement (Second) of Contracts,* Section 370.

11. *Restatement (Second) of Contracts,* Section 359.

CASE 18.3 Stainbrook v. Low

Court of Appeals of Indiana, 2006. 842 N.E.2d 386.

• **Background and Facts** In April 2004, Howard Stainbrook agreed to sell to Trent Low forty acres of land in Jennings County, Indiana, for $45,000. Thirty-two of the acres were wooded and eight were tillable. Under the agreement, Low was to pay for a survey of the property and other costs, including a tax payment due in November. Low gave Stainbrook a check for $1,000 to show his intent to fulfill the contract. They agreed to close the deal on May 11, and Low made financial arrangements to meet his obligations. On May 8, a tractor rolled over on Stainbrook, and he died. Howard's son David became the executor of Stainbrook's estate. David asked Low to withdraw his offer to buy the forty acres. Low refused and filed a suit against David in an Indiana state court, seeking to enforce the contract. The court ordered specific performance. David appealed to a state intermediate appellate court, arguing, among other things, that his father's contract with Low was "ambiguous and inequitable."

• **Decision and Rationale** The state intermediate appellate court held that specific performance was an appropriate remedy in this case and affirmed the lower court's order. Stainbrook's son, David, the executor of the estate, argued that specific performance was not appropriate because Low did not prove full and complete performance for his part of the contract. The court pointed out that while Low did not pay the November 2004 property taxes, he offered to make the tax payment, and David refused his offer. In reality, in this case, "specific performance is an appropriate remedy to a party who has *substantially* performed under the terms of the contract." In addition, David's contention that the agreement was unfair was not convincing to the court. Stainbrook, although old, was competent at the time of the making of the contract. He consulted a lawyer regarding the agreement, and he insisted on several handwritten changes to the contract that benefited his own interest.

• **The Ethical Dimension** *Should a party who seeks specific performance of a contract be required to prove that he or she has performed, substantially performed, or offered to perform his or her contract obligations? Why or why not?*

• **The Global Dimension** *Suppose that Stainbrook and Low had been citizens and residents of other countries. Would the location of the land that was the subject of their contract have been sufficient to support the Indiana state court's jurisdiction and award in this case? Discuss.*

Contracts for Personal Services

Personal-service contracts require one party to work personally for another party. Courts normally refuse to grant specific performance of personal-service contracts because to order a party to perform personal services against his or her will amounts to a type of involuntary servitude.[12]

Moreover, the courts do not want to have to monitor a service contract if supervision would be difficult—as it would be if the contract required the exercise of personal judgment or talent. For example, if you contracted with a brain surgeon to perform brain surgery on you and the surgeon refused to perform, the court would not compel (and you certainly would not want) the surgeon to perform under those circumstances. A court cannot assure meaningful performance in such a situation.[13] If a contract is not deemed personal, the remedy at law of monetary damages may be adequate if substantially identical service (for example, lawn mowing) is available from other persons.

12. Involuntary servitude, or slavery, is contrary to the public policy expressed in the Thirteenth Amendment to the U.S. Constitution. A court can, however, enter an order (injunction) prohibiting a person who breached a personal-service contract from engaging in similar contracts for a period of time in the future.

13. Similarly, courts often refuse to order specific performance of construction contracts because courts are not set up to operate as construction supervisors or engineers.

SECTION 4 Reformation

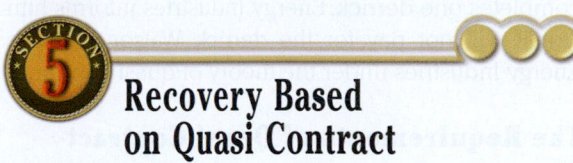

Reformation is an equitable remedy used when the parties have *imperfectly* expressed their agreement in writing. Reformation allows a court to rewrite the contract to reflect the parties' true intentions.

When Fraud or Mutual Mistake Is Present

Courts order reformation most often when fraud or mutual mistake (for example, a clerical error) is present. Typically, a party seeks reformation so that some other remedy may then be pursued. For example, if Keshan contracts to buy a certain parcel of land from Malboa but their contract mistakenly refers to a parcel of land different from the one being sold, the contract does not reflect the parties' intentions. Accordingly, a court can reform the contract so that it conforms to the parties' intentions and accurately refers to the parcel of land being sold. Keshan can then, if necessary, show that Malboa has breached the contract as reformed. She can at that time request an order for specific performance.

Oral Contracts and Covenants Not to Compete

Courts also frequently reform contracts in two other situations. The first involves two parties who have made a binding oral contract. They further agree to put the oral contract in writing, but in doing so, they make an error in stating the terms. Normally, a court will allow into evidence the correct terms of the oral contract, thereby reforming the written contract.

The second situation occurs when the parties have executed a written covenant not to compete (discussed in Chapter 13). If the covenant is for a valid and legitimate purpose (such as the sale of a business) but the area or time restraints of the covenant are unreasonable, some courts will reform the restraints by making them reasonable and will enforce the entire contract as reformed. Other courts, however, will throw out the entire restrictive covenant as illegal.

Exhibit 18–2 graphically summarizes the remedies, including reformation, that are available to the nonbreaching party.

SECTION 5 Recovery Based on Quasi Contract

Recall from Chapter 10 that quasi contract is not a true contract but rather a fictional contract that is imposed on the parties to prevent unjust enrichment. Hence, quasi contract provides a basis for relief when no enforceable contract exists. The legal obligation arises because the law considers that the party accepting the benefits has made an implied promise to pay for them. Generally, when one party has conferred a benefit on another party, justice requires the party receiving the benefit to pay the reasonable value for it. The party conferring the benefit can recover in *quantum meruit*, which means "as much as he or she deserves" (see Chapter 10).

When Quasi Contracts Are Used

In addition to being used when there is no actual contract or agreement between the parties, quasi contract may be available when the parties have a contract, but it is unenforceable for some reason. Quasi-contractual recovery is often granted when one party has partially

EXHIBIT 18–2 • Remedies for Breach of Contract

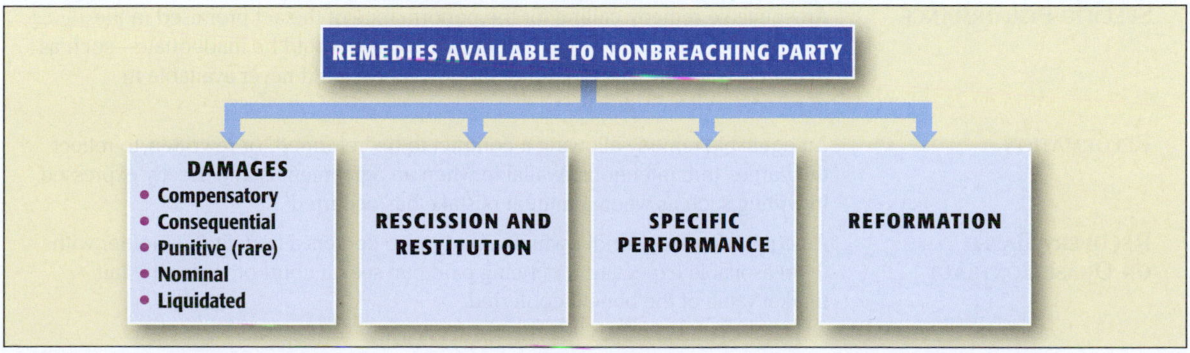

performed under a contract that is unenforceable. It provides an alternative to suing for damages and allows the party to recover the reasonable value of the partial performance, measured in some cases according to the benefit received and in others according to the detriment suffered.

Suppose that Watson contracts to build two oil derricks for Energy Industries. The derricks are to be built over a period of three years, but the parties do not make a written contract. The Statute of Frauds will thus bar the enforcement of the contract.[14] After Watson completes one derrick, Energy Industries informs him that it will not pay for the derrick. Watson can sue Energy Industries under the theory of quasi contract.

The Requirements of Quasi Contract

To recover under the theory of quasi contract, the party seeking recovery must show the following:

1. The party has conferred a benefit on the other party.
2. The party conferred the benefit with the reasonable expectation of being paid.
3. The party did not act as a volunteer in conferring the benefit.
4. The party receiving the benefit would be unjustly enriched by retaining the benefit without paying for it.

14. Contracts that by their terms cannot be performed within one year must be in writing to be enforceable (see Chapter 15).

In the example just given, Watson can sue in quasi contract because all of the conditions for quasi-contractual recovery have been fulfilled. Watson conferred a benefit on Energy Industries with the reasonable expectation of being paid. The derrick conferred an obvious benefit on Energy Industries. Allowing Energy Industries to retain the derrick without paying Watson would enrich the company unjustly. Therefore, Watson should be able to recover in *quantum meruit* the reasonable value of the oil derrick, which is ordinarily equal to its fair market value. (*Concept Summary 18.1* reviews all of the equitable remedies, including quasi contract, that may be available in the event that a contract is breached.)

SECTION 6 Election of Remedies

In many cases, a nonbreaching party has several remedies available. When the remedies are inconsistent with one another, the common law of contracts

CONCEPT SUMMARY 18.1
Equitable Remedies

Remedy	Description
Rescission and Restitution	1. *Rescission*—A remedy whereby a contract is canceled and the parties are restored to the original positions that they occupied prior to the transaction. 2. *Restitution*—When a contract is rescinded, both parties must make restitution to each other by returning the goods, property, or funds previously conveyed.
Specific Performance	An equitable remedy calling for the performance of the act promised in the contract. Only available when monetary damages would be inadequate—such as in contracts for the sale of land or unique goods—and never available in personal-service contracts.
Reformation	An equitable remedy allowing a contract to be "reformed," or rewritten, to reflect the parties' true intentions. Available when an agreement is imperfectly expressed in writing, such as when a mutual mistake has occurred.
Recovery Based on Quasi Contract	An equitable theory under which a party who confers a benefit on another with the reasonable expectation of being paid can seek a court order for the fair market value of the benefit conferred.

requires the party to choose which remedy to pursue. This is called *election of remedies.*

The Purpose of the Doctrine

The purpose of the doctrine of election of remedies is to prevent double recovery. Suppose that McCarthy agrees in writing to sell his land to Tally. Then McCarthy changes his mind and repudiates the contract. Tally can sue for compensatory damages *or* for specific performance. If Tally could seek compensatory damages in addition to specific performance, she would recover twice for the same breach of contract. The doctrine of election of remedies requires Tally to choose the remedy she wants, and it eliminates any possibility of double recovery. In other words, the election doctrine represents the legal embodiment of the adage "You can't have your cake and eat it, too."

The doctrine has often been applied in a rigid and technical manner, leading to some harsh results. For example, Beacham is fraudulently induced to buy a parcel of land for $150,000. He spends an additional $10,000 moving onto the land and then discovers the fraud. Instead of suing for damages, Beacham sues to rescind the contract. The court allows Beacham to recover the purchase price of $150,000 in restitution, but not the additional $10,000 in moving expenses (because the seller did not receive this payment, he or she will not be required to return it). So Beacham suffers a net loss of $10,000 on the transaction. If Beacham had elected to sue for damages instead of seeking the remedy of rescission and restitution, he could have recovered the $10,000 as well as the $150,000.

The UCC's Rejection of the Doctrine

Because of the many problems associated with the doctrine of election of remedies, the UCC expressly rejects it.[15] As will be discussed in Chapter 22, remedies under the Uniform Commercial Code (UCC) are not exclusive but are cumulative in nature and include all the available remedies for breach of contract.

Pleading in the Alternative

Although the nonbreaching party must ultimately elect which remedy to pursue, modern court procedures do allow plaintiffs to plead their cases "in the alternative" (pleadings were discussed in Chapter 3). In other words, when the plaintiff originally files a lawsuit, he or she can ask the court to order either rescission (and restitution) or damages, for example. Then, as the case progresses to trial, the party can elect the remedy that is most beneficial or appropriate, or the judge can order one remedy and not another. This process still prevents double recovery because the party can be awarded only one of the remedies that was requested.

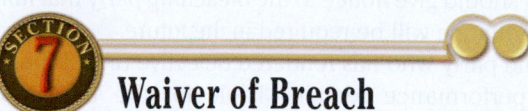

SECTION 7 Waiver of Breach

Under certain circumstances, a nonbreaching party may be willing to accept a defective performance of the contract. This knowing relinquishment of a legal right (that is, the right to require satisfactory and full performance) is called a **waiver.**

Consequences of a Waiver of Breach

When a waiver of a breach of contract occurs, the party waiving the breach cannot take any later action on it. In effect, the waiver erases the past breach; the contract continues as if the breach had never occurred. Of course, the waiver of breach of contract extends only to the matter waived and not to the whole contract.

Reasons for Waiving a Breach

Businesspersons often waive breaches of contract to get whatever benefit is still possible out of the contract. For example, a seller contracts with a buyer to deliver to the buyer ten thousand tons of coal on or before November 1. The contract calls for the buyer to pay by November 10 for coal delivered. Because of a coal miners' strike, coal is hard to find. The seller breaches the contract by not tendering delivery until November 5. The buyer will likely choose to waive the seller's breach, accept delivery of the coal, and pay as contracted.

Waiver of Breach and Subsequent Breaches

Ordinarily, the waiver by a contracting party will not operate to waive subsequent, additional, or future breaches of contract. This is always true when the subsequent breaches are unrelated to the first breach. For example, an owner who waives the right to sue for late

15. See UCC 2–703 and 2–711.

completion of a stage of construction does not waive the right to sue for failure to comply with engineering specifications on the same job. A waiver will be extended to subsequent defective performance, however, if a reasonable person would conclude that similar defective performance in the future will be acceptable. Therefore, a *pattern of conduct* that waives a number of successive breaches will operate as a continued waiver. To change this result, the nonbreaching party should give notice to the breaching party that full performance will be required in the future.

The party who has rendered defective or less-than-full performance remains liable for the damages caused by the breach of contract. In effect, the waiver operates to keep the contract going. The waiver prevents the nonbreaching party from calling the contract to an end or rescinding the contract. The contract continues, but the nonbreaching party can recover damages caused by the defective or less-than-full performance.

SECTION 8

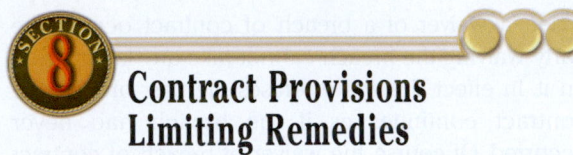

Contract Provisions Limiting Remedies

A contract may include provisions stating that no damages can be recovered for certain types of breaches or that damages will be limited to a maximum amount. The contract may also provide that the only remedy for breach is replacement, repair, or refund of the purchase price. Provisions stating that no damages can be recovered are called *exculpatory clauses* (see Chapter 13). Provisions that affect the availability of certain remedies are called *limitation-of-liability clauses.*

The UCC Allows Sales Contracts to Limit Remedies

The UCC provides that in a contract for the sale of goods, remedies can be limited. We will examine the UCC provisions on limited remedies in Chapter 22, in the context of the remedies available on the breach of a contract for the sale or lease of goods.[16]

Enforceability of Limitation-of-Liability Clauses

Whether a limitation-of-liability clause in a contract will be enforced depends on the type of breach that is excused by the provision. For example, a provision excluding liability for fraudulent or intentional injury will not be enforced. Likewise, a clause excluding liability for illegal acts or violations of law will not be enforced.

A clause excluding liability for negligence may be enforced in certain situations, however. When an exculpatory clause for negligence is contained in a contract made between parties who have roughly equal bargaining positions, the clause usually will be enforced.[17]

16. See UCC 2–719(1).

17. See, for example, *Asch Webhosting, Inc. v. Adelphia Business Solutions Investment, LLC*, __ F.Supp.2d __ (D.N.J. 2007); and *Lucier v. Williams*, 366 N.J.Super. 485, 841 A.2d 907 (2004).

REVIEWING Breach of Contract and Remedies

Kyle Bruno enters a contract with X Entertainment to be a stuntman in a movie. Bruno is widely known as the best motorcycle stuntman in the business, and the movie to be produced, *Xtreme Riders,* has numerous scenes involving high-speed freestyle street-bike stunts. Filming is set to begin August 1 and end by December 1 so that the film can be released the following summer. Both parties to the contract have stipulated that the filming must end on time to capture the profits from the summer movie market. The contract states that Bruno will be paid 10 percent of the net proceeds from the movie for his stunts. The contract also includes a liquidated damages provision, which specifies that if Bruno breaches the contract, he will owe X Entertainment $1 million. In addition, the contract includes a limitation-of-liability clause stating that if Bruno is injured during filming, X Entertainment's

REVIEWING Breach of Contract and Remedies, Continued

liability is limited to nominal damages. Using the information presented in the chapter, answer the following questions.

1. One day, while Bruno is preparing for a difficult stunt, he gets into an argument with the director and refuses to perform any stunts at all. Can X Entertainment seek specific performance of the contract? Why or why not?
2. Suppose that while performing a high-speed wheelie on a motorcycle, Bruno is injured by the intentionally reckless act of an X Entertainment employee. Will a court be likely to enforce the limitation-of-liability clause? Why or why not?
3. What factors would a court consider to determine whether the $1 million liquidated damages provision constitutes valid damages or is a penalty?
4. Suppose that the contract had no liquidated damages provision (or the court refused to enforce it) and X Entertainment breached the contract. The breach caused the release of the film to be delayed until the fall. Could Bruno seek consequential (special) damages for lost profits from the summer movie market in that situation? Explain.

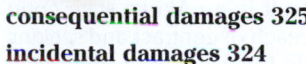

TERMS AND CONCEPTS

consequential damages 325
incidental damages 324
liquidated damages 328
mitigation of damages 327
nominal damages 327
penalty 328
reformation 331
restitution 329
specific performance 329
waiver 333

QUESTIONS AND CASE PROBLEMS

18–1. Cohen contracts to sell his house and lot to Windsor for $100,000. The terms of the contract call for Windsor to pay 10 percent of the purchase price as a deposit toward the purchase price, or a down payment. The terms further stipulate that if the buyer breaches the contract, Cohen will retain the deposit as liquidated damages. Windsor pays the deposit, but because her expected financing of the $90,000 balance falls through, she breaches the contract. Two weeks later Cohen sells the house and lot to Ballard for $105,000. Windsor demands her $10,000 back, but Cohen refuses, claiming that Windsor's breach and the contract terms entitle him to keep the deposit. Discuss who is correct.

18–2. QUESTION WITH SAMPLE ANSWER

In which of the following situations would specific performance be an appropriate remedy? Discuss fully.

(a) Thompson contracts to sell her house and lot to Cousteau. Then, on finding another buyer willing to pay a higher purchase price, she refuses to deed the property to Cousteau.

(b) Amy contracts to sing and dance in Fred's nightclub for one month, beginning May 1. She then refuses to perform.

(c) Hoffman contracts to buy a rare coin owned by Erikson, who is breaking up his coin collection. At the last minute, Erikson decides to keep his collection intact and refuses to deliver the coin to Hoffman.

(d) ABC Corp. has three shareholders: Panozzo, who owns 48 percent of the stock; Chang, who owns another 48 percent; and Ryan, who owns 4 percent. Ryan contracts to sell her 4 percent to Chang. Later, Ryan refuses to transfer the shares to Chang.

• **For a sample answer to Question 18–2, go to Appendix I at the end of this text.**

18–3. Ken owns and operates a famous candy store and makes most of the candy sold in the store. Business is particularly heavy during the Christmas season. Ken contracts with Sweet, Inc., to purchase ten thousand pounds of sugar to be delivered on or before November 15. Ken has informed Sweet that this particular order is to be used for the Christmas season business. Because of problems at the refinery, the sugar is not tendered to Ken until December 10, at which time Ken refuses it as being too late. Ken has been unable to purchase the quantity of sugar needed to meet his Christmas orders and has had to turn down numerous regular customers, some of whom have indicated that they will purchase candy elsewhere in the future. The sugar Ken has been able to purchase has cost him 10 cents per pound above the price contracted for with Sweet. Ken sues Sweet for breach of contract, claiming as damages the higher price paid for sugar from others, lost profits from this year's lost Christmas sales, future lost profits from customers who have indicated that they will discontinue doing business with him, and punitive damages for failure to meet the contracted delivery date. Sweet claims Ken is limited to compensatory damages only. Discuss who is correct, and why.

18–4. Mitigation of Damages. William West, an engineer, worked for Bechtel Corp., an organization of about 150 engineering and construction companies, which is headquartered in San Francisco, California, and operates worldwide. Except for a two-month period in 1985, Bechtel employed West on long-term assignments or short-term projects for thirty years. In October 1997, West was offered a position on a project with Saudi Arabian Bechtel Co. (SABCO), which West understood would be for two years. In November, however, West was terminated for what he believed was his "age and lack of display of energy." After his return to California, West received numerous offers from Bechtel for work that suited his abilities and met his salary expectations, but he did not accept any of them and did not look for other work. Three months later, he filed a suit in a California state court against Bechtel, alleging, in part, breach of contract and seeking the salary he would have earned during two years with SABCO. Bechtel responded, in part, that, even if there had been a breach, West had failed to mitigate his damages. Is Bechtel correct? Discuss. [*West v. Bechtel Corp.*, 96 Cal.App.4th 966, 117 Cal.Rptr.2d 647 (1 Dist. 2002)]

18–5. Liquidated Damages versus Penalties. Every homeowner in the Putnam County, Indiana, subdivision of Stardust Hills must be a member of the Stardust Hills Owners Association, Inc., and must pay annual dues of $200 for the maintenance of common areas and other community services. Under the association's rules, dues paid more than ten days late "shall bear a delinquent fee at a rate of $2.00 per day." Phyllis Gaddis owned a Stardust Hills lot on which she failed to pay the dues. Late fees began to accrue. Nearly two months later, the association filed a suit in an Indiana state court to collect the unpaid dues and the late fees. Gaddis argued in response that the delinquent fee was an unenforceable penalty. What questions should be considered in determining the status of this fee? Should the association's rule regarding assessment of the fee be enforced? Explain. [*Gaddis v. Stardust Hills Owners Association, Inc.*, 804 N.E.2d 231 (Ind.App. 2004)]

18–6. CASE PROBLEM WITH SAMPLE ANSWER

Tyna Ek met Russell Peterson in Seattle, Washington. Peterson persuaded Ek to buy a boat that he had once owned, the *O'Hana Kai*, which was in Juneau, Alaska. Ek paid $43,000 for the boat, and in January 2000, the parties entered into a contract. In the contract, Peterson agreed to make the vessel seaworthy so that within one month it could be transported to Seattle, where he would pay its moorage costs. He would also renovate the boat at his own expense in return for a portion of the profit on its resale in 2001. At the time of the resale, Ek would recover her costs, after which she would reimburse Peterson for his expenses. Ek loaned Peterson her cell phone so that they could communicate while he prepared the vessel for the trip to Seattle. In March, Peterson, who was still in Alaska, borrowed $4,000 from Ek. Two months later, Ek began to receive unanticipated, unauthorized bills for vessel parts and moorage, the use of her phone, and charges on her credit card. She went to Juneau to take possession of the boat. Peterson moved it to Petersburg, Alaska, where he registered it under a false name, and then to Taku Harbor, where the police seized it. Ek filed a suit in an Alaska state court against Peterson, alleging breach of contract and seeking damages. If the court finds in Ek's favor, what should her damages include? Discuss. [*Peterson v. Ek*, 93 P.3d 458 (Alaska 2004)]

- **To view a sample answer for Problem 18–6, go to this book's Web site at www.cengage.com/blaw/jentz, select "Chapter 18," and click on "Case Problem with Sample Answer."**

18–7. Waiver of Breach. In May 1998, RDP Royal Palm Hotel, L.P., contracted with Clark Construction Group, Inc., to build the Royal Palms Crowne Plaza Resort in Miami Beach, Florida. The deadline for "substantial completion" was February 28, 2000, but RDP could ask for changes, and the date would be adjusted accordingly. During construction, Clark faced many setbacks, including a buried seawall, contaminated soil, the unforeseen deterioration of the existing hotel, and RDP's issue of hundreds of change orders. Clark requested extensions of the deadline, and RDP agreed, but the parties never specified a date. After the original deadline passed, RDP continued to issue change orders, Clark continued to perform, and RDP accepted the work. In March 2002, when the resort was substantially complete, RDP stopped paying Clark. Clark stopped working. RDP hired another contractor to finish the resort, which opened in May. RDP filed a suit in a federal district court against Clark, alleging, among other things, breach of contract for the two-year delay in the resort's completion. In whose favor should the court rule, and why? Discuss. [*RDP Royal Palm Hotel, L.P. v. Clark Construction Group, Inc.*, __ F.3d __ (11th Cir. 2006)]

18–8. Remedies. On July 7, 2000, Frances Morelli agreed to sell to Judith Bucklin a house at 126 Lakedell Drive in Warwick, Rhode Island, for $77,000. Bucklin made a deposit on the house. The closing at which the parties would exchange the deed for the price was scheduled for September 1. The agreement did not state that "time is of the essence," but it did provide, in "Paragraph 10," that "[i]f Seller is unable to [convey good, clear, insurable, and marketable title], Buyer shall have the option to: (a) accept such title as Seller is able to convey without abatement or reduction of the Purchase Price, or (b) cancel this Agreement and receive a return of all Deposits." An examination of the public records revealed that the house did not have marketable title. Wishing to be flexible, Bucklin offered Morelli time to resolve the problem, and the closing did not occur as scheduled. Morelli decided "the deal is over" and offered to return the deposit. Bucklin refused and, in mid-October, decided to exercise her option under Paragraph 10(a). She notified Morelli, who did not respond. Bucklin filed a suit in a Rhode Island state court against Morelli. In whose favor should the court rule? Should damages be awarded? If not, what is the appropriate remedy? Why? [*Bucklin v. Morelli,* 912 A.2d 931 (R.I. 2007)]

18–9. A QUESTION OF ETHICS

*In 2004, Tamara Cohen, a real estate broker, began showing property in Manhattan to Steven Galistinos, who represented comedian Jerry Seinfeld and his wife, Jessica. According to Cohen, she told Galistinos that her commission would be 5 or 6 percent, and he agreed. According to Galistinos, there was no such agreement. Cohen spoke with Maximillan Sanchez, another broker, about a townhouse owned by Ray and Harriet Mayeri. According to Cohen, Sanchez said that the commission would be 6 percent, which they agreed to split equally. Sanchez later acknowledged that they agreed to split the fee, but claimed that they did not discuss a specific amount. On a Friday in February 2005, Cohen showed the townhouse to Jessica. According to Cohen, she told Jessica that the commission would be 6 percent, with the Seinfelds paying half, and Jessica agreed. According to Jessica, there was no such conversation. Later that day, Galistinos asked Cohen to arrange for the Seinfelds to see the premises again. Cohen told Galistinos that her religious beliefs prevented her from showing property on Friday evenings or Saturdays before sundown. She suggested the following Monday or Tuesday, but Galistinos said that Jerry would not be available and asked her to contact Carolyn Liebling, Jerry's business manager. Cohen left Liebling a message. Over the weekend, the Seinfelds toured the building on their own and agreed to buy the property for $3.95 million. Despite repeated attempts, they were unable to contact Cohen. [*Cohen v. Seinfeld, *15 Misc.3d 1118(A), 839 N.Y.S.2d 432 (Sup. 2007)]*

(a) The contract between the Seinfelds and the Mayeris stated that the sellers would pay Sanchez's fee and the "buyers will pay buyer's real estate broker's fees." The Mayeris paid Sanchez $118,500, which is 3 percent of $3.95 million. The Seinfelds refused to pay Cohen. She filed a suit in a New York state court against them, asserting, among other things, breach of contract. Should the court order the Seinfelds to pay Cohen? If so, is she entitled to a full commission even though she was not available to show the townhouse when the Seinfelds wanted to see it? Explain.

(b) What obligation do parties involved in business deals owe to each other with respect to their religious beliefs? How might the situation in this case have been avoided?

18–10. VIDEO QUESTION

Go to this text's Web site at **www.cengage.com/blaw/jentz** and select "Chapter 18." Click on "Video Questions" and view the video titled *Midnight Run.* Then answer the following questions.

(a) In the video, Eddie (Joe Pantoliano) and Jack (Robert De Niro) negotiate a contract for Jack to find the Duke, a mob accountant who embezzled funds, and bring him back for trial. Assume that the contract is valid. If Jack breaches the contract by failing to bring in the Duke, what kinds of remedies, if any, can Eddie seek? Explain your answer.

(b) Would the equitable remedy of specific performance be available to either Jack or Eddie in the event of a breach? Why or why not?

(c) Now assume that the contract between Eddie and Jack is unenforceable. Nevertheless, Jack performs his side of the bargain (brings in the Duke). Does Jack have any legal recourse in this situation? Why or why not?

LAW ON THE WEB

For updated links to resources available on the Web, as well as a variety of other materials, visit this text's Web site at

www.cengage.com/blaw/jentz

For a summary of how contracts may be breached and other information on contract law, go to Lawyers.com's Web page at

contracts.lawyers.com

The following sites offer information on contract law, including breach of contract and remedies:

www.nolo.com

www.law.cornell.edu/wex/index.php/Contracts

Legal Research Exercises on the Web

Go to **www.cengage.com/blaw/jentz**, the Web site that accompanies this text. Select "Chapter 18" and click on "Internet Exercises." There you will find the following Internet research exercises that you can perform to learn more about the topics covered in this chapter.

Internet Exercise 18–1: Legal Perspective
Contract Damages and Contract Theory

Internet Exercise 18–2: Management Perspective
The Duty to Mitigate

CHAPTER 19

E-Contracts and E-Signatures

The basic principles of contract law that were covered in previous chapters evolved over an extended period of time. Certainly, they were formed long before cyberspace and electronic contracting became realities. Therefore, new legal theories, new adaptations of existing laws, and new laws are needed to govern **e-contracts,** or contracts entered into electronically. To date, however, most courts have adapted traditional contract law principles and, when applicable, provisions of the Uniform Commercial Code (UCC) to cases involving e-contract disputes. Although an e-contract has the same basic requirements to be valid—agreement, consideration, capacity, and legality—certain aspects of forming e-contracts are unique, such as the method by which the offer and acceptance are communicated.

In the first part of this chapter, we look at how traditional laws are being applied to contracts formed online. We then examine some new laws that have been enacted to apply in situations that are not readily encompassed by the traditional laws governing contracts. For example, traditional laws governing signature and writing requirements are not easily adapted to contracts formed in the online environment. Thus, new laws have been created to address these issues.

SECTION 1 Online Contract Formation

Today, numerous contracts are being formed online. Although these contracts are being generated through a new medium, the age-old problems attending contract formation still exist. Disputes concerning contracts formed online continue to center around contract terms and whether the parties voluntarily assented to those terms.

Note that online contracts may be formed not only for the sale of goods and services but also for the purpose of *licensing*. The "sale" of software generally involves a license, or a right to use the software, rather than the passage of title (ownership rights) from the seller to the buyer. For example, Galynn wants to obtain software that will allow her to work on spreadsheets on her BlackBerry. She goes online and purchases GridMagic. During the transaction, she has to click on several on-screen "I agree" boxes to indicate that she understands that she is purchasing only the right to use the software and will not obtain any ownership rights. After she agrees to these terms (the licensing agreement), she can download the software to her BlackBerry. Although in this chapter we typically refer to the offeror and offeree as a *seller* and a *buyer*, in many transactions these parties would be more accurately described as a *licensor* and a *licensee*.

Online Offers

Sellers doing business via the Internet can protect themselves against contract disputes and legal liability by creating offers that clearly spell out the terms that will govern their transactions if the offers are accepted. Significant terms should be conspicuous and easy to view.

Displaying the Offer The seller's Web site should include a hypertext link to a page containing the full contract so that potential buyers are made aware of the terms to which they are assenting. The contract generally must be displayed online in a readable format such as a twelve-point typeface. For example, Netquip sells a variety of heavy equipment, such as trucks and trailers, online at its Web site. Netquip must include its full pricing schedule on the Web site with explanations of all complex provisions. In addition, the terms of the sale (such as any warranties and Netquip's refund policy) must be fully disclosed.

Is an online contract enforceable if the offeror requires an offeree to scroll down or print the contract to read its terms, which are otherwise readily accessible and clear? That was the question in the following case.

CASE 19.1 Feldman v. Google, Inc.

United States District Court, Eastern District of Pennsylvania, 2007. 513 F.Supp.2d 229.

• **Company Profile** In the mid-1990s, Larry Page and Sergey Brin, Stanford University graduate students in computer science, began work on an Internet search engine called "BackRub." Renamed "Google" after the mathematical term for a 1 followed by 100 zeros, the engine was made available in 1998. In less than a year, the service was acquiring major clients, receiving achievement awards, being included on many "Top Web Site" lists, and handling millions of queries per day. By 2000, Google had become the world's largest search engine. According to Google, Inc.'s Web site at www.google.com, its mission is to organize the world's information and make it universally accessible and useful. The company's revenue derives from keyword-targeted advertising.

• **Background and Facts** In Google, Inc.'s AdWords program, when an Internet user searches on www.google.com using key words that an advertiser has identified, an ad appears. If the user clicks on it, Google charges the advertiser. Google requires an advertiser to agree to certain terms before placing an ad. These terms—set out in a preamble and seven paragraphs—are displayed online in a window with a scroll bar. A link to a printer-friendly version of the terms is at the top of the window. At the bottom of the page, viewable without scrolling, are the words, "Yes, I agree to the above terms and conditions," and a box on which an advertiser must click to proceed. Among the terms, a forum-selection clause provides that any dispute over the program is to be "adjudicated in Santa Clara County, California." Lawrence Feldman, a lawyer, participated in the program by selecting key words, including "Vioxx," "Bextra," and "Celebrex," to trigger a showing of his ad to potential clients. In a subsequent suit between Feldman and Google in a federal district court in Pennsylvania, Feldman claimed that at least 20 percent of the clicks for which he was charged $100,000 between January 2003 and January 2006 were fraudulent.[a] Feldman filed a motion for summary judgment. Google asked the court to transfer the case to a court in Santa Clara County, California.

• **Decision and Rationale** The court denied Feldman's motion for summary judgment and granted Google's motion to transfer the case. The court held that "the requirements of an express contract for reasonable notice of terms and mutual assent are satisfied" in this situation. Feldman and Google were bound to the terms. The court pointed out that the contract at issue was a click-wrap agreement (or *click-on agreement*, to be discussed shortly in this chapter) that appeared on an Internet Web page. "Even though they are electronic, click-wrap agreements are considered to be writings because they are printable and storable. * * * Absent a showing of fraud, failure to read an enforceable click-wrap agreement, as with any binding contract, will not excuse compliance with its terms." By clicking "Yes," Feldman agreed to all of the terms. Without clicking the "Yes" button, Feldman could not have engaged in an agreement with the defendant.

• **The Ethical Dimension** *With respect to click fraud, which was the heart of Feldman's claim in this case, what circumstances might suggest unethical behavior by Google?*

• **The E-Commerce Dimension** *Under what different facts might the court have held that the plaintiff did not have reasonable notice of the terms of the agreement and thus did not assent to them?*

a. Feldman was alleging that *click fraud* had taken place. Click fraud occurs when someone, such as a competitor or a prankster with no interest in an advertiser's goods or services, clicks repeatedly on an ad, driving up the ad's cost to the advertiser without generating a sale. For more on click fraud, see the *Insight into Ethics* feature on pages 270 and 271.

Provisions to Include An important rule to keep in mind is that the offeror controls the offer and thus the resulting contract. Therefore, the seller should anticipate the terms that he or she wants to include in a contract and provide for them in the offer. At a minimum, an online offer should include the following provisions:

1. A clause that clearly indicates what constitutes the buyer's agreement to the terms of the offer, such as a box containing the words "I accept" that the buyer can click on to indicate acceptance. (Mechanisms for accepting online offers are discussed in detail later in the chapter.)
2. A provision specifying how payment for the goods and of any applicable taxes must be made.
3. A statement of the seller's refund and return policies.
4. Disclaimers of liability for certain uses of the goods. For example, an online seller of business forms may add a disclaimer that the seller does not accept responsibility for the buyer's reliance on the forms rather than on an attorney's advice.
5. A provision specifying the remedies available to the buyer if the goods are found to be defective or if the contract is otherwise breached. Any limitation of remedies should be clearly spelled out.
6. A statement indicating how the seller will use the information gathered about the buyer.
7. Provisions relating to dispute settlement, such as an arbitration clause or a *forum-selection clause* (discussed next).

Dispute-Settlement Provisions Online offers frequently include provisions relating to dispute settlement. An arbitration clause might be included, indicating that any dispute arising under the contract will be arbitrated in a specified forum. Many online contracts also contain a **forum-selection clause,** which indicates the forum, or place (such as the court or jurisdiction), for the resolution of any dispute arising under the contract. These clauses can help online sellers avoid having to appear in court in many distant jurisdictions when customers are dissatisfied with their purchases.

Suppose that a California buyer purchases defective goods sold online by a company located in New York. Unable to obtain a refund or adequate replacement goods from the seller, the California buyer files a suit against the seller in a California state court. If the New York seller meets the "minimum-contacts" requirement (discussed in Chapter 2) for the California court to exercise jurisdiction over the dispute, the New York seller will need to travel to California—or at least hire an attorney in California—to defend against the lawsuit. Forum-selection clauses in online contracts offer a way for sellers to avoid this problem. Forum-selection clauses are also routinely included in contracts for the international sale of goods (see Chapter 20).

Online Acceptances

The *Restatement (Second) of Contracts*—a compilation of common law contract principles—states that parties may agree to a contract "by written or spoken words or by other action or by failure to act."[1] Similarly, Section 2–204 of the UCC states that any contract for the sale of goods "may be made in any manner sufficient to show agreement, including conduct by both parties which recognizes the existence of such a contract."

Click-On Agreements The courts have used these provisions to conclude that a binding contract can be created by conduct, including the act of clicking on a box indicating "I accept" or "I agree" to accept an online offer. When an online buyer indicates his or her assent to be bound by the terms of the offer by clicking on some on-screen prompt, a **click-on agreement** (sometimes referred to as a *click-on license* or *click-wrap agreement*) is formed. Exhibit 19–1 on the following page shows a portion of a click-on agreement that accompanies a package of software made and marketed by Microsoft.

Generally, the law does not require that all of the parties to a contract must actually have read all of its terms for the contract to be effective. Clicking on a button or box that states "I agree" to certain terms can be enough. The terms may be contained on a Web site through which the buyer is obtaining goods or services, or they may appear on a computer screen when software is loaded from a CD-ROM or DVD or downloaded from the Internet.

In the following case, the court considered the enforceability of a click-wrap software licensing agreement that included a forum-selection clause.

1. *Restatement (Second) of Contracts,* Section 19.

EXHIBIT 19–1 • A Click-On Agreement

This exhibit illustrates an online offer to form a contract. To accept the offer, the user simply scrolls down the page and clicks on the "Accept" box.

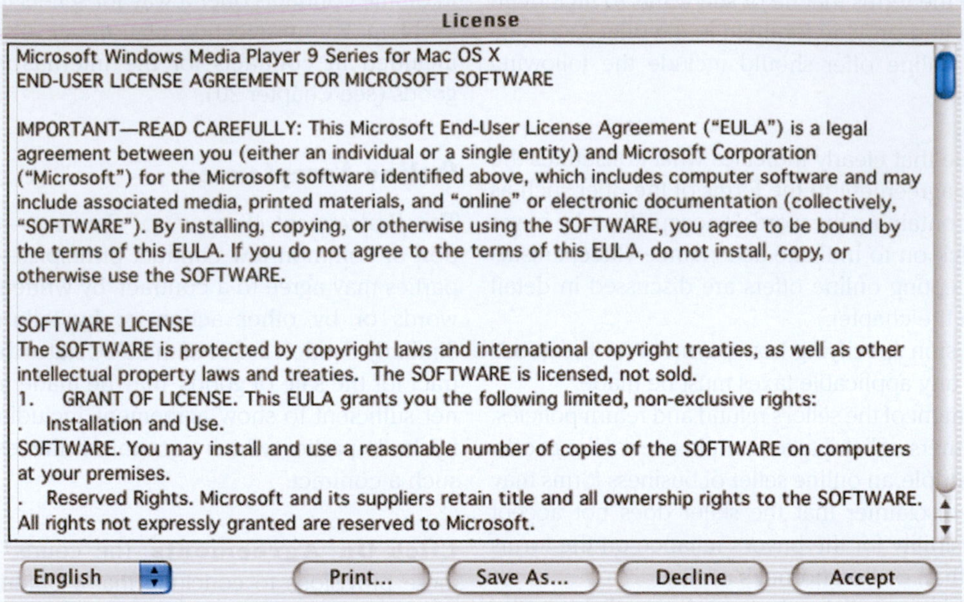

CASE 19.2 Mortgage Plus, Inc. v. DocMagic, Inc.

United States District Court, District of Kansas, 2004. __ F.Supp.2d __.

Background and Facts In 1997, Mortgage Plus, Inc., a mortgage lender in Kansas, asked DocMagic, Inc., a California firm, for software to prepare and manage loan documents and for document preparation services. DocMagic sent Mortgage Plus a CD-ROM containing the software, which had to be loaded onto a computer. Before it could be installed, however, a window displayed a "Software License and User Agreement" on the screen. The agreement asked, "Do you accept all terms of the preceding License Agreement? If you choose No, Setup will close." A click on a "Yes" button was needed to continue. The agreement also included a clause designating California as the venue for the resolution of any disputes. To prepare loan documents, the software asked for certain information, which it used to create a worksheet. The worksheet was e-mailed to DocMagic, which completed the documents and returned them via e-mail. Over the next six years, Mortgage Plus borrowers filed claims against the firm, alleging that the firm had made mistakes that cost the borrowers $150,000 to resolve. Mortgage Plus filed a suit in a federal district court against DocMagic, alleging that its software failed to produce documents that met certain legal requirements. The defendant filed a motion to transfer the suit to a federal court in California based on the clause in the click-on agreement.

Decision and Rationale The court concluded that the software licensing agreement was a valid contract because a user had to agree to its terms before the software could be installed and used. The forum-selection clause was thus enforceable, and the court ordered the suit to be transferred to a federal district court in California. Mortgage Plus argued that the parties had negotiated and entered into a contract before DocMagic shipped the software and that the forum-selection clause was a later, improper attempt to modify this contract. The court, however, found no evidence of this purported "original contractual agreement." Mortgage Plus then argued that it was not aware of, and thus did not accept, the licensing agreement, claiming that "a clickwrap agreement consisting of a window entitled 'Software Licensing Agreement' appearing prior to installation of software cannot be construed as a legally binding contract." The court rejected this argument and explained, "The software required users to accept the terms by clicking through a series of screens before they could access and subsequently install the software." Because

CASE 19.2 CONTINUED Mortgage Plus had a choice as to whether to download the software and utilize the related services, "installation and use of the software with the attached license constituted an affirmative acceptance of the license terms."

- **What If the Facts Were Different?** *Suppose that the individual who clicked on the "Yes" button and installed the software was not authorized to do so. Would the result have been different?*

- **The E-Commerce Dimension** *If DocMagic had e-mailed the forum-selection clause to Mortgage Plus and Mortgage Plus had not responded, could the "silence" be construed as an acceptance of the clause? Explain your answer.*

Shrink-Wrap Agreements In many ways, click-on agreements are the Internet equivalents of *shrink-wrap agreements* (or *shrink-wrap licenses,* as they are sometimes called). A **shrink-wrap agreement** is an agreement whose terms are expressed inside a box in which the goods are packaged. (The term *shrink-wrap* refers to the plastic that covers the box.) Usually, the party who opens the box is told that she or he agrees to the terms by keeping whatever is in the box.

Similarly, when the purchaser opens a software package, he or she agrees to abide by the terms of the limited license agreement. Suppose that Garcia orders a new computer from a national company, which ships the computer to Garcia. Along with the computer, the box contains an agreement setting forth the terms of the sale, including what remedies are available. The document also states that Garcia's retention of the computer for longer than thirty days will be construed as an acceptance of the terms.

In most instances, a shrink-wrap agreement is not between a retailer and a buyer, but between the manufacturer of the hardware or software and the ultimate buyer-user of the product. The terms generally concern warranties, remedies, and other issues associated with the use of the product.

Shrink-Wrap Agreements—Enforceable Contract Terms. In many cases, the courts have treated the terms of shrink-wrap agreements as just as enforceable as the terms of other contracts. These courts reason that by including the terms with the product, the seller proposes a contract that the buyer can accept by using the product after having an opportunity to read the terms. Thus, a buyer's failure to object to terms contained within a shrink-wrapped software package (or an online offer) may constitute an acceptance of the terms by conduct.[2] Additionally, it seems practical from a business's point of view to enclose a full statement of the legal terms of a sale with the product rather than to read the statement over the phone, for example, when a buyer calls in an order for the product.

Shrink-Wrap Terms That May Not Be Enforced. Nevertheless, the courts have not enforced all of the terms included in shrink-wrap agreements. One important consideration is whether the parties form their contract before or after the seller communicates the terms of the shrink-wrap agreement to the buyer. If a court finds that the buyer learned of the shrink-wrap terms *after* the parties entered into a contract, the court may conclude that those terms were proposals for additional terms and were not part of the contract unless the buyer expressly agreed to them.[3]

Businesspersons should be aware that courts have sometimes refused to enforce shrink-wrap terms on the ground that the parties did not expressly agree to the terms at the time of entering into the contract. To ensure that contract terms are enforceable, businesspersons should consider avoiding shrink-wrap terms altogether, particularly in transactions with consumers. By structuring an offer as a click-on agreement, they can prevent many potential problems that have arisen with shrink-wrap agreements.

If the purchase transaction cannot take place online, then they should consider whether it is feasible to require the buyer to register the goods online after receipt. If the goods being sold include software, for example, then a seller can require a buyer to register the purchase online. At that time, the buyer can be informed of all the contract terms and be required to click on a box to show her or his agreement to those terms. As long as a buyer has to indicate her or his assent to the terms in some fashion, the courts generally will uphold the terms.

2. For a leading case on this issue, see *ProCD, Inc. v. Zeidenberg,* 86 F.3d 1447 (7th Cir. 1996).

3. See, for example, *Klocek v. Gateway, Inc.,* 104 F.Supp.2d 1332 (D.Kans. 2000).

Browse-Wrap Terms Like the terms of a click-on agreement, **browse-wrap terms** can occur in a transaction conducted over the Internet. Unlike a click-on agreement, however, browse-wrap terms do not require an Internet user to assent to the terms before, say, downloading or using certain software. In other words, a person can install the software without clicking "I agree" to the terms of a license. Offerors of browse-wrap terms generally assert that the terms are binding without the user's active consent.

Critics contend that browse-wrap terms are not enforceable because they do not satisfy the basic elements of contract formation. Some argue that a user must at least be presented with the terms before indicating agreement in order to form a valid online contract. With respect to a browse-wrap term, this would require that a user navigate past it and agree to it before being able to obtain whatever is being sold.

For example, Netscape Communications Corporation provided free downloadable software called "SmartDownload" on its Web site to those who indicated, by clicking on a designated box, that they wished to obtain it. On the Web site's download page was a reference to a license agreement that was visible only by scrolling to the next screen. In other words, the user did not have to agree to the terms of the license before downloading the software. One of the terms in the license required all disputes to be submitted to arbitration in California. When a group of users filed a lawsuit against Netscape in New York, however, the court held that the arbitration clause in the browse-wrap license agreement was unenforceable because users were not required to indicate their assent to the agreement.[4]

SECTION 2 E-Signatures

In many instances, a contract cannot be enforced unless it is signed by the party against whom enforcement is sought. In the days when many people could not write, documents were signed with an "X." Then handwritten signatures became common, followed by typed signatures, printed signatures, and, most recently, digital signatures that are transmitted electronically. Throughout the evolution of signature technology, the question of what constitutes a valid signature has arisen frequently, and with good reason—without some consensus on what constitutes a valid signature, little business or legal work could be accomplished. In this section, we look at how electronic signatures, or *e-signatures*, can be created and verified on e-contracts, as well as how the parties can enter into agreements that prevent disputes concerning e-signatures.

E-Signature Technologies

Today, numerous technologies allow electronic documents to be signed. An **e-signature** has been defined as "an electronic sound, symbol, or process attached to or logically associated with a record and executed or adopted by a person with the intent to sign the record."[5] Thus, e-signatures include encrypted digital signatures, names (intended as signatures) at the ends of e-mail messages, and "clicks" on a Web page if the click includes the identification of the person. Various forms of e-signatures have been—or are now being—developed, but most e-signatures used today fall into one of two categories, *digitized handwritten signatures* and *public-key infrastructure–based digital signatures*.

Digitized Handwritten Signatures A digitized signature is a graphical image of a handwritten signature that is often created using a digital pen and pad, such as an ePad, and special software. For security reasons, the strokes of a person's signature can be measured by software to authenticate the person signing (this is referred to as *signature dynamics*).

Examples of digitized signatures are abundant. When United Parcel Service (UPS) delivers a package to your office, for example, the delivery person asks you to sign a digital pad to verify receipt. Similarly, when you pick up a prescription, some pharmacies ask you to sign an electronic pad to confirm that the pharmacist has informed you of the potential side effects of the prescribed medications.

Public-Key Infrastructure Digital Signatures In a public-key infrastructure (such as an *asymmetric cryptosystem*), two mathematically linked but different keys are generated—a private signing key and a public validation key. A digital signature is created when the signer uses the private key to create a unique mark on an electronic document. With the

4. *Specht v. Netscape Communications Corp.*, 306 F.3d 17 (2d Cir. 2002).

5. This definition is from the Uniform Electronic Transactions Act, which will be discussed later in this chapter.

appropriate software, the recipient of the document can use the public key to verify the identity of the signer. A **cybernotary**—a legally recognized certification authority—issues the key pair, identifies the owner of the keys, and certifies the validity of the public key. The cybernotary also serves as a repository for public keys.

State Laws Governing E-Signatures

Most states have laws governing e-signatures. The problem is that state e-signature laws are not uniform. Some states—California is a notable example—prohibit many types of documents from being signed with e-signatures, whereas other states are more permissive. Additionally, some states recognize only digital signatures as valid, while others permit other types of e-signatures.

In an attempt to create more uniformity among the states, in 1999 the National Conference of Commissioners on Uniform State Laws and the American Law Institute promulgated the Uniform Electronic Transactions Act (UETA). To date, the UETA has been adopted, at least in part, by forty-eight states. Among other things, the UETA declares that a signature may not be denied legal effect or enforceability solely because it is in electronic form.[6] (The provisions of the UETA will be discussed in more detail shortly.)

6. Many states have also included a similar provision in their versions of the UCC.

Federal Law on E-Signatures and E-Documents

In 2000, Congress enacted the Electronic Signatures in Global and National Commerce Act (E-SIGN Act),[7] which provides that no contract, record, or signature may be "denied legal effect" solely because it is in electronic form. In other words, under this law, an electronic signature is as valid as a signature on paper, and an e-document can be as enforceable as a paper one.

For an e-signature to be enforceable, the contracting parties must have agreed to use electronic signatures. For an electronic document to be valid, it must be in a form that can be retained and accurately reproduced.

The E-SIGN Act does not apply to all types of documents, however. Contracts and documents that are exempt include court papers, divorce decrees, evictions, foreclosures, health-insurance terminations, prenuptial agreements, and wills. Also, the only agreements governed by the UCC that fall under this law are those covered by Articles 2 and 2A and UCC 1–107 and 1–206. Despite these limitations, the E-SIGN Act significantly expanded the possibilities for contracting online. For a discussion of e-signature laws and e-commerce issues worldwide, see this chapter's *Insight into the Global Environment* feature on page 347.

In the case that follows, the court applied a variety of contract principles to determine the legal effect of an exchange of e-mails, plus a phone call.

7. 15 U.S.C. Sections 7001 *et seq.*

CASE 19.3 Amber Chemical, Inc. v. Reilly Industries, Inc.

United States District Court, Eastern District of California, 2007. __ F.Supp.2d __.

• **Background and Facts** Amber Chemical, Inc., a California corporation, sells chemicals to oil companies and agricultural businesses. In the fall of each year, Amber agreed to buy a minimum quantity of potassium chloride from Reilly Industries, Inc., an Indiana firm, at a price set by Reilly. Based on this price, Amber entered into contracts with its own customers. Amber then submitted periodic purchase orders to Reilly to process. In the fall of 2003, through e-mails between Reilly employee Brett Wilhelm and Amber employee Bob Brister, Reilly agreed to sell potassium chloride throughout 2004 for $122.50 per ton as long as the quantity of Amber's purchases met or exceeded the quantity of its purchases in 2003. In a phone call from Wilhelm, Brister orally confirmed that Amber would buy as much or more as it had the previous year. In mid-March 2004, Reilly sold its potassium chloride business, and the shipments to Amber stopped. In a suit between the parties in a federal district court, Amber alleged breach of contract. Reilly filed a motion for

CASE CONTINUES

CASE 19.3 CONTINUED summary judgment, claiming that the parties did not have a written contract, as the Statute of Frauds required. Amber responded by asserting the doctrine of promissory estoppel.

- **Decision and Rationale** The court denied Reilly's motion for summary judgment. "In sum, viewing the evidence in the light most favorable to [Amber, a] contract was formed; * * * and unconscionable injury occurred." The court acknowledged that the transaction between Amber and Reilly involved a sale of goods for a price of $500 or more and thus was subject to the writing requirement of the Statute of Frauds. The court interpreted Wilhelm's e-mail as an invitation to negotiate—to "discuss this proposal" and "work out a contract"—not an offer. Similarly, Brister's e-mailed reply to "please work the contract up" did not constitute an acceptance. And no written contract was otherwise prepared. Amber contended, however, that Reilly made a promise on which Amber relied to its detriment. The court concluded that the e-mails and phone call between Brister and Wilhelm "resulted in a two-way promise, pursuant to which Reilly promised to provide Amber a firm price for 2004, in exchange for Amber's commitment * * * to purchase at least as much potassium chloride as it had in 2003." Also, Wilhelm knew that Amber would use Reilly's price to enter into contracts to supply its own customers, and "it is undisputed that Amber suffered financial damages as a result of the alleged breach, because Amber purchased potassium chloride from other sources at unfavorable prices" to supply those customers after the shipments from Reilly stopped.

- **The Legal Environment Dimension** *Under the Uniform Commercial Code, a contract for a sale of goods normally must state a quantity so that a court will have a basis for determining a remedy. Here, Amber's alleged oral contract did not include a specific quantity. On what basis, then, could the court in this case determine a remedy?*

- **The E-Commerce Dimension** *Reilly included with each shipment a standard invoice stating that it constituted the parties' entire agreement and that its "Standard Terms" could be modified only in a writing signed by the parties. This, Reilly asserted, made those terms "a complete expression of the parties' agreement." Should the court agree with Reilly and apply the* parol evidence rule *(see Chapter 15)? If so, what would be its effect? If not, why not?*

Partnering Agreements

One way that online sellers and buyers can prevent disputes over signatures, as well as disputes over the terms and conditions of their e-contracts, is to form partnering agreements. In a **partnering agreement,** a seller and a buyer who frequently do business with each other agree in advance on the terms and conditions that will apply to all transactions subsequently conducted electronically. The partnering agreement can also establish special access and identification codes to be used by the parties when transacting business electronically.

A partnering agreement reduces the likelihood that disputes will arise under the contract because the buyer and the seller have agreed in advance to the terms and conditions that will accompany each sale. Furthermore, if a dispute does arise, a court or arbitration forum will be able to refer to the partnering agreement when determining the parties' intent with respect to subsequent contracts. Of course, even with a partnering agreement, fraud remains a possibility. If an unauthorized person uses a purchaser's designated access number and identification code, it may be some time before the problem is discovered.[8]

SECTION 3

The Uniform Electronic Transactions Act

As noted earlier, the Uniform Electronic Transactions Act (UETA) was promulgated in 1999. It represented one of the first comprehensive efforts to create uniform laws pertaining to e-commerce.

The primary purpose of the UETA is to remove barriers to e-commerce by giving the same legal effect to electronic records and signatures as is given to paper documents and signatures. As mentioned earlier, the UETA broadly defines an *e-signature* as "an electronic

8. See, for example, *AET, Inc. v. C5 Communications, LLC,* ___ F.Supp.2d ___ (S.D.Tex. 2007).

INSIGHT INTO THE GLOBAL ENVIRONMENT
International Use and Regulation of the Internet

Today, most e-commerce conducted on a worldwide basis involves buyers, sellers, and enablers from the United States. Not surprisingly, then, U.S. law is often used to resolve legal issues related to global e-commerce. The preeminence of U.S. law in this area is likely to be challenged in the future, however, as Internet use continues to expand around the globe. Already, several international organizations have created their own codes of conduct, rules, and regulations for global Internet transactions. We examine a selection of them here.

A United Nations Convention

An important step toward creating international rules for Internet transactions was taken in 2005, when the United Nations Convention on the Use of Electronic Communications in International Contracts was completed. This convention will go into effect as soon as enough countries ratify it, which may have happened by the time you read this. A major goal of the convention is to improve commercial certainty by determining an Internet user's location for legal purposes. The convention also establishes standards for creating functional equivalence between electronic communciations and paper documents. Like the E-SIGN Act discussed in the text, the convention provides that e-signatures should be treated as the equivalent of signatures on paper documents. The drafters also attempted to codify the proper use of automated message systems for contract formation.

Choice of Court

Another recent treaty that will help to foster international trade is the Convention on the Choice of Court Agreements, completed by the Hague Conference on Private International Law on June 30, 2005. Although this convention does not specifically address e-commerce and applies only to business-to-business transactions, not business-to-consumer transactions, it will provide more certainty regarding jurisdiction and recognition of judgments by other nations' courts. Such matters are important to both offline and online transactions, so the convention should enhance e-commerce as well.

The Choice of Court Convention was designed to promote international trade and investment by providing more certainty in resolving international contract disputes. It governs business agreements that designate a single court, or the courts of a single country, to be the forum for resolving disputes. One of its goals is to offer parties entering into international trade contracts a balanced choice between litigation and arbitration when selecting a method of settling disputes. In this sense, the convention is similar to the United Nations Convention on the Recognition and Enforcement of Foreign Arbitral Awards of 1958, commonly referred to as the New York Arbitration Convention (see Chapter 2 for further discussion of this convention).

Fighting International Cyber Crime

Unfortunately, cyber crime has expanded along with the Internet, but steps are beginning to be taken to combat cyber crime on an international basis. At the beginning of this decade, the Council of Europe created the Cyber-Crime Convention, which has been signed by thirty nations including the United States. This treaty provides mechanisms for international cooperation in the battle against Internet-related crime. It prohibits the unauthorized access of an Internet computer system, the unauthorized interception of Internet data, Internet fraud and forgery, and copyright infringement through the use of the Internet.

CRITICAL THINKING

INSIGHT INTO POLITICS

There are about two hundred sovereign nations in the world today, but only thirty have signed the Cyber-Crime Convention. Why do you think so many nations' governments have been reluctant to be bound by the convention?

sound, symbol, or process attached to or logically associated with a record and executed or adopted by a person with the intent to sign the record."[9] A **record** is "information that is inscribed on a tangible medium or that is stored in an electronic or other medium and is retrievable in perceivable [visual] form."[10]

9. UETA 102(8).

10. UETA 102(15).

The Scope and Applicability of the UETA

The UETA does not create new rules for electronic contracts but rather establishes that records, signatures, and contracts may not be denied enforceability solely due to their electronic form. The UETA does not apply to all writings and signatures but only to electronic records and electronic signatures *relating to a transaction.* A *transaction* is defined as an interaction between two or more people relating to business, commercial, or governmental activities.[11]

The act specifically does *not* apply to wills or testamentary trusts (see Chapter 50) or to transactions governed by the UCC (other than those covered in Articles 2 and 2A).[12] In addition, the provisions of the UETA allow the states to exclude its application to other areas of law.

As described earlier, Congress passed the E-SIGN Act in 2000, a year after the UETA was presented to the states for adoption. Thus, a significant issue is whether and to what extent the federal E-SIGN Act preempts the UETA as adopted by the states.

The Federal E-SIGN Act and the UETA

The E-SIGN Act refers explicitly to the UETA and provides that if a state has enacted the uniform version of the UETA, it is not preempted by the E-SIGN Act.[13] In other words, if the state has enacted the UETA without modification, state law will govern. The problem is that many states have enacted nonuniform (modified) versions of the UETA, largely for the purpose of excluding other areas of state law from the UETA's terms. The E-SIGN Act specifies that those exclusions will be preempted to the extent that they are inconsistent with the E-SIGN Act's provisions.

The E-SIGN Act, however, explicitly allows the states to enact alternative procedures or requirements for the use or acceptance of electronic records or electronic signatures. Generally, however, the procedures or requirements must be consistent with the provisions of the E-SIGN Act, and the state must not give greater legal status or effect to one specific type of technology. Additionally, if a state enacted alternative procedures or requirements *after* the E-SIGN Act was adopted, the state law must specifically refer to the E-SIGN Act. The relationship between the UETA and the E-SIGN Act is illustrated in Exhibit 19–2.

11. UETA 2(12) and 3.
12. UETA 3(b).
13. 15 U.S.C. Section 7002(2)(A)(i).

Highlights of the UETA

We look next at selected provisions of the UETA. Our discussion is, of course, based on the act's uniform provisions. Keep in mind that the states that have enacted the UETA may have adopted slightly different versions.

The Parties Must Agree to Conduct Transactions Electronically The UETA will not apply to a transaction unless each of the parties has previously agreed to conduct transactions by electronic means. The agreement need not be explicit, however, and it may be implied by the conduct of the parties and the surrounding circumstances.[14] In the comments that accompany the UETA, the drafters stated that it may be reasonable to infer that a person who gives out a business card with an e-mail address on it has consented to transact business electronically.[15] The party's agreement may also be inferred from a letter or other writing, as well as from some verbal communication. Nothing in the UETA requires that the agreement to conduct transactions electronically be made electronically.

Note, however, that some courts have required that the parties' agreement to conduct transactions electronically be clear and unambiguous. For example, in one Louisiana case, the fact that the parties had *negotiated* the terms of previous contracts via e-mail was not sufficient evidence (by itself) to show that the parties had *agreed* to transact business electronically.[16]

A person who has previously agreed to an electronic transaction can withdraw his or her consent and refuse to conduct further business electronically. Additionally, the act expressly gives parties the power to vary the UETA's provisions by contract. In other words, *parties can opt out of some or all of the terms of the UETA.* If the parties do not opt out of the terms of the UETA, however, the UETA will govern their electronic transactions.

Attribution In the context of electronic transactions, the term *attribution* refers to the procedures that may be used to ensure that the person sending an electronic record is the same person whose e-signature accompanies the record. Under the UETA, if an electronic record or signature was the act of a particular person, the record or signature may be attrib-

14. UETA 5(b).
15. UETA 5, Comment 4B.
16. See, for example, *EPCO Carbondioxide Products, Inc. v. Bank One, N.A.*, ___ F.Supp.2d ___ (W.D.La. 2007).

EXHIBIT 19–2 • The E-SIGN Act and the UETA

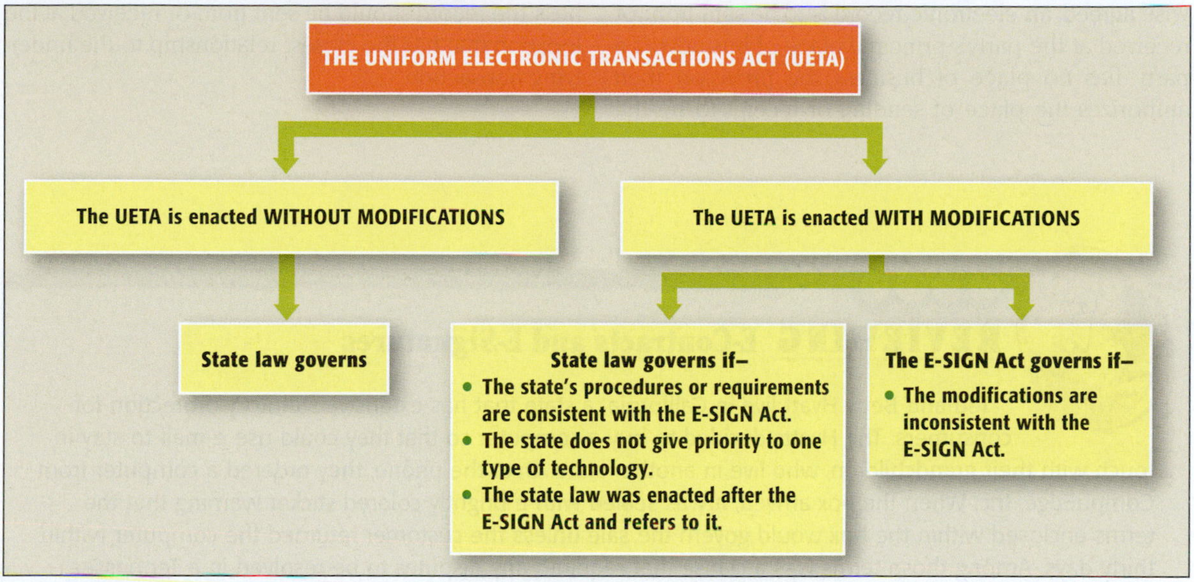

uted to that person. If a person types her or his name at the bottom of an e-mail purchase order, that name will qualify as a "signature" and be attributed to the person whose name appears. Just as in paper contracts, one may use any relevant evidence to prove that the record or signature is or is not the act of the person.[17]

Note that even if an individual's name does not appear on a record (a voice-mail message, for example), the UETA states that the effect of the record is to be determined from the context and surrounding circumstances. In other words, a record may have legal effect even if no one has signed it. For instance, a fax that contains a letterhead identifying the sender may, depending on the circumstances, be attributed to that sender.

Notarization If existing state law requires a document to be notarized, the UETA provides that this requirement is satisfied by the electronic signature of a notary public or other person authorized to verify signatures. For example, if a person intends to accept an offer to purchase real estate via e-mail, the requirement is satisfied if a notary public is present to verify the person's identity and affix an electronic signature to the e-mail acceptance.

The Effect of Errors Section 10 of the UETA encourages, but does not require, the use of security procedures (such as encryption) to verify changes to electronic documents and to correct errors. If the parties have agreed to a security procedure and one party fails to detect an error because of not following the procedure, the other party can legally avoid the effect of the change or error. If the parties have not agreed to use a security procedure, then other state laws (including contract law governing mistakes—see Chapter 14) will determine the effect of the error on the parties' agreement.

To avoid the effect of errors, a party must promptly notify the other party of the error and of her or his intent not to be bound by the error. In addition, the party must take reasonable steps to return any benefit or consideration received. Parties cannot avoid a transaction from which they have benefited.

Timing Section 15 of the UETA sets forth provisions relating to the sending and receiving of electronic records. These provisions apply unless the parties agree to different terms. Under Section 15, an electronic record is considered *sent* when it is properly directed to the intended recipient in a form readable by the recipient's computer system. Once the electronic record leaves the control of the sender or comes under the control of the recipient, the UETA deems it to have been sent. An electronic record is considered *received* when it enters the recipient's processing system in a readable form—*even if no individual is aware of its receipt.*

17. UETA 9.

Additionally, the UETA provides that, unless otherwise agreed, an electronic record is to be sent from or received at the party's principal place of business. If a party has no place of business, the provision then authorizes the place of sending or receipt to be the party's residence. If a party has multiple places of business, the record should be sent from or received at the location that has the closest relationship to the underlying transaction.

REVIEWING E-Contracts and E-Signatures

Ted and Betty Hyatt live in California, a state that has extensive statutory protection for consumers. The Hyatts decided to buy a computer so that they could use e-mail to stay in touch with their grandchildren, who live in another state. Over the phone, they ordered a computer from CompuEdge, Inc. When the box arrived, it was sealed with a brightly colored sticker warning that the terms enclosed within the box would govern the sale unless the customer returned the computer within thirty days. Among those terms was a clause that required any disputes to be resolved in a Tennessee state court. The Hyatts then signed up for Internet service through CyberTool, an Internet service provider. They downloaded CyberTool's software and clicked on the "quick install" box that allowed them to bypass CyberTool's "Terms of Service" page. It was possible to read this page by scrolling to the next screen, but the Hyatts did not realize this. The terms included a clause that stated that all disputes were to be submitted to a Virginia state court. As soon as the Hyatts attempted to e-mail their grandchildren, they experienced problems using CyberTool's e-mail service, which continually stated that the network was busy. They also were unable to receive the photos sent by their grandchildren. Using the information presented in the chapter, answer the following questions.

1. Did the Hyatts accept the list of contract terms included in the computer box? Why or why not? What is the name used for this type of e-contract?
2. What type of agreement did the Hyatts form with CyberTool?
3. Suppose that the Hyatts experienced trouble with the computer's components after they had used the computer for two months. What factors will a court consider in deciding whether to enforce the forum-selection clause? Would a court be likely to enforce the clause in this contract? Why or why not?
4. Are the Hyatts bound by the contract terms specified on CyberTool's "Terms of Service" page that they did not read? Which of the required elements for contract formation might the Hyatts' claim lack? How might a court rule on this issue?

TERMS AND CONCEPTS

browse-wrap terms 344
click-on agreement 341
cybernotary 345
e-contract 339
e-signature 344
forum-selection clause 341
partnering agreement 346
record 347
shrink-wrap agreement 343

QUESTIONS AND CASE PROBLEMS

19–1. Paul is a financial analyst for King Investments, Inc., a brokerage firm. He uses the Internet to investigate the background and activities of companies that might be good investments for King's customers. While visiting the Web site of Business Research, Inc., Paul sees on his screen a message that reads, "Welcome to businessresearch.com. By visiting our site, you have been entered as a subscriber to our e-publication, *Companies Unlimited.* This publication will be sent to you daily at a cost of $7.50 per week. An invoice will be included with *Companies Unlimited* every four weeks. You may cancel your subscription at any time." Has Paul entered into an enforceable contract to pay for *Companies Unlimited?* Why or why not?

19–2. QUESTION WITH SAMPLE ANSWER

Anne is a reporter for *Daily Business Journal,* a print publication consulted by investors and other businesspersons. She often uses the Internet to conduct research for the articles that she writes for the publication. While visiting the Web site of Cyberspace Investments Corp., Anne reads a pop-up window that states, "Our business newsletter, *E-Commerce Weekly,* is available at a one-year subscription rate of $5 per issue. To subscribe, enter your e-mail address below and click 'SUBSCRIBE.' By subscribing, you agree to the terms of the subscriber's agreement. To read this agreement, click 'AGREEMENT.' " Anne enters her e-mail address, but does not click on "AGREEMENT" to read the terms. Has Anne entered into an enforceable contract to pay for *E-Commerce Weekly?* Explain.

- **For a sample answer to Question 19–2, go to Appendix I at the end of this text.**

19–3. Bob, a sales representative for Central Computer Co., occasionally uses the Internet to obtain information about his customers and to look for new sales leads. While visiting the Web site of Marketing World, Inc., Bob is presented with an on-screen message that offers, "To improve your ability to make deals, read our monthly online magazine, *Sales Genius,* available at a subscription rate of $15 a month. To subscribe, fill in your name, company name, and e-mail address below, and click 'YES!' By clicking 'YES!' you agree to the terms of the subscription contract. To read this contract, click 'TERMS.' " Among those terms is a clause that allows Marketing World to charge interest for subscription bills not paid within a certain time. The terms also prohibit subscribers from copying or distributing part or all of *Sales Genius* in any form. Bob subscribes without reading the terms. Marketing World later files a suit against Bob based on his failure to pay for his subscription. Should the court hold that Bob is obligated to pay interest on the amount? Explain.

19–4. Browse-Wrap Terms. Ticketmaster Corp. operates a Web site that allows customers to buy tickets to concerts, ball games, and other events. On the site's home page are instructions and an index to internal pages (one page per event). Each event page provides basic information (a short description of the event, with the date, time, place, and price) and a description of how to order tickets over the Internet, by telephone, by mail, or in person. The home page contains—if a customer scrolls to the bottom—"terms and conditions" that proscribe, among other things, linking to Ticketmaster's internal pages. A customer need not view these terms to go to an event page. Tickets.Com, Inc., operates a Web site that also publicizes special events. Tickets.Com's site includes links to Ticketmaster's internal events pages. These links bypass Ticketmaster's home page. Ticketmaster filed a suit in a federal district court against Tickets.Com, alleging, in part, breach of contract on the ground that Tickets.Com's linking violated Ticketmaster's terms and conditions. Tickets.Com filed a motion to dismiss. Was Tickets.Com bound by the terms and conditions posted on Ticketmaster's home page? Why or why not? How should the court rule on the motion? [*Ticketmaster Corp. v. Tickets.Com, Inc.,* __ F.Supp.2d __ (C.D.Cal. 2000)]

19–5. Shrink-Wrap Agreements. 1-A Equipment Co. signed a sales order to lease Accware 10 User NT software, which is made and marketed by ICode, Inc. Just above the signature line, the order stated: "Thank you for your order. No returns or refunds will be issued for software license and/or services. All sales are final. Please read the End User License and Service Agreement." The software was delivered in a sealed envelope inside a box. On the outside of the envelope, an "End User Agreement" provided, in part, "BY OPENING THIS PACKAGING, CLICKING YOUR ACCEPTANCE OF THE AGREEMENT DURING DOWNLOAD OR INSTALLATION OF THIS PRODUCT, OR BY USING ANY PART OF THIS PRODUCT, YOU AGREE TO BE LEGALLY BOUND BY THE TERMS OF THE AGREEMENT. . . . This agreement will be governed by the laws in force in the Commonwealth of Virginia . . . and exclusive venue for any litigation shall be in Virginia." Later, dissatisfied with the software, 1-A filed a suit in a Massachusetts state court against ICode, alleging breach of contract and misrepresentation. ICode asked the court to dismiss the case on the basis of the "End User Agreement." Is the agreement enforceable? Should the court dismiss the suit? Why or why not? [*1-A Equipment Co. v. ICode, Inc.,* __ N.E.2d __ (Mass.Dist. 2000)]

19–6. Click-On Agreements. America Online, Inc. (AOL), provided e-mail service to Walter Hughes and other members under a click-on agreement titled "Terms of Service." This agreement consisted of three parts: a "Member Agreement," "Community Guidelines," and a "Privacy Policy." The Member Agreement included a forum-selection clause that read, "You expressly agree that exclusive jurisdiction for any claim or dispute with AOL or relating in any way to your membership or your use of AOL resides in the courts of Virginia." When Officer Thomas McMenamon of the Methuen, Massachusetts, Police Department received threatening e-mail sent from an AOL account, he requested and obtained from AOL Hughes's name and other personal information. Hughes filed a suit in a federal district court against AOL, which filed a motion to dismiss on the basis of the forum-selection clause. Considering that the clause was a click-on provision, is it enforceable? Explain. [*Hughes v. McMenamon*, 204 F.Supp.2d 178 (D.Mass. 2002)]

19–7. CASE PROBLEM WITH SAMPLE ANSWER

Stewart Lamle invented "Farook," a board game similar to "Tic Tac Toe." In May 1996, Lamle began negotiating with Mattel, Inc., to license Farook for distribution outside the United States. On June 11, 1997, the parties met and agreed on many terms, including a three-year duration, the geographic scope of the agreement, a schedule for payment, and a royalty percentage. On June 26, Mike Bucher, a Mattel employee, sent Lamle an e-mail titled "Farook Deal" that repeated these terms and added that they "ha[ve] been agreed [to] . . . by . . . Mattel subject to contract. . . . Best regards Mike Bucher." Lamle faxed Mattel a more formal draft of the terms, but Mattel did not sign it. Mattel displayed Farook at its Pre-Toy Fair in August. After the fair, Mattel sent Lamle a fax saying that it no longer wished to license his game. Lamle filed a suit in a federal district court against Mattel, asserting, in part, breach of contract. One of the issues was whether the parties had entered into a contract. Could Bucher's name on the June 26 e-mail be considered a valid signature under the Uniform Electronic Transactions Act (UETA)? Could it be considered a valid signature outside the UETA? Why or why not? [*Lamle v. Mattel, Inc.*, 394 F.3d 1355 (Fed.Cir. 2005)]

- **To view a sample answer for Problem 19–7, go to this book's Web site at www.cengage.com/blaw/jentz, select "Chapter 19," and click on "Case Problem with Sample Answer."**

19–8. Shrink-Wrap Agreements and Browse-Wrap Terms. Mary DeFontes bought a computer and a service contract from Dell Computers Corp. DeFontes was charged $950.51, of which $13.51 was identified on the invoice as "tax." This amount was paid to the state of Rhode Island. DeFontes and other Dell customers filed a suit in a Rhode Island state court against Dell, claiming that Dell was overcharging its customers by collecting a tax on service contracts and transportation costs. Dell asked the court to order DeFontes to submit the dispute to arbitration. Dell cited its "Terms and Conditions Agreement," which provides, in part, that by accepting delivery of Dell's products or services, a customer agrees to submit any dispute to arbitration. Customers can view this agreement through an *inconspicuous* link at the bottom of Dell's Web site, and Dell encloses a copy with each order when it is shipped. Dell argued that DeFontes accepted these terms by failing to return her purchase within thirty days, although the agreement did not state this. Is DeFontes bound to the "Terms and Conditions Agreement"? Should the court grant Dell's request? Why or why not? [*DeFontes v. Dell Computers Corp.*, __ A.2d __ (R.I. 2004)]

19–9. Online Acceptances. Internet Archive (IA) is devoted to preserving a record of resources on the Internet for future generations. IA uses the "Wayback Machine" to automatically browse Web sites and reproduce their contents in an archive. IA does not ask the owners' permission before copying their material but will remove it on request. Suzanne Shell, a resident of Colorado, owns **www.profane-justice.org**, which is dedicated to providing information to individuals accused of child abuse or neglect. The site warns, "IF YOU COPY OR DISTRIBUTE ANYTHING ON THIS SITE YOU ARE ENTERING INTO A CONTRACT." The terms, which can be accessed only by clicking on a link, include, among other charges, a fee of $5,000 for each page copied "in advance of printing." Neither the warning nor the terms require a user to indicate assent. When Shell discovered that the Wayback Machine had copied the contents of her site—approximately eighty-seven times between May 1999 and October 2004—she asked IA to remove the copies from its archive and pay her $100,000. IA removed the copies and filed a suit in a federal district court against Shell, who responded, in part, with a counterclaim for breach of contract. IA filed a motion to dismiss this claim. Did IA contract with Shell? Explain. [*Internet Archive v. Shell*, 505 F.Supp.2d 755 (D.Colo. 2007)]

19–10. A QUESTION OF ETHICS

*In 2000 and 2001, Dewayne Hubbert, Elden Craft, Chris Grout, and Rhonda Byington bought computers from Dell Corp. through its Web site. Before buying, Hubbert and the others configured their own computers. To make a purchase, each buyer completed forms on five Web pages. On each page, Dell's "Terms and Conditions of Sale" were accessible by clicking on a blue hyperlink. A statement on three of the pages read, "All sales are subject to Dell's Term[s] and Conditions of Sale," but a buyer was not required to click an assent to the terms to complete a purchase. The terms were also printed on the backs of the invoices and on separate documents contained in the shipping boxes with the computers. Among those terms was a "Binding Arbitration" clause. The computers contained Pentium 4 microprocessors, which Dell advertised as the fastest, most powerful Intel Pentium processor available. In 2002, Hubbert and the others filed a suit in an Illinois state court against Dell, alleging that this marketing was false, misleading, and deceptive. The plaintiffs claimed that the Pentium 4 microprocessor was slower and less powerful, and provided less performance, than either a Pentium III or an AMD Athlon, and at a greater cost. Dell asked the court to compel arbitration. [*Hubbert v. Dell Corp., *359 Ill.App.3d 976, 835 N.E.2d 113, 296 Ill.Dec. 258 (5 Dist. 2005)]*

(a) Should the court enforce the arbitration clause in this case? If you were the judge, how would you rule on this issue?

(b) In your opinion, do shrink-wrap, click-on, and browse-wrap terms impose too great a burden on purchasers? Why or why not?

(c) An ongoing complaint about shrink-wrap, click-on, and browse-wrap terms is that sellers (often large corporations) draft them and buyers (typically individual consumers) do not read them. Should purchasers be bound in contract by terms that they have not even read? Why or why not?

19–11. VIDEO QUESTION

Go to this text's Web site at **www.cengage.com/blaw/jentz** and select "Chapter 19." Click on "Video Questions" and view the video titled *E-Contracts: Agreeing Online*. Then answer the following questions.

(a) According to the instructor in the video, what is the key factor in determining whether a particular term in an online agreement is enforceable?

(b) Suppose that you click on "I accept" in order to download software from the Internet. You do not read the terms of the agreement before accepting it, even though you know that such agreements often contain forum-selection and arbitration clauses. The software later causes irreparable harm to your computer system, and you want to sue. When you go to the Web site and view the agreement, however, you discover that a choice-of-law clause in the contract specifies that the law of Nigeria controls. Is this term enforceable? Is it a term that should be reasonably expected in an online contract?

(c) Does it matter what the term actually says if it is a type of term that one could reasonably expect to be in the contract? What arguments can be made for and against enforcing a choice-of-law clause in an online contract?

LAW ON THE WEB

For updated links to resources available on the Web, as well as a variety of other materials, visit this text's Web site at

www.cengage.com/blaw/jentz

You can access the UCC, including Article 2, at the Web site of Cornell University Law School. Go to

www.law.cornell.edu/ucc/ucc.table.html

The Web site of the National Conference of Commissioners on Uniform State Laws provides the draft and final versions of the UETA, lists the states that have adopted it, and offers information on why states should adopt it, at

www.nccusl.org

Legal Research Exercises on the Web

Go to **www.cengage.com/blaw/jentz**, the Web site that accompanies this text. Select "Chapter 19" and click on "Internet Exercises." There you will find the following Internet research exercises that you can perform to learn more about the topics covered in this chapter.

Internet Exercise 19–1: Legal Perspective
E-Contract Formation

Internet Exercise 19–2: Management Perspective
E-Signatures

UNIT THREE · FOCUS ON ETHICS

Contract Law and the Application of Ethics

Generally, as you read in Chapter 5, a responsible business manager will evaluate a business transaction on the basis of three criteria—legality, profitability, and ethics. But what does acting ethically mean in the area of contracts? If an individual with whom you enter into a contract fails to look after her or his own interests, is that your fault? Should you be doing something about it? If the contract happens to be to your advantage and to the other party's detriment, do you have a responsibility to correct the situation?

Suppose that your neighbor puts a "For sale" sign on her car, offering to sell it for $6,000. You learn that she is moving to another state and needs the extra cash to help finance the move. You know that she could easily get $10,000 for the car, and you are considering purchasing it and then reselling it at a profit. But you also discover that your neighbor is completely unaware that she has priced the car significantly below its *Blue Book* value. Are you ethically obligated to tell her that she is essentially giving away $4,000 if she sells you the car for only $6,000?

This kind of situation, transplanted into the world of commercial transactions, raises an obvious question: At what point should the sophisticated businessperson cease looking after his or her own economic welfare and become "his brother's keeper," so to speak?

Freedom of Contract and Freedom from Contract

The answer to the question just raised is not simple. On the one hand, a common ethical assumption in our society is that individuals should be held responsible for the consequences of their own actions, including their contractual promises. This principle is expressed in the legal concept of freedom of contract. On the other hand, another common assumption in our society is that individuals should not harm one another by their actions. This is the basis of both tort law and criminal law.

In the area of contract law, ethical behavior often involves balancing these principles. In the above example, if you purchased the car and your neighbor later learned its true value and sued you for the difference, very likely no court of law would find that the contract should be rescinded. At times, however, courts will hold that the principle of freedom *of* contract should give way to the principle of freedom *from* contract, a doctrine based on the assumption that people should not be harmed by the actions of others. We look next at some examples of situations in which parties to contracts may be excused from performance under their contracts to prevent injustice.

Impossibility of Performance The doctrine of impossibility of performance is based to some extent on the ethical question of whether one party should suffer economic loss when it is impossible to perform a contract. The rule that one is "bound by his or her contracts" is not followed when performance becomes impossible. This doctrine, however, is applied only when the parties themselves did not consciously assume the risk of the events that rendered performance impossible. Furthermore, this doctrine rests on the assumption that the party claiming the defense of impossibility has acted ethically.

A contract is discharged, for example, if it calls for the delivery of a particular car and, through no fault of either party, this car is stolen and completely demolished in an accident. Yet the doctrine would not excuse performance if the party agreeing to sell the car caused its destruction by her or his negligence.

Before the late nineteenth century, courts were reluctant to discharge a contract even when performance was literally impossible. Just as society's ethics changes with the passage of time, however, the law also changes to reflect society's new perceptions of ethical behavior.[1] Today, courts are much more willing to discharge a contract when its performance has become literally impossible. Holding a party in breach of contract, when performance has become impossible through no fault of that party, no longer coincides with society's notions of fairness.

Unconscionability The doctrine of unconscionability is a good example of how the law attempts to enforce ethical behavior. Under this doctrine, a contract may be deemed to be so unfair to one party as to be unenforceable—even though that party voluntarily agreed to the contract's terms.

1. A leading English case in which the court held that a defendant was discharged from the duty to perform due to impossibility of performance is *Taylor v. Caldwell,* 122 Eng.Rep. 309 (K.B. [King's Bench] 1863).

Unconscionable action, like unethical action, defies precise definition. Information about the particular facts and specific circumstances surrounding the contract is essential. For example, a court might find that a contract made with a marginally literate consumer was unfair and unenforceable but might uphold the same contract made with a major business firm.

Section 2–302 of the Uniform Commercial Code, which incorporates the common law concept of unconscionability, similarly does not define the concept with any precision. Rather, it leaves it to the courts to determine when a contract is so one sided and unfair to one party as to be unconscionable and thus unenforceable.

Usually, courts will do all that they can to save contracts rather than render them unenforceable. Only in extreme situations, as when a contract or clause is so one sided as to "shock the conscience" of the court, will a court hold a contract or contractual clause unconscionable.

Exculpatory Clauses In some situations, courts have also refused to enforce exculpatory clauses on the ground that they are unconscionable or contrary to public policy. An *exculpatory clause* attempts to excuse a party from liability in the event of monetary or physical injury, no matter who is at fault. In some situations, such clauses are upheld. For example, a health club can require its members to sign a clause releasing the club from any liability for injuries the members might incur while using the club's equipment and facilities. The law permits parties to assume, by express agreement, the risks inherent in certain activities. In such situations, exculpatory clauses make it possible for a firm's owner to stay in business—by shifting some of the liability risks from the business to the customer.

Nonetheless, some jurisdictions take a dubious view of exculpatory clauses, particularly when the agreement is between parties with unequal bargaining power, such as a landlord and a tenant or an employer and an employee. An exculpatory clause that attempts to exempt an employer from *all* liability for negligence toward its employees frequently is held to be against public policy and thus void.[2] The courts reason that disparity in bargaining power and economic necessity force the employee to accept the employer's terms.

2. See, for example, *City of Santa Barbara v. Superior Court,* 62 Cal.Rptr.3d 527, 161 P.3d 1095 (2007); and *Health Net of California, Inc. v. Department of Health Services,* 113 Cal.App.4th 224, 6 Cal.Rptr.3d 235 (2003).

FOCUS on ETHICS

Covenants Not to Compete

In today's complicated, technological business world, knowledge learned on the job, including trade secrets, has become a valuable commodity. To prevent this knowledge from falling into the hands of competitors, more and more employers are requiring their employees to sign covenants not to compete. The increasing number of lawsuits over noncompete clauses in employment contracts has caused many courts to reconsider the reasonableness of these covenants.

Should Courts Reform Unreasonable Noncompete Covenants? In a number of jurisdictions, if a court finds that a restraint in a noncompete covenant is not reasonable in light of the circumstances, it will reform the unreasonable provision and then enforce it. For example, a court might rewrite an unreasonable restriction by reducing the time period during which a former employee cannot compete from three years to one year, and then enforce the reformed agreement.[3]

Other jurisdictions are not so "employer friendly" and refuse to enforce unreasonable covenants. As one observer noted, the farther west you go from the Mississippi River, the harder it is to enforce a covenant not to compete. Under California law, covenants not to compete are illegal, and other western states tend to regard such covenants with suspicion. For example, the Washington Supreme Court has refused to reform noncompete covenants that are unreasonable and lacking in consideration.[4] Courts in Arizona and Texas have reached similar conclusions.[5]

Some commentators argue that when the courts modify and then enforce unreasonable covenants, this only encourages employers to continue to create unreasonable covenants—for two reasons: (1) most noncompete covenants are never challenged in court, and (2) if a covenant is

3. See, for example, *Estee Lauder Companies, Inc. v. Batra,* 430 F.Supp.2d 158 (S.D.N.Y. 2006); *National Café Services, Ltd. v. Podaras,* 148 S.W.3d 194 (Tex.App.—Waco 2004); *Pathfinder Communications Corp. v. Macy,* 795 N.E.2d 1103 (Ind.App. 2003); and *Health Care Enterprises, Inc. v. Levy,* 715 So.2d 341 (Fla.App.4th 1998).

4. See, for example, *Labriola v. Pollard Group, Inc.,* 152 Wash.2d 828, 100 P.3d 791 (2004).

5. *Hardy v. Mann Frankfort Stein & Lipp Advisors, Inc.* ___ S.W.3d ___ (Tex.App.—Houston [1 Dist.] 2007); and *Varsity Gold, Inc. v. Porzio,* 202 Ariz. 355, 45 P.3d 352 (2002).

(Continued)

contested, the worst that can happen is that the court will modify, and then enforce, the covenant.

Do Noncompete Covenants Stifle Innovation? One of the reasons that the courts usually look closely at covenants not to compete and evaluate them on a case-by-case basis is the strong public policy favoring competition in this country. Even so, claim some scholars, covenants not to compete, regardless of their "reasonability," may stifle competition and innovation.

Consider, for example, the argument put forth by Ronald Gilson, a Stanford University professor of law and business. He contends that California's prohibition on covenants not to compete may help to explain why technological innovation and economic growth have skyrocketed in California's Silicon Valley, while technological development along Massachusetts's Route 128 has languished. According to Gilson, "The different legal rules governing postemployment covenants not to compete in California and Massachusetts help explain the difference in employee job mobility and therefore the knowledge transfer that [is] a critical factor in explaining the differential performance of Silicon Valley and Route 128."[6] For this and for other reasons, some scholars contend that covenants not to compete may not survive the cyber age.[7] Certainly, such covenants present new types of challenges for the courts in deciding what restrictions are reasonable in the context of the Internet.[8]

Oral Contracts and Promissory Estoppel

Oral contracts are made every day. Many—if not most—of them are carried out, and no problems arise. Occasionally, however, oral contracts are not performed, and one party decides to sue the other. Sometimes, to prevent injustice, the courts will enforce oral contracts under the theory of promissory estoppel if detrimental reliance can be shown. The court may even use this theory to remove a contract from the Statute of Frauds—that is, render the oral contract enforceable.

In addition, ethical standards certainly underlie the doctrine of *promissory estoppel,* under which a person who has reasonably relied on the promise of another to his or her detriment can often obtain some measure of recovery. Essentially, promissory estoppel allows a variety of promises to be enforced even though they lack what is formally regarded as consideration.

An oral promise made by an insurance agent to a business owner, for example, may be binding if the owner relies on that promise to her or his detriment. Employees who rely to their detriment on an employer's promise may be able to recover under the doctrine of promissory estoppel. A contractor who, when bidding for a job, relies on a subcontractor's promise to perform certain construction work at a certain price may be able to recover, on the basis of promissory estoppel, any damages sustained because of the subcontractor's failure to perform. These are but a few of the many examples in which the courts, in the interests of fairness and justice, have estopped a promisor from denying that a contract existed.

Oral Contracts and the Statute of Frauds

As you learned in Chapter 15, the Statute of Frauds was originally enacted in England in 1677. The act was intended to prevent harm to innocent parties by requiring written evidence of agreements concerning important transactions.

Until the Statute of Frauds was passed, the English courts had enforced oral contracts on the strength of oral testimony by witnesses. Under these conditions, it was not too difficult to evade justice by procuring "convincing" witnesses to support the claim that a contract had been created and then breached. The possibility of fraud in such actions was enhanced by the fact that seventeenth-century English courts did not allow oral testimony to be given by the parties to a lawsuit—or by any parties with an interest in the litigation, such as husbands or wives. Defense against actions for breach of contract was thus limited to written evidence or the testimony of third parties.

Detrimental Reliance Under the Statute of Frauds, if a contract is oral when it is required to be in writing, it will not, as a rule, be enforced by the courts. An exception to this rule is made if a party has reasonably relied, to his or her detriment, on the oral contract. Enforcing an oral contract on the basis of a party's reliance arguably undercuts the

6. Ronald J. Gilson, "The Legal Infrastructure of High Technology Industrial Districts: Silicon Valley, Route 128, and Covenants Not to Compete," 575 *New York University Law Review* 579 (June 1999).

7. See, for example, Robert C. Welsh, Larry C. Drapkin, and Samantha C. Grant, "Are Noncompete Clauses Kaput?" *The National Law Journal,* August 14, 2000, pp. B13–B14.

8. For an example of a dispute in the Internet context, see *EarthWeb v. Schlack,* 71 F.Supp.2d 299 (S.D.N.Y. 1999).

essence of the Statute of Frauds. The reason that such an exception is made is to prevent the statute—which was created to prevent injustice—from being used to promote injustice. Nevertheless, this use of the doctrine is controversial—as is the Statute of Frauds itself.

Criticisms of the Statute of Frauds Since its inception more than three hundred years ago, the statute has been criticized by some because, although it was created to protect the innocent, it can also be used as a technical defense by a party breaching a genuine, mutually agreed-on oral contract—if the contract falls within the Statute of Frauds. For this reason, some legal scholars believe the act has caused more injustice than it has prevented. Thus, exceptions are sometimes made—such as under the doctrine of promissory estoppel—to prevent unfairness and inequity. Generally, the courts are slow to apply the statute if doing so will result in obvious injustice. In some instances, this has required a good deal of inventiveness on the part of the courts.

FOCUS on ETHICS

DISCUSSION QUESTIONS

1. Suppose that you contract to purchase steel at a fixed price per ton. Before the contract is performed, a lengthy steelworkers' strike causes the price of steel to triple from the price specified in the contract. If you demand that the supplier fulfill the contract, the supplier will go out of business. What are your ethical obligations in this situation? What are your legal rights?
2. Many countries have no Statute of Frauds, and even England, the country that created the original act, has repealed it. Should the United States do likewise? What are some of the costs and benefits to society of the Statute of Frauds?
3. In determining whether an exculpatory clause should be enforced, why does it matter whether the contract containing the clause involves essential services (such as transportation) or nonessential services (such as skiing or other leisure-time activities)?
4. Employers often include covenants not to compete in employment contracts to protect their trade secrets. What effect, if any, will the growth in e-commerce have on the reasonability of covenants not to compete?

UNIT FOUR

Domestic and International Sales and Lease Contracts

CONTENTS

CHAPTER 20

The Formation of Sales and Lease Contracts

When we turn to contracts for the sale and lease of goods, we move away from common law principles and into the area of statutory law. State statutory law governing sales and lease transactions is based on the Uniform Commercial Code (UCC), which, as mentioned in Chapter 1, has been adopted as law by all of the states.[1]

The UCC is widely viewed as one of the most important legal developments in the United States. We open this chapter with a discussion of the UCC's historical significance as a legal landmark. We then look at the scope of the UCC's Article 2 (on sales) and Article 2A (on leases) as a background to the topic of this chapter, which is the formation of contracts for the sale and lease of goods. The goal of the UCC is to simplify and streamline commercial transactions, allowing parties to form contracts without observing the same degree of formality used in forming other types of contracts.

Today, businesses often engage in sales and lease transactions on a global scale. Because international sales transactions are increasingly commonplace, we conclude the chapter with an examination of the United Nations Convention on Contracts for the International Sale of Goods (CISG), which governs international sales contracts. The CISG is a model uniform law that applies only when a nation has adopted it, just as the UCC applies only to the extent it has been adopted by a state.

1. Louisiana has not adopted Articles 2 and 2A, however.

SECTION 1 The Uniform Commercial Code

In the early years of this nation, sales law varied from state to state, and this lack of uniformity complicated the formation of multistate sales contracts. The problems became especially troublesome in the late nineteenth century as multistate contracts became the norm. For this reason, numerous attempts were made to produce a uniform body of laws relating to commercial transactions. The National Conference of Commissioners on Uniform State Laws (NCCUSL) drafted two uniform ("model") acts that were widely adopted by the states: the Uniform Negotiable Instruments Law (1896) and the Uniform Sales Act (1906). Several other proposed uniform acts followed, although most were not as widely adopted.

In the 1940s, the NCCUSL recognized the need to integrate the half dozen or so uniform acts covering commercial transactions into a single, comprehensive body of statutory law. The NCCUSL developed the Uniform Commercial Code (UCC) to serve that purpose. First issued in 1949, the UCC facilitates commercial transactions by making the laws governing sales and lease contracts clearer, simpler, and more readily applicable to the numerous difficulties that can arise during such transactions.

Comprehensive Coverage of the UCC

The UCC is the single most comprehensive codification of the broad spectrum of laws involved in a total commercial transaction. The UCC views the entire "commercial transaction for the sale of and payment for goods" as a single legal occurrence having numerous facets.

You can gain an idea of the UCC's comprehensiveness by looking at the titles of the articles of the UCC in Appendix C. As you will note, Article 1, titled "General Provisions," sets forth definitions and general principles applicable to commercial transactions, including an obligation to perform in "good faith" all contracts falling under the UCC [UCC 1–304]. Article 1 thus provides the basic groundwork for the remaining articles, each of which focuses on a particular aspect of commercial transactions.

A Single, Integrated Framework for Commercial Transactions

The UCC attempts to provide a consistent and integrated framework of rules to deal with all the phases *ordinarily arising* in a commercial sales transaction from start to finish. A simple example will illustrate how several articles of the UCC can apply to a single commercial transaction. Suppose that a consumer—a person who purchases goods primarily for personal or household use—buys a stainless steel, bottom-freezer refrigerator from an appliance store. The consumer agrees to pay for the refrigerator on an installment plan.

Because the transaction involves a contract for the sale of goods, Article 2 will apply. If the consumer gives a check as the down payment on the purchase price, it will be negotiated and ultimately passed through one or more banks for collection. This process is the subject matter of Article 3, Negotiable Instruments, and Article 4, Bank Deposits and Collections. If the appliance store extends credit to the consumer through an installment plan, it may retain a *lien* (a legal right or interest) on the refrigerator (the collateral, which is the property pledged as security against a debt). If so, then Article 9, Secured Transactions, will be applicable (*secured transactions* will be discussed in detail in Chapter 29).

Suppose, in addition, that the appliance company must obtain the refrigerator from the manufacturer's warehouse before shipping it by common carrier to the consumer. The storage and shipment of goods are the subject matter of Article 7, Documents of Title. To pay the manufacturer, which is located in another state, for the refrigerator supplied, the appliance company may use a letter of credit—the subject matter of Article 5.

Periodic Revisions of the UCC

Various articles and sections of the UCC are periodically revised or supplemented to clarify certain rules or to establish new rules when changes in business customs have rendered the existing UCC provisions inapplicable. For example, because of the increasing importance of leases of goods in the commercial context, Article 2A, governing leases, was added to the UCC. To clarify the rights of parties to commercial fund transfers, particularly electronic fund transfers, Article 4A was issued.

Articles 3 and 4, covering negotiable instruments and banking, underwent a significant revision in the 1990s, as did Articles 5, 8, and 9. Because of other changes in business practices and in the law, the NCCUSL has recommended the repeal of Article 6 (on bulk transfers) and has offered a revised Article 6 to those states that prefer not to repeal it. Article 1 was revised in 2001, and the NCCUSL approved amendments to Articles 3 and 4 in 2002. In 2003, the NCCUSL approved amendments to Articles 2 and 2A, and to Article 7, in an attempt to update the UCC to accommodate electronic commerce and electronic documents of title. Although the majority of the states have adopted the 2003 amendments to Article 7, *no* state has enacted the 2003 amendments to Articles 2 and 2A.[2] Nevertheless, you need to be aware of potential changes in the law. Exhibit 20–1 on the next page summarizes the most significant modifications that would occur if a state adopted the amendments to Article 2.

SECTION 2

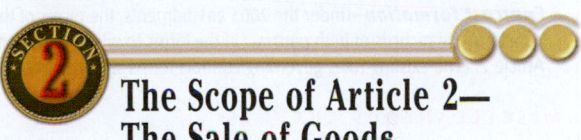

The Scope of Article 2—The Sale of Goods

Article 2 of the UCC (as adopted by state statutes) governs **sales contracts,** or contracts for the sale of goods. To facilitate commercial transactions, Article 2 modifies some of the common law contract requirements that were discussed in the previous chapters. To the extent that it has not been modified by the UCC, however, the common law of contracts also applies to sales contracts. For example, the common law requirements for a valid contract—agreement (offer and acceptance), consideration, capacity, and legality—that were summarized in Chapter 10 and discussed at length in Chapters 11 through 13 are also applicable to sales contracts. Thus, you should reexamine these common law principles when studying the law of sales.

In general, the rule is that whenever a conflict arises between a common law contract rule and the state statutory law based on the UCC, the UCC controls. In other words, when a UCC provision addresses a certain issue, the UCC rule governs; when the UCC is silent, the common law governs. The relationship between general contract law and the law governing sales of goods is illustrated in Exhibit 20–2 on page 363.

2. Because no state has adopted the 2003 amendments to Articles 2 and 2A, we base our discussion of sales and lease contracts in this text on the law *prior* to the 2003 amendments.

EXHIBIT 20–1 • The 2003 Amendments to UCC Article 2: Selected Provisions*

GENERAL CHANGES

- ***Electronic contracting***–The 2003 amendments reflect the rise of electronic contracting (for example, the word *record* is substituted for the word *writing*) and the provisions of the federal law governing e-signatures (see Chapter 19).
- ***New protections for buyers***–There would be some new protections for buyers, and some provisions would be applicable only to buyers who qualify as consumers. For example, specific language would be required to disclaim implied warranties (discussed in Chapter 23).
- ***Remedies***–The amendments in UCC 2–703 and 2–711 give a complete list of the remedies available to buyers and sellers, respectively, on a breach of contract (see Chapter 22).

SOME IMPORTANT SPECIFIC CHANGES

- ***Shipping and delivery terms***–The amendments would completely eliminate UCC 2–319 through 2–324, which deal with shipping and delivery terms (F.O.B., C.I.F., and others listed in Chapter 21 in Exhibit 21–1 on page 392). Additionally, risk of loss relating to goods to be delivered without movement (discussed in Chapter 22) would now pass on the buyer's receipt of the goods regardless of the seller's status as a merchant or nonmerchant.
- ***New sections on express warranties***–With respect to *new goods only,* two new sections would extend to remote purchasers any express warranties made by a seller or lessor in an advertisement or in a record accompanying goods.
- ***Remedial promises***–Added to the sections on express warranties would be a seller's obligation to honor a "remedial promise"–defined as a promise to repair, replace, or refund all or part of the price on the happening of a specified event.
- ***Seller's right to cure***–This right would be extended (except in consumer contracts) to allow sellers, in some circumstances, to cure even after the time for performance has expired (the right to cure is discussed in Chapter 22).
- ***Contract formation***–Under the 2003 amendments, the terms of the contract, subject to the parol evidence rule, are (1) the terms that appear in the records of both parties, (2) the terms to which both parties agree, and (3) the terms supplied or incorporated under UCC Article 2. (The existing rules governing contract terms when an acceptance states additional terms are discussed later in this chapter.)

MISCELLANEOUS CHANGES

- ***Statute of Frauds***–The Statute of Frauds threshold amount would increase from $500 to $5,000, and the one-year rule would be repealed for contracts for the sale of goods [UCC 2–201].
- ***Assignment and delegation***–Rules governing assignment and delegation [UCC 2–210] would be modified to conform to the revised Article 9, which deals with secured transactions (discussed in Chapter 29).
- ***Buyer's acceptance of nonconforming goods***–When a buyer has accepted nonconforming goods [UCC 2–607(3)], the failure of the buyer to notify the seller of the breach would no longer operate as a bar to further recovery. Failure to give timely notice would prevent a remedy "only to the extent that the seller is prejudiced by the failure" (discussed in Chapters 22 and 23).
- ***Consequential damages***–A seller would be able to recover consequential damages resulting from a buyer's breach under UCC 2–710. Under existing law, the seller is limited to incidental damages (see Chapter 22).
- ***Statute of limitations***–The statute of limitations [UCC 2–725] would be modified to, among other things, clarify when a breach or cause of action accrues and to provide added protection for consumers (the statute of limitations is discussed in Chapter 23).

*This exhibit lists only selected changes made by the 2003 amendments. As of this writing, the amendments have not been adopted by any state.

In regard to Article 2, you should keep two points in mind. First, Article 2 deals with the sale of *goods;* it does not deal with real property (real estate), services, or intangible property such as stocks and bonds. Thus, if the subject matter of a dispute is goods, the UCC governs. If it is real estate or services, the common law applies. Second, in some situations, the rules may vary quite a bit, depending on whether the buyer or the seller is a *merchant.* We look now at how the UCC defines a *sale, goods,* and *merchant status.*

What Is a Sale?

The UCC defines a **sale** as "the passing of title [evidence of ownership rights] from the seller to the buyer for a price" [UCC 2–106(1)]. The price may be payable in cash (or its equivalent) or in other goods or services.

What Are Goods?

To be characterized as a *good,* an item of property must be *tangible,* and it must be *movable.* **Tangible property** has physical existence—it can be touched or seen. Intangible property—such as corporate stocks and bonds, patents and copyrights, and ordinary contract rights—has only conceptual existence and thus does not come under Article 2. A *movable* item can be carried from place to place. Hence, real estate is excluded from Article 2.

Two areas in particular give rise to disputes over whether the object of a contract is goods and thus

EXHIBIT 20–2 • The Law Governing Contracts

This exhibit graphically illustrates the relationship between general contract law and statutory law (UCC Articles 2 and 2A) governing contracts for the sale and lease of goods. Sales contracts are not governed exclusively by Article 2 of the UCC but are also governed by general contract law whenever it is relevant and has not been modified by the UCC.

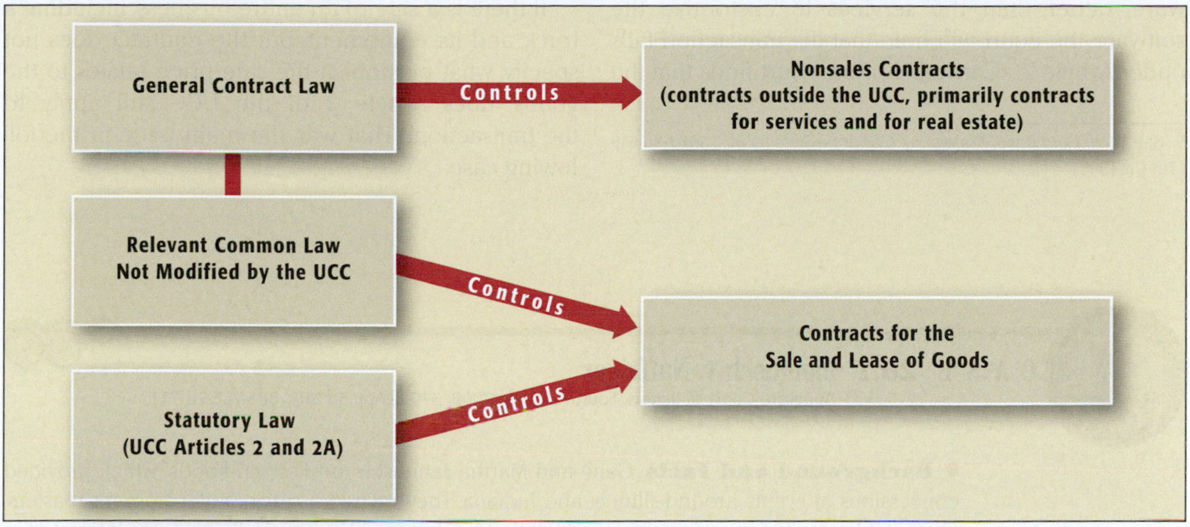

whether Article 2 is applicable. One problem concerns *goods associated with real estate,* such as crops or timber, and the other concerns contracts involving a combination of *goods and services.*

Goods Associated with Real Estate Goods associated with real estate often fall within the scope of Article 2. Section 2–107 provides the following rules:

1. A contract for the sale of minerals or the like (including oil and gas) or a structure (such as a building) is a contract for the sale of goods if *severance, or separation, is to be made by the seller.* If the *buyer* is to sever (separate) the minerals or structures from the land, the contract is considered to be a sale of real estate governed by the principles of real property law, not the UCC.
2. A sale of growing crops (such as potatoes, carrots, wheat, and the like) or timber to be cut is a contract for the sale of goods *regardless of who severs them.*
3. Other "things attached" to real property but capable of severance without material harm to the land are considered to be goods *regardless of who severs them.*[3] Examples of "things attached" that are severable without harm to realty are a window air conditioner in a house and tables and stools in a restaurant. Thus, a sale of these items would be considered a sale of goods. The test is whether removal will cause substantial harm to the real property to which the item is attached.

Goods and Services Combined In cases involving contracts in which goods and services are combined, courts have reached different results. For example, is providing blood to a patient during an operation a "sale of goods" or the "performance of a medical service"? Some courts say it is a good; others say it is a service. Because the UCC does not provide the answers to such questions, the courts generally use the **predominant-factor test** to determine whether a contract is primarily for the sale of goods or for the sale of services.[4] This determination is important because if a court decides that a mixed contract is primarily a goods contract, *any* dispute, even a dispute over the service portion, will be decided under the UCC. Likewise, any disagreement over a predominantly services contract will not be decided using the UCC, even if the dispute involves the goods portion of the contract.

For example, an Indiana company contracts to purchase customized software from Dharma Systems. The

3. The UCC avoids the term *fixtures* here because of the numerous definitions of the word. A fixture is anything so firmly or permanently attached to land or to a building as to become a part of it. Once personal property becomes a fixture, real estate law governs. See Chapter 47.

4. UCC 2–314(1) does stipulate that serving food or drinks is a "sale of goods" for purposes of the implied warranty of merchantability, as will be discussed in Chapter 23. The UCC also specifies that selling unborn animals or rare coins qualifies as a "sale of goods."

contract states that half of the purchase price is for Dharma Systems' professional services and the other half is for the goods (the software). If the court determines that the contract is predominantly for the software, rather than the services to customize the software, the court will hold that the transaction falls under Article 2.[5] Conversely, if the court finds that the services are predominant, it will hold that the transaction is not governed by the UCC. If the transaction is not covered by the UCC, then UCC provisions, including those relating to implied warranties, will not apply.

If there is a sale of an entire business, including a truck and its equipment, but the contract does not specify what portion of the sale price relates to the goods, does Article 2 of the UCC still apply to the transaction? That was the main issue in the following case.

5. See *Micro Data Base Systems, Inc. v. Dharma Systems, Inc.*, 148 F.3d 649 (7th Cir. 1998).

CASE 20.1 Jannusch v. Naffziger

Appellate Court of Illinois, Fourth District, 2008. 379 Ill.App.3d 381, 883 N.E.2d 711.

- **Background and Facts** Gene and Martha Jannusch ran Festival Foods, which provided concessions at events around Illinois and Indiana. They owned a truck, trailer, freezers, roasters, chairs, tables, fountain service, signs, and lighting. Lindsey and Louann Naffziger were interested in buying the concessions business. They met with the Jannusches and orally agreed to a price of $150,000. The Naffzigers paid $10,000 down with the balance to come from a bank loan. They took possession of the equipment and began to use it immediately in Festival Foods operations at various events, even though Gene Jannusch kept the titles to the truck and trailer in his name. Gene Jannusch was paid to attend two events with the Naffzigers to provide advice about running the operation. After six events, and at the end of the outdoor season, the Naffzigers returned the truck and all the equipment to its storage location and wanted out of the deal. They said the business did not generate as much income as they expected. The Jannusches sued the Naffzigers for the balance due on the purchase price. The trial court held that the Uniform Commercial Code (UCC) governed the case but that there was not enough evidence to show that the parties had a sufficient meeting of the minds to form a contract. The Jannusches appealed.

- **Decision and Rationale** The Appellate Court of Illinois reversed the trial court's decision. The reviewing court ruled that a contract was formed and breached. The oral agreement for the sale of the business was predominantly one for the sale of goods and therefore was within Article 2 of the UCC. The oral agreement was sufficiently definite to form a sales contract, even though it did not specify the price of each item being sold or distinguish between the value of the equipment and the value of the goodwill of the business. The Naffzigers made a payment, took possession of the business, and operated it as their own. While some terms of the contract were missing, it was definite enough to be enforced. The fact that it was not in writing does not preclude enforcement of a specific promise. The Naffzigers breached the contract and were liable for damages.

- **What If the Facts Were Different?** *Suppose that the contract had stated that the truck and other equipment were worth $50,000 and the goodwill value of the business was worth $100,000. Would that have changed the outcome of this case? Why or why not?*

- **The Ethical Dimension** *Given that the business was not what the Naffzigers expected it to be, and that they returned everything, was it fair for the Jannuschs to demand full payment? Explain your answer.*

Who Is a Merchant?

Article 2 governs the sale of goods in general. It applies to sales transactions between all buyers and sellers. In a limited number of instances, though, the UCC presumes that special business standards ought to be imposed because of merchants' relatively high degree of commercial expertise.[6] Such standards do not apply to the casual or inexperienced seller or buyer ("consumer"). Section 2–104 sets forth three ways in which merchant status can arise:

1. A merchant is a person who *deals in goods of the kind* involved in the sales contract. Thus, a retailer, a wholesaler, or a manufacturer is a merchant of the goods sold in the particular business. A merchant for one type of goods is not necessarily a merchant for another type. For example, a sporting goods retailer is a merchant when selling tennis rackets but not when selling a used computer.
2. A merchant is a person who, by occupation, holds himself or herself out as having knowledge and skill unique to the practices or goods involved in the transaction. This broad definition may include banks or universities as merchants.
3. A person who *employs a merchant as a broker, agent, or other intermediary* has the status of merchant in that transaction. Hence, if a "gentleman farmer" who ordinarily does not run the farm hires a broker to purchase or sell livestock, the farmer is considered a merchant in the transaction.

In summary, a person is a **merchant** when she or he, acting in a mercantile capacity, possesses or uses an expertise specifically related to the goods being sold. This basic distinction is not always clear-cut. For example, state courts appear to be split on whether farmers should be considered merchants.[7] In some states, farmers are considered merchants because they sell products or livestock on a regular basis. In other states, courts have held that the drafters of the UCC did not intend to include farmers as merchants.

6. The provisions that apply only to merchants deal principally with the Statute of Frauds, firm offers, confirmatory memoranda, warranties, and contract modification. These special rules reflect expedient business practices commonly known to merchants in the commercial setting. They will be discussed later in this chapter.

7. See the court's discussion of this issue in *R. F. Cunningham & Co. v. Driscoll,* 7 Misc.3d 234, 790 N.Y.S.2d 368 (2005).

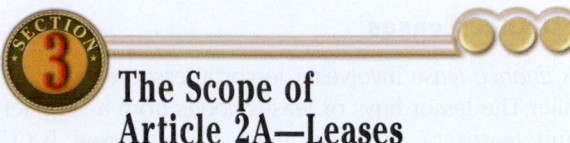

SECTION 3 The Scope of Article 2A—Leases

In the past few decades, leases of personal property (goods) have become increasingly common. Consumers and business firms lease automobiles, industrial equipment, items for use in the home (such as floor polishers), and many other types of goods. Article 2A of the UCC was created to fill the need for uniform guidelines in this area. Article 2A covers any transaction that creates a lease of goods or a sublease of goods [UCC 2A–102, 2A–103(1)(k)]. Article 2A is essentially a repetition of Article 2, except that it applies to leases of goods rather than sales of goods and thus varies to reflect differences between sales and lease transactions. (Note that Article 2A is not concerned with leases of real property, such as land or buildings. The laws governing these types of transactions will be examined in Chapter 48.)

Definition of a Lease Agreement

Article 2A defines a **lease agreement** as a lessor and lessee's bargain with respect to the lease of goods, as found in their language and as implied by other circumstances [UCC 2A–103(1)(k)]. A **lessor** is one who transfers the right to the possession and use of goods under a lease [UCC 2A–103(1)(p)]. A **lessee** is one who acquires the right to the possession and use of goods under a lease [UCC 2A–103(1)(o)]. In other words, the lessee is the party who is leasing the goods from the lessor. Article 2A applies to all types of leases of goods. Special rules apply to certain types of leases, however, including consumer leases and finance leases.

Consumer Leases

A *consumer lease* involves three elements: (1) a lessor who regularly engages in the business of leasing or selling; (2) a lessee (except an organization) who leases the goods "primarily for a personal, family, or household purpose"; and (3) total lease payments that are less than $25,000 [UCC 2A–103(1)(e)]. In the interest of providing special protection for consumers, certain provisions of Article 2A apply only to consumer leases. For example, one provision states that a consumer may recover attorneys' fees if a court determines that a term in a consumer lease contract is unconscionable [UCC 2A–108(4)(a)].

Finance Leases

A *finance lease* involves a lessor, a lessee, and a supplier. The lessor buys or leases goods from a supplier and leases or subleases them to the lessee [UCC 2A–103(1)(g)]. Typically, in a finance lease, the lessor is simply financing the transaction. For example, Marlin Corporation wants to lease a crane for use in its construction business. Marlin's bank agrees to purchase the equipment from Jennco, Inc., and lease the equipment to Marlin. In this situation, the bank is the lessor-financer, Marlin is the lessee, and Jennco is the supplier.

Article 2A, unlike ordinary contract law, makes the lessee's obligations under a finance lease irrevocable and independent from the financer's obligations [UCC 2A–407]. In other words, the lessee must perform and continue to make lease payments even if the leased equipment turns out to be defective. The lessee must look almost entirely to the supplier for any recovery.

For example, American Transit Insurance Company (ATIC) arranged to lease telephone equipment through a finance lease. Siemens Credit Corporation obtained the equipment from the manufacturer and then leased the equipment to ATIC for a five-year term at $2,314 per month. When the equipment turned out to be defective, ATIC stopped making the lease payments. Siemens then sued ATIC for the lease payments due. ATIC alleged, among other things, that requiring it to make payments on defective equipment was unconscionable. According to the court, though, the lease clearly qualified as a finance lease under Article 2A, and thus ATIC was obligated to make all payments due under the lease regardless of the condition or performance of the leased equipment. The court stated that ATIC's claims could be brought only against the manufacturer, not against the lessor (Siemens).[8]

SECTION 4

The Formation of Sales and Lease Contracts

In regard to the formation of sales and lease contracts, the UCC modifies the common law in several ways. We look here at how Articles 2 and 2A of the UCC modify common law contract rules. Remember, though, that parties to sales contracts are free to establish whatever terms they wish. The UCC comes into play when the parties fail to provide in their contract for a contingency that later gives rise to a dispute. The UCC makes this very clear time and again by its use of such phrases as "unless the parties otherwise agree" and "absent a contrary agreement by the parties."

Offer

In general contract law, the moment a definite offer is met by an unqualified acceptance, a binding contract is formed. In commercial sales transactions, the verbal exchanges, correspondence, and actions of the parties may not reveal exactly when a binding contractual obligation arises. The UCC states that an agreement sufficient to constitute a contract can exist even if the moment of its making is undetermined [UCC 2–204(2), 2A–204(2)].

Open Terms According to general contract law, an offer must be definite enough for the parties (and the courts) to ascertain its essential terms when it is accepted. In contrast, the UCC states that a sales or lease contract will not fail for indefiniteness even if one or more terms are left open as long as (1) the parties intended to make a contract and (2) there is a reasonably certain basis for the court to grant an appropriate remedy [UCC 2–204(3), 2A–204(3)].

Suppose that Mike agrees to lease from CompuQuik a highly specialized computer work station. Mike and one of CompuQuik's sales representatives sign a lease agreement that leaves some of the details blank, to be "worked out" the following week, when the leasing manager will be back from her vacation. In the meantime, CompuQuik obtains the necessary equipment from one of its suppliers and spends several days modifying the equipment to suit Mike's needs. When the leasing manager returns, she calls Mike and tells him that his work station is ready. Mike says he is no longer interested in the work station, as he has arranged to lease the same equipment for a lower price from another firm. CompuQuik sues Mike to recover its costs in obtaining and modifying the equipment, and one of the issues before the court is whether the parties had an enforceable contract. The court will likely hold that they did, based on their intent and conduct, despite the blanks in their written agreement.

Relative to the common law of contracts, the UCC has radically lessened the requirement of definiteness of terms. Keep in mind, though, that if too many terms

8. *Siemens Credit Corp. v. American Transit Insurance Co.*, 2001 WL 40775 (S.D.N.Y. 2001).

are left open, a court may find that the parties did not intend to form a contract.

Open Price Term. If the parties have not agreed on a price, the court will determine a "reasonable price at the time for delivery" [UCC 2–305(1)]. If either the buyer or the seller is to determine the price, the price is to be fixed in good faith [UCC 2–305(2)]. Under the UCC, *good faith* means honesty in fact and the observance of reasonable commercial standards of fair dealing in the trade [UCC 2–103(1)(b)]. The concepts of *good faith* and *commercial reasonableness* permeate the UCC. (The obligations of good faith and commercial reasonableness in sales and lease contracts will be discussed in detail in Chapter 22.)

Sometimes, the price fails to be fixed through the fault of one of the parties. In that situation, the other party can treat the contract as canceled or fix a reasonable price. For example, Perez and Merrick enter into a contract for the sale of goods and agree that Perez will fix the price. Perez refuses to specify the price. Merrick can either treat the contract as canceled or set a reasonable price [UCC 2–305(3)].

Open Payment Term. When the parties do not specify payment terms, payment is due at the time and place at which the buyer is to receive the goods [UCC 2–310(a)]. The buyer can tender payment using any commercially normal or acceptable means, such as a check or credit card. If the seller demands payment in cash, however, the buyer must be given a reasonable time to obtain it [UCC 2–511(2)]. This is especially important when the contract states a definite and final time for performance.

Open Delivery Term. When no delivery terms are specified, the buyer normally takes delivery at the seller's place of business [UCC 2–308(a)]. If the seller has no place of business, the seller's residence is used. When goods are located in some other place and both parties know it, delivery is made there. If the time for shipment or delivery is not clearly specified in the sales contract, then the court will infer a "reasonable" time for performance [UCC 2–309(1)].

Duration of an Ongoing Contract. A single contract might specify successive performances but not indicate how long the parties are required to deal with each other. In this situation, either party may terminate the ongoing contractual relationship. Nevertheless, principles of good faith and sound commercial practice call for reasonable notification before termination so as to give the other party sufficient time to seek a substitute arrangement [UCC 2–309(2), (3)].

Options and Cooperation with Regard to Performance. When specific shipping arrangements have not been made but the contract contemplates shipment of the goods, the *seller* has the right to make these arrangements in good faith, using commercial reasonableness in the situation [UCC 2–311].

When terms relating to an assortment of goods are omitted from a sales contract, the buyer can specify the assortment. For example, Harley and Babcock contract for the sale of one thousand pens. The pens come in a variety of colors, but the contract is silent as to which colors are ordered. Babcock, the buyer, has the right to take whatever colors he wishes. Babcock, however, must exercise good faith and commercial reasonableness in making the selection [UCC 2–311].

Open Quantity Term. Normally, if the parties do not specify a quantity, a court will have no basis for determining a remedy. This is because there is almost no way to determine objectively what is a reasonable quantity of goods for someone to purchase (whereas a court can objectively determine a reasonable price for particular goods by looking at the market). The UCC recognizes two exceptions in requirements and output contracts [UCC 2–306(1)].

In a **requirements contract,** the buyer agrees to purchase and the seller agrees to sell all or up to a stated amount of what the buyer *needs* or *requires.* There is implicit consideration in a requirements contract because the buyer gives up the right to buy from any other seller, and this forfeited right creates a legal detriment. Requirements contracts are common in the business world and are normally enforceable. If, however, the buyer promises to purchase only if he or she *wishes* to do so, or if the buyer reserves the right to buy the goods from someone other than the seller, the promise is illusory (without consideration) and unenforceable by either party.[9]

In an **output contract,** the seller agrees to sell and the buyer agrees to buy all or up to a stated amount of what the seller *produces.* Again, because the seller essentially forfeits the right to sell goods to another buyer, there is implicit consideration in an output contract.

9. See, for example, *In re Anchor Glass Container Corp.*, 345 Bankr. 765 (M.D.Fla. 2006).

The UCC imposes a *good faith limitation* on requirements and output contracts. The quantity under such contracts is the amount of requirements or the amount of output that occurs during a *normal* production period. The actual quantity purchased or sold cannot be unreasonably disproportionate to normal or comparable prior requirements or output [UCC 2–306].

Businesspersons should be aware that if they leave certain terms of a sales or lease contract open, the UCC allows a court to supply the missing terms. Although this can sometimes be advantageous (to establish that a contract existed, for instance), it can also be a major disadvantage. If a business engaged in selling goods fails to state a price in its contract offer, for example, a court will impose a reasonable price by looking at the market price of similar goods *at the time of delivery.* In other words, instead of receiving its standard price for the goods, the business will receive what a court considers a reasonable price when the goods are delivered.

Allowing the court to supply a price term can thus reduce one of the potential benefits of contracting—profit realized by the sale of goods at the contract price, despite a subsequent decline in the market price of the goods being sold. Therefore, when drafting contracts for the sale or lease of goods, businesspersons should make sure that the contract clearly states any terms that are essential to the bargain, particularly price. It is often better for the business owner or manager to establish the terms of the contracts rather than to leave it up to a court to determine what terms are reasonable after a dispute has arisen.

Merchant's Firm Offer Under regular contract principles, an offer can be revoked at any time before acceptance. The major common law exception is an *option contract* (discussed in Chapter 11), in which the offeree pays consideration for the offeror's irrevocable promise to keep the offer open for a stated period. The UCC creates a second exception, which applies only to firm offers for the sale or lease of goods made by a merchant (regardless of whether or not the offeree is a merchant).

When a Merchant's Firm Offer Arises. A **firm offer** arises when a merchant-offeror gives *assurances in a signed writing* that the offer will remain open. The merchant's firm offer is irrevocable without the necessity of consideration[10] for the stated period or, if no definite period is stated, a reasonable period (neither to exceed three months) [UCC 2–205, 2A–205].

To illustrate: Osaka, a used-car dealer, writes a letter to Bennett on January 1 stating, "I have a used 2007 Suzuki on the lot that I'll sell you for $20,500 any time between now and January 31." By January 18, Osaka has heard nothing from Bennett, so he sells the Suzuki to another person. On January 23, Bennett tenders $20,500 to Osaka and asks for the car. When Osaka tells him the car has already been sold, Bennett claims that Osaka has breached a valid contract. Bennett is right. Osaka is a merchant of used cars and assured Bennett in a signed writing that he would keep his offer open until the end of January. Thus, Bennett's acceptance on January 23 created a contract, which Osaka breached.

The Offer Must Be in Writing and Signed by the Offeror. It is necessary that the offer be both *written* and *signed* by the offeror.[11] When a firm offer is contained in a form contract prepared by the offeree, the offeror must also sign a separate assurance of the firm offer. This requirement ensures that the offeror will be made aware of the offer. For instance, an offeree might respond to an initial offer by sending its own form contract containing a clause stating that the offer will remain open for three months. If the firm offer is buried amid copious language in one of the pages of the offeree's form contract, the offeror may inadvertently sign the contract without realizing that it contains a firm offer. This would defeat the purpose of the rule—which is to give effect to a merchant's deliberate intent to be bound to a firm offer.

Acceptance

Under the UCC, acceptance of an offer to buy, sell, or lease goods generally may be made in any reasonable manner and by any reasonable means. We examine the UCC's provisions governing acceptance in detail in the subsections that follow.

Methods of Acceptance The general common law rule is that an offeror can specify, or authorize, a particular means of acceptance, making that means

10. If the offeree pays consideration, then an option contract (not a merchant's firm offer) is formed.

11. *Signed* includes any symbol executed or adopted by a party with a present intention to authenticate a writing [UCC 1–201(37)]. A complete signature is not required.

the only one effective for contract formation. Under the common law, if the offer is accepted by an improper means of communication, normally it is considered a counteroffer rather than an acceptance. (For a review of the requirements relating to the mode and timeliness of acceptance, see Chapter 11.) Only when the offeror does not specify an authorized means of acceptance will courts applying general contract law consider whether the acceptance was by reasonable means. The UCC, in contrast, gives effect to all acceptances communicated by reasonable means.

Any Reasonable Means. When the offeror does not specify a means of acceptance, the UCC provides that acceptance can be made by any means of communication that is reasonable under the circumstances [UCC 2–206(1), 2A–206(1)]. This is also the basic rule under the common law of contracts (see Chapter 11).

For example, Anodyne Corporation writes a letter to Bethlehem Industries offering to lease $5,000 worth of goods. The offer states that Anodyne will keep the offer open for only ten days from the date of the letter. Before the ten days have lapsed, Bethlehem sends Anodyne an acceptance by fax. The fax is misdirected by someone at Anodyne's offices and does not reach the right person at Anodyne until after the ten-day deadline has passed. Has a valid contract been formed? The answer is probably yes, because acceptance by fax appears to be a commercially reasonable mode of acceptance under the circumstances. Acceptance would be effective on Bethlehem's transmission of the fax, which occurred before the offer lapsed.

Promise to Ship or Prompt Shipment. The UCC permits an offeree to accept an offer to buy goods "either by a prompt promise to ship or by the prompt or current shipment of conforming or nonconforming goods" [UCC 2–206(1)(b)]. Conforming goods are goods that accord with the contract's terms; nonconforming goods do not. The seller's prompt shipment of *nonconforming goods* constitutes both an *acceptance* (a contract) and a *breach* of that contract. This rule does not apply if the seller **seasonably** (within a reasonable amount of time) notifies the buyer that the nonconforming shipment is offered only as an *accommodation,* or as a favor. The notice of accommodation must clearly indicate to the buyer that the shipment does not constitute an acceptance and that therefore no contract has been formed.

Suppose that Barrymore orders one thousand *black* fans from Stroh. Stroh ships one thousand *blue* fans to Barrymore, notifying Barrymore that these are sent as an accommodation because Stroh has only blue fans in stock. The shipment of blue fans is not an acceptance but a counteroffer, and a contract will be formed only if Barrymore accepts the blue fans. If, however, Stroh ships one thousand blue fans instead of black *without* notifying Barrymore that the goods are being shipped as an accommodation, Stroh's shipment acts as both an acceptance of Barrymore's offer and a breach of the resulting contract. Barrymore may sue Stroh for any appropriate damages.

Communication of Acceptance Under the common law, because a unilateral offer invites acceptance by performance, the offeree need not notify the offeror of performance unless the offeror would not otherwise know about it. In other words, beginning the requested performance is an implied acceptance. The UCC is more stringent than the common law in this regard. Under the UCC, if the offeror is not notified within a reasonable time that the offeree has accepted the contract by beginning performance, then the offeror can treat the offer as having lapsed before acceptance [UCC 2–206(2), 2A–206(2)].

Additional Terms Under the common law, if Alderman makes an offer to Beale, and Beale in turn accepts but adds some slight modification, there is no contract. Recall from Chapter 11 that the so-called *mirror image rule* requires that the terms of the acceptance exactly match those of the offer. The UCC dispenses with the mirror image rule. Generally, the UCC takes the position that if the offeree's response indicates a *definite* acceptance of the offer, a contract is formed, *even if the acceptance includes terms additional to or different from those contained in the offer* [UCC 2–207(1)]. What happens to these additional terms? The answer to this question depends, in part, on whether the parties are nonmerchants or merchants.

Rules When One Party or Both Parties Are Nonmerchants. If one (or both) of the parties is a *nonmerchant,* the contract is formed according to the terms of the original offer and not according to the additional terms of the acceptance [UCC 2–207(2)]. For example, Tolsen offers in writing to sell his laptop computer and printer to Valdez for $1,500. Valdez e-mails a reply to Tolsen, stating, "I accept your offer to purchase your laptop and printer for $1,500. I *would* *like* a box of laser printer paper and two extra toner cartridges to be included in the purchase price." Valdez has given Tolsen a definite expression of acceptance (creating a contract), even though the acceptance also *suggests* an added term for the offer. Because Tolsen is not a merchant, the additional term is merely a proposal (suggestion), and Tolsen is not legally obligated to comply with that term.

Rules When Both Parties Are Merchants. The drafters of the UCC created a special rule for merchants that is designed to avoid the "battle of the forms," which occurs when two merchants exchange standard forms containing different contract terms. Under UCC 2–207(2), in contracts *between merchants,* the additional terms *automatically* become part of the contract *unless:*

1. The original offer expressly limited acceptance to its terms,
2. The new or changed terms materially alter the contract, or
3. The offeror objects to the new or changed terms within a reasonable period of time.

What constitutes a material alteration of the contract is usually a question of fact that only a court can decide. Generally, if the modification involves no unreasonable element of surprise or hardship for the offeror, a court is likely to hold that the modification did not materially alter the contract.

Courts frequently consider the parties' prior dealings when determining whether the alteration is material. Suppose that Woolf has ordered meat from Tupman sixty-four times over a two-year period. Each time, Woolf placed the order over the phone, and Tupman mailed first a confirmation form, and then an invoice, to Woolf. Tupman's confirmation form and invoice have always included an arbitration clause. If Woolf places another order and fails to pay for the meat, the court will likely hold that the additional term—the arbitration provision—did not materially alter the contract because Woolf should not have been surprised by the term. The result might be different, however, if the parties had dealt with each other only on two prior occasions, and the arbitration clause was not in the confirmation form but was included only on the back of a faxed invoice.[12]

In the following case, the court observed that the UCC's principles on additional terms had created a "revolutionary change in contract law."

12. See, for example, *Sibcoimtrex, Inc. v. American Foods Group, Inc.,* 241 F.Supp.2d 104 (D.Mass. 2003).

CASE 20.2 Sun Coast Merchandise Corp. v. Myron Corp.

Superior Court of New Jersey, Appellate Division, 2007. 393 N.J.Super. 55, 922 A.2d 782.
lawlibrary.rutgers.edu/search.shtml[a]

• **Background and Facts** Sun Coast Merchandise Corporation, a California firm, designs and sells products that businesses distribute as promotional items. Myron Corporation, a New Jersey firm, asked Sun about a flip-top calculator on which Myron could engrave the names of its customers. In December 2000, Myron began to submit purchase orders for about 400,000 of what the parties referred to as "Version I" calculators. In April 2001, Sun redesigned the flip-top. Over the next few weeks, the parties discussed terms for the making and shipping of four million of the "Version II" calculators before the Christmas season. By May 27, Myron had faxed four orders with specific delivery dates. Two days later, Sun announced a delayed schedule and asked Myron to submit revised orders. Unwilling to agree to the new dates, Myron did not honor this request. The parties attempted to negotiate the issue but were unsuccessful. Finally, Sun filed a suit in a New Jersey state court against Myron, claiming, among other things, breach of contract. The court entered a judgment in Sun's favor. On appeal to a state intermediate appellate court, Myron argued, among other things, that the judge's instruction to the jury regarding Sun's claim was inadequate.

• **Decision and Rationale** The state intermediate appellate court reversed the lower court's judgment and remanded the case for a new trial. The court pointed out that "no longer are communicating parties left to debate whether an acceptance perfectly meets the terms of an offer,

a. In the "SEARCH THE N.J. COURTS DECISIONS" section, type "Sun Coast" in the box, and click on "Search!" In the result, click on the case name to access the opinion.

CASE 20.2 CONTINUED but instead the existence of a binding contract may be based on words or conduct, which need not mirror an offer, so long as they reveal the parties' intention to be bound." Thus, the jury could have found that a contract was formed. Nonetheless, the court accepted the possibility that the jury could also have found that the parties' "inability to agree on certain terms reveals the lack of an intent to be bound; in other words, that their communications constituted new negotiations that never ripened into a contract." Therefore, the reviewing court concluded that the trial judge's instructions to the jury with respect to the question of whether Sun and Myron had formed a contract were "fundamentally flawed" and "provided insufficient guidance for the jury's resolution of the issues." Hence, the trial court's decision was reversed.

- **The Ethical Dimension** *How does the UCC's obligation of good faith relate to the application of the principles concerning additional terms?*

- **The Legal Environment Dimension** *Applying the correct principles to the facts in this case, how would you have decided the issue? Explain.*

Conditioned on Offeror's Assent. Regardless of merchant status, the UCC provides that the offeree's expression cannot be construed as an acceptance if it contains additional or different terms that are expressly *conditioned* on the offeror's assent to those terms [UCC 2–207(1)]. For example, Philips offers to sell Hundert 650 pounds of turkey thighs at a specified price and with specified delivery terms. Hundert responds, "I accept your offer for 650 pounds of turkey thighs *on the condition that you agree to give me ninety days to pay for them.*" Hundert's response will be construed not as an acceptance but as a counteroffer, which Philips may or may not accept.

Additional Terms May Be Stricken. The UCC provides yet another option for dealing with conflicting terms in the parties' writings. Section 2–207(3) states that conduct by both parties that recognizes the existence of a contract is sufficient to establish a contract for sale even though the writings of the parties do not otherwise establish a contract. In this situation, "the terms of the particular contract will consist of those terms on which the writings of the parties agree, together with any supplementary terms incorporated under any other provisions of this Act." In a dispute over contract terms, this provision allows a court simply to strike from the contract those terms on which the parties do not agree.

Suppose that SMT Marketing orders goods over the phone from Brigg Sales, Inc., which ships the goods with an acknowledgment form (confirming the order) to SMT. SMT accepts and pays for the goods. The parties' writings do not establish a contract, but there is no question that a contract exists. If a dispute arises over the terms, such as the extent of any warranties, UCC 2–207(3) provides the governing rule.

As noted previously, the fact that a merchant's acceptance frequently contains additional terms or even terms that conflict with those of the offer is often referred to as the "battle of the forms." Although the UCC tries to eliminate this battle, the problem of differing contract terms still arises in commercial settings, particularly when contracts are based on the merchants' standard forms, such as order forms and confirmation forms.

Consideration

The common law rule that a contract requires consideration also applies to sales and lease contracts. Unlike the common law, however, the UCC does not require a contract modification to be supported by new consideration. The UCC states that an agreement modifying a contract for the sale or lease of goods "needs no consideration to be binding" [UCC 2–209(1), 2A–208(1)].

Modifications Must Be Made in Good Faith

Of course, any contract modification must be made in good faith [UCC 1–304]. Suppose that Allied agrees to lease certain goods to Louise for a stated price. Subsequently, a sudden shift in the market makes it difficult for Allied to lease the items to Louise at the given price without suffering a loss. Allied tells Louise of the situation, and she agrees to pay an additional sum for leasing the goods. Later, Louise reconsiders and refuses to pay more than the original price. Under the UCC, Louise's promise to modify the contract needs no consideration to be binding. Hence, Louise is bound by the modified contract.

In this example, a shift in the market is a *good faith* reason for contract modification. What if there really was no shift in the market, however, and Allied knew that Louise needed the goods immediately but refused to deliver them unless Louise agreed to pay an additional amount? This sort of extortion of a modification without a legitimate commercial reason would violate the duty of good faith, and Allied would not be permitted to enforce the higher price.

When Modification Does Require a Writing

In some situations, an agreement to modify a sales or lease contract without consideration must be in writing to be enforceable. For example, if the contract itself prohibits any changes to the contract unless they are in a signed writing, only those changes agreed to in a signed writing are enforceable. If a consumer (nonmerchant buyer) is dealing with a merchant and the merchant supplies the form that contains the prohibition against oral modification, the consumer must sign a separate acknowledgment of the clause [UCC 2–209(2), 2A–208(2)].

Also, under Article 2, any modification that brings a sales contract under the Statute of Frauds must usually be in writing to be enforceable. Thus, if an oral contract for the sale of goods priced at $400 is modified so that the goods are priced at $600, the modification must be in writing to be enforceable [UCC 2–209(3)]. (This is because the UCC's Statute of Frauds provision, as you will read shortly, requires a written record of sales contracts for goods priced at $500 or more.) Nevertheless, if the buyer accepts delivery of the goods after the oral modification, he or she is bound to the $600 price [UCC 2–201(3)(c)]. (Unlike Article 2, Article 2A does not say whether a lease as modified needs to satisfy the Statute of Frauds.)

The Statute of Frauds

As discussed in Chapter 15, the Statute of Frauds requires that certain types of contracts, to be enforceable, must be in writing or be evidenced by a written memorandum or record. The UCC contains Statute of Frauds provisions covering sales and lease contracts. Under these provisions, sales contracts for goods priced at $500 or more and lease contracts requiring total payments of $1,000 or more must be in writing to be enforceable [UCC 2–201(1), 2A–201(1)]. (Note that these low threshold amounts may eventually be raised.)

Sufficiency of the Writing The UCC has greatly relaxed the requirements for the sufficiency of a writing to satisfy the Statute of Frauds. A writing or a memorandum will be sufficient as long as it indicates that the parties intended to form a contract and as long as it is signed by the party (or agent of the party) against whom enforcement is sought. The contract normally will not be enforceable beyond the quantity of goods shown in the writing, however. All other terms can be proved in court by oral testimony. For leases, the writing must reasonably identify and describe the goods leased and the lease term.

Special Rules for Contracts between Merchants Once again, the UCC provides a special rule for merchants.[13] Merchants can satisfy the requirements of a writing for the Statute of Frauds if, after the parties have agreed orally, one of the merchants sends a signed written confirmation to the other merchant. The communication must indicate the terms of the agreement, and the merchant receiving the confirmation must have reason to know of its contents. Unless the merchant who receives the confirmation gives written notice of objection to its contents within ten days after receipt, the writing is sufficient against the receiving merchant, even though she or he has not signed anything [UCC 2–201(2)].

Suppose that Alfonso is a merchant-buyer in Cleveland. He contracts over the telephone to purchase $6,000 worth of spare aircraft parts from Goldstein, a merchant-seller in New York City. Two days later, Goldstein sends a written confirmation detailing the terms of the oral contract, and Alfonso subsequently receives it. If Alfonso does not give Goldstein written notice of objection to the contents of the written confirmation within ten days of receipt, Alfonso cannot raise the Statute of Frauds as a defense against the enforcement of the oral contract.

Note that the written confirmation need not be a traditional paper document with a handwritten signature. Courts have held that an e-mail confirming the order and including the company's typed name was sufficient to satisfy the UCC's Statute of Frauds.[14]

13. Note that this rule applies only to sales (under Article 2); there is no corresponding rule that applies to leases (under Article 2A). According to the comments accompanying UCC 2A–201 (Article 2A's Statute of Frauds), the "between merchants" provision was not included because "the number of such transactions involving leases, as opposed to sales, was thought to be modest."

14. See, for example, *Bazak International Corp. v. Tarrant Apparel Group*, 378 F.Supp.2d 377 (S.D.N.Y. 2005); *Lachira v. Sutton*, 2007 WL 1346913 (D.Conn. 2007); and *Great White Bear, LLC v. Mervyns, LLC*, 2007 WL 1295747 (S.D.N.Y. 2007).

Exceptions The UCC defines three exceptions to the writing requirements of the Statute of Frauds. An oral contract for the sale of goods priced at $500 or more or the lease of goods involving total payments of $1,000 or more will be enforceable despite the absence of a writing in the circumstances described next [UCC 2–201(3), 2A–201(4)].

Specially Manufactured Goods. An oral contract is enforceable if (1) it is for goods that are *specially manufactured* for a particular buyer or specially manufactured or obtained for a particular lessee, (2) these goods are *not suitable for resale or lease* to others in the ordinary course of the seller's or lessor's business, and (3) the seller or lessor has *substantially started to manufacture* the goods or has made commitments for the manufacture or procurement of the goods. In these situations, once the seller or lessor has taken action, the buyer or lessee cannot repudiate the agreement claiming the Statute of Frauds as a defense.

Assume that Womach orders custom-made draperies for her new boutique. The price is $9,000, and the contract is oral. When the merchant-seller manufactures the draperies and tenders delivery to Womach, she refuses to pay for them even though the job has been completed on time. Womach claims that she is not liable because the contract was oral. Clearly, if the unique style and color of the draperies make it improbable that the seller can find another buyer, Womach is liable to the seller. Note that the seller must have made a substantial beginning in manufacturing the specialized item prior to the buyer's repudiation. (Here, the manufacture was completed.) Of course, the court must still be convinced by evidence of the terms of the oral contract.

Admissions. An oral contract for the sale or lease of goods is enforceable if the party against whom enforcement is sought admits in pleadings, testimony, or other court proceedings that a sales or lease contract was made. In this situation, the contract will be enforceable even though it was oral, but enforceability will be limited to the quantity of goods admitted.

For example, Lane and Salazar negotiate an agreement over the telephone. During the negotiations, Lane requests a delivery price for five hundred gallons of gasoline and a separate price for seven hundred gallons of gasoline. Salazar replies that the price would be the same per gallon. Lane orally orders five hundred gallons. Salazar honestly believes that Lane ordered seven hundred gallons and tenders that amount. Lane refuses the shipment of seven hundred gallons, and Salazar sues for breach. In his pleadings and testimony, Lane admits that an oral contract was made, but only for five hundred gallons. Because Lane admits the existence of the oral contract, Lane cannot plead the Statute of Frauds as a defense. The contract is enforceable, however, only to the extent of the quantity admitted (five hundred gallons).

Partial Performance. An oral contract for the sale or lease of goods is enforceable if payment has been made and accepted or goods have been received and accepted. This is the "partial performance" exception. The oral contract will be enforced at least to the extent that performance *actually* took place.

Suppose that Allan orally contracts to lease Wolfgang ten thousand chairs at $5 each to be used during a one-day rock concert. Before delivery, Wolfgang sends Allan a check for $25,000, which Allan cashes. Later, when Allan attempts to deliver the chairs, Wolfgang refuses delivery, claiming the Statute of Frauds as a defense, and demands the return of his $25,000. Under the UCC's partial performance rule, Allan can enforce the oral contract by tender of delivery of five thousand chairs for the $25,000 accepted. Similarly, if Wolfgang had made no payment but had accepted the delivery of five thousand chairs from Allan, the oral contract would have been enforceable against Wolfgang for $25,000 (the lease payment due for the five thousand chairs delivered).

The exceptions just discussed and other ways in which sales law differs from general contract law are summarized in Exhibit 20–3 on the following page.

Parol Evidence

If the parties intended the terms as set forth in the contract as a complete and final expression of their agreement, then the terms of the contract cannot be contradicted by evidence of any prior agreements or contemporaneous oral agreements. As discussed in Chapter 15, this principle of law is known as the parol evidence rule. If, however, the writing contains only some of the terms that the parties agreed on and not others, then the contract is not fully integrated.

When a court finds that the terms of the agreement are not fully integrated, then the court may allow evidence of *consistent additional terms* to explain or supplement the terms stated in the contract. The court may also allow the parties to submit evidence of *course of dealing, usage of trade,* and *course of performance* when the contract was only partially integrated [UCC 2–202, 2A–202]. A court will not under any

EXHIBIT 20–3 • Major Differences between Contract Law and Sales Law

	Contract Law	Sales Law
Contract Terms	Contract must contain all material terms.	Open terms are acceptable if parties intended to form a contract, but contract is not enforceable beyond quantity term.
Acceptance	Mirror image rule applies. If additional terms are added in acceptance, counteroffer is created.	Additional terms will not negate acceptance unless acceptance is expressly conditioned on assent to the additional terms.
Contract Modification	Modification requires consideration.	Modification does not require consideration.
Irrevocable Offers	Option contracts (with consideration).	Merchants' firm offers (without consideration).
Statute of Frauds Requirements	All material terms must be included in the writing.	Writing is required only for sale of goods of $500 or more, but contract is not enforceable beyond quantity specified. Merchants can satisfy the writing requirement by a confirmatory memorandum evidencing their agreement. *Exceptions:* 1. Specially manufactured goods. 2. Admissions by party against whom enforcement is sought. 3. Partial performance.

circumstances allow the parties to submit evidence that contradicts the stated terms (this is also the rule under the common law of contracts).

Course of Dealing and Usage of Trade Under the UCC, the meaning of any agreement, evidenced by the language of the parties and by their actions, must be interpreted in light of commercial practices and other surrounding circumstances. In interpreting a commercial agreement, the court will assume that the course of prior dealing between the parties and the general usage of trade were taken into account when the agreement was phrased.

A **course of dealing** is a sequence of previous actions and communications between the parties to a particular transaction that establishes a common basis for their understanding [UCC 1–303(b)]. A course of dealing is restricted to the sequence of conduct between the parties in their transactions previous to the agreement.

Usage of trade is defined as any practice or method of dealing having such regularity of observance in a place, vocation, or trade as to justify an expectation that it will be observed with respect to the transaction in question [UCC 1–303(c)]. The express terms of an agreement and an applicable course of dealing or usage of trade will be construed to be consistent with each other whenever reasonable. When such a construction is *unreasonable,* however, the express terms in the agreement will prevail [UCC 1–303(e)].

Course of Performance The conduct that occurs under the terms of a particular agreement is called a **course of performance** [UCC 1–303(a)]. Presumably, the parties themselves know best what they meant by their words, and the course of performance actually undertaken under their agreement is the best indication of what they meant [UCC 2–208(1), 2A–207(1)].

For example, Janson's Lumber Company contracts with Barrymore to sell Barrymore a specified number of two-by-fours. The lumber in fact does not measure 2 inches by 4 inches but rather 1⅞ inches by 3¾ inches. Janson's agrees to deliver the lumber in five deliveries, and Barrymore, without objection, accepts the lumber in the first three deliveries. On the fourth delivery, however, Barrymore objects that the two-by-fours do not measure 2 inches by 4 inches.

The course of performance in this transaction—that is, the fact that Barrymore accepted three deliveries without objection under the agreement—is relevant in determining that here a "two-by-four" actually means a "1⅞-by-3¾." Janson's can also prove that two-by-fours need not be exactly 2 inches by 4 inches by applying usage of trade, course of dealing, or both. Janson's can, for example, show that in previous transactions, Barrymore took 1⅞-inch-by-3¾-inch lumber without objection. In addition, Janson's can show that in the trade, two-by-fours are commonly 1⅞ inches by 3¾ inches.

Rules of Construction The UCC provides *rules of construction* for interpreting contracts. Express terms, course of performance, course of dealing, and usage of trade are to be construed together when they do not contradict one another. When such a construction is unreasonable, however, the following order of priority controls: (1) express terms, (2) course of performance, (3) course of dealing, and (4) usage of trade [UCC 1–303(e), 2–208(2), 2A–207(2)].

Unconscionability

As discussed in Chapters 13 and 14, an unconscionable contract is one that is so unfair and one sided that it would be unreasonable to enforce it. The UCC allows a court to evaluate a contract or any clause in a contract, and if the court deems it to have been unconscionable *at the time it was made*, the court can do any of the following [UCC 2–302, 2A–108]:

1. Refuse to enforce the contract.
2. Enforce the remainder of the contract without the unconscionable part.
3. Limit the application of the unconscionable term to avoid an unconscionable result.

The following landmark case illustrates an early application of the UCC's unconscionability provisions.

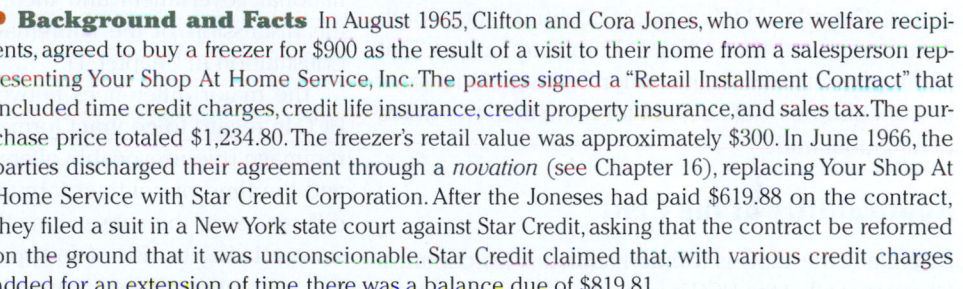

CASE 20.3 Jones v. Star Credit Corp.

Supreme Court of New York, Nassau County, 1969. 59 Misc.2d 189, 298 N.Y.S.2d 264.

• **Background and Facts** In August 1965, Clifton and Cora Jones, who were welfare recipients, agreed to buy a freezer for $900 as the result of a visit to their home from a salesperson representing Your Shop At Home Service, Inc. The parties signed a "Retail Installment Contract" that included time credit charges, credit life insurance, credit property insurance, and sales tax. The purchase price totaled $1,234.80. The freezer's retail value was approximately $300. In June 1966, the parties discharged their agreement through a *novation* (see Chapter 16), replacing Your Shop At Home Service with Star Credit Corporation. After the Joneses had paid $619.88 on the contract, they filed a suit in a New York state court against Star Credit, asking that the contract be reformed on the ground that it was unconscionable. Star Credit claimed that, with various credit charges added for an extension of time, there was a balance due of $819.81.

• **Decision and Rationale** The state trial court ruled in favor of the Joneses. The contract was reformed so that they were required to make no further payments. The court relied on UCC 2–302(1), which states that if "the court as a matter of law finds the contract or any clause of the contract to have been unconscionable at the time it was made the court may * * * so limit the application of any unconscionable clause as to avoid any unconscionable result." The court considered the disparity between the $900 purchase price and the $300 retail value, the fact that the credit charges alone exceeded the retail value, and the seller's knowledge of the buyers' limited resources sufficient to declare the contract unconscionable.

• **Impact of This Case on Today's Law** *This early case illustrates the approach that many courts take today when deciding whether a sales contract is unconscionable—an approach that*

CASE CONTINUES

CASE 20.3 CONTINUED *focuses on "excessive" price and unequal bargaining power. Most of the litigants who have used UCC 2–302 successfully could demonstrate both an absence of meaningful choice and that the contract terms were unreasonably favorable to the other party.*

- **The Ethical Dimension** *Why would the seller's knowledge of the buyers' limited resources support a finding of unconscionability? Explain.*
- **The Legal Environment Dimension** *Why didn't the court rule that the Joneses, as adults, had made a decision of their own free will and therefore were bound by the terms of the contract, regardless of the difference between the freezer's contract price and its retail value?*

Concept Summary 20.1 reviews the concepts and rules related to the formation of sales and lease contracts that we have discussed in this chapter.

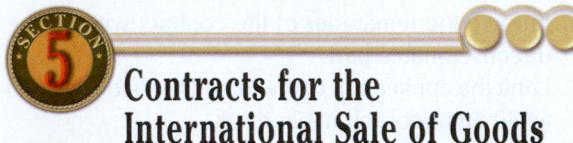

SECTION 5 Contracts for the International Sale of Goods

International sales contracts between firms or individuals located in different countries may be governed by the 1980 United Nations Convention on Contracts for the International Sale of Goods (CISG). The CISG governs international contracts only if the countries of the parties to the contract have ratified the CISG and if the parties have not agreed that some other law will govern their contract. As of 2008, the CISG had been adopted by seventy countries, including the United States, Canada, Mexico, some Central and South American countries, and most European nations. That means that the CISG is the uniform international sales law of countries that account for more than two-thirds of all global trade.

Applicability of the CISG

Essentially, the CISG is to international sales contracts what Article 2 of the UCC is to domestic sales contracts. As discussed in this chapter, in domestic transactions the UCC applies when the parties to a contract for a sale of goods have failed to specify in writing some important term concerning price, delivery, or the like. Similarly, whenever the parties to international transactions have failed to specify in writing the precise terms of a contract, the CISG will be applied. Unlike the UCC, the CISG does not apply to consumer sales, and neither the UCC nor the CISG applies to contracts for services.

Businesspersons must take special care when drafting international sales contracts to avoid problems caused by distance, including language differences and differences in national laws. The appendix following this chapter (pages 383–386) shows an actual international sales contract used by Starbucks Coffee Company. The contract illustrates many of the special terms and clauses that are typically contained in international contracts for the sale of goods. Annotations in the appendix explain the meaning and significance of specific clauses in the contract. (See Chapter 52 for a discussion of other laws that frame global business transactions.)

A Comparison of CISG and UCC Provisions

The provisions of the CISG, although similar for the most part to those of the UCC, differ from them in some respects. In the event that the CISG and the UCC are in conflict, the CISG applies (because it is a treaty of the national government and therefore is supreme—see the discussion of the supremacy clause of the U.S. Constitution in Chapter 4).

The major differences between the CISG and the UCC in regard to contract formation concern the mirror image rule, irrevocable offers, the Statute of Frauds, and the time of contract formation. We discuss these differences in the subsections that follow. CISG provisions relating to risk of loss, performance, remedies, and warranties will be discussed in the following chapters as those topics are examined.

The Mirror Image Rule Under the UCC, a definite expression of acceptance that contains additional terms can still result in the formation of a contract, unless the additional terms are conditioned on the assent of the offeror. In other words, the UCC does away with the mirror image rule in domestic sales contracts.

Article 19 of the CISG provides that a contract can be formed even though the acceptance contains additional terms, unless the additional terms materially alter the contract. Under the CISG, however, the definition of

CONCEPT SUMMARY 20.1
The Formation of Sales and Lease Contracts

Concept	Description
OFFER AND ACCEPTANCE	1. *Offer—* a. Not all terms have to be included for a contract to be formed. b. The price does not have to be included for a contract to be formed. c. Particulars of performance can be left open. d. An offer by a merchant in a signed writing with assurances that the offer will not be withdrawn is irrevocable without consideration (for up to three months). 2. *Acceptance—* a. Acceptance may be made by any reasonable means of communication; it is effective when dispatched. b. The acceptance of a unilateral offer can be made by a promise to ship or by the shipment of conforming or nonconforming goods. c. Acceptance by performance requires notice within a reasonable time; otherwise, the offer can be treated as lapsed. d. A definite expression of acceptance creates a contract even if the terms of the acceptance modify the terms of the offer.
CONSIDERATION	A modification of a contract for the sale of goods does not require consideration.
REQUIREMENTS UNDER THE STATUTE OF FRAUDS	1. All contracts for the sale of goods priced at $500 or more must be in writing. A writing is sufficient as long as it indicates a contract between the parties and is signed by the party against whom enforcement is sought. A contract is not enforceable beyond the quantity shown in the writing. 2. When written confirmation of an oral contract between merchants is not objected to in writing by the receiver within ten days, the oral contract is enforceable. 3. Exceptions to the requirement of a writing exist in the following situations: a. When the oral contract is for specially manufactured or obtained goods not suitable for resale or lease to others and the seller or lessor has made commitments for the manufacture or procurement of the goods. b. If the defendant admits in pleadings, testimony, or other court proceedings that an oral contract for the sale or lease of goods was made, then the contract will be enforceable to the extent of the quantity of goods admitted. c. The oral agreement will be enforceable to the extent that payment has been received and accepted or to the extent that goods have been received and accepted.
PAROL EVIDENCE RULE	1. The terms of a clearly and completely worded written contract cannot be contradicted by evidence of prior agreements or contemporaneous oral agreements. 2. Evidence is admissible to clarify the terms of a writing in the following situations: a. If the contract terms are ambiguous. b. If evidence of course of dealing, usage of trade, or course of performance is necessary to learn or to clarify the intentions of the parties to the contract.

a "material alteration" includes virtually any change in the terms. If an additional term relates to payment, quality, quantity, price, time and place of delivery, extent of one party's liability to the other, or the settlement of disputes, the CISG considers the added term a material alteration. In effect, then, the CISG requires that the terms of the acceptance mirror those of the offer.

Therefore, as a practical matter, businesspersons undertaking international sales transactions should not use the sale or purchase forms that they customarily use for transactions within the United States. Instead, they should draft specific forms to suit the needs of the particular transactions.

Irrevocable Offers UCC 2–205 provides that a merchant's firm offer is irrevocable, even without consideration, if the merchant gives assurances in a signed writing. In contrast, under the CISG, an offer can become irrevocable without a signed writing. Article 16(2) of the CISG provides that an offer will be irrevocable if the offeror simply states orally that the offer is irrevocable or if the offeree reasonably relies on the offer as being irrevocable. In both of these situations, the offer will be irrevocable even without a writing and without consideration.

The Statute of Frauds As mentioned previously, the UCC's Statute of Frauds provision [UCC 2–201] requires that contracts for the sale of goods priced at $500 or more be evidenced by a written record signed by the party against whom enforcement is sought. Article 11 of the CISG, however, states that a contract of sale "need not be concluded in or evidenced by writing and is not subject to any other requirements as to form. It may be proved by any means, including witnesses." Article 11 of the CISG accords with the legal customs of most nations, which no longer require contracts to meet certain formal or writing requirements to be enforceable.

Time of Contract Formation Under the common law of contracts, an acceptance is effective on dispatch, so a contract is created when the acceptance is transmitted. The UCC does not alter this so-called mailbox rule. Under the CISG, in contrast, a contract is created not at the time the acceptance is transmitted but only on its *receipt* by the offeror. (The offer becomes *irrevocable,* however, when the acceptance is sent.) Article 18(2) states that an acceptance by return promise "becomes effective at the moment the indication of assent reaches the offeror." Under Article 18(3), the offeree may also bind the offeror by performance even without giving any notice to the offeror. The acceptance becomes effective "at the moment the act is performed." Thus, the rule is that it is the offeree's reliance, rather than the communication of acceptance to the offeror, that creates the contract.

Special Provisions in International Contracts

Language and legal differences among nations can create special problems for parties to international contracts when disputes arise. It is possible to avoid these problems by including in a contract special provisions relating to choice of language, choice of forum, choice of law, and the types of events that may excuse the parties from performance.

Choice of Language A deal struck between a U.S. company and a company in another country frequently involves two languages. One party may not understand complex contractual terms that are written in the other party's language. Translating the terms poses its own problems, as typically many phrases are not readily translatable into another language. To make sure that no disputes arise out of this language problem, an international sales contract should have a **choice-of-language clause** designating the official language by which the contract will be interpreted in the event of disagreement. The clause might also specify that the agreement is to be translated into, say, Spanish; that the translation is to be ratified by both parties; and that the foreign company can rely on the translation. If arbitration is anticipated, an additional clause must be added to indicate the official language that will be used at the arbitration proceeding.

Choice of Forum As discussed in Chapter 19, a forum-selection clause designates the *forum* (place, or court) in which any disputes that arise under the contract will be litigated. Including a forum-selection clause in an international contract is especially important because when several countries are involved, litigation may be sought in courts in different nations. There are no universally accepted rules regarding the jurisdiction of a particular court over subject matter or parties to a dispute, although the adoption of the 2005 Choice of Court Convention (discussed in Chapter 19's *Insight into the Global Environment* feature on page 347) should help resolve certain issues. A forum-selection clause should indicate the specific court that will have jurisdiction. The forum does not necessarily have to be within the geographic boundaries of either party's nation.

Under certain circumstances, a forum-selection clause will not be valid. Specifically, if the clause denies one party an effective remedy, is the product of fraud or unconscionable conduct, causes substantial inconvenience to one of the parties to the contract, or violates public policy, the clause will not be enforced.

Choice of Law A contractual provision designating the applicable law, called a **choice-of-law clause,** is typically included in every international contract. At common law (and in European civil law systems—see Chapter 52), parties are allowed to choose the law that will govern their contractual relationship, provided that the law chosen is the law of a jurisdiction that has a substantial relationship to the parties and to the business transaction.

Under the UCC, parties may choose the law that will govern the contract as long as the choice is "reasonable." Article 6 of the CISG, however, imposes no limitation on the parties in their choice of what law will govern the contract, and the 1986 Hague Convention on the Law Applicable to Contracts for the International Sale of Goods—often referred to as the Choice-of-Law Convention—allows unlimited autonomy in the choice of law. Whenever a choice of law is not specified in a contract, the Hague Convention indicates that the law of the country where the seller's place of business is located will govern.

***Force Majeure* Clause** Every contract, and particularly those involving international transactions, should have a ***force majeure* clause.** The meaning of the French term *force majeure* is "impossible or irresistible force"—sometimes loosely defined as "an act of God." *Force majeure* clauses commonly stipulate that in addition to acts of God, a number of other eventualities (such as governmental orders or regulations, embargoes, or extreme shortages of materials) may excuse a party from liability for nonperformance.

REVIEWING The Formation of Sales and Lease Contracts

Guy Holcomb owns and operates Oasis Goodtime Emporium, an adult entertainment establishment. Holcomb wanted to create an adult Internet system for Oasis that would offer customers adult theme videos and "live" chat room programs using performers at the club. On May 10, Holcomb signed a work order authorizing Thomas Consulting Group (TCG) "to deliver a working prototype of a customer chat system, demonstrating the integration of live video and chatting in a Web browser." In exchange for creating the prototype, Holcomb agreed to pay TCG $64,697. On May 20, Holcomb signed an additional work order in the amount of $12,943 for TCG to install a customized firewall system. The work orders stated that Holcomb would make monthly installment payments to TCG, and both parties expected the work would be finished by September. Due to unforeseen problems largely attributable to system configuration and software incompatibility, completion of the project required more time than anticipated. By the end of the summer, the Web site was still not ready, and Holcomb had fallen behind in his payments to TCG. TCG was threatening to cease work and file a suit for breach of contract unless the bill was paid. Rather than make further payments, Holcomb wanted to abandon the Web site project. Using the information presented in the chapter, answer the following questions.

1. Would a court be likely to decide that the transaction between Holcomb and TCG was covered by the Uniform Commercial Code (UCC)? Why or why not?
2. Would a court be likely to consider Holcomb a merchant under the UCC? Why or why not?
3. Did the parties have a valid contract under the UCC? Were any terms left open in the contract? If so, which terms? How would a court deal with open terms?
4. Suppose that Holcomb and TCG meet in October in an attempt to resolve their problems. At that time, the parties reach an oral agreement that TCG will continue to work without demanding full payment of the past due amounts and Holcomb will pay TCG $5,000 per week. Assuming the contract falls under the UCC, is the oral agreement enforceable? Why or why not?

TERMS AND CONCEPTS

choice-of-language clause 378
choice-of-law clause 379
course of dealing 374
course of performance 374
firm offer 368
***force majeure* clause 379**
lease agreement 365
lessee 365
lessor 365
merchant 365
output contract 367
predominant-factor test 363
requirements contract 367
sale 362
sales contract 361
seasonably 369
tangible property 362
usage of trade 374

QUESTIONS AND CASE PROBLEMS

20–1. Strike offers to sell Bailey one thousand shirts for a stated price. The offer declares that shipment will be made by the Dependable Truck Line. Bailey replies, "I accept your offer for one thousand shirts at the price quoted. Delivery to be by Yellow Express Truck Line." Both Strike and Bailey are merchants. Three weeks later, Strike ships the shirts by the Dependable Truck Line, and Bailey refuses shipment. Strike sues for breach of contract. Bailey claims (a) that there never was a contract because the reply, which included a modification of carriers, did not constitute an acceptance and (b) that even if there had been a contract, Strike would have been in breach owing to having shipped the shirts by Dependable, contrary to the contract terms. Discuss fully Bailey's claims.

20–2. QUESTION WITH SAMPLE ANSWER

Flint, a retail seller of television sets, orders one hundred Color-X sets from manufacturer Martin. The order specifies the price and that the television sets are to be shipped by Hummingbird Express on or before October 30. Martin receives the order on October 5. On October 8, Martin writes Flint a letter indicating that the order was received and that the sets will be shipped as directed, at the specified price. Flint receives this letter on October 10. On October 28, Martin, in preparing the shipment, discovers it has only ninety Color-X sets in stock. Martin ships the ninety Color-X sets and ten television sets of a different model, stating clearly on the invoice that the ten are being shipped only as an accommodation. Flint claims Martin is in breach of contract. Martin claims that the shipment was not an acceptance and therefore no contract was formed. Explain who is correct, and why.

- **For a sample answer to Question 20–2, go to Appendix I at the end of this text.**

20–3. Shane has a requirements contract with Sky that obligates Sky to supply Shane with all the gasoline Shane needs for his delivery trucks for one year at $2.30 per gallon. A clause inserted in small print in the contract by Shane, and not noticed by Sky, states, "The buyer reserves the right to reject any shipment for any reason without liability." For six months, Shane orders and Sky delivers under the contract without any controversy. Then, because of a war in the Middle East, the price of gasoline to Sky increases substantially. Sky contacts Shane and tells Shane he cannot possibly fulfill the requirements contract unless Shane agrees to pay $2.50 per gallon. Shane, in need of the gasoline, agrees in writing to modify the contract. Later that month, Shane learns he can buy gasoline at $2.40 per gallon from Collins. Shane refuses delivery of his most recent order from Sky, claiming (a) that the contract allows him to do so without liability, and (b) that he is required to pay only $2.30 per gallon if he accepts the delivery. Discuss fully Shane's contentions.

20–4. Goods Associated with Real Estate. Heatway Radiant Floors and Snowmelting Corp. sells parts for underground radiant heating systems. These systems circulate warm fluid under indoor flooring as an alternative to conventional heating systems or under driveways and sidewalks to melt snow and ice. Goodyear Tire and Rubber Co. made and sold a hose, Entran II, that Heatway used in its radiant systems. Between 1989 and 1993, 25 million feet of Entran II was made by Goodyear and installed by Heatway. In 1992, homeowners began complaining about hardening of the hose and leaks in the systems. Linda Loughridge and other homeowners filed a suit in a federal district court against Goodyear and Heatway, alleging a variety of contract breaches under Colorado's version of the Uniform Commercial Code (UCC). Goodyear filed a motion for summary judgment, arguing, in part, that because Entran II was used in the construction of underground systems that were covered by flooring or cement, the hose was not a "good" and thus the UCC did not apply. Should the court agree with this interpretation of the scope of Article 2? Explain. [*Loughridge v. Goodyear Tire and Rubber Co.*, 192 F.Supp.2d 1175 (D.Colo. 2002)]

20–5. Statute of Frauds. Quality Pork International is a Nebraska firm that makes and sells custom pork products. Rupari Food Services, Inc., buys and sells food products from and to retail operations and food brokers. In November 1999, Midwest Brokerage arranged an oral contract between Quality and Rupari, under which Quality would ship three orders to Star Food Processing, Inc., and Rupari would pay for the products. Quality shipped the goods to Star and sent invoices to Rupari. In turn, Rupari billed Star for all three orders but paid Quality only for the first two (for $43,736.84 and $47,467.80, respectively), not for the third. Quality filed a suit in a Nebraska state court against Rupari, alleging breach of contract, to recover $44,051.98, the cost of the third order. Rupari argued that because the parties did not have a written agreement, as required by Section 2–201 of the Uniform Commercial Code (UCC), there was no enforceable contract. What are the exceptions to the UCC's writing requirement? Do any of those exceptions apply here? Explain. [*Quality Pork International v. Rupari Food Services, Inc.*, 267 Neb. 474, 675 N.W.2d 642 (2004)]

20–6. CASE PROBLEM WITH SAMPLE ANSWER

Propulsion Technologies, Inc., a Louisiana firm doing business as (dba) PowerTech Marine Propellers, markets small steel boat propellers that are made by a unique tooling method. Attwood Corp., a Michigan firm, operated a foundry (a place where metal is cast) in Mexico. In 1996, Attwood offered to produce castings of the propellers. Attwood promised to maintain quality, warrant the castings against defects, and obtain insurance to cover liability. In January 1997, the parties signed a letter that expressed these and other terms—Attwood was to be paid per casting, and twelve months' notice was required to terminate the deal—but the letter did not state a quantity. PowerTech provided the tooling. Attwood produced rough castings, which PowerTech refined by checking each propeller's pitch; machining its interior; grinding, balancing, and polishing the propeller; and adding serial numbers and a rubber clutch. In October, Attwood told PowerTech that the foundry was closing. PowerTech filed a suit in a federal district court against Attwood, alleging, among other things, breach of contract. One of the issues was whether their deal was subject to Article 2 of the Uniform Commercial Code (UCC). What type of transactions does Article 2 cover? Does the arrangement between PowerTech and Attwood qualify? Explain. [*Propulsion Technologies, Inc. v. Attwood Corp.*, 369 F.3d 896 (5th Cir. 2004)]

- **To view a sample answer for Problem 20–6, go to this book's Web site at www.cengage.com/blaw/jentz, select "Chapter 20," and click on "Case Problem with Sample Answer."**

20–7. Offer. In 1998, Johnson Controls, Inc. (JCI), began buying auto parts from Q.C. Onics Ventures, LP. For each part, JCI would inform Onics of its need and ask the price. Onics would analyze the specifications, contact its suppliers, and respond with a formal quotation. A quote listed a part's number and description, the price per unit, and an estimate of units available for a given year. A quote did not state payment terms, an acceptance date, timing of performance, warranties, or quantities. JCI would select a supplier and issue a purchase order for a part. The purchase order required the seller to supply all of JCI's requirements for the part but gave the buyer the right to end the deal at any time. Using this procedure, JCI issued hundreds of purchase orders. In July 2001, JCI terminated its relationship with Onics and began buying parts through another supplier. Onics filed a suit in a federal district court against Johnson, alleging breach of contract. Which documents—the price quotations or the purchase orders—constituted offers? Which were acceptances? What effect would the answers to these questions have on the result in this case? Explain. [*Q.C. Onics Ventures, LP v. Johnson Controls, Inc.*, __ F.Supp.2d __ (N.D.Ind. 2006)]

20–8. Parol Evidence. Clear Lakes Trout Co. operates a fish hatchery in Idaho. Rodney and Carla Griffith are trout growers. Clear Lakes agreed to sell "small trout" to the Griffiths, who agreed to sell the trout back when they had grown to "market size." At the time, in the trade "market size" referred to fish approximating one-pound live weight. The parties did business without a written agreement until September 1998 when they executed a contract with a six-year duration. The contract did not define "market size." All went well until September 11, 2001, after which there was a demand for larger fish. Clear Lakes began taking deliveries later and in smaller loads, leaving the Griffiths with overcrowded ponds and other problems. In 2003, the Griffiths refused to accept more fish and filed a suit in an Idaho state court against Clear Lakes, alleging breach of contract. Clear Lakes argued that there was no contract because the parties had different interpretations of "market size." Clear Lakes claimed that "market size" varied according to whatever its customers demanded. The Griffiths asserted that the term referred to fish of about one-pound live weight. Is outside evidence admissible to explain the terms of a contract? Are there any exceptions that could apply in this case? If so, what is the likely result? Explain. [*Griffith v. Clear Lakes Trout Co.*, 143 Idaho 733, 152 P.3d 604 (2007)]

20–9. A QUESTION OF ETHICS

Daniel Fox owned Fox and Lamberth Enterprises, Inc., a kitchen and bath remodeling business, in Dayton, Ohio. Fox leased a building from Carl and Bellulah Hussong. Craftsmen Home Improvement, Inc., also remodeled baths and kitchens. When Fox planned to close his business, Craftsmen expressed an interest in buying his showroom assets. Fox set a price of $50,000. Craftsmen's owners agreed and gave Fox a list of *the desired items and "A Bill of Sale" that set the terms for payment. The parties did not discuss Fox's arrangement with the Hussongs, but Craftsmen expected to negotiate a new lease and extensively modified the premises, including removing some of the displays to its own showroom. When the Hussongs and Craftsmen could not agree on new terms, Craftsmen told Fox that the deal was off. [*Fox & Lamberth Enterprises, Inc. v. Craftsmen Home Improvement, Inc., *__ N.E.2d __ (Ohio App., 2 Dist. 2006)]*

(a) In Fox's suit in an Ohio state court for breach of contract, Craftsmen raised the Statute of Frauds as a defense. What are the requirements of the Statute of Frauds? Did the deal between Fox and Craftsmen meet these requirements? Did it fall under one of the exceptions? Explain.
(b) Craftsmen also claimed that the "predominant factor" of its agreement with Fox was a lease for the Hussongs' building. What is the predominant-factor test? Does it apply here? In any event, is it fair to hold a party to a contract to buy a business's assets when the buyer cannot negotiate a favorable lease of the premises on which the assets are located? Discuss.

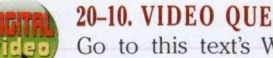

20–10. VIDEO QUESTION

Go to this text's Web site at **www.cengage.com/blaw/jentz** and select "Chapter 20." Click on "Video Questions" and view the video titled *Sales and Lease Contracts: Price as a Term.* Then answer the following questions.

(a) Is Anna correct in assuming that a contract can exist even though the sales price for the computer equipment was not specified? Explain.
(b) According to the Uniform Commercial Code (UCC), what conditions must be satisfied in order for a contract to be formed when certain terms are left open? What terms (in addition to price) can be left open?
(c) Are the e-mail messages that Anna refers to sufficient proof of the contract?
(d) Would parol evidence be admissible?

LAW ON THE WEB

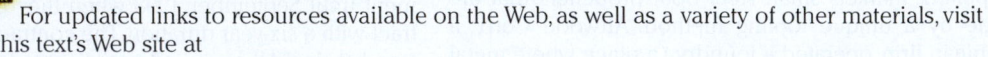

For updated links to resources available on the Web, as well as a variety of other materials, visit this text's Web site at

www.cengage.com/blaw/jentz

To view the text of the Uniform Commercial Code (UCC)—and keep up to date on its various revisions—go to the Web site of the National Conference of Commissioners on Uniform State Laws (NCCUSL) at

www.nccusl.org

Cornell University's Legal Information Institute also offers online access to the UCC, as well as to UCC articles as enacted by particular states and proposed revisions to articles, at

www.law.cornell.edu/ucc/index.htm

The Pace University School of Law's Institute of International Commercial Law maintains a Web site that contains the full text of the CISG, as well as relevant cases and discussions of the law. Go to

cisgw3.law.pace.edu/cisg/text/treaty.html

Legal Research Exercises on the Web

Go to **www.cengage.com/blaw/jentz**, the Web site that accompanies this text. Select "Chapter 20" and click on "Internet Exercises." There you will find the following Internet research exercises that you can perform to learn more about the topics covered in this chapter.

Internet Exercise 20–1: Legal Perspective
Is It a Contract?

Internet Exercise 20–2: Management Perspective
A Checklist for Sales Contracts

An Example of a Contract for the International Sale of Coffee

1

OVERLAND COFFEE IMPORT CONTRACT
OF THE
GREEN COFFEE ASSOCIATION
OF
NEW YORK CITY, INC.*

Contract Seller's No.: 504617
Buyer's No.: P9264
Date: 10/11/09

2

SOLD BY: XYZ Co.
TO: Starbucks

3

QUANTITY: Five Hundred (500) Bags Tons of Mexican coffee weighing about 152.117 lbs. per bag.

4

PACKAGING: Coffee must be packed in clean sound bags of uniform size made of sisal, henequen, jute, burlap, or similar woven material, without inner lining or outer covering of any material properly sewn by hand and/or machine.
Bulk shipments are allowed if agreed by mutual consent of Buyer and Seller.

5

DESCRIPTION: High grown Mexican Altura

PRICE: At Ten/$10.00 dollars U.S. Currency, per lb. net, (U.S. Funds)
Upon delivery in Bonded Public Warehouse at Laredo, TX
(City and State)

6

PAYMENT: Cash against warehouse receipts

Bill and tender to DATE when all import requirements and governmental regulations have been satisfied, and coffee delivered or discharged (as per contract terms). Seller is obliged to give the Buyer two (2) calendar days free time in Bonded Public Warehouse following but not including date of tender.

7

ARRIVAL: During December (Period) via truck (Method of Transportation)
from Mexico (Country of Exportation) for arrival at Laredo, TX, USA (Country of Importation)
Partial shipments permitted.

ADVICE OF ARRIVAL: Advice of arrival with warehouse name and location, together with the quantity, description, marks and place of entry, must be transmitted directly, or through Seller's Agent/Broker, to the Buyer or his Agent/Broker. Advice will be given as soon as known but not later than the fifth business day following arrival at the named warehouse. Such advice may be given verbally with written confirmation to be sent the same day.

8

WEIGHTS: (1) DELIVERED WEIGHTS: Coffee covered by this contract is to be weighed at location named in tender. Actual tare to be allowed.
(2) SHIPPING WEIGHTS: Coffee covered by this contract is sold on shipping weights. Any loss in weight exceeding 1/2 percent at location named in tender is for account of Seller at contract price.
(3) Coffee is to be weighed within fifteen (15) calendar days after tender. Weighing expenses, if any, for account of Seller (Seller or Buyer)

9

MARKINGS: Bags to be branded in English with the name of Country of Origin and otherwise to comply with laws and regulations of the Country of Importation, in effect at the time of entry, governing marking of import merchandise. Any expense incurred by failure to comply with these regulations to be borne by Exporter/Seller.

10

RULINGS: The "Rulings on Coffee Contracts" of the Green Coffee Association of New York City, Inc., in effect on the date this contract is made, is incorporated for all purposes as a part of this agreement, and together herewith, constitute the entire contract. No variation or addition hereto shall be valid unless signed by the parties to the contract.
Seller guarantees that the terms printed on the reverse hereof, which by reference are made a part hereof, are identical with the terms as printed in By-Laws and Rules of the Green Coffee Association of New York City, Inc., heretofore adopted.
Exceptions to this guarantee are:

11

ACCEPTED:
XYZ Co.
Seller
BY DM
Agent

COMMISSION TO BE PAID BY:
Seller

12

Starbucks
Buyer
BY [signature]
Agent

ABC Brokerage
Broker(s)

13

When this contract is executed by a person acting for another, such person hereby represents that he is fully authorized to commit his principal.

* Reprinted with permission of The Green Coffee Association of New York City, Inc.

(Continued)

1 This is a contract for a sale of coffee to be *imported* internationally. If the parties have their principal places of business located in different countries, the contract may be subject to the United Nations Convention on Contracts for the International Sale of Goods (CISG). If the parties' principal places of business are located in the United States, the contract may be subject to the Uniform Commercial Code (UCC).

2 Quantity is one of the most important terms to include in a contract. Without it, a court may not be able to enforce the contract. See Chapter 20.

3 Weight per unit (bag) can be exactly stated or approximately stated. If it is not so stated, usage of trade in international contracts determines standards of weight.

4 Packaging requirements can be conditions for acceptance and payment. Bulk shipments are not permitted without the consent of the buyer.

5 A description of the coffee and the "Markings" constitute express warranties. Warranties in contracts for domestic sales of goods are discussed generally in Chapter 23. International contracts rely more heavily on descriptions and models or samples.

6 Under the UCC, parties may enter into a valid contract even though the price is not set. Under the CISG, a contract must provide for an exact determination of the price.

7 The terms of payment may take one of two forms: credit or cash. Credit terms can be complicated. A cash term can be simple, and payment can be made by any means acceptable in the ordinary course of business (for example, a personal check or a letter of credit). If the seller insists on actual cash, the buyer must be given a reasonable time to get it. See Chapter 22.

8 *Tender* means the seller has placed goods that conform to the contract at the buyer's disposition. What constitutes a valid tender is explained in Chapter 22. This contract requires that the coffee meet all import regulations and that it be ready for pickup by the buyer at a "Bonded Public Warehouse." (A *bonded warehouse* is a place in which goods can be stored without paying taxes until the goods are removed.)

9 The delivery date is significant because, if it is not met, the buyer may hold the seller in breach of the contract. Under this contract, the seller can be given a "period" within which to deliver the goods, instead of a specific day, which could otherwise present problems. The seller is also given some time to rectify goods that do not pass inspection (see the "Guarantee" clause on page two of the contract). For a discussion of the remedies of the buyer and seller, see Chapter 22.

10 As part of a proper tender, the seller (or its agent) must inform the buyer (or its agent) when the goods have arrived at their destination. The responsibilities of agents are set out in Chapters 31 and 32.

11 In some contracts, delivered and shipped weights can be important. During shipping, some loss can be attributed to the type of goods (spoilage of fresh produce, for example) or to the transportation itself. A seller and buyer can agree on the extent to which either of them will bear such losses. See Chapter 47 for a discussion of the liability of common carriers for loss during shipment.

12 Documents are often incorporated in a contract by reference, because including them word for word can make a contract difficult to read. If the document is later revised, the entire contract might have to be reworked. Documents that are typically incorporated by reference include detailed payment and delivery terms, special provisions, and sets of rules, codes, and standards.

13 In international sales transactions, and for domestic deals involving certain products, brokers are used to form the contracts. When so used, the brokers are entitled to a commission. See Chapter 31.

TERMS AND CONDITIONS

14

ARBITRATION: All controversies relating to, in connection with, or arising out of this contract, its modification, making or the authority or obligations of the signatories hereto, and whether involving the principals, agents, brokers, or others who actually subscribe hereto, shall be settled by arbitration in accordance with the "Rules of Arbitration" of the Green Coffee Association of New York City, Inc., as they exist at the time of the arbitration (including provisions as to payment of fees and expenses). Arbitration is the sole remedy hereunder, and it shall be held in accordance with the law of New York State, and judgment of any award may be entered in the courts of that State, or in any other court of competent jurisdiction. All notices or judicial service in reference to arbitration or enforcement shall be deemed given if transmitted as required by the aforesaid rules.

15

GUARANTEE: (a) If all or any of the coffee is refused admission into the country of importation by reason of any violation of governmental laws or acts, which violation existed at the time the coffee arrived at Bonded-Public Warehouse, seller is required, as to the amount not admitted and as soon as possible, to deliver replacement coffee in conformity to all terms and conditions of this contract, excepting only the Arrival terms, but not later than thirty (30) days after the date of the violation notice. Any payment made and expenses incurred for any coffee denied entry shall be refunded within ten (10) calendar days of denial of entry, and payment shall be made for the replacement delivery in accordance with the terms of this contract. Consequently, if Buyer removes the coffee from the Bonded Public Warehouse, Seller's responsibility as to such portion hereunder ceases.

(b) Contracts containing the overstamp "No Pass-No Sale" on the face of the contract shall be interpreted to mean: If any or all of the coffee is not admitted into the country of Importation in its original condition by reason of failure to meet requirements of the government's laws or Acts, the contract shall be deemed null and void as to that portion of the coffee which is not admitted in its original condition. Any payment made and expenses incurred for any coffee denied entry shall be refunded within ten (10) calendar days of denial of entry.

CONTINGENCY: This contract is not contingent upon any other contract.

16

CLAIMS: Coffee shall be considered accepted as to quality unless within *fifteen* (15) calendar days after delivery at Bonded Public Warehouse or within *fifteen* (15) calendar days after all Government clearances have been received, whichever is later, either:

(a) Claims are settled by the parties hereto, or,

(b) Arbitration proceedings have been filed by one of the parties in accordance with the provisions hereof.

(c) If neither (a) nor (b) has been done in the stated period or if any portion of the coffee has been removed from the Bonded Public Warehouse before representative sealed samples have been drawn by the Green Coffee Association of New York City, Inc., in accordance with its rules, Seller's responsibility for quality claims ceases for that portion so removed.

(d) Any question of quality submitted to arbitration shall be a matter of allowance only, unless otherwise provided in the contract.

17

18

DELIVERY: (a) No more than three (3) chops may be tendered for each lot of 250 bags.

(b) Each chop of coffee tendered is to be uniform in grade and appearance. All expense necessary to make coffee uniform shall be for account of seller.

(c) Notice of arrival and/or sampling order constitutes a tender, and must be given not later than the fifth business day following arrival at Bonded Public Warehouse stated on the contract.

19

INSURANCE: Seller is responsible for any loss or damage, or both, until Delivery and Discharge of coffee at the Bonded Public Warehouse in the Country of Importation.

All Insurance Risks, costs and responsibility are for Seller's Account until Delivery and Discharge of coffee at the Bonded Public Warehouse in the Country of Importation.

Buyer's insurance responsibility begins from the day of importation or from the day of tender, whichever is later.

FREIGHT: Seller to provide and pay for all transportation and related expenses to the Bonded Public Warehouse in the Country of Importation.

20

EXPORT DUTIES/TAXES: Exporter is to pay all Export taxes, duties or other fees or charges, if any, levied because of exportation.

IMPORT DUTIES/TAXES: Any Duty or Tax whatsoever, imposed by the government or any authority of the Country of Importation, shall be borne by the Importer/Buyer.

21

INSOLVENCY OR FINANCIAL FAILURE OF BUYER OR SELLER: If, at any time before the contract is fully executed, either party hereto shall meet with creditors because of inability generally to make payment of obligations when due, or shall suspend such payments, fail to meet his general trade obligations in the regular course of business, shall file a petition in bankruptcy or, for an arrangement, shall become insolvent, or commit an act of bankruptcy, then the other party may at his option, expressed in writing, declare the aforesaid to constitute a breach and default of this contract, and may, in addition to other remedies, decline to deliver further or make payment or may sell or purchase for the defaulter's account, and may collect damage for any injury or loss, or shall account for the profit, if any, occasioned by such sale or purchase.

This clause is subject to the provisions of (11 USC 365 (e) 1) if invoked.

22

BREACH OR DEFAULT OF CONTRACT: In the event either party hereto fails to perform, or breaches or repudiates this agreement, the other party shall subject to the specific provisions of this contract be entitled to the remedies and relief provided for by the Uniform Commercial Code of the State of New York. The computation and ascertainment of damages, or the determination of any other dispute as to relief, shall be made by the arbitrators in accordance with the Arbitration Clause herein.

Consequential damages shall not, however, be allowed.

23

(Continued)

14 Arbitration is the settling of a dispute by submitting it to a disinterested party (other than a court) that renders a decision. The procedures and costs can be provided for in an arbitration clause or incorporated through other documents. To enforce an award rendered in an arbitration, the winning party can "enter" (submit) the award in a court "of competent jurisdiction." For a general discussion of arbitration and other forms of dispute resolution (other than courts), see Chapter 2.

15 When goods are imported internationally, they must meet certain import requirements before being released to the buyer. Because of this, buyers frequently want a guaranty clause that covers the goods not admitted into the country and that either requires the seller to replace the goods within a stated time or allows the contract for those goods not admitted to be void. See Chapter 17.

16 In the "Claims" clause, the parties agree that the buyer has a certain time within which to reject the goods. The right to reject is a right by law and does not need to be stated in a contract. If the buyer does not exercise the right within the time specified in the contract, the goods will be considered accepted. See Chapter 22.

17 Many international contracts include definitions of terms so that the parties understand what they mean. Some terms are used in a particular industry in a specific way. Here, the word *chop* refers to a unit of like-grade coffee bean. The buyer has a right to inspect ("sample") the coffee. If the coffee does not conform to the contract, the seller must correct the nonconformity. See Chapter 22.

18 The "Delivery," "Insurance," and "Freight" clauses, with the "Arrival" clause on page one of the contract, indicate that this is a destination contract. The seller has the obligation to deliver the goods to the destination, not simply deliver them into the hands of a carrier. Under this contract, the destination is a "Bonded Public Warehouse" in a specific location. The seller bears the risk of loss until the goods are delivered at their destination. Typically, the seller will have bought insurance to cover the risk. See Chapter 21 for a discussion of delivery terms and the risk of loss and Chapter 49 for a general discussion of insurance.

19 Delivery terms are commonly placed in all sales contracts. Such terms determine who pays freight and other costs and, in the absence of an agreement specifying otherwise, who bears the risk of loss. International contracts may use these delivery terms or they may use INCOTERMS, which are published by the International Chamber of Commerce. For example, the INCOTERM DDP (delivered duty paid) requires the seller to arrange shipment, obtain and pay for import or export permits, and get the goods through customs to a named destination.

20 Exported and imported goods are subject to duties, taxes, and other charges imposed by the governments of the countries involved. International contracts spell out who is responsible for these charges.

21 This clause protects a party if the other party should become financially unable to fulfill the obligations under the contract. Thus, if the seller cannot afford to deliver, or the buyer cannot afford to pay, for the stated reasons, the other party can consider the contract breached. This right is subject to "11 USC 365(e)(1)," which refers to a specific provision of the U.S. Bankruptcy Code dealing with executory contracts. Bankruptcy provisions are covered in Chapter 30.

22 In the "Breach or Default of Contract" clause, the parties agreed that the remedies under this contract are the remedies (except for consequential damages) provided by the UCC, as in effect in the state of New York. The amount and "ascertainment" of damages, as well as other disputes about relief, are to be determined by arbitration. Breach of contract and contractual remedies in general are explained in Chapter 22. Arbitration is discussed in Chapter 2.

23 Three clauses frequently included in international contracts (see Chapter 20) are omitted here. There is no choice-of-language clause designating the official language to be used in interpreting the contract terms. There is no choice-of-forum clause designating the place in which disputes will be litigated, except for arbitration (law of New York State). Finally, there is no *force majeure* clause relieving the sellers or buyers from nonperformance due to events beyond their control.

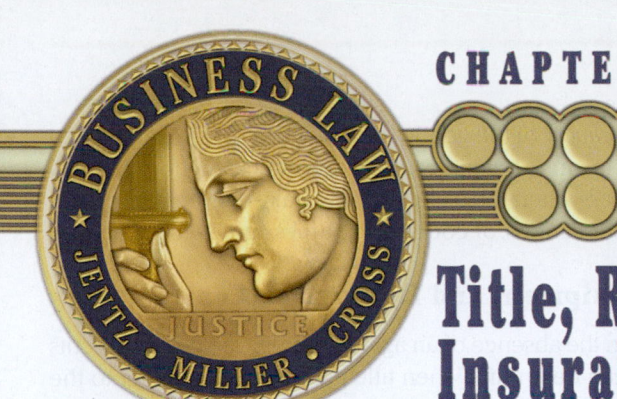

CHAPTER 21

Title, Risk, and Insurable Interest

Before the creation of the Uniform Commercial Code (UCC), *title*—the right of ownership—was the central concept in sales law, controlling all issues of rights and remedies of the parties to a sales contract. There were numerous problems with this concept, however. For example, it was frequently difficult to determine when title actually passed from the seller to the buyer, and therefore it was also difficult to predict which party a court would decide had title at the time of a loss. Because of such problems, the UCC divorced the question of title as completely as possible from the question of the rights and obligations of buyers, sellers, and third parties (such as subsequent purchasers, creditors, or the tax collector).

In some situations, title is still relevant under the UCC, and the UCC has special rules for locating title. These rules will be discussed in the sections that follow. In most situations, however, the UCC has replaced the concept of title with three other concepts: (1) identification, (2) risk of loss, and (3) insurable interest.

In lease contracts, of course, the lessor-owner of the goods retains title. Hence, the UCC's provisions relating to passage of title do not apply to leased goods. Other concepts discussed in this chapter, though, including identification, risk of loss, and insurable interest, relate to lease contracts as well as to sales contracts.

SECTION 1 Identification

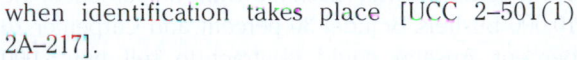

Before any interest in specific goods can pass from the seller or lessor to the buyer or lessee, the goods must be (1) in existence and (2) identified as the specific goods designated in the contract. **Identification** takes place when specific goods are designated as the subject matter of a sales or lease contract. Title and risk of loss cannot pass to the buyer from the seller unless the goods are identified to the contract [UCC 2–105(2)]. (As mentioned, title to leased goods remains with the lessor—or, if the owner is a third party, with that party.) Identification is significant because it gives the buyer or lessee the right to insure (or to have an insurable interest in) the goods and the right to recover from third parties who damage the goods.

Once the goods are in existence, the parties can agree in their contract on when identification will take place. If they do not so specify, the UCC will determine when identification takes place [UCC 2–501(1), 2A–217].

Existing Goods

If the contract calls for the sale or lease of specific and ascertained goods that are already in existence, identification takes place at the time the contract is made. For example, you contract to purchase or lease a fleet of five cars by the vehicle identification numbers of the cars.

Future Goods

If a sale or lease involves unborn animals to be born within twelve months after contracting, identification takes place when the animals are conceived. If a sale involves crops that are to be harvested within twelve months (or the next harvest season occurring after contracting, whichever is longer), identification takes place when the crops are planted; otherwise, identification takes place when the crops begin to grow. In a sale or lease of any other future goods, identification occurs when the goods are shipped, marked, or otherwise designated by the seller or lessor as the goods to which the contract refers.

Goods That Are Part of a Larger Mass

Goods that are part of a larger mass are identified when the goods are marked, shipped, or somehow designated by the seller or lessor as the particular goods to pass under the contract. Suppose that a buyer orders one thousand cases of beans from a lot of ten thousand cases. Until the seller separates the thousand cases of beans from the ten-thousand-case lot, title and risk of loss remain with the seller.

A common exception to this rule deals with fungible goods. **Fungible goods** are goods that are alike naturally, by agreement, or by trade usage. Typical examples are specific grades or types of wheat, oil, and wine, usually stored in large containers. If the owners of these goods hold title as tenants in common (owners having shares undivided from the entire mass jointly owned—see Chapter 47), a seller-owner can pass title and risk of loss to the buyer without actually separating the goods. The buyer replaces the seller as an owner in common [UCC 2–105(4)].

For example, Anselm, Braudel, and Carpenter are farmers. They deposit, respectively, 5,000 bushels, 3,000 bushels, and 2,000 bushels of grain of the same grade and quality in a grain elevator. The three become owners in common, with Anselm owning 50 percent of the 10,000 bushels, Braudel 30 percent, and Carpenter 20 percent. Anselm could contract to sell her 5,000 bushels of grain to Treyton and, because the goods are fungible, pass title and risk of loss to Treyton without physically separating the 5,000 bushels. Treyton now becomes an owner in common with Braudel and Carpenter.

SECTION 2 When Title Passes

Once goods exist and are identified, the provisions of UCC 2–401 apply to the passage of title. Unless the parties explicitly agree,[1] title passes to the buyer at the time and the place the seller performs the *physical delivery* of the goods [UCC 2–401(2)]. For example, if a person is buying cattle at a livestock auction, title will pass when the cattle are physically delivered to him or her (unless, of course, the parties agree otherwise).[2]

Shipment and Destination Contracts

In the absence of an agreement, delivery arrangements can determine when title passes from the seller to the buyer. In a **shipment contract,** the seller is required or authorized to ship goods by carrier, such as a trucking company. Under a shipment contract, the seller is required only to deliver the goods into the hands of a carrier, and title passes to the buyer at the time and place of shipment [UCC 2–401(2)(a)]. *Generally, all contracts are assumed to be shipment contracts if nothing to the contrary is stated in the contract.*

In a **destination contract,** the seller is required to deliver the goods to a particular destination, usually directly to the buyer, but sometimes to another party designated by the buyer. Title passes to the buyer when the goods are *tendered* at that destination [UCC 2–401(2)(b)]. (As you will read in Chapter 22, *tender of delivery* occurs when the seller places or holds conforming goods at the buyer's disposal—with any necessary notice—enabling the buyer to take possession [UCC 2–503(1)].)

Delivery without Movement of the Goods

When a sales contract does not call for the seller to ship or deliver the goods (when the buyer is to pick up the goods), the passage of title depends on whether the seller must deliver a **document of title,** such as a bill of lading or a warehouse receipt, to the buyer. A *bill of lading*[3] is a receipt for goods that is signed by a carrier and serves as a contract for the transportation of the goods. A *warehouse receipt* is a receipt issued by a warehouser for goods stored in a warehouse.

When a document of title is required, title passes to the buyer *when and where the document is delivered.* Thus, if the goods are stored in a warehouse, title passes to the buyer when the appropriate documents are delivered to the buyer. The goods never move. In fact, the buyer can choose to leave the goods at the same warehouse for a period of time, and the buyer's title to those goods will be unaffected.

1. In many sections of the UCC, the phrase "unless otherwise explicitly agreed" appears, meaning that any explicit agreement between the buyer and the seller determines the rights, duties, and liabilities of the parties, including when title passes.

2. See, for example, *In re Stewart,* 274 Bankr. 503 (2002).

3. The term *bill of lading* has been used by international carriers for many years and is derived from *bill,* which historically referred to a schedule of costs for services, and the verb *to lade,* which means to load cargo onto a ship or other form of transportation.

When no document of title is required, and delivery is made without moving the goods, title passes at the time and place the sales contract is made, if the goods have already been identified. If the goods have not been identified, title does not pass until identification occurs. For example, Juan sells lumber to Bodan. They agree that Bodan will pick up the lumber at the yard. If the lumber has been identified (segregated, marked, or in any other way distinguished from all other lumber), title passes to Bodan when the contract is signed. If the lumber is still in large storage bins at the mill, title does not pass to Bodan until the particular pieces of lumber to be sold under this contract are identified [UCC 2–401(3)].

Sales or Leases by Nonowners

Problems occur when persons who acquire goods with imperfect titles attempt to sell or lease them. Sections 2–402 and 2–403 of the UCC deal with the rights of two parties who lay claim to the same goods sold with imperfect titles. Generally, a buyer acquires at least whatever title the seller has to the goods sold.

These same UCC sections also protect lessees. Obviously, a lessee does not acquire whatever title the lessor has to the goods; rather, the lessee acquires a right to possess and use the goods—that is, a *leasehold interest.* A lessee acquires whatever leasehold interest the lessor has or has the power to transfer, subject to the lease contract [UCC 2A–303, 2A–304, 2A–305].

Void Title A buyer may unknowingly purchase goods from a seller who is not the owner of the goods. If the seller is a thief, the seller's title is void—legally, no title exists. Thus, the buyer acquires no title, and the real owner can reclaim the goods from the buyer. If the goods were leased instead, the same result would occur because the lessor would have no leasehold interest to transfer.

For example, if Jin steals goods owned by Maren, Jin has a *void title* to those goods. If Jin sells the goods to Shidra, Maren can reclaim them from Shidra even though Shidra acted in good faith and honestly was not aware that the goods were stolen. (Note that Shidra may file a tort claim against Jin under these circumstances, but here we are only discussing the title to goods.) Article 2A contains similar provisions for leases.

Voidable Title A seller has a *voidable title* if the goods that he or she is selling were obtained by fraud, paid for with a check that is later dishonored, purchased from a minor, or purchased on credit when the seller was *insolvent.* (Under the UCC, a person is **insolvent** when that person ceases to pay "his [or her] debts in the ordinary course of business or cannot pay his [or her] debts as they become due or is insolvent within the meaning of federal bankruptcy law" [UCC 1–201(23)].)

Good Faith Purchasers. In contrast to a seller with void title, a seller with voidable title has the power to transfer good title to a good faith purchaser for value. A **good faith purchaser** is one who buys without knowledge of circumstances that would make a person of ordinary prudence inquire about the validity of the seller's title to the goods. One who purchases *for value* gives legally sufficient consideration (value) for the goods purchased. The real owner normally cannot recover goods from a good faith purchaser for value [UCC 2–403(1)].[4] If the buyer of the goods is not a good faith purchaser for value, then the actual owner of the goods can reclaim them from the buyer (or from the seller, if the goods are still in the seller's possession).

The dispute in the following case arose from the transfer of a car without its document of title to a third party who never suspected that the seller would turn out to be a thief.

4. The real owner could, of course, sue the person who initially obtained voidable title to the goods.

CASE 21.1 Empire Fire and Marine Insurance Co. v. Banc Auto, Inc.

Pennsylvania Superior Court, 2006. 897 A.2d 1247.

• **Background and Facts** In July 2001, Euro Motorcars, an auto dealership in Bethesda, Maryland, agreed to sell a used 2000 Mercedes-Benz S430 for $56,500 to Patrick Figueroa, whose job was to buy and sell cars among dealers. The parties understood that Euro would turn over a document of title to the Mercedes when the price was paid. Banc Auto, Inc., a dealer in Manheim, Pennsylvania, agreed to buy the car from Figueroa for $56,500, plus a percentage of Banc's profit in reselling the vehicle. Banc issued a check to Figueroa. Figueroa cashed the check. Figueroa did not

CASE CONTINUES

CASE 21.1 CONTINUED pay Euro, however, and consequently Euro refused to deliver the document of title. Figueroa was convicted of stealing the check and paid Banc $10,000 in restitution. Empire Fire and Marine Insurance Company, Banc's insurer, filed a suit in a Pennsylvania state court against Banc and Euro, asking the court to determine Empire's obligation to its insured. The court ordered the Mercedes to be sold and awarded Banc the $40,000 in proceeds. Euro appealed to a state intermediate appellate court, asserting that Banc was not entitled to the funds because Euro still possessed the document of title.

• **Decision and Rationale** The state intermediate appellate court held that because Euro had given possession of the Mercedes to Figueroa with the intent of later providing the document of title, Figueroa had obtained voidable title to the car. Because Figueroa had a voidable title when he transferred the car to Banc, Banc was a good faith purchaser and was entitled to the damages awarded. The court affirmed the lower court's ruling in Banc's favor. The state intermediate appellate court pointed out that under UCC 2–401(2), "title passes to the buyer at the time and place at which the seller completes his performance with reference to the physical delivery of the goods * * * even though a document of title is to be delivered at a different time." Under UCC 2–403, "a person with voidable title has power to transfer a good title to a good faith purchaser for value * * * even though * * * the delivery was procured through fraud punishable as larcenous [theft] under the criminal law." Applying these principles to the case, the court concluded that when Euro delivered the Mercedes to Figueroa, he obtained voidable title to the car and was free to sell it to Banc or any other buyer in good faith. The court noted that a person who obtains goods through the assent of the original owner obtains a voidable title, whereas a person who obtains the goods without the original owner's consent has a void title. It was immaterial that Figueroa obtained the car through criminal fraud, because there was no evidence that Banc knew or had any reason to suspect Figueroa of fraud in the transaction.

• **The Ethical Dimension** *Given that Euro Motorcars had had prior dealings with Figueroa on a number of occasions and did not suspect that Figueroa would commit theft, was the result in this case fair? Why or why not?*

• **The E-Commerce Dimension** *If automobile title documents were available online, would that have helped Euro to avoid loss in this situation? What problems might arise from the online availability of title documents?*

Voidable Title and Leases. The same rules apply in situations involving leases. A lessor with voidable title has the power to transfer a valid leasehold interest to a good faith lessee for value. The real owner cannot recover the goods, except as permitted by the terms of the lease. The real owner can, however, receive all proceeds arising from the lease, as well as a transfer of all rights, title, and interest as the lessor under the lease, including the lessor's interest in the return of the goods when the lease expires [UCC 2A–305(1)].

The Entrustment Rule According to UCC 2–403(2), entrusting goods to a merchant *who deals in goods of that kind* gives the merchant the power to transfer all rights to *a buyer in the ordinary course of business.* This is known as the **entrustment rule.** A buyer in the ordinary course of business is a person who—in good faith and without knowledge that the sale violates the rights of another party—buys goods in the ordinary course from a merchant (other than a pawnbroker) in the business of selling goods of that kind [UCC 1–201(9)].

In Sales Contracts. The entrustment rule basically allows innocent buyers to obtain legitimate title to goods purchased from merchants even if the merchants do not have good title. Consider an example. Jan leaves her watch with a jeweler to be repaired. The jeweler sells both new and used watches. The jeweler sells Jan's watch to Kim, a customer who does not know that the jeweler has no right to sell it. Kim, as a good faith buyer, gets good title against Jan's claim of ownership.[5]

5. Jan, of course, can sue the jeweler for the tort of conversion (or trespass to personal property) to obtain damages equivalent to the cash value of the watch (see Chapter 6).

Note, however, that Kim obtains only those rights held by the person entrusting the goods (here, Jan). Suppose instead that Jan had stolen the watch from Greg and then left it with the jeweler to be repaired. The jeweler then sold it to Kim. Kim would obtain good title against Jan, who entrusted the watch to the jeweler, but not against Greg (the real owner), who neither entrusted the watch to Jan nor authorized Jan to entrust it.

Red Elvis, an artwork by Andy Warhol, was at the center of the dispute over title in the following case.

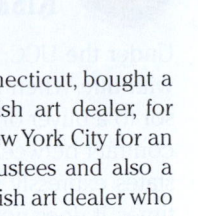

CASE 21.2 Lindholm v. Brant

Supreme Court of Connecticut, 2007. 283 Conn. 65, 925 A.2d 1048.

- **Background and Facts** In 1987, Kerstin Lindholm of Greenwich, Connecticut, bought a silkscreen by Andy Warhol titled *Red Elvis* from Anders Malmberg, a Swedish art dealer, for $300,000. In 1998, Lindholm loaned *Red Elvis* to the Guggenheim Museum in New York City for an exhibition to tour Europe. Peter Brant, who was on the museum's board of trustees and also a Greenwich resident, believed that Lindholm was the owner. Stellan Holm, a Swedish art dealer who had bought and sold other Warhol works with Brant, told him, however, that Malmberg had bought it and would sell it for $2.9 million. Malmberg refused Brant's request to provide a copy of an invoice between Lindholm and himself on the ground that such documents normally and customarily are not disclosed in art deals. To determine whether Malmberg had good title, Brant hired an attorney to search the Art Loss Register (an international database of stolen and missing artworks) and other sources. No problems were found, but Brant was cautioned that this provided only "minimal assurances." Brant's attorney drafted a formal contract, which conditioned payment on the delivery of *Red Elvis* to a warehouse in Denmark. The exchange took place in April 2000.[a] Lindholm filed a suit in a Connecticut state court against Brant, alleging conversion, among other things. The court issued a judgment in Brant's favor. Lindholm appealed to the Connecticut Supreme Court.

- **Decision and Rationale** The Connecticut Supreme Court affirmed the judgment of the lower court. The appellate court pointed out that "a person buys goods in good faith if there is honesty in fact and the observance of reasonable commercial standards of fair dealing in the conduct or transaction concerned." In most art transactions, the buyer has no reason for concern about the seller's ability to convey good title; such transactions are completed by a handshake and an invoice exchange. Sophisticated buyers and sellers normally do not obtain signed invoices from the original seller to the dealer prior to a transaction. "Nor is it an ordinary or customary practice to request the underlying invoice corroborating [substantiating] information as to a dealer's authority to convey title." In sum, it is customary to rely on representations made by "respected dealers regarding their authority to sell works of art." The state supreme court concluded that "on the basis of all the circumstances surrounding this sale," Brant was a buyer in the ordinary course of business and therefore took all rights to *Red Elvis* under UCC 2–403(2).

- **The Ethical Dimension** *How did the "usual and customary" methods of dealing in the art business help Malmberg deceive the other parties in this case? What additional steps might those parties have taken to thwart this deceit?*

- **The Global Dimension** *Considering the international locales in this case, why was Lindholm able to bring an action against Brant in Connecticut?*

a. Unaware of this deal, Lindholm accepted a Japanese buyer's offer of $4.6 million for *Red Elvis.* The funds were wired to Malmberg, who kept them. Lindholm filed a criminal complaint against Malmberg in Sweden. In 2003, a Swedish court convicted Malmberg of "gross fraud embezzlement." The court awarded Lindholm $4.6 million and other relief.

In Lease Contracts. Article 2A provides a similar rule for leased goods. If a lessor entrusts goods to a lessee-merchant who deals in goods of that kind, and the merchant transfers the goods to a buyer or sublessee in the ordinary course of business, the buyer or sublessee acquires all of the rights that the lessor had in the goods [UCC 2A–305(2)].[6]

SECTION 3

Risk of Loss

Under the UCC, risk of loss does not necessarily pass with title. When risk of loss passes from a seller or lessor to a buyer or lessee is generally determined by the contract between the parties. Sometimes, the contract states expressly when the risk of loss passes. At other times, it does not, and a court must interpret the existing terms to ascertain whether the risk has passed. When no provision in the contract indicates when risk passes, the UCC provides special rules, based on delivery terms, to guide the courts.

Delivery with Movement of the Goods

When the agreement does not specify when risk passes, the following rules apply in situations involving movement of the goods (so-called *carrier cases*).

6. This rule is consistent with the common law of *bailments* (see Chapter 47). For an illustration of the entrustment rule in lease contracts, see *Bank One, N.A. v. Americani,* 271 Ga.App. 483, 610 S.E.2d 103 (2005). (The initials *N.A.* stand for National Association.)

Contract Terms Specific delivery terms in the contract can help determine when risk of loss passes to the buyer. These terms relate generally to the determination of which party will bear the costs of delivery, as well as which party will bear the risk of loss. The terms that have traditionally been used in contracts are listed and defined in Exhibit 21–1. *Unless the parties agree otherwise,* these terms will determine which party will pay the costs of delivering the goods and who will bear the risk of loss.

Shipment Contracts In a shipment contract, if the seller or lessor is required or authorized to ship goods by carrier (but is not required to deliver them to a particular destination), risk of loss passes to the buyer or lessee when the goods are duly delivered to the carrier [UCC 2–509(1)(a), 2A–219(2)(a)].

For example, a seller in Texas sells five hundred cases of grapefruit to a buyer in New York, F.O.B. Houston (free on board in Houston, which means that the buyer pays the transportation charges from Houston—see Exhibit 21–1). The contract authorizes shipment by carrier; it does not require that the seller tender the grapefruit in New York. Risk passes to the buyer when conforming goods are properly placed in the possession of the carrier. If the goods are damaged in transit, the loss is the buyer's. (Actually, buyers have recourse against carriers, subject to certain limitations, and they may insure the goods from the time the goods leave the seller.)

The following case illustrates how the application of a contract's delivery term can affect a buyer's recovery for goods damaged in transit.

EXHIBIT 21–1 • Contract Terms—Definitions

The contract terms listed and defined in this exhibit help to determine which party will bear the costs of delivery and when risk of loss will pass from the seller to the buyer.

F.O.B. (free on board)—Indicates that the selling price of goods includes transportation costs to the specific F.O.B. place named in the contract. The seller pays the expenses and carries the risk of loss to the F.O.B. place named [UCC 2–319(1)]. If the named place is the place from which the goods are shipped (for example, the seller's city or place of business), the contract is a shipment contract. If the named place is the place to which the goods are to be shipped (for example, the buyer's city or place of business), the contract is a destination contract.

F.A.S. (free alongside)—Requires that the seller, at his or her own expense and risk, deliver the goods alongside the carrier before risk passes to the buyer [UCC 2–319(2)].

C.I.F. or **C.&F.** (cost, insurance, and freight or just cost and freight)—Requires, among other things, that the seller "put the goods in possession of a carrier" before risk passes to the buyer [UCC 2–320(2)]. (These are basically pricing terms, and the contracts remain shipment contracts, not destination contracts.)

Delivery ex-ship (delivery from the carrying vessel)—Means that risk of loss does not pass to the buyer until the goods are properly unloaded from the ship or other carrier [UCC 2–322].

CASE 21.3 Spray-Tek, Inc. v. Robbins Motor Transportation, Inc.

United States District Court, Western District of Wisconsin, 2006. 426 F.Supp.2d 875.

• **Background and Facts** Spray-Tek, Inc., is engaged in the business of commercial dehydration of food-flavoring, pharmaceutical, and chemical products. In 2003, Spray-Tek contracted with Niro, Inc., for the design and manufacture of a customized dryer for $1,161,500. Niro agreed to ship the dryer "F.O.B. points of manufacture in the U.S.A." from its facility in Hudson, Wisconsin, to Spray-Tek's facility in Bethlehem, Pennsylvania. Niro arranged for Robbins Motor Transportation, Inc., to pick up the dryer on October 18, 2004. Robbins acknowledged in the bill of lading that it received the dryer "in apparent good order." On October 28, while in transit through Baltimore, Maryland, the dryer struck an overpass and fell off Robbins's truck. It was declared a total loss. Niro made a replacement, delivered it, and billed Spray-Tek an additional $233,100. Spray-Tek filed a suit in a federal district court against Robbins Motor under a federal statute known as the "Carmack Amendment"[a] to recover the replacement cost and other expenses. A plaintiff must show three elements to recover under the Carmack Amendment: (1) delivery of goods to a carrier in good condition, (2) their arrival in damaged condition, and (3) proof of the amount of damages. Spray-Tek filed a motion for summary judgment. Robbins argued, in part, that Spray-Tek was not entitled to recovery because it did not own the dryer during its transport.

• **Decision and Rationale** The court issued a summary judgment in Spray-Tek's favor on the question of when the dryer became the buyer's property. "The drying chamber became plaintiff's property once it was placed on board the delivery truck at its point of manufacture in Hudson, Wisconsin." The court concluded, however, that other issues, including a possible contractual limitation on the amount of damages, involved genuine questions of material fact to be resolved at trial. The court determined that there was no dispute as to the first and second elements required for recovery under the Carmack Amendment: the dryer was delivered in good condition to Robbins, and on its "arrival," it was damaged. The question was whether, at the time the damage occurred, the title and the risk of loss had passed to Spray-Tek. The court held that the contract between Spray-Tek and Niro established Spray-Tek as the owner of the dryer when it was damaged. One clause in the contract provided that Spray-Tek would bear the risk of loss of the dryer after its delivery to the shipping point if delivery "F.O.B. shipping point" was specified. Another of the contract's terms of sale specified "F.O.B. points of manufacture in the U.S.A." Thus, "here the shipping point and the manufacturing point were identical. Accordingly, the F.O.B. points of manufacture language contained within plaintiff's contract demonstrates that plaintiff bore the risk of loss once the drying chamber departed from Niro's Hudson, Wisconsin facility." Although Robbins argued that Spray-Tek had not satisfied the third element, failing to show what "it is obligated to pay for the dryer," the court pointed out that Niro's invoice for the replacement dryer established the amount of damages.

• **What If the Facts Were Different?** *Would the result have been different if the contract between Spray-Tek and Niro had specified "F.O.B. Bethlehem, Pennsylvania"? Explain.*

• **The Legal Environment Dimension** *One of the elements required to establish a carrier's liability is to show that the goods arrived in damaged condition. Should Robbins Motor Transportation have been absolved of liability in this case on the ground that the drying chamber never arrived at its final destination? Why or why not?*

a. The Carmack Amendment is part of the Interstate Commerce Act and can be found at 49 U.S.C. Section 14706. Its purpose is to remove some of the uncertainty surrounding a carrier's liability when an interstate shipment of goods is damaged.

Destination Contracts In a destination contract, the risk of loss passes to the buyer or lessee when the goods are tendered to the buyer or lessee at the specified destination [UCC 2–509(1)(b), 2A–219(2)(b)]. In the preceding example involving cases of grapefruit, if the contract had been a destination contract, F.O.B. New York (see Exhibit 21–1), risk of loss during transit to New York would have been the seller's. Risk of loss would not have passed to the buyer until the carrier tendered the goods to the buyer in New York.

Whether a contract is a shipment contract or a destination contract can have significant consequences for the parties. When an agreement is ambiguous as to whether it is a shipment or a destination contract, courts will presume that it is a shipment contract. The parties must use clear and explicit language to overcome this presumption and create a destination contract.

Whether a contract is a shipment contract or a destination contract can have significant consequences for the parties if the goods are damaged in transit. When the terms of an agreement are ambiguous, under the UCC there is a strong presumption favoring shipment contracts. To overcome this presumption, the parties must have explicitly agreed to terms satisfying the requirements of a destination contract. Because of this presumption, businesspersons should always clearly state that they are forming a destination contract when that is what they desire. In fact, it is advisable to state explicitly whether a contract is a shipment or destination contract, and which party will bear the risk of loss.

Managers should avoid leaving the determination up to the default rules in the UCC. By drafting their contract carefully at the outset, the parties can avert future costly legal disputes if a shipment of goods is damaged—particularly when the contract involves more than one shipment of goods.

Delivery without Movement of the Goods

In many contracts, the seller or lessor is not required to ship or deliver the goods to a particular destination. Frequently, the buyer or lessee is to pick up the goods from the seller or lessor, or the goods are to be held by a bailee. A *bailment* is a temporary delivery of personal property, without passage of title, into the care of another, called a *bailee*. Under the UCC, a bailee is a party who—by a bill of lading, warehouse receipt, or other document of title—acknowledges possession of goods and/or contracts to deliver them. A warehousing company, for example, or a trucking company that normally issues documents of title for the goods it receives is a bailee.[7]

Goods Held by the Seller If the goods are held by the seller, a document of title usually is not used. If the seller is not a merchant, the risk of loss to goods held by the seller passes to the buyer on *tender of delivery* [UCC 2–509(3)]. If the seller is a merchant, risk of loss to goods held by the seller passes to the buyer when the buyer *actually takes physical possession of the goods* [UCC 2–509(3)]. For example, Henry Ganno purchases lumber at a lumberyard, and an employee at the lumberyard loads it onto Ganno's truck with a forklift. Once the truck is loaded, the risk of loss passes to Ganno because he has taken physical possession of the goods. In the event that Ganno suffers a loss driving away from the lumberyard, he—not the lumberyard—will bear the burden of that loss.[8]

In respect to leases, the risk of loss passes to the lessee on the lessee's receipt of the goods if the lessor—or supplier, in a finance lease (see Chapter 20)—is a merchant. Otherwise, the risk passes to the lessee on tender of delivery [UCC 2A–219(2)(c)]. For example, Erikson Crane leases a helicopter from Jevis, Ltd., which is in the business of renting aircraft. While Erikson's pilot is on the way to Idaho to pick up the particular helicopter, the helicopter is damaged during an unexpected storm. In this situation, Jevis is a merchant-lessor, so it would bear the risk of loss to the leased helicopter until Erikson took possession of the helicopter.

Goods Held by a Bailee When a bailee is holding goods that are to be delivered under a contract without being moved, the goods are usually represented by a negotiable or nonnegotiable document of title (a bill of lading or a warehouse receipt).[9] Risk of loss passes to the buyer when (1) the buyer receives a negotiable document of title for the goods, (2) the bailee acknowledges the buyer's right to possess the goods, or (3) the buyer receives a nonnegotiable document of title or a writing (record) directing the bailee to hand over the goods *and* the buyer has had a *reasonable time* to present the document to the bailee and demand the goods. Obviously, if the bailee refuses to honor the document, the risk of loss remains with the seller [UCC 2–503(4)(b), 2–509(2)].

With respect to leases, if goods held by a bailee are to be delivered without being moved, the risk of loss passes to the lessee on acknowledgment by the bailee of the lessee's right to possession of the goods [UCC 2A–219(2)(b)]. (*Concept Summary 21.1* reviews the rules for when title and risk of loss pass to the buyer or

7. See Chapter 47 for a detailed discussion of the law of bailments.

8. *Ganno v. Lanoga Corp.*, 119 Wash.App. 310, 80 P.3d 180 (2003).

9. A negotiable document of title actually stands for the goods it covers, so any transfer of the goods requires the surrender of the document. In contrast, a nonnegotiable document of title merely serves as evidence of the goods' existence.

CONCEPT SUMMARY 21.1
Delivery without Movement of the Goods

Concept	Description
GOODS NOT REPRESENTED BY A DOCUMENT OF TITLE	Unless otherwise agreed, if the goods are not represented by a document of title, title and risk pass as follows: 1. Title passes on the formation of the contract [UCC 2–401(3)(b)]. 2. Risk of loss passes to the buyer or lessee: a. If the seller or lessor is a merchant, risk passes on the buyer's or lessee's *receipt of the goods.* b. If the seller or lessor is a nonmerchant, risk passes to the buyer or lessee on the seller's or lessor's *tender* of delivery of the goods [UCC 2–509(3), 2A–219(2)(c)].
GOODS REPRESENTED BY A DOCUMENT OF TITLE	Unless otherwise agreed, if the goods are represented by a document of title, title and risk pass to the buyer when: 1. The buyer receives a negotiable document of title for the goods, or 2. The bailee acknowledges the buyer's right to possess the goods, or 3. The buyer receives a nonnegotiable document of title or a writing (record) directing the bailee to hand over the goods and the buyer has had a reasonable time to present the document to the bailee and demand the goods [UCC 2–503(4)(b), 2–509(2)].
LEASED GOODS HELD BY A BAILEE	If leased goods held by a bailee are to be delivered without being moved, the risk of loss passes to the lessee on acknowledgment by the bailee of the lessee's right to possession of the goods [UCC 2A–219(2)(b)].

lessee when the seller or lessor is not required to ship or deliver the goods.)

Conditional Sales

Buyers and sellers can form sales contracts that are conditioned either on the buyer's approval of the goods or on the buyer's resale of the goods. Under such contracts, the buyer is in possession of the goods, and disputes sometimes arise as to which party should bear the loss if, for example, the goods are damaged or stolen.

Sale or Return A **sale or return** is a type of contract by which the buyer (usually a merchant) purchases goods primarily for resale, but has the right to return part or all of the goods (undo the sale) in lieu of payment if the goods fail to be resold. Basically, a sale or return is a sale of goods in the present, which may be undone at the buyer's option within a specified time period. When the buyer receives possession at the time of the sale, title and risk of loss pass to the buyer. Title and risk of loss remain with the buyer until the buyer returns the goods to the seller within the time period specified. If the buyer fails to return the goods within this time period, the sale is finalized. The return of the goods is made at the buyer's risk and expense. Goods held under a sale-or-return contract are subject to the claims of the buyer's creditors while they are in the buyer's possession.

The UCC treats a **consignment** as a sale or return. Under a consignment, the owner of goods (the *consignor*) delivers them to another (the *consignee*) to be sold or kept. If the consignee sells the goods, the consignee must pay the consignor for them. If the consignee does not sell or keep the goods, they may simply be returned to the consignor. While the goods are in the possession of the consignee, the consignee holds title to them, and creditors of the consignee will prevail over the consignor in any action to repossess the goods [UCC 2–326(2)].

Sale on Approval When a seller offers to sell goods to a buyer and sends the goods to the buyer on a trial basis, a **sale on approval** is made. Essentially, the seller in such contracts delivers the goods primarily so that the prospective buyer (usually not a merchant) can use the goods and be convinced of their appearance or performance. The term *sale* here is misleading, however, because only an *offer* to sell has been made, along with a bailment created by the buyer's possession.

Therefore, title and risk of loss (from causes beyond the buyer's control) remain with the seller until the buyer accepts (approves) the offer. Acceptance can be made expressly, by any act inconsistent with the *trial* purpose or the seller's ownership, or by the buyer's election not to return the goods within the trial period. If the buyer does not wish to accept, the buyer may notify the seller of that fact within the trial period, and the return is made at the seller's expense and risk [UCC 2–327(1)]. Goods held on approval are not subject to the claims of the buyer's creditors until acceptance.

Risk of Loss When a Sales or Lease Contract Is Breached

A sales or lease contract can be breached in many ways, and the transfer of risk operates differently depending on which party breaches. Generally, the party in breach bears the risk of loss.

When the Seller or Lessor Breaches If the goods are so nonconforming that the buyer has the right to reject them, the risk of loss does not pass to the buyer until the defects are *cured* (that is, until the goods are repaired, replaced, or discounted in price by the seller—see Chapter 22) or until the buyer accepts the goods in spite of their defects (thus waiving the right to reject). For example, a buyer orders blue file cabinets from a seller, F.O.B. seller's plant. The seller ships black file cabinets instead. The black cabinets (nonconforming goods) are damaged in transit. The risk of loss falls on the seller. Had the seller shipped blue cabinets (conforming goods) instead, the risk would have fallen on the buyer [UCC 2–510(1)].

If a buyer accepts a shipment of goods and later discovers a defect, acceptance can be revoked. The revocation allows the buyer to pass the risk of loss back to the seller, at least to the extent that the buyer's insurance does not cover the loss [UCC 2–510(2)].

In regard to leases, Article 2A states a similar rule. If the tender or delivery of goods is so nonconforming that the lessee has the right to reject them, the risk of loss remains with the lessor (or the supplier) until cure or acceptance [UCC 2A–220(1)(a)]. If the lessee, after acceptance, rightfully revokes her or his acceptance of the goods, the risk of loss passes back to the lessor or supplier to the extent that the lessee's insurance does not cover the loss [UCC 2A–220(1)(b)].

When the Buyer or Lessee Breaches The general rule is that when a buyer or lessee breaches a contract, the risk of loss *immediately* shifts to the buyer or lessee. This rule has three important limitations [UCC 2–510(3), 2A–220(2)]:

1. The seller or lessor must already have identified the contract goods.
2. The buyer or lessee bears the risk for only a *commercially reasonable time* after the seller or lessor has learned of the breach.
3. The buyer or lessee is liable only to the extent of any deficiency in the seller's or lessor's insurance coverage.

(See *Concept Summary 21.2* for a summary of the rules on who bears the risk of loss when a contract is breached.)

SECTION 4 Insurable Interest

Parties to sales and lease contracts often obtain insurance coverage to protect against damage, loss, or destruction of goods. Any party purchasing insurance, however, must have a sufficient interest in the insured item to obtain a valid policy. Insurance laws—not the UCC—determine sufficiency. The UCC is helpful, however, because it contains certain rules regarding insurable interests in goods.

Insurable Interest of the Buyer or Lessee

A buyer or lessee has an **insurable interest** in identified goods. The moment the contract goods are *identified* by the seller or lessor, the buyer or lessee has a special property interest that allows the buyer or lessee to obtain necessary insurance coverage for those goods even before the risk of loss has passed [UCC 2–501(1), 2A–218(1)]. Identification can be made at any time and in any manner agreed to by the parties. If the parties do not explicitly agree on identification, then the UCC provisions apply.

For example, in March a farmer sells a cotton crop that she hopes to harvest in October. If the contract does not specify otherwise, the buyer acquires an

CONCEPT SUMMARY 21.2
Risk of Loss When a Sales or Lease Contract Is Breached

Concept	Description
When the Seller or Lessor Breaches the Contract	If the seller or lessor breaches by tendering nonconforming goods that the buyer or lessee has a right to reject, the risk of loss does not pass to the buyer or lessee until the defects are cured or the buyer accepts the goods (thus waiving the right to reject) [UCC 2–510(1), 2A–220(1)].
When the Buyer or Lessee Breaches the Contract	If the buyer or lessee breaches the contract, the risk of loss to identified goods immediately shifts to the buyer or lessee. Limitations to this rule are as follows [UCC 2–510(3), 2A–220(2)]: 1. The seller or lessor must already have identified the contract goods. 2. The buyer or lessee bears the risk for only a commercially reasonable time after the seller or lessor has learned of the breach. 3. The buyer or lessee is liable only to the extent of any deficiency in the seller's or lessor's insurance coverage.

insurable interest in the crop when it is planted because the goods (the cotton crop) are identified to the sales contract. The rule stated in UCC 2–501(1)(c) is that the buyer obtains an insurable interest in crops when the crops are planted or otherwise become growing crops, provided that the crops will "be harvested within twelve months or the next normal harvest season after contracting, whichever is longer."

Insurable Interest of the Seller or Lessor

A seller has an insurable interest in goods as long as he or she retains title to the goods. Even after title passes to a buyer, a seller who has a security interest in the goods (a right to secure payment—see Chapter 29) still has an insurable interest and can insure the goods [UCC 2–501(2)]. Thus, both the buyer and the seller can have an insurable interest in identical goods at the same time. Of course, the buyer or seller must sustain an actual loss to have the right to recover from an insurance company. In regard to leases, the lessor retains an insurable interest in leased goods unless the lessee exercises an option to buy, in which event the risk of loss passes to the lessee [UCC 2A–218(3)].

PREVENTING LEGAL DISPUTES

As just explained, a seller who has a security interest in goods can still insure those goods, even though title has passed to the buyer. In today's business world, sellers frequently retain a security interest in goods because the buyer has not yet paid for the goods at the time of delivery. A business that sells and ships goods should usually maintain adequate insurance on all goods sold at least until it is assured that the buyer will pay for the goods. Losses can still occur after the goods have been delivered to the buyer. Sellers should not assume that the buyer's insurance will pay for losses the seller sustains. Insurance is essential to protect against loss.

REVIEWING Title, Risk, and Insurable Interest

In December, Mendoza agreed to buy the broccoli grown on one hundred acres of Willow Glen's one-thousand-acre broccoli farm. The sales contract specified F.O.B. Willow

REVIEWING CONTINUES

REVIEWING Title, Risk, and Insurable Interest, Continued

Glen's field by Falcon Trucking. The broccoli was to be planted in February and harvested in March of the following year. Using the information presented in the chapter, answer the following questions.

1. At what point is a crop of broccoli identified to the contract under the Uniform Commercial Code (UCC)? Explain. Why is identification significant?
2. When does title to the broccoli pass from Willow Glen to Mendoza under the terms of this contract? Why?
3. Suppose that while in transit, Falcon's truck overturns and spills the entire load. Who bears the loss, Mendoza or Willow Glen?
4. Suppose that instead of buying fresh broccoli, Mendoza had contracted with Willow Glen to purchase one thousand cases of frozen broccoli from Willow Glen's processing plant. The highest grade of broccoli is packaged under the "FreshBest" label, and everything else is packaged under the "FamilyPac" label. Further suppose that although the contract specified that Mendoza was to receive FreshBest broccoli, Falcon Trucking delivered FamilyPac broccoli to Mendoza. If Mendoza refuses to accept the broccoli, who bears the loss?

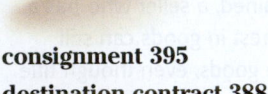

TERMS AND CONCEPTS

consignment 395
destination contract 388
document of title 388
entrustment rule 390
fungible goods 388
good faith purchaser 389
identification 387
insolvent 389
insurable interest 396
sale on approval 395
sale or return 395
shipment contract 388

QUESTIONS AND CASE PROBLEMS

21-1. Mackey orders from Pride one thousand cases of Greenie brand peas from lot A at list price to be shipped F.O.B. Pride's city via Fast Freight Lines. Pride receives the order and immediately sends Mackey an acceptance of the order with a promise to ship promptly. Pride later separates the one thousand cases of Greenie peas and prints Mackey's name and address on each case. The peas are placed on Pride's dock, and Fast Freight is notified to pick up the shipment. The night before the pickup by Fast Freight, through no fault of Pride's, a fire destroys the one thousand cases of peas. Pride claims that title passed to Mackey at the time the contract was made and that risk of loss passed to Mackey when the goods were marked with Mackey's name and address. Discuss Pride's contentions.

21-2. QUESTION WITH SAMPLE ANSWER

On May 1, Sikora goes into Carson's retail clothing store to purchase a suit. Sikora finds a suit he likes for $190 and buys it. The suit needs alterations. Sikora is to pick up the altered suit at Carson's store on May 10. Consider the following separate sets of circumstances:

(a) One of Carson's major creditors obtains a judgment on the debt Carson owes and has the court issue a writ of execution (a court order to seize a debtor's property to satisfy a debt) to collect on that judgment all clothing in Carson's possession. Discuss Sikora's rights in the suit under these circumstances.

(b) On May 9, through no fault of Carson's, the store burns down, and all contents are a total loss. Between Carson and Sikora, who suffers the loss of the suit destroyed by the fire? Explain.

• **For a sample answer to Question 21-2, go to Appendix I at the end of this text.**

21-3. Zeke, who sells lawn mowers, tells Stasio, a regular customer, about a special promotional campaign. On receipt of a $50 down payment, Zeke will sell Stasio a new Universal lawn mower for $200, even though it normally sells for $350. Zeke further tells Stasio that if Stasio does not like the performance of the lawn mower, he can return it within thirty days, and Zeke will refund the $50 down payment. Stasio pays the $50 and takes the mower. On the tenth day, the lawn mower is stolen through no fault of Stasio's. Stasio calls Zeke and demands the return of his $50. Zeke claims that Stasio should suffer the risk of loss and that he still owes Zeke the remainder of the purchase price, $150. Discuss who is correct, Stasio or Zeke.

21–4. Risk of Loss. H.S.A. II, Inc., made parts for motor vehicles. Under an agreement with Ford Motor Co., Ford provided steel to H.S.A. to make Ford parts. Ford's purchase orders for the parts contained the term "FOB Carrier Supplier's [Plant]." GMAC Business Credit, L.L.C., loaned money to H.S.A. under terms that guaranteed payment would be made—if the funds were not otherwise available—from H.S.A.'s inventory, raw materials, and finished goods. H.S.A. filed for bankruptcy on February 2, 2000, and ceased operations on June 20, when it had in its plant more than $1 million in finished goods for Ford. Ford sent six trucks to H.S.A. to pick up the goods. GMAC halted the removal. The parties asked the bankruptcy court to determine whose interest had priority. GMAC contended, among other things, that Ford did not have an interest in the goods because there had not yet been a sale. Ford responded that under its purchase orders, title and risk of loss transferred on completion of the parts. In whose favor should the court rule, and why? [*In re H.S.A. II, Inc.*, 271 Bankr. 534 (E.D.Mich. 2002)]

21–5. Conditional Sales. Corvette Collection of Boston, Inc. (CCB), was a used-Corvette dealership located (despite its name) in Pompano Beach, Florida. In addition to selling used Corvettes, CCB serviced Corvettes and sold Corvette parts. CCB owned some of its inventory and held the rest on consignment, although there were no signs indicating the consignments. In November 2001, CCB filed a petition for bankruptcy in a federal district court. At the time, CCB possessed six Corvettes that were consigned by Chester Finley and The Corvette Experience, Inc. (TCE), neither of which had a security interest in the goods. Robert Furr, on CCB's behalf, asked the court to declare that CCB held the goods under a contract for a sale or return. Finley and TCE asserted that the goods were held under a contract for a sale on approval. What difference does it make? Under what circumstances would the court rule in favor of Finley and TCE? How should the court rule under the facts as stated? Why? [*In re Corvette Collection of Boston, Inc.*, 294 Bankr. 409 (S.D.Fla. 2003)]

21–6. CASE PROBLEM WITH SAMPLE ANSWER

William Bisby gave an all-terrain vehicle (ATV) to Del City Cycle in Enid, Oklahoma, to sell on his behalf. Joseph Maddox bought the ATV but paid for it with a check written on a closed checking account. The bank refused to honor the check. Before Del City or Bisby could reclaim the ATV, however, Maddox sold it to Aaron Jordan, who sold it to Shannon Skaggs. In November 2003, the Enid Police Department seized the ATV from Skaggs. Bisby filed a suit in an Oklahoma state court against the state and Skaggs, claiming that he was the owner of the ATV and asking the court to return it to him. Skaggs objected. Is there a distinction between the ownership interests of a party who steals an item and those of a party who acquires the item with a check that is not paid? What was the status of Skaggs's title, if any, to the ATV? Among the many parties involved in this case, which one should the court rule is the owner of "good" title to the ATV? Why? [*State v. Skaggs*, 140 P.3d 576 (Okla.Civ.App. Div. 3 2006)]

- **To view a sample answer for Problem 21–6, go to this book's Web site at www.cengage.com/blaw/jentz, select "Chapter 21," and click on "Case Problem with Sample Answer."**

21–7. Shipment and Destination Contracts. In 2003, Karen Pearson and Steve and Tara Carlson agreed to buy a 2004 Dynasty recreational vehicle (RV) from DeMartini's RV Sales in Grass Valley, California. On September 29, Pearson, the Carlsons, and DeMartini's signed a contract providing that "seller agrees to deliver the vehicle to you on the date this contract is signed." The buyers made a payment of $145,000 on the total price of $356,416 the next day, when they also signed a form acknowledging that the RV had been inspected and accepted. They agreed to return later to have the RV transported out of state for delivery (to avoid paying state sales tax on the purchase). On October 7, Steve Carlson returned to DeMartini's to ride with the seller's driver to Nevada to consummate the out-of-state delivery. When the RV developed problems, Pearson and the Carlsons filed a suit in a federal district court against the RV's manufacturer, Monaco Coach Corp., alleging, in part, breach of warranty under state law. The applicable statute is expressly limited to goods sold in California. Monaco argued that this RV had been sold in Nevada. How does the Uniform Commercial Code (UCC) define a sale? What does the UCC provide with respect to the passage of title? How do these provisions apply here? Discuss. [*Carlson v. Monaco Coach Corp.*, 486 F.Supp.2d 1127 (E.D.Cal. 2007)]

21–8. A QUESTION OF ETHICS

Kenneth West agreed to sell his car, a 1975 Corvette, to a man representing himself as Robert Wilson. In exchange for a cashier's check, West signed over the Corvette's title to Wilson and gave him the car. Ten days later, when West learned that the cashier's check was a forgery, he filed a stolen vehicle report with the police. The police could not immediately locate Wilson or the Corvette, however, and the case grew cold. Nearly two and a half years later, the police found the Corvette in the possession of Tammy Roberts, who also had the certificate of title. She said that she had bought the car from her brother, who had obtained it through an ad in the newspaper. West filed a suit *in a Colorado state court against Roberts to reclaim the car. The court applied Colorado Revised Statutes Section 4-2-403 (Colorado's version of UCC 2–403) to determine the vehicle's rightful owner. [*West v. Roberts, *143 P.3d 1037 (Colo. 2006)]*

(a) Under UCC 2–403, what title, if any, to the Corvette did "Wilson" acquire? What was the status of Roberts's title, if any, assuming that she bought the car without knowledge of circumstances that would make a person of ordinary prudence inquire about the validity of the seller's title? In whose favor should the court rule? Explain.

(b) If the original owner of a vehicle relinquishes it due to fraud, should he or she be allowed to recover the vehicle from a good faith purchaser? If not, which party or parties might the original owner sue for recovery? What is the ethical principle underlying your answer to these questions? Discuss.

21–9. VIDEO QUESTION

Go to this text's Web site at **www.cengage.com/blaw/jentz** and select "Chapter 21." Click on "Video Questions" and view the video titled *Risk of Loss.* Then answer the following questions.

(a) Does Oscar have a right to refuse the shipment because the lettuce is wilted? Why or why not? What type of contract is involved in this video?

(b) Does Oscar have a right to refuse the shipment because the lettuce is not organic butter crunch lettuce? Why or why not?

(c) Assume that you are in Oscar's position—that is, you are buying produce for a supermarket. What different approaches might you take to avoid having to pay for a delivery of wilted produce?

LAW ON THE WEB

For updated links to resources available on the Web, as well as a variety of other materials, visit this text's Web site at

www.cengage.com/blaw/jentz

To find information on the UCC, including the UCC provisions discussed in this chapter, refer to the Web sites listed in the *Law on the Web* feature in Chapter 20.

For more information on shipment and destination contracts and a list of related commercial law Web links, go to

www.legalmatch.com/law-library/article/merchandise-risk-of-loss.html

For an overview of bills of lading, access the following Web site:

www.law.cornell.edu/ucc/7/overview.html

Legal Research Exercises on the Web

Go to **www.cengage.com/blaw/jentz**, the Web site that accompanies this text. Select "Chapter 21" and click on "Internet Exercises." There you will find the following Internet research exercises that you can perform to learn more about the topics covered in this chapter.

Internet Exercise 21–1: Legal Perspective
The Entrustment Rule

Internet Exercise 21–2: Management Perspective
Passage of Title

CHAPTER 22

Performance and Breach of Sales and Lease Contracts

The performance that is required of the parties under a sales or lease contract consists of the duties and obligations each party has under the terms of the contract. The basic obligation of the seller or lessor is to transfer and deliver the goods as stated in the contract, and the basic duty of the buyer or lessee is to accept and pay for the goods.

Keep in mind that "duties and obligations" under the terms of the contract include those specified by the agreement, by custom, and by the Uniform Commercial Code (UCC). Thus, parties to a sales or lease contract may be bound not only by terms they expressly agreed on, but also by terms implied by custom, such as a customary method of weighing or measuring particular goods. In addition, the UCC sometimes imposes terms on parties to a sales contract, such as the requirement that a seller find a substitute carrier to deliver goods to the buyer if the agreed-on carrier becomes unavailable. In this chapter, we examine the performance obligations of the parties under a sales or lease contract.

Sometimes, circumstances make it difficult for a person to carry out the promised performance, leading to a breach of the contract. When a breach occurs, the aggrieved party looks for remedies—which we examine in the second half of the chapter. The UCC provides a range of possible remedies, from retaining the goods to requiring the breaching party's performance under the contract. Generally, these remedies are designed to put the aggrieved party "in as good a position as if the other party had fully performed." Note that in contrast to the common law of contracts, remedies under the UCC are *cumulative* in nature. In other words, an innocent party to a breached sales or lease contract is not limited to one exclusive remedy.

SECTION 1 Performance Obligations

As discussed in previous chapters, the obligations of good faith and commercial reasonableness underlie every sales and lease contract.

The UCC's Good Faith Provision

The UCC's good faith provision, which can never be disclaimed, reads as follows: "Every contract or duty within this Act imposes an obligation of good faith in its performance or enforcement" [UCC 1–304]. *Good faith* means honesty in fact. For a merchant, it means honesty in fact and the observance of reasonable commercial standards of fair dealing in the trade [UCC 2–103(1)(b)]. In other words, merchants are held to a higher standard of performance or duty than are nonmerchants.

Good Faith and Contract Performance

The principle of good faith applies to both parties and provides a framework for the entire agreement. If a sales contract leaves open some particulars of performance, for instance, the parties must exercise good faith and commercial reasonableness when later specifying the details. The *Focus on Ethics* feature on pages 443 and 444 explores the ethical implications of the UCC's good faith standard.

In performing a sales or lease contract, the basic obligation of the seller or lessor is to *transfer and deliver conforming goods*. The basic obligation of the buyer or lessee is to *accept and pay for conforming goods* in accordance with the contract [UCC

2–301, 2A–516(1)]. Overall performance of a sales or lease contract is controlled by the agreement between the parties. When the contract is unclear and disputes arise, the courts look to the UCC and impose standards of good faith and commercial reasonableness. For a discussion of the importance of good faith in contract performance, see this chapter's *Business Application* feature.

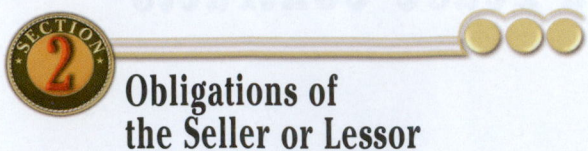

SECTION 2 Obligations of the Seller or Lessor

As stated, the basic duty of the seller or lessor is to deliver the goods called for under the contract to the buyer or lessee.

Tender of Delivery

Goods that conform to the contract description in every way are called **conforming goods.** To fulfill the contract, the seller or lessor must either deliver or tender delivery of conforming goods to the buyer or lessee. **Tender of delivery** occurs when the seller or lessor makes conforming goods available to the buyer or lessee and gives the buyer or lessee whatever notification is reasonably necessary to enable the buyer or lessee to take delivery [UCC 2–503(1), 2A–508(1)].

Tender must occur at a *reasonable hour* and in a *reasonable manner.* For example, a seller cannot call the buyer at 2:00 A.M. and say, "The goods are ready. I'll give you twenty minutes to get them." Unless the parties have agreed otherwise, the goods must be tendered for delivery at a reasonable hour and kept available for a reasonable period of time to enable the buyer to take possession of them [UCC 2–503(1)(a)].

Normally, all goods called for by a contract must be tendered in a single delivery—unless the parties have agreed that the goods may be delivered in several lots or *installments* (to be discussed shortly) [UCC 2–307, 2–612, 2A–510]. Hence, an order for 1,000 shirts cannot be delivered two shirts at a time. If, however, the parties agree that the shirts will be delivered in four orders of 250 each as they are produced (for summer, fall, winter, and spring stock), then tender of delivery may occur in this manner.

Place of Delivery

The buyer and seller (or lessor and lessee) may agree that the goods will be delivered to a particular destination where the buyer or lessee will take possession. If the contract does not designate the place of delivery, then the goods must be made available to the buyer at the *seller's place of business* or, if the seller has none, at the *seller's residence* [UCC 2–308]. If, at the time of contracting, the parties know that the goods identified to the contract are located somewhere other than the seller's business, then the *location of the goods* is the place for their delivery [UCC 2–308].

For example, Li Wan and Boyd both live in San Francisco. In San Francisco, Li Wan contracts to sell Boyd five used trucks, which both parties know are located in a Chicago warehouse. If nothing more is specified in the contract, the place of delivery for the trucks is Chicago. Li Wan may tender delivery either by giving Boyd a negotiable or nonnegotiable document of title or by obtaining the bailee's (warehouser's) acknowledgment that the buyer is entitled to possession.[1]

Delivery via Carrier

In many instances, attendant circumstances or delivery terms in the contract (such as F.O.B. or F.A.S. terms, shown in Exhibit 21–1 on page 392) make it apparent that the parties intend that a carrier be used to move the goods. In contracts involving a carrier, a seller can complete performance of the obligation to deliver the goods in two ways—through a shipment contract or through a destination contract.

Shipment Contracts Recall from Chapter 21 that a *shipment contract* requires or authorizes the seller to ship goods by a carrier. The contract does not require the seller to deliver the goods at a particular destination [UCC 2–319, 2–509]. Unless otherwise agreed, the seller must do the following:

1. Place the goods into the hands of the carrier.
2. Make a contract for their transportation that is reasonable according to the nature of the goods and their value. (For example, certain types of goods need refrigeration in transit.)
3. Obtain and promptly deliver or tender to the buyer any documents necessary to enable the buyer to obtain possession of the goods from the carrier.

1. If the seller delivers a nonnegotiable document of title or merely instructs the bailee in a writing (record) to release the goods to the buyer without the bailee's acknowledgment of the buyer's rights, this is also a sufficient tender, unless the buyer objects [UCC 2–503(4)]. Risk of loss, however, does not pass until the buyer has had a reasonable amount of time in which to present the document or the instructions. See Chapter 21.

BUSINESS APPLICATION
Good Faith and Fair Dealing

MANAGEMENT FACES A LEGAL ISSUE

As discussed elsewhere, all contracts governed by the Uniform Commercial Code (UCC) must meet the requirements of good faith and fair dealing. Yet do these requirements supersede the written terms of a contract? In other words, if a party adheres strictly to the express, written terms of a contract, can that party nonetheless face liability for breaching the UCC's good faith requirements?

WHAT THE COURTS SAY

Generally, the courts take the good faith provisions of the UCC very seriously. Some courts have held that good faith can be breached even when the parties have equal bargaining power. In one case, for example, the court held that, although the plaintiffs were sophisticated businesspersons who had the assistance of highly competent counsel, they could still maintain an action for breach of good faith and fair dealing. The court reasoned that "the presence of bad faith is to be found in the eye of the beholder or, more to the point, in the eye of the trier of fact," indicating that it was up to a jury to determine whether the parties had performed in good faith.[a]

Courts even apply the implied covenant of good faith and fair dealing with respect to individuals who form partnerships. In one case, two individuals who had jointly bought properties for development over a ten-year period had a "falling out." One of them filed a complaint alleging breach of this implied good faith covenant. The reviewing court in this case stated that the "implied covenant of good faith and fair dealing is present in every contract." Further, "the duty imposed by this covenant prohibits either party from doing anything that would have the effect of injuring the other party's right to receive the fruits of the contract." That is why juries are entitled to afford great weight to the conduct of the parties when determining the meaning of a contract.[b]

IMPLICATIONS FOR MANAGERS

The message for business owners and managers involved in sales contracts (and even other contracts) is clear: compliance with the literal terms of a contract is not enough—the standards of good faith and fair dealing must also be met. While the specific standards of good faith performance are still evolving, the overriding principle is that a party to a contract should do nothing to injure or destroy the rights of the other party to receive the fruits of the contract.

a. *Seidenberg v. Summit Bank*, 348 N.J.Super. 243, 791 A.2d 1068 (2002).

b. *Stankovits v. Schrager*, __ A.2d __, 2007 WL 4410247 (N.J.Super.A.D. 2007).

4. Promptly notify the buyer that shipment has been made [UCC 2–504].

If the seller does not make a reasonable contract for transportation or fails to notify the buyer of the shipment, the buyer can reject the goods, but only if a *material loss* of the goods or a significant *delay* results. Suppose that a contract involves the shipment of fresh fruit, such as strawberries, but the seller does not arrange for refrigerated transportation. In this situation, if the fruit spoils during transport, a material loss would likely result. (Of course, the parties are free to make agreements that alter the UCC's rules and allow the buyer to reject goods for other reasons.)

Destination Contracts In a *destination contract,* the seller agrees to deliver conforming goods to the buyer at a particular destination. The goods must be tendered at a reasonable hour and held at the buyer's disposal for a reasonable length of time. The seller must also give the buyer appropriate notice. In addition, the seller must provide the buyer with any documents of title necessary to enable the buyer to obtain delivery from the carrier. Sellers often do this by tendering the documents through ordinary banking channels [UCC 2–503].

The Perfect Tender Rule

As previously noted, the seller or lessor has an obligation to ship or tender *conforming goods,* which the buyer or lessee is then obligated to accept and pay for according to the terms of the contract [UCC 2–507]. Under the common law, the seller was obligated to deliver goods that conformed with the terms of the contract in every detail. This was called the **perfect tender rule.** The UCC preserves the perfect tender doctrine by stating that if goods or tender of delivery fails *in any respect* to conform to the contract, the buyer or lessee has the right to accept the goods, reject the entire shipment, or accept part and reject part [UCC 2–601, 2A–509].

For example, a lessor contracts to lease fifty Comclear monitors to be delivered at the lessee's place of business on or before October 1. On September 28, the lessor discovers that it has only thirty Comclear monitors in inventory but will have another twenty Comclear monitors within the next two weeks. The lessor tenders delivery of the thirty Comclear monitors on October 1, with the promise that the other monitors will be delivered within two weeks. Because the lessor has failed to make a perfect tender of fifty Comclear monitors, the lessee has the right to reject the entire shipment and hold the lessor in breach.

Exceptions to the Perfect Tender Rule

Because of the rigidity of the perfect tender rule, several exceptions to the rule have been created, some of which we discuss here.

Agreement of the Parties Exceptions to the perfect tender rule may be established by agreement. If the parties have agreed, for example, that defective goods or parts will not be rejected if the seller or lessor is able to repair or replace them within a reasonable period of time, the perfect tender rule does not apply.

Cure The UCC does not specifically define the term **cure,** but it refers to the right of the seller or lessor to repair, adjust, or replace defective or nonconforming goods [UCC 2–508, 2A–513]. When any delivery is rejected because of nonconforming goods and the time for performance has not yet expired, the seller or lessor can attempt to "cure" the defect *within the contract time for performance* [UCC 2–508(1), 2A–513(1)]. To do so, the seller or lessor must seasonably (timely) notify the buyer or lessee of the intention to cure.

Reasonable Grounds Required When Time for Performance Has Expired. Once the time for performance under the contract has expired, the seller or lessor can still exercise the right to cure if he or she has *reasonable grounds to believe that the nonconforming tender will be acceptable to the buyer or lessee* [UCC 2–508(2), 2A–513(2)]. For example, if in the past a buyer frequently accepted a particular substitute for a good when the good ordered was not available, the seller has reasonable grounds to believe the buyer will again accept the substitute. Even if the buyer rejects the substitute good on a particular occasion, the seller nonetheless had reasonable grounds to believe that the substitute would be acceptable. A seller or lessor will sometimes tender nonconforming goods with some type of price allowance, which can serve as the "reasonable grounds" to believe that the buyer or lessee will accept the nonconforming tender.

A Restriction on the Buyer's or Lessee's Right of Rejection. The right to cure substantially restricts the right of the buyer or lessee to reject goods. For example, if a lessee refuses a tender of goods as nonconforming but does not disclose the nature of the defect to the lessor, the lessee cannot later assert the defect as a defense if the defect is one that the lessor could have cured. Generally, buyers and lessees must act in good faith and state specific reasons for refusing to accept goods [UCC 2–605, 2A–514].

Substitution of Carriers When an agreed-on manner of delivery (such as the use of a particular carrier to transport the goods) becomes impracticable or unavailable through no fault of either party, but a commercially reasonable substitute is available, this substitute performance is sufficient tender to the buyer and must be used [UCC 2–614(1)]. For example, a sales contract calls for the delivery of a large piece of machinery to be shipped by ABC Truck Lines on or before June 1. The contract terms clearly state the importance of the delivery date. The employees of ABC Truck Lines go on strike. The seller must make a reasonable substitute tender, perhaps by another trucking firm or by rail, if it is available. Note that the seller normally is responsible for any additional shipping costs, unless contrary arrangements have been made in the sales contract.

Installment Contracts An **installment contract** is a single contract that requires or authorizes delivery in two or more separate lots to be accepted and paid for separately. With an installment contract, a buyer or lessee can reject an installment *only if the nonconformity substantially impairs the value* of the installment and cannot be cured [UCC 2–307, 2–612(2), 2A–510(1)]. If the buyer or lessee fails to notify the seller or lessor of the rejection, however, and subsequently accepts a nonconforming installment, the contract is reinstated [UCC 2–612(3), 2A–510(2)].

The entire installment contract is breached only when one or more nonconforming installments *substantially* impair the value of the *whole contract.*

The UCC strictly limits rejection to cases of *substantial* nonconformity. Suppose that an installment contract involves parts of a machine. The first part is necessary for the operation of the machine, but when it is delivered, it is irreparably defective. The failure of this first installment will be a breach of the whole contract because the machine will not operate without the first part. The situation would likely be different, however, if the contract had called for twenty carloads of plywood and only 9 percent of one of the carloads of plywood had deviated from the thickness specifications in the contract.

The point to remember is that the UCC significantly alters the right of the buyer or lessee to reject the entire contract if the contract requires delivery to be made in several installments. The UCC strictly limits rejection to cases of *substantial* nonconformity (unless the parties agree that breach of an installment constitutes a breach of the entire contract).

Commercial Impracticability As stated in Chapter 17, occurrences unforeseen by either party when a contract was made may make performance commercially impracticable. When this occurs, the perfect tender rule no longer applies. According to UCC 2–615(a) and 2A–405(a), a delay in delivery or nondelivery in whole or in part is not a breach if performance has been made impracticable "by the occurrence of a contingency the nonoccurrence of which was a basic assumption on which the contract was made." The seller or lessor must, however, notify the buyer or lessee as soon as practicable that there will be a delay or nondelivery.

Foreseeable versus Unforeseeable Contingencies. The doctrine of commercial impracticability does not extend to problems that could have been foreseen. An increase in cost resulting from inflation, for instance, does not in and of itself excuse performance, as this kind of risk is ordinarily assumed by a seller or lessor conducting business. The nonoccurrence of the contingency must have been a basic assumption on which the contract was made [UCC 2–615, 2A–405].

For example, an oil company that receives its oil from the Middle East has a contract to supply a buyer with 100,000 barrels of oil. Because of an oil embargo by the Organization of Petroleum Exporting Countries (OPEC), the seller cannot secure oil from the Middle East or any other source to meet the terms of the contract. This situation comes fully under the commercial impracticability exception to the perfect tender doctrine.

Can unanticipated increases in a seller's costs that make performance "impracticable" constitute a valid defense to performance on the basis of commercial impracticability? The court dealt with this question in the following case.

CASE 22.1 Maple Farms, Inc. v. City School District of Elmira

Supreme Court of New York, 1974. 76 Misc.2d 1080, 352 N.Y.S.2d 784.

Background and Facts On June 15, 1973, Maple Farms, Inc., formed an agreement with the city school district of Elmira, New York, to supply the school district with milk for the 1973–1974 school year. The agreement was in the form of a requirements contract, under which Maple Farms would sell to the school district all the milk the district required at a fixed price—which was the June market price of milk. By December 1973, the price of raw milk had increased by 23 percent over the price specified in the contract. This meant that if the terms of the contract were fulfilled, Maple Farms would lose $7,350. Because it had similar contracts with other school districts, Maple Farms stood to lose a great deal if it was held to the price stated in the contracts. When the school district would not agree to release Maple Farms from its contract, Maple Farms brought an action in a New York state court for a declaratory judgment (a determination of the parties' rights under a contract). Maple Farms contended that the substantial increase in the price of raw milk was an event not contemplated by the parties when the contract was formed and that, given the increased price, performance of the contract was commercially impracticable.

Decision and Rationale The state trial court ruled that inflation and fluctuating prices did not render performance in this case impracticable and granted summary judgment in favor of

CASE CONTINUES

CASE 22.1 CONTINUED the school district. Commercial impracticability arises when an event occurs that is totally unexpected and unforeseeable by the parties. An increase in the price of milk was not unexpected because the previous year the price had risen 10 percent and the price of milk had traditionally varied. Also, general inflation should have been anticipated. Maple Farms had reason to know these facts and could have provided "in the contract an exculpatory clause to excuse it from performance in the event of a substantial rise in the price of raw milk." The court also noted that the school district's primary purpose in forming the contract was to protect itself (for budgeting reasons) against price fluctuations.

- **Impact of This Case on Today's Law** *This case is a classic illustration of the UCC's commercial impracticability doctrine as courts still apply it today. Under this doctrine, increased cost alone does not excuse performance unless the rise in cost is due to some unforeseen contingency that alters the essential nature of the performance.*

- **What If the Facts Were Different?** *Suppose that the court had ruled in the plaintiff's favor. How might that ruling have affected the plaintiff's contracts with other parties?*

Partial Performance. Sometimes, the unforeseen event only *partially* affects the capacity of the seller or lessor to perform. When the seller or lessor can *partially* fulfill the contract but cannot tender total performance, the seller or lessor is required to allocate in a fair and reasonable manner any remaining production and deliveries among its regular customers and those to whom it is contractually obligated to deliver the goods [UCC 2–615(b), 2A–405(b)]. The buyer or lessee must receive notice of the allocation and has the right to accept or reject it [UCC 2–615(c), 2A–405(c)].

For example, a Florida orange grower, Best Citrus, Inc., contracts to sell this season's production to a number of customers, including Martin's grocery chain. Martin's contracts to purchase two thousand crates of oranges. Best Citrus has sprayed *some* of its orange groves with a chemical called Karmoxin. The U.S. Department of Agriculture discovers that persons who eat products sprayed with Karmoxin may develop cancer and issues an order prohibiting the sale of these products. Best Citrus picks all the oranges not sprayed with Karmoxin, but the quantity is insufficient to meet all the contracted-for deliveries. In this situation, Best Citrus is required to allocate its production, so it notifies Martin's that it cannot deliver the full quantity agreed on in the contract and specifies the amount it will be able to deliver under the circumstances. Martin's can either accept or reject the allocation, but Best Citrus has no further contractual liability.

Destruction of Identified Goods Sometimes, an unexpected event, such as a fire, totally destroys goods through no fault of either party and before risk passes to the buyer or lessee. In such a situation, *if the goods were identified at the time the contract was formed,* the parties are excused from performance [UCC 2–613, 2A–221]. If the goods are only partially destroyed, however, the buyer or lessee can inspect them and either treat the contract as void or accept the damaged goods with a reduction in the contract price.

Consider an example. Atlas Sporting Equipment agrees to lease to River Bicycles sixty bicycles of a particular model that has been discontinued. No other bicycles of that model are available. River specifies that it needs the bicycles to rent to tourists. Before Atlas can deliver the bicycles, they are destroyed by a fire. In this situation, Atlas is not liable to River for failing to deliver the bicycles. Through no fault of either party, the goods were destroyed before the risk of loss passed to the lessee. The loss was total, so the contract is avoided. Clearly, Atlas has no obligation to tender the bicycles, and River has no obligation to pay for them.

Assurance and Cooperation Two other exceptions to the perfect tender doctrine apply equally to both parties to sales and lease contracts: the right of assurance and the duty of cooperation.

The Right of Assurance. The UCC provides that if one of the parties to a contract has "reasonable grounds" to believe that the other party will not perform as contracted, she or he may *in writing* "demand adequate assurance of due performance" from the other party. Until such assurance is received, she or he may "suspend" further performance without liability. What constitutes "reasonable grounds" is determined by commercial standards. If such assurances are not forthcoming within a reasonable time (not to exceed thirty days), the failure to respond may be treated as a *repudiation* of the contract [UCC 2–609, 2A–401].

For example, two companies that make road-surfacing materials, Koch Materials and Shore Slurry Seal, Inc., enter into a contract. Koch obtains a license to use Novachip, a special material made by Shore, and Shore agrees to buy all of its asphalt from Koch for the next seven years. A few years into the contract term, Shore notifies Koch that it is planning to sell its assets to Asphalt Paving Systems, Inc. Koch demands assurances that Asphalt Paving will continue the deal, but Shore refuses to provide assurances. In this situation, Koch can treat Shore's failure to give assurances as a repudiation and file suit against Shore for breach of contract.[2]

A businessperson who has doubts about the other party's ability or willingness to perform a sales contract should always demand adequate assurances. The UCC comes to the aid of a party who has reasonable grounds to suspect that the other party to a contract will not perform as promised. Rather than having to "wait and see" (and possibly incur significant losses as a result), the party with such suspicions may seek adequate assurance of performance from the other party.

The failure to give such assurance can be treated as an anticipatory repudiation (breach) of the contract, thus entitling the nonbreaching party to seek damages (*anticipatory repudiation* will be discussed shortly). Perhaps more important, this failure allows the nonbreaching party to suspend its performance, which can save a business from sustaining substantial losses that could be recovered only through litigation. Ultimately, it may be better simply to withdraw from a deal when the other party will not provide assurances than to continue with a contract that is likely to be breached anyway and then bring a lawsuit.

The Duty of Cooperation. Sometimes, the performance of one party depends on the cooperation of the other. The UCC provides that when such cooperation is not forthcoming, the other party can suspend his or her own performance without liability and hold the uncooperative party in breach or proceed to perform the contract in any reasonable manner [UCC 2–311(3)(b)].

For example, Amati is required by contract to deliver twelve hundred model Z washing machines to locations in the state of California to be specified later by Farrell. Deliveries are to be made on or before October 1. Amati has repeatedly requested the delivery locations, but Farrell has not responded. The twelve hundred model Z machines are ready for shipment on October 1, but Farrell still refuses to give Amati the delivery locations. Amati does not ship on October 1. Can Amati be held liable? The answer is no. Amati is excused for any resulting delay of performance because of Farrell's failure to cooperate.

SECTION 3 Obligations of the Buyer or Lessee

The main obligation of the buyer or lessee under a sales or lease contract is to pay for the goods tendered in accordance with the contract. Once the seller or lessor has adequately tendered delivery, the buyer or lessee is obligated to accept the goods and pay for them according to the terms of the contract.

Payment

In the absence of any specific agreements, the buyer or lessee must make payment at the time and place the goods are *received* [UCC 2–310(a), 2A–516(1)]. When a sale is made on credit, the buyer is obliged to pay according to the specified credit terms (for example, 60, 90, or 120 days), not when the goods are received. The credit period usually begins on the *date of shipment* [UCC 2–310(d)].

Payment can be made by any means agreed on between the parties—cash or any other method generally acceptable in the commercial world. If the seller demands cash when the buyer offers a check, credit card, or the like, the seller must permit the buyer reasonable time to obtain legal tender [UCC 2–511].

Right of Inspection

Unless the parties otherwise agree, or for C.O.D. (collect on delivery) transactions, the buyer or lessee has an absolute right to inspect the goods before making payment. This right allows the buyer or lessee to verify that the goods tendered or delivered conform to the

2. *Koch Materials Co. v. Shore Slurry Seal, Inc.*, 205 F.Supp.2d 324 (D.N.J. 2002).

contract. If the goods are not as ordered, the buyer or lessee has no duty to pay. *An opportunity for inspection is therefore a condition precedent to the right of the seller or lessor to enforce payment* [UCC 2–513(1), 2A–515(1)].

Inspection can take place at any reasonable place and time and in any reasonable manner. Generally, what is reasonable is determined by custom of the trade, past practices of the parties, and the like. The buyer bears the costs of inspecting the goods but can recover the costs from the seller if the goods do not conform and are rejected [UCC 2–513(2)].

Acceptance

A buyer or lessee manifests acceptance of the delivered goods by doing any of the following:

1. When the buyer or lessee has had a reasonable opportunity to inspect the goods and indicates to the seller or lessor that the goods either are conforming or that he or she will retain them in spite of their nonconformity, the buyer or lessee has accepted [UCC 2–606(1)(a), 2A–515(1)(a)].
2. If the buyer or lessee has had a reasonable opportunity to inspect the goods and has *failed to reject* them within a reasonable period of time, then acceptance is presumed [UCC 2–602(1), 2–606(1)(b), 2A–515(1)(b)].
3. In sales contracts, if the buyer *performs any act inconsistent with the seller's ownership,* then the buyer will be deemed to have accepted the goods. For example, any use or resale of the goods—except for the limited purpose of testing or inspecting the goods—generally constitutes an acceptance [UCC 2–606(1)(c)].

Partial Acceptance

If some of the goods delivered do not conform to the contract and the seller or lessor has failed to cure, the buyer or lessee can make a *partial* acceptance [UCC 2–601(c), 2A–509(1)]. The same is true if the nonconformity was not reasonably discoverable before acceptance. (In the latter situation, the buyer or lessee may be able to revoke the acceptance, as will be discussed later in this chapter.)

A buyer or lessee cannot accept less than a single commercial unit, however. The UCC defines a *commercial unit* as a unit of goods that, by commercial usage, is viewed as a "single whole" for purposes of sale and that cannot be divided without materially impairing the character of the unit, its market value, or its use [UCC 2–105(6), 2A–103(1)(c)]. A commercial unit can be a single article (such as a machine), a set of articles (such as a suite of furniture), a quantity (such as a bale, a gross, or a carload), or any other unit treated in the trade as a single whole. (See *Concept Summary 22.1* for a review of the obligations of both parties to a sales or lease contract.)

SECTION 4 Anticipatory Repudiation

What if, before the time for contract performance, one party clearly communicates to the other the intention *not* to perform? Such an action is a breach of the contract by *anticipatory repudiation.*[3]

Suspension of Performance Obligations

When anticipatory repudiation occurs, the nonbreaching party has a choice of two responses: (1) treat the repudiation as a final breach by pursuing a remedy or (2) wait to see if the repudiating party will decide to honor the contract despite the avowed intention to renege [UCC 2–610, 2A–402]. In either situation, the nonbreaching party may suspend performance.

A Repudiation May Be Retracted

The UCC permits the breaching party to "retract" his or her repudiation (subject to some limitations). This can be done by any method that clearly indicates the party's intent to perform. Once retraction is made, the rights of the repudiating party under the contract are reinstated. There can be no retraction, however, if since the time of the repudiation the other party has canceled or materially changed position or otherwise indicated that the repudiation is final [UCC 2–611, 2A–403].

For example, Cora, who owns a small inn, purchases a suite of furniture from Horton's Furniture Warehouse on April 1. The contract states that "delivery must be made on or before May 1." On April 10, Horton informs Cora that he cannot make delivery until May 10 and asks her to consent to the modified delivery date. In this situation, Cora has the option of either treating Horton's notice of late delivery as a final breach of contract and pursuing a remedy or agreeing to the later delivery date. Suppose that Cora does neither for two weeks. On

3. Refer back to Chapter 17 for a discussion of the common law origins and application of the doctrine of anticipatory repudiation.

CONCEPT SUMMARY 22.1
Performance of Sales and Lease Contracts

Concept	Description
Obligations of the Seller or Lessor	1. The seller or lessor must tender *conforming* goods to the buyer or lessee at a *reasonable hour* and in a *reasonable manner.* Under the perfect tender doctrine, the seller or lessor must tender goods that conform exactly to the terms of the contract [UCC 2–503(1), 2A–508(1)]. 2. If the seller or lessor tenders nonconforming goods and the buyer or lessee rejects them, the seller or lessor may *cure* (repair or replace the goods) within the contract time for performance [UCC 2–508(1), 2A–513(1)]. Even if the time for performance under the contract has expired, the seller or lessor has a reasonable time to substitute conforming goods without liability if the seller or lessor has reasonable grounds to believe the nonconforming tender will be acceptable to the buyer or lessee [UCC 2–508(2), 2A–513(2)]. 3. If the agreed-on means of delivery becomes impracticable or unavailable, the seller must substitute an alternative means (such as a different carrier) if a reasonable one is available [UCC 2–614(1)]. 4. If a seller or lessor tenders nonconforming goods in any one installment under an installment contract, the buyer or lessee may reject the installment only if the nonconformity substantially impairs its value and cannot be cured. The entire installment contract is breached only when one or more installments *substantially* impair the value of the *whole* contract [UCC 2–612, 2A–510]. 5. When performance becomes commercially impracticable owing to circumstances unforeseen when the contract was formed, the perfect tender rule no longer applies [UCC 2–615, 2A–405].
Obligations of the Buyer or Lessee	1. On tender of delivery by the seller or lessor, the buyer or lessee must pay for the goods at the time and place the goods are *received,* unless the sale is made on credit. Payment can be made by any method generally acceptable in the commercial world, but the seller can demand cash [UCC 2–310, 2–511]. 2. Unless otherwise agreed or in C.O.D. shipments, the buyer or lessee has an absolute right to inspect the goods before acceptance [UCC 2–513(1), 2A–515(1)]. 3. The buyer or lessee can manifest acceptance of delivered goods in words or by conduct, such as by failing to reject the goods after having had a reasonable opportunity to inspect them. A buyer will be deemed to have accepted goods if he or she performs any act inconsistent with the seller's ownership [UCC 2–606(1), 2A–515(1)].

April 24, Horton informs Cora that he will be able to deliver the furniture by May 1 after all. In effect, Horton has retracted his repudiation, reinstating the rights and obligations of the parties under the original contract. Note that if Cora had indicated after Horton's repudiation that she was canceling the contract, Horton would not have been able to retract his repudiation.

SECTION 5 Remedies of the Seller or Lessor

Numerous remedies are available under the UCC to a seller or lessor when the buyer or lessee is in breach. Generally, the remedies available to the seller or lessor depend on the circumstances existing at the time of the breach. The most pertinent considerations are which party has possession of the goods, whether the goods are in transit, and whether the buyer or lessee has rejected or accepted the goods.

When the Goods Are in the Possession of the Seller or Lessor

Under the UCC, if the buyer or lessee breaches the contract before the goods have been delivered to her or him, the seller or lessor has the right to pursue the following remedies:

1. Cancel (rescind) the contract.
2. Resell the goods and sue to recover damages.
3. Sue to recover the purchase price or lease payments due.
4. Sue to recover damages for the buyer's nonacceptance.

The Right to Cancel the Contract If the buyer or lessee breaches the contract, the seller or lessor can choose to simply cancel the contract [UCC 2–703(f), 2A–523(1)(a)]. The seller or lessor must notify the buyer or lessee of the cancellation, and at that point all remaining obligations of the seller or lessor are discharged. The buyer or lessee is not discharged from all remaining obligations, however; he or she is in breach, and the seller or lessor can pursue remedies available under the UCC for breach.

The Right to Withhold Delivery In general, sellers and lessors can withhold delivery or discontinue performance of their obligations under sales or lease contracts when the buyers or lessees are in breach. This is true whether a buyer or lessee has wrongfully rejected or revoked acceptance of contract goods (which will be discussed later in this chapter), failed to make a payment, or repudiated the contract [UCC 2–703(a), 2A–523(1)(c)]. The seller or lessor can also refuse to deliver the goods to a buyer or lessee who is insolvent (unable to pay debts as they become due) unless the buyer or lessee pays in cash [UCC 2–702(1), 2A–525(1)].

The Right to Resell or Dispose of the Goods When a buyer or lessee breaches or repudiates the contract while the seller or lessor is in possession of the goods, the seller or lessor can resell or dispose of the goods. The seller or lessor can retain any profits made as a result of the sale and can hold the buyer or lessee liable for any loss [UCC 2–703(d), 2–706(1), 2A–523(1)(e), 2A–527(1)].

The seller must give the original buyer reasonable notice of the resale, unless the goods are perishable or will rapidly decline in value [UCC 2–706(2), (3)]. A good faith purchaser in a resale takes the goods free of any of the rights of the original buyer, even if the seller fails to comply with this requirement [UCC 2–706(5)]. The UCC encourages the resale of the goods because although the buyer is liable for any deficiency, the seller is not accountable to the buyer for any profits made on the resale [UCC 2–706(6)].

Unfinished Goods. When the goods contracted for are unfinished at the time of the breach, the seller or lessor can do one of two things: (1) cease manufacturing the goods and resell them for scrap or salvage value or (2) complete the manufacture and resell or dispose of the goods, holding the buyer or lessee liable for any deficiency. In choosing between these two alternatives, the seller or lessor must exercise reasonable commercial judgment in order to mitigate the loss and obtain maximum value from the unfinished goods [UCC 2–704(2), 2A–524(2)]. Any resale of the goods must be made in good faith and in a commercially reasonable manner.

Measure of Damages. In sales transactions, the seller can recover any deficiency between the resale price and the contract price, along with *incidental damages,* defined as those costs to the seller resulting from the breach [UCC 2–706(1), 2–710]. The resale can be private or public, and the goods can be sold as a unit or in parcels.

In lease transactions, the lessor may lease the goods to another party and recover from the original lessee, as damages, any unpaid lease payments up to the beginning date of the lease term under the new lease. The lessor can also recover any deficiency between the lease payments due under the original lease contract and those under the new lease contract, along with incidental damages [UCC 2A–527(2)].

The Right to Recover the Purchase Price or Lease Payments Due Under the UCC, an unpaid seller or lessor can bring an action to recover the purchase price or the payments due under the lease contract, plus incidental damages [UCC 2–709(1), 2A–529(1)]. If a seller or lessor is unable to resell or dispose of the goods and sues for the contract price or lease payments due, the goods must be held for the buyer or lessee. The seller or lessor can resell the goods at any time prior to collecting the judgment from the buyer or lessee, but the net proceeds from the sale must be credited to the buyer or lessee. This illustrates the duty to mitigate damages.

Suppose that Southern Realty contracts with Gem Point, Inc., to purchase one thousand pens with Southern Realty's name inscribed on them. Gem Point tenders delivery of the pens, but Southern Realty wrongfully refuses to accept them. In this situation, Gem Point can bring an action for the purchase price because it delivered conforming goods, and Southern Realty refused to accept or pay for the goods. Gem Point obviously cannot resell the pens inscribed with the buyer's business name, so this situation falls under UCC 2–709. Gem Point is required to hold onto the pens for Southern Realty, but can resell them (in the event that it can find a buyer) at any time prior to collecting the judgment from Southern Realty.

The Right to Recover Damages for the Buyer's Nonacceptance If a buyer or lessee repudiates a contract or wrongfully refuses to accept the goods, a seller or lessor can maintain an action to recover the damages sustained. Ordinarily, the amount of damages equals the difference between the contract price or lease payments and the market price or lease payments at the time and place of tender of the goods, plus incidental damages [UCC 2–708(1), 2A–528(1)]. When the ordinary measure of damages is inadequate to put the seller or lessor in as good a position as the buyer's or lessee's performance would have, the UCC provides an alternative. In that situation, the proper measure of damages is the lost profits of the seller or lessor, including a reasonable allowance for overhead and other expenses [UCC 2–708(2), 2A–528(2)].

When the Goods Are in Transit

When the seller or lessor has delivered the goods to a carrier or a bailee but the buyer or lessee has not yet received them, the goods are said to be *in transit*. If, while the goods are in transit, the seller or lessor learns that the buyer or lessee is insolvent, the seller or lessor can stop the carrier or bailee from delivering the goods, regardless of the quantity of goods shipped. If the buyer or lessee is in breach but is not insolvent, the seller or lessor can stop the goods in transit only if the quantity shipped is at least a carload, a truckload, a planeload, or a larger shipment [UCC 2–705(1), 2A–526(1)].

To stop delivery, the seller or lessor must *timely notify* the carrier or other bailee that the goods are to be returned or held for the seller or lessor. If the carrier has sufficient time to stop delivery, the goods must be held and delivered according to the instructions of the seller or lessor, who is liable to the carrier for any additional costs incurred [UCC 2–705(3), 2A–526(3)].

The seller or lessor has the right to stop delivery of the goods under UCC 2–705(2) and 2A–526(2) until the time when:

1. The buyer or lessee receives the goods.
2. The carrier or the bailee acknowledges the rights of the buyer or lessee in the goods (by reshipping or holding the goods for the buyer or lessee, for example).
3. A negotiable document of title covering the goods has been properly transferred to the buyer in a sales transaction, giving the buyer ownership rights in the goods [UCC 2–705(2)].

Once the seller or lessor reclaims the goods in transit, she or he can pursue the remedies allowed to sellers and lessors when the goods are in their possession.

When the Goods Are in the Possession of the Buyer or Lessee

When the buyer or lessee has breached a sales or lease contract and the goods are in his or her possession, the seller or lessor can sue to recover the purchase price of the goods or the lease payments due, plus incidental damages [UCC 2–709(1), 2A–529(1)]. In some situations, a seller may also have a right to reclaim the goods from the buyer. For example, in a sales contract, if the buyer has received the goods on credit and the seller discovers that the buyer is insolvent, the seller can demand return of the goods [UCC 2–702(2)]. Ordinarily, the demand must be made within ten days of the buyer's receipt of the goods.[4] The seller's right to reclaim the goods is subject to the rights of a good faith purchaser or other subsequent buyer in the ordinary course of business who purchases the goods from the buyer before the seller reclaims them.

In regard to lease contracts, if the lessee is in default (fails to make payments that are due, for example), the lessor may reclaim the leased goods that are in the lessee's possession [UCC 2A–525(2)].

4. The seller can demand and reclaim the goods at any time, though, if the buyer misrepresented his or her solvency in writing within three months prior to the delivery of the goods.

SECTION 6

Remedies of the Buyer or Lessee

When the seller or lessor breaches the contract, the buyer or lessee has numerous remedies available under the UCC. Like the remedies available to sellers and lessors, the remedies available to buyers and lessees depend on the circumstances existing at the time of the breach.

When the Seller or Lessor Refuses to Deliver the Goods

If the seller or lessor refuses to deliver the goods to the buyer or lessee, the basic remedies available to the buyer or lessee include the right to:

1. Cancel (rescind) the contract.
2. Recover goods that have been paid for if the seller or lessor is insolvent.
3. Sue to obtain specific performance if the goods are unique or damages are an inadequate remedy.
4. Buy other goods (obtain cover) and recover damages from the seller.
5. Sue to obtain identified goods held by a third party (replevy goods).
6. Sue to recover damages.

The Right to Cancel the Contract When a seller or lessor fails to make proper delivery or repudiates the contract, the buyer or lessee can cancel, or rescind, the contract. The buyer or lessee is relieved of any further obligations under the contract but retains all rights to other remedies against the seller or lessor [UCC 2–711(1), 2A–508(1)(a)]. (The right to cancel the contract is also available to a buyer or lessee who has rightfully rejected goods or revoked acceptance, as will be discussed shortly.)

The Right to Recover the Goods If a buyer or lessee has made a partial or full payment for goods that remain in the possession of the seller or lessor, the buyer or lessee can recover the goods if the seller or lessor becomes insolvent within ten days after receiving the first payment and if the goods are identified to the contract. To exercise this right, the buyer or lessee must tender to the seller or lessor any unpaid balance of the purchase price or lease payments [UCC 2–502, 2A–522].

The Right to Obtain Specific Performance A buyer or lessee can obtain specific performance if the goods are unique or the remedy at law (monetary damages) is inadequate [UCC 2–716(1), 2A–521(1)]. Ordinarily, an award of damages is sufficient to place a buyer or lessee in the position she or he would have occupied if the seller or lessor had fully performed. When the contract is for the purchase of a particular work of art or a similarly unique item, however, damages may not be sufficient. Under these circumstances, equity requires that the seller or lessor perform exactly by delivering the particular goods identified to the contract (the remedy of specific performance).

The Right of Cover In certain situations, buyers and lessees can protect themselves by obtaining **cover**—that is, by buying or leasing substitute goods for those that were due under the contract. This option is available when the seller or lessor repudiates the contract or fails to deliver the goods. (Cover is also available when a buyer or lessee has rightfully rejected goods or revoked acceptance, to be discussed shortly.)

In obtaining cover, the buyer or lessee must act in good faith and without unreasonable delay [UCC 2–712, 2A–518]. After purchasing or leasing substitute goods, the buyer or lessee can recover from the seller or lessor the difference between the cost of cover and the contract price (or lease payments), plus incidental and consequential damages, less the expenses (such as delivery costs) that were saved as a result of the breach [UCC 2–712, 2–715, 2A–518]. Consequential damages are any losses suffered by the buyer or lessee that the seller or lessor had reason to know about at the time of contract formation. Consequential damages can also include any injury to the buyer's or lessee's person or property proximately resulting from the contract's breach [UCC 2–715(2), 2A–520(2)].

Buyers and lessees are not required to cover, and failure to do so will not bar them from using any other remedies available under the UCC. A buyer or lessee who fails to cover, however, risks not being able to collect consequential damages that could have been avoided had he or she purchased or leased substitute goods.

The Right to Replevy Goods Buyers and lessees also have the right to replevy goods. **Replevin**[5] is an action to recover identified goods in the hands of

5. Pronounced ruh-*pleh*-vun, derived from the Old French word *plevir,* meaning "to pledge."

a party who is unlawfully withholding them. At common law, *replevin* refers to a legal proceeding to recover specific personal property that has been unlawfully taken. Under the UCC, a buyer or lessee can replevy goods identified to the contract if the seller or lessor has repudiated or breached the contract. To maintain an action to replevy goods, buyers and lessees must usually show that they were unable to cover for the goods after making a reasonable effort [UCC 2–716(3), 2A–521(3)].

The Right to Recover Damages If a seller or lessor repudiates the contract or fails to deliver the goods, the buyer or lessee can sue for damages. The measure of recovery is the difference between the contract price (or lease payments) and the market price of the goods (or lease payments that could be obtained for the goods) at the time the buyer (or lessee) *learned* of the breach. The market price or market lease payments are determined at the place where the seller or lessor was supposed to deliver the goods. The buyer or lessee can also recover incidental and consequential damages less the expenses that were saved as a result of the breach [UCC 2–713, 2A–519].

Consider an example. Schilling orders 10,000 bushels of wheat from Valdone for $25.00 per bushel, with delivery due on June 14 and payment due on June 20. Valdone does not deliver on June 14. On June 14, the market price of wheat is $25.50 per bushel. Schilling chooses to do without the wheat. He sues Valdone for damages for nondelivery. Schilling can recover $0.50 × 10,000, or $5,000, plus any expenses the breach has caused him. The measure of damages is the market price on the day Schilling was to have received delivery less the contract price. (Any expenses Schilling saved by the breach would be deducted from the damages.)

When the Seller or Lessor Delivers Nonconforming Goods

When the seller or lessor delivers nonconforming goods, the buyer or lessee has several remedies available under the UCC.

The Right to Reject the Goods If either the goods or the tender of the goods by the seller or lessor fails to conform to the contract in any respect, the buyer or lessee can reject all of the goods or any commercial unit of the goods [UCC 2–601, 2A–509]. If the buyer or lessee rejects the goods, she or he may then obtain cover or cancel the contract, and may seek damages just as if the seller or lessor had refused to deliver the goods (see the earlier discussion of these remedies).

In the following case, the buyer of a piano that was represented to be new rejected the instrument on its delivery in an "unacceptable" condition and brought an action against the seller, seeking damages.

CASE 22.2 Jauregui v. Bobb's Piano Sales & Service, Inc.

District Court of Appeal of Florida, Third District, 2006. 922 So.2d 303.

• **Background and Facts** In November 2001, Jorge Jauregui contracted to buy a Kawai RX5 piano (Serial No. 2392719a) for $24,282 from Bobb's Piano Sales and Service, Inc., in Miami, Florida. The piano was represented to be in new condition and to qualify for the manufacturer's "new piano" warranty. Bobb's did not mention that the piano had been in storage for almost a year and had been moved at least six times. The piano was delivered with "unacceptable damage," according to Jauregui, who videotaped its condition. He sent a letter of complaint to the state department of consumer services, identifying at least four "necessary repairs." He then filed a suit in a Florida state court against Bobb's, claiming breach of contract. Bobb's admitted that the piano needed repair. The court concluded that Bobb's was in breach of the parties' contract and that specific performance was not possible, but ruled that Jauregui "takes nothing in damages." Jauregui appealed to a state intermediate appellate court.

• **Decision and Rationale** The state intermediate appellate court agreed with the lower court's conclusion that the defendant had breached the parties' contract but not with the ruling that the plaintiff should not obtain damages. The appellate court awarded Jauregui the contract

CASE CONTINUES

CASE 22.2 CONTINUED price with interest, the amounts of the sales tax and delivery charge, and attorneys' fees. The court also ordered Bobb's to remove the piano. The appellate court stated that the lower court's ruling was "erroneous as a matter of law." The lower court had reasoned that even in a defective condition, the piano as delivered was worth as much or more than Jauregui had paid for it, and thus no damages had been sustained. The appellate court explained, however, that "in a case such as this one, the purchaser of non-conforming goods like the offending piano retains the option to claim either the difference in value or, as plaintiff clearly did in this case, in effect, to cancel the deal and get his money back. This principle is based on the common sense idea that the purchaser is entitled to receive what he wanted to buy and pay for and that the seller is not free to supply any non-conforming item [he or] she wishes just so long as the deviant goods are worth just as much."

- **What If the Facts Were Different?** *If Bobb's had delivered the piano in new condition and Jauregui had refused to pay for it only out of "buyer's remorse," how might the outcome in this case have been different?*

- **The Legal Environment Dimension** *What might a buyer who prevails in a dispute such as the one in this case be awarded in addition to the contract price with interest?*

Timeliness and Reason for Rejection Required. The buyer or lessee must reject the goods within a reasonable amount of time after delivery or tender of delivery and must seasonably (timely) notify the seller or lessor [UCC 2–602(1), 2A–509(2)]. If the buyer or lessee fails to reject the goods within a reasonable amount of time, acceptance will be presumed. The buyer or lessee must also designate defects that are ascertainable by reasonable inspection. Failure to do so precludes the buyer or lessee from using such defects to justify rejection or to establish breach when the seller or lessor could have cured the defects if they had been disclosed seasonably [UCC 2–605, 2A–514].

Duties of Merchant Buyers and Lessees When Goods Are Rejected. Suppose that a *merchant buyer* or *lessee* rightfully rejects goods and the seller or lessor has no agent or business at the place of rejection. What should the buyer or lessee do in that situation? Under the UCC, the merchant buyer or lessee has a good faith obligation to follow any reasonable instructions received from the seller or lessor with respect to the goods [UCC 2–603, 2A–511]. The buyer or lessee is entitled to be reimbursed for the care and cost entailed in following the instructions. The same requirements hold if the buyer or lessee rightfully revokes her or his acceptance of the goods at some later time [UCC 2–608(3), 2A–517(5)]. (Revocation of acceptance will be discussed shortly.)

If no instructions are forthcoming and the goods are perishable or threaten to decline in value quickly, the buyer or lessee can resell the goods in good faith, taking appropriate reimbursement and a selling commission (not to exceed 10 percent of the gross proceeds) from the proceeds [UCC 2–603(1), (2); 2A–511(1)]. If the goods are not perishable, the buyer or lessee may store them for the seller or lessor or reship them to the seller or lessor [UCC 2–604, 2A–512].

Revocation of Acceptance Acceptance of the goods precludes the buyer or lessee from exercising the right of rejection, but it does not necessarily prevent the buyer or lessee from pursuing other remedies. In certain circumstances, a buyer or lessee is permitted to *revoke* his or her acceptance of the goods.

Acceptance of a lot or a commercial unit can be revoked if the nonconformity *substantially* impairs the value of the lot or unit *and* if one of the following factors is present:

1. Acceptance was predicated on the reasonable assumption that the nonconformity would be cured, and it has not been cured within a reasonable period of time [UCC 2–608(1)(a), 2A–517(1)(a)].
2. The buyer or lessee did not discover the nonconformity before acceptance, either because it was difficult to discover before acceptance or because assurances made by the seller or lessor that the goods were conforming kept the buyer or lessee from inspecting the goods [UCC 2–608(1)(b), 2A–517(1)(b)].

Revocation of acceptance is not effective until notice is given to the seller or lessor. Notice must occur within a reasonable time after the buyer or lessee either discovers or *should have discovered* the grounds for revocation. Additionally, revocation must occur before the goods have undergone any substantial change (such as spoilage) not caused by their own defects [UCC 2–608(2), 2A–517(4)]. Once acceptance is revoked, the buyer or lessee can pursue remedies, just as if the goods had been rejected.

The Right to Recover Damages for Accepted Goods A buyer or lessee who has accepted nonconforming goods may also keep the goods and recover for any loss "resulting in the ordinary course of events . . . as determined in any manner which is reasonable" [UCC 2–714(1), 2A–519(3)]. The buyer or lessee, however, must notify the seller or lessor of the breach within a reasonable time after the defect was or should have been discovered. Failure to give notice of the defects (breach) to the seller or lessor bars the buyer or lessee from pursuing any remedy [UCC 2–607(3), 2A–516(3)]. In addition, the parties to a sales or lease contract can insert a provision requiring the buyer or lessee to give notice of any defects in the goods within a prescribed period.

When the goods delivered are not as warranted, the measure of damages equals the difference between the value of the goods as accepted and their value if they had been delivered as warranted, unless special circumstances show proximately caused damages of a different amount [UCC 2–714(2), 2A–519(4)]. The buyer or lessee is also entitled to incidental and consequential damages when appropriate [UCC 2–714(3), 2A–519]. The UCC further permits the buyer or lessee, with proper notice to the seller or lessor, to deduct all or any part of the damages from the price or lease payments still due under the contract [UCC 2–717, 2A–516(1)].

Is two years after a sale of goods a reasonable time period in which to discover a defect in those goods and notify the seller or lessor of a breach? That was the question in the following case.

CASE 22.3 Fitl v. Strek

Supreme Court of Nebraska, 2005. 269 Neb. 51, 690 N.W.2d 605.
www.findlaw.com/11stategov/ne/neca.html[a]

Background and Facts Over the Labor Day weekend in 1995, James Fitl attended a sports card show in San Francisco, California, where he met Mark Strek, doing business as Star Cards of San Francisco, an exhibitor at the show. Later, on Strek's representation that a certain 1952 Mickey Mantle Topps baseball card was in near-mint condition, Fitl bought the card from Strek for $17,750. Strek delivered it to Fitl in Omaha, Nebraska, and Fitl placed it in a safe-deposit box. In May 1997, Fitl sent the card to Professional Sports Authenticators (PSA), a sports-cards grading service. PSA told Fitl that the card was ungradable because it had been discolored and doctored. Fitl complained to Strek, who replied that Fitl should have initiated a return of the card within "a typical grace period for the unconditional return of a card, . . . 7 days to 1 month" of its receipt. In August, Fitl sent the card to ASA Accugrade, Inc. (ASA), another grading service, for a second opinion of the card's value. ASA also concluded that the card had been refinished and trimmed. Fitl filed a suit in a Nebraska state court against Strek, seeking damages. The court awarded Fitl $17,750, plus his court costs. Strek appealed to the Nebraska Supreme Court.

Decision and Rationale The state supreme court affirmed the decision of the lower court. UCC 2–607(3)(a) states, "Where a tender has been accepted * * * the buyer must within a reasonable time after he discovers or should have discovered any breach notify the seller of breach or be barred from any remedy." Under UCC 1–205(a), "what is a reasonable time for taking any action depends on the nature, purpose and circumstances of such action." In the circumstances of this case, the state supreme court concluded that notice of a defect in the goods two years after their purchase was reasonable. The buyer (Fitl) had reasonably relied on the seller's (Strek's) representation that the goods were "authentic," which they were not, and when their

a. In the "Supreme Court Opinions" section, in the "2005" row, click on "January." In the result, click on the appropriate link next to the name of the case to access the opinion.

CASE CONTINUES

CASE 22.3 CONTINUED defects were discovered, Fitl had given a timely notice. The court reasoned that "the policies behind the notice requirement, to allow the seller to correct a defect, to prepare for negotiation and litigation, and to protect against stale claims at a time beyond which an investigation can be completed, were not unfairly prejudiced by the lack of an earlier notice to Strek. Any problem Strek may have had with the party from whom he obtained the baseball card was a separate matter from his transaction with Fitl, and an investigation into the source of the altered card would not have minimized Fitl's damages."

- **What If the Facts Were Different?** *Suppose that Fitl and Strek had included in their deal a clause requiring Fitl to give notice of any defect in the card within "7 days to 1 month" of its receipt. Would the result have been different? Why or why not?*
- **The Legal Environment Dimension** *What might a buyer who prevails in a dispute such as the one in this case be awarded?*

SECTION 7

Additional Provisions Affecting Remedies

The parties to a sales or lease contract can vary their respective rights and obligations by contractual agreement. For example, a seller and buyer can expressly provide for remedies in addition to those provided in the UCC. They can also specify remedies in lieu of those provided in the UCC, or they can change the measure of damages. As under the common law of contracts, they may also include clauses in their contracts providing for liquidated damages in the event of a breach or a delay in performance (see Chapter 18).

Additionally, a seller can stipulate that the buyer's only remedy on the seller's breach will be repair or replacement of the item, or the seller can limit the buyer's remedy to return of the goods and refund of the purchase price. In sales and lease contracts, an agreed-on remedy is in addition to those provided in the UCC unless the parties expressly agree that the remedy is exclusive of all others [UCC 2–719(1), 2A–503(1)]. State "lemon-law" statutes also provide additional remedies to buyers of automobiles.

Exclusive Remedies

If the parties state that a remedy is *exclusive,* then it is the sole remedy. Suppose that Standard Tool Company agrees to sell a pipe-cutting machine to United Pipe & Tubing Corporation. The contract limits United's remedy exclusively to repair or replacement of any defective parts. Thus, repair or replacement of defective parts is the buyer's only remedy under this contract.

When circumstances cause an exclusive remedy to fail in its essential purpose, however, it is no longer exclusive, and the buyer or lessee may pursue other remedies available under the UCC [UCC 2–719(2), 2A–503(2)]. In the example just given, suppose that Standard Tool Company was unable to repair a defective part, and no replacement parts were available. In this situation, because the exclusive remedy failed in its essential purpose, the buyer could pursue other remedies available under the UCC.

Consequential Damages

As discussed in Chapter 18, *consequential damages* are special damages that compensate for indirect losses (such as lost profits) resulting from a breach of contract that were reasonably foreseeable. Under the UCC, parties to a contract can limit or exclude consequential damages, provided the limitation is not unconscionable. When the buyer or lessee is a consumer, any limitation of consequential damages for personal injuries resulting from consumer goods is *prima facie* (presumptively) unconscionable. The limitation of consequential damages is not necessarily unconscionable when the loss is commercial in nature—for example, lost profits and property damage [UCC 2–719(3), 2A–503(3)].

Lemon Laws

Purchasers of defective automobiles—called "lemons"—may have remedies in addition to those offered by the UCC. All of the states and the District of Columbia have enacted *lemon laws.* Basically, lemon laws provide that if an automobile under warranty possesses a defect that significantly affects the vehicle's value or use, and the defect has not been remedied by the seller within a specified number of opportunities (usually three or four), the buyer is entitled to a new car, replacement of defective parts, or return of all consideration paid.

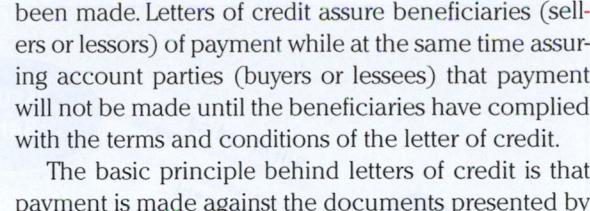

In most states, lemon laws require an aggrieved new-car owner to notify the dealer or manufacturer of the problem and to provide the dealer or manufacturer with an opportunity to solve it. If the problem remains, the owner must then submit complaints to the arbitration program specified in the manufacturer's warranty before taking the case to court. Decisions by arbitration panels are binding on the manufacturer (that is, cannot be appealed by the manufacturer to the courts) but usually are not binding on the purchaser. All arbitration boards must meet state and/or federal standards of impartiality, and some states have established mandatory government-sponsored arbitration programs for lemon-law disputes.

SECTION 8 Dealing with International Contracts

Because buyers and sellers (or lessees and lessors) engaged in international business transactions may be separated by thousands of miles, special precautions are often taken to ensure performance under international contracts. Sellers and lessors want to avoid delivering goods for which they might not be paid. Buyers and lessees desire the assurance that sellers and lessors will not be paid until there is evidence that the goods have been shipped. Thus, **letters of credit** are frequently used to facilitate international business transactions.

Letter-of-Credit Transactions

In a simple letter-of-credit transaction, the *issuer* (a bank) agrees to issue a letter of credit and to ascertain whether the *beneficiary* (seller or lessor) performs certain acts. In return, the *account party* (buyer or lessee) promises to reimburse the issuer for the amount paid to the beneficiary. The transaction may also involve an *advising bank* that transmits information and a *paying bank* that expedites payment under the letter of credit. See Exhibit 22–1 on the following page for an illustration of a letter-of-credit transaction.

Under a letter of credit, the issuer is bound to pay the beneficiary (seller or lessor) when the beneficiary has complied with the terms and conditions of the letter of credit. The beneficiary looks to the issuer, not to the account party (buyer or lessee), when it presents the documents required by the letter of credit. Typically, the letter of credit will require that the beneficiary deliver a *bill of lading* to prove that shipment has been made. Letters of credit assure beneficiaries (sellers or lessors) of payment while at the same time assuring account parties (buyers or lessees) that payment will not be made until the beneficiaries have complied with the terms and conditions of the letter of credit.

The basic principle behind letters of credit is that payment is made against the documents presented by the beneficiary and not against the facts that the documents purport to reflect. Thus, in a letter-of-credit transaction, the issuer (bank) does not police the underlying contract; the letter of credit is independent of the underlying contract between the buyer and the seller. Eliminating the need for the bank (issuer) to inquire into whether actual conditions have been satisfied greatly reduces the costs of letters of credit.

Remedies for Breach of International Sales Contracts

The United Nations Convention on Contracts for the International Sale of Goods (CISG) provides international sellers and buyers with remedies very similar to those available under the UCC. Article 74 of the CISG provides for money damages, including foreseeable consequential damages, on a contract's breach. As under the UCC, the measure of damages is normally the difference between the contract price and the market price of the goods.

Under Article 49, the buyer is permitted to avoid obligations under the contract if the seller breaches the contract or fails to deliver the goods during the time specified in the contract or later agreed on by the parties. Similarly, under Article 64, the seller can avoid obligations under the contract if the buyer breaches the contract, fails to accept delivery of the goods, or fails to pay for the goods.

The CISG also allows for specific performance as a remedy under Article 28, which provides that "one party is entitled to require performance of any obligation by the other party." This statement is then qualified, however. Article 28 goes on to state that a court may grant specific performance as a remedy only if it would do so "under its own law in respect of similar contracts of sale not governed by this Convention." As already discussed, in the United States the equitable remedy of specific performance will normally be granted only if no adequate remedy at law (money damages) is available and the goods are unique in nature. In other countries, however, such as Germany, specific performance is a commonly granted remedy for breach of contract.

EXHIBIT 22–1 • A Letter-of-Credit Transaction

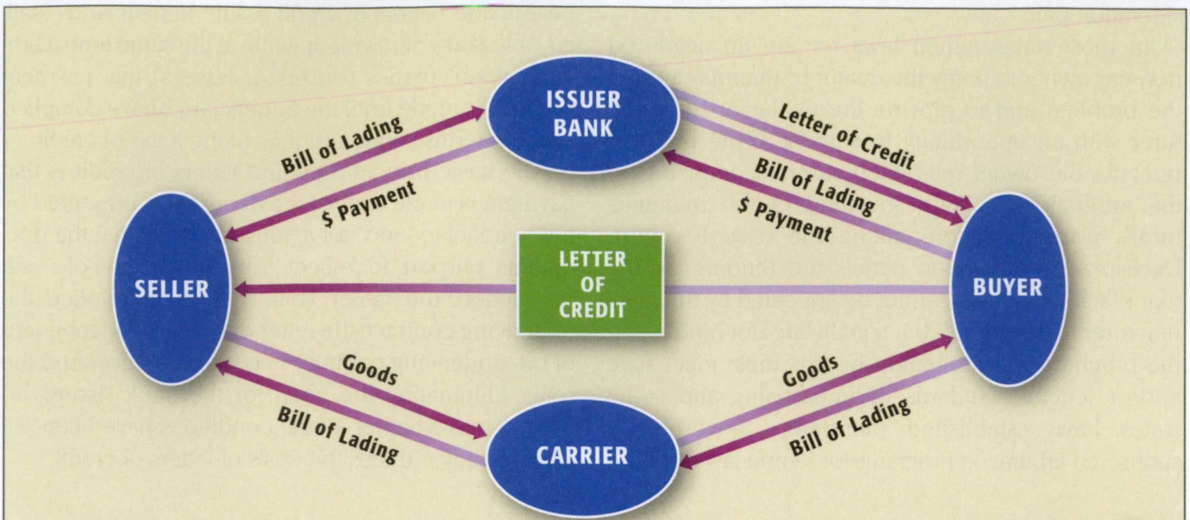

CHRONOLOGY OF EVENTS

1. **Buyer contracts with issuer bank to issue a letter of credit; this sets forth the bank's obligation to pay on the letter of credit and buyer's obligation to pay the bank.**
2. **Letter of credit is sent to seller informing seller that on compliance with the terms of the letter of credit (such as presentment of necessary documents—in this example, a bill of lading), the bank will issue payment for the goods.**
3. **Seller delivers goods to carrier and receives a bill of lading.**
4. **Seller delivers the bill of lading to issuer bank and, if the document is proper, receives payment.**
5. **Issuer bank delivers the bill of lading to buyer.**
6. **Buyer delivers the bill of lading to carrier.**
7. **Carrier delivers the goods to buyer.**
8. **Buyer settles with issuer bank.**

REVIEWING Performance and Breach of Sales and Lease Contracts

GFI, Inc., a Hong Kong company, makes audio decoder chips, one of the essential components used in the manufacture of MP3 players. Egan Electronics contracts with GFI to buy 10,000 chips on an installment contract, with 2,500 chips to be shipped every three months, F.O.B. Hong Kong, via Air Express. At the time for the first delivery, GFI delivers only 2,400 chips but explains to Egan that although the shipment is less than 5 percent short, the chips are of a higher quality than those specified in the contract and are worth 5 percent more than the contract price. Egan accepts the shipment and pays GFI the contract price. At the time for the second shipment, GFI makes a shipment identical to the first. Egan again accepts and pays for the chips. At the time for the third shipment, GFI ships 2,400 of the same chips, but this time GFI sends them via Hong Kong Air instead of Air Express. While in transit, the chips are destroyed. When it is time for the fourth shipment, GFI again sends 2,400 chips, but this time Egan rejects the chips without explanation. Using the information presented in the chapter, answer the following questions.

REVIEWING Performance and Breach of Sales and Lease Contracts, Continued

1. Did GFI have a legitimate reason to expect that Egan would accept the fourth shipment? Why or why not?
2. Did the substitution of carriers in the third shipment constitute a breach of the contract by GFI? Explain.
3. Suppose that the silicon used for the chips becomes unavailable for a period of time. Consequently, GFI cannot manufacture enough chips to fulfill the contract but does ship as many as it can to Egan. Under what doctrine might a court release GFI from further performance of the contract?
4. Under the UCC, does Egan have a right to reject the fourth shipment? Why or why not?

TERMS AND CONCEPTS

conforming goods 402
cover 412
cure 404
installment contract 404
letter of credit 417
perfect tender rule 403
replevin 412
tender of delivery 402

QUESTIONS AND CASE PROBLEMS

22–1. Ames contracts to ship to Curley one hundred model Z television sets. The terms of delivery are F.O.B. Ames's city, by Green Truck Lines, with delivery on or before April 30. On April 15, Ames discovers that because of an error in inventory control, all model Z sets have been sold, and the stock has not been replenished. Ames has model X, a similar but slightly more expensive unit, in stock. On April 16, Ames ships one hundred model X sets, with notice that Curley will be charged the model Z price. Curley (in a proper manner) rejects the model X sets when they are tendered on April 18. Ames does not wish to be held in breach of contract, even though he has tendered nonconforming goods. Discuss Ames's options.

22–2. QUESTION WITH SAMPLE ANSWER

Topken has contracted to sell Lorwin five hundred washing machines of a certain model at list price. Topken is to ship the goods on or before December 1. Topken produces one thousand washing machines of this model but has not yet prepared Lorwin's shipment. On November 1, Lorwin repudiates the contract. Discuss the remedies available to Topken.

• **For a sample answer to Question 22–2, go to Appendix I at the end of this text.**

22–3. Lehor collects antique cars. He contracts to purchase spare parts for a 1938 engine from Beem. These parts are not made anymore and are scarce. To obtain the contract with Beem, Lehor agrees to pay 50 percent of the purchase price in advance. On May 1, Lehor sends the payment, which is received on May 2. On May 3, Beem, having found another buyer willing to pay substantially more for the parts, informs Lehor that he will not deliver as contracted. That same day, Lehor learns that Beem is insolvent. Discuss fully any possible remedies available to Lehor to enable him to take possession of these parts.

22–4. Remedies of the Buyer or Lessee. Mississippi Chemical Corp. (MCC) produces ammonia at its fertilizer plant in Yazoo City, Mississippi. The production of ammonia involves the compression of gas in special equipment called a compressor train. In 1989, MCC bought from Dresser-Rand Co. a specially designed train that included a "high-case compressor" and a "low-case compressor." The contract expressly guaranteed that the train would be free from defects and would conform to certain technical specifications, but it did not work as promised. When the high-case compressor broke in 1990, MCC wrote to Dresser, "This letter constitutes notice by MCC that [Dresser] is in breach" of the contract. The same defects caused the low-case compressor to break in 1993 and 1996. In 1997, MCC filed a suit in a federal district court against Dresser, asserting a number of claims based on the contract. Dresser argued, in part, that it had never received written notice of the defects in the low-case compressor and thus was entitled to judgment as a matter of law. Was there sufficient notice to Dresser for MCC to recover for damages caused by defects in the train? Discuss. [*Mississippi Chemical Corp. v. Dresser-Rand Co.*, 287 F.3d 359 (5th Cir. 2002)]

22–5. Acceptance. In April 1996, Excalibur Oil Group, Inc., applied for credit and opened an account with Standard Distributors, Inc., to obtain snack foods and other items for Excalibur's convenience stores. For three months, Standard delivered the goods and Excalibur paid the invoices. In July, Standard was dissolved and its assets were distributed to J. F. Walker Co. Walker continued to deliver the goods to Excalibur, which continued to pay the invoices until November, when the firm began to experience financial difficulties. By January 1997, Excalibur owed Walker $54,241.77. Walker then dealt with Excalibur solely on a collect-on-delivery basis until Excalibur's stores closed in 1998. Walker filed a suit in a Pennsylvania state court against Excalibur and its owner to recover amounts due on the unpaid invoices. To successfully plead its case, Walker had to show that there was a contract between the parties. One question was whether Excalibur had manifested acceptance of the goods delivered by Walker. How does a buyer manifest acceptance? Was there an acceptance in this case? In whose favor should the court rule, and why? [*J. F. Walker Co. v. Excalibur Oil Group, Inc.*, 792 A.2d 1269 (Pa.Super. 2002)]

22–6. CASE PROBLEM WITH SAMPLE ANSWER

Eaton Corp. bought four air-conditioning units from Trane Co., an operating division of American Standard, Inc., in 1998. The contract stated in part, "NEITHER PARTY SHALL BE LIABLE FOR . . . CONSEQUENTIAL DAMAGES." Trane was responsible for servicing the units. During the last ten days of March 2003, Trane's employees serviced and inspected the units, changed the filters and belts, and made a materials list for repairs. On April 3, a fire occurred at Eaton's facility, extensively damaging the units and the facility, although no one was hurt. Alleging that the fire started in the electric motor of one of the units, and that Trane's faulty servicing of the units caused the fire, Eaton filed a suit in a federal district court against Trane. Eaton asserted a breach of contract, among other claims, seeking consequential damages. Trane filed a motion for summary judgment, based on the limitation-of-remedies clause. What are consequential damages? Can these be limited in some circumstances? Is the clause valid in this case? Explain. [*Eaton Corp. v. Trane Carolina Plains*, 350 F.Supp.2d 699 (D.S.C. 2004)]

- **To view a sample answer for Problem 22–6, go to this book's Web site at www.cengage.com/blaw/jentz, select "Chapter 22," and click on "Case Problem with Sample Answer."**

22–7. Perfect Tender. Advanced Polymer Sciences, Inc. (APS), based in Ohio, makes polymers and resins for use as protective coatings in industrial applications. APS also owns the technology for equipment used to make certain composite fibers. *SAVA gumarska in kemijska industria d.d.* (SAVA), based in Slovenia, makes rubber goods. In 1999, SAVA and APS contracted to form *SAVA Advanced Polymers proizvodno podjetje d.o.o.* (SAVA AP) to make and distribute APS products in Eastern Europe. Their contract provided for, among other things, the alteration of a facility to make the products using specially made equipment to be sold by APS to SAVA. Disputes arose between the parties, and in August 2000, SAVA stopped work on the new facility. APS then notified SAVA that it was stopping the manufacture of the equipment and "insist[ed] on knowing what is SAVA's intention towards this venture." In October, SAVA told APS that it was canceling their contract. In subsequent litigation, SAVA claimed that APS had repudiated the contract when it stopped making the equipment. What might APS assert in its defense? How should the court rule? Explain. [*SAVA gumarska in kemijska industria d.d. v. Advanced Polymer Sciences, Inc.*, 128 S.W.3d 304 (Tex.App.—Dallas 2004)]

22–8. Remedies of the Buyer. L.V.R.V., Inc., sells recreational vehicles (RVs) in Las Vegas, Nevada, as Wheeler's Las Vegas RV. In September 1997, Wheeler's sold a Santara RV made by Coachmen Recreational Vehicle Co. to Arthur and Roswitha Waddell. The Waddells hoped to spend two or three years driving around the country, but almost immediately—and repeatedly—they experienced problems with the RV. Its entry door popped open. Its cooling and heating systems did not work properly. Its batteries did not maintain a charge. Most significantly, its engine overheated when ascending a moderate grade. The Waddells took the RV to Wheeler's service department for repairs. Over the next year and a half, the RV spent more than seven months at Wheeler's. In March 1999, the Waddells filed a complaint in a Nevada state court against the dealer to revoke their acceptance of the RV. What are the requirements for a buyer's revocation of acceptance? Were the requirements met in this case? In whose favor should the court rule? Why? [*Waddell v. L.V.R.V., Inc.*, 122 Nev. 15, 125 P.3d 1160 (2006)]

22–9. Additional Provisions Affecting Remedies. Nomo Agroindustrial Sa De CV is a farm company based in Mexico that grows tomatoes, cucumbers, and other vegetables to sell in the United States. In the early 2000s, Nomo had problems when its tomato plants contracted a disease: tomato spotted wilt virus (TSWV). To obtain a crop that was resistant to TSWV, Nomo contacted Enza Zaden North America, Inc., an international corporation that manufactures seeds. Enza's brochures advertised—and Enza told Nomo—that its Caiman variety was resistant to TSWV. Based on these assurances, Nomo bought Caiman seeds. The invoice, which Nomo's representative signed, limited any damages to the purchase price of the seeds. The plants germinated from the Caiman seeds contracted TSWV, destroying Nomo's entire tomato crop.

Nomo filed a suit in a federal district court against Enza, seeking to recover for the loss. Enza argued, in part, that any damages were limited to the price of the seeds. Can parties agree to limit their remedies under the UCC? If so, what are Nomo's best arguments against the enforcement of the limitations clause in Enza's invoice? What should the court rule on this issue? Why? [*Nomo Agroindustrial Sa De CV v. Enza Zaden North America, Inc.*, 492 F.Supp.2d 1175 (D.Ariz. 2007)]

22-10. A QUESTION OF ETHICS

Scotwood Industries, Inc., sells calcium chloride flake for use in ice melt products. Between July and September 2004, Scotwood delivered thirty-seven shipments of flake to Frank Miller & Sons, Inc. After each delivery, Scotwood billed Miller, which paid thirty-five of the invoices and processed 30 to 50 percent of the flake. In August, Miller began complaining about the quality. Scotwood assured Miller that it would remedy the situation. Finally, in October, Miller told Scotwood, "[T]his is totally unacceptable. We are willing to discuss Scotwood picking up the material." Miller claimed that the flake was substantially defective because it was chunked. Calcium chloride maintains its purity for up to five years but chunks if it is exposed to and absorbs moisture, making it unusable. In response to Scotwood's suit to collect payment on the unpaid invoices, Miller filed a counterclaim in a federal district court for breach of contract, seeking to recover based on revocation of acceptance, among other things. [Scotwood Industries, Inc. v. Frank Miller & Sons, Inc., *435 F.Supp.2d 1160 (D.Kan. 2006)]*

(a) What is revocation of acceptance? How does a buyer effectively exercise this option? Do the facts in this case support this theory as a ground for Miller to recover damages? Why or why not?

(b) Is there an ethical basis for allowing a buyer to revoke acceptance of goods and recover damages? If so, is there an ethical limit to this right? Discuss.

22-11. VIDEO QUESTION

Go to this text's Web site at **www.cengage.com/blaw/jentz** and select "Chapter 22." Click on "Video Questions" and view the video titled *International: Letter of Credit.* Then answer the following questions.

(a) Do banks always require the same documents to be presented in letter-of-credit transactions? If not, who dictates what documents will be required in the letter of credit?

(b) At what point does the seller receive payment in a letter-of-credit transaction?

(c) What assurances does a letter of credit provide to the buyer and the seller involved in the transaction?

LAW ON THE WEB

For updated links to resources available on the Web, as well as a variety of other materials, visit this text's Web site at

www.cengage.com/blaw/jentz

To find information on the UCC, including the UCC provisions discussed in this chapter, refer to the Web sites listed in the *Law on the Web* section in Chapter 20.

For access to materials and articles concerning the United Nations Convention on Contracts for the International Sale of Goods (CISG), go to the Institute of International Commercial Law's Web site at

www.cisg.law.pace.edu/cisg/text/cisgint.html

Legal Research Exercises on the Web

Go to **www.cengage.com/blaw/jentz**, the Web site that accompanies this text. Select "Chapter 22" and click on "Internet Exercises." There you will find the following Internet research exercises that you can perform to learn more about the topics covered in this chapter.

Internet Exercise 22–1: Legal Perspective
International Performance Requirements

Internet Exercise 22–2: Social Perspective
Lemon Laws

Internet Exercise 22–3: Management Perspective
The Right to Reject Goods

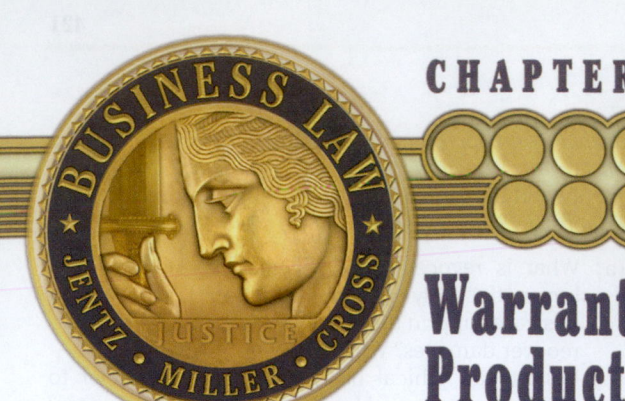

CHAPTER 23

Warranties and Product Liability

Warranty is an age-old concept. In sales and lease law, a warranty is an assurance by one party of the existence of a fact on which the other party can rely. Article 2 (on sales) and Article 2A (on leases) of the Uniform Commercial Code (UCC) designate several types of warranties that can arise in a sales or lease contract. These warranties include warranties of title, express warranties, and implied warranties. We examine each of these types of warranties in this chapter.

Because a warranty imposes a duty on the seller or lessor, a breach of warranty is a breach of the seller's or lessor's promise. Assuming that the parties have not agreed to limit or modify the remedies available, if the seller or lessor breaches a warranty, the buyer or lessee can sue to recover damages from the seller or lessor. Under some circumstances, a breach of warranty can allow the buyer or lessee to rescind (cancel) the agreement.[1]

Breach of warranty actions are a subset of product liability claims. Product liability encompasses the contract theory of warranty, as well as the tort theories of negligence, misrepresentation, and strict liability (discussed in Chapters 6 and 7). Manufacturers and sellers of goods can be held liable for products that are defective or unreasonably dangerous. Goods can be defective in a number of ways, including manufacturing defects, design defects, and inadequate warnings. We examine product liability in the second part of the chapter. Because warranty law protects buyers, some of whom are consumers, warranty law is also part of the broad body of consumer protection law that will be discussed in Chapter 44.

1. *Rescission* restores the parties to the positions they were in before the contract was made.

SECTION 1 Types of Warranties

Most goods are covered by some type of warranty designed to protect buyers. Articles 2 and 2A of the UCC designate several types of warranties that can arise in a sales or lease contract, including warranties of title, express warranties, and implied warranties. We discuss these types of warranties in the following subsections, as well as a federal statute that is designed to prevent deception and make warranties more understandable.

Warranties of Title

Title warranty arises automatically in most sales contracts. The UCC imposes the three types of warranties of title discussed here [UCC 2–312, 2A–211].

Good Title In most sales, sellers warrant that they have good and valid title to the goods sold and that the transfer of the title is rightful [UCC 2–312(1)(a)]. Suppose that Alexis steals goods from Camden and sells them to Ona, who does not know that they are stolen. If Camden discovers that Ona has the goods, then he has the right to reclaim them from Ona. When Alexis sold Ona the goods, Alexis *automatically* warranted to Ona that the title conveyed was valid and that its transfer was rightful. Because a thief has no title to stolen goods, Alexis breached the warranty of title imposed by UCC 2–312(1)(a) and became liable to the buyer for appropriate damages. (See Chapter 21 on pages 389–392 for a detailed discussion of sales by nonowners.)

No Liens A second warranty of title protects buyers who are *unaware* of any encumbrances (claims, charges, or liabilities—usually called *liens*[2]) against goods at the time the contract is made [UCC 2–312(1)(b)]. This warranty protects buyers who, for example, unknowingly purchase goods that are subject to a creditor's security interest (a *security interest* in this context is an interest in the goods that secures payment or performance of an obligation—see Chapter 29). If a creditor legally repossesses the goods from a buyer *who had no actual knowledge of the security interest,* the buyer can recover from the seller for breach of warranty. (A buyer who has *actual knowledge of a security interest* has no recourse against a seller.)

Consider an example. Henderson buys a used boat from Loring for cash. A month later, Barish proves that she has a valid security interest in the boat and that Loring, who has missed five payments, is in default. Barish then repossesses the boat from Henderson. Henderson demands his cash back from Loring. Under Section 2–312(1)(b), Henderson has legal grounds to recover from Loring because the seller of goods warrants that the goods are delivered free from any security interest or other lien of which the buyer has no knowledge.

Article 2A affords similar protection for lessees. Section 2A–211(1) provides that during the term of the lease, no claim of any third party will interfere with the lessee's enjoyment of the leasehold interest.

No Infringements A merchant-seller is also deemed to warrant that the goods delivered are free from any copyright, trademark, or patent claims of a third person[3] [UCC 2–312(3), 2A–211(2)]. If this warranty is breached and the buyer is sued by the party holding copyright, trademark, or patent rights in the goods, the buyer *must notify the seller* of the litigation within a reasonable time to enable the seller to decide whether to defend the lawsuit. If the seller states in a writing (or record) that she or he has decided to defend and agrees to bear all expenses, then the buyer must turn over control of the litigation to the seller; otherwise, the buyer is barred from any remedy against the seller for liability established by the litigation [UCC 2–607(3)(b), 2–607(5)(b)].

In situations that involve leases rather than sales, Article 2A provides for the same notice of infringement litigation [UCC 2A–516(3)(b), 2A–516(4)(b)]. There is an exception for leases to individual consumers for personal, family, or household purposes. A consumer who fails to notify the lessor within a reasonable time does not lose his or her remedy against the lessor for whatever liability is established in the litigation [UCC 2A–516(3)(b)].

Disclaimer of Title Warranty In an ordinary sales transaction, the title warranty can be disclaimed or modified only by *specific language* in a contract. For example, sellers may assert that they are transferring only such rights, title, and interest as they have in the goods. In a lease transaction, the disclaimer must "be specific, be by a writing, and be conspicuous" [UCC 2A–214(4)].[4]

In certain situations, the circumstances surrounding the sale are sufficient to indicate clearly to a buyer that no assurances as to title are being made. The classic example is a sheriff's sale; in this situation, buyers know that the goods have been seized to satisfy debts and that the sheriff cannot guarantee title [UCC 2–312(2)].

Express Warranties

A seller or lessor can create an **express warranty** by making representations concerning the quality, condition, description, or performance potential of the goods. Under UCC 2–313 and 2A–210, express warranties arise when a seller or lessor indicates any of the following:

1. That the goods conform to any *affirmation* (declaration) of fact or *promise* that the seller or lessor makes to the buyer or lessee about the goods. Such affirmations or promises are usually made during the bargaining process. Statements such as "these drill bits will *easily* penetrate stainless steel—and without dulling" are express warranties.
2. That the goods conform to any *description* of them. For example, a label that reads "Crate contains one

2. Pronounced *leens*. Liens will be discussed in detail in Chapter 28.

3. Recall from Chapter 20 that a *merchant* is defined in UCC 2–104(1) as a person who deals in goods of the kind involved in the sales contract or who, by occupation, presents himself or herself as having knowledge or skill peculiar to the goods involved in the transaction.

4. Note that although the 2003 amendments to Articles 2 and 2A have not been adopted in any state, some states, such as Connecticut, have passed legislation that expressly allows warranty disclaimers via electronic record. See Connecticut Statutes Section 42a-2A-214. Even in states that have not passed such legislation, electronic records are likely to satisfy the writing requirement for disclaimers (under the Uniform Electronic Transactions Act, discussed in Chapter 19).

150-horsepower diesel engine" or a contract that calls for the delivery of a "wool coat" creates an express warranty that the content of the goods sold conforms to the description.

3. That the goods conform to any *sample or model* of the goods shown to the buyer or lessee.

Express warranties can be found in a seller's or lessor's advertisement, brochure, or promotional materials, in addition to being made orally or in an express warranty provision in a sales or lease contract.

Basis of the Bargain To create an express warranty, a seller or lessor does not have to use formal words such as *warrant* or *guarantee.* It is only necessary that a reasonable buyer or lessee would regard the representation as being part of the basis of the bargain [UCC 2–313(2), 2A–210(2)]. Just what constitutes the basis of the bargain is hard to say. The UCC does not define the concept, and it is a question of fact in each case whether a representation was made at such a time and in such a way that it induced the buyer or lessee to enter into the contract. Therefore, if an express warranty is not intended, the marketing agent or salesperson should not promise too much.

Businesspersons engaged in selling or leasing goods should be careful about the words they use with customers, in writing and orally. Express warranties can be found in a seller's or lessor's advertisement, brochure, or promotional materials, in addition to being made orally or in an express warranty provision in a contract. Avoiding unintended warranties is crucial in preventing legal disputes, and all employees should be instructed on how the promises they make to buyers during a sale can create warranties.

Statements of Opinion and Value Only statements of fact create express warranties. A seller or lessor who makes a statement merely relating to the value or worth of the goods, or states an opinion about or recommends the goods, is not creating an express warranty [UCC 2–313(2), 2A–210(2)].

Suppose that a seller claims that "this is the best used car to come along in years; it has four new tires and a 250-horsepower engine just rebuilt this year." The seller has made several *affirmations of fact* that can create a warranty: the automobile has an engine; it has a 250-horsepower engine; the engine was rebuilt this year; there are four tires on the automobile; and the tires are new. The seller's *opinion* that the vehicle is "the best used car to come along in years," however, is known as "puffery" and creates no warranty. (*Puffery* is an expression of opinion by a seller or lessor that is not made as a representation of fact.) A statement relating to the value of the goods, such as "it's worth a fortune" or "anywhere else you'd pay $10,000 for it," usually does not create a warranty.

An Exception for Statements of Opinion by Experts. Although an ordinary seller or lessor can give an opinion that is not a warranty, if the seller or lessor is an expert and gives an opinion as an expert to a layperson, then a warranty may be created. For example, Saul is an art dealer and an expert in seventeenth-century paintings. If Saul states to Lauren, a purchaser, that in his opinion a particular painting is a Rembrandt, Saul has warranted the accuracy of his opinion.

Puffery versus Express Warranties. It is not always easy to determine what constitutes an express warranty and what constitutes puffery. The reasonableness of the buyer's or lessee's reliance appears to be the controlling criterion in many cases. Suppose that a salesperson's statements that a ladder will "never break" and will "last a lifetime" are so clearly improbable that no reasonable buyer should rely on them. Additionally, the context in which a statement is made may be relevant in determining the reasonableness of a buyer's or lessee's reliance. A reasonable person is more likely to rely on a written statement made in an advertisement than on a statement made orally by a salesperson.

For example, in one case a tobacco farmer had read an ad stating that Chlor-O-Pic was a chemical fumigant that would suppress black shank disease, a fungal disease that destroys tobacco crops. The ad specifically indicated how much of the product should be applied per acre and stated that, if applied as directed, Chlor-O-Pic would give "season-long control with application in fall, winter, or spring." The farmer bought eight thousand pounds of Chlor-O-Pic and applied it as directed to 143 acres of his tobacco crop. Nonetheless, the crop developed black shank disease, resulting in an estimated loss of three thousand pounds of tobacco per acre. When the farmer sued the manufacturer of Chlor-O-Pic, he argued that he had purchased the product in reliance on what he assumed to be a "strong promise" of "season-long control." In this case, the jury agreed with the farmer. The manufacturer had indeed made a strong promise—one that created an express warranty.[5]

Implied Warranties

An **implied warranty** is one that *the law derives* by inference from the nature of the transaction or the relative situations or circumstances of the parties. Under the UCC, merchants impliedly warrant that the goods they sell or lease are merchantable and, in certain circumstances, fit for a particular purpose. In addition, an implied warranty may arise from a course of dealing or usage of trade. We examine these three types of implied warranties in the following subsections.

Implied Warranty of Merchantability Every sale or lease of goods made by a merchant who deals in goods of the kind sold or leased automatically gives rise to an **implied warranty of merchantability** [UCC 2–314, 2A–212]. Thus, a merchant who is in the business of selling ski equipment makes an implied warranty of merchantability every time he sells a pair of skis. A neighbor selling her skis at a garage sale does not (because she is not in the business of selling goods of this type).

Merchantable Goods. To be *merchantable*, goods must be "reasonably fit for the ordinary purposes for which such goods are used." They must be of at least average, fair, or medium-grade quality. The quality must be comparable to quality that will pass without objection in the trade or market for goods of the same description. To be merchantable, the goods must also be adequately packaged and labeled, and they must conform to the promises or affirmations of fact made on the container or label, if any.

The warranty of merchantability may be breached even though the merchant did not know or could not have discovered that a product was defective (not merchantable). Suppose that Christianson contracts to purchase a log home package from Milde, a log home dealer. The dealer provides the logs and other materials and constructs the home. Immediately after Christianson moves into the house, she finds that the exterior walls leak when it rains, staining and discoloring the interior walls, due to a defective waterproofing product used on the logs. Even though Milde did not know that the waterproofing product was defective, he can be held liable because the waterproofing product was not reasonably fit for its ordinary purpose (making the house waterproof).

Of course, merchants are not absolute insurers against *all* accidents arising in connection with the goods. For example, a bar of soap is not unmerchantable merely because a user could slip and fall by stepping on it.

If the buyer of a product that requires a significant number of repairs sells the item before filing a complaint against its manufacturer, is the sale evidence of the good's merchantability? That was the question in the following case.

5. *Triple E, Inc. v. Hendrix & Dail, Inc.*, 344 S.C. 186, 543 S.E.2d 245 (2001). See also *Nomo Agroindustrial Sa De CV v. Enza Zaden North America, Inc.*, 492 F.Supp.2d 1175 (D.Ariz. 2007).

CASE 23.1 Shoop v. DaimlerChrysler Corp.

Appellate Court of Illinois, First District, Fourth Division, 2007.
371 Ill.App.3d 1058, 864 N.E.2d 785, 309 Ill.Dec. 544.

• **Company Profile** In 1920, Walter Chrysler, the head of manufacturing operations for General Motors Corporation (GMC), was dissatisfied with its management and quit. He took over Maxwell Motor Company and renamed it Chrysler Corporation. For most of its history, Chrysler has ranked third in vehicle sales among the "Big 3" U.S. automakers—GMC, Ford Motor Company, and Chrysler. In 1998, the German company Daimler-Benz AG, maker of Mercedes-Benz vehicles, bought Chrysler and created DaimlerChrysler AG. The new entity proved less successful than its investors hoped, and in 2007, Chrysler was sold to Cerberus Capital Management, which renamed it Chrysler, LLC (**www.chrysler.com**). Its vehicles are made and sold under the Chrysler, Dodge, Jeep, and Mopar brands.

• **Background and Facts** In April 2002, Darrell Shoop bought a 2002 Dodge Dakota truck for $28,000 from Dempsey Dodge in Chicago, Illinois. DaimlerChrysler Corporation had manufactured

CASE CONTINUES

CASE 23.1 CONTINUED the Dakota. Problems with the truck arose almost immediately. Defects in the engine, suspension, steering, transmission, and other components required repairs twelve times within the first eighteen months, including at least five times for the same defect, which remained uncorrected. In May 2005, after having driven the Dakota 39,000 miles, Shoop accepted $16,500 for the trade-in value of the truck as part of a purchase of a new vehicle. At the time, a comparable vehicle in average condition would have had an average trade-in value of $14,425 and an average retail value of $17,225. Shoop filed a suit in an Illinois state court against DaimlerChrysler, alleging, among other things, a breach of the implied warranty of merchantability. DaimlerChrysler countered, in part, that Shoop's sale of the Dakota was evidence of its merchantability. The court issued a summary judgment in DaimlerChrysler's favor. Shoop appealed to a state intermediate appellate court.

- **Decision and Rationale** The state appellate court reversed the lower court's summary judgment and remanded the case for trial. For automobiles, fitness for the ordinary purpose of driving implies that the vehicle should be in safe condition and free from defects. The reviewing court stated that, in addition, "breach of an implied warranty of merchantability may also occur when the warrantor has unsuccessfully attempted to repair or replace defective parts. Whether an implied warranty has been breached is a question of fact." The facts in this case were clear: the plaintiff was required to take the truck to the Chrysler dealership twelve times within eighteen months. The dealership was unable to cure the defects after a reasonable number of attempts. The state intermediate appellate court concluded that "a genuine issue of material fact existed as to whether Chrysler breached the implied warranty of merchantability."

- **The Ethical Dimension** *Should Shoop's trade-in of the Dakota truck preclude his recovery in this case? Why or why not?*

- **The Legal Environment Dimension** *If Shoop is allowed to recover damages for breach of warranty, what should be the measure of those damages?*

Merchantable Food. The UCC treats the serving of food or drink to be consumed on or off the premises as a sale of goods subject to the implied warranty of merchantability [UCC 2–314(1)]. "Merchantable" food is food that is fit to eat on the basis of consumer expectations. For example, the courts assume that consumers should reasonably expect to find on occasion bones in fish fillets, cherry pits in cherry pie, a nutshell in a package of shelled nuts, and the like—because such substances are natural to the ingredients or the finished food product. In contrast, consumers would not reasonably expect to find an inchworm in a can of peas or a piece of glass in a soft drink—because these substances are *not* natural to the food product. In the following classic case, the court had to determine whether one should reasonably expect to find a fish bone in fish chowder.

CASE 23.2 Webster v. Blue Ship Tea Room, Inc.

Supreme Judicial Court of Massachusetts, 1964. 347 Mass. 421, 198 N.E.2d 309.

- **Background and Facts** Blue Ship Tea Room, Inc., was located in Boston in an old building overlooking the ocean. Webster, who had been born and raised in New England, went to the restaurant and ordered fish chowder. The chowder was milky in color. After three or four spoonfuls, she felt something lodged in her throat. As a result, she underwent two esophagoscopies; in the second esophagoscopy, a fish bone was found and removed. Webster filed a suit against the restaurant in a Massachusetts state court for breach of the implied warranty of merchantability. The jury rendered a verdict for Webster, and the restaurant appealed to the state's highest court.

- **Decision and Rationale** The Supreme Judicial Court of Massachusetts "sympathized with a plaintiff who has suffered a peculiarly New England injury," but entered a judgment for Blue

CASE 23.2 CONTINUED Ship Tea Room. The court concluded that no breach of warranty had occurred. The question was whether a fish bone made chowder unfit for eating. "The joys of life in New England include the ready availability of fresh fish chowder. We should be prepared to cope with the hazards of fish bones, the occasional presence of which in chowders is, it seems to us, to be anticipated, and which, in the light of a hallowed tradition, do not impair their fitness or merchantability."

• **Impact of This Case on Today's Law** *This classic case, phrased in memorable language, was an early application of the UCC's implied warranty of merchantability to food products. The case established the rule that consumers should expect to find, on occasion, elements of food products that are natural to the product (such as fish bones in fish chowder). Courts today still apply this rule.*

• **The E-Commerce Dimension** *If Webster had made the chowder herself from a recipe that she had found on the Internet, could she have successfully brought an action against its author for a breach of the implied warranty of merchantability? Explain.*

Implied Warranty of Fitness for a Particular Purpose The **implied warranty of fitness for a particular purpose** arises when *any* seller or lessor (merchant or nonmerchant) knows the particular purpose for which a buyer or lessee will use the goods *and* knows that the buyer or lessee is relying on the skill and judgment of the seller or lessor to select suitable goods [UCC 2–315, 2A–213].

Particular versus Ordinary Purpose. A "particular purpose" of the buyer or lessee differs from the "ordinary purpose for which goods are used" (merchantability). Goods can be merchantable but unfit for a particular purpose. Assume that you need a gallon of paint to match the color of your living room walls—a light shade somewhere between coral and peach. You take a sample to your local hardware store and request a gallon of paint of that color. Instead, you are given a gallon of bright blue paint. Here, the salesperson has not breached any warranty of implied merchantability—the bright blue paint is of high quality and suitable for interior walls—but she or he has breached an implied warranty of fitness for a particular purpose.

Knowledge and Reliance Requirements. A seller or lessor need not have actual knowledge of the buyer's or lessee's particular purpose. It is sufficient if a seller or lessor "has reason to know" the purpose. For an implied warranty to be created, however, the buyer or lessee must have *relied* on the skill or judgment of the seller or lessor in selecting or furnishing suitable goods. Moreover, the seller or lessor must have reason to know that the buyer or lessee is relying on her or his judgment or skill.

For example, Bloomberg leases a computer from Future Tech, a lessor of technical business equipment. Bloomberg tells the clerk that she wants a computer that will run a complicated new engineering graphics program at a realistic speed. Future Tech leases Bloomberg an Architex One computer with a CPU speed of only 2.4 gigahertz, even though a speed of at least 3.8 gigahertz would be required to run Bloomberg's graphics program at a "realistic speed." After discovering that it takes forever to run her program, Bloomberg wants a full refund. Here, because Future Tech has breached the implied warranty of fitness for a particular purpose, Bloomberg normally will be able to recover. The clerk knew specifically that Bloomberg wanted a computer with enough speed to run certain software and was relying on the clerk's judgment. Furthermore, Bloomberg relied on the clerk to furnish a computer that would fulfill this purpose. Because Future Tech did not do so, the warranty was breached.

Other Implied Warranties Implied warranties can also arise (or be excluded or modified) as a result of course of dealing or usage of trade [UCC 2–314(3), 2A–212(3)]. In the absence of evidence to the contrary, when both parties to a sales or lease contract have knowledge of a well-recognized trade custom, the courts will infer that both parties intended for that custom to apply to their contract. For example, if it is an industry-wide custom to lubricate a new car before it is delivered and a dealer fails to do so, the dealer can be held liable to a buyer for damages resulting from the breach of an implied warranty. (This, of course, would also be negligence on the part of the dealer.)

Third Party Beneficiaries of Warranties

One of the general principles of contract law is that unless you are one of the parties to a contract, you have no rights under the contract. In other words, *privity of contract* must exist between a plaintiff and a defendant before any action based on a contract can be maintained. In Chapter 16, you learned about two notable exceptions to the rule of privity—assignments and third party beneficiary contracts. Another exception is made under warranty laws so that third parties can recover for harms suffered as a result of breached warranties, both express and implied.

There has been sharp disagreement among state courts as to how far warranty liability should extend, however. In view of this disagreement, the UCC offers three alternatives for liability to third parties [UCC 2–318, 2A–216]. All three alternatives are intended to eliminate the privity requirement with respect to certain types of injuries (personal versus property) to certain beneficiaries, such as household members or bystanders. For example, in some jurisdictions if the injured plaintiff was a guest in the home of the person who purchased the warranted product, the privity requirement is waived.

Magnuson-Moss Warranty Act

The Magnuson-Moss Warranty Act of 1975[6] was designed to prevent deception in warranties by making them easier to understand. The Federal Trade Commission (FTC) primarily enforces the act (the FTC's role in protecting consumers will be discussed in Chapter 44). Additionally, the attorney general or a consumer who has been injured can enforce the act if informal procedures for settling disputes prove to be ineffective. The act modifies UCC warranty rules to some extent when *consumer* transactions are involved. The UCC, however, remains the primary codification of warranty rules for commercial transactions.

Under the Magnuson-Moss Warranty Act, no seller is *required* to give a written warranty for consumer goods sold. If a seller chooses to make an express written warranty, however, and the cost of the consumer goods is more than $25, the warranty must be labeled as either "full" or "limited." In addition, the warrantor must make certain disclosures fully and conspicuously in a single document in "readily understood language." These disclosures state the names and addresses of the warrantor(s), what specifically is warranted, procedures for enforcing the warranty, any limitations on warranty relief, and that the buyer has legal rights.

Full Warranty Although a *full warranty* may not cover every aspect of the consumer product sold, what it does cover ensures some type of consumer satisfaction in the event that the product is defective. A full warranty requires free repair or replacement of any defective part; if the product cannot be repaired within a reasonable time, the consumer has the choice of either a refund or a replacement without charge. There is frequently no time limit on a full warranty. Any limitation on consequential damages must be *conspicuously* stated. Additionally, the warrantor need not perform warranty services if the problem with the product was caused by damage to the product or unreasonable use by the consumer.

Limited Warranty A *limited warranty* arises when the written warranty fails to meet one of the minimum requirements of a full warranty. The fact that only a limited warranty is being given must be conspicuously disclosed. If the only difference between a limited warranty and a full warranty is a time limitation, the Magnuson-Moss Warranty Act allows the warrantor to identify the warranty as a full warranty by such language as "full twelve-month warranty."

Implied Warranties Implied warranties do not arise under the Magnuson-Moss Warranty Act; they continue to be created according to UCC provisions. Implied warranties may not be disclaimed under the Magnuson-Moss Warranty Act, however. A warrantor can impose a time limit on the duration of an implied warranty, but it must correspond to the duration of the express warranty.[7] (See *Concept Summary 23.1* for a review of the various types of warranties.)

SECTION 2 Overlapping Warranties

Sometimes, two or more warranties are made in a single transaction. An implied warranty of merchantability, an implied warranty of fitness for a particular purpose, or both can exist in addition to an express warranty. For example, when a sales contract for a new car states that "this car engine is warranted to be free

6. 15 U.S.C. Sections 2301–2312.

7. This time limit must, of course, be reasonable, conscionable, and set forth in clear and conspicuous language on the face of the warranty.

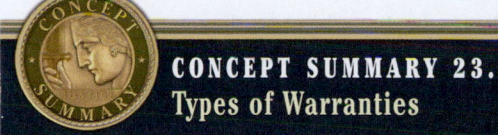

CONCEPT SUMMARY 23.1
Types of Warranties

Concept	Description
WARRANTIES OF TITLE	The UCC provides for the following warranties of title [UCC 2–312, 2A–211]: 1. *Good title*—A seller warrants that he or she has the right to pass good and rightful title to the goods. 2. *No liens*—A seller warrants that the goods sold are free of any encumbrances (claims, charges, or liabilities—usually called *liens*). A lessor warrants that the lessee will not be disturbed in her or his possession of the goods by the claims of a third party. 3. *No infringements*—A merchant-seller warrants that the goods are free of infringement claims (claims that a patent, trademark, or copyright has been infringed) by third parties. Lessors make similar warranties.
EXPRESS WARRANTIES	An express warranty arises under the UCC when a seller or lessor indicates any of the following as part of the sale or bargain [UCC 2–313, 2A–210]: 1. An affirmation or promise of fact. 2. A description of the goods. 3. A sample or model shown as conforming to the contract goods.
IMPLIED WARRANTY OF MERCHANTABILITY	When a seller or lessor is a merchant who deals in goods of the kind sold or leased, the seller or lessor warrants that the goods sold or leased are properly packaged and labeled, are of proper quality, and are reasonably fit for the ordinary purposes for which such goods are used [UCC 2–314, 2A–212].
IMPLIED WARRANTY OF FITNESS FOR A PARTICULAR PURPOSE	An implied warranty of fitness for a particular purpose arises when the buyer's or lessee's purpose or use is known by the seller or lessor, and the buyer or lessee purchases or leases the goods in reliance on the seller's or lessor's selection [UCC 2–315, 2A–213].
OTHER IMPLIED WARRANTIES	Other implied warranties can arise as a result of course of dealing or usage of trade [UCC 2–314(3), 2A–212(3)].
MAGNUSON-MOSS WARRANTY ACT	Express written warranties covering consumer goods priced at more than $25, *if made,* must be labeled as either a full warranty or a limited warranty. A full warranty requires free repair or replacement of defective parts and refund or replacement for goods that cannot be repaired in a reasonable time. A limited warranty arises when less than a full warranty is being offered.

from defects for 36,000 miles or thirty-six months, whichever occurs first," there is an express warranty against all defects, as well as an implied warranty that the car will be fit for normal use.

When the Warranties Are Consistent

The rule under the UCC is that express and implied warranties are construed as *cumulative* if they are consistent with one another [UCC 2–317, 2A–215]. In other words, courts interpret two or more warranties as being in agreement with each other unless this construction is unreasonable. If it is unreasonable for the two warranties to be consistent, then the court looks at the intention of the parties to determine which warranty is dominant.

Conflicting Warranties If the warranties are *inconsistent,* the courts usually apply the following rules to interpret which warranty is most important:

1. *Express* warranties displace inconsistent *implied* warranties, except implied warranties of fitness for a particular purpose.
2. Samples take precedence over inconsistent general descriptions.

3. Exact or technical specifications displace inconsistent samples or general descriptions.

In the example presented earlier on page 427, suppose that when Bloomberg leases the computer at Future Tech, the contract contains an express warranty concerning the speed of the CPU and the application programs that the computer is capable of running. Bloomberg does not realize that the speed expressly warranted in the contract is insufficient for her needs until she tries to run the software and the computer slows to a crawl. Bloomberg later claims that Future Tech has breached the implied warranty of fitness for a particular purpose because she made it clear that she was leasing the computer to perform certain tasks. Although the express warranty on CPU speed takes precedence over the implied warranty of merchantability, it normally does not take precedence over an implied warranty of fitness for a particular purpose. Bloomberg normally will prevail.

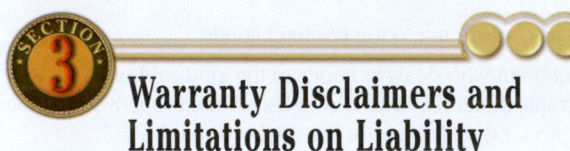

SECTION 3 Warranty Disclaimers and Limitations on Liability

The UCC generally permits warranties to be disclaimed or limited by specific and unambiguous language, provided that this is done in a manner that protects the buyer or lessee from surprise. Because each type of warranty is created in a different way, the manner in which a seller or lessor can disclaim warranties varies with the type of warranty.

Express Warranties

As already stated, any affirmation of fact or promise, description of the goods, or use of samples or models by a seller or lessor creates an express warranty. Obviously, then, express warranties can be excluded if the seller or lessor carefully refrains from making any promise or affirmation of fact relating to the goods, describing the goods, or using a sample or model. In addition, a written (or an electronic record) disclaimer in language that is clear and conspicuous, and called to a buyer's or lessee's attention, can negate all oral express warranties not included in the written sales or lease contract [UCC 2–316(1), 2A–214(1)]. This allows the seller or lessor to avoid false allegations that oral warranties were made, and it ensures that only representations made by properly authorized individuals are included in the bargain.

Note, however, that a buyer or lessee must be made aware of any warranty disclaimers or modifications *at the time the contract is formed.* In other words, any oral or written warranties—or disclaimers—made during the bargaining process cannot be modified at a later time by the seller or lessor without the consent of the buyer or lessee.

Implied Warranties

Generally speaking, unless circumstances indicate otherwise, the implied warranties of merchantability and fitness are disclaimed by the expressions "as is," "with all faults," and other similar phrases that in common understanding for *both* parties call the buyer's or lessee's attention to the fact that there are no implied warranties [UCC 2–316(3)(a), 2A–214(3)(a)]. (Note, however, that some states have passed consumer protection statutes forbidding "as is" sales or making it illegal to disclaim warranties of merchantability on consumer goods.)

Disclaimer of the Implied Warranty of Merchantability The UCC also permits a seller or lessor to specifically disclaim an implied warranty either of merchantability or of fitness. A merchantability disclaimer must specifically mention *merchantability.* It need not be written; but if it is, the writing (or record) must be conspicuous [UCC 2–316(2), 2A–214(4)]. Under the UCC, a term or clause is conspicuous when it is written or displayed in such a way that a reasonable person would notice it. For example, terms can be made conspicuous by using capital letters, a larger font size, or a different color that sets them off from the surrounding text.

Disclaimer of the Implied Warranty of Fitness To disclaim an implied warranty of fitness for a particular purpose, the disclaimer must be in writing and be conspicuous. The writing does not have to mention the word *fitness;* it is sufficient if, for example, the disclaimer states, "THERE ARE NO WARRANTIES THAT EXTEND BEYOND THE DESCRIPTION ON THE FACE HEREOF."

Buyer's or Lessee's Examination or Refusal to Inspect

If a buyer or lessee actually examines the goods (or a sample or model) as fully as desired before entering into a contract, or refuses to examine the goods on the seller's or lessor's request that he or she do so, *there is no implied warranty with respect to defects that a reason-*

able examination would reveal or defects that are found on examination [UCC 2–316(3)(b), 2A–214(2)(b)].

Suppose that Joplin buys a lamp at Gershwin's Home Store. No express warranties are made. Gershwin asks Joplin to inspect the lamp before buying it, but she refuses. Had Joplin inspected the lamp, she would have noticed that the base of the lamp was obviously cracked and the electrical cord was loose. If the lamp later cracks or starts a fire in Joplin's home and causes damage, she normally will not be able to hold Gershwin's liable for breach of the warranty of merchantability. Because Joplin refused to examine the lamp when asked by Gershwin, Joplin will be deemed to have assumed the risk that it was defective.

Unconscionability

The UCC sections dealing with warranty disclaimers do not refer specifically to unconscionability as a factor. Ultimately, however, the courts will test warranty disclaimers with reference to the UCC's unconscionability standards [UCC 2–302, 2A–108]. Such things as lack of bargaining position, take-it-or-leave-it choices, and a buyer's or lessee's failure to understand or know of a warranty disclaimer will be relevant to the issue of unconscionability.

Statute of Limitations

A cause of action for breach of contract under the UCC must be commenced *within four years after the cause of action accrues*—that is, within four years after the breach occurs. The parties can reduce this period to not less than one year in their original agreement, but they *cannot* extend it beyond four years [UCC 2–725(1), 2A–506(1)]. An action for breach of warranty accrues when the seller or lessor *tenders* delivery, even if the aggrieved party is unaware of the breach at that time [UCC 2–725(2), 2A–506(2)]. In addition, the aggrieved party usually must notify the breaching party within a reasonable time after discovering the breach or be barred from pursuing any remedy [UCC 2–607(3)(a), 2A–516(3)].

SECTION 4 Product Liability

Those who make, sell, or lease goods can be held liable for physical harm or property damage caused by those goods to a consumer, user, or bystander. This is called **product liability.** Because one particular product may cause harm to a number of consumers, product liability actions are sometimes filed by a group of plaintiffs acting together. (For a discussion of a law that requires claims filed by a large group of plaintiffs to be heard in federal courts, see this chapter's *Emerging Trends* feature on the following two pages.)

Product liability may be based on the warranty theories just discussed, as well as on the theories of negligence, misrepresentation, and strict liability. We look here at product liability based on negligence and on misrepresentation.

Product Liability Based on Negligence

In Chapter 7, *negligence* was defined as the failure to exercise the degree of care that a reasonable, prudent person would have exercised under the circumstances. If a manufacturer fails to exercise "due care" to make a product safe, a person who is injured by the product may sue the manufacturer for negligence.

Due Care Must Be Exercised Due care must be exercised in designing the product, selecting the materials, using the appropriate production process, assembling and testing the product, and placing adequate warnings on the label informing the user of dangers of which an ordinary person might not be aware. The duty of care also extends to the inspection and testing of any purchased components that are used in the product sold by the manufacturer.

Privity of Contract Not Required A product liability action based on negligence does not require the injured plaintiff and the negligent defendant-manufacturer to be in *privity of contract* (see Chapter 16). In other words, the plaintiff and the defendant need not be directly involved in a contractual relationship (that is, in privity). Thus, any person who is injured by a product may bring a negligence suit even though he or she was not the one who actually purchased the product. A manufacturer, seller, or lessor is liable for failure to exercise due care to *any person* who sustains an injury proximately caused by a negligently made (defective) product. Relative to the long history of the common law, this exception to the privity requirement is a fairly recent development, dating to the early part of the twentieth century.[8]

8. A landmark case in this respect is *MacPherson v. Buick Motor Co.*, 217 N.Y. 382, 111 N.E. 1050 (1916).

EMERGING TRENDS IN BUSINESS LAW

Removing Class-Action Lawsuits to the Federal Courts

Many product liability actions are class actions. A *class action* is a lawsuit in which a single person or a small group of people represents the interests of a larger group. Women allegedly injured by silicone breast implants, for example, sued the manufacturers as a class, as did many of those allegedly injured by asbestos and tobacco. The idea behind class actions is that an individual consumer who has been injured by a product is unlikely to have the financial means to pursue complex litigation against a large corporation. A class action allows all those injured by a product to pool their resources and obtain competent legal counsel to bring a single lawsuit on their behalf.

Federal courts have always had specific requirements for class actions. For example, the class (the group of plaintiffs) must be so large that individual suits would be impracticable, and the case must involve legal or factual issues common to all members of the class. Until 2005, however, any state or federal court could hear class actions.

The Class Action Fairness Act of 2005

The Class Action Fairness Act (CAFA) of 2005[a] significantly changed the way class actions are tried. Though it affects all class actions, the CAFA was primarily designed to shift large, interstate product liability and tort class-action suits from the state courts to the federal courts. Under the act, federal district courts now have original (trial) jurisdiction over any civil action in which there are one hundred plaintiffs from multiple states and the damages sought exceed $5 million.

Under the CAFA, a state court can retain jurisdiction over a case *only* if more than two-thirds of the plaintiffs and at least one principal defendant are citizens of the state and the injuries were incurred in that state. If more than one-third but less than two-thirds of the plaintiffs live in a state, the act allows a federal judge to decide (based on specified considerations) whether the trial should be held in state or federal court.

In addition, the act makes it easier for a defendant to remove (transfer) a case from a state court to a federal court, even if the defendant is a citizen of the state where the action was filed. In cases involving multiple defendants, the CAFA also allows one defendant to remove the case to federal court without the consent of all the defendants (as was previously required). In sum, the act encourages all class actions to be heard in federal courts, which have historically been less sympathetic to consumers' product liability claims than state courts have been.

Goals of the Act

One of the main goals of the CAFA was to prevent plaintiffs' lawyers from "forum shopping," or looking for the state court that is most likely to be sympathetic to their claims. Corporate lawyers and business groups have long complained that class actions are often brought in states and counties where the judges and juries have a reputation for awarding large verdicts against corporate defendants. Sometimes, cases are even brought in states where only a small number of the plaintiffs reside. According to these critics, the CAFA will prevent such practices and help cut down on frivolous lawsuits. Not only will the business community benefit, but consumers will gain as well because businesses will no longer have to bear the costs of frivolous suits and will therefore be able to lower prices. President George W. Bush said that the act marks a critical step toward ending the "lawsuit culture in our country."[b]

Critics of the act contend, however, that class actions are the only way that individual consumers

a. Pub. L. No. 109-2, 119 Stat. 4 (February 18, 2005), codified at 28 U.S.C. Sections 1711 *et seq.*

b. Presidential press release, "President Signs Class-Action Fairness Act of 2005," February 18, 2005.

Product Liability Based on Misrepresentation

When a fraudulent misrepresentation has been made to a user or consumer and that misrepresentation ultimately results in an injury, the basis of liability may be the tort of fraud. In this situation, the misrepresentation must have been made knowingly or with reckless disregard for the facts. For example, the intentional mislabeling of packaged cosmetics and the intentional concealment of a product's defects would constitute fraudulent misrepresentation. The misrepresentation must be of a material fact, and the seller must have had the intent to induce the buyer's reliance on the misrepresentation. Misrepresentation on a label or advertisement is enough to show an intent to induce the reliance of anyone who may use the product. In addition, the buyer must have relied on the misrepresentation.

can obtain redress for injuries suffered from defective products. They say that by making it more difficult to pursue class actions, the CAFA is making it harder for injured parties to hold large corporations accountable for their wrongful acts and harmful products.

Even with the CAFA, Removing a Class Action to Federal Court Is Not Always Easy

The CAFA contains numerous ambiguities that the courts are still interpreting as they try to establish the new "rules of engagement" under the act. PepsiCo, Inc., found this out when it tried to remove a class-action suit from a New Jersey state court to a federal district court under the CAFA. The plaintiff had brought the suit against PepsiCo "for herself and on behalf of all persons in New Jersey who, within the past four years, purchased beverages with the tendency to contain benzene." The federal court held, however, that the case did not meet the CAFA's requirement that the amount in controversy exceed $5 million.[c]

Alabama Power Company suffered a similar fate when it also tried to remove a class action to a federal district court. When it appealed to the U.S. Court of Appeals for the Eleventh Circuit, the court denied the company's request in a seventy-seven-page ruling that addressed not only the $5 million threshold requirement but a number of other unresolved issues raised by the CAFA as well.[d]

In essence, the Eleventh Circuit raised the burden of proof for defendants seeking to remove cases to federal court. To do so, defendants must now prove that the amount-in-controversy requirement is a legal certainty. Prior to this ruling, traditionally a "preponderance of the evidence" standard was used.

IMPLICATIONS FOR THE BUSINESSPERSON

1. Product liability actions may still be tried in state courts. The CAFA applies only to class actions in which the plaintiffs seek damages of more than $5 million.
2. Businesspersons should be aware that even though a law appears to change only procedural rules, such as where and how a dispute is litigated, it may have consequences that affect substantive rights, including a party's ability to litigate.

FOR CRITICAL ANALYSIS

1. Do you agree that the CAFA will be effective in curtailing frivolous lawsuits? What other methods can you suggest to stop plaintiffs from filing suits that have no merit?
2. Critics of the CAFA argue that this legislation deprives Americans of "their day in court" when they are wronged by powerful corporations. Under what circumstances could this criticism be justified?

RELEVANT WEB SITES

To locate information on the Web concerning the issues discussed in this feature, go to this text's Web site at **www.cengage.com/blaw/jentz**, select "Chapter 23," and click on "Emerging Trends."

c. *Lamond v. PepsiCo, Inc.,* ___ F.Supp.2d ___ (D.N.J. 2007).

d. *Lowery v. Alabama Power Co.,* 483 F.3d 1184 (11th Cir. 2007).

SECTION 5 Strict Product Liability

Under the doctrine of *strict liability* (discussed in Chapter 7), people may be liable for the results of their acts regardless of their intentions or their exercise of reasonable care. In addition, liability does not depend on privity of contract. The injured party does not have to be the buyer or a third party beneficiary (see Chapter 16), as required under contract warranty theory. In the 1960s, courts applied the doctrine of strict liability in several landmark cases involving manufactured goods, and it has since become a common method of holding manufacturers liable.

Strict Product Liability and Public Policy

The law imposes strict product liability as a matter of public policy. This public policy rests on the threefold assumption that (1) consumers should be protected against unsafe products; (2) manufacturers and distributors should not escape liability for faulty products simply because they are not in privity of contract with the ultimate user of those products; and (3) manufacturers, sellers, and lessors of products are in a better position to bear the costs associated with injuries caused by their products—costs that they can ultimately pass on to all consumers in the form of higher prices.

California was the first state to impose strict product liability in tort on manufacturers. In a landmark 1962 decision, *Greenman v. Yuba Power Products, Inc.*,[9] the California Supreme Court set out the reason for applying tort law rather than contract law (including laws governing warranties) in cases involving consumers who were injured by defective products. According to the *Greenman* court, the "purpose of such liability is to [e]nsure that the costs of injuries resulting from defective products are borne by the manufacturers . . . rather than by the injured persons who are powerless to protect themselves." Today, the majority of states recognize strict product liability, although some state courts limit its application to situations involving personal injuries (rather than property damage).

The Requirements for Strict Product Liability

The courts often look to the *Restatements of the Law* for guidance, even though the *Restatements* are not binding authorities. Section 402A of the *Restatement (Second) of Torts,* which was originally issued in 1964, has become a widely accepted statement of the liabilities of sellers of goods (including manufacturers, processors, assemblers, packagers, bottlers, wholesalers, distributors, retailers, and lessors).

The bases for an action in strict liability, which are set forth in Section 402A of the *Restatement (Second) of Torts* and commonly applied by the courts, can be summarized as a series of six requirements, which are listed here. Depending on the jurisdiction, if these requirements are met, a manufacturer's liability to an injured party can be virtually unlimited.

1. The product must be in a *defective condition* when the defendant sells it.
2. The defendant must normally be engaged in the *business of selling* (or otherwise distributing) that product.
3. The product must be *unreasonably dangerous* to the user or consumer because of its defective condition (in most states).
4. The plaintiff must incur *physical harm* to self or property by use or consumption of the product.
5. The defective condition must be the *proximate cause* of the injury or damage.
6. The goods *must not have been substantially changed* from the time the product was sold to the time the injury was sustained.

Proving a Defective Condition Under these requirements, in any action against a manufacturer, seller, or lessor the plaintiff need not show why or in what manner the product became defective. The plaintiff does, however, have to prove that the product was defective at the time it left the hands of the seller or lessor and that this defective condition makes it "unreasonably dangerous" to the user or consumer. Unless evidence can be presented to support the conclusion that the product was defective when it was sold or leased, the plaintiff will not succeed. If the product was delivered in a safe condition and subsequent mishandling made it harmful to the user, the seller or lessor is normally not strictly liable.

Unreasonably Dangerous Products The *Restatement* recognizes that many products cannot be made entirely safe for all uses; thus, sellers or lessors are liable only for products that are *unreasonably* dangerous. A court could consider a product so defective as to be an **unreasonably dangerous product** in either of the following situations:

1. The product was dangerous beyond the expectation of the ordinary consumer.
2. A less dangerous alternative was *economically* feasible for the manufacturer, but the manufacturer failed to produce it.

As will be discussed next, a product may be unreasonably dangerous due to a flaw in the manufacturing process, a design defect, or an inadequate warning.

Product Defects

Because Section 402A of the *Restatement (Second) of Torts* did not clearly define such terms as *defective* and *unreasonably dangerous,* these terms have been subject to different interpretations by different courts. In

9. 59 Cal.2d 57, 377 P.2d 897, 27 Cal.Rptr. 697 (1962).

1997, to address these concerns, the American Law Institute (ALI) issued the *Restatement (Third) of Torts: Products Liability.* This *Restatement* defines the three types of product defects that have traditionally been recognized in product liability law—manufacturing defects, design defects, and inadequate warnings.

Manufacturing Defects According to Section 2(a) of the *Restatement (Third) of Torts,* a product "contains a manufacturing defect when the product departs from its intended design even though all possible care was exercised in the preparation and marketing of the product." Basically, a manufacturing defect is a departure from a product's design specifications. A glass bottle that is made too thin and explodes in a consumer's face is an example of a manufacturing defect. Liability is imposed on the manufacturer (and on the wholesaler and retailer) regardless of whether the manufacturer's quality control efforts were "reasonable." The idea behind holding defendants strictly liable for manufacturing defects is to encourage greater investment in product safety and stringent quality control standards. Cases involving allegations of a manufacturing defect are often decided based on the opinions and testimony of experts.[10]

Design Defects Unlike a product with a manufacturing defect, a product with a design defect is made in conformity with the manufacturer's design specifications but nevertheless results in injury to the user because the design itself was improper. The product's design creates an unreasonable risk to the user. A product "is defective in design when the foreseeable risks of harm posed by the product could have been reduced or avoided by the adoption of a reasonable alternative design by the seller or other distributor, or a predecessor in the commercial chain of distribution, and the omission of the alternative design renders the product not reasonably safe."[11]

Test for Design Defects. To successfully assert a design defect, a plaintiff has to show that a reasonable alternative design was available and that the defendant's failure to adopt the alternative design rendered the product not reasonably safe. In other words, a manufacturer or other defendant is liable only when the harm was reasonably preventable. In one case, for example, Gillespie, who cut off several of his fingers while operating a table saw, alleged that the blade guards on the saw were defectively designed. At the trial, however, an expert testified that the alternative design for blade guards used for table saws could not have been used for the particular cut that Gillespie was performing at the time he was injured. The court found that Gillespie's claim that the blade guards were defective failed because there was no proof that a guard with a "better" design would have prevented his injury.[12]

Factors to Be Considered. According to the *Restatement,* a court can consider a broad range of factors, including the magnitude and probability of the foreseeable risks, and the relative advantages and disadvantages of the product as it was designed and as it could have been designed. Basically, most courts engage in a risk-utility analysis, determining whether the risk of harm from the product as designed outweighs its utility to the user and to the public.

Suppose that a nine-year-old child finds rat poison in a cupboard at the local boys' club and eats it, thinking that it is candy. The child dies, and his parents file a suit against the manufacturer alleging that the rat poison was defectively designed because it looked like candy and was supposed to be placed in cupboards. In this situation, a court would probably consider factors such as the foreseeability that a child would think the rat poison was candy, the gravity of the potential harm from consumption, the availability of an alternative design, and the usefulness of the product. If the parents could offer sufficient evidence for a reasonable person to conclude that the harm was reasonably preventable, then the manufacturer could be held liable.

In the following case, a smoker who developed lung cancer sued a cigarette manufacturer claiming, among other things, that there was a defect in the design of its cigarettes.

10. See, for example, *Derienzo v. Trek Bicycle Corp.,* 376 F.Supp.2d 537 (S.D.N.Y. 2005).

11. *Restatement (Third) of Torts: Products Liability,* Section 2(b).

12. *Gillespie v. Sears, Roebuck & Co.,* 386 F.3d 21 (1st Cir. 2004).

CASE 23.3 Bullock v. Philip Morris USA, Inc.

Court of Appeal of California, Second District, Division 3, 2008.
159 Cal.App.4th 655, 71 Cal.Rptr.3d 775.

• **Company Profile** Philip Morris started as a tobacco products shop in London in 1847. Philip Morris & Co., Ltd., was incorporated in New York in 1902. It introduced the famous Marlboro cigarette in 1924. From 1954 on, it established itself on a worldwide basis. It is the largest seller of cigarettes in the United States. The company, along with other cigarette makers, has been the object of numerous lawsuits.

• **Background and Facts** Jodie Bullock smoked cigarettes manufactured by Philip Morris for forty-five years from 1956, when she was seventeen years old, until she was diagnosed with lung cancer in 2001. By the late 1950s, scientific professionals in the United States had proved that cigarette smoking caused lung cancer. Nonetheless, Philip Morris issued full-page announcements stating that there was no proof that cigarette smoking caused cancer and that "numerous scientists" questioned "the validity of the statistics themselves." Philip Morris's chief executive officer, Joseph Cullman III, stated on the television news program *Face the Nation* (CBS, January 3, 1971), "We do not believe that cigarettes are hazardous; we don't accept that." Jodie Bullock sued Philip Morris in April 2001 seeking to recover damages for personal injuries based on product liability, among other claims. At trial, the jury found that there was a defect in the design of the cigarettes and that they were negligently designed. It awarded Bullock $850,000 in compensatory damages, including $100,000 in noneconomic damages for pain and suffering, and later awarded her $28 million in punitive damages. Philip Morris appealed.

• **Decision and Rationale** The California Court of Appeal for the Second District affirmed the trial court's judgment as to the finding of liability. At trial, Philip Morris contended that there was no evidence showing that a design defect existed because there was no evidence that a safer alternative cigarette design had been available. The reviewing court pointed out that "a product is defective in design for purposes of tort liability if the benefits of the design do not outweigh the risk of danger inherent in the design, or if the product, used in an intended or reasonably foreseeable manner, failed to perform as safely as an ordinary consumer would expect." In this case, the jury instructions were broad ranging. The jury was instructed to consider the gravity of the danger posed by the design, as well as the likelihood that the danger would cause damage. Philip Morris failed to show any error with respect to its liability based on a design defect.

• **What If the Facts Were Different?** *Assume that Philip Morris had never publicly denied the scientific link between smoking and lung cancer. In other words, the company simply sold cigarettes without saying anything about the medical consequences of smoking. Do you think the jury award would have been the same? Explain your answer.*

• **The Ethical Dimension** *Under what circumstances, if any, could Philip Morris have justified its continuing campaign to discredit the scientific arguments that linked smoking with lung cancer?*

Inadequate Warnings A product may also be deemed defective because of inadequate instructions or warnings. A product will be considered defective "when the foreseeable risks of harm posed by the product could have been reduced or avoided by the provision of reasonable instructions or warnings by the seller or other distributor, or a predecessor in the commercial chain of distribution, and the omission of the instructions or warnings renders the product not reasonably safe."[13]

Important factors for a court to consider include the risks of a product, the "content and comprehensibility" and "intensity of expression" of warnings and instructions, and the "characteristics of expected user

13. *Restatement (Third) of Torts: Products Liability,* Section 2(c).

groups."[14] A "reasonableness" test applies to determine if the warnings adequately alert consumers to the product's risks. For example, children would likely respond readily to bright, bold, simple warning labels, whereas educated adults might need more detailed information.

Obvious Risks. There is no duty to warn about risks that are obvious or commonly known. Warnings about such risks do not add to the safety of a product and could even detract from it by making other warnings seem less significant. As will be discussed later in the chapter, the obviousness of a risk and a user's decision to proceed in the face of that risk may be a defense in a product liability suit based on an inadequate warning. Nevertheless, risks that may seem obvious to some users will not be obvious to all users, especially when the users are likely to be children. Suppose that an eleven-year-old child dives into a shallow, above-ground pool, hits the bottom, and is paralyzed as a result. She later sues the pool maker. The manufacturer cannot escape liability for failing to warn about the hazards of diving into a pool simply by claiming that the risk was obvious.[15]

Foreseeable Misuses. Generally, a seller must warn those who purchase its product of the harm that can result from the foreseeable misuse of the product as well. The key is the foreseeability of the misuse. Sellers are not required to take precautions against every conceivable misuse of a product, just those that are foreseeable.

Market-Share Liability

Ordinarily, in all product liability claims, a plaintiff must prove that the defective product that caused his or her injury was the product of a specific defendant. In a few situations, however, courts have dropped this requirement when plaintiffs could not prove which of many distributors of a harmful product supplied the particular product that caused the injuries. For example, in one case a plaintiff who was a hemophiliac received injections of a blood protein known as antihemophiliac factor (AHF) concentrate. The plaintiff later tested positive for the AIDS (acquired immune deficiency syndrome) virus. Because it was not known which manufacturer was responsible for the particular AHF received by the plaintiff, the court held that all of the manufacturers of AHF could be held liable under the theory of **market-share liability.**[16]

Courts in many jurisdictions do not recognize this theory of liability, believing that it deviates too significantly from traditional legal principles.[17] In jurisdictions that do recognize market-share liability, it is usually applied in cases involving drugs or chemicals, when it is difficult or impossible to determine which company made a particular product.

Other Applications of Strict Product Liability

Virtually all courts extend the strict liability of manufacturers and other sellers to injured bystanders. Thus, if a defective forklift that will not go into reverse injures a passerby, that individual can sue the manufacturer for product liability (and possibly bring a negligence action against the forklift operator as well).

Strict product liability also applies to suppliers of component parts. For example, General Motors buys brake pads from a subcontractor and puts them in Chevrolets without changing their composition. If those pads are defective, both the supplier of the brake pads and General Motors will be held strictly liable for the damages caused by the defects.

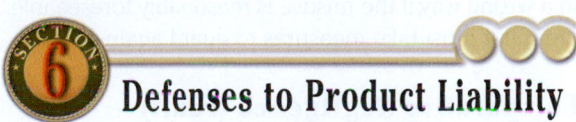

SECTION 6 Defenses to Product Liability

Defendants in product liability suits can raise a number of defenses. One defense, of course, is to show that there is no basis for the plaintiff's claim. For example, in a product liability case based on negligence, if a defendant can show that the plaintiff has *not* met the requirements (such as causation) for an action in negligence, generally the defendant will not be liable. In regard to strict product liability, a defendant can claim that the plaintiff failed to meet one of the requirements for an action in strict liability. For example, if the defendant establishes that the goods

14. *Restatement (Third) of Torts: Products Liability,* Section 2, Comment h.

15. *Bunch v. Hoffinger Industries, Inc.,* 123 Cal.App.4th 1278, 20 Cal.Rptr.3d 780 (2004).

16. *Smith v. Cutter Biological, Inc.,* 72 Haw. 416, 823 P.2d 717 (1991); *Sutowski v. Eli Lilly & Co.,* 82 Ohio St.3d 347, 696 N.E.2d 187 (1998); and *In re Methyl Tertiary Butyl Ether ("MTBE") Products Liability Litigation,* 447 F.Supp.2d 289 (S.D.N.Y. 2006).

17. For the Illinois Supreme Court's position on market-share liability, see *Smith v. Eli Lilly & Co.,* 137 Ill.2d 222, 560 N.E.2d 324 (1990). Pennsylvania law also does not recognize market-share liability. See *Bortell v. Eli Lilly & Co.,* 406 F.Supp.2d 1 (D.D.C. 2005).

have been subsequently altered, normally the defendant will not be held liable.[18] Defendants may also assert the defenses discussed next.

Assumption of Risk

Assumption of risk can sometimes be used as a defense in a product liability action. To establish such a defense, the defendant must show that (1) the plaintiff knew and appreciated the risk created by the product defect and (2) the plaintiff voluntarily assumed the risk, even though it was unreasonable to do so. For example, if a buyer failed to heed a seller's product recall, the buyer may be deemed to have assumed the risk of the product defect that the seller offered to cure. (See Chapter 7 for a more detailed discussion of assumption of risk.)

Product Misuse

Similar to the defense of voluntary assumption of risk is that of **product misuse,** which occurs when a product is used for a purpose for which it was not intended. Here, in contrast to assumption of risk, the injured party *does not know that the product is dangerous for a particular use.* The courts have severely limited this defense, however. Even if the injured party does not know about the inherent danger of using the product in a wrong way, if the misuse is reasonably foreseeable, the seller must take measures to guard against it.

Comparative Negligence (Fault)

Developments in the area of comparative negligence, or fault (discussed in Chapter 7), have also affected the doctrine of strict liability. In the past, the plaintiff's conduct was never a defense to liability for a defective product. Today, courts in many jurisdictions will consider the negligent or intentional actions of both the plaintiff and the defendant when apportioning liability and damages.[19] This means that a defendant may be able to limit at least some of its liability if it can show that the plaintiff's misuse of the product contributed to his or her injuries. When proved, comparative negligence does not completely absolve the defendant of liability (as do other defenses), but it can reduce the total amount of damages that will be awarded to the plaintiff.

Note that some jurisdictions allow only intentional conduct to affect a plaintiff's recovery, whereas other states allow ordinary negligence to be used as a defense to product liability. For example, Dan Smith, a mechanic in Alaska, was not wearing a hard hat at work when he was asked to start the diesel engine of an air compressor. Because the compressor was an older model, he had to prop open a door to start it. When he got the engine started, the door fell from its position and hit Smith's head. The injury caused him to suffer from seizures and epilepsy. Smith sued the manufacturer, claiming that the engine was defectively designed. The manufacturer contended that Smith had been negligent by failing to wear a hard hat and propping open the door in an unsafe manner. Smith's attorney argued that ordinary negligence could not be used as a defense in product liability cases. The Alaska Supreme Court ruled that defendants in product liability actions can raise the plaintiff's ordinary negligence to reduce their liability proportionately.[20]

Commonly Known Dangers

The dangers associated with certain products (such as matches and sharp knives) are so commonly known that, as already mentioned, manufacturers need not warn users of those dangers. If a defendant succeeds in convincing the court that a plaintiff's injury resulted from a *commonly known danger,* the defendant will not be liable.

A classic case on this issue involved a plaintiff who was injured when an elastic exercise rope she had purchased slipped off her foot and struck her in the eye, causing a detachment of the retina. The plaintiff claimed that the manufacturer should be liable because it had failed to warn users that the exerciser might slip off a foot in such a manner. The court stated that to hold the manufacturer liable in these circumstances "would go beyond the reasonable dictates of justice in fixing the liabilities of manufacturers." After all, stated the court, "[a]lmost every physical object can be inherently dangerous or potentially dangerous in a sense. . . . A manufacturer cannot manufacture a knife that will not cut or a hammer that will not mash a thumb or a stove that will not burn a finger.

18. See, for example, *Edmondson v. Macclesfield L-P Gas Co.,* 642 S.E.2d 265 (N.C.App. 2007); and *Pichardo v. C. S. Brown Co.,* 35 A.D.3d 303, 827 N.Y.S.2d 131 (N.Y.App. 2006).

19. See, for example, *State Farm Insurance Companies v. Premier Manufactured Systems, Inc.,* 213 Ariz. 419, 142 P.3d 1232 (2006); and *Ready v. United/Goedecke Services, Inc.,* 367 Ill.App.3d 272, 854 N.E.2d 758 (2006).

20. *Smith v. Ingersoll-Rand Co.,* 14 P.3d 990 (Alaska 2000).

The law does not require [manufacturers] to warn of such common dangers."[21]

Knowledgeable User

A related defense is the *knowledgeable user* defense. If a particular danger (such as electrical shock) is or should be commonly known by particular users of a product (such as electricians), the manufacturer need not warn these users of the danger.

In one case, for example, the parents of a group of teenagers who had become overweight and developed health problems filed a product liability suit against McDonald's. The teenagers claimed that the well-known fast-food chain should be held liable for failing to warn customers of the adverse health effects of eating its food products. The court rejected this claim, however, based on the *knowledgeable user defense.* The court found that it is well known that the food at McDonald's contains high levels of cholesterol, fat, salt, and sugar and is therefore unhealthful. The court's opinion, which thwarted future lawsuits against fast-food restaurants, stated: "If consumers know (or reasonably should know) the potential ill health effects of eating at McDonald's, they cannot blame McDonald's if they, nonetheless, choose to satiate their appetite with a surfeit [excess] of supersized McDonald's products."[22]

Statutes of Limitations and Repose

As previously discussed, statutes of limitations restrict the time within which an action may be brought. The statute of limitations for product liability cases varies according to state law, and unlike warranty claims, product liability claims are not subject to the UCC's limitation period. Usually, the injured party must bring a product liability claim within two to four years. Often, the running of the prescribed period is *tolled* (that is, suspended) until the party suffering an injury has discovered it or should have discovered it. To ensure that sellers and manufacturers will not be left vulnerable to lawsuits indefinitely, many states have passed laws, called **statutes of repose,** that place *outer* time limits on product liability actions. For example, a statute of repose may require that claims be brought within twelve years from the date of sale or manufacture of the defective product. If the plaintiff does not bring an action before the prescribed period expires, the seller cannot be held liable.

21. *Jamieson v. Woodward & Lothrop,* 247 F.2d 23 (D.C.Cir. 1957).

22. *Pelman v. McDonald's Corp.,* 237 F.Supp.2d 512 (S.D.N.Y. 2003).

REVIEWING Warranties and Product Liability

Shalene Kolchek bought a Great Lakes Spa from Val Porter, a dealer who was selling spas at the state fair. Porter told Kolchek that Great Lakes spas are "top of the line" and "the Cadillac of spas" and indicated that the spa she was buying was "fully warranted for three years." Kolchek signed an installment contract; then Porter handed her the manufacturer's paperwork and arranged for the spa to be delivered and installed for her. Three months later, Kolchek noticed that one corner of the spa was leaking onto her new deck and causing damage. She complained to Porter, but he did nothing about the problem. Kolchek's family continued to use the spa. Using the information presented in the chapter, answer the following questions.

1. Did Porter's statement that the spa was "top of the line" and "the Cadillac of spas" create any type of warranty? Why or why not?
2. If the paperwork provided to Kolchek after her purchase indicated that the spa had no warranty, would this be an effective disclaimer under the Uniform Commercial Code? Explain.
3. One night, Kolchek's six-year-old daughter, Litisha, was in the spa with her mother. Litisha's hair became entangled in the spa's drain and she was sucked down and held underwater for a prolonged period, causing her to suffer brain damage. Under which theory or theories of product liability can Kolchek sue Porter to recover for Litisha's injuries?
4. If Kolchek had negligently left Litisha alone in the spa prior to the incident described in the previous question, what defense to liability might Porter assert?

TERMS AND CONCEPTS

- express warranty 423
- implied warranty 425
- implied warranty of fitness for a particular purpose 427
- implied warranty of merchantability 425
- market-share liability 437
- product liability 431
- product misuse 438
- statute of repose 439
- unreasonably dangerous product 434

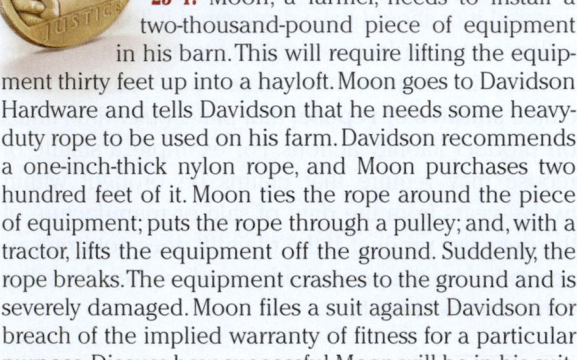

QUESTIONS AND CASE PROBLEMS

23–1. Moon, a farmer, needs to install a two-thousand-pound piece of equipment in his barn. This will require lifting the equipment thirty feet up into a hayloft. Moon goes to Davidson Hardware and tells Davidson that he needs some heavy-duty rope to be used on his farm. Davidson recommends a one-inch-thick nylon rope, and Moon purchases two hundred feet of it. Moon ties the rope around the piece of equipment; puts the rope through a pulley; and, with a tractor, lifts the equipment off the ground. Suddenly, the rope breaks. The equipment crashes to the ground and is severely damaged. Moon files a suit against Davidson for breach of the implied warranty of fitness for a particular purpose. Discuss how successful Moon will be in his suit.

23–2. QUESTION WITH SAMPLE ANSWER

Colt manufactures a new pistol. The firing of the pistol depends on an enclosed high-pressure device. The pistol has been thoroughly tested in two laboratories in the Midwest, and its design and manufacture are in accord with current technology. Wayne purchases one of the new pistols from Hardy's Gun and Rifle Emporium. When he uses the pistol in the high altitude of the Rockies, the difference in pressure causes the pistol to misfire, resulting in serious injury to Wayne. Colt can prove that all due care was used in the manufacturing process, and it refuses to pay for Wayne's injuries. Discuss Colt's liability in tort.

- **For a sample answer to Question 23–2, go to Appendix I at the end of this text.**

23–3. Baxter manufactures electric hair dryers. Julie purchases a Baxter dryer from her local Ace Drugstore. Cox, a friend and guest in Julie's home, has taken a shower and wants to dry her hair. Julie tells Cox to use the new Baxter hair dryer that she has just purchased. As Cox plugs in the dryer, sparks fly out from the motor, and sparks continue to fly as she operates it. Despite this, Cox begins drying her hair. Suddenly, the entire dryer ignites into flames, severely burning Cox's scalp. Cox sues Baxter on the basis of negligence and strict liability in tort. Baxter admits that the dryer was defective but denies liability, particularly because Cox was not the person who purchased the dryer. In other words, Cox had no contractual relationship with Baxter. Discuss the validity of Baxter's defense. Are there any other defenses that Baxter might assert to avoid liability? Discuss fully.

23–4. Implied Warranties. Shalom Malul contracted with Capital Cabinets, Inc., in August 1999 for new kitchen cabinets made by Holiday Kitchens. The price was $10,900. On Capital's recommendation, Malul hired Barry Burger to install the cabinets for $1,600. Burger finished the job in March 2000, and Malul contracted for more cabinets at a price of $2,300, which Burger installed in April. Within a couple of weeks, the doors on several of the cabinets began to "melt," as the laminate (surface covering) began to pull away from the substrate (the material underneath the surface). Capital replaced several of the doors, but the problem occurred again, involving a total of six out of thirty doors. A Holiday Kitchens representative inspected the cabinets and concluded that the melting was due to excessive heat, the result of the doors being placed too close to the stove. Malul filed a suit in a New York state court against Capital alleging, among other things, a breach of the implied warranty of merchantability. Were these goods "merchantable"? Why or why not? [*Malul v. Capital Cabinets, Inc.*, 191 Misc.2d 399, 740 N.Y.S.2d 828 (N.Y.City Civ.Ct. 2002)]

23–5. Product Liability. In January 1999, John Clark of Clarksdale, Mississippi, bought a paintball gun. Clark practiced with the gun and knew how to screw in the carbon dioxide cartridge, pump the gun, and use its safety and trigger. He hunted and had taken a course in hunter safety education. He knew that protective eyewear was available for purchase, but he chose not to buy it. Clark also understood that it was "common sense" not to shoot anyone in the face. Chris Rico, another Clarksdale resident, owned a paintball gun made by Brass Eagle, Inc. Rico was similarly familiar with the gun's use and its risks. At that time and place, Clark, Rico, and their friends played a game that involved shooting paintballs at cars whose occupants also had the guns. One night, while Clark and Rico were cruising with their guns, Rico shot at Clark's car but hit Clark in the eye. Clark filed a suit in a Mississippi state court against Brass Eagle to recover for the injury, alleging, among other things, that its gun was defectively designed. During the trial, Rico testified that his gun "never malfunctioned." In whose favor should the court rule? Why? [*Clark v. Brass Eagle, Inc.*, 866 So.2d 456 (Miss. 2004)]

23-6. CASE PROBLEM WITH SAMPLE ANSWER

Mary Jane Boerner began smoking in 1945 at the age of fifteen. For a short time, she smoked Lucky Strikes (a brand of cigarettes) before switching to the Pall Mall brand, which she smoked until she quit altogether in 1981. Pall Malls had higher levels of carcinogenic tar than other cigarettes and lacked effective filters, which would have reduced the amount of tar inhaled into the lungs. In 1996, Mary Jane developed lung cancer. She and her husband, Henry Boerner, filed a suit in a federal district court against Brown & Williamson Tobacco Co., the maker of Pall Malls. The Boerners claimed, among other things, that Pall Malls contained a design defect. Mary Jane died in 1999. According to Dr. Peter Marvin, her treating physician, she died from the effects of cigarette smoke. Henry continued the suit, offering evidence that Pall Malls featured a filter that actually increased the amount of tar taken into the body. When is a product defective in design? Does this product meet the requirements? Why or why not? [*Boerner v. Brown & Williamson Tobacco Co.*, 394 F.3d 594 (8th Cir. 2005)]

- **To view a sample answer for Problem 23–6, go to this book's Web site at www.cengage.com/blaw/jentz, select "Chapter 23," and click on "Case Problem with Sample Answer."**

23-7. Express Warranties. Videotape is recorded magnetically. The magnetic particles that constitute the recorded image are bound to the tape's polyester base. The binder that holds the particles to the base breaks down over time. This breakdown, which is called sticky shed syndrome, causes the image to deteriorate. The Walt Disney Co. made many of its movies available on tape. Buena Vista Home Entertainment, Inc., sold the tapes, which it described as part of a "Gold Collection" or "Masterpiece Collection." The advertising included such statements as "Give Your Children The Memories Of A Lifetime—Collect Each Timeless Masterpiece!" and "Available For A Limited Time Only!" Charmaine Schreib and others who bought the tapes filed a suit in an Illinois state court against Disney and Buena Vista, alleging, among other things, breach of warranty. The plaintiffs claimed that the defendants' marketing promised the tapes would last for generations. In reality, the tapes were as subject to sticky shed syndrome as other tapes. Did the ads create an express warranty? In whose favor should the court rule on this issue? Explain. [*Schreib v. The Walt Disney Co.*, __ N.E.2d __ (Ill.App. 1 Dist. 2006)]

23-8. Product Liability. Bret D'Auguste was an experienced skier when he rented equipment to ski at Hunter Mountain Ski Bowl, Inc., owned by Shanty Hollow Corp., in New York. The adjustable retention/release value for the bindings on the rented equipment was set at a level that, according to skiing industry standards, was too low—meaning that the skis would be released too easily—given D'Auguste's height, weight, and ability. When D'Auguste entered a "double black diamond," or extremely difficult, trail, he noticed immediately that the surface consisted of ice and virtually no snow. He tried to exit the steeply declining trail by making a sharp right turn, but in the attempt, his left ski snapped off. D'Auguste lost his balance, fell, and slid down the mountain, striking his face and head against a fence along the trail. According to a report by a rental shop employee, one of the bindings on D'Auguste's skis had a "cracked heel housing." D'Auguste filed a suit in a New York state court against Shanty Hollow and others, including the bindings' manufacturer, on a theory of strict product liability. The manufacturer filed a motion for summary judgment. On what basis might the court *grant* the motion? On what basis might the court *deny* the motion? How should the court rule? Explain. [*D'Auguste v. Shanty Hollow Corp.*, 26 A.D.3d 403, 809 N.Y.S.2d 555 (2 Dept. 2006)]

23-9. Implied Warranties. Peter and Tanya Rothing operate Diamond R Stables near Belgrade, Montana, where they bred, trained, and sold horses. Arnold Kallestad owns a ranch in Gallatin County, Montana, where he grows hay and grain, and raises Red Angus cattle. For more than twenty years, Kallestad has sold between three hundred and one thousand tons of hay annually, sometimes advertising it for sale in the *Bozeman Daily Chronicle*. In 2001, the Rothings bought hay from Kallestad for $90 a ton. They received delivery on April 23. In less than two weeks, at least nine of the Rothings' horses exhibited symptoms of poisoning that was diagnosed as botulism. Before the outbreak was over, nineteen animals died. Robert Whitlock, associate professor of medicine and the director of the Botulism Laboratory at the University of Pennsylvania, concluded that Kallestad's hay was the source. The Rothings filed a suit in a Montana state court against Kallestad, claiming, in part, breach of the implied warranty of merchantability. Kallestad asked the court to dismiss this claim on the ground that, if botulism had been present, it had been in no way foreseeable. Should the court grant this request? Why or why not? [*Rothing v. Kallestad*, 337 Mont. 193, 159 P.3d 222 (2007)]

23-10. A QUESTION OF ETHICS

Susan Calles lived with her four daughters, Amanda, age 11, Victoria, age 5, and Jenna and Jillian, age 3. In March 1998, Calles bought an Aim N Flame utility lighter, which she stored on the top shelf of her kitchen cabinet. A trigger can ignite the Aim N Flame after an "ON/OFF" switch is slid to the "on" position. On the night of March 31, Calles and Victoria left to get videos.

*Jenna and Jillian were in bed, and Amanda was watching television. Calles returned to find fire trucks and emergency vehicles around her home. Robert Finn, a fire investigator, determined that Jenna had started a fire using the lighter. Jillian suffered smoke inhalation, was hospitalized, and died on April 21. Calles filed a suit in an Illinois state court against Scripto-Tokai Corp., which distributed the Aim N Flame, and others. In her suit, which was grounded, in part, in strict liability claims, Calles alleged that the lighter was an "unreasonably dangerous product." Scripto filed a motion for summary judgment. [*Calles v. Scripto-Tokai Corp., *224 Ill.2d 247, 864 N.E.2d 249, 309 Ill.Dec. 383 (2007)]*

(a) A product is "unreasonably dangerous" when it is dangerous beyond the expectation of the ordinary consumer. Whose expectation—Calles's or Jenna's—applies here? Why? Does the lighter pass this test? Explain.

(b) A product is also "unreasonably dangerous" when a less dangerous alternative was economically feasible for its maker, who failed to produce it. Scripto contended that because its product was "simple" and the danger was "obvious," it should be excepted from this test. Do you agree? Why or why not?

(c) Calles presented evidence as to the likelihood and seriousness of injury from lighters that do not have child-safety devices. Scripto argued that the Aim N Flame is a useful, inexpensive, alternative source of fire and is safer than a match. Calles admitted that she was aware of the dangers presented by lighters in the hands of children. Scripto admitted that it had been a defendant in at least twenty-five suits for injuries that occurred under similar circumstances. With these factors in mind, how should the court rule? Why?

23–11. VIDEO QUESTION

Go to this text's Web site at **www.cengage.com/blaw/jentz** and select "Chapter 23." Click on "Video Questions" and view the video titled *Warranties*. Then answer the following questions.

(a) Discuss whether the grocery store's label of a "Party Platter for Twenty" creates an express warranty under the Uniform Commercial Code that the platter will actually serve twenty people.

(b) List and describe any implied warranties discussed in the chapter that apply to this scenario.

(c) How would a court determine whether Oscar had breached any express or implied warranties concerning the quantity of food on the platter?

LAW ON THE WEB

For updated links to resources available on the Web, as well as a variety of other materials, visit this text's Web site at

www.cengage.com/blaw/jentz

The Federal Trade Commission posts *A Businessperson's Guide to Federal Warranty Law* at

www.ftc.gov/bcp/conline/pubs/buspubs/warranty.htm

The Web site of The Center for Auto Safety provides information and links to every state's lemon laws at

www.autosafety.org/lemonlaws.php

For information on product liability suits against tobacco companies, go to the Web site of the Library & Center for Knowledge Management, which is maintained by the University of California–San Francisco, at

library.ucsf.edu/tobacco/litigation

Legal Research Exercises on the Web

Go to **www.cengage.com/blaw/jentz**, the Web site that accompanies this text. Select "Chapter 23" and click on "Internet Exercises." There you will find the following Internet research exercises that you can perform to learn more about the topics covered in this chapter.

Internet Exercise 23–1: Legal Perspective
Product Liability Litigation

Internet Exercise 23–2: Management Perspective
The Duty to Warn

Internet Exercise 23–3: Social Perspective
Warranties

UNIT FOUR
FOCUS ON ETHICS

Domestic and International Sales and Lease Contracts

Transactions involving the sale or lease of goods make up a great deal of the business activity in the commercial and manufacturing sectors of our economy. Articles 2 and 2A of the Uniform Commercial Code (UCC) govern the sale or lease of goods in every state except Louisiana. Many of the UCC's provisions express our ethical standards.

Good Faith and Commercial Reasonableness

The concepts of good faith and commercial reasonableness permeate the UCC and help to prevent unethical behavior by businesspersons. These two key concepts are read into every contract and impose certain duties on all parties. Additionally, reasonability in the formation, performance, and termination of contracts underlies virtually all of the UCC's provisions.

As an example, consider the UCC's approach to open terms. Section 2–311(1) states that when a term is to be specified by one of the parties, "[a]ny such specification must be made in good faith and within limits set by commercial reasonableness." The requirement of commercial reasonableness means that the term subsequently supplied by one party should not come as a surprise to the other. The party filling in the missing term may not take advantage of the opportunity to add a term that will be beneficial to himself or herself (and detrimental to the other party) and then demand contractual performance of the other party that was totally unanticipated. Under the UCC, the party filling in the missing term is not allowed to deviate from what is commercially reasonable in the context of the transaction. Courts frequently look to course of dealing, usage of trade, and the surrounding circumstances in determining what is commercially reasonable in a given situation.

Good Faith in Output and Requirements Contracts The obligation of good faith is particularly important in so-called output and requirements contracts. UCC 2–306 states that "quantity" in these contracts "means such actual output or requirements as may occur in good faith." For example, Mandrow's Machines has fifty employees assembling personal computers. Mandrow's has a requirements contract with Advanced Tech Circuit Boards, under which Advanced Tech is to supply Mandrow's with all of the circuit boards it needs. If Mandrow's suddenly quadruples the size of its business, it cannot insist that Advanced Tech supply it with all of its requirements, as specified in the original contract.

Consider another example. Assume that the market price of the goods subject to a requirements contract rises rapidly and dramatically because of an extreme shortage of materials necessary to their production. The buyer could claim that her needs are equivalent to the seller's entire output. Then, after buying all of the seller's output at the contract price (which is substantially below the market price), the buyer could turn around and sell the goods that she does not need at the higher market price. Under the UCC, this type of unethical behavior is prohibited, even though the buyer in this instance has not technically breached the contract.

Bad Faith Not Required A party can breach the obligation of good faith under the UCC even if the party did not show "bad faith"—that is, even when there is no proof that the party was dishonest. For example, in one case a large manufacturer of recreational boats, Genmar Holdings, Inc., purchased Horizon, a small company that produced a particular type of "deep-V" fishing boat. Genmar bought Horizon to expand into the southern boat market and to prevent Horizon from becoming a potential future competitor. At the time of the sale, Genmar executives promised that Horizon boats would be the "champion" of the facility and vowed to keep Horizon's key employees (including the founder and his family) on as managers. The contract required Genmar to pay Horizon a lump sum in cash and also to pay "earn-out consideration" under a specified formula for five years. The "earn-out" amount would depend on the number of Horizon brand boats sold and on the annual gross revenues of the facility.

One year after the sale, Genmar renamed the Horizon brand of boats "Nova" and told employees at the facility to give priority to producing the original Genmar brand of boats over the Nova boats. Because the Genmar boats were more difficult and time consuming to make than the Nova boats, the facility's gross revenues and production decreased, and Genmar was not required to pay the "earn-out" amounts. Eventually, Genmar fired the former

(Continued)

Horizon employees and stopped manufacturing the Nova brand of boats entirely. The former employees filed a suit alleging that Genmar had breached the implied covenant of good faith and fair dealing. The defendants argued that they could not have violated good faith because there was no proof that they had engaged in fraud, deceit, or misrepresentation. The court held for the plaintiffs, however, and the decision was affirmed on appeal.[1] It is possible for a party to breach its good faith obligations under the UCC even if the party did not engage in fraud, deceit, or misrepresentation.

Commercial Reasonableness Under the UCC, the concept of good faith is closely linked to commercial reasonableness. All commercial actions—including the performance and enforcement of contract obligations—must display commercial reasonableness. A merchant is expected to act in a reasonable manner according to reasonable commercial customs.

The concept of commercial reasonableness is clearly expressed in the doctrine of commercial impracticability. Under this doctrine, which is related to the common law doctrine of impossibility of performance, a party's nonperformance of a contractual obligation may be excused when, because of unforeseen circumstances, performance of the contract becomes impracticable. The courts make clear, however, that before performance will be excused under this doctrine, the nonperforming party must have made every reasonable effort to fulfill his or her obligations.

The Concept of the Good Faith Purchaser

The concept of the good faith purchaser reflects the UCC's emphasis on protecting innocent parties. Suppose that you innocently and in good faith purchase a boat from someone who appears to have good title and who demands and receives from you a fair market price. The UCC believes that you should be protected from the possibility that the real owner—from whom the seller may have fraudulently obtained the boat—will later appear and demand his boat back. (Nothing, however, prevents the true owner from bringing suit against the party who defrauded him.)

Ethical questions arise, however, when the purchaser is not quite so innocent. Suppose that the purchaser has reason to suspect that the seller may not have good title to the goods being sold but nonetheless goes ahead with the transaction because it is a "good deal." At what point does the buyer, in this situation, cross over the boundary that separates the good faith purchaser from one who purchases in bad faith? This boundary is a significant one in the law of sales because the UCC will not be a refuge for those who purchase in bad faith. The term *good faith purchaser* means just that—one who enters into a contract for the purchase of goods without knowing, or having any reason to know, that there is anything shady or illegal about the deal.

Unconscionability

The doctrine of unconscionability represents a good example of how the law attempts to enforce ethical behavior. This doctrine suggests that some contracts may be so unfair to one party as to be unenforceable, even though that party originally agreed to the contract's terms. Section 2–302 of the UCC provides that a court will consider the fairness of contracts and may hold that a contract or any clause of a contract was unconscionable at the time it was made. If so, the court may refuse to enforce the contract, enforce the contract without the unconscionable clause, or limit the application of the clause so as to avoid an unconscionable result.

The Test for Unconscionability The UCC does not define the term *unconscionability.* The drafters of the UCC, however, have added explanatory comments to the relevant sections, and these comments serve as guidelines for applying the UCC. Comment 1 to Section 2–302 suggests that the basic test for unconscionability is whether, under the circumstances existing at the time of the contract's formation, the clause in question was so one sided as to be unconscionable. This test is to be applied against the general commercial background of the contract. For example, a court might find that a contract between a merchant-seller and a marginally literate consumer was unfair and unenforceable, but the court might uphold the same contract when it was made between two merchants.

Unconscionability—A Case Example In one case applying Section 2–302, a New York appellate court held that an arbitration clause was

1. *O'Tool v. Genmar Holdings, Inc.,* 387 F.3d 1188 (10th Cir. 2004).

unconscionable and refused to enforce it. Gateway 2000, Inc., which sold computers and software directly to consumers, included in its retail agreements a clause specifying that any dispute arising out of the contract had to be arbitrated in Chicago, Illinois, in accordance with the arbitration rules of the International Chamber of Commerce (ICC).

A number of consumers who had purchased Gateway products became incensed when they learned that ICC rules governing arbitration required advance fees of $4,000 (more than the cost of most Gateway products), of which the $2,000 registration fee was nonrefundable—even if the consumer prevailed at the arbitration. Additionally, the consumers would have to pay travel expenses to Chicago. In the class-action litigation against Gateway that followed, the New York court agreed with the consumers that the "egregiously [flagrantly] oppressive" arbitration clause was unconscionable: "Barred from resorting to the courts by the arbitration clause in the first instance, the designation of a financially prohibitive forum effectively bars consumers from this forum as well; consumers are thus left with no forum at all in which to resolve a dispute."[2]

Warranties

A seller or lessor has not only a legal obligation to provide safe products but also an ethical one. When faced with the possibility of increasing safety at no extra cost, every ethical businessperson will certainly opt for a safer product. An ethical issue arises, however, when producing a safer product means higher costs. To some extent, our warranty laws serve to protect consumers from sellers who may be tempted to neglect ethical concerns if what they are doing is both legal and profitable.

Express and Implied Warranties Both express and implied warranties are recognized by the UCC. Under UCC 2–314 and 2A–212, goods sold by a merchant or leased by a lessor must be fit for the ordinary purposes for which such goods are used, be of proper quality, and be properly labeled and packaged. The UCC injects greater fairness into contractual situations by recognizing descriptions as express warranties. Hence, a seller or lessor of goods may be held to have breached a contract if the goods fail to conform to the description. In this way, the UCC acknowledges that a buyer or lessee may often reasonably believe that a seller or lessor is warranting his or her product, even though the seller or lessor may not use a formal word such as *warrant* or *guarantee.* Thus, the law imposes an ethical obligation on sellers and lessors in a statutory form.

Warranty Disclaimers The UCC requirement that warranty disclaimers be sufficiently conspicuous to catch the eye of a reasonable purchaser is based on the ethical premise that sellers of goods should not take advantage of unwary consumers, who may not—in the excitement of making a new purchase—always read the "fine print" on standard purchase order forms. As discussed in Chapter 23, if a seller or lessor, when attempting to disclaim warranties, fails to meet the specific requirements imposed by the UCC, the warranties will not be effectively disclaimed. Before the UCC was adopted by the states, purchasers of automobiles frequently signed standard-form purchase agreements drafted by the auto manufacturer without learning the meaning of all the fine print until later.

Freedom of Contract versus Freedom from Contract—Revisited Although freedom of contract reflects a basic ethical principle in our society, courts have made it clear that when such freedom leads to gross unfairness, it should be curbed. (Several examples of the exceptions to freedom of contract that courts will make were offered in the *Focus on Ethics* feature at the end of Unit Three.) Nonetheless, before the UCC was in effect, courts generally would not intervene in cases involving warranty disclaimers in fine print or otherwise "hidden" in a standard purchase order form. Exceptions were made only when the resulting unfairness "shocked the conscience" of the court. By obligating sellers and lessors to meet specific requirements when disclaiming warranties, the UCC has made dealing fairly with buyers and lessees—already an ethical obligation of all sellers and lessors of goods—a legal obligation as well.

Today, if a warranty disclaimer unfairly "surprises" a purchaser or a lessee, chances are that the disclaimer was not sufficiently conspicuous. In this situation, the unfairness of the bargain need not be so great as to "shock the court's conscience" before a remedy will be granted.

2. *Brower v. Gateway 2000, Inc.,* 246 A.D.2d 246, 676 N.Y.S.2d 659 (1998). See also *Gill v. World Inspection Network International, Inc.,* 2006 WL 2166821 (E.D.N.Y. 2006).

(Continued)

The Battle of the Forms

UCC Section 2–207 provides that a contract can be entered into even though the acceptance includes additional terms. Conflicts often arise because whether a form is defined as an offer or an acceptance can have significant consequences for the parties. Indeed, one of the results of Section 2–207 is that buyers and sellers go to great lengths to draft their responses as "offers" or "counteroffers" (instead of acceptances) so that their terms will control any resulting contracts. Remember that under UCC 2–207(2), between merchants additional terms in an acceptance that materially alter the contract do not become part of the contract—the terms of the offer control.

Some courts have taken a different approach in resolving contract disputes when the parties are in fundamental disagreement over a material term. Rather than looking to UCC 2–207(2), they apply the rule expressed in UCC 2–207(3). This rule provides that when the parties' conduct and communications clearly indicate that a contract was formed, any conflicting material terms may simply be stricken from the contract. This rule is sometimes referred to, aptly enough, as the "knock-out rule." Thus, this UCC provision leaves it to the discretion of the courts to determine whether, under the circumstances, a contract has been formed and what the terms of the contract are—which will be the terms on which the parties agree.

DISCUSSION QUESTIONS

1. Review the UCC provisions that apply to the topics discussed in Chapters 20 through 23. Discuss fully how various UCC provisions, excluding the provisions discussed above, reflect social values and ethical standards.
2. How can a court objectively measure good faith and commercial reasonableness?
3. Generally, the courts determine what constitutes "reasonable" behavior in disputes between contract parties over this issue. Should the UCC be more specific in defining what will be deemed reasonable in specific circumstances so that the courts do not have to decide the issue? Why or why not?
4. Why does the UCC protect innocent persons (good faith purchasers) who buy goods from sellers with voidable title but not innocent persons who buy goods from sellers with void title?

UNIT FIVE

Negotiable Instruments

CONTENTS

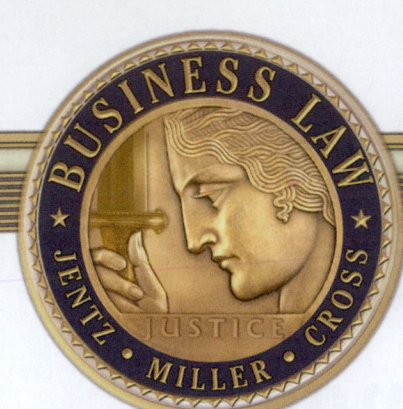

CHAPTER 24

The Function and Creation of Negotiable Instruments

A **negotiable instrument** is a signed writing (or record) that contains an unconditional promise or order to pay an exact amount of money, either on demand or at a specific future time. The checks you write to pay for groceries, rent, your monthly car payment, insurance premiums, and other items are negotiable instruments.

Most commercial transactions that take place in the modern business world would be inconceivable without negotiable instruments. A negotiable instrument can function as a substitute for cash or as an extension of credit. For example, when a buyer writes a check to pay for goods, the check serves as a substitute for cash. When a buyer gives a seller a promissory note in which the buyer promises to pay the seller the purchase price within sixty days, the seller has essentially extended credit to the buyer for a sixty-day period. For a negotiable instrument to operate *practically* as either a substitute for cash or a credit device, or both, it is essential that the instrument be *easily transferable without danger of being uncollectible.* This is a fundamental function of negotiable instruments. Each rule described in the following pages can be examined in light of this function.

The law governing negotiable instruments grew out of commercial necessity. In the medieval world, merchants engaging in foreign trade used *bills of exchange* to finance and conduct their affairs, rather than risk transporting gold or coins. Because the English king's courts of those times did not recognize the validity of these bills of exchange, the merchants developed their own set of rules, which were enforced by "fair" or "borough" courts. Eventually, the decisions of these courts became a distinct set of laws known as the *Lex Mercatoria* (Law Merchant). The Law Merchant was codified in England in the Bills of Exchange Act of 1882. In 1896, in the United States, the National Conference of Commissioners on Uniform State Laws (NCCUSL) drafted the Uniform Negotiable Instruments Law. This law was the forerunner of Article 3 of the Uniform Commercial Code (UCC).

SECTION 1 Articles 3 and 4 of the UCC

Negotiable instruments are governed by Articles 3 and 4 of the UCC. In this chapter and in Chapters 25 and 26, we will focus on the law as established by Article 3. You will learn about the different types of negotiable instruments, the requirements that all negotiable instruments must meet, the process of *negotiation* (transferring an instrument from one party to another), and the responsibilities of parties to negotiable instruments. Note that UCC 3–104(b) defines an *instrument* as a "negotiable instrument." For that reason, whenever the term *instrument* is used in this book, it refers to a negotiable instrument. Article 4 governs bank deposits and collections as well as bank-customer relationships—topics that we will examine in Chapter 27.

The 1990 Revision of Articles 3 and 4

In 1990, a revised version of Article 3 was issued for adoption by the states. Many of the changes to Article 3 simply clarified old sections; some, however, significantly altered the former provisions. As of this writing, all of the states except New York and South Carolina have adopted the revised article. Therefore, all references to Article 3 in this chapter and in the following chapters are to the *revised* Article 3. When the revisions to Article 3 have made important changes in the law, however, we discuss the previous law in footnotes. Article 4 was also revised in 1990. In part, these changes were necessary because the changes in Article 3 affected Article 4 provisions. The revised Articles 3 and 4 are included in their entirety in Appendix C.

The 2002 Amendments to Articles 3 and 4

In 2002, the NCCUSL and the American Law Institute approved a number of amendments to Articles 3 and 4 of the UCC. One of the purposes of the amendments was to update the law with respect to e-commerce. For example, the amended versions of the articles implement the policy of the Uniform Electronic Transactions Act (see Chapter 19) by removing unnecessary obstacles to electronic communications. Additionally, the word *writing* has been replaced with the term *record* throughout the articles. Other amendments relate to such topics as telephone-generated checks and the payment and discharge of negotiable instruments.

Most states have not yet adopted these amendments. Therefore, in this text we provide footnotes discussing the amendments only if they will significantly alter existing law. Keep in mind, however, that even when the changes are not substantive, some section numbers may change slightly once a state has adopted the amendments to Article 3 (subsection 9 may become subsection 12, for example).

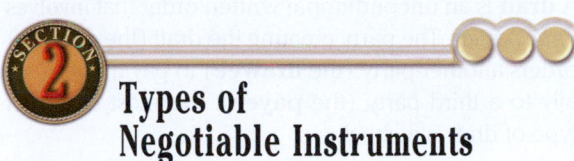

SECTION 2 Types of Negotiable Instruments

The UCC specifies four types of negotiable instruments: *drafts, checks, notes,* and *certificates of deposit* (CDs). These instruments, which are summarized briefly in Exhibit 24–1, are frequently divided into the two classifications that we will discuss in the following subsections: *orders to pay* (drafts and checks) and *promises to pay* (promissory notes and CDs).

Negotiable instruments may also be classified as either demand instruments or time instruments. A *demand instrument* is payable on demand—that is, it is payable immediately after it is issued and thereafter for

EXHIBIT 24–1 • Basic Types of Negotiable Instruments

Instruments	Characteristics	Parties
ORDERS TO PAY		
Draft	An order by one person to another person or to bearer [UCC 3–104(e)].	*Drawer*—The person who signs or makes the order to pay [UCC 3–103(a)(3)].
Check	A draft drawn on a bank and payable on demand [UCC 3–104(f)].[a] (With certain types of checks, such as cashier's checks, the bank is both the drawer and the drawee—see Chapter 27 for details.)	*Drawee*—The person to whom the order to pay is made [UCC 3–103(a)(2)]. *Payee*—The person to whom payment is ordered.
PROMISES TO PAY		
Promissory note	A promise by one party to pay money to another party or to bearer [UCC 3–104(e)].	*Maker*—The person who promises to pay [UCC 3–103(a)(5)].
Certificate of deposit	A note made by a bank acknowledging a deposit of funds made payable to the holder of the note [UCC 3–104(j)].	*Payee*—The person to whom the promise is made.

a. Under UCC 4–105(1), banks include savings banks, savings and loan associations, credit unions, and trust companies.

a reasonable period of time.[1] **Issue** is "the first delivery of an instrument by the maker or drawer . . . for the purpose of giving rights on the instrument to any person" [UCC 3–105]. All checks are demand instruments because, by definition, they must be payable on demand. A *time instrument* is payable at a future date.

Drafts and Checks (Orders to Pay)

A **draft** is an unconditional written order that involves *three parties.* The party creating the draft (the **drawer**) orders another party (the **drawee**) to pay money, usually to a third party (the **payee**). The most common type of draft is a check.

Time Drafts and Sight Drafts A *time draft* is payable at a definite future time. A *sight draft* (or demand draft) is payable on sight—that is, when it is presented for payment. A sight draft may be payable on acceptance. **Acceptance** is the drawee's written promise to pay the draft when it comes due. An instrument is usually accepted by writing the word *accepted* across the face of the instrument, followed by the date of acceptance and the signature of the drawee. A draft can be both a time and a sight draft; such a draft is payable at a stated time after sight.

Exhibit 24–2 shows a typical time draft. For the drawee to be obligated to honor the order, the drawee must be obligated to the drawer either by agreement or through a debtor-creditor relationship. For example, on January 16, Ourtown Real Estate orders $1,000 worth of office supplies from Eastman Supply Company, with payment due April 16. Also on January 16, Ourtown sends Eastman a draft drawn on its account with the First National Bank of Whiteacre as payment. In this scenario, the drawer is Ourtown, the drawee is Ourtown's bank (First National Bank of Whiteacre), and the payee is Eastman Supply Company. First National Bank is obligated to honor the draft because of its account agreement with Ourtown Real Estate.

Trade Acceptances A trade acceptance is a type of draft that is frequently used in the sale of goods. In a **trade acceptance,** the seller of the goods is both the drawer and the payee. Essentially, the draft orders the buyer to pay a specified amount to the seller, usually at a stated time in the future.

For example, Midwestern Style Fabrics sells $50,000 worth of fabric to D&F Clothiers, Inc., each spring on terms requiring payment to be made in ninety days. One year, Midwestern Style needs cash, so it draws a *trade acceptance* that orders D&F to pay $50,000 to the order of Midwestern Style Fabrics ninety days hence. Midwestern Style presents the draft to D&F, which

1. "A promise or order is 'payable on demand' if it (i) states that it is payable on demand or at sight, or otherwise indicates that it is payable at the will of the holder, or (ii) does not state any time of payment" [UCC 3–108(a)]. The UCC defines a *holder* as "the person in possession if a negotiable instrument is payable either to bearer or to an identified person [who] is the person in possession" [see UCC 1–201(21)(A)]. The term *bearer* will be defined later in this chapter.

EXHIBIT 24–2 • A Typical Time Draft

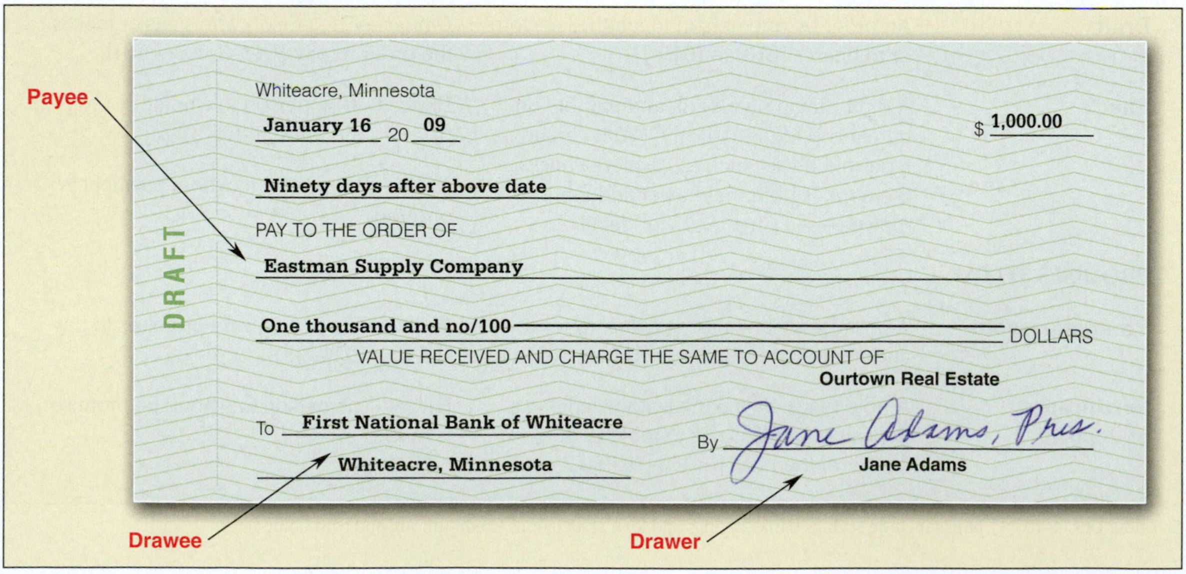

accepts the draft by signing and dating the face of the instrument. D&F then returns the draft to Midwestern Style Fabrics. D&F's acceptance creates an enforceable promise to pay the draft when it comes due in ninety days. Midwestern Style can now obtain the cash it needs by selling the trade acceptance in the *commercial money market* (a financial market for short-term borrowing that businesses use). Trade acceptances are the standard credit instruments in sales transactions (see Exhibit 24–3).

When the draft orders the buyer's bank to pay, it is called a banker's acceptance. A **banker's acceptance** is commonly used in international trade.

Checks As mentioned, the most commonly used type of draft is a **check.** The writer of the check is the drawer, the bank on which the check is drawn is the drawee, and the person to whom the check is made payable is the payee. As mentioned earlier, checks are demand instruments because they are payable on demand. (Do other countries always consider checks to be negotiable instruments? For a discussion of this issue, see this chapter's *Insight into the Global Environment* feature on the next page.)

Checks will be discussed more fully in Chapter 27, but it should be noted here that with certain types of checks, such as *cashier's checks,* the bank is both the drawer and the drawee. The bank customer purchases a cashier's check from the bank—that is, pays the bank the amount of the check—and indicates to whom the check should be made payable. The bank, not the customer, is the drawer of the check, as well as the drawee. The idea behind a cashier's check is that it functions the same as cash, so there is no question of whether the check will be paid—the bank has committed itself to paying the stated amount on demand.

Promissory Notes and CDs (Promises to Pay)

A **promissory note** is a written promise made by one person (the **maker** of the promise to pay) to another (usually a payee). A promissory note, which is often referred to simply as a *note,* can be made payable at a definite time or on demand. It can name a specific payee or merely be payable to bearer (*bearer instruments* are discussed later in this chapter). For example, on April 30, Laurence and Margaret Roberts sign a writing unconditionally promising to pay "to the order of" the First National Bank of Whiteacre $3,000 (with 8 percent interest) on or before June 29. This writing is a promissory note. A typical promissory note is shown in Exhibit 24–4 on page 453.

Promissory notes are used in a variety of credit transactions. Often a promissory note will carry the name of the transaction involved. For example, suppose that a note is secured by personal property, such as an automobile. This type of note is referred to as a *collateral note* because the property pledged as security for the satisfaction of the debt is called *collateral.*[2]

2. To minimize the risk of loss when making a loan, a creditor often requires the debtor to provide some *collateral,* or security, beyond a promise that the debt will be repaid. When this security takes the form of personal property (such as a motor vehicle), the creditor has an interest in the property known as a *security interest.* Security interests will be discussed in detail in Chapter 29.

EXHIBIT 24–3 • A Typical Trade Acceptance

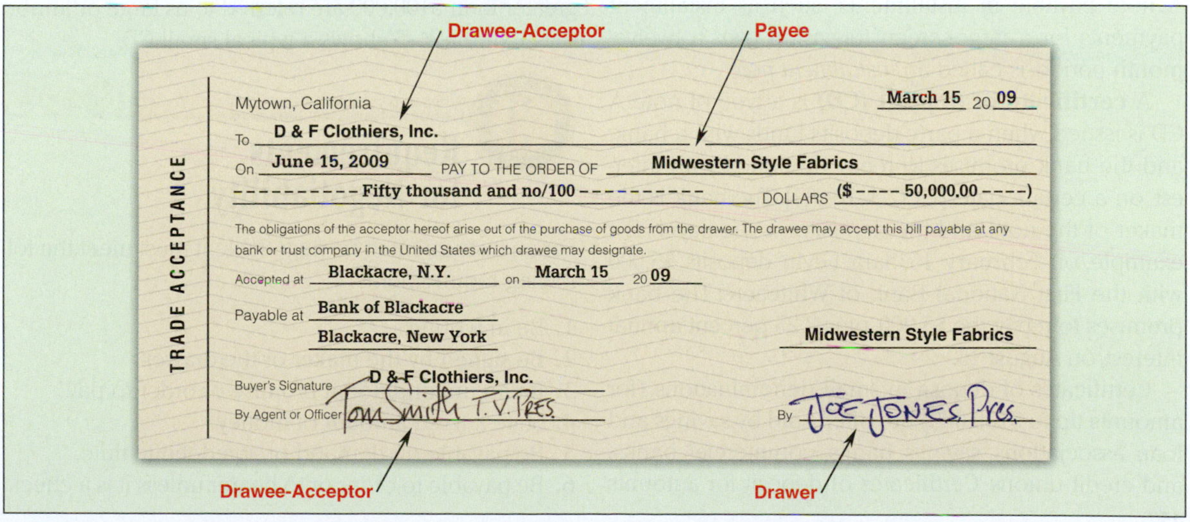

TRADE ACCEPTANCE

Mytown, California March 15 2009

To D & F Clothiers, Inc.

On June 15, 2009 PAY TO THE ORDER OF Midwestern Style Fabrics

Fifty thousand and no/100 DOLLARS ($ 50,000.00)

The obligations of the acceptor hereof arise out of the purchase of goods from the drawer. The drawee may accept this bill payable at any bank or trust company in the United States which drawee may designate.

Accepted at Blackacre, N.Y. on March 15 2009

Payable at Bank of Blackacre, Blackacre, New York

Midwestern Style Fabrics

Buyer's Signature D & F Clothiers, Inc.

By Agent or Officer Tom Smith T.V.Pres.

By Joe Jones Pres.

INSIGHT INTO THE GLOBAL ENVIRONMENT
The Negotiability of Checks in Other Nations

Checks have a long history of being accepted the "same as cash" in the United States. Indeed, for many people in the United States, checks are the ultimate negotiable instrument. In many other countries, however, checks are disappearing as a means of payment.

Where Checks Are Rarely Used Today

In many European nations, including Austria, Germany, and the Netherlands, people rarely write checks today. Instead, they rely on direct bank transfers and electronic payments (both of which will be discussed in Chapter 27). For most Europeans, for example, recurring monthly bills, such as phone bills, utility bills, and mortgage payments, are paid through automatic bank transfers—payments are automatically transferred from customers' bank accounts directly to the billing companies' accounts.

In Great Britain, where checks have been used even longer than in the United States, checks are rapidly becoming a thing of the past. Since 2001 British businesses have received more payments electronically than by check. Now many businesses are trying to phase out checks altogether. In 2006, ASDA, Britain's second largest supermarket chain and a subsidiary of Wal-Mart, announced that, beginning in the London area and extending soon to all Britain, it would no longer accept checks as payment. Boots, the country's largest pharmacy chain, has instituted a similar policy, and British utility companies are also discouraging the use of checks by charging an extra fee to customers who pay by check.

The shift away from checks in Europe has been spurred by the European Union's low-cost electronic payment system, which is much faster and more efficient than the systems available in the United States. The combination of lower costs and better protection from identity theft has led many Europeans to abandon their checks.

Even When Used, Checks Are Often Nonnegotiable

Another reason Europeans have been willing to give up their checks is that the checks often are not actually negotiable. In France, for example, some people still use checks, but, unlike in the United States, the payee named on a check cannot indorse the check to a third party. (As will be discussed briefly later in this chapter and in detail in Chapter 25, by *indorsing,* or signing, a check, the payee can transfer her or his ownership rights in it to a third party.) Furthermore, the payee cannot walk into any bank in France and cash the check. In France, a check can only be deposited into the payee's account at a bank. Considering the inconvenience a check presents, it is no wonder that more and more shops in France are refusing to accept checks.

CRITICAL THINKING

INSIGHT INTO THE SOCIAL ENVIRONMENT
What are the disadvantages of not being able to indorse checks to other parties?

A note payable in installments, such as installment payments for a large-screen television over a twelve-month period, is called an *installment note.*

A **certificate of deposit (CD)** is a type of note. A CD is issued when a party deposits funds with a bank, and the bank promises to repay the funds, with interest, on a certain date [UCC 3–104(j)]. The bank is the maker of the note, and the depositor is the payee. For example, on February 15, Sara Levin deposits $5,000 with the First National Bank of Whiteacre. The bank promises to repay the $5,000, plus 3.25 percent annual interest, on August 15.

Certificates of deposit in small denominations (for amounts up to $100,000) are often sold by savings and loan associations, savings banks, commercial banks, and credit unions. Certificates of deposit for amounts greater than $100,000 are referred to as large or jumbo CDs. Exhibit 24–5 shows a typical small CD.

SECTION 3 Requirements for Negotiability

For an instrument to be negotiable, it must meet the following requirements:

1. Be in writing.
2. Be signed by the maker or the drawer.
3. Be an unconditional promise or order to pay.
4. State a fixed amount of money.
5. Be payable on demand or at a definite time.
6. Be payable to order or to bearer, unless it is a check.

EXHIBIT 24–4 • A Typical Promissory Note

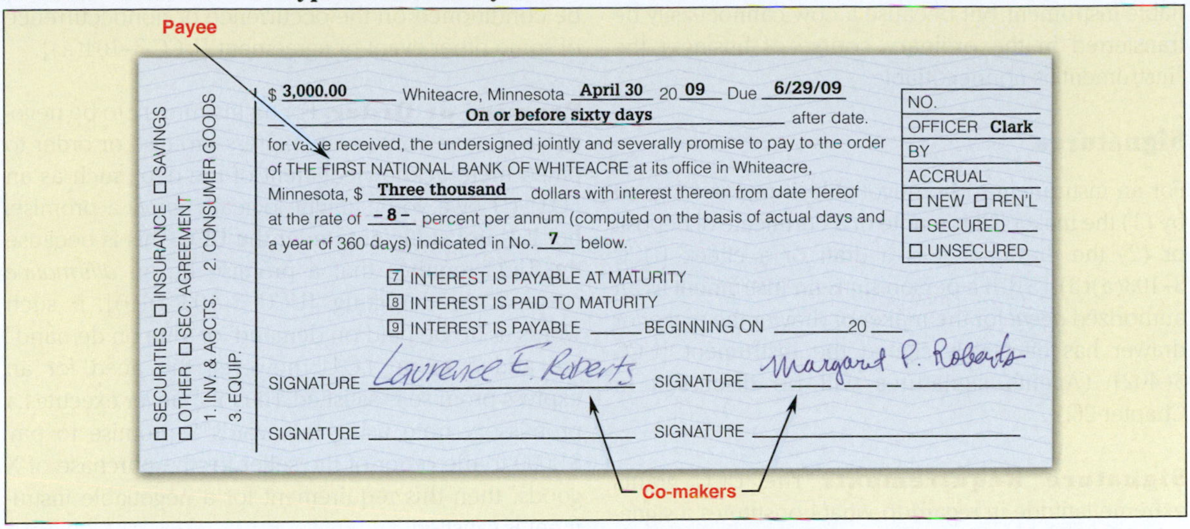

Written Form

Negotiable instruments normally must be in written form.[3] Clearly, an oral promise can create the danger of fraud or make it difficult to determine liability. The writing must be on material that lends itself to *permanence*. Promises carved in blocks of ice or inscribed in the sand or on other impermanent surfaces would not qualify as negotiable instruments. The UCC nevertheless gives considerable leeway as to what can be a negotiable instrument. Checks and notes have been written on napkins, menus, tablecloths, shirts, and a variety of other materials.

The writing must also have *portability*. Although the UCC does not explicitly state this requirement, if an instrument is not movable, it obviously cannot meet the requirement that it be freely transferable. Suppose that Cullen writes on the side of a cow, "I, Cullen, promise to pay to Merrill or her order $500 on demand."

3. UCC Section 3–104, which defines negotiable instruments, does not explicitly require a writing. The writing requirement comes from the UCC's definitions of an *order* (as a written instruction) and a *promise* (as a written undertaking) [UCC 3–103(a)(6), (9)]. Note, however, that since the widespread adoption of the Uniform Electronic Transactions Act (UETA), discussed in Chapter 19, an electronic record may be sufficient evidence of a written instruction to constitute a negotiable instrument (see UETA Section 16). Additionally, a handful of states have adopted the 2002 amendments to Article 3 of the UCC, which, as explained earlier, were issued explicitly to authorize electronic records. Thus, these states allow electronic negotiable instruments.

EXHIBIT 24–5 • A Typical Small Certificate of Deposit

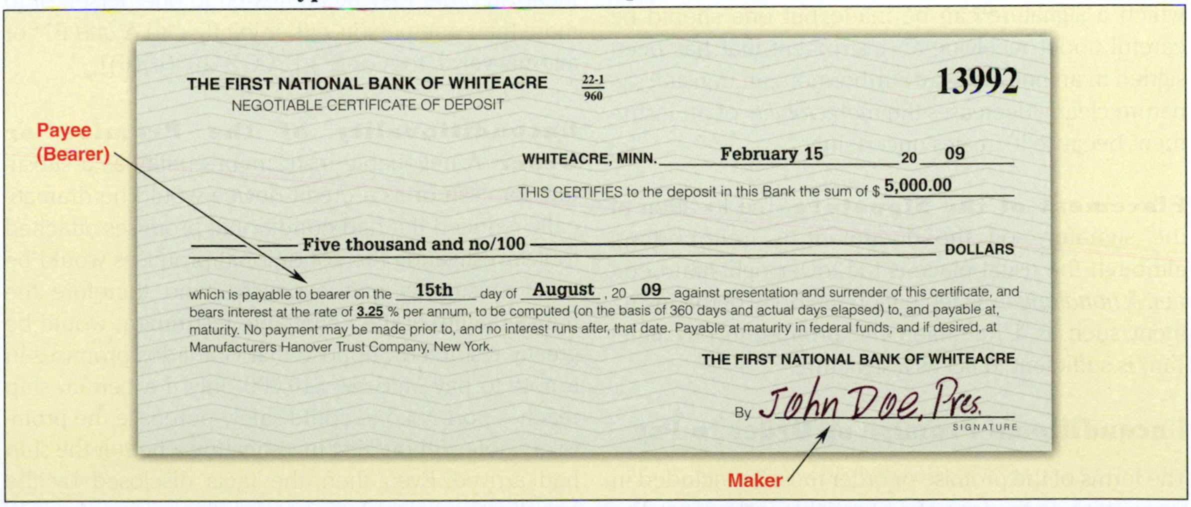

Technically, this meets the requirements of a negotiable instrument, but because a cow cannot easily be transferred in the ordinary course of business, the "instrument" is nonnegotiable.

Signatures

For an instrument to be negotiable, it must be signed by (1) the maker if it is a note or a certificate of deposit or (2) the drawer if it is a draft or a check [UCC 3–103(a)(3), (5)]. If a person signs an instrument as an authorized *agent* for the maker or drawer, the maker or drawer has effectively signed the instrument [UCC 3–402]. (Agents' signatures will be discussed in Chapter 26.)

Signature Requirements The UCC grants extreme latitude in regard to what constitutes a signature. UCC 1–201(39) provides that a **signature** may include "any symbol executed or adopted by a party with present intention to authenticate a writing." UCC 3–401(b) expands on this by stating that a "signature may be made (i) manually or by means of a device or machine, and (ii) by the use of any name, including a trade or assumed name, or by a word, mark, or symbol executed or adopted by a person with present intention to authenticate a writing." Thus, initials, an X (if the writing is also signed by a witness), or a thumbprint will suffice as a signature. A trade name or an assumed name is also sufficient. Signatures that are placed onto instruments by means of rubber stamps are permitted and frequently used in the business world. If necessary, parol evidence (discussed in Chapter 15) is admissible to identify the signer. When the signer is identified, the signature becomes effective.

There are virtually no limitations on the manner in which a signature can be made, but one should be careful about receiving an instrument that has been signed in an unusual way. Furthermore, an unusual signature clearly decreases the *marketability* of an instrument because it creates uncertainty.

Placement of the Signature The location of the signature on the document is unimportant, although the usual place is the lower right-hand corner. A *handwritten* statement on the body of the instrument, such as "I, Kammie Orlik, promise to pay Janel Tan," is sufficient to act as a signature.

Unconditional Promise or Order to Pay

The terms of the promise or order must be included in the writing on the face of a negotiable instrument. The terms must also be *unconditional*—that is, they cannot be conditioned on the occurrence or nonoccurrence of some other event or agreement [UCC 3–104(a)].

Promise or Order For an instrument to be negotiable, it must contain an express promise or order to pay. A mere acknowledgment of the debt, such as an I.O.U. ("I owe you"), might logically *imply* a promise, but it is not sufficient under the UCC. This is because the UCC requires that a promise be an *affirmative* (express) undertaking [UCC 3–103(a)(9)]. If such words as "to be paid on demand" or "due on demand" are added to an I.O.U., however, the need for an express promise is satisfied. Thus, if a buyer executes a promissory note using the words "I promise to pay $1,000 to the order of the seller for the purchase of X goods," then this requirement for a negotiable instrument is satisfied.

A certificate of deposit is exceptional in this respect. No express promise is required in a CD because the bank's acknowledgment of the deposit and the other terms of the instrument clearly indicate a promise by the bank to repay the sum of money [UCC 3–104(j)].

An *order* is associated with three-party instruments, such as trade acceptances, checks, and drafts. An order directs a third party to pay the instrument as drawn. In the typical check, for example, the word *pay* (to the order of a payee) is a command to the drawee bank to pay the check when presented, and thus it is an order. A command, such as "pay," is mandatory even if it is accompanied by courteous words, as in "Please pay" or "Kindly pay." Generally, the language used must indicate that a command, or order, is being given. Stating "I wish you would pay" does not fulfill this requirement. An order may be addressed to one person or to more than one person, either jointly ("to A *and* B") or alternatively ("to A *or* B") [UCC 3–103(a)(6)].

Unconditionality of the Promise or Order A negotiable instrument's utility as a substitute for cash or as a credit device would be dramatically reduced if it had conditional promises attached to it. Investigating the conditional promises would be time consuming and expensive, and therefore the transferability of the negotiable instrument would be greatly restricted. Suppose that Granados promises in a note to pay McGraw $10,000 only if a certain ship reaches port. No one could safely purchase the promissory note without first investigating whether the ship had arrived. Even then, the facts disclosed by the investigation might be incorrect. To avoid such problems, the UCC provides that only instruments with *unconditional* promises or orders can be negotiable [UCC 3–104(a)].

A promise or order is conditional (and *not* negotiable) if it states (1) an express condition to payment, (2) that the promise or order is subject to or governed by another writing, or (3) that the rights or obligations with respect to the promise or order are stated in another writing. A mere *reference* to another writing, however, does not of itself make the promise or order conditional [UCC 3–106(a)]. For example, including the phrase "as per contract" or "This debt arises from the sale of goods X and Y" does not render an instrument nonnegotiable.

Payment Out of a Particular Fund. Similarly, a statement in the instrument that payment can be made only out of a particular fund or source will not render the instrument nonnegotiable [UCC 3–106(b)(ii)]. Thus, for example, terms in a note that include the condition that payment will be made out of the proceeds of next year's cotton crop will not make the note nonnegotiable. (The payee of such a note, however, may find the note commercially unacceptable and refuse to take it.)

Note Secured by a Mortgage. Finally, a simple statement in an otherwise negotiable note indicating that the note is secured by a mortgage does not destroy its negotiability [UCC 3–106(b)(i)]. Actually, such a statement might even make the note more acceptable in commerce. Realize, though, that the statement that a note is secured by a mortgage must not stipulate that the maker's promise to pay is *subject to* the terms and conditions of the mortgage [UCC 3–106(a)(ii)].

As when drafting contracts, businesspersons should use clear language when creating negotiable instruments to avoid potential misunderstandings. To create an order instrument, generally the language used must indicate that a command, or order, is being given. Business owners and managers can be polite (and say "Please pay") if they like, provided that they include a clear command. Also, businesspersons should make certain that they do not use any words that could be interpreted as making the promise conditional. They should not refer to any terms in another document or contract controlling the instrument. If in doubt, they need to contact an attorney.

A Fixed Amount of Money

Negotiable instruments must state with certainty a fixed amount of money, with or without interest or other charges described in the promise or order, to be paid at the time the instrument is payable [UCC 3–104(a)]. This requirement ensures that the value of the instrument can be determined with clarity and certainty.

Fixed Amount The term *fixed amount* means that the amount must be ascertainable from the face of the instrument. Interest may be stated as a fixed or variable rate. A demand note payable with 10 percent interest meets the requirement of a fixed amount because its amount can be determined at the time it is payable [UCC 3–104(a)].

The rate of interest may also be determined with reference to information that is not contained in the instrument if that information is readily ascertainable by reference to a formula or a source described in the instrument [UCC 3–112(b)]. For example, an instrument that is payable at the *legal rate of interest* (a rate of interest fixed by statute) is negotiable. Mortgage notes tied to a variable rate of interest (a rate that fluctuates as a result of market conditions) can also be negotiable.

Payable in Money UCC 3–104(a) provides that a fixed amount is to be *payable in money*. The UCC defines money as "a medium of exchange authorized or adopted by a domestic or foreign government as a part of its currency" [UCC 1–201(24)].

Suppose that the maker of a note promises "to pay on demand $1,000 in U.S. gold." Because gold is not a medium of exchange adopted by the U.S. government, the note is not payable in money. The same result occurs if the maker promises "to pay $1,000 and fifty magnums of 1994 Chateau Lafite-Rothschild wine" because the instrument is not payable *entirely* in money. An instrument payable in government bonds or in shares of IBM stock is not negotiable because neither is a medium of exchange recognized by the U.S. government. The statement "Payable in $1,000 U.S. currency or an equivalent value in gold" renders the instrument nonnegotiable because the maker reserved the option of paying in money *or* gold. Any instrument payable in the United States with a face amount stated in a foreign currency can be paid in the foreign money or in the equivalent in U.S. dollars [UCC 3–107].

Payable on Demand or at a Definite Time

A negotiable instrument must "be payable on demand or at a definite time" [UCC 3–104(a)(2)]. Clearly, to ascertain the value of a negotiable instrument, it is essential to know when the maker, drawee, or *acceptor* is required to pay (an **acceptor** is a drawee who has accepted, or agreed to pay, an instrument when it is presented later for payment). It is also necessary to know when the obligations of secondary parties, such as *indorsers*,[4] will arise. Furthermore, it is necessary to know when an instrument is due in order to calculate when the statute of limitations may apply [UCC 3–118(a)]. Finally, with an interest-bearing instrument, it is necessary to know the exact interval during which the interest will accrue to determine the instrument's value at the present time.

4. We should note that because the UCC uses the spelling *indorse* (*indorsement*, and the like), rather than the more common spelling *endorse* (*endorsement*, and the like), we adopt the UCC's spelling here and in other chapters in this text. Indorsers will be discussed in Chapter 25.

Payable on Demand Instruments that are payable on demand include those that contain the words "Payable at sight" or "Payable upon presentment." When a person takes the instrument to the appropriate party for payment or acceptance, *presentment* occurs. **Presentment** means a demand made by or on behalf of a person entitled to enforce an instrument to either pay or accept the instrument [UCC 3–501].

The very nature of the instrument may indicate that it is payable on demand. For example, a check, by definition, is payable on demand [UCC 3–104(f)]. If no time for payment is specified and the person responsible for payment must pay on the instrument's presentment, the instrument is payable on demand [UCC 3–108(a)].

At the center of the dispute in the following case was a note that required payments in monthly installments beginning several months before the note was executed. Was this a demand note?

CASE 24.1 Gowin v. Granite Depot, LLC[a]

Supreme Court of Virginia, 2006. 272 Va. 246, 634 S.E.2d 714.

Background and Facts In 1998, John Stathis began a granite countertop business, which was organized the following year as Granite Depot, LLC. Stathis offered Patrick Gowin a job and promised that within two years, he would become a Granite Depot member.[b] Gowin accepted the offer, and in November 2000, he became a member with a 20 percent interest in the firm. Stathis held the other 80 percent. Gowin's capital contribution to the firm was to be $12,500, for which he signed a note. The note was dated January 15, 2000, and payable to Granite Depot "in twenty-four (24) monthly installments . . . commencing on February 1, 2000." Stathis told Gowin "not to worry about [the note], the company would take care of it." Gowin made no payments on the note, and Granite Depot made no demands for payment. The relationship between Stathis and Gowin deteriorated, however, and Gowin quit his job in May 2002. Stathis, as the firm's majority member, eliminated Gowin as a member for failing "to make his required contribution to the Company." Gowin filed a suit in a Virginia state court against Granite Depot and Stathis, claiming, among other things, that the note was a demand note and asserting that because no demand for payment had been made, he had not failed to make his contribution. The court dismissed the suit. Gowin appealed to the Virginia Supreme Court.

Decision and Rationale The state supreme court reversed the lower court's judgment and remanded the case for further proceedings. The reviewing court held that the note was a demand note and agreed with Gowin that because no demand for payment had been made, his obligation to make a payment had not arisen. The termination of his membership in Granite Depot was thus improper, and Gowin was still a member of the firm. The state supreme court emphasized

a. An *LLC* is a limited liability company, which is a form of business organization discussed in detail in Chapter 37.
b. A member in an LLC has many of the same rights as a partner in a partnership but is not personally liable for the obligations of the firm. See Chapters 36 and 37.

CASE 24.1 CONTINUED that the note was dated January 15, 2000, with its first payment due on February 1, but that it was not signed until November, "making compliance with the stated dates impossible." The parties agreed that the payment dates were not correct, but no one contended that this mistake invalidated the note. The court reasoned that the note effectively did not state a date for its payment and was therefore a demand note under UCC 3–108(a). According to UCC 3–304(a)(1) and (3), a demand note does not become overdue until the day after demand is made or the note has been outstanding for an "unreasonably long [time]," whichever occurs first. Under the circumstances in this case, the note never became overdue because payment was never demanded.

- **The Ethical Dimension** *Did the statement "not to worry, the company will take care of it," which was made about the $12,500 note, imply that the company did not require a capital contribution by Gowin? Why might the company have made such a statement?*

- **The Legal Environment Dimension** *Why is a note with no stated time for payment considered a demand note rather than an unenforceable note?*

Payable at a Definite Time If an instrument is not payable on demand, to be negotiable it must be payable at a definite time. An instrument is payable at a definite time if it states that it is payable (1) on a specified date, (2) within a definite period of time (such as thirty days) after being presented for payment, or (3) on a date or time readily ascertainable at the time the promise or order is issued [UCC 3–108(b)]. The maker or drawee is under no obligation to pay until the specified time.

When an instrument is payable by the maker or drawer *on or before* a stated date, it is clearly payable at a definite time. The maker or drawer has the *option* of paying before the stated maturity date, but the holder can still rely on payment being made by the maturity date. The option to pay early does not violate the definite-time requirement. For example, John gives Ernesto an instrument dated May 1, 2009, that indicates on its face that it is payable *on or before* May 1, 2010. This instrument satisfies the definite-time requirement.

In contrast, an instrument that is undated and made payable "one month after date" is clearly nonnegotiable. There is no way to determine the maturity date from the face of the instrument. Whether the time period is a month or a year, if the date is uncertain, the instrument is not payable at a definite time. Thus, an instrument that states, "One year after the death of my grandfather, Jeremy Adams, I promise to pay to the order of Lucy Harmon $5,000. [Signed] Jacqueline Wells," is nonnegotiable.

Acceleration Clause An **acceleration clause** allows a payee or other holder of a time instrument to demand payment of the entire amount due, with interest, if a certain event occurs, such as a default in payment of an installment when due. (Under the UCC, a **holder** is any person in possession of a negotiable instrument that is payable either to the bearer or to an identified person that is the person in possession [UCC 1–201(20)].)

Assume that Martin lends $1,000 to Ruth, who makes a negotiable note promising to pay $100 per month for eleven months. The note contains an acceleration provision that permits Martin or any holder to immediately demand all the payments plus the interest owed to date if Ruth fails to pay an installment in any given month. If, for example, Ruth fails to make the third payment and Martin accelerates the unpaid balance, the note will be due and payable in full. Ruth will owe Martin the remaining principal plus any unpaid interest to that date.

Under the UCC, instruments that include acceleration clauses are negotiable, regardless of the reason for the acceleration, because (1) the exact value of the instrument can be ascertained and (2) the instrument will be payable on a specified date if the event allowing acceleration does not occur [UCC 3–108(b)(ii)]. Thus, the specified date is the outside limit used to determine the value of the instrument.

In the following case, the question was whether a party entitled to installment payments on a promissory note that contained an acceleration clause waived the right to exercise this provision when the party accepted late payments from the maker.

CASE 24.2 Foundation Property Investments, LLC v. CTP, LLC

Court of Appeals of Kansas, 2007. 37 Kan.App.2d 890, 159 P.3d 1042.
www.kscourts.org/Cases-and-Opinions/opinions[a]

• **Background and Facts** In April 2004, CTP, LLC, bought a truck stop in South Hutchinson, Kansas. As part of the deal, CTP borrowed $96,000 from Foundation Property Investments, LLC. The loan was evidenced by a promissory note, which provided that CTP was to make monthly payments of $673.54 between June 1, 2004, and June 1, 2009. The note stated that on default in any payment, "the whole amount then unpaid shall become immediately due and payable at the option of the holder without notice." CTP paid the first four installments on or before the due dates, but beginning in October 2004, CTP paid the next ten installments late. In July 2005, citing the late payments, Foundation demanded full payment of the note by the end of the month. CTP responded that the parties' course of dealing permitted payments to be made beyond their due dates. Foundation filed a suit in a Kansas state court against CTP to collect the note's full amount. CTP asserted that Foundation had waived its right to accelerate the note by its acceptance of late payments. The court determined that Foundation was entitled to payment of the note in full, plus interest and attorneys' fees and costs, for a total of $110,975.58, and issued a summary judgment in Foundation's favor. CTP appealed to a state intermediate appellate court.

• **Decision and Rationale** The appellate court reversed the lower court's ruling and remanded the case with instructions to enter a judgment in CTP's favor. The plaintiff argued at trial that the provisions of the acceleration clause in the note should be strictly construed against CTP. The reviewing court looked, nonetheless, to the plaintiff's actions. *Course of dealing* is defined as "a sequence of previous conduct between the parties to a particular transaction which is fairly to be regarded as a establishing a common basis of understanding for interpreting their expressions and other conduct." The reviewing court pointed out that Foundation Property Investments never objected to CTP's late payments during the nine-month period. The action of accepting late payments "was inconsistent with [Foundation's] claim or right to receive prompt payments. Accordingly, the trial court incorrectly determined that Foundation's conduct did not constitute a wavier of its right of acceleration." The acceptance of late payments did constitute a waiver. CTP was not required to pay the note in full, plus interest and attorneys' fees and costs.

• **The E-Commerce Dimension** *If Foundation had sent CTP an e-mail threatening to accelerate the note each time CTP's payment was late, would this have been sufficient to support the holder's eventual demand for full payment? Why or why not?*

• **The Global Dimension** *Suppose that Foundation was an entity based outside the United States. Could it have successfully claimed, in attempting to enforce the acceleration clause, that it had not given CTP notice because it had not been aware of Kansas law? Discuss.*

a. In the menu at the left, click on "Search by Docket Number." In the result, in the right column, click on "96000–96999." On the next page, scroll to "96697" and click on the number to access the opinion. The Kansas courts, Washburn University School of Law Library, and University of Kansas School of Law Library maintain this Web site.

Extension Clause The reverse of an acceleration clause is an **extension clause,** which allows the date of maturity to be extended into the future [UCC 3–108(b)(iii), (iv)]. To keep the instrument negotiable, the interval of the extension must be specified if the right to extend the time of payment is given to the maker or the drawer of the instrument. If, however, the holder of the instrument can extend the time of payment, the extended maturity date need not be specified.

Suppose that Alek executes a note that reads, "The maker has the right to postpone the time of payment of this note beyond its definite maturity date of January 1, 2010. This extension, however, shall be for no more than a reasonable time." A note with this language is not negotiable because it does not satisfy the definite-time requirement. The right to extend is the maker's, and the maker has not indicated when the note will become due after the extension.

In contrast, suppose that Alek's note reads, "The holder of this note at the date of maturity, January 1, 2010, can extend the time of payment until the following June 1 or later, if the holder so wishes." This note is a negotiable instrument. The length of the extension does not have to be specified because the option to extend is solely that of the holder. After January 1, 2010, the note is, in effect, a demand instrument.

Payable to Order or to Bearer

Because one of the functions of a negotiable instrument is to serve as a substitute for cash, freedom to transfer is essential. To ensure a proper transfer, the instrument must be "payable to order or to bearer" at the time it is issued or first comes into the possession of the holder [UCC 3–104(a)(1)]. An instrument is not negotiable unless it meets this requirement.

Order Instruments An **order instrument** is an instrument that is payable (1) "to the order of an identified person" or (2) "to an identified person or order" [UCC 3–109(b)]. An identified person is the person "to whom the instrument is initially payable" as determined by the intent of the maker or drawer [UCC 3–110(a)]. The identified person, in turn, may transfer the instrument to whomever he or she wishes. Thus, the maker or drawer is agreeing to pay either the person specified on the instrument or whomever that person might designate. In this way, the instrument retains its transferability. Suppose that an instrument states, "Payable to the order of James Crawford" or "Pay to James Crawford or order." Clearly, the maker or drawer has indicated that payment will be made to Crawford or to whomever Crawford designates. The instrument is negotiable.

Except for bearer instruments (explained in the following subsection), the person specified must be named with *certainty* because the transfer of an order instrument requires an indorsement. An **indorsement** is a signature placed on an instrument, such as on the back of a check, generally for the purpose of transferring one's ownership rights in the instrument. Indorsements will be discussed at length in Chapter 25.

If an instrument states, "Payable to the order of my nicest cousin," the instrument is nonnegotiable because a holder could not be sure that the person who indorsed the instrument was actually the "nicest cousin" who was supposed to have indorsed it.

Bearer Instruments A **bearer instrument** is an instrument that does not designate a specific payee [UCC 3–109(a)]. The term **bearer** refers to a person in possession of an instrument that is payable to bearer or indorsed in blank (with a signature only, as will be discussed in Chapter 25) [UCC 1–201(5), 3–109(a), 3–109(c)]. This means that the maker or drawer agrees to pay anyone who presents the instrument for payment. Any instrument containing terms such as the following is a bearer instrument:

1. "Payable to the order of bearer."
2. "Payable to Simon Reed or bearer."
3. "Payable to bearer."
4. "Pay cash."
5. "Pay to the order of cash."

In addition, an instrument that "indicates that it is not payable to an identified person" is a bearer instrument [UCC 3–109(a)(3)]. Thus, an instrument that is "payable to X" can be negotiated as a bearer instrument, as though it were payable to cash. The UCC does not accept an instrument issued to a nonexistent organization as payable to bearer, however [UCC 3–109, Comment 2]. Therefore, an instrument "payable to the order of the Camrod Company," if no such company exists, is not a bearer instrument or an order instrument and, in fact, does not qualify as a negotiable instrument. (See *Concept Summary 24.1* on the following page for a convenient summary of the basic rules governing negotiability.)

SECTION 4 Factors Not Affecting Negotiability

Certain ambiguities or omissions will not affect the negotiability of an instrument. Article 3's rules for interpreting ambiguous terms include the following:

1. Unless the date of an instrument is necessary to determine a definite time for payment, the fact that an instrument is undated does not affect its negotiability. A typical example is an undated check, which is still negotiable. If a check is not dated, under the UCC its date is the date of its issue, meaning the date on which the drawer first delivers the check to another person to give that person rights on the check [UCC 3–113(b)].
2. Antedating or postdating an instrument does not affect its negotiability [UCC 3–113(a)]. *Antedating* occurs when a party puts a date on an instrument that precedes the actual calendar date. *Postdating*

CONCEPT SUMMARY 24.1
Requirements for Negotiability

Requirements	Basic Rules
MUST BE IN WRITING UCC 3–103(6), (9)	A writing can be on anything that is readily transferable and that has a degree of permanence.
MUST BE SIGNED BY THE MAKER OR DRAWER UCC 1–201(39) UCC 3–103(a)(3), (5) UCC 3–401(b) UCC 3–402	1. The signature can be anywhere on the face of the instrument. 2. It can be in any form (such as a word, mark, or rubber stamp) that purports to be a signature and authenticates the writing. 3. A signature may be made in a representative capacity.
MUST BE A DEFINITE PROMISE OR ORDER UCC 3–103(a)(6), (9) UCC 3–104(a)	1. A promise must be more than a mere acknowledgment of a debt. 2. The words "I/We promise" or "Pay" meet this criterion.
MUST BE UNCONDITIONAL UCC 3–106	1. Payment cannot be expressly conditional on the occurrence of an event. 2. Payment cannot be made subject to or governed by another agreement.
MUST BE AN ORDER OR PROMISE TO PAY A FIXED AMOUNT UCC 3–104(a) UCC 3–107 UCC 3–112(b)	An amount may be considered a fixed sum even if payable in installments, with a fixed or variable rate of interest, or at a foreign exchange rate.
MUST BE PAYABLE IN MONEY UCC 3–104(a)	1. Any medium of exchange recognized as the currency of a government is money. 2. The maker or drawer cannot retain the option to pay the instrument in money *or* something else.
MUST BE PAYABLE ON DEMAND OR AT A DEFINITE TIME UCC 3–104(a)(2) UCC 3–108(a), (b), (c)	1. Any instrument that is payable on sight, presentment, or issue or that does not state any time for payment is a demand instrument. 2. An instrument is still payable at a definite time, even if it is payable on or before a stated date or within a fixed period after sight or if the drawer or maker has the option to extend the time for a definite period. 3. Acceleration clauses do not affect the negotiability of the instrument.
MUST BE PAYABLE TO ORDER OR TO BEARER UCC 3–104(a)(1) UCC 3–109 UCC 3–110(a)	1. An order instrument must identify the payee with reasonable certainty. 2. An instrument whose terms intend payment to no particular person is payable to bearer.

occurs when a party puts a date on an instrument that is after the actual date. Suppose that Crenshaw draws a check on his account at First Bank, payable to Sung Imports. Crenshaw postdates the check by fifteen days. Sung Imports can immediately negotiate the check, and, unless Crenshaw tells First Bank otherwise, the bank can charge the amount of the check to Crenshaw's account [UCC 4–401(c)].

3. Handwritten terms outweigh typewritten and printed terms (preprinted terms on forms, for example), and typewritten terms outweigh printed terms

[UCC 3–114]. For example, if your check is printed "Pay to the order of," and in handwriting you insert in the blank "Anita Delgado or bearer," the check is a bearer instrument.

4. Words outweigh figures unless the words are ambiguous [UCC 3–114]. This rule becomes important when the numerical amount and the written amount on a check differ. Suppose that Paruzzo issues a check payable to Cheaper Appliance Company. For the amount, she fills in the number "$100" but writes out the words "One thousand and 00/100" dollars. The check is payable in the amount of $1,000.

5. When an instrument simply states "with interest" and does not specify a particular interest rate, the interest rate is the judgment rate of interest (a rate of interest fixed by statute that is applied to a monetary judgment awarded by a court until the judgment is paid or terminated) [UCC 3–112(b)].

6. A check is negotiable even if there is a notation on it stating that it is "nonnegotiable" or "not governed by Article 3." Any other instrument, however, can be made nonnegotiable by the maker's or drawer's conspicuously noting on it that it is "nonnegotiable" or "not governed by Article 3" [UCC 3–104(d)].

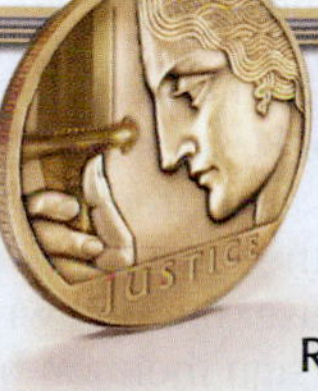

REVIEWING The Function and Creation of Negotiable Instruments

Robert Durbin, a student, borrowed funds from a bank for his education and signed a promissory note for its repayment. The bank lent the funds under a federal program designed to assist students at postsecondary institutions. Under this program, repayment ordinarily begins nine to twelve months after the student borrower fails to carry at least one-half of the normal full-time course load at his or her school. The federal government guarantees that the note will be fully repaid. If the student defaults on the repayment, the lender presents the current balance—principal, interest, and costs—to the government. When the government pays the balance, it becomes the lender, and the borrower owes the government directly. After Durbin defaulted on his note, the government paid the lender the balance due and took possession of the note. Durbin then refused to pay the government, claiming that the government was not the holder of the note. The government filed a suit in a federal district court against Durbin to collect the amount due. Using the information presented in the chapter, answer the following questions.

1. Using the categories discussed in the chapter, what type of negotiable instrument was the note that Durbin signed (an order to pay or a promise to pay)? Explain.
2. Suppose that the note did not state a specific interest rate but instead referred to a statute that established the maximum interest rate for government-guaranteed school loans. Would the note fail to meet the requirements for negotiability in that situation? Why or why not?
3. How does a party who is not named by a negotiable instrument (in this situation, the government) obtain a right to enforce the instrument?
4. Suppose that in court, Durbin argues that because the school closed down before he could finish his education, there was a failure of consideration: he did not get something of value in exchange for his promise to pay. Assuming that the government is a holder of the promissory note, would this argument likely be successful against it? Why or why not?

TERMS AND CONCEPTS

acceleration clause 457
acceptance 450
acceptor 456
banker's acceptance 451
bearer 459
bearer instrument 459
certificate of deposit (CD) 452
check 451
draft 450
drawee 450
drawer 450
extension clause 458
holder 457
indorsement 459
issue 450
maker 451
negotiable instrument 448
order instrument 459
payee 450
presentment 456
promissory note 451
signature 454
trade acceptance 450

QUESTIONS AND CASE PROBLEMS

24–1. Sabrina Runyan writes the following note on a sheet of paper: "I, the undersigned, do hereby acknowledge that I owe Leo Woo one thousand dollars, with interest, payable out of the proceeds of the sale of my horse, Lightning, next month. Payment is to be made on or before six months from date." Discuss specifically why this is not a negotiable instrument.

24–2. QUESTION WITH SAMPLE ANSWER

Juan Sanchez writes the following note on the back of an envelope: "I, Juan Sanchez, promise to pay Kathy Martin or bearer $500 on demand." Is this a negotiable instrument? Discuss fully.

- **For a sample answer to Question 24–2, go to Appendix I at the end of this text.**

24–3. A college student, Austin Keynes, wished to purchase a new entertainment system from Friedman Electronics, Inc. Because Keynes did not have the cash to pay for the entertainment system, he offered to sign a note promising to pay $150 per month for the next six months. Friedman Electronics, eager to sell the system to Keynes, agreed to accept the promissory note, which read, "I, Austin Keynes, promise to pay to Friedman Electronics or its order the sum of $150 per month for the next six months." The note was signed by Austin Keynes. About a week later, Friedman Electronics, which was badly in need of cash, signed the back of the note and sold it to the First National Bank of Halston. Give the specific designation of each of the three parties on this note.

24–4. Adam's checks are imprinted with the words "Pay to the order of" followed by a blank. Adam fills in an amount on one of the checks and signs it, but he does not write anything in the blank following the "Pay to the order of" language. Adam gives this check to Beth. On another check, Adam writes in the blank "Carl or bearer." Which, if either, of these checks is a bearer instrument, and why?

24–5. Negotiability. In October 1998, Somerset Valley Bank notified Alfred Hauser, president of Hauser Co., that the bank had begun to receive what appeared to be Hauser Co. payroll checks. None of the payees were Hauser Co. employees, however, and Hauser had not written the checks or authorized anyone to sign them on his behalf. Automatic Data Processing, Inc., provided payroll services for Hauser Co. and used a facsimile signature on all its payroll checks. Hauser told the bank not to cash the checks. In early 1999, Robert Triffin, who deals in negotiable instruments, bought eighteen of the checks, totaling more than $8,800, from various check-cashing agencies. The agencies stated that they had cashed the checks expecting the bank to pay them. Each check was payable to a bearer for a fixed amount, on demand, and did not state any undertaking by the person promising payment other than the payment of money. Each check bore a facsimile drawer's signature stamp identical to Hauser Co.'s authorized stamp. Each check had been returned to an agency marked "stolen check" and stamped "do not present again." When the bank refused to cash the checks, Triffin filed a suit in a New Jersey state court against Hauser Co. Were the checks negotiable instruments? Why or why not? [*Triffin v. Somerset Valley Bank*, 343 N.J.Super. 73, 777 A.2d 993 (2001)]

24–6. Negotiability. In October 1996, Robert Hildebrandt contracted with Harvey and Nancy Anderson to find a tenant for the Andersons' used-car lot. The Andersons agreed to pay Hildebrandt "a commission equal in amount to five percent up to first three years of lease." On December 12, Paramount Automotive, Inc., agreed to lease the premises for three years at $7,500 per month, and the Andersons signed a promissory note, which stated that they would pay Hildebrandt $13,500, plus interest, in consecutive monthly installments of $485 until the total sum was paid. The note contained an acceleration clause. In a separate agreement, Paramount promised to pay $485 of its monthly rent directly to Hildebrandt. Less than a year later, Paramount stopped making payments to all parties. To enforce the note, Hildebrandt filed a suit in an Oregon state court against the Andersons. One issue in the case was whether the note was a negotiable instrument. The Andersons claimed that it was not, because it was not "unconditional," arguing that their obligation to make payments on the note was conditioned on their receipt of rent from Paramount. Are the Andersons correct? Explain. [*Hildebrandt v. Anderson,* 180 Or.App. 192, 42 P.3d 355 (2002)]

24-7. CASE PROBLEM WITH SAMPLE ANSWER

In July 1981, Southeast Bank in Miami, Florida, issued five cashier's checks, totaling $450,000, to five payees, including Roberto Sanchez. Two months later, in Colombia, South America, Sanchez gave the checks to Juan Diaz. In 1991, Southeast failed. Under federal law, notice must be mailed to a failed bank's depositors, who then have eighteen months to file a claim for their funds. Under an "Assistance Agreement," First Union National Bank agreed to assume Southeast's liability for outstanding cashier's checks and other items. First Union received funds to pay these items but was required to return the funds if, within eighteen months after Southeast's closing, payment for any item had been not claimed. In 1996, in Colombia, Diaz gave the five cashier's checks that he had received from Sanchez to John Acevedo in payment of a debt. In 2001, Acevedo tendered these checks to First Union for payment. Does First Union have to pay? Would it make any difference if the required notice had not been mailed? Why or why not? [*Acevedo v. First Union National Bank,* 357 F.3d 1244 (11th Cir. 2004)]

- **To view a sample answer for Problem 24–7, go to this book's Web site at www.cengage.com/blaw/jentz, select "Chapter 24," and click on "Case Problem with Sample Answer."**

24-8. Negotiability. In September 2001, Cory Babcock and Honest Air Conditioning & Heating, Inc., bought a new 2001 Chevrolet Corvette from Cox Chevrolet in Sarasota, Florida. Their retail installment sales contract (RISC) required monthly payments until $52,516.20 was paid. The RISC imposed many other conditions on the buyers and seller with respect to the payment for, and handling of, the Corvette. Cox assigned the RISC to General Motors Acceptance Corp. (GMAC). In August 2002, the buyers sold the car to Florida Auto Brokers, which agreed to pay the balance due on the RISC. The check to GMAC for this amount was dishonored for insufficient funds, however, after the vehicle's title had been forwarded. GMAC filed a suit in a Florida state court against Honest Air and Babcock, seeking $35,815.26 as damages for breach of contract. The defendants argued that the RISC was a negotiable instrument. A ruling in their favor on this point would reduce any damages due GMAC to less than the Corvette's current value. What are the requirements for an instrument to be negotiable? Does the RISC qualify? Explain. [*General Motors Acceptance Corp. v. Honest Air Conditioning & Heating, Inc.,* 933 So.2d 34 (Fla.App. 2 Dist. 2006)]

24-9. A QUESTION OF ETHICS

*In November 2000, Monay Jones signed a promissory note in favor of a mortgage company in the amount of $261,250, using the deed to her home in Denver, Colorado, as collateral. Fifth Third Bank soon became the holder of the note. After Jones defaulted on the payment, in September 2001 she and the bank agreed to raise the note's balance to $280,231.23. She again defaulted. In November, the bank received a check from a third party as payment on Jones's note. It was the bank's policy to refuse personal checks in payoff of large debts. The bank representative who worked on Jones's account noted receipt of the check in the bank's records and forwarded it to the "payoff department." A week later, the bank discovered that the check had been lost without having been posted to Jones's account or submitted for payment. The bank notified Jones, and both parties searched, without success, for a copy of the check or evidence of the identity of its maker, the drawee bank, or the amount. In late 2002, the bank filed a suit in a Colorado state court to foreclose on Jones's home. She insisted that the note had been paid in full by a cashier's check issued by an Arkansas bank at the request of her deceased aunt. [*Fifth Third Bank v. Jones, *168 P.3d 1 (Colo.App. 2007)*]*

(a) What evidence supports a finding that Jones gave the bank a check? Does it seem more likely that the check was a cashier's check or a personal check? Would it be fair for a court to find that the check had paid the note in full?

(b) Under UCC 3–310, if a cashier's check or other certified check "is taken for an obligation, the obligation is discharged." The bank argued that it had not "taken [Jones's check] for an obligation" because the bank's internal administrative actions were still pending when the check was lost. Would it be fair for the court to rule in the bank's favor based on this argument? Why or why not?

24-10. VIDEO QUESTION

Go to this text's Web site at www.cengage/com/blaw/jentz and select "Chapter 24." Click on "Video Questions" and view the video titled *Negotiable Instruments.* Then answer the following questions.

(a) Who is the maker of the promissory note discussed in the video?
(b) Is the note in the video payable on demand or at a definite time?
(c) Does the note contain an unconditional promise or order to pay?
(d) If the note does not meet the requirements of negotiability, can Onyx assign the note (assignment was discussed in Chapter 16) to the bank in exchange for cash?

LAW ON THE WEB

For updated links to resources available on the Web, as well as a variety of other materials, visit this text's Web site at

www.cengage.com/blaw/jentz

The National Conference of Commissioners on Uniform State Laws, in association with the University of Pennsylvania Law School, now offers an official site for in-process and final drafts of uniform and model acts. For an index of final acts, including UCC Articles 3 and 4, go to

www.law.upenn.edu/bll/archives/ulc/ulc_final.htm

Cornell University's Legal Information Institute offers online access to the UCC, as well as to UCC articles as enacted by particular states and proposed revisions to articles, at

www.law.cornell.edu/ucc/ucc.table.html

Legal Research Exercises on the Web

Go to **www.cengage.com/blaw/jentz**, the Web site that accompanies this text. Select "Chapter 24" and click on "Internet Exercises." There you will find the following Internet research exercises that you can perform to learn more about the topics covered in this chapter.

Internet Exercise 24–1: Legal Perspective
Overview of Negotiable Instruments

Internet Exercise 24–2: Management Perspective
Banks and Bank Accounts

CHAPTER 25

Transferability and Holder in Due Course

Once issued, a negotiable instrument can be transferred to others by *assignment* or by *negotiation*. Recall from Chapter 16 that an assignment is a transfer of rights under a contract. Under general contract principles, a transfer by assignment to an assignee gives the assignee only those rights that the assignor possessed. Any defenses that can be raised against an assignor can normally be raised against the assignee. This same principle applies when a negotiable instrument, such as a promissory note, is transferred by assignment to an assignee.

Under the Uniform Commercial Code (UCC), **negotiation** is the transfer of an instrument in such form that the transferee (the person to whom the instrument is transferred) becomes a *holder* [UCC 3–201(a)]. A holder receives, at the very least, the rights of the previous possessor [UCC 3–203(b), 3–305]. Unlike an assignment, a transfer by negotiation can make it possible for a holder to receive *more* rights in the instrument than the prior possessor had [UCC 3–305]. A holder who receives greater rights is known as a *holder in due course*, a concept we discuss in this chapter. First, though, we look at the requirements for negotiation and examine the various types of *indorsements* that are used when order instruments are negotiated.

SECTION 1 Negotiation

There are two methods of negotiating an instrument so that the receiver becomes a holder. The method used depends on whether the instrument is an *order instrument* or a *bearer instrument*.

Negotiating Order Instruments

An order instrument contains the name of a payee capable of indorsing, as in "Pay to the order of Elliot Goodseal." If an instrument is an order instrument, it is negotiated by delivery with any necessary indorsements (*indorsements* will be discussed shortly). For example, the Carrington Corporation issues a payroll check "to the order of Elliot Goodseal." Goodseal takes the check to the bank, signs his name on the back (an indorsement), gives it to the teller (a delivery), and receives cash. Goodseal has negotiated the check to the bank [UCC 3–201(b)].

Negotiating order instruments requires both delivery and indorsement. If Goodseal had taken the check to the bank and delivered it to the teller without signing it, the transfer would not qualify as a negotiation. In that situation, the transfer would be treated as an assignment, and the bank would become an assignee rather than a holder.

Negotiating Bearer Instruments

If an instrument is payable to bearer, it is negotiated by delivery—that is, by transfer into another person's possession. Indorsement is not necessary [UCC 3–201(b)]. The use of bearer instruments thus involves a greater risk of loss or theft than the use of order instruments.

Assume that Alonzo Cruz writes a check payable to "cash," thus creating a bearer instrument. Cruz then hands the check to Blaine Parrington (a delivery). Parrington puts the check in his wallet, which is subsequently stolen. The thief now has possession of the check. At this point, the thief has no rights in the check.

If the thief "delivers" the check to an innocent third person, however, negotiation will be complete. All rights to the check will pass *absolutely* to that third person, and Parrington will lose all right to recover the proceeds of the check from that person [UCC 3–306]. Of course, Parrington can recover his funds from the thief if the thief can be found.

SECTION 2 Indorsements

As just described, an indorsement is required whenever an order instrument is negotiated. An *indorsement* is a signature with or without additional words or statements. It is most often written on the back of the instrument itself. If there is no room on the instrument, the indorsement can be written on a separate piece of paper, called an **allonge,**[1] and affixed to the instrument. A paper affixed to a negotiable instrument is part of the instrument [UCC 3–204(a)].

A person who transfers a note or a draft by signing (indorsing) it and delivering it to another person is an **indorser.** The person to whom the check is indorsed and delivered is the **indorsee.** Suppose that Luisa Parks receives a graduation check for $100. She can transfer the check to her mother (or to anyone) by signing it on the back. Luisa is an indorser. If Luisa indorses the check by writing "Pay to Aretha Parks," Aretha Parks is the indorsee.

We examine here four categories of indorsements: blank indorsements, special indorsements, qualified indorsements, and restrictive indorsements.

Blank Indorsements

A **blank indorsement** specifies no particular indorsee and can consist of a mere signature [UCC 3–205(b)]. Hence, a check payable "to the order of Mark Deitsch" can be indorsed in blank simply by writing Deitsch's signature on the back of the check. Exhibit 25–1 shows a blank indorsement.

EXHIBIT 25–1 • A Blank Indorsement

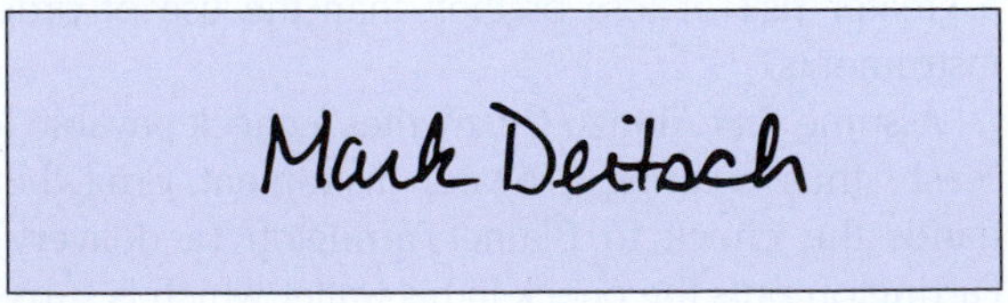

1. Pronounced uh-*lohnj*.

An instrument payable to order and indorsed in blank becomes a bearer instrument and can be negotiated by delivery alone [UCC 3–205(b)]. In other words, as will be discussed later, a blank indorsement converts an order instrument to a bearer instrument, which anybody can cash. Suppose that Rita Chou indorses in blank a check payable to her order and then loses it on the street. If Coker finds the check, he can sell it to Duncan for value without indorsing it. This constitutes a negotiation because Coker has made delivery of a bearer instrument (which was an order instrument until it was indorsed in blank).

Special Indorsements

A **special indorsement** identifies the person to whom the indorser intends to make the instrument payable; that is, it names the indorsee [UCC 3–205(a)]. For example, words such as "Pay to the order of Russell Clay" or "Pay to Russell Clay," followed by the signature of the indorser, are sufficient. When an instrument is indorsed in this way, it is an order instrument.

To avoid the risk of loss from theft, a holder may convert a blank indorsement to a special indorsement. This changes the bearer instrument back to an order instrument. A holder may "convert a blank indorsement that consists only of a signature into a special indorsement by writing, above the signature of the indorser, words identifying the person to whom the instrument is made payable" [UCC 3–205(c)].

For example, a check is made payable to Hal Cohen. He signs his name on the back of the check—a blank indorsement—and negotiates the check to William Hunter. Hunter is not able to cash the check immediately but wants to avoid any risk should he lose the check. He therefore writes "Pay to William Hunter" above Cohen's blank indorsement. In this manner, Hunter has converted Cohen's blank indorsement into a special indorsement. Further negotiation now requires William Hunter's indorsement, plus delivery. Exhibit 25–2 shows a special indorsement.

EXHIBIT 25–2 • A Special Indorsement

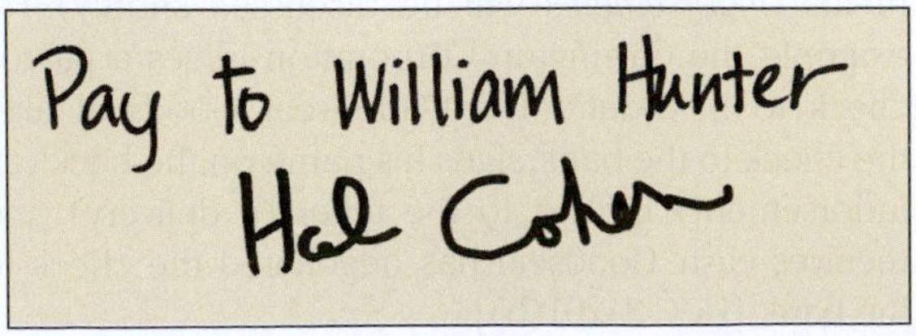

Qualified Indorsements

Generally, an indorser, *merely by indorsing,* impliedly promises to pay the holder, or any subsequent indorser, the amount of the instrument in the event that the drawer or maker defaults on the payment [UCC 3–415(a)]. Usually, then, indorsements are *unqualified indorsements.* In other words, the indorser is guaranteeing payment of the instrument in addition to transferring title to it. An indorser who does not wish to be liable on an instrument can use a **qualified indorsement** to disclaim this liability [UCC 3–415(b)]. The notation "without recourse" is commonly used to create a qualified indorsement.

Suppose that a check is made payable to the order of Sarah Jacobs. Sarah wants to negotiate the check to Allison Jong but does not want to assume liability for the check's payment. Sarah could create a qualified indorsement by indorsing the check as follows: "Pay to Allison Jong, without recourse, [signed] Sarah Jacobs" (see Exhibit 25–3).

EXHIBIT 25–3 • A Qualified Indorsement

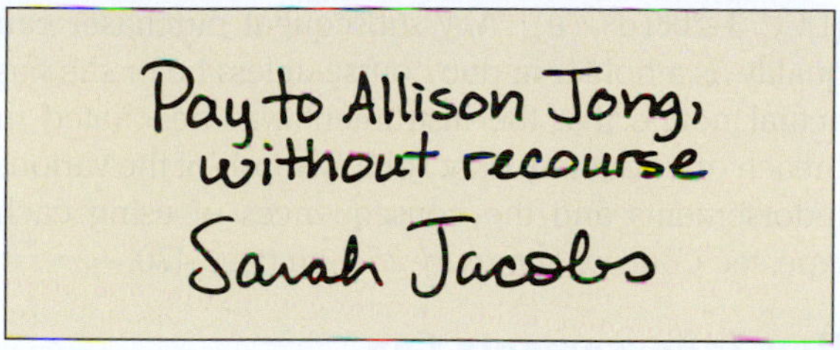
Pay to Allison Jong,
without recourse
Sarah Jacobs

The Effect of Qualified Indorsements

Qualified indorsements are often used by persons acting in a representative capacity. For example, insurance agents sometimes receive checks payable to them that are really intended as payment to the insurance company. The agent is merely indorsing the payment through to the insurance company and should not be required to make good on a check if it is later dishonored. The "without recourse" indorsement relieves the agent from any liability on the check. If the instrument is dishonored, the holder cannot obtain recovery from the agent who indorsed "without recourse" unless the indorser has breached one of the transfer warranties that will be discussed in Chapter 26. These warranties relate to good title, authorized signature, no material alteration, and other requirements.

Special versus Blank Qualified Indorsements A qualified indorsement ("without recourse") can be accompanied by either a special indorsement or a blank indorsement. A special qualified indorsement includes the name of the indorsee as well as the words "without recourse," as in Exhibit 25–3. The special indorsement makes the instrument an order instrument, and it requires an indorsement, plus delivery, for negotiation. A blank qualified indorsement makes the instrument a bearer instrument, and only delivery is required for negotiation. In either situation, the instrument still transfers title to the indorsee and can be further negotiated.

Restrictive Indorsements

A **restrictive indorsement** requires the indorsee to comply with certain instructions regarding the funds involved but does not prohibit further negotiation of the instrument [UCC 3–206(a)]. Restrictive indorsements come in many forms, some of which we discuss here.

Indorsements Prohibiting Further Indorsement An indorsement such as "Pay to Julie Thrush only, [signed] Thomas Fasulo" does not destroy negotiability. Thrush can negotiate the paper to a holder just as if it had read "Pay to Julie Thrush, [signed] Thomas Fasulo" [UCC 3–206(a)]. If the holder gives value, this type of restrictive indorsement has the same legal effect as a special indorsement.

Conditional Indorsements When payment depends on the occurrence of some event specified in the indorsement, the instrument has a conditional indorsement [UCC 3–204(a)]. For example, Ken Barton indorses a check as follows: "Pay to Lars Johansen if he completes the renovation of my kitchen by June 1, 2009, [signed] Ken Barton." Article 3 states that an indorsement conditioning the right to receive payment "does not affect the right of the indorsee to enforce the instrument" [UCC 3–206(b)]. A person paying or taking an instrument for value (*taking for value* will be discussed later in the chapter) can disregard the condition without liability.

A conditional indorsement (on the back of the instrument) does not prevent further negotiation of the instrument. If conditional language appears on the *face* (front) of an instrument, however, the instrument is not negotiable because it does not meet the requirement that a negotiable instrument must contain an unconditional promise to pay.

Indorsements for Deposit or Collection A common type of restrictive indorsement makes the indorsee (almost always a bank) a collecting agent of the indorser [UCC 3–206(c)]. Exhibit 25–4 illustrates this type of indorsement on a check payable and issued to Marcel Dumont. In particular, the indorsements "For deposit only" and "For collection only" have the effect of locking the instrument into the bank collection process. Only a bank can acquire the rights of a holder following one of these indorsements until the item has been specially indorsed by a bank to a person who is not a bank [UCC 3–206(c), 4–201(b)]. A bank's liability for payment of an instrument with a restrictive indorsement of this kind will be discussed in Chapter 27.

EXHIBIT 25–4 • "For Deposit Only" and "For Collection Only" Indorsements

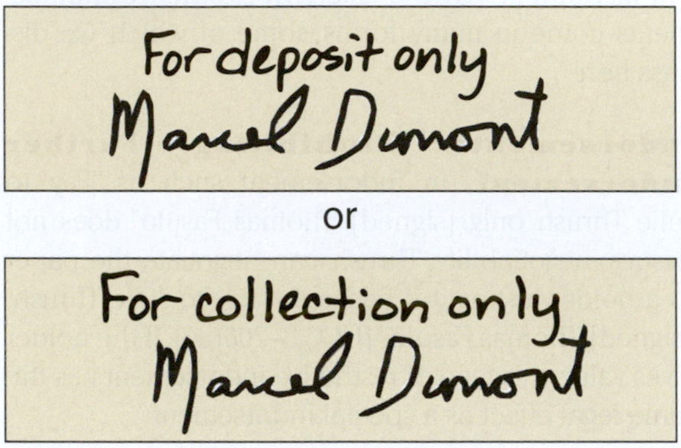
For deposit only
Marcel Dumont
or
For collection only
Marcel Dumont

Trust (Agency) Indorsements Indorsements to persons who are to hold or use the funds for the benefit of the indorser or a third party are called **trust indorsements** (also known as *agency indorsements*) [UCC 3–206(d), (e)]. Assume that Ralph Zimmer asks his accountant, Stephanie Contento, to pay some bills for him while he is out of the country. He indorses a check, drawn by a friend, to Stephanie Contento "as agent for Ralph Zimmer." This trust (agency) indorsement obligates Contento to use the funds from the friend's check only for the benefit of Zimmer.

The result of a trust indorsement is that legal rights in the instrument are transferred to the original indorsee. To the extent that the original indorsee pays or applies the proceeds consistently with the indorsement (for example, in an indorsement stating "Pay to Ellen Cook in trust for Roger Callahan"), the indorsee is a holder and can become a holder in due course (a status that will be described shortly). Sample trust (agency) indorsements are shown in Exhibit 25–5.

EXHIBIT 25–5 • Trust (Agency) Indorsements

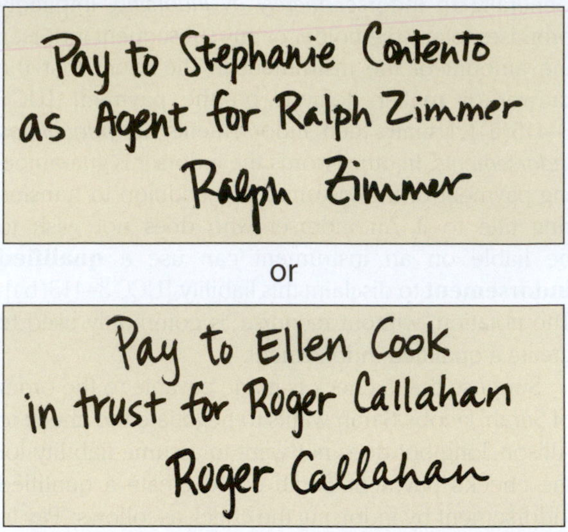
Pay to Stephanie Contento
as Agent for Ralph Zimmer
Ralph Zimmer
or
Pay to Ellen Cook
in trust for Roger Callahan
Roger Callahan

The fiduciary restrictions—restrictions mandated by a relationship involving trust and loyalty—on the instrument do not reach beyond the original indorsee [UCC 3–206(d), (e)]. Any subsequent purchaser can qualify as a holder in due course unless he or she has actual notice that the instrument was negotiated in breach of a fiduciary duty. For a synopsis of the various indorsements and the consequences of using each type, see *Concept Summary 25.1* on page 470.

How Indorsements Can Convert Order Instruments to Bearer Instruments and Vice Versa

As we saw earlier, order instruments and bearer instruments are negotiated differently. The method used for negotiation depends on the character of the instrument *at the time the negotiation takes place.* Indorsement can convert an order instrument into a bearer instrument. For example, a check originally payable to "cash" but subsequently indorsed with the words "Pay to Arnold" must be negotiated as an order instrument (by indorsement and delivery), even though it was previously a bearer instrument [UCC 3–205(a)].

As mentioned earlier, an instrument payable to the order of a named payee and indorsed in blank becomes a bearer instrument [UCC 3–205(b)]. For example, a check made payable to the order of Jessie Arnold is issued to Arnold, and Arnold indorses it by signing her name on the back. The instrument, which is now a bearer instrument, can be negotiated by delivery without indorsement. Arnold can negotiate the check to whomever she wishes merely by delivery, and that person can negotiate by delivery without indorsement. If Arnold loses the check after she indorses it, anyone who finds the check can negotiate it further.

Similarly, a bearer instrument can be converted into an order instrument through indorsement. Suppose that Arnold takes the check that she indorsed in blank (now a bearer instrument) and negotiates it, by delivery, to Jonas Tolling. Tolling indorses the check "Pay to Mark Hyatt, [signed] Jonas Tolling." By adding this special indorsement, Tolling has converted the check into an order instrument. The check can be further negotiated only by indorsement (by Mark Hyatt) and delivery [UCC 3–205(b)]. Exhibit 25–6 illustrates how an indorsement can convert an order instrument into a bearer instrument and vice versa.

SECTION 3 Miscellaneous Indorsement Problems

Of course, a significant problem occurs when an indorsement is forged or unauthorized. The UCC rules concerning unauthorized or forged signatures and indorsements will be discussed in Chapter 26 in the context of signature liability. These rules will be examined again in Chapter 27 in the context of the bank's liability for payment of an instrument containing an unauthorized signature. Here we look at some other difficulties that may arise with indorsements.

Misspelled Names

An indorsement should be identical to the name that appears on the instrument. A payee or indorsee whose name is misspelled can indorse with the misspelled name, the correct name, or both [UCC 3–204(d)]. For example, if Marie Ellison receives a check payable to the order of Mary Ellison, she can indorse the check either "Marie Ellison" or "Mary Ellison." The usual practice is to indorse with the name as it appears on the instrument followed by the correct name.

Instruments Payable to Entities

A negotiable instrument can be drawn payable to a entity such as an estate, a partnership, or an organization. In this situation, an authorized representative of the entity can negotiate the instrument. For example, a check may read "Pay to the order of the Red Cross." An authorized representative of the Red Cross can negotiate this check. Similarly, negotiable paper can be payable to a public officer. For example, checks reading "Pay to the order of the County Tax Collector" or "Pay to the order of Larry White, Receiver of Taxes" can be negotiated by whoever holds the office [UCC 3–110(c)].

Alternative or Joint Payees

An instrument payable to two or more persons *in the alternative* (for example, "Pay to the order of Ying or Mifflin") requires the indorsement of only one of the payees [UCC 3–110(d)]. If, however, an instrument is made payable to two or more persons *jointly* (for

EXHIBIT 25–6 • Converting an Order Instrument to a Bearer Instrument and Vice Versa

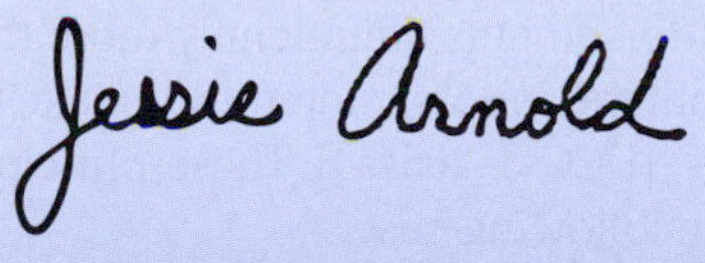

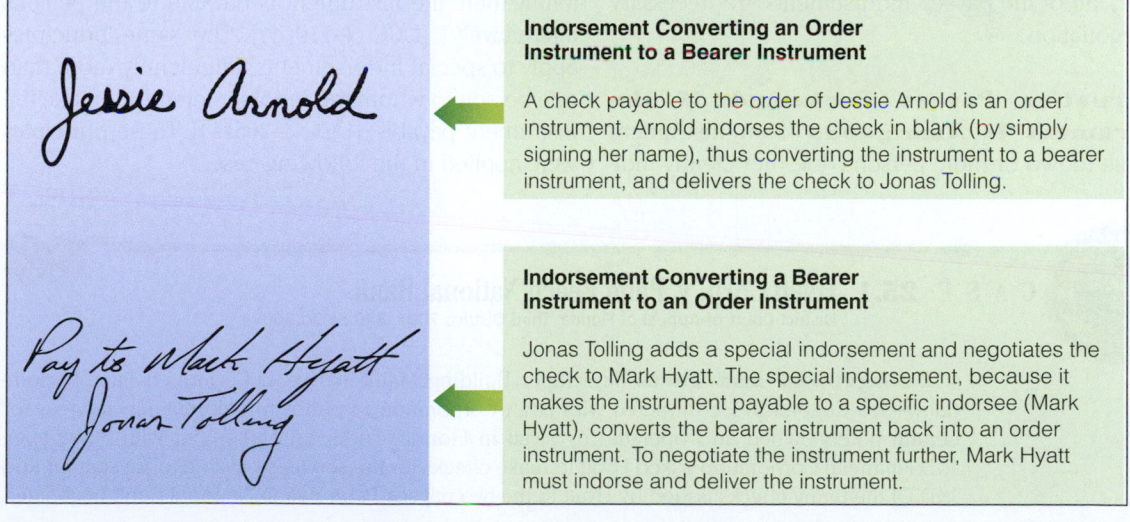

Indorsement Converting an Order Instrument to a Bearer Instrument

A check payable to the order of Jessie Arnold is an order instrument. Arnold indorses the check in blank (by simply signing her name), thus converting the instrument to a bearer instrument, and delivers the check to Jonas Tolling.

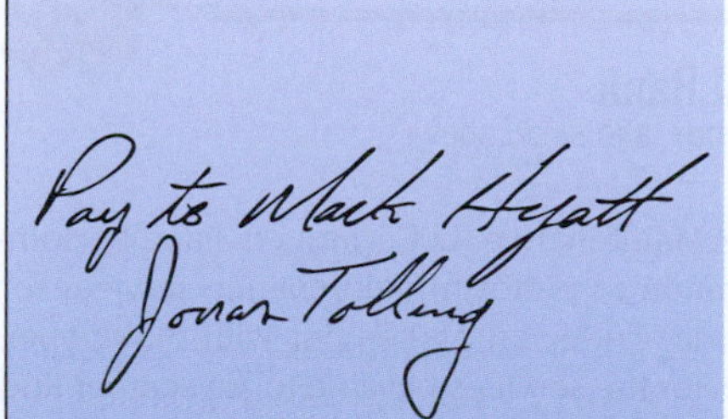

Indorsement Converting a Bearer Instrument to an Order Instrument

Jonas Tolling adds a special indorsement and negotiates the check to Mark Hyatt. The special indorsement, because it makes the instrument payable to a specific indorsee (Mark Hyatt), converts the bearer instrument back into an order instrument. To negotiate the instrument further, Mark Hyatt must indorse and deliver the instrument.

CONCEPT SUMMARY 25.1
Types of Indorsements and Their Effect

Type of Indorsement	Description	Examples	Legal Effect
BLANK INDORSEMENTS	Indorser does not identify the person to whom the instrument is payable; can consist of a mere signature.	"Elana Guiterrez" "Mark Deitsch"	Creates a bearer instrument, which can be negotiated by delivery alone.
SPECIAL INDORSEMENTS	Indorser identifies the person to whom the instrument is payable.	"Pay to the order of Russell Clay" "Pay to William Hunter"	Creates an order instrument; negotiation requires delivery and indorsement.
QUALIFIED INDORSEMENTS	Indorser includes words indicating that he or she is not guaranteeing or assuming liability for payment.	"Without recourse, Elana Guitterez" (blank qualified indorsement) "Pay to Allison Jong without recourse, Sarah Jacobs" (special qualified indorsement, which creates an order instrument)	Relieves indorser of any liability for payment of the instrument; frequently used by agents or others acting on behalf of another.
RESTRICTIVE INDORSEMENTS	Indorser includes specific instructions regarding the funds involved or states a condition to the right of the indorsee to receive payment.	"For deposit only" "For collection only"	Only a bank can become a holder of instruments that are indorsed for deposit or collection.
		"Pay to Stephanie Contento as agent for Ralph Zimmer" "Pay to Ellen Cook in trust for Roger Callahan"	In a trust indorsement, the third party agent or trustee has the rights of a holder but has fiduciary duties to use the funds consistently with the indorsement.

example, "Pay to the order of Bridgette and Tony Van Horn"), all of the payees' indorsements are necessary for negotiation.

Alternative Payees Presumed If the Instrument Is Ambiguous If an instrument payable to two or more persons does not clearly indicate whether it is payable in the alternative or payable jointly, then "the instrument is payable to the persons alternatively" [UCC 3–110(d)]. The same principles apply to special indorsements that identify more than one person to whom the indorser intends to make the instrument payable [UCC 3–205(a)]. These principles were applied in the following case.

CASE 25.1 Hyatt Corp. v. Palm Beach National Bank

District Court of Appeal of Florida, Third District, 2003. 840 So.2d 300.

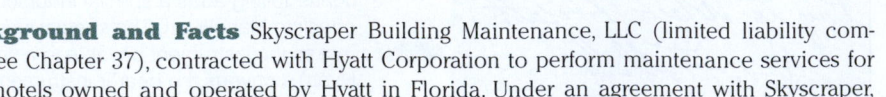

• **Background and Facts** Skyscraper Building Maintenance, LLC (limited liability company—see Chapter 37), contracted with Hyatt Corporation to perform maintenance services for certain hotels owned and operated by Hyatt in Florida. Under an agreement with Skyscraper, J&D Financial Corporation asked Hyatt to make checks for the services payable to Skyscraper and J&D. Of the many checks issued by Hyatt to the two payees, Palm Beach National Bank negotiated

CASE 25.1 CONTINUED two that were indorsed only by Skyscraper. These two checks were made payable to "J&D Financial Corp. Skyscraper Building Maint." Parties listed in this manner are referred to as "stacked payees." J&D filed a suit in a Florida state court against Hyatt, the bank, and others, seeking, among other things, full repayment of the two checks. J&D and Hyatt asserted that the checks were payable jointly, requiring indorsement by both payees. The bank argued that the checks were payable to J&D and Skyscraper alternatively and thus negotiable on only one payee's indorsement. The court issued a summary judgment in the bank's favor. J&D and Hyatt appealed to a state intermediate appellate court.

● **Decision and Rationale** The state intermediate appellate court affirmed the lower court's judgment, holding that the bank properly negotiated the checks even though they were indorsed by only one of the two payees. The appellate court pointed out that UCC 3–110(d) provides, "If an instrument payable to two or more persons is ambiguous as to whether it is payable to the persons alternatively, the instrument is payable to the persons alternatively." The court acknowledged that under the previous version of this provision, "if an ambiguity existed as to whether multiple payees were intended as joint or alternative payees, they were deemed joint payees," but noted that the statute had been amended and the amendment "reverses the prior rule." The court concluded that when a check lists two payees without the use of the word *and* or *or*, the nature of the payees, as to whether they are alternative or joint, is ambiguous. "Therefore, the UCC amendment prevails and they are to be treated as alternative payees, thus requiring only one of the payees' signatures." In other words, a check payable to stacked payees is payable alternatively. "Consequently," the court stated, "the bank could negotiate the check when it was endorsed by only one of the two payees, thereby escaping liability."

● **The Legal Environment Dimension** *Other than negotiation, what is the significance of the UCC provision at issue in this case?*

● **The Ethical Dimension** *If an instrument made payable to two persons without specifying* and *or* or *(a stacked-payee designation) was considered unambiguous and payable jointly before the amendment of this provision of the UCC, should that same payee designation be considered unambiguous after the amendment? Explain.*

Suspension of the Drawer's Obligation

When a drawer gives one alternative or joint payee a check, the drawer's obligation on the check to other payees is suspended [UCC 3–310(b)(1)]. The payee who has possession of the check holds it for the benefit of all of the payees.

On the check's negotiation, is the drawer obliged to ensure that the funds are disbursed between the payees? In the following case, one of the parties—a payee on a "co-payable" check—contended in effect that a drawer has such a duty.

CASE 25.2 Graves v. Johnson

Court of Appeals of Indiana, 2007. 862 N.E.2d 716.

● **Background and Facts** Vernon and Shirley Graves owned a commercial building and the property on which it was located in Kokomo, Indiana. The Graveses leased the premises to John and Tamara Johnson, who operated Johnson's Towing & Recovery on the property. The Johnsons insured the property and their business through Westport Insurance Company. A fire destroyed the building in November 2003. Westport hired Claims Management Services, Inc. (CMS), to investigate and pay the claim. On CMS's behalf, Robert Davis met with Vernon, who was acting as the rebuilding contractor, and agreed that Westport would pay $98,000 in three "progress payments" with the

CASE CONTINUES

CASE 25.2 CONTINUED checks to be "co-payable" to Johnson's Towing and Vernon. Westport issued two checks, for $30,000 and $29,000, respectively, and delivered them to Vernon, who deposited them into his account. A third check for $68,037.42 was tendered to the Johnsons. They did not remit the funds to the Graveses, however, who subsequently filed a suit in an Indiana state court against the Johnsons and Westport.[a] The court entered a summary judgment in Westport's favor. The Graveses appealed to a state intermediate appellate court.

• **Decision and Rationale** The state intermediate appellate court affirmed the judgment of the lower court. The reviewing court pointed out that when there are joint payees to a check, "payment to and possession by one joint payee is constructive possession by the other joint payee." Thereafter, the obligations of the check's issuer are suspended with respect to the other joint payee. Any underlying debt for which the check constitutes a discharge is extinguished even when a jointly payable check is sent to just one co-payee and that co-payee embezzles the funds, as occurred in this case. The insurance company's tender of the last check to the Johnsons suspended the insurance company's obligation to both payees.

• **The Ethical Dimension** *Does a drawer who acts as Westport did—consulting with, and delivering the first two checks to, the Graveses—create an ethical obligation with respect to the delivery of the third check? Why or why not?*

• **The Legal Environment Dimension** *Is there a method, other than payment, that would have discharged Westport's obligation as the drawer of the check? Explain.*

a. The Johnsons filed for bankruptcy, which automatically suspended the Graveses' suit against them.

SECTION 4

Holder versus Holder in Due Course

The rules contained in Article 3 of the UCC govern a party's right to payment of a check, draft, note, or certificate of deposit.[2] Problems arise when a holder seeking payment of a negotiable instrument learns that a defense to payment exists or that another party has a prior claim to the instrument. In such situations, it becomes important for the person seeking payment to have the rights of a *holder in due course* (HDC). An HDC takes a negotiable instrument free of all claims and most defenses of other parties.

Status of an Ordinary Holder

As pointed out in Chapter 24, the UCC defines a *holder* as "the person in possession of a negotiable instrument that is payable either to bearer or to an identified person that is the person in possession" [UCC 1–201(21)(A)]. An ordinary holder obtains only those rights that the transferor had in the instrument. In this respect, a holder has the same status as an assignee (see Chapter 16). A holder normally is subject to the same defenses that could be asserted against the transferor, just as an assignee is subject to the defenses that could be asserted against the assignor.

Status of a Holder in Due Course (HDC)

In contrast, a **holder in due course (HDC)** is a holder who, by meeting certain acquisition requirements (to be discussed shortly), takes an instrument free of most of the defenses and claims to which the transferor was subject. Stated another way, an HDC can normally acquire a higher level of immunity than can an ordinary holder in regard to defenses against payment on the instrument or ownership claims to the instrument by other parties.

An example will help to clarify the distinction between the rights of an ordinary holder and the rights of an HDC. Debby Morrison signs a $10,000 note payable to Alex Jerrod in payment for goods. Jerrod negotiates the note to Beverly Larson, who promises to

2. The rights and liabilities on checks, drafts, notes, and certificates of deposit are determined under Article 3 of the UCC. Other kinds of documents, such as stock certificates, bills of lading, and other documents of title, meet the requirements of negotiable instruments, but the rights and liabilities of the parties on these documents are covered by Articles 7 and 8 of the UCC. See Chapter 47, on bailments, for information about Article 7.

pay Jerrod for it in thirty days. During the next month, Larson learns that Jerrod has breached his contract with Morrison by delivering defective goods and that, for this reason, Morrison will not honor the $10,000 note. Whether Larson can hold Morrison liable on the note depends on whether Larson has met the requirements for HDC status. If Larson has met these requirements and thus has HDC status, she is entitled to payment on the note. If Larson has not met these requirements, she has the status of an ordinary holder, and Morrison's defense against payment to Jerrod will also be effective against Larson.

SECTION 5 Requirements for HDC Status

The basic requirements for attaining HDC status are set forth in UCC 3–302. An HDC must first be a holder of a negotiable instrument and must have taken the instrument (1) for value; (2) in good faith; and (3) without notice that it is overdue, that it has been dishonored, that any person has a defense against it or a claim to it, or that the instrument contains unauthorized signatures or alterations or is so irregular or incomplete as to call into question its authenticity. We now examine each of these requirements.

Taking for Value

An HDC must have given value for the instrument [UCC 3–302(a)(2)(i), 3–303]. A person who receives an instrument as a gift or inherits it has *not* met the requirement of value. In these situations, the person normally becomes an ordinary holder and does not possess the rights of an HDC.

How an Instrument Is Taken for Value Under UCC 3–303(a), a holder takes an instrument for value if the holder has done any of the following:

1. Performed the promise for which the instrument was issued or transferred.
2. Acquired a security interest or other lien in the instrument (other than a lien obtained by a judicial proceeding).[3]
3. Taken the instrument in payment of, or as security for, an **antecedent** (preexisting) **claim.** For example, Zon owes Dwyer $2,000 on a past-due account. If Zon negotiates a $2,000 note signed by Gordon to Dwyer and Dwyer accepts it to discharge the overdue account balance, Dwyer has given value for the instrument.
4. Given a negotiable instrument as payment. Suppose that Martin has issued a $5,000 negotiable promissory note to Paulene. The note is due six months from the date issued. Paulene needs funds and does not want to wait until the maturity date to collect. She negotiates the note to her friend Kristen, who pays her $2,000 in cash and writes her a check—a negotiable instrument—for the balance of $3,000. Kristen has given full value for the note by paying $2,000 in cash and issuing Paulene the check for $3,000.
5. Given an irrevocable commitment (such as a letter of credit described in Chapter 22 on page 417) as payment.

The Concept of Value in Negotiable Instruments Law The concept of value in the law of negotiable instruments is not the same as the concept of consideration in the law of contracts. An executory promise (a promise to give value in the future) is clearly valid consideration to support a contract [UCC 1–201(44)]. In contrast, it normally does not constitute sufficient value to make the promisor an HDC. UCC 3–303(a)(1) provides that a holder takes the instrument for value only to the extent that the promise has been performed. Therefore, if the holder plans to pay for the instrument later or plans to perform the required services at some future date, the holder has not yet given value. In that situation, the holder is not yet an HDC.

In the Morrison-Jerrod-Larson example presented earlier, Larson is not an HDC because she did not take the instrument (Morrison's note) for value—she has not yet paid Jerrod for the note. Thus, Morrison's defense of breach of contract is valid against Larson as well as against Jerrod. If Larson had paid Jerrod for the note at the time of transfer (which would mean she had given value for the instrument), she would be an HDC. As an HDC, she could hold Morrison liable on the note even though Morrison has a valid defense against Jerrod on the basis of breach of contract. Exhibit 25–7 on page 474 illustrates these concepts.

Exceptions In a few situations, the holder may pay for the instrument but does not acquire HDC status. For example, when the instrument is purchased at a judicial sale, such as a bankruptcy or creditor's sale, the holder will not be an HDC. Similarly, if the instrument is acquired as a result of taking over a trust or estate (as administrator), or as part of a corporate purchase

3. Security interests will be discussed in Chapter 29. Other liens will be discussed in Chapter 28.

EXHIBIT 25–7 • Taking for Value

By exchanging defective goods for the note, Jerrod breached his contract with Morrison. Morrison could assert this defense if Jerrod presented the note to her for payment. Jerrod exchanged the note for Larson's promise to pay in thirty days, however. Because Larson did not take the note for value, she is not a holder in due course. Thus, Morrison can assert against Larson the defense of Jerrod's breach when Larson submits the note to Morrison for payment. If Larson had taken the note for value, Morrison could not assert that defense and would be liable to pay the note.

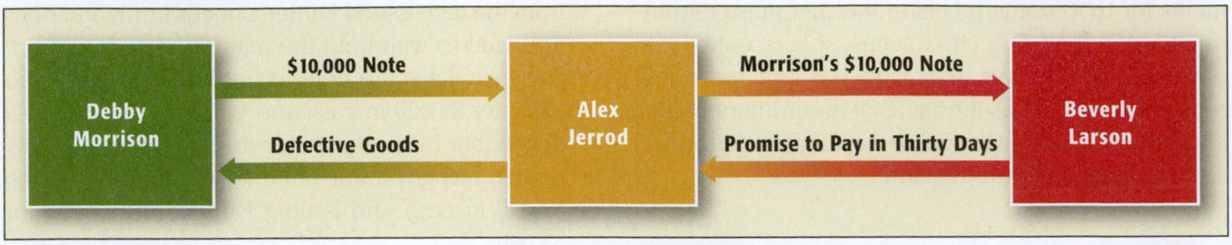

of assets, the holder will have only the rights of an ordinary holder [UCC 3–302(c)].

Taking in Good Faith

The second requirement for HDC status is that the holder take the instrument in *good faith* [UCC 3–302(a)(2)(ii)]. Under Article 3, *good faith* is defined as "honesty in fact and the observance of reasonable commercial standards of fair dealing" [UCC 3–103(a)(4)].[4] The good faith requirement applies only to the *holder.* It is immaterial whether the transferor acted in good faith. Thus, a person who in good faith takes a negotiable instrument from a thief may become an HDC.

The good faith requirement means that the purchaser, when acquiring the instrument, must honestly believe that it is not defective. If a person purchases a $10,000 note for $300 from a stranger on a street corner, the issue of good faith can be raised on the grounds of both the suspicious circumstances and the grossly inadequate consideration (value). In the following case, the court had to deal with the meaning of accepting a check in good faith.

4. Before the revision of Article 3, the applicable definition of *good faith* was "honesty in fact in the conduct or transaction concerned" [UCC 1–201(19)].

CASE 25.3 Georg v. Metro Fixtures Contractors, Inc.

Supreme Court of Colorado, 2008. 178 P.3d 1209.

• **Background and Facts** Clinton Georg employed Cassandra Demery as a bookkeeper at his business, Freestyle, until he discovered she had embezzled more than $200,000 and had failed to pay $240,000 in state and federal taxes owed by Freestyle. Georg fired Demery and said that if she did not repay the embezzled funds, he would notify the authorities. Demery went to work for Metro Fixtures, a company owned by her parents, as a bookkeeper. She wrote a check to Freestyle for $189,000 out of Metro's account and deposited it to Freestyle's checking account. She told Georg it was a loan to her from her family to repay him. Georg used the funds to pay his back taxes. Two years later, Metro discovered Demery's theft and sued Georg and Freestyle for *conversion* (see Chapter 6), as Demery had no authority to take the funds. The trial court held that Freestyle was a holder in due course and granted summary judgment. Metro appealed. The appeals court reversed, holding that because Demery deposited the check directly into Freestyle's account, Freestyle could not have been a holder in due course as it never had actual possession of the check. Georg and Freestyle appealed.

• **Decision and Rationale** Colorado's highest court reversed the appellate court's decision, finding that the payee, Freestyle, was a holder in due course based on its constructive posses-

CASE 25.3 CONTINUED sion of the check. Even though Metro did not authorize Demery to issue the check for $189,000, she had authority to issue checks for Metro. Georg had no reason to know that Demery had lied when she said her parents, who owned the company, had loaned her the funds. Freestyle took the check in good faith. The UCC intends to protect the party least able to protect itself. So, as in this case, when two innocent parties suffer because of wrongdoing, the loss falls on the party who has created the circumstances that enabled the third party to engage in wrongdoing. Metro gave Demery authority to write checks on its account, so it bears the loss.

- **What If the Facts Were Different?** *Suppose that Demery had gone to work for a company with which she had no relationship and stole funds from it to pay Georg. Would Georg then be the more innocent party? Why or why not?*

- **The Ethical Dimension** *Was it right for Georg to let the loss fall on Metro, and was it reasonable for him to believe that Demery's parents had loaned her the funds? Explain your answer.*

Taking without Notice

The final requirement for HDC status concerns notice of defects. A person cannot be a HDC if she or he knows or has reason to know that the instrument is defective in any one of the following ways [UCC 3–302(a)]:

1. It is overdue.
2. It has been dishonored.
3. It is part of a series of which at least one instrument has an uncured (uncorrected) default.
4. The instrument contains an unauthorized signature or has been altered.
5. There is a defense against the instrument or a claim to the instrument.
6. The instrument is so incomplete or irregular as to call into question its authenticity.[5]

What Constitutes Notice? Notice of a defective instrument is given whenever the holder (1) has actual knowledge of the defect; (2) has received a notice of the defect (such as a letter from a bank identifying the serial numbers of stolen checks); or (3) has reason to know that a defect exists, given all the facts and circumstances known at the time in question [UCC 1–201(25)]. The holder must also have received the notice "at a time and in a manner that gives a reasonable opportunity to act on it" [UCC 3–302(f)]. A purchaser's knowledge of certain facts, such as insolvency proceedings against the maker or drawer of the instrument, does not constitute notice that the instrument is defective [UCC 3–302(b)].

Overdue Instruments What constitutes notice that an instrument is overdue depends on whether it is a demand instrument (payable on demand) or a time instrument (payable at a definite time).

Demand Instruments. A purchaser has notice that a *demand instrument* is overdue if he or she either takes the instrument knowing that demand has been made or takes the instrument an unreasonable length of time after its date. For a check, a "reasonable time" is ninety days after the date of the check. For all other demand instruments, what will be considered a reasonable time depends on the circumstances [UCC 3–304(a)].

Time Instruments. Normally, a *time instrument* is overdue on the day after its due date; hence, anyone who takes a time instrument after the due date is on notice that it is overdue [UCC 3–304(b)].[6] Thus, if a promissory note due on May 15 is purchased on May 16, the purchaser will be an ordinary holder, not an HDC. If an instrument states that it is "Payable in thirty days," counting begins the day after the instrument is dated. For example, a note dated December 1 that is payable in thirty days is due by midnight on December 31. If the payment date falls on a Sunday or holiday, the instrument is payable on the next business day.

A series of notes issued at the same time with successive maturity dates is overdue when any note in the series is overdue. This serves to notify prospective purchasers that they cannot qualify as HDCs [UCC 3–302(a)(2)(iii)].

5. Section 302(1)(c) of the unrevised Article 3 provided that HDC protection is lost if a holder has notice that an instrument is overdue or has been dishonored or if there is a claim to or a defense against it.

6. A time instrument also becomes overdue the day after an accelerated due date, unless the purchaser has no reason to know that the due date has been accelerated [UCC 3–302(a)(2)(iii), 3–304(b)(3)].

If the principal is to be paid in installments, the default or nonpayment of any one installment will make the instrument overdue and provide notice to prospective purchasers of the default. The instrument will remain overdue until the default is cured [UCC 3–304(b)(1)]. An instrument does not become overdue if there is a default on a payment of interest only [UCC 3–304(c)]. Most installment notes provide that any payment shall be applied first to interest and the balance to the principal. This serves as notice that any installment payment for less than the full amount results in a default on an installment payment toward the principal.

Dishonored Instruments An instrument is *dishonored* when the party to whom the instrument is presented refuses to pay it. If a holder knows or has reason to know that an instrument has been dishonored, the holder is on notice and cannot claim HDC status [UCC 3–302(a)(2)]. Thus, a person who takes a check clearly stamped "insufficient funds" is put on notice.

For example, Gonzalez holds a demand note dated September 1 on Apex, Inc., a local business firm. On September 17, she demands payment, and Apex refuses (that is, dishonors the instrument). On September 22, Gonzalez negotiates the note to Brenner, a purchaser who lives in another state. Brenner does not know, and has no reason to know, that the note has been dishonored. Because Brenner is *not* put on notice, Brenner can become an HDC.

Notice of Claims or Defenses A holder cannot become an HDC if he or she has notice of any claim to the instrument or defense against it [UCC 3–302(a)(2)(v), (vi)]. Knowledge of claims or defenses can be imputed (attributed) to the purchaser if these claims or defenses are apparent on the face of the instrument or if the purchaser otherwise had reason to know of them from facts surrounding the transaction.[7]

Knowledge of a Defense. It stands to reason that a purchaser cannot be an HDC if she or he knows that a party to an instrument has a defense that entitles that party to avoid the obligation. For example, a potential purchaser who knows that the maker of a note has breached the underlying contract with the payee cannot thereafter purchase the note as an HDC.

Knowledge of one defense precludes a holder from asserting HDC status in regard to all other defenses. For example, Litton, knowing that the note he has taken has a forged indorsement, presents it to the maker for payment. The maker refuses to pay on the ground of breach of the underlying contract. The maker can assert this defense against Litton even though Litton had no knowledge of the breach, because Litton's knowledge of the forgery alone prevents him from being an HDC in *all* circumstances.

Knowledge of Wrongful Negotiation by a Fiduciary. Knowledge that a fiduciary has wrongfully negotiated an instrument is sufficient notice of a claim against the instrument to preclude HDC status. Suppose that O'Banion, a university trustee, improperly writes a check on the university trust account to pay a personal debt. Lewis knows that the check has been improperly drawn on university funds, but she accepts it anyway. Lewis cannot claim to be an HDC. When a purchaser knows that a fiduciary is acting in breach of duty, HDC status is denied [UCC 3–307(b)].

Incomplete Instruments A purchaser cannot become an HDC of an instrument so incomplete on its face that an element of negotiability is lacking (for example, the amount is not filled in) [UCC 3–302(a)(1)]. Minor omissions (such as the omission of the date—see Chapter 24) are permissible because these do not call into question the validity of the instrument [UCC 3–113(b)].

Similarly, when a person accepts an instrument that has been completed without knowing that it was incomplete when issued, the person can take it as an HDC [UCC 3–115(b), 3–302(a)(1)]. Even if an instrument that is originally incomplete is later completed in an unauthorized manner, an HDC can still enforce the instrument as completed [UCC 3–407(c)].

To illustrate: Peyton asks Brittany to buy a textbook for him when she goes to the campus bookstore. Peyton writes a check payable to the campus store, leaves the amount blank, and tells Brittany to fill in the price of the textbook. The cost of the textbook is $85. If Brittany fills in the check for $150 before she gets to the bookstore, the bookstore cashier sees only a properly completed instrument. Therefore, because the

7. If an instrument contains a statement required by a statute or an administrative rule to the effect that the rights of a holder or transferee are subject to the claims or defenses that the issuer could assert against the original payee, the instrument is negotiable, but there cannot be an HDC of the instrument. See UCC 3–106(d) and the discussion of federal limitations on HDC rights in Chapter 26.

bookstore had no notice that the check was incomplete when it was issued, the bookstore can take the check for $150 and become an HDC. (Material alterations will be discussed in Chapter 26.)

Irregular Instruments Any irregularity on the face of an instrument (such as an obvious forgery or alteration) that calls into question its validity or ownership, or that creates an ambiguity as to the party to pay, will bar HDC status. A difference between the handwriting used in the body of a check and that used in the signature will not in and of itself make an instrument irregular. Antedating or postdating a check or stating the amount in digits but failing to write out the numbers normally will not make a check irregular [UCC 3–113(a)].[8] Visible evidence of forgery of a maker's or drawer's signature, however, will disqualify a purchaser from HDC status. Conversely, a good forgery of a signature or a careful alteration can go undetected by reasonable examination; therefore, the purchaser can qualify as an HDC [UCC 3–302(a)(1)].

Losses that result from well-crafted forgeries usually fall on the party to whom the forger transferred the instrument (assuming, of course, that the forger cannot be found). This means that a bank that accepts checks for deposit despite apparent evidence on the faces of the checks that they were irregular will bear the loss if the checks later turn out to be forged.[9]

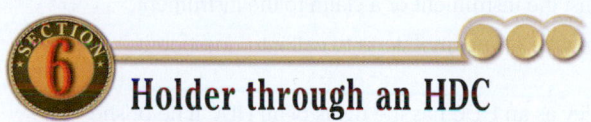

SECTION 6 Holder through an HDC

A person who does not qualify as an HDC but who derives his or her title through an HDC can acquire the rights and privileges of an HDC. This rule, which is called the **shelter principle,** is set out in UCC 3–203(b):

> Transfer of an instrument, whether or not the transfer is a negotiation, vests in the transferee any right of the transferor to enforce the instrument, including any right as a holder in due course, but the transferee cannot acquire rights of a holder in due course by a transfer, directly or indirectly, from a holder in due course if the transferee engaged in fraud or illegality affecting the instrument.

The Purpose of the Shelter Principle

The shelter principle extends the benefits of HDC status and is designed to aid the HDC in readily disposing of the instrument. Anyone, no matter how far removed from an HDC, who can ultimately trace her or his title back to an HDC comes within the shelter principle. Normally, a person who acquires an instrument from an HDC or from someone with HDC rights receives HDC rights on the legal theory that the transferee of an instrument receives at least the rights that the transferor had. By extending the benefits of HDC status, the shelter principle promotes the marketability and free transferability of negotiable instruments.

Limitations on the Shelter Principle

Nevertheless, there are some limitations on the shelter principle. Certain persons who formerly held instruments cannot improve their positions by later reacquiring the instruments from HDCs [UCC 3–203(b)]. Therefore, if a holder was a party to fraud or illegality affecting the instrument or if, as a prior holder, he or she had notice of a claim or defense against the instrument, that holder is not allowed to improve his or her status by repurchasing the instrument from a later HDC.

To illustrate: Matthew and Carla collaborate to defraud Lorena. Lorena is induced to give Carla a negotiable note payable to Carla's order. Carla then specially indorses the note for value to Larry, an HDC. Matthew and Carla split the proceeds. Larry negotiates the note to Stuart, another HDC. Stuart then negotiates the note for value to Matthew. Matthew, even though he obtained the note through an HDC, is not a holder through an HDC, because he participated in the original fraud and can never acquire HDC rights in this note.

See *Concept Summary 25.2* on the following page for a review of the requirements for HDC status.

8. Note that some courts have held that the postdating of a check may raise substantial suspicions about its authenticity, particularly if it is a commercial check. See, for example, *Bay Shore Check Cashing Corp. v. Landscapes by North East Construction Corp.,* 776 N.Y.S.2d 742 (N.Y.Dist. 2004).

9. See, for example, *Firstar Bank, N.A. v. First Star Title Agency, Inc.*, 2004 WL 1906851 (Ohio App. 2004).

CONCEPT SUMMARY 25.2
Rules and Requirements for HDC Status

Basic Requirements	Rules
MUST BE A *HOLDER*	A *holder* is defined as a person in possession of an instrument "if the instrument is payable to bearer or, in the cases of an instrument payable to an identified person, if the identified person is in possession" [UCC 1–201(20)].
MUST TAKE *FOR VALUE*	A holder gives *value* by doing any of the following [UCC 3–303]: 1. Performing the promise for which the instrument was issued or transferred. 2. Acquiring a security interest or other lien in the instrument (other than a lien obtained by a judicial proceeding). 3. Taking the instrument in payment of, or as security for, an antecedent debt. 4. Giving a negotiable instrument as payment. 5. Giving an irrevocable commitment as payment.
MUST TAKE *IN GOOD FAITH*	*Good faith* is defined for purposes of revised Article 3 as "honesty in fact and the observance of reasonable commercial standards of fair dealing" [UCC 3–103(a)(4)].
MUST TAKE *WITHOUT NOTICE*	A holder must not be *on notice* that the instrument is defective in any of the following ways [UCC 3–302, 3–304]: 1. The instrument is overdue. 2. The instrument has been dishonored. 3. There is an uncured (uncorrected) default with respect to another instrument issued as part of the same series. 4. The instrument contains an unauthorized signature or has been altered. 5. There is a defense against the instrument or a claim to the instrument. 6. The instrument is so irregular or incomplete as to call into question its authenticity.
SHELTER PRINCIPLE—HOLDER THROUGH A HOLDER IN DUE COURSE	A holder who cannot qualify as an HDC has the rights of an HDC if he or she derives title through an HDC [UCC 3–203(b)].

REVIEWING Transferability and Holder in Due Course

The Brown family owns several companies, including the J. H. Stevedoring Company and Penn Warehousing and Distribution, Inc. Many aspects of the companies' operations and management are intertwined. Dennis Bishop began working for J. H. and Penn in 1999. By 2008, Bishop was financial controller at J. H., where he was responsible for approving invoices for payment and reconciling the corporate checkbook. In December 2008, Bishop began stealing from Penn and J. H. by writing checks on the corporate accounts and using the funds for his own benefit (committing the crime of embezzlement). Several members of the Brown family signed the checks for Bishop without hesitation because he was a longtime, trusted employee. Over the next two years, Bishop embezzled $1,209,436, of which $670,632 was used to buy horses from the Fasig-Tipton Company and Fasig-Tipton

REVIEWING Transferability and Holder in Due Course, Continued

Midlantic, Inc., with Penn and J. H. checks made payable to those firms. When Bishop's fraud was revealed, J. H. and Penn filed a suit in a federal district court against the Fasig-Tipton firms (the defendants) to recover the amounts of the checks made payable to them. Using the information presented in the chapter, answer the following questions.

1. What method was most likely used to negotiate the instruments described here?
2. Suppose that all of the checks issued to the defendants were made payable to "Fasig-Tipton Co., Fasig-Tipton Midlantic, Inc." Under the Uniform Commercial Code, were the instruments payable jointly or in the alternative? Why is this significant?
3. Do the defendants in this situation (the two Fasig-Tipton firms) meet the requirements of an HDC? Why or why not?
4. In whose favor should the court rule and why?

TERMS AND CONCEPTS

allonge 466
antecedent claim 473
blank indorsement 466
holder in due course (HDC) 472
indorsee 466
indorser 466
negotiation 465
qualified indorsement 467
restrictive indorsement 467
shelter principle 477
special indorsement 466
trust indorsement 468

QUESTIONS AND CASE PROBLEMS

25-1. A check drawn by Cullen for $500 is made payable to the order of Jordan and issued to Jordan. Jordan owes his landlord $500 in rent and transfers the check to his landlord with the following indorsement: "For rent paid, [signed] Jordan." Jordan's landlord has contracted to have Deborah do some landscaping on the property. When Deborah insists on immediate payment, the landlord transfers the check to Deborah without indorsement. Later, to pay for some palm trees purchased from Better-Garden Nursery, Deborah transfers the check with the following indorsement: "Pay to Better-Garden Nursery, without recourse, [signed] Deborah." Better-Garden Nursery sends the check to its bank indorsed "For deposit only, [signed] Better-Garden Nursery."

(a) Classify each of these indorsements.
(b) Was the transfer from Jordan's landlord to Deborah, without indorsement, an assignment or a negotiation? Explain.

25-2. QUESTION WITH SAMPLE ANSWER

Celine issues a ninety-day negotiable promissory note payable to the order of Hayden. The amount of the note is left blank, pending a determination of the amount that Hayden will need to purchase a used car for Celine. Celine authorizes any amount not to exceed $2,000. Hayden, without authority, fills in the note in the amount of $5,000 and thirty days later sells the note to First National Bank of Oklahoma for $4,850. Hayden does not buy the car and leaves the state. First National Bank has no knowledge that the instrument was incomplete when issued or that Hayden had no authority to complete the instrument in the amount of $5,000.

(a) Does the bank qualify as a holder in due course? If so, for what amount? Explain.
(b) If Hayden had sold the note to a stranger in a bar for $500, would the stranger qualify as a holder in due course? Explain.

- **For a sample answer to Question 25–2, go to Appendix I at the end of this text.**

25–3. Through negotiation, Emilio has received from dishonest payees two checks with the following histories:

(a) The drawer issued a check to the payee for $9. The payee cleverly altered the numeral on the check from $9 to $90 and the written word from "nine" to "ninety."

(b) The drawer issued a check to the payee without filling in the amount. The drawer authorized the payee to fill in the amount for no more than $90. The payee filled in the amount of $900.

Discuss whether Emilio, by giving value to the payees, can qualify as a holder in due course of these checks.

25–4. Bertram writes a check for $200 payable to "cash." He puts the check in his pocket and drives to the bank to cash the check. As he gets out of his car in the bank's parking lot, the check slips out of his pocket and falls to the pavement. Jerrod walks by moments later, picks up the check, and later that day delivers it to Amber, to whom he owes $200. Amber indorses the check "For deposit only, [signed] Amber Dowel" and deposits it into her checking account. In light of these circumstances, answer the following questions:

(a) Is the check a bearer instrument or an order instrument?

(b) Did Jerrod's delivery of the check to Amber constitute a valid negotiation? Why or why not?

(c) What type of indorsement did Amber make?

(d) Does Bertram have a right to recover the $200 from Amber? Explain.

25–5. Transfer of Instruments. In July 1988, Chester Crow executed a promissory note payable "to the order of THE FIRST NATIONAL BANK OF SHREVEPORT or BEARER" in the amount of $21,578.42 at an interest rate of 3 percent per year above the "prime rate in effect at The First National Bank of Shreveport" in Shreveport, Louisiana, until paid. The note was a standard preprinted promissory note. In 1999, Credit Recoveries, Inc., filed a suit in a Louisiana state court against Crow, alleging that he owed $7,222.57 on the note, plus interest. Crow responded that the debt represented by the note had been canceled by the bank in September 1994. He also contended that, in any event, to collect on the note Credit Recoveries had to prove its legitimate ownership of it. When no evidence of ownership was forthcoming, Crow filed a motion to dismiss the suit. Is the note an order instrument or a bearer instrument? How might it have been transferred to Credit Recoveries? With this in mind, should the court dismiss the suit on the basis of Crow's contention? [*Credit Recoveries, Inc. v. Crow,* 862 So.2d 1146 (La.App. 2 Cir. 2003)]

25–6. Alternative or Joint Payees. Hartford Mutual Insurance Co. issued a check for $60,150 payable to "Andrew Michael Bogdan, Jr., Crystal Bogdan, Oceanmark Bank FSB, Goodman-Gable-Gould Company." The check was to pay a claim related to the Bogdans' commercial property. Besides the Bogdans, the payees were the mortgage holder (Oceanmark) and the insurance agent who adjusted the claim. The Bogdans and the agent indorsed the check and cashed it at Provident Bank of Maryland. Meanwhile, Oceanmark sold the mortgage to Pelican National Bank, which asked Provident to pay it the amount of the check. Provident refused. Pelican filed a suit in a Maryland state court against Provident, arguing that the check had been improperly negotiated. Was this check payable jointly or in the alternative? Whose indorsements were required to cash it? In whose favor should the court rule? Explain. [*Pelican National Bank v. Provident Bank of Maryland,* 381 Md. 327, 849 A.2d 475 (2004)]

25–7. CASE PROBLEM WITH SAMPLE ANSWER

In February 2001, New York Linen Co., a party rental company, agreed to buy 550 chairs from Elite Products. On delivery of the chairs, New York Linen issued a check (dated February 27) for $13,300 to Elite. Elite's owner, Meir Shmeltzer, transferred the check to General Credit Corp., a company in the business of buying instruments from payees for cash. Meanwhile, after recounting the chairs, New York Linen discovered that delivery was not complete and stopped payment of the check. The next day, New York Linen drafted a second check, reflecting an adjusted payment of $11,275, and delivered it to Elite. A notation on the second check indicated that it was a replacement for the first check. When the first check was dishonored, General Credit filed a suit in a New York state court against New York Linen to recover the amount. New York Linen argued in part that General Credit was not a holder in due course because of the notation on the second check. In whose favor should the court rule? Why? [*General Credit Corp. v. New York Linen Co.,* __ Misc.2d __ (N.Y. City Civ.Ct. 2002)]

- **To view a sample answer for Problem 25–7, go to this book's Web site at www.cengage.com/blaw/jentz, select "Chapter 25," and click on "Case Problem with Sample Answer."**

25–8. Holder in Due Course. Robert Triffin bought a number of dishonored checks from McCall's Liquor Corp., Community Check Cashing II, LLC (CCC), and other licensed check-cashing businesses in New Jersey. Seventeen of the checks had been dishonored as counterfeit. In an attempt to recover on the items, Triffin met with the drawer, Automatic Data Processing, Inc. (ADP). At the meeting, Triffin said that he knew the checks were counterfeit. When ADP refused to pay, Triffin filed suits in New Jersey state courts to collect, asserting claims totaling $11,021.33. With each complaint were copies of assignment agreements corresponding to each check. Each agreement stated, among other things, that the seller was a holder in due course (HDC) and had assigned its rights in the check to Triffin. ADP had not previously seen these agreements. A private investigator determined that the forms attached to the McCall's and CCC checks had not been signed by their sellers but that

Triffin had scanned the signatures into his computer and pasted them onto the agreements. ADP claimed fraud. Does Triffin qualify as an HDC? If not, did he acquire the rights of an HDC under the shelter principle? As for the fraud claim, which element of fraud would ADP be least likely to prove? [*Triffin v. Automatic Data Processing, Inc.*, 394 N.J.Super. 237, 926 A.2d 362 (App.Div. 2007)]

25–9. A QUESTION OF ETHICS

*As an assistant comptroller for Interior Crafts, Inc., in Chicago, Illinois, Todd Leparski was authorized to receive checks from Interior's customers and deposit the checks into Interior's account. Between October 2000 and February 2001, Leparski stole more than $500,000 from Interior by indorsing the checks "Interior Crafts—For Deposit Only" but depositing some of them into his own account at Marquette Bank through an automated teller machine owned by Pan American Bank. Marquette alerted Interior, which was able to recover about $250,000 from Leparski. Interior also recovered $250,000 under its policy with American Insurance Co. To collect the rest of the missing funds, Interior filed a suit in an Illinois state court against Leparski and the banks. The court ruled in favor of Interior, and Pan American appealed to a state intermediate appellate court. [*Interior Crafts, Inc. v. Leparski*, 366 Ill.App.3d 1148, 853 N.E.2d 1244, 304 Ill.Dec. 878 (3 Dist. 2006)]*

(a) What type of indorsement is "Interior Crafts—For Deposit Only"? What is the obligation of a party that receives a check with this indorsement? Does the fact that Interior authorized Leparski to indorse its checks but not to deposit those checks into his own account absolve Pan American of liability? Explain.

(b) From an ethical perspective, how might a business firm such as Interior discourage an employee's thievery such as Leparski's acts in this case? Discuss.

25–10. VIDEO QUESTION

Go to this text's Web site at **www.cengage.com/blaw/jentz** and select "Chapter 25." Click on "Video Questions" and view the video titled *Negotiability & Transferability: Indorsing Checks*. Then answer the following questions.

(a) According to the instructor in the video, what are the two reasons why banks generally require a person to indorse a check that is made out to cash (a bearer instrument), even when the check is signed in the presence of the teller?

(b) Suppose that your friend makes out a check payable to cash, signs it, and hands it to you. You take the check to your bank and indorse the check with your name and the words "without recourse." What type of indorsement is this? How does this indorsement affect the bank's rights?

(c) Now suppose that you go to your bank and write a check on your account payable to cash for $500. The teller gives you the cash without asking you to indorse the check. After you leave, the teller slips the check into his pocket. Later, the teller delivers it (without an indorsement) to his friend Carol in payment for a gambling debt. Carol takes your check to her bank, indorses it, and deposits the money. Discuss whether Carol is a holder in due course.

LAW ON THE WEB

For updated links to resources available on the Web, as well as a variety of other materials, visit this text's Web site at

www.cengage.com/blaw/jentz

To find information on the UCC, including the Article 3 provisions discussed in this chapter, refer to the Web sites listed in the *Law on the Web* section in Chapter 24.

Legal Research Exercises on the Web

Go to **www.cengage.com/blaw/jentz**, the Web site that accompanies this text. Select "Chapter 25" and click on "Internet Exercises." There you will find the following Internet research exercises that you can perform to learn more about the topics covered in this chapter.

Internet Exercise 25–1: Legal Perspective
Electronic Negotiable Instruments

Internet Exercise 25–2: Management Perspective
Holder in Due Course

CHAPTER 26

Liability, Defenses, and Discharge

Two kinds of liability are associated with negotiable instruments: signature liability and warranty liability. *Signature liability* relates to signatures on instruments. Those who sign negotiable instruments are potentially liable for payment of the amount stated on the instrument. *Warranty liability,* in contrast, extends to both signers and nonsigners. A breach of warranty can occur when the instrument is transferred or presented for payment.

Note that the focus is on liability on the *instrument itself or on warranties connected with the transfer or presentment of the instrument* as opposed to liability on any underlying contract. Suppose that Donna agrees to buy one thousand compact discs from Luis and issues a check to Luis in payment. The liability discussed in this chapter does not relate directly to the contract (for instance, whether the compact discs are of proper quality or fit for the purpose for which they are intended). The liability discussed here is the liability arising in connection with the *check* (such as what recourse Luis will have if Donna's bank refuses to pay the check due to insufficient funds in Donna's account or Donna's order to her bank to stop payment on the check).

The first part of this chapter covers the liability of the parties who sign instruments—for example, drawers of drafts and checks, makers of notes and certificates of deposit, and indorsers. It also covers the liability of accommodation parties and the warranty liability of those who transfer instruments and present instruments for payment. The chapter then examines the defenses that can be raised to avoid liability on an instrument. The final section in the chapter looks at some of the ways in which parties can be *discharged* from liability on negotiable instruments.

SECTION 1 Signature Liability

The key to liability on a negotiable instrument is a signature. As discussed in Chapter 24, the Uniform Commercial Code (UCC) broadly defines a signature as any name, word, mark, or symbol executed or adopted by a person with the present intention to authenticate a writing [UCC 1–209(39), 3–401(b)]. A signature can be made manually or by use of any device or machine.

The general rule is as follows: "A person is not liable on an instrument unless (i) the person signed the instrument, or (ii) the person is represented by an agent or representative who signed the instrument and the signature is binding on the represented person" [UCC 3–401(a)]. Essentially, this means that every person, except a qualified indorser,[1] who signs a negotiable instrument is either primarily or secondarily liable for payment of that instrument when it comes due. The following subsections discuss these two types of liability, as well as the conditions that must be met before liability can arise.

Primary Liability

A person who is primarily liable on a negotiable instrument is absolutely required to pay the instrument—unless, of course, he or she has a valid defense to

1. A qualified indorser—one who indorses "without recourse"—undertakes no obligation to pay [UCC 3–415(b)]. A qualified indorser merely assumes warranty liability, which will be discussed later in this chapter.

payment. Liability is immediate when the instrument is signed or issued. No action by the holder of the instrument is required. *Makers* and *acceptors* are primarily liable [UCC 3–412, 3–413].

Makers The maker of a promissory note promises to pay the instrument according to its terms. It is the maker's promise to pay that renders the instrument negotiable. If the instrument was incomplete when the maker signed it, the maker is obligated to pay it according to either its stated terms or terms that were agreed on and later filled in to complete the instrument [UCC 3–115, 3–407, 3–412]. For example, Tristan executes a preprinted promissory note to Sharon, without filling in the due-date blank. If Sharon does not complete the form by adding the date, the note will be payable on demand. If Sharon subsequently writes in a due date that Tristan authorized, the note is payable on the stated due date. In either situation, Tristan (the maker) is obligated to pay the note.

Acceptors An *acceptor* is a drawee that promises to pay an instrument when it is presented later for payment, as mentioned in Chapter 24. When a drawee *accepts* a draft (usually by writing "accepted" across its face), the drawee becomes primarily liable to all subsequent holders of the instrument. In other words, the drawee's acceptance is a promise to pay that places the drawee in virtually the same position as the maker of a promissory note [UCC 3–413]. A drawee that refuses to accept a draft that requires the drawee's acceptance (such as a trade acceptance) has dishonored the instrument. (**Dishonor** of an instrument occurs when payment or acceptance of the instrument, whichever is required, is refused even though the instrument is presented in a timely and proper manner.)

Acceptance of a check is called *certification,* as will be discussed in Chapter 27. Certification is not necessary on checks, and a bank is under no obligation to certify checks. If it does certify a check, however, the drawee bank occupies the position of an acceptor and is primarily liable on the check to any holder [UCC 3–409(d)].

Secondary Liability

Drawers and *indorsers* have secondary liability. On a negotiable instrument, secondary liability is similar to the liability of a guarantor in a simple contract (described in Chapter 28) in the sense that it is *contingent liability.* In other words, a drawer or an indorser will be liable only if the party that is responsible for paying the instrument refuses to do so (dishonors the instrument). With respect to drafts and checks, a drawer's secondary liability does not arise until the drawee fails to pay or to accept the instrument, whichever is required. In regard to notes, an indorser's secondary liability does not arise until the maker, who is primarily liable, has defaulted on the instrument [UCC 3–412, 3–415].

Dishonor of an instrument thus triggers the liability of parties who are secondarily liable on the instrument—that is, the drawer and *unqualified* indorsers. Suppose that Lamar writes a check for $1,000 on her account at Western Bank payable to the order of Carerra. Carerra indorses and delivers the check, for value, to Deere. Deere deposits the check into his account at Universal Bank, but the bank returns the check to Deere marked "insufficient funds," thus dishonoring the check. The question for Deere is whether the drawer (Lamar) or the indorser (Carerra) can be held liable on the check after the bank has dishonored it. The answer to the question depends on whether certain conditions for secondary liability have been satisfied.

Parties who are secondarily liable on a negotiable instrument promise to pay on that instrument *only if* the following events occur:[2]

1. The instrument is properly and timely presented.
2. The instrument is dishonored.
3. Timely notice of dishonor is given.[3]

Proper and Timely Presentment As discussed in Chapter 24, *presentment* is the formal demand for the payment or acceptance of a negotiable instrument. The UCC requires that a holder present the instrument to the appropriate party, in a timely fashion, and in a proper manner (providing reasonable identification if requested) [UCC 3–414(f), 3–415(e), 3–501]. The party to whom the instrument must be presented depends on the type of instrument involved. A note or certificate of deposit (CD) must be presented to the maker for payment. A draft is presented to the drawee for acceptance, payment, or both.

2. An instrument can be drafted to include a waiver of the presentment and notice of dishonor requirements [UCC 3–504]. Presume, for simplicity's sake, that such waivers have *not* been incorporated into the instruments described in this chapter.

3. Note that these requirements are necessary for a secondarily liable party to have *signature* liability on a negotiable instrument, but they are not necessary for a secondarily liable party to have *warranty* liability (to be discussed later in this chapter).

A check is presented to the drawee (bank) for payment [UCC 3–501(a), 3–502(b)].

Presentment can be made by any commercially reasonable means, including oral, written, or electronic communication [UCC 3–501(b)]. It can also be made at the place specified in the instrument. Ordinarily, presentment is effective when the demand for payment or acceptance is received (if presentment takes place after an established cutoff hour, however, it may be treated as occurring the next business day).

One of the most crucial criteria for proper presentment is timeliness [UCC 3–414(f), 3–415(e), 3–501(b)(4)]. Failure to present within a reasonable time is a common reason for improper presentment and can lead to the instrument's dishonor and potentially discharge parties from secondary liability. A reasonable time for presentment is determined by the nature of the instrument, any usage of banking or trade, and the facts of the particular case. If the instrument is payable on demand, the holder should present it for payment or acceptance within a reasonable time.

For domestic, uncertified checks, the UCC establishes a presumptively reasonable time period [UCC 3–414(f), 3–415(e)]. An ordinary check should be presented for payment within thirty days of its date or the date that it was indorsed. A drawer is *not* automatically discharged from liability for checks presented after thirty days, but the holder must be able to prove that the presentment after that time was reasonable.[4] The time for proper presentment for different types of instruments is shown in Exhibit 26–1.

4. For a seminal case in which a state's highest court held that presentment more than thirty days after the date of an uncertified check did not discharge the liability of the drawer, see *Grist v. Osgood,* 90 Nev. 165, 521 P.2d 368 (1974).

Dishonor As mentioned earlier, an instrument is dishonored when payment or acceptance of the instrument is refused in spite of proper and timely presentment. An instrument is also dishonored when the required presentment is excused (as it would be, for example, if the maker had died) and the instrument is not properly accepted or paid [UCC 3–502(e), 3–504].

In certain situations, a delay in payment or a refusal to pay an instrument will *not* dishonor the instrument. When presentment is made after an established cutoff hour (not earlier than 2:00 P.M.), for instance, a bank can postpone payment until the following business day without dishonoring the instrument [UCC 3–501(b)(4)]. In addition, when the holder refuses to exhibit the instrument, to give reasonable identification, or to sign a receipt for the payment on the instrument, a bank's refusal to pay does not dishonor the instrument [UCC 3–501(b)(2)]. Returning an instrument because it lacks a proper indorsement also is not a dishonor [UCC 3–501(b)(3)(i)].

Proper Notice Once an instrument has been dishonored, proper notice must be given to secondary parties (drawers and indorsers) for them to be held liable. Notice may be given in any reasonable manner, including an oral, written, or electronic communication, as well as by writing or stamping on the instrument itself [UCC 3–503(b)].[5] If the party giving notice is a bank, it must give any necessary notice before its midnight deadline (midnight of the next banking day

5. Note that written notice is preferable, as oral notice makes it possible for a secondary party to claim that notice was not received. Also, to give proper notice of the dishonor of a foreign draft (a draft drawn in one country and payable in another country), a formal notice called a *protest* is required [UCC 3–505(b)].

EXHIBIT 26–1 • Time for Proper Presentment

Type of Instrument	For Acceptance	For Payment
Time	On or before due date.	On due date.
Demand	Within a reasonable time (after date of issue or after secondary party becomes liable on the instrument).	Within a reasonable time.
Check	No stated time limit.	Within thirty days of its date, to hold drawer secondarily liable. Within thirty days of indorsement, to hold indorser secondarily liable.

after receipt) [UCC 3–503(c)]. If the party giving notice is not a bank, the party must give notice within thirty days following the day of dishonor or the day on which the person receives notice of dishonor [UCC 3–503(c)].

Accommodation Parties

An **accommodation party** is one who signs an instrument for the purpose of lending his or her name as credit to another party on the instrument [UCC 3–419(a)]. Requiring an accommodation party is one way to secure against nonpayment of a negotiable instrument. When one person (such as a parent) cosigns a promissory note with the maker (such as the parent's son or daughter), the cosigner is an accommodation party, and the maker is the accommodated party.

If the accommodation party signs on behalf of the *maker,* he or she is an *accommodation maker* and is primarily liable on the instrument.[6] For example, if Alex takes out a loan to purchase a car and his uncle cosigns the note, the uncle becomes primarily liable on the instrument. In other words, Alex's uncle is guaranteeing payment, and the bank can seek payment directly from the uncle.

If, however, the accommodation party signs on behalf of a *payee or other holder* (usually to make the instrument more marketable), she or he is an *accommodation indorser* and, as an indorser, is secondarily liable. Suppose that Frank Huston applies to Northeast Bank for a $20,000 loan to start a small business. Huston's lender (who has possession of the note) has Finch Smith, who has invested in Huston's business, sign the note. In this situation, Smith is an indorser and his liability is secondary; that is, the lender must pursue Huston first before seeking payment from Smith. If Smith ends up paying the amount due on the note, he has a right to reimbursement from Huston (the accommodated party) [UCC 3–419(e)].

Authorized Agents' Signatures

The general law of agency, covered in Chapters 31 and 32, applies to negotiable instruments. Questions often arise as to the liability on an instrument signed by an agent. An **agent** is a person who agrees to represent or act for another, called the **principal.** Agents can sign negotiable instruments, just as they can sign contracts, and thereby bind their principals [UCC 3–401(a)(ii), 3–402(a)]. Without such a rule, all corporate commercial business would stop, as every corporation can and must act through its agents. Certain requirements must be met, however, before the principal becomes liable on the instrument. A basic requirement to hold the principal liable on the instrument is that the agent be *authorized* to sign the instrument on the principal's behalf.

Liability of the Principal Generally, an authorized agent binds a principal on an instrument if the agent *clearly names* the principal in the signature (by writing, mark, or some symbol). In this situation, the UCC presumes that the signature is authorized and genuine [UCC 3–308(a)]. The agent may or may not add his or her own name, but if the signature shows clearly that it is made on behalf of the principal, the agent is not liable on the instrument [UCC 3–402(b)(1)]. For example, either of the following signatures by Sandra Binney as agent for Bob Aronson will bind Aronson on the instrument:

1. Aronson, by Binney, agent.
2. Aronson.

If Binney (the agent) signs just her own name, however, she will be personally liable to a holder in due course who has no notice of her agency status. An agent can escape liability to ordinary holders if the agent proves that the original parties did not intend the agent to be liable on the instrument [UCC 3–402(a), (b)(2)].[7] In either situation, the principal is bound if the party entitled to enforce the instrument can prove the agency relationship.

Liability of the Agent An authorized agent may be held personally liable on a negotiable instrument in two other situations. An agent can be personally liable when the instrument is signed in both the agent's name and the principal's name but nothing on the instrument indicates the agency relationship. For instance, if Binney signs the instrument "Sandra Binney, Bob Aronson" or "Aronson, Binney," she may be held personally liable because it is not clear that there is an agency relationship. When the agent indicates agency

6. A 2002 amendment to UCC Article 3 expressly provides that an accommodation party is primarily liable if the party indicates on the instrument that he or she guarantees payment or "does not unambiguously indicate an intention to guarantee collection rather than payment" [Amended UCC 3–419(e)]. Recall from Chapter 24, however, that as yet only a few states have adopted the 2002 amendments to Article 3.

7. See UCC 3–402, Comment 1.

status in signing a negotiable instrument but fails to name the principal (for example, "Sandra Binney, agent"), the agent may also be liable [UCC 3–402(b)(2)]. Because the above forms of signing are ambiguous, however, parol evidence is admissible to prove the agency relationship.

An important exception to the rules on agent liability is made for checks that are signed by agents. If an agent signs his or her own name on a *check that is payable from the account of the principal,* and the principal is identified on the check, the agent will not be personally liable on the check [UCC 3–402(c)]. Suppose that Binney, who is *authorized* to draw checks on Aronson Company's account, signs a check that is preprinted with Aronson Company's name. The signature reads simply "Sandra Binney." In this situation, Binney will not be personally liable on the check.

Unauthorized Signatures

Unauthorized signatures arise in two situations—when a person forges another person's name on a negotiable instrument and when an agent who lacks the authority signs an instrument on behalf of a principal. The general rule is that an unauthorized signature is wholly inoperative and will not bind the person whose name is signed or forged. For example, Pablo finds Veronica's checkbook lying on the street, writes out a check to himself, and forges Veronica's signature. If a bank negligently fails to ascertain that Veronica's signature is not genuine and cashes the check for Pablo, the bank generally will be liable to Veronica for the amount. (The liability of banks for paying instruments with forged signatures will be discussed further in Chapter 27.)

If an agent lacks the authority to sign the principal's name or has exceeded the authority given by the principal, the signature does not bind the principal but will bind the "unauthorized signer" [UCC 3–403(a)]. Assume that Maya Campbell is the principal and Lena Shem is her agent. Shem, without authority, signs a promissory note as follows: "Maya Campbell, by Lena Shem, agent." Because Maya Campbell's "signature" is unauthorized, Campbell cannot be held liable, but Shem is liable to a holder of the note. This would be true even if Shem had signed the note "Maya Campbell," without indicating any agency relationship. In either situation, the unauthorized signer, Shem, is liable on the instrument.

Exceptions to the General Rule There are two exceptions to the general rule that an unauthorized signature will not bind the person whose name is signed:

1. When the person whose name is signed *ratifies* (affirms) the signature, he or she will be bound [UCC 3–403(a)]. For example, a principal can ratify an unauthorized signature made by an agent, either expressly (by affirming the validity of the signature) or impliedly (by other conduct, such as keeping any benefits received in the transaction or failing to repudiate the signature). The parties involved need not be principal and agent. Thus, a mother may ratify her daughter's signature forging the mother's name so that the daughter will not be prosecuted for forgery.
2. When the negligence of the person whose name was forged substantially contributed to the forgery, a court may not allow the person to deny the effectiveness of an unauthorized signature [UCC 3–115, 3–406, 4–401(d)(2)]. Assume that Rob, the owner of a business, leaves his signature stamp and a blank check on an office counter. An employee, using the stamp, fills in and cashes the check. Rob can be estopped (prevented), on the basis of his negligence, from denying liability for payment of the check [UCC 3–115, 3–406, 4–401(d)(2)]. Whatever loss occurs may be allocated, however, between certain parties on the basis of *comparative negligence* [UCC 3–406(b)]. If Rob, in this example, can demonstrate that the bank was negligent in paying the check, the bank may bear a portion of the loss. The liability of the parties in this type of situation will be discussed further in Chapter 27.

When the Holder Is a Holder in Due Course A person who forges a check or signs an instrument without authorization can be held personally liable for payment by a holder in due course, or HDC [UCC 3–403(a)]. This is true even if the name of the person signing the instrument without authorization does not appear on the instrument. If Michel Vuillard signs "Paul Richaud" without Richaud's authorization, Vuillard is personally liable just as if he had signed his own name. Vuillard's liability is limited, however, to persons who in good faith pay the instrument or take it for value. A holder who knew the signature was unauthorized would not qualify as an HDC and thus could not recover from Vuillard on the instrument. (The defenses that are effective against ordinary holders versus HDCs will be discussed in detail later in this chapter.)

PREVENTING LEGAL DISPUTES

Businesspersons should be aware that although an unauthorized signature on a negotiable instrument is ineffective against the person whose name was signed, the signer remains liable. While this rule may not be of great consequence with forgeries (because persons who commit forgery are likely to be difficult to locate and have limited financial resources), it can be very significant when dealing with unauthorized agents.

A corporate agent, for instance, may have exceeded her or his authority when signing on behalf of a corporation. If you accepted an instrument from this person in good faith and paid value for it, you should be able to collect from the unauthorized agent what you cannot collect from the corporation. Because persons acting on behalf of a corporation typically have access to financial resources, pursuing this avenue may be your best chance of obtaining payment in some situations.

Special Rules for Unauthorized Indorsements

Generally, when an indorsement is forged or unauthorized, the burden of loss falls on the first party to take the instrument with the forged or unauthorized indorsement. This general rule is premised on the concept that the first party to take an instrument is in the best position to prevent the loss.

For example, Jenny Nilson steals a check drawn on Universal Bank and payable to the order of Inga Leed. Nilson indorses the check "Inga Leed" and presents the check to Universal Bank for payment. The bank, without asking Nilson for identification, pays the check, and Nilson disappears. In this situation, Leed will not be liable on the check because her indorsement was forged. The bank will bear the loss, which it might have avoided if it had requested identification from Nilson.

This general rule has two important exceptions. These exceptions arise when an indorsement is made by an imposter or by a fictitious payee. We look at these two situations here.

Imposters An **imposter** is one who uses mail, Internet, telephone, or other means to induce a maker or drawer to issue an instrument in the name of an impersonated payee. If the maker or drawer believes the imposter to be the named payee at the time of issue, the indorsement by the imposter is not treated as unauthorized when the instrument is transferred to an innocent party. This is because the maker or drawer *intended* the imposter to receive the instrument. In this situation, under the UCC's *imposter rule,* the imposter's indorsement will be effective—that is, not considered a forgery—insofar as the drawer or maker is concerned [UCC 3–404(a)].

Suppose that Kayla impersonates Donna and induces Edward to write a check payable to the order of Donna. Kayla, continuing to impersonate Donna, negotiates the check to First National Bank. In this situation, Kayla's signature will be considered effective, and Edward, as the drawer of the check, is liable for its amount to First National. (The state can still file criminal charges against Kayla for her conduct, of course.)

The comparative negligence standard mentioned previously also applies to situations involving imposters [UCC 3–404(d)]. Thus, if a bank fails to exercise ordinary care in cashing a check made out to an imposter, the drawer may be able to recover a portion of the loss from the bank.

Fictitious Payees When a person causes an instrument to be issued to a payee who will have *no interest* in the instrument, the payee is referred to as a **fictitious payee.** A fictitious payee can be a person or firm that does not truly exist, or it may be an identifiable party that will not acquire any interest in the instrument. Under the UCC's *fictitious payee rule,* the payee's indorsement is not treated as a forgery, and an innocent holder can hold the maker or drawer liable on the instrument [UCC 3–404(b), 3–405].

Situations involving fictitious payees most often arise when (1) a dishonest employee deceives the employer into signing an instrument payable to a party with no right to receive payment on the instrument or (2) a dishonest employee or agent has the authority to issue an instrument on behalf of the employer and issues a check to a party who has no interest in the instrument.

How a Fictitious Payee Can Be Created—An Example. Assume that Goldstar Aviation, Inc., gives its bookkeeper, Leslie Rose, general authority to issue company checks drawn on First State Bank so that Rose can pay employees' wages and other corporate bills. Rose decides to cheat Goldstar out of $10,000 by issuing a check payable to the Del Rey Company, a supplier of aircraft parts. Rose does not intend Del Rey to receive any of the funds, nor is Del Rey entitled to the payment. Rose indorses the check in Del Rey's name and deposits the check in an account that she opened in West National Bank in the name "Del Rey Co." West National Bank accepts the check and collects payment from the drawee bank, First State Bank. First State Bank charges Goldstar's account $10,000. Rose transfers $10,000 out of the Del Rey account and closes the account. Goldstar discovers the fraud and demands that the account be recredited.

Who Bears the Loss? According to the UCC's fictitious payee rule, Rose's indorsement in the name of a payee with no interest in the instrument is "effective," so there is no "forgery" [UCC 3–404(b)(2)]. Under this provision, West National Bank is protected in paying on the check, and the drawee bank is protected in charging Goldstar's account. Thus, the employer-drawer, Goldstar, will bear the loss. Of course, Goldstar has recourse against Rose, if she has not absconded with the funds. Additionally, if Goldstar can prove that West National Bank's failure to exercise reasonable care contributed substantially to the loss, the bank may be required to bear a proportionate share of the loss under the UCC's comparative negligence standard [UCC 3–404(d)]. Thus, West National Bank could be liable for a portion of the loss if it failed to exercise ordinary care in its dealings with Rose.

Whether a dishonest employee actually signs the check or merely supplies his or her employer with names of fictitious creditors (or with true names of creditors having fictitious debts), the result is the same under the UCC. Assume that Dan Symes draws up the payroll list from which employees' salary checks are written. He fraudulently adds the name Penny Trip (a real person but a fictitious employee) to the payroll, thereby causing checks to be issued to her. Trip cashes the checks and shares the proceeds with Symes. Again, it is the employer-drawer who bears the loss. For a synopsis of the rules relating to signature liability, see *Concept Summary 26.1.*

SECTION 2 Warranty Liability

In addition to the signature liability discussed in the preceding section, transferors make certain implied warranties regarding the instruments that they are negotiating. Liability under these warranties is not subject to the conditions of proper presentment, dishonor, and notice of dishonor. These warranties arise even when a transferor does not indorse the instrument (as in delivery of a bearer instrument). Warranty liability is particularly important when a holder cannot hold a party liable on her or his signature.

Warranties fall into two categories: those that arise from the *transfer* of a negotiable instrument and those that arise on *presentment* [UCC 3–416, 3–417]. Both transfer and presentment warranties attempt to shift liability back to the wrongdoer or to the person who dealt face to face with the wrongdoer and thus was in the best position to prevent the wrongdoing.

Transfer Warranties

The UCC describes five **transfer warranties** [UCC 3–416]. For transfer warranties to arise, an instrument *must be transferred for consideration.* For example, Quality Products Corporation sells goods to Royal Retail Stores, Inc., and receives in payment Royal Retail's note. Quality then sells the note, for value, to Superior Finance Company. In this situation, the instrument has been transferred for consideration. One who transfers an instrument for consideration makes the following transfer warranties to all subsequent transferees and holders who take the instrument in good faith (with some exceptions, as will be noted shortly):

1. The transferor is entitled to enforce the instrument.
2. All signatures are authentic and authorized.
3. The instrument has not been altered.
4. The instrument is not subject to a defense or claim of any party that can be asserted against the transferor.
5. The transferor has no knowledge of any bankruptcy proceedings against the maker, the acceptor, or the drawer of the instrument.[8]

Parties to Whom Warranty Liability Extends The manner of transfer and the type of negotiation that are used determine how far and to

8. A 2002 amendment to UCC 3–416(a) adds a sixth warranty: "with respect to a remotely created consumer item, that the person on whose account the item is drawn authorized the issuance of the item in the amount for which the item is drawn." UCC 3–103(16) defines a "remotely created consumer item" as an item, such as a check, drawn on a consumer account, that is not created by the payor bank and does not contain the drawer's handwritten signature. Suppose that a telemarketer submits an instrument to a bank for payment, claiming that the consumer on whose account the instrument purports to be drawn authorized it over the phone. Under this amendment, a bank that accepts and pays the instrument warrants to the next bank in the collection chain that the consumer authorized the item in that amount.

CONCEPT SUMMARY 26.1
Signature Liability

Concept	Description
Primary and Secondary Liability	Every party (except a qualified indorser) who signs a negotiable instrument is either primarily or secondarily liable for payment of the instrument when it comes due. 1. *Primary liability*—Makers and acceptors are primarily liable [UCC 3–409, 3–412, 3–413]. 2. *Secondary liability*—Drawers and indorsers are secondarily liable [UCC 3–414, 3–415, 3–501, 3–502, 3–503]. Parties who are secondarily liable on an instrument promise to pay on that instrument only if the following events occur: a. The instrument is properly and timely presented. b. The instrument is dishonored. c. Timely notice of dishonor is given.
Accommodation Parties	An *accommodation party* is one who signs an instrument for the purpose of lending his or her name as credit to another party on the instrument [UCC 3–419]. Accommodation *makers* are primarily liable; accommodation *indorsers* are secondarily liable.
Agents' Signatures	An *agent* is a person who agrees to represent or act for another, called the *principal*. Agents can sign negotiable instruments and thereby bind their principals. Liability on the instrument depends on whether the agent is authorized and on whether the agent's representative capacity and the principal's identity are both indicated on the instrument [UCC 3–401, 3–402, 3–403]. Agents need not indicate their representative capacity on *checks*—provided the checks clearly identify the principal and are drawn on the principal's account.
Unauthorized Signatures	An unauthorized signature is wholly inoperative as the signature of the person whose name is signed *unless:* 1. The person whose name is signed ratifies (affirms) it or is precluded from denying it [UCC 3–115, 3–403, 3–406, 4–401]. 2. The instrument has been negotiated to a holder in due course [UCC 3–403].
Special Rules for Unauthorized Indorsements	An unauthorized indorsement will not bind the maker or drawer of the instrument except in the following circumstances: 1. When an imposter induces the maker or drawer of an instrument to issue it to the imposter *(imposter rule)* [UCC 3–404(a)]. 2. When a person causes an instrument to be issued to a payee who will have *no interest* in the instrument *(fictitious payee rule)* [UCC 3–404(b), 3–405].

whom a transfer warranty will run. Transfer of an order instrument by indorsement and delivery extends warranty liability to any subsequent holder who takes the instrument in good faith. The warranties of a person who, for consideration, transfers *without indorsement* (by delivery of a bearer instrument), however, will extend only to the immediate transferee [UCC 3–416(a)].

Suppose that Wylie forges Kim's name as a maker of a promissory note. The note is made payable to Wylie. Wylie indorses the note in blank, negotiates it for consideration to Bret, and then leaves the country. Bret, without indorsement, delivers the note for consideration to Fern. Fern, also without indorsement, delivers the note for consideration to Rick. On Rick's presentment of the note to Kim, the forgery is discovered. Rick

CONCEPT SUMMARY 26.2
Transfer Warranty Liability for Transferors Who Receive Consideration

Transferors	Transferees to Whom Warranties Extend If Consideration Is Received
INDORSERS WHO RECEIVE CONSIDERATION	Five transfer warranties extend to *all* subsequent holders: 1. The transferor is entitled to enforce the instrument. 2. All signatures are authentic and authorized. 3. The instrument has not been altered. 4. The instrument is not subject to a defense or claim of any party that can be asserted against the transferor. 5. The transferor has no knowledge of insolvency proceedings against the maker, acceptor, or drawer of the instrument.
NONINDORSERS WHO RECEIVE CONSIDERATION	Same as for indorsers, but warranties extend *only* to the *immediate transferee.*

can hold Fern (the immediate transferor) liable for breach of the warranty that all signatures are genuine. Rick cannot hold Bret liable because Bret is not Rick's immediate transferor; rather, Bret is a prior nonindorsing transferor.

Note that if Wylie had added a special indorsement ("Payable to Bret") instead of a blank indorsement, the instrument would have remained an order instrument. In that situation, Bret would have had to indorse the instrument to negotiate it to Fern, and his transfer warranties would extend to all subsequent holders, including Rick. This example shows the importance of the distinction between transfer by indorsement and delivery (of an order instrument) and transfer by delivery only, without indorsement (of a bearer instrument). For a synopsis of the rules on transfer warranty liability, see *Concept Summary 26.2.*

Recovery for Breach of Warranty A transferee or holder who takes an instrument in good faith can sue on the basis of breach of a warranty as soon as he or she has reason to know of the breach [UCC 3–416(d)]. Notice of a claim for breach of warranty must be given to the warrantor within thirty days after the transferee or holder has reason to know of the breach and the identity of the warrantor, or the warrantor is not liable for any loss caused by a delay [UCC 3–416(c)]. The transferee or holder can recover damages for the breach in an amount equal to the loss suffered (but not more than the amount of the instrument), plus expenses and any loss of interest caused by the breach [UCC 3–416(b)].

These warranties can be disclaimed with respect to any instrument except a check [UCC 3–416(c)]. In the check-collection process, banks rely on these warranties. For all other instruments, the immediate parties can agree to a disclaimer, and an indorser can disclaim by including in the indorsement such words as "without warranties."

Presentment Warranties

Any person who presents an instrument for payment or acceptance makes the following **presentment warranties** to any other person who in good faith pays or accepts the instrument [UCC 3–417(a), (d)]:

1. The person obtaining payment or acceptance is entitled to enforce the instrument or is authorized to obtain payment or acceptance on behalf of a person who is entitled to enforce the instrument. (This is, in effect, a warranty that there are no missing or unauthorized indorsements.)
2. The instrument has not been altered.
3. The person obtaining payment or acceptance has no knowledge that the signature of the drawer of the instrument is unauthorized.[9]

These warranties are referred to as *presentment warranties* because they protect the person to whom the instrument is presented. The second and third war-

9. As discussed in footnote 8, the 2002 amendments to Article 3 of the UCC provide additional protection for "remotely created" consumer items, such as a check drawn on a personal account that the account holder authorized over the phone but did not physically sign.

ranties do not apply in certain circumstances (to certain parties). It is assumed, for example, that a drawer will recognize her or his own signature and that a maker or an acceptor will recognize whether an instrument has been materially altered.

Presentment warranties cannot be disclaimed with respect to checks, and a claim for breach must be given to the warrantor within thirty days after the claimant knows or has reason to know of the breach and the identity of the warrantor, or the warrantor is not liable for any loss caused by a delay [UCC 3–417(e)].

How should these warranties apply when two banks dispute whether a check was altered and its paper copy has been destroyed, leaving only its digital image? That was the question in the following case.

CASE 26.1 Wachovia Bank, N.A. v. Foster Bancshares, Inc.

United States Court of Appeals, Seventh Circuit, 2006. 457 F.3d 619.

Background and Facts Sunjin Choi deposited in her account at Foster Bank in Chicago, Illinois, a check for $133,026, on which she appeared to be the payee. The check was drawn on the account of MediaEdge, LLC, at Wachovia Bank, N.A., in Charlotte, North Carolina. Foster presented the check to Wachovia, which paid it and debited MediaEdge's account. Wachovia then made a digital copy of the check and destroyed the paper copy. The payee of the check as originally issued was not Choi, however, but CMP Media, Inc. Before MediaEdge learned that CMP had not received the check, Choi withdrew the funds from her account and disappeared. MediaEdge asked Wachovia to recredit its account. Wachovia filed a suit in a federal district court against Foster, seeking the amount of the check on the basis of the presentment warranty that an instrument has not been altered. The court issued a summary judgment in Wachovia's favor. Foster appealed to the U.S. Court of Appeals for the Seventh Circuit. Because only the digital copy of the check existed and there was no way to determine from it whether the paper copy had been altered, Foster argued that it should be assumed that the check was forged. Under that assumption, Wachovia, not Foster, would be liable for the loss. (Liability on a forged check will be discussed in detail in Chapter 27.)

Decision and Rationale The U.S. Court of Appeals for the Seventh Circuit affirmed the lower court's judgment. "Changing the payee's name is the classic alteration. It can with modern technology be effected by forging a check rather than by altering an original check, but since this is a novel method, the presenting bank must do more than merely assert the possibility of it." The appellate court stated that a bank in which a check is deposited may reasonably suspect the payee's name has been altered even if there is no visible evidence such as traces of a chemical wash. "The size of the check may be a warning flag that induces the bank to delay making funds deposited by the check available for withdrawal." The court also emphasized what Foster did *not* prove: that keeping a paper copy of the check would have been "a reasonable method of determining whether the drawee bank or the presenting bank should be liable for the loss"; that the forgery of checks was a more common method of bank fraud than their alteration; that banks normally contract for a different allocation of liability than the UCC provides; or that Choi's *modus operandi* (usual method of operation) was to forge checks instead of to alter them. Here, the check deposited with Foster "was for a hefty $133,000, and there is no evidence that Choi had previously deposited large checks. We do not suggest that Foster was careless in deciding to make the money available for withdrawal when it did. But the uncertainties that the bank has made no effort to dispel counsel against [making the assumption] that it urges."

The E-Commerce Dimension *How might the principles in this case have been applied if there had never been a paper copy of the check—if, for example, Choi's deposit and withdrawal of funds had occurred entirely online?*

The Legal Environment Dimension *What is the practical basis for the warranty that a check presented for payment has not been altered since its issuance? (Hint: Presentment warranties often shift liability back to the party that was in the best position to prevent the wrongdoing.)*

SECTION 3

Defenses

Depending on whether a holder or a holder in due course (HDC)—or a holder through an HDC—makes the demand for payment, certain defenses can bar collection from persons who would otherwise be liable on an instrument. There are two general categories of defenses—*universal defenses* and *personal defenses*, which are discussed below and summarized in Exhibit 26–2.

Universal Defenses

Universal defenses (also called *real defenses*) are valid against *all* holders, including HDCs and holders through HDCs. Universal defenses include those described in the following subsections.

Forgery Forgery of a maker's or drawer's signature cannot bind the person whose name is used unless that person ratifies (approves or validates) the signature or is precluded from denying it (because the forgery was made possible by the maker's or drawer's negligence, for example) [UCC 3–401(a), 3–403(a)]. Thus, when a person forges an instrument, the person whose name is forged has no liability to pay any holder or any HDC the value of the forged instrument.

Fraud in the Execution If a person is deceived into signing a negotiable instrument, believing that she or he is signing something other than a negotiable instrument (such as a receipt), *fraud in the execution* (or inception) is committed against the signer [UCC 3–305(a)(1)(iii)]. Suppose that Gerard, a salesperson, asks Javier, a customer, to sign a paper, which Gerard says is a receipt for the delivery of goods that Javier is picking up from the store. In fact, the paper is a promissory note, but Javier is unfamiliar with the English language and does not realize this. In this situation, even if the note is negotiated to an HDC, Javier has a valid defense against payment.

This defense cannot be raised, however, if a reasonable inquiry would have revealed the nature and terms of the instrument. Thus, the signer's age, experience, and intelligence are relevant because they frequently determine whether the signer should have understood the nature of the transaction before signing.

Material Alteration An alteration is *material* if it changes the contract terms between two parties *in any way*. Examples of material alterations include completing an instrument, adding words or numbers, or making any other unauthorized change that relates to a party's obligation [UCC 3–407(a)]. Any change in the amount, the date, or the rate of interest—even if the change is only one penny, one day, or 1 percent—is

EXHIBIT 26–2 • Defenses against Liability on Negotiable Instruments

UNIVERSAL (REAL) DEFENSES	PERSONAL (LIMITED) DEFENSES
Valid against all holders, including holders in due course	**Valid against ordinary holders but not against holders in due course**
1. Forgery.	1. Breach of contract (including breach of contract warranties).
2. Fraud in the execution.	2. Lack or failure of consideration.
3. Material alteration.	3. Fraud in the inducement.
4. Discharge in bankruptcy.	4. Illegality, incapacity (other than minority), or duress, if the contract is voidable.
5. Minority, if the contract is voidable.	5. Previous payment or cancellation of the instrument.
6. Illegality, incapacity, or duress, if the contract is void under state law.	6. Unauthorized completion of an incomplete instrument.

material. It is not a material alteration, however, to correct the maker's address, to draw a red line across the instrument to indicate that an auditor has checked it, or to correct the total final payment due when a mathematical error is discovered in the original computation. If the alteration is not material, any holder is entitled to enforce the instrument according to its original terms.

Material alteration is a *complete defense* against an ordinary holder but only a *partial defense* against an HDC. An ordinary holder can recover nothing on an instrument that has been materially altered [UCC 3–407(b)]. In contrast, when the holder is an HDC and an original term, such as the monetary amount payable, has been *altered,* the HDC can enforce the instrument against the maker or drawer according to the original terms but not for the altered amount [UCC 3–407(c)(i)]. If the instrument was originally incomplete and was later completed in an unauthorized manner, alteration can no longer be claimed as a defense against an HDC, and the HDC can enforce the instrument as completed [UCC 3–407(b), (c)]. This is because a drawer or maker who has issued an incomplete instrument normally will be held responsible for such an alteration, which could have been avoided by the exercise of greater care. If the alteration is readily apparent (such as a number changed on the face of a check), then obviously the holder has notice of some defect or defense and therefore cannot be an HDC [UCC 3–302(a)(1), (2)(iv)].

Is a note that allows for an extension of the time for payment materially altered when, on its expiration, its maker and payee execute a second note that the payee insists is only an extension of the time for payment but that in reality increases the balance due? That was the question in the following case.

CASE 26.2 Keesling v. T.E.K. Partners, LLC

Indiana Court of Appeals, 2007. 861 N.E.2d 1246.

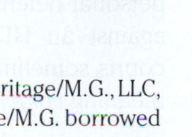

Background and Facts In January 1998, two separate entities formed Heritage/M.G., LLC, in order to develop a residential neighborhood. A year and a half later, Heritage/M.G. borrowed $300,000 to partially finance the development. Final payment on the note was due on June 1, 2001. The signatories included Thomas McMullen, on behalf of Heritage/M.G., and Larry and Vivian Keesling. Heritage/M.G. did not complete the payments by the original deadline. By January 3, 2002, the balance was just below $50,000. Without the knowledge or consent of the Keeslings, Heritage/M.G. borrowed another $102,000 on which no payments were ever made. The original lenders assigned both the first and the second note to T.E.K. Partners, LLC. The trial court concluded that T.E.K. Partners was entitled to a judgment of $375,905.07. The Keeslings appealed.

Decision and Rationale The Indiana Court of Appeals reversed the trial court's judgment against the Keeslings. The reviewing court agreed with T.E.K. Partners that a guarantee is a promise to answer for the debt, default, or miscarriage of another person. It is an "agreement collateral to the debt itself and represents a conditional promise whereby the guarantor promises to pay only if the principal debtor fails to pay." Nonetheless, "when parties cause material alteration of an underlying obligation without the consent of the guarantor, the guarantor is discharged from future liability." In this case, the change increased the risk of loss to the guarantor. Initially, the Keeslings guaranteed the original note; they were accommodation parties. McMullen, on behalf of Heritage/M.G., executed the second note for $102,000 without consulting the accommodation parties (the Keeslings). This "second note not only added new debt but increased the total principle draws beyond the $300,000 face amount of the original note." This second note constituted a material alteration of the original obligation. The Keeslings were discharged from their personal liability on the original note. "And they have no liability for the additional sums advanced under the second note, which they did not sign."

What If the Facts Were Different? *If the court had affirmed the judgment in favor of T.E.K. Partners, against whom might the Keeslings have had a right of recourse?*

The Legal Environment Dimension *What might the parties who executed the second note have done at the time to avoid the outcome in this case?*

Discharge in Bankruptcy Discharge in bankruptcy (see Chapter 30) is an absolute defense on any instrument regardless of the status of the holder [UCC 3–305(a)(1)(iv)]. This defense exists because the purpose of bankruptcy is to finally settle all of the insolvent party's debts.

Minority Minority, or infancy, is a universal defense only to the extent that state law recognizes it as a defense to a simple contract. Because state laws on minority vary, so do determinations of whether minority is a universal defense against an HDC [UCC 3–305(a)(1)(i)]. (See Chapter 13 for further discussion of the contractual liability of minors.)

Illegality Certain types of illegality constitute universal defenses, whereas others are personal defenses. If a statute provides that an illegal transaction is void, then the defense is universal—that is, absolute against both an ordinary holder and an HDC. If the law merely makes the instrument voidable, then the illegality is a personal defense against an ordinary holder, but not against an HDC [UCC 3–305(a)(1)(ii)]. Note that courts sometimes treat the word *void* in a statute as meaning *voidable* to protect an HDC.

Mental Incapacity If a court has declared a person to be mentally incompetent, then any instrument issued by that person is void. The instrument is void *ab initio* (from the beginning) and unenforceable by any holder or HDC [UCC 3–305(a)(1)(ii)]. Mental incapacity in these circumstances is a universal defense. If a court has not declared a person to be mentally incompetent, then mental incapacity operates as a personal defense against ordinary holders but not HDCs.

Extreme Duress When a person signs and issues a negotiable instrument under such extreme duress as an immediate threat of force or violence (for example, at gunpoint), the instrument is void and unenforceable by any holder or HDC [UCC 3–305(a)(1)(ii)]. (Ordinary duress is a personal, rather than a universal, defense.)

Personal Defenses

Personal defenses, such as those described next, are used to avoid payment to an ordinary holder of a negotiable instrument, but not to an HDC or a holder through an HDC.

Breach of Contract or Breach of Warranty When there is a breach of the underlying contract for which the negotiable instrument was issued, the maker of a note can refuse to pay it, or the drawer of a check can stop payment. Breach of warranty can also be claimed as a defense to liability on the instrument.

For example, Elias purchases two dozen pairs of athletic shoes from De Soto. The shoes are to be delivered in six weeks. Elias gives De Soto a promissory note for $1,000, which is the price of the shoes. The shoes arrive, but many of them are stained, and the soles of several pairs are coming apart. Elias has a defense to liability on the note on the basis of breach of contract and breach of warranty. (Recall from Chapter 23 that a seller impliedly promises that the goods being sold are at least merchantable.) If, however, the note is no longer in the hands of the payee-seller (De Soto) but is presented for payment by an HDC, the maker-buyer (Elias) will not be able to plead breach of contract or warranty as a defense against liability on the note.

Lack or Failure of Consideration The absence of consideration may be a successful defense in some instances [UCC 3–303(b), 3–305(a)(2)]. Suppose that Tony gives Cleo, as a gift, a note that states, "I promise to pay you $100,000," and Cleo accepts the note. No consideration is given in return for Tony's promise, and a court will not enforce the promise.

Similarly, if delivery of goods becomes impossible, a party who has issued a draft or note under the contract has a defense for not paying it. Thus, in the hypothetical athletic-shoe transaction described previously, if delivery of the shoes became impossible due to their loss in an accident, De Soto could not subsequently enforce Elias's promise to pay the $1,000 promissory note. If the note was in the hands of an HDC, however, Elias's defense would not be available against the HDC.

Fraud in the Inducement (Ordinary Fraud) A person who issues a negotiable instrument based on false statements by the other party will be able to avoid payment on that instrument, unless the holder is an HDC. To illustrate: Gerhard agrees to purchase Carla's used tractor for $26,500. Carla, knowing her statements to be false, tells Gerhard that the tractor is in good working order and that it has been used for only one harvest. In addition, she tells Gerhard that she owns the tractor free and clear of all claims. Gerhard pays Carla $4,500 in cash and issues a negotiable promissory note for the balance. As it turns out, Carla still owes the original seller $10,000 on the purchase of the tractor, and the tractor is subject to a valid security interest (discussed in Chapter 29). In addition, the tractor is three years old and has been used in three harvests.

In this situation, Gerhard can refuse to pay the note if it is held by an ordinary holder. If, however, Carla has negotiated the note to an HDC, Gerhard must pay the HDC. Of course, Gerhard can then sue Carla to recover the funds.

Illegality As mentioned, if a statute provides that an illegal transaction is void, a universal defense exists. If, however, the statute provides that an illegal transaction is voidable, the defense is personal. For example, a state may make gambling contracts illegal and void but be silent on the payment of gambling debts. Thus, an instrument given in payment of a gambling debt becomes voidable and is a personal defense.

Mental Incapacity As mentioned, if a maker or drawer has been declared by a court to be mentally incompetent, mental incapacity is a universal defense [UCC 3–305(a)(1)(ii)]. If a maker or drawer issues a negotiable instrument while mentally incompetent but before a formal court hearing has declared him or her to be so, however, the instrument is voidable. In this situation, mental incapacity can serve only as a personal defense.

Other Personal Defenses A number of other personal defenses can be used to avoid payment to an ordinary holder, but not an HDC, of a negotiable instrument, including the following:

1. Discharge by payment or cancellation [UCC 3–601(b), 3–602(a), 3–603, 3–604].
2. Unauthorized completion of an incomplete instrument [UCC 3–115, 3–302, 3–407, 4–401(d)(2)].
3. Nondelivery of the instrument [UCC 1–201(14), 3–105(b), 3–305(a)(2)].
4. Ordinary duress or undue influence rendering the contract voidable [UCC 3–305(a)(1)(ii)].

Federal Limitations on HDC Rights

The federal government limits HDC rights in certain circumstances because the HDC doctrine sometimes has harsh effects on consumers. Consider an example. A consumer purchases a used car under an express warranty from an automobile dealer. The consumer pays $5,000 down and signs a promissory note to the dealer for the remaining $10,000 due on the car. The dealer sells the bank this promissory note, which is a negotiable instrument, and the bank then becomes the creditor, to whom the consumer makes payments.

The car, however, does not perform as warranted. The consumer returns the car and requests a refund of the down payment and cancellation of the contract. Even if the dealer refunds the $5,000, however, under the traditional HDC rule, the consumer would normally still owe the remaining $10,000 because the consumer's claim of breach of warranty is a personal defense and the bank is an HDC.

Thus, the traditional HDC rule leaves consumers who have purchased defective products liable to HDCs. To protect consumers, in 1976 the Federal Trade Commission (FTC) issued Rule 433,[10] which effectively abolished the HDC doctrine in consumer credit transactions.

Requirements of FTC Rule 433 FTC Rule 433, entitled "Preservation of Consumers' Claims and Defenses," limits an HDC's rights in an instrument that evidences a debt arising out of a consumer credit transaction. The rule attempts to prevent a consumer from being required to make payment for a defective product to a third party (the bank, in the previous example) who is an HDC of a promissory note that formed part of the contract with the dealer who sold the defective good.

FTC Rule 433 applies to any seller of goods or services who takes or receives a consumer credit contract. The rule also applies to a seller who accepts as full or partial payment for a sale the proceeds of any purchase-money loan[11] made in connection with any consumer credit contract. Under this rule, these parties must include in the consumer credit contract the following provision:

NOTICE

ANY HOLDER OF THIS CONSUMER CREDIT CONTRACT IS SUBJECT TO ALL CLAIMS AND DEFENSES WHICH THE DEBTOR COULD ASSERT AGAINST THE SELLER OF GOODS OR SERVICES OBTAINED PURSUANT HERETO OR WITH THE PROCEEDS HEREOF. RECOVERY HEREUNDER BY THE DEBTOR SHALL NOT EXCEED AMOUNTS PAID BY THE DEBTOR HEREUNDER.

---

10. 16 C.F.R. Section 433.2. The rule was enacted in 1976 pursuant to the FTC's authority under the Federal Trade Commission Act, 15 U.S.C. Sections 41–58.

11. A *purchase-money loan* is one in which a seller or lessor advances funds to a buyer or lessee through a credit contract to purchase or lease the goods, as will be discussed in Chapter 29.

Effect of the Rule FTC Rule 433 allows a consumer who is a party to a consumer credit transaction to bring any defense she or he has against the seller of a product against a subsequent holder as well. In essence, the rule places an HDC of the instrument in the position of a contract assignee. The rule makes the buyer's duty to pay conditional on the seller's full performance of the contract. Both the seller and the creditor are responsible for the seller's misconduct. The rule also clearly reduces the degree of transferability of negotiable instruments resulting from consumer credit contracts. An instrument that contains this notice or a similar statement required by law may remain negotiable, but there cannot be an HDC of such an instrument [UCC 3–106(d)].

What if the seller does not include the notice in a promissory note and then sells the note to a third party, such as a bank? Although the seller has violated the rule, the bank has not. Because the FTC rule does not prohibit third parties from purchasing notes or credit contracts that do *not* contain the required rule, the third party does not become subject to the buyer's defenses against the seller. Thus, some consumers remain unprotected by the FTC rule.[12]

SECTION 4 Discharge

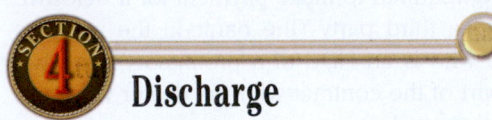

Discharge from liability on an instrument can occur in several ways, including by payment, by cancellation, and, as previously discussed, by material alteration. Discharge can also occur if a party reacquires an instrument, if a holder impairs another party's right of recourse, or if a holder surrenders collateral without consent.

Discharge by Payment or Tender of Payment

All parties to a negotiable instrument will be discharged when the party primarily liable on it pays to a holder the amount due in full [UCC 3–602, 3–603].[13] The liability of all parties is also discharged if the drawee of an unaccepted draft or check makes payment in good faith to the holder. Payment by any other party (for example, an indorser) discharges only the liability of that party and subsequent parties. The party making such a payment still has the right to recover on the instrument from any prior parties.[14]

A party will not be discharged when paying in bad faith to a holder who acquired the instrument by theft or who obtained the instrument from someone else who acquired it by theft (unless, of course, the person has the rights of an HDC) [UCC 3–602(b)(2)].

If a tender of payment is made to a person entitled to enforce the instrument and the tender is refused, indorsers and accommodation parties with a right of recourse against the party making the tender are discharged to the extent of the amount of the tender [UCC 3–603(b)]. If a tender of payment of an amount due on an instrument is made to a person entitled to enforce the instrument, the obligor's obligation to pay interest after the due date on the amount tendered is discharged [UCC 3–603(c)].

Discharge by Cancellation or Surrender

Intentional cancellation of an instrument discharges the liability of all parties [UCC 3–604]. Intentionally writing "Paid" across the face of an instrument cancels it. Intentionally tearing up an instrument cancels it. If a holder intentionally crosses out a party's signature, that party's liability and the liability of subsequent indorsers who have already indorsed the instrument are discharged. Materially altering an instrument may discharge the liability of all parties, as previously discussed [UCC 3–407(b)]. (An HDC may be able to enforce a materially altered instrument against its maker or drawer according to the instrument's *original* terms, however.)

Destruction or mutilation of a negotiable instrument is considered cancellation only if it is done with the intention of eliminating obligation on the instrument [UCC 3–604(a)(i)]. Thus, if destruction or mutilation occurs by accident, the instrument is not discharged, and the original terms can be established by parol evidence [UCC 3–309]. A note's holder may

12. Under a 2002 amendment to UCC 3–305(e), a third party holder in possession of a note or other instrument that is required to include this notice would be subject to a buyer's defenses against a seller even if the instrument did not include the notice.

13. This is true even if the payment is made with knowledge of a claim to the instrument by another person unless the payor knows that "payment is prohibited by injunction or similar process of a court of competent jurisdiction" or, in most situations, "the party making payment accepted, from a person having a claim to the instrument, indemnity against loss resulting from refusal to pay the person entitled to enforce the instrument" [UCC 3–602(a), (b)(1)].

14. Under the 2002 amendment to UCC 3–602(b), when a party entitled to enforce an instrument transfers it without giving notice to the parties obligated to pay it, and one of those parties pays the transferor, that payment is effective. Suppose that Roberto borrows $5,000 from Consumer Finance Company on a note payable to the lender. Consumer Finance transfers the note to Delta Investment Corporation but continues to collect payments from Roberto. Under this amendment, those payments effectively discharge Roberto to the extent of their amount.

also discharge the obligation by surrendering the note to the person to be discharged [UCC 3–604(a)(i)].

Discharge by Reacquisition

A person who reacquires an instrument that he or she held previously discharges all intervening indorsers against subsequent holders who do not qualify as HDCs [UCC 3–207]. Of course, the person reacquiring the instrument may be liable to subsequent holders if the instrument is dishonored.

Discharge by Impairment of Recourse

Discharge can also occur when a party's right of recourse is impaired [UCC 3–605]. A *right of recourse* is a right to seek reimbursement. Ordinarily, when a holder collects the amount of an instrument from an indorser, the indorser has a right of recourse against prior indorsers, the maker or drawer, and accommodation parties. If the holder has adversely affected the indorser's right to seek reimbursement from these other parties, however, the indorser is not liable on the instrument (to the extent that the indorser's right of recourse is impaired). This occurs when, for example, the holder releases or agrees not to sue a party against whom the indorser has a right of recourse. It also occurs when a holder agrees to an extension of the instrument's due date or to some other material modification that results in a loss to the indorser with respect to the right of recourse [UCC 3–605(c), (d)].[15]

Discharge by Impairment of Collateral

Sometimes, a party to an instrument gives collateral as security that her or his performance will occur. When a holder "impairs the value" of that collateral without the consent of the parties who would benefit from the collateral in the event of nonpayment, those parties to the instrument are discharged to the extent of the impairment [UCC 3–605(e), (f)].

For example, Jerome and Myra sign a note as co-makers, putting up Jerome's property as collateral. The note is payable to Montessa. Montessa is required by law to file a financing statement with the state to put others on notice of her interest in Jerome's property as collateral for the note. If Montessa fails to file the statement and Jerome goes through bankruptcy—which results in his property's being sold to pay other debts and leaves him unable to pay anything on the note—Montessa has impaired the value of the collateral to Myra, who is discharged to the extent of that impairment.

In other words, when Jerome goes through bankruptcy, Montessa's earlier failure to file the statement prevents her from taking possession of the collateral, selling it, and crediting the amount owed on the note. Myra, as co-maker, is then responsible only for any remaining indebtedness, instead of the entire unpaid balance. Thus, Myra is discharged to the extent that the proceeds from the sale of the collateral would have discharged her liability on the note.

15. The 2002 amendments to UCC 3–605 essentially apply the principles of suretyship and guaranty (to be discussed in Chapter 28) to circumstances that involve the impairment of the right of recourse of "secondary obligors," which include indorsers and accommodation parties. One important difference from the principles of suretyship and guaranty, however, is that under amended UCC 3–605(a), the release of a principal obligor by a person entitled to enforce a check grants a complete discharge to an indorser of the check without requiring proof of harm.

REVIEWING Liability, Defenses, and Discharge

Nancy Mahar was the office manager at Golden Years Nursing Home, Inc. She was given a signature stamp to issue checks to the nursing home's employees for up to $100 as advances on their pay. The checks were drawn on Golden Years' account at First National Bank. Over a seven-year period, Mahar wrote a number of checks to employees exclusively for the purpose of embezzling funds for herself. She forged the employees' indorsements on the checks, signed her name as a second indorser, and deposited the checks in her personal account at Star Bank. The employees whose names were on the checks never actually requested them. When the scheme was uncovered,

REVIEWING CONTINUES

REVIEWING Liability, Defenses, and Discharge, Continued

Golden Years filed a suit against Mahar, Star Bank, and others to recover the funds. Using the information presented in the chapter, answer the following questions.

1. With regard to signature liability, which provision of the Uniform Commercial Code (UCC) discussed in this chapter applies to this scenario?
2. What is the rule set forth by that provision?
3. Under the UCC, which party, Golden Years or Star Bank, must bear the loss in this situation? Why?
4. Based on these facts, describe any transfer or presentment warranties that Mahar may have violated.

TERMS AND CONCEPTS

accommodation party 485
agent 485
dishonor 483
fictitious payee 487
imposter 487
personal defense 494
presentment warranty 490
principal 485
transfer warranty 488
universal defense 492

QUESTIONS AND CASE PROBLEMS

26-1. What are the exceptions to the rule that a bank will be liable for paying a check over an unauthorized indorsement?

26-2. Waldo makes out a negotiable promissory note payable to the order of Grace. Grace indorses the note by writing on it "Without recourse, Grace" and transfers the note for value to Adam. Adam, in need of cash, negotiates the note to Keith by indorsing it with the words "Pay to Keith, Adam." On the due date, Keith presents the note to Waldo for payment, only to learn that Waldo has filed for bankruptcy and will have all debts (including the note) discharged. Discuss fully whether Keith can hold Waldo, Grace, or Adam liable on the note.

26-3. QUESTION WITH SAMPLE ANSWER

Niles sold Kennedy a small motorboat for $1,500, maintaining to Kennedy that the boat was in excellent condition. Kennedy gave Niles a check for $1,500, which Niles indorsed and gave to Frazier for value. When Kennedy took the boat for a trial run, she discovered that the boat leaked, needed to be painted, and required a new motor. Kennedy stopped payment on her check, which had not yet been cashed. Niles has disappeared. Can Frazier recover from Kennedy as a holder in due course? Discuss.

• **For a sample answer to Question 26-3, go to Appendix I at the end of this text.**

26-4. Williams purchased a used car from Stein for $1,000. Williams paid for the car with a check (written in pencil) payable to Stein for $1,000. Stein, through careful erasures and alterations, changed the amount on the check to read $10,000 and negotiated the check to Boz. Boz took the check for value, in good faith, and without notice of the alteration and thus met the Uniform Commercial Code's requirements for the status of a holder in due course. Can Williams successfully raise the universal (real) defense of material alteration to avoid payment on the check? Explain.

26-5. Gil makes out a $900 negotiable promissory note payable to Ben. By special indorsement, Ben transfers the note for value to Jess. By blank indorsement, Jess transfers the note for value to Pam. By special indorsement, Pam transfers the note for value to Adrien. In need of cash, Adrien transfers the instrument for value by blank indorsement back to Jess. When told that Ben has left the country, Jess strikes out Ben's indorsement. Later she learns that Ben is a wealthy restaurant owner in

Baltimore and that Gil is financially unable to pay the note. Jess contends that, as a holder in due course, she can hold Ben, Pam, or Adrien liable on the note. Discuss fully Jess's contentions.

26–6. Unauthorized Indorsements. Telemedia Publications, Inc., publishes *Cablecast* magazine, a weekly guide to the listings of the cable television programming in Baton Rouge, Louisiana. Cablecast hired Jennifer Pennington as a temporary employee. Pennington's duties included indorsing subscription checks received in the mail with the Cablecast deposit stamp, preparing the deposit slip, and taking the checks to be deposited to City National Bank. John McGregor, the manager of Cablecast, soon noticed shortages in revenues coming into Cablecast. When he learned that Pennington had taken checks payable to Cablecast and deposited them into her personal account at Premier Bank, N.A., he confronted her. She admitted to taking $7,913.04 in Cablecast checks. Cablecast filed a suit in a Louisiana state court against Premier Bank. The bank responded in part that Cablecast was solely responsible for losses caused by the fraudulent indorsements of its employees. At trial, Cablecast failed to prove that Premier Bank had not acted in good faith or that it had not exercised ordinary care in its handling of the checks. What rule should the court apply here? Why? [*Cablecast Magazine v. Premier Bank, N.A.*, 729 So.2d 1165 (La.App. 1 Cir. 1999)]

26–7. Agents' Signatures. Robert Helmer and Percy Helmer, Jr., were authorized signatories on the corporate checking account of Event Marketing, Inc. The Helmers signed a check drawn on Event Marketing's account and issued to Rumarson Technologies, Inc. (RTI), in the amount of $24,965. The check was signed on July 13, 1998, but dated August 14. When RTI presented the check for payment, it was dishonored due to insufficient funds. RTI filed a suit in a Georgia state court against the Helmers to collect the amount of the check. Claiming that the Helmers were personally liable on Event Marketing's check, RTI filed a motion for summary judgment. Can an authorized signatory on a corporate account be held personally liable for corporate checks returned for insufficient funds? Are the Helmers liable in this case? Discuss. [*Helmer v. Rumarson Technologies, Inc.*, 245 Ga.App. 598, 538 S.E.2d 504 (2000)]

26–8. Defenses. On September 13, 1979, Barbara Shearer and Barbara Couvion signed a note for $22,500, with interest at 11 percent, payable in monthly installments of $232.25 to Edgar House and Paul Cook. House and Cook assigned the note to Southside Bank in Kansas City, Missouri. In 1997, the note was assigned to Midstates Resources Corp., which assigned the note to The Cadle Co. in 2000. According to the payment history that Midstates gave to Cadle, the interest rate on the note was 12 percent. A Cadle employee noticed the discrepancy and recalculated the payments at 11 percent. When Shearer and Couvion refused to make further payments on the note, Cadle filed a suit in a Missouri state court against them to collect. Couvion and Shearer responded that they had made timely payments on the note, that Cadle and the previous holders had failed to accurately apply the payments to the reduction of principal and interest, and that the note "is either paid in full and satisfied or very close to being paid in full and satisfied." Is the makers' answer sufficient to support a verdict in their favor? If so, on what ground? If not, why not? [*The Cadle Co. v. Shearer*, 69 S.W.3d 122 (Mo.App.W.D. 2002)]

26–9. CASE PROBLEM WITH SAMPLE ANSWER

Ameripay, LLC, is a payroll services company that, among other things, issues payroll checks to the employees of its clients. In July 2002, Nu Tribe Radio Networks, Inc. (NTRN), based in New York City, hired Ameripay. Under their agreement, Ameripay set up an account on NTRN's behalf at Commerce Bank. NTRN agreed to deposit funds in the account to cover its payroll obligations. Arthur Piacentini, an owner of Ameripay, was an authorized signatory on the account. On the checks, NTRN was the only identified company, and Piacentini's signature appeared without indicating his status. At the end of the month, four NTRN employees cashed their payroll checks, which Piacentini had signed, at A-1 Check Cashing Emporium, Inc. The checks were returned dishonored. Ameripay had stopped their payment because it had not received the funds from NTRN. A-1 assigned its interest in the checks to Robert Triffin, who filed a suit in a New Jersey state court against Ameripay. What principles determine who, between a principal and an agent, is liable for the amount of an unpaid instrument? How do those principles apply in this case? Is Ameripay liable? Why or why not? [*Triffin v. Ameripay, LLC*, 368 N.J.Super. 587, 847 A.2d 628 (App.Div. 2004)]

- **To view a sample answer for Problem 26–9, go to this book's Web site at www.cengage.com/blaw/jentz, select "Chapter 26," and click on "Case Problem with Sample Answer."**

26–10. Accommodation Parties. Donald Goosic, a building contractor in Nebraska, did business as "Homestead" builders. To construct a house on "spec" (without a preconstruction buyer), Donald obtained materials from Sack Lumber Co. on an open account. When Donald "got behind in his payments," his wife, Frances, cosigned a note payable to Sack for $43,000, the outstanding balance on the account. Donald made payments on the note until he obtained a discharge of his debts in a bankruptcy proceeding to which Frances was not a party. Less than a year later, Sack filed a suit in a Nebraska state court against Frances to collect on the note. She contended that she was an accommodation party, not a maker, and thus was not liable because the applicable statute of limitations had run. She testified that Donald "made more debt than . . . money" and that she was "paying the bills out of [her] income." The Goosics' most recent tax returns showed only losses relating to Homestead. Under the Uniform Commercial Code, a person receiving only an indirect benefit from a transaction can qualify as an accommodation party. How would you rule on this question of fact? Why? [*Sack Lumber Co. v. Goosic*, 15 Neb.App. 529, 732 N.W.2d 690 (2007)]

26-11. A QUESTION OF ETHICS

Clarence Morgan, Jr., owned Easy Way Automotive, a car dealership in D'Lo, Mississippi. Easy Way sold a truck to Loyd Barnard, who signed a note for the amount of the price payable to Trustmark National Bank in six months. Before the note came due, Barnard returned the truck to Easy Way, which sold it to another buyer. Using some of the proceeds from the second sale, Easy Way sent a check to Trustmark to pay Barnard's note. Meanwhile, Barnard obtained another truck from Easy Way, financed through another six-month note payable to Trustmark. After eight of these deals, some of which involved more than one truck, an Easy Way check to Trustmark was dishonored. In a suit in a Mississippi state court, Trustmark sought to recover the amounts of two of the notes from Barnard. Trustmark had not secured titles to two of the trucks covered by the notes, however, and this complicated Barnard's efforts to reclaim the vehicles from the later buyers. [Trustmark National Bank v. Barnard, *930 So.2d 1281 (Miss.App. 2006)*]

(a) On what basis might Barnard be liable on the Trustmark notes? Would he be primarily or secondarily liable? Could this liability be discharged on the theory that Barnard's right of recourse had been impaired when Trustmark did not secure titles to the trucks covered by the notes? Explain.

(b) Easy Way's account had been subject to other recent overdrafts, and a week after the check to Trustmark was returned for insufficient funds, Morgan committed suicide. At the same time, Barnard was unable to obtain a mortgage because the unpaid notes affected his credit rating. How do the circumstances of this case underscore the importance of practicing business ethics?

LAW ON THE WEB

For updated links to resources available on the Web, as well as a variety of other materials, visit this text's Web site at

www.cengage.com/blaw/jentz

To find information on the UCC, including the Article 3 provisions discussed in this chapter, refer to the Web sites listed in the *Law on the Web* section in Chapter 24.

Legal Research Exercises on the Web

Go to **www.cengage.com/blaw/jentz,** the Web site that accompanies this text. Select "Chapter 26" and click on "Internet Exercises." There you will find the following Internet research exercises that you can perform to learn more about the topics covered in this chapter.

Internet Exercise 26–1: Legal Perspective
Fictitious Payees

Internet Exercise 26–2: Management Perspective
FTC Rule 433

CHAPTER 27

Checks and Banking in the Digital Age

Checks are the most common type of negotiable instruments governed by the Uniform Commercial Code (UCC). Although debit cards now account for more retail payments than checks, commercial checks remain an integral part of the U.S. economic system. Issues relating to checks are governed by Articles 3 and 4 of the UCC. As noted in the preceding chapters, Article 3 establishes the requirements that all negotiable instruments, including checks, must meet. Article 3 also sets forth the rights and responsibilities of parties to negotiable instruments. Article 4 establishes a framework for deposit and checking agreements between a bank and its customers. Article 4 also governs the relationships of banks with one another as they process checks for payment. A check therefore may fall within the scope of Article 3 and yet be subject to the provisions of Article 4 while in the course of collection. If a conflict arises between Article 3 and Article 4, Article 4 controls [UCC 4–102(a)].

In this chapter, we first identify the legal characteristics of checks and the legal duties and liabilities that arise when a check is issued. Then we examine the collection process. Increasingly, credit cards, debit cards, and other devices and methods for transferring funds electronically are being used to pay for goods and services. In the latter part of this chapter, we look at the law governing electronic fund transfers.

SECTION 1 Checks

A **check** is a special type of draft that is drawn on a bank, ordering the bank to pay a fixed amount of money on demand [UCC 3–104(f)]. Article 4 defines a *bank* as "a person engaged in the business of banking, including a savings bank, savings and loan association, credit union or trust company" [UCC 4–105(1)].[1] If any other nonbank institution (such as a brokerage firm) handles a check for payment or for collection, the check is not covered by Article 4.

Recall from the preceding chapters that a person who writes a check is called the *drawer.* The drawer is usually a depositor in the bank on which the check is drawn. The person to whom the check is payable is the *payee.* The bank or financial institution on which the check is drawn is the *drawee.* Thus, if Anne Tomas writes a check on her checking account to pay her college tuition, she is the drawer, her bank is the drawee, and her college is the payee.

Between the time a check is drawn and the time it reaches the drawee, the effectiveness of the check may be altered by some event—for example, the drawer may die or order payment not to be made, or the account on which the check is drawn may be depleted. To avoid this problem, a payee may insist on payment by an instrument that has already been accepted by the drawee. Such an instrument may be a cashier's check, a traveler's check, or a certified check.

Cashier's Checks

Checks are usually three-party instruments, but on some checks, the bank serves as both the drawer *and* the drawee. For example, when a bank draws a check on itself, the check is called a **cashier's check** and is

1. The unrevised Article 4 does not define the term *bank,* except to distinguish among banks that deposit, collect, and pay instruments. The term was generally considered to include only commercial banks, which at the time the unrevised Article 4 was written were the only banks that could offer checking accounts. Revised Article 4's definition makes it clear that other depositary institutions now have the authority to issue and otherwise deal with checks.

a negotiable instrument on issue (see Exhibit 27–1) [UCC 3–104(g)]. Normally, a cashier's check indicates a specific payee. In effect, with a cashier's check, the bank assumes responsibility for paying the check, thus making the check more readily acceptable in commerce.

For example, Blake needs to pay a moving company $7,000 for moving his household goods to a new home in another state. The moving company requests payment in the form of a cashier's check. Blake goes to a bank (he need not have an account at the bank) and purchases a cashier's check, payable to the moving company, in the amount of $7,000. Blake has to pay the bank the $7,000 for the check, plus a small service fee. He then gives the check to the moving company.

Cashier's checks are sometimes used in the business community as nearly the equivalent of cash. Except in very limited circumstances, the issuing bank must honor its cashier's checks when they are presented for payment. If a bank wrongfully dishonors a cashier's check, a holder can recover from the bank all expenses incurred, interest, and consequential damages [UCC 3–411]. This same rule applies if a bank wrongfully dishonors a certified check (to be discussed shortly) or a teller's check. (A **teller's check** is usually drawn by a bank on another bank; when drawn on a nonbank, it is payable at or through a bank [UCC 3–104(h)].) For example, when a credit union issues a check to withdraw funds from its account at another financial institution, and the teller at the credit union signs the check, it is a teller's check.)

Traveler's Checks

A **traveler's check** is an instrument that is payable on demand, drawn on or payable at a financial institution (such as a bank), and designated as a traveler's check. The issuing institution is directly obligated to accept and pay its traveler's check according to the check's terms. Traveler's checks are designed as a safe substitute for cash when a person is on vacation or traveling and are issued for a fixed amount, such as $20, $50, or $100. The purchaser is required to sign the check at the time it is purchased and again at the time it is used [UCC 3–104(i)]. Most major banks today do not issue traveler's checks; rather, they purchase and issue American Express traveler's checks for their customers (see Exhibit 27–2).

Certified Checks

A **certified check** is a check that has been *accepted* by the bank on which it is drawn [UCC 3–409(d)]. When a drawee bank agrees to certify a check, it immediately charges the drawer's account with the amount of the check and transfers those funds to its own certified-check account. In effect, the bank is agreeing in advance to accept that check when it is presented for payment and to make payment from those funds reserved in the certified-check account.

EXHIBIT 27–1 • A Cashier's Check

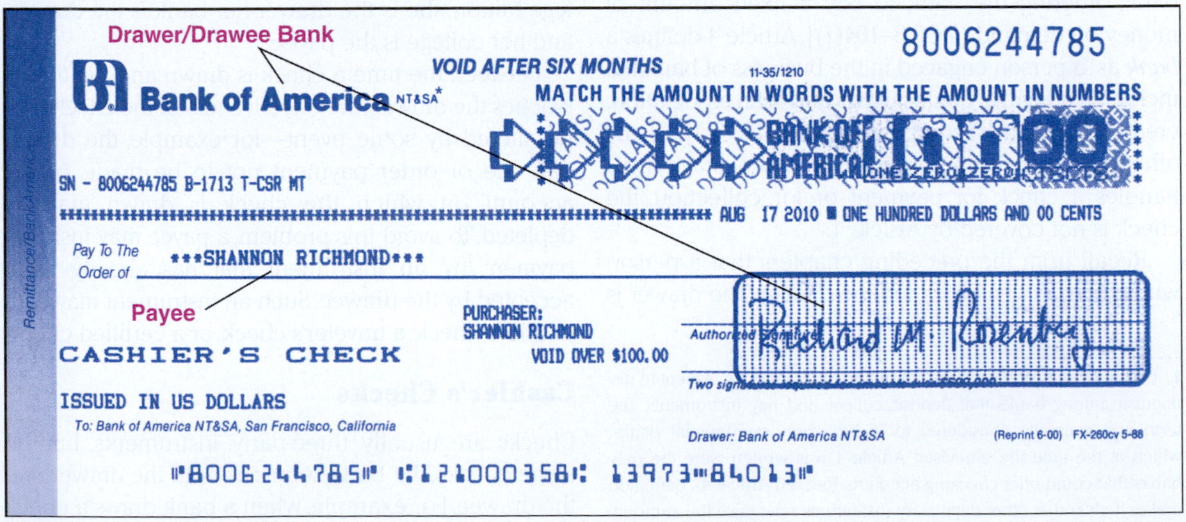

*The abbreviation *NT&SA* stands for National Trust and Savings Association. The Bank of America NT&SA is a subsidiary of Bank of America Corporation, which is engaged in financial services, insurance, investment management, and other businesses.

EXHIBIT 27–2 • An American Express Traveler's Check

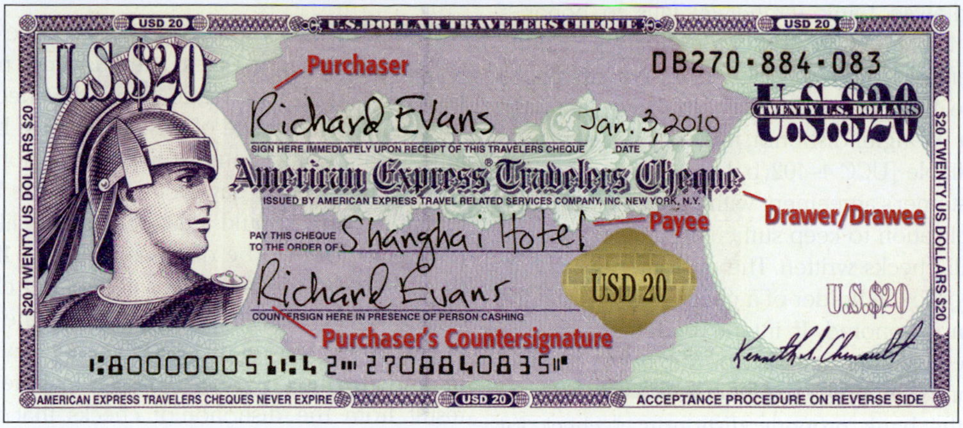

Essentially, certification prevents the bank from denying liability. It is a promise that sufficient funds are on deposit and *have been set aside* to cover the check.

To certify a check, the bank writes or stamps the word *certified* on the face of the check and typically writes the amount that it will pay.[2] Either the drawer or the holder (payee) of a check can request certification, but the drawee bank is not required to certify a check. A bank's refusal to certify a check is not a dishonor of the check [UCC 3–409(d)]. Once a check is certified, the drawer and any prior indorsers are completely discharged from liability on the check [UCC 3–414(c), 3–415(d)]. Only the certifying bank is required to pay the instrument.

SECTION 2 The Bank-Customer Relationship

The bank-customer relationship begins when the customer opens a checking account and deposits funds that the bank will use to pay for checks written by the customer. The rights and duties of the bank and the customer are contractual and depend on the nature of the transaction. Essentially, three types of relationships come into being, as discussed next.

Creditor-Debtor Relationship

A creditor-debtor relationship is created between a customer and a bank when, for example, the customer makes cash deposits into a checking account. When a customer makes a deposit, the customer becomes a creditor, and the bank a debtor, for the amount deposited.

Agency Relationship

An agency relationship also arises between the customer and the bank when the customer writes a check on his or her account. In effect, the customer is ordering the bank to pay the amount specified on the check to the holder when the holder presents the check to the bank for payment. In this situation, the bank becomes the customer's agent and is obligated to honor the customer's request. Similarly, if the customer deposits a check into his or her account, the bank, as the customer's agent, is obligated to collect payment on the check from the bank on which the check was drawn.

Contractual Relationship

Whenever a bank-customer relationship is established, certain contractual rights and duties arise. The rights and duties of the bank and the customer are contractual and depend on the nature of the transaction. The respective rights and duties of banks and their customers will be discussed in detail in the following pages.

SECTION 3 Honoring Checks

When a banking institution provides checking services, it agrees to honor the checks written by its customers, with the usual stipulation that sufficient funds

2. If the certification does not state an amount, and the amount is later increased and the instrument negotiated to a holder in due course (HDC), the obligation of the certifying bank is the amount of the instrument when it was taken by the HDC [UCC 3–413(b)].

must be available in the account to pay each check. When a drawee bank *wrongfully* fails to honor a check, it is liable to its customer for damages resulting from its refusal to pay. The UCC does not attempt to specify the theory under which the customer may recover for wrongful dishonor; it merely states that the drawee is liable [UCC 4–402(b)].

The customer's agreement with the bank includes a general obligation to keep sufficient funds on deposit to cover all checks written. The customer is liable to the payee or to the holder of a check in a civil suit if a check is not honored. If intent to defraud can be proved, the customer can also be subject to criminal prosecution for writing a bad check.

When the bank properly dishonors a check for insufficient funds, it has no liability to the customer. The bank may rightfully refuse payment on a customer's check in other circumstances as well. We look here at the rights and duties of both the bank and its customers in relation to specific situations.

Overdrafts

When the bank receives an item properly payable from its customer's checking account but the account contains insufficient funds to cover the amount of the check, the bank has two options. It can either (1) dishonor the item or (2) pay the item and charge the customer's account, thus creating an **overdraft,** providing that the customer has authorized the payment and the payment does not violate any bank-customer agreement [UCC 4–401(a)].[3] The bank can subtract the difference from the customer's next deposit because the check carries with it an enforceable implied promise to reimburse the bank.

When a check "bounces," a holder can resubmit the check, hoping that at a later date sufficient funds will be available to pay it. The holder must notify any indorsers on the check of the first dishonor, however; otherwise, they will be discharged from their signature liability, as discussed in Chapter 26.

A bank can expressly agree with a customer to accept overdrafts through what is sometimes called an "overdraft protection agreement." If such an agreement is formed, any failure of the bank to honor a check because it would create an overdraft breaches this agreement and is treated as a wrongful dishonor [UCC 4–402(a), (b)].

3. When customers have a joint account, the bank cannot hold any customer on the account liable for payment of an overdraft unless that customer has signed the check or has benefited from the proceeds of the check [UCC 4–401(b)].

Postdated Checks

A bank may also charge a postdated check against a customer's account, unless the customer notifies the bank, in a timely manner, not to pay the check until the stated date. The notice of postdating must be given in time to allow the bank to act on the notice before committing itself to pay on the check. The UCC states that the bank should treat the notice like a stop-payment order (to be discussed shortly). If the bank fails to act on the customer's notice and charges the customer's account before the date on the postdated check, the bank may be liable for any damages incurred by the customer. Damages include those that result from the dishonor of checks that are subsequently presented for payment and are dishonored for insufficient funds [UCC 4–401(c)].

Stale Checks

Commercial banking practice regards a check that is presented for payment more than six months from its date as a **stale check.** A bank is not obligated to pay an uncertified check presented more than six months from its date [UCC 4–404]. When receiving a stale check for payment, the bank has the option of paying or not paying the check. If a bank pays a stale check in good faith without consulting the customer, the bank has the right to charge the customer's account for the amount of the check.

Death or Incompetence of a Customer

Neither the death nor the incompetence of a customer revokes a bank's authority to pay an item until the bank knows of the situation and has had reasonable time to act on the notice [UCC 4–405]. Thus, if, at the time a check is issued or its collection is undertaken, a bank does not know that the customer who wrote the check has been declared incompetent, the bank can pay the item without incurring liability. Even when a bank knows of the death of its customer, for ten days after the *date of death* it can pay or certify checks drawn on or before the date of death. Without this provision, banks would constantly be required to verify the continued life and competence of their drawers. An exception to the rule is made if a person claiming an interest in the account of the deceased customer, such as an heir or an executor of the estate (see Chapter 50), orders the bank to stop payment.

Stop-Payment Orders

A **stop-payment order** is an order by a customer to her or his bank not to pay a certain check.[4] Only a customer or a "person authorized to draw on the account" can order the bank not to pay the check when it is presented for payment [UCC 4–403(a)]. A customer has no right to stop payment on a check that has already been certified (or accepted) by a bank, however. Also, a stop-payment order must be received within a reasonable time and in a reasonable manner to permit the bank to act on it [UCC 4–403(a)]. Although a stop-payment order can be given orally, usually by phone, the order is binding on the bank for only fourteen calendar days unless confirmed in writing.[5] A written stop-payment order (see Exhibit 27–3) or an oral order confirmed in writing is effective for six months, at which time it must be renewed in writing [UCC 4–403(b)].

Bank's Liability for Wrongful Payment If the bank pays the check over the customer's properly instituted stop-payment order, the bank will be obligated to recredit the customer's account. In addition, if the bank's payment over a stop-payment order causes subsequent checks written on the drawer's account to "bounce," the bank will be liable for the resultant costs the drawer incurs. The bank is liable only for the amount of the actual loss suffered by the drawer because of the wrongful payment, however [UCC 4–403(c)].

Assume that Toshio Murano orders one hundred cellular telephones from Advanced Communications, Inc., at $50 each. Murano pays in advance for the phones with a check for $5,000. Later that day, Advanced Communications tells Murano that it will not deliver the phones as arranged. Murano immediately calls the bank and stops payment on the check. Two days later, in spite of this stop-payment order, the bank inadvertently honors Murano's check to Advanced Communications for the undelivered phones. The bank will be liable to Murano for the full $5,000.

The result would be different, however, if Advanced Communications had delivered and Murano had accepted ninety-nine phones. Because Murano would have owed Advanced Communications $4,950 for the goods delivered, Murano's actual loss would be only $50. Consequently, the bank would be liable to Murano for only $50.

Customer's Liability for Wrongful Stop-Payment Order A stop-payment order has its risks for a customer. The drawer must have a *valid legal*

4. Note that although this discussion focuses on checks, the right to stop payment is not limited to checks; it extends to any item payable by any bank. See Official Comment 3 to UCC 4–403.

5. Some states do not recognize oral stop-payment orders; the orders must be in writing.

EXHIBIT 27–3 • A Stop-Payment Order

Bank of America

Checking Account Stop-Payment Order

To: Bank of America NT&SA
I want to stop payment on the following check(s).

ACCOUNT NUMBER: ______ – ______

SPECIFIC STOP

*ENTER DOLLAR AMOUNT: ______ *CHECK NUMBER: ______

THE CHECK WAS SIGNED BY: ______

THE CHECK IS PAYABLE TO: ______

THE REASON FOR THIS STOP PAYMENT IS: ______

STOP RANGE (Use for lost or stolen check(s) only.)

DOLLAR AMOUNT: 000

*ENTER STARTING CHECK NUMBER: ______ *END CHECK NUMBER: ______

THE REASON FOR THIS STOP PAYMENT IS: ______

BANK USE ONLY

TRANCODE:

☐ 21—ENTER STOP PAYMENT (SEE OTHER SIDE TO REMOVE)

NON READS: ______
UNPROC. STMT HIST: ______
PRIOR STMT CYCLE: ______
HOLDS ON COOLS: ______
REJECTED CHKS: ______
LARGE ITEMS: ______
FEE COLLECTED: ______
DATE ACCEPTED: ______
TIME ACCEPTED: ______

I agree that this order (1) is effective only if the above check(s) has (have) not yet been cashed or paid against my account, (2) will end six months from the date it is delivered to you unless I renew it in writing, and (3) is not valid if the check(s) was (were) accepted on the strength of my Bank of America courtesy-check guarantee card by a merchant participating in that program. I also agree (1) to notify you immediately to cancel this order if the reason for the stop payment no longer exists or (2) that closing the account on which the check(s) is (are) drawn automatically cancels this order.

IF ANOTHER BRANCH OF THIS BANK OR ANOTHER PERSON OR ENTITY BECOMES A "HOLDER IN DUE COURSE" OF THE ABOVE CHECK, I UNDERSTAND THAT PAYMENT MAY BE ENFORCED AGAINST THE CHECK'S MAKER (SIGNER).

*I CERTIFY THE AMOUNT AND CHECK NUMBER(S) ABOVE ARE CORRECT.

☐ I have written a replacement check (number and date of check).

______

(Optional—please circle one: Mr., Ms., Mrs., Miss) CUSTOMER'S SIGNATURE **X** ______ DATE ______ *ground* for issuing such an order; otherwise, the holder can sue the drawer for payment. Moreover, defenses sufficient to refuse payment to a payee may not be valid grounds to prevent payment to a subsequent holder in due course [UCC 3–305, 3–306]. A person who wrongfully stops payment on a check not only will be liable to the payee for the amount of the check but also may be liable for consequential damages incurred by the payee as a result of the wrongful stop-payment order.

Checks Bearing Forged Signatures

When a bank pays a check on which the drawer's signature is forged, generally the bank suffers the loss.[6] A bank may be able to recover at least some of the loss from the customer, however, if the customer's negligence substantially contributed to the forgery. A bank may also obtain partial recovery from the forger of the check (if he or she can be found) or from the holder who presented the check for payment (if the holder knew that the signature was forged).

The General Rule A forged signature on a check has no legal effect as the signature of a drawer [UCC 3–403(a)]. For this reason, banks require a signature card from each customer who opens a checking account so that the bank can determine whether the signature on a customer's check is genuine. The general rule is that the bank must recredit the customer's account when it pays on a forged signature. (Note that banks today normally verify signatures only on checks that exceed a certain threshold, such as $1,000, $2,500, or some higher amount. Even though a bank sometimes incurs liability costs when it has paid forged checks, the costs involved in verifying the signature on every check signature would be much higher.)

Note that a bank may contractually shift to the customer the risk of forged checks created by the use of facsimile or other nonmanual signatures. For example, the contract might stipulate that the customer is solely responsible for maintaining security over any device affixing a signature. The contract might also provide that any nonmanual signature is effective as the customer's signature regardless of whether the person who affixed the signature was authorized to do so.[7]

Customer Negligence When a customer's negligence substantially contributes to a forgery, the bank normally will not be obligated to recredit the customer's account for the amount of the check [UCC 3–406(a)]. If negligence on the part of the bank (or other "person") paying the instrument or taking it for value or for collection substantially contributed to the customer's loss, however, the customer's liability may be reduced by the amount of the loss caused by the bank's negligence [UCC 3–406(b)].[8]

Suppose that CompuNet, Inc., uses a check-writing machine to write its payroll and business checks. A CompuNet employee uses the machine to create a check payable to himself for $10,000, and CompuNet's bank subsequently honors it. CompuNet requests the bank to recredit $10,000 to its account for incorrectly paying on a forged check. If the bank can show that CompuNet failed to take reasonable care in controlling access to the check-writing equipment, the bank will not be required to recredit its account for the amount of the forged check. If CompuNet can show that negligence on the part of the bank (or another person) contributed substantially to the loss, however, then CompuNet's liability may be reduced proportionately.

In the following case, an employee opened a bogus bank account and fraudulently deposited his employer's checks in it for years. The court had to determine if the bank should have requested written authorization from the company before opening the account.

6. Each year, check fraud costs banks many billions of dollars—more than the combined losses from credit-card fraud, theft from automated teller machines, and armed robberies.

7. *Lor-Mar/Toto, Inc. v. 1st Constitution Bank,* 376 N.J.Super. 520, 871 A.2d 110 (2005).

8. The unrevised Article 3 does not include a similar provision.

CASE 27.1 Auto-Owners Insurance Co. v. Bank One

Supreme Court of Indiana, 2008. 879 N.E.2d 1086.

• **Background and Facts** Kenneth Wulf worked in the claims department of Auto-Owners Insurance Company for ten years. When the department received a check, a staff member would note it for the files and send it on to headquarters. Wulf opened a checking account at Bank One in the name of "Auto-Owners, Kenneth B. Wulf." Over eight years, he deposited $546,000 worth of

CASE 27.1 CONTINUED checks that he had stolen from Auto-Owners and had indorsed with a stamp that read "Auto-Owners Insurance Deposit Only." When the scam was finally discovered, Auto-Owners sued Bank One, contending that it had failed to exercise ordinary care in opening the account because it had not asked for documentation to show that Wulf was authorized to open an account in the name of Auto-Owners. The trial courts rejected that argument and granted summary judgment for Bank One. After an intermediate appellate court upheld the summary judgment, Auto-Owners appealed to the Indiana Supreme Court.

• **Decision and Rationale** Indiana's highest court affirmed the lower courts' decisions, finding that Bank One's conduct did not "substantially contribute" to bringing about the losses suffered by Auto-Owners. The bank breached no duty to the insurance company by opening Wulf's checking account. In such cases, the courts consider all of the facts surrounding the transactions that occurred. Here, the major reason for the losses suffered by Auto-Owners was its weak internal monitoring of its own files and the lack of controls in the handling of company checks. The bank did not worsen the situation by allowing Wulf to have a checking account.

• **The E-Commerce Dimension** *Would the situation have been different if Wulf had handled his account electronically rather than manually? Why or why not?*

• **The Legal Environment Dimension** *What reasonable steps could Auto-Owners have taken to prevent such internal fraud?*

Timely Examination of Bank Statements Required. Banks typically send or make available to their customers monthly statements detailing the activity of the customers' checking accounts. Banks are not obligated to include the original canceled checks themselves with the statement sent to the customer. If the bank does not send the canceled checks, however, it must provide the customer with information (check number, amount, and date of payment) on the statement that will allow the customer to reasonably identify each check that the bank has paid [UCC 4–406(a), (b)]. Sometimes, banks send photocopies of the canceled checks with the statement. If the bank retains the canceled checks, it must keep the checks—or legible copies of them—for seven years [UCC 4–406(b)]. The customer may obtain a canceled check (or a copy of the check) from the bank during this period of time.

The customer has a duty to promptly examine bank statements (and canceled checks or photocopies, if they are included with the statements) with reasonable care when the statements are received or made available to determine whether any payment was not authorized [UCC 4–406(c)]. The customer must report any alterations or forged signatures, including forged signatures of indorsers if discovered (to be discussed later). If the customer fails to fulfill this duty and the bank suffers a loss as a result, the customer will be liable for the loss [UCC 4–406(d)].

Consequences of Failing to Detect Forgeries. When a series of forgeries by the same wrongdoer has taken place, the UCC provides that the customer, to recover for all of the forged items, must have discovered and reported the first forged check to the bank within thirty calendar days of the receipt or availability of the bank statement (and canceled checks or copies, if they are included) [UCC 4–406(d)(2)]. Failure to notify the bank within this time period discharges the bank's liability for all forged checks that it pays prior to notification.

For example, Joseph Montanez, an employee and bookkeeper for Espresso Roma Corporation, used stolen computer software and blank checks to generate company checks on his home computer. The series of forged checks spanned a period of more than two years and totaled more than $330,000. When the bank statements containing the forged checks arrived in the mail, Montanez sorted through the statements and removed the checks so that the forgeries would go undetected. Eventually, Espresso Roma did discover the forgeries and asked the bank to recredit its account. The bank refused and litigation ensued. The court held that the bank was not liable for the forged checks because Espresso Roma failed to report the first forgeries within the UCC's time period of thirty days.[9]

9. *Espresso Roma Corp. v. Bank of America, N.A.,* 100 Cal.App.4th 525, 124 Cal.Rptr.2d 549 (2002).

When the Bank Is Also Negligent. In one situation, a bank customer can escape liability, at least in part, for failing to notify the bank of forged or altered checks within the required thirty-day period. If the customer can prove that the bank was also negligent—that is, that the bank failed to exercise ordinary care—then the bank will also be liable, and the loss will be allocated between the bank and the customer on the basis of comparative negligence [UCC 4–406(e)]. In other words, even though a customer may have been negligent, the bank may still have to recredit the customer's account for a portion of the loss if the bank failed to exercise ordinary care.

Section 3–103(a)(7) of the UCC defines *ordinary care* as the "observance of reasonable commercial standards, prevailing in the area in which [a] person is located, with respect to the business in which that person is engaged." As mentioned earlier, it is customary in the banking industry to manually examine signatures only on checks over a certain amount (such as $1,000, $2,500, or some higher amount). Thus, if a bank, in accordance with prevailing banking standards, fails to examine a signature on a particular check, the bank may or may not have breached its duty to exercise ordinary care.

Regardless of the degree of care exercised by the customer or the bank, the UCC places an absolute time limit on the liability of a bank for paying a check with a forged customer signature. A customer who fails to report her or his forged signature within one year from the date that the statement was made available for inspection loses the legal right to have the bank recredit her or his account [UCC 4–406(f)].

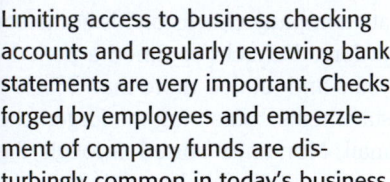

Limiting access to business checking accounts and regularly reviewing bank statements are very important. Checks forged by employees and embezzlement of company funds are disturbingly common in today's business world. One of the best ways to avoid significant losses due to forgery or embezzlement, and to prevent litigation over a bank's liability for forged items, is to keep a watchful eye on business accounts and always be on the lookout for suspicious transactions. Business owners and managers should limit the number of persons who have access to the bank accounts and bank statements of their business. Company checkbooks or signature stamps should never be left in public or unsecured areas. Passwords should be used to limit access to computerized check-writing software. Businesspersons should also review monthly bank statements in a timely fashion and report any discrepancies to the bank.

The UCC's rules pertaining to a series of forged checks are not flexible—by failing to report forgeries within thirty days of the first statement in which a forged item appears, the account holder loses the right to hold the bank liable. Businesspersons should be careful not to do anything that could be construed as negligence contributing to a forgery (or to a subsequent alteration of a check, to be discussed shortly).

Other Parties from Whom the Bank May Recover As noted earlier, a forged signature on a check has no legal effect as the signature of a drawer; a forged signature, however, is effective as the signature of the unauthorized signer [UCC 3–403(a)]. Therefore, when a bank pays a check on which the drawer's signature is forged, the bank has a right to recover from the party who forged the signature. The bank may also have a right to recover from a party (its customer or a collecting bank—to be discussed later in this chapter) who transferred a check bearing a forged drawer's signature and received payment (see the discussion of transfer warranties discussed in Chapter 26). This right is limited, however, in that the bank cannot recover from a person who took the check in good faith and for value or who in good faith changed position in reliance on the payment or acceptance [UCC 3–418(c)].

Checks Bearing Forged Indorsements

A bank that pays a customer's check bearing a forged indorsement must recredit the customer's account or be liable to the customer (drawer) for breach of contract. Suppose that Carlo issues a $500 check "to the order of Sophia." Marcello steals the check, forges Sophia's indorsement, and cashes the check. When the check reaches Carlo's bank, the bank pays it and debits Carlo's account. The bank must recredit Carlo's account for the $500 because it failed to carry out Carlo's order to pay "to the order of Sophia" [UCC 4–401(a)]. (Carlo's bank will in turn recover—under the principle of breach of warranty—from the bank that cashed the check [UCC 4–207(a)(2)].)

Eventually, *the loss usually falls on the first party to take the instrument bearing the forged indorsement* because, as discussed in Chapter 26, a forged indorsement does not transfer title. Thus, whoever takes an instrument with a forged indorsement cannot become a holder.

The customer, in any event, has a duty to report forged indorsements promptly on discovery or notice. Failure to report forged indorsements, whether discovered or not, within a three-year period after the forged items become available to the customer relieves the bank of liability [UCC 4–111].[10]

Altered Checks

The customer's instruction to the bank is to pay the exact amount on the face of the check to the holder. The bank has an implicit duty to examine checks before making final payments. If it fails to detect an alteration, it is liable to its customer for the loss because it did not pay as the customer ordered. The loss is the difference between the original amount of the check and the amount actually paid. Suppose that a check written for $11 is raised to $111. The customer's account will be charged $11 (the amount the customer ordered the bank to pay). The bank will normally be responsible for the $100 [UCC 4–401(d)(1)].

Customer Negligence As in a situation involving a forged drawer's signature, a customer's negligence can shift the loss when payment is made on an altered check (unless the bank was also negligent). A common example occurs when a person carelessly writes a check, leaving large gaps around the numbers and words where additional numbers and words can be inserted (see Exhibit 27–4).

Similarly, a person who signs a check and leaves the dollar amount for someone else to fill in is barred from protesting when the bank unknowingly and in good faith pays whatever amount is shown [UCC 4–401(d)(2)]. Finally, if the bank can trace its loss on successive altered checks to the customer's failure to discover the initial alteration, then the bank can reduce its liability for reimbursing the customer's account [UCC 4–406].[11] The law governing the customer's duty to examine monthly statements and canceled checks, and to discover and report alterations to the bank, is the same as that applied to a forged drawer's signature.

In every situation involving a forged drawer's signature or an alteration, a bank must observe reasonable commercial standards of care in paying on a customer's checks [UCC 4–406(e)]. The customer's contributory negligence can be asserted only if the bank has exercised ordinary care.

10. This is a general statute of limitations for all actions under Article 4; it provides that any lawsuit must be begun within three years of the time that the cause of action arises.

11. The bank's defense is the same whether the successive payments were made on a forged drawer's signature or on altered checks. The bank must prove that prompt notice would have prevented its loss. For example, notification might have alerted the bank not to pay further items or might have enabled it to catch the forger.

EXHIBIT 27–4 • A Poorly Filled-Out Check

XYZ CORPORATION
10 INDUSTRIAL PARK
ST. PAUL, MINNESOTA 56561

2206

June 8 20 09

22-1/960

PAY TO THE ORDER OF John Doe $ 100.00

One hundred and 00/100 DOLLARS

THE FIRST NATIONAL BANK OF MYTOWN
332 MINNESOTA STREET
MYTOWN, MINNESOTA 55555

Stephanie Roe, President

⑈94⑈ 77577⑈ 0885

Other Parties from Whom the Bank May Recover The bank is entitled to recover the amount of loss (including expenses and any loss of interest) from the transferor who, by presenting the check for payment, warrants that the check has not been altered.[12]

There are two exceptions, however. If the bank is the drawer (as it is on a cashier's check and a teller's check), it cannot recover on this ground from the presenting party if the party is a holder in due course (HDC) acting in good faith [UCC 3–417(a)(2), 4–208(a)(2)]. The reason is that an instrument's drawer is in a better position than an HDC to know whether the instrument has been altered.

Similarly, an HDC, acting in good faith in presenting a certified check for payment, does not warrant to the check's certifier that the check was not altered before the HDC acquired it [UCC 3–417(a)(2), 4–208(a)(2)]. Consider an example. Alan, the drawer, draws a check for $500 payable to Pam, the payee. Pam alters the amount to $5,000. National City Bank, the drawee, certifies the check for $5,000. Pam negotiates the check to Don, an HDC. The drawee bank pays Don $5,000. On discovering the mistake, the bank cannot recover from Don the $4,500 paid by mistake, even though the bank was not in a superior position to detect the alteration. This is in accord with the purpose of certification, which is to obtain the definite obligation of a bank to honor a definite instrument. For a synopsis of the rules governing the honoring of checks, see *Concept Summary 27.1.*

SECTION 4 Accepting Deposits

A bank has a duty to its customer to accept the customer's deposits of cash and checks. When checks are deposited, the bank must make the funds represented by those checks available within certain time frames. A bank also has a duty to collect payment on any checks payable or indorsed to its customer and deposited by the customer into his or her account. Cash deposits made in U.S. currency are received into the customer's account without being subject to further collection procedures.

Availability Schedule for Deposited Checks

The Expedited Funds Availability Act of 1987[13] and Regulation CC,[14] which was issued by the Federal Reserve Board of Governors (the *Federal Reserve System* will be discussed shortly) to implement the act, require that any local check deposited must be available for withdrawal by check or as cash within one business day from the date of deposit. A check is classified as a local check if the first bank to receive the check for payment and the bank on which the check is drawn are located in the same check-processing region (regions are designated by the Federal Reserve Board of Governors). For nonlocal checks, the funds must be available for withdrawal within not more than five business days. (Note that eventually, under the Check 21 Act discussed later in this chapter, a bank will have to credit a customer's account as soon as the bank receives the funds.)

In addition, the act requires the following:

1. That funds be available on the next business day for cash deposits and wire transfers, government checks, the first $100 of a day's check deposits, cashier's checks, certified checks, and checks for which the banks receiving and paying the checks are branches of the same institution.
2. That the first $100 of any deposit be available for cash withdrawal on the opening of the *next business day* after deposit. If a local check is deposited, the next $400 is to be available for withdrawal by no later than 5:00 P.M. on the next business day. If, for example, you deposit a local check for $500 on Monday, you can withdraw $100 in cash at the opening of the business day on Tuesday, and an additional $400 must be available for withdrawal by no later than 5:00 P.M. on Wednesday.

A different availability schedule applies to deposits made at *nonproprietary* automated teller machines (ATMs). These are ATMs that are not owned or operated by the bank receiving the deposits. Basically, a five-day hold is permitted on all deposits, including cash deposits, that are made at nonproprietary ATMs. Other exceptions also exist. For example, a banking

12. Usually, the party presenting an instrument for payment is the payee, a holder, a bank customer, or a collecting bank. A bank's customers include its account holders, which may include other banks [UCC 4–104(a)(5)]. As will be discussed later in this chapter, a *collecting bank* is any bank handling an item for collection except the bank on which the check is drawn [UCC 4–105(5)].

13. 12 U.S.C. Sections 4001–4010.

14. 12 C.F.R. Sections 229.1–229.42.

institution has eight days to make funds available in new accounts (those open less than thirty days) and has an extra four days on deposits that exceed $5,000 (except deposits of government and cashier's checks).

Interest-Bearing Accounts

Under the Truth-in-Savings Act (TISA) of 1991[15] and Regulation DD,[16] the act's implementing regulation, banks must pay interest based on the full balance of a customer's interest-bearing account each day. For example, Vogel has an interest-bearing checking account with First National Bank. Vogel keeps a $500 balance in the account for most of the month but withdraws all but $50 the day before the bank posts the interest. The bank cannot pay interest on just the $50. The interest must be adjusted to account for the entire month, including those days when Vogel's balance was higher.

Before opening a deposit account, new customers must be provided certain information in a brochure, pamphlet, or other handout. The information, which

15. 12 U.S.C. Sections 4301–4313.
16. 12 C.F.R. Sections 230.1–230.9.

CONCEPT SUMMARY 27.1
Honoring Checks

Situation	Basic Rules
WRONGFUL DISHONOR [UCC 4–402]	The bank is liable to its customer for actual damages proved if it wrongfully dishonors a check due to mistake.
OVERDRAFT [UCC 4–401]	The bank has a right to charge a customer's account for any item properly payable, even if the charge results in an overdraft.
POSTDATED CHECK [UCC 4–401]	The bank may charge a postdated check against a customer's account, unless the customer notifies the bank of the postdating in time to allow the bank to act on the notice before the bank commits itself to pay on the check.
STALE CHECK [UCC 4–404]	The bank is not obligated to pay an uncertified check presented more than six months after its date, but the bank may do so in good faith without liability.
DEATH OR INCOMPETENCE OF A CUSTOMER [UCC 4–405]	So long as the bank does not know of the death or incompetence of a customer, the bank can pay an item without liability. Even with knowledge of a customer's death, a bank can honor or certify checks (in the absence of a stop-payment order) for ten days after the date of the customer's death.
STOP-PAYMENT ORDER [UCC 4–403]	The customer (or a "person authorized to draw on the account") must institute a stop-payment order in time for the bank to have a reasonable opportunity to act. Oral orders (if allowed) are binding for only fourteen days unless they are confirmed in writing. Written orders are effective for only six months, unless renewed in writing. The bank is liable for wrongful payment over a timely stop-payment order to the extent that the customer suffers a loss. A customer has no right to stop payment on a certified check or an accepted draft and can be held liable for stopping payment on any check without a valid legal ground.
FORGED SIGNATURE OR ALTERATION [UCC 4–406]	The customer has a duty to examine account statements with reasonable care on receipt and to notify the bank promptly of any unauthorized signatures or alterations. On a series of unauthorized signatures or alterations by the same wrongdoer, examination and report must be made within thirty calendar days of receipt of the first statement containing a forged or altered item. The customer's failure to comply with these rules releases the bank from liability unless the bank failed to exercise reasonable care; in that event, liability may be apportioned according to a comparative negligence standard. Regardless of care or lack of care, the customer is *estopped* (prevented) from holding the bank liable after one year for unauthorized customer signatures or alterations and after three years for unauthorized indorsements.

must also appear in all advertisements, includes the following:

1. The minimum balance required to open an account and to be paid interest.
2. The interest, stated in terms of the annual percentage yield on the account.
3. How interest is calculated.
4. Any fees, charges, and penalties and how they are calculated.

Also, under the TISA and Regulation DD, a customer's monthly statement must declare the interest earned on the account, any fees that were charged, how the fees were calculated, and the number of days that the statement covers.

The Traditional Collection Process

Usually, deposited checks involve parties who do business at different banks, but sometimes checks are written between customers of the same bank. Either situation brings into play the bank collection process as it operates within the statutory framework of Article 4 of the UCC. Note that the check-collection process described in the following subsections will be modified in the future as the banking industry implements the Check Clearing in the 21st Century Act,[17] also known as the Check 21 Act, which will be discussed shortly.

Designations of Banks Involved in the Collection Process The first bank to receive a check for payment is the **depositary bank.**[18] For example, when a person deposits a tax-refund check from the Internal Revenue Service into a personal checking account at the local bank, that bank is the depositary bank. The bank on which a check is drawn (the drawee bank) is called the **payor bank.** Any bank except the payor bank that handles a check during some phase of the collection process is a **collecting bank.** Any bank except the payor bank or the depositary bank to which an item is transferred in the course of this collection process is called an **intermediary bank.**

During the collection process, any bank can take on one or more of the various roles of depositary, payor, collecting, or intermediary bank. To illustrate: A buyer in New York writes a check on her New York bank and sends it to a seller in San Francisco. The seller deposits the check in her San Francisco bank account. The seller's bank is both a *depositary bank* and a *collecting bank.* The buyer's bank in New York is the *payor bank.* As the check travels from San Francisco to New York, any *collecting bank* handling the item in the collection process (other than the ones acting as depositary bank and payor bank) is also called an *intermediary bank.* Exhibit 27–5 illustrates how various banks function in the collection process.

Check Collection between Customers of the Same Bank An item that is payable by the depositary bank that receives it (which in this situation is also the payor bank) is called an "on-us item." If the bank does not dishonor the check by the opening of the second banking day following its receipt, the check is considered paid [UCC 4–215(e)(2)]. For example, Oswald and Martin both have checking accounts at First State Bank. On Monday morning, Martin deposits into his own checking account a $300 check from Oswald. That same day, the bank issues Martin a "provisional credit" for $300. When the bank opens on Wednesday, Oswald's check is considered honored, and Martin's provisional credit becomes a final payment.

Check Collection between Customers of Different Banks Once a depositary bank receives a check, it must arrange to present the check, either directly or through intermediary banks, to the appropriate payor bank. Each bank in the collection chain must pass the check on before midnight of the next banking day following its receipt [UCC 4–202(b)].[19] A "banking day" is any part of a day that the bank is open to carry on substantially all of its banking functions. Thus, if only a bank's drive-through facilities are open, a check deposited on Saturday would not trigger a bank's midnight deadline until the following Monday. When the check reaches the payor bank, that bank is liable for the face amount of the check, unless the payor bank dishonors the check or

17. 12 U.S.C. Sections 5001–5018.

18. All definitions in this section are found in UCC 4–105. The terms *depositary* and *depository* have different meanings in the banking context. A depository bank refers to a *physical place* (a bank or other institution) in which deposits or funds are held or stored.

19. A bank may take a "reasonably longer time" in certain circumstances, such as when the bank's computer system is down because of a power failure [UCC 4–202(b)].

EXHIBIT 27–5 • The Traditional Check-Collection Process

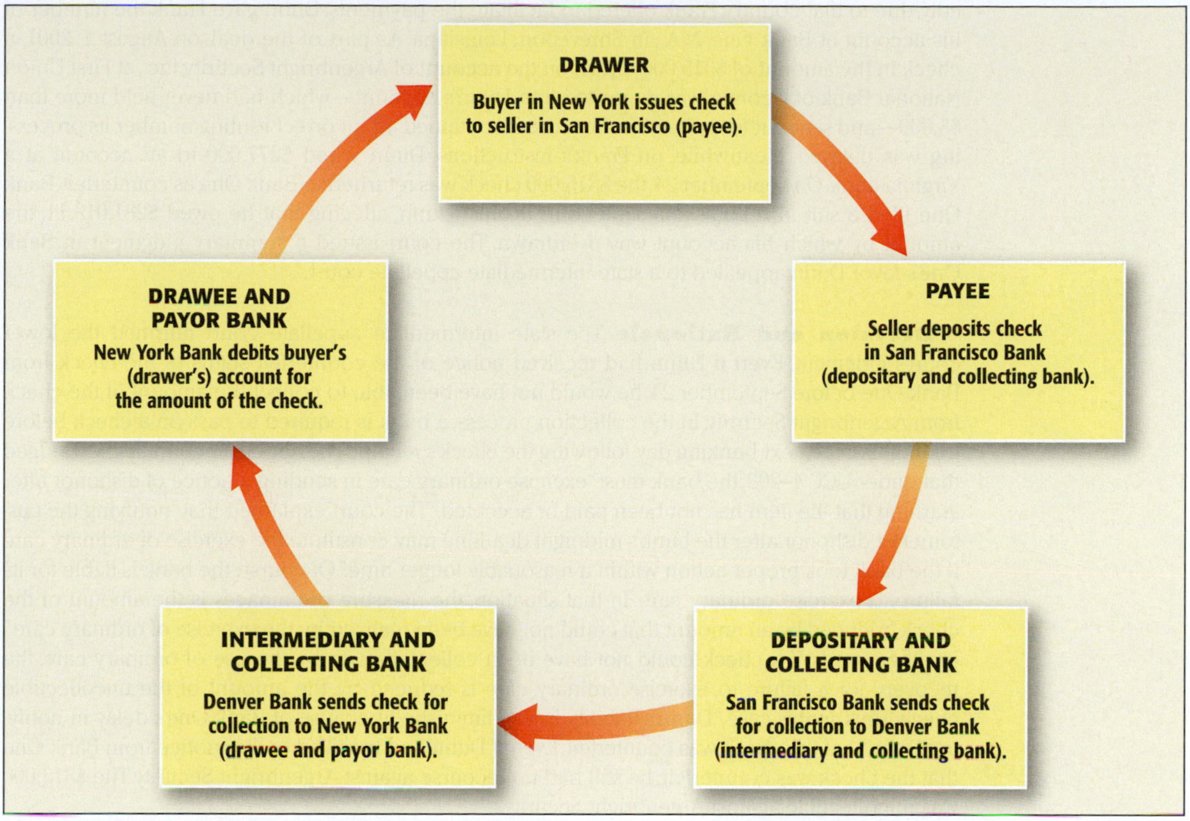
DRAWER
Buyer in New York issues check to seller in San Francisco (payee).
PAYEE
Seller deposits check in San Francisco Bank (depositary and collecting bank).
DEPOSITARY AND COLLECTING BANK
San Francisco Bank sends check for collection to Denver Bank (intermediary and collecting bank).
INTERMEDIARY AND COLLECTING BANK
Denver Bank sends check for collection to New York Bank (drawee and payor bank).
DRAWEE AND PAYOR BANK
New York Bank debits buyer's (drawer's) account for the amount of the check.

returns it by midnight of the next banking day following receipt [UCC 4–302].[20]

Because of this deadline and because banks need to maintain an even work flow in the many items they handle daily, the UCC permits what is called *deferred posting*. According to UCC 4–108, "a bank may fix an afternoon hour of 2:00 P.M. or later as a cutoff hour for the handling of money and items and the making of entries on its books." Any checks received after that hour "may be treated as being received at the opening of the next banking day." Thus, if a bank's "cutoff hour" is 3:00 P.M., a check received by a payor bank at 4:00 P.M. on Monday will be deferred for posting until Tuesday. In this situation, the payor bank's deadline will be midnight Wednesday.

Does a delay of more than one month in a bank's notice to its customer that a check deposited in his account is counterfeit reduce the customer's liability for overdrafts in the account? That was the customer's contention in the following case.

20. Most checks are cleared by a computerized process, and communication and computer facilities may fail because of electrical outages, equipment malfunction, or other conditions. If such conditions arise and a bank fails to meet its midnight deadline, the bank is "excused" from liability if the bank has exercised "such diligence as the circumstances require" [UCC 4–109(d)].

CASE 27.2 Bank One, N.A. v. Dunn

Court of Appeal of Louisiana, Second Circuit, 2006. 927 So.2d 645.

• Background and Facts Floyd Dunn, a U.S. citizen, was hired to lobby in the United States for Zaire (now named the Democratic Republic of the Congo). After three years of efforts on Zaire's behalf, Dunn submitted a bill for $500,000. Instead of paying, Zaire agreed to trade computers to Dunn, who was to sell them to Nigeria for $32.1 million. "Senator Frank," who claimed to be

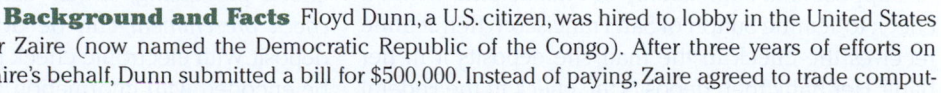

CASE CONTINUES

CASE 27.2 CONTINUED from Nigeria, told Dunn that he would receive his $32.1 million after he paid "back taxes" supposedly due to that country. Frank offered to facilitate the payments. Dunn gave Frank the number of his account at Bank One, N.A., in Shreveport, Louisiana. As part of the deal, on August 1, 2001, a check in the amount of $315,000 drawn on the account of Argenbright Security, Inc., at First Union National Bank of Georgia was deposited into Dunn's account—which had never held more than $5,000—and sent out for collection. Because it contained an incorrect routing number, its processing was delayed. Meanwhile, on Frank's instructions, Dunn wired $277,000 to an account at a Virginia bank. On September 24, the $315,000 check was returned to Bank One as counterfeit. Bank One filed a suit in a Louisiana state court against Dunn, alleging that he owed $281,019.11, the amount by which his account was overdrawn. The court issued a summary judgment in Bank One's favor. Dunn appealed to a state intermediate appellate court.

- **Decision and Rationale** The state intermediate appellate court affirmed the lower court's judgment. Even if Dunn had received notice of the counterfeit status of the check from Bank One before September 24, he would not have been able to collect the amount of the check from Argenbright Security. In the collection process, a bank is required to pass on a check before midnight of the next banking day following the check's receipt. The appellate court acknowledged that under UCC 4–202, the bank must "exercise ordinary care in sending a notice of dishonor after learning that the item has not been paid or accepted." The court explained that "notifying the customer of dishonor after the bank's midnight deadline may constitute the exercise of ordinary care if the bank took proper action within a reasonably longer time." Of course, the bank is liable for its failure to exercise ordinary care. In that situation, the measure of damages is the amount of the check "reduced by an amount that could not have been realized by the exercise of ordinary care." In other words, if a check could not have been collected even by the use of ordinary care, the recovery for a failure to exercise ordinary care is reduced by the amount of the uncollectible check. Thus, in this case, "Dunn's liability is not diminished because of Bank One's delay in notifying Dunn that the check was counterfeit. Even if Dunn had received earlier notice from Bank One that the check was counterfeit, he still had no recourse against Argenbright Security. The $315,000 was uncollectible against Argenbright Security."

- **The Ethical Dimension** *Does a bank have a duty to protect its customers from their own naïveté, as exemplified in this case by Dunn's trusting someone he did not know with his bank account information? Why or why not?*

- **The E-Commerce Dimension** *How would electronic check presentment (to be discussed shortly) have affected the timeliness of the events in this case and ultimately the outcome?*

How the Federal Reserve System Clears Checks The **Federal Reserve System** is a network of twelve district banks, which are located around the country and headed by the Federal Reserve Board of Governors. Most banks in the United States have Federal Reserve accounts. The Federal Reserve System has greatly simplified the check-collection process by acting as a **clearinghouse—**a system or a place where banks exchange checks and drafts drawn on each other and settle daily balances.

Suppose that Pamela Moy of Philadelphia writes a check to Jeanne Sutton of San Francisco. When Jeanne receives the check in the mail, she deposits it in her bank. Her bank then deposits the check in the Federal Reserve Bank of San Francisco, which transfers it to the Federal Reserve Bank of Philadelphia. That Federal Reserve bank then sends the check to Moy's bank, which deducts the amount of the check from Moy's account.

Electronic Check Presentment In the past, most checks were processed manually—the employees of each bank in the collection chain would physically handle each check that passed through the bank for collection or payment. Today, however, most checks are processed electronically. In contrast to manual check processing, which can take days, *electronic check presentment* can be done on the day of the deposit. With electronic check presentment, items may be encoded with information (such as the amount of the check) that can be read and processed by other banks' computers. In some situations, a check is retained at its place of deposit, and only its image or description is presented for payment under an electronic presentment agreement [UCC 4–110].[21]

A person who encodes information on an item after the item has been issued warrants to any subsequent bank or payor that the encoded information is correct [UCC 4–209]. This is also true for a person who retains an item while transmitting its image or information describing it as presentation for payment. This person warrants that the retention and presentment of the item comply with a Federal Reserve or other agreement.

Regulation CC provides that a returned check must be encoded with the routing number of the depositary bank, the amount of the check, and other information and adds that this "does not affect a paying bank's responsibility to return a check within the deadlines required by the UCC." What happens when a payor bank fails to properly encode an item and thereby causes the check to be returned to the depositary bank after the required deadline? That was the question in the following case.

21. UCC 4–110 assumes that no bank will participate in an electronic presentment program without an express agreement (which is no longer true since Check 21 went into effect).

CASE 27.3 NBT Bank, N.A. v. First National Community Bank

United States Court of Appeals, Third Circuit, 2004. 393 F.3d 404.

Background and Facts A small group of Pennsylvania business entities developed a scheme of "check kiting"—that is, they wrote checks on one account, drawing on nonexistent funds, and then covered these overdrafts with checks drawn on another account, which also lacked sufficient funds. The checks were deposited in NBT Bank, which then presented them for payment to First National Community Bank (FNCB). A dispute arose concerning one check for $706,000 drawn on an FNCB account drafted by an entity called Human Services Consultants, Inc. Someone associated with Human Services physically deposited the check at NBT, which gave provisional credit to the depositor for the full amount of the check. The check was then transmitted to a Federal Reserve bank for presentment to FNCB. FNCB did not pay because of the absence of sufficient funds in the account. FNCB attempted to return the check via the Federal Reserve bank. FNCB physically delivered that check prior to the midnight deadline. Simultaneously, FNCB sent a notice of dishonor to NBT, indicating that it would not pay the disputed check. NBT received the notice on the same day that the disputed check was physically delivered to the Federal Reserve bank. The problem was that FNCB erroneously coded the returned check with another bank's routing number. That error caused NBT to receive the check three days later. NBT brought a suit against FNCB, claiming that FNCB had failed to return the disputed check prior to the midnight deadline as required by the UCC. The district court ruled in favor of FNCB. NBT Bank appealed.

Decision and Rationale The Court of Appeals for the Third Circuit affirmed the district court's decision. The appellate court pointed out that Federal Reserve "Regulation CC" complemented, but did not replace, the requirements of Article 4 of the UCC. In other words, Federal Reserve regulations may vary the terms of the UCC. Regulation CC outlines the measure of damages when a bank fails to exercise ordinary care. These damages are calculated by the amount of the loss incurred, up to the amount of the check, reduced by the amount of the loss that the plaintiff bank would have incurred even if the defendant bank had exercised ordinary care. The plaintiff bank, NBT, suffered no loss as a result of FNCB's encoding error. Therefore, NBT could not recover from FNCB.

What If the Facts Were Different? *How might the result in this case have been different if NBT had committed the encoding error and FNCB had suffered the loss?*

The Ethical Dimension *If a bank warrants that the information it encoded on an item is correct and FNCB committed an error in encoding, then why did the court not hold FNCB liable for the amount of the check?*

Check Clearing and the Check 21 Act

In the traditional collection process, paper checks had to be physically transported before they could be cleared. To streamline this costly and time-consuming process and to improve the overall efficiency of the nation's payment system, Congress passed the Check Clearing in the 21st Century Act[22] (Check 21).

Purpose of Check 21 Prior to the implementation of Check 21, banks had to present the original paper check for payment in the absence of an agreement for presentment in some other form. Although the UCC authorizes banks to use other means of presentment, such as electronic presentment, a broad-based system of electronic presentment failed to develop because it required agreements among individual banks. Check 21 has changed this situation by creating a new negotiable instrument called a *substitute check*. Although the act did not require any bank to change its current check-collection practices, the creation of substitute checks will certainly facilitate the use of electronic check processing over time.

What Is a Substitute Check? A substitute check is a paper reproduction of the front and back of an original check that contains all of the same information required on checks for automated processing. Banks create a substitute check from a digital image of an original check. Every substitute check must include the following statement somewhere on it: "This a legal copy of your check. You can use it in the same way you would use the original check."

In essence, those financial institutions that exchange digital images of checks do not have to send the original paper checks. They can simply transmit the information electronically and replace the original checks with the paper reproductions—the substitute checks. Banks that do not exchange checks electronically are required to accept substitute checks in the same way that they accept original checks.

The Gradual Elimination of Paper Checks Because financial institutions must accept substitute checks as if they were original checks, the original checks will no longer be needed and will probably be destroyed after their digital images are created. By eliminating the original check after a substitute check is created, the financial system can prevent the check from being paid twice. Also, eliminating original checks and retaining only digital images will reduce the expense of storage and retrieval. Nevertheless, at least for quite a while, not all checks will be converted to substitute checks. That means that if a bank returns canceled checks to deposit holders at the end of each month, some of those returned checks may be substitute checks, and some may be original canceled paper checks.

Since the passage of Check 21, financial institution customers cannot demand an original canceled check. Check 21 is a federal law and applies to all financial institutions, other businesses, and individuals in the United States. In other words, no customers can opt out of Check 21 and demand that their original canceled checks be returned with their monthly statements. Also, businesses and individuals must accept a substitute check as proof of payment because it is the legal equivalent of the original check.

Reduced "Float" Time Sometimes, individuals and businesses write checks even though they have insufficient funds in their accounts to cover those checks. Such check writers are relying on "float," or the time between when a check is written and when the amount is actually deducted from their account. When all checks had to be physically transported, the float time could be several days, but as Check 21 is implemented, the time required to process checks will be substantially reduced—and so will float time. Thus, account holders who plan to cover their checks after writing them may experience unexpected overdrafts.

Though consumers and businesses will no longer be able to rely on float time, they may benefit in another way from Check 21. The Expedited Funds Availability Act (mentioned earlier in this chapter) requires that the Federal Reserve Board revise the availability schedule for funds from deposited checks to correspond to reductions in check-processing time. Therefore, as the speed of check processing increases under Check 21, the Federal Reserve Board will reduce the maximum time that a bank can hold funds from deposited checks before making them available to the depositor. Thus, account holders will have faster access to their deposited funds.

SECTION 5 Electronic Fund Transfers

The application of computer technology to banking, in the form of electronic fund transfer systems, has helped to relieve banking institutions of the burden of

22. 12 U.S.C. Section 5001, Pub. L. No. 108-100.

having to move mountains of paperwork to process fund transfers. An **electronic fund transfer (EFT)** is a transfer of funds made by the use of an electronic terminal, a telephone, a computer, or magnetic tape. The law governing EFTs depends on the type of transfer involved. Consumer fund transfers are governed by the Electronic Fund Transfer Act (EFTA) of 1978.[23] Commercial fund transfers are governed by Article 4A of the UCC.

The benefits of electronic banking are obvious. Automatic payments, direct deposits, and other fund transfers are now made electronically; no physical transfers of cash, checks, or other negotiable instruments are involved. Not surprisingly, though, electronic banking can also pose difficulties. For example, it is difficult to issue stop-payment orders with electronic banking. In addition, fewer records are available to prove or disprove that a transaction took place, and the possibilities for tampering with a person's private banking information have increased.

Types of EFT Systems

Most banks today offer EFT services to their customers. The following are the four most common types of EFT systems used by bank customers:

1. *Automated teller machines* (ATMs)—The machines are connected online to the bank's computers. A customer inserts a **debit card** (a plastic card, also called an *ATM card*) issued by the bank and keys in a *personal identification number* (PIN) to access her or his accounts and conduct banking transactions.
2. *Point-of-sale systems*—Online terminals allow consumers to transfer funds to merchants to pay for purchases using a debit card.
3. *Direct deposits and withdrawals*—Customers can authorize the bank to allow another party, such as the government or an employer, to make direct deposits into their accounts. Similarly, a customer can request the bank to make automatic payments to a third party at regular, recurrent intervals from the customer's funds (insurance premiums or loan payments, for example).
4. *Internet payment systems*—Many financial institutions permit their customers to access the institution's computer system via the Internet and direct a transfer of funds between accounts or pay a particular bill, such as a utility bill. Payments can be made on a onetime or a recurring basis.

23. 15 U.S.C. Sections 1693–1693r. The EFTA amended Title IX of the Consumer Credit Protection Act.

Consumer Fund Transfers

The Electronic Fund Transfer Act (EFTA) provides a basic framework for the rights, liabilities, and responsibilities of users of EFT systems. Additionally, the act gave the Federal Reserve Board authority to issue rules and regulations to help implement the act's provisions. The Federal Reserve Board's implemental regulation is called **Regulation E.**

The EFTA governs financial institutions that offer electronic transfers of funds involving customer accounts. The types of accounts covered include checking accounts, savings accounts, and any other asset accounts established for personal, family, or household purposes. Telephone transfers are covered by the EFTA only if they are made in accordance with a prearranged plan under which periodic or recurring transfers are contemplated.

Disclosure Requirements The EFTA is essentially a disclosure law benefiting consumers. The act requires financial institutions to inform consumers of their rights and responsibilities, including those listed here, with respect to EFT systems.

1. If a customer's debit card is lost or stolen and used without her or his permission, the customer may be required to pay no more than $50. The customer, however, must notify the bank of the loss or theft within two days of learning about it. Otherwise, the customer's liability increases to $500. The customer may be liable for more than $500 if she or he does not report the unauthorized use within sixty days after it appears on the customer's statement.
2. The customer has sixty days to discover and notify the bank of any error on the monthly statement. The bank then has ten days to investigate and must report its conclusions to the customer in writing. If the bank takes longer than ten days to do so, it must return the disputed amount to the customer's account until it finds the error. If there is no error, however, the customer must return the funds to the bank.
3. The bank must furnish receipts for transactions made through computer terminals, but it is not obligated to do so for telephone transfers.
4. The bank must provide a monthly statement for every month in which there is an electronic transfer of funds. Otherwise, the bank must provide a statement every quarter. The statement must show the amount and date of the transfer, the names of the retailers or other third parties involved, the

location or identification of the terminal, and the fees. Additionally, the statement must give an address and a phone number for inquiries and error notices.

5. Any preauthorized payment for utility bills and insurance premiums can be stopped three days before the scheduled transfer if the customer notifies the financial institution orally or in writing. (The institution may require the customer to provide written confirmation within fourteen days of an oral notification.) For other EFT transactions, however, the EFTA does not provide for the reversal of an electronic transfer of funds once the transfer has occurred.

Unauthorized Transfers Because of the vulnerability of EFT systems to fraudulent activities, the EFTA clearly defined what constitutes an unauthorized transfer. Under the act, a transfer is unauthorized if (1) it is initiated by a person who has no actual authority to initiate the transfer, (2) the consumer receives no benefit from it, and (3) the consumer did not furnish the person "with the card, code, or other means of access" to his or her account. Gaining unauthorized access to an EFT system constitutes a federal felony, and those convicted may be fined up to $10,000 and sentenced to as long as ten years in prison.

Violations and Damages Banks are held to strict compliance with the terms of the EFTA. If they fail to adhere to the letter of the law of the EFTA, they will be held liable for the violation. For a bank's violation of the EFTA, a consumer may recover both actual damages (including attorneys' fees and costs) and punitive damages of not less than $100 and not more than $1,000. In a class-action suit, the punitive-damages award can be up to $500,000 or 1 percent of the institution's net worth. (Unlike actual damages, punitive damages are assessed to punish a defendant or to deter similar wrongdoers.) Failure to investigate an error in good faith makes the bank liable for treble damages (three times the amount of damages). Even when a customer has sustained no actual damage, the bank may be liable for legal costs and punitive damages if it fails to follow the proper procedures outlined by the EFTA in regard to error resolution.

Commercial Fund Transfers

Funds are also transferred electronically "by wire" between commercial parties. In fact, the dollar volume of payments made via wire transfers is more than $1 trillion a day—an amount that far exceeds the dollar volume of payments made by other means. The two major wire payment systems are the Federal Reserve wire transfer network (Fedwire) and the New York Clearing House Interbank Payments Systems (CHIPS).

Commercial wire transfers are governed by Article 4A of the UCC, which has been adopted by most of the states. Article 4A uses the term *funds transfer* rather than *wire transfer* to describe the overall payment transaction. The full text of Article 4A is presented in Appendix C.

As an example of the type of funds transfer covered by Article 4A, assume that American Industries, Inc., owes $5 million to Chandler Corporation. Instead of sending Chandler a check or some other instrument that would enable Chandler to obtain payment, American Industries tells its bank, North Bank, to credit $5 million to Chandler's account in South Bank. North Bank debits American Industries' North Bank account and wires $5 million to South Bank with instructions to credit $5 million to Chandler's South Bank account. In more complex transactions, additional banks would be involved.

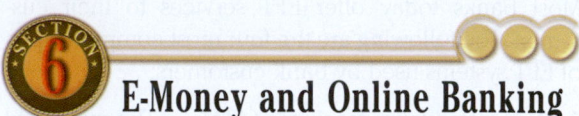

SECTION 6 E-Money and Online Banking

New forms of electronic payments (e-payments) have the potential to replace *physical* cash—coins and paper currency—with *virtual* cash in the form of electronic impulses. This is the unique promise of **digital cash,** which consists of funds stored on microchips and other computer devices. Digital cash is increasingly being used to launder money, as discussed in this chapter's *Emerging Trends* feature on pages 520 and 521.

Various forms of electronic money, or **e-money,** are emerging. The simplest kind of e-money system uses *stored-value cards.* These are plastic cards embossed with magnetic strips containing magnetically encoded data. In some applications, a stored-value card can be used only to purchase specific goods and services offered by the card issuer.

Another form of e-money is the smart card. **Smart cards** are plastic cards containing computer microchips that can hold much more information than magnetic strips. A smart card carries and processes security programming. This capability gives smart cards a technical advantage over stored-value cards. The microprocessors on smart cards can also authenticate the validity of transactions. Retailers can program electronic cash registers to confirm the authenticity of a smart card by examining a unique digital signature stored on its microchip. (Digital signatures were discussed in Chapter 19.)

Online Banking Services

Increasingly, many bank customers are conducting at least part of their banking online. Today, most online bank customers use three kinds of services. One of the most popular is bill consolidation and payment. Another is transferring funds among accounts (which may often also be accomplished by phone or through an ATM). The third is applying for loans, which many banks permit customers to do via the Internet. Customers typically must appear in person to finalize the terms of a loan, however.

Two important banking activities generally are not yet available online: depositing and withdrawing funds. With smart cards, people could transfer funds on the Internet, thereby effectively transforming their personal computers into ATMs. Many observers believe that people will eventually be introduced to e-money and smart cards through online banking.

Since the late 1990s, several banks have operated exclusively on the Internet. These "virtual banks" have no physical branch offices. Because few individuals are equipped to send funds to virtual banks via smart-card technology, the virtual banks have accepted deposits through physical delivery systems, such as the U.S. Postal Service, FedEx, UPS, or DHL.

Regulatory Compliance

Banks have an interest in promoting the widespread use of online banking because it has significant potential for reducing costs and thus increasing profits. As in other areas of cyberspace, however, determining how laws apply to online banking activities can be difficult.

The Home Mortgage Disclosure Act[24] and the Community Reinvestment Act (CRA) of 1977,[25] for example, require a bank to define its market area and also to provide information about its deposits and loans. Under the CRA, banks establish market areas situated next to their branch offices. The banks map these areas using boundaries defined by counties or standard metropolitan areas and annually review the maps. The purpose of these requirements is to prevent discrimination in lending practices.

How does a successful "cyberbank" delineate its community? If, for example, Bank of Internet becomes a tremendous success, does it really have any physical communities? Will the Federal Reserve Board simply allow a written description of a cybercommunity for Internet customers? Such regulatory issues are new, challenging, and certain to become more complicated as Internet banking widens its scope internationally.

Privacy Protection

At the present time, it is not clear which, if any, laws apply to the security of e-money payment information and e-money issuers' financial records. This is partly because it is not clear whether e-money issuers fit within the traditional definition of a financial institution.

E-Money Payment Information The Federal Reserve has decided not to impose Regulation E, which governs certain electronic fund transfers, on e-money transactions. Federal laws prohibiting unauthorized access to electronic communications might apply, however. For example, the Electronic Communications Privacy Act of 1986[26] prohibits any person from knowingly divulging to any other person the contents of an electronic communication while that communication is in transmission or in electronic storage.

E-Money Issuers' Financial Records Under the Right to Financial Privacy Act of 1978,[27] before a financial institution may give financial information about you to a federal agency, you must explicitly consent. If you do not, a federal agency wishing to access your financial records normally must obtain a warrant. A digital cash issuer may be subject to this act if that issuer is deemed to be (1) a bank by virtue of its holding customer funds or (2) any entity that issues a physical card similar to a credit or debit card.

Consumer Financial Data In 1999, Congress passed the Financial Services Modernization Act,[28] also known as the Gramm-Leach-Bliley Act, in an attempt to delineate how financial institutions can treat customer data. In general, the act and its rules[29] place restrictions and obligations on financial institutions to protect consumer data and privacy. Every financial institution must provide its customers with information on its privacy policies and practices. No financial institution can disclose nonpublic personal information about a consumer to an unaffiliated third party unless the act's disclosure and opt-out requirements are met.

24. 12 U.S.C. Sections 2801–2810.
25. 12 U.S.C. Sections 2901–2908.
26. 18 U.S.C. Sections 2510–2521.
27. 12 U.S.C. Sections 3401 *et seq.*
28. 12 U.S.C. Sections 24a, 248b, 1820a, 1828b, and others.
29. 12 C.F.R. Part 40.

EMERGING TRENDS IN BUSINESS LAW
Using Digital Cash Facilitates Money Laundering

As Chapter 9 pointed out, criminals often engage in money laundering to make their illegitimate funds appear legitimate. Profits illegally obtained—through drug trafficking, for example—are processed through a series of financial transactions that conceals their criminal origin. For example, Colombian drug cartels have used some of their profits to buy the most advanced computers and programming available so that they can engage in digital money laundering using secret Web sites. At a typical encrypted private Web site operated by a drug cartel, black market money changers bid on cash in U.S. and other currencies and eventually enable it to be converted to Colombian pesos.

Investigators for the U.S. Treasury Department estimate that these private Web sites can launder as much as $3 billion per year. Although most countries have legislation against money laundering, it is estimated that worldwide more than $600 billion in drug-trafficking profits is laundered every year—an amount equal to between 2 and 5 percent of the world's gross domestic product.[a]

Reporting Requirements for Cash Transfers

Under current law, U.S. financial institutions must report transactions or fund transfers involving more than $10,000 in cash.[b] In the past, to avoid running afoul of these reporting requirements, drug traffickers—and terrorist groups—had to move their cash a little at a time in numerous transactions or smuggle bundles of cash across borders. Now the advent of digital cash has given them new options.

a. This statistic was taken from the Web site of the U.S. Department of Justice, **www.usdoj.gov/dea/programs/money.htm**.

b. The Bank Secrecy Act of 1970, 18 U.S.C. Sections 1956–1957, as amended by the Money Laundering Control Act of 1986, 31 C.F.R. Section 103.22(a)(1); and as modified by Title III of the Patriot Act of 2001.

Laundering Money through Prepaid ATM Cards

Today, many drug traffickers, terrorist groups, and other criminals who must move large amounts of cash are turning to prepaid ATM cards. From a would-be money launderer's perspective, a prepaid ATM card offers several advantages over a standard ATM or debit card issued by a bank. Any bank-issued card is linked to the customer's bank account. Thus, using such a card creates a paper trail (albeit electronically) that can be easily traced.

In contrast, a prepaid ATM card has no link to a bank account. It is essentially a *stored-value card*. The purchaser simply pays a specific amount to the card provider, and that amount is loaded onto the card. The user can then access those funds anywhere in the world without having to provide identification or have a bank account. Students and travelers use prepaid ATM cards as a convenient and safe substitute for cash. So, too, do about 75 million

REVIEWING Checks and Banking in the Digital Age

RPM Pizza, Inc., issued a check for $96,000 to Systems Marketing for an advertising campaign. A few days later, RPM decided not to go through with the deal and placed a written stop-payment order on the check. RPM and Systems had no further contact for many months. Three weeks after the stop-payment order expired, however, Toby Rierson, an employee at Systems, cashed the check. Bank One Cambridge, RPM's bank, paid the check with funds from RPM's account. Because of the amount of the check, and because the check was more than six months old (stale), the signature on the check should have been specially verified according to standard banking procedures and Bank One's own policies, but it was not. RPM filed a suit in a federal district court against Bank One to recover the amount of the check. Using the information presented in the chapter, answer the following questions.

residents of the United States who do not have bank accounts. More important for money laundering purposes is that prepaid ATM cards can be purchased anonymously at retail and check-cashing stores across the nation—businesses that are not yet subject to the government's reporting requirements. Thus, drug traffickers and terrorist groups can pay for the cards with large amounts of cash and then use the cards to move funds across the border—a much easier process than smuggling physical cash.

Using Virtual Gaming Currency to Launder Money

The growing popularity of virtual gaming has opened the door to cyber laundering—and provided money launderers with a new source of prepaid ATM cards. For years, gamers in virtual worlds have been selling their digital monies, goods, and properties for real-world compensation. Initally, players were able to convert their virtual dollars or credits to real-world cash only by selling them on online auction sites, such as eBay. Now, however, gamers can go to various Web sites and exchange their virtual currency for real-world ATM cards. In 2006, for example, the makers of Entropia Universe began offering prepaid ATM cards in exchange for virtual assets.

With these new types of ATM cards, a gamer can instantly convert his or her virtual-world assets into physical currency and withdraw "real" cash from any Versatel brand ATM in the world. This means that a person can generate and hold financial assets anonymously in the virtual world without having to report the proceeds to the government or pay taxes on them. More importantly, these assets can be purchased, transferred, and accessed from any place in the world and are completely unregulated and unreported. Once the funds are withdrawn from a virtual account, they are "clean" and cannot be traced to an identifiable source. Hence, the virtual world holds great appeal for those who wish to hide their assets from the government's view and transfer funds internationally without risking detection.

IMPLICATIONS FOR THE BUSINESSPERSON

1. Be aware that all banks are required to report any wire transfers of more than $10,000 to the U.S. Treasury.
2. Be prepared for increased government regulation of digital cash transactions.

FOR CRITICAL ANALYSIS

1. Should only banks and regulated financial institutions be allowed to issue ATM cards? Why or why not?
2. How else might the government regulate digital funds to reduce the potential for cyber laundering?

RELEVANT WEB SITES

To locate information on the Web concerning the issues discussed in this feature, go to this text's Web site at **www.cengage.com/blaw/jentz**, select "Chapter 27," and click on "Emerging Trends."

REVIEWING Checks and Banking in the Digital Age, Continued

1. How long is a written stop-payment order effective? What else could RPM have done to prevent this check from being cashed?
2. What would happen if it turned out that RPM did not have a legitimate reason for stopping payment on the check?
3. What are a bank's obligations with respect to stale checks? Should Bank One have contacted RPM before paying the check? Why or why not?
4. Assume that Rierson's indorsement on the check was a forgery. Would a court be likely to hold the bank liable for the amount of the check because it failed to verify the signature on the check? Why or why not?

TERMS AND CONCEPTS

cashier's check 501
certified check 502
check 501
clearinghouse 514
collecting bank 512
debit card 517
depositary bank 512
digital cash 518
electronic fund transfer (EFT) 517
e-money 518
Federal Reserve System 514
intermediary bank 512
overdraft 504
payor bank 512
Regulation E 517
smart card 518
stale check 504
stop-payment order 505
teller's check 502
traveler's check 502

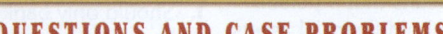

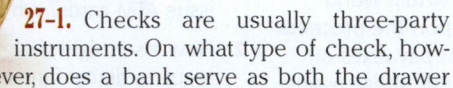

QUESTIONS AND CASE PROBLEMS

27-1. Checks are usually three-party instruments. On what type of check, however, does a bank serve as both the drawer and the drawee? What type of check does a bank agree in advance to accept when the check is presented for payment?

27-2. QUESTION WITH SAMPLE ANSWER

Gary goes grocery shopping and carelessly leaves his checkbook in his shopping cart. His checkbook, with two blank checks remaining, is stolen by Dolores. On May 5, Dolores forges Gary's name on a check for $10 and cashes the check at Gary's bank, Citizens Bank of Middletown. Gary has not reported the loss of his blank checks to his bank. On June 1, Gary receives his monthly bank statement and copies of canceled checks from Citizens Bank, including the forged check, but he does not examine the canceled checks. On June 20, Dolores forges Gary's last check. This check is for $1,000 and is cashed at Eastern City Bank, a bank with which Dolores has previously done business. Eastern City Bank puts the check through the collection process, and Citizens Bank honors it. On July 1, on receipt of his bank statement and canceled checks covering June transactions, Gary discovers both forgeries and immediately notifies Citizens Bank. Dolores cannot be found. Gary claims that Citizens Bank must recredit his account for both checks, as his signature was forged. Discuss fully Gary's claim.

- **For a sample answer to Question 27-2, go to Appendix I at the end of this text.**

27-3. On January 5, Brian drafts a check for $3,000 drawn on Southern Marine Bank and payable to his assistant, Shanta. Brian puts last year's date on the check by mistake. On January 7, before Shanta has had a chance to go to the bank, Brian is killed in an automobile accident. Southern Marine Bank is aware of Brian's death. On January 10, Shanta presents the check to the bank, and the bank honors the check by payment to Shanta. Later, Brian's widow, Joyce, claims that because the bank knew of Brian's death and also because the check was by date over one year old, the bank acted wrongfully when it paid Shanta. Joyce, as executor of Brian's estate and sole heir by his will, demands that Southern Marine Bank recredit Brian's estate for the check paid to Shanta. Discuss fully Southern Marine's liability in light of Joyce's demand.

27-4. Yannuzzi has a checking account at Texas Bank. She frequently uses her access card to obtain cash from the bank's automated teller machines. She always withdraws $50 when she makes a withdrawal, but she never withdraws more than $50 in any one day. When she received the April statement on her account, she noticed that on April 13 two withdrawals for $50 each had been made from the account. Believing this to be a mistake, she went to her bank on May 10 to inform it of the error. A bank officer told her that the bank would investigate and advise her as to the result. On May 26, the bank officer called her and said that bank personnel were having trouble locating the error but would continue to try to find it. On June 20, the bank sent her a full written report telling her that no error had been made. Yannuzzi, unhappy with the bank's explanation, filed suit against the bank, alleging that it had violated the Electronic Fund Transfer Act. What was the outcome of the suit? Would it matter if the bank could show that on the day in question it deducted $50 from Yannuzzi's account to cover a check that cleared the bank on that day—a check that Yannuzzi had written to a local department store?

27-5. Forged Signatures. Visiting Nurses Association of Telfair County, Inc. (VNA), maintained a checking account at Security State Bank in Valdosta, Georgia. Wanda Williamson, a VNA clerk, was responsible for making VNA bank deposits, but she was not a signatory on the association's account. Over a four-year period, Williamson embezzled more than $250,000 from VNA by forging its indorsement on checks, cashing them at the bank, and keeping a portion of the proceeds. Williamson was arrested, convicted, sentenced to a prison term, and ordered to pay restitution. VNA filed a suit in a Georgia state court against the bank, alleging, among other things, negligence. The bank filed a motion for summary judgment on the ground that VNA was precluded by Section 4–406(f) of the Uniform Commercial Code from recovering on checks with forged indorsements. Should the court grant the motion? Explain. [*Security State Bank v. Visiting Nurses Association of Telfair County, Inc.*, 568 S.E.2d 491 (Ga.App. 2002)]

27–6. Forged Signatures. Cynthia Stafford worked as an administrative professional at Gerber & Gerber, P.C. (professional corporation), a law firm, for more than two years. During that time, she stole ten checks payable to Gerber & Gerber (G&G), which she indorsed in blank by forging one of the attorney's signatures. She then indorsed the forged checks in her name and deposited them in her account at Regions Bank. Over the same period, G&G deposited in its accounts at Regions Bank thousands of checks amounting to $300 million to $400 million. Each G&G check was indorsed with a rubber stamp for deposit into the G&G account. The thefts were made possible, in part, because G&G kept unindorsed checks in an open file accessible to all employees and Stafford was sometimes the person assigned to stamp the checks. When the thefts were discovered, G&G filed a suit in a Georgia state court against Regions Bank to recover the stolen funds, alleging, among other things, negligence. Regions Bank filed a motion for summary judgment. What principles apply to attribute liability between these parties? How should the court rule on the bank's motion? Explain. [*Gerber & Gerber, P.C. v. Regions Bank*, 266 Ga.App. 8, 596 S.E.2d 174 (2004)]

27–7. CASE PROBLEM WITH SAMPLE ANSWER

In December 1999, Jenny Triplett applied for a bookkeeping position with Spacemakers of America, Inc., in Atlanta, Georgia. Spacemakers hired Triplett and delegated to her all responsibility for maintaining the company checkbook and reconciling it with the monthly statements from SunTrust Bank. Triplett also handled invoices from vendors. Spacemakers' president, Dennis Rose, reviewed the invoices and signed the checks to pay them, but no other employee checked Triplett's work. By the end of her first full month of employment, Triplett had forged six checks totaling more than $22,000, all payable to Triple M Entertainment, which was not a Spacemakers vendor. By October 2000, Triplett had forged fifty-nine more checks, totaling more than $475,000. A SunTrust employee became suspicious of an item that required sight inspection under the bank's fraud detection standards, which exceeded those of other banks in the area. Triplett was arrested. Spacemakers filed a suit in a Georgia state court against SunTrust. The bank filed a motion for summary judgment. On what basis could the bank avoid liability? In whose favor should the court rule, and why? [*Spacemakers of America, Inc. v. SunTrust Bank*, 271 Ga.App. 335, 609 S.E.2d 683 (2005)]

- **To view a sample answer for Problem 27–7, go to this book's Web site at www.cengage.com/blaw/jentz, select "Chapter 27," and click on "Case Problem with Sample Answer."**

27–8. Forged Indorsements. In 1994, Brian and Penny Grieme bought a house in Mandan, North Dakota. They borrowed for the purchase through a loan program financed by the North Dakota Housing Finance Agency (NDHFA). The Griemes obtained insurance for the house from Center Mutual Insurance Co. When a hailstorm damaged the house in 2001, Center Mutual determined that the loss was $4,378 and issued a check for that amount, drawn on Bremer Bank, N.A. The check's payees included Brian Grieme and the NDHFA. Grieme presented the check for payment to Wells Fargo Bank of Tempe, Arizona. The back of the check bore his signature and in hand-printed block letters the words "ND Housing Finance." The check was processed for collection and paid, and the canceled check was returned to Center Mutual. By the time the insurer learned that NDHFA's indorsement had been forged, the Griemes had canceled their policy, defaulted on their loan, and filed for bankruptcy. The NDHFA filed a suit in a North Dakota state court against Center Mutual for the amount of the check. Who is most likely to suffer the loss in this case? Why? [*State ex rel. North Dakota Housing Finance Agency v. Center Mutual Insurance Co.*, 720 N.W.2d 425 (N.Dak. 2006)]

27–9. A QUESTION OF ETHICS

*From the 1960s, James Johnson served as Bradley Union's personal caretaker and assistant, and was authorized by Union to handle his banking transactions. Louise Johnson, James's wife, wrote checks on Union's checking account to pay his bills, normally signing the checks "Brad Union." Branch Banking & Trust Co. (BB&T) managed Union's account. In December 2000, on the basis of Union's deteriorating mental and physical condition, a North Carolina state court declared him incompetent. Douglas Maxwell was appointed as Union's guardian. Maxwell "froze" Union's checking account and asked BB&T for copies of the canceled checks, which were provided by July 2001. Maxwell believed that Union's signature on the checks had been forged. In August 2002, Maxwell contacted BB&T, which refused to recredit Union's account. Maxwell filed a suit on Union's behalf in a North Carolina state court against BB&T. [*Union v. Branch Banking & Trust Co.*, *176 N.C.App. 711, 627 S.E.2d 276 (2006)]*

(a) Before Maxwell's appointment, BB&T sent monthly statements and canceled checks to Union, and Johnson reviewed them, but no unauthorized signatures were ever reported. On whom can liability be imposed in the case of a forged drawer's signature on a check? What are the limits set by Section

4–406(f) of the Uniform Commercial Code? Should Johnson's position, Union's incompetence, or Maxwell's appointment affect the application of these principles? Explain.

(b) Why was this suit brought against BB&T? Is BB&T liable? If not, who is? Why? Regardless of any violations of the law, did anyone act unethically in this case? If so, who and why?

LAW ON THE WEB

For updated links to resources available on the Web, as well as a variety of other materials, visit this text's Web site at

www.cengage.com/blaw/jentz

You can obtain extensive information on banking regulation from the Federal Deposit Insurance Corporation (FDIC) at

www.fdic.gov

Additional information about banking can be obtained from the Federal Reserve System at

www.federalreserveonline.org

The American Bankers Association is the largest banking trade association in the United States. To learn more about the banking industry, go to

www.aba.com

Legal Research Exercises on the Web

Go to **www.cengage.com/blaw/jentz**, the Web site that accompanies this text. Select "Chapter 27" and click on "Internet Exercises." There you will find the following Internet research exercises that you can perform to learn more about the topics covered in this chapter.

Internet Exercise 27–1: Legal Perspective
Smart Cards

Internet Exercise 27–2: Management Perspective
Check Fraud

Negotiable Instruments

Articles 3 and 4 of the Uniform Commercial Code (UCC), which deal with negotiable instruments, constitute an important part of the law governing commercial transactions. These articles reflect several fundamental ethical principles. One principle is that individuals should be protected against harm caused by the misuse of negotiable instruments. Another basic principle—and one that underlies the entire concept of negotiable instruments—is that the laws governing the use of negotiable instruments should be practical and reasonable to encourage the free flow of commerce.

Here, we look first at some of the ethical implications of the concept of a holder in due course (HDC). We then examine some other ethical issues that frequently arise in relation to these instruments.

Ethics, the HDC Concept, and *Ort v. Fowler*

The drafters of Article 3 did not create the HDC concept out of thin air. Indeed, under the common law, courts had often restricted the extent to which defenses could successfully be raised against a good faith holder of a negotiable instrument. As an example, consider a classic 1884 case, *Ort v. Fowler*.[1]

Case Background Ort, a farmer, was working alone in his field one day, when he was approached by a stranger who claimed to be the statewide agent for a manufacturer of iron posts and wire fencing. The two men conversed for some time, and eventually the stranger persuaded the farmer to act as an area representative for the manufacturer. The stranger then completed two documents for Ort to sign, telling him that they were identical copies of an agreement in which Ort agreed to represent the manufacturer.

Because the farmer did not have his glasses with him and could read only with great difficulty, he asked the stranger to read the document to him. The stranger then purported to do so, not mentioning that the document was a promissory note. Both men signed each document. The stranger later negotiated the promissory note he had fraudulently obtained from Ort to a party that today we would refer to as an HDC. When this party brought suit against him, Ort attempted to defend on the basis of fraud in the execution.

The Court's Decision The Kansas court deciding the issue entertained three possible views. One was that because Ort never *intended* to execute a note, he should not be held liable for doing so. A second view was that the jury should decide, as a question of fact, whether Ort was guilty of negligence under the circumstances. The third view was that because Ort possessed all of his faculties and was able to read the English language, signing a promissory note solely in reliance on a stranger's assurances that it was a different instrument constituted negligence.

This third view was the one adopted by the court in 1884. The court held that Ort's negligence had contributed to the fraud and that such negligence precluded Ort from raising fraud as a defense against payment on the note. Today, the UCC expresses essentially the same reasoning: fraud is a defense against an HDC only if the injured party signed the instrument "with neither knowledge nor a reasonable opportunity to learn of its character or its essential terms" [UCC 3–305(a)(1)(iii)].

The Reasoning Underlying the HDC Concept Although it may not seem fair that an innocent victim should have to suffer the consequences of another's fraudulent act, the UCC assumes that it would be even less fair if an HDC could not collect payment. The reasoning behind this assumption is that an HDC, as a third party, is less likely to have been responsible for—or to have had an opportunity to protect against—the fraud in the underlying transaction.

In general, the HDC doctrine, like other sections of the UCC, reflects the philosophy that when two or more innocent parties are at risk, the burden should fall on the party that was in the best position to prevent the loss. For businesspersons, the HDC doctrine means that they should exercise caution when issuing and accepting commercial paper in order to protect against the risk of loss through fraud.

Good Faith in Negotiable Instruments Law

Clearly, the principle of good faith reflects ethical principles. The most notable application of the good

1. 31 Kan. 478, 2 P. 580 (1884).

(Continued)

faith requirement in negotiable instruments law is, of course, the HDC doctrine. Traditionally, to acquire the protected status of an HDC, a holder must have acquired an instrument in good faith. Yet other transactions subject to Articles 3 and 4 also require good faith—as, indeed, do all transactions governed by the UCC.

The Importance of Good Faith A party that acts in bad faith may be precluded from seeking shelter under UCC provisions that would otherwise apply. This point was emphasized by a Pennsylvania court's decision with respect to the fictitious payee rule. The bank in this case had accepted 882 payroll checks generated and indorsed by Dorothy Heck, a payroll clerk employed by Pavex, Inc. The checks were made payable to various current and former Pavex employees, indorsed by Heck with the payees' names, and deposited into Heck's personal checking account at her bank.

Although the indorsements on the checks that Heck deposited did not exactly match the names of the payees—as was required by the bank's policy—the bank allowed Heck to deposit the checks anyway. Because the bank failed to follow its own policy, the court held that the bank had acted in bad faith and could not assert the fictitious payee rule as a defense. The bank was therefore liable for approximately $170,000 of the $250,000 loss suffered by Pavex.[2]

A different court reached a very different result in another case when a dishonest insurance agent took 279 checks written to his employer, Brooks Insurance; indorsed them; and deposited them into his own bank account. The bank in this case had a policy that any checks written to a business entity should be deposited into an account with that business's name. Although the bank violated its own policy when it allowed the agent to deposit the checks into an account with a different name, the court decided that this was not enough to show bad faith. Even though the bank may have acted negligently, the court allowed the bank to assert the fictitious payee rule and avoid liability.[3]

How Should Good Faith Be Tested? There has long been a division of opinion as to how good faith should be measured or tested. At one end of the spectrum of views is the position that the test of good faith should be subjective in nature. In other words, as long as a person acts honestly, no matter how negligent or foolish the conduct may be, that person is acting in good faith. At the other end of the spectrum is the "objective" test of good faith. Under this test, honesty in itself is not enough. A party must also act reasonably under the circumstances. Whereas a fool might pass the subjective test, he or she would not meet the objective test.

Over time, the pendulum seems to have swung from one end of the spectrum to the other. When the UCC was initially drafted, the definition of *good faith* set forth in UCC 1–201(19) established a subjective test for good faith. It defined *good faith* as "honesty in fact in the conduct or transaction concerned." The only UCC article that incorporated a more objective test for good faith was Article 2. Section 2–103(1)(b) defined good faith as both honesty in fact *and* the observance of reasonable commercial standards of fair dealing in the trade. Under this test, a person who acts honestly in fact but does not observe reasonable commercial standards of fair dealing will not meet the good faith requirement.

This more objective measure of good faith has since been incorporated into other articles of the UCC, including Articles 3, 4, and 4A.

Criticisms of the Objective Standard Some critics claim that while the subjective test of "honesty in fact" is manageable, the objective test that requires the "observance of reasonable commercial standards" opens the door to potentially endless litigation. After all, it is difficult to determine what is commercially reasonable in a given context until you hear what others in that commercial situation have to say. Thus, parties to a dispute can nearly always make some kind of good faith argument, and any time the issue is raised, litigation can result.

How Good Faith Standards Can Affect HDC Status Whether the objective or the subjective standard of good faith is used has considerable impact on HDC status, as an example will illustrate. Mitchell was a farmer who operated a multistate farming operation on leased property. Runnells, a grain broker, had sold Mitchell's 2001 grain crop. Mitchell instructed Runnells to use the crop proceeds to draw checks payable to Mitchell's various landlords in fulfillment

2. *Pavex, Inc. v. York Federal Savings and Loan Association*, 716 A.2d 640 (Pa.Super.Ct. 1998).

3. *Continental Casualty Co. v. Fifth/Third Bank*, 418 F.Supp.2d 964 (N.D. Ohio 2006).

of his rent obligations. The checks totaled more than $153,000. The landlords accepted the checks in payment of the farmer's rent—completely unaware that Mitchell had already pledged the proceeds from the sale of his crops as collateral for a loan from Agriliance (security interests will be discussed in Chapter 29). Agriliance filed a lawsuit in a federal court against Runnells and the various landlords for conversion (wrongful taking of personal property—see Chapter 6).

According to the UCC, an HDC takes a negotiable instrument free of any claim to the instrument, including claims of prior secured parties. Thus, the outcome of the case depended on whether Runnells and the landlords were HDCs. Under the subjective standard, the landlords would be HDCs because they had taken the checks without actual knowledge of Agriliance's claim to the crop proceeds. The objective standard, however, dictated a different result. Because it is common for farmers to put their crops up as collateral for loans, the court held that reasonable commercial standards of fair dealing required Mitchell's creditors (Runnells and the landlords) to conduct a search of the public records. Such a search would have revealed the existence of Agriliance's prior secured claim. Runnells and the landlords in this case could not be HDCs because they failed to meet the objective element of good faith. The court, therefore, ruled that Agriliance was entitled to the crop proceeds.[4]

Efficiency versus Due Care

A major problem faced by today's banking institutions is how to verify customer signatures on the billions of checks that are processed by the banking system each month. If a bank fails to verify a signature on a check it receives for payment and the check turns out to be forged, the bank will normally be held liable to its customer for the amount paid. But how can banks possibly examine, item by item, each signature on every check that they pay?

The banks' solution to this problem is simply to not examine all signatures. Instead, computers are programmed to verify signatures only on checks exceeding a certain threshold amount, such as $1,000 or $2,500 or perhaps some higher figure. Checks for less than the threshold amount are selected for signature verification only on a random basis. In other words, serious attention is restricted to serious matters. As a result, many, if not most, checks are paid without signature verification. This practice, which has become an acceptable standard in today's banking industry, is economically efficient for banks. Even though liability costs are sometimes incurred—when forged checks are paid—the total costs involved in verifying the authenticity of each and every signature would be far higher.

Some people have argued that banks using such procedures are not exercising due care in handling their customers' accounts. Under the UCC, banks are held to a standard of "ordinary care." At one time in the banking industry, ordinary care was generally interpreted to mean that a bank had a duty to inspect *all* signatures on checks. But what constitutes ordinary care in today's world? Does a bank exercise ordinary care if it follows the prevailing industry practice of examining signatures on only a few, randomly selected checks payable for under a certain amount? Or does ordinary care still mean that a bank should examine each signature?

DISCUSSION QUESTIONS

1. Because the UCC offers special protection to HDCs, innocent makers of notes or drawers of checks in fraudulent transactions often have no legal recourse. From an ethical standpoint, how could you justify to the "losers" in such situations the provisions of the UCC that fail to protect them? Can you think of a way in which such problems could be handled more fairly or ethically than they are under the UCC?
2. What do you think would result if the law was changed to allow personal defenses to be successfully raised against HDCs? Who would lose, and who would gain? How would such a change in the law affect the flow of commerce in this country?
3. Do you think that the UCC's provisions have struck an appropriate balance between the interests of banks and those of bank customers? Why or why not?

4. *Agriliance, L.L.C. v. Runnells Grain Elevator, Inc.*, 272 F.Supp.2d 800 (S.D. Iowa 2003).

UNIT SIX

Creditors' Rights and Bankruptcy

CONTENTS

CHAPTER 28

Creditors' Rights and Remedies

Normally, creditors have no problem collecting the debts owed to them. When disputes arise over the amount owed, however, or when the debtor simply cannot or will not pay, what happens? What remedies are available to creditors when a debtor **defaults** (fails to pay as promised)? In this chapter, we focus on some basic laws that assist the debtor and creditor in resolving their dispute without the debtor's having to resort to bankruptcy—a topic to be discussed in Chapter 30. In Chapter 29, we will discuss the remedies that are available only to secured creditors (those whose loans are supported or backed by collateral) under Article 9 of the Uniform Commercial Code (UCC).

SECTION 1 Laws Assisting Creditors

Both the common law and statutory laws other than Article 9 of the UCC create various rights and remedies for creditors. We discuss here some of these rights and remedies, including liens, garnishment, creditors' composition agreements, and mortgage foreclosure.

Liens

A **lien** is a claim against a debtor's property that must be satisfied before the property (or its proceeds) is available to satisfy the claims of other creditors. As mentioned, liens may arise under the common law or under statutory law. Statutory liens include *mechanic's liens*, whereas *artisan's liens* were recognized at common law. *Judicial liens* are those that represent a creditor's efforts to collect on a debt before or after a judgment is entered by a court. Liens are a very important tool for creditors because they generally take priority over other claims against the same property (priority of claims will be discussed in depth in Chapter 29).

Mechanic's Liens When a person contracts for labor, services, or materials to be furnished for the purpose of making improvements on real property but does not immediately pay for the improvements, the creditor can place a **mechanic's lien** on the property. This creates a special type of debtor-creditor relationship in which the real estate itself becomes security for the debt.

For example, a painter agrees to paint a house for a homeowner for an agreed-on price to cover labor and materials. If the homeowner cannot pay or pays only a portion of the charges, a mechanic's lien against the property can be created. The painter is the lienholder, and the real property is encumbered (burdened) with the mechanic's lien for the amount owed. If the homeowner does not pay the lien, the property can be sold to satisfy the debt. Notice of the *foreclosure* (the enforcement of the lien) must be given to the debtor in advance, however.

Note that state law governs the procedures that must be followed to create a mechanic's lien. Generally, the lienholder has to file a written notice of lien against the particular property involved. The notice of lien must be filed within a specific time period, measured from the last date on which materials or labor was provided (usually within 60 to 120 days). If the property owner fails to pay the debt, the lienholder is entitled to foreclose on the real estate on which the improvements were made and to sell it to satisfy the amount of the debt. Of course, as mentioned, the lienholder is required by statute to give notice to the owner of the property prior to foreclosure and sale. The sale proceeds are used to pay the debt and the costs of the legal proceedings; the surplus, if any, is paid to the former owner.

Artisan's Liens An **artisan's lien** is a device created at common law through which a creditor can recover payment from a debtor for labor and materials furnished in the repair of personal property. In contrast to a mechanic's lien, an artisan's lien is *possessory*. This means that the lienholder ordinarily must have retained possession of the property and have expressly or impliedly agreed to provide the services on a cash, not a credit, basis. The lien remains in existence as long as the lienholder maintains possession, and the lien is terminated once possession is voluntarily surrendered—unless the surrender is only temporary.

For example, Whitney leaves her diamond ring at the jewelry shop to be repaired and to have her initials engraved on the band. In the absence of an agreement, the jeweler can keep the ring until Whitney pays for the services that the jeweler provides. Should Whitney fail to pay, the jeweler has a lien on Whitney's ring for the amount of the bill and can sell the ring in satisfaction of the lien.

Modern statutes permit the holder of an artisan's lien to foreclose and sell the property subject to the lien to satisfy payment of the debt. As with a mechanic's lien, the lienholder is required to give notice to the owner of the property prior to foreclosure and sale. The sale proceeds are used to pay the debt and the costs of the legal proceedings, and the surplus, if any, is paid to the former owner.[1]

Judicial Liens When a debt is past due, a creditor can bring a legal action against the debtor to collect the debt. If the creditor is successful in the action, the court awards the creditor a judgment against the debtor (usually for the amount of the debt plus any interest and legal costs incurred in obtaining the judgment). Frequently, however, the creditor is unable to collect the awarded amount.

To ensure that a judgment in the creditor's favor will be collectible, the creditor is permitted to request that certain nonexempt property of the debtor be seized to satisfy the debt. (As will be discussed later in this chapter, under state or federal statutes, some kinds of property are exempt from attachment by creditors.) If the court orders the debtor's property to be seized prior to a judgment in the creditor's favor, the court's order is referred to as a *writ of attachment.* If the court orders the debtor's property to be seized following a judgment in the creditor's favor, the court's order is referred to as a *writ of execution.*

Writ of Attachment. In the context of judicial liens, **attachment** refers to a court-ordered seizure and taking into custody of property prior to the securing of a judgment for a past-due debt. (As you will read in Chapter 29, this word has a different meaning in the context of secured transactions. Under UCC 9–203, *attachment* refers to the process through which a security interest becomes effective and enforceable against a debtor with respect to the debtor's collateral.) Normally, attachment is a *prejudgment* remedy, occurring either at the time a lawsuit is filed or immediately thereafter. In order to attach *before* a judgment, a creditor must comply with the specific state's statutory restrictions. The due process clause of the Fourteenth Amendment to the U.S. Constitution also applies and requires that the debtor be given notice and an opportunity to be heard (see Chapter 4).

The creditor must have an enforceable right to payment of the debt under law and must follow certain procedures. Otherwise, the creditor can be liable for damages for wrongful attachment. Typically, the creditor must file with the court an *affidavit* (a written or printed statement, made under oath or sworn to) stating that the debtor has failed to pay and delineating the statutory grounds under which attachment is sought. The creditor must also post a bond to cover at least the court costs, the value of the property attached, and the value of the loss of use of that property suffered by the debtor. When the court is satisfied that all the requirements have been met, it issues a **writ of attachment,** which directs the sheriff or other officer to seize nonexempt property. If the creditor prevails at trial, the seized property can be sold to satisfy the judgment.

Writ of Execution. If a creditor obtains a judgment against the debtor and the debtor will not or cannot pay the judgment, the creditor is entitled to go back to the court and request a writ of execution. A **writ of execution** is an order that directs the sheriff to seize (levy) and sell any of the debtor's nonexempt real or personal property that is within the court's geographic jurisdiction (usually the county in which the courthouse is located). The proceeds of the sale are used to pay the judgment, accrued interest, and the costs of the sale. Any excess is paid to the debtor. The debtor can

1. An artisan's lien has priority over a filed statutory lien (such as a title lien on an automobile or a lien filed under Article 9 of the UCC) and a bailee's lien (such as a storage lien).

pay the judgment and redeem the nonexempt property at any time before the sale takes place. (Because of exemption laws and bankruptcy laws, however, many judgments are virtually uncollectible.)

Garnishment

An order for **garnishment** permits a creditor to collect a debt by seizing property of the debtor that is being held by a third party. In a garnishment proceeding, the third party—the person or entity on whom the garnishment judgment is served—is called the *garnishee*. Typically, the garnishee is the debtor's employer, and the creditor is seeking a judgment so that part of the debtor's usual paycheck will be paid to the creditor. In some situations, however, the garnishee is a third party that holds funds belonging to the debtor (such as a bank) or who has possession of, or exercises control over, funds or other types of property belonging to the debtor. Almost all types of property can be garnished, including tax refunds, pensions, and trust funds—so long as the property is not exempt from garnishment and is in the possession of a third party.

Garnishment Proceedings State law governs garnishment actions, so the specific procedures vary from state to state. According to the laws in many states, the judgment creditor needs to obtain only one order of garnishment, which will then apply continuously to the judgment debtor's weekly wages until the entire debt is paid. Garnishment can be a prejudgment remedy, requiring a hearing before a court, or a postjudgment remedy.

Laws Limiting the Amount of Wages Subject to Garnishment Both federal and state laws limit the amount that can be taken from a debtor's weekly take-home pay through garnishment proceedings.[2] Federal law provides a minimal framework to protect debtors from losing all their income to pay judgment debts.[3] State laws also provide dollar exemptions, and these amounts are often larger than those provided by federal law. Under federal law, an employer cannot dismiss an employee because his or her wages are being garnished.

The question in the following case was whether payments to an independent contractor for services performed could be garnished.

2. A few states (such as Texas) do not permit garnishment of wages by private parties except under a child-support order.

3. For example, the federal Consumer Credit Protection Act, 15 U.S.C. Sections 1601–1693r, provides that a debtor can retain either 75 percent of his or her disposable earnings per week or an amount equivalent to thirty hours of work paid at federal minimum wage rates, whichever is greater.

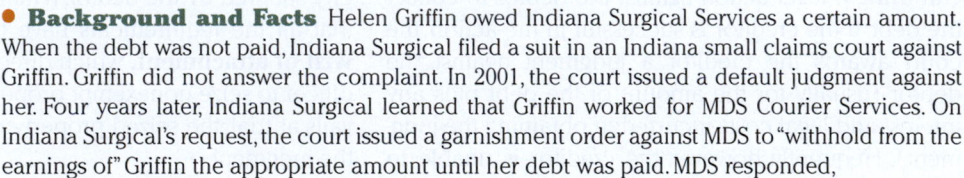

CASE 28.1 Indiana Surgical Specialists v. Griffin

Court of Appeals of Indiana, 2007. 867 N.E.2d 260.

Background and Facts Helen Griffin owed Indiana Surgical Services a certain amount. When the debt was not paid, Indiana Surgical filed a suit in an Indiana small claims court against Griffin. Griffin did not answer the complaint. In 2001, the court issued a default judgment against her. Four years later, Indiana Surgical learned that Griffin worked for MDS Courier Services. On Indiana Surgical's request, the court issued a garnishment order against MDS to "withhold from the earnings of" Griffin the appropriate amount until her debt was paid. MDS responded,

> MDS Courier Services, Inc. employs drivers on a "contract" basis, therefore, drivers are not actual employees, but rather "contracted" to do a particular job. Because of this, we are not responsible for any payroll deductions including garnishments.

Indiana Surgical asked the court to hold MDS in contempt. Dawn Klingenberger, an MDS manager, testified that Griffin was a subcontractor of MDS, called as needed, compensated per job at "thirty-five percent of whatever she does," and paid on a biweekly basis. The court ruled that "the judgment debtor is a subcontractor, and not an employee," and that her earnings could not be garnished. Indiana Surgical appealed to a state intermediate appellate court.

Decision and Rationale The Indiana Court of Appeals reversed the decision of the lower court and remanded the case. The reviewing court pointed out that garnishment in the state of Indiana is applied to "the earnings of an individual." In that state, *earnings* are defined as "com-

CASE 28.1 CONTINUED pensation paid or payable for personal services, whether it be denominated as wages, salary, commissions, bonus, or otherwise." Griffin received periodic payments of compensation for her personal services as a courier. The state intermediate appellate court held that payments for the services of an independent contractor fall within the applicable definition of earnings. Thus, Griffin's earnings as an independent contractor could be garnished.

- **The Ethical Dimension** *Should some persons be exempt from garnishment orders? Explain.*

- **The Legal Environment Dimension** *Building contractors and subcontractors are typically classified as independent contractors. Could payments to these parties also fall within the definition of earnings applied in this case? Discuss.*

Creditors' Composition Agreements

Creditors may contract with the debtor for discharge of the debtor's liquidated debts (debts that are definite, or fixed, in amount) on payment of a sum less than that owed. These agreements are referred to as *composition agreements* or **creditors' composition agreements** and are usually held to be enforceable unless they are formed under duress.

Mortgages

A **mortgage** is a written instrument giving a creditor an interest in (lien on) the debtor's real property as security for the payment of a debt. Financial institutions grant mortgage loans for the purchase of property—usually a dwelling (real property will be discussed in Chapter 48). Given the relatively large sums that many individuals borrow to purchase a home, defaults are not uncommon. Mortgages are recorded with the county in the state where the property is located. Recording ensures that the creditor is officially on record as holding an interest in the property. As a further precaution, most creditors require mortgage life insurance for debtors who do not pay at least 20 percent of the purchase price as a down payment at the time of the transaction.

Mortgage Foreclosure In the event of a debtor's default, the entire mortgage debt becomes due and payable. If the debtor cannot pay, the mortgage holder has the right to foreclose on the mortgaged property. The usual method of foreclosure is by judicial sale of the property, although the statutory methods of foreclosure vary from state to state. If the proceeds of the foreclosure sale are sufficient to cover both the costs of the foreclosure and the mortgage debt, any surplus goes to the debtor. If the sale proceeds are insufficient to cover the foreclosure costs and the mortgage debt, however, the **mortgagee** (the creditor-lender) can seek to recover the difference from the **mortgagor** (the debtor) by obtaining a *deficiency judgment.*

The mortgagee obtains a deficiency judgment in a separate legal action that is pursued subsequent to the foreclosure action. The deficiency judgment entitles the creditor to recover from other property owned by the debtor. Some states do not permit deficiency judgments for certain types of real estate interests.

Redemption Rights Before the foreclosure sale, a defaulting mortgagor can redeem the property by paying the full amount of the debt, plus any interest and costs that have accrued. This is known as the **right of redemption.** Some states even allow a mortgagor to redeem the property within a certain period of time after the foreclosure sale—called a *statutory period of redemption.* In states that allow redemption after the sale, the deed to the property usually is not delivered to the purchaser until the statutory period has expired. *Concept Summary 28.1* on the next page provides a synopsis of the remedies available to creditors.

Mortgage-Lending Practices and Declining Housing Prices Mortgage lenders usually extend credit to high-risk borrowers at higher-than-normal interest rates (involving what are called subprime mortgages) and adjustable-rate mortgages (ARMs). The widespread use of subprime mortgages and ARMs in recent years resulted in some borrowers becoming overextended and therefore unable to pay their loan payments as they came due. In addition, housing prices in the United States dropped, which meant that some borrowers were unable to sell their homes for the amount they owed on the mortgage (sometimes called "being underwater"). As a consequence, there was a sharp increase in the number of home foreclosures in 2007 and 2008, prompting debate about whether the government should step in to rescue debtors from foreclosure.

In 2008, Congress took that step and passed historic and controversial legislation designed to help borrowers facing foreclosure and to bolster the housing market.[4] The law raised the national debt ceiling to $10.6 trillion (an increase of $800 billion) and authorized the U.S. Treasury to rescue the two mortgage company giants, Fannie Mae and Freddie Mac. (These two companies own or guarantee half of the nation's $12 trillion in mortgages and had been experiencing declining stock prices.)

One important provision expanded the Federal Housing Administration (FHA) loan guarantee programs to $300 billion. This was intended to help troubled borrowers refinance, but the FHA can only guarantee new fixed-rate loans if the existing lenders agree to write down loan balances to 90 percent of the homes' current appraised value. Other eligibility rules apply as well, which limit the number of homeowners who benefit from the new law and make implementing its provisions more difficult. Even optimistic forecasts suggest that the law will help only about 400,000 of the estimated 3 million homeowners who will likely lose their homes by the end of 2009.[5]

4. House Resolution 3221. A bill to provide needed housing reform and for other purposes, also known as the Foreclosure Prevention Act of 2008.

SECTION 2 Suretyship and Guaranty

When a third person promises to pay a debt owed by another in the event that the debtor does not pay, either a *suretyship* or a *guaranty* relationship is created. Exhibit 28–1 illustrates these relationships. The third person's credit becomes the security for the debt owed. At common law, there were significant differences in the liability of a *surety* and a *guarantor,* as will be discussed in the following subsections. Today, however, the distinctions outlined here have been abolished in some states.

5. Ron Scherer, "Big housing bill: no rescues soon," *The Christian Science Monitor,* August 1, 2008. David M. Herszenhorn, "Bush Signs Sweeping Housing Bill," *The New York Times,* July 31, 2008; Jeanne Sahadi, "Senate passes landmark housing bill," *CNNMoney.com,* July 26, 2008.

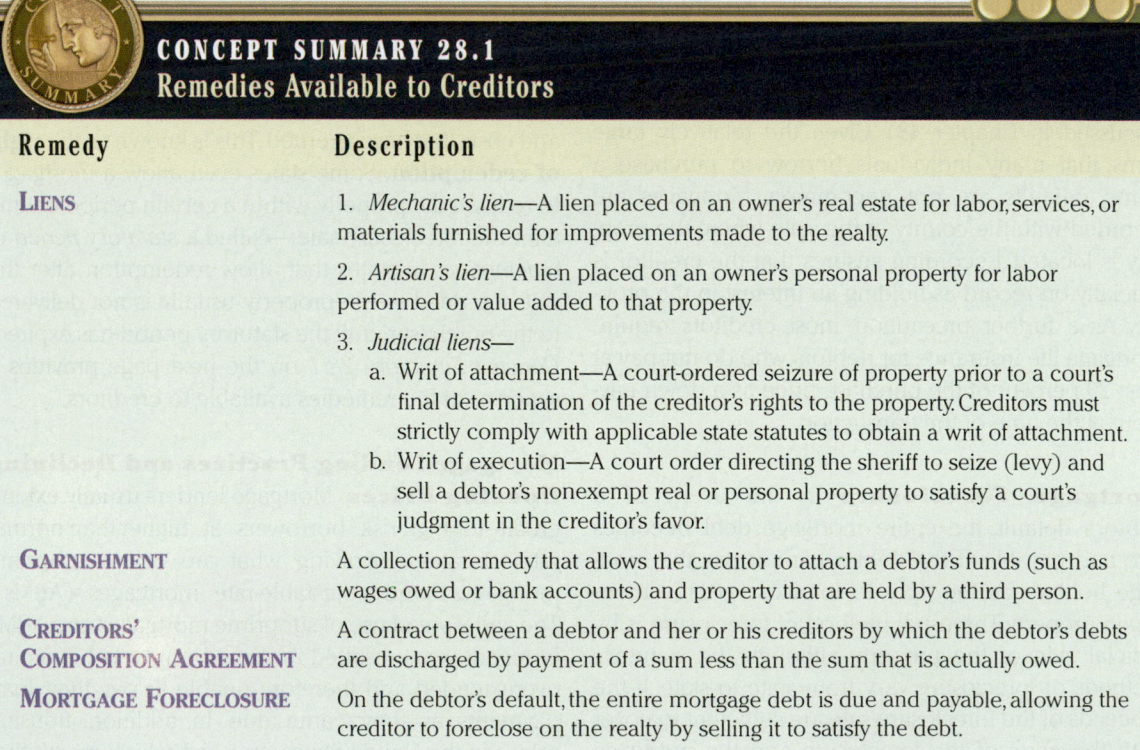

CONCEPT SUMMARY 28.1
Remedies Available to Creditors

Remedy	Description
LIENS	1. *Mechanic's lien*—A lien placed on an owner's real estate for labor, services, or materials furnished for improvements made to the realty. 2. *Artisan's lien*—A lien placed on an owner's personal property for labor performed or value added to that property. 3. *Judicial liens*— a. Writ of attachment—A court-ordered seizure of property prior to a court's final determination of the creditor's rights to the property. Creditors must strictly comply with applicable state statutes to obtain a writ of attachment. b. Writ of execution—A court order directing the sheriff to seize (levy) and sell a debtor's nonexempt real or personal property to satisfy a court's judgment in the creditor's favor.
GARNISHMENT	A collection remedy that allows the creditor to attach a debtor's funds (such as wages owed or bank accounts) and property that are held by a third person.
CREDITORS' COMPOSITION AGREEMENT	A contract between a debtor and her or his creditors by which the debtor's debts are discharged by payment of a sum less than the sum that is actually owed.
MORTGAGE FORECLOSURE	On the debtor's default, the entire mortgage debt is due and payable, allowing the creditor to foreclose on the realty by selling it to satisfy the debt.

EXHIBIT 28–1 • Suretyship and Guaranty Parties

In a suretyship or guaranty arrangement, a third party promises to be responsible for a debtor's obligations. A third party who agrees to be responsible for the debt even if the primary debtor does not default is known as a surety; a third party who agrees to be *secondarily* responsible for the debt—that is, responsible only if the primary debtor defaults—is known as a guarantor. As noted in Chapter 15, normally a promise of guaranty (a collateral, or secondary, promise) must be in writing to be enforceable.

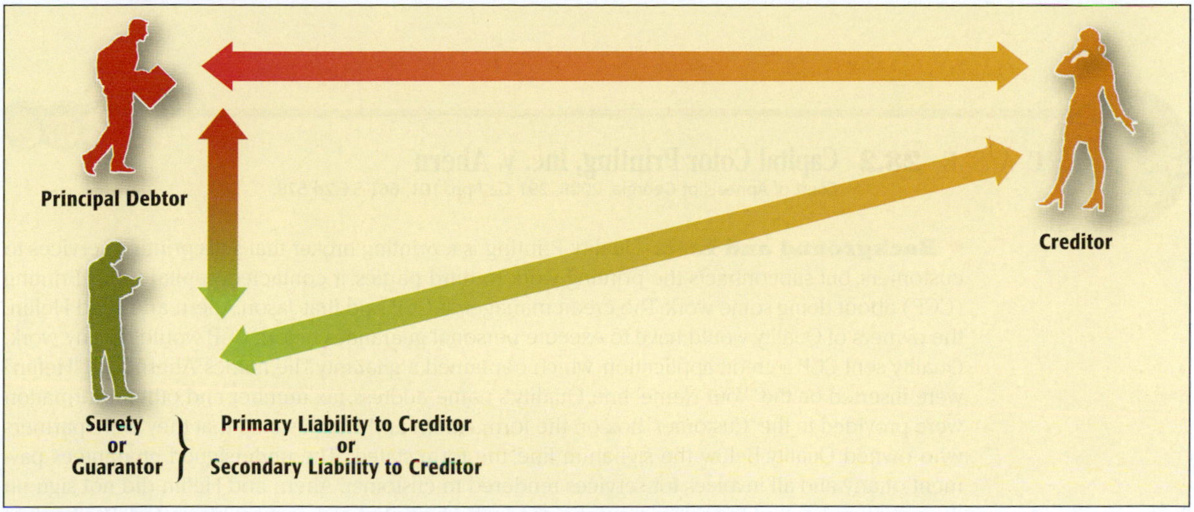

Suretyship

A contract of **suretyship** is a promise made by a third person to be responsible for the debtor's obligation. It is an express contract between the **surety** (the third party) and the creditor. In the strictest sense, the surety is primarily liable for the debt of the principal. This means that the creditor can demand payment from the surety from the moment the debt is due and that the creditor need not exhaust all legal remedies against the principal debtor before holding the surety responsible for payment. Thus, a suretyship contract is not a form of indemnity; that is, it is not merely a promise to make good any loss that a creditor may incur as a result of the debtor's failure to pay. Moreover, a surety agreement does not have to be in writing to be enforceable, although usually such agreements are in writing.

For example, Jason Oller wants to borrow funds from the bank to buy a used car. Because Jason is still in college, the bank will not lend him the funds unless his father, Stuart Oller, who has dealt with the bank before, will cosign the note (add his signature to the note, thereby becoming jointly liable for payment of the debt). When Mr. Oller cosigns the note, he becomes primarily liable to the bank. On the note's due date, the bank can seek payment from Jason Oller, Stuart Oller, or both jointly.

Guaranty

A guaranty contract is similar to a suretyship contract in that it includes a promise to answer for the debt or default of another. There are some significant differences between these two types of contracts, however.

Suretyship versus Guaranty With a suretyship arrangement, the surety is *primarily* liable for the debtor's obligation. With a guaranty arrangement, the **guarantor**—the third person making the guaranty—is *secondarily* liable. The guarantor can be required to pay the obligation only after the principal debtor defaults, and usually only after the creditor has made an attempt to collect from the debtor.

For example, a corporation, BX Enterprises, needs to borrow to meet its payroll. The bank is skeptical about the creditworthiness of BX and requires Dawson, its president, who is a wealthy businessperson and owner of 70 percent of BX Enterprises, to sign an agreement making herself personally liable for payment if BX does not pay off the loan. As a guarantor of the loan, Dawson cannot be held liable until BX Enterprises is in default.

Under the Statute of Frauds, a guaranty contract between the guarantor and the creditor must be in writing to be enforceable unless the *main purpose* exception (discussed in Chapter 15) applies.[6] A suretyship agreement, by contrast, need not be in writing to be enforceable. In other words, surety agreements can be oral, whereas guaranty contracts must be written.

In the following case, the issue was whether a guaranty form for the debt of a partnership was actually made out in the guarantors' names and whether the guarantors signed this form.

6. Briefly, the main purpose exception provides that if the main purpose of the guaranty agreement is to benefit the guarantor, then the contract need not be in writing to be enforceable.

CASE 28.2 Capital Color Printing, Inc. v. Ahern

Court of Appeals of Georgia, 2008. 291 Ga.App. 101, 661 S.E.2d 578.

• **Background and Facts** Quality Printing is a printing broker that sells printing services to customers, but subcontracts the printing work to third parties. It contacted Capital Color Printing (CCP) about doing some work. The credit manager at CCP said that Jason Ahern and Todd Heflin, the owners of Quality, would have to execute personal guaranties before CCP would do any work. Quality sent CCP a credit application, which contained a guaranty. The names "Ahern" and "Heflin" were inserted on the "Your Name" line. Quality's name, address, tax number, and other information were provided in the "Customer" box on the form. Ahern and Heflin stated that they were partners who owned Quality. Below the signature line, the form stated: "The undersigned guarantees payment of any and all invoices for services rendered to customer." Ahern and Heflin did not sign on the signature line, but their names were signed where printed names were requested. The back of the form stated that the guarantors agreed to be liable for any unpaid bills. When Quality did not pay CCP $76,000 for work it had done, CCP sued Ahern, Heflin, and Quality. Ahern and Heflin moved for summary judgment as to CCP's claims against them, contending that the guaranty failed to specifically identify the principal debtor (Quality) and thus was unenforceable as a matter of law because it violated the Statute of Frauds (see Chapter 15). Ahern claimed that he was not liable because he quit working with Heflin and that Heflin put his name on the guaranty without his permission. The trial court agreed with the defendants and dismissed the claim. CCP appealed.

• **Decision and Rationale** The appeals court reversed the lower court's ruling, holding that CCP was entitled to summary judgment against Heflin as guarantor of payment for services performed for Quality. Other issues would be resolved at trial. The partners claimed that the Statute of Frauds was violated because the guaranty did not specify the name of the principal debtor, Quality. That would be true if the document failed to identify Quality at all, but elements of the form taken as a whole were sufficient to identify Quality as the customer that would be the principal debtor. The law does not require a specific format for such forms, only the ability to identify the roles of the parties identified in the document. While no signatures were on the form, the evidence indicated that Heflin filled in both his and Ahern's names as guarantors. Ahern claimed that was forgery and that he had ended his business dealings with Heflin. A jury could explore the details of the business relationship. If forgery had occurred, only Heflin might be liable. If Heflin had apparent authority to bind Ahern to the obligation to CCP, which performed $76,000 in printing services for Quality, then Ahern would also be liable on the guaranty.

• **The Global Dimension** *If a firm was attempting to obtain a guaranty from third parties to a contract with a company in another country, what steps might be taken?*

• **The Ethical Dimension** *At the time that Ahern and Heflin were partners, was it improper for Heflin to insert Ahern's name as a guarantor on the contract with CCP, or was that an acceptable business practice? Explain.*

The Extent and Time of the Guarantor's Liability The guaranty contract terms determine the extent and time of the guarantor's liability. For example, the guaranty can be *continuing,* designed to cover a series of transactions by the debtor. Also, the guaranty can be *unlimited* or *limited* as to time and amount. In addition, the guaranty can be *absolute* or *conditional.* When a guaranty is absolute, the guarantor becomes liable immediately on the debtor's default. With a conditional guaranty, the guarantor becomes liable only on the happening of a certain event. For example, Days Inns of America, Inc., entered into a contract that licensed P&N Enterprises, Inc., to operate a guest lodging facility in Connecticut. The president of P&N Enterprises, Paul Yeh, signed the licensing contract and also signed a guaranty contract, in his individual capacity. Yeh personally guaranteed P&N's obligations under the license agreement, "provided that P&N's tangible net worth was less than $1,000,000 at the time of payment or performance." The condition of that promise (the guaranty) was the tangible net worth requirement.[7]

Businesspersons should be careful when signing guaranty contracts and should explicitly indicate if they are signing on behalf of a company rather than personally. If a corporate officer or director, for example, signs her or his name on a guaranty for a third party without indicating that she or he is signing as a representative of the corporation, that individual might be held personally liable as the guarantor. Although a guaranty contract may be preferable to a suretyship contract in many situations because it creates secondary rather than primary liability, there is still substantial risk involved.

Moreover, depending on the wording used in a guaranty contract, the extent of the guarantor's liability may be unlimited or may continue over a series of transactions. Businesspersons should be absolutely clear about the potential liability before agreeing to serve as a guarantor, and they should contact an attorney for guidance.

Defenses of the Surety and the Guarantor

The defenses of the surety and the guarantor are basically the same. Therefore, the following discussion applies to both, although it refers only to the surety.

Actions Releasing the Surety Certain actions will release the surety from the obligation. If the principal obligation is paid by the debtor or by another person on behalf of the debtor, the surety is discharged from the obligation. Similarly, if valid tender of payment is made, and the creditor for some reason rejects it with knowledge of the surety's existence, then the surety is released from any obligation on the debt.

In addition, if a creditor surrenders the collateral to the debtor or impairs the collateral while knowing of the surety and without the surety's consent, the surety is released to the extent of any loss suffered as a result of the creditor's actions. The primary reason for this requirement is to protect a surety who agreed to become obligated only because the debtor's collateral was in the possession of the creditor.

Finally, making any material modification in the terms of the original contract between the principal debtor and the creditor can operate to discharge a surety's obligations. For example, a gratuitous surety will be completely discharged if the principal debtor and the creditor materially modify the contract without first obtaining the surety's consent. (A *gratuitous surety* is one who receives no consideration in return for acting as a surety, such as a father who agrees to assume responsibility for his daughter's debt obligation.) A surety who is compensated (such as a venture capitalist who will profit from a loan made to the principal debtor) will be discharged from the contract only if the modification is actually or potentially detrimental to the surety.

Defenses of the Principal Debtor Generally, the surety can use any defenses available to the principal debtor to avoid liability on the obligation to the creditor. The ability of the surety to assert any defenses the debtor may have against the creditor is the most important concept in suretyship. It means that most of the defenses available to the debtor are also those of the surety. A few exceptions do exist, however. The surety cannot assert the principal debtor's incapacity or bankruptcy as a defense, nor can the surety assert the statute of limitations as a defense.

7. *Days Inns of America, Inc. v. P&N Enterprises, Inc.,* 2006 WL 2801248 (D.Conn. 2006). For another example of a conditional guaranty, see *Express Recovery Services, Inc. v. Rice,* 2005 UT App 495, 125 P.3d 108 (2005).

Obviously, a surety may also have his or her own defenses—for example, incapacity or bankruptcy. If the creditor fraudulently induced the surety to guarantee the debt, the surety can assert fraud as a defense. In most states, the creditor has a legal duty to inform the surety, prior to the formation of the suretyship contract, of material facts known by the creditor that would substantially increase the surety's risk. Failure to so inform is fraud and makes the suretyship obligation voidable.

Rights of the Surety and the Guarantor

Generally, when the surety or guarantor pays the debt owed to the creditor, the surety or guarantor is entitled to certain rights. Because the rights of the surety and the guarantor are basically the same, the following discussion applies to both.

The Right of Subrogation First, the surety has the legal **right of subrogation.** Simply stated, this means that any right the creditor had against the debtor now becomes the right of the surety. Included are creditor rights in bankruptcy and rights to judgments obtained by the creditor. In short, the surety now stands in the shoes of the creditor and may pursue any remedies that were available to the creditor against the debtor.

The Right of Reimbursement Second, the surety has a **right of reimbursement** from the debtor. Basically, the surety is entitled to receive from the debtor all outlays made on behalf of the suretyship arrangement. Such outlays can include expenses incurred as well as the actual amount of the debt paid to the creditor.

The Right of Contribution Third, in the situation of **co-sureties** (two or more sureties on the same obligation owed by the debtor), a surety who pays more than her or his proportionate share on a debtor's default is entitled to recover from the co-sureties the amount paid above the surety's obligation. This is the **right of contribution.** Generally, a co-surety's liability either is determined by agreement or, in the absence of agreement, is set at the maximum liability under the suretyship contract.

For example, two co-sureties are obligated under a suretyship contract to guarantee the debt of a debtor. Together, the sureties' maximum liability is $25,000. Surety A's maximum liability is $15,000, and surety B's is $10,000. The debtor owes $10,000 and is in default. Surety A pays the creditor the entire $10,000. In the absence of agreement, surety A can recover $4,000 from surety B ($\$10,000/\$25,000 \times \$10,000 = \$4,000$, surety B's obligation).

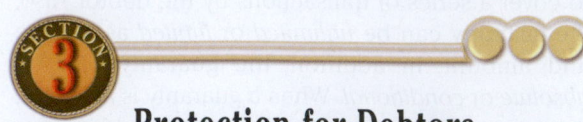

SECTION 3

Protection for Debtors

The law protects debtors as well as creditors. Certain property of the debtor, for example, is exempt under state law from creditors' actions. Consumer protection statutes (see Chapter 44) also protect debtors' rights. Of course, bankruptcy laws, which will be discussed in Chapter 30, are designed specifically to assist debtors in need of help.

In most states, certain types of real and personal property are exempt from execution or attachment. State exemption statutes usually include both real and personal property.

Exempted Real Property

Probably the most familiar exemption is the **homestead exemption.** Each state permits the debtor to retain the family home, either in its entirety or up to a specified dollar amount, free from the claims of unsecured creditors or trustees in bankruptcy. (Note that federal bankruptcy laws after 2005 place a cap of $125,000 for debtors in bankruptcy who have recently moved and are seeking to use state homestead exemptions—see Chapter 30 for details.)

Suppose that Beere owes Veltman $40,000. The debt is the subject of a lawsuit, and the court awards Veltman a judgment of $40,000 against Beere. Beere's homestead is valued at $50,000, and the homestead exemption is $25,000. There are no outstanding mortgages or other liens on his homestead. To satisfy the judgment debt, Beere's family home is sold at public auction for $45,000. The proceeds of the sale are distributed as follows:

1. Beere is given $25,000 as his homestead exemption.
2. Veltman is paid $20,000 toward the judgment debt, leaving a $20,000 deficiency judgment (that is, "leftover debt") that can be satisfied from any other nonexempt property (personal or real) that Beere may own, if permitted by state law.

In a few states, statutes allow the homestead exemption only if the judgment debtor has a family. If a judgment debtor does not have a family, a creditor may be entitled to collect the full amount realized from the sale of the debtor's home.

Exempted Personal Property

Personal property that is most often exempt from satisfaction of judgment debts includes the following:

1. Household furniture up to a specified dollar amount.
2. Clothing and certain personal possessions, such as family pictures or a Bible.
3. A vehicle (or vehicles) for transportation (at least up to a specified dollar amount).
4. Certain classified animals, usually livestock but including pets.
5. Equipment that the debtor uses in a business or trade, such as tools or professional instruments, up to a specified dollar amount.

REVIEWING Creditors' Rights and Remedies

Air Ruidoso, Ltd., operated a commuter airline and air charter service between Ruidoso, New Mexico, and airports in Albuquerque and El Paso. Executive Aviation Center, Inc., provided services for airlines at the Albuquerque International Airport. When Air Ruidoso failed to pay more than $10,000 that it owed on its account for fuel, oil, and oxygen, Executive Aviation took possession of Air Ruidoso's plane, claiming that it had a lien on the plane. Using the information presented in the chapter, answer the following questions.

1. Can Executive Aviation establish an artisan's lien on the plane? Why or why not?
2. Suppose that Executive Aviation files a lawsuit in court against Air Ruidoso for the $10,000 past-due debt. What two methods discussed in this chapter would allow the court to seize Air Ruidoso's plane to satisfy the debt?
3. Suppose that Executive Aviation discovers that Air Ruidoso has sufficient assets in one of its bank accounts to pay the past-due amount. How might Executive Aviation attempt to obtain access to these funds?
4. Suppose that a clause in the contract between Air Ruidoso and Executive Aviation provides that "if the airline becomes insolvent, Braden Fasco, the chief executive officer of Air Ruidoso, agrees to cover its outstanding debts." Is this a suretyship or a guaranty agreement?

TERMS AND CONCEPTS

artisan's lien 531
attachment 531
co-surety 538
creditors' composition agreement 533
default 530
garnishment 532
guarantor 535
homestead exemption 538
lien 530
mechanic's lien 530
mortgage 533
mortgagee 533
mortgagor 533
right of contribution 538
right of redemption 533
right of reimbursement 538
right of subrogation 538
surety 535
suretyship 535
writ of attachment 531
writ of execution 531

QUESTIONS AND CASE PROBLEMS

28–1. Sylvia takes her car to Caleb's Auto Repair Shop. A sign in the window states that all repairs must be paid for in cash unless credit is approved in advance. Sylvia and Caleb agree that Caleb will repair Sylvia's car engine and put in a new transmission. No mention is made of credit. Because Caleb is not sure how much engine repair will be necessary, he refuses to give Sylvia an estimate. He repairs the engine and puts in a new transmission. When Sylvia comes to pick up her car, she learns that the bill is $2,500. Sylvia is furious, refuses to pay Caleb that amount, and demands possession of her car. Caleb insists on payment. Discuss the rights of both parties in this matter.

28–2. QUESTION WITH SAMPLE ANSWER

Kanahara is employed part-time by the Cross-Bar Packing Corp. and earns take-home pay of $400 per week. He is $2,000 in debt to the Holiday Department Store for goods purchased on credit over the past eight months. Most of this property is nonexempt and is now in Kanahara's apartment. Kanahara is in default on his payments to Holiday. Holiday learns that Kanahara has a girlfriend in another state and that he plans on giving her most of this property for Christmas. Discuss what actions are available to and should be taken by Holiday to collect the debt owed by Kanahara.

- **For a sample answer to Question 28–2, go to Appendix I at the end of this text.**

28–3. Natalie is a student at Slippery Stone University. In need of funds to pay for tuition and books, she asks West Bank for a short-term loan. The bank agrees to make a loan if Natalie will have someone who is financially responsible guarantee the loan payments. Sheila, a well-known businessperson and a friend of Natalie's family, calls the bank and agrees to pay the loan if Natalie cannot. Because of Sheila's reputation, the loan is made. Natalie is making the payments, but because of illness she is unable to work for one month. She requests that West Bank extend the loan for three months. West Bank agrees, raising the interest rate for the extended period. Sheila is not notified of the extension (and thus does not consent to it). One month later, Natalie drops out of school. All attempts to collect from Natalie fail. West Bank wants to hold Sheila liable. Discuss the validity of West Bank's claim against Sheila.

28–4. Grant is the owner of a relatively old home valued at $45,000. He notices that the bathtubs and fixtures in both bathrooms are leaking and need to be replaced. He contracts with Jane's Plumbing to replace the bathtubs and fixtures. Jane replaces them, and on June 1 she submits her bill of $4,000 to Grant. Because of financial difficulties, Grant does not pay the bill. Grant's only asset is his home, but his state's homestead exemption is $40,000. Discuss fully Jane's remedies in this situation.

28–5. Guaranty. In 1988, Jamieson-Chippewa Investment Co. entered into a five-year commercial lease with TDM Pharmacy, Inc., for certain premises in Ellisville, Missouri, on which TDM intended to operate a small drugstore. Dennis and Tereasa McClintock ran the pharmacy business. The lease granted TDM three additional five-year options to renew. The lease was signed by TDM and by the McClintocks individually as guarantors. The lease did not state that the guaranty was continuing; in fact, there were no words of guaranty in the lease other than the single word "Guarantors" on the signature page. In 1993, Dennis McClintock, acting as the president of TDM, exercised TDM's option to renew the lease for one term. Three years later, when the pharmacy failed, TDM defaulted on the lease. Jamieson-Chippewa filed a suit in a Missouri state court against the McClintocks for the rent for the rest of the term, based on their guaranty. The McClintocks filed a motion for summary judgment, contending that they had not guaranteed any rent payments beyond the initial five-year term. How should the court rule? Why? [*Jamieson-Chippewa Investment Co. v. McClintock*, 996 S.W.2d 84 (Mo.App.E.D. 1999)]

28–6. Garnishment. Susan Guinta is a real estate salesperson. Smythe Cramer Co. went to an Ohio state court and obtained a garnishment order to attach Guinta's personal earnings. The order was served on Russell Realtors to attach sales commissions that Russell owed to Guinta. Russell objected, arguing that commissions are not personal earnings and are therefore exempt from attachment under a garnishment of personal earnings. An Ohio statute defines *personal earnings* as "money, or any other consideration or thing of value, that is paid or due to a person in exchange for work, labor, or personal services provided by the person to an employer." An *employer* is "a person who is required to withhold taxes out of payments of personal earnings made to a judgment debtor." Russell does not withhold taxes from its salespersons' commissions. Under a federal statute, *earnings* means "compensation paid or payable for personal services, whether denominated as wages, salary, commission, bonus, or otherwise." When the federal definition is more restrictive and results in a smaller garnishment, that definition is controlling. Property other than personal earnings may be subject to garnishment without limits. How should the court rule regarding Russell's objection? Why? [*Smythe Cramer Co. v. Guinta*, 116 Ohio Misc.2d 20, 762 N.E.2d 1083 (2001)]

28–7. CASE PROBLEM WITH SAMPLE ANSWER

Karen and Gerald Baldwin owned property in Rapid City, South Dakota, which they leased to Wyoming Alaska Corp. (WACO) for use as a gas station and convenience store. The lease obligated the Baldwins to make repairs, but WACO was authorized to make necessary repairs. After seventeen years, the property was run-down. The store's customers were tripping over chunks of concrete in the parking lot. An underground gasoline storage tank was leaking. The store's manager hired Duffield Construction, Inc., to install a new tank and make other repairs. The Baldwins saw the new tank sitting on the property before the work began. When WACO paid only a small portion of the cost, Duffield filed a mechanic's lien and asked a South Dakota state court to foreclose on the property. The Baldwins disputed the lien, arguing that they had not requested the work. What is the purpose of a mechanic's lien? Should property owners who do not contract for improvements be liable for the cost under such a lien? How might property owners protect themselves against a lien for work that they do not request? Explain. [*Duffield Construction, Inc. v. Baldwin,* 679 N.W.2d 477 (S.D. 2004)]

- **To view a sample answer for Problem 28-7, go to this book's Web site at www.cengage.com/blaw/jentz, select "Chapter 28," and click on "Case Problem with Sample Answer."**

28-8. Guaranty. In 1981, in Troy, Ohio, Willis and Mary Jane Ward leased a commercial building to Buckeye Pizza Corp. to operate a pizza parlor. Two years later, Buckeye assigned its interest in the building to Ohio, Ltd. In 1985, Ohio sold its pizza business, including its lease of the Wards' building, to NR Dayton Mall, Inc., an Indiana corporation and a subsidiary of Noble Roman's, Inc. As part of the deal, Noble Roman's agreed that it "unconditionally guarantees the performance by N.R. DAYTON MALL, INC., of all its obligations under the . . . Assumption Undertaking." In the "Assumption Undertaking," NR agreed to accept assignment of the Ward lease and to pay Buckeye's and Ohio's expenses if they were sued under it. A dozen years later, NR defaulted on the lease and abandoned the premises. The Wards filed a suit in an Indiana state court against Noble Roman's and others, contending that the firm was liable for NR's default. Noble Roman's argued that it had guaranteed only to indemnify Buckeye and Ohio. The Wards filed a motion for summary judgment. Should the court grant the motion? Explain. [*Noble Roman's, Inc. v. Ward,* 760 N.E.2d 1132 (Ind.App. 2002)]

28-9. Attachment. In 2004 and 2005, Kent Avery, on behalf of his law firm—the Law Office of Kent Avery, LLC—contracted with Marlin Broadcasting, LLC, to air commercials on WCCC-FM, 106.9 "The Rock." Avery, who was the sole member of his firm, helped to create the ads, which solicited direct contact with "defense attorney Kent Avery," featured his voice, and repeated his name and experience to make potential clients familiar with him. When WCCC was not paid for the broadcasts, Marlin filed a suit in a Connecticut state court against Avery and his firm, alleging an outstanding balance of $35,250. Pending the court's hearing of the suit, Marlin filed a request for a writ of attachment. Marlin offered in evidence the parties' contracts, the ads' transcripts, and WCCC's invoices. Avery contended that he could not be held personally liable for the cost of the ads. Marlin countered that the ads unjustly enriched Avery by conferring a personal benefit on him to Marlin's detriment. What is the purpose of attachment? What must a creditor prove to obtain a writ of attachment? Did Marlin meet this test? Explain. [*Marlin Broadcasting, LLC v. Law Office of Kent Avery, LLC,* 101 Conn.App. 638, 922 A.2d 1131 (2007)]

28-10. A QUESTION OF ETHICS

In January 2003, Gary Ryder and Washington Mutual Bank, F.A., executed a note in which Ryder promised to pay $2,450,000, plus interest at a rate that could vary from month to month. The amount of the first payment was $10,933. The note was to be paid in full by February 1, 2033. A mortgage on Ryder's real property at 345 Round Hill Road in Greenwich, Connecticut, in favor of the bank secured his obligations under the note. The note and mortgage required that he pay the taxes on the property, which he did not do in 2004 and 2005. The bank notified him that he was in default and, when he failed to act, paid $50,095.92 in taxes, penalties, interest, and fees. Other disputes arose between the parties, and Ryder filed a suit in a federal district court against the bank, alleging, in part, breach of contract. He charged, among other things, that some of his timely payments were not processed and were subjected to incorrect late fees, forcing him to make excessive payments and ultimately resulting in "non-payment by Ryder." [Ryder v. Washington Mutual Bank, F.A., *501 F.Supp.2d 311 (D.Conn. 2007)*]

(a) The bank filed a counterclaim, seeking to foreclose on the mortgage. What should a creditor be required to prove to foreclose on mortgaged property? What would be a debtor's most effective defense? Which party in this case is likely to prevail on the bank's counterclaim? Why?

(b) The parties agreed to a settlement that released the bank from Ryder's claims and required him to pay the note by January 31, 2007. The court dismissed the suit, but when Ryder did not make the payment, the bank asked the court to reopen the case. The bank then asked for a judgment in its favor on Ryder's complaint, arguing that the settlement had "immediately" released the bank from his claims. Does this seem fair? Why or why not?

LAW ON THE WEB

For updated links to resources available on the Web, as well as a variety of other materials, visit this text's Web site at

www.cengage.com/blaw/jentz

The Legal Information Institute at Cornell University offers a collection of law materials concerning debtor-creditor relationships, including federal statutes and recent Supreme Court decisions on this topic, at

www.law.cornell.edu/wex/index.php/Debtor_and_creditor

The U.S. Department of Labor's Web site contains a page on garnishment and employees' rights in relation to garnishment proceedings at

www.dol.gov/dol/topic/wages/garnishments.htm

Legal Research Exercises on the Web

Go to **www.cengage.com/blaw/jentz**, the Web site that accompanies this text. Select "Chapter 28" and click on "Internet Exercises." There you will find the following Internet research exercises that you can perform to learn more about the topics covered in this chapter.

Internet Exercise 28–1: Legal Perspective
Debtor-Creditor Relations

Internet Exercise 28–2: Management Perspective
Mechanic's Liens

CHAPTER 29

Secured Transactions

Whenever the payment of a debt is guaranteed, or *secured,* by personal property owned by the debtor or in which the debtor has a legal interest, the transaction becomes known as a **secured transaction.** The concept of the secured transaction is as basic to modern business practice as the concept of credit. Logically, sellers and lenders do not want to risk nonpayment, so they usually will not sell goods or lend funds unless the promise of payment is somehow guaranteed. Indeed, business as we know it could not exist without laws permitting and governing secured transactions.

Article 9 of the Uniform Commercial Code (UCC) governs secured transactions as applied to personal property, *fixtures* (certain property that is attached to land—see Chapter 47), accounts, instruments, commercial assignments of $1,000 or more, *chattel paper* (any writing evidencing a debt secured by personal property), agricultural liens, and what are called general intangibles (such as patents and copyrights). Article 9 does not cover the creditor devices, such as liens and mortgages, that were discussed in Chapter 28. Because the revised version of Article 9 has now been adopted by all of the states, we base this chapter's discussion of secured transactions entirely on the provisions of the revised version.

In this chapter, we first look at the terminology of secured transactions. We then discuss how the rights and duties of creditors and debtors are created and enforced under Article 9. As will become evident, the law of secured transactions tends to favor the rights of creditors; to a lesser extent, however, it offers debtors some protections as well.

SECTION 1 The Terminology of Secured Transactions

The UCC's terminology is now uniformly adopted in all documents used in situations involving secured transactions. A brief summary of the UCC's definitions of terms relating to secured transactions follows.

1. A **secured party** is any creditor who has a *security interest* in the *debtor's collateral.* This creditor can be a seller, a lender, a cosigner, or even a buyer of accounts or chattel paper [UCC 9–102(a)(72)].
2. A **debtor** is the party who *owes payment* or other performance of a secured obligation [UCC 9–102(a)(28)].
3. A **security interest** is the *interest* in the collateral (such as personal property, fixtures, or accounts) that *secures payment or performance of an obligation* [UCC 1–201(37)].
4. A **security agreement** is an *agreement* that *creates* or provides for a *security interest* [UCC 9–102(a)(73)].
5. **Collateral** is the *subject* of the *security interest* [UCC 9–102(a)(12)].
6. A **financing statement**—referred to as the UCC-1 form—is the *document that is normally filed* to give *public notice* to *third parties* of the *secured party's security interest* [UCC 9–102(a)(39)].

Together, these definitions form the concept by which a debtor-creditor relationship becomes a secured transaction relationship (see Exhibit 29–1 on the next page).

EXHIBIT 29–1 • Secured Transactions—Concept and Terminology

In a security agreement, a debtor and a creditor agree that the creditor will have a security interest in collateral in which the debtor has rights. In essence, the collateral secures the loan and ensures the creditor of payment should the debtor default.

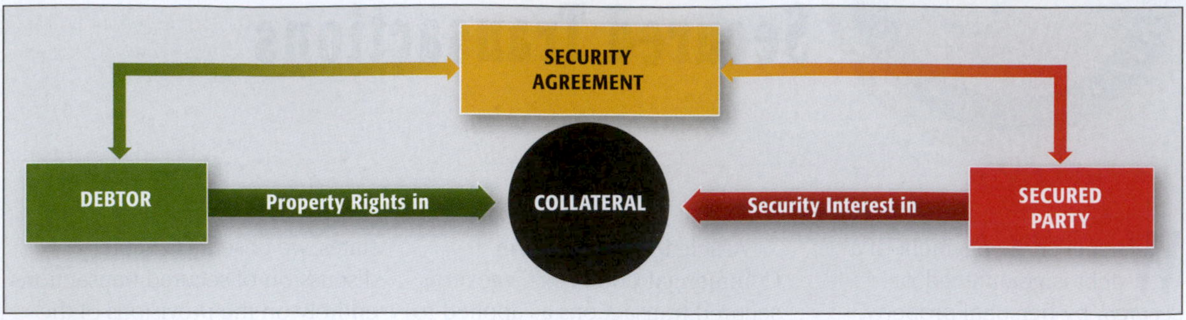

SECTION 2 Creating a Security Interest

A creditor has two main concerns if the debtor defaults: (1) Can the debt be satisfied through the possession and (usually) sale of the collateral? (2) Will the creditor have priority over any other creditors or buyers who may have rights in the same collateral? These two concerns are met through the creation and perfection of a security interest. We begin by examining how a security interest is created.

To become a secured party, the creditor must obtain a security interest in the collateral of the debtor. Three requirements must be met for a creditor to have an enforceable security interest:

1. Either (a) the collateral must be in the possession of the secured party in accordance with an agreement, or (b) there must be a written or authenticated security agreement that describes the collateral subject to the security interest and is signed or authenticated by the debtor.
2. The secured party must give the debtor something of value.
3. The debtor must have rights in the collateral.

Once these requirements have been met, the creditor's rights are said to *attach* to the collateral. **Attachment** gives the creditor an enforceable security interest in the collateral [UCC 9–203].[1]

Written or Authenticated Security Agreement

When the collateral is *not* in the possession of the secured party, the security agreement must be either written or authenticated, and it must describe the collateral. Note here that **authentication** means to sign, execute, or adopt any symbol on an electronic record verifying that the person signing has the intent to adopt or accept the record [UCC 9–102(a)(7)]. If the security agreement is in writing or authenticated, *only the debtor's signature or authentication* is required to create the security interest. The reason authentication is acceptable is to provide for electronic filing (the filing process will be discussed later).

A security agreement must contain a description of the collateral that reasonably identifies it. Generally, such phrases as "all the debtor's personal property" or "all the debtor's assets" would *not* constitute a sufficient description [UCC 9–108(c)].

Secured Party Must Give Value

The secured party must give the debtor something of value. Under the UCC, value can take any of several forms, including a binding commitment to extend credit and, in general, any consideration sufficient to support a simple contract [UCC 1–201(44)]. Normally, the value given by a secured party involves a direct loan or a commitment to sell goods on credit.

Debtor Must Have Rights in the Collateral

The debtor must have rights in the collateral; that is, the debtor must have some ownership interest or right to obtain possession of that collateral. The debtor's rights

1. Note that the term *attachment* has a different meaning in secured transactions than it does in the context of judicial liens, as was mentioned in Chapter 28. In the context of judicial liens, attachment refers to a court-ordered seizure and taking into custody of property prior to the securing of a court judgment for a past-due debt.

can represent either a current or a future legal interest in the collateral. For example, a retail seller–debtor can give a secured party a security interest not only in existing inventory owned by the retailer but also in *future* inventory to be acquired by the retailer.

One common misconception about having rights in the collateral is that the debtor must hold title to it. This is not a requirement. A beneficial interest in a trust (*trusts* will be discussed in Chapter 50), when the trustee holds title to the trust property, can be the subject of a security interest for a loan that a creditor makes to the beneficiary.

SECTION 3 Perfecting a Security Interest

Perfection is the legal process by which secured parties protect themselves against the claims of third parties who may wish to have their debts satisfied out of the same collateral. Whether a secured party's security interest is perfected or unperfected may have serious consequences for the secured party if, for example, the debtor defaults on the debt or files for bankruptcy. What if the debtor has borrowed from two different creditors, using the same property as collateral for both loans? If the debtor defaults on both loans, which of the two creditors has first rights to the collateral? In this situation, the creditor with a perfected security interest will prevail.

Perfection is usually accomplished by filing a financing statement with the office of the appropriate government official. In some circumstances, however, a security interest becomes perfected without the filing of a financing statement.

Where or how to perfect a security interest sometimes depends on the classification or definition of the collateral. Collateral is generally divided into two classifications: *tangible collateral* (collateral that can be seen, felt, and touched) and *intangible collateral* (collateral that consists of or generates rights). Exhibit 29–2 on the following two pages summarizes the various classifications of collateral and the methods of perfecting a security interest in collateral falling within each of those classifications.[2]

2. There are additional classifications, such as agricultural liens, commercial tort claims, and investment property. For definitions of these types of collateral, see UCC 9–102(a)(5), (a)(13), and (a)(49).

Perfection by Filing

The most common means of perfection is by filing a *financing statement*—a document that gives public notice to third parties of the secured party's security interest—with the office of the appropriate government official. The security agreement itself can also be filed to perfect the security interest. The financing statement must provide the names of the debtor and the secured party, and must indicate the collateral covered by the financing statement. A uniform financing statement form (see Exhibit 29–3 on page 548) is now used in all states [UCC 9–521].

Communication of the financing statement to the appropriate filing office, together with the correct filing fee, or the acceptance of the financing statement by the filing officer constitutes a filing [UCC 9–516(a)]. The word *communication* means that the filing can be accomplished electronically [UCC 9–102(a)(18)]. Once completed, filings are indexed in the name of the debtor so that they can be located by subsequent searchers. A financing statement may be filed even before a security agreement is made or a security interest attaches [UCC 9–502(d)].

The Debtor's Name The UCC requires that a financing statement be filed under the name of the debtor [UCC 9–502(a)(1)]. Slight variations in names normally will not be considered misleading if a search of the filing office's records, using a standard computer search engine routinely used by that office, would disclose the filings [UCC 9–506(c)].[3] If the debtor is identified by the correct name at the time of the filing of a financing statement, the secured party's interest retains its priority even if the debtor's name later changes. Because most states use electronic filing systems, UCC 9–503 sets out detailed rules for determining when the debtor's name as it appears on a financing statement is sufficient.

Specific Types of Debtors. For corporations, which are organizations that have registered with the state, the debtor's name on the financing statement must be "the name of the debtor indicated on the public record of the debtor's jurisdiction of organization" [UCC 9–503(a)(1)]. If the debtor is a trust or a

3. If the name listed in the financing statement is so inaccurate that a search using the standard search engine will not disclose the debtor's name, then it is deemed seriously misleading under UCC 9–506. See also UCC 9–507, which governs the effectiveness of financing statements found to be seriously misleading.

trustee with respect to property held in trust, the filed financing statement must disclose this information and must provide the trust's name as specified in its official documents [UCC 9–503(a)(3)]. For all others, the filed financing statement must disclose "the individual or organizational name of the debtor" [UCC 9–503(a)(4)(A)]. As used here, the word *organization* includes unincorporated associations, such as clubs and some churches, as well as joint ventures and general partnerships. If an organizational debtor does not have a group name, the names of the individuals in the group must be listed.

Trade Names. In general, providing only the debtor's trade name (or a fictitious name) in a financing statement is *not* sufficient for perfection [UCC 9–503(c)]. Assume that a loan is being made to a sole proprietorship owned by Peter Jones. The trade, or fictitious, name is Pete's Plumbing. A financing statement filed in the trade name Pete's Plumbing would *not* be sufficient because it does not identify Peter Jones as the actual debtor. As will be discussed in Chapter 35, a sole proprietorship (such as Pete's Plumbing) is not a legal entity distinct from the person who owns it. The reason for this rule is to ensure that the debtor's name on a

EXHIBIT 29–2 • Types of Collateral and Methods of Perfection

Tangible Collateral All things that are movable at the time the security interest attaches (such as livestock) or that are attached to the land, including timber to be cut and growing crops.		Method of Perfection
1. Consumer Goods [UCC 9–301, 9–303, 9–309(1), 9–310(a), 9–313(a)]	Goods used or bought primarily for personal, family, or household purposes—for example, household furniture [UCC 9–102(a)(23)].	For purchase-money security interest, attachment (that is, the creation of a security interest) is sufficient; for boats, motor vehicles, and trailers, filing or compliance with a certificate-of-title statute is required; for other consumer goods, general rules of filing or possession apply.
2. Equipment [UCC 9–301, 9–310(a), 9–313(a)]	Goods bought for or used primarily in business (and not part of inventory or farm products)—for example, a delivery truck [UCC 9–102(a)(33)].	Filing or (rarely) possession by secured party.
3. Farm Products [UCC 9–301, 9–310(a), 9–313(a)]	Crops (including aquatic goods), livestock, or supplies produced in a farming operation—for example, ginned cotton, milk, eggs, and maple syrup [UCC 9–102(a)(34)].	Filing or (rarely) possession by secured party.
4. Inventory [UCC 9–301, 9–310(a), 9–313(a)]	Goods held by a person for sale or under a contract of service or lease; raw materials held for production and work in progress [UCC 9–102(a)(48)].	Filing or (rarely) possession by secured party.
5. Accessions [UCC 9–301, 9–310(a), 9–313(a)]	Personal property that is so attached, installed, or fixed to other personal property (goods) that it becomes a part of these goods—for example, a DVD player installed in an automobile [UCC 9–102(a)(1)].	Filing or (rarely) possession by secured party (same as personal property being attached).

EXHIBIT 29–2 • **Types of Collateral and Methods of Perfection, Continued**

Intangible Collateral Nonphysical property that exists only in connection with something else.		Method of Perfection
1. Chattel Paper [UCC 9–301, 9–310(a), 9–312(a), 9–313(a), 9–314(a)]	A writing or writings (records) that evidence both a monetary obligation and a security interest in goods and software used in goods—for example, a security agreement or a security agreement and promissory note. *Note:* If the record or records consist of information stored in an electronic medium, the collateral is called *electronic chattel paper.* If the information is inscribed on a tangible medium, it is called *tangible chattel paper* [UCC 9–102(a)(11), (a)(31), and (a)(78)].	Filing or possession or control by secured party.
2. Instruments [UCC 9–301, 9–309(4), 9–310(a), 9–312(a) and (e), 9–313(a)]	A negotiable instrument, such as a check, note, certificate of deposit, or draft, or other writing that evidences a right to the payment of money and is not a security agreement or lease but rather a type that can ordinarily be transferred (after indorsement, if necessary) by delivery [UCC 9–102(a)(47)].	Except for temporary perfected status, filing or possession. For the sale of promissory notes, perfection can be by attachment (automatically on the creation of the security interest).
3. Accounts [UCC 9–301, 9–309(2) and (5), 9–310(a)]	Any right to receive payment for the following: (a) any property, real or personal, sold, leased, licensed, assigned, or otherwise disposed of, including intellectual licensed property; (b) services rendered or to be rendered, such as contract rights; (c) policies of insurance; (d) secondary obligations incurred; (e) use of a credit card; (f) winnings of a government-sponsored or government-authorized lottery or other game of chance; and (g) health-care insurance receivables, defined as an interest or claim under a policy of insurance to payment for health-care goods or services provided [UCC 9–102(a)(2) and (a)(46)].	Filing required except for certain assignments that can be perfected by attachment (automatically on the creation of the security interest).
4. Deposit Accounts [UCC 9–104, 9–304, 9–312(b), 9–314(a)]	Any demand, time, savings, passbook, or similar account maintained with a bank [UCC 9–102(a)(29)].	Perfection by control, such as when the secured party is the bank in which the account is maintained or when the parties have agreed that the secured party can direct the disposition of funds in a particular account.
5. General Intangibles [UCC 9–301, 9–309(3), 9–310(a) and (b)(8)]	Any personal property (or debtor's obligation to make payments on such) other than that defined above [UCC 9–102(a)(42)], including software that is independent from a computer or other good [UCC 9–102(a)(44), (a)(61), and (a)(75)].	Filing only (for copyrights, with the U.S. Copyright Office), except a sale of a payment intangible by attachment (automatically on the creation of the security interest).

EXHIBIT 29–3 • The Uniform Financing Statement

UCC FINANCING STATEMENT

FOLLOW INSTRUCTIONS (front and back) CAREFULLY

A. NAME & PHONE OF CONTACT AT FILER (optional)

B. SEND ACKNOWLEDGEMENT TO: (Name and Address)

THE ABOVE SPACE IS FOR FILING OFFICE USE ONLY

1. DEBTOR'S EXACT FULL LEGAL NAME - Insert only one debtor name (1a or 1b) - do not abbreviate or combine names

1a. ORGANIZATION'S NAME				
OR 1b. INDIVIDUAL'S LAST NAME	FIRST NAME		MIDDLE NAME	SUFFIX
1c. MAILING ADDRESS	CITY	STATE	POSTAL CODE	COUNTRY
1d. TAX ID# SSN OR EIN / ADDL INFO RE ORGANIZATION DEBTOR / 1e. TYPE OF ORGANIZATION	1f. JURISDICTION OF ORGANIZATION	1g. ORGANIZATIONAL ID #, if any		☐ NONE

2. ADDITIONAL DEBTOR'S EXACT FULL LEGAL NAME - Insert only one debtor name (2a or 2b) - do not abbreviate or combine names

2a. ORGANIZATION'S NAME				
OR 2b. INDIVIDUAL'S LAST NAME	FIRST NAME		MIDDLE NAME	SUFFIX
2c. MAILING ADDRESS	CITY	STATE	POSTAL CODE	COUNTRY
2d. TAX ID# SSN OR EIN / ADDL INFO RE ORGANIZATION DEBTOR / 2e. TYPE OF ORGANIZATION	2f. JURISDICTION OF ORGANIZATION	2g. ORGANIZATIONAL ID #, if any		☐ NONE

3. SECURED PARTY'S NAME - (or NAME of TOTAL ASSIGNOR S/P) Insert only one secured party name (3a or 3b)

3a. ORGANIZATION'S NAME				
OR 3b. INDIVIDUAL'S LAST NAME	FIRST NAME		MIDDLE NAME	SUFFIX
3c. MAILING ADDRESS	CITY	STATE	POSTAL CODE	COUNTRY

4. This FINANCING STATEMENT covers the following collateral:

5. ALTERNATIVE DESIGNATION (if applicable) ☐ LESSEE/LESSOR ☐ CONSIGNEE/CONSIGNOR ☐ BAILEE/BAILOR ☐ SELLER/BUYER ☐ AG. LIEN ☐ NON-UCC FILING

6. ☐ This FINANCING STATEMENT is to be filed [for record] (or recorded) in the REAL ESTATE RECORDS. Attach Addendum (if applicable)

7. Check to REQUEST SEARCH REPORT(S) on Debtor(s) (ADDITIONAL FEE) (optional) ☐ All Debtors ☐ Debtor 1 ☐ Debtor 2

OPTIONAL FILER REFERENCE DATA

NATIONAL UCC FINANCING STATEMENT (FORM UCC1) (REV. 07/29/98) financing statement is one that prospective lenders can locate and recognize in future searches.

Changes in the Debtor's Name If the debtor's name changes, the financing statement remains effective for collateral the debtor acquired before or within four months after the name change. Unless an amendment to the financing statement is filed within this four-month period, collateral acquired by the debtor after the four-month period is unperfected [UCC 9–507(b) and (c)]. A one-page uniform financing statement amendment form is available for filing name changes and for other purposes (see the discussion of amendments later in this chapter) [UCC 9–521].

In today's business climate, debtors frequently change their trade names. This can make it difficult to find out whether the debtor's collateral is subject to a prior perfected security interest. Businesspersons should keep this in mind when making loans or extending credit to a customer. When searching the records, find out if the prospective debtor has used any other names in the past and include those former names in your search. Remember that the key to determining if a security interest has been perfected is whether the financing statement adequately notifies other potential creditors that a security interest exists. If a search of the records using the debtor's correct name would disclose the interest, the filing generally is sufficient. Making sure that no other creditor has a prior interest in the property being used as collateral, and filing the financing statement under the correct name, are basic steps that can prevent disputes.

Description of the Collateral The UCC requires that both the security agreement and the financing statement contain a description of the collateral in which the secured party has a security interest. The security agreement must describe the collateral because no security interest in goods can exist unless the parties agree on which goods are subject to the security interest. The financing statement must also describe the collateral to provide public notice of the fact that certain goods of the debtor are subject to a security interest. Other parties who might later wish to lend funds to the debtor or buy the collateral can thus learn of the security interest by checking with the state or local office in which a financing statement for that type of collateral would be filed. For land-related security interests, a legal description of the realty is also required [UCC 9–502(b)].

Sometimes, the descriptions in the two documents vary, with the description in the security agreement being more precise than the description in the financing statement, which is allowed to be more general. For example, a security agreement for a commercial loan to a manufacturer may list all of the manufacturer's equipment subject to the loan by serial number, whereas the financing statement may simply state "all equipment owned or hereafter acquired." The UCC permits broad, general descriptions in the financing statement, such as "all assets" or "all personal property." Usually, whenever the description in a financing statement accurately describes the agreement between the secured party and the debtor, the description is sufficient [UCC 9–504].

Where to File In most states, a financing statement must be filed centrally in the appropriate state office, such as the office of the secretary of state, in the state where the debtor is located. Filing in the county where the collateral is located is required only when the collateral consists of timber to be cut; fixtures; or items to be extracted, such as oil, coal, gas, and minerals [UCC 9–301(3) and (4), 9–502(b)].

The state in which a financing statement should be filed depends on the *debtor's location,* not the location of the collateral (as was required under the unrevised Article 9) [UCC 9–301]. The debtor's location is determined as follows [UCC 9–307]:

1. For an *individual debtor,* it is the state of the debtor's principal residence.
2. For an organization registered with the state, such as a corporation or limited liability company, it is the state in which the organization is registered. For example, if a debtor is incorporated in Delaware and has its chief executive office in New York, a secured party would file the financing statement in Delaware because that is where the debtor's business is registered.
3. For all other entities, it is the state in which the business is located or, if the debtor has more than one office, the place from which the debtor manages its business operations and affairs (its chief executive offices).

Consequences of an Improper Filing Any improper filing renders the secured party unperfected and reduces the secured party's claim in bankruptcy to that of an unsecured creditor. For example, if the debtor's name on the financing statement is inaccurate or if the collateral is not sufficiently described on the filing statement, the filing may not be effective. The following case provides an illustration.

CASE 29.1 Corona Fruits & Veggies, Inc. v. Frozsun Foods, Inc.

Court of Appeal of California, Second District, Division 6, 2006.
143 Cal.App.4th 319, 48 Cal.Rptr.3d 868.

Background and Facts In July 2001, Corona Fruits & Veggies, Inc., and Corona Marketing Company sublet farmland in Santa Barbara County, California, to Armando Munoz Juarez, a strawberry farmer. The Corona companies also loaned funds to Juarez for payroll and production expenses. The sublease and other documents involved in the transaction set out Juarez's full name, but Juarez generally went by the name "Munoz" and signed the sublease "Armando Munoz." The Coronas filed UCC-1 financing statements that identified the debtor as "Armando Munoz." In December, Juarez contracted to sell strawberries to Frozsun Foods, Inc., which advanced funds secured by a financing statement that identified the debtor as "Armando Juarez." By the next July, Juarez owed the Coronas $230,482.52 and Frozsun $19,648.52. When Juarez did not repay the Coronas, they took possession of the farmland, harvested and sold the strawberries, and kept the proceeds. The Coronas and Frozsun filed a suit in a California state court against Juarez to collect the rest of his debt. The court ruled that Frozsun's interest took priority because only its financing statement was recorded properly. The Coronas appealed to a state intermediate appellate court.

Decision and Rationale The state intermediate appellate court affirmed the lower court's ruling. "Shakespeare asked, 'What's in a name?' We supply an answer * * * : Everything when the last name is true and nothing when the last name is false." The appellate court recognized that "minor errors in a UCC financing statement do not affect the effectiveness of the financing statement." It is only when "errors render the document seriously misleading to other creditors" that the effectiveness of a statement is undercut. "When a creditor files a UCC-1 financing statement, the debtor's true last name is crucial because the financing statements are indexed by last names. A subsequent creditor who loans [funds] to a debtor with the same name is put on notice that its lien is secondary." In this case, Juarez's identification cards and tax returns stated his true, full name, and the Coronas identified him by this name in their contracts, business records, and checks, and even in their pleadings filed with the court. The Coronas could have used this name in their financing statements, too, to protect the priority of their security interests, but they did not. Frozsun searched the UCC records under the name "Juarez" and did not find the Coronas' statements. For these reasons, Frozsun's interest was superior.

The Legal Environment Dimension *Under what circumstances might a financing statement be considered effective even if it does not identify the debtor correctly?*

The Global Dimension *In most Latin American countries, a person's surname consists of the father's name followed by the mother's name. Should this fact have changed the result in this case? Why or why not?*

Perfection without Filing

In two types of situations, security interests can be perfected without filing a financing statement. The first occurs when the collateral is transferred into the possession of the secured party. The second occurs when the security interest is one of a limited number under the UCC that can be perfected on attachment (without a filing and without having to possess the goods) [UCC 9–309]. The phrase *perfected on attachment* means that these security interests are automatically perfected at the time of their creation. Two of the most common security interests that are perfected on attachment are a *purchase-money security interest* in consumer goods (defined and explained below) and an assignment of a beneficial interest in a decedent's estate [UCC 9–309(1), (13)].

Perfection by Possession In the past, one of the most frequently used means of obtaining financing under the common law was to **pledge** certain collateral as security for the debt and transfer the collateral into the creditor's possession. When the debt was paid, the collateral was returned to the debtor. Although the debtor usually entered into a written security agreement, oral security agreements were also enforceable as long as the secured party possessed the collateral. Article 9 of the UCC retained the common law pledge and the principle that the security agreement need not be in writing to be enforceable if the collateral is transferred to the secured party [UCC 9–310, 9–312(b), 9–313].

For most collateral, possession by the secured party is impractical because it denies the debtor the right to use or derive income from the property to pay off the debt. Suppose that a farmer takes out a loan to finance the purchase of a piece of heavy farm equipment needed to harvest crops and uses the equipment as collateral. Clearly, the purpose of the purchase would be defeated if the farmer transferred the collateral into the creditor's possession. Certain items, however, such as stocks, bonds, instruments, and jewelry, are commonly transferred into the creditor's possession when they are used as collateral for loans.

Perfection by Attachment—The Purchase-Money Security Interest in Consumer Goods Under the UCC, fourteen types of security interests are perfected automatically at the time they are created [UCC 9–309]. The most common of these is the **purchase-money security interest (PMSI).** A PMSI in consumer goods is created when a person buys goods primarily for personal, family, or household purposes, and the seller or lender agrees to extend credit for part or all of the purchase price of the goods. The entity that extends the credit and obtains the PMSI can be either the seller (a store, for example) or a financial institution that lends the buyer the funds with which to purchase the goods [UCC 9–102(a)(2)].

Automatic Perfection. A PMSI in consumer goods is perfected automatically at the time of a credit sale—that is, at the time the PMSI is created. Suppose that Jamie wants to purchase a new high-definition television set from ABC Television, Inc. The purchase price is $2,500. Not being able to pay the entire amount in cash, Jamie signs a purchase agreement to pay $1,000 down and $100 per month until the balance plus interest is fully paid. ABC is to retain a security interest in the purchased goods until full payment has been made. Because the security interest was created as part of the purchase agreement, it is a PMSI. ABC does not need to do anything else to perfect its security interest.

Exceptions to the Rule of Automatic Perfection. There are two exceptions to this rule of automatic perfection for PMSIs. First, certain types of security interests that are subject to other federal or state laws may require additional steps to be perfected [UCC 9–311]. For example, many jurisdictions have certificate-of-title statutes that establish perfection requirements for security interests in certain goods, including automobiles, trailers, boats, mobile homes, and farm tractors. If a consumer in these jurisdictions purchases a boat, for example, the secured party will need to file a certificate of title with the appropriate state official to perfect the PMSI. A second exception involves PMSIs in nonconsumer goods, such as livestock or a business's inventory, which are not automatically perfected (these types of PMSIs are discussed later in this chapter in the context of priorities) [UCC 9–324].

Effective Time Duration of Perfection

A financing statement is effective for five years from the date of filing [UCC 9–515]. If a **continuation statement** is filed *within six months prior to* the expiration date, the effectiveness of the original statement is continued for another five years, starting with the expiration date of the first five-year period [UCC 9–515(d), (e)]. The effectiveness of the statement can be continued in the same manner indefinitely. Any attempt to file a continuation statement outside the six-month window will render the continuation ineffective, and the perfection will lapse at the end of the five-year period.

If a financing statement lapses, the security interest that had been perfected by the filing now becomes unperfected. A purchaser for value can take the property that was used as collateral as if the security interest had never been perfected [UCC 9–515(c)]. For a synopsis of the rules for creating and perfecting a security interest, see *Concept Summary 29.1* on the next page.

CONCEPT SUMMARY 29.1
Creating and Perfecting a Security Interest

Concept	Description
Creating a Security Interest	1. Unless the creditor has possession of the collateral, there must be a written or authenticated security agreement signed or authenticated by the debtor and describing the collateral subject to the security interest. 2. The secured party must give value to the debtor. 3. The debtor must have rights in the collateral—some ownership interest or right to obtain possession of the specified collateral.
Perfecting a Security Interest	1. *Perfection by filing*—The most common method of perfection is by filing a financing statement containing the names of the secured party and the debtor and indicating the collateral covered by the financing statement. a. Communication of the financing statement to the appropriate filing office, together with the correct filing fee, constitutes a filing. b. The financing statement must be filed under the name of the debtor; fictitious (trade) names normally are not sufficient. 2. *Perfection without filing*— a. By transfer of collateral—The debtor can transfer possession of the collateral to the secured party. For example, a *pledge* is this type of transfer. b. By attachment—A limited number of security interests are perfected by attachment, such as a purchase-money security interest (PMSI) in consumer goods. If the secured party has a PMSI in consumer goods (bought for personal, family, or household purposes), the secured party's security interest is perfected automatically.

SECTION 4

The Scope of a Security Interest

In addition to covering collateral already in the debtor's possession, a security agreement can cover various other types of property, including the proceeds of the sale of collateral, after-acquired property, and future advances.

Proceeds

Proceeds means whatever is received when collateral is sold or disposed of in some other way [UCC 9–102(a)(64)]. A security interest in the collateral gives the secured party a security interest in the proceeds acquired from the sale of that collateral. For example, suppose that a bank has a perfected security interest in the inventory of a retail seller of heavy farm machinery. The retailer sells a tractor out of this inventory to a farmer, who is by definition *a buyer in the ordinary course of business.* The farmer agrees, in a security agreement, to make monthly payments to the retailer for a period of twenty-four months. If the retailer should go into default on the loan from the bank, the bank is entitled to the remaining payments the farmer owes to the retailer as proceeds.

A security interest in proceeds perfects automatically on the *perfection* of the secured party's security interest in the original collateral and remains perfected for twenty days after the debtor receives the proceeds. One way to extend the twenty-day automatic perfection period is to provide for such extended coverage in the original security agreement [UCC 9–315(c), (d)]. This is typically done when the collateral is the type that is likely to be sold, such as a retailer's inventory—for example, of computers or DVD players. The UCC also permits a security interest in identifiable cash proceeds to remain perfected after twenty days [UCC 9–315(d)(2)].

After-Acquired Property

After-acquired property is property that the debtor acquired after the execution of the security agreement. The security agreement may provide for a security interest in after-acquired property [UCC 9–204(1)]. This is particularly useful for inventory financing arrangements because a secured party whose security interest is in existing inventory knows that the debtor will sell that inventory, thereby reducing the collateral subject to the security interest.

Generally, the debtor will purchase new inventory to replace the inventory sold. The secured party wants this newly acquired inventory to be subject to the original security interest. Thus, the after-acquired property clause continues the secured party's claim to any inventory acquired thereafter. This is not to say that the original security interest will take priority over the rights of all other creditors with regard to this after-acquired inventory, as will be discussed later.

To illustrate: Amato buys factory equipment from Bronson on credit, giving as security an interest in all of her equipment—both what she is buying and what she already owns. The security agreement with Bronson contains an after-acquired property clause. Six months later, Amato pays cash to another seller of factory equipment for additional equipment. Six months after that, Amato goes out of business before she has paid off her debt to Bronson. Bronson has a security interest in all of Amato's equipment, even the equipment bought from the other seller.

Future Advances

Often, a debtor will arrange with a bank to have a *continuing line of credit* under which the debtor can borrow funds intermittently. Advances against lines of credit can be subject to a properly perfected security interest in certain collateral. The security agreement may provide that any future advances made against that line of credit are also subject to the security interest in the same collateral [UCC 9–204(c)]. Future advances need not be of the same type or otherwise related to the original advance to benefit from this type of **cross-collateralization.**[4] Cross-collateralization occurs when an asset that is not the subject of a loan is used to collateralize that loan.

For example, Stroh is the owner of a small manufacturing plant with equipment valued at $1 million. He has an immediate need for $40,000 of working capital, so he obtains a loan from Midwestern Bank and signs a security agreement, putting up all of his equipment as security. The bank properly perfects its security interest. The security agreement provides that Stroh can borrow up to $500,000 in the future, using the same equipment as collateral for any future advances. In this situation, Midwestern Bank does not have to execute a new security agreement and perfect a security interest in the collateral each time an advance is made, up to a cumulative total of $500,000. For priority purposes, each advance is perfected as of the date of the *original* perfection.

The Floating-Lien Concept

A security agreement that provides for a security interest in proceeds, in after-acquired property, or in collateral subject to future advances by the secured party (or in all three) is often characterized as a **floating lien.** This type of security interest continues in the collateral or proceeds even if the collateral is sold, exchanged, or disposed of in some other way.

A Floating Lien in Inventory Floating liens commonly arise in the financing of inventories. A creditor is not interested in specific pieces of inventory, which are constantly changing, so the lien "floats" from one item to another, as the inventory changes.

Consider an example. Cascade Sports, Inc., a corporation formed in Oregon, operates as a cross-country ski dealer and has a line of credit with Portland First Bank to finance an inventory of cross-country skis. Cascade and Portland First enter into a security agreement that provides for coverage of proceeds, after-acquired inventory, present inventory, and future advances. Portland First perfects its security interest in the inventory by filing centrally with the office of the secretary of state in Oregon. One day, Cascade sells a new pair of the latest cross-country skis and receives a used pair in trade. That same day, Cascade purchases two new pairs of cross-country skis from a local manufacturer for cash. Later that day, to meet its payroll, Cascade borrows $8,000 from Portland First Bank under the security agreement.

Portland First gets a perfected security interest in the used pair of skis under the proceeds clause, has a perfected security interest in the two new pairs of skis purchased from the local manufacturer under the after-acquired property clause, and has the new

4. See Official Comment 5 to UCC 9–204.

amount of funds advanced to Cascade secured on all of the above collateral by the future-advances clause. All of this is accomplished under the original perfected security interest. The various items in the inventory have changed, but Portland First still has a perfected security interest in Cascade's inventory. Hence, it has a floating lien on the inventory.

A Floating Lien in a Shifting Stock of Goods The concept of the floating lien can also apply to a shifting stock of goods. The lien can start with raw materials; follow them as they become finished goods and inventories; and continue as the goods are sold and are turned into accounts receivable, chattel paper, or cash.

SECTION 5 Priorities

When more than one party claims an interest in the same collateral, which has priority? The UCC sets out detailed rules to answer this question. Although in many situations the party who has a perfected security interest will have priority, there are exceptions that give priority rights to another party, such as a buyer in the ordinary course of business.

General Rules of Priority

The basic rule is that when more than one security interest has been perfected in the same collateral, the first security interest to be perfected (or filed) has priority over any security interests that are perfected later. If only one of the conflicting security interests has been perfected, then that security interest has priority. If none of the security interests have been perfected, then the first security interest that attaches has priority. The UCC's rules of priority can be summarized as follows:

1. *A perfected security interest has priority over unsecured creditors and unperfected security interests.* When two or more parties have claims to the same collateral, a perfected secured party's interest has priority over the interests of most other parties [UCC 9–322(a)(2)]. This includes priority to the proceeds from a sale of collateral resulting from a bankruptcy (giving the perfected secured party rights superior to those of the bankruptcy trustee as discussed in Chapter 30).
2. *Conflicting perfected security interests.* When two or more secured parties have perfected security interests in the same collateral, generally the first to perfect (by filing or taking possession of the collateral) has priority [UCC 9–322(a)(1)].
3. *Conflicting unperfected security interests.* When two conflicting security interests are unperfected, the first to attach (be created) has priority [UCC 9–322(a)(3)]. This is sometimes called the "first-in-time" rule.

Exceptions to the General Rule

Under some circumstances, on the debtor's default, the perfection of a security interest will not protect a secured party against certain other third parties having claims to the collateral. For example, the UCC provides that in some instances a PMSI, properly perfected,[5] will prevail over another security interest in after-acquired collateral, even though the other was perfected first. We discuss several significant exceptions to the general rules of priority in the following subsections.

Buyers in the Ordinary Course of Business Under the UCC, a person who buys "in the ordinary course of business" takes the goods free from any security interest created by the seller *even if the security interest is perfected and the buyer knows of its existence* [UCC 9–320(a)]. In other words, a buyer in the ordinary course will have priority even if a previously perfected security interest exists as to the goods. The rationale for this rule is obvious: if buyers could not obtain the goods free and clear of any security interest the merchant had created, for example, in inventory, the unfettered flow of goods in the marketplace would be hindered. Note that the buyer can know about the existence of a perfected security interest, so long as he or she does not know that buying the goods violates the rights of any third party.

The UCC defines a *buyer in the ordinary course of business* as any person who in good faith, and without knowledge that the sale violates the rights of another in the goods, buys in ordinary course from a person in the business of selling goods of that kind [UCC 1–201(9)]. For example, on August 1 West Bank perfects a security interest in all of Best Television's existing inventory and any inventory thereafter acquired. On September 1, Carla, a student at Central University, purchases one of the television sets in

5. Recall that, with some exceptions (such as motor vehicles), a PMSI in *consumer goods* is automatically perfected—no filing is necessary. A PMSI that is *not* in consumer goods must still be perfected, however.

Best's inventory. If, on December 1, Best goes into default, can West Bank repossess the television set sold to Carla? The answer is no, because Carla is a buyer in the ordinary course of business (Best is in the business of selling goods of that kind) and takes the television free and clear of West Bank's perfected security interest. This is true even if Carla knew that West Bank had a security interest in Best's inventory when she purchased the TV.

PMSI in Goods Other Than Inventory and Livestock An important exception to the first-in-time rule involves certain types of collateral, such as equipment, that is not inventory (or livestock) and in which one of the secured parties has a perfected PMSI [UCC 9–324(a)]. Suppose that Sandoval borrows funds from West Bank, signing a security agreement in which she puts up all of her present and after-acquired equipment as security. On May 1, West Bank perfects this security interest (which is not a PMSI). On July 1, Sandoval purchases a new piece of equipment from Zylex Company on credit, signing a security agreement. The delivery date for the new equipment is August 1.

Zylex thus has a PMSI in the new equipment (that is not part of its inventory), but the PMSI is not in consumer goods and thus is not automatically perfected. If Sandoval defaults on her payments to both West Bank and Zylex, which of them has priority with regard to the new piece of equipment? Generally, West Bank would have priority because its interest perfected first in time. In this situation, however, Zylex has a PMSI, and provided that Zylex perfected its interest in the equipment within twenty days after Sandoval took possession on August 1, Zylex has priority.

PMSI in Inventory Another important exception to the first-in-time rule has to do with security interests in inventory [UCC 9–324(b)]. For example, on May 1, SNS Television borrows funds from West Bank. SNS signs a security agreement, putting up all of its present inventory and any inventory thereafter acquired as collateral. West Bank perfects its interest (not a PMSI) on that date. On June 10, SNS buys new inventory from Martin, Inc., a manufacturer, to use for its Fourth of July sale. SNS makes a down payment for the new inventory and signs a security agreement giving Martin a PMSI in the new inventory as collateral for the remaining debt. Martin delivers the inventory to SNS on June 28. Because of a hurricane in the area, SNS's Fourth of July sale is a disaster, and most of its inventory remains unsold. In August, SNS defaults on its payments to both West Bank and Martin.

Does West Bank or Martin have priority with respect to the new inventory delivered to SNS on June 28? If Martin has not perfected its security interest by June 28, West Bank's after-acquired collateral clause has priority because it was the first to be perfected. If, however, Martin has perfected *and* gives proper notice of its security interest to West Bank before SNS takes possession of the goods on June 28, Martin has priority.

Buyers of the Collateral The UCC recognizes that there are certain types of buyers whose interest in purchased goods could conflict with those of a perfected secured party on the debtor's default. These include buyers in the ordinary course of business (as discussed), as well as buyers of farm products, instruments, documents, or securities. The UCC sets down special rules of priority for these types of buyers. Exhibit 29–4 on the next page describes various rules regarding the priority of claims to a debtor's collateral.

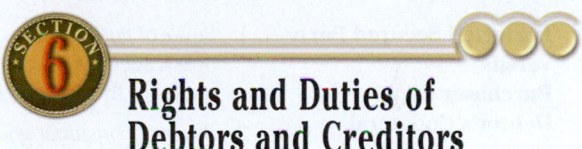

SECTION 6 Rights and Duties of Debtors and Creditors

The security agreement itself determines most of the rights and duties of the debtor and the secured party. The UCC, however, imposes some rights and duties that are applicable in the absence of a valid security agreement that states the contrary.

Information Requests

Under UCC 9–523(a), a secured party has the option, when making the filing, of furnishing a *copy* of the financing statement being filed to the filing officer and requesting that the filing officer make a note of the file number, the date, and the hour of the original filing on the copy. The filing officer must send this copy to the person designated by the secured party or to the debtor, if the debtor makes the request. Under UCC 9–523(c) and (d), a filing officer must also give information to a person who is contemplating obtaining a security interest from a prospective debtor. The filing officer must issue a certificate that provides information on possible perfected financing statements with respect to the named debtor. The filing officer will charge a fee for the certification and for any information copies provided [UCC 9–525(d)].

EXHIBIT 29–4 • Priority of Claims to a Debtor's Collateral

Parties	Priority
Perfected Secured Party versus Unsecured Parties and Creditors	A perfected secured party's interest has priority over the interests of most other parties, including unsecured creditors, unperfected secured parties, subsequent lien creditors, trustees in bankruptcy, and buyers who do not purchase the collateral in the ordinary course of business.
Perfected Secured Party versus Perfected Secured Party	Between two perfected secured parties in the same collateral, the general rule is that the first in time of perfection is the first in right to the collateral [UCC 9–322(a)(1)].
Perfected Secured Party versus Perfected PMSI	A PMSI, even if second in time of perfection, has priority providing that the following conditions are met: 1. *Other collateral*—A PMSI has priority, providing it is perfected within twenty days after the debtor takes possession [UCC 9–324(a)]. 2. *Inventory*—A PMSI has priority if it is perfected and proper written or authenticated notice is given to the other security-interest holder *on* or *before* the time the debtor takes possession [UCC 9–324(b)]. 3. *Software*—Applies to a PMSI in software only if used in goods subject to a PMSI. If the goods are inventory, priority is determined the same as for inventory; if they are not, priority is determined as for goods other than inventory [UCC 9–103(c), 9–324(f)].
Perfected Secured Party versus Purchaser of Debtor's Collateral	1. *Buyer of goods in the ordinary course of the seller's business*—Buyer prevails over a secured party's security interest, even if perfected and even if the buyer knows of the security interest [UCC 9–320(a)]. 2. *Buyer of consumer goods purchased outside the ordinary course of business*—Buyer prevails over a secured party's interest, even if perfected by attachment, providing the buyer purchased as follows: a. For value. b. Without actual knowledge of the security interest. c. For use as a consumer good. d. Prior to the secured party's perfection by *filing* [UCC 9–320(b)]. 3. *Buyer of chattel paper*—Buyer prevails if the buyer: a. Gave new value in making the purchase. b. Took possession in the ordinary course of the buyer's business. c. Took without knowledge of the security interest [UCC 9–330]. 4. *Buyer of instruments, documents, or securities*—Buyer who is a holder in due course, a holder to whom negotiable documents have been duly negotiated, or a bona fide purchaser of securities has priority over a previously perfected security interest [UCC 9–330(d), 9–331(a)]. 5. *Buyer of farm products*—Buyer from a farmer takes free and clear of perfected security interests unless, where permitted, a secured party files centrally an effective financing statement (EFS) or the buyer receives proper notice of the security interest before the sale.
Unperfected Secured Party versus Unsecured Creditor	An unperfected secured party prevails over unsecured creditors and creditors who have obtained judgments against the debtor but who have not begun the legal process to collect on those judgments [UCC 9–201(a)].

Release, Assignment, and Amendment

A secured party can release all or part of any collateral described in the financing statement, thereby terminating its security interest in that collateral. The release is recorded by filing a uniform amendment form [UCC 9–512, 9–521(b)]. A secured party can also assign all or part of the security interest to a third party (the assignee). The assignee becomes the secured party of record if the assignment is filed by use of a uniform amendment form [UCC 9–514, 9–521(a)].

If the debtor and the secured party agree, they can amend the filing—by adding or substituting new collateral, for example—by filing a uniform amendment form that indicates the file number of the initial financing statement [UCC 9–512(a)]. The amendment does not extend the time period of perfection, but if new collateral is added, the perfection date (for priority purposes) for the new collateral begins on the date the amendment is filed [UCC 9–512(b), (c)].

Confirmation or Accounting Request by Debtor

The debtor may believe that the amount of the unpaid debt or the listing of the collateral subject to the security interest is inaccurate. The debtor has the right to request a confirmation of the unpaid debt or listing of collateral. The secured party must either approve or correct this confirmation request [UCC 9–210].

The secured party must comply with the debtor's confirmation request by authenticating and sending to the debtor an accounting within fourteen days after the request is received. Otherwise, the secured party will be held liable for any loss suffered by the debtor, plus $500 [UCC 9–210, 9–625(f)].

Termination Statement

If the secured party perfected its interest in the collateral by filing, the debtor is entitled to have a termination statement filed once the debt has been fully paid. Such a statement demonstrates to the public that the filed perfected security interest has been terminated [UCC 9–513].

Whenever consumer goods are involved, the secured party *must* file a termination statement (or, alternatively, a release) within one month of the final payment or within twenty days of receiving the debtor's authenticated demand, whichever is earlier [UCC 9–513(b)].

When the collateral is other than consumer goods, on an authenticated demand by the debtor, the secured party must either send a termination statement to the debtor or file such a statement within twenty days [UCC 9–513(c)]. Otherwise, when the collateral is other than consumer goods, the secured party is not required to file or to send a termination statement. Whenever a secured party fails to file or send the termination statement as requested, the debtor can recover $500 plus any additional loss suffered [UCC 9–625(e)(4), (f)].

SECTION 7 Default

Article 9 defines the rights, duties, and remedies of the secured party and of the debtor on the debtor's default. Should the secured party fail to comply with his or her duties, the debtor is afforded particular rights and remedies.

The topic of default is one of great concern to secured lenders and to the lawyers who draft security agreements. What constitutes *default* is not always clear. In fact, Article 9 does not define the term. Consequently, parties are encouraged in practice—and by the UCC—to include in their security agreements certain standards to be applied in determining when default has actually occurred. In so doing, parties can stipulate the conditions that will constitute a default [UCC 9–601, 9–603]. Often, these critical terms are shaped by the creditor in an attempt to provide the maximum protection possible. The ultimate terms, however, cannot go beyond the limitations imposed by the good faith requirement and the unconscionability provisions of the UCC.

Any breach of the terms of the security agreement can constitute default. Nevertheless, default occurs most commonly when the debtor fails to meet the scheduled payments that the parties have agreed on or when the debtor becomes bankrupt.

Basic Remedies

The rights and remedies of secured parties under Article 9 are *cumulative* [UCC 9–601(c)]. Therefore, if a creditor is unsuccessful in enforcing rights by one method, she or he can pursue another method.[6]

6. See James J. White and Robert S. Summers, *Uniform Commercial Code*, 5th ed. (St. Paul: West Publishing Co., 2000), pp. 908–909.

Generally, a secured party's remedies can be divided into the two basic categories discussed next.

Repossession of the Collateral On the debtor's default, a secured party can take peaceful or judicial possession of the collateral covered by the security agreement [UCC 9–609(b)]. This provision, because it allows the secured party to take peaceful possession of the collateral without the use of the judicial process, is often referred to as the "self-help" provision of Article 9. This provision has been controversial, largely because the UCC does not define what constitutes *peaceful possession*. The general rule, however, is that the collateral has been taken peacefully if the secured party has taken it without committing (1) trespass onto realty, (2) assault and/or battery, or (3) breaking and entering. On taking possession, the secured party may either retain the collateral for satisfaction of the debt [UCC 9–620] or resell the goods and apply the proceeds toward the debt [UCC 9–610].

Judicial Remedies Alternatively, a secured party can relinquish the security interest and use any judicial remedy available, such as obtaining a judgment on the underlying debt, followed by execution and levy. (**Execution** is the implementation of a court's decree or judgment. **Levy** is the obtaining of funds by legal process through the seizure and sale of nonsecured property, usually done after a writ of execution has been issued. These writs were discussed in Chapter 28.) Execution and levy are rarely undertaken unless the collateral is no longer in existence or has declined so much in value that it is worth substantially less than the amount of the debt and the debtor has other assets available that may be legally seized to satisfy the debt [UCC 9–601(a)].[7]

If a customer finances a purchase through a bank loan, returns the item, and refuses to make the loan payments, and the seller then resells the returned item to another customer, what are the rights of the secured party (the bank)? That was one of the issues in the following case.

7. Some assets are exempt from creditors' claims under state statutes (as was discussed in Chapter 28) or bankruptcy laws (to be described in Chapter 30).

CASE 29.2 First National Bank of Litchfield v. Miller

Supreme Court of Connecticut, 2008. 285 Conn. 294, 939 A.2d 572.

• **Background and Facts** The Millers wanted to buy a boat from Norwest Marine, so they made a $3,500 deposit and signed a form contract. Title and ownership would pass when the Millers made full payment, although delivery would occur earlier, as often happens. The agreement stated that the Millers had inspected and accepted the boat and that the document constituted the entire agreement between Norwest and the Millers. Because the Millers needed financing, Norwest contacted First National Bank of Litchfield to begin the loan process. The Millers signed a loan agreement with the bank, which sent Norwest full payment for the boat. The bank received title to the boat. When the Millers took delivery of the boat, it did not run properly, so they returned it to Norwest for repairs, which took a couple of days. The repairs were performed under warranty. The Millers then refused to accept the boat, claiming that it was not satisfactory. They returned the payment coupons and told the bank that they did not desire the loan because they did not want the boat. Norwest had sent most of the funds it had received from the bank to pay the boat manufacturer. With the permission of all parties, Norwest then sold the boat for $15,000 less to another party. The bank sued, contending that the Millers had breached the retail contract by refusing to make monthly payments, and that Norwest had breached the security interest in the boat because it had warranted that the boat had been delivered to the Millers. Norwest filed a cross-claim against the Millers for failing to take possession of the boat. The Millers filed claims against the bank and Norwest asserting that they had committed fraud. The trial court held for the bank, awarding it the full amount owed under the loan contract, plus attorneys' fees. The Millers appealed, and the appellate court reversed and remanded. The case was certified to the state's highest court for review.

• **Decision and Rationale** The state supreme court reinstated the verdict of the trial court, holding that the Millers had accepted delivery of the boat under the UCC. They had signed a pur-

CASE 29.2 CONTINUED chase agreement that stated that they had inspected the boat and were satisfied with it. Additionally, they had signed a retail installment contract with the bank stating that they had already accepted delivery of the boat and that it was registered in their names. Norwest acted in good faith by performing warranty repair work that solved the boat's mechanical problem. Norwest also installed some equipment on the boat that was specifically requested by the Millers. The Millers could not claim they had never taken delivery of the boat, and they were therefore responsible for the loan they had accepted.

- **The Ethical Dimension** *Should the bank have attempted to resolve the consumer problem suffered by the Millers rather than suing them for full payment on the loan? Why or why not?*

- **The Legal Environment Dimension** *How could Norwest and the bank have avoided the problem that arose in this case?*

Disposition of Collateral

Once default has occurred and the secured party has obtained possession of the collateral, the secured party can retain the collateral in full satisfaction of the debt (subject to limitations, discussed next) or sell, lease, or otherwise dispose of the collateral in any commercially reasonable manner [UCC 9–602(7), 9–603, 9–610(a), 9–620]. Any sale is always subject to procedures established by state law.

Retention of Collateral by the Secured Party The UCC acknowledges that parties are sometimes better off if they do not sell the collateral. Therefore, a secured party may retain the collateral unless it consists of consumer goods and the debtor has paid 60 percent or more of the purchase price in a PMSI or debt in a non-PMSI (as will be discussed shortly) [UCC 9–620(e)].

This general right, however, is subject to several conditions. The secured party must send notice of the proposal to the debtor if the debtor has not signed a statement renouncing or modifying her or his rights *after default* [UCC 9–620(a), 9–621]. If the collateral is consumer goods, the secured party does not need to give any other notice. In all other situations, the secured party must also send notice to any other secured party from whom the secured party has received written or authenticated notice of a claim of interest in the collateral in question. The secured party must also send notice to any **junior lienholder** (one holding a lien that is subordinate to one or more other liens on the same property) who has filed a statutory lien (such as a mechanic's lien—see Chapter 28) or a security interest in the collateral ten days before the debtor consented to the retention [UCC 9–621].

If, within twenty days after the notice is sent, the secured party receives an objection sent by a person entitled to receive notification, the secured party must sell or otherwise dispose of the collateral in accordance with the provisions of UCC 9–602, 9–603, 9–610, and 9–613 (disposition procedures will be discussed shortly). If no such written objection is forthcoming, the secured party may retain the collateral in full or partial satisfaction of the debtor's obligation [UCC 9–620(a), 9–621].

Consumer Goods When the collateral is consumer goods and the debtor has paid 60 percent of the purchase price on a PMSI, or 60 percent of the debt on a non-PMSI, the secured party must sell or otherwise dispose of the repossessed collateral within ninety days [UCC 9–620(e), (f)]. Failure to comply opens the secured party to an action for conversion or other liability under UCC 9–625(b) and (c) unless the consumer-debtor signed a written statement *after default* renouncing or modifying the right to demand the sale of the goods [UCC 9–624].

Disposition Procedures A secured party who does not choose to retain the collateral or who is required to sell it must resort to the disposition procedures prescribed under UCC 9–602(7), 9–603, 9–610(a), and 9–613. The UCC allows a great deal of flexibility with regard to disposition. UCC 9–610(a) states that after default, a secured party may sell, lease, license, or otherwise dispose of any or all of the collateral in its present condition or following any commercially reasonable preparation or processing. The secured party may also purchase the collateral at a public sale, but not at a private sale—unless the collateral is of a kind customarily sold on a recognized market or is the subject of widely distributed standard price quotations [UCC 9–610(c)].

A Commercially Reasonable Manner. One of the major limitations on the disposition of collateral is that it must be accomplished in a commercially reasonable manner. UCC 9–610(b) states as follows:

> Every aspect of a disposition of collateral, including the method, manner, time, place, and other terms, must be commercially reasonable. If commercially reasonable, a secured party may dispose of collateral by public or private proceedings, by one or more contracts, as a unit or in parcels, and at any time and place and on any terms.

Whenever the secured party fails to conduct a disposition in a commercially reasonable manner or to give proper notice, the deficiency of the debtor is reduced to the extent that such failure affected the price received at the disposition [UCC 9–626(a)(3)].

The issue in the following case was whether it was commercially reasonable on a debtor's default for the creditor to delay in selling the debtor's stock, which served as the collateral for the parties' loan. Between the time of the default and the sale of the stock, the stock's market value declined significantly.

CASE 29.3 Layne v. Bank One, Kentucky, N.A.

United States Court of Appeals, Sixth Circuit, 2005. 395 F.3d 271.

Background and Facts Charles Johnson was the chief executive officer of PurchasePro.com, Inc. Geoff Layne was the company's marketing director. Johnson and Layne entered into two separate loan agreements with Bank One, Kentucky, N.A., and Banc One Securities Corporation (collectively, Bank One), secured by their shares of PurchasePro.com stock. Layne's agreement included a loan-to-value (LTV) ratio of 50 percent. This meant that the market value of the stock had to be at least twice the outstanding balance on the loan. Johnson's agreement had a 40 percent LTV ratio, which meant that the stock's market value had to be two and one-half times the balance. If the market value dropped, Layne and Johnson had five days to provide more collateral or pay off the loans. Otherwise, they would be in default, and Bank One could sell the stock. In February 2001, the price of the stock fell below these limits. After months of unsuccessful negotiations, Bank One sold Johnson's shares in July, recovering $524,757.39 in proceeds to pay down his debt but leaving an unpaid balance of approximately $2.2 million. Layne and Johnson filed a suit in a federal district court against Bank One, alleging, among other things, breach of contract. Bank One filed counterclaims against Johnson and Layne, seeking payment on the loans. The court issued a summary judgment in Bank One's favor. Johnson appealed to the U.S. Court of Appeals for the Sixth Circuit.

Decision and Rationale The U.S. Court of Appeals for the Sixth Circuit affirmed the judgment of the lower court. UCC 9–610 requires that "every aspect of a disposition of collateral * * * must be commercially reasonable." The purpose is to protect the debtor's interest by ensuring he or she receives the market price of the collateral. A sale on a "recognized market" is commercially reasonable because the price represents the fair market value of the collateral. Bank One disposed of the PurchasePro shares through a sale on the National Association of Securities Dealers Automated Quotations (NASDAQ).[a] Johnson argued that the timing was commercially unreasonable because the price of the shares was low. UCC 9–610 "does not impose an obligation on a lender to liquidate and sell the collateral stock at a specific time during the life of the loan," but only states "*how* the disposition should occur. * * * The sale of the stock was on the NASDAQ, a recognized market, and thus ensured that Johnson received the fair market value for his stock shortly after the decision to liquidate was made, which is all that [UCC 9–610] requires."

What If the Facts Were Different? *If Bank One had refused to negotiate with Johnson and Layne, and had sold their stock as soon as their loans were in default, would the result in this case have been different? Why or why not?*

a. *NASDAQ* is an automated information system that gives price quotations on publicly traded securities, including stock traded among stockbrokers and others.

CASE 29.3 CONTINUED

- **The Legal Environment Dimension** *Should a court's scrutiny of the price paid for collateral be different when the purchaser is the secured party or someone related to the secured party? Explain.*

Notification Requirements. Unless the collateral is perishable or will decline rapidly in value or is a type customarily sold on a recognized market, a secured party must send to the debtor and other identified persons "a reasonable authenticated notification of disposition" [UCC 9–611(b), (c)]. The debtor may waive the right to receive this notice, but only after default [UCC 9–624(a)].

Proceeds from Disposition Proceeds from the disposition of collateral after default on the underlying debt are distributed in the following order:

1. Expenses incurred by the secured party in repossessing, storing, and reselling the collateral.
2. Balance of the debt owed to the secured party.
3. Junior lienholders who have made written or authenticated demands.
4. Unless the collateral consists of accounts, payment intangibles, promissory notes, or chattel paper, any surplus goes to the debtor [UCC 9–608(a); 9–615(a), (e)].

Noncash Proceeds Whenever the secured party receives noncash proceeds from the disposition of collateral after default, the secured party must make a value determination and apply this value in a commercially reasonable manner [UCC 9–608(a)(3), 9–615(c)].

Deficiency Judgment Often, after proper disposition of the collateral, the secured party still has not collected all that the debtor owes. Unless otherwise agreed, the debtor is liable for any deficiency, and the creditor can obtain a **deficiency judgment** from a court to collect the deficiency. Note, however, that if the underlying transaction was, for example, a sale of accounts or of chattel paper, the debtor is entitled to any surplus or is liable for any deficiency only if the security agreement so provides [UCC 9–615(d) and (e)].

Redemption Rights At any time before the secured party disposes of the collateral or enters into a contract for its disposition, or before the debtor's obligation has been discharged through the secured party's retention of the collateral, the debtor or any other secured party can exercise the right of *redemption* of the collateral. The debtor or other secured party can do this by tendering performance of all obligations secured by the collateral and by paying the expenses reasonably incurred by the secured party in retaking and maintaining the collateral [UCC 9–623]. *Concept Summary 29.2* provides a review of the secured party's remedies on the debtor's default.

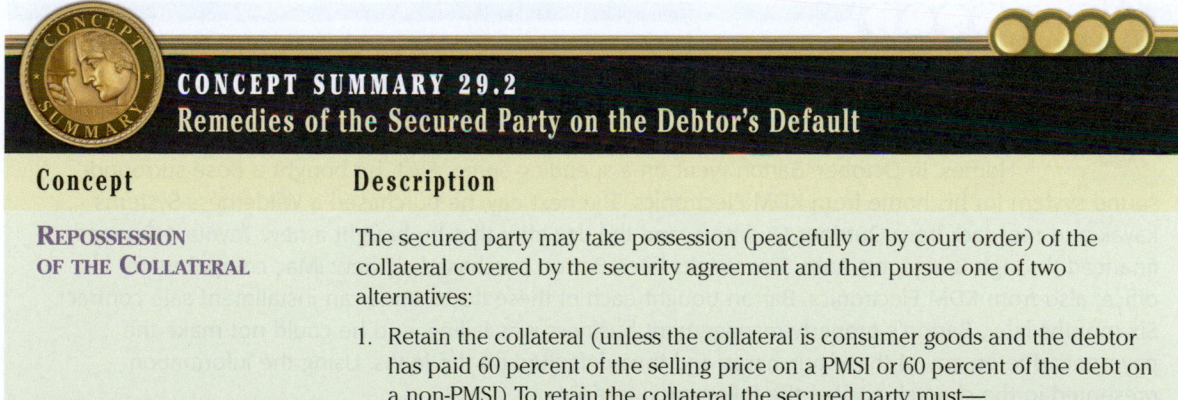

CONCEPT SUMMARY 29.2
Remedies of the Secured Party on the Debtor's Default

Concept	Description
REPOSSESSION OF THE COLLATERAL	The secured party may take possession (peacefully or by court order) of the collateral covered by the security agreement and then pursue one of two alternatives: 1. Retain the collateral (unless the collateral is consumer goods and the debtor has paid 60 percent of the selling price on a PMSI or 60 percent of the debt on a non-PMSI). To retain the collateral, the secured party must— a. Give notice to the debtor if the debtor has not signed a statement renouncing or modifying his or her rights after default. With consumer goods, no other notice is necessary.

CONCEPT SUMMARY CONTINUES

CONCEPT SUMMARY 29.2
Remedies of the Secured Party on the Debtor's Default, Continued

Concept	Description
Repossession of the Collateral (Continued)	b. Send notice to any other secured party who has given written or authenticated notice of a claim to the same collateral or who has filed a security interest or a statutory lien ten days before the debtor consented to the retention. If an objection is received within twenty days from the debtor or any other secured party given notice, the creditor must dispose of the collateral according to the requirements of UCC 9–602, 9–603, 9–610, and 9–613. Otherwise, the creditor may retain the collateral in full or partial satisfaction of the debt. 2. Dispose of the collateral in accordance with the requirements of UCC 9–602(7), 9–603, 9–610(a), and 9–613. To do so, the secured party must— a. Dispose of (sell, lease, or license) the goods in a commercially reasonable manner. b. Notify the debtor and (except in sales of consumer goods) other identified persons, including those who have given notice of claims to the collateral to be sold (unless the collateral is perishable or will decline rapidly in value). c. Apply the proceeds in the following order: (1) Expenses incurred by the secured party in repossessing, storing, and reselling the collateral. (2) The balance of the debt owed to the secured party. (3) Junior lienholders who have made written or authenticated demands. (4) Surplus to the debtor (unless the collateral consists of accounts, payment intangibles, promissory notes, or chattel paper).
Judicial Remedies	The secured party may relinquish the security interest and proceed with any judicial remedy available, such as obtaining a judgment on the underlying debt, followed by execution and levy on the nonexempt assets of the debtor.

REVIEWING Secured Transactions

Paul Barton owned a small property-management company, doing business as Brighton Homes. In October, Barton went on a spending spree. First, he bought a Bose surround-sound system for his home from KDM Electronics. The next day, he purchased a Wilderness Systems kayak and roof rack from Outdoor Outfitters, and the day after that he bought a new Toyota 4-Runner financed through Bridgeport Auto. Two weeks later, Barton purchased six new iMac computers for his office, also from KDM Electronics. Barton bought each of these items under an installment sale contract. Six months later, Barton's property-management business was failing, and he could not make the payments due on any of these purchases and thus defaulted on the loans. Using the information presented in the chapter, answer the following questions.

1. For which of Barton's purchases (the surround-sound system, the kayak, the 4-Runner, and the six iMacs) would the creditor need to file a financing statement to perfect its security interest?

REVIEWING Secured Transactions, Continued

2. Suppose that Barton's contract for the office computers mentioned only the name *Brighton Homes*. What would be the consequences if KDM Electronics filed a financing statement that listed only Brighton Homes as the debtor's name?
3. Which of these purchases would qualify as a PMSI in consumer goods?
4. Suppose that after KDM Electronics repossesses the surround-sound system, it decides to keep the system rather than sell it. Can KDM do this under Article 9? Why or why not?

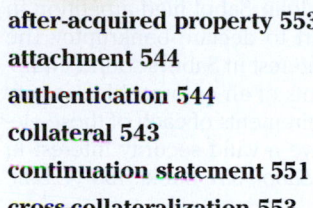

TERMS AND CONCEPTS

after-acquired property 553
attachment 544
authentication 544
collateral 543
continuation statement 551
cross-collateralization 553
debtor 543
deficiency judgment 561
execution 558
financing statement 543
floating lien 553
junior lienholder 559
levy 558
perfection 545
pledge 551
proceeds 552
purchase-money security interest (PMSI) 551
secured party 543
secured transaction 543
security agreement 543
security interest 543

QUESTIONS AND CASE PROBLEMS

29–1. Redford is a seller of electric generators. He purchases a large quantity of generators from a manufacturer, Mallon Corp., by making a down payment and signing an agreement to make the balance of payments over a period of time. The agreement gives Mallon Corp. a security interest in the generators and the proceeds. Mallon Corp. properly files a financing statement on its security interest. Redford receives the generators and immediately sells one of them to Garfield on an installment contract, with payment to be made in twelve equal installments. At the time of the sale, Garfield knows of Mallon's security interest. Two months later, Redford goes into default on his payments to Mallon. Discuss Mallon's rights against Garfield in this situation.

29–2. Marsh has a prize horse named Arabian Knight. Marsh is in need of working capital. She borrows $50,000 from Mendez, who takes possession of Arabian Knight as security for the loan. No written agreement is signed. Discuss whether, in the absence of a written agreement, Mendez has a security interest in Arabian Knight. If Mendez does have a security interest, is it a perfected security interest?

29–3. QUESTION WITH SAMPLE ANSWER

Delgado is a retail seller of television sets. He sells a color television set to Cummings for $600. Cummings cannot pay cash, so she signs a security agreement, paying $100 down and agreeing to pay the balance in twelve equal installments of $50 each. The security agreement gives Delgado a security interest in the television set sold. Cummings makes six payments on time; then she goes into default because of unexpected financial problems. Delgado repossesses the set and wants to keep it in full satisfaction of the debt. Discuss Delgado's rights and duties in this matter.

- **For a sample answer to Question 29–3, go to Appendix I at the end of this text.**

29–4. Purchase-Money Security Interest. When a customer opens a credit-card account with Sears, Roebuck & Co., the customer fills out an application and sends it to Sears for review; if the application is approved, the customer receives a Sears card. The application contains a security agreement, a copy of which is also sent with the card. When a customer buys an item using the card, the customer signs a sales receipt that describes the merchandise and contains language granting Sears a purchase-money security interest (PMSI) in the merchandise. Dayna Conry bought a variety of consumer goods from Sears on her card. When she did not make payments on her account, Sears filed a suit against her in an Illinois state court to repossess the goods. Conry filed for bankruptcy and was granted a discharge. Sears then filed a suit against her to obtain possession of the goods through its PMSI, but it could not find Conry's credit-card application to offer into evidence. Is a signed Sears sales receipt sufficient proof of its security interest? In whose favor should the court rule? Explain. [*Sears, Roebuck & Co. v. Conry,* 321 Ill.App.3d 997, 748 N.E.2d 1248, 255 Ill.Dec. 178 (3 Dist. 2001)]

29–5. Priorities. PC Contractors, Inc., was an excavating business in Kansas City, Missouri. Union Bank made loans to PC, subject to a perfected security interest in its equipment and other assets, including "after-acquired property." In late 1997, PC leased heavy construction equipment from Dean Machinery Co. The lease agreements required monthly payments, which PC often made late or missed completely. After eighteen months, Dean demanded that PC either return the equipment or buy it. While attempting to obtain financing for the purchase, PC continued to make monthly payments. In November 2000, Dean, which had not filed a financing statement to cover the transaction, demanded full payment of the amount due. Before paying the price, PC went out of business and surrendered its assets to Union, which prepared to sell them. Dean filed a suit in a Missouri state court against Union to recover the equipment, claiming, in part, that the bank's security interest had not attached to the equipment because PC had not paid for it. In whose favor should the court rule, and why? [*Dean Machinery Co. v. Union Bank,* 106 S.W.3d 510 (Mo.App.W.D. 2003)]

29–6. CASE PROBLEM WITH SAMPLE ANSWER

In St. Louis, Missouri, in August 2000, Richard Miller orally agreed to loan Jeff Miller $35,000 in exchange for a security interest in a 1999 Kodiak dump truck. The Millers did not put anything in writing concerning the loan, its repayment terms, or Richard's security interest or rights in the truck. Jeff used the amount of the loan to buy the truck, which he kept in his possession. In June 2004, Jeff filed a petition to obtain a discharge of his debts in bankruptcy. Richard claimed that he had a security interest in the truck and thus was entitled to any proceeds from its sale. What are a creditor's main concerns on a debtor's default? How does a creditor satisfy these concerns? What are the requirements for a creditor to have an enforceable security interest? Have these requirements been met in this case? Considering these points, what is the court likely to rule with respect to Richard's claim? [*In re Miller,* 320 Bankr. 911 (E.D.Mo. 2005)]

- **To view a sample answer for Problem 29–6, go to this book's Web site at www.cengage.com/blaw/jentz, select "Chapter 29," and click on "Case Problem with Sample Answer."**

29–7. Creating a Security Interest. In 2002, Michael Sabol, doing business in the recording industry as Sound Farm Productions, applied to Morton Community Bank in Bloomington, Illinois, for a $58,000 loan to expand his business. Besides the loan application, Sabol signed a promissory note that referred to the bank's rights in "any collateral." Sabol also signed a letter that stated, "the undersigned does hereby authorize Morton Community Bank to execute, file and record all financing statements, amendments, termination statements and all other statements authorized by Article 9 of the Illinois Uniform Commercial Code, as to any security interest." Sabol did not sign any other documents, including the financing statement, which did, however, contain a description of the collateral. Less than three years later, without having repaid the loan, Sabol filed a petition in a federal bankruptcy court to declare bankruptcy. The bank claimed a security interest in Sabol's sound equipment. What are the elements of an enforceable security interest? What are the requirements of each of those elements? Does the bank have a valid security interest in this case? Explain. [*In re Sabol,* 337 Bankr. 195 (C.D.Ill. 2006)]

29–8. A QUESTION OF ETHICS

*In 1995, Mark Denton cosigned a $101,250 loan that the First Interstate Bank (FIB) in Missoula, Montana, issued to Denton's friend Eric Anderson. Denton's business assets—a mini-warehouse operation—secured the loan. On his own, Anderson obtained a $260,000 U.S. Small Business Administration (SBA) loan from FIB at the same time. The purpose of both loans was to buy logging equipment with which Anderson could start a business. In 1997, the business failed. As a consequence, FIB repossessed and sold the equipment and applied the proceeds to the SBA loan. FIB then asked Denton to pay the other loan's outstanding balance ($98,460) plus interest. When Denton refused, FIB initiated proceedings to obtain his business assets. Denton filed a suit in a Montana state court against FIB, claiming, in part, that Anderson's equipment was the collateral for the loan that FIB was attempting to collect from Denton. [*Denton v. First Interstate Bank of Commerce, *2006 MT 193, 333 Mont. 169, 142 P.3d 797 (2006)]*

(a) Denton's assets served as the security for Anderson's loan because Anderson had nothing to offer. When the loan was obtained, Dean Gillmore, FIB's loan officer, explained to them that if Anderson defaulted, the proceeds from the sale of the logging equipment would be applied to the SBA loan first.

Under these circumstances, is it fair to hold Denton liable for the unpaid balance of Anderson's loan? Why or why not?

(b) Denton argued that the loan contract was unconscionable and constituted a "contract of adhesion." What makes a contract unconscionable? Did the transaction between the parties in this case qualify? What is a "contract of adhesion"? Was this deal unenforceable on that basis? Explain.

29-9. VIDEO QUESTION

Go to this text's Web site at **www.cengage.com/blaw/jentz** and select "Chapter 29." Click on "Video Questions" and view the video titled *Secured Transactions*. Then answer the following questions.

(a) This chapter lists three requirements for creating a security interest. In the video, which requirement does Laura assert has not been met?

(b) What, if anything, must the bank have done to perfect its interest in the editing equipment?

(c) If the bank exercises its self-help remedy to repossess Onyx's editing equipment, does Laura have any chance of getting it back? Explain.

(d) Assume that the bank had a perfected security interest and repossessed the editing equipment. Also assume that the purchase price (and the loan amount) for the equipment was $100,000, of which Onyx has paid $65,000. Discuss the rights and duties of the bank with regard to the collateral in this situation.

LAW ON THE WEB

For updated links to resources available on the Web, as well as a variety of other materials, visit this text's Web site at

www/cengage.com/blaw/jentz

To find Article 9 of the UCC as modified by a particular state on adoption, go to

www.law.cornell.edu/ucc/ucc.table.html

For an overview of secured transactions law and links to UCC provisions and case law on this topic, go to

www.law.cornell.edu/wex/index.php/Secured_transactions

Legal Research Exercises on the Web

Go to **www.cengage.com/blaw/jentz**, the Web site that accompanies this text. Select "Chapter 29" and click on "Internet Exercises." There you will find the following Internet research exercises that you can perform to learn more about the topics covered in this chapter.

Internet Exercise 29–1: Legal Perspective
Repossession

Internet Exercise 29–2: Management Perspective
Filing Financial Statements

CHAPTER 30

Bankruptcy Law

Historically, debtors had few rights. Today, in contrast, debtors have numerous rights. Some of these rights were discussed in Chapters 28 and 29. In this chapter, we look at another significant right of debtors: the right to petition for bankruptcy relief under federal law. Article I, Section 8, of the U.S. Constitution gave Congress the power to establish "uniform Laws on the subject of Bankruptcies throughout the United States." Bankruptcy law in the United States has two goals—to protect a debtor by giving him or her a fresh start, free from creditors' claims, and to ensure equitable treatment to creditors who are competing for a debtor's assets. Federal bankruptcy legislation was first enacted in 1898 and has undergone several modifications since that time, most recently in 2005 as a result of the Bankruptcy Reform Act.[1] This act significantly overhauled certain provisions of the Bankruptcy Code for the first time in twenty-five years.

1. The full title of the act is the Bankruptcy Abuse Prevention and Consumer Protection Act of 2005, Pub. L. No. 109-8, 119 Stat. 23.

SECTION 1 Bankruptcy Proceedings

Bankruptcy proceedings are held in federal bankruptcy courts, which are under the authority of the U.S. district courts, and rulings from bankruptcy courts can be appealed to the district courts. Although bankruptcy law is federal law, state laws on secured transactions, liens, judgments, and exemptions also play a role in federal bankruptcy proceedings.

The Role of the Bankruptcy Courts

Essentially, a bankruptcy court fulfills the role of an administrative court for the federal district court concerning matters in bankruptcy. The bankruptcy court holds proceedings dealing with the procedures required to administer the estate of the debtor in bankruptcy (the *estate* consists of the debtor's assets, as will be discussed shortly). A bankruptcy court can conduct a jury trial if the appropriate district court has authorized it and the parties to the bankruptcy consent.

Types of Bankruptcy Relief

Title 11 of the *United States Code* encompasses the Bankruptcy Code, which has eight chapters. Chapters 1, 3, and 5 of the Code contain general definitional provisions, as well as provisions governing case administration, creditors, the debtor, and the estate. These three chapters normally apply to all kinds of bankruptcies. The next five chapters of the Code set forth the different types of relief that debtors may seek. Chapter 7 provides for **liquidation** proceedings (the selling of all nonexempt assets and the distribution of the proceeds to the debtor's creditors). Chapter 9 governs the adjustment of a municipality's debts. Chapter 11 governs reorganizations. Chapters 12 and 13 provide for the adjustment of debts by parties with regular incomes (family farmers and family fishermen under Chapter 12 and individuals under Chapter 13).[2] A

2. There are no Chapters 2, 4, 6, 8, or 10 in Title 11. Such "gaps" are not uncommon in the *United States Code*. This is because chapter numbers (or other subdivisional unit numbers) are sometimes reserved for future use when a statute is enacted. (A gap may also appear if a law has been repealed.)

debtor (except for a municipality) does not have to be insolvent[3] to file for bankruptcy relief under any chapter of the Bankruptcy Code. Anyone obligated to a creditor can declare bankruptcy.

In this chapter, we deal first with liquidation proceedings under Chapter 7 of the Code. We then examine the procedures required for Chapter 11 reorganizations and Chapter 12 and 13 plans. (The latter three chapters of the Code are known as "rehabilitation" chapters.)

Special Treatment of Consumer-Debtors

To ensure that consumer-debtors are fully informed of the various types of relief available, the Code requires that the clerk of the bankruptcy court provide certain information to all consumer-debtors before they file for bankruptcy. (Recall from Chapter 29 that a consumer-debtor is a debtor whose debts result primarily from the purchase of goods for personal, family, or household use.) First, the clerk must give consumer-debtors written notice of the general purpose, benefits, and costs of each chapter of the Bankruptcy Code under which they might proceed. Second, the clerk must provide consumer-debtors with informational materials on the types of services available from credit counseling agencies.

SECTION 2

Liquidation Proceedings

Liquidation under Chapter 7 of the Bankruptcy Code is generally the most familiar type of bankruptcy proceeding and is often referred to as an *ordinary,* or *straight, bankruptcy.* Put simply, a debtor in a liquidation bankruptcy turns all assets over to a **trustee.** The trustee sells the nonexempt assets and distributes the proceeds to creditors. With certain exceptions, the remaining debts are then **discharged** (extinguished), and the debtor is relieved of the obligation to pay the debts.

Any "person"—defined as including individuals, partnerships, and corporations[4]—may be a debtor in a liquidation proceeding. Railroads, insurance companies, banks, savings and loan associations, investment companies licensed by the Small Business Administration, and credit unions cannot be debtors in a liquidation bankruptcy, however. Other chapters of the Bankruptcy Code or other federal or state statutes apply to them. A husband and wife may file jointly for bankruptcy under a single petition.

A straight bankruptcy may be commenced by the filing of either a voluntary or an involuntary **petition in bankruptcy—**the document that is filed with a bankruptcy court to initiate bankruptcy proceedings. If a debtor files the petition, it is a voluntary bankruptcy. If one or more creditors file a petition to force the debtor into bankruptcy, it is called an involuntary bankruptcy. We discuss both voluntary and involuntary bankruptcy proceedings under Chapter 7 in the following subsections.

Voluntary Bankruptcy

To bring a voluntary petition in bankruptcy, the debtor files official forms designated for that purpose in the bankruptcy court. Under the Bankruptcy Reform Act of 2005, before debtors can file a petition, they must receive credit counseling from an approved nonprofit agency within the 180-day period preceding the date of filing. The act outlined detailed criteria for the **U.S. trustee**—a government official who performs appointment and other administrative tasks that a bankruptcy judge would otherwise have to perform—to approve nonprofit budget and counseling agencies and to make the list of approved agencies available to the public. A debtor filing a Chapter 7 petition must include a certificate proving that he or she received individual or group briefing from an approved counseling agency within the last 180 days (roughly six months).

The Code requires a consumer-debtor who has opted for liquidation bankruptcy proceedings to confirm the accuracy of the petition's contents. The debtor must also state in the petition, at the time of filing, that he or she understands the relief available under other chapters of the Code and has chosen to proceed under Chapter 7. If an attorney is representing the consumer-debtor, the attorney must file an affidavit

3. The inability to pay debts as they become due is known as *equitable* insolvency. A *balance sheet* insolvency, which exists when a debtor's liabilities exceed assets, is not the test. Thus, it is possible for debtors to voluntarily petition for bankruptcy or to be forced into involuntary bankruptcy even though their assets far exceed their liabilities. This may occur when a debtor's cash flow problems become severe.

4. The definition of *corporation* includes unincorporated companies and associations. It also covers labor unions.

stating that she or he has informed the debtor of the relief available under each chapter of the Bankruptcy Code. In addition, the Code requires the attorney to reasonably attempt to verify the accuracy of the consumer-debtor's petition and schedules (described below). Failure to do so is considered perjury.

Chapter 7 Schedules The voluntary petition must contain the following schedules:

1. A list of both secured and unsecured creditors, their addresses, and the amount of debt owed to each.
2. A statement of the financial affairs of the debtor.
3. A list of all property owned by the debtor, including property that the debtor claims is exempt.
4. A list of current income and expenses.
5. A certificate of credit counseling (as discussed previously).
6. Proof of payments received from employers within sixty days prior to the filing of the petition.
7. A statement of the amount of monthly income, itemized to show how the amount is calculated.
8. A copy of the debtor's federal income tax return for the most recent year ending immediately before the filing of the petition.

As previously noted, the official forms must be completed accurately, sworn to under oath, and signed by the debtor. To conceal assets or knowingly supply false information on these schedules is a crime under the bankruptcy laws.

With the exception of tax returns, failure to file the required schedules within forty-five days after the filing of the petition (unless an extension of up to forty-five days is granted) will result in an automatic dismissal of the petition. The debtor has up to seven days before the date of the first creditors' meeting to provide a copy of the most recent tax returns to the trustee.

Additional Information May Be Required At the request of the court, the trustee, or any party in interest, the debtor must file tax returns at the end of each tax year while the case is pending and provide copies to the court. This requirement also applies to Chapter 11 and 13 bankruptcies (discussed later in this chapter). Also, if requested by the trustee, the debtor must provide a photo document establishing his or her identity (such as a driver's license or passport) or other such personal identifying information.

Substantial Abuse Prior to 2005, a bankruptcy court could dismiss a Chapter 7 petition for relief (discharge of debts) if the use of Chapter 7 would constitute a "substantial abuse" of that chapter. The Bankruptcy Reform Act of 2005 established a new system of "means testing" (the debtor's income) to determine whether a debtor's petition is presumed to be a "substantial abuse" of Chapter 7.

When Abuse Will Be Presumed. If the debtor's family income is greater than the median family income in the state in which the petition is filed, the trustee or any party in interest (such as a creditor) can bring a motion to dismiss the Chapter 7 petition. State median incomes vary from state to state and are calculated and reported by the U.S. Bureau of the Census.

The debtor's current monthly income is calculated using the last six months' average income, less certain "allowed expenses" reflecting the basic needs of the debtor. The monthly amount is then multiplied by twelve. If the resulting income exceeds the state median income by $6,000 or more,[5] abuse is presumed, and the trustee or any creditor can file a motion to dismiss the petition. A debtor can rebut (refute) the presumption of abuse "by demonstrating special circumstances that justify additional expenses or adjustments of current monthly income for which there is no reasonable alternative." (An example might be anticipated medical costs not covered by health insurance.) These additional expenses or adjustments must be itemized and their accuracy attested to under oath by the debtor.

When Abuse Will Not Be Presumed. If the debtor's income is below the state median (or if the debtor has successfully refuted the means-test presumption), abuse will not be presumed. In these situations, the court may still find substantial abuse, but the creditors will not have standing (see Chapter 2) to file a motion to dismiss. Basically, this leaves intact the prior law on substantial abuse, allowing the court to consider such factors as the debtor's bad faith or circumstances indicating substantial abuse.

Can a debtor seeking relief under Chapter 7 exclude voluntary contributions to a retirement plan as a reasonably necessary expense in calculating her income? The Code does not disallow the contributions, but whether their exclusion constitutes substantial abuse requires a review of the debtor's circumstances, as in the following case.

5. This amount ($6,000) is the equivalent of $100 per month for five years, indicating that the debtor could pay at least $100 per month under a Chapter 13 five-year repayment plan.

CASE 30.1 Hebbring v. U.S. Trustee

United States Court of Appeals, Ninth Circuit, 2006. 463 F.3d 902.

• **Background and Facts** In 2003, Lisa Hebbring owned a single-family home in Reno, Nevada, valued at $160,000, on which she owed $154,103. She also owned a 2001 Volkswagen Beetle valued at $14,000, on which she owed $18,839, and other personal property valued at $1,775. She earned $49,000 per year as a customer service representative for SBC Nevada. In June, Hebbring filed a Chapter 7 petition in a federal bankruptcy court, seeking relief from $11,124 in credit-card debt. Her petition listed monthly net income of $2,813 and expenditures of $2,897, for a deficit of $84. In calculating her income, Hebbring excluded a $232 monthly pretax deduction for a contribution to a retirement plan maintained by her employer and an $81 monthly after-tax deduction for a contribution to her own retirement savings. At the time, Hebbring was thirty-three years old. The U.S. trustee assigned to oversee her case filed a motion to dismiss her petition for substantial abuse, arguing, in part, that the retirement savings contributions should be disallowed. According to the trustee, these and other adjustments would leave Hebbring $615 per month in disposable income, which would be enough to repay 100 percent of her credit-card debt over three years. The court dismissed her petition. She appealed to a federal district court, which affirmed the dismissal. Hebbring appealed to the U.S. Court of Appeals for the Ninth Circuit.

• **Decision and Rationale** The U.S. Court of Appeals for the Ninth Circuit affirmed the lower court's decision, "finding that Hebbring's retirement contributions are not reasonably necessary based on her age and financial circumstances, and that she is therefore capable of paying her unsecured debts." The appellate court emphasized the facts of Hebbring's situation. She was thirty-three years old, earning $49,000 per year, making mortgage payments on a house, and contributing about 8 percent of her income toward her retirement savings. "In light of these circumstances, the bankruptcy court's conclusion that Hebbring's retirement contributions are not a reasonably necessary expense is not clearly erroneous." Furthermore, based on the information that Hebbring provided on the schedules she submitted with her bankruptcy petition, even excluding her voluntary retirement plan contributions, she "has $172 per month in disposable income, sufficient to repay 56% of her unsecured [credit-card] debt over three years or 93% over five years * * * . The bankruptcy court thus did not err in finding that Hebbring is able to [pay at least] a substantial portion of the unsecured claims."

• **The Ethical Dimension** *Is it fair for the court to treat retirement contributions differently depending on a person's age? Why or why not?*

• **The E-Commerce Environment** *Is it likely to have made a difference to the result in this case that the debtor's retirement contributions were automatically and electronically deducted from her pay? Explain.*

Additional Grounds for Dismissal As noted, a debtor's voluntary petition for Chapter 7 relief may be dismissed for substantial abuse or for failing to provide the necessary documents (such as schedules and tax returns) within the specified time. In addition, a motion to dismiss a Chapter 7 filing might be granted in two other situations under the Bankruptcy Reform Act of 2005. First, if the debtor has been convicted of a violent crime or a drug-trafficking offense, the victim can file a motion to dismiss the voluntary petition.[6] Second, if the debtor fails to pay postpetition domestic-support obligations (which include child and spousal support), the court may dismiss the debtor's Chapter 7 petition.

Order for Relief If the voluntary petition for bankruptcy is found to be proper, the filing of the petition will itself constitute an **order for relief.** (An order for relief is a court's grant of assistance to a petitioner.) Once a consumer-debtor's voluntary petition has been filed, the clerk of the court or other appointee must give the trustee and creditors notice of the order for relief by mail not more than twenty days after entry of the order.

6. Note that the court may not dismiss a case on this ground if the debtor's bankruptcy is necessary to satisfy a claim for a domestic-support obligation.

Involuntary Bankruptcy

An involuntary bankruptcy occurs when the debtor's creditors force the debtor into bankruptcy proceedings. An involuntary case cannot be commenced against a farmer[7] or a charitable institution. For an involuntary action to be filed against other debtors, the following requirements must be met: If the debtor has twelve or more creditors, three or more of these creditors having unsecured claims totaling at least $13,475 must join in the petition. If a debtor has fewer than twelve creditors, one or more creditors having a claim of $13,475 may file.

If the debtor challenges the involuntary petition, a hearing will be held, and the bankruptcy court will enter an order for relief if it finds either of the following:

1. The debtor is generally not paying debts as they become due.
2. A general receiver, assignee, or custodian took possession of, or was appointed to take charge of, substantially all of the debtor's property within 120 days before the filing of the petition.

If the court grants an order for relief, the debtor will be required to supply the same information in the bankruptcy schedules as in a voluntary bankruptcy.

An involuntary petition should not be used as an everyday debt-collection device, and the Code provides penalties for the filing of frivolous petitions against debtors. Judgment may be granted against the petitioning creditors for the costs and attorneys' fees incurred by the debtor in defending against an involuntary petition that is dismissed by the court. If the petition is filed in bad faith, damages can be awarded for injury to the debtor's reputation. Punitive damages may also be awarded.

Automatic Stay

The moment a petition, either voluntary or involuntary, is filed, an **automatic stay,** or suspension, of virtually all actions by creditors against the debtor or the debtor's property normally goes into effect. In other words, once a petition has been filed, creditors cannot contact the debtor by phone or mail or start any legal proceedings to recover debts or to repossess property. A secured creditor or other party in interest, however, may petition the bankruptcy court for relief from the automatic stay. The Code provides that if a creditor knowingly violates the automatic stay (a willful violation), any injured party, including the debtor, is entitled to recover actual damages, costs, and attorneys' fees, and may be awarded punitive damages as well.

Underlying the Code's automatic-stay provision for a secured creditor is a concept known as *adequate protection*. The **adequate protection doctrine,** among other things, protects secured creditors from losing their security as a result of the automatic stay. The bankruptcy court can provide adequate protection by requiring the debtor or trustee to make periodic cash payments or a one-time cash payment (or to provide additional collateral or replacement liens) to the extent that the stay may actually cause the value of the property to decrease.

Exceptions to the Automatic Stay There are several exceptions to the automatic stay. The 2005 Bankruptcy Reform Act created a new exception for domestic-support obligations, which includes any debt owed to or recoverable by a spouse, former spouse, or child of the debtor; a child's parent or guardian; or a governmental unit. In addition, proceedings against the debtor related to divorce, child custody or visitation, domestic violence, and support enforcement are not stayed. Also excepted are investigations by a securities regulatory agency, the creation or perfection of statutory liens for property taxes or special assessments on real property, eviction actions on judgments obtained prior to filing the petition, and withholding from the debtor's wages for repayment of a retirement account loan.

Limitations on the Automatic Stay Under the Code, if a creditor or other party in interest requests relief from the stay, the stay will automatically terminate sixty days after the request, unless the court grants an extension[8] or the parties agree otherwise. Also, the automatic stay on secured debts (see Chapter 29) will terminate thirty days after the petition is filed if the debtor had filed a bankruptcy petition that was dismissed within the prior year. Any party in interest can request the court to extend the stay by showing that the filing is in good faith.

7. The definition of *farmer* includes persons who receive more than 50 percent of their gross income from farming operations, such as tilling the soil, dairy farming, ranching, or the production or raising of crops, poultry, or livestock. Corporations and partnerships may qualify under certain conditions.

8. The court might grant an extension, for example, on a motion by the trustee that the property is of value to the estate.

If two or more bankruptcy petitions were dismissed during the prior year, the Code presumes bad faith, and the automatic stay does not go into effect until the court determines that the filing was made in good faith. In addition, if the petition is subsequently dismissed because the debtor failed to file the required documents within thirty days of filing, for example, the stay is terminated. Finally, the automatic stay on secured property terminates forty-five days after the creditors' meeting (to be discussed shortly) unless the debtor redeems or reaffirms certain debts (*reaffirmation* is discussed later in this chapter). In other words, the debtor cannot keep the secured property (such as a financed automobile), even if she or he continues to make payments on it, without reinstating the rights of the secured party to collect on the debt.

Property of the Estate

On the commencement of a liquidation proceeding under Chapter 7, an *estate in property* is created. The estate consists of all the debtor's legal and equitable interests in property currently held, wherever located, together with community property (property jointly owned by a husband and wife in certain states—see Chapter 48), property transferred in a transaction voidable by the trustee, proceeds and profits from the property of the estate, and certain after-acquired property. Interests in certain property—such as gifts, inheritances, property settlements (from divorce), and life insurance death proceeds—to which the debtor becomes entitled *within 180 days after filing* may also become part of the estate. Withholdings for employee benefit plan contributions are excluded from the estate. Generally, though, the filing of a bankruptcy petition fixes a dividing line: property acquired prior to the filing of the petition becomes property of the estate, and property acquired after the filing of the petition, except as just noted, remains the debtor's.

Creditors' Meeting and Claims

Within a reasonable time after the order for relief has been granted (not less than twenty days or more than forty days), the trustee must call a meeting of the creditors listed in the schedules filed by the debtor. The bankruptcy judge does not attend this meeting, but the debtor is required to attend and to submit to examination under oath by the creditors and the trustee. At the meeting, the trustee ensures that the debtor is aware of the potential consequences of bankruptcy and of his or her ability to file for bankruptcy under a different chapter of the Bankruptcy Code.

To be entitled to receive a portion of the debtor's estate, each creditor normally files a *proof of claim* with the bankruptcy court clerk within ninety days of the creditors' meeting.[9] The proof of claim lists the creditor's name and address, as well as the amount that the creditor asserts is owed to the creditor by the debtor. A proof of claim is necessary if there is any dispute concerning the claim. Generally, any legal obligation of the debtor is a claim (except claims for breach of employment contracts or real estate leases for terms longer than one year).

Exemptions

The trustee takes control over the debtor's property, but an individual debtor is entitled to exempt certain property from the bankruptcy. The Bankruptcy Code exempts the following property:[10]

1. Up to $20,200 in equity in the debtor's residence and burial plot (the homestead exemption).
2. Interest in a motor vehicle up to $3,225.
3. Interest, up to $525 for a particular item, in household goods and furnishings, wearing apparel, appliances, books, animals, crops, and musical instruments (the aggregate total of all items is limited, however, to $10,775).[11]
4. Interest in jewelry up to $1,350.
5. Interest in any other property up to $1,075, plus any unused part of the $20,200 homestead exemption up to $10,125.
6. Interest in any tools of the debtor's trade up to $2,025.
7. Life insurance contracts owned by the debtor.
8. Certain interests in accrued dividends and interest under life insurance contracts owned by the debtor, not to exceed $10,775.
9. Professionally prescribed health aids.

9. This ninety-day rule applies in Chapter 12 and Chapter 13 bankruptcies as well.

10. The dollar amounts stated in the Bankruptcy Code are adjusted automatically every three years on April 1 based on changes in the Consumer Price Index. The adjusted amounts are rounded to the nearest $25. The amounts stated in this chapter are in accordance with those computed on April 1, 2007.

11. The 2005 Bankruptcy Reform Act clarified that "household goods and furnishings" includes, for example, one computer, one radio, one television, and one videocassette recorder. Other items, such as works of art, electronic entertainment equipment with a fair market value of more than $500, and antiques and jewelry (except wedding rings) valued at more than $500, are not included.

10. The right to receive Social Security and certain welfare benefits, alimony and support, certain retirement funds and pensions, and education savings accounts held for specific periods of time.
11. The right to receive certain personal-injury and other awards up to $20,200.

Individual states have the power to pass legislation precluding debtors from using the federal exemptions within the state; a majority of the states have done this (see Chapter 28). In those states, debtors may use only state, not federal, exemptions. In the rest of the states, an individual debtor (or a husband and wife filing jointly) may choose either the exemptions provided under state law or the federal exemptions.

The Homestead Exemption

The 2005 Bankruptcy Reform Act significantly changed the law for those debtors seeking to use state homestead exemption statutes (which were discussed in Chapter 28). Under prior law, the homestead exemptions of six states, including Florida and Texas, allowed debtors petitioning for bankruptcy to shield *unlimited* amounts of equity in their homes from creditors. The 2005 act places limits on the amount that can be claimed as exempt in bankruptcy. Also, a debtor must have lived in a state for two years prior to filing the petition to be able to use the state homestead exemption (the prior law required only six months).

In general, if the debtor acquired the homestead within three and a half years preceding the date of filing, the maximum equity exempted is $136,875, even if state law would permit a higher amount. Moreover, the debtor may not claim the homestead exemption if he or she has committed any criminal act, intentional tort, or willful or reckless misconduct that caused serious physical injury or death to another individual in the preceding five years. Similarly, a debtor who has been convicted of a felony may not be able to claim the exemption.

The Trustee

Promptly after the order for relief in the liquidation proceeding has been entered, a trustee is appointed. The basic duty of the trustee is to collect the debtor's available estate and reduce it to cash for distribution, preserving the interests of both the debtor and unsecured creditors. This requires that the trustee be accountable for administering the debtor's estate. To enable the trustee to accomplish this duty, the Code gives the trustee certain powers, stated in both general and specific terms. These powers must be exercised within two years of the order for relief.

The trustee has additional duties with regard to means testing debtors and protecting domestic-support creditors. The trustee is required to promptly review all materials filed by the debtor to determine if there is substantial abuse. Within ten days after the first meeting of the creditors, the trustee must file a statement indicating whether the case is presumed to be an abuse under the means test. The trustee must provide all creditors with a copy of this statement. When there is a presumption of abuse, the trustee must either file a motion to dismiss the petition (or convert it to a Chapter 13 case) or file a statement setting forth the reasons why a motion would not be appropriate. If the debtor owes a domestic-support obligation (such as child support), the trustee is required to provide written notice of the bankruptcy to the claim holder (such as a former spouse).

The Trustee's Powers The trustee occupies a position *equivalent* in rights to that of certain other parties. For example, the trustee has the same rights as a creditor who could have obtained a judicial lien or levy execution on the debtor's property. This means that a trustee has priority over an unperfected secured party (see Chapter 29) as to the debtor's property.[12] This right of a trustee, which is equivalent to that of a lien creditor, is known as the *strong-arm power.* A trustee also has power equivalent to that of a *bona fide purchaser* of real property from the debtor.

The Right to Possession of the Debtor's Property The trustee has the power to require persons holding the debtor's property at the time the petition is filed to deliver the property to the trustee. (Usually, though, the trustee takes constructive, rather than actual, possession of the debtor's property. To obtain control of a debtor's business inventory, for instance, a trustee might change the locks on the doors to the business and hire a security guard.)

Avoidance Powers The trustee also has specific powers of *avoidance*—that is, the trustee can set aside a sale or other transfer of the debtor's property, taking it back as a part of the debtor's estate. These powers include any voidable rights available to the debtor,

12. Nevertheless, in most states a creditor with an unperfected purchase-money security interest may prevail against a trustee if the creditor perfects (files) within twenty days of the debtor's receipt of the collateral. This is normally true even if the debtor files a bankruptcy petition before the creditor perfects.

preferences, certain statutory liens, and fraudulent transfers by the debtor. Each of these powers is discussed in more detail below. Note that under the Code, the trustee no longer has the power to avoid any transfer that was a bona fide payment of a domestic-support debt.

The debtor shares most of the trustee's avoidance powers. Thus, if the trustee does not take action to enforce one of the rights mentioned above, the debtor in a liquidation bankruptcy can still enforce that right.[13]

Voidable Rights A trustee steps into the shoes of the debtor. Thus, any reason that a debtor can use to obtain the return of her or his property can be used by the trustee as well. These grounds include fraud, duress, incapacity, and mutual mistake.

For example, Ben sells his boat to Tara. Tara gives Ben a check, knowing that she has insufficient funds in her bank account to cover the check. Tara has committed fraud. Ben has the right to avoid that transfer and recover the boat from Tara. Once an order for relief under Chapter 7 of the Code has been entered for Ben, the trustee can exercise the same right to recover the boat from Tara, and the boat becomes a part of the debtor's estate.

Preferences A debtor is not permitted to transfer property or to make a payment that favors—or gives a **preference** to—one creditor over others. The trustee is allowed to recover payments made both voluntarily and involuntarily to one creditor in preference over another. If a **preferred creditor** (one who has received a preferential transfer from the debtor) has sold the property to an innocent third party, the trustee cannot recover the property from the innocent party. The preferred creditor, however, generally can be held accountable for the value of the property.

To have made a preferential payment that can be recovered, an *insolvent* debtor generally must have transferred property, for a *preexisting* debt, within *ninety days* prior to the filing of the bankruptcy petition. The transfer must have given the creditor more than the creditor would have received as a result of the bankruptcy proceedings. The trustee need not prove insolvency, as the Code presumes that the debtor is insolvent during this ninety-day period.

13. Under a Chapter 11 bankruptcy (to be discussed later), for which no trustee other than the debtor generally exists, the debtor has the same avoidance powers as a trustee under Chapter 7. Under Chapters 12 and 13 (also to be discussed later), a trustee must be appointed.

Preferences to Insiders. Sometimes, the creditor receiving the preference is an **insider**—an individual, a partner, a partnership, a corporation, or an officer or a director of a corporation (or a relative of one of these) who has a close relationship with the debtor. In this situation, the avoidance power of the trustee is extended to transfers made within *one year* before filing; however, the *presumption* of insolvency is confined to the ninety-day period. Therefore, the trustee must prove that the debtor was insolvent at the time of a transfer that occurred prior to the ninety-day period.

Transfers That Do Not Constitute Preferences. Not all transfers are preferences. To be a preference, the transfer must be made for something other than current consideration. Most courts generally assume that payment for services rendered within fifteen days prior to the payment is not a preference. If a creditor receives payment in the ordinary course of business from an individual or business debtor, such as payment of last month's telephone bill, the trustee in bankruptcy cannot recover the payment. To be recoverable, a preference must be a transfer for an antecedent (preexisting) debt, such as a year-old printing bill. In addition, the Code permits a consumer-debtor to transfer any property to a creditor up to a total value of $5,475, without the transfer's constituting a preference. (This amount is increased periodically under the law.) Payment of domestic-support debts does not constitute a preference.

Liens on Debtor's Property The trustee has the power to avoid certain statutory liens against the debtor's property, such as a landlord's lien for unpaid rent. The trustee can avoid statutory liens that first became effective against the debtor when the bankruptcy petition was filed or when the debtor became insolvent. The trustee can also avoid any lien against a good faith purchaser that was not perfected or enforceable on the date of the bankruptcy filing.

Fraudulent Transfers The trustee may avoid fraudulent transfers or obligations if they were made within two years of the filing of the petition or if they were made with actual intent to hinder, delay, or defraud a creditor. Transfers made for less than a reasonably equivalent consideration are also vulnerable if by making them, the debtor became insolvent or intended to incur debts that he or she could not pay. Similarly, a transfer that left a debtor engaged in business with an unreasonably small amount of capital may be considered fraudulent. When a fraudulent transfer is made outside the Code's two-year limit, creditors may seek alternative relief under state laws. Some state laws often allow creditors to recover for transfers made up to three years prior to the filing of a petition.

Distribution of Property

The Code provides specific rules for the distribution of the debtor's property to secured and unsecured creditors. (We will examine these distributions shortly.) Anything remaining after the priority classes of creditors have been satisfied is turned over to the debtor. Exhibit 30–1 illustrates graphically the collection and distribution of property in most voluntary bankruptcies.

In a bankruptcy case in which the debtor has no assets (called "no-asset cases"), creditors are notified of the debtor's petition for bankruptcy but are instructed not to file a claim. In no-asset cases, the unsecured creditors will receive no payment, and most, if not all, of these debts will be discharged.

Distribution to Secured Creditors The rights of perfected secured creditors were discussed in Chapter 29. The Code provides that a consumer-debtor must file with the clerk a statement of intention with respect to the secured collateral. The statement must be filed within thirty days of filing a liquidation petition or before the date of the first meeting of the creditors (whichever is first). The statement must indicate whether the debtor will redeem the collateral (make a single payment equal to the current value of the property), reaffirm the debt (continue making payments on the debt), or surrender the property to the secured party.[14] The trustee is obligated to enforce the debtor's statement within forty-five days after the meeting of the creditors. As noted previously, failure of the debtor to redeem or reaffirm within forty-five days terminates the automatic stay.

If the collateral is surrendered to the perfected secured party, the secured creditor can either accept the property in full satisfaction of the debt or foreclose on the collateral and use the proceeds to pay off the debt. Thus, the perfected secured party has priority over unsecured parties as to the proceeds from the disposition of the collateral. When the proceeds from sale of the collateral exceed the amount of the perfected secured party's claim, the secured party also has priority to an amount that will cover the reasonable fees and costs incurred. Any excess over this amount is returned to the trustee and used to satisfy the claims of unsecured creditors. If the collateral is insufficient to cover the secured debt owed, the secured creditor becomes an unsecured creditor for the difference.

14. Also, if applicable, the debtor must specify whether the collateral will be claimed as exempt property.

EXHIBIT 30–1 • Collection and Distribution of Property in Most Voluntary Bankruptcies

This exhibit illustrates the property that might be collected in a debtor's voluntary bankruptcy and how it might be distributed to creditors. Involuntary bankruptcies and some voluntary bankruptcies could include additional types of property and other creditors.

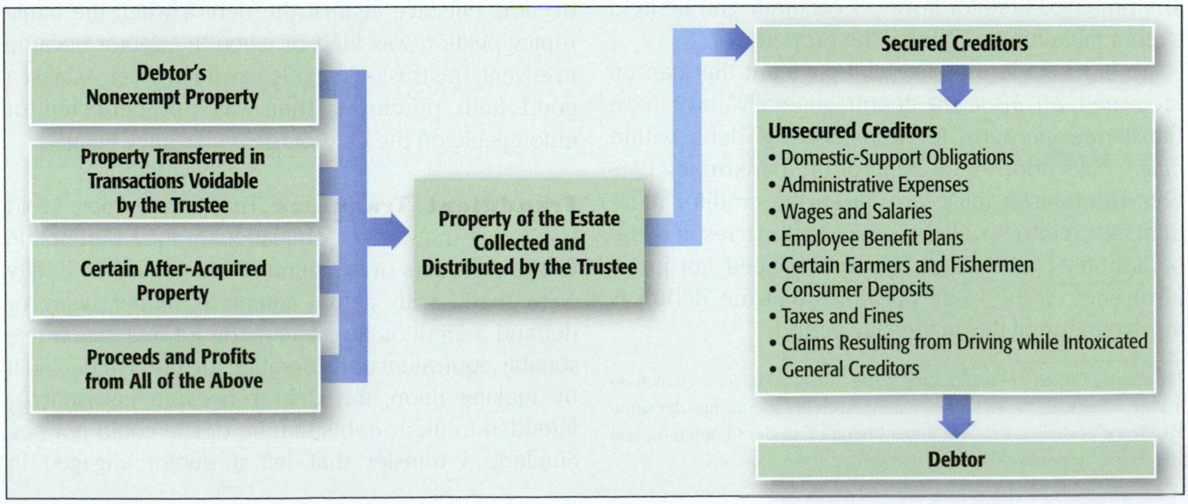

Distribution to Unsecured Creditors Bankruptcy law establishes an order of priority for classes of debts owed to *unsecured* creditors, and they are paid in the order of their priority. Each class must be fully paid before the next class is entitled to any of the remaining proceeds. If there are insufficient proceeds to pay fully all the creditors in a class, the proceeds are distributed *proportionately* to the creditors in that class, and classes lower in priority receive nothing.

The 2005 act elevated domestic-support (mainly child-support) obligations to the highest priority of unsecured claims—so these are the first debts to be paid. After that, administrative expenses related to the bankruptcy (such as court costs, trustee fees, and attorneys' fees) are paid; next come any expenses that a debtor in an involuntary bankruptcy incurs in the ordinary course of business. Unpaid wages, salaries, and commissions earned within ninety days prior to the petition are paid next, followed by certain claims for contributions to employee benefit plans, claims by some farmers and fishermen, consumer deposits, and certain taxes. Claims of general creditors rank last in the order of priority, which is why these unsecured creditors often receive little, if anything, in a Chapter 7 bankruptcy.

Discharge

From the debtor's point of view, the primary purpose of liquidation is to obtain a fresh start through a discharge of debts.[15] As mentioned earlier, once the debtor's assets have been distributed to creditors as permitted by the Code, the debtor's remaining debts are then discharged, meaning that the debtor is not obligated to pay them. Any judgments on the debts are voided, and creditors are enjoined (prevented) from bringing any actions to collect them. A discharge does not affect the liability of a co-debtor.

Certain debts, however, are not dischargeable in bankruptcy. Also, certain debtors may not qualify to have all debts discharged in bankruptcy. These situations are discussed next.

15. Discharges are granted under Chapter 7 only to individuals, not to corporations or partnerships. The latter may use Chapter 11, or they may terminate their existence under state law.

Exceptions to Discharge Discharge of a debt may be denied because of the nature of the claim or the conduct of the debtor. A court will not discharge claims that are based on a debtor's willful or malicious conduct or fraud,[16] or claims related to property or funds that the debtor obtained by false pretenses, embezzlement, or larceny. Any monetary judgment against the debtor for driving while intoxicated cannot be discharged in bankruptcy. When a debtor fails to list a creditor on the bankruptcy schedules (and thus the creditor is not notified of the bankruptcy), that creditor's claims are not dischargeable.

Claims that are not dischargeable in a liquidation bankruptcy include amounts due to the government for taxes, fines, or penalties.[17] Additionally, amounts borrowed by the debtor to pay these taxes will not be discharged. Domestic-support obligations and property settlements arising from a divorce or separation cannot be discharged. Certain student loans and educational debts are not dischargeable (unless payment of the loans imposes an undue hardship on the debtor and the debtor's dependents),[18] nor are amounts due on a retirement account loan. Consumer debts for purchasing luxury items worth more than $550 and cash advances totaling more than $825 generally are not dischargeable.

In the following case, the court considered whether to order the discharge of a debtor's student loan obligations. What does a debtor have to prove to show "undue hardship"?

16. Even if a debtor who is sued for fraud settles the lawsuit, the United States Supreme Court has held that the amount due under the settlement agreement may not be discharged in bankruptcy because of the underlying fraud. See *Archer v. Warner,* 538 U.S. 314, 123 S.Ct. 1462, 155 L.Ed.2d 454 (2003).

17. Taxes accruing within three years prior to bankruptcy are nondischargeable, including federal and state income taxes, employment taxes, taxes on gross receipts, property taxes, excise taxes, customs duties, and any other taxes for which the government claims the debtor is liable in some capacity. See 11 U.S.C. Sections 507(a)(8), 523(a)(1).

18. For a case discussing whether a student loan should be discharged because of undue hardship, see *In re Savage,* 311 Bankr. 835 (1st Cir. 2004).

CASE 30.2 In re Mosley

United States Court of Appeals, Eleventh Circuit, 2007. 494 F.3d 1320.

• **Background and Facts** Keldric Mosley incurred student loans while attending Georgia's Alcorn State University between 1989 and 1994. At Alcorn, Mosley joined the U.S. Army Reserve

CASE CONTINUES

CASE 30.2 CONTINUED Officers' Training Corps. During training in 1993, Mosley fell from a tank and injured his hip and back. Medical problems from his injuries led him to resign his commission. He left Alcorn to live with his mother in Atlanta from 1994 to 1999. He worked briefly for several employers, but depressed and physically limited by his injury, he was unable to keep any of the jobs. He tried to return to school but could not obtain financial aid because of the debt he had incurred at Alcorn. In 1999, a federal bankruptcy court granted him a discharge under Chapter 7, but it did not include the student loans. In 2000, after a week at the Georgia Regional Hospital, a state-supported mental-health facility, Mosley was prescribed medication through the U.S. Department of Veterans Affairs for depression, back pain, and other problems. By 2004, his monthly income consisted primarily of $210 in disability benefits from the Veterans Administration. Homeless and in debt for $45,000 to Educational Credit Management Corporation, Mosley asked the bankruptcy court to reopen his case. The court granted him a discharge of his student loans on the basis of undue hardship. Educational Credit appealed to the U.S. Court of Appeals for the Eleventh Circuit.

• **Decision and Rationale** The U.S. Court of Appeals for the Eleventh Circuit affirmed the lower court's discharge of the debtor's student loans. To establish undue hardship, the court required "that the debtor cannot maintain, based on current income and expenses, a 'minimal' standard of living * * * if forced to repay the loans; that additional circumstances exist indicating that this state of affairs is likely to persist for a significant portion of the repayment period of the student loans; and that the debtor has made good faith efforts to repay the loans." The plaintiff, Educational Credit, claimed that the bankruptcy court was too lax in its acceptance of the evidence purportedly showing that Mosley would remain in the same financial situation for a long period of time. Moreover, Educational Credit argued that the record did not support a conclusion of undue hardship. In contrast, the U.S. Court of Appeals for the Eleventh Circuit reasoned that Mosley's medical problems, lack of skills, and dire living conditions made it unlikely that he would be able to hold a job and repay the loans. Furthermore, Mosley had made good faith efforts to repay his student loans and "would suffer undue hardship if they were excepted from [bankruptcy] discharge."

• **The Ethical Dimension** *Should a debtor be required to attempt to negotiate a repayment plan with a creditor to demonstrate good faith? Why or why not?*

• **The Global Dimension** *If this debtor were to relocate to a country with a lower cost of living than the United States, should his change in circumstances be a ground for revoking the discharge? Explain your answer.*

Objections to Discharge In addition to the exceptions to discharge previously discussed, a bankruptcy court may also deny the discharge of the *debtor* (as opposed to the debt). In the latter situation, the assets of the debtor are still distributed to the creditors, but the debtor remains liable for the unpaid portion of all claims. Grounds for the denial of discharge of the debtor include the following:

1. The debtor's concealment or destruction of property with the intent to hinder, delay, or defraud a creditor.
2. The debtor's fraudulent concealment or destruction of financial records.
3. The granting of a discharge to the debtor within eight years of the filing of the petition.
4. The debtor's failure to complete the required consumer education course (unless such a course is unavailable).
5. Proceedings in which the debtor could be found guilty of a felony (basically, a court may not discharge any debt until the completion of felony proceedings against the debtor).

Revocation of Discharge On petition by the trustee or a creditor, the bankruptcy court can, within one year, revoke the discharge decree. The discharge decree will be revoked if it is discovered that the debtor acted fraudulently or dishonestly during the bankruptcy proceedings. The revocation renders the discharge void, allowing creditors not satisfied by the distribution of the debtor's estate to proceed with their claims against the debtor.

Reaffirmation of Debt

An agreement to pay a debt dischargeable in bankruptcy is called a **reaffirmation agreement.** A debtor may wish to pay a debt—for example, a debt owed to a family member, physician, bank, or some other creditor—even though the debt could be discharged in bankruptcy. Also, as noted previously, a debtor cannot retain secured property while continuing to pay without entering into a reaffirmation agreement.

Reaffirmation Procedures To be enforceable, reaffirmation agreements must be made before the debtor is granted a discharge. The agreement must be signed and filed with the court (along with certain required disclosures, described next). Court approval is required unless the debtor is represented by an attorney during the negotiation of the reaffirmation and submits the proper documents and certifications. Even when the debtor is represented by an attorney, court approval may be required if it appears that the reaffirmation will result in undue hardship on the debtor.[19] When court approval is required, a separate hearing will take place. The court will approve the reaffirmation only if it finds that the agreement will not result in undue hardship to the debtor and that the reaffirmation is consistent with the debtor's best interests.

Reaffirmation Disclosures To discourage creditors from engaging in abusive reaffirmation practices, there are more requirements for reaffirmation. The Code provides specific language for several pages of disclosures that must be given to debtors entering reaffirmation agreements. Among other things, these disclosures explain that the debtor is not required to reaffirm any debt, but that liens on secured property, such as mortgages and cars, will remain in effect even if the debt is not reaffirmed.

The reaffirmation agreement must disclose the amount of the debt reaffirmed, the rate of interest, the date payments begin, and the right to rescind. The disclosures also caution the debtor: "Only agree to reaffirm a debt if it is in your best interest. Be sure you can afford the payments you agree to make." The original disclosure documents must be signed by the debtor, certified by the debtor's attorney, and filed with the court at the same time as the reaffirmation agreement. A reaffirmation agreement that is not accompanied by the original signed disclosures will not be effective.

SECTION 3 Reorganizations

The type of bankruptcy proceeding most commonly used by corporate debtors is the Chapter 11 *reorganization*. In a reorganization, the creditors and the debtor formulate a plan under which the debtor pays a portion of the debts and is discharged of the remainder. The debtor is allowed to continue in business. Although this type of bankruptcy is generally a corporate reorganization, any debtors (including individuals but excluding stockbrokers and commodities brokers) who are eligible for Chapter 7 relief are eligible for relief under Chapter 11.[20] In 1994, Congress established a "fast-track" Chapter 11 procedure for small-business debtors whose liabilities do not exceed $2.19 million and who do not own or manage real estate. This allows bankruptcy proceedings without the appointment of committees and can save time and costs.

The same principles that govern the filing of a liquidation (Chapter 7) petition apply to reorganization (Chapter 11) proceedings. The case may be brought either voluntarily or involuntarily. The same guidelines govern the entry of the order for relief. The automatic-stay and adequate protection provisions are applicable in reorganizations as well. The Code's exceptions to the automatic stay also apply to Chapter 11 proceedings, as do the provisions regarding substantial abuse and additional grounds for dismissal (or conversion) of bankruptcy petitions. Additionally, there are specific rules and limitations for *individual* debtors who file a Chapter 11 petition. For example, an individual debtor's postpetition acquisitions and earnings become the property of the bankruptcy estate.

19. If the debtor's monthly income minus the debtor's monthly expenses as shown on her or his completed and signed statement is less than the scheduled payments on the reaffirmed debt, undue hardship will be presumed. The debtor can rebut the presumption by providing a statement that explains and identifies additional sources of funds from which the debtor will make the agreed-on payments.

20. In addition, railroads are eligible for Chapter 11 relief.

Must Be in the Best Interests of the Creditors

Under Section 305(a) of the Bankruptcy Code, a court, after notice and a hearing, may dismiss or suspend all proceedings in a case at any time if dismissal or suspension would better serve the interests of the creditors. Section 1112 also allows a court, after notice and a hearing, to dismiss a case under reorganization "for cause." Cause includes the absence of a reasonable likelihood of rehabilitation, the inability to effect a plan, and an unreasonable delay by the debtor that is prejudicial to (may harm the interests of) creditors.[21]

Workouts

In some instances, creditors may prefer private, negotiated adjustments of creditor-debtor relations, also known as **workouts,** to bankruptcy proceedings. Often, these out-of-court workouts are much more flexible and thus more conducive to a speedy settlement. Speed is critical because delay is one of the most costly elements in any bankruptcy proceeding. Another advantage of workouts is that they avoid the various administrative costs of bankruptcy proceedings.

Debtor in Possession

On entry of the order for relief, the debtor generally continues to operate the business as a **debtor in possession (DIP).** The court, however, may appoint a trustee (often referred to as a *receiver*) to operate the debtor's business if gross mismanagement of the business is shown or if appointing a trustee is in the best interests of the estate.

The DIP's role is similar to that of a trustee in a liquidation. The DIP is entitled to avoid preferential payments made to creditors and fraudulent transfers of assets. The DIP has the power to decide whether to cancel or assume prepetition executory contracts (those that are not yet performed) or unexpired leases. The DIP can also exercise a trustee's strong-arm powers.

Creditors' Committees

As soon as practicable after the entry of the order for relief, a creditors' committee of unsecured creditors is appointed. If the debtor has filed a reorganization plan accepted by the creditors, however, the trustee may decide not to call a meeting of the creditors. The committee may consult with the trustee or the DIP concerning the administration of the case or the formulation of the plan. Additional creditors' committees may be appointed to represent special interest creditors. A court may order the trustee to change the membership of a committee or to increase the number of committee members to include a small-business concern if the court deems it necessary to ensure adequate representation of the creditors.

Orders affecting the estate generally will be entered only with the consent of the committee or after a hearing in which the judge is informed of the position of the committee. As mentioned earlier, businesses with debts of less than $2.19 million that do not own or manage real estate can avoid creditors' committees. In these cases, orders can be entered without a committee's consent.

The Reorganization Plan

A reorganization plan to rehabilitate the debtor is a plan to conserve and administer the debtor's assets in the hope of an eventual return to successful operation and solvency.

Filing the Plan Only the debtor may file a plan within the first 120 days after the date of the order for relief. The 120-day period may be extended but not beyond eighteen months from the date of the order for relief. If the debtor does not meet the 120-day deadline or obtain an extension, and if the debtor fails to procure the required creditor consent (discussed below) within 180 days, any party may propose a plan up to twenty months from the date of the order for relief. (In other words, the 180-day period cannot be extended beyond twenty months past the date of the order for relief.) For a small-business debtor, the time for the debtor's filing is 180 days.

The plan must be fair and equitable and must do the following:

1. Designate classes of claims and interests.
2. Specify the treatment to be afforded the classes. (The plan must provide the same treatment for all claims in a particular class.)
3. Provide an adequate means for execution. (Individual debtors must utilize postpetition assets as necessary to execute the plan.)
4. Provide for payment of tax claims over a five-year period.

Acceptance and Confirmation of the Plan Once the plan has been developed, it is submitted to

21. See 11 U.S.C. Section 1112(b). Debtors are not prohibited from filing successive petitions, however. A debtor whose petition is dismissed, for example, can file a new Chapter 11 petition (which may be granted unless it is filed in bad faith).

each class of creditors for acceptance. Each class must accept the plan unless the class is not adversely affected by it. A class has accepted the plan when a majority of the creditors, representing two-thirds of the amount of the total claim, vote to approve it. Confirmation is conditioned on the debtor certifying that all postpetition domestic-support obligations have been paid in full. For small-business debtors, if the plan meets the listed requirements, the court must confirm the plan within forty-five days (unless this period is extended).

Even when all classes of creditors accept the plan, the court may refuse to confirm it if it is not "in the best interests of the creditors."[22] A former spouse or child of the debtor can block the plan if it does not provide for payment of her or his claims in cash. If an unsecured creditor objects to the plan, specific rules apply to the value of property to be distributed under the plan. The plan can also be modified on the request of the debtor, a trustee, or a holder of the unsecured claim. Tax claims must be paid over a five-year period.

Even if only one class of creditors has accepted the plan, the court may still confirm the plan under the Code's so-called **cram-down provision.** In other words, the court may confirm the plan over the objections of a class of creditors. Before the court can exercise this right of cram-down confirmation, it must be demonstrated that the plan is fair and equitable, and does not discriminate unfairly against any creditors.

Discharge The plan is binding on confirmation; however, confirmation of a plan does not discharge an individual debtor. Individual debtors must complete the plan prior to discharge, unless the court orders otherwise. For all other debtors, the court may order discharge at any time after the plan is confirmed. The debtor is given a reorganization discharge from all claims not protected under the plan. This discharge does not apply to any claims that would be denied discharge under liquidation.

SECTION 4

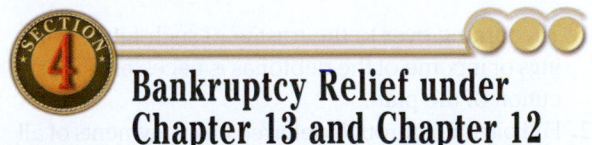

Bankruptcy Relief under Chapter 13 and Chapter 12

In addition to bankruptcy relief through liquidation and reorganization, the Code also provides for individuals' repayment plans (Chapter 13) and family-farmer and family-fishermen debt adjustments (Chapter 12).

Individuals' Repayment Plan

Chapter 13 of the Bankruptcy Code provides for "Adjustment of Debts of an Individual with Regular Income." Individuals (not partnerships or corporations) with regular income who owe fixed (liquidated) unsecured debts of less than $336,900 or fixed secured debts of less than $1,010,650 may take advantage of bankruptcy repayment plans. Among those eligible are salaried employees; sole proprietors; and individuals who live on welfare, Social Security, fixed pensions, or investment income. Many small-business debtors have a choice of filing under either Chapter 11 or Chapter 13. Repayment plans offer several advantages, however. One advantage is that they are less expensive and less complicated than reorganization proceedings or, for that matter, even liquidation proceedings.

Filing the Petition A Chapter 13 repayment plan case can be initiated only by the filing of a voluntary petition by the debtor or by the conversion of a Chapter 7 petition (because of a finding of substantial abuse under the means test, for example). Certain liquidation and reorganization cases may be converted to repayment plan cases with the consent of the debtor.[23] A trustee, who will make payments under the plan, must be appointed. On the filing of a repayment plan petition, the automatic stay previously discussed takes effect. Although the stay applies to all or part of the debtor's consumer debt, it does not apply to any business debt incurred by the debtor. The automatic stay also does not apply to domestic-support obligations.

The Bankruptcy Code imposes the requirement of good faith on a debtor at both the time of the filing of the petition and the time of the filing of the plan. The Code does not define good faith—it is determined in each case through a consideration of "the totality of the circumstances." Bad faith can be cause for the dismissal of a Chapter 13 petition, as the following case illustrates.

22. The plan need not provide for full repayment to unsecured creditors. Instead, creditors receive a percentage of each dollar owed to them by the debtor.

23. A Chapter 13 repayment plan may be converted to a Chapter 7 liquidation either at the request of the debtor or, under certain circumstances, "for cause" by a creditor. A Chapter 13 case may be converted to a Chapter 11 case after a hearing.

CASE 30.3 In re Buis

United States Bankruptcy Court, Northern District of Florida, Pensacola Division, 2006.
337 Bankr. 243.

• **Background and Facts** In 2000, Roger and Pauline Buis bought an air show business, including a helicopter, a trailer, and props, from Robert and Annette Hosking. The price was $275,000, which the Buises agreed to pay in installments. The Buises formed Otto Airshows and decorated the helicopter as "Otto the Clown." They performed in air shows and took passengers on flights for a fee. In 2003, the Buises began accusing a competitor, Army Aviation Heritage Foundation and Museum, Inc. (AAHF), of safety lapses. AAHF filed a suit in a federal district court against the Buises and their company, alleging *defamation* (see Chapter 6). The court issued a summary judgment in AAHF's favor. While the amount of the damages was being determined, the Buises stopped doing business as Otto Airshows. They formed a new firm, Prop and Rotor Aviation, Inc., to which they leased the Otto equipment. Within a month, they filed a bankruptcy petition under Chapter 13. The plan and the schedules did not mention AAHF, the Prop and Rotor lease, a settlement that the Buises received in an unrelated suit, and other items. AAHF filed a motion to dismiss the case, asserting, among other things, that the Buises filed their petition in bad faith.

• **Decision and Rationale** The court dismissed the Buises' petition. The debtors had not included all of their assets and liabilities on their initial petition and had timed its filing to avoid payment on the judgment to AAHF. They had also attempted to transfer interests in some of their assets in preference to certain creditors. In particular, "the debtors failed to list AAHF as a creditor, which is especially hard for the court to comprehend when the debtor admitted that it was AAHF's judgment that pushed them into bankruptcy." The Buises also failed to "report any income from leases in their statement of financial affairs or list any agreement with Prop and Rotor anywhere in their schedules." They did not disclose the $55,000 that they had obtained in their unrelated suit, as well as "a Kubota lawn tractor worth $10,000 and their generator, worth $400." The debtors filed their petition "after they were found liable in the District Court Action and after an unsuccessful mediation with AAHF, but before a final judgment could be entered." The court saw this as an attempt to "keep the debtors eligible to file for relief under Chapter 13, because the debts owed to AAHF would be dischargeable." The court interpreted the Buises' transfers of assets to creditors as "suspect," because the debtors granted the interests and "waited 90 days so they would 'stick,' then filed their petition." Besides, "the debtor admitted that he began planning to avoid AAHF's judgment through a Chapter 13 bankruptcy shortly after the adverse ruling."

• **What If the Facts Were Different?** *If AAHF had lost its defamation suit against the Buises, would the result in this case have been the same? Why or why not?*

• **The Global Dimension** *Could the Buises have shipped their assets to Canada or Mexico to prevent them from being included in the bankruptcy estate? Explain.*

The Repayment Plan Only the debtor may file the repayment plan. This plan may provide either for payment of all obligations in full or for payment of a lesser amount.[24] The plan must provide for the following:

1. The turning over to the trustee of such future earnings or income of the debtor as is necessary for execution of the plan.
2. Full payment through deferred cash payments of all claims entitled to priority, such as taxes.[25]
3. Identical treatment of all claims within a particular class. (The Code permits the debtor to list co-

24. A plan under Chapter 13 or Chapter 12 (to be discussed shortly) may propose to pay less than 100 percent of prepetition domestic-support obligations that were assigned, but only if disposable income is dedicated to a five-year plan. Disposable income is also redefined to exclude the amounts reasonably necessary to pay current domestic-support obligations.

25. As with a Chapter 11 reorganization plan, full repayment of all claims is not always required.

debtors, such as guarantors or sureties, as a separate class.)

Time Allowed for Repayment. Prior to the 2005 act, the time for repayment under a plan was usually three years unless the court approved an extension for up to five years. Today, the length of the payment plan (three or five years) is determined by the debtor's family income. If the debtor's family income is greater than the state median family income under the means test (previously discussed), the proposed plan must be for five years.[26] The term may not exceed five years, however.

The Code requires the debtor to make "timely" payments from her or his disposable income, and the trustee must ensure that the debtor commences these payments. The debtor must begin making payments under the proposed plan within thirty days after the plan has been *filed*. Failure of the debtor to make timely payments or to commence payments within the thirty-day period will allow the court to convert the case to a liquidation bankruptcy or to dismiss the petition.

Confirmation of the Plan. After the plan is filed, the court holds a confirmation hearing, at which interested parties (such as creditors) may object to the plan. The hearing must be held at least twenty days, but no more than forty-five days, after the meeting of the creditors. Confirmation of the plan is dependent on the debtor's certification that postpetition domestic-support obligations have been paid in full and that all prepetition tax returns have been filed. The court will confirm a plan with respect to each claim of a secured creditor under any of the following circumstances:

1. If the secured creditors have accepted the plan.
2. If the plan provides that secured creditors retain their liens until there is payment in full or until the debtor receives a discharge.
3. If the debtor surrenders the property securing the claims to the creditors.

In addition, for confirmation, the plan must provide that a creditor with a purchase-money security interest (PMSI—see Chapter 29) retains its lien until payment of the entire debt for a motor vehicle purchased within 910 days before filing the petition. For PMSIs on other personal property, the payment plan must cover debts incurred within a one-year period preceding the filing.

Objection to the Plan. Unsecured creditors do not have the power to confirm a repayment plan, but they can object to it. The court can approve a plan over the objection of the trustee or any unsecured creditor only in either of the following situations:

1. When the value of the property (replacement value as of the date of filing) to be distributed under the plan is at least equal to the amount of the claims.
2. When all of the debtor's projected disposable income to be received during the plan period will be applied to making payments. Disposable income is all income received less amounts needed to pay domestic-support obligations and/or amounts needed to meet ordinary expenses to continue the operation of a business. Also excluded from disposable income are charitable contributions up to 15 percent of the debtor's gross income and the reasonable and necessary costs for health insurance for the debtor and his or her dependents.

Modification of the Plan. Prior to completion of payments, the plan may be modified at the request of the debtor, the trustee, or an unsecured creditor. If any interested party objects to the modification, the court must hold a hearing to determine whether the modified plan will be approved.

Discharge After the debtor has completed all payments, the court grants a discharge of all debts provided for by the repayment plan. Except for allowed claims not provided for by the plan, certain long-term debts provided for by the plan, certain tax claims, payments on retirement accounts, and claims for domestic-support obligations, all other debts are dischargeable. Under prior law, a discharge of debts under a Chapter 13 repayment plan was sometimes referred to as a "superdischarge" because it allowed the discharge of fraudulently incurred debt and claims resulting from malicious or willful injury.

The 2005 Bankruptcy Reform Act, however, deleted most of the "superdischarge" provisions, especially for debts based on fraud. Today, debts for trust fund taxes, taxes for which returns were never filed or filed late (within two years of filing), domestic-support payments, student loans, and injury or property damage from driving under the influence of alcohol or drugs are nondischargeable. The law also excludes fraudulent tax obligations, criminal fines and restitution,

26. See 11 U.S.C. Section 1322(d) for details on when the court will find that the Chapter 13 plan should extend to a five-year period.

fraud by a person acting in a fiduciary capacity, and restitution for willfully and maliciously causing personal injury or death.

Even if the debtor does not complete the plan, a hardship discharge may be granted if failure to complete the plan was due to circumstances beyond the debtor's control and if the value of the property distributed under the plan was greater than what would have been paid in a liquidation. A discharge can be revoked within one year if it was obtained by fraud.

Family Farmers and Fishermen

In 1986, to help relieve economic pressure on small farmers, Congress created Chapter 12 of the Bankruptcy Code. In 2005, Congress extended this protection to family fishermen,[27] modified its provisions somewhat, and made it a permanent chapter in the Bankruptcy Code (previously, the statutes authorizing Chapter 12 had to be periodically renewed by Congress).

Definitions For purposes of Chapter 12, a *family farmer* is one whose gross income is at least 50 percent farm dependent and whose debts are at least 50 percent farm related. The total debt for a family farmer must not exceed $3,544,525. A partnership or closely held corporation (see Chapter 38) at least 50 percent owned by the farm family can also qualify as a family farmer.

A *family fisherman* is defined as one whose gross income is at least 50 percent dependent on commercial fishing operations[28] and whose debts are at least 80 percent related to commercial fishing. The total debt for a family fisherman must not exceed $1,642,500. As with family farmers, a partnership or closely held corporation can also qualify.

Filing the Petition The procedure for filing a family-farmer or family-fisherman bankruptcy plan is very similar to the procedure for filing a repayment plan under Chapter 13. The debtor must file a plan not later than ninety days after the order for relief. The filing of the petition acts as an automatic stay against creditors' and co-obligors' actions against the estate.

A farmer or fisherman who has already filed a reorganization or repayment plan may convert it to a Chapter 12 plan. The debtor may also convert a Chapter 12 plan to a liquidation plan.

Content and Confirmation of the Plan The content of a plan under Chapter 12 is basically the same as that of a Chapter 13 repayment plan. The plan can be modified by the debtor but, except for cause, must be confirmed or denied within forty-five days of filing.

Court confirmation of the plan is the same as for a repayment plan. In summary, the plan must provide for payment of secured debts at the value of the collateral. If the secured debt exceeds the value of the collateral, the remaining debt is unsecured. For unsecured debtors, the plan must be confirmed if either (1) the value of the property to be distributed under the plan equals the amount of the claim, or (2) the plan provides that all of the debtor's disposable income to be received in a three-year period (or longer, by court approval) will be applied to making payments. Disposable income is all income received less amounts needed to support the farmer or fisherman and his or her family and to continue the farming or commercial fishing operation. Completion of payments under the plan discharges all debts provided for by the plan. See *Concept Summary 30.1* for a comparison of bankruptcy procedures under Chapters 7, 11, 12, and 13.

27. Although the Code uses the terms *fishermen* and *fisherman,* Chapter 12 provisions apply equally to men and women.

28. Commercial fishing operations include catching, harvesting, or aquaculture raising fish, shrimp, lobsters, urchins, seaweed, shellfish, or other aquatic species or products.

CONCEPT SUMMARY 30.1
Forms of Bankruptcy Relief Compared

Issue	Chapter 7	Chapter 11	Chapters 12 and 13
PURPOSE	Liquidation.	Reorganization.	Adjustment.
WHO CAN PETITION	Debtor (voluntary) or creditors (involuntary).	Debtor (voluntary) or creditors (involuntary).	Debtor (voluntary) only.

CONCEPT SUMMARY 30.1
Forms of Bankruptcy Relief Compared, Continued

Issue	Chapter 7	Chapter 11	Chapters 12 and 13
Who Can Be a Debtor	Any "person" (including partnerships, corporations, and municipalities) *except* railroads, insurance companies, banks, savings and loan institutions, investment companies licensed by the Small Business Administration, and credit unions. Farmers and charitable institutions also cannot be involuntarily petitioned. If the court finds the petition to be a substantial abuse of the use of Chapter 7, the debtor may be required to convert to a Chapter 13 repayment plan.	Any debtor eligible for Chapter 7 relief; railroads are also eligible. Individuals have specific rules and limitations.	*Chapter 12*—Any family farmer (one whose gross income is at least 50 percent farm dependent and whose debts are at least 50 percent farm related) or family fisherman (one whose gross income is at least 50 percent dependent on commercial fishing operations and whose debts are at least 80 percent related to commercial fishing) or any partnership or closely held corporation at least 50 percent owned by a family farmer or fisherman, when total debt does not exceed a specified amount ($3,544,525 for farmers and $1,642,500 for fishermen). *Chapter 13*—Any individual (not partnerships or corporations) with regular income who owes fixed (liquidated) unsecured debts of less than $336,900 or fixed secured debts of less than $1,010,650.
Procedure Leading to Discharge	Nonexempt property is sold with proceeds to be distributed (in order) to priority groups. Dischargeable debts are terminated.	Plan is submitted; if it is approved and followed, debts are discharged.	Plan is submitted and must be approved if the value of the property to be distributed equals the amount of the claims or if the debtor turns over disposable income for a three-year or five-year period; if the plan is followed, debts are discharged.
Advantages	On liquidation and distribution, most debts are discharged, and the debtor has an opportunity for a fresh start.	Debtor continues in business. Creditors can either accept the plan, or it can be "crammed down" on them. The plan allows for the reorganization and liquidation of debts over the plan period.	Debtor continues in business or possession of assets. If the plan is approved, most debts are discharged after the plan period.

REVIEWING Bankruptcy Law

Three months ago, Janet Hart's husband of twenty years died of cancer. Although he had medical insurance, he left Janet with outstanding medical bills of more than $50,000. Janet has worked at the local library for the past ten years, earning $1,500 per month. Since her husband's death, Janet also receives $1,500 in Social Security benefits and $1,100 in life insurance proceeds every month, for a total monthly income of $4,100. After she pays the mortgage payment of $1,500 and the amounts due on other debts, Janet has barely enough left over to buy groceries for her family (she has two teenage daughters at home). She decides to file for Chapter 7 bankruptcy, hoping for a fresh start. Using the information presented in the chapter, answer the following questions.

1. Under the Bankruptcy Code what must Janet do before filing a petition for relief under Chapter 7?
2. How much time does Janet have after filing the bankruptcy petition to submit the required schedules? What happens if Janet does not meet the deadline?
3. Assume that Janet files a petition under Chapter 7. Further assume that the median family income in the state in which Janet lives is $49,300. What steps would a court take to determine whether Janet's petition is presumed to be "substantial abuse" using the means test?
4. Suppose that the court determines that no *presumption* of substantial abuse applies in Janet's case. Nevertheless, the court finds that Janet does have the ability to pay at least a portion of the medical bills out of her disposable income. What would the court likely order in that situation?

TERMS AND CONCEPTS

adequate protection doctrine 570
automatic stay 570
cram-down provision 579
debtor in possession (DIP) 578
discharge 567
insider 573
liquidation 566
order for relief 569
petition in bankruptcy 567
preference 573
preferred creditor 573
reaffirmation agreement 577
trustee 567
U.S. trustee 567
workout 578

QUESTIONS AND CASE PROBLEMS

30–1. Burke has been a rancher all her life, raising cattle and crops. Her ranch is valued at $500,000, almost all of which is exempt under state law. Burke has eight creditors and a total indebtedness of $70,000. Two of her largest creditors are Oman ($30,000 owed) and Sneed ($25,000 owed). The other six creditors have claims of less than $5,000 each. A drought has ruined all of Burke's crops and forced her to sell many of her cattle at a loss. She cannot pay off her creditors.

(a) Under the Bankruptcy Code, can Burke, with a $500,000 ranch, voluntarily petition herself into bankruptcy? Explain.

(b) Could either Oman or Sneed force Burke into involuntary bankruptcy? Explain.

30–2. QUESTION WITH SAMPLE ANSWER

Peaslee is not known for his business sense. He started a greenhouse and nursery business two years ago, and because of his lack of experience, he soon was in debt to a number of creditors. On February 1, Peaslee borrowed $5,000 from his father to pay some of these creditors. On May 1, Peaslee paid back the $5,000, depleting his entire working capital. One creditor, the Cool Springs Nursery Supply Corp., extended credit to Peaslee on numerous purchases. Cool Springs pressured

Peaslee for payment, and on July 1, Peaslee paid Cool Springs half the amount owed. On September 1, Peaslee voluntarily petitioned himself into bankruptcy. The trustee in bankruptcy claims that Peaslee's father and Cool Springs must turn over to the debtor's estate the amounts Peaslee paid to them. Discuss the trustee's claims.

- **For a sample answer to Question 30–2, go to Appendix I at the end of this text.**

30–3. Montoro petitioned himself into voluntary bankruptcy. There were three major claims against his estate. One was made by Carlton, a friend who held Montoro's negotiable promissory note for $2,500; one was made by Elmer, an employee who was owed three months' back wages of $4,500; and one was made by the United Bank of the Rockies on an unsecured loan of $5,000. In addition, Dietrich, an accountant retained by the trustee, was owed $500, and property taxes of $1,000 were owed to Rock County. Montoro's nonexempt property was liquidated, with proceeds of $5,000. Discuss fully what amount each party will receive, and why.

30–4. Discharge in Bankruptcy. Between 1980 and 1987, Craig Hanson borrowed funds from Great Lakes Higher Education Corp. to finance his education. Hanson defaulted on the debt in 1989, and Great Lakes obtained a judgment against him for $31,583.77. Three years later, Hanson filed a bankruptcy petition under Chapter 13. Great Lakes timely filed a proof of claim in the amount of $35,531.08. Hanson's repayment plan proposed to pay $135 monthly to Great Lakes over sixty months, which in total was only 19 percent of the claim, but said nothing about discharging the remaining balance. The plan was confirmed without objection. After Hanson completed the payments under the plan, without any additional proof or argument being offered, the court granted a discharge of his student loans. In 2003, Educational Credit Management Corp. (ECMC), which had taken over Great Lakes' interest in the loans, filed a motion for relief from the discharge. What is the requirement for the discharge of a student loan obligation in bankruptcy? Did Hanson meet this requirement? Should the court grant ECMC's motion? Discuss. [*In re Hanson,* 397 F.3d 482 (7th Cir. 2005)]

30–5. Exceptions to Discharge. Between 1988 and 1992, Lorna Nys took out student loans, totaling about $30,000, to finance an associate of arts degree in drafting from the College of the Redwoods and a bachelor of arts degree from Humboldt State University (HSU) in California. In 1996, Nys began working at HSU as a drafting technician. As a "Drafter II," the highest-paying drafting position at HSU, Nys's gross income in 2002 was $40,244. She was fifty-one years old, Her net monthly income was $2,299.33, and she had $2,295.05 in monthly expenses, including saving $140 for her retirement, which she planned for age sixty-five. When Educational Credit Management Corp. (ECMC) began to collect payments on Nys's student loans, she filed a Chapter 7 petition in a federal bankruptcy court, seeking a discharge of the loans. ECMC argued that Nys did not show any "additional circumstances" that would impede her ability to repay. What is the standard for the discharge of student loans under Chapter 7? Does Nys meet that standard? Explain. [*In re Nys,* 446 F.3d 938 (9th Cir. 2006)]

30–6. CASE PROBLEM WITH SAMPLE ANSWER

James Stout, a professor of economics and business at Cornell College in Iowa City, Iowa, filed a petition in bankruptcy under Chapter 7, seeking to discharge about $95,000 in credit-card debts. At the time, Stout had been divorced for ten years and had custody of his children: Z. S., who attended college, and G. S., who was twelve years old. Stout's ex-wife did not contribute child support. According to Stout, G. S. was an "elite" ice-skater who practiced twenty hours a week and had placed between first and third at more than forty competitive events. He had decided to home school G. S., whose achievements were average for her grade level despite her frequent absences from public school. His petition showed monthly income of $4,227 and expenses of $4,806. The expenses included annual home school costs of $8,400 and annual skating expenses of $6,000. They did not include Z. S.'s college costs, such as airfare for his upcoming studies in Europe, and other items. The trustee allowed monthly expenses of $3,227—with nothing for skating—and asked the court to dismiss the petition. Can the court grant this request? Should it? If so, what might it encourage Stout to do? Explain. [*In re Stout,* 336 Bankr. 138 (N.D. Iowa 2006)]

- **To view a sample answer for Problem 30–6, go to this book's Web site at www.cengage.com/blaw/jentz, select "Chapter 30," and click on "Case Problem with Sample Answer."**

30–7. Discharge in Bankruptcy. Rhonda Schroeder married Gennady Shvartsshteyn (Gene) in 1997. Gene worked at Royal Courier and Air Domestic Connect in Illinois, where Melissa Winyard also worked in 1999 and 2000. During this time, Gene and Winyard had an affair. A year after leaving Royal, Winyard filed a petition in a federal bankruptcy court under Chapter 7 and was granted a discharge of her debts. Sometime later, in a letter to Schroeder, who had learned of the affair, Winyard wrote, "I never intentionally wanted any of this to happen. I never wanted to disrupt your marriage." Schroeder obtained a divorce and, in 2005, filed a suit in an Illinois state court against Winyard, alleging "alienation of affection." Schroeder claimed that there had been "mutual love and affection" in her marriage until Winyard engaged in conduct intended to alienate her husband's affection. Schroeder charged that Winyard "caused him to have sexual intercourse with her," resulting in "the destruction of the marital relationship." Winyard filed a motion for summary judgment on the ground that any liability on her part had been discharged in her bankruptcy. Is there an exception to discharge for "willful and malicious conduct"? If so, does Schroeder's claim qualify? Discuss. [*Schroeder v.*

Winyard, 375 Ill.App.3d 358, 873 N.E.2d 35, 313 Ill.Dec. 740 (2 Dist. 2007)]

30–8. A QUESTION OF ETHICS

In October 1994, Charles Edwards formed ETS Payphones, Inc., to sell and lease pay phones as investment opportunities—an investor would buy a phone from ETS, which would lease it back. ETS promised returns of 14 to 15 percent but consistently lost money. To meet its obligations to existing investors, ETS had to continually attract new investors. Eventually, ETS defrauded thousands of investors of more than $300 million. Edwards transferred the funds from ETS to himself. In 2000, ETS filed a petition in a federal bankruptcy court to declare bankruptcy. Darryl Laddin was appointed trustee. On the debtor's behalf, Laddin filed a suit against Reliance Trust Co. and others, alleging, among other things, that the defendants helped defraud investors by "ignoring the facts" and "funneling" the investors' funds to ETS, causing it to "incur millions of dollars in additional debt." Laddin sought treble (triple) damages. [Official Committee of Unsecured Creditors of PSA, Inc. v. Edwards, *437 F.3d 1145 (11th Cir. 2006)*]

(a) The defendants argued, in part, that the doctrine of *in pari delicto,* which provides that a wrongdoer may not profit from his or her wrongful acts, barred Laddin's claim. Who should be considered ethically responsible for the investors' losses? Explain.

(b) Laddin contended that his actions, as trustee on behalf of the debtor, should not be subject to the doctrine of *in pari delicto* because that doctrine depends on the "personal malfeasance of the individual seeking to recover." The defendants filed a motion to dismiss Laddin's complaint. Do you think that the court should rule in favor of Laddin or the defendants? Why?

30–9. VIDEO QUESTION

Go to this text's Web site at **www.cengage.com/blaw/jentz** and select "Chapter 30." Click on "Video Questions" and view the video titled *The River.* Then answer the following questions.

(a) In the video, a crowd (including Mel Gibson) is gathered at a farm auction in which the farming goods of a neighbor are being sold. The people in the crowd, who are upset because they believe that the bank is selling out the farmer, begin chanting "no sale, no sale." In an effort to calm the situation, the farmer tells the crowd that "they've already foreclosed" on his farm. What does he mean?

(b) Assume that the auction is a result of Chapter 7 bankruptcy proceedings. Was the farmer's petition for bankruptcy voluntary or involuntary? Explain.

(c) Suppose that the farmer purchased the homestead three years prior to filing a petition for bankruptcy and that the current market value of the farm is $215,000. What is the maximum amount of equity the farmer could claim as exempt?

(d) Compare the results of a Chapter 12 bankruptcy as opposed to a Chapter 7 bankruptcy for the farmer in the video.

LAW ON THE WEB

For updated links to resources available on the Web, as well as a variety of other materials, visit this text's Web site at

www.cengage.com/blaw/jentz

The U.S. Bankruptcy Code is online at

www.law.cornell.edu:80/uscode/11

For information and news on bankruptcy law and cases, go to the site maintained by Bankruptcy Media at

www.bankruptcymedia.com

Another good resource for bankruptcy information is the American Bankruptcy Institute (ABI) at

www.abiworld.org

Legal Research Exercises on the Web

Go to **www.cengage.com/blaw/jentz**, the Web site that accompanies this text. Select "Chapter 30" and click on "Internet Exercises." There you will find the following Internet research exercises that you can perform to learn more about the topics covered in this chapter.

Internet Exercise 30–1: Legal Perspective
Bankruptcy

Internet Exercise 30–2: Management Perspective
Bankruptcy Alternatives

UNIT SIX FOCUS ON ETHICS

Creditors' Rights and Bankruptcy

We have certainly come a long way from the period in our history when debtors' prisons existed. Today, debtors are in a much more favorable position—they can file for protection under bankruptcy law. Indeed, after the Bankruptcy Reform Act of 1978 was passed, some claimed that we had gone too far toward protecting debtors and had made it too easy for them to avoid paying what they legally owed. Critics of the 2005 Bankruptcy Reform Act are concerned that the pendulum has swung too far in the opposite direction—favoring creditors' interests and making it too difficult for debtors to obtain a fresh start. Clearly, it is hard to protect the rights of both debtors and creditors at the same time, and laws governing debtor-creditor relationships have traditionally been perceived, by one group or another, as being unfair.

It is obviously not possible for the law to protect both debtors and creditors at all times under all circumstances. Attempts to balance the rights of both groups necessarily raise questions of fairness and justice. In this *Focus on Ethics* feature, we look at several aspects of debtor-creditor relationships that frequently involve issues of fairness, and we examine the ethical ramifications of the 2005 Bankruptcy Reform Act for debtors and creditors.

"Self-Help" Repossession

Section 9–503 of the Uniform Commercial Code (UCC) states that "[u]nless otherwise agreed, a secured party has on default the right to take possession of the collateral. In taking possession, a secured party may proceed without judicial process if this can be done without breach of the peace." The underlying rationale for this "self-help" provision of Article 9 is that it simplifies the process of repossession for creditors and reduces the burden on the courts. Because the UCC does not define "breach of the peace," however, it is not always easy to predict what behavior will constitute such a breach.

One problem is that the debtor may not realize what is happening when agents of the creditor show up to repossess the collateral. Often, to avoid confrontation with the debtor and any potential violence or breach of the peace, a secured creditor will arrange to have the collateral repossessed during the night or in the early-morning hours, when the repossession effort is least likely to be observed. But a debtor who awakens in the night and sees his or her car being towed away may not realize that it is being repossessed.

At the same time, repossession can be risky for the creditor; if the repossession results in a breach of the peace, the creditor may be liable for substantial damages. Inevitably, repossession attempts will occasionally result in confrontations with the debtor. Indeed, some contend that the self-help provision encourages violence by providing an incentive for debtors to incite creditors to breach the peace, which may entitle the debtors to damages.

Ethics and Bankruptcy

As we have seen, the first goal of bankruptcy law is to provide relief and protection to debtors. Society has generally concluded that everyone should be given the chance to start over. But how far should society go in allowing debtors to avoid obligations that they voluntarily incurred? This question has been debated for some time, and it is certainly at the forefront of the issues raised by the 2005 Bankruptcy Reform Act.

Consider the concept of bankruptcy from the point of view of the creditor. The creditor has extended a transfer of purchasing power from herself or himself to the debtor. That transfer of purchasing power represents a transfer of an asset for an asset. The debtor obtains the asset of funds, goods, or services, and the creditor obtains the asset of a *secured* or *unsecured* legal obligation to repay. Once the debtor is in bankruptcy, voluntarily or involuntarily, the asset that the creditor owns most often has a diminished value. Indeed, in many circumstances, that asset has no value. Yet the easier it becomes for debtors to discharge their debts under bankruptcy laws, the greater will be the incentive for debtors to use such laws to avoid paying amounts that are legally owed.

Clearly, bankruptcy law is a balancing act between providing a second chance for debtors and ensuring that creditors are given reasonable protection. Understandably, ethical issues arise in the process.

Bankruptcy and Economics

Among other things, the increasing number of bankruptcies since the early 1990s meant that creditors incurred higher risks in making loans—because bankruptcy shifts the cost of the debt from the debtor to the creditor. To compensate for these higher risks, creditors take one or more of the following actions: increase the interest rates charged to everyone, require additional security (collateral), or be more selective in granting credit.

(Continued)

Thus, with more lenient bankruptcy laws, debtors who find themselves in bankruptcy will be better off, but those debtors who will never be in bankruptcy will be worse off. Ethical concerns regarding this trade-off must be matched with the economic concerns of other groups of individuals affected by the law.

Consequences of Bankruptcy Under the 2005 Bankruptcy Reform Act, filing for personal bankruptcy (particularly under Chapter 7) has become more difficult. Although the stigma attached to bankruptcy today is less than it once was, bankruptcy is never easy for debtors. Many debtors feel a sense of shame and failure when they petition for bankruptcy. After all, bankruptcy is a matter of public record, and there is no way to avoid a certain amount of publicity. In one case, for example, a couple who filed for Chapter 7 bankruptcy wanted to use their attorney's mailing address in another town on their bankruptcy schedules in an effort to prevent an elderly parent and one of their employers from learning about the bankruptcy. The court, however, held that debtors are not entitled to be protected from publicity surrounding the filing of their cases.[1]

A court in another case held that the public interest in information involving a particular bankruptcy debtor (Gitto Global Corporation) was important enough to justify disclosing a previously sealed report from a bankruptcy examiner. In essence, the court gave the media access to the bankruptcy examiner's report on the misconduct of more than 120 individuals at the debtor company.[2]

Bankruptcy also has other consequences for debtors, including blemished credit ratings for up to ten years and higher interest charges for new debts, such as those incurred through the purchase of cars or homes. Some private employers may even refuse to hire a job applicant who has filed for bankruptcy. The courts provide little relief for applicants who are denied a job for this reason.[3]

Thus, bankruptcy can have adverse effects for both debtors and creditors. Because of the consequences of bankruptcy, debtors do not always get the fresh start promised by bankruptcy law. At the same time, creditors rarely are able to recover all that is owed them once a debtor petitions for bankruptcy.

Is It Fair to Increase the Costs for Debtors Seeking Bankruptcy Relief? The 2005 Bankruptcy Reform Act increased the costs of filing for bankruptcy. Not only did the filing fee for Chapter 7 bankruptcies increase from $155 to $200, but attorneys' fees also increased in many instances. Attorneys' fees, rather than filing fees, typically constitute the major expense for bankruptcy filings. Many attorneys have raised the fees they charge to handle bankruptcy cases in the wake of the 2005 act because they are assuming greater risk. Under the 2005 law, the debtor's attorney must certify the accuracy of all factual allegations in the bankruptcy petition and schedules under the penalty of perjury. In other words, attorneys may be subject to sanctions (fines) if there are any factual inaccuracies.

Because attorneys are held accountable for factual inaccuracies, the debtor's attorney may decide to independently investigate the truth of the facts stated in the petition and schedules. This may entail hiring private investigators, appraisers, and auditors for assistance in accounting for all of the debtor's income and assets. If the debtor enters a reaffirmation agreement, it will not be enforceable unless the attorney certifies that the debtor is capable of making the payments due under the agreement. Thus, another round of investigations may be needed before the attorney will sign the certification. Obviously, the debtor ends up paying these costs. Is this fair considering that a main goal of bankruptcy is to give debtors a fresh start?

DISCUSSION QUESTIONS

1. Do you think that the law favors debtors at the expense of creditors or vice versa? Is there any way to achieve a better balance between the interests of creditors and those of debtors?
2. So long as a breach of the peace does not result, a lender may repossess goods on the debtor's default under the self-help provision of Article 9. Do you think that debtors have a right to be told in advance about a planned repossession? Some observers argue that the self-help remedy under Article 9 should be abolished. Do you agree? Why or why not?
3. Is it unethical to avoid paying one's debts by going into bankruptcy? Does a person have a moral responsibility to pay his or her debts?
4. Are borrowers better off as a result of the 2005 Bankruptcy Reform Act? Why or why not? Do credit-card companies have a duty to reduce the interest rates they charge to all consumers if their costs fall? Should they?

1. *In the Matter of Laws,* 223 Bankr. 714 (D.Neb. 1998).
2. *In re Gitto Global Corp.,* 2005 WL 10273348 (D.Mass. 2005).
3. See, for example, *In re Potter,* 354 Bankr. 301 (D.Ala. 2006); and *In re Stinson,* 285 Bankr. 239 (W.D.Va. 2002).

UNIT SEVEN

Agency and Employment

CONTENTS

CHAPTER 31

Agency Formation and Duties

One of the most common, important, and pervasive legal relationships is that of **agency.** As discussed in Chapter 26, in an agency relationship involving two parties, one of the parties, called the *agent,* agrees to represent or act for the other, called the *principal.* The principal has the right to control the agent's conduct in matters entrusted to the agent. By using agents, a principal can conduct multiple business operations simultaneously in various locations. Thus, for example, contracts that bind the principal can be made at different places with different persons at the same time.

A familiar example of an agent is a corporate officer who serves in a representative capacity for the owners of the corporation. In this capacity, the officer has the authority to bind the principal (the corporation) to a contract. Indeed, agency law is essential to the existence and operation of a corporate entity because only through its agents can a corporation function and enter into contracts.

Most employees are also considered to be agents of their employers. Thus, some of the concepts that you will learn about in Chapters 33 and 34, on employment law, are based on agency law. Generally, agency relationships permeate the business world. For that reason, an understanding of the law of agency is crucial to understanding business law.

SECTION 1 Agency Relationships

Section 1(1) of the *Restatement (Second) of Agency*[1] defines *agency* as "the fiduciary relation [that] results from the manifestation of consent by one person to another that the other shall act in his [or her] behalf and subject to his [or her] control, and consent by the other so to act." The term **fiduciary** is at the heart of agency law. The term can be used both as a noun and as an adjective. When used as a noun, it refers to a person having a duty created by his or her undertaking to act primarily for another's benefit in matters connected with the undertaking. When used as an adjective, as in the phrase "fiduciary relationship," it means that the relationship involves trust and confidence.

Agency relationships commonly exist between employers and employees. Agency relationships may sometimes also exist between employers and independent contractors who are hired to perform special tasks or services.

Employer-Employee Relationships

Normally, all employees who deal with third parties are deemed to be agents. A salesperson in a department store, for instance, is an agent of the store's owner (the principal) and acts on the owner's behalf. Employment laws (state and federal) apply only to the employer-employee relationship. Statutes governing Social Security, withholding taxes, workers' compensation, unemployment compensation, workplace safety, employment discrimination, and other aspects of employment (see Chapters 33 and 34) are applicable

1. The *Restatement (Second) of Agency* is an authoritative summary of the law of agency and is often referred to by judges in their decisions and opinions.

only when an employer-employee relationship exists. *These laws do not apply to an independent contractor.*

Because employees who deal with third parties are normally deemed to be agents of their employers, agency law and employment law overlap considerably. Agency relationships, though, as will become apparent, can exist outside an employer-employee relationship, and thus agency law has a broader reach than employment law does.

Employer-Independent Contractor Relationships

Independent contractors are not employees because, by definition, those who hire them have no control over the details of their work performance. Section 2 of the *Restatement (Second) of Agency* defines an **independent contractor** as follows:

> [An independent contractor is] a person who contracts with another to do something for him [or her] but who is not controlled by the other nor subject to the other's right to control with respect to his [or her] physical conduct in the performance of the undertaking. He [or she] may or may not be an agent.

Building contractors and subcontractors are independent contractors; a property owner who hires a contractor and subcontractors to complete a project does not control the details of the way they perform their work. Truck drivers who own their vehicles and hire out on a per-job basis are independent contractors, but truck drivers who drive company trucks on a regular basis usually are employees.

The relationship between a principal and an independent contractor may or may not involve an agency relationship. To illustrate: An owner of real estate who hires a real estate broker to negotiate the sale of her property not only has contracted with an independent contractor (the real estate broker) but also has established an agency relationship for the specific purpose of selling the property. Another example is an insurance agent, who is both an independent contractor and an agent of the insurance company for which he or she sells policies. (Note that an insurance *broker*, in contrast, normally is an agent of the person obtaining insurance and not of the insurance company.)

Determining Employee Status

The courts are frequently asked to determine whether a particular worker is an employee or an independent contractor. How a court decides this issue can have a significant effect on the rights and liabilities of the parties. For example, employers are required to pay certain taxes, such as Social Security and unemployment taxes, for employees but not for independent contractors. Those who hire independent contractors may also do so in an effort to avoid liability for the negligence of those independent contractors. (See this chapter's *Business Application* feature on the following page for more details on this issue.)

Criteria Used by the Courts In deciding whether a worker is categorized as an employee or an independent contractor, courts often consider the following questions:

1. How much control does the employer exercise over the details of the work? (If the employer exercises considerable control over the details of the work and the day-to-day activities of the worker, this indicates employee status. This is perhaps the most important factor weighed by the courts in determining employee status.)
2. Is the worker engaged in an occupation or business distinct from that of the employer? (If so, this points to independent-contractor, not employee, status.)
3. Is the work usually done under the employer's direction or by a specialist without supervision? (If the work is usually done under the employer's direction, this indicates employee status.)
4. Does the employer supply the tools at the place of work? (If so, this indicates employee status.)
5. For how long is the person employed? (If the person is employed for a long period of time, this indicates employee status.)
6. What is the method of payment—by time period or at the completion of the job? (Payment by time period, such as once every two weeks or once a month, indicates employee status.)
7. What degree of skill is required of the worker? (If a great degree of skill is required, this may indicate that the person is an independent contractor hired for a specialized job and not an employee.)

Sometimes, workers may benefit from having employee status—for tax purposes and to be protected under certain employment laws, for example. As mentioned earlier, federal statutes governing employment discrimination apply only when an employer-employee relationship exists. The question in the following case was whether, for the purpose of applying one of these statutes, a television show's co-host was an employee or an independent contractor.

BUSINESS APPLICATION
Independent-Contractor Negligence

MANAGEMENT FACES A LEGAL ISSUE

It is common for managers to hire independent contractors. They do so for a variety of reasons, such as reducing paperwork and avoiding certain tax liabilities. More important, business managers wish to reduce negligence lawsuits. As a general rule, employers are not liable for torts (wrongs) that an independent contractor commits against third parties. Nevertheless, there are exceptions. If an employer exercises significant control over the work activity of an independent contractor, that contractor may be considered an employee. Consequently, the employer can be liable for the contractor's torts.

WHAT THE COURTS SAY

In a case involving a trucking company, which hired independent contractors to make deliveries, a motorist was killed in a collision with one of the company's independent-contractor drivers. At trial, the defendant (the trucking company) prevailed. The plaintiff argued that the trucking company failed to investigate the background, qualifications, or experience of the driver. The appellate court pointed out that an employer of an independent contractor has no control over the manner in which the work is done. The plaintiff failed to offer any proof as to why the trucking company should have investigated the truck driver.[a]

In another case, a tenant whose hand was injured sued the building's owner. An independent contractor, hired by the owner to perform repair work on the outside of the building, attempted to close the tenant's balcony door when the tenant's hand got caught, causing her injury. The appellate court ultimately held that the building's owner and its managing agent could not be held liable for the independent contractor's alleged negligence. As in the previous case, the court noted that the employer (the building's owner) had no right to control the manner in which the independent contractor did his work. The tenant suffered harm because of the independent contractor's actions not because the premises were in disrepair.[b]

Finally, another issue that sometimes arises is the liability of a business owner for injuries to employees of independent contractors that the owner has hired. In one case, two employees of an independent subcontractor suffered electrical burns while working on a construction project. They sued the owner of the project as well as the electric utility. The defendants prevailed at trial, and on appeal, the court agreed.[c]

IMPLICATIONS FOR MANAGERS

In any contract with independent contractors, it is best to require that the contractors assume liability for any harm they cause to a third party through their own negligence. Managers should insist that independent contractors carry liability insurance and ensure that the liability insurance policy is current. Additionally, business managers should refrain from doing anything that would lead a third party to believe that an independent contractor is an employee. And, of course, they cannot maintain control over an independent contractor's actions.

a. *Stander v. Dispoz-O-Products, Inc.*, 973 So.2d 603 (Fla.App. 2008).

b. *Stagno v. 143-50 Hoover Owners Corp.*, 48 A.D.3d 548, 853 N.Y.S.2d 85 (2008).

c. *Dalton v. 933 Peachtree, LP*, 291 Ga.App. 123, 661 S.E.2d 156 (2008).

CASE 31.1 Alberty-Vélez v. Corporación de Puerto Rico para la Difusión Pública

United States Court of Appeals, First Circuit, 2004. 361 F.3d 1.

www.ca1.uscourts.gov[a]

Background and Facts In July 1993, Victoria Lis Alberty-Vélez (Alberty) began to co-host a new television show, *Desde Mi Pueblo,* on WIPR, a television station in Puerto Rico. The show profiled Puerto Rican cities and towns. Instead of signing a single contract, Alberty signed a new contract for each episode. Each contract obligated her to work a certain number of days. She was not obliged to do other work for WIPR, and WIPR was not obliged to contract with her for other work.

a. In the right-hand column, click on "Opinions." When that page opens, under "General Search," type "02-2187" in the "Opinion Number begins with" box and click on "Submit Search." In the result, click on the appropriate link to access the opinion. The U.S. Court of Appeals for the First Circuit maintains this Web site.

CASE 31.1 CONTINUED During the filming, Alberty was responsible for providing her own clothing, shoes, accessories, hairstylist, and other services and materials. She was paid a lump sum, ranging from $400 to $550, for each episode. WIPR did not withhold income or Social Security taxes and did not provide health insurance, life insurance, a retirement plan, paid sick leave, maternity leave, or vacation pay. Alberty became pregnant, and after November 1994, WIPR stopped contracting with her. She filed a suit in a federal district court against WIPR's owner, Corporación de Puerto Rico para la Difusión Pública, alleging, among other things, discrimination on the basis of her pregnancy in violation of a federal statute. The court issued a judgment in the defendant's favor. Alberty appealed to the U.S. Court of Appeals for the First Circuit.

• **Decision and Rationale** The U.S. Court of Appeals for the First Circuit affirmed the lower court's judgment in WIPR's favor. To determine whether a party is an independent contractor, a court considers the employer's right to control the manner and means by which the party does the job for which he or she is hired. Important factors include the required skills; the source of the tools for the job; the location of the work; the duration of the relationship between the parties; whether the employer has the right to assign other projects to the hired party; the parties' discretion over when and how long the work is done; the method of payment; whether the work is part of the employer's regular business; whether the employer is in business; the provision of employee benefits; and the tax treatment of the hired party. In this case, "the parties structured their relationship through the use of set length contracts that permitted Alberty the freedom to pursue other opportunities and assured WIPR that it would not have to pay Alberty for the weeks that it was not filming. Further, the lack of benefits, the method of payment, and the parties' own description of their relationship in tax documents all indicate independent contractor status."

• **What If the Facts Were Different?** *Suppose that Alberty had been a full-time, hourly worker and that such status was common among television hosts, but WIPR had manipulated the benefits and tax withholdings to favor independent-contractor status. How might the result have been different?*

• **The Global Dimension** *Would Alberty have been defined as an employee if she had been a foreign correspondent who reported on stories from international locations and WIPR had paid her travel and related expenses? Explain.*

Criteria Used by the IRS Businesspersons should be aware that the Internal Revenue Service (IRS) has established its own criteria for determining whether a worker is an independent contractor or an employee. Although the IRS once considered twenty factors in determining a worker's status, guidelines in effect since 1997 encourage IRS examiners to look closely at just one of those factors—the degree of control the business exercises over the worker.

The IRS tends to scrutinize closely a firm's classification of a worker as an independent contractor rather than an employee because employers can avoid certain tax liabilities by hiring independent contractors instead of employees. Even when a firm has classified a worker as an independent contractor, if the IRS decides that the worker is actually an employee, the employer will be responsible for paying any applicable Social Security, withholding, and unemployment taxes. For example, in one widely publicized case, Microsoft Corporation was ordered to pay back payroll taxes for hundreds of temporary workers who had contractually agreed to work for Microsoft as independent contractors.[2]

Employee Status and "Works for Hire" Under the Copyright Act of 1976, any copyrighted work created by an employee within the scope of her or his employment at the request of the employer is a "work for hire," and the employer owns the copyright to the work. In contrast, when an employer hires an independent contractor—a freelance artist, writer, or computer programmer, for example—the independent contractor normally owns the copyright. In this situation, the employer can own the copyright only if the parties agree in writing that the work is a "work for hire" and the work falls into one of nine specific categories, including audiovisual and other works.

2. *Vizcaino v. U.S. District Court for the Western District of Washington*, 173 F.3d 713 (9th Cir. 1999).

In one case, for example, Graham marketed CD-ROM discs containing compilations of software programs that are available free to the public. Graham hired James to create a file-retrieval program that allowed users to access the software on the CDs. James built into the final version of the program a notice stating that he was the author of the program and owned the copyright. Graham removed the notice. When James sold the program to another CD-ROM publisher, Graham filed a suit claiming that James's file-retrieval program was a "work for hire" and that Graham owned the copyright to the program. The court, however, decided that James—a skilled computer programmer who controlled the manner and method of his work—was an independent contractor and not an employee for hire. Thus, James owned the copyright to the file-retrieval program.[3]

SECTION 2

Formation of the Agency Relationship

Agency relationships normally are *consensual;* in other words, they come about by voluntary consent and agreement between the parties. Generally, the agreement need not be in writing,[4] and consideration is not required.

A person must have contractual capacity to be a principal.[5] Those who cannot legally enter into contracts directly should not be allowed to do so indirectly through an agent. Any person can be an agent, however, regardless of whether he or she has the capacity to contract. Because an agent derives the authority to enter into contracts from the principal and because a contract made by an agent is legally viewed as a contract of the principal, it is immaterial whether the agent personally has the legal capacity to make that contract. Thus, even a minor or a person who is legally incompetent can be appointed as an agent.

An agency relationship can be created for any legal purpose. An agency relationship created for a purpose that is illegal or contrary to public policy is unenforceable. If LaSalle (as principal) contracts with Burke (as agent) to sell illegal narcotics, the agency relationship is unenforceable because selling illegal narcotics is a felony and is contrary to public policy. It is also illegal for physicians and other licensed professionals to employ unlicensed agents to perform professional actions.

Generally, an agency relationship can arise in four ways: by agreement of the parties, by ratification, by estoppel, and by operation of law. We look here at each of these possibilities.

Agency by Agreement

Most agency relationships are based on an express or implied agreement that the agent will act for the principal and that the principal agrees to have the agent so act. An agency agreement can take the form of an express written contract. For example, Henchen enters into a written agreement with Vogel, a real estate agent, to sell Henchen's house. An agency relationship exists between Henchen and Vogel for the sale of the house and is detailed in a document that both parties sign.

Many express agency relationships are created by oral agreement and are not based on a written contract. Suppose that Henchen asks Grace, a gardener, to contract with others for the care of his lawn on a regular basis. If Grace agrees, an agency relationship exists between Henchen and Grace for the lawn care.

An agency agreement can also be implied by conduct. For example, a hotel expressly allows only Hans Cooper to park cars, but Hans has no employment contract there. The hotel's manager tells Hans when to work, as well as where and how to park the cars. The hotel's conduct manifests a willingness to have Hans park its customers' cars, and Hans can infer from the hotel's conduct that he has authority to act as a parking valet. Thus, there is an implied agreement that Hans is an agent for the hotel and provides valet parking services for hotel guests.

Agency by Ratification

On occasion, a person who is in fact not an agent may make a contract on behalf of another (a principal). If the principal approves or affirms that contract by word or by action, an agency relationship is created by ratification. Ratification involves a question of intent, and intent can be expressed by either words or conduct.

3. *Graham v. James,* 144 F.3d 229 (2d Cir. 1998).

4. There are two main exceptions to the statement that agency agreements need not be in writing. An agency agreement must be in writing (1) whenever agency authority empowers the agent to enter into a contract that the Statute of Frauds requires to be in writing (this is called the *equal dignity rule,* to be discussed in the next chapter) and (2) whenever an agent is given power of attorney.

5. Note that some states allow a minor to be a principal. When a minor is permitted to be a principal, however, any resulting contracts will be voidable by the minor principal but *not* by the adult third party.

The basic requirements for ratification will be discussed in Chapter 32.

Agency by Estoppel

When a principal causes a third person to believe that another person is the principal's agent, and the third person acts to his or her detriment in reasonable reliance on that belief, the principal is "estopped to deny" (prevented from denying) the agency relationship. In such a situation, the principal's actions have created the *appearance* of an agency that does not in fact exist. The third person must prove that he or she *reasonably* believed that an agency relationship existed, however.[6]

Suppose that Jayden accompanies Grant, a seed sales representative, to call on a customer, Palko, who owns a seed store. Jayden has performed independent sales work but has never signed an employment agreement with Grant. Grant boasts to Palko that he wishes he had three more assistants "just like Jayden." By making this representation, Grant creates the impression that Jayden is his agent and has authority to solicit orders. Palko has reason to believe from Grant's statements that Jayden is an agent for Grant. Palko then places seed orders with Jayden. If Grant does not correct the impression that Jayden is an agent, Grant will be bound to fill the orders just as if Jayden were really his agent. Grant's representation to Palko has created the impression that Jayden is Grant's agent and has authority to solicit orders.

Note that the acts or declarations of a purported *agent* in and of themselves do not create an agency by estoppel. Rather, it is the deeds or statements *of the principal* that create an agency by estoppel. If Jayden walked into Palko's store and claimed to be Grant's agent, when in fact he was not, and Grant had no knowledge of Jayden's representations, Grant would not be bound to any deal struck by Jayden and Palko.

Under what other circumstances might a third party reasonably believe that a person is an agent of and has the authority to act for a principal when the person does not actually have this authority? The following case provides an illustration.

6. These concepts also apply when a person who is in fact an agent undertakes an action that is beyond the scope of her or his authority, as will be discussed in Chapter 32.

CASE 31.2 Motorsport Marketing, Inc. v. Wiedmaier, Inc.

Missouri Court of Appeals, Western District, 2006. 195 S.W.3d 492.
www.courts.mo.gov[a]

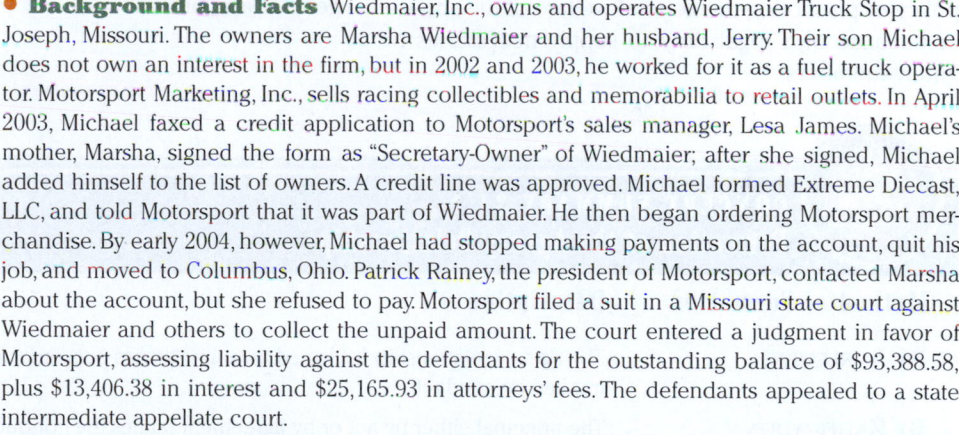

• **Background and Facts** Wiedmaier, Inc., owns and operates Wiedmaier Truck Stop in St. Joseph, Missouri. The owners are Marsha Wiedmaier and her husband, Jerry. Their son Michael does not own an interest in the firm, but in 2002 and 2003, he worked for it as a fuel truck operator. Motorsport Marketing, Inc., sells racing collectibles and memorabilia to retail outlets. In April 2003, Michael faxed a credit application to Motorsport's sales manager, Lesa James. Michael's mother, Marsha, signed the form as "Secretary-Owner" of Wiedmaier; after she signed, Michael added himself to the list of owners. A credit line was approved. Michael formed Extreme Diecast, LLC, and told Motorsport that it was part of Wiedmaier. He then began ordering Motorsport merchandise. By early 2004, however, Michael had stopped making payments on the account, quit his job, and moved to Columbus, Ohio. Patrick Rainey, the president of Motorsport, contacted Marsha about the account, but she refused to pay. Motorsport filed a suit in a Missouri state court against Wiedmaier and others to collect the unpaid amount. The court entered a judgment in favor of Motorsport, assessing liability against the defendants for the outstanding balance of $93,388.58, plus $13,406.38 in interest and $25,165.93 in attorneys' fees. The defendants appealed to a state intermediate appellate court.

• **Decision and Rationale** The state intermediate appellate court affirmed the judgment of the lower court, echoing the conclusion that "Michael acted as an apparent agent of Wiedmaier, Inc., in its dealings with Motorsport." The appellate court emphasized that "the credit application

a. In the "Quick Links" box, click on "Opinion & Minutes." When that page opens, click on the "Missouri Court of Appeals, Western District opinions" link. At the bottom of the next page, click on the "Search Opinions" link. In that page's "Search for" box, type "Wiedmaier" and click on "Search." In the result, click on the name of the case to access the opinion. The Missouri state courts maintain this Web site.

CASE CONTINUES

CASE 31.2 CONTINUED constituted a direct communication from Wiedmaier, Inc. (through Marsha) to Motorsport causing Motorsport to reasonably believe that Michael had authority to act for Wiedmaier, Inc." Marsha signed the application, on which Michael was listed as an owner. The defendants argued that Michael paid Motorsport with checks drawn on Extreme Diecast's account, which should have led Motorsport to investigate further. In response, the court pointed out that, as Motorsport was aware, "it is a common practice for a truck stop to have a separate division with a separate name to handle its diecast and other related merchandise, and that Michael represented that this is exactly what Extreme Diecast was." In good faith reliance on the credit application and Michael's representations, Motorsport extended credit to Wiedmaier and filled Michael's orders. "If the transaction[s] executed by Michael [do] not bind Wiedmaier, Inc., Motorsport will suffer the loss of the balance due on the account."

- **What If the Facts Were Different?** *Suppose that Motorsport's sales manager had telephoned Marsha Wiedmaier. Further suppose that Marsha had vouched for Michael's creditworthiness but informed Motorsport that she and her husband owned Wiedmaier and that Michael worked for them. How might the outcome of this case have been different in that situation?*

- **The E-Commerce Dimension** *Should the court have applied the law differently in this case if Michael had done business with Motorsport entirely online? Explain.*

Agency by Operation of Law

The courts may find an agency relationship in the absence of a formal agreement in other situations as well. This may occur in family relationships. Suppose that one spouse purchases certain basic necessaries (such as food or clothing—see Chapter 13) and charges them to the other spouse's charge account. The courts will often rule that the latter is liable for payment for the necessaries, either because of a social policy of promoting the general welfare of the spouse or because of a legal duty to supply necessaries to family members.

Agency by operation of law may also occur in emergency situations, when the agent's failure to act outside the scope of her or his authority would cause the principal substantial loss. If the agent is unable to contact the principal, the courts will often grant this emergency power. For example, a railroad engineer may contract on behalf of his or her employer for medical care for an injured motorist hit by the train. *Concept Summary 31.1* reviews the various ways that agencies are formed.

CONCEPT SUMMARY 31.1
Formation of the Agency Relationship

Method of Formation	Description
BY AGREEMENT	The agency relationship is formed through express consent (oral or written) or implied by conduct.
BY RATIFICATION	The principal either by act or by agreement ratifies the conduct of a person who is not in fact an agent.
BY ESTOPPEL	The principal causes a third person to believe that another person is the principal's agent, and the third person acts to his or her detriment in reasonable reliance on that belief.
BY OPERATION OF LAW	The agency relationship is based on a social duty (such as the need to support family members) or formed in emergency situations when the agent is unable to contact the principal and failure to act outside the scope of the agent's authority would cause the principal substantial loss.

SECTION 3

Duties of Agents and Principals

Once the principal-agent relationship has been created, both parties have duties that govern their conduct. As discussed previously, the principal-agent relationship is *fiduciary*—one of trust. In a fiduciary relationship, each party owes the other the duty to act with the utmost good faith. In this section, we examine the various duties of agents and principals.

Agent's Duties to the Principal

Generally, the agent owes the principal five duties—performance, notification, loyalty, obedience, and accounting.

Performance An implied condition in every agency contract is the agent's agreement to use reasonable diligence and skill in performing the work. When an agent fails to perform his or her duties, liability for breach of contract may result. The degree of skill or care required of an agent is usually that expected of a reasonable person under similar circumstances. Generally, this is interpreted to mean ordinary care. If an agent has represented herself or himself as possessing special skills, however, the agent is expected to exercise the degree of skill or skills claimed. Failure to do so constitutes a breach of the agent's duty.

Not all agency relationships are based on contract. In some situations, an agent acts gratuitously—that is, without payment. A gratuitous agent cannot be liable for breach of contract, as there is no contract; he or she is subject only to tort liability. Once a gratuitous agent has begun to act in an agency capacity, he or she has the duty to continue to perform in that capacity in an acceptable manner and is subject to the same standards of care and duty to perform as other agents.

For example, Bower's friend Alcott is a real estate broker. Alcott offers to sell Bower's farm at no charge. If Alcott never attempts to sell the farm, Bower has no legal cause of action to force her to do so. If Alcott does find a buyer, however, but negligently fails to follow through with the sales contract, causing the buyer to seek other property, then Bower can sue Alcott for negligence.

Notification An agent is required to notify the principal of all matters that come to her or his attention concerning the subject matter of the agency. This is the *duty of notification*, or the duty to inform. For example, Lang, an artist, is about to negotiate a contract to sell a series of paintings to Barber's Art Gallery for $25,000. Lang's agent learns that Barber is insolvent and will be unable to pay for the paintings. Lang's agent has a duty to inform Lang of Barber's insolvency because it is relevant to the subject matter of the agency—the sale of Lang's paintings. Generally, the law assumes that the principal is aware of any information acquired by the agent that is relevant to the agency—regardless of whether the agent actually passes on this information to the principal. It is a basic tenet of agency law that notice to the agent is notice to the principal.

Loyalty Loyalty is one of the most fundamental duties in a fiduciary relationship. Basically stated, the agent has the duty to act *solely for the benefit of his or her principal* and not in the interest of the agent or a third party. For example, an agent cannot represent two principals in the same transaction unless both know of the dual capacity and consent to it. The duty of loyalty also means that any information or knowledge acquired through the agency relationship is confidential. It is a breach of loyalty to disclose such information either during the agency relationship or after its termination. Typical examples of confidential information are trade secrets and customer lists compiled by the principal (see Chapters 8 and 13).

In short, the agent's loyalty must be undivided. The agent's actions must be strictly for the benefit of the principal and must not result in any secret profit for the agent. For example, Don Cousins contracts with Leo Hodgins, a real estate agent, to negotiate the purchase of an office building as an investment. While working for Cousins, Hodgins discovers that the property owner will sell the building only as a package deal with another parcel. If Hodgins then forms a limited partnership with his brother to buy the two properties and resell the building to Cousins, has he breached his fiduciary duties? The answer is yes, because as a real estate agent, Hodgins had a duty to communicate all offers to his principal and not to secretly purchase the property and then resell it to his principal. Hodgins is required to act in Cousins's best interests and can become the purchaser in this situation only with Cousins's knowledge and approval.[7]

Obedience When an agent is acting on behalf of the principal, the agent has a duty to follow all lawful and clearly stated instructions given by the principal. Any deviation from such instructions is a violation of

7. *Cousins v. Realty Ventures, Inc.*, 844 So.2d 860 (La.App. 5 Cir. 2003).

this duty. During emergency situations, however, when the principal cannot be consulted, the agent may deviate from the instructions without violating this duty. Whenever instructions are not clearly stated, the agent can fulfill the duty of obedience by acting in good faith and in a manner reasonable under the circumstances.

Accounting Unless an agent and a principal agree otherwise, the agent has a duty to keep and make available to the principal an account of all property and funds received and paid out on behalf of the principal. The agent has a duty to maintain separate accounts for the principal's funds and the agent's personal funds, and the agent must not intermingle the funds in these accounts. Whenever a licensed professional (such as an attorney) violates this duty to account, he or she may be subject to disciplinary proceedings carried out by the appropriate regulatory institution (such as the state bar association) in addition to being liable to the principal (the professional's client) for failure to account.

Principal's Duties to the Agent

The principal also has certain duties to the agent. These duties relate to compensation, reimbursement and indemnification, cooperation, and safe working conditions.

Compensation In general, when a principal requests certain services from an agent, the agent reasonably expects payment. The principal therefore has a duty to pay the agent for services rendered. For example, when an accountant or an attorney is asked to act as an agent, an agreement to compensate the agent for this service is implied. The principal also has a duty to pay that compensation in a timely manner. Except in a gratuitous agency relationship, in which the agent does not act in exchange for payment, the principal must pay the agreed-on value for the agent's services. If no amount has been expressly agreed on, then the principal owes the agent the customary compensation for such services.

Many disputes arise because the principal and agent did not specify how much the agent would be paid. To avoid such disputes, businesspersons should always state in advance, and in writing, the amount or rate of compensation that they will pay their agents. Even when dealing with salespersons, such as real estate agents, who customarily are paid a percentage of the value of the sale, it is best to explicitly state the rate of compensation. When the parties are clear up front about the terms of their agency relationship, a dispute is less likely to surface.

Reimbursement and Indemnification Whenever an agent disburses funds to fulfill the request of the principal or to pay for necessary expenses in the course of a reasonable performance of her or his agency duties, the principal has the duty to reimburse the agent for these payments.[8] Agents cannot recover for expenses incurred by their own misconduct or negligence, though.

Subject to the terms of the agency agreement, the principal has the duty to *indemnify* (compensate) an agent for liabilities incurred because of authorized and lawful acts and transactions. For example, if the agent, on the principal's behalf, forms a contract with a third party, and the principal fails to perform the contract, the third party may sue the agent for damages. In this situation, the principal is obligated to compensate the agent for any costs incurred by the agent as a result of the principal's failure to perform the contract.

Additionally, the principal must indemnify the agent for the value of benefits that the agent confers on the principal. The amount of indemnification is usually specified in the agency contract. If it is not, the courts will look to the nature of the business and the type of benefits to determine the amount. Note that this rule applies to acts by gratuitous agents as well.

Cooperation A principal has a duty to cooperate with the agent and to assist the agent in performing his or her duties. The principal must do nothing to prevent that performance. For example, when a principal grants an agent an exclusive territory, creating an *exclusive agency*, the principal cannot compete with the agent or appoint or allow another agent to so compete in violation of the exclusive agency. If the principal does so, she or he will be exposed to liability for the agent's lost sales or profits.

Safe Working Conditions The common law requires the principal to provide safe working prem-

8. This principle applies to acts by gratuitous agents as well. If a finder of a dog that becomes sick takes the dog to a veterinarian and pays the required fees for the veterinarian's services, the agent is entitled to be reimbursed by the owner of the dog for those fees.

ises, equipment, and conditions for all agents and employees. The principal has a duty to inspect working areas and to warn agents and employees about any unsafe situations. When the agent is an employee, the employer's liability is frequently covered by state workers' compensation insurance, and federal and state statutes often require the employer to meet certain safety standards (see Chapter 33).

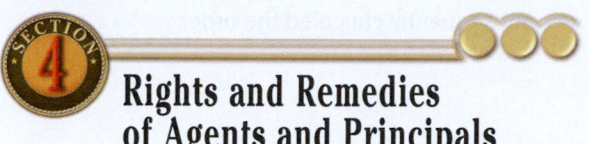

SECTION 4 Rights and Remedies of Agents and Principals

It is said that every wrong has its remedy. In business situations, disputes between agents and principals may arise out of either contract or tort law and carry corresponding remedies. These remedies include monetary damages, termination of the agency relationship, an injunction, and required accountings.

Agent's Rights and Remedies against the Principal

For every duty of the principal, the agent has a corresponding right. Therefore, the agent has the right to be compensated, reimbursed, and indemnified and to work in a safe environment. An agent also has the right to perform agency duties without interference by the principal.

Tort and Contract Remedies Remedies of the agent for breach of duty by the principal follow normal contract and tort remedies. For example, Aaron Hart, a builder who has just constructed a new house, contracts with a real estate agent, Fran Boller, to sell the house. The contract calls for the agent to have an exclusive, ninety-day listing and to receive 6 percent of the selling price when the home is sold. Boller holds several open houses and shows the home to a number of potential buyers. One month before the ninety-day listing terminates, Hart agrees to sell the house to another buyer—not one to whom Boller has shown the house—after the ninety-day listing expires. Hart and the buyer agree that Hart will reduce the price of the house by 3 percent because he will sell it directly and thus will not have to pay Boller's commission. In this situation, if Boller learns of Hart's actions, she can terminate the agency relationship and sue Hart for damages—including the 6 percent commission she should have earned on the sale of the house.

Demand for an Accounting An agent can also withhold further performance and demand that the principal give an accounting. For example, a sales agent may demand an accounting if the agent and principal disagree on the amount of commissions the agent should have received for sales made during a specific period of time.

No Right to Specific Performance When the principal-agent relationship is not contractual, the agent has no right to specific performance. An agent can recover for past services and future damages but cannot force the principal to allow him or her to continue acting as an agent.

Principal's Rights and Remedies against the Agent

In general, a principal has contract remedies for an agent's breach of fiduciary duties. The principal also has tort remedies if the agent commits misrepresentation, negligence, deceit, libel, slander, or trespass. In addition, any breach of a fiduciary duty by an agent may justify the principal's termination of the agency. The main actions available to the principal are constructive trust, avoidance, and indemnification.

Constructive Trust Anything that an agent obtains by virtue of the employment or agency relationship belongs to the principal. An agent commits a breach of fiduciary duty if he or she secretly retains benefits or profits that, by right, belong to the principal. For example, Andrews, a purchasing agent for Metcalf, receives cash rebates from a customer. If Andrews keeps the rebates for himself, he violates his fiduciary duty to his principal, Metcalf. On finding out about the cash rebates, Metcalf can sue Andrews and recover them.

Avoidance When an agent breaches the agency agreement or agency duties under a contract, the principal has a right to avoid any contract entered into with the agent. This right of avoidance is at the election of the principal.

Indemnification In certain situations, when a principal is sued by a third party for an agent's negligent conduct, the principal can sue the agent for an equal amount of damages. This is called *indemnification.* The same holds true if the agent violates the principal's instructions. For example, Parke (the principal) owns a used-car lot where Moore (the agent) works as a salesperson. Parke tells Moore to make no warranties for the used cars. Moore is eager to make a sale to Walters, a customer, and adds a 50,000-mile warranty for the car's engine. Parke may still be liable to Walters for engine failure, but if Walters sues Parke, Parke normally can then sue Moore for indemnification for violating his instructions.

Sometimes, it is difficult to distinguish between instructions of the principal that limit an agent's authority and those that are merely advice. For example, Gutierrez (the principal) owns an office supply company; Logan (the agent) is the manager. Gutierrez tells Logan, "Don't purchase any more inventory this month." Gutierrez goes on vacation. A large order comes in from a local business, and the inventory on hand is insufficient to meet it. What is Logan to do? In this situation, Logan probably has the inherent authority to purchase more inventory despite Gutierrez's command. It is unlikely that Logan would be required to indemnify Gutierrez in the event that the local business subsequently canceled the order.

REVIEWING Agency Formation and Duties

James Blatt hired Marilyn Scott to sell insurance for the Massachusetts Mutual Life Insurance Company. Their contract stated, "Nothing in this contract shall be construed as creating the relationship of employer and employee." The contract was terminable at will by either party. Scott financed her own office and staff, was paid according to performance, had no taxes withheld from her checks, and could legally sell products of Massachusetts Mutual's competitors. But when Blatt learned that Scott was simultaneously selling insurance for Perpetual Life Insurance Corporation, one of Massachusetts Mutual's fiercest competitors, Blatt withheld client contact information from Scott that would have assisted her insurance sales for Massachusetts Mutual. Scott complained to Blatt that he was inhibiting her ability to sell insurance for Massachusetts Mutual. Blatt subsequently terminated their contract. Scott filed a suit in a New York state court against Blatt and Massachusetts Mutual. Scott claimed that she had lost sales for Massachusetts Mutual—and her commissions—as a result of Blatt's withholding contact information from her. Using the information presented in the chapter, answer the following questions.

1. Who is the principal, and who is the agent in this scenario? By which method was an agency relationship formed between Scott and Blatt?
2. What facts would the court consider the most important in determining whether Scott was an employee or an independent contractor?
3. How would the court most likely rule on Scott's employee status?
4. Which of the four duties that Blatt owed Scott in their agency relationship has probably been breached?

TERMS AND CONCEPTS

agency 590 **fiduciary 590** **independent contractor 591**

QUESTIONS AND CASE PROBLEMS

31–1. Paul Gett is a well-known, wealthy financial expert. Adam Wade, Gett's friend, tells Timothy Brown that he is Gett's agent for the purchase of rare coins and shows Brown a local newspaper clipping mentioning Gett's interest in coin collecting. Brown, knowing of Wade's friendship with Gett, contracts with Wade to sell a rare coin valued at $25,000 to Gett. Wade takes the coin and disappears with it. On the payment due date, Brown seeks to collect from Gett. Gett denies liability and claims that Wade was never his agent. Discuss fully whether an agency was in existence at the time the contract for the rare coin was made.

31–2. QUESTION WITH SAMPLE ANSWER

Peter hires Alice as an agent to sell a piece of property he owns. The price is to be at least $30,000. Alice discovers that the fair market value of Peter's property is actually at least $45,000 and could be higher because a shopping mall is going to be built nearby. Alice forms a real estate partnership with her cousin Carl, and she prepares for Peter's signature a contract for the sale of the property to Carl for $32,000. Peter signs the contract. Just before closing and passage of title, Peter learns about the shopping mall and the increased fair market value of his property. Peter refuses to deed the property to Carl. Carl claims that Alice, as agent, solicited a price above that agreed on when the agency was created and that the contract is therefore binding and enforceable. Discuss fully whether Peter is bound to this contract.

- **For a sample answer to Question 31–2, go to Appendix I at the end of this text.**

31–3. Ankir is hired by Jamison as a traveling salesperson. Ankir not only solicits orders but also delivers the goods and collects payments from his customers. Ankir deposits all payments in his private checking account and at the end of each month draws sufficient cash from his bank to cover the payments made. Jamison is totally unaware of this procedure. Because of a slowdown in the economy, Jamison tells all his salespeople to offer 20 percent discounts on orders. Ankir solicits orders, but he offers only 15 percent discounts, pocketing the extra 5 percent paid by customers. Ankir has not lost any orders by this practice, and he is rated as one of Jamison's top salespersons. Jamison learns of Ankir's actions. Discuss fully Jamison's rights in this matter.

31–4. Agency Formation. Ford Motor Credit Co. is a subsidiary of Ford Motor Co. with its own offices, officers, and directors. Ford Credit buys contracts and leases of automobiles entered into by dealers and consumers. Ford Credit also provides inventory financing for dealers' purchases of Ford and non-Ford vehicles and makes loans to Ford and non-Ford dealers. Dealers and consumers are not required to finance their purchases or leases of Ford vehicles through Ford Credit. Ford Motor is not a party to the agreements between Ford Credit and its customers and does not directly receive any payments under those agreements. Also, Ford Credit is not subject to any agreement with Ford Motor "restricting or conditioning" its ability to finance the dealers' inventories or the consumers' purchases or leases of vehicles. A number of plaintiffs filed a product liability suit in a Missouri state court against Ford Motor. Ford Motor claimed that the court did not have venue. The plaintiffs asserted that Ford Credit, which had an office in the jurisdiction, acted as Ford's "agent for the transaction of its usual and customary business" there. Is Ford Credit an agent of Ford Motor? Discuss. [*State ex rel. Ford Motor Co. v. Bacon,* 63 S.W.3d 641 (Mo. 2002)]

31–5. Agent's Duties to Principal. Sam and Theresa Daigle decided to build a home in Cameron Parish, Louisiana. To obtain financing, they contacted Trinity United Mortgage Co. At a meeting with Joe Diez on Trinity's behalf, on July 18, 2001, the Daigles signed a temporary loan agreement with Union Planters Bank. Diez assured them that they did not need to make payments on this loan until their house was built and that permanent financing had been secured. Because the Daigles did not make payments on the Union loan, Trinity declined to make the permanent loan. Meanwhile, Diez left Trinity's employ. On November 1, the Daigles moved into their new house. They tried to contact Diez at Trinity but were told that he was unavailable and would get back to them. Three weeks later, Diez came to the Daigles' home and had them sign documents that they believed were to secure a permanent loan but that were actually an application with Diez's new employer. Union filed a suit in a Louisiana state court against the Daigles for failing to pay on its loan. The Diagles paid Union, obtained permanent financing through another source, and filed a suit against Trinity to recover the cost. Who should have told the Daigles that Diez was no longer Trinity's agent? Could Trinity be liable to the Daigles on this basis? Explain. [*Daigle v. Trinity United Mortgage, L.L.C.,* 890 So.2d 583 (La.App. 3 Cir. 2004)]

31–6. Principal's Duties to Agent. Josef Boehm was an officer and the majority shareholder of Alaska Industrial Hardware, Inc. (AIH), in Anchorage, Alaska. In August 2001, Lincolnshire Management, Inc., in New York, created AIH Acquisition Corp. to buy AIH. The three firms signed a "commitment letter" to negotiate "a definitive stock purchase agreement" (SPA). In September, Harold Snow and Ronald Braley began to work, on Boehm's behalf, with Vincent Coyle, an agent for AIH Acquisition, to produce an SPA. They exchanged many drafts and dozens of e-mails. Finally, in February 2002, Braley told Coyle that Boehm would sign the SPA "early next week." That did not occur, however, and at the end of March, after more negotiations and drafts, Boehm demanded more money. AIH Acquisition agreed and, following more work by the agents, another SPA was drafted. In April, the parties met in Anchorage. Boehm still refused to sign. AIH Acquisition and others filed a suit in a federal district court against AIH. Did Boehm violate any of the duties that principals owe to their agents? If so, which duty, and how was it violated? Explain. [*AIH Acquisition Corp., LLC v. Alaska Industrial Hardware, Inc.,* __ F.Supp.2d __ (S.D.N.Y. 2004)]

31-7. CASE PROBLEM WITH SAMPLE ANSWER

In July 2001, John Warren viewed a condominium in Woodland Hills, California, as a potential buyer. Hildegard Merrill was the agent for the seller. Because Warren's credit rating was poor, Merrill told him he needed a co-borrower to obtain a mortgage at a reasonable rate. Merrill said that her daughter Charmaine would "go on title" until the loan and sale were complete if Warren would pay her $10,000. Merrill also offered to defer her commission on the sale as a loan to Warren so that he could make a 20 percent down payment on the property. He agreed to both plans. Merrill applied for and secured the mortgage in Charmaine's name alone by misrepresenting her daughter's address, business, and income. To close the sale, Merrill had Warren remove his name from the title to the property. In October, Warren moved into the condominium, repaid Merrill the amount of her deferred commission, and began paying the mortgage. Within a few months, Merrill had Warren evicted. Warren filed a suit in a California state court against Merrill and Charmaine. Who among these parties was in an agency relationship? What is the basic duty that an agent owes a principal? Was the duty breached here? Explain. [*Warren v. Merrill,* 143 Cal.App.4th 96, 49 Cal.Rptr.3d 122 (2 Dist. 2006)]

- **To view a sample answer for Problem 31–7, go to this book's Web site at www.cengage.com/blaw/jentz, select "Chapter 31," and click on "Case Problem with Sample Answer."**

31–8. Agent's Duties to Principal. Su Ru Chen owned the Lucky Duck Fortune Cookie Factory in Everett, Massachusetts, which made Chinese-style fortune cookies for restaurants. In November 2001, Chen listed the business for sale with Bob Sun, a real estate broker, for $35,000. Sun's daughter Frances and her fiancé, Chiu Chung Chan, decided that Chan would buy the business. Acting as a broker on Chen's (the seller's) behalf, Frances asked about the Lucky Duck's finances. Chen said that each month the business sold at least 1,000 boxes of cookies at a $2,000 profit. Frances negotiated a price of $23,000, which Chan (her fiancé) paid. When Chan began to operate the Lucky Duck, it became clear that the demand for the cookies was actually about 500 boxes per month—a rate at which the business would suffer losses. Less than two months later, the factory closed. Chan filed a suit in a Massachusetts state court against Chen, alleging fraud, among other things. Chan's proof included Frances's testimony as to what Chen had said to her. Chen objected to the admission of this testimony. What is the basis for this objection? Should the court admit the testimony? Why or why not? [*Chan v. Chen,* 70 Mass.App.Ct. 79, 872 N.E.2d 1153 (2007)]

31-9. A QUESTION OF ETHICS

*Emergency One, Inc. (EO), makes fire and rescue vehicles. Western Fire Truck, Inc., contracted with EO to be its exclusive dealer in Colorado and Wyoming through December 2003. James Costello, a Western salesperson, was authorized to order EO vehicles for his customers. Without informing Western, Costello e-mailed EO about Western's difficulties in obtaining cash to fund its operations. He asked about the viability of Western's contract and his possible employment with EO. On EO's request, and in disregard of Western's instructions, Costello sent some payments for EO vehicles directly to EO. In addition, Costello, with EO's help, sent a competing bid to a potential Western customer. EO's representative e-mailed Costello, "You have my permission to kick [Western's] ass." In April 2002, EO terminated its contract with Western, which, after reviewing Costello's e-mail, fired Costello. Western filed a suit in a Colorado state court against Costello and EO, alleging, among other things, that Costello breached his duty as an agent and that EO aided and abetted the breach. [*Western Fire Truck, Inc. v. Emergency One, Inc.,* *134 P.3d 570 (Colo.App. 2006)]*

(a) Was there an agency relationship between Western and Costello? In determining whether an agency relationship exists, is the *right* to control or the *fact* of control more important? Explain.

(b) Did Costello owe Western a duty? If so, what was the duty? Did Costello breach it? How?

(c) A Colorado state statute allows a court to award punitive damages in "circumstances of fraud, malice, or willful and wanton conduct." Did any of these circumstances exist in this case? Should punitive damages be assessed against either defendant? Why or why not?

31-10. VIDEO QUESTION

Go to this text's Web site at **www.cengage.com/blaw/jentz** and select "Chapter 31." Click on "Video Questions" and view the video titled *Fast Times at Ridgemont High.* Then answer the following questions.

(a) Recall from the video that Brad (Judge Reinhold) is told to deliver an order of Captain Hook Fish and Chips to IBM. Is Brad an employee or an independent contractor? Why?

(b) Assume that Brad is an employee and agent of Captain Hook Fish and Chips. What duties does he owe Captain Hook? What duties does Captain Hook, as principal, owe Brad?

(c) In the video, Brad throws part of his uniform and several bags of the food that he is supposed to deliver out of his car window while driving. Assuming Brad is an agent-employee of Captain Hook Fish and Chips, did these actions violate any of his duties as an agent? Explain.

LAW ON THE WEB

For updated links to resources available on the Web, as well as a variety of other materials, visit this text's Web site at

www.cengage.com/blaw/jentz

The Legal Information Institute (LII) at Cornell University is an excellent source for information on agency law, including court cases involving agency concepts. You can access the LII's Web page on this topic at

www.law.cornell.edu/wex/index.php/Agency

Legal Research Exercises on the Web

Go to **www.cengage.com/blaw/jentz**, the Web site that accompanies this text. Select "Chapter 31" and click on "Internet Exercises." There you will find the following Internet research exercises that you can perform to learn more about the topics covered in this chapter.

Internet Exercise 31–1: Legal Perspective
Employees or Independent Contractors?

Internet Exercise 31–2: Management Perspective
Problems with Using Independent Contractors

CHAPTER 32

Liability to Third Parties and Termination

As discussed in the previous chapter, the law of agency focuses on the special relationship that exists between a principal and an agent—how the relationship is formed and the duties the principal and agent assume once the relationship is established. This chapter deals with another important aspect of agency law—the liability of principals and agents to third parties.

We look first at the liability of principals for contracts formed by agents with third parties. Generally, the liability of the principal will depend on whether the agent was authorized to form the contracts. The second part of the chapter deals with an agent's liability to third parties in contract and tort, and the principal's liability to third parties because of an agent's torts. The chapter concludes with a discussion of how agency relationships are terminated.

SECTION 1 Scope of Agent's Authority

The liability of a principal to third parties with whom an agent contracts depends on whether the agent had the authority to enter into legally binding contracts on the principal's behalf. An agent's authority can be either *actual* (express or implied) or *apparent.* If an agent contracts outside the scope of his or her authority, the principal may still become liable by ratifying the contract.

Express Authority

Express authority is authority declared in clear, direct, and definite terms. Express authority can be given orally or in writing. In most states, the **equal dignity rule** requires that if the contract being executed is or must be in writing, then the agent's authority must also be in writing. Failure to comply with the equal dignity rule can make a contract voidable *at the option of the principal.* The law regards the contract at that point as a mere offer. If the principal decides to accept the offer, the acceptance must be ratified, or affirmed, in writing.

Assume that Pattberg (the principal) orally asks Austin (the agent) to sell a ranch that Pattberg owns. Austin finds a buyer and signs a sales contract (a contract for an interest in realty must be in writing) on behalf of Pattberg to sell the ranch. The buyer cannot enforce the contract unless Pattberg subsequently ratifies Austin's agency status in writing. Once the contract is ratified, either party can enforce rights under the contract.

Modern business practice allows an exception to the equal dignity rule. An executive officer of a corporation, when acting for the corporation in an ordinary business situation, is not required to obtain written authority from the corporation. In addition, the equal dignity rule does not apply when the agent acts in the presence of the principal or when the agent's act of signing is merely perfunctory. Thus, if Healy (the principal) negotiates a contract but is called out of town the day it is to be signed and orally authorizes Scougall to sign, the oral authorization is sufficient.

Power of Attorney Giving an agent a **power of attorney** confers express authority.[1] The power of attorney is a written document and is usually notarized. (A document is notarized when a **notary public**—a public official authorized to attest to the

1. An agent who holds a power of attorney is called an *attorney-in-fact* for the principal. The holder does not have to be an attorney-at-law (and often is not).

authenticity of signatures—signs and dates the document and imprints it with her or his seal of authority.) Most states have statutory provisions for creating a power of attorney. A power of attorney can be special (permitting the agent to perform specified acts only), or it can be general (permitting the agent to transact all business for the principal). Because of the extensive authority granted to an agent by a general power of attorney (see Exhibit 32–1), it should be used with great caution and usually only in exceptional circumstances. Ordinarily, a power of attorney terminates on the incapacity or death of the person giving the power.[2]

Implied Authority

An agent has the **implied authority** to do what is reasonably necessary to carry out express authority and

2. A *durable* power of attorney, however, continues to be effective despite the principal's incapacity. An elderly person, for example, might grant a durable power of attorney to provide for the handling of property and investments or specific health-care needs should he or she become incompetent (see Chapter 50).

EXHIBIT 32–1 • A Sample General Power of Attorney

GENERAL POWER OF ATTORNEY

Know All Men by These Presents:

That I, __________, hereinafter referred to as PRINCIPAL, in the County of __________
State of __________, do(es) appoint __________ as my true and lawful attorney.

In principal's name, and for principal's use and benefit, said attorney is authorized hereby;

(1) To demand, sue for, collect, and receive all money, debts, accounts, legacies, bequests, interest, dividends, annuities, and demands as are now or shall hereafter become due, payable, or belonging to principal, and take all lawful means, for the recovery thereof and to compromise the same and give discharges for the same;
(2) To buy and sell land, make contracts of every kind relative to land, any interest therein or the possession thereof, and to take possession and exercise control over the use thereof;
(3) To buy, sell, mortgage, hypothecate, assign, transfer, and in any manner deal with goods, wares and merchandise, choses in action, certificates or shares of capital stock, and other property in possession or in action, and to make, do, and transact all and every kind of business of whatever nature;
(4) To execute, acknowledge, and deliver contracts of sale, escrow instructions, deeds, leases including leases for minerals and hydrocarbon substances and assignments of leases, covenants, agreements and assignments of agreements, mortgages and assignments of mortgages, conveyances in trust, to secure indebtedness or other obligations, and assign the beneficial interest thereunder, subordinations of liens or encumbrances, bills of lading, receipts, evidences of debt, releases, bonds, notes, bills, requests to reconvey deeds of trust, partial or full judgments, satisfactions of mortgages, and other debts, and other written instruments of whatever kind and nature, all upon such terms and conditions as said attorney shall approve.

GIVING AND GRANTING to said attorney full power and authority to do all and every act and thing whatsoever requisite and necessary to be done relative to any of the foregoing as fully to all intents and purposes as principal might or could do if personally present.

All that said attorney shall lawfully do or cause to be done under the authority of this power of attorney is expressly approved.

Dated: __________ /s/__________

State of __________ } SS.
County of __________

On __________, before me, the undersigned, a Notary Public in and for said State, personally appeared __________
____
known to me to be the person __________ whose name __________ subscribed to the within instrument and acknowledged that __________ executed the same.

Witness my hand and official seal. (Seal) __________
Notary Public in and for said State.

accomplish the objectives of the agency. Authority can also be implied by custom or inferred from the position the agent occupies. For example, Carlson is employed by Packard Grocery to manage one of its stores. Packard has not expressly stated that Carlson has authority to contract with third persons. Nevertheless, authority to manage a business implies authority to do what is reasonably required (as is customary or can be inferred from a manager's position) to operate the business. This includes making contracts for hiring personnel, for buying merchandise and equipment, and even for advertising the products sold in the store.

In general, implied authority is authority customarily associated with the position occupied by the agent or authority that can be inferred from the express authority given to the agent to perform fully his or her duties. For instance, an agent who has authority to solicit orders for goods sold by the principal generally would not have the authority to collect payments for the goods unless the agent possesses the goods. The test is whether it was reasonable for the agent to believe that she or he had the authority to enter into the contract in question.

Also note that an agent's implied authority cannot contradict his or her express authority. Thus, if a principal has limited an agent's authority—such as by forbidding a manager to enter into contracts to hire additional workers—then the fact that managers customarily would have such authority is irrelevant.

Apparent Authority and Estoppel

Actual authority (express or implied) arises from what the principal makes clear *to the agent.* Apparent authority, in contrast, arises from what the principal causes a third party to believe. An agent has **apparent authority** when the principal, by either word or action, causes a *third party* reasonably to believe that the agent has authority to act, even though the agent has no express or implied authority. If the third party changes his or her position in reliance on the principal's representations, the principal may be *estopped* (prevented) from denying that the agent had authority.

Apparent authority usually comes into existence through a principal's pattern of conduct over time. Suppose that Bain is a traveling salesperson with the authority to solicit orders for a principal's goods. Because she does not carry any goods with her, she normally would not have the implied authority to collect payments from customers on behalf of the principal. Assume that she does accept payments from Corgley Enterprises, however, and submits them to the principal's accounting department for processing. If the principal does nothing to stop Bain from continuing this practice, a pattern develops over time, and the principal confers apparent authority on Bain to accept payments from Corgley.

At issue in the following case was a question of apparent authority or, as the court referred to it, "ostensible agency."

CASE 32.1 Ermoian v. Desert Hospital

Court of Appeal of California, Fourth District, Division 2, 2007.
152 Cal.App.4th 475, 61 Cal.Rptr.3d 754.

• **Background and Facts** In 1990, Desert Hospital in California established a comprehensive perinatal services program (CPSP) to provide obstetrical care to women who were uninsured. (*Perinatal* is often defined as relating to the period from about the twenty-eighth week of pregnancy to around one month after birth.) The CPSP was set up in an office suite across from the hospital and named "Desert Hospital Outpatient Maternity Services Clinic." The hospital contracted with a corporation controlled by Dr. Morton Gubin, which employed Dr. Masami Ogata, to provide obstetrical services. In January 1994, Jackie Shahan went to the hospital's emergency room because of cramping and other symptoms. The emergency room physician told Shahan that she was pregnant and referred her to the clinic. Shahan visited the clinic throughout her pregnancy. On May 15, Shahan's baby, Amanda Ermoian, was born with brain abnormalities that left her severely mentally retarded and unable to care for herself. Her conditions could not have been prevented, treated, or cured in utero. Through a guardian, Amanda filed a suit in a California state court against the hospital and others, alleging "wrongful life." She claimed that the defendants negligently failed to inform her mother of her abnormalities before her birth, depriving her mother of the opportunity to make an informed choice to terminate the pregnancy. The court ruled in the defendants' favor, holding, among other things, that the hospital was not liable because Gubin and Ogata

CASE 32.1 CONTINUED were not its employees. Amanda appealed to a state intermediate appellate court, contending, in part, that the physicians were the hospital's "ostensible [apparent] agents."

• **Decision and Rationale** The state intermediate appellate court decided that, contrary to the lower court's finding, the physicians, Gubin and Ogata, were "ostensible agents of the Hospital." The appellate court affirmed the lower court's ruling, however, on Amanda's (Jackie Shahan's baby's) "wrongful life" claim, concluding that the physicians were not negligent in failing to advise Shahan to have an elective abortion. This court pointed out that ostensible agency (apparent agency) can be implied when a principal "by his acts has led others to believe that he has conferred authority upon an agent." Liability for an act of an ostensible agent rests on a doctrine of estoppel. The court noted that a person dealing with an agent must believe in the agent's authority. In this case, the hospital "held out the clinic and the personnel in the clinic as part of the hospital." The clinic used the same name as the hospital and labeled itself as an outpatient clinic. Moreover, personnel in the hospital's emergency room referred Shahan specifically to Gubin. When Shahan called the hospital, the receptionist told her "that she was calling the Hospital outpatient clinic which was the clinic of Dr. Gubin." The appellate court ruled that the hospital, and those associated with it, created the appearance to Shahan that the hospital was the provider of obstetrical care.

• **The Ethical Dimension** *Does a principal have an ethical responsibility to inform an unaware third party that an apparent (ostensible) agent does not in fact have authority to act on the principal's behalf?*

• **The E-Commerce Dimension** *Could Amanda have established Drs. Gubin and Ogata's apparent authority if Desert Hospital had maintained a Web site that advertised the services of the CPSP clinic and stated clearly that the physicians were not its employees? Explain.*

Emergency Powers

When an unforeseen emergency demands action by the agent to protect or preserve the property and rights of the principal, but the agent is unable to communicate with the principal, the agent has emergency power. For example, Fulsom is an engineer for Pacific Drilling Company. While Fulsom is acting within the scope of his employment, he is severely injured in an accident at an oil rig many miles from home. Dudley, the rig supervisor, directs Thompson, a physician, to give medical aid to Fulsom and to charge Pacific for the medical services. Dudley, an agent, has no express or implied authority to bind the principal, Pacific Drilling, for Thompson's medical services. Because of the emergency situation, however, the law recognizes Dudley as having authority to act appropriately under the circumstances.

Ratification

Ratification occurs when the principal affirms, or accepts responsibility for, an agent's *unauthorized* act. When ratification occurs, the principal is bound to the agent's act, and the act is treated as if it had been authorized by the principal *from the outset.* Ratification can be either express or implied.

If the principal does not ratify the contract, the principal is not bound, and the third party's agreement with the agent is viewed as merely an unaccepted offer. Because the third party's agreement is an unaccepted offer, the third party can revoke it at any time, without liability, before the principal ratifies the contract. The agent, however, may be liable to the third party for misrepresenting her or his authority.

The requirements for ratification can be summarized as follows:

1. The agent must have acted on behalf of an identified principal who subsequently ratifies the action.
2. The principal must know all of the material facts involved in the transaction. If a principal ratifies a contract without knowing all of the facts, the principal can rescind (cancel) the contract.[3]
3. The principal must affirm the agent's act in its entirety.
4. The principal must have the legal capacity to authorize the transaction at the time the agent engages in the act and at the time the principal

3. If the third party has changed position in reliance on the apparent contract, however, the principal can rescind but must reimburse the third party for any costs.

ratifies. The third party must also have the legal capacity to engage in the transaction.

5. The principal's affirmation (ratification) must occur before the third party withdraws from the transaction.
6. The principal must observe the same formalities when approving the act done by the agent as would have been required to authorize it initially.

Concept Summary 32.1 summarizes the rules concerning an agent's authority to bind the principal and a third party.

SECTION 2

Liability for Contracts

Liability for contracts formed by an agent depends on how the principal is classified and on whether the actions of the agent were authorized or unauthorized. Principals are classified as disclosed, partially disclosed, or undisclosed.

A **disclosed principal** is a principal whose identity is known by the third party at the time the contract is made by the agent. A **partially disclosed principal** is a principal whose identity is not known by the third party, but the third party knows that the agent is or may be acting for a principal at the time the contract is made. An **undisclosed principal** is a principal whose identity is totally unknown by the third party, and the third party has no knowledge that the agent is acting in an agency capacity at the time the contract is made.

Authorized Acts

If an agent acts within the scope of her or his authority, normally the principal is obligated to perform the contract regardless of whether the principal was disclosed, partially disclosed, or undisclosed. Whether the agent may also be held liable under the contract, however, depends on the disclosed, partially disclosed, or undisclosed status of the principal.

Disclosed or Partially Disclosed Principal

A disclosed or partially disclosed principal is liable to a third party for a contract made by the agent. If the principal is disclosed, an agent has no contractual liability for the nonperformance of the principal or the third party. If the principal is partially disclosed, in most states the agent is also treated as a party to the contract, and the third party can hold the agent liable for contractual nonperformance.[4]

4. *Restatement (Second) of Agency,* Section 321.

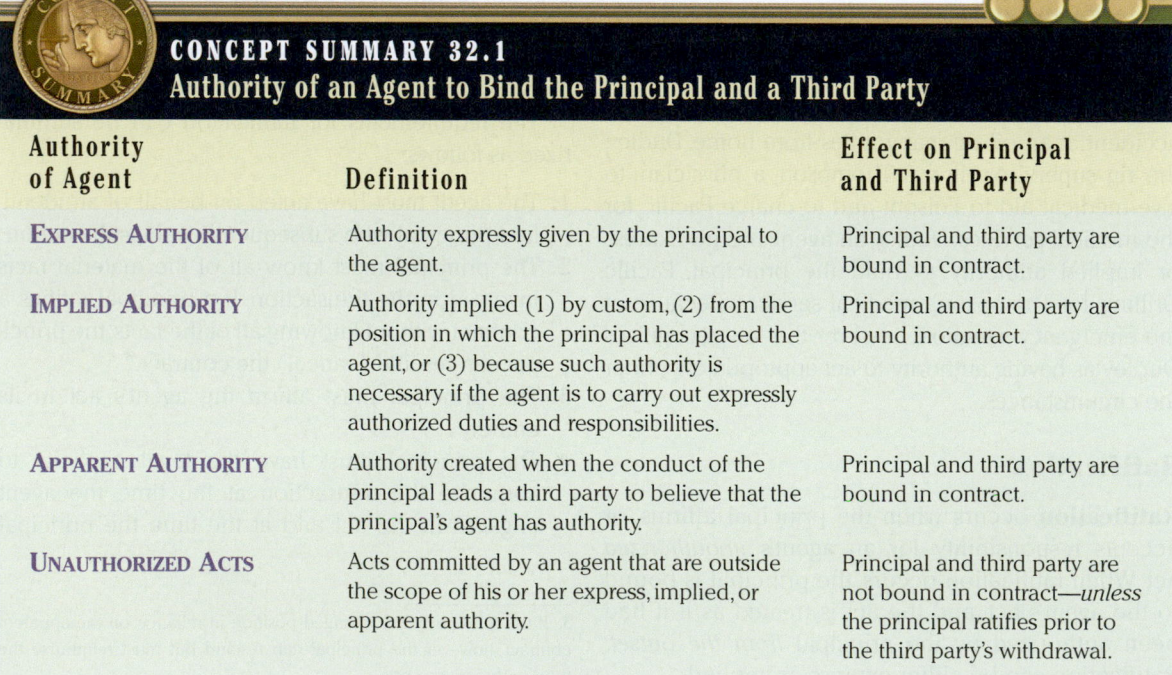

CONCEPT SUMMARY 32.1
Authority of an Agent to Bind the Principal and a Third Party

Authority of Agent	Definition	Effect on Principal and Third Party
EXPRESS AUTHORITY	Authority expressly given by the principal to the agent.	Principal and third party are bound in contract.
IMPLIED AUTHORITY	Authority implied (1) by custom, (2) from the position in which the principal has placed the agent, or (3) because such authority is necessary if the agent is to carry out expressly authorized duties and responsibilities.	Principal and third party are bound in contract.
APPARENT AUTHORITY	Authority created when the conduct of the principal leads a third party to believe that the principal's agent has authority.	Principal and third party are bound in contract.
UNAUTHORIZED ACTS	Acts committed by an agent that are outside the scope of his or her express, implied, or apparent authority.	Principal and third party are not bound in contract—*unless* the principal ratifies prior to the third party's withdrawal.

Undisclosed Principal When neither the fact of an agency relationship nor the identity of the principal is disclosed, the undisclosed principal is bound to perform just as if the principal had been fully disclosed at the time the contract was made.

When a principal's identity is undisclosed and the agent is forced to pay the third party, the agent is entitled to be *indemnified* (compensated) by the principal. The principal had a duty to perform, even though his or her identity was undisclosed, and failure to do so will make the principal ultimately liable. Once the undisclosed principal's identity is revealed, the third party generally can elect to hold either the principal or the agent liable on the contract.

Conversely, the undisclosed principal can require the third party to fulfill the contract, *unless* (1) the undisclosed principal was expressly excluded as a party in the written contract; (2) the contract is a negotiable instrument signed by the agent with no indication of signing in a representative capacity;[5] or (3) the performance of the agent is personal to the contract, allowing the third party to refuse the principal's performance.

Unauthorized Acts

If an agent has no authority but nevertheless contracts with a third party, the principal cannot be held liable on the contract. It does not matter whether the principal was disclosed, partially disclosed, or undisclosed. The agent is liable, however. Suppose that Scammon signs a contract for the purchase of a truck, purportedly acting as an agent under authority granted by Johnson. In fact, Johnson has not given Scammon any such authority. Johnson refuses to pay for the truck, claiming that Scammon had no authority to purchase it. The seller of the truck is entitled to hold Scammon liable for payment.

If the principal is disclosed or partially disclosed, the agent is liable as long as the third party relied on the agency status. The agent's liability here is based on the theory of breach of the *implied warranty of authority,* not on breach of the contract itself.[6] The agent's implied warranty of authority can be breached intentionally or by a good faith mistake.[7] For example, Kilmer (the principal) is a reclusive artist who hires Higgs (the agent) to solicit offers for particular paintings from various galleries, but does not authorize him to enter into sales agreements. Olaf, a gallery owner, desires to buy two of Kilmer's paintings right away for an upcoming show. Higgs tells Olaf that he will draw up a sales contract. By doing so, Higgs impliedly warrants that he has the authority to enter into sales contracts on behalf of Kilmer. If it later turns out that Kilmer does not wish to ratify the sales contract signed by Higgs, Olaf cannot hold Kilmer liable, but he can hold Higgs liable for breaching the implied warranty of authority.

Note that if the third party knows at the time the contract is made that the agent does not have authority, then the agent is not liable. Similarly, if the agent expresses to the third party *uncertainty* as to the extent of her or his authority, the agent is not personally liable.

Actions by E-Agents

Although standard agency principles once applied only to *human* agents, today these same agency principles are being applied to e-agents. An electronic agent, or **e-agent,** is a semiautonomous computer program that is capable of executing specific tasks. E-agents used in e-commerce include software that can search through many databases and retrieve only relevant information for the user.

The Uniform Electronic Transactions Act (UETA), which has been adopted at least in part by the majority of the states (see Chapter 19), includes several provisions relating to the principal's liability for the actions of e-agents. Section 15 of the UETA states that e-agents may enter into binding agreements on behalf of their principals. Presumably, then—at least in those states that have adopted the act—the principal will be bound by the terms in a contract entered into by an e-agent. Thus, if you place an order over the Internet, the company (principal) whose system took the order via an e-agent cannot claim that it did not receive your order.

The UETA also stipulates that if an e-agent does not provide an opportunity to prevent errors at the time of the transaction, the other party to the transaction can avoid the transaction. Therefore, if an e-agent fails to provide an on-screen confirmation of a purchase or sale, the other party can avoid the effect of any errors. For example, Finig wants to purchase three each of three different items (a total of nine items). The e-agent mistakenly records an order for thirty-three of a single item and does not provide an on-screen verification of

5. Under the Uniform Commercial Code (UCC), only the agent is liable if the instrument neither names the principal nor shows that the agent signed in a representative capacity [UCC 3–402(b)(2)].

6. The agent is not liable on the contract because the agent was never intended personally to be a party to the contract.

7. If the agent intentionally misrepresents his or her authority, then the agent can also be liable in tort for fraud.

the order. If thirty-three items are then sent to Finig, he can avoid the contract to purchase them.

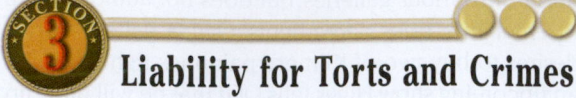

SECTION 3
Liability for Torts and Crimes

Obviously, any person, including an agent, is liable for his or her own torts and crimes. Whether a principal can also be held liable for an agent's torts and crimes depends on several factors, which we examine here. In some situations, a principal may be held liable not only for the torts of an agent but also for the torts committed by an independent contractor.

Principal's Tortious Conduct

A principal conducting an activity through an agent may be liable for harm resulting from the principal's own negligence or recklessness. Thus, a principal may be liable for giving improper instructions, authorizing the use of improper materials or tools, or establishing improper rules that result in the agent's committing a tort. For instance, if Jack knows that Lucy cannot drive but nevertheless tells her to use the company truck to deliver some equipment to a customer, he will be liable for his own negligence to anyone injured by her negligent driving.

Principal's Authorization of Agent's Tortious Conduct

Similarly, a principal who authorizes an agent to commit a tort may be liable to persons or property injured thereby, because the act is considered to be the principal's. For example, Selkow directs his agent, Warren, to cut the corn on specific acreage, which neither of them has the right to do. The harvest is therefore a trespass (a tort), and Selkow is liable to the owner of the corn.

Note that an agent acting at the principal's direction can be liable as a *tortfeasor* (one who commits a wrong, or tort), along with the principal, for committing the tortious act even if the agent was unaware that the act was wrong. Assume that in the above example Warren, the agent, did not know that Selkow lacked the right to harvest the corn. Warren can still be held liable to the owner of the field for damages, along with Selkow, the principal.

Liability for Agent's Misrepresentation

A principal is exposed to tort liability whenever a third person sustains a loss due to the agent's misrepresentation. The principal's liability depends on whether the agent was actually or apparently authorized to make representations and whether the representations were made within the scope of the agency. The principal is always directly responsible for an agent's misrepresentation made within the scope of the agent's authority.

Suppose that Bassett is a demonstrator for Moore's products. Moore sends Bassett to a home show to demonstrate the products and to answer questions from consumers. Moore has given Bassett authority to make statements about the products. If Bassett makes only true representations, all is fine; but if he makes false claims, Moore will be liable for any injuries or damages sustained by third parties in reliance on Bassett's false representations.

Apparent Implied Authority When a principal has placed an agent in a position of apparent authority—making it possible for the agent to defraud a third party—the principal may also be liable for the agent's fraudulent acts. For example, Frendak is a loan officer at First Security Bank. In the ordinary course of the job, Frendak approves and services loans and has access to the credit records of all customers. Frendak falsely represents to a borrower, McMillan, that the bank feels insecure about McMillan's loan and intends to call it in unless McMillan provides additional collateral, such as stocks and bonds. McMillan gives Frendak numerous stock certificates, which Frendak keeps in her own possession and later uses to make personal investments. The bank is liable to McMillan for losses sustained on the stocks even though the bank was unaware of the fraudulent scheme.

If, in contrast, Frendak had been a recently hired junior bank teller rather than a loan officer when she told McMillan that the bank required additional security for the loan, McMillan would not have been justified in relying on her representation. In that situation, the bank normally would not be liable to McMillan for the losses sustained.

Innocent Misrepresentation Tort liability based on fraud requires proof that a material misstatement was made knowingly and with the intent to deceive. An agent's innocent mistakes occurring in a contract transaction or involving a warranty contained in the contract can provide grounds for the third party's rescission of the contract and the award of damages. Moreover, justice dictates that when a principal knows that an agent is not accurately advised of facts but does not correct either the agent's or the third party's impressions, the principal is directly responsible to the third party for resulting damages. The point is that the principal is always directly responsible for an agent's misrepresentation made within the scope of authority.

Liability for Agent's Negligence

Under the doctrine of ***respondeat superior,***[8] the principal-employer is liable for any harm caused to a third party by an agent-employee within the scope of employment. This doctrine imposes **vicarious liability,** or indirect liability, on the employer—that is, liability without regard to the personal fault of the employer for torts committed by an employee in the course or scope of employment.[9] Third parties injured through the negligence of an employee can sue either that employee or the employer, if the employee's negligent conduct occurred while the employee was acting within the scope of employment.

Rationale Underlying the Doctrine of *Respondeat Superior* At early common law, a servant (employee) was viewed as the master's (employer's) property. The master was deemed to have absolute control over the servant's acts and was held strictly liable for them no matter how carefully the master supervised the servant. The rationale for the doctrine of *respondeat superior* is based on the social duty that requires every person to manage his or her affairs, whether accomplished by the person or through agents, so as not to injure another. Liability is imposed on employers because they are deemed to be in a better financial position to bear the loss. The superior financial position carries with it the duty to be responsible for damages.

Generally, public policy requires that an injured person be afforded effective relief, and a business enterprise is usually better able to provide that relief than is an individual employee. Employers normally carry liability insurance to cover any damages awarded as a result of such lawsuits. They are also able to spread the cost of risk over the entire business enterprise.

The doctrine of *respondeat superior,* which the courts have applied for nearly two centuries, continues to have practical implications in all situations involving principal-agent (employer-employee) relationships. Today, the small-town grocer with one clerk and the multinational corporation with thousands of employees are equally subject to the doctrinal demand of "let the master respond." (Keep this principle in mind as you read through Chapters 33 and 34.)

When an agent commits a negligent act, can the agent, as well as the principal, be held liable? That was the issue in the following case.

8. Pronounced ree-*spahn*-dee-uht soo-*peer*-ee-your. The doctrine of *respondeat superior* applies not only to employer-employee relationships but also to other principal-agent relationships in which the principal has the right of control over the agent.

9. The theory of *respondeat superior* is similar in this respect to the theory of strict liability covered in Chapter 7.

CASE 32.2 Warner v. Southwest Desert Images, LLC

Court of Appeals of Arizona, Divisions 2, Department A, 2008.
218 Ariz. 121, 180 P.3d 986.

Background and Facts Aegis Communications hired Southwest Desert Images (SDI) to provide landscaping services for its property. SDI employee David Hoggatt was spraying an herbicide to control weeds around the Aegis building one day when he was told that the spray was being sucked into the building by the air-conditioning system and making people sick. The building was evacuated and employees were treated for breathing problems and itchy eyes. Aegis employee Catherine Warner, who had suffered two heart attacks previously, was taken to the hospital. It was determined that she had suffered a heart attack. She continued experiencing health complications that she blamed on exposure to the spray. Warner sued SDI and Hoggatt for negligence. The trial judge dismissed the suit against Hoggatt. The jury found SDI alone to be liable for Warner's injuries. She was awarded $3,825 in damages. She appealed the decision.

Decision and Rationale The appeals court held that Hoggatt should not have been dismissed from the lawsuit. The fact that Hoggatt was an agent/employee of SDI did not excuse him from liability for his negligence in spraying. There was evidence that Hoggatt ignored instructions provided by the company that sold SDI the spray. In doing so, he was negligent. An agent (Hoggatt)

CASE CONTINUES

CASE 32.2 CONTINUED is not excused from responsibility for tortious conduct just because he is working for a principal (SDI). The jury found SDI completely responsible, but denied Warner the right to collect from Hoggatt as a joint tortfeasor in this situation. The appeals court ruled, however, that Warner should be able to collect from Hoggatt as well.

- **The Ethical Dimension** *Assume that Hoggatt was following the instructions of his employer, SDI, in applying the spray. Should Hoggatt be personally liable in such a situation, given that the employer is better able financially to pay the judgment and may have insurance that covers the matter? Explain your answer.*

- **The Legal Environment Dimension** *How could SDI reduce the likelihood of similar lawsuits occurring in the future?*

Determining the Scope of Employment The key to determining whether a principal may be liable for the torts of an agent under the doctrine of *respondeat superior* is whether the torts are committed within the scope of the agency or employment. The *Restatement (Second) of Agency,* Section 229, outlines the following general factors that courts will consider in determining whether a particular act occurred within the course and scope of employment:

1. Whether the employee's act was authorized by the employer.
2. The time, place, and purpose of the act.
3. Whether the act was one commonly performed by employees on behalf of their employers.
4. The extent to which the employer's interest was advanced by the act.
5. The extent to which the private interests of the employee were involved.
6. Whether the employer furnished the means or instrumentality (for example, a truck or a machine) by which an injury was inflicted.
7. Whether the employer had reason to know that the employee would perform the act in question and whether the employee had done it before.
8. Whether the act involved the commission of a serious crime.

The Distinction between a "Detour" and a "Frolic" A useful insight into the concept of "scope of employment" may be gained from Judge Baron Parke's classic distinction between a "detour" and a "frolic" in the case of *Joel v. Morison* (1834).[10] In this case, the English court held that if a servant merely took a detour from his master's business, the master will be responsible. If, however, the servant was on a "frolic of his own" and not in any way "on his master's business," the master will not be liable.

Consider an example. Mandel, a traveling salesperson, while driving his employer's vehicle to call on a customer, decides to stop at the post office—which is one block off his route—to mail a personal letter. As Mandel approaches the post office, he negligently runs into a parked vehicle owned by Chan. In this situation, because Mandel's detour from the employer's business is not substantial, he is still acting within the scope of employment, and the employer is liable. The result would be different, though, if Mandel had decided to pick up a few friends for cocktails in another city and in the process had negligently run his vehicle into Chan's. In that circumstance, the departure from the employer's business would be substantial, and the employer normally would not be liable to Chan for damages. Mandel would be considered to have been on a "frolic" of his own.

Employee Travel Time An employee going to and from work or to and from meals is usually considered to be outside the scope of employment. In contrast, all travel time of traveling salespersons or others whose jobs require them to travel is normally considered to be within the scope of employment for the duration of the business trip, including the return trip home, unless there is a significant departure from the employer's business.

Notice of Dangerous Conditions The employer is charged with knowledge of any dangerous conditions discovered by an employee and pertinent to the employment situation. Suppose that Brad, a maintenance employee in an apartment building, notices a lead pipe protruding from the ground in the building's courtyard. Brad neglects either to fix the pipe or to inform his employer of the danger. John falls

10. 6 Car. & P. 501, 172 Eng. Rep. 1338 (1834).

on the pipe and is injured. The employer is charged with knowledge of the dangerous condition regardless of whether Brad actually informed the employer. That knowledge is imputed to the employer by virtue of the employment relationship.

Borrowed Servants Employers sometimes lend the services of their employees to other employers. Suppose that an employer leases ground-moving equipment to another employer and sends along an employee to operate the machinery. Who is liable for injuries caused by the employee's negligent actions on the job site? Liability turns on *which employer had the primary right to control* the employee at the time the injuries occurred. Generally, the employer who rents out the equipment is presumed to retain control over her or his employee. If the rental is for a relatively long period of time, however, control may be deemed to pass to the employer who is renting the equipment and presumably controlling and directing the employee.

Liability for Agent's Intentional Torts

Most intentional torts that employees commit have no relation to their employment; thus, their employers will not be held liable. Nevertheless, under the doctrine of *respondeat superior,* the employer can be liable for intentional torts of the employee that are committed within the course and scope of employment, just as the employer is liable for negligence. For instance, an employer is liable when an employee (such as a bouncer at a nightclub or a security guard at a department store) commits the tort of assault and battery or false imprisonment while acting within the scope of employment.

In addition, an employer who knows or should know that an employee has a propensity for committing tortious acts is liable for the employee's acts even if they ordinarily would not be considered within the scope of employment. For example, if an employer hires a bouncer knowing that he has a history of arrests for criminal assault and battery, the employer may be liable if the employee viciously attacks a patron in the parking lot after hours.

An employer is also liable for permitting an employee to engage in reckless actions that can injure others. Assume that an employer observes an employee smoking while filling containerized trucks with highly flammable liquids. Failure to stop the employee will cause the employer to be liable for any injuries that result if a truck explodes. Needless to say, most employers purchase liability insurance to cover their potential liability for employee conduct in many situations (see Chapter 49).

Liability for Independent Contractor's Torts

Generally, an employer is not liable for physical harm caused to a third person by the negligent act of an independent contractor in the performance of the contract. This is because the employer does not have *the right to control* the details of an independent contractor's performance. Exceptions to this rule are made in certain situations, though, such as when the contract involves unusually hazardous activities—for example, blasting operations, the transportation of highly volatile chemicals, or the use of poisonous gases. In these situations, an employer cannot be shielded from liability merely by using an independent contractor. Strict liability is imposed on the employer-principal as a matter of law. Also, in some states, strict liability may be imposed by statute.

Liability for Agent's Crimes

An agent is liable for his or her own crimes. A principal or employer is not liable for an agent's or employee's crime simply because the agent or employee committed the crime while otherwise acting within the scope of authority or employment. An exception to this rule is made when the principal or employer participated in the crime by conspiracy or other action. In some jurisdictions, under specific statutes, a principal may be liable for an agent's violating, in the course and scope of employment, such regulations as those governing sanitation, prices, weights, and the sale of liquor.

SECTION 4

Termination of an Agency

Agency law is similar to contract law in that both an agency and a contract may be terminated by an act of the parties or by operation of law. Once the relationship between the principal and the agent has ended, the agent no longer has the right (*actual* authority) to bind the principal. For an agent's *apparent* authority to be terminated, though, third persons may also need to be notified that the agency has been terminated.

Termination by Act of the Parties

An agency relationship may be terminated by act of the parties in a number of ways, including those discussed here.

Lapse of Time An agency agreement may specify the time period during which the agency relationship will exist. If so, the agency ends when that time expires. For example, Akers signs an agreement of agency with Janz "beginning January 1, 2009, and ending December 31, 2010." The agency is automatically terminated on December 31, 2010. If no definite time is stated, then the agency continues for a reasonable time and can be terminated at will by either party. What constitutes a reasonable time depends on the circumstances and the nature of the agency relationship.

Purpose Achieved An agent can be employed to accomplish a particular objective, such as the purchase of stock for a cattle rancher. In that situation, the agency automatically ends after the cattle have been purchased. If more than one agent is employed to accomplish the same purpose, such as the sale of real estate, the first agent to complete the sale automatically terminates the agency relationship for all the others.

Occurrence of a Specific Event An agency can be created to terminate on the happening of a certain event. For instance, if Posner appoints Rubik to handle her business affairs while she is away, the agency automatically terminates when Posner returns.

Mutual Agreement Recall from basic contract law that parties can rescind (cancel) a contract by mutually agreeing to terminate the contractual relationship at any time. The same holds true in agency law regardless of whether the agency contract is in writing or whether it is for a specific duration.

At the Option of One Party As a *general* rule, either party can terminate the agency relationship—because agency is a consensual relationship, and thus neither party can be compelled to continue in the relationship. The agent's act is said to be a *renunciation* of authority. The principal's act is a *revocation* of authority. Although both parties may have the *power* to terminate the agency, they may not possess the *right* to terminate and may therefore be liable for breach of contract.

Wrongful Termination. Wrongful termination can subject the canceling party to a lawsuit for breach of contract. Suppose that Rawlins has a one-year employment contract with Munro to act as agent in return for $65,000. Munro has the *power* to discharge Rawlins before the contract period expires. If Munro discharges Rawlins, though, he can be sued for breaching the contract and will be liable to Rawlins for damages because he had no *right* to terminate the agency.

Even in an agency at will—that is, an agency that either party may terminate at any time—the principal who wishes to terminate must give the agent *reasonable* notice. The notice must be at least sufficient to allow the agent to recoup his or her expenses and, in some situations, to make a normal profit.

Agency Coupled with an Interest. A special rule applies in an *agency coupled with an interest.* This type of agency is not an agency in the usual sense because it is created for the agent's benefit instead of for the principal's benefit. Suppose that Julie borrows $5,000 from Rob, giving Rob some of her jewelry and signing a letter authorizing him to sell the jewelry as her agent if she fails to repay the loan. After Julie receives the $5,000 from Rob, she attempts to revoke his authority to sell the jewelry as her agent. Julie will not succeed in this attempt because a principal cannot revoke an agency created for the agent's benefit.

An agency coupled with an interest should not be confused with a situation in which the agent merely derives proceeds or profits from the sale of the subject matter. For example, an agent who merely receives a commission from the sale of real property does not have a beneficial interest in the property itself.

Notice of Termination When an agency has been terminated by act of the parties, it is the principal's duty to inform any third parties who know of the existence of the agency that it has been terminated (notice of the termination may be given by others, however).

Although an agent's actual authority ends when the agency is terminated, an agent's *apparent authority* continues until the third party receives notice (from any source) that such authority has been terminated. If the principal knows that a third party has dealt with the agent, the principal is expected to notify that person *directly*. For third parties who have heard about the agency but have not yet dealt with the agent, *constructive notice* is sufficient.[11]

11. With *constructive notice* of a fact, knowledge of the fact is imputed by law to a person if he or she could have discovered the fact by proper diligence. Constructive notice is often accomplished by publication in a newspaper.

No particular form is required for notice of termination of the principal-agent relationship to be effective. The principal can personally notify the agent, or the agent can learn of the termination through some other means. Assume that Manning bids on a shipment of steel, and Stone is hired as an agent to arrange transportation of the shipment. When Stone learns that Manning has lost the bid, Stone's authority to make the transportation arrangement terminates. If the agent's authority is written, however, normally it must be revoked in writing (unless the written document contained an expiration date).

Termination by Operation of Law

Certain events will terminate agency authority automatically because their occurrence makes it impossible for the agent to perform or improbable that the principal would continue to want performance. We look at these events here. Note that when an agency terminates by operation of law, there is no duty to notify third persons—unless the agent's authority is coupled with an interest.

Death or Insanity The general rule is that the death or insanity of either the principal or the agent automatically and immediately terminates an ordinary agency relationship.[12] Knowledge of the death or insanity is not required. For example, Grey sends Bosley to Japan to purchase a rare book. Before Bosley makes the purchase, Grey dies. Bosley's agent status is terminated at the moment of Grey's death, even though Bosley does not know that Grey has died. (Some states, however, have changed the common law by statute to make knowledge of the principal's death a requirement for agency termination.)

An agent's transactions that occur after the death of the principal are not binding on the principal's estate. Assume that Bosley is hired by Grey to collect a debt from Cochran (a third party). Grey dies, but Bosley, not knowing of Grey's death, still collects the debt from Cochran. Cochran's payment to Bosley is no longer legally sufficient to discharge the debt to Grey because Bosley no longer has Grey's authority to collect the funds. If Bosley absconds with the funds, Cochran must pay the debt again to Grey's estate.

Impossibility When the specific subject matter of an agency is destroyed or lost, the agency terminates. Assume that Gonzalez employs Raich to sell Gonzalez's house. Prior to any sale, the house is destroyed by fire. Raich's agency and authority to sell the house terminate. Similarly, when it is impossible for the agent to perform the agency lawfully because of a change in the law, the agency terminates.

Changed Circumstances When an event occurs that has such an unusual effect on the subject matter of the agency that the agent can reasonably infer that the principal will not want the agency to continue, the agency terminates. Suppose that Baird hires Joslen to sell a tract of land for $40,000. Subsequently, Joslen learns that there is oil under the land and that the land is therefore worth $1 million. The agency and Joslen's authority to sell the land for $40,000 are terminated.

Bankruptcy If either the principal or the agent petitions for bankruptcy, the agency is *usually* terminated. In certain circumstances, such as when the agent's financial status is irrelevant to the purpose of the agency, the agency relationship may continue. *Insolvency* (defined as the inability to pay debts when they come due or when liabilities exceed assets), as distinguished from bankruptcy, does not necessarily terminate the relationship.

War When the principal's country and the agent's country are at war with each other, the agency is terminated. In this situation, the agency is automatically suspended or terminated because there is no way to enforce the legal rights and obligations of the parties. See *Concept Summary 32.2* on the next page for a synopsis of the rules governing the termination of an agency.

12. There is an exception to this rule in banking. Under UCC 4–405, when a bank has knowledge of a customer's death, it has authority for ten days after the death to pay checks (but not notes or drafts) drawn by the customer unless it receives a stop-payment order from someone who has an interest in the account, such as an heir.

CONCEPT SUMMARY 32.2
Termination of an Agency

Method of Termination	Rules	Termination of Agent's Authority
ACT OF THE PARTIES		
1. Lapse of time.	Automatic at end of the stated time.	
2. Purpose achieved.	Automatic on the completion of the purpose.	
3. Occurrence of a specific event.	Normally automatic on the happening of the event.	**Notice to Third Parties Required—**
4. Mutual agreement.	Mutual consent required.	1. Direct to those who have dealt with agency.
5. At the option of one party (revocation, if by principal; renunciation, if by agent).	Either party normally has a right to terminate the agency but may lack the power to do so, which can lead to liability for breach of contract.	2. Constructive to all others.
OPERATION OF LAW		
1. Death or insanity.	Automatic on the death or insanity of either the principal or the agent (except when the agency is coupled with an interest).	
2. Impossibility—destruction of the specific subject matter.	Applies any time the agency cannot be performed because of an event beyond the parties' control.	**No Notice Required—**
3. Changed circumstances.	Events so unusual that it would be inequitable to allow the agency to continue to exist.	Automatic on the happening of the event.
4. Bankruptcy.	A bankruptcy decree (not mere insolvency) usually terminates the agency.	
5. War between principal's country and agent's country.	Automatically suspends or terminates the agency—no way to enforce legal rights.	

REVIEWING Liability to Third Parties and Termination

Lynne Meyer, on her way to a business meeting and in a hurry, stopped at a Buy-Mart store for a new pair of nylons to wear to the meeting. There was a long line at one of the checkout counters, but a cashier, Valerie Watts, opened another counter and began loading the cash drawer. Meyer told Watts that she was in a hurry and asked Watts to work faster. Instead, Watts only slowed her pace. At this point, Meyer hit Watts. It is not clear from the record whether Meyer hit Watts intentionally or, in an attempt to retrieve the nylons, hit her inadvertently. In response, Watts grabbed Meyer by the hair and hit her repeatedly in the back of the head, while Meyer screamed for help. Management personnel separated the two women and questioned them about the incident. Watts was immediately fired for violating the store's no-fighting policy. Meyer subsequently sued Buy-Mart, alleging that the store was liable for the tort (assault and battery) committed by its employee. Using the information presented in the chapter, answer the following questions.

REVIEWING Liability to Third Parties and Termination, Continued

1. Under what doctrine discussed in this chapter might Buy-Mart be held liable for the tort committed by Watts?
2. What is the key factor in determining whether Buy-Mart is liable under this doctrine?
3. How is Buy-Mart's potential liability affected depending on whether Watts's behavior constituted an intentional tort or a tort of negligence?
4. Suppose that when Watts applied for the job at Buy-Mart, she disclosed in her application that she had previously been convicted of felony assault and battery. Nevertheless, Buy-Mart hired Watts as a cashier. How might this fact affect Buy-Mart's liability for Watts's actions?

TERMS AND CONCEPTS

apparent authority 606
disclosed principal 608
e-agent 609
equal dignity rule 604
express authority 604
implied authority 605
notary public 604
partially disclosed principal 608
power of attorney 604
ratification 607
***respondeat superior* 611**
undisclosed principal 608
vicarious liability 611

QUESTIONS AND CASE PROBLEMS

32–1. Adam is a traveling salesperson for Peter Petri Plumbing Supply Corp. Adam has express authority to solicit orders from customers and to offer a 5 percent discount if payment is made within thirty days of delivery. Petri has said nothing to Adam about extending credit. Adam calls on a new prospective customer, John's Plumbing Firm. John tells Adam that he will place a large order for Petri products if Adam will give him a 10 percent discount with payment due in equal installments thirty, sixty, and ninety days from delivery. Adam says he has authority to make such a contract. John calls Petri and asks if Adam is authorized to make contracts giving a discount. No mention is made of payment terms. Petri replies that Adam has authority to give discounts on purchase orders. On the basis of this information, John orders $10,000 worth of plumbing supplies and fixtures. The goods are delivered and are being sold. One week later, John receives a bill for $9,500, due in thirty days. John insists he owes only $9,000 and can pay it in three equal installments, at thirty, sixty, and ninety days from delivery. Discuss the liability of Petri and John only.

32–2. QUESTION WITH SAMPLE ANSWER
Alice Adams is a purchasing agent-employee for the A&B Coal Supply partnership. Adams has authority to purchase the coal needed by A&B to satisfy the needs of its customers. While Adams is leaving a coal mine from which she has just purchased a large quantity of coal, her car breaks down. She walks into a small roadside grocery store for help. While there, she runs into Will Wilson, who owns 360 acres back in the mountains with all mineral rights. Wilson, in need of cash, offers to sell Adams the property for $1,500 per acre. On inspection of the property, Adams forms the opinion that the subsurface contains valuable coal deposits. Adams contracts to purchase the property for A&B Coal Supply, signing the contract "A&B Coal Supply, Alice Adams, agent." The closing date is August 1. Adams takes the contract to the partnership. The managing partner is furious, as A&B is not in the property business. Later, just before closing, both Wilson and the partnership learn that the value of the land is at least $15,000 per acre. Discuss the rights of A&B and Wilson concerning the land contract.

- **For a sample answer to Question 32–2, go to Appendix I at the end of this text.**

32–3. Paula Enterprises hires Able to act as its agent to purchase a one-thousand-acre tract of land from Thompson for $1,000 per acre. Paula Enterprises does not wish Thompson to know that it is the principal or that Able is its agent. Paula wants the land for a new country housing development, and Thompson may not sell the land for that purpose or may demand a premium price. Able makes the contract for the purchase, signing only his name as purchaser and not disclosing the agency relationship to Thompson. The closing and transfer of deed are to take place on September 1.

(a) If Thompson learns of Paula's identity on August 1, can Thompson legally refuse to deed the property on September 1? Explain.
(b) Paula gives Able the funds for the closing, but Able absconds with the funds, causing a breach of Able's contract at the date of closing. Thompson then learns of Paula's identity and wants to enforce the contract. Discuss fully Thompson's rights under these circumstances.

32–4. ABC Tire Corp. hires Arnez as a traveling salesperson and assigns him a geographic area and time schedule in which to solicit orders and service customers. Arnez is given a company car to use in covering the territory. One day, Arnez decides to take his personal car to cover part of his territory. It is 11:00 A.M., and Arnez has just finished calling on all customers in the city of Tarrytown. His next appointment is at 2:00 P.M. in the city of Austex, twenty miles down the road. Arnez starts out for Austex, but halfway there he decides to visit a former college roommate who runs a farm ten miles off the main highway. Arnez is enjoying his visit with his former roommate when he realizes that it is 1:45 P.M. and that he will be late for the appointment in Austex. Driving at a high speed down the country road to reach the main highway, Arnez crashes his car into Thomas's tractor, severely injuring Thomas, a farmer. Thomas claims that he can hold ABC Tire Corp. liable for his injuries. Discuss fully ABC's liability in this situation.

32–5. Liability for Employee's Acts. Federated Financial Reserve Corp. leases consumer and business equipment. As part of its credit-approval and debt-collection practices, Federated hires credit collectors and authorizes them to obtain credit reports on its customers. Janice Caylor, a Federated collector, used this authority to obtain a report on Karen Jones, who was not a Federated customer but who was the former wife of Caylor's roommate, Randy Lind. When Jones discovered that Lind had her address and how he had obtained it, she filed a suit in a federal district court against Federated and the others. Jones claimed, in part, that they had violated the Fair Credit Reporting Act, the goal of which is to protect consumers from the improper use of credit reports. Under what theory might an employer be held liable for an employee's violation of a statute? Does that theory apply in this case? Explain. [*Jones v. Federated Financial Reserve Corp.*, 144 F.3d 961 (6th Cir. 1998)]

32–6. Liability for Independent Contractor's Torts. Greif Brothers Corp., a steel drum manufacturer, owned and operated a manufacturing plant in Youngstown, Ohio. In 1987, Lowell Wilson, the plant superintendent, hired Youngstown Security Patrol, Inc. (YSP), a security company, to guard Greif property and "deter thieves and vandals." Some YSP security guards, as Wilson knew, carried firearms. Eric Bator, a YSP security guard, was not certified as an armed guard but nevertheless took his gun, in a briefcase, to work. While working at the Greif plant on August 12, 1991, Bator fired his gun at Derrell Pusey, in the belief that Pusey was an intruder. The bullet struck and killed Pusey. Pusey's mother filed a suit in an Ohio state court against Greif and others, alleging, in part, that her son's death was the result of YSP's negligence, for which Greif was responsible. Greif filed a motion for a directed verdict. What is the plaintiff's best argument that Greif is responsible for YSP's actions? What is Greif's best defense? Explain. [*Pusey v. Bator,* 94 Ohio St.3d 275, 762 N.E.2d 968 (2002)]

32–7. CASE PROBLEM WITH SAMPLE ANSWER

In 1998, William Larry Smith signed a lease for certain land in Chilton County, Alabama, owned by Sweet Smitherman. The lease stated that it was between "Smitherman, and WLS, Inc., d/b/a [doing business as] S&H Mobile Homes" and the signature line identified the lessee as "WLS, Inc. d/b/a S&H Mobile Homes . . . By: William Larry Smith, President." The amount of the rent was $5,000, payable by the tenth of each month. All of the checks that Smitherman received for the rent identified the owner of the account as "WLS Corporation d/b/a S&H Mobile Homes." Nearly four years later, Smitherman filed a suit in an Alabama state court against William Larry Smith, alleging that he owed $26,000 in unpaid rent. Smith responded, in part, that WLS was the lessee and that he was not personally responsible for the obligation to pay the rent. Is Smith a principal, an agent, both a principal and an agent, or neither? In any event, in the lease, is the principal disclosed, partially disclosed, or undisclosed? With the answers to these questions in mind, who is liable for the unpaid rent, and why? Discuss. [*Smith v. Smitherman,* 887 So.2d 285 (Ala.Civ.App. 2004)]

- **To view a sample answer for Problem 32–7, go to this book's Web site at www.cengage.com/blaw/jentz, select "Chapter 32," and click on "Case Problem with Sample Answer."**

32–8. Apparent Authority. Lee Dennegar and Mark Knutson lived in Dennegar's house in Raritan, New Jersey.

Dennegar paid the mortgage and other household expenses. With Dennegar's consent, Knutson managed their household's financial affairs and the "general office functions concerned with maintaining the house." Dennegar allowed Knutson to handle the mail and "to do with it as he chose." Knutson wrote checks for Dennegar to sign, although Knutson signed Dennegar's name to many of the checks with Dennegar's consent. AT&T Universal issued a credit card in Dennegar's name in February 2001. Monthly statements were mailed to Dennegar's house, and payments were sometimes made on those statements. Knutson died in June 2003. The unpaid charges on the card of $14,752.93 were assigned to New Century Financial Services, Inc. New Century filed a suit in a New Jersey court against Dennegar to collect the unpaid amount. Dennegar claimed that he never applied for or used the card and knew nothing about it. Under what theory could Dennegar be liable for the charges? Explain. [*New Century Financial Services, Inc. v. Dennegar,* 394 N.J.Super. 595, 928 A.2d 48 (A.D. 2007)]

32-9. A QUESTION OF ETHICS

Warren Davis lived with Renee Brandt in a house that Davis owned in Virginia Beach, Virginia. At Davis's request, attorney Leigh Ansell prepared, and Davis acknowledged, a durable power of attorney appointing Ansell to act as Davis's attorney-in-fact. Ansell was authorized to sign "any . . . instrument of . . . deposit" and "any contract . . . relating to . . . personal property." Ansell could act "in any circumstances as fully and effectively as I could do as part of my normal, everyday business affairs if acting personally." A few days later, at Davis's direction, Ansell prepared, and Davis signed, a will that gave Brandt the right to occupy, rent-free, the house in which she and Davis lived "so long as she lives in the premises." The will's other chief beneficiaries were Davis's daughters, Sharon Jones and Jody Clark. According to Ansell, Davis intended to "take care of [Brandt] outside of this will" and asked Ansell to designate Brandt the beneficiary "payable on death" (POD) of Davis's $250,000 certificate of deposit (CD). The CD had no other named beneficiary. Less than two months later, Davis died. A suit between Brandt and Davis's daughters ensued in a Virginia state court. [Jones v. Brandt, *645 S.E.2d 312 (Va. 2007)*]

(a) Should the language in a power of attorney be interpreted broadly or strictly? Why?

(b) In this case, did Ansell have the authority under the power of attorney to change the beneficiary of Davis's CD? Explain.

(c) Ansell advised Davis by letter that he had complied with the instruction to designate Brandt the beneficiary of the CD. Davis made no objection. On these facts, what theory might apply to validate the designation?

LAW ON THE WEB

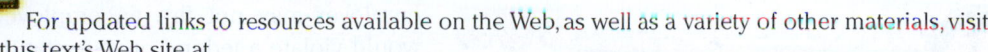

For updated links to resources available on the Web, as well as a variety of other materials, visit this text's Web site at

www.cengage.com/blaw/jentz

There are now numerous "shopping bots" (e-agents) that will search the Web to obtain the best prices for specified products. You can obtain the latest reviews on the merits of various shopping bots by going to

www.botspot.com

Legal Research Exercises on the Web

Go to **www.cengage.com/blaw/jentz**, the Web site that accompanies this text. Select "Chapter 32" and click on "Internet Exercises." There you will find the following Internet research exercises that you can perform to learn more about the topics covered in this chapter.

Internet Exercise 32–1: Legal Perspective
Power of Attorney

Internet Exercise 32–2: Management Perspective
Liability in Agency Relationships

CHAPTER 33

Employment and Labor Law

Traditionally, employment relationships in the United States were governed primarily by the common law. Today, in contrast, the workplace is regulated extensively by federal and state statutes. Recall from Chapter 1 that common law doctrines apply only to areas *not* covered by statutory law. Common law doctrines have thus been displaced to a significant extent by statutory law. In this chapter, we look at the most significant laws regulating employment relationships. We examine other important laws regulating the workplace—those prohibiting employment discrimination—in the next chapter.

Keep in mind, however, that certain aspects of employment relationships are still governed by common law rules, including the rules under contract, tort, and agency law discussed in previous chapters of this text. Given that many employees (those who deal with third parties) normally are deemed to be agents of their employer, agency concepts are especially relevant in the employment context, as is the distinction between employees and independent contractors. Generally, the laws discussed in this chapter and in Chapter 34 apply only to the employer-employee relationship and not to independent contractors. Here, we begin our discussion by examining one other common law doctrine that has not been entirely displaced by statutory law—that of employment at will.

SECTION 1 Employment at Will

Traditionally, employment relationships have generally been governed by the common law doctrine of **employment at will.** Under this doctrine, either the employer or the employee may terminate an employment contract at any time and for any reason, unless the contract specifically provides to the contrary. This doctrine is still in widespread use, and only one state (Montana) does not apply it. Indeed, as discussed in the *Contemporary Legal Debates* feature in Chapter 12 on pages 240 and 241, the legal status of the majority of American workers is "employee at will." Nonetheless, as has occurred in many other areas of employment law, federal and state statutes have partially displaced the common law and now prevent this doctrine from being applied in a number of circumstances. Today, an employer may not fire an employee if to do so would violate a federal or state statute, such as one prohibiting termination of employment for discriminatory reasons (see Chapter 34).

Exceptions to the Employment-at-Will Doctrine

Under the employment-at-will doctrine, as mentioned, an employer may hire and fire employees at will (regardless of the employees' performance) without liability, unless the decision violates the terms of an employment contract or statutory law. Because of the harsh effects of the employment-at-will doctrine for employees, courts have carved out various exceptions to this doctrine. These exceptions are based on contract theory, tort theory, and public policy.

Exceptions Based on Contract Theory Some courts have held that an *implied* employment contract exists between the employer and the employee. If the employee is fired outside the terms of the implied contract, he or she may succeed in an action for breach of contract even though no written employment contract exists.

For example, an employer's manual or personnel bulletin may state that, as a matter of policy, workers will be dismissed only for good cause. If the employee is aware of this policy and continues to work for the employer, a court may find that there is an implied contract based on the terms stated in the manual or bulletin. Generally, the key consideration in determining whether an employment manual creates an implied contractual obligation is the employee's reasonable expectations.

Oral promises that an employer makes to employees regarding discharge policy may also be considered part of an implied contract. If the employer fires a worker in a manner contrary to what was promised, a court may hold that the employer has violated the implied contract and is liable for damages. Most state courts will consider this claim and judge it by traditional contract standards. In some cases, courts have held that an implied employment contract existed even though the employees agreed in writing to be employees at will.[1] In a few states, courts have gone further and held that all employment contracts contain an implied covenant of good faith. In those states, if an employer fires an employee for an arbitrary or unjustified reason, the employee can claim that the covenant of good faith was breached and the contract violated.

Exceptions Based on Tort Theory In some situations, the discharge of an employee may give rise to an action for wrongful discharge under tort theories. Abusive discharge procedures may result in intentional infliction of emotional distress or defamation. In addition, some courts have permitted workers to sue their employers under the tort theory of fraud. Under this theory, an employer may be held liable for making false promises to a prospective employee if the person detrimentally relies on the employer's representations by taking the job.

Suppose that an employer induces a prospective employee to leave a lucrative position and move to another state by offering "a long-term job with a thriving business." In fact, the employer is having significant financial problems. Furthermore, the employer is planning a merger that will result in the elimination of the position offered to the prospective employee. If the person takes the job in reliance on the employer's representations and is laid off shortly thereafter, he or she may be able to bring an action against the employer for fraud.[2]

Exceptions Based on Public Policy

Another common law exception to the employment-at-will doctrine is made on the basis of public policy. Courts may apply this exception when an employer fires a worker for reasons that violate a fundamental public policy of the jurisdiction.

Generally, the courts require that the public policy involved be expressed clearly in the statutory law governing the jurisdiction. The public policy against employment discrimination, for instance, is expressed clearly in federal and state statutes. Thus, if a worker is fired for discriminatory reasons but has no cause of action under statutory law (because, for example, the workplace has too few employees to be covered by the statute), that worker may succeed in a suit against the employer for wrongful discharge in violation of public policy.[3] Firing an employee for filing a workers' compensation claim (discussed later in this chapter) is another example of the strong public policy that must exist for a court to find an exception to the employment-at-will doctrine.[4]

Occasionally, a discharge can violate public policy if it is done in retaliation for an employee's refusing to engage in criminal conduct or **whistleblowing**—that is, reporting to government officials, upper management authorities, or the media that an employer is involved in some unsafe or illegal activity. Does the public-policy exception apply to a nursing home employee who is fired for reporting the abuse of a patient as required by a state statute? That was the question in the following case.

1. See, for example, *Kuest v. Regent Assisted Living, Inc.,* 111 Wash.App.36, 43 P.3d 23 (2002).

2. See, for example, *Lazar v. Superior Court of Los Angeles Co.,* 12 Cal.4th 631, 909 P.2d 981, 49 Cal.Rptr.2d 377 (1996); and *Helmer v. Bingham Toyota Isuzu,* 129 Cal.App.4th 1121, 29 Cal.Rptr.3d 136 (2005).

3. See, for example, *Wholey v. Sears Roebuck,* 370 Md. 38, 803 A.2d 482 (2002).

4. Note that some states, such as Ohio, have limited an employee's ability to sue for wrongful discharge based on the public-policy exception. See, for example, *Bickers v. W.&S. Life Insurance Co.,* 116 Ohio St.3d 351, 879 N.E.2d 201 (2007).

CASE 33.1 Wendeln v. The Beatrice Manor, Inc.

Supreme Court of Nebraska, 2006. 271 Neb. 373, 712 N.W.2d 226.

Background and Facts Rebecca Wendeln, a twenty-one-year-old certified nursing assistant, worked as a staffing coordinator at The Beatrice Manor, Inc., in Beatrice, Nebraska. One of the patients at Beatrice Manor was wheelchair-bound. Moving the patient required two persons and a gait belt (an ambulatory aid used to transfer or mobilize patients). In December 2001, two medical aides told Wendeln that the patient had been improperly moved and had been injured. Wendeln reported the incident to the Nebraska Department of Health and Human Services, as required under the state Adult Protective Services Act (APSA). A few days later, Wendeln's supervisor angrily confronted her about the report. Intimidated, Wendeln asked for a day off, which was granted. On her return, she was fired. She filed a suit in a Nebraska state court against Beatrice Manor, alleging, among other things, that her discharge was a violation of the state's public policy. A jury returned a verdict in her favor, awarding damages of $79,000. Beatrice Manor appealed to the Nebraska Supreme Court.

Decision and Rationale The state supreme court affirmed the trial court's judgment. The appellate court recognized an exception to the employment-at-will doctrine "for wrongful discharge when the motivation for the firing contravenes public policy." The state supreme court acknowledged that "unless constitutionally, statutorily, or contractually prohibited," an employer can terminate an at-will employee at any time with or without cause. The right of an employer to discharge employees at will is limited, however, in "instances where a very clear mandate of public policy has been violated." The court cited as an example the state workers' compensation law, under which an employee could bring an action against an employer who discharged the employee for filing a claim. If there was no exception to the employment-at-will doctrine under the state workers' compensation law, its rights "could simply be circumvented by the employer's threatening to discharge the employee if he or she exercised those rights." Similarly, "the purpose of the APSA would be circumvented" if the employees who are required to report possible patient abuse could be discharged for filing their reports. The state legislature "articulates public policy when it declares certain conduct to be in violation of the criminal law. The APSA makes a clear public policy statement by utilizing the threat of criminal sanction to ensure the implementation of the reporting provisions set forth to protect the vulnerable adults with which the APSA is concerned."

The Ethical Dimension *Is it fair to sanction an employer for discharging an employee who reports on the employer's unsafe or illegal actions to government authorities or others? Discuss.*

The Global Dimension *In many countries, discharging an employee is more difficult and costly for the employer than it is in the United States. Why?*

Wrongful Discharge

Whenever an employer discharges an employee in violation of an employment contract or a statutory law protecting employees, the employee may bring an action for **wrongful discharge.** Even if an employer's actions do not violate any express employment contract or statute, the employer may still be subject to liability under a common law doctrine, such as a tort theory or agency. Suppose that an employer discharges a female employee and publicly discloses private facts about her sex life to her co-workers. In that situation, the employee could bring a wrongful discharge claim against the employer based on the tort of invasion of privacy (see Chapter 6).

SECTION 2 Wage and Hour Laws

In the 1930s, Congress enacted several laws regulating the wages and working hours of employees. In 1931, Congress passed the Davis-Bacon Act,[5] which requires the payment of "prevailing wages" to employees of

5. 40 U.S.C. Sections 276a–276a-5.

contractors and subcontractors working on government construction projects. In 1936, the Walsh-Healey Act[6] was passed. This act requires that a minimum wage, as well as overtime pay at 1.5 times regular pay rates, be paid to employees of manufacturers or suppliers entering into contracts with agencies of the federal government.

In 1938, with the passage of the Fair Labor Standards Act[7] (FLSA), Congress extended wage-hour requirements to cover all employers engaged in interstate commerce or in the production of goods for interstate commerce. Here, we examine the FLSA's provisions in regard to child labor, maximum hours, minimum wages, and overtime exemptions.

Child Labor

The FLSA prohibits oppressive child labor. Children under fourteen years of age are allowed to do certain types of work, such as deliver newspapers, work for their parents, and be employed in the entertainment and (with some exceptions) agricultural areas. Children who are fourteen or fifteen years of age are allowed to work, but not in hazardous occupations. There are also numerous restrictions on how many hours per day and per week they can work. For example, minors under the age of sixteen cannot work during school hours, for more than three hours on a school day (or eight hours on a nonschool day), for more than eighteen hours during a school week (or forty hours during a nonschool week), or before 7 A.M. or after 7 P.M. (9 P.M. during the summer). Most states require persons under sixteen years of age to obtain work permits.

Working times and hours are not restricted for persons between the ages of sixteen and eighteen, but they cannot be employed in hazardous jobs or in jobs detrimental to their health and well-being. None of these restrictions apply to those over the age of eighteen.

Hours and Wages

The FLSA provides that a **minimum wage** of a specified amount ($7.25 per hour as of 2009) must be paid to employees in covered industries. Congress periodically revises this minimum wage.[8] Under the FLSA, the term *wages* includes the reasonable costs of the employer in furnishing employees with board, lodging, and other facilities if they are customarily furnished by that employer.

Under the FLSA, any employee who works more than forty hours per week must be paid no less than 1.5 times her or his regular pay for all hours over forty. Note that the FLSA overtime provisions apply only after an employee has worked more than forty hours per *week*. Thus, employees who work for ten hours a day, four days per week, are not entitled to overtime pay because they do not work more than forty hours per week.

Overtime Exemptions

Certain employees—usually executive, administrative, and professional employees; outside salespersons; and computer programmers—are exempt from the overtime provisions of the FLSA. Employers are not required to pay overtime wages to exempt employees. In order for an exemption to apply, an employee's specific job duties and salary must meet all the requirements of the U.S. Department of Labor (DOL) regulations. In the past, because the salary limits were low and the duties tests were complex and confusing, some employers were able to avoid paying overtime wages to their employees. This prompted the DOL to substantially revise the overtime regulations in 2004 for the first time in more than fifty years. The revisions effectively expanded the number of workers eligible for overtime by nearly tripling the salary threshold.[9]

Employers can continue to pay overtime to ineligible employees if they want to do so, but they cannot waive or reduce the overtime requirements of the FLSA. The exemptions to the overtime-pay requirement do not apply to manual laborers or other workers who perform tasks involving repetitive operations with their hands (such as nonmanagement production-line employees, for example). The exemptions also do not apply to police, firefighters, licensed nurses, and other public-safety workers. White-collar workers who earn more than $100,000 per year, computer programmers, dental hygienists, and insurance adjusters are typically exempt—though they must also meet certain other criteria. An employer cannot deny overtime wages to an employee based solely on the employee's job title.[10] (Does the FLSA require

6. 41 U.S.C. Sections 35–45.

7. 29 U.S.C. Sections 201–260.

8. Note that many state and local governments also have minimum-wage laws; these laws may provide for higher minimum-wage rates than that required by the federal government.

9. 29 C.F.R. Section 541.

10. See, for example, *In re Wal-Mart Stores, Inc.*, 395 F.3d 1177 (10th Cir. 2005); and *Martin v. Indiana Michigan Power Co.*, 381 F.3d 574 (6th Cir. 2004).

EMERGING TRENDS IN BUSINESS LAW

Paying Overtime in the Virtual Workforce

According to WorldatWork, a research organization for human resources professionals, nearly 46 million U.S. workers perform at least part of their job at home, and close to 13 million of them are full-time *telecommuters,* meaning that they work at home or off-site by means of an electronic linkup to the central workplace. Just because employees work at a remote location does not mean that they are automatically exempt from overtime-pay requirements (or minimum-wage laws). Federal (and sometimes state and local) wage and hour laws often apply to the virtual workforce, as many businesses are finding out the unfortunate way—through litigation.

Telecommuters and Overtime-Pay Requirements

As described in the text, the U.S. Department of Labor revised its regulations in 2004 to clarify how overtime exemptions apply to employees in various occupations. The new regulations established a primary duty test to be used in classifying workers.[a] In general, workers whose primary duty involves the exercise of discretion and independent judgment are more likely to be exempt from the overtime-pay requirements. So are those whose positions require advanced knowledge or specialized instructions, such as computer systems analysts and software engineers.

Although the regulations appear detailed, they do not specifically address how these exemptions apply to telecommuters. Since the new rules went into effect in 2004, telecommuters have filed a barrage of lawsuits claiming that their employers violated the Fair Labor Standards Act by failing to pay them for overtime work and to compensate them for work-related tasks.

An Increasing Number of Cases and Settlements

To date, more cases have been filed in California than in any other state—mostly by telecommuting information technology workers, pharmaceutical sales representatives, and insurance company employees. Suits are also pending in Colorado, the District of Columbia, Illinois, Missouri, New Jersey, New York, and Ohio.

Some defendants with large numbers of employees have decided to settle before the case goes to trial. Computer Sciences Corporation in El Segundo, California, for example, paid $24 million to settle a case brought by telecommuters and call-center

a. See 29 C.F.R. Sections 541.203 and 541.400.

employers to pay overtime wages to workers who telecommute? See this chapter's *Emerging Trends* feature for a discussion of this issue.)

Under the overtime-pay regulations, an employee qualifies for the executive exemption if, among other requirements, his or her "primary duty" is management. This requirement was the focus of the dispute in the following case.

CASE 33.2 Mims v. Starbucks Corp.

United States District Court, Southern District of Texas, 2007. __ F.Supp.2d __.

● **Company Profile** Starbucks Corporation (**www.starbucks.com**) is the largest and best-known purveyor of specialty coffees and coffee products in North America. Named after the first mate in Herman Melville's *Moby Dick,* Starbucks does business in more than 10,000 retail locations in the United States and forty-one foreign countries and territories. Starbucks also supplies premium, fresh-roasted coffee to bookstores, grocery stores, restaurants, airlines, sports and entertainment venues, movie theaters, hotels, and cruise ship lines throughout the world. Starbucks's success is predicated on the consistently high quality of its coffees and the other products and services it provides. Starbucks has a reputation for excellence and is recognized for its knowledgeable staff and service.

● **Background and Facts** In Starbucks Corporation's stores, baristas wait on customers, make drinks for customers, serve customers, operate the cash register, clean the store, and maintain its equipment. In each store, a manager supervises and motivates six to thirty employees, including employees,[b] and International Business Machines Corporation (IBM) settled a similar suit for $65 million.[c] Other defendants have refused to settle. Farmers Insurance Exchange went to trial but lost and faced a significant jury verdict. On appeal to the U.S. Court of Appeals for the Ninth Circuit, however, the company prevailed.[d] In contrast, Advanced Business Integrators, Inc., had to pay nearly $50,000 in overtime compensation to a computer consultant who had spent the majority of his work time at customers' sites training their employees in the use of his employer's software.[e]

b. *Computer Sciences Corp.*, No. 03-08201 (C.D.Cal., settled in 2005).

c. *International Business Machines Corp.*, No. 06-00430 (N.D.Cal., settled in 2006).

d. *In re Farmers Insurance Exchange, Claims Representatives' Overtime Pay Litigation*, 481 F.3d 1119 (9th Cir. 2007).

e. *Eicher v. Advanced Business Integrators, Inc.*, 151 Cal.App.4th 1363, 61 Cal.Rptr.3d 114 (2007).

IMPLICATIONS FOR THE BUSINESSPERSON

1. The litigation discussed here illustrates the importance of properly tracking hours worked for compensation purposes. Even though recording the hours worked by telecommuters may be difficult, allowing employees to work from home without an accounting of how many hours they actually work may lead to class-action claims for overtime pay.
2. Businesspersons may consider whether a particular job is appropriate for telecommuting and then allow only exempt employees to telecommute.

FOR CRITICAL ANALYSIS

1. Why might telecommuting employees sometimes accept being wrongly classified as "executives" or "professionals" under the overtime-pay requirements and thus be exempt from overtime pay?
2. If more class-action lawsuits claiming overtime pay for telecommuters are successful, what do you think will be the effect on telecommuting? Why?

RELEVANT WEB SITES

To locate information on the Web concerning the issues discussed in this feature, go to this text's Web site at www.cengage.com/blaw/jentz, select "Chapter 33," and click on "Emerging Trends."

CASE 33.2 CONTINUED baristas, shift supervisors, and assistant managers. The manager oversees customer service and processes employee records, payrolls, and inventory counts. He or she also develops strategies to increase revenues, control costs, and comply with corporate policies. Kevin Keevican was hired as a barista in March 2000. Keevican was subsequently promoted to shift supervisor, assistant manager, and, in November 2001, manager. During his tenure, Keevican doubled pastry sales at one store, nearly tripled revenues at another, and won sales awards at both. As a manager, Keevican worked seventy hours a week for $650 to $800, a 10 to 20 percent bonus, and fringe benefits that were not available to baristas, such as paid sick leave. Keevican resigned in 2004. He and other former managers, including Kathleen Mims, filed a suit in a federal district court against Starbucks, seeking unpaid overtime and other amounts. The plaintiffs admitted that they performed many managerial tasks, but argued that they spent 70 to 80 percent of their time on barista chores. Starbucks filed a motion for summary judgment.

• **Decision and Rationale** The court issued a summary judgment in Starbucks's favor and dismissed the claims of the plaintiffs, who were exempt from the FLSA's overtime provisions as executive employees. The court held that an employee's "primary duty" is "what the employee does that is of principal value to the employer, not the collateral tasks that she may also perform, even if they consume more than half her time." The determining factors are "(1) the relative importance of managerial duties compared to other duties; (2) the frequency with which the employee makes discretionary decisions; (3) the employee's relative freedom from supervision; and (4) the relationship between the employee's salary and the wages paid to employees who perform relevant nonexempt work." In this case, the barista chores "quite obviously were of minor importance to Defendant when compared to the significant management responsibilities * * * that directly

CASE CONTINUES

CASE 33.2 CONTINUED influenced the ultimate commercial and financial success or failure of the store." Also, each plaintiff was "the single highest-ranking employee in his [or her] particular store and was responsible on site for that store's day-to-day overall operations." He or she was "vested with enough discretionary power and freedom from supervision to qualify for the executive exemption." Finally, the "marked disparity in pay and benefits between Plaintiffs and the non-exempt employees is a hallmark of exempt status."

- **What If the Facts Were Different?** *Suppose that Keevican's job title had been "glorified barista" instead of "manager." Would the result have been different? Explain.*

- **The Legal Environment Dimension** *What might the court have concluded if the stores could have operated successfully without the "managerial" functions performed by the plaintiffs?*

SECTION 3

Labor Unions

In the 1930s, in addition to wage-hour laws, Congress enacted several other laws regulating employment relationships. These laws protect employees' rights to join labor unions, to bargain with management over the terms and conditions of employment, and to conduct strikes.

Federal Labor Laws

Federal labor laws governing union-employer relations have developed considerably since the first law was enacted in 1932. Initially, the laws were concerned with protecting the rights and interests of workers. Subsequent legislation placed some restraints on unions and granted rights to employers. We look here at four major federal statutes regulating union-employer relations.

Norris-LaGuardia Act Congress protected peaceful strikes, picketing, and boycotts in 1932 in the Norris-LaGuardia Act.[11] The statute restricted the power of federal courts to issue injunctions against unions engaged in peaceful strikes. In effect, this act declared a national policy permitting employees to organize.

National Labor Relations Act One of the foremost statutes regulating labor is the National Labor Relations Act (NLRA) of 1935.[12] The purpose of the NLRA was to secure for employees the rights to organize; to bargain collectively through representatives of their own choosing; and to engage in concerted activities for organizing, collective bargaining, and other purposes. The NLRA specifically defined a number of employer practices as unfair to labor:

1. Interference with the efforts of employees to form, join, or assist labor organizations or to engage in concerted activities for their mutual aid or protection.
2. An employer's domination of a labor organization or contribution of financial or other support to it.
3. Discrimination in the hiring of or the awarding of tenure to employees for reason of union affiliation.
4. Discrimination against employees for filing charges under the act or giving testimony under the act.
5. Refusal to bargain collectively with the duly designated representative of the employees.

To ensure that employees' rights would be protected, the NLRA established the National Labor Relations Board (NLRB). The NLRB has the authority to investigate employees' charges of unfair labor practices and to file complaints against employers in response to these charges. When violations are found, the NLRB may also issue **cease-and-desist orders**—orders compelling employers to stop engaging in the unfair practices. Cease-and-desist orders can be enforced by a federal appellate court if necessary. Disputes over alleged unfair labor practices are first decided by the NLRB and may then be appealed to a federal court.

To be protected under the NLRA, an individual must be an employee or a job applicant (otherwise, the NLRA's ban on discrimination in regard to hiring would mean little). Additionally, the United States Supreme Court has held that individuals who are hired by a union to organize a company (union organizers) are to be considered employees of the company for NLRA purposes.[13]

11. 29 U.S.C. Sections 101–110, 113–115.
12. 20 U.S.C. Sections 151–169.
13. *NLRB v. Town & Country Electric, Inc.*, 516 U.S. 85, 116 S.Ct. 450, 133 L.Ed.2d 371 (1995).

Labor-Management Relations Act The Labor-Management Relations Act (LMRA) of 1947[14] was passed to proscribe certain unfair union practices, such as the *closed shop*. A **closed shop** is a firm that requires union membership by its workers as a condition of employment. Although the act made the closed shop illegal, it preserved the legality of the union shop. A **union shop** is a firm that does not require union membership as a prerequisite for employment but can, and usually does, require that workers join the union after a specified amount of time on the job.

The LMRA also prohibited unions from refusing to bargain with employers, engaging in certain types of picketing, and *featherbedding* (causing employers to hire more employees than necessary). In addition, the act allowed individual states to pass their own **right-to-work laws**—laws making it illegal for union membership to be required for *continued* employment in any establishment. Thus, union shops are technically illegal in the twenty-two states that have right-to-work laws.

Labor-Management Reporting and Disclosure Act The Labor-Management Reporting and Disclosure Act (LMRDA) of 1959[15] established an employee bill of rights and reporting requirements for union activities. The act strictly regulates unions' internal business procedures, including elections. For example, the LMRDA requires unions to hold regularly scheduled elections of officers using secret ballots. Former convicts are prohibited from holding union office. Moreover, union officials are accountable for union property and funds. Members have the right to attend and to participate in union meetings, to nominate officers, and to vote in most union proceedings.

The act also outlawed **hot-cargo agreements,** in which employers voluntarily agree with unions not to handle, use, or deal in goods of other employers produced by nonunion employees. The act made all such boycotts (called **secondary boycotts**) illegal.

Union Organization

Forming a union requires support from a majority of the employees in a defined bargaining unit, such as all of the workers at a specific automotive plant or all of the nurses employed by a particular hospital. Typically, the first step union organizers (unionizers) take is to have the workers that the union is seeking to represent sign authorization cards. An **authorization card** usually states that the worker desires to have a certain union, such as the United Auto Workers, represent the workforce. If a majority of the workers sign authorization cards, the organizers can present the cards to the employer and ask for formal recognition of the union. The employer is not required to recognize the union at this point, but it may do so voluntarily on a showing of majority support. (Under legislation that was proposed in 2007, the employer would have been required to recognize the union as soon as a majority of the workers had signed authorization cards—without holding an election, as described next.[16])

Union Elections If the employer refuses to voluntarily recognize the union after a majority of the workers sign authorization cards—or if fewer than 50 percent of the workers sign authorization cards—the union organizers can petition the NLRB for an election. For an election to be held, the NLRB requires that unionizers demonstrate that at least 30 percent of the workers to be represented support a union or an election on unionization. The NLRB supervises the election and ensures that the voting is secret and that the voters are eligible. If the proposed union receives majority support (more than 50 percent of the votes) in a fair election, the NLRB certifies the union as the bargaining representative for the employees.

Union Election Campaigns Many disputes between labor and management arise during union election campaigns. Generally, the employer has control over unionizing activities that take place on company property and during working hours. The employer can limit union solicitation activities to nonwork areas, such as the cafeteria or parking lot, and to nonwork hours, such as lunch hours, coffee breaks, and before and after work. The employer must have a legitimate business reason for limiting the union solicitation activities and cannot discriminate against the union in its policies on solicitation. (The *Business Application* feature on the following page for this chapter discusses how employers can now restrict unions from using the company's e-mail system to communicate with its members.)

14. 29 U.S.C. Sections 141 *et seq.*

15. 29 U.S.C. Sections 401 *et seq.*

16. The U.S. House of Representatives passed the Employee Free Choice Act, also known as the Card Check Bill (H.R. 800), in March 2007, but the bill (S 1041) was defeated in the U.S. Senate in June 2007. Because this pro-labor measure enjoyed wide support, similar legislation is likely to be proposed in the future.

BUSINESS APPLICATION
Restricting Union Communications via Corporate E-Mail Systems

MANAGEMENT FACES A LEGAL ISSUE

Most companies have e-mail policies for their employees. Some prohibit any personal use of a company's e-mail system, while others are specific about what types of personal e-mails may be sent, such as requests for charitable contributions from other employees. Most companies prohibit solicitations by outside organizations or groups that wish to use the company's e-mail system to sell products or to induce group action. The legal issue that has faced managers is how to avoid discrimination in deciding which communications are and are not allowed on a company's e-mail system. In particular, some employers have attempted to stop any union-related communications from going through their company's e-mail system. Routinely, the National Labor Relations Board (NLRB) has prevented employers from enforcing such restrictions. As long as a company officially or unofficially allows nonwork-related e-mail communications—such as invitations to bridal showers or recruiting for fantasy sports leagues—that company cannot ban or prohibit union-related e-mail communications.

WHAT THE COURTS SAY

In its most recent ruling, the NLRB established a precedent that now allows companies to restrict union-related communications from their e-mail systems. The Eugene (Oregon) Newspaper Guild sued the Guard Publishing Company (doing business as *The Register-Guard*). *The Register-Guard* has a policy that prohibits employees from using the newspaper's e-mail system for "nonjob-related solicitations." The newspaper's policy applies to commercial ventures, outside organizations, and religious and political causes. When the president of the newspaper's union sent out several e-mails to employees using the corporate e-mail system, *The Register-Guard* sent her two written warnings. The union claimed discriminatory restriction. The newspaper argued that it was not discriminatory because it did not permit any outside groups or organizations to use its e-mail system to distribute propaganda or induce group action.

The NLRB reversed a determination against the newspaper by an *administrative law judge* (see Chapter 43) because the NLRB reasoned that the newspaper's policy did not regulate traditional face-to-face solicitation that the United States Supreme Court held was protected in 1945.[a] The NLRB further reasoned that even though an employee is rightfully on an employer's premises, that employee does not automatically have an additional right to use the employer's equipment.[b]

IMPLICATIONS FOR MANAGERS

The latest NLRB ruling most likely does *not* require that *current* corporate e-mail policies be changed. Those companies establishing e-mail policies for the first time (or revising their existing policies) can impose broad prohibitions such as allowing e-mail only for work-related purposes. Nonetheless, any new or revised e-mail policy should be based on a real justification—for example, preventing loss of productivity or protecting against computer viruses. Finally, companies can discipline their employees who use the corporate e-mail system to send union-related communications, if such communications violate the company's general e-mail policy. Such discipline must be meted out evenly for all violations of company e-mail policy, however.

a. *Republic Aviation Corp. v. NLRB,* 324 U.S. 793, 65 S.Ct. 892, 89 L.Ed. 1372 (1945).

b. The Guard Publishing Company, doing business as *The Register-Guard* and Eugene Newspaper Guild, CWA Local 37194.

Suppose that a union is seeking to organize clerks at a department store owned by Amanti Enterprises. Amanti can prohibit all union solicitation in areas of the store open to the public because the unionizing activities could interfere with the store's business. It can also restrict union-related activities to coffee breaks and lunch hours. Amanti cannot, however, allow solicitation for charitable causes during work hours or in the public part of the store if it prohibits union-related solicitation.

An employer may campaign among its workers against the union, but the NLRB carefully monitors and regulates the tactics used by management. Otherwise, management might use its economic power to coerce the workers to vote not to unionize. If the employer issues threats ("If the union wins, you'll all be fired") or engages in other unfair labor practices, the NLRB can issue a cease-and-desist order. The NLRB may also ask a court to order a new election, or it may certify the union even though it lost the election. Like an employer, a union and its supporters may not engage in unfair labor practices during a union election campaign.[17]

Collective Bargaining

If the NLRB certifies the union, the union becomes the *exclusive bargaining representative* of the workers. The central legal right of a union is to engage in collective bargaining on the members' behalf. **Collective bargaining** is the process by which labor and management negotiate the terms and conditions of employment, including wages, benefits, working conditions, and other matters. Collective bargaining allows union representatives elected by the union members to speak on their behalf at the bargaining table.

When a union is officially recognized, it may demand to bargain with the employer and negotiate new terms or conditions of employment. In collective bargaining, as in most other business negotiations, each side uses its economic power to pressure or persuade the other side to grant concessions.

Bargaining does not mean that one side must give in to the other or that compromises must be made. It does mean that a demand to bargain with the employer must be taken seriously and that both sides must bargain in "good faith." Good faith bargaining requires that management, for example, be willing to meet with union representatives and consider the union's wishes when negotiating a contract. Examples of bad faith bargaining on the part of management include engaging in a campaign among workers to undermine the union, constantly shifting positions on disputed contract terms, and sending bargainers who lack authority to commit the company to a contract. If an employer (or a union) refuses to bargain in good faith without justification, it has committed an unfair labor practice, and the other party may petition the NLRB for an order requiring good faith bargaining.

Strikes

Even when labor and management have bargained in good faith, they may be unable to reach a final agreement. When extensive collective bargaining has been conducted and an impasse results, the union may call a strike against the employer to pressure it into making concessions. A **strike** occurs when the unionized employees leave their jobs and refuse to work. The workers also typically picket the workplace, walking or standing outside the facility with signs stating their complaints.

A strike is an extreme action. Striking workers lose their right to be paid, and management loses production and may lose customers, if it cannot fill their orders. Labor law regulates the circumstances and conduct of strikes. A union may strike when the employer has engaged in unfair labor practices, but most strikes are "economic strikes," which are initiated because the union wants a better contract. For example, in 2007, the United Auto Workers engaged in an economic strike when General Motors (GM) proposed that its workers accept wage cuts and pay much higher monthly premiums for health care. Approximately 73,000 GM employees walked off the job, shutting down several plants in the United States and Canada. Although the strike was settled quickly, it nevertheless resulted in lost production and profits for the company, its suppliers, and its contractors, as well as lost wages for the strikers.

The Right to Strike The right to strike is guaranteed by the NLRA, within limits, and strike activities, such as picketing, are protected by the free speech guarantee of the First Amendment to the U.S. Constitution. Nonworkers have a right to participate in picketing an employer. The NLRA also gives workers the right to refuse to cross a picket line of fellow workers who are engaged in a lawful strike. Employers are permitted to hire replacement workers to substitute for the striking workers.

The Rights of Strikers after a Strike Ends An important issue concerns the rights of strikers after a strike ends. In a typical economic strike, the employer has a right to hire permanent replacements during the strike and need not terminate the replacement workers when the economic strikers seek to return to work. In other words, striking workers are not guaranteed the right to return to their jobs after the strike if satisfactory replacement workers have been found.

If the employer has not hired replacement workers to fill the strikers' positions, however, then the employer must rehire the economic strikers to fill any vacancies. Employers may not discriminate against former economic strikers, and those who are rehired retain their seniority rights. Different rules apply when a union strikes because the employer has engaged in unfair labor practices. In this situation, the employer may still hire replacements but must give the strikers back their jobs once the strike is over.

17. See, for example, *Associated Rubber Co. v. NLRB*, 296 F.3d 1055 (11th Cir. 2002).

SECTION 4

Worker Health and Safety

Under the common law, employees injured on the job had to rely on tort law, contract law, or agency law principles (discussed in Chapters 31 and 32) to seek recovery from their employers. Today, numerous state and federal statutes protect employees from the risk of accidental injury, death, or disease resulting from their employment. This section discusses the primary federal statute governing health and safety in the workplace, along with state workers' compensation acts.

The Occupational Safety and Health Act

At the federal level, the primary legislation protecting employees' health and safety is the Occupational Safety and Health Act of 1970.[18] Congress passed this act in an attempt to ensure safe and healthful working conditions for practically every employee in the country. The act not only imposes a general duty on employers to keep workplaces safe but also requires them to meet specific standards.

Enforcement Agencies Three federal agencies develop and enforce the standards set by the Occupational Safety and Health Act. The Occupational Safety and Health Administration (OSHA), which is part of the U.S. Department of Labor, has the authority to promulgate standards, make inspections, and enforce the act. OSHA has issued safety standards governing many workplace details, such as the structural stability of ladders and the requirements for railings. OSHA also establishes standards that protect employees against exposure to substances that may be harmful to their health.

The National Institute for Occupational Safety and Health is part of the U.S. Department of Health and Human Services. It conducts research on safety and health problems and recommends standards for OSHA to adopt. Finally, the Occupational Safety and Health Review Commission is an independent agency set up to handle appeals from actions taken by OSHA administrators.

Procedures and Violations OSHA compliance officers may enter and inspect the facilities of any establishment covered by the Occupational Safety and Health Act.[19] Employees may also file complaints of violations. Under the act, an employer cannot discharge an employee who files a complaint or who, in good faith, refuses to work in a high-risk area if bodily harm or death might result.

Employers with eleven or more employees are required to keep occupational injury and illness records for each employee. Each record must be made available for inspection when requested by an OSHA inspector. Whenever a work-related injury or disease occurs, employers must make reports directly to OSHA. Whenever an employee is killed in a work-related accident or when five or more employees are hospitalized in one accident, the employer must notify the Department of Labor within forty-eight hours. If the company fails to do so, it will be fined. Following the accident, a complete inspection of the premises is mandatory.

Criminal penalties for willful violation of the Occupational Safety and Health Act are limited. Employers may be prosecuted under state laws, however. In other words, the act does not preempt state and local criminal laws.[20]

State Workers' Compensation Laws

State **workers' compensation laws** establish an administrative procedure for compensating workers injured on the job. Instead of suing, an injured worker files a claim with the administrative agency or board that administers the local workers' compensation claims.

Employees Who Are Covered by Workers' Compensation Most workers' compensation statutes are similar. No state covers all employees. Typically, domestic workers, agricultural workers, temporary employees, and employees of common carriers (companies that provide transportation services to the public) are excluded, but minors are covered. Usually, the statutes allow employers to purchase insurance from a private insurer or a state fund to pay

18. 29 U.S.C. Sections 553, 651–678.

19. In 1978, the United States Supreme Court held that warrantless inspections violated the warrant clause of the Fourth Amendment to the U.S. Constitution. See *Marshall v. Barlow's, Inc.*, 436 U.S. 307, 98 S.Ct. 1816, 56 L.Ed.2d 305 (1978). Although this case has not been overruled, the Supreme Court subsequently indicated that statutory inspection programs can provide a constitutionally adequate substitute for a warrant. See *Donovan v. Dewey*, 452 U.S. 594, 101 S.Ct. 2534, 69 L.Ed.2d 262 (1981).

20. *Pedraza v. Shell Oil Co.*, 942 F.2d 48 (1st Cir. 1991); *cert.* denied, 502 U.S. 1082, 112 S.Ct. 993, 117 L.Ed.2d 154 (1992). See also *In re Welding Fume Products Liability Litigation*, 364 F. Supp.2d 669 (N.D. Ohio 2005).

workers' compensation benefits in the event of a claim. Most states also allow employers to be *self-insured*—that is, employers that show an ability to pay claims do not need to buy insurance.

Requirements for Receiving Workers' Compensation In general, the right to recover benefits is predicated wholly on the existence of an employment relationship and the fact that the worker's injury was *accidental* and *occurred on the job or in the course of employment,* regardless of fault. Intentionally inflicted self-injury, for example, would not be considered accidental and hence would not be covered. If an injury occurs while an employee is commuting to or from work, it usually will not be considered to have occurred on the job or in the course of employment and hence will not be covered.

An employee must notify his or her employer of an injury promptly (usually within thirty days of the injury's occurrence). Generally, an employee must also file a workers' compensation claim with the appropriate state agency or board within a certain period (sixty days to two years) from the time the injury is first noticed, rather than from the time of the accident.

Workers' Compensation versus Litigation An employee who accepts workers' compensation benefits is prohibited from suing for injuries caused by the employer's negligence. By barring lawsuits for negligence, workers' compensation laws also prevent employers from raising common law defenses to negligence, such as contributory negligence or assumption of risk, to avoid liability. A worker may sue an employer who *intentionally* injures the worker, however.

SECTION 5 Income Security, Pension, and Health Plans

Federal and state governments participate in insurance programs designed to protect employees and their families from the financial impact of retirement, disability, death, hospitalization, and unemployment. The key federal law on this subject is the Social Security Act of 1935.[21]

Social Security

The Social Security Act of 1935 provides for old-age (retirement), survivors', and disability insurance. The act is therefore often referred to as OASDI. Both employers and employees must "contribute" under the Federal Insurance Contributions Act (FICA)[22] to help pay for benefits that will partially make up for the employees' loss of income on retirement.

The basis for the employee's and the employer's contribution is the employee's annual wage base—the maximum amount of the employee's wages that is subject to the tax. The employer withholds the employee's FICA contribution from the employee's wages and then matches this contribution. The annual wage base increases each year to take into account the rising cost of living. In 2008, employers were required to withhold 6.2 percent of each employee's wages, up to a maximum wage base of $102,000, and to match this contribution.

Retired workers are eligible to receive monthly payments from the Social Security Administration, which administers the Social Security Act. Social Security benefits are fixed by statute but increase automatically with increases in the cost of living.

Medicare

Medicare, a federal government health-insurance program, is administered by the Social Security Administration for people sixty-five years of age and older and for some under age sixty-five who have a disability. It originally had two parts, one pertaining to hospital costs and the other to nonhospital medical costs, such as visits to physicians' offices. People who have Medicare hospital insurance can obtain additional federal medical insurance if they pay small monthly premiums, which increase as the cost of medical care rises.

As with Social Security contributions, both the employer and the employee "contribute" to Medicare, but unlike Social Security, there is no cap on the amount of wages subject to the Medicare tax. In 2008, both the employer and the employee were required to pay 1.45 percent of *all* wages and salaries to finance Medicare. Thus, for Social Security and Medicare together, in 2008 the employer and employee each paid 7.65 percent of the first $102,000 of income (6.2 percent for Social Security + 1.45 percent for Medicare), for a combined total of 15.3 percent. In addition, all wages and salaries above $102,000 were

21. 42 U.S.C. Sections 301–1397e.

22. 26 U.S.C. Sections 3101–3125.

taxed at a combined (employer and employee) rate of 2.9 percent for Medicare. Self-employed persons pay both the employer and the employee portions of the Social Security and Medicare taxes (15.3 percent of income up to $102,000 and 2.9 percent of income above that amount in 2008).

Private Pension Plans

The Employee Retirement Income Security Act (ERISA) of 1974[23] is the major federal act regulating employee retirement plans set up by employers to supplement Social Security benefits. This statute empowers the Labor Management Services Administration of the U.S. Department of Labor to enforce its provisions governing employers who have private pension funds for their employees. ERISA does not require an employer to establish a pension plan. When a plan exists, however, ERISA provides standards for its management.

A key provision of ERISA concerns vesting. **Vesting** gives an employee a legal right to receive pension benefits at some future date when she or he stops working. Before ERISA was enacted, some employees who had worked for companies for as long as thirty years received no pension benefits when their employment terminated because those benefits had not vested. ERISA establishes complex vesting rules. Generally, however, all of an employee's contributions to a pension plan vest immediately, and the employee's rights to the employer's contributions vest after five years of employment.

In an attempt to prevent mismanagement of pension funds, ERISA has established rules on how they must be invested. Managers must choose investments cautiously and must diversify the plan's investments to minimize the risk of large losses. ERISA also includes detailed record-keeping and reporting requirements.

Unemployment Compensation

To ease the financial impact of unemployment, the United States has a system of unemployment insurance. The Federal Unemployment Tax Act (FUTA) of 1935[24] created a state-administered system that provides unemployment compensation to eligible individuals. Under this system, employers pay into a fund, and the proceeds are paid out to qualified unemployed workers. FUTA and state laws require employers that fall under the provisions of the act to pay unemployment taxes at regular intervals.

FUTA generally determines covered employment and imposes certain requirements on state unemployment programs, but the states determine individual eligibility requirements and benefit amounts. To be eligible for unemployment compensation, a worker must be willing and able to work and be actively seeking employment. Workers who have been fired for misconduct or who have left their jobs without good cause normally are not eligible for benefits.

COBRA

Federal legislation also addresses the issue of health insurance for workers who have lost their jobs and are no longer eligible for group health-insurance plans. Employers who have twenty or more employees and provide a group health plan must comply with the requirements of the Consolidated Omnibus Budget Reconciliation Act (COBRA) of 1985.[25] COBRA basically gives employees a right to continue the group health benefits provided by their employers for a limited time after the voluntary or involuntary loss of employment. The act also applies to workers who are no longer eligible for coverage under the employer's health plan because their hours have been decreased. Spouses, former spouses, and dependent children who were covered under the plan also have the right to continue health coverage.

Procedures under COBRA An employer must notify an employee of COBRA's provisions if the worker faces termination or a reduction of hours that would affect her or his eligibility for coverage under the plan. The worker has sixty days (beginning with the date that the group coverage would stop) to decide whether to continue with the employer's group insurance plan. If the worker chooses to discontinue the coverage, then the employer has no further obligation. If the worker chooses to continue coverage, the employer is obligated to keep the policy active for up to eighteen months but is not required to pay for the coverage.[26]

Usually, the worker (or beneficiary) must pay the premiums for continued coverage, plus an additional

23. 29 U.S.C. Sections 1001 *et seq.*
24. 26 U.S.C. Sections 3301–3310.
25. 29 U.S.C. Sections 1161–1169.
26. Certain events, such as a disability, can extend the period of COBRA coverage. Also, COBRA does not prohibit health plans from offering continuation health coverage that goes beyond COBRA periods.

2 percent administrative fee. The coverage provided must be the same as that enjoyed by the worker prior to the termination or reduction of employment. If family members were originally included, for example, COBRA prohibits their exclusion.

Employer's Obligations under COBRA

The employer is relieved of the responsibility to provide COBRA coverage if the worker fails to pay the premium, becomes eligible for Medicare, or is covered under another health plan (such as a spouse's or new employer's). The employer is also relieved of the obligation if the employer completely cancels its group benefit plan for all employees. An employer that fails to comply with COBRA risks substantial penalties, such as a tax of up to 10 percent of the annual cost of the group plan or $500,000, whichever is less.

Employer-Sponsored Group Health Plans

The Health Insurance Portability and Accountability Act (HIPAA),[27] which was discussed in Chapter 4 in the context of its privacy protections, contains provisions that affect employer-sponsored group health plans. HIPAA does not require employers to provide health insurance, but it does establish requirements for those that do. One provision of HIPAA limits an employer's ability to exclude persons from coverage for "preexisting conditions" to conditions for which medical treatment was received within the previous six months (excluding pregnancy). Another provision requires that an employee be given credit for previous health coverage (including COBRA coverage) to decrease any waiting period before coverage becomes effective.

In addition, employers that are plan sponsors have significant responsibilities regarding the manner in which they collect, use, and disclose the health information of employees and their families. Employers must comply with numerous administrative, technical, and procedural safeguards (such as training employees, designating privacy officials, and distributing privacy notices) to ensure that employees' health information is not disclosed to unauthorized parties. Failure to comply with HIPAA regulations can result in civil penalties of up to $100 per person per violation (with a cap of $25,000 per year). The employer is also subject to criminal prosecution for certain types of HIPAA violations and can face up to $250,000 in criminal fines and imprisonment for up to ten years if convicted.

27. 29 U.S.C.A. Sections 1181 *et seq.*

SECTION 6 Family and Medical Leave

In 1993, Congress passed the Family and Medical Leave Act (FMLA)[28] to protect employees who need time off work for family or medical reasons. A majority of the states also have legislation allowing for a leave from employment for family or medical reasons, and many employers maintain private family-leave plans for their workers.

Coverage and Application of the FMLA

The FMLA requires employers who have fifty or more employees to provide an employee with up to twelve weeks of unpaid family or medical leave during any twelve-month period. Generally, an employee may take family leave to care for a newborn baby, an adopted child, or a foster child, and medical leave when the employee or the employee's spouse, child, or parent has a "serious health condition" requiring care.[29] Employees suffering from certain chronic health conditions, such as asthma, diabetes, and pregnancy, may take FMLA leave for their own incapacities that require absences of fewer than three days.

The employer must continue the worker's health-care coverage and guarantee employment in the same position or a comparable position when the employee returns to work. An important exception to the FMLA, however, allows the employer to avoid reinstating a *key employee*—defined as an employee whose pay falls within the top 10 percent of the firm's workforce. (The employer must continue to maintain health benefits for the key employee during the leave, however.) Also, the act does not apply to part-time or newly hired employees (those who have worked for less than one year).

Employees suffering from addiction to drugs and alcohol pose a special problem under the FMLA. Under what circumstances do days off because of the addiction, as opposed to days off for treatment in a medical facility, count as part of protected leave? That was the issue in the following case.

28. 29 U.S.C. Sections 2601, 2611–2619, 2651–2654.

29. The foster care must be state sanctioned before such an arrangement falls within the coverage of the FMLA.

CASE 33.3 Darst v. Interstate Brands Corp.

United States Court of Appeals, Seventh Circuit, 2008. 512 F.3d 903.

Background and Facts Krzysztof Chalimoniuk worked for Interstate Brands Corporation (IBC) for fifteen years before he was fired for excessive absenteeism. Chalimoniuk, an alcoholic, sought treatment for his condition. He requested leave under the Family and Medical Leave Act (FMLA) from July 29 to August 14, 2000, to deal with the problem. From August 4 to 11, he was hospitalized for treatment of alcohol dependence and withdrawal. When he failed to return to work on August 15, he was fired for being absent. IBC noted that he was also absent July 29 to August 3, when he was not hospitalized, and those days were counted as improper absences as he was already over the limit for the number of days he could miss under the company's leave policy. Chalimoniuk sued, contending that IBC had violated his FMLA rights. During the course of litigation, Chalimoniuk filed for bankruptcy, and his claim against IBC became part of the bankruptcy estate. Richard Darst, as trustee for the estate, continued to prosecute the claim. The district court granted summary judgment in favor of IBC. Darst appealed to the U.S. Court of Appeals for the Seventh Circuit.

Decision and Rationale The appeals court affirmed that IBC had not violated Chalimoniuk's rights under the FMLA. Chalimoniuk was entitled to FMLA leave to obtain treatment, but not because he was incapacitated by the alcoholism and could not or would not come to work. Absence from work because of an employee's use of a substance, rather than for treatment of a serious health condition, does not qualify for FMLA leave. Further, contrary to Chalimoniuk's assertion, IBC had the right to determine the dates during which Chalmoniuk was to receive treatment for alcoholism. This employer right is allowed unless it interferes with or denies the worker's exercise of his or her rights under the FMLA.

The Ethical Dimension *Did IBC take unfair advantage of the "letter of the law" by not granting Chalimoniuk a little more leave time as he was, in fact, dealing with his problem? Explain your answer.*

The Legal Environment Dimension *Although IBC won this lawsuit, defending the case was costly. How can employers avoid such litigation?*

Remedies for Violations of the FMLA

Remedies for violations of the FMLA can include (1) damages for lost benefits, denied compensation, and actual monetary losses (such as the cost of providing for care of the family member) up to an amount equivalent to the employee's wages for twelve weeks; (2) job reinstatement; and (3) promotion, if a promotion had been denied. A successful plaintiff is entitled to court costs, attorneys' fees, and—in cases involving bad faith on the part of the employer—two times the amount of damages awarded by a judge or jury. Supervisors may also be subject to personal liability, as employers, for violations of the act when the supervisor exercises sufficient control over the employee's leave.[30]

Employers generally are required to notify employees when an absence will be counted against leave authorized under the act. If an employer fails to provide such notice, and the employee consequently suffers an injury because he or she did not receive notice, the employer may be sanctioned.[31]

Interaction with Other Laws

The FMLA does not affect any other federal or state law that prohibits discrimination. Nor does it supersede any state or local law that provides more generous family- or medical-leave protection. For example, if a California state law allows employees who are disabled by pregnancy to take up to four months of unpaid leave, an employer in California would have to

30. See, for example, *Rupnow v. TRC, Inc.*, 999 F.Supp. 1047 (N.D. Ohio 1998); and *Mueller v. J. P. Morgan Chase & Co.*, 2007 WL 915160 (N.D. Ohio 2007).

31. *Ragsdale v. Wolverine World Wide, Inc.*, 535 U.S. 81, 122 S.Ct. 1155, 152 L.Ed.2d 167 (2002); and *Mondaine v. American Drug Stores, Inc.*, 408 F.Supp.2d 1169 (D.Kan. 2006).

comply with that law (in addition to the provisions of the FMLA). Also, an employer who is obligated to provide more extensive leave under a collective bargaining agreement must do so, regardless of the FMLA.

SECTION 7 Employee Privacy Rights

In the last thirty years, concerns about the privacy rights of employees have arisen in response to the sometimes invasive tactics used by employers to monitor and screen workers. Perhaps the greatest privacy concern in today's employment arena has to do with electronic monitoring of employees' activities. Clearly, employers need to protect themselves from liability for their employees' online activities. They also have a legitimate interest in monitoring the productivity of their workers. At the same time, employees expect to have a certain zone of privacy in the workplace. Indeed, many lawsuits have alleged that employers' intrusive monitoring practices violate employees' privacy rights.

Electronic Monitoring in the Workplace

According to the American Management Association, more than two-thirds of employers engage in some form of electronic monitoring of their employees. Types of monitoring include monitoring workers' Web site connections, reviewing employees' e-mail and computer files, video recording of employee job performance, and recording and reviewing telephone conversations and voice mail.

Various specially designed software products have made it easier for an employer to track employees' Internet use. Software allows an employer to track almost every move an employee makes on the Internet, including the specific Web sites visited and the time spent surfing the Web. Filtering software, which was discussed in Chapter 4, can be used to prevent access to certain Web sites, such as sites containing sexually explicit images. Other filtering software may be used to screen incoming e-mail for viruses and to block junk e-mail (spam).

Although the use of filtering software by public employers (government agencies) has led to charges that blocking access to Web sites violates employees' rights to free speech, this issue does not arise in private businesses. This is because the First Amendment's protection of free speech applies only to *government* restraints on speech, not restraints imposed in the private sector.

Employee Privacy Protection under Constitutional and Tort Law Recall from Chapter 4 that the United States Supreme Court has inferred a personal right to privacy from the constitutional guarantees provided by the First, Third, Fourth, Fifth, and Ninth Amendments to the Constitution. Tort law (see Chapters 6 and 7), state constitutions, and a number of state and federal statutes also provide for privacy rights.

When determining whether an employer should be held liable for violating an employee's privacy rights, the courts generally weigh the employer's interests against the employee's reasonable expectation of privacy. Normally, if employees are informed that their communications are being monitored, they cannot reasonably expect those communications to be private. If employees are not informed that certain communications are being monitored, however, the employer may be held liable for invading their privacy. For this reason, today most employers that engage in electronic monitoring notify their employees about the monitoring.

For the most part, courts have held that an employer's monitoring of electronic communications in the workplace does not violate employees' privacy rights. Even if employees are not informed that their e-mail will be monitored, courts generally have concluded that employees have no expectation of privacy if the employer provided the e-mail system.[32] Courts have even found that employers have a right to monitor the e-mail of an independent contractor (such as an insurance agent) when the employer provided the e-mail service and was authorized to access stored messages.[33]

The Electronic Communications Privacy Act The major statute with which employers must comply is the Electronic Communications Privacy Act (ECPA) of 1986.[34] This act amended existing federal wiretapping law to cover electronic forms of communications, such as communications via cellular telephones or e-mail. The ECPA prohibits the intentional interception of any wire or electronic communication or the intentional disclosure or use of the information obtained by the interception. Excluded from coverage, however, are any electronic communications through devices that are "furnished to the subscriber or user by

32. For a leading case on this issue, see *Smyth v. Pillsbury Co.*, 914 F.Supp. 97 (E.D.Pa. 1996).

33. See *Fraser v. Nationwide Mutual Insurance Co.*, 352 F.3d 107 (3d Cir. 2004).

34. 18 U.S.C. Sections 2510–2521.

a provider of wire or electronic communication service" and that are being used by the subscriber or user, or by the provider of the service, "in the ordinary course of its business."

This "business-extension exception" to the ECPA permits an employer to monitor employees' electronic communications in the ordinary course of business. It does not, however, permit an employer to monitor employees' personal communications. Under another exception to the ECPA, however, an employer may avoid liability under the act if the employees consent to having their electronic communications intercepted by the employer. Thus, an employer may be able to avoid liability under the ECPA by simply requiring employees to sign forms indicating that they consent to such monitoring.

Business owners and managers should realize that although courts generally have sided with employers in monitoring cases, employers do not have *carte blanche* to monitor all employee activities and conversations. Courts have penalized some employers who have gone too far in recording personal conversations among employees or videotaped employees in bathrooms, locker rooms, or dressing rooms. In fact, a few courts have allowed videotaping of employees only when no audio recording is involved.

To avoid legal disputes, managers should exercise caution when monitoring employees and ensure that any monitoring is conducted in a reasonable place and manner. They should establish written policies, notify employees of how and when they may be monitored, and inform employees of the reasons for the monitoring. Specifically, business owners and managers need to explain what the concern is, what job repercussions could result, and what recourse employees have in the event that a negative action is taken against them. By providing more privacy protection to employees than is legally required, a business can both avoid potential privacy complaints and give employees a sense that they retain some degree of privacy in their workplace. An enhanced sense of privacy can lead to greater job satisfaction, and improved employee morale can have financial benefits for employers (such as less turnover, fewer absences, and higher productivity).

Other Types of Monitoring

In addition to monitoring their employees' online activities, employers also engage in other types of employee screening and monitoring practices. The practices discussed below have often been challenged as violations of employee privacy rights.

Lie-Detector Tests At one time, many employers required employees or job applicants to take polygraph examinations (lie-detector tests). To protect the privacy interests of employees and job applicants, in 1988 Congress passed the Employee Polygraph Protection Act.[35] The act prohibits employers from (1) requiring or causing employees or job applicants to take lie-detector tests or suggesting or requesting that they do so; (2) using, accepting, referring to, or asking about the results of lie-detector tests taken by employees or applicants; and (3) taking or threatening negative employment-related action against employees or applicants based on results of lie-detector tests or on their refusal to take the tests.

Employers excepted from these prohibitions include federal, state, and local government employers; certain security service firms; and companies manufacturing and distributing controlled substances. Other employers may use polygraph tests when investigating losses attributable to theft, including embezzlement and the theft of trade secrets.

Drug Testing In the interests of public safety and to reduce unnecessary costs, many employers, including the government, require their employees to submit to drug testing.

Public Employers. Government (public) employers, of course, are constrained in drug testing by the Fourth Amendment to the U.S. Constitution, which prohibits unreasonable searches and seizures (see Chapter 4). Drug testing of public employees is allowed by statute for transportation workers and is normally upheld by the courts when drug use in a particular job may threaten public safety.[36] The Federal Aviation Administration also requires drug and alcohol testing of all employees and contractors (including employees of foreign air carriers) who perform

35. 29 U.S.C. Sections 2001 *et seq.*

36. Omnibus Transportation Employee Testing Act of 1991, Pub. L. No. 102-143, Title V, 105 Stat. 917 (1991).

safety-related functions.[37] When there is a reasonable basis for suspecting public employees of drug use, courts often find that drug testing does not violate the Fourth Amendment.

Private Employers. The Fourth Amendment does not apply to drug testing conducted by private employers.[38] Hence, the privacy rights and drug testing of private-sector employees are governed by state law, which varies from state to state. When testing is not allowed by state statute, employees sometimes file suit against their employers for the tort of invasion of privacy, although such claims have not met with much success.

Many states have statutes that allow drug testing by private employers but put restrictions on when and how the testing may be performed. A collective bargaining agreement may also provide protection against drug testing (or authorize drug testing under certain conditions). The permissibility of a private employee's drug test often hinges on whether the employer's testing was reasonable. Random drug tests and even "zero-tolerance" policies (that deny a "second chance" to employees who test positive for drugs) have been held to be reasonable.[39]

SECTION 8 The Law Governing Immigration

Both legal and illegal immigration have been surging in recent decades, as illustrated in Exhibit 33–1. The expansion of immigration has made an understanding of related legal requirements for business steadily more important. Employers must take steps to avoid hiring illegal immigrants or face serious penalties.

Law and Illegal Immigration

Today, there are an estimated 11 to 12 million illegal immigrants living in the United States. The overwhelming majority of these immigrants hold jobs, and they are the subject of considerable political controversy. Many contend that the immigrants take jobs from American citizens or hold down wages for such jobs. The Immigration Reform and Control Act (IRCA) of 1986[40] was intended to prevent this and made it illegal to hire, recruit, or refer for a fee someone not authorized to work in the country. The federal government—through Immigration and Customs Enforcement officers—conducts random compliance audits and has engaged in enforcement actions against employers who hire illegal immigrants. This section sets out the compliance requirements for companies.

EXHIBIT 33–1 • Foreign-Born Population and Illegal Aliens, 1960–2010

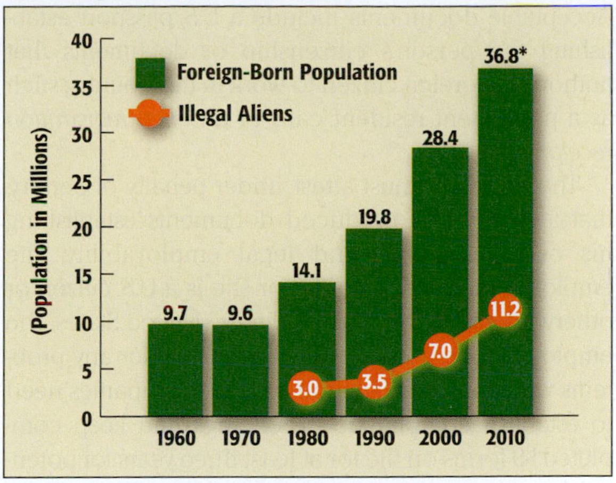

*Authors' estimates.
Source: U.S. Census Bureau, Center for Immigration Studies.

I-9 Employment Verification

To comply with current law (based on the 1986 act), employers must perform **I-9 verifications** for new hires, including even those hired as "contractors" or "day workers" if they work under the employer's direct supervision. Form I-9, Employment Eligibility Verification, available from the U.S. Citizenship and Immigration Services,[41] must be completed within three days of a worker's commencement of employment. The three-day period is to allow the employer to verify the worker's documents and the form's accuracy. The I-9 form requires employers to review and verify

37. Antidrug and Alcohol Misuse Prevention Program for Personnel Engaged in Specified Aviation Activities, 71 *Federal Register* 1666 (January 10, 2006), enacted pursuant to 49 U.S.C. Section 45102(a)(1).

38. See *Chandler v. Miller,* 520 U.S. 305, 117 S.Ct. 1295, 137 L.Ed.2d 513 (1997).

39. See *CITGO Asphalt Refining Co. v. Paper, Allied-Industrial, Chemical, and Energy Workers International Union Local No. 2-991,* 385 F.3d 809 (3d Cir. 2004).

40. This act amended various provisions of the McCarran-Walter Act, including 8 U.S.C. Sections 1160, 1187, 1188, 1255a, 1324a, 1324b, 1364, and 1365.

41. The U.S. Citizenship and Immigration Services is a federal agency that is part of the U.S. Department of Homeland Security.

documents establishing the prospective worker's identity and eligibility for employment in the United States. Acceptable documents include a U.S. passport establishing the person's citizenship or documents that authorize a foreign citizen to work in this country, such as a permanent resident card or an *alien registration receipt*.

The employer must attest, under penalty of perjury, that an employee produced documents establishing his or her identity and legal employability. The employee must state that he or she is a U.S. citizen or otherwise authorized to work in the United States. The employer is the party legally responsible for any problems with the I-9 verification process. Companies need to establish compliance procedures and keep completed I-9 forms on file for at least three years for potential future government inspection.

The 1986 act prohibits only "knowing" violations, but these include situations in which an employer "should have known" that the worker was unauthorized. Good faith is a defense under the statute, and employers are legally entitled to rely on documentation of authorization to work that reasonably appears on its face to be genuine, even if it is later established to be counterfeit. Good faith is not a defense, however, to the failure to possess the proper paperwork. Moreover, if an employer subsequently learns that an employee is not authorized to work in this country, it must promptly discharge that employee or be in violation of the law.

Enforcement

The U.S. Immigration and Customs Enforcement (ICE) was established in 2003 as the largest investigative arm of the U.S. Department of Homeland Security. ICE has a General Inspection Program that conducts random compliance audits. Other audits may occur after the agency receives a written complaint alleging an employer's violations. Government inspections involve a review of an employer's file of I-9 forms. The government need not obtain a subpoena or a warrant to conduct such an inspection.

Administrative Actions After investigation and discovery of a possible violation, ICE will bring an administrative action and issue a Notice of Intent to Fine, which sets out the charges against the employer. The employer has a right to a hearing on the enforcement action, if it files a request within thirty days. This hearing is conducted before an *administrative law judge* (see Chapter 43), and the employer has a right to counsel and to *discovery* (see Chapter 3). The typical defense in such actions is good faith or substantial compliance with the documentation provisions.

In past years, the threat of enforcement was regarded as minimal, but the federal government has substantially increased its enforcement activities as demonstrated by the ICE data presented in Exhibit 33–2. In 2007, ICE raided and identified hundreds of illegal workers at plants owned by companies including Fresh Del Monte Produce, Jones Industrial Network, Koch Foods, and Tarrasco Steel.

Criminal Actions ICE has increasingly sought criminal punishment for acts such as harboring an alien or illegally inducing illegal immigration. In January 2008, an employee of George's Processing, Inc., was convicted by a Missouri federal jury after an ICE raid resulted in the arrests of 136 illegal aliens at the plant. The convicted management employee was in the human resources department of the company and was involved in the hiring process. Evidence suggested that she helped applicants complete their I-9 forms, knowing that they had fraudulently obtained identity documents and Social Security numbers.

Private Actions U.S. immigration laws do not contain any provision allowing individuals who might be

EXHIBIT 33–2 • Worksite Enforcement Arrests by the U.S. Immigration and Customs Enforcement

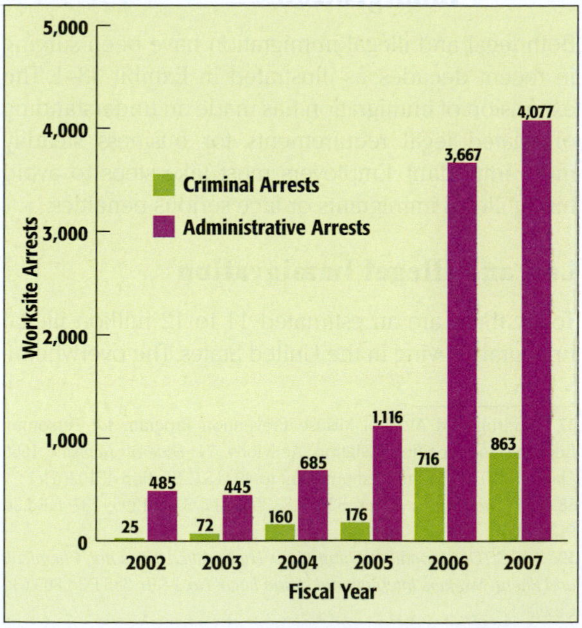

Source: U.S. Immigration and Customs Enforcement, 2008.

injured as a result of the hiring of illegal workers to sue for damages. Nevertheless, an increasing number of civil lawsuits are being brought against those who violate immigration laws under the Racketeering Influenced and Corrupt Organizations Act (RICO). As discussed in Chapter 9, RICO requires a pattern of illegal conduct, such as a pattern of hiring illegal immigrants. Thus, employers who have a history of hiring illegal immigrants, bringing them into the United States, or helping them find lodging, risk being sued by their legal employees under RICO. In addition, because RICO authorizes treble (triple) damages, legal workers potentially could receive three times the amount of their actual damages from the employer.[42]

Penalties

In general, the federal government (through ICE) enforces the current immigration laws. An employer who violates the law by hiring an unauthorized alien is subject to substantial penalties. A first offense can result in a civil fine of up to $2,200 for each unauthorized employee. Fines rise to $5,000 per employee for a second offense and up to $11,000 for subsequent offenses by the same employer. Criminal penalties apply to employers who have engaged in a "pattern or practice of violations," and these penalties include additional fines and imprisonment for up to ten years. A company may also be barred from future government contracts for violations.

ICE regulations provide a list of circumstances that may warrant the mitigation or aggravation of penalties. Considerations include whether the company is a small business and the relative cooperation of the employer in the investigation. In determining the amount of the penalty, ICE also considers the seriousness of the violation (such as intentional falsification of documents) and the employer's past compliance.

Antidiscrimination Provisions

The passage of the Immigration Reform and Control Act (ICRA) of 1986 led to concerns about discrimination based on national origin. Some employers reportedly refused to hire Latinos out of concern for violating the statute. Amendments to the act established prohibitions on unfair immigration-related employment practices. The ICRA now provides that it is an unfair immigration-related practice for an employer to discriminate against any individual (other than an unauthorized alien) with respect to hiring or discharging the individual from employment.[43] Companies must exercise reasonable care to evaluate the required I-9 documents in a fair and consistent manner. They may not require greater proof from some prospective employees or reject apparently sufficient documentation of work authorization or citizenship.

A prospective employee who believes that he or she has been subject to discrimination may file a charge with the Office of Special Counsel for Immigration Related Unfair Employment Practices (OSC). The OSC investigates the charge and may file a complaint with an administrative law judge if it finds the complaint has merit. If the OSC fails to file such a complaint within 120 days, the private party may bring a private action for discrimination. The standards and procedures for evaluating the action parallel those of Title VII of the Civil Rights Act, which will be discussed in Chapter 34.

Law and Legal Immigration

The immigration laws of this country are very elaborate, and individuals can seek authorization to enter the country under numerous different provisions, such as those permitting refugees who can demonstrate certain persecution from their home country's government. This section focuses on the rules for those who immigrate in order to work in the United States. U.S. businesses can benefit from hiring immigrants who have abilities surpassing those of available domestic workers. Our immigration laws have long made provisions for businesses to hire especially qualified foreign workers. The Immigration Act of 1990 placed caps on the number of visas (entry permits) that can be issued to immigrants each year.

Most temporary visas are set aside for workers who can be characterized as "persons of extraordinary ability," members of the professions holding advanced degrees, or other skilled workers and professionals. To hire these individuals, employers must submit a petition to the Citizenship and Immigration Services, which determines whether the job candidate meets the legal standards. Each visa is for a specific job, and there are legal limits on the employee's ability to switch jobs once in the United States.

42. See, for example, *Williams v. Mohawk Industries, Inc.*, 465 F.3d 1277 (11th Cir. 2006); *cert.* denied __ U.S. __, 127, S.Ct. 1381, 167 L.Ed.2d 174 (2007). (This case was discussed in Chapter 9 on page 189.) See also *Hernandez v. Balakian*, 480 F.Supp.2d 1198 (E.D. Cal. 2007).

43. 8 U.S.C. Section 1324b.

Self-Authorized Immigrant Job Candidates A company seeking to hire a noncitizen worker may do so, if the worker is self-authorized. This means that either the worker (1) is a lawful permanent resident or (2) has a valid temporary Employment Authorization Document (EAD). Lawful permanent residents can prove their status to an employer by presenting an **I-551 Alien Registration Receipt,** known as a "green card," or a properly stamped foreign passport.

When an Immigrant Is Not Self-Authorized Many workers are not already self-authorized, though, and employers may obtain a labor certification, or green card, for those immigrants whom they wish to hire. Fifty thousand new green-card immigrants are authorized each year. To take advantage of this authority, the job must be for a permanent, full-time position.

To gain such authorization for hiring a foreign worker, the employer must show that no American worker is qualified, willing, and able to take the job. This requires publication of the bona fide job opening in suitable newspapers or professional journals within six months of the hiring action. The government has detailed regulations governing the nature of this publication.[44] Any U.S. applicants must be interviewed and hired for the position if they meet its stated qualifications. The qualifications are also evaluated for their business necessity. A group of administrative law judges rejected one company's notice for hiring kitchen supervisors, because the company required that the applicants speak Spanish.[45]

The employer must also determine from a state agency what the "prevailing wage" for the position is in the location and must offer the immigrating worker at least 100 percent of that prevailing wage. The prevailing wage rate is defined as the average wage paid to similarly employed workers in the requested occupation in the area of intended employment. Fringe benefits are also considered in this calculation.

A separate authorization system provides for the temporary entry and hiring of nonimmigrant visa workers. These are individuals who enter the country for a period of time and who are restricted to an activity consistent with their visas. Applicants must express an intention to depart the country at the expiration of their requested stay, though they may apply for an extension of the stay.

The H-1B Visa Program The most common and controversial visa program today involves the H-1B visa system. These individuals may stay and work in the country for three to six years and work only for the sponsoring employer. The recipients of these visas include many high-tech workers. Sixty-five thousand slots for new immigrants were initially set aside for H-1B visas; the number was temporarily increased to 195,000, but that law expired and the cap returned to 65,000 in 2004. The available slots go quickly, and many businesses, such as Microsoft, have lobbied Congress to expand the number of H1-B visas offered to immigrants. In recent years, the total allotment of H1-B visas has been filled within the first few weeks of the year, leaving no slots available for the remaining eleven months.

The criteria for such a visa include the potential employee's "specialty occupation," which is defined as having highly specialized knowledge and the attainment of a bachelor's or higher degree or its equivalent. Qualifying jobs may include computer programmers, electronics specialists, complex business managers, engineers, professionals, and other jobs. In one 2006 ruling, ICE found that the position of "accountant" did not qualify as a specialty occupation because the American Council for Accountancy and Taxation did not require a degree for an individual to be credentialed as such.

Labor Certification Before an employer can submit an H-1B application, it must obtain a Labor Certification application filed on a form known as ETA 9035. The employer must agree to provide a wage level at least equal to that offered to other individuals with similar experience and qualifications and attest that the hiring will not adversely affect other workers similarly employed. The employer must inform U.S. workers of the intent to hire a foreign worker by posting the form. The U.S. Department of Labor reviews the applications and may reject them for incompleteness or inaccuracies.

In 2002, a former employee of Sun Microsystems complained to the U.S. Department of Justice that the company was discriminating against U.S. workers in favor of H-1B visa holders. Sun had laid off nearly four thousand domestic workers while applying for thousands of temporary visa employees. The court ultimately found that Sun had violated only minor

44. The most relevant regulations can be found at 20 C.F.R. 655 (for temporary employment) and 20 C.F.R. 656 (for permanent employment).

45. *In the matter of Malnati Organization, Inc.*, 2007-INA-00035 (Bd. Alien Lab. Cert. App. 2007).

technical requirements and ordered it merely to change its posting practices for applicants for open positions.

H-2, O, L, and E Visas Other specialty temporary nonimmigrant visas are available for other categories of employees. H-2 visas provide for workers performing agricultural labor of a seasonal nature. O visas provide entry for persons who have "extraordinary ability in the sciences, arts, education, business or athletics which has been demonstrated by sustained national or international acclaim." L visas allow companies to bring some of their foreign managers or executives to work inside the country. E visas permit the entry of certain foreign investors or entrepreneurs.

REVIEWING Employment and Labor Law

Rick Saldona began working as a traveling salesperson for Aimer Winery in 1979. Sales constituted 90 percent of Saldona's work time. Saldona worked an average of fifty hours per week but received no overtime pay. In June 2009, Saldona's new supervisor, Caesar Braxton, claimed that Saldona had been inflating his reported sales calls and required Saldona to submit to a polygraph test. Saldona reported Braxton to the U.S. Department of Labor, which prohibited Aimer from requiring Saldona to take a polygraph test for this purpose. In August 2009, Saldona's wife, Venita, fell from a ladder and sustained a head injury while employed as a full-time agricultural harvester. Saldona delivered to Aimer's Human Resources Department a letter from his wife's physician indicating that she would need daily care for several months, and Saldona took leave until December 2009. Aimer had sixty-three employees at that time. When Saldona returned to Aimer, he was informed that his position had been eliminated because his sales territory had been combined with an adjacent territory. Using the information presented in the chapter, answer the following questions.

1. Would Saldona have been legally entitled to receive overtime pay at a higher rate? Why or why not?
2. What is the maximum length of time Saldona would have been allowed to take leave to care for his injured spouse?
3. Under what circumstances would Aimer have been allowed to require an employee to take a polygraph test?
4. Would Aimer likely be able to avoid reinstating Saldona under the *key employee* exception? Why or why not?

TERMS AND CONCEPTS

I-551 Alien Registration Receipt 640
I-9 verification 637
authorization card 627
cease-and-desist order 626
closed shop 627
collective bargaining 629
employment at will 620
hot-cargo agreement 627
minimum wage 623
right-to-work law 627
secondary boycott 627
strike 629
union shop 627
vesting 632
whistleblowing 621
workers' compensation law 630
wrongful discharge 622

QUESTIONS AND CASE PROBLEMS

33–1. Calzoni Boating Co. is an interstate business engaged in manufacturing and selling boats. The company has five hundred nonunion employees. Representatives of these employees are requesting a four-day, ten-hours-per-day workweek, and Calzoni is concerned that this would require paying time and a half after eight hours per day. Which federal act is Calzoni thinking of that might require this? Will the act in fact require paying time and a half for all hours worked over eight hours per day if the employees' proposal is accepted? Explain.

33–2. QUESTION WITH SAMPLE ANSWER

Denton and Carlo were employed at an appliance plant. Their job required them to perform occasional maintenance work while standing on a wire mesh twenty feet above the plant floor. Other employees had fallen through the mesh, and one of them had been killed by the fall. When Denton and Carlo were asked by their supervisor to perform tasks that would likely require them to walk on the mesh, they refused because of their fear of bodily harm or death. Because of their refusal to do the requested work, the two employees were fired from their jobs. Was their discharge wrongful? If so, under what federal employment law? To what federal agency or department should they turn for assistance?

- **For a sample answer to Question 33–2, go to Appendix I at the end of this text.**

33–3. Suppose that Consolidated Stores is undergoing a unionization campaign. Prior to the union election, management states that the union is unnecessary to protect workers. Management also provides bonuses and wage increases to the workers during this period. The employees reject the union. Union organizers protest that the wage increases during the election campaign unfairly prejudiced the vote. Should these wage increases be regarded as an unfair labor practice? Discuss.

33–4. Unfair Labor Practice. The New York Department of Education's e-mail policy prohibits the use of the e-mail system for unofficial purposes, except that officials of the New York Public Employees Federation (PEF), the union representing state employees, can use the system for some limited communications, including the scheduling of union meetings and activities. In 1998, Michael Darcy, an elected PEF official, began sending mass, union-related e-mails to employees, including a summary of a union delegates' convention, a union newsletter, a criticism of proposed state legislation, and a criticism of the state governor and the Governor's Office of Employee Relations. Richard Cate, the department's chief operating officer, met with Darcy and reiterated the department's e-mail policy. When Darcy refused to stop his use of the e-mail system, Cate terminated his access to it. Darcy filed a complaint with the New York Public Employment Relations Board, alleging an unfair labor practice. Do the circumstances support Cate's action? Why or why not? [*Benson v. Cuevas,* 293 A.D.2d 927, 741 N.Y.S.2d 310 (3 Dept. 2002)]

33–5. Collective Bargaining. Verizon New York, Inc. (VNY), provides telecommunications services. VNY and the Communications Workers of America (CWA) are parties to collective bargaining agreements covering installation and maintenance employees. At one time, VNY supported annual blood drives. VNY, CWA, and charitable organizations jointly set dates, arranged appointments, and adjusted work schedules for the drives. For each drive, about a thousand employees, including managers, spent up to four hours traveling to a donor site, giving blood, recovering, and returning to their jobs. Employees received full pay for the time. In 2001, VNY told CWA that it would no longer allow employees to participate "on Company time," claiming that it experienced problems meeting customer requests for service during the drives. CWA filed a complaint with the National Labor Relations Board (NLRB), asking that VNY be ordered to bargain over the decision. Did VNY commit an unfair labor practice? Should the NLRB grant CWA's request? Why or why not? [*Verizon New York, Inc. v. National Labor Relations Board,* 360 F.3d 206 (D.C.Cir. 2004)]

33–6. Workers' Compensation Laws. The Touch of Class Lounge is in a suburban shopping plaza, or strip mall, in Omaha, Nebraska. Patricia Bauer, the Lounge's owner, does not own the parking lot, which is provided for the common use of all of the businesses in the plaza. Stephanie Zoucha was a bartender at the Lounge. Her duties ended when she locked the door after closing. On June 4, 2001, at 1:15 A.M., Zoucha closed the bar and locked the door from the inside. An hour later, she walked to her car in the parking lot, where she was struck with "[l]ike a tire iron on the back of my head." Zoucha sustained a skull fracture and other injuries, including significant cognitive damage (impairment of speech and thought formation). Her purse, containing her tip money, was stolen. She identified her attacker as William Nunez, who had been in the Lounge earlier that night. Zoucha filed a petition in a Nebraska state court to obtain workers' compensation. What are the requirements for receiving workers' compensation? Should Zoucha's request be granted or denied? Why? [*Zoucha v. Touch of Class Lounge,* 269 Neb. 89, 690 N.W.2d 610 (2005)]

33–7. CASE PROBLEM WITH SAMPLE ANSWER

Jennifer Willis worked for Coca Cola Enterprises, Inc. (CCE), in Louisiana as a senior account manager. On a Monday in May 2003, Willis called her supervisor to tell him that she was sick and would not be able to work that day. She also said that she was pregnant, but she did not say she was sick *because* of the pregnancy. On Tuesday, she called to ask where to report to work and was told that she could not return without a doctor's release. She said that she had a doctor's appointment on "Wednesday," which her supervisor understood to be the next day. Willis meant the *following* Wednesday. More than a week later, during which time Willis did not contact CCE, she was told that she had violated CCE's "No Call/No Show" policy. Under this policy, "an employee absent from work for three consecutive days without notifying the supervisor during that period will be considered to have voluntarily resigned." She was fired. Willis filed a suit in a federal district court against CCE under the Family and Medical Leave Act (FMLA). To be eligible for FMLA leave, an employee must inform an employer of the reason for the leave. Did Willis meet this requirement? Did CCE's response to Willis's absence violate the FMLA? Explain. [*Willis v. Coca Cola Enterprises, Inc.*, 445 F.3d 413 (5th Cir. 2006)]

- **To view a sample answer for Problem 33–7, go to this book's Web site at www.cengage.com/blaw/jentz, select "Chapter 33," and click on "Case Problem with Sample Answer."**

33–8. Unemployment Insurance. Mary Garas, a chemist, sought work in Missouri through Kelly Services, Inc. Kelly is a staffing agency that places individuals in jobs of varying duration with other companies. Through Kelly, Garas worked at Merial Co. from April 2005 to February 2006. After the assignment ended, Garas asked Kelly for more work. Meanwhile, she filed a claim for unemployment benefits with the Missouri Division of Employment Security (DES). In March, Kelly recruiter Rebecca Cockrum told Garas about a temporary assignment with Celsis Laboratory. Garas said that she would prefer a "more stable position," but later asked Cockrum to submit her résumé to Celsis. Before the employer responded, Kelly told the DES that Garas had refused suitable work. Under a Missouri state statute, a claim for unemployment benefits must be denied if "the claimant failed without good cause . . . to accept suitable work when offered the claimant . . . by an employer by whom the individual was formerly employed." The DES denied Garas's claim for benefits. She filed an appeal with a state court. Was the DES's denial right or wrong? Why? [*Garas v. Kelly Services, Inc.*, 211 S.W.3d 149 (Mo.App.E.D. 2007)]

33–9. A QUESTION OF ETHICS

*Beverly Tull had worked for Atchison Leather Products, Inc., in Kansas for ten years when, in 1999, she began to complain of hand, wrist, and shoulder pain. Atchison recommended that she contact a certain physician, who in April 2000 diagnosed the condition as carpal tunnel syndrome "severe enough" for surgery. In August, Tull filed a claim with the state workers' compensation board. Because Atchison changed workers' compensation insurance companies every year, a dispute arose as to which company should pay Tull's claim. Fearing liability, no insurer would authorize treatment, and Tull was forced to delay surgery until December. The board granted her temporary total disability benefits for the subsequent six weeks that she missed work. On April 23, 2002, Berger Co. bought Atchison. The new employer adjusted Tull's work so that it was less demanding and stressful, but she continued to suffer pain. In July, a physician diagnosed her condition as permanent. The board granted her permanent partial disability benefits. By May 2005, the bickering over the financial responsibility for Tull's claim involved five insurers—four of which had each covered Atchison for a single year and one of which covered Berger. [*Tull v. Atchison Leather Products, Inc.*, *37 Kan.App.2d 87, 150 P.3d 316 (2007)]*

(a) When an injured employee files a claim for workers' compensation, a proceeding is held to assess the injury and determine the amount of compensation. Should a dispute between insurers over the payment of the claim be resolved in the same proceeding? Why or why not?
(b) The board designated April 23, 2002, as the date of Tull's injury. What is the reason for determining the date of a worker's injury? Should the board in this case have selected this date or a different date? Why?
(c) How should the board assess liability for the payment of Tull's medical expenses and disability benefits? Would it be appropriate to impose joint and several liability on the insurers (holding each of them responsible for the full amount of damages), or should the individual liability of each of them be determined? Explain.

33–10. VIDEO QUESTION

Go to this text's Web site at **www.cengage.com/blaw/jentz** and select "Chapter 33." Click on "Video Questions" and view the video titled *Employment at Will.* Then answer the following questions.

(a) In the video, Laura asserts that she can fire Ray "for any reason; for no reason." Is this true? Explain your answer.
(b) What exceptions to the employment-at-will doctrine are discussed in the chapter? Does Ray's situation fit into any of these exceptions?
(c) Would Ray be protected from wrongful discharge under whistleblowing statutes? Why or why not?
(d) Assume that you are the employer in this scenario. What arguments can you make that Ray should not be able to sue for wrongful discharge in this situation?

LAW ON THE WEB

For updated links to resources available on the Web, as well as a variety of other materials, visit this text's Web site at

www.cengage.com/blaw/jentz

The U.S. Department of Labor offers an FLSA Overtime Calculator and a variety of other information to assist both employers and workers at

www.dol.gov/elaws

The American Federation of Labor–Congress of Industrial Organizations (AFL-CIO) provides links to labor-related resources at

www.aflcio.org

The National Labor Relations Board is online at

www.nlrb.gov

Legal Research Exercises on the Web

Go to **www.cengage.com/blaw/jentz**, the Web site that accompanies this text. Select "Chapter 33" and click on "Internet Exercises." There you will find the following Internet research exercises that you can perform to learn more about the topics covered in this chapter.

Internet Exercise 33–1: Legal Perspective
Workers' Compensation

Internet Exercise 33–2: Management Perspective
Workplace Monitoring and Surveillance

Internet Exercise 33–3: Historical Perspective
Labor Unions and Labor Law

CHAPTER 34

Employment Discrimination

Out of the 1960s civil rights movement to end racial and other forms of discrimination grew a body of law protecting employees against discrimination in the workplace. This protective legislation further eroded the employment-at-will doctrine, which was discussed in Chapter 33. In the past several decades, judicial decisions, administrative agency actions, and legislation have restricted the ability of employers, as well as unions, to discriminate against workers on the basis of race, color, religion, national origin, gender, age, or disability. A class of persons defined by one or more of these criteria is known as a **protected class.**

Several federal statutes prohibit **employment discrimination** against members of protected classes. The most important statute is Title VII of the Civil Rights Act of 1964.[1] Title VII prohibits employment discrimination on the basis of race, color, religion, national origin, and gender. The Age Discrimination in Employment Act of 1967[2] and the Americans with Disabilities Act of 1990[3] prohibit discrimination on the basis of age and disability, respectively. The protections afforded under these laws extend to U.S. citizens who are working abroad for U.S. firms or for companies that are controlled by U.S. firms—*unless* to do so would violate the laws of the countries in which their workplaces are located. This "foreign laws exception" prevents employers from being subjected to conflicting laws.

This chapter focuses on the kinds of discrimination prohibited by these federal statutes. Note, however, that discrimination against employees on the basis of any of the above-mentioned criteria may also violate state human rights statutes or other state laws prohibiting discrimination.

1. 42 U.S.C. Sections 2000e–2000e-17.
2. 29 U.S.C. Sections 621–634.
3. 42 U.S.C. Sections 12102–12118.

SECTION 1 Title VII of the Civil Rights Act of 1964

Title VII of the Civil Rights Act of 1964 and its amendments prohibit job discrimination against employees, applicants, and union members on the basis of race, color, national origin, religion, and gender at any stage of employment. It prohibits discrimination in decisions concerning hiring, firing, promotion, demotion, discipline, compensation, opportunities for additional job training, and any other term and condition of employment.

Title VII expressly applies to employers affecting interstate commerce with fifteen or more employees, labor unions with fifteen or more members, labor unions that operate hiring halls (to which members go regularly to be rationed jobs as they become available), employment agencies, and state and local governing units or agencies. A special section of the act prohibits discrimination in most federal government employment. When Title VII applies to the employer, any employee—including an undocumented (alien) worker—can bring an action for employment discrimination. Moreover, an employer with fewer than fifteen employees is not automatically shielded from a lawsuit filed under Title VII.[4]

4. The United States Supreme Court has held that courts still have jurisdiction to hear an employee's Title VII claim against his or her employer, even if that employer has fewer than fifteen employees. See *Arbaugh v. Y&H Corp.*, 546 U.S. 500, 126 S.Ct. 1235, 163 L.Ed.2d 1097 (2006).

The Equal Employment Opportunity Commission

The Equal Employment Opportunity Commission (EEOC) monitors compliance with Title VII. A victim of alleged discrimination, before bringing a suit against the employer, must first file a claim with the EEOC. The EEOC may investigate the dispute and attempt to obtain the parties' voluntary consent to an out-of-court settlement. If voluntary agreement cannot be reached, the EEOC may then file a suit against the employer on the employee's behalf. If the EEOC decides not to investigate the claim, the victim may bring his or her own lawsuit against the employer.

The EEOC does not investigate every claim of employment discrimination. Generally, it takes only "priority cases," such as cases that affect many workers, cases involving retaliatory discharge (firing an employee in retaliation for submitting a claim with the EEOC), and cases involving types of discrimination that are of particular concern to the EEOC. In recent years, the EEOC has been receiving and investigating an increasing number of claims of religious discrimination in the workplace.[5]

Intentional and Unintentional Discrimination

Title VII of the Civil Rights Act of 1964 prohibits both intentional and unintentional discrimination.

Intentional Discrimination Intentional discrimination by an employer against an employee is known as **disparate-treatment discrimination.** Because intent may sometimes be difficult to prove, courts have established certain procedures for resolving disparate-treatment cases. Suppose that a woman applies for employment with a construction firm and is rejected. If she sues on the basis of disparate-treatment discrimination in hiring, she must show that (1) she is a member of a protected class, (2) she applied and was qualified for the job in question, (3) she was rejected by the employer, and (4) the employer continued to seek applicants for the position or filled the position with a person not in a protected class.

If the woman can meet these relatively easy requirements, she makes out a ***prima facie* case** of illegal discrimination. Making out a *prima facie* case of discrimination means that the plaintiff has met her initial burden of proof and will win in the absence of a legally acceptable employer defense. (Defenses to claims of employment discrimination will be discussed later in this chapter.) The burden then shifts to the employer-defendant, who must articulate a legal reason for not hiring the plaintiff. For example, the employer might say that the plaintiff was not hired because she lacked sufficient experience or training. To prevail, the plaintiff must then show that the employer's reason is a *pretext* (not the true reason) and that discriminatory intent actually motivated the employer's decision.

Unintentional Discrimination Employers often use interviews and testing procedures to choose from among a large number of applicants for job openings. Minimum educational requirements are also common. Employer practices, such as those involving educational requirements, may have an unintended discriminatory impact on a protected class. **Disparate-impact discrimination** occurs when a protected group of people is adversely affected by an employer's practices, procedures, or tests, even though they do not appear to be discriminatory. In a disparate-impact discrimination case, the complaining party must first show statistically that the employer's practices, procedures, or tests are discriminatory in effect. The plaintiff must show a causal link between the practice and the discriminatory effect. Once the plaintiff has made out a *prima facie* case, the burden of proof shifts to the employer to show that the practices or procedures in question were justified. There are two ways of proving that disparate-impact discrimination exists, as discussed next.

Pool of Applicants. A plaintiff can prove a disparate impact by comparing the employer's workforce to the pool of qualified individuals available in the local labor market. The plaintiff must show that as a result of educational or other job requirements or hiring procedures, the percentage of nonwhites, women, or members of other protected classes in the employer's workforce does not reflect the percentage of that group in the pool of qualified applicants. If a person challenging an employment practice can show a connection between the practice and the disparity, she or he makes out a *prima facie* case and need not provide evidence of discriminatory intent.

Rate of Hiring. Disparate-impact discrimination can also occur when an educational or other job require-

5. Dick Dahl, "EEOC Reports 10 Percent Increase in Charges," *Lawyers USA*, February 26, 2007.

ment or hiring procedure excludes members of a protected class from an employer's workforce at a substantially higher rate than nonmembers, regardless of the racial balance in the employer's workforce. This "rates analysis" compares the selection rate for whites with that for nonwhites (or other members of a protected class). The plaintiff does not have to prove that the workforce does not reflect the percentage of qualified nonwhite persons available in the local labor market.

The EEOC has devised a test, called the "four-fifths rule" or the "80 percent rule," to determine whether an employment examination is discriminatory on its face. Under this rule, a selection rate for protected classes that is less than four-fifths, or 80 percent, of the rate for the group with the highest rate will generally be regarded as evidence of disparate impact. To illustrate: One hundred majority-group applicants take an employment test, and fifty pass the test and are hired. One hundred minority-group applicants take the test, and twenty pass the test and are hired. Because twenty is less than four-fifths (80 percent) of fifty, the test would be considered discriminatory under the EEOC guidelines.

Discrimination Based on Race, Color, and National Origin

Title VII prohibits employers from discriminating against employees or job applicants on the basis of race, color, or national origin. If an employer's standards or policies for selecting or promoting employees have a discriminatory effect on employees or job applicants in these protected classes, then a presumption of illegal discrimination arises. To avoid liability, the employer must then show that its standards or policies have a substantial, demonstrable relationship to realistic qualifications for the job in question.

Suppose that a city fires Cheng Mai, a Chinese American, who has worked in the city's planning department for two years. Mai claims that he was fired because of his national origin and presents evidence that the city's "residents only" policy has a discriminatory effect on Chinese Americans. The policy requires all city employees to become residents of the city within a reasonable time after being hired. Cheng Mai has not moved to the city but instead has continued to live with his wife and children in a nearby town that has a small population of Chinese Americans. Although residency requirements sometimes violate antidiscrimination laws, if the city can show that its residency requirement has a substantial, demonstrable relationship to realistic qualifications for the job in question, then normally it will not be illegal.

Reverse Discrimination Note that discrimination based on race can also take the form of *reverse discrimination,* or discrimination against "majority" individuals, such as white males. For example, in one Pennsylvania case, an African American woman fired four white men from their management positions at a school district. The men filed a lawsuit for racial discrimination alleging that the woman was trying to eliminate white males from the department. The woman claimed that the terminations were part of a reorganization plan to cut costs in the department. The jury sided with the men and awarded them nearly $3 million in damages. The verdict was upheld on appeal (though the damages award was reduced slightly).[6]

Potential "Section 1981" Claims Victims of racial or ethnic discrimination may also have a cause of action under 42 U.S.C. Section 1981. This section, which was enacted as part of the Civil Rights Act of 1866 to protect the rights of freed slaves, prohibits discrimination on the basis of race or ethnicity in the formation or enforcement of contracts. Because employment is often a contractual relationship, Section 1981 can provide an alternative (and potentially advantageous) basis for a plaintiff's action.[7] Unlike Title VII, Section 1981 does not place a cap on damages (see the discussion of Title VII remedies later in this chapter). Thus, if an employee can prove that he or she was discriminated against in the formation or enforcement of a contract, the employee may be able to obtain a larger damages award under Section 1981 than would be available under Title VII.

Discrimination Based on Religion

Title VII of the Civil Rights Act of 1964 also prohibits government employers, private employers, and unions from discriminating against persons because of their religion. An employer must "reasonably accommodate" the religious practices of its employees, unless to do so would cause undue hardship to the employer's business. For example, if an employee's religion prohibits him from working on a certain day of the week or at a certain type of job, the employer must make a

6. *Johnston v. School District of Philadelphia,* 2006 WL 999966 (E.D.Pa. 2006).

7. See, for example, *E.E.O.C. v. Sephora USA, LLC,* 419 F.Supp.2d 408 (S.D.N.Y. 2005).

reasonable attempt to accommodate these religious requirements. Employers must reasonably accommodate an employee's religious belief even if the belief is not based on the doctrines of a traditionally recognized religion, such as Christianity or Judaism, or a denomination, such as Baptist. The only requirement is that the belief be sincerely held by the employee.[8]

Discrimination Based on Gender

Under Title VII, as well as under other federal acts (including those discussed here), employers are forbidden from discriminating against employees on the basis of gender. Employers are prohibited from classifying jobs as male or female and from advertising in help-wanted columns that are designated male or female unless the employer can prove that the gender of the applicant is essential to the job. Furthermore, employers cannot have separate male and female seniority lists. Generally, to succeed in a suit for gender discrimination, a plaintiff must demonstrate that gender was a determining factor in the employer's decision to hire, fire, or promote him or her. Typically, this involves looking at all of the surrounding circumstances.

The Equal Pay Act of 1963[9] prohibits employers from engaging in gender-based wage discrimination. For the act's equal pay requirements to apply, the male and female employees must work at the same establishment doing similar work. The work need not be identical, provided there is substantial equality of skill, effort, responsibility, and working conditions. To determine whether the Equal Pay Act has been violated, a court will look to the primary duties of the two jobs. It is the job content rather than the job description that controls.[10] If a court finds that the wage differential is due to any factor other than gender, such as a seniority or merit system, then it does not violate the Equal Pay Act.

The Pregnancy Discrimination Act of 1978,[11] which amended Title VII, expanded the definition of gender discrimination to include discrimination based on pregnancy. Women affected by pregnancy, childbirth, or related medical conditions must be treated—for all employment-related purposes, including the provision of benefits under employee benefit programs—the same as other persons not so affected but similar in ability to work.

Constructive Discharge

The majority of Title VII complaints involve unlawful discrimination in decisions to hire or fire employees. In some situations, however, employees who leave their jobs voluntarily can claim that they were "constructively discharged" by the employer. **Constructive discharge** occurs when the employer causes the employee's working conditions to be so intolerable that a reasonable person in the employee's position would feel compelled to quit.

Proving Constructive Discharge The plaintiff must present objective proof of intolerable working conditions, which the employer knew or had reason to know about yet failed to correct within a reasonable time period. Courts generally also require the employee to show causation—that the employer's unlawful discrimination caused the working conditions to be intolerable. Put a different way, the employee's resignation must be a foreseeable result of the employer's discriminatory action.

For example, Khalil's employer humiliates him by informing him in front of his co-workers that he is being demoted to an inferior position. Khalil's co-workers then continually insult, harass, and make derogatory remarks to him about his national origin (he is from Iraq). The employer is aware of this discriminatory treatment but does nothing to remedy the situation, despite repeated complaints from Khalil. After several months, Khalil quits his job and files a Title VII claim. In this situation, Khalil would likely have sufficient evidence to maintain an action for constructive discharge in violation of Title VII. Although courts weigh the facts on a case-by-case basis, employee demotion is one of the most frequently cited reasons for a finding of constructive discharge, particularly when the employee was subjected to humiliation.

Applies to All Title VII Discrimination Note that constructive discharge is a theory that plaintiffs can use to establish any type of discrimination claims under Title VII, including race, color, national origin, religion, gender, pregnancy, and sexual harassment. Constructive discharge has also been successfully used in situations that involve discrimination based

8. *Frazee v. Illinois Department of Employment Security,* 489 U.S. 829, 109 S.Ct. 1514, 103 L.Ed.2d 914 (1989); and *Watts v. Florida International University,* 495 F.3d 1289 (11th Cir. 2007).

9. 29 U.S.C. Section 206(d).

10. For an illustration of the factors courts consider in wage-discrimination claims under the Equal Pay Act, see *Beck-Wilson v. Principi,* 441 F.3d 353 (6th Cir. 2006).

11. 42 U.S.C. Section 2000e(k).

on age or disability (both of which will be discussed later in this chapter). Constructive discharge is most commonly asserted in cases involving sexual harassment, however.

Sexual Harassment

Title VII also protects employees against **sexual harassment** in the workplace. Sexual harassment can take two forms: *quid pro quo* harassment and hostile-environment harassment. *Quid pro quo* is a Latin phrase that is often translated as "something in exchange for something else." *Quid pro quo* harassment occurs when sexual favors are demanded in return for job opportunities, promotions, salary increases, or other benefits. Hostile-environment claims, in contrast, arise when a person is subjected to unwelcome sexual advances, requests for sexual favors, and other verbal or physical conduct or communication of a sexual nature. The United States Supreme Court has stated that hostile-environment harassment occurs when "the workplace is permeated with discriminatory intimidation, ridicule, and insult, that is sufficiently severe or pervasive to alter the conditions of the victim's employment and create an abusive working environment."[12]

The courts determine whether the sexually offensive conduct was sufficiently severe or pervasive as to create a hostile environment on a case-by-case basis. Typically, a single incident of sexually offensive conduct is not enough to permeate the work environment (although there have been exceptions when the conduct was particularly severe). For example, if a male supervisor makes suggestive gestures and tells a female employee on one occasion that he would like to have sexual relations with her, that may not be enough to make the work environment hostile.[13] If a supervisor repeatedly makes sexually offensive comments, however, or asks for specific details about the sexual conduct of a co-worker on several occasions, this may be enough to create a hostile environment.[14]

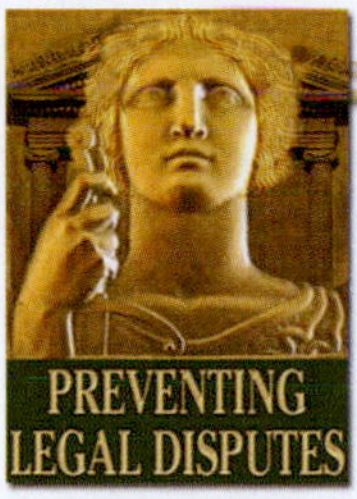

It is essential for business owners and managers to be familiar with the laws pertaining to sexual harassment and gender discrimination and to understand what constitutes a hostile environment. Harassment in the workplace can take many forms and be based on many characteristics (such as gender, race, national origin, religion, age, and disability), but sexual harassment must be on the basis of an employee's gender. Managers should establish written policies and review them annually.

Any complaint should be taken seriously and investigated. Some employment specialists even suggest that employers and managers assume that hostile-environment harassment has occurred if an employee claims that it has. Prompt remedial action is key, but it must not include any immediate adverse action (such as termination) against the person who has made the complaint. Most importantly, managers should quickly seek the advice of counsel when a complaint arises.

Harassment by Supervisors For an employer to be held liable for a supervisor's sexual harassment, the supervisor must have taken a *tangible employment action* against the employee. A **tangible employment action** is a significant change in employment status, such as firing or failing to promote an employee, reassigning the employee to a position with significantly different responsibilities, or effecting a significant change in employment benefits.

Only a supervisor, or another person acting with the authority of the employer, can cause this sort of injury. A co-worker can sexually harass another employee, and anyone who has regular contact with an employee can inflict psychological injuries by offensive conduct. A co-worker cannot dock another's pay, demote her or him, or set conditions for continued employment, however.

Supreme Court Guidelines. In 1998, in two separate cases, the United States Supreme Court issued some significant guidelines relating to the liability of employers for their supervisors' harassment of employees in the workplace. In *Faragher v. City of Boca Raton,*[15] the Court held that an employer (a city) could be held liable for a supervisor's harassment of employees even though the employer was unaware of

12. *Harris v. Forklift Systems,* 510 U.S. 17, 114 S.Ct. 367, 126 L.Ed.2d 295 (1993). See also *Baker v. Via Christi Regional Medical Center,* 491 F.Supp.2d 1040 (D.Kan. 2007).

13. *Pomales v. Celulares Telefonica, Inc.,* 447 F.3d 79 (1st Cir. 2006); and *Fontanez-Nunez v. Janssen Ortho, LLC,* 447 F.3d 50 (1st Cir. 2006).

14. See, for example, *Fye v. Oklahoma Corp. Commission,* 2006 WL 895237 (10th Cir. 2006).

15. 524 U.S. 775, 118 S.Ct. 2275, 141 L.Ed.2d 662 (1998).

the behavior. The Court reached this conclusion primarily because, although the city had a written policy against sexual harassment, the policy had not been distributed to city employees. Additionally, the city had not established any procedures that could be followed by employees who felt that they were victims of sexual harassment. In *Burlington Industries, Inc. v. Ellerth*,[16] the Court ruled that a company could be held liable for the harassment of an employee by one of its vice presidents even though the employee suffered no adverse job consequences.

In these two cases, the Court set forth some commonsense guidelines on liability for harassment in the workplace that are helpful to employers and employees alike. On the one hand, employees benefit by the ruling that employers may be held liable for their supervisors' harassment even though the employers were unaware of the actions and even though the employees suffered no adverse job consequences. On the other hand, the Court made it clear in both decisions that employers have an affirmative defense against liability for their supervisors' harassment of employees if the employers can show the following:

1. That they have taken "reasonable care to prevent and correct promptly any sexually harassing behavior" (by establishing effective harassment policies and complaint procedures, for example).
2. That the employees suing for harassment failed to follow these policies and procedures.

In 2004, the Supreme Court further clarified the tangible employment action requirement as it applies in constructive discharge cases. The Court held that "[t]o establish constructive discharge, a plaintiff alleging sexual harassment must show that the work environment became so intolerable that resignation was a fitting response. An employer may then assert the *Ellerth/Faragher* affirmative defense unless the plaintiff quit in reasonable response to a tangible employment action."[17]

Retaliation by Employer. Charges of sexual harassment by supervisors—and other claims under Title VII as well—have sometimes resulted in attempts by the employer to retaliate against the employee bringing the claim by demoting him or her or by making some other change in his or her employment status. Title VII includes an antiretaliation provision that makes it unlawful for an employer to "discriminate against" an employee or applicant who has "opposed" a practice that Title VII prohibits. In a *retaliation claim*, the individual asserts that she or he has suffered a harm as a result of making a charge, testifying, or participating in a Title VII investigation or proceeding.

The courts disagreed, however, on what the plaintiff had to show to prove retaliation. Some courts required a plaintiff to show that the challenged action resulted in an adverse effect on the terms or conditions of *employment*. Other courts required a plaintiff to show only that the challenged action would have been material to a reasonable employee. In the following case, the United States Supreme Court considered whether Title VII's ban on retaliation covers acts that are not job related.

16. 524 U.S. 742, 118 S.Ct. 2257, 141 L.Ed.2d 633 (1998).

17. *Pennsylvania State Police v. Suders*, 542 U.S. 129, 124 S.Ct. 2342, 159 L.Ed.2d 204 (2004).

CASE 34.1 Burlington Northern and Santa Fe Railway Co. v. White

Supreme Court of the United States, 2006. 548 U.S. 53, 126 S.Ct. 2405, 165 L.Ed.2d 345.

• **Background and Facts** Sheila White worked in the maintenance department of the Burlington Northern and Santa Fe Railway Company's Tennessee yard. She was the only female worker in that department. She complained to Burlington officials that her supervisor, Bill Joiner, had repeatedly said that women should not be working in the maintenance department. White was reassigned from forklift duty to "track laborer" duties. Joiner was disciplined for his remarks. White's supervisor in her new job complained to Burlington officials that White had been insubordinate. She was suspended without pay but was later reinstated after an investigation. She was awarded back pay for the period of the suspension. Among other actions, White then filed a Title VII suit in federal district court, claiming that Burlington's acts of changing her job responsibilities and suspending her without pay amounted to unlawful retaliation. The jury found in White's favor and awarded her $43,500 in damages. On appeal to the U.S. Court of Appeals for the Sixth Circuit, the district court's judgment was affirmed. Burlington then appealed to the United States Supreme Court.

CASE 34.1 CONTINUED

- **Decision and Rationale** The United States Supreme Court affirmed the appellate court's judgment. The Court pointed out that "the anti-retaliation provision [of Title VII] seeks to secure that primary objective by preventing an employer from interfering (through retaliation) with an employee's efforts to secure or advance enforcement of the Act's basic guarantees. * * * The anti-retaliation provision seeks to prevent harm to individuals based on what they do, i.e., their conduct." All that a plaintiff in an anti-retaliation case must do is to show that a reasonable employee would have found the challenged action materially adverse. In this case, "the track labor duties were by all accounts more arduous and dirtier." Additionally, the forklift operator position required more qualifications, which was an indication of prestige. Finally, the forklift operator position was objectively considered a better job, and the male employees resented White for occupying it. "Based on this record, a jury could reasonably conclude that the reassignment of responsibilities would have been materially adverse to a reasonable employee."

- **What If the Facts Were Different?** *Assume that White had been reassigned to another job within Burlington that was considered to be of equal "prestige" and was no "dirtier" than her previous job as a forklift operator. Would the outcome of this case have been the same? Why or why not?*

- **The Ethical Dimension** *How might Burlington have avoided the initial problem of the supervisor's overt vocal animosity toward White because he did not want any females working in the maintenance department?*

Harassment by Co-Workers and Nonemployees Often, employees alleging harassment complain that the actions of co-workers, not supervisors, are responsible for creating a hostile working environment. In such cases, the employee still has a cause of action against the employer. Generally, though, the employer will be held liable only if it knew or should have known about the harassment and failed to take immediate remedial action.

Employers may also be liable for harassment by *nonemployees* under certain conditions. Suppose that a restaurant owner or manager knows that a particular customer repeatedly harasses a waitress and permits the harassment to continue. In this situation, the restaurant owner may be liable under Title VII even though the customer is not an employee of the restaurant. The issue turns on the control that the employer exerts over a nonemployee. In one case, the owner of a Pizza Hut franchise was held liable for the harassment of a waitress by two male customers because no steps were taken to prevent the harassment.[18]

In another case, a female sales representative at Merck & Company, Inc., was temporarily assigned to work in Mexico at Merck-Mexico (a subsidiary of Merck & Company). She claimed that she was being sexually harassed and informed the supervisor in Mexico, who allegedly warned her not to report the harassment to Merck's U.S. headquarters. When she filed a lawsuit, Merck argued that it should not be liable because the alleged harassers were employed by Merck-Mexico and not by the U.S.-based Merck & Company. Although the trial court granted a summary judgment in Merck's favor, an appellate court reversed that decision. The appellate court held that there was a sufficient issue of fact as to whether Merck and its corporate affiliate in Mexico could be considered a single employer for purposes of a Title VII claim. In other words, the court ruled that there was enough evidence of Merck's control over the alleged harassers for the employee to take her case to a jury trial.[19]

Same-Gender Harassment The courts have also had to address the issue of whether men who are harassed by other men, or women who are harassed by other women, are also protected by laws that prohibit gender-based discrimination in the workplace. For example, what if the male president of a firm demands sexual favors from a male employee? Does this action qualify as sexual harassment? For some time, the courts were widely split on this question. In 1998, in *Oncale v. Sundowner Offshore Services, Inc.*,[20] the Supreme Court resolved the issue by holding that Title VII protection extends to situations in which individuals are harassed by members of the same gender.

Nonetheless, it can be difficult to prove that the harassment in same-gender harassment cases is "based on sex." Suppose that a gay man is harassed by another man at the workplace. The harasser is not a homosexual and does not treat all men with

18. *Lockard v. Pizza Hut, Inc.*, 162 F.3d 1062 (10th Cir. 1998).

19. *Torres-Negron v. Merck & Co.*, 488 F.3d 34 (1st Cir. 2007).

20. 523 U.S. 75, 118 S.Ct. 998, 140 L.Ed.2d 207 (1998).

EMERGING TRENDS IN BUSINESS LAW

New Issues in Online Privacy and Employment Discrimination

As computers come to be used for more aspects of both personal and professional life, the line between personal use and work-related use is becoming blurred. As this chapter has explained, employers are legally required to prevent discrimination in the workplace, including a hostile environment created by workers' online activities. That employers have a right—or even obligation—to monitor their employees' computer use to this end is generally established. Indeed, as discussed in Chapter 33, courts generally have held that employees have no expectation of privacy in their workplace computers when a private employer supplies the equipment. The limits of this privacy exception are still being tested, however, as a number of issues related to computers, privacy, and employment discrimination remain unresolved. A new issue that is just emerging is whether employers can obtain information about job applicants by conducting online searches when asking for the same information on a job application or in an interview might be illegal.

Searches of Workplace Computers

An employee who uses his or her workplace computer to view sexually explicit photographs may create a hostile environment if the photographs can be seen by other employees. Furthermore, if the photographs involve children, the employee's activities may be illegal. Courts generally have held that employers can search a workplace computer for evidence of employee misconduct[a] and that they can also consent to a search by government officials. If the computer is in a locked office, however, does the employee have a greater expectation of privacy? In *United States v. Ziegler*[b] in 2007, the court had to answer this question.

The Internet service provider for Frontline Processing Corporation informed the Federal Bureau of Investigation (FBI) that one of Frontline's computers had been used to access child-pornography Web sites in violation of federal criminal law. The FBI investigated and determined that Jeffrey Ziegler, Frontline's director of operations, had used the computer in his office to search for and view online photos of "very young girls in various states of undress." Frontline agreed to cooperate with the FBI, and at some point, corporate employees entered Ziegler's locked office and made a backup copy of the hard drive on his computer without his consent.

Ziegler appealed his subsequent conviction for possessing child pornography on the ground that the search of his computer violated his Fourth Amendment rights against unreasonable search and seizure. The U.S. Court of Appeals for the Ninth Circuit first held that Ziegler had no reasonable expectation of privacy, but on rehearing, the court changed its ruling and held that Ziegler did have a reasonable expectation of privacy in the contents of the computer in his locked office. Because the employer (Frontline) owned the computer, however, the court held that Frontline's consent validated the search. According to the court, a "computer is the type of workplace property that remains within control of the employer 'even if the employee has placed personal items in it.' "

Unresolved Issues

Certainly, the trend is clearly toward limiting employees' expectations of privacy in employer-owned computers in the workplace, but several questions still remain open.

What expectations of privacy does an employee have in a laptop computer that is provided by the company but is used by the

a. See, for example, *Twymon v. Wells Fargo & Co.*, 462 F.3d 925 (8th Cir. 2006); and *Griffis v. Pinal County*, 213 Ariz. 300, 141 P.3d 780 (2006).

b. 474 F.3d 1184 (9th Cir. 2007). See also *Doe v. XYC Corp.*, 382 N.J.Super. 122, 887 A.2d 1156 (2005).

hostility—just this one man. Does the victim in this situation have a cause of action under Title VII? A court may find that the harasser's conduct does not qualify as sexual harassment under Title VII because it was based on the employee's sexual orientation, not on his "sex."[21]

Note that although Title VII does not prohibit discrimination or harassment based on a person's sexual orientation, a growing number of companies are voluntarily establishing nondiscrimination policies that include sexual orientation. According to some reports, at the end of 2006, approximately 80 percent of the companies in the Fortune 500 had banned workplace discrimination on the basis of sexual orientation.[22] In addition, an increasing number of states have passed legislation that explicitly prohibits sexual orientation discrimination in the workplace.[23]

21. See, for example, *McCown v. St. John's Health System*, 349 F.3d 540 (8th Cir. 2003); and *Rene v. MGM Grand Hotel, Inc.*, 305 F.3d 1061 (9th Cir. 2002).

22. Marc Gunther, "Corporate America backs gay rights: Gay rights are good business, no matter the politics," April 26, 2006, as reported on *Plugged In*, a daily column by writers of *Fortune* magazine.

23. See, for example, 775 Illinois Compiled Statutes 5/1–103.

employee at home or on the road? Similarly, if the employee works at home on an employer-owned computer, to what degree can the employer justify monitoring the employee's online activities? Although computers in remote locations could be used to send harassing e-mail, other employees are unlikely to view offensive material on such computers, so that justification for monitoring Internet use seems less valid.

Other issues have to do with whether employers must tell employees that their computer use will be monitored and the degree to which employers should monitor employees' online activities that are mostly personal. To date, only two states (Connecticut and Delaware) have passed laws specifically requiring private employers to inform employees that their workplace Internet activities will be monitored. Personal blogs raise an even more complex issue: Does an employer have the right to monitor its employees' personal blogs? If an employee's personal blog contains racially or sexually offensive comments about co-workers, what should the employer do? Thus far, in most of the cases involving employees dismissed for computer misuse, the employer had a written Internet policy and presented evidence that the employee knew about and disregarded the policy. According to recent surveys, however, most organizations do not have policies on employees' blogs.

Facebook, MySpace, and Job Applications

Even more problematic is another issue that is just emerging. Today, many college students and recent graduates belong to social networking sites such as Facebook.com and MySpace.com, at which they can post photographs, comments, blogs, or even videos about themselves. Some of this material is sexually suggestive, to say the least. A number of employers have begun to use search engines to search for information on job applicants. A search may turn up photos that the applicant intended to be viewed only by close friends. Such searches may reveal information about the applicant's marital status, sexual orientation, or political or religious views that the employer could not ask for on a job application or discuss in a job interview. Nevertheless, this information is now readily available to employers.

Some colleges and employment counselors are beginning to advise job seekers to make sure that they remove any information they do not want a prospective employer to see, but the issue of whether employers have a right to search for this information is likely to persist.

IMPLICATIONS FOR THE BUSINESSPERSON

1. Employers should explicitly inform all employees that their company-provided computers, even if used at home, can be monitored by the employer.
2. It is not illegal for employers to conduct an online search for information about job applicants, including their blogs and their postings at social networks such as Facebook and MySpace.

FOR CRITICAL ANALYSIS

1. Suppose that an employee writes a message to like-minded persons concerning religious beliefs or political views. Can the employee be fired in that situation? Who decides what is acceptable Internet activity when there is no written policy?
2. How might an employee avoid the possibility that his or her employer will discover objectionable items on the employee's computer?

RELEVANT WEB SITES

To locate information on the Web concerning the issues discussed in this feature, go to this text's Web site at **www.cengage.com/blaw/jentz**, select "Chapter 34," and click on "Emerging Trends."

Online Harassment

Employees' online activities can create a hostile working environment in many ways. Racial jokes, ethnic slurs, or other comments contained in e-mail may become the basis for a claim of hostile-environment harassment or other forms of discrimination. A worker who regularly sees sexually explicit images on a co-worker's computer screen may find the images offensive and claim that they create a hostile working environment. For a discussion of some new areas in which an employer may potentially be liable for an employee's online conduct, see this chapter's *Emerging Trends* feature.

Nevertheless, employers may be able to avoid liability for online harassment by taking prompt remedial action. For example, in one case Angela Daniels, an employee under contract to WorldCom Corporation, received racially harassing e-mailed jokes from another employee. After receiving the jokes, Daniels complained to WorldCom managers. Shortly afterward, the company issued a warning to the offending employee about the proper use of the e-mail system and held two meetings to discuss company policy on the use of the system. In Daniels's discrimination suit against WorldCom, a federal district court concluded that the employer was not liable for its employee's racially harassing e-mails because the employer took prompt remedial action.[24]

Remedies under Title VII

Employer liability under Title VII may be extensive. If the plaintiff successfully proves that unlawful discrimination occurred, he or she may be awarded reinstatement, back pay, retroactive promotions, and damages. Compensatory damages are available only in cases of intentional discrimination. Punitive damages may be recovered against a private employer only if the employer acted with malice or reckless indifference to an individual's rights. The statute limits the total amount of compensatory and punitive damages that the plaintiff can recover from specific employers (ranging from $50,000 against employers with one hundred or fewer employees to $300,000 against employers with more than five hundred employees).

SECTION 2 Discrimination Based on Age

Age discrimination is potentially the most widespread form of discrimination, because anyone—regardless of race, color, national origin, or gender—could be a victim at some point in life. The Age Discrimination in Employment Act (ADEA) of 1967, as amended, prohibits employment discrimination on the basis of age against individuals forty years of age or older. The act also prohibits mandatory retirement for nonmanagerial workers. The United States Supreme Court has made it clear that the text and the legislative history of the ADEA show that it was meant to protect relatively old workers from discrimination that gives an unfair advantage to the relatively young. Therefore, the ADEA does not necessarily prohibit an employer from eliminating a health-insurance benefits program for workers under age fifty but retaining the program for workers over fifty.[25]

For the act to apply, an employer must have twenty or more employees, and the employer's business activities must affect interstate commerce. The EEOC administers the ADEA, but the act also permits private causes of action against employers for age discrimination.

Procedures under the ADEA

The burden-shifting procedure under the ADEA is similar to that under Title VII. If a plaintiff can establish that he or she (1) was a member of the protected age group, (2) was qualified for the position from which he or she was discharged, and (3) was discharged under circumstances that give rise to an inference of discrimination, the plaintiff has established a *prima facie* case of unlawful age discrimination. The burden then shifts to the employer, who must articulate a legitimate reason for the discrimination. If the plaintiff can prove that the employer's reason is only a pretext and that the plaintiff's age was a determining factor in the employer's decision, the employer will be held liable under the ADEA.

Sometimes, large companies go through what they call a restructuring, during which they reduce the size of their overall workforce by, say, two thousand employees. When a laid-off worker subsequently files a suit against the company for age discrimination, a trial may ensue. In the following case, the question before the United States Supreme Court was what type of testimony should be allowed at trial.

24. *Daniels v. WorldCom Corp.*, 1998 WL 91261 (N.D.Tex. 1998). See also *Musgrove v. Mobil Oil Corp.*, 2003 WL 21653125 (N.D.Tex. 2003).

25. *General Dynamics Land Systems, Inc. v. Cline*, 540 U.S. 581, 124 S.Ct. 1236, 157 L.Ed.2d 1094 (2004).

CASE 34.2 Sprint/United Management Co. v. Mendelsohn

Supreme Court of the United States, 2008. ___ U.S. ___, 128 S.Ct. 1140, 170 L.Ed.2d 1.

• **Background and Facts** Ellen Mendelsohn worked for Sprint/United Management Company (Sprint) from 1989 to 2002, when Sprint fired her during a companywide reduction in the workforce. Mendelsohn, who was fifty-one years old at the time, sued under the Age Discrimination in Employment Act (ADEA), alleging disparate treatment based on her age. Five other former Sprint employees testified that they had also suffered discrimination based on age.

CASE 34.2 CONTINUED Three of these employees said that they had heard managers make remarks belittling older workers and indicating that age was a planning factor in who was fired during the workforce reduction. None of the five witnesses worked in the same part of the company as Mendelsohn and could not testify about her supervisors. The district court excluded their testimony as to the impact on Mendelsohn because the witnesses were not "similarly situated" in the company. The district court, nonetheless, held that these witnesses could testify about the workforce reduction being a pretext for age discrimination in general by the employer. The appeals court held that the testimony was *per se* not relevant and had to be excluded. Mendelsohn appealed to the United States Supreme Court.

• **Decision and Rationale** The United States Supreme Court held that the appeals court had gone too far in excluding all testimony offered by the witnesses. It should have allowed the district court to have more control over the evidence. The trial court should have allowed the evidence provided by the witnesses to be studied in more detail to see if the witnesses were providing credible evidence of a discriminatory policy at Sprint that was played out through the reduction in the workforce. The courts had to assess the value of such evidence. They could not simply reject evidence that did not directly address the attitude of Mendelsohn's immediate supervisors.

• **What If the Facts Were Different?** *In this case, supervisors in other parts of the company were reported to have made the negative comments about older workers. Assume that a witness testified that one of Mendelsohn's supervisors had made such comments. How might the result of this case been different with this testimony?*

• **The Legal Environment Dimension** *What steps should employers take within an organization to reduce the likelihood of such age discrimination lawsuits?*

Replacing Older Workers with Younger Workers

Numerous age discrimination cases have been brought against employers who, to cut costs, replaced older, higher-salaried employees with younger, lower-salaried workers. Whether a firing is discriminatory or simply part of a rational business decision to prune the company's ranks is not always clear. Companies typically defend a decision to discharge a worker by asserting that the worker could no longer perform her or his duties or that the worker's skills were no longer needed.

The employee must prove that the discharge was motivated, at least in part, by age bias. Proof that qualified older employees are generally discharged before employees who are younger or that co-workers continually made unflattering age-related comments about the discharged worker may be enough. The plaintiff does not need to prove that she or he was replaced by a person "outside the protected class" (under the age of forty years), so long as the replacement is younger (or substantially younger) than the plaintiff. Nevertheless, the bigger the age gap, the more likely the individual is to succeed in showing age discrimination.

State Employees Not Covered by the ADEA

Generally, the states are immune under the Eleventh Amendment from lawsuits brought by private individuals in federal court—unless a state consents to the suit. For example, in separate cases, professors and librarians contended that their employers—two Florida state universities—denied them salary increases and other benefits because they were getting old and their successors could be hired at lower cost. The universities claimed that as agencies of a sovereign state, they could not be sued without the state's consent. The cases ultimately reached the United States Supreme Court, which held that the Eleventh Amendment bars private parties from suing state employers for violations of the ADEA.[26]

State immunity under the Eleventh Amendment is not absolute, however, as the Supreme Court explained in 2004. In some situations, such as when fundamental rights are at stake, Congress has the power to abrogate

26. *Kimel v. Florida Board of Regents,* 528 U.S. 62, 120 S.Ct. 631, 145 L.Ed.2d 522 (2000).

(abolish) state immunity to private suits through legislation that unequivocally shows Congress's intent to subject states to private suits.[27] Generally, though, the Court has found that state employers are immune from private suits brought by employees under the ADEA (for age discrimination), the Americans with Disabilities Act (for disability-based discrimination),[28] and the Fair Labor Standards Act (the wage and hour laws that were discussed in Chapter 33).[29] As explained in Chapter 33, state employers are not immune from the requirements of the Family and Medical Leave Act (FMLA).[30]

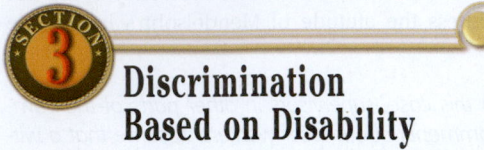

SECTION 3 Discrimination Based on Disability

The Americans with Disabilities Act (ADA) of 1990 is designed to eliminate discriminatory employment practices that prevent otherwise qualified workers with disabilities from fully participating in the national labor force. Prior to 1990, the major federal law providing protection to those with disabilities was the Rehabilitation Act of 1973. That act protected only federal government employees and those employed under federally funded programs. The ADA extends federal protection against disability-based discrimination to all workplaces with fifteen or more workers (with the exception of state government employers, who are generally immune under the Eleventh Amendment, as just discussed). Basically, the ADA requires that employers "reasonably accommodate" the needs of persons with disabilities unless to do so would cause the employer to suffer an "undue hardship."

Procedures under the ADA

To prevail on a claim under the ADA, a plaintiff must show that he or she (1) has a disability, (2) is otherwise qualified for the employment in question, and (3) was excluded from the employment solely because of the disability. As in Title VII cases, a claim alleging violation of the ADA may be commenced only after the plaintiff has pursued the claim through the EEOC, which administers the provisions of the act relating to disability-based discrimination in the employment context. The EEOC may decide to investigate and perhaps even sue the employer on behalf of the employee. The EEOC can bring a suit on behalf of the employee under the ADA even if the employee signed an arbitration agreement with the employer.[31]

If the EEOC decides not to sue, then the employee may do so. Plaintiffs in lawsuits brought under the ADA may seek many of the same remedies that are available under Title VII. These include reinstatement, back pay, a limited amount of compensatory and punitive damages (for intentional discrimination), and certain other forms of relief. Repeat violators may be ordered to pay fines of up to $100,000.

What Is a Disability?

The ADA broadly defines *persons with disabilities* as persons with physical or mental impairments that "substantially limit" their everyday activities. More specifically, the ADA defines a *disability* as "(1) a physical or mental impairment that substantially limits one or more of the major life activities of such individuals; (2) a record of such impairment; or (3) being regarded as having such an impairment."

Health conditions that have been considered disabilities under federal law include blindness, alcoholism, heart disease, cancer, muscular dystrophy, cerebral palsy, paraplegia, diabetes, acquired immune deficiency syndrome (AIDS), testing positive for the human immunodeficiency virus (HIV, the virus that causes AIDS), and morbid obesity (which exists when an individual's weight is two times that of a normal person). The ADA excludes from coverage certain conditions, such as kleptomania (the obsessive desire to steal).

Although the ADA's definition of disability is broad, starting in 1999, the United States Supreme Court has issued a series of decisions narrowing the definition of what constitutes a disability under the act.

Correctable Conditions In 1999, the Supreme Court reviewed a case raising the issue of whether severe myopia, or nearsightedness, which can be corrected with lenses, qualifies as a disability under the ADA. The Supreme Court ruled that it does not.[32] The determination of whether a person is substantially lim-

27. *Tennessee v. Lane,* 541 U.S. 509, 124 S.Ct. 1978, 158 L.Ed.2d 820 (2004).
28. *Board of Trustees of the University of Alabama v. Garrett,* 531 U.S. 356, 121 S.Ct. 955, 148 L.Ed.2d 866 (2001).
29. *Alden v. Maine,* 527 U.S. 706, 119 S.Ct. 2240, 144 L.Ed.2d 636 (1999).
30. *Nevada Department of Human Resources v. Hibbs,* 538 U.S. 721, 123 S.Ct. 1972, 155 L.Ed.2d 953 (2003).
31. This was the Supreme Court's ruling in *EEOC v. Waffle House, Inc.,* 534 U.S. 279, 122 S.Ct. 754, 151 L.Ed.2d 755 (2002).
32. *Sutton v. United Airlines, Inc.,* 527 U.S. 471, 119 S.Ct. 2139, 144 L.Ed.2d 450 (1999).

ited in a major life activity is based on how the person functions when taking medication or using corrective devices, not on how the person functions without these measures.

In a similar case in 2002, a federal appellate court held that a pharmacist suffering from diabetes, which could be corrected by insulin, did not have a cause of action against his employer under the ADA.[33] In other cases decided in the early 2000s, the courts have held that plaintiffs with bipolar disorder, epilepsy, and other such conditions do *not* fall under the ADA's protections if the conditions can be corrected.

Repetitive-Stress Injuries For some time, the courts were divided on the issue of whether carpal tunnel syndrome (or any other repetitive-stress injury) constitutes a disability under the ADA. Carpal tunnel syndrome is a condition of pain and weakness in the hand caused by repetitive compression of a nerve in the wrist. In 2002, in a case involving this issue, the Supreme Court unanimously held that it does not. The Court stated that although the employee could not perform the manual tasks associated with her job, the condition did not constitute a disability under the ADA because it did not "substantially limit" the major life activity of performing manual tasks.[34]

Reasonable Accommodation

If a job applicant or an employee with a disability can perform essential job functions with reasonable accommodation, the employer must make the accommodation. Required modifications may include installing ramps for a wheelchair, establishing flexible working hours, creating or modifying job assignments, and designing or improving training materials and procedures.

Generally, employers should give primary consideration to employees' preferences in deciding what accommodations should be made. If an applicant or employee fails to let the employer know how his or her disability can be accommodated, the employer may avoid liability for failing to hire or retain the individual on the ground that the individual has failed to meet the "otherwise qualified" requirement.

Undue Hardship Employers who do not accommodate the needs of persons with disabilities must demonstrate that the accommodations would cause *undue hardship*. Generally, the law offers no uniform standards for identifying what is an undue hardship other than the imposition of a "significant difficulty or expense" on the employer.

Usually, the courts decide whether an accommodation constitutes an undue hardship on a case-by-case basis. Suppose that Bryan Lockhart works for a cell phone company that provides parking to its employees. Lockhart, who uses a wheelchair, informs the company supervisors that the parking spaces are so narrow that he is unable to extend the ramp on his van that allows him to get in and out of the vehicle. Lockhart therefore requests that the company reasonably accommodate his needs by paying a monthly fee for him to use a larger parking space in an adjacent lot. In this situation, a court would likely find that it would not be an undue hardship for the employer to pay for additional parking for Lockhart.

Job Applications and Preemployment Physical Exams Employers must modify their job-application and selection process so that those with disabilities can compete for jobs with those who do not have disabilities. A job announcement that has only a phone number, for example, would discriminate against potential job applicants with hearing impairments. Thus, the job announcement must also provide another way for applicants to contact the prospective employer. Employers are also restricted in the kinds of questions they may ask on job-application forms and during preemployment interviews. (For a discussion on interviewing job applicants with disabilities, see this chapter's *Business Application* feature on page 658.)

Additionally, employers cannot require persons with disabilities to submit to preemployment physicals unless such exams are required of all other applicants. An employer can condition an offer of employment on the applicant's successfully passing a medical examination, but can disqualify the applicant only if the medical problems discovered would render the applicant unable to perform the job. For example, when filling the position of delivery truck driver, a company cannot screen out all applicants who are unable to meet the U.S. Department of Transportation's hearing standard. The company would first have to prove that drivers who are deaf are not qualified to perform the essential job function of driving safely and pose a higher risk of accidents than drivers who are not deaf.[35]

33. *Orr v. Walmart Stores, Inc.*, 297 F.3d 720 (8th Cir. 2002).
34. *Toyota Motor Manufacturing, Kentucky, Inc. v. Williams*, 534 U.S. 184, 122 S.Ct. 681, 151 L.Ed.2d 615 (2002).
35. *Bates v. United Parcel Service, Inc.*, 465 F.3d 1069 (9th Cir. 2006).

BUSINESS APPLICATION
Interviewing Job Applicants with Disabilities

MANAGEMENT FACES A LEGAL ISSUE

Many employers have been held liable under the Americans with Disabilities Act (ADA) because they have asked the wrong questions when interviewing job applicants with disabilities. The Equal Employment Opportunity Commission (EEOC) has issued guidelines about which questions employers may or may not ask job applicants with disabilities. For example, an interviewer may ask a job applicant whether he or she can meet the company's attendance requirements. In contrast, the interviewer cannot ask how many days a person was sick in the previous year. An employer can ask applicants whether they can do the job. An employer, however, cannot ask how an applicant would do the job *unless* the disability is obvious, the applicant brings up the subject during the interview, or the employer asks the question of all applicants for that particular job. After a job offer is made, employers are allowed to ask the applicant questions concerning her or his disability, including questions about previous workers' compensation claims or the extent of, say, a drinking or drug problem.

WHAT THE COURTS SAY

In one case, the job applicant suffered from a hearing disability. He alleged that the potential employer discriminated against him because of his deafness disability when he applied for a position as an information technology specialist. At trial, one of the key issues was how the interview was performed. The interviewer claimed that he had no concerns about the applicant's deafness. But at one point during the interview, the interviewer passed a handwritten note asking the applicant, "How do you communicate in offices where no one can sign?" The applicant responded, "I have no problem with writing as my basic communication." The court pointed out that the interviewer did not ask this question of any other applicant. Although the applicant ultimately did not prevail at trial, the court made it clear that the interviewer should not have asked any special questions of the applicant.[a]

In another case, an applicant sued the federal government after applying for the position of bank examiner. He claimed that during an interview, there was an improper inquiry about his perceived disability. In fact, the applicant had previously suffered a stroke and slurred his words when he spoke. During the interview, he was asked what was wrong with his arm and whether his disability affected his mental coherence. Ultimately, the applicant lost his case because he had lied on his résumé. Nonetheless, the defendants would have had an easier time at trial had the interviewer followed the EEOC guidelines.[b]

IMPLICATIONS FOR MANAGERS

Most managers should consult with an attorney who specializes in employment regulation when preparing for job interviews. In particular, they should review the kinds of questions typically asked of job applicants during interviews or following employment offers. Any questions that increase the risk of a lawsuit from an applicant with disabilities must be altered. All questions should be consistent with EEOC guidelines. Anyone who interviews job applicants should be informed of what questions can and cannot be asked of candidates with disabilities. It is important to note, however, that a manager is allowed to ask a candidate who has been offered a job for his or her medical documents in order to verify the nature of the applicant's disability.

a. *Adeyemi v. District of Columbia,* __ F.Supp.2d __, 2007 WL 1020754 (D.D.C. 2007).

b. *Strong v. Paulson,* __ F.3d __, 2007 WL 2859789 (7th Cir. 2007). See also, *Lorah v. Tetra Tech, Inc.,* 541 F.Supp.2d 629 (D.Del. 2008).

Substance Abusers Drug addiction is considered a disability under the ADA because it is a substantially limiting impairment. Note that the ADA only protects persons with *former* drug addictions—those who have completed a supervised drug-rehabilitation program or who are currently participating in a supervised rehabilitation program. Those who are currently using illegal drugs are not protected by the act, nor are persons who have used drugs casually in the past. They are not considered addicts and therefore do not have a disability (addiction).

People suffering from alcoholism are protected by the ADA. Employers cannot legally discriminate against employees simply because they suffer from alcoholism and must treat them the same way other employees are treated. For example, an employee with alcoholism who comes to work late because she or he was drinking excessively the night before cannot be disciplined any differently than an employee who comes to work late for another reason. Of course, employers have the right to prohibit the use of alcohol in the workplace and can require that employees not be under the influence of alcohol while working. Employers can also fire or refuse to hire a person with alcoholism if he or she poses a substantial risk of harm either to himself or herself or to others and the risk cannot be reduced by reasonable accommodation.

Health-Insurance Plans Workers with disabilities must be given equal access to any health insurance provided to other employees. Nevertheless, employers can exclude from coverage preexisting health conditions and certain types of diagnostic or surgical procedures. An employer can also put a limit, or cap, on health-care payments under its particular group health policy as long as the cap is applied equally to all insured employees and does not discriminate on the basis of disability. Whenever a group health-care plan makes a disability-based distinction in its benefits, the plan violates the ADA (unless the employer can justify its actions under the business necessity defense, as will be discussed later in this chapter).

Association Discrimination

The ADA contains an "association provision" that protects qualified individuals from employment discrimination based on a known disability of a person with whom the qualified individual is known to have a relationship or an association.[36] The purpose of this provision is to prevent employers from taking adverse employment actions based on stereotypes or assumptions about individuals who associate with people who have disabilities. An employer cannot, for instance, refuse to hire the parent of a child with a disability based on the assumption that the person will miss work too often or be unreliable.

To establish a *prima facie* case of association discrimination under the ADA, the plaintiff must show that she or he (1) was qualified for the job, (2) was subjected to adverse employment action, and (3) was known by her or his employer to have a relative or an associate with a disability. In addition, the plaintiff must show that the adverse employment action occurred under circumstances raising a reasonable inference that the disability of the relative or associate was a determining factor in the employer's decision.

In the following case, a man claimed that his employer unlawfully discriminated against him based on his wife's disability. Although the case involved a state law that offers slightly more protection than the ADA, the opinion shows how courts analyze association discrimination claims.

36. 42 U.S.C. Section 12112(b)(4).

CASE 34.3 Francin v. Mosby, Inc.

Missouri Court of Appeals, Eastern District, Division Three, 2008. 248 S.W.3d 619.
www.courts.mo.gov[a]

Background and Facts Randall Francin began working at Mosby, Inc., (doing business as Elsevier) in 1991. He worked as a production assistant until March 2002, when his position was eliminated within the company due to organizational restructuring. Francin was rehired a few months later as an associate database publishing editor. In his new position, Francin updated drug information and proofread information contained in drug inserts. In 2003, Francin's wife was diagnosed with amyotrophic lateral sclerosis (ALS). He discussed his potential rights for leave under the Family and Medical Leave Act (discussed in Chapter 33) with a representative from the human resources department at Elsevier. Francin received a "merit award increase" in salary in January 2004. Later in 2004, Francin's supervisor resigned. During an interview with a new boss, Francin mentioned his wife's illness. On September 21, 2004, Francin was fired. Francin filed a suit under the Missouri Human Rights Act (MHRA), alleging that Elsevier had discriminated against him because

a. Click on "Opinions & Minutes" under the "Quick Links" menu. Select the link for opinions from the Missouri Court of Appeals, Eastern District, and scroll down to the listings under the date 1/8/08. Find the plaintiff's name "Randall Francin" and click on it to access the opinion (the line ends with the case number ED89814). This is the official Web site of the Missouri courts.

CASE CONTINUES

CASE 34.3 CONTINUED of his association with a person with a disability. Elsevier filed a motion for summary judgment, which was granted by the trial court. Francin appealed to a state intermediate appellate court.

- **Decision and Rationale** The Missouri Court of Appeals, Eastern District, reversed the trial court's decision and remanded the case for further proceedings. The reviewing court said that claims for discrimination because of association with a person protected by Missouri's version of the Americans with Disabilities Act do not require that the employee actually take leave under the Family and Medical Leave Act. Francin argued on appeal that there was a "genuine issue of material fact concerning whether his wife's disability was a contributing factor causing his termination with the company." Francin pointed out that the evidence showed that he had satisfactory job performance ratings. Moreover, there was a suspiciously close timing between his termination and his discussions with his new boss about his wife's condition. The trial court erred in granting summary judgment in favor of Elsevier.

- **What If the Facts Were Different?** *Assume that Francin had only discussed his wife's illness with a human resources officer in the company and never mentioned it to his new boss. Would the outcome of the appeal have been different? Explain.*

- **The Ethical Dimension** *Did Elsevier have any ethical duty to keep Francin employed, even if he did indicate he might take time off under the Family and Medical Leave Act? Why or why not?*

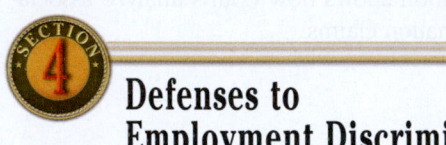

SECTION 4 Defenses to Employment Discrimination

The first line of defense for an employer charged with employment discrimination is, of course, to assert that the plaintiff has failed to meet his or her initial burden of proof—proving that discrimination did in fact occur. As noted, plaintiffs bringing cases under the ADA may find it difficult to meet this initial burden because they must prove that their alleged disabilities are disabilities covered by the ADA. Furthermore, plaintiffs in ADA cases must prove that they were otherwise qualified for the job.

Once a plaintiff succeeds in proving that discrimination occurred, then the burden shifts to the employer to justify the discriminatory practice. Often, employers attempt to justify the discrimination by claiming that it was the result of a business necessity, a bona fide occupational qualification, or a seniority system. Alternatively, they may assert that employee misconduct should limit their liability. In some situations, as noted earlier, an effective antiharassment policy and prompt remedial action when harassment occurs may shield employers from liability for sexual harassment under Title VII.

Business Necessity

An employer may defend against a claim of *disparate-impact* (unintentional) discrimination by asserting that a practice that has a discriminatory effect is a **business necessity.** If requiring a high school diploma, for example, is shown to have a discriminatory effect, an employer might argue that a high school education is required for workers to perform the job at a required level of competence. If the employer can demonstrate to the court's satisfaction that a definite connection exists between a high school education and job performance, then the employer normally will succeed in this business necessity defense.

Bona Fide Occupational Qualification

Another defense applies when discrimination against a protected class is essential to a job—that is, when a particular trait is a **bona fide occupational qualification (BFOQ).** Race, color, and national origin, however, can never be justified as a BFOQ.

Generally, courts have restricted the BFOQ defense to instances in which the employee's gender or religion is essential to the job. For example, a women's clothing boutique might legitimately hire only female salespersons if part of a salesperson's job involves assisting clients in the boutique's dressing rooms. Similarly, a state prison might legitimately respond to prior complaints of sexual abuse of female prisoners by hiring only female staff to work in the prison units housing women.[37]

Seniority Systems

An employer with a history of discrimination may have no members of protected classes in upper-level positions. Even if the employer now seeks to be unbiased, it may face a lawsuit seeking a court order that members of protected classes be promoted ahead of schedule to compensate for past discrimination. If no present intent to discriminate is shown, however, and if promotions or other job benefits are distributed according to a fair **seniority system** (in which workers with more years of service are promoted first or laid off last), the employer normally has a good defense against the suit.

According to the United States Supreme Court, this defense may also apply to claims of discrimination under the ADA. If an employee with a disability requests an accommodation (such as an assignment to a particular position) that conflicts with an employer's seniority system, the accommodation will generally not be considered "reasonable" under the act.[38]

After-Acquired Evidence of Employee Misconduct

In some situations, employers have attempted to avoid liability for employment discrimination on the basis of "after-acquired evidence" of an employee's misconduct. Suppose that an employer fires a worker, who then sues the employer for employment discrimination. During pretrial investigation, the employer learns that the employee made material misrepresentations on his employment application—misrepresentations that, had the employer known about them, would have served as a ground to fire the individual. Can this after-acquired evidence be used as a defense?

According to the United States Supreme Court, after-acquired evidence of wrongdoing cannot be used to shield an employer entirely from liability for employment discrimination. It may, however, be used to limit the amount of damages for which the employer is liable.[39]

SECTION 5 Affirmative Action

The laws discussed in this chapter were designed to reduce or eliminate discriminatory practices with respect to hiring, retaining, and promoting employees. **Affirmative action** programs go a step further and attempt to "make up" for past patterns of discrimination by giving members of protected classes preferential treatment in hiring or promotion. During the 1960s, all federal and state government agencies, private companies that contracted to do business with the federal government, and institutions that received federal funding were required to implement affirmative action policies.

Title VII of the Civil Rights Act of 1964 neither requires nor prohibits affirmative action. Thus, most private companies and organizations have not been required to implement affirmative action policies, though many have done so voluntarily.

Affirmative action programs have aroused much controversy during the last forty years, particularly when they result in *reverse discrimination*, which as mentioned previously, is discrimination against members of a majority group, such as white males. At issue is whether affirmative action programs, because of their inherently discriminatory nature, violate employee rights or the equal protection clause of the Fourteenth Amendment to the U.S. Constitution.

The *Bakke* Case

An early case addressing this issue outside the employment context, *Regents of the University of California v. Bakke*,[40] involved an affirmative action program implemented by the University of California at Davis. Allan Bakke, who had been turned down for medical school at the Davis campus, sued the university for reverse discrimination after he discovered that his academic record was better than the records of some of the minority applicants who had been admitted to the program.

37. *Everson v. Michigan Department of Corrections*, 391 F.3d 737 (6th Cir. 2004).

38. *U.S. Airways, Inc. v. Barnett*, 535 U.S. 391, 122 S.Ct. 1516, 152 L.Ed.2d 589 (2002).

39. *McKennon v. Nashville Banner Publishing Co.*, 513 U.S. 352, 115 S.Ct. 879, 130 L.Ed.2d 852 (1995). See also *EEOC v. Dial Corp.*, 469 F.3d 735 (8th Cir. 2006).

40. 438 U.S. 265, 98 S.Ct. 2733, 57 L.Ed.2d 750 (1978).

The United States Supreme Court held that affirmative action programs were subject to intermediate scrutiny. Recall from the discussion of the equal protection clause in Chapter 4 that any law or action evaluated under a standard of intermediate scrutiny, to be constitutionally valid, must be substantially related to important government objectives. Applying this standard, the Court held that the university could give favorable weight to minority applicants as part of a plan to increase minority enrollment so as to achieve a more culturally diverse student body. The Court stated, however, that the use of a quota system, in which a certain number of places are explicitly reserved for minority applicants, violated the equal protection clause of the Fourteenth Amendment.

The *Adarand* Case

Although the *Bakke* case and later court decisions alleviated the harshness of the quota system, today's courts are going even further in questioning the constitutional validity of affirmative action programs. In 1995, in its landmark decision in *Adarand Constructors, Inc. v. Peña,*[41] the United States Supreme Court held that any federal, state, or local affirmative action program that uses racial or ethnic classifications as the basis for making decisions is subject to strict scrutiny by the courts.

In effect, the Court's ruling in *Adarand* means that an affirmative action program is constitutional only if it attempts to remedy past discrimination and does not make use of quotas or preferences. Furthermore, once such a program has succeeded in the goal of remedying past discrimination, it must be changed or dropped. Since then, other federal courts have followed the Supreme Court's lead by declaring affirmative action programs invalid unless they attempt to remedy past or current discrimination.

The *Hopwood* Case

In 1996, in *Hopwood v. State of Texas,*[42] the U.S. Court of Appeals for the Fifth Circuit held that an affirmative action program at the University of Texas School of Law in Austin violated the equal protection clause. In that case, two white law school applicants sued the university when they were denied admission. The court decided that the affirmative action policy unlawfully discriminated in favor of minority applicants. In its decision, the court directly challenged the *Bakke* decision by stating that the use of race even as a means of achieving diversity on college campuses "undercuts the Fourteenth Amendment." The United States Supreme Court declined to hear the case, thus letting the lower court's decision stand. Federal appellate court decisions since then have been divided on whether such programs are constitutional.[43]

Subsequent Court Decisions

In 2003, the United States Supreme Court reviewed two cases involving issues similar to that in the *Hopwood* case. Both cases involved admissions programs at the University of Michigan. In *Gratz v. Bollinger,*[44] two white applicants who were denied undergraduate admission to the university alleged reverse discrimination. The school's admission policy gave each applicant a score based on a number of factors, including grade point average, standardized test scores, and personal achievements. The system *automatically* awarded every "underrepresented" minority (African American, Hispanic, and Native American) applicant twenty points—one-fifth of the points needed to guarantee admission. The Court held that this policy violated the equal protection clause.

In contrast, in *Grutter v. Bollinger,*[45] the Court held that the University of Michigan Law School's admission policy was constitutional. In that case, the Court concluded that "[u]niversities can, however, consider race or ethnicity more flexibly as a 'plus' factor in the context of individualized consideration of each and every applicant." The significant difference between the two admissions policies, in the Court's view, was that the law school's approach did not apply a mechanical formula giving "diversity bonuses" based on race or ethnicity.

In 2007, the United States Supreme Court ruled on two more cases involving racial classifications used in assigning students to schools in Seattle, Washington, and Jefferson County, Kentucky. Both school districts had adopted student assignment plans that relied on race to determine which schools certain children attended. The Seattle school district plan classified children as white or nonwhite and used the racial classifications as a "tiebreaker" to determine the particular

41. 515 U.S. 200, 115 S.Ct. 2097, 132 L.Ed.2d 158 (1995).

42. 84 F.3d 720 (5th Cir. 1996).

43. See, for example, *Johnson v. Board of Regents of the University of Georgia,* 263 F.3d 1234 (11th Cir. 2001); and *Smith v. University of Washington School of Law,* 233 F.3d 1188 (9th Cir. 2000).

44. 539 U.S. 244, 123 S.Ct. 2411, 156 L.Ed.2d 257 (2003).

45. 539 U.S. 306, 123 S.Ct. 2325, 156 L.Ed.2d 304 (2003).

high school students attended. The school district in Jefferson County classified students as black or other to assign children to elementary schools. A group of parents from the relevant public schools filed lawsuits claiming that the school districts' racial preferences violated the equal protection clause. The Supreme Court applied strict scrutiny and held that the school districts failed to show that use of racial classifications in their student assignment plans was necessary to achieve their stated goal of racial diversity.[46]

SECTION 6 State Laws Prohibiting Discrimination

Although the focus of this chapter is on federal legislation, most states also have statutes that prohibit employment discrimination. Generally, the same kinds of discrimination are prohibited under federal and state legislation. In addition, state statutes often provide protection for certain individuals who are not protected under federal laws. For example, a New Jersey appellate court held that anyone over the age of eighteen was entitled to sue for age discrimination under the state law, which specified no threshold age limit.[47]

Furthermore, state laws prohibiting discrimination may apply to firms with fewer employees than the threshold number required under federal statutes, thus offering protection to more workers. Even when companies are too small to be covered by state statutes, state courts may uphold employees' rights against discrimination in the workplace for public-policy reasons.[48] State laws may also provide for additional damages, such as damages for emotional distress, that are not provided for under federal statutes.[49] Finally, some states, such as California and Washington, have passed laws that end affirmative action programs in those states or modify admission policies at state-sponsored universities.

46. The Court consolidated the two cases and issued only one opinion to address the issues presented by both cases. *Parents Involved in Community Schools v. Seattle School Dist. No. 1*, ___ U.S. ___, 127 S.Ct. 2738, 168 L.Ed.2d 508 (2007).

47. *Bergen Commercial Bank v. Sisler*, 307 N.J.Super. 333, 704 A.2d 1017 (1998).

48. See, for example, *Roberts v. Dudley, D.V.M.*, 92 Wash.App. 652, 966 P.2d 377 (1998); and *Insignia Residential Corp. v. Ashton*, 359 Md. 560, 755 A.2d 1080 (2000).

49. For a reverse discrimination case in which a former police officer was awarded nearly $80,000 in emotional distress damages based on a violation of New Jersey's Law Against Discrimination, see *Klawitter v. City of Trenton*, 395 N.J.Super. 302, 928 A.2d 900 (2007).

REVIEWING Employment Discrimination

Amaani Lyle, an African American woman, was hired by Warner Brothers Television Productions to be a scriptwriters' assistant for the writers of *Friends,* a popular, adult-oriented television series. One of her essential job duties was to type detailed notes for the scriptwriters during brainstorming sessions in which they discussed jokes, dialogue, and story lines. The writers then combed through Lyle's notes after the meetings for script material. During these meetings, the three male scriptwriters told lewd and vulgar jokes and made sexually explicit comments and gestures. They often talked about their personal sexual experiences and fantasies, and some of these conversations were then used in episodes of *Friends.*

Lyle never complained that she found the writers' conduct during the meetings offensive. After four months, Lyle was fired because she could not type fast enough to keep up with the writers' conversations during the meetings. She filed a suit against Warner Brothers, alleging sexual harassment and claiming that her termination was based on racial discrimination. Using the information presented in the chapter, answer the following questions.

1. Would Lyle's claim of racial discrimination be for intentional (disparate-treatment) or unintentional (disparate-impact) discrimination? Explain.

REVIEWING CONTINUES

REVIEWING Employment Discrimination, Continued

2. Can Lyle establish a *prima facie* case of racial discrimination? Why or why not?
3. When Lyle was hired, she was told that typing speed was extremely important to the position. At the time, she maintained that she could type eighty words per minute, so she was not given a typing test. It later turned out that Lyle could type only fifty words per minute. What impact might typing speed have on Lyle's lawsuit?
4. Lyle's sexual-harassment claim is based on the hostile work environment created by the writers' sexually offensive conduct at meetings that she was required to attend. The writers, however, argue that their behavior was essential to the "creative process" of writing for *Friends,* a show that routinely contained sexual innuendos and adult humor. Which defense discussed in the chapter might Warner Brothers assert using this argument?

TERMS AND CONCEPTS

affirmative action 661
bona fide occupational qualification (BFOQ) 660
business necessity 660
constructive discharge 648
disparate-impact discrimination 646
disparate-treatment discrimination 646
employment discrimination 645
***prima facie* case 646**
protected class 645
seniority system 661
sexual harassment 649
tangible employment action 649

QUESTIONS AND CASE PROBLEMS

34–1. Discuss fully whether either of the following actions would constitute a violation of Title VII of the 1964 Civil Rights Act, as amended:

(a) Tennington, Inc., is a consulting firm and has ten employees. These employees travel on consulting jobs in seven states. Tennington has an employment record of hiring only white males.

(b) Novo Films is making a movie about Africa and needs to employ approximately one hundred extras for this picture. Novo advertises in all major newspapers in Southern California for the hiring of these extras. The ad states that only African Americans need apply.

34–2. QUESTION WITH SAMPLE ANSWER

Chinawa, a major processor of cheese sold throughout the United States, employs one hundred workers at its principal processing plant. The plant is located in Heartland Corners, which has a population that is 50 percent white and 25 percent African American, with the balance Hispanic American, Asian American, and others. Chinawa requires a high school diploma as a condition of employment for its cleaning crew. Three-fourths of the white population complete high school, compared with only one-fourth of those in the minority groups. Chinawa has an all-white cleaning crew. Has Chinawa violated Title VII of the Civil Rights Act of 1964? Explain.

• **For a sample answer to Question 34–2, go to Appendix I at the end of this text.**

34–3. Discrimination Based on Disability. PGA Tour, Inc., sponsors professional golf tournaments. A player may enter in several ways, but the most common method is to compete successfully in a three-stage qualifying tournament known as the "Q-School." Anyone may enter the Q-School by submitting two letters of recommendation and paying $3,000 to cover greens fees and the cost of a golf cart, which is permitted during the first two stages, but is prohibited during the third stage. The rules governing the events include the "Rules of Golf," which apply at all levels of amateur and professional golf and do not prohibit the use of golf carts, and the "hard card," which applies specifically to the PGA tour and requires the players to walk the course during most of a tournament. Casey Martin is a talented golfer with a degenerative circulatory disorder that prevents him from walking golf courses. Martin entered the Q-School and asked for permission to use a cart during the third stage. PGA refused. Martin filed a suit in a federal district court against PGA, alleging a violation of the Americans with Disabilities Act. Is a golf cart in these circumstances a "reasonable accommodation" under the ADA? Why or why not? [*PGA Tour, Inc. v. Martin,* 531 U.S. 1049, 121 S.Ct. 652, 148 L.Ed.2d 556 (2001)]

34–4. Discrimination Based on Age. The United Auto Workers (UAW) is the union that represents the employees of General Dynamics Land Systems, Inc. In 1997, a collective bargaining agreement between UAW and General Dynamics eliminated the company's obligation to provide health insurance to employees who retired after the date of the agreement, except for current workers at least fifty years of age. Dennis Cline and 194 other employees over the age of forty but under age fifty objected to this term. They complained to the Equal Employment Opportunity Commission, claiming that the agreement violated the Age Discrimination in Employment Act (ADEA) of 1967. The ADEA forbids discriminatory preference for the "young" over the "old." Does the ADEA also prohibit favoring the old over the young? How should the court rule? Explain. [*General Dynamics Land Systems, Inc. v. Cline,* 540 U.S. 581, 124 S.Ct. 1236, 157 L.Ed.2d 1094 (2004)]

34–5. CASE PROBLEM WITH SAMPLE ANSWER

Kimberly Cloutier began working at the Costco store in West Springfield, Massachusetts, in July 1997. Cloutier had multiple earrings and four tattoos, but no facial piercings. In June 1998, Costco promoted Cloutier to cashier. Over the next two years, she engaged in various forms of body modification, including facial piercing and cutting. In March 2001, Costco revised its dress code to prohibit all facial jewelry except earrings. Cloutier was told that she would have to remove her facial jewelry. She asked for a complete exemption from the code, asserting that she was a member of the Church of Body Modification and that eyebrow piercing was part of her religion. She was told to remove the jewelry, cover it, or go home. She went home and was later discharged for her absence. Cloutier filed a suit in a federal district court against Costco, alleging religious discrimination in violation of Title VII. Does an employer have an obligation to accommodate its employees' religious practices? If so, to what extent? How should the court rule in this case? Discuss. [*Cloutier v. Costco Wholesale Corp.,* 390 F.3d 126 (1st Cir. 2004)]

- **To view a sample answer for Problem 34–5, go to this book's Web site at www.cengage.com/blaw/jentz, select "Chapter 34," and click on "Case Problem with Sample Answer."**

34–6. Discrimination Based on Gender. For twenty years, Darlene Jespersen worked as a bartender at Harrah's Casino in Reno, Nevada. In 2000, Harrah's implemented a "Personal Best" program that included new grooming standards. Among other requirements, women were told to wear makeup "applied neatly in complimentary colors." Jespersen, who never wore makeup off the job, felt so uncomfortable wearing it on the job that it interfered with her ability to perform. Unwilling to wear makeup and not qualifying for another position at Harrah's with similar compensation, Jespersen quit the casino. She filed a suit in a federal district court against Harrah's Operating Co., the casino's owner, alleging that the makeup policy discriminated against women in violation of Title VII of the Civil Rights Act of 1964. Harrah's argued that any burdens under the new program fell equally on both genders, citing the "Personal Best" short-hair standard that applied only to men. Jespersen responded by describing her personal reaction to the makeup policy and emphasizing her exemplary record during her tenure at Harrah's. In whose favor should the court rule? Why? [*Jespersen v. Harrah's Operating Co.,* 444 F.3d 1104 (9th Cir. 2006)]

34–7. Discrimination Based on Disability. Cerebral palsy limits Steven Bradley's use of his legs. He uses forearm crutches for short-distance walks and a wheelchair for longer distances. Standing for more than ten or fifteen minutes is difficult. With support, however, Bradley can climb stairs and get on and off a stool. His condition also restricts the use of his fourth finger to, for example, type, but it does not limit his ability to write—he completed two years of college. His grip strength is normal, and he can lift heavy objects. In 2001, Bradley applied for a "greeter" or "cashier" position at a Wal-Mart Stores, Inc., Supercenter in Richmond, Missouri. The job description stated, "No experience or qualification is required." Bradley indicated that he was available for full- or part-time work from 4:00 P.M. to 10:00 P.M. any evening. His employment history showed that he currently worked as a proofreader and that he had previously worked as an administrator. His application was rejected, according to Janet Daugherty, the personnel manager, based on his "work history" and the "direct threat" that he posed to the safety of himself and others. Bradley claimed, however, that the store refused to hire him due to his disability. What steps must Bradley follow to pursue his claim? What does he need to show to prevail? Is he likely to meet these requirements? Discuss. [*EEOC v. Wal-Mart Stores, Inc.,* 477 F.3d 561 (8th Cir. 2007)]

34–8. A QUESTION OF ETHICS

Titan Distribution, Inc., employed Quintak, Inc., to run its tire mounting and distribution operation *in Des Moines, Iowa. Robert Chalfant worked for Quintak as a second shift supervisor at Titan. He suffered a heart attack in 1992 and underwent heart bypass surgery in 1997. He also had arthritis. In July 2002, Titan decided to terminate Quintak. Chalfant applied to work at Titan. On his application, he described himself as disabled. After a physical exam, Titan's physician concluded that Chalfant could work in his current capacity, and he was notified that he would be hired. Despite the notice, Nadis Barucic, a Titan employee, wrote "not pass px" at the top of his application, and he was not hired. He took a job with AMPCO Systems, a parking ramp management company. This work involved walking up to five miles a day and lifting more weight than he had at Titan. In September, Titan eliminated its second shift. Chalfant filed a suit in a federal district court against Titan, in part, under the Americans with Disabilities Act (ADA). Titan argued that it had not hired Chalfant because he did not pass the physical, but no one—including Barucic—could explain why she had written "not pass px" on his application. Later, Titan claimed that Chalfant was not hired because the entire second shift was going to be eliminated. [*Chalfant v. Titan Distribution, Inc.*, *475 F.3d 982 (8th Cir. 2007)]*

(a) What must Chalfant establish to make his case under the ADA? Can he meet these requirements? Explain.

(b) In employment-discrimination cases, punitive damages can be appropriate when an employer acts with malice or reckless indifference in regard to an employee's protected rights. Would an award of punitive damages to Chalfant be appropriate in this case? Discuss.

34–9. VIDEO QUESTION

Go to this text's Web site at **www.cengage.com/blaw/jentz** and select "Chapter 34." Click on "Video Questions" and view the video titled *Parenthood*. Then answer the following questions.

(a) In the video, Gil (Steve Martin) threatens to leave his job when he discovers that his boss is promoting another person to partner instead of him. His boss (Dennis Dugan) laughs and tells him that the threat is not realistic because if Gil leaves, he will be competing for positions with workers who are younger than he is and willing to accept lower salaries. If Gil takes his employer's advice and stays in his current position, can he sue his boss for age discrimination based on the boss's statements? Why or why not?

(b) Suppose that Gil leaves his current position and applies for a job at another firm. The prospective employer refuses to hire him based on his age. What would Gil have to prove to establish a *prima facie* case of age discrimination? Explain your answer.

(c) What defenses might Gil's current employer raise if Gil sues for age discrimination?

LAW ON THE WEB

For updated links to resources available on the Web, as well as a variety of other materials, visit this text's Web site at

www.cengage.com/blaw/jentz

The Employment Law Information Network provides access to many articles on age discrimination and other employment issues at

www.elinfonet.com/fedindex/2

The New York State Governor's Office of Employee Relations maintains an interactive site on sexual harassment and how to prevent sexual harassment in the workplace. Go to

www.goer.state.ny.us/Train/onlinelearning/SH/intro.html

An abundance of helpful information on disability-based discrimination, including the text of the Americans with Disabilities Act of 1990, can be found at the following Web site:

www.jan.wvu.edu/links/adalinks.htm

An excellent source for information on various forms of employment discrimination is the Equal Employment Opportunity Commission's Web site at

www.eeoc.gov

Legal Research Exercises on the Web

Go to **www.cengage.com/blaw/jentz**, the Web site that accompanies this text. Select "Chapter 34" and click on "Internet Exercises." There you will find the following Internet research exercises that you can perform to learn more about the topics covered in this chapter.

Internet Exercise 34–1: Legal Perspective
Americans with Disabilities

Internet Exercise 34–2: Management Perspective
Equal Employment Opportunity

Internet Exercise 34–3: Social Perspective
Religious and National-Origin Discrimination

UNIT SEVEN · FOCUS ON ETHICS

Agency and Employment

Ethical principles—and challenging ethical issues—pervade the areas of agency and employment. As you read in Chapter 31, when one person agrees to act on behalf of another, as an agent does in an agency relationship, that person assumes certain ethical responsibilities. Similarly, the principal also assumes certain ethical duties. In essence, agency law gives legal force to the ethical duties arising in an agency relationship. Although agency law also focuses on the rights of agents and principals, those rights are framed by the concept of duty—that is, an agent's duty becomes a right for the principal, and vice versa. Significantly, many of the duties of the principal and agent are negotiable when they form their contract. In forming a contract, the principal and the agent can extend or abridge many of the ordinary duties owed in such a relationship.

Employees who deal with third parties are also deemed to be agents and thus share the ethical (and legal) duties imposed under agency law. In the employment context, however, it is not always possible for an employee to negotiate favorable employment terms. Often, an employee who is offered a job must either accept the job on the employer's terms or look elsewhere for a position. Although numerous federal and state statutes protect employees, in some situations employees still have little recourse against their employers. At the same time, employers complain that statutes regulating employment relationships impose so many requirements that they find it hard to exercise a reasonable amount of control over their workplaces.

In the following paragraphs, we focus on the ethical dimensions of selected issues in agency and employment law.

The Agent's Duty to the Principal

The very nature of the principal-agent relationship is one of trust, which we call a fiduciary relationship. Because of the nature of this relationship, an agent is considered to owe certain duties to the principal. These duties include being loyal and obedient, informing the principal of important facts concerning the agency, accounting to the principal for property or funds received, and performing with reasonable diligence and skill.

Thus, ethical conduct would prevent an agent from representing two principals in the same transaction, making a secret profit from the agency relationship, or failing to disclose the agent's interest in property being purchased by the principal. The expected ethical conduct of the agent has evolved into rules that, if breached, cause the agent to be held legally liable.

Does an Agent Also Have a Duty to Society? A question that sometimes arises is whether an agent's obligation extends beyond the duty to the principal and includes a duty to society as well. Consider, for example, the situation faced by an employee who knows that her employer is engaging in an unethical—or even illegal—practice, such as marketing an unsafe product. Does the employee's duty to the principal include keeping silent about this practice, which may harm users of the product? Does the employee have a duty to protect consumers by disclosing this information to the public, even if she loses her job as a result? Some scholars have argued that many of the greatest evils in the past thirty years have been accomplished in the name of duty to the principal.

Does an Agent's Breach of Loyalty Terminate the Agent's Authority? Suppose that an employee-agent who is authorized to access company trade secrets contained in computer files takes those secrets to a competitor for whom the employee is about to begin working. Clearly, in this situation the agent has violated the ethical—and legal—duty of loyalty to the principal. Does this breach of loyalty mean that the employee's act of accessing the trade secrets was unauthorized? The question has significant implications because if the act was unauthorized, the employee will be subject to state and federal laws prohibiting unauthorized access to computer information and data. If the act was authorized, the employee will not be subject to such laws. Although one court has held that the moment the employee accessed trade secrets for the purpose of divulging them to a competitor, the employee's authority as an agent terminated,[1] most courts have held that an agent's authority continues.

In one case, for example, three employees of Lockheed Martin Corporation copied confidential information and trade secrets from Lockheed's computer network onto compact discs and BlackBerries (personal digital assistants). Lockheed had authorized the employee-agents to access these

1. *Shurgard Storage Centers, Inc. v. Safeguard Self Storage, Inc.*, 119 F.Supp.2d 1121 (W.D.Wash. 2000).

files but was understandably upset when the three resigned and went to work for a competitor taking the trade secrets with them. Lockheed sued the former agents under the Computer Fraud and Abuse Act (discussed in Chapter 6), arguing that they accessed the data without authorization. The federal district court, however, held that the individuals did have authorization to access the computer network and did not lose this authorization when they breached the duty of loyalty. Therefore, the court dismissed the case.[2]

The Principal's Duty to the Agent

Just as agents owe certain duties to their principals, so do principals owe duties to their agents, such as compensation and reimbursement for job-related expenses. Principals also owe their agents a duty of cooperation. One might expect principals to cooperate with their agents out of self-interest, but this does not always happen. Suppose that a principal hires an agent on commission to sell a building, and the agent puts considerable time and expense into finding a buyer. If the principal changes his mind and decides to retain the building, he may try to prevent the agent from completing the sale. Is such action ethical? Does it violate the principal's duty of cooperation? What alternatives would the principal have?

Although a principal is legally obligated to fulfill certain duties to the agent, these duties do not include any specific duty of loyalty. Some argue that employers' failure to be loyal to their employees has resulted in a reduction in employee loyalty to employers. After all, they maintain, why should an employee be loyal to an employer's interests over the years when the employee knows that the employer has no corresponding legal duty to be loyal to the employee's interests? Employers who do show a sense of loyalty toward their employees—for example, by not laying off longtime, faithful employees when business is slow or when those employees could be replaced by younger workers at lower cost—base that loyalty primarily on ethical, not legal, considerations.

Apparent Authority and Agency by Estoppel

Agency law is designed to enforce the ethical or fiduciary duties that arise once an agency relationship is established. To perhaps an even greater extent, agency law is designed to protect third parties—people outside the agency relationship. The doctrines of apparent authority and agency by estoppel stem primarily from ethical considerations that arise when third parties suffer a loss from an apparent agency relationship.

Sometimes, for example, a third party may be led by the actions of the principal to believe that an individual is acting in the capacity of an agent, when in fact the individual is not an agent at all. For instance, a patient treated by a physician in a hospital's emergency room may assume that the physician is an agent of the hospital, even though the physician is an independent contractor and has no agency relationship with the hospital. If the patient suffers harm because of the physician's negligence and sues the hospital, some courts may hold the hospital liable under a theory of apparent agency.

For example, in one case a man and his wife were shopping at a mall when the man experienced signs and symptoms of a stroke. His wife called an ambulance and asked the driver to take her husband to a hospital that could render emergency services for a stroke. He was taken to Kenner Regional Medical Center in Louisiana and seen by Dr. Roland LeBlanc. After many hours of waiting at Kenner Regional, the man's family had him transferred to another hospital for treatment of a stroke. Later, the family filed a lawsuit against Kenner Regional based on Dr. LeBlanc's negligent failure to render emergency services for the stroke in a timely manner. Because Dr. LeBlanc was not an employee but only an independent contractor at the hospital, the trial court granted a summary judgment dismissing Kenner Regional from the lawsuit. The appellate court reversed, however, reasoning that the man was entitled to assume that the treating physician at the emergency room was an employee of the hospital.[3] It would be unethical to allow the hospital to avoid liability for the negligent conduct of the physicians it has working in its emergency room simply because of the physicians' status as independent contractors.

Respondeat Superior

Another legal concept that addresses the effect of agency relationships on third parties is the doctrine of *respondeat superior.* This doctrine raises a significant

2. *Lockheed Martin Corp. v. Speed,* 2006 WL 2683058 (M.D.Fla. 2006). See also *Cenveo Corp. v. CelumSolutions Software GMBH & Co. KG,* 504 F.Supp.2d 574 (D.Minn. 2007).

3. *Arroyo v. East Jefferson General Hospital,* 956 So.2d 661 (La.App. 2007); see also the case presented in Chapter 32 as Case 32.1 *Ermoian v. Desert Hospital,* 152 Cal.App.4th 475, 61 Cal.Rptr.3d 754 (2007).

(Continued)

ethical question: Why should innocent employers be required to assume responsibility for the tortious, or wrongful, actions of their agent-employees? Again, the answer has to do with the courts' perception that when one of two innocent parties must suffer a loss, the party in the best position to prevent that loss should bear the burden. In an employment relationship, for example, the employer has more control over the employee's behavior than a third party to the relationship does.

Another reason for retaining the doctrine of *respondeat superior* in our laws is based on the employer's assumed ability to pay any damages that are incurred by a third party. One of our society's shared beliefs is that an injured party should be afforded the most effective relief possible. Thus, even though an employer may be absolutely innocent, the employer has "deeper pockets" than the employee and will be more likely to have the funds necessary to make the injured party whole.

Should an Employee Who Participates in Fraud Be Rewarded for Whistleblowing?

Many whistleblowing statutes reward employees who report their employers' wrongdoing with a percentage of the funds recovered after a lawsuit. In other words, employees have a strong financial incentive to offer up their employers for civil litigation. But what if the employee is somehow involved in the wrongdoing? Should the employee still receive a share of the proceeds?

Consider, for example, the largest Medicaid fraud settlement in U.S. history, involving a deal between Bayer Corporation and Kaiser Permanente, a health-maintenance organization. As one of Bayer's biggest customers, Kaiser demanded a discount price on Cipro, an antibiotic manufactured by Bayer. By law, however, Bayer could not sell the antibiotic to Kaiser for less than it sold Cipro to the federal government for use in the Medicaid program. (Medicaid helps low-income persons pay for necessary medical services.) If Bayer lowered the price of Cipro to Kaiser, it would have to refund millions of dollars to Medicaid. Therefore, Bayer "privately labeled" the same antibiotic using a different name and sold it to Kaiser at a 40 percent discount. Ironically, the person who blew the whistle on the fraudulent scheme—George Couto—was the marketing manager who actually negotiated the private labeling deal with Kaiser. Although Couto did not initiate the labeling scheme—and had suspected that it was illegal—he was instrumental in its success. Even though Couto had been a prime mover in the fraudulent scheme on behalf of Bayer, he was given 24 percent of the government's share of the $257 million settlement.[4]

Whistleblower statutes exist to encourage employees to report the wrongdoing of their employers with the ultimate objective of inhibiting such wrongdoing. But is it fair for an employee who participates in the employer's wrongdoing to benefit financially to such a large degree? Will this practice effectively inhibit, or could it even encourage, wrongful acts?

DISCUSSION QUESTIONS

1. How much obedience and loyalty does an agent-employee owe to an employer? What if the employer engages in an activity—or requests that the employee engage in an activity—that violates the employee's ethical standards but does not necessarily violate any public policy or law? In such a situation, does an employee's duty to abide by her or his own ethical standards override the employee's duty of loyalty to the employer?
2. When an agent acts in violation of his or her ethical or legal duty to the principal, should that action terminate the agent's authority to act on behalf of the principal? Why or why not?
3. If an agent-employee injures a third party during the course of employment, under the doctrine of *respondeat superior,* the employer may be held liable for the employee's action even though the employer did not authorize the action and was not even aware of it. Is it fair to hold the employer liable in this situation? Would it be more equitable if the employee alone was held liable for his or her tortious (legally wrongful) actions to third parties, even when the actions were committed within the scope of employment?
4. Should an employee who is involved in but later "blows the whistle" on an employer's wrongdoing be allowed to collect a financial reward under whistleblower statutes? Why or why not?

4. Peter Aronson, "A Rogue to Catch a Rogue," *The National Law Journal,* August 18–25, 2003.

UNIT EIGHT

Business Organizations

CONTENTS

CHAPTER 35

Sole Proprietorships and Franchises

Anyone who starts a business must first decide which form of business organization will be most appropriate for the new endeavor. In making this decision, the **entrepreneur** (one who initiates and assumes the financial risk of a new enterprise) needs to consider a number of factors, especially (1) ease of creation, (2) the liability of the owners, (3) tax considerations, and (4) the need for capital. In studying this unit, keep these factors in mind as you read about the various business organizational forms available to entrepreneurs. You may also find it helpful to refer to Exhibit 40–4 on pages 767 and 768 in Chapter 40, which compares the major business forms in use today with respect to these and other factors.

Traditionally, entrepreneurs have relied on three major business forms—the sole proprietorship, the partnership, and the corporation. In this chapter, we examine the sole proprietorship and the franchise, which, though not really a separate business organizational form, is widely used today by entrepreneurs. In Chapter 36, we will examine the second major traditional business form, the partnership, as well as some newer variations on partnerships. The third major traditional form—the corporation—will be discussed in detail in Chapters 38 through 41. We will also look at the limited liability company (LLC), a relatively new and increasingly popular form of business enterprise, and other special forms of business in Chapter 37. We conclude this unit with a chapter (Chapter 42) discussing practical legal information that all businesspersons should know, particularly those operating small businesses.

SECTION 1 Sole Proprietorships

The simplest form of business organization is a **sole proprietorship.** In this form, the owner is the business; thus, anyone who does business without creating a separate business organization has a sole proprietorship. More than two-thirds of all American businesses are sole proprietorships. They are usually small enterprises—about 99 percent of the sole proprietorships in the United States have revenues of less than $1 million per year. Sole proprietors can own and manage any type of business from an informal, home-office undertaking to a large restaurant or construction firm.

Advantages of the Sole Proprietorship

A major advantage of the sole proprietorship is that the proprietor owns the entire business and receives all of the profits (because she or he assumes all of the risk). In addition, starting a sole proprietorship is often easier and less costly than starting any other kind of business, as few legal formalities are required.[1] No documents need to be filed with the government to start a sole proprietorship (though a state business license may be required to operate certain businesses).

This type of business organization also provides more flexibility than does a partnership or a corporation. The sole proprietor is free to make any decision he or she wishes concerning the business—such as whom to hire, when to take a vacation, and what kind of business to pursue. In addition, the proprietor can sell or transfer all or part of the business to another party at

1. Although starting a sole proprietorship involves fewer legal formalities than other business organizational forms, even small sole proprietorships may need to comply with zoning requirements, obtain licenses, and the like.

any time and does not need approval from anyone else (as would be required from partners in a partnership or normally from shareholders in a corporation).

A sole proprietor pays only personal income taxes (including Social Security and Medicare taxes) on the business's profits, which are reported as personal income on the proprietor's personal income tax return. Sole proprietors are also allowed to establish certain tax-exempt retirement accounts.

Disadvantages of the Sole Proprietorship

The major disadvantage of the sole proprietorship is that, as sole owner, the proprietor alone bears the burden of any losses or liabilities incurred by the business enterprise. In other words, the sole proprietor has unlimited liability, or legal responsibility, for all obligations that arise in doing business. Any lawsuit against the business or its employees can lead to unlimited personal liability for the owner of a sole proprietorship. Creditors can go after the owner's personal assets to satisfy any business debts. This unlimited liability is a major factor to be considered in choosing a business form.

The sole proprietorship also has the disadvantage of lacking continuity on the death of the proprietor. When the owner dies, so does the business—it is automatically dissolved. Another disadvantage is that in raising capital, the proprietor is limited to his or her personal funds and any personal loans that he or she can obtain.

The personal liability of the owner of a sole proprietorship was at issue in the following case. The case involved the federal Cable Communications Act, which prohibits a commercial establishment from broadcasting television programs to its patrons without authorization. The court had to decide whether the owner of a sole proprietorship that installed a satellite television system was personally liable for violating this act by identifying a restaurant as a "residence" for billing purposes.

CASE 35.1 Garden City Boxing Club, Inc. v. Dominguez

United States District Court, Northern District of Illinois, Eastern Division, 2006. __ F.Supp.2d __.

Background and Facts Garden City Boxing Club, Inc. (GCB), which is based in San Jose, California, owned the exclusive right to broadcast via closed-circuit television several prizefights, including the match between Oscar De La Hoya and Fernando Vargas on September 14, 2002. GCB sold the right to receive the broadcasts to bars and other commercial venues. The fee was $20 multiplied by an establishment's maximum fire code occupancy. Antenas Enterprises in Chicago, Illinois, sells and installs satellite television systems under a contract with DISH Network. After installing a system, Antenas sends the buyer's address and other identifying information to DISH. In January 2002, Luis Garcia, an Antenas employee, identified a new customer as Jose Melendez at 220 Hawthorn Commons in Vernon Hills. The address was a restaurant—Mundelein Burrito—but Garcia designated the account as residential. Mundelein's patrons watched the De La Hoya–Vargas match on September 14, as well as three other fights on other dates, for which the restaurant paid only the residential rate to DISH and nothing to GCB. GCB filed a suit in a federal district court against Luis Dominguez, the sole proprietor of Antenas, to collect the fee.

Decision and Rationale The court issued a summary judgment in GCB's favor, holding that the plaintiff was entitled to the amount of the fee, plus damages and attorneys' fees. The court found that Mundelein was clearly a commercial establishment. "The structure of the building, an exterior identification sign, and its location in a strip mall made this obvious." Under the Cable Communications Act, "an authorized intermediary of a communication violates the Act when it divulges communication through an electronic channel to one other than the addressee." Antenas's improper designation of Mundelein as residential allowed the unauthorized broadcast of four prizefights to the restaurant. Antenas is a sole proprietorship. A sole proprietorship has no legal identity apart from that of the individual who owns it. Furthermore, a sole proprietor is personally responsible for the acts that his or her employees commit within the scope of their

CASE CONTINUES

CASE 35.1 CONTINUED employment. Dominguez owns Antenas, and Garcia is Dominguez's employee. "Accordingly, Dominguez is personally liable for the damages caused by the violation of * * * the [Cable Communications] Act."

- **What If the Facts Were Different?** *If Mundelein had identified itself as a residence when ordering the satellite system, how might the result in this case have been different?*
- **The Global Dimension** *Because the Internet has made it possible for sole proprietorships to do business worldwide without greatly increasing their costs, should they be considered, for some purposes, the equivalent of other business forms? Why or why not?*

SECTION 2

Franchises

Instead of setting up a business form for marketing their own products or services, many entrepreneurs opt to purchase a franchise. A **franchise** is an arrangement in which the owner of a trademark, a trade name, or a copyright licenses others to use the trademark, trade name, or copyright in the selling of goods or services. A **franchisee** (a purchaser of a franchise) is generally legally independent of the **franchisor** (the seller of the franchise). At the same time, the franchise is economically dependent on the franchisor's integrated business system. In other words, a franchisee can operate as an independent businessperson but still obtain the advantages of a regional or national organization. Today, franchising companies and their franchisees account for a significant portion of all retail sales in this country. Well-known franchises include McDonald's, 7-Eleven, and Holiday Inn.

Types of Franchises

Many different kinds of businesses now sell franchises, and numerous types of franchises are available. Generally, though, franchises fall into one of three classifications: distributorships, chain-style business operations, and manufacturing or processing-plant arrangements.

Distributorship With a *distributorship,* a manufacturing concern (franchisor) licenses a dealer (franchisee) to sell its product. Often, a distributorship covers an exclusive territory. An example is an automobile dealership or beer distributorship, such as Anheuser-Busch.

Chain-Style Business Operation In a *chain-style business operation,* a franchise operates under a franchisor's trade name and is identified as a member of a select group of dealers that engage in the franchisor's business. The franchisee is generally required to follow standardized or prescribed methods of operation. Often, the franchisor insists that the franchisee maintain certain standards of performance. In addition, the franchisee may be required to obtain materials and supplies exclusively from the franchisor. McDonald's and most other fast-food chains are examples of this type of franchise. Chain-style franchises are also common in service-related businesses, including real estate brokerage firms, such as Century 21, and tax-preparing services, such as H & R Block, Inc.

A Manufacturing or Processing-Plant Arrangement With a *manufacturing* or *processing-plant arrangement,* the franchisor transmits to the franchisee the essential ingredients or formula to make a particular product. The franchisee then markets the product either at wholesale or at retail in accordance with the franchisor's standards. Examples of this type of franchise include Coca-Cola and other soft-drink bottling companies.

Laws Governing Franchising

Because a franchise relationship is primarily a contractual relationship, it is governed by contract law. If the franchise exists primarily for the sale of products manufactured by the franchisor, the law governing sales contracts as expressed in Article 2 of the Uniform Commercial Code applies (see Chapters 20 through 23). Additionally, the federal government and most states have enacted laws governing certain aspects of franchising. Generally, these laws are designed to protect prospective franchisees from dishonest franchisors and to prevent franchisors from terminating franchises without good cause.

Federal and state laws control the franchising relationship. Ultimately, it falls to the courts to interpret the laws and determine whether a franchise relationship exists. In some cases, courts have held that even though the parties signed a franchising agreement, the franchisees are in fact employees because of the degree of control exercised over them by the franchisors. In other cases, courts have held that a franchising relationship exists even in the absence of a franchising contract. Because of the myriad of federal laws that apply, and because state laws on franchising vary dramatically, business owners and managers should seek the advice of counsel within the state before entering into a franchising relationship.

Federal Regulation of Franchises in Certain Industries The federal government has enacted laws that protect franchisees in certain industries, such as automobile dealerships and service stations. These laws protect the franchisee from unreasonable demands and bad faith terminations of the franchise by the franchisor. If an automobile manufacturer–franchisor terminates a franchise because of a dealer-franchisee's failure to comply with unreasonable demands (for example, failure to attain an unrealistically high sales quota), the manufacturer may be liable for damages.[2] Similarly, federal law prescribes the conditions under which a franchisor of service stations can terminate the franchise.[3] Federal antitrust laws (to be discussed in Chapter 46) also apply in certain circumstances to prohibit certain types of anticompetitive agreements.

The Franchise Rule In 1978, the Federal Trade Commission (FTC) issued the Franchise Rule, which requires franchisors to disclose material facts that a prospective franchisee needs to make an informed decision concerning the purchase of a franchise.[4] The rule was designed to enable potential franchisees to weigh the risks and benefits of an investment. Basically, the rule requires the franchisor to make numerous written disclosures to prospective franchisees.

For example, a franchisor is required to disclose whether the projected earnings figures are based on actual data or hypothetical examples. If a franchisor makes sales or earnings projections based on actual data for a specific franchise location, the franchisor must disclose the number and percentage of its actual franchises that have achieved this result. All representations made to a prospective franchisee must have a reasonable basis. Franchisors are also required to explain termination, cancellation, and renewal provisions of the franchise contract to potential franchisees before the agreement is signed. Those who violate the Franchise Rule are subject to substantial civil penalties, and the FTC can sue on behalf of injured parties to recover damages.

Online Disclosure Allowed Amendments to the Franchise Rule that went into effect in 2007 allow franchisors to provide disclosure documents via the Internet as long as they meet certain requirements. For example, prospective franchisees must be able to download or save all electronic disclosure documents. The amendments also bring the federal rule into closer alignment with state franchise disclosure laws (discussed next) and require additional disclosures on lawsuits that the franchisor has filed against franchisees and settlement agreements that it has entered into with them.

State Protection for Franchisees State legislation varies but often is aimed at protecting franchisees from unfair practices and bad faith terminations by franchisors. Approximately fifteen states have laws similar to the federal rules requiring franchisors to provide presale disclosures to prospective franchisees.[5] Some states also require a disclosure document (known as a *Uniform Franchise Offering Circular*, or UFOC) to be filed with a state official. To protect franchisees, a state law might require the

2. Automobile Dealers' Franchise Act of 1965, also known as the Automobile Dealers' Day in Court Act, 15 U.S.C. Sections 1221 *et seq.*

3. Petroleum Marketing Practices Act (PMPA) of 1979, 15 U.S.C. Sections 2801 *et seq.*

4. 16 C.F.R. Section 436.1.

5. These states include California, Hawaii, Illinois, Indiana, Maryland, Michigan, Minnesota, New York, North Dakota, Oregon, Rhode Island, South Dakota, Virginia, Washington, and Wisconsin.

disclosure of information such as the actual costs of operation, recurring expenses, and profits earned, along with facts substantiating these figures. To protect franchisees against arbitrary or bad faith terminations, the law might also require that certain procedures be followed in terminating a franchising relationship. State deceptive trade practices acts (see Chapter 44) may also prohibit certain types of actions on the part of franchisors.

For example, the Illinois Franchise Disclosure Act prohibits any untrue statement of a material fact in connection with the offer or sale of any franchise. If Miyamoto, a franchisor of bagel stores, understates the start-up costs and exaggerates the anticipated yearly profits from operating a bagel shop to a franchisee, he has violated state law.[6]

The Franchise Contract

The franchise relationship is defined by a contract between the franchisor and the franchisee. The franchise contract specifies the terms and conditions of the franchise and spells out the rights and duties of the franchisor and the franchisee. If either party fails to perform its contractual duties, that party may be subject to a lawsuit for breach of contract. Furthermore, if a franchisee is induced to enter into a franchise contract by the franchisor's fraudulent misrepresentation, the franchisor may be liable for damages. Generally, statutes and the case law governing franchising tend to emphasize the importance of good faith and fair dealing in franchise relationships.

Because each type of franchise relationship has its own characteristics, it is difficult to describe the broad range of details a franchising contract may include. We look next at some of the major issues that typically are addressed in a franchise contract.

Payment for the Franchise The franchisee ordinarily pays an initial fee or lump-sum price for the franchise license (the privilege of being granted a franchise). This fee is separate from the various products that the franchisee purchases from or through the franchisor. In some industries, the franchisor relies heavily on the initial sale of the franchise for realizing a profit. In other industries, the continued dealing between the parties brings profit to both. In most situations, the franchisor receives a stated percentage of the annual sales or annual volume of business done by the franchisee. The franchise agreement may also require the franchisee to pay a percentage of the franchisor's advertising costs and certain administrative expenses.

Business Premises The franchise agreement may specify whether the premises for the business must be leased or purchased outright. Sometimes, a building must be constructed to meet the terms of the agreement. Certainly, the agreement will specify whether the franchisor or the franchisee is responsible for supplying equipment and furnishings for the premises.

Location of the Franchise Typically, the franchisor determines the territory to be served. Some franchise contracts give the franchisee exclusive rights, or "territorial rights," to a certain geographic area. Other franchise contracts, while defining the territory allotted to a particular franchise, either specifically state that the franchise is nonexclusive or are silent on the issue of territorial rights.

Many franchise cases involve disputes over territorial rights, and the implied covenant of good faith and fair dealing often comes into play in this area of franchising. Suppose that the franchise contract either does not give the franchisee exclusive territorial rights or is silent on the issue. If the franchisor allows a competing franchise to be established nearby, the first franchisee may suffer a significant loss in profits. In this situation, a court may hold that the franchisor's actions breached an implied covenant of good faith and fair dealing.

Business Organization The franchisee's business organization is of great concern to the franchisor. As part of the franchise agreement, the franchisor may require that the business have a particular form and capital structure. The franchise agreement may also provide standards of operation in such aspects of the business as sales quotas, quality, and record keeping. Additionally, a franchisor may retain stringent control over the training of personnel involved in the operation and over administrative aspects of the business.

Quality Control Although the day-to-day operation of the franchise business normally is left up to the franchisee, the franchise agreement may provide for some degree of supervision and control by the franchisor so that it can protect the franchise's name and

6. *Bixby's Food Systems, Inc. v. McKay*, 193 F.Supp.2d 1053 (N.D.Ill. 2002).

reputation. When the franchise is a service operation, such as a motel, the contract often states that the franchisor will establish certain standards for the facility and will be permitted to make periodic inspections to ensure that the standards are being maintained.

As a general rule, the validity of a provision permitting the franchisor to establish and enforce certain quality standards is unquestioned. Because the franchisor has a legitimate interest in maintaining the quality of the product or service to protect its name and reputation, it can exercise greater control in this area than would otherwise be tolerated. Increasingly, however, franchisors are finding that if they exercise too much control over the operations of their franchisees, they may incur *vicarious (indirect) liability* under agency theory for the acts of their franchisees' employees (see Chapter 32). The actual exercise of control, or at least the right to control, is the key consideration. If the franchisee controls the day-to-day operations of the business to a significant degree, the franchisor may be able to avoid liability, as the following case illustrates.

CASE 35.2 Kerl v. Dennis Rasmussen, Inc.

Wisconsin Supreme Court, 2004. 2004 WI 86, 273 Wis.2d 106, 682 N.W.2d 328.

Background and Facts Arby's, Inc., is a national franchisor of fast-food restaurants. Dennis Rasmussen, Inc. (DRI), is an Arby's franchisee. Under the terms of their franchise contract, DRI agreed to follow Arby's specifications for several aspects of operating the business. DRI hired Cathy Propp as manager for its Arby's restaurant in 1994. In early 1999, Propp hired Harvey Pierce, a local county jail inmate with work-release privileges after a conviction for sexual assault. On June 11, Pierce left his shift at the restaurant without permission, walked half a mile to a discount store parking lot, and shot his former girlfriend Robin Kerl, her fiancé, David Jones, and himself. Pierce and Jones died. Kerl survived, but suffered a permanent disability. Kerl and others filed a suit in a Wisconsin state court against DRI and Arby's, claiming in part that Arby's was vicariously (indirectly) liable for DRI's allegedly negligent hiring and supervision of Pierce. Arby's filed a motion for summary judgment, which the court granted. The plaintiffs appealed this judgment to a state intermediate appellate court.

Decision and Rationale The state intermediate appellate court affirmed the lower court's summary judgment in Arby's favor, concluding that Arby's did not have a right of control, or actual control, over DRI's allegedly negligent actions and thus was not vicariously liable for DRI's actions. The court held that "in an action seeking to impose vicarious liability on a franchisor for the negligent actions of a franchisee, a franchisor's general right to control several aspects of a franchisee's operations is not enough. Rather, the decisive factor is whether the franchisor controls the daily operations of the franchisee such that it exercises a considerable degree of control over the instrumentality [particular operation] at issue." In this case, the franchise contract assigned responsibility for the employees to DRI, who "shall hire, train, maintain, and properly supervise sufficient, qualified, and courteous personnel." Under the contract, Arby's remedy for DRI's failure to comply was limited to "giving DRI thirty days to cure the problem and then terminating the franchise agreement if DRI does not rectify the situation within the deadline. Nothing in the agreement gives Arby's the right to supervise directly how DRI handles personnel issues."

The Ethical Dimension *Should a franchisor be allowed to control the operation of its franchisee without liability for the franchisee's conduct? Explain your answer.*

The Legal Environment Dimension *What would constitute the "right to control" under a franchise contract?*

Pricing Arrangements Franchises provide the franchisor with an outlet for the firm's goods and services. Depending on the nature of the business, the franchisor may require the franchisee to purchase certain supplies from the franchisor at an established price.[7] A franchisor cannot, however, set the prices at which the franchisee will resell the goods because such price setting may be a violation of state or federal antitrust laws, or both. A franchisor can suggest retail prices but cannot mandate them.

SECTION 3 Franchise Termination

The duration of the franchise is a matter to be determined between the parties. Generally, a franchise relationship starts with a short trial period, such as a year, so that the franchisee and the franchisor can determine whether they want to stay in business with one another. Usually, the franchise agreement specifies that termination must be "for cause," such as the death or disability of the franchisee, insolvency of the franchisee, breach of the franchise agreement, or failure to meet specified sales quotas. Most franchise contracts provide that notice of termination must be given. If no set time for termination is specified, then a reasonable time, with notice, is implied. A franchisee must be given reasonable time to wind up the business—that is, to do the accounting and return the copyright or trademark or any other property of the franchisor.

Wrongful Termination

Because a franchisor's termination of a franchise often has adverse consequences for the franchisee, much franchise litigation involves claims of wrongful termination. Generally, the termination provisions of contracts are more favorable to the franchisor than to the franchisee. This means that the franchisee, who normally invests a substantial amount of time and financial resources in making the franchise operation successful, may receive little or nothing for the business on termination. The franchisor owns the trademark and hence the business.

It is in this area that statutory and case law become important. The federal and state laws discussed earlier attempt, among other things, to protect franchisees from the arbitrary or unfair termination of their franchises by the franchisors. Generally, both statutory and case law emphasize the importance of good faith and fair dealing in terminating a franchise relationship.

The Importance of Good Faith and Fair Dealing

In determining whether a franchisor has acted in good faith when terminating a franchise agreement, the courts generally try to balance the rights of both parties. If a court perceives that a franchisor has arbitrarily or unfairly terminated a franchise, the franchisee will be provided with a remedy for wrongful termination. If a franchisor's decision to terminate a franchise was made in the normal course of the franchisor's business operations, however, and reasonable notice of termination was given to the franchisee, normally a court will not consider the termination wrongful.

At issue in the following case was whether General Motors Corporation acted wrongfully in terminating its franchise with a motor vehicle dealer in Connecticut.

7. Although a franchisor can require franchisees to purchase supplies from it, requiring a franchisee to purchase exclusively from the franchisor may violate federal antitrust laws (see Chapter 46). For two landmark cases in these areas, see *United States v. Arnold, Schwinn & Co.*, 388 U.S. 365, 87 S.Ct. 1956, 18 L.Ed.2d 1249 (1967); and *Fortner Enterprises, Inc. v. U.S. Steel Corp.*, 394 U.S. 495, 89 S.Ct. 1252, 22 L.Ed.2d 495 (1969).

CASE 35.3 Chic Miller's Chevrolet, Inc. v. General Motors Corp.

United States District Court, District of Connecticut, 2005. 352 F.Supp.2d 251.

Background and Facts Chapin Miller began work as a mail clerk with General Motors Acceptance Corporation (GMAC). By 1967, Miller had succeeded sufficiently within the organization to acquire Chic Miller's (no relation) Chevrolet, a General Motors Corporation (GM) dealership, in Bristol, Connecticut. As part of its operations, Chic Miller's entered into lending agreements, commonly known as *floor plan financing*, to enable it to buy new vehicles from GM. At first, the dealership had floor plan financing through GMAC. In 2001, however, Miller felt that GMAC was charging interest "at an inappropriately high rate" and negotiated a lower rate from Chase Manhattan Bank. In November 2002, Chase declined to provide further financing. Unable to obtain a loan from any other lender, Chic Miller's contacted GMAC, which also refused to make a deal. Under the parties' "Dealer Sales and Service Agreement," GM could terminate a dealership for "Failure of Dealer to

CASE 35.3 CONTINUED

maintain the line of credit." GM sent several notices of termination, but Chic Miller's remained open until March 2004, when it closed for seven days. GM sent a final termination notice. Chic Miller's filed a suit in a federal district court against GM, alleging, among other things, a failure to act in good faith in terminating the franchise. GM filed a motion for summary judgment.

• **Decision and Rationale** The court granted GM's motion for summary judgment. The court stated that to terminate a franchise under the Connecticut Franchise Act, "a franchisor must: provide notice that complies with statutory requirements; have 'good cause' for the termination; and act 'in good faith.'" The court explained that there is "good cause" under the statute "if there is a failure by the dealer to comply with a provision of the franchise which is both reasonable and of material significance to the franchise relationship." In this case, the court concluded that GM acted in good faith, with good cause under the statute to terminate Chic Miller's franchise. The dealer failed to maintain floor plan financing, a material requirement under the franchise agreement. "Without floor plan financing, a dealership is unable to purchase motor vehicle inventory, which, in turn, severely limits a dealership's ability to earn income from vehicle sales." The dealership "will eventually lose its ability to generate revenues and become financially insolvent, and will not be able to conduct customary sales and service operations." Here, the dealer also failed to conduct sales and service operations for seven consecutive business days, another material requirement under the parties' contract.

• **What If the Facts Were Different?** *Suppose that in March 2004, Chic Miller's had placed one newspaper ad promoting its services and had sold one car. Would the result have been different?*

• **The Global Dimension** *Should General Motors Corporation, or any domestic franchisor, be allowed to impose different contract terms on franchisees in foreign countries than it does on franchisees in the United States? Why or why not?*

REVIEWING Sole Proprietorships and Franchises

Carlos Del Rey decided to open a Mexican fast-food restaurant and signed a franchise contract with a national chain called La Grande Enchilada. The contract required the franchisee to strictly follow the franchisor's operating manual and stated that failure to do so would be grounds for terminating the franchise contract. The manual set forth detailed operating procedures and safety standards, and provided that a La Grande Enchilada representative would inspect the restaurant monthly to ensure compliance. Nine months after Del Rey began operating his restaurant, a spark from the grill ignited an oily towel in the kitchen. No one was injured, but by the time firefighters were able to put out the fire, the kitchen had sustained extensive damage. The cook told the fire department that the towel was "about two feet from the grill" when it caught fire, which was in compliance with the franchisor's manual that required towels be placed at least one foot from the grills. Nevertheless, the next day La Grande Enchilada notified Del Rey that his franchise would terminate in thirty days for failure to follow the prescribed safety procedures. Using the information presented in the chapter, answer the following questions.

1. What type of franchise was Del Rey's La Grande Enchilada restaurant?
2. If Del Rey operates the restaurant as a sole proprietorship, who bears the loss for the damaged kitchen? Explain.
3. Assume that Del Rey files a lawsuit against La Grande Enchilada, claiming that his franchise was wrongfully terminated. What is the main factor that a court would consider in determining whether the franchise was wrongfully terminated?
4. Would a court be likely to rule that La Grande Enchilada had good cause to terminate Del Rey's franchise in this situation? Why or why not?

TERMS AND CONCEPTS

- entrepreneur 672
- franchise 674
- franchisee 674
- franchisor 674
- sole proprietorship 672

QUESTIONS AND CASE PROBLEMS

35–1. Maria, Pablo, and Vicky are recent college graduates who would like to go into business for themselves. They are considering purchasing a franchise. If they enter into a franchising arrangement, they would have the support of a large company that could answer any questions they might have. Also, a firm that has been in business for many years would be experienced in dealing with some of the problems that novice businesspersons might encounter. These and other attributes of franchises can lessen some of the risks of the marketplace. What other aspects of franchising—positive and negative—should Maria, Pablo, and Vicky consider before committing themselves to a particular franchise?

35–2. QUESTION WITH SAMPLE ANSWER

National Foods, Inc., sells franchises to its fast-food restaurants, known as Chicky-D's. Under the franchise agreement, franchisees agree to hire and train employees strictly according to Chicky-D's standards. Chicky-D's regional supervisors are required to approve all job candidates before they are hired and all general policies affecting those employees. Chicky-D's reserves the right to terminate a franchise for violating the franchisor's rules. In practice, however, Chicky-D's regional supervisors routinely approve new employees and individual franchisees' policies. After several incidents of racist comments and conduct by Tim, a recently hired assistant manager at a Chicky-D's, Sharon, a counterperson at the restaurant, resigns. Sharon files a suit in a federal district court against National. National files a motion for summary judgment, arguing that it is not liable for harassment by franchise employees. Will the court grant National's motion? Why or why not?

- **For a sample answer to Question 35–2, go to Appendix I at the end of this text.**

35–3. Otmar has secured a particular high-quality ice cream franchise. The franchise agreement calls for Otmar to sell the ice cream only at a specific location; to buy all the ice cream from the franchisor; to order and sell all the flavors produced by the franchisor; and to refrain from selling any ice cream stored for more than two weeks after delivery by the franchisor, as the quality of the ice cream declines after that period of time. After two months of operation, Otmar believes that he can increase his profits by moving the store to another part of the city. He refuses to order even a limited quantity of the "fruit delight" flavor because of its higher cost, and he has sold ice cream that has been stored longer than two weeks without customer complaint. Otmar maintains that the franchisor has no right to restrict him in these practices. Discuss his claims.

35–4. Omega Computers, Inc., is a franchisor that grants exclusive geographic territories to its franchisees with retail locations, including Pete's Digital Products. After selling more than two hundred franchises, Omega establishes an interactive Web site. On the site, a customer can order Omega's products directly from the franchisor. When Pete's sets up a Web site through which a customer can also order Omega's products, Omega and Pete's file suits against each other, each alleging that the other is in violation of the franchise agreement. To decide this issue, what factors should the court consider? How might the parties have avoided this conflict? Discuss.

35–5. Franchise Termination. In 1985, Bruce Byrne, with his sons Scott and Gordon, opened Lone Star R.V. Sales, Inc., a motor home dealership in Houston, Texas. In 1994, Lone Star became a franchised dealer for Winnebago Industries, Inc., a manufacturer of recreational vehicles. The parties renewed the franchise in 1995, but during the next year, their relationship began to deteriorate. Lone Star did not maintain a current inventory, its sales did not meet the goals agreed to by the parties, and Lone Star disparaged Winnebago products to consumers and otherwise failed to actively promote them. Several times, the Byrnes subjected Winnebago employees to verbal abuse. During one phone conversation, Bruce threatened to throw a certain Winnebago sales manager off Lone Star's lot if he appeared at the dealership. Bruce was physically incapable of carrying out the threat, however. In 1998, Winnebago terminated the franchise, claiming, among many other things, that it was concerned for the safety of its employees. Lone Star filed a protest with the Texas Motor Vehicle Board. Did Winnebago have good cause to terminate Lone Star's franchise? Discuss. [*Lone Star R.V. Sales, Inc. v. Motor Vehicle Board of the Texas Department of Transportation,* 49 S.W.3d 492 (Tex.App.—Austin 2001)]

35–6. Franchise Termination. In the automobile industry, luxury-car customers are considered the most demanding segment of the market with respect to customer service. Jaguar Cars, a division of Ford Motor Co., is the exclusive U.S. distributor of Jaguar luxury cars. Jaguar Cars distributes its products through franchised dealers. In April 1999, Dave Ostrem Imports, Inc., an authorized Jaguar dealer in Des Moines, Iowa, contracted to sell its dealership to Midwest Automotive III, LLC. A Jaguar franchise generally cannot be sold without Jaguar Cars' permission. Jaguar Cars asked Midwest Auto to submit three years of customer satisfaction index (CSI) data for all franchises with which its owners had been associated. (CSI data are intended to measure how well dealers treat their customers and satisfy their customers' needs. Jaguar Cars requires above-average CSI ratings for its dealers.) Most of Midwest Auto's scores fell below the national average. Jaguar Cars rejected Midwest Auto's application and sought to terminate the franchise, claiming that a transfer of the dealership would be "substantially detrimental" to the distribution of Jaguar vehicles in the community. Was Jaguar Cars' attempt to terminate this franchise reasonable? Why or why not? [*Midwest Automotive III, LLC v. Iowa Department of Transportation,* 646 N.W.2d 417 (Iowa 2002)]

35–7. CASE PROBLEM WITH SAMPLE ANSWER

Walik Elkhatib, a Palestinian Arab, emigrated to the United States in 1971 and became an American citizen. Eight years later, Elkhatib bought a Dunkin' Donuts, Inc., franchise in Bellwood, Illinois. Dunkin' Donuts began offering breakfast sandwiches with bacon, ham, or sausage through its franchises in 1984, but Elkhatib refused to sell these items at his store on the ground that his religion forbade the handling of pork. In 1995, Elkhatib opened a second franchise in Berkeley, Illinois, at which he also refused to sell pork products. The next year, Elkhatib began selling meatless sandwiches at both locations. In 1998, Elkhatib opened a third franchise in Westchester, Illinois. When he proposed to relocate this franchise, Dunkin' Donuts refused to approve the new location and added that it would not renew any of his franchise agreements because he did not carry the full sandwich line. Elkhatib filed a suit in a federal district court against Dunkin' Donuts and others. The defendants filed a motion for summary judgment. Did Dunkin' Donuts act in good faith in its relationship with Elkhatib? Explain. [*Elkhatib v. Dunkin' Donuts, Inc.,* __ F.Supp.2d __ (N.D.Ill. 2004)]

- **To view a sample answer for Problem 35–7, go to this book's Web site at www.cengage.com/blaw/jentz, select "Chapter 35," and click on "Case Problem with Sample Answer."**

35–8. The Franchise Contract. On August 23, 1995, Climaco Guzman entered into a commercial janitorial services franchise agreement with Jan-Pro Cleaning Systems, Inc., in Rhode Island for a franchise fee of $3,285. In the agreement, Jan-Pro promised to furnish Guzman with "one (1) or more customer account(s) . . . amounting to $8,000.00 gross volume per year. . . . No portion of the franchise fee is refundable except and to the extent that the Franchisor, within 120 business days following the date of execution of the Franchise Agreement, fails to provide accounts." By February 19, Guzman had not received any accounts and demanded a full refund. Jan-Pro then promised "two accounts grossing $12,000 per year in income." Despite its assurances, Jan-Pro did not have the ability to furnish accounts that met the requirements. In September, Guzman filed a suit in a Rhode Island state court against Jan-Pro, alleging, in part, fraudulent misrepresentation. Should the court rule in Guzman's favor? Why or why not? [*Guzman v. Jan-Pro Cleaning Systems, Inc.,* 839 A.2d 504 (R.I. 2003)]

35–9. Sole Proprietorship. James Ferguson operates "Jim's 11-E Auto Sales" in Jonesborough, Tennessee, as a sole proprietorship. In 1999, Consumers Insurance Co. issued a policy to "Jim Ferguson, Jim's 11E Auto Sales" covering "Owned 'Autos' Only." *Auto* was defined to include "a land motor vehicle," which was not further explained in the policy. Coverage extended to damage caused by the owner or driver of an underinsured motor vehicle. In 2000, Ferguson bought and titled in his own name a 1976 Harley-Davidson motorcycle, intending to repair and sell the cycle through his dealership. In October 2001, while riding the motorcycle, Ferguson was struck by an auto driven by John Jenkins. Ferguson filed a suit in a Tennessee state court against Jenkins, who was underinsured with respect to Ferguson's medical bills, and Consumers. The insurer argued, among other things, that because the motorcycle was bought and titled in Ferguson's own name, and he was riding it at the time of the accident, it was his personal vehicle and thus was not covered under the dealership's policy. What is the relationship between a sole proprietor and a sole proprietorship? How might this status affect the court's decision in this case? [*Ferguson v. Jenkins,* 204 S.W.3d 779 (Tenn.App. 2006)]

35–10. A QUESTION OF ETHICS

In August 2004, Ralph Vilardo contacted Travel Center, Inc., in Cincinnati, Ohio, to buy a trip to Florida in December for his family to celebrate his fiftieth wedding anniversary. Vilardo paid $6,900 to David Sheets, the sole proprietor of Travel Center. Vilardo also paid $195 to Sheets for a separate trip to Florida in February 2005. Sheets assured Vilardo that everything was set, but in fact *no arrangements were made. Later, two unauthorized charges for travel services totaling $1,182.35 appeared on Vilardo's credit-card statement. Vilardo filed a suit in an Ohio state court against Sheets and his business, alleging, among other things, fraud and violations of the state consumer protection law. Vilardo served Sheets and Travel Center with copies of the complaint, the summons, a request for admissions, and other documents filed with the court, including a motion for summary judgment. Each of these filings asked for a response within a certain time period. Sheets responded once on his own behalf with a denial of all of Vilardo's claims. Travel Center did not respond. [*Vilardo v. Sheets, *__ N.E.2d __ (Ohio App. 12 Dist. 2006)]*

(a) Almost four months after Vilardo filed his complaint, Sheets decided that he was unable to adequately represent himself and retained an attorney who asked the court for more time. Should the court grant this request? Why or why not? Ultimately, what should the court rule in this case?

(b) Sheets admitted that "Travel Center, Inc." was a sole proprietorship. He also argued that liability might be imposed on his business but not on himself. How would you rule with respect to this argument? Why? Would there be anything unethical about allowing Sheets to avoid liability on this basis? Explain.

LAW ON THE WEB

For updated links to resources available on the Web, as well as a variety of other materials, visit this text's Web site at

www.cengage.com/blaw/jentz

To learn how the U.S. Small Business Administration assists in forming, financing, and operating businesses, go to

www.sbaonline.sba.gov

For information about FTC regulations on franchising, as well as state laws regulating franchising, go to

www.ftc.gov/bcp/franchise/netfran.htm

A good source of information on the purchase and sale of franchises is Franchising.org, which is online at

www.franchising.org

Legal Research Exercises on the Web

Go to **www.cengage.com/blaw/jentz**, the Web site that accompanies this text. Select "Chapter 35" and click on "Internet Exercises." There you will find the following Internet research exercises that you can perform to learn more about the topics covered in this chapter.

Internet Exercise 35–1: Legal Perspective
Starting a Business

Internet Exercise 35–2: Management Perspective
Franchises

CHAPTER 36

Partnerships and Limited Liability Partnerships

Traditionally, one of the most common forms of business organization selected by two or more persons is the *partnership.* A **partnership** arises from an agreement, express or implied, between two or more persons to carry on a business for a profit. Partners are co-owners of a business and have joint control over its operation and the right to share in its profits. In this chapter, we examine several forms of partnership.

We begin the chapter with an examination of ordinary partnerships, or *general partnerships,* and the rights and duties of partners in this traditional business entity. We then examine some special forms of partnerships known as *limited partnerships* and *limited liability partnerships,* which receive a different treatment under the law.

SECTION 1 Basic Partnership Concepts

Partnerships are governed both by common law concepts (in particular, those relating to agency) and by statutory law. As in so many other areas of business law, the National Conference of Commissioners on Uniform State Laws has drafted uniform laws for partnerships, and these have been widely adopted by the states.

Agency Concepts and Partnership Law

When two or more persons agree to do business as partners, they enter into a special relationship with one another. To an extent, their relationship is similar to an agency relationship because each partner is deemed to be the agent of the other partners and of the partnership. The agency concepts that were discussed in Chapters 31 and 32 thus apply—specifically, the imputation of knowledge of, and responsibility for, acts carried out within the scope of the partnership relationship. In their relationship to one another, partners are also bound by the fiduciary ties that bind an agent and principal under agency law.

Partnership law is distinct from agency law in one significant way, however. A partnership is based on a voluntary contract between two or more competent persons who agree to place some or all of their funds or other assets, labor, and skills in a business with the understanding that profits and losses will be shared. In a nonpartnership agency relationship, the agent usually does not have an ownership interest in the business, nor is he or she obligated to bear a portion of ordinary business losses.

The Uniform Partnership Act

The Uniform Partnership Act (UPA) governs the operation of partnerships *in the absence of express agreement* and has done much to reduce controversies in the law relating to partnerships. Except for Louisiana, all of the states, as well as the District of Columbia, have adopted the UPA. A majority of the states have enacted the most recent version of the UPA, which was adopted in 1994 and amended in 1997 to provide limited liability for partners in a limited liability partnership.[1] Excerpts from the latest version of the UPA, including the 1997 amendments, are presented in Appendix E.

1. At the time this book went to press, more than half of the states, as well as the District of Columbia, Puerto Rico, and the U.S. Virgin Islands, had adopted the UPA with the 1997 amendments. We therefore base our discussion of the UPA on the 1997 version and refer to older versions of the UPA in footnotes when necessary.

When Does a Partnership Exist?

Parties sometimes find themselves in conflict over whether their business enterprise is a legal partnership, especially in the absence of a formal, written partnership agreement. The UPA defines the term *partnership* as "an association of two or more persons to carry on as co-owners a business for profit" [UPA 101(6)]. The *intent* to associate is a key element of a partnership, and one cannot join a partnership unless all other partners consent [UPA 401(i)].

In resolving disputes over whether a partnership exists, courts usually look for the following three essential elements of partnership implicit in the UPA's definition:

1. A sharing of profits or losses.
2. A joint ownership of the business.
3. An equal right to participate in the management of the business.

If the evidence in a particular case is insufficient to establish all three factors, the UPA provides a set of guidelines to be used. For example, the sharing of profits and losses from a business creates a presumption that a partnership exists. No presumption is made, however, if the profits were received as payment of any of the following [UPA 202(c)(3)]:

1. A debt by installments or interest on a loan.
2. Wages of an employee or for the services of an independent contractor.
3. Rent to a landlord.
4. An annuity to a surviving spouse or representative of a deceased partner.
5. A sale of the goodwill of a business or property.

To illustrate: A debtor owes a creditor $5,000 on an unsecured debt. To repay the debt, the debtor agrees to pay (and the creditor, to accept) 10 percent of the debtor's monthly business profits until the loan with interest has been paid. Although the creditor is sharing profits from the business, the debtor and creditor are not presumed to be partners.

Joint Property Ownership and Partnership Status

Joint ownership of property does not in and of itself create a partnership. Therefore, the fact that, say, MacPherson and Bunker own real property as *joint tenants* or as *tenants in common* (forms of joint ownership that will be discussed in Chapter 47) does not by itself establish a partnership. In fact, the sharing of gross returns and even profits from such ownership "does not by itself establish a partnership" [UPA 202(c)(1) and (2)].[2] Thus, if MacPherson and Bunker jointly own a piece of farmland and lease it to a farmer for a share of the profits from the farming operation in lieu of set rental payments, the sharing of the profits ordinarily will not make MacPherson, Bunker, and the farmer partners.

Note, though, that while the sharing of profits from ownership of property does not prove the existence of a partnership, sharing *both profits and losses* usually does. For example, two sisters, Zoe and Cienna, buy a restaurant together, open a joint bank account from which they pay for supplies and expenses, and share the proceeds that the restaurant generates. Zoe manages the restaurant and Cienna handles the bookkeeping. After eight years, Cienna stops keeping the books and does no other work for the restaurant. Zoe, who is now operating the restaurant by herself, no longer wants to share the profits with Cienna. She offers to buy her sister out, but the two cannot agree on a fair price. When Cienna files a lawsuit, a question arises as to whether the two sisters were partners in the restaurant. In this situation, a court would find that a partnership existed because the sisters shared management responsibilities, had joint accounts, and shared the profits and the losses of the restaurant equally.

Entity versus Aggregate

A partnership is sometimes called a *company* or a *firm*, terms that suggest that the partnership is an entity separate and apart from its aggregate members. The law of partnership recognizes the independent entity for most purposes but may treat the partnership as a composite of its individual partners for some purposes.

Partnership as an Entity At common law, a partnership was never treated as a separate legal entity. Thus, a common law suit could never be brought by or against the firm in its own name; each individual partner had to sue or be sued. Today, most states provide specifically that a partnership can be treated as an entity for certain purposes. These usually include the capacity to sue or be sued, to collect judgments, and to have all accounting procedures carried out in the name of the partnership. In addition, the UPA clearly states, "A partnership is an entity" and "A partnership may sue and be sued in the name of the partnership" [UPA 201 and 307(a)]. As an entity, a partnership may hold the title to real or personal

2. See, for example, *In re Estate of Ivanchak*, 169 Ohio App.3d 140, 862 N.E.2d 151 (2006).

property in its name rather than in the names of the individual partners. Finally, federal procedural laws frequently permit a partnership to be treated as an entity in such matters as lawsuits in federal courts and bankruptcy proceedings.

Partnership as an Aggregate In one circumstance, the partnership is not regarded as a separate legal entity but is treated as an aggregate of the individual partners. For federal income tax purposes, a partnership is not a taxpaying entity. The income and losses it incurs are "passed through" the partnership framework and attributed to the partners on their individual tax returns. The partnership itself has no tax liability and is responsible only for filing an **information return** with the Internal Revenue Service. In other words, the firm itself pays no taxes. A partner's profit from the partnership (whether distributed or not) is taxed as individual income to the individual partner.

SECTION 2

Partnership Formation

As a general rule, agreements to form a partnership can be *oral, written,* or *implied by conduct.* Some partnership agreements, however, must be in writing to be legally enforceable within the Statute of Frauds (see Chapter 15 for details). For example, a partnership agreement that authorizes the partners to deal in transfers of real property must be evidenced by a sufficient writing (or record).

The Partnership Agreement

A partnership agreement, called **articles of partnership,** can include virtually any terms that the parties wish, so long as the terms are not illegal or contrary to public policy or statute [UPA 103]. The terms commonly included in a partnership agreement are listed in Exhibit 36–1 on the next page.

Duration of the Partnership

The partnership agreement can specify the duration of the partnership by stating that it will continue until a designated date or until the completion of a particular project. This is called a *partnership for a term.* If this type of partnership is dissolved (broken up) without the consent of all of the partners prior to the expiration of the partnership term, the dissolution constitutes a breach of the agreement. The responsible partner can be held liable for any resulting losses.

If no fixed duration is specified, the partnership is a *partnership at will.* Any partner can dissolve this type of partnership at any time without violating the agreement and without incurring liability for losses to other partners that result from the termination.

A Corporation as Partner

In a general partnership, the partners are personally liable for the debts incurred by the partnership. If one of the general partners is a corporation, however, what does personal liability mean? Basically, the capacity of corporations to contract is a question of corporate law. At one time, many states had restrictions on corporations becoming partners, although such restrictions have become less common over the years.

The Revised Model Business Corporation Act (see Appendix G) allows corporations generally to make contracts and incur liabilities. The UPA specifically permits a corporation to be a partner. By definition, "a partnership is an association of two or more persons," and the UPA defines *person* as including corporations [UPA 101(10)].

Partnership by Estoppel

Sometimes, persons who are not partners nevertheless hold themselves out as partners and make representations that third parties rely on in dealing with them. In such a situation, a court may conclude that a **partnership by estoppel** exists and impose liability—but not partnership *rights*—on the alleged partner or partners. Similarly, a partnership by estoppel may be imposed when a partner represents, expressly or impliedly, that a nonpartner is a member of the firm. Whenever a third person has reasonably and detrimentally relied on the representation that a nonpartner was part of the partnership, partnership by estoppel is deemed to exist. When this occurs, the nonpartner is regarded as an agent whose acts are binding on the partnership [UPA 308].

SECTION 3

Partnership Operation

The rights and duties of partners are governed largely by the specific terms of their partnership agreement. In the absence of provisions to the contrary in the partnership agreement, the law imposes the rights and duties discussed in the following subsections. The character and nature of the partnership business generally influence the application of these rights and duties.

EXHIBIT 36–1 • Terms Commonly Included in a Partnership Agreement

Basic Structure	1. Name of the partnership. 2. Names of the partners. 3. Location of the business and the state law under which the partnership is organized. 4. Purpose of the partnership. 5. Duration of the partnership.
Capital Contributions	1. Amount of capital that each partner is contributing. 2. The agreed-on value of any real or personal property that is contributed instead of cash. 3. How losses and gains on contributed capital will be allocated, and whether contributions will earn interest.
Sharing of Profits and Losses	1. Percentage of the profits and losses of the business that each partner will receive. 2. When distributions of profit will be made and how net profit will be calculated.
Management and Control	1. How management responsibilities will be divided among the partners. 2. Name(s) of the managing partner or partners, and whether other partners have voting rights.
Accounting and Partnership Records	1. Name of the bank in which the partnership will maintain its business and checking accounts. 2. Statement that an accounting of partnership records will be maintained and that any partner or her or his agent can review these records at any time. 3. The dates of the partnership's fiscal year and when the annual audit of the books will take place.
Dissociation and Dissolution	1. Events that will cause the dissociation of a partner or dissolve the partnership, such as the retirement, death, or incapacity of any partner. 2. How partnership property will be valued and apportioned on dissociation and dissolution. 3. Whether an arbitrator will determine the value of partnership property on dissociation and dissolution and whether that determination will be binding.
Arbitration	Whether arbitration is required for any dispute relating to the partnership agreement.

Rights of Partners

The rights of partners in a partnership relate to the following areas: management, interest in the partnership, compensation, inspection of books, accounting, and property.

Management In a general partnership, "All partners have equal rights in the management and conduct of partnership business" [UPA 401(f)]. Unless the partners agree otherwise, each partner has one vote in management matters *regardless of the proportional size of his or her interest in the firm.* In a large partnership, partners often agree to delegate daily management responsibilities to a management committee made up of one or more of the partners.

The majority rule controls decisions on ordinary matters connected with partnership business, unless otherwise specified in the agreement. Decisions that significantly affect the nature of the partnership or that are not apparently for carrying on the ordinary course of the partnership business, or business of the kind, however, require the *unanimous* consent of the partners [UPA 301(2), 401(i), 401(j)]. Unanimous consent is likely to be required for a decision to undertake any of the following actions:[3]

1. Altering the essential nature of the firm's business as expressed in the partnership agreement or altering the capital structure of the partnership.

3. The previous version of the UPA specifically listed most of these actions as requiring unanimous consent. The current version of the UPA omits the list entirely to allow the courts more flexibility. The Official Comments explain that most of these acts, except for submitting a claim to arbitration, will likely still remain outside the apparent authority of an individual partner.

2. Admitting new partners or engaging in a completely new business.
3. Assigning partnership property to a trust for the benefit of creditors.
4. Disposing of the partnership's goodwill.
5. Confessing judgment against the partnership or submitting partnership claims to arbitration. (A **confession of judgment** is an act by a debtor permitting a judgment to be entered against him or her by a creditor, for an agreed sum, without the institution of legal proceedings.)
6. Undertaking any act that would make further conduct of partnership business impossible.
7. Amending the terms of the partnership agreement.

Interest in the Partnership Each partner is entitled to the proportion of business profits and losses that is designated in the partnership agreement. If the agreement does not apportion profits (indicate how the profits will be shared), the UPA provides that profits will be shared equally. If the agreement does not apportion losses, losses will be shared in the same ratio as profits [UPA 401(b)].

For example, Rico and Brett form a partnership. The partnership agreement provides for capital contributions of $60,000 from Rico and $40,000 from Brett, but it is silent as to how they will share profits or losses. In this situation, they will share both profits and losses equally. If their partnership agreement had provided that they would share profits in the same ratio as capital contributions, however, 60 percent of the profits would go to Rico, and 40 percent would go to Brett. If the agreement was silent as to losses, losses would be shared in the same ratio as profits (60 percent and 40 percent, respectively).

Compensation Devoting time, skill, and energy to partnership business is a partner's duty and generally is not a compensable service. Partners can, of course, agree otherwise. For example, the managing partner of a law firm often receives a salary in addition to her or his share of profits for performing special duties, such as managing the office or personnel.

Inspection of Books Partnership books and records must be kept accessible to all partners. Each partner has the right to receive (and the corresponding duty to produce) full and complete information concerning the conduct of all aspects of partnership business [UPA 403]. Each firm retains books for recording and securing such information. Partners contribute the information, and a bookkeeper typically has the duty to preserve it. The books must be kept at the firm's principal business office (unless the partners agree otherwise). Every partner, whether active or inactive, is entitled to inspect all books and records on demand and can make copies of the materials. The personal representative of a deceased partner's estate has the same right of access to partnership books and records that the decedent would have had [UPA 403].

Accounting of Partnership Assets or Profits An accounting of partnership assets or profits is required to determine the value of each partner's share in the partnership. An accounting can be performed voluntarily, or it can be compelled by court order. At common law, an accounting was generally not available to partners prior to the dissolution of the partnership. Under UPA 405(b), in contrast, a partner has the right to bring an action for an accounting during the term of the partnership, as well as on the firm's dissolution and winding up.[4] The UPA also provides partners with access to the courts during the term of the partnership to resolve various claims against the partnership and the other partners.

Property Rights Property acquired *by* a partnership is the property of the partnership and not of the partners individually [UPA 203]. Partnership property includes all property that was originally contributed to the partnership and anything later purchased by the partnership or in the partnership's name (except in rare circumstances) [UPA 204]. A partner may use or possess partnership property only on behalf of the partnership [UPA 401(g)]. A partner is *not* a co-owner of partnership property and has no right to sell, mortgage, or transfer partnership property to another [UPA 501].[5]

In other words, partnership property is owned by the partnership as an entity and not by the individual partners. Thus, a creditor of an individual partner cannot seek to use partnership property to satisfy the partner's debt. Such a creditor can, however, petition a court for a **charging order** to attach the individual partner's *interest* in the partnership (her or his proportionate

4. Under the previous version of the UPA, a partner could bring an action for an accounting only if the partnership agreement provided for an accounting, the partner was wrongfully excluded from the business or its property or books, another partner was in breach of his or her fiduciary duty, or other circumstances rendered it "just and reasonable."

5. Under the previous version of the UPA, partners were *tenants in partnership*. This meant that every partner was a co-owner with all other partners of the partnership property. The current UPA does not recognize this concept.

share of the profits and losses and right to receive distributions) to satisfy the partner's obligation [UPA 502]. (A partner can also assign her or his right to a share of the partnership profits to another to satisfy a debt.)

Duties and Liabilities of Partners

The duties and liabilities of partners that we examine here are basically derived from agency law. Each partner is an agent of every other partner and acts as both a principal and an agent in any business transaction within the scope of the partnership agreement. Each partner is also a general agent of the partnership in carrying out the usual business of the firm "or business of the kind carried on by the partnership" [UPA 301(1)]. Thus, every act of a partner concerning partnership business and "business of the kind" and every contract signed in the partnership's name bind the firm. The UPA affirms general principles of agency law that pertain to the authority of a partner to bind a partnership in contract or tort.

Fiduciary Duties The fiduciary duties that a partner owes to the partnership and the other partners are the duty of care and the duty of loyalty [UPA 404(a)].

Duty of Care. A partner's duty of care is limited to refraining from "grossly negligent or reckless conduct, intentional misconduct, or a knowing violation of law" [UPA 404(c)].[6] A partner is not liable to the partnership for simple negligence or honest errors in judgment in conducting partnership business, but is liable for any grossly negligent or reckless conduct that causes damage to the firm.

Duty of Loyalty. The duty of loyalty requires a partner to account to the partnership for "any property, profit, or benefit" derived by the partner in the conduct of the partnership's business or from the use of its property. A partner must also refrain from dealing with the firm as an adverse party or competing with the partnership in business [UPA 404(b)]. The duty of loyalty can be breached by self-dealing, misusing partnership property, disclosing trade secrets, or usurping a partnership business opportunity.

A classic example is the 1928 case of *Meinhard v. Salmon.*[7] Salmon leased a building on Fifth Avenue in New York City for twenty years. The building had been a hotel, and Salmon wanted to convert it into a commercial building and lease it out to shops and offices. Salmon formed a partnership with Meinhard, who put up half of the capital. Both men received a percentage of the profits and shared the losses equally, but Salmon had the sole power to manage the building. A few months before the lease was set to expire, the property owner approached Salmon about leasing several adjacent properties and constructing a $3 million building on them.

Salmon did not inform Meinhard about this business opportunity and instead signed a new lease in the name of his own business (in which Meinhard was not an owner). The new lease covered the adjacent properties and the original development. In the lawsuit that followed, the court held that Salmon had breached his fiduciary duty by failing to inform Meinhard of a business opportunity and secretly taking advantage of the opportunity himself. The court granted Meinhard a 50 percent interest in the new lease.

Breach and Waiver of Fiduciary Duties. A partner's fiduciary duties may not be waived or eliminated in the partnership agreement, and in fulfilling them, each partner must act consistently with the obligation of good faith and fair dealing [UPA 103(b), 404(d)]. Note that a partner may pursue his or her own interests without automatically violating these duties [UPA 404(e)]. The key is whether the partner has disclosed the interest to the other partners.

For example, a partner who owns a shopping mall may vote against a partnership proposal to open a competing mall, provided that the partner has fully disclosed her interest in the shopping mall to the other partners at the firm. Similarly, suppose that in the case *Meinhard v. Salmon* discussed previously, Salmon had informed Meinhard about the opportunity of leasing and developing the additional properties. If Meinhard was not interested in extending the partnership's lease to cover the nearby properties, then Salmon would have been able to take advantage of the opportunity on his own. A partner cannot make secret profits or put self-interest before his or her duty to the interest of the partnership, however.

Authority of Partners The UPA affirms general principles of agency law that pertain to a partner's authority to bind a partnership in contract. A partner may also subject the partnership to tort liability under agency principles. When a partner is carrying on part-

6. The previous version of the UPA touched only briefly on the duty of loyalty and left the details of the partners' fiduciary duties to be developed under the law of agency.

7. 249 N.Y. 458, 164 N.E. 545 (N.Y.App. 1928).

nership business or business of the kind with third parties in the usual way, apparent authority exists, and both the partner and the firm share liability.

The partnership will not be liable, however, if the third parties *know* that the partner has no such authority. For example, Patricia, a partner in the partnership of Heise, Green, and Stevens, applies for a loan on behalf of the partnership without authorization from the other partners. The bank manager knows that Patricia has no authority to do so. If the bank manager grants the loan, Patricia will be personally bound, but the firm will not be liable.

A partnership may file a "statement of partnership authority" to limit a partner's capacity to act as the firm's agent or transfer property on its behalf [UPA 105, 303]. Any limit on a partner's authority, however, normally does not affect a third party who does not know about the statement. Statements limiting the partners' authority to transfer real property that are filed with the appropriate state records office (the office that records real property transfers—see Chapter 48) will bind third parties, whether or not they know about the limitation.

The agency concepts relating to apparent authority, actual authority, and ratification that were discussed in Chapter 32 also apply to partnerships. The extent of *implied authority* is generally broader for partners than for ordinary agents, however.

The Scope of Implied Powers. The character and scope of the partnership business and the customary nature of the particular business operation determine the implied powers of partners. For example, a partnership business that has goods in inventory and makes profits buying and selling those goods is known as a *trading partnership.* In a trading partnership, each partner has a wide range of implied powers, such as to advertise products, hire employees, and extend the firm's credit by issuing or signing checks.

In an ordinary partnership, the partners can exercise all implied powers reasonably necessary and customary to carry on that particular business. Such powers include the authority to make warranties on goods in the sales business and the power to enter into contracts consistent with the firm's regular course of business. Most partners also have the implied authority to make admissions and representations concerning partnership affairs. A partner might also have the implied power to convey (transfer) real property in the firm's name when such conveyances are part of the ordinary course of partnership business.

Authorized versus Unauthorized Actions. If a partner acts within the scope of authority, the partnership is legally bound to honor the partner's commitments to third parties. For example, a partner's authority to sell partnership products carries with it the implied authority to transfer title and to make usual warranties. Hence, in a partnership that operates a retail tire store, any partner negotiating a contract with a customer for the sale of a set of tires can warrant that "each tire will be warranted for normal wear for 40,000 miles."

This same partner, however, does not have the authority to sell office equipment, fixtures, or the partnership's retail facility without the consent of all of the other partners. In addition, because partnerships are formed to generate profits, a partner generally does not have the authority to make charitable contributions without the consent of the other partners. Such actions are not binding on the partnership unless they are ratified by all of the other partners.

Liability of Partners One significant disadvantage associated with a traditional partnership is that the partners are *personally* liable for the debts of the partnership. Moreover, the liability is essentially unlimited because the acts of one partner in the ordinary course of business subject the other partners to personal liability [UPA 305]. The following subsections explain the rules on a partner's liability.

Joint Liability. Each partner in a partnership is jointly liable for the partnership's obligations. **Joint liability** means that a third party must sue all of the partners as a group, but each partner can be held liable for the full amount. Under the prior version of the UPA, which is still in effect in a few states, partners were subject to joint liability on partnership debts and contracts, but not on partnership debts arising from torts.[8] If, for example, a third party sues a partner on a partnership contract, the partner has the right to demand that the other partners be sued with her or him. In fact, if the third party does not sue all of the partners, the assets of the partnership cannot be used to satisfy the judgment. Under the theory of joint liability, the partnership's assets must be exhausted before creditors can reach the partners' individual assets.[9]

8. Under the previous version of the UPA, the partners were subject to *joint and several liability,* which is discussed next, on debts arising from torts. States that still follow this rule include Connecticut, West Virginia, and Wyoming.

9. For a case applying joint liability to partnerships, see *Shar's Cars, LLC v. Elder,* 97 P.3d 724 (Utah App. 2004).

Joint and Several Liability. In the majority of the states, under UPA 306(a), partners are both jointly and severally (separately, or individually) liable for all partnership obligations, including contracts, torts, and breaches of trust. **Joint and several liability** means that a third party has the option of suing all of the partners together (jointly) or one or more of the partners separately (severally). This is true even if a partner did not participate in, ratify, or know about whatever it was that gave rise to the cause of action. Normally, though, the partnership's assets must be exhausted before a creditor can enforce a judgment against a partner's separate assets [UPA 307(d)].

A judgment against one partner severally (separately) does not extinguish the others' liability. Those not sued in the first action normally may be sued subsequently, unless the first action was conclusive on the question of liability. Suppose that Renalt brings a malpractice (professional negligence) action against one partner in a firm and then discovers that another partner was involved in the negligence. Normally, he may also file a lawsuit against the second partner (unless the court held that no one at the firm breached the standard of care with regard to Renalt).

If a plaintiff is successful in a suit against a partner or partners, he or she may collect on the judgment only against the assets of those partners named as defendants. A partner who commits a tort is required to indemnify (reimburse) the partnership for any damages it pays. The question in the following case was whether a partnership must indemnify a partner for liability that results from negligent conduct occurring in the ordinary course of the partnership's business.

CASE 36.1 Moren v. Jax Restaurant

Minnesota Court of Appeals, 2004. 679 N.W.2d 165.
www.lawlibrary.state.mn.us/archive/cap1st.html[a]

Background and Facts "Jax Restaurant" is a partnership that operates Jax Restaurant in Foley, Minnesota. One afternoon in October 2000, Nicole Moren, one of the partners, finished her shift at the restaurant at 4:00 P.M. and picked up her two-year-old son, Remington, from day care. About 5:30 P.M., Moren returned to the restaurant with Remington after Amy Benedetti, the other partner and Moren's sister, asked for help. Moren's husband offered to pick up Remington in twenty minutes. Because Moren did not want Remington running around the restaurant, she brought him into the kitchen with her, set him on top of the counter, and began rolling out pizza dough using a dough-pressing machine. While she was making pizzas, Remington reached his hand into the dough press. His hand was crushed, causing permanent injuries. Through his father, Remington filed a suit in a Minnesota state court against the partnership, alleging negligence. The partnership filed a complaint against Moren, arguing that it was entitled to indemnity (compensation or reimbursement) from Moren for her negligence. The court issued a summary judgment in favor of Moren on the complaint. The partnership appealed this judgment to a state intermediate appellate court.

Decision and Rationale The state intermediate appellate court affirmed the lower court's judgment. The appellate court pointed out that under the UPA, a partnership is liable for an injury caused by a partner who, while acting in the ordinary course of the firm's business, commits a wrongful act or omission, or engages in other misconduct. Thus, according to the court, the firm must indemnify a partner for liability incurred by the partner in the ordinary course of the partnership's business. The court also explained that "the conduct of a partner may be partly motivated by personal reasons and still occur in the ordinary course of business of the partnership." In this case, Moren was acting for the benefit of the partnership by making pizzas when her son was injured. Even though she was simultaneously acting in her role as a mother, the court concluded that her conduct remained in the ordinary course of the partnership business. Therefore "liability for Nicole Moren's negligence rested with the partnership, even if the partner's conduct partly served her personal interests." For this reason, said the court, "her conduct bound the partnership and it owes indemnity to her for her negligence."

a. In the "Published" section, click on "M–O." On that page, scroll to the name of the case and click on the docket number to access the opinion. The Minnesota State Law Library maintains this Web site.

CASE 36.1 CONTINUED

- **What If the Facts Were Different?** *Suppose that Moren's predominant motive in bringing her son to the restaurant had been to benefit herself by feeding him free pizza. Would the result have been different? Why or why not?*
- **The Legal Environment Dimension** *What seems to have occurred in this case that might have served as an alternative basis for imposing liability on the partnership? (Hint: Who besides Moren had the authority to act on behalf of the partnership?)*

Liability of Incoming Partners. A partner newly admitted to an existing partnership is not personally liable for any partnership obligation incurred before the person became a partner [UPA 306(b)]. In other words, the new partner's liability to existing creditors of the partnership is limited to her or his capital contribution to the firm. Suppose that Smartclub is a partnership with four members. Alex Jaff, a newly admitted partner, contributes $100,000 to the partnership. Smartclub has about $600,000 in debt at the time Jaff joins the firm. Although Jaff's capital contribution of $100,000 can be used to satisfy Smartclub's obligations, Jaff is not personally liable for partnership debts that were incurred before he became a partner. Thus, his personal assets cannot be used to satisfy the partnership's antecedent (prior) debt. If, however, the managing partner at Smartclub borrows funds for the partnership after Jaff becomes a partner, Jaff will be personally liable for those amounts.

SECTION 4

Dissociation of a Partner

Dissociation occurs when a partner ceases to be associated in the carrying on of the partnership business. Although a partner always has the *power* to dissociate from the firm, he or she may not have the *right* to dissociate. Dissociation normally entitles the partner to have his or her interest purchased by the partnership, and terminates his or her actual authority to act for the partnership and to participate with the partners in running the business. Otherwise, the partnership can continue to do business without the dissociating partner.[10]

Events Causing Dissociation

Under UPA 601, a partner can be dissociated from a partnership in any of the following ways:

1. By the partner's voluntarily giving notice of an "express will to withdraw." (Note that when a partner gives notice of her or his intent to withdraw, the remaining partners must decide whether to continue or give up the partnership business. If they do not agree to continue the partnership, the voluntary dissociation of a partner will dissolve the firm [UPA 801(1)].)
2. By the occurrence of an event agreed to in the partnership agreement.
3. By a unanimous vote of the other partners under certain circumstances, such as when a partner transfers substantially all of her or his interest in the partnership, or when it becomes unlawful to carry on partnership business with that partner.
4. By order of a court or arbitrator if the partner has engaged in wrongful conduct that affects the partnership business, breached the partnership agreement or violated a duty owed to the partnership or the other partners, or engaged in conduct that makes it "not reasonably practicable to carry on the business in partnership with the partner" [UPA 601(5)].
5. By the partner's declaring bankruptcy, assigning his or her interest in the partnership for the benefit of creditors, or becoming physically or mentally incapacitated, or by the partner's death. Note that although the bankruptcy or death of a partner represents that partner's "dissociation" from the partnership, it is not an *automatic* ground for the partnership's dissolution (*dissolution* will be discussed shortly).

Wrongful Dissociation

As mentioned, a partner has the power to dissociate from a partnership at any time, but a partner's dissociation can be wrongful in a few circumstances [UPA 602].

10. Under the previous version of the UPA, when a partner withdrew from a partnership, the partnership was considered dissolved, its business had to be wound up, and the proceeds had to be distributed to creditors and among partners. The new UPA provisions dramatically changed the law governing partnership breakups and dissolution by no longer requiring that the partnership end if one partner dissociates.

When a partner's dissociation is in breach of a partnership agreement, for instance, it is wrongful. For example, a partnership agreement states that it is a breach of the partnership agreement for any partner to assign partnership property to a creditor without the consent of the others. If a partner, Janik, makes such an assignment, she has not only breached the agreement but has also wrongfully dissociated from the partnership. Similarly, if a partner refuses to perform duties required by the partnership agreement—such as accounting for profits earned from the use of partnership property—this breach can be treated as wrongful dissociation.

With regard to a partnership for a definite term or a particular undertaking, dissociation that occurs before the expiration of the term or the completion of the undertaking can be wrongful. In such partnerships, the dissociation normally is considered wrongful if the partner withdraws by express will, is expelled by a court or an arbitrator, or declares bankruptcy [UPA 602].

A partner who wrongfully dissociates is liable to the partnership and to the other partners for damages caused by the dissociation. This liability is in addition to any other obligation of the partner to the partnership or to the other partners. Thus, a wrongfully dissociating partner would be liable to the partnership not only for any damage caused by the breach of the partnership agreement, but also for costs incurred to replace the partner's expertise or to obtain new financing.

Effects of Dissociation

Dissociation (rightful or wrongful) terminates some of the rights of the dissociated partner, requires that the partnership purchase his or her interest, and alters the liability of the parties to third parties.

Rights and Duties On a partner's dissociation, his or her right to participate in the management and conduct of the partnership business terminates [UPA 603]. The partner's duty of loyalty also ends. A partner's other fiduciary duties, including the duty of care, continue only with respect to events that occurred before dissociation, unless the partner participates in winding up the partnership's business (discussed later in this chapter). For example, Debbie Pearson is a partner who is leaving an accounting firm, Bubb & Pearson. Pearson can immediately compete with the firm for new clients. She must exercise care in completing ongoing client transactions, however, and must account to the firm for any fees received from the old clients based on those transactions.

After a partner's dissociation, his or her interest in the partnership must be purchased according to the rules in UPA 701. The **buyout price** is based on the amount that would have been distributed to the partner if the partnership had been wound up on the date of dissociation. Offset against the price are amounts owed by the partner to the partnership, including damages for wrongful dissociation.

In the following case, the court had to decide how the buyout price of a partner's interest should be determined on his dissociation from his family's ranch business, which had been operated as a partnership for more than twenty years.

CASE 36.2 Warnick v. Warnick

Supreme Court of Wyoming, 2006. 2006 WY 58, 133 P.3d 997.

• **Background and Facts** In 1978, Wilbur and Dee Warnick and their son Randall Warnick bought a ranch in Sheridan County, Wyoming, for $335,000. To operate the ranch, they formed a partnership—Warnick Ranches. The partners' initial capital contributions totaled $60,000, of which Wilbur paid 36 percent, Dee paid 30 percent, and Randall paid 34 percent. Wilbur and Dee moved onto the ranch in 1981. Randall lived and worked on the ranch during the 1981 and 1982 summer haying seasons and again from 1991 to 1998. The partners each contributed funds to the operation and received cash distributions from the partnership. In the summer of 1999, Randall dissociated from the partnership. When the parties could not agree on a buyout price, Randall filed a suit in a Wyoming state court against the other partners and the partnership to recover what he believed to be a fair price. The court awarded Randall $115,783.13—the amount of his cash contributions, plus 34 percent of the partnership assets' increase in value above all partners' cash contributions, with interest from the date of his dissociation. The defendants appealed to the Wyoming Supreme Court,

CASE 36.2 CONTINUED arguing that, in the calculation, $50,000 should be deducted from the appraised value of the ranch, its livestock, and its equipment for the estimated expenses of selling these assets.

● **Decision and Rationale** The court affirmed the judgment of the lower court, holding that "purely hypothetical costs of sale are not a required deduction in valuing partnership assets." The state supreme court explained that under Wyoming Statutes Section 17-21-701 (Wyoming's version of UPA 701) the buyout price is "the amount that would have been paid to the dissociating partner following a settlement of partnership accounts upon the winding up of the partnership, if, on the date of dissociation, the assets of the partnership were sold at a price equal to the greater of the liquidation value or the value based on a sale of the business as a going concern without the dissociating partner." The first step in the calculation is to value the partnership's assets according to the two methods. In making the determination in this case, the defendants "assume that the liquidation value of the ranch is the amount of cash that would remain following a sale." But liquidation value refers to the prices of assets if they are sold separately, as opposed to the value of the business as a whole. For this purpose, an asset's price is the amount that "a willing and informed buyer would pay a willing and informed seller, with neither being under any compulsion to deal." Such a seller would factor the cost of a sale into the price, as the appraiser and the lower court likely did here. Besides "the assets of this partnership were not, in fact, liquidated. Instead, * * * the assets were retained by Warnick Ranches."

● **The Ethical Dimension** *Was it unethical for Randall to file a suit against his parents to obtain what he regarded as a fair price for his interest? Why or why not?*

● **The Legal Environment Dimension** *How and why might the value of a partnership interest in a going concern differ from the value of the same interest as a result of a liquidation?*

Liability to Third Parties For two years after a partner dissociates from a continuing partnership, the partnership may be bound by the acts of the dissociated partner based on apparent authority [UPA 702]. In other words, the partnership may be liable to a third party with whom a dissociated partner enters into a transaction if the third party reasonably believed that the dissociated partner was still a partner. Similarly, a dissociated partner may be liable for partnership obligations entered into during a two-year period following dissociation [UPA 703].

To avoid this possible liability, a partnership should notify its creditors, customers, and clients of a partner's dissociation. Also, either the partnership or the dissociated partner can file a statement of dissociation in the appropriate state office to limit the dissociated partner's authority to ninety days after the filing [UPA 704]. Filing this statement helps to minimize the firm's potential liability for the former partner and vice versa.

SECTION 5 Partnership Termination

The same events that cause dissociation can result in the end of the partnership if the remaining partners no longer wish to (or are unable to) continue the partnership business. Not every type of dissociation will cause dissolution of the partnership, though. Only certain departures of a partner will trigger dissolution, and generally the partnership can continue if the remaining partners consent [UPA 801].

The termination of a partnership is referred to as **dissolution,** which essentially means the commencement of the winding up process. **Winding up** is the actual process of collecting, liquidating, and distributing the partnership assets.[11] We discuss here the dissolution and winding up of partnership business.

Dissolution

Dissolution of a partnership generally can be brought about by the acts of the partners, by operation of law, and by judicial decree [UPA 801]. Any partnership (including one for a fixed term) can be dissolved by the partners' agreement. Similarly, if the partnership agreement states that it will dissolve on a certain event, such as a partner's death or bankruptcy, then the

11. Although "winding down" would seem to describe more accurately the process of settling accounts and liquidating the assets of a partnership, English and U.S. statutory and case law have traditionally used "winding up" to denote this final stage of a partnership's existence.

occurrence of that event will dissolve the partnership. A partnership for a fixed term or a particular undertaking is dissolved by operation of law at the expiration of the term or on the completion of the undertaking.

Any event that makes it unlawful for the partnership to continue its business will result in dissolution [UPA 801(4)]. Under the UPA, a court may order dissolution when it becomes obviously impractical for the firm to continue—for example, if the business can only be operated at a loss [UPA 801(5)]. Additionally, a partner's impropriety involving partnership business (for example, fraud perpetrated on the other partners) or improper behavior reflecting unfavorably on the firm may provide grounds for a judicial decree of dissolution. Finally, if dissension between partners becomes so persistent and harmful as to undermine the confidence and cooperation necessary to carry on the firm's business, a court may grant a decree of dissolution.

Winding Up and Distribution of Assets

After dissolution, the partnership continues for the limited purpose of the winding up process.[12] The partners cannot create new obligations on behalf of the partnership. They have authority only to complete transactions begun but not finished at the time of dissolution and to wind up the business of the partnership [UPA 803, 804(1)].

Winding up includes collecting and preserving partnership assets, discharging liabilities (paying debts), and accounting to each partner for the value of his or her interest in the partnership. Partners continue to have fiduciary duties to one another and to the firm during this process. UPA 401(h) provides that a partner is entitled to compensation for services in winding up partnership affairs (and reimbursement for expenses incurred in the process) above and apart from his or her share in the partnership profits.

Both creditors of the partnership and creditors of the individual partners can make claims on the partnership's assets. In general, partnership creditors share proportionately with the partners' individual creditors in the partners' assets, which include their interests in the partnership. A partnership's assets are distributed according to the following priorities [UPA 807]:

1. Payment of debts, including those owed to partner and nonpartner creditors.
2. Return of capital contributions and distribution of profits to partners.[13]

If the partnership's liabilities are greater than its assets, the partners bear the losses—in the absence of a contrary agreement—in the same proportion in which they shared the profits (rather than, for example, in proportion to their contributions to the partnership's capital).

Partnership Buy-Sell Agreements

Usually, when people enter into partnerships, they are getting along with one another. To prepare for the possibility that the situation might change and they may become unable to work together amicably, the partners should make express arrangements during the formation of the partnership to provide for its smooth dissolution. A **buy-sell agreement,** sometimes called simply a *buyout agreement,* provides for one or more partners to buy out the other or others, should the situation warrant. Agreeing beforehand on who buys what, under what circumstances, and, if possible, at what price may eliminate costly negotiations or litigation later. Alternatively, the agreement may specify that one or more partners will determine the value of the interest being sold and that the other or others will decide whether to buy or sell.

Under UPA 701(a), if a partner's dissociation does not result in a dissolution of the partnership, a buyout of the partner's interest is mandatory. The UPA contains an extensive set of buyout rules that apply when the partners do not have a buyout agreement. Basically, a withdrawing partner receives the same amount through a buyout that he or she would receive if the business were winding up [UPA 701(b)].

SECTION 6 Limited Liability Partnerships

The **limited liability partnership (LLP)** is a hybrid form of business designed mostly for professionals who normally do business as partners in a partnership. The major advantage of the LLP is that it allows a partnership to continue as a pass-through entity for tax purposes but limits the personal liability of the partners.

12. Note that at any time after dissolution but before winding up is completed, all of the partners may decide to continue the partnership business and waive the right to have the business wound up [UPA 802].

13. Under the previous version of the UPA, creditors of the partnership had priority over creditors of the individual partners. Also, in distributing partnership assets, third party creditors were paid before partner creditors, and capital contributions were returned before profits.

The first state to enact an LLP statute was Texas, in 1991. Other states quickly followed suit, and by 1997, virtually all of the states had enacted LLP statutes. LLPs must be formed and operated in compliance with state statutes, which may include provisions of the UPA. The appropriate form must be filed with a central state agency, usually the secretary of state's office, and the business's name must include either "Limited Liability Partnership" or "LLP" [UPA 1001, 1002]. In addition, an LLP must file an annual report with the state to remain qualified as an LLP in that state [UPA 1003]. In most states, it is relatively easy to convert a traditional partnership into an LLP because the firm's basic organizational structure remains the same. Additionally, all of the statutory and common law rules governing partnerships still apply (apart from those modified by the LLP statute). Normally, LLP statutes are simply amendments to a state's already existing partnership law.

The LLP is especially attractive for two categories of enterprises: professional services and family businesses. Professional service firms include law firms and accounting firms. *Family limited liability partnerships* are basically business organizations in which the majority of the partners are related to each other.

Liability in an LLP

Traditionally, many professionals, such as attorneys and accountants, have worked together using the partnership business form. As previously discussed, a major disadvantage of the general partnership is the unlimited personal liability of its owner-partners. Each partner in a general partnership is exposed to potential liability for the malpractice of another partner.

The LLP allows professionals to avoid personal liability for the malpractice of other partners. A partner in an LLP is still liable for her or his own wrongful acts, such as negligence, however. Also liable is the partner who supervised the party who committed a wrongful act. This is generally true for all types of partners and partnerships, not just LLPs.

Although LLP statutes vary from state to state, generally each state statute limits the liability of partners in some way. For example, Delaware law protects each innocent partner from the "debts and obligations of the partnership arising from negligence, wrongful acts, or misconduct." In North Carolina, Texas, and Washington, D.C., the statutes protect innocent partners from obligations arising from "errors, omissions, negligence, incompetence, or malfeasance." The UPA more broadly exempts partners from personal liability for any partnership obligation, "whether arising in contract, tort, or otherwise" [UPA 306(c)]. Even though the language of these statutes may seem to apply specifically to attorneys, virtually any group of professionals can use the LLP (depending on the state statute). LLPs are especially popular in the accounting field. All of the "Big Four" firms—the four largest international accountancy and professional services firms—are organized as LLPs, including PricewaterhouseCoopers, LLP, and Deloitte Development, LLP.

Family Limited Liability Partnerships

A **family limited liability partnership (FLLP)** is a limited liability partnership in which the majority of the partners are persons related to each other, essentially as spouses, parents, grandparents, siblings, cousins, nephews, or nieces. A person acting in a fiduciary capacity for persons so related can also be a partner. All of the partners must be natural persons or persons acting in a fiduciary capacity for the benefit of natural persons.

Probably the most significant use of the FLLP form of business organization is in agriculture. Family-owned farms sometimes find this form to their benefit. The FLLP offers the same advantages as other LLPs with certain additional advantages, such as, in Iowa, an exemption from real estate transfer taxes when partnership real estate is transferred among partners.[14]

SECTION 7 Limited Partnerships

We now look at a business organizational form that limits the liability of *some* of its owners—the **limited partnership.** Limited partnerships originated in medieval Europe and have been in existence in the United States since the early 1800s. In many ways, limited partnerships are like the general partnerships discussed at the beginning of this chapter, but they differ from general partnerships in several ways. Because of this, they are sometimes referred to as *special partnerships.*

A limited partnership consists of at least one **general partner** and one or more **limited partners.** A general partner assumes management responsibility

14. Iowa Statutes Section 428A.2.

for the partnership and has full responsibility for the partnership and for all its debts. A limited partner contributes cash or other property and owns an interest in the firm but does not undertake any management responsibilities and is not personally liable for partnership debts beyond the amount of his or her investment. A limited partner can forfeit limited liability by taking part in the management of the business. A comparison of the characteristics of general partnerships and limited partnerships appears in Exhibit 36–2.[15]

Until 1976, the law governing limited partnerships in all states except Louisiana was the Uniform Limited Partnership Act (ULPA). Since 1976, most states and the District of Columbia have adopted the revised version of the ULPA, known as the Revised Uniform Limited Partnership Act (RULPA). Because the RULPA is the dominant law governing limited partnerships in the United States, we refer to the RULPA in the following discussion. Note, however, that in 2001 the National Conference of Commissioners on Uniform State Laws adopted a new, more flexible version of this law (ULPA 2001), which has been adopted in a minority of states.

Formation of a Limited Partnership

In contrast to the informal, private, and voluntary agreement that usually suffices for a general partnership, the formation of a limited partnership is formal and public. The parties must follow specific statutory requirements and file a certificate with the state. In this regard, a limited partnership resembles a corporation more than it does a general partnership. A limited partnership must have at least one general partner and one limited partner, as mentioned previously. Additionally, the partners must sign a **certificate of limited partnership,** which requires information similar to that found in a corporate charter (see Chapter 38), such as the name, mailing address, and capital contribution of each general and limited partner. The certificate must be filed with the designated state official—under the RULPA, the secretary of state. The certificate is usually open to public inspection.

Rights and Liabilities of Partners

General partners, unlike limited partners, are personally liable to the partnership's creditors; thus, at least one general partner is necessary in a limited partnership so that someone has personal liability. This policy can be circumvented in states that allow a corporation to be the general partner in a partnership. Because the corporation has limited liability by virtue of corporation statutes, if a corporation is the general partner, no one in the limited partnership has personal liability.

Rights of Limited Partners Subject to the limitations that will be discussed shortly, limited partners have essentially the same rights as general partners, including the right of access to partnership books and the right to other information regarding partnership business. On dissolution of the partnership, limited partners are entitled to a return of their contributions in accordance with the partnership certificate [RULPA 201(a)(10)]. They can also assign their interests subject to the certificate [RULPA 702, 704].

The RULPA provides that a limited partner has the right to sue an outside party on behalf of the firm if the general partners with authority to do so have refused to file suit [RULPA 1001].[16] In addition, investor protection legislation, such as securities laws (discussed in Chapter 41), may give some protection to limited partners.

Liabilities of Limited Partners In contrast to the personal liability of general partners, the liability of a limited partner is limited to the capital that she or he contributes or agrees to contribute to the partnership [RULPA 502].

A limited partnership is formed by good faith compliance with the requirements for signing and filing the certificate, even if it is incomplete or defective. When a limited partner discovers a defect in the formation of the limited partnership, he or she can avoid future liability by filing the appropriate amendment or correction with the state or by renouncing an interest in the profits of the partnership [RULPA 304]. If the limited partner takes neither of these actions on discovery of the defect, however, the firm's creditors can hold the partner personally liable [RULPA 207].

Limited Partners and Management Limited partners enjoy limited liability so long as they do not participate in management [RULPA 303].[17] A limited partner who participates in management will be just as liable as a general partner to any creditor who trans-

15. Under the UPA, a general partnership can be converted into a limited partnership and vice versa [UPA 902, 903]. The UPA also provides for the merger of a general partnership with one or more general or limited partnerships [UPA 905].

16. For a case from a jurisdiction that does *not* follow the RULPA in this respect, see *Energy Investors Fund, L.P. v. Metric Constructors, Inc.,* 351 N.C. 331, 525 S.E.2d 441 (2000).

17. Note that the 2001 version of this law (which has been adopted in a minority of states) provides limited liability to limited partners for entity obligations "even if the limited partner participates in the management and control of the limited partnership" [ULPA 2001, Section 303].

EXHIBIT 36–2 • A Comparison of General Partnerships and Limited Partnerships

Characteristic	General Partnership (UPA)	Limited Partnership (RULPA)
Creation	By agreement of two or more persons to carry on a business as co-owners for profit.	By agreement of two or more persons to carry on a business as co-owners for profit. Must include one or more general partners and one or more limited partners. Filing of a certificate with the secretary of state is required.
Sharing of Profits and Losses	By agreement; or, in the absence of agreement, profits are shared equally by the partners, and losses are shared in the same ratio as profits.	Profits are shared as required in the certificate agreement, and losses are shared likewise, up to the amount of the limited partners' capital contributions. In the absence of a provision in the certificate agreement, profits and losses are shared on the basis of percentages of capital contributions.
Liability	Unlimited personal liability of all partners.	Unlimited personal liability of all general partners; limited partners liable only to the extent of their capital contributions.
Capital Contribution	No minimum or mandatory amount; set by agreement.	Set by agreement.
Management	By agreement, or in the absence of agreement, all partners have an equal voice.	General partner or partners only. Limited partners have no voice or else are subject to liability as general partners (but *only* if a third party has reason to believe that the limited partner is a general partner). A limited partner may act as an agent or employee of the partnership and vote on amending the certificate or on the sale or dissolution of the partnership.
Duration	Terminated by agreement of the partners, but can continue to do business even when a partner dissociates from the partnership.	Terminated by agreement in the certificate or by retirement, death, or mental incompetence of a general partner in the absence of the right of the other general partners to continue the partnership. Death of a limited partner, unless he or she is the only remaining limited partner, does not terminate the partnership.
Distribution of Assets on Liquidation—Order of Priorities	1. Payment of debts, including those owed to partner and nonpartner creditors. 2. Return of capital contributions and distribution of profit to partners.	1. Outside creditors and partner creditors. 2. Partners and former partners entitled to distributions or partnership assets. 3. Unless otherwise agreed, return of capital contributions and distribution of profit to partners.

acts business with the limited partnership and believes, based on the limited partner's conduct, that the limited partner is a general partner [RULPA 303]. The degree to which a limited partner can participate—by, for example, reviewing partnership operations or providing advice—before being exposed to liability is an unsettled question.[18] A limited partner who knowingly permits his or her name to be used in

18. The question is unsettled partly because state laws differ on this issue. Factors to be considered under the RULPA are listed in RULPA 303(b), (c).

the name of the limited partnership is liable to creditors who extend credit to the limited partnership without knowledge that the limited partner is not a general partner [RULPA 102, 303(d)].

Although limited partners cannot participate in management, this does not mean that the general partners are totally free of restrictions in running the business. The general partners in a limited partnership have fiduciary obligations to the partnership and to the limited partners. Suppose that a limited partnership is formed to build and operate a shopping mall. The parties reach an agreement under which the limited partners have several options for handling their 15 percent interest in the mall. If the general partner transfers the partnership's interests in the mall into a trust vehicle (see Chapter 50) without informing the limited partners or obtaining their consent, the general partner has violated his fiduciary duties to the limited partners.[19]

Dissociation and Dissolution

A general partner has the power to voluntarily dissociate, or withdraw, from a limited partnership unless the partnership agreement specifies otherwise. A limited partner theoretically can withdraw from the partnership by giving six months' notice unless the partnership agreement specifies a term, which most do. Also, some states have passed laws prohibiting the withdrawal of limited partners.

In a limited partnership, a general partner's voluntary dissociation from the firm normally will lead to dissolution *unless* all partners agree to continue the business. Similarly, the bankruptcy, retirement, death, or mental incompetence of a general partner will cause the dissociation of that partner and the dissolution of the limited partnership unless the other members agree to continue the firm [RULPA 801]. Bankruptcy of a limited partner, however, does not dissolve the partnership unless it causes the bankruptcy of the firm. Death or an assignment of the interest of a limited partner does not dissolve a limited partnership [RULPA 702, 704, 705]. A limited partnership can be dissolved by court decree [RULPA 802].

On dissolution, creditors' claims, including those of partners who are creditors, take first priority. After that, partners and former partners receive unpaid distributions of partnership assets and, except as otherwise agreed, amounts representing returns on their contributions and amounts proportionate to their shares of the distributions [RULPA 804].

In the following case, two limited partners wanted the business of the partnership to be sold on its dissolution, while another limited partner and the general partner wanted it to continue.

19. *Smith v. Fairfax Realty, Inc.*, 82 P.3d 1064 (Utah Sup.Ct. 2003).

CASE 36.3 In re Dissolution of Midnight Star Enterprises, L.P.

Supreme Court of South Dakota, 2006. 2006 SD 98, 724 N.W.2d 334.

• **Background and Facts** Midnight Star Enterprises, Limited Partnership, consists of a casino, bar, and restaurant in Deadwood, South Dakota. The owners are Midnight Star Enterprises, Limited (MSEL), the general partner, which owns 22 partnership units; actor Kevin Costner, a limited partner, who owns 71.5 partnership units; and Carla and Francis Caneva, limited partners, who own 3.25 partnership units each. Costner also owns MSEL and thus controls 93.5 partnership units. The Canevas were the business's managers, for which they received salaries and bonuses. When MSEL voiced concerns about the management, communication among the partners broke down. MSEL filed a petition in a South Dakota state court to dissolve the partnership. MSEL hired Paul Thorstenson, an accountant, to determine the firm's fair market value, which he calculated to be \$3.1 million. The Canevas solicited a competitor's offer to buy the business for \$6.2 million, which the court ruled was the appropriate amount. At the Canevas' request, the court ordered MSEL and Costner to buy the business for that price within ten days or sell it on the open market to the highest bidder. MSEL appealed to the South Dakota Supreme Court.

• **Decision and Rationale** The South Dakota Supreme Court reversed the judgment of the lower court and remanded the case to allow MSEL and Costner to pay the Canevas the value of their 6.5 partnership units after a revaluation of the partnership. The state supreme court concluded that the partnership agreement did not require the business to be sold on the open market on the partnership's dissolution. Under the agreement, during liquidation, the firm's property could be distributed in kind among the partners if it was first offered for sale to a third party. In other

CASE 36.3 CONTINUED words, only a decision to make an in-kind distribution of assets required that the business be offered for sale on the open market. The court also concluded that the correct value of the business was the accountant's figure, which was based on a fair market value analysis using a hypothetical buyer. This analysis provided a reasonable basis for determining value "by removing the irrationalities, strategies, and emotions" that exist in an actual offer. Besides, the partnership agreement required a "fair market value" of the assets. Finally, "since it was error for the [lower] court to value Midnight Star at $6.2 million, it was also error to force the general partners to buy the business for $6.2 million or sell the business." The state supreme court reasoned that "forced sales typically end up in economic waste." A buyout is an acceptable alternative, as long as the partners receive the fair value of their property interest. "Instead of ordering the majority partners to purchase the whole partnership for the appraised value, the majority partners should only be required to pay any interests the withdrawing partner is due."

- **The Legal Environment Dimension** *Why did the court hold that a forced sale of the property of the limited partnership was not appropriate in this case?*

- **The Ethical Dimension** *Under what circumstances might a forced sale of the property of a limited partnership on its dissolution be appropriate?*

Limited Liability Limited Partnerships

A **limited liability limited partnership (LLLP)** is a type of limited partnership. An LLLP differs from a limited partnership in that a general partner in an LLLP has the same liability as a limited partner in a limited partnership. In other words, the liability of all partners is limited to the amount of their investments in the firm.

A few states provide expressly for LLLPs.[20] In states that do not provide for LLLPs but do allow for limited partnerships and limited liability partnerships, a limited partnership should probably still be able to register with the state as an LLLP.

20. See, for example, Colorado Revised Statutes Annotated Section 7-62-109. Other states that provide expressly for limited liability limited partnerships include Delaware, Florida, Georgia, Kentucky, Maryland, Nevada, Texas, and Virginia.

REVIEWING Partnerships and Limited Liability Partnerships

Grace Tarnavsky and her sons, Manny and Jason, bought a ranch known as the Cowboy Palace in March 2006, and the three verbally agreed to share the business for five years. Grace contributed 50 percent of the investment, and each son contributed 25 percent. Manny agreed to handle the livestock, and Jason agreed to handle the bookkeeping. The Tarnavskys took out joint loans and opened a joint bank account into which they deposited the ranch's proceeds and from which they made payments toward property, cattle, equipment, and supplies. In September 2008, Manny severely injured his back while baling hay and became permanently unable to handle livestock. Manny therefore hired additional laborers to tend the livestock, causing the Cowboy Palace to incur significant debt. In September 2009, Al's Feed Barn filed a lawsuit against Jason to collect $32,400 in unpaid debts. Using the information presented in the chapter, answer the following questions.

1. Was this relationship a partnership for a term or a partnership at will?
2. Did Manny have the authority to hire additional laborers to work at the ranch after his injury? Why or why not?
3. Under the current UPA, can Al's Feed Barn bring an action against Jason individually for the Cowboy Palace's debt? Why or why not?
4. Suppose that after his back injury in 2008, Manny sent his mother and brother a notice indicating his intent to withdraw from the partnership. Can he still be held liable for the debt to Al's Feed Barn? Why or why not?

TERMS AND CONCEPTS

articles of partnership 685
buyout price 692
buy-sell agreement 694
certificate of limited partnership 696
charging order 687
confession of judgment 687
dissociation 691
dissolution 693
family limited liability partnership (FLLP) 695
general partner 695
information return 685
joint and several liability 690
joint liability 689
limited liability limited partnership (LLLP) 699
limited liability partnership (LLP) 694
limited partner 695
limited partnership 695
partnership 683
partnership by estoppel 685
winding up 693

QUESTIONS AND CASE PROBLEMS

36–1. Daniel is the owner of a chain of shoe stores. He hires Rubya to be the manager of a new store, which is to open in Grand Rapids, Michigan. Daniel, by written contract, agrees to pay Rubya a monthly salary and 20 percent of the profits. Without Daniel's knowledge, Rubya represents himself to Classen as Daniel's partner, showing Classen the agreement to share profits. Classen extends credit to Rubya. Rubya defaults. Discuss whether Classen can hold Daniel liable as a partner.

36–2. QUESTION WITH SAMPLE ANSWER

Dorinda, Luis, and Elizabeth form a limited partnership. Dorinda is a general partner, and Luis and Elizabeth are limited partners. Consider each of the separate events below, and discuss fully which event(s) constitute(s) a dissolution of the limited partnership.

(a) Luis assigns his partnership interest to Ashley.
(b) Elizabeth is petitioned into involuntary bankruptcy.
(c) Dorinda dies.

- **For a sample answer to Question 36–2, go to Appendix I at the end of this text.**

36–3. Meyer, Knapp, and Cavanna establish a partnership to operate a window-washing service. Meyer contributes $10,000 to the partnership, and Knapp and Cavanna contribute $1,000 each. The partnership agreement is silent as to how profits and losses will be shared. One month after the partnership begins operation, Knapp and Cavanna vote, over Meyer's objection, to purchase another truck for the firm. Meyer believes that because he contributed $10,000, the partnership cannot make any major commitment to purchase over his objection. In addition, Meyer claims that in the absence of any provision in the agreement, profits must be divided in the same ratio as capital contributions. Discuss Meyer's contentions.

36–4. Liability of Partners. Frank Kolk was the manager of Triples American Grill, a sports bar and restaurant. Kolk and John Baines opened bank accounts in the name of the bar, each signing the account signature cards as "owner." Baines was often at the bar and had free access to its office. Baines told others that he was "an owner" and "a partner." Kolk told Steve Mager, the president of Cheesecake Factory, Inc., that Baines was a member of a partnership that owned Triples. On this basis, Cheesecake delivered its goods to Triples on credit. In fact, the bar was owned by a corporation. When the unpaid account totaled more than $20,000, Cheesecake filed a suit in a New Mexico state court against Baines to collect. On what basis might Baines be liable to Cheesecake? What does Cheesecake have to show to win its case? [*Cheesecake Factory, Inc. v. Baines,* 125 N.M. 622, 964 P.2d 183 (1998)]

36–5. Indications of Partnership. In August 1998, Jea Yu contacted Cameron Eppler, president of Design88, Ltd., to discuss developing a Web site that would cater to investors and provide services to its members for a fee. Yu and Patrick Connelly invited Eppler and Ha Tran, another member of Design88, to a meeting to discuss the site. The parties agreed that Design88 would perform certain Web design, implementation, and maintenance functions for 10 percent of the profits from the site, which would be called "The Underground Trader." They signed a "Master Partnership Agreement," which was later amended to include Power Uptik Productions, LLC (PUP). The parties often referred to themselves as partners. From Design88's offices in Virginia, Design88 designed and hosted the site, solicited members through Internet and national print campaigns, processed member applications, provided technical support, monitored access to the site, and negotiated and formed business alliances on the site's behalf. When relations among the parties soured, PUP withdrew. Design88 filed a suit against PUP and the others. Did a partnership exist among these parties? Explain.

[*Design88 Ltd. v. Power Uptik Productions, LLC,* 133 F.Supp.2d 873 (W.D.Va. 2001)]

36–6. Fiduciary Duties. Charles Chaney and Lawrence Burdett were equal partners in a partnership in Georgia known as BMW Partners. Their agreement was silent as to the effect of a partner's death on the firm. The partnership's sole asset was real property, which the firm leased in 1987 to a corporation that the partners co-owned. Under the lease, the corporation was to pay the partnership $8,000 per month, but after a few years, the corporation began paying $9,000 per month. Chaney died on April 15, 1998. Burdett wanted to continue the partnership business and offered to buy Chaney's estate's interest in it. Meanwhile, claiming that the real property's fair rental value was $4,500 (not $9,000) and that the corporation had overpaid the rent by $80,000, Burdett adjusted the rental payments to recoup this amount. Bonnie Chaney, Charles's widow and his estate's legal representative, filed a suit in a Georgia state court against Burdett, alleging, in part, that he had breached his fiduciary duty by adjusting the amount of the rent. Did Burdett's fiduciary duty expire on Chaney's death? Explain. [*Chaney v. Burdett,* 274 Ga. 805, 560 S.E.2d 21 (2002)]

36–7. CASE PROBLEM WITH SAMPLE ANSWER

At least six months before the 1996 Summer Olympic Games in Atlanta, Georgia, Stafford Fontenot, Steve Turner, Mike Montelaro, Joe Sokol, and Doug Brinsmade agreed to sell Cajun food at the Games and began making preparations. Calling themselves "Prairie Cajun Seafood Catering of Louisiana," on May 19 the group applied for a license with the Fulton County, Georgia, Department of Public Health–Environmental Health Services. Later, Ted Norris received for the sale of a mobile kitchen an $8,000 check drawn on the "Prairie Cajun Seafood Catering of Louisiana" account and two promissory notes, one for $12,000 and the other for $20,000. The notes, which were dated June 12, listed only Fontenot "d/b/a [doing business as] Prairie Cajun Seafood" as the maker. On July 31, Fontenot and his friends signed a partnership agreement, which listed specific percentages of profits and losses. They drove the mobile kitchen to Atlanta, but business was "disastrous." When the notes were not paid, Norris filed a suit in a Louisiana state court against Fontenot, seeking payment. What are the elements of a partnership? Was there a partnership among Fontenot and the others? Who is liable on the notes? Explain. [*Norris v. Fontenot,* 867 So.2d 179 (La.App. 3 Cir. 2004)]

- **To view a sample answer for Problem 36–7, go to this book's Web site at www.cengage.com/blaw/jentz, select "Chapter 36," and click on "Case Problem with Sample Answer."**

36–8. Partnership Status. Charlie Waugh owned and operated an auto parts junkyard in Georgia. Charlie's son, Mack, started working in the business part-time as a child and full-time when he left school at the age of sixteen. Mack oversaw the business's finances, depositing the profits in a bank. Charlie gave Mack a one-half interest in the business, telling him that if "something happened" to Charlie, the entire business would be his. In 1994, Charlie and his wife, Alene, transferred to Mack the land on which the junkyard was located. Two years later, however, Alene and her daughters, Gail and Jewel, falsely convinced Charlie, whose mental competence had deteriorated, that Mack had cheated him. Mack was ordered off the land. Shortly thereafter, Charlie died. Mack filed a suit in a Georgia state court against the rest of the family, asserting, in part, that he and Charlie had been partners and that he was entitled to Charlie's share of the business. Was the relationship between Charlie and Mack a partnership? Is Mack entitled to Charlie's "share"? Explain. [*Waugh v. Waugh,* 265 Ga.App. 799, 595 S.E.2d 647 (2004)]

36–9. Indications of Partnership. In August 2003, Tammy Duncan began working as a waitress at Bynum's Diner, which was owned by her mother, Hazel Bynum, and her stepfather, Eddie Bynum, in Valdosta, Georgia. Less than a month later, the three signed an agreement under which Eddie was to relinquish his management responsibilities, allowing Tammy to be co-manager. At the end of this six-month period, Eddie would revisit this agreement and could then extend it for another six-month period. The diner's bank account was to remain in Eddie's name. There was no provision with regard to the diner's profit, if any, and the parties did not change the business's tax information. Tammy began doing the bookkeeping, as well as waiting tables and performing other duties. On October 30, she slipped off a ladder and injured her knees. At the end of the six-month term, Tammy quit working at the diner. The Georgia State Board of Workers' Compensation determined that she had been the diner's employee and awarded her benefits under the diner's workers' compensation policy with Cypress Insurance Co. Cypress filed a suit in a Georgia state court against Tammy, arguing that she was not an employee, but a co-owner. What are the essential elements of a partnership? Was Tammy a partner in the business of the diner? Explain. [*Cypress Insurance Co. v. Duncan,* 281 Ga.App. 469, 636 S.E.2d 159 (2006)]

36–10. A QUESTION OF ETHICS

In 1991, Hassan Mardanlou and Ali Ghaffarian signed a lease for 3960 South State Street in Salt Lake City, Utah. Ghaffarian paid $6,000 for the first and last months' rent, and said to Mardanlou, "We are in this together, partner." Mardanlou bought business cards for "Access Auto" with his and Ghaffarian's names on the cards. Both men were listed on Access Auto's insurance policy. Mardanlou bought the firm's furniture. Ghaffarian did the bookkeeping and bought the inventory. Mardanlou did not have access to the books but wrote checks on the firm's account, sold its inventory, and managed the sales staff. In March 1993, Ghaffarian gave Mardanlou a check *for $10,000. Otherwise, Mardanlou was paid a fixed amount each month. Later that year, without telling Mardanlou, Ghaffarian bought the leased property with the firm's funds but titled it in his name. In 1995, Mardanlou learned of this deal and confronted Ghaffarian, who said, "Don't worry, we're partners." Ghaffarian filed the firm's tax returns in his name only, despite Mardanlou's repeated objections. Finally, in 1997, Mardanlou quit the firm and filed a suit in a Utah state court against Ghaffarian to dissolve the partnership and obtain a share of the profits.* [Mardanlou v. Ghaffarian, *2006 UT App 165, 135 P.3d 904 (2006)*]

(a) What factors indicate that Mardanlou and Ghaffarian were partners? What factors indicate that they were not partners? If you were the judge, how would you resolve this dispute?
(b) Is Mardanlou entitled to a share of the value of the real property that Ghaffarian bought in his own name? If so, how much? From an ethical point of view, what solution appears to be the fairest? Discuss.
(c) Is Mardanlou entitled to a share of Access Auto's profits? Why or why not?

LAW ON THE WEB

For updated links to resources available on the Web, as well as a variety of other materials, visit this text's Web site at

www.cengage.com/blaw/jentz

For some of the advantages and disadvantages of doing business as a partnership, go to the following page, which is part of the U.S. Small Business Administration's Web site. Click on "Forms of Ownership" and then scroll down to "Partnerships."

www.sba.gov/smallbusinessplanner/start/chooseastructure/index.html

Legal Research Exercises on the Web

Go to **www.cengage.com/blaw/jentz**, the Web site that accompanies this text. Select "Chapter 36" and click on "Internet Exercises." There you will find the following Internet research exercises that you can perform to learn more about the topics covered in this chapter.

Internet Exercise 36–1: Legal Perspective
Liability of Dissociated Partners

Internet Exercise 36–2: Economic Perspective
Taxation of Partnerships

Internet Exercise 36–3: Management Perspective
Limited Partnerships and Limited Liability Partnerships

CHAPTER 37

Limited Liability Companies and Special Business Forms

In the preceding chapters, we have examined sole proprietorships, partnerships, and several forms of limited partnerships. Before we discuss corporations, one of the most prevalent business forms, we pause to examine a relatively new form of business organization called the **limited liability company (LLC).** The LLC is a hybrid form that combines the limited liability aspects of the corporation and the tax advantages of a partnership. Increasingly, LLCs are becoming an organizational form of choice among businesspersons—a trend encouraged by state statutes permitting their use.

In this chapter, we begin by examining the LLC. After looking at the LLC form of business in some detail, we describe a number of business forms that can be used for special types of business ventures.

SECTION 1 Limited Liability Companies

Limited liability companies (LLCs) are governed by state LLC statutes. These laws vary, of course, from state to state. In an attempt to create more uniformity among the states in this respect, in 1995 the National Conference of Commissioners on Uniform State Laws issued the Uniform Limited Liability Company Act (ULLCA). To date, fewer than one-fourth of the states have adopted the ULLCA, and thus the law governing LLCs remains far from uniform.[1] Some provisions are common to most state statutes, however, and we base our discussion of LLCs in this section on these common elements.

Evolution of the LLC

In 1977, Wyoming became the first state to pass legislation authorizing the creation of an LLC. Although LLCs emerged in the United States only in 1977, they have been used for more than a century in various foreign jurisdictions, including several European and South American nations. For example, the South American *limitada* is a form of business organization that operates more or less as a partnership but provides limited liability for the owners.

Taxation of the LLC In the United States, after Wyoming's adoption of an LLC statute, it still was not known how the Internal Revenue Service (IRS) would treat the LLC for tax purposes. In 1988, however, the IRS ruled that Wyoming LLCs would be taxed as partnerships instead of corporations, providing that certain requirements were met. Prior to this ruling, only one additional state—Florida, in 1982—had authorized LLCs. The 1988 ruling encouraged other states to enact LLC statutes, and in less than a decade, all states had done so.

IRS rules that went into effect on January 1, 1997, also encouraged more widespread use of LLCs in the business world. Under these rules, an unincorporated business will automatically be taxed as a partnership unless it indicates otherwise on the tax form. The exceptions involve publicly traded companies,

1. Note that the ULLCA was revised in 2006, but no state has yet adopted the revised version of this uniform act.

companies formed under a state incorporation statute, and certain foreign-owned companies. If a business chooses to be taxed as a corporation, it can indicate this preference by checking a box on the Internal Revenue Service (IRS) form.

Foreign Entities May Be LLC Members Part of the impetus behind creating LLCs in this country is that foreign investors are allowed to become LLC members. Thus, in an era increasingly characterized by global business efforts and investments, the LLC offers U.S. firms and potential investors from other countries flexibility and the opportunity for limited liability and increased tax benefits.

The Nature of the LLC

LLCs share many characteristics with corporations. Like corporations, LLCs are creatures of the state. In other words, they must be formed and operated in compliance with state law. Like the shareholders of a corporation, the owners of an LLC, who are called **members,** enjoy limited liability [ULLCA 303].[2] Also like corporations, LLCs are legal entities apart from their owners. As a legal person, the LLC can sue or be sued, enter into contracts, and hold title to property [ULLCA 201]. The terminology used to describe LLCs formed in other states or nations is also similar to that used in corporate law. For example, an LLC formed in one state but doing business in another state is referred to in the second state as a *foreign LLC.*

Can a member, manager, or agent of an LLC be held responsible for its contractual obligations or tort liability based solely on the individual's position in the LLC? That was the question in the following case.

2. Members of an LLC can also bring derivative actions, which you will read about in Chapter 39, on behalf of the LLC [ULLCA 101]. As with a corporate shareholder's derivative suit, any damages recovered go to the LLC, not to the members personally. See, for example, *PacLink Communications International, Inc. v. Superior Court,* 90 Cal.App.4th 958, 109 Cal.Rptr.2d 436 (2001).

CASE 37.1 McFarland v. Virginia Retirement Services of Chesterfield, LLC

United States District Court, Eastern District of Virginia, 2007. 477 F.Supp.2d 727.

• **Background and Facts** Virginia Retirement Services of Chesterfield, LLC, does business as Magnolias of Chesterfield (Magnolia), a retirement community. In May 2005, Penny McFarland became Magnolia's activities director and office manager. McFarland was responsible for coordinating and conducting activities for the residents. In June 2006, Effie Stovall, McFarland's supervisor, told the staff to take the residents outside for a walk. The temperature was 95 degrees. Out of concern for the residents, someone complained to the state licensing board. An inspector contacted McFarland, who immediately told Stovall. When Mary Dunmoyer, Magnolia's executive director, learned of the contact, she had Stovall discharge McFarland for trying to "sabotage" the community. McFarland filed a suit in a federal district court against Virginia Retirement Services, Dunmoyer, and other individual defendants, alleging, among other things, wrongful discharge—that she was terminated because she provided information regarding the health and safety of Magnolia's residents in response to the inspector's inquiry. The individual defendants, who were members, managers, or agents of Magnolia, filed a motion to be dismissed from the suit.

• **Decision and Rationale** The district court dismissed the individual defendants from McFarland's suit—except for Dunmoyer—because they were not alleged to have personally participated in discharging McFarland. The court noted that under the Virginia Limited Liability Company Act "no member, manager, organizer or other agent of a limited liability company shall have any personal obligation for any liabilities of a limited liability company, whether such liabilities arise in contract, tort or otherwise, solely by reason of being a member, manager, organizer or agent of a limited liability company." Because Magnolia is indeed a limited liability company, "its members, managers, and agents can have no personal obligation for any liabilities" solely by virtue of their positions. In this case, only one member—the manager, Mary Dunmoyer—contributed to McFarland's alleged wrongful termination. Thus, the lawsuit could proceed only against Dunmoyer and Magnolia.

• **The Ethical Dimension** *Did any of Magnolia's members, managers, or agents act unethically? Explain.*

CASE 37.1 CONTINUED

• **The Legal Environment Dimension** *Why is the liability of the members of an LLC limited with respect to the firm's debts and other obligations?*

LLC Formation

As mentioned, LLCs are creatures of statute and thus must follow state statutory requirements. To form an LLC, **articles of organization** must be filed with a central state agency—usually the secretary of state's office [ULLCA 202]. Typically, the articles are required to include such information as the name of the business, its principal address, the name and address of a registered agent, the names of the owners, and information on how the LLC will be managed [ULLCA 203]. The business's name must include the words *Limited Liability Company* or the initials *LLC* [ULLCA 105(a)]. In addition to filing the articles of organization, a few states require that a notice of the intention to form an LLC be published in a local newspaper. Although a majority of the states permit one-member LLCs, some states require at least two members.

Businesspersons sometimes enter into contracts on behalf of a business organization that is not yet formed. For example, as you will read in Chapter 38, persons forming a corporation may enter into contracts during the process of incorporation but before the corporation becomes a legal entity. These contracts are referred to as preincorporation contracts. Once the corporation is formed and adopts the preincorporation contract (by means of a *novation,* discussed in Chapter 17), it can then enforce the contract terms.

In the following case, the question was whether the same principle extends to LLCs. A person in the process of forming an LLC entered into a preorganization contract under which it would be obligated to purchase the Park Plaza Hotel in Hollywood, California. Once the LLC legally existed, the owners of the hotel refused to sell the property to the LLC, claiming that the contract was unenforceable.

CASE 37.2 02 Development, LLC v. 607 South Park, LLC

Court of Appeal, Second District, Division 1, California, 2008.
159 Cal.App.4th 609, 71 Cal.Rptr.3d 608.

• **Background and Facts** In March 2004, 607 South Park, LLC, entered into a written agreement to sell Park Plaza Hotel to 607 Park View Associates, Ltd., for $8.7 million. The general partner of 607 Park View Associates was Creative Environments of Hollywood, Inc. In February 2005, Creative Environments assigned the rights to the hotel purchase to another company, 02 Development, LLC. At the time, 02 Development did not yet exist; it was legally created several months later. 02 Development sued 607 South Park for breach of the hotel purchase agreement. 607 South Park moved for summary judgment, arguing that no enforceable contract existed because at the time of the assignment, 02 Development did not yet legally exist. Furthermore, 607 South Park argued that 02 Development suffered no damages because it was "not ready, willing, and able to fund the purchase of the hotel." The trial court granted the motion and entered judgment in favor of 607 South Park. 02 Development appealed.

• **Decision and Rationale** The Court of Appeal for the Second District in California reversed the judgment and directed the trial court to enter an order denying 607 South Park's motion for summary judgment. The reviewing court pointed out that limited liability companies should be treated the same as corporations with respect to preincorporation contracts. "When the assignment agreement was executed, 02 Development did not exist so it was not then a party to the agreement. But once 02 Development came into existence, it could enforce any preorganization contract made on its behalf, such as the assignment agreement, if it adopted or ratified it." The

CASE CONTINUES

CASE 37.2 CONTINUED court also dismissed 607 South Park's argument that 02 Development had to present admissible evidence that it would have been financially able to close the transaction. "607 South Park presented no evidence that 02 Development would have been unable to arrange for the necessary funding to close the transaction on time if 607 South Park had given it the opportunity instead of repudiating a contract in advance." Consequently, the trial court erred when it granted 607 South Park's motion for summary judgment.

- **The Legal Environment Dimension** *Why was it unimportant to the appellate court that 02 Development did not have to prove that it had funding commitments for $8.7 million?*
- **The Ethical Dimension** *Presumably, 607 South Park repudiated the real estate purchase agreement because it either had, or believed it could obtain, a better offer for the property. Are there any circumstances under which this reason could justify 607 South Park's behavior?*

Jurisdictional Requirements

One of the significant differences between LLCs and corporations has to do with federal jurisdictional requirements. Under the federal jurisdiction statute, a corporation is deemed to be a citizen of the state where it is incorporated and maintains its principal place of business. The statute does not mention the state citizenship of partnerships, LLCs, and other unincorporated associations, but the courts have tended to regard these entities as citizens of every state in which their members are citizens.

The state citizenship of an LLC may come into play when a party sues the LLC based on diversity of citizenship. Remember from Chapter 2 that when parties to a lawsuit are from different states and the amount in controversy exceeds $75,000, a federal court can exercise diversity jurisdiction. *Total* diversity of citizenship must exist, however. For example, Fong, a citizen of New York, wishes to bring a suit against Skycel, an LLC formed under the laws of Connecticut. One of Skycel's members also lives in New York. Fong will not be able to bring a suit against Skycel in federal court on the basis of diversity jurisdiction because the defendant LLC is also a citizen of New York. The same would be true if Fong was bringing a suit against multiple defendants and one of the defendants lived in New York.

Advantages and Disadvantages of the LLC

The LLC offers many advantages, and relatively few disadvantages, to businesspersons.

Advantages A key advantage of the LLC is that the members are not personally liable for the debts or obligations of the entity: their risk of loss is limited to the amount of their investments. An LLC also offers flexibility in regard to both taxation and management, as will be discussed shortly. Another advantage is that an LLC is an enduring business entity that exists beyond the illness or death of its members. In addition, as mentioned earlier, an LLC can include foreign investors.

An LLC that has *two or more members* can choose to be taxed as either a partnership or a corporation. As will be discussed in Chapter 38, a corporate entity must pay income taxes on its profits, and the shareholders pay personal income taxes on profits distributed as dividends. An LLC that wants to distribute profits to the members may prefer to be taxed as a partnership to avoid the double taxation that occurs with corporate entities. Unless an LLC indicates that it wishes to be taxed as a corporation, the IRS automatically taxes it as a partnership. This means that, as in a partnership, the LLC as an entity pays no taxes but "passes through" its profits to the members, who then personally pay taxes on the profits. If an LLC's members want to reinvest profits in the business, however, rather than distribute the profits to members, they may prefer to be taxed as a corporation. Corporate income tax rates may be lower than personal tax rates.

An LLC that has only *one member* cannot be taxed as a partnership, however. For federal income tax purposes, one-member LLCs are automatically taxed as sole proprietorships unless they indicate that they wish to be taxed as corporations. With respect to state taxes, most states follow the IRS rules, but a few states tax LLCs even though they do not tax partnerships.

Disadvantages The main disadvantage of the LLC is that state LLC statutes are not uniform. Therefore, businesses that operate in more than one state may not receive consistent treatment. Generally, though, most states will apply to a foreign LLC (an LLC formed in another state) the law of the state where the LLC was formed.

The LLC Operating Agreement

As mentioned, an advantage of the LLC form of business is the flexibility it offers in terms of operation and management. The members get to decide who will participate in the management and operation of their business, and how other issues will be resolved. Members normally do this by forming an **operating agreement** [ULLCA 103(a)]. Operating agreements typically contain provisions relating to management, how profits will be divided, the transfer of membership interests, whether the LLC will be dissolved on the death or departure of a member, and other important issues.

In many states, an operating agreement need not be in writing and indeed need not even be formed for an LLC to exist. Generally, though, LLC members should protect their interests by forming a written operating agreement. As with any business arrangement, disputes may arise over any number of issues. If there is no agreement covering the topic under dispute, such as how profits will be divided, the state LLC statute will govern the outcome. For example, most LLC statutes provide that if the members have not specified how profits will be divided, they will be divided equally among the members. Generally, when an issue is not covered by an operating agreement or by an LLC statute, the principles of partnership law are applied.

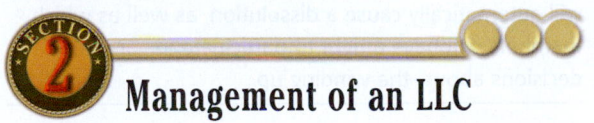

SECTION 2 Management of an LLC

Basically, the members have two options for managing an LLC—the members may decide in their operating agreement to be either a "member-managed" LLC or a "manager-managed" LLC. Most state LLC statutes and the ULLCA provide that unless the articles of organization specify otherwise, an LLC is assumed to be member managed [ULLCA 203(a)(6)].

Participation in Management

In a *member-managed* LLC, all of the members participate in management, and decisions are made by majority vote [ULLCA 404(a)]. In a *manager-managed* LLC, the members designate a group of persons to manage the firm. The management group may consist of only members, both members and nonmembers, or only nonmembers. Managers in a manager-managed LLC owe fiduciary duties to the LLC and its members, including the duty of loyalty and the duty of care [ULLCA 409(a), 409(h)], just as corporate directors and officers owe fiduciary duties to the corporation and its shareholders.

Operating Procedures

The members of an LLC can include provisions governing decision-making procedures in their operating agreement. For instance, the agreement can include procedures for choosing or removing managers. Although most LLC statutes are silent on this issue, the ULLCA provides that members may choose and remove managers by majority vote [ULLCA 404(b)(3)].

The members are also free to include in the agreement provisions designating when and for what purposes they will hold formal members' meetings. Most state LLC statutes have no provisions regarding members' meetings, which is in contrast to most state laws governing corporations, as you will read in Chapter 38.

Members may also specify in their agreement how voting rights will be apportioned. If they do not, LLC statutes in most states provide that voting rights are apportioned according to each member's capital contributions.[3] Some states provide that, in the absence of an agreement to the contrary, each member has one vote.

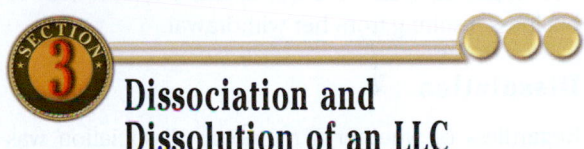

SECTION 3 Dissociation and Dissolution of an LLC

Recall from Chapter 36 that in the context of partnerships, *dissociation* occurs when a partner ceases to be associated in the carrying on of the partnership business. The same concept applies to LLCs. A member of an LLC has the *power* to dissociate from the LLC at any time, but he or she may not have the *right* to dissociate. Under the ULLCA, the events that trigger a member's dissociation from an LLC are similar to the events

3. This is similar to partnership law in the sense that partners in a partnership generally have equal rights in management and equal voting rights, unless otherwise specified in a partnership agreement. See Section 401(f) of the Uniform Partnership Act.

causing a partner to be dissociated under the Uniform Partnership Act (UPA). These include voluntary withdrawal, expulsion by other members or by court order, bankruptcy, incompetence, and death. Generally, even if a member dies or otherwise dissociates from an LLC, the other members may continue to carry on the LLC business, unless the operating agreement has contrary provisions.

Effect of Dissociation

When a member dissociates from an LLC, he or she loses the right to participate in management and the right to act as an agent for the LLC. His or her duty of loyalty to the LLC also terminates, and the duty of care continues only with respect to events that occurred before dissociation. Generally, the dissociated member also has a right to have his or her interest in the LLC bought out by the other members of the LLC. The LLC's operating agreement may contain provisions establishing a buyout price, but if it does not, the member's interest is usually purchased at a fair value. In states that have adopted the ULLCA, the LLC must purchase the interest at "fair" value within 120 days after the dissociation.

If the member's dissociation violates the LLC's operating agreement, it is considered legally wrongful, and the dissociated member can be held liable for damages caused by the dissociation. Suppose that Chadwick and Barrel are members in an LLC. Chadwick manages the accounts, and Barrel, who has many connections in the community and is a skilled investor, brings in the business. If Barrel wrongfully dissociates from the LLC, the LLC's business will suffer, and Chadwick can hold Barrel liable for the loss of business resulting from her withdrawal.

Dissolution

Regardless of whether a member's dissociation was wrongful or rightful, normally the dissociated member has no right to force the LLC to dissolve. The remaining members can opt to either continue or dissolve the business. Members can also stipulate in their operating agreement that certain events will cause dissolution, or they can agree that they have the power to dissolve the LLC by vote. As with partnerships, a court can order an LLC to be dissolved in certain circumstances, such as when the members have engaged in illegal or oppressive conduct, or when it is no longer feasible to carry on the business.

When an LLC is dissolved, any members who did not wrongfully dissociate may participate in the winding up process. To wind up the business, members must collect, liquidate, and distribute the LLC's assets. Members may preserve the assets for a reasonable time to optimize their return, and they continue to have the authority to perform reasonable acts in conjunction with winding up. In other words, the LLC will be bound by the reasonable acts of its members during the winding up process. Once all of the LLC's assets have been sold, the proceeds are distributed to pay off debts to creditors first (including debts owed to members who are creditors of the LLC). The member's capital contributions are returned next, and any remaining amounts are then distributed to members in equal shares or according to their operating agreement.

Because disputes often arise among members of an LLC during dissociation and dissolution, those forming an LLC should carefully draft their operating agreement. Stipulate the events that will cause dissociation and how the fair-value buyout price will be calculated. Set a time limit by which the LLC must pay the dissociated member (or her or his estate) in the event that she or he withdraws, becomes disabled, or dies. Include provisions that clearly limit the authority of dissociated members to act on behalf of the LLC and provide a right to seek damages from members who exceed the agreed-on parameters. Also, managers should notify third parties if any member dissociates and file a notice of dissociation with the state to limit the extent of the former member's apparent authority to act on behalf of the LLC. It is also advisable to set forth in the operating agreement any events that will automatically cause a dissolution, as well as which members will have a right to participate in—or make decisions about—the winding up.

SECTION 4

Special Business Forms

In addition to the LLC and the other traditional business forms discussed in this unit, several other forms can be used to organize a business. For the most part, these special business forms are hybrid organizations—that is, they have characteristics similar to those of partnerships or corporations, or combine features of both. These forms include joint ventures, syndicates, joint stock companies, business trusts, and cooperatives.

Joint Venture

A **joint venture** is a relationship in which two or more persons or business entities combine their efforts or their property for a single transaction or project or a related series of transactions or projects. Unless otherwise agreed, joint venturers share profits and losses equally and have an equal voice in controlling the project. For instance, when several contractors combine their resources to build and sell houses in a single development, their relationship is a joint venture.

Joint ventures range in size from very small activities to huge, multimillion-dollar joint actions carried out by some of the world's largest corporations. Large organizations often undertake new products or services by forming joint ventures with other enterprises. For example, Intel Corporation and Micron Technology, Inc., formed a joint venture to manufacture NAND flash memory, a data-storage chip widely used in digital cameras, cell phones, and portable music players including some iPods made by Apple, Inc. Also, Mitsubishi Chemical Corporation formed a joint venture with Exxon Chemical Corporation to start Mytex Polymers, a company that produces certain plastic compounds used by automakers in the United States and Japan.

Similarities to Partnerships The joint venture resembles a partnership and is taxed like a partnership. The main difference is that a joint venture is typically created for a single project or series of transactions, whereas a partnership usually (though not always) involves an ongoing business. For this reason, most courts apply the same principles to joint ventures as they apply to partnerships. For instance, the joint venturers owe to each other the same fiduciary duties, including the duty of loyalty, that partners owe each other.

Like partners, the joint venturers have equal rights to manage the activities of the enterprise. Control of the operation may be given to one of the members, however, without affecting the status of the relationship.[4]

The question in the following case was whether two vintage aircraft makers had formed a joint venture.

4. See, for example, *PGI, Inc. v. Rathe Productions, Inc.*, 265 Va. 438, 576 S.E.2d 438 (2003).

CASE 37.3 SPW Associates, LLP v. Anderson

Supreme Court of North Dakota, 2006. 2006 ND 159, 718 N.W.2d 580.
www.ndcourts.com/search/opinions.asp[a]

• **Background and Facts** Murdo Cameron is a commercial airline pilot interested in vintage P-51 Mustang planes. He developed graphite body parts and other components to make replicas of the P-51 and placed ads in aviation magazines for someone to design and make other parts and build the planes. Douglas Anderson answered the ad, and in 1996, they agreed in writing to collaborate on the manufacture of one P-51 for each of them. They agreed orally to make additional P-51s to sell. For the first plane, which Anderson would build, Cameron would provide an engine, which Anderson would pay for after the plane's first flight. In 1997, to finance the making of the P-51s, Anderson borrowed funds from SPW Associates, LLP, using the first plane as the security for the loan. Anderson did not tell SPW about his deal with Cameron nor did he tell Cameron about his deal with SPW. Anderson built one plane before defaulting on the loan. SPW filed a suit in a North Dakota state court against Anderson, Cameron, and others, asking the court to declare that SPW was entitled to the aircraft. The court ruled, among other things, that Anderson and Cameron had entered into a joint venture, the plane was the venture's property, Anderson was authorized to grant SPW a security interest in it, and SPW was entitled to its possession. Cameron appealed to the North Dakota Supreme Court, arguing, in part, that there was no joint venture.

• **Decision and Rationale** The state supreme court affirmed the conclusions of the lower court. The state supreme court identified four elements that must exist for an enterprise to

a. In the "Title:" box, type "SPW" and click on "Execute." In the result, click on the name of the case to access the opinion. The North Dakota Supreme Court maintains this Web site.

CASE CONTINUES

CASE 37.3 CONTINUED constitute a joint venture: (1) a contract showing that the parties agreed to engage in a common undertaking; (2) the parties' contribution of funds, property, time, or skill to further the undertaking; (3) an interest in, and mutual right to control, the property of the venture; and (4) an agreement to share its profits. In this case, there was no dispute that Anderson and Cameron had contracted in writing to build two P-51s; that they had contributed funds, property, time, and skill to this purpose; and that they each had exerted control over the planes' components. As for evidence of an agreement to share profits, Anderson and Cameron's written contract referred to "future aircraft purchases" and "multiple year production runs," and they admitted that they intended to build additional planes to sell to the public. The court recognized that the principles of partnership law apply to joint ventures. Under those principles, "a partner is an agent of, and may bind, the partnership." Applying that rule to this case, the court found that Anderson, as a joint venturer, had the authority to grant a security interest in the venture's property—the first P-51—for the loan from SPW, which was thus entitled to keep the plane in satisfaction of the debt on Anderson's default.

- **The Legal Environment Dimension** *On what basis might Cameron maintain a suit against Anderson?*

- **What If the Facts Were Different?** *How might the outcome of this case have been different if Cameron had been merely an aircraft parts supplier, with his only profit to be from the sale of components to Anderson?*

Differences from Partnerships Joint ventures differ from partnerships in several important ways. The members of a joint venture have less implied and apparent authority than the partners in a partnership. As discussed in Chapter 36, each partner is treated as an agent of the other partners. Because the activities of a joint venture are more limited than the business of a partnership, the members of a joint venture are presumed to have less power to bind their co-venturers. In addition, the death of a joint venturer ordinarily does not terminate a joint venture, whereas the death of a partner causes dissociation and potentially terminates the firm. A joint venture normally terminates when the project or transaction for which it was formed is completed, unless the members have otherwise agreed.

Syndicate

A group of individuals or firms that get together to finance a particular project, such as the building of a shopping center or the purchase of a professional basketball franchise, is called a **syndicate,** or an *investment group.* The form of such groups varies considerably. A syndicate may be organized as a corporation or as a general or limited partnership. In some instances, the members merely own property jointly and have no legally recognized business arrangement.

Joint Stock Company

A **joint stock company** is a true hybrid of a partnership and a corporation. It has many characteristics of a corporation in that (1) its ownership is represented by transferable shares of stock, (2) it is usually managed by directors and officers of the company or association, and (3) it can have a perpetual existence. Most of its other features, however, are more characteristic of a partnership, and it is usually treated as a partnership. Like a partnership, a joint stock company is formed by agreement (not statute); property is usually held in the names of the members; shareholders have personal liability; and generally the company is not treated as a legal entity for purposes of a lawsuit. In a joint stock company, however, shareholders are not considered to be agents of each other, as they would be in a true partnership.

Business Trust

A **business trust** is created by a written trust agreement that sets forth the interests of the beneficiaries and the obligations and powers of the trustees. With a business trust, legal ownership and management of the trust's property stay with one or more of the trustees, and the profits are distributed to the beneficiaries.

The business trust form of business was started in Massachusetts in an attempt to obtain the limited liability advantage of corporate status while avoiding certain restrictions on a corporation's ownership and development of real property. A business trust resembles a corporation in many respects. Beneficiaries of the trust, for example, are not personally responsible for the trust's debts or obligations. In fact, in a number of states, business trusts must pay corporate taxes.

Cooperative

A **cooperative** is an association that is organized to provide an economic service to its members (or shareholders); it may or may not be incorporated. Most cooperatives are governed by state statutes for cooperatives, general business corporations, or LLCs. Generally, an incorporated cooperative will distribute dividends, or profits, to its owners on the basis of their transactions with the cooperative rather than on the basis of the amount of capital they contributed. Members of incorporated cooperatives have limited liability, as do shareholders of corporations or members of LLCs. Cooperatives that are unincorporated are often treated like partnerships. The members have joint liability for the cooperative's acts.

The cooperative form of business is generally adopted by groups of individuals who wish to pool their resources to gain some advantage in the marketplace. Consumer purchasing co-ops are formed to obtain lower prices through quantity discounts. Seller marketing co-ops are formed to control the market and thereby obtain higher retail prices from consumers. Co-ops range in size from small, local consumer cooperatives to national businesses such as Ace Hardware and Land O'Lakes, the well-known producer of dairy products.

REVIEWING Limited Liability Companies and Special Business Forms

A bridge on a prominent public roadway in the city of Papagos, Arizona, was deteriorating and in need of repair. The city posted notices seeking proposals for an artistic bridge design and reconstruction. Davidson Masonry, LLC, which was owned and managed by Carl Davidson and his wife, Marilyn Rowe, decided to submit a bid for a decorative concrete project that incorporated artistic metalwork. They contacted Shana Lafayette, a local sculptor who specialized in large-scale metal forms, to help them design the bridge. The city selected their bridge design and awarded them the contract for a commission of $184,000. Davidson Masonry and Lafayette then entered into an agreement to work together on the bridge project. Davidson Masonry agreed to install and pay for concrete and structural work, and Lafayette agreed to install the metalwork at her expense. They agreed that overall profits would be split, with 25 percent going to Lafayette and 75 percent going to Davidson Masonry. Lafayette designed numerous metal sculptures of salmon that were incorporated into colorful decorative concrete forms designed by Rowe, while Davidson performed the structural engineering. The group worked together successfully until the project was completed. Using the information presented in the chapter, answer the following questions.

1. Would Davidson Masonry automatically be taxed as a partnership or a corporation?
2. Is Davidson Masonry member managed or manager managed?
3. When Davidson Masonry and Lafayette entered an agreement to work together, what kind of special business form was created? Explain.
4. Suppose that during construction, Lafayette had entered into an agreement to rent space in a warehouse that was close to the bridge so that she could work on her sculptures near the site where they would eventually be installed. She entered into the contract without the knowledge or consent of Davidson Masonry. In this situation, would a court be likely to hold that Davidson Masonry was bound by the contract that Lafayette entered? Why or why not?

TERMS AND CONCEPTS

articles of organization 705
business trust 710
cooperative 711
joint stock company 710
joint venture 709
limited liability company (LLC) 703
member 704
operating agreement 707
syndicate 710

QUESTIONS AND CASE PROBLEMS

37–1. John, Lesa, and Tabir form a limited liability company. John contributes 60 percent of the capital, and Lesa and Tabir each contribute 20 percent. Nothing is decided about how profits will be divided. John assumes that he will be entitled to 60 percent of the profits, in accordance with his contribution. Lesa and Tabir, however, assume that the profits will be divided equally. A dispute over the question arises, and ultimately a court has to decide the issue. What law will the court apply? In most states, what will result? How could this dispute have been avoided in the first place? Discuss fully.

37–2. QUESTION WITH SAMPLE ANSWER

Bateson Corp. is considering entering into two contracts—one with a joint stock company that distributes home products east of the Mississippi River and the other with a business trust formed by a number of sole proprietors who are sellers of home products on the West Coast. Both contracts will require Bateson to make large capital outlays in order to supply the businesses with restaurant equipment. In both business organizations, at least two shareholders or beneficiaries are personally wealthy, but both organizations have limited financial resources. The owner-managers of Bateson are not familiar with either form of business organization. Because each form resembles a corporation, they are concerned about potential limits on liability in the event that either business organization breaches the contract by failing to pay for the equipment. Discuss fully Bateson's concern.

- **For a sample answer to Question 37–2, go to Appendix I at the end of this text.**

37–3. Joe, a resident of New Jersey, wants to open a restaurant. He asks Kay, his friend, an experienced attorney and a New Yorker, for her business and legal advice in exchange for a 20 percent ownership interest in the restaurant. Kay helps Joe negotiate a lease for the restaurant premises and advises Joe to organize the business as a limited liability company (LLC). Joe forms Café Olé, LLC, and with Kay's help, obtains financing. Then, the night before the restaurant opens, Joe tells Kay that he is "cutting her out of the deal." The restaurant proves to be a success. Kay wants to file a suit in a federal district court against Joe and the LLC. Can a federal court exercise jurisdiction over the parties based on diversity of citizenship? Explain.

37–4. Limited Liability Companies. Gloria Duchin, a Rhode Island resident, was the sole shareholder and chief executive officer of Gloria Duchin, Inc. (Duchin, Inc.), which manufactured metallic Christmas ornaments and other novelty items. The firm was incorporated in Rhode Island. Duchin Realty, Inc., also incorporated in Rhode Island, leased real estate to Duchin, Inc. The Duchin entities hired Gottesman Co. to sell Duchin, Inc., and to sign with the buyer a consulting agreement for Gloria Duchin and a lease for Duchin Realty's property. Gottesman negotiated a sale, a consulting agreement, and a lease with Somerset Capital Corp. James Mitchell, a resident of Massachusetts, was the chairman and president of Somerset, and Mary Mitchell, also a resident of Massachusetts, was the senior vice president. The parties agreed that to buy Duchin, Inc., Somerset would create a new limited liability company, JMTR Enterprises, L.L.C., in Rhode Island, with the Mitchells as its members. When the deal fell apart, JMTR filed a suit in a Massachusetts state court against the Duchin entities, alleging, among other things, breach of contract. When the defendants tried to remove the case to a federal district court, JMTR argued that the court did not have jurisdiction because there was no diversity of citizenship between the parties: all of the plaintiffs and defendants were citizens of Rhode Island. Is JMTR correct? Why or why not? [*JMTR Enterprises, L.L.C. v. Duchin*, 42 F.Supp.2d 87 (D.Mass. 1999)]

37–5. Foreign Limited Liability Companies. Walter Matjasich and Cary Hanson organized Capital Care, LLC, in Utah. Capital Care operated, and Matjasich and Hanson managed, Heartland Care Center in Topeka,

Kansas. LTC Properties, Inc., held a mortgage on the Heartland facilities. When Heartland failed as a business, its residents were transferred to other facilities. Heartland employees who provided care to the residents for five days during the transfers were not paid wages. The employees filed claims with the Kansas Department of Human Resources for the unpaid wages. Kansas state law provides that a *corporate* officer or manager may be liable for a firm's unpaid wages, but protects limited liability company (LLC) members from personal liability generally and states that an LLC cannot be construed as a corporation. Under Utah state law, however, the members of an LLC can be personally liable for wages due the LLC's employees. Should Matjasich and Hanson be held personally liable for the unpaid wages? Explain. [*Matjasich v. Department of Human Resources*, 271 Kan. 246, 21 P.3d 985 (2001)]

37–6. Limited Liability Companies. Michael Collins entered into a three-year employment contract with E-Magine, LLC. E-Magine was in business for only a brief time, during which it incurred considerable losses. In terminating operations, which ceased before the term of the contract with Collins expired, E-Magine also terminated Collins's services. In exchange for a payment of $24,240, Collins signed a "final payment agreement," which purported to be a settlement of any claims that he might have against E-Magine. Collins filed a suit in a New York state court against E-Magine, its members and managers, and others, alleging, among other things, breach of his employment contract. Collins claimed that signing the "final payment agreement" was the only means for him to obtain what he was owed for past sales commissions and asked the court to impose personal liability on the members and managers of E-Magine for breach of contract. Should the court grant this request? Why or why not? [*Collins v. E-Magine, LLC*, 291 A.D.2d 350, 739 N.Y.S.2d 121 (1 Dept. 2002)]

37–7. Joint Ventures. In 1993, TOG Acquisition Co. attempted to acquire the Orleander Group, a manufacturer of bicycle accessories, but failed for lack of financing. Orleander then granted to Herrick Co. an exclusive right to negotiate for the sale of the business. In August, representatives of TOG, Herrick, and SCS Communications, Inc., signed a letter in which they agreed "to work together to acquire the business of the Orleander Group." The "letter agreement" provided that the parties would contribute "equal amounts of capital" and that all of the terms of the acquisition required the approval of each party. On November 19, TOG and SCS told Herrick that it was out of the deal and, ten days later, acquired Orleander without Herrick. Herrick filed a suit in a federal district court against SCS and others, alleging, among other things, that the "letter agreement" was a contract to establish a joint venture, which TOG and SCS had breached. The defendants filed a motion for summary judgment. In whose favor should the court rule? Why? [*SCS Communications, Inc. v. Herrick Co.*, 360 F.3d 329 (2d Cir. 2004)]

37–8. CASE PROBLEM WITH SAMPLE ANSWER

Westbury Properties, Inc., and others (collectively, the Westbury group) owned, managed, and developed real property. Jerry Stoker and the Stoker Group, Inc. (the Stokers), also developed real property. The Westbury group entered into agreements with the Stokers concerning a large tract of property in Houston County, Georgia. The parties formed limited liability companies (LLCs), including Bellemeade, LLC (the LLC group), to develop various parcels of the tract for residential purposes. The operating agreements provided that "no Member shall be accountable to the [LLC] or to any other Member with respect to [any other] business or activity even if the business or activity competes with the [LLC's] business." The Westbury group entered into agreements with other parties to develop additional parcels within the tract in competition with the LLC group. The Stokers filed a suit in a Georgia state court against the Westbury group, alleging, among other things, breach of fiduciary duty. What duties do the members of an LLC owe to each other? Under what principle might the terms of an operating agreement alter these duties? In whose favor should the court rule? Discuss. [*Stoker v. Bellemeade, LLC*, 272 Ga.App. 817, 615 S.E.2d 1 (2005)]

- **To view a sample answer for Problem 37–8, go to this book's Web site at www.cengage.com/blaw/jentz, select "Chapter 37," and click on "Case Problem with Sample Answer."**

37–9. Limited Liability Companies. A "Certificate of Formation" (CF) for Grupo Dos Chiles, LLC, was filed with the Delaware secretary of state in February 2000. The CF named Jamie Rivera as the "initial member." The next month, Jamie's mother, Yolanda Martinez, and Alfred Shriver, who had a personal relationship with Martinez at the time, signed an "LLC Agreement" for Grupo, naming themselves "managing partners." Grupo's business was the operation of Dancing Peppers Cantina, a restaurant in Alexandria, Virginia. Identifying themselves as Grupo's owners, Shriver and Martinez borrowed funds from Advanceme, Inc., a restaurant lender. In June 2003, Grupo lost its LLC status in Delaware for failing to pay state taxes, and by the end of July, Martinez and Shriver had ended their relationship. Shriver filed a suit in a Virginia state court against Martinez to wind up Grupo's affairs. Meanwhile, without consulting Shriver, Martinez paid Grupo's back taxes. Shriver filed a suit in a Delaware state court against Martinez, asking the court to dissolve the firm. What effect did the LLC Agreement have on the CF? Did Martinez's unilateral act reestablish Grupo's LLC status?

Should the Delaware court grant Shriver's request? Why or why not? [*In re Grupo Dos Chiles, LLC,* __ A.2d __ (Del.Ch. 2006)]

37–10. A QUESTION OF ETHICS

*Blushing Brides, L.L.C., a publisher of wedding planning magazines in Columbus, Ohio, opened an account with Gray Printing Co. in July 2000. On behalf of Blushing Brides, Louis Zacks, the firm's member-manager, signed a credit agreement that identified the firm as the "purchaser" and required payment within thirty days. Despite the agreement, Blushing Brides typically took up to six months to pay the full amount for its orders. Gray printed and shipped 10,000 copies of a fall/winter 2001 issue for Blushing Brides but had not been paid when the firm ordered 15,000 copies of a spring/summer 2002 issue. Gray refused to print the new order without an assurance of payment. On May 22, Zacks signed a promissory note payable to Gray within thirty days for $14,778, plus interest at 6 percent per year. Gray printed the new order but by October had been paid only $7,500. Gray filed a suit in an Ohio state court against Blushing Brides and Zacks to collect the balance. [*Gray Printing Co. v. Blushing Brides, L.L.C., __ N.E.2d __ (Ohio App. 10 Dist. 2006)]

(a) Under what circumstances is a member of an LLC liable for the firm's debts? In this case, is Zacks personally liable under the credit agreement for the unpaid amount on Blushing Brides' account? Did Zacks's promissory note affect the parties' liability on the account? Explain.

(b) Should a member of an LLC assume an ethical responsibility to meet the obligations of the firm? Discuss.

(c) Gray shipped only 10,000 copies of the spring/summer 2002 issue of Blushing Brides' magazine, waiting for the publisher to identify a destination for the other 5,000 copies. The magazine had a retail price of $4.50 per copy. Did Gray have a legal or ethical duty to "mitigate the damages" by attempting to sell or otherwise distribute these copies itself? Why or why not?

LAW ON THE WEB

For updated links to resources available on the Web, as well as a variety of other materials, visit this text's Web site at

www.cengage.com/blaw/jentz

LLRX.com, a Web site for legal professionals, provides information on LLCs on its Web journal. Go to

www.llrx.com/features/llc.htm

You can find information on filing fees for LLCs at

www.bizcorp.com

Legal Research Exercises on the Web

Go to **www.cengage.com/blaw/jentz**, the Web site that accompanies this text. Select "Chapter 37" and click on "Internet Exercises." There you will find the following Internet research exercises that you can perform to learn more about the topics covered in this chapter.

Internet Exercise 37–1: Legal Perspective
Limited Liability Companies

Internet Exercise 37–2: Management Perspective
Joint Ventures

CHAPTER 38

CORPORATIONS—Formation and Financing

The corporation is a creature of statute. A corporation is an artificial being, existing only in law and neither tangible nor visible. Its existence generally depends on state law, although some corporations, especially public organizations, are created under federal law. Each state has its own body of corporate law, and these laws are not entirely uniform.

The Model Business Corporation Act (MBCA) is a codification of modern corporation law that has been influential in the codification of state corporation statutes. Today, the majority of state statutes are guided by the most recent version of the MBCA, often referred to as the Revised Model Business Corporation Act (RMBCA). Excerpts from the RMBCA are included in Appendix G of this text. Keep in mind, however, that there is considerable variation among the regulations of the states that have used the MBCA or the RMBCA as a basis for their statutes, and several states do not follow either act. Consequently, individual state corporation laws should be relied on to determine corporate law rather than the MBCA or RMBCA.

In this chapter, we examine the nature of the corporate form of business enterprise and the various classifications of corporations. We then discuss the formation and financing of today's corporation.

SECTION 1 The Nature and Classification of Corporations

A corporation is a legal entity created and recognized by state law. It can consist of one or more *natural persons* (as opposed to the artificial *legal person* of the corporation) identified under a common name. The corporation substitutes itself for its shareholders in conducting corporate business and in incurring liability, yet its authority to act and the liability for its actions are separate and apart from the individuals who own it.

Corporate Personnel

When an individual purchases a share of stock in a corporation, that person becomes a shareholder and an owner of the corporation. The shareholders elect a *board of directors* who are responsible for the overall management of the corporation. The directors make all policy decisions and hire the *corporate officers* and other employees to run the daily business operations of the corporation.

Unlike the members in a partnership, the body of shareholders can change constantly without affecting the continued existence of the corporation. A shareholder can sue the corporation, and the corporation can sue a shareholder. Additionally, under certain circumstances, a shareholder can sue on behalf of a corporation. The rights and duties of all corporate personnel will be examined in Chapter 39.

The Limited Liability of Shareholders

One of the key advantages of the corporate form is the limited liability of its owners (shareholders). Corporate shareholders normally are not personally liable for the obligations of the corporation beyond the extent of their investments. In certain limited situations, however, the "corporate veil" can be pierced and liability for the corporation's obligations extended to shareholders—a concept that will be explained later in this chapter. Additionally, to enable the firm to obtain credit, shareholders in small companies sometimes voluntarily assume personal liability, as guarantors, for corporate obligations.

Corporate Taxation

Corporate profits are taxed by various levels of government. Corporations can do one of two things with corporate profits—retain them or pass them on to shareholders in the form of dividends. The corporation normally receives no tax deduction for dividends distributed to shareholders. Dividends are again taxable (except when they represent distributions of capital) to the shareholder receiving them. This double-taxation feature of the corporation is one of its major disadvantages.[1]

1. Congress enacted a law in 2003 that mitigated this double-taxation feature to some extent by providing a reduced federal tax rate on qualifying dividends. The Jobs Growth Tax Relief Reconciliation Act of 2003, Pub. L. No. 108-27, May 28, 2003, is codified at 26 U.S.C.A. Section 6429.

Retained Earnings Profits that are not distributed are retained by the corporation. These **retained earnings,** if invested properly, will yield higher corporate profits in the future and thus cause the price of the company's stock to rise. Individual shareholders can then reap the benefits of these retained earnings in the capital gains they receive when they sell their shares.

Offshore Low-Tax Jurisdictions In recent years, some U.S. corporations have been using holding companies to reduce—or at least defer—their U.S. income taxes. At its simplest, a **holding company** (sometimes referred to as a *parent company*) is a company whose business activity consists of holding shares in another company. Typically, the holding company is established in a low-tax or no-tax offshore jurisdiction, such as those shown in Exhibit 38–1. Among the best known are the Cayman Islands, Dubai, Hong Kong, Luxembourg, Monaco, and Panama.

Sometimes, a major U.S. corporation sets up an investment holding company in a low-tax offshore environment. The corporation then transfers its cash, bonds, stocks, and other investments to the holding company. In general, any profits received by the holding company on these investments are taxed at the rate of the offshore jurisdiction in which the company is registered, not the U.S. tax rates applicable to the U.S.

EXHIBIT 38–1 • Offshore Low-Tax Jurisdictions

corporation or its shareholders. Thus, deposits of cash, for example, may earn interest that is taxed at only a minimal rate. Once the profits are brought "onshore," though, they are taxed at the federal corporate income tax rate, and any payments received by the shareholders are also taxable at the full U.S. rates.

Constitutional Rights of Corporations

A corporation is recognized under state and federal law as a "person," and it enjoys many of the same rights and privileges that natural persons who are U.S. citizens enjoy. The Bill of Rights guarantees persons certain protections, and corporations are considered persons in most instances. Accordingly, a corporation as an entity has a right of access to the courts and can sue or be sued. It also has a right to due process before denial of life (corporate existence), liberty, or property, as well as freedom from unreasonable searches and seizures and from double jeopardy.

Under the First Amendment, corporations are entitled to freedom of speech. As we pointed out in Chapter 4, however, commercial speech (such as advertising) and political speech (such as contributions to political causes or candidates) receive significantly less protection than noncommercial speech.

Generally, a corporation is not entitled to claim the Fifth Amendment privilege against self-incrimination. Therefore, agents or officers of the corporation cannot refuse to produce corporate records on the ground that it might incriminate them.[2] Additionally, the privileges and immunities clause of the U.S. Constitution (Article IV, Section 2) does not protect corporations, nor does it protect unincorporated associations. This clause requires each state to treat citizens of other states equally with respect to certain rights, such as access to the courts and travel rights. This constitutional clause does not apply to corporations because corporations are legal persons only, not natural citizens.

Torts and Criminal Acts

A corporation is liable for the torts committed by its agents or officers within the course and scope of their employment. This principle applies to a corporation exactly as it applies to the ordinary agency relationships discussed in Chapter 32. It follows the doctrine of *respondeat superior.*

Under modern criminal law, a corporation may also be held liable for the criminal acts of its agents and employees, provided the punishment is one that can be applied to the corporation. Although corporations cannot be imprisoned, they can be fined. (Of course, corporate directors and officers can be imprisoned, and in recent years, many have faced criminal penalties for their own actions or for the actions of employees under their supervision.)

The question in the following case was whether a corporation could be convicted for its employee's criminal negligence.

2. *Braswell v. United States,* 487 U.S. 99, 108 S.Ct. 2284, 101 L.Ed. 98 (1988). A court might allow an officer or employee to assert the Fifth Amendment privilege against self-incrimination in only a few circumstances. See, for example, *In re Three Grand Jury Subpoenas Duces Tecum Dated January 29, 1999,* 191 F.3d 173 (2d Cir. 1999); and *United States v. Bedell & Co.,* 2006 WL 3813792 (E.D.N.Y. 2006).

CASE 38.1 Commonwealth v. Angelo Todesca Corp.

Supreme Judicial Court of Massachusetts, 2006. 446 Mass. 128, 842 N.E.2d 930.
www.findlaw.com/11stategov/ma/maca.html[a]

Background and Facts Brian Gauthier worked as a truck driver for Angelo Todesca Corporation, a trucking and paving company. During 2000, Gauthier drove a ten-wheel tri-axle dump truck, which was designated AT-56. Angelo's safety manual required its trucks to be equipped with back-up alarms, which were to sound automatically whenever the vehicles were in reverse gear. In November, Gauthier discovered that AT-56's alarm was missing. Angelo ordered a new alarm. Meanwhile, Gauthier continued to drive AT-56. On December 1, Angelo assigned Gauthier to haul asphalt to a work site in Centerville, Massachusetts. At the site, as Gauthier backed up AT-56 to dump its load, he struck a police officer who was directing traffic through the site and facing away from the truck. The officer died of his injuries. The commonwealth of Massachusetts charged

a. In the "Supreme Court Opinions" section, in the "2006" row, click on "March." When that page opens, scroll to the name of the case and click on its docket number to access the opinion.

CASE CONTINUES

CASE 38.1 CONTINUED Gauthier and Angelo in a Massachusetts state court with, among other wrongful acts, motor vehicle homicide. Angelo was convicted and fined $2,500. On Angelo's appeal, a state intermediate appellate court reversed Angelo's conviction. The state appealed to the Massachusetts Supreme Judicial Court, the state's highest court.

- **Decision and Rationale** The Massachusetts Supreme Judicial Court affirmed Angelo's conviction. The court identified three elements required to prove a corporation guilty of a criminal offense: (1) an individual commits a criminal offense; (2) at the time of commission, the individual is engaged in corporate business; and (3) the corporation vested the individual with the authority to engage in that business on its behalf. The focus in this case was on the first element, with the defendant arguing that a "corporation" could not be guilty of vehicular homicide because it cannot "operate" a vehicle. The court recognized that a corporation is not a "living person" but pointed out that it can act through its agents, which may include its employees. The court reasoned that if an employee commits a crime "while engaged in corporate business that the employee has been authorized to conduct," a corporation can be held liable for the crime. The defendant also contended that operating a truck without a back-up alarm is not a crime. The court conceded this point but explained that "the criminal conduct was Gauthier's negligent operation of the defendant's truck, resulting in the victim's death."

- **What If the Facts Were Different?** *If Gauthier had been an independent contractor rather than Angelo's employee, would the result in this case have been different? Explain.*

- **The Legal Environment Dimension** *Under what circumstances might an employee's supervisor, or even a corporate officer or director, be held liable for the employee's crime?*

Corporate Sentencing Guidelines

Recall from Chapter 9 that the U.S. Sentencing Commission created standardized sentencing guidelines for federal crimes. These guidelines went into effect in 1987. The commission subsequently created specific sentencing guidelines for crimes committed by corporate employees (white-collar crimes).[3] The net effect of the guidelines has been a significant increase in the penalties for crimes committed by corporate personnel. Penalties depend on such factors as the seriousness of the offense, the amount involved, and the extent to which top company executives are implicated. Corporate lawbreakers can face fines amounting to hundreds of millions of dollars, though the guidelines allow judges to impose less severe penalties in certain circumstances.

When a company has taken substantial steps to prevent, investigate, and punish wrongdoing, such as by establishing and enforcing crime prevention standards, a court may impose less serious penalties. Many states' corporate laws now require corporations to have adequate systems for detecting and reporting misconduct that can be attributed to corporations. Corporate sentencing guidelines that became effective in 2004 require corporations to train employees on how to comply with relevant laws. Additionally, corporate directors have a fiduciary duty to prevent employee misconduct, which means that if they discover an employee has committed a crime, they have a duty to promptly report it. As will be discussed in Chapters 41 and 51, the Sarbanes-Oxley Act also requires corporate attorneys to report possible corporate misconduct (both civil and criminal) to officials within the corporation. (For a detailed discussion of corporate governance and compliance issues, see Chapter 41.)

Classification of Corporations

Corporations can be classified in several ways. The classification of a corporation normally depends on its location, purpose, and ownership characteristics, as described in the following subsections.

Domestic, Foreign, and Alien Corporations

A corporation is referred to as a **domestic corporation** by its home state (the state in which it incorporates). A corporation formed in one state but doing business in another is referred to in the second state

3. The Sarbanes-Oxley Act of 2002 stiffened the penalties for certain types of corporate crime and ordered the U.S. Sentencing Commission to revise the sentencing guidelines accordingly—see Chapter 41.

as a **foreign corporation.** A corporation formed in another country (say, Mexico) but doing business in the United States is referred to in the United States as an **alien corporation.**

A corporation does not have an automatic right to do business in a state other than its state of incorporation. In some instances, it must obtain a *certificate of authority* in any state in which it plans to do business. Once the certificate has been issued, the corporation generally can exercise in that state all of the powers conferred on it by its home state. If a foreign corporation does business in a state without obtaining a certificate of authority, the state can impose substantial fines and sanctions on the corporation, and sometimes even on its officers, directors, or agents.

Note that most state statutes specify certain activities, such as soliciting orders via the Internet, that are not considered "doing business" within the state. Thus, a foreign corporation normally does not need a certificate of authority to sell goods or services via the Internet or by mail.

Public and Private Corporations A public corporation is one formed by the government to meet some political or governmental purpose. Cities and towns that incorporate are common examples. In addition, many federal government organizations, such as the U.S. Postal Service, the Tennessee Valley Authority, and AMTRAK, are public corporations. Note that a public corporation is not the same as a *publicly held* corporation (often called a *public company*). A publicly held corporation is any corporation whose shares are publicly traded in a securities market, such as the New York Stock Exchange or the over-the-counter market.

In contrast to public corporations (*not* public companies), private corporations are created either wholly or in part for private benefit. Most corporations are private. Although they may serve a public purpose, as a public electric or gas utility does, they are owned by private persons rather than by the government.[4]

Nonprofit Corporations Corporations formed for purposes other than making a profit are called *nonprofit* or *not-for-profit* corporations. Private hospitals, educational institutions, charities, and religious organizations, for example, are frequently organized as nonprofit corporations. The nonprofit corporation is a convenient form of organization that allows various groups to own property and to form contracts without exposing the individual members to personal liability.

Close Corporations In terms of numbers, not size, most corporate enterprises in the United States fall into the category of close corporations. A **close corporation** is one whose shares are held by members of a family or by relatively few persons. Close corporations are also referred to as *closely held, family*, or *privately held* corporations. Usually, the members of the small group constituting a close corporation are personally known to each other. Because the number of shareholders is so small, there is no trading market for the shares.

In practice, a close corporation is often operated like a partnership. Some states have enacted special statutory provisions that apply to close corporations. These provisions expressly permit close corporations to depart significantly from certain formalities required by traditional corporation law.[5]

Additionally, a provision added to the RMBCA in 1991 gives a close corporation considerable flexibility in determining its rules of operation [RMBCA 7.32]. If all of a corporation's shareholders agree in writing, the corporation can operate without directors, bylaws, annual or special shareholders' or directors' meetings, stock certificates, or formal records of shareholders' or directors' decisions.[6]

Management of Close Corporations. A close corporation has a single shareholder or a closely knit group of shareholders, who usually hold the positions of directors and officers. Management of a close corporation resembles that of a sole proprietorship or a partnership. As a corporation, however, the firm must meet all specific legal requirements set forth in state statutes.

To prevent a majority shareholder from dominating a close corporation, the corporation may require that more than a simple majority of the directors approve any action taken by the board. Typically, this would apply only to extraordinary actions, such as changing

4. The United States Supreme Court first recognized the property rights of private corporations and clarified the distinction between public and private corporations in the landmark case *Trustees of Dartmouth College v. Woodward,* 17 U.S. (4 Wheaton) 518, 4 L.Ed. 629 (1819).

5. For example, in some states (such as Maryland), a close corporation need not have a board of directors.

6. Shareholders cannot agree, however, to eliminate certain rights of shareholders, such as the right to inspect corporate books and records or the right to bring *derivative actions* (lawsuits on behalf of the corporation—see Chapter 39).

the amount of dividends or dismissing an employee-shareholder, and not to ordinary business decisions.

Misappropriation of Close Corporation Finances. Sometimes, a majority shareholder in a close corporation takes advantage of her or his position to engage in misappropriation of company funds. In so doing, this shareholder clearly injures the minority shareholders. In such situations, possible remedies include many of those available to shareholders of regular corporations, including an appraisal of the minority shareholders' shares. In the following case, two wronged minority shareholders pursued an additional remedy.

CASE 38.2 Williams v. Stanford

District Court of Appeal of Florida, First District, 2008. 977 So.2d 722.

- **Background and Facts** Two brothers, Paul and James Williams, together held 30 percent of the stock in Brown and Standard (B&S), Inc., a construction company. John Stanford owned the other 70 percent of the close corporation shares. The Williams brothers worked for B&S for five years when they became suspicious of Stanford's financial management. Stanford reported net losses for the company. The brothers asked to see the B&S books and were fired. Later, it was shown that Stanford had misappropriated at least $250,000 in B&S funds for his personal use. The Williams brothers brought a *shareholder's derivative suit* (see Chapter 39) on behalf of B&S, naming Stanford as the defendant and accusing him of breach of fiduciary duty. Before trial, Stanford resigned from B&S and closed the company. He gave the assets and liabilities of B&S to a new company he formed and owned, J. C. Stanford & Sons. He offered the Williams brothers $25,000 each for their stock in B&S. They responded with a request for $125,000 each. The district court held that by law the Williams brothers, by making a counteroffer, gave up their rights to bring a suit against the company and granted summary judgment to Stanford. The Williams brothers appealed.

- **Decision and Rationale** The appellate court reversed in favor of the Williams brothers, holding that they were entitled to a trial on their allegations that their shares were worth more than the $25,000 Stanford offered. When dissenting shareholders seek more than the appraisal of their shares in the wake of dubious transactions, the courts must balance the principle that an adequate remedy should exist for the shareholders against the desire to prevent the courts from becoming bogged down in disputes about the fairness of cash-out prices offered to minority shareholders. When shareholders point to specific acts of self-dealing or misrepresentation, they are entitled to equitable remedies beyond the normal appraisal option that dissenting shareholders must accept.

- **The Ethical Dimension** *Was it acceptable for the Williams brothers to demand $125,000 each for their shares? Why or why not?*

- **The Legal Environment Dimension** *What could have been done in B&S to reduce the likelihood that this kind of problem would arise?*

Transfer of Shares in Close Corporations. By definition, a close corporation has a small number of shareholders. Thus, the transfer of one shareholder's shares to someone else can cause serious management problems. The other shareholders may find themselves required to share control with someone they do not know or like.

Suppose that three brothers, Terry, Damon, and Henry Johnson, are the only shareholders of Johnson's Car Wash, Inc. Terry and Damon do not want Henry to sell his shares to an unknown third person. To avoid this situation, the corporation could restrict the transferability of shares to outside persons. Shareholders could be required to offer their shares to the corporation or the other shareholders before selling them to an outside purchaser. In fact, a few states have statutes that prohibit the transfer of close corporation shares unless certain persons—including shareholders, family members, and the corporation—are first given the opportunity to purchase the shares for the same price.

Control of a close corporation can also be stabilized through the use of a *shareholder agreement.* A shareholder agreement can provide that when one of the original shareholders dies, her or his shares of stock in the corporation will be divided in such a way that the proportionate holdings of the survivors, and thus their proportionate control, will be maintained. Courts are generally reluctant to interfere with private agreements, including shareholder agreements.

S Corporations A close corporation that meets the qualifying requirements specified in Subchapter S of the Internal Revenue Code can operate as an **S corporation.** If a corporation has S corporation status, it can avoid the imposition of income taxes at the corporate level while retaining many of the advantages of a corporation, particularly limited liability.

Qualification Requirements for S Corporations. Among the numerous requirements for S corporation status, the following are the most important:

1. The corporation must be a domestic corporation.
2. The corporation must not be a member of an affiliated group of corporations.
3. The shareholders of the corporation must be individuals, estates, or certain trusts. Nonqualifying trusts and partnerships cannot be shareholders. Corporations can be shareholders under certain circumstances.
4. The corporation must have no more than one hundred shareholders.
5. The corporation must have only one class of stock, although all shareholders do not need to have the same voting rights.
6. No shareholder of the corporation may be a nonresident alien.

Benefits of S Corporations. At times, it is beneficial for a regular corporation to elect S corporation status. Benefits include the following:

1. When the corporation has losses, the S election allows the shareholders to use the losses to offset other taxable income.
2. When the shareholder's tax bracket is lower than the tax bracket for regular corporations, the S election causes the corporation's entire income to be taxed in the shareholder's bracket (because it is taxed as personal income), whether or not it is distributed. This is particularly attractive when the corporation wants to accumulate earnings for some future business purpose.

In the past, many close corporations opted for S corporation status to obtain these tax benefits. Today, however, the limited liability partnership and the limited liability company (discussed in Chapters 36 and 37, respectively) offer similar advantages plus additional benefits, including more flexibility in forming and operating the business. Hence, the S corporation has lost some of its appeal.

Professional Corporations Professionals such as physicians, lawyers, dentists, and accountants can incorporate. Professional corporations are typically identified by the letters *P.C.* (professional corporation), *S.C.* (service corporation), or *P.A.* (professional association). In general, the laws governing professional corporations are similar to those governing ordinary business corporations, but there are a few differences with regard to liability that deserve mention.

First, there is generally no limitation on liability for acts of malpractice or obligations incurred because of a breach of duty to a client or patient of the professional corporation. In other words, each shareholder in a professional corporation can be held liable for any malpractice liability incurred by the others within the scope of the corporate business. The reason for this rule is that professionals, in contrast to shareholders in other types of corporations, should not be allowed to avoid liability for their wrongful acts simply by incorporating. Second, in many states, professional persons are liable not only for their own negligent acts, but also for the misconduct of persons under their direct supervision who render professional services on behalf of the corporation. Third, a shareholder in a professional corporation is generally protected from contractual liability and cannot be held liable for the torts—other than malpractice or a breach of duty to clients or patients—that are committed by other professionals at the firm. See *Concept Summary 38.1* on the next page for a review of corporation classifications.

SECTION 2

Corporate Formation

Up to this point, we have discussed some of the general characteristics of corporations. We now examine the process by which corporations come into existence.

CONCEPT SUMMARY 38.1
Classification of Corporations

Classification	Description
Domestic, Foreign, and Alien Corporations	A corporation is referred to as a *domestic corporation* in its home state (the state in which it incorporates). A corporation is referred to as a *foreign corporation* by any state that is not its home state. A corporation is referred to as an *alien corporation* if it originates in another country but does business in the United States.
Public and Private Corporations	A *public corporation* is formed by a government (for example, a city, town, or public project). A *private corporation* is formed wholly or in part for private benefit. Most corporations are private corporations.
Nonprofit Corporation	A corporation formed without a profit-making purpose (for example, charitable, educational, and religious organizations and hospitals).
Close Corporation	A corporation owned by a family or a relatively small number of individuals; because the number of shareholders is small and the transfer of shares is usually restricted, the shares are not traded in a public securities market.
S Corporation	A small domestic corporation (must have no more than one hundred shareholders) that, under Subchapter S of the Internal Revenue Code, is given special tax treatment. S corporations allow shareholders to enjoy the limited legal liability of the corporate form but avoid its double-taxation feature (shareholders pay taxes on the income at personal income tax rates, and the S corporation is not taxed separately).
Professional Corporation	A corporation formed by professionals (for example, physicians or lawyers) to obtain the advantages of incorporation (such as tax benefits and limited liability). In most situations, the professional corporation is treated like other corporations, but sometimes the courts will disregard the corporate form and treat the shareholders as partners, especially with regard to malpractice liability.

Incorporating a business is much simpler today than it was twenty years ago, and many states allow businesses to incorporate online.

One of the most common reasons for creating a corporation is the need for additional capital to finance expansion. Many of the Fortune 500 companies started as sole proprietorships or partnerships and then converted to a corporate entity. A sole proprietor in need of funds can seek partners who will bring capital with them. Although a partnership may be able to secure more funds from potential lenders than the sole proprietor could, the amount is still limited. When a firm wants significant growth, continuing to add partners can result in so many partners that the firm can no longer operate effectively. Therefore, incorporation may be the best choice for an expanding business organization because a corporation can obtain more capital by issuing shares of stock. (Corporate financing is discussed later in this chapter.)

Promotional Activities

In the past, preliminary steps were taken to organize and promote the business prior to incorporating. Contracts were made with investors and others on behalf of the future corporation. Today, however, due to the relative ease of forming a corporation in most states, persons incorporating their business rarely, if ever, engage in preliminary promotional activities. Nevertheless, it is important for businesspersons to understand that they are personally liable for all preincorporation contracts made with investors, accountants, or others on behalf of the future corporation. This personal liability continues until the corporation assumes the preincorporation contracts by *novation* (discussed in Chapter 17).

Incorporation Procedures

Exact procedures for incorporation differ among states, but the basic steps are as follows: (1) select a state of incorporation, (2) secure the corporate name, (3) prepare the articles of incorporation, and (4) file the articles of incorporation with the secretary of state. These steps are discussed in more detail in the following subsections.

Selecting the State of Incorporation The first step in the incorporation process is to select a state in which to incorporate. Because state laws differ, individuals may look for the states that offer the most advantageous tax or incorporation provisions. Another consideration is the fee that a particular state charges to incorporate as well as the annual fees and the fees for specific transactions (such as stock transfers).

Delaware has historically had the least restrictive laws as well as provisions that favor corporate management. Consequently, many corporations, including a number of the largest, have incorporated there. Delaware's statutes permit firms to incorporate in that state and conduct business and locate their operating headquarters elsewhere. Most other states now permit this as well. Generally, though, closely held corporations, particularly those of a professional nature, incorporate in the state where their principal shareholders live and work. For reasons of convenience and cost, businesses often choose to incorporate in the state in which most of the corporation's business will be conducted.

Securing the Corporate Name The choice of a corporate name is subject to state approval to ensure against duplication or deception. State statutes usually require that the secretary of state run a check on the proposed name in the state of incorporation. In some states, the persons incorporating a firm must do the check themselves at their own expense. Specialized Internet search engines are available for checking corporate names, and many companies will perform this service for a fee. Once cleared, a name can be reserved for a short time, for a fee, pending the completion of the articles of incorporation. All states require the corporation name to include the word *Corporation (Corp.), Incorporated (Inc.), Company (Co.),* or *Limited (Ltd.)*.

A new corporation's name cannot be the same as (or deceptively similar to) the name of an existing corporation doing business within the state (see Chapter 8). The name should also be one that can be used as the business's Internet domain name. Suppose that an existing corporation is named Digital Synergy, Inc. A new corporation cannot choose the name Digital Synergy Company because that name is deceptively similar to the first, and the state will be unlikely to allow it. In addition, the new firm would not want to choose the name Digital Synergy Company because it would be unable to acquire an Internet domain name using the name of the business.

If those incorporating a firm contemplate doing business in other states—or over the Internet—they need to check on existing corporate names in those states as well. Otherwise, if the firm does business under a name that is the same as or deceptively similar to an existing company's name, it may be liable for trade name infringement.

PREVENTING LEGAL DISPUTES

Businesspersons should be cautious when choosing a corporate name. Even if a particular state does not require the incorporator to run a name check, doing so is always advisable and can help prevent future disputes. Many states provide online search capabilities, but these searches are usually limited and will only compare the proposed name to the names of active corporations within that state. Trade name disputes, however, are not limited to corporations. Thus, using a business name that is deceptively similar to the name of a partnership or limited liability company can also lead to a dispute.

Disputes are even more likely to arise among firms that do business over the Internet. Business owners should always check on the availability of a particular domain name before selecting a corporate name. This is an area in which it pays to be overly cautious and incur some additional cost to hire an attorney or specialized firm to conduct a name search. If owners learn that another business is using a similar name, they can contact that business and ask for its consent to the proposed name.

Preparing the Articles of Incorporation The primary document needed to incorporate a business is the **articles of incorporation.** (For a sample form of articles of incorporation, see Exhibit 38–2.)[7] The articles include basic information about the corporation and serve as a primary source of authority for its future organization and business functions. The person or persons who execute (sign) the articles are called *incorporators.* Generally, the articles of incorporation *must* include the following information [RMBCA 2.02].

1. The name of the corporation.
2. The number of shares the corporation is authorized to issue.
3. The name and address of the corporation's initial registered agent.
4. The name and address of each incorporator.

In addition, the articles *may* set forth other information, such as the names and addresses of the initial board of directors, the duration and purpose of the corporation, a par value of shares of the corporation, and any other information pertinent to the rights and duties

7. In some states, the articles of incorporation may be referred to as the *corporate charter,* especially after the state has approved or granted its authority for the existence of the corporation. Under some circumstances, such as when a corporation fails to pay taxes, a state can revoke the firm's corporate charter, or status as a corporation. See, for example, *Bullington v. Palangio,* 345 Ark. 320, 45 S.W.3d 834 (2001).

EXHIBIT 38–2 • Articles of Incorporation

ARTICLE ONE The name of the corporation is ______________________________.

ARTICLE TWO The period of its duration is __________ (may be a number of years or until a certain date).

ARTICLE THREE The purpose (or purposes) for which the corporation is organized is (are) ______________________________
____
______________________________.

ARTICLE FOUR The aggregate number of shares that the corporation shall have the authority to issue is _____ with the par value of __________ dollar(s) each (or without par value).

ARTICLE FIVE The corporation will not commence business until it has received for the issuance of its shares consideration of the value of $1,000 (can be any sum not less than $1,000).

ARTICLE SIX The address of the corporation's registered office is ______________________________, and the name of its registered agent at such address is ______________________________
______________________________.

ARTICLE SEVEN The number of initial directors is __________, and the names and addresses of the directors are ______________________________
______________________________.

ARTICLE EIGHT The names and addresses of the incorporators are

__________ (name)	__________ (address)	__________ (signature)
__________ (name)	__________ (address)	__________ (signature)
__________ (name)	__________ (address)	__________ (signature)

Sworn to on __________ (date) by the above-named incorporators.

____
Notary Public

(Notary Seal)

of the corporation's shareholders and directors. Articles of incorporation vary widely depending on the jurisdiction and the size and type of the corporation. Frequently, the articles do not provide much detail about the firm's operations, which are spelled out in the company's **bylaws** (internal rules of management adopted by the corporation at its first organizational meeting).

Shares of the Corporation. The articles must specify the number of shares of stock the corporation is authorized to issue [RMBCA 2.02(a)]. For instance, a company might state that the aggregate number of shares that the corporation has the authority to issue is five thousand. Large corporations often state a par value of each share, such as $.20 per share, and specify the various types or classes of stock authorized for issuance (see the discussion of *common* and *preferred stock* later in this chapter). Sometimes, the articles set forth the capital structure of the corporation and other relevant information concerning equity, shares, and credit.

Registered Office and Agent. The corporation must indicate the location and address of its registered office within the state. Usually, the registered office is also the principal office of the corporation. The corporation must also give the name and address of a specific person who has been designated as an *agent* and who can receive legal documents (such as orders to appear in court) on behalf of the corporation.

Incorporators. Each incorporator must be listed by name and address. The incorporators need not have any interest at all in the corporation, and sometimes signing the articles is their only duty. Many states do not have residency or age requirements for incorporators. In some states, only one incorporator is needed, but other states require as many as three. Incorporators frequently participate in the first organizational meeting of the corporation.

Duration and Purpose. A corporation has perpetual existence unless the articles state otherwise. The owners may want to prescribe a maximum duration, however, after which the corporation must formally renew its existence.

The RMBCA does not require a specific statement of purpose to be included in the articles. A corporation can be formed for any lawful purpose. Some incorporators include a general statement of purpose "to engage in any lawful act or activity," while others specify the intended business activities (such as "to engage in the production and sale of agricultural products"). The trend is toward allowing corporate articles to state that the corporation is organized for "any legal business," with no mention of specifics, to avoid the need for future amendments to the corporate articles [RMBCA 2.02(b)(2)(i), 3.01].

Some states prohibit certain licensed professionals, such as physicians or lawyers, from forming a general business corporation and require them instead to incorporate as a professional corporation (discussed previously).[8] Also, in some states, businesses in certain industries—such as banks, insurance companies, or public utilities—cannot be operated in the general corporate form and are governed by special incorporation statutes.

Internal Organization. The articles can describe the corporation's internal management structure, although this is usually included in the bylaws adopted after the corporation is formed. The articles of incorporation commence the corporation; the bylaws are formed after commencement by the board of directors. Bylaws cannot conflict with the incorporation statute or the articles of incorporation [RMBCA 2.06].

Under the RMBCA, shareholders may amend or repeal the bylaws. The board of directors may also amend or repeal the bylaws unless the articles of incorporation or provisions of the incorporation statute reserve this power to the shareholders exclusively [RMBCA 10.20]. Typical bylaw provisions describe such matters as voting requirements for shareholders, the election of the board of directors, the methods of replacing directors, and the manner and time of holding shareholders' and board meetings (these corporate activities will be discussed in Chapter 39).

Filing the Articles with the State Once the articles of incorporation have been prepared and signed by the incorporators, they are sent to the appropriate state official, usually the secretary of state, along with the required filing fee. In most states, the secretary of state then stamps the articles "Filed" and returns a copy of the articles to the incorporators. Once this occurs, the corporation officially exists. (Note that some states issue a *certificate of incorporation,* or *corporate charter,* which is similar to articles of incorporation, representing the state's authorization for the

8. See, for example, New Jersey Statutes Annotated Titles 14A:17-1 *et seq.*

corporation to conduct business. This procedure was typical under the unrevised MBCA.)

First Organizational Meeting to Adopt Bylaws

After incorporation, the first organizational meeting must be held. Usually, the most important function of this meeting is the adoption of bylaws—the internal rules of management for the corporation. If the articles of incorporation named the initial board of directors, then the directors, by majority vote, call the meeting to adopt the bylaws and complete the company's organization. If the articles did not name the directors (as is typical), then the incorporators hold the meeting to elect the directors, adopt bylaws, and complete the routine business of incorporation (authorizing the issuance of shares and hiring employees, for example). The business transacted depends on the requirements of the state's incorporation statute, the nature of the corporation, the provisions made in the articles, and the desires of the incorporators.

SECTION 3 Defects in Formation and Corporate Status

The procedures for incorporation are very specific. If they are not followed precisely, others may be able to challenge the existence of the corporation. Errors in incorporation procedures can become important when, for example, a third party who is attempting to enforce a contract or bring suit for a tort injury learns of them. On the basis of improper incorporation, the plaintiff could seek to make the would-be shareholders personally liable. Additionally, when the corporation seeks to enforce a contract against a defaulting party, that party may be able to avoid liability on the ground of a defect in the incorporation procedure.

To prevent injustice, the courts will sometimes attribute corporate existence to an improperly formed corporation by holding it to be a *de jure* corporation or a *de facto* corporation, as discussed below. Occasionally, a corporation may be held to exist by estoppel.

De Jure and *De Facto* Corporations

If a corporation has substantially complied with all conditions precedent to incorporation, a corporation is said to have *de jure* (rightful and lawful) existence. In most states and under RMBCA 2.03(b), the secretary of state's filing of the articles of incorporation is conclusive proof that all mandatory statutory provisions have been met [RMBCA 2.03(b)]. Because a *de jure* corporation is one that is properly formed, neither the state nor a third party can attack its existence.[9] If, for example, the articles listed an incorrect address for an incorporator, the corporation was improperly formed, but most courts will uphold its *de jure* status.

Sometimes, there is a defect in complying with statutory mandates—for example, the corporation failed to hold an organizational meeting. Under these circumstances, the corporation may have *de facto* (actual) status, meaning that it will be treated as a legal corporation despite the defect in its formation. A corporation with *de facto* status cannot be challenged by third persons (only by the state). In other words, the shareholders of a *de facto* corporation are still protected by limited liability (provided they are unaware of the defect). The following elements are required for *de facto* status:

1. There must be a state statute under which the corporation can be validly incorporated.
2. The parties must have made a good faith attempt to comply with the statute.
3. The enterprise must already have undertaken to do business as a corporation.

Corporation by Estoppel

If a business holds itself out to others as being a corporation but has made no attempt to incorporate, the firm normally will be estopped (prevented) from denying corporate status in a lawsuit by a third party. This usually occurs when a third party contracts with an entity that claims to be a corporation but has not filed articles of incorporation. It can also occur when a third party contracts with a person claiming to be an agent of a corporation that does not in fact exist. When justice requires, the courts treat an alleged corporation as if it were an actual corporation for the purpose of determining the rights and liabilities of its officers and directors in particular circumstances. A corporation by estoppel is thus determined by the situation. Recognition of its corporate status does not extend beyond the resolution of the problem at hand.

9. There is an exception: a few states allow state authorities, in a *quo warranto* proceeding, to bring an action against the corporation for noncompliance with a condition subsequent to incorporation. This might occur if the corporation fails to file annual reports, for example.

SECTION 4 Corporate Powers

Under modern law, a corporation generally can engage in any act and enter into any contract available to a natural person in order to accomplish the purposes for which it was formed. When a corporation is created, the express and implied powers necessary to achieve its purpose also come into existence.

Express Powers

The express powers of a corporation are found in its articles of incorporation, in the law of the state of incorporation, and in the state and federal constitutions.

Corporate bylaws and the resolutions of the corporation's board of directors also grant or restrict certain powers. Because state corporation statutes frequently provide default rules that apply if the company's bylaws are silent on an issue, it is important that the bylaws set forth the specific operating rules of the corporation. In addition, after the bylaws are adopted, the corporation's board of directors will pass resolutions that also grant or restrict corporate powers.

The following order of priority is used if a conflict arises among the various documents involving a corporation:

1. U.S. Constitution.
2. Constitution of the state of incorporation.
3. State statutes.
4. Articles of incorporation.
5. Bylaws.
6. Resolutions of the board of directors.

Implied Powers

Certain implied powers arise when a corporation is created. Barring express constitutional, statutory, or charter prohibitions, the corporation has the implied power to perform all acts reasonably appropriate and necessary to accomplish its corporate purposes. For this reason, a corporation has the implied power to borrow funds within certain limits, to lend funds, and to extend credit to those with whom it has a legal or contractual relationship.

To borrow funds, the corporation acts through its board of directors to authorize the loan. Most often, the president or chief executive officer (see Chapter 39) of the corporation will execute the necessary papers on behalf of the corporation. Corporate officers such as these have the implied power to bind the corporation in matters directly connected with the *ordinary* business affairs of the enterprise. A corporate officer does not have the authority to bind the corporation to an action that will greatly affect the corporate purpose or undertaking, such as the sale of substantial corporate assets, however.

Ultra Vires Doctrine

The term ***ultra vires*** means "beyond the power." In corporate law, acts of a corporation that are beyond its express or implied powers are *ultra vires* acts. Most cases dealing with *ultra vires* acts have involved contracts made for unauthorized purposes. For example, Suarez is the chief executive officer of SOS Plumbing, Inc. He enters into a contract with Carlini for the purchase of twenty cases of brandy. It is difficult to see how this contract is reasonably related to the conduct and furtherance of the corporation's stated purpose of providing plumbing installation and services. Hence, a court would probably find the contract to be *ultra vires*.

In some states, when a contract is entirely executory (not yet performed by either party), either party can use a defense of *ultra vires* to prevent enforcement of the contract. Under Section 3.04 of the RMBCA, the shareholders can seek an injunction from a court to prevent the corporation from engaging in *ultra vires* acts. The attorney general in the state of incorporation can also bring an action to obtain an injunction against the *ultra vires* transactions or to institute dissolution proceedings against the corporation on the basis of *ultra vires* acts. The corporation or its shareholders (on behalf of the corporation) can seek damages from the officers and directors who were responsible for the *ultra vires* acts.

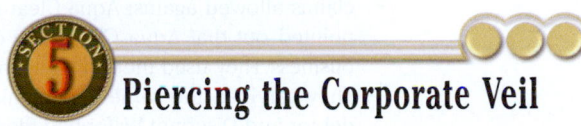

SECTION 5 Piercing the Corporate Veil

Occasionally, the owners use a corporate entity to perpetrate a fraud, circumvent the law, or in some other way accomplish an illegitimate objective. In these situations, the court will ignore the corporate structure and **pierce the corporate veil,** exposing the shareholders to personal liability [RMBCA 2.04]. Generally, when the corporate privilege is abused for personal benefit or when the corporate business is treated so carelessly that the corporation and the controlling shareholder are no longer separate entities, the court will require the owner to assume personal liability to creditors for the corporation's debts.

In short, when the facts show that great injustice would result from the use of a corporation to avoid individual responsibility, a court will look behind the corporate structure to the individual shareholder. The following are some of the factors that frequently cause the courts to pierce the corporate veil:

1. A party is tricked or misled into dealing with the corporation rather than the individual.
2. The corporation is set up never to make a profit or always to be insolvent, or it is too "thinly" capitalized—that is, it has insufficient capital at the time it is formed to meet its prospective debts or potential liabilities.
3. Statutory corporate formalities, such as holding required corporation meetings, are not followed.
4. Personal and corporate interests are mixed together, or **commingled,** to the extent that the corporation has no separate identity.

In the following case, when a corporation's creditors sought payment of its debts, the owners took for themselves the small value in the business, filed a bankruptcy petition for the firm, and incorporated under a new name to continue the business. Could the court recover the business assets from the new corporation for distribution to the original firm's creditors?

CASE 38.3 In re Aqua Clear Technologies, Inc.

United States Bankruptcy Court, Southern District of Florida, 2007. 361 Bankr. 567.

• **Background and Facts** Harvey and Barbara Jacobson owned Aqua Clear Technologies, Inc., a small Florida business that installed and serviced home water-softening systems. Barbara was Aqua Clear's president, and Sharon, the Jacobsons' daughter, was an officer, but neither participated in the business. Although Harvey controlled the day-to-day operations, he was not an Aqua Clear officer, director, or employee, but an independent contractor in service to it. Aqua Clear had no compensation agreement with the Jacobsons. Instead, whenever Harvey decided that there were sufficient funds, they took funds out of the business for their personal expenses, including the maintenance of their home and payments for their cars, health-insurance premiums, and charges on their credit cards. In December 2004, Aqua Clear filed a bankruptcy petition in a federal bankruptcy court. Three weeks later, Harvey incorporated Discount Water Services, Inc., and continued to service water-softening systems for Aqua Clear's customers. Discount appropriated Aqua Clear's equipment and inventory without a formal transfer and advertised Aqua Clear's phone number as Discount's own. Kenneth Welt, Aqua Clear's trustee, initiated a proceeding against Discount, seeking, among other things, to recover Aqua Clear's assets. The trustee contended that Discount was Aqua Clear's alter ego. (An *alter ego* is the double of something—in this case, the original company.)

• **Decision and Rationale** The court issued a judgment against Discount, and in the trustee's favor, for $108,732.64, which represented the amount of the claims listed in Aqua Clear's bankruptcy schedules. The court also agreed to add the administrative expenses and all other claims allowed against Aqua Clear once those amounts were determined. The bankruptcy court pointed out that Aqua Clear—the debtor—and Discount Water "were in substantially the same business. They used the same telephone number. They operated from the same business location. They serviced the same geographic area and many of the same customers." Furthermore, the debtor and Discount Water had identical officers and directors. Consequently, "the Court may presume fraud when a transfer occurs between two corporations controlled by the same officers and directors." The court then pointed out that Aqua Clear had sent a letter to its health-insurance carrier stating that it was simply changing its name to Discount Water Services, Inc. Most of the Jacobsons' actions were designed to interfere with the collection efforts of judgment creditors. " * * * The bottom line question is whether each entity has run its own race, or whether there has been a relay-style passing of the baton from one to the other."

• **The Ethical Dimension** *Was the Jacobsons' disregard for corporate formalities unethical? Why or why not?*

• **The Global Dimension** *If the scope of the Jacobsons' business had been global, should the court have issued a different judgment? Explain.*

The Commingling of Personal and Corporate Assets

The potential for corporate assets to be used for personal benefit is especially great in a close corporation, in which the shares are held by a single person or by only a few individuals, usually family members. In such a situation, the separate status of the corporate entity and the sole shareholder (or family-member shareholders) must be carefully preserved. Certain practices invite trouble for the one-person or family-owned corporation: the commingling of corporate and personal funds; the failure to remit taxes, including payroll and sales taxes; and the shareholders' continuous personal use of corporate property (for example, vehicles).

For example, Donald Park incorporated three sports companies—SSP, SSI, and SSII. His mother was the president of SSP and SSII but did not participate in their operations. Park handled most of the corporations' activities out of his apartment and drew funds from their accounts as needed to pay his personal expenses. None of the three corporations had any employees, issued stock or paid dividends, maintained corporate records, or followed other corporate formalities. Park—misrepresenting himself as the president of SSP and the vice president of SSII—obtained loans on behalf of SSP from Dimmitt & Owens Financial, Inc. When the loans were not paid, Dimmitt filed a suit in a federal district court, seeking, among other things, to impose personal liability on Park. Because Park had commingled corporate funds with his personal funds and failed to follow corporate formalities, the court "pierced the corporate veil" and held him personally responsible for the debt.[10]

Loans to the Corporation

Corporation laws usually do not specifically prohibit a shareholder from lending funds to her or his corporation. When an officer, director, or majority shareholder lends the corporation funds and takes back security in the form of corporate assets, however, the courts will scrutinize the transaction closely. Any such transaction must be made in good faith and for fair value.

SECTION 6

Corporate Financing

Corporations are financed by the issuance and sale of corporate securities. **Securities** (stocks and bonds) evidence the obligation to pay funds or the right to participate in earnings and the distribution of corporate assets. **Stocks,** or *equity securities,* represent the purchase of ownership in the business firm. **Bonds** (debentures), or *debt securities,* represent the borrowing of funds by firms (and governments). Of course, not all debt is in the form of debt securities. For example, some debt is in the form of accounts payable and notes payable, which typically are short-term debts. Bonds are simply a way for corporations to split up their long-term debt so that they can market it more easily.

Bonds

Bonds are issued by business firms and by governments at all levels as evidence of the funds they are borrowing from investors. Bonds almost always have a designated *maturity date*—the date when the principal, or face amount, of the bond (or loan) is returned to the investor—and are sometimes referred to as *fixed-income securities* because their owners receive fixed-dollar interest payments during the period of time prior to maturity.

The characteristics of corporate bonds vary widely, in part because corporations differ in their ability to generate the earnings and cash flow necessary to make interest payments and to repay the principal amount of the bonds at maturity. Furthermore, corporate bonds are only a part of the total debt and the overall financial structure of a corporate business. The different types of corporate bonds are described in Exhibit 38–3 on the following page.

Stocks

Issuing stocks is another way for corporations to obtain financing [RMBCA 6.01]. The ways in which stocks differ from bonds are summarized in Exhibit 38–4 on the next page. Basically, stocks represent ownership in a business firm, whereas bonds represent borrowing by the firm.

Exhibit 38–5 on page 731 offers a summary of the types of stocks issued by corporations. The two major types are *common stock* and *preferred stock.*

Common Stock The true ownership of a corporation is represented by **common stock.** Common stock provides a proportionate interest in the corporation with regard to (1) control, (2) earnings, and (3) net assets. A shareholder's interest is generally in proportion to the number of shares he or she owns out of the total number of shares issued.

10. *Dimmitt & Owens Financial, Inc. v. Superior Sports Products, Inc.,* 196 F.Supp.2d 731 (N.D.Ill. 2002).

EXHIBIT 38–3 • Types of Corporate Bonds

Type	Definition
Debenture Bonds	Bonds for which no specific assets of the corporation are pledged as backing. Rather, the bonds are backed by the general credit rating of the corporation, plus any assets that can be seized if the corporation allows the debentures to go into default.
Mortgage Bonds	Bonds that pledge specific property. If the corporation defaults on the bonds, the bondholders can foreclose on the property.
Convertible Bonds	Bonds that can be exchanged for a specified number of shares of stock under certain conditions.
Callable Bonds	Bonds that may be called in and the principal repaid at specified times or under conditions stipulated in the bonds when they are issued.

Any person who purchases common stock acquires voting rights—one vote per share held. Voting rights in a corporation apply to the election of the firm's board of directors and to any proposed changes in the ownership structure of the firm. For example, a holder of common stock generally has the right to vote in a decision on a proposed merger, as mergers can change the proportion of ownership. State corporation law specifies the types of actions for which shareholder approval must be obtained.

Holders of common stock are investors who assume a *residual* position in the overall financial structure of the business. In terms of receiving returns on their investments, they are last in line. They are entitled to earnings only after the corporation pays all other groups—suppliers, employees, managers, bankers, governments, bondholders, and holders of preferred stock—what is due them. Once those groups are paid, the owners of common stock may be entitled to *all* the remaining earnings. (The board of directors normally is not under any duty to declare the remaining earnings as dividends, however.)

Preferred Stock **Preferred stock** is an equity security with *preferences*. Usually, this means that holders of preferred stock have priority over holders of common stock as to dividends and to payment on dissolution of the corporation. The preferences must be stated in the articles of incorporation. Preferred stockholders may or may not have the right to vote. Sometimes, there is more

EXHIBIT 38–4 • How Do Stocks and Bonds Differ?

Stocks	Bonds
1. Stocks represent ownership.	1. Bonds represent debt.
2. Stocks (common) do not have a fixed dividend rate.	2. Interest on bonds must always be paid, whether or not any profit is earned.
3. Stockholders can elect the board of directors, which controls the corporation.	3. Bondholders usually have no voice in or control over management of the corporation.
4. Stocks do not have a maturity date; the corporation usually does not repay the stockholder.	4. Bonds have a maturity date, when the corporation is to repay the bondholder the face value of the bond.
5. All corporations issue or offer to sell stocks. This is the usual definition of a corporation.	5. Corporations do not necessarily issue bonds.
6. Stockholders have a claim against the property and income of the corporation after all creditors' claims have been met.	6. Bondholders have a claim against the property and income of the corporation that must be met before the claims of stockholders.

EXHIBIT 38–5 • Types of Stocks

Type	Definition
Common Stock	Voting shares that represent ownership interest in a corporation. Common stock has the lowest priority with respect to payment of dividends and distribution of assets on the corporation's dissolution.
Preferred Stock	Shares of stock that have priority over common-stock shares as to payment of dividends and distribution of assets on dissolution. Dividend payments are usually a fixed percentage of the face value of the share. Preferred shares may or may not be nonvoting shares.
Cumulative Preferred Stock	Preferred shares for which required dividends not paid in a given year must be paid in a subsequent year before any common-stock dividends can be paid.
Participating Preferred Stock	Preferred shares entitling the owner to receive (1) the preferred-stock dividend and (2) additional dividends after the corporation has paid dividends on common stock.
Convertible Preferred Stock	Preferred shares entitling the owner to convert his or her shares into a specified number of common shares either in the issuing corporation or, sometimes, in another corporation.
Redeemable, or Callable, Preferred Stock	Preferred shares issued with the express condition that the issuing corporation has the right to repurchase the shares as specified.

than one class of preferred stock (see Exhibit 38–5), and one class is given preferences over another class.

Preferred stock is not included among the liabilities of a business because it is equity. Like other equity securities, preferred shares have no fixed maturity date on which the firm must pay them off. Although firms occasionally buy back preferred stock, they are not legally obligated to do so. Investors who hold preferred stock have assumed a rather cautious position in their relationship to the corporation. They have a stronger position than common shareholders with respect to dividends and claims on assets, but they will not share in the full prosperity of the firm if it grows successfully over time. This is because preferred shares will not rise as rapidly in value as common shares during a period of financial success. Preferred stockholders do receive fixed dividends periodically, however, and they may benefit to some extent from changes in the market price of the shares.

From an investment standpoint, preferred stock is more similar to bonds than to common stock, even though preferred stock appears in the ownership section of the firm's balance sheet. As a result, preferred stock is often categorized with corporate bonds as a fixed-income security, even though the legal status is not the same.

Venture Capital and Private Equity Capital

As discussed, corporations traditionally obtain financing through issuing and selling securities (stocks and bonds) in the capital market. In reality, however, many investors do not want to purchase stock in a business that lacks a track record, and banks are generally reluctant to extend loans to high-risk enterprises. Numerous corporations fail because they are undercapitalized. Therefore, to obtain sufficient financing, many entrepreneurs seek alternative financing.

Venture Capital Start-up businesses and high-risk enterprises often obtain venture capital financing. **Venture capital** is capital provided by professional, outside investors (*venture capitalists,* usually groups of wealthy investors and investment banks) to new business ventures. Venture capital investments are high risk—the investors must be willing to lose their invested funds—but offer the potential for well-above-average returns at some point in the future.

To obtain venture capital financing, the start-up business typically gives up a share of its ownership to the venture capitalists. In addition to funding, venture capitalists may provide managerial and technical expertise, and nearly always are given some control over the new company's decisions. Many Internet-based companies, such as Google and Amazon, were initially financed by venture capital.

Private Equity Capital In recent years, private equity firms have been playing a larger role in corporate financing. These firms obtain their capital from wealthy investors in private markets—hence, the name *private equity*. The firms use their **private equity capital** to invest in existing—often, publicly traded—corporations. Usually, they buy an entire corporation and then reorganize it. Sometimes, divisions of the purchased company are sold off to pay down debt. Ultimately, the private equity firm may sell shares in the reorganized (and perhaps more profitable) company to the public in an *initial public offering* (usually called an IPO—see Chapter 41). In this way, the private equity firm can make profits by selling its shares in the company to the public. When DaimlerChrysler wanted to sell its less-than-successful Chrysler division, it sold 80 percent of it to the private equity firm Cerberus Capital Management, LP.

Locating Potential Investors Online

Today, the Internet allows anyone to access, easily and inexpensively, a large number of potential investors. A number of online "matching services" are available to match potential investors with companies or future companies that are seeking investors. Online matching services enable entrepreneurs to reach a wide group of potential investors quickly and with relatively little effort. An incorporator or a small company seeking capital investment can pay a fee to one of these services, which will then include a description of the company in a list that it makes available to investors, also for a fee.

Some matching services specialize in matching entrepreneurs in specific industries with potential investors. Other services focus on matching start-up companies with foreign investors or restrict their operations to firms within a certain region, such as the Pacific Northwest. These companies sometimes also assist businesspersons in creating effective business plans or managing financial issues.

REVIEWING CORPORATIONS—Formation and Financing

William Sharp was the sole shareholder and manager of Chickasaw Club, Inc., an S corporation that operated a popular nightclub of the same name in Columbus, Georgia. Sharp maintained a corporate checking account but paid the club's employees, suppliers, and entertainers in cash out of the club's proceeds. Sharp owned the property on which the club was located. He rented it to the club but made mortgage payments out of the club's proceeds and often paid other personal expenses with Chickasaw corporate funds. At 12:45 A.M. on July 31, 2005, eighteen-year-old Aubrey Lynn Pursley, who was already intoxicated, entered the Chickasaw Club. A city ordinance prohibited individuals under the age of twenty-one from entering nightclubs, but Chickasaw employees did not check Pursley's identification to verify her age. Pursley drank more alcohol at Chickasaw and was visibly intoxicated when she left the club at 3:00 A.M. with a beer in her hand. Shortly afterward, Pursley lost control of her car, struck a tree, and was killed. Joseph Dancause, Pursley's stepfather, filed a tort lawsuit in a Georgia state court against Chickasaw Club, Inc., and William Sharp, seeking damages. Using the information presented in the chapter, answer the following questions.

1. Under what theory might the court in this case make an exception to the limited liability of shareholders and hold Sharp personally liable for the damages? What factors would be relevant to the court's decision?
2. Suppose that Chickasaw's articles of incorporation failed to describe the corporation's purpose or management structure as required by state law. Would the court be likely to rule that Sharp is personally liable to Dancause on that basis?
3. Suppose that the club extended credit to its regular patrons in an effort to maintain a loyal clientele, although neither the articles of incorporation nor the corporate bylaws authorized this practice. Would the corporation likely have the power to engage in this activity? Explain.
4. How would the court classify the Chickasaw Club corporation—domestic or foreign, public or private?

TERMS AND CONCEPTS

alien corporation 719
articles of incorporation 724
bonds 729
bylaws 725
close corporation 719
commingle 728
common stock 729
domestic corporation 718
foreign corporation 719
holding company 716
pierce the corporate veil 727
preferred stock 730
private equity capital 732
retained earnings 716
S corporation 721
securities 729
stocks 729
ultra vires 727
venture capital 731

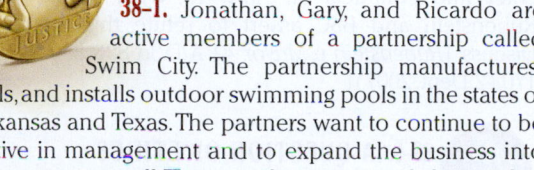

QUESTIONS AND CASE PROBLEMS

38–1. Jonathan, Gary, and Ricardo are active members of a partnership called Swim City. The partnership manufactures, sells, and installs outdoor swimming pools in the states of Arkansas and Texas. The partners want to continue to be active in management and to expand the business into other states as well. They are also concerned about rather large recent judgments entered against swimming pool companies throughout the United States. Based on these facts only, discuss whether the partnership should incorporate.

38–2. QUESTION WITH SAMPLE ANSWER

Cummings, Okawa, and Taft are recent college graduates who want to form a corporation to manufacture and sell personal computers. Peterson tells them he will set in motion the formation of their corporation. First, Peterson makes a contract with Owens for the purchase of a piece of land for $20,000. Owens does not know of the prospective corporate formation at the time the contract is signed. Second, Peterson makes a contract with Babcock to build a small plant on the property being purchased. Babcock's contract is conditional on the corporation's formation. Peterson secures all necessary subscription agreements and capitalization, and he files the articles of incorporation. A charter is issued.

(a) Discuss whether the newly formed corporation, Peterson, or both are liable on the contracts with Owens and Babcock.

(b) Discuss whether the corporation is automatically liable to Babcock on formation.

- **For a sample answer to Question 38–2, go to Appendix I at the end of this text.**

38–3. Oya Paka and two business associates formed a corporation called Paka Corp. for the purpose of selling computer services. Oya, who owned 50 percent of the corporate shares, served as the corporation's president. Oya wished to obtain a personal loan from her bank for $250,000, but the bank required the note to be cosigned by a third party. Oya cosigned the note in the name of the corporation. Later, Oya defaulted on the note, and the bank sued the corporation for payment. The corporation asserted, as a defense, that Oya had exceeded her authority when she cosigned the note on behalf of the corporation. Had she? Explain.

38–4. Disregarding the Corporate Entity. Steven and Janis Gimbert leased a warehouse to a manufacturing business owned by Manzar Zuberi. Zuberi signed the lease as the purported representative of "ATM Manufacturing, Inc.," which was a nonexistent corporation. Zuberi was actually the president of two existing corporations, ATM Enterprises, Inc., and Ameri-Pak International. Under the Ameri-Pak name, Zuberi manufactured a household cleaning product in the Gimberts' warehouse. The hydrochloric acid used in the operations severely damaged the premises, and the Gimberts filed a suit in a Georgia state court against Zuberi personally to collect for the damage. On what basis might Zuberi be held personally liable? Discuss fully. [*Zuberi v. Gimbert,* 230 Ga.App. 471, 496 S.E.2d 741 (1998)]

38–5. Corporate Powers. InterBel Telephone Cooperative, Inc., is a Montana corporation organized under the Montana Rural Electric and Telephone Cooperative Act. This statute limits the purposes of such corporations to providing "adequate telephone service" but adds that this "enumeration . . . shall not be deemed to exclude like or similar objects, purposes, powers, manners, methods, or things." Mooseweb Corp. is an Internet service provider that has been owned and operated by Fred Weber since 1996. Mooseweb provides Web site hosting, modems, computer installation, technical support, and dial-up access to customers in Lincoln County, Montana. InterBel began to offer Internet service in 1999, competing with Mooseweb in Lincoln County. Weber filed a suit in a Montana state court against InterBel, alleging that its Internet service was *ultra vires.* Both parties filed motions for summary judgment. In whose favor should the court rule, and why? [*Weber v. InterBel Telephone Cooperative, Inc.*, 2003 MT 320, 318 Mont. 295, 80 P.3d 88 (2003)]

38–6. Torts and Criminal Acts. Greg Allen is an employee, shareholder, and director of Greg Allen Construction Co., and its president. In 1996, Daniel and Sondra Estelle hired Allen's firm to renovate a home they owned in Ladoga, Indiana. To finance the cost, they obtained a line of credit from Banc One, Indiana, which required periodic inspections before it would disburse funds. Allen was on the job every day and supervised all of the work. He designed all of the structural changes, including a floor system for the bedroom over the living room, the floor system of the living room, and the stairway to the second floor. He did all of the electrical, plumbing, and carpentry work and installed all of the windows. He did most of the drywall taping and finishing and most of the painting. The Estelles found much of this work to be unacceptable, and the bank's inspector agreed that it was of poor quality. When Allen failed to act on the Estelles' complaints, they filed a suit in an Indiana state court against Allen Construction and Allen personally, alleging, in part, that his individual work on the project was negligent. Can both Allen and his corporation be held liable for this tort? Explain. [*Greg Allen Construction Co. v. Estelle*, 798 N.E.2d 171 (Ind. 2004)]

38–7. CASE PROBLEM WITH SAMPLE ANSWER

Thomas Persson and Jon Nokes founded Smart Inventions, Inc., in 1991 to market household consumer products. The success of their first product, the Smart Mop, continued with later products, which were sold through infomercials and other means. Persson and Nokes were the firm's officers and equal shareholders, with Persson responsible for product development and Nokes in charge of day-to-day operations. By 1998, they had become dissatisfied with each other's efforts. Nokes represented the firm as financially "dying," "in a grim state, . . . worse than ever," and offered to buy all of Persson's shares for $1.6 million. Persson accepted. On the day that they signed the agreement to transfer the shares, Smart Inventions began marketing a new product—the Tap Light—which was an instant success, generating millions of dollars in revenues. In negotiating with Persson, Nokes had intentionally kept the Tap Light a secret. Persson filed a suit in a California state court against Smart Inventions and others, asserting fraud and other claims. Under what principle might Smart Inventions be liable for Nokes's fraud? Is Smart Inventions liable in this case? Explain. [*Persson v. Smart Inventions, Inc.*, 125 Cal.App.4th 1141, 23 Cal.Rptr.3d 335 (2 Dist. 2005)]

- **To view a sample answer for Problem 38–7, go to this book's Web site at www.cengage.com/blaw/jentz, select "Chapter 38," and click on "Case Problem with Sample Answer."**

38–8. Improper Incorporation. Denise Rubenstein and Christopher Mayor agreed to form Bayshore Sunrise Corp. (BSC) in New York to rent certain premises and operate a laundromat. BSC entered into a twenty-year commercial lease with Bay Shore Property Trust on April 15, 1999. Mayor signed the lease as the president of BSC. The next day—April 16—BSC's certificate of incorporation was filed with New York's secretary of state. Three years later, BSC defaulted on the lease, which resulted in its termination. Rubenstein and BSC filed a suit in a New York state court against Mayor, his brother-in-law Thomas Castellano, and Planet Laundry, Inc., claiming wrongful interference with a contractual relationship. The plaintiffs alleged that Mayor and Castellano conspired to squeeze Rubenstein out of BSC and arranged the default on the lease so that Mayor and Castellano could form and operate their own business, Planet Laundry, at the same address. The defendants argued that they could not be liable on the plaintiffs' claim because there had never been an enforceable lease—BSC lacked the capacity to enter into contracts on April 15. What theory might Rubenstein and BSC assert to refute this argument? Discuss. [*Rubenstein v. Mayor*, 41 A.D.3d 826, 839 N.Y.S.2d 170 (2 Dept. 2007)]

38–9. A QUESTION OF ETHICS

Mike Lyons incorporated Lyons Concrete, Inc., in Montana, but did not file its first annual report, so the state involuntarily dissolved the firm in 1996. Unaware of the dissolution, Lyons continued to do business as Lyons Concrete. In 2003, he signed a written contract with William Weimar to form and pour a certain amount of concrete on Weimar's property in Lake County for $19,810. Weimar was in a rush to complete the entire project, and he and Lyons orally agreed to additional work on a time-and-materials basis. When scheduling conflicts arose, Weimar had his own employees set some of the forms, which proved deficient. Weimar also directed Lyons to pour concrete in the rain, which undercut its quality. In mid-project, Lyons submitted an invoice for $14,389, which Weimar paid. After the work was complete, Lyons invoiced Weimar for $25,731, but he refused to pay, claiming that the $14,389 covered everything. To recover the unpaid amount, Lyons filed a mechanic's lien as "Mike Lyons d/b/a Lyons Concrete, Inc." against Weimar's property. Weimar filed a suit in a Montana state court to strike the lien, which Lyons filed a counterclaim to reassert. [Weimar v. Lyons, *338 Mont. 242, 164 P.3d 922 (2007)*]

(a) Before the trial, Weimar asked for a change of venue on the ground that a sign on the courthouse lawn advertised "Lyons Concrete." How might the sign affect a trial on the parties' dispute? Should the court grant this request?

(b) Weimar asked the court to dismiss the counterclaim on the ground that the state had dissolved Lyons Concrete in 1996. Lyons immediately filed new articles of incorporation for "Lyons Concrete, Inc." Under what doctrine might the court rule that Weimar could not deny the existence of Lyons Concrete? What ethical values underlie this doctrine? Should the court make this ruling?

(c) At the trial, Weimar argued in part that there was no "fixed price" contract between the parties and that even if there was, the poor quality of the work, which required repairs, amounted to a breach, excusing Weimar's further performance. Should the court rule in Weimar's favor on this basis?

38–10. VIDEO QUESTION

Go to this text's Web site at **www.cengage.com/blaw/jentz** and select "Chapter 38." Click on "Video Questions" and view the video titled *Corporation or LLC: Which Is Better?* Then answer the following questions.

(a) Compare the liability that Anna and Caleb would be exposed to as shareholders/owners of a corporation versus as members of a limited liability company (LLC).

(b) How does the taxation of corporations and LLCs differ?

(c) Given that Anna and Caleb conduct their business (Wizard Internet) over the Internet, can you think of any drawbacks to forming an LLC?

(d) If you were in the position of Anna and Caleb, would you choose to create a corporation or an LLC? Why?

LAW ON THE WEB

For updated links to resources available on the Web, as well as a variety of other materials, visit this text's Web site at

www.cengage.com/blaw/jentz

Cornell University's Legal Information Institute has links to state corporation statutes at

topics.law.cornell.edu/wex/state_statutes.html

The Center for Corporate Law at the University of Cincinnati College of Law is a good source of information on corporate law. Go to

www.law.uc.edu/CCL

Legal Research Exercises on the Web

Go to **www.cengage.com/blaw/jentz**, the Web site that accompanies this text. Select "Chapter 38" and click on "Internet Exercises." There you will find the following Internet research exercises that you can perform to learn more about the topics covered in this chapter.

Internet Exercise 38–1: Legal Perspective
Corporate Law

Internet Exercise 38–2: Management Perspective
Online Incorporation

CHAPTER 39

CORPORATIONS—Directors, Officers, and Shareholders

A corporation joins the efforts and resources of a large number of individuals for the purpose of producing greater returns than those persons could have obtained individually. Corporate directors, officers, and shareholders all play different roles within the corporate entity. Sometimes, actions that may benefit the corporation as a whole do not coincide with the separate interests of the individuals making up the corporation. In such situations, it is important to know the rights and duties of all participants in the corporate enterprise. This chapter focuses on these rights and duties and the ways in which conflicts among corporate participants are resolved.

SECTION 1 The Roles of Directors and Officers

The board of directors is the ultimate authority in every corporation. Directors have responsibility for all policymaking decisions necessary to the management of all corporate affairs. Just as shareholders cannot act individually to bind the corporation, the directors must act as a body in carrying out routine corporate business. The board selects and removes the corporate officers, determines the capital structure of the corporation, and declares dividends. Each director has one vote, and customarily the majority rules. The general areas of responsibility of the board of directors are shown in Exhibit 39–1.

Directors are sometimes inappropriately characterized as *agents* because they act on behalf of the corporation. No individual director, however, can act as an agent to bind the corporation; and as a group, directors collectively control the corporation in a way that no agent is able to control a principal. In addition, although directors occupy positions of trust and control over the corporation, they are not *trustees* because they do not hold title to property for the use and benefit of others.

Few qualifications are required for directors. Only a handful of states impose minimum age and residency requirements. A director may be a shareholder, but that is not necessary (unless the articles of incorporation or bylaws require ownership).

Election of Directors

Subject to statutory limitations, the number of directors is set forth in the corporation's articles or bylaws. Historically, the minimum number of directors has been three, but today many states permit fewer. Normally, the incorporators appoint the first board of directors at the time the corporation is created, or the corporation itself names the directors in the articles. The initial board serves until the first annual shareholders' meeting. Subsequent directors are elected by a majority vote of the shareholders.

A director usually serves for a term of one year—from annual meeting to annual meeting. Longer and staggered terms are permissible under most state

EXHIBIT 39–1 • Directors' Management Responsibilities

Authorize Major Corporate Policy Decisions	Select and Remove Corporate Officers and Other Managerial Employees, and Determine Their Compensation	Make Financial Decisions
Examples:	*Examples:*	*Examples:*
—Oversee major contract negotiations and management-labor negotiations. —Initiate negotiations on sale or lease of corporate assets outside the regular course of business. —Decide whether to pursue new product lines or business opportunities.	—Search for and hire corporate executives and determine the elements of their compensation packages, including stock options. —Supervise managerial employees and make decisions regarding their termination.	—Make decisions regarding the issuance of authorized shares and bonds. —Decide when to declare dividends to be paid to shareholders.

statutes. A common practice is to elect one-third of the board members each year for a three-year term. In this way, there is greater management continuity.

Removal of Directors A director can be removed *for cause*—that is, for failing to perform a required duty—either as specified in the articles or bylaws or by shareholder action. Even the board of directors itself may be given power to remove a director for cause, subject to shareholder review. In most states, a director cannot be removed without cause unless the shareholders have reserved the right to do so at the time of election. Whether shareholders should be able to remove a director without cause is part of an ongoing debate about the balance of power between a corporation and its shareholders.

Vacancies on the Board of Directors Vacancies can occur on the board of directors because of death or resignation or when a new position is created through amendment of the articles or bylaws. In these situations, either the shareholders or the board itself can fill the position, depending on state law or on the provisions of the bylaws. Note, however, that even when the bylaws appear to authorize an election, a court can invalidate an election if the directors were attempting to diminish the shareholders' influence in it.

For example, the bylaws of Liquid Audio, a Delaware corporation, authorized a board of five directors. Two directors on the board were elected each year. Another company had offered to buy all of Liquid Audio's stock, but the board of directors rejected this offer. An election was coming up, and the directors feared that the shareholders would elect new directors who would go through with the sale. The directors therefore amended the bylaws to increase the number of directors to seven, thereby diminishing the shareholders' influence in the vote. The shareholders filed an action challenging the election. The Delaware Supreme Court ruled that the directors' action was illegal because they had attempted to diminish the shareholders' right to vote effectively in an election of directors.[1]

Compensation of Directors

In the past, corporate directors rarely were compensated, but today they are often paid at least nominal sums and may receive more substantial compensation in large corporations because of the time, work, effort, and especially risk involved. Most states permit the corporate articles or bylaws to authorize compensation for directors. In fact, the Revised Model Business Corporation Act (RMBCA) states that unless the articles or bylaws provide otherwise, the board of directors may set their own compensation [RMBCA 8.11]. Directors also gain through indirect benefits, such as business contacts and prestige, and other rewards, such as stock options.

In many corporations, directors are also chief corporate officers (president or chief executive officer, for

1. *MM Companies, Inc. v. Liquid Audio, Inc.*, 813 A.2d 1118 (Del.Sup.Ct. 2003).

example) and receive compensation in their managerial positions. A director who is also an officer of the corporation is referred to as an **inside director,** whereas a director who does not hold a management position is an **outside director.** Typically, a corporation's board of directors includes both inside and outside directors.

Board of Directors' Meetings

The board of directors conducts business by holding formal meetings with recorded minutes. The dates of regular meetings are usually established in the articles or bylaws or by board resolution, and no further notice is customarily required. Special meetings can be called, with notice sent to all directors. Today, most states allow directors to participate in board of directors' meetings from remote locations via telephone or Web conferencing, provided that all the directors can simultaneously hear each other during the meeting [RMBCA 8.20].

Unless the articles of incorporation or bylaws specify a greater number, a majority of the board of directors normally constitutes a quorum [RMBCA 8.24]. (A **quorum** is the minimum number of members of a body of officials or other group that must be present for business to be validly transacted.) Some state statutes specifically allow corporations to set a quorum as less than a majority but not less than one-third of the directors.[2]

Once a quorum is present, the directors transact business and vote on issues affecting the corporation. Each director present at the meeting has one vote.[3] Ordinary matters generally require a simple majority vote; certain extraordinary issues may require a greater-than-majority vote. In other words, the affirmative vote of a majority of the directors present at a meeting binds the board of directors with regard to most decisions.

Rights of Directors

A corporate director must have certain rights to function properly in that position. The *right to participation* means that directors are entitled to participate in all board of directors' meetings and have a right to be notified of these meetings. As mentioned earlier, the dates of regular board meetings are usually preestablished and no notice of these meetings is required. If special meetings are called, however, notice is required unless waived by the director [RMBCA 8.23].

A director also has a *right of inspection,* which means that each director can access the corporation's books and records, facilities, and premises. Inspection rights are essential for directors to make informed decisions and to exercise the necessary supervision over corporate officers and employees. This right of inspection is virtually absolute and cannot be restricted (by the articles, bylaws, or any act of the board of directors).

When a director becomes involved in litigation by virtue of her or his position or actions, the director may also have a *right to indemnification* (reimbursement) for the legal costs, fees, and damages incurred. Most states allow corporations to indemnify and purchase liability insurance for corporate directors [RMBCA 8.51].

Whenever businesspersons serve as corporate directors or officers, they may at some point become involved in litigation as a result of their positions. To protect against personal liability, directors or officers should take several steps. First, they should make sure that the corporate bylaws explicitly give them a right to indemnification (reimbursement) for any costs incurred as a result of litigation, as well as any judgments or settlements stemming from a lawsuit. Second, they should have the corporation purchase directors' and officers' liability insurance (D&O insurance). Having D&O insurance policies enables the corporation to avoid paying the substantial costs involved in defending a particular director or officer. The D&O policies offered by most private insurance companies have maximum coverage limits, so ensuring that the corporation is required to indemnify directors and officers in the event that the costs exceed the policy limits is very important.

Committees of the Board of Directors

When a board of directors has a large number of members and must deal with a myriad of complex business issues, meetings can become unwieldy. Therefore, the boards of large, publicly held corpora-

2. See, for example, Delaware Code Annotated Title 8, Section 141(b); and New York Business Corporation Law, Section 707.

3. Except in Louisiana, which allows a director to vote by proxy under certain circumstances.

tions typically create committees, appoint directors to serve on individual committees, and delegate certain tasks to these committees. Committees focus on individual subjects and increase the efficiency of the board. The most common types of committees include the following:

1. *Executive committee.* The board members often elect an executive committee of directors to handle the interim management decisions between board of directors' meetings. The executive committee is limited to making management decisions about ordinary business matters and conducting preliminary investigations into proposals. It cannot declare dividends, authorize the issuance of shares, amend the bylaws, or initiate any actions that require shareholder approval.
2. *Audit committee.* The audit committee is responsible for the selection, compensation, and oversight of the independent public accountants who audit the corporation's financial records. The Sarbanes-Oxley Act of 2002 requires all publicly held corporations to have an audit committee (as discussed in Chapters 41 and 51).
3. *Nominating committee.* This committee chooses the candidates for the board of directors that management wishes to submit to the shareholders in the next election. The committee cannot select directors to fill vacancies on the board, however [RMBCA 8.25].
4. *Compensation committee.* The compensation committee reviews and decides the salaries, bonuses, stock options, and other benefits that are given to the corporation's top executives. The committee may also determine the compensation of directors.
5. *Litigation committee.* This committee decides whether the corporation should pursue requests by shareholders to file a lawsuit against some party that has allegedly harmed the corporation. The committee members investigate the allegations and weigh the costs and benefits of litigation.

In addition to appointing committees, the board of directors can also delegate some of its functions to corporate officers. In doing so, the board is not relieved of its overall responsibility for directing the affairs of the corporation. Instead, corporate officers and managerial personnel are empowered to make decisions relating to ordinary, daily corporate activities within well-defined guidelines.

Corporate Officers and Executives

Officers and other executive employees are hired by the board of directors. At a minimum, most corporations have a president, one or more vice presidents, a secretary, and a treasurer. In most states, an individual can hold more than one office, such as president and secretary, and can be both an officer and a director of the corporation. In addition to carrying out the duties articulated in the bylaws, corporate and managerial officers act as agents of the corporation, and the ordinary rules of agency (discussed in Chapters 31 and 32) normally apply to their employment.

Corporate officers and other high-level managers are employees of the company, so their rights are defined by employment contracts. Regardless of the terms of an employment contract, however, the board of directors normally can remove a corporate officer at any time with or without cause—although the officer may then seek damages from the corporation for breach of contract.

The duties of corporate officers are the same as those of directors because both groups are involved in decision making and are in similar positions of control. Hence, officers and directors are viewed as having the same fiduciary duties of care and loyalty in their conduct of corporate affairs, a subject to which we now turn. For a synopsis of the roles of directors and officers, see *Concept Summary 39.1* on page 740.

SECTION 2

The Duties and Liabilities of Directors and Officers

Directors and officers are deemed to be fiduciaries of the corporation because their relationship with the corporation and its shareholders is one of trust and confidence. As fiduciaries, directors and officers owe ethical—and legal—duties to the corporation and the shareholders as a whole. These fiduciary duties include the duty of care and the duty of loyalty.

Duty of Care

Directors and officers must exercise due care in performing their duties. The standard of *due care* has been variously described in judicial decisions and codified in many state corporation codes. Generally, directors and officers are required to act in good faith, to exercise the care that an ordinarily prudent person would

CONCEPT SUMMARY 39.1
Roles of Directors and Officers

Aspect	Description
Election of Directors	The incorporators usually appoint the first board of directors; thereafter, shareholders elect the directors. Directors usually serve a one-year term, although the term can be longer. Few qualifications are required; a director can be a shareholder but is not required to be. Compensation is usually specified in the corporate articles or bylaws.
Board of Directors' Meetings	The board of directors conducts business by holding formal meetings with recorded minutes. The dates of regular meetings are usually established in the corporate articles or bylaws; special meetings can be called, with notice sent to all directors. Usually, a quorum is a majority of the corporate directors. Once a quorum is present, each director has one vote, and the majority normally rules in ordinary matters.
Rights of Directors	Directors' rights include the rights of participation, inspection, compensation, and indemnification.
Board of Directors' Committees	Directors may appoint committees and delegate some of their responsibilities to the committees and to corporate officers and executives. Common committees include the *executive committee,* which handles ordinary, interim management decisions between board of directors' meetings; the *audit committee,* which hires and supervises the independent public accountants who audit the corporation's financial records; the *nominating committee,* which chooses the candidates for the board of directors to be put to a shareholder vote; the *compensation committee,* which reviews and decides management's salaries, bonuses, stock options, and other benefits; and the *litigation committee,* which decides whether the corporation should pursue lawsuits requested by the shareholders.
Role of Corporate Officers and Executives	The board of directors normally hires the corporate officers and other executive employees. In most states, a person can hold more than one office and can be both an officer and a director of a corporation. The rights of corporate officers and executives are defined by employment contracts.

exercise in similar circumstances, and to do what they believe is in the best interests of the corporation [RMBCA 8.30(a), 8.42(a)]. Directors and officers whose failure to exercise due care results in harm to the corporation or its shareholders can be held liable for negligence (unless the business judgment rule applies).

Duty to Make Informed and Reasonable Decisions Directors and officers are expected to be informed on corporate matters and to conduct a reasonable investigation of the situation before making a decision. This means that they must do what is necessary to keep adequately informed: attend meetings and presentations, ask for information from those who have it, read reports, and review other written materials. In other words, directors and officers must investigate, study, and discuss matters and evaluate alternatives before making a decision. They cannot decide on the spur of the moment without adequate research.

Although directors and officers are expected to act in accordance with their own knowledge and training, they are also normally entitled to rely on information given to them by certain other persons. Most states and Section 8.30(b) of the RMBCA allow a director to make decisions in reliance on information furnished by competent officers or employees, professionals such as attorneys and accountants, and committees of the board of directors (on which the director does not serve). The reliance must be in good faith, of course, to insulate a director from liability if the information later proves to be inaccurate or unreliable.

Duty to Exercise Reasonable Supervision Directors are also expected to exercise a reasonable amount of supervision when they delegate work to corporate officers and employees. Suppose that Dale, a corporate bank director, fails to attend any board of directors' meetings for five years. In addition, Dale never inspects any of the corporate books or records and generally fails to supervise the efforts of the bank president and the loan committee. Meanwhile, Brennan, the bank president, who is a corporate officer, makes various improper loans and permits large overdrafts. In this situation, Dale (the corporate director) can be held liable to the corporation for losses resulting from the unsupervised actions of the bank president and the loan committee.

Dissenting Directors Directors are expected to attend board of directors' meetings, and their votes should be entered into the minutes. Sometimes, an individual director disagrees with the majority's vote (which becomes an act of the board of directors). Unless a dissent is entered in the minutes, the director is presumed to have assented. If a decision later leads to the directors being held liable for mismanagement, dissenting directors are rarely held individually liable to the corporation. For this reason, a director who is absent from a given meeting sometimes registers with the secretary of the board a dissent to actions taken at the meeting.

The Business Judgment Rule Directors and officers are expected to exercise due care and to use their best judgment in guiding corporate management, but they are not insurers of business success. Under the **business judgment rule,** a corporate director or officer will not be liable to the corporation or to its shareholders for honest mistakes of judgment and bad business decisions. Courts give significant deference to the decisions of corporate directors and officers, and consider the reasonableness of a decision at the time it was made, without the benefit of hindsight. Thus, corporate decision makers are not subjected to second-guessing by shareholders or others in the corporation.

The business judgment rule will apply as long as the director or officer (1) took reasonable steps to become informed about the matter, (2) had a rational basis for his or her decision, and (3) did not have a conflict of interest between his or her personal interest and that of the corporation. In fact, unless there is evidence of bad faith, fraud, or a clear breach of fiduciary duties, most courts will apply the rule and protect directors and officers who make bad business decisions from liability for those choices. Consequently, if there is a reasonable basis for a business decision, a court is unlikely to interfere with that decision, even if the corporation suffers as a result.

Duty of Loyalty

Loyalty can be defined as faithfulness to one's obligations and duties. In the corporate context, the duty of loyalty requires directors and officers to subordinate their personal interests to the welfare of the corporation.

For example, directors may not use corporate funds or confidential corporate information for personal advantage. Similarly, they must refrain from putting their personal interests above those of the corporation. For instance, a director should not oppose a transaction that is in the corporation's best interest simply because pursuing it may cost the director her or his position. Cases dealing with the duty of loyalty typically involve one or more of the following:

1. Competing with the corporation.
2. Usurping (taking personal advantage of) a corporate opportunity.
3. Having an interest that conflicts with the interest of the corporation.
4. Engaging in *insider trading* (using information that is not public to make a profit trading securities, as discussed in Chapter 41).
5. Authorizing a corporate transaction that is detrimental to minority shareholders.
6. Selling control over the corporation.

The following classic case illustrates the conflict that can arise between a corporate official's personal interest and his or her duty of loyalty.

CASE 39.1 Guth v. Loft, Inc.

Supreme Court of Delaware, 1939. 23 Del.Ch. 255, 5 A.2d 503.

• **Background and Facts** Loft, Inc., made and sold candies, syrups, beverages, and food from its offices and plant in Long Island City, New York. Loft operated 115 retail outlets in several states and also sold its products wholesale. Charles Guth was Loft's president. Guth and his family

CASE CONTINUES

CASE 39.1 CONTINUED owned Grace Company, which made syrups for soft drinks in a plant in Baltimore, Maryland. Coca-Cola Company supplied Loft with cola syrup. Unhappy with what he felt was Coca-Cola's high price, Guth entered into an agreement with Roy Megargel to acquire the trademark and formula for Pepsi-Cola and form Pepsi-Cola Corporation. Neither Guth nor Megargel could finance the new venture, however, and Grace was insolvent. Without the knowledge of Loft's board, Guth used Loft's capital, credit, facilities, and employees to further the Pepsi enterprise. At Guth's direction, Loft made the concentrate for the syrup, which was sent to Grace to add sugar and water. Loft charged Grace for the concentrate but allowed forty months' credit. Grace charged Pepsi for the syrup but also granted substantial credit. Grace sold the syrup to Pepsi's customers, including Loft, which paid on delivery or within thirty days. Loft also paid for Pepsi's advertising. Finally, losing profits at its stores as a result of switching from Coca-Cola, Loft filed a suit in a Delaware state court against Guth, Grace, and Pepsi, seeking their Pepsi stock and an accounting. The court entered a judgment in the plaintiff's favor. The defendants appealed to the Delaware Supreme Court.

Decision and Rationale The Delaware Supreme Court upheld the judgment of the lower court. The court pointed out that the officers and directors of a corporation stand in a fiduciary relation to that corporation and to its shareholders. Corporate officers and directors must protect the corporation's interest at all times. They must also "refrain from doing anything that works injury to the corporation." In other words, corporate officers and directors must provide undivided and unselfish loyalty to the corporation, meaning "that there should be no conflict between duty and self-interest." Whenever an opportunity is presented to the corporation, officers and directors with knowledge of that opportunity cannot seize it for themselves. "The corporation may elect to claim all of the benefits of the transaction for itself, and the law will impress a trust in favor of the corporation upon the property, interest, and profits so acquired." Guth clearly created a conflict between his self-interest and his duty to Loft—the corporation of which he was president and director. Guth illegally appropriated the Pepsi-Cola opportunity for himself and thereby placed himself in a competitive position with the company for which he worked. The state supreme court was "convinced that the opportunity to acquire the Pepsi-Cola trademark and formula, goodwill and business belonged to [Loft], and that Guth, as its president, had no right to appropriate the opportunity to himself."

Impact of This Case on Today's Law *This early Delaware decision was one of the first to set forth a test for determining when a corporate officer or director has breached the duty of loyalty. The test has two basic parts—whether the opportunity was reasonably related to the corporation's line of business, and whether the corporation was financially able to undertake the opportunity. The court also considered whether the corporation had an interest or expectancy in the opportunity and recognized that when the corporation had "no interest or expectancy, the officer or director is entitled to treat the opportunity as his own."*

What If the Facts Were Different? *Suppose that Loft's board of directors had approved Pepsi-Cola's use of its personnel and equipment. Would the court's decision have been different? Discuss.*

Conflicts of Interest

Corporate directors often have many business affiliations, and a director may sit on the board of more than one corporation. Of course, directors are precluded from entering into or supporting businesses that operate in direct competition with corporations on whose boards they serve. Their fiduciary duty requires them to make a full disclosure of any potential conflicts of interest that might arise in any corporate transaction [RMBCA 8.60].

Disclosure Requirements Sometimes, a corporation enters into a contract or engages in a transaction in which an officer or director has a personal interest. The director or officer must make a *full disclosure* of that interest and must abstain from voting on the proposed transaction.

For example, Ballo Corporation needs office space. Stephan Colson, one of its five directors, owns the building adjoining the corporation's headquarters. He negotiates a lease with Ballo for the space, making a full disclosure to Ballo and the other four directors. The lease arrangement is fair and reasonable, and it is unanimously approved by the other members of the corporation's board of directors. Under these circumstances, the contract is valid. The rule is one of reason; otherwise, directors would be prevented from ever having financial dealings with the corporations they serve.

State statutes set different standards for corporate contracts. Generally, though, a contract will not be voidable if it was fair and reasonable to the corporation at the time it was made, there was a full disclosure of the interest of the officers or directors involved in the transaction, and the contract was approved by a majority of the disinterested directors or shareholders [RMBCA 8.62].

Corporations with Common Directors

Often, contracts are negotiated between corporations having one or more directors who are members of both boards. Such transactions require great care, as they are closely scrutinized by the courts. (As will be discussed in Chapter 46, in certain circumstances—if two large corporations are competing with each other, for example—having a director sit on the boards of both companies may constitute a violation of antitrust laws.)

Liability of Directors and Officers

Directors and officers are exposed to liability on many fronts. They can be liable for negligence in certain circumstances, as previously discussed. Corporate directors and officers may be held liable for the crimes and torts committed by themselves or by corporate employees under their supervision, as discussed in Chapters 9 and 38. Additionally, if shareholders perceive that the corporate directors are not acting in the best interests of the corporation, they may sue the directors, in what is called a *shareholder's derivative suit,* on behalf of the corporation. (This type of action is discussed later in this chapter, in the context of shareholders' rights.) In addition, directors and officers can be held personally liable under a number of statutes, such as statutes enacted to protect consumers or the environment (see Chapters 44 and 45). See *Concept Summary 39.2* for a review of the duties and liabilities of directors and officers.

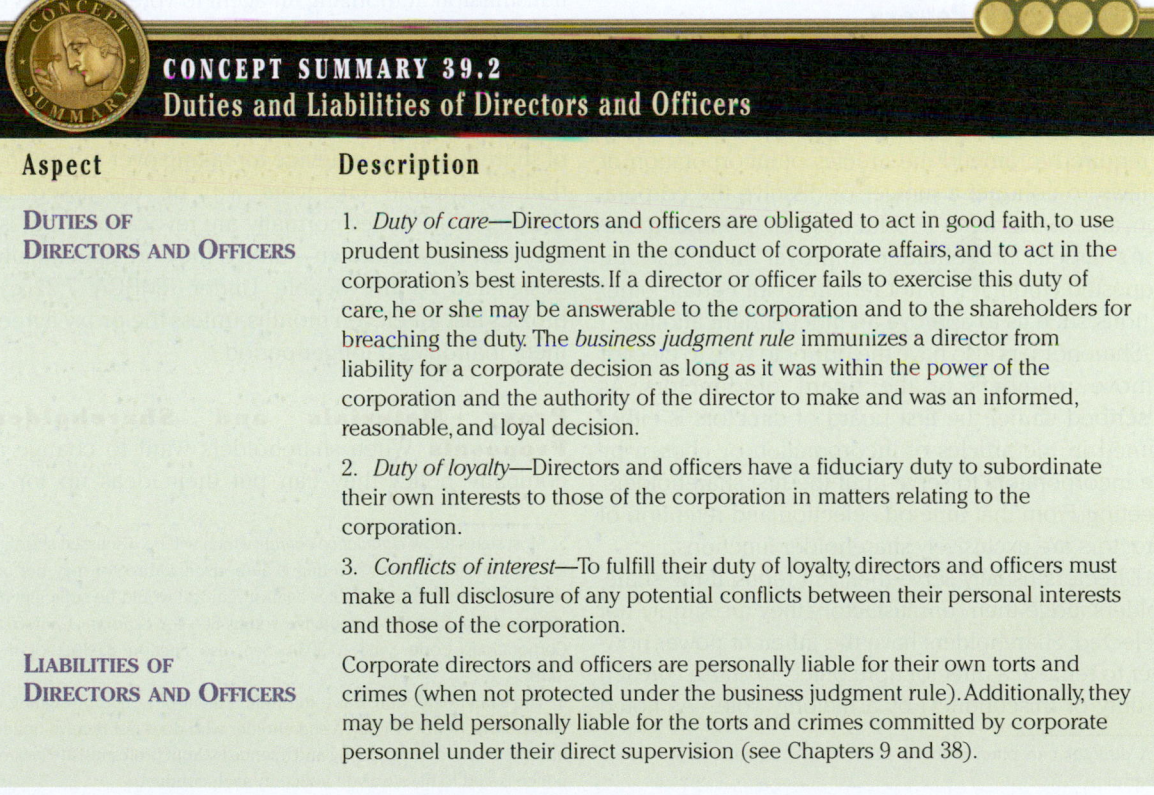

CONCEPT SUMMARY 39.2
Duties and Liabilities of Directors and Officers

Aspect	Description
DUTIES OF DIRECTORS AND OFFICERS	1. *Duty of care*—Directors and officers are obligated to act in good faith, to use prudent business judgment in the conduct of corporate affairs, and to act in the corporation's best interests. If a director or officer fails to exercise this duty of care, he or she may be answerable to the corporation and to the shareholders for breaching the duty. The *business judgment rule* immunizes a director from liability for a corporate decision as long as it was within the power of the corporation and the authority of the director to make and was an informed, reasonable, and loyal decision. 2. *Duty of loyalty*—Directors and officers have a fiduciary duty to subordinate their own interests to those of the corporation in matters relating to the corporation. 3. *Conflicts of interest*—To fulfill their duty of loyalty, directors and officers must make a full disclosure of any potential conflicts between their personal interests and those of the corporation.
LIABILITIES OF DIRECTORS AND OFFICERS	Corporate directors and officers are personally liable for their own torts and crimes (when not protected under the business judgment rule). Additionally, they may be held personally liable for the torts and crimes committed by corporate personnel under their direct supervision (see Chapters 9 and 38).

SECTION 3 The Role of Shareholders

The acquisition of a share of stock makes a person an owner of and a shareholder in a corporation. Shareholders own the corporation but have no right to manage it. Basically, the shareholders' ownership control is limited to voting to elect or remove members of the board of directors and deciding whether to approve fundamental changes in the corporation. Shareholders are not agents of the corporation, nor do they have legal title to the corporation's property, such as its buildings and equipment: they simply have an *equitable* (ownership) interest in the firm.

Ordinarily, corporate officers and other employees owe no direct duty to individual shareholders (unless some contract or special relationship exists between them in addition to the corporate relationship). The officers' duty is to act in the best interests of the corporation and its shareholder-owners *as a whole*. In addition, as you will read later in this chapter, controlling shareholders owe a fiduciary duty to minority shareholders.

In this section, we look at the powers of shareholders, which may be established in the articles of incorporation and under the state's general corporation law.

Shareholders' Powers

Shareholders must approve fundamental changes affecting the corporation before the changes can be implemented. Hence, shareholder approval normally is required to amend the articles of incorporation or bylaws, to conduct a merger or dissolve the corporation, and to sell all or substantially all of the corporation's assets. Shareholder approval may also be requested (though it is not required) for certain other actions, such as to approve an independent auditor.

Shareholders also have the power to vote to elect or remove members of the board of directors. As described earlier, the first board of directors is either named in the articles of incorporation or chosen by the incorporators to serve until the first shareholders' meeting. From that time on, selection and retention of directors are exclusively shareholder functions.

Directors usually serve their full terms; if the shareholders judge them unsatisfactory, they are simply not reelected. Shareholders have the inherent power, however, to remove a director from office *for cause* (breach of duty or misconduct) by a majority vote.[4] As noted earlier in this chapter, some state statutes (and some articles of incorporation) permit removal of directors without cause by the vote of a majority of the shareholders entitled to vote.[5]

Shareholders' Meetings

Shareholders' meetings must occur at least annually. In addition, special meetings can be called to deal with urgent matters.

Notice of Meetings A corporation must notify its shareholders of the date, time, and place of an annual or special shareholders' meeting at least ten days, but not more than sixty days, before the meeting date [RMBCA 7.05].[6] (The date and time of the annual meeting can be specified in the bylaws, however.) Notices of special meetings must include a statement of the purpose of the meeting; business transacted at a special meeting is limited to that purpose.

Proxies It usually is not practical for owners of only a few shares of stock of publicly traded corporations to attend a shareholders' meeting. Therefore, the law allows stockholders to either vote in person or appoint another person as their agent to vote their shares at the meeting. The signed appointment form or electronic transmission authorizing an agent to vote the shares is called a **proxy** (from the Latin *procurare,* meaning "to manage, take care of"). Management often solicits proxies, but any person can solicit proxies to concentrate voting power. Proxies have been used by groups of shareholders as a device for taking over a corporation (corporate takeovers will be discussed in Chapter 40). Proxies normally are revocable—that is, they can be withdrawn—unless they are specifically designated as irrevocable. Under RMBCA 7.22(c), proxies last for eleven months, unless the proxy agreement mandates a longer period.

Proxy Materials and Shareholder Proposals When shareholders want to change a company policy, they can put their ideas up for a

4. A director can often demand court review of removal for cause, however.

5. Most states allow *cumulative voting* (which will be discussed shortly) for directors. If cumulative voting is authorized, a director may not be removed if the number of votes against removal would be sufficient to elect a director under cumulative voting. See, for example, California Corporations Code Section 303A. See also Section 8.08(c) of the RMBCA.

6. The shareholder can waive the requirement of notice by signing a waiver form [RMBCA 7.06]. A shareholder who does not receive notice but who learns of the meeting and attends without protesting the lack of notice is said to have waived notice by such conduct.

shareholder vote. They do this by submitting a shareholder proposal to the board of directors and asking the board to include the proposal in the proxy materials that are sent to all shareholders before meetings. (See this chapter's *Contemporary Legal Debates* feature on pages 746 and 747 for a discussion of a proposal that would increase shareholders' access to the proxy process.)

The Securities and Exchange Commission (SEC), which regulates the purchase and sale of securities (see Chapter 41), has special provisions relating to proxies and shareholder proposals. SEC Rule 14a-8 provides that all shareholders who own stock worth at least $1,000 are eligible to submit proposals for inclusion in corporate proxy materials. The corporation is required to include information on whatever proposals will be considered at the shareholders' meeting along with proxy materials. Only those proposals that relate to significant policy considerations rather than ordinary business operations must be included. Under the SEC's e-proxy rules that went into effect in 2007,[7] companies may furnish proxy materials to shareholders by posting them on a Web site (see the discussion of these rules in the *Insight into E-Commerce* feature on pages 774–775 in Chapter 41).

Proxy Materials Concerning Executive Pay The issue of executive compensation has become increasingly contentious in recent years. In particular, shareholders have complained about "excessive" executive pay when the returns to shareholders declined during the same period that top executives received tens (or hundreds) of millions of dollars in compensation. Activist shareholders argue that shareholders in general should have a say in what top management earns.

Shareholder Voting

Shareholders exercise ownership control through the power of their votes. Corporate business matters are presented in the form of resolutions, which shareholders vote to approve or disapprove. Each common shareholder is entitled to one vote per share, although the voting techniques discussed below all enhance the power of the shareholder's vote. The articles of incorporation can exclude or limit voting rights, particularly to certain classes of shares. For example, owners of preferred shares are usually denied the right to vote [RMBCA 7.21]. If a state statute requires specific voting procedures, the corporation's articles or bylaws must be consistent with the statute.

Quorum Requirements For shareholders to act during a meeting, a quorum must be present. Generally, this condition is met when shareholders holding more than 50 percent of the outstanding shares are in attendance. In some states, obtaining the unanimous written consent of shareholders is a permissible alternative to holding a shareholders' meeting [RMBCA 7.25].

Once a quorum is present, voting can proceed. A majority vote of the shares represented at the meeting is usually required to pass resolutions. Assume that Novo Pictures, Inc., has 10,000 outstanding shares of voting stock. Its articles of incorporation set the quorum at 50 percent of outstanding shares and provide that a majority vote of the shares present is necessary to pass ordinary matters. Therefore, for this firm, at the shareholders' meeting, a quorum of stockholders representing 5,000 outstanding shares must be present to conduct business, and a vote of at least 2,501 of those shares is needed to pass ordinary resolutions. Thus, if 6,000 shares are represented, a vote of 3,001 will be necessary.

At times, more than a simple majority vote will be required either by statute or by the articles of incorporation. Extraordinary corporate matters, such as a merger, a consolidation, or the dissolution of the corporation (see Chapter 40), require approval by a higher percentage of the representatives of all corporate shares entitled to vote, not just a majority of those present at that particular meeting [RMBCA 7.27].

Voting Lists The RMBCA requires a corporation to maintain an alphabetical voting list of shareholders. The corporation prepares the voting list before each shareholders' meeting. Ordinarily, only persons whose names appear on the corporation's stockholder records as owners are entitled to vote.[8] The voting list contains the name and address of each shareholder as shown on the corporate records on a given cutoff date, or *record date.* (Under RMBCA 7.07, the bylaws or board of directors may fix a record date that is as much as seventy days before the meeting.) The voting list also includes the number of voting shares held by each owner. The list is usually kept at the corporate

7. 17 C.F.R. Parts 240, 249, and 274.

8. When the legal owner is deceased, bankrupt, mentally incompetent, or in some other way under a legal disability, his or her vote can be cast by a person designated by law to control and manage the owner's property.

CONTEMPORARY LEGAL DEBATES

A Shareholder Access Rule

Although shareholders elect the board of directors, shareholders who own a relatively small percentage of the outstanding shares of a corporation are unlikely to be successful even in nominating candidates for director positions. Enter the possibility of a "shareholder access" rule that would make it easier for dissident shareholders to use the proxy process to elect their candidates to the board of directors of a publicly held company. The Securities and Exchange Commission (SEC) made a modest attempt to allow such shareholder access in the early 2000s, but the proposed change was highly controversial and died in 2003.

Recently, however, it has been resurrected. Until late 2006, the SEC interpreted its own rule as specifically allowing a corporation to refuse to include in its proxy materials any shareholder proposal that "relates to an election for membership on the company's board of directors."[a] Now the U.S. Court of Appeals for the Second Circuit has rejected the SEC's interpretation.[b] The court ruled that a corporation could not exclude from its proxy materials a shareholder proposal that, if adopted by the majority of shareholders, would amend the bylaws to require the corporation to publish the names of shareholder-nominated candidates for director positions, in addition to the candidates nominated by the corporation's board of directors.

a. Rule 14a-8(i)8; 17 C.F.R. Section 240.14a-8.

b. *American Federation of State, County, & Municipal Employees v. American International Group, Inc.*, 462 F.3d 121 (2d Cir. 2006). Note that the SEC disagreed with the court in this case and has since proposed a change to clarify its rules. 72 *Federal Register* 43488-01 (August 3, 2007).

Investor Activists Are in Favor of Shareholder Access

Whatever action the SEC takes on this interpretation of its rule in the wake of this court decision, shareholder access will remain controversial. Investor activists have always claimed that without a shareholder access rule, directors have little incentive to pay attention to the concerns of their shareholders. Furthermore, the current system not only discourages shareholders from trying to take an active role in guiding the corporation but also leads to litigation. Because shareholders have no way to engage in dialogue with the corporation to alter what they regard as questionable behavior, they have no choice but to resort to lawsuits against the company. The media have also generally applauded shareholder access as a way to level the playing field between small shareholders and giant corporations.

headquarters and must be made available for shareholder inspection [RMBCA 7.20].

Cumulative Voting Most states permit, and some require, shareholders to elect directors by *cumulative voting*, a voting method designed to allow minority shareholders to be represented on the board of directors.[9] With cumulative voting, each shareholder is entitled to a total number of votes equal to the number of board members to be elected multiplied by the number of voting shares that the shareholder owns. The shareholder can cast all of these votes for one candidate or split them among several nominees for director. All nominees stand for election at the same time. When cumulative voting is not required by statute or under the articles, the entire board can be elected by a majority of shares at a shareholders' meeting.

Suppose that a corporation has 10,000 shares issued and outstanding. The minority shareholders hold 3,000 shares, and the majority shareholders hold the other 7,000 shares. Three members of the board are to be elected. The majority shareholders' nominees are Alomon, Beasley, and Caravel. The minority shareholders' nominee is Dovrik. Can Dovrik be elected to the board by the minority shareholders?

If cumulative voting is allowed, the answer is yes. The minority shareholders have 9,000 votes among them (the number of directors to be elected times the number of shares, or $3 \times 3{,}000 = 9{,}000$ votes). All of these votes can be cast to elect Dovrik. The majority shareholders have 21,000 votes ($3 \times 7{,}000 = 21{,}000$ votes), but these votes must be distributed among three nominees. The principle of cumulative voting is that no matter how the majority shareholders cast their

9. See, for example, California Corporations Code Section 708. Under RMBCA 7.28, however, no cumulative voting rights exist unless the articles of incorporation so provide.

Shareholder Access May Mean Lower Returns for Shareholders

Others are not so sure that shareholder access will benefit shareholders. Opponents of shareholder access, such as law professor Lynn A. Stout of the UCLA-Sloan Research Program on Business Organizations, argue that such a rule is unnecessary because shareholders today have more influence and power over top management and directors than ever before. Shareholders can join in class-action lawsuits against corporations, and they gained additional protections under the Sarbanes-Oxley Act of 2002. Moreover, small investors can purchase their shares through mutual funds, which wield much more power than individual shareholders.

Furthermore, says Professor Stout, shareholder access would dramatically accelerate "an already dangerous trend: 'the flight of corporations away from public investors into the arms of private equity.'" As Chapter 38 described, an increasing number of public corporations are going private because they have been purchased by private equity firms. A shareholder access rule could enhance this process because the rule would impose additional costs on publicly held companies. As the costs of having public shareholders increase, more top managers may decide that the corporation should eliminate the shareholders. In other words, more publicly held companies will let private equity firms know that they are for sale. When a company is taken private, its public shareholders receive a small premium over the market value of their shares, but once the company goes private, of course, they are no longer shareholders and are unable to benefit from the company's growth under new management (if that growth materializes). Consequently, in the long run public shareholders may earn lower returns if a shareholder access rule is adopted.

WHERE DO YOU STAND?

Several dozen managers and directors of foreign-based pension plans and insurance companies—which invest in U.S. securities—wrote a joint letter to the head of the SEC. In that letter, they stated that "experience in the United Kingdom, Australia, and the Netherlands has shown that boards whose members may be removed by shareholders are much more sensitive to shareholder opinion and are much more likely to engage in a meaningful dialogue with the institutions that hold their shares." How important is such a dialogue? What might be some of the topics of such a dialogue?

21,000 votes, they will not be able to elect all three directors if the minority shareholders cast all of their 9,000 votes for Dovrik, as illustrated in Exhibit 39–2.

Other Voting Techniques A group of shareholders can agree in writing prior to a shareholders' meeting, in a *shareholder voting agreement,* to vote their shares together in a specified manner. Such agreements usually are held to be valid and enforceable. A shareholder can also appoint a voting agent and vote by proxy, as mentioned previously.

In the following case, corporate management was concerned about losing a proxy contest. The corporation's chief executive officer then entered into an

EXHIBIT 39–2 • Results of Cumulative Voting

Ballot	Majority Shareholder Votes			Minority Shareholder Votes	Directors Elected
	Alomon	*Beasley*	*Caravel*	*Dovrik*	
1	10,000	10,000	1,000	9,000	Alomon, Beasley, Dovrik
2	9,001	9,000	2,999	9,000	Alomon, Beasley, Dovrik
3	6,000	7,000	8,000	9,000	Beasley, Caravel, Dovrik

agreement with a shareholder who would support management's candidates in return for a seat on the board of directors. A shareholder who opposed the deal filed a lawsuit claiming that this agreement was illegal and a breach of the officer's fiduciary duty.

CASE 39.2 Portnoy v. Cryo-Cell International, Inc.

Court of Chancery of Delaware, 2008. 940 A.2d 43.

Background and Facts Cryo-Cell International, Inc., a small public company, was struggling to succeed. Several of its stockholders considered mounting a proxy contest to replace the board of directors. One of those shareholders, Andrew Filipowski, apparently used management's fear of being replaced to create a deal for himself—that is, he would be included in management's slate of directors at an upcoming stockholders' annual meeting. Another shareholder, David Portnoy, filed an opposing slate of directors. The company's chief executive officer (CEO), Mercedes Walton, created a plan that would allow management and Filipowski to win the proxy contest. This plan involved Walton as a "matchmaker" who would find stockholders willing to sell their shares to Filipowski. Walton promised Filipowski that if management's slate of directors won, Cryo-Cell's board of directors would then add another board seat that a Filipowski designee would fill. This side deal created by Walton, however, was not made public to the shareholders when they voted. In other words, they did not know that they were in fact electing an additional member to the board of directors when the management slate won. After the election, Walton prepared to add Filipowski's designee to the board of directors. At this time, the dissenting shareholder group lead by Portnoy filed a lawsuit claiming that the election results should be overturned. Portnoy argued that the side agreement with Filipowski was not created in the best interests of the company or its shareholders. Portnoy claimed that all of the dealings between the company and Filipowski were tainted by fiduciary misconduct. Indeed, Portnoy claimed that the agreement to add Filipowski to the management slate in exchange for his support in the proxy fight constituted an "illegal vote-buying arrangement."

Decision and Rationale The court ruled that the incumbent board's actions and the side agreement with the company's CEO (Walton) did constitute serious breaches of fiduciary duty and therefore tainted the election. The remedy "that vindicates the interests of Cryo-Cell stockholders as a class is to order a prompt special meeting at which a new election will be held and presided over by a special master." The court did not find the addition of Filipowski to the management slate of directors to be improper, though. "When stockholders can decide for themselves whether to seat a candidate who obtained a place on a management slate by way of [bargaining with management], it seems unwise to formulate a standard that involves the potential for excessive and imprecise judicial involvement." Such an arrangement is not vote buying; in contrast, making a side agreement that guaranteed Filipowski's designee an additional seat on the board raised questions of impropriety. Walton had promised "she and her incumbent colleagues would use their powers as directors of Cryo-Cell to increase the size of the board and to seat [Filipowski's designee]. This was therefore a promise that would not be, for the duration of the term, subject to prior approval by the electorate." Thus, it was improper.

The Legal Environment Dimension *Why was it acceptable to add Filipowski to the management slate of proposed directors but not to agree to increase the board membership by one director, with that director being Filipowski's designee?*

The Ethical Dimension *If Filipowski had promised to bring additional funding to keep Cryo-Cell from failing due to lack of capital, would the actions described in this case have been considered ethical? Explain your answer.*

Another technique is for shareholders to enter into a *voting trust.* A **voting trust** is an agreement (a trust contract) under which a shareholder transfers the shares to a trustee, usually for a specified period of time. The trustee is then responsible for voting the shares on behalf of the beneficiary-shareholder. The agreement can specify how the trustee is to vote, or it can allow the trustee to use his or her discretion. The trustee takes physical possession of the stock certificate and in return gives the shareholder a *voting trust certificate.* The shareholder retains other rights of ownership (for example, the right to receive dividend payments) except the power to vote the shares [RMBCA 7.30].

SECTION 4 Rights of Shareholders

Shareholders possess numerous rights. A significant right—the right to vote their shares—has already been discussed. We now look at some additional rights of shareholders in the following subsections.

Stock Certificates

A **stock certificate** is a certificate issued by a corporation that evidences ownership of a specified number of shares in the corporation. In jurisdictions that require the issuance of stock certificates, shareholders have the right to demand that the corporation issue certificates and record their names and addresses in the corporate stock record books. In most states and under RMBCA 6.26, the board of directors may provide that shares of stock will be uncertificated (that is, no actual, physical stock certificates will be issued). When shares are uncertificated, the corporation may be required to send each shareholder a letter or some other notice containing the same information that is required to be included on the face of stock certificates.

Stock is intangible personal property, and the ownership right exists independently of the certificate itself. If a stock certificate is lost or destroyed, ownership is not destroyed with it. A new certificate can be issued to replace the one that was lost or destroyed.[10] Notice of shareholders' meetings, dividends, and operational and financial reports are all distributed according to the recorded ownership listed in the corporation's books, not on the basis of possession of the certificate.

Preemptive Rights

Sometimes, the articles of incorporation grant preemptive rights to shareholders [RMBCA 6.30]. With **preemptive rights,** a shareholder receives a preference over all other purchasers to subscribe to or purchase a prorated share of a new issue of stock. In other words, a shareholder who is given preemptive rights can purchase the same percentage of the new shares being issued as she or he already holds in the company. This right does not apply to **treasury shares**—shares that are authorized but have not been issued.

The Purpose of Preemptive Rights Preemptive rights allow each shareholder to maintain her or his proportionate control, voting power, or financial interest in the corporation. Generally, preemptive rights apply only to additional, newly issued stock sold for cash, and the preemptive rights must be exercised within a specified time period, which is usually thirty days.

For example, Tron Corporation authorizes and issues 1,000 shares of stock, and Omar Loren purchases 100 shares, making him the owner of 10 percent of the company's stock. Subsequently, Tron, by vote of its shareholders, authorizes the issuance of another 1,000 shares (by amending the articles of incorporation). This increases its capital stock to a total of 2,000 shares. If preemptive rights have been provided, Loren can purchase one additional share of the new stock being issued for each share he already owns—or 100 additional shares. Thus, he can own 200 of the 2,000 shares outstanding, and his relative position as a shareholder will be maintained. If preemptive rights are not reserved, his proportionate control and voting power will be diluted from that of a 10 percent shareholder to that of a 5 percent shareholder because the additional 1,000 shares were issued.

Preemptive Rights in Close Corporations Preemptive rights are most important in close corporations because each shareholder owns a relatively small number of shares but controls a substantial interest in the corporation. Without preemptive rights, it would be possible for a shareholder to lose his or her proportionate control over the firm.

10. For a lost or destroyed certificate to be reissued, a shareholder normally must furnish an *indemnity bond,* which is a written promise to reimburse the holder for any actual or claimed loss caused by the issuer's or some other person's conduct. The bond protects the corporation against potential loss should the original certificate reappear at some future time in the hands of a bona fide purchaser. See Sections 8–302 and 8–405(2) of the Uniform Commercial Code.

Stock Warrants

Stock warrants are rights to buy stock at a stated price by a specified date that are given by the company. Usually, when preemptive rights exist and a corporation is issuing additional shares, it gives its shareholders stock warrants. Warrants are often publicly traded on securities exchanges.

Dividends

As mentioned in Chapter 38, a **dividend** is a distribution of corporate profits or income *ordered by the directors* and paid to the shareholders in proportion to their respective shares in the corporation. Dividends can be paid in cash, property, stock of the corporation that is paying the dividends, or stock of other corporations.[11]

Sources of Funds for Dividends State laws vary, but every state determines the general circumstances and legal requirements under which dividends are paid. State laws also control the sources of revenue to be used; only certain funds are legally available for paying dividends. Once declared, a cash dividend becomes a corporate debt enforceable at law like any other debt. Depending on state law, dividends may be paid from the following sources:

1. *Retained earnings.* All states allow dividends to be paid from the undistributed net profits earned by the corporation, including capital gains from the sale of fixed assets. As mentioned in Chapter 38, the undistributed net profits are called *retained earnings.*
2. *Net profits.* A few states allow dividends to be issued from current net profits without regard to deficits in prior years.
3. *Surplus.* A number of states allow dividends to be paid out of any kind of surplus.

Directors' Failure to Declare a Dividend When directors fail to declare a dividend, shareholders can ask a court to compel the directors to meet and declare a dividend. To succeed, the shareholders must show that the directors have acted so unreasonably in withholding the dividend that their conduct is an abuse of their discretion.

Often, a corporation accumulates large cash reserves for a legitimate corporate purpose, such as expansion or research. The mere fact that the firm has sufficient earnings or surplus available to pay a dividend is not enough to compel the directors to distribute funds that, in the board's opinion, should not be distributed.[12] The courts are hesitant to interfere with corporate operations and will not compel directors to declare dividends unless abuse of discretion is clearly shown.

Inspection Rights

Shareholders in a corporation enjoy both common law and statutory inspection rights. The RMBCA provides that every shareholder is entitled to examine specified corporate records [RMBCA 16.02]. This includes inspecting voting lists, as discussed earlier [RMBCA 7.20]. A shareholder who is denied the right of inspection can seek a court order to compel the inspection. The shareholder's right of inspection is limited, however, to the inspection and copying of corporate books and records for a *proper purpose,* provided the request is made in advance. The shareholder may inspect in person, or an attorney, accountant, or other authorized assistant may do so as the shareholder's agent.

The power of inspection is fraught with potential abuses, and the corporation is allowed to protect itself from them. For example, a shareholder can properly be denied access to corporate records to prevent harassment or to protect trade secrets or other confidential corporate information.[13] Some states require that a shareholder must have held her or his shares for a minimum period of time immediately preceding the demand to inspect or must hold a minimum number of outstanding shares.

Transfer of Shares

Corporate stock represents an ownership right in intangible personal property. The law generally recognizes the right of an owner to transfer property to another person unless there are valid restrictions on its transferability. Although stock certificates are negotiable and freely transferable by indorsement and delivery, transfer of stock in closely held corporations (see Chapter 38) is usually restricted. These restrictions must be reasonable and may be found in the bylaws or

11. On one occasion, a distillery declared and paid a "dividend" in bonded whiskey.

12. A striking exception to this rule was made in *Dodge v. Ford Motor Co.,* 204 Mich. 459, 170 N.W. 668 (1919), when Henry Ford, the president and major stockholder of Ford Motor Company, refused to declare a dividend notwithstanding the firm's large capital surplus. The court, holding that Ford had abused his discretion, ordered the company to declare a dividend.

13. See, for example, *Disney v. Walt Disney Co.,* 857 A.2d 444 (Del.Ch. 2004).

stated in a shareholder agreement. The existence of any restrictions on transferability must always be indicated on the face of the stock certificate.

When shares are transferred, a new entry is made in the corporate stock book to indicate the new owner. Until the corporation is notified and the entry is complete, all rights—including voting rights, notice of shareholders' meetings, and the right to dividend distributions—remain with the current record owner.

Rights on Dissolution

When a corporation is dissolved and its outstanding debts and the claims of its creditors have been satisfied, the remaining assets are distributed on a pro rata basis among the shareholders. The articles of incorporation may provide that certain classes of preferred stock will be given priority. If no class of stock has been given preferences in the distribution of assets, all of the stockholders share the remaining assets. In some circumstances, such as when the board of directors is mishandling corporate assets or is allowing a deadlock to irreparably injure the corporation, shareholders can petition a court to have the corporation dissolved [RMBCA 1430].

The Shareholder's Derivative Suit

When the corporation is harmed by the actions of a third party, the directors can bring a lawsuit in the name of the corporation against that party. If the corporate directors fail to bring a lawsuit, shareholders can do so "derivatively" in what is known as a **shareholder's derivative suit.** A shareholder cannot bring a derivative suit until ninety days after making a written demand on the corporation (the board of directors) to take suitable action [RMBCA 7.40]. Only if the directors refuse to take appropriate action can the derivative suit go forward.

The right of shareholders to bring a derivative action is especially important when the wrong suffered by the corporation results from the actions of the corporate directors. This is because the directors and officers would probably be unwilling to take any action against themselves. Nevertheless, a court will dismiss a derivative suit if the majority of directors or an independent panel determines in good faith that the lawsuit is not in the best interests of the corporation [RMBCA 7.44].

When shareholders bring a derivative suit, they are not pursuing rights or benefits for themselves personally but are acting as guardians of the corporate entity. Therefore, if the suit is successful, any damages recovered normally go into the corporation's treasury, not to the shareholders personally. (The shareholders may be entitled to reimbursement for reasonable expenses of the lawsuit, including attorneys' fees.)

SECTION 5 Liability of Shareholders

One of the hallmarks of the corporate organization is that shareholders are not personally liable for the debts of the corporation. If the corporation fails, the shareholders can lose their investments, but that is generally the limit of their liability. As discussed in Chapter 38, however, in certain instances of fraud, undercapitalization, or careless observance of corporate formalities, a court will *pierce the corporate veil* (disregard the corporate entity) and hold the shareholders individually liable. But these situations are the exception, not the rule.

A shareholder can also be personally liable in certain other rare instances. One relates to *watered stock.* Also, in some instances, a majority shareholder who engages in oppressive conduct or attempts to exclude minority shareholders from receiving certain benefits can be held personally liable.

Watered Stock

When a corporation issues shares for less than their fair market value, the shares are referred to as **watered stock.**[14] Usually, the shareholder who receives watered stock must pay the difference to the corporation (the shareholder is personally liable). In some states, the shareholder who receives watered stock may be liable to creditors of the corporation for unpaid corporate debts.

Suppose that during the formation of a corporation, Gomez, one of the incorporators, transfers his property, Sunset Beach, to the corporation for 10,000 shares of stock at a par value of $100 per share for a total price of $1 million. After the property is transferred and the shares are issued, Sunset Beach is carried on the corporate books at a value of $1 million. On appraisal, it is discovered that the market value of the property at the time of transfer was only $500,000. The shares issued to Gomez are therefore watered stock, and he is liable to

14. The phrase *watered stock* was originally used to describe cattle that were kept thirsty during a long drive and then were allowed to drink large quantities of water just prior to their sale. The increased weight of the "watered stock" allowed the seller to reap a higher profit.

CONCEPT SUMMARY 39.3
Role of Shareholders

Aspect	Description
Shareholders' Powers	Shareholders' powers include approval of all fundamental changes affecting the corporation and election of the board of directors.
Shareholders' Meetings	Shareholders' meetings must occur at least annually; special meetings can be called when necessary. Notice of the time and place of a meeting (and its purpose, if the meeting is specially called) must be sent to shareholders. A minimum number of shareholders (quorum) must be present to vote.
Shareholders' Rights	Shareholders have numerous rights, which may include the following: 1. Voting rights. 2. The right to receive stock certificates (depending on the jurisdiction). 3. Preemptive rights (depending on the corporate articles). 4. The right to receive dividends (at the discretion of the directors). 5. The right to inspect the corporate records. 6. The right to transfer shares (this right may be restricted in close corporations). 7. The right to receive a share of corporate assets when the corporation is dissolved. 8. The right to sue on behalf of the corporation (bring a shareholder's derivative suit) when the directors fail to do so.
Shareholders' Liability	Shareholders may be liable for watered stock. In certain situations, majority shareholders may be regarded as having a fiduciary duty to minority shareholders and will be liable if that duty is breached.

the corporation for the difference between the value of the shares and the value of the property. *Concept Summary 39.3* reviews the role played by shareholders in a corporation.

Duties of Majority Shareholders

In some instances, a majority shareholder is regarded as having a fiduciary duty to the corporation and to the minority shareholders. This occurs when a single shareholder (or a few shareholders acting in concert) owns a sufficient number of shares to exercise *de facto* (actual) control over the corporation. In these situations, the majority shareholders owe a fiduciary duty to the minority shareholders.

A common example of a breach of fiduciary duty occurs when the majority shareholders "freeze out" the minority shareholders and exclude them from certain benefits of participating in the firm. For example, Brodie, Jordan, and Barbuto formed a close corporation to operate a machine shop. Each owned one-third of the shares in the company, and all three were directors. Brodie served as the corporate president for twelve years but thereafter met with the other shareholders only a few times a year. After disagreements arose, Brodie asked the company to purchase his shares, but his requests were refused. A few years later, Brodie died and his wife inherited his shares in the company. Jordan and Barbuto refused to perform a valuation of the company, denied her access to the corporate information she requested, did not declare any dividends, and refused to elect her as a director. In this situation, a court found that the majority shareholders had violated their fiduciary duty to Brodie's wife.[15]

A breach of fiduciary duties by those who control a closely held corporation normally constitutes what is known as *oppressive conduct.* The court in the following case examined a pattern of conduct by those in control to determine whether it was oppressive.

15. *Brodie v. Jordan,* 447 Mass. 866, N.E.2d 1076 (2006).

CASE 39.3 Kaplan v. First Hartford Corp.

United States District Court, District of Maine, 2007. 484 F.Supp.2d 131.

• **Background and Facts** First Hartford Corporation (FHC) was incorporated in Maine in 1909 to compete in the textile industry. As textiles declined, FHC focused on buying, developing, and managing real estate. During the 1980s and 1990s, FHC struggled to stay in business. The company went through bankruptcy and downsized from 143 employees to 21. It held no board or shareholders' meetings and issued no audited financial statements. During this time, Ned Ellis managed FHC. He had been a director since 1966 and president since 1968, and owned about 43 percent of FHC's stock. Ellis also owned and operated Green Manor Corporation, which owned still other companies. Ellis treated FHC as part of a common enterprise with his other companies, often failing to document their transactions, which included interest-free loans, property exchanges, forgiveness of debts, and other deals, totaling millions of dollars. By 2000, FHC had grown profitable, chiefly through Ellis's efforts. A market began to develop for its stock, and the firm began to hold shareholders' meetings. Ellis's nephew, Richard Kaplan, owned about 19 percent of the stock. After several lawsuits in which Kaplan sought information about the deals between FHC and Ellis's companies, Kaplan filed a suit in a federal district court against FHC and Ellis, alleging that Ellis had operated the company oppressively for his own benefit.

• **Decision and Rationale** The district court concluded that Ellis had "contributed greatly to the corporation (it undoubtedly would not have survived without his efforts)" but that he had "also engaged in oppressive conduct with respect to minority shareholders" and thus Kaplan was entitled to relief. The court gave the parties further time to present their positions on an appropriate remedy. The court agreed that Ellis had treated FHC as his own property, "moving money back and forth among his various companies, including FHC, as he thinks beneficial." Ellis clearly disregarded corporate formalities. "He inadequately documented self-interested transactions. * * * It is the pattern of abusive conduct that establishes oppression." In spite of the fact that Kaplan had successfully sued FHC four times, Ellis's pattern of oppressive conduct continued. Even though FHC would not have survived without Ellis's leadership, he was obligated to operate FHC appropriately, "not treating the company as part of his general family assets, but as an independent entity of which he was a director (and controlling shareholder) with statutory and fiduciary obligations to others. Whatever good intentions he had originally, his actions cumulatively demonstrated a pattern of peremptory and oppressive treatment of minority shareholders."

• **The Ethical Dimension** *Were Ellis's treatment of FHC and his conduct with respect to Kaplan unethical? Explain.*

• **What If the Facts Were Different?** *Would the court's decision in this case likely have been different if FHC had been engaged in the more volatile technology industry rather than real estate? Why or why not?*

REVIEWING CORPORATIONS—Directors, Officers, and Shareholders

David Brock is on the board of directors of Firm Body Fitness, Inc., which owns a string of fitness clubs in New Mexico. Brock owns 15 percent of the Firm Body stock and is also employed as a tanning technician at one of the fitness clubs. After the January financial report showed that Firm Body's tanning division was operating at a substantial net loss, the board of directors, led by Marty Levinson,

REVIEWING CONTINUES

REVIEWING CORPORATIONS—Directors, Officers, and Shareholders, Continued

discussed the possibility of terminating the tanning operations. Brock successfully convinced a majority of the board that the tanning division was necessary to market the clubs' overall fitness package. By April, the tanning division's financial losses had risen. The board hired a business analyst, who conducted surveys and determined that the tanning operations did not significantly increase membership. A shareholder, Diego Peñada, discovered that Brock owned stock in Sunglow, Inc., the company from which Firm Body purchased its tanning equipment. Peñada notified Levinson, who privately reprimanded Brock. Shortly thereafter Brock and Mandy Vail, who owned 37 percent of the Firm Body stock and also held shares of Sunglow, voted to replace Levinson on the board of directors. Using the information presented in the chapter, answer the following questions.

1. What duties did Brock, as a director, owe to Firm Body?
2. Does the fact that Brock owned shares in Sunglow establish a conflict of interest? Why or why not?
3. Suppose that Firm Body brought an action against Brock claiming that he had breached the duty of loyalty by not disclosing his interest in Sunglow to the other directors. What theory might Brock use in his defense?
4. Now suppose that Firm Body did not bring an action against Brock. What type of lawsuit might Peñada be able to bring based on these facts?

TERMS AND CONCEPTS

business judgment rule 741
dividend 750
inside director 738
outside director 738
preemptive rights 749
proxy 744
quorum 738
shareholder's derivative suit 751
stock certificate 749
stock warrant 750
treasury share 749
voting trust 749
watered stock 751

QUESTIONS AND CASE PROBLEMS

39–1. Oxy Corp. is negotiating with the Wick Construction Co. for the renovation of the Oxy corporate headquarters. Wick, the owner of the Wick Construction Co., is also one of the five members of the board of directors of Oxy. The contract terms are standard for this type of contract. Wick has previously informed two of the other directors of his interest in the construction company. Oxy's board approves the contract by a three-to-two vote, with Wick voting with the majority. Discuss whether this contract is binding on the corporation.

39–2. QUESTION WITH SAMPLE ANSWER

AstroStar, Inc., has a board of directors consisting of three members (Eckhart, Dolan, and Macero) and has approximately five hundred shareholders. At a regular board meeting, the board selects Galiard as president of the corporation by a two-to-one vote, with Eckhart dissenting. The minutes of the meeting do not register Eckhart's dissenting vote. Later, an audit discovers that Galiard is a former convict and has embezzled $500,000 from the corporation that is not covered by insurance. Can the corporation hold directors Eckhart, Dolan, and Macero personally liable? Discuss.

• **For a sample answer to Question 39–2, go to Appendix I at the end of this text.**

39–3. Superal Corp. authorized 100,000 shares and issued all of them during its first six months in operation. Avril purchased 10,000 of the shares (10 percent). Later, Superal reacquired 10,000 of the shares it originally issued. With shareholder approval, Superal has now amended its articles so as to authorize and issue another 100,000 shares. It has also, by a resolution of the board of directors, made plans to reissue the 10,000 shares of treasury stock (the shares reacquired by the corporation). The corporate articles do not include a provision dealing with shareholders' preemptive rights. Because of her ownership of 10 percent of Superal, Avril claims that she has the preemptive right to purchase 10,000 shares of the new issue and 1,000 shares of the stock being reissued. Discuss her claims.

39–4. Lucia has acquired one share of common stock of a multimillion-dollar corporation with more than 500,000 shareholders. Lucia's ownership interest is so small that she is not sure what her rights are as a shareholder. For example, she wants to know whether this one share entitles her to (1) attend and vote at shareholders' meetings, (2) inspect the corporate books, and (3) receive yearly dividends. Discuss Lucia's rights in these three matters.

39–5. Inspection Rights. Craig Johnson founded Distributed Solutions, Inc. (DSI), in 1991 to make software and provide consulting services, including payroll services for small companies. Johnson was the sole officer and director and the majority shareholder. Jeffrey Hagen was a minority shareholder. In 1993, Johnson sold DSI's payroll services to himself and a few others and set up Distributed Payroll Solutions, Inc. (DPSI). In 1996, DSI had revenues of $739,034 and assets of $541,168. In 1997, DSI's revenues were $934,532. Within a year, however, all of DSI's assets were sold, and Johnson told Hagen that he was dissolving the firm because, among other things, it conducted no business and had no prospects for future business. Hagen asked for corporate records to determine the value of DSI's stock, DSI's financial condition, and "whether unauthorized and oppressive acts had occurred in connection with the operation of the corporation which impacted the value of" the stock. When there was no response, Hagen filed a suit in an Illinois state court against DSI and Johnson, seeking an order to compel the inspection. The defendants filed a motion to dismiss, arguing that Hagen had failed to plead a proper purpose. Should the court grant Hagen's request? Discuss. [*Hagen v. Distributed Solutions, Inc.,* 328 Ill.App.3d 132, 764 N.E.2d 1141, 262 Ill.Dec. 24 (1 Dist. 2002)]

39–6. Duty of Loyalty. Digital Commerce, Ltd., designed software to enable its clients to sell their products or services over the Internet. Kevin Sullivan served as a Digital vice president until 2000, when he became president. Sullivan was dissatisfied that his compensation did not include stock in Digital, but he was unable to negotiate a deal that included equity (shares of ownership in the company). In May, Sullivan solicited ASR Corp.'s business for Digital while he investigated employment opportunities with ASR for himself. When ASR would not include an "equity component" in a job offer, Sullivan refused to negotiate further on Digital's behalf. A few months later, Sullivan began to form his own firm to compete with Digital, conducting organizational and marketing activities on Digital's time, including soliciting ASR's business. In August, Sullivan resigned after having all e-mail pertaining to the new firm deleted from Digital's computers. ASR signed a contract with Sullivan's new firm and paid it $400,000 for work through October 2001. Digital filed a suit in a federal district court against Sullivan, claiming that he had usurped a corporate opportunity. Did Sullivan breach his fiduciary duty to Digital? Explain. [*In re Sullivan,* 305 Bankr. 809 (W.D.Mich. 2004)]

39–7. CASE PROBLEM WITH SAMPLE ANSWER

In 1978, David Brandt and Dean Somerville incorporated Posilock Puller, Inc. (PPI), to make and market bearing pullers. Each received half of the stock. Initially operating out of McHenry, North Dakota, PPI moved to Cooperstown, North Dakota, in 1984 into a building owned by Somerville. After the move, Brandt's participation in PPI diminished, and Somerville's increased. In 1998, Somerville formed PL MFG as his own business to make components for the bearing pullers and sell the parts to PPI. The start-up costs included a $450,000 loan from Sheyenne Valley Electric Cooperative. PPI executed the loan documents and indorsed the check. The proceeds were deposited into an account for PL MFG, which did not sign a promissory note payable to PPI until 2000. When Brandt learned of PL MFG and the loan, he filed a suit in a North Dakota state court against Somerville, alleging, in part, a breach of fiduciary duty. What fiduciary duty does a director owe to his or her corporation? What does this duty require? Should the court hold Somerville liable? Why or why not? [*Brandt v. Somerville,* 2005 ND 35, 692 N.W.2d 144 (2005)]

- **To view a sample answer for Problem 39–7, go to this book's Web site at www.cengage.com/blaw/jentz, select "Chapter 39," and click on "Case Problem with Sample Answer."**

39–8. Duties of Majority Shareholders. Steve and Marie Venturini were involved in the operation of Steve's Sizzling Steakhouse in Carlstadt, New Jersey, from the day their parents opened it in the 1930s. By the 1980s, Steve, Marie, and her husband Joe were running it. The business was a corporation with Steve and Marie each owning half of the stock. Steve died in 2001, leaving his stock in equal shares to his sons Steve and Gregg. Son Steve had never worked there. Gregg did occasional maintenance work until his father's death. Despite their lack of participation, the sons were paid more than $750 per week each. In 2002, Marie's son Blaise, who had obtained a college degree in restaurant management while working part-time at the steakhouse, took over its management. When his cousins became threatening, he denied them access to the business and its books. Marie refused Gregg and Steve's offer of about $1.4 million for her stock in the restaurant, and they refused her offer of about $800,000 for theirs. They filed a suit in a New Jersey state court against her, claiming, among other things, a breach of fiduciary duty. Should the court order the aunt to buy out the nephews or the nephews to buy out the aunt, or neither? Why? [*Venturini v. Steve's Steakhouse, Inc.*, __ A.2d __ (N.J.Super. Ch. Div. 2006)]

39–9. Fiduciary Duties and Liabilities. Harry Hoaas and Larry Griffiths were shareholders in Grand Casino, Inc., which owned and operated a casino in Watertown, South Dakota. Griffiths owned 51 percent of the stock and Hoaas 49 percent. Hoaas managed the casino, which Griffiths typically visited once a week. At the end of 1997, an accounting showed that the cash on hand was less than the amount posted in the casino's books. Later, more shortfalls were discovered. In October 1999, Griffiths did a complete audit. Hoaas was unable to account for $135,500 in missing cash. Griffiths then kept all of the casino's most recent profits, including Hoaas's $9,447.20 share, and, without telling Hoaas, sold the casino for $100,000 and kept all of the proceeds. Hoaas filed a suit in a South Dakota state court against Griffiths, asserting, among other things, a breach of fiduciary duty. Griffiths countered with evidence of Hoaas's misappropriation of corporate cash. What duties did these parties owe each other? Did either Griffiths or Hoaas, or both of them, breach those duties? How should their dispute be resolved? How should their finances be reconciled? Explain. [*Hoaas v. Griffiths*, 2006 SD 27, 714 N.W.2d 61 (2006)]

39–10. A QUESTION OF ETHICS

*New Orleans Paddlewheels, Inc. (NOP), is a Louisiana corporation formed in 1982 when James Smith, Sr., and Warren Reuther were its only shareholders, with each holding 50 percent of the stock. NOP is part of a sprawling enterprise of tourism and hospitality companies in New Orleans. The positions on the board of each company were split equally between the Smith and Reuther families. At Smith's request, his son James Smith, Jr. (JES), became involved in the businesses. In 1999, NOP's board elected JES as president, to be in charge of day-to-day operations, and Reuther as chief executive officer (CEO), to be in charge of marketing and development. Over the next few years, animosity developed between Reuther and JES. In October 2001, JES terminated Reuther as CEO and denied him access to the offices and books of NOP and the other companies, literally changing the locks on the doors. At the next meetings of the boards of NOP and the overall enterprise, deadlock ensued, with the directors voting along family lines on every issue. Complaining that the meetings were a "waste of time," JES began to run the entire enterprise by taking advantage of an unequal balance of power on the companies' executive committees. In NOP's subsequent bankruptcy proceeding, Reuther filed a motion for the appointment of a trustee to formulate a plan for the firm's reorganization, alleging, among other things, misconduct by NOP's management. [*In re New Orleans Paddlewheels, Inc., *350 Bankr. 667 (E.D.La. 2006)]*

(a) Was Reuther legally entitled to have access to the books and records of NOP and the other companies? JES maintained, among other things, that NOP's books were "a mess." Was JES's denial of that access unethical? Explain.

(b) How would you describe JES's attempt to gain control of NOP and the other companies? Were his actions deceptive and self-serving in the pursuit of personal gain or legitimate and reasonable in the pursuit of a business goal? Discuss.

LAW ON THE WEB

For updated links to resources available on the Web, as well as a variety of other materials, visit this text's Web site at

www.cengage.com/blaw/jentz

One of the best sources on the Web for information on corporations, including their directors, is the EDGAR database of the Securities and Exchange Commission (SEC) at

www.sec.gov/edgar.shtml

Legal Research Exercises on the Web

Go to **www.cengage.com/blaw/jentz**, the Web site that accompanies this text. Select "Chapter 39" and click on "Internet Exercises." There you will find the following Internet research exercises that you can perform to learn more about the topics covered in this chapter.

Internet Exercise 39–1: Legal Perspective
Liability of Directors and Officers

Internet Exercise 39–2: Management Perspective
D&O Insurance

CHAPTER 40

CORPORATIONS—Merger, Consolidation, and Termination

A corporation typically extends its operations by combining with another corporation through a merger, a consolidation, a purchase of assets, or a purchase of a controlling interest in the other corporation. This chapter examines these four types of corporate expansion. Dissolution and winding up are the combined processes by which a corporation terminates its existence. The last part of this chapter discusses some of the typical reasons for terminating a corporation's existence and the methods used in the termination process.

SECTION 1 Merger and Consolidation

The terms *merger* and *consolidation* traditionally referred to two legally distinct proceedings. Today, however, the term *consolidation* generally is used as a generic term to refer to all types of combinations, including mergers (discussed below) and acquisitions (discussed later in this chapter). Whether a combination is a merger, a consolidation, or a share exchange, the rights and liabilities of shareholders, the corporation, and the corporation's creditors are the same. Note also that the power to merge, consolidate, and exchange shares is conferred by statute, and thus state law establishes the specific procedures.

Merger

A **merger** involves the legal combination of two or more corporations. After a merger, only one of the corporations continues to exist. For example, Corporation A and Corporation B decide to merge. They agree that A will absorb B. Therefore, after the merger, B ceases to exist as a separate entity, and A continues as the **surviving corporation.** Exhibit 40–1 illustrates this process.

After the merger, A is recognized as a single corporation possessing all of the rights, privileges, and powers of itself and B. Corporation A automatically acquires all of B's property and assets without the necessity of a formal transfer. Corporation A also becomes liable for all of B's debts and obligations. Finally, A's articles of incorporation are deemed amended to include any changes that are stated in the *articles of merger.*

In a merger, the surviving corporation inherits the disappearing corporation's preexisting legal rights and obligations. For example, if the disappearing corporation had a right of action against a third party, the surviving corporation can bring a suit after the merger to recover the disappearing corporation's damages.

EXHIBIT 40–1 • Merger

In this illustration, Corporation A and Corporation B decide to merge. They agree that A will absorb B, so after the merger, B no longer exists as a separate entity, and A continues as the surviving corporation.

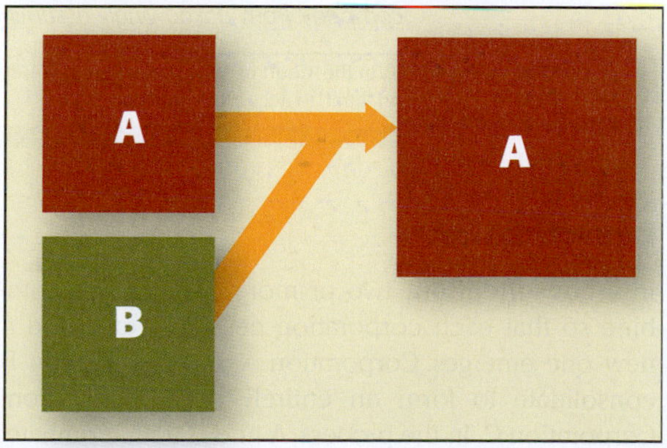

Similarly, following a merger, a third party who had a right of action against the disappearing corporation normally will now have the right to bring an action against the successor (surviving) corporation. The court applied these principles regarding successor liability in the following case.

CASE 40.1 Rodriguez v. Tech Credit Union Corp.

Court of Appeals of Indiana, 2005. 824 N.E.2d 442.
www.findlaw.com/11stategov/in/inca.html[a]

Background and Facts In January 2000, Catalina Rodriguez became the general manager of LTV Steel Employees Federal Credit Union in East Chicago, Indiana, subject to an employment contract. At the time, LTV was in poor financial condition, with a large number of delinquent and unpaid loans. In January 2002, LTV's board of directors terminated Rodriguez's employment for, among other things, extending loan payment periods for individuals with whom she had personal relationships and directing some of LTV's insurance business to Airey Insurance and Financial Services, Inc., which employed her son as a sales representative. On April 27, Tech Credit Union Corporation acquired LTV. The "Agreement of Merger" stated, "The LTV Steel Employees Federal Credit Union shall be merged into Tech Credit Union under the name and charter of Tech Credit Union." The agreement was silent as to whether Tech acquired LTV's liabilities. LTV dissolved. Later, Rodriguez filed a suit in an Indiana state court against Tech and others, alleging, among other things, breach of contract. Tech filed a motion for summary judgment, which the court granted. Rodriguez appealed to a state intermediate appellate court.

Decision and Rationale The state intermediate appellate court affirmed the judgment of the lower court. The appellate court held that Tech succeeded to the liabilities of LTV. The court pointed out that the document under which Tech acquired LTV was titled "Agreement of Merger" and that it repeatedly referred to the transaction as a merger. Following a merger between two firms, the surviving corporation succeeds to all the rights, powers, liabilities, and obligations of the merging corporation. Thus, Tech, as the surviving corporation, acquired LTV's liabilities. Because neither LTV nor its board acted wrongfully with respect to Rodriguez, however, there was no basis for assessing liability against Tech. LTV was failing financially when Rodriguez became the general manager and "things did not improve on her watch." There were "questionable loans and extensions" and "collections efforts were ineffective. In addition, Rodriguez signed a contract with Airey, then presented it to the Board of Directors as a proposal rather than as an existing contract," without revealing her son's employment with Airey. In terminating Rodriguez, the members of the board "exercised their business judgment in good faith and acted in the best interest of the corporation. Thus, the Board Members committed no wrongdoing."

What If the Facts Were Different? *Suppose that the document under which Tech acquired LTV was not titled "Agreement of Merger" and that it did not refer to the transaction as a "merger." Would the result have been different? Explain.*

The E-Commerce Dimension *How might the Internet prevent a prospective acquiring company from unknowingly assuming the liabilities of the disappearing firm on their merger?*

a. In the "Court of Appeals" section, in the "2005" row, click on "March." In the result, scroll to the name of the case and click on "html" to access the opinion.

Consolidation

In a **consolidation,** two or more corporations combine so that each corporation ceases to exist and a new one emerges. Corporation A and Corporation B consolidate to form an entirely new organization, Corporation C. In the process, A and B both terminate. Corporation C comes into existence as an entirely new entity. Exhibit 40–2 illustrates this process.

The results of a consolidation are similar to those of a merger—only one company remains—but it is an entirely new entity (the *consolidated corporation*). C is a new corporation and a single entity; A and B

EXHIBIT 40–2 • Consolidation

In this illustration, Corporation A and Corporation B consolidate to form an entirely new organization, Corporation C. In the process, A and B terminate, and C comes into existence as an entirely new entity.

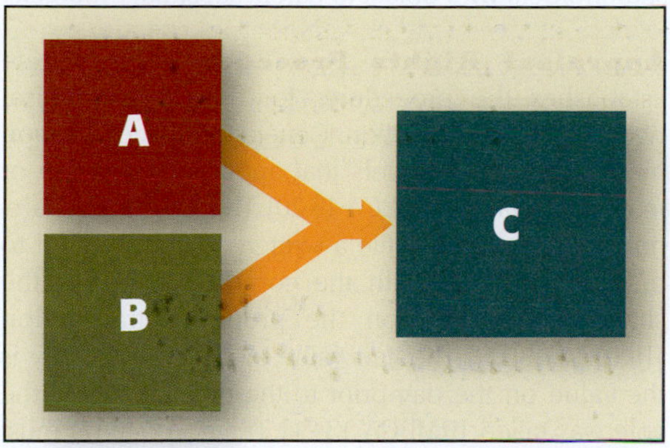

cease to exist. C inherits all of the rights, privileges, and powers previously held by A and B. Title to any property and assets owned by A and B passes to C without a formal transfer. C assumes liability for all debts and obligations owed by A and B. The *articles of consolidation* take the place of A's and B's original corporate articles and are thereafter regarded as C's corporate articles.

When a merger or a consolidation takes place, the surviving corporation or newly formed corporation will issue shares or pay some fair consideration to the shareholders of the corporation or corporations that cease to exist. True consolidations have become less common among for-profit corporations because it is often advantageous for one of the firms to survive. In contrast, nonprofit corporations and associations may prefer consolidation because it suggests a new beginning in which neither of the two initial entities is dominant.

Share Exchange

In a **share exchange,** some or all of the shares of one corporation are exchanged for some or all of the shares of another corporation, but both corporations continue to exist. Share exchanges are often used to create *holding companies* (companies that own part or all of other companies' outstanding stock—see Chapter 38). For example, UAL Corporation is a large holding company that owns United Airlines. If one corporation owns *all* of the shares of another corporation, it is referred to as the *parent corporation,* and the wholly owned company is the *subsidiary corporation.*

Merger, Consolidation, and Share Exchange Procedures

All states have statutes authorizing mergers, consolidations, and share exchanges for domestic (in-state) and foreign (out-of-state) corporations. The procedures vary somewhat among jurisdictions. In some states, a consolidation resulting in an entirely new corporation simply follows the initial incorporation procedures discussed in Chapter 38, whereas other business combinations must follow the procedures outlined below.

The Revised Model Business Corporation Act (RMBCA) sets forth the following basic requirements [RMBCA 11.01–11.07]:

1. The board of directors of *each* corporation involved must adopt a plan of merger or share exchange.
2. The plan must specify any terms and conditions of the merger. It also must state the basis of valuing the shares of each merging corporation and how they will be converted into shares or other securities, cash, property, or other interests in another corporation.
3. The majority of the shareholders of *each* corporation must vote to approve the plan at a shareholders' meeting. If any class of stock is entitled to vote as a separate group, the majority of each separate voting group must approve the plan. Although RMBCA 11.04(e) requires the approval of only a simple majority of the shareholders entitled to vote once a quorum is present, frequently a corporation's articles of incorporation or bylaws require a higher level of approval. In addition, some state statutes require the approval of two-thirds of the outstanding shares of voting stock, and others require a four-fifths approval.
4. Once approved by the directors and the shareholders of both corporations, the surviving corporation files the plan (articles of merger, consolidation, or share exchange) with the appropriate official, usually the secretary of state.
5. When state formalities are satisfied, the state issues a certificate of merger to the surviving corporation or a certificate of consolidation to the newly consolidated corporation.

Short-Form Mergers

RMBCA 11.04 provides a simplified procedure for the merger of a substantially owned subsidiary corporation into its parent corporation. Under these provisions, a **short-form merger**—also referred to as a **parent-subsidiary merger**—can be accomplished *without* the approval of the shareholders of either corporation. The short-form merger can be used only when the parent corporation owns at least 90 percent of the outstanding shares of each class of stock of the subsidiary corporation. Once the board of directors of the parent corporation approves the plan, it is filed with the state, and copies are sent to each shareholder of record in the subsidiary corporation.

Shareholder Approval

As mentioned, except in a short-form merger, the shareholders of both corporations must approve a merger or other plan of consolidation. Shareholders invest in a corporation with the expectation that the board of directors will manage the enterprise and make decisions on *ordinary* business matters. For *extraordinary* matters, normally both the board of directors and the shareholders must approve of the transaction.

Mergers and other combinations are extraordinary business matters, meaning that the board of directors must normally obtain the shareholders' approval and provide appraisal rights (discussed next). Amendments to the articles of incorporation and the dissolution of the corporation also generally require shareholder approval. Sometimes, a transaction can be structured in such a way that shareholder approval is not required, but if the shareholders challenge the transaction, a court might require shareholder approval. For this reason, the board of directors may request shareholder approval even when it might not be legally required.

Appraisal Rights

What if a shareholder disapproves of a merger or a consolidation but is outvoted by the other shareholders? The law recognizes that a dissenting shareholder should not be forced to become an unwilling shareholder in a corporation that is new or different from the one in which the shareholder originally invested. Dissenting shareholders therefore are given a statutory right to be paid the fair value of the number of shares they held on the date of the merger or consolidation. This right is referred to as the shareholder's **appraisal right.** So long as the transaction does not involve fraud or other illegal conduct, appraisal rights are the exclusive remedy for a shareholder who is dissatisfied with the price received for the stock.

Appraisal rights normally extend to regular mergers, consolidations, share exchanges, short-form mergers, and sales of substantially all of the corporate assets not in the ordinary course of business. Such rights can be particularly important in a short-form merger because the minority stockholders do not receive advance notice of the merger, the directors do not consider or approve it, and there is no vote.[1] Appraisal rights are often the only recourse available to shareholders who object to parent-subsidiary mergers.

Appraisal Rights Procedures Each state establishes the procedures for asserting appraisal rights in that jurisdiction. Generally, the corporation must notify shareholders that appraisal rights are or may be available [RMBCA 13.20]. The dissenting shareholders usually must file a written notice of intent to demand payment with the corporation, before the shareholders' vote on the proposed transaction [RMBCA 13.21]. The "fair value of shares" normally is the value on the day prior to the date on which the vote was taken [RMBCA 13.21]. The corporation must make a written offer to purchase a dissenting shareholder's stock, accompanying the offer with a current balance sheet and income statement for the corporation. If the shareholder and the corporation do not agree on the fair value, a court will determine it.

Shareholders may lose their appraisal rights if they do not adhere precisely to the procedures prescribed by statute. When they lose the right to an appraisal, dissenting shareholders must go along with the transaction despite their objections.

Appraisal Rights and Shareholder Status Under the RMBCA, once a dissenting shareholder elects appraisal rights, the shareholder loses her or his shareholder status [RMBCA 13.23]. Without that status, the shareholder cannot vote, receive dividends, or sue to enjoin whatever action prompted the dissent. In some jurisdictions (and under the RMBCA), shareholder status may be reinstated if the shareholder decides to withdraw from the appraisal process. In other jurisdictions, shareholder status may not be reinstated until the appraisal is concluded.

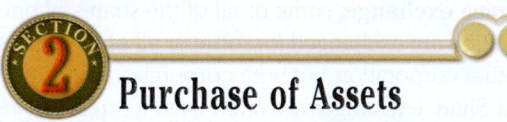

SECTION 2 Purchase of Assets

When a corporation acquires all or substantially all of the assets of another corporation by direct purchase, the purchasing, or *acquiring,* corporation simply extends its ownership and control over more assets. Because no change in the legal entity occurs, the

1. See, for example, *Glassman v. Unocal Exploration Corp.*, 777 A.2d 242 (Del.Sup.Ct. 2001).

acquiring corporation usually does not need to obtain shareholder approval for the purchase.[2]

Both the U.S. Department of Justice and the Federal Trade Commission, however, have issued guidelines that significantly constrain and often prohibit mergers that could result from a purchase of assets. (These guidelines are part of the federal antitrust laws that will be discussed in Chapter 46.)

Sales of Corporate Assets

Note that the corporation that is *selling* all of its assets is substantially changing its business position and perhaps its ability to carry out its corporate purposes. For that reason, the corporation whose assets are being sold must obtain approval from both its board of directors and its shareholders [RMBCA 12.02]. In most states and under RMBCA 13.02, dissenting shareholders of the selling corporation can demand appraisal rights.

Successor Liability in Purchases of Assets

Generally, a corporation that purchases the assets of another corporation is not automatically responsible for the liabilities of the selling corporation. Exceptions to this rule are made in the following circumstances:

1. When the purchasing corporation impliedly or expressly assumes the seller's liabilities.
2. When the sale transaction is actually a merger or consolidation of the two companies.[3]
3. When the purchasing corporation is merely a continuation of the selling corporation—that is, the buyer continues operating the seller's business in the same manner and retains the same personnel (same directors, officers, and shareholders).
4. When the sale is entered into fraudulently for the purpose of escaping liability.

In any of these situations, the acquiring corporation will be held to have assumed both the assets and the liabilities of the selling corporation.

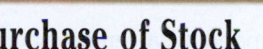

SECTION 3 Purchase of Stock

An alternative to the purchase of another corporation's assets is the purchase of a substantial number of the voting shares of its stock. This enables the acquiring corporation to gain control of the acquired corporation, or **target corporation.** The process of acquiring control over a corporation in this way is commonly referred to as a corporate **takeover.**

Tender Offers

In seeking to purchase the stock of the target corporation, the acquiring corporation deals directly with the target's shareholders by making a *tender offer*. A **tender offer** is a proposal to buy shares of stock from a target corporation's shareholders either for cash or for some type of corporate security of the acquiring company. The tender offer can be conditioned on the receipt of a specified number of outstanding shares by a certain date. As a means of inducing shareholders to accept the offer, the tender price offered generally is higher than the market price of the target's stock prior to the announcement of the tender offer. For example, in the 2006 merger of AT&T and BellSouth, BellSouth shareholders received approximately $37.09 per share—a 16 percent premium over the market price of the stock.

Federal securities laws strictly control the terms, duration, and circumstances under which most tender offers are made. Generally, the offering corporation does not need to notify the Securities and Exchange Commission (SEC) or the target corporation's management until after the tender offer is made. The offeror must then disclose to the SEC the source of the funds used in the offer, the purpose of the offer, and the acquiring corporation's plans for the firm if the takeover is successful.

In addition, a majority of states have passed antitakeover statutes. Although some of these state statutes have been found to violate the commerce clause of the U.S. Constitution, others have been upheld as constitutional.[4]

2. Shareholder approval may be required in a few situations. If the acquiring corporation plans to pay for the assets with its own corporate stock but not enough authorized unissued shares are available, then shareholders must vote to approve an amendment to the corporate articles. Also, if the acquiring corporation is a company whose stock is traded on a national stock exchange and it will be issuing a significant number (at least 20 percent) of its outstanding shares, shareholders must approve.

3. See, for example, *Cargo Partner AG v. Albatrans, Inc.*, 352 F.3d 41 (2d Cir. 2003) applying New York law on *de facto* mergers; and *Village Builders 96, L.P. v. U.S. Laboratories, Inc.*, 121 Nev. 261, 112 P.3d 1082 (2005).

4. For a leading case in which the United States Supreme Court ruled that a state antitakeover statute was constitutional, see *CTS Corp. v. Dynamics Corp. of America*, 481 U.S. 69, 107 S.Ct. 1637, 95 L.Ed.2d 67 (1987). For a case in which a federal district court found that Arizona's statute was unconstitutional, see *Rocket Acquisition Corp. v. Ventana Medical Systems, Inc.*, __ F.Supp.2d __ (D.Ariz. 2007).

Responses to Tender Offers

A firm may respond to a tender offer in numerous ways. If the target firm's board of directors views the tender offer as favorable, the board will recommend that the shareholders accept it. Frequently, though, the target corporation's management opposes the proposed takeover.

To resist a takeover, a target company may make a *self-tender,* in which it offers to acquire stock from its own shareholders and thereby retain corporate control. The target corporation may also engage in a media campaign to persuade its shareholders that the tender offer is not in their best interests. Another possible defense is for the target firm to issue additional stock, thereby increasing the number of shares that the acquiring corporation must purchase to gain control.

Alternatively, a target corporation might resort to one of several other tactics to resist a takeover (see Exhibit 40–3). In one commonly used tactic, known as a poison pill, a target company gives its shareholders rights to purchase additional shares at low prices when there is a takeover attempt. A poison pill is an attempt to prevent a takeover by making it prohibitively expensive.

Concept Summary 40.1 reviews all of the ways in which a corporation may expand its operations.

Takeover Defenses and Directors' Fiduciary Duties

As mentioned, the board of directors of the target corporation often opposes the takeover. Clearly, board members have an interest in keeping their jobs and control, but they also have a fiduciary duty to the corporation and its shareholders to act in the best interests of the company. In a hostile takeover attempt, sometimes directors' duties of care and loyalty collide with their self-interest. Then the shareholders, who would have received a premium for their shares as a result of the takeover, file lawsuits alleging that the directors breached their fiduciary duties in defending against the tender offer.

In this situation, courts apply the *business judgment* rule (discussed in Chapter 39) to analyze whether the directors acted reasonably in resisting the takeover attempt. The directors must show that they had reasonable grounds to believe that the tender offer posed a danger to the corporation's policies and effectiveness. In addition, the board's response must have been

EXHIBIT 40–3 • The Terminology of Takeover Defenses

Type	Definition
Crown Jewel	When threatened with a takeover, management makes the company less attractive to the raider by selling to a third party the company's most valuable asset (the "crown jewel").
Golden Parachute	When a takeover is successful, top management is usually changed. With this in mind, a company may establish special termination or retirement benefits that must be paid to top managers if they are "retired." In other words, a departing high-level manager's parachute will be "golden" when he or she is forced to "bail out" of the company.
Greenmail	To regain control, a target company may pay a higher-than-market price to repurchase all of the stock bought by the acquiring corporation. When a takeover is attempted through a gradual accumulation of target stock rather than a tender offer, the intent may be to induce the target company to buy back the shares at a premium price—a concept similar to blackmail.
Pac-Man	Named after the Atari video game, this is an aggressive defense in which the target corporation attempts its own takeover of the acquiring corporation.
Poison Pill	The target corporation issues to its stockholders rights to purchase additional shares at low prices when there is a takeover attempt. This makes the takeover undesirably or even prohibitively expensive for the acquiring corporation.
White Knight	The target corporation solicits a merger with a third party, which then makes a better (often simply a higher) tender offer to the target's shareholders. The third party that "rescues" the target is the "white knight."

CONCEPT SUMMARY 40.1
Methods of Expanding Corporate Operations and Interests

Method	Description
MERGER AND CONSOLIDATION	1. *Merger*—The legal combination of two or more corporations, with the result that the surviving corporation acquires all of the assets and obligations of the other corporation, which then ceases to exist. 2. *Consolidation*—The legal combination of two or more corporations, with the result that each corporation ceases to exist and a new one emerges. The new corporation assumes all of the assets and obligations of the former corporations. 3. *Share exchange*—A form of business combination in which some or all of the shares of one corporation are exchanged for some or all of the shares of another corporation, but both firms continue to exist. 4. *Procedure*—Determined by state statutes. Basic requirements are the following: a. The board of directors of each corporation involved must approve the plan of merger, consolidation, or share exchange. b. The shareholders of each corporation must approve the merger or other consolidation plan at a shareholders' meeting. c. Articles of merger or consolidation (the plan) must be filed, usually with the secretary of state. d. The state issues a certificate of merger (or consolidation) to the surviving (or newly consolidated) corporation. 5. *Short-form merger (parent-subsidiary merger)*—When the parent corporation owns at least 90 percent of the outstanding shares of each class of stock of the subsidiary corporation, shareholder approval is not required for the two firms to merge. 6. *Appraisal rights*—Statutory rights of dissenting shareholders to receive the *fair value* for their shares when a merger or consolidation takes place. If the shareholder and the corporation do not agree on the fair value, a court will determine it.
PURCHASE OF ASSETS	A purchase of assets occurs when one corporation acquires all or substantially all of the assets of another corporation. 1. *Acquiring corporation*—The acquiring (purchasing) corporation is not required to obtain shareholder approval; the corporation is merely increasing its assets, and no fundamental business change occurs. 2. *Acquired corporation*—The acquired (purchased) corporation is required to obtain the approval of both its directors and its shareholders for the sale of its assets because the sale will substantially change the corporation's business position.
PURCHASE OF STOCK	A purchase of stock occurs when one corporation acquires a substantial number of the voting shares of the stock of another (target) corporation. 1. *Tender offer*—A public offer to all shareholders of the target corporation to purchase their stock at a price generally higher than the market price of the target stock prior to the announcement of the tender offer. Federal and state securities laws strictly control the terms, duration, and circumstances under which most tender offers are made. 2. *Target responses*—The ways in which target corporations respond to takeover bids include self-tender (the target firm's offer to acquire its own shareholders' stock) and numerous other strategies (see Exhibit 40–3).

rational in relation to the threat posed.[5] Basically, the defensive tactics used must have been reasonable, and the board of directors must have been trying to protect the corporation and its shareholders from a perceived danger. If the directors' actions were reasonable under the circumstances, then they are not liable for breaching their fiduciary duties.

Takeovers and Antitrust Law

Sometimes, a target corporation will seek an injunction against an aggressor on the ground that the attempted takeover violates antitrust laws. This defense may succeed if a court finds that the takeover would result in a substantial increase in the acquiring corporation's market power. Because antitrust laws are designed to protect competition rather than competitors, incumbent managers who are able to avoid a takeover by resorting to the use of private antitrust actions are unintended beneficiaries of the laws.

As will be discussed in Chapter 46, antitrust challenges to mergers may also be brought by the government rather than by private parties. Hence, the antitrust considerations involved in a proposed takeover can exist apart from the consideration of defense tactics.

SECTION 4 Termination

The termination of a corporation's existence has two phases—dissolution and winding up. **Dissolution** is the legal death of the artificial "person" of the corporation. *Winding up* is the process by which corporate assets are *liquidated,* or converted into cash and distributed among creditors and shareholders according to specific rules of preference.[6]

Voluntary Dissolution

Dissolution can be brought about voluntarily by the directors and the shareholders. State incorporation statutes establish the required procedures for voluntarily dissolving a corporation. Basically, there are two possible methods: by the shareholders' unanimous vote to initiate dissolution proceedings,[7] or by a proposal of the board of directors that is submitted to the shareholders at a shareholders' meeting.

When a corporation is dissolved voluntarily, the corporation must file *articles of dissolution* with the state and notify its creditors of the dissolution. The corporation must also establish a date (at least 120 days after the date of dissolution) by which all claims against the corporation must be received [RMBCA 14.06].

A corporation's creditors want to be notified when the firm is dissolved so that they can file claims for payment. If a corporation is dissolved and its assets are liquidated without notice to a party who has a claim against the firm, who is liable for the debt? That was the question in the following case.

5. For a landmark Delaware Supreme Court case applying the business judgment rule to hostile takeovers, see *Unocal Corp. v. Mesa Petroleum Co.,* 493 A.2d 946 (Del.Sup.Ct. 1985). See also *Shaper v. Bryan,* 371 Ill.App.3d 1079, 864 N.E.2d 876, 309 Ill.Dec. 635 (2007).

6. Some prefer to call this phase *liquidation,* but we use the term *winding up* to mean all acts needed to bring the legal and financial affairs of the business to an end, including liquidating the assets and distributing them among creditors and shareholders. See RMBCA 14.05.

7. Only some states allow shareholders to initiate corporation dissolution. See, for example, Delaware Code Annotated Title 8, Section 275(c).

CASE 40.2 Parent v. Amity Autoworld, Ltd.

New York District Court, Suffolk County, Third District, 2007. 15 Misc.3d 633, 832 N.Y.S.2d 775.

Background and Facts Christine Parent leased an automobile from Amity Autoworld, Ltd. Soon thereafter, Amity sold all of the assets of its automobile franchise to another company called J S Autoworld, Ltd., which used the name Atlantic. Parent made a written claim for monetary damages to Amity one month after the sale of its assets. Parent then commenced a small claims action against Amity and obtained a $2,643 judgment. The sheriff's department was unable to execute collection of the award against Amity because it had been sold to Atlantic. Underlying that transaction was the fact that Amity's principal shareholder, John Staluppi, Jr., was the son of Atlantic's principal shareholder, John Staluppi, Sr. Staluppi, Jr., was listed as the chairman, chief executive officer, executive officer, and agent for process for Amity.

CASE 40.2 CONTINUED

Decision and Rationale The court authorized Parent to amend her complaint to include John Staluppi, Jr., as a defendant. The court directed the clerk of the court to serve a copy of the amended summons and of the court's decision on John Staluppi, Jr. A trial was to follow. "Even in the absence of fraud, it is a violation of a duty on the part of the directors of the corporation to divest itself of all of its property without affording a reasonable opportunity to its creditors to present and enforce their claims before the transfer becomes effective." After the return of an unsatisfied execution against a corporation that no longer exists, any creditor may maintain "an action against a shareholder to reach assets received by him. Directors incur derivative personal liability when they undertake to divest a corporation of all of its property and in reality dissolve it without undertaking the proceedings for voluntary dissolution." The court pointed out that when a corporation is informally dissolved, its directors cannot shield themselves against corporate creditor liability. Amity was liquidated and dissolved without any notice to creditors. Its sole shareholder, John Staluppi, Jr., personally received more than $4 million from the transaction.

The Legal Environment Dimension *A corporation may do business under a variety of names—the name of one of its owners or officers, the name under which it is incorporated, or the name on a sign at its business premises, for example. How strictly should the law require a judgment to be issued against a corporation in its "true" name?*

The Ethical Dimension *Could a corporation's former directors or shareholders, or its successors, avoid liability following its informal dissolution by claiming that they did all they felt was necessary to protect its creditors? Why or why not?*

Involuntary Dissolution

Because corporations are creatures of statute, the state can also dissolve a corporation in certain circumstances. The secretary of state or the state attorney general can bring an action to dissolve a corporation that has failed to pay its annual taxes or to submit required annual reports, for example [RMBCA 14.20]. A state court can also dissolve a corporation that has engaged in *ultra vires* acts or committed fraud or misrepresentation to the state during incorporation. Courts can also dissolve a corporation for mismanagement [RMBCA 14.30].

In some circumstances, a shareholder or a group of shareholders may petition a court to have the corporation dissolved. The RMBCA permits any shareholder to initiate an action for dissolution in any of the following circumstances [RMBCA 14.30]:

1. The directors are deadlocked in the management of corporate affairs, the shareholders are unable to break the deadlock, and the corporation is suffering irreparable injury as a result or is about to do so.
2. The acts of the directors or those in control of the corporation are illegal, oppressive, or fraudulent.
3. Corporate assets are being misapplied or wasted.
4. The shareholders are deadlocked in voting power and have failed, for a specified period (usually two annual meetings), to elect successors to directors whose terms have expired or would have expired with the election of successors.

As noted above, a court may dissolve a corporation if the controlling shareholders or directors have engaged in fraudulent, illegal, or oppressive conduct. For example, Mt. Princeton Trout Club, Inc. (MPTC), was formed to own land in Colorado and provide fishing and other recreational benefits to its shareholders. The articles of incorporation prohibited MPTC from selling or leasing any of the property and assets of the corporation without the approval of a majority of the directors. Despite this provision, MPTC officers entered into leases and contracts to sell corporate property without even notifying the directors. When a shareholder, Sam Colt, petitioned for dissolution, the court dissolved MPTC based on a finding that its officers had engaged in illegal, oppressive, and fraudulent conduct.[8]

The issue in the following case was whether the circumstances satisfied the statutory requirements for a court to dissolve a trucking corporation.

8. *Colt v. Mt. Princeton Trout Club, Inc.*, 78 P.3d 1115 (Colo. App. 2003).

CASE 40.3 Sartori v. S&S Trucking, Inc.

Supreme Court of Montana, 2006. 2006 MT 164, 332 Mont. 503, 139 P.3d 806.

• **Background and Facts** Tony Stacy approached his friend Justin Sartori about buying a trucking business and operating it together. Sartori agreed, and because he had a good credit rating and Stacy did not, Sartori borrowed $78,493.68 from First Interstate Bank in Eureka, Montana, to buy the business. In September 2003, they formed S&S Trucking, Inc., and agreed to be its only directors, officers, and shareholders, with each owning an equal number of shares. Within weeks, however, they realized that they were incompatible. For example, Sartori often did not show up when and where Stacy expected, and they differed over the payment of earnings from S&S's income. In October, Sartori incorporated Brimstone Enterprise to undermine S&S. He had S&S's mail forwarded to Brimstone, transferred S&S's licenses to Brimstone, and attempted to attract S&S's customers to Brimstone. In mid-November, he quit working for S&S and filed a suit in a Montana state court against S&S and Stacy, demanding that the firm be dissolved. The court set a deadline for the dissolution. The defendants appealed to the Montana Supreme Court.

• **Decision and Rationale** The Montana Supreme Court affirmed the decision of the lower court, holding that the order for the dissolution of S&S was correct. The state supreme court pointed out that under Montana Code Section 35-1-938(2)(a), a court can dissolve a corporation in a proceeding by a shareholder if "the directors are deadlocked in the management of the corporate affairs, the shareholders are unable to break the deadlock, and irreparable injury to the corporation is threatened or being suffered or the business and affairs of the corporation can no longer be conducted to the advantage of the shareholders generally because of the deadlock." The court conceded that S&S had not suffered an "irreparable injury," but reasoned that the deadlock between Sartori and Stacy had led Sartori to sabotage the corporation. "As a result, the business and affairs of S&S could no longer be conducted to the advantage of the shareholders."

• **The Ethical Dimension** *Did Sartori or Stacy behave unethically toward each other or toward the corporation? Discuss.*

• **The Legal Environment Dimension** *At the time of the defendants' appeal, S&S had twelve employees and, according to Stacy, its business was thriving. Should the court have taken these factors into consideration when deciding whether to order the dissolution of the firm? Explain.*

Winding Up

When dissolution takes place by voluntary action, the members of the board of directors act as trustees of the corporate assets. As trustees, they are responsible for winding up the affairs of the corporation for the benefit of corporate creditors and shareholders. This makes the board members personally liable for any breach of their fiduciary trustee duties.

When the dissolution is involuntary—or if board members do not wish to act as trustees of the assets—the court will appoint a **receiver** to wind up the corporate affairs and liquidate corporate assets. Courts may also appoint a receiver when shareholders or creditors can show that the board of directors should not be permitted to act as trustees of the corporate assets. On dissolution, the liquidated assets are first used to pay creditors. Any remaining assets are distributed to shareholders according to their respective stock rights; preferred stock has priority over common stock. Generally, the preferences are stated in the corporate articles.

SECTION 5 Major Business Forms Compared

As mentioned in Chapter 35, when deciding which form of business organization to choose, businesspersons normally consider several factors, including ease of creation, the liability of the owners, tax considerations, and the need for capital. Each major form of business organization offers distinct advantages and disadvantages with respect to these and other factors. Exhibit 40–4 on pages 767 and 768 summarizes the essential advantages and disadvantages of each of the forms of business organization discussed in Chapters 35 through 40.

EXHIBIT 40–4 • Major Forms of Business Compared

Characteristic	Sole Proprietorship	Partnership	Corporation
Method of Creation	Created at will by owner.	Created by agreement of the parties.	Authorized by the state under the state's corporation law.
Legal Position	Not a separate entity; owner is the business.	A traditional partnership is a separate legal entity in most states.	Always a legal entity separate and distinct from its owners—a legal fiction for the purposes of owning property and being a party to litigation.
Liability	Unlimited liability.	Unlimited liability.	Limited liability of shareholders—shareholders are not liable for the debts of the corporation.
Duration	Determined by owner; automatically dissolved on owner's death.	Terminated by agreement of the partners, but can continue to do business even when a partner dissociates from the partnership.	Can have perpetual existence.
Transferability of Interest	Interest can be transferred, but individual's proprietorship then ends.	Although partnership interest can be assigned, assignee does not have full rights of a partner.	Shares of stock can be transferred.
Management	Completely at owner's discretion.	Each partner has a direct and equal voice in management unless expressly agreed otherwise in the partnership agreement.	Shareholders elect directors, who set policy and appoint officers.
Taxation	Owner pays personal taxes on business income.	Each partner pays income taxes in proportion to her or his share of the net profits, whether or not they are distributed.	Double taxation—corporation pays income tax on net profits, with no deduction for dividends, and shareholders pay income tax on disbursed dividends they receive.
Organizational Fees, Annual License Fees, and Annual Reports	None or minimal.	None or minimal.	All required.
Transaction of Business in Other States	Generally no limitation.	Generally no limitation.[a]	Normally must file a foreign qualification form to do business in another state.

a. A few states have enacted statutes requiring that foreign partnerships qualify to do business there.

EXHIBIT CONTINUES

EXHIBIT 40–4 • **Major Forms of Business Compared, Continued**

Characteristic	Limited Partnership	Limited Liability Company	Limited Liability Partnership
Method of Creation	Created by agreement to carry on a business for profit. At least one party must be a general partner and the other(s) limited partner(s). Certificate of limited partnership is filed. Charter must be issued by the state.	Created by an agreement of the member-owners of the company. Articles of organization are filed. Charter must be issued by the state.	Created by agreement of the partners. A statement of qualification for the limited liability partnership is filed.
Legal Position	Treated as a legal entity.	Treated as a legal entity.	Generally, treated same as a traditional partnership.
Liability	Unlimited liability of all general partners; limited partners are liable only to the extent of capital contributions.	Member-owners' liability is limited to the amount of capital contributions or investments.	Varies, but under the Uniform Partnership Act, liability of a partner for acts committed by other partners is limited.
Duration	By agreement in certificate, or by termination of the last general partner (retirement, death, and the like) or last limited partner.	Unless a single-member LLC, can have perpetual existence (same as a corporation).	Remains in existence until cancellation or revocation.
Transferability of Interest	Interest can be assigned (same as a traditional partnership), but if assignee becomes a member with consent of other partners, certificate must be amended.	Member interests are freely transferable.	Interest can be assigned same as in a traditional partnership.
Management	General partners have equal voice or by agreement. Limited partners may not retain limited liability if they actively participate in management.	Member-owners can fully participate in management or can designate a group of persons to manage on behalf of the members.	Same as a traditional partnership.
Taxation	Generally taxed as a partnership.	LLC is not taxed, and members are taxed personally on profits "passed through" the LLC.	Same as a traditional partnership.
Organizational Fees, Annual License Fees, and Annual Reports	Organizational fee required; usually not others.	Organizational fee required; others vary with states.	Fees are set by each state for filing statements of qualification, foreign qualification, and annual reports.
Transaction of Business in Other States	Generally no limitations.	Generally no limitation, but may vary depending on state.	Must file a statement of foreign qualification before doing business in another state.

REVIEWING CORPORATIONS—Merger, Consolidation, and Termination

In November 2002, Mario Bonsetti and Rico Sanchez incorporated Gnarly Vulcan Gear, Inc. (GVG), to manufacture windsurfing equipment. Bonsetti owned 60 percent and Sanchez owned 40 percent of the corporation's stock, and both men served on the board of directors. In January 2006, Hula Boards, Inc., owned solely by Mai Jin Li, made a public offer to Bonsetti and Sanchez to buy GVG stock. Hula offered 30 percent more than the market price per share for the GVG stock, and Bonsetti and Sanchez each sold 20 percent of their stock to Hula. Jin Li became the third member of the GVG board of directors. In April 2008, an irreconcilable dispute arose between Bonsetti and Sanchez over design modifications of their popular Baked Chameleon board. Sanchez and Jin Li voted to merge GVG with Hula Boards under the latter name, despite Bonsetti's dissent. Gnarly Vulcan Gear was dissolved and production of the Baked Chameleon ceased. Using the information presented in the chapter, answer the following questions.

1. What rights does Bonsetti have (in most states) as a minority shareholder dissenting to the merger of GVG and Hula Boards?
2. Could the parties have used a short-form merger procedure in this situation? Why or why not?
3. What is the term used for Hula's offer to purchase GVG stock? By what method did Hula acquire control over GVG?
4. Suppose that after the merger, a person who was injured on a Baked Chameleon board sued Hula (the surviving corporation). Can Hula be held liable for an injury? Why or why not?

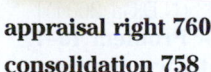

TERMS AND CONCEPTS

appraisal right 760
consolidation 758
dissolution 764
merger 757
parent-subsidiary merger 759
receiver 766
share exchange 759
short-form merger 759
surviving corporation 757
takeover 761
target corporation 761
tender offer 761

QUESTIONS AND CASE PROBLEMS

40–1. Gretz is the chair of the board of directors of Faraday, Inc., and Williams is the chair of the board of directors of Firebrand, Inc. Faraday is a manufacturing corporation, and Firebrand is a transportation corporation. Gretz and Williams meet to discuss the possibility of combining their corporations and activities into a single corporate entity. They consider two alternative courses of action: (1) Faraday acquires all of the stock and assets of Firebrand, or (2) the two corporations combine to form a new corporation, Farabrand, Inc. Both chairs are concerned about the necessity of a formal transfer of property, liability for existing debts, and the need to amend the articles of incorporation. Explain what the two proposed combinations are called, and discuss the legal effect each has on the transfer of property, the liabilities of the combined corporations, and the need to amend the articles of incorporation.

40–2. QUESTION WITH SAMPLE ANSWER

Alir owns 10,000 shares of Ajax Corp. Her shares represent a 10 percent ownership in Ajax. Zeta Corp. is interested in acquiring Ajax in a merger, and the board of directors of each corporation has approved the merger. The shareholders of Zeta have already approved the acquisition, and Ajax has called for a shareholders' meeting to approve the merger. Alir disapproves of the merger and does not want to accept Zeta shares for the Ajax shares she holds. The market price of Ajax shares is $20 per share the day before the shareholder vote and drops to $16 on the day the shareholders of Ajax approve the merger. Discuss Alir's rights in this matter, beginning with the notice of the proposed merger.

- **For a sample answer to Question 40–2, go to Appendix I at the end of this text.**

40–3. Alitech Corp. is a small midwestern business that owns a valuable patent. Alitech has approximately 1,000 shareholders with 100,000 authorized and outstanding shares. Block Corp. would like to have the use of the patent, but Alitech refuses to give Block a license. Block has tried to acquire Alitech by purchasing Alitech's assets, but Alitech's board of directors has refused to approve the acquisition. Alitech's shares are selling for $5 per share. Discuss how Block Corp. might proceed to gain the control and use of Alitech's patent.

40–4. Saunders Corp. has been experiencing losses for several years but still has valuable fixed assets. The shareholders see little hope that the corporation will ever make a profit. Another corporation, Topway Corp., has not paid state taxes for several years or filed annual reports as required by statute. In addition, Topway is accused of committing gross and persistent *ultra vires* acts. Discuss whether these corporations will be terminated and how the assets of each would be handled on dissolution.

40–5. Successor Liability. In 1996, Robert McClellan, a licensed contractor doing business as McClellan Design and Construction, entered into a contract with Peppertree North Condominium Association, Inc., to do earthquake repair work on Peppertree's seventy-six-unit condominium complex in Northridge, California. McClellan completed the work, but Peppertree failed to pay. In an arbitration proceeding against Peppertree to collect the amount due, McClellan was awarded $141,000, plus 10 percent interest, attorneys' fees, and costs. McClellan filed a suit in a California state court against Peppertree to confirm the award. Meanwhile, the Peppertree board of directors filed articles of incorporation for Northridge Park Townhome Owners Association, Inc., and immediately transferred Peppertree's authority, responsibilities, and assets to the new association. Two weeks later, the court issued a judgment against Peppertree. When McClellan learned about the new association, he filed a motion asking the court to add Northridge as a debtor to the judgment. Should the court grant the motion? Why or why not? [*McClellan v. Northridge Park Townhome Owners Association, Inc.*, 89 Cal.App.4th 746, 107 Cal.Rptr.2d 702 (2 Dist. 2001)]

40–6. Corporate Dissolution. Trans-System, Inc. (TSI), is an interstate trucking business. In 1994, to provide a source of well-trained drivers, TSI formed Northwestern Career Institute, Inc., a school for persons interested in obtaining a commercial driver's license. Tim Scott, who had worked for TSI since 1987, was named chief administrative officer and director. Scott, a Northwestern shareholder, disagreed with James Williams, the majority shareholder of both TSI and Northwestern, over four equipment leases between the two firms under which the sum of the payments exceeded the value of the equipment by not more than $3,000. Under four other leases, payments were $40,000 less than the value of the equipment. Scott also disputed TSI's one-time use, for purposes unrelated to the driving school, of $125,000 borrowed by Northwestern. Scott was terminated in 1998. He filed a suit in a Washington state court against TSI, seeking, among other things, the dissolution of Northwestern on the ground that the directors of the two firms had acted in an oppressive manner and misapplied corporate assets. Should the court grant this relief? If not, what remedy might be appropriate? Discuss. [*Scott v. Trans-System, Inc.*, 148 Wash.2d 701, 64 P.3d 1 (2003)]

40–7. CASE PROBLEM WITH SAMPLE ANSWER

In January 1999, General Star Indemnity Co. agreed to insure Indianapolis Racing League (IRL) race cars against damage during on-track accidents. In connection with the insurance, General Star deposited $400,000 with G Force LLC (GFCO), a Colorado firm, to enable it to buy and provide parts for damaged cars without delay. GFCO agreed to return any unspent funds. Near the end of the season, Elan Motorsports Technologies (EMT) acquired GFCO. In 2000, EMT incorporated G Force LLC in Georgia (GFGA), and GFCO ceased to exist. GFGA renewed the arrangement with General Star and engaged in the same operations as GFCO, but EMT employees conducted GFGA's business at EMT's offices. In 2002, EMT assumed ownership of GFGA's assets and continued the business. EMT also assumed GFGA's liabilities, except for the obligation to return General Star's unspent funds. General Star filed a suit in a Georgia state court against EMT, seeking to recover its deposit. What is the rule concerning the liability of a corporation that buys the assets of another? Are there exceptions? Which principles apply in this case? Explain. [*General Star Indemnity Co. v. Elan Motorsports Technologies, Inc.*, 356 F.Supp.2d 1333 (N.D.Ga. 2004)]

- **To view a sample answer for Problem 40–7, go to this book's Web site at www.cengage.com/blaw/jentz, select "Chapter 40," and click on "Case Problem with Sample Answer."**

40–8. Purchase of Assets. Paradise Pools, Inc. (PPI), also known as "Paradise Pools and Spas," was incorporated in 1981. In 1994, PPI entered into a contract with Bromanco, Inc., to build a pool in Vicksburg, Mississippi, as part of a Days Inn Hotel project being developed by Amerihost Development, Inc. PPI built the pool, but Bromanco, the general contractor, defaulted on other parts of the project, and Amerihost completed the construction itself. Litigation ensued in Mississippi state courts, and Amerihost was awarded $12,656.46 against PPI. Meanwhile, Paradise Corp. (PC) was incorporated in 1995 with the same management as PPI, but different shareholders. PC acquired PPI's assets in 1996, without assuming its liabilities, and soon became known as "Paradise Pools and Spas." Amerihost obtained a writ of garnishment against PC to enforce the judgment against PPI. PC filed a motion to dismiss the writ on the basis that it was "not a party to the proceeding." Should the court dismiss the case? Why or why not? [*Paradise Corp. v. Amerihost Development, Inc.*, 848 So.2d 177 (Miss. 2003)]

40–9. Dissolution. Clara Mahaffey operated Mahaffey's Auto Salvage, Inc., in Dayton, Ohio, as a sole proprietorship. In 1993, Kenneth Stumpff and Mahaffey's son, Richard Harris, joined the firm. Stumpff ran the wrecker and bought the vehicles for salvage. Harris handled the day-to-day operations and the bookkeeping. They became the company's equal 50 percent shareholders on Mahaffey's death in 2002. Harris, who inherited the land on which the firm was located, increased the rent to $1,500 per month. Within two years of Mahaffey's death, and without consulting Stumpff, Harris raised the rent to $2,500. Stumpff's wife died, and he took a leave of absence, during which the company paid him $2,500 a month and provided health insurance. After two years, Harris stopped the payments, discontinued the health benefits, and fired Stumpff, threatening to call the police if he came on the premises. Stumpff withdrew $16,000 from the firm's account, leaving a balance of $113. Harris offered to buy Stumpff's interest in the business, but Stumpff refused and filed a suit in an Ohio state court against Harris. A state statute permits the dissolution of a corporation if the owners are deadlocked in its management. Should the court order the dissolution of Mahaffey's? Why or why not? [*Stumpff v. Harris*, __ N.E.2d __ (Ohio App. 2 Dist. 2006)]

40–10. A QUESTION OF ETHICS

Topps Co. makes baseball and other cards, including the Pokemon collection, and distributes Bazooka bubble gum and other confections. Arthur Shorin, the son of Joseph Shorin, one of Topps's founders and the inspiration for "Bazooka Joe" (a character in the comic strip wrapped around each piece of gum), worked for Topps for fifty years and had served as its board chairman and chief executive officer since 1980. Shorin's son-in-law, Scott Silverstein, served as Topps's president and chief operating officer. When Topps's financial performance began to lag, the board considered selling the company. Michael Eisner (formerly head of Disney Studios) offered to pay $9.75 per share and to retain Topps's management in a merger with his company. Upper Deck Co., Topps's chief competitor in the sports-card business, offered $10.75 per share but did not offer to retain the managers. Topps demanded that Upper Deck not reveal its bid publicly, but Topps publicized the offer, without accurately representing Upper Deck's interest and disparaging its seriousness. Upper Deck asked Topps to allow it to tell its side of events and to make a tender offer to Topps's shareholders. Topps refused and scheduled a shareholder vote on the Eisner offer. Topps's shareholders filed a suit in a Delaware state court against their firm, asking the court to prevent the vote. [In re Topps Co. Shareholders Litigation, *926 A.2d 58 (Del. Ch. 2007)*]

(a) The shareholders contended that Topps's conduct had "tainted the vote." What factors support this contention? How might these factors affect the vote?

(b) Why might Topps's board and management be opposed to either of the offers for the company? Is this opposition ethical? Should the court enjoin (prevent) the scheduled vote? Explain.

LAW ON THE WEB

For updated links to resources available on the Web, as well as a variety of other materials, visit this text's Web site at

www.cengage.com/blaw/jentz

The court opinions of Delaware's Court of Chancery, which is widely considered to be the nation's premier trial court for corporate law, are available on the Web in a searchable database offered by the Delaware state courts. Go to

courts.state.de.us

Legal Research Exercises on the Web

Go to **www.cengage.com/blaw/jentz**, the Web site that accompanies this text. Select "Chapter 40" and click on "Internet Exercises." There you will find the following Internet research exercises that you can perform to learn more about the topics covered in this chapter.

Internet Exercise 40–1: Legal Perspective
Mergers

Internet Exercise 40–2: Management Perspective
Golden Parachutes

CHAPTER 41

CORPORATIONS—Securities Law and Corporate Governance

The stock market crash of October 29, 1929, and the ensuing economic depression caused the public to focus on the importance of securities markets for the economic well-being of the nation. Congress was pressured to regulate securities trading, and the result was the Securities Act of 1933[1] and the Securities Exchange Act of 1934.[2] Both acts were designed to provide investors with more information to help them make buying and selling decisions about securities—generally defined as any instruments evidencing corporate ownership (stock) or debts (bonds)—and to prohibit deceptive, unfair, and manipulative practices in the purchase and sale of securities.

This chapter discusses the nature of federal securities regulation and its effect on the business world. We begin by looking at the federal administrative agency that regulates securities transactions, the Securities and Exchange Commission. Next, we examine the major traditional laws governing securities offerings and trading. We then discuss corporate governance and the Sarbanes-Oxley Act, which significantly affects certain types of securities transactions. In the concluding pages of this chapter, we look at how securities laws are being adapted to the online environment.

1. 15 U.S.C. Sections 77a–77aa.
2. 15 U.S.C. Sections 78a–78mm.

SECTION 1 The Securities and Exchange Commission

The 1934 act created the Securities and Exchange Commission (SEC) as an independent regulatory agency that would administer the 1933 and 1934 acts. The SEC plays a key role in interpreting the provisions of these acts (and their amendments) and in creating regulations governing the purchase and sale of securities. The basic functions of the SEC are listed in Exhibit 41–1.

Organization of the SEC

The SEC's broad responsibilities are organized into four divisions—Corporate Finance, Market Regulation, Investment Management, and Enforcement. Each divi-

EXHIBIT 41–1 • Basic Functions of the Securities and Exchange Commission

1. Interprets federal securities laws and investigates securities law violations.
2. Issues new rules and amends existing rules.
3. Oversees the inspection of securities firms, brokers, investment advisers, and ratings agencies.
4. Oversees private regulatory organizations in the securities, accounting, and auditing fields.
5. Coordinates U.S. securities regulation with federal, state, and foreign authorities.

sion handles different aspects of securities regulation in coordination with the other divisions.

The Division of Corporate Finance reviews the documents that publicly held corporations are required to file with the SEC, including registration statements for new stock issues, quarterly and annual filings, and proxy materials. The Division of Market Regulation provides day-to-day oversight of the major securities market participants, including the national and regional securities exchanges and securities firms (brokers, dealers, and others). The Division of Investment Management interprets the laws affecting investment companies and supervises the activities of mutual fund companies.

The SEC is a law enforcement agency, and the Division of Enforcement carries out this function. This division investigates alleged securities law violations and recommends whether the agency should pursue civil or criminal sanctions against a violator and whether the action should be brought before an administrative law judge or in a federal court.

Updating the Regulatory Process

The SEC is working to make the regulatory process more efficient and more relevant to today's securities trading practices. To this end, the SEC has embraced modern technology and communications methods, especially the Internet, more completely than many other federal agencies have. For example, the agency now requires—not just allows—companies to file certain information electronically so that it can be posted on the SEC's EDGAR (Electronic Data Gathering, Analysis, and Retrieval) database. The EDGAR database includes material on initial public offerings (IPOs), proxy statements, corporations' annual reports, registration statements, and other documents that have been filed with the SEC. Investors can access the database via the Internet to obtain information that can be used to make investment decisions. (See the *Law on the Web* section at the end of this chapter for instructions on how to access the EDGAR database.)

In another example of how the SEC is adapting to the growing use of the Internet, in 2007 the agency issued new rules allowing companies to post their proxy materials on their Web sites rather than mailing the materials to shareholders (see the *Insight into E-Commerce* feature on pages 774 and 775 for a discussion of these new rules). Of course, the online environment can be used to perpetrate fraud as well as to disseminate information, and the SEC is taking steps to combat online securities fraud, as described later in this chapter.

SECTION 2 The Securities Act of 1933

The Securities Act of 1933 governs initial sales of stock by businesses. The act was designed to prohibit various forms of fraud and to stabilize the securities industry by requiring that investors receive financial and other significant information concerning the securities being offered for public sale. Basically, the purpose of this act is to require disclosure. The 1933 act provides that all securities transactions must be registered with the SEC unless they are specifically exempt from the registration requirements.

What Is a Security?

Section 2(1) of the Securities Act of 1933 contains a broad definition of securities, which generally include the following:[3]

1. Instruments and interests commonly known as securities, such as preferred and common stocks, treasury stocks, bonds, debentures, and stock warrants.
2. Any interests commonly known as securities, such as stock options, puts, calls, or other types of privilege on a security or on the right to purchase a security or a group of securities in a national security exchange.
3. Notes, instruments, or other evidence of indebtedness, including certificates of interest in a profit-sharing agreement and certificates of deposit.
4. Any fractional undivided interest in oil, gas, or other mineral rights.
5. Investment contracts, which include interests in limited partnerships and other investment schemes.

In interpreting the act, the United States Supreme Court has held that an **investment contract** is any transaction in which a person (1) invests (2) in a common enterprise (3) reasonably expecting profits (4) derived *primarily* or *substantially* from others' managerial or entrepreneurial efforts. Known as the *Howey* test, this definition continues to guide the determination

3. 15 U.S.C. Section 77b(1). Amendments in 1982 added stock options.

INSIGHT INTO E-COMMERCE
Moving Company Information to the Internet

Anyone who has ever owned shares in a public company knows that such companies often are required to mail voluminous paper documents that relate to proxies. As of July 1, 2007, publicly held companies can now voluntarily utilize *e-proxies.*

Notice and Access: E-Proxy Rules

New Security and Exchange Commission (SEC) rules[a] allow publicly held companies to furnish proxy materials to shareholders by posting them on a Web site and notifying the shareholders that the proxy materials are available online. This is called the "notice and access" model. (The SEC has also proposed an amendment to the proxy rules that would *require* publicly held companies to use e-proxies.)

The notice and access model involves the following steps:

1. The company posts the proxy materials on its publicly accessible Web site.
2. Subsequently, the company sends a (paper) notice to each shareholder at least forty calendar days prior to the date of the shareholders' meeting for which the proxy is being solicited.
3. No other materials can be sent along with the initial notice (unless the proxy is being combined with the meeting notice required by state law).
4. The notice must be written in plain English, and it must include a prominent statement of the following: the date, time, and location of the shareholders' meeting; the specific Web site at which shareholders can access the proxy materials; an explanation of how they can obtain paper copies of the proxy materials at no cost; and a clear and impartial description of each matter to be considered at the shareholders' meeting.
5. Next, the company must wait at least ten days before sending a "paper" proxy card to the shareholders. This ten-day waiting period provides shareholders with sufficient time to access the proxy materials online or to request paper copies.
6. If a shareholder requests paper proxy materials, the company must send them within three business days.
7. After receiving the initial paper notice, a shareholder can permanently elect to receive all future proxy materials on paper or by e-mail.

a. 17 C.F.R. Parts 240, 249, and 274.

---

of what types of contracts can be considered securities.[4]

For our purposes, it is convenient to think of securities in their most common form—stocks and bonds issued by corporations. Bear in mind, though, that securities can take many forms, including interests in whiskey, cosmetics, worms, beavers, boats, vacuum cleaners, muskrats, and cemetery lots. Almost any stake in the ownership or debt of a company can be considered a security. Investment contracts in condominiums, franchises, limited partnerships in real estate, oil or gas or other mineral rights, pay-phone programs, and farm animals accompanied by care agreements have qualified as securities.[5]

PREVENTING LEGAL DISPUTES

Businesspersons should be aware that securities are not limited to stocks and bonds but can encompass a wide variety of legal claims. The analysis hinges on the nature of the transaction rather than the instrument or substance involved. Because Congress enacted securities laws to regulate *investments,* in whatever form and by whatever name they are called, virtually any type of security that might be sold as an investment can be subject to securities laws. When in doubt about whether an investment transaction involves securities, businesspersons and managers should always seek the advice of an attorney.

Registration Statement

Section 5 of the Securities Act of 1933 broadly provides that if a security does not qualify for an exemption, that security must be *registered* before it is offered to the

4. *SEC v. W. J. Howey Co.,* 328 U.S. 293, 66 S.Ct. 1100, 90 L.Ed. 1244 (1946).
5. See, for example, *SEC v. Alpha Telcom, Inc.,* 187 F.Supp.2d 1250 (D.Or. 2002); and *SEC v. Edwards,* 540 U.S. 389, 124 S.Ct. 892, 157 L.Ed.2d 813 (2004).

Internet Postings and Blogs

Some commentators want the SEC to go even further in allowing information to be delivered online. On September 25, 2006, Jonathan Schwartz, the chief executive officer (CEO) of Sun Micosystems, Inc., sent a letter to the chair of the SEC arguing that the company should be able to use its Web site to disseminate information required by the SEC. Schwartz pointed out that Sun's Web site receives nearly one million hits per day and is a "tremendous vehicle for the broad delivery of timely and robust information." In his blog, which appears on the company's Web site, Schwartz lamented that until the SEC changed its rules, companies would still be "consuming trees with press releases."

The SEC's current rule, Regulation Fair Disclosure, or Regulation FD,[b] does not allow significant information about a publicly held corporation to be distributed on the company's Web site or in its CEO's blog. Regulation FD was created in an attempt to ensure that some investors do not have more information than the general public. Under Regulation FD, when a company gives "material nonpublic information" about its prospects to certain individuals or entities, it must disclose that information to the public. To comply with the regulation, corporate executives typically first meet with stock market analysts, either in person or by teleconference, and then hold a press conference to disseminate the information to the public. Schwartz contends that "the proliferation of the Internet supports a new policy that online communications fully satisfy Regulation FD's broad distribution requirement."[c]

So far, though, the SEC has not budged. Professor Adam Pritchard, who teaches securities law at the University of Michigan Law School, thinks that Schwartz's idea is commendable. He even suggests that a public company could just go ahead and use the corporate blog for disclosure, as nothing in the current SEC rules prohibits such use.

CRITICAL THINKING
INSIGHT INTO ENVIRONMENTAL ISSUES

Clearly, continuing to use paper proxy materials and press releases printed on paper has an impact on the environment. Even when the paper is recycled, the sludge from the ink presents a problem. What might be preventing the SEC from mandating the use of online proxy materials to prevent the waste of so much paper?

b. 17 C.F.R. Section 243.101(e)(2).

c. Schwartz's letter is posted with a short article titled "One Small Step for the Blogosphere" at **blogs.sun.com/jonathan/entry/one_small_step_for_the**.

public. Issuing corporations must file a *registration statement* with the SEC and must provide all investors with a *prospectus*. A **prospectus** is a written disclosure document that describes the security being sold, the financial operations of the issuing corporation, and the investment or risk attaching to the security. The 1933 act requires a prospectus to be delivered to investors, and issuers use this document as a selling tool. A company can also deliver a prospectus to investors electronically via the Internet.[6] In principle, the registration statement and the prospectus supply sufficient information to enable unsophisticated investors to evaluate the financial risk involved.

Contents of the Registration Statement

The registration statement must be written in plain English and fully describe the following:

1. The securities being offered for sale, including their relationship to the registrant's other capital securities.
2. The corporation's properties and business (including a financial statement certified by an independent public accounting firm).
3. The management of the corporation, including managerial compensation, stock options, pensions, and other benefits. Any interests of directors or officers in any material transactions with the corporation must be disclosed.
4. How the corporation intends to use the proceeds of the sale.
5. Any pending lawsuits or special risk factors.

All companies, both domestic and foreign, must file their registration statements electronically. As mentioned previously, electronic filing enables the SEC to include the information in its electronic database, EDGAR, so that investors can access the information via the Internet.

6. Basically, an electronic prospectus must meet the same requirements as a printed prospectus. The SEC has special rules that address situations in which the graphics, images, or audio files in a printed prospectus cannot be reproduced in an electronic form. 17 C.F.R. Section 232.304.

Registration Process The registration statement does not become effective until after it has been reviewed and approved by the SEC. The 1933 act restricts the types of activities that an issuer can engage in at each stage of the registration process. If an issuer violates the restrictions discussed here, investors can rescind their contracts to purchase the securities. During the *prefiling period* (thirty days before filing the registration statement), the issuer cannot sell or offer to sell the securities. Advertising of an upcoming securities offering is not allowed during the prefiling period.

Waiting Period. Once the registration statement has been filed, a waiting period of at least twenty days begins during which the SEC reviews the registration statement for completeness. Typically, the staff members at the SEC who review the registration statement ask the registrant to make numerous changes and additions, which can extend the length of the waiting period.[7]

During the waiting period, the securities can be offered for sale but cannot be sold by the issuing corporation. Only certain types of offers are allowed. All issuers can distribute a *preliminary prospectus,* called a **red herring prospectus.**[8] A red herring prospectus contains most of the information that will be included in the final prospectus but often does not include a price. General advertising is permitted, such as a **tombstone ad,** so named because historically the format resembled a tombstone. Such ads simply tell the investor where and how to obtain a prospectus.[9]

In 2005, the SEC, in recognition of modern communications technologies, reformed its rules to authorize the use of a *free-writing prospectus* during this period.[10] A **free-writing prospectus** is any type of written, electronic, or graphic offer that describes the issuer or its securities and includes a legend indicating that the investor may obtain the prospectus at the SEC's Web site. The issuer normally must file the free-writing prospectus with the SEC no later than the first date it is used. Certain inexperienced issuers are required to file a *preliminary prospectus* prior to the filing of a free-writing prospectus.

Posteffective Period. Once the SEC has reviewed and approved the registration statement and the twenty-day period has elapsed, the registration is effective. The issuer can now offer and sell the securities without restrictions. If the company issued a preliminary prospectus to investors, it must provide those investors with a final prospectus either prior to or at the time they purchase the securities. The issuer can require investors to download the final prospectus from a Web site, but it must notify investors of the Internet address at which they can access the prospectus.

To review the entire process, suppose that Delphia, Inc., wants to make a public offering of its common stock. The firm files a registration statement and a prospectus with the SEC. On the same day, the company can make *offers* to sell the stock and start using a free-writing prospectus, but it cannot actually sell any of its stock. Delphia and its attorneys continue to work with the SEC and provide additional information to it for nearly six months. When the SEC finally indicates that it has all the necessary information for the registration statement to be approved, Delphia can request an acceleration of the twenty-day waiting period. Only *after* the SEC declares the registration to be effective and the waiting period has elapsed or been accelerated can Delphia sell the first shares in the issue.

Exempt Securities

A number of specific securities are exempt from the registration requirements of the Securities Act of 1933. These securities—which can also generally be resold without being registered—include the following:[11]

1. Government-issued securities.
2. Bank and financial institution securities, which are regulated by banking authorities.
3. Short-term notes and drafts (negotiable instruments that have a maturity date that does not exceed nine months).
4. Securities of nonprofit, educational, and charitable organizations.

7. It is common for the SEC to require a registrant to provide additional information more than once. Only after the registration statement has gone through several rounds of changes does the SEC give its approval. In these circumstances, because the process may have taken months to complete, registrants frequently request an acceleration of the twenty-day waiting period. If the SEC grants the request, registration can become effective without the issuer having to wait the full twenty days.

8. The name *red herring* comes from the legend printed in red across the prospectus stating that the registration has been filed but has not become effective.

9. During the waiting period, the SEC also allows *road shows,* in which a corporate executive travels around speaking to institutional investors and securities analysts, as well as electronic road shows, which are viewed via real-time communications methods, such as Web casting.

10. See SEC Rules 164 and 433. Note also that companies that qualify as "well-known seasoned issuers" under the SEC's rules (large corporations with at least $700 million of value of stock in the hands of the public) can even use a free-writing prospectus during the prefiling period.

11. 15 U.S.C. Section 77c.

5. Securities issued by common carriers (railroads and trucking companies).
6. Any insurance, endowment, or annuity contract issued by a state-regulated insurance company.
7. Securities issued in a corporate reorganization in which one security is exchanged for another or in a bankruptcy proceeding.
8. Securities issued in stock dividends and stock splits.

Exhibit 41–2 summarizes the securities and the transactions (discussed next) that are exempt from the registration requirements under the Securities Act of 1933 and SEC regulations.

Exempt Transactions

In addition to the exempt securities listed in the previous subsection, certain *transactions* are exempt from registration requirements. The most important exemptions to the 1933 act are the transaction exemptions, which are very broad and can enable an issuer to avoid the high cost and complicated procedures associated with registration. Because the coverage of the exemptions overlaps somewhat, an offering may qualify for more than one. Therefore, many sales of securities occur without registration. Even when a transaction is exempt from the registration requirements, the offering is still subject to the antifraud provisions of the 1933 act (as well as those of the 1934 act, to be discussed later in this chapter).

Regulation A Offerings Securities issued by an issuer that has offered less than $5 million in securities during any twelve-month period are exempt from registration.[12] Under Regulation A,[13] the issuer must file with the SEC a notice of the issue and an offering circular, which must also be provided to investors before

12. 15 U.S.C. Section 77c(b).
13. 17 C.F.R. Sections 230.251–230.263.

EXHIBIT 41–2 • Exemptions for Securities Offerings under the 1933 Act

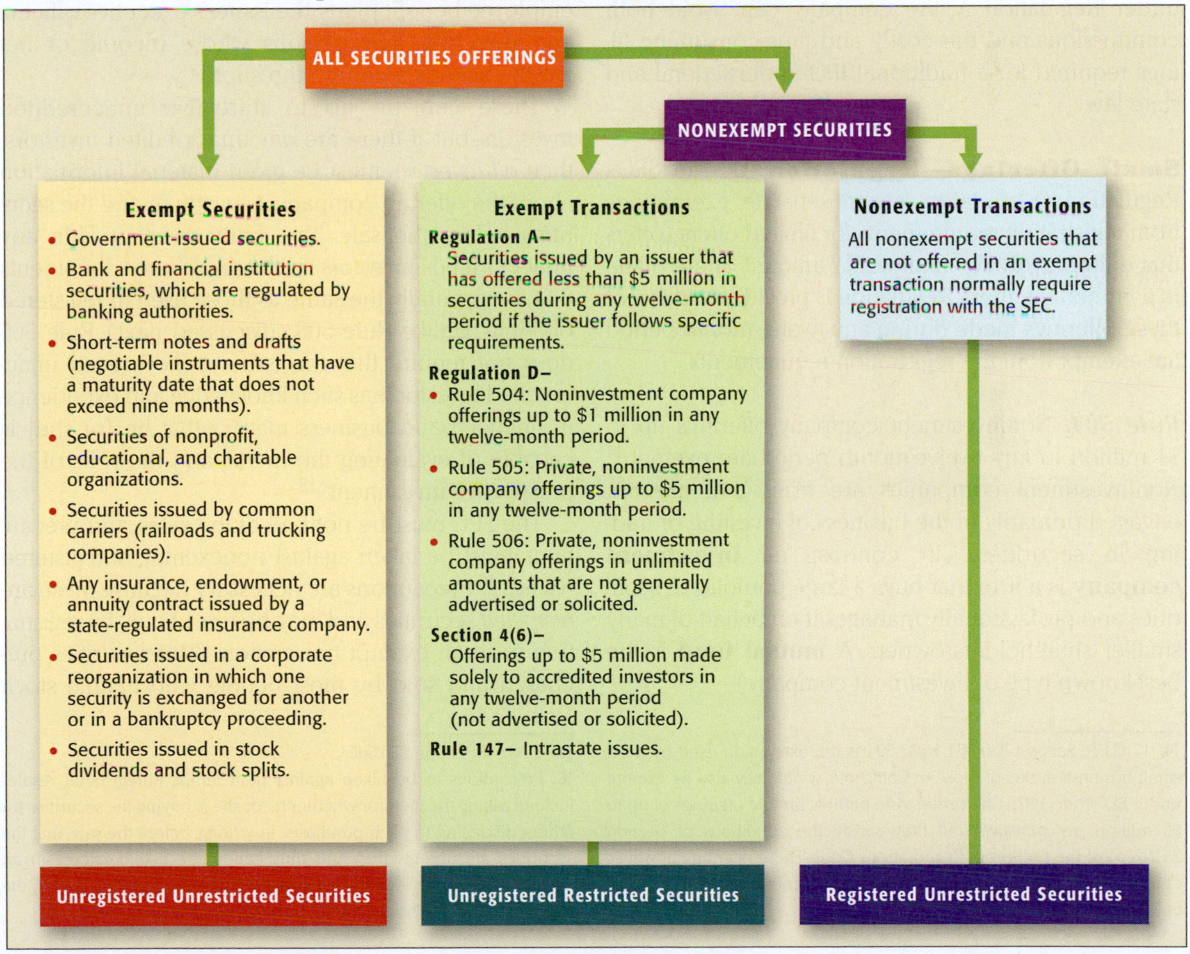
ALL SECURITIES OFFERINGS
NONEXEMPT SECURITIES
Exempt Securities
• Government-issued securities.
• Bank and financial institution securities, which are regulated by banking authorities.
• Short-term notes and drafts (negotiable instruments that have a maturity date that does not exceed nine months).
• Securities of nonprofit, educational, and charitable organizations.
• Securities issued by common carriers (railroads and trucking companies).
• Any insurance, endowment, or annuity contract issued by a state-regulated insurance company.
• Securities issued in a corporate reorganization in which one security is exchanged for another or in a bankruptcy proceeding.
• Securities issued in stock dividends and stock splits.
Exempt Transactions
Regulation A– Securities issued by an issuer that has offered less than $5 million in securities during any twelve-month period if the issuer follows specific requirements.
Regulation D–
• Rule 504: Noninvestment company offerings up to $1 million in any twelve-month period.
• Rule 505: Private, noninvestment company offerings up to $5 million in any twelve-month period.
• Rule 506: Private, noninvestment company offerings in unlimited amounts that are not generally advertised or solicited.
Section 4(6)– Offerings up to $5 million made solely to accredited investors in any twelve-month period (not advertised or solicited).
Rule 147– Intrastate issues.
Nonexempt Transactions
All nonexempt securities that are not offered in an exempt transaction normally require registration with the SEC.
Unregistered Unrestricted Securities
Unregistered Restricted Securities
Registered Unrestricted Securities

the sale. This process is much simpler and less expensive than the procedures associated with full registration. Companies are allowed to "test the waters" for potential interest before preparing the offering circular. To *test the waters* means to determine potential interest without actually selling any securities or requiring any commitment on the part of those who express interest. Small-business issuers (companies with annual revenues of less than $25 million) can also use an integrated registration and reporting system that requires simpler forms than the full registration system.

Some companies have sold their securities via the Internet using Regulation A. In 1996, the Spring Street Brewing Company became the first company to sell securities via an online initial public offering (IPO). Spring Street raised about $1.6 million—without having to pay any commissions to brokers or underwriters. Such online IPOs are particularly attractive to small companies and start-up ventures that may find it difficult to raise capital from institutional investors or through underwriters. By making the offering online under Regulation A, the company can avoid both commissions and the costly and time-consuming filings required for a traditional IPO under federal and state law.

Small Offerings—Regulation D The SEC's Regulation D contains several separate exemptions from registration requirements for limited offers (offers that either involve a small dollar amount or are made in a limited manner). Regulation D provides that any of these offerings made during any twelve-month period are exempt from the registration requirements.

Rule 504. Noninvestment company offerings up to $1 million in any twelve-month period are exempt.[14] Noninvestment companies are firms that are not engaged primarily in the business of investing or trading in securities. (In contrast, an **investment company** is a firm that buys a large portfolio of securities and professionally manages it on behalf of many smaller shareholders/owners. A **mutual fund** is the best-known type of investment company.)

For example, Beta, L.P., is a limited partnership that develops commercial property. Beta intends to offer $600,000 of its limited partnership interests for sale between June 1 and next May 31. The buyers will become limited partners in Beta. Because an interest in a limited partnership meets the definition of a security (discussed earlier in this chapter), its sale is subject to the registration and prospectus requirements of the Securities Act of 1933. Under Rule 504, however, the sales of Beta's interests are exempt from these requirements because Beta is a noninvestment company making an offering of less than $1 million in a twelve-month period. Therefore, Beta can sell its interests without filing a registration statement with the SEC or issuing a prospectus to any investor.

Rule 505. Private, noninvestment company offerings up to $5 million in any twelve-month period are exempt. Under this exemption, the offer may be made to an unlimited number of *accredited investors*. **Accredited investors** are defined to include banks, insurance companies, investment companies, employee benefit plans, the issuer's executive officers and directors, and persons whose income or net worth exceeds a certain threshold.

There can be up to thirty-five unaccredited investors, but if there are *any* unaccredited investors, then *all* investors must be given material information about the offering company, its business, and the securities before the sale. The issuer must provide any unaccredited investors with disclosure documents that are generally the same as those used in registered offerings. Unlike Rule 506 (discussed next), Rule 505 does not require that the issuer believe each unaccredited investor "has such knowledge and experience in financial and business matters that he [or she] is capable of evaluating the merits and the risks of the prospective investment."[15]

The SEC must be notified of the sales, and precautions must be taken against nonexempt, unregistered resales.[16] Precautions are necessary because these are *restricted* securities and may be resold only by registration or in an exempt transaction. (The securities purchased and sold by most people who handle stock

14. 17 C.F.R. Section 230.504. Rule 504 is the exemption used by most small businesses, except those in California, which may also be exempt under SEC Rule 1001. California's rule permits limited offerings of up to $5 million *per transaction* if they satisfy the conditions of Section 25102(n) of the California Corporations Code. These offerings, however, can be made only to "qualified purchasers" (knowledgeable, sophisticated investors).

15. 17 C.F.R. Section 230.505.

16. Precautions to be taken against nonexempt, unregistered resales include asking the investor whether he or she is buying the securities for others; disclosing to each purchaser in writing, before the sale, that the securities are unregistered and thus cannot be resold, except in an exempt transaction, without first being registered; and indicating on the certificates that the securities are unregistered and restricted.

transactions are called, in contrast, *unrestricted* securities.) The purchasers must buy for investment and may not sell the securities for at least a year. No general solicitation or advertising is allowed.

Rule 506. Private, noninvestment company offerings in unlimited amounts that are not generally solicited or advertised are exempt if the SEC is notified of the sales and precaution is taken against nonexempt, unregistered resales. As with Rule 505, there can be an unlimited number of accredited investors and up to thirty-five unaccredited investors. The issuer must provide any unaccredited investors with disclosure documents that are generally the same as those used in registered offerings. In contrast to Rule 505, the issuer must believe that each unaccredited investor has sufficient knowledge or experience in financial matters to be capable of evaluating the investment's merits and risks.[17]

This exemption is perhaps the most important one for those firms that want to raise funds through the sale of securities without registering them. It is often referred to as the *private placement* exemption because it exempts "transactions not involving any public offering."[18] This provision applies to private offerings to a limited number of persons who are sufficiently sophisticated and able to assume the risk of the investment (and who thus have no need for federal registration protection). It also applies to private offerings to similarly sophisticated institutional investors.

For example, Citco Corporation needs to raise capital to expand its operations. Citco decides to make a private $10 million offering of its common stock directly to two hundred accredited investors and a group of thirty highly sophisticated, but unaccredited, investors. Citco provides all of these investors with a prospectus and material information about the firm, including its most recent financial statements. As long as Citco notifies the SEC of the sale, this offering will likely qualify as an exempt transaction under Rule 506. The offering is nonpublic and not generally advertised. There are fewer than thirty-five unaccredited investors, and each of them possesses sufficient knowledge and experience to evaluate the risks involved. The issuer has provided all purchasers with the material information. Thus, Citco will *not* be required to comply with the registration requirements of the Securities Act of 1933.

Small Offerings—Section 4(6) Under Section 4(6) of the Securities Act of 1933, an offer made *solely* to accredited investors is exempt if it does not exceed $5 million. Any number of accredited investors may participate, but no unaccredited investors may do so. No general solicitation or advertising may be used; the SEC must be notified of all sales; and precautions must be taken against nonexempt, unregistered resales. Like other restricted securities, securities sold under Section 4(6) may be resold only by registration or in an exempt transaction.[19]

Intrastate Offerings—Rule 147 Also exempt are intrastate transactions involving purely local offerings.[20] This exemption applies to most offerings that are restricted to residents of the state in which the issuing company is organized and doing business. For nine months after the last sale, virtually no resales may be made to nonresidents, and precautions must be taken against this possibility. These offerings remain subject to applicable laws in the state of issue.

Resales Most securities can be resold without registration (although some resales may be subject to restrictions, as discussed above in connection with specific exemptions). The Securities Act of 1933 provides exemptions for resales by most persons other than issuers or underwriters. The average investor who sells shares of stock need not file a registration statement with the SEC. Resales of restricted securities acquired under Rule 505, Rule 506, or Section 4(6), however, trigger the registration requirements unless the party selling them complies with Rule 144 or Rule 144A. These rules are sometimes referred to as "safe harbors."

Rule 144. Rule 144 exempts restricted securities from registration on resale if there is adequate current public information about the issuer, the person selling the securities has owned them for at least one year, they are sold in certain limited amounts in unsolicited brokers' transactions, and the SEC is given notice of the resale.[21] "Adequate current public information" consists of the reports that certain companies are required to file under the Securities Exchange Act of 1934. A person who has owned the securities for at least two years is subject to none of these requirements, unless the person is an affiliate. An *affiliate* is one who

17. 17 C.F.R. Section 230.506.
18. 15 U.S.C. Section 77d(2).
19. 15 U.S.C. Section 77d(6).
20. 15 U.S.C. Section 77c(a)(11); 17 C.F.R. Section 230.147.
21. 17 C.F.R. Section 230.144.

controls, is controlled by, or is in common control with the issuer.

Rule 144A. Securities that at the time of issue are not of the same class as securities listed on a national securities exchange or quoted in a U.S. automated interdealer quotation system may be resold under Rule 144A.[22] They may be sold only to a qualified institutional buyer (an institution, such as an insurance company or a bank, that owns and invests at least $100 million in securities). The seller must take reasonable steps to ensure that the buyer knows that the seller is relying on the exemption under Rule 144A. A sample restricted stock certificate is shown in Exhibit 41–3.

Violations of the 1933 Act

It is a violation of the Securities Act of 1933 to intentionally defraud investors by misrepresenting or omitting facts in a registration statement or prospectus. Liability is also imposed on those who are negligent for not discovering the fraud. Selling securities before the effective date of the registration statement or under an exemption for which the securities do not qualify results in liability.

Criminal Penalties The U.S. Department of Justice brings criminal actions against those who willfully violate the 1933 act. Violators may be penalized by fines up to $10,000, imprisonment up to five years, or both.

Civil Sanctions The SEC is authorized to impose civil sanctions against those who willfully violate the 1933 act. It can request an injunction to prevent further sales of the securities involved or ask a court to grant other relief, such as ordering a violator to refund profits.

Private parties who purchase securities and suffer harm as a result of false or omitted statements or other violations may bring a suit in a federal court to recover their losses and additional damages. If a registration statement or a prospectus contains material false statements or omissions, for example, damages may be recovered from those who signed the statement or

22. 17 C.F.R. Section 230.144A.

EXHIBIT 41–3 • A Sample Restricted Stock Certificate

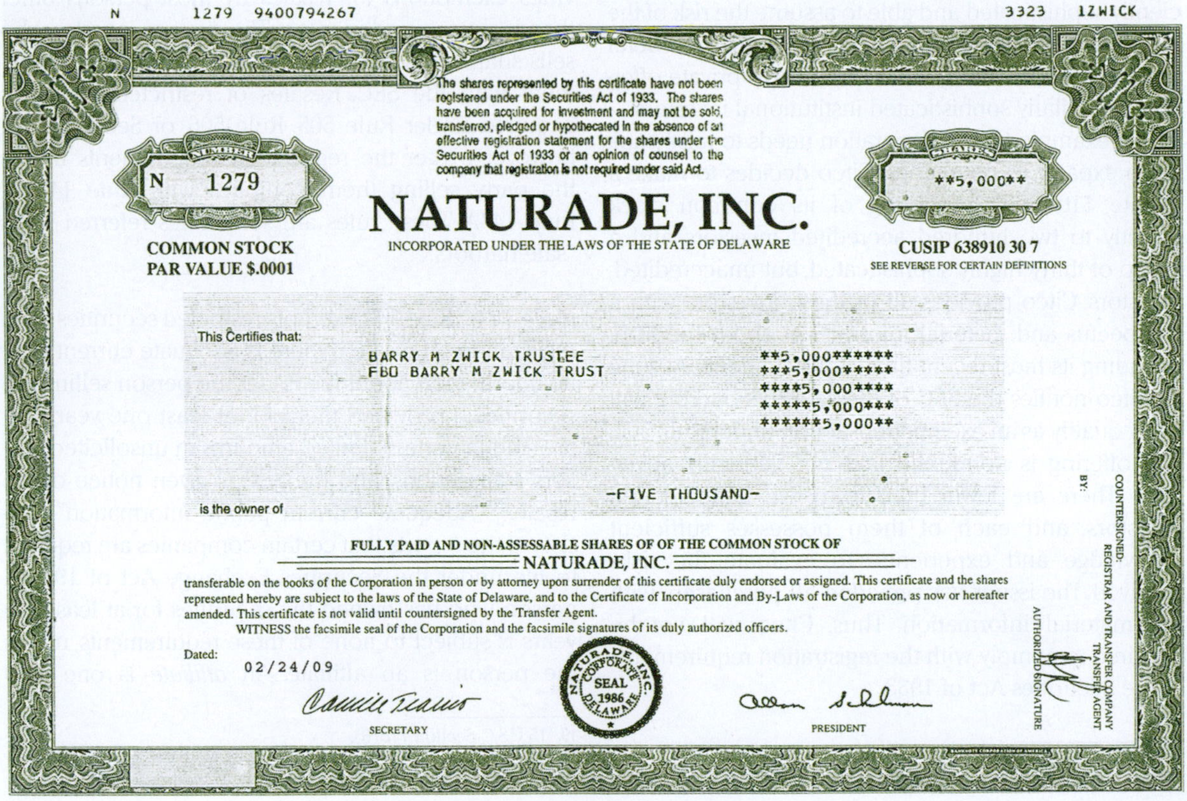
N 1279 9400794267 3323 1ZWICK

The shares represented by this certificate have not been registered under the Securities Act of 1933. The shares have been acquired for investment and may not be sold, transferred, pledged or hypothecated in the absence of an effective registration statement for the shares under the Securities Act of 1933 or an opinion of counsel to the company that registration is not required under said Act.

N 1279

5,000

NATURADE, INC.

INCORPORATED UNDER THE LAWS OF THE STATE OF DELAWARE

COMMON STOCK
PAR VALUE $.0001

CUSIP 638910 30 7
SEE REVERSE FOR CERTAIN DEFINITIONS

This Certifies that:

BARRY M ZWICK TRUSTEE
FBO BARRY M ZWICK TRUST

is the owner of

-FIVE THOUSAND-

FULLY PAID AND NON-ASSESSABLE SHARES OF OF THE COMMON STOCK OF
NATURADE, INC.

transferable on the books of the Corporation in person or by attorney upon surrender of this certificate duly endorsed or assigned. This certificate and the shares represented hereby are subject to the laws of the State of Delaware, and to the Certificate of Incorporation and By-Laws of the Corporation, as now or hereafter amended. This certificate is not valid until countersigned by the Transfer Agent.

WITNESS the facsimile seal of the Corporation and the facsimile signatures of its duly authorized officers.

Dated: 02/24/09

NATURADE, INC. CORPORATE SEAL 1986 DELAWARE

SECRETARY PRESIDENT

COUNTERSIGNED:
REGISTRAR AND TRANSFER COMPANY
TRANSFER AGENT
BY:
AUTHORIZED SIGNATURE

those who provided information used in preparing the statement (such as accountants and other experts—see Chapter 51).

Defenses There are three basic defenses to charges of violations under the 1933 act. First, even if a statement was not true or a fact was left out of the registration statement, a defendant can avoid liability if he or she can prove that the statement or omission was not material. Second, a defendant can avoid liability by proving that the plaintiff knew about the misrepresentation and bought the stock anyway.

The third and most important is the *due diligence* defense, which can be asserted by any defendant, except the issuer of the stock. This defense requires the defendant to prove that she or he reasonably believed, at the time the registration statement became effective, that the statements in it were true and there were no omissions of material facts. (This defense will be discussed further in Chapter 51, in the context of the liability of accountants.)

SECTION 3 The Securities Exchange Act of 1934

The Securities Exchange Act of 1934 provides for the regulation and registration of securities exchanges, brokers, dealers, and national securities associations, such as the National Association of Securities Dealers (NASD). Unlike the 1933 act, which is a one-time disclosure law, the 1934 act provides for continuous periodic disclosures by publicly held corporations to enable the SEC to regulate subsequent trading.

The Securities Exchange Act of 1934 applies to companies that have assets in excess of $10 million and five hundred or more shareholders. These corporations are referred to as Section 12 companies because they are required to register their securities under Section 12 of the 1934 act. Section 12 companies are required to file reports with the SEC annually and quarterly, and sometimes even monthly if specified events occur (such as a merger).

The act also authorizes the SEC to engage in market surveillance to deter undesirable market practices such as fraud, market manipulation, and misrepresentation. In addition, the act provides for the SEC's regulation of proxy solicitations for voting (discussed in Chapter 39).

Section 10(b), SEC Rule 10b-5, and Insider Trading

Section 10(b) is one of the most important sections of the Securities Exchange Act of 1934. This section prohibits the use of any manipulative or deceptive device in violation of SEC rules and regulations. Among the rules that the SEC has promulgated pursuant to the 1934 act is **SEC Rule 10b-5,** which prohibits the commission of fraud in connection with the purchase or sale of any security.

Applicability of SEC Rule 10b-5 SEC Rule 10b-5 applies in virtually all cases concerning the trading of securities, whether on organized exchanges, in over-the-counter markets, or in private transactions. The rule covers, among other things, notes, bonds, agreements to form a corporation, and joint-venture agreements. Generally, it covers just about any form of security. It is immaterial whether a firm has securities registered under the 1933 act for the 1934 act to apply.

Although SEC Rule 10b-5 is applicable only when the requisites of federal jurisdiction—such as the use of the mails, stock exchange facilities, or any instrumentality of interstate commerce—are present, virtually no commercial transaction can be completed without such contact. In addition, the states have corporate securities laws, many of which include provisions similar to SEC Rule 10b-5.

Insider Trading One of the major goals of Section 10(b) and SEC Rule 10b-5 is to prevent so-called **insider trading,** which occurs when persons buy or sell securities on the basis of information that is not available to the public. Corporate directors, officers, and others, such as majority shareholders, often have advance inside information that can affect the future market value of the corporate stock. Obviously, if they act on this information, their positions give them a trading advantage over the general public and other shareholders.

The 1934 Securities Exchange Act defines inside information and extends liability to those who take advantage of such information in their personal transactions when they know that the information is unavailable to those with whom they are dealing. Section 10(b) of the 1934 act and SEC Rule 10b-5 apply to anyone who has access to or receives information of a nonpublic nature on which trading is based—not just to corporate "insiders."

Disclosure under SEC Rule 10b-5 Any material omission or misrepresentation of material facts in connection with the purchase or sale of a security may violate Section 10(b) of the 1934 act and SEC Rule 10b-5. The key to liability (which can be civil or criminal) under this rule is whether the information omitted or misrepresented is *material.*

The following are some examples of material facts calling for disclosure under SEC Rule 10b-5:

1. Fraudulent trading in the company stock by a broker-dealer.
2. A dividend change (whether up or down).
3. A contract for the sale of corporate assets.
4. A new discovery, a new process, or a new product.
5. A significant change in the firm's financial condition.
6. Potential litigation against the company.

Note that any one of these facts, by itself, is not *automatically* considered material. Rather, it will be regarded as a material fact only if it is significant enough that it would likely affect an investor's decision as to whether to purchase or sell the company's securities. For example, Tron Corporation is involved in a product liability lawsuit. Tron's attorney, Paula Frasier, advises the firm's directors, officers, and accountants that the company likely will be required to pay damages as a result of the suit. If Tron wants to make a stock offering before the end of the trial, it must disclose its potential liability in the litigation and the financial consequences to the firm. These facts are significant enough that they would likely affect an investor's decision as to whether to purchase Tron's stock.

The case that follows is a landmark decision interpreting SEC Rule 10b-5. The SEC sued several of Texas Gulf Sulphur Company's directors, officers, and employees under SEC Rule 10b-5 after they purchased large amounts of the company's stock prior to the announcement of a rich ore discovery by the corporation. At issue was whether the ore discovery was a material fact that had to be disclosed under Rule 10b-5.

CASE 41.1 SEC v. Texas Gulf Sulphur Co.

United States Court of Appeals, Second Circuit, 1968. 401 F.2d 833.

• **Background and Facts** Texas Gulf Sulphur Company (TGS) conducted aerial geophysical surveys over more than 15,000 square miles of eastern Canada. The operations indicated concentrations of commercially exploitable minerals. At one site near Timmins, Ontario, TGS drilled a hole that appeared to yield a core with an exceedingly high mineral content. TGS kept secret the results of the core sample. Officers and employees of the company made substantial purchases of TGS's stock or accepted stock options (rights to purchase stock) after learning of the ore discovery, even though further drilling was necessary to establish whether there was enough ore to be mined commercially. Several months later, TGS announced that the strike was expected to yield at least 25 million tons of ore. Subsequently, the price of TGS stock rose substantially. The Securities and Exchange Commission (SEC) brought a suit against the officers and employees of TGS for violating SEC Rule 10b-5. The officers and employees argued that the information on which they had traded had not been material at the time of their trades because the mine had not then been commercially proved. The trial court held that most of the defendants had not violated SEC Rule 10b-5, and the SEC appealed.

• **Decision and Rationale** The U.S. Court of Appeals for the Second Circuit reversed the decision of the trial court and remanded the case. The appellate court ruled in favor of the SEC, concluding that all of the trading by insiders who knew of the mineral find before its true extent had been publicly announced violated SEC Rule 10b-5. The court held that the test of "materiality" of a fact is whether the information would affect the judgment of reasonable investors. The court stated, "A major factor in determining whether the * * * discovery was a material fact is the importance attached to the drilling results by those who knew about it. * * * The timing by those who knew of it of their stock purchases * * * virtually compels the inference that the insiders were influenced by the drilling results."

• **Impact of This Case on Today's Law** *This landmark case affirmed the principle that the test of whether information is "material," for SEC Rule 10b-5 purposes, is whether it would affect the*

CASE 41.1 CONTINUED *judgment of reasonable investors. The corporate insiders' purchases of stock and stock options indicated that they were influenced by the drilling results and that the information about the drilling results was material. The courts continue to cite this case when applying SEC Rule 10b-5 to cases of alleged insider trading.*

• **What If the Facts Were Different?** *Suppose that further drilling revealed that there was not enough ore at this site for it to be mined commercially. Would the defendants still have been liable for violating SEC Rule 10b-5? Why or why not?*

The Private Securities Litigation Reform Act of 1995 One of the unintended effects of SEC Rule 10b-5 was to deter disclosure of forward-looking information. To understand why, consider an example. A company announces that its projected earnings in a certain time period will be X amount. It turns out that the forecast is wrong. The earnings are in fact much lower, and the price of the company's stock is affected—negatively. The shareholders then bring a class-action suit against the company, alleging that the directors violated SEC Rule 10b-5 by disclosing misleading financial information.

In an attempt to rectify this problem and promote disclosure, Congress passed the Private Securities Litigation Reform Act of 1995. Among other things, the act provides a "safe harbor" for publicly held companies that make forward-looking statements, such as financial forecasts. Those who make such statements are protected against liability for securities fraud as long as the statements are accompanied by "meaningful cautionary statements identifying important factors that could cause actual results to differ materially from those in the forward-looking statement."[23]

After the 1995 act was passed, a number of class-action suits involving securities were filed in state courts to skirt the requirements of the 1995 federal act. In response to this problem, Congress passed the Securities Litigation Uniform Standards Act of 1998 (SLUSA).[24] The act placed stringent limits on the ability of plaintiffs to bring class-action suits in state courts against firms whose securities are traded on national stock exchanges.

23. 15 U.S.C. Sections 77z-2, 78u-5.

Outsiders and SEC Rule 10b-5 The traditional insider-trading case involves true insiders—corporate officers, directors, and majority shareholders who have access to (and trade on) inside information. Increasingly, however, liability under Section 10(b) of the 1934 act and SEC Rule 10b-5 has been extended to include certain "outsiders"—those who trade on inside information acquired indirectly. Two theories have been developed under which outsiders may be held liable for insider trading: the *tipper/tippee theory* and the *misappropriation theory*.

In the following case, the plaintiffs attempted to assert a third theory of liability—scheme liability—in a case argued before the United States Supreme Court. Can Section 10(b) and SEC Rule 10b-5 apply to outsiders—suppliers and customers—who seemingly "aid and abet" a scheme to "cook the books" in order to show inflated sales revenue figures for another publicly traded company? That was the main issue in the case here.

24. Pub. L. No. 105-353. This act amended many sections of Title 15 of the *United States Code*.

CASE 41.2 Stoneridge Investment Partners, LLC v. Scientific-Atlanta, Inc.

Supreme Court of the United States, 2008. ___ U.S. ___, 128 S.Ct. 761, 169 L.Ed.2d 627.
www.supremecourtus.gov/opinions/opinions.html[a]

• **Background and Facts** In 2000, the cable operator Charter Communications wanted to keep its stock price high by satisfying stock analysts' expectations about its revenue growth. When it became apparent that revenues were not growing as projected, management at Charter devised an accounting scheme that would artificially inflate its reported revenues. The scheme involved its

a. Click on "2007 Term Opinions of the Court" and scroll down to 1/15/08. Click on the case name to access the opinion.

CASE CONTINUES

CASE 41.2 CONTINUED digital cable converter (set top) box suppliers, Scientific-Atlanta and Motorola. They agreed to overcharge Charter for the cable-boxes in exchange for additional advertising on Charter's cable network. A group of investors, represented in this case by Stoneridge Investment Partners, sued Scientific-Atlanta and Motorola, alleging violation of Section 10(b) of the Securities Exchange Act of 1934 and of SEC Rule 10b-5. At trial, the district court dismissed the case. On appeal, the U.S. Court of Appeals for the Eighth Circuit upheld this ruling. Stoneridge then appealed to the United States Supreme Court.

Decision and Rationale The United States Supreme Court affirmed the federal appellate court's decision. The Court pointed out that Scientific-Atlanta and Motorola had no role in preparing or disseminating Charter's financial statements. The financial statements of both Scientific-Atlanta and Motorola were correct. The $20 per cable set top box that they received from Charter was offset by their agreeing to spend the equivalent of $20 per cable set top box in additional advertising. They "booked the transactions as a wash, under generally accepted accounting practices." To bring a Section 10(b) private action, the plaintiff must have relied upon the defendant's deceptive acts. There has to be the "requisite causal connection between a defendant's misrepresentation and a plaintiff's injury in order to access liability against the defendant." But neither Scientific-Atlanta nor Motorola had a duty to disclose because no member "of the investing public had knowledge, either actual or presumed, of [their] deceptive acts during the relevant times." As a result, Stoneridge was unable to show reliance upon any of the actions of Scientific-Atlanta and Motorola "except in an indirect chain that we find too remote for liability." Section 10(b)'s right of private action cannot be applied to a supplier or customer.

The Ethical Dimension *As suppliers to Charter, Scientific-Atlanta and Motorola engaged in an accounting fiction that, as the Court pointed out, was merely a "wash." Hence, these two companies conformed to generally accepted accounting rules. Nonetheless, was their behavior ethical? Why or why not?*

The Global Dimension *The Court noted that if it had ruled in favor of the investors bringing the suit, foreign companies might have been deterred from doing business within the United States. Explain the logic behind this line of reasoning.*

Tipper/Tippee Theory. Anyone who acquires inside information as a result of a corporate insider's breach of his or her fiduciary duty can be liable under SEC Rule 10b-5. This liability extends to **tippees** (those who receive "tips" from insiders) and even remote tippees (tippees of tippees).

The key to liability under this theory is that the inside information must be obtained as a result of someone's breach of a fiduciary duty to the corporation whose shares are traded. The tippee is liable under this theory only if (1) there is a breach of a duty not to disclose inside information, (2) the disclosure is in exchange for personal benefit, and (3) the tippee knows (or should know) of this breach and benefits from it.[25]

25. See, for example, *Chiarella v. United States*, 445 U.S. 222, 100 S.Ct. 1108, 63 L.Ed.2d 348 (1980); and *Dirks v. SEC*, 463 U.S. 646, 103 S.Ct. 3255, 77 L.Ed.2d 911 (1983).

Misappropriation Theory. Liability for insider trading may also be established under the misappropriation theory. Under this theory, an individual who wrongfully obtains (misappropriates) inside information and trades on it for her or his personal gain is held liable because the individual stole information rightfully belonging to another.

The misappropriation theory has been controversial because it significantly extends the reach of SEC Rule 10b-5 to outsiders who ordinarily would not be deemed fiduciaries of the corporations in whose stock they trade. For example, in one landmark case, James O'Hagan was a partner at the law firm of Dorsey & Whitney. A large corporation hired the firm to assist in a takeover of the Pillsbury Company. O'Hagan bought shares of Pillsbury stock. After the tender offer was announced, the stock price increased by more than 35 percent, and O'Hagan sold his shares for a profit of more than $4 million. The SEC prosecuted O'Hagan for securities fraud in violation of Rule 10b-5 under the misappropriation theory. Ultimately, the United States Supreme Court upheld O'Hagan's conviction under the misappropriation theory because he secretly converted the client-corporation's inside information for personal gain.[26]

Insider Reporting and Trading—Section 16(b) Section 16(b) of the 1934 act provides for the recapture by the corporation of all profits realized by certain insiders on any purchase and sale or sale and purchase of the corporation's stock within any six-month period. It is irrelevant whether the insider actually uses inside information; *all such short-swing profits must be returned to the corporation.* In this context, *insiders* means officers, directors, and large stockholders of Section 12 corporations (those owning 10 percent of the class of equity securities registered under Section 12 of the 1934 act).[27] To discourage such insiders from using nonpublic information about their companies to their personal benefit in the stock market, they must file reports with the SEC concerning their ownership and trading of the corporation's securities.

Section 16(b) applies not only to stock but also to warrants, options, and securities convertible into stock. In addition, the courts have fashioned complex rules for determining profits. Note that the SEC exempts a number of transactions under Rule 16b-3.[28] For all of these reasons, corporate insiders should seek the advice of competent counsel before trading in the corporation's stock. Exhibit 41–4 compares the effects of SEC Rule 10b-5 and Section 16(b).

Regulation of Proxy Statements

Section 14(a) of the Securities Exchange Act of 1934 regulates the solicitation of proxies (see Chapter 39) from shareholders of Section 12 companies. The SEC regulates the content of proxy statements. Whoever solicits a proxy must fully and accurately disclose in the proxy statement all of the facts that are pertinent to the matter on which the shareholders are to vote. SEC Rule 14a-9 is similar to the antifraud provisions of SEC Rule 10b-5. Remedies for violations are extensive,

26. *United States v. O'Hagan,* 521 U.S. 642, 117 S.Ct. 2199, 138 L.Ed.2d 724 (1997).

27. 15 U.S.C. Section 78*l*. Note that Section 403 of the Sarbanes-Oxley Act of 2002 shortened the reporting deadlines specified in Section 16(b).

28. 17 C.F.R. Section 240.16b-3.

EXHIBIT 41–4 • Comparison of Coverage, Application, and Liability under SEC Rule 10b-5 and Section 16(b)

Area of Comparison	SEC Rule 10b-5	Section 16(b)
What is the subject matter of the transaction?	Any security (does not have to be registered).	Any security (does not have to be registered).
What transactions are covered?	Purchase or sale.	Short-swing purchase and sale or short-swing sale and purchase.
Who is subject to liability?	Virtually anyone with inside information under a duty to disclose—including officers, directors, controlling shareholders, and tippees.	Officers, directors, and certain 10 percent shareholders.
Is omission or misrepresentation necessary for liability?	Yes.	No.
Are there any exempt transactions?	No.	Yes, there are a number of exemptions.
Who may bring an action?	A person transacting with an insider, the SEC, or a purchaser or seller damaged by a wrongful act.	A corporation or a shareholder by derivative action.

ranging from injunctions to prevent a vote from being taken to monetary damages.

Violations of the 1934 Act

As mentioned earlier, violations of Section 10(b) of the Securities Exchange Act of 1934 and SEC Rule 10b-5, including insider trading, may lead to both criminal and civil liability. For either criminal or civil sanctions to be imposed, however, *scienter* must exist—that is, the violator must have had an intent to defraud or knowledge of his or her misconduct (see Chapter 14). *Scienter* can be proved by showing that the defendant made false statements or wrongfully failed to disclose material facts.

Violations of Section 16(b) include the sale by insiders of stock acquired less than six months before the time of sale (or less than six months after the sale if selling short). These violations are subject to civil sanctions. Liability under Section 16(b) is strict liability. Neither *scienter* nor negligence is required.

Criminal Penalties For violations of Section 10(b) and Rule 10b-5, an individual may be fined up to $5 million, imprisoned for up to twenty years, or both. A partnership or a corporation may be fined up to $25 million. Under Section 807 of the Sarbanes-Oxley Act of 2002, for a *willful* violation of the 1934 act the violator can be imprisoned for up to twenty-five years (in addition to being subject to a fine). In a criminal prosecution under the securities laws, a jury is not allowed to speculate about whether a defendant acted willfully—the prosecution must prove beyond a reasonable doubt that the defendant knew he or she was acting wrongfully.[29]

In criminal prosecutions under Sections 10(b) and 14(a), the standard for assessing the materiality of a defendant's false statements to shareholders is the perspective of the reasonable investor. The issue in the following case was whether that standard also applies to statements in documents filed with the SEC.

29. See, for example, *United States v. Stewart*, 305 F.Supp.2d 368 (S.D.N.Y. 2004), a case involving Martha Stewart, founder of a well-known media and homemaking empire, who was later convicted on other charges.

CASE 41.3 United States v. Berger

United States Court of Appeals, Ninth Circuit, 2007. 473 F.3d 1080.

• **Background and Facts** Craig Consumer Electronics, Inc., bought car stereos, compact music centers, and small personal stereos from its offices in Hong Kong and sold the goods from its offices in California to retail stores. Richard Berger was Craig's president, chief executive officer, and board chairman. In 1994, Craig entered into a $50 million loan agreement with BT Commercial Corporation and other lenders. Under the agreement, Craig could borrow up to 85 percent of the value of its accounts receivable (the amount owed to it by retail stores) and up to 65 percent of the value of its inventory. Each business day, Craig provided the lenders with a "Borrowing Certificate" to report the amount of its accounts receivables and inventory. By early 1995, Craig lacked sufficient receivables and inventory to borrow funds for its operations. To hide these facts, Berger and others falsified the information in the certificates. They also hid Craig's true financial condition in reports filed with the Securities and Exchange Commission (SEC). In 1997, owing the banks more than $8.4 million, Craig filed for bankruptcy. Berger and others were convicted in a federal district court of, among other things, criminal violations of the Securities Exchange Act of 1934 for the false statements in the reports filed with the SEC. Berger was sentenced to six months in prison, fined $1.25 million, and ordered to pay the banks $3.14 million in restitution. Berger appealed to the U.S. Court of Appeals for the Ninth Circuit.

• **Decision and Rationale** The U.S. Court of Appeals for the Ninth Circuit held that the materiality of false statements in reports filed with the SEC "must be assessed from the perspective of the reasonable investor" and affirmed Berger's conviction and the restitution order. The court vacated the prison term and fine, however, on the ground that certain factors were omitted or mistakenly applied, and it remanded the case for reconsideration of the sentence. Berger had argued that there was an issue concerning materiality with respect to the falsehoods generated for the use of Craig's creditors in order to obtain continued funding for the business. Specifically, Berger con-

CASE 41.3 CONTINUED tended that the court "should review materiality from the perspective of the SEC" and that in this case, there was insufficient evidence that the falsehoods were material to the SEC. In other words, Berger contended that the falsehoods should not be judged from the reasonable investor's perspective, but only in the context of SEC's own regulatory decisions. The appeals court rejected this argument: "The purpose of the 1934 Act was to benefit and protect investors, with proper agency decision making as a secondary concern." Further, "materiality should be assessed from the reasonable investor's perspective."

- **The Ethical Dimension** *Assuming that Craig's default on the loan was inevitable, what did Berger do that was unethical? Explain.*

- **The Global Dimension** *Considering that Craig bought goods overseas to sell in the United States, how much blame should the court have attributed to global electronics markets for the banks' losses?*

Civil Sanctions The SEC can also bring a suit in a federal district court against anyone violating, or aiding in a violation of, the 1934 act or SEC rules by purchasing or selling a security while in the possession of material nonpublic information.[30] The violation must occur on or through the facilities of a national securities exchange or from or through a broker or dealer.[31] The court may assess as a penalty as much as triple the profits gained or the loss avoided by the guilty party. Profit or loss is defined as "the difference between the purchase or sale price of the security and the value of that security as measured by the trading price of the security at a reasonable period of time after public dissemination of the nonpublic information."[32]

The Insider Trading and Securities Fraud Enforcement Act of 1988 enlarged the class of persons who may be subject to civil liability for insider-trading violations. This act also gave the SEC authority to award **bounty payments** (rewards given by government officials for acts beneficial to the state) to persons providing information leading to the prosecution of insider-trading violations.[33]

Private parties may also sue violators of Section 10(b) and Rule 10b-5. A private party may obtain rescission (cancellation) of a contract to buy securities or damages to the extent of the violator's illegal profits. Those found liable have a right to seek contribution from those who share responsibility for the violations, including accountants, attorneys, and corporations.[34] (The liability of accountants and attorneys for violations of the securities laws is discussed in Chapter 51.) For violations of Section 16(b), a corporation can bring an action to recover the short-swing profits.

SECTION 4 Corporate Governance

Corporate governance can be narrowly defined as the relationship between a corporation and its shareholders. The international Organisation of Economic Co-operation and Development (OECD), based in France, provides a broader definition:

> Corporate governance is the system by which business corporations are directed and controlled. The corporate governance structure specifies the distribution of rights and responsibilities among different participants in the corporation, such as the board of directors, managers, shareholders, and other stakeholders, and spells out the rules and procedures for making decisions on corporate affairs.[35]

Although this definition has no legal value, it does set the tone for the ways in which modern corporations should be governed. In other words, effective corporate governance requires more than compliance with laws and regulations.

30. 15 U.S.C. Section 78u(d)(2)(A).

31. Transactions pursuant to a public offering by an issuer of securities are excepted.

32. 15 U.S.C. Section 78u(d)(2)(C).

33. 15 U.S.C. Section 78u-1.

34. The Supreme Court has held that a private cause of action under Section 10(b) and SEC Rule 10b-5 cannot be brought against accountants, attorneys, and others who "aid and abet" violations of the act. Only the SEC can bring actions against so-called aiders and abettors. *Central Bank of Denver, N.A. v. First Interstate Bank of Denver, N.A.*, 511 U.S. 164, 114 S.Ct. 1439, 128 L.Ed.2d 119 (1994).

35. *Governance in the 21st Century: Future Studies* (OECD, 2001).

The Need for Effective Corporate Governance

The need for effective corporate governance arises in large corporations because corporate ownership (by shareholders) is separated from corporate control (by officers and managers). In the real world, officers and managers are tempted to advance their own interests, even when such interests conflict with those of the shareholders. The collapse of Enron Corporation and other well-publicized scandals in the corporate world in the early 2000s provide a clear illustration of the reasons for concern about managerial opportunism.

Attempts at Aligning the Interests of Officers with Those of Shareholders

Some corporations have sought to align the financial interests of their officers with those of the company's shareholders by providing the officers with **stock options,** which enable them to purchase shares of the corporation's stock at a set price. When the market price rises above that level, the officers can sell their shares for a profit. Because a stock's market price generally increases as the corporation prospers, the options give the officers a financial stake in the corporation's well-being and supposedly encourage them to work hard for the benefit of the shareholders.

Options have turned out to be an imperfect device for providing effective governance, however. Executives in some companies have been tempted to "cook" the company's books in order to keep share prices high so that they could sell their stock for a profit. Executives in other corporations have experienced no losses when share prices dropped; instead, their options were "repriced" so that they did not suffer from the share price decline and could still profit from future increases above the lowered share price. Thus, although stock options theoretically can motivate officers to protect shareholder interests, stock option plans have sometimes become a way for officers to take advantage of shareholders.

With stock options generally failing to work as planned and numerous headline-making scandals occurring within major corporations, there has been an outcry for more "outside" directors (see Chapter 39). The theory is that outside, independent directors will more closely monitor the actions of corporate officers. Hence, today we see more boards with outside directors. Note, though, that outside directors may not be truly independent of corporate officers; they may be friends or business associates of the leading officers. A study of board appointments found that the best way to increase one's probability of appointment was to "suck up" to the chief executive officer.[36]

Corporate Governance and Corporate Law

Effective corporate governance standards are designed to address problems (such as those briefly discussed above) and to motivate officers to make decisions to promote the financial interests of the company's shareholders. Generally, corporate governance entails corporate decision-making structures that monitor employees (particularly officers) to ensure that they are acting for the benefit of the shareholders. Thus, corporate governance involves, at a minimum:

1. The audited reporting of financial conditions at the corporation so that managers can be evaluated.
2. Legal protections for shareholders so that violators of the law, who attempt to take advantage of shareholders, can be punished for misbehavior and victims may recover damages for any associated losses.

The Practical Significance of Effective Corporate Governance Effective corporate governance may have considerable practical significance. A study by researchers at Harvard University and the Wharton School of Business found that firms providing greater shareholder rights had higher profits, higher sales growth, higher firm value, and other economic advantages.[37] Better corporate governance in the form of greater accountability to investors may therefore offer the opportunity to enhance institutional wealth considerably.

Governance and Corporation Law Corporate governance is the essential purpose of corporation law in the United States. These statutes set up the legal framework for corporate governance. Under the corporate law of Delaware, where most major companies incorporate, all corporations must have in place certain structures of corporate governance. The key structure of corporate law is, of course, the board of directors. Directors make the most important decisions about the future of the corporation and monitor

36. Jennifer Reingold, "Suck Up and Move Fast," *Fast Company*, January 2005, p. 34.

37. Paul A. Gompers, Joy L. Ishii, and Andrew Metrick, "Corporate Governance and Equity Prices," *Quarterly Journal of Economics*, Vol. 118 (2003), p. 107.

the actions of corporate officers. Directors are elected by shareholders to look out for their best interests.

The Board of Directors Some argue that shareholder democracy is key to improving corporate governance. If shareholders could vote on major corporate decisions, shareholders could presumably have more control over the corporation. Essential to shareholder democracy is the concept of electing the board of directors, usually at the corporation's annual meeting. Under corporate law, a corporation must have a board of directors elected by the shareholders. Virtually anyone can become a director, though some organizations, such as the New York Stock Exchange, require certain standards of service for directors of their listed corporations.

Directors have the responsibility of ensuring that officers are operating wisely and in the exclusive interest of shareholders. Directors receive reports from the officers and give them managerial directions. The board in theory controls the compensation of officers (presumably tied to performance). The reality, though, is that corporate directors devote a relatively small amount of time to monitoring officers.

Ideally, shareholders would monitor the directors' supervision of officers. As one leading board monitor commented, "Boards of directors are like subatomic particles—they behave differently when they are observed." Consequently, monitoring directors, and holding them responsible for corporate failings, can induce the directors to do a better job of monitoring officers and ensuring that the company is being managed in the interest of shareholders. Although the directors can be sued for failing to do their jobs effectively, directors are rarely held personally liable.

Importance of the Audit Committee As mentioned in Chapter 39, the board of directors normally creates an *audit committee* (and it is required for publicly held corporations). The audit committee plays a crucial role in overseeing the corporation's accounting and financial reporting processes, including both internal and outside auditors. Unless the committee members have sufficient expertise and are willing to spend the time to carefully examine the corporation's bookkeeping methods, however, the audit committee may be ineffective.

The audit committee also oversees the corporation's "internal controls." These are the measures taken—largely by the company's internal auditing staff—to ensure that reported results are accurate. For example, these controls help to determine whether a corporation's debts are collectible. If the debts are not collectible, it is up to the audit committee to make sure that the corporation's financial officers do not simply pretend that payment will eventually be made.

The Role of the Compensation Committee Another important committee mentioned in Chapter 39 is the *compensation committee,* which determines the compensation to be paid to the company's officers. As part of this process, the committee is responsible for assessing the officers' performance and for designing a compensation system that will better align the officers' interests with those of the shareholders.

The Sarbanes-Oxley Act of 2002

As discussed in Chapter 5, in 2002, following a series of corporate scandals, Congress passed the Sarbanes-Oxley Act (see Appendix H for excerpts and explanatory comments). Generally, the act attempts to increase corporate accountability by imposing strict disclosure requirements and harsh penalties for violations of securities laws. Among other things, the act requires chief corporate executives to take personal responsibility for the accuracy of financial statements and reports that are filed with the SEC.

Additionally, certain financial and stock-transaction reports must now be filed with the SEC earlier than was required under the previous rules. The act also created a new entity, called the Public Company Accounting Oversight Board, that regulates and oversees public accounting firms. Other provisions of the act created new private civil actions and expanded the SEC's remedies in administrative and civil actions.

Because of the importance of this act, we present some of its key provisions relating to corporate accountability in Exhibit 41–5 on the next page. (Provisions of the act that relate to public accounting firms and accounting practices will be discussed in Chapter 51, in the context of the liability of accountants.)

More Internal Controls and Accountability The Sarbanes-Oxley Act includes some traditional securities law provisions but also introduces direct *federal* corporate governance requirements for public companies (companies whose shares are traded in the public securities markets). The law addresses many of the corporate governance procedures just discussed and creates new requirements in an attempt to make the system work more effectively. The

EXHIBIT 41–5 • Some Key Provisions of the Sarbanes-Oxley Act of 2002 Relating to Corporate Accountability

Certification Requirements—Under Section 906 of the Sarbanes-Oxley Act, the chief executive officers (CEOs) and chief financial officers (CFOs) of most major companies listed on public stock exchanges must now certify financial statements that are filed with the SEC. For virtually all filed financial reports, CEOs and CFOs have to certify that such reports "fully comply" with SEC requirements and that all of the information reported "fairly represents, in all material respects, the financial conditions and results of operations of the issuer."

Under Section 302 of the act, for each quarterly and annual filing with the SEC, CEOs and CFOs of reporting companies are required to certify that a signing officer reviewed the report and that it contains no untrue statements of material fact. Also, the signing officer or officers must certify that they have established an internal control system to identify all material information and that any deficiencies in the system were disclosed to the auditors.

Loans to Directors and Officers—Section 402 prohibits any reporting company, as well as any private company that is filing an initial public offering, from making personal loans to directors and executive officers (with a few limited exceptions, such as for certain consumer and housing loans).

Protection for Whistleblowers—Section 806 protects *whistleblowers*—those employees who report ("blow the whistle" on) securities violations by their employers—from being fired or in any way discriminated against by their employers.

Blackout Periods—Section 306 prohibits certain types of securities transactions during *blackout periods*—periods during which the issuer's ability to purchase, sell, or otherwise transfer funds in individual account plans (such as pension funds) is suspended.

Enhanced Penalties for—

- *Violations of Section 906 Certification Requirements*—A CEO or CFO who certifies a financial report or statement filed with the SEC knowing that the report or statement does not fulfill all of the requirements of Section 906 will be subject to criminal penalties of up to $1 million in fines, ten years in prison, or both. *Willful* violators of the certification requirements may be subject to $5 million in fines, twenty years in prison, or both.
- *Violations of the Securities Exchange Act of 1934*—Penalties for securities fraud under the 1934 act were also increased (as discussed earlier in this chapter). Individual violators may be fined up to $5 million, imprisoned for up to twenty years, or both. *Willful* violators may be imprisoned for up to twenty-five years in addition to being fined.
- *Destruction or Alteration of Documents*—Anyone who alters, destroys, or conceals documents or otherwise obstructs any official proceeding will be subject to fines, imprisonment for up to twenty years, or both.
- *Other Forms of White-Collar Crime*—The act stiffened the penalties for certain criminal violations, such as federal mail and wire fraud, and ordered the U.S. Sentencing Commission to revise the sentencing guidelines for white-collar crimes (see Chapter 9).

Statute of Limitations for Securities Fraud—Section 804 provides that a private right of action for securities fraud may be brought no later than two years after the discovery of the violation or five years after the violation, whichever is earlier.

requirements deal with independent monitoring of company officers by both the board of directors and auditors.

Sections 302 and 404 of the act require high-level managers (the most senior officers) to establish and maintain an effective system of internal controls. Moreover, senior management must reassess the system's effectiveness on an annual basis. Some companies already had strong and effective internal control systems in place before the passage of the act, but others had to take expensive steps to bring their internal controls up to the new federal standard. These include "disclosure controls and procedures" to ensure that company financial reports are accurate and timely. Assessment must involve documenting financial results and accounting policies before reporting the results. By the beginning of 2008, hundreds of listed publicly held companies had reported that they had identified and corrected shortcomings in their internal control systems.

Certification and Monitoring As described in Exhibit 41–5, Section 906 requires that chief executive officers and chief financial officers certify the accuracy of the information in the corporate financial statements. These corporate officers are subject to both civil and criminal penalties for violations of this section. This requirement makes the officers directly accountable for the accuracy of their financial reporting and precludes any "ignorance defense" if shortcomings are later discovered.

Another requirement is to improve directors' monitoring of officers' activities. All members of the corporate audit committee for public companies must be outside directors. The New York Stock Exchange has a similar rule that also extends to the board's compensation committee. The audit committee must have a written charter that sets out its duties and provides for performance appraisal. At least one "financial expert" must serve on the audit committee, which must hold executive meetings without company officers being present. The audit committee must also establish procedures to encourage *whistleblowers* (see Chapter 33) to report violations. In addition to reviewing the internal controls, the committee also monitors the actions of the outside auditor.

SECTION 5 State Securities Laws

Today, all states have their own corporate securities laws, or **blue sky laws,** that regulate the offer and sale of securities within individual state borders. (The phrase *blue sky laws* dates to a 1917 United States Supreme Court decision in which the Court declared that the purpose of such laws was to prevent "speculative schemes which have no more basis than so many feet of 'blue sky.'"[38]) Article 8 of the Uniform Commercial Code, which has been adopted by all of the states, also imposes various requirements relating to the purchase and sale of securities.

Requirements under State Securities Laws

Despite some differences in philosophy, all state blue sky laws have certain features. Typically, state laws have disclosure requirements and antifraud provisions, many of which are patterned after Section 10(b) of the Securities Exchange Act of 1934 and SEC Rule 10b-5. State laws also provide for the registration or qualification of securities offered or issued for sale within the state and impose disclosure requirements. Unless an exemption from registration is applicable, issuers must register or qualify their stock with the appropriate state official, often called a *corporations commissioner.* Additionally, most state securities laws regulate securities brokers and dealers.

Concurrent Regulation

State securities laws apply mainly to intrastate transactions. Since the adoption of the 1933 and 1934 federal securities acts, the state and federal governments have regulated securities concurrently. Issuers must comply with both federal and state securities laws, and exemptions from federal law are not necessarily exemptions from state laws.

The dual federal and state system has not always worked well, particularly during the early 1990s, when there was considerable expansion of the securities markets. In response, Congress passed the National Securities Markets Improvement Act of 1996, which preempted state power to regulate many aspects of securities. The National Conference of Commissioners on Uniform State Laws then substantially revised the Uniform Securities Act and recommended it to the states for adoption in 2002. Unlike the previous version of this law, the new act is designed to coordinate state and federal securities regulation and enforcement efforts. Since 2002, thirteen states have adopted the Uniform Securities Act, and several other states are considering adoption.[39]

SECTION 6 Online Securities Fraud

A major problem facing the SEC today is how to enforce the antifraud provisions of the securities laws in the online environment. In 1999, in the first cases involving illegal online securities offerings, the SEC filed suit against three individuals for illegally offering securities on an Internet auction site.[40] In essence, all three indicated that their companies would soon go public and attempted to sell unregistered securities via

38. *Hall v. Geiger-Jones Co.,* 242 U.S. 539, 37 S.Ct. 217, 61 L.Ed. 480 (1917).

39. At the time this book went to press, the 2002 version of the Uniform Securities Act had been adopted in Hawaii, Idaho, Indiana, Iowa, Kansas, Maine, Michigan, Minnesota, Missouri, Oklahoma, South Carolina, South Dakota, and Vermont, as well as in the U.S. Virgin Islands. Adoption legislation was pending in the District of Columbia and Washington. You can find current information on state adoptions at **www.nccusl.org**.

40. *In re Davis,* SEC Administrative File No. 3-10080 (October 20, 1999); *In re Haas,* SEC Administrative File No. 3-10081 (October 20, 1999); and *In re Sitaras,* SEC Administrative File No. 3-10082 (October 20, 1999).

the Web auction site. All of these actions were in violation of Sections 5, 17(a)(1), and 17(a)(3) of the 1933 Securities Act. Since then, the SEC has brought a variety of Internet-related fraud cases, including cases involving investment scams and the manipulation of stock prices in Internet chat rooms. The SEC regularly issues interpretive releases to explain how securities laws apply in the online environment and revises its rules to address new issues that arise in the Internet context.

Investment Scams

An ongoing concern for the SEC is how to curb investment scams. One fraudulent investment scheme involved twenty thousand investors, who lost, in all, more than $3 million. Some cases have involved false claims about the earnings potential of home businesses, such as the claim that one could "earn $4,000 or more each month." Others have concerned claims of "guaranteed credit repair."

Using Chat Rooms to Manipulate Stock Prices

"Pumping and dumping" occurs when a person who has purchased a particular stock heavily promotes ("pumps up") that stock—thereby creating a great demand for it and driving up its price—and then sells ("dumps") it. The practice of pumping up a stock and then dumping it is quite old. In the online world, however, the process can occur much more quickly and efficiently.

A famous example in this area involved Jonathan Lebed, a fifteen-year-old from New Jersey, who became the first minor ever charged with securities fraud by the SEC. The SEC charged that Lebed bought thinly traded stocks. After purchasing a stock, he would flood stock-related chat rooms with messages touting the stock's virtues. He used numerous false names so that no one would know that a single person was posting the messages. He would say that the stock was the most "undervalued stock in history" and that its price would jump by 1,000 percent "very soon." When other investors bought the stock, the price would go up quickly, and Lebed would sell out. The SEC forced the teenager to repay almost $300,000 in gains plus interest but allowed him to keep about $500,000 of his profits.

The SEC has been bringing an increasing number of cases against those who manipulate stock prices in this way. Many of these online investment scams are perpetrated through mass e-mails (spam) and online newsletters, as well as chat rooms.

Hacking into Online Stock Accounts

The last few years have seen the emergence of a new form of "pumping and dumping" stock that involves hackers who break into existing online stock accounts and make unauthorized transfers. Millions of people now buy and sell investments online through online brokerage companies such as E*Trade and Ameritrade. Sophisticated hackers have learned to use online investing to their advantage.

By installing keystroke-monitoring software on computer terminals in public places, such as hotels, libraries, and airports, hackers can gain access to online account information. They simply wait for a person to access an online trading account and then monitor the next several dozen keystrokes to determine the customer's account number and password. Once they have the log-in information, they can access the customer's account and liquidate her or his existing stock holdings. The hackers then use the customer's funds to purchase thinly traded, microcap securities, also known as penny stocks. The goal is to boost the price of a stock that the hacker has already purchased at a lower price. Then, when the stock price goes up, the hacker sells all the stock and wires the funds to either an offshore account or a dummy corporation, making it difficult for the SEC to trace the transactions and prosecute the offender.

For example, Aleksey Kamardin, a twenty-one-year-old Florida student, purchased 55,000 shares of stock in Fuego Entertainment using an E*Trade account in his own name. Kamardin then hacked into other customers' accounts at E*Trade, Ameritrade, Schwab, and other brokerage companies, and used their funds to purchase a total of 458,000 shares of Fuego stock. When the stock price rose from $.88 per share to $1.28 per share, Kamardin sold all of his shares of Fuego, making a profit of $9,164.28 in about three hours. Kamardin did this with other thinly traded stocks as well, allegedly making $82,960 in about five weeks and prompting the SEC to file charges against him in January 2007.[41]

So far, the brokerage companies have been covering their customers' losses from this new wave of frauds, but the potential for loss is substantial. E*Trade and Ameritrade have also increased security measures and are changing their software to prevent further intrusions into customers' online stock accounts.

41. You can read the SEC's complaint against Kamardin by going to the SEC's Web site at **www.sec.gov**, clicking on the link to litigation releases, and selecting LR-19981. The case had not been resolved by the time this book went to press.

REVIEWING CORPORATIONS—Securities Law and Corporate Governance

Dale Emerson served as the chief financial officer for Reliant Electric Company, a distributor of electricity serving portions of Montana and North Dakota. Reliant was in the final stages of planning a takeover of Dakota Gasworks, Inc., a natural gas distributor that operated solely within North Dakota. Emerson went on a weekend fishing trip with his uncle, Ernest Wallace. Emerson mentioned to Wallace that he had been putting in a lot of extra hours at the office planning a takeover of Dakota Gasworks. On returning from the fishing trip, Wallace met with a broker from Chambers Investments and purchased $20,000 of Reliant stock. Three weeks later, Reliant made a tender offer to Dakota Gasworks stockholders and purchased 57 percent of Dakota Gasworks stock. Over the next two weeks, the price of Reliant stock rose 72 percent before leveling out. Wallace then sold his Reliant stock for a gross profit of $14,400. Using the information presented in the chapter, answer the following questions.

1. Would registration with the SEC be required for Dakota Gasworks securities? Why or why not?
2. Did Emerson violate Section 10(b) of the Securities Exchange Act of 1934 and SEC Rule 10b-5? Why or why not?
3. What theory or theories might a court use to hold Wallace liable for insider trading?
4. Under the Sarbanes-Oxley Act of 2002, who would be required to certify the accuracy of the financial statements Reliant filed with the SEC?

TERMS AND CONCEPTS

accredited investor 778
blue sky laws 791
bounty payment 787
corporate governance 787
free-writing prospectus 776
insider trading 781
investment company 778
investment contract 773
mutual fund 778
prospectus 775
red herring prospectus 776
SEC Rule 10b-5 781
stock options 788
tippee 784
tombstone ad 776

QUESTIONS AND CASE PROBLEMS

41-1. Estrada Hermanos, Inc., a corporation incorporated and doing business in Florida, decides to sell $1 million worth of its common stock to the public. The stock will be sold only within the state of Florida. José Estrada, the chair of the board, says the offering need not be registered with the Securities and Exchange Commission. His brother, Gustavo, disagrees. Who is right? Explain.

41-2. QUESTION WITH SAMPLE ANSWER

Huron Corp. has 300,000 common shares outstanding. The owners of these outstanding shares live in several different states. Huron has decided to split the 300,000 shares two for one. Will Huron Corp. have to file a registration statement and prospectus on the 300,000 new shares to be issued as a result of the split? Explain.

- **For a sample answer to Question 41-2, go to Appendix I at the end of this text.**

41-3. Violations of the 1934 Act. 2TheMart.com, Inc., was conceived in January 1999 to launch an auction Web site to compete with eBay, Inc. On January 19, 2TheMart announced that its Web site was in its "final development" stages and expected to be active by the end of July as a "preeminent" auction site, and that the company had "retained the services of leading Web site design and architecture consultants to design and construct" the site.

Based on the announcement, investors rushed to buy 2TheMart's stock, causing a rapid increase in the price. On February 3, 2TheMart entered into an agreement with IBM to take preliminary steps to plan the site. Three weeks later, 2TheMart announced that the site was "currently in final development." On June 1, 2TheMart signed a contract with IBM to design, build, and test the site, with a target delivery date of October 8. When 2TheMart's site did not debut as announced, Mary Harrington and others who had bought the stock filed a suit in a federal district court against the firm's officers, alleging violations of the Securities Exchange Act of 1934. The defendants responded, in part, that any alleged misrepresentations were not material and asked the court to dismiss the suit. How should the court rule, and why? [*In re 2TheMart.com, Inc. Securities Litigation,* 114 F.Supp.2d 955 (C.D.Cal. 2000)]

41–4. Insider Reporting and Trading. Ronald Bleakney, an officer at Natural Microsystems Corp. (NMC), a Section 12 corporation, directed NMC sales in North America, South America, and Europe. In November 1998, Bleakney sold more than 7,500 shares of NMC stock. The following March, Bleakney resigned from the firm, and the next month, he bought more than 20,000 shares of its stock. NMC provided some guidance to employees concerning the rules of insider trading, and with regard to Bleakney's transactions, the corporation said nothing about potential liability. Richard Morales, an NMC shareholder, filed a suit against NMC and Bleakney to compel recovery, under Section 16(b) of the Securities Exchange Act of 1934, of Bleakney's profits from the purchase and sale of his shares. (When Morales died, his executor, Deborah Donoghue, became the plaintiff.) Bleakney argued that he should not be liable because he relied on NMC's advice. Should the court order Bleakney to return his profits to the corporation? Explain. [*Donoghue v. Natural Microsystems Corp.,* 198 F.Supp.2d 487 (S.D.N.Y. 2002)]

41–5. CASE PROBLEM WITH SAMPLE ANSWER

Scott Ginsburg was chief executive officer (CEO) of Evergreen Media Corp., which owned and operated radio stations. In 1996, Evergreen became interested in acquiring EZ Communications, Inc., which also owned radio stations. To initiate negotiations, Ginsburg met with EZ's CEO, Alan Box, on Friday, July 12. Two days later, Scott phoned his brother Mark, who, on Monday, bought 3,800 shares of EZ stock. Mark discussed the deal with their father Jordan, who bought 20,000 EZ shares on Thursday. On July 25, the day before the EZ bid was due, Scott phoned his parents' home, and Mark bought another 3,200 EZ shares. The same routine was followed over the next few days, with Scott periodically phoning Mark or Jordan, both of whom continued to buy EZ shares. Evergreen's bid was refused, but on August 5, EZ announced its merger with another company. The price of EZ stock rose 30 percent, increasing the value of Mark's and Jordan's shares by $664,024 and $412,875, respectively. The Securities and Exchange Commission (SEC) filed a civil suit in a federal district court against Scott. What was the most likely allegation? What is required to impose sanctions for this offense? Should the court hold Scott liable? Why or why not? [*SEC v. Ginsburg,* 362 F.3d 1292 (11th Cir. 2004)]

- **To view a sample answer for Problem 41–5, go to this book's Web site at www.cengage.com/blaw/jentz, select "Chapter 41," and click on "Case Problem with Sample Answer."**

41–6. Securities Laws. In 1997, WTS Transnational, Inc., required financing to develop a prototype of an unpatented fingerprint-verification system. At the time, WTS had no revenue, $655,000 in liabilities, and only $10,000 in assets. Thomas Cavanagh and Frank Nicolois, who operated an investment banking company called U.S. Milestone (USM), arranged the financing using Curbstone Acquisition Corp. Curbstone had no assets but had registered approximately 3.5 million shares of stock with the Securities and Exchange Commission (SEC). Under the terms of the deal, Curbstone acquired WTS, and the resulting entity was named Electro-Optical Systems Corp. (EOSC). New EOSC shares were issued to all of the WTS shareholders. Only Cavanagh and others affiliated with USM could sell EOSC stock to the public, however. Over the next few months, these individuals issued false press releases, made small deceptive purchases of EOSC shares at high prices, distributed hundreds of thousands of shares to friends and relatives, and sold their own shares at inflated prices through third party companies they owned. When the SEC began to investigate, the share price fell to its actual value, and innocent investors lost more than $15 million. Were any securities laws violated in this case? If so, what might be an appropriate remedy? [*SEC v. Cavanagh,* 445 F.3d 105 (2d Cir. 2006)]

41–7. Securities Trading. Between 1994 and 1998, Richard Svoboda, a credit officer for NationsBank N.A., in Dallas, Texas, evaluated and approved his employer's extensions of credit to clients. These responsibilities gave Svoboda access to nonpublic information about the clients' earnings, performance, acquisitions, and business plans in confidential memos, e-mail, credit applications, and other sources. Svoboda devised a scheme with Michael Robles, an independent accountant, to use this information to trade securities. Pursuant to their scheme, Robles traded in the securities of more than twenty different companies and profited by more than $1 million. Despite their agreement that Robles would do all of the trading, Svoboda also executed trades on his own and made profits of more than $200,000. Aware that their scheme violated NationsBank's policy, they attempted to conduct their trades so as to avoid suspicion. When NationsBank questioned Svoboda about his actions, he lied, refused to cooperate, and was fired. Did Svoboda or Robles commit any crimes? Are they subject to civil liability? If so, who could file a suit and on what ground? What are the possible sanctions? What might be a defense? How should a court rule? Discuss. [*SEC v. Svoboda,* 409 F.Supp.2d 331 (S.D.N.Y. 2006)]

41–8. A QUESTION OF ETHICS

*Melvin Lyttle told John Montana and Paul Knight about a "Trading Program" that purportedly would buy and sell securities in deals that were fully insured, as well as monitored and controlled by the Federal Reserve. Without checking the details or even verifying whether the Program existed, Montana and Knight, with Lyttle's help, began to sell interests in the Program to investors. For a minimum investment of $1 million, the investors were promised extraordinary rates of return—from 10 percent to as much as 100 percent per week—without risk. They were told, among other things, that the Program would "utilize banks that can ensure full bank integrity of The Transaction whose undertaking[s] are in complete harmony with international banking rules and protocol and who guarantee maximum security of a Funder's Capital Placement Amount." Nothing was required but the investors' funds and their silence—the Program was to be kept secret. Over a four-month period in 1999, Montana raised approximately $23 million from twenty-two investors. The promised gains did not accrue, however. Instead, Montana, Lyttle, and Knight depleted investors' funds in high-risk trades or spent the funds on themselves. [*SEC v. Montana, *464 F.Supp.2d 772 (S.D.Ind. 2006)]*

(a) The Securities and Exchange Commission (SEC) filed a suit in a federal district court against Montana and the others, seeking an injunction, civil penalties, and refund of profits with interest. The SEC alleged, among other things, violations of Section 10(b) of the Securities Exchange Act of 1934 and SEC Rule 10b-5. What is required to establish such violations? Describe how and why the facts in this case meet, or fail to meet, these requirements.

(b) It is often remarked, "There's a sucker born every minute!" Does that phrase describe the Program's investors? Ultimately, about half of the investors recouped the amount they invested. Should the others be considered at least partly responsible for their own losses? Why or why not?

41–9. VIDEO QUESTION

Go to this text's Web site at **www.cengage.com/blaw/jentz** and select "Chapter 41." Click on "Video Questions" and view the video titled *Mergers and Acquisitions.* Then answer the following questions.

(a) Was the purchase of Onyx Advertising a material fact that the Quigley Co. had a duty to disclose under SEC Rule 10b-5? Why or why not?

(b) Does it matter whether Quigley knew about or authorized the company spokesperson's statements? Why or why not?

(c) Which case discussed in the chapter presented issues that are very similar to those presented in the video? Under the holding of that case, would Onyx Advertising be able to maintain a suit against the Quigley Co. for violation of SEC Rule 10b-5?

(d) Who else might be able to bring a suit against the Quigley Co. for insider trading under SEC Rule 10b-5?

LAW ON THE WEB

For updated links to resources available on the Web, as well as a variety of other materials, visit this text's Web site at

www.cengage.com/blaw/jentz

To access the SEC's EDGAR database, go to

www.sec.gov/edgar.shtml

The Center for Corporate Law at the University of Cincinnati College of Law examines many of the laws discussed in this chapter, including the Securities Act of 1933 and the Securities Exchange Act of 1934. Go to

www.law.uc.edu/CCL

Legal Research Exercises on the Web

Go to **www.cengage.com/blaw/jentz**, the Web site that accompanies this text. Select "Chapter 41" and click on "Internet Exercises." There you will find the following Internet research exercises that you can perform to learn more about the topics covered in this chapter.

Internet Exercise 41–1: Legal Perspective
Electronic Delivery

Internet Exercise 41–2: Management Perspective
The SEC's Role

CHAPTER 42

Law for Small Businesses

Small businesses create much of the wealth and many of the new jobs in the United States. According to the Census Bureau, there are around 5 million firms with ten or fewer employees. The Small Business Administration (SBA) reports that small businesses employ half of all private-sector employees in the country, generate more than half of the nation's gross domestic product, and obtain a disproportionate number of patents. The SBA also reports, however, that more than half of small businesses fail within four years. A lack of understanding of legal issues and how to respond to them is one of the reasons that new businesses fail.

Some relatively new companies, such as Google, have become highly successful. Understanding business law and the legal environment has often been crucial to business success. Consider that Google's growth is grounded to some extent in the smart decisions about contracts that the company made in its early days.

For the most part, the laws of particular interest to small-business owners are the same general business laws covered throughout this text, and this chapter provides a review of some of those laws. In this chapter, we examine a number of the options and legal requirements faced by those who wish to start their own small businesses. We also indicate how the general legal principles discussed throughout this book apply in the context of a small-business enterprise. Because legal compliance is crucial for any venture, we begin with a discussion of the importance of obtaining legal counsel.

SECTION 1 The Importance of Legal Counsel

Nearly everyone who starts a business enterprise faces the following question: "Do I need an attorney?" The answer to this question will likely be "yes." Today, it is virtually impossible for nonexperts to keep up with the myriad rules and regulations that govern the conduct of business in the United States. Indeed, businesspersons sometimes incur penalties for violating laws or regulations of which they are totally unaware, as noted in Chapter 5. Obtaining competent legal counsel can help a small business avoid a number of pitfalls. An attorney may be very helpful when a business undertakes certain types of transactions, including the following:

- Negotiating a franchise agreement.
- Creating standard business forms, such as purchase orders and contract confirmations.
- Buying or selling real property or a business.
- Negotiating agreements to license intellectual property rights.
- Obtaining new outside investors.

Relevant questions thus include how to find the right attorney for your needs and how to hold down legal costs as much as possible.

Although attorneys may seem expensive, the cautious business owner will make sure that he or she is not "penny wise and pound foolish." The consultation fee paid to an attorney may be a drop in the bucket compared with the potential liability facing a businessperson for violating a statutory law or regulation. Also, outside legal help may be essential for certain tasks associated with forming a new business, such as drafting and filing the documents necessary for incorporation. Failure to comply with specific state incorporation requirements may subject the owners of the new enterprise to personal liability for contracts or other obligations. Exhibit 42–1 provides estimated average attorneys' fees for a few basic small-business transactions. Of course, these amounts will vary depending on the complexity of the job and the geographic area where the business is located.

Finding an Attorney

In selecting an attorney, most businesspersons rely on referrals from friends, business associates, and other local entities. Business networks, such as chambers of commerce and bar organizations, may also help identify knowledgeable attorneys. Attorneys and their areas of specialty are often listed in the Yellow Pages of the telephone book. A good source of information is the *Martindale-Hubbell Law Directory,* which can be found at most law libraries. (It is also accessible online at **www.martindale.com**.) This directory lists the names, addresses, telephone numbers, areas of legal practice, and other information for more than 900,000 attorneys and law firms in the United States. A number of lawyers specialize in small-business law. Many states now have certification programs that identify specialists in various legal areas.

Retaining an Attorney

Retaining an experienced attorney will yield benefits beyond the resolution of legal problems. Many attorneys have beneficial contacts, including potential investors in your enterprise. An attorney may also have valuable business expertise. Furthermore, because the law protects the confidentiality of attorney-client communications, an attorney provides a useful sounding board for business plans.

At the start-up stage, you may not have the financial resources to pay a lawyer, especially one who charges a high hourly rate. Attorneys have responded to this situation by offering innovative fee arrangements, especially in such hotbeds of entrepreneurship as Silicon Valley, south of San Francisco. Most attorneys will not charge for an initial consultation, and some will provide a substantial amount of service in exchange for a promise of future legal business after the venture is established. Some attorneys may accept an equity (ownership) stake in the new business in lieu of a cash payment. As a client, you often have the opportunity to negotiate your attorney's compensation system to suit your needs.

Some small-business owners keep an attorney on **retainer.** This means that the client pays the attorney a fixed amount every month, and the attorney handles all necessary legal business that arises during the month. The amount of the retainer is negotiated with an eye toward expected legal needs. Thus, this approach probably will not save much overall, but it will make your legal costs stable and predictable over time.

EXHIBIT 42–1 • Average Attorneys' Fees for Selected Small-Business Transactions

Legal Task	Fee Range
Partnership creation	$450–$1,000
Lease-option contract	$250–$350
Trademark application	$250–$450
Employee handbook analysis	$750–$1,000

Retaining an Accountant

In a new business, the proper management of accounts receivable and accounts payable is critical. There are software accounting programs to handle this job, but many small businesses hire professional accountants to do their bookkeeping. Although it is more expensive, having an accountant adds to your credibility with potential investors and lenders. Bookkeeping accuracy is also legally important, as errors often provoke litigation.

SECTION 2 Selecting an Appropriate Business Form

The various forms of business organization available to businesspersons were discussed in detail in Chapters 35 through 41; we will review them here in the context of small businesses. In the earliest stages, a small business may operate as a sole proprietorship, which requires few legal formalities. The law considers all new, single-owner businesses to be sole proprietorships unless the owner affirmatively adopts some other form. Once business is under way, however, the sole proprietorship form may become problematic if additional investors are needed or the personal financial risks of the business become too great. You and the additional investors (owners) may then want to establish a more formal organization, such as a limited partnership, a corporation, a limited liability company (LLC), or a limited liability partnership (LLP).

Each business form has its own particular advantages and disadvantages. Factors to consider when choosing a business form include liability, taxation, continuity of life, and the legal formalities and costs associated with starting the business. In addition, there may be other considerations for businesses that are contemplating doing business over the Internet—see the *Insight into the Global Environment* feature for a discussion of these issues.

Limitations on Liability

A key consideration in starting a business is whether the business form chosen will limit the owner's personal liability for business debts and obligations. If you form a limited liability entity, such as a corporation, you can normally avoid personal liability if, say, a customer slips and breaks his ankle in your store, sues your store, and is awarded damages by a court. Although the business entity may be liable for damages, you and the other owners often will not be personally liable beyond the extent of your contributions to the firm. Legal limited liability is generally necessary for those who wish to raise outside capital.

All corporate business forms offer limited liability to the shareholder-owners. In a general partnership, however, there is no limited liability—each partner is personally liable for the debts and obligations of the partnership. In a limited partnership, the limited partners have limited liability. A limited partnership requires at least one general partner, however, who remains personally liable for the partnership's obligations. Note that limited personal liability does not obviate the need to obtain insurance for significant business liability risks (see Chapter 49). Limited liability organizations protect only personal assets, and a substantial uninsured liability can bankrupt the business and cause the owner to lose her or his entire investment. Moreover, limited personal liability may be lost by contract (such as by giving a personal guarantee) or by failure to comply with the rules for a business form.

All states now permit businesspersons to conduct their business operations as limited liability companies (LLCs). Also, many states now provide for limited liability partnerships (LLPs). These increasingly popular business forms also offer the advantage of limited personal liability for business debts and obligations (see Chapters 36 and 37 for a more detailed discussion of this aspect of LLCs and LLPs).

Tax Considerations

Taxes are another critical factor to be considered in choosing a small-business form. A sole proprietorship is not a separate legal entity, and the owner pays taxes on business income as an individual. All revenues are taxable, but business expenses can be deducted, so the owner is taxed only once on the business's profits.

All corporations must pay certain state and local taxes—such as **franchise taxes** (annual taxes imposed for the privilege of doing business in a state)—but the key consideration involves corporate income taxes. The corporate form entails what is known as *double taxation*. The company must pay a corporate income tax on its profits, and the shareholder-owners must also pay individual income tax on any distributions of the remaining profits that they receive from the corporation. Double taxation is limited to distributions of profits, though, so corporations are taxed only once on retained earnings. (See Chapter 38 for a complete discussion of corporate taxation.) Partnerships, LLCs, and LLPs avoid double taxation and provide for "pass-through" taxation, in which profits are passed through to the partners or members and are taxed only on their individual returns, not at the business level.

Continuity of Life

Continuity of life is another concern in selecting a business form. Businesses may fail to prepare for the possibility that an owner may die, resign, be expelled, or become incapacitated. Corporations have continuity of life—that is, they survive their owners—except in the unusual event that the corporate documents provide otherwise. On the death of a corporate shareholder-owner, normally that shareholder's ownership interest simply passes to his or her heirs.

In many states, a partnership will not terminate on the death or withdrawal of a partner, unless the partners have expressly provided otherwise. (In those states that have not adopted the most recent version of the Uniform Partnership Act, however, the death of a partner will automatically dissolve the partnership—

INSIGHT INTO THE GLOBAL ENVIRONMENT

Moving Your Small Business Online: Seller Beware

Today, almost every small business seems to have a Web site. Before you set up a Web site, though, you need to consider some of the implications of establishing an all-inclusive online presence for your business.

Jurisdictional Problems

A small-business owner who creates a Web site that allows individuals to purchase goods or services may run into jurisdictional issues. Because the Internet is a worldwide communications device, there is no way that you can effectively prevent your Web site from being viewed by almost everyone with Internet access throughout the world. Even within the United States, you cannot put a disclaimer on your Web site stating that you will sell your goods or services only within the state where your business has its principal office. Thus, if any customers are not satisfied with your products, they may attempt to bring lawsuits against you in other states or even other countries.

You may encounter other problems in foreign countries as well. If you are an online book seller, for example, you can legally sell a copy of Adolf Hitler's *Mein Kampf* to anyone in the United States. But if you ship that same book to a resident of Germany, you will have violated German law. Similarly, you may run afoul of Germany's strict antidiscrimination laws if you ship certain novels by Charles Dickens to German customers because many view these novels as anti-Semitic. If you start an online auction site and allow Nazi memorabilia to be offered for sale on the site, you will be violating French law if you allow the site to be viewed by French citizens.[a]

a. *Yahoo! Inc. v. La Ligue Contre le Racisme et l'Antisemitisme*, 379 F.3d 1120 (9th Cir. 2004); *cert.* denied, __ U.S. __, 126 S.Ct. 2332, 164 L.Ed.2d 841 (2006). This case was previously discussed in Chapter 2 on page 33.

Regulation of Informational Content on Web Sites

Suppose that you establish an online business that provides information, such as summaries of current news articles, events of the day, book reviews, and scholarly articles. If some of the content appears to insult Islam, the government of Malaysia may attempt to prosecute you. If one of the articles on your site expresses a negative view of the government of Zimbabwe, you may find yourself being tried *in absentia* (without being present) by that government. If your site includes an article that appears to deny the Holocaust,[b] the German government may prosecute both you and the author of the article.

Trademark Issues

Before the advent of the Internet, an entrepreneur starting a new business would only have to check the state in which she or he was doing business to make sure that the business's name did not infringe on the name of an established business. Now a business's name often becomes part of its Web site address. Consequently, an entrepreneur will want to choose a business name that can also be purchased for use in the Web address. That means selecting a name that does not infringe on some other company's trademark, even if that company is based in Europe or Asia.

CRITICAL THINKING

INSIGHT INTO TECHNOLOGY

Researchers are attempting to create technology that would allow Web site operators to screen out users from certain geographic areas. What global issues discussed in this feature might be less of a problem if such technology becomes cheap and effective?

b. This is the general term used for all of Hitler's actions to exterminate Jews during World War II (1939–1945).

see Chapter 36.) By definition, a sole proprietorship terminates with the death of the sole proprietor.

Legal Formality and Expense

Businesspersons also need to consider the legal formalities and expenses involved in starting a business. The requirements and costs associated with forming and operating as a corporation can be considerable. The expense of establishing a limited partnership may also be significant. For these reasons, some individuals initially undertake business operations as sole proprietorships or general partnerships—and run considerable financial risk because of the personal liability associated with each of these business forms. Start-up formalities and costs are generally less extensive for LLCs than for corporations or limited partnerships.

Requirements for All Businesses Although sole proprietorships and general partnerships avoid the legal formalities associated with incorporating or creating a limited partnership, sole proprietors and partners must still comply with many laws. Any business, whatever its form, has to meet a variety of legal requirements, which typically relate to the following:

- Business name registration.
- Occupational licensing.
- State tax registration (for example, to obtain permits for collecting and remitting sales taxes).
- Health and environmental permits.
- Zoning and building codes.
- Import/export regulations.

If the business has employees, the owner must also comply with a host of laws governing the workplace. (We will look at many of these laws in the final section of this chapter.)

Formalizing the Business The owner should not overlook the potential benefits that may be gained by establishing a more formal business arrangement than a sole proprietorship. Consider a family business that is owned and operated by a husband and wife. At the outset, the spouses should consider the possibility that they may have a falling-out in the future. If they run their enterprise as a sole proprietorship, it may be difficult to establish their respective ownership rights in the business should a dispute arise.

If they form a partnership, however, they can specify in a written partnership agreement how profits and losses will be shared, as well as the extent of each partner's ownership interest in the partnership. Alternatively, the spouses could incorporate and draw up a shareholder agreement providing for various eventualities (shareholder agreements are discussed later in this chapter) and permitting the company's continuation. Formalizing the business is critical to its potential expansion as well.

SECTION 3 The Limited Liability Company

For most new small businesses, the LLC has become the preferred choice of organization. The LLC structure offers a small business the benefit of limited liability without the double taxation associated with a corporation. In addition, although forming an LLC involves filing a certificate with the state and paying a fee, the process is far less complex than that required for a corporation.

The Basic LLC Structure

The structure of an LLC roughly parallels that of a corporation. Instead of articles of incorporation, though, an LLC has an *operating agreement* that serves as the organization's charter. The owners of an LLC are called *members*, not shareholders. A member need not be a natural person but may be a separate corporation or other organized entity. Those who run the day-to-day operations of an LLC are known as *managers*. Two important aspects of an LLC's structure are its flexibility and the fiduciary duties of its members and managers.

Flexibility in Determining Members' Rights Under state law, LLCs have much more legal flexibility than corporations enjoy. Whereas corporations must comply with numerous requirements, LLCs are generally given the flexibility to alter the statutory rules in their operating agreements. Generally, the state statute includes default rules that will govern an LLC unless its operating agreement provides otherwise. For example, default rules typically provide that profits, voting rights, and assets on liquidation will be apportioned according to the value of each member's contribution. An LLC's operating agreement, however, may apportion the members' voting rights equally or according to their financial contributions or some other criteria. Similarly, the operating agreement may provide for profits and losses, and distributions to members, to be allocated on some other basis.

As another example, state statutes typically presume that an LLC's members will be its managers, but the agreement may provide otherwise. Usually, LLC membership interests cannot be transferred, and new memberships may not be issued, without the consent of all existing members. These default rules may also be modified by the agreement. Unlike a corporation, an LLC is not required by law to hold a formal annual meeting, but the agreement may require such a meeting. One leading case even found that the agreement could require all disputes among an LLC's members to be resolved by arbitration, disallowing any court challenges.[1]

The following case demonstrates how the rights of a terminated LLC member can be limited by the operating agreement.

1. *Elf Atochem North America, Inc. v. Jaffari*, 727 A.2d 286 (Del. 1999).

CASE 42.1 Mixon v. Iberia Surgical, LLC

Court of Appeal of Louisiana, Third Circuit, 2007. 956 So.2d 76.

• **Background and Facts** A group of physicians in Louisiana created Iberia Surgical, LLC. The members included Dr. Tynes Mixon, who became the managing partner. Within a year, Iberia Surgical formed the New Iberia Surgical Center, LLC. Mixon became dissatisfied with the operation of the new facility and the management practices of his fellow physicians. By unanimous vote of the membership, Iberia Surgical terminated Mixon's membership and employment. The LLC's operating agreement provided that a member could be terminated without cause by a unanimous vote of the remaining members of the company. The company paid Mixon $71,536.85. Mixon asserted that the termination of his membership was an abuse of right and violated moral rules, good faith, and elementary fairness. He argued that the termination was done to cause harm. Additionally, he argued that the payment was not in accord with the fair market value of his membership, which he valued at almost $500,000. The trial court granted summary judgment in favor of Iberia Surgical, LLC.

• **Decision and Rationale** The Court of Appeal of Louisiana for the Third Circuit affirmed the trial court's decision. This reviewing court pointed out that Mixon had negotiated and signed the LLC's operating agreement, which gave its members the right to terminate another member without cause. "Dr. Mixon has provided no evidence to suggest the termination was done to cause him harm or for any other reason than a legitimate business reason. * * * There is no evidence to suggest the terms of the Operating Agreement violate moral rules, good faith, or elementary fairness." With respect to the payment made to Mixon, the court pointed out that the operating agreement called for the use of "book value" in determining the monetary value of a member's interest. "The book value of a business has a well-defined meaning, is unambiguous, and is susceptible of only one construction. It is the value as shown by the books of the business, and no other value. Book value is calculated by measuring the assets of the business against its liabilities." The company correctly calculated book value in determining its payment to Mixon.

• **The Legal Environment Dimension** *What might Mixon and the other members of Iberia Surgical have done to avoid the litigation and its ultimate result in this case?*

• **The Ethical Dimension** *Does the outcome in this case underscore the advantages or the disadvantages of the LLC form of business organization? Explain.*

Extent of Fiduciary Duties A key element of corporate law involves the fiduciary duties of directors and officers to shareholders. The nature and scope of these duties are not as fully defined for LLCs, but the states have imposed some requirements of fair and honest dealing by members and managers. Like many other aspects of the LLC, however, the duties of members and managers may be set out and limited in the LLC agreement.

Converting an LLC into a Corporation

If a small business begins as an LLC and thrives, the owners may wish to convert it to a corporation. By incorporating, the larger business can attract more outside capital, and because it will be retaining its earnings to fund future growth, rather than distributing them to the owners, it will not experience the double-taxation disadvantage of the corporate form. In addition, the corporate structure facilitates equity-based employee incentive plans and a more expansive management structure.

If the LLC agreement does not provide otherwise, this conversion may require the unanimous consent of the members. The LLC must then file articles of dissolution with the state. The members will agree on a process to assign ownership interests in the new corporation by shareholdings. Then, they will go about forming the successor corporation, a procedure discussed in the next section.

SECTION 4 Creating the Business Entity

As explained earlier in this chapter, the different forms of business organization differ considerably in the formalities and expenses required to create a business. There are no special legal requirements for creating a sole proprietorship, and a general partnership requires only an agreement between the partners. Forming an LLC involves slightly more legal work. Forming a limited partnership is more complicated. The limited partnership agreement, often called a certificate of limited partnership, must be prepared and recorded with the appropriate governmental authority. State laws also regulate the names of limited partnerships, require certain record keeping, and govern other aspects of the business. The procedures required for the creation of a corporation are perhaps the most complicated of all, so the remainder of this section is devoted to them.

Choosing a Corporate Name

To incorporate, you first must choose a corporate name and file it with the appropriate state office, usually the office of the secretary of state. The name must be different from those used by existing businesses (even unincorporated businesses). Although private databases can be used to check names, the secretary of state's office should have all of the information necessary. The name of your new company should also include the word *Corporation*, *Company*, or *Incorporated* (abbreviated *Corp.*, *Co.*, and *Inc.*, respectively).

Note that filing a name with the appropriate state official will protect the name as a trade name only within the state. Therefore, businesspersons who anticipate doing business nationally—via the Internet, for example—will want to make sure that their trade names will be protected under trademark law (to be discussed shortly).

Articles of Incorporation, Bylaws, and Initial Meeting

The second key step in incorporation is preparing and filing the articles of incorporation. Other steps involve drafting the corporate bylaws and holding the initial board of directors' meeting.

Articles of Incorporation As discussed in Chapter 38, states have different requirements as to the provisions that must be included in the articles. For example, some states require a minimum number of incorporators or directors, or a minimum capital contribution. As mentioned, entrepreneurs typically engage an attorney to help them draft and file the documents necessary to incorporate, including the articles of incorporation.

Drafting Corporate Bylaws Another important step in the incorporation process is drafting the bylaws, which become the company's governing rules. The bylaws establish the dates on which annual meetings will be held, the number required for a voting quorum, and other rules. The articles of incorporation should not include all of the corporate rules because the articles are relatively difficult to change. Bylaws are binding, but they are more easily modified. Usually, bylaws can be changed by a majority vote of the shareholders; in some states, the bylaws can be modified by the board of directors.

Holding the Initial Board of Directors' Meeting The corporation then holds its first board of directors' meeting. The initial corporate directors are designated in the articles of incorporation. The directors adopt the agreed-on bylaws, appoint corporate officers and define their respective authority, issue stock, open a bank account, and take other necessary actions. The directors will continue to meet periodically and must stand for election at annual shareholders' meetings.

Creating a Corporate Records Book

The next step is to establish a corporate records book in which the corporation's important documents, such as the articles of incorporation and the minutes of directors' and shareholders' meetings, will be kept. If the state requires stock certificates, they will have to be printed and distributed to the owners. The corporation may also need a corporate seal because banks and other institutions sometimes require that seals be placed on certain documents. Again, an attorney typically handles these tasks as part of the incorporation process.

SECTION 5 Intellectual Property

Protecting rights in intellectual property is the central concern for some businesses. For example, software companies depend on their copyrights and patents to protect their investments in the research and development required to create new programs. Without copyright or patent protection, a competitor or a customer could simply copy the software. Laws governing rights in intellectual property were discussed in detail in Chapter 8. Here, we examine some aspects of intellectual property law that individuals should consider at the outset of any business venture.

Choosing and Protecting a Trademark

Choosing a trademark or service mark and making sure that it can be protected under trademark law can be crucial to the success of a new business venture. A factor to consider in choosing a name for your business entity is whether you will use your business name as a trademark. Assume that you plan to incorporate your business. When the firm is incorporated, the secretary of state (or other state agency with which the business name is filed) approves your company's name only as a trade name—the name that you can use on checks, invoices, and letterhead stationery. You have legal ownership of your trade name only in that state.

If you decide to use your business (trade) name as a trademark, then you need to follow the principles of trademark law. The general rule is that your trademark cannot be the same as or so similar to another's mark that a customer might think that your product was produced by someone else.

Historically, the first business that actually used a trademark in the marketplace owned it. Today, for national trademark protection, the business must be the first to register the trademark with the U.S. Patent and Trademark Office (PTO) in Washington, D.C. First use still takes some precedence over federal registration, however. Suppose that you have used a particular trademark for two years but have not registered the mark with the PTO. If another company then registers the same mark with the PTO, you will probably have the traditional common law right to continue using that mark but only in the geographic region in which you have been operating. Outside that region, the federal registrant will own the mark.

Choosing a Trademark A trademark should be distinctive. Use of your name or a mere description of your product will probably receive, at most, only weak protection. If you have started a new online company, you cannot call it "Internet" and expect to receive protection. Although using a slight twist on the word may be tempting, this may lead to confusion—thousands of companies already have the word *net* as part of their names. A distinctive made-up word (such as *Exxon* or *Kodak*) may be a good choice.

Once you have chosen a mark, you should do a trademark search to ensure that the mark is not too similar to existing marks. You can hire a trademark search firm or do the search yourself. Sources to consult include the Yellow Pages in any area in which you do business and the *Gale Trade Names Directory* (available in your local library). You can also look at the federal trademark register, as well as the trademark register in your state. (Go to **www.uspto.gov** to check the PTO's online federal trademark register.) Other trademark databases, such as TrademarkScan, are also available on the Internet.

Registering a Trademark After selecting a trademark that appears to be available and that is not confusingly similar to an existing mark, you should register the mark with both the state government and the federal government. As explained earlier, registration is not required, but if you do not register, your protection may be limited to the area in which you do business. Federal registration gives your trademark nationwide protection, provided that the trademark is already in use or will be used within six months. Even if your current business is only local, registration for national protection is important to protect long-term corporate growth.

To register your trademark with the PTO, you must submit an application that includes a specimen (picture) of your trademark, a list of marked goods and/or services, and the date on which you first used the trademark. You may want to register more than one mark. If your logo consists of a distinctive name as well as a graphic, you can register each item independently. For example, Apple, Inc., uses a rainbow-colored apple as a registered logo and the name *Apple* as a trademark. The apple logo and the Apple name could be registered separately to get independent protection. The PTO now allows online filing through the Trademark Electronic Application System, available at **www.uspto.gov/teas**.

Protecting a Trademark After registering your trademark, you must take care of it. If your mark is federally registered, you may use the symbol® with your mark; this puts others on notice of your registration. Even if you have not registered, you can use the symbol™ with your mark. Five years after you initially register your mark, you should renew your registration with the PTO. Thereafter, you can renew at ten-year intervals. Filing for renewal informs the PTO that your mark is still in use and ensures that others cannot contest its validity.

Protecting your mark also entails remaining alert to possible trademark infringement. If another company uses your trademark or a mark very similar to yours, you should take prompt action by sending a letter of complaint and consider filing a lawsuit for trademark infringement. If you ignore the problem, you may lose rights in your trademark. If, for example, a media outlet improperly refers to your trademark as if it were a generic word, send a letter of correction and keep a copy in your files. You may at some point need to demonstrate that you have consistently sought to enforce your rights in the mark, or it may be deemed abandoned.

Protecting Trade Secrets

Much of the value of a business may lie in its trade secrets. As discussed in Chapter 8, trade secrets are business secrets that have value and might be appropriated by another company, such as a competitor. Trade secrets may include information concerning product development, production processes and techniques, or customer lists.

As a practical matter, trade secrets must be divulged to key employees, and thus any business runs the risk that those employees might disclose the secrets to competitors—or even set up competing businesses themselves. Generally, protecting against the possibility that valuable trade secrets will fall into the hands of others, especially competitors, presents an ongoing challenge for businesses, including new enterprises.

Nondisclosure and Noncompete Agreements To protect their trade secrets, companies may require employees who have access to trade secrets to agree in their employment contracts never to divulge those secrets. A company may also include a covenant not to compete in an employment contract. A noncompete covenant will help to protect against the possibility that a key employee may go to work for a competitor or set up a competing business—situations in which the company's trade secrets will likely be disclosed.

Misappropriation of Trade Secrets As discussed in Chapter 8, trade secrets are protected under the common law.[2] Thus, a company can sue an individual or a firm that has misappropriated its trade secrets. In one case, for example, two engineers who had developed new software for their company left to work at a new, smaller firm. After the engineers developed a similar product for their new employer, the first company sued for infringement of trade secrets and prevailed in court. The new company was prohibited from selling any of the contested products for three years.[3]

SECTION 6 Raising Financial Capital

Raising financial capital is critical to the growth of most small businesses. In the early days of a business, the sole proprietor or partners may be able to contribute sufficient capital, but if the business becomes successful, more funds may be needed. The owner or owners may want to raise capital from external sources to expand the business. One way to do this is to borrow funds. Another is to exchange equity (ownership rights) in the company in return for funds, either through private arrangements or through public stock offerings.

Loans

A small business may find it beneficial to obtain a bank loan because raising capital in this way allows the founder to retain full ownership and control of the business (though the bank may place some restrictions on future business decisions as a condition of granting the loan). Bank loans may not be available for some businesses, however. Banks are usually reluctant to lend significant sums to businesses that are not yet established. Even if a bank is willing to make such a loan, the bank may require personal guaranty contracts from the owners, putting their personal assets at risk (see Chapter 28).

Loans with desirable terms may be available from the federal Small Business Administration (SBA). One SBA program provides loans of up to $25,000 to businesspersons who are women, low-income individuals, or members of minority groups. Be aware that the SBA requires business owners to put some of their own

2. The theft of trade secrets is also a federal crime under the Economic Espionage Act of 1996 (see Chapter 9).

3. *Scully Signal Co. v. Joyal,* 881 F.Supp. 727 (D.R.I. 1995).

funds at risk in the business. Some entrepreneurs have even used their credit cards to obtain initial capital.

Venture Capital

As discussed in Chapter 38, many new businesses raise needed capital by exchanging certain ownership rights (equity) in the firm for venture capital. In other words, an outsider contributes funds in exchange for an ownership interest in the company. **Venture capitalists,** often organized into major firms, seek out promising enterprises and fund them in exchange for equity stakes. Akin to venture capitalists are "angels," individuals who typically invest somewhat smaller sums in new businesses.

According to the U.S. National Venture Capital Association, U.S. venture capitalists invested $25.5 billion in 2,978 deals in 2007 (although these numbers were dramatically lower during the business slowdown in 2008). On average, a venture capitalist invests about $5 million to $10 million in a company. In addition to providing needed financing, venture capitalists offer other advantages for businesses. Venture capitalists are often experienced managers who can provide invaluable assistance to entrepreneurs with respect to strategic business decisions, marketing, and important business contacts. Obtaining this assistance may be crucial to a new company's success. The disadvantage is that a venture capitalist with a substantial equity stake will demand a corresponding degree of operational control over the company and a similar proportion of future profits.

To attract outside venture capital, you will need a **business plan** that describes the company, its products, and its anticipated future performance. The plan should be relatively concise (fewer than fifty pages). After considering your plan, a venture capitalist may decide to investigate your venture further. This step may require you to disclose trade secrets, and you should insist that the potential investor sign a confidentiality agreement. If all goes well, you will then negotiate the terms of financing. A key point to be negotiated is how much ownership and control the venture capitalist will receive in exchange for the capital contribution. Exhibit 42–2 on the following page summarizes some key issues that may arise in negotiations with venture capitalists.

Although venture capital may be crucial to a small business's growth, accepting venture capital sometimes carries certain risks, as the following case illustrates.

CASE 42.2 InfoSAGE, Inc. v. Mellon Ventures, LP

Superior Court of Pennsylvania, 2006. 896 A.2d 616.

• **Background and Facts** InfoSAGE, Inc., a software development company, funded its initial development with $5 million from its founders and two rounds of venture capital financing that provided another $5 million. Mellon Ventures, LP, furnished the initial round of venture capital financing. InfoSAGE prepared a business plan predicated on a third round of venture capital financing to be used for its marketing efforts. After the additional financing did not materialize, InfoSAGE's board voted to enter into a so-called bridge loan contract with Mellon. The company contacted numerous venture capital firms but was never able to obtain a third round of financing. It filed for Chapter 11 proceedings in bankruptcy court. The founders of InfoSAGE accused Mellon of interfering with their efforts to obtain the third round of financing and filed a lawsuit, alleging tortious interference with business relations and breach of fiduciary duty on the part of Mellon's director appointee (Charles Billerbeck). The trial court granted summary judgment for Mellon, and InfoSAGE appealed.

• **Decision and Rationale** The appellate court affirmed the summary judgment in favor of Mellon. The reviewing court reasoned that just showing suspicious behavior on Billerbeck's part was not sufficient. InfoSAGE "would have had to establish that its prospective contractual relations with the venture capital firms had progressed to a point showing, or were based on, a reasonable likelihood or probability that these relations would result in a contract." The court could not merely assume that this would happen. Additionally, the evidence presented by InfoSAGE did not show that Billerbeck or Mellon was unjustly enriched as a result of their actions during the company's attempt at obtaining a third round of outside financing.

CASE CONTINUES

CASE 42.2 CONTINUED

- **The Ethical Dimension** *Although the court did not find Mellon legally liable to InfoSAGE, could Mellon's actions be interpreted as unethical? Explain.*

- **The Legal Environment Dimension** *What fact missing from the circumstances of this case was most important to InfoSAGE's cause of action and could have led to a different result if it had existed?*

Securities Regulation

Anyone raising capital needs to be aware of the regulations that govern securities. Many small-business owners raise funds from friends or business acquaintances instead of from venture capitalists. Whatever method is used, the investor exchanges capital for an interest in the enterprise. If this interest consists of shares of stock (or otherwise qualifies as a security under federal or state law), the business may become subject to extraordinarily detailed regulatory requirements. The securities may have to be registered with the Securities and Exchange Commission (SEC) or with the state in which the offering is made, unless the offering falls within an exemption to the securities laws.

Private Offerings In certain circumstances, legal exemptions are available so that businesspersons need not worry about full registration or compliance with all of the securities regulations. (Securities regulations and exemptions were discussed in detail in Chapter 41.) In short, the exemptions permit you to raise a limited amount of funds from a limited number of investors in what is sometimes called a *private offering.* If your offering qualifies, you need not register your shares as securities with the SEC. States have separate regulatory schemes and different terms for their exemptions from registration. In a private offering, capital is typically raised through a private placement memorandum distributed to selected potential investors.

Public Offerings If your business proves especially successful, you may make a public offering in which a certain number of your shares are offered for purchase by members of the public at a price that you

EXHIBIT 42–2 • Venture Capital Issues

Type and Quantity of Stock	The venture capitalists will negotiate the *amount of stock* (which will determine their ownership share of the enterprise) and the *type of stock* (which will usually be preferred stock).
Stock Preferences	If the venture capitalists receive preferred shares, the shares will generally (1) provide for an annual per-share dividend to be paid before common stockholders receive any dividends and (2) give the venture capitalists priority among shareholders in the event of the firm's liquidation.
Conversion and Antidilution Rights	The preferred shares will be convertible into common stock at the option of the venture capitalists, and the company will be restrained from issuing new stock in an amount that would materially dilute the venture capitalists' ownership interests.
Board of Directors	The venture capitalists will define their proportionate representation on the board of directors.
Registration Rights	Should the company conduct a public offering or register its shares at a later date, the venture capitalists will have the right to have their shares registered also ("piggybacked"), making those shares more marketable.
Representations and Warranties	The owner will be required to make representations about the firm's capital structure, its possession of necessary government authorizations, its financial statements, and other material facts.

have set. Public offerings are highly regulated, but they may allow you to raise very large amounts of capital. Securities issued through public offerings must be registered with the SEC and applicable state regulatory agencies.

Full registration is complex, but the states and the SEC have jointly created a simplified securities registration process for small businesses. The Small Corporate Offering Registration (SCOR), which requires a form with only fifty questions, can be used for small offerings. Forty-three states have adopted the SCOR process, but with varying laws relating to use of the form.

SECTION 7 Buy-Sell Agreements and Key-Person Insurance

In the excitement of forming a new business, it is easy to overlook the possibility that partners or shareholders may die or become disabled or that disputes among partners or shareholders may make business decision making impossible. At the outset of any enterprise involving two or more owners, the owners should decide—and put in writing—how such problems will be resolved.

Shareholder Agreements

Even if a new company has only two owners, they should have a shareholder agreement that defines their relative ownership rights and interests. Such agreements are vital for small, closely held companies, in large part because shares in such entities cannot be readily sold to outsiders. This means that an owner may be locked into the investment against her or his will with little return.

Buy-Sell Agreements A key aspect of the shareholder agreement is a *buy-sell agreement.* (This type of agreement was discussed in Chapter 36 in the context of a partnership agreement.) In a corporate shareholder agreement, a buy-sell agreement provides for the buyout of a shareholder and establishes criteria for the price to be paid for that shareholder's ownership interest. The death of a shareholder might trigger a buy-sell agreement, enabling the decedent's heirs to cash out the investment. Other common triggering events include a shareholder's bankruptcy, a shareholder's divorce, and the legal attachment of a shareholder's shares for other reasons.

Provisions in Buy-Sell Agreements The buy-sell agreement should include a provision for pricing the shares that will be sold. The price may be a set price or be calculated according to a formula. Buy-sell agreements can also resolve serious deadlocks that may develop between co-owners as the business grows. The agreement might provide that one owner has an option to buy out the others in the event that such a deadlock occurs. Alternatively, all co-owners might submit sealed bids to buy each other out, with the highest bidder being allowed to buy out the others.

A buy-sell agreement might also include a provision for a *right of first refusal,* which restricts the transferability of the shares for a specified duration. Such a provision will prevent an owner from selling to a third party without first giving the other owners an opportunity to buy out his or her interest. An alternative to the right of first refusal is a provision for a "take-along right," which allows an investor to participate in any sale of shares to a third party. This right can protect relatively passive investors from the possibility that managing shareholders may "bail out" of the corporation by selling their shares to third parties.

Key-Person Insurance

Much of the value of a small enterprise may rest in the skills of one or a few employees (such as a software designer or a top management executive). To protect against the risk that these key persons may become disabled or die, business enterprises typically obtain *key-person insurance* (see Chapter 49). The proceeds of a key-person insurance policy can help cover the losses caused by the death or disability of essential employees. Venture capitalists or other investors may require that the company take out a key-person insurance policy as a condition of investing in the corporation.

SECTION 8 Contract Law and Small Businesses

Any business venture will require that contracts be formed and signed. For example, if you lease business premises, you will need to sign a lease contract. Any purchases or sales of equipment will also involve contracts. Understanding the basic contract law principles that were covered in Chapters 10 through 19 can help to ensure that any contracts you form will be valid and enforceable. As a general rule, you should make sure that any contractual agreement is in writing. Then, should a dispute arise, there will be written evidence of the contract's terms. Additionally, as discussed in Chapter 15, some contracts—such as contracts for the sale of goods priced at $500 or more[4]—fall under the Statute of Frauds, which means that they must be evidenced by a writing to be enforceable.

Creating Contract Forms

Small-business owners often consult with their attorneys in creating contract forms for specific purposes. For example, a business may wish to provide a warranty for its products but also limit the scope of that warranty. This decision is best made through the mutual judgment of the businessperson and her or his attorney to ensure that both business and legal concerns are addressed.

4. There was an attempt in 2003 to raise this amount to $5,000 in a new version of Article 2 of the Uniform Commercial Code, but no state adopted the newer version, so, for the moment, the relatively low $500 figure remains in force.

Avoiding Potential Personal Liability

Contract law contains traps, and the businessperson should be aware of them. If you incorporate, you will want to enter contracts as an agent of the corporation, not in your individual capacity. Otherwise, you may be personally liable on the contracts. This principle applies to negotiable instruments as well. For example, if you sign a promissory note on behalf of the corporation, you should indicate that you are signing in a representative capacity (see Chapter 26 for further details on signature liability with respect to negotiable instruments). The same advice applies to partners and partnerships. Ultimately, though, liability is simply a matter of contract interpretation, as demonstrated by the following case.

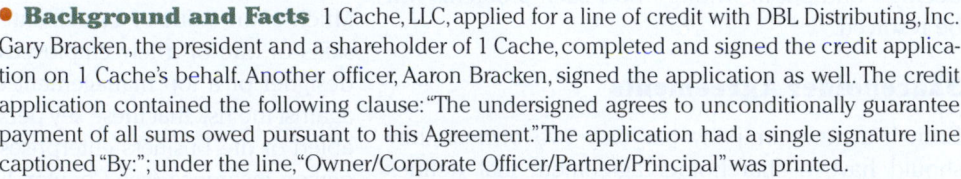

CASE 42.3 DBL Distributing, Inc. v. 1 Cache, LLC

Court of Appeals of Utah, 2006. 147 P.3d 478.

Background and Facts 1 Cache, LLC, applied for a line of credit with DBL Distributing, Inc. Gary Bracken, the president and a shareholder of 1 Cache, completed and signed the credit application on 1 Cache's behalf. Another officer, Aaron Bracken, signed the application as well. The credit application contained the following clause: "The undersigned agrees to unconditionally guarantee payment of all sums owed pursuant to this Agreement." The application had a single signature line captioned "By:"; under the line, "Owner/Corporate Officer/Partner/Principal" was printed.

Near the beginning of 2001, DBL updated its credit application form. The updated form modified the guarantee language as follows: "The undersigned agrees to personally guarantee payment of all sums owed pursuant to this Agreement." The updated application also altered the signature block section to include separate lines for the applicant's firm name, signature, and title. DBL apparently sought to have each of its existing customers complete an updated application. On April 24, 2001, the Brackens completed and signed an updated application on behalf of 1 Cache. This time, Gary added the handwritten notation "president, only in his representative capacity" next to his signature in the space for his title.

1 Cache filed for Chapter 7 bankruptcy on August 26, 2002. Two years later, on August 4, 2004, DBL filed a complaint against 1 Cache and Gary Bracken, asserting, among other things, that Bracken was personally liable for the outstanding debt incurred by 1 Cache. Bracken filed a motion to dismiss, and DBL moved for summary judgment. The trial court granted Bracken's motion to dismiss and denied the motion for summary judgment, and DBL appealed.

Decision and Rationale The appellate court reversed the dismissal of DBL's claims but affirmed the denial of DBL's motion for summary judgment. It remanded the case for further proceedings, potentially including a trial on the contested factual issues. In general, a corporate signatory is not individually liable on an instrument he or she signs in a representative capacity. The reviewing court noted, though, that "to relieve an individual signer from liability, the signer's corporate capacity must be clear from the form of the signature." The 2001 updated credit application presented a conflict between "the substance of the documents, each of which specifically indicates personal liability against whoever signs it, and the signatures themselves, which suggest only corporate liability." Some previous cases addressed this conflict, and courts held that the clear lan-

CASE 42.3 CONTINUED guage of personal guarantee on a document can result in personal liability despite a corporate signature. It might be up to a jury to decide the contested factual issues.

- **What If the Facts Were Different?** *Suppose that Bracken had signed the credit application "Gary Bracken, president, for 1 Cache, LLC." Would he have been personally liable for the debt to DBL? Why or why not?*

- **The E-Commerce Dimension** *If Bracken had submitted the application online, with "Gary Bracken, president, for 1 Cache, LLC" typed in the space for a signature, would either he or 1 Cache have been bound to repay the debt? Explain.*

SECTION 9

Employment Issues

Small businesses are exempt from some employment laws. For example, businesses with fewer than fifteen employees are exempt from federal laws prohibiting employment discrimination and certain other federal acts, such as the Family and Medical Leave Act of 1993.[5] Some state statutes have similar exemptions for small businesses. Nevertheless, even the smallest businesses are subject to many employment laws, so a knowledge of employment law is crucial for entrepreneurs starting up businesses.

For example, the rather detailed regulations of the federal Occupational Safety and Health Administration have no small-business exemptions. Small businesses may be less likely to be inspected for violations, but if enforcement and penalties are applied, they can be far more disastrous for start-up companies than for larger, established firms that are in a better position to absorb these costs. Similarly, just one successful lawsuit against a small business can mean bankruptcy for the business, as indicated earlier in this chapter.

Hiring Employees

Hiring good employees can be crucial to business success. You should keep several legal issues in mind during this process.

- Be sure that the person you hire will not be disclosing any protected trade secrets of a former employer.
- Do not make promises of job security unless you are sure you can keep them. If you promise that an employee's job will be permanent and the employee relies on your assurances, you may find it difficult to fire her or him.
- Determine what screening tests are appropriate for the job. In some circumstances, you may be able to require the applicant to take a drug test.
- Comply with all of the requirements imposed by federal immigration laws with respect to verifying whether workers are U.S. citizens and whether those who are not citizens are authorized to work in this country.

Employment Contracts Generally, you should put all employment agreements in writing. This is generally done in an offer letter that sets forth the basic terms of employment, including wages and benefits. An employment contract might specify that the contract is for at-will employment (see Chapter 33), meaning that you can fire the employee at any time for any reason, provided that no employment laws are violated. In new businesses, an employee might want stock or options in lieu of part of his or her salary. Although granting equity to an employee saves scarce cash, it dilutes the other owners' interests. For high-level employees at least, you would be wise to consult an attorney regarding what contractual provisions should be included before awarding an equity interest in the firm.

Verifying Applicants' Credentials and Job Experience It goes without saying that you should contact former employers of job applicants and verify the applicants' credentials and job experience. You should also make sufficient inquiries to avoid a negligent-hiring lawsuit. Suppose that you hire a person who has been convicted twice for criminal assault. If that employee attacks a customer, the customer could sue your business for negligence in screening the worker's background during the hiring process. You therefore should check to see if a job applicant has any history of criminal conduct. You should also check a job applicant's driving record if the job involves driving a vehicle for business purposes. Additionally, actions of dishonest employees

5. 29 U.S.C. Sections 2601, 2611–2619, 2651–2654.

can cause a small business to suffer substantial economic losses. Thorough screening procedures will help you to avoid such problems.

Workers' Compensation

Most states require that employers carry workers' compensation insurance. If one of your employees is injured in the course of employment, the employee will be compensated for the injury by the state workers' compensation fund. That employee generally cannot sue you for further damages.

Workers' compensation insurance premiums are often high, and they may constitute one of a small business's greatest expenses. Premiums are initially based on the size of your payroll and the amount of risk involved in the business that you operate. After some time, your rates may be raised or lowered, depending on the safety record of your company. The fewer claims made against you, the lower your workers' compensation insurance costs will be.

Firing Employees

At one time or another, a small-business owner will probably find it necessary to fire a worker. Unless otherwise specified in employment contracts, your employees are presumptively at-will employees, and you can fire them without having to give any reason for doing so. Nevertheless, it is generally advisable to document good cause for terminating a worker—otherwise, he or she may succeed in a lawsuit against you for unlawful discrimination or some other legal violation.

Employee Files Generally, you should keep a file on each employee that includes the employee's application, performance reviews, and other relevant information. If you fire the employee, full documentation of why she or he was fired should be added to the file. Realize, though, that nearly half of the states have laws that allow employees to have access to their personnel records.

Severance Pay If you fire a worker, you might want to offer **severance pay,** which is a payment in addition to the employee's wages owed on termination. As a condition of receiving the severance pay, you might ask the employee to sign a release promising not to sue. Severance pay may be especially appropriate if the termination is not the employee's fault. Normally, you are not required to give severance pay (unless you have previously promised to do so or a union contract requires it). Most states have laws governing when you must provide the employee with his or her final paycheck, however.

Wrongful Discharge Some states recognize a legal action for wrongful discharge, but these actions are generally limited to terminations in bad faith. You must be aware of any promises you made to an employee in a written contract, in an employee handbook, or even orally. These promises may prevent you from firing the employee without due process, good cause, or whatever else you may have promised.

Using Independent Contractors

Independent contractors are not considered to be employees. As explained in Chapter 31, according to the *Restatement (Second) of Agency,* an independent contractor is "a person who contracts with another to do something for him [or her] but who is not controlled by the other nor subject to the other's right to control with respect to his [or her] physical conduct in the performance of the undertaking."

Benefits of Using Independent Contractors The use of independent contractors offers many advantages to small businesses. For one thing, you need not withhold income taxes and Social Security and Medicare taxes from payments made to independent contractors, as you are required to do when you pay wages to employees. Furthermore, you need not match the amount withheld for Social Security and Medicare taxes, which can be costly for an employer. Additionally, you need not pay premiums for workers' compensation insurance or unemployment insurance with respect to independent contractors.

Another important benefit of hiring workers as independent contractors rather than employees is that you are not subject to laws governing employment relationships, including laws prohibiting discrimination. Normally, a court will not permit an independent contractor to bring a suit against you for age discrimination, for example, or for any other type of discrimination prohibited by federal or state laws governing employment relationships—because these laws protect only *employees,* not independent contractors.

Liability for Misclassification of Workers Of course, the trade-off in using independent contractors is that you cannot exercise a significant amount of control over how they perform their work. If you do, the Internal Revenue Service (IRS) or another government agency may decide that they are, in fact, employees and not independent contractors. Misclassification of an employee as an independent contractor can subject you to considerable tax liability, including penalties.

Microsoft Corporation certainly realized the potential seriousness of misclassification in 1999. In a tax audit, the IRS concluded that Microsoft exercised significant control over workers who had been designated by the company as independent contractors. The IRS reclassified them as employees. The company accepted the ruling and paid overdue employment taxes. Then several hundred independent contractors sued the company to recover the benefits that Microsoft had made available to its employees but not to the independent contractors. The court held that the workers were entitled to participate in Microsoft's stock-purchase plan and other employee benefits—benefits worth millions of dollars.[6]

6. *Vizcaino v. U.S. District Court for the Western District of Washington*, 173 F.3d 713 (9th Cir. 1999). This case was also mentioned in Chapter 31 in the discussion of the IRS criteria for determining when an agent is an employee.

REVIEWING Law for Small Businesses

APC, Inc., is a venture capital firm that invests in new businesses to help them grow. Wyatt Newmark owns and serves as a chef at "Earp's," a restaurant with a Western design that he operates as a sole proprietorship. Newmark has five employees at his restaurant–three servers, another chef, and a janitor. Newmark has had great success and hopes to expand or franchise the business. Newmark, who has not even retained an attorney for his small business, has approached APC for an investment. Using the information presented in the chapter, answer the following questions.

1. What approaches may APC take in order to invest in the restaurant, and what are the legal implications of each approach?
2. If APC takes an equity interest, the restaurant will need a new legal organizational form. What form would you recommend? Why?
3. In order to preserve the opportunity for growth and a possible franchise, what legal filings should Newmark's entity undertake?
4. What is the difference between employee status and independent-contractor status? Which form of employment relationship would be more advantageous to Newmark? Why should employers be cautious when designating workers as independent contractors?

TERMS AND CONCEPTS

business plan 805
franchise taxes 798
retainer 797
severance pay 810
venture capitalist 805

QUESTIONS AND CASE PROBLEMS

42–1. George Overton has plans for establishing a new business with Elena Costanza. They will both be managers, and each will take an annual salary of $50,000. The company will have other expenses of $175,000. They expect to take in $375,000 in the first year of operation and share the profits equally. George and Elena have not yet decided whether to incorporate the new business or run it as a partnership. What are the tax differences between the two approaches?

42–2. QUESTION WITH SAMPLE ANSWER

Amy forms Best Properties, LLC (BP), to own real estate as a long-term investment. BP acquires a 40,000-square-foot warehouse for $500,000, with the financing arranged for, and guaranteed by, Amy. Later, Carl and Dave become BP members. They sign a "member's agreement," which states, "Amy shall own a 50 percent interest in the capital, profits, and losses of BP and shall have 50 percent of the voting rights. Carl and Dave, collectively, shall own a 50 percent interest in the capital, profits, and losses of BP and shall have 50 percent of the voting rights." BP's sole asset is the warehouse. When relations among the members become strained, Amy executes a deed transferring the warehouse to Excel, LLC, for $500,000. Excel has two members—Amy, with a 60 percent interest, and Carl, with 40 percent. Neither Amy nor Carl discuss the warehouse transfer with Dave, but Amy mails him a check that purports to represent his 25 percent interest in the warehouse. Dave files a suit against Amy and Carl, alleging that the transfer was unfair. On what basis might the court rule in favor of the defendants? Why might the court decide in Dave's favor? Explain.

- **For a sample answer to Question 42–2, go to Appendix I at the end of this text.**

42–3. Owner Liability. Gregory and Dale Stires and Stanley Hall owned and operated the Elk Valley Game Ranch as partners. Hall bought thirty-eight head of elk from Martin Carelli and signed a promissory note agreeing to pay $36,000. Hall also signed a security agreement identifying the elk as collateral. Both the note and the security agreement referred to Hall but not to the Stireses. The elk were kept at the ranch. After Hall quit the partnership, the Stireses continued to operate the ranch. When the note was not paid, Carelli filed a suit in a Montana state court against Hall and the Stireses. The court ruled in Carelli's favor. The Stireses appealed, claiming that Hall was personally liable and they were not. What will the appellate court decide? Why? [*Carelli v. Hall*, 926 P.2d 756 (Mont. 1996)]

42–4. Owner Liability. Harry Lipson was the president of The Folktree Concertmakers, Inc. To obtain concert advertising in the *Boston Globe*, Lipson completed the newspaper's "Standard Application for Credit." He signed the application "Harry Lipson as President of Folktree Concertmakers, Inc." The application package also contained a form called a Guaranty, which he signed simply as "Harry Lipson." Between 1970 and 1995, Folktree placed about $67,000 in advertising with the paper but failed to pay bills totaling $8,556.55. The Boston Globe Newspaper Co. sued both Folktree and Lipson, and the trial court granted summary judgment for the newspaper. Lipson appealed on the ground that he was not personally liable for the debt. Can Lipson be held personally liable for the debt? What should the appellate court decide? Discuss fully. [*The Boston Globe Newspaper Co. v. The Folktree Concertmakers, Inc.*, 1998 Mass.App.Div. 206 (1998)]

42–5. CASE PROBLEM WITH SAMPLE ANSWER

Carol Anstett was a salaried, at-will employee of the Plastics Division of Eagle-Picher Industries, Inc. The Plastics Division had an express severance policy under which "[s]alaried employees terminated other than for cause or voluntary separation" were entitled to certain benefits. In July 1997, Eagle-Picher sold the Plastics Division to Cambridge Industries, Inc. Eagle-Picher notified the Plastics Division employees of what was happening to their health insurance and retirement benefits on "termination of service." Cambridge immediately reemployed nearly all of the Plastics Division personnel, including Anstett. The employees believed that the sale of the division triggered an application of the severance policy and asked Eagle-Picher to pay. The company refused, claiming that the employees had not been terminated. Anstett and others filed a suit in a federal district court against Eagle-Picher, seeking the separation benefits. Eagle-Picher responded that the policy was intended only to cover employees who suffered a loss of income, not to cover a corporate asset sale in which the purchaser immediately rehired the employees. How should the court rule? Explain. [*Anstett v. Eagle-Picher Industries, Inc.*, 203 F.3d 501 (7th Cir. 2000)]

- **To view a sample answer for Problem 42–5, go to this book's Web site at www.cengage.com/blaw/jentz, select "Chapter 42," and click on "Case Problem with Sample Answer."**

42–6. Trade Secrets. J. K. Harris & Co. was a small business that was established to help taxpayers settle delinquent accounts. Harris hired Vicki Dye on February 6, 2001. After several weeks, she was given a "Confidentiality/Non-Disclosure, Non-Solicitation and Non-Compete Agreement" to sign. The company fired Dye on October 2, 2001. Dye subsequently went to work for another small tax-resolution business and sent multiple letters to her former clients. Harris informed Dye that her actions were a serious breach of the confidentiality and noncompete agreement and later filed a suit against her in a federal district court. Harris sought an injunction preventing Dye from contacting former clients and offering tax-resolution services. How would you settle this dispute? Explain. [*J. K. Harris & Co., LLC v. Dye*, __ F.Supp.2d __ (D.Minn. 2001)]

42–7. Trademarks. National Distillers Products Co. was founded to market and sell a vodka called *Teton Glacier*, and the company registered this mark with the U.S. Patent and Trademark Office. National Distillers sought to market the product as an ultrapremium vodka, but it was not very successful. Within a year, Refreshment Brands, Inc. (RBI), began advertising that it would be selling a new vodka product called *Glacier Bay*. After RBI produced the product, National Distillers sued for trademark infringement. Should the plaintiff prevail? [*National Distillers Products Co., L.L.C v. Refreshment Brands, Inc.*, 198 F.Supp.2d 474 (S.D.N.Y. 2002)]

42-8. A QUESTION OF ETHICS

Sean McNamee was the owner of an accounting firm, W. F. McNamee & Co., LLC (WFM), which he founded and formed in Connecticut as a limited liability company (LLC). For federal tax purposes, an LLC can elect to be treated as a corporation or as a sole proprietorship by checking the appropriate box on a certain tax form. A corporation's income is subject to double taxation—the corporation is taxed directly, and its shareholders are taxed on dividends paid to them from the income—but its owners normally are not liable if the firm does not pay its taxes. A sole proprietorship is taxed only once—the owner pays an individual's income tax on the business's income—but its owner is liable if the tax is not paid. In 2000, an LLC with a single owner that did not elect corporate treatment was taxed as a sole proprietorship. McNamee did not elect to have WFM treated as a corporation. During the last six months of 2000 and all of 2001, WFM employed an average of six persons but did not pay any payroll taxes. The unpaid total was $64,736.18. WFM went out of business in 2002. The U.S. Department of the Treasury, through the Internal Revenue Service (IRS), assessed the amount of the unpaid tax against McNamee personally. [McNamee v. Department of the Treasury, *488 F.3d 100 (2d Cir. 2007)*]

(a) McNamee objected to the IRS's attempt to collect the tax from him, pointing to Connecticut statutes under which the members of an LLC are not personally liable for its debts. He argued that the IRS's action was "in direct conflict with the right of an LLC member." How would the IRS likely respond to this objection? Do you agree with McNamee or the IRS? Why? What might McNamee have done to avoid this dispute?

(b) In October 2005, the IRS proposed to amend the check-the-box regulation to relieve the owner of a single-member LLC from the possibility of personal liability for the LLC's payroll tax liability. Does this proposal show that the check-the-box regulation under which McNamee was personally assessed with the amount of the unpaid taxes was "unethical" or "wrong"? Why or why not?

LAW ON THE WEB

For updated links to resources available on the Web, as well as a variety of other materials, visit this text's Web site at

www.cengage.com/blaw/jentz

A number of Web sites can provide valuable assistance for a small business. Lawyers.com maintains a site with helpful advice on various subjects, such as hiring an attorney, at

www.lawyers.com

Court TV and FindLaw jointly operate a wide-ranging site, including a small-business law center that includes legal forms and guidance, at

www.courttv.findlaw.com

Answers to many basic legal questions about running a small business and brief guidance documents can be found at

business-law.freeadvice.com

To obtain tax information and forms, go to the Web site of the Internal Revenue Service at

www.irs.gov

Legal Research Exercises on the Web

Go to **www.cengage.com/blaw/jentz**, the Web site that accompanies this text. Select "Chapter 42" and click on "Internet Exercises." There you will find the following Internet research exercises that you can perform to learn more about the topics covered in this chapter.

Internet Exercise 42–1: Legal Perspective
The Entrepreneur's Options

Internet Exercise 42–2: Management Perspective
Financing a Business

UNIT EIGHT · FOCUS ON ETHICS

Business Organizations

Every now and then, scandals in the business world rock the nation. Certainly, this was true in the early 2000s when the activities of Enron Corporation and a number of other companies came to light. As noted in several chapters in this unit, Congress responded to public outcry in 2002 by passing the Sarbanes-Oxley Act, which imposed stricter requirements on corporations with respect to accounting practices and statements made in documents filed with the Securities and Exchange Commission. The lesson for the business world is, of course, that if business leaders do not behave ethically (and legally), the government will create new laws and regulations that force them to do so. We offered suggestions on how business decision makers can create an ethical workplace in Chapter 5. Here, we look at selected areas in which the relationships within specific business organizational forms may raise ethical issues.

The Emergence of Corporate Governance

The well-publicized corporate abuses of the last ten years have fueled the impetus for businesspersons to create their own internal rules for corporate governance (discussed in Chapter 41). In a few situations, officers have blatantly stolen from the corporation and its shareholders. More frequently, though, officers receive benefits or "perks" of office that are excessive. To illustrate: Tyco International bought a $6,000 shower curtain and a $15,000 umbrella stand for its chief executive officer's apartment.

Corporate officers may be given numerous benefits that they may or may not deserve. A leading corporate officer can receive compensation of $50 million or more in a year when the company's share price is actually declining. Even if corporate officers are scrupulously honest and have modest personal tastes, their behavior may still raise concerns: they may not be good managers, and they may make incompetent corporate choices. They may be a little lazy and fail to do the hard work necessary to investigate corporate decisions. Alternatively, officers may simply fail to appreciate the concerns of shareholders on certain matters, such as maximizing short-term versus long-term results.

Corporate governance controls are meant to ensure that officers receive only the benefits they earn. Governance monitors the actions taken by officers to make sure they are wise and in the best interests of the company. In this way, the corporation can be confident that it is acting ethically toward its shareholders.

Fiduciary Duties Revisited

As outlined in Chapters 31 and 32, the law of agency permeates virtually all relationships within any partnership or corporation. An important duty that arises in the law of agency, and applies to all partners and corporate directors, officers, and management personnel, is the duty of loyalty. As caretakers of the shareholders' wealth, corporate directors and officers also have a fiduciary duty to exercise care when making decisions affecting the corporate enterprise.

The Duty of Loyalty Every individual has his or her own personal interests, which may at times conflict with the interests of the partnership or corporation with which he or she is affiliated. In particular, a partner or a corporate director may face a conflict between personal interests and the interests of the business entity. Corporate officers and directors may find themselves in a position to acquire assets that would also benefit the corporation if acquired in the corporation's name. If an officer does purchase the asset without offering the opportunity to the corporation, however, she or he may be liable for usurping a corporate opportunity.[1]

Most courts also hold that a corporate officer or director has a fiduciary duty to disclose improper conduct to the corporation. The Supreme Court of Arkansas weighed in on this issue in 2007. Thomas Coughlin was a top executive in theft prevention at Wal-Mart who held several other high-level positions prior to becoming a member of the corporation's board of directors. He retired in 2005 and entered into a retirement agreement and release of claims with Wal-Mart under which he was to receive millions of dollars in benefits over the years.

Then Wal-Mart discovered that Coughlin, prior to retiring, had been abusing his position of authority and conspiring with subordinates to misappropriate hundreds of thousands of dollars in property and cash through various fraudulent schemes. Wal-Mart filed a lawsuit alleging that Coughlin had breached his fiduciary duty of loyalty by failing to disclose his misconduct before entering a self-dealing contract. Ultimately, the state's highest court agreed and held that the director's fiduciary duty obligated him to

1. For a landmark case on this issue, see *Guth v. Loft, Inc.*, 5 A.2d 503 (Del. 1939), presented as Case 39.1 in Chapter 39.

divulge material facts of *past* fraud to the corporation before entering the contract. The court stated, "[W]e are persuaded, in addition, that the majority view is correct, which is that the failure of a fiduciary to disclose material facts of his fraudulent conduct to his corporation prior to entering into a self-dealing contract with that corporation will void that contract."[2]

The Duty of Care In addition to the duty of loyalty, every corporate director or officer owes a duty of care. *Due care* means that officers and directors must keep themselves informed and make businesslike judgments. Officers have a duty to disclose material information that shareholders need for competent decision making. Some courts have even suggested that corporate directors have a duty to detect and "ferret out" wrongdoing within the corporation.[3] In fact, a number of courts applying Delaware law have recognized that directors may be held liable for failing to exercise proper oversight.[4] Corporate law also creates other structures to protect shareholder interests, such as the right to inspect books and records.

Although traditionally the duty of care did not require directors to monitor the behavior of corporate employees to detect and prevent wrongdoing, the tide may be changing. Since the corporate sentencing guidelines were issued in 1991, courts have the power to impose substantial penalties on corporations and corporate directors for criminal wrongdoing. The guidelines allow these penalties to be mitigated, though, if a company can show that it has an effective compliance program in place to detect and prevent wrongdoing by corporate personnel. Since the Sarbanes-Oxley Act of 2002 required the sentencing commission to revise these guidelines, the penalties for white-collar crimes, such as federal mail and wire fraud, have increased dramatically.

Fiduciary Duties to Creditors It is a long-standing principle that corporate directors ordinarily owe fiduciary duties only to a corporation's shareholders.

Focus on Ethics

Directors who favor the interests of other corporate "stakeholders," such as creditors, over those of the shareholders have been held liable for breaching these duties. The picture changes, however, when a corporation approaches insolvency. At this point, the shareholders' equity interests in the corporation may be worthless, while the interests of creditors become paramount. In this situation, do the fiduciary duties of loyalty and care extend to the corporation's creditors as well as to the shareholders? The answer to this question, according to some courts, is yes. In a leading case on this issue, a Delaware court noted that "[t]he possibility of insolvency can do curious things to incentives, exposing creditors to risks of opportunistic behavior and creating complexities for directors." The court held that when a corporation is on the brink of insolvency, the directors assume a fiduciary duty to other stakeholders that sustain the corporate entity, including creditors.[5]

Online Chat Rooms and Securities Fraud

The Securities and Exchange Commission (SEC) typically claims that fraud occurs when a false statement of fact is made. Many statements about stock, however, such as "this stock is headed for $20," are simply opinions. Opinions can never be labeled true or false at the time they are made; otherwise, they would not be opinions. As long as a person has a "genuine belief" that an opinion is true, then presumably no fraud is involved. Yet what if negative "opinions" about a certain company cause the price of its stock to drop? Does the company have any legal recourse against those expressing the opinions?

The Problem Facing GTMI Consider the problem facing Global Telemedia International, Inc. (GTMI). In March 2000, GTMI's stock was trading at $4.70 per share. That month, persons using various aliases began to post messages in the GTMI chat room on the Raging Bull Web site. (Raging Bull is a financial service Web site that organizes chat rooms dedicated to publicly traded companies.) The messages were critical of GTMI and its officers. Over the next six months, GTMI's stock price declined significantly—by October, the stock was closing at

2. *Wal-Mart Stores, Inc. v. Coughlin,* 369 Ark. 365, ___ S.W.3d ___ (2007).

3. *In re Caremark International, Inc. Derivative Litigation,* 698 A.2d 959 (Del.Ch. 1996); also *Forsythe v. ESC Fund Management Co. (U.S.), Inc.,* 2007 WL 2982247 (Del.Ch. 2007).

4. See, for example, *McCall v. Scott,* 239 F.3d 808 (6th Cir. 2001); *Guttman v. Huang,* 823 A.2d 492 (Del.Ch. 2003); *Landy v. D'Alessandro,* 316 F.Supp.2d 49 (D.Mass. 2004); and *Miller v. U.S. Foodservice, Inc.,* 361 F.Supp.2d 470 (D.Md. 2005).

5. *Credit Lyonnais Bank Nederland N.V. v. Pathe Communications Corp.,* 1991 WL 277613 (Del.Ch. 1991). See also *Production Resources Group, LLC v. NCT Group, Inc.,* 863 A.2d 772 (Del.Ch. 2004); and *In re Amcast Industrial Corp.,* 365 Bankr. 91 (S.D. Ohio 2007).

(Continued)

$0.25 a share. In an attempt to recoup damages, GTMI sued the "John Does" for defamation (see Chapter 6).

Had Defamation Occurred? The court noted that defamation of a publicly traded company requires a "false statement of fact made with malice that caused damage." The defendants (those who posted the messages) asserted that their online statements were not actionable because they were statements of opinion, not statements of fact. Ultimately, the court agreed with the defendants.

In reaching its decision, the court looked at the "totality of the circumstances," including the context and format of the statements, as well as the expectations of the audience in that particular situation. Here, said the court, the context and format of the statements—anonymous postings "in the general cacophony of an Internet chat room in which about 1,000 messages a week are posted about GTMI"— strongly suggested that the postings constituted opinion, not fact.[6]

The Sarbanes-Oxley Act and Insider Trading

The attorney-client privilege generally prevents lawyers from disclosing confidential client information—even when the client has committed an unlawful act. The idea is to encourage clients to be open and honest with their attorneys to ensure competent representation. The Sarbanes-Oxley Act of 2002, however, requires attorneys to report any material violations of securities laws to the corporation's highest authority.[7] The act does not require that the lawyer break client confidences, though, because the lawyer is still reporting to officials within the corporation.

In August 2003, the SEC went one step further than the Sarbanes-Oxley Act to permit attorneys to disclose confidential information to the SEC without the corporate client's consent in certain circumstances.[8] Although the American Bar Association modified its ethics rules to allow attorneys to break confidence with a client to report possible corporate fraud, not all state ethics codes allow attorneys to disclose client information to the SEC. Thus, by reporting possible violations of securities law to the SEC, corporate lawyers may violate the state ethics code of their profession.

DISCUSSION QUESTIONS

1. Three decades ago, corporations and corporate directors were rarely prosecuted for crimes, and penalties for corporate crimes were relatively light. Today, this is no longer true. Under the corporate sentencing guidelines and the Sarbanes-Oxley Act, corporate wrongdoers can receive strict penalties. Do these developments mean that corporations are committing more crimes today than in the past? Will stricter laws be effective in curbing corporate criminal activity? How can a company avoid liability for crimes committed by its employees?
2. Do you agree that when a corporation is approaching insolvency, the directors' fiduciary obligations should extend to the corporation's creditors as well as to the shareholders? Why or why not?
3. "When opinions about a company's reputation are exchanged in Internet chat rooms and those opinions cause the price of the company's stock to decline, the company may have a cause of action for defamation." How would you argue in favor of this proposition? How would you argue against it?
4. Should corporate lawyers who become aware that someone at the client corporation may have violated securities laws report their suspicions only to persons within the corporation, or should they report their concerns to the SEC? Explain.

6. *Global Telemedia International, Inc. v. Does,* 132 F.Supp.2d 1261 (C.D.Cal. 2001). See also *Troy Group, Inc. v. Tilson,* 364 F.Supp.2d 1149 (C.D.Cal. 2005), which involved allegations of defamation against an investor based on statements in an e-mail message.

7. See Section 307 of the Sarbanes-Oxley Act.

8. See 17 C.F.R. Part 205.3.

UNIT NINE

Government Regulation

CONTENTS

CHAPTER 43

Administrative Law

Government agencies established to administer the law have a great impact on the day-to-day operations of the government and the economy. Administrative agencies issue rules covering virtually every aspect of a business's activities. At the federal level, the Securities and Exchange Commission regulates a firm's capital structure and financing, as well as its financial reporting. The National Labor Relations Board oversees relations between a firm and any unions with which it may deal. The Equal Employment Opportunity Commission also regulates employer-employee relationships. The Environmental Protection Agency and the Occupational Safety and Health Administration affect the way a firm manufactures its products, and the Federal Trade Commission influences the way it markets those products.

Added to this layer of federal regulation is a second layer of state regulation that, when not preempted, may cover many of the same activities as federal regulation or regulate independently the activities that federal regulation does not cover. Finally, agency regulations at the county or municipal level also affect certain types of business activities.

The rules, orders, and decisions of administrative agencies make up the body of *administrative law*. You were introduced briefly to some of the main principles of administrative law in Chapter 1. In the following pages, we look at these principles in much greater detail.

SECTION 1 The Practical Significance of Administrative Law

Unlike statutory law, administrative law is created by administrative agencies, not by legislatures, but it is nevertheless of paramount significance for businesses. When Congress—or a state legislature—enacts legislation, it typically adopts a rather general statute and leaves its implementation to an administrative agency, which then creates the detailed rules and regulations necessary to carry out the statute. The administrative agency, with its specialized personnel, has the time, resources, and expertise to make the detailed decisions required for regulation. For example, when Congress enacted the Clean Air Act, it provided only general directions for the prevention of air pollution. The specific pollution-control requirements imposed on business are almost entirely the product of decisions made by the Environmental Protection Agency (EPA).

Legislation and regulations have great benefits—in the example of the Clean Air Act, a much cleaner environment than existed in decades past. At the same time, these benefits entail costs for business. The EPA has estimated the costs of compliance with the Clean Air Act at tens of billions of dollars yearly. Although the agency has calculated that the overall benefits of its regulations often exceed their costs, the burden on business is substantial. The U.S. Small Business Administration has estimated the costs of regulation to business, by size of business, and produced the figures shown in Exhibit 43–1.[1] These costs are averages and vary considerably by type of business (for example,

1. W. Mark Crain, "The Impact of Regulatory Costs on Small Firms," Small Business Research Summary No. 264, September 2005.

EXHIBIT 43–1 • Costs of Regulation to Businesses

Type of Regulation	Cost per Employee (<20 Employees)	Cost per Employee (500+ Employees)
All federal regulations	$7,647	$5,283
Environmental	$3,296	$ 710
Economic	$2,127	$2,952
Workplace	$ 920	$ 841
Tax compliance	$1,304	$ 780

retail or manufacturing). The costs are proportionately higher for small businesses because they cannot take advantage of the economies of scale available to larger operations. Clearly, the costs of regulation to business are considerable and are significantly higher today than they were in 2005 when the estimates were made.

Given the costs that regulation entails, business has a strong incentive to try to influence the regulatory environment. Whenever new regulations are proposed, as happens constantly, companies may lobby the agency to try to persuade it not to adopt a particular regulation or to adopt one that is more cost-effective. These lobbying efforts consist mainly of providing information to regulators about the costs and problems that the rule may pose for business. At the same time, public-interest groups may be lobbying in favor of more stringent regulation. The rulemaking process, including these lobbying efforts, is governed by administrative law. If persuasion fails, administrative law also provides a tool by which businesses or other groups may challenge the legality of the new regulation.

SECTION 2 Agency Creation and Powers

To create an administrative agency, Congress passes **enabling legislation,** which specifies the name, purposes, functions, and powers of the agency being created. Federal administrative agencies may exercise only those powers that Congress has delegated to them in enabling legislation. Through similar enabling acts, state legislatures create state administrative agencies, which commonly parallel federal agencies.

An agency's enabling statute defines its legal authority. An agency cannot regulate beyond the powers granted by the statute, and it may be required to take some regulatory action by the terms of that statute.

Enabling Legislation—An Example

Consider the enabling legislation for the Federal Trade Commission (FTC). The enabling statute for this agency is the Federal Trade Commission Act of 1914.[2] The act prohibits unfair methods of competition and deceptive trade practices. It also describes the procedures that the FTC must follow to charge persons or organizations with violations of the act, and it provides for judicial review of agency orders. The act grants the FTC the power to do the following:

1. Create "rules and regulations for the purpose of carrying out the Act."
2. Conduct investigations of business practices.
3. Obtain reports from interstate corporations concerning their business practices.
4. Investigate possible violations of federal antitrust statutes.[3]
5. Publish findings of its investigations.
6. Recommend new legislation.
7. Hold trial-like hearings to resolve certain kinds of trade disputes that involve FTC regulations or federal antitrust laws.

The authorizing statute for the FTC allows it to prevent the use of "unfair methods of competition," but does not define *unfairness.* Congress delegated that authority to the commission, thereby providing it with considerable discretion in regulating competition.

2. 15 U.S.C. Sections 41–58.
3. The FTC shares enforcement of the Clayton Act with the Antitrust Division of the U.S. Department of Justice.

When regulated groups oppose a rule adopted by an agency, they often bring a lawsuit arguing that the rule was not authorized by the enabling statute and is therefore void. Conversely, a group may file a suit claiming that an agency has illegally *failed* to pursue regulation required by the enabling statute.

Types of Agencies

As discussed in Chapter 1, there are two basic types of administrative agencies: executive agencies and independent regulatory agencies. Federal *executive agencies* include the cabinet departments of the executive branch, which were formed to assist the president in carrying out executive functions, and the subagencies within the cabinet departments. The Occupational Safety and Health Administration, for example, is a subagency within the U.S. Department of Labor. Exhibit 43–2 on page 822 lists the cabinet departments and some of their most important subagencies.

All administrative agencies are part of the executive branch of government, but *independent regulatory agencies* are outside the major executive departments. The Federal Trade Commission and the Securities and Exchange Commission are examples of independent regulatory agencies. These and other selected independent regulatory agencies, as well as their principal functions, are listed in Exhibit 43–3 on page 823.

The accountability of the regulators is the most significant difference between the two types of agencies. Agencies that are considered part of the executive branch are subject to the authority of the president, who has the power to appoint and remove federal officers. The president could give orders to the head of an executive agency and fire him or her for failing to carry them out. This power is less pronounced in regard to independent agencies, whose officers serve for fixed terms and cannot be removed without just cause. In practice, however, the president's ability to exert influence over independent regulatory agencies is often considerable because the president has the authority to appoint the members of the agencies.

All three branches of government exercise certain controls over agency powers and functions, as will be discussed later in this chapter, but in many ways administrative agencies function independently. None of the other branches, including the presidency, has the time and resources necessary to monitor the multitude of administrative actions constantly under way. For this reason, administrative agencies, which constitute the **bureaucracy,** are sometimes referred to as the "fourth branch" of the U.S. government.

SECTION 3 The Administrative Procedure Act

All federal agencies must follow specific procedural requirements in their rulemaking, adjudication, and other functions. Sometimes, Congress specifies certain procedural requirements in an agency's enabling legislation. In the absence of any directives from Congress concerning a particular agency procedure, the Administrative Procedure Act (APA) of 1946[4] applies.

The Arbitrary and Capricious Test

One of Congress's goals in enacting the APA was to provide for more judicial control over administrative agencies, which had assumed greater powers during the expansion of government that had taken place as a result of the Great Depression of the 1930s and World War II (1939–1945). To that end, the APA provides that courts should "hold unlawful and set aside" agency actions found to be "arbitrary, capricious, an abuse of discretion, or otherwise not in accordance with law."[5] Under this standard, parties can challenge regulations as contrary to law or so irrational as to be arbitrary and capricious.

The definition of what makes a rule arbitrary and capricious is a vague one, but it includes factors such as whether the agency has done any of the following:

1. Failed to provide a rational explanation for its decision.
2. Changed its prior policy without justification.
3. Considered legally inappropriate factors.
4. Entirely failed to consider a relevant factor.
5. Rendered a decision plainly contrary to the evidence.

The following case considers the application of the arbitrary and capricious standard.

4. 5 U.S.C. Sections 551–706.
5. 5 U.S.C. Section 706(2)(A).

CASE 43.1 Fox Television Stations, Inc. v. Federal Communications Commission

United States Court of Appeals, Second Circuit, 2007. 489 F.3d 444.

- **Background and Facts** Since 1975, the Federal Communications Commission (FCC) has exercised its statutory authority to sanction indecent (but nonobscene) speech. The FCC defines such speech as "language that describes, in terms patently offensive as measured by contemporary community standards for the broadcast medium, sexual or excretory activities and organs." In 2003, the FCC held that any variant of "the F-Word has inherent sexual connotation" and therefore fell within the scope of the indecency definition, even if used "fleetingly" on television or radio. On February 21, 2006, the FCC determined that Fox Television Stations, Inc.'s broadcasts of several Billboard Musical Awards shows were "indecent and profane." Fox filed a petition for review of the FCC's order in the U.S. Court of Appeals for the Second Circuit.

- **Decision and Rationale** The appellate court granted Fox's petition for review. It vacated the FCC's order and remanded the matter to the FCC for further proceedings. The court observed that the FCC had permitted "fleeting expletives" in previous years but justified its current crackdown with the "first blow" theory. This theory holds that because indecent material on television can enter "the home uninvited and without warning," saying that viewers can avoid further offense by turning off the television when they hear indecent language is "like saying that the remedy for an assault is to run away after the first blow." The appellate court was not persuaded. It pointed out that the FCC waited thirty years to change its perception of "fleeting expletives." The so-called first blow theory "bears no rational connection to the Commission's actual policy regarding fleeting expletives." Moreover, "even top leaders of our government have used variants of these expletives in a manner that no reasonable person would believe referenced 'sexual or excretory organs or activities.'" The court noted several occasions when the U.S. president and vice president had used questionable words in public.

- **The Legal Environment Dimension** *According to the court's opinion in this case, is an administrative agency locked into its first interpretation of a statute?*

- **The Ethical Dimension** *Were the agency's reasons for its actions rejected in this case because the court disagreed with those reasons? Explain.*

Rulemaking Procedures

Today, the major function of an administrative agency is **rulemaking**—the formulation of new regulations, or rules, as they are often called. The APA defines a *rule* as "an agency statement of general or particular applicability and future effect designed to implement, interpret, or prescribe law and policy."[6] Regulations are sometimes said to be *quasi-legislative* because, like statutes, they have a binding effect. Like those who violate statutes, violators of agency rules may be punished. Because agency rules have such great legal force, the APA established procedures for agencies to follow in creating rules. Many rules must be adopted using the APA's *notice-and-comment rulemaking* procedure.

Notice-and-comment rulemaking involves three basic steps: notice of the proposed rulemaking, a comment period, and the final rule. The APA recognizes some limited exceptions to these procedural requirements, but they are seldom invoked. If the required procedures are violated, the resulting rule may be invalid. The impetus for rulemaking may come from various sources, including Congress, the agency itself, or private parties who may petition an agency to begin a rulemaking (or repeal a rule). For example, environmental groups have petitioned for stricter pollution controls to combat global warming.

Notice of the Proposed Rulemaking When a federal agency decides to create a new rule, the agency publishes a notice of the proposed rulemaking proceedings in the *Federal Register*, a daily publication

6. 5 U.S.C. Section 551(4).

EXHIBIT 43–2 • Executive Departments and Important Subagencies

Department and Date Formed	Selected Subagencies
State (1789)	Passport Office; Bureau of Diplomatic Security; Foreign Service; Bureau of Human Rights and Humanitarian Affairs; Bureau of Consular Affairs; Bureau of Intelligence and Research
Treasury (1789)	Internal Revenue Service; U.S. Mint
Interior (1849)	U.S. Fish and Wildlife Service; National Park Service; Bureau of Indian Affairs; Bureau of Land Management
Justice (1870)[a]	Federal Bureau of Investigation; Drug Enforcement Administration; Bureau of Prisons; U.S. Marshals Service
Agriculture (1889)	Soil Conservation Service; Agricultural Research Service; Food Safety and Inspection Service; Forest Service
Commerce (1913)[b]	Bureau of the Census; Bureau of Economic Analysis; Minority Business Development Agency; U.S. Patent and Trademark Office; National Oceanic and Atmospheric Administration
Labor (1913)[b]	Occupational Safety and Health Administration; Bureau of Labor Statistics; Employment Standards Administration; Office of Labor-Management Standards; Employment and Training Administration
Defense (1949)[c]	National Security Agency; Joint Chiefs of Staff; Departments of the Air Force, Navy, Army; service academies
Housing and Urban Development (1965)	Office of Community Planning and Development; Government National Mortgage Association; Office of Fair Housing and Equal Opportunity
Transportation (1967)	Federal Aviation Administration; Federal Highway Administration; National Highway Traffic Safety Administration; Federal Transit Administration
Energy (1977)	Office of Civilian Radioactive Waste Management; Office of Nuclear Energy; Energy Information Administration
Health and Human Services (1980)[d]	Food and Drug Administration; Centers for Medicare and Medicaid Services; Centers for Disease Control and Prevention; National Institutes of Health
Education (1980)[d]	Office of Special Education and Rehabilitation Services; Office of Elementary and Secondary Education; Office of Postsecondary Education; Office of Vocational and Adult Education
Veterans Affairs (1989)	Veterans Health Administration; Veterans Benefits Administration; National Cemetery System
Homeland Security (2002)	U.S. Citizenship and Immigration Services; U.S. Customs and Border Protection; Transportation Security Administration; U.S. Coast Guard; Federal Emergency Management Agency

a. Formed from the Office of the Attorney General (created in 1789).
b. Formed from the Department of Commerce and Labor (created in 1903).
c. Formed from the Department of War (created in 1789) and the Department of the Navy (created in 1798).
d. Formed from the Department of Health, Education, and Welfare (created in 1953).

EXHIBIT 43–3 • Selected Independent Regulatory Agencies

Name and Date Formed	Principal Duties
Federal Reserve System Board of Governors (Fed) (1913)	Determines policy with respect to interest rates, credit availability, and the money supply.
Federal Trade Commission (FTC) (1914)	Prevents businesses from engaging in unfair trade practices; stops the formation of monopolies in the business sector; protects consumer rights.
Securities and Exchange Commission (SEC) (1934)	Regulates the nation's stock exchanges, in which shares of stock are bought and sold; enforces the securities laws, which require full disclosure of the financial profiles of companies that wish to sell stock and bonds to the public.
Federal Communications Commission (FCC) (1934)	Regulates all communications by telegraph, cable, telephone, radio, satellite, and television.
National Labor Relations Board (NLRB) (1935)	Protects employees' rights to join unions and bargain collectively with employers; attempts to prevent unfair labor practices by both employers and unions.
Equal Employment Opportunity Commission (EEOC) (1964)	Works to eliminate discrimination in employment based on religion, gender, race, color, disability, national origin, or age; investigates claims of discrimination.
Environmental Protection Agency (EPA) (1970)	Undertakes programs aimed at reducing air and water pollution; works with state and local agencies to help fight environmental hazards.
Nuclear Regulatory Commission (NRC) (1975)	Ensures that electricity-generating nuclear reactors in the United States are built and operated safely; regularly inspects operations of such reactors.

of the executive branch that prints government orders, rules, and regulations. The notice states where and when the proceedings will be held, the agency's legal authority for making the rule (usually its enabling legislation), and the terms or subject matter of the proposed rule. Courts have ruled that the APA requires an agency to make available to the public certain information, such as the key scientific data underlying the proposal.

Comment Period Following the publication of the notice of the proposed rulemaking proceedings, the agency must allow ample time for persons to comment in writing on the proposed rule. The purpose of this comment period is to give interested parties the opportunity to express their views on the proposed rule in an effort to influence agency policy. The comments may be in writing or, if a hearing is held, may be given orally.

The agency need not respond to all comments, but it must respond to any significant comments that bear directly on the proposed rule. The agency responds by either modifying its final rule or explaining, in a statement accompanying the final rule, why it did not make any changes. In some circumstances, particularly when the procedure being used in a specific instance is less formal, an agency may accept comments after the comment period is closed. The agency should summarize these *ex parte*[7] comments in the record for possible review.

The Final Rule After the agency reviews the comments, it drafts the final rule and publishes it in the *Federal Register*. Such a final rule must contain a "concise general statement of . . . basis and purpose" that describes the reasoning behind the rule.[8]

7. In Latin, *ex parte* means "from the part." In the law, it refers to one of the parties taking some action on his or her own, such as communicating with a judge or bringing a motion, without notifying the other party or giving the other party a chance to respond.
8. 5 U.S.C. Section 555(c).

The final rule may change the terms of the proposed rule, in light of the public comments, but cannot change the proposal too radically, or a new proposal and a new opportunity for comment are required. The final rule is later compiled along with the rules and regulations of other federal administrative agencies in the *Code of Federal Regulations* (C.F.R.). Final rules have binding legal effect unless the courts later overturn them. For this reason, they are often referred to as legislative rules. *Legislative rules* are substantive in that they affect legal rights, whereas *interpretive rules* issued by agencies simply declare policy and do not affect legal rights or obligations (see the discussion of informal agency actions later in this chapter).

The court in the following case considered whether to enforce rules that were issued outside the rulemaking procedure.

CASE 43.2 Hemp Industries Association v. Drug Enforcement Administration

United States Court of Appeals, Ninth Circuit, 2004. 357 F.3d 1012.

• **Background and Facts** The members of the Hemp Industries Association (HIA) import and distribute sterilized hemp seed and oil and cake derived from hemp seed. They also make and sell food and cosmetic products made from hemp seed and oil. These products contain only nonpsychoactive trace amounts of tetrahydrocannabinols (THC).[a] On October 9, 2001, the U.S. Drug Enforcement Administration (DEA) published an interpretive rule declaring that "any product that contains any amount of THC is a Schedule I controlled substance."[b] On the same day, the DEA proposed two legislative rules. One rule—DEA-205F—amended the listing of THC in Schedule I to include natural, as well as synthetic, THC. The second rule—DEA-206F—exempted from control nonpsychoactive hemp products that contain trace amounts of THC not intended to enter the human body. On March 21, 2003, without following formal rulemaking procedures, the DEA declared that these rules were final. This effectively banned the possession and sale of the food products of the HIA's members. The HIA petitioned the U.S. Court of Appeals for the Ninth Circuit to review the rules, asserting that they should not be enforced.

• **Decision and Rationale** The U.S. Court of Appeals for the Ninth Circuit held that DEA-205F and DEA-206F "are inconsistent with the unambiguous meaning of the CSA definitions of marijuana and THC, and the DEA did not use the appropriate scheduling procedures to add nonpsychoactive hemp to the list of controlled substances." The court issued an injunction against the enforcement of the rules with respect to nonpsychoactive hemp or products containing it. The DEA argued that THC in the parts of the hemp plant "excluded from the definition of 'marijuana' have always been included under the listing for 'THC' " in the applicable statutes. The court explained that those statutes provided otherwise. Congress's "intent to exclude nonpyschoactive hemp from regulation is entirely clear." About the DEA's attempted rulemaking, the court stated, "Formal rulemaking requires hearings on the record, and [the Administrative Procedures Act] invites parties to submit proposed findings and oppose the stated bases of tentative agency decisions, and requires the agency to issue formal rulings on each finding, conclusion, or exception on the record." The court pointed out that in this case, "the DEA did not and does not claim to have followed formal rulemaking procedures" nor did the agency make the required findings to issue the rules.

• **What If the Facts Were Different?** *Suppose that the statutory definitions of THC and marijuana covered naturally occurring THC and nonpsychoactive hemp. Would the result in this case have been different? Explain.*

• **The E-Commerce Dimension** *How might the Internet expedite formal rulemaking procedures such as those required by the U.S. Court of Appeals for the Ninth Circuit in this case? Discuss.*

a. A *nonpsychoactive substance* is one that does not affect a person's mind or behavior. Nonpsychoactive hemp is derived from industrial hemp plants grown in Canada and in Europe, the flowers of which contain only a trace amount of the THC contained in marijuana varieties grown for psychoactive use.

b. A *controlled substance* is a drug whose availability is restricted by law.

Informal Agency Actions

Rather than take the time to conduct notice-and-comment rulemaking, agencies have increasingly been using more informal methods of policymaking. These include issuing interpretive rules, which are specifically exempted from the APA's requirements. Such rules simply declare the agency's interpretation of its enabling statute's meaning, and they impose no direct and legally binding obligations on regulated parties. In addition, agencies issue various other materials, such as "guidance documents," that advise the public on the agencies' legal and policy positions.

Such informal actions are exempt from the APA's requirements because they do not establish legal rights—a party cannot be directly prosecuted for violating an interpretive rule or a guidance document. Nevertheless, an agency's informal action can be of practical importance because it warns regulated entities that the agency may engage in formal rulemaking if they fail to heed the positions taken informally by the agency.

SECTION 4 Judicial Deference to Agency Decisions

When asked to review agency decisions, courts historically granted some deference (significant weight) to the agency's judgment, often citing the agency's great expertise in the subject area of the regulation. This deference seems especially appropriate when applied to an agency's analysis of factual questions, but should it also extend to an agency's interpretation of its own legal authority? In *Chevron U.S.A., Inc. v. Natural Resources Defense Council, Inc.*,[9] the United States Supreme Court held that it should, thereby creating a standard of broadened deference to agencies on questions of legal interpretation.

The Holding of the *Chevron* Case

At issue in the *Chevron* case was whether the courts should defer to an agency's interpretation of a statute giving it authority to act. The Environmental Protection Agency (EPA) had interpreted the phrase "stationary source" in the Clean Air Act as referring to an entire manufacturing plant, and not to each facility within a plant. The agency's interpretation enabled it to adopt the so-called bubble policy that allowed companies to offset increases in emissions in part of a plant with decreases elsewhere in the plant—an interpretation that reduced the pollution-control compliance costs faced by manufacturers. An environmental group challenged the legality of the EPA's interpretation.

The Supreme Court held that the courts should defer to an agency's interpretation of *law* as well as fact. The Court found that the agency's interpretation of the statute was reasonable and upheld the bubble policy. The Court's decision in the *Chevron* case created a new standard for courts to use when reviewing agency interpretations of law, which involves the following two questions:

1. Did Congress directly address the issue in dispute in the statute? If so, the statutory language prevails.
2. If the statute is silent or ambiguous, is the agency's interpretation "reasonable"? If it is, a court should uphold the agency's interpretation even if the court would have interpreted the law differently.

When Courts Will Give *Chevron* Deference to Agency Interpretation

The notion that courts should defer to agencies on matters of law was controversial. Under the holding of the *Chevron* case, when the meaning of a particular statute's language is unclear and an agency interprets it, the court must follow the agency's interpretation as long as it is reasonable. This led to considerable discussion and litigation to test the boundaries of the *Chevron* holding. For instance, are courts required to give deference to all agency interpretations or only to those interpretations that result from adjudication or formal rulemaking procedures? The United States Supreme Court has held that in order for agency interpretations to be assured of *Chevron* deference, they must meet the formal legal standards for notice-and-comment rulemaking.[10] Nevertheless, there are still gray areas, and many agency interpretations are challenged in court.

In the case that follows, an environmental organization brought an action challenging the U.S. Forest Service's decision to issue a special use permit to a

9. 467 U.S. 837, 104 S.Ct. 2778, 81 L.Ed.2d 694 (1984).

10. *United States v. Mead Corp.*, 533 U.S. 218, 121 S.Ct. 2164, 150 L.Ed.2d 292 (2001).

business that conducts helicopter-skiing operations in two national forests. As you will read in Chapter 45, the National Environmental Policy Act requires federal agencies to prepare an *environmental impact statement* (EIS) that considers every significant aspect of the environmental impact of a proposed action. Although the Forest Service prepared an EIS before issuing the use permit to the helicopter-skiing operation, environmental groups claimed that the EIS did not sufficiently analyze increasing recreational pressures in the forests. The groups sought to have the court invalidate the permit.

CASE 43.3 Citizens' Committee to Save Our Canyons v. Krueger

United States Court of Appeals, Tenth Circuit, 2008. 513 F.3d 1169.

• **Background and Facts** Under the National Forest Management Act (NFMA), the U.S. Forest Service manages national forests pursuant to forest plans periodically developed for each forest. The plans for two national forests—the Wasatch-Cache and Uinta forests—were initially adopted in 1985 and revised in 2003. The Forest Service interpreted the 1985 forest plans as requiring the forests to allow helicopter skiing, and the plans expressly recognized helicopter skiing as a legitimate use of the national forests. Wasatch Powderbird Guides (WPG) has continuously operated a guided helicopter-skiing business in the Wasatch-Cache and Uinta national forests since 1973. It operates pursuant to special use permits periodically issued by the Forest Service. Citizens' Committee to Save Our Canyons and Utah Environmental Congress (referred to collectively as SOC) are nonprofit organizations composed of members who use the areas in which WPG operates for nonmotorized uses such as backcountry skiing, snowshoeing, hiking, and camping. They claim that their recreational opportunities and experiences are diminished by WPG's operations and argue that the Forest Service failed to comply with relevant laws when issuing WPG's most recent permit. The district court upheld the Forest Service permit, and SOC appealed to the U.S. Court of Appeals for the Tenth Circuit.

• **Decision and Rationale** The U.S. Court of Appeals for the Tenth Circuit affirmed the decision of the district court upholding the Forest Service permit allowing WPG to conduct helicopter-skiing operations in two national forests. The appeals court pointed out that it will set aside an agency's action *only* if it is "arbitrary, capricious, an abuse of discretion, or otherwise not in accordance with law, or" if that agency has failed to follow required procedures. "The duty of a court reviewing agency action under the 'arbitrary or capricious' standard is to ascertain whether the agency examined the relevant data and articulated a rational connection between facts found and the decision made. * * * The reviewing court must determine whether the agency considered all relevant factors * * *." The court stated that the Forest Service's environmental impact statement fully disclosed and considered the impact of its decision to issue a special use permit to a helicopter-skiing service. The court further noted that there had been an extensive period for public comment and that the Forest Service had imposed reasonable restrictions on the helicopter-skiing service operations "designed to minimize conflict among forest users." The Forest Service's procedure considered all relevant factors and allowed for public comment. The permit was in compliance with federal laws.

• **What If the Facts Were Different?** *Suppose that the Forest Service had granted WPG a permit for its helicopter-skiing operations on national forest land without preparing an EIS or soliciting public comment. How might that have changed the court's ruling in this case?*

• **The Ethical Dimension** *If it turned out that the helicopter-skiing operation had paid a substantial sum to the Forest Service official who prepared the EIS to influence its findings, would the court have been able to consider this fact and invalidate the permit? Why or why not?*

SECTION 5

Agency Enforcement and Adjudication

Although rulemaking is the most prominent agency activity, enforcement of the rules is also critical. Often, an agency itself enforces its rules. It identifies alleged violators and pursues civil remedies against them in a proceeding held by the agency rather than in federal court, although the agency's determinations are reviewable in court.

Investigation

After final rules are issued, agencies conduct investigations to monitor compliance with those rules or the terms of the enabling statute. A typical agency investigation of this kind might begin when a citizen reports a possible violation to the agency. Many agency rules also require considerable compliance reporting from regulated entities, and such a report may trigger an enforcement investigation. For example, environmental regulators often require reporting of emissions, and the Occupational Safety and Health Administration (OSHA) requires companies to report any work-related deaths.

Inspections Many agencies gather information through on-site inspections. Sometimes, inspecting an office, a factory, or some other business facility is the only way to obtain the evidence needed to prove a regulatory violation. Administrative inspections and tests cover a wide range of activities, including safety inspections of underground coal mines, safety tests of commercial equipment and automobiles, and environmental monitoring of factory emissions. An agency may also ask a firm or individual to submit certain documents or records to the agency for examination. For example, the Federal Trade Commission often asks to inspect corporate records for compliance.

Normally, business firms comply with agency requests to inspect facilities or business records because it is in any firm's interest to maintain a good relationship with regulatory bodies. In some instances, however, such as when a firm thinks an agency's request is unreasonable and may be detrimental to the firm's interest, the firm may refuse to comply with the request. In such situations, an agency may resort to the use of a subpoena or a search warrant.

Subpoenas There are two basic types of subpoenas. The subpoena *ad testificandum* (to testify) is an ordinary subpoena. It is a writ, or order, compelling a witness to appear at an agency hearing. The subpoena *duces tecum*[11] (bring it with you) compels an individual or organization to hand over books, papers, records, or documents to the agency. An administrative agency may use either type of subpoena to obtain testimony or documents.

There are limits on the information that an agency can demand. To determine whether an agency is abusing its discretion in its pursuit of information as part of an investigation, a court may consider such factors as the following:

1. *The purpose of the investigation.* An investigation must have a legitimate purpose. Harassment is an example of an improper purpose. An agency may not issue an administrative subpoena to inspect business records if the agency's motive is to harass or pressure the business into settling an unrelated matter.
2. *The relevance of the information being sought.* Information is relevant if it reveals that the law is being violated or if it assures the agency that the law is not being violated.
3. *The specificity of the demand for testimony or documents.* A subpoena must, for example, adequately describe the material being sought.
4. *The burden of the demand on the party from whom the information is sought.* In responding to a request for information, a party must bear the costs of, for example, copying the documents that must be handed over; a business is generally protected from revealing such information as trade secrets, however.

Searches during Site Inspections As mentioned, agency investigations often involve on-site inspections. The Environmental Protection Agency (EPA) frequently conducts inspections to enforce environmental laws. For example, the EPA may inspect a site to determine if hazardous wastes are being stored properly or to sample a facility's wastewater to ensure that it complies with the Clean Water Act. Usually, companies do not resist such inspections, although in some circumstances they may do so.

The Fourth Amendment protects against unreasonable searches and seizures by requiring that in most

11. Pronounced *doo*-suhs *tee*-kum.

instances a physical search for evidence must be conducted under the authority of a search warrant. An agency's search warrant is an order directing law enforcement officials to search a specific place for a specific item and present it to the agency. Although it was once thought that administrative inspections were exempt from the warrant requirement, the United States Supreme Court held in *Marshall v. Barlow's, Inc.*,[12] that the requirement does apply to the administrative process.

Agencies can conduct warrantless searches in several situations. Warrants are not required to conduct searches in highly regulated industries. Firms that sell firearms or liquor, for example, are automatically subject to inspections without warrants. Sometimes, a statute permits warrantless searches of certain types of hazardous operations, such as coal mines. Also, a warrantless inspection in an emergency situation is normally considered reasonable.

Adjudication

After conducting an investigation of a suspected rule violation, an agency may begin to take administrative action against an individual or organization. Most administrative actions are resolved through negotiated settlements at their initial stages, without the need for formal **adjudication** (the process of resolving a dispute by presenting evidence and arguments before a neutral third party decision maker).

Negotiated Settlements Depending on the agency, negotiations may take the form of a simple conversation or a series of informal conferences. Whatever form the negotiations take, their purpose is to rectify the problem to the agency's satisfaction and eliminate the need for additional proceedings.

Settlement is an appealing option to firms for two reasons: to avoid appearing uncooperative and to avoid the expense involved in formal adjudication proceedings and in possible later appeals. Settlement is also an attractive option for agencies. To conserve their own resources and avoid formal actions, administrative agencies devote a great deal of effort to giving advice and negotiating solutions to problems.

Formal Complaints If a settlement cannot be reached, the agency may issue a formal complaint against the suspected violator. If the EPA, for example, finds that a factory is polluting groundwater in violation of federal pollution laws, the EPA will issue a complaint against the violator in an effort to bring the plant into compliance with federal regulations. This complaint is a public document, and a press release may accompany it. The factory charged in the complaint will respond by filing an answer to the EPA's allegations. If the factory and the EPA cannot agree on a settlement, the case will be adjudicated.

Agency adjudication may involve a trial-like arbitration procedure before an **administrative law judge (ALJ).** The Administrative Procedure Act (APA) requires that before the hearing takes place, the agency must issue a notice that includes the facts and law on which the complaint is based, the legal authority for the hearing, and its time and place. The administrative adjudication process is described below and illustrated graphically in Exhibit 43–4.

The Role of the Administrative Law Judge

The ALJ presides over the hearing and has the power to administer oaths, take testimony, rule on questions of evidence, and make determinations of fact. Although technically, the ALJ is not an independent judge and works for the agency prosecuting the case (in our example, the EPA), the law requires an ALJ to be an unbiased adjudicator (judge).

Certain safeguards prevent bias on the part of the ALJ and promote fairness in the proceedings. For example, the APA requires that the ALJ be separate from an agency's investigative and prosecutorial staff. The APA also prohibits *ex parte* (private) communications between the ALJ and any party to an agency proceeding, such as the EPA or the factory. Finally, provisions of the APA protect the ALJ from agency disciplinary actions unless the agency can show good cause for such an action.

Hearing Procedures Hearing procedures vary widely from agency to agency. Administrative agencies generally exercise substantial discretion over the type of procedure that will be used. Frequently, disputes are resolved through informal adjudication proceedings. For example, the parties, their counsel, and the ALJ may simply meet at a table in a conference room to attempt to settle the dispute.

A formal adjudicatory hearing, in contrast, resembles a trial in many respects. Prior to the hearing, the parties are permitted to undertake discovery—involving depositions, interrogatories, and requests for documents or other information, as described in Chapter 3—although the discovery process is not quite as extensive

12. 436 U.S. 307, 98 S.Ct. 1816, 56 L.Ed.2d 305 (1978).

EXHIBIT 43–4 • The Process of Formal Administrative Adjudication

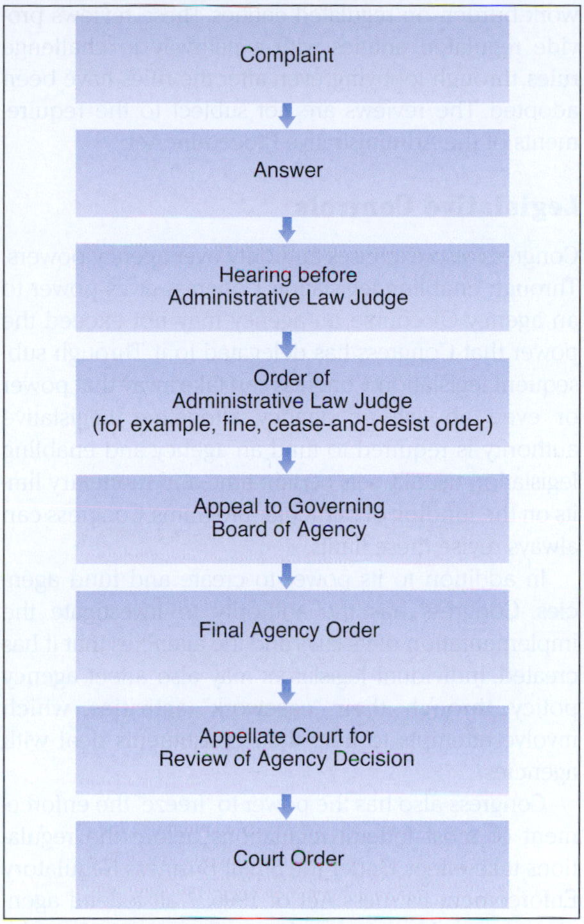

as it would be in a court proceeding. The hearing itself must comply with the procedural requirements of the APA and must also meet the constitutional standards of due process. During the hearing, the parties may give testimony, present other evidence, and cross-examine adverse witnesses. A significant difference between a trial and an administrative agency hearing, though, is that normally much more information, including hearsay (secondhand information), can be introduced as evidence during an administrative hearing. The burden of proof in an enforcement proceeding is placed on the agency.

Agency Orders Following a hearing, the ALJ renders an **initial order,** or decision, on the case. Either party can appeal the ALJ's decision to the board or commission that governs the agency. If the factory in the previous example is dissatisfied with the ALJ's decision, it can appeal the decision to the EPA. If the factory is dissatisfied with the commission's decision, it can appeal the decision to a federal court of appeals. If no party appeals the case, the ALJ's decision becomes the **final order** of the agency. The ALJ's decision also becomes final if a party appeals and the commission and the court decline to review the case. If a party appeals and the case is reviewed, the final order comes from the commission's decision or (if that decision is appealed to a federal appellate court) that of the court.

SECTION 6 Limitations on Agency Powers

Combining the functions normally divided among the three branches of government into an administrative agency concentrates considerable power in a single organization. Because of this concentration of authority, one of the major policy objectives of the government is to control the risks of arbitrariness and overreaching by administrative agencies without hindering the effective use of agency power to deal with particular problem areas, as Congress intends.

The judicial branch of the government exercises control over agency powers through the courts' review of agency actions. The executive and legislative branches of government also exercise control over agency authority.

Judicial Controls

As described earlier, the Administrative Procedure Act provides for judicial review of most agency decisions. Agency actions are not automatically subject to judicial review, however. Procedural doctrines such as exhaustion and ripeness may limit the opportunity of judicial review.

The Exhaustion Doctrine The *exhaustion doctrine* requires that a regulated party use all of its potential administrative remedies before going to court, even though the party might prefer to go straight to the independent federal courts, rather than going through the administrative adjudication process. Requiring the administrative process first allows the agency to evaluate the argument and enables a court to take advantage of the agency's own fact-finding capabilities before ruling. The exhaustion of administrative remedies is not required, though, if the party can demonstrate that those remedies are inadequate to address its challenge.

In the classic exhaustion case, a company was served with a complaint from the National Labor Relations Board (NLRB) alleging that it had engaged in unfair labor practices.[13] The company argued that because it was not operating in interstate commerce, the NLRB had no jurisdiction. The United States Supreme Court rejected this argument and held that the company was required to first use administrative procedures to challenge the complaint.

The Ripeness Doctrine Under what is known as the *ripeness doctrine,* a court will not review an administrative agency's decision until the case is "ripe for review." Generally, a case is ripe for review if the parties can demonstrate that they have met certain requirements. The party bringing the action must have *standing to sue* the agency (the party must have a direct stake in the outcome of the judicial proceeding), and there must be an *actual controversy* at issue. Recall from Chapter 2 that these are basic judicial requirements that must be met before any court will hear a case.

Standing requires that a plaintiff have an actual injury, that the injury be causally connected with the challenged action, and that the injury be one that can be successfully redressed by a judicial resolution of the case. The rationale for this doctrine is to prevent courts from entangling themselves in abstract disagreements over administrative policies. The doctrine also protects agencies from judicial interference until an administrative decision has been formalized and its effects are clear. The court can then evaluate both the appropriateness of an issue for judicial resolution and the hardship that the plaintiff will suffer if the court refuses to hear the case.

Executive Controls

The executive branch of government exercises control over agencies both through the president's power to appoint federal officers and through the president's veto power. The president may veto enabling legislation presented by Congress or congressional attempts to modify an existing agency's authority. In addition, the president has created a process whereby the Office of Information and Regulatory Affairs (OIRA) of the Office of Management and Budget reviews the cost-effectiveness of agency rules. The OIRA also reviews agencies' compliance with the Paperwork Reduction Act,[14] which requires agencies to minimize the paperwork burden on regulated entities. These reviews provide regulated entities with a pathway to challenge rules, through lobbying, even after the rules have been adopted. The reviews are not subject to the requirements of the Administrative Procedure Act.

Legislative Controls

Congress also exercises authority over agency powers. Through enabling legislation, Congress gives power to an agency. Of course, an agency may not exceed the power that Congress has delegated to it. Through subsequent legislation, Congress can take away that power or even abolish an agency altogether. Legislative authority is required to fund an agency, and enabling legislation usually sets certain time and monetary limits on the funding of particular programs. Congress can always revise these limits.

In addition to its power to create and fund agencies, Congress has the authority to investigate the implementation of its laws and the agencies that it has created. Individual legislators may also affect agency policy through their "casework" activities, which involve attempts to help their constituents deal with agencies.

Congress also has the power to "freeze" the enforcement of most federal regulations before the regulations take effect. Under the Small Business Regulatory Enforcement Fairness Act of 1996,[15] all federal agencies must submit final rules to Congress before the rules become effective. If, within sixty days, Congress passes a joint resolution disapproving of a rule, its enforcement is frozen while the rule is reviewed by congressional committees.

Another legislative check on agency actions is the Administrative Procedure Act, discussed earlier in this chapter. Additionally, the laws discussed in the next section provide certain checks on the actions of administrative agencies.

SECTION 7 Public Accountability

As a result of growing public concern over the powers exercised by administrative agencies, Congress passed several laws to make agencies more accountable

13. *Myers v. Bethlehem Shipbuilding Corp.,* 303 U.S. 41, 58 S.Ct. 459, 82 L.Ed. 638 (1938).

14. Pub. L. No. 104-13, May 22, 1995, 109 Stat. 163, amending 44 U.S.C. Sections 3501 *et seq.*

15. 5 U.S.C. Sections 801–808.

through public scrutiny. We discuss here the most significant of these laws.

Freedom of Information Act

Enacted in 1966, the Freedom of Information Act (FOIA)[16] requires the federal government to disclose certain records to any person or entity on written request. The FOIA exempts certain types of records, such as those pertaining to national security, and records containing information that is confidential or personal.

A request that complies with the FOIA procedures need only contain a reasonably specific description of the information sought. Many agencies now accept requests via e-mail, as well as by fax. The agency has twenty working days to answer a request and must notify the individual if the information sought is being withheld and which exemptions apply. The agency typically charges the person requesting the information a fee for research, copying, and other services.

An agency's failure to comply with an FOIA request may be challenged in a federal district court. The media, industry trade associations, public-interest groups, and even companies seeking information about competitors rely on these FOIA provisions to obtain information from government agencies.

Under a 1996 amendment to the FOIA, all federal government agencies must make their records available electronically on the Internet, on CD-ROMs, and in other electronic formats. Any document an agency creates must be accessible by computer within a year after its creation. Agencies must also provide a clear index to all of their documents.

Government in the Sunshine Act

Congress passed the Government in the Sunshine Act,[17] or open meeting law, in 1976. It requires that "every portion of every meeting of an agency" be open to "public observation." The act also requires the establishment of procedures to ensure that the public is provided with adequate advance notice of scheduled meetings and agendas. Like the FOIA, the Sunshine Act contains certain exceptions. Closed meetings are permitted when (1) the subject of the meeting concerns accusing any person of a crime, (2) an open meeting would frustrate the implementation of agency actions, or (3) the subject of the meeting involves matters relating to future litigation or rulemaking. Courts interpret these exceptions to allow open access whenever possible.

Regulatory Flexibility Act

Concern over the effects of regulation on the efficiency of businesses, particularly smaller ones, led Congress to pass the Regulatory Flexibility Act[18] in 1980. Under this act, whenever a new regulation will have a "significant impact upon a substantial number of small entities," the agency must conduct a regulatory flexibility analysis. The analysis must measure the cost that the rule would impose on small businesses and must consider less burdensome alternatives. The act also contains provisions to alert small businesses—through advertising in trade journals, for example—about forthcoming regulations. The act reduces some record-keeping burdens for small businesses, especially with regard to hazardous waste management.

Small Business Regulatory Enforcement Fairness Act

As mentioned earlier, the Small Business Regulatory Enforcement Fairness Act (SBREFA) of 1996 allows Congress to review new federal regulations for at least sixty days before they take effect. This period gives opponents of the rules time to present their arguments to Congress.

The SBREFA also authorizes the courts to enforce the Regulatory Flexibility Act. This helps to ensure that federal agencies, such as the Internal Revenue Service, will consider ways to reduce the economic impact of new regulations on small businesses. Federal agencies are required to prepare guides that explain in "plain English" how small businesses can comply with federal regulations.

The SBREFA also set up the National Enforcement Ombudsman at the Small Business Administration to receive comments from small businesses about their dealings with federal agencies. Based on these comments, Regional Small Business Fairness Boards rate the agencies and publicize their findings.

Finally, the SBREFA allows small businesses to recover their expenses and legal fees from the government when an agency makes demands for fines or penalties that a court considers excessive.

16. 5 U.S.C. Section 552.

17. 5 U.S.C. Section 552b.

18. 5 U.S.C. Sections 601–612.

REVIEWING Administrative Law

Assume that the Securities and Exchange Commission (SEC) has a rule that it will enforce statutory provisions prohibiting insider trading only when the insiders make monetary profits for themselves. Then the SEC makes a new rule, declaring that it will now bring enforcement actions against individuals for insider trading even if the individuals did not personally profit from the transactions. In making the new rule, the SEC does not conduct a rulemaking procedure but simply announces its decision. A stockbrokerage firm objects and says that the new rule was unlawfully developed without opportunity for public comment. The brokerage firm challenges the rule in an action that ultimately is reviewed by a federal appellate court. Using the information presented in the chapter, answer the following questions.

1. Is the SEC an executive agency or an independent regulatory agency? Does it matter to the outcome of this dispute? Explain.
2. Suppose that the SEC asserts that it has always had the statutory authority to pursue persons for insider trading regardless of whether they personally profited from the transaction. This is the only argument the SEC makes to justify changing its enforcement rules. Would a court be likely to find that the SEC's action was arbitrary and capricious under the Administrative Procedure Act (APA)? Why or why not?
3. Would a court be likely to give *Chevron* deference to the SEC's interpretation of the law on insider trading? Why or why not?
4. Now assume that a court finds that the new rule is merely "interpretive." What effect would this determination have on whether the SEC had to follow the APA's rulemaking procedures?

TERMS AND CONCEPTS

adjudication 828
administrative law judge (ALJ) 828
bureaucracy 820
enabling legislation 819
final order 829
initial order 829
notice-and-comment rulemaking 821
rulemaking 821

QUESTIONS AND CASE PROBLEMS

43–1. For decades, the Federal Trade Commission (FTC) resolved fair trade and advertising disputes through individual adjudications. In the 1960s, the FTC began promulgating rules that defined fair and unfair trade practices. In cases involving violations of these rules, the due process rights of participants were more limited and did not include cross-examination. Although anyone found violating a rule would receive a full adjudication, the legitimacy of the rule itself could not be challenged in the adjudication. Any party charged with violating a rule was almost certain to lose the adjudication. Affected parties complained to a court, arguing that their rights before the FTC were unduly limited by the new rules. What will the court examine to determine whether to uphold the new rules?

43-2. QUESTION WITH SAMPLE ANSWER

Assume that the Food and Drug Administration (FDA), using proper procedures, adopts a rule describing its future investigations. This new rule covers all future circumstances in which the FDA wants to regulate food additives. Under the new rule, the FDA is not to regulate food additives without giving food companies an opportunity to cross-examine witnesses. At a subsequent time, the FDA wants to regulate methylisocyanate, a food additive. The FDA undertakes an informal rulemaking procedure, without cross-examination, and regulates methylisocyanate. Producers protest, saying that the FDA promised them the opportunity for cross-examination. The FDA responds that the Administrative Procedure Act does not require such cross-examination and that it is free to withdraw the promise made in its new rule. If the producers challenge the FDA in court, on what basis would the court rule in their favor?

- **For a sample answer to Question 43–2, go to Appendix I at the end of this text.**

43-3. Rulemaking. The Occupational Safety and Health Administration (OSHA) is part of the U.S. Department of Labor. OSHA issued a "Directive" under which each employer in selected industries was to be inspected unless it adopted a "Comprehensive Compliance Program (CCP)"—a safety and health program designed to meet standards that in some respects exceeded those otherwise required by law. The Chamber of Commerce of the United States objected to the Directive and filed a petition for review with the U.S. Court of Appeals for the District of Columbia Circuit. The Chamber claimed, in part, that OSHA did not use proper rulemaking procedures in issuing the Directive. OSHA argued that it was not required to follow those procedures because the Directive itself was a "rule of procedure." OSHA claimed that the rule did not "alter the rights or interests of parties, although it may alter the manner in which the parties present themselves or their viewpoints to the agency." What are the steps of the most commonly used rulemaking procedure? Which steps are missing in this case? In whose favor should the court rule and why? [*Chamber of Commerce of the United States v. U.S. Department of Labor,* 174 F.3d 206 (D.C.Cir. 1999)]

43-4. Arbitrary and Capricious Test. Lion Raisins, Inc., is a family-owned, family-operated business that grows raisins and markets them to private enterprises. In the 1990s, Lion also successfully bid on more than fifteen contracts awarded by the U.S. Department of Agriculture (USDA). In May 1999, a USDA investigation reported that Lion appeared to have falsified inspectors' signatures, given false moisture content, and changed the grade of raisins on three USDA raisin certificates issued between 1996 and 1998. Lion was subsequently awarded five more USDA contracts. Then, in November 2000, the company was the low bidder on two new USDA contracts for school lunch programs. In January 2001, however, the USDA awarded these contracts to other bidders and, on the basis of the May 1999 report, suspended Lion from participating in government contracts for one year. Lion filed a suit in the U.S. Court of Federal Claims against the USDA, seeking, in part, lost profits on the school lunch contracts on the ground that the USDA's suspension was arbitrary and capricious. What reasoning might the court employ to grant a summary judgment in Lion's favor? [*Lion Raisins, Inc. v. United States,* 51 Fed.Cl. 238 (2001)]

43-5. Investigation. Maureen Droge began working for United Air Lines, Inc. (UAL), as a flight attendant in 1990. In 1995, she was assigned to Paris, France, where she became pregnant. Because UAL does not allow its flight attendants to fly during their third trimester of pregnancy, Droge was placed on involuntary leave. She applied for temporary disability benefits through the French social security system, but her request was denied because UAL does not contribute to the French system on behalf of its U.S.-based flight attendants. Droge filed a charge of discrimination with the U.S. Equal Employment Opportunity Commission (EEOC), alleging that UAL had discriminated against her and other Americans. The EEOC issued a subpoena, asking UAL to detail all benefits received by all UAL employees living outside the United States. UAL refused to provide the information, in part, on the grounds that it was irrelevant and compliance would be unduly burdensome. The EEOC filed a suit in a federal district court against UAL. Should the court enforce the subpoena? Why or why not? [*Equal Employment Opportunity Commission v. United Air Lines, Inc.,* 287 F.3d 643 (7th Cir. 2002)]

43-6. Judicial Controls. Under federal law, when accepting bids on a contract, an agency must hold "discussions" with all offerors. An agency may ask a single offeror for "clarification" of its proposal, however, without holding "discussions" with the others. Regulations define *clarifications* as "limited exchanges." In March 2001, the U.S. Air Force asked for bids on a contract. The winning contractor would examine, assess, and develop means of integrating national intelligence assets with the U.S. Department of Defense space systems, to enhance the capabilities of the Air Force's Space Warfare Center. Among the bidders were Information Technology and Applications Corp. (ITAC) and RS Information Systems, Inc. (RSIS). The Air Force asked the parties for more information on their subcontractors but did not allow them to change their proposals. Determining that there were weaknesses in ITAC's bid, the Air Force awarded the contract to RSIS. ITAC filed a suit in the U.S. Court of Federal Claims against the government, contending that the post-proposal requests to RSIS, and its responses, were improper "discussions." Should the court rule in ITAC's favor? Why or why not? [*Information Technology & Applications Corp. v. United States,* 316 F.3d 1312 (Fed.Cir. 2003)]

43-7. CASE PROBLEM WITH SAMPLE ANSWER

Riverdale Mills Corp. makes plastic-coated steel wire products in Northbridge, Massachusetts. Riverdale uses a water-based cleaning process that generates acidic and alkaline wastewater. To meet federal clean-water requirements, Riverdale has a system within its plant to treat the water. It then flows through a pipe that opens into a manhole-covered test pit outside the plant in full view of Riverdale's employees. Three hundred feet away, the pipe merges into the public sewer system. In October 1997, the U.S. Environmental Protection Agency (EPA) sent Justin Pimpare and Daniel Granz to inspect the plant. Without a search warrant and without Riverdale's express consent, the agents took samples from the test pit. Based on the samples, Riverdale and James Knott, the company's owner, were charged with criminal violations of the federal Clean Water Act. The defendants filed a suit in a federal district court against the EPA agents and others, alleging violations of the Fourth Amendment. What right does the Fourth Amendment provide in this context? This right is based on a "reasonable expectation of privacy." Should the agents be held liable? Why or why not? [*Riverdale Mills Corp. v. Pimpare,* 392 F.3d 55 (1st Cir. 2004)]

- **To view a sample answer for Problem 43–7, go to this book's Web site at www.cengage.com/blaw/jentz, select "Chapter 43," and click on "Case Problem with Sample Answer."**

43-8. Rulemaking. The Investment Company Act of 1940 prohibits a mutual fund from engaging in certain transactions in which there may be a conflict of interest between the manager of the fund and its shareholders. Under rules issued by the Securities and Exchange Commission (SEC), however, a fund that meets certain conditions may engage in an otherwise prohibited transaction. In June 2004, the SEC added two new conditions. A year later, the SEC reconsidered the new conditions in terms of the costs that they would impose on the funds. Within eight days, and without asking for public input, the SEC readopted the conditions. The Chamber of Commerce of the United States—which is both a mutual fund shareholder and an association with mutual fund managers among its members—asked the U.S. Court of Appeals for the Second Circuit to review the new rules. The Chamber charged, in part, that in readopting the rules, the SEC relied on materials not in the "rulemaking record" without providing an opportunity for public comment. The SEC countered that the information was otherwise "publicly available." In adopting a rule, should an agency consider information that is not part of the rulemaking record? Why or why not? [*Chamber of Commerce of the United States v. Securities and Exchange Commission,* 443 F.3d 890 (D.C.Cir. 2006)]

43-9. Agency Powers. A well-documented rise in global temperatures has coincided with a significant increase in the concentration of carbon dioxide in the atmosphere. Some scientists believe that the two trends are related, because when carbon dioxide is released into the atmosphere, it produces a greenhouse effect, trapping solar heat. Under the Clean Air Act (CAA) of 1963, the Environmental Protection Agency (EPA) is authorized to regulate "any" air pollutants "emitted into . . . the ambient air" that in its "judgment cause, or contribute to, air pollution." Calling global warming "the most pressing environmental challenge of our time," a group of private organizations asked the EPA to regulate carbon dioxide and other "greenhouse gas" emissions from new motor vehicles. The EPA refused, stating, among other things, that Congress last amended the CAA in 1990 without authorizing new, binding auto emissions limits. The petitioners—nineteen states, including Massachusetts, and others—asked the U.S. Court of Appeals for the District of Columbia Circuit to review the EPA's denial. Did the EPA have the authority to regulate greenhouse gas emissions from new motor vehicles? If so, was its stated reason for refusing to do so consistent with that authority? Discuss. [*Massachusetts v. Environmental Protection Agency,* __ U.S. __, 127 S.Ct. 1438, 167 L.Ed.2d 248 (2007)]

43-10. A QUESTION OF ETHICS

*To ensure highway safety and protect driver health, Congress charged federal agencies with regulating the hours of service of commercial motor vehicle operators. Between 1940 and 2003, the regulations that applied to long-haul truck drivers were mostly unchanged. (Long-haul drivers are those who operate beyond a 150-mile radius of their base.) In 2003, the Federal Motor Carrier Safety Administration (FMCSA) revised the regulations significantly, increasing the number of daily and weekly hours that drivers could work. The agency had not considered the impact of the changes on the health of the drivers, however, and the revisions were overturned. The FMCSA then issued a notice that it would reconsider the revisions and opened them up for public comment. The agency analyzed the costs to the industry and the crash risks due to driver fatigue under different options and concluded that the safety benefits of not increasing the hours did not outweigh the economic costs. In 2005, the agency issued a rule that was nearly identical to the 2003 version. Public Citizen, Inc., and others, including the Owner-Operator Independent Drivers Association, asked the U.S. Court of Appeals for the District of Columbia Circuit to review the 2005 rule as it applied to long-haul drivers. [*Owner-Operator Independent Drivers Association, Inc. v. Federal Motor Carrier Safety Administration, *494 F.3d 188 (D.C.Cir. 2007)]*

(a) The agency's cost-benefit analysis included new methods that were not disclosed to the public in time for comments. Was this unethical? Should the agency have disclosed the new methodology sooner? Why or why not?

(b) The agency created a graph to show the risk of a crash as a function of the time a driver spent on the job. The graph plotted the first twelve hours of a day individually, but the rest of the time was depicted with an aggregate figure at the seventeenth hour. This made the risk at those hours appear to be lower. Is it unethical for an agency to manipulate data? Explain.

LAW ON THE WEB

For updated links to resources available on the Web, as well as a variety of other materials, visit this text's Web site at

www.cengage.com/blaw/jentz

To view the text of the Administrative Procedure Act of 1946, go to

www.oalj.dol.gov/libapa.htm

For information on the Freedom of Information Act and sample request letters, go to

www.nist.gov/admin/foia/foia.htm

The U.S. Government Printing Office provides a searchable online database of the *Code of Federal Regulations* at

www.gpoaccess.gov/cfr/index.html

Legal Research Exercises on the Web

Go to **www.cengage.com/blaw/jentz**, the Web site that accompanies this text. Select "Chapter 43" and click on "Internet Exercises." There you will find the following Internet research exercises that you can perform to learn more about the topics covered in this chapter.

Internet Exercise 43–1: Legal Perspective
The Freedom of Information Act

Internet Exercise 43–2: Management Perspective
Agency Inspections

CHAPTER 44

Consumer Law

All statutes, agency rules, and common law judicial decisions that serve to protect the interests of consumers are classified as **consumer law.** Traditionally, in disputes involving consumers, it was assumed that the freedom to contract carried with it the obligation to live by the deal made. Over time, this attitude has changed considerably. Today, myriad federal and state laws protect consumers from unfair trade practices, unsafe products, discriminatory or unreasonable credit requirements, and other problems related to consumer transactions. Nearly every agency and department of the federal government has an office of consumer affairs, and most states have one or more such offices to help consumers. Also, typically the attorney general's office assists consumers at the state level.

In this chapter, we examine some of the major laws and regulations protecting consumers. Because of the wide variation among state consumer protection laws, our primary focus in this chapter is on federal legislation. Realize, though, that state laws often provide more sweeping and significant protections for the consumer than do federal laws. Exhibit 44–1 indicates many of the areas of consumer law that are regulated by federal statutes.

SECTION 1 Deceptive Advertising

One of the earliest federal consumer protection laws—and still one of the most important—was the Federal Trade Commission Act of 1914 (mentioned in Chapter 43).[1] The act created the Federal Trade Commission (FTC) to carry out the broadly stated goal of preventing unfair and deceptive trade practices, including deceptive advertising.[2]

1. 15 U.S.C. Sections 41–58.
2. 15 U.S.C. Section 45.

EXHIBIT 44–1 • Selected Areas of Consumer Law Regulated by Statutes

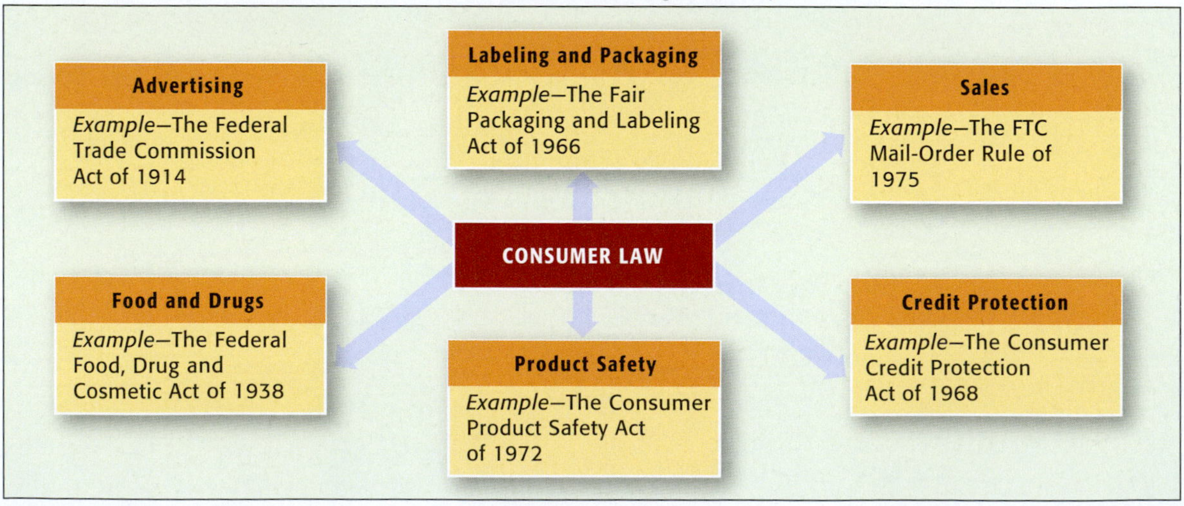

Generally, **deceptive advertising** occurs if a reasonable consumer would be misled by the advertising claim. Vague generalities and obvious exaggerations are permissible. These claims are known as *puffery*. When a claim takes on the appearance of literal authenticity, however, it may create problems. Advertising that *appears* to be based on factual evidence but in fact is not reasonably supported by some evidence will be deemed deceptive.

Some advertisements contain "half-truths," meaning that the presented information is true but incomplete and therefore leads consumers to a false conclusion. For example, the makers of Campbell's soups advertised that "most" Campbell's soups were low in fat and cholesterol and thus were helpful in fighting heart disease. What the ad did not say was that Campbell's soups are high in sodium, and high-sodium diets may increase the risk of heart disease. The FTC ruled that Campbell's claims were thus deceptive. Advertising that contains an endorsement by a celebrity may be deemed deceptive if the celebrity does not actually use the product.

In the following case brought by the FTC, *WIRED* magazine had already put the product in question on its list of the top ten "Snake-Oil Gadgets."

CASE 44.1 Federal Trade Commission v. QT, Inc.

United States Court of Appeals, Seventh Circuit, 2008. 512 F.3d 858.
www.ca7.uscourts.gov[a]

Background and Facts QT, Inc., and assorted related companies, heavily promoted the Q-Ray Ionized Bracelet on television infomercials as well as on its Web site. In its promotions, the company made many claims about the pain-relief powers of these bracelets. The bracelet offered immediate, significant, or complete pain relief and could cure chronic pain. At trial in the U.S. District Court for the Northern District of Illinois, the presiding judge labeled all such claims as fraudulent, forbade further promotional claims, and ordered the company to pay $16 million, plus interest, into a fund to be distributed to all customers. QT, Inc., appealed.

Decision and Rationale The U.S. Court of Appeals for the Seventh Circuit affirmed the district court's decision. QT, Inc., was required to stop its deceptive advertising and to pay the $16 million, plus interest, so that its customers could be reimbursed. The appellate court stated that "almost everything that defendants have said about the bracelet is false." It had no therapeutic effect. No bracelet had a memory cycle specific to each individual wearer. The judge presiding over the trial "did not commit a clear error, or abuse his discretion, in concluding that the defendants set out to bilk unsophisticated persons who found themselves in pain from arthritis and other chronic conditions." All statements about how the product worked were pure fiction. "Proof is what separates an effect new to science from a swindle." Although the defendants told customers that the bracelet's efficiency had been "test proven," it had not. What remained were testimonials, which are not a form of proof. "Physicians know how to treat pain. Why pay $200 for a Q-Ray Ionized Bracelet when you can get relief from an aspirin tablet that costs [one cent]?"

What If the Facts Were Different? *Assume that the defendant had actually conducted scientific studies, but they were inconclusive. How might the judge have ruled in that situation?*

The Ethical Dimension *Most people have seen infomercials. Do the fraudulent promotional claims of QT, Inc., in such infomercials mean that all products "pitched" on television are suspect? Why or why not?*

a. Click on "Opinions" in the left-hand column. In the box for the case number, type "07" and "1662" and then click on "List Case." Follow the links to access the opinion. The U.S. Court of Appeals for the Seventh Circuit maintains this Web site.

Bait-and-Switch Advertising

The FTC has issued rules that govern specific advertising techniques. One of the most important rules is contained in the FTC's "Guides Against Bait Advertising,"[3] issued in 1968. The rule seeks to prevent **bait-and-switch advertising**—that is, advertising a very low price for a particular item that will likely be unavailable to the consumer, who will then be encouraged to purchase a more expensive item. The low price is the "bait" to lure the consumer into the store. The salesperson is instructed to "switch" the consumer to a different, more expensive item. Under the FTC guidelines, bait-and-switch advertising occurs if the seller refuses to show the advertised item, fails to have a reasonable quantity of the item in stock, fails to promise to deliver the advertised item within a reasonable time, or discourages employees from selling the item.

Online Deceptive Advertising

Deceptive advertising may occur in the online environment as well. The FTC has been quite active in monitoring online advertising and has identified hundreds of Web sites that have made false or deceptive advertising claims for products ranging from medical treatments for various diseases to exercise equipment and weight-loss aids.

The FTC has issued guidelines to help online businesses comply with existing laws prohibiting deceptive advertising.[4] These guidelines include three basic requirements. First, all ads—both online and offline—must be truthful and not misleading. Second, any claims made in an ad must be substantiated; that is, advertisers must have evidence to back up their claims. Third, ads cannot be "unfair," which the FTC defines as "caus[ing] or . . . likely to cause substantial consumer injury that consumers could not reasonably avoid and that is not outweighed by the benefit to consumers or competition."

The guidelines also call for "clear and conspicuous" disclosure of any qualifying or limiting information. The FTC suggests that advertisers should assume that consumers will not read an entire Web page. Therefore, to satisfy the "clear and conspicuous" requirement, online advertisers should place the disclosure as close as possible to the claim being qualified or include the disclosure within the claim itself. If such placement is not feasible, the next-best location is on a section of the page to which a consumer can easily scroll. Generally, hyperlinks to a disclosure are recommended only for lengthy disclosures or for disclosures that must be repeated in a variety of locations on the Web page.

FTC Actions against Deceptive Advertising

The FTC receives complaints from many sources, including competitors of alleged violators, consumers, consumer organizations, trade associations, Better Business Bureaus, government organizations, and state and local officials. When the agency receives numerous and widespread complaints about a particular problem, it will investigate. If the FTC concludes that a given advertisement is unfair or deceptive, it drafts a formal complaint, which is sent to the alleged offender. The company may agree to settle the complaint without further proceedings; if not, the FTC can conduct a hearing in which the company can present its defense (see Chapter 43).

If the FTC succeeds in proving that an advertisement is unfair or deceptive, it usually issues a **cease-and-desist order** requiring the company to stop the challenged advertising. It might also impose a sanction known as **counteradvertising** by requiring the company to advertise anew—in print, on the Internet, on radio, and on television—to inform the public about the earlier misinformation. The FTC may institute **multiple product orders,** which require a firm to cease and desist from false advertising in regard to all of its products, not just the product that was the subject of the action.

Telemarketing and Electronic Advertising

The Telephone Consumer Protection Act (TCPA)[5] prohibits telephone solicitation using an automatic telephone dialing system or a prerecorded voice. Most states also have statutes regulating telephone solicitation. The TCPA also makes it illegal to transmit ads via fax without first obtaining the recipient's permission. (Similar issues have arisen with respect to junk e-mail, called *spam*—see Chapters 6 and 9.)

The Federal Communications Commission (FCC) enforces the TCPA. The FCC imposes substantial fines ($11,000 each day) on companies that violate the junk fax provisions of the act and has even fined one com-

3. 16 C.F.R. Part 238.

4. *Advertising and Marketing on the Internet: Rules of the Road,* September 2000.

5. 47 U.S.C. Sections 227 *et seq.*

pany as much as $5.4 million.[6] The TCPA also provides for a private right of action under which consumers can recover actual losses resulting from a violation of the act or receive $500 in damages for each violation, whichever is greater. If a court finds that a defendant willfully or knowingly violated the act, the court has the discretion to treble (triple) the amount of damages awarded.

The Telemarketing and Consumer Fraud and Abuse Prevention Act of 1994[7] directed the FTC to establish rules governing telemarketing and to bring actions against fraudulent telemarketers. The FTC's Telemarketing Sales Rule of 1995[8] requires a telemarketer to identify the seller's name, describe the product being sold, and disclose all material facts related to the sale (such as the total cost of the goods being sold). The rule makes it illegal for telemarketers to misrepresent information or facts about their goods or services. A telemarketer must also remove a consumer's name from its list of potential contacts if the customer so requests. An amendment to the Telemarketing Sales Rule established the national Do Not Call Registry. Telemarketers must refrain from calling those consumers who have placed their names on the list.

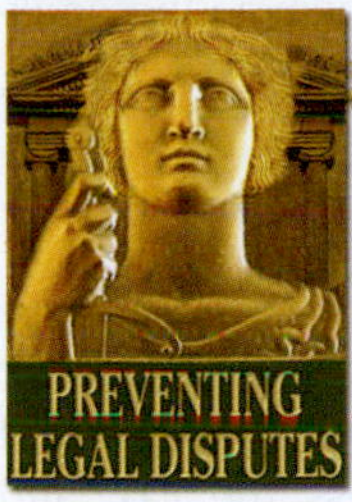

Advertising is essential to business. Business owners and managers who advertise via faxes and phone calls, however, must know and follow all applicable rules, such as the federal Telephone Consumer Protection Act. The Federal Communications Commission aggressively enforces these rules. Business owners and managers should educate and train their employees about such laws. Procedures to incorporate would include not sending faxes without the recipient's permission and developing effective opt-out programs so those wanting to refuse faxes can do so. Keeping reliable records of the faxes sent and maintaining these records for four years is an important procedure as well. Managers should not purchase lists of fax or phone numbers from outsiders. Avoiding consumer complaints about unwanted faxes and phone calls is the best strategy for avoiding potentially significant liability.

SECTION 2 Labeling and Packaging Laws

A number of federal and state laws deal specifically with the information given on labels and packages. In general, labels must be accurate, and they must use words that are easily understood by the ordinary consumer. For example, a box of cereal cannot be labeled "giant" if that would exaggerate the amount of cereal contained in the box.

In some instances, labels must specify the raw materials used in the product, such as the percentage of cotton, nylon, or other fiber used in a garment. In other instances, the product must carry a warning. Cigarette packages and advertising, for example, must include one of several warnings about the health hazards associated with smoking.[9]

Federal Statutes

There are numerous federal laws regulating the labeling and packaging of products. These include the Wool Products Labeling Act of 1939,[10] the Fur Products Labeling Act of 1951,[11] the Flammable Fabrics Act of 1953,[12] and the Fair Packaging and Labeling Act of 1966.[13] The Comprehensive Smokeless Tobacco Health Education Act of 1986,[14] for example, requires that producers, packagers, and importers of smokeless tobacco label their product with one of several warnings about the use of smokeless tobacco.

Food Labeling

Because the quality and safety of food are so important to consumers, several statutes deal specifically with food labeling. The Fair Packaging and Labeling Act requires that food product labels identify (1) the product; (2) the net quantity of the contents and, if the number of servings is stated, the size of the serving; (3) the manufacturer; and (4) the packager or distributor. The act includes additional requirements concerning descriptions on packages, savings claims, components of nonfood products, and standards for the partial filling of packages.

Food products must bear labels detailing the nutritional content, including how much fat the food contains and what kind of fat it is. The Nutrition Labeling

6. See *Missouri ex rel. Nixon v. American Blast Fax, Inc.*, 323 F.3d 649 (8th Cir. 2003); *cert.* denied, 540 U.S. 1104, 124 S.Ct. 1043, 157 L.Ed.2d 888 (2004).
7. 15 U.S.C. Sections 6101–6108.
8. 16 C.F.R. Sections 310.1–310.8.
9. 15 U.S.C. Sections 1331–1341.
10. 15 U.S.C. Section 68.
11. 15 U.S.C. Section 69.
12. 15 U.S.C. Section 1191.
13. 15 U.S.C. Sections 1451 *et seq.*
14. 15 U.S.C. Sections 4401–4408.

and Education Act of 1990[15] requires standard nutrition facts (including fat content) on food labels; regulates the use of such terms as *fresh* and *low fat;* and authorizes certain health claims, subject to the federal Food and Drug Administration's approval.

SECTION 3 Sales

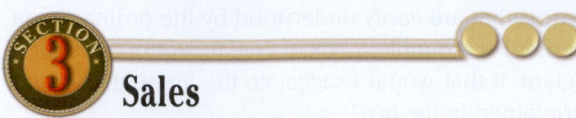

A number of statutes protect consumers by requiring the disclosure of certain terms in sales transactions and providing rules governing unsolicited merchandise and various forms of sales, such as door-to-door sales, mail-order sales, and referral sales. The FTC has regulatory authority in this area, as do other federal agencies. The Federal Reserve Board of Governors, for example, has issued **Regulation Z,**[16] which governs credit provisions associated with sales contracts, as discussed later in this chapter.

Many states have also enacted laws governing consumer sales transactions. Moreover, states have protected consumers to a certain extent through adopting the Uniform Commercial Code (discussed in Chapters 20 through 23) and, in a few states, the Uniform Consumer Credit Code.

Door-to-Door Sales

Door-to-door sales are singled out for special treatment in the laws of most states, largely because of the potential for high-pressure sales tactics. Repeat purchases are not as likely as they are in stores, so the seller has less incentive to cultivate the goodwill of the purchaser. Furthermore, the seller is unlikely to present alternative products and their prices. Thus, a number of states have passed "cooling-off" laws that permit the buyers of goods sold door to door to cancel their contracts within a specified period of time, usually two to three business days after the sale.

An FTC regulation also requires sellers to give consumers three days to cancel any door-to-door sale, and this rule applies in addition to any state law. The FTC rule further requires that consumers be notified in Spanish of this right if the oral negotiations for the sale were in that language.

Telephone and Mail-Order Sales

The FTC Mail or Telephone Order Merchandise Rule of 1993, which amended the FTC Mail-Order Rule of 1975,[17] provides specific protections for consumers who purchase goods over the phone or through the mail. The 1993 rule extended the 1975 rule to include sales orders transmitted using computers, fax machines, or other means involving a telephone line. Among other things, the rule requires merchants to ship orders within the time promised in their catalogues or advertisements and to notify consumers when orders cannot be shipped on time. Merchants must also issue a refund within a specified period of time when a consumer cancels an order.

In addition, under the Postal Reorganization Act of 1970,[18] a consumer who receives *unsolicited* merchandise sent by U.S. mail can keep it, throw it away, or dispose of it in any manner that she or he sees fit. The recipient will not be obligated to the sender. Suppose that Serena receives a copy of the "Cookbook of the Month" from a company via U.S. mail, even though she did not order the cookbook. She gives it to her friend, Vaya, who loves to cook. The following month, Serena receives a bill for $49.99 from the company that sent the cookbook. Under the 1970 act, because the cookbook was sent to her unsolicited through the U.S. mail, Serena is not obligated to pay the bill.

Online Sales

Protecting consumers from fraudulent and deceptive sales practices conducted via the Internet has proved to be a challenging task. Nonetheless, the FTC and other federal agencies have brought a number of enforcement actions against those who perpetrate online fraud. Additionally, the federal statute prohibiting wire fraud that was discussed in Chapter 9 applies to online transactions.

Some states have amended their consumer protection statutes to cover Internet transactions as well. For example, the California legislature revised its Business and Professions Code to include transactions conducted over the Internet or by "any other electronic means of communication." Previously, that code covered only telephone, mail-order catalogue, radio, and television sales. Now any entity selling over the Internet in California must explicitly create an on-screen notice indicating its refund and return policies, where its busi-

15. 21 U.S.C. Section 343.1.
16. 12 C.F.R. Sections 226.1–226.30.
17. 16 C.F.R. Sections 435.1–435.2.
18. 39 U.S.C. Section 3009.

ness is physically located, its legal name, and a number of other details. Various states are also setting up information sites to help consumers protect themselves.

SECTION 4

Credit Protection

Because of the extensive use of credit by American consumers, credit protection has become an especially important area of consumer protection legislation. A key statute regulating the credit and credit-card industries is Title I of the Consumer Credit Protection Act (CCPA),[19] which is commonly referred to as the Truth-in-Lending Act (TILA).

The Truth-in-Lending Act

The TILA is basically a *disclosure law.* It is administered by the Federal Reserve Board and requires sellers and lenders to disclose credit terms or loan terms so that individuals can shop around for the best financing arrangements. TILA requirements apply only to persons who, in the ordinary course of business, lend funds, sell on credit, or arrange for the extension of credit. Thus, sales or loans made between two consumers do not come under the protection of the act. Additionally, this law protects only debtors who are natural persons (as opposed to the artificial "person" of a corporation); it does not extend to other legal entities.

The disclosure requirements are contained in Regulation Z, which was promulgated (publicized) by the Federal Reserve Board. If the contracting parties are subject to the TILA, the requirements of Regulation Z apply to any transaction involving an installment sales contract that calls for payment to be made in more than four installments. Transactions subject to Regulation Z typically include installment loans, retail and installment sales, car loans, home-improvement loans, and certain real estate loans if the amount of financing is less than $25,000.

Under the provisions of the TILA, all of the terms of a credit instrument must be clearly and conspicuously disclosed. The TILA provides for contract rescission (cancellation) if a creditor fails to follow *exactly* the procedures required by the act.[20] TILA requirements are strictly enforced.

Equal Credit Opportunity In 1974, Congress enacted the Equal Credit Opportunity Act (ECOA)[21] as an amendment to the TILA. The ECOA prohibits the denial of credit solely on the basis of race, religion, national origin, color, gender, marital status, or age. The act also prohibits credit discrimination on the basis of whether an individual receives certain forms of income, such as public-assistance benefits.

Under the ECOA, a creditor may not require the signature of an applicant's spouse, other than as a joint applicant, on a credit instrument if the applicant qualifies under the creditor's standards of creditworthiness for the amount and terms of the credit request. For example, Tonja, an African American, applied for financing with a used-car dealer. The dealer looked at Tonja's credit report and, without submitting the application to the lender, decided that she would not qualify. Instead of informing Tonja that she did not qualify, the dealer told her that she needed a cosigner on the loan to purchase the car. According to a federal appellate court in 2004, the dealer qualified as a creditor in this situation because the dealer unilaterally denied the credit and thus could be held liable under the ECOA.[22]

Credit-Card Rules The TILA also contains provisions regarding credit cards. One provision limits the liability of a cardholder to $50 per card for unauthorized charges made before the creditor is notified that the card has been lost. Another provision prohibits a credit-card company from billing a consumer for any unauthorized charges if the credit card was improperly issued by the company. Suppose that a consumer receives an unsolicited credit card in the mail and the card is later stolen and used by the thief to make purchases. In this situation, the consumer to whom the card was sent will not be liable for the unauthorized charges.

Other provisions of the act set out specific procedures for both the credit-card company and its cardholder to use in settling disputes related to credit-card purchases. These procedures would be used if, for example, a cardholder thinks that an error has occurred in billing or wishes to withhold payment for a faulty product purchased by credit card.

Consumer Leases The Consumer Leasing Act (CLA) of 1988[23] amended the TILA to provide protection for consumers who lease automobiles and other

19. 15 U.S.C. Sections 1601–1693r.

20. Note, however, that amendments to the TILA enacted in 1995 prevent borrowers from rescinding loans because of minor clerical errors in closing documents [15 U.S.C. Sections 1605, 1631, 1635, 1640, and 1641].

21. 15 U.S.C. Sections 1691–1691f.

22. *Treadway v. Gateway Chevrolet Oldsmobile, Inc.*, 362 F.3d 971 (7th Cir. 2004).

23. 15 U.S.C. Sections 1667–1667e.

goods. The CLA applies to those who lease or arrange to lease consumer goods in the ordinary course of their business. The act applies only if the goods are priced at $25,000 or less and if the lease term exceeds four months. The CLA and its implementing regulation, Regulation M,[24] require lessors to disclose in writing (or by electronic record) all of the material terms of the lease.

The Fair Credit Reporting Act

In 1970, to protect consumers against inaccurate credit reporting, Congress enacted the Fair Credit Reporting Act (FCRA).[25] The act provides that consumer credit reporting agencies may issue credit reports to users only for specified purposes, including the extension of credit, the issuance of insurance policies, and compliance with a court order, and in response to a consumer's request for a copy of his or her own credit report. The act further provides that whenever a consumer is denied credit or insurance on the basis of her or his credit report, or is charged more than others ordinarily would be for credit or insurance, the consumer must be notified of that fact and of the name and address of the credit reporting agency that issued the credit report.

Under the FCRA, consumers may request the source of any information being given out by a credit agency, as well as the identity of anyone who has received an agency's report. Consumers are also permitted to access the information about them contained in a credit reporting agency's files. If a consumer discovers that an agency's files contain inaccurate information about his or her credit standing, the agency, on the consumer's written request, must investigate the matter and delete any unverifiable or erroneous information within a reasonable period of time. As part of its investigation, the agency should systematically examine its records and contact the creditor whose information the consumer disputes.[26] An agency that fails to comply with the act is liable for actual damages, plus additional damages not to exceed $1,000 and attorneys' fees.[27] The FCRA allows an award of punitive damages for a "willful" violation.[28]

Fair and Accurate Credit Transactions Act

In an effort to combat identity theft (discussed in Chapter 9), Congress passed the Fair and Accurate Credit Transactions Act (FACT Act) of 2003.[29] The act established a national fraud alert system so that consumers who suspect that they have been or may be victimized by identity theft can place an alert on their credit files. The act also requires the major credit reporting agencies to provide consumers with free copies of their own credit reports every twelve months. Another provision requires account numbers on credit-card receipts to be truncated (shortened) so that merchants, employees, or others who may have access to the receipts do not have the consumers' names and full credit-card numbers. The act further mandates that financial institutions work with the Federal Trade Commission to identify "red flag" indicators of identity theft and to develop rules for disposing of sensitive credit information.

The FACT Act gives consumers who have been victimized by identity theft some assistance in rebuilding their credit reputations. For example, credit reporting agencies must stop reporting allegedly fraudulent account information once the consumer establishes that identify theft has occurred. Business owners and creditors are required to provide consumers with copies of any records that can help the consumer prove that the particular account or transaction is fraudulent (records showing that an account was created by a fraudulent signature, for example). In addition, the act allows consumers to report the accounts affected by identity theft directly to creditors in order to help prevent the spread of erroneous credit information.

24. 12 C.F.R. Part 213.
25. 15 U.S.C. Sections 1681–1681t.
26. See, for example, *Johnson v. MBNA America Bank, N.A.*, 357 F.3d 426 (4th Cir. 2004).
27. 15 U.S.C. Section 1681n.
28. Under the FCRA, if an insurance company *raises* a customer's rates because of a credit score, the insurance company is required to notify the individual. In 2007, the United States Supreme Court held that even the failure to notify *new* customers that they are paying higher insurance rates as a result of their credit scores is an adverse action that can be considered a *willful* violation of the FCRA. *Safeco Insurance Co. of America v. Burr*, ___ U.S. ___, 127 S.Ct. 2201, 167 L.Ed.2d 1045 (2007).
29. Pub. L. No. 108-159, 117 Stat. 1952 (December 4, 2003).

The Fair Debt Collection Practices Act

In 1977, Congress enacted the Fair Debt Collection Practices Act (FDCPA)[30] in an attempt to curb what were perceived to be abuses by collection agencies. The act applies only to specialized debt-collection agencies that regularly attempt to collect debts on behalf of someone else, usually for a percentage of the amount owed. Creditors attempting to collect debts are not covered by the act unless, by misrepresenting themselves, they cause debtors to believe they are collection agencies.

Requirements under the Act The act explicitly prohibits a collection agency from using any of the following tactics:

1. Contacting the debtor at the debtor's place of employment if the debtor's employer objects.
2. Contacting the debtor during inconvenient or unusual times (for example, calling the debtor at three o'clock in the morning) or at any time if the debtor is being represented by an attorney. (If a collection agency is not aware that a debtor is represented by an attorney, will contacting the debtor about a debt subject the collection agency to liability? For the answer to this question, see this chapter's *Business Application* feature on page 845.)
3. Contacting third parties other than the debtor's parents, spouse, or financial adviser about payment of a debt unless a court authorizes such action.
4. Using harassment or intimidation (for example, using abusive language or threatening violence) or employing false or misleading information (for example, posing as a police officer).
5. Communicating with the debtor at any time after receiving notice that the debtor is refusing to pay the debt, except to advise the debtor of further action to be taken by the collection agency.

The FDCPA also requires a collection agency to include a **validation notice** whenever it initially contacts a debtor for payment of a debt or within five days of that initial contact. The notice must state that the debtor has thirty days in which to dispute the debt and to request a written verification of the debt from the collection agency. The debtor's request for debt validation must be in writing.

The following case involved the prohibition against contacting a third party other than the debtor's parents, spouse, or financial adviser about the payment of a debt. A consumer alleged that a debt-collection company violated Colorado's fair debt collection statute when it hired a third party to send her the required validation notice. Although the case was brought under Colorado's fair debt collection statute, the state statute parallels the relevant portions of the FDCPA, and both prohibit communications between a debt collector and third parties.

30. 15 U.S.C. Section 1692.

CASE 44.2 Flood v. Mercantile Adjustment Bureau, LLC

Supreme Court of Colorado, 2008. 176 P.3d 769.
www.courts.state.co.us/supct/supctopinion.htm[a]

• **Background and Facts** In January 2000, Elizabeth Flood purchased a used automobile, which she subsequently financed through Citi Financial Transouth. Shortly thereafter, she discovered that the car had been damaged. When she returned it to the dealership, the dealer refused to give her a refund. Instead, he provided Flood with a replacement vehicle. Several months later, the replacement vehicle exhibited electrical problems and finally broke down. Flood unsuccessfully attempted to rescind the sale. Flood then lost her job and missed several payments. Transouth repossessed her car and sold it for less than the amount owed. Transouth transferred Flood's delinquent account to Mercantile Adjustment Bureau (MAB). In 2004, MAB caused a written debt-collection communication to be sent to Flood. MAB electronically transmitted the necessary information to a mailing service company, Unimail, which then used a mechanized process to print the letters, stuff the envelopes, and mail them. Flood filed a suit against MAB for, among other claims, impermissibly communicating with a third party in violation of a section of Colorado's Fair Debt Collection

a. Click on "Supreme Court Case Announcements by Date," then click on "2008," and then on "01/22/08."

CASE CONTINUES

CASE 44.2 CONTINUED Practices Act, which is modeled after the federal Fair Debt Collection Practices Act of 1977. At trial, MAB prevailed. Flood appealed to the Supreme Court of Colorado.

• **Decision and Rationale** The Supreme Court of Colorado held that Mercantile Adjustment Bureau did not violate Colorado's statute prohibiting communication with a third party about an outstanding debt. The state supreme court affirmed the lower court's opinion on this issue, but reversed the decision on other grounds (because the letter sent contained contradictory language and failed to effectively convey the required notices regarding the debtor's rights). The state's highest court agreed that the statute prohibits communications between a debt collector and third parties. The federal and state statutes have as their purpose "to protect a consumer's reputation and privacy as well as to prevent loss of jobs resulting from a debt collector's communication with a consumer's employer concerning the collection of the debt." In this case, the collection agency electronically transmitted its collection information to Unimail. Unimail then printed the collection communications, which were mechanically stuffed into envelopes. Under no circumstances could this process involve a family member, employer, friend, or other third party being contacted about the debt-collection efforts. The automated mailing service cannot reasonably be perceived as a threat to the consumer's privacy or reputation.

• **What If the Facts Were Different?** *Assume that Unimail had spotcheckers who randomly pulled printed communications to debtors prior to mailing. These checkers read the letters to make sure that they were accurate. Would the court have still ruled in favor of Mercantile Adjustment Bureau? Why or why not?*

• **The Legal Environment Dimension** *Why might this ruling actually benefit debtors in the long run?*

Enforcement of the Act The enforcement of the FDCPA is primarily the responsibility of the Federal Trade Commission. The act provides that a debt collector who fails to comply with the act is liable for actual damages, plus additional damages not to exceed $1,000[31] and attorneys' fees.

Cases brought under the FDCPA sometimes raise questions as to who qualifies as a debt collector or debt-collection agency subject to the act. For example, in the past courts were issuing conflicting opinions on whether attorneys who attempted to collect debts owed to their clients were subject to the FDCPA's provisions. In 1995, however, the United States Supreme Court resolved this issue when it held that an attorney who regularly tries to obtain payment of consumer debts through legal proceedings meets the FDCPA's definition of "debt collector."[32]

31. According to the U.S. Court of Appeals for the Sixth Circuit, the $1,000 limit on damages applies to each lawsuit, not to each violation. See *Wright v. Finance Service of Norwalk, Inc.*, 22 F.3d 647 (6th Cir. 1994).

32. *Heintz v. Jenkins*, 514 U.S. 291, 115 S.Ct. 1489, 131 L.Ed.2d 395 (1995).

Garnishment of Wages

Despite the increasing number of protections afforded debtors, creditors are not without means of securing payment on debts. One of these is the right to garnish a debtor's wages after the debt has gone unpaid for a prolonged period. Recall from Chapter 28 that in a *garnishment* process, a creditor directly attaches, or seizes, a portion of the debtor's assets (such as wages) that are in the possession of a third party (such as an employer).

State law governs the garnishment process, but the law varies among the states as to how easily garnishment can be obtained. Indeed, a few states, such as Texas, prohibit garnishment of wages except for child support and court-approved spousal maintenance. Constitutional due process and federal legislation under the TILA also provide certain protections against abuse.[33] In general, the debtor is entitled to notice and an opportunity to be heard. Moreover, wages cannot be garnished beyond 25 percent of the debtor's after-tax earnings, and the garnishment must leave the debtor with at least a specified minimum income.

33. 15 U.S.C. Sections 1671–1677.

BUSINESS APPLICATION
Dealing with the Fair Debt Collection Practices Act's Requirements

MANAGEMENT FACES A LEGAL ISSUE

Collection agencies are, as the term indicates, in the business of collecting debts. Yet as you read elsewhere in this chapter, owners and managers of such agencies are constrained in the tactics they can use when collecting debts by the requirements of the Fair Debt Collection Practices Act (FDCPA). One of these requirements is that a collection agency is prohibited from contacting a debtor about an overdue debt "if the debt collector knows the consumer is represented by an attorney." Problem situations arise, however. Consider just one: What happens if a collection agency is not aware that the debtor has hired an attorney to represent him or her? In this situation, if the agency contacts the debtor directly, will the agency be in violation of the FDCPA?

WHAT THE COURTS SAY

This question has come before the courts on a number of occasions. For example, in a case involving a debt owed by Paul Schmitt to First Bank USA, Schmitt retained an attorney and was considering the possibility of filing for bankruptcy. The attorney advised the bank that Schmitt was unable to pay the debt and that if the account was turned over to a collection agency, the bank should let the agency know of the attorney's representation. The bank later transferred Schmitt's account to FMA Alliance, a collection agency, but it did not inform the agency about the legal representation. When FMA sent a letter directly to Schmitt seeking immediate payment of the debt, Schmitt brought an action against FMA, alleging that the agency had violated the FDCPA. FMA responded that it could not be liable under the act because FMA did not *know* of the legal representation. Schmitt countered that even if FMA did not have *actual* knowledge of Schmitt's legal representation, FMA had *implied* knowledge of the representation—because, as the bank's agent, such knowledge could be imputed to FMA.

When Schmitt's case ultimately reached the U.S. Court of Appeals for the Eighth Circuit, the court stated that Schmitt's argument contradicted established agency law (see Chapters 31 and 32). The court noted that although under agency law, the agent's knowledge is imputed to the principal, the reverse is not true—a principal's knowledge cannot be imputed to an agent. The court thus held that FMA had not violated the FDCPA because FMA did not have knowledge of the debtor's legal representation.[a]

Now consider yet another case in which a law firm regularly attempted to collect consumer debts. A debtor did not pay a credit-card company that the law firm represented. The law firm filed a petition in a U.S. district court in Missouri. In the meantime, the debtor contracted with American Mediation, a mediation service, and signed a power of attorney. American Mediation attempted to find a mediated resolution. The attorney for the credit-card company (the creditor) faxed a letter to American Mediation addressed to the debtor (the plaintiff). The letter confirmed a telephone conversation in which the debtor had agreed to make payments of $175 per month to the creditor until the debt was paid. Soon after, though, the debtor hired an attorney to represent him. The debtor's attorney addressed a letter to the creditor's law firm (the defendants), stating that the debtor was suing, but would drop the suit if the law firm paid the debtor $5,000. Ultimately, the law firm acting for the creditor prevailed because the court reasoned that any misconceptions were attributable to American Mediation. There was no violation of the FDCPA.[b]

IMPLICATIONS FOR MANAGERS

The courts have come down on both sides of this important issue. Thus, managers of collection agencies would be wise to (1) always check with their creditor-clients to find out if the relevant debtors are represented by attorneys and (2) learn how courts in their jurisdictions have ruled on this issue.

a. *Schmitt v. FMA Alliance,* 398 F.3d 995 (8th Cir. 2005). For another case in which the court held that a creditor's knowledge cannot be imputed to debt collectors, see *Randolph v. IMBS, Inc.,* 368 F.3d 726 (7th Cir. 2004).

b. *Anderson v. Gamache & Myers, P.C.,* __ F.Supp.2d __ , 2007 WL 4365745 (E.D.Mo. 2007).

SECTION 5 Consumer Health and Safety

The laws discussed earlier regarding the labeling and packaging of products go a long way toward promoting consumer health and safety. There is a significant distinction, however, between regulating the information dispensed about a product and regulating the actual content of the product. The classic example is tobacco products. Producers of tobacco products are required to warn consumers about the hazards associated with the use of their products, but the sale of tobacco products has not been subjected to significant restrictions or banned outright despite the obvious dangers to health.[34] We now examine various laws that regulate the actual products made available to consumers.

The Federal Food, Drug and Cosmetic Act

The first federal legislation regulating food and drugs was enacted in 1906 as the Pure Food and Drugs Act. That law, as amended in 1938, exists today as the Federal Food, Drug and Cosmetic Act (FDCA).[35] The act protects consumers against adulterated and misbranded foods and drugs. As to foods, in its present form, the act establishes food standards, specifies safe levels of potentially hazardous food additives, and sets classifications of foods and food advertising. Most of these statutory requirements are monitored and enforced by the Food and Drug Administration (FDA).

The FDCA also charges the FDA with the responsibility of ensuring that drugs are safe before they are marketed to the public. Under an extensive set of procedures established by the FDA, drugs must be shown to be effective as well as safe, and the use of some food additives suspected of being carcinogenic is prohibited. A 1976 amendment to the FDCA[36] authorizes the FDA to regulate medical devices, such as pacemakers and other health devices and equipment, and to withdraw from the market any such device that is mislabeled.

The question in the following case was whether the U.S. Constitution provides terminally ill patients with a right of access to experimental drugs that have passed limited safety trials but have not been proved safe and effective.

34. We are ignoring recent civil litigation concerning the liability of tobacco product manufacturers for injuries that arise from the use of tobacco. See, for example, *Philip Morris USA v. Williams*, ___ U.S.___, 127 S.Ct. 1057, 166 L.Ed.2d 940 (2007).

35. 21 U.S.C. Sections 301–393.

36. 21 U.S.C. Sections 352(o), 360(j), 360(k), and 360c–360k.

CASE 44.3 Abigail Alliance for Better Access to Developmental Drugs v. von Eschenbach

United States Court of Appeals, District of Columbia Circuit, 2007. 495 F.3d 695.

Background and Facts The Food and Drug Administration (FDA) and Congress have created programs to provide terminally ill patients with access to promising experimental drugs before the completion of the clinical-testing process—which can be lengthy. The Abigail Alliance for Better Access to Developmental Drugs (Alliance), an organization of terminally ill patients and their supporters, asked the FDA to expand this access. The FDA responded that, among other things, "a reasonably precise estimate of response rate" and "enough experience to detect serious adverse effects" are "critical" in determining when experimental drugs should be made available. Accordingly, "it does not serve patients well to make drugs too widely available before there is a reasonable assessment of such risks to guide patient decisions, and experience in managing them." Accepting Alliance's proposal "would upset the appropriate balance * * * by giving almost total weight to the goal of early availability and giving little recognition to the importance of marketing drugs with reasonable knowledge for patients and physicians of their likely clinical benefit and their toxicity." Alliance filed a suit in a federal district court against FDA commissioner Andrew von Eschenbach and others, arguing that the Constitution provides terminally ill patients with a fundamental right of access to experimental drugs. The court ruled in the defendants' favor. Alliance appealed to the U.S. Court of Appeals for the District of Columbia Circuit.

Decision and Rationale The U.S. Court of Appeals for the District of Columbia Circuit affirmed the lower court's decision, holding that terminally ill patients do not have a fundamental constitutional right of access to experimental drugs. The court pointed out that the Food, Drug and Cosmetic Act as amended in 1962 explicitly requires that the Food and Drug Administration (FDA) approve only drugs "deemed effective for public use." No group can override "current FDA regulations simply by insisting that drugs which have completed [some] testing are safe enough for terminally ill patients. Current law bars public access to drugs undergoing clinical testing on safety grounds. The fact that a drug * * * is safe for limited clinical testing in a controlled and closely

CASE 44.3 CONTINUED monitored environment after detailed scrutiny of each trial participant does not mean that a drug is safe for use beyond supervised trials." Here, the government's restrictions bear a rational relationship to a legitimate state interest. That interest is one of "protecting patients, including the terminally ill, from potentially unsafe drugs with unknown therapeutic effects."

- **The Global Dimension** *Should the court have ruled that as long as a drug has been approved for use in any country, terminally ill patients in the United States should be given access to it? Explain.*
- **The Legal Environment Dimension** *In light of the analysis in this case, what option is left to those who believe that terminally ill patients—not the government—should make the decision about whether to accept the risk associated with experimental drugs?*

The Consumer Product Safety Act

Consumer product-safety legislation began in 1953 with the passage of the Flammable Fabrics Act, which prohibits the sale of highly flammable clothing or materials. Over the next two decades, Congress enacted legislation regarding the design or composition of specific classes of products. Then, in 1972, Congress enacted the Consumer Product Safety Act,[37] creating the first comprehensive scheme of regulation over matters of consumer safety. The act also established the Consumer Product Safety Commission (CPSC), which has far-reaching authority over consumer safety.

The CPSC's Authority The CPSC conducts research on the safety of individual consumer products and maintains a clearinghouse on the risks associated with various products. The Consumer Product Safety Act authorizes the CPSC to set standards for consumer products and to ban the manufacture and sale of any product that it deems to be potentially hazardous to consumers. The CPSC also has authority to remove from the market any products it believes to be imminently hazardous and to require manufacturers to report on any products already sold or intended for sale if the products have proved to be dangerous. The CPSC also has authority to administer other product-safety legislation, such as the Child Protection and Toy Safety Act of 1969[38] and the Federal Hazardous Substances Act of 1960.[39]

The CPSC's authority is sufficiently broad to allow it to ban any product that it believes poses an "unreasonable risk" to consumers. This includes the authority to ban the importation of hazardous products into the United States. Some of the products that the CPSC has banned include various types of fireworks, cribs, and toys, as well as many products containing asbestos or vinyl chloride.

Notification Requirements The Consumer Product Safety Act requires the distributors of consumer products to notify the CPSC immediately if they receive information that a product "contains a defect which . . . creates a substantial risk to the public" or "an unreasonable risk of serious injury or death."

For example, Aroma Housewares Company had been distributing a particular model of juicer for just over a year when it began receiving letters from customers. They complained that during operation the juicer had suddenly exploded, sending pieces of glass and razor-sharp metal across the room. The company received twenty-three letters from angry consumers about the exploding juicer but waited more than six months before notifying the CPSC that the product posed a significant risk to the public. In a suit filed by the federal government, the court held that when a company first receives information regarding a threat, the company is required to report the problem within twenty-four hours to the CPSC. The court also found that even if the company had to investigate the allegations, it should not have taken more than ten days to verify the information and report the problem. The court therefore held that the company had violated the law and ordered it to pay damages.[40]

37. 15 U.S.C. Sections 2051–2083.
38. This act consists of amendments to 15 U.S.C. Sections 1261, 1262, and 1274.
39. 15 U.S.C. Sections 1261–1277.
40. *United States v. Miram Enterprises, Inc.*, 185 F.Supp.2d 1148 (S.D.Cal. 2002).

REVIEWING Consumer Law

Leota Sage saw a local motorcycle dealer's newspaper advertisement for a MetroRider EZ electric scooter for $1,699. When she went to the dealership, however, she learned that the EZ model had been sold out. The salesperson told Sage that he still had the higher-end MetroRider FX model in stock for $2,199 and would offer her one for $1,999. Sage was disappointed but decided to purchase the FX model. When Sage said that she wished to purchase the scooter on credit, she was directed to the dealer's credit department. As she filled out the credit forms, the clerk told Sage, who is an African American, that she would need a cosigner to obtain a loan. Sage could not understand why she would need a cosigner and asked to speak to the store manager. The manager apologized, told her that the clerk was mistaken, and said that he would "speak to" the clerk about that. The manager completed Sage's credit application, and Sage then rode the scooter home. Seven months later, Sage received a letter from the manufacturer informing her that a flaw had been discovered in the scooter's braking system and that the model had been recalled. Using the information presented in the chapter, answer the following questions.

1. Had the dealer engaged in deceptive advertising? Why or why not?
2. Suppose that Sage had ordered the scooter through the dealer's Web site but the dealer had been unable to deliver it by the date promised. What would the FTC have required the merchant to do in that situation?
3. Assuming that the clerk had required a cosigner based on Sage's race or gender, what act prohibits such credit discrimination?
4. What organization has the authority to ban the sale of scooters based on safety concerns?

TERMS AND CONCEPTS

bait-and-switch advertising 838
cease-and-desist order 838
consumer law 836
counteradvertising 838
deceptive advertising 837
multiple product orders 838
Regulation Z 840
validation notice 843

QUESTIONS AND CASE PROBLEMS

44–1. Andrew, a resident of California, received an advertising circular in the U.S. mail announcing a new line of regional cookbooks distributed by the Every-Kind Cookbook Co. Andrew didn't want any books and threw the circular away. Two days later, Andrew received in the mail an introductory cookbook entitled *Lower Mongolian Regional Cookbook,* as announced in the circular, on a "trial basis" from Every-Kind. Andrew was not interested but did not go to the trouble to return the cookbook. Every-Kind demanded payment of $20.95 for the *Lower Mongolian Regional Cookbook*. Discuss whether Andrew can be required to pay for the book.

44–2. Maria Ochoa receives two new credit cards on May 1. She had solicited one of them from Midtown Department Store, and the other arrived unsolicited from High-Flying Airlines. During the month of May, Ochoa makes numerous credit-card purchases from Midtown Department Store, but she does not use the High-Flying Airlines card. On May 31, a burglar breaks into Ochoa's home and steals both credit cards, along with other items. Ochoa notifies the Midtown Department Store of the theft on June 2, but she fails to notify High-Flying Airlines. Using the Midtown credit card, the burglar makes a $500 purchase on June 1 and a $200 purchase on June 3. The burglar then charges a vacation flight on the High-Flying Airlines card for $1,000 on June 5. Ochoa receives the bills for these charges and refuses to pay them. Discuss Ochoa's liability in these situations.

44–3. QUESTION WITH SAMPLE ANSWER

On June 28, a salesperson for Renowned Books called on the Gonchars at their home. After a very persuasive sales pitch by the agent, the Gonchars agreed in writing to purchase a twenty-volume set of historical encyclopedias from Renowned Books for a total of $299. A down payment of $35 was required, with the remainder of the cost to be paid in monthly payments over a one-year period. Two days later, the Gonchars, having second thoughts, contacted the book company and stated that they had decided to rescind the contract. Renowned Books said this would be impossible. Has Renowned Books violated any consumer law by not allowing the Gonchars to rescind their contract? Explain.

- **For a sample answer to Question 44–3, go to Appendix I at the end of this text.**

44–4. Fair Debt Collection. CrossCheck, Inc., provides check-authorization services to retail merchants. When a customer presents a check, the merchant contacts CrossCheck, which estimates the probability that the check will clear the bank. If the check is within an acceptable statistical range, CrossCheck notifies the merchant. If the check is dishonored, the merchant sends it to CrossCheck, which pays it. CrossCheck then attempts to redeposit the check. If this fails, CrossCheck takes further steps to collect the amount. CrossCheck attempts to collect on more than two thousand checks per year and spends $2 million on these efforts, which involve about 7 percent of its employees and 6 percent of its total expenses. William Winterstein took his truck to C&P Auto Service Center, Inc., for a tune-up and paid for the service with a check. C&P contacted CrossCheck and, on its recommendation, accepted the check. When the check was dishonored, C&P mailed it to CrossCheck, which reimbursed C&P and sent a letter to Winterstein requesting payment. Winterstein filed a suit in a federal district court against CrossCheck, asserting that the letter violated the Fair Debt Collection Practices Act. CrossCheck filed a motion for summary judgment. On what ground might the court grant the motion? Explain. [*Winterstein v. CrossCheck, Inc.*, 149 F.Supp.2d 466 (N.D.Ill. 2001)]

44–5. Fair Credit Reporting Act. Source One Associates, Inc., is based in Poughquag, New York. Peter Easton, Source One's president, is responsible for its daily operations. Between 1995 and 1997, Source One received requests from persons in Massachusetts seeking financial information about individuals and businesses. To obtain this information, Easton first obtained the targeted individuals' credit reports through Equifax Consumer Information Services by claiming that the reports would be used only in connection with credit transactions involving the consumers. From the reports, Easton identified financial institutions at which the targeted individuals held accounts. He then called the institutions to learn the account balances by impersonating either officers of the institutions or the account holders. The information was then provided to Source One's customers for a fee. Easton did not know why the customers wanted the information. The state ("commonwealth") of Massachusetts filed a suit in a Massachusetts state court against Source One and Easton, alleging, among other things, violations of the Fair Credit Reporting Act (FCRA). Did the defendants violate the FCRA? Explain. [*Commonwealth v. Source One Associates, Inc.*, 436 Mass. 118, 763 N.E.2d 42 (2002)]

44–6. Deceptive Advertising. "Set Up & Ready to Make Money in Minutes Guaranteed!" the ads claimed. "The Internet Treasure Chest (ITC) will give you everything you need to start your own exciting Internet business including your own worldwide Web site all for the unbelievable price of only $59.95." The ITC "contains virtually everything you need to quickly and easily get your very own worldwide Internet business up, running, stocked with products, able to accept credit cards and ready to take orders almost immediately." What ITC's marketers—Damien Zamora and end70 Corp.—did not disclose were the significant additional costs required to operate the business: domain name registration fees, monthly Internet access and hosting charges, monthly fees to access the ITC product warehouse, and other "upgrades." The Federal Trade Commission filed a suit in a federal district court against end70 and Zamora, seeking an injunction and other relief. Are the defendants' claims "deceptive advertising"? If so, what might the court order the defendants to do to correct any misrepresentations? [*Federal Trade Commission v. end70 Corp.*, __ F.Supp.2d __ (N.D.Tex. 2003)]

44–7. CASE PROBLEM WITH SAMPLE ANSWER

One of the products that McDonald's Corp. sells is the Happy Meal®, which consists of a McDonald's food entree, a small order of french fries, a small drink, and a toy. In the early 1990s, McDonald's began to aim its Happy Meal marketing at children aged one to three. In 1995, McDonald's began making nutritional information for its food products available in documents known as "McDonald's Nutrition Facts." Each document lists each food item that the restaurant serves and provides a nutritional breakdown, but the Happy Meal is not included. Marc Cohen filed a suit in an Illinois state court against McDonald's, alleging, among other things, that the defendant had violated a state law prohibiting consumer fraud and deceptive business practices by failing to adhere to the National Labeling and Education Act

(NLEA) of 1990. The NLEA sets out different requirements for products specifically intended for children under the age of four—generally, the products cannot declare the percent of daily value of nutritional components. Would this requirement be readily understood by a consumer who is not familiar with nutritional standards? Why or why not? Should a state court impose such regulations? Explain. [*Cohen v. McDonald's Corp.*, 347 Ill.App.3d 627, 808 N.E.2d 1,283 Ill.Dec.451 (1 Dist. 2004)]

- **To view a sample answer for Problem 44–7, go to this book's Web site at www.cengage.com/blaw/jentz, select "Chapter 44," and click on "Case Problem with Sample Answer."**

44–8. Debt Collection. 55th Management Corp. in New York City owns residential property that it leases to various tenants. In June 2000, claiming that one of the tenants, Leslie Goldman, owed more than $13,000 in back rent, 55th retained Jeffrey Cohen, an attorney, to initiate nonpayment proceedings. Cohen filed a petition in a New York state court against Goldman, seeking recovery of the unpaid rent and at least $3,000 in attorneys' fees. After receiving notice of the petition, Goldman filed a suit in a federal district court against Cohen. Goldman contended that the notice of the petition constituted an initial contact that, under the Fair Debt Collection Practices Act (FDCPA), required a validation notice. Because Cohen did not give Goldman a validation notice at the time, or within five days, of the notice of the petition, Goldman argued that Cohen was in violation of the FDCPA. Should the filing of a suit in a state court be considered "communication," requiring a debt collector to provide a validation notice under the FDCPA? Why or why not? [*Goldman v. Cohen,* 445 F.3d 152 (2d Cir. 2006)]

44–9. A QUESTION OF ETHICS

After graduating from law school—and serving time in prison for attempting to collect debts by posing as an FBI agent—Barry Sussman theorized that if a debt-collection business collected only debts that it owned as a result of buying checks written on accounts with insufficient funds (NSF checks), it would not be subject to the Federal Debt Collection Practices Act (FDCPA). Sussman formed Check Investors, Inc., to act on his theory. Check Investors bought more than 2.2 million NSF checks, with an estimated face value of about $348 million, for pennies on the dollar. Check Investors added a fee of $125 or $130 to the face amount of each check (which exceeds the legal limit in most states) and aggressively pursued its drawer to collect. The firm's employees were told to accuse drawers of being criminals and to threaten them with arrest and prosecution. The threats were false. Check Investors never took steps to initiate a prosecution. The employees contacted the drawers' family members and used "saturation phoning"—phoning a drawer numerous times in a short period. They used abusive language, referring to drawers as "deadbeats," "retards," "thieves," and "idiots." Between January 2000 and January 2003, Check Investors netted more than $10.2 million from its efforts. [Federal Trade Commission v. Check Investors, Inc., *502 F.3d 159 (3d Cir. 2007)*]

(a) The Federal Trade Commission filed a suit in a federal district court against Check Investors and others, alleging, in part, violations of the FDCPA. Was Check Investors a "debt collector," collecting "debts," within the meaning of the FDCPA? If so, did its methods violate the FDCPA? Were its practices unethical? What might Check Investors argue in its defense? Discuss.

(b) Are "deadbeats" the primary beneficiaries of laws such as the FDCPA? If not, how would you characterize debtors who default on their obligations?

44–10. VIDEO QUESTION

Go to this text's Web site at **www.cengage.com/blaw/jentz** and select "Chapter 44." Click on "Video Questions" and view the video titled *Advertising Communication Law: Bait and Switch.* Then answer the following questions.

(a) Is the auto dealership's advertisement for the truck in the video deceptive? Why or why not?

(b) Is the advertisement for the truck an offer to which the dealership is bound? Does it matter if Betty detrimentally relied on the advertisement?

(c) Is Tony committed to buying Betty's trade-in truck for $3,000 because that is what he told her over the phone?

LAW ON THE WEB

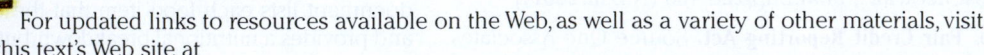

For updated links to resources available on the Web, as well as a variety of other materials, visit this text's Web site at

www.cengage.com/blaw/jentz

For a government-sponsored Web site containing reports on consumer issues, go to

www.consumer.gov

The Federal Trade Commission (FTC) offers extensive information on consumer protection laws, consumer problems, enforcement issues, and other topics relevant to consumer law at its Web site. Go to

www.ftc.gov

and click on "Consumer Protection."

To learn more about the FTC's "cooling-off" rule, you can access it directly by going to the following URL:

www.ftc.gov/bcp/edu/pubs/consumer/products/pro03.shtm

Legal Research Exercises on the Web

Go to **www.cengage.com/blaw/jentz**, the Web site that accompanies this text. Select "Chapter 44" and click on "Internet Exercises." There you will find the following Internet research exercises that you can perform to learn more about the topics covered in this chapter.

Internet Exercise 44–1: Legal Perspective
The Food and Drug Administration

Internet Exercise 44–2: Management Perspective
Internet Advertising and Marketing

CHAPTER 45

Environmental Law

Concerns over the degradation of the environment have increased over time in response to the environmental effects of population growth, urbanization, and industrialization. Environmental protection is not without a price, however. For many businesses, the costs of complying with environmental regulations are high, and for some they may seem too high. A constant tension exists between the desire to increase profits and productivity and the need to protect the environment. In this chapter, we discuss **environmental law,** which consists of all laws and regulations designed to protect and preserve our environmental resources.

SECTION 1 Common Law Actions

Common law remedies against environmental pollution originated centuries ago in England. Those responsible for operations that created dirt, smoke, noxious odors, noise, or toxic substances were sometimes held liable under common law theories of nuisance or negligence. Today, injured individuals continue to rely on the common law to obtain damages and injunctions against business polluters.

Nuisance

Under the common law doctrine of **nuisance,** persons may be held liable if they use their property in a manner that unreasonably interferes with others' rights to use or enjoy their own property. Courts typically balance the equities between the harm caused by the pollution and the costs of stopping it. Courts have often denied injunctive relief on the ground that the hardships that would be imposed on the polluter and on the community are greater than the hardships suffered by the plaintiff. For example, a factory that causes neighboring landowners to suffer from smoke, soot, and vibrations may be left in operation if it is the core of the local economy. The injured parties may be awarded only monetary damages, which may include compensation for the decline in the value of their property caused by the factory's operation.

A property owner may be given relief from pollution if he or she can identify a distinct harm separate from that affecting the general public. This harm is referred to as a "private" nuisance. Under the common law, individuals were denied *standing* (access to the courts—see Chapter 2) unless they suffered a harm distinct from the harm suffered by the public at large. Some states still require this. For example, in one case a group of individuals who made their living by commercial fishing in a major river in New York filed a suit seeking damages and an injunction against a company that was polluting the river. The New York court found that the plaintiffs had standing because they were particularly harmed by the pollution in the river.[1] A public authority (such as a state's attorney general), however, can sue to abate a "public" nuisance.

Negligence and Strict Liability

An injured party may sue a business polluter in tort under the negligence and strict liability theories discussed in Chapters 6 and 7. The basis for a negligence action is a business's alleged failure to use reasonable care toward a party whose injury was foreseeable and was caused by the lack of reasonable care. For example, employees might sue an employer whose failure to use proper pollution controls contaminated

1. *Lee v. General Electric Co.,* 538 N.Y.S.2d 844, 145 A.D.2d 291 (1989).

the air, causing the employees to suffer respiratory illnesses. A developing area of tort law involves **toxic torts**—actions against toxic polluters.

Businesses that engage in ultrahazardous activities—such as the transportation of radioactive materials—are strictly liable for any injuries the activities cause. In a strict liability action, the injured party need not prove that the business failed to exercise reasonable care.

SECTION 2

Federal, State, and Local Regulation

All levels of government in the United States regulate some aspect of the environment. In this section, we look at the various ways in which the federal, state, and local governments control business activities and land use in the interests of environmental preservation and protection.

Federal Regulation

Congress has passed a number of statutes to control the impact of human activities on the environment. Exhibit 45–1 on the next page lists and summarizes the major federal environmental statutes, most of which are discussed in this chapter. Some of these statutes were passed in an attempt to improve air and water quality. Others specifically regulate toxic chemicals, including pesticides, herbicides, and hazardous wastes.

Environmental Regulatory Agencies The primary federal agency regulating environmental law is the Environmental Protection Agency (EPA), which was created in 1970 to coordinate federal environmental responsibilities. Other federal agencies with authority for regulating specific environmental matters include the Department of the Interior, the Department of Defense, the Department of Labor, the Food and Drug Administration, and the Nuclear Regulatory Commission. These regulatory agencies—and all other agencies of the federal government—must take environmental factors into consideration when making significant decisions.

Most federal environmental laws provide that private parties can sue to enforce environmental regulations if government agencies fail to do so—or can sue to protest agency enforcement actions if they believe that these actions go too far. Typically, a threshold hurdle in such suits is meeting the requirements for standing to sue (see Chapter 2).

State and local regulatory agencies also play a significant role in carrying out federal environmental legislation. Typically, the federal government relies on state and local governments to implement federal environmental statutes and regulations such as those regulating air quality.

Environmental Impact Statements The National Environmental Policy Act (NEPA) of 1969[2] requires that an **environmental impact statement (EIS)** be prepared for every major federal action that significantly affects the quality of the environment. An EIS must analyze (1) the impact on the environment that the action will have, (2) any adverse effects on the environment and alternative actions that might be taken, and (3) irreversible effects the action might generate.

An action qualifies as "major" if it involves a substantial commitment of resources (monetary or otherwise). An action is "federal" if a federal agency has the power to control it. Construction by a private developer of a ski resort on federal land, for example, may require an EIS. Building or operating a nuclear plant, which requires a federal permit, or constructing a dam as part of a federal project requires an EIS. If an agency decides that an EIS is unnecessary, it must issue a statement supporting this conclusion. EISs have become instruments for private individuals, consumer interest groups, businesses, and others to challenge federal agency actions on the basis that the actions improperly threaten the environment.

State and Local Regulation

Many states regulate the degree to which the environment may be polluted. Thus, for example, even when state zoning laws permit a business's proposed development, the proposal may have to be altered to lessen the development's impact on the environment. State laws may restrict a business's discharge of chemicals into the air or water or regulate its disposal of toxic wastes. States may also regulate the disposal or recycling of other wastes, including glass, metal, and plastic containers and paper. Additionally, states may restrict the emissions from motor vehicles.

City, county, and other local governments oversee certain aspects of the environment. For instance, local zoning laws control some land use. These laws may be

2. 42 U.S.C. Sections 4321–4370d.

EXHIBIT 45–1 • Major Federal Environmental Statutes

Popular Name	Purpose	Statute Reference
Rivers and Harbors Appropriations Act (1899)	To prohibit ships and manufacturers from discharging and depositing refuse in navigable waterways.	33 U.S.C. Sections 401–418.
Federal Insecticide, Fungicide, and Rodenticide Act (1947)	To control the use of pesticides and herbicides.	7 U.S.C. Sections 136–136y.
Federal Water Pollution Control Act (1948)	To eliminate the discharge of pollutants from major sources into navigable waters.	33 U.S.C. Sections 1251–1387.
Clean Air Act (1963, 1970)	To control air pollution from mobile and stationary sources.	42 U.S.C. Sections 7401–7671q.
National Environmental Policy Act (1969)	To limit environmental harm from federal government activities.	42 U.S.C. Sections 4321–4370d.
Endangered Species Act (1973)	To protect species that are threatened with extinction.	16 U.S.C. Sections 1531–1544.
Safe Drinking Water Act (1974)	To regulate pollutants in public drinking water systems.	42 U.S.C. Sections 300f to 300j-25.
Resource Conservation and Recovery Act (1976)	To establish standards for hazardous waste disposal.	42 U.S.C. Sections 6901–6986.
Toxic Substances Control Act (1976)	To regulate toxic chemicals and chemical compounds.	15 U.S.C. Sections 2601–2692.
Comprehensive Environmental Response, Compensation, and Liability Act (1980)	To regulate the clean-up of hazardous waste–disposal sites.	42 U.S.C. Sections 9601–9675.
Oil Pollution Act (1990)	To establish liability for the clean-up of navigable waters after oil-spill disasters.	33 U.S.C. Sections 2701–2761.
Small Business Liability Relief and Brownfields Revitalization Act (2002)	To allow developers who comply with state voluntary clean-up programs to avoid federal liability for the properties that they decontaminate and develop.	42 U.S.C. Section 9628.

designed to inhibit or direct the growth of cities and suburbs or to protect the natural environment. In the interest of safeguarding the environment, such laws may prohibit certain land uses.

Other aspects of the environment may also be subject to local regulation. Methods of waste and garbage removal and disposal, for example, can have a substantial impact on a community. The appearance of buildings and other structures, including advertising signs and billboards, may affect traffic safety, property values, or local aesthetics. Noise generated by a business or its customers may be annoying, disruptive, or damaging to its neighbors. The location and condition of parks, streets, and other public uses of land subject to local control affect the environment and can also affect business.

SECTION 3 Air Pollution

Federal involvement with air pollution goes back to the 1950s and 1960s, when Congress authorized funds for air-pollution research and passed the Clean Air Act.[3] The act focused on multistate air pollution and pro-

3. 42 U.S.C. Sections 7401–7671q.

vided assistance to the states. Amendments to the Clean Air Act, particularly those made in 1970, 1977, and 1990, strengthened the government's authority to regulate air quality. These laws provide the basis for issuing regulations to control pollution coming primarily from mobile sources (such as automobiles) and stationary sources (such as electric utilities and industrial plants).

Mobile Sources

Automobiles and other vehicles are referred to as mobile sources of pollution. The EPA has issued regulations specifying standards for mobile sources of pollution, as well as for service stations. The agency periodically updates these standards in light of new developments and data.

Motor Vehicles Regulations governing air pollution from automobiles and other mobile sources specify pollution standards and time schedules for meeting these standards. For example, the 1990 amendments to the Clean Air Act required automobile manufacturers to cut new automobiles' exhaust emissions of nitrogen oxide by 60 percent and emissions of other pollutants by 35 percent by 1998. Regulations that became effective beginning with 2004 model cars called for nitrogen oxide tailpipe emissions to be cut by nearly 10 percent by 2007. For the first time, sport-utility vehicles (SUVs) and light trucks were required to meet the same emission standards as automobiles. The amendments also required service stations to sell gasoline with a higher oxygen content in certain cities, and to sell even cleaner-burning gasoline in the most polluted urban areas.

When individuals or groups oppose regulations, they often file lawsuits in an attempt to *prevent* an agency from taking some regulatory action. As mentioned earlier, however, private parties also sometimes file lawsuits in an effort to *compel* an agency to take action in an area in which it has failed to act. A group of private organizations and several states recently took such an action when they sued to require the EPA to adopt rules to regulate carbon dioxide emissions from automobiles under the Clean Air Act. For a discussion of the Supreme Court's decision in this case, see the *Contemporary Legal Debates* feature on pages 856 and 857.

Updating Pollution-Control Standards As mentioned, the EPA attempts to update pollution-control standards when new scientific information becomes available. For example, studies conducted in the 1990s concluded that very small particles (2.5 microns, or millionths of a meter) of soot affect our health as significantly as larger particles. Based on this evidence, in 1997 the EPA issued new particulate standards for motor vehicle exhaust systems and other sources of pollution. The EPA also set a more rigorous standard for ozone (the basic ingredient of smog), which is formed when sunlight combines with pollutants from cars and other sources.

The EPA's particulate standards and ozone standard were challenged in court by a number of business groups that claimed that the EPA had exceeded its authority under the Clean Air Act by issuing the stricter rules. Additionally, the groups claimed that the EPA had to take economic costs into account when developing new regulations. In 2001, however, the United States Supreme Court upheld the EPA's authority under the Clean Air Act to issue the standards. The Court also held that the EPA did not have to take economic costs into account when creating new rules.[4]

In 2006, the EPA again reevaluated its particulate standards and found that more than two hundred counties were not meeting the standards set in 1997. The EPA issued new regulations for daily (twenty-four hour) exposure to particles of soot but did not change the annual particulate standards.[5]

Stationary Sources

The Clean Air Act also authorizes the EPA to establish air-quality standards for stationary sources (such as manufacturing plants) but recognizes that the primary responsibility for implementing these standards rests with state and local governments. The standards are aimed at controlling hazardous air pollutants—that is, those likely to cause death or serious irreversible or incapacitating illness such as cancer or neurological and reproductive damage.

Listing of Regulated Hazardous Air Pollutants When Congress amended the Clean Air Act in 1970, it required the EPA to list all regulated hazardous air pollutants (HAPs) on a prioritized schedule. The EPA listed only eight substances for the next eighteen years. In 1990, Congress again amended the act and required the EPA to list more substances as HAPs. In all, 189 substances, including asbestos, benzene, beryllium, cadmium, and vinyl chloride, have been classified as hazardous. They are emitted from stationary sources by a variety of business activities,

4. *Whitman v. American Trucking Associations,* 531 U.S. 457, 121 S.Ct. 903, 149 L.Ed.2d 1 (2001).
5. 40 C.F.R. Part 50.

CONTEMPORARY LEGAL DEBATES

Should the EPA Take the Threat of Global Warming into Account?

For some time, environmental groups have argued that Congress should take action to curb emissions of so-called greenhouse gases, including carbon dioxide, which build up in the atmosphere and supposedly create a "greenhouse effect," leading to global warming. They wanted Congress to mandate that the Environmental Protection Agency (EPA) consider global warming effects when instituting regulations, particularly with respect to carbon dioxide emissions from automobiles.

If Congress Won't Act, Go to Court to Force the EPA to Act

In 1999, frustrated by Congress's apparent lack of concern about global warming, environmental groups went directly to the EPA and petitioned the agency to use its authority under the Clean Air Act to regulate greenhouse gases, including carbon dioxide emissions from motor vehicles. In 2003, however, the EPA denied their petition, stating, among other things, that the Clean Air Act did not authorize it to address global climate change or to regulate carbon dioxide emissions. As a result of the EPA's refusal to take action, the environmental groups and several states brought a lawsuit to force the EPA to act. At issue in the case was not only whether the EPA has the authority to regulate carbon dioxide under the Clean Air Act but also whether the plaintiffs had *standing* to bring their case at all.

The Supreme Court Agrees

In 2007, in *Massachusetts v. Environmental Protection Agency,*[a] the United States Supreme Court issued what may turn out to be a landmark decision supporting the plaintiffs. As to whether the plaintiffs had standing to sue, recall from the discussion earlier in this chapter that ordinarily a plaintiff must have suffered a particularized harm that is distinct from that experienced by the public at large. In this case, Massachusetts asserted that it had standing because its coastline, including lands owned by the state, faced an imminent threat from rising sea levels caused by global warming. The Court agreed, declaring that "the harm associated with climate changes is serious and well recognized," including "severe and irreversible changes to natural ecosystems" and "a precipitate rise in sea levels." The EPA had argued that because global warming has widespread effects, an individual plaintiff could not show the particularized harm that standing requires, but the Court said that the fact that these effects are widely shared does not minimize their

a. ___ U.S. ___, 127 S.Ct. 1438, 167 L.Ed.2d 248 (2007).

including smelting (melting ore to produce metal), dry cleaning, house painting, and commercial baking.

Mercury is one of the listed hazardous substances. The EPA attempted nonetheless to remove mercury from its list of designated HAPs emitted from electric utility steam-generating units. In the following case, New Jersey and others challenged this delisting.

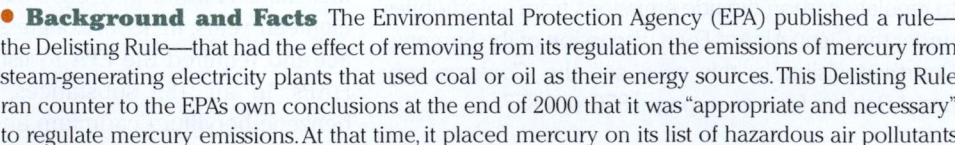

CASE 45.1 State of New Jersey v. Environmental Protection Agency

United States Court of Appeals, District of Columbia, 2008. 517 F.3d 574.

www.cadc.uscourts.gov/bin/opinions/allopinions.asp[a]

Background and Facts The Environmental Protection Agency (EPA) published a rule—the Delisting Rule—that had the effect of removing from its regulation the emissions of mercury from steam-generating electricity plants that used coal or oil as their energy sources. This Delisting Rule ran counter to the EPA's own conclusions at the end of 2000 that it was "appropriate and necessary" to regulate mercury emissions. At that time, it placed mercury on its list of hazardous air pollutants

a. This is the opinions page of the U.S. Court of Appeals for the District of Columbia. Select "February" and "2008" from the drop-down menus for "Month" and "Year" and click on "Go!" Scroll down to the listing for case number "05-1097" and click on the link to access the opinion.

impact on Massachusetts. Hence, Massachusetts had standing to bring a lawsuit to force the EPA to take action to protect the state and its residents.

The Court also found that the Clean Air Act gives the EPA the authority to regulate carbon dioxide. The agency had contended that the statutory language did not include carbon dioxide, but the Court pointed out that the statute defines an air pollutant as "any physical, chemical, . . . substance which is emitted into or otherwise enters the ambient air"—a definition that would include all airborne compounds. Thus, the statute's mandate that the EPA should regulate "any air pollutant" from cars that might "endanger public health or welfare" provides authority to regulate carbon dioxide.

But Others Are Critical

Although environmental groups hailed the decision, others were highly critical. Many observers questioned the Court's ruling on standing. They pointed out that Massachusetts had presented no exhibits to support witnesses' statements that Massachusetts would actually lose coastal land as a result of rising sea levels. Hence, there was no imminent harm—and thus no case or controversy, as required by Article III of the U.S. Constitution. To date, at least two federal courts have declined to extend the ruling to other subjects.[b]

The Court's interpretation of the Clean Air Act has also been controversial. Critics have pointed out that when Congress last amended the Clean Air Act in 1990, there were already major studies on global warming. Nevertheless, Congress did not include amendments that would have forced the EPA to set carbon dioxide emission standards. If Congress chose not to force the EPA to act, why should the Court do so? In his dissent, Justice Antonin Scalia also criticized the majority's broad definition of "pollutant." He pointed out that the dictionary defines "pollute" as "to make or render impure or unclean," a definition that hardly applies to carbon dioxide, which, after all, is the principal product of human respiration.

WHERE DO YOU STAND?

Some argue that the requirement that plaintiffs have standing is one of the self-restraints on the power of the federal courts. Do you think that the Supreme Court's decision in the *Massachusetts* case diluted the standards for standing? Why or why not? Will the Supreme Court's new approach to standing increase or decrease the role of the courts in U.S. public life? Why?

---

b. See *United States v. Genendo Pharmaceutical, N.V.,* 485 F.3d 958 (7th Cir. 2007); and *American Civil Liberties Union v. National Security Agency,* 493 F.3d 644 (6th Cir. 2007).

CASE 45.1 CONTINUED (HAPs) to be monitored at electricity-generating sites. New Jersey and fourteen additional states, plus various state agencies, challenged the EPA's action.

• **Decision and Rationale** The U.S. Court of Appeals for the District of Columbia Circuit ruled in favor of New Jersey and the other plaintiffs. The EPA was required to rescind its delisting of mercury. Congress required the EPA to regulate more than one hundred HAPs, including mercury and nickel compounds. "In seeking to ensure that regulation of HAPs reflects the 'maximum reduction in emissions which can be achieved by application of [the] best available controlled technology,' Congress imposed specific, pollution-control requirements on both new and existing sources of HAPs." The court rejected the EPA's argument that it had previously removed listed sources without satisfying the requirements of the statute. "But previous statutory violations cannot excuse the one now before the court." The court stated that it could not see how "applying an unreasonable statutory interpretation for several years can transform it into a reasonable interpretation." Mercury could not be delisted.

• **What If the Facts Were Different?** *Assume that the EPA had carried out scientific tests that showed mercury was relatively harmless as a by-product of electricity generation. How might this have affected the court's ruling?*

• **The Global Dimension** *Because air pollution knows no borders, how did this ruling affect our neighboring countries?*

Air Pollution-Control Standards The EPA sets primary and secondary levels of ambient standards—that is, the maximum levels of certain pollutants—and the states formulate plans to achieve those standards. Different standards apply depending on whether the sources of pollution are located in clean areas or polluted areas and whether they are already existing sources or major new sources. Major new sources include existing sources modified by a change in a method of operation that increases emissions. Performance standards for major sources require the use of the *maximum achievable control technology,* or MACT, to reduce emissions. The EPA issues guidelines as to what equipment meets this standard.[6]

Violations of the Clean Air Act

For violations of emission limits under the Clean Air Act, the EPA can assess civil penalties of up to $25,000 per day. Additional fines of up to $5,000 per day can be assessed for other violations, such as failing to maintain the required records. To penalize those who find it more cost-effective to violate the act than to comply with it, the EPA is authorized to impose a penalty equal to the violator's economic benefits from noncompliance. Persons who provide information about violators may be paid up to $10,000. Private citizens can also sue violators.

Those who knowingly violate the act may be subject to criminal penalties, including fines of up to $1 million and imprisonment for up to two years (for false statements or failure to report violations). Corporate officers are among those who may be subject to these penalties.

SECTION 4

Water Pollution

Water pollution stems mostly from industrial, municipal, and agricultural sources. Pollutants entering streams, lakes, and oceans include organic wastes, heated water, sediments from soil runoff, nutrients (including fertilizers and human and animal wastes), and toxic chemicals and other hazardous substances. We look here at laws and regulations governing water pollution.

Navigable Waters

Federal regulations governing water pollution can be traced back to the Rivers and Harbors Appropriations Act of 1899.[7] These regulations prohibited ships and manufacturers from discharging or depositing refuse in navigable waterways. Once limited to waters actually used for navigation, the term *navigable waters* is today interpreted to include intrastate lakes and streams used by interstate travelers and industries, as well as coastal and freshwater wetlands (*wetlands* will be defined shortly).

The Clean Water Act In 1948, Congress passed the Federal Water Pollution Control Act (FWPCA),[8] but its regulatory system and enforcement powers proved to be inadequate. In 1972, amendments to the FWPCA—known as the Clean Water Act—established the following goals: (1) make waters safe for swimming, (2) protect fish and wildlife, and (3) eliminate the discharge of pollutants into the water. The act requires municipal and industrial polluters to apply for permits before discharging wastes into navigable waters. The Clean Water Act also set specific schedules, which were extended by amendment in 1977 and by the Water Quality Act of 1987.[9] Under these schedules, the EPA establishes limits for discharges of various types of pollutants based on the technology available for controlling them.

Standards for Equipment Regulations, for the most part, specify that the *best available control technology,* or BACT, be installed. The EPA issues guidelines as to what equipment meets this standard; essentially, the guidelines require the most effective pollution-control equipment available. New sources must install BACT equipment before beginning operations. Existing sources are subject to timetables for the installation of BACT equipment and must immediately install equipment that utilizes the *best practical control technology,* or BPCT. The EPA also issues guidelines as to what equipment meets this standard.

Wetlands The Clean Water Act prohibits the filling or dredging of wetlands unless a permit is obtained from the Army Corps of Engineers. The EPA defines **wetlands** as "those areas that are inundated or saturated by surface or ground water at a frequency and

6. The EPA has also issued rules to regulate hazardous air pollutants emitted by landfills. 40 C.F.R. Sections 60.750–759.

7. 33 U.S.C. Sections 401–418.
8. 33 U.S.C. Sections 1251–1387.
9. This act amended 33 U.S.C. Section 1251.

duration sufficient to support, and that under normal circumstances do support, a prevalence of vegetation typically adapted for life in saturated soil conditions." The EPA's broad interpretation of what constitutes a wetland for purposes of regulation by the federal government has generated substantial controversy.

The Migratory Bird Rule. One of the most controversial regulations was the "migratory bird rule" issued by the Army Corps of Engineers. Under this rule, any bodies of water that could affect interstate commerce, including seasonal ponds or waters "used or suitable for use by migratory birds" that fly over state borders, were "navigable waters" subject to federal regulation under the Clean Water Act as wetlands. The rule was challenged in a case brought by a group of communities that wanted to build a landfill in a tract of land northwest of Chicago. The Army Corps of Engineers refused to grant a permit for the landfill on the ground that the shallow ponds on the property formed a habitat for migratory birds.

Ultimately, the United States Supreme Court held that the Army Corps of Engineers had exceeded its authority under the Clean Water Act. The Court stated that it was not prepared to hold that isolated and seasonable ponds, puddles, and "prairie potholes" become "navigable waters of the United States" simply because they serve as a habitat for migratory birds.[10]

Seasonal Bodies of Water. The United States Supreme Court revisited the issue of wetlands in 2006, again scaling back the reach of the Clean Water Act. Two disputes had arisen as to whether certain properties in Michigan could be developed by the owners or were protected as wetlands, and the Court consolidated the cases on appeal. One involved property deemed to be wetlands because it was near an unnamed ditch that flowed into the Sutherland-Oemig Drain, which ultimately connected to Lake St. Clair. The other involved acres of marshy land, some of which was adjacent to a creek that flowed into a river, which flowed into yet another river, eventually reaching Saginaw Bay. Although the lower courts had concluded that both properties were wetlands under the Clean Water Act, the Supreme Court reversed these decisions. The Court held that the act covers "only those wetlands with a continuous surface connection to bodies that are waters of the United States in their own right." The Court further held that navigable waters under the act include only relatively permanent, standing or flowing bodies of water—not intermittent or temporary flows of water.[11]

In the following case, an appellate court had to deal with the meaning of *wetlands* and how it involved saturated land adjacent to so-called navigable-in-fact waters.

10. *Solid Waste Agency of Northern Cook County v. U.S. Army Corps of Engineers*, 531 U.S. 159, 121 S.Ct. 675, 148 L.Ed.2d 576 (2001).

11. *Rapanos v. United States*, 547 U.S. 715, 126 S.Ct. 2208, 165 L.Ed.2d 159 (2006).

CASE 45.2 United States v. Lucas

United States Court of Appeals, Fifth District, 2008. 516 F.3d 316.

Background and Facts Robert Lucas owned Big Hill Acres, Inc., and Consolidated Investments, Inc. Through these companies, he and others acquired a large parcel of land in Jackson County, Mississippi. He subdivided the property and sold mobile-home lots under long-term installment plans. Because the property was not connected to a municipal waste system, he was allowed to install individual septic systems on each lot under the condition that they be certified by the county. A Mississippi Department of Health engineer initially approved the septic systems. Later, he withdrew these approvals when it was discovered that the lots were on water-saturated soils. In conjunction with the U.S. Army Corps of Engineers, the Mississippi Department of Environmental Quality, and the U.S. Environmental Protection Agency (EPA), the Mississippi Department of Health became concerned that Lucas was selling house lots and installing septic systems on wetlands. These agencies issued cease-and-desist orders. Additionally, the EPA sent letters to residents warning them about where the wetlands were located. The federal government filed a forty-one-count indictment against Lucas, charging him and others with the filling of wetlands without a permit from the

CASE CONTINUES

CASE 45.2 CONTINUED U.S. Army Corps of Engineers. A jury convicted Lucas and others on all counts. The U.S. District Court for the Southern District of Mississippi sentenced Lucas and two other defendants to prison terms, as well as ordering them to pay restitution and fines. The defendants appealed.

● **Decision and Rationale** The court of appeals found that the district court did not abuse its discretion as to jury instructions concerning the Clean Water Act offenses so described. The reviewing court looked at the most significant question about whether the property at issue was subject to the Clean Water Act. The defendants argued that the jury instructions should have required the jury to "find that the wetlands were 'waters of the United States.'" Indeed, the jury instructions provided a definition of the term *wetlands* to mean "those areas that are inundated or saturated by surface or ground water at a frequency and duration sufficient to support, and that under normal circumstances do support, a prevalence of vegetation typically adapted for life in saturated soil conditions * * *." The jury instructions further pointed out that wetlands are to be considered "waters of the United States" if they are adjacent to a navigable body of open water. The issue in the jury instructions involved a "significant" connection between the wetlands in question and a navigable-in-fact waterway. The jury was to examine flow rates of surface waters from the wetlands into a navigable body of water. The government showed at trial that there was a significant connection between the wetlands on Big Hill Acres and navigable-in-fact waters. It showed that the waters from the surface of Big Hill Acres drain in three directions, all of which end up in navigable waters. The government successfully proved that on the edge of the property in question, there was a merger between the property wetlands and flowing open water.

● **What If the Facts Were Different?** *Assume that during most of the year, there was a solid strip of land around the property in question that remained completely dry. Would the outcome of this case have been the same? Why or why not?*

● **The Ethical Dimension** *Does it seem appropriate to put businesspersons in prison when they violate the Clean Water Act? Explain your answer.*

Violations of the Clean Water Act Under the Clean Water Act, violators are subject to a variety of civil and criminal penalties. Depending on the violation, civil penalties range from $10,000 to $25,000 per day, but not more than $25,000 per violation. Criminal penalties, which apply only if an act was intentional, range from a fine of $2,500 per day and imprisonment for up to one year to a fine of $1 million and fifteen years' imprisonment. Injunctive relief and damages can also be imposed. The polluting party can be required to clean up the pollution or pay for the cost of the clean-up.

Drinking Water

Another statute governing water pollution is the Safe Drinking Water Act.[12] Passed in 1974, this act requires the EPA to set maximum levels for pollutants in public water systems. Operators of public water supply systems must come as close as possible to meeting the EPA's standards by using the best available technology that is economically and technologically feasible. The EPA is particularly concerned about contamination from underground sources. Pesticides and wastes leaked from landfills or disposed of in underground injection wells are among the more than two hundred pollutants known to exist in groundwater used for drinking in at least thirty-four states. Many of these substances are associated with cancer and may cause damage to the central nervous system, liver, and kidneys.

The act was amended in 1996 to give the EPA greater flexibility in setting regulatory standards governing drinking water. These amendments also imposed requirements on suppliers of drinking water. Each supplier must send to every household it supplies with water an annual statement describing the source of its water, the level of any contaminants con-

12. 42 U.S.C. Sections 300f to 300j-25.

tained in the water, and any possible health concerns associated with the contaminants.

Ocean Dumping

The Marine Protection, Research, and Sanctuaries Act of 1972[13] (known popularly as the Ocean Dumping Act) regulates the transportation and dumping of material (pollutants) into ocean waters. It prohibits entirely the ocean dumping of radiological, chemical, and biological warfare agents and high-level radioactive waste.

The act also established a permit program for transporting and dumping other materials, and designated certain areas as marine sanctuaries. Each violation of any provision or permit requirement in the Ocean Dumping Act may result in a civil penalty of up to $50,000. A knowing violation is a criminal offense that may result in a $50,000 fine, imprisonment for not more than a year, or both. A court may also grant an injunction to prevent an imminent or continuing violation.

Oil Pollution

In response to the worst oil spill in North American history—more than 10 million gallons of oil that leaked into Alaska's Prince William Sound from the *Exxon Valdez* supertanker—Congress passed the Oil Pollution Act of 1990.[14] Under this act, any onshore or offshore oil facility, oil shipper, vessel owner, or vessel operator that discharges oil into navigable waters or onto an adjoining shore may be liable for clean-up costs, as well as damages. The act created an oil clean-up and economic compensation fund, and required oil tankers using U.S. ports to be double hulled by the year 2011 (to limit the severity of accidental spills).

Under the act, damage to natural resources, private property, and the local economy, including the increased cost of providing public services, is compensable. The penalties range from $2 million to $350 million, depending on the size of the vessel and on whether the oil spill came from a vessel or an offshore facility. The party held responsible for the clean-up costs can bring a civil suit for contribution from other potentially liable parties.

13. 16 U.S.C. Sections 1401–1445.
14. 33 U.S.C. Sections 2701–2761.

SECTION 5 Toxic Chemicals

Originally, most environmental clean-up efforts were directed toward reducing smog and making water safe for fishing and swimming. Today, control of toxic chemicals used in agriculture and in industry has become increasingly important.

Pesticides and Herbicides

The Federal Insecticide, Fungicide, and Rodenticide Act (FIFRA) of 1947[15] regulates pesticides and herbicides. Under FIFRA, pesticides and herbicides must be (1) registered before they can be sold, (2) certified and used only for approved applications, and (3) used in limited quantities when applied to food crops. The EPA can cancel or suspend registration of substances that are identified as harmful and may also inspect factories where the chemicals are made. Under 1996 amendments to FIFRA, there must be no more than a one-in-a-million risk to people of developing cancer from any kind of exposure to the substance, including eating food that contains pesticide residues.[16]

It is a violation of FIFRA to sell a pesticide or herbicide that is either unregistered or has had its registration canceled or suspended. It is also a violation to sell a pesticide or herbicide with a false or misleading label or to destroy or deface any labeling required under the act. For example, it is an offense to sell a substance that has a chemical strength different from the concentration declared on the label. Penalties for commercial dealers include imprisonment for up to one year and a fine up to $25,000 (producers can be fined up to $50,000). Farmers and other private users of pesticides or herbicides who violate the act are subject to a $1,000 fine and incarceration for up to thirty days.

Can a state regulate the sale and use of federally registered pesticides? Tort suits against pesticide manufacturers were common long before the enactment of FIFRA in 1947 and continued to be a feature of the legal landscape at the time FIFRA was amended. Until it heard the following case, however, the United States Supreme Court had never considered whether the statute preempts claims arising under state law.

15. 7 U.S.C. Sections 136–136y.
16. 21 U.S.C. Section 346a.

CASE 45.3 Bates v. Dow Agrosciences, LLC

Supreme Court of the United States, 2005. 544 U.S. 431, 125 S.Ct. 1788, 161 L.Ed.2d 687.
www.findlaw.com/casecode/supreme.html[a]

• **Background and Facts** The Environmental Protection Agency (EPA) conditionally registered Strongarm, a new weed-killing pesticide, on March 8, 2000.[b] Dow Agrosciences, LLC, immediately sold Strongarm to Texas peanut farmers, who normally plant their crops around May 1. The label stated, "Use of Strongarm is recommended in all areas where peanuts are grown." When the farmers applied Strongarm to their fields, the pesticide damaged their crops while failing to control the growth of weeds. After unsuccessfully attempting to negotiate with Dow, the farmers announced their intent to sue Strongarm's maker for violations of Texas state law. Dow filed a suit in a federal district court against the peanut farmers, asserting that the Federal Insecticide, Fungicide, and Rodenticide Act (FIFRA) preempted their claims. The court issued a summary judgment in Dow's favor. The farmers appealed to the U.S. Court of Appeals for the Fifth Circuit, which affirmed the lower court's judgment. The farmers appealed to the United States Supreme Court.

• **Decision and Rationale** The United States Supreme Court vacated the lower court's judgment and remanded the case for further proceedings as to whether the requirements under Texas state law conflicted with the FIFRA standard, an issue on which the Court had "not received sufficient briefing." The Court acknowledged that "nothing in the text of FIFRA would prevent a State from making the violation of a federal labeling or packaging requirement a state offense." In fact, under a specific provision of FIFRA, a state can regulate the sale and use of federally registered pesticides to the extent that it does not permit anything that FIFRA prohibits. Under the same provision, though, as the Court pointed out, a state cannot impose any requirements for labeling or packaging in addition to or different from those that FIFRA requires. "Imagine 50 different labeling regimes prescribing the color, font size, and wording of warnings." The Court stated, "That Congress added [this] provision is evidence of its intent to draw a distinction between state labeling requirements that are pre-empted and those that are not."

• **What If the Facts Were Different?** *Suppose that FIFRA required Strongarm's label to include the word* CAUTION, *and the Texas peanut farmers filed their claims under a state regulation that required the label to use the word* DANGER. *Would the result have been different?*

• **The Legal Environment Dimension** *According to the Court's interpretation, what is required for a state regulation or rule to be preempted under FIFRA? Why is this significant?*

a. In the "Browsing" section, click on "2005 Decisions." In the result, click on the name of the case to access the opinion.
b. Strongarm might more commonly be called an herbicide, but FIFRA classifies it as a pesticide.

Toxic Substances

The first comprehensive law covering toxic substances was the Toxic Substances Control Act of 1976.[17] The act was passed to regulate chemicals and chemical compounds that are known to be toxic—such as asbestos and polychlorinated biphenyls, popularly known as PCBs—and to institute investigation of any possible harmful effects from new chemical compounds. The regulations authorize the EPA to require that manufacturers, processors, and other entities planning to use chemicals first determine their effects on human health and the environment. The EPA can regulate substances that may pose an imminent hazard or an unreasonable risk of injury to health or the environment. The EPA may require special labeling, limit the use of a substance, set production quotas, or prohibit the use of a substance altogether.

17. 15 U.S.C. Sections 2601–2692.

SECTION 6

Hazardous Wastes

Some industrial, agricultural, and household wastes pose more serious threats than others. If not properly disposed of, these toxic chemicals may present a substantial danger to human health and the environment. If released into the environment, they may contaminate public drinking water resources.

Resource Conservation and Recovery Act

In 1976, Congress passed the Resource Conservation and Recovery Act (RCRA)[18] in reaction to a growing concern about the effects of hazardous waste materials on the environment. The RCRA required the EPA to establish regulations to determine which forms of solid waste should be considered hazardous and to establish regulations to monitor and control hazardous waste disposal. The act also requires all producers of hazardous waste materials to label and package properly any hazardous waste to be transported. The RCRA was amended in 1984 and 1986 to decrease the use of land containment in the disposal of hazardous waste and to require smaller generators of hazardous waste to comply with the act.

Under the RCRA, a company may be assessed a civil penalty of up to $25,000 for each violation.[19] The penalty is based on the seriousness of the violation, the probability of harm, and the extent to which the violation deviates from RCRA requirements. Criminal penalties include fines up to $50,000 for each day of violation, imprisonment for up to two years (in most instances), or both. Criminal fines and the time of imprisonment can be doubled for certain repeat offenders.

Superfund

In 1980, Congress passed the Comprehensive Environmental Response, Compensation, and Liability Act (CERCLA),[20] commonly known as Superfund. The basic purpose of Superfund is to regulate the clean-up of disposal sites in which hazardous waste is leaking into the environment. A special federal fund was created for that purpose.

Superfund provides that when a release or a threatened release of hazardous chemicals from a site occurs, the EPA can clean up the site and recover the cost of the clean-up from the following persons: (1) the person who generated the wastes disposed of at the site, (2) the person who transported the wastes to the site, (3) the person who owned or operated the site at the time of the disposal, or (4) the current owner or operator. A person falling within one of these categories is referred to as a **potentially responsible party (PRP).**

Liability under Superfund is usually joint and several—that is, a PRP who generated *only a fraction of the hazardous waste* disposed of at the site may nevertheless be liable for *all* of the clean-up costs. CERCLA authorizes a party who has incurred clean-up costs to bring a "contribution action" against any other person who is liable or potentially liable for a percentage of the costs.

Purchasers of property can be held liable under Superfund for the cost of cleaning up hazardous wastes dumped by previous owners. It is therefore important for businesspersons to research the property that they are interested in buying to find out whether it has been contaminated by hazardous wastes. It is up to the purchaser to raise environmental issues before signing any agreements—sellers, title insurance companies, and real estate brokers will rarely pursue such matters. Although current property owners who pay clean-up costs can sue previous owners for contribution, litigation is expensive and its outcome uncertain. Clearly, a more prudent course is to investigate the history of the land's use before buying the property. When feasible, a prospective purchaser should hire a private environmental site inspector to determine, at a minimum, whether the land has any obvious signs of former contamination. Generally, companies that perform good faith environmental inspections on property also receive lighter penalties and fines in the event that a violation later surfaces.

18. 42 U.S.C. Sections 6901–6986.
19. 42 U.S.C. Section 6928(a).
20. 42 U.S.C. Sections 9601–9675.

REVIEWING Environmental Law

In the late 1980s, residents of Lake Caliopa, Minnesota, began noticing an unusually high number of lung ailments among their population. A group of concerned local citizens pooled their resources and commissioned a study of the frequency of these health conditions per capita as compared to national averages. The study concluded that residents of Lake Caliopa experienced four to seven times the frequency of asthma, bronchitis, and emphysema as the population nationwide. During the study period, citizens began expressing concerns about the large volumes of smog emitted by the Cotton Design apparel manufacturing plant on the outskirts of town. The plant had opened its production facility two miles east of town beside the Tawakoni River in 1997 and employed seventy full-time workers by 2008.

Just downstream on the Tawakoni River, the city of Lake Caliopa operated a public water works facility, which supplied all city residents with water. In August 2008, the Minnesota Pollution Control Agency required Cotton Design to install new equipment to control air and water pollution. In May 2009, thirty citizens brought a class-action lawsuit in a Minnesota state court against Cotton Design for various respiratory ailments allegedly caused or compounded by smog from Cotton Design's factory. Using the information presented in the chapter, answer the following questions.

1. Under the common law, what would each plaintiff be required to identify in order to be given relief by the court?
2. Are air-quality regulations typically overseen by federal, state, or local governments?
3. What standard for limiting emissions into the air does Cotton Design's pollution-control equipment have to meet?
4. What information must the city send to every household that the city supplies with water?

TERMS AND CONCEPTS

environmental impact statement (EIS) 853
environmental law 852
nuisance 852
potentially responsible party (PRP) 863
toxic tort 853
wetlands 858

QUESTIONS AND CASE PROBLEMS

45–1. Some scientific knowledge indicates that there is no safe level of exposure to a cancer-causing agent. In theory, even one molecule of such a substance has the potential for causing cancer. Section 112 of the Clean Air Act requires that all cancer-causing substances be regulated to ensure a margin of safety. Some environmental groups have argued that all emissions of such substances must be eliminated to attain such a margin of safety. Total elimination would likely shut down many major U.S. industries.

Should the Environmental Protection Agency totally forbid all emissions of cancer-causing chemicals? Discuss.

45–2. QUESTION WITH SAMPLE ANSWER

Fruitade, Inc., is a processor of a soft drink called Freshen Up. Fruitade uses returnable bottles, which it cleans with a special acid to allow for further beverage processing. The acid is diluted with water and then allowed to pass into a navigable stream. Fruitade crushes its broken bottles and throws the crushed glass into the stream. Discuss fully any environmental laws that Fruitade has violated.

- **For a sample answer to Question 45–2, go to Appendix I at the end of this text.**

45–3. Moonbay is a home-building corporation that primarily develops retirement communities. Farmtex owns a number of feedlots in Sunny Valley. Moonbay purchased 20,000 acres of farmland in the same area and began building and selling homes on this acreage. In the meantime, Farmtex continued to expand its feedlot business, and eventually only 500 feet separated the two operations. Because of the odor and flies from the feedlots, Moonbay found it difficult to sell the homes in its development. Moonbay wants to enjoin (prevent) Farmtex from operating its feedlot in the vicinity of the retirement home development. Under what common law theory would Moonbay file this action? Has Farmtex violated any federal environmental laws? Discuss.

45–4. Clean Water Act. Attique Ahmad owned the Spin-N-Market, a convenience store and gas station. The gas pumps were fed by underground tanks, one of which had a leak at its top that allowed water to enter. Ahmad emptied the tank by pumping its contents into a storm drain and a sewer system. Through the storm drain, gasoline flowed into a creek, forcing the city to clean the water. Through the sewer system, gasoline flowed into a sewage treatment plant, forcing the city to evacuate the plant and two nearby schools. Ahmad was charged with discharging a pollutant without a permit, which is a criminal violation of the Clean Water Act. The act provides that a person who "knowingly violates" the act commits a felony. Ahmad claimed that he had believed he was discharging only water. Did Ahmad commit a felony? Why or why not? Discuss fully. [*United States v. Ahmad,* 101 F.3d 386 (5th Cir. 1996)]

45–5. Environmental Impact Statement. Greers Ferry Lake is in Arkansas, and its shoreline is under the management of the U.S. Army Corps of Engineers, which is part of the U.S. Department of Defense (DOD). The Corps's 2000 Shoreline Management Plan (SMP) rezoned numerous areas along the lake, authorized the Corps to issue permits for the construction of new boat docks in the rezoned areas, increased by 300 percent the area around habitable structures that could be cleared of vegetation, and instituted a Wildlife Enhancement Permit to allow limited modifications of the shoreline. In relation to the SMP's adoption, the Corps issued a Finding of No Significant Impact, which declared that no environmental impact statement (EIS) was necessary. The Corps issued thirty-two boat dock construction permits under the SMP before Save Greers Ferry Lake, Inc., filed a suit in a federal district court against the DOD, asking the court to, among other things, stop the Corps from acting under the SMP and order it to prepare an EIS. What are the requirements for an EIS? Is an EIS needed in this case? Explain. [*Save Greers Ferry Lake, Inc. v. Department of Defense,* 255 F.3d 498 (8th Cir. 2001)]

45–6. CERCLA. Beginning in 1926, Marietta Dyestuffs Co. operated an industrial facility in Marietta, Ohio, to make dyes and other chemicals. In 1944, Dyestuffs became part of American Home Products Corp. (AHP), which sold the Marietta facility to American Cyanamid Co. in 1946. In 1950, AHP sold the rest of the Dyestuffs assets and all of its stock to Goodrich Co., which immediately liquidated the acquired corporation. Goodrich continued to operate the dissolved corporation's business, however. Cyanamid continued to make chemicals at the Marietta facility, and in 1993, it created Cytec Industries, Inc., which expressly assumed all environmental liabilities associated with Cyanamid's ownership and operation of the facility. Cytec spent nearly $25 million on clean-up costs and filed a suit in a federal district court against Goodrich to recover, under CERCLA, a portion of the costs attributable to the clean-up of hazardous wastes that may have been discarded at the site between 1926 and 1946. Cytec filed a motion for summary judgment in its favor. Should the court grant Cytec's motion? Explain. [*Cytec Industries, Inc. v. B. F. Goodrich Co.,* 196 F.Supp.2d 644 (S.D. Ohio 2002)]

45–7. CASE PROBLEM WITH SAMPLE ANSWER

William Gurley was the president and majority stockholder in Gurley Refining Co. (GRC). GRC bought used oil, treated it, and sold it. The refining process created a by-product residue of oily waste. GRC disposed of this waste by dumping it at, among other locations, a landfill in West Memphis, Arkansas. In February 1992, after detecting hazardous chemicals at the site, the Environmental Protection Agency (EPA) asked Gurley about his assets, the generators of the material disposed of at the landfill, site operations, and the structure of GRC. Gurley refused to respond, except to suggest that the EPA ask GRC. In October, the EPA placed the site on its clean-up list and again asked Gurley for information. When he still refused to respond, the EPA filed a suit in a federal district court against him, asking the court to impose a civil penalty. In February 1999, Gurley finally answered the EPA's questions. Under CERCLA, a court may impose a civil penalty "not to exceed

$25,000 for each day of noncompliance against any person who unreasonably fails to comply" with an information request. Should the court assess a penalty in this case? Why or why not? [*United States v. Gurley,* 384 F.3d 316 (6th Cir. 2004)]

- **To view a sample answer for Problem 45–7, go to this book's Web site at www.cengage.com/blaw/jentz, select "Chapter 45," and click on "Case Problem with Sample Answer."**

45–8. Clean Water Act. The Anacostia River, which flows through Washington, D.C., is one of the ten most polluted rivers in the country. For bodies of water such as the Anacostia, the Clean Water Act requires states (which, under the act, include the District of Columbia) to set a "total maximum daily load" (TMDL) for pollutants. A TMDL is to be set "at a level necessary to implement the applicable water-quality standards with seasonal variations." The Anacostia contains biochemical pollutants that consume oxygen, putting the river's aquatic life at risk for suffocation. In addition, the river is murky, stunting the growth of plants that rely on sunlight and impairing recreational use. The Environmental Protection Agency (EPA) approved one TMDL limiting the *annual* discharge of oxygen-depleting pollutants and a second limiting the *seasonal* discharge of pollutants contributing to turbidity. Neither TMDL limited daily discharges. Friends of the Earth, Inc. (FoE), asked a federal district court to review the TMDLs. What is FoE's best argument in this dispute? What is the EPA's likely response? What should the court rule, and why? [*Friends of the Earth, Inc. v. Environmental Protection Agency,* 446 F.3d 140 (D.C.Cir. 2006)]

45–9. Environmental Impact Statement. The fourth largest crop in the United States is alfalfa, of which 5 percent is exported to Japan. RoundUp Ready alfalfa is genetically engineered to resist glyphosate, the active ingredient in the herbicide RoundUp. The U.S. Department of Agriculture (USDA) regulates genetically engineered agricultural products through the Animal and Plant Health Inspection Service (APHIS). APHIS concluded that RoundUp Ready alfalfa does not have any harmful health effects on humans or livestock and deregulated it. Geertson Seed Farms and others filed a suit in a federal district court against Mike Johanns (the secretary of the USDA) and others, asserting that APHIS's decision required the preparation of an environmental impact statement (EIS). The plaintiffs argued, among other things, that the introduction of RoundUp Ready alfalfa might significantly decrease the availability of, or even eliminate, all nongenetically engineered varieties. The plaintiffs were concerned that the RoundUp Ready alfalfa might contaminate standard alfalfa because alfalfa is pollinated by bees, which can travel as far as two miles from a pollen source. If contamination occurred, farmers would not be able to market "contaminated" varieties as "organic," which would affect the sales of "organic" livestock and exports to Japan, which does not allow the import of glyphosate-resistant alfalfa. Should an EIS be prepared in this case? Why or why not? [*Geertson Seed Farms v. Johanns,* __ F.Supp.2d __ (N.D.Cal. 2007)]

45–10. A QUESTION OF ETHICS

*In the Clean Air Act, Congress allowed California, which has particular problems with clean air, to adopt its own standard for emissions from cars and trucks, subject to the approval of the Environmental Protection Agency (EPA) according to certain criteria. Congress also allowed other states to adopt California's standard after the EPA's approval. In 2004, in an effort to address global warming, the California Air Resources Board amended the state's standard to attain "the maximum feasible and cost-effective reduction of GHG [greenhouse gas] emissions from motor vehicles." The regulation, which applies to new passenger vehicles and light-duty trucks for 2009 and later, imposes decreasing limits on emissions of carbon dioxide through 2016. While EPA approval was pending, Vermont and other states adopted similar standards. Green Mountain Chrysler Plymouth Dodge Jeep and other auto dealers, automakers, and associations of automakers filed a suit in a federal district court against George Crombie (secretary of the Vermont Agency of Natural Resources) and others, seeking relief from the state regulations. [*Green Mountain Chrysler Plymouth Dodge Jeep v. Crombie, *508 F.Supp.2d 295 (D.Vt. 2007)]*

(a) Under the Environmental Policy and Conservation Act (EPCA) of 1975, the National Highway Traffic Safety Administration sets fuel economy standards for new cars. The plaintiffs argued, among other things, that the EPCA, which prohibits states from adopting separate fuel economy standards, preempts Vermont's GHG regulation. Do the GHG rules equate to the fuel economy standards? Discuss.

(b) Do Vermont's rules tread on the efforts of the federal government to address global warming internationally? Who should regulate GHG emissions? The federal government? The state governments? Both? Neither? Why?

(c) The plaintiffs claimed that they would go bankrupt if they were forced to adhere to the state's GHG standards. Should they be granted relief on this basis? Does history support their claim? Explain.

LAW ON THE WEB

For updated links to resources available on the Web, as well as a variety of other materials, visit this text's Web site at

www.cengage.com/blaw/jentz

For information on the standards, guidelines, and regulations of the Environmental Protection Agency (EPA), go to the EPA's Web site at

www.epa.gov

To learn about the Resource Conservation and Recovery Act's "buy-recycled" requirements and other steps that the federal government has taken toward "greening the environment," go to

www.epa.gov/cpg

The Law Library of the Indiana University School of Law provides numerous links to online environmental law sources. Go to

www.law.indiana.edu/library/services/onl_env.shtml

Legal Research Exercises on the Web

Go to **www.cengage.com/blaw/jentz**, the Web site that accompanies this text. Select "Chapter 45" and click on "Internet Exercises." There you will find the following Internet research exercises that you can perform to learn more about the topics covered in this chapter.

Internet Exercise 45–1: Legal Perspective
Nuisance Law

Internet Exercise 45–2: Management Perspective
Complying with Environmental Regulation

Internet Exercise 45–3: Ethical Perspective
Environmental Justice

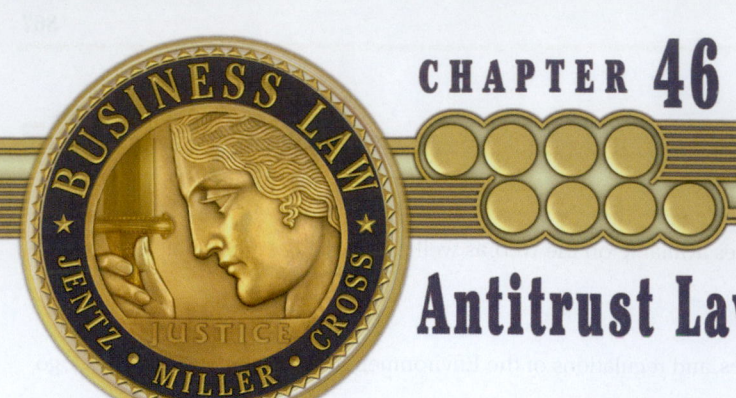

CHAPTER 46

Antitrust Law

Today's antitrust laws are the direct descendants of common law actions intended to limit **restraints of trade** (agreements between firms that have the effect of reducing competition in the marketplace). Concern over monopolistic practices arose following the Civil War with the growth of large corporate enterprises and their attempts to reduce or eliminate competition. They did this by legally tying themselves together in a *business trust,* a type of business entity described in Chapter 37 on page 710. The participants in the most famous trust—the Standard Oil trust in the late 1800s—transferred their stock to a trustee and received trust certificates in exchange. The trustee then made decisions fixing prices, controlling production, and determining the control of exclusive geographic markets for all of the oil companies that were in the Standard Oil trust. Some argued that the trust wielded so much economic power that corporations outside the trust could not compete effectively.

Many states attempted to control such monopolistic behavior by enacting statutes outlawing the use of trusts. That is why all of the laws that regulate economic competition today are referred to as **antitrust laws.** At the national level, Congress recognized the problem in 1887 and passed the Interstate Commerce Act,[1] followed by the Sherman Antitrust Act[2] in 1890. In 1914, Congress passed the Clayton Act[3] and the Federal Trade Commission Act[4] to further curb anticompetitive or unfair business practices. Since their passage, the 1914 acts have been amended by Congress to broaden and strengthen their coverage, and they continue to be an important element in the legal environment in which businesses operate.

1. 49 U.S.C. Sections 501–526.
2. 15 U.S.C. Sections 1–7.
3. 15 U.S.C. Sections 12–27.
4. 15 U.S.C. Sections 41–58.

SECTION 1 The Sherman Antitrust Act

The author of the Sherman Antitrust Act of 1890, Senator John Sherman, was the brother of the famed Civil War general and a recognized financial authority. He had been concerned for years about what he saw as diminishing competition within U.S. industry and the emergence of monopolies. He told Congress that the Sherman Act "does not announce a new principle of law, but applies old and well-recognized principles of the common law."[5]

The common law regarding trade regulation was not always consistent. Certainly, it was not very familiar to the members of Congress. The public concern over large business integrations and trusts was familiar, however, and in 1890 Congress passed "An Act to Protect Trade and Commerce against Unlawful Restraints and Monopolies"—more commonly referred to as the Sherman Antitrust Act, or simply the Sherman Act.

5. 21 *Congressional Record* 2456 (1890).

Major Provisions of the Sherman Act

Sections 1 and 2 contain the main provisions of the Sherman Act:

> 1: Every contract, combination in the form of trust or otherwise, or conspiracy, in restraint of trade or commerce among the several States, or with foreign nations, is hereby declared to be illegal [and is a felony punishable by fine and/or imprisonment].

2: Every person who shall monopolize, or attempt to monopolize, or combine or conspire with any other person or persons, to monopolize any part of the trade or commerce among the several States, or with foreign nations, shall be deemed guilty of a felony [and is similarly punishable].

Differences between Section 1 and Section 2

These two sections of the Sherman Act are quite different. Section 1 requires two or more persons, as a person cannot contract, combine, or conspire alone. Thus, the essence of the illegal activity is *the act of joining together.* Section 2 can apply either to one person or to two or more persons because it refers to "[e]very person." Thus, unilateral conduct can result in a violation of Section 2.

The cases brought to the courts under Section 1 of the Sherman Act differ from those brought under Section 2. Section 1 cases are often concerned with finding an agreement (written or oral) that leads to a restraint of trade. Section 2 cases deal with the structure of a monopoly that exists in the marketplace. The term **monopoly** generally is used to describe a market in which there is a single seller or a very limited number of sellers. Whereas Section 1 focuses on agreements that are restrictive—that is, agreements that have a wrongful purpose—Section 2 looks at the so-called misuse of **monopoly power** in the marketplace.

Monopoly power exists when a firm has an extreme amount of **market power**—the power to affect the market price of its product. Both Section 1 and Section 2 seek to curtail firms' market practices that result in undesired monopoly pricing and output behavior. For a case to be brought under Section 2, however, it must involve a market in which the "threshold" or "necessary" amount of monopoly power already exists.

Jurisdictional Requirements

The Sherman Act applies only to restraints that have a significant impact on interstate commerce. Courts have generally held that any activity that substantially affects interstate commerce falls within the scope of the Sherman Act. As will be discussed later in this chapter, the Sherman Act also extends to U.S. nationals abroad who are engaged in activities that have an effect on U.S. foreign commerce. State laws regulate local restraints on competition.

SECTION 2 Section 1 of the Sherman Act

The underlying assumption of Section 1 of the Sherman Act is that society's welfare is harmed if rival firms are permitted to join in an agreement that consolidates their market power or otherwise restrains competition. The types of trade restraints that Section 1 of the Sherman Act prohibits generally fall into two broad categories: *horizontal restraints* and *vertical restraints,* both of which will be discussed shortly. First, though, we look at the rules that the courts may apply when assessing the anticompetitive impact of alleged restraints of trade.

Per Se Violations versus the Rule of Reason

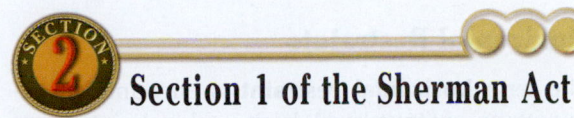

Some restraints are so blatantly and substantially anticompetitive that they are deemed ***per se* violations**—illegal *per se* (on their face, or inherently)—under Section 1. Other agreements, however, even though they result in enhanced market power, do not *unreasonably* restrain trade and are therefore lawful. Using what is called the **rule of reason,** the courts analyze anticompetitive agreements that allegedly violate Section 1 of the Sherman Act to determine whether they may, in fact, constitute reasonable restraints of trade.

The need for a rule-of-reason analysis of some agreements in restraint of trade is obvious—if the rule of reason had not been developed, virtually any business agreement could conceivably be held to violate the Sherman Act. Justice Louis Brandeis effectively phrased this sentiment in *Chicago Board of Trade v. United States,* a case decided in 1918:

> Every agreement concerning trade, every regulation of trade, restrains. To bind, to restrain, is of their very essence. The true test of legality is whether the restraint imposed is such as merely regulates and perhaps thereby promotes competition or whether it is such as may suppress or even destroy competition.[6]

When analyzing an alleged Section 1 violation under the rule of reason, a court will consider several factors. These factors include the purpose of the agreement, the parties' power to implement the agreement to achieve that purpose, and the effect or potential effect of the agreement on competition. A court might also consider whether the parties could have relied on less restrictive means to achieve their purpose.

6. 246 U.S. 231, 38 S.Ct. 242, 62 L.Ed. 683 (1918).

Horizontal Restraints

The term **horizontal restraint** is encountered frequently in antitrust law. A horizontal restraint is any agreement that in some way restrains competition between rival firms competing in the same market.

Price Fixing Any agreement among competitors to fix prices, or **price-fixing agreement,** constitutes a *per se* violation of Section 1 of the Sherman Act. Perhaps the definitive case regarding price-fixing agreements is still the 1940 case of *United States v. Socony-Vacuum Oil Co.*[7] In that case, a group of independent oil producers in Texas and Louisiana were caught between falling demand due to the Great Depression of the 1930s and increasing supply from newly discovered oil fields in the region. In response to these conditions, a group of the major refining companies agreed to buy "distress" gasoline (excess supplies) from the independents so as to dispose of it in an "orderly manner." Although there was no explicit agreement as to price, it was clear that the purpose of the agreement was to limit the supply of gasoline on the market and thereby raise prices.

There may have been good reasons for the agreement. Nonetheless, the United States Supreme Court recognized the potentially adverse effects that such an agreement could have on open and free competition. The Court held that the reasonableness of a price-fixing agreement is never a defense; any agreement that restricts output or artificially fixes price is a *per se* violation of Section 1.

A case involving two pharmaceutical companies provides a modern illustration. The manufacturer of the prescription drug Cardizem CD, which can help prevent heart attacks, was about to lose its patent on the drug. Another company developed a generic version in anticipation of the patent expiring. After the two firms became involved in litigation over the patent, the first company agreed to pay the second company $40 million per year not to market the generic version until their dispute was resolved. This agreement was held to be a *per se* violation of the Sherman Act because it restrained competition between rival firms and delayed the entry of generic versions of Cardizem into the market.[8]

Group Boycotts A **group boycott** is an agreement by two or more sellers to refuse to deal with (boycott) a particular person or firm. Traditionally, the courts have considered group boycotts to constitute *per se* violations of Section 1 of the Sherman Act because they involve concerted action. To prove a violation of Section 1, the plaintiff must demonstrate that the boycott or joint refusal to deal was undertaken with the intention of eliminating competition or preventing entry into a given market. Although most boycotts are illegal, a few, such as group boycotts against a supplier for political reasons, may be protected under the First Amendment right to freedom of expression.

Horizontal Market Division It is a *per se* violation of Section 1 of the Sherman Act for competitors to divide up territories or customers. For example, manufacturers A, B, and C compete against one another in the states of Kansas, Nebraska, and Iowa. They agree that A will sell products only in Kansas, B only in Nebraska, and C only in Iowa. This concerted action reduces costs and allows each of the three (assuming there is no other competition) to raise the price of the goods sold in its own state. The same violation would take place if A, B, and C agreed that A would sell only to institutional purchasers (such as school districts, universities, state agencies and departments, and cities) in the three states, B only to wholesalers, and C only to retailers.

Trade Associations Businesses in the same general industry or profession frequently organize trade associations to pursue common interests. A trade association may engage in various joint activities such as exchanging information, representing the members' business interests before governmental bodies, conducting advertising campaigns, and setting regulatory standards to govern the industry or profession. Generally, the rule of reason is applied to many of these horizontal actions. If a court finds that a trade association practice or agreement that restrains trade is nonetheless sufficiently beneficial both to the association and to the public, it may deem the restraint reasonable.

Joint Ventures Joint ventures undertaken by competitors are also subject to antitrust laws. As discussed in Chapter 37, a *joint venture* is an undertaking by two or more individuals or firms for a specific purpose. If a joint venture does not involve price fixing or market divisions, the agreement will be analyzed under the rule of reason. Whether the venture will then be upheld under Section 1 depends on an overall assessment of the purposes of the venture, a strict analysis of the potential benefits relative to the likely harms, and, in

7. 310 U.S. 150, 60 S.Ct. 811, 84 L.Ed. 1129 (1940).

8. *In re Cardizem CD Antitrust Litigation,* 332 F.3d 896 (6th Cir. 2003).

some cases, an assessment of whether there are less restrictive alternatives for achieving the same goals.[9]

Vertical Restraints

A **vertical restraint** of trade results from an agreement between firms at different levels in the manufacturing and distribution process. In contrast to horizontal relationships, which occur at the same level of operation, vertical relationships encompass the entire chain of production: the purchase of inputs, basic manufacturing, distribution to wholesalers, and eventual sale of a product at the retail level. For some products, these distinct phases are carried on by different firms. In other instances, a single firm carries out two or more of the separate functional phases. Such enterprises are considered to be **vertically integrated firms.**

Even though firms operating at different functional levels are not in direct competition with one another, they are in competition with other firms. Thus, agreements between firms standing in a vertical relationship may affect competition. Some vertical restraints are *per se* violations of Section 1; others are judged under the rule of reason.

Territorial or Customer Restrictions In arranging for the distribution of its products, a manufacturing firm often wishes to insulate dealers from direct competition with other dealers selling its products. To this end, the manufacturer may institute territorial restrictions or attempt to prohibit wholesalers or retailers from reselling the products to certain classes of buyers, such as competing retailers.

A firm may have legitimate reasons for imposing such territorial or customer restrictions. For example, a computer manufacturer may wish to prevent a dealer from reducing costs and undercutting rivals by offering computers without promotion or customer service, while relying on a nearby dealer to provide these services. In this situation, the cost-cutting dealer reaps the benefits (sales of the product) paid for by other dealers who undertake promotion and arrange for customer service. By not providing customer service, the cost-cutting dealer may also harm the manufacturer's reputation.

Territorial and customer restrictions are judged under a rule of reason. In *United States v. Arnold, Schwinn & Co.*,[10] a case decided in 1967, a bicycle manufacturer, Schwinn, was assigning specific territories to its wholesale distributors and authorizing certain retail dealers only if they agreed to advertise Schwinn bikes and give them the same prominence as other brands. The United States Supreme Court held that these vertical territorial and customer restrictions were *per se* violations of Section 1 of the Sherman Act. Ten years later, however, the Court overturned the *Schwinn* decision.[11]

Resale Price Maintenance Agreements An agreement between a manufacturer and a distributor or retailer in which the manufacturer specifies what the retail prices of its products must be is known as a **resale price maintenance agreement.** Such agreements were once considered to be *per se* violations of Section 1 of the Sherman Act, but in 1997 the United States Supreme Court ruled that *maximum* resale price maintenance agreements should be judged under the rule of reason.[12] In these agreements, the manufacturer sets a maximum price that retailers and distributors can charge for its products.

The question before the Supreme Court in the following case was whether *minimum* resale price maintenance agreements should be treated as *per se* unlawful.

9. For a classic example of how courts judge joint ventures under the rule of reason, see *United States v. Morgan*, 118 F.Supp. 621 (S.D.N.Y. 1953).

10. 388 U.S. 365, 87 S.Ct. 1856, 18 L.Ed.2d 1249 (1967).

11. *Continental T.V., Inc. v. GTE Sylvania, Inc.*, 433 U.S. 36, 97 S.Ct. 2549, 53 L.Ed.2d 568 (1977).

12. *State Oil Co. v. Khan*, 522 U.S. 3, 118 S.Ct. 275, 139 L.Ed.2d 199 (1997).

CASE 46.1 Leegin Creative Leather Products, Inc. v. PSKS, Inc.

Supreme Court of the United States, 2007. __ U.S. __, 127 S.Ct. 2705, 168 L.Ed.2d 623.
supct.law.cornell.edu/supct/index.html[a]

Background and Facts Leegin Creative Leather Products, Inc., designs, manufactures, and distributes leather goods and accessories. One of its brand names is Brighton. Kay's Kloset, owned by PSKS, Inc., started purchasing Brighton goods from Leegin in 1995. Leegin required resellers of Brighton goods to charge customers a minimum price. This minimum price formed part of a resale

a. In the "Archive of Decisions" section, in the "By party" subsection, click on "1990-present." In the result, in the "2006-2007" row, click on "1st party." On the next page, scroll to the name of the case and click on it. On the next page, click on the appropriate link to access the opinion.

CASE CONTINUES

CASE 46.1 CONTINUED price maintenance program that Leegin had instituted. When Leegin discovered that Kay's Kloset had been discounting Brighton products by 20 percent, Leegin stopped selling Brighton products to the store. PSKS sued Leegin in federal court. It claimed that Leegin had violated antitrust law when it imposed minimum prices. The U.S. District Court for the Eastern District of Texas entered a judgment against Leegin in the amount of almost $4 million. The U.S. Court of Appeals for the Fifth Circuit affirmed.

● **Decision and Rationale** The United States Supreme Court reversed the judgment of the court of appeals and remanded the case for proceedings consistent with its opinion. The Court pointed out that a *per se* rule should be confined to restraints of trade that "would always or almost always tend to restrict competition and decrease output. To justify a *per se* prohibition, a restraint must have manifestly anticompetitive effects, and lack * * * any redeeming virtue." In the case of minimum resale prices, the Court did not believe that a *per se* rule should apply. "Minimum resale price maintenance can stimulate interbrand competition * * * by reducing intrabrand competition * * *. Resale price maintenance * * * has the potential to give consumers more options so that they can choose among low-price, low-service brands; high-price, high-service brands; and brands that fall in between." Consequently, the Court felt that resale price maintenance did not necessarily restrict competition and decrease output. "As the [*per se*] rule would proscribe a significant amount of procompetitive conduct, these agreements appear ill suited for *per se* condemnation."

● **The Legal Environment Dimension** *Should the Court have applied the doctrine of* stare decisis *to hold that minimum resale price maintenance agreements are still subject to the* per se *rule? Why or why not?*

● **The Global Dimension** *If a product or line of products is in competition with products provided by major foreign companies, is there more or less chance that resale price maintenance would lessen competition and restrict output? Explain.*

SECTION 3

Section 2 of the Sherman Act

Section 1 of the Sherman Act proscribes certain concerted, or joint, activities that restrain trade. In contrast, Section 2 condemns "every person who shall monopolize, or attempt to monopolize." Thus, two distinct types of behavior are subject to sanction under Section 2: *monopolization* and *attempts to monopolize*. A tactic that may be involved in either offense is predatory pricing. **Predatory pricing** occurs when one firm (the predator) attempts to drive its competitors from the market by selling its product at prices substantially *below* the normal costs of production. Once the competitors are eliminated, the predator will raise its prices far above their competitive levels to recapture its losses and earn high profits.

Monopolization

The United States Supreme Court has defined **monopolization** as involving the following two elements: "(1) the possession of monopoly power in the relevant market and (2) the willful acquisition or maintenance of the power as distinguished from growth or development as a consequence of a superior product, business acumen, or historic accident."[13] A violation of Section 2 requires that both of these elements—monopoly power and an *intent* to monopolize—be established.

Monopoly Power The Sherman Act does not define *monopoly*. In economic parlance, monopoly refers to control of a specific market by a single entity. It is well established in antitrust law, however, that a firm may be a monopolist even though it is not the sole seller in a market. Additionally, size alone does not determine whether a firm is a monopoly. For example, a "mom and pop" grocery located in an isolated desert town is a monopolist if it is the only grocery serving that particular market. Size in relation to the market is what matters because monopoly involves the power to affect prices and output.

Monopoly power may be proved by direct evidence that the firm used its power to control prices and restrict output.[14] Usually, however, there is not

13. *United States v. Grinnell Corp.*, 384 U.S. 563, 86 S.Ct. 1698, 16 L.Ed.2d 778 (1966).

14. See, for example, *Broadcom Corp. v. Qualcomm, Inc.*, 501 F.3d 297 (3d Cir. 2007).

enough evidence to show that the firm was intentionally controlling prices, so the plaintiff has to offer indirect, or circumstantial, evidence of monopoly power. To prove monopoly power indirectly, the plaintiff must show that the firm has a dominant share of the relevant market and that there are significant barriers for new competitors entering that market.

Relevant Market Before a court can determine whether a firm has a dominant market share, it must define the relevant market. The relevant market consists of two elements: (1) a relevant product market and (2) a relevant geographic market.

Relevant Product Market. The relevant product market includes all products that, although produced by different firms, have identical attributes, such as sugar. It also includes products that are reasonably interchangeable for the purpose for which they are produced. Products will be considered reasonably interchangeable if consumers treat them as acceptable substitutes.[15]

What should the relevant product market include? This is often the key issue in monopolization cases because the way the market is defined may determine whether a firm has monopoly power. For example, in 2007, the Federal Trade Commission (FTC) filed a Section 2 claim against Whole Foods Market, Inc., which owns a nationwide chain of natural and organic food stores. The FTC was seeking to prevent Whole Foods from merging with Wild Oats Markets, Inc., its main competitor in nationwide high-end organic food supermarkets.

The FTC argued that the relevant product market consisted of only "premium natural and organic supermarkets (PNOS)" rather than all supermarkets. By defining the product market narrowly, the degree of a firm's market power is enhanced. A federal court disagreed with the FTC, however, and held that the relevant product market was all supermarkets, not just PNOS. Because the proposed merger would not create a monopoly or substantially lessen competition in all supermarkets, the FTC could not block the merger.[16]

Relevant Geographic Market. The second component of the relevant market is the geographic area in which the firm and its competitors sell the product or services. For products that are sold nationwide, the geographic boundaries of the market can encompass the entire United States. If a producer and its competitors sell in only a limited area (one in which customers have no access to other sources of the product), then the geographic market is limited to that area. A national firm may thus compete in several distinct areas and have monopoly power in one geographic area but not in another.

Consider one such example: Clear Channel Communications, Inc., owns numerous radio stations and promotes and books concert tours. Malinda Heerwagen, who had attended various rock concerts in Chicago, Illinois, filed a lawsuit against Clear Channel alleging violations of Section 2. Heerwagen claimed that the company had used anticompetitive practices to acquire and maintain monopoly power in a national ticket market for live rock concerts, causing audiences to pay inflated prices for the tickets. Heerwagen argued that because Clear Channel sold tickets nationwide, the geographic market was the entire United States. The court, however, ruled that even though Clear Channel sold tickets nationally, the relevant market for concert tickets was local. The court reasoned that "[a] purchaser of a concert ticket is hardly likely to look outside of her own area, even if the price for tickets has increased inside her region and decreased for the same tour in other places."[17]

The Intent Requirement Monopoly power, in and of itself, does not constitute the offense of monopolization under Section 2 of the Sherman Act. The offense also requires an *intent* to monopolize. A dominant market share may be the result of good business judgment or the development of a superior product. It may simply be the result of historical accident. In these situations, the acquisition of monopoly power is not an antitrust violation.

If, however, a firm possesses market power as a result of carrying out some purposeful act to acquire or maintain that power through anticompetitive means, then it is in violation of Section 2. In most monopolization cases, intent may be inferred from evidence that the firm had monopoly power and engaged in anticompetitive behavior.

When Navigator, the first popular graphical Internet browser, used Java technology that was able to run on a variety of platforms, Microsoft Corporation perceived a threat to its dominance in the operating-system

15. See, for example, *Linzer Products Corp. v. Sekar,* 499 F.Supp.2d 540 (S.D.N.Y. 2007); and *HDC Medical, Inc. v. Minntech Corp.,* 474 F.3d 543 (8th Cir. 2007).

16. *FTC v. Whole Foods Market, Inc.,* 502 F.Supp.2d 1 (D.D.C. 2007).

17. *Heerwagen v. Clear Channel Communications,* 435 F.3d 219 (2d Cir. 2006).

market. Microsoft developed a competing browser, Internet Explorer, and then began to require computer makers that wanted to install Windows to also install Explorer and exclude Navigator. Microsoft also included codes in Windows that would cripple the operating system if Explorer was deleted and paid Internet service providers to distribute Explorer and exclude Navigator. Because of this pattern of exclusionary conduct, a court found that Microsoft was guilty of monopolization. The court reasoned that Microsoft's pattern of conduct could be rational only if the firm knew that it possessed monopoly power.[18]

Because exclusionary conduct can have legitimate efficiency-enhancing effects, it can be difficult to determine when conduct will be viewed as anticompetitive and a violation of Section 2 of the Sherman Act. Thus, a business that possesses monopoly power must be careful that its actions cannot be inferred to be evidence of intent to monopolize. Even if a business does not have a dominant market share, owners and managers would be wise to take precautions. They should articulate clear, legitimate reasons for the particular conduct or contract and not provide any direct evidence (damaging e-mails, for example) of an intent to exclude competitors. A court will be less likely to infer the intent to monopolize if the specific conduct was aimed at increasing output and lowering per-unit costs, improving product quality, or protecting a patented technology or innovation. Exclusionary conduct and agreements that have no redeeming qualities are much more likely to be deemed illegal.

Refusals to Deal As discussed previously, joint refusals to deal (group boycotts) are subject to close scrutiny under Section 1 of the Sherman Act. A single manufacturer acting unilaterally, though, normally is free to deal, or not to deal, with whomever it wishes. In vertical arrangements, a manufacturer can refuse to deal with retailers or dealers that cut prices to levels substantially below the manufacturer's suggested retail prices.[19]

Nevertheless, in some instances, a unilateral refusal to deal will violate antitrust laws. These instances involve offenses proscribed under Section 2 of the Sherman Act and occur only if (1) the firm refusing to deal has—or is likely to acquire—monopoly power and (2) the refusal is likely to have an anticompetitive effect on a particular market. For example, the owner of three of the four major downhill ski areas in Aspen, Colorado, refused to continue participating in a jointly offered six-day "all Aspen" lift ticket. The Supreme Court ruled that the owner's refusal to cooperate with its smaller competitor was a violation of Section 2 of the Sherman Act. Because the company owned three-fourths of the local ski areas, it had monopoly power, and thus its unilateral refusal had an anticompetitive effect on the market.[20]

Attempts to Monopolize

Section 2 also prohibits **attempted monopolization** of a market. Any action challenged as an attempt to monopolize must have been specifically intended to exclude competitors and garner monopoly power. The attempt must also have had a "dangerous" probability of success—only *serious* threats of monopolization are condemned as violations. The probability cannot be dangerous unless the alleged offender possesses some degree of market power.[21]

As mentioned earlier, predatory pricing is a form of anticompetitive conduct that is commonly used by firms that are attempting to monopolize. In 2007, the United States Supreme Court ruled that *predatory bidding,* which is similar but involves the exercise of market power on the market's buy, or input, side, should be analyzed under the same standards as predatory pricing.[22] In predatory bidding, a firm deliberately bids up the prices of inputs to prevent its competitors from obtaining sufficient supplies to manufacture their products. To succeed in a predatory pricing (or predatory bidding) claim, a plaintiff must prove that the

18. *United States v. Microsoft Corp.,* 253 F.3d 34 (D.C.Cir. 2001). Microsoft has faced numerous antitrust claims and has settled a number of lawsuits in which it was accused of antitrust violations and anticompetitive tactics.

19. For a classic case in this area, see *United States v. Colgate & Co.,* 250 U.S. 300, 39 S.Ct. 465, 63 L.Ed. 992 (1919).

20. *Aspen Skiing Co. v. Aspen Highlands Skiing Corp.,* 472 U.S. 585, 105 S.Ct. 2847, 86 L.Ed.2d 467 (1985). See also *America Channel, LLC v. Time Warner Cable, Inc.,* 2007 WL 142173 (D.Minn. 2007); and *Z-Tel Communications, Inc. v. SBC Communications, Inc.,* 331 F.Supp.2d 513 (E.D.Tex. 2004).

21. See, for example, *Nobody in Particular Presents, Inc. v. Clear Channel Communications, Inc.,* 311 F.Supp.2d 1048 (D.Colo. 2004); and *City of Moundridge, KS v. Exxon Mobil Corp.,* 471 F.Supp.2d 20 (D.D.C. 2007).

22. *Weyerhaeuser Co. v. Ross-Simmons Hardwood Lumber Co., Inc.,* ___ U.S. ___, 127 S.Ct. 1069, 166 L.Ed.2d 911 (2007). See also *Brooke Group, Ltd. v. Brown & Williamson Tobacco Corp.,* 509 U.S. 209, 113 S.Ct. 2578, 125 L.Ed.2d 168 (1993).

alleged predator has a "dangerous probability of recouping its investment in below-cost pricing" because low prices alone often stimulate competition. (Note that predatory pricing may also lead to claims of price discrimination, to be discussed shortly.)

SECTION 4 The Clayton Act

In 1914, Congress enacted the Clayton Act. The Clayton Act was aimed at specific anticompetitive or monopolistic practices that the Sherman Act did not cover. The substantive provisions of the act deal with four distinct forms of business behavior, which are declared illegal but not criminal. For each of the four provisions, the act states that the behavior is illegal only if it tends to substantially lessen competition or to create monopoly power. The major offenses under the Clayton Act are set out in Sections 2, 3, 7, and 8 of the act.

Price Discrimination

Section 2 of the Clayton Act prohibits **price discrimination,** which occurs when a seller charges different prices to competing buyers for identical goods or services. Congress strengthened this section by amending it with the passage of the Robinson-Patman Act in 1936. As amended, Section 2 prohibits direct and indirect price discrimination that cannot be justified by differences in production costs, transportation costs, or cost differences due to other reasons. In short, a seller is prohibited from reducing a price to one buyer below the price charged to that buyer's competitor.

Required Elements To violate Section 2, the seller must be engaged in interstate commerce, the goods must be of like grade and quality, and goods must have been sold to two or more purchasers. In addition, the effect of the price discrimination must be to substantially lessen competition, to tend to create a monopoly, or to otherwise injure competition. Without proof of an actual injury resulting from the price discrimination, the plaintiff cannot recover damages.

Note that price discrimination claims can arise from discounts, offsets, rebates, or allowances given to one buyer over another. Moreover, giving favorable credit terms, delivery, or freight charges to only some buyers can also lead to allegations of price discrimination. For example, offering goods to different customers at the same price but including free delivery for certain buyers may violate Section 2 in some circumstances.

Defenses There are several statutory defenses to liability for price discrimination.

1. *Cost justification.* If the seller can justify the price reduction by demonstrating that a particular buyer's purchases saved the seller costs in producing and selling the goods, the seller will not be liable for price discrimination.
2. *Meeting the price of competition.* If the seller charged the lower price in a good faith attempt to meet an equally low price of a competitor, the seller will not be liable for price discrimination. For example, Water Craft was a retail dealership of Mercury Marine outboard motors in Baton Rouge, Louisiana. Mercury Marine also sold its motors to other dealers in the Baton Rouge area. When Water Craft discovered that Mercury was selling its outboard motors at a substantial discount to Water Craft's largest competitor, it filed a price discrimination lawsuit against Mercury. In this situation, the court held that Mercury Marine had shown that the discounts given to Water Craft's competitor were made in good faith to meet the low price charged by another manufacturer of marine motors.[23]
3. *Changing market conditions.* A seller may lower its price on an item in response to changing conditions affecting the market for or the marketability of the goods concerned. Sellers are allowed to readjust their prices to meet the realities of the market without liability for price discrimination. Thus, if an advance in technology makes a particular product less marketable than it was previously, a seller can lower the product's price.

Exclusionary Practices

Under Section 3 of the Clayton Act, sellers or lessors cannot sell or lease goods "on the condition, agreement or understanding that the . . . purchaser or lessee thereof shall not use or deal in the goods . . . of a competitor or competitors of the seller." In effect, this section prohibits two types of vertical agreements involving exclusionary practices—exclusive-dealing contracts and tying arrangements.

Exclusive-Dealing Contracts A contract under which a seller forbids a buyer to purchase

23. *Water Craft Management, LLC v. Mercury Marine,* 457 F.3d 484 (5th Cir. 2006).

products from the seller's competitors is called an **exclusive-dealing contract.** A seller is prohibited from making an exclusive-dealing contract under Section 3 if the effect of the contract is "to substantially lessen competition or tend to create a monopoly."

The United States Supreme Court's 1949 decision in the case of *Standard Oil Co. of California v. United States* provides a classic illustration of exclusive dealing.[24] In this case, the then-largest gasoline seller in the nation made exclusive-dealing contracts with independent stations in seven western states. The contracts involved 16 percent of all retail outlets, whose sales were approximately 7 percent of all retail sales in that market. The Court noted that the market was substantially concentrated because the seven largest gasoline suppliers all used exclusive-dealing contracts with their independent retailers and together controlled 65 percent of the market. Looking at market conditions after the arrangements were instituted, the Court found that market shares were extremely stable, and entry into the market was apparently restricted. Thus, the Court held that the Clayton Act had been violated because competition was "foreclosed in a substantial share" of the relevant market.

Note that since the Supreme Court's 1949 decision in the *Standard Oil* case, a number of subsequent decisions have called the holding in this case into doubt.[25] Today, it is clear that to violate antitrust law, the effect of an exclusive-dealing agreement (or a tying arrangement, discussed next) must qualitatively and substantially harm competition. To prevail, a plaintiff must present affirmative evidence that the performance of the agreement will foreclose competition and harm consumers.

Tying Arrangements In a **tying arrangement,** or *tie-in sales agreement,* a seller conditions the sale of a product (the tying product) on the buyer's agreement to purchase another product (the tied product) produced or distributed by the same seller. The legality of a tie-in agreement depends on many factors, particularly the purpose of the agreement and the agreement's likely effect on competition in the relevant markets (the market for the tying product and the market for the tied product).

In 1936, for example, the United States Supreme Court held that International Business Machines and Remington Rand had violated Section 3 of the Clayton Act by requiring the purchase of their own machine cards (the tied product) as a condition to the leasing of their tabulation machines (the tying product). Because only these two firms sold completely automated tabulation machines, the Court concluded that each possessed market power sufficient to "substantially lessen competition" through the tying arrangements.[26]

Section 3 of the Clayton Act has been held to apply only to commodities, not to services. Tying arrangements, however, can also be considered agreements that restrain trade in violation of Section 1 of the Sherman Act. Thus, cases involving tying arrangements of services have been brought under Section 1 of the Sherman Act. Although earlier cases condemned tying arrangements as illegal *per se,* courts now evaluate tying agreements under the rule of reason.

When an arrangement ties patented and unpatented products, can the relevant market and the patent holder's power in that market be presumed without proof? That was the question in the following case.

24. 337 U.S. 293, 69 S.Ct. 1051, 93 L.Ed. 1371 (1949).

25. See, for example, *Illinois Tool Works, Inc. v. Independent Ink, Inc.,* which is presented as Case 46.2; *Stop & Shop Supermarket Co. v. Blue Cross & Blue Shield of R.I.,* 373 F.3d 57 (1st Cir. 2004); *Texas Instruments, Inc. v. Hyundai Electronics Industries Co.,* 49 F.Supp.2d 893 (E.D.Tex. 1999); and *Yeager's Fuel, Inc. v. Pennsylvania Power & Light Co.,* 953 F.Supp. 617 (E.D.Pa. 1997).

26. *International Business Machines Corp. v. United States,* 298 U.S. 131, 56 S.Ct. 701, 80 L.Ed. 1085 (1936).

CASE 46.2 Illinois Tool Works, Inc. v. Independent Ink, Inc.

Supreme Court of the United States, 2006. 547 U.S. 28, 126 S.Ct. 1281, 164 L.Ed.2d 26.
www.findlaw.com/casecode/supreme.html[a]

Background and Facts Illinois Tool Works, Inc., in Glenview, Illinois, owns Trident, Inc. The firms make printing systems that include three components: a patented inkjet printhead; a patented ink container that attaches to the printhead; and specially designed, but unpatented, ink. They sell the systems to original equipment manufacturers (OEMs) that incorporate the systems into printers that are sold to other companies to use in printing bar codes on packaging materials. As part of each deal,

a. In the "Browsing" section, click on "2006 Decisions." When that page opens, scroll to the name of the case and click on it to read the opinion.

CASE 46.2 CONTINUED the OEMs agree to buy ink exclusively from Illinois and Trident and not to refill the patented containers with ink of any kind. Independent Ink, Inc., in Gardena, California, sells ink with the same chemical composition as Illinois and Trident's product at lower prices. Independent filed a suit in a federal district court against Illinois and Trident, alleging, among other things, that they were engaged in illegal tying in violation of the Sherman Act. Independent filed a motion for summary judgment, arguing that because the defendants owned patents in their products, market power could be presumed. The court issued a summary judgment in the defendants' favor, holding that market power could not be presumed. The U.S. Court of Appeals for the Federal Circuit reversed this judgment. Illinois and Trident appealed to the United States Supreme Court.

• **Decision and Rationale** The United States Supreme Court vacated the judgment of the appellate court and remanded the case to the trial court to give Independent "a fair opportunity" to offer evidence of the relevant market and the defendants' power within it. The Court ruled that a plaintiff that alleges an illegal tying arrangement involving a patented product must prove that the defendant has market power in the tying product. The Court pointed out that the presumption that a company automatically possesses market power in a patented product arose outside the area of antitrust law as part of the patent misuse doctrine. The assumption was that "by tying the purchase of unpatented goods to the sale of [a] patented good, the patentee was restraining competition or securing a limited monopoly of an unpatented material." The patent misuse doctrine "presumed the requisite economic power over the tying product such that the patentee could extend its economic control to unpatented products." Over the years, however, Congress "chipp[ed] away at the assumption in the patent misuse context" and finally amended the patent laws to eliminate the presumption in that context. "Given the fact that the patent misuse doctrine provided the basis for the market power presumption, it would be anomalous to preserve the presumption in antitrust after Congress has eliminated its foundation." Instead, tying arrangements involving patented products should be evaluated according to such factors as those that apply in a rule-of-reason analysis.

• **The Ethical Dimension** *What are the ethical values underpinning antitrust laws, and why are those laws applied to tying arrangements in particular?*

• **The Legal Environment Dimension** *In light of the factors that a court considers under the rule of reason, how might the court rule on remand in the Illinois case? Explain.*

Mergers

Under Section 7 of the Clayton Act, a person or business organization cannot hold stock or assets in more than one business when "the effect . . . may be to substantially lessen competition." Section 7 is the statutory authority for preventing mergers that could result in monopoly power or a substantial lessening of competition in the marketplace. Section 7 applies to both horizontal and vertical mergers, as discussed in the following subsections.

A crucial consideration in most merger cases is **market concentration.** Determining market concentration involves allocating percentage market shares among the various companies in the relevant market. When a small number of companies share a large part of the market, the market is concentrated. For example, if the four largest grocery stores in Chicago accounted for 80 percent of all retail food sales, the market clearly would be concentrated in those four firms. Competition is not necessarily diminished solely as a result of market concentration, however, and other factors must be considered to determine if a merger violates Section 7. One factor of particular importance is whether the merger will make it more difficult for *potential* competitors to enter the relevant market.

Horizontal Mergers Mergers between firms that compete with each other in the same market are called **horizontal mergers.** If a horizontal merger creates an entity with a resulting significant market share, the merger may be presumed illegal. This is because of the United States Supreme Court's interpretation that Congress, in amending Section 7 of the Clayton Act in 1950, intended to prevent mergers that increase market concentration.[27] Three other factors

27. *Brown Shoe v. United States,* 370 U.S. 294, 82 S.Ct. 1502, 8 L.Ed.2d 510 (1962).

that the courts also consider in analyzing the legality of a horizontal merger are the overall concentration of the relevant market, the relevant market's history of tending toward concentration, and whether the merger is apparently designed to establish market power or restrict competition.

Market Share and Market Concentration. The Federal Trade Commission and the U.S. Department of Justice (DOJ) have established guidelines indicating which mergers will be challenged. Under the guidelines, the first factor to be considered is the degree of concentration in the relevant market. In determining market concentration, the FTC and the DOJ employ what is known as the **Herfindahl-Hirschman Index (HHI).** The HHI is computed by summing the squares of the percentage market shares of the firms in the relevant market. For example, if there are four firms with shares of 30 percent, 30 percent, 20 percent, and 20 percent, respectively, then the HHI equals 2,600 (900 + 900 + 400 + 400 = 2,600). If the premerger HHI is less than 1,000, then the market is unconcentrated, and the merger is unlikely to be challenged. If the premerger HHI is between 1,000 and 1,800, the industry is moderately concentrated, and the merger will be challenged only if it increases the HHI by 100 points or more.[28] If the HHI is greater than 1,800, the market is highly concentrated. In a highly concentrated market, a merger that produces an increase in the HHI of between 50 and 100 points raises significant competitive concerns. Mergers that produce an increase in the HHI of more than 100 points in a highly concentrated market are deemed likely to enhance market power. HHI figures were a factor in the following case.

28. Compute the change in the index by doubling the product of the merging firms' premerger market shares. For example, a merger between a firm with a 5 percent share and one with a 6 percent share will increase the HHI by $2 \times (5 \times 6) = 60$.

CASE 46.3 Chicago Bridge & Iron Co. v. Federal Trade Commission

United States Court of Appeals, Fifth Circuit, 2008. __ F.3d __.
www.ca5.uscourts.gov[a]

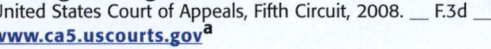

• **Background and Facts** Chicago Bridge & Iron Company, and its U.S. subsidiary of the same name, is a company that designs, engineers, and constructs industrial-storage tanks for liquefied natural gas (LNG), liquefied petroleum gas (LPG), and liquid atmospheric gases, such as nitrogen, oxygen, and argon (LIN/LOX), as well as thermal vacuum chambers (TVCs) for testing aerospace satellites. In these four separate markets, Chicago Bridge and another company, Pitt-Des Moines, Inc., have been the dominant firms. In 2001, Chicago Bridge acquired all of Pitt-Des Moines's assets for $84 million. The Federal Trade Commission (FTC) charged that Chicago Bridge's acquisition violated Section 7 of the Clayton Act and Section 5 of the Federal Trade Commission Act. An administrative law judge concurred, finding that the acquisition resulted in an undue increase in Chicago Bridge's market power that would not be constrained by timely entry of new competitors. At issue was the use of the Herfindahl-Hirschman Index (HHI). The FTC calculated the HHI over a several-year period rather than on an annualized basis. Chicago Bridge appealed to the U.S. Court of Appeals for the Fifth Circuit.

• **Decision and Rationale** The U.S. Court of Appeals for the Fifth Circuit affirmed the Federal Trade Commission's ruling that Chicago Bridge divest itself of its former competitor, Pitt-Des Moines. The reviewing court pointed out that merger guidelines create a presumption of adverse competitive consequences when the postmerger HHI exceeds 1,088 and the merger produces an increase in the HHI of more than one hundred points. When Chicago Bridge purchased the assets of Pitt-Des Moines, the postmerger *increases* in the HHI ranged from a low of 2,635 for the LIN/LOX storage-tank market to a high of almost 5,000 for the TVC storage-tank market. Indeed, if the merger were to be approved, the latter market would have a complete monopoly along with the LNG market. The reviewing court was unimpressed with Chicago Bridge's contention that the FTC should not have used sales data over an eleven-year period. "When sales data are sporadic, a longer historical perspective may be necessary."

a. On the left, click on "Opinions Page" and then in "Search for opinions where:" type "Chicago Bridge" in the "Title contains text:" box. Then click on the docket number listed.

CASE 46.3 CONTINUED The court stated, "We find that the record contains substantial evidence to support the Commission's finding that the HHIs are not completely irrelevant in three of the four markets. Instead of ignoring HHIs, we agree with the Commission that they should be viewed with caution and within the larger picture of long-term trends in the market." Further, "the Government's other evidence favors what the HHIs also indicate; the proposed merger will substantially lessen competition."

- **The Global Dimension** *Assume that just prior to Chicago Bridge's acquisition of its only U.S. competitor, a multinational company based in Indonesia announced that it intended to enter all four of the markets mentioned in this case. How might this announcement affect the reasoning behind this case, if at all?*
- **The Legal Environment Dimension** *What are some of the problems with attempting to measure industry concentration?*

Other Factors. Other factors to be considered include the ease of entry into the relevant market, economic efficiency, the financial condition of the merging firms, and the nature and price of the product or products involved. If a firm is a leading one—having at least a 35 percent share and twice that of the next leading firm—any merger with a firm having as little as a 1 percent share will be closely scrutinized.

Vertical Mergers A **vertical merger** occurs when a company at one stage of production acquires a company at a higher or lower stage of production. An example of a vertical merger is a company merging with one of its suppliers or retailers. Courts in the past have almost exclusively focused on "foreclosure" in assessing vertical mergers. *Foreclosure* occurs when competitors of the merging firms lose opportunities to either sell products to or buy products from the merging firms.

In one early case, for example, du Pont was challenged for acquiring a considerable amount of General Motors (GM) stock. The United States Supreme Court held that the transaction was illegal. The Court noted that the stock acquisition would enable du Pont to prevent other sellers of fabrics and finishes from selling to GM, which then accounted for 50 percent of all auto fabric and finishes purchases.[29]

Today, whether a vertical merger will be deemed illegal generally depends on several factors, such as whether the merger creates a single firm that controls an undue percentage share of the relevant market. The courts also analyze whether the merger results in a significant increase in the concentration of firms in that market, barriers to entry into the market, and the apparent intent of the merging parties. Mergers that do not prevent competitors of either of the merging firms from competing in a segment of the market will not be condemned as foreclosing competition and are legal.

Interlocking Directorates

Section 8 of the Clayton Act deals with *interlocking directorates*—that is, the practice of having individuals serve as directors on the boards of two or more competing companies simultaneously. Specifically, no person may be a director for two or more competing corporations at the same time if either of the corporations has capital, surplus, or undivided profits aggregating more than $24,001,000 or competitive sales of $2,400,100 or more. The threshold amounts are adjusted each year by the Federal Trade Commission. (The amounts given here are those announced by the commission in 2007.)

SECTION 5 Enforcement of Antitrust Laws

The federal agencies that enforce the federal antitrust laws are the U.S. Department of Justice (DOJ) and the Federal Trade Commission (FTC). The FTC was established by the Federal Trade Commission Act of 1914. Section 5 of that act is its sole substantive provision. Among other things, Section 5 provides as follows: "Unfair methods of competition in or affecting commerce, and unfair or deceptive acts or practices in or affecting commerce are hereby declared illegal." Section 5 condemns all forms of anticompetitive behavior that are not covered under other federal antitrust laws.

29. *United States v. E.I. du Pont de Nemours & Co.,* 353 U.S. 586, 77 S.Ct. 872, 1 L.Ed.2d 1057 (1957).

Only the DOJ can prosecute violations of the Sherman Act as either criminal or civil violations. Violations of the Clayton Act are not crimes, and either the DOJ or the FTC can enforce that statute through civil proceedings. The DOJ or the FTC may ask the courts to impose various remedies including **divestiture** (making a company give up one or more of its operations) and dissolution. A group of meat packers, for example, might be forced to divest itself of control or ownership of butcher shops.

The FTC has sole authority to enforce violations of Section 5 of the Federal Trade Commission Act. FTC actions are effected through administrative orders, but if a firm violates an FTC order, the FTC can seek court sanctions for the violation.

Private Actions

A private party who allegedly has been injured as a result of a violation of the Sherman Act or the Clayton Act can sue for damages and attorneys' fees. In some instances, private parties may also seek injunctive relief to prevent antitrust violations. The courts have determined that the ability to sue depends on the directness of the injury suffered by the would-be plaintiff. Thus, a person wishing to sue under the Sherman Act must prove (1) that the antitrust violation either caused or was a substantial factor in causing the injury that was suffered and (2) that the unlawful actions of the accused party affected business activities of the plaintiff that were protected by the antitrust laws.

In 2007, the United States Supreme Court issued a decision that limited the ability of private parties to pursue antitrust lawsuits without presenting some evidence of facts that suggest that an illegal agreement was made. A group of plaintiffs who were subscribers of local telephone and high-speed Internet services filed a class-action lawsuit against several regional telecommunication companies (including Bell Atlantic). The plaintiffs claimed that the companies had conspired with one another and engaged in *parallel conduct*—offering similar services and pricing—over a period of years to prevent other companies from entering the market and competing. The Supreme Court, however, found that "without more, parallel conduct does not suggest conspiracy" and dismissed the case, finding that a bare assertion of conspiracy is not enough to allow the antitrust lawsuit to go forward.[30] The Court noted that more specificity is necessary to avoid potentially "massive" discovery costs, especially when the class is as large as in the current case.

Treble Damages

In recent years, more than 90 percent of all antitrust actions have been brought by private plaintiffs. One reason for this is that successful plaintiffs may recover treble damages—three times the damages that they have suffered as a result of the violation. Such recoveries by private plaintiffs for antitrust violations have been rationalized as encouraging people to act as "private attorneys general" who will vigorously pursue antitrust violators on their own initiative. In a situation involving a price-fixing agreement, normally each competitor is jointly and severally liable for the total amount of any damages, including treble damages if they are imposed.

SECTION 6 Exemptions from Antitrust Law

There are many legislative and constitutional limitations on antitrust enforcement. Most statutory and judicially created exemptions to the antitrust laws apply to the following areas or activities:

1. *Labor.* Section 6 of the Clayton Act generally permits labor unions to organize and bargain without violating antitrust laws.[31] Section 20 of the Clayton Act specifies that strikes and other labor activities are not violations of any law of the United States. A union can lose its exemption, however, if it combines with a nonlabor group rather than acting simply in its own self-interest.
2. *Agricultural associations and fisheries.* Section 6 of the Clayton Act (along with the Cooperative Marketing Associations Act of 1922[32]) exempts agricultural cooperatives from the antitrust laws. The Fisheries Cooperative Marketing Act of 1976 exempts from antitrust legislation individuals in the fishing industry who collectively catch, produce, and prepare their products for market. Both exemptions allow members of such co-ops to combine and set prices for a particular product but do not

30. *Bell Atlantic Corp. v. Twombly,* ___ U.S. ___, 127 S.Ct. 1955, 167 L.Ed.2d 929 (2007).

31. See, for example, *Clarett v. National Football League,* 369 F.3d 124 (2d Cir. 2004).

32. 7 U.S.C. Sections 291–292.

allow them to engage in exclusionary practices or restraints of trade directed at competitors.

3. *Insurance.* The McCarran-Ferguson Act of 1945[33] exempts the insurance business from the antitrust laws whenever state regulation exists. This exemption does not cover boycotts, coercion, or intimidation on the part of insurance companies.
4. *Foreign trade.* Under the provisions of the 1918 Webb-Pomerene Act,[34] U.S. exporters may engage in cooperative activity to compete with similar foreign associations. This type of cooperative activity may not, however, restrain trade within the United States or injure other U.S. exporters. The Export Trading Company Act of 1982[35] broadened the Webb-Pomerene Act by permitting the Department of Justice to certify properly qualified export trading companies. Any activity within the scope described by the certificate is exempt from public prosecution under the antitrust laws.
5. *Professional baseball.* In 1922, the United States Supreme Court held that professional baseball was not within the reach of federal antitrust laws because it did not involve "interstate commerce."[36] The Curt Flood Act of 1998 modified some of the effects of this decision, however. Essentially, the act allows players the option of suing team owners for anticompetitive practices if, for example, the owners collude to "blacklist" players, hold down players' salaries, or force players to play for specific teams.[37]
6. *Oil marketing.* The 1935 Interstate Oil Compact allows states to determine quotas on oil that will be marketed in interstate commerce.
7. *Cooperative research and production.* Cooperative research among small-business firms is exempt under the Small Business Act of 1958.[38] Research or production of a product, process, or service by joint ventures consisting of competitors is exempt under special federal legislation, including the National Cooperative Research Act of 1984,[39] as amended.
8. *Joint efforts by businesspersons to obtain legislative or executive action.* This is often referred to as the *Noerr-Pennington* doctrine.[40] For example, DVD producers might jointly lobby Congress to change the copyright laws without being held liable for attempting to restrain trade. Though selfish rather than purely public-minded conduct is permitted, there is an exception: an action will not be protected if it is clear that the action is "objectively baseless in the sense that no reasonable [person] could reasonably expect success on the merits" and it is an attempt to make anticompetitive use of government processes.[41]
9. *Other exemptions.* Other activities exempt from antitrust laws include activities approved by the president in furtherance of the defense of the nation (under the Defense Production Act of 1950[42]); state actions, when the state policy is clearly articulated and the policy is actively supervised by the state; and activities of regulated industries (such as the transportation, communication, and banking industries) when federal agencies (such as the Federal Communications Commission) have primary regulatory authority.

SECTION 7 U.S. Antitrust Laws in the Global Context

U.S. antitrust laws have a broad application. Not only may persons in foreign nations be subject to their provisions, but the laws may also be applied to protect foreign consumers and competitors from violations committed by U.S. business firms. Consequently, *foreign persons,* a term that by definition includes foreign governments, may sue under U.S. antitrust laws in U.S. courts.

The Extraterritorial Application of U.S. Antitrust Laws

Section 1 of the Sherman Act provides for the extraterritorial effect of the U.S. antitrust laws. The United States is a major proponent of free competition in the global economy, and thus any conspiracy that has a

33. 15 U.S.C. Sections 1011–1015.
34. 15 U.S.C. Sections 61–66.
35. 15 U.S.C. Sections 4001–4003.
36. *Federal Baseball Club of Baltimore, Inc. v. National League of Professional Baseball Clubs,* 259 U.S. 200, 42 S.Ct. 465, 66 L.Ed. 898 (1922).
37. Note that in 2003, a federal appellate court held that because baseball was exempt from federal antitrust laws, it was also exempt from the reach of state antitrust laws due to the supremacy clause of the U.S. Constitution. *Major League Baseball v. Crist,* 331 F.3d 1177 (11th Cir. 2003).
38. 15 U.S.C. Sections 631–657.
39. 15 U.S.C. Sections 4301–4306.
40. See *Eastern Railroad Presidents Conference v. Noerr Motor Freight, Inc.,* 365 U.S. 127, 81 S.Ct. 523, 5 L.Ed.2d 464 (1961); and *United Mine Workers of America v. Pennington,* 381 U.S. 657, 85 S.Ct. 1585, 14 L.Ed.2d 626 (1965).
41. *Professional Real Estate Investors, Inc. v. Columbia Pictures Industries, Inc.,* 508 U.S. 49, 113 S.Ct. 1920, 123 L.Ed.2d 611 (1993).
42. 50 App. U.S.C. Sections 2061–2171.

substantial effect on U.S. commerce is within the reach of the Sherman Act. The violation may even occur outside the United States, and foreign governments as well as individuals can be sued for violation of U.S. antitrust laws. Before U.S. courts will exercise jurisdiction and apply antitrust laws, it must be shown that the alleged violation had a substantial effect on U.S. commerce. U.S. jurisdiction is automatically invoked, however, when a *per se* violation occurs.

If a domestic firm, for example, joins a foreign cartel to control the production, price, or distribution of goods, and this cartel has a *substantial effect* on U.S. commerce, a *per se* violation may exist. Hence, both the domestic firm and the foreign cartel could be sued for violation of the U.S. antitrust laws. Likewise, if a foreign firm doing business in the United States enters into a price-fixing or other anticompetitive agreement to control a portion of U.S. markets, a *per se* violation may exist.

The Application of Foreign Antitrust Laws

Many other nations also have laws that promote competition and prohibit trade restraints. For example, Japanese antitrust laws forbid unfair trade practices, monopolization, and restrictions that unreasonably restrain trade. Several nations in Southeast Asia, including Indonesia, Malaysia, and Vietnam, have enacted statutes protecting competition. Argentina, Brazil, Chile, Peru, and several other Latin American countries have adopted modern antitrust laws as well. Most of the antitrust laws apply extraterritorially, as U.S. antitrust laws do. This means that a U.S. company may be subject to another nation's antitrust laws if the company's conduct has a substantial effect on that nation's commerce.

Several U.S. corporations have faced antitrust actions in the European Union (EU), which has laws that are stricter, at least with respect to fines, than those of the United States. The EU blocked a bid by General Electric Company to acquire Honeywell International, Inc., in 2001. The EU entered into its own antitrust settlement with Microsoft Corporation, with remedies (including fines of $613 million as of 2008) that went beyond those imposed in the United States. The EU has also threatened additional fines for Microsoft's alleged failure to comply with requirements that it offer Windows without its private Media Player video and music applications.

REVIEWING Antitrust Law

The Internet Corporation for Assigned Names and Numbers (ICANN) is a nonprofit entity organizing Internet domain names. It is governed by a board of directors elected by various groups with commercial interests in the Internet. One of ICANN's functions is to authorize an entity as a registry for certain "Top Level Domains" (TLDs). ICANN entered into an agreement with VeriSign to serve as registry for the ".com" TLD to provide registry services in accordance with ICANN's specifications. VeriSign complained that ICANN was restricting the services that it could make available as a registrar and blocking new services, imposing unnecessary conditions on those services, and setting prices at which the services were offered. VeriSign claimed that ICANN's control of the registry services for domain names violated Section 1 of the Sherman Act. Using the information presented in the chapter, answer the following questions.

1. Should ICANN's actions be judged under the rule of reason or be deemed a *per se* violation of Section 1 of the Sherman Act?
2. Should ICANN's actions be viewed as a horizontal or a vertical restraint of trade?
3. Does it matter that ICANN's leadership is chosen by those with a commercial interest in the Internet?
4. If the dispute is judged under the rule of reason, what might be ICANN's defense for having a standardized set of registry services that must be used?

TERMS AND CONCEPTS

antitrust law 868
attempted monopolization 874
divestiture 880
exclusive-dealing contract 876
group boycott 870
Herfindahl-Hirschman Index 878
horizontal merger 877
horizontal restraint 870
market concentration 877
market power 869
monopolization 872
monopoly 869
monopoly power 869
***per se* violation 869**
predatory pricing 872
price discrimination 875
price-fixing agreement 870
resale price maintenance agreement 871
restraint of trade 868
rule of reason 869
tying arrangement 876
vertical merger 879
vertical restraint 871
vertically integrated firm 871

QUESTIONS AND CASE PROBLEMS

46–1. Jorge's Appliance Corp. was a new retail seller of appliances in Sunrise City. Because of its innovative sales techniques and financing, Jorge's caused the appliance department of No-Glow Department Store, a large chain store with a great deal of buying power, to lose a substantial amount of sales. No-Glow told a number of appliance manufacturers from whom it made large-volume purchases that if they continued to sell to Jorge's, No-Glow would stop buying from them. The manufacturers immediately stopped selling appliances to Jorge's. Jorge's filed a suit against No-Glow and the manufacturers, claiming that their actions constituted an antitrust violation. No-Glow and the manufacturers were able to prove that Jorge's was a small retailer with a small market share. They claimed that because the relevant market was not substantially affected, they were not guilty of restraint of trade. Discuss fully whether there was an antitrust violation.

46–2. QUESTION WITH SAMPLE ANSWER

Instant Foto Corp. is a manufacturer of photography film. At the present time, Instant Foto has approximately 50 percent of the market. Instant Foto advertises that the purchase price for Instant Foto film includes photo processing by Instant Foto Corp. Instant Foto claims that its film processing is specially designed to improve the quality of photos taken with Instant Foto film. Is Instant Foto's combination of film purchase and film processing an antitrust violation? Explain.

- **For a sample answer to Question 46–2, go to Appendix I at the end of this text.**

46–3. Monopolization. Moist snuff is a smokeless tobacco product sold in small round cans from racks, which include point-of-sale (POS) ads. POS ads are critical because tobacco advertising is restricted and the number of people who use smokeless tobacco products is relatively small. In the moist snuff market in the United States, there are only four competitors, including U.S. Tobacco Co. and its affiliates (USTC) and Conwood Co. In 1990, USTC, which held 87 percent of the market, began to convince major retailers, including Wal-Mart Stores, Inc., to use USTC's "exclusive racks" to display its products and those of all other snuff makers. USTC agents would then destroy competitors' racks. USTC also began to provide retailers with false sales data to convince them to maintain its poor-selling items and drop competitors' less expensive products. Conwood's Wal-Mart market share fell from 12 percent to 6.5 percent. In stores in which USTC did not have rack exclusivity, however, Conwood's market share increased to 25 percent. Conwood filed a suit in a federal district court against USTC, alleging, in part, that USTC used its monopoly power to exclude competitors from the moist snuff market. Should the court rule in Conwood's favor? What is USTC's best defense? Discuss. [*Conwood Co., L.P. v. U.S. Tobacco Co.*, 290 F.3d 768 (6th Cir. 2002)]

46–4. Restraint of Trade. Visa U.S.A., Inc., MasterCard International, Inc., American Express (Amex), and Discover are the four major credit- and charge-card networks in the United States. Visa and MasterCard are joint ventures, owned by the thousands of banks that are their members. The banks issue the cards, clear transactions, and collect fees from the merchants who accept the cards. By contrast, Amex and Discover themselves issue cards to customers, process transactions, and collect fees. Since 1995, Amex has asked banks to issue its cards. No bank has been willing to do so, however, because it would have to stop issuing Visa and MasterCard cards under those networks' rules barring member banks from issuing cards on rival networks. The U.S. Department of Justice filed a suit in a federal district court against Visa and MasterCard, alleging, in part, that the rules were illegal restraints of trade under the Sherman Act. Do the rules harm competition? If so, how? What relief might the court order to stop any anticompetitiveness? [*United States v. Visa U.S.A., Inc.*, 344 F.3d 229 (2d Cir. 2003)]

46-5. Sherman Act. Dentsply International, Inc., is one of a dozen manufacturers of artificial teeth for dentures and other restorative devices. Dentsply sells its teeth to twenty-three dealers of dental products. The dealers supply the teeth to dental laboratories, which fabricate dentures for sale to dentists. There are hundreds of other dealers who compete with each other on the basis of price and service. Some manufacturers sell directly to the laboratories. There are also thousands of laboratories that compete with each other on the basis of price and service. Because of advances in dental medicine, however, artificial tooth manufacturing is marked by low growth potential, and Dentsply dominates the industry. Dentsply's market share is greater than 75 percent and is about fifteen times larger than that of its next-closest competitor. Dentsply prohibits its dealers from marketing competitors' teeth unless they were selling the teeth before 1993. The federal government filed a suit in a federal district court against Dentsply, alleging, among other things, a violation of Section 2 of the Sherman Act. What must the government show to succeed in its suit? Are those elements present in this case? What should the court rule? Explain. [*United States v. Dentsply International, Inc.*, 399 F.3d 181 (3d Cir. 2005)]

46-6. Price Fixing. Texaco, Inc., and Shell Oil Co. are competitors in the national and international oil and gasoline markets. They refine crude oil into gasoline and sell it to service station owners and others. Between 1998 and 2002, Texaco and Shell engaged in a joint venture, Equilon Enterprises, to consolidate their operations in the western United States and a separate venture, Motiva Enterprises, for the same purpose in the eastern United States. This ended their competition in the domestic refining and marketing of gasoline. As part of the ventures, Texaco and Shell agreed to pool their resources and share the risks and profits of their joint activities. The Federal Trade Commission and several states approved the formation of these entities without restricting the pricing of their gasoline, which the ventures began to sell at a single price under the original Texaco and Shell brand names. Fouad Dagher and other station owners filed a suit in a federal district court against Texaco and Shell, alleging that the defendants were engaged in illegal price fixing. Do the circumstances in this case fit the definition of a price-fixing agreement? Explain. [*Texaco Inc. v. Dagher*, 547 U.S. 1, 126 S.Ct. 1276, 164 L.Ed.2d 1 (2006)]

46-7. CASE PROBLEM WITH SAMPLE ANSWER

In 1999, residents of the city of Madison, Wisconsin, became concerned that overconsumption of liquor seemed to be increasing near the campus of the University of Wisconsin–Madison (UW), leading to more frequent use of detoxification facilities and calls for police services in the campus area. Under pressure from UW, which shared these concerns, the city initiated a new policy, imposing conditions on area taverns to discourage price reduction "specials" believed to encourage high-volume and dangerous drinking. In 2002, the city began to draft an ordinance to ban all drink specials. Tavern owners responded by announcing that they had "voluntarily" agreed to discontinue drink specials on Friday and Saturday nights after 8 P.M. The city put its ordinance on hold. UW student Nic Eichenseer and others filed a suit in a Wisconsin state court against the Madison–Dane County Tavern League, Inc. (an association of local tavern owners), and others, alleging violations of antitrust law. On what might the plaintiffs base a claim for relief? Are the defendants in this case exempt from the antitrust laws? What should the court rule? Why? [*Eichenseer v. Madison–Dane County Tavern League, Inc.*, 2006 WI App 226, 725 N.W.2d 274 (2006)]

- **To view a sample answer for Problem 46–7, go to this book's Web site at www.cengage.com/blaw/jentz, select "Chapter 46," and click on "Case Problem with Sample Answer."**

46-8. Price Discrimination. The customers of Sodexho, Inc., and Feesers, Inc., are institutional food service facilities such as school, hospital, and nursing home cafeterias. Feesers is a distributor that buys unprepared food from suppliers for resale to customers who run their own cafeterias. Sodexho is a food service management company that buys unprepared food from suppliers, prepares the food, and sells the meals to the facilities, which it also operates, under contracts with its clients. Sodexho uses a distributor, such as Sysco Corp., to buy the food from a supplier, such as Michael Foods, Inc. Sysco pays Michael's list price and sells the food to Sodexho at a lower price—which Sodexho has negotiated with Michael—plus an agreed mark-up. Sysco invoices Michael for the difference. Sodexho resells the food to its facilities at its cost, plus a "procurement fee." In sum, Michael charges Sysco less for food resold to Sodexho than it charges Feesers for the same products, and thus Sodexho's customers pay less than Feesers's customers for these products. Feesers filed a suit in a federal district court against Michael and others, alleging price discrimination. To establish its claim, what does Feesers have to show? What might be the most difficult element to prove? How should the court rule? Why? [*Feesers, Inc. v. Michael Foods, Inc.*, 498 F.3d 206 (3d Cir. 2007)]

46–9. A QUESTION OF ETHICS

*In the 1990s, DuCoa, LP, made choline chloride, a B-complex vitamin essential for the growth and development of animals. The U.S. market for choline chloride was divided into thirds among DuCoa, Bioproducts, Inc., and Chinook Group, Ltd. To stabilize the market and keep the price of the vitamin higher than it would otherwise have been, the companies agreed to fix the price and allocate market share by deciding which of them would offer the lowest price to each customer. At times, however, the companies disregarded the agreement. During an increase in competitive activity in August 1997, Daniel Rose became president of DuCoa. The next month, a subordinate advised him of the conspiracy. By February 1998, Rose had begun to implement a strategy to persuade DuCoa's competitors to rejoin the conspiracy. By April, the three companies had reallocated their market shares and increased their prices. In June, the U.S. Department of Justice began to investigate allegations of price fixing in the vitamin market. Ultimately, a federal district court convicted Rose of conspiracy to violate Section 1 of the Sherman Act. [*United States v. Rose, *449 F.3d 627 (5th Cir. 2006)]*

(a) The court "enhanced" Rose's sentence to thirty months' imprisonment, one year of supervised release, and a $20,000 fine based, among other things, on his role as "a manager or supervisor" in the conspiracy. Rose appealed this enhancement to the U.S. Court of Appeals for the Fifth Circuit. Was it fair to increase Rose's sentence on this ground? Why or why not?

(b) Was Rose's participation in the conspiracy unethical? If so, how might Rose have behaved ethically instead? If not, could any of the participants' conduct be considered unethical? Explain.

LAW ON THE WEB

For updated links to resources available on the Web, as well as a variety of other materials, visit this text's Web site at

www.cengage.com/blaw/jentz

You can access the Antitrust Division of the U.S. Department of Justice online at

www.usdoj.gov

To see the American Bar Association's Web page on antitrust law, go to

www.abanet.org/antitrust

The Federal Trade Commission offers an abundance of information on antitrust law, including *A Plain English Guide to Antitrust Laws,* which is available at

www.ftc.gov/bc/compguide/index.html

Legal Research Exercises on the Web

Go to **www.cengage.com/blaw/jentz**, the Web site that accompanies this text. Select "Chapter 46" and click on "Internet Exercises." There you will find the following Internet research exercises that you can perform to learn more about the topics covered in this chapter.

Internet Exercise 46–1: Legal Perspective
The Standard Oil Trust

Internet Exercise 46–2: Management Perspective
Avoiding Antitrust Problems

UNIT NINE FOCUS ON ETHICS

Government Regulation

If this text had been written a hundred years ago, it would have had little to say about federal government regulation. Today, in contrast, virtually every area of economic activity is regulated by the government. Ethical issues in government regulation arise because regulation, by its very nature, means that some traditional rights and freedoms must be given up to ensure that other rights and freedoms are protected. Essentially, government regulation brings two ethical principles into conflict. On the one hand, deeply embedded in American culture is the idea that the government should play a limited role in directing our lives. On the other hand, one of the basic functions of government is to protect the welfare of individuals and the environment in which they live.

Ultimately, virtually every law or rule regulating business represents a decision to give up certain rights in order to protect other perceived rights. In this *Focus on Ethics* feature, we look at some of the ethical aspects of government regulation.

Telemarketing and Consumers' Privacy Rights

A good example of how the rights of one group may conflict with those of another is the debate over the Do Not Call Registry discussed in Chapter 44. The do-not-call list allows consumers to register their telephone numbers with the Federal Trade Commission to protect themselves from unwanted phone solicitations. Consumers, who had long complained about receiving unsolicited sales calls, have welcomed the Do Not Call Registry and the reduced number of calls that they receive as a result.

Telemarketers, in contrast, have strongly objected to the list. Business has sagged for numerous companies, causing jobs to be lost. Many firms have continued to contact individuals on the registry, making themselves vulnerable to fines of up to $11,000 whenever they dial a phone number on the list. Thus, protecting consumers' privacy rights has entailed significant restrictions on an industry's ability to conduct its business.

Recently, some members of Congress have suggested that a Do Not Spam bill, similar to the Do Not Call legislation, be enacted. While the idea holds promise in principle, in practice it would be hard to enforce. Most spammers use offshore Internet servers to avoid being regulated by U.S. authorities. For the moment, there is no practical way to limit the large quantity of spam that fills e-mail inboxes each minute of every day.

Credit Reporting Agencies and "Blacklisting"

Today, some consumer credit reporting agencies will also investigate and report a person's litigation history online. Physicians and landlords frequently use such services to learn whether prospective patients or tenants have a prior history of suing their physicians or their landlords. One service, for example, allows physicians, for a fee, to perform more than two hundred online name searches to find out if a person was a plaintiff in a previous malpractice suit.

Users say that these services are an ideal way to screen out undesirable patients and applicants and reduce the risk of being sued. Consumer rights advocates, however, claim that the sale of such information is akin to "blacklisting"—discriminating against potential patients or tenants on the basis of previous litigation history. In the last decade, these practices have led to complaints of unfairness as well as lawsuits against reporting agencies.

By and large, though, consumers have little recourse unless what is being reported about them is inaccurate. Under the Fair Credit Reporting Act (FCRA) of 1970, companies that sell consumer information must report the information accurately and must provide a remedy for consumers who seek to dispute the information. If no remedy is provided, the agency will be in violation of the FCRA.[1]

Consumer Safety

Recently, many consumers have become concerned about the safety of the products they buy, especially children's toys. Many of the toys—and other goods—sold in the United States are imported, often from China. Domestic manufacturers are unable or unwilling to compete with Chinese toy makers. Wal-Mart, for example, buys millions of Chinese toys each year. After some well-publicized safety lapses with such imports, many Americans have called for increased regulation of products from low-cost Chinese producers. Indeed, Wal-Mart criticized its Chinese suppliers. Later, though, Wal-Mart publicly apologized to the government of China for exaggerating the cause of the toy defects. It turned out that the Chinese suppliers had followed Wal-Mart's specifications, which were at the basis of the safety problems.

The economic and even ethical trade-off here is obvious: accept lower-priced, less-than-perfect

1. See, for example, *Decker v. U.D. Registry, Inc.,* 105 Cal.App.4th 1382, 129 Cal.Rptr.2d 892 (2003).

products from foreign low-cost producers or impose stricter scrutiny on such imports and have the U.S. consumer pay a higher price.

Environmental Law

Questions of fairness inevitably arise in regard to environmental law. Has the government gone too far—or not far enough—in regulating businesses in the interest of protecting the environment? At what point do the costs of environmental regulations become too burdensome for society to bear? Consider the problem of toxic waste. Although everybody is in favor of cleaning up America's toxic waste dumps, nobody has the slightest idea what this task will ultimately cost. Moreover, there is no agreed-on standard as to how clean a site must be before it no longer poses any threat. Must 100 percent of the contamination be removed, or would removal of some lesser amount achieve a reasonable degree of environmental quality?

Global Environmental Issues

Pollution does not respect geographic borders. Indeed, one of the reasons that the federal government became involved in environmental protection was that state regulation alone apparently could not solve the problem of air or water pollution. Pollutants generated in one state move in the air and water to other states. Neither does pollution respect national borders. Environmental issues, perhaps more than any others, bring home to everyone the fact that the world today is truly a global community. What one country does or does not do with respect to environmental preservation may be felt by citizens in countries thousands of miles away.

Another challenging—and controversial—issue is potential global warming. The fear is that emissions, largely from combustion of fossil fuels, will remain in the atmosphere and create a "greenhouse effect" by preventing heat from radiating outward. Concerns over this issue have led to many attempts to force all world polluters to "clean up their acts." For example, leaders of 160 nations have already agreed to reduce emissions of greenhouse gases in their respective countries. They did this when they ratified the Kyoto Protocol, which was drawn up at a world summit meeting held in Kyoto, Japan, in 1997. The Kyoto Protocol, which is often referred to as the global warming treaty, established different rates of reduction in emissions of greenhouse gases for different countries or regions. Most nations, however, including the United States, will not meet the treaty's objectives. Indeed, the Bush administration told the world in early 2001 that the treaty was a dead letter because it did not address the problem of curbing greenhouse gases from most of the developing world.

Is Economic Development the Answer?

Economists have shown that economic development is the quickest way to reduce pollution worldwide. After a nation reaches a certain per capita income level, the more economic growth the nation experiences, the lower the pollution output. This occurs because richer nations have the resources to pay for pollution reduction. For example, industries in the United States pollute much less per unit of output than do industries in developing nations—because we are willing to pay for pollution abatement. Even among developed nations, the United States is a leader in curbing pollution. Indeed, from 2001 to 2007, the United States saw a much smaller increase in greenhouse gases than did the European Union (EU). Most members of the EU had signed the Kyoto Protocol.

DISCUSSION QUESTIONS

1. Does the national Do Not Call Registry adversely affect the way that business is conducted in this country? If so, how? Should Congress enact a Do Not Spam law? Why or why not?
2. If 90 percent of the toxic waste at a given site can be removed for $50,000, but removing the last 10 percent will cost $2 million, is it reasonable to require that the last 10 percent be removed? How would you address this question?
3. Assume that removing all asbestos from every public building in the nation would save ten lives per year and that the cost of the asbestos removal would be $250 billion (or $25 billion per life saved). Is this too high of a price to pay? Should cost ever be a consideration when human lives are at stake?
4. Can you think of a better way that the law can address the problem of global warming, which is clearly not just a national issue? Explain.

UNIT TEN

Property

CONTENTS

CHAPTER 47

Personal Property and Bailments

Property consists of the legally protected rights and interests a person has in anything with an ascertainable value that is subject to ownership. Property would have little value (and the word would have little meaning) if the law did not define the rights of owners to use, sell, dispose of, control, and prevent others from trespassing on their property rights. In the United States, a substantial body of law protects the rights of property owners, but that protection is not absolute. As you will read in this chapter and the next, property owners may have to prove that their ownership rights in a particular item of property are superior to the claims of others. In addition, through its police powers, the government can impose regulations and taxes on property, and can take or seize private property under certain circumstances.

In the first part of this chapter, we examine the differences between personal and real property. We then look at the methods of acquiring ownership of personal property and issues relating to mislaid, lost, and abandoned personal property. In the second part of the chapter, we examine bailment relationships. A *bailment* is created when personal property is temporarily delivered into the care of another without a transfer of title, such as when you take an item of clothing to the dry cleaner. The fact that there is no passage of title and no intent to transfer title is what distinguishes a bailment from a sale or a gift.

SECTION 1 Personal Property versus Real Property

Real property (sometimes called *realty* or *real estate*) means the land and everything permanently attached to it, including structures and anything attached permanently to the structures. Everything else is **personal property** (sometimes referred to in case law as *personalty* or **chattel**). In essence, real property is immovable, whereas personal property is capable of being moved.

Personal property can be tangible or intangible. Tangible personal property, such as a television set, heavy construction equipment, or a car, has physical substance. Intangible personal property represents some set of rights and interests, but it has no real physical existence. Stocks and bonds are intangible personal property. So, too, are patents, trademarks, and copyrights, as discussed in Chapter 8.

Both personal property and real property can be owned by an individual person or by an entity. When two or more persons own real or personal property together, concurrent ownership exists.

Why Is the Distinction Important?

The distinction between real and personal property is important for several reasons. First, the two types of property are usually subject to different types of taxes. Generally, each state assesses property taxes on real property. Typically, the tax rate is based on the market value of the real property and the various services provided by the city, state, and county in which the property is located (such as schools, roads, and libraries). Businesses usually pay taxes (both federal and state) on the personal property they own, use, or lease, including office or farm equipment and supplies. Individuals may pay sales tax when purchasing personal property, but generally they are not required to pay annual taxes on personal property that is not used for business.

Another reason for distinguishing between real and personal property has to do with the way the property is acquired or transferred. Personal property can be transferred with a minimum of formality, but real property transfers generally involve a written sales contract and a *deed* that is recorded with the state (deeds and real property transfers are discussed in Chapter 48). Similarly, establishing ownership rights is simpler for personal property than for real property. For example, if Mia gives Shawn an iPod as a gift, Shawn does not need to have any paperwork evidencing title (the ways to acquire ownership of personal property will be discussed shortly).

Converting Real to Personal Property

Sometimes, real property can be turned into personal property by detaching it from the land. For instance, the trees, bushes, and plants growing on land are considered part of the real property. If the property is sold, all the vegetation growing on the land normally is transferred to the new owner of the real property. Once the items are severed (removed) from the land, however, they become personal property. If the trees are cut from the land, the timber is personal property. If apples, grapes, or raspberries are picked from trees or vines growing on real property, they become personal property. (Note, however, that some crops that must be planted every year, such as corn and wheat, are considered to be personal property.) Similarly, if land contains minerals (including oil) or other natural resources such as silica or marble, the resources are part of the real property. But once removed, they become personal property. Conversely, personal property may be converted into real property by attaching it to the real property, as discussed next.

SECTION 2 Fixtures

Certain personal property can become so closely associated with the real property to which it is attached that the law views it as real property. Such property is known as a **fixture—**a thing affixed to realty. A thing is affixed to realty when it is attached to the realty by roots; embedded in it; or permanently attached by means of cement, plaster, bolts, nails, or screws. The fixture can be physically attached to real property or attached to another fixture; it can even be an item, such as a statue, that is not physically attached to the land, as long as the owner *intends* the property to be a fixture.

Fixtures are included in the sale of land if the sales contract does not provide otherwise. The sale of a house includes the land and the house and garage on it, as well as the cabinets, plumbing, and windows. Because these are permanently affixed to the property, they are considered to be a part of it. Unless otherwise agreed, however, the curtains and throw rugs are not included. Items such as drapes and window-unit air conditioners are difficult to classify. Thus, a contract for the sale of a house or commercial property should indicate which items of this sort are included in the sale.

The issue of whether an item is a fixture (and thus real estate) or not a fixture (and thus personal property) often arises with respect to land sales, real property taxation, insurance coverage, and divorces. How the issue is resolved can have important consequences for the parties involved.

The Role of Intent

Generally, when the courts need to determine whether a certain item is a fixture, they examine the intention of the party who placed the object on the real property. If the facts indicate that the person intended the item to be a fixture, then it will normally be considered a fixture. When the intent of the party who placed the item on the realty is in dispute, the courts will usually deem that the item is a fixture if either or both of the following are true:

1. The property attached cannot be removed without causing substantial damage to the remaining realty.
2. The property attached is so adapted to the rest of the realty as to become a part of it.

Certain items can only be attached to property permanently; such items are fixtures—it is assumed that the owner intended them to be fixtures because they had to be permanently attached to the property. A tile floor, cabinets, and carpeting are examples. Also, when an item of property is custom-made for installation on real property, as storm windows are, the item is usually classified as a fixture. In addition, an item that is firmly attached to the land and integral to its use, such as a complex irrigation system bolted to a cement slab on a farm, may be considered a fixture.[1] The courts assume that owners, in making such

1. See, for example, *In re Sand & Sage Farm & Ranch, Inc.*, 266 Bankr. 507 (D.Kan. 2001).

installations, intend the objects to become part of their real property.

Trade Fixtures

Trade fixtures are an exception to the rule that fixtures are a part of the real property. A trade fixture is personal property that is installed for a commercial purpose by a tenant (one who rents real property from the owner, or landlord). Trade fixtures remain the property of the tenant, unless removal would irreparably damage the building or realty. A walk-in cooler, for example, purchased and installed by a tenant who uses the premises for a restaurant, is a trade fixture. The tenant can remove the cooler from the premises when the lease terminates but ordinarily must repair any damage that the removal causes or compensate the landlord for the damage.

SECTION 3 Acquiring Ownership of Personal Property

The most common way of acquiring personal property is by purchasing it. We have already discussed the purchase and sale of personal property (goods) in Chapters 20 through 23. Often, property is acquired by will or inheritance, a topic we cover in Chapter 50. Here we look at additional ways in which ownership of personal property can be acquired, including acquisition by possession, production, gift, accession, and confusion.

Possession

One example of acquiring ownership through possession is the capture of wild animals. Wild animals belong to no one in their natural state, and the first person to take possession of a wild animal normally owns it. The killing of a wild animal amounts to assuming ownership of it. Merely being in hot pursuit does not give title, however. This basic rule has two exceptions. First, any wild animals captured by a trespasser are the property of the landowner, not the trespasser. Second, if wild animals are captured or killed in violation of wild game statutes, the state, not the capturer, obtains title to the animals.

Those who find lost or abandoned property can also acquire ownership rights through mere possession of the property, as will be discussed later in this chapter. (Ownership rights in real property can also be acquired through *adverse possession*—to be discussed in Chapter 48.)

Production

Production is another means of acquiring ownership of personal property. For instance, writers, inventors, manufacturers, and others who produce personal property may thereby acquire title to it. (In some situations, though, as when a researcher is hired to invent a new product or technique, the researcher may not own what is produced—see Chapter 31.)

Gift

A **gift** is another fairly common means of acquiring or transferring ownership of property. A gift is essentially a *voluntary* transfer of property ownership for which no consideration is given. As discussed in Chapter 12, the presence of consideration is what distinguishes a contract from a gift. Gifts can be made during a person's lifetime or in a last will and testament. A gift made by will is called a *testamentary* gift.

For a gift to be effective, three requirements must be met—donative intent on the part of the *donor* (the one giving the gift), delivery, and acceptance by the *donee* (the one receiving the gift). We examine each of these requirements here. Until these three requirements are met, no effective gift has been made. For example, your aunt tells you that she is going to give you a new Mercedes-Benz for your next birthday. This is simply a promise to make a gift. It is not considered a gift until the Mercedes-Benz is delivered and accepted.

Donative Intent Donative intent (the intent to make a gift) is determined from the language of the donor and the surrounding circumstances. When a gift is challenged in court, for example, the court may look at the relationship between the parties and the size of the gift in relation to the donor's other assets. A court might question donative intent when a person made the gift to her or his enemy. Similarly, when a person has given away a large portion of her or his assets, the court will carefully scrutinize the transactions to determine whether the donor was mentally competent or whether fraud or duress was involved.

Delivery The gift must be delivered to the donee. Delivery can be accomplished by the donor or by means of a third person who is acting as an agent for either the donor or the donee. Delivery is obvious in most cases, but some objects cannot be relinquished physically. Then the question of delivery depends on the surrounding circumstances.

Constructive Delivery. When the physical object itself cannot be delivered, a symbolic, or constructive, delivery will be sufficient. **Constructive delivery** does not confer actual possession of the object in question, only the right to take actual possession. It is a general term for all of those acts that the law holds to be equivalent to acts of real delivery.

Suppose that you want to make a gift of various rare coins that you have stored in a safe-deposit box at your bank. You certainly cannot deliver the box itself to the donee, and you do not want to take the coins out of the bank. Instead, you can simply deliver the key to the box to the donee and authorize the donee's access to the box and its contents. This constitutes symbolic, or constructive, delivery of the contents of the box.

Delivery of intangible personal property—such as stocks, bonds, insurance policies, and contracts, for example—must always be accomplished by constructive delivery. This is because the documents represent rights and are not, in themselves, the true property.

Relinquishing Dominion and Control. An effective delivery also requires giving up *complete dominion*[2] *and control* over the subject matter of the gift. The outcome of disputes often turns on whether control has actually been relinquished. The Internal Revenue Service scrutinizes transactions between relatives when one has given income-producing property to the other. A relative who does not relinquish complete control over a piece of property will have to pay taxes on the income from that property.

In the following classic case, the court focused on the requirement that a donor must relinquish complete control and dominion over property before a gift can be effectively delivered.

2. The term *dominion* in this sense refers to absolute ownership rights in, and control over, property. One who has dominion over property both possesses and has title to the property.

CASE 47.1 In re Estate of Piper

Missouri Court of Appeals, 1984. 676 S.W.2d 897.

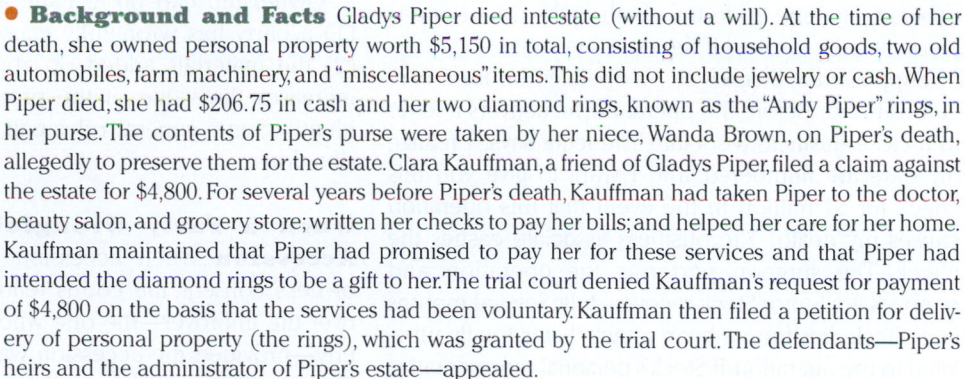

• **Background and Facts** Gladys Piper died intestate (without a will). At the time of her death, she owned personal property worth $5,150 in total, consisting of household goods, two old automobiles, farm machinery, and "miscellaneous" items. This did not include jewelry or cash. When Piper died, she had $206.75 in cash and her two diamond rings, known as the "Andy Piper" rings, in her purse. The contents of Piper's purse were taken by her niece, Wanda Brown, on Piper's death, allegedly to preserve them for the estate. Clara Kauffman, a friend of Gladys Piper, filed a claim against the estate for $4,800. For several years before Piper's death, Kauffman had taken Piper to the doctor, beauty salon, and grocery store; written her checks to pay her bills; and helped her care for her home. Kauffman maintained that Piper had promised to pay her for these services and that Piper had intended the diamond rings to be a gift to her. The trial court denied Kauffman's request for payment of $4,800 on the basis that the services had been voluntary. Kauffman then filed a petition for delivery of personal property (the rings), which was granted by the trial court. The defendants—Piper's heirs and the administrator of Piper's estate—appealed.

• **Decision and Rationale** The state intermediate appellate court reversed the judgment of the trial court, ruling that no effective gift of the rings had been made because Piper had never actually delivered them to Kauffman. The appellate court held that one of the essential elements to make a gift is "a delivery of the property by the donor to the donee." The court stated, "While no particular form is necessary to effect a delivery, and while the delivery may be actual, constructive, or symbolical, there must be some evidence to support a delivery theory." The court concluded that "language, written or spoken, expressing an intention to give, does not constitute a gift, unless the intention is executed by a complete and unconditional delivery of the subject matter, or delivery of a proper written instrument evidencing a gift. There is no evidence in this case to prove delivery, and, for such reason, the trial court's judgment is erroneous."

CASE CONTINUES

CASE 47.1 CONTINUED

- **Impact of This Case on Today's Law** *This classic case clearly illustrates the delivery requirement when making a gift. Assuming that Piper did, indeed, intend for Kauffman to have the rings, it was unfortunate that Kauffman had no right to receive them after Piper's death. Yet the alternative could lead to perhaps even more unfairness. The policy behind the delivery requirement is to protect alleged donors and their heirs from fraudulent claims based solely on parol evidence. If not for this policy, an alleged donee could easily claim that a gift was made when, in fact, it was not.*

- **What If the Facts Were Different?** *Suppose that Piper had told Kauffman that she was giving the rings to Kauffman but wished to keep them in her possession for a few more days. Would this have affected the court's decision in this case? Explain.*

Acceptance The final requirement of a valid gift is acceptance by the donee. This rarely presents any problems because most donees readily accept their gifts. The courts generally assume acceptance unless shown otherwise.

Gifts *Inter Vivos* and Gifts *Causa Mortis*

A gift made during the donor's lifetime is called a **gift *inter vivos*.** A **gift *causa mortis*** is made in contemplation of imminent death. To be effective, a gift *causa mortis* must meet the three requirements of intent, delivery, and acceptance. Gifts *causa mortis* do not become absolute until the donor dies from the contemplated illness or disease. A gift *causa mortis* is revocable at any time up to the death of the donor and is automatically revoked if the donor recovers.

Suppose that Steck is to be operated on for a cancerous tumor. Before the operation, he delivers a letter to a close business associate. The letter says, "I realize my days are numbered, and I want to give you this check for $1 million in the event that this operation causes my death." The business associate cashes the check. The surgeon performs the operation and removes the tumor. Steck recovers fully. Several months later, Steck dies from a heart attack that is totally unrelated to the operation. If Steck's personal representative (the party charged with administering Steck's estate) tries to recover the $1 million, normally she will succeed. The gift *causa mortis* is automatically revoked if the donor recovers. The *specific event* that was contemplated in making the gift was death caused by a particular operation. Because Steck's death was not the result of this event, the gift is revoked, and the $1 million passes to Steck's estate.[3]

3. *Brind v. International Trust Co.*, 66 Colo. 60, 179 P. 148 (1919).

Accession

Accession means "something added." Accession occurs when someone adds value to a piece of personal property by the use of either labor or materials. Generally, there is no dispute about who owns the property after accession occurs, especially when the accession is accomplished with the owner's consent. For example, a Corvette-customizing specialist comes to Hoshi's house. Hoshi has all the materials necessary to customize the car. The specialist uses the materials and his labor to add a unique bumper to Hoshi's Corvette. Hoshi simply pays the customizer for the value of the labor, obviously retaining title to the property.

Ownership can be at issue after an accession if (1) a party has wrongfully caused the accession or (2) the materials added or labor expended greatly increases the value of the property or changes its identity. Some general rules can be applied in these situations.

When a Party Wrongfully Causes the Accession When accession occurs without the owner's consent, the courts tend to favor the owner over the improver—the one who improved the property—provided the accession was done in bad faith. This is true even if the accession increased the value of the property substantially. In addition, many courts will deny the improver (wrongdoer) any compensation for the value added. For example, Shalynn steals a car and puts expensive new tires on it. Obviously, the rightful owner is entitled to recover the car and is not required to pay the thief for the value of the new tires.

Increased Property Value Due to a Good Faith Accession If the accession is performed in good faith, however, even without the owner's consent, ownership of the improved item most often depends on whether the accession has increased the value of the property or changed its identity. The greater the increase in value, the more likely that ownership will pass to the improver. If ownership does pass, the improver must compensate the original owner for the value of the property prior to the accession. If the increase in value is not sufficient for ownership to pass to the improver, most courts require the owner to compensate the improver for the value added.

Confusion

Confusion is the commingling (mixing together) of goods so that one person's personal property cannot be distinguished from another's. It frequently involves goods that are fungible.[4] *Fungible goods* are goods consisting of identical particles, such as grain or oil. For example, if two farmers put their number 2–grade winter wheat into the same storage bin, confusion occurs. When goods are confused due to a wrongful and willful act and the wrongdoer is unable to prove what percentage of the confused goods belongs to him or her, then the innocent party ordinarily acquires title to the whole.

If confusion occurs as a result of agreement, an honest mistake, or the act of some third party, the owners share ownership in the commingled goods in proportion to the amount each contributed. For example, five farmers in a small Iowa community agree that they will harvest the same amount of number 2–grade yellow corn every fall and store it in cooperative silos. Each farmer thus owns one-fifth of the total corn in the silos. If anything happens to the corn, each farmer will bear the loss in equal proportions of one-fifth. If one farmer harvests and stores more corn than the others in the cooperative silos and wants to claim a greater ownership interest, that farmer must keep careful records. Otherwise, the courts will presume that each farmer has an equal interest in the corn. *Concept Summary 47.1* on the next page provides a review of the various ways of acquiring personal property.

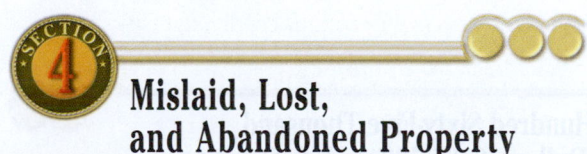

SECTION 4 Mislaid, Lost, and Abandoned Property

As already noted, one of the methods of acquiring ownership of property is to possess it. Simply finding something and holding onto it, however, does not *necessarily* give the finder any legal rights in the property. Different rules apply, depending on whether the property was mislaid, lost, or abandoned.

Mislaid Property

Property that has been voluntarily placed somewhere by the owner and then inadvertently forgotten is **mislaid property.** Suppose that you go to a movie theater. While paying for popcorn at the concession stand, you set your iPhone on the counter and then leave it there. The phone is mislaid property, and the theater owner is entrusted with the duty of reasonable care for the goods. When mislaid property is found, the finder does not obtain title to the goods.[5] Instead, the owner of the place where the property was mislaid becomes the caretaker of the property because it is highly likely that the true owner will return.[6]

Lost Property

Property that is *involuntarily* left is **lost property.** A finder of lost property can claim title to the property against the whole world, *except the true owner.* If the true owner demands that the lost property be returned, the finder must return it. If a third party attempts to take possession of lost property from a finder, the third party cannot assert a better title than the finder. For example, while walking across a courtyard one evening, Khalia finds a gold ring with precious stones. She takes the ring to a jeweler to have it appraised. While pretending to weigh the jewelry, the jeweler's employee removes several of the stones. If Khalia brings an action to recover the stones from the jeweler, she normally will win because she found lost property and holds valid title against everyone *except the true owner.*[7]

Conversion of Lost Property When a finder of lost property knows the true owner and fails to return the property to that person, the finder is guilty of the tort of *conversion* (see Chapter 6). In the example just mentioned, suppose that Khalia knows that the gold ring she found belongs to Geneva. If Khalia does not return Geneva's ring in that situation, she is guilty of conversion. Many states require the finder to make a reasonably diligent search to locate the true owner of lost property.

4. See Section 1–201(17) of the Uniform Commercial Code (UCC).

5. The finder is an *involuntary bailee*—see the discussion of bailments later in this chapter.

6. The owner of the place where property is mislaid is a bailee with right of possession against all except the true owner.

7. For a landmark English case establishing finders' rights in property, see *Armory v. Delamirie,* 93 Eng.Rep. 664 (K.B. [King's Bench] 1722).

CONCEPT SUMMARY 47.1
Acquisition of Personal Property

Type of Acquisition	How Acquisition Occurs
By Purchase or by Will	The most common means of acquiring ownership in personal property is by purchasing it (see Chapters 20 through 23). Another way in which personal property is often acquired is by will or inheritance (see Chapter 50).
Possession	Ownership may be acquired by possession if no other person has ownership title (for example, capturing wild animals or finding abandoned property).
Production	Any product or item produced by an individual (with minor exceptions) becomes the property of that individual.
Gift	An effective gift is made when the following three requirements are met: 1. *Intent*—There is evidence of *intent* to make a gift of the property in question. 2. *Delivery*—The gift is delivered (physically or constructively) to the donee or the donee's agent. 3. *Acceptance*—The gift is accepted by the donee or the donee's agent.
Accession	When someone adds value to a piece of property by use of labor or materials, the added value generally becomes the property of the owner of the original property (when accessions are made in bad faith or wrongfully). Good faith accessions that substantially increase the property's value or change the identity of the property may cause title to pass to the improver.
Confusion	In the case of fungible goods, if a person wrongfully and willfully commingles goods with those of another in order to render them indistinguishable, the innocent party acquires title to the whole. Otherwise, the owners share ownership of the commingled goods in proportion to the amount each contributed.

Estray Statutes Many states have **estray statutes,** which encourage and facilitate the return of property to its true owner and then reward the finder for honesty if the property remains unclaimed. These laws provide an incentive for finders to report their discoveries by making it possible for them, after passage of a specified period of time, to acquire legal title to the property they have found.

Estray statutes usually require the county clerk to advertise the property in an attempt to help the owner recover what has been lost. Generally, the item must be lost property, not merely mislaid property, for the estray statute to apply. When the situation indicates that the property was probably lost and not mislaid or abandoned, loss is presumed as a matter of public policy, and the estray statute applies.

In the following case, the court considered whether two railroad employees were entitled to the $165,580 that they found in a duffel bag by the railroad tracks in the Maine woods.

CASE 47.2 United States v. One Hundred Sixty-Five Thousand Five Hundred Eighty Dollars ($165,580) in U.S. Currency

United States District Court, District of Maine, 2007. 502 F.Supp.2d 114.

• **Background and Facts** In Maine, the St. John River forms the border with Canada. The river freezes in the winter, allowing travel by foot or snowmobile to and from Canada. Drug smugglers use this route to bring drugs into the United States and to transport U.S. cash back to Canada. On February 4, 2005, Daniel Madore and Traves LaPointe, two railroad employees, found a black duffel bag in some bushes along the north side of the tracks where they were working. The bag con-

CASE 47.2 CONTINUED tained $165,580 in cash. Madore and LaPointe presented the bag to senior patrol agents of the U.S. government. A drug-sniffing dog responded positively to the bag for the scent of drugs. On March 1, 2006, the federal government filed this complaint against the $165,580. Madore and LaPointe filed answers to the complaint, arguing that they were the legal owners of the lost property.

- **Decision and Rationale** The U.S. District Court for the District of Maine ruled in favor of the U.S. government. The court first looked at state law. Maine requires that whoever finds lost cash or goods must give notice in writing to the clerk of the town where the cash or goods were found and post a notification thereof in some public place in that town. This notice must be given within seven days of finding the property. For sums larger than ten dollars, the claimant must also publish a notice in some newspaper in that town. Madore and LaPointe did neither. Furthermore, federal law provides that "illicit cash is forfeited to the Government." Because "the money in this case is the other side of an illegal drug deal," it is by definition "illicit." The court further stated that "Simply because [Madore and LaPointe] found the money on the side of the railroad tracks does not legitimize the case or their claim to it."

- **The Legal Environment Dimension** *Could the claimants have successfully argued that because they briefly possessed the currency, they had an ownership interest in it? Explain.*

- **What If the Facts Were Different?** *If the claimants had refuted the government's assertion that the cash was "illicit," would the result in this case have been different? Why or why not?*

Abandoned Property

Property that has been *discarded* by the true owner, with *no intention* of reclaiming title to it, is **abandoned property.** Someone who finds abandoned property acquires title to it, and such title is good against the whole world, *including the original owner.* The owner of lost property who eventually gives up any further attempt to find it is frequently held to have abandoned the property.

For example, Aleka is driving with the windows down in her car. Somewhere along her route, a valuable scarf blows out the window. She retraces her route and looks for the scarf but cannot find it. She finally decides that further search is futile and proceeds to her destination five hundred miles away. Six months later, Frye, a hitchhiker, finds the scarf. Frye has acquired title, which is good even against Aleka. By completely giving up her search, Aleka abandoned the scarf just as effectively as if she had intentionally discarded it.

Note that if a person finds abandoned property while trespassing on the property of another, that person will not acquire title. In that situation, the owner of the real property on which the abandoned property was found will acquire title to it. See *Concept Summary 47.2* for a comparison of mislaid, lost, and abandoned property.

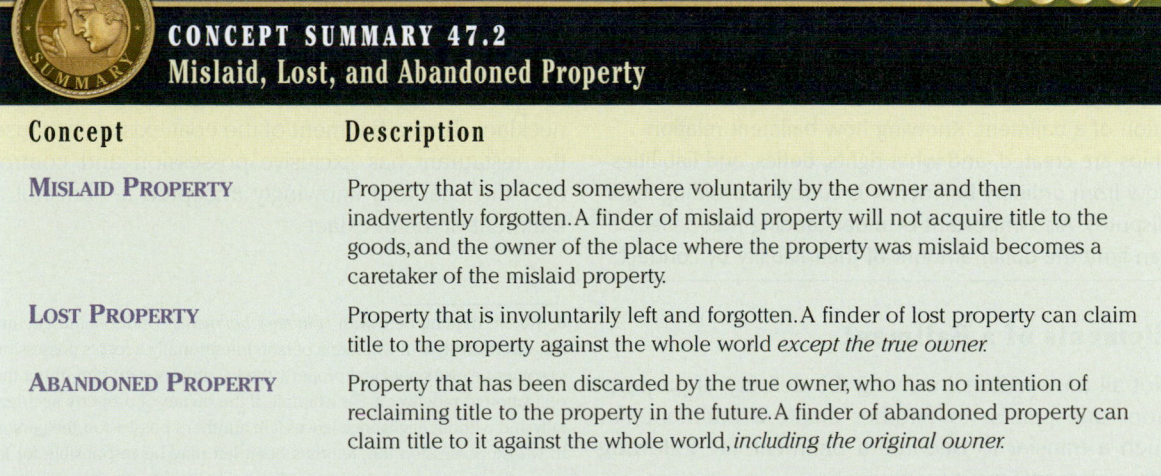

CONCEPT SUMMARY 47.2
Mislaid, Lost, and Abandoned Property

Concept	Description
MISLAID PROPERTY	Property that is placed somewhere voluntarily by the owner and then inadvertently forgotten. A finder of mislaid property will not acquire title to the goods, and the owner of the place where the property was mislaid becomes a caretaker of the mislaid property.
LOST PROPERTY	Property that is involuntarily left and forgotten. A finder of lost property can claim title to the property against the whole world *except the true owner.*
ABANDONED PROPERTY	Property that has been discarded by the true owner, who has no intention of reclaiming title to the property in the future. A finder of abandoned property can claim title to it against the whole world, *including the original owner.*

SECTION 5

Bailments

Sometimes, the owner of personal property allows another party to use or possess the property temporarily. Many routine personal and business transactions involve bailments. A **bailment** is formed by the delivery of personal property, without transfer of title, by one person (called a **bailor**) to another (called a **bailee**). Bailment agreements usually are made for a particular purpose—for example, to loan, lease, store, repair, or transport the property. On completion of the purpose, the bailee is obligated to return the bailed property in the same or better condition to the bailor or a third person or to dispose of it as directed.

Although bailments typically arise by agreement, not all of the elements of a contract must necessarily be present (such as mutual assent and consideration). For example, if you lend your business law text to a friend, a bailment is created, but not by contract, because there is no consideration. Nevertheless, many commercial bailments, such as the delivery of your suit to the cleaners for dry cleaning, do involve contracts.

A bailment differs from a sale or a gift in that possession is transferred without passage of title or intent to transfer title. In a sale or a gift, title is transferred from the seller or donor to the buyer or donee.

PREVENTING LEGAL DISPUTES

Businesspersons need to be aware that the law of bailments applies to many routine personal and business transactions. Indeed, a vast number of bailments are created daily in the business community. When dealing with bailments, whether you realize it or not, you are subject to the obligations and duties that arise from the bailment relationship. Consequently, every person should understand the elements necessary for the creation of a bailment. Knowing how bailment relationships are created, and what rights, duties, and liabilities flow from ordinary bailments, is critical in avoiding legal disputes. Also important is understanding that bailees can limit the dollar amount of their liability by contract.

Elements of a Bailment

Not all transactions involving the delivery of property from one person to another create a bailment. For such a transfer to become a bailment, the following three elements must be present:

1. Personal property.
2. Delivery of possession (without title).
3. Agreement that the property will be returned to the bailor or otherwise disposed of according to its owner's directions.

Personal Property Requirement Only personal property can be bailed; there can be no bailment of persons. Although a bailment of your luggage is created when it is transported by an airline, as a passenger you are not the subject of a bailment. Also, you cannot bail realty; thus, leasing your house to a tenant is not a bailment. Although bailments commonly involve *tangible* items—jewelry, cattle, automobiles, and the like—*intangible* personal property, such as promissory notes and shares of corporate stock, may also be bailed.

Delivery of Possession *Delivery of possession* means transfer of possession of the property to the bailee. For delivery to occur, the bailee must be given *exclusive possession and control* over the property, and the bailee must *knowingly* accept the personal property.[8] In other words, the bailee must *intend* to exercise control over it.

If either delivery of possession or knowing acceptance is lacking, there is no bailment relationship. For example, Yang is hurrying to catch his plane and wants to check a package at the airport. He arrives at the airport check-in station, but the person in charge has gone on a coffee break. Yang decides to leave the package on the counter. Even though there has clearly been a physical transfer of the package, the person in charge of the check-in station has not knowingly accepted the personal property. Therefore, there has not been an effective delivery.

The result is the same if, for example, Delacroix goes to a restaurant and checks her coat, leaving a $20,000 diamond necklace in the coat pocket. In accepting the coat, the bailee does not *knowingly* also accept the necklace. Thus, a bailment of the coat exists—because the restaurant has exclusive possession and control over the coat and knowingly accepted it—but not a bailment of the necklace.

---

8. We are dealing here with *voluntary bailments.* Under some circumstances, regardless of whether a person intentionally accepts possession of someone else's personal property, the law imposes on him or her the obligation to redeliver it. For example, if the owner of property accidentally and without negligence leaves it in another's possession, the person in whose possession the item has been left may be responsible for its return. This is referred to as an *involuntary bailment.*

Physical versus Constructive Delivery. Either *physical* or *constructive* delivery will result in the bailee's exclusive possession of and control over the property. As discussed earlier, in the context of gifts, constructive delivery is a substitute, or symbolic, delivery. What is delivered to the bailee is not the actual property bailed (such as a car) but something so related to the property (such as the car keys) that the requirement of delivery is satisfied.

Involuntary Bailments. In certain situations, a bailment is found despite the apparent lack of the requisite elements of control and knowledge. One example of such a situation occurs when the bailee acquires the property accidentally or by mistake—as in finding someone else's lost or mislaid property. A bailment is created even though the bailor did not voluntarily deliver the property to the bailee. Such bailments are referred to as *constructive* or *involuntary* bailments (see footnote 8).

Suppose that several corporate managers attend a meeting at the law firm of Jacobs & Matheson. One of the corporate officers, Kyle Gustafson, inadvertently leaves his briefcase at the firm at the conclusion of the meeting. In this situation, a court could find that an involuntary bailment was created even though Gustafson did not voluntarily deliver the briefcase and the law firm did not intentionally accept it. If an involuntary bailment exists, the firm is responsible for taking care of the briefcase and returning it to Gustafson.

The Bailment Agreement

A bailment agreement can be *express* or *implied*. Although a written agreement is not required for bailments of less than one year (that is, the Statute of Frauds does not apply—see Chapter 15), it is a good idea to have a written contract, especially when valuable property is involved.

The bailment agreement expressly or impliedly provides for the return of the bailed property to the bailor, or to a third person, or for disposal of the property by the bailee. The agreement presupposes that the bailee will return the identical goods originally given by the bailor. In certain types of bailments, though, such as bailments of fungible goods,[9] only equivalent property must be returned.

For example, if Hobson stores his grain (fungible goods) in Kwam's grain elevator, a bailment is created. But at the end of the storage period, the grain elevator company is not obligated to return to Hobson exactly the same grain that was stored. As long as the company returns grain of the same type, grade, and quantity, the bailee company has performed its obligation.

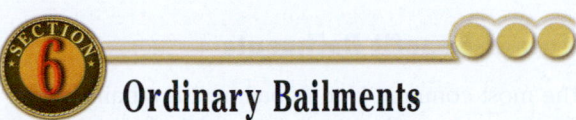

9. As mentioned earlier, *fungible goods* are goods that consist of identical particles, such as wheat. Fungible goods are defined in UCC 1–201(17).

SECTION 6 Ordinary Bailments

Bailments are either *ordinary* or *special (extraordinary)*. There are three types of ordinary bailments. They are distinguished according to *which party receives a benefit from the bailment*. This factor will dictate the rights and liabilities of the parties, and the courts may use it to determine the standard of care required of the bailee in possession of the personal property. The three types of ordinary bailments are listed below and described in the following subsections:

- *Bailment for the sole benefit of the bailor.*
- *Bailment for the sole benefit of the bailee.*
- *Bailment for the mutual benefit of the bailee and the bailor.*

Bailment for the Sole Benefit of the Bailor

A bailment for the sole benefit of the bailor is a type of *gratuitous bailment*—meaning that it involves no consideration. The bailment is for the convenience and benefit of the bailor. Basically, the bailee is caring for the bailor's property as a favor; therefore, the bailee owes only a slight duty of care and will be liable only if grossly negligent in caring for the property. (Negligence was discussed in Chapter 7.) For example, Allen asks his friend, Sumi, to store his car in her garage while he is away. If Sumi agrees to do so, then a gratuitous bailment exists because the bailment of the car is for the sole benefit of the bailor (Allen). If the car is damaged while in Sumi's garage, Sumi will not be responsible for the damage unless it was caused by her gross negligence.

Bailment for the Sole Benefit of the Bailee

Typically, in a bailment for the sole benefit of the bailee, the bailor lends an article to a person (the bailee) solely for that person's convenience and benefit. Because the bailee is borrowing the item for her or his own benefit, the bailee owes a duty to exercise the utmost care and will be liable for even slight negligence. Suppose that Allen asks to borrow Sumi's boat so that he can take his girlfriend sailing over the weekend. The bailment of the boat is for Allen's (the bailee's) sole benefit. If Allen fails to pay attention and runs the boat aground, damaging its hull, he is liable for the costs of repairing the boat.

Mutual-Benefit Bailments

The most common kind of bailment is a bailment for the mutual benefit of the bailee and the bailor. Mutual-benefit bailments involve some form of compensation for storing items or holding property. Because this type of bailment is contractual, it is often referred to as a *bailment for hire.* In a bailment for hire, the bailee must exercise ordinary care, which is the care that a reasonably prudent person would use under the circumstances. If the bailee fails to exercise reasonable care, he or she will be liable for ordinary negligence. For example, Allen leaves his car at a service station for an oil change. Because the service station will be paid to change Allen's oil, this is a mutual-benefit bailment. If the service station fails to put the correct amount of oil back into Allen's car and the engine is damaged as a result, the service station will be liable for failure to exercise reasonable care. Many lease arrangements that involve goods (leases were discussed in Chapters 20 through 23) also fall into this category of bailment once the lessee takes possession.

Rights of the Bailee

Certain rights are implicit in the bailment agreement. Generally, the bailee has the right to take possession, to utilize the property for accomplishing the purpose of the bailment, to receive some form of compensation (unless the bailment is intended to be gratuitous), and to limit her or his liability for the bailed goods. These rights of the bailee are present (with some limitations) in varying degrees in all bailment transactions.

Right of Possession A hallmark of the bailment agreement is that the bailee acquires the *right to control and possess the property temporarily.* The duration of a bailment depends on the terms of the agreement. If the bailment agreement specifies a particular period, then the bailment is continuous for that time period. Earlier termination by the bailor is a breach of contract (if the bailment involves consideration), and the bailee can recover damages from the bailor. If no duration is specified, the bailment ends when either the bailor or the bailee so demands and possession of the bailed property is returned to the bailor.

A bailee's right of possession, even though temporary, permits the bailee to recover damages from any third parties for damage or loss to the property. For example, No-Spot Dry Cleaners sends all suede leather garments to Cleanall Company for special processing. If Cleanall loses or damages any leather goods, No-Spot has the right to recover against Cleanall.

Right to Use Bailed Property Depending on the type of bailment and the terms of the bailment agreement, a bailee may also have a right to use the bailed property. When no provision is made, the extent of use depends on how necessary it is for the goods to be at the bailee's disposal for the ordinary purpose of the bailment to be carried out. When leasing drilling machinery, for example, the bailee is expected to use the equipment to drill. In contrast, when providing long-term storage for a car, the bailee is not expected to use the car because the ordinary purpose of a storage bailment does not include use of the property (unless an emergency dictates such use to protect the car).

Right of Compensation Except in a gratuitous bailment, a bailee has a right to be compensated as provided for in the bailment agreement, to be reimbursed for costs and services rendered in keeping the bailed property, or both. In mutual-benefit bailments, the amount of compensation is often stated in the bailment contract. For example, in the rental (bailment) of a car, the contract provides for charges on the basis of time, mileage, or a combination of the two, plus other possible charges. In nonrental bailments, such as when a car is left at a gas station for an oil change, the bailee earns a service charge for the work performed.

Gratuitous Bailments. Even in a gratuitous bailment, a bailee has a right to be reimbursed or compensated for costs incurred in keeping the bailed property. For example, Hetta loses her pet dog, which is found by Jesse. Jesse takes Hetta's dog to his home and feeds it. Even though he takes good care of the dog, it becomes ill, and he takes it to a veterinarian. Jesse pays the bill for the veterinarian's services and the medicine. He is normally entitled to be reimbursed by Hetta for these reasonable costs incurred in keeping her dog.

The Bailee's Lien. To enforce the right of compensation, the bailee has a right to place a *possessory lien* (claim) on the specific bailed property until she or he has been fully compensated. This lien on specific bailed property is sometimes referred to as a **bailee's lien,** or artisan's lien (discussed in Chapter 28). If the bailor refuses to pay or cannot pay the charges (compensation), in most states the bailee is entitled to foreclose on the lien. This means that the bailee can sell the property and be paid the amount owed for the bailment out of the proceeds, returning any excess to the bailor.

For example, Sarito takes his car to a parking garage to be stored while he is out of the country. He pays storage fees for two months in advance. When he returns six months later, the garage tenders Sarito his car, but because he is now unemployed, he cannot pay the fee. The garage has a right to retain possession of Sarito's car, exercising a bailee's lien. Unless Sarito can arrange for payment, the garage will normally be entitled to sell the car to obtain compensation for the storage.

Right to Limit Liability In ordinary bailments, bailees have the right to limit their liability as long as the limitations are called to the attention of the bailor and are not against public policy. It is essential that the bailor be informed of the limitation in some way. Thus, a sign in Nikolai's garage stating that Nikolai will not be responsible "for loss due to theft, fire, or vandalism" may or may not be held to be notice to the bailor. Whether the notice will be effective will depend on the size of the sign, its location, and any other circumstances affecting the likelihood that customers will see it.

Even when the bailor knows of the limitation, courts consider certain types of disclaimers of liability to be against public policy and therefore illegal. The courts carefully scrutinize *exculpatory clauses,* which limit a person's liability for her or his own wrongful acts, and in bailments they are often held to be illegal. This is particularly true in bailments for the mutual benefit of the bailor and the bailee. For example, the receipt from a parking garage—the bailee—expressly disclaims liability for any damage to parked cars, regardless of the cause. Because the bailee has attempted to exclude liability for the bailee's own negligence, including the parking attendant's negligence, the clause will likely be deemed unenforceable because it is against public policy.

Duties of the Bailee

The bailee has two basic responsibilities: (1) to take appropriate care of the property and (2) to surrender or dispose of the property at the end of the bailment. The bailee's duties are based on a mixture of tort law and contract law.

The Duty of Care The bailee must exercise reasonable care in preserving the bailed property (the duty of care was discussed in Chapter 7). As discussed earlier, what constitutes reasonable care in a bailment situation normally depends on the nature and specific circumstances of the bailment. In a bailment for the sole benefit of the bailor, for example, the bailee need exercise only a slight degree of care, whereas in a bailment for the sole benefit of the bailee, the bailee must exercise great care. Exhibit 47–1 illustrates the degree of care required of bailees in bailment relationships. Determining whether a bailee exercised an appropriate degree of care is usually a question of fact for the jury or judge (in a nonjury trial). A bailee's failure to exercise appropriate care in handling the bailor's property results in tort liability.

Duty to Return Bailed Property At the end of the bailment, the bailee normally must hand over the original property to either the bailor or someone the bailor designates or must otherwise dispose of it as directed.[10] This is usually a *contractual* duty arising from the bailment agreement (contract). Failure to give up possession at the time the bailment ends is a breach of contract and could result in the tort of conversion or an action based on bailee negligence. If the bailed property has been lost or is returned damaged,

10. If the bailment involves *fungible goods,* such as grain, then the bailee is not required to return the exact same goods to the bailor, but must return the same quantity of goods that are of like quality and grade.

EXHIBIT 47–1 • Degree of Care Required of a Bailee

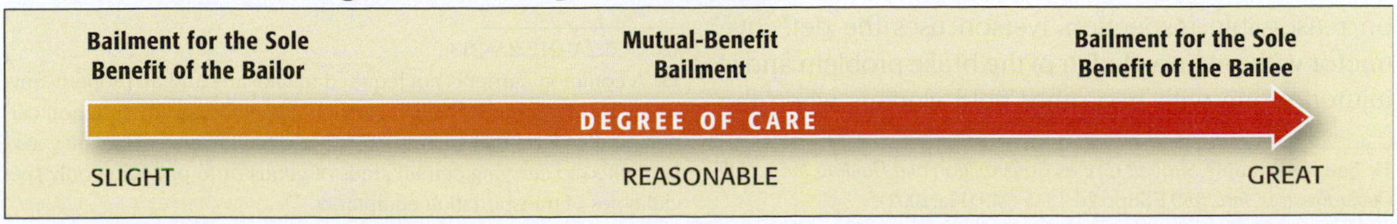

a court will presume that the bailee was negligent. The bailee's obligation is excused, however, if the goods or other tangible personal property were destroyed, lost, or stolen through no fault of the bailee (or claimed by a third party with a superior claim).

Because the bailee has a duty to return the bailed goods to the bailor, a bailee may be liable if the goods are given to the wrong person. Hence, a bailee must be satisfied that the person (other than the bailor) to whom the goods are being delivered is the actual owner or has authority from the owner to take possession of the goods. Should the bailee deliver in error, then the bailee may be liable for conversion or misdelivery.[11]

Duties of the Bailor

The duties of a bailor are essentially the same as the rights of a bailee. Obviously, a bailor has a duty to compensate the bailee either as agreed or as reimbursement for costs incurred by the bailee in keeping the bailed property. A bailor also has an all-encompassing duty to provide the bailee with goods or chattels that are free from known defects that could cause injury to the bailee.

Bailor's Duty to Reveal Defects The bailor's duty to reveal defects to the bailee translates into two rules:

1. In a *mutual-benefit bailment*, the bailor must notify the bailee of all known defects and any hidden defects that the bailor knows of or could have discovered with reasonable diligence and proper inspection.
2. In a *bailment for the sole benefit of the bailee*, the bailor must notify the bailee of any known defects.

The bailor's duty to reveal defects is based on a negligence theory of tort law. A bailor who fails to give the appropriate notice is liable to the bailee and to any other person who might reasonably be expected to come into contact with the defective article. Suppose that Rentco (the bailor) rents a tractor to Hal Iverson. The brake mechanism on the tractor is defective at the time the bailment is made. Although Rentco was unaware of the defect, it would have been discovered on reasonable inspection. Iverson uses the defective tractor without knowledge of the brake problem and is injured along with two other field workers when the tractor rolls out of control. In this situation, Rentco is liable for the injuries sustained by Iverson and the two others because it negligently failed to discover the defect and notify Iverson.

Warranty Liability for Defective Goods A bailor can also incur warranty liability based on contract law (see Chapter 23) for injuries resulting from the bailment of defective articles. Property leased by a bailor must be *fit for the intended purpose of the bailment.* The bailor's knowledge of or ability to discover any defects is immaterial. Warranties of fitness arise by law in sales contracts and have been applied by judicial interpretation in cases involving bailments "for hire." Article 2A of the Uniform Commercial Code (UCC) extends the implied warranties of merchantability and fitness for a particular purpose to bailments whenever those bailments include rights to use the bailed goods.[12]

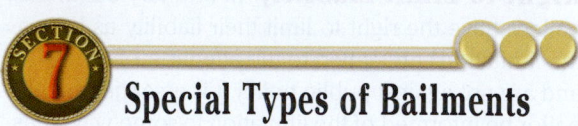

SECTION 7

Special Types of Bailments

Up to this point, our discussion has concerned ordinary bailments, in which bailees are expected to exercise ordinary care in the handling of bailed property. Some bailment transactions warrant special consideration. In these bailments, the bailee's duty of care is *extraordinary*—that is, the bailee's liability for loss or damage to the property is absolute—as is generally true for common carriers and innkeepers. Warehouse companies have the same duty of care as ordinary bailees; but like carriers, they are subject to extensive federal and state laws, including Article 7 of the UCC.

Common Carriers

Common carriers are publicly licensed to provide transportation services to the general public. In contrast, private carriers operate transportation facilities for a select clientele. A private carrier is not required to provide service to every person or company making a request. A common carrier, however, must arrange carriage for all who apply, within certain limitations.[13]

11. See, for example, *Sunbelt Cranes Construction and Hauling, Inc. v. Gulf Coast Erectors, Inc.*, 189 F.Supp.2d 1341 (M.D.Fla. 2002).

12. UCC 2A–212, 2A–213.

13. A common carrier is not required to take any and all property anywhere in all instances. Public regulatory agencies govern common carriers, and carriers may be restricted to geographic areas. They may also be limited to carrying certain kinds of goods or to providing only special types of transportation equipment.

The delivery of goods to a common carrier creates a bailment relationship between the shipper (bailor) and the common carrier (bailee). Unlike ordinary bailees, the common carrier is held to a standard of care based on *strict liability,* rather than reasonable care, in protecting the bailed personal property. This means that the common carrier is absolutely liable, regardless of due care, for all loss or damage to goods except damage caused by one of the following common law exceptions: (1) an act of God, (2) an act of a public enemy, (3) an order of a public authority, (4) an act of the shipper, or (5) the inherent nature of the goods.

Common carriers cannot contract away their liability for damaged goods. Subject to government regulations, however, they are permitted to limit their dollar liability to an amount stated on the shipment contract or rate filing.[14] This point is illustrated in the following case.

14. Federal laws require common carriers to offer shippers the opportunity to obtain higher dollar limits for loss by paying a higher fee for the transport.

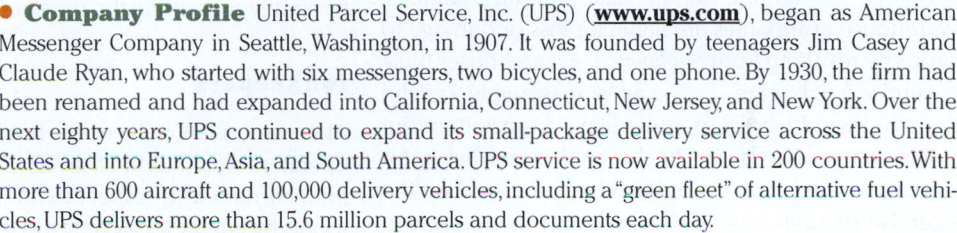

CASE 47.3 Treiber & Straub, Inc. v. United Parcel Service, Inc.

United States Court of Appeals, Seventh Circuit, 2007. 474 F.3d 379.

• **Company Profile** United Parcel Service, Inc. (UPS) (**www.ups.com**), began as American Messenger Company in Seattle, Washington, in 1907. It was founded by teenagers Jim Casey and Claude Ryan, who started with six messengers, two bicycles, and one phone. By 1930, the firm had been renamed and had expanded into California, Connecticut, New Jersey, and New York. Over the next eighty years, UPS continued to expand its small-package delivery service across the United States and into Europe, Asia, and South America. UPS service is now available in 200 countries. With more than 600 aircraft and 100,000 delivery vehicles, including a "green fleet" of alternative fuel vehicles, UPS delivers more than 15.6 million parcels and documents each day.

• **Background and Facts** Michael Straub is the president of Treiber & Straub, Inc., a fine-jewelry store in Wisconsin. To return a diamond ring to Norman Silverman Company, a wholesaler in California, Straub chose United Parcel Service, Inc. (UPS), and, through **www.ups.com**, arranged to ship the ring via "Next Day Air." To ship a package using the Web site, a customer has to click on two on-screen boxes to agree to "My UPS Terms and Conditions." Among these terms, UPS and its insurer, UPS Capital Insurance Agency, Inc., limit their liability and the amount of insurance coverage on packages to $50,000. UPS refuses to ship items of "unusual value"—those worth more than $50,000. The carrier and its insurer disclaim liability entirely for such items. The ring was worth $105,000. Undeterred, Straub opted for the maximum coverage and indicated on the air bill that the value was "$50,000 or less." UPS lost the ring. Treiber reimbursed the wholesaler for the full loss and filed a suit in a federal district court against UPS and its insurer to recover $50,000 under the insurance policy. The court issued a summary judgment in the defendants' favor based on the disclaimer. The plaintiff appealed to the U.S. Court of Appeals for the Seventh Circuit, arguing, among other things, that the disclaimer was "literally buried among all the other extensive terms and conditions on the vast UPS Web site."

• **Decision and Rationale** The U.S. Court of Appeals for the Seventh Circuit affirmed the judgment of the lower court. The appellate court held that the carrier's disclaimer was prominent enough. The court examined the relevant pages on the UPS Web site. On those pages, UPS initially limits its liability to $100 but offers customers an opportunity to buy insurance for coverage up to $50,000. If a customer wants to ship a package with a value of more than $50,000, UPS refuses to accept it or to insure it. UPS does not explain all of the details about these limits on a single page, but the court ruled that this "does not call for a different result in light of everything else that was available to the shipper." The limitation and the disclaimer are repeated several times on the Web site. This ensures "clear and reasonable notice" of the terms, to which a customer has to click twice in agreement to arrange a shipment. Further, the court reasoned that if UPS accepted packages

CASE CONTINUES

CASE 47.3 CONTINUED with values greater than $50,000 but insured them for no more than that amount,"it would distort the mix of claims it is insuring, skewing it toward the high-value end, necessitating a significant change in premiums. The risk of theft would also increase for packages with higher declared values." The court also pointed out that in this case, "by indicating on the air bill the insured value (of $50,000 or less) rather than the actual value" of the ring, "Treiber [& Straub] effectively breached the shipping contract."

- **What If the Facts Were Different?** *If Straub had claimed that he had not read the terms, would the result in this case have been different? Why or why not?*
- **The E-Commerce Dimension** *Did the fact that Treiber and UPS entered into their contract online affect the outcome in this case? What does their contract indicate about the use of the Internet to do business?*

Warehouse Companies

Warehousing is the business of providing storage of property for compensation. Like ordinary bailees, warehouse companies are liable for loss or damage to property resulting from *negligence.* A warehouser must "exercise such care . . . as a reasonably careful [person] would exercise under like circumstances but unless otherwise agreed he [or she] is not liable for damages which could not have been avoided by the exercise of such care."[15] A warehouse company can limit the dollar amount of liability, but the bailor must be given the option of paying an increased storage rate for a higher liability limit.[16]

Unlike ordinary bailees, a warehouse company can issue *documents of title*—in particular, *warehouse receipts*—and is subject to extensive government regulation, including Article 7 of the UCC.[17] A warehouse receipt describes the bailed property and the terms of the bailment contract. It can be negotiable or nonnegotiable, depending on how it is written. It is negotiable if its terms provide that the warehouse company will deliver the goods "to the bearer" of the receipt or "to the order of" a person named on the receipt.[18] The warehouse receipt represents the goods (that is, it indicates title) and hence has value and utility in financing commercial transactions.

For example, Ossip delivers 6,500 cases of canned corn to Chaney, the owner of a warehouse. Chaney issues a negotiable warehouse receipt payable "to bearer" and gives it to Ossip. Ossip sells and delivers the warehouse receipt to Better Foods, Inc. Better Foods is now the owner of the corn and can obtain the cases by simply presenting the warehouse receipt to Chaney.

Innkeepers

At common law, innkeepers, hotel owners, and similar operators were held to the same strict liability as common carriers with respect to property brought into the rooms by guests. Today, only those who provide lodging to the public for compensation as a *regular* business are covered under this rule of strict liability. Moreover, the rule applies only to those who are *guests,* as opposed to *lodgers.* A lodger is a permanent resident of the hotel or inn, whereas a guest is a traveler.

In many states, innkeepers can avoid strict liability for loss of guests' valuables and cash by providing a safe in which to keep them. Each guest must be clearly notified of the availability of such a safe. Statutes often limit the liability of innkeepers with regard to articles that are not kept in the safe or are of such a nature that they are not ordinarily kept in a safe. These statutes may limit the amount of monetary damages or even provide that the innkeeper incurs no liability in the absence of negligence. Commonly, hotels notify guests of the state laws governing the liability of innkeepers by posting a notice on the inside of the door of the hotel room or in some other prominent place within the room.

Normally, the innkeeper assumes no responsibility for the safety of a guest's automobile because the guest usually retains possession and control. If, however, the innkeeper provides parking facilities, and the guest's car is entrusted to the innkeeper or to an employee, the rules governing ordinary bailments will apply. *Concept Summary 47.3* reviews the rights and duties of bailees and bailors.

15. UCC 7–204(1).
16. UCC 7–204(2).
17. A *document of title* is defined in UCC 1–201(15) as any "document which in the regular course of business or financing is treated as adequately evidencing that the person in possession of it is entitled to receive, hold, and dispose of the document and the goods it covers." A *warehouse receipt* is a document of title issued by a person engaged in the business of storing goods for hire.
18. UCC 7–104.

CONCEPT SUMMARY 47.3
Rights and Duties of the Bailee and the Bailor

Concept	Description
RIGHTS OF A BAILEE (DUTIES OF A BAILOR)	1. The right of possession allows actions against third parties who damage or convert the bailed property and allows actions against the bailor for wrongful breach of the bailment. 2. A bailee has the right to be compensated or reimbursed for keeping bailed property. This right is based in contract or quasi contract. 3. If the compensation or reimbursement is not paid, the bailee has a right to place a possessory lien on the bailed property and to foreclose on the lien. 4. A bailee has the right to limit his or her liability. An ordinary bailee can limit the types of risk, monetary amount, or both, provided proper notice is given and the limitation is not against public policy. In special bailments, limitations on the types of risk are usually not allowed, but limitations on the monetary amount of loss are permitted by regulation.
DUTIES OF A BAILEE (RIGHTS OF A BAILOR)	1. A bailee must exercise reasonable care over property entrusted to her or him. A common carrier (special bailee) is held to a standard of care based on strict liability unless the bailed property is lost or destroyed due to (a) an act of God, (b) an act of a public enemy, (c) an act of a government authority, (d) an act of the shipper, or (e) the inherent nature of the goods. 2. Bailed goods in a bailee's possession must be returned to the bailor or be disposed of according to the bailor's directions. Failure to return the property gives rise to a presumption of negligence. 3. A bailee cannot use or profit from bailed goods except by agreement or in situations in which the use is implied to further the bailment purpose.

REVIEWING Personal Property and Bailments

Vanessa Denai purchased forty acres of land in rural Louisiana with a 1,600-square-foot house on it and a metal barn near the house. Denai later met Lance Finney, who had been seeking a small plot of rural property to rent. After several meetings, Denai invited Finney to live on a corner of her property in exchange for Finney's assistance in cutting wood and tending her property. Denai agreed to store Finney's sailboat in her barn. With Denai's consent, Finney constructed a concrete and oak foundation on Denai's property. Finney then purchased a 190-square-foot dome from Dome Baja for $3,395. The dome was shipped by Doty Express, a transportation company licensed to serve the public. When it arrived, Finney installed the dome frame and fabric exterior so that the dome was detachable from the foundation. A year after Finney installed the dome, Denai wrote Finney a note stating, "I've decided to give you four acres of land surrounding your dome as drawn on this map." This gift violated no local land-use restrictions. Using the information presented in the chapter, answer the following questions.

1. Is the dome real property or personal property? Explain.
2. Is Denai's gift of land to Finney a testamentary gift, a gift *causa mortis,* or a gift *inter vivos?*
3. What type of bailment relationship was created when Denai agreed to store Finney's boat? What degree of care was Denai required to exercise in storing the boat?
4. What standard of care applied to the shipment of the dome by Doty Express?

TERMS AND CONCEPTS

abandoned property 897
accession 894
bailee 898
bailee's lien 901
bailment 898
bailor 898
chattel 890
confusion 895
constructive delivery 893
estray statute 896
fixture 891
gift 892
gift *causa mortis* 894
gift *inter vivos* 894
lost property 895
mislaid property 895
personal property 890
property 890
real property 890
trade fixture 892

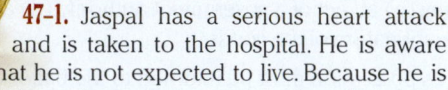

QUESTIONS AND CASE PROBLEMS

47-1. Jaspal has a serious heart attack and is taken to the hospital. He is aware that he is not expected to live. Because he is a bachelor with no close relatives nearby, Jaspal gives his car keys to his close friend, Friedrich, telling Friedrich that he is expected to die and that the car is Friedrich's. Jaspal survives the heart attack, but two months later he dies from pneumonia. Jaspal's uncle, Sam, the executor of Jaspal's estate, wants Friedrich to return the car. Friedrich refuses, claiming that the car was given to him by Jaspal as a gift. Discuss whether Friedrich will be required to return the car to Jaspal's estate.

47-2. QUESTION WITH SAMPLE ANSWER

Curtis is an executive on a business trip to the West Coast. He has driven his car on this trip and checks into the Hotel Ritz. The hotel has a guarded underground parking lot. Curtis gives his car keys to the parking lot attendant but fails to notify the attendant that his wife's $10,000 fur coat is in a box in the trunk. The next day, on checking out, he discovers that his car has been stolen. Curtis wants to hold the hotel liable for both the car and the coat. Discuss the probable success of his claim.

- **For a sample answer to Question 47-2, go to Appendix I at the end of this text.**

47-3. Bill Heise is a janitor for the First Mercantile Department Store. While walking to work, Bill finds an expensive watch lying on the curb. Bill gives the watch to his son, Otto. Two weeks later, Martin Avery, the true owner of the watch, discovers that Bill found the watch and demands it back from Otto. Explain who is entitled to the watch, and why.

47-4. Discuss the standard of care required from the bailee for the bailed property in the following situations, and determine whether the bailee breached that duty.

(a) Benedetto borrows Tom's lawn mower because his own lawn mower needs repair. Benedetto mows his front yard. To mow the backyard, he needs to move some hoses and lawn furniture. He leaves the mower in front of his house while doing so. When he returns, he discovers that the mower has been stolen.

(b) Atka owns a valuable speedboat. She is going on vacation and asks her neighbor, Regina, to store the boat in one stall of Regina's double garage. Regina consents, and the boat is moved into the garage. Regina, in need of some grocery items for dinner, drives to the store. When doing so, she leaves the garage door open, as is her custom. While she is at the store, the speedboat is stolen.

47-5. Orlando borrows a gasoline-driven lawn edger from his neighbor, Max. Max has not used the lawn edger for two years. Orlando has never owned a lawn edger and is not familiar with its use. Max previously used this edger often, and if he had made a reasonable inspection, he would have discovered that the blade was loose. Orlando is injured when the blade becomes detached while he is edging his yard.

(a) Can Orlando hold Max liable for his injuries?

(b) Would your answer be different if Orlando had rented the edger from Max and paid a fee? Explain.

47–6. Raul, David, and Javier immigrated to the United States from Colima, Mexico, to find jobs and help their families. When they learned that a mutual friend, Francisco, planned to travel to Colima, they asked him to deliver various sums, totaling more than $25,000, to their families. During customs inspections at the border, Francisco told U.S. customs officials that he was not carrying more than $10,000, when in fact, he carried more than $35,000. The government seized the cash and arrested Francisco. Raul, David, and Javier requested the government to return their cash, arguing that Francisco was a gratuitous bailee and that they still retained title. Are they right? Explain fully.

47–7. Gifts *Inter Vivos*. Thomas Stafford owned four promissory notes. Payments on the notes were deposited into a bank account in the names of Stafford and his daughter, June Zink, jointly with a note on the account indicating that if either Stafford or Zink should die, ownership would pass automatically to the survivor. Stafford kept control of the notes and would not allow Zink to spend any of the proceeds. He also kept the interest on the account. On one note, Stafford indorsed "Pay to the order of Thomas J. Stafford or June S. Zink, or the survivor." The payee on each of the other notes was "Thomas J. Stafford and June S. Zink, or the survivor." When Stafford died, Zink took possession of the notes, claiming that she was now the owner of the notes. Stafford's son, also Thomas, filed a suit in a Virginia state court against Zink, claiming that the notes were partly his. Thomas argued that their father had not made a valid gift *inter vivos* of the notes to Zink. In whose favor will the court rule? Why? [*Zink v. Stafford*, 509 S.E.2d 833 (Va. 1999)]

47–8. CASE PROBLEM WITH SAMPLE ANSWER

A. D. Lock owned Lock Hospitality, Inc., which in turn owned the Best Western Motel in Conway, Arkansas. Joe Terry and David Stocks were preparing the motel for renovation. As they were removing the ceiling tiles in room 118, with Lock present in the room, they noticed a dusty cardboard box near the heating and air-supply vent where it had apparently been concealed. Terry climbed a ladder to reach the box, opened it, and handed it to Stocks. The box was filled with more than $38,000 in old currency. Lock took possession of the box and its contents. Terry and Stocks filed a suit in an Arkansas state court against Lock and his corporation to obtain the money. Should the money be characterized as lost, mislaid, or abandoned property? To whom should the court award it? Explain. [*Terry v. Lock*, 37 S.W.3d 202 (Ark. 2001)]

- **To view a sample answer for Problem 47–8, go to this book's Web site at www.cengage.com/blaw/jentz, select "Chapter 47," and click on "Case Problem with Sample Answer."**

47–9. A QUESTION OF ETHICS

*Jason Crippen and Catharyn Campbell of Knoxville, Tennessee, were involved in a romantic relationship for many months. Their relationship culminated in an engagement on December 25, 2005, when Crippen placed an engagement ring on Campbell's finger and simultaneously proposed marriage. Campbell accepted the proposal, and the parties were engaged to be married. The engagement did not last, however. The parties broke up, their romantic relationship ended, and neither had any intent to marry the other. Crippen asked Campbell to return the ring. She refused. Crippen filed a suit in a Tennessee state court against Campbell to recover the ring. Both parties filed motions for summary judgment. The court ruled in Campbell's favor. Crippen appealed to a state intermediate appellate court. [*Crippen v. Campbell, *__ S.W.2d __ (Tenn.App. 2007)]*

(a) Under what reasoning could the court affirm the award of the ring to Campbell? On what basis could the court reverse the judgment and order Campbell to return the ring? (Hint: Is an engagement ring a completed gift immediately on its delivery?) Which principles do you support and why?

(b) Should the court determine who was responsible for breaking off the engagement before awarding ownership of the ring? Explain.

(c) If, instead of Crippen, one of his creditors had sought the ring in satisfaction of one of his debts, how should the court have ruled? Why?

47–10. VIDEO QUESTION

Go to this text's Web site at **www.cengage.com/blaw/jentz** and select "Chapter 47." Click on "Video Questions" and view the video titled *Personal Property and Bailments*. Then answer the following questions.

(a) What type of bailment is discussed in the video?

(b) What were Vinny's duties with regard to the rug-cleaning machine? What standard of care should apply?

(c) Did Vinny exercise the appropriate degree of care? Why or why not? How would a court decide this issue?

LAW ON THE WEB

For updated links to resources available on the Web, as well as a variety of other materials, visit this text's Web site at

www.cengage.com/blaw/jentz

To learn about whether a married person has ownership rights in a gift received by his or her spouse, go to Scott Law Firm's Web page at

www.scottlawfirm.com/property.htm

For a discussion of the origins of the term *bailment* and how bailment relationships have been defined, go to

www.lectlaw.com/def/b005.htm

Legal Research Exercises on the Web

Go to **www.cengage.com/blaw/jentz**, the Web site that accompanies this text. Select "Chapter 47" and click on "Internet Exercises." There you will find the following Internet research exercises that you can perform to learn more about the topics covered in this chapter.

Internet Exercise 47–1: Legal Perspective
Lost Property

Internet Exercise 47–2: Management Perspective
Bailments

CHAPTER 48

Real Property and Landlord-Tenant Relationships

From the earliest times, property has provided a means for survival. Primitive peoples lived off the fruits of the land, eating the vegetation and wildlife. Later, as the wildlife was domesticated and the vegetation cultivated, property provided pastures and farmland. In the twelfth and thirteenth centuries, the power of feudal lords was exemplified by the amount of land that they held. After the age of feudalism passed, property continued to be an indicator of family wealth and social position. In the Western world, the protection of an individual's right to his or her property has become one of our most important rights.

In this chapter, we first look at the nature of ownership rights in real property. We then examine the legal requirements involved in the transfer of real property, including the kinds of rights that are transferred by various types of deeds; the procedures used in the sale of real estate; and a way in which real property can, under certain conditions, be transferred merely by possession. Realize that real property rights are never absolute. There is a higher right—that of the government to take, for compensation, private land for public use. This chapter discusses this right, as well as other restrictions on the ownership of property. We conclude the chapter with a discussion of landlord-tenant relationships.

SECTION 1 The Nature of Real Property

As discussed in Chapter 47, *real property* consists of land and the buildings, plants, and trees that it contains. Personal property is movable; real property is immovable. Real property usually means land and structures, but it also includes airspace and subsurface rights, plant life and vegetation, and fixtures (as discussed in Chapter 47).

Land and Structures

Land includes the soil on the surface of the earth and the natural products or artificial structures that are attached to it. Land further includes all the waters contained on or under its surface and much, but not necessarily all, of the airspace above it. The exterior boundaries of land extend down to the center of the earth and up to the farthest reaches of the atmosphere (subject to certain qualifications).

Airspace and Subsurface Rights

The owner of real property has relatively exclusive rights to both the airspace above the land and the soil and minerals underneath it. Any limitations on either airspace rights or subsurface rights, called *encumbrances*, normally must be indicated on the document that transfers title at the time of purchase. The ways in which ownership rights in real property can be limited will be examined in detail later in this chapter.

Airspace Rights Early cases involving airspace rights dealt with such matters as whether a telephone wire could be run across a person's property when the wire did not touch any of the property[1] and whether a bullet shot over a person's land constituted trespass.[2] Today, disputes concerning airspace rights may involve the right of commercial and private planes to fly over property and the right of individuals and governments to seed clouds and produce artificial rain. Flights over private land normally do not violate property rights unless the flights are so low and so frequent that they directly interfere with the owner's enjoyment and use of the land.

Subsurface Rights In many states, land ownership can be separated from ownership of its subsurface. In other words, the owner of the surface may sell subsurface rights to another person. Subsurface rights can be extremely valuable, as these rights include the ownership of minerals, oil, or natural gas. But a subsurface owner's rights would be of little value if he or she could not use the surface to exercise those rights. Hence, a subsurface owner will have a right (called a *profit*, discussed later in this chapter) to go onto the surface of the land to, for example, find and remove minerals.

When the ownership is separated into surface and subsurface rights, each owner can pass title to what she or he owns without the consent of the other owner. Of course, conflicts may arise between surface and subsurface owners when attempts are made to excavate below the surface. One party's interest may become subservient (secondary) to the other party's interest either by statute or case law. At common law and generally today, if the owners of the subsurface rights excavate, they are absolutely liable if their excavation causes the surface to collapse. Depending on the circumstances, the excavators may also be liable for any damage to structures on the land. Many states have statutes that extend excavators' liability to include damage to structures on the property. Typically, these statutes provide exact guidelines as to the requirements for excavations of various depths.

Plant Life and Vegetation

Plant life, both natural and cultivated, is also considered to be real property. In many instances, the natural vegetation, such as trees, adds greatly to the value of realty. When a parcel of land is sold and the land has growing crops on it, the sale includes the crops, unless otherwise specified in the sales contract. When crops are sold by themselves, however, they are considered to be personal property or goods, as noted in Chapter 47. Consequently, the sale of crops is a sale of goods and thus is governed by the Uniform Commercial Code (UCC) rather than by real property law.

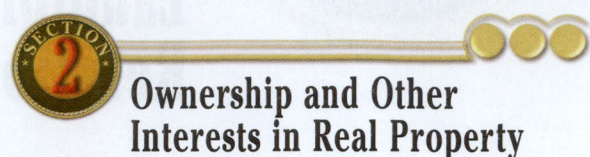

SECTION 2 Ownership and Other Interests in Real Property

Ownership of property is an abstract concept that cannot exist independently of the legal system. No one can actually possess, or *hold,* a piece of land, the air above, the earth below, and all the water contained on it. One can only possess *rights* in real property. Numerous rights are involved in real property ownership, which is why property ownership is often viewed as a bundle of rights. These rights include the right to possess the property and the right to dispose of the property—by sale, gift, rental, and lease, for example. Traditionally, ownership interests in real property were referred to as *estates in land,* which include fee simple estates, life estates, and leasehold estates. We examine these estates in land, forms of concurrent ownership, and certain other interests in real property that is owned by others in the following subsections.

Ownership in Fee Simple

A person who holds the entire bundle of rights is said to be the owner in **fee simple absolute.** In a fee simple absolute, the owner has the greatest aggregation of rights, privileges, and power possible. The owner can give the property away or dispose of the property by deed (the instrument used to transfer property, as discussed later in this chapter) or by will (discussed in Chapter 50). When there is no will, the fee simple passes to the owner's legal heirs on her or his death. A fee simple absolute is potentially infinite in duration and is assigned forever to a person and her or his heirs without limitation or condition.[3] The

1. *Butler v. Frontier Telephone Co.,* 186 N.Y. 486, 79 N.E. 716 (1906). Stringing a wire across someone's property violates the airspace rights of that person. Leaning walls and projecting eave spouts and roofs also violate the airspace rights of the property owner.

2. *Herrin v. Sutherland,* 74 Mont. 587, 241 P. 328 (1925). Shooting over a person's land normally constitutes trespass.

3. Note that in *fee simple defeasible,* ownership in fee simple will automatically terminate if a stated event occurs, such as when property is conveyed (transferred) to a school board only as long as it is used for school purposes. In addition, the fee simple may be subject to a *condition subsequent,* meaning that if a stated event occurs, the prior owner of the property can bring an action to regain possession of the property.

owner has the right of *exclusive* possession and use of the property.

The rights that accompany a fee simple absolute include the right to use the land for whatever purpose the owner sees fit. Of course, other laws, including applicable zoning, noise, and environmental laws, may limit the owner's ability to use the property in certain ways.

In the following case, the court had to decide whether the noise—rock and roll music, conversation, and clacking pool balls—coming from a local bar (called a "saloon" during the days of cowboys in the United States) unreasonably interfered with a neighboring property owner's rights.

CASE 48.1 Biglane v. Under the Hill Corp.

Mississippi Supreme Court, 2007. 949 So.2d 9.
www.mssc.state.ms.us[a]

Background and Facts In 1967, Nancy and James Biglane bought and refurbished a building at 27 Silver Street in Natchez, Mississippi, and opened the lower portion as a gift shop. In 1973, Andre Farish and Paul O'Malley bought the building next door, at 25 Silver Street, and opened the Natchez Under the Hill Saloon. Later, the Biglanes converted the upper floors of their building into an apartment and moved in. Despite installing insulated walls and windows, locating the bedroom on the side of the building away from the Saloon, and placing the air-conditioning unit on the side nearest the Saloon, the Biglanes had a problem: the noise of the Saloon kept them wide awake at night. During the summer, the Saloon, which had no air-conditioning, opened its windows and doors, and live music echoed up and down the street. The Biglanes asked the Saloon to turn the music down, and it was. Thicker windows were installed, the loudest band was replaced, and the other bands were asked to keep their output below a certain level of decibels. Still dissatisfied, the Biglanes filed a suit in a Mississippi state court against the Saloon. The court enjoined the defendant from opening doors or windows when music was playing and ordered it to prevent its patrons from loitering in the street. Both parties appealed to the Mississippi Supreme Court.

Decision and Rationale The Mississippi Supreme Court affirmed the lower court's injunction: "One landowner may not use his land so as to unreasonably annoy, inconvenience, or harm others." The state supreme court pointed out that an owner may be subject to liability when the owner's conduct is "an invasion of another's interest in the private use and enjoyment of land and that invasion is * * * intentional and unreasonable." Reasonable use of property does not include "obnoxious noises, which in turn result in a material injury to owners of property in the vicinity, causing them to suffer substantial annoyance, inconvenience, and discomfort." An owner does not have to be driven from his or her property. The interference can be sufficient if "the enjoyment of life and property is rendered materially uncomfortable and annoying." Each case is to be decided on its own facts, including the location of the property and the surrounding circumstances. Here, the court balanced the interests of the Biglanes and the Saloon "in a quest for an equitable remedy that allowed the couple to enjoy their private apartment * * * while protecting a popular business and tourist attraction from over-regulation."

The Ethical Dimension *At one point in their dispute, the Biglanes blocked off two parking lots that served the Saloon. Was this an unreasonable interference with the Saloon's rights? Explain.*

The Legal Environment Dimension *Could repulsive odors emanating from a neighbor's property constitute unreasonable interference with a property owner's rights? Why or why not?*

a. In the right-hand column, under "Supreme Court," click on "Decisions." When that page opens, in the pull-down menu under "Select Year," select "2007." Under "Alphabetical Party (by Party Last Name)," select "B," and click on "Submit." Scroll down the list and click on the case name to access the opinion.

Life Estates

A **life estate** is an estate that lasts for the life of some specified individual. A **conveyance,** or transfer of real property, "to A for his life" creates a life estate.[4] In a life estate, the life tenant's ownership rights cease to exist on the life tenant's death. The life tenant has the right to use the land, provided no **waste** (injury to the land) is committed. In other words, the life tenant cannot use the land in a manner that would adversely affect its value. The life tenant can use the land to harvest crops or, if mines and oil wells are already on the land, can extract minerals and oil from it, but the life tenant cannot exploit the land by creating new wells or mines.

The life tenant has the right to mortgage the life estate and create liens, *easements* (giving others the right to use the property, as discussed on page 914), and leases; but none can extend beyond the life of the tenant. In addition, with few exceptions, the owner of a life estate has an exclusive right to possession during his or her lifetime.

Along with these rights, the life tenant also has some duties—to keep the property in repair and to pay property taxes. In sum, the owner of the life estate has the same rights as a fee simple owner except that she or he must maintain the value of the property during her or his tenancy, less the decrease in value resulting from the normal use of the property allowed by the life tenancy.

Concurrent Ownership

Persons who share ownership rights simultaneously in particular property (including real property and personal property) are said to be concurrent owners. There are two principal types of **concurrent ownership:** *tenancy in common* and *joint tenancy.* Concurrent ownership rights can also be held in a tenancy by the entirety or as community property, although these types of concurrent ownership are less common.

Tenancy in Common The term **tenancy in common** refers to a form of co-ownership in which each of two or more persons owns an undivided interest in the property. The interest is undivided because each tenant has rights in the whole property. On the death of a tenant in common, that tenant's interest in the property passes to her or his heirs.

For example, four friends purchase a condominium unit in Hawaii together as tenants in common. This means that each of them has an ownership interest (one-fourth) in the whole. If one of the four owners, Trey, dies a year after the purchase, his ownership interest passes to his heirs (his wife and children, for example) rather than to the other tenants in common.

Unless the co-tenants have agreed otherwise, a tenant in common can transfer her or his interest in the property to another without the consent of the remaining co-owners. Generally, it is presumed that a co-tenancy is a tenancy in common unless there is a clear intention to establish a joint tenancy (discussed next).

Joint Tenancy In a **joint tenancy,** each of two or more persons owns an undivided interest in the property, but a deceased joint tenant's interest passes to the surviving joint tenant or tenants. The right of a surviving joint tenant to inherit a deceased joint tenant's ownership interest—referred to as a *right of survivorship*—distinguishes a joint tenancy from a tenancy in common. Suppose that Jerrold and Eva are married and purchase a house as joint tenants. The title to the house clearly expresses the intent to create a joint tenancy because it says "to Jerrold and Eva as joint tenants with right of survivorship." Jerrold has three children from a prior marriage. If Jerrold dies, his interest in the house automatically passes to Eva rather than to his children from the prior marriage.

Although a joint tenant can transfer her or his rights by sale or gift to another without the consent of the other joint tenants, doing so terminates the joint tenancy. In such a situation, the person who purchases the property or receives it as a gift becomes a tenant in common, not a joint tenant. For example, three brothers, Brody, Saul, and Jacob, own a parcel as joint tenants. Brody is experiencing financial difficulties and sells his interest in the property to Beth. The sale terminates the joint tenancy, and now Beth, Saul, and Jacob hold the property as tenants in common.

A joint tenant's interest can also be levied against (seized by court order) to satisfy the tenant's judgment creditors. If this occurs, the joint tenancy terminates, and the remaining owners hold the property as tenants in common. (Judgment creditors can also seize the interests of tenants in a tenancy in common.)

Tenancy by the Entirety A **tenancy by the entirety** is a less common form of ownership that typically is created by a conveyance (transfer) of real property to a husband and wife. It differs from a joint

4. A less common type of life estate is created by the conveyance "to A for the life of B." This is known as an estate *pur autre vie*—that is, an estate for the duration of the life of another.

tenancy in that neither spouse may separately transfer his or her interest during his or her lifetime unless the other spouse consents. In some states in which statutes give the wife the right to convey her property, this form of concurrent ownership has effectively been abolished. A divorce, either spouse's death, or mutual agreement will terminate a tenancy by the entirety.

Community Property Only a limited number of states[5] allow property to be owned by a married couple as **community property.** If property is held as community property, each spouse technically owns an undivided one-half interest in the property. This type of ownership applies to most property acquired by the husband or the wife during the course of the marriage. It generally does not apply to property acquired prior to the marriage or to property acquired by gift or inheritance during the marriage. After a divorce, community property is divided equally in some states and according to the discretion of the court in other states.

Leasehold Estates

A **leasehold estate** is created when a real property owner or lessor (landlord) agrees to convey the right to possess and use the property to a lessee (tenant) for a certain period of time. In every leasehold estate, the tenant has a *qualified* right to exclusive, though *temporary*, possession (qualified by the landlord's right to enter onto the premises to ensure that the tenant is not causing damage to the property). The tenant can use the land—for example, by harvesting crops—but cannot injure it by such activities as cutting down timber for sale or extracting oil.

The respective rights and duties of the landlord and tenant that arise under a lease agreement will be discussed in detail later in this chapter. Here, we look at the types of leasehold estates, or tenancies, that can be created when real property is leased.

Fixed-Term Tenancy or Tenancy for Years A **fixed-term tenancy,** also called a *tenancy for years*, is created by an express contract by which property is leased for a specified period of time, such as a month, a year, or a period of years. Signing a one-year lease to occupy an apartment, for instance, creates a tenancy for years. Note that the term need not be specified by date and can be conditioned on the occurrence of an event, such as leasing a cabin for the summer or an apartment during Mardi Gras. At the end of the period specified in the lease, the lease ends (without notice), and possession of the property returns to the lessor. If the tenant dies during the period of the lease, the lease interest passes to the tenant's heirs as personal property. Often, leases include renewal or extension provisions.

Periodic Tenancy A **periodic tenancy** is created by a lease that does not specify how long it is to last but does specify that rent is to be paid at certain intervals. This type of tenancy is automatically renewed for another rental period unless properly terminated. For example, Jewel, LLC, enters into a lease with Capital Properties. The lease states, "Rent is due on the tenth day of every month." This provision creates a periodic tenancy from month to month. This type of tenancy can also extend from week to week or from year to year. A periodic tenancy sometimes arises when a landlord allows a tenant under a tenancy for years to *hold over* (retain possession after the lease term ends) and continue paying monthly or weekly rent.

Under the common law, to terminate a periodic tenancy, the landlord or tenant must give at least one period's notice to the other party. If the tenancy is month to month, for example, one month's notice must be given. State statutes often require a different period for notice of termination in a periodic tenancy, however.

Tenancy at Will In a **tenancy at will,** either the landlord or the tenant can terminate the tenancy without notice. This type of tenancy can arise if a landlord rents property to a tenant "for as long as both agree" or allows a person to live on the premises without paying rent. Tenancy at will is rare today because most state statutes require a landlord to provide some period of notice to terminate a tenancy (as previously noted). States may also require a landowner to have sufficient cause (reason) to end a residential tenancy. Certain events, such as the death of either party or the voluntary commission of *waste* (harm to the premises) by the tenant, automatically terminate a tenancy at will.

Tenancy at Sufferance The mere possession of land without right is called a **tenancy at sufferance.** A tenancy at sufferance is not a true tenancy because it is created when a tenant *wrongfully* retains possession of property. Whenever a tenancy for years or a

5. These states include Alaska, Arizona, California, Idaho, Louisiana, Nevada, New Mexico, Texas, Washington, and Wisconsin. Puerto Rico allows property to be owned as community property as well.

periodic tenancy ends and the tenant continues to retain possession of the premises without the owner's permission, a tenancy at sufferance is created.

Nonpossessory Interests

In contrast to the types of property interests just described, some interests in land do not include any rights to possess the property. These interests, known as **nonpossessory interests,** include *easements, profits,* and *licenses.* Nonpossessory interests are basically interests in real property owned by others.

An **easement** is the right of a person to make limited use of another person's real property without taking anything from the property. An easement, for example, can be the right to walk across another's property. In contrast, a **profit** is the right to go onto land owned by another and take away some part of the land itself or some product of the land. For example, Akmed, the owner of Sandy View, gives Ann the right to go there and remove all the sand and gravel that she needs for her cement business. Ann has a profit.

Easements and profits can be classified as either *appurtenant* or *in gross.* Because easements and profits are similar and the same rules apply to both, we discuss them together.

Easement or Profit Appurtenant An easement or profit *appurtenant* arises when the owner of one piece of land has a right to go onto (or remove things from) an adjacent piece of land owned by another. The land that is benefited by the easement is called the *dominant estate,* and the land that is burdened is called the *servient estate.* Because easements appurtenant are intended to *benefit the land,* they run with (are conveyed with) the land when it is transferred.[6] Suppose that Owen has a right to drive his car across Green's land, which is adjacent to Owen's property. This right-of-way over Green's property is an easement appurtenant to Owen's land and can be used only by Owen. If Owen sells his land, the easement runs with the land to benefit the new owner.

Easement or Profit in Gross An easement or profit *in gross* exists when someone who does not own an adjacent tract of land has a right to use or take things from another's land. These easements are intended to *benefit a particular person or business,* not a particular piece of land, and cannot be transferred. For example, Avery owns a parcel of land with a marble quarry. Avery conveys to Classic Stone Corporation the right to come onto her land and remove up to five hundred pounds of marble per day. Classic Stone owns a profit in gross and cannot transfer this right to another. Similarly, when a utility company is granted an easement to run its power lines across another's property, it obtains an easement in gross.

Creation of an Easement or Profit Most easements and profits are created by an express grant in a contract, deed, or will. This allows the parties to include terms defining the extent and length of time of use. In some situations, an easement or profit can also be created without an express agreement.

An easement or profit may arise by *implication* when the circumstances surrounding the division of a parcel of property imply its creation. For example, Barrow divides a parcel of land that has only one well for drinking water. If Barrow conveys the half without a well to Dean, a profit by implication arises because Dean needs drinking water.

An easement may also be created by *necessity.* An easement by necessity does not require division of property for its existence. A person who rents an apartment, for example, has an easement by necessity in the private road leading up to the dwelling.

An easement arises by *prescription* when one person exercises an easement, such as a right-of-way, on another person's land without the landowner's consent, and the use is apparent and continues for a period of time equal to the applicable statute of limitations. (In much the same way, title to property may be obtained by *adverse possession,* which is discussed later in this chapter.)

Termination of an Easement or Profit An easement or profit can be terminated or extinguished in several ways. The simplest way is to deed it back to the owner of the land that is burdened by it. Another way is to abandon it and create evidence of intent to relinquish the right to use it. Mere nonuse will not extinguish an easement or profit *unless the nonuse is accompanied by an overt act showing the intent to abandon.* Also, if the owner of an easement or profit becomes the owner of the property burdened by it, then it is merged into the property.

6. See, for example, *Webster v. Ragona,* 7 A.D.3d 850, 776 N.Y.S.2d 347 (2004).

CONCEPT SUMMARY 48.1
Interests in Real Property

Type of Interest	Description
Ownership Interests	1. *Fee simple absolute*—The most complete form of ownership. 2. *Life estate*—An estate that lasts for the life of a specified individual. 3. *Concurrent interests*—When two or more persons hold title to property together, concurrent ownership exists. a. A tenancy in common exists when two or more persons own an undivided interest in property; on a tenant's death, that tenant's property interest passes to his or her heirs. b. A joint tenancy exists when two or more persons own an undivided interest in property, with a right of survivorship; on the death of a joint tenant, that tenant's property interest transfers to the remaining tenant(s), not to the heirs of the deceased. c. A tenancy by the entirety is a form of co-ownership between a husband and wife that is similar to a joint tenancy, except that a spouse cannot separately transfer her or his interest during her or his lifetime. d. Community property is a form of co-ownership between a husband and wife in which each spouse technically owns an undivided one-half interest in property acquired during the marriage. This type of ownership occurs in only a few states.
Leasehold Interests	A leasehold interest, or estate, is an interest in real property that is held for only a limited period of time, as specified in the lease agreement. Types of tenancies relating to leased property include the following: 1. *Fixed-term tenancy (tenancy for years)*—Tenancy for a period of time stated by express contract. 2. *Periodic tenancy*—Tenancy for a period determined by the frequency of rent payments; automatically renewed unless proper notice is given. 3. *Tenancy at will*—Tenancy for as long as both parties agree; no notice of termination is required. 4. *Tenancy at sufferance*—Possession of land without legal right.
Nonpossessory Interests	Interests that involve the right to use real property but not to possess it. Easements, profits, and licenses are nonpossessory interests.

Licenses In the context of real property, a **license** is the revocable right of a person to come onto another person's land. It is a personal privilege that arises from the consent of the owner of the land and can be revoked by the owner. A ticket to attend a movie at a theater is an example of a license. Assume that a Broadway theater owner issues a ticket to see a play to Alena. If Alena is refused entry because she is improperly dressed, she has no right to force her way into the theater. The ticket is only a revocable license, not a conveyance of an interest in property. (See *Concept Summary 48.1* for a review of the interests that can exist in real property.)

In essence, a license grants a person the authority to enter the land of another and perform a specified act or series of acts without obtaining any permanent interest in the land. What happens when a person with a license exceeds the authority granted and undertakes an action that is not permitted? That was the central issue in the following case.

CASE 48.2 Roman Catholic Church of Our Lady of Sorrows v. Prince Realty Management, LLC

New York Supreme Court, Appellate Division, Second Department, 2008.
47 A.D.3d 909, 850 N.Y.S.2d 569.

- **Background and Facts** The Roman Catholic Church of Our Lady of Sorrows (the Church) and Prince Realty Management, LLC (Prince), own adjoining property in Queens County, New York. On August 19, 2005, the parties entered into an agreement by which the Church granted Prince a three-month license to use a three-foot strip of its property immediately adjacent to Prince's property. The license specifically authorized Prince to remove an existing chainlink fence on the licensed strip and to "put up plywood panels surrounding the construction site, including the [licensed strip]." The license also required that Prince restore the boundary line between the properties with a new brick fence. The purpose of the license was to allow Prince to erect a temporary plywood fence in order to protect Prince's property during the construction of a new building. During the term of the license, Prince installed structures consisting of steel piles and beams on the licensed property. The Church objected to the installation of these structures and repeatedly demanded that they be removed. The Church commenced an action to recover damages for breach of the license and for trespass. The trial court concluded that the Church had made a *prima facie* case showing that the structures were placed on its property by the defendant in violation of the license, and that Prince had failed to dispute the plaintiff's claim that it had violated the agreement. Prince appealed.

- **Decision and Rationale** The New York appellate court held that the license did not permit the adjoining property owner to install structures consisting of steel piles and beams on the licensed strip of property. The reviewing court pointed out that "a license, within the context of real property law, grants the licensee a revocable non-assignable privilege to do one or more acts upon the land of a licensor, without granting possession of any interest herein. A license is the authority to do a particular act or series of acts upon another's land, which would amount to a trespass without such permission." The evidence was clear that the license allowed only for temporary structures. The defendant nonetheless installed structures consisting of steel piles and beams on the licensed property. "The plaintiff * * * established as a matter of law that the defendant's installation of these structures constituted a trespass regardless of whether they were subsequently removed."

- **The Ethical Dimension** *When the Church requested that the steel piles and beams be removed, the defendant resisted, but eventually did remove them. Was it still appropriate for the Church to file this lawsuit? Explain your answer.*

- **The Legal Environment Dimension** *The Church sued for damages. What would be an appropriate calculation of those damages?*

SECTION 3 Transfer of Ownership

Ownership of real property can pass from one person to another in a number of ways. Commonly, ownership interests in land are transferred by sale, and the terms of the transfer are specified in a real estate sales contract. Often, real estate brokers or agents who are licensed by the state assist the buyers and sellers during the sales transaction. Real property ownership can also be transferred by gift, by will or inheritance, by possession, or by eminent domain. In the subsections that follow, we focus primarily on voluntary sales of real property. We then consider adverse possession, which is an involuntary method of transferring title to real property. Eminent domain is discussed later in this chapter, and transfers by will or inheritance on the death of the owner will be discussed in Chapter 50.

Listing Agreements

In a typical real estate transaction, the seller employs a real estate agent to find a buyer for the property by entering into a listing agreement with the agent. The listing agreement specifies the duration of the listing with that real estate agent, the terms under which the seller will sell the property, and the amount of commission the seller will pay. There are different types of listing agreements. If the contract gives the agent an exclusive right to sell the property, then only that real estate agent is authorized to sell the property for a specified period of time. For example, a seller might give the agent thirty days of exclusive agency. If a buyer is found within the thirty-day period, the agent will be paid the full amount of the commission even if the agent was not responsible for finding that buyer. After the thirty-day period ends, if another real estate agent procures a buyer, the listing agent may have to split the commission. In an open listing, the seller agrees to pay a commission to the real estate agent who brings in a buyer. An open listing is nonexclusive, and thus agents with other real estate firms may attempt to find a buyer and share in the commission with the listing agent.

Although many sales of real estate involve listing agreements, it is not necessary for a property owner to list the property with a real estate agent. Many owners offer their properties for sale directly without an agent. The ability to advertise real properties for sale via the Internet has made it easier for an owner to find a buyer without using an agent. Because an agent is not essential, listing agreements are not shown in Exhibit 48–1, which summarizes the steps involved in any sale of real property.

Real Estate Sales Contracts

The sale of real estate is in some ways similar to the sale of goods because it involves a transfer of ownership, often with specific warranties. In a sale of real estate, however, certain formalities are observed that are not required in a sale of goods. The sale of real

EXHIBIT 48–1 • Steps Involved in the Sale of Real Estate

BUYER'S PURCHASE OFFER
Buyer offers to purchase Seller's property. The offer may be conditioned on Buyer's ability to obtain financing, on satisfactory inspections of the premises, on title examination, and the like. Included with the offer is earnest money, which will be placed in an escrow account.

SELLER'S RESPONSE
If Seller accepts Buyer's offer, then a contract is formed. Seller could also reject the offer or make a counteroffer that modifies Buyer's terms. Buyer may accept or reject Seller's counteroffer or make a counteroffer that modifies Seller's terms.

PURCHASE AND SALE AGREEMENT
Once an offer or a counteroffer is accepted, a purchase and sale agreement is formed.

TITLE EXAMINATION AND INSURANCE
The examiner investigates and verifies Seller's rights in the property and discloses any claims or interests held by others. Buyer (and/or Seller) may purchase title insurance to protect against a defect in title.

FINANCING
Buyer may seek a mortgage loan to finance the purchase. Buyer agrees to grant lender an interest in the property as security for Buyer's indebtedness.

INSPECTION
Buyer has the property inspected for any physical problems, such as major structural or mechanical defects and insect infestation.

ESCROW
Buyer's purchase funds (including earnest money) are held in an escrow account by an escrow agent (such as a title company or a bank). This agent holds the deed transferring title received from Seller and any funds received from Buyer until all conditions of the sale have been met.

CLOSING
The escrow agent transfers the deed to Buyer and the proceeds of the sale to Seller. The proceeds are the purchase price less any amount already paid by Buyer and any closing costs to be paid by Seller. Included in the closing costs are fees charged for services performed by the lender, escrow agent, and title examiner. The purchase and sale of the property are complete.

estate is a complicated transaction. Usually, after substantial negotiation between the parties (offers, counteroffers, responses), the parties enter into a detailed contract setting forth their agreement. A contract for a sale of land includes such terms as the purchase price, the type of deed the buyer will receive, the condition of the premises, and any items that will be included.

Contingencies Unless the buyer pays cash for the property, the buyer must obtain financing through a mortgage loan. (As discussed in Chapter 29, a *mortgage* is a loan made by an individual or institution, such as a banking institution or trust company, for which the property is given as security.) Real estate sales contracts are often made contingent on the buyer obtaining financing at or below a specified rate of interest. The contract may also be contingent on the buyer selling other real property, the seller obtaining a survey and title insurance, and the property passing one or more inspections. Normally, the buyer is responsible for having the premises inspected for physical or mechanical defects and for insect infestation.

Closing Date and Escrow The contract usually fixes a date for performance, or **closing,** that is frequently four to twelve weeks after the contract is signed. On this day, the seller conveys the property to the buyer by delivering the deed to the buyer in exchange for payment of the purchase price. Deposits toward the purchase price normally are held in a special account, called an **escrow account,** until all of the conditions of sale have been met. Once the closing takes place, the funds remaining in the escrow account (after payments have been made to the escrow agency, title insurance company, and lien holders) are transferred to the seller. The *escrow agent,* which may be a title company, bank, or special escrow company, acts as a neutral party in the sales transaction and facilitates the sale by allowing the buyer and seller to close the transaction without having to exchange documents and funds.

Implied Warranties in the Sale of New Homes The common law rule of *caveat emptor* ("let the buyer beware") held that the seller of a home made no warranty as to its soundness or fitness (unless the contract or deed stated otherwise). Today, however, most states imply a warranty—the **implied warranty of habitability**—in the sale of new homes. The seller of a new house warrants that it will be fit for human habitation even if the deed or contract of sale does not include such a warranty.

Essentially, the seller is warranting that the house is in reasonable working order and is of reasonably sound construction. To recover damages for breach of the implied warranty of habitability, the purchaser of the house is required to prove only that it is somehow defective and that the defect caused the damage. Thus, under this theory, the seller of a new home is in effect a guarantor of its fitness. In some states, the warranty protects not only the first purchaser but any subsequent purchaser as well.

Seller's Duty to Disclose Hidden Defects In most jurisdictions, courts impose on sellers a duty to disclose any known defect that materially affects the value of the property and that the buyer could not reasonably discover. Failure to disclose such a material defect gives the buyer a right to rescind the contract and to sue for damages based on fraud or misrepresentation.

A dispute may arise over whether the seller knew of the defect before the sale, and there is normally a limit to the time within which the buyer can bring a suit against the seller based on the defect. For example, in Louisiana, where the following case was decided, the prescribed limit for a suit against a seller who knew, or can be presumed to have known, of the defect is one year from the day that the buyer discovered it. If the seller did not know of the defect, the limit is one year from the date of the sale.

CASE 48.3 Whitehead v. Humphrey

Court of Appeal of Louisiana, Second Circuit, 2007. 954 So.2d 859.

• **Background and Facts** Matthew Humphrey paid $44,000 for a home in Webster Parish, Louisiana, in the fall of 2003 and partially renovated it. Among other things, he replaced rotten wood underneath a bedroom window, leveled the porch, painted the interior, replaced sheetrock, tore out a wall, replaced a window, dug up eighty feet of field line for the septic system, and pumped out the septic tank. In February 2004, Terry and Tabitha Whitehead bought the house for $67,000. A few

CASE 48.3 CONTINUED months after they moved in, problems began to develop with the air-conditioning unit, the fireplace, the septic system, and the plumbing in the bathrooms. In May 2005, they discovered rotten wood behind the tile in the bathroom and around the front porch. In October, the Whiteheads filed a suit in a Louisiana state court against Humphrey, seeking to rescind the sale. The court awarded the plaintiffs the cost of repairing the fireplace ($1,675) and replacing some of the bad wood ($7,695). The Whiteheads appealed to a state intermediate appellate court.

● **Decision and Rationale** The Court of Appeal of Louisiana for the Second Circuit upheld the trial court's refusal to rescind the sale. Further, the reviewing court accepted the trial court's awarding of the cost of repairing the defects in the fireplace and the rotten wood. The court pointed out that before the sale, both the buyer and the seller were aware of a problem regarding the sewer system. "Corrective actions were taken, and no problems concerning the flushing of the toilets and flowage through the underground system prevented the Whiteheads from completing their purchase. From this evidence, the ruling of the trial court * * * can be upheld from the view that neither side understood that a latent defect remained unresolved." Moreover, the buyers failed to file a suit within one year of the discovery of that problem. Therefore, the limitations for filing ran against their claim. In contrast, it was not until May 2005 that the Whiteheads first discovered the problem of the rotten boards and sills beneath the house that the seller had improperly repaired. They filed their lawsuit timely and must be compensated by the seller.

● **The Ethical Dimension** *Should the court have rescinded the sale despite the running of the limitations period on the Whiteheads' sewer claim? Why or why not?*

● **The Legal Environment Dimension** *In Louisiana, a seller who knows of a defect and does not inform a buyer can be liable for the buyer's attorneys' fees in a suit based on that defect. Did Humphrey qualify as such a "bad faith" seller in this case? Explain.*

Deeds

Possession and title to land are passed from person to person by means of a **deed**—the instrument of conveyance of real property. A deed is a writing signed by an owner of real property by which title to it is transferred to another.[7] Deeds must meet certain requirements, but unlike a contract, a deed does not have to be supported by legally sufficient consideration. Gifts of real property are common, and they require deeds even though there is no consideration for the gift. To be valid, a deed must include the following:

1. The names of the *grantor* (the giver or seller) and the *grantee* (the donee or buyer).
2. Words evidencing the intent to convey (for example, "I hereby bargain, sell, grant, or give"). No specific words are necessary, and if the deed does *not* specify the estate being transferred, it presumptively transfers it in fee simple absolute.
3. A legally sufficient description of the land. (The description must include enough detail to distinguish the property being conveyed from every other parcel of land. The property can be identified by reference to an official survey or recorded plat map, or each boundary can be described by *metes and bounds*. **Metes and bounds** is a system of measuring boundary lines by the distance between two points, often using physical features of the local geography. For example, "beginning at the southwesterly intersection of Court and Main Streets, then West 40 feet to the fence, then South 100 feet, then Northeast approximately 120 feet back to the beginning.")
4. The grantor's (and usually his or her spouse's) signature.
5. Delivery of the deed.

Warranty Deeds Different types of deeds provide different degrees of protection against defects of title. A **warranty deed** makes the greatest number of warranties and thus provides the most extensive protection against defects of title. In most states, special language is required to create a warranty deed.

7. Note that in some states when a person purchases real property, the bank or lender receives a *trust deed* on the property until the homeowner pays off the mortgage. Despite its name, a trust deed is not used to transfer property. Instead, it is similar to a mortgage in that the lender holds the property as security for a loan.

Warranty deeds include a number of *covenants,* or promises, that the grantor makes to the grantee. These covenants include a covenant that the grantor has the title to, and the power to convey, the property; a covenant of quiet enjoyment (a warranty that the buyer will not be disturbed in her or his possession of the land); and a covenant that transfer of the property is made without knowledge of adverse claims of third parties.

Generally, the warranty deed makes the grantor liable for all defects of title by the grantor and previous titleholders. For example, Julio sells a two-acre lot and office building by warranty deed. Subsequently, a third person appears, shows that she has better title than Julio had, and forces the buyer off the property. Here, the covenant of quiet enjoyment has been breached, and the buyer can sue Julio to recover the purchase price of the land, plus any other damages incurred as a result.

Special Warranty Deed In contrast to the warranty deed, the **special warranty deed,** which is frequently referred to as a *limited warranty deed,* warrants only that the grantor or seller held good title during his or her ownership of the property. In other words, the grantor is not warranting that there were no defects of title when the property was held by previous owners.

If the special warranty deed discloses all liens or other encumbrances, the seller will not be liable to the buyer if a third person subsequently interferes with the buyer's ownership. If the third person's claim arises out of, or is related to, some act of the seller, however, the seller will be liable to the buyer for damages.

Quitclaim Deed A **quitclaim deed** offers the least amount of protection against defects in the title. Basically, a quitclaim deed conveys to the grantee whatever interest the grantor had; so, if the grantor had no interest, then the grantee receives no interest. Naturally, if the grantor had a defective title or no title at all, a conveyance by warranty deed or special warranty deed would not cure the defects. Such deeds, however, will give the buyer a cause of action to sue the seller.

A quitclaim deed can and often does serve as a release of the grantor's interest in a particular parcel of property. For instance, Sandor owns a strip of waterfront property on which he wants to build condominiums. Lanz has an easement on a portion of the property, which might interfere with Sandor's plans for the development. Sandor can negotiate with Lanz to deed the easement back to Sandor. Lanz's signing of a quitclaim deed would constitute such a transfer.

Grant Deed With a **grant deed,** the grantor simply states, "I grant the property to you" or "I convey, or bargain and sell, the property to you." By state statute, grant deeds carry with them an implied warranty that the grantor owns the property and has not previously transferred it to someone else or encumbered it, except as set out in the deed.

Sheriff's Deed A **sheriff's deed** is a document giving ownership rights to a buyer of property at a sheriff's sale, which is a sale held by a sheriff when the owner of the property has failed to pay a court judgment against her or him. Typically, the property was subject to a mortgage or tax payments, and the owner defaulted on the payments. After a statutory period of time during which the defaulting owner can redeem the property (see Chapter 28), the deed is delivered to the purchaser.

Recording Statutes

Once the seller delivers the deed to the buyer (at closing), legal title to the property is conveyed. Nevertheless, the buyer should promptly record the deed with the state records office to establish superior ownership rights against any third parties who might make a claim to the property. Every state has a **recording statute,** which allows deeds to be recorded in the public record. Recording a deed involves a fee, which the buyer typically pays because he or she is the one who will be protected by recording the deed.

Recording a deed gives notice to the public that a certain person is now the owner of a particular parcel of real estate. Putting everyone on notice as to the true owner is intended to prevent the previous owners from fraudulently conveying the land to other purchasers. Deeds are generally recorded in the county in which the property is located. Many state statutes require that the grantor sign the deed in the presence of two witnesses before it can be recorded.

Marketable Title The question of title to a particular parcel of property is especially important to the buyer. A grantor (seller) is obligated to transfer **marketable title,** or good title, to the grantee (buyer). Marketable title means that the grantor's ownership is free from encumbrances (except those disclosed by the grantor) and free of defects. If the buyer signs a real estate sales contract and then discovers that the seller does not have a marketable title, the buyer can withdraw from the contract. For example, Chan enters an agreement to buy Fortuna Ranch from Hal. Chan then discovers that Hal has previously given Pearl an unexpired option to purchase the ranch. In this situation, the title is not marketable because Pearl could exercise the option and Hal would be compelled to sell the ranch to her. Therefore, Chan can withdraw from the contract to buy the property.

Title Search Because each document affecting ownership of property is recorded, recording provides a chronological public record of all transactions concerning the property. Systematically examining this record for transactions creating interests or rights in a specific parcel of real property is called a **title search.** A prospective buyer or lender generally performs a title search to determine whether the seller truly owns the interest that he or she is attempting to convey and whether anyone else has an interest in the property. A title search should—but does not always—reveal encumbrances on the property and the existence of an easement or lien.

Methods of Ensuring Good Title To ensure that the title is marketable, a grantee has several options depending on the state. The grantee may hire an attorney to examine an *abstract of title* (history of what the public records show regarding the title to the property) and provide an opinion as to whether the title is marketable. If the title is defective, the attorney's opinion will specify the nature of the defects. The attorney is liable to the grantee for any loss caused by her or his negligence.

An alternative method available in a few states is the *Torrens system* of title registration. Under this system, the title is registered in a judicial proceeding; all parties claiming an interest in the property are notified of the proceeding and are given an opportunity to assert their claims. After the hearing, the court issues a certificate of title, which is similar to an automobile title, to the person found to be the owner. All encumbrances are noted on the certificate, and when the property is sold, the certificate is transferred to the grantee along with the deed.

The most common method of assuring title is through **title insurance,** which insures the grantee against loss from defects in title to real property. When financing the purchase of real property, many lenders require title insurance to protect their interests in the collateral for the loan. Title insurance is becoming less significant because title information and records are now available electronically and thus are easy to access.

Adverse Possession

A person who wrongfully possesses (by occupying or using) the real property of another may eventually acquire title to it through **adverse possession.** Adverse possession is a means of obtaining title to land without delivery of a deed and without the consent of—or payment to—the true owner. Thus, adverse possession is a method of involuntarily transferring title to the property from the true owner to the adverse possessor.

Essentially, when one person possesses the real property of another for a certain statutory period of time (three to thirty years, with ten years being most common), that person acquires title to the land. For property to be held adversely, four elements must be satisfied:

1. Possession must be *actual and exclusive*—that is, the possessor must physically occupy the property. This requirement is clearly met if the possessor lives on the property, but it may also be met if the possessor builds fences, erects structures, plants crops, or even grazes animals on the land.
2. The possession must be *open, visible, and notorious,* not secret or clandestine. The possessor must occupy the land for all the world to see. This requirement of obviousness ensures that the true owner is on notice that someone is possessing the owner's property wrongfully.
3. Possession must be *continuous and peaceable for the required period of time.* This requirement means that the possessor must not be interrupted in the occupancy by the true owner or by the courts. *Continuous* does not mean constant—it simply means that the possessor has continuously occupied the property in some fashion for the statutory time and has not used force to possess the land.
4. Possession must be *hostile and adverse.* In other words, the possessor cannot be living on the property with the owner's permission and must claim the property as against the whole world.

There are a number of public-policy reasons for the adverse possession doctrine. These include society's interest in resolving boundary disputes, in quieting (determining) title when title to property is in question, and in ensuring that real property remains in the stream of commerce. More fundamentally, policies behind the doctrine include punishing owners who do not take action when they see adverse possession and rewarding possessors for putting land to productive use.

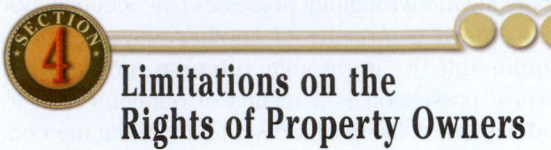

SECTION 4 Limitations on the Rights of Property Owners

No ownership rights in real property can ever really be absolute; that is, an owner of real property cannot always do whatever she or he wishes on or with the property. Nuisance and environmental laws, for example, restrict certain types of activities. Holding the property is also conditional on the payment of property taxes. Zoning laws and building permits frequently restrict one's use of the realty. In addition, if a property owner fails to pay debts, the property may be seized to satisfy judgment creditors. In short, the rights of every property owner are subject to certain conditions and limitations. We look here at some of the important ways in which owners' rights in real property can be limited.

Eminent Domain

Even ownership in real property in fee simple absolute is limited by a superior ownership. Just as the king was the ultimate landowner in medieval England, today the government has an ultimate ownership right in all land in the United States. This right, known as **eminent domain,** is sometimes referred to as the *condemnation power* of government to take land for public use. It gives the government the right to acquire possession of real property in the manner directed by the U.S. Constitution and the laws of the state whenever the public interest requires it. Property may be taken only for public use, not for private benefit.

For example, when a new public highway is to be built, the government decides where to build it and how much land to condemn. After the government determines that a particular parcel of land is necessary for public use, it will first offer to buy the property. If the owner refuses the offer, the government brings a judicial **(condemnation)** proceeding to obtain title to the land. Then, in another proceeding, the court determines the *fair value* of the land, which is usually approximately equal to its market value.

When the government takes land owned by a private party for public use, it is referred to as a **taking,** and the government must compensate the private party. Under the so-called *takings clause* of the Fifth Amendment to the U.S. Constitution, the government may not take private property for public use without "just compensation." State constitutions contain similar provisions.

Can the power of eminent domain be used to further economic development? That was the question in the following case.

CASE 48.4 Kelo v. City of New London, Connecticut

Supreme Court of the United States, 2005. 545 U.S. 469, 125 S.Ct. 2655, 162 L.Ed.2d 439.
www.findlaw.com/casecode/supreme.html[a]

Background and Facts After decades of economic decline, the city of New London was designated as a "distressed municipality" by a Connecticut state agency in 1990, but conditions continued to deteriorate. In 1996, the federal government closed the Naval Undersea Warfare Center, which had been located in the Fort Trumbull area of the city and had employed more than 1,500 people. Within two years, the city's unemployment rate was nearly double that of the state. In 1998, Pfizer, Inc., announced that it would build a $300 million research facility on a site next to Fort Trumbull. Hoping that this would draw new business to the city, the city council approved a plan to redevelop the area that once housed the federal facility. The city bought most of the land for the project, but negotiations with some of the property owners fell through, and the city began condemnation proceedings. Susette Kelo and other affected owners filed a suit in a Connecticut

a. In the "Browsing" section, click on "2005 Decisions." In the result, click on "Kelo v. New London" to access the opinion.

CASE 48.4 CONTINUED state court against the city and others. The plaintiffs claimed, among other things, that the taking of their property would violate the "public use" restriction in the U.S. Constitution's Fifth Amendment. The court issued a ruling partly in favor of both sides. On appeal, the Connecticut Supreme Court held that all of the city's proposed takings were valid. The owners appealed to the United States Supreme Court.

• **Decision and Rationale** The United States Supreme Court affirmed the lower court's judgment. The Court held that economic development can constitute a "public use" within the meaning of the Fifth Amendment's takings clause to justify a local government's exercise of its power of eminent domain. The Court concluded that the city's plan "unquestionably serves a public purpose," even though it would also benefit private parties. The Court explained, "Viewed as a whole, our jurisprudence has recognized that the needs of society have varied between different parts of the Nation, just as they have evolved over time in response to changed circumstances. Our earliest cases in particular embodied a strong theme of federalism, emphasizing the great respect that we owe to state legislatures and state courts in discerning local public needs. For more than a century, our public use jurisprudence has wisely eschewed rigid formulas and intrusive scrutiny in favor of affording legislatures broad latitude in determining what public needs justify the use of the takings power." Thus, the city's "determination that the area was sufficiently distressed to justify a program of economic rejuvenation is entitled to our deference. The City has carefully formulated an economic development plan that it believes will provide appreciable benefits to the community. * * * Because that plan unquestionably serves a public purpose, the takings challenged here satisfy the public use requirement of the Fifth Amendment."

• **The Legal Environment Dimension** *What did the Court hold with respect to the principal issue in this case?*

• **The Ethical Dimension** *Considering the impact of the majority's ruling, what are some arguments against this decision?*

Legislation Prohibiting Takings for Economic Development

The increasingly widespread use of eminent domain for economic development has generated substantial controversy. Although the United States Supreme Court approved this type of taking in the *Kelo* case (just discussed), the Court also recognized that individual states have the right to pass laws that prohibit takings for economic development. By mid-2008, more than forty states had done exactly that. By either amending their constitutions or by passing special legislation, these states have effectively limited the government's ability to take private property and give it to developers. On a local level, community activists have stopped dozens of projects that abused eminent domain for private development.

Restrictive Covenants

A private restriction on the use of land is known as a **restrictive covenant.** If the restriction is binding on the party who purchases the property originally and on subsequent purchasers as well, it is said to "run with the land." A covenant running with the land must be in writing (usually it is in the deed), and subsequent purchasers must have reason to know about it. Suppose that in the course of developing a fifty-lot suburban subdivision, Levitt records a declaration of restrictions that effectively limits construction on each lot to one single-family house. Each lot's deed includes a reference to the declaration with a provision that the purchaser and her or his successors are bound to those restrictions. Thus, each purchaser assumes ownership with notice of the restrictions. If an owner attempts to build a duplex (or any structure that does not comply with the restrictions) on a lot, the other owners may obtain a court order enjoining the construction.

In fact, Levitt might simply have included the restrictions on the subdivision's map, filed the map in the appropriate public office, and included a reference to the map in each deed. In this way, each owner would also have been held to have constructive notice of the restrictions.

SECTION 5 Landlord-Tenant Relationships

The property interest involved in a landlord-tenant relationship is known as a *leasehold estate,* as discussed earlier in this chapter. The owner of the property is the landlord, or **lessor;** the party assuming temporary possession is the tenant, or **lessee;** and their rental agreement is the lease contract, or, more simply, the **lease.** The *temporary* nature of possession, under a lease, is what distinguishes a tenant from a purchaser, who acquires title to the property. The *exclusivity* of possession distinguishes a tenant from a licensee, who acquires the temporary right to a *nonexclusive* use, such as sitting in a theater seat.

In the past thirty years, landlord-tenant relationships have become much more complex, as have the laws governing them. Generally, the law has come to apply contract doctrines, such as those providing for implied warranties and unconscionability, to the landlord-tenant relationship. Increasingly, landlord-tenant relationships have become subject to specific state and local statutes and ordinances as well. In 1972, in an effort to create more uniformity in the law governing landlord-tenant relationships, the National Conference of Commissioners on Uniform State Laws approved the Uniform Residential Landlord and Tenant Act (URLTA) for adoption by the states. More than one-fourth of the states have adopted variations of the URLTA.

Creation of the Landlord-Tenant Relationship

A landlord-tenant relationship is established by a lease contract. As mentioned, a lease contract arises when a property owner (landlord) agrees to give another party (the tenant) the exclusive right to possess the property—usually for a price and for a specified term. A lease contract may be oral or written. In most states, statutes require leases for terms exceeding one year to be in writing. The lease should describe the property and indicate the length of the term, the amount of the rent, and how and when it is to be paid.

State or local law often dictates permissible lease terms. For example, a statute or ordinance might prohibit the leasing of a structure that is in a certain physical condition or is not in compliance with local building codes. Similarly, a statute may prohibit the leasing of property for a particular purpose. For instance, a state law might prohibit gambling houses. Thus, if a landlord and tenant intend that the leased premises be used only to house an illegal betting operation, their lease is unenforceable.

Because of the many laws pertaining to lease terms and prohibiting discriminatory treatment, as a businessperson you would be wise to exercise caution when renting out property. Find out what the laws are in your state, and investigate the background of prospective tenants. Hire an attorney to draft a lease agreement that complies with state laws rather than using a preprinted lease form, which may contain provisions not allowed in your state. Also, make sure that you understand what it takes to evict a tenant who does not pay rent in your state. Do not tell prospective renters more than they need to know about the selection process, why one prospective renter was selected over another, or to whom the property was ultimately leased. Never reveal any bias on your part against persons with children, disabilities, or other characteristics, or against persons of another race. Mistakes in this area can be costly in terms of legal fees and lost rent.

Parties' Rights and Duties

The rights and duties of landlords and tenants generally pertain to four broad areas of concern—the possession, use, maintenance, and, of course, rent of leased property.

Possession A landlord is obligated to give a tenant possession of the property that the tenant has agreed to lease. Whether the landlord must provide actual physical possession (making sure that the previous tenant leaves) or the legal right to possession (leaving it to the new tenant to oust the previous tenant) depends on the particular state. After obtaining possession, the tenant retains the property exclusively until the lease expires, unless the lease states otherwise.

The covenant of quiet enjoyment mentioned previously also applies to leased premises. Under this covenant, the landlord promises that during the lease term, neither the landlord nor anyone having a superior title to the property will disturb the tenant's use and enjoyment of the property. This covenant forms the essence of the landlord-tenant relationship, and if it is breached, the tenant can terminate the lease and sue for damages.

If the landlord deprives the tenant of possession of the leased property or interferes with the tenant's use or enjoyment of it, an **eviction** occurs. An eviction occurs, for instance, when the landlord changes the lock and refuses to give the tenant a new key. A **constructive eviction** occurs when the landlord wrongfully performs or fails to perform any of the duties the lease requires, thereby making the tenant's further use and enjoyment of the property exceedingly difficult or impossible. Examples of constructive eviction include a landlord's failure to provide heat in the winter, light, or other essential utilities.

Use and Maintenance of the Premises If the parties do not limit by agreement the uses to which the property may be put, the tenant may make any use of it, as long as the use is legal and reasonably relates to the purpose for which the property is adapted or ordinarily used and does not injure the landlord's interest.

The tenant is responsible for any damage to the premises that he or she causes, intentionally or negligently, and the tenant may be held liable for the cost of returning the property to the physical condition it was in at the lease's inception. Also, the tenant is not entitled to create a *nuisance* by substantially interfering with others' quiet enjoyment of their property rights (the tort of nuisance was discussed in Chapter 45). The tenant usually is not responsible for ordinary wear and tear and the property's consequent depreciation in value.

In some jurisdictions, landlords of residential property are required by statute to maintain the premises in good repair. Landlords must also comply with applicable state statutes and city ordinances regarding maintenance and repair of commercial buildings.

Implied Warranty of Habitability A landlord who leases residential property is required to ensure that the premises are habitable—that is, in a condition that is safe and suitable for people to live in. Also, the landlord must make repairs to maintain the premises in that condition for the lease's duration. Some state legislatures have enacted this warranty into law. In other jurisdictions, courts have based the warranty on the existence of a landlord's statutory duty to keep leased premises in good repair, or they have simply applied it as a matter of public policy.

Generally, this warranty applies to major, or *substantial*, physical defects that the landlord knows or should know about and has had a reasonable time to repair—for example, a large hole in the roof. An unattractive or annoying feature, such as a crack in the wall, may be unpleasant, but unless the crack is a structural defect or affects the residence's heating capabilities, it is probably not sufficiently substantial to make the place uninhabitable.

Rent *Rent* is the tenant's payment to the landlord for the tenant's occupancy or use of the landlord's real property. Usually, the tenant must pay the rent even if she or he refuses to occupy the property or moves out, as long as the refusal or the move is unjustified and the lease is in force. Under the common law, if the leased premises were destroyed by fire or flood, the tenant still had to pay rent. Today, however, most states' statutes provide that if an apartment building burns down, tenants are not required to continue to pay rent.

In some situations, such as when a landlord breaches the implied warranty of habitability, a tenant may be allowed to withhold rent as a remedy. When rent withholding is authorized under a statute, the tenant must usually put the amount withheld into an *escrow account*. This account is held in the name of the depositor (the tenant) and an *escrow agent* (usually, the court or a government agency), and the funds are returned to the depositor if the third party (the landlord) fails to make the premises habitable. Generally, the tenant may withhold an amount equal to the amount by which the defect rendering the premises unlivable reduces the property's rental value. How much that is may be determined in different ways, and the tenant who withholds more than is legally permissible is liable to the landlord for the excess amount withheld.

Transferring Rights to Leased Property

Either the landlord or the tenant may wish to transfer her or his rights to the leased property during the term of the lease.

Transferring the Landlord's Interest Just as any other real property owner can sell, give away, or otherwise transfer his or her property, so can a landlord—who is, of course, the leased property's owner. If complete title to the leased property is transferred, the tenant becomes the tenant of the new owner. The new owner may collect subsequent rent but must abide by the terms of the existing lease agreement.

Transferring the Tenant's Interest The tenant's transfer of his or her entire interest in the leased property to a third person is an *assignment of the lease.* The tenant's transfer of all or part of the premises for a period shorter than the lease term is a *sublease.*

Assignment. A lease assignment is an agreement to transfer all rights, title, and interest in the lease to the assignee. It is a complete transfer. Many leases require that the assignment have the landlord's written consent. An assignment that lacks consent can be avoided (nullified) by the landlord. State statutes may specify that the landlord may not unreasonably withhold such consent, though. Also, a landlord who knowingly accepts rent from the assignee may be held to have waived the consent requirement.

When an assignment is valid, the assignee acquires all of the tenant's rights under the lease. An assignment, however, does not release the assigning tenant from the obligation to pay rent should the assignee default. Also, if the assignee exercises an option under the original lease to extend the term, the assigning tenant remains liable for the rent during the extension, unless the landlord agrees otherwise.

Subleases. As mentioned, the tenant's transfer of all or part of the premises for a period shorter than the lease term is a **sublease.** The same restrictions that apply to an assignment of the tenant's interest in leased property apply to a sublease. If the landlord's consent is required, a sublease without such permission is ineffective. Also, a sublease does not release the tenant from her or his obligations under the lease any more than an assignment does.

For example, Derek, a student, leases an apartment for a two-year period. Although Derek had planned on attending summer school, he is offered a job in Europe for the summer months, and he accepts. Because he does not wish to pay three months' rent for an unoccupied apartment, Derek subleases the apartment to Adva, who becomes a sublessee. (Derek may have to obtain his landlord's consent for this sublease if the lease requires it.) Adva is bound by the same terms of the lease as Derek was. As in a lease assignment, the landlord can hold Derek liable if Adva violates the lease terms.

Termination of the Lease

Usually, a lease terminates when its term ends. The tenant surrenders the property to the landlord, who retakes possession. If the lease states the time it will end, the landlord is not required to give the tenant notice. The lease terminates automatically. In contrast, a *periodic tenancy* (a tenancy from month to month, for example) will renew automatically unless one of the parties gives timely notice (usually, one rental period) of termination. If the lease does not contain an option for renewal and the parties have not agreed that the tenant may stay on, the tenant has no right to remain. If the lease is renewable and the tenant decides to exercise the option, the tenant must comply with any conditions requiring notice to the landlord of the tenant's decision.

A lease may also be terminated in several other ways. For example, the landlord may agree that the tenant will purchase the leased property during the term or at its end, thus terminating the lease. The parties may agree to end a tenancy before it would otherwise terminate. The tenant may also *abandon* the premises—move out completely with no intention of returning before the lease term expires.

At common law and in many states, when a tenant abandons leased property, the tenant remains obligated to pay the rent for the remainder of the lease term—however long that might be. The landlord may refuse to lease the premises to an acceptable new tenant and let the property stand vacant. In a growing number of jurisdictions, however, the landlord is required to *mitigate* his or her damages—that is, the landlord is required to make a reasonable attempt to lease the property to another party. In these jurisdictions, the tenant's liability for unpaid rent is restricted to the period of time that the landlord would reasonably need to lease the property to another tenant.[8] Damages may also be allowed for the landlord's costs in leasing the property again. What is considered a reasonable period of time with respect to leasing the property to another party varies with the type of lease and the location of the leased premises.

8. See, for example, *Frenchtown Square Partnership v. Lemstone, Inc.,* 99 Ohio St.3d 254, 791 N.E.2d 417 (2003). For a fuller discussion of mitigation of damages, see Chapter 17.

REVIEWING Real Property and Landlord-Tenant Relationships

Vern Shoepke purchased a two-story home from Walter and Eliza Bruster in the town of Roche, Maine. The warranty deed did not specify what covenants would be included in the conveyance. The property was adjacent to a public park that included a popular Frisbee golf course. (Frisbee golf is a sport similar to golf but using Frisbees.) Wayakichi Creek ran along the north end of the park and along Shoepke's property. The deed allowed Roche citizens the right to walk across a five-foot-wide section of the lot beside Wayakichi Creek as part of a two-mile public trail system. Teenagers regularly threw Frisbee golf discs from the walking path behind Shoepke's property over his yard to the adjacent park. Shoepke habitually shouted and cursed at the teenagers, demanding that they not throw objects over his yard. Two months after moving into his Roche home, Shoepke leased the second floor to Lauren Slater for nine months. (The lease agreement did not specify that Shoepke's consent would be required to sublease the second floor.) After three months of tenancy, Slater sublet the second floor to a local artist, Javier Indalecio. Over the remaining six months, Indalecio's use of oil paints damaged the carpeting in Shoepke's home. Using the information presented in the chapter, answer the following questions.

1. What is the term for the right of Roche citizens to walk across Shoepke's land on the trail?
2. In the warranty deed that was used in the property transfer from the Brusters to Shoepke, what covenants would be inferred by most courts?
3. Suppose that Shoepke wants to file a trespass lawsuit against some teenagers who continually throw Frisbees over his land. Shoepke discovers, however, that when the city put in the Frisbee golf course, the neighborhood homeowners signed an agreement that limited their right to complain about errant Frisbees. What is this type of promise or agreement called in real property law?
4. Can Shoepke hold Slater financially responsible for the damage to the carpeting caused by Indalecio?

TERMS AND CONCEPTS

adverse possession 921
closing 918
community property 913
concurrent ownership 912
condemnation 922
constructive eviction 925
conveyance 912
deed 919
easement 914
eminent domain 922
escrow account 918
eviction 925
fee simple absolute 910
fixed-term tenancy 913
grant deed 920
implied warranty of habitability 918
joint tenancy 912
lease 924
leasehold estate 913
lessee 924
lessor 924
license 915
life estate 912
marketable title 920
metes and bounds 919
nonpossessory interest 914
periodic tenancy 913
profit 914
quitclaim deed 920
recording statute 920
restrictive covenant 923
sheriff's deed 920
special warranty deed 920
sublease 926
taking 922
tenancy at sufferance 913
tenancy at will 913
tenancy by the entirety 912
tenancy in common 912
title insurance 921
title search 921
warranty deed 919
waste 912

QUESTIONS AND CASE PROBLEMS

48–1. Madison owned a tract of land, but he was not sure that he had full title to the property. When Rafael expressed an interest in buying the land, Madison sold it to Rafael and executed a quitclaim deed. Rafael properly recorded the deed immediately. Several months later, Madison learned that he had had full title to the tract of land. He then sold the land to Linda by warranty deed. Linda knew of the earlier purchase by Rafael but took the deed anyway and later sued to have Rafael evicted from the land. Linda claimed that because she had a warranty deed, her title to the land was better than that conferred by Rafael's quitclaim deed. Will Linda succeed in claiming title to the land? Explain.

48–2. James owns a three-story building. He leases the ground floor to Juan's Mexican restaurant. The lease is to run for a five-year period and contains an express covenant of quiet enjoyment. One year later, James leases the top two stories to the Upbeat Club, a discotheque. The club's hours run from 5:00 P.M. to 11:00 P.M. The noise from the Upbeat Club is so loud that it is driving customers away from Juan's restaurant. Juan has notified James of the interference and has called the police on a number of occasions. James refuses to talk to the owners of the Upbeat Club or to do anything to remedy the situation. Juan abandons the premises. James files suit for breach of the lease agreement and for the rental payments still due under the lease. Juan claims that he was constructively evicted and files a countersuit for damages. Discuss who will be held liable.

48–3. QUESTION WITH SAMPLE ANSWER

Wilfredo and Patricia are neighbors. Wilfredo's lot is extremely large, and his present and future use of it will not involve the entire area. Patricia wants to build a single-car garage and driveway along the present lot boundary. Because ordinances require buildings to be set back fifteen feet from an owner's property line, however, the placement of Patricia's existing structures prevents her from building the garage. Patricia contracts to purchase ten feet of Wilfredo's property along their boundary line for $3,000. Wilfredo is willing to sell but will give Patricia only a quitclaim deed, whereas Patricia wants a warranty deed. Discuss the differences between these deeds as they would affect the rights of the parties if the title to this ten feet of land later proves to be defective.

- **For a sample answer to Question 48–3, go to Appendix I at the end of this text.**

48–4. Sarah has rented a house from Frank. The house is only two years old, but the roof leaks every time it rains. The water that has accumulated in the attic has caused plaster to fall off ceilings in the upstairs bedrooms, and one ceiling has started to sag. Sarah has complained to Frank and asked him to have the roof repaired. Frank says that he has caulked the roof, but the roof still leaks. Frank claims that because Sarah has sole control of the leased premises, she has the duty to repair the roof. Sarah insists that repairing the roof is Frank's responsibility. Discuss fully who is responsible for repairing the roof and, if the responsibility belongs to Frank, what remedies are available to Sarah.

48–5. Glenn is the owner of a lakeside house and lot. He deeds the house and lot "to my wife, Livia, for life, then to my daughter, Sarina." What is Livia's interest called? Is there any limitation on her rights to use the property as she wishes? Discuss.

48–6. Easements. The Wallens family owned a cabin on Lummi Island in the state of Washington. A driveway ran from the cabin across their property to South Nugent Road. In 1952, Floyd Massey bought the adjacent lot and built a cabin. To gain access to his property, he used a bulldozer to extend the driveway without the Wallenses' permission but also without their objection. In 1975, the Wallenses sold their property to Wright Fish Co. Massey continued to use and maintain the driveway without permission or objection. In 1984, Massey sold his property to Robert Drake. Drake and his employees continued to use and maintain the driveway without permission or objection, although Drake knew it was located largely on Wright's property. In 1997, Wright sold its lot to Robert Smersh. The next year, Smersh told Drake to stop using the driveway. Drake filed a suit in a Washington state court against Smersh, claiming an easement by prescription (which is created by meeting the same requirements as adverse possession). Does Drake's use of the driveway meet all of the requirements? What should the court rule? Explain. [*Drake v. Smersh,* 122 Wash.App. 147, 89 P.3d 726 (Div. 1 2004)]

48–7. CASE PROBLEM WITH SAMPLE ANSWER

The Hope Partnership for Education, a religious organization, proposed to build a private independent middle school in a blighted neighborhood in Philadelphia, Pennsylvania. In 2002, the Hope Partnership asked the Redevelopment Authority of the City of Philadelphia to acquire specific land for the project and sell it to the Hope Partnership for a nominal price. The land included a house at 1839 North Eighth Street owned by Mary Smith, whose daughter Veronica lived there with her family. The Authority offered Smith $12,000 for the house and initiated a taking of the property. Smith filed a suit in a Pennsylvania state court against the Authority, admitting that the house was a "substandard structure in a blighted area," but arguing that the taking was unconstitutional because its beneficiary was private. The Authority asserted that only the public purpose of the taking should be considered, not the status of the property's developer. On what basis can a government entity use the power of eminent domain to take property? What are the limits to this power? How should the court rule? Why? [*Redevelopment Authority of City of Philadelphia v. New Eastwick Corp.,* 588 Pa. 789, 906 A.2d 1197 (2006)]

- **To view a sample answer for Problem 48–7, go to this book's Web site at www.cengage.com/blaw/jentz, select "Chapter 48," and click on "Case Problem with Sample Answer."**

48–8. Ownership in Fee Simple. Thomas and Teresa Cline built a house on a seventy-six-acre parcel of real estate next to Roy Berg's home and property in Augusta County, Virginia. The homes were about 1,800 feet apart but in view of each other. After several disagreements between the parties, Berg equipped an eleven-foot tripod with motion sensors and floodlights that intermittently illuminated the Clines' home. Berg also installed surveillance cameras that tracked some of the movement on the Clines' property. The cameras transmitted on an open frequency, which could be received by any television within range. The Clines asked Berg to turn off, or at least redirect, the lights. When he refused, they erected a fence for two hundred feet along the parties' common property line. The thirty-two-foot-high fence consisted of twenty utility poles spaced ten feet apart with plastic wrap stretched between the poles. This effectively blocked the lights and cameras. Berg filed a suit against the Clines in a Virginia state court, complaining that the fence interfered unreasonably with his use and enjoyment of his property. He asked the court to order the Clines to take the fence down. What are the limits on an owner's use of property? How should the court rule in this case? Why? [*Cline v. Berg,* 273 Va. 142, 639 S.E.2d 231 (2007)]

48–9. A QUESTION OF ETHICS

In 1999, Stephen and Linda Kailin bought the Monona Center, a mall in Madison, Wisconsin, from Perry Armstrong for $760,000. The contract provided, "Seller represents to Buyer that as of the date of acceptance Seller had no notice or knowledge of conditions affecting the Property or transaction" other than certain items disclosed at the time of the offer. Armstrong told the Kailins of the Center's eight tenants, their lease expiration dates, and the monthly and annual rent due under each lease. One of the lessees, Ring's All-American Karate, occupied about a third of the Center's space under a five-year lease. Because of Ring's financial difficulties, Armstrong had agreed to reduce its rent for nine months in 1997. By the time of the sale to the Kailins, Ring owed $13,910 in unpaid rent, but Armstrong did not tell the Kailins, who did not ask. Ring continued to fail to pay rent and finally vacated the Center. The Kailins filed a suit in a Wisconsin state court against Armstrong and others, alleging, among other things, misrepresentation. [Kailin v. Armstrong, *2002 WI App 70, 252 Wis.2d 676, 643 N.W.2d 132 (2002)*]

(a) Did Armstrong have a duty to disclose Ring's delinquency and default to the Kailins? Explain.

(b) What obligation, if any, did Ring have to the Kailins or Armstrong after failing to pay the rent and eventually defaulting on the lease? Why?

LAW ON THE WEB

For updated links to resources available on the Web, as well as a variety of other materials, visit this text's Web site at

www.cengage.com/blaw/jentz

For links to numerous sources relating to real property, go to

www.findlaw.com/01topics/index.html

and click on "Property Law & Real Estate."

For information on condemnation procedures and rules under one state's (California's) law, go to

www.eminentdomainlaw.net/propertyguide.html

Legal Research Exercises on the Web

Go to **www.cengage.com/blaw/jentz**, the Web site that accompanies this text. Select "Chapter 48" and click on "Internet Exercises." There you will find the following Internet research exercises that you can perform to learn more about the topics covered in this chapter.

Internet Exercise 48–1: Legal Perspective
Eminent Domain

Internet Exercise 48–2: Management Perspective
Fair Housing

Internet Exercise 48–3: Social Perspective
The Rights of Tenants

Unit Ten · Focus on Ethics

Property

Property rights have long been given extensive legal protection under both English and U.S. law. In the United States, the right to own property is closely associated with liberty, the pursuit of happiness, and other concepts that have played an integral role in American life. At the same time, conflicts often arise over who owns what and over how property should be used. In this *Focus on Ethics* feature, we explore some of the ethical dimensions of property laws and disputes over property ownership rights.

Finders' Rights

The children's adage "finders keepers, losers weepers" is actually written into law—provided that the loser (the rightful owner) cannot be found, that is. A finder may acquire good title to found personal property against everyone *except the true owner.*

An early English case, *Armory v. Delamirie,*[1] is a landmark in Anglo-American jurisprudence concerning actions in *trover*—an early form of recovery of damages for the conversion of property. The plaintiff in this case was Armory, a chimney sweep who found a jewel in its setting during the course of his work. He took the jewel to a goldsmith to have it appraised. The goldsmith refused to return the jewel to Armory, claiming that Armory was not the rightful owner of the property. The court held that the finder, as prior possessor of the item, had rights to the jewel superior to those of all others except the rightful owner. The court said, "The finder of a jewel, though he does not by such finding acquire an absolute property or ownership, yet . . . has such a property as will enable him to keep it against all but the rightful owner, and consequently maintain trover."

The *Armory* case illustrates the doctrine of the *relativity of title.* Under this doctrine, if two contestants, neither of whom can claim absolute title to the property, are before the court, the one who can claim prior possession will likely have established sufficient rights to the property to win the case.

Bailee's Duty of Care

The standard of care expected of a bailee clearly illustrates how property law reflects ethical principles. For example, a friend asks to borrow your business law text for the weekend. You agree to loan your friend the book. In this situation, which is a bailment for the sole benefit of the bailee (your friend), most people would agree that your friend has an ethical obligation to take great care of your book. After all, if your friend lost your book, you would incur damages. You would have to purchase another one, and if you could not, you might find it difficult to do well on your homework assignments and examinations.

The situation would be different if you had loaned your book to your friend totally for your own benefit. Suppose that you are leaving town during the summer, and your friend offers to store several boxes of books for you until you return in the fall. In this situation, a bailment for the sole benefit of the bailor (you) exists. If your books are destroyed through the bailee's (your friend's) negligence and you sue the bailee for damages, a court will likely take into consideration the fact that the bailee was essentially doing you a favor by storing the books. Although bailees generally have a duty to exercise reasonable care over bailed property, what constitutes reasonable care in a specific situation normally depends on the surrounding circumstances, including the reason for the bailment and who stood to benefit from the arrangement.

Bailee's Liability

The law of bailments also clearly expresses ethical principles in its rules governing the liability of bailees. On the one hand, the law permits bailees to limit their liability for bailed goods by monetary amount or type of risk, as explained in Chapter 47. On the other hand, the law does not permit bailees to exclude liability for harm caused by their own negligence. Exculpatory clauses in bailment contracts that attempt to relieve the bailee of liability for negligence will normally be closely scrutinized by the courts, particularly if the contract is between a member of the public and a bailee providing quasi-public services, such as a warehouser.

Consider an example. Lisa Gonzalez leased short-term storage space from a warehouser and placed an assortment of electronic equipment, furniture, family memorabilia, and other items in the space. Seven weeks later, when she returned to retrieve her property, she discovered that the space had been inundated with water and that her stored possessions had been either destroyed or damaged. When she sued the warehouser for negligence, the warehouser pointed to the exculpatory clause in the bailment (rental) contract. The lengthy clause stated, among other things, that the owner (warehouser) "shall not be liable to Occupant for any loss or

1. 93 Eng.Rep. 664 (K.B. [King's Bench] 1722).

damage that may be occasioned by or through Owner's acts, omissions to act, or negligence." The court, stating that the exculpatory clause was "outrageous," deemed it unconscionable and thus void and unenforceable.[2]

Note, however, that self-service storage facilities are not necessarily considered warehouses or bailees in all situations. In New Jersey, for example, under a statute enacted after the *Gonzalez* case was decided, a self-storage facility is not considered a warehouse unless the owner of the facility takes some kind of title to the property stored at the facility.[3] In 2007, a court applying New Jersey law held that the owner of a self-storage facility was neither a warehouser nor a bailee of the goods stored in the unit. The dispute involved two parties whose goods were damaged by a leak in the roof at a U-Haul self-storage facility. Both had signed contracts with U-Haul that stated that the facility was not a bailee of the property and that the customer bore the risk of loss to the property. The facility had offered both parties insurance coverage when they signed the rental agreement, which contained an exculpatory clause. The court found that the exculpatory clause was valid and held in favor of the storage facility. According to the court, the contract for the self-storage units was similar to a lease for commercial property, and thus the exculpatory clause was not against public policy or unconscionable.[4]

Fair Housing versus Religious Freedom

Numerous restraints are imposed on landlords by federal and state antidiscrimination laws, but sometimes these laws conflict with other constitutional rights, such as freedom of religion. For example, suppose that a landlord feels that it would violate his religious principles to rent an apartment to an unmarried couple. Should the law, in the interest of preventing discrimination in housing, compel the landlord to violate his conscience?

This issue brings into conflict two fundamental ethical principles—one promoting freedom from discrimination and the other promoting freedom of religion. It is simply not possible to develop an objective rule to determine which principle should prevail in all cases, and the courts have reached different conclusions.

In one case, for example, the Minnesota Supreme Court held that a landlord had a right to refuse, for religious reasons, to rent a house to a woman who planned to share the house with her fiancé. The court concluded that the landlord's right to exercise his religion outweighed the tenant's interest in cohabiting on the property with her fiancé prior to their marriage.[5] In a case with similar facts, however, the California Supreme Court held that a landlord's refusal to rent commercial property to an unmarried couple for religious reasons violated a state statute that prohibited discrimination based on "marital status." The court stated that enforcing the law would not "substantially burden" the landlord's freedom of religion under either the U.S. Constitution or the California state constitution.[6]

Land-Use Regulations and the "Takings Clause"

Regulations to control land use, including environmental regulations, are prevalent throughout the United States. Generally, these laws reflect the public's interest in preserving natural resources and habitats for wildlife. At times, their goal is to enable the public to have access to and enjoy limited natural resources, such as coastal areas. Although few would disagree with the rationale underlying these laws, the owners of the private property directly affected by the laws often feel that they should be compensated for the limitations imposed on their right to do as they wish with their land.

Remember from Chapter 48 that the Fifth Amendment to the U.S. Constitution gives the government the power to "take" private property for public use. The Fifth Amendment attaches an important condition to this power, however: when private land is taken for public use, the landowner must be given "just compensation."

No General Rule In cases alleging that a "regulatory taking" has occurred, the courts have largely decided the issue on a case-by-case basis. In other words, there is no general rule that indicates whether a specific situation will be deemed a taking. In one case, the city of Monterey, California, in the interests of protecting various forms of coastal wildlife, would not allow an owner of oceanfront property to build a residential development. In effect, the city's actions

2. *Gonzalez v. A-1 Self Storage, Inc.,* 350 N.J.Super. 403, 795 A.2d 885 (2000).
3. Self-Service Storage Act, New Jersey Statutes 2A:44-188 (2006).
4. *Kane v. U-Haul International, Inc.,* 2007 WL 412466 (3d Cir. 2007).
5. *State by Cooper v. French,* 460 N.W.2d 2 (Minn. 1990).
6. *Smith v. Fair Employment and Housing Commission,* 12 Cal.4th 1143, 913 P.2d 909, 51 Cal.Rptr.2d 700 (1996).

(Continued)

meant that the entire property had to be left in its natural state, thus making the owner's planned use of the land impossible. When the landowner challenged the city's action as an unconstitutional taking without compensation, the United States Supreme Court ultimately agreed, and the landowner had to be compensated.[7]

In another case, however, the Supreme Court held for the regulators. In an attempt to curb pollution in Lake Tahoe, located on the California-Nevada border, a regional planning agency issued a moratorium on (a temporary suspension of) the construction of housing in certain areas around the lake. The moratorium was extended time and again until, some twenty years later, a number of landowners sued the agency. The landowners claimed that a regulatory taking had occurred for which they should be compensated. The Supreme Court disagreed. Because the agency's actions had not deprived the owners of their property for too long a time, no taking had occurred. How long is "too long"? The Court said that no categorical rule could be stated; the answer always depends on "the facts presented."[8]

A Question of Fairness The question of whether private landowners should be compensated when their land is essentially "taken" for public use by environmental and land-use regulations clearly involves issues of fairness. On the one hand, states, cities, and other local governments want to preserve their natural resources and need some authority to regulate land use to achieve this goal. On the other hand, private property owners complain that they alone should not have to bear the costs of creating a benefit, such as environmental preservation, that all members of the public enjoy.

7. *City of Monterey v. Del Monte Dunes at Monterey, Ltd.,* 526 U.S. 687, 119 S.Ct. 1624, 143 L.Ed.2d 882 (1999). See also *Vulcan Materials Co. v. The City of Tehuacana,* 369 F.3d 882 (5th Cir. 2004).

8. *Tahoe-Sierra Preservation Council v. Tahoe Regional Planning Agency,* 535 U.S. 302, 122 S.Ct. 1465, 152 L.Ed.2d 517 (2002).

Discrimination in Housing

The Fair Housing Act also presents issues of fairness. The act prohibits mortgage lenders from refusing to lend funds for the purchase of homes in certain areas. Prohibiting this practice, known as *redlining,* severely restricts lenders' ability to choose freely where (or where not) to invest their money. Should lenders be coerced by law into lending funds toward the purchase of homes that are located in neighborhoods where criminal activity is on the rise and property values are rapidly declining? The lender is in business to make a profit on its loan; it is not a charitable organization. The public policy expressed in the Fair Housing Act protects disadvantaged borrowers, in this context, by making more housing available to them. Lenders, however, are forced to extend credit in areas that may increase their risk of loss.

DISCUSSION QUESTIONS

1. Do you think that the law strikes a fair balance between the rights of parties with respect to found property? Why or why not?
2. Why do different standards of care apply to bailed goods? Do these standards reflect underlying ethical values? If so, how? Should bailees be able to contract away liability for their own negligence with respect to bailed goods? Why or why not?
3. In your opinion, has the government gone too far in protecting tenants' rights? Or should tenants have even greater protection? When tenants' rights, such as the right to be free of discrimination, conflict with a landlord's constitutionally protected rights, such as the free exercise of religion, which rights should prevail?
4. Do you believe that it is fair for courts to decide whether a regulatory taking has occurred on a case-by-case basis and not to articulate a general rule on which landowners can rely? Why or why not?

UNIT ELEVEN

Special Topics

CONTENTS

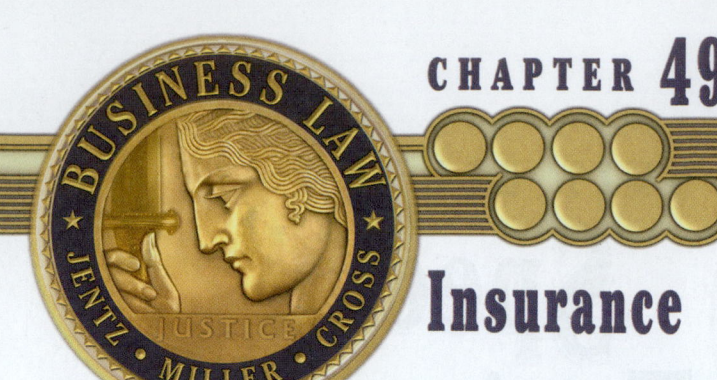

CHAPTER 49

Insurance

Protecting against loss is a foremost concern of all property owners. No one can predict whether an accident or a fire will occur, so individuals and businesses typically protect their personal and financial interests by obtaining insurance.

Insurance is a contract in which the insurance company (the insurer) promises to pay a sum of money or give something of value to another (either the insured or the beneficiary) to compensate the other for a particular, stated loss. Insurance protection may provide for compensation for the injury or death of the insured or another, for damage to the insured's property, or for other types of losses, such as those resulting from lawsuits. Basically, insurance is an arrangement for *transferring and allocating risk.* In general, **risk** can be described as a prediction concerning potential loss based on known and unknown factors.

Risk management normally involves the transfer of certain risks from the individual to the insurance company by a contractual agreement. We examine the insurance contract and its provisions in this chapter. First, however, we look at some basic insurance terminology and concepts.

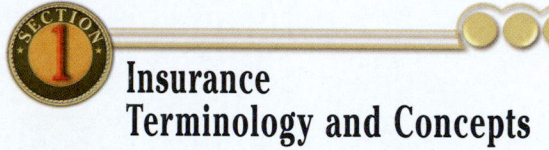

SECTION 1 Insurance Terminology and Concepts

Like other legal areas, insurance has its own special concepts and terminology, a knowledge of which is essential to an understanding of insurance law.

Insurance Terminology

An insurance contract is called a **policy;** the consideration paid to the insurer is called a **premium;** and the insurance company is sometimes called an **underwriter.** The parties to an insurance policy are the *insurer* (the insurance company) and the *insured* (the person covered by its provisions).

Insurance contracts are usually obtained through an *agent,* who normally works for the insurance company, or through a *broker,* who is ordinarily an independent contractor. When a broker deals with an applicant for insurance, the broker is, in effect, the applicant's agent (and not an agent of the insurance company). In contrast, an insurance agent is an agent of the insurance company, not an agent of the applicant. As a general rule, the insurance company is bound by the acts of its agents when they act within the scope of the agency relationship (see Chapters 31 and 32). In most situations, state law determines the status of all parties writing or obtaining insurance.

Classifications of Insurance

Insurance is classified according to the nature of the risk involved. For example, fire insurance, casualty insurance, life insurance, and title insurance apply to different types of risk. Furthermore, policies of these types protect different persons and interests. This is reasonable because the types of losses that are expected and the types that are foreseeable or unforeseeable vary with the nature of the activity. Exhibit 49–1 provides a list of various insurance classifications.

EXHIBIT 49–1 • Insurance Classifications

Type of Insurance	Coverage
Accident	Covers expenses, losses, and suffering incurred by the insured because of accidents causing physical injury and any consequent disability; sometimes includes a specified payment to heirs of the insured if death results from an accident.
All-risk	Covers all losses that the insured may incur except those that are specifically excluded. Typical exclusions are losses due to war, pollution, earthquakes, and floods.
Automobile	May cover damage to automobiles resulting from specified hazards or occurrences (such as fire, vandalism, theft, or collision); normally provides protection against liability for personal injuries and property damage resulting from the operation of the vehicle.
Casualty	Protects against losses incurred by the insured as a result of being held liable for personal injuries or property damage sustained by others.
Credit	Pays to a creditor the balance of a debt on the disability, death, insolvency, or bankruptcy of the debtor; often offered by lending institutions.
Decreasing-term life	Provides life insurance; requires uniform payments over the life (term) of the policy, but with a decreasing face value (amount of coverage).
Employer's liability	Insures employers against liability for injuries or losses sustained by employees during the course of their employment; covers claims not covered under workers' compensation insurance.
Fidelity or guaranty	Provides indemnity against losses in trade or losses caused by the dishonesty of employees, the insolvency of debtors, or breaches of contract.
Fire	Covers losses to the insured caused by fire.
Floater	Covers movable property, as long as the property is within the territorial boundaries specified in the contract.
Group	Provides individual life, medical, or disability insurance coverage but is obtainable through a group of persons, usually employees. The policy premium is paid either entirely by the employer or partially by the employer and partially by the employee.
Health	Covers expenses incurred by the insured resulting from physical injury or illness and other expenses relating to health and life maintenance.
Homeowners'	Protects homeowners against some or all risks of loss to their residences and the residences' contents or liability arising from the use of the property.
Key-person	Protects a business in the event of the death or disability of a key employee.
Liability	Protects against liability imposed on the insured as a result of injuries to the person or property of another.
Life	Covers the death of the policyholder; on the death of the insured, the insurer pays the amount specified in the policy to the insured's beneficiary.

EXHIBIT CONTINUES

EXHIBIT 49–1 • Insurance Classifications, Continued

Type of Insurance	Coverage
Major medical	Protects the insured against major hospital, medical, or surgical expenses.
Malpractice	Protects professionals (physicians, lawyers, and others) against malpractice claims brought against them by their patients or clients; a form of liability insurance.
Marine	Covers movable property (including ships, freight, and cargo) against certain perils or navigation risks during a specific voyage or time period.
Mortgage	Covers a mortgage loan; the insurer pays the balance of the mortgage to the creditor on the death or disability of the debtor.
No-fault auto	Covers personal injuries and (sometimes) property damage resulting from automobile accidents. The insured submits his or her claims to his or her own insurance company, regardless of who was at fault. A person may sue the party at fault or that party's insurer only in cases involving serious medical injury and consequent high medical costs. Governed by state "no-fault" statutes.
Term life	Provides life insurance for a specified period of time (term) with no cash surrender value; usually renewable.
Title	Protects against any defects in title to real property and any losses incurred as a result of existing claims against or liens on the property at the time of purchase.

Insurable Interest

A person can insure anything in which she or he has an **insurable interest.** Without this insurable interest, there is no enforceable contract, and a transaction to purchase insurance coverage would have to be treated as a wager. The existence of an insurable interest is a primary concern in determining liability under an insurance policy.

Life Insurance In regard to life insurance, one must have a reasonable expectation of benefit from the continued life of another to have an insurable interest in that person's life. The insurable interest must exist *at the time the policy is obtained.* The benefit may be pecuniary (monetary), or it may be founded on the relationship between the parties (by blood or affinity). Close family relationships give a person an insurable interest in the life of another. Generally, blood or marital relationships fit this category. A husband can take out an insurance policy on his wife and vice versa; parents can take out life insurance policies on their children; brothers and sisters, on each other; and grandparents, on grandchildren—as all these are close family relationships. A policy that a person takes out on his or her spouse remains valid even if they divorce, unless a specific provision in the policy calls for its termination on divorce.

Key-Person Life Insurance *Key-person insurance* is insurance obtained by an organization on the life of a person who is important to that organization. Because the organization expects to experience some pecuniary gain from the continuation of the key person's life or some financial loss from the key person's death, the organization has an insurable interest. Typically, a partnership will insure the life of each partner because the firm will sustain some degree of loss if any partner dies. Similarly, a corporation has an insurable interest in the life of a key executive whose death would result in financial loss to the company. If a firm insures a key person's life and then that person leaves the firm and subsequently dies, the firm can collect on the insurance policy, provided it has continued to pay the premiums.

Property Insurance An insurable interest exists in real or personal property when the insured derives a pecuniary benefit from the property's preservation and continued existence. In other words, a person has an insurable interest in property if the person stands to suffer a financial loss if the property is destroyed or damaged. The owner of the property clearly has an insurable interest, but a party need not be the owner to have an insurable interest. Both a mortgagor and a mortgagee, for example, have an insurable interest in the mortgaged property, as do a landlord and a tenant in leased property, and a partner in partnership property. A secured party has an insurable interest in the property in which he or she has a security interest.

The existence of an insurable interest is a primary concern in determining liability under an insurance policy. The insurable interest in property must exist when the loss occurs. Whether a party had an insurable interest in property was at issue in the following case.

CASE 49.1 Zurich American Insurance Co. v. ABM Industries, Inc.

United States Court of Appeals, Second Circuit, 2005. 397 F.3d 158.

Background and Facts ABM Industries, Inc., is an engineering, lighting, and janitorial service contractor that, in 2001, occupied office and storage space in the World Trade Center (WTC) in New York City. This space included a call center to which WTC tenants reported problems. ABM operated the heating, ventilating, and air-conditioning (HVAC) systems for the WTC, essentially running the physical plant, and serviced the common areas of the complex. At the time, ABM employed more than 800 persons at the WTC. Zurich American Insurance Company insured ABM against losses resulting from "business interruption * * * caused by direct physical loss or damage * * * to property owned, controlled, used, leased, or intended for use by the Insured." After the terrorist attacks on the WTC on September 11, ABM filed a claim with Zurich to recover for the loss of all income derived from ABM's operations at the WTC. Zurich asked a federal district court for a declaratory judgment on the extent of its liability. The court issued a summary judgment in Zurich's favor, limiting the amount of ABM's recovery to the income it lost from "the destruction of the [WTC] space that ABM itself occupied or caused by the destruction of ABM's own supplies and equipment." ABM appealed to the U.S. Court of Appeals for the Second Circuit.

Decision and Rationale The U.S. Court of Appeals for the Second Circuit reversed the ruling of the lower court and awarded a summary judgment in ABM's favor. The appellate court stated, "The only prerequisite to coverage mandated by New York law is that an entity have an insurable interest in the property it insures." The court pointed out that under the applicable New York state statute, this term includes "any lawful and substantial economic interest in the safety or preservation of property from loss, destruction, or pecuniary [monetary] damage." The court emphasized that in this case, the insurance "policy's scope expressly includes real or personal property that the insured 'used,' 'controlled,' or 'intended for use.'" Because ABM's income depends on "the common areas and leased premises in the WTC complex, * * * ABM meets New York's requirement of having an insurable interest in that property."

The Legal Environment Dimension *On what issue was the court asked to rule in this case?*

The Ethical Dimension *On what did the court base its reasoning for its ruling on this issue?*

SECTION 2 The Insurance Contract

An insurance contract is governed by the general principles of contract law, although the insurance industry is heavily regulated by the states.[1] Customarily, a party offers to purchase insurance by submitting an application to the insurance company. The company can either accept or reject the offer. Sometimes, the insurance company's acceptance is conditional—on the results of a life insurance applicant's medical examination, for example. For the insurance contract to be binding, consideration (in the form of a premium) must be given, and the parties forming the

1. The states were given authority to regulate the insurance industry by the McCarran-Ferguson Act of 1945, 15 U.S.C. Sections 1011–1015.

contract must have the required contractual capacity to do so.

Application for Insurance

The filled-in application form for insurance is usually attached to the policy and made a part of the insurance contract. Thus, an insurance applicant is bound by any false statements that appear in the application (subject to certain exceptions). Because the insurance company evaluates the risk based on the information included in the insurance application, misstatements or misrepresentations can void a policy, especially if the insurance company can show that it would not have extended insurance if it had known the facts.

Effective Date

The effective date of an insurance contract—that is, the date on which the insurance coverage begins—is important. In some instances, the insurance applicant is not protected until a formal written policy is issued. In other situations, coverage begins when a binder is written (to be discussed shortly) or, depending on the terms of the contract, after a certain period of time has elapsed or a specified condition is met.

Brokers versus Agents A broker is the agent of an applicant. Therefore, if the broker fails to procure a policy, the applicant normally is not insured. According to general principles of agency law, if the broker fails to obtain policy coverage and the applicant is harmed as a result, then the broker is liable to the harmed applicant-principal for the loss.

Binders A person who seeks insurance from an insurance company's agent is usually protected from the moment the application is made, provided—for life insurance—that some form of premium has been paid. Between the time the company receives the application and the time it is either rejected or accepted, the applicant is covered (possibly subject to certain conditions, such as passing a physical examination). Usually, the agent will write a memorandum, or **binder,** indicating that a policy is pending and stating its essential terms.

Conditions Agreed to by the Parties If the parties agree that the policy will be issued and delivered at a later time, the contract is not effective until the policy is issued and delivered or sent to the applicant, depending on the agreement. Thus, any loss sustained between the time of application and the delivery of the policy is not covered. An insurance contract may also include a clause stating that the applicant must be "still insurable" on the effective date of the policy.

Parties may agree that a life insurance policy will be binding at the time the insured pays the first premium, or the policy may be expressly contingent on the applicant's passing a physical examination. If the applicant pays the premium and passes the examination, then the policy coverage is continuously in effect. If the applicant pays the premium but dies before having the physical examination, then in order to collect, the applicant's estate normally must show that the applicant would have passed the examination had he or she not died.

Provisions and Clauses

Some of the important provisions and clauses contained in insurance contracts are discussed in the following subsections and listed in Exhibit 49–2.

Provisions Mandated by Statute If a statute mandates that a certain provision be included in insurance contracts, a court will deem that an insurance policy contains the provision regardless of whether the parties actually included it in the language of their contract. If a statute requires that any limitations regarding coverage be stated in the contract, a court will not allow an insurer to avoid liability for a claim through reliance on an unexpressed restriction.

Incontestability Clauses Statutes commonly require that a policy for life or health insurance provide that after the policy has been in force for a specified length of time—often two or three years—the insurer cannot contest statements made in the application. This is known as an **incontestability clause.** Once a policy becomes incontestable, the insurer cannot later avoid a claim on the basis of, for example, fraud on the part of the insured, unless the clause provides an exception for that circumstance. The clause does not prevent an insurer from refusing or reducing payment for a claim due to nonpayment of premiums, failure to file proof of death within a certain period, or lack of an insurable interest.

Coinsurance Clauses Often, when taking out fire insurance policies, property owners insure their property for less than full value because most fires do

EXHIBIT 49–2 • Insurance Contract Provisions and Clauses

Antilapse clause	An antilapse clause provides that a life insurance policy will not automatically lapse if no payment is made on the date due. Ordinarily, under such a provision, the insured has a *grace period* of thirty or thirty-one days within which to pay an overdue premium before the policy is canceled.
Appraisal clause	Insurance policies frequently provide that if the parties cannot agree on the amount of a loss covered under the policy or the value of the property lost, an appraisal, or estimate, by an impartial and qualified third party can be demanded.
Arbitration clause	Many insurance policies include clauses that call for arbitration of any disputes that arise between the insurer and the insured concerning the settlement of claims.
Coinsurance clause	Many property insurance policies include a coinsurance clause that applies in the event of a partial loss and determines what percentage of the value of the property must be insured for an owner to be fully reimbursed for a loss. If the owner insures the property up to a specified percentage (typically 80 percent) of its value, she or he will recover any loss up to the face amount of the policy.
Incontestability clause	An incontestability clause provides that after a policy has been in force for a specified length of time—usually two or three years—the insurer cannot contest statements made in the application.
Multiple insurance clause	Many insurance policies include a clause providing that if the insured has multiple insurance policies that cover the same property and the amount of coverage exceeds the loss, the loss will be shared proportionately by the insurance companies.

not result in a total loss. To encourage owners to insure their property for an amount as close to full value as possible, fire insurance policies generally include a coinsurance clause. Typically, a *coinsurance clause* provides that if the owner insures the property up to a specified percentage—usually 80 percent—of its value, she or he will recover any loss up to the face amount of the policy. If the insurance is for less than the fixed percentage, the owner is responsible for a proportionate share of the loss. In effect, the owner becomes a coinsurer.

Coinsurance applies only in instances of partial loss. The amount of the recovery is calculated by using the following formula.

$$\text{loss} \times \left(\frac{\text{amount of insurance coverage}}{\text{coininsurance percentage} \times \text{property value}} \right) = \text{amount of recovery}$$

Thus, if the owner of property valued at $200,000 takes out a policy in the amount of $100,000 and suffers a loss of $80,000, the recovery will be $50,000. The owner will be responsible for (coinsure) the balance of the loss, or $30,000.

$$\$80{,}000 \times \left(\frac{\$100{,}000}{0.8 \times \$200{,}000} \right) = \$50{,}000$$

If the owner had taken out a policy in the amount of 80 percent of the value of the property, or $160,000, then according to the same formula, the owner would have recovered the full amount of the loss (the face amount of the policy).

Appraisal and Arbitration Clauses Most fire insurance policies provide that if the parties cannot agree on the amount of a loss covered under the policy or on the value of the property lost, an *appraisal* can be demanded. An appraisal is an estimate of the property's value determined by a suitably qualified individual who has no interest in the property. Typically, two appraisers are used, one being appointed by each party. A third party, or umpire, may be called on to resolve differences. Other types of insurance policies also contain provisions for appraisal and arbitration when the insured and insurer disagree on the value of a loss.

Multiple Insurance Coverage If an insured has *multiple insurance coverage*—that is, policies with several companies covering the same insurable interest—and the amount of coverage exceeds the loss, the insured can collect from each insurer only the company's proportionate share of the liability, relative to the total amount of insurance. Many fire insurance policies include a pro rata clause, which requires that any loss be shared proportionately by all carriers. For example, if Grumbling insured $50,000 worth of property with two companies and each policy had a liability limit of $40,000, then on the property's total destruction Grumbling could collect only $25,000 from each insurer.

Antilapse Clauses A life insurance policy may provide, or a statute may require a policy to provide, that it will not automatically lapse if no payment is made on the date due. Ordinarily, under an *antilapse provision*, the insured has a *grace period* of thirty or thirty-one days within which to pay an overdue premium. If the insured fails to pay a premium altogether, there are alternatives to cancellation:

1. The insurer may be required to extend the insurance for a period of time.
2. The insurer may issue a policy with less coverage to reflect the amount of the payments made.
3. The insurer may pay to the insured the policy's **cash surrender value**—the amount the insurer has agreed to pay on the policy's cancellation before the insured's death. (In determining this value, the following factors are considered: the period that the policy has already run, the amount of the premium, the insured's age and life expectancy, and amounts to be repaid on any outstanding loans taken out against the policy.)

When the insurance contract states that the insurer cannot cancel the policy, these alternatives are important.

Interpreting Provisions of an Insurance Contract

The courts recognize that most people do not have the special training necessary to understand the intricate terminology used in insurance policies. Therefore, when disputes arise, the courts will interpret the words used in an insurance contract according to their ordinary meanings in light of the nature of the coverage involved.

Ambiguity When there is an ambiguity in the policy, the provision generally is interpreted against the insurance company. Also, when it is unclear whether an insurance contract actually exists because the written policy has not been delivered, the uncertainty normally is resolved against the insurance company. The court presumes that the policy is in effect unless the company can show otherwise. Similarly, an insurer must make sure that the insured is adequately notified of any change in coverage under an existing policy.

Disputes over insurance often focus on the interpretation of an ambiguous provision in the policy, as the following case illustrates.

CASE 49.2 Cary v. United of Omaha Life Insurance Co.

Supreme Court of Colorado, 2005. 108 P.3d 288.

• **Background and Facts** Fourteen-year-old Dena Cary shot herself under the chin in an unsuccessful suicide attempt because she suffered a major depressive episode of her diagnosed bipolar disorder. Her injuries required extensive medical treatment. Dena's father, Thomas Cary, sought payment for these costs under his medical insurance covering injury and illness, but the insurer denied the claim. The insurer argued that coverage was excluded under a provision reading: "Injury. Injury means accidental bodily injury which occurs independently of Illness. Injury does not include self-inflicted bodily injury, either while sane or insane." The Carys filed an action in a Colorado state court for bad faith denial of coverage. The trial court found that the injury was covered by the policy, but the state intermediate appellate court reversed. The Carys appealed to the state supreme court.

CASE 49.2 CONTINUED

• **Decision and Rationale** The Colorado Supreme Court reversed the decision of the appellate court, with instructions to return the case to the trial court for proceedings consistent with the state supreme court's opinion. The state supreme court reasoned that "the plan is ambiguous because it is susceptible to * * * equally reasonable interpretation[s]." The court construed the policy's definition of *injury*, and its explanation of the term and its exclusions, according to two interpretations. Under one interpretation, the second sentence limited the first sentence's phrase "accidental bodily injury which occurs independently of Illness," so that "injuries that occur as a result of illness, even if self-inflicted, are defined out of the 'injury' definition and are covered by the Plan's promise to provide coverage for treatment of an Illness." Under a second interpretation, both sentences were of "equal" value, with neither limiting the other, so that "if an injury is accidental or is the result of an illness, it nonetheless would be excluded from coverage if it is self-inflicted." Because ambiguities in insurance policies are resolved in favor of coverage, "Dena's injuries are covered."

• **What If the Facts Were Different?** *Suppose that there had not been an ambiguity in this policy and that it had been subject to only one reasonable interpretation. Would the result have been different? Explain.*

• **The Legal Environment Dimension** *Should insurance policy provisions be interpreted to avoid ambiguities if possible? Why or why not?*

Cancellation The insured can cancel a policy at any time, and the insurer can cancel under certain circumstances. When an insurance company can cancel its insurance contract, the policy or a state statute usually requires that the insurer give advance written notice of the cancellation.[2] The same requirement applies when only part of a policy is canceled. Any premium paid in advance and not yet earned may be refundable on the policy's cancellation. The insured may also be entitled to a life insurance policy's cash surrender value.

The insurer may cancel an insurance policy for various reasons, depending on the type of insurance. For example, automobile insurance can be canceled for nonpayment of premiums or suspension of the insured's driver's license. Property insurance can be canceled for nonpayment of premiums or for other reasons, including the insured's fraud or misrepresentation, gross negligence, or conviction for a crime that increases the risk assumed by the insurer. Life and health policies can be canceled because of false statements made by the insured in the application, but the cancellation must take place only before the effective date of an incontestability clause. An insurer cannot cancel—or refuse to renew—a policy because of the national origin or race of an applicant or because the insured has appeared as a witness in a case brought against the company.

Duties and Obligations of the Parties

Both parties to an insurance contract are responsible for the obligations they assume under the contract (contract law was discussed in Chapters 10 through 19). In addition, both the insured and the insurer have an implied duty to act in good faith.

Duties of the Insured Good faith requires the party who is applying for insurance to reveal everything necessary for the insurer to evaluate the risk. In other words, the applicant must disclose all material facts, including all facts that an insurer would consider in determining whether to charge a higher premium or to refuse to issue a policy altogether.

Once the insurance policy is issued, the insured has three basic duties under the contract: (1) to pay the premiums as stated in the contract, (2) to notify the insurer within a reasonable time if an event occurs that gives rise to a claim, and (3) to cooperate with the insurer during any investigation or litigation.

Duties of the Insurer Once the insurer has accepted the risk, and some event occurs that gives rise to a claim, the insurer has a *duty to investigate* to

2. At issue in one case was whether a notification of cancellation included on a disc sent to the insured constituted "written notice" of cancellation. The court held that the computerized document, which could be printed out as "hard copy," constituted written notice. See *Clyburn v. Allstate Insurance Co.*, 826 F.Supp. 955 (D.S.C. 1993).

determine the facts. When a policy provides insurance against third party claims, the insurer is obligated to make reasonable efforts to settle such a claim. If a settlement cannot be reached, then regardless of the claim's merit, the insurer has a *duty to defend* any suit against the insured. The insurer also owes a *duty to pay* any legitimate claims up to the face amount of the policy.

An insurer has a duty to provide or pay an attorney to defend its insured when a complaint against the insured alleges facts that could, if proved, impose liability on the insured within the policy's coverage. In the following case, the question was whether a policy covered a dentist's potential liability arising from a practical joke that he played on an employee while performing a dental procedure.

CASE 49.3 Woo v. Fireman's Fund Insurance Co.

Supreme Court of Washington, 2007. 161 Wash.2d 43, 164 P.3d 454.

Background and Facts Tina Alberts worked for Robert Woo as a dental surgical assistant. Her family also raised potbellied pigs, and she often talked about them at work. Sometimes, Woo mentioned the pigs, intending to encourage a "friendly working environment." Alberts interpreted the comments as offensive. Alberts asked Woo to replace two of her teeth with implants. The procedure required the installation of temporary partial bridges called "flippers." While Alberts was anesthetized, Woo installed a set of flippers shaped like boar tusks, as a joke, and took photos. Before Alberts regained consciousness, he inserted the normal flippers. A month later, Woo's staff gave Alberts the photos at a gathering to celebrate her birthday. Stunned, Alberts refused to return to work. Woo tried to apologize. Alberts filed a suit in a Washington state court against him, alleging battery and other torts. He asked Fireman's Fund Insurance Company to defend him, claiming coverage under his policy. The insurer refused. Woo settled the suit with Alberts for $250,000 and filed a suit against Fireman's, claiming that it had breached its duty to defend him. The court awarded him $750,000 in damages, plus the amount of the settlement and attorneys' fees and costs. A state intermediate appellate court reversed the award. Woo appealed to the Supreme Court of Washington.

Decision and Rationale The state supreme court reversed the decision of the lower court. The Supreme Court of Washington held that Fireman's had a duty to defend Woo under the professional liability provision of his policy. The court pointed out that the professional liability provision in Fireman's policy stated that it would defend any claim brought against the insured "even if the allegations of the claim are groundless, false or fraudulent." Further, the policy defines *dental services* as "all services which are performed in the practice of the dentistry profession as defined in the business and professional codes of the state where [the dentist is licensed]." The court was unimpressed with Fireman's attempt to establish that Woo's practical joke was not connected to treating Alberts's condition. "In addition to covering the rendering of dental services, the professional liability provision covers ownership, maintenance, or operation of an office for the practice of dentistry and Alberts' [s] complaints alleged Woo's practical joke took place while Woo was conducting his dental practice. The insertion of boar tusk flippers was also intertwined with Woo's dental practice because it involved an interaction with an employee."

The Ethical Dimension *Are the acts of the principal parties—Woo, Alberts, and Fireman's—ethically justifiable in the circumstances of this case? Discuss.*

The Legal Environment Dimension *In determining if an insurer has a duty to defend an insured, should a court ask whether the insured had a "reasonable expectation" of coverage? Explain.*

Bad Faith Actions Although the law of insurance generally follows contract law, most states now recognize a "bad faith" tort action against insurers. Thus, if an insurer in bad faith denies coverage of a claim, the insured may recover in tort an amount exceeding the policy's coverage limits and may even recover millions of dollars in punitive damages. Some courts have held insurers liable for a bad faith refusal to settle claims for reasonable amounts within the policy limits.[3]

3. See, for example, *Columbia National Insurance Co. v. Freeman*, 347 Ark. 423, 64 S.W.3d 720 (2002).

Defenses against Payment

An insurance company can raise any of the defenses that would be valid in an ordinary action on a contract, as well as a few additional defenses. If the insurance company can show that the policy was procured through fraud or misrepresentation, for example, it may have a valid defense for not paying on a claim. (The insurance company may also have the right to disaffirm or rescind an insurance contract.) An absolute defense exists if the insurer can show that the insured lacked an insurable interest—thus rendering the policy void from the beginning. Improper actions, such as those that are against public policy or that are otherwise illegal, can also give the insurance company a defense against the payment of a claim or allow it to rescind the contract.

In some situations, the insurance company may be prevented, or estopped, from asserting defenses that normally are available. For example, an insurance company ordinarily cannot escape payment on the death of an insured on the ground that the person's age was stated incorrectly on the application. Also, incontestability clauses prevent the insurer from asserting certain defenses.

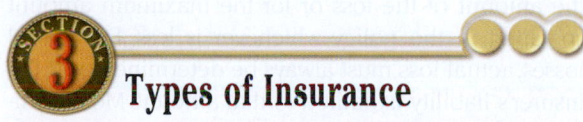

SECTION 3 Types of Insurance

There are four general types of insurance coverage: life insurance, fire and homeowners' insurance, automobile insurance, and business liability insurance. We now examine briefly the coverage available under each of these types of insurance.

Life Insurance

There are five basic types of life insurance:

1. **Whole life,** sometimes referred to as straight life, ordinary life, or cash-value insurance, provides protection with a cumulated cash surrender value that can be used as collateral for a loan. The insured pays premiums during his or her entire lifetime, and the beneficiary receives a fixed payment on the death of the insured.
2. **Limited-payment life** is a type of policy under which premiums are paid for a stated number of years; after that time, the policy is paid up and fully effective during the insured's life. For example, a policy might call for twenty payments. Naturally, premiums are higher than for whole life. This insurance also has a cash surrender value.
3. **Term insurance** is a type of policy for which premiums are paid for a specified term. Payment on the policy is due only if death occurs within the term period. Premiums are lower than for whole life or limited-payment life, and there usually is no cash surrender value. Frequently, this type of insurance can be converted to another type of life insurance.
4. **Endowment insurance** involves fixed premium payments that are made for a definite term. At the end of the term, a fixed amount is paid to the insured or, on the death of the insured during the specified period, to a beneficiary. Thus, this type of insurance represents both term insurance and a form of **annuity** (the right to receive fixed, periodic payments for life or—as in this instance—for a term of years). Endowment insurance has a rapidly increasing cash surrender value, but premiums are high because a payment must be made at the end of the term even if the insured is still living.
5. **Universal life** combines aspects of both term insurance and whole life insurance. From every payment, usually called a "contribution," the issuing life insurance company makes two deductions: the first is a charge for term insurance protection; the second is for company expenses and profit. The funds that remain after these deductions earn interest for the policyholder at a rate determined by the company. The interest-earning amount is called the policy's *cash value,* but that term does not mean the same thing as it does for a traditional whole life insurance policy. With a universal life policy, the cash value grows at a variable interest rate rather than at a predetermined rate.

The rights and liabilities of the parties to life insurance contracts are basically dependent on the specific contract. A few features deserve special attention.

Liability The life insurance contract determines not only the extent of the insurer's liability but also, generally, whether the insurer is liable on the death of the insured. Most life insurance contracts exclude liability for death caused by suicide, military action during war, execution by a state or federal government, and even an event that occurs while the insured is a passenger in a commercial vehicle. In the absence of contractual exclusion, most courts today construe any cause of death to be one of the insurer's risks.

Adjustment Due to Misstatement of Age The insurance policy constitutes the agreement between the parties. The application for insurance is part of the policy and is usually attached to the policy. When the insured misstates his or her age on the application, an error is introduced, particularly as to the amount of premiums paid. As mentioned, misstatement of age is not a material error sufficient to allow the insurer to void the policy. Instead, on discovery of the error, the insurer will adjust the premium payments and/or benefits accordingly.

Assignment Most life insurance policies allow the insured to change beneficiaries. When this is permitted, in the absence of any prohibition or notice requirement, the insured can assign the rights to the policy (for example, as security for a loan) without the consent of the insurer or the beneficiary. If the beneficiary's right is *vested*—that is, has become absolute, entitling the beneficiary to payment of the proceeds—the policy cannot be assigned without the beneficiary's consent. For the most part, life insurance contracts permit assignment and require notice only to the insurer to be effective.

Creditors' Rights Unless insurance proceeds are exempt under state law, the insured's interest in life insurance is an asset that is subject to the rights of judgment creditors. These creditors generally can reach insurance proceeds payable to the insured's estate, proceeds payable to anyone if the payment of premiums constituted a fraud on creditors, and proceeds payable to a named beneficiary unless the beneficiary's rights have vested. Creditors, however, cannot compel the insured to make available the cash surrender value of the policy or to change the named beneficiary to that of the creditor. Almost all states exempt at least a part of the proceeds of life insurance from creditors' claims.

Termination Although the insured can cancel and terminate the policy, the insurer generally cannot do so. Therefore, termination usually takes place only if one of the following occurs:

1. Default in premium payments that causes the policy to lapse.
2. Death and payment of benefits.
3. Expiration of the term of the policy.
4. Cancellation by the insured.

Fire and Homeowners' Insurance

There are basically two types of insurance policies for a home—standard fire insurance policies and homeowners' policies.

Standard Fire Insurance Policies The standard fire insurance policy protects the homeowner against fire and lightning, as well as damage from smoke and water caused by the fire or the fire department. Most fire insurance policies are classified according to the type of property covered and the extent (amount) of the issuer's liability. Exhibit 49–3 lists typical fire insurance policies, and the following subsections discuss specific features and provisions.

Liability. The insurer's liability is determined from the terms of the policy. Most policies, however, limit recovery to losses resulting from *hostile* fires—basically, those that break out or begin in places where no fire was intended to burn. A *friendly* fire—one burning in a place where it was intended to burn—is not covered. Therefore, smoke from a fireplace is not covered, but smoke from a fire caused by a defective electrical outlet is covered. Sometimes, owners add "extended coverage" to the fire policy to cover losses from "friendly" fires.

If the policy is a *valued* policy (see Exhibit 49–3) and the subject matter is completely destroyed, the insurer is liable for the amount specified in the policy. If it is an *open* policy, then the extent of the actual loss must be determined, and the insurer is liable only for the amount of the loss or for the maximum amount specified in the policy, whichever is less. For partial losses, actual loss must always be determined, and the insurer's liability is limited to that amount. Most insurance policies permit the insurer to either restore or replace the property destroyed or to pay for the loss.

Proof of Loss. As a condition for recovery, fire insurance policies require the insured to file a proof of loss with the insurer within a specified period or immediately (within a reasonable time). Failure to comply *could* allow the insurance carrier to avoid liability. Courts vary somewhat on the enforcement of such clauses.

Occupancy Clause. Most standard policies require that the premises be occupied at the time of the loss. The relevant clause states that if the premises become vacant or unoccupied for a given period, unless consent by the insurer is given, the coverage is suspended until the premises are reoccupied. Persons going on extended vacations should check their policies regarding this point.

Assignment. Before a loss has occurred, a fire insurance policy is not assignable without the consent of the

EXHIBIT 49–3 • Typical Fire Insurance Policies

Type of Policy	Coverage
Blanket	Covers a class of property rather than specific property, because the property is expected to shift or vary in nature. A policy covering the inventory of a business is an example.
Floater	Usually supplements a specific policy. It is intended to cover property that may change in either location or quantity. To illustrate, if the painting mentioned below under "specific policy" is to be exhibited during the year at numerous locations throughout the state, a floater policy would be desirable.
Open	A policy that does not state an agreed-on value for the property. The policy usually provides for a maximum liability of the insurer, but payment for loss is restricted to the fair market value of the property at the time of loss or to the insurer's limit, whichever is less.
Specific	Covers a specific item of property at a specific location. An example is a particular painting located in a residence or a piece of machinery located in a factory or business.
Valued	A policy that, by agreement, places a specific value on the subject to be insured to cover the eventuality of its total loss.

insurer. The theory is that the fire insurance policy is a personal contract between the insured and the insurer. The nonassignability of a policy is extremely important when a house is purchased. The purchaser must procure his or her own insurance. If the purchaser wishes to assume the seller's remaining period of insurance coverage, the insurer's consent is essential.

To illustrate: Ann is selling her home and lot to Jeff. Ann has a one-year fire policy with Ajax Insurance Company, with six months of coverage remaining at the date on which the sale is to close. Ann agrees to assign the balance of her policy, but Ajax has not given its consent. One day after passage of the deed, a fire totally destroys the house. Can Jeff recover from Ajax?

The answer is no, as the policy is actually voided on the closing of the transaction and the deeding of the property. The reason the policy is voided is that Ann no longer has an insurable interest at the time of loss, and Jeff has no rights in a nonassignable policy.

Homeowners' Policies A homeowners' policy provides protection against a number of risks under a single policy, allowing the policyholder to avoid the cost of buying each protection separately. There are two basic types of homeowners' coverage:

1. *Property coverage* includes the garage, house, and other private buildings on the policyholder's lot. It also includes the personal possessions and property of the policyholder at home, while traveling, or at work. It pays additional expenses for living away from home because of a fire or some other covered peril.
2. *Liability coverage* is for personal liability in the event that someone is injured on the insured's property, the insured damages someone else's property, or the insured injures someone else (unless the injury involves an automobile, which would be covered by automobile insurance, discussed next).

Property Coverage. Perils insured under property coverage often include fire, lightning, wind, hail, vandalism, and theft (of personal property). Standard homeowners' insurance typically does not cover flood damage. Personal property that is typically not included under property coverage, in the absence of a specific provision, includes such items as motor vehicles, farm equipment, airplanes, and boats. Coverage for other property, such as jewelry and securities, is usually limited to a specified dollar amount.

Liability Coverage. Liability coverage under a homeowners' policy applies when others are injured or property is damaged because of the unsafe condition of the policyholder's premises. It also applies when the policyholder is negligent. It normally does not apply, however, if the liability arises from business or professional activities or from the operation of a motor vehicle, which are subjects for separate policies. Also excluded is liability arising from intentional misconduct. Similar to liability coverage is coverage for the medical payments of others who are injured on the policyholder's property and for the property of others that is damaged by a member of the policyholder's family.

Renters' Policies. Renters also take out insurance policies to protect against losses to personal property. Renters' insurance covers personal possessions against various perils and includes coverage for additional living expenses and liability.

Automobile Insurance

There are two basic kinds of automobile insurance: liability insurance and collision and comprehensive insurance.

Liability Insurance Automobile liability insurance covers liability for bodily injury and property damage. Liability limits are usually described by a series of three numbers, such as 100/300/50. This means that, for one accident, the policy will pay a maximum of $100,000 for bodily injury to one person, a maximum of $300,000 for bodily injury to more than one person, and a maximum of $50,000 for property damage. Many insurance companies offer liability coverage in amounts up to $500,000 and sometimes higher.

Individuals who are dissatisfied with the maximum liability limits offered by regular automobile insurance coverage can purchase separate coverage under an *umbrella policy.* Umbrella limits sometimes go as high as $10 million. Umbrella policies also cover personal liability in excess of the liability limits of a homeowners' policy.

Collision and Comprehensive Insurance Collision insurance covers damage to the insured's car in any type of collision. Usually, it is not advisable to purchase full collision coverage (otherwise known as *zero deductible*). The price per year is relatively high because it is likely that some small repair jobs will be required each year. Most people prefer to take out policies with a deductible of $100, $250, or $500, which costs substantially less than zero-deductible coverage.

Comprehensive insurance covers loss, damage, and destruction due to fire, hurricane, hail, vandalism, and theft. It can be obtained separately from collision insurance.

Other Automobile Insurance Other types of automobile insurance coverage include the following:

1. *Uninsured motorist coverage.* Uninsured motorist coverage insures the driver and passengers against injury caused by any driver without insurance or by a hit-and-run driver. Some states require that it be included in all auto insurance policies sold.
2. *Accidental death benefits.* Sometimes referred to as *double indemnity,* accidental death benefits provide for a payment of twice the policy's face amount if the policyholder dies in an accident. This coverage generally costs very little, but it may not be necessary if the insured has a sufficient amount of life insurance.
3. *Medical payment coverage.* Medical payment coverage provided by an auto insurance policy pays hospital and other medical bills and sometimes funeral expenses. This type of insurance protects all the passengers in the insured's car when the insured is driving.
4. *Other-driver coverage.* An **omnibus clause,** or *other-driver clause,* protects the vehicle owner who has taken out the insurance and anyone who drives the vehicle with the owner's permission. This coverage may be held to extend to a third party who drives the vehicle with the permission of the person to whom the owner gave permission.
5. *No-fault insurance.* Under no-fault statutes, claims arising from an accident are made against the claimant's own insurer, regardless of whose fault the accident was. In some situations—for example, when injuries require expensive medical treatment—an injured party may seek recovery from another party or insurer. In those instances, the injured party may collect the maximum amount of no-fault insurance and still sue for total damages from the party at fault, although usually, on winning an award, the injured party must reimburse the insurer for its no-fault payments.

Business Liability Insurance

A business may be vulnerable to all sorts of risks. A key employee may die or become disabled; a customer may be injured when using a manufacturer's product; the patron of an establishment selling liquor may leave the premises and injure a third party in an automobile accident; or a professional may overlook some important detail, causing liability for malpractice. Should the first situation arise (for instance, if the company president dies), the firm may have some protection under a key-person insurance policy, discussed earlier. In the other circumstances, other types of insurance may apply.

General Liability Comprehensive general liability insurance can encompass virtually as many risks as the insurer agrees to cover. For example, among the types of coverage that a business might wish to acquire is protection from liability for injuries arising from on-premises events not otherwise covered, such as company social functions. Some specialized establishments, such as taverns, may be subject to liability in particular circumstances, and policies can be drafted to meet their needs. In many jurisdictions, for example, statutes impose liability on a seller of liquor when a buyer of the liquor becomes intoxicated as a result of the sale and injures a third party. Legal protection may extend not only to the immediate consequences of an injury, such as quadriplegia resulting from an automobile accident, but also to the loss of financial support suffered by a family because of the injuries. Insurance can provide coverage for these injuries and financial losses.

Product Liability Manufacturers may be subject to liability for injuries that their products cause, and product liability insurance can be written to match specific products' risks. Coverage can be procured under a comprehensive general liability policy or under a separate policy. The coverage may include payment for expenses involved in recalling and replacing a product that has proved to be defective. (For a comprehensive discussion of product liability, see Chapter 23.)

Professional Malpractice Attorneys, physicians, architects, engineers, and other professionals have increasingly become the targets of negligence suits. Professionals purchase malpractice insurance to protect themselves against such claims. The large judgments in some malpractice suits have received considerable publicity and are sometimes cited in what has been called "the insurance crisis," because they have contributed to a significant increase in malpractice insurance premiums.

Workers' Compensation Workers' compensation insurance covers payments to employees who are injured in accidents arising out of and in the course of employment—that is, on the job. State statutes govern workers' compensation, as discussed in detail in Chapter 33.

REVIEWING Insurance

Provident Insurance, Inc., issued an insurance policy to a company providing an employee, Steve Matlin, with disability insurance. Soon thereafter, Matlin was diagnosed with "panic disorder and phobia of returning to work." He lost his job and sought disability coverage. Provident denied coverage, doubting the diagnosis of disability. Matlin and his employer sued Provident. During pretrial discovery, the insurer learned that Matlin had stated on the policy application that he had never been treated for any "emotional, mental, nervous, urinary, or digestive disorder" or any kind of heart disease. In fact, before Matlin filled out the application, he had visited a physician for chest pains and general anxiety, and the physician had prescribed an antidepressant and recommended that Matlin stop smoking. Using the information presented in the chapter, answer the following questions.

1. Did Matlin commit a misrepresentation on his policy application?
2. If there was any ambiguity on the application, should it be resolved in favor of the insured or the insurer?
3. Assuming that the policy is valid, does Matlin's situation fall within the terms of the disability policy?
4. If Matlin is covered by the policy but is also disqualified by his misrepresentation on the application for coverage, might the insurer still be liable for bad faith denial of coverage? Explain.

TERMS AND CONCEPTS

annuity 943
binder 938
cash surrender value 940
endowment insurance 943
incontestability clause 938
insurable interest 936
insurance 934
limited-payment life 943
omnibus clause 946
policy 934
premium 934
risk 934
risk management 934
term insurance 943
underwriter 934
universal life 943
whole life 943

QUESTIONS AND CASE PROBLEMS

49–1. Adia owns a house and has an elderly third cousin living with her. Adia decides she needs fire insurance on the house and a life insurance policy on her third cousin to cover funeral and other expenses that will result from her cousin's death. Adia takes out a fire insurance policy from Ajax Insurance Co. and a $10,000 life insurance policy from Beta Insurance Co. on her third cousin. Six months later, Adia sells the house to John and transfers title to him. Adia and her cousin move into an apartment. With two months remaining on the Ajax policy, a fire totally destroys the house; at the same time, Adia's third cousin dies. Both insurance companies claim they have no liability under the insurance contracts, as Adia did not have an insurable interest, and tender back (return) the premiums. Discuss their claims.

49–2. QUESTION WITH SAMPLE ANSWER

Patrick contracts with an Ajax Insurance Co. agent for a $50,000 ordinary life insurance policy. The application form is filled in to show Patrick's age as thirty-two. In addition, the application form asks whether Patrick has ever had any heart ailments or problems. Patrick answers no, forgetting that as a young child he was diagnosed as having a slight heart murmur. A policy is issued. Three years later, Patrick becomes seriously ill and dies. A review of the policy discloses that Patrick was actually thirty-three at the time of the application and the issuance of the policy and that he erred in answering the question about a history of heart ailments. Discuss whether Ajax can void the policy and escape liability on Patrick's death.

• **For a sample answer to Question 49–2, go to Appendix I at the end of this text.**

49–3. Sapata has an ordinary life insurance policy on her life and a fire insurance policy on her house. Both policies have been in force for a number of years. Sapata's life insurance names her son, Rory, as beneficiary. Sapata has specifically removed her right to change beneficiaries, and the life insurance policy is silent on the right of assignment. Sapata is going on a one-year European vacation and borrows money from Leonard to finance the trip. Leonard takes an assignment of the life insurance policy as security for the loan, as the policy has accumulated a substantial cash surrender value. Sapata also rents out her house to Leonard and assigns her fire insurance policy to him. Discuss fully whether Sapata's assignment of these policies is valid.

49–4. Fritz has an open fire insurance policy on his home for a maximum liability of $60,000. The policy has a number of standard clauses, including the right of the insurer to restore or rebuild the property in lieu of a monetary payment, and it has a standard coinsurance clause. A fire in Fritz's house virtually destroys a utility room and part of the kitchen. The fire was caused by the overheating of an electric water heater. The total damage to the property is $10,000. The property at the time of loss is valued at $100,000. Fritz files a proof-of-loss claim for $10,000. Discuss the insurer's liability in this situation.

49–5. Insurer's Defenses. In 1990, the city of Worcester, Massachusetts, adopted an ordinance that required rooming houses to be equipped with automatic sprinkler systems no later than September 25, 1995. In Worcester, James and Mark Duffy owned a forty-eight-room lodging house with two retail stores on the first floor. In 1994, the Duffys applied with General Star Indemnity Co. for an insurance policy to cover the premises. The application indicated that the premises had sprinkler systems. General issued a policy that required, among other safety features, a sprinkler system. Within a month, the premises were inspected on behalf of General. On the inspection form forwarded to the insurer, in the list of safety systems, next to the word *sprinkler* the inspector had inserted only a hyphen. In

July 1995, when the premises sustained more than $100,000 in fire damage, General learned that there was no sprinkler system. The insurer filed a suit in a federal district court against the Duffys to rescind the policy, alleging misrepresentation in their insurance application about the presence of sprinklers. How should the court rule, and why? [*General Star Indemnity Co. v. Duffy*, 191 F.3d 55 (1st Cir. 1999)]

49–6. Interpreting Provisions. Valley Furniture & Interiors, Inc., bought an insurance policy from Transportation Insurance Co. (TIC). The policy provided coverage of $50,000 for each occurrence of property loss caused by employee dishonesty. An "occurrence" was defined as "a single act or series of related acts." Valley allowed its employees to take pay advances and to buy discounted merchandise, with the advances and the cost of the merchandise deducted from their paychecks. The payroll manager was to notify the payroll company to make the deductions. Over a period of six years, without notifying the payroll company, the payroll manager issued advances to other employees and herself and bought merchandise for herself, in amounts totaling more than $200,000. Valley filed claims with TIC for three "occurrences" of employee theft. TIC considered the acts a "series of related acts" and paid only $50,000. Valley filed a suit in a Washington state court against TIC, alleging, in part, breach of contract. What is the standard for interpreting an insurance clause? How should this court define "series of related acts"? Why? [*Valley Furniture & Interiors, Inc. v. Transportation Insurance Co.*, 107 Wash.App. 104, 26 P.3d 952 (Div. 1 2001)]

49–7. Cancellation. James Mitchell bought a building in Los Angeles, California, in February 2000 and applied to United National Insurance Co. for a fire insurance policy. The application stated, among other things, that the building measured 3,420 square feet, it was to be used as a video production studio, the business would generate $300,000 in revenue, and the building had no uncorrected fire code violations. In fact, the building measured less than 2,000 square feet; it was used to film only one music video over a two-day period; the business generated only $6,500 in revenue; and the city had cited the building for combustible debris, excessive weeds, broken windows, missing doors, damaged walls, and other problems. In November, Mitchell met Carl Robinson, who represented himself as a business consultant. Mitchell gave Robinson the keys to the property to show it to a prospective buyer. On November 22, Robinson set fire to the building and was killed in the blaze. Mitchell filed a claim for the loss. United denied the claim and rescinded the policy. Mitchell filed a suit in a California state court against United. Can an insurer cancel a policy? If so, on what ground might United have justifiably canceled Mitchell's policy? What might Mitchell argue to oppose a cancellation? What should the court rule? Explain. [*Mitchell v. United National Insurance Co.*, 127 Cal.App.4th 457, 25 Cal.Rptr.3d 627 (2 Dist. 2005)]

49–8. CASE PROBLEM WITH SAMPLE ANSWER

Richard Vanderbrook's home in New Orleans, Louisiana, was insured through Unitrin Preferred Insurance Co. His policy excluded coverage for, among other things, "[f]lood, surface water, waves, tidal water, overflow of a body of water, or spray from any of these, whether or not driven by wind." The policy did not define the term *flood.* In August 2005, Hurricane Katrina struck along the coast of the Gulf of Mexico, devastating portions of Louisiana. In New Orleans, some of the most significant damage occurred when the levees along three canals—the 17th Street Canal, the Industrial Canal, and the London Avenue Canal—ruptured, and water submerged about 80 percent of the city, including Vanderbrook's home. He filed a claim for the loss, but Unitrin refused to pay. Vanderbrook and others whose policies contained similar exclusions asked a federal district court to order their insurers to pay. They contended that their losses were due to the negligent design, construction, and maintenance of the levees and that the policies did not clearly exclude coverage for an inundation of water induced by negligence. On what does a decision in this case hinge? What reasoning supports a ruling in the plaintiffs' favor? In the defendants' favor? [*In re Katrina Canal Breaches Litigation*, 495 F.3d 191 (5th Cir. 2007)]

- **To view a sample answer for Problem 49–8, go to this book's Web site at www.cengage.com/blaw/jentz, select "Chapter 49," and click on "Case Problem with Sample Answer."**

49–9. A QUESTION OF ETHICS

Paul and Julie Leonard's two-story home in Pascagoula, Mississippi, is only twelve feet above sea level and less than two hundred yards from the Gulf of Mexico. In 1989, the Leonards bought a homeowners' insurance policy from Jay Fletcher, an agent for Nationwide Mutual Insurance Co. The policy covered any damage caused by wind. It excluded all damage caused by water, including flooding. With each annual renewal, Nationwide reminded the Leonards that their policy did not cover flood damage, but that such coverage was available. The policy also contained an anticoncurrent-causation (ACC) clause that excluded coverage for damage caused by the synergistic action of a covered peril such as wind and an excluded peril such as water. In August 2005, Hurricane Katrina battered Pascagoula with torrential rain and sustained winds in excess of one hundred miles per hour. Wind damage to the Leonards' home was modest, but the storm drove ashore a seventeen-foot storm surge that flooded the ground floor. When Nationwide refused to pay for the damage to the ground floor, the Leonards filed a suit in a federal *district court against the insurer. [*Leonard v. Nationwide Mutual Insurance Co., *499 F.3d 419 (5th Cir. 2007)]*

(a) Nationwide argued that the storm surge was a concurrently caused peril—a wall of water pushed ashore by hurricane winds—and thus its damage was excluded under the ACC clause. How would you rule on this point? Should a court "enlarge" an insurer's policy obligations? Why or why not?

(b) When the Leonards bought their policy in 1989, Fletcher told them that all hurricane damage was covered. Ten years later, Fletcher told Paul Leonard that they did not need additional flood coverage. Did these statements materially misrepresent or alter the policy? Were they unethical? Discuss.

49-10. VIDEO QUESTION

Go to this text's Web site at **www.cengage.com/blaw/jentz** and select "Chapter 49." Click on "Video Questions" and view the video titled *Double Indemnity*. Then answer the following questions.

(a) Recall from the video that Mrs. Dietrichson (Barbara Stanwyck) is attempting to take out an "accident insurance" policy (similar to life insurance) on her husband without his knowledge. Does Mrs. Dietrichson have an insurable interest in the life of her husband? Why or why not?

(b) Why would Walter (Fred MacMurray), the insurance agent, refuse to sell Mrs. Dietrichson an insurance policy covering her husband's life without her husband's knowledge?

(c) Suppose that Mrs. Dietrichson contacts a different insurance agent and does not tell the agent that she wants to obtain insurance on her husband without his knowledge. Instead, she asks the agent to leave an insurance application for her husband to sign. Without her husband's knowledge, Mrs. Dietrichson then fills out the application for insurance, which includes a two-year incontestability clause, and forges Mr. Dietrichson's signature. Mr. Dietrichson dies three years after the policy is issued. Will the insurance company be obligated to pay on the policy? Why or why not?

LAW ON THE WEB

For updated links to resources available on the Web, as well as a variety of other materials, visit this text's Web site at

www.cengage.com/blaw/jentz

For a summary of the law governing insurance contracts in the United States, including rules of interpretation, go to

www.consumerlawpage.com/article/insureds.shtml

For more information on business insurance, visit AllBusiness.com's Insurance Center Web page at

www.allbusiness.com/business-finance/business-insurance/2986834-1.html

Legal Research Exercises on the Web

Go to **www.cengage.com/blaw/jentz**, the Web site that accompanies this text. Select "Chapter 49" and click on "Internet Exercises." There you will find the following Internet research exercises that you can perform to learn more about the topics covered in this chapter.

Internet Exercise 49–1: Legal Perspective
Disappearing Decisions

Internet Exercise 49–2: Management Perspective
Risk Management in Cyberspace

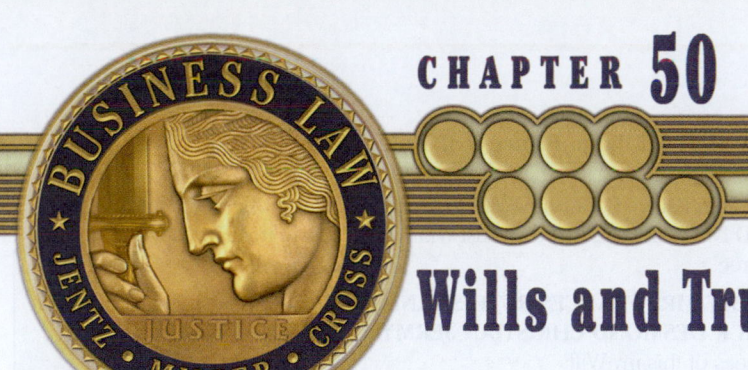

CHAPTER 50

Wills and Trusts

As the old adage states, "You can't take it with you." After you die, all of the real and personal property that you own will be transferred to others. A person can direct the passage of his or her property after death by *will*, subject to certain limitations imposed by the state. If no valid will has been executed, the decedent is said to have died **intestate,** and state **intestacy laws** prescribe the distribution of the property among heirs or next of kin. If no heirs or kin can be found, the property will **escheat**[1] (title will be transferred to the state). In addition, a person can transfer property through a *trust*. In a trust arrangement, the owner (who may be called the *grantor*, or the *settlor*) of the property transfers legal title to a trustee, who has a duty imposed by law to hold the property for the use or benefit of another (the beneficiary).

Wills and trusts are two basic devices used in the process of **estate planning—**determining in advance how one's property and obligations should be transferred on death. In this chapter, we examine wills and trusts in some detail. Estate planning may also involve powers of attorney and living wills, which we discuss at the conclusion of this chapter. Other estate-planning devices include life insurance (discussed in Chapter 49) and joint-tenancy arrangements (described in Chapter 48). Typically, estate planning involves consultations with professionals, including attorneys, accountants, and financial planners.

1. Pronounced is-*cheet*.

SECTION 1 Wills

A **will** is the final declaration of how a person desires to have her or his property disposed of after death. It is a formal instrument that must follow exactly the requirements of state law to be effective. One who makes a will is known as a **testator** (from the Latin *testari*, "to make a will"). A will is referred to as a *testamentary disposition* of property, and one who dies after having made a valid will is said to have died **testate.**

A will can serve other purposes besides the distribution of property. It can appoint a guardian for minor children or incapacitated adults. It can also appoint a personal representative to settle the affairs of the deceased. An **executor** is a personal representative named in a will. An **administrator** is a personal representative appointed by the court for a decedent who dies without a will, fails to name an executor in the will, names an executor lacking the capacity to serve, or writes a will that the court refuses to admit to probate. Exhibit 50–1 on the following page presents excerpts from the will of Diana, Princess of Wales, who died in an automobile accident in 1997. Princess Diana left behind a substantial fortune, most of which was bequeathed to her sons, Prince William and Prince Henry, to be held in trust until they reached the age of majority.

Laws Governing Wills

Laws governing wills come into play when a will is probated. To **probate** (prove) a will means to establish its validity and carry out the administration of the estate through a process supervised by a probate court. Probate laws vary from state to state. In 1969, to promote more uniformity among the states, the American Bar Association and the National Conference of Commissioners on Uniform State Laws issued the Uniform Probate Code (UPC).

The UPC codifies general principles and procedures for the resolution of conflicts in settling estates and relaxes some of the requirements for a valid will

EXHIBIT 50–1 • Excerpts from the Will of Diana, Princess of Wales

I **DIANA PRINCESS OF WALES** of Kensington Palace London W8 HEREBY REVOKE all former Wills and testamentary dispositions made by me AND DECLARE this to be my last Will which I make this First day of June One thousand nine hundred and ninety three

1 I APPOINT my mother **THE HONOURABLE MRS FRANCES RUTH SHAND KYDD** of Callinesh Isle of Seil Oban Scotland and **COMMANDER PATRICK DESMOND CHRISTIAN JERMY JEPHSON** of St James's Palace London SW1 to be the Executors and Trustees of this my Will

2 I WISH to be buried

3 SHOULD any child of mine be under age at the date of the death of the survivor of myself and my husband I APPOINT my mother and my brother **EARL SPENCER** to be the guardians of that child and I express the wish that should I predecease my husband he will consult with my mother with regard to the upbringing education and welfare of our children

. . . .

5 SUBJECT to the payment or discharge of my funeral testamentary and administration expenses and debts and other liabilities I GIVE all my property and assets of every kind and wherever situate to my Executors and Trustees Upon trust either to retain (if they think fit without being liable for loss) all or any part in the same state as they are at the time of my death or to sell whatever and wherever they decide with power when they consider it proper to invest trust monies and to vary investments in accordance with the powers contained in the Schedule to this my Will and to hold the same UPON TRUST for such of them my children **PRINCE WILLIAM** and **PRINCE HENRY** as are living three months after my death and attain the age of twenty-five years if more than one in equal shares PROVIDED THAT if either child of mine dies before me or within three months after my death and issue of that child are living three months after my death and attain the age of twenty-one years such issue shall take by substitution if more than one in equal shares *per stirpes* the share that the deceased child of mine would have taken had he been living three months after my death but so that no issue shall take whose parent is then living and so capable of taking

. . . .

(Signed by HER ROYAL HIGHNESS)
(in our joint presence and)
(then by us in her presence)

contained in earlier state laws. Almost half of the states have enacted some part of the UPC and incorporated it into their own probate codes. For this reason, references to its provisions will be included in this chapter. Nonetheless, succession and inheritance laws still vary widely among the states, and one should always check the particular laws of the state involved.[2]

Gifts by Will

A gift of real estate by will is generally called a **devise,** and a gift of personal property under a will is called a **bequest,** or **legacy.** The recipient of a gift by will is a *devisee* or a *legatee,* depending on whether the gift was a devise or a legacy.

Types of Gifts Gifts by will can be specific, general, or residuary. A *specific* devise or bequest (legacy) describes particular property (such as "Eastwood Estate" or "my gold pocket watch") that can be distinguished from the rest of the testator's property. A *general* devise or bequest (legacy) uses less restrictive terminology. For example, "I devise all my lands" is a general devise. A general bequest often specifies a sum of cash instead of a particular item of property, such as a watch or an automobile. For example, "I give to my nephew, Carleton, $30,000" is a general bequest.

Sometimes, a will provides that any assets remaining after specific gifts have been made and debts have been paid—called the *residuary* (or *residuum*) of the estate—are to be given to the testator's spouse, distributed to the testator's descendants, or disposed of in some other way. If the testator has not indicated what party or parties should receive the residuary of the estate, the residuary passes according to state laws of intestacy.

If a gift is conditioned on the commission of an illegal act or an act that is legally impossible to fulfill, the

2. For example, California law differs substantially from the UPC.

gift will be invalid. For example, in one case a testator made a gift of $29 million to a nursing home on the condition that the funds be used only to help "white" patients. Because this condition was impossible to fulfill without violating laws prohibiting discrimination, the gift was invalidated.[3]

Abatement If the assets of an estate are insufficient to pay in full all general bequests provided for in the will, an *abatement* takes place, meaning that the legatees receive reduced benefits. For example, Julie's will leaves "$15,000 each to my children, Tamara and Lynn." On Julie's death, only $10,000 is available to honor these bequests. By abatement, each child will receive $5,000. If bequests are more complicated, abatement may be more complex. The testator's intent, as expressed in the will, controls.

Lapsed Legacies If a legatee dies prior to the death of the testator or before the legacy is payable, a *lapsed legacy* results. At common law, the legacy failed. Today, the legacy may not lapse if the legatee is in a certain blood relationship to the testator (such as a child, grandchild, brother, or sister) and has left a child or other surviving descendant.

Requirements for a Valid Will

A will must comply with statutory formalities designed to ensure that the testator understood his or her actions at the time the will was made. These formalities are intended to help prevent fraud. Unless they are followed, the will is declared void, and the decedent's property is distributed according to the laws of intestacy of that state.

Although the required formalities vary among jurisdictions, most states uphold certain basic requirements for executing a will. We now look at the basic requirements for a valid will, including references to the UPC when appropriate.

3. *Home for Incurables of Baltimore City v. University of Maryland Medical System Corp.*, 369 Md. 67, 797 A.2d 746 (2002).

Testamentary Capacity and Intent For a will to be valid, the testator must have testamentary capacity—that is, the testator must be of legal age and sound mind *at the time the will is made.* The legal age for executing a will varies, but in most states and under the UPC, the minimum age is eighteen years [UPC 2–501]. Thus, the will of a twenty-one-year-old decedent written when the person was sixteen is invalid if, under state law, the legal age for executing a will is eighteen.

The "Sound-Mind" Requirement. The concept of "being of sound mind" refers to the testator's ability to formulate and to comprehend a personal plan for the disposition of property. Generally, a testator must (1) intend the document to be his or her last will and testament, (2) comprehend the kind and character of the property being distributed, and (3) comprehend and remember the "natural objects of his or her bounty" (usually, family members and persons for whom the testator has affection).

Intent. A valid will is one that represents the maker's intention to transfer and distribute her or his property. When it can be shown that the decedent's plan of distribution was the result of fraud or undue influence, the will is declared invalid. A court may sometimes infer undue influence when the named beneficiary was in a position to influence the making of the will. Suppose that the testator ignored blood relatives and named as a beneficiary a nonrelative who was in constant close contact with the testator. For example, if a nurse or friend caring for the testator at the time of death was named as beneficiary to the exclusion of all family members, the family might challenge the validity of the will. In that situation, a court might infer undue influence and declare the will invalid.

A testator's disposition of his or her property passes all of the property that he or she was entitled to dispose of at the time of death. The corollary principle is that property a testator does not own at the time of death is not subject to transfer by will. These principles were applied in the following case.

CASE 50.1 Shaw Family Archives, Ltd. v. CMG Worldwide, Inc.

United States District Court, Southern District of New York, 2007. 486 F.Supp.2d 309.

• **Background and Facts** The actress Marilyn Monroe, a New York resident, died in California on August 5, 1962. Her will gave her estate's residuary assets to Lee Strasberg and two other beneficiaries. Lee died in 1982. On the death of Aaron Frosch (the executor of Monroe's estate), Lee's widow,

CASE CONTINUES

CASE 50.1 CONTINUED Anna, was appointed administrator. In 2001, the residuary assets were transferred to Marilyn Monroe, LLC (MMLLC), which Anna formed to manage those assets. During Monroe's life, photographer Sam Shaw took photos of her. After his death, the photos descended to the Shaw Family Archives (SFA). With Bradford Licensing Associates, SFA maintained a Web site through which they licensed Monroe's picture, image, and likeness for commercial use. In 2006, T-shirts that bore her picture and SFA's inscription on the label were offered for sale in Indiana. MMLLC asserted that under Indiana's Right of Publicity Act (which creates a right of publicity that survives for one hundred years after a person's death) it owned a right of publicity bequeathed by the residuary clause of Monroe's will and that SFA had violated this right. SFA and others filed a suit in a federal district court against MMLLC and CMG Worldwide, Inc., contending that MMLLC did not own such a right. Both parties filed motions for summary judgment.

● **Decision and Rationale** The court issued a summary judgment in SFA's favor, holding that MMLLC had not become the owner of a right of publicity in Marilyn Monroe's name, likeness, and persona through her will. The court pointed out that in 1962, when Marilyn Monroe died, inheritable after-death publicity rights were not recognized in California, Indiana, or New York. "To this day New York law does not recognize any common law right of publicity and limits its statutory publicity rights to living persons." California did not pass its inheritable after-death publicity rights law until twenty-two years following Monroe's death. Indiana did so only in 1994. "Thus, at the time of her death * * * Ms. Monroe did not have any postmortem right of publicity under the law of any relevant state. As a result, any publicity rights she enjoyed during her lifetime were extinguished at her death by operation of law." California and New York were the only two states in which Monroe could have conceivably been domiciled. In 1962, when she died, neither permitted a "testator to dispose by will of a property she does not own at the time of her death." Further, the court stated, no case or statute "stands for the proposition that any intent on the part of the testator can overcome his testamentary incapacity to devise property he does not own at the time of his death."

● **The E-Commerce Dimension** *Did SFA and Bradford's online offer of licenses for the commercial use of Monroe's image have any effect on the court's decision in this case? Why or why not?*

● **The Legal Environment Dimension** *How might the court have ruled if Monroe had phrased her residuary clause to clearly state an intent to devise property she did not then own? (Hint: Can people—during or after their lives—transfer property that they do not own?)*

Writing Requirements Generally, a will must be in writing. The writing itself can be informal as long as it substantially complies with the statutory requirements. In some states, a will can be handwritten in crayon or ink. It can be written on a sheet or scrap of paper, on a paper bag, or on a piece of cloth. A will that is completely in the handwriting of the testator is called a **holographic will** (sometimes referred to as an *olographic will*).

In some instances, a court may find an oral will valid. A **nuncupative will** is an oral will made before witnesses. It is not permitted in most states. Where authorized by statute, such wills are generally valid only if made during the last illness of the testator and are therefore sometimes referred to as *deathbed wills*. Normally, only personal property can be transferred by a nuncupative will. Statutes frequently permit military personnel to make nuncupative wills when on active duty.

Signature Requirements A fundamental requirement is that the testator's signature must appear, generally at the end of the will. Each jurisdiction dictates by statute and court decision what constitutes a signature. Initials, an X or other mark, and words such as "Mom" have all been upheld as valid when it was shown that the testators *intended* them to be signatures.

Witness Requirements A will normally must be attested (sworn to) by two, and sometimes three, witnesses. The number of witnesses, their qualifications, and the manner in which the witnessing must be done are generally set out in a statute. A witness may be required to be disinterested—that is, not a beneficiary under the will. The UPC, however, allows even interested witnesses to attest to a will [UPC 2–505]. There are no age requirements for witnesses, but they must be mentally competent.

The purpose of witnesses is to verify that the testator actually executed (signed) the will and had the requisite intent and capacity at the time. A witness need not read the contents of the will. Usually, the testator and all witnesses must sign in the sight or the presence of one another, but there are exceptions.[4] The UPC does not require all parties to sign in the presence of one another and deems it sufficient if the testator acknowledges her or his signature to the witnesses [UPC 2–502].

Publication Requirements The maker of a will *publishes* the will by orally declaring to the witnesses that the document they are about to sign is his or her "last will and testament." Publication is becoming an unnecessary formality in most states, and it is not required under the UPC.

Revocation of Wills

An executed will is revocable by the maker at any time during the maker's lifetime. The maker may revoke a will by a physical act, such as tearing up the will, or by a subsequent writing. Wills can also be revoked by operation of law. Revocation can be partial or complete, and it must follow certain strict formalities.

Revocation by a Physical Act of the Maker The testator may revoke a will by intentionally burning, tearing, canceling, obliterating, or destroying it or by having someone else do so in the presence of the testator and at the testator's direction.[5] In some states, partial revocation by physical act of the maker is recognized. Thus, those portions of a will lined out or torn away are dropped, and the remaining parts of the will are valid. At no time, however, can a provision be crossed out and an additional or substitute provision written in. Such altered portions require reexecution (signing again) and reattestation (rewitnessing).

To revoke a will by physical act, it is necessary to follow the mandates of a state statute exactly. When a state statute prescribes the specific methods for revoking a will by physical act, those are the only methods that will revoke the will.

If the original of a will cannot be found after the testator's death, it is generally presumed that the testator must have destroyed it with the intent to revoke it. Whether the testator had destroyed the original of her will was at issue in the following case.

4. See, for example, *Slack v. Truitt*, 368 Md. 2, 791 A.2d 129 (2000).

5. The destruction cannot be inadvertent. The maker's intent to revoke must be shown. When a will has been burned or torn accidentally, it is normally recommended that the maker have a new document created so that it will not falsely appear that the maker intended to revoke the will.

CASE 50.2 In re Estate of Pallister

Supreme Court of South Carolina, 2005. 363 S.C. 437, 611 S.E.2d 250.
www.judicial.state.sc.us/opinions/indexSCPub.cfm[a]

Background and Facts Mary Pallister grew up in South Carolina but spent most of the last two decades of her life in New Mexico, where she executed two wills. The beneficiaries of both wills included her husband's sister, Ruth Diem, and Diem's daughter, Ann Patton. Pallister had been close friends with Diem for more than fifty years and maintained a similar relationship with Patton. After Pallister's husband died, she moved to Methodist Manor in Florence, South Carolina, near the family of her brother's son, James Reames. In 1999, Pallister executed a new will, expressly revoking the others. Again, the beneficiaries were Diem and Patton. The will also stated that James was to inherit the estate if Diem and Patton died before Pallister. Otherwise, he would inherit nothing. In March 2001, Pallister was admitted to a hospital and died the next month, leaving an estate with a value of more than $1.4 million. The original of the 1999 will could not be found. Diem and Patton petitioned a

a. In the right-hand column, click on "2005" and then on "March." In the result, scroll to the name of the case and click on the appropriate link to access the opinion. The South Carolina Judicial Department maintains this Web site.

CASE CONTINUES

CASE 50.2 CONTINUED South Carolina probate court to accept a copy of the original. James and others opposed the petition, arguing that because the original could not be found, Pallister must have destroyed it with the intent to revoke it.[b] A jury issued a verdict in favor of the petitioners (Diem and Patton). James (and others) appealed. The South Carolina Supreme Court agreed to review the case.

- **Decision and Rationale** The South Carolina Supreme Court affirmed the decision of the lower court, which had accepted for probate a copy of Pallister's will despite the loss of the original. The state supreme court stated, "The person asserting that an original will was, in fact, valid but mistakenly lost or destroyed by another, bears the burden of presenting clear and convincing evidence to rebut the presumption the testator destroyed the will with an intent to revoke it." The court ruled that in this case "clear and convincing" evidence supported the conclusion that the original existed at the time of Pallister's death, and had been lost after her death or destroyed by a third party without her knowledge or consent. The court pointed out that the beneficiaries were the same persons named in her prior wills and that there was no evidence she wanted to change or revoke the current will. The court also noted that Pallister's nephew James knew about the will, admitted he was displeased with its terms, called her attorney to complain about it, had access to her apartment, knew where she kept important records, and had transferred about $713,000 in her assets to himself three days before her death after obtaining her signature on the required forms.

- **What If the Facts Were Different?** *Suppose that shortly before Pallister's death, she had asked James to tear up her will, and he had done it. Would the result have been different? Explain.*

- **The E-Commerce Dimension** *How might the availability of a secure online repository for a person's will affect a challenge to the will?*

b. As explained later in this chapter, if Pallister died without a will, her estate would be distributed according to the applicable intestacy laws. In that circumstance, James would inherit part of the estate.

Revocation by a Subsequent Writing A will may also be wholly or partially revoked by a **codicil,** a written instrument separate from the will that amends or revokes provisions in the will. A codicil eliminates the necessity of redrafting an entire will merely to add to it or amend it. A codicil can also be used to revoke an entire will. The codicil must be executed with the same formalities required for a will, and it must refer expressly to the will. In effect, it updates a will because the will is "incorporated by reference" into the codicil.

A new will (second will) can be executed that may or may not revoke the first or a prior will, depending on the language used. To revoke a prior will, the second will must use language specifically revoking other wills, such as, "This will hereby revokes all prior wills." If the second will is otherwise valid and properly executed, it will revoke all prior wills. If the express *declaration of revocation* is missing, then both wills are read together. If any of the dispositions made in the second will are inconsistent with the prior will, the second will controls.

Revocation by Operation of Law Revocation by operation of law occurs when marriage, divorce or annulment, or the birth of a child takes place after a will has been executed. In most states, when a testator marries after executing a will that does not include the new spouse, on the testator's death the spouse can still receive the amount he or she would have taken had the testator died intestate—that is, without a will (how an intestate's property is distributed under state laws will be discussed shortly). In effect, this revokes the will to the point of providing the spouse with an intestate share. The rest of the estate is passed under the will [UPC 2–301, 2–508]. If, however, the new spouse is otherwise provided for in the will (or by transfer of property outside the will), the new spouse will not be given an intestate amount.

At common law and under the UPC, divorce does not necessarily revoke the entire will. A divorce or an annulment occurring after a will has been executed will revoke those dispositions of property made under the will to the former spouse [UPC 2–508].

If a child is born after a will has been executed and if it appears that the deceased parent would have made a provision for the child, that child may be entitled to a portion of the estate. The child is entitled to receive whatever portion of the estate she or he would have received if the decedent had died intestate in that state. Most state laws allow a child (born before or after execution of the will) to receive some portion of a parent's estate even if no provision is made in the parent's will. This is true unless it is clear from the will's terms that the testator intended to disinherit the child. Under the UPC, the rule is the same.

Rights under a Will

The law imposes certain limitations on the way a person can dispose of property in a will. For example, a married person who makes a will generally cannot avoid leaving a certain portion of the estate to the surviving spouse (unless there is a valid prenuptial agreement—see Chapter 15). In most states, this is called an elective share, a forced share, or a widow's (or widower's) share, and it is often one-third of the estate or an amount equal to a spouse's share under intestacy laws.

Beneficiaries under a will have rights as well. A beneficiary can renounce (disclaim) his or her share of the property given under a will. Further, a surviving spouse can renounce the amount given under a will and elect to take the forced share when the forced share is larger than the amount of the gift—this is the widow's (or widower's) election, or right of election. State statutes provide the methods by which a surviving spouse accomplishes renunciation. The purpose of these statutes is to allow the spouse to obtain whichever distribution would be more advantageous. The revised UPC gives the surviving spouse an elective right to take a percentage of the total estate determined by the length of time that the spouse and the decedent were married to each other [UPC 2–201].

Probate Procedures

Typically, probate procedures vary, depending on the size of the decedent's estate.

Informal Probate Proceedings For smaller estates, most state statutes provide for the distribution of assets without formal probate proceedings. Faster and less expensive methods are then used. Property can be transferred by *affidavit* (a written statement taken in the presence of a person who has authority to affirm it), and problems or questions can be handled during an administrative hearing. Some states allow title to cars, savings and checking accounts, and certain other property to be transferred simply by filling out forms.

A majority of states also provide for *family settlement agreements,* which are private agreements among the beneficiaries. Once a will is admitted to probate, the family members can agree to settle among themselves the distribution of the decedent's assets. Although a family settlement agreement speeds the settlement process, a court order is still needed to protect the estate from future creditors and to clear title to the assets involved. The use of these and other types of summary procedures in estate administration can save time and expenses.

Formal Probate Proceedings For larger estates, formal probate proceedings are normally undertaken, and the probate court supervises every aspect of the settlement of the decedent's estate. Additionally, in some situations—such as when a guardian for minor children must be appointed—more formal probate procedures cannot be avoided. Formal probate proceedings may take anywhere from six months to two years to complete, depending on the size and complexity of the estate. The length of probate depends on factors such as the types of assets owned, the form of ownership, tax issues, the difficulty in locating the beneficiaries who inherit under the will, and marital property issues. When the will is contested or anyone objects to the actions of the personal representative (regardless of whether the person is the executor named in the will or an administrator appointed by the court), the duration of probate is extended. As a result, a sizable portion of the decedent's assets (as much as 10 percent) may go to pay the fees charged by attorneys and personal representatives, as well as court costs.

Property Transfers outside the Probate Process

In the ordinary situation, a person can employ various **will substitutes** to avoid the cost of probate—for example, *living* trusts (discussed later in this chapter), life insurance policies, or individual retirement accounts (IRAs) with named beneficiaries. One method of transferring property outside the probate process is by making gifts to children or others while one is still living.

Another method of accomplishing a property transfer without a will is through the joint ownership of property. For example, a person can hold title to certain real or personal property as a joint tenant with a spouse or other person. Recall from Chapter 48 that in a joint tenancy, when one joint tenant dies, the other joint tenant or tenants automatically inherit the deceased tenant's share of the property. This is true even if the deceased tenant has provided otherwise in her or his will. See *Concept Summary 50.1* for a review of basic information about wills.

CONCEPT SUMMARY 50.1
Wills

Concept	Description
Terminology	1. *Intestate*—Describes one who dies without a valid will. 2. *Testator*—A person who makes a will. 3. *Personal representative*—A person appointed in a will or by a court to settle the affairs of a decedent. A personal representative named in the will is an *executor;* a personal representative appointed by the court for an intestate decedent is an *administrator.* 4. *Devise*—A gift of real estate by will; may be general or specific. The recipient of a devise is a *devisee.* 5. *Bequest, or legacy*—A gift of personal property by will; may be general or specific. The recipient of a bequest (legacy) is a *legatee.*
Requirements for a Valid Will	1. The testator must have testamentary capacity (be of legal age and sound mind at the time the will is made). 2. A will must be in writing (except for nuncupative wills). 3. A will must be signed by the testator; what constitutes a signature varies from jurisdiction to jurisdiction. 4. A nonholographic (not handwritten) will normally must be witnessed in the manner prescribed by state statute. 5. A will may have to be *published*—that is, the testator may be required to announce to witnesses that this is his or her "last will and testament." Not required under the UPC.
Revocation of Wills	1. *By physical act of the maker*—Tearing up, canceling, obliterating, or deliberately destroying part or all of a will. 2. *By subsequent writing*— a. Codicil—A formal, separate document that amends or revokes an existing will. b. Second will, or new will—A new, properly executed will expressly revoking the existing will. 3. *By operation of law*— a. Marriage—Generally revokes a will written before the marriage to the extent of providing for the spouse. b. Divorce or annulment—Revokes dispositions of property made to the former spouse under a will made before the divorce or annulment. c. Subsequently born child—It is inferred that the child is entitled to receive the portion of the estate granted under intestacy distribution laws.
Probate Procedures	To *probate* a will means to establish its validity and to carry out the administration of the estate through a court process. Probate laws vary from state to state. Probate procedures may be informal or formal, depending on the size of the estate and other factors, such as whether a guardian for minor children must be appointed.

PREVENTING LEGAL DISPUTES

For most people, estate planning involves not only ensuring that, after they die, their property goes to the intended recipients, but also avoiding probate and maximizing their estates. To this end, many choose to set up a living trust, arrange for a joint tenancy, or name beneficiaries of a retirement account or an insurance policy. If you use these will substitutes, though, be aware that a court will not apply the same principles in reviewing a transfer outside the probate process as it would apply to a testamentary transfer. Therefore, any such arrangements must be carefully drafted by your attorney and must comply with all legal requirements. To avoid disputes between beneficiaries after your death, make sure that your words and actions in such property transfers are clear and represent the final expression of your intent.

SECTION 2 Intestacy Laws

Each state regulates by statute how property will be distributed when a person dies intestate (without a valid will). These statutes are called statutes of descent and distribution or, more simply, intestacy laws, as mentioned in this chapter's introduction. Intestacy laws attempt to carry out the likely intent and wishes of the decedent. These laws assume that deceased persons would have intended that their natural heirs (spouses, children, grandchildren, or other family members) inherit their property. Therefore, intestacy statutes set out rules and priorities under which these heirs inherit the property. If no heirs exist, the state will assume ownership of the property.

The rules of descent vary widely from state to state. It is thus important to refer to the exact terms of the applicable state statutes when addressing any problem of intestacy distribution.

Surviving Spouse and Children

Usually, state statutes provide that first the debts of the decedent must be satisfied out of the estate; then the remaining assets pass to the surviving spouse and to the children. A surviving spouse usually receives only a share of the estate—typically, one-half if there is also a surviving child and one-third if there are two or more children.[6] Only if no children or grandchildren survive the decedent will a surviving spouse receive the entire estate.

Assume that Allen dies intestate and is survived by his wife, Betty, and his children, Duane and Tara. Allen's property passes according to intestacy laws. After his outstanding debts are paid, Betty will receive the homestead (either in fee simple or as a life estate) and ordinarily a one-third to one-half interest in all other property. The remaining real and personal property will pass to Duane and Tara in equal portions. Under most state intestacy laws and under the UPC, in-laws do not share in an estate. If a child dies before his or her parents, the child's spouse will not receive an inheritance on the parents' death. For example, if Duane died before his father (Allen), Duane's spouse would not inherit Duane's share of Allen's estate.

When there is no surviving spouse or child, the order of inheritance is grandchildren, then parents of the decedent. These relatives are usually called *lineal descendants.* If there are no lineal descendants, then *collateral heirs*—brothers and sisters, nieces and nephews, and aunts and uncles of the decedent—are the next groups that share. If there are no survivors in any of these groups, most statutes provide for the property to be distributed among the next of kin of the collateral heirs.

Stepchildren, Adopted Children, and Illegitimate Children

Under intestacy laws, stepchildren are not considered kin. Legally adopted children, however, are recognized as lawful heirs of their adoptive parents. Statutes vary from state to state in regard to the inheritance rights of illegitimate children. Generally, an illegitimate child is treated as the child of the mother and can inherit from her and her relatives. Traditionally, the child was not regarded as the legal child of the father with the right of inheritance unless paternity was established through some legal proceeding prior to the father's death. The United States Supreme Court has held that state statutes may limit the inheritance rights of illegitimate children, provided that the statutes bear

6. UPC 2–102 has a formula for computing a surviving spouse's share that is contingent on the number of surviving children and parents. For example, if the decedent has no surviving children and one surviving parent, the surviving spouse takes the first $200,000, plus three-fourths of any balance of the intestate estate. UPC 2–102(2).

some reasonable relationship to a legitimate state purpose.[7]

Given the dramatic increase in the number of children born out of wedlock in society today, many states have relaxed their laws of inheritance. A majority of states now consider a child born of any union that has the characteristics of a formal marriage relationship (such as unmarried parents who cohabit) to be legitimate. Under the revised UPC, a child is the child of his or her natural (biological) parents, regardless of their marital status, as long as the natural parent has openly treated the child as his or hers [UPC 2–114]. Although illegitimate children may have inheritance rights in most states, their rights are not necessarily identical to those of legitimate children.

Distribution to Grandchildren

Usually, a will provides for how the decedent's estate will be distributed to descendants of deceased children (grandchildren). If a will does not include such a provision—or if a person dies intestate—the question arises as to what share the grandchildren of the decedent will receive. Each state designates one of two methods of distributing the assets of intestate decedents.

One method of dividing an intestate's estate is ***per stirpes.*** Under this method, within a class or group of distributees (for example, grandchildren), the children of any one descendant take the share that their deceased parent *would have been* entitled to inherit. For example, Michael, a widower, has two children, Scott and Jillian. Scott has two children (Becky and Holly), and Jillian has one child (Paul). Scott and Jillian die before their father. When Michael dies, if his estate is distributed *per stirpes,* Becky and Holly each receive one-fourth of the estate (dividing Scott's one-half share). Paul receives one-half of the estate (taking Jillian's one-half share). Exhibit 50–2 illustrates the *per stirpes* method of distribution.

An estate may also be distributed on a ***per capita*** basis—that is, each person in a class or group takes an equal share of the estate. If Michael's estate is distributed *per capita,* Becky, Holly, and Paul will each receive a one-third share. Exhibit 50–3 illustrates the *per capita* method of distribution.

7. In a landmark ruling in *Trimble v. Gordon,* 430 U.S. 762, 97 S.Ct. 1459, 52 L.Ed.2d 31 (1977), however, the United States Supreme Court ruled that an Illinois illegitimacy statute was unconstitutional because it did not bear a rational relationship to a legitimate state purpose.

SECTION 3 Trusts

A **trust** is any arrangement by which property is transferred from one person to a trustee to be administered for the transferor's or another party's benefit. It can also be defined as a right of property (real or personal) held by one party for the benefit of another. A trust can be created to become effective during a person's lifetime or after a person's death. Trusts may be established for any purpose that is not illegal or against public policy.

Essential Elements of a Trust

The essential elements of a trust are as follows:

1. A designated beneficiary (except in charitable trusts, discussed shortly).

EXHIBIT 50–2 • *Per Stirpes* Distribution

Under this method of distribution, an heir takes the share that his or her deceased parent would have been entitled to inherit, had the parent lived. This may mean that a class of distributees—the grandchildren in this example—will not inherit in equal portions. Note that Becky and Holly receive only one-fourth of Michael's estate while Paul inherits one-half.

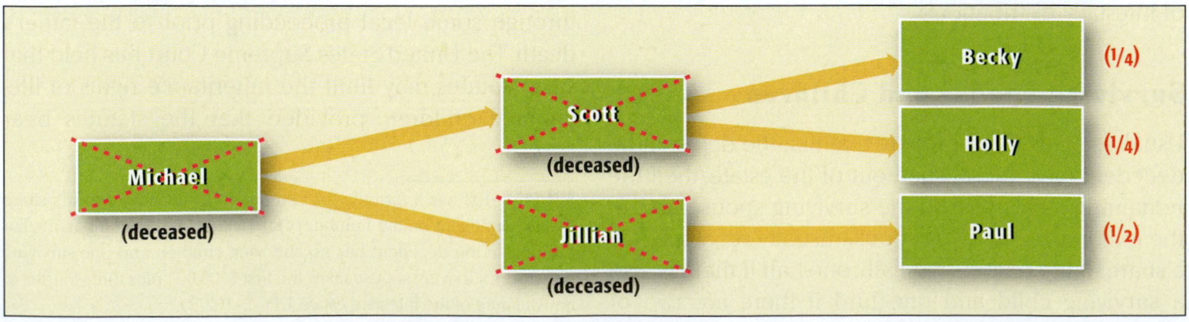

EXHIBIT 50–3 • *Per Capita* Distribution

Under this method of distribution, all heirs in a certain class—in this example, the grandchildren—inherit equally. Note that Becky and Holly in this situation each inherit one-third, as does Paul.

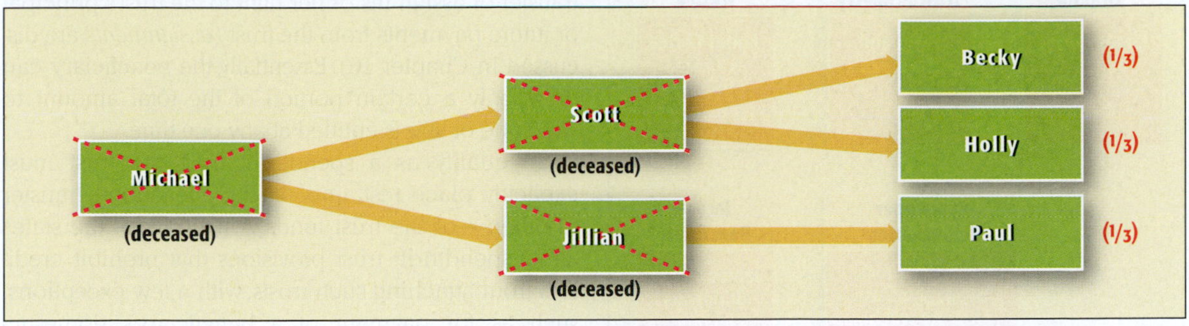

2. A designated trustee.
3. A fund sufficiently identified to enable title to pass to the trustee.
4. Actual delivery by the *grantor* (the person creating the trust) to the trustee with the intention of passing title.

Express Trusts

An express trust is created or declared in explicit terms, usually in writing. There are numerous types of express trusts, each with its own special characteristics.

Living Trusts A living trust—or ***inter vivos* trust** (*inter vivos* is Latin for "between or among the living")—is a trust created by a grantor during her or his lifetime. Living trusts have become a popular estate-planning option because at the grantor's death, assets held in a living trust can pass to the heirs without going through probate. Note, however, that living trusts do not necessarily shelter assets from estate taxes, and the grantor may still have to pay income taxes on trust earnings—depending on whether the trust is revocable or irrevocable.

Revocable Living Trusts. Living trusts can be revocable or irrevocable. In a *revocable* living trust, which is the most common type, the grantor retains control over the trust property during her or his lifetime. The grantor deeds the property to the trustee but retains the power to amend, alter, or revoke the trust during her or his lifetime. The grantor may also serve as a trustee or co-trustee, and can arrange to receive income earned by the trust assets during her or his lifetime. Because the grantor is in control of the funds, she or he is required to pay income taxes on the trust earnings. Unless the trust is revoked, the principal of the trust is transferred to the trust beneficiary on the grantor's death.

Suppose that James Cortez owns a large farm. After his wife dies, James decides to create a living trust for the benefit of his three children, Alicia, Emma, and Jayden. He contacts his attorney who prepares the documents creating the trust, executes a deed conveying the farm to the trust, and transfers the farm's bank accounts into the name of the trust. The trust designates James as the trustee and names his son Jayden as the *successor trustee,* who will take over the management of the trust when James dies or becomes incapacitated. James is the beneficiary during his lifetime and will receive an income from the trust (hence, he is called the *income beneficiary*). On James's death, the farm will pass to his three children without having to go through probate (the children are referred to as *remainder beneficiaries*). By holding the property in a revocable living trust, James still has control over the farm and accounts: he can make changes to the trust or end the trust at any time during his life. After his death, the trust becomes irrevocable and Jayden, as trustee, must manage and distribute the trust property according to the trust's terms. This trust arrangement is illustrated in Exhibit 50–4 on page 962.

Irrevocable Living Trusts. In an *irrevocable* living trust, in contrast, the grantor permanently gives up control over the property to the trustee. The grantor executes a trust deed, and legal title to the trust property passes to the named trustee. The trustee has a duty to administer the property as directed by the grantor for the benefit and in the interest of the beneficiaries. The trustee must preserve the trust property;

EXHIBIT 50–4 • A Revocable Living Trust Arrangement

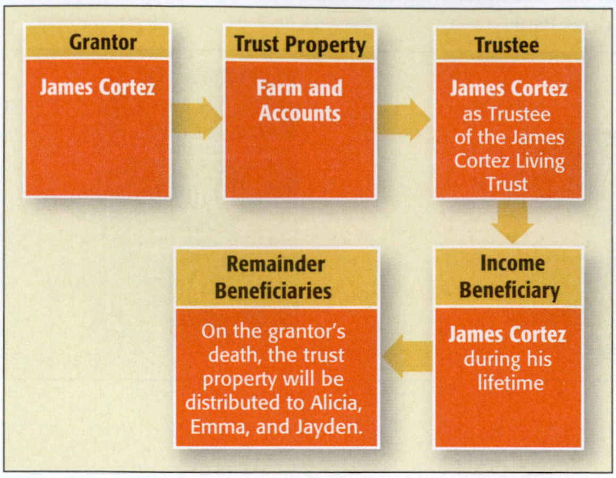

make it productive; and, if required by the terms of the trust agreement, pay income to the beneficiaries, all in accordance with the terms of the trust. Because the grantor has, in effect, given over the property for the benefit of the beneficiaries, he or she is no longer responsible for paying income taxes on the trust earnings.

Testamentary Trusts A **testamentary trust** is created by will and comes into existence on the grantor's death. Although a testamentary trust has a trustee who maintains legal title to the trust property, actions of the trustee are subject to judicial approval. This trustee can be named in the will or appointed by the court. Thus, a testamentary trust does not fail when the will does not name a trustee. The legal responsibilities of the trustee are the same as in an *inter vivos* trust.

If a court finds that the will setting up a testamentary trust is invalid, then the trust will also be invalid. The property that was supposed to be in the trust will then pass according to intestacy laws, not according to the terms of the trust.

Charitable Trusts A **charitable trust** is an express trust designed for the benefit of a segment of the public or the public in general. It differs from other types of trusts in that the identities of the beneficiaries are uncertain and it can be established to last indefinitely. Usually, to be deemed a charitable trust, a trust must be created for charitable, educational, religious, or scientific purposes.

Spendthrift Trusts A **spendthrift trust** is created to provide for the maintenance of a beneficiary by preventing him or her from being careless with the bestowed funds. Unlike the beneficiaries of other trusts, the beneficiary in a spendthrift trust is not permitted to transfer or assign his or her right to the trust's principal or future payments from the trust (*assignments* are discussed in Chapter 16). Essentially, the beneficiary can draw only a certain portion of the total amount to which he or she is entitled at any one time.

To qualify as a spendthrift trust, the trust must explicitly place restraints on the alienation—transfer to others—of the trust funds. A majority of the states allow spendthrift trust provisions that prohibit creditors from attaching such trusts, with a few exceptions, such as for payment of a beneficiary's domestic-support obligations. Additionally, creditors that have provided *necessaries* (see Chapter 13) to spendthrift trust recipients may request a court to compel payment from the trust income or principal.

Totten Trusts A **Totten trust**[8] is created when a grantor deposits funds into an account in her or his own name with instructions that in the event of the grantor's death, whatever is in that account should go to a specific beneficiary. This type of trust is revocable at will until the depositor dies or completes the gift in her or his lifetime (by delivering the funds to the intended beneficiary, for example). The beneficiary has no access to the funds until the depositor's death, when the beneficiary obtains property rights to the balance on hand.

Implied Trusts

Sometimes, a trust is imposed (implied) by law, even in the absence of an express trust. Implied trusts include constructive trusts and resulting trusts.

Constructive Trusts A **constructive trust** arises by operation of law in the interests of equity and fairness. In a constructive trust, the owner of the property is declared to be a trustee for the parties who are, in equity, actually entitled to the benefits that flow from the trust. If someone wrongfully holds legal title to property—because the property was obtained through fraud or in breach of a legal duty, for example—a court may impose a constructive trust.

In the following case, a pizzeria was at the heart of a dispute over the imposition of a constructive trust.

8. This type of trust derives its unusual name from *In the Matter of Totten*, 179 N.Y. 112, 71 N.E. 748 (1904).

CASE 50.3 Cinquemani v. Lazio

New York Supreme Court, Appellate Division, Third Department, 2007.
37 A.D.3d 882, 829 N.Y.S.2d 265.

• **Background and Facts** Francesco and Eleonora Lazio emigrated from Italy to the United States and started two pizzerias in New York, one in the city of Sherrill and the other in the village of Sylvan Beach. In 1985, they paid $40,000 for the Sylvan Beach premises. At the Lazios' urging, Eleonora's brother Guiseppe Cinquemani and his wife, Marie, also emigrated from Italy. The Cinquemanis took over the operation of the Sylvan Beach pizzeria, which they continued to run for more than ten years. They paid Francesco $250 per week and also paid him an amount sufficient to cover the pizzeria's sales tax receipts, income tax withholding, and workers' compensation fees. Over the period the Cinquemanis operated the pizzeria, they paid a total of $178,250. They also repaired and improved the premises at their expense. After Guiseppe died in 2003, the Lazios tried to exclude Marie from the Sylvan Beach pizzeria. Marie filed a suit in a New York state court against the Lazios, claiming, among other things, that Francesco had promised to transfer the business and its building to the Cinquemanis. The court awarded the pizzeria to Marie and imposed a constructive trust. The Lazios appealed to a state intermediate appellate court.

• **Decision and Rationale** The state intermediate appellate court affirmed the lower court's award. The appellate court identified the requirements for the imposition of a constructive trust: a confidential or fiduciary relationship, a promise, a transfer in reliance on the promise, and unjust enrichment. In this case, familial ties led the Lazios to encourage the Cinquemanis to come to New York and operate the Sylvan Beach pizzeria, to guarantee the financing for the Cinquemanis' purchase of a home, to become the godparents of the Cinquemanis' children, and to celebrate holidays with the Cinquemanis. This pattern of behavior established the confidential relationship. Marie and others testified that Francesco had said he would convey the Sylvan Beach pizzeria and its premises to the Cinquemanis after they "made sufficient monthly payments to equate to its value." This was the promise. In reliance, the Cinquemanis made monthly payments to Francesco, repaired and improved the pizzeria's premises, and operated the business "exclusively and continuously for more than ten years." As for the unjust enrichment, "the proof of payment together with the circumstances of the repair, improvement and operation of the premises by Cinquemani and plaintiff supports the court's conclusion that defendants would unfairly benefit if they were allowed to retain the pizzeria."

• **The Legal Environment Dimension** *What are the basic elements of any trust, and what makes up each of those elements in this case?*

• **What If the Facts Were Different?** *Assume that the Lazios had never reported the income or paid the sales taxes from the Sylvan Beach pizzeria and had never obtained workers' compensation insurance for its employees. How might these facts have affected the court's decision?*

Resulting Trusts A **resulting trust** arises from the conduct of the parties. Here, the trust results, or is created, when circumstances raise an inference that the party holding legal title to the property does so for the benefit of another, unless the inference is refuted.

To illustrate: Glenda wants to sell one acre of land she owns. Because she is going out of the country for two years and will not be available to deed the property to a buyer during that period, she conveys the property to her good friend Oscar. Oscar can then attempt to sell the property while Glenda is gone. Because the intent of the transaction in which Glenda conveyed the property to Oscar is neither a sale nor a gift, the property will be held in a trust—a resulting trust—by Oscar for the benefit of Glenda. Therefore, on Glenda's return, Oscar will be required to deed back the property to Glenda or, if the property has been sold, to turn over the proceeds (held in trust) to her. *Concept Summary 50.2* on the next page provides a synopsis of basic information about trusts.

CONCEPT SUMMARY 50.2
Trusts

Concept	Description
Definition and Essential Elements	A trust is any arrangement by which property is transferred from one person to a trustee to be administered for another's benefit. The essential elements of a trust are (1) a designated beneficiary, (2) a designated trustee, (3) a fund sufficiently identified to enable title to pass to the trustee, and (4) actual delivery to the trustee with the intention of passing title.
Types of Trusts	1. *Living (inter vivos) trust*—A trust executed by a grantor during his or her lifetime. A living trust may be revocable or irrevocable. 2. *Testamentary trust*—A trust created by will and coming into existence on the death of the grantor. 3. *Charitable trust*—A trust designed for the benefit of a segment of the public or the public in general. 4. *Spendthrift trust*—A trust created to provide for the maintenance of a beneficiary by allowing only a certain portion of the total amount to be received by the beneficiary at any one time. 5. *Totten trust*—A trust created when one person deposits funds in his or her own name with instructions that the funds should go to a beneficiary on the depositor's death.
Implied Trusts	Implied trusts, which are imposed by law in the interests of fairness and justice, include the following: 1. *Constructive trust*—Arises by operation of law when a transaction occurs in which the person who takes title to property is, in equity, not entitled to enjoy the benefits from it. 2. *Resulting trust*—Arises from the conduct of the parties when an *apparent intention* to create a trust is present.

The Trustee

The trustee is the person holding the trust property. Anyone legally capable of holding title to, and dealing in, property can be a trustee. If the settlor of a trust fails to name a trustee, or if a named trustee cannot or will not serve, the trust does not fail—an appropriate court can appoint a trustee.

Trustee's Duties A trustee must act with honesty, good faith, and prudence in administering the trust and must exercise a high degree of loyalty toward the trust beneficiary. The general standard of care is the degree of care a prudent person would exercise in his or her personal affairs.[9] The duty of loyalty requires that the trustee act in the exclusive interest of the beneficiary.

Among specific duties, a trustee must keep clear and accurate accounts of the trust's administration and furnish complete and correct information to the beneficiary. A trustee must keep trust assets separate from her or his own assets. A trustee has a duty to pay to an income beneficiary the net income of the trust assets at reasonable intervals. A trustee also has a duty

9. Revised Uniform Principal and Income Act, Section 2(a)(3), which has been adopted by a majority of the states. See also *Restatement (Third) of Trusts, (Prudent Investor Rule)* Section 227.

to limit the risk of loss from investments by reasonable diversification and to dispose of assets that do not represent prudent investments. Depending on the particular circumstances, prudent investment choices might include federal, state, or municipal bonds; corporate bonds; and shares of preferred or common stock.

Trustee's Powers When a grantor creates a trust, he or she may prescribe the trustee's powers and performance. Generally, state law[10] applies in the absence of specific terms in the trust documents.[11] When state law does apply, it is most likely to restrict the trustee's investment of trust funds. Typically, statutes confine trustees to investments in conservative debt securities such as government, utility, and railroad bonds and first-mortgage loans on realty. Frequently, though, a grantor gives a trustee discretionary investment power. In that circumstance, any statute may be considered only advisory, with the trustee's decisions subject in most states to the prudent person rule.

A difficult question arises when the trust income proves to be insufficient to provide for the income beneficiary in an appropriate manner. In that situation, to what extent does the trustee have discretion to "invade" the principal and distribute it to the beneficiary? Conversely, if the trust income turns out to be more than adequate to provide for the beneficiary, can the trustee retain a portion of the income and add it to the principal? Generally, the answer to both questions is that the income beneficiary should be provided with a somewhat predictable annual income, but with a view to the safety of the principal. Thus, a trustee may make individualized adjustments in annual distributions.

Of course, a trustee is responsible for carrying out the purposes of the trust. If the trustee fails to comply with the terms of the trust or the controlling statute, he or she is personally liable for any loss.

Allocations between Principal and Income Often, a grantor will provide one beneficiary with a life estate and another beneficiary with the remainder interest in the trust. A farmer, for example, may create a testamentary trust providing that the farm's income be paid to her surviving spouse and that, on the surviving spouse's death, the farm be given to their children. In this example, the surviving spouse has a *life estate* in the farm's income, and the children have a *remainder interest* in the farm (the principal). When a trust is set up in this manner, questions may arise among the income and principal beneficiaries as to how the receipts and expenses for the farm's management and the trust's administration should be allocated between income and principal. Even when the income and principal beneficiaries are the same, these questions may come up.

When a trust instrument does not provide instructions, a trustee must refer to applicable state law. The general rule is that ordinary receipts and expenses are chargeable to the income beneficiary, whereas extraordinary receipts and expenses are allocated to the principal beneficiaries.[12] To illustrate: The receipt of rent from trust realty would be ordinary, as would the expense of paying the property's taxes. The cost of long-term improvements and proceeds from the property's sale, however, would be extraordinary.

Trust Termination

The terms of a trust should expressly state the event on which the grantor wishes it to terminate—for example, the beneficiary's or the trustee's death. If the trust instrument does not provide for termination on the beneficiary's death, the beneficiary's death will not end the trust. Similarly, without an express provision, a trust will not terminate on the trustee's death.

Typically, a trust instrument specifies a termination date. For example, a trust created to educate the grantor's child may provide that the trust ends when the beneficiary reaches the age of twenty-five. If the trust's purpose is fulfilled before that date, a court may order the trust's termination. If no date is specified, a trust will terminate when its purpose has been fulfilled. Of course, if a trust's purpose becomes impossible or illegal, the trust will terminate.

10. As mentioned, a majority of the states have adopted the Revised Uniform Principal and Income Act. Other uniform acts may also apply—for instance, about twenty states have adopted the Uniform Trust Code, issued in 2000 and amended in 2001 and 2003.

11. Revised Uniform Principal and Income Act, Section 2(a)(1); and *Restatement (Second) of Trusts,* Section 164.

12. Revised Uniform Principal and Income Act, Section 3, 6, 8, and 13; and *Restatement (Second) of Trusts,* Section 233.

SECTION 4 Other Estate-Planning Issues

Estate planning involves making difficult decisions about the future, such as who will inherit the family home and other assets and who will take care of minor children. It also involves preparing in advance for other contingencies, such as what happens if you become incapacitated and cannot make your own decisions? Who will take care of your finances and other affairs? Do you want to be kept alive by artificial means, and who do you trust to make decisions about your health care in the event that you cannot? Preparing in advance for situations involving illness and incapacity can significantly ease the problems faced by family members. In this section, we discuss powers of attorney and living wills, both of which are frequently executed in conjunction with a will or trust.

Power of Attorney

As discussed in Chapter 32, a power of attorney is frequently used in business situations to give a person (an agent) authority to act on another's behalf. The powers often are limited to a specific context, such as negotiating a deal with a buyer or entering various contracts necessary to achieve a particular objective. Powers of attorney are also commonly used in estate planning.

Durable Power of Attorney One method of providing for future disability is to use a durable power of attorney. A **durable power of attorney** authorizes an individual to act on behalf of a person when he or she becomes incapacitated. It can be drafted to take effect immediately or only after a physician certifies that the person is incapacitated. The person to whom the power is given can then write checks, collect insurance proceeds, and otherwise manage the incapacitated person's affairs, including health care.

For example, adult children may seek a durable power of attorney from their aging parents, particularly if the parents are becoming mentally incompetent or afflicted by Alzheimer's disease. A husband and wife may give each other power of attorney to make decisions in the event that one of them is hospitalized and cannot speak for himself or herself. A person who is undergoing an operation may sign a durable power of attorney to a loved one who can take over his or her affairs in the event of incapacity.

If you become incapacitated without having executed a durable power of attorney, a court may need to appoint a conservator to handle your financial affairs. Although a spouse may have some ability to write checks on joint accounts, for example, her or his power is often significantly limited. In most situations, it is better to have named a person you wish to handle your affairs in the event that you cannot.

Health-Care Power of Attorney A **health-care power of attorney** designates a person who will have the power to choose what type of and how much medical treatment a person who is unable to make such decisions will receive. The health-care power of attorney is growing in importance as medical technology allows physicians and hospitals to keep people technically alive but in a so-called vegetative state for ever-increasing periods of time. Consider the situation faced by the husband of Terri Schiavo, a Florida woman who was in a vegetative state from 1990 to 2005. It took more than twenty court hearings for the husband to convince the court that he had a right—against the wishes of Schiavo's mother and sister—to remove her feeding tube and let her die. If Schiavo had given her husband a health-care power of attorney, he would have had the right to make the decision to remove the feeding tube for her without going to court.

Living Will

A living will is not a will in the usual sense—that is, it does not appoint an estate representative, dispose of property, or establish a trust. Rather, a **living will** is an advance health directive that allows a person to control what medical treatment may be used after a serious accident or illness. Through a living will, a person can indicate whether he or she wants certain lifesaving procedures to be undertaken in situations in which the treatment will not result in a reasonable quality of life.

Most states have enacted statutes permitting living wills, and it is important that the requirements of state law be followed exactly in creating such wills. Typically, state statutes require physicians to abide by the terms of living wills, and living wills are often included with a patient's medical records.

REVIEWING Wills and Trusts

In June 2007, Bernard Ramish set up a $48,000 trust fund through West Plains Credit Union to provide tuition for his nephew, Nathan Covacek, to attend Tri-State Polytechnic Institute. The trust was established under Ramish's control and went into effect that August. In December, Ramish suffered a brain aneurysm that caused frequent, severe headaches but no other symptoms. Shortly thereafter, Ramish met with an attorney to formalize in writing that he wanted no artificial life-support systems to be used should he suffer a serious illness. Ramish designated his cousin, Lizzie Johansen, to act on his behalf, including choosing his medical treatment, should he become incapacitated. In August 2009, Ramish developed heatstroke on the golf course at La Prima Country Club. After recuperating at the clubhouse, Ramish quickly wrote his will on the back of a wine list. It stated, "My last will and testament: Upon my death, I give all of my personal property to my friend Steve Eshom and my home to Lizzie Johansen." He signed the will at the bottom in the presence of five men in the La Prima clubhouse, and all five men signed as witnesses. A week later, Ramish suffered a second aneurysm and died in his sleep. He was survived by his mother, Dorris Ramish; his son-in-law, Bruce Lupin; and his granddaughter, Tori Lupin. Using the information presented in the chapter, answer the following questions.

1. What type of trust did Ramish create for the benefit of Covacek? Was it revocable or irrevocable?
2. Would Ramish's testament on the back of the wine list meet the requirements for a valid will?
3. What would the order of inheritance have been if Ramish had died intestate?
4. Was Johansen granted a durable power of attorney or a health-care power of attorney for Ramish? Explain. Had Ramish created a living will?

TERMS AND CONCEPTS

administrator 951
bequest 952
charitable trust 962
codicil 956
constructive trust 962
devise 952
durable power of attorney 966
escheat 951
estate planning 951
executor 951
health-care power of attorney 966
holographic will 954
***inter vivos* trust 961**
intestacy laws 951
intestate 951
legacy 952
living will 966
nuncupative will 954
***per capita* 960**
***per stirpes* 960**
probate 951
resulting trust 963
spendthrift trust 962
testamentary trust 962
testate 951
testator 951
Totten trust 962
trust 960
will 951
will substitutes 957

QUESTIONS AND CASE PROBLEMS

50–1. Benjamin is a widower who has two married children, Edward and Patricia. Patricia has two children, Perry and Paul. Edward has no children. Benjamin dies, and his typewritten will leaves all of his property equally to his children, Edward and Patricia, and provides that should a child predecease him, the grandchildren are to take *per stirpes*. The will was witnessed by Patricia and by Benjamin's lawyer and was signed by Benjamin in their presence. Patricia has predeceased Benjamin. Edward claims the will is invalid.

(a) Discuss whether the will is valid.
(b) Discuss the distribution of Benjamin's estate if the will is invalid.
(c) Discuss the distribution of Benjamin's estate if the will is valid.

50–2. Gary Mendel drew up a will in which he left his favorite car, a 1966 red Ferrari, to his daughter, Roberta. A year prior to his death, Mendel sold the 1966 Ferrari and purchased a 1969 Ferrari. Discuss whether Roberta will inherit the 1969 Ferrari under the terms of her father's will.

50–3. QUESTION WITH SAMPLE ANSWER

While single, James made out a will naming his mother, Carol, as sole beneficiary. Later, James married Lisa.

(a) If James died while married to Lisa without changing his will, would the estate go to his mother, Carol? Explain.
(b) Assume that James made out a new will on his marriage to Lisa, leaving his entire estate to Lisa. Later, he divorced Lisa and married Mandis, but he did not change his will. Discuss the rights of Lisa and Mandis to his estate after his death.
(c) Assume that James divorced Lisa, married Mandis, and changed his will, leaving his estate to Mandis. Later, a daughter, Claire, was born. James died without having included Claire in his will. Discuss fully whether Claire has any rights in the estate.

- **For a sample answer to Question 50–3, go to Appendix I at the end of this text.**

50–4. Merlin Winters had three sons. Merlin and his youngest son, Abraham, had a falling out in 1994 and stopped speaking to each other. Merlin made a formal will in 1996, leaving all of his property to the two older sons and deliberately excluding Abraham. Merlin's health began to deteriorate, and by 1997, he was under the full-time care of a nurse, Julia. In 1998, he made a new will expressly revoking the 1996 will and leaving all of his property to Julia. On Merlin's death, the two older sons contest the 1998 will, claiming that Julia exercised undue influence over their father. Abraham claims that both wills are invalid because the first will was revoked by the second will, and the second will is invalid on the ground of undue influence. Is Abraham's contention correct? Explain.

50–5. Rohan, an eighty-three-year-old invalid, employs a nurse, Sarah, to care for him. Prior to Sarah's employment, Rohan executed a will leaving his entire estate to his only living relative—his great-grandson, Leon. Sarah convinces Rohan that Leon is dead and gets Rohan to change his will, naming Sarah as his sole beneficiary. After Rohan's death, Leon appears and contests the will. Discuss the probable success of Leon's action.

50–6. Intestacy Laws. In January 1993, three and a half years after Lauren and Warren Woodward were married, they were informed that Warren had leukemia. At the time, the couple had no children, and the doctors told the Woodwards that the leukemia treatment might leave Mr. Woodward sterile. The couple arranged for Mr. Woodward's sperm to be collected and placed in a sperm bank for later use. In October 1993, Warren Woodward died. Two years later, Lauren Woodward gave birth to twin girls who had been conceived through artificial insemination using Mr. Woodward's sperm. The following year, Mrs. Woodward applied for Social Security survivor benefits for the two children. The Social Security Administration (SSA) rejected her application, on the ground that she had not established that the twins were the husband's children within the meaning of the Social Security Act of 1935. Mrs. Woodward then filed a paternity action in Massachusetts, and the probate court determined that Warren Woodward was the twins' father. Mrs. Woodward resubmitted her application to the SSA but was again refused survivor benefits for the twins. She then filed an action in a federal district court to determine the inheritance rights, under Massachusetts's intestacy law, of children conceived from the sperm of a deceased individual and his surviving spouse. How should the court resolve this case? Should children conceived after a parent's death (by means of artificial insemination or *in vitro* fertilization) still inherit under intestate succession laws? Why or why not? [*Woodward v. Commissioner of Social Security,* 435 Mass. 536, 760 N.E.2d 257 (2002)]

50–7. Wills. In 1944, Benjamin Feinberg bought a plot in Beth Israel Cemetery in Plattsburgh, New York. A mausoleum was built on the plot to contain six crypts. In 1954, Feinberg's spouse died and was interred in one of the crypts. Feinberg, his only son, one of his two daughters, and the daughter's son, Julian Bergman, began using the mausoleum regularly as a place of prayer and meditation. When Feinberg died, he was interred in the mausoleum. His two daughters were interred in two of the remaining crypts on their deaths. Feinberg's son died in 2001 and was interred in the fifth crypt. His widow, Laurie, then changed the locks on the mausoleum and refused access to Julian, who filed a suit in a New York state court against her to obtain a key. Feinberg and all of his children died testate, but none of them made a specific bequest of their interest in the plot to anyone. Each person's will included a residuary clause, however. Who owns the plot, who has access to it, and why? [*Bergman v. Feinberg,* 6 A.D.3d 1031, 776 N.Y.S.2d 611 (3 Dept. 2004)]

50–8. CASE PROBLEM WITH SAMPLE ANSWER

Alma Zeigler, a resident of Georgia, died in June 2001. Zeigler's will named as executor her granddaughter, Stacey Hatchett. Hatchett, who was teaching and attending graduate school in Illinois, filed a petition to probate the will in a Georgia state court, which confirmed her as executor in January 2002. The estate's main asset was a brick, three-bedroom house in Savannah. Hatchett sold the house for $65,000, without obtaining an appraisal, and deposited the proceeds in her personal account. Meanwhile, Zeigler's adopted son took the furnishings from the house and placed them in storage. By August 2003, Hatchett had not inventoried these items, did not know their location, and knew only that the son lived "somewhere in Florida." Also unaccounted for was a diamond ring that had been on Zeigler's finger at the time of her death and a van that Zeigler had owned. Rita Williams, to whom the will devised certain real property, filed a petition with the court, asking that Hatchett, who had not been in Georgia since filing the petition to probate the will, be removed as executor. What are the duties of an executor, or personal representative? Did Hatchett violate these duties? Explain. [*In re Estate of Zeigler,* 273 Ga.App. 269, 614 S.E.2d 799 (2005)]

- **To view a sample answer for Problem 50–8, go to this book's Web site at www.cengage.com/blaw/jentz, select "Chapter 50," and click on "Case Problem with Sample Answer."**

50–9. Wills. James Lillard's first wife had a child whom James adopted when he married that child's mother. James fathered other children with her until they divorced in the early 1970s. In 1975, James married his second wife. During this marriage, each spouse's biological children remained the other's stepchildren because neither spouse adopted the other's children. James's second wife died in 2002, and he was diagnosed with terminal cancer in January 2004. In February, he executed a will that divided his property equally among all of his children and stepchildren. By October, James was living with his children, who managed his finances and administered his prescribed drugs, which impaired him mentally and physically. A hospice worker noted that on October 5 James had difficulty completing sentences and was forgetful. A visitor two days later described him as "morphined up." On this same day, he tore his first will in half and executed a new will that left most of his property to his children. James died on October 19. His children submitted the second will to a Georgia state court for probate. His stepchildren objected, alleging, among other things, that at the time of its execution, James lacked testamentary capacity. His children responded that the first will had been validly revoked. Which will should be declared valid? Why? [*Lillard v. Owens,* 281 Ga. 619, 641 S.E.2d 511 (2007)]

50–10. A QUESTION OF ETHICS

*Vickie Lynn Smith, an actress and model also known as Anna Nicole Smith, met J. Howard Marshall II in 1991. During their courtship, J. Howard lavished gifts and large sums of money on Anna Nicole, and they married on June 27, 1994. J. Howard died on August 4, 1995. According to Anna Nicole, J. Howard intended to provide for her financial security through a trust, but under the terms of his will, all of his assets were transferred to a trust for the benefit of E. Pierce Marshall, one of J. Howard's sons. While J. Howard's estate was subject to probate proceedings in a Texas state court, Anna Nicole filed for bankruptcy in a federal bankruptcy court. Pierce filed a claim in the bankruptcy proceeding, alleging that Anna Nicole had defamed him when her lawyers told the media that Pierce had engaged in forgery and fraud to gain control of his father's assets. Anna Nicole filed a counterclaim, alleging that Pierce prevented the transfer of his father's assets to a trust for her by, among other things, imprisoning J. Howard against his wishes, surrounding him with security guards to prevent contact with her, and transferring property against his wishes. [*Marshall v. Marshall, *547 U.S. 293, 126 S.Ct. 1735, 164 L.Ed.2d 480 (2006)]*

(a) What is the purpose underlying the requirements for a valid will? Which of these requirements might be at issue in this case? How should it apply here? Why?
(b) State courts generally have jurisdiction over the probate of a will and the administration of an estate. Does the Texas state court thus have the sole authority to adjudicate all of the claims in this case? Why or why not?
(c) How should Pierce's claim against Anna Nicole and her counterclaim be resolved?
(d) Anna Nicole executed her will in 2001. The beneficiary—Daniel, her son, who was not J. Howard's child—died in 2006, shortly after Anna Nicole gave birth to a daughter, Dannielynn. In 2007, before executing a new will, Anna Nicole died. What happens if a will's beneficiary dies before the testator? What happens if a child is born after a will is executed?

LAW ON THE WEB

For updated links to resources available on the Web, as well as a variety of other materials, visit this text's Web site at

www.cengage.com/blaw/jentz

The SeniorLaw Web site offers information on a variety of topics, including estate planning and trusts. The URL for this site is

www.seniorlaw.com

You can find the Uniform Probate Code, as well as links to various state probate statutes, at Cornell University's Legal Information Institute. Go to

www.law.cornell.edu/uniform/probate.html

A number of tools, including wills and trusts, that can be used in estate planning are described by the National Association of Financial and Estate Planning on its Web site at

www.nafep.com

Legal Research Exercises on the Web

Go to **www.cengage.com/blaw/jentz**, the Web site that accompanies this text. Select "Chapter 50" and click on "Internet Exercises." There you will find the following Internet research exercises that you can perform to learn more about the topics covered in this chapter.

Internet Exercise 50–1: Legal Perspective
Wills and Trusts

Internet Exercise 50–2: Management Perspective
Social Security

CHAPTER 51

Professional Liability and Accountability

Professionals such as accountants, attorneys, physicians, architects, and others are increasingly faced with the threat of liability. One of the reasons for this is that the public has become more aware that professionals are required to deliver competent services and are obligated to adhere to standards of performance commonly accepted within their professions.

Certainly, the dizzying collapse of Enron Corporation and the failure of other major companies, including WorldCom, Inc., in the early 2000s called attention to the importance of abiding by professional accounting standards. Arthur Andersen, LLP, one of the world's leading public accounting firms, ended up being indicted on criminal charges for its role in thwarting the government's investigation into Enron's accounting practices.[1] As a result, that company ceased to exist and roughly 85,000 employees lost their jobs. Moreover, under the Sarbanes-Oxley Act of 2002, which Congress passed in response to these events, public accounting firms throughout the nation will feel the effects for years to come. Among other things, the act imposed stricter regulation and oversight on the public accounting industry.

Considering the many potential sources of legal liability that they face, accountants, attorneys, and other professionals should be very aware of their legal obligations. In this chapter, we look at the potential liability of professionals under both the common law and statutory law. The chapter concludes with a brief examination of the relationships of professionals, particularly accountants and attorneys, with their clients.

1. Although Arthur Andersen, LLP, was subsequently convicted in a federal district court on the charge of obstructing justice, the United States Supreme Court reversed and remanded the case in 2005 due to erroneous jury instructions. *Arthur Andersen, LLP v. United States,* 544 U.S. 696, 125 S.Ct. 2129, 161 L.Ed.2d 1008 (2005).

SECTION 1 Potential Liability to Clients

Under the common law, professionals may be liable to clients for breach of contract, negligence, or fraud.

Liability for Breach of Contract

Accountants and other professionals face liability for any breach of contract under the common law. A professional owes a duty to her or his client to honor the terms of the contract and to perform the contract within the stated time period. If the professional fails to perform as agreed in the contract, then she or he has breached the contract, and the client has the right to recover damages from the professional. Damages include expenses incurred by the client to hire another party to provide the contracted-for services and any other reasonable and foreseeable losses that arise from the professional's breach. For example, if the client had to pay liquidated damages or penalties for failing to meet deadlines, the court may order the professional to pay an equivalent amount in damages to the client.

Liability for Negligence

Accountants and other professionals may also be held liable for negligence in the performance of their services. Recall from Chapter 7 that to establish negligence, the plaintiff must prove four elements: duty, breach, causation, and damages. These elements must also be proved in negligence cases against professionals, which often focus on the standard of care exercised by the professional.

All professionals are subject to the standards of conduct and the ethical codes established by their profession, by state statutes, and by judicial decisions. They are also governed by the contracts they enter into with their clients. In performance of their contracts, professionals must exercise the established standards of care, knowledge, and judgment generally accepted by members of their professional group. Here, we look at the duty of care owed by two groups of professionals that frequently perform services for business firms: accountants and attorneys.

Accountant's Duty of Care Accountants play a major role in a business's financial system. Accountants have the necessary expertise and experience in establishing and maintaining accurate financial records to design, control, and audit recordkeeping systems; to prepare reliable statements that reflect an individual's or a business's financial status; and to give tax advice and prepare tax returns.

Standard of Care. Generally, an accountant must possess the skills that an ordinarily prudent accountant would have and must exercise the degree of care that an ordinarily prudent accountant would exercise. The level of skill expected of accountants and the degree of care that they should exercise in performing their services are reflected in what are known as **generally accepted accounting principles (GAAP)** and **generally accepted auditing standards (GAAS).** The Financial Accounting Standards Board (FASB, usually pronounced "faz-bee") determines what accounting conventions, rules, and procedures constitute GAAP at a given point in time. GAAS are standards concerning an auditor's professional qualities and the judgment that he or she exercises in auditing financial records. GAAS are established by the American Institute of Certified Public Accountants. GAAP and GAAS are also reflected in the rules established by the Securities and Exchange Commission (see Chapter 41).

As long as an accountant conforms to GAAP and acts in good faith, the accountant normally will not be held liable to the client for a mistake in judgment. An accountant is not required to discover every impropriety, **defalcation**[2] (embezzlement), or fraud, in a client's books. If, however, the impropriety, defalcation, or fraud has gone undiscovered because of the accountant's negligence or failure to perform an express or implied duty, the accountant will be liable for any resulting losses suffered by the client and perhaps by third parties. Therefore, an accountant who uncovers suspicious financial transactions and fails to investigate the matter fully or to inform the client of the discovery can be held liable to the client for the resulting loss.

Violations of GAAP and GAAS. A violation of GAAP and GAAS will be considered *prima facie* evidence of negligence on the part of the accountant. Compliance with GAAP and GAAS, however, does not necessarily relieve an accountant from potential legal liability. An accountant may be held to a higher standard of conduct established by state statute and by judicial decisions.

Audits, Qualified Opinions, and Disclaimers. One of the most important tasks that an accountant may perform for a business is an audit. An *audit* is a systematic inspection, by analyses and tests, of a business's financial records. The purpose of an audit is to provide the auditor with evidence to support an opinion on the reliability of the business's financial statements. A normal audit is not intended to uncover fraud or other misconduct. Nevertheless, an accountant may be liable for failing to detect misconduct if a normal audit would have revealed it. Also, if the auditor agreed to examine the records for evidence of fraud or other obvious misconduct and then failed to detect it, he or she may be liable. After performing an audit, the auditor issues an opinion letter stating whether, in his or her opinion, the financial statements fairly present the business's financial position.

In issuing an opinion letter, an auditor may qualify the opinion or include a disclaimer. An opinion that disclaims any liability for false or misleading financial statements is too general, however. A qualified opinion or a disclaimer must be specific and identify the reason for the qualification or disclaimer. For example, an auditor of a corporation might qualify the opinion by stating that there is uncertainty about how a lawsuit against the firm will be resolved. In that situation, the auditor will not be liable if the outcome of the suit is bad for the firm. The auditor could still be liable, however, for failing to discover other problems that an audit in compliance with GAAS and GAAP would have revealed. In a disclaimer, the auditor is basically stating that she or he does not have sufficient information to issue an opinion. Again, the auditor must identify what the problem is and what information is lacking.

2. This term, pronounced deh-ful-*kay*-shun, is derived from the Latin *de* ("off") and *falx* ("sickle"—a tool for cutting grain or tall grass). In law, the term refers to the act of a defaulter or of an embezzler. As used here, it means embezzlement.

Unaudited Financial Statements. Sometimes, accountants are hired to prepare unaudited financial statements. (A financial statement is considered unaudited if incomplete auditing procedures have been used in its preparation or if insufficient procedures have been used to justify an opinion.) Accountants may be subject to liability for failing, in accordance with standard accounting procedures, to designate a balance sheet as "unaudited." An accountant will also be held liable for failure to disclose to a client the facts or circumstances that give reason to believe that misstatements have been made or that a fraud has been committed.

Defenses to Negligence. As this discussion has described, an accountant may be held liable to a client for losses resulting from the accountant's negligence in performing various accounting services. An accountant facing a cause of action for damages based on negligence, however, has several possible defenses, including the following:

1. That the accountant was not negligent.
2. That if the accountant was negligent, this negligence was not the proximate cause of the client's losses.[3]
3. That the client was also negligent (depending on whether state law allows contributory negligence or comparative negligence as a defense—see Chapter 7).

3. See, for example, *Oregon Steel Mills, Inc. v. Coopers & Lybrand, LLP*, 336 Or. 329, 83 P.3d 322 (2004).

Attorney's Duty of Care The conduct of attorneys is governed by rules established by each state and by the American Bar Association's Model Rules of Professional Conduct. All attorneys owe a duty to provide competent and diligent representation. Attorneys are required to be familiar with well-settled principles of law applicable to a case and to find law that can be discovered through a reasonable amount of research. The lawyer must also investigate and discover facts that could materially affect the client's legal rights.

Standard of Care. In judging an attorney's performance, the standard used will normally be that of a reasonably competent general practitioner of ordinary skill, experience, and capacity. If an attorney holds himself or herself out as having expertise in a special area of law (for example, intellectual property), then the attorney's standard of care in that area is higher than for attorneys without such expertise.

Misconduct. Generally, a state's rules of professional conduct for attorneys provide that committing a criminal act that reflects adversely on the person's "honesty or trustworthiness, or fitness as a lawyer in other respects" is professional misconduct. The rules often further provide that a lawyer should not engage in conduct involving "dishonesty, fraud, deceit, or misrepresentation."

Such rules were in force in Wisconsin when the events in the following case took place.

CASE 51.1 In re Disciplinary Proceedings against Inglimo

Supreme Court of Wisconsin, 2007. 2007 WI 126, 305 Wis.2d 71, 740 N.W.2d 125.

• **Background and Facts** A little more than a decade after Michael Inglimo was admitted to the practice of law in Wisconsin, he started occasionally using marijuana with one of his clients. Inglimo represented this client in a criminal case in 2000 and 2001. He was under the influence of drugs during that trial and was not prepared for it. Later, he wrote checks from bank accounts that he maintained in trust for his clients to purchase a car for himself. He also maintained personal funds in these trust accounts and did not keep a running balance of receipts, disbursements, and the amount remaining in the trust account for each client. He did not record the deposits in the trust account checkbook register. In 2003, he was convicted for misdemeanor possession of marijuana. The state's Office of Legal Regulation (OLR) filed a complaint against him. A referee concluded that he had violated the state's rules of professional conduct for attorneys and recommended that he be suspended from the practice of law for eighteen months. Both Inglimo and the OLR appealed to the Wisconsin Supreme Court.

CASE CONTINUES

CASE 51.1 CONTINUED

• **Decision and Rationale** The state's highest court concluded that a three-year suspension was necessary to protect the public. It agreed with the Office of Legal Regulation that the referee's recommendation of an eighteen-month suspension was too lenient. "An eighteen-month suspension in the current case, given the number and nature of ethical violations, would unduly depreciate the seriousness of attorney Inglimo's professional misconduct." The reviewing court was unimpressed with Inglimo's contention that he had removed "from his life both controlled substances and the persons who connected him to that lifestyle." Unconvinced, the court stated that "a substantial period of suspension is necessary in this case to impress upon attorney Inglimo and other lawyers in this state the seriousness of the professional misconduct at issue here and to protect the public from similar misconduct in the future."

• **The Legal Environment Dimension** *The standards for defining professional misconduct appear to focus on an act's impact on third parties rather than its effect on the professional. Is this the appropriate focus? Why or why not?*

• **The Ethical Dimension** *Should an attorney's misbehavior be considered a violation of the rules of professional conduct even if he or she is not convicted of a crime? Discuss.*

Liability for Malpractice. When an attorney fails to exercise reasonable care and professional judgment, she or he breaches the duty of care and can be held liable for *malpractice* (professional negligence). In malpractice cases—as in all cases involving allegations of negligence—the plaintiff must prove that the attorney's breach of the duty of care actually caused the plaintiff to suffer some injury. For example, attorney Colette Boehmer allows the statute of limitations to lapse on the claim of Sufi Carn, her client. Boehmer can be held liable for malpractice because Carn can no longer file a cause of action in this case and has lost a potential award of damages.

Liability for Fraud

Recall from Chapter 14 that fraud, or misrepresentation, involves the following elements:

1. A misrepresentation of a material fact has occurred.
2. There is an intent to deceive.
3. The innocent party has justifiably relied on the misrepresentation.
4. For damages, the innocent party must have been injured.

A professional may be held liable for *actual* fraud when he or she intentionally misstates a material fact to mislead his or her client and the client justifiably relies on the misstated fact to his or her injury. A material fact is one that a reasonable person would consider important in deciding whether to act.

In contrast, a professional may be held liable for *constructive* fraud whether or not he or she acted with fraudulent intent. Constructive fraud may be found when an accountant is grossly negligent in performing his or her duties. For example, Paula, an accountant, is conducting an audit of National Computing Company (NCC). Paula accepts the explanations of Ron, an NCC officer, regarding certain financial irregularities, despite evidence that contradicts those explanations and indicates that the irregularities may be illegal. Paula's conduct could be characterized as an intentional failure to perform a duty in reckless disregard of the consequences of such failure. This would constitute gross negligence and could be held to be constructive fraud. Both actual and constructive fraud may potentially lead to an accountant or other professional being held liable to a client for losses resulting from the fraud.

Limiting Professionals' Liability

Accountants and other professionals can limit their liability to some extent by disclaiming it. Depending on the circumstances, a disclaimer that does not meet certain requirements will not be effective, however; and in some situations, a disclaimer may not be effective at all.

Professionals may be able to limit their liability for the misconduct of other professionals with whom they work by organizing the business as a professional corporation (P.C.) or a limited liability partnership (LLP). In some states, a professional who is a member of a P.C. is not personally liable for a co-member's misconduct unless she or he participated in it or supervised the member who acted wrongly. The innocent professional is liable only to the extent of his or her interest in the assets of the firm. This is also true for professionals who are partners in an LLP. P.C.s were discussed in more detail in Chapter 38. LLPs were covered in Chapter 36.

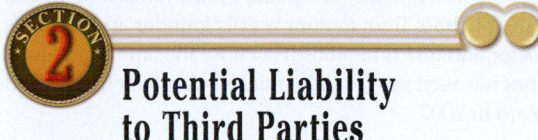

SECTION 2 Potential Liability to Third Parties

Traditionally, an accountant or other professional owed a duty only to those with whom she or he had a direct contractual relationship—that is, those with whom she or he was in *privity of contract.* A professional's duty was only to her or his client. Violations of statutory laws, fraud, and other intentional or reckless acts of wrongdoing were the only exceptions to this general rule.

Today, numerous third parties—including investors, shareholders, creditors, corporate managers and directors, regulatory agencies, and others—rely on the opinions of auditors (accountants) when making decisions. In view of this extensive reliance, many courts have all but abandoned the privity requirement in regard to accountants' liability to third parties.

In this section, we focus primarily on the potential liability of auditors to third parties. Understanding an auditor's common law liability to third parties is critical because often, when a business fails, its independent auditor (accountant) may be one of the few potentially solvent (able to pay expenses and debts) defendants. The majority of courts now hold that auditors can be held liable to third parties for negligence, but the standard for the imposition of this liability varies. There are generally three different views of accountants' liability to third parties, each of which we discuss below.

The *Ultramares* Rule

The traditional rule regarding an accountant's liability to third parties was enunciated by Chief Judge Benjamin Cardozo in *Ultramares Corp. v. Touche,*[4] a case decided in 1931. In the *Ultramares* case, Fred Stern & Company had hired the public accounting firm of Touche, Niven & Company to review Stern's financial records and prepare a balance sheet for the year ending December 31, 1923.[5] Touche prepared the balance sheet and supplied Stern with thirty-two certified copies. According to the certified balance sheet, Stern had a net worth (assets exceed liabilities) of $1,070,715.26. In reality, however, Stern's liabilities exceeded its assets—the company's records had been falsified by insiders at Stern to reflect a positive net worth. In reliance on the certified balance sheets, a lender, Ultramares Corporation, loaned substantial amounts to Stern. After Stern was declared bankrupt, Ultramares brought an action against Touche for negligence in an attempt to recover damages.

The Requirement of Privity The New York Court of Appeals (that state's highest court) refused to impose liability on Touche and concluded that Touche's accountants owed a duty of care only to those persons for whose "primary benefit" the statements were intended. In this case, the statements were intended only for the primary benefit of Stern. The court held that in the absence of privity or a relationship "so close as to approach that of privity," a party could not recover from an accountant. The court's requirement of privity has since been referred to as the *Ultramares* rule, or the New York rule.

Modification to Allow "Near Privity" The *Ultramares* rule was restated and somewhat modified in a 1985 New York case, *Credit Alliance Corp. v. Arthur Andersen & Co.*[6] In that case, the court held that if a third party has a sufficiently close relationship or nexus (link or connection) with an accountant, then the *Ultramares* privity requirement may be satisfied without the establishment of an accountant-client relationship. The rule enunciated in the *Credit Alliance* case is often referred to as the "near privity" rule. Only a minority of states have adopted this rule of accountants' liability to third parties.

Under this rule, does an accountant who is aware that a nonclient might rely on the accountant's work owe the nonclient a duty of care when preparing reports on that party's financial status for his manager? Does the accountant have a duty to advise the nonclient on other financial transactions? These were the questions in the following case.

4. 255 N.Y. 170, 174 N.E. 441 (1931).

5. Banks, creditors, stockholders, purchasers, and sellers often rely on balance sheets when making decisions relating to a company's business.

6. 65 N.Y.2d 536, 483 N.E.2d 110 (1985). A "relationship sufficiently intimate to be equated with privity" is enough for a third party to sue another's accountant for negligence.

CASE 51.2 Reznor v. J. Artist Management, Inc.

United States District Court, Southern District of New York, 2005. 365 F.Supp.2d 565.

• **Company Profile** In 1988, an assistant engineer and janitor at a recording studio in Cleveland, Ohio, asked its owner for permission to record demos of his own songs while the studio was not being used. The owner agreed. Because the songwriter could not find a band to play the music as he wanted it to sound, he played all of the instruments, except the drums, himself. So began the rock band Nine Inch Nails (**www.nin.com**). Michael Trent Reznor was its founder and is still its chief producer, singer, songwriter, musical director, and instrumentalist. He chose the name Nine Inch Nails because it abbreviates easily. The band has released several influential albums, which have sold more than 20 million copies, including Year Zero in 2007.

• **Background and Facts** Michael Trent Reznor met John Malm, Jr., a part-time promoter of local rock bands, in Cleveland, Ohio, in 1985. Malm became Reznor's manager and formed J. Artist Management, Inc. (JAM). Reznor became the lead singer in the band Nine Inch Nails (NIN), which performed its first show in 1988. Reznor and Malm signed a management agreement, under which JAM was to receive 20 percent of Reznor's gross compensation. Over the next few years, Reznor and Malm created other companies to sell NIN's merchandise and perform various services. In 1996, Malm hired accountant Richard Szekelyi and his firm, Navigent Group, to provide financial consulting services to JAM and the jointly owned companies. Szekelyi did not provide services to Reznor personally, but his duties included examining Reznor's financial records. Szekelyi discovered that the accounting among the parties was flawed, with Malm, for example, receiving tax benefits that should have gone to Reznor. According to Szekelyi, by 2003, Reznor owed JAM $1.56 million, and the jointly owned companies owed Reznor $5.5 million, which (as later became clear) was unlikely to be repaid. Reznor fired Malm and filed a suit in a federal district court against JAM and others, including Szekelyi and Navigent.

• **Decision and Rationale** The court granted the motion of Szekelyi and Navigent for summary judgment and dismissed them from the case. The court recognized that an accountant can be liable to a nonclient for fraud if the accountant knows of the falsity of a client's statements, or recklessly disregards circumstances that cast doubt on the truth of the statements, and knows that the nonclient is reasonably relying on the accountant. Applying this principle, the court reasoned that "since Reznor was not Szekelyi's client, Szekelyi would be liable to Reznor for malpractice only where he was aware that the nonclient would rely on his work for a particular purpose. Szekelyi's presentations to Reznor in 2002 and 2003 meet this standard, and so Szekelyi is liable for any malpractice he may have committed in preparing and presenting these reports of Reznor's financial status. However, there is no evidence that Szekelyi breached any standard of care in preparing and presenting these reports." Furthermore, "because Szekelyi was not Reznor's accountant or business manager, he owed Reznor in his individual capacity no such duty with respect to other transactions." Also, "there is no evidence that * * * Szekelyi knew or should have known of any impropriety" in this case involving fraud. "Indeed, there is no evidence that Szekelyi did anything but attempt to correct the only clearly flawed accounting in evidence, [that is,] the improper tax treatment."

• **What If the Facts Were Different?** *If Szekelyi had also been Reznor's accountant, would the result have been different? Why or why not?*

• **The Legal Environment Dimension** *How might Reznor, or anyone in a similar position, have avoided the negative impact of the result in this case?*

The *Restatement* Rule

The *Ultramares* rule has been severely criticized. Auditors perform much of their work for use by persons who are not parties to the contract; thus, it is asserted that they owe a duty to these third parties. Consequently, there has been an erosion of the *Ultramares* rule, and accountants have increasingly been exposed to potential liability to third parties. The majority of courts have adopted the position taken by the *Restatement (Second) of Torts.* Under the *Restatement,* accountants are subject to liability for negligence not only to their clients but also to foreseen, or known, users—and users within a foreseen class of users—of their reports or financial statements.

Under Section 552(2) of the *Restatement (Second) of Torts,* an accountant's liability extends to:

1. Persons for whose benefit and guidance the accountant intends to supply the information or knows that the recipient intends to supply it, and
2. Persons whom the accountant intends the information to influence or knows that the recipient so intends.

For example, Steve, an accountant, prepares a financial statement for Tech Software, Inc., a client, knowing that the client will submit that statement to First National Bank to secure a loan. If Steve makes negligent misstatements or omissions in the statement, the bank may hold Steve liable because he knew that the bank would rely on his work product when deciding whether to make the loan.

Liability to Reasonably Foreseeable Users

A small minority of courts hold accountants liable to any users whose reliance on an accountant's statements or reports was *reasonably foreseeable.* This standard has been criticized as extending liability too far because it means that accountants can be liable even in circumstances in which they are unaware of how their opinions will be used.[7]

The majority of courts have concluded that the *Restatement*'s approach is the more reasonable one because it allows accountants to control their exposure to liability. Liability is "fixed by the accountants' particular knowledge at the moment the audit is published," not by the foreseeability of the harm that might occur to a third party after the report is released. Even the California courts, which for years relied on reasonable foreseeability as the standard for determining an auditor's liability to third parties, have changed their positions.[8]

7. See, for example, the North Carolina Supreme Court's criticisms of this rule in *Raritan River Steel Co. v. Cherry, Bekaert & Holland,* 322 N.C. 200, 367 S.E.2d 609 (1988).

8. *Bily v. Arthur Young & Co.,* 3 Cal.4th 370, 834 P.2d 745, 11 Cal.Rptr.2d 51 (1992).

Liability of Attorneys to Third Parties

Like accountants, attorneys may be held liable under the common law to third parties who rely on legal opinions to their detriment. Generally, an attorney is not liable to a nonclient unless the attorney has committed fraud (or malicious conduct). The liability principles stated in Section 552 of the *Restatement (Second) of Torts,* however, may apply to attorneys as well as to accountants.[9]

Concept Summary 51.1 on the next page reviews the common law rules under which accountants, attorneys, and other professionals may be held liable.

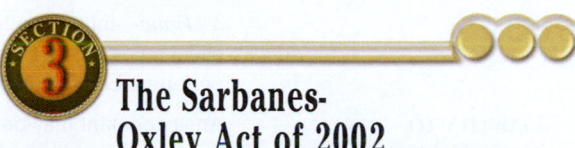

SECTION 3 The Sarbanes-Oxley Act of 2002

As previously mentioned, in 2002 Congress enacted the Sarbanes-Oxley Act, which became effective on August 29, 2002. The act imposes a number of strict requirements on both domestic and foreign public accounting firms that provide auditing services to companies ("issuers") whose securities are sold to public investors. The act defines the term *issuer* as a company that has securities that are registered under Section 12 of the Securities Exchange Act of 1934, that is required to file reports under Section 15(d) of the 1934 act, or that has filed a registration statement that has not yet become effective under the Securities Act of 1933.

The Public Company Accounting Oversight Board

Among other things, the Sarbanes-Oxley Act calls for an increased degree of government oversight of public accounting practices. To this end, the act created the Public Company Accounting Oversight Board, which reports to the Securities and Exchange Commission. The board consists of a chair and four other members. The purpose of the board is to oversee the audit of public companies that are subject to securities laws in order to protect public investors and to ensure that public accounting firms comply with the provisions of the Sarbanes-Oxley Act.

9. See, for example, *North Fork Bank v. Cohen & Krassner,* 843 N.Y.S.2d 575, 44 A.D.3d 375 (N.Y.A.D. 1 Dept. 2007); and *Kastner v. Jenkins & Gilchrist, P.C.,* 231 S.W.3d 571 (Tex.App.—Dallas 2007).

CONCEPT SUMMARY 51.1
Common Law Liability of Accountants and Other Professionals

Concept	Nature of Liability
Liability to Clients	1. *Breach of contract*—An accountant or other professional who fails to perform according to his or her contractual obligations can be held liable for breach of contract and resulting damages. 2. *Negligence*—An accountant or other professional, in performance of her or his duties, must use the care, knowledge, and judgment generally used by professionals in the same or similar circumstances. Failure to do so is negligence. An accountant's violation of generally accepted accounting principles and generally accepted auditing standards is *prima facie* evidence of negligence. 3. *Fraud*—Intentionally misrepresenting a material fact to a client, when the client relies on the misrepresentation, is actual fraud. Gross negligence in performance of duties is constructive fraud.
Liability to Third Parties	An accountant may be liable for negligence to any third person the accountant knows or should have known will benefit from the accountant's work. The standard for imposing this liability varies, but generally courts follow one of the following rules: 1. *Ultramares rule*—An accountant owes a duty of care to those persons for whose primary benefit the accountant's statements were intended. Liability will be imposed only if the accountant is in privity, or near privity, with the third party. 2. *Restatement rule*—Extends liability to third parties whose reliance is foreseen or known and to third parties in a class of foreseen or known users. This includes persons for whose benefit and guidance the accountant intends to supply the information, and persons whom the accountant intends the information to influence. The majority of courts have adopted this rule. 3. *"Reasonably foreseeable user" rule*—Liability will be imposed if the third party's use was reasonably foreseeable. 4. *Liability of attorneys*—An attorney generally is not liable to a nonclient unless the attorney committed fraud or other malicious conduct, although in some situations an attorney may be liable to persons whose reliance is foreseen or known.

Applicability to Public Accounting Firms

Titles I and II of the act set forth the key provisions relating to the duties of the oversight board and the requirements relating to public accounting firms—defined by the act as firms and associated persons that are "engaged in the practice of public accounting or preparing or issuing audit reports." These provisions are summarized in Exhibit 51–1. (Provisions of the act that are more directly concerned with corporate fraud and the responsibilities of corporate officers and directors were listed and described in Exhibit 41–5 in Chapter 41 on page 790.)

Requirements for Maintaining Working Papers

While performing an audit for a client, an accountant accumulates **working papers**—the various documents used and developed during the audit. These include notes, computations, memoranda, copies, and other papers that make up the work prod-

EXHIBIT 51–1 • Key Provisions of the Sarbanes-Oxley Act of 2002 Relating to Public Accounting Firms

AUDITOR INDEPENDENCE

To help ensure that auditors remain independent of the firms that they audit, Title II of the Sarbanes-Oxley Act does the following:

- Makes it unlawful for Registered Public Accounting Firms (RPAFs) to perform both audit and nonaudit services for the same company at the same time. Nonaudit services include the following:
  1. Bookkeeping or other services related to the accounting records or financial statements of the audit client.
  2. Financial information systems design and implementation.
  3. Appraisal or valuation services.
  4. Fairness opinions.
  5. Management functions.
  6. Broker or dealer, investment adviser, or investment banking services.
- Requires preapproval for most auditing services from the issuer's (the corporation's) audit committee.
- Requires audit partner rotation by prohibiting RPAFs from providing audit services to an issuer if either the lead audit partner or the audit partner responsible for reviewing the audit has provided such services to that corporation in each of the prior five years.
- Requires RPAFs to make timely reports to the audit committees of the corporations. The report must indicate all critical accounting policies and practices to be used; all alternative treatments of financial information within generally accepted accounting principles that have been discussed with the corporation's management officials, the ramifications of the use of such alternative treatments, and the treatment preferred by the auditor; and other material written communications between the auditor and the corporation's management.
- Makes it unlawful for an RPAF to provide auditing services to an issuer if the corporation's chief executive officer, chief financial officer, chief accounting officer, or controller was previously employed by the auditor and participated in any capacity in the audit of the corporation during the one-year period preceding the date that the audit began.

DOCUMENT RETENTION AND DESTRUCTION

- The Sarbanes-Oxley Act provides that anyone who destroys, alters, or falsifies records with the intent to obstruct or influence a federal investigation or in relation to bankruptcy proceedings can be criminally prosecuted and sentenced to a fine, imprisonment for up to twenty years, or both.
- The act also requires accountants who audit or review publicly traded companies to retain all working papers related to the audit or review for a period of five years (now amended to seven years). Violators can be sentenced to a fine, imprisonment for up to ten years, or both.

uct of an accountant's services to a client. Under the common law and the statutory law in a number of states, working papers remain the accountant's property. It is important for accountants to retain such records in the event that they need to defend against lawsuits for negligence or other actions in which their competence is challenged. The client also has a right to access an accountant's working papers because they reflect the client's financial situation. On a client's request, an accountant must return to the client any of the client's records or journals, and failure to do so may result in liability.

Section 802(a)(1) of the Sarbanes-Oxley Act provided that accountants must maintain working papers relating to an audit or review for five years—subsequently increased to seven years—from the end of the fiscal period in which the audit or review was concluded. An accountant who knowingly violates this requirement may be fined, imprisoned for up to ten years, or both.

SECTION 4

Potential Liability of Accountants under Securities Laws

Both civil and criminal liability may be imposed on accountants under the Securities Act of 1933, the Securities Exchange Act of 1934, and the Private Securities Litigation Reform Act of 1995.[10]

Liability under the Securities Act of 1933

The Securities Act of 1933 requires registration statements to be filed with the Securities and Exchange Commission (SEC) prior to an offering of securities (see Chapter 41).[11] Accountants frequently prepare and certify the issuer's financial statements that are included in the registration statement.

Liability under Section 11 Section 11 of the Securities Act of 1933 imposes civil liability on accountants for misstatements and omissions of material facts in registration statements. An accountant may be held liable if he or she prepared any financial statements included in the registration statement that "contained an untrue statement of a material fact or omitted to state a material fact required to be stated therein or necessary to make the statements therein not misleading."[12]

An accountant may be liable to anyone who acquires a security covered by the registration statement. A purchaser of a security need only demonstrate that she or he has suffered a loss on the security. Proof of reliance on the materially false statement or misleading omission ordinarily is not required, nor is there a requirement of privity between the accountant and the security purchaser.

The Due Diligence Standard. Section 11 imposes a duty on accountants to use **due diligence** in preparing financial statements included in the filed registration statements. After the purchaser has proved a loss on the security, the accountant has the burden of showing that he or she exercised due diligence in preparing the financial statements. Proving due diligence requires an accountant to demonstrate that she or he did not commit negligence or fraud. To avoid liability, the accountant must show that he or she had, "after reasonable investigation, reasonable grounds to believe and did believe, at the time such part of the registration statement became effective, that the statements therein were true and that there was no omission of a material fact required to be stated therein or necessary to make the statements therein not misleading."[13] Failure to follow GAAP and GAAS is proof of a lack of due diligence.

In particular, the due diligence standard places a burden on accountants to verify information furnished by a corporation's officers and directors. Merely asking questions is not always sufficient to satisfy the requirement of due diligence. Accountants may be held liable, for example, for failing to detect danger signals in materials that, under GAAS, required further investigation under the circumstances, especially when the documents were furnished by corporate officers.[14]

PREVENTING LEGAL DISPUTES

When "danger signals" exist, accountants and others must investigate the situation further. Remember that persons other than accountants, such as corporate directors, officers, and managers, can also be liable for failing to perform due diligence. Courts are more likely to impose liability when someone has ignored warning signs or red flags that suggest accounting errors or misstatements are present. Therefore, to avoid liability, businesspersons should always investigate the facts underlying financial statements that appear "too good to be true." They should compare recent financial statements to earlier ones, read minutes of shareholders' and directors' meetings, and inspect changes in material contracts, bad debts, and newly discovered liabilities. Additionally, they need to know what is required to meet due diligence standards in the particular jurisdiction and conduct themselves in a manner that is above reproach.

10. Civil and criminal liability may also be imposed on accountants and other professionals under other statutes, including the Racketeer Influenced and Corrupt Organizations Act (RICO). RICO was discussed in Chapter 9.

11. Many securities and transactions are expressly exempted from the 1933 act.

12. 15 U.S.C. Section 77k(a).

13. 15 U.S.C. Section 77k(b)(3).

14. See, for example, *Escott v. BarChris Construction Corp.*, 283 F.Supp. 643 (S.D.N.Y. 1968); *In re Cardinal Health, Inc. Securities Litigation*, 426 F.Supp.2d 688 (S.D. Ohio 2006); and *In re WorldCom, Inc. Securities Litigation*, 352 F.Supp.2d 472 (S.D.N.Y. 2005).

Defenses to Liability. Besides proving that he or she has acted with due diligence, an accountant may raise the following defenses to Section 11 liability:

1. There were no misstatements or omissions.
2. The misstatements or omissions were not of material facts.
3. The misstatements or omissions had no causal connection to the plaintiff's loss.
4. The plaintiff-purchaser invested in the securities knowing of the misstatements or omissions.

Liability under Section 12(2) Section 12(2) of the Securities Act of 1933 imposes civil liability for fraud in relation to offerings or sales of securities.[15] Liability is based on communication to an investor, whether orally or in the written prospectus,[16] of an untrue statement or omission of a material fact.

Penalties and Sanctions for Violations Those who purchase securities and suffer harm as a result of a false or omitted statement, or some other violation, may bring a suit in a federal court to recover their losses and other damages. The U.S. Department of Justice brings criminal actions against those who commit willful violations. The penalties include fines up to $10,000, imprisonment up to five years, or both. The SEC is authorized to seek an injunction against a willful violator to prevent further violations. The SEC can also ask a court to grant other relief, such as an order to a violator to refund profits derived from an illegal transaction.

Liability under the Securities Exchange Act of 1934

Under Sections 18 and 10(b) of the Securities Exchange Act of 1934 and SEC Rule 10b-5, an accountant may be found liable for fraud. A plaintiff has a substantially heavier burden of proof under the 1934 act than under the 1933 act because under the 1934 act, an accountant does not have to prove due diligence to escape liability. The 1934 act relieves an accountant from liability if the accountant acted in "good faith."

Liability under Section 18 Section 18 of the 1934 act imposes civil liability on an accountant who makes or causes to be made in any application, report, or document a statement that at the time and in light of the circumstances was false or misleading with respect to any material fact.[17] Liability is narrow under Section 18 in that it applies only to applications, reports, documents, and registration statements filed with the SEC. In addition, it applies only to sellers and purchasers. Under Section 18, a seller or purchaser must prove one of the following:

1. The false or misleading statement affected the price of the security.
2. The purchaser or seller relied on the false or misleading statement in making the purchase or sale and was not aware of the inaccuracy of the statement.

An accountant will not be liable for violating Section 18 if he or she acted in good faith in preparing the financial statement. To demonstrate good faith, an accountant must show that he or she had no knowledge that the financial statement was false or misleading and that he or she lacked any intent to deceive, manipulate, defraud, or seek unfair advantage over another party. (Note that "mere" negligence in preparing a financial statement does not lead to liability under the 1934 act. This differs from the 1933 act, under which an accountant is liable for all negligent acts.)

In addition to the good faith defense, accountants can escape liability by proving that the buyer or seller of the security in question knew the financial statement was false and misleading. Sellers and purchasers must bring a cause of action "within one year after the discovery of the facts constituting the cause of action and within three years after such cause of action accrued."[18] In addition to awarding damages to a successful plaintiff, a court also has the discretion to assess reasonable costs, including attorneys' fees, against accountants who violate this section.

Liability under Section 10(b) and SEC Rule 10b-5 Accountants also face potential legal liability under the antifraud provisions contained in the Securities Exchange Act of 1934 and SEC Rule 10b-5. The scope of these antifraud provisions is very broad and allows private parties to bring civil actions against violators.

Section 10(b) makes it unlawful for any person, including accountants, to use, in connection with the purchase or sale of any security, any manipulative or deceptive device or plan that is counter to SEC rules and regulations.[19] Rule 10b-5 further makes it unlawful

15. 15 U.S.C. Section 77*l*.
16. As discussed in Chapter 38, a *prospectus* contains financial disclosures about the corporation for the benefit of potential investors.
17. 15 U.S.C. Section 78r(a).
18. 15 U.S.C. Section 17r(c).
19. 15 U.S.C. Section 78j(b).

INSIGHT INTO ETHICS
An Auditor's Duty to Correct Certified Opinions

As explained earlier, an accountant concludes an audit by issuing an opinion letter stating whether, in his or her opinion, the financial statements accurately reflect the business's financial position. All auditors know that both the law and today's accounting standards require that their certified opinions be based on complete and accurate information. But what if an auditor discovers (or should have discovered) that the certified opinions it issued in the past were based on inaccurate data? Considering that investors often rely on these opinions in making investment decisions, does the auditor have a legal or ethical duty to disclose the problems and correct the previous opinions?

The Duty to Speak

The issue first arose in 1980 in *ITT v. Cornfeld.*[a] In that case, the court ruled that an accountant's duty to "speak" was limited to "those statements that the accountant actually prepared and certified." Over the next years, other courts followed that reasoning, holding that only those individuals who have an underlying duty to speak can become liable for their silence.

Then, in 1994, in *Central Bank of Denver v. First Interstate Bank of Denver,*[b] the United States Supreme Court appeared to open the door to potential liability for accountants and auditors who fail to disclose. Although the Court did not specifically address an accountant's duty to correct past mistakes, it did hold that any secondary actor "including a lawyer, accountant, or bank, who . . . makes a material misstatement (or omission) on which a purchaser or seller of securities relies may be liable as a primary violator under [Rule] 10b-5."

Now Accountants Sometimes Do Have a Duty to Correct

In 2007, the U.S. Court of Appeals for the Second Circuit extended this ruling, stating that, under certain

a. 619 F.2d 909 (2d Cir. 1980)

b. 511 U.S. 164, 114 S.Ct. 1439, 128 L.Ed.2d 119 (1994).

for any person, by use of any means or instrumentality of interstate commerce, to do the following:

1. Employ any device, scheme, or strategy to defraud.
2. Make any untrue statement of a material fact or omit to state a material fact necessary to make the statements made, in light of the circumstances, not misleading.
3. Engage in any act, practice, or course of business that operates or would operate as a fraud or deceit on any person, in connection with the purchase or sale of any security.[20]

The Scope of Accountants' Liability under Section 10(b) and Rule 10b-5. Accountants may be held liable only to sellers or purchasers of securities under Section 10(b) and Rule 10b-5, but privity is not necessary. An accountant may be liable not only for fraudulent misstatements of material facts in written material filed with the SEC, but also for any fraudulent oral statements or omissions made in connection with the purchase or sale of any security.

Requirements for Recovering Damages. For a plaintiff to succeed in recovering damages under these antifraud provisions, he or she must prove intent *(scienter)* to commit the fraudulent or deceptive act. Ordinary negligence is not enough. Do accountants have a duty to correct misstatements that they discover in *previous* financial statements if they know that potential investors are relying on those statements? For a discussion of this issue, see this chapter's *Insight into Ethics* feature.

The Private Securities Litigation Reform Act of 1995

The Private Securities Litigation Reform Act of 1995 made some changes to the potential liability of accountants and other professionals in securities fraud cases. Among other things, the act imposed a statutory obligation on accountants. An auditor must use adequate procedures in an audit to detect any illegal acts of the company being audited. If something illegal is detected, the auditor must disclose it to the company's board of directors, the audit committee, or the SEC, depending on the circumstances.[21]

20. 17 C.F.R. Section 240.10b-5.

21. 15 U.S.C. Section 78j-1.

circumstances, an accountant has a legal (and, presumably, ethical) duty to correct a past certified opinion of a company's financial statements.[c] The case was brought by David Overton, who had loaned $1.5 million to Direct Brokerage, Inc., and invested $500,000 in the company. Overton claimed that, in doing so, he relied on Direct Brokerage's 2002 financial statements. From 1999 through 2002, the financial statements had been audited and certified by Todman & Company. According to Overton, the auditors ignored several "red flags" that should have made them suspicious of the financial statements starting in 1998. Allegedly, the auditors failed to notice gross discrepancies in the payroll taxes reported on the certified financial statements from 1998 through 2002. In 1998, the statements reported that the company owed $248,899 in payroll taxes. Yet for 1999 and 2000, the certified statements reflected a payroll tax liability of zero. The auditors never investigated the discrepancies and failed to detect these errors in the 2001 and 2002 audits.

Although the trial court dismissed the case, Overton prevailed on appeal. The court ruled that "an accountant violates 'the duty to correct' and becomes primarily liable under [Section] 10(b) and Rule 10b-5 when it (1) makes a statement in its certified opinion that is false or misleading when made; (2) subsequently learns or was reckless in not learning that the earlier statement was false and misleading; (3) knows or should know that potential investors are relying on the opinion and financial statements; yet (4) fails to take reasonable steps to correct or withdraw its opinion and/or the financial statements."

c. *Overton v. Todman & Co., CPAs*, 478 F.3d 479 (2007).

CRITICAL THINKING

INSIGHT INTO CULTURE

Some people, particularly Europeans, argue that the United States has a "lawsuit culture." In other words, whenever someone does not like the outcome of something, he or she sues. Do you think that the *Overton* case outlined above was just part of our "lawsuit culture," or did David Overton have a valid reason to sue Direct Brokerage's auditors? Explain your answer.

Proportionate Liability The 1995 act provides that, in most situations, a party is liable only for the proportion of damages for which he or she is responsible.[22] In other words, the parties are subject to proportionate liability rather than joint and several liability. Only if an accountant knowingly participated in defrauding investors will he or she be liable for the entire amount of the loss. Suppose that accountant Nina Chavez assisted the president and owner of Midstate Trucking Company in drafting financial statements that misrepresented Midstate's financial condition. If Nina did not knowingly participate in the fraud, she will be liable only for the proportion of damages for which she was responsible.

Aiding and Abetting The 1995 act also provides that aiding and abetting a violation of the Securities Exchange Act of 1934 is a violation in itself. Accountants aid and abet when they are generally aware that they are participating in an activity that is improper and knowingly assist the activity. Silence may constitute aiding.

If an accountant knowingly aids and abets a primary violator, the SEC can seek an injunction or monetary damages. For example, Smith & Jones, an accounting firm, performs an audit for Belco Sales Company that is so inadequate as to constitute gross negligence. Belco uses the financial statements provided by Smith & Jones as part of a scheme to defraud investors. When the scheme is uncovered, the SEC can bring an action against Smith & Jones for aiding and abetting on the ground that the firm knew or should have known that its audited statements contained material misrepresentations on which investors were likely to rely.

22. 15 U.S.C. Section 78u-4(g).

SECTION 5 Potential Criminal Liability of Accountants

An accountant may be found criminally liable for violations of the Securities Act of 1933, the Securities Exchange Act of 1934, and the Internal Revenue Code. In addition, in most states, criminal penalties may be imposed for such actions as knowingly certifying false or fraudulent reports; falsifying, altering, or destroying books of account; and obtaining property or credit through the use of false financial statements.

Criminal Violations of Securities Laws

Under both the 1933 act and the 1934 act, accountants may be subject to criminal penalties for *willful* violations—imprisonment for up to five years and/or a fine of up to $10,000 under the 1933 act and up to ten years and $100,000 under the 1934 act. Under the Sarbanes-Oxley Act of 2002, for a securities filing that is accompanied by an accountant's false or misleading certified audit statement, the accountant may be fined up to $5 million, imprisoned for up to twenty years, or both.

Criminal Violations of Tax Laws

The Internal Revenue Code makes aiding or assisting in the preparation of a false tax return a felony punishable by a fine of $100,000 ($500,000 for a corporation's return) and imprisonment for up to three years.[23] This provision applies to anyone who prepares tax returns for others for compensation, not just to accountants.[24] A penalty of $250 per tax return is levied on tax preparers for negligent understatement of the client's tax liability. For willful understatement of tax liability or reckless or intentional disregard of rules or regulations, a penalty of $1,000 is imposed.[25]

A tax preparer may also be subject to penalties for failing to furnish the taxpayer with a copy of the return, failing to sign the return, or failing to furnish the appropriate tax identification numbers.[26] In addition, those who prepare tax returns for others may be fined $1,000 per document for aiding and abetting another's understatement of tax liability (the penalty is increased to $10,000 for corporate returns).[27] The tax preparer's liability is limited to one penalty per taxpayer per tax year.

Concept Summary 51.2 outlines the potential statutory liability of accountants and other professionals.

SECTION 6 Confidentiality and Privilege

Professionals are restrained by the ethical tenets of their professions to keep all communications with their clients confidential.

23. 26 U.S.C. Section 7206(2).
24. 26 U.S.C. Section 7701(a)(36).
25. 26 U.S.C. Section 6694.
26. 26 U.S.C. Section 6695.
27. 26 U.S.C. Section 6701.

Attorney-Client Relationships

The confidentiality of attorney-client communications is protected by law, which confers a *privilege* on such communications. This privilege exists because of the need for full disclosure to the attorney of the facts of a client's case.

To encourage frankness, confidential attorney-client communications relating to representation are normally held in strictest confidence and protected by law. The attorney and her or his employees may not discuss the client's case with anyone—even under court order—without the client's permission. The client holds the privilege, and only the client may waive it—by disclosing privileged information to someone outside the privilege, for example.

Note, however, that since the Sarbanes-Oxley Act was enacted in 2002, the SEC has implemented new rules requiring attorneys who become aware that a client has violated securities laws to report the violation to the SEC. Reporting a client's misconduct could be a breach of the attorney-client privilege and has caused much controversy in the legal community (see the *Focus on Ethics* feature at the end of Unit 8 on pages 814–816 for more details).

Accountant-Client Relationship

In a few states, accountant-client communications are privileged by state statute. In these states, accountant-client communications may not be revealed even in court or in court-sanctioned proceedings without the client's permission. The majority of states, however, abide by the common law, which provides that, if a court so orders, an accountant must disclose information about his or her client to the court. Physicians and other professionals may similarly be compelled to disclose in court information given to them in confidence by patients or clients.

Communications between professionals and their clients—other than those between an attorney and her or his client—are not privileged under federal law. In cases involving federal law, state-provided rights to confidentiality of accountant-client communications are not recognized. Thus, in those cases, in response to a court order, an accountant must provide the information sought.

CONCEPT SUMMARY 51.2
Statutory Liability of Accountants and Other Professionals

Statute	Nature of Liability
SARBANES-OXLEY ACT OF 2002	See Exhibit 51–1 on page 979 for the provisions of the act on auditor independence. Additionally, under Section 802(a)(1) of the act, accountants are required, in some circumstances, to maintain working papers relating to an audit or review for five years (now amended to seven years) from the end of the fiscal period in which the audit or review was concluded. A knowing violation of this requirement will subject the accountant to a fine, imprisonment for up to ten years, or both.
SECURITIES ACT OF 1933, SECTIONS 11 AND 12(2)	Under Section 11 of the 1933 Securities Act, an accountant who makes a false statement or omits a material fact in audited financial statements required for registration of securities under the law may be liable to anyone who acquires securities covered by the registration statement. The accountant's defense is basically the use of due diligence and the reasonable belief that the work was complete and correct. The burden of proof is on the accountant. Willful violations of this act may be subject to criminal penalties. Section 12(2) of the 1933 act imposes civil liability for fraud on anyone who makes an untrue statement or omits a material fact when offering or selling a security to any purchaser of the security.
SECURITIES EXCHANGE ACT OF 1934, SECTIONS 10(B) AND 18	Under Sections 10(b) and 18 of the 1934 Securities Exchange Act, accountants are held liable for false and misleading applications, reports, and documents required under the act. The burden is on the plaintiff, and the accountant has numerous defenses, including good faith and lack of knowledge that what was submitted was false. Willful violations of this act may be subject to criminal penalties.
INTERNAL REVENUE CODE	1. Aiding or assisting in the preparation of a false tax return is a felony. Aiding and abetting an individual's understatement of tax liability is a separate crime. 2. Tax preparers who negligently or willfully understate a client's tax liability or who recklessly or intentionally disregard Internal Revenue Code rules or regulations are subject to penalties. 3. Tax preparers who fail to provide a taxpayer with a copy of the return, fail to sign the return, or fail to furnish the appropriate tax identification numbers may also be subject to penalties.

REVIEWING Professional Liability and Accountability

Superior Wholesale Corporation planned to purchase Regal Furniture, Inc., and wished to determine Regal's net worth. Superior hired Lynette Shuebke, of the accounting firm Shuebke Delgado, to review an audit that had been prepared by Norman Chase, the accountant for Regal. Shuebke advised Superior that Chase had performed a high-quality audit and that Regal's

REVIEWING CONTINUES

REVIEWING Professional Liability and Accountability, Continued

inventory on the audit dates was stated accurately on the general ledger. As a result of these representations, Superior went forward with its purchase of Regal. After the purchase, Superior discovered that the audit by Chase had been materially inaccurate and misleading, primarily because the inventory had been grossly overstated on the balance sheet. Later, a former Regal employee who had begun working for Superior exposed an e-mail exchange between Chase and former Regal chief executive officer Buddy Gantry. The exchange revealed that Chase had cooperated in overstating the inventory and understating Regal's tax liability. Using the information presented in the chapter, answer the following questions.

1. If Shuebke's review was conducted in good faith and conformed to generally accepted accounting principles, could Superior hold Shuebke Delgado liable for negligently failing to detect material omissions in Chase's audit? Why or why not?
2. According to the rule adopted by the majority of courts to determine accountants' liability to third parties, could Chase be liable to Superior?
3. Generally, what requirements must be met before Superior can recover damages under Section 10(b) of the Securities Exchange Act of 1934 and SEC Rule 10b-5? Could Superior meet these requirements?
4. Suppose that a court determined that Chase had aided Regal in willfully understating its tax liability. What is the maximum penalty that could be imposed on Chase?

TERMS AND CONCEPTS

defalcation 972
due diligence 980
generally accepted accounting principles (GAAP) 972
generally accepted auditing standards (GAAS) 972
working papers 978

QUESTIONS AND CASE PROBLEMS

51–1. Larkin, Inc., retains Howard Patterson to manage its books and prepare its financial statements. Patterson, a certified public accountant, lives in Indiana and practices there. After twenty years, Patterson has become a bit bored with the format of generally accepted accounting principles (GAAP) and has become creative in his accounting methods. Now, though, Patterson has a problem, as he is being sued by Molly Tucker, one of Larkin's creditors. Tucker alleges that Patterson either knew or should have known that Larkin's financial statements would be distributed to various individuals. Furthermore, she asserts that these financial statements were negligently prepared and seriously inaccurate. What are the consequences of Patterson's failure to follow GAAP? Under the traditional *Ultramares* rule, can Tucker recover damages from Patterson? Explain.

51–2. QUESTION WITH SAMPLE ANSWER

The accounting firm of Goldman, Walters, Johnson & Co. prepared financial statements for Lucy's Fashions, Inc. After reviewing the various financial statements, Happydays State Bank agreed to loan Lucy's Fashions $35,000 for expansion. When Lucy's Fashions declared bankruptcy under Chapter 11 six months later, Happydays State Bank promptly filed an action against Goldman, Walters, Johnson & Co., alleging negligent preparation of financial statements. Assuming that the court has abandoned the *Ultramares* approach, what is the result? What are the policy reasons for holding accountants liable to third parties with whom they are not in privity?

- **For a sample answer to Question 51–2, go to Appendix I at the end of this text.**

51-3. In early 2009, Bennett, Inc., offered a substantial number of new common shares to the public. Harvey Helms had a long-standing interest in Bennett because his grandfather had once been president of the company. On receiving a prospectus prepared and distributed by Bennett, Helms was dismayed by the pessimism it embodied. Helms decided to delay purchasing stock in the company. Later, Helms asserted that the prospectus prepared by the accountants was overly pessimistic and contained materially misleading statements. Discuss fully how successful Helms would be in bringing a cause of action under Rule 10b-5 against the accountants of Bennett, Inc.

51-4. Accountant's Liability to Third Parties. In June 1993, Sparkomatic Corp. agreed to negotiate a sale of its Kenco Engineering division to Williams Controls, Inc. At the end of July, Sparkomatic asked its accountants, Parente, Randolph, Orlando, Carey & Associates, to audit Kenco's financial statements for the previous three years and to certify interim and closing balance sheets to be included with the sale's closing documents. All of the parties knew that these documents would serve as a basis for setting the sale price. Within a few days, Williams signed an "Asset Purchase Agreement" that promised access to Parente's records with respect to Kenco. The sale closed in mid-August. In September, Williams was given the financial statements for Kenco's previous three years and the interim and closing balance sheets, all of which were certified by Parente. Williams's accountant found no errors in the closing balance sheet but did not review any of the other documents. The parties set a final purchase price. Later, however, Williams filed a suit in a federal district court against Parente, claiming negligent misrepresentation, among other things, in connection with Parente's preparation of the financial documents. Parente responded with a motion for summary judgment, asserting that the parties lacked privity. Under the *Restatement (Second) of Torts,* Section 552, how should the court rule? Explain. [*Williams Controls, Inc. v. Parente, Randolph, Orlando, Carey & Associates,* 39 F.Supp.2d 517 (M.D.Pa. 1999)]

51-5. Accountant's Liability. In 1995, JTD Health Systems, Inc., hired Tammy Heiby as accounting coordinator. Apparently overwhelmed by the duties of the position, Heiby failed to make payroll tax payments to the Internal Revenue Service (IRS) in 1995 and 1996. Heiby tried to hide this omission by falsifying journal entries and manually writing three checks out of sequence, totaling $1.7 million and payable to a bank, from JTD's cash account (to dispose of excess funds that should have been paid in taxes). JTD hired Pricewaterhouse Coopers, LLP, to review JTD's internal accounting procedures and audit its financial statements for 1995. Coopers's inexperienced auditor was aware that the cash account had not been balanced in months and knew about the checks but never questioned them. The auditor instead mistakenly explained that the unbalanced account was due to changes in Medicaid/Medicare procedures and recommended no further investigation. In 1996, the IRS asked JTD to remit the unpaid taxes, plus interest and penalties. JTD filed a suit in an Ohio state court against Coopers, alleging common law negligence and breach of contract. Should Coopers be held liable to JTD on these grounds? Why or why not? [*JTD Health Systems, Inc. v. Pricewaterhouse Coopers, LLP,* 141 Ohio App.3d 280, 750 N.E.2d 1177 (Ohio App. 3 Dist. 2001)]

51-6. Accountant's Liability under the Private Securities Litigation Reform Act. Solucorp Industries, Ltd., a corporation headquartered in New York, develops and markets products for use in environmental clean-ups. Solucorp's financial statements for the six months ending December 31, 1997, recognized $1.09 million in license fees payable by Smart International, Ltd. The fees comprised about 50 percent of Solucorp's revenue for the period. At the time, however, the parties had a license agreement only "in principle," and Smart had made only one payment of $150,000. Glenn Ohlhauser, an accountant asked to audit the statements, objected to the inclusion of the fees. In February 1998, Solucorp showed Ohlhauser a license agreement backdated to September 1997 but refused to provide any financial information about Smart. Ohlhauser issued an unqualified opinion on the 1997 statements, which were included with forms filed with the Securities and Exchange Commission (SEC). The SEC filed a suit in a federal district court against Ohlhauser and others. What might be the basis in the Private Securities Litigation Reform Act for the SEC's suit against Ohlhauser? What might be Ohlhauser's defense? Discuss. [*Securities and Exchange Commission v. Solucorp Industries, Ltd.,* 197 F.Supp.2d 4 (S.D.N.Y. 2002)]

51-7. CASE PROBLEM WITH SAMPLE ANSWER

In October 1993, Marilyn Greenen, a licensed certified public accountant (CPA), began working at the Port of Vancouver, Washington (the Port), as an account manager. She was not directly engaged in public accounting at the Port, but she oversaw the preparation of financial statements and supervised employees with accounting duties. At the start of her employment, she enrolled her husband for benefits under the Port's medical plan. Her marriage was dissolved in November, but she did not notify the Port of the change. In May 1998 and April 1999, the Port confronted her about the divorce, but she did not update her insurance information. After she was terminated, she reimbursed the Port for the additional premiums it had paid for unauthorized coverage for her former spouse. The Washington State Board of

Accountancy imposed sanctions on Greenen for "dishonesty and misleading representations" while, in the words of an applicable state statute, "representing oneself as a CPA." Greenen asked a Washington state court to review the case. What might be an appropriate sanction in this case? What might be Greenen's best argument against the board's action? On what reasoning might the court uphold the decision? [*Greenen v. Washington State Board of Accountancy,* 824 Wash.App. 126, 110 P.3d 224 (Div. 2 2005)]

- **To view a sample answer for Problem 51–7, go to this book's Web site at www.cengage.com/blaw/jentz, select "Chapter 51," and click on "Case Problem with Sample Answer."**

51–8. Confidentiality and Privilege. Napster, Inc., offered a service that allowed its users to browse digital music files on other users' computers and download selections for free. Music industry principals filed a suit in a federal district court against Napster, alleging copyright infringement. The court ordered Napster to remove from its service files that were identified as infringing. Napster failed to comply and was shut down in July 2001. In October, Bertelsmann AG, a German corporation, loaned Napster $85 million to fund its anticipated transition to a licensed digital music distribution system. The terms allowed Napster to spend the loan on "general, administrative and overhead expenses." In an e-mail, Hank Barry, Napster's chief executive officer, referred to a "side deal" under which Napster could use up to $10 million of the loan to pay litigation expenses. Napster failed to launch the new system before declaring bankruptcy in June 2002. Some of the plaintiffs filed a suit in a federal district court against Bertelsmann, charging that, by its loan, it prolonged Napster's infringement. The plaintiffs asked the court to order the disclosure of all attorney-client communications related to the loan. What principle could Bertelsmann assert to protect these communications? What is the purpose of this protection? Should this principle protect a client who consults an attorney for advice that will help the client commit fraud? Should the court grant the plaintiffs' request? Discuss. [*In re Napster, Inc. Copyright Litigation,* 479 F.3d 1078 (9th Cir. 2007)]

51–9. A QUESTION OF ETHICS

*Portland Shellfish Co. processes live shellfish in Maine. As one of the firm's two owners, Frank Wetmore held 300 voting and 150 nonvoting shares of the stock. Donna Holden held the other 300 voting shares. Donna's husband Jeff managed the company's daily operations, including production, procurement, and sales. The board of directors consisted of Frank and Jeff. In 2001, disagreements arose over the company's management. The Holdens invoked the "Shareholders' Agreement," which provided that "in the event of a deadlock, the directors shall hire an accountant at [Macdonald, Page, Schatz, Fletcher & Co., LLC] to determine the value of the outstanding shares. . . . [E]ach shareholder shall have the right to buy out the other shareholder(s)' interest." Macdonald Page estimated the stock's "fair market value" to be $1.09 million. Donna offered to buy Frank's shares at a price equal to his proportionate share. Frank countered by offering $1.25 million for Donna's shares. Donna rejected Frank's offer and insisted that he sell his shares to her or she would sue. In the face of this threat, Frank sold his shares to Donna for $750,705. Believing the stock to be worth more than twice Macdonald Page's estimate, Frank filed a suit in a federal district court against the accountant. [*Wetmore v. Macdonald, Page, Schatz, Fletcher & Co., LLC, *476 F.3d 1 (1st Cir. 2007)]*

(a) Frank claimed that in valuing the stock, the accountant disregarded "commonly accepted and reliable methods of valuation in favor of less reliable methods." He alleged negligence, among other things. Macdonald Page filed a motion to dismiss the complaint. What are the elements that establish negligence? Which is the most critical element in this case?

(b) Macdonald Page evaluated the company's stock by identifying its "fair market value," defined as "the price at which the property would change hands between a willing buyer and a willing seller, neither being under a compulsion to buy or sell and both having reasonable knowledge of relevant facts." The accountant knew that the shareholders would use its estimate to determine the price that one would pay to the other. Under these circumstances, was Frank's injury foreseeable?

(c) What factor might have influenced Frank to sell his shares to Donna even though he thought that Macdonald Page's "fair market value" figure was less than half of what it should have been? Does this factor represent an unfair, or unethical, advantage?

51–10. VIDEO QUESTION

Go to this text's Web site at **www.cengage.com/blaw/jentz** and select "Chapter 51." Click on "Video Questions" and view the video titled *Accountant's Liability.* Then answer the following questions.

(a) Should Ray prepare a financial statement that values a list of assets provided by the advertising firm without verifying that the firm actually owns these assets?

(b) Discuss whether Ray is in privity with the company interested in buying Laura's advertising firm.

(c) Under the *Ultramares* rule, to whom does Ray owe a duty?

(d) Assume that Laura did not tell Ray that she intended to give the financial statement to the potential acquirer. Would this fact change Ray's liability under the *Ultramares* rule? Explain.

LAW ON THE WEB

For updated links to resources available on the Web, as well as a variety of other materials, visit this text's Web site at

www.cengage.com/blaw/jentz

The Web site for the Financial Accounting Standards Board can be found at

www.fasb.org

For information on the accounting profession, including links to the Sarbanes-Oxley Act of 2002 and articles concerning the act's impact on the accounting profession, go to the Web site of the American Institute of Certified Public Accountants (AICPA) at

aicpa.org

Legal Research Exercises on the Web

Go to **www.cengage.com/blaw/jentz**, the Web site that accompanies this text. Select "Chapter 51" and click on "Internet Exercises." There you will find the following Internet research exercises that you can perform to learn more about the topics covered in this chapter.

Internet Exercise 51–1: Legal Perspective
The Sarbanes-Oxley Act of 2002

Internet Exercise 51–2: Management Perspective
Avoiding Legal Liability

CHAPTER 52

International Law in a Global Economy

International business transactions are not unique to the modern world. What is new in our day is the dramatic growth in world trade and the emergence of a global business community. Because the exchange of goods, services, and ideas (intellectual property) on a worldwide level is now routine, students of business law and the legal environment should be familiar with the laws pertaining to international business transactions.

Laws affecting the international legal environment of business include both international law and national law. **International law** can be defined as a body of law—formed as a result of international customs, treaties, and organizations—that governs relations among or between nations. International law may be public, creating standards for the nations themselves; or it may be private, establishing international standards for private transactions that cross national borders. **National law** is the law of a particular nation, such as Brazil, Germany, Japan, or the United States. In this chapter, we examine how both international law and national law frame business operations in the international context.

SECTION 1 International Law

The major difference between international law and national law is that government authorities can enforce national law. What government, however, can enforce international law? By definition, a *nation* is a sovereign entity—which means that there is no higher authority to which that nation must submit. If a nation violates an international law and persuasive tactics fail, other countries or international organizations have no recourse except to take coercive actions—from severance of diplomatic relations and boycotts to, as a last resort, war—against the violating nation.

In essence, international law is the result of centuries-old attempts to reconcile the traditional need of each country to be the final authority over its own affairs with the desire of nations to benefit economically from trade and harmonious relations with one another. Sovereign nations can, and do, voluntarily agree to be governed in certain respects by international law for the purpose of facilitating international trade and commerce, as well as civilized discourse. As a result, a body of international law has evolved. In this section, we examine the primary sources and characteristics of that body of law, as well as some important legal principles and doctrines that have been developed over time to facilitate dealings among nations.

Sources of International Law

Basically, there are three sources of international law: international customs, treaties and international agreements, and international organizations and conferences. We look at each of these sources here.

International Customs One important source of international law consists of the international customs that have evolved among nations in their relations with one another. Article 38(1) of the Statute of the International Court of Justice refers to an international custom as "evidence of a general practice accepted as law." The legal principles and doctrines that you will read about shortly are rooted in international customs and traditions that have evolved over time in the international arena.

Treaties and International Agreements Treaties and other explicit agreements between or among foreign nations provide another important source of international law. A **treaty** is an agreement or contract between two or more nations that must be authorized and ratified by the supreme power of each nation. Under Article II, Section 2, of the U.S. Constitution, the president has the power "by and with the Advice and Consent of the Senate, to make Treaties, provided two-thirds of the Senators present concur."

A *bilateral* agreement, as the term implies, is an agreement formed by two nations to govern their commercial exchanges or other relations with one another. A *multilateral* agreement is formed by several nations. For example, regional trade associations such as the European Union (EU, which is discussed later in this chapter) are the result of multilateral trade agreements. Other regional trade associations that have been created through multilateral agreements include the Association of Southeast Asian Nations (ASEAN) and the Andean Common Market (ANCOM).

International Organizations In international law, the term **international organization** generally refers to an organization composed mainly of officials of member nations and usually established by treaty. The United States is a member of more than one hundred multilateral and bilateral organizations, including at least twenty through the United Nations. These organizations adopt resolutions, declarations, and other types of standards that often require nations to behave in a particular manner. The General Assembly of the United Nations, for example, has adopted numerous nonbinding resolutions and declarations that embody principles of international law. Disputes with respect to these resolutions and declarations may be brought before the International Court of Justice. That court, however, normally has authority to settle legal disputes only when nations voluntarily submit to its jurisdiction.

The United Nations Commission on International Trade Law has made considerable progress in establishing uniformity in international law as it relates to trade and commerce. One of the commission's most significant creations to date is the 1980 Convention on Contracts for the International Sale of Goods (CISG). Recall from Chapters 20 through 23, which cover contracts for the sale of goods, that the CISG is similar to Article 2 of the Uniform Commercial Code in that it is designed to settle disputes between parties to sales contracts. It spells out the duties of international buyers and sellers that will apply if the parties have not agreed otherwise in their contracts. The CISG governs only sales contracts between trading partners in nations that have ratified the CISG, however.

Common Law and Civil Law Systems

Companies operating in foreign nations are subject to the laws of those nations. In addition, international disputes often are resolved through the court systems of foreign nations. Therefore, businesspersons should understand that legal systems around the globe generally are divided into *common law* and *civil law* systems. As discussed in Chapter 1, in a common law system, the courts independently develop the rules governing certain areas of law, such as torts and contracts. These common law rules apply to all areas not covered by statutory law. Although the common law doctrine of *stare decisis* obligates judges to follow precedential decisions in their jurisdictions, courts may modify or even overturn precedents when deemed necessary.

In contrast to common law countries, most of the European nations, as well as nations in Latin America, Africa, and Asia, base their legal systems on Roman civil law, or "code law." The term *civil law,* as used here, refers not to civil as opposed to criminal law but to *codified* law—an ordered grouping of legal principles enacted into law by a legislature or other governing body. In a **civil law system,** the only official source of law is a statutory code. Courts interpret the code and apply the rules to individual cases, but courts may not depart from the code and develop their own laws. In theory, the law code sets forth all of the principles needed for the legal system. Trial procedures also differ in civil law systems. Unlike judges in common law systems, judges in civil systems often actively question witnesses. Exhibit 52–1 on the following page lists some of the nations that use civil law systems and some that use common law systems.

International Principles and Doctrines

Over time, a number of legal principles and doctrines have evolved and have been employed—to a greater or lesser extent—by the courts of various nations to resolve or reduce conflicts that involve a foreign element. The three important legal principles discussed

EXHIBIT 52–1 • **The Legal Systems of Selected Nations**

Civil Law		Common Law	
Argentina	Indonesia	Australia	Nigeria
Austria	Iran	Bangladesh	Singapore
Brazil	Italy	Canada	United Kingdom
Chile	Japan	Ghana	United States
China	Mexico	India	Zambia
Egypt	Poland	Israel	
Finland	South Korea	Jamaica	
France	Sweden	Kenya	
Germany	Tunisia	Malaysia	
Greece	Venezuela	New Zealand	

below are based primarily on courtesy and respect, and are applied in the interests of maintaining harmonious relations among nations.

The Principle of Comity Under what is known as the principle of **comity,** one nation will defer and give effect to the laws and judicial decrees of another country, as long as they are consistent with the law and public policy of the accommodating nation. For example, a Swedish seller and a U.S. buyer have formed a contract, which the buyer breaches. The seller sues the buyer in a Swedish court, which awards damages. The buyer's assets, however, are in the United States and cannot be reached unless the judgment is enforced by a U.S. court. In this situation, if a U.S. court determines that the procedures and laws applied in the Swedish court are consistent with U.S. national law and policy, the U.S. court will likely defer to, and enforce, the foreign court's judgment.

One way to understand the principle of comity (and the *act of state doctrine,* which will be discussed shortly) is to consider the relationships among the states in our federal form of government. Each state honors (gives "full faith and credit" to) the contracts, property deeds, wills, and other legal obligations formed in other states, as well as judicial decisions with respect to such obligations. On a worldwide basis, nations similarly attempt to honor judgments rendered in other countries when it is feasible to do so. Of course, in the United States the states are constitutionally required to honor other states' actions, whereas, internationally, nations are not *required* to honor the actions of other nations.

The Act of State Doctrine The **act of state doctrine** is a judicially created doctrine that provides that the judicial branch of one country will not examine the validity of public acts committed by a recognized foreign government within the latter's own territory. This doctrine is premised on the theory that the U.S. judicial branch will not sit in judgment of foreign acts when to do so would upset our international relations with that foreign nation.

When a Foreign Government Takes Private Property. The act of state doctrine can have important consequences for individuals and firms doing business with, and investing in, other countries. This doctrine is frequently employed in cases involving **expropriation,** which occurs when a government seizes a privately owned business or privately owned goods for a proper public purpose and awards just compensation. When a government seizes private property for an illegal purpose and without just compensation, the taking is referred to as a **confiscation.** The line between these two forms of taking is sometimes blurred because of differing interpretations of what is illegal and what constitutes just compensation.

For example, Flaherty, Inc., a U.S. company, owns a mine in Brazil. The government of Brazil seizes the mine for public use and claims that the profits Flaherty has already realized from the mine constitute just compensation. Flaherty disagrees, but the act of state doctrine may prevent that company's recovery in a U.S. court. Note that in a case alleging that a foreign government has wrongfully taken the plaintiff's property, the defendant government has the burden of proving that the taking was an expropriation, not a confiscation.

Doctrine May Immunize a Foreign Government's Actions. When applicable, both the act of state doctrine and the doctrine of *sovereign immunity,* which we discuss next, tend to shield foreign nations from the jurisdiction of U.S. courts. As a result, firms or individuals who own property overseas generally have little legal protection against government actions in the countries where they operate.

The Doctrine of Sovereign Immunity

When certain conditions are satisfied, the doctrine of **sovereign immunity** exempts foreign nations from the jurisdiction of the U.S. courts. In 1976, Congress codified this rule in the Foreign Sovereign Immunities Act (FSIA).[1] The FSIA exclusively governs the circumstances in which an action may be brought in the United States against a foreign nation, including attempts to attach a foreign nation's property. Because the law is jurisdictional in nature, a plaintiff generally has the burden of showing that a defendant is not entitled to sovereign immunity.

Section 1605 of the FSIA sets forth the major exceptions to the jurisdictional immunity of a foreign state. A foreign state is not immune from the jurisdiction of U.S. courts in the following situations:

1. When the foreign state has waived its immunity either explicitly or by implication.
2. When the foreign state has engaged in commercial activity within the United States or in commercial activity outside the United States that has "a direct effect in the United States."[2]
3. When the foreign state has committed a tort in the United States or has violated certain international laws.

In applying the FSIA, questions frequently arise as to whether an entity is a "foreign state" and what constitutes a "commercial activity." Under Section 1603 of the FSIA, a *foreign state* includes both a political subdivision of a foreign state and an instrumentality (department or agency of any branch of a government) of a foreign state. Section 1603 broadly defines a *commercial activity* as a commercial activity that is carried out by a foreign state within the United States, but it does not describe the particulars of what constitutes a commercial activity. Thus, the courts are left to decide whether a particular activity is governmental or commercial in nature.

1. 28 U.S.C. Sections 1602–1611.
2. See, for example, *Keller v. Central Bank of Nigeria,* 277 F.3d 811 (6th Cir. 2002), in which the court held that failure to pay promised funds to an account in a bank in Cleveland, Ohio, was an action having a direct effect in the United States.

SECTION 2 Doing Business Internationally

A U.S. domestic firm can engage in international business transactions in a number of ways. The simplest way is to seek out foreign markets for domestically produced products or services. In other words, U.S. firms can **export** their goods and services to markets abroad. Alternatively, a U.S. firm can establish foreign production facilities to be closer to the foreign market or markets in which its products are sold. The advantages may include lower labor costs, fewer government regulations, and lower taxes and trade barriers. A domestic firm can also obtain revenues by licensing its technology to an existing foreign company or by selling franchises to overseas entities.

Exporting

Exporting can take two forms: direct exporting and indirect exporting. In *direct exporting,* a U.S. company signs a sales contract with a foreign purchaser that provides for the conditions of shipment and payment for the goods. (International contracts for the purchase and sale of goods, and the use of letters of credit to make payments in international transactions, were discussed in Chapters 20 through 23.) If sufficient business develops in a foreign country, a U.S. company may establish a specialized marketing organization there by appointing a foreign agent or a foreign distributor. This is called *indirect exporting.*

When a U.S. firm wishes to limit its involvement in an international market, it will typically establish an agency relationship with a foreign firm. Recall that in an agency relationship, one person (the agent) agrees to act on behalf of, or instead of, another (the principal) (see Chapter 31). The foreign agent is empowered to enter into contracts in the agent's country on behalf of the U.S. principal.

When a foreign country represents a substantial market, a U.S. firm may wish to appoint a distributor located in that country. The U.S. firm and the distributor enter into a **distribution agreement**—a contract setting out the terms and conditions of the distributorship, such as price, currency of payment, guarantee of supply availability, and method of payment. Disputes concerning distribution agreements may involve jurisdictional or other issues, as well as contract law, however.

Manufacturing Abroad

An alternative to direct or indirect exporting is the establishment of foreign manufacturing facilities. Typically, U.S. firms establish manufacturing plants abroad when they believe that by doing so they will reduce costs—particularly for labor, shipping, and raw materials—and thereby be able to compete more effectively in foreign markets. Foreign firms have done the same in the United States. Sony, Nissan, and other Japanese manufacturers have established U.S. plants to avoid import duties that the U.S. Congress may impose on Japanese products entering this country.

A U.S. firm can conduct manufacturing operations in other countries in several ways. They include licensing, franchising, and investing in a wholly owned subsidiary or a joint venture.

Licensing A U.S. firm can obtain business abroad by licensing a foreign manufacturing company to use its copyrighted, patented, or trademarked intellectual property or trade secrets. Like any other licensing agreement (see Chapters 8 and 19), a licensing agreement with a foreign-based firm calls for a payment of royalties on some basis—such as so many cents per unit produced or a certain percentage of profits from units sold in a particular geographic territory. For example, the Coca-Cola Bottling Company licenses firms worldwide to use (and keep confidential) its secret formula for the syrup used in its soft drink; in return, the company receives a percentage of the income gained from the sale of Coca-Cola by those firms.

The licensing of intellectual property rights benefits all parties to the transaction. The firm that receives the license can take advantage of an established reputation for quality. The firm that grants the license receives income from the foreign sales of its products and also establishes a global reputation. Also, once a firm's trademark is known worldwide, the demand for other products manufactured or sold by that firm may increase—obviously, an important consideration.

Franchising Franchising is a well-known form of licensing. Recall from Chapter 35 that in a franchise arrangement the owner of a trademark, trade name, or copyright (the franchisor) licenses another (the franchisee) to use the trademark, trade name, or copyright, under certain conditions or limitations, in the selling of goods or services. In return, the franchisee pays a fee, which is usually based on a percentage of gross or net sales. Examples of international franchises include Holiday Inn and Hertz.

Investing in a Wholly Owned Subsidiary or a Joint Venture Another way to expand into a foreign market is to establish a wholly owned subsidiary firm in a foreign country. In many European countries, a subsidiary would likely take the form of a *société anonyme (S.A.)*, which is similar to a U.S. corporation. In German-speaking nations, it would be called an *Aktiengesellschaft (A.G.)*. When a wholly owned subsidiary is established, the parent company, which remains in the United States, retains complete ownership of all of the facilities in the foreign country, as well as total authority and control over all phases of the operation.

A U.S. firm can also expand into international markets through a joint venture. In a joint venture, the U.S. company owns only part of the operation; the rest is owned either by local owners in the foreign country or by another foreign entity. All of the firms involved in a joint venture share responsibilities, as well as profits and liabilities. (See Chapter 37 for a more detailed discussion of joint ventures.)

SECTION 3 Regulation of Specific Business Activities

Doing business abroad can affect the economies, foreign policies, domestic politics, and other national interests of the countries involved. For this reason, nations impose laws to restrict or facilitate international business. Controls may also be imposed by international agreements.

Investing

Firms that invest in foreign nations face the risk that the foreign government may expropriate the investment property. Expropriation, as mentioned earlier in this chapter, occurs when property is taken and the owner is paid just compensation for what is taken. This does not violate generally observed principles of international law. Confiscating property without compensation (or without adequate compensation), however, normally violates these principles. Few remedies are available for confiscation of property by a foreign government. Claims are often resolved by lump-sum settlements after negotiations between the United States and the taking nation.

To counter the deterrent effect that the possibility of confiscation may have on potential investors, many countries guarantee compensation to foreign investors if property is taken. A guaranty can be in the form of national constitutional or statutory laws or provisions in international treaties. As further protection for foreign investments, some countries provide insurance for their citizens' investments abroad.

Export Controls

The U.S. Constitution provides in Article I, Section 9, that "No Tax or Duty shall be laid on Articles exported from any State." Thus, Congress cannot impose any export taxes. Congress can, however, use a variety of other devices to restrict or encourage exports. Congress may set export quotas on various items, such as grain being sold abroad. Under the Export Administration Act of 1979,[3] the flow of technologically advanced products and technical data can be restricted. In recent years, the U.S. Department of Commerce has made a controversial attempt to restrict the export of encryption software.

While restricting certain exports, the United States (and other nations) also use incentives and subsidies to stimulate other exports and thereby aid domestic businesses. The Revenue Act of 1971,[4] for instance, promoted exports by exempting from taxes the income earned by firms marketing their products overseas through certain foreign sales corporations. Under the Export Trading Company Act of 1982,[5] U.S. banks are encouraged to invest in export trading companies, which are formed when exporting firms join together to export a line of goods.

Import Controls

All nations have restrictions on imports, and the United States is no exception. Restrictions include strict prohibitions, quotas, and tariffs. Under the Trading with the Enemy Act of 1917,[6] for example, no goods may be imported from nations that have been designated enemies of the United States. Other laws prohibit the importation of illegal drugs, books that urge insurrection against the United States, and agricultural products that pose dangers to domestic crops or animals.

Importing goods that infringe U.S. patents is also prohibited. The International Trade Commission is an independent agency of the U.S. government that, among other duties, investigates allegations that imported goods infringe U.S. patents and imposes penalties if necessary. In the following case, the court considered an appeal from a party fined more than $13.5 million for importing certain disposable cameras.

3. 50 U.S.C. Sections 2401–2420.
4. 26 U.S.C. Sections 991–994.
5. 15 U.S.C. Sections 4001, 4003.
6. 12 U.S.C. Section 95a.

CASE 52.1 Fuji Photo Film Co. v. International Trade Commission

United States Court of Appeals, Federal Circuit, 2007. 474 F.3d 1281.

Background and Facts Fuji Photo Film Company owns fifteen patents for "lens-fitted film packages" (LFFPs), popularly known as disposable cameras. An LFFP consists of a plastic shell preloaded with film. To develop the film, a consumer gives the LFFP to a film processor and receives back the negatives and prints, but not the shell. Fuji makes and sells LFFPs. Jazz Photo Corporation collected used LFFP shells in the United States, shipped them abroad to insert new film, and imported refurbished shells back into the United States for sale. The International Trade Commission (ITC) determined that Jazz's resale of shells originally sold outside the United States infringed Fuji's patents. In 1999, the ITC issued a cease-and-desist order to stop the imports. While the order was being disputed at the ITC and in the courts, between August 2001 and December 2003 Jazz imported and sold 27 million refurbished LFFPs. Fuji complained to the ITC, which fined Jazz more than $13.5 million. Jack Benun, Jazz's chief operating officer, appealed to the U.S. Court of Appeals for the Federal Circuit.

CASE CONTINUES

CASE 52.1 CONTINUED

• **Decision and Rationale** The U.S. Court of Appeals for the Federal Circuit affirmed the ITC's decision. The court held, among other things, that "substantial evidence supports the finding that the majority of the cameras were first sold abroad." The court explained that to determine Jazz's violations of Fuji's patents, the ITC had used identifying numbers printed on Fuji's LFFPs and Fuji's production and shipping databases to pinpoint where Jazz's refurbished LFFPs were first sold. Against this evidence, Benun asserted that Jazz utilized its own "informed compliance program" to track the LFFP shells from their collection to their sale. Benun argued that this tracking system ensured that only shells collected from the United States were refurbished for sale here. The court reasoned, however, that this tracking program would ensure "at most" only that Jazz refurbished LFFPs collected from the United States, not that Jazz refurbished LFFPs first sold here. Besides, Jazz's tracking program was "too incomplete and disorganized to be credible." Because "there was no suggestion that the incomplete and disorganized nature of the program was due to Fuji's actions, this ground alone was sufficient to justify a conclusion that Benun" did not prove the refurbished LFFPs had been sold first in the United States.

• **What If the Facts Were Different?** *Suppose that, after this decision, Jazz fully compensated Fuji for the infringing sales of LFFPs. Would Jazz have acquired the right to refurbish those LFFPs in the future? Explain.*

• **The Global Dimension** *How does prohibiting the importing of goods that infringe U.S. patents protect those patents outside the United States?*

Quotas and Tariffs Limits on the amounts of goods that can be imported are known as **quotas.** At one time, the United States had legal quotas on the number of automobiles that could be imported from Japan. Today, Japan "voluntarily" restricts the number of automobiles exported to the United States. **Tariffs** are taxes on imports. A tariff is usually a percentage of the value of the import, but it can be a flat rate per unit (such as per barrel of oil). Tariffs raise the prices of imported goods, causing some consumers to purchase more domestically manufactured goods.

Antidumping Duties The United States has specific laws directed at what it sees as unfair international trade practices. **Dumping,** for example, is the sale of imported goods at "less than fair value." *Fair value* is usually determined by the price of those goods in the exporting country. Foreign firms that engage in dumping in the United States hope to undersell U.S. businesses to obtain a larger share of the U.S. market. To prevent this, an extra tariff—known as an *antidumping duty*—may be assessed on the imports.

The procedure for imposing antidumping duties involves two U.S. government agencies: the International Trade Commission (ITC) and the International Trade Administration (ITA). The ITC assesses the effects of dumping on domestic businesses and then makes recommendations to the president concerning temporary import restrictions. The ITA, which is part of the Department of Commerce, decides whether imports were sold at less than fair value. The ITA's determination establishes the amount of antidumping duties, which are set to equal the difference between the price charged in the United States and the price charged in the exporting country. A duty may be retroactive to cover past dumping.

Minimizing Trade Barriers through Trade Agreements

Restrictions on imports are also known as *trade barriers.* The elimination of trade barriers is sometimes seen as essential to the world's economic well-being. Most of the world's leading trading nations are members of the World Trade Organization (WTO), which was established in 1995. To minimize trade barriers among nations, each member country of the WTO is required to grant **normal trade relations (NTR) status** (formerly known as *most-favored-nation status*) to other member countries. This means that each member is obligated to treat other members at least as well as it treats the country that receives its most favorable treatment with regard to imports or exports. Various regional trade agreements and associations also help to minimize trade barriers between nations.

The European Union The European Union (EU) arose out of the 1957 Treaty of Rome, which created the Common Market, a free trade zone comprising the nations of Belgium, France, Italy, Luxembourg, the Netherlands, and West Germany. Today, the EU is a single integrated trading unit made up of twenty-seven European nations.

The EU has its own governing authorities. These include the Council of Ministers, which coordinates economic policies and includes one representative from each nation; a commission, which proposes regulations to the council; and an elected assembly, which oversees the commission. The EU also has its own court, the European Court of Justice, which can review each nation's judicial decisions and is the ultimate authority on EU law.

The EU has gone a long way toward creating a new body of law to govern all of the member nations—although some of its efforts to create uniform laws have been confounded by nationalism. The council and the commission issue regulations, or directives, that define EU law in various areas, and these requirements normally are binding on all member countries. EU directives govern such issues as environmental law, product liability, anticompetitive practices, and laws governing corporations. The EU directive on product liability, for example, states that a "producer of an article shall be liable for damages caused by a defect in the article, whether or not he [or she] knew or could have known of the defect." Liability extends to anyone who puts a trademark or other identifying feature on an article, and liability may not be excluded, even by contract.

The North American Free Trade Agreement The North American Free Trade Agreement (NAFTA), which became effective on January 1, 1994, created a regional trading unit consisting of Canada, Mexico, and the United States. The goal of NAFTA was to eliminate tariffs among these three nations on substantially all goods by reducing the tariffs incrementally over a period of time. NAFTA gives the three countries a competitive advantage by retaining tariffs on goods imported from countries outside the NAFTA trading unit. Additionally, NAFTA provided for the elimination of barriers that traditionally have prevented the cross-border movement of services, such as financial and transportation services. NAFTA also attempts to eliminate citizenship requirements for the licensing of accountants, attorneys, physicians, and other professionals.

The Central America–Dominican Republic–United States Free Trade Agreement A more recent trade agreement, the Central America–Dominican Republic–United States Free Trade Agreement (CAFTA-DR), was signed into law by President George W. Bush in 2005. This agreement was formed by Costa Rica, the Dominican Republic, El Salvador, Guatemala, Honduras, Nicaragua, and the United States. Its purpose was to reduce trade tariffs and improve market access among all of the signatory nations, including the United States. As of 2008, legislatures from all seven countries had approved the CAFTA-DR, despite significant opposition in certain nations, including Costa Rica, where nationwide strikes erupted in response to legislation adopting the treaty.

SECTION 4

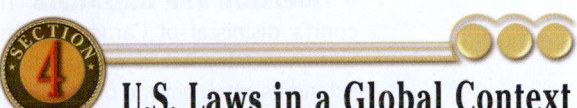

U.S. Laws in a Global Context

The internationalization of business raises questions about the extraterritorial application of a nation's laws—that is, the effect of the country's laws outside its boundaries. To what extent do U.S. domestic laws apply to other nations' businesses? To what extent do U.S. domestic laws apply to U.S. firms doing business abroad? Here, we discuss the extraterritorial application of certain U.S. laws, including the Sarbanes-Oxley Act and laws prohibiting employment discrimination.

The Sarbanes-Oxley Act

The Sarbanes-Oxley Act of 2002, which was discussed in Chapters 5, 41, and 51, is designed to improve the quality and clarity of financial reporting and auditing of public companies. The act prescribes the issuance of codes of ethics, increases the criminal penalties for securities fraud, and utilizes other means to hold public companies to higher reporting standards.

Three provisions protect whistleblowers. One section requires public companies to adopt procedures that encourage employees to expose "questionable" accounting. Another section imposes criminal sanctions for retaliation against anyone who reports the commission of any federal offense to law enforcement officers.

A third section—18 U.S.C. Section 1514A—creates an administrative complaint procedure and a federal civil cause of action for employees who report violations of the federal laws relating to fraud against the shareholders of public companies. The extraterritorial application of this section was at issue in the following case.

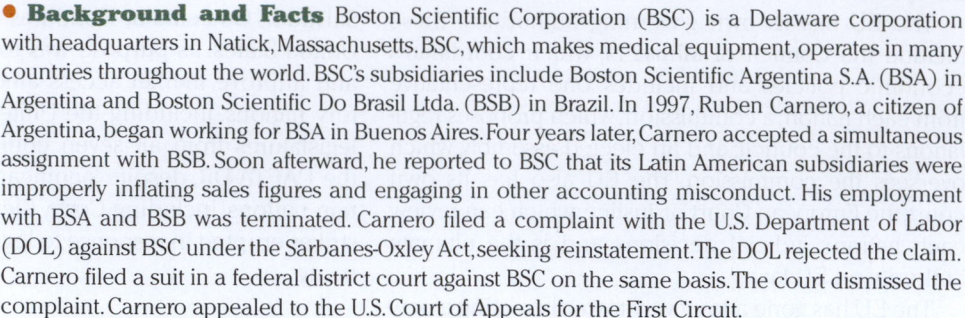

CASE 52.2 Carnero v. Boston Scientific Corp.

United States Court of Appeals, First Circuit, 2006. 433 F.3d 1.
www.ca1.uscourts.gov[a]

- **Background and Facts** Boston Scientific Corporation (BSC) is a Delaware corporation with headquarters in Natick, Massachusetts. BSC, which makes medical equipment, operates in many countries throughout the world. BSC's subsidiaries include Boston Scientific Argentina S.A. (BSA) in Argentina and Boston Scientific Do Brasil Ltda. (BSB) in Brazil. In 1997, Ruben Carnero, a citizen of Argentina, began working for BSA in Buenos Aires. Four years later, Carnero accepted a simultaneous assignment with BSB. Soon afterward, he reported to BSC that its Latin American subsidiaries were improperly inflating sales figures and engaging in other accounting misconduct. His employment with BSA and BSB was terminated. Carnero filed a complaint with the U.S. Department of Labor (DOL) against BSC under the Sarbanes-Oxley Act, seeking reinstatement. The DOL rejected the claim. Carnero filed a suit in a federal district court against BSC on the same basis. The court dismissed the complaint. Carnero appealed to the U.S. Court of Appeals for the First Circuit.

- **Decision and Rationale** The U.S. Court of Appeals for the First Circuit affirmed the lower court's dismissal of Carnero's complaint under 18 U.S.C. Section 1514A. This section of the Sarbanes-Oxley Act "does not reflect the necessary clear expression of congressional intent to extend its reach beyond our nation's borders." The appellate court pointed out that "when a statute is silent as to its territorial reach, and no contrary congressional intent clearly appears, there is generally a presumption against its extraterritorial application." This presumption recognizes that Congress is chiefly focused on domestic situations and prevents "unintended clashes" with other nations' laws. In this case, the Sarbanes-Oxley Act is silent as to the application of 18 U.S.C. Section 1514A abroad. The enforcement of this section is the responsibility of the DOL, whose jurisdiction and resources are entirely domestic. The section's venue provisions (which establish the appropriate location to file a civil lawsuit) apply only to plaintiffs and violations within U.S. borders, "with no corresponding basis being provided for venue as to foreign complainants claiming violations in foreign countries." The legislative history of the statute also reveals that Congress did not consider "the possibility or the problems of overseas application" of this section. In contrast, other sections of the statute were expressly tailored for "extraterritorial enforcement."

- **What If the Facts Were Different?** *Suppose that Carnero had been an American working for BSA and BSB. Would the result in this case have been the same? Discuss.*

- **The Legal Environment Dimension** *How might the court's decision in this case frustrate the basic purpose of the Sarbanes-Oxley Act, which is to protect investors in U.S. securities markets and the integrity of those markets?*

a. In the right-hand column, click on "Opinions." When that page opens, in the "Short Title *contains*" box, type "Carnero" and click on "Submit Search." In the result, in the "Click for Opinion" column, click on one of the numbers to access the opinion.

Antidiscrimination Laws

As explained in Chapter 34, federal laws in the United States prohibit discrimination on the basis of race, color, national origin, religion, gender, age, and disability. These laws, as they affect employment relationships, generally apply extraterritorially. Since 1984, for example, the Age Discrimination in Employment Act of 1967 has covered U.S. employees working abroad for U.S. employers. The Americans with Disabilities Act of 1990, which requires employers to accommodate the needs of workers with disabilities, also applies to U.S. nationals working abroad for U.S. firms.

For some time, it was uncertain whether the major U.S. law regulating discriminatory practices in the workplace, Title VII of the Civil Rights Act of 1964, applied extraterritorially. The Civil Rights Act of 1991 addressed this issue. The act provides that Title VII applies extraterritorially to all U.S. employees working for U.S. employers abroad. Generally, U.S. employers must abide by U.S. discrimination laws unless to do so would violate the laws of the country where their workplaces are located. This "foreign laws exception" allows employers to avoid being subjected to conflicting laws.

International Tort Claims

The international application of tort liability is growing in significance and controversy. An increasing number of U.S. plaintiffs are suing foreign (or U.S.) entities for torts that these entities have allegedly committed overseas. Often, these cases involve human rights violations by foreign governments. The Alien Tort Claims Act (ATCA),[7] adopted in 1789, allows even foreign citizens to bring civil suits in U.S. courts for injuries caused by violations of the law of nations or a treaty of the United States.

Since 1980, plaintiffs have increasingly used the ATCA to bring actions against companies operating in other countries. ATCA actions have been brought against companies doing business in nations such as Colombia, Ecuador, Egypt, Guatemala, India, Indonesia, Nigeria, and Saudi Arabia. Some of these cases have involved alleged environmental destruction. In addition, mineral companies in Southeast Asia have been sued for collaborating with oppressive government regimes.

The following case involved claims against "hundreds" of corporations that allegedly "aided and abetted" the government of South Africa in maintaining its apartheid (racially discriminatory) regime.

7. 28 U.S.C. Section 1350.

CASE 52.3 Khulumani v. Barclay National Bank, Ltd.

United States Court of Appeals, Second Circuit, 2007. 504 F.3d 254.

• **Background and Facts** The Khulumani plaintiffs, along with other plaintiff groups, filed class-action claims on behalf of victims of the apartheid-related atrocities, human rights violations, crimes against humanity, and unfair and discriminatory forced-labor practices committed by the South African government. The plaintiffs brought these actions under the Alien Tort Claims Act (ATCA) against more than fifty corporate defendants and others. These corporations included Bank of America, Barclay National Bank, Citigroup, Credit Suisse Group, General Electric, and IBM. The plaintiffs filed separate actions in multiple federal district courts. All of the actions were transferred to a federal district court in the Southern District of New York. The defendants filed motions to dismiss. The district court held that the plaintiffs failed to establish subject-matter jurisdiction under the ATCA. The district court dismissed the plaintiffs' complaints in their entirety. The plaintiffs appealed to the U.S. Court of Appeals for the Second Circuit.

• **Decision and Rationale** The court of appeals vacated the district court's dismissal of the plaintiffs' claims and remanded the case for further proceedings. The reviewing court declared that the district court "erred in holding that aiding and abetting violations of customary international law cannot provide a basis for ATCA jurisdiction. We hold that * * * a plaintiff may plead a theory of aiding and abetting liability under the ATCA." The reviewing court further stated that "the determination whether a norm is sufficiently definite to support a cause of action should (and, indeed, inevitably must) involve an element of judgment about the practical consequences of making that cause available to litigants in the federal courts." The court further declined to accept the defendants' argument that an adjudication of the case by the U.S. court "would offend amicable working relationships with a foreign country." (In 2008, the United States Supreme Court did not have a quorum to decide this case, so the lawsuit against the named corporations was allowed to proceed.)

• **The Legal Environment Dimension** *What are the ramifications of the ruling for the defendants in this case?*

• **The Ethical Dimension** *Should the companies cited as defendants in this case have refused all business dealings with South Africa while that country's white government imposed unjust restrictions on the majority black African population during apartheid?*

REVIEWING International Law in a Global Economy

Robco, Inc., was a Florida arms dealer. The armed forces of Honduras contracted to purchase weapons from Robco over a six-year period. After the government was replaced and a democracy installed, the Honduran government sought to reduce the size of its military, and its relationship with Robco deteriorated. Honduras refused to honor the contract and purchase the inventory of arms, which Robco could sell only at a much lower price. Robco filed a suit in a federal district court in the United States to recover damages for this breach of contract by the government of Honduras. Using the information presented in the chapter, answer the following questions.

1. Should the Foreign Sovereign Immunities Act (FSIA) preclude this lawsuit? Why or why not?
2. Does the act of state doctrine bar Robco from seeking to enforce the contract? Explain.
3. Suppose that prior to this lawsuit, the new government of Honduras had enacted a law making it illegal to purchase weapons from foreign arms dealers. What doctrine of deference might lead a U.S. court to dismiss Robco's case in that situation?
4. Now suppose that the U.S. court hears the case and awards damages to Robco, but the government of Honduras has no assets in the United States that can be used to satisfy the judgment. Under which doctrine might Robco be able to collect the damages by asking another nation's court to enforce the U.S. judgment?

TERMS AND CONCEPTS

act of state doctrine 992
civil law system 991
comity 992
confiscation 992
distribution agreement 993
dumping 996
export 993
expropriation 992
international law 990
international organization 991
national law 990
normal trade relations (NTR) status 996
quota 996
sovereign immunity 993
tariff 996
treaty 991

QUESTIONS AND CASE PROBLEMS

52–1. In 1995, France implemented a law making the use of the French language mandatory in certain legal documents. Documents relating to securities offerings, such as prospectuses, for example, must be written in French. So must instruction manuals and warranties for goods and services offered for sale in France. Additionally, all agreements entered into with French state or local authorities, with entities controlled by state or local authorities, and with private entities carrying out a public service (such as providing utilities) must be written in French. What kinds of problems might this law pose for U.S. businesspersons who wish to form contracts with French individuals or business firms?

52–2. QUESTION WITH SAMPLE ANSWER

As China and formerly Communist nations move toward free enterprise, they must develop a new set of business laws. If you could start from scratch, what kind of business law system would you adopt, a civil law system or a common law system? What kind of business regulations would you impose?

- **For a sample answer to Question 52–2, go to Appendix I at the end of this text.**

52–3. Sovereign Immunity. Tonoga, Ltd., doing business as Taconic Plastics, Ltd., is a manufacturer incorporated in Ireland with its principal place of business in New York. In 1997, Taconic entered into a contract with a German construction company to supply special material for a tent project designed to shelter religious pilgrims visiting holy sites in Saudi Arabia. Most of the material was made in, and shipped from, New York. The company did not pay Taconic and eventually filed for bankruptcy. Another German firm, Werner Voss Architects and Engineers, acting as an agent for the government of Saudi Arabia, guaranteed the payments due Taconic to induce it to complete the project. When Taconic received all but the final payment, the firm filed a suit in a federal district court against the government of Saudi Arabia, claiming a breach of the guaranty and seeking to collect, in part, about $3 million. The defendant filed a motion to dismiss based on the doctrine of sovereign immunity, among other things. Under what circumstances does this doctrine apply? What are its exceptions? Should this suit be dismissed under the "commercial activity" exception? Explain. [*Tonoga, Ltd. v. Ministry of Public Works and Housing of Kingdom of Saudi Arabia,* 135 F.Supp.2d 350 (N.D.N.Y. 2001)]

52–4. Import Controls. DaimlerChrysler Corp. made and marketed motor vehicles. DaimlerChrysler assembled the 1993 and 1994 model years of its trucks at plants in Mexico. Assembly involved sheet metal components sent from the United States. DaimlerChrysler subjected some of the parts to a complicated treatment process, which included the application of coats of paint to prevent corrosion, impart color, and protect the finish. Under federal law, goods that are assembled abroad using U.S.-made parts can be imported tariff free. A federal statute provides that painting is "incidental" to assembly and does not affect the status of the goods. A federal regulation states that "painting primarily intended to enhance the appearance of an article or to impart distinctive features or characteristics" is not incidental. The U.S. Customs Service levied a tariff on the trucks. DaimlerChrysler filed a suit in the U.S. Court of International Trade, challenging the levy. Should the court rule in DaimlerChrysler's favor? Why or why not? [*DaimlerChrysler Corp. v. United States,* 361 F.3d 1378 (Fed.Cir. 2004)]

52–5. Comity. E&L Consulting, Ltd., is a U.S. corporation that sells lumber products in New Jersey, New York, and Pennsylvania. Doman Industries, Ltd., is a Canadian corporation that also sells lumber products, including green hem-fir, a durable product used for home building. Doman supplies more than 95 percent of the green hem-fir for sale in the northeastern United States. In 1990, Doman contracted to sell green hem-fir through E&L, which received monthly payments plus commissions. In 1998, Sherwood Lumber Corp., a New York firm and an E&L competitor, approached E&L about a merger. The negotiations were unsuccessful. According to E&L, Sherwood and Doman then conspired to monopolize the green hem-fir market in the United States. When Doman terminated its contract with E&L, the latter filed a suit in a federal district court against Doman, alleging violations of U.S. antitrust law. Doman filed for bankruptcy in a Canadian court and asked the U.S. court to dismiss E&L's suit, in part, under the principle of comity. What is the "principle of comity"? On what basis would it apply in this case? What would be the likely result? Discuss. [*E&L Consulting, Ltd. v. Doman Industries, Ltd.,* 360 F.Supp.2d 465 (E.D.N.Y. 2005)]

52–6. Dumping. A newspaper printing press system is more than a hundred feet long, stands four or five stories tall, and weighs 2 million pounds. Only about ten of the systems are sold each year in the United States. Because of the size and cost, a newspaper may update its system, rather than replace it, by buying "additions." By the 1990s, Goss International Corp. was the only domestic maker of the equipment in the United States and represented the entire U.S. market. Tokyo Kikai Seisakusho (TKSC), a Japanese corporation, makes the systems in Japan. In the 1990s, TKSC began to compete in the U.S. market, forcing Goss to cut its prices below cost. TKSC's tactics included offering its customers "secret" rebates on prices that were ultimately substantially less than the products' actual market value in Japan. According to TKSC office memos, the goal was to "win completely this survival game" against Goss, the "enemy." Goss filed a suit in a federal district court against TKSC and others, alleging illegal dumping. At what point does a foreign firm's attempt to compete with a domestic manufacturer in the United States become illegal dumping? Was that point reached in this case? Discuss. [*Goss International Corp. v. Man Roland Druckmaschinen Aktiengesellschaft,* 434 F.3d 1081 (8th Cir. 2006)]

52–7. CASE PROBLEM WITH SAMPLE ANSWER

Jan Voda, M.D., a resident of Oklahoma City, Oklahoma, owns three U.S. patents related to guiding catheters for use in interventional cardiology, as well as corresponding foreign patents issued by the European Patent Office, Canada, France, Germany, and Great Britain. Voda filed a suit in a federal district court against Cordis Corp., a U.S. firm, alleging infringement of the U.S. patents under U.S. patent law and of the corresponding foreign patents under the patent law of the various foreign countries. Cordis admitted, "[T]he XB catheters have been sold domestically and internationally since 1994. The XB catheters were manufactured in Miami Lakes, from 1993 to 2001 and have been manufactured in Juarez, Mexico, since 2001." Cordis argued, however, that Voda could not assert infringement claims under foreign patent law because the court did not have jurisdiction over such claims. Which of the important international legal principles discussed in this chapter would be most likely to apply in this case? How should the court apply it? Explain. [*Voda v. Cordis Corp.,* 476 F.3d 887 (Fed.Cir. 2007)]

- **To view a sample answer for Problem 52–7, go to this book's Web site at www.cengage.com/blaw/jentz, select "Chapter 52," and click on "Case Problem with Sample Answer."**

52-8. A QUESTION OF ETHICS

*On December 21, 1988, Pan Am Flight 103 exploded 31,000 feet in the air over Lockerbie, Scotland, killing all 259 passengers and crew on board and 11 people on the ground. Among those killed was Roger Hurst, a U.S. citizen. An investigation determined that a portable radio-cassette player packed in a brown Samsonite suitcase smuggled onto the plane was the source of the explosion. The explosive device was constructed with a digital timer specially made for, and bought by, Libya. Abdel Basset Ali Al-Megrahi, a Libyan government official and an employee of the Libyan Arab Airline (LAA), was convicted by the Scottish High Court of Justiciary on criminal charges that he planned and executed the bombing in association with members of the Jamahiriya Security Organization (JSO) (an agency of the Libyan government that performs security and intelligence functions) or the Libyan military. Members of the victims' families filed a suit in a U.S. federal district court against the JSO, the LAA, Al-Megrahi, and others. The plaintiffs claimed violations of U.S. federal law, including the Anti-Terrorism Act, and state law, including the intentional infliction of emotional distress. [*Hurst v. Socialist People's Libyan Arab Jamahiriya*, 474 F.Supp.2d 19 (D.D.C. 2007)]*

(a) Under what doctrine, codified in which federal statute, might the defendants claim to be immune from the jurisdiction of a U.S. court? Should this law include an exception for "state-sponsored terrorism"? Why or why not?

(b) The defendants agreed to pay $2.7 billion, or $10 million per victim, to settle all claims for "compensatory death damages." The families of eleven victims, including Hurst, were excluded from the settlement because they were "not wrongful death beneficiaries under applicable state law." These plaintiffs continued the suit. The defendants filed a motion to dismiss. Should the motion be granted on the ground that the settlement bars the plaintiffs' claims? Explain.

LAW ON THE WEB

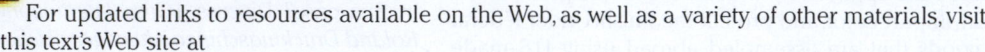

For updated links to resources available on the Web, as well as a variety of other materials, visit this text's Web site at

www.cengage.com/blaw/jentz

FindLaw, which is now a part of West Group, includes an extensive array of links to international doctrines and treaties, as well as to the laws of other nations, on its Web site. Go to

www.findlaw.com/12international

For information on the legal requirements of doing business internationally, a good source is the Internet Law Library's collection of laws of other countries. You can access this source at

www.lawguru.com/ilawlib/?id=52

Legal Research Exercises on the Web

Go to **www.cengage.com/blaw/jentz**, the Web site that accompanies this text. Select "Chapter 52" and click on "Internet Exercises." There you will find the following Internet research exercises that you can perform to learn more about the topics covered in this chapter.

Internet Exercise 52–1: Legal Perspective
The World Trade Organization

Internet Exercise 52–2: Management Perspective
Overseas Business Opportunities

Special Topics

Unique situations present particular ethical problems. In this final *Focus on Ethics* feature, we consider some of the ethical dimensions of the special legal topics discussed in the chapters of this unit.

Insurance

A number of ethical issues arise in the area of insurance, some of which we examine here.

Insurance Agents and Fiduciary Duties When a person applies for insurance coverage through an insurance company's agent, is the agent obligated to advise that person as to what coverage she or he should obtain? If the agent does not advise a client about certain types of coverage, has the agent breached a fiduciary duty owed to the applicant? For example, suppose that someone applies for auto insurance, and the insurance agent does not advise her that she should obtain uninsured motorist coverage. Later, the client is involved in an accident with an uninsured motorist, and the insurance company refuses to compensate her for her injuries and losses. The client claims that the insurance agent was negligent in not advising her to sign up for uninsured motorist coverage. Was the agent negligent? Did the agent breach a duty owed to the client?

The answer to this question is no. As mentioned in Chapter 49, an insurance agent is an agent of the insurer (the insurance company), not of the party who applies for insurance. As such, the agent owes fiduciary duties to the insurer, but not to the insured. The agent's only duties to the insured are contractual in nature. Although this rule may seem unfair to insurance applicants, who may know less about the need for certain types of insurance coverage than the agent does, a contrary rule might create even more unfairness. An insurance agent could be held liable for failure to advise a client of every possible insurance option, and the insured would be relieved of any burden to take care of his or her own financial needs and expectations. Also, as one court noted, if the state legislature does not require such coverage, why should the courts require insurance companies to offer or explain available optional coverage?[1]

1. *Jones v. Kennedy*, 108 S.W.3d 203 (Mo.App. 2003). See also *Auto-Owners Insurance Co. v. Midwest Agency*, 2007 WL 2885345 (E.D.Mo. 2007).

Insurance and Computer "Downtime" As noted in Chapter 49, traditional business insurance policies usually do not specifically cover the risks associated with computer "downtime." Thus, in a number of cases, insurers have defended against payment by claiming that these kinds of losses are not covered.

For example, in one case an employment agency's computer system was attacked by a computer virus that caused all data to be lost. The agency's business insurance policy provided coverage for "accidental direct physical loss to business personal property" and for the replacement of valuable "papers or records, including those which exist on electronic or magnetic media." When the agency filed a claim with its insurer, the insurer denied coverage—claiming that the loss was neither "accidental" (because the hacker intended to infect the computer system) nor "physical" (because data are not tangible—capable of being touched). The court, however, concluded that the agency had in no way intentionally caused the computer system to be damaged, and therefore the loss was accidental. The court also noted that the policy expressly covered electronic records and storage media. Therefore, the data loss was "physical" as a matter of law.[2]

In another case, an insurance policy insured against "direct physical loss or damage from any cause" to "property, business income, and operations." A power outage caused the insured company to lose all of its programming information. The insurer refused to pay for the costs associated with the computer downtime, contending that no "physical loss or damage" had been sustained. Although many courts would likely have agreed with the insurance company, in this case the court sided with the insured. The court concluded that "[a]t a time when computer technology dominates our professional as well as our personal lives," the term should not be "restricted to the physical destruction or harm of computer circuitry" but should also include "loss of access, loss of use, and loss of functionality."[3]

Inheritance Rights

New applications of technology often present thorny issues for the courts, from both a legal and an ethical perspective. A challenging issue has to

2. *Lambrecht & Associates, Inc. v. State Farm Lloyd's*, 119 S.W.3d 16 (Tex.App. 2003).

3. *American Guarantee & Liability Insurance Co. v. Ingram Micro, Inc.*, ___ F.Supp.2d ___ (D.Ariz. 2000).

(Continued)

do with the inheritance rights of posthumously conceived children—children conceived through the use of a decedent's sperm that had been previously collected and stored in a sperm bank. Do such children have inheritance rights under state intestacy laws? Should they?[4]

Generally, the laws on this issue vary from state to state. Courts in four states (Arizona, Massachusetts, New Jersey, and New York) have held that posthumously conceived children are heirs who are entitled to benefits under the Social Security Act.[5] Several states (including Colorado, Delaware, Texas, Virginia, and Washington) have amended their intestacy laws to allow posthumously conceived children to inherit.

Liability of Accountants

Society has obviously deemed it fair that accountants abide by certain professional standards. This view is reflected in common law principles governing the liability of accountants, as well as in statutory law. Today, accountants face potential liability on many fronts.

Liability of Accountants under the Common Law A long-standing principle under the common law is that accountants should be held to a duty of care and that they should stand prepared to compensate clients and others for violating that duty. Still, many consider it unfair that there are no uniform, well-defined limits to the potential liability of accountants. Negligence suits brought against accountants by third parties often raise a question with obvious ethical implications: How far should an accountant's liability extend? As discussed in Chapter 51, courts in different jurisdictions have reached different conclusions on this issue.

At one end of the spectrum are a minority of courts that hold that accountants are liable only to third parties who are in privity or "near privity" with the accountants. At the other end are a minority of courts that have ruled that accountants may be held liable to third parties whose reliance on the accountants' statements or reports was "reasonably foreseeable." In the eyes of many, accountants' liability to third parties is too restricted in the former jurisdictions and too extensive in the latter. For accountants, the courts' varying approaches to liability to third parties pose a significant problem: How can accountants predict, and control, the extent of their liability?

Liability under State Consumer Protection Statutes As you read in Chapter 51, accountants face potential liability, and significant penalties, under the Sarbanes-Oxley Act of 2002. Further complicating the extent of accountants' statutory liability is the possibility that they may be liable to third parties under consumer protection statutes. For example, the Texas Supreme Court has held that a "consumer," as a third party, can sue an accounting firm for violations of the state Deceptive Trade Practices Act (DTPA).[6] The Texas DTPA, which is similar to statutes in many other states, allows the successful plaintiff to recover treble damages as well as attorneys' fees. The burden of proof under the DTPA is relatively light for the plaintiff: to recover damages, the plaintiff need only show that there was a "knowing" violation of the statute. The statute also imposes strict liability on defendants.

International Transactions

Conducting business internationally presents unique challenges, including, at times, ethical challenges. This is understandable, given that laws and cultures vary from one country to another. Consider the role of women. In the United States, equal employment opportunity is a fundamental public policy. This policy is clearly expressed in Title VII of the Civil Rights Act of 1964 (discussed in Chapter 34), which prohibits discrimination against women in the employment context. Some other countries, however, largely reject any professional role for women. Consequently, U.S. women conducting business transactions in those countries may encounter difficulties. For example, when the World Bank sent a delegation that included women to negotiate with the Central Bank of Korea, the

---

4. See, for example, *Woodward v. Commissioner of Social Security,* 435 Mass. 536, 760 N.E.2d 257 (2002), which was presented as Case Problem 50–6.

5. See *In re Martin B.,* 17 Misc.3d 198, 841 N.Y.S.2d 207 (N.Y.Sur. 2007); *Gillett-Netting v. Barnhart,* 371 F.3d 593 (9th Cir. 2004); *In re Estate of Kolacy,* 332 N.J.Super. 593, 753 A.2d 1257 (Ch.Div. 2000); and the *Woodward* case cited in footnote 4.

6. *Arthur Andersen & Co. v. Perry Equipment Corp.,* 945 S.W.2d 812 (Tex. 1997). See also *Export Worldwide, Ltd. v. Alfred Knight,* 2007 WL 1300468 (W.D.Tex. 2007); and *Swinnea v. ERI Consulting Engineers, Inc.,* 236 S.W.3d 825 (Tex.App.—Tyler 2007).

Koreans were surprised and offended. They thought that the presence of women meant that the Koreans were not being taken seriously.

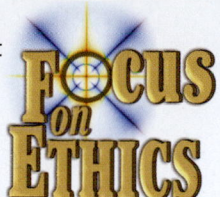

There are also some important ethical differences among nations. In Islamic countries, for example, the consumption of alcohol and certain foods is forbidden by the Islamic religion. Thus, it would be thoughtless and imprudent to invite a Saudi Arabian business contact out for a drink. Additionally, in many foreign nations, gift giving is a common practice between contracting companies or between companies and government officials. To Americans, such gift giving may look suspiciously like an unethical (and possibly illegal) bribe. This cultural difference has been an important source of friction in international business, particularly since the U.S. Congress passed the Foreign Corrupt Practices Act in 1977 (discussed in Chapters 5 and 9). This act prohibits U.S. business firms from offering certain side payments to foreign officials to secure favorable contracts.

DISCUSSION QUESTIONS

1. Should the law impose a duty on agents for insurance companies to advise insurance applicants as to what types of coverage would best suit their needs?
2. Should posthumously conceived children have inheritance rights under state intestacy laws? What arguments can be made for and against such children obtaining inheritance rights?
3. At one time, most courts held that accountants could not be held liable to third parties in negligence lawsuits. Why do the majority of courts today hold that accountants can be held liable to third parties?
4. Generally, what public policies must the courts balance in determining whether third parties can recover from accountants for losses caused by the accountants' negligence?

APPENDIX A

How to Brief Cases and Analyze Case Problems

How to Brief Cases

To fully understand the law with respect to business, you need to be able to read and understand court decisions. To make this task easier, you can use a method of case analysis that is called *briefing*. There is a fairly standard procedure that you can follow when you "brief" any court case. You must first read the case opinion carefully. When you feel you understand the case, you can prepare a brief of it.

Although the format of the brief may vary, typically it will present the essentials of the case under headings such as those listed below.

1. **Citation.** Give the full citation for the case, including the name of the case, the date it was decided, and the court that decided it.
2. **Facts.** Briefly indicate (a) the reasons for the lawsuit; (b) the identity and arguments of the plaintiff(s) and defendant(s), respectively; and (c) the lower court's decision—if appropriate.
3. **Issue.** Concisely phrase, in the form of a question, the essential issue before the court. (If more than one issue is involved, you may have two—or even more—questions here.)
4. **Decision.** Indicate here—with a "yes" or "no," if possible—the court's answer to the question (or questions) in the *Issue* section above.
5. **Reason.** Summarize as briefly as possible the reasons given by the court for its decision (or decisions) and the case or statutory law relied on by the court in arriving at its decision.

An Example of a Briefed Sample Court Case

As an example of the format used in briefing cases, we present here a briefed version of the sample court case that was presented in Exhibit 1–6 on pages 24 and 25.

BERGER V. CITY OF SEATTLE
United States Court of Appeals,
Ninth Circuit, 2008.
512 F.3d 582.

FACTS The Seattle Center is an entertainment "zone" in downtown Seattle, Washington, that attracts nearly ten million tourists each year. The center encompasses theaters, arenas, museums, exhibition halls, conference rooms, outdoor stadiums, and restaurants, and features street performers. Under the authority of the city, the center's director issued rules in 2002 to address safety concerns and other matters. Among other things, street performers were required to obtain permits and wear badges. After members of the public filed numerous complaints of threatening behavior by street performer and balloon artist Michael Berger, Seattle Center staff cited Berger for several rules violations. He filed a suit in a federal district court against the city and others, alleging, in part, that the rules violated his free speech rights under the First Amendment to the U.S. Constitution. The court issued a judgment in the plaintiff's favor. The city appealed to the U.S. Court of Appeals for the Ninth Circuit.

ISSUE Did the rules issued by the Seattle Center under the city's authority meet the requirements for valid restrictions on speech under the First Amendment?

DECISION Yes. The U.S. Court of Appeals for the Ninth Circuit reversed the decision of the lower court and remanded the case for further proceedings. "Such content neutral and narrowly tailored rules * * * must be upheld."

REASON The court concluded first that the rules requiring permits and badges were "content neutral." Time, place, and manner restrictions do not violate the First Amendment if they burden all expression equally and do not allow officials to treat different messages differently. In this case, the rules met this test and thus did not discriminate based on content. The court also concluded that the rules were "narrowly tailored" to "promote a substantial government interest that would be achieved less effectively" otherwise. With the rules, the city was trying to "reduce territorial disputes among performers, deter patron harassment, and facilitate the identification and apprehension of offending performers." This was pursuant to the valid governmental objective of protecting the safety and convenience of the other performers and the public generally. The public's complaints about Berger and others showed that unregulated street performances posed a threat to these interests. The court was "satisfied that the city's permit scheme was designed to further valid governmental objectives."

Review of Sample Court Case

Here, we provide a review of the briefed version to indicate the kind of information that is contained in each section.

CITATION The name of the case is *Berger v. City of Seattle.* Berger is the plaintiff; the City of Seattle is the defendant. The U.S. Court of Appeals for the Ninth Circuit decided this case in 2008. The citation states that this case can be found in volume 512 of the *Federal Reporter, Third Series,* on page 582.

FACTS The *Facts* section identifies the plaintiff and the defendant, describes the events leading up to this suit, the allegations made by the plaintiff in the initial suit, and (because this case is an appellate court decision) the lower court's ruling and the party appealing. The party appealing's argument on appeal is also sometimes included here.

ISSUE The *Issue* section presents the central issue (or issues) decided by the court. In this case, the U.S. Court of Appeals for the Ninth Circuit considered whether certain rules imposed on street performers by local government authorities satisfied the requirements for valid restrictions on speech under the First Amendment to the U.S. Constitution.

DECISION The *Decision* section includes the court's decision on the issues before it. The decision reflects the opinion of the judge or justice hearing the case. Decisions by appellate courts are frequently phrased in reference to the lower court's decision. In other words, the appellate court may "affirm" the lower court's ruling or "reverse" it. Here, the court determined that Seattle's rules were "content neutral" and "narrowly tailored" to "promote a substantial government interest that would otherwise be achieved less effectively." The court found in favor of the city and reversed the lower court's ruling in the plaintiff's (Berger's) favor.

REASON The *Reason* section includes references to the relevant laws and legal principles that the court applied in coming to its conclusion in the case. The relevant law in the *Berger* case included the requirements under the First Amendment for evaluating the purpose and effect of government regulation with respect to expression. This section also explains the court's application of the law to the facts in this case.

Analyzing Case Problems

In addition to learning how to brief cases, students of business law and the legal environment also find it helpful to know how to analyze case problems. Part of the study of business law and the legal environment usually involves analyzing case problems, such as those included in this text at the end of each chapter.

For each case problem in this book, we provide the relevant background and facts of the lawsuit and the issue before the court. When you are assigned one of these problems, your job will be to determine how the court should decide the issue, and why. In other words, you will need to engage in legal analysis and reasoning. Here, we offer some suggestions on how to make this task less daunting. We begin by presenting a sample problem:

> While Janet Lawson, a famous pianist, was shopping in Quality Market, she slipped and fell on a wet floor in one of the aisles. The floor had recently been mopped by one of the store's employees, but there were no signs warning customers that the floor in that area was wet. As a result of the fall, Lawson injured her right arm and was unable to perform piano concerts for the next six months. Had she been able to perform the scheduled concerts, she would have earned approximately $60,000 over that period of time. Lawson sued Quality Market for this amount, plus another $10,000 in medical expenses. She claimed that the store's failure to warn customers of the wet floor constituted negligence and therefore the market was liable for her injuries. Will the court agree with Lawson? Discuss.

Understand the Facts

This may sound obvious, but before you can analyze or apply the relevant law to a specific set of facts, you must clearly understand those facts. In other words, you should read through the case problem carefully—more than once, if necessary—to make sure you understand the identity of the plaintiff(s) and defendant(s) in the case and the progression of events that led to the lawsuit.

In the sample case problem just given, the identity of the parties is fairly obvious. Janet Lawson is the one bringing the suit; therefore, she is the plaintiff. Quality Market, against whom she is bringing the suit, is the defendant. Some of the case problems you may work on have multiple plaintiffs or defendants. Often, it is helpful to use abbreviations for the parties. To indicate a reference to a plaintiff, for example, the *pi* symbol—π—is often used, and a defendant is denoted by a *delta*—Δ—a triangle.

The events leading to the lawsuit are also fairly straightforward. Lawson slipped and fell on a wet floor, and she contends that Quality Market should be liable for her injuries because it was negligent in not posting a sign warning customers of the wet floor.

When you are working on case problems, realize that the facts should be accepted as they are given. For example, in our sample problem, it should be accepted that the floor was wet and that there was no sign. In other words, avoid making conjectures, such as "Maybe the floor wasn't too wet," or "Maybe an employee was getting a sign to put up," or "Maybe someone stole the sign." Questioning the facts as they are presented only adds confusion to your analysis.

Legal Analysis and Reasoning

Once you understand the facts given in the case problem, you can begin to analyze the case. Recall from Chapter 1 that the IRAC method is a helpful tool to use in the legal analysis and reasoning process. IRAC is an acronym for **I**ssue, **R**ule, **A**pplication, **C**onclusion. Applying this method to our sample problem would involve the following steps:

1. First, you need to decide what legal **issue** is involved in the case. In our sample case, the basic issue is whether Quality Market's failure to warn customers of the wet floor constituted negligence. As discussed in Chapter 6, negligence is a *tort*—a civil wrong. In a tort lawsuit, the plaintiff seeks to be compensated for another's wrongful act. A defendant will be deemed negligent if he or she breached a duty of care owed to the plaintiff and the breach of that duty caused the plaintiff to suffer harm.
2. Once you have identified the issue, the next step is to determine what **rule of law** applies to the issue. To make this determination, you will want to review carefully the text of the chapter in which the relevant rule of law for the problem appears. Our sample case problem involves the tort of negligence, which is covered in Chapter 6. The applicable rule of law is the tort law principle that business owners owe a duty to exercise reasonable care to protect their customers ("business invitees"). Reasonable care, in this context, includes either removing—or warning customers of—*foreseeable* risks about which the owner *knew* or *should have known*. Business owners need not warn customers of "open and obvious" risks, however. If a business owner breaches this duty of care (fails to exercise the appropriate degree of care toward customers), and the breach of duty causes a customer to be injured, the business owner will be liable to the customer for the customer's injuries.
3. The next—and usually the most difficult—step in analyzing case problems is the **application** of the relevant rule of law to the specific facts of the case you are studying. In our sample problem, applying the tort law principle just discussed presents few difficulties. An employee of the store had mopped the floor in the aisle where Lawson slipped and fell, but no sign was present indicating that the floor was wet. That a customer might fall on a wet floor is clearly a foreseeable risk. Therefore, the failure to warn customers about the wet floor was a breach of the duty of care owed by the business owner to the store's customers.
4. Once you have completed Step 3 in the IRAC method, you should be ready to draw your **conclusion.** In our sample problem, Quality Market is liable to Lawson for her injuries, because the market's breach of its duty of care caused Lawson's injuries.

The fact patterns in the case problems presented in this text are not always as simple as those presented in our sample problem. Often, for example, a case has more than one plaintiff or defendant. A case may also involve more than one issue and have more than one applicable rule of law. Furthermore, in some case problems the facts may indicate that the general rule of law should not apply. For example, suppose that a store employee advised Lawson not to walk on the floor in the aisle because it was wet, but Lawson decided to walk on it anyway. This fact could alter the outcome of the case because the store could then raise the defense of *assumption of risk* (see Chapter 7). Nonetheless, a careful review of the chapter should always provide you with the knowledge you need to analyze the problem thoroughly and arrive at accurate conclusions.

APPENDIX B

The Constitution of the United States

Preamble

We the People of the United States, in Order to form a more perfect Union, establish Justice, insure domestic Tranquility, provide for the common defence, promote the general Welfare, and secure the Blessings of Liberty to ourselves and our Posterity, do ordain and establish this Constitution for the United States of America.

Article I

Section 1. All legislative Powers herein granted shall be vested in a Congress of the United States, which shall consist of a Senate and House of Representatives.

Section 2. The House of Representatives shall be composed of Members chosen every second Year by the People of the several States, and the Electors in each State shall have the Qualifications requisite for Electors of the most numerous Branch of the State Legislature.

No Person shall be a Representative who shall not have attained to the Age of twenty five Years, and been seven Years a Citizen of the United States, and who shall not, when elected, be an Inhabitant of that State in which he shall be chosen.

Representatives and direct Taxes shall be apportioned among the several States which may be included within this Union, according to their respective Numbers, which shall be determined by adding to the whole Number of free Persons, including those bound to Service for a Term of Years, and excluding Indians not taxed, three fifths of all other Persons. The actual Enumeration shall be made within three Years after the first Meeting of the Congress of the United States, and within every subsequent Term of ten Years, in such Manner as they shall by Law direct. The Number of Representatives shall not exceed one for every thirty Thousand, but each State shall have at Least one Representative; and until such enumeration shall be made, the State of New Hampshire shall be entitled to chuse three, Massachusetts eight, Rhode Island and Providence Plantations one, Connecticut five, New York six, New Jersey four, Pennsylvania eight, Delaware one, Maryland six, Virginia ten, North Carolina five, South Carolina five, and Georgia three.

When vacancies happen in the Representation from any State, the Executive Authority thereof shall issue Writs of Election to fill such Vacancies.

The House of Representatives shall chuse their Speaker and other Officers; and shall have the sole Power of Impeachment.

Section 3. The Senate of the United States shall be composed of two Senators from each State, chosen by the Legislature thereof, for six Years; and each Senator shall have one Vote.

Immediately after they shall be assembled in Consequence of the first Election, they shall be divided as equally as may be into three Classes. The Seats of the Senators of the first Class shall be vacated at the Expiration of the second Year, of the second Class at the Expiration of the fourth Year, and of the third Class at the Expiration of the sixth Year, so that one third may be chosen every second Year; and if Vacancies happen by Resignation, or otherwise, during the Recess of the Legislature of any State, the Executive thereof may make temporary Appointments until the next Meeting of the Legislature, which shall then fill such Vacancies.

No Person shall be a Senator who shall not have attained to the Age of thirty Years, and been nine Years a Citizen of the United States, and who shall not, when elected, be an Inhabitant of that State for which he shall be chosen.

The Vice President of the United States shall be President of the Senate, but shall have no Vote, unless they be equally divided.

The Senate shall chuse their other Officers, and also a President pro tempore, in the Absence of the Vice President, or when he shall exercise the Office of President of the United States.

The Senate shall have the sole Power to try all Impeachments. When sitting for that Purpose, they shall be on Oath or Affirmation. When the President of the United States is tried, the Chief Justice shall preside: And no Person shall be convicted without the Concurrence of two thirds of the Members present.

Judgment in Cases of Impeachment shall not extend further than to removal from Office, and disqualification to hold and enjoy any Office of honor, Trust, or Profit under the United States: but the Party convicted shall nevertheless be liable and subject to Indictment, Trial, Judgment, and Punishment, according to Law.

Section 4. The Times, Places and Manner of holding Elections for Senators and Representatives, shall be prescribed in each State by the Legislature thereof; but the Congress may at any time by Law make or alter such Regulations, except as to the Places of chusing Senators.

The Congress shall assemble at least once in every Year, and such Meeting shall be on the first Monday in December, unless they shall by Law appoint a different Day.

Section 5. Each House shall be the Judge of the Elections, Returns, and Qualifications of its own Members, and a Majority of each shall constitute a Quorum to do Business; but a smaller Number may adjourn from day to day, and may be authorized to compel the Attendance of absent Members, in such Manner, and under such Penalties as each House may provide.

Each House may determine the Rules of its Proceedings, punish its Members for disorderly Behavior, and, with the Concurrence of two thirds, expel a Member.

Each House shall keep a Journal of its Proceedings, and from time to time publish the same, excepting such Parts as may in their Judgment require Secrecy; and the Yeas and Nays of the Members of either House on any question shall, at the Desire of one fifth of those Present, be entered on the Journal.

Neither House, during the Session of Congress, shall, without the Consent of the other, adjourn for more than three days, nor to any other Place than that in which the two Houses shall be sitting.

Section 6. The Senators and Representatives shall receive a Compensation for their Services, to be ascertained by Law, and paid out of the Treasury of the United States. They shall in all Cases, except Treason, Felony and Breach of the Peace, be privileged from Arrest during their Attendance at the Session of their respective Houses, and in going to and returning from the same; and for any Speech or Debate in either House, they shall not be questioned in any other Place.

No Senator or Representative shall, during the Time for which he was elected, be appointed to any civil Office under the Authority of the United States, which shall have been created, or the Emoluments whereof shall have been increased during such time; and no Person holding any Office under the United States, shall be a Member of either House during his Continuance in Office.

Section 7. All Bills for raising Revenue shall originate in the House of Representatives; but the Senate may propose or concur with Amendments as on other Bills.

Every Bill which shall have passed the House of Representatives and the Senate, shall, before it become a Law, be presented to the President of the United States; If he approve he shall sign it, but if not he shall return it, with his Objections to the House in which it shall have originated, who shall enter the Objections at large on their Journal, and proceed to reconsider it. If after such Reconsideration two thirds of that House shall agree to pass the Bill, it shall be sent together with the Objections, to the other House, by which it shall likewise be reconsidered, and if approved by two thirds of that House, it shall become a Law. But in all such Cases the Votes of both Houses shall be determined by Yeas and Nays, and the Names of the Persons voting for and against the Bill shall be entered on the Journal of each House respectively. If any Bill shall not be returned by the President within ten Days (Sundays excepted) after it shall have been presented to him, the Same shall be a Law, in like Manner as if he had signed it, unless the Congress by their Adjournment prevent its Return in which Case it shall not be a Law.

Every Order, Resolution, or Vote, to which the Concurrence of the Senate and House of Representatives may be necessary (except on a question of Adjournment) shall be presented to the President of the United States; and before the Same shall take Effect, shall be approved by him, or being disapproved by him, shall be repassed by two thirds of the Senate and House of Representatives, according to the Rules and Limitations prescribed in the Case of a Bill.

Section 8. The Congress shall have Power To lay and collect Taxes, Duties, Imposts and Excises, to pay the Debts and provide for the common Defence and general Welfare of the United States; but all Duties, Imposts and Excises shall be uniform throughout the United States;

To borrow Money on the credit of the United States;

To regulate Commerce with foreign Nations, and among the several States, and with the Indian Tribes;

To establish an uniform Rule of Naturalization, and uniform Laws on the subject of Bankruptcies throughout the United States;

To coin Money, regulate the Value thereof, and of foreign Coin, and fix the Standard of Weights and Measures;

To provide for the Punishment of counterfeiting the Securities and current Coin of the United States;

To establish Post Offices and post Roads;

To promote the Progress of Science and useful Arts, by securing for limited Times to Authors and Inventors the exclusive Right to their respective Writings and Discoveries;

To constitute Tribunals inferior to the supreme Court;

To define and punish Piracies and Felonies committed on the high Seas, and Offenses against the Law of Nations;

To declare War, grant Letters of Marque and Reprisal, and make Rules concerning Captures on Land and Water;

To raise and support Armies, but no Appropriation of Money to that Use shall be for a longer Term than two Years;

To provide and maintain a Navy;

To make Rules for the Government and Regulation of the land and naval Forces;

To provide for calling forth the Militia to execute the Laws of the Union, suppress Insurrections and repel Invasions;

To provide for organizing, arming, and disciplining, the Militia, and for governing such Part of them as may be employed in the Service of the United States, reserving to the States respectively, the Appointment of the Officers, and the Authority of training the Militia according to the discipline prescribed by Congress;

To exercise exclusive Legislation in all Cases whatsoever, over such District (not exceeding ten Miles square) as may, by Cession of particular States, and the Acceptance of Congress, become the Seat of the Government of the United States, and to exercise like Authority over all Places purchased by the Consent of the Legislature of the State in which the Same shall be, for the Erection of Forts, Magazines, Arsenals, dock-Yards, and other needful Buildings;—And

To make all Laws which shall be necessary and proper for carrying into Execution the foregoing Powers, and all other Powers vested by this Constitution in the Government of the United States, or in any Department or Officer thereof.

Section 9. The Migration or Importation of such Persons as any of the States now existing shall think proper to admit, shall not be prohibited by the Congress prior to the Year one thousand eight hundred and eight, but a Tax or duty may be imposed on such Importation, not exceeding ten dollars for each Person.

The privilege of the Writ of Habeas Corpus shall not be suspended, unless when in Cases of Rebellion or Invasion the public Safety may require it.

No Bill of Attainder or ex post facto Law shall be passed.

No Capitation, or other direct, Tax shall be laid, unless in Proportion to the Census or Enumeration herein before directed to be taken.

No Tax or Duty shall be laid on Articles exported from any State.

No Preference shall be given by any Regulation of Commerce or Revenue to the Ports of one State over those of another: nor shall Vessels bound to, or from, one State be obliged to enter, clear, or pay Duties in another.

No Money shall be drawn from the Treasury, but in Consequence of Appropriations made by Law; and a regular Statement and Account of the Receipts and Expenditures of all public Money shall be published from time to time.

No Title of Nobility shall be granted by the United States: And no Person holding any Office of Profit or Trust under them, shall, without the Consent of the Congress, accept of any present, Emolument, Office, or Title, of any kind whatever, from any King, Prince, or foreign State.

Section 10. No State shall enter into any Treaty, Alliance, or Confederation; grant Letters of Marque and Reprisal; coin Money; emit Bills of Credit; make any Thing but gold and silver Coin a Tender in Payment of Debts; pass any Bill of Attainder, ex post facto Law, or Law impairing the Obligation of Contracts, or grant any Title of Nobility.

No State shall, without the Consent of the Congress, lay any Imposts or Duties on Imports or Exports, except what may be absolutely necessary for executing its inspection Laws: and the net Produce of all Duties and Imposts, laid by any State on Imports or Exports, shall be for the Use of the Treasury of the United States; and all such Laws shall be subject to the Revision and Controul of the Congress.

No State shall, without the Consent of Congress, lay any Duty of Tonnage, keep Troops, or Ships of War in time of Peace, enter into any Agreement or Compact with another State, or with a foreign Power, or engage in War, unless actually invaded, or in such imminent Danger as will not admit of delay.

Article II

Section 1. The executive Power shall be vested in a President of the United States of America. He shall hold his Office during the Term of four Years, and, together with the Vice President, chosen for the same Term, be elected, as follows:

Each State shall appoint, in such Manner as the Legislature thereof may direct, a Number of Electors, equal to the whole Number of Senators and Representatives to which the State may be entitled in the Congress; but no Senator or Representative, or Person holding an Office of Trust or Profit under the United States, shall be appointed an Elector.

The Electors shall meet in their respective States, and vote by Ballot for two Persons, of whom one at least shall not be an Inhabitant of the same State with themselves. And they shall make a List of all the Persons voted for, and of the Number of Votes for each; which List they shall sign and certify, and transmit sealed to the Seat of the Government of the United States, directed to the President of the Senate. The President of the Senate shall, in the Presence of the Senate and House of Representatives, open all the Certificates, and the Votes shall then be counted. The Person having the greatest Number of Votes shall be the President, if such Number be a Majority of the whole Number of Electors appointed; and if there be more than one who have such Majority, and have an equal Number of Votes, then the House of Representatives shall immediately chuse by Ballot one of them for President; and if no Person have a Majority, then from the five highest on the List the said House shall in like Manner chuse the President. But in chusing the President, the Votes shall be taken by States, the Representation from each State having one Vote; A quorum for this Purpose shall consist of a Member or Members from two thirds of the States, and a Majority of all the States shall be necessary to a Choice. In every Case, after the Choice of the President, the Person having the greater Number of Votes of the Electors shall be the Vice President. But if there should remain two or more who have equal Votes, the Senate shall chuse from them by Ballot the Vice President.

The Congress may determine the Time of chusing the Electors, and the Day on which they shall give their Votes; which Day shall be the same throughout the United States.

No person except a natural born Citizen, or a Citizen of the United States, at the time of the Adoption of this Constitution, shall be eligible to the Office of President; neither shall any Person be eligible to that Office who shall not have attained to the Age of thirty five Years, and been fourteen Years a Resident within the United States.

In Case of the Removal of the President from Office, or of his Death, Resignation or Inability to discharge the

Powers and Duties of the said Office, the same shall devolve on the Vice President, and the Congress may by Law provide for the Case of Removal, Death, Resignation or Inability, both of the President and Vice President, declaring what Officer shall then act as President, and such Officer shall act accordingly, until the Disability be removed, or a President shall be elected.

The President shall, at stated Times, receive for his Services, a Compensation, which shall neither be increased nor diminished during the Period for which he shall have been elected, and he shall not receive within that Period any other Emolument from the United States, or any of them.

Before he enter on the Execution of his Office, he shall take the following Oath or Affirmation: "I do solemnly swear (or affirm) that I will faithfully execute the Office of President of the United States, and will to the best of my Ability, preserve, protect and defend the Constitution of the United States."

Section 2. The President shall be Commander in Chief of the Army and Navy of the United States, and of the Militia of the several States, when called into the actual Service of the United States; he may require the Opinion, in writing, of the principal Officer in each of the executive Departments, upon any Subject relating to the Duties of their respective Offices, and he shall have Power to grant Reprieves and Pardons for Offenses against the United States, except in Cases of Impeachment.

He shall have Power, by and with the Advice and Consent of the Senate to make Treaties, provided two thirds of the Senators present concur; and he shall nominate, and by and with the Advice and Consent of the Senate, shall appoint Ambassadors, other public Ministers and Consuls, Judges of the supreme Court, and all other Officers of the United States, whose Appointments are not herein otherwise provided for, and which shall be established by Law; but the Congress may by Law vest the Appointment of such inferior Officers, as they think proper, in the President alone, in the Courts of Law, or in the Heads of Departments.

The President shall have Power to fill up all Vacancies that may happen during the Recess of the Senate, by granting Commissions which shall expire at the End of their next Session.

Section 3. He shall from time to time give to the Congress Information of the State of the Union, and recommend to their Consideration such Measures as he shall judge necessary and expedient; he may, on extraordinary Occasions, convene both Houses, or either of them, and in Case of Disagreement between them, with Respect to the Time of Adjournment, he may adjourn them to such Time as he shall think proper; he shall receive Ambassadors and other public Ministers; he shall take Care that the Laws be faithfully executed, and shall Commission all the Officers of the United States.

Section 4. The President, Vice President and all civil Officers of the United States, shall be removed from Office on Impeachment for, and Conviction of, Treason, Bribery, or other high Crimes and Misdemeanors.

Article III

Section 1. The judicial Power of the United States, shall be vested in one supreme Court, and in such inferior Courts as the Congress may from time to time ordain and establish. The Judges, both of the supreme and inferior Courts, shall hold their Offices during good Behaviour, and shall, at stated Times, receive for their Services a Compensation, which shall not be diminished during their Continuance in Office.

Section 2. The judicial Power shall extend to all Cases, in Law and Equity, arising under this Constitution, the Laws of the United States, and Treaties made, or which shall be made, under their Authority;—to all Cases affecting Ambassadors, other public Ministers and Consuls;—to all Cases of admiralty and maritime Jurisdiction;—to Controversies to which the United States shall be a Party;—to Controversies between two or more States;—between a State and Citizens of another State;—between Citizens of different States;—between Citizens of the same State claiming Lands under Grants of different States, and between a State, or the Citizens thereof, and foreign States, Citizens or Subjects.

In all Cases affecting Ambassadors, other public Ministers and Consuls, and those in which a State shall be a Party, the supreme Court shall have original Jurisdiction. In all the other Cases before mentioned, the supreme Court shall have appellate Jurisdiction, both as to Law and Fact, with such Exceptions, and under such Regulations as the Congress shall make.

The Trial of all Crimes, except in Cases of Impeachment, shall be by Jury; and such Trial shall be held in the State where the said Crimes shall have been committed; but when not committed within any State, the Trial shall be at such Place or Places as the Congress may by Law have directed.

Section 3. Treason against the United States, shall consist only in levying War against them, or, in adhering to their Enemies, giving them Aid and Comfort. No Person shall be convicted of Treason unless on the Testimony of two Witnesses to the same overt Act, or on Confession in open Court.

The Congress shall have Power to declare the Punishment of Treason, but no Attainder of Treason shall work Corruption of Blood, or Forfeiture except during the Life of the Person attainted.

Article IV

Section 1. Full Faith and Credit shall be given in each State to the public Acts, Records, and judicial Proceedings of every other State. And the Congress may by general Laws prescribe the Manner in which such Acts, Records and Proceedings shall be proved, and the Effect thereof.

Section 2. The Citizens of each State shall be entitled to all Privileges and Immunities of Citizens in the several States.

A Person charged in any State with Treason, Felony, or other Crime, who shall flee from Justice, and be found in another State, shall on Demand of the executive Authority of the State from which he fled, be delivered up, to be removed to the State having Jurisdiction of the Crime.

No Person held to Service or Labour in one State, under the Laws thereof, escaping into another, shall, in Consequence of any Law or Regulation therein, be discharged from such Service or Labour, but shall be delivered up on Claim of the Party to whom such Service or Labour may be due.

Section 3. New States may be admitted by the Congress into this Union; but no new State shall be formed or erected within the Jurisdiction of any other State; nor any State be formed by the Junction of two or more States, or Parts of States, without the Consent of the Legislatures of the States concerned as well as of the Congress.

The Congress shall have Power to dispose of and make all needful Rules and Regulations respecting the Territory or other Property belonging to the United States; and nothing in this Constitution shall be so construed as to Prejudice any Claims of the United States, or of any particular State.

Section 4. The United States shall guarantee to every State in this Union a Republican Form of Government, and shall protect each of them against Invasion; and on Application of the Legislature, or of the Executive (when the Legislature cannot be convened) against domestic Violence.

Article V

The Congress, whenever two thirds of both Houses shall deem it necessary, shall propose Amendments to this Constitution, or, on the Application of the Legislatures of two thirds of the several States, shall call a Convention for proposing Amendments, which, in either Case, shall be valid to all Intents and Purposes, as part of this Constitution, when ratified by the Legislatures of three fourths of the several States, or by Conventions in three fourths thereof, as the one or the other Mode of Ratification may be proposed by the Congress; Provided that no Amendment which may be made prior to the Year One thousand eight hundred and eight shall in any Manner affect the first and fourth Clauses in the Ninth Section of the first Article; and that no State, without its Consent, shall be deprived of its equal Suffrage in the Senate.

Article VI

All Debts contracted and Engagements entered into, before the Adoption of this Constitution shall be as valid against the United States under this Constitution, as under the Confederation.

This Constitution, and the Laws of the United States which shall be made in Pursuance thereof; and all Treaties made, or which shall be made, under the Authority of the United States, shall be the supreme Law of the Land; and the Judges in every State shall be bound thereby, any Thing in the Constitution or Laws of any State to the Contrary notwithstanding.

The Senators and Representatives before mentioned, and the Members of the several State Legislatures, and all executive and judicial Officers, both of the United States and of the several States, shall be bound by Oath or Affirmation, to support this Constitution; but no religious Test shall ever be required as a Qualification to any Office or public Trust under the United States.

Article VII

The Ratification of the Conventions of nine States shall be sufficient for the Establishment of this Constitution between the States so ratifying the Same.

Amendment I [1791]

Congress shall make no law respecting an establishment of religion, or prohibiting the free exercise thereof; or abridging the freedom of speech, or of the press; or the right of the people peaceably to assembly, and to petition the Government for a redress of grievances.

Amendment II [1791]

A well regulated Militia, being necessary to the security of a free State, the right of the people to keep and bear Arms, shall not be infringed.

Amendment III [1791]

No Soldier shall, in time of peace be quartered in any house, without the consent of the Owner, nor in time of war, but in a manner to be prescribed by law.

Amendment IV [1791]

The right of the people to be secure in their persons, houses, papers, and effects, against unreasonable searches and seizures, shall not be violated, and no Warrants shall issue, but upon probable cause, supported by Oath or affirmation, and particularly describing the place to be searched, and the persons or things to be seized.

Amendment V [1791]

No person shall be held to answer for a capital, or otherwise infamous crime, unless on a presentment or indictment of a Grand Jury, except in cases arising in the land or naval forces, or in the Militia, when in actual service in time of War or public danger; nor shall any person be subject for the same offence to be twice put in jeopardy of life or limb; nor shall be compelled in any criminal case to be a witness against himself, nor be deprived of life, liberty, or property, without due process of law; nor shall private property be taken for public use, without just compensation.

Amendment VI [1791]

In all criminal prosecutions, the accused shall enjoy the right to a speedy and public trial, by an impartial jury of the State and district wherein the crime shall have been committed, which district shall have been previously ascertained by law, and to be informed of the nature and cause of the accusation; to be confronted with the witnesses against him; to have compulsory process for obtaining witnesses in his favor, and to have the Assistance of Counsel for his defence.

Amendment VII [1791]

In Suits at common law, where the value in controversy shall exceed twenty dollars, the right of trial by jury shall be preserved, and no fact tried by jury, shall be otherwise re-examined in any Court of the United States, than according to the rules of the common law.

Amendment VIII [1791]

Excessive bail shall not be required, nor excessive fines imposed, nor cruel and unusual punishments inflicted.

Amendment IX [1791]

The enumeration in the Constitution, of certain rights, shall not be construed to deny or disparage others retained by the people.

Amendment X [1791]

The powers not delegated to the United States by the Constitution, nor prohibited by it to the States, are reserved to the States respectively, or to the people.

Amendment XI [1798]

The Judicial power of the United States shall not be construed to extend to any suit in law or equity, commenced or prosecuted against one of the United States by Citizens of another State, or by Citizens or Subjects of any Foreign State.

Amendment XII [1804]

The Electors shall meet in their respective states, and vote by ballot for President and Vice-President, one of whom, at least, shall not be an inhabitant of the same state with themselves; they shall name in their ballots the person voted for as President, and in distinct ballots the person voted for as Vice-President, and they shall make distinct lists of all persons voted for as President, and of all persons voted for as Vice-President, and of the number of votes for each, which lists they shall sign and certify, and transmit sealed to the seat of the government of the United States, directed to the President of the Senate;—The President of the Senate shall, in the presence of the Senate and House of Representatives, open all the certificates and the votes shall then be counted;—The person having the greatest number of votes for President, shall be the President, if such number be a majority of the whole number of Electors appointed; and if no person have such majority, then from the persons having the highest numbers not exceeding three on the list of those voted for as President, the House of Representatives shall choose immediately, by ballot, the President. But in choosing the President, the votes shall be taken by states, the representation from each state having one vote; a quorum for this purpose shall consist of a member or members from two-thirds of the states, and a majority of all states shall be necessary to a choice. And if the House of Representatives shall not choose a President whenever the right of choice shall devolve upon them, before the fourth day of March next following, then the Vice-President shall act as President, as in the case of the death or other constitutional disability of the President.—The person having the greatest number of votes as Vice-President, shall be the Vice-President, if such number be a majority of the whole number of Electors appointed, and if no person have a majority, then from the two highest numbers on the list, the Senate shall choose the Vice-President; a quorum for the purpose shall consist of two-thirds of the whole number of Senators, and a majority of the whole number shall be necessary to a choice. But no person constitutionally ineligible to the office of President shall be eligible to that of Vice-President of the United States.

Amendment XIII [1865]

Section 1. Neither slavery nor involuntary servitude, except as a punishment for crime whereof the party shall have been duly convicted, shall exist within the United States, or any place subject to their jurisdiction.

Section 2. Congress shall have power to enforce this article by appropriate legislation.

Amendment XIV [1868]

Section 1. All persons born or naturalized in the United States, and subject to the jurisdiction thereof, are citizens of the United States and of the State wherein they reside. No State shall make or enforce any law which shall abridge the privileges or immunities of citizens of the United States; nor shall any State deprive any person of life, liberty, or property, without due process of law; nor deny to any person within its jurisdiction the equal protection of the laws.

Section 2. Representatives shall be apportioned among the several States according to their respective numbers, counting the whole number of persons in each State, excluding Indians not taxed. But when the right to vote at any election for the choice of electors for President and Vice President of the United States, Representatives in Congress, the Executive and Judicial officers of a State, or the members of the Legislature thereof, is denied to any of the male inhabitants of such State, being twenty-one years of age, and citizens of the United States, or in any way abridged, except for participation in rebellion, or other crime, the basis of representation therein shall be reduced in the proportion which the number of such male citizens shall bear to the whole number of male citizens twenty-one years of age in such State.

Section 3. No person shall be a Senator or Representative in Congress, or elector of President and Vice President, or hold any office, civil or military, under the United States, or under any State, who having previously taken an oath, as a member of Congress, or as an officer of the United States, or as a member of any State legislature, or as an executive or judicial officer of any State, to support the Constitution of the United States, shall have engaged in insurrection or rebellion against the same, or given aid or comfort to the enemies thereof. But Congress may by a vote of two-thirds of each House, remove such disability.

Section 4. The validity of the public debt of the United States, authorized by law, including debts incurred for payment of pensions and bounties for services in suppressing insurrection or rebellion, shall not be questioned. But neither the United States nor any State shall assume or pay any debt or obligation incurred in aid of insurrection or rebellion against the United States, or any claim for the loss or emancipation of any slave; but all such debts, obligations and claims shall be held illegal and void.

Section 5. The Congress shall have power to enforce, by appropriate legislation, the provisions of this article.

Amendment XV [1870]

Section 1. The right of citizens of the United States to vote shall not be denied or abridged by the United States or by any State on account of race, color, or previous condition of servitude.

Section 2. The Congress shall have power to enforce this article by appropriate legislation.

Amendment XVI [1913]

The Congress shall have power to lay and collect taxes on incomes, from whatever source derived, without apportionment among the several States, and without regard to any census or enumeration.

Amendment XVII [1913]

Section 1. The Senate of the United States shall be composed of two Senators from each State, elected by the people thereof, for six years; and each Senator shall have one vote. The electors in each State shall have the qualifications requisite for electors of the most numerous branch of the State legislatures.

Section 2. When vacancies happen in the representation of any State in the Senate, the executive authority of such State shall issue writs of election to fill such vacancies: *Provided,* That the legislature of any State may empower the executive thereof to make temporary appointments until the people fill the vacancies by election as the legislature may direct.

Section 3. This amendment shall not be so construed as to affect the election or term of any Senator chosen before it becomes valid as part of the Constitution.

Amendment XVIII [1919]

Section 1. After one year from the ratification of this article the manufacture, sale, or transportation of intoxicating liquors within, the importation thereof into, or the exportation thereof from the United States and all territory subject to the jurisdiction thereof for beverage purposes is hereby prohibited.

Section 2. The Congress and the several States shall have concurrent power to enforce this article by appropriate legislation.

Section 3. This article shall be inoperative unless it shall have been ratified as an amendment to the Constitution by the legislatures of the several States, as provided in the Constitution, within seven years from the date of the submission hereof to the States by the Congress.

Amendment XIX [1920]

Section 1. The right of citizens of the United States to vote shall not be denied or abridged by the United States or by any State on account of sex.

Section 2. Congress shall have power to enforce this article by appropriate legislation.

Amendment XX [1933]

Section 1. The terms of the President and Vice President shall end at noon on the 20th day of January, and the terms of Senators and Representatives at noon on the 3d day of January, of the years in which such terms would have ended if this article had not been ratified; and the terms of their successors shall then begin.

Section 2. The Congress shall assemble at least once in every year, and such meeting shall begin at noon on the 3d day of January, unless they shall by law appoint a different day.

Section 3. If, at the time fixed for the beginning of the term of the President, the President elect shall have died, the Vice President elect shall become President. If the President shall not have been chosen before the time fixed for the beginning of his term, or if the President elect shall have failed to qualify, then the Vice President elect shall act as President until a President shall have qualified; and the Congress may by law provide for the case wherein neither a President elect nor a Vice President elect shall have qualified, declaring who shall then act as President, or the manner in which one who is to act shall be selected, and such person shall act accordingly until a President or Vice President shall have qualified.

Section 4. The Congress may by law provide for the case of the death of any of the persons from whom the House of Representatives may choose a President whenever the right of choice shall have devolved upon them, and for the case of the death of any of the persons from whom the Senate may choose a Vice President whenever the right of choice shall have devolved upon them.

Section 5. Sections 1 and 2 shall take effect on the 15th day of October following the ratification of this article.

Section 6. This article shall be inoperative unless it shall have been ratified as an amendment to the Constitution by the legislatures of three-fourths of the several States within seven years from the date of its submission.

Amendment XXI [1933]

Section 1. The eighteenth article of amendment to the Constitution of the United States is hereby repealed.

Section 2. The transportation or importation into any State, Territory, or possession of the United States for delivery or use therein of intoxicating liquors, in violation of the laws thereof, is hereby prohibited.

Section 3. This article shall be inoperative unless it shall have been ratified as an amendment to the Constitution by conventions in the several States, as provided in the Constitution, within seven years from the date of the submission hereof to the States by the Congress.

Amendment XXII [1951]

Section 1. No person shall be elected to the office of the President more than twice, and no person who has held the office of President, or acted as President, for more than two years of a term to which some other person was elected President shall be elected to the office of President more than once. But this Article shall not apply to any person holding the office of President when this Article was proposed by the Congress, and shall not prevent any person who may be holding the office of President, or acting as President, during the term within which this Article becomes operative from holding the office of President or acting as President during the remainder of such term.

Section 2. This article shall be inoperative unless it shall have been ratified as an amendment to the Constitution by the legislatures of three-fourths of the several States within seven years from the date of its submission to the States by the Congress.

Amendment XXIII [1961]

Section 1. The District constituting the seat of Government of the United States shall appoint in such manner as the Congress may direct:

A number of electors of President and Vice President equal to the whole number of Senators and Representatives in Congress to which the District would be entitled if it were a State, but in no event more than the least populous state; they shall be in addition to those appointed by the states, but they shall be considered, for the purposes of the election of President and Vice President, to be electors appointed by a state; and they shall meet in the District and perform such duties as provided by the twelfth article of amendment.

Section 2. The Congress shall have power to enforce this article by appropriate legislation.

Amendment XXIV [1964]

Section 1. The right of citizens of the United States to vote in any primary or other election for President or Vice President, for electors for President or Vice President, or for Senator or Representative in Congress, shall not be denied or abridged by the United States, or any State by reason of failure to pay any poll tax or other tax.

Section 2. The Congress shall have power to enforce this article by appropriate legislation.

Amendment XXV [1967]

Section 1. In case of the removal of the President from office or of his death or resignation, the Vice President shall become President.

Section 2. Whenever there is a vacancy in the office of the Vice President, the President shall nominate a Vice President who shall take office upon confirmation by a majority vote of both Houses of Congress.

Section 3. Whenever the President transmits to the President pro tempore of the Senate and the Speaker of the House of Representatives his written declaration that he is unable to discharge the powers and duties of his office, and until he transmits to them a written declaration to the contrary, such powers and duties shall be discharged by the Vice President as Acting President.

Section 4. Whenever the Vice President and a majority of either the principal officers of the executive departments or of such other body as Congress may by law provide, transmit to the President pro tempore of the Senate and the Speaker of the House of Representatives their written declaration that the President is unable to discharge the powers and duties of his office, the Vice President shall immediately assume the powers and duties of the office as Acting President.

Thereafter, when the President transmits to the President pro tempore of the Senate and the Speaker of the House of Representatives his written declaration that no inability exists, he shall resume the powers and duties of his office unless the Vice President and a majority of either the principal officers of the executive department or of such other body as Congress may by law provide, transmit within four days to the President pro tempore of the Senate and the Speaker of the House of Representatives their written declaration that the President is unable to discharge the powers and duties of his office. Thereupon Congress shall decide the issue, assembling within forty-eight hours for that purpose if not in session. If the Congress, within twenty-one days after receipt of the latter written declaration, or, if Congress is not in session, within twenty-one days after Congress is required to assemble, determines by two-thirds vote of both Houses that the President is unable to discharge the powers and duties of his office, the Vice President shall continue to discharge the same as Acting President; otherwise, the President shall resume the powers and duties of his office.

Amendment XXVI [1971]

Section 1. The right of citizens of the United States, who are eighteen years of age or older, to vote shall not be denied or abridged by the United States or by any State on account of age.

Section 2. The Congress shall have power to enforce this article by appropriate legislation.

Amendment XXVII [1992]

No law, varying the compensation for the services of the Senators and Representatives, shall take effect, until an election of Representatives shall have intervened.

APPENDIX C

The Uniform Commercial Code

(Adopted in fifty-two jurisdictions; all fifty States, although Louisiana has adopted only Articles 1, 3, 4, 7, 8, and 9; the District of Columbia; and the Virgin Islands.)

The Code consists of the following articles:

Art.

1. General Provisions
2. Sales

2A. Leases

3. Negotiable Instruments
4. Bank Deposits and Collections

4A. Funds Transfers

5. Letters of Credit
6. Repealer of Article 6—Bulk Transfers and [Revised] Article 6—Bulk Sales
7. Warehouse Receipts, Bills of Lading and Other Documents of Title
8. Investment Securities
9. Secured Transactions
10. Effective Date and Repealer
11. Effective Date and Transition Provisions

Article 1
GENERAL PROVISIONS

Part 1 General Provisions

§ 1–101. Short Titles.

(a) This [Act] may be cited as Uniform Commercial Code.

(b) This article may be cited as Uniform Commercial Code-Uniform Provisions.

§ 1–102. Scope of Article.

This article applies to a transaction to the extent that it is governed by another article of [the Uniform Commercial Code].

§ 1–103. Construction of [Uniform Commercial Code] to Promote Its Purpose and Policies; Applicability of Supplemental Principles of Law.

(a) [The Uniform Commercial Code] must be liberally construed and applied to promote its underlying purposes and policies, which are:

(1) to simplify, clarify, and modernize the law governing commercial transactions;

(2) to permit the continued expansion of commercial practices through custom, usage, and agreement of the parties; and

(3) to make uniform the law among the various jurisdictions.

(b) Unless displaced by the particular provisions of [the Uniform Commercial Code], the principles of law and equity, including the law merchant and the law relative to capacity to contract, principal and agent, estoppel, fraud, misrepresentation, duress, coercion, mistake, bankruptcy, and other validating or invalidating cause, supplement its provisions.

§ 1–104. Construction Against Implicit Repeal.

This Act being a general act intended as a unified coverage of its subject matter, no part of it shall be deemed to be impliedly repealed by subsequent legislation if such construction can reasonably be avoided.

§ 1–105. Severability.

If any provision or clause of [the Uniform Commercial Code] or its application to any person or circumstance is held invalid, the invalidity does not affect other provisions or applications of [the Uniform Commercial Code] which can be given effect without the invalid provision or application, and to this end the provisions of [the Uniform Commercial Code] are severable.

§ 1–106. Use of Singular and Plural; Gender.

In [the Uniform Commercial Code], unless the statutory context otherwise requires:

(1) words in the singular number include the plural, and those in the plural include the singular; and

(2) words of any gender also refer to any other gender.

§ 1–107. Section Captions.

Section captions are part of [the Uniform Commercial Code].

§ 1–108. Relation to Electronic Signatures in Global and National Commerce Act.

This article modifies, limits, and supersedes the Federal Electronic Signatures in Global and National Commerce Act, 15 U.S.C. Sections 7001 *et seq.*, except that nothing in this article modifies, limits, or supersedes section 7001(c) of that act or authorizes electronic delivery of any of the notices described in section 7003(b) of that Act.

Part 2 General Definitions and Principles of Interpretation

§ 1–201. General Definitions.

Subject to additional definitions contained in the subsequent Articles of this Act which are applicable to specific Articles or Parts thereof, and unless the context otherwise requires, in this Act:

(1) "Action", in the sense of a judicial proceeding, includes recoupment, counterclaim, set-off, suit in equity, and any other proceedings in which rights are determined.

(2) "Aggrieved party" means a party entitled to resort to a remedy.

(3) "Agreement", as distinguished from "contract", means the bargain of the parties in fact, as found in their language or by implication from other circumstances, including course of performance, course of dealing, or usage of trade as provided in Section 1-303.

(4) "Bank" means a person engaged in the business of banking and includes a savings bank, savings and loan association, credit union, and trust company.

(5) "Bearer" means a person in control of a negotiable electronic document of title or a person in possession of a negotiable instrument, negotiable tangible document of title, or certificated security that is payable to bearer or indorsed in blank.

(6) "Bill of lading" means a document of title evidencing the receipt of goods for shipment issued by a person engaged in the business of directly or indirectly transporting or forwarding goods. The term does not include a warehouse receipt.

(7) "Branch" includes a separately incorporated foreign branch of a bank.

(8) "Burden of establishing" a fact means the burden of persuading the trier of fact that the existence of the fact is more probable than its nonexistence.

(9) "Buyer in ordinary course of business" means a person that buys goods in good faith, without knowledge that the sale violates the rights of another person in the goods, and in the ordinary course from a person, other than a pawnbroker, in the business of selling goods of that kind. A person buys goods in the ordinary course if the sale to the person comports with the usual or customary practices in the kind of business in which the seller is engaged or with the seller's own usual or customary practices. A person that sells oil, gas, or other minerals at the wellhead or minehead is a person in the business of selling goods of that kind. A buyer in ordinary course of business may buy for cash, by exchange of other property, or on secured or unsecured credit, and may acquire goods or documents of title under a pre-existing contract for sale. Only a buyer that takes possession of the goods or has a right to recover the goods from the seller under Article 2 may be a buyer in ordinary course of business. A person that acquires goods in a transfer in bulk or as security for or in total or partial satisfaction of a money debt is not a buyer in ordinary course of business.

(10) "Conspicuous", with reference to a term, means so written, displayed, or presented that a reasonable person against which it is to operate ought to have noticed it. Whether a term is "conspicuous" or not is a decision for the court. Conspicuous terms include the following:

(A) a heading in capitals equal to or greater in size than the surrounding text, or in contrasting type, font, or color to the surrounding text of the same or lesser size; and

(B) language in the body of a record or display in larger type than the surrounding text, or in contrasting type, font, or color to the surrounding text of the same size, or set off from surrounding text of the same size by symbols or other marks that call attention to the language.

(11) "Consumer" means an individual who enters into a transaction primarily for personal, family, or household purposes.

(12) "Contract", as distinguished from "agreement", means the total legal obligation that results from the parties' agreement as determined by [the Uniform Commercial Code] as supplemented by any other laws.

(13) "Creditor" includes a general creditor, a secured creditor, a lien creditor and any representative of creditors, including an assignee for the benefit of creditors, a trustee in bankruptcy, a receiver in equity and an executor or administrator of an insolvent debtor's or assignor's estate.

(14) "Defendant" includes a person in the position of defendant in a counterclaim, cross-action, or third-party claim.

(15) "Delivery" with respect to an electronic document of title means voluntary transfer of control and with respect to an instrument, a tangible document of title, or chattel paper means voluntary transfer of possession.

(16) "Document of title" means a record (i) that in regular course of business or financing is treated as adequately evidencing that the person in possession or control of the record is entitled to receive, control, hold, and dispose of the record and the goods the record covers and (ii) that purports to be issued by or addressed to a bailee and to cover goods in the bailee's possession

which are either identified or are fungible portions of an identified mass. The term includes a bill of lading, transport document, dock warrant, dock receipt, warehouse receipt, and order for delivery of goods. An electronic document of title means a document of title evidenced by a record consisting of information stored in an electronic medium. A tangible document of title means a document of title evidenced by a record consisting of information that is inscribed on a tangible medium.

(17) "Fault" means a default, breach, or wrongful act or omission.

(18) "Fungible goods" means:

(A) goods of which any unit, by nature or usage of trade, is the equivalent of any other like unit; or

(B) goods that by agreement are treated as equivalent.

(19) "Genuine" means free of forgery or counterfeiting.

(20) "Good faith," except as otherwise provided in Article 5, means honesty in fact and the observance of reasonable commercial standards of fair dealing.

(21) "Holder" means:

(A) the person in possession of a negotiable instrument that is payable either to bearer or to an identified person that is the person in possession;

(B) the person in possession of a negotiable tangible document of title if the goods are deliverable either to bearer or to the order of the person in possession; or

(C) the person in control of a negotiable electronic document of title.

(22) "Insolvency proceeding" includes an assignment for the benefit of creditors or other proceeding intended to liquidate or rehabilitate the estate of the person involved.

(23) "Insolvent" means:

(A) having generally ceased to pay debts in the ordinary course of business other than as a result of bona fide dispute;

(B) being unable to pay debts as they become due; or

(C) being insolvent within the meaning of federal bankruptcy law.

(24) "Money" means a medium of exchange currently authorized or adopted by a domestic or foreign government. The term includes a monetary unit of account established by an intergovernmental organization or by agreement between two or more countries.

(25) "Organization" means a person other than an individual.

(26) "Party", as distinguished from "third party", means a person that has engaged in a transaction or made an agreement subject to [the Uniform Commercial Code].

(27) "Person" means an individual, corporation, business trust, estate, trust, partnership, limited liability company, association, joint venture, government, governmental subdivision, agency, or instrumentality, public corporation, or any other legal or commercial entity.

(28) "Present value" means the amount as of a date certain of one or more sums payable in the future, discounted to the date certain by use of either an interest rate specified by the parties if that rate is not manifestly unreasonable at the time the transaction is entered into or, if an interest rate is not so specified, a commercially reasonable rate that takes into account the facts and circumstances at the time the transaction is entered into.

(29) "Purchase" means taking by sale, lease, discount, negotiation, mortgage, pledge, lien, security interest, issue or reissue, gift, or any other voluntary transaction creating an interest in property.

(30) "Purchaser" means a person that takes by purchase.

(31) "Record" means information that is inscribed on a tangible medium or that is stored in an electronic or other medium and is retrievable in perceivable form.

(32) "Remedy" means any remedial right to which an aggrieved party is entitled with or without resort to a tribunal.

(33) "Representative" means a person empowered to act for another, including an agent, an officer of a corporation or association, and a trustee, executor, or administrator of an estate.

(34) "Right" includes remedy.

(35) "Security interest" means an interest in personal property or fixtures which secures payment or performance of an obligation. "Security interest" includes any interest of a consignor and a buyer of accounts, chattel paper, a payment intangible, or a promissory note in a transaction that is subject to Article 9. "Security interest" does not include the special property interest of a buyer of goods on identification of those goods to a contract for sale under Section 2-401, but a buyer may also acquire a "security interest" by complying with Article 9. Except as otherwise provided in Section 2-505, the right of a seller or lessor of goods under Article 2 or 2A to retain or acquire possession of the goods is not a "security interest", but a seller or lessor may also acquire a "security interest" by complying with Article 9. The retention or reservation of title by a seller of goods notwithstanding shipment or delivery to the buyer under Section 2-401 is limited in effect to a reservation of a "security interest." Whether a transaction in the form of a lease creates a "security interest" is determined pursuant to Section 1-203.

(36) "Send" in connection with a writing, record, or notice means:

(A) to deposit in the mail or deliver for transmission by any other usual means of communication with postage or cost of transmission provided for and properly addressed and, in the case of an instrument, to an address specified thereon or otherwise agreed, or if there be none to any address reasonable under the circumstances; or

(B) in any other way to cause to be received any record or notice within the time it would have arrived if properly sent.

(37) "Signed" includes using any symbol executed or adopted with present intention to adopt or accept a writing.

(38) "State" means a State of the United States, the District of Columbia, Puerto Rico, the United States Virgin Islands, or any territory or insular possession subject to the jurisdiction of the United States.

(39) "Surety" includes a guarantor or other secondary obligor.

(40) "Term" means a portion of an agreement that relates to a particular matter.

(41) "Unauthorized signature" means a signature made without actual, implied, or apparent authority. The term includes a forgery.

(42) "Warehouse receipt" means a document of title issued by a person engaged in the business of storing goods for hire.

(43) "Writing" includes printing, typewriting, or any other intentional reduction to tangible form. "Written" has a corresponding meaning.

As amended in 2003.

* * * *

§ 1–205. Reasonable Time; Seasonableness.

(a) Whether a time for taking an action required by [the Uniform Commercial Code] is reasonable depends on the nature, purpose, and circumstances of the action.

(b) An action is taken seasonably if it is taken at or within the time agreed or, if no time is agreed, at or within a reasonable time.

* * * *

Part 3 Territorial Applicability and General Rules

* * * *

§ 1–303. Course of Performance, Course of Dealing, and Usage of Trade.

(a) A "course of performance" is a sequence of conduct between the parties to a particular transaction that exists if:

(1) the agreement of the parties with respect to the transaction involves repeated occasions for performance by a party; and

(2) the other party, with knowledge of the nature of the performance and opportunity for objection to it, accepts the performance or acquiesces in it without objection.

(b) A "course of dealing" is a sequence of conduct concerning previous transactions between the parties to a particular transaction that is fairly to be regarded as establishing a common basis of understanding for interpreting their expressions and other conduct.

(c) A "usage of trade" is any practice or method of dealing having such regularity of observance in a place, vocation, or trade as to justify an expectation that it will be observed with respect to the transaction in question. The existence and scope of such a usage must be proved as facts. If it is established that such a usage is embodied in a trade code or similar record, the interpretation of the record is a question of law.

(d) A course of performance or course of dealing between the parties or usage of trade in the vocation or trade in which they are engaged or of which they are or should be aware is relevant in ascertaining the meaning of the parties' agreement, may give particular meaning to specific terms of the agreement, and may supplement or qualify the terms of the agreement. A usage of trade applicable in the place in which part of the performance under the agreement is to occur may be so utilized as to that part of the performance.

(e) Except as otherwise provided in subsection (f), the express terms of an agreement and any applicable course of performance, course of dealing, or usage of trade must be construed whenever reasonable as consistent with each other. If such a construction is unreasonable:

(1) express terms prevail over course of performance, course of dealing, and usage of trade;

(2) course of performance prevails over course of dealing and usage of trade; and

(3) course of dealing prevails over usage of trade.

(f) Subject to Section 2-209 and Section 2A-208, a course of performance is relevant to show a waiver or modification of any term inconsistent with the course of performance.

(g) Evidence of a relevant usage of trade offered by one party is not admissible unless that party has given the other party notice that the court finds sufficient to prevent unfair surprise to the other party.

§ 1–304. Obligation of Good Faith.

Every contract or duty within [the Uniform Commercial Code] imposes an obligation of good faith in its performance and enforcement.

* * * *

§ 1–309. Option to Accelerate at Will.

A term providing that one party or that party's successor in interest may accelerate payment or performance or require collateral or additional collateral "at will" or when the party "deems itself insecure," or words of similar import, means that the party has power to do so only if that party in good faith believes that the prospect of payment or performance is impaired. The burden of establishing lack of good faith is on the party against which the power has been exercised.

§ 1–310. Subordinated Obligations.

An obligation may be issued as subordinated to performance of another obligation of the person obligated, or a creditor may subordinate its right to performance of an obligation by agreement with either the person obligated or another creditor of the person obligated. Subordination does not create a security interest as against either the common debtor or a subordinated creditor.

Article 2 SALES

Part 1 Short Title, General Construction and Subject Matter

§ 2–101. Short Title.

This Article shall be known and may be cited as Uniform Commercial Code—Sales.

§ 2–102. Scope; Certain Security and Other Transactions Excluded From This Article.

Unless the context otherwise requires, this Article applies to transactions in goods; it does not apply to any transaction which although in the form of an unconditional contract to sell or present sale is intended to operate only as a security transaction nor does this Article impair or repeal any statute regulating sales to consumers, farmers or other specified classes of buyers.

§ 2–103. Definitions and Index of Definitions.

(1) In this Article unless the context otherwise requires

(a) "Buyer" means a person who buys or contracts to buy goods.

(b) "Good faith" in the case of a merchant means honesty in fact and the observance of reasonable commercial standards of fair dealing in the trade.

(c) "Receipt" of goods means taking physical possession of them.

(d) "Seller" means a person who sells or contracts to sell goods.

(2) Other definitions applying to this Article or to specified Parts thereof, and the sections in which they appear are:

"Acceptance". Section 2–606.
"Banker's credit". Section 2–325.
"Between merchants". Section 2–104.
"Cancellation". Section 2–106(4).
"Commercial unit". Section 2–105.
"Confirmed credit". Section 2–325.
"Conforming to contract". Section 2–106.
"Contract for sale". Section 2–106.
"Cover". Section 2–712.
"Entrusting". Section 2–403.
"Financing agency". Section 2–104.
"Future goods". Section 2–105.
"Goods". Section 2–105.
"Identification". Section 2–501.
"Installment contract". Section 2–612.
"Letter of Credit". Section 2–325.
"Lot". Section 2–105.
"Merchant". Section 2–104.
"Overseas". Section 2–323.
"Person in position of seller". Section 2–707.
"Present sale". Section 2–106.
"Sale". Section 2–106.
"Sale on approval". Section 2–326.
"Sale or return". Section 2–326.
"Termination". Section 2–106.

(3) The following definitions in other Articles apply to this Article:

"Check". Section 3–104.
"Consignee". Section 7–102.
"Consignor". Section 7–102.
"Consumer goods". Section 9–109.
"Dishonor". Section 3–507.
"Draft". Section 3–104.

(4) In addition Article 1 contains general definitions and principles of construction and interpretation applicable throughout this Article.

As amended in 1994 and 1999.

§ 2–104. Definitions: "Merchant"; "Between Merchants"; "Financing Agency".

(1) "Merchant" means a person who deals in goods of the kind or otherwise by his occupation holds himself out as having knowledge or skill peculiar to the practices or goods involved in the transaction or to whom such knowledge or skill may be attributed by his employment of an agent or broker or other intermediary who by his occupation holds himself out as having such knowledge or skill.

(2) "Financing agency" means a bank, finance company or other person who in the ordinary course of business makes advances against goods or documents of title or who by arrangement with either the seller or the buyer intervenes in ordinary course to make or collect payment due or claimed under the contract for sale, as by purchasing or paying the seller's draft or making advances against it or by merely taking it for collection whether or not documents of title accompany the draft. "Financing agency" includes also a bank or other person who similarly intervenes between persons who are in the position of seller and buyer in respect to the goods (Section 2–707).

(3) "Between merchants" means in any transaction with respect to which both parties are chargeable with the knowledge or skill of merchants.

§ 2–105. Definitions: Transferability; "Goods"; "Future" Goods; "Lot"; "Commercial Unit".

(1) "Goods" means all things (including specially manufactured goods) which are movable at the time of identification to the contract for sale other than the money in which the price is to be paid, investment securities (Article 8) and things in action. "Goods" also includes the unborn young of animals and growing crops and other identified things attached to realty as described in the section on goods to be severed from realty (Section 2–107).

(2) Goods must be both existing and identified before any interest in them can pass. Goods which are not both existing and identified are "future" goods. A purported present sale of future goods or of any interest therein operates as a contract to sell.

(3) There may be a sale of a part interest in existing identified goods.

(4) An undivided share in an identified bulk of fungible goods is sufficiently identified to be sold although the

quantity of the bulk is not determined. Any agreed proportion of such a bulk or any quantity thereof agreed upon by number, weight or other measure may to the extent of the seller's interest in the bulk be sold to the buyer who then becomes an owner in common.

(5) "Lot" means a parcel or a single article which is the subject matter of a separate sale or delivery, whether or not it is sufficient to perform the contract.

(6) "Commercial unit" means such a unit of goods as by commercial usage is a single whole for purposes of sale and division of which materially impairs its character or value on the market or in use. A commercial unit may be a single article (as a machine) or a set of articles (as a suite of furniture or an assortment of sizes) or a quantity (as a bale, gross, or carload) or any other unit treated in use or in the relevant market as a single whole.

§ 2–106. Definitions: "Contract"; "Agreement"; "Contract for Sale"; "Sale"; "Present Sale"; "Conforming" to Contract; "Termination"; "Cancellation".

(1) In this Article unless the context otherwise requires "contract" and "agreement" are limited to those relating to the present or future sale of goods. "Contract for sale" includes both a present sale of goods and a contract to sell goods at a future time. A "sale" consists in the passing of title from the seller to the buyer for a price (Section 2–401). A "present sale" means a sale which is accomplished by the making of the contract.

(2) Goods or conduct including any part of a performance are "conforming" or conform to the contract when they are in accordance with the obligations under the contract.

(3) "Termination" occurs when either party pursuant to a power created by agreement or law puts an end to the contract otherwise than for its breach. On "termination" all obligations which are still executory on both sides are discharged but any right based on prior breach or performance survives.

(4) "Cancellation" occurs when either party puts an end to the contract for breach by the other and its effect is the same as that of "termination" except that the cancelling party also retains any remedy for breach of the whole contract or any unperformed balance.

§ 2–107. Goods to Be Severed From Realty: Recording.

(1) A contract for the sale of minerals or the like (including oil and gas) or a structure or its materials to be removed from realty is a contract for the sale of goods within this Article if they are to be severed by the seller but until severance a purported present sale thereof which is not effective as a transfer of an interest in land is effective only as a contract to sell.

(2) A contract for the sale apart from the land of growing crops or other things attached to realty and capable of severance without material harm thereto but not described in subsection (1) or of timber to be cut is a contract for the sale of goods within this Article whether the subject matter is to be severed by the buyer or by the seller even though it forms part of the realty at the time of contracting, and the parties can by identification effect a present sale before severance.

(3) The provisions of this section are subject to any third party rights provided by the law relating to realty records, and the contract for sale may be executed and recorded as a document transferring an interest in land and shall then constitute notice to third parties of the buyer's rights under the contract for sale.

As amended in 1972.

Part 2 Form, Formation and Readjustment of Contract

§ 2–201. Formal Requirements; Statute of Frauds.

(1) Except as otherwise provided in this section a contract for the sale of goods for the price of $500 or more is not enforceable by way of action or defense unless there is some writing sufficient to indicate that a contract for sale has been made between the parties and signed by the party against whom enforcement is sought or by his authorized agent or broker. A writing is not insufficient because it omits or incorrectly states a term agreed upon but the contract is not enforceable under this paragraph beyond the quantity of goods shown in such writing.

(2) Between merchants if within a reasonable time a writing in confirmation of the contract and sufficient against the sender is received and the party receiving it has reason to know its contents, its satisfies the requirements of subsection (1) against such party unless written notice of objection to its contents is given within ten days after it is received.

(3) A contract which does not satisfy the requirements of subsection (1) but which is valid in other respects is enforceable

(a) if the goods are to be specially manufactured for the buyer and are not suitable for sale to others in the ordinary course of the seller's business and the seller, before notice of repudiation is received and under circumstances which reasonably indicate that the goods are for the buyer, has made either a substantial beginning of their manufacture or commitments for their procurement; or

(b) if the party against whom enforcement is sought admits in his pleading, testimony or otherwise in court that a contract for sale was made, but the contract is not enforceable under this provision beyond the quantity of goods admitted; or

(c) with respect to goods for which payment has been made and accepted or which have been received and accepted (Sec. 2–606).

§ 2–202. Final Written Expression: Parol or Extrinsic Evidence.

Terms with respect to which the confirmatory memoranda of the parties agree or which are otherwise set forth in a writing intended by the parties as a final expression of their agreement with respect to such terms as are included therein may not be contradicted by evidence of any prior agreement or of a contemporaneous oral agreement but may be explained or supplemented

(a) by course of dealing or usage of trade (Section 1–205) or by course of performance (Section 2–208); and

(b) by evidence of consistent additional terms unless the court finds the writing to have been intended also as a complete and exclusive statement of the terms of the agreement.

§ 2–203. Seals Inoperative.

The affixing of a seal to a writing evidencing a contract for sale or an offer to buy or sell goods does not constitute the writing a sealed instrument and the law with respect to sealed instruments does not apply to such a contract or offer.

§ 2–204. Formation in General.

(1) A contract for sale of goods may be made in any manner sufficient to show agreement, including conduct by both parties which recognizes the existence of such a contract.

(2) An agreement sufficient to constitute a contract for sale may be found even though the moment of its making is undetermined.

(3) Even though one or more terms are left open a contract for sale does not fail for indefiniteness if the parties have intended to make a contract and there is a reasonably certain basis for giving an appropriate remedy.

§ 2–205. Firm Offers.

An offer by a merchant to buy or sell goods in a signed writing which by its terms gives assurance that it will be held open is not revocable, for lack of consideration, during the time stated or if no time is stated for a reasonable time, but in no event may such period of irrevocability exceed three months; but any such term of assurance on a form supplied by the offeree must be separately signed by the offeror.

§ 2–206. Offer and Acceptance in Formation of Contract.

(1) Unless other unambiguously indicated by the language or circumstances

(a) an offer to make a contract shall be construed as inviting acceptance in any manner and by any medium reasonable in the circumstances;

(b) an order or other offer to buy goods for prompt or current shipment shall be construed as inviting acceptance either by a prompt promise to ship or by the prompt or current shipment of conforming or nonconforming goods, but such a shipment of nonconforming goods does not constitute an acceptance if the seller seasonably notifies the buyer that the shipment is offered only as an accommodation to the buyer.

(2) Where the beginning of a requested performance is a reasonable mode of acceptance an offeror who is not notified of acceptance within a reasonable time may treat the offer as having lapsed before acceptance.

§ 2–207. Additional Terms in Acceptance or Confirmation.

(1) A definite and seasonable expression of acceptance or a written confirmation which is sent within a reasonable time operates as an acceptance even though it states terms additional to or different from those offered or agreed upon, unless acceptance is expressly made conditional on assent to the additional or different terms.

(2) The additional terms are to be construed as proposals for addition to the contract. Between merchants such terms become part of the contract unless:

(a) the offer expressly limits acceptance to the terms of the offer;

(b) they materially alter it; or

(c) notification of objection to them has already been given or is given within a reasonable time after notice of them is received.

(3) Conduct by both parties which recognizes the existence of a contract is sufficient to establish a contract for sale although the writings of the parties do not otherwise establish a contract. In such case the terms of the particular contract consist of those terms on which the writings of the parties agree, together with any supplementary terms incorporated under any other provisions of this Act.

§ 2–208. Course of Performance or Practical Construction.

(1) Where the contract for sale involves repeated occasions for performance by either party with knowledge of the nature of the performance and opportunity for objection to it by the other, any course of performance accepted or acquiesced in without objection shall be relevant to determine the meaning of the agreement.

(2) The express terms of the agreement and any such course of performance, as well as any course of dealing and usage of trade, shall be construed whenever reasonable as consistent with each other; but when such construction is unreasonable, express terms shall control course of performance and course of performance shall control both course of dealing and usage of trade (Section 1–303).

(3) Subject to the provisions of the next section on modification and waiver, such course of performance shall be relevant to show a waiver or modification of any term inconsistent with such course of performance.

§ 2–209. Modification, Rescission and Waiver.

(1) An agreement modifying a contract within this Article needs no consideration to be binding.

(2) A signed agreement which excludes modification or rescission except by a signed writing cannot be otherwise modified or rescinded, but except as between merchants such a requirement on a form supplied by the merchant must be separately signed by the other party.

(3) The requirements of the statute of frauds section of this Article (Section 2–201) must be satisfied if the contract as modified is within its provisions.

(4) Although an attempt at modification or rescission does not satisfy the requirements of subsection (2) or (3) it can operate as a waiver.

(5) A party who has made a waiver affecting an executory portion of the contract may retract the waiver by reasonable notification received by the other party that strict performance will be required of any term waived, unless the retraction would be unjust in view of a material change of position in reliance on the waiver.

§ 2–210. Delegation of Performance; Assignment of Rights.

(1) A party may perform his duty through a delegate unless otherwise agreed or unless the other party has a substantial interest in having his original promisor perform or control the acts required by the contract. No delegation of performance relieves the party delegating of any duty to perform or any liability for breach.

(2) Except as otherwise provided in Section 9–406, unless otherwise agreed, all rights of either seller or buyer can be assigned except where the assignment would materially change the duty of the other party, or increase materially the burden or risk imposed on him by his contract, or impair materially his chance of obtaining return performance. A right to damages for breach of the whole contract or a right arising out of the assignor's due performance of his entire obligation can be assigned despite agreement otherwise.

(3) The creation, attachment, perfection, or enforcement of a security interest in the seller's interest under a contract is not a transfer that materially changes the duty of or increases materially the burden or risk imposed on the buyer or impairs materially the buyer's chance of obtaining return performance within the purview of subsection (2) unless, and then only to the extent that, enforcement actually results in a delegation of material performance of the seller. Even in that event, the creation, attachment, perfection, and enforcement of the security interest remain effective, but (i) the seller is liable to the buyer for damages caused by the delegation to the extent that the damages could not reasonably by prevented by the buyer, and (ii) a court having jurisdiction may grant other appropriate relief, including cancellation of the contract for sale or an injunction against enforcement of the security interest or consummation of the enforcement.

(4) Unless the circumstances indicate the contrary a prohibition of assignment of "the contract" is to be construed as barring only the delegation to the assignee of the assignor's performance.

(5) An assignment of "the contract" or of "all my rights under the contract" or an assignment in similar general terms is an assignment of rights and unless the language or the circumstances (as in an assignment for security) indicate the contrary, it is a delegation of performance of the duties of the assignor and its acceptance by the assignee constitutes a promise by him to perform those duties. This promise is enforceable by either the assignor or the other party to the original contract.

(6) The other party may treat any assignment which delegates performance as creating reasonable grounds for insecurity and may without prejudice to his rights against the assignor demand assurances from the assignee (Section 2–609).

As amended in 1999.

Part 3 General Obligation and Construction of Contract

§ 2–301. General Obligations of Parties.

The obligation of the seller is to transfer and deliver and that of the buyer is to accept and pay in accordance with the contract.

§ 2–302. Unconscionable Contract or Clause.

(1) If the court as a matter of law finds the contract or any clause of the contract to have been unconscionable at the time it was made the court may refuse to enforce the contract, or it may enforce the remainder of the contract without the unconscionable clause, or it may so limit the application of any unconscionable clause as to avoid any unconscionable result.

(2) When it is claimed or appears to the court that the contract or any clause thereof may be unconscionable the parties shall be afforded a reasonable opportunity to present evidence as to its commercial setting, purpose and effect to aid the court in making the determination.

§ 2–303. Allocations or Division of Risks.

Where this Article allocates a risk or a burden as between the parties "unless otherwise agreed", the agreement may not only shift the allocation but may also divide the risk or burden.

§ 2–304. Price Payable in Money, Goods, Realty, or Otherwise.

(1) The price can be made payable in money or otherwise. If it is payable in whole or in part in goods each party is a seller of the goods which he is to transfer.

(2) Even though all or part of the price is payable in an interest in realty the transfer of the goods and the seller's obligations with reference to them are subject to this Article, but not the transfer of the interest in realty or the transferor's obligations in connection therewith.

§ 2–305. Open Price Term.

(1) The parties if they so intend can conclude a contract for sale even though the price is not settled. In such a case the price is a reasonable price at the time for delivery if

(a) nothing is said as to price; or

(b) the price is left to be agreed by the parties and they fail to agree; or

(c) the price is to be fixed in terms of some agreed market or other standard as set or recorded by a third person or agency and it is not so set or recorded.

(2) A price to be fixed by the seller or by the buyer means a price for him to fix in good faith.

(3) When a price left to be fixed otherwise than by agreement of the parties fails to be fixed through fault of one party the other may at his option treat the contract as cancelled or himself fix a reasonable price.

(4) Where, however, the parties intend not to be bound unless the price be fixed or agreed and it is not fixed or agreed there is no contract. In such a case the buyer must return any goods already received or if unable so to do must pay their reasonable value at the time of delivery and the seller must return any portion of the price paid on account.

§ 2–306. Output, Requirements and Exclusive Dealings.

(1) A term which measures the quantity by the output of the seller or the requirements of the buyer means such actual output or requirements as may occur in good faith, except that no quantity unreasonably disproportionate to any stated estimate or in the absence of a stated estimate to any normal or otherwise comparable prior output or requirements may be tendered or demanded.

(2) A lawful agreement by either the seller or the buyer for exclusive dealing in the kind of goods concerned imposes unless otherwise agreed an obligation by the seller to use best efforts to supply the goods and by the buyer to use best efforts to promote their sale.

§ 2–307. Delivery in Single Lot or Several Lots.

Unless otherwise agreed all goods called for by a contract for sale must be tendered in a single delivery and payment is due only on such tender but where the circumstances give either party the right to make or demand delivery in lots the price if it can be apportioned may be demanded for each lot.

§ 2–308. Absence of Specified Place for Delivery.

Unless otherwise agreed

(a) the place for delivery of goods is the seller's place of business or if he has none his residence; but

(b) in a contract for sale of identified goods which to the knowledge of the parties at the time of contracting are in some other place, that place is the place for their delivery; and

(c) documents of title may be delivered through customary banking channels.

§ 2–309. Absence of Specific Time Provisions; Notice of Termination.

(1) The time for shipment or delivery or any other action under a contract if not provided in this Article or agreed upon shall be a reasonable time.

(2) Where the contract provides for successive performances but is indefinite in duration it is valid for a reasonable time but unless otherwise agreed may be terminated at any time by either party.

(3) Termination of a contract by one party except on the happening of an agreed event requires that reasonable notification be received by the other party and an agreement dispensing with notification is invalid if its operation would be unconscionable.

§ 2–310. Open Time for Payment or Running of Credit; Authority to Ship Under Reservation.

Unless otherwise agreed

(a) payment is due at the time and place at which the buyer is to receive the goods even though the place of shipment is the place of delivery; and

(b) if the seller is authorized to send the goods he may ship them under reservation, and may tender the documents of title, but the buyer may inspect the goods after their arrival before payment is due unless such inspection is inconsistent with the terms of the contract (Section 2–513); and

(c) if delivery is authorized and made by way of documents of title otherwise than by subsection (b) then payment is due at the time and place at which the buyer is to receive the documents regardless of where the goods are to be received; and

(d) where the seller is required or authorized to ship the goods on credit the credit period runs from the time of shipment but post-dating the invoice or delaying its dispatch will correspondingly delay the starting of the credit period.

§ 2–311. Options and Cooperation Respecting Performance.

(1) An agreement for sale which is otherwise sufficiently definite (subsection (3) of Section 2–204) to be a contract is not made invalid by the fact that it leaves particulars of performance to be specified by one of the parties. Any such specification must be made in good faith and within limits set by commercial reasonableness.

(2) Unless otherwise agreed specifications relating to assortment of the goods are at the buyer's option and except as otherwise provided in subsections (1)(c) and (3) of Section 2–319 specifications or arrangements relating to shipment are at the seller's option.

(3) Where such specification would materially affect the other party's performance but is not seasonably made or where one party's cooperation is necessary to the agreed performance of the other but is not seasonably forthcoming, the other party in addition to all other remedies

(a) is excused for any resulting delay in his own performance; and

(b) may also either proceed to perform in any reasonable manner or after the time for a material part of his own performance treat the failure to specify or to cooperate as a breach by failure to deliver or accept the goods.

§ 2–312. Warranty of Title and Against Infringement; Buyer's Obligation Against Infringement.

(1) Subject to subsection (2) there is in a contract for sale a warranty by the seller that

(a) the title conveyed shall be good, and its transfer rightful; and

(b) the goods shall be delivered free from any security interest or other lien or encumbrance of which the buyer at the time of contracting has no knowledge.

(2) A warranty under subsection (1) will be excluded or modified only by specific language or by circumstances which give the buyer reason to know that the person selling does not claim title in himself or that he is purporting to sell only such right or title as he or a third person may have.

(3) Unless otherwise agreed a seller who is a merchant regularly dealing in goods of the kind warrants that the goods shall be delivered free of the rightful claim of any third person by way of infringement or the like but a buyer who furnishes specifications to the seller must hold the seller harmless against any such claim which arises out of compliance with the specifications.

§ 2–313. Express Warranties by Affirmation, Promise, Description, Sample.

(1) Express warranties by the seller are created as follows:

(a) Any affirmation of fact or promise made by the seller to the buyer which relates to the goods and becomes part of the basis of the bargain creates an express warranty that the goods shall conform to the affirmation or promise.

(b) Any description of the goods which is made part of the basis of the bargain creates an express warranty that the goods shall conform to the description.

(c) Any sample or model which is made part of the basis of the bargain creates an express warranty that the whole of the goods shall conform to the sample or model.

(2) It is not necessary to the creation of an express warranty that the seller use formal words such as "warrant" or "guarantee" or that he have a specific intention to make a warranty, but an affirmation merely of the value of the goods or a statement purporting to be merely the seller's opinion or commendation of the goods does not create a warranty.

§ 2–314. Implied Warranty: Merchantability; Usage of Trade.

(1) Unless excluded or modified (Section 2–316), a warranty that the goods shall be merchantable is implied in a contract for their sale if the seller is a merchant with respect to goods of that kind. Under this section the serving for value of food or drink to be consumed either on the premises or elsewhere is a sale.

(2) Goods to be merchantable must be at least such as

(a) pass without objection in the trade under the contract description; and

(b) in the case of fungible goods, are of fair average quality within the description; and

(c) are fit for the ordinary purposes for which such goods are used; and

(d) run, within the variations permitted by the agreement, of even kind, quality and quantity within each unit and among all units involved; and

(e) are adequately contained, packaged, and labeled as the agreement may require; and

(f) conform to the promises or affirmations of fact made on the container or label if any.

(3) Unless excluded or modified (Section 2–316) other implied warranties may arise from course of dealing or usage of trade.

§ 2–315. Implied Warranty: Fitness for Particular Purpose.

Where the seller at the time of contracting has reason to know any particular purpose for which the goods are required and that the buyer is relying on the seller's skill or judgment to select or furnish suitable goods, there is unless excluded or modified under the next section an implied warranty that the goods shall be fit for such purpose.

§ 2–316. Exclusion or Modification of Warranties.

(1) Words or conduct relevant to the creation of an express warranty and words or conduct tending to negate or limit warranty shall be construed wherever reasonable as consistent with each other; but subject to the provisions of this Article on parol or extrinsic evidence (Section 2–202) negation or limitation is inoperative to the extent that such construction is unreasonable.

(2) Subject to subsection (3), to exclude or modify the implied warranty of merchantability or any part of it the language must mention merchantability and in case of a writing must be conspicuous, and to exclude or modify any implied warranty of fitness the exclusion must be by a writing and conspicuous. Language to exclude all implied warranties of fitness is sufficient if it states, for example, that "There are no warranties which extend beyond the description on the face hereof."

(3) Notwithstanding subsection (2)

(a) unless the circumstances indicate otherwise, all implied warranties are excluded by expressions like "as is", "with all faults" or other language which in common understanding calls the buyer's attention to the exclusion of warranties and makes plain that there is no implied warranty; and

(b) when the buyer before entering into the contract has examined the goods or the sample or model as fully as he desired or has refused to examine the goods there is no implied warranty with regard to defects which an examination ought in the circumstances to have revealed to him; and

(c) an implied warranty can also be excluded or modified by course of dealing or course of performance or usage of trade.

(4) Remedies for breach of warranty can be limited in accordance with the provisions of this Article on liquidation or limitation of damages and on contractual modification of remedy (Sections 2–718 and 2–719).

§ 2–317. Cumulation and Conflict of Warranties Express or Implied.

Warranties whether express or implied shall be construed as consistent with each other and as cumulative, but if such construction is unreasonable the intention of the parties shall determine which warranty is dominant. In ascertaining that intention the following rules apply:

(a) Exact or technical specifications displace an inconsistent sample or model or general language of description.

(b) A sample from an existing bulk displaces inconsistent general language of description.

(c) Express warranties displace inconsistent implied warranties other than an implied warranty of fitness for a particular purpose.

§ 2–318. Third Party Beneficiaries of Warranties Express or Implied.

Note: If this Act is introduced in the Congress of the United States this section should be omitted. (States to select one alternative.)

Alternative A

A seller's warranty whether express or implied extends to any natural person who is in the family or household of his buyer or who is a guest in his home if it is reasonable to expect that such person may use, consume or be affected by the goods and who is injured in person by breach of the warranty. A seller may not exclude or limit the operation of this section.

Alternative B

A seller's warranty whether express or implied extends to any natural person who may reasonably be expected to use, consume or be affected by the goods and who is injured in person by breach of the warranty. A seller may not exclude or limit the operation of this section.

Alternative C

A seller's warranty whether express or implied extends to any person who may reasonably be expected to use, consume or be affected by the goods and who is injured by breach of the warranty. A seller may not exclude or limit the operation of this section with respect to injury to the person of an individual to whom the warranty extends.

As amended 1966.

§ 2–319. F.O.B. and F.A.S. Terms.

(1) Unless otherwise agreed the term F.O.B. (which means "free on board") at a named place, even though used only in connection with the stated price, is a delivery term under which

(a) when the term is F.O.B. the place of shipment, the seller must at that place ship the goods in the manner provided in this Article (Section 2–504) and bear the expense and risk of putting them into the possession of the carrier; or

(b) when the term is F.O.B. the place of destination, the seller must at his own expense and risk transport the goods to that place and there tender delivery of them in the manner provided in this Article (Section 2–503);

(c) when under either (a) or (b) the term is also F.O.B. vessel, car or other vehicle, the seller must in addition at his own expense and risk load the goods on board. If the term is F.O.B. vessel the buyer must name the vessel and in an appropriate case the seller must comply with the provisions of this Article on the form of bill of lading (Section 2–323).

(2) Unless otherwise agreed the term F.A.S. vessel (which means "free alongside") at a named port, even though used only in connection with the stated price, is a delivery term under which the seller must

(a) at his own expense and risk deliver the goods alongside the vessel in the manner usual in that port or on a dock designated and provided by the buyer; and

(b) obtain and tender a receipt for the goods in exchange for which the carrier is under a duty to issue a bill of lading.

(3) Unless otherwise agreed in any case falling within subsection (1)(a) or (c) or subsection (2) the buyer must seasonably give any needed instructions for making delivery, including when the term is F.A.S. or F.O.B. the loading berth of the vessel and in an appropriate case its name and sailing date. The seller may treat the failure of needed instructions as a failure of cooperation under this Article (Section 2–311). He may also at his option move the goods in any reasonable manner preparatory to delivery or shipment.

(4) Under the term F.O.B. vessel or F.A.S. unless otherwise agreed the buyer must make payment against tender of the required documents and the seller may not tender nor the buyer demand delivery of the goods in substitution for the documents.

§ 2–320. C.I.F. and C. & F. Terms.

(1) The term C.I.F. means that the price includes in a lump sum the cost of the goods and the insurance and freight to the named destination. The term C. & F. or C.F. means that the price so includes cost and freight to the named destination.

(2) Unless otherwise agreed and even though used only in connection with the stated price and destination, the term C.I.F. destination or its equivalent requires the seller at his own expense and risk to

(a) put the goods into the possession of a carrier at the port for shipment and obtain a negotiable bill or bills of lading covering the entire transportation to the named destination; and

(b) load the goods and obtain a receipt from the carrier (which may be contained in the bill of lading) showing that the freight has been paid or provided for; and

(c) obtain a policy or certificate of insurance, including any war risk insurance, of a kind and on terms then current at the port of shipment in the usual amount, in the currency of the contract, shown to cover the same goods covered by the bill of lading and providing for payment of loss to the order of the buyer or for the account of whom it may concern; but the seller may add to the price the amount of the premium for any such war risk insurance; and

(d) prepare an invoice of the goods and procure any other documents required to effect shipment or to comply with the contract; and

(e) forward and tender with commercial promptness all the documents in due form and with any indorsement necessary to perfect the buyer's rights.

(3) Unless otherwise agreed the term C. & F. or its equivalent has the same effect and imposes upon the seller the same obligations and risks as a C.I.F. term except the obligation as to insurance.

(4) Under the term C.I.F. or C. & F. unless otherwise agreed the buyer must make payment against tender of the required documents and the seller may not tender nor the buyer demand delivery of the goods in substitution for the documents.

§ 2–321. C.I.F. or C. & F.: "Net Landed Weights"; "Payment on Arrival"; Warranty of Condition on Arrival.

Under a contract containing a term C.I.F. or C. & F.

(1) Where the price is based on or is to be adjusted according to "net landed weights", "delivered weights", "out turn" quantity or quality or the like, unless otherwise agreed the seller must reasonably estimate the price. The payment due on tender of the documents called for by the contract is the amount so estimated, but after final adjustment of the price a settlement must be made with commercial promptness.

(2) An agreement described in subsection (1) or any warranty of quality or condition of the goods on arrival places upon the seller the risk of ordinary deterioration, shrinkage and the like in transportation but has no effect on the place or time of identification to the contract for sale or delivery or on the passing of the risk of loss.

(3) Unless otherwise agreed where the contract provides for payment on or after arrival of the goods the seller must before payment allow such preliminary inspection as is feasible; but if the goods are lost delivery of the documents and payment are due when the goods should have arrived.

§ 2–322. Delivery "Ex-Ship".

(1) Unless otherwise agreed a term for delivery of goods "ex-ship" (which means from the carrying vessel) or in equivalent language is not restricted to a particular ship and requires delivery from a ship which has reached a place at the named port of destination where goods of the kind are usually discharged.

(2) Under such a term unless otherwise agreed

(a) the seller must discharge all liens arising out of the carriage and furnish the buyer with a direction which puts the carrier under a duty to deliver the goods; and

(b) the risk of loss does not pass to the buyer until the goods leave the ship's tackle or are otherwise properly unloaded.

§ 2–323. Form of Bill of Lading Required in Overseas Shipment; "Overseas".

(1) Where the contract contemplates overseas shipment and contains a term C.I.F. or C. & F. or F.O.B. vessel, the seller unless otherwise agreed must obtain a negotiable bill of lading stating that the goods have been loaded on board or, in the case of a term C.I.F. or C. & F., received for shipment.

(2) Where in a case within subsection (1) a bill of lading has been issued in a set of parts, unless otherwise agreed if the documents are not to be sent from abroad the buyer may demand tender of the full set; otherwise only one part of the bill of lading need be tendered. Even if the agreement expressly requires a full set

(a) due tender of a single part is acceptable within the provisions of this Article on cure of improper delivery (subsection (1) of Section 2–508); and

(b) even though the full set is demanded, if the documents are sent from abroad the person tendering an incomplete set may nevertheless require payment upon furnishing an indemnity which the buyer in good faith deems adequate.

(3) A shipment by water or by air or a contract contemplating such shipment is "overseas" insofar as by usage of trade or agreement it is subject to the commercial, financing or shipping practices characteristic of international deep water commerce.

§ 2–324. "No Arrival, No Sale" Term.

Under a term "no arrival, no sale" or terms of like meaning, unless otherwise agreed,

(a) the seller must properly ship conforming goods and if they arrive by any means he must tender them on arrival but he assumes no obligation that the goods will arrive unless he has caused the non-arrival; and

(b) where without fault of the seller the goods are in part lost or have so deteriorated as no longer to conform to the contract or arrive after the contract time, the buyer may proceed as if there had been casualty to identified goods (Section 2–613).

§ 2–325. "Letter of Credit" Term; "Confirmed Credit".

(1) Failure of the buyer seasonably to furnish an agreed letter of credit is a breach of the contract for sale.

(2) The delivery to seller of a proper letter of credit suspends the buyer's obligation to pay. If the letter of credit is dishonored, the seller may on seasonable notification to the buyer require payment directly from him.

(3) Unless otherwise agreed the term "letter of credit" or "banker's credit" in a contract for sale means an irrevocable credit issued by a financing agency of good repute

and, where the shipment is overseas, of good international repute. The term "confirmed credit" means that the credit must also carry the direct obligation of such an agency which does business in the seller's financial market.

§ 2–326. Sale on Approval and Sale or Return; Rights of Creditors.

(1) Unless otherwise agreed, if delivered goods may be returned by the buyer even though they conform to the contract, the transaction is

(a) a "sale on approval" if the goods are delivered primarily for use, and

(b) a "sale or return" if the goods are delivered primarily for resale.

(2) Goods held on approval are not subject to the claims of the buyer's creditors until acceptance; goods held on sale or return are subject to such claims while in the buyer's possession.

(3) Any "or return" term of a contract for sale is to be treated as a separate contract for sale within the statute of frauds section of this Article (Section 2–201) and as contradicting the sale aspect of the contract within the provisions of this Article or on parol or extrinsic evidence (Section 2–202).

As amended in 1999.

§ 2–327. Special Incidents of Sale on Approval and Sale or Return.

(1) Under a sale on approval unless otherwise agreed

(a) although the goods are identified to the contract the risk of loss and the title do not pass to the buyer until acceptance; and

(b) use of the goods consistent with the purpose of trial is not acceptance but failure seasonably to notify the seller of election to return the goods is acceptance, and if the goods conform to the contract acceptance of any part is acceptance of the whole; and

(c) after due notification of election to return, the return is at the seller's risk and expense but a merchant buyer must follow any reasonable instructions.

(2) Under a sale or return unless otherwise agreed

(a) the option to return extends to the whole or any commercial unit of the goods while in substantially their original condition, but must be exercised seasonably; and

(b) the return is at the buyer's risk and expense.

§ 2–328. Sale by Auction.

(1) In a sale by auction if goods are put up in lots each lot is the subject of a separate sale.

(2) A sale by auction is complete when the auctioneer so announces by the fall of the hammer or in other customary manner. Where a bid is made while the hammer is falling in acceptance of a prior bid the auctioneer may in his discretion reopen the bidding or declare the goods sold under the bid on which the hammer was falling.

(3) Such a sale is with reserve unless the goods are in explicit terms put up without reserve. In an auction with reserve the auctioneer may withdraw the goods at any time until he announces completion of the sale. In an auction without reserve, after the auctioneer calls for bids on an article or lot, that article or lot cannot be withdrawn unless no bid is made within a reasonable time. In either case a bidder may retract his bid until the auctioneer's announcement of completion of the sale, but a bidder's retraction does not revive any previous bid.

(4) If the auctioneer knowingly receives a bid on the seller's behalf or the seller makes or procures such as bid, and notice has not been given that liberty for such bidding is reserved, the buyer may at his option avoid the sale or take the goods at the price of the last good faith bid prior to the completion of the sale. This subsection shall not apply to any bid at a forced sale.

Part 4 Title, Creditors and Good Faith Purchasers

§ 2–401. Passing of Title; Reservation for Security; Limited Application of This Section.

Each provision of this Article with regard to the rights, obligations and remedies of the seller, the buyer, purchasers or other third parties applies irrespective of title to the goods except where the provision refers to such title. Insofar as situations are not covered by the other provisions of this Article and matters concerning title became material the following rules apply:

(1) Title to goods cannot pass under a contract for sale prior to their identification to the contract (Section 2–501), and unless otherwise explicitly agreed the buyer acquires by their identification a special property as limited by this Act. Any retention or reservation by the seller of the title (property) in goods shipped or delivered to the buyer is limited in effect to a reservation of a security interest. Subject to these provisions and to the provisions of the Article on Secured Transactions (Article 9), title to goods passes from the seller to the buyer in any manner and on any conditions explicitly agreed on by the parties.

(2) Unless otherwise explicitly agreed title passes to the buyer at the time and place at which the seller completes his performance with reference to the physical delivery of the goods, despite any reservation of a security interest and even though a document of title is to be delivered at a different time or place; and in particular and despite any reservation of a security interest by the bill of lading

(a) if the contract requires or authorizes the seller to send the goods to the buyer but does not require him to deliver them at destination, title passes to the buyer at the time and place of shipment; but

(b) if the contract requires delivery at destination, title passes on tender there.

(3) Unless otherwise explicitly agreed where delivery is to be made without moving the goods,

(a) if the seller is to deliver a document of title, title passes at the time when and the place where he delivers such documents; or

(b) if the goods are at the time of contracting already identified and no documents are to be delivered, title passes at the time and place of contracting.

(4) A rejection or other refusal by the buyer to receive or retain the goods, whether or not justified, or a justified revocation of acceptance revests title to the goods in the seller. Such revesting occurs by operation of law and is not a "sale".

§ 2–402. Rights of Seller's Creditors Against Sold Goods.

(1) Except as provided in subsections (2) and (3), rights of unsecured creditors of the seller with respect to goods which have been identified to a contract for sale are subject to the buyer's rights to recover the goods under this Article (Sections 2–502 and 2–716).

(2) A creditor of the seller may treat a sale or an identification of goods to a contract for sale as void if as against him a retention of possession by the seller is fraudulent under any rule of law of the state where the goods are situated, except that retention of possession in good faith and current course of trade by a merchant-seller for a commercially reasonable time after a sale or identification is not fraudulent.

(3) Nothing in this Article shall be deemed to impair the rights of creditors of the seller

(a) under the provisions of the Article on Secured Transactions (Article 9); or

(b) where identification to the contract or delivery is made not in current course of trade but in satisfaction of or as security for a pre-existing claim for money, security or the like and is made under circumstances which under any rule of law of the state where the goods are situated would apart from this Article constitute the transaction a fraudulent transfer or voidable preference.

§ 2–403. Power to Transfer; Good Faith Purchase of Goods; "Entrusting".

(1) A purchaser of goods acquires all title which his transferor had or had power to transfer except that a purchaser of a limited interest acquires rights only to the extent of the interest purchased. A person with voidable title has power to transfer a good title to a good faith purchaser for value. When goods have been delivered under a transaction of purchase the purchaser has such power even though

(a) the transferor was deceived as to the identity of the purchaser, or

(b) the delivery was in exchange for a check which is later dishonored, or

(c) it was agreed that the transaction was to be a "cash sale", or

(d) the delivery was procured through fraud punishable as larcenous under the criminal law.

(2) Any entrusting of possession of goods to a merchant who deals in goods of that kind gives him power to transfer all rights of the entruster to a buyer in ordinary course of business.

(3) "Entrusting" includes any delivery and any acquiescence in retention of possession regardless of any condition expressed between the parties to the delivery or acquiescence and regardless of whether the procurement of the entrusting or the possessor's disposition of the goods have been such as to be larcenous under the criminal law.

(4) The rights of other purchasers of goods and of lien creditors are governed by the Articles on Secured Transactions (Article 9), Bulk Transfers (Article 6) and Documents of Title (Article 7).

As amended in 1988.

Part 5 Performance

§ 2–501. Insurable Interest in Goods; Manner of Identification of Goods.

(1) The buyer obtains a special property and an insurable interest in goods by identification of existing goods as goods to which the contract refers even though the goods so identified are non-conforming and he has an option to return or reject them. Such identification can be made at any time and in any manner explicitly agreed to by the parties. In the absence of explicit agreement identification occurs

(a) when the contract is made if it is for the sale of goods already existing and identified;

(b) if the contract is for the sale of future goods other than those described in paragraph (c), when goods are shipped, marked or otherwise designated by the seller as goods to which the contract refers;

(c) when the crops are planted or otherwise become growing crops or the young are conceived if the contract is for the sale of unborn young to be born within twelve months after contracting or for the sale of crops to be harvested within twelve months or the next normal harvest season after contracting whichever is longer.

(2) The seller retains an insurable interest in goods so long as title to or any security interest in the goods remains in him and where the identification is by the seller alone he may until default or insolvency or notification to the buyer that the identification is final substitute other goods for those identified.

(3) Nothing in this section impairs any insurable interest recognized under any other statute or rule of law.

§ 2–502. Buyer's Right to Goods on Seller's Insolvency.

(1) Subject to subsections (2) and (3) and even though the goods have not been shipped a buyer who has paid a part or all of the price of goods in which he has a special property under the provisions of the immediately

preceding section may on making and keeping good a tender of any unpaid portion of their price recover them from the seller if:

(a) in the case of goods bought for personal, family, or household purposes, the seller repudiates or fails to deliver as required by the contract; or

(b) in all cases, the seller becomes insolvent within ten days after receipt of the first installment on their price.

(2) The buyer's right to recover the goods under subsection (1)(a) vests upon acquisition of a special property, even if the seller had not then repudiated or failed to deliver.

(3) If the identification creating his special property has been made by the buyer he acquires the right to recover the goods only if they conform to the contract for sale.

As amended in 1999.

§ 2–503. Manner of Seller's Tender of Delivery.

(1) Tender of delivery requires that the seller put and hold conforming goods at the buyer's disposition and give the buyer any notification reasonably necessary to enable him to take delivery. The manner, time and place for tender are determined by the agreement and this Article, and in particular

(a) tender must be at a reasonable hour, and if it is of goods they must be kept available for the period reasonably necessary to enable the buyer to take possession; but

(b) unless otherwise agreed the buyer must furnish facilities reasonably suited to the receipt of the goods.

(2) Where the case is within the next section respecting shipment tender requires that the seller comply with its provisions.

(3) Where the seller is required to deliver at a particular destination tender requires that he comply with subsection (1) and also in any appropriate case tender documents as described in subsections (4) and (5) of this section.

(4) Where goods are in the possession of a bailee and are to be delivered without being moved

(a) tender requires that the seller either tender a negotiable document of title covering such goods or procure acknowledgment by the bailee of the buyer's right to possession of the goods; but

(b) tender to the buyer of a non-negotiable document of title or of a written direction to the bailee to deliver is sufficient tender unless the buyer seasonably objects, and receipt by the bailee of notification of the buyer's rights fixes those rights as against the bailee and all third persons; but risk of loss of the goods and of any failure by the bailee to honor the non-negotiable document of title or to obey the direction remains on the seller until the buyer has had a reasonable time to present the document or direction, and a refusal by the bailee to honor the document or to obey the direction defeats the tender.

(5) Where the contract requires the seller to deliver documents

(a) he must tender all such documents in correct form, except as provided in this Article with respect to bills of lading in a set (subsection (2) of Section 2–323); and

(b) tender through customary banking channels is sufficient and dishonor of a draft accompanying the documents constitutes non-acceptance or rejection.

§ 2–504. Shipment by Seller.

Where the seller is required or authorized to send the goods to the buyer and the contract does not require him to deliver them at a particular destination, then unless otherwise agreed he must

(a) put the goods in the possession of such a carrier and make such a contract for their transportation as may be reasonable having regard to the nature of the goods and other circumstances of the case; and

(b) obtain and promptly deliver or tender in due form any document necessary to enable the buyer to obtain possession of the goods or otherwise required by the agreement or by usage of trade; and

(c) promptly notify the buyer of the shipment.

Failure to notify the buyer under paragraph (c) or to make a proper contract under paragraph (a) is a ground for rejection only if material delay or loss ensues.

§ 2–505. Seller's Shipment under Reservation.

(1) Where the seller has identified goods to the contract by or before shipment:

(a) his procurement of a negotiable bill of lading to his own order or otherwise reserves in him a security interest in the goods. His procurement of the bill to the order of a financing agency or of the buyer indicates in addition only the seller's expectation of transferring that interest to the person named.

(b) a non-negotiable bill of lading to himself or his nominee reserves possession of the goods as security but except in a case of conditional delivery (subsection (2) of Section 2–507) a non-negotiable bill of lading naming the buyer as consignee reserves no security interest even though the seller retains possession of the bill of lading.

(2) When shipment by the seller with reservation of a security interest is in violation of the contract for sale it constitutes an improper contract for transportation within the preceding section but impairs neither the rights given to the buyer by shipment and identification of the goods to the contract nor the seller's powers as a holder of a negotiable document.

§ 2–506. Rights of Financing Agency.

(1) A financing agency by paying or purchasing for value a draft which relates to a shipment of goods acquires to the extent of the payment or purchase and in addition to its own rights under the draft and any document of title securing it any rights of the shipper in the goods includ-

ing the right to stop delivery and the shipper's right to have the draft honored by the buyer.

(2) The right to reimbursement of a financing agency which has in good faith honored or purchased the draft under commitment to or authority from the buyer is not impaired by subsequent discovery of defects with reference to any relevant document which was apparently regular on its face.

§ 2–507. Effect of Seller's Tender; Delivery on Condition.

(1) Tender of delivery is a condition to the buyer's duty to accept the goods and, unless otherwise agreed, to his duty to pay for them. Tender entitles the seller to acceptance of the goods and to payment according to the contract.

(2) Where payment is due and demanded on the delivery to the buyer of goods or documents of title, his right as against the seller to retain or dispose of them is conditional upon his making the payment due.

§ 2–508. Cure by Seller of Improper Tender or Delivery; Replacement.

(1) Where any tender or delivery by the seller is rejected because non-conforming and the time for performance has not yet expired, the seller may seasonably notify the buyer of his intention to cure and may then within the contract time make a conforming delivery.

(2) Where the buyer rejects a non-conforming tender which the seller had reasonable grounds to believe would be acceptable with or without money allowance the seller may if he seasonably notifies the buyer have a further reasonable time to substitute a conforming tender.

§ 2–509. Risk of Loss in the Absence of Breach.

(1) Where the contract requires or authorizes the seller to ship the goods by carrier

(a) if it does not require him to deliver them at a particular destination, the risk of loss passes to the buyer when the goods are duly delivered to the carrier even though the shipment is under reservation (Section 2–505); but

(b) if it does require him to deliver them at a particular destination and the goods are there duly tendered while in the possession of the carrier, the risk of loss passes to the buyer when the goods are there duly so tendered as to enable the buyer to take delivery.

(2) Where the goods are held by a bailee to be delivered without being moved, the risk of loss passes to the buyer

(a) on his receipt of a negotiable document of title covering the goods; or

(b) on acknowledgment by the bailee of the buyer's right to possession of the goods; or

(c) after his receipt of a non-negotiable document of title or other written direction to deliver, as provided in subsection (4)(b) of Section 2–503.

(3) In any case not within subsection (1) or (2), the risk of loss passes to the buyer on his receipt of the goods if the seller is a merchant; otherwise the risk passes to the buyer on tender of delivery.

(4) The provisions of this section are subject to contrary agreement of the parties and to the provisions of this Article on sale on approval (Section 2–327) and on effect of breach on risk of loss (Section 2–510).

§ 2–510. Effect of Breach on Risk of Loss.

(1) Where a tender or delivery of goods so fails to conform to the contract as to give a right of rejection the risk of their loss remains on the seller until cure or acceptance.

(2) Where the buyer rightfully revokes acceptance he may to the extent of any deficiency in his effective insurance coverage treat the risk of loss as having rested on the seller from the beginning.

(3) Where the buyer as to conforming goods already identified to the contract for sale repudiates or is otherwise in breach before risk of their loss has passed to him, the seller may to the extent of any deficiency in his effective insurance coverage treat the risk of loss as resting on the buyer for a commercially reasonable time.

§ 2–511. Tender of Payment by Buyer; Payment by Check.

(1) Unless otherwise agreed tender of payment is a condition to the seller's duty to tender and complete any delivery.

(2) Tender of payment is sufficient when made by any means or in any manner current in the ordinary course of business unless the seller demands payment in legal tender and gives any extension of time reasonably necessary to procure it.

(3) Subject to the provisions of this Act on the effect of an instrument on an obligation (Section 3–310), payment by check is conditional and is defeated as between the parties by dishonor of the check on due presentment.

As amended in 1994.

§ 2–512. Payment by Buyer Before Inspection.

(1) Where the contract requires payment before inspection non-conformity of the goods does not excuse the buyer from so making payment unless

(a) the non-conformity appears without inspection; or

(b) despite tender of the required documents the circumstances would justify injunction against honor under this Act (Section 5–109(b)).

(2) Payment pursuant to subsection (1) does not constitute an acceptance of goods or impair the buyer's right to inspect or any of his remedies.

As amended in 1995.

§ 2–513. Buyer's Right to Inspection of Goods.

(1) Unless otherwise agreed and subject to subsection (3), where goods are tendered or delivered or identified to the contract for sale, the buyer has a right before payment or acceptance to inspect them at any reasonable place and time and in any reasonable manner. When the seller is required or authorized to send the goods to the buyer, the inspection may be after their arrival.

(2) Expenses of inspection must be borne by the buyer but may be recovered from the seller if the goods do not conform and are rejected.

(3) Unless otherwise agreed and subject to the provisions of this Article on C.I.F. contracts (subsection (3) of Section 2–321), the buyer is not entitled to inspect the goods before payment of the price when the contract provides

(a) for delivery "C.O.D." or on other like terms; or

(b) for payment against documents of title, except where such payment is due only after the goods are to become available for inspection.

(4) A place or method of inspection fixed by the parties is presumed to be exclusive but unless otherwise expressly agreed it does not postpone identification or shift the place for delivery or for passing the risk of loss. If compliance becomes impossible, inspection shall be as provided in this section unless the place or method fixed was clearly intended as an indispensable condition failure of which avoids the contract.

§ 2–514. When Documents Deliverable on Acceptance; When on Payment.

Unless otherwise agreed documents against which a draft is drawn are to be delivered to the drawee on acceptance of the draft if it is payable more than three days after presentment; otherwise, only on payment.

§ 2–515. Preserving Evidence of Goods in Dispute.

In furtherance of the adjustment of any claim or dispute

(a) either party on reasonable notification to the other and for the purpose of ascertaining the facts and preserving evidence has the right to inspect, test and sample the goods including such of them as may be in the possession or control of the other; and

(b) the parties may agree to a third party inspection or survey to determine the conformity or condition of the goods and may agree that the findings shall be binding upon them in any subsequent litigation or adjustment.

Part 6 Breach, Repudiation and Excuse

§ 2–601. Buyer's Rights on Improper Delivery.

Subject to the provisions of this Article on breach in installment contracts (Section 2–612) and unless otherwise agreed under the sections on contractual limitations of remedy (Sections 2–718 and 2–719), if the goods or the tender of delivery fail in any respect to conform to the contract, the buyer may

(a) reject the whole; or

(b) accept the whole; or

(c) accept any commercial unit or units and reject the rest.

§ 2–602. Manner and Effect of Rightful Rejection.

(1) Rejection of goods must be within a reasonable time after their delivery or tender. It is ineffective unless the buyer seasonably notifies the seller.

(2) Subject to the provisions of the two following sections on rejected goods (Sections 2–603 and 2–604),

(a) after rejection any exercise of ownership by the buyer with respect to any commercial unit is wrongful as against the seller; and

(b) if the buyer has before rejection taken physical possession of goods in which he does not have a security interest under the provisions of this Article (subsection (3) of Section 2–711), he is under a duty after rejection to hold them with reasonable care at the seller's disposition for a time sufficient to permit the seller to remove them; but

(c) the buyer has no further obligations with regard to goods rightfully rejected.

(3) The seller's rights with respect to goods wrongfully rejected are governed by the provisions of this Article on Seller's remedies in general (Section 2–703).

§ 2–603. Merchant Buyer's Duties as to Rightfully Rejected Goods.

(1) Subject to any security interest in the buyer (subsection (3) of Section 2–711), when the seller has no agent or place of business at the market of rejection a merchant buyer is under a duty after rejection of goods in his possession or control to follow any reasonable instructions received from the seller with respect to the goods and in the absence of such instructions to make reasonable efforts to sell them for the seller's account if they are perishable or threaten to decline in value speedily. Instructions are not reasonable if on demand indemnity for expenses is not forthcoming.

(2) When the buyer sells goods under subsection (1), he is entitled to reimbursement from the seller or out of the proceeds for reasonable expenses of caring for and selling them, and if the expenses include no selling commission then to such commission as is usual in the trade or if there is none to a reasonable sum not exceeding ten per cent on the gross proceeds.

(3) In complying with this section the buyer is held only to good faith and good faith conduct hereunder is neither acceptance nor conversion nor the basis of an action for damages.

§ 2–604. Buyer's Options as to Salvage of Rightfully Rejected Goods.

Subject to the provisions of the immediately preceding section on perishables if the seller gives no instructions within a reasonable time after notification of rejection the buyer may store the rejected goods for the seller's account or reship them to him or resell them for the seller's account with reimbursement as provided in the preceding section. Such action is not acceptance or conversion.

§ 2–605. Waiver of Buyer's Objections by Failure to Particularize.

(1) The buyer's failure to state in connection with rejection a particular defect which is ascertainable by reason-

able inspection precludes him from relying on the unstated defect to justify rejection or to establish breach

(a) where the seller could have cured it if stated seasonably; or

(b) between merchants when the seller has after rejection made a request in writing for a full and final written statement of all defects on which the buyer proposes to rely.

(2) Payment against documents made without reservation of rights precludes recovery of the payment for defects apparent on the face of the documents.

§ 2–606. What Constitutes Acceptance of Goods.

(1) Acceptance of goods occurs when the buyer

(a) after a reasonable opportunity to inspect the goods signifies to the seller that the goods are conforming or that he will take or retain them in spite of their nonconformity; or

(b) fails to make an effective rejection (subsection (1) of Section 2–602), but such acceptance does not occur until the buyer has had a reasonable opportunity to inspect them; or

(c) does any act inconsistent with the seller's ownership; but if such act is wrongful as against the seller it is an acceptance only if ratified by him.

(2) Acceptance of a part of any commercial unit is acceptance of that entire unit.

§ 2–607. Effect of Acceptance; Notice of Breach; Burden of Establishing Breach After Acceptance; Notice of Claim or Litigation to Person Answerable Over.

(1) The buyer must pay at the contract rate for any goods accepted.

(2) Acceptance of goods by the buyer precludes rejection of the goods accepted and if made with knowledge of a non-conformity cannot be revoked because of it unless the acceptance was on the reasonable assumption that the non-conformity would be seasonably cured but acceptance does not of itself impair any other remedy provided by this Article for non-conformity.

(3) Where a tender has been accepted

(a) the buyer must within a reasonable time after he discovers or should have discovered any breach notify the seller of breach or be barred from any remedy; and

(b) if the claim is one for infringement or the like (subsection (3) of Section 2–312) and the buyer is sued as a result of such a breach he must so notify the seller within a reasonable time after he receives notice of the litigation or be barred from any remedy over for liability established by the litigation.

(4) The burden is on the buyer to establish any breach with respect to the goods accepted.

(5) Where the buyer is sued for breach of a warranty or other obligation for which his seller is answerable over

(a) he may give his seller written notice of the litigation. If the notice states that the seller may come in and defend and that if the seller does not do so he will be bound in any action against him by his buyer by any determination of fact common to the two litigations, then unless the seller after seasonable receipt of the notice does come in and defend he is so bound.

(b) if the claim is one for infringement or the like (subsection (3) of Section 2–312) the original seller may demand in writing that his buyer turn over to him control of the litigation including settlement or else be barred from any remedy over and if he also agrees to bear all expense and to satisfy any adverse judgment, then unless the buyer after seasonable receipt of the demand does turn over control the buyer is so barred.

(6) The provisions of subsections (3), (4) and (5) apply to any obligation of a buyer to hold the seller harmless against infringement or the like (subsection (3) of Section 2–312).

§ 2–608. Revocation of Acceptance in Whole or in Part.

(1) The buyer may revoke his acceptance of a lot or commercial unit whose non-conformity substantially impairs its value to him if he has accepted it

(a) on the reasonable assumption that its nonconformity would be cured and it has not been seasonably cured; or

(b) without discovery of such non-conformity if his acceptance was reasonably induced either by the difficulty of discovery before acceptance or by the seller's assurances.

(2) Revocation of acceptance must occur within a reasonable time after the buyer discovers or should have discovered the ground for it and before any substantial change in condition of the goods which is not caused by their own defects. It is not effective until the buyer notifies the seller of it.

(3) A buyer who so revokes has the same rights and duties with regard to the goods involved as if he had rejected them.

§ 2–609. Right to Adequate Assurance of Performance.

(1) A contract for sale imposes an obligation on each party that the other's expectation of receiving due performance will not be impaired. When reasonable grounds for insecurity arise with respect to the performance of either party the other may in writing demand adequate assurance of due performance and until he receives such assurance may if commercially reasonable suspend any performance for which he has not already received the agreed return.

(2) Between merchants the reasonableness of grounds for insecurity and the adequacy of any assurance offered shall be determined according to commercial standards.

(3) Acceptance of any improper delivery or payment does not prejudice the party's right to demand adequate assurance of future performance.

(4) After receipt of a justified demand failure to provide within a reasonable time not exceeding thirty days such assurance of due performance as is adequate under the circumstances of the particular case is a repudiation of the contract.

§ 2–610. Anticipatory Repudiation.

When either party repudiates the contract with respect to a performance not yet due the loss of which will substantially impair the value of the contract to the other, the aggrieved party may

(a) for a commercially reasonable time await performance by the repudiating party; or

(b) resort to any remedy for breach (Section 2–703 or Section 2–711), even though he has notified the repudiating party that he would await the latter's performance and has urged retraction; and

(c) in either case suspend his own performance or proceed in accordance with the provisions of this Article on the seller's right to identify goods to the contract notwithstanding breach or to salvage unfinished goods (Section 2–704).

§ 2–611. Retraction of Anticipatory Repudiation.

(1) Until the repudiating party's next performance is due he can retract his repudiation unless the aggrieved party has since the repudiation cancelled or materially changed his position or otherwise indicated that he considers the repudiation final.

(2) Retraction may be by any method which clearly indicates to the aggrieved party that the repudiating party intends to perform, but must include any assurance justifiably demanded under the provisions of this Article (Section 2–609).

(3) Retraction reinstates the repudiating party's rights under the contract with due excuse and allowance to the aggrieved party for any delay occasioned by the repudiation.

§ 2–612. "Installment Contract"; Breach.

(1) An "installment contract" is one which requires or authorizes the delivery of goods in separate lots to be separately accepted, even though the contract contains a clause "each delivery is a separate contract" or its equivalent.

(2) The buyer may reject any installment which is non-conforming if the non-conformity substantially impairs the value of that installment and cannot be cured or if the non-conformity is a defect in the required documents; but if the non-conformity does not fall within subsection (3) and the seller gives adequate assurance of its cure the buyer must accept that installment.

(3) Whenever non-conformity or default with respect to one or more installments substantially impairs the value of the whole contract there is a breach of the whole. But the aggrieved party reinstates the contract if he accepts a non-conforming installment without seasonably notifying of cancellation or if he brings an action with respect only to past installments or demands performance as to future installments.

§ 2–613. Casualty to Identified Goods.

Where the contract requires for its performance goods identified when the contract is made, and the goods suffer casualty without fault of either party before the risk of loss passes to the buyer, or in a proper case under a "no arrival, no sale" term (Section 2–324) then

(a) if the loss is total the contract is avoided; and

(b) if the loss is partial or the goods have so deteriorated as no longer to conform to the contract the buyer may nevertheless demand inspection and at his option either treat the contract as voided or accept the goods with due allowance from the contract price for the deterioration or the deficiency in quantity but without further right against the seller.

§ 2–614. Substituted Performance.

(1) Where without fault of either party the agreed berthing, loading, or unloading facilities fail or an agreed type of carrier becomes unavailable or the agreed manner of delivery otherwise becomes commercially impracticable but a commercially reasonable substitute is available, such substitute performance must be tendered and accepted.

(2) If the agreed means or manner of payment fails because of domestic or foreign governmental regulation, the seller may withhold or stop delivery unless the buyer provides a means or manner of payment which is commercially a substantial equivalent. If delivery has already been taken, payment by the means or in the manner provided by the regulation discharges the buyer's obligation unless the regulation is discriminatory, oppressive or predatory.

§ 2–615. Excuse by Failure of Presupposed Conditions.

Except so far as a seller may have assumed a greater obligation and subject to the preceding section on substituted performance:

(a) Delay in delivery or non-delivery in whole or in part by a seller who complies with paragraphs (b) and (c) is not a breach of his duty under a contract for sale if performance as agreed has been made impracticable by the occurrence of a contingency the nonoccurrence of which was a basic assumption on which the contract was made or by compliance in good faith with any applicable foreign or domestic governmental regulation or order whether or not it later proves to be invalid.

(b) Where the causes mentioned in paragraph (a) affect only a part of the seller's capacity to perform, he must allocate production and deliveries among his customers but may at his option include regular customers not then under contract as well as his own requirements for further manufacture. He may so allocate in any manner which is fair and reasonable.

(c) The seller must notify the buyer seasonably that there will be delay or non-delivery and, when allocation is required under paragraph (b), of the estimated quota thus made available for the buyer.

§ 2–616. Procedure on Notice Claiming Excuse.

(1) Where the buyer receives notification of a material or indefinite delay or an allocation justified under the preceding section he may by written notification to the seller as to any delivery concerned, and where the prospective deficiency substantially impairs the value of the whole contract under the provisions of this Article relating to breach of installment contracts (Section 2–612), then also as to the whole,

(a) terminate and thereby discharge any unexecuted portion of the contract; or

(b) modify the contract by agreeing to take his available quota in substitution.

(2) If after receipt of such notification from the seller the buyer fails so to modify the contract within a reasonable time not exceeding thirty days the contract lapses with respect to any deliveries affected.

(3) The provisions of this section may not be negated by agreement except in so far as the seller has assumed a greater obligation under the preceding section.

Part 7 Remedies

§ 2–701. Remedies for Breach of Collateral Contracts Not Impaired.

Remedies for breach of any obligation or promise collateral or ancillary to a contract for sale are not impaired by the provisions of this Article.

§ 2–702. Seller's Remedies on Discovery of Buyer's Insolvency.

(1) Where the seller discovers the buyer to be insolvent he may refuse delivery except for cash including payment for all goods theretofore delivered under the contract, and stop delivery under this Article (Section 2–705).

(2) Where the seller discovers that the buyer has received goods on credit while insolvent he may reclaim the goods upon demand made within ten days after the receipt, but if misrepresentation of solvency has been made to the particular seller in writing within three months before delivery the ten day limitation does not apply. Except as provided in this subsection the seller may not base a right to reclaim goods on the buyer's fraudulent or innocent misrepresentation of solvency or of intent to pay.

(3) The seller's right to reclaim under subsection (2) is subject to the rights of a buyer in ordinary course or other good faith purchaser under this Article (Section 2–403). Successful reclamation of goods excludes all other remedies with respect to them.

§ 2–703. Seller's Remedies in General.

Where the buyer wrongfully rejects or revokes acceptance of goods or fails to make a payment due on or before delivery or repudiates with respect to a part or the whole, then with respect to any goods directly affected and, if the breach is of the whole contract (Section 2–612), then also with respect to the whole undelivered balance, the aggrieved seller may

(a) withhold delivery of such goods;

(b) stop delivery by any bailee as hereafter provided (Section 2–705);

(c) proceed under the next section respecting goods still unidentified to the contract;

(d) resell and recover damages as hereafter provided (Section 2–706);

(e) recover damages for non-acceptance (Section 2–708) or in a proper case the price (Section 2–709);

(f) cancel.

§ 2–704. Seller's Right to Identify Goods to the Contract Notwithstanding Breach or to Salvage Unfinished Goods.

(1) An aggrieved seller under the preceding section may

(a) identify to the contract conforming goods not already identified if at the time he learned of the breach they are in his possession or control;

(b) treat as the subject of resale goods which have demonstrably been intended for the particular contract even though those goods are unfinished.

(2) Where the goods are unfinished an aggrieved seller may in the exercise of reasonable commercial judgment for the purposes of avoiding loss and of effective realization either complete the manufacture and wholly identify the goods to the contract or cease manufacture and resell for scrap or salvage value or proceed in any other reasonable manner.

§ 2–705. Seller's Stoppage of Delivery in Transit or Otherwise.

(1) The seller may stop delivery of goods in the possession of a carrier or other bailee when he discovers the buyer to be insolvent (Section 2–702) and may stop delivery of carload, truckload, planeload or larger shipments of express or freight when the buyer repudiates or fails to make a payment due before delivery or if for any other reason the seller has a right to withhold or reclaim the goods.

(2) As against such buyer the seller may stop delivery until

(a) receipt of the goods by the buyer; or

(b) acknowledgment to the buyer by any bailee of the goods except a carrier that the bailee holds the goods for the buyer; or

(c) such acknowledgment to the buyer by a carrier by reshipment or as warehouseman; or

(d) negotiation to the buyer of any negotiable document of title covering the goods.

(3) (a) To stop delivery the seller must so notify as to enable the bailee by reasonable diligence to prevent delivery of the goods.

(b) After such notification the bailee must hold and deliver the goods according to the directions of the seller but the seller is liable to the bailee for any ensuing charges or damages.

(c) If a negotiable document of title has been issued for goods the bailee is not obliged to obey a notification to stop until surrender of the document.

(d) A carrier who has issued a non-negotiable bill of lading is not obliged to obey a notification to stop received from a person other than the consignor.

§ 2–706. Seller's Resale Including Contract for Resale.

(1) Under the conditions stated in Section 2–703 on seller's remedies, the seller may resell the goods concerned or the undelivered balance thereof. Where the resale is made in good faith and in a commercially reasonable manner the seller may recover the difference between the resale price and the contract price together with any incidental damages allowed under the provisions of this Article (Section 2–710), but less expenses saved in consequence of the buyer's breach.

(2) Except as otherwise provided in subsection (3) or unless otherwise agreed resale may be at public or private sale including sale by way of one or more contracts to sell or of identification to an existing contract of the seller. Sale may be as a unit or in parcels and at any time and place and on any terms but every aspect of the sale including the method, manner, time, place and terms must be commercially reasonable. The resale must be reasonably identified as referring to the broken contract, but it is not necessary that the goods be in existence or that any or all of them have been identified to the contract before the breach.

(3) Where the resale is at private sale the seller must give the buyer reasonable notification of his intention to resell.

(4) Where the resale is at public sale

(a) only identified goods can be sold except where there is a recognized market for a public sale of futures in goods of the kind; and

(b) it must be made at a usual place or market for public sale if one is reasonably available and except in the case of goods which are perishable or threaten to decline in value speedily the seller must give the buyer reasonable notice of the time and place of the resale; and

(c) if the goods are not to be within the view of those attending the sale the notification of sale must state the place where the goods are located and provide for their reasonable inspection by prospective bidders; and

(d) the seller may buy.

(5) A purchaser who buys in good faith at a resale takes the goods free of any rights of the original buyer even though the seller fails to comply with one or more of the requirements of this section.

(6) The seller is not accountable to the buyer for any profit made on any resale. A person in the position of a seller (Section 2–707) or a buyer who has rightfully rejected or justifiably revoked acceptance must account for any excess over the amount of his security interest, as hereinafter defined (subsection (3) of Section 2–711).

§ 2–707. "Person in the Position of a Seller".

(1) A "person in the position of a seller" includes as against a principal an agent who has paid or become responsible for the price of goods on behalf of his principal or anyone who otherwise holds a security interest or other right in goods similar to that of a seller.

(2) A person in the position of a seller may as provided in this Article withhold or stop delivery (Section 2–705) and resell (Section 2–706) and recover incidental damages (Section 2–710).

§ 2–708. Seller's Damages for Non-Acceptance or Repudiation.

(1) Subject to subsection (2) and to the provisions of this Article with respect to proof of market price (Section 2–723), the measure of damages for non-acceptance or repudiation by the buyer is the difference between the market price at the time and place for tender and the unpaid contract price together with any incidental damages provided in this Article (Section 2–710), but less expenses saved in consequence of the buyer's breach.

(2) If the measure of damages provided in subsection (1) is inadequate to put the seller in as good a position as performance would have done then the measure of damages is the profit (including reasonable overhead) which the seller would have made from full performance by the buyer, together with any incidental damages provided in this Article (Section 2–710), due allowance for costs reasonably incurred and due credit for payments or proceeds of resale.

§ 2–709. Action for the Price.

(1) When the buyer fails to pay the price as it becomes due the seller may recover, together with any incidental damages under the next section, the price

(a) of goods accepted or of conforming goods lost or damaged within a commercially reasonable time after risk of their loss has passed to the buyer; and

(b) of goods identified to the contract if the seller is unable after reasonable effort to resell them at a reasonable price or the circumstances reasonably indicate that such effort will be unavailing.

(2) Where the seller sues for the price he must hold for the buyer any goods which have been identified to the contract and are still in his control except that if resale becomes possible he may resell them at any time prior to the collection of the judgment. The net proceeds of any such resale must be credited to the buyer and payment of the judgment entitles him to any goods not resold.

(3) After the buyer has wrongfully rejected or revoked acceptance of the goods or has failed to make a payment due or has repudiated (Section 2–610), a seller who is held not entitled to the price under this section shall nevertheless be awarded damages for non-acceptance under the preceding section.

§ 2–710. Seller's Incidental Damages.

Incidental damages to an aggrieved seller include any commercially reasonable charges, expenses or commissions incurred in stopping delivery, in the transportation, care and custody of goods after the buyer's breach, in connection with return or resale of the goods or otherwise resulting from the breach.

§ 2–711. Buyer's Remedies in General; Buyer's Security Interest in Rejected Goods.

(1) Where the seller fails to make delivery or repudiates or the buyer rightfully rejects or justifiably revokes acceptance then with respect to any goods involved, and with respect to the whole if the breach goes to the whole contract (Section 2–612), the buyer may cancel and whether or not he has done so may in addition to recovering so much of the price as has been paid

(a) "cover" and have damages under the next section as to all the goods affected whether or not they have been identified to the contract; or

(b) recover damages for non-delivery as provided in this Article (Section 2–713).

(2) Where the seller fails to deliver or repudiates the buyer may also

(a) if the goods have been identified recover them as provided in this Article (Section 2–502); or

(b) in a proper case obtain specific performance or replevy the goods as provided in this Article (Section 2–716).

(3) On rightful rejection or justifiable revocation of acceptance a buyer has a security interest in goods in his possession or control for any payments made on their price and any expenses reasonably incurred in their inspection, receipt, transportation, care and custody and may hold such goods and resell them in like manner as an aggrieved seller (Section 2–706).

§ 2–712. "Cover"; Buyer's Procurement of Substitute Goods.

(1) After a breach within the preceding section the buyer may "cover" by making in good faith and without unreasonable delay any reasonable purchase of or contract to purchase goods in substitution for those due from the seller.

(2) The buyer may recover from the seller as damages the difference between the cost of cover and the contract price together with any incidental or consequential damages as hereinafter defined (Section 2–715), but less expenses saved in consequence of the seller's breach.

(3) Failure of the buyer to effect cover within this section does not bar him from any other remedy.

§ 2–713. Buyer's Damages for Non-Delivery or Repudiation.

(1) Subject to the provisions of this Article with respect to proof of market price (Section 2–723), the measure of damages for non-delivery or repudiation by the seller is the difference between the market price at the time when the buyer learned of the breach and the contract price together with any incidental and consequential damages provided in this Article (Section 2–715), but less expenses saved in consequence of the seller's breach.

(2) Market price is to be determined as of the place for tender or, in cases of rejection after arrival or revocation of acceptance, as of the place of arrival.

§ 2–714. Buyer's Damages for Breach in Regard to Accepted Goods.

(1) Where the buyer has accepted goods and given notification (subsection (3) of Section 2–607) he may recover as damages for any non-conformity of tender the loss resulting in the ordinary course of events from the seller's breach as determined in any manner which is reasonable.

(2) The measure of damages for breach of warranty is the difference at the time and place of acceptance between the value of the goods accepted and the value they would have had if they had been as warranted, unless special circumstances show proximate damages of a different amount.

(3) In a proper case any incidental and consequential damages under the next section may also be recovered.

§ 2–715. Buyer's Incidental and Consequential Damages.

(1) Incidental damages resulting from the seller's breach include expenses reasonably incurred in inspection, receipt, transportation and care and custody of goods rightfully rejected, any commercially reasonable charges, expenses or commissions in connection with effecting cover and any other reasonable expense incident to the delay or other breach.

(2) Consequential damages resulting from the seller's breach include

(a) any loss resulting from general or particular requirements and needs of which the seller at the time of contracting had reason to know and which could not reasonably be prevented by cover or otherwise; and

(b) injury to person or property proximately resulting from any breach of warranty.

§ 2–716. Buyer's Right to Specific Performance or Replevin.

(1) Specific performance may be decreed where the goods are unique or in other proper circumstances.

(2) The decree for specific performance may include such terms and conditions as to payment of the price, damages, or other relief as the court may deem just.

(3) The buyer has a right of replevin for goods identified to the contract if after reasonable effort he is unable to

effect cover for such goods or the circumstances reasonably indicate that such effort will be unavailing or if the goods have been shipped under reservation and satisfaction of the security interest in them has been made or tendered. In the case of goods bought for personal, family, or household purposes, the buyer's right of replevin vests upon acquisition of a special property, even if the seller had not then repudiated or failed to deliver.

As amended in 1999.

§ 2–717. Deduction of Damages From the Price.

The buyer on notifying the seller of his intention to do so may deduct all or any part of the damages resulting from any breach of the contract from any part of the price still due under the same contract.

§ 2–718. Liquidation or Limitation of Damages; Deposits.

(1) Damages for breach by either party may be liquidated in the agreement but only at an amount which is reasonable in the light of the anticipated or actual harm caused by the breach, the difficulties of proof of loss, and the inconvenience or nonfeasibility of otherwise obtaining an adequate remedy. A term fixing unreasonably large liquidated damages is void as a penalty.

(2) Where the seller justifiably withholds delivery of goods because of the buyer's breach, the buyer is entitled to restitution of any amount by which the sum of his payments exceeds

(a) the amount to which the seller is entitled by virtue of terms liquidating the seller's damages in accordance with subsection (1), or

(b) in the absence of such terms, twenty per cent of the value of the total performance for which the buyer is obligated under the contract or $500, whichever is smaller.

(3) The buyer's right to restitution under subsection (2) is subject to offset to the extent that the seller establishes

(a) a right to recover damages under the provisions of this Article other than subsection (1), and

(b) the amount or value of any benefits received by the buyer directly or indirectly by reason of the contract.

(4) Where a seller has received payment in goods their reasonable value or the proceeds of their resale shall be treated as payments for the purposes of subsection (2); but if the seller has notice of the buyer's breach before reselling goods received in part performance, his resale is subject to the conditions laid down in this Article on resale by an aggrieved seller (Section 2–706).

§ 2–719. Contractual Modification or Limitation of Remedy.

(1) Subject to the provisions of subsections (2) and (3) of this section and of the preceding section on liquidation and limitation of damages,

(a) the agreement may provide for remedies in addition to or in substitution for those provided in this Article and may limit or alter the measure of damages recoverable under this Article, as by limiting the buyer's remedies to return of the goods and repayment of the price or to repair and replacement of nonconforming goods or parts; and

(b) resort to a remedy as provided is optional unless the remedy is expressly agreed to be exclusive, in which case it is the sole remedy.

(2) Where circumstances cause an exclusive or limited remedy to fail of its essential purpose, remedy may be had as provided in this Act.

(3) Consequential damages may be limited or excluded unless the limitation or exclusion is unconscionable. Limitation of consequential damages for injury to the person in the case of consumer goods is prima facie unconscionable but limitation of damages where the loss is commercial is not.

§ 2–720. Effect of "Cancellation" or "Rescission" on Claims for Antecedent Breach.

Unless the contrary intention clearly appears, expressions of "cancellation" or "rescission" of the contract or the like shall not be construed as a renunciation or discharge of any claim in damages for an antecedent breach.

§ 2–721. Remedies for Fraud.

Remedies for material misrepresentation or fraud include all remedies available under this Article for nonfraudulent breach. Neither rescission or a claim for rescission of the contract for sale nor rejection or return of the goods shall bar or be deemed inconsistent with a claim for damages or other remedy.

§ 2–722. Who Can Sue Third Parties for Injury to Goods.

Where a third party so deals with goods which have been identified to a contract for sale as to cause actionable injury to a party to that contract

(a) a right of action against the third party is in either party to the contract for sale who has title to or a security interest or a special property or an insurable interest in the goods; and if the goods have been destroyed or converted a right of action is also in the party who either bore the risk of loss under the contract for sale or has since the injury assumed that risk as against the other;

(b) if at the time of the injury the party plaintiff did not bear the risk of loss as against the other party to the contract for sale and there is no arrangement between them for disposition of the recovery, his suit or settlement is, subject to his own interest, as a fiduciary for the other party to the contract;

(c) either party may with the consent of the other sue for the benefit of whom it may concern.

§ 2–723. Proof of Market Price: Time and Place.

(1) If an action based on anticipatory repudiation comes to trial before the time for performance with respect to some or all of the goods, any damages based on market price (Section 2–708 or Section 2–713) shall be determined according to the price of such goods pre-

vailing at the time when the aggrieved party learned of the repudiation.

(2) If evidence of a price prevailing at the times or places described in this Article is not readily available the price prevailing within any reasonable time before or after the time described or at any other place which in commercial judgment or under usage of trade would serve as a reasonable substitute for the one described may be used, making any proper allowance for the cost of transporting the goods to or from such other place.

(3) Evidence of a relevant price prevailing at a time or place other than the one described in this Article offered by one party is not admissible unless and until he has given the other party such notice as the court finds sufficient to prevent unfair surprise.

§ 2–724. Admissibility of Market Quotations.

Whenever the prevailing price or value of any goods regularly bought and sold in any established commodity market is in issue, reports in official publications or trade journals or in newspapers or periodicals of general circulation published as the reports of such market shall be admissible in evidence. The circumstances of the preparation of such a report may be shown to affect its weight but not its admissibility.

§ 2–725. Statute of Limitations in Contracts for Sale.

(1) An action for breach of any contract for sale must be commenced within four years after the cause of action has accrued. By the original agreement the parties may reduce the period of limitation to not less than one year but may not extend it.

(2) A cause of action accrues when the breach occurs, regardless of the aggrieved party's lack of knowledge of the breach. A breach of warranty occurs when tender of delivery is made, except that where a warranty explicitly extends to future performance of the goods and discovery of the breach must await the time of such performance the cause of action accrues when the breach is or should have been discovered.

(3) Where an action commenced within the time limited by subsection (1) is so terminated as to leave available a remedy by another action for the same breach such other action may be commenced after the expiration of the time limited and within six months after the termination of the first action unless the termination resulted from voluntary discontinuance or from dismissal for failure or neglect to prosecute.

(4) This section does not alter the law on tolling of the statute of limitations nor does it apply to causes of action which have accrued before this Act becomes effective.

Article 2A
LEASES

Part 1 General Provisions

§ 2A–101. Short Title.

This Article shall be known and may be cited as the Uniform Commercial Code—Leases.

§ 2A–102. Scope.

This Article applies to any transaction, regardless of form, that creates a lease.

§ 2A–103. Definitions and Index of Definitions.

(1) In this Article unless the context otherwise requires:

(a) "Buyer in ordinary course of business" means a person who in good faith and without knowledge that the sale to him [or her] is in violation of the ownership rights or security interest or leasehold interest of a third party in the goods buys in ordinary course from a person in the business of selling goods of that kind but does not include a pawnbroker. "Buying" may be for cash or by exchange of other property or on secured or unsecured credit and includes receiving goods or documents of title under a pre-existing contract for sale but does not include a transfer in bulk or as security for or in total or partial satisfaction of a money debt.

(b) "Cancellation" occurs when either party puts an end to the lease contract for default by the other party.

(c) "Commercial unit" means such a unit of goods as by commercial usage is a single whole for purposes of lease and division of which materially impairs its character or value on the market or in use. A commercial unit may be a single article, as a machine, or a set of articles, as a suite of furniture or a line of machinery, or a quantity, as a gross or carload, or any other unit treated in use or in the relevant market as a single whole.

(d) "Conforming" goods or performance under a lease contract means goods or performance that are in accordance with the obligations under the lease contract.

(e) "Consumer lease" means a lease that a lessor regularly engaged in the business of leasing or selling makes to a lessee who is an individual and who takes under the lease primarily for a personal, family, or household purpose [, if the total payments to be made under the lease contract, excluding payments for options to renew or buy, do not exceed $______].

(f) "Fault" means wrongful act, omission, breach, or default.

(g) "Finance lease" means a lease with respect to which:

(i) the lessor does not select, manufacture or supply the goods;

(ii) the lessor acquires the goods or the right to possession and use of the goods in connection with the lease; and

(iii) one of the following occurs:

(A) the lessee receives a copy of the contract by which the lessor acquired the goods or the right to possession and use of the goods before signing the lease contract;

(B) the lessee's approval of the contract by which the lessor acquired the goods or the right to possession and use of the goods is a condition to effectiveness of the lease contract;

(C) the lessee, before signing the lease contract, receives an accurate and complete statement designating the promises and warranties, and any disclaimers of warranties, limitations or modifications of remedies, or liquidated damages, including those of a third party, such as the manufacturer of the goods, provided to the lessor by the person supplying the goods in connection with or as part of the contract by which the lessor acquired the goods or the right to possession and use of the goods; or

(D) if the lease is not a consumer lease, the lessor, before the lessee signs the lease contract, informs the lessee in writing (a) of the identity of the person supplying the goods to the lessor, unless the lessee has selected that person and directed the lessor to acquire the goods or the right to possession and use of the goods from that person, (b) that the lessee is entitled under this Article to any promises and warranties, including those of any third party, provided to the lessor by the person supplying the goods in connection with or as part of the contract by which the lessor acquired the goods or the right to possession and use of the goods, and (c) that the lessee may communicate with the person supplying the goods to the lessor and receive an accurate and complete statement of those promises and warranties, including any disclaimers and limitations of them or of remedies.

(h) "Goods" means all things that are movable at the time of identification to the lease contract, or are fixtures (Section 2A–309), but the term does not include money, documents, instruments, accounts, chattel paper, general intangibles, or minerals or the like, including oil and gas, before extraction. The term also includes the unborn young of animals.

(i) "Installment lease contract" means a lease contract that authorizes or requires the delivery of goods in separate lots to be separately accepted, even though the lease contract contains a clause "each delivery is a separate lease" or its equivalent.

(j) "Lease" means a transfer of the right to possession and use of goods for a term in return for consideration, but a sale, including a sale on approval or a sale or return, or retention or creation of a security interest is not a lease. Unless the context clearly indicates otherwise, the term includes a sublease.

(k) "Lease agreement" means the bargain, with respect to the lease, of the lessor and the lessee in fact as found in their language or by implication from other circumstances including course of dealing or usage of trade or course of performance as provided in this Article. Unless the context clearly indicates otherwise, the term includes a sublease agreement.

(l) "Lease contract" means the total legal obligation that results from the lease agreement as affected by this Article and any other applicable rules of law. Unless the context clearly indicates otherwise, the term includes a sublease contract.

(m) "Leasehold interest" means the interest of the lessor or the lessee under a lease contract.

(n) "Lessee" means a person who acquires the right to possession and use of goods under a lease. Unless the context clearly indicates otherwise, the term includes a sublessee.

(o) "Lessee in ordinary course of business" means a person who in good faith and without knowledge that the lease to him [or her] is in violation of the ownership rights or security interest or leasehold interest of a third party in the goods, leases in ordinary course from a person in the business of selling or leasing goods of that kind but does not include a pawnbroker. "Leasing" may be for cash or by exchange of other property or on secured or unsecured credit and includes receiving goods or documents of title under a pre-existing lease contract but does not include a transfer in bulk or as security for or in total or partial satisfaction of a money debt.

(p) "Lessor" means a person who transfers the right to possession and use of goods under a lease. Unless the context clearly indicates otherwise, the term includes a sublessor.

(q) "Lessor's residual interest" means the lessor's interest in the goods after expiration, termination, or cancellation of the lease contract.

(r) "Lien" means a charge against or interest in goods to secure payment of a debt or performance of an obligation, but the term does not include a security interest.

(s) "Lot" means a parcel or a single article that is the subject matter of a separate lease or delivery, whether or not it is sufficient to perform the lease contract.

(t) "Merchant lessee" means a lessee that is a merchant with respect to goods of the kind subject to the lease.

(u) "Present value" means the amount as of a date certain of one or more sums payable in the future, discounted to the date certain. The discount is determined by the interest rate specified by the parties if the rate was not manifestly unreasonable at the time the transaction was entered into; otherwise, the discount is determined by a commercially reasonable rate that takes into account the facts and circumstances of each case at the time the transaction was entered into.

(v) "Purchase" includes taking by sale, lease, mortgage, security interest, pledge, gift, or any other voluntary transaction creating an interest in goods.

(w) "Sublease" means a lease of goods the right to possession and use of which was acquired by the lessor as a lessee under an existing lease.

(x) "Supplier" means a person from whom a lessor buys or leases goods to be leased under a finance lease.

(y) "Supply contract" means a contract under which a lessor buys or leases goods to be leased.

(z) "Termination" occurs when either party pursuant to a power created by agreement or law puts an end to the lease contract otherwise than for default.

(2) Other definitions applying to this Article and the sections in which they appear are:

"Accessions". Section 2A–310(1).

"Construction mortgage". Section 2A–309(1)(d).

"Encumbrance". Section 2A–309(1)(e).

"Fixtures". Section 2A–309(1)(a).

"Fixture filing". Section 2A–309(1)(b).

"Purchase money lease". Section 2A–309(1)(c).

(3) The following definitions in other Articles apply to this Article:

"Accounts". Section 9–106.

"Between merchants". Section 2–104(3).

"Buyer". Section 2–103(1)(a).

"Chattel paper". Section 9–105(1)(b).

"Consumer goods". Section 9–109(1).

"Document". Section 9–105(1)(f).

"Entrusting". Section 2–403(3).

"General intangibles". Section 9–106.

"Good faith". Section 2–103(1)(b).

"Instrument". Section 9–105(1)(i).

"Merchant". Section 2–104(1).

"Mortgage". Section 9–105(1)(j).

"Pursuant to commitment". Section 9–105(1)(k).

"Receipt". Section 2–103(1)(c).

"Sale". Section 2–106(1).

"Sale on approval". Section 2–326.

"Sale or return". Section 2–326.

"Seller". Section 2–103(1)(d).

(4) In addition Article 1 contains general definitions and principles of construction and interpretation applicable throughout this Article.

As amended in 1990 and 1999.

§ 2A–104. Leases Subject to Other Law.

(1) A lease, although subject to this Article, is also subject to any applicable:

(a) certificate of title statute of this State: (list any certificate of title statutes covering automobiles, trailers, mobile homes, boats, farm tractors, and the like);

(b) certificate of title statute of another jurisdiction (Section 2A–105); or

(c) consumer protection statute of this State, or final consumer protection decision of a court of this State existing on the effective date of this Article.

(2) In case of conflict between this Article, other than Sections 2A–105, 2A–304(3), and 2A–305(3), and a statute or decision referred to in subsection (1), the statute or decision controls.

(3) Failure to comply with an applicable law has only the effect specified therein.

As amended in 1990.

§ 2A–105. Territorial Application of Article to Goods Covered by Certificate of Title.

Subject to the provisions of Sections 2A–304(3) and 2A–305(3), with respect to goods covered by a certificate of title issued under a statute of this State or of another jurisdiction, compliance and the effect of compliance or noncompliance with a certificate of title statute are governed by the law (including the conflict of laws rules) of the jurisdiction issuing the certificate until the earlier of (a) surrender of the certificate, or (b) four months after the goods are removed from that jurisdiction and thereafter until a new certificate of title is issued by another jurisdiction.

§ 2A–106. Limitation on Power of Parties to Consumer Lease to Choose Applicable Law and Judicial Forum.

(1) If the law chosen by the parties to a consumer lease is that of a jurisdiction other than a jurisdiction in which the lessee resides at the time the lease agreement becomes enforceable or within 30 days thereafter or in which the goods are to be used, the choice is not enforceable.

(2) If the judicial forum chosen by the parties to a consumer lease is a forum that would not otherwise have jurisdiction over the lessee, the choice is not enforceable.

§ 2A–107. Waiver or Renunciation of Claim or Right After Default.

Any claim or right arising out of an alleged default or breach of warranty may be discharged in whole or in part without consideration by a written waiver or renunciation signed and delivered by the aggrieved party.

§ 2A–108. Unconscionability.

(1) If the court as a matter of law finds a lease contract or any clause of a lease contract to have been unconscionable at the time it was made the court may refuse to enforce the lease contract, or it may enforce the remainder of the lease contract without the unconscionable clause, or it may so limit the application of any unconscionable clause as to avoid any unconscionable result.

(2) With respect to a consumer lease, if the court as a matter of law finds that a lease contract or any clause of a lease contract has been induced by unconscionable conduct or that unconscionable conduct has occurred in the collection of a claim arising from a lease contract, the court may grant appropriate relief.

(3) Before making a finding of unconscionability under subsection (1) or (2), the court, on its own motion or that of a party, shall afford the parties a reasonable opportunity

to present evidence as to the setting, purpose, and effect of the lease contract or clause thereof, or of the conduct.

(4) In an action in which the lessee claims unconscionability with respect to a consumer lease:

(a) If the court finds unconscionability under subsection (1) or (2), the court shall award reasonable attorney's fees to the lessee.

(b) If the court does not find unconscionability and the lessee claiming unconscionability has brought or maintained an action he [or she] knew to be groundless, the court shall award reasonable attorney's fees to the party against whom the claim is made.

(c) In determining attorney's fees, the amount of the recovery on behalf of the claimant under subsections (1) and (2) is not controlling.

§ 2A–109. Option to Accelerate at Will.

(1) A term providing that one party or his [or her] successor in interest may accelerate payment or performance or require collateral or additional collateral "at will" or "when he [or she] deems himself [or herself] insecure" or in words of similar import must be construed to mean that he [or she] has power to do so only if he [or she] in good faith believes that the prospect of payment or performance is impaired.

(2) With respect to a consumer lease, the burden of establishing good faith under subsection (1) is on the party who exercised the power; otherwise the burden of establishing lack of good faith is on the party against whom the power has been exercised.

Part 2 Formation and Construction of Lease Contract

§ 2A–201. Statute of Frauds.

(1) A lease contract is not enforceable by way of action or defense unless:

(a) the total payments to be made under the lease contract, excluding payments for options to renew or buy, are less than $1,000; or

(b) there is a writing, signed by the party against whom enforcement is sought or by that party's authorized agent, sufficient to indicate that a lease contract has been made between the parties and to describe the goods leased and the lease term.

(2) Any description of leased goods or of the lease term is sufficient and satisfies subsection (1)(b), whether or not it is specific, if it reasonably identifies what is described.

(3) A writing is not insufficient because it omits or incorrectly states a term agreed upon, but the lease contract is not enforceable under subsection (1)(b) beyond the lease term and the quantity of goods shown in the writing.

(4) A lease contract that does not satisfy the requirements of subsection (1), but which is valid in other respects, is enforceable:

(a) if the goods are to be specially manufactured or obtained for the lessee and are not suitable for lease or sale to others in the ordinary course of the lessor's business, and the lessor, before notice of repudiation is received and under circumstances that reasonably indicate that the goods are for the lessee, has made either a substantial beginning of their manufacture or commitments for their procurement;

(b) if the party against whom enforcement is sought admits in that party's pleading, testimony or otherwise in court that a lease contract was made, but the lease contract is not enforceable under this provision beyond the quantity of goods admitted; or

(c) with respect to goods that have been received and accepted by the lessee.

(5) The lease term under a lease contract referred to in subsection (4) is:

(a) if there is a writing signed by the party against whom enforcement is sought or by that party's authorized agent specifying the lease term, the term so specified;

(b) if the party against whom enforcement is sought admits in that party's pleading, testimony, or otherwise in court a lease term, the term so admitted; or

(c) a reasonable lease term.

§ 2A–202. Final Written Expression: Parol or Extrinsic Evidence.

Terms with respect to which the confirmatory memoranda of the parties agree or which are otherwise set forth in a writing intended by the parties as a final expression of their agreement with respect to such terms as are included therein may not be contradicted by evidence of any prior agreement or of a contemporaneous oral agreement but may be explained or supplemented:

(a) by course of dealing or usage of trade or by course of performance; and

(b) by evidence of consistent additional terms unless the court finds the writing to have been intended also as a complete and exclusive statement of the terms of the agreement.

§ 2A–203. Seals Inoperative.

The affixing of a seal to a writing evidencing a lease contract or an offer to enter into a lease contract does not render the writing a sealed instrument and the law with respect to sealed instruments does not apply to the lease contract or offer.

§ 2A–204. Formation in General.

(1) A lease contract may be made in any manner sufficient to show agreement, including conduct by both parties which recognizes the existence of a lease contract.

(2) An agreement sufficient to constitute a lease contract may be found although the moment of its making is undetermined.

(3) Although one or more terms are left open, a lease contract does not fail for indefiniteness if the parties have

intended to make a lease contract and there is a reasonably certain basis for giving an appropriate remedy.

§ 2A–205. Firm Offers.

An offer by a merchant to lease goods to or from another person in a signed writing that by its terms gives assurance it will be held open is not revocable, for lack of consideration, during the time stated or, if no time is stated, for a reasonable time, but in no event may the period of irrevocability exceed 3 months. Any such term of assurance on a form supplied by the offeree must be separately signed by the offeror.

§ 2A–206. Offer and Acceptance in Formation of Lease Contract.

(1) Unless otherwise unambiguously indicated by the language or circumstances, an offer to make a lease contract must be construed as inviting acceptance in any manner and by any medium reasonable in the circumstances.

(2) If the beginning of a requested performance is a reasonable mode of acceptance, an offeror who is not notified of acceptance within a reasonable time may treat the offer as having lapsed before acceptance.

§ 2A–207. Course of Performance or Practical Construction.

(1) If a lease contract involves repeated occasions for performance by either party with knowledge of the nature of the performance and opportunity for objection to it by the other, any course of performance accepted or acquiesced in without objection is relevant to determine the meaning of the lease agreement.

(2) The express terms of a lease agreement and any course of performance, as well as any course of dealing and usage of trade, must be construed whenever reasonable as consistent with each other; but if that construction is unreasonable, express terms control course of performance, course of performance controls both course of dealing and usage of trade, and course of dealing controls usage of trade.

(3) Subject to the provisions of Section 2A–208 on modification and waiver, course of performance is relevant to show a waiver or modification of any term inconsistent with the course of performance.

§ 2A–208. Modification, Rescission and Waiver.

(1) An agreement modifying a lease contract needs no consideration to be binding.

(2) A signed lease agreement that excludes modification or rescission except by a signed writing may not be otherwise modified or rescinded, but, except as between merchants, such a requirement on a form supplied by a merchant must be separately signed by the other party.

(3) Although an attempt at modification or rescission does not satisfy the requirements of subsection (2), it may operate as a waiver.

(4) A party who has made a waiver affecting an executory portion of a lease contract may retract the waiver by reasonable notification received by the other party that strict performance will be required of any term waived, unless the retraction would be unjust in view of a material change of position in reliance on the waiver.

§ 2A–209. Lessee under Finance Lease as Beneficiary of Supply Contract.

(1) The benefit of the supplier's promises to the lessor under the supply contract and of all warranties, whether express or implied, including those of any third party provided in connection with or as part of the supply contract, extends to the lessee to the extent of the lessee's leasehold interest under a finance lease related to the supply contract, but is subject to the terms warranty and of the supply contract and all defenses or claims arising therefrom.

(2) The extension of the benefit of supplier's promises and of warranties to the lessee (Section 2A–209(1)) does not: (i) modify the rights and obligations of the parties to the supply contract, whether arising therefrom or otherwise, or (ii) impose any duty or liability under the supply contract on the lessee.

(3) Any modification or rescission of the supply contract by the supplier and the lessor is effective between the supplier and the lessee unless, before the modification or rescission, the supplier has received notice that the lessee has entered into a finance lease related to the supply contract. If the modification or rescission is effective between the supplier and the lessee, the lessor is deemed to have assumed, in addition to the obligations of the lessor to the lessee under the lease contract, promises of the supplier to the lessor and warranties that were so modified or rescinded as they existed and were available to the lessee before modification or rescission.

(4) In addition to the extension of the benefit of the supplier's promises and of warranties to the lessee under subsection (1), the lessee retains all rights that the lessee may have against the supplier which arise from an agreement between the lessee and the supplier or under other law.

As amended in 1990.

§ 2A–210. Express Warranties.

(1) Express warranties by the lessor are created as follows:

(a) Any affirmation of fact or promise made by the lessor to the lessee which relates to the goods and becomes part of the basis of the bargain creates an express warranty that the goods will conform to the affirmation or promise.

(b) Any description of the goods which is made part of the basis of the bargain creates an express warranty that the goods will conform to the description.

(c) Any sample or model that is made part of the basis of the bargain creates an express warranty that the whole of the goods will conform to the sample or model.

(2) It is not necessary to the creation of an express warranty that the lessor use formal words, such as "warrant" or

"guarantee," or that the lessor have a specific intention to make a warranty, but an affirmation merely of the value of the goods or a statement purporting to be merely the lessor's opinion or commendation of the goods does not create a warranty.

§ 2A–211. Warranties Against Interference and Against Infringement; Lessee's Obligation Against Infringement.

(1) There is in a lease contract a warranty that for the lease term no person holds a claim to or interest in the goods that arose from an act or omission of the lessor, other than a claim by way of infringement or the like, which will interfere with the lessee's enjoyment of its leasehold interest.

(2) Except in a finance lease there is in a lease contract by a lessor who is a merchant regularly dealing in goods of the kind a warranty that the goods are delivered free of the rightful claim of any person by way of infringement or the like.

(3) A lessee who furnishes specifications to a lessor or a supplier shall hold the lessor and the supplier harmless against any claim by way of infringement or the like that arises out of compliance with the specifications.

§ 2A–212. Implied Warranty of Merchantability.

(1) Except in a finance lease, a warranty that the goods will be merchantable is implied in a lease contract if the lessor is a merchant with respect to goods of that kind.

(2) Goods to be merchantable must be at least such as

(a) pass without objection in the trade under the description in the lease agreement;

(b) in the case of fungible goods, are of fair average quality within the description;

(c) are fit for the ordinary purposes for which goods of that type are used;

(d) run, within the variation permitted by the lease agreement, of even kind, quality, and quantity within each unit and among all units involved;

(e) are adequately contained, packaged, and labeled as the lease agreement may require; and

(f) conform to any promises or affirmations of fact made on the container or label.

(3) Other implied warranties may arise from course of dealing or usage of trade.

§ 2A–213. Implied Warranty of Fitness for Particular Purpose.

Except in a finance of lease, if the lessor at the time the lease contract is made has reason to know of any particular purpose for which the goods are required and that the lessee is relying on the lessor's skill or judgment to select or furnish suitable goods, there is in the lease contract an implied warranty that the goods will be fit for that purpose.

§ 2A–214. Exclusion or Modification of Warranties.

(1) Words or conduct relevant to the creation of an express warranty and words or conduct tending to negate or limit a warranty must be construed wherever reasonable as consistent with each other; but, subject to the provisions of Section 2A–202 on parol or extrinsic evidence, negation or limitation is inoperative to the extent that the construction is unreasonable.

(2) Subject to subsection (3), to exclude or modify the implied warranty of merchantability or any part of it the language must mention "merchantability", be by a writing, and be conspicuous. Subject to subsection (3), to exclude or modify any implied warranty of fitness the exclusion must be by a writing and be conspicuous. Language to exclude all implied warranties of fitness is sufficient if it is in writing, is conspicuous and states, for example, "There is no warranty that the goods will be fit for a particular purpose".

(3) Notwithstanding subsection (2), but subject to subsection (4),

(a) unless the circumstances indicate otherwise, all implied warranties are excluded by expressions like "as is" or "with all faults" or by other language that in common understanding calls the lessee's attention to the exclusion of warranties and makes plain that there is no implied warranty, if in writing and conspicuous;

(b) if the lessee before entering into the lease contract has examined the goods or the sample or model as fully as desired or has refused to examine the goods, there is no implied warranty with regard to defects that an examination ought in the circumstances to have revealed; and

(c) an implied warranty may also be excluded or modified by course of dealing, course of performance, or usage of trade.

(4) To exclude or modify a warranty against interference or against infringement (Section 2A–211) or any part of it, the language must be specific, be by a writing, and be conspicuous, unless the circumstances, including course of performance, course of dealing, or usage of trade, give the lessee reason to know that the goods are being leased subject to a claim or interest of any person.

§ 2A–215. Cumulation and Conflict of Warranties Express or Implied.

Warranties, whether express or implied, must be construed as consistent with each other and as cumulative, but if that construction is unreasonable, the intention of the parties determines which warranty is dominant. In ascertaining that intention the following rules apply:

(a) Exact or technical specifications displace an inconsistent sample or model or general language of description.

(b) A sample from an existing bulk displaces inconsistent general language of description.

(c) Express warranties displace inconsistent implied warranties other than an implied warranty of fitness for a particular purpose.

§ 2A–216. Third-Party Beneficiaries of Express and Implied Warranties.

Alternative A

A warranty to or for the benefit of a lessee under this Article, whether express or implied, extends to any natural person who is in the family or household of the lessee or who is a guest in the lessee's home if it is reasonable to expect that such person may use, consume, or be affected by the goods and who is injured in person by breach of the warranty. This section does not displace principles of law and equity that extend a warranty to or for the benefit of a lessee to other persons. The operation of this section may not be excluded, modified, or limited, but an exclusion, modification, or limitation of the warranty, including any with respect to rights and remedies, effective against the lessee is also effective against any beneficiary designated under this section.

Alternative B

A warranty to or for the benefit of a lessee under this Article, whether express or implied, extends to any natural person who may reasonably be expected to use, consume, or be affected by the goods and who is injured in person by breach of the warranty. This section does not displace principles of law and equity that extend a warranty to or for the benefit of a lessee to other persons. The operation of this section may not be excluded, modified, or limited, but an exclusion, modification, or limitation of the warranty, including any with respect to rights and remedies, effective against the lessee is also effective against the beneficiary designated under this section.

Alternative C

A warranty to or for the benefit of a lessee under this Article, whether express or implied, extends to any person who may reasonably be expected to use, consume, or be affected by the goods and who is injured by breach of the warranty. The operation of this section may not be excluded, modified, or limited with respect to injury to the person of an individual to whom the warranty extends, but an exclusion, modification, or limitation of the warranty, including any with respect to rights and remedies, effective against the lessee is also effective against the beneficiary designated under this section.

§ 2A–217. Identification.

Identification of goods as goods to which a lease contract refers may be made at any time and in any manner explicitly agreed to by the parties. In the absence of explicit agreement, identification occurs:

(a) when the lease contract is made if the lease contract is for a lease of goods that are existing and identified;

(b) when the goods are shipped, marked, or otherwise designated by the lessor as goods to which the lease contract refers, if the lease contract is for a lease of goods that are not existing and identified; or

(c) when the young are conceived, if the lease contract is for a lease of unborn young of animals.

§ 2A–218. Insurance and Proceeds.

(1) A lessee obtains an insurable interest when existing goods are identified to the lease contract even though the goods identified are nonconforming and the lessee has an option to reject them.

(2) If a lessee has an insurable interest only by reason of the lessor's identification of the goods, the lessor, until default or insolvency or notification to the lessee that identification is final, may substitute other goods for those identified.

(3) Notwithstanding a lessee's insurable interest under subsections (1) and (2), the lessor retains an insurable interest until an option to buy has been exercised by the lessee and risk of loss has passed to the lessee.

(4) Nothing in this section impairs any insurable interest recognized under any other statute or rule of law.

(5) The parties by agreement may determine that one or more parties have an obligation to obtain and pay for insurance covering the goods and by agreement may determine the beneficiary of the proceeds of the insurance.

§ 2A–219. Risk of Loss.

(1) Except in the case of a finance lease, risk of loss is retained by the lessor and does not pass to the lessee. In the case of a finance lease, risk of loss passes to the lessee.

(2) Subject to the provisions of this Article on the effect of default on risk of loss (Section 2A–220), if risk of loss is to pass to the lessee and the time of passage is not stated, the following rules apply:

(a) If the lease contract requires or authorizes the goods to be shipped by carrier

(i) and it does not require delivery at a particular destination, the risk of loss passes to the lessee when the goods are duly delivered to the carrier; but

(ii) if it does require delivery at a particular destination and the goods are there duly tendered while in the possession of the carrier, the risk of loss passes to the lessee when the goods are there duly so tendered as to enable the lessee to take delivery.

(b) If the goods are held by a bailee to be delivered without being moved, the risk of loss passes to the lessee on acknowledgment by the bailee of the lessee's right to possession of the goods.

(c) In any case not within subsection (a) or (b), the risk of loss passes to the lessee on the lessee's receipt of the goods if the lessor, or, in the case of a finance lease, the supplier, is a merchant; otherwise the risk passes to the lessee on tender of delivery.

§ 2A–220. Effect of Default on Risk of Loss.

(1) Where risk of loss is to pass to the lessee and the time of passage is not stated:

(a) If a tender or delivery of goods so fails to conform to the lease contract as to give a right of rejection, the risk of their loss remains with the lessor, or, in the case of a finance lease, the supplier, until cure or acceptance.

(b) If the lessee rightfully revokes acceptance, he [or she], to the extent of any deficiency in his [or her] effective insurance coverage, may treat the risk of loss as having remained with the lessor from the beginning.

(2) Whether or not risk of loss is to pass to the lessee, if the lessee as to conforming goods already identified to a lease contract repudiates or is otherwise in default under the lease contract, the lessor, or, in the case of a finance lease, the supplier, to the extent of any deficiency in his [or her] effective insurance coverage may treat the risk of loss as resting on the lessee for a commercially reasonable time.

§ 2A–221. Casualty to Identified Goods.

If a lease contract requires goods identified when the lease contract is made, and the goods suffer casualty without fault of the lessee, the lessor or the supplier before delivery, or the goods suffer casualty before risk of loss passes to the lessee pursuant to the lease agreement or Section 2A–219, then:

(a) if the loss is total, the lease contract is avoided; and

(b) if the loss is partial or the goods have so deteriorated as to no longer conform to the lease contract, the lessee may nevertheless demand inspection and at his [or her] option either treat the lease contract as avoided or, except in a finance lease that is not a consumer lease, accept the goods with due allowance from the rent payable for the balance of the lease term for the deterioration or the deficiency in quantity but without further right against the lessor.

Part 3 Effect of Lease Contract

§ 2A–301. Enforceability of Lease Contract.

Except as otherwise provided in this Article, a lease contract is effective and enforceable according to its terms between the parties, against purchasers of the goods and against creditors of the parties.

§ 2A–302. Title to and Possession of Goods.

Except as otherwise provided in this Article, each provision of this Article applies whether the lessor or a third party has title to the goods, and whether the lessor, the lessee, or a third party has possession of the goods, notwithstanding any statute or rule of law that possession or the absence of possession is fraudulent.

§ 2A–303. Alienability of Party's Interest Under Lease Contract or of Lessor's Residual Interest in Goods; Delegation of Performance; Transfer of Rights.

(1) As used in this section, "creation of a security interest" includes the sale of a lease contract that is subject to Article 9, Secured Transactions, by reason of Section 9–109(a)(3).

(2) Except as provided in subsections (3) and Section 9–407, a provision in a lease agreement which (i) prohibits the voluntary or involuntary transfer, including a transfer by sale, sublease, creation or enforcement of a security interest, or attachment, levy, or other judicial process, of an interest of a party under the lease contract or of the lessor's residual interest in the goods, or (ii) makes such a transfer an event of default, gives rise to the rights and remedies provided in subsection (4), but a transfer that is prohibited or is an event of default under the lease agreement is otherwise effective.

(3) A provision in a lease agreement which (i) prohibits a transfer of a right to damages for default with respect to the whole lease contract or of a right to payment arising out of the transferor's due performance of the transferor's entire obligation, or (ii) makes such a transfer an event of default, is not enforceable, and such a transfer is not a transfer that materially impairs the propsect of obtaining return performance by, materially changes the duty of, or materially increases the burden or risk imposed on, the other party to the lease contract within the purview of subsection (4).

(4) Subject to subsection (3) and Section 9–407:

(a) if a transfer is made which is made an event of default under a lease agreement, the party to the lease contract not making the transfer, unless that party waives the default or otherwise agrees, has the rights and remedies described in Section 2A–501(2);

(b) if paragraph (a) is not applicable and if a transfer is made that (i) is prohibited under a lease agreement or (ii) materially impairs the prospect of obtaining return performance by, materially changes the duty of, or materially increases the burden or risk imposed on, the other party to the lease contract, unless the party not making the transfer agrees at any time to the transfer in the lease contract or otherwise, then, except as limited by contract, (i) the transferor is liable to the party not making the transfer for damages caused by the transfer to the extent that the damages could not reasonably be prevented by the party not making the transfer and (ii) a court having jurisdiction may grant other appropriate relief, including cancellation of the lease contract or an injunction against the transfer.

(5) A transfer of "the lease" or of "all my rights under the lease", or a transfer in similar general terms, is a transfer of rights and, unless the language or the circumstances, as in a transfer for security, indicate the contrary, the transfer is a delegation of duties by the transferor to the transferee. Acceptance by the transferee constitutes a promise by the transferee to perform those duties. The promise is enforceable by either the transferor or the other party to the lease contract.

(6) Unless otherwise agreed by the lessor and the lessee, a delegation of performance does not relieve the transferor as against the other party of any duty to perform or of any liability for default.

(7) In a consumer lease, to prohibit the transfer of an interest of a party under the lease contract or to make a

transfer an event of default, the language must be specific, by a writing, and conspicuous.

As amended in 1990 and 1999.

§ 2A–304. Subsequent Lease of Goods by Lessor.

(1) Subject to Section 2A–303, a subsequent lessee from a lessor of goods under an existing lease contract obtains, to the extent of the leasehold interest transferred, the leasehold interest in the goods that the lessor had or had power to transfer, and except as provided in subsection (2) and Section 2A–527(4), takes subject to the existing lease contract. A lessor with voidable title has power to transfer a good leasehold interest to a good faith subsequent lessee for value, but only to the extent set forth in the preceding sentence. If goods have been delivered under a transaction of purchase the lessor has that power even though:

(a) the lessor's transferor was deceived as to the identity of the lessor;

(b) the delivery was in exchange for a check which is later dishonored;

(c) it was agreed that the transaction was to be a "cash sale"; or

(d) the delivery was procured through fraud punishable as larcenous under the criminal law.

(2) A subsequent lessee in the ordinary course of business from a lessor who is a merchant dealing in goods of that kind to whom the goods were entrusted by the existing lessee of that lessor before the interest of the subsequent lessee became enforceable against that lessor obtains, to the extent of the leasehold interest transferred, all of that lessor's and the existing lessee's rights to the goods, and takes free of the existing lease contract.

(3) A subsequent lessee from the lessor of goods that are subject to an existing lease contract and are covered by a certificate of title issued under a statute of this State or of another jurisdiction takes no greater rights than those provided both by this section and by the certificate of title statute.

As amended in 1990.

§ 2A–305. Sale or Sublease of Goods by Lessee.

(1) Subject to the provisions of Section 2A–303, a buyer or sublessee from the lessee of goods under an existing lease contract obtains, to the extent of the interest transferred, the leasehold interest in the goods that the lessee had or had power to transfer, and except as provided in subsection (2) and Section 2A–511(4), takes subject to the existing lease contract. A lessee with a voidable leasehold interest has power to transfer a good leasehold interest to a good faith buyer for value or a good faith sublessee for value, but only to the extent set forth in the preceding sentence. When goods have been delivered under a transaction of lease the lessee has that power even though:

(a) the lessor was deceived as to the identity of the lessee;

(b) the delivery was in exchange for a check which is later dishonored; or

(c) the delivery was procured through fraud punishable as larcenous under the criminal law.

(2) A buyer in the ordinary course of business or a sublessee in the ordinary course of business from a lessee who is a merchant dealing in goods of that kind to whom the goods were entrusted by the lessor obtains, to the extent of the interest transferred, all of the lessor's and lessee's rights to the goods, and takes free of the existing lease contract.

(3) A buyer or sublessee from the lessee of goods that are subject to an existing lease contract and are covered by a certificate of title issued under a statute of this State or of another jurisdiction takes no greater rights than those provided both by this section and by the certificate of title statute.

§ 2A–306. Priority of Certain Liens Arising by Operation of Law.

If a person in the ordinary course of his [or her] business furnishes services or materials with respect to goods subject to a lease contract, a lien upon those goods in the possession of that person given by statute or rule of law for those materials or services takes priority over any interest of the lessor or lessee under the lease contract or this Article unless the lien is created by statute and the statute provides otherwise or unless the lien is created by rule of law and the rule of law provides otherwise.

§ 2A–307. Priority of Liens Arising by Attachment or Levy on, Security Interests in, and Other Claims to Goods.

(1) Except as otherwise provided in Section 2A–306, a creditor of a lessee takes subject to the lease contract.

(2) Except as otherwise provided in subsection (3) and in Sections 2A–306 and 2A–308, a creditor of a lessor takes subject to the lease contract unless the creditor holds a lien that attached to the goods before the lease contract became enforceable.

(3) Except as otherwise provided in Sections 9–317, 9–321, and 9–323, a lessee takes a leasehold interest subject to a security interest held by a creditor of the lessor.

As amended in 1990 and 1999.

§ 2A–308. Special Rights of Creditors.

(1) A creditor of a lessor in possession of goods subject to a lease contract may treat the lease contract as void if as against the creditor retention of possession by the lessor is fraudulent under any statute or rule of law, but retention of possession in good faith and current course of trade by the lessor for a commercially reasonable time after the lease contract becomes enforceable is not fraudulent.

(2) Nothing in this Article impairs the rights of creditors of a lessor if the lease contract (a) becomes enforceable, not in current course of trade but in satisfaction of or as security for a pre-existing claim for money, security, or the

like, and (b) is made under circumstances which under any statute or rule of law apart from this Article would constitute the transaction a fraudulent transfer or voidable preference.

(3) A creditor of a seller may treat a sale or an identification of goods to a contract for sale as void if as against the creditor retention of possession by the seller is fraudulent under any statute or rule of law, but retention of possession of the goods pursuant to a lease contract entered into by the seller as lessee and the buyer as lessor in connection with the sale or identification of the goods is not fraudulent if the buyer bought for value and in good faith.

§ 2A–309. Lessor's and Lessee's Rights When Goods Become Fixtures.

(1) In this section:

(a) goods are "fixtures" when they become so related to particular real estate that an interest in them arises under real estate law;

(b) a "fixture filing" is the filing, in the office where a mortgage on the real estate would be filed or recorded, of a financing statement covering goods that are or are to become fixtures and conforming to the requirements of Section 9–502(a) and (b);

(c) a lease is a "purchase money lease" unless the lessee has possession or use of the goods or the right to possession or use of the goods before the lease agreement is enforceable;

(d) a mortgage is a "construction mortgage" to the extent it secures an obligation incurred for the construction of an improvement on land including the acquisition cost of the land, if the recorded writing so indicates; and

(e) "encumbrance" includes real estate mortgages and other liens on real estate and all other rights in real estate that are not ownership interests.

(2) Under this Article a lease may be of goods that are fixtures or may continue in goods that become fixtures, but no lease exists under this Article of ordinary building materials incorporated into an improvement on land.

(3) This Article does not prevent creation of a lease of fixtures pursuant to real estate law.

(4) The perfected interest of a lessor of fixtures has priority over a conflicting interest of an encumbrancer or owner of the real estate if:

(a) the lease is a purchase money lease, the conflicting interest of the encumbrancer or owner arises before the goods become fixtures, the interest of the lessor is perfected by a fixture filing before the goods become fixtures or within ten days thereafter, and the lessee has an interest of record in the real estate or is in possession of the real estate; or

(b) the interest of the lessor is perfected by a fixture filing before the interest of the encumbrancer or owner is of record, the lessor's interest has priority over any conflicting interest of a predecessor in title of the encumbrancer or owner, and the lessee has an interest of record in the real estate or is in possession of the real estate.

(5) The interest of a lessor of fixtures, whether or not perfected, has priority over the conflicting interest of an encumbrancer or owner of the real estate if:

(a) the fixtures are readily removable factory or office machines, readily removable equipment that is not primarily used or leased for use in the operation of the real estate, or readily removable replacements of domestic appliances that are goods subject to a consumer lease, and before the goods become fixtures the lease contract is enforceable; or

(b) the conflicting interest is a lien on the real estate obtained by legal or equitable proceedings after the lease contract is enforceable; or

(c) the encumbrancer or owner has consented in writing to the lease or has disclaimed an interest in the goods as fixtures; or

(d) the lessee has a right to remove the goods as against the encumbrancer or owner. If the lessee's right to remove terminates, the priority of the interest of the lessor continues for a reasonable time.

(6) Notwithstanding paragraph (4)(a) but otherwise subject to subsections (4) and (5), the interest of a lessor of fixtures, including the lessor's residual interest, is subordinate to the conflicting interest of an encumbrancer of the real estate under a construction mortgage recorded before the goods become fixtures if the goods become fixtures before the completion of the construction. To the extent given to refinance a construction mortgage, the conflicting interest of an encumbrancer of the real estate under a mortgage has this priority to the same extent as the encumbrancer of the real estate under the construction mortgage.

(7) In cases not within the preceding subsections, priority between the interest of a lessor of fixtures, including the lessor's residual interest, and the conflicting interest of an encumbrancer or owner of the real estate who is not the lessee is determined by the priority rules governing conflicting interests in real estate.

(8) If the interest of a lessor of fixtures, including the lessor's residual interest, has priority over all conflicting interests of all owners and encumbrancers of the real estate, the lessor or the lessee may (i) on default, expiration, termination, or cancellation of the lease agreement but subject to the agreement and this Article, or (ii) if necessary to enforce other rights and remedies of the lessor or lessee under this Article, remove the goods from the real estate, free and clear of all conflicting interests of all owners and encumbrancers of the real estate, but the lessor or lessee must reimburse any encumbrancer or owner of the real estate who is not the lessee and who has not otherwise agreed for the cost of repair of any physical injury, but not for any diminution in value of the real estate caused by the absence of the goods removed or by any necessity of replacing them. A person entitled to reimbursement may refuse permission to remove until the

party seeking removal gives adequate security for the performance of this obligation.

(9) Even though the lease agreement does not create a security interest, the interest of a lessor of fixtures, including the lessor's residual interest, is perfected by filing a financing statement as a fixture filing for leased goods that are or are to become fixtures in accordance with the relevant provisions of the Article on Secured Transactions (Article 9).

As amended in 1990 and 1999.

§ 2A–310. Lessor's and Lessee's Rights When Goods Become Accessions.

(1) Goods are "accessions" when they are installed in or affixed to other goods.

(2) The interest of a lessor or a lessee under a lease contract entered into before the goods became accessions is superior to all interests in the whole except as stated in subsection (4).

(3) The interest of a lessor or a lessee under a lease contract entered into at the time or after the goods became accessions is superior to all subsequently acquired interests in the whole except as stated in subsection (4) but is subordinate to interests in the whole existing at the time the lease contract was made unless the holders of such interests in the whole have in writing consented to the lease or disclaimed an interest in the goods as part of the whole.

(4) The interest of a lessor or a lessee under a lease contract described in subsection (2) or (3) is subordinate to the interest of

(a) a buyer in the ordinary course of business or a lessee in the ordinary course of business of any interest in the whole acquired after the goods became accessions; or

(b) a creditor with a security interest in the whole perfected before the lease contract was made to the extent that the creditor makes subsequent advances without knowledge of the lease contract.

(5) When under subsections (2) or (3) and (4) a lessor or a lessee of accessions holds an interest that is superior to all interests in the whole, the lessor or the lessee may (a) on default, expiration, termination, or cancellation of the lease contract by the other party but subject to the provisions of the lease contract and this Article, or (b) if necessary to enforce his [or her] other rights and remedies under this Article, remove the goods from the whole, free and clear of all interests in the whole, but he [or she] must reimburse any holder of an interest in the whole who is not the lessee and who has not otherwise agreed for the cost of repair of any physical injury but not for any diminution in value of the whole caused by the absence of the goods removed or by any necessity for replacing them. A person entitled to reimbursement may refuse permission to remove until the party seeking removal gives adequate security for the performance of this obligation.

§ 2A–311. Priority Subject to Subordination.

Nothing in this Article prevents subordination by agreement by any person entitled to priority.

As added in 1990.

Part 4 Performance of Lease Contract: Repudiated, Substituted and Excused

§ 2A–401. Insecurity: Adequate Assurance of Performance.

(1) A lease contract imposes an obligation on each party that the other's expectation of receiving due performance will not be impaired.

(2) If reasonable grounds for insecurity arise with respect to the performance of either party, the insecure party may demand in writing adequate assurance of due performance. Until the insecure party receives that assurance, if commercially reasonable the insecure party may suspend any performance for which he [or she] has not already received the agreed return.

(3) A repudiation of the lease contract occurs if assurance of due performance adequate under the circumstances of the particular case is not provided to the insecure party within a reasonable time, not to exceed 30 days after receipt of a demand by the other party.

(4) Between merchants, the reasonableness of grounds for insecurity and the adequacy of any assurance offered must be determined according to commercial standards.

(5) Acceptance of any nonconforming delivery or payment does not prejudice the aggrieved party's right to demand adequate assurance of future performance.

§ 2A–402. Anticipatory Repudiation.

If either party repudiates a lease contract with respect to a performance not yet due under the lease contract, the loss of which performance will substantially impair the value of the lease contract to the other, the aggrieved party may:

(a) for a commercially reasonable time, await retraction of repudiation and performance by the repudiating party;

(b) make demand pursuant to Section 2A–401 and await assurance of future performance adequate under the circumstances of the particular case; or

(c) resort to any right or remedy upon default under the lease contract or this Article, even though the aggrieved party has notified the repudiating party that the aggrieved party would await the repudiating party's performance and assurance and has urged retraction. In addition, whether or not the aggrieved party is pursuing one of the foregoing remedies, the aggrieved party may suspend performance or, if the aggrieved party is the lessor, proceed in accordance with the provisions of this Article on the lessor's right to identify goods to the lease contract notwithstanding default or to salvage unfinished goods (Section 2A–524).

§ 2A–403. Retraction of Anticipatory Repudiation.

(1) Until the repudiating party's next performance is due, the repudiating party can retract the repudiation unless,

since the repudiation, the aggrieved party has cancelled the lease contract or materially changed the aggrieved party's position or otherwise indicated that the aggrieved party considers the repudiation final.

(2) Retraction may be by any method that clearly indicates to the aggrieved party that the repudiating party intends to perform under the lease contract and includes any assurance demanded under Section 2A–401.

(3) Retraction reinstates a repudiating party's rights under a lease contract with due excuse and allowance to the aggrieved party for any delay occasioned by the repudiation.

§ 2A–404. Substituted Performance.

(1) If without fault of the lessee, the lessor and the supplier, the agreed berthing, loading, or unloading facilities fail or the agreed type of carrier becomes unavailable or the agreed manner of delivery otherwise becomes commercially impracticable, but a commercially reasonable substitute is available, the substitute performance must be tendered and accepted.

(2) If the agreed means or manner of payment fails because of domestic or foreign governmental regulation:

(a) the lessor may withhold or stop delivery or cause the supplier to withhold or stop delivery unless the lessee provides a means or manner of payment that is commercially a substantial equivalent; and

(b) if delivery has already been taken, payment by the means or in the manner provided by the regulation discharges the lessee's obligation unless the regulation is discriminatory, oppressive, or predatory.

§ 2A–405. Excused Performance.

Subject to Section 2A–404 on substituted performance, the following rules apply:

(a) Delay in delivery or nondelivery in whole or in part by a lessor or a supplier who complies with paragraphs (b) and (c) is not a default under the lease contract if performance as agreed has been made impracticable by the occurrence of a contingency the nonoccurrence of which was a basic assumption on which the lease contract was made or by compliance in good faith with any applicable foreign or domestic governmental regulation or order, whether or not the regulation or order later proves to be invalid.

(b) If the causes mentioned in paragraph (a) affect only part of the lessor's or the supplier's capacity to perform, he [or she] shall allocate production and deliveries among his [or her] customers but at his [or her] option may include regular customers not then under contract for sale or lease as well as his [or her] own requirements for further manufacture. He [or she] may so allocate in any manner that is fair and reasonable.

(c) The lessor seasonably shall notify the lessee and in the case of a finance lease the supplier seasonably shall notify the lessor and the lessee, if known, that there will be delay or nondelivery and, if allocation is required under paragraph (b), of the estimated quota thus made available for the lessee.

§ 2A–406. Procedure on Excused Performance.

(1) If the lessee receives notification of a material or indefinite delay or an allocation justified under Section 2A–405, the lessee may by written notification to the lessor as to any goods involved, and with respect to all of the goods if under an installment lease contract the value of the whole lease contract is substantially impaired (Section 2A–510):

(a) terminate the lease contract (Section 2A–505(2)); or

(b) except in a finance lease that is not a consumer lease, modify the lease contract by accepting the available quota in substitution, with due allowance from the rent payable for the balance of the lease term for the deficiency but without further right against the lessor.

(2) If, after receipt of a notification from the lessor under Section 2A–405, the lessee fails so to modify the lease agreement within a reasonable time not exceeding 30 days, the lease contract lapses with respect to any deliveries affected.

§ 2A–407. Irrevocable Promises: Finance Leases.

(1) In the case of a finance lease that is not a consumer lease the lessee's promises under the lease contract become irrevocable and independent upon the lessee's acceptance of the goods.

(2) A promise that has become irrevocable and independent under subsection (1):

(a) is effective and enforceable between the parties, and by or against third parties including assignees of the parties, and

(b) is not subject to cancellation, termination, modification, repudiation, excuse, or substitution without the consent of the party to whom the promise runs.

(3) This section does not affect the validity under any other law of a covenant in any lease contract making the lessee's promises irrevocable and independent upon the lessee's acceptance of the goods.

As amended in 1990.

Part 5 Default

A. In General

§ 2A–501. Default: Procedure.

(1) Whether the lessor or the lessee is in default under a lease contract is determined by the lease agreement and this Article.

(2) If the lessor or the lessee is in default under the lease contract, the party seeking enforcement has rights and remedies as provided in this Article and, except as limited by this Article, as provided in the lease agreement.

(3) If the lessor or the lessee is in default under the lease contract, the party seeking enforcement may reduce the

party's claim to judgment, or otherwise enforce the lease contract by self-help or any available judicial procedure or nonjudicial procedure, including administrative proceeding, arbitration, or the like, in accordance with this Article.

(4) Except as otherwise provided in Section 1–106(1) or this Article or the lease agreement, the rights and remedies referred to in subsections (2) and (3) are cumulative.

(5) If the lease agreement covers both real property and goods, the party seeking enforcement may proceed under this Part as to the goods, or under other applicable law as to both the real property and the goods in accordance with that party's rights and remedies in respect of the real property, in which case this Part does not apply.

As amended in 1990.

§ 2A–502. Notice After Default.

Except as otherwise provided in this Article or the lease agreement, the lessor or lessee in default under the lease contract is not entitled to notice of default or notice of enforcement from the other party to the lease agreement.

§ 2A–503. Modification or Impairment of Rights and Remedies.

(1) Except as otherwise provided in this Article, the lease agreement may include rights and remedies for default in addition to or in substitution for those provided in this Article and may limit or alter the measure of damages recoverable under this Article.

(2) Resort to a remedy provided under this Article or in the lease agreement is optional unless the remedy is expressly agreed to be exclusive. If circumstances cause an exclusive or limited remedy to fail of its essential purpose, or provision for an exclusive remedy is unconscionable, remedy may be had as provided in this Article.

(3) Consequential damages may be liquidated under Section 2A–504, or may otherwise be limited, altered, or excluded unless the limitation, alteration, or exclusion is unconscionable. Limitation, alteration, or exclusion of consequential damages for injury to the person in the case of consumer goods is prima facie unconscionable but limitation, alteration, or exclusion of damages where the loss is commercial is not prima facie unconscionable.

(4) Rights and remedies on default by the lessor or the lessee with respect to any obligation or promise collateral or ancillary to the lease contract are not impaired by this Article.

As amended in 1990.

§ 2A–504. Liquidation of Damages.

(1) Damages payable by either party for default, or any other act or omission, including indemnity for loss or diminution of anticipated tax benefits or loss or damage to lessor's residual interest, may be liquidated in the lease agreement but only at an amount or by a formula that is reasonable in light of the then anticipated harm caused by the default or other act or omission.

(2) If the lease agreement provides for liquidation of damages, and such provision does not comply with subsection (1), or such provision is an exclusive or limited remedy that circumstances cause to fail of its essential purpose, remedy may be had as provided in this Article.

(3) If the lessor justifiably withholds or stops delivery of goods because of the lessee's default or insolvency (Section 2A–525 or 2A–526), the lessee is entitled to restitution of any amount by which the sum of his [or her] payments exceeds:

(a) the amount to which the lessor is entitled by virtue of terms liquidating the lessor's damages in accordance with subsection (1); or

(b) in the absence of those terms, 20 percent of the then present value of the total rent the lessee was obligated to pay for the balance of the lease term, or, in the case of a consumer lease, the lesser of such amount or $500.

(4) A lessee's right to restitution under subsection (3) is subject to offset to the extent the lessor establishes:

(a) a right to recover damages under the provisions of this Article other than subsection (1); and

(b) the amount or value of any benefits received by the lessee directly or indirectly by reason of the lease contract.

§ 2A–505. Cancellation and Termination and Effect of Cancellation, Termination, Rescission, or Fraud on Rights and Remedies.

(1) On cancellation of the lease contract, all obligations that are still executory on both sides are discharged, but any right based on prior default or performance survives, and the cancelling party also retains any remedy for default of the whole lease contract or any unperformed balance.

(2) On termination of the lease contract, all obligations that are still executory on both sides are discharged but any right based on prior default or performance survives.

(3) Unless the contrary intention clearly appears, expressions of "cancellation," "rescission," or the like of the lease contract may not be construed as a renunciation or discharge of any claim in damages for an antecedent default.

(4) Rights and remedies for material misrepresentation or fraud include all rights and remedies available under this Article for default.

(5) Neither rescission nor a claim for rescission of the lease contract nor rejection or return of the goods may bar or be deemed inconsistent with a claim for damages or other right or remedy.

§ 2A–506. Statute of Limitations.

(1) An action for default under a lease contract, including breach of warranty or indemnity, must be commenced within 4 years after the cause of action accrued. By the original lease contract the parties may reduce the period of limitation to not less than one year.

(2) A cause of action for default accrues when the act or omission on which the default or breach of warranty is

based is or should have been discovered by the aggrieved party, or when the default occurs, whichever is later. A cause of action for indemnity accrues when the act or omission on which the claim for indemnity is based is or should have been discovered by the indemnified party, whichever is later.

(3) If an action commenced within the time limited by subsection (1) is so terminated as to leave available a remedy by another action for the same default or breach of warranty or indemnity, the other action may be commenced after the expiration of the time limited and within 6 months after the termination of the first action unless the termination resulted from voluntary discontinuance or from dismissal for failure or neglect to prosecute.

(4) This section does not alter the law on tolling of the statute of limitations nor does it apply to causes of action that have accrued before this Article becomes effective.

§ 2A–507. Proof of Market Rent: Time and Place.

(1) Damages based on market rent (Section 2A–519 or 2A–528) are determined according to the rent for the use of the goods concerned for a lease term identical to the remaining lease term of the original lease agreement and prevailing at the times specified in Sections 2A–519 and 2A–528.

(2) If evidence of rent for the use of the goods concerned for a lease term identical to the remaining lease term of the original lease agreement and prevailing at the times or places described in this Article is not readily available, the rent prevailing within any reasonable time before or after the time described or at any other place or for a different lease term which in commercial judgment or under usage of trade would serve as a reasonable substitute for the one described may be used, making any proper allowance for the difference, including the cost of transporting the goods to or from the other place.

(3) Evidence of a relevant rent prevailing at a time or place or for a lease term other than the one described in this Article offered by one party is not admissible unless and until he [or she] has given the other party notice the court finds sufficient to prevent unfair surprise.

(4) If the prevailing rent or value of any goods regularly leased in any established market is in issue, reports in official publications or trade journals or in newspapers or periodicals of general circulation published as the reports of that market are admissible in evidence. The circumstances of the preparation of the report may be shown to affect its weight but not its admissibility.

As amended in 1990.

B. Default by Lessor

§ 2A–508. Lessee's Remedies.

(1) If a lessor fails to deliver the goods in conformity to the lease contract (Section 2A–509) or repudiates the lease contract (Section 2A–402), or a lessee rightfully rejects the goods (Section 2A–509) or justifiably revokes acceptance of the goods (Section 2A–517), then with respect to any goods involved, and with respect to all of the goods if under an installment lease contract the value of the whole lease contract is substantially impaired (Section 2A–510), the lessor is in default under the lease contract and the lessee may:

(a) cancel the lease contract (Section 2A–505(1));

(b) recover so much of the rent and security as has been paid and is just under the circumstances;

(c) cover and recover damages as to all goods affected whether or not they have been identified to the lease contract (Sections 2A–518 and 2A–520), or recover damages for nondelivery (Sections 2A–519 and 2A–520);

(d) exercise any other rights or pursue any other remedies provided in the lease contract.

(2) If a lessor fails to deliver the goods in conformity to the lease contract or repudiates the lease contract, the lessee may also:

(a) if the goods have been identified, recover them (Section 2A–522); or

(b) in a proper case, obtain specific performance or replevy the goods (Section 2A–521).

(3) If a lessor is otherwise in default under a lease contract, the lessee may exercise the rights and pursue the remedies provided in the lease contract, which may include a right to cancel the lease, and in Section 2A–519(3).

(4) If a lessor has breached a warranty, whether express or implied, the lessee may recover damages (Section 2A–519(4)).

(5) On rightful rejection or justifiable revocation of acceptance, a lessee has a security interest in goods in the lessee's possession or control for any rent and security that has been paid and any expenses reasonably incurred in their inspection, receipt, transportation, and care and custody and may hold those goods and dispose of them in good faith and in a commercially reasonable manner, subject to Section 2A–527(5).

(6) Subject to the provisions of Section 2A–407, a lessee, on notifying the lessor of the lessee's intention to do so, may deduct all or any part of the damages resulting from any default under the lease contract from any part of the rent still due under the same lease contract.

As amended in 1990.

§ 2A–509. Lessee's Rights on Improper Delivery; Rightful Rejection.

(1) Subject to the provisions of Section 2A–510 on default in installment lease contracts, if the goods or the tender or delivery fail in any respect to conform to the lease contract, the lessee may reject or accept the goods or accept any commercial unit or units and reject the rest of the goods.

(2) Rejection of goods is ineffective unless it is within a reasonable time after tender or delivery of the goods and the lessee seasonably notifies the lessor.

§ 2A–510. Installment Lease Contracts: Rejection and Default.

(1) Under an installment lease contract a lessee may reject any delivery that is nonconforming if the nonconformity substantially impairs the value of that delivery and cannot be cured or the nonconformity is a defect in the required documents; but if the nonconformity does not fall within subsection (2) and the lessor or the supplier gives adequate assurance of its cure, the lessee must accept that delivery.

(2) Whenever nonconformity or default with respect to one or more deliveries substantially impairs the value of the installment lease contract as a whole there is a default with respect to the whole. But, the aggrieved party reinstates the installment lease contract as a whole if the aggrieved party accepts a nonconforming delivery without seasonably notifying of cancellation or brings an action with respect only to past deliveries or demands performance as to future deliveries.

§ 2A–511. Merchant Lessee's Duties as to Rightfully Rejected Goods.

(1) Subject to any security interest of a lessee (Section 2A–508(5)), if a lessor or a supplier has no agent or place of business at the market of rejection, a merchant lessee, after rejection of goods in his [or her] possession or control, shall follow any reasonable instructions received from the lessor or the supplier with respect to the goods. In the absence of those instructions, a merchant lessee shall make reasonable efforts to sell, lease, or otherwise dispose of the goods for the lessor's account if they threaten to decline in value speedily. Instructions are not reasonable if on demand indemnity for expenses is not forthcoming.

(2) If a merchant lessee (subsection (1)) or any other lessee (Section 2A–512) disposes of goods, he [or she] is entitled to reimbursement either from the lessor or the supplier or out of the proceeds for reasonable expenses of caring for and disposing of the goods and, if the expenses include no disposition commission, to such commission as is usual in the trade, or if there is none, to a reasonable sum not exceeding 10 percent of the gross proceeds.

(3) In complying with this section or Section 2A–512, the lessee is held only to good faith. Good faith conduct hereunder is neither acceptance or conversion nor the basis of an action for damages.

(4) A purchaser who purchases in good faith from a lessee pursuant to this section or Section 2A–512 takes the goods free of any rights of the lessor and the supplier even though the lessee fails to comply with one or more of the requirements of this Article.

§ 2A–512. Lessee's Duties as to Rightfully Rejected Goods.

(1) Except as otherwise provided with respect to goods that threaten to decline in value speedily (Section 2A–511) and subject to any security interest of a lessee (Section 2A–508(5)):

(a) the lessee, after rejection of goods in the lessee's possession, shall hold them with reasonable care at the lessor's or the supplier's disposition for a reasonable time after the lessee's seasonable notification of rejection;

(b) if the lessor or the supplier gives no instructions within a reasonable time after notification of rejection, the lessee may store the rejected goods for the lessor's or the supplier's account or ship them to the lessor or the supplier or dispose of them for the lessor's or the supplier's account with reimbursement in the manner provided in Section 2A–511; but

(c) the lessee has no further obligations with regard to goods rightfully rejected.

(2) Action by the lessee pursuant to subsection (1) is not acceptance or conversion.

§ 2A–513. Cure by Lessor of Improper Tender or Delivery; Replacement.

(1) If any tender or delivery by the lessor or the supplier is rejected because nonconforming and the time for performance has not yet expired, the lessor or the supplier may seasonably notify the lessee of the lessor's or the supplier's intention to cure and may then make a conforming delivery within the time provided in the lease contract.

(2) If the lessee rejects a nonconforming tender that the lessor or the supplier had reasonable grounds to believe would be acceptable with or without money allowance, the lessor or the supplier may have a further reasonable time to substitute a conforming tender if he [or she] seasonably notifies the lessee.

§ 2A–514. Waiver of Lessee's Objections.

(1) In rejecting goods, a lessee's failure to state a particular defect that is ascertainable by reasonable inspection precludes the lessee from relying on the defect to justify rejection or to establish default:

(a) if, stated seasonably, the lessor or the supplier could have cured it (Section 2A–513); or

(b) between merchants if the lessor or the supplier after rejection has made a request in writing for a full and final written statement of all defects on which the lessee proposes to rely.

(2) A lessee's failure to reserve rights when paying rent or other consideration against documents precludes recovery of the payment for defects apparent on the face of the documents.

§ 2A–515. Acceptance of Goods.

(1) Acceptance of goods occurs after the lessee has had a reasonable opportunity to inspect the goods and

(a) the lessee signifies or acts with respect to the goods in a manner that signifies to the lessor or the supplier that the goods are conforming or that the lessee will take or retain them in spite of their nonconformity; or

(b) the lessee fails to make an effective rejection of the goods (Section 2A–509(2)).

(2) Acceptance of a part of any commercial unit is acceptance of that entire unit.

§ 2A–516. Effect of Acceptance of Goods; Notice of Default; Burden of Establishing Default after Acceptance; Notice of Claim or Litigation to Person Answerable Over.

(1) A lessee must pay rent for any goods accepted in accordance with the lease contract, with due allowance for goods rightfully rejected or not delivered.

(2) A lessee's acceptance of goods precludes rejection of the goods accepted. In the case of a finance lease, if made with knowledge of a nonconformity, acceptance cannot be revoked because of it. In any other case, if made with knowledge of a nonconformity, acceptance cannot be revoked because of it unless the acceptance was on the reasonable assumption that the nonconformity would be seasonably cured. Acceptance does not of itself impair any other remedy provided by this Article or the lease agreement for nonconformity.

(3) If a tender has been accepted:

(a) within a reasonable time after the lessee discovers or should have discovered any default, the lessee shall notify the lessor and the supplier, if any, or be barred from any remedy against the party notified;

(b) except in the case of a consumer lease, within a reasonable time after the lessee receives notice of litigation for infringement or the like (Section 2A–211) the lessee shall notify the lessor or be barred from any remedy over for liability established by the litigation; and

(c) the burden is on the lessee to establish any default.

(4) If a lessee is sued for breach of a warranty or other obligation for which a lessor or a supplier is answerable over the following apply:

(a) The lessee may give the lessor or the supplier, or both, written notice of the litigation. If the notice states that the person notified may come in and defend and that if the person notified does not do so that person will be bound in any action against that person by the lessee by any determination of fact common to the two litigations, then unless the person notified after seasonable receipt of the notice does come in and defend that person is so bound.

(b) The lessor or the supplier may demand in writing that the lessee turn over control of the litigation including settlement if the claim is one for infringement or the like (Section 2A–211) or else be barred from any remedy over. If the demand states that the lessor or the supplier agrees to bear all expense and to satisfy any adverse judgment, then unless the lessee after seasonable receipt of the demand does turn over control the lessee is so barred.

(5) Subsections (3) and (4) apply to any obligation of a lessee to hold the lessor or the supplier harmless against infringement or the like (Section 2A–211).

As amended in 1990.

§ 2A–517. Revocation of Acceptance of Goods.

(1) A lessee may revoke acceptance of a lot or commercial unit whose nonconformity substantially impairs its value to the lessee if the lessee has accepted it:

(a) except in the case of a finance lease, on the reasonable assumption that its nonconformity would be cured and it has not been seasonably cured; or

(b) without discovery of the nonconformity if the lessee's acceptance was reasonably induced either by the lessor's assurances or, except in the case of a finance lease, by the difficulty of discovery before acceptance.

(2) Except in the case of a finance lease that is not a consumer lease, a lessee may revoke acceptance of a lot or commercial unit if the lessor defaults under the lease contract and the default substantially impairs the value of that lot or commercial unit to the lessee.

(3) If the lease agreement so provides, the lessee may revoke acceptance of a lot or commercial unit because of other defaults by the lessor.

(4) Revocation of acceptance must occur within a reasonable time after the lessee discovers or should have discovered the ground for it and before any substantial change in condition of the goods which is not caused by the nonconformity. Revocation is not effective until the lessee notifies the lessor.

(5) A lessee who so revokes has the same rights and duties with regard to the goods involved as if the lessee had rejected them.

As amended in 1990.

§ 2A–518. Cover; Substitute Goods.

(1) After a default by a lessor under the lease contract of the type described in Section 2A–508(1), or, if agreed, after other default by the lessor, the lessee may cover by making any purchase or lease of or contract to purchase or lease goods in substitution for those due from the lessor.

(2) Except as otherwise provided with respect to damages liquidated in the lease agreement (Section 2A–504) or otherwise determined pursuant to agreement of the parties (Sections 1–102(3) and 2A–503), if a lessee's cover is by lease agreement substantially similar to the original lease agreement and the new lease agreement is made in good faith and in a commercially reasonable manner, the lessee may recover from the lessor as damages (i) the present value, as of the date of the commencement of the term of the new lease agreement, of the rent under the new lease agreement applicable to that period of the new lease term which is comparable to the then remaining term of the original lease agreement minus the present value as of the same date of the total rent for the then remaining lease term of the original lease agreement, and (ii) any incidental or consequential damages, less expenses saved in consequence of the lessor's default.

(3) If a lessee's cover is by lease agreement that for any reason does not qualify for treatment under subsection

(2), or is by purchase or otherwise, the lessee may recover from the lessor as if the lessee had elected not to cover and Section 2A–519 governs.

As amended in 1990.

§ 2A–519. Lessee's Damages for Non-Delivery, Repudiation, Default, and Breach of Warranty in Regard to Accepted Goods.

(1) Except as otherwise provided with respect to damages liquidated in the lease agreement (Section 2A–504) or otherwise determined pursuant to agreement of the parties (Sections 1–102(3) and 2A–503), if a lessee elects not to cover or a lessee elects to cover and the cover is by lease agreement that for any reason does not qualify for treatment under Section 2A–518(2), or is by purchase or otherwise, the measure of damages for non-delivery or repudiation by the lessor or for rejection or revocation of acceptance by the lessee is the present value, as of the date of the default, of the then market rent minus the present value as of the same date of the original rent, computed for the remaining lease term of the original lease agreement, together with incidental and consequential damages, less expenses saved in consequence of the lessor's default.

(2) Market rent is to be determined as of the place for tender or, in cases of rejection after arrival or revocation of acceptance, as of the place of arrival.

(3) Except as otherwise agreed, if the lessee has accepted goods and given notification (Section 2A–516(3)), the measure of damages for non-conforming tender or delivery or other default by a lessor is the loss resulting in the ordinary course of events from the lessor's default as determined in any manner that is reasonable together with incidental and consequential damages, less expenses saved in consequence of the lessor's default.

(4) Except as otherwise agreed, the measure of damages for breach of warranty is the present value at the time and place of acceptance of the difference between the value of the use of the goods accepted and the value if they had been as warranted for the lease term, unless special circumstances show proximate damages of a different amount, together with incidental and consequential damages, less expenses saved in consequence of the lessor's default or breach of warranty.

As amended in 1990.

§ 2A–520. Lessee's Incidental and Consequential Damages.

(1) Incidental damages resulting from a lessor's default include expenses reasonably incurred in inspection, receipt, transportation, and care and custody of goods rightfully rejected or goods the acceptance of which is justifiably revoked, any commercially reasonable charges, expenses or commissions in connection with effecting cover, and any other reasonable expense incident to the default.

(2) Consequential damages resulting from a lessor's default include:

(a) any loss resulting from general or particular requirements and needs of which the lessor at the time of contracting had reason to know and which could not reasonably be prevented by cover or otherwise; and

(b) injury to person or property proximately resulting from any breach of warranty.

§ 2A–521. Lessee's Right to Specific Performance or Replevin.

(1) Specific performance may be decreed if the goods are unique or in other proper circumstances.

(2) A decree for specific performance may include any terms and conditions as to payment of the rent, damages, or other relief that the court deems just.

(3) A lessee has a right of replevin, detinue, sequestration, claim and delivery, or the like for goods identified to the lease contract if after reasonable effort the lessee is unable to effect cover for those goods or the circumstances reasonably indicate that the effort will be unavailing.

§ 2A–522. Lessee's Right to Goods on Lessor's Insolvency.

(1) Subject to subsection (2) and even though the goods have not been shipped, a lessee who has paid a part or all of the rent and security for goods identified to a lease contract (Section 2A–217) on making and keeping good a tender of any unpaid portion of the rent and security due under the lease contract may recover the goods identified from the lessor if the lessor becomes insolvent within 10 days after receipt of the first installment of rent and security.

(2) A lessee acquires the right to recover goods identified to a lease contract only if they conform to the lease contract.

C. Default by Lessee

§ 2A–523. Lessor's Remedies.

(1) If a lessee wrongfully rejects or revokes acceptance of goods or fails to make a payment when due or repudiates with respect to a part or the whole, then, with respect to any goods involved, and with respect to all of the goods if under an installment lease contract the value of the whole lease contract is substantially impaired (Section 2A–510), the lessee is in default under the lease contract and the lessor may:

(a) cancel the lease contract (Section 2A–505(1));

(b) proceed respecting goods not identified to the lease contract (Section 2A–524);

(c) withhold delivery of the goods and take possession of goods previously delivered (Section 2A–525);

(d) stop delivery of the goods by any bailee (Section 2A–526);

(e) dispose of the goods and recover damages (Section 2A–527), or retain the goods and recover damages (Section 2A–528), or in a proper case recover rent (Section 2A–529)

(f) exercise any other rights or pursue any other remedies provided in the lease contract.

(2) If a lessor does not fully exercise a right or obtain a remedy to which the lessor is entitled under subsection (1), the lessor may recover the loss resulting in the ordinary course of events from the lessee's default as determined in any reasonable manner, together with incidental damages, less expenses saved in consequence of the lessee's default.

(3) If a lessee is otherwise in default under a lease contract, the lessor may exercise the rights and pursue the remedies provided in the lease contract, which may include a right to cancel the lease. In addition, unless otherwise provided in the lease contract:

(a) if the default substantially impairs the value of the lease contract to the lessor, the lessor may exercise the rights and pursue the remedies provided in subsections (1) or (2); or

(b) if the default does not substantially impair the value of the lease contract to the lessor, the lessor may recover as provided in subsection (2).

As amended in 1990.

§ 2A–524. Lessor's Right to Identify Goods to Lease Contract.

(1) After default by the lessee under the lease contract of the type described in Section 2A–523(1) or 2A–523(3)(a) or, if agreed, after other default by the lessee, the lessor may:

(a) identify to the lease contract conforming goods not already identified if at the time the lessor learned of the default they were in the lessor's or the supplier's possession or control; and

(b) dispose of goods (Section 2A–527(1)) that demonstrably have been intended for the particular lease contract even though those goods are unfinished.

(2) If the goods are unfinished, in the exercise of reasonable commercial judgment for the purposes of avoiding loss and of effective realization, an aggrieved lessor or the supplier may either complete manufacture and wholly identify the goods to the lease contract or cease manufacture and lease, sell, or otherwise dispose of the goods for scrap or salvage value or proceed in any other reasonable manner.

As amended in 1990.

§ 2A–525. Lessor's Right to Possession of Goods.

(1) If a lessor discovers the lessee to be insolvent, the lessor may refuse to deliver the goods.

(2) After a default by the lessee under the lease contract of the type described in Section 2A–523(1) or 2A–523(3)(a) or, if agreed, after other default by the lessee, the lessor has the right to take possession of the goods. If the lease contract so provides, the lessor may require the lessee to assemble the goods and make them available to the lessor at a place to be designated by the lessor which is reasonably convenient to both parties. Without removal, the lessor may render unusable any goods employed in trade or business, and may dispose of goods on the lessee's premises (Section 2A–527).

(3) The lessor may proceed under subsection (2) without judicial process if that can be done without breach of the peace or the lessor may proceed by action.

As amended in 1990.

§ 2A–526. Lessor's Stoppage of Delivery in Transit or Otherwise.

(1) A lessor may stop delivery of goods in the possession of a carrier or other bailee if the lessor discovers the lessee to be insolvent and may stop delivery of carload, truckload, planeload, or larger shipments of express or freight if the lessee repudiates or fails to make a payment due before delivery, whether for rent, security or otherwise under the lease contract, or for any other reason the lessor has a right to withhold or take possession of the goods.

(2) In pursuing its remedies under subsection (1), the lessor may stop delivery until

(a) receipt of the goods by the lessee;

(b) acknowledgment to the lessee by any bailee of the goods, except a carrier, that the bailee holds the goods for the lessee; or

(c) such an acknowledgment to the lessee by a carrier via reshipment or as warehouseman.

(3) (a) To stop delivery, a lessor shall so notify as to enable the bailee by reasonable diligence to prevent delivery of the goods.

(b) After notification, the bailee shall hold and deliver the goods according to the directions of the lessor, but the lessor is liable to the bailee for any ensuing charges or damages.

(c) A carrier who has issued a nonnegotiable bill of lading is not obliged to obey a notification to stop received from a person other than the consignor.

§ 2A–527. Lessor's Rights to Dispose of Goods.

(1) After a default by a lessee under the lease contract of the type described in Section 2A–523(1) or 2A–523(3)(a) or after the lessor refuses to deliver or takes possession of goods (Section 2A–525 or 2A–526), or, if agreed, after other default by a lessee, the lessor may dispose of the goods concerned or the undelivered balance thereof by lease, sale, or otherwise.

(2) Except as otherwise provided with respect to damages liquidated in the lease agreement (Section 2A–504) or otherwise determined pursuant to agreement of the parties (Sections 1–102(3) and 2A–503), if the disposition is by lease agreement substantially similar to the original lease agreement and the new lease agreement is made in good faith and in a commercially reasonable manner, the lessor may recover from the lessee as damages (i) accrued and unpaid rent as of the date of the commencement of the term of the new lease agreement, (ii) the pre-

sent value, as of the same date, of the total rent for the then remaining lease term of the original lease agreement minus the present value, as of the same date, of the rent under the new lease agreement applicable to that period of the new lease term which is comparable to the then remaining term of the original lease agreement, and (iii) any incidental damages allowed under Section 2A–530, less expenses saved in consequence of the lessee's default.

(3) If the lessor's disposition is by lease agreement that for any reason does not qualify for treatment under subsection (2), or is by sale or otherwise, the lessor may recover from the lessee as if the lessor had elected not to dispose of the goods and Section 2A–528 governs.

(4) A subsequent buyer or lessee who buys or leases from the lessor in good faith for value as a result of a disposition under this section takes the goods free of the original lease contract and any rights of the original lessee even though the lessor fails to comply with one or more of the requirements of this Article.

(5) The lessor is not accountable to the lessee for any profit made on any disposition. A lessee who has rightfully rejected or justifiably revoked acceptance shall account to the lessor for any excess over the amount of the lessee's security interest (Section 2A–508(5)).

As amended in 1990.

§ 2A–528. Lessor's Damages for Non-acceptance, Failure to Pay, Repudiation, or Other Default.

(1) Except as otherwise provided with respect to damages liquidated in the lease agreement (Section 2A–504) or otherwise determined pursuant to agreement of the parties (Section 1–102(3) and 2A–503), if a lessor elects to retain the goods or a lessor elects to dispose of the goods and the disposition is by lease agreement that for any reason does not qualify for treatment under Section 2A–527(2), or is by sale or otherwise, the lessor may recover from the lessee as damages for a default of the type described in Section 2A–523(1) or 2A–523(3)(a), or if agreed, for other default of the lessee, (i) accrued and unpaid rent as of the date of the default if the lessee has never taken possession of the goods, or, if the lessee has taken possession of the goods, as of the date the lessor repossesses the goods or an earlier date on which the lessee makes a tender of the goods to the lessor, (ii) the present value as of the date determined under clause (i) of the total rent for the then remaining lease term of the original lease agreement minus the present value as of the same date of the market rent as the place where the goods are located computed for the same lease term, and (iii) any incidental damages allowed under Section 2A–530, less expenses saved in consequence of the lessee's default.

(2) If the measure of damages provided in subsection (1) is inadequate to put a lessor in as good a position as performance would have, the measure of damages is the present value of the profit, including reasonable overhead, the lessor would have made from full performance by the lessee, together with any incidental damages allowed under Section 2A–530, due allowance for costs reasonably incurred and due credit for payments or proceeds of disposition.

As amended in 1990.

§ 2A–529. Lessor's Action for the Rent.

(1) After default by the lessee under the lease contract of the type described in Section 2A–523(1) or 2A–523(3)(a) or, if agreed, after other default by the lessee, if the lessor complies with subsection (2), the lessor may recover from the lessee as damages:

(a) for goods accepted by the lessee and not repossessed by or tendered to the lessor, and for conforming goods lost or damaged within a commercially reasonable time after risk of loss passes to the lessee (Section 2A–219), (i) accrued and unpaid rent as of the date of entry of judgment in favor of the lessor (ii) the present value as of the same date of the rent for the then remaining lease term of the lease agreement, and (iii) any incidental damages allowed under Section 2A–530, less expenses saved in consequence of the lessee's default; and

(b) for goods identified to the lease contract if the lessor is unable after reasonable effort to dispose of them at a reasonable price or the circumstances reasonably indicate that effort will be unavailing, (i) accrued and unpaid rent as of the date of entry of judgment in favor of the lessor, (ii) the present value as of the same date of the rent for the then remaining lease term of the lease agreement, and (iii) any incidental damages allowed under Section 2A–530, less expenses saved in consequence of the lessee's default.

(2) Except as provided in subsection (3), the lessor shall hold for the lessee for the remaining lease term of the lease agreement any goods that have been identified to the lease contract and are in the lessor's control.

(3) The lessor may dispose of the goods at any time before collection of the judgment for damages obtained pursuant to subsection (1). If the disposition is before the end of the remaining lease term of the lease agreement, the lessor's recovery against the lessee for damages is governed by Section 2A–527 or Section 2A–528, and the lessor will cause an appropriate credit to be provided against a judgment for damages to the extent that the amount of the judgment exceeds the recovery available pursuant to Section 2A–527 or 2A–528.

(4) Payment of the judgment for damages obtained pursuant to subsection (1) entitles the lessee to the use and possession of the goods not then disposed of for the remaining lease term of and in accordance with the lease agreement.

(5) After default by the lessee under the lease contract of the type described in Section 2A–523(1) or Section 2A–523(3)(a) or, if agreed, after other default by the lessee, a lessor who is held not entitled to rent under this

section must nevertheless be awarded damages for nonacceptance under Sections 2A–527 and 2A–528.

As amended in 1990.

§ 2A–530. Lessor's Incidental Damages.

Incidental damages to an aggrieved lessor include any commercially reasonable charges, expenses, or commissions incurred in stopping delivery, in the transportation, care and custody of goods after the lessee's default, in connection with return or disposition of the goods, or otherwise resulting from the default.

§ 2A–531. Standing to Sue Third Parties for Injury to Goods.

(1) If a third party so deals with goods that have been identified to a lease contract as to cause actionable injury to a party to the lease contract (a) the lessor has a right of action against the third party, and (b) the lessee also has a right of action against the third party if the lessee:

(i) has a security interest in the goods;

(ii) has an insurable interest in the goods; or

(iii) bears the risk of loss under the lease contract or has since the injury assumed that risk as against the lessor and the goods have been converted or destroyed.

(2) If at the time of the injury the party plaintiff did not bear the risk of loss as against the other party to the lease contract and there is no arrangement between them for disposition of the recovery, his [or her] suit or settlement, subject to his [or her] own interest, is as a fiduciary for the other party to the lease contract.

(3) Either party with the consent of the other may sue for the benefit of whom it may concern.

§ 2A–532. Lessor's Rights to Residual Interest.

In addition to any other recovery permitted by this Article or other law, the lessor may recover from the lessee an amount that will fully compensate the lessor for any loss of or damage to the lessor's residual interest in the goods caused by the default of the lessee.

As added in 1990.

Revised Article 3
NEGOTIABLE INSTRUMENTS

Part 1 General Provisions and Definitions

§ 3–101. Short Title.

This Article may be cited as Uniform Commercial Code–Negotiable Instruments.

§ 3–102. Subject Matter.

(a) This Article applies to negotiable instruments. It does not apply to money, to payment orders governed by Article 4A, or to securities governed by Article 8.

(b) If there is conflict between this Article and Article 4 or 9, Articles 4 and 9 govern.

(c) Regulations of the Board of Governors of the Federal Reserve System and operating circulars of the Federal Reserve Banks supersede any inconsistent provision of this Article to the extent of the inconsistency.

§ 3–103. Definitions.

(a) In this Article:

(1) "Acceptor" means a drawee who has accepted a draft.

(2) "Drawee" means a person ordered in a draft to make payment.

(3) "Drawer" means a person who signs or is identified in a draft as a person ordering payment.

(4) "Good faith" means honesty in fact and the observance of reasonable commercial standards of fair dealing.

(5) "Maker" means a person who signs or is identified in a note as a person undertaking to pay.

(6) "Order" means a written instruction to pay money signed by the person giving the instruction. The instruction may be addressed to any person, including the person giving the instruction, or to one or more persons jointly or in the alternative but not in succession. An authorization to pay is not an order unless the person authorized to pay is also instructed to pay.

(7) "Ordinary care" in the case of a person engaged in business means observance of reasonable commercial standards, prevailing in the area in which the person is located, with respect to the business in which the person is engaged. In the case of a bank that takes an instrument for processing for collection or payment by automated means, reasonable commercial standards do not require the bank to examine the instrument if the failure to examine does not violate the bank's prescribed procedures and the bank's procedures do not vary unreasonably from general banking usage not disapproved by this Article or Article 4.

(8) "Party" means a party to an instrument.

(9) "Promise" means a written undertaking to pay money signed by the person undertaking to pay. An acknowledgment of an obligation by the obligor is not a promise unless the obligor also undertakes to pay the obligation.

(10) "Prove" with respect to a fact means to meet the burden of establishing the fact (Section 1–201(8)).

(11) "Remitter" means a person who purchases an instrument from its issuer if the instrument is payable to an identified person other than the purchaser.

(b) [Other definitions' section references deleted.]

(c) [Other definitions' section references deleted.]

(d) In addition, Article 1 contains general definitions and principles of construction and interpretation applicable throughout this Article.

§ 3–104. Negotiable Instrument.

(a) Except as provided in subsections (c) and (d), "negotiable instrument" means an unconditional promise or order to pay a fixed amount of money, with or without interest or other charges described in the promise or order, if it:

(1) is payable to bearer or to order at the time it is issued or first comes into possession of a holder;

(2) is payable on demand or at a definite time; and

(3) does not state any other undertaking or instruction by the person promising or ordering payment to do any act in addition to the payment of money, but the promise or order may contain (i) an undertaking or power to give, maintain, or protect collateral to secure payment, (ii) an authorization or power to the holder to confess judgment or realize on or dispose of collateral, or (iii) a waiver of the benefit of any law intended for the advantage or protection of an obligor.

(b) "Instrument" means a negotiable instrument.

(c) An order that meets all of the requirements of subsection (a), except paragraph (1), and otherwise falls within the definition of "check" in subsection (f) is a negotiable instrument and a check.

(d) A promise or order other than a check is not an instrument if, at the time it is issued or first comes into possession of a holder, it contains a conspicuous statement, however expressed, to the effect that the promise or order is not negotiable or is not an instrument governed by this Article.

(e) An instrument is a "note" if it is a promise and is a "draft" if it is an order. If an instrument falls within the definition of both "note" and "draft," a person entitled to enforce the instrument may treat it as either.

(f) "Check" means (i) a draft, other than a documentary draft, payable on demand and drawn on a bank or (ii) a cashier's check or teller's check. An instrument may be a check even though it is described on its face by another term, such as "money order."

(g) "Cashier's check" means a draft with respect to which the drawer and drawee are the same bank or branches of the same bank.

(h) "Teller's check" means a draft drawn by a bank (i) on another bank, or (ii) payable at or through a bank.

(i) "Traveler's check" means an instrument that (i) is payable on demand, (ii) is drawn on or payable at or through a bank, (iii) is designated by the term "traveler's check" or by a substantially similar term, and (iv) requires, as a condition to payment, a countersignature by a person whose specimen signature appears on the instrument.

(j) "Certificate of deposit" means an instrument containing an acknowledgment by a bank that a sum of money has been received by the bank and a promise by the bank to repay the sum of money. A certificate of deposit is a note of the bank.

§ 3–105. Issue of Instrument.

(a) "Issue" means the first delivery of an instrument by the maker or drawer, whether to a holder or nonholder, for the purpose of giving rights on the instrument to any person.

(b) An unissued instrument, or an unissued incomplete instrument that is completed, is binding on the maker or drawer, but nonissuance is a defense. An instrument that is conditionally issued or is issued for a special purpose is binding on the maker or drawer, but failure of the condition or special purpose to be fulfilled is a defense.

(c) "Issuer" applies to issued and unissued instruments and means a maker or drawer of an instrument.

§ 3–106. Unconditional Promise or Order.

(a) Except as provided in this section, for the purposes of Section 3–104(a), a promise or order is unconditional unless it states (i) an express condition to payment, (ii) that the promise or order is subject to or governed by another writing, or (iii) that rights or obligations with respect to the promise or order are stated in another writing. A reference to another writing does not of itself make the promise or order conditional.

(b) A promise or order is not made conditional (i) by a reference to another writing for a statement of rights with respect to collateral, prepayment, or acceleration, or (ii) because payment is limited to resort to a particular fund or source.

(c) If a promise or order requires, as a condition to payment, a countersignature by a person whose specimen signature appears on the promise or order, the condition does not make the promise or order conditional for the purposes of Section 3–104(a). If the person whose specimen signature appears on an instrument fails to countersign the instrument, the failure to countersign is a defense to the obligation of the issuer, but the failure does not prevent a transferee of the instrument from becoming a holder of the instrument.

(d) If a promise or order at the time it is issued or first comes into possession of a holder contains a statement, required by applicable statutory or administrative law, to the effect that the rights of a holder or transferee are subject to claims or defenses that the issuer could assert against the original payee, the promise or order is not thereby made conditional for the purposes of Section 3–104(a); but if the promise or order is an instrument, there cannot be a holder in due course of the instrument.

§ 3–107. Instrument Payable in Foreign Money.

Unless the instrument otherwise provides, an instrument that states the amount payable in foreign money may be paid in the foreign money or in an equivalent amount in dollars calculated by using the current bank-offered spot rate at the place of payment for the purchase of dollars on the day on which the instrument is paid.

§ 3–108. Payable on Demand or at Definite Time.

(a) A promise or order is "payable on demand" if it (i) states that it is payable on demand or at sight, or otherwise indicates that it is payable at the will of the holder, or (ii) does not state any time of payment.

(b) A promise or order is "payable at a definite time" if it is payable on elapse of a definite period of time after sight or acceptance or at a fixed date or dates or at a time or times readily ascertainable at the time the promise or order is issued, subject to rights of (i) prepayment, (ii) acceleration, (iii) extension at the option of the holder, or (iv) extension to a further definite time at the option of the maker or acceptor or automatically upon or after a specified act or event.

(c) If an instrument, payable at a fixed date, is also payable upon demand made before the fixed date, the instrument is payable on demand until the fixed date and, if demand for payment is not made before that date, becomes payable at a definite time on the fixed date.

§ 3–109. Payable to Bearer or to Order.

(a) A promise or order is payable to bearer if it:

(1) states that it is payable to bearer or to the order of bearer or otherwise indicates that the person in possession of the promise or order is entitled to payment;

(2) does not state a payee; or

(3) states that it is payable to or to the order of cash or otherwise indicates that it is not payable to an identified person.

(b) A promise or order that is not payable to bearer is payable to order if it is payable (i) to the order of an identified person or (ii) to an identified person or order. A promise or order that is payable to order is payable to the identified person.

(c) An instrument payable to bearer may become payable to an identified person if it is specially indorsed pursuant to Section 3–205(a). An instrument payable to an identified person may become payable to bearer if it is indorsed in blank pursuant to Section 3–205(b).

§ 3–110. Identification of Person to Whom Instrument Is Payable.

(a) The person to whom an instrument is initially payable is determined by the intent of the person, whether or not authorized, signing as, or in the name or behalf of, the issuer of the instrument. The instrument is payable to the person intended by the signer even if that person is identified in the instrument by a name or other identification that is not that of the intended person. If more than one person signs in the name or behalf of the issuer of an instrument and all the signers do not intend the same person as payee, the instrument is payable to any person intended by one or more of the signers.

(b) If the signature of the issuer of an instrument is made by automated means, such as a check-writing machine, the payee of the instrument is determined by the intent of the person who supplied the name or identification of the payee, whether or not authorized to do so.

(c) A person to whom an instrument is payable may be identified in any way, including by name, identifying number, office, or account number. For the purpose of determining the holder of an instrument, the following rules apply:

(1) If an instrument is payable to an account and the account is identified only by number, the instrument is payable to the person to whom the account is payable. If an instrument is payable to an account identified by number and by the name of a person, the instrument is payable to the named person, whether or not that person is the owner of the account identified by number.

(2) If an instrument is payable to:

(i) a trust, an estate, or a person described as trustee or representative of a trust or estate, the instrument is payable to the trustee, the representative, or a successor of either, whether or not the beneficiary or estate is also named;

(ii) a person described as agent or similar representative of a named or identified person, the instrument is payable to the represented person, the representative, or a successor of the representative;

(iii) a fund or organization that is not a legal entity, the instrument is payable to a representative of the members of the fund or organization; or

(iv) an office or to a person described as holding an office, the instrument is payable to the named person, the incumbent of the office, or a successor to the incumbent.

(d) If an instrument is payable to two or more persons alternatively, it is payable to any of them and may be negotiated, discharged, or enforced by any or all of them in possession of the instrument. If an instrument is payable to two or more persons not alternatively, it is payable to all of them and may be negotiated, discharged, or enforced only by all of them. If an instrument payable to two or more persons is ambiguous as to whether it is payable to the persons alternatively, the instrument is payable to the persons alternatively.

§ 3–111. Place of Payment.

Except as otherwise provided for items in Article 4, an instrument is payable at the place of payment stated in the instrument. If no place of payment is stated, an instrument is payable at the address of the drawee or maker stated in the instrument. If no address is stated, the place of payment is the place of business of the drawee or maker. If a drawee or maker has more than one place of business, the place of payment is any place of business of the drawee or maker chosen by the person entitled to enforce the instrument. If the drawee or maker has no place of business, the place of payment is the residence of the drawee or maker.

§ 3–112. Interest.

(a) Unless otherwise provided in the instrument, (i) an instrument is not payable with interest, and (ii) interest on an interest-bearing instrument is payable from the date of the instrument.

(b) Interest may be stated in an instrument as a fixed or variable amount of money or it may be expressed as a fixed or variable rate or rates. The amount or rate of interest may be stated or described in the instrument in any manner and may require reference to information not contained in the instrument. If an instrument provides for interest, but the amount of interest payable cannot be ascertained from the description, interest is payable at the judgment rate in effect at the place of payment of the instrument and at the time interest first accrues.

§ 3–113. Date of Instrument.

(a) An instrument may be antedated or postdated. The date stated determines the time of payment if the instrument is payable at a fixed period after date. Except as provided in Section 4–401(c), an instrument payable on demand is not payable before the date of the instrument.

(b) If an instrument is undated, its date is the date of its issue or, in the case of an unissued instrument, the date it first comes into possession of a holder.

§ 3–114. Contradictory Terms of Instrument.

If an instrument contains contradictory terms, typewritten terms prevail over printed terms, handwritten terms prevail over both, and words prevail over numbers.

§ 3–115. Incomplete Instrument.

(a) "Incomplete instrument" means a signed writing, whether or not issued by the signer, the contents of which show at the time of signing that it is incomplete but that the signer intended it to be completed by the addition of words or numbers.

(b) Subject to subsection (c), if an incomplete instrument is an instrument under Section 3–104, it may be enforced according to its terms if it is not completed, or according to its terms as augmented by completion. If an incomplete instrument is not an instrument under Section 3–104, but, after completion, the requirements of Section 3–104 are met, the instrument may be enforced according to its terms as augmented by completion.

(c) If words or numbers are added to an incomplete instrument without authority of the signer, there is an alteration of the incomplete instrument under Section 3–407.

(d) The burden of establishing that words or numbers were added to an incomplete instrument without authority of the signer is on the person asserting the lack of authority.

§ 3–116. Joint and Several Liability; Contribution.

(a) Except as otherwise provided in the instrument, two or more persons who have the same liability on an instrument as makers, drawers, acceptors, indorsers who indorse as joint payees, or anomalous indorsers are jointly and severally liable in the capacity in which they sign.

(b) Except as provided in Section 3–419(e) or by agreement of the affected parties, a party having joint and several liability who pays the instrument is entitled to receive from any party having the same joint and several liability contribution in accordance with applicable law.

(c) Discharge of one party having joint and several liability by a person entitled to enforce the instrument does not affect the right under subsection (b) of a party having the same joint and several liability to receive contribution from the party discharged.

§ 3–117. Other Agreements Affecting Instrument.

Subject to applicable law regarding exclusion of proof of contemporaneous or previous agreements, the obligation of a party to an instrument to pay the instrument may be modified, supplemented, or nullified by a separate agreement of the obligor and a person entitled to enforce the instrument, if the instrument is issued or the obligation is incurred in reliance on the agreement or as part of the same transaction giving rise to the agreement. To the extent an obligation is modified, supplemented, or nullified by an agreement under this section, the agreement is a defense to the obligation.

§ 3–118. Statute of Limitations.

(a) Except as provided in subsection (e), an action to enforce the obligation of a party to pay a note payable at a definite time must be commenced within six years after the due date or dates stated in the note or, if a due date is accelerated, within six years after the accelerated due date.

(b) Except as provided in subsection (d) or (e), if demand for payment is made to the maker of a note payable on demand, an action to enforce the obligation of a party to pay the note must be commenced within six years after the demand. If no demand for payment is made to the maker, an action to enforce the note is barred if neither principal nor interest on the note has been paid for a continuous period of 10 years.

(c) Except as provided in subsection (d), an action to enforce the obligation of a party to an unaccepted draft to pay the draft must be commenced within three years after dishonor of the draft or 10 years after the date of the draft, whichever period expires first.

(d) An action to enforce the obligation of the acceptor of a certified check or the issuer of a teller's check, cashier's check, or traveler's check must be commenced within three years after demand for payment is made to the acceptor or issuer, as the case may be.

(e) An action to enforce the obligation of a party to a certificate of deposit to pay the instrument must be commenced within six years after demand for payment is made to the maker, but if the instrument states a due date and the maker is not required to pay before that date, the six-year period begins when a demand for payment is in effect and the due date has passed.

(f) An action to enforce the obligation of a party to pay an accepted draft, other than a certified check, must be commenced (i) within six years after the due date or dates stated in the draft or acceptance if the obligation of the acceptor is payable at a definite time, or (ii) within six years after the date of the acceptance if the obligation of the acceptor is payable on demand.

(g) Unless governed by other law regarding claims for indemnity or contribution, an action (i) for conversion of an instrument, for money had and received, or like action based on conversion, (ii) for breach of warranty, or (iii) to enforce an obligation, duty, or right arising under this Article and not governed by this section must be commenced within three years after the [cause of action] accrues.

§ 3–119. Notice of Right to Defend Action.

In an action for breach of an obligation for which a third person is answerable over pursuant to this Article or Article 4, the defendant may give the third person written notice of the litigation, and the person notified may then give similar notice to any other person who is answerable over. If the notice states (i) that the person notified may come in and defend and (ii) that failure to do so will bind the person notified in an action later brought by the person giving the notice as to any determination of fact common to the two litigations, the person notified is so bound unless after seasonable receipt of the notice the person notified does come in and defend.

Part 2 Negotiation, Transfer, and Indorsement

§ 3–201. Negotiation.

(a) "Negotiation" means a transfer of possession, whether voluntary or involuntary, of an instrument by a person other than the issuer to a person who thereby becomes its holder.

(b) Except for negotiation by a remitter, if an instrument is payable to an identified person, negotiation requires transfer of possession of the instrument and its indorsement by the holder. If an instrument is payable to bearer, it may be negotiated by transfer of possession alone.

§ 3–202. Negotiation Subject to Rescission.

(a) Negotiation is effective even if obtained (i) from an infant, a corporation exceeding its powers, or a person without capacity, (ii) by fraud, duress, or mistake, or (iii) in breach of duty or as part of an illegal transaction.

(b) To the extent permitted by other law, negotiation may be rescinded or may be subject to other remedies, but those remedies may not be asserted against a subsequent holder in due course or a person paying the instrument in good faith and without knowledge of facts that are a basis for rescission or other remedy.

§ 3–203. Transfer of Instrument; Rights Acquired by Transfer.

(a) An instrument is transferred when it is delivered by a person other than its issuer for the purpose of giving to the person receiving delivery the right to enforce the instrument.

(b) Transfer of an instrument, whether or not the transfer is a negotiation, vests in the transferee any right of the transferor to enforce the instrument, including any right as a holder in due course, but the transferee cannot acquire rights of a holder in due course by a transfer, directly or indirectly, from a holder in due course if the transferee engaged in fraud or illegality affecting the instrument.

(c) Unless otherwise agreed, if an instrument is transferred for value and the transferee does not become a holder because of lack of indorsement by the transferor, the transferee has a specifically enforceable right to the unqualified indorsement of the transferor, but negotiation of the instrument does not occur until the indorsement is made.

(d) If a transferor purports to transfer less than the entire instrument, negotiation of the instrument does not occur. The transferee obtains no rights under this Article and has only the rights of a partial assignee.

§ 3–204. Indorsement.

(a) "Indorsement" means a signature, other than that of a signer as maker, drawer, or acceptor, that alone or accompanied by other words is made on an instrument for the purpose of (i) negotiating the instrument, (ii) restricting payment of the instrument, or (iii) incurring indorser's liability on the instrument, but regardless of the intent of the signer, a signature and its accompanying words is an indorsement unless the accompanying words, terms of the instrument, place of the signature, or other circumstances unambiguously indicate that the signature was made for a purpose other than indorsement. For the purpose of determining whether a signature is made on an instrument, a paper affixed to the instrument is a part of the instrument.

(b) "Indorser" means a person who makes an indorsement.

(c) For the purpose of determining whether the transferee of an instrument is a holder, an indorsement that transfers a security interest in the instrument is effective as an unqualified indorsement of the instrument.

(d) If an instrument is payable to a holder under a name that is not the name of the holder, indorsement may be made by the holder in the name stated in the instrument or in the holder's name or both, but signature in both names may be required by a person paying or taking the instrument for value or collection.

§ 3–205. Special Indorsement; Blank Indorsement; Anomalous Indorsement.

(a) If an indorsement is made by the holder of an instrument, whether payable to an identified person or payable to bearer, and the indorsement identifies a person to whom it makes the instrument payable, it is a "special indorsement." When specially indorsed, an instrument becomes payable to the identified person and may be negotiated only by the indorsement of that person. The principles stated in Section 3–110 apply to special indorsements.

(b) If an indorsement is made by the holder of an instrument and it is not a special indorsement, it is a "blank indorsement." When indorsed in blank, an instrument becomes payable to bearer and may be negotiated by transfer of possession alone until specially indorsed.

(c) The holder may convert a blank indorsement that consists only of a signature into a special indorsement by writing, above the signature of the indorser, words identifying the person to whom the instrument is made payable.

(d) "Anomalous indorsement" means an indorsement made by a person who is not the holder of the instrument. An anomalous indorsement does not affect the manner in which the instrument may be negotiated.

§ 3-206. Restrictive Indorsement.

(a) An indorsement limiting payment to a particular person or otherwise prohibiting further transfer or negotiation of the instrument is not effective to prevent further transfer or negotiation of the instrument.

(b) An indorsement stating a condition to the right of the indorsee to receive payment does not affect the right of the indorsee to enforce the instrument. A person paying the instrument or taking it for value or collection may disregard the condition, and the rights and liabilities of that person are not affected by whether the condition has been fulfilled.

(c) If an instrument bears an indorsement (i) described in Section 4–201(b), or (ii) in blank or to a particular bank using the words "for deposit," "for collection," or other words indicating a purpose of having the instrument collected by a bank for the indorser or for a particular account, the following rules apply:

(1) A person, other than a bank, who purchases the instrument when so indorsed converts the instrument unless the amount paid for the instrument is received by the indorser or applied consistently with the indorsement.

(2) A depositary bank that purchases the instrument or takes it for collection when so indorsed converts the instrument unless the amount paid by the bank with respect to the instrument is received by the indorser or applied consistently with the indorsement.

(3) A payor bank that is also the depositary bank or that takes the instrument for immediate payment over the counter from a person other than a collecting bank converts the instrument unless the proceeds of the instrument are received by the indorser or applied consistently with the indorsement.

(4) Except as otherwise provided in paragraph (3), a payor bank or intermediary bank may disregard the indorsement and is not liable if the proceeds of the instrument are not received by the indorser or applied consistently with the indorsement.

(d) Except for an indorsement covered by subsection (c), if an instrument bears an indorsement using words to the effect that payment is to be made to the indorsee as agent, trustee, or other fiduciary for the benefit of the indorser or another person, the following rules apply:

(1) Unless there is notice of breach of fiduciary duty as provided in Section 3–307, a person who purchases the instrument from the indorsee or takes the instrument from the indorsee for collection or payment may pay the proceeds of payment or the value given for the instrument to the indorsee without regard to whether the indorsee violates a fiduciary duty to the indorser.

(2) A subsequent transferee of the instrument or person who pays the instrument is neither given notice nor otherwise affected by the restriction in the indorsement unless the transferee or payor knows that the fiduciary dealt with the instrument or its proceeds in breach of fiduciary duty.

(e) The presence on an instrument of an indorsement to which this section applies does not prevent a purchaser of the instrument from becoming a holder in due course of the instrument unless the purchaser is a converter under subsection (c) or has notice or knowledge of breach of fiduciary duty as stated in subsection (d).

(f) In an action to enforce the obligation of a party to pay the instrument, the obligor has a defense if payment would violate an indorsement to which this section applies and the payment is not permitted by this section.

§ 3-207. Reacquisition.

Reacquisition of an instrument occurs if it is transferred to a former holder, by negotiation or otherwise. A former holder who reacquires the instrument may cancel indorsements made after the reacquirer first became a holder of the instrument. If the cancellation causes the instrument to be payable to the reacquirer or to bearer, the reacquirer may negotiate the instrument. An indorser whose indorsement is canceled is discharged, and the discharge is effective against any subsequent holder.

Part 3 Enforcement of Instruments

§ 3-301. Person Entitled to Enforce Instrument.

"Person entitled to enforce" an instrument means (i) the holder of the instrument, (ii) a nonholder in possession of the instrument who has the rights of a holder, or (iii) a person not in possession of the instrument who is entitled to enforce the instrument pursuant to Section 3–309 or 3–418(d). A person may be a person entitled to enforce the instrument even though the person is not the owner of the instrument or is in wrongful possession of the instrument.

§ 3-302. Holder in Due Course.

(a) Subject to subsection (c) and Section 3–106(d), "holder in due course" means the holder of an instrument if:

(1) the instrument when issued or negotiated to the holder does not bear such apparent evidence of forgery or alteration or is not otherwise so irregular or incomplete as to call into question its authenticity; and

(2) the holder took the instrument (i) for value, (ii) in good faith, (iii) without notice that the instrument

is overdue or has been dishonored or that there is an uncured default with respect to payment of another instrument issued as part of the same series, (iv) without notice that the instrument contains an unauthorized signature or has been altered, (v) without notice of any claim to the instrument described in Section 3–306, and (vi) without notice that any party has a defense or claim in recoupment described in Section 3–305(a).

(b) Notice of discharge of a party, other than discharge in an insolvency proceeding, is not notice of a defense under subsection (a), but discharge is effective against a person who became a holder in due course with notice of the discharge. Public filing or recording of a document does not of itself constitute notice of a defense, claim in recoupment, or claim to the instrument.

(c) Except to the extent a transferor or predecessor in interest has rights as a holder in due course, a person does not acquire rights of a holder in due course of an instrument taken (i) by legal process or by purchase in an execution, bankruptcy, or creditor's sale or similar proceeding, (ii) by purchase as part of a bulk transaction not in ordinary course of business of the transferor, or (iii) as the successor in interest to an estate or other organization.

(d) If, under Section 3–303(a)(1), the promise of performance that is the consideration for an instrument has been partially performed, the holder may assert rights as a holder in due course of the instrument only to the fraction of the amount payable under the instrument equal to the value of the partial performance divided by the value of the promised performance.

(e) If (i) the person entitled to enforce an instrument has only a security interest in the instrument and (ii) the person obliged to pay the instrument has a defense, claim in recoupment, or claim to the instrument that may be asserted against the person who granted the security interest, the person entitled to enforce the instrument may assert rights as a holder in due course only to an amount payable under the instrument which, at the time of enforcement of the instrument, does not exceed the amount of the unpaid obligation secured.

(f) To be effective, notice must be received at a time and in a manner that gives a reasonable opportunity to act on it.

(g) This section is subject to any law limiting status as a holder in due course in particular classes of transactions.

§ 3–303. Value and Consideration.

(a) An instrument is issued or transferred for value if:

(1) the instrument is issued or transferred for a promise of performance, to the extent the promise has been performed;

(2) the transferee acquires a security interest or other lien in the instrument other than a lien obtained by judicial proceeding;

(3) the instrument is issued or transferred as payment of, or as security for, an antecedent claim against any person, whether or not the claim is due;

(4) the instrument is issued or transferred in exchange for a negotiable instrument; or

(5) the instrument is issued or transferred in exchange for the incurring of an irrevocable obligation to a third party by the person taking the instrument.

(b) "Consideration" means any consideration sufficient to support a simple contract. The drawer or maker of an instrument has a defense if the instrument is issued without consideration. If an instrument is issued for a promise of performance, the issuer has a defense to the extent performance of the promise is due and the promise has not been performed. If an instrument is issued for value as stated in subsection (a), the instrument is also issued for consideration.

§ 3–304. Overdue Instrument.

(a) An instrument payable on demand becomes overdue at the earliest of the following times:

(1) on the day after the day demand for payment is duly made;

(2) if the instrument is a check, 90 days after its date; or

(3) if the instrument is not a check, when the instrument has been outstanding for a period of time after its date which is unreasonably long under the circumstances of the particular case in light of the nature of the instrument and usage of the trade.

(b) With respect to an instrument payable at a definite time the following rules apply:

(1) If the principal is payable in installments and a due date has not been accelerated, the instrument becomes overdue upon default under the instrument for nonpayment of an installment, and the instrument remains overdue until the default is cured.

(2) If the principal is not payable in installments and the due date has not been accelerated, the instrument becomes overdue on the day after the due date.

(3) If a due date with respect to principal has been accelerated, the instrument becomes overdue on the day after the accelerated due date.

(c) Unless the due date of principal has been accelerated, an instrument does not become overdue if there is default in payment of interest but no default in payment of principal.

§ 3–305. Defenses and Claims in Recoupment.

(a) Except as stated in subsection (b), the right to enforce the obligation of a party to pay an instrument is subject to the following:

(1) a defense of the obligor based on (i) infancy of the obligor to the extent it is a defense to a simple contract, (ii) duress, lack of legal capacity, or illegality of the transaction which, under other law, nullifies the obligation of the obligor, (iii) fraud that induced the obligor to sign the instrument with neither knowledge nor reasonable opportunity to learn of its char-

acter or its essential terms, or (iv) discharge of the obligor in insolvency proceedings;

(2) a defense of the obligor stated in another section of this Article or a defense of the obligor that would be available if the person entitled to enforce the instrument were enforcing a right to payment under a simple contract; and

(3) a claim in recoupment of the obligor against the original payee of the instrument if the claim arose from the transaction that gave rise to the instrument; but the claim of the obligor may be asserted against a transferee of the instrument only to reduce the amount owing on the instrument at the time the action is brought.

(b) The right of a holder in due course to enforce the obligation of a party to pay the instrument is subject to defenses of the obligor stated in subsection (a)(1), but is not subject to defenses of the obligor stated in subsection (a)(2) or claims in recoupment stated in subsection (a)(3) against a person other than the holder.

(c) Except as stated in subsection (d), in an action to enforce the obligation of a party to pay the instrument, the obligor may not assert against the person entitled to enforce the instrument a defense, claim in recoupment, or claim to the instrument (Section 3–306) of another person, but the other person's claim to the instrument may be asserted by the obligor if the other person is joined in the action and personally asserts the claim against the person entitled to enforce the instrument. An obligor is not obliged to pay the instrument if the person seeking enforcement of the instrument does not have rights of a holder in due course and the obligor proves that the instrument is a lost or stolen instrument.

(d) In an action to enforce the obligation of an accommodation party to pay an instrument, the accommodation party may assert against the person entitled to enforce the instrument any defense or claim in recoupment under subsection (a) that the accommodated party could assert against the person entitled to enforce the instrument, except the defenses of discharge in insolvency proceedings, infancy, and lack of legal capacity.

§ 3–306. Claims to an Instrument.

A person taking an instrument, other than a person having rights of a holder in due course, is subject to a claim of a property or possessory right in the instrument or its proceeds, including a claim to rescind a negotiation and to recover the instrument or its proceeds. A person having rights of a holder in due course takes free of the claim to the instrument.

§ 3–307. Notice of Breach of Fiduciary Duty.

(a) In this section:

(1) "Fiduciary" means an agent, trustee, partner, corporate officer or director, or other representative owing a fiduciary duty with respect to an instrument.

(2) "Represented person" means the principal, beneficiary, partnership, corporation, or other person to whom the duty stated in paragraph (1) is owed.

(b) If (i) an instrument is taken from a fiduciary for payment or collection or for value, (ii) the taker has knowledge of the fiduciary status of the fiduciary, and (iii) the represented person makes a claim to the instrument or its proceeds on the basis that the transaction of the fiduciary is a breach of fiduciary duty, the following rules apply:

(1) Notice of breach of fiduciary duty by the fiduciary is notice of the claim of the represented person.

(2) In the case of an instrument payable to the represented person or the fiduciary as such, the taker has notice of the breach of fiduciary duty if the instrument is (i) taken in payment of or as security for a debt known by the taker to be the personal debt of the fiduciary, (ii) taken in a transaction known by the taker to be for the personal benefit of the fiduciary, or (iii) deposited to an account other than an account of the fiduciary, as such, or an account of the represented person.

(3) If an instrument is issued by the represented person or the fiduciary as such, and made payable to the fiduciary personally, the taker does not have notice of the breach of fiduciary duty unless the taker knows of the breach of fiduciary duty.

(4) If an instrument is issued by the represented person or the fiduciary as such, to the taker as payee, the taker has notice of the breach of fiduciary duty if the instrument is (i) taken in payment of or as security for a debt known by the taker to be the personal debt of the fiduciary, (ii) taken in a transaction known by the taker to be for the personal benefit of the fiduciary, or (iii) deposited to an account other than an account of the fiduciary, as such, or an account of the represented person.

§ 3–308. Proof of Signatures and Status as Holder in Due Course.

(a) In an action with respect to an instrument, the authenticity of, and authority to make, each signature on the instrument is admitted unless specifically denied in the pleadings. If the validity of a signature is denied in the pleadings, the burden of establishing validity is on the person claiming validity, but the signature is presumed to be authentic and authorized unless the action is to enforce the liability of the purported signer and the signer is dead or incompetent at the time of trial of the issue of validity of the signature. If an action to enforce the instrument is brought against a person as the undisclosed principal of a person who signed the instrument as a party to the instrument, the plaintiff has the burden of establishing that the defendant is liable on the instrument as a represented person under Section 3–402(a).

(b) If the validity of signatures is admitted or proved and there is compliance with subsection (a), a plaintiff producing the instrument is entitled to payment if the plaintiff proves entitlement to enforce the instrument under Section 3–301, unless the defendant proves a defense or claim in recoupment. If a defense or claim in recoupment is proved, the right to payment of the plaintiff is subject to the defense or claim, except to the extent the plaintiff proves that the plaintiff has rights of a holder in due course which are not subject to the defense or claim.

§ 3–309. Enforcement of Lost, Destroyed, or Stolen Instrument.

(a) A person not in possession of an instrument is entitled to enforce the instrument if (i) the person was in possession of the instrument and entitled to enforce it when loss of possession occurred, (ii) the loss of possession was not the result of a transfer by the person or a lawful seizure, and (iii) the person cannot reasonably obtain possession of the instrument because the instrument was destroyed, its whereabouts cannot be determined, or it is in the wrongful possession of an unknown person or a person that cannot be found or is not amenable to service of process.

(b) A person seeking enforcement of an instrument under subsection (a) must prove the terms of the instrument and the person's right to enforce the instrument. If that proof is made, Section 3–308 applies to the case as if the person seeking enforcement had produced the instrument. The court may not enter judgment in favor of the person seeking enforcement unless it finds that the person required to pay the instrument is adequately protected against loss that might occur by reason of a claim by another person to enforce the instrument. Adequate protection may be provided by any reasonable means.

§ 3–310. Effect of Instrument on Obligation for Which Taken.

(a) Unless otherwise agreed, if a certified check, cashier's check, or teller's check is taken for an obligation, the obligation is discharged to the same extent discharge would result if an amount of money equal to the amount of the instrument were taken in payment of the obligation. Discharge of the obligation does not affect any liability that the obligor may have as an indorser of the instrument.

(b) Unless otherwise agreed and except as provided in subsection (a), if a note or an uncertified check is taken for an obligation, the obligation is suspended to the same extent the obligation would be discharged if an amount of money equal to the amount of the instrument were taken, and the following rules apply:

(1) In the case of an uncertified check, suspension of the obligation continues until dishonor of the check or until it is paid or certified. Payment or certification of the check results in discharge of the obligation to the extent of the amount of the check.

(2) In the case of a note, suspension of the obligation continues until dishonor of the note or until it is paid. Payment of the note results in discharge of the obligation to the extent of the payment.

(3) Except as provided in paragraph (4), if the check or note is dishonored and the obligee of the obligation for which the instrument was taken is the person entitled to enforce the instrument, the obligee may enforce either the instrument or the obligation. In the case of an instrument of a third person which is negotiated to the obligee by the obligor, discharge of the obligor on the instrument also discharges the obligation.

(4) If the person entitled to enforce the instrument taken for an obligation is a person other than the obligee, the obligee may not enforce the obligation to the extent the obligation is suspended. If the obligee is the person entitled to enforce the instrument but no longer has possession of it because it was lost, stolen, or destroyed, the obligation may not be enforced to the extent of the amount payable on the instrument, and to that extent the obligee's rights against the obligor are limited to enforcement of the instrument.

(c) If an instrument other than one described in subsection (a) or (b) is taken for an obligation, the effect is (i) that stated in subsection (a) if the instrument is one on which a bank is liable as maker or acceptor, or (ii) that stated in subsection (b) in any other case.

§ 3–311. Accord and Satisfaction by Use of Instrument.

(a) If a person against whom a claim is asserted proves that (i) that person in good faith tendered an instrument to the claimant as full satisfaction of the claim, (ii) the amount of the claim was unliquidated or subject to a bona fide dispute, and (iii) the claimant obtained payment of the instrument, the following subsections apply.

(b) Unless subsection (c) applies, the claim is discharged if the person against whom the claim is asserted proves that the instrument or an accompanying written communication contained a conspicuous statement to the effect that the instrument was tendered as full satisfaction of the claim.

(c) Subject to subsection (d), a claim is not discharged under subsection (b) if either of the following applies:

(1) The claimant, if an organization, proves that (i) within a reasonable time before the tender, the claimant sent a conspicuous statement to the person against whom the claim is asserted that communications concerning disputed debts, including an instrument tendered as full satisfaction of a debt, are to be sent to a designated person, office, or place, and (ii) the instrument or accompanying communication was not received by that designated person, office, or place.

(2) The claimant, whether or not an organization, proves that within 90 days after payment of the instrument, the claimant tendered repayment of the amount of the instrument to the person against whom the claim is asserted. This paragraph does not

apply if the claimant is an organization that sent a statement complying with paragraph (1)(i).

(d) A claim is discharged if the person against whom the claim is asserted proves that within a reasonable time before collection of the instrument was initiated, the claimant, or an agent of the claimant having direct responsibility with respect to the disputed obligation, knew that the instrument was tendered in full satisfaction of the claim.

§ 3–312. Lost, Destroyed, or Stolen Cashier's Check, Teller's Check, or Certified Check.*

(a) In this section:

(1) "Check" means a cashier's check, teller's check, or certified check.

(2) "Claimant" means a person who claims the right to receive the amount of a cashier's check, teller's check, or certified check that was lost, destroyed, or stolen.

(3) "Declaration of loss" means a written statement, made under penalty of perjury, to the effect that (i) the declarer lost possession of a check, (ii) the declarer is the drawer or payee of the check, in the case of a certified check, or the remitter or payee of the check, in the case of a cashier's check or teller's check, (iii) the loss of possession was not the result of a transfer by the declarer or a lawful seizure, and (iv) the declarer cannot reasonably obtain possession of the check because the check was destroyed, its whereabouts cannot be determined, or it is in the wrongful possession of an unknown person or a person that cannot be found or is not amenable to service of process.

(4) "Obligated bank" means the issuer of a cashier's check or teller's check or the acceptor of a certified check.

(b) A claimant may assert a claim to the amount of a check by a communication to the obligated bank describing the check with reasonable certainty and requesting payment of the amount of the check, if (i) the claimant is the drawer or payee of a certified check or the remitter or payee of a cashier's check or teller's check, (ii) the communication contains or is accompanied by a declaration of loss of the claimant with respect to the check, (iii) the communication is received at a time and in a manner affording the bank a reasonable time to act on it before the check is paid, and (iv) the claimant provides reasonable identification if requested by the obligated bank. Delivery of a declaration of loss is a warranty of the truth of the statements made in the declaration. If a claim is asserted in compliance with this subsection, the following rules apply:

(1) The claim becomes enforceable at the later of (i) the time the claim is asserted, or (ii) the 90th day following the date of the check, in the case of a cashier's check or teller's check, or the 90th day following the date of the acceptance, in the case of a certified check.

(2) Until the claim becomes enforceable, it has no legal effect and the obligated bank may pay the check or, in the case of a teller's check, may permit the drawee to pay the check. Payment to a person entitled to enforce the check discharges all liability of the obligated bank with respect to the check.

(3) If the claim becomes enforceable before the check is presented for payment, the obligated bank is not obliged to pay the check.

(4) When the claim becomes enforceable, the obligated bank becomes obliged to pay the amount of the check to the claimant if payment of the check has not been made to a person entitled to enforce the check. Subject to Section 4–302(a)(1), payment to the claimant discharges all liability of the obligated bank with respect to the check.

(c) If the obligated bank pays the amount of a check to a claimant under subsection (b)(4) and the check is presented for payment by a person having rights of a holder in due course, the claimant is obliged to (i) refund the payment to the obligated bank if the check is paid, or (ii) pay the amount of the check to the person having rights of a holder in due course if the check is dishonored.

(d) If a claimant has the right to assert a claim under subsection (b) and is also a person entitled to enforce a cashier's check, teller's check, or certified check which is lost, destroyed, or stolen, the claimant may assert rights with respect to the check either under this section or Section 3–309.

Added in 1991.

Part 4 Liability of Parties

§ 3–401. Signature.

(a) A person is not liable on an instrument unless (i) the person signed the instrument, or (ii) the person is represented by an agent or representative who signed the instrument and the signature is binding on the represented person under Section 3–402.

(b) A signature may be made (i) manually or by means of a device or machine, and (ii) by the use of any name, including a trade or assumed name, or by a word, mark, or symbol executed or adopted by a person with present intention to authenticate a writing.

§ 3–402. Signature by Representative.

(a) If a person acting, or purporting to act, as a representative signs an instrument by signing either the name of the represented person or the name of the signer, the represented person is bound by the signature to the same extent the represented person would be bound if the signature were on a simple contract. If the represented

* [Section 3–312 was not adopted as part of the 1990 Official Text of Revised Article 3. It was officially approved and recommended for enactment in all states in August 1991 by the National Conference of Commissioners on Uniform State Laws.]

person is bound, the signature of the representative is the "authorized signature of the represented person" and the represented person is liable on the instrument, whether or not identified in the instrument.

(b) If a representative signs the name of the representative to an instrument and the signature is an authorized signature of the represented person, the following rules apply:

(1) If the form of the signature shows unambiguously that the signature is made on behalf of the represented person who is identified in the instrument, the representative is not liable on the instrument.

(2) Subject to subsection (c), if (i) the form of the signature does not show unambiguously that the signature is made in a representative capacity or (ii) the represented person is not identified in the instrument, the representative is liable on the instrument to a holder in due course that took the instrument without notice that the representative was not intended to be liable on the instrument. With respect to any other person, the representative is liable on the instrument unless the representative proves that the original parties did not intend the representative to be liable on the instrument.

(c) If a representative signs the name of the representative as drawer of a check without indication of the representative status and the check is payable from an account of the represented person who is identified on the check, the signer is not liable on the check if the signature is an authorized signature of the represented person.

§ 3–403. Unauthorized Signature.

(a) Unless otherwise provided in this Article or Article 4, an unauthorized signature is ineffective except as the signature of the unauthorized signer in favor of a person who in good faith pays the instrument or takes it for value. An unauthorized signature may be ratified for all purposes of this Article.

(b) If the signature of more than one person is required to constitute the authorized signature of an organization, the signature of the organization is unauthorized if one of the required signatures is lacking.

(c) The civil or criminal liability of a person who makes an unauthorized signature is not affected by any provision of this Article which makes the unauthorized signature effective for the purposes of this Article.

§ 3–404. Impostors; Fictitious Payees.

(a) If an impostor, by use of the mails or otherwise, induces the issuer of an instrument to issue the instrument to the impostor, or to a person acting in concert with the impostor, by impersonating the payee of the instrument or a person authorized to act for the payee, an indorsement of the instrument by any person in the name of the payee is effective as the indorsement of the payee in favor of a person who, in good faith, pays the instrument or takes it for value or for collection.

(b) If (i) a person whose intent determines to whom an instrument is payable (Section 3–110(a) or (b)) does not intend the person identified as payee to have any interest in the instrument, or (ii) the person identified as payee of an instrument is a fictitious person, the following rules apply until the instrument is negotiated by special indorsement:

(1) Any person in possession of the instrument is its holder.

(2) An indorsement by any person in the name of the payee stated in the instrument is effective as the indorsement of the payee in favor of a person who, in good faith, pays the instrument or takes it for value or for collection.

(c) Under subsection (a) or (b), an indorsement is made in the name of a payee if (i) it is made in a name substantially similar to that of the payee or (ii) the instrument, whether or not indorsed, is deposited in a depositary bank to an account in a name substantially similar to that of the payee.

(d) With respect to an instrument to which subsection (a) or (b) applies, if a person paying the instrument or taking it for value or for collection fails to exercise ordinary care in paying or taking the instrument and that failure substantially contributes to loss resulting from payment of the instrument, the person bearing the loss may recover from the person failing to exercise ordinary care to the extent the failure to exercise ordinary care contributed to the loss.

§ 3–405. Employer's Responsibility for Fraudulent Indorsement by Employee.

(a) In this section:

(1) "Employee" includes an independent contractor and employee of an independent contractor retained by the employer.

(2) "Fraudulent indorsement" means (i) in the case of an instrument payable to the employer, a forged indorsement purporting to be that of the employer, or (ii) in the case of an instrument with respect to which the employer is the issuer, a forged indorsement purporting to be that of the person identified as payee.

(3) "Responsibility" with respect to instruments means authority (i) to sign or indorse instruments on behalf of the employer, (ii) to process instruments received by the employer for bookkeeping purposes, for deposit to an account, or for other disposition, (iii) to prepare or process instruments for issue in the name of the employer, (iv) to supply information determining the names or addresses of payees of instruments to be issued in the name of the employer, (v) to control the disposition of instruments to be issued in the name of the employer, or (vi) to act otherwise with respect to instruments in a responsible capacity. "Responsibility" does not include authority that merely allows an employee to have access to instruments or blank or incomplete instrument forms

that are being stored or transported or are part of incoming or outgoing mail, or similar access.

(b) For the purpose of determining the rights and liabilities of a person who, in good faith, pays an instrument or takes it for value or for collection, if an employer entrusted an employee with responsibility with respect to the instrument and the employee or a person acting in concert with the employee makes a fraudulent indorsement of the instrument, the indorsement is effective as the indorsement of the person to whom the instrument is payable if it is made in the name of that person. If the person paying the instrument or taking it for value or for collection fails to exercise ordinary care in paying or taking the instrument and that failure substantially contributes to loss resulting from the fraud, the person bearing the loss may recover from the person failing to exercise ordinary care to the extent the failure to exercise ordinary care contributed to the loss.

(c) Under subsection (b), an indorsement is made in the name of the person to whom an instrument is payable if (i) it is made in a name substantially similar to the name of that person or (ii) the instrument, whether or not indorsed, is deposited in a depositary bank to an account in a name substantially similar to the name of that person.

§ 3–406. Negligence Contributing to Forged Signature or Alteration of Instrument.

(a) A person whose failure to exercise ordinary care substantially contributes to an alteration of an instrument or to the making of a forged signature on an instrument is precluded from asserting the alteration or the forgery against a person who, in good faith, pays the instrument or takes it for value or for collection.

(b) Under subsection (a), if the person asserting the preclusion fails to exercise ordinary care in paying or taking the instrument and that failure substantially contributes to loss, the loss is allocated between the person precluded and the person asserting the preclusion according to the extent to which the failure of each to exercise ordinary care contributed to the loss.

(c) Under subsection (a), the burden of proving failure to exercise ordinary care is on the person asserting the preclusion. Under subsection (b), the burden of proving failure to exercise ordinary care is on the person precluded.

§ 3–407. Alteration.

(a) "Alteration" means (i) an unauthorized change in an instrument that purports to modify in any respect the obligation of a party, or (ii) an unauthorized addition of words or numbers or other change to an incomplete instrument relating to the obligation of a party.

(b) Except as provided in subsection (c), an alteration fraudulently made discharges a party whose obligation is affected by the alteration unless that party assents or is precluded from asserting the alteration. No other alteration discharges a party, and the instrument may be enforced according to its original terms.

(c) A payor bank or drawee paying a fraudulently altered instrument or a person taking it for value, in good faith and without notice of the alteration, may enforce rights with respect to the instrument (i) according to its original terms, or (ii) in the case of an incomplete instrument altered by unauthorized completion, according to its terms as completed.

§ 3–408. Drawee Not Liable on Unaccepted Draft.

A check or other draft does not of itself operate as an assignment of funds in the hands of the drawee available for its payment, and the drawee is not liable on the instrument until the drawee accepts it.

§ 3–409. Acceptance of Draft; Certified Check.

(a) "Acceptance" means the drawee's signed agreement to pay a draft as presented. It must be written on the draft and may consist of the drawee's signature alone. Acceptance may be made at any time and becomes effective when notification pursuant to instructions is given or the accepted draft is delivered for the purpose of giving rights on the acceptance to any person.

(b) A draft may be accepted although it has not been signed by the drawer, is otherwise incomplete, is overdue, or has been dishonored.

(c) If a draft is payable at a fixed period after sight and the acceptor fails to date the acceptance, the holder may complete the acceptance by supplying a date in good faith.

(d) "Certified check" means a check accepted by the bank on which it is drawn. Acceptance may be made as stated in subsection (a) or by a writing on the check which indicates that the check is certified. The drawee of a check has no obligation to certify the check, and refusal to certify is not dishonor of the check.

§ 3–410. Acceptance Varying Draft.

(a) If the terms of a drawee's acceptance vary from the terms of the draft as presented, the holder may refuse the acceptance and treat the draft as dishonored. In that case, the drawee may cancel the acceptance.

(b) The terms of a draft are not varied by an acceptance to pay at a particular bank or place in the United States, unless the acceptance states that the draft is to be paid only at that bank or place.

(c) If the holder assents to an acceptance varying the terms of a draft, the obligation of each drawer and indorser that does not expressly assent to the acceptance is discharged.

§ 3–411. Refusal to Pay Cashier's Checks, Teller's Checks, and Certified Checks.

(a) In this section, "obligated bank" means the acceptor of a certified check or the issuer of a cashier's check or teller's check bought from the issuer.

(b) If the obligated bank wrongfully (i) refuses to pay a cashier's check or certified check, (ii) stops payment of a teller's check, or (iii) refuses to pay a dishonored teller's check, the person asserting the right to enforce the check is entitled to compensation for expenses and loss of interest resulting from the nonpayment and may recover consequential damages if the obligated bank refuses to pay after receiving notice of particular circumstances giving rise to the damages.

(c) Expenses or consequential damages under subsection (b) are not recoverable if the refusal of the obligated bank to pay occurs because (i) the bank suspends payments, (ii) the obligated bank asserts a claim or defense of the bank that it has reasonable grounds to believe is available against the person entitled to enforce the instrument, (iii) the obligated bank has a reasonable doubt whether the person demanding payment is the person entitled to enforce the instrument, or (iv) payment is prohibited by law.

§ 3–412. Obligation of Issuer of Note or Cashier's Check.

The issuer of a note or cashier's check or other draft drawn on the drawer is obliged to pay the instrument (i) according to its terms at the time it was issued or, if not issued, at the time it first came into possession of a holder, or (ii) if the issuer signed an incomplete instrument, according to its terms when completed, to the extent stated in Sections 3–115 and 3–407. The obligation is owed to a person entitled to enforce the instrument or to an indorser who paid the instrument under Section 3–415.

§ 3–413. Obligation of Acceptor.

(a) The acceptor of a draft is obliged to pay the draft (i) according to its terms at the time it was accepted, even though the acceptance states that the draft is payable "as originally drawn" or equivalent terms, (ii) if the acceptance varies the terms of the draft, according to the terms of the draft as varied, or (iii) if the acceptance is of a draft that is an incomplete instrument, according to its terms when completed, to the extent stated in Sections 3–115 and 3–407. The obligation is owed to a person entitled to enforce the draft or to the drawer or an indorser who paid the draft under Section 3–414 or 3–415.

(b) If the certification of a check or other acceptance of a draft states the amount certified or accepted, the obligation of the acceptor is that amount. If (i) the certification or acceptance does not state an amount, (ii) the amount of the instrument is subsequently raised, and (iii) the instrument is then negotiated to a holder in due course, the obligation of the acceptor is the amount of the instrument at the time it was taken by the holder in due course.

§ 3–414. Obligation of Drawer.

(a) This section does not apply to cashier's checks or other drafts drawn on the drawer.

(b) If an unaccepted draft is dishonored, the drawer is obliged to pay the draft (i) according to its terms at the time it was issued or, if not issued, at the time it first came into possession of a holder, or (ii) if the drawer signed an incomplete instrument, according to its terms when completed, to the extent stated in Sections 3–115 and 3–407. The obligation is owed to a person entitled to enforce the draft or to an indorser who paid the draft under Section 3–415.

(c) If a draft is accepted by a bank, the drawer is discharged, regardless of when or by whom acceptance was obtained.

(d) If a draft is accepted and the acceptor is not a bank, the obligation of the drawer to pay the draft if the draft is dishonored by the acceptor is the same as the obligation of an indorser under Section 3–415(a) and (c).

(e) If a draft states that it is drawn "without recourse" or otherwise disclaims liability of the drawer to pay the draft, the drawer is not liable under subsection (b) to pay the draft if the draft is not a check. A disclaimer of the liability stated in subsection (b) is not effective if the draft is a check.

(f) If (i) a check is not presented for payment or given to a depositary bank for collection within 30 days after its date, (ii) the drawee suspends payments after expiration of the 30-day period without paying the check, and (iii) because of the suspension of payments, the drawer is deprived of funds maintained with the drawee to cover payment of the check, the drawer to the extent deprived of funds may discharge its obligation to pay the check by assigning to the person entitled to enforce the check the rights of the drawer against the drawee with respect to the funds.

§ 3–415. Obligation of Indorser.

(a) Subject to subsections (b), (c), and (d) and to Section 3–419(d), if an instrument is dishonored, an indorser is obliged to pay the amount due on the instrument (i) according to the terms of the instrument at the time it was indorsed, or (ii) if the indorser indorsed an incomplete instrument, according to its terms when completed, to the extent stated in Sections 3–115 and 3–407. The obligation of the indorser is owed to a person entitled to enforce the instrument or to a subsequent indorser who paid the instrument under this section.

(b) If an indorsement states that it is made "without recourse" or otherwise disclaims liability of the indorser, the indorser is not liable under subsection (a) to pay the instrument.

(c) If notice of dishonor of an instrument is required by Section 3–503 and notice of dishonor complying with that section is not given to an indorser, the liability of the indorser under subsection (a) is discharged.

(d) If a draft is accepted by a bank after an indorsement is made, the liability of the indorser under subsection (a) is discharged.

(e) If an indorser of a check is liable under subsection (a) and the check is not presented for payment, or given to a depositary bank for collection, within 30 days after the day the indorsement was made, the liability of the indorser under subsection (a) is discharged.

As amended in 1993.

§ 3–416. Transfer Warranties.

(a) A person who transfers an instrument for consideration warrants to the transferee and, if the transfer is by indorsement, to any subsequent transferee that:

(1) the warrantor is a person entitled to enforce the instrument;

(2) all signatures on the instrument are authentic and authorized;

(3) the instrument has not been altered;

(4) the instrument is not subject to a defense or claim in recoupment of any party which can be asserted against the warrantor; and

(5) the warrantor has no knowledge of any insolvency proceeding commenced with respect to the maker or acceptor or, in the case of an unaccepted draft, the drawer.

(b) A person to whom the warranties under subsection (a) are made and who took the instrument in good faith may recover from the warrantor as damages for breach of warranty an amount equal to the loss suffered as a result of the breach, but not more than the amount of the instrument plus expenses and loss of interest incurred as a result of the breach.

(c) The warranties stated in subsection (a) cannot be disclaimed with respect to checks. Unless notice of a claim for breach of warranty is given to the warrantor within 30 days after the claimant has reason to know of the breach and the identity of the warrantor, the liability of the warrantor under subsection (b) is discharged to the extent of any loss caused by the delay in giving notice of the claim.

(d) A [cause of action] for breach of warranty under this section accrues when the claimant has reason to know of the breach.

§ 3–417. Presentment Warranties.

(a) If an unaccepted draft is presented to the drawee for payment or acceptance and the drawee pays or accepts the draft, (i) the person obtaining payment or acceptance, at the time of presentment, and (ii) a previous transferor of the draft, at the time of transfer, warrant to the drawee making payment or accepting the draft in good faith that:

(1) the warrantor is, or was, at the time the warrantor transferred the draft, a person entitled to enforce the draft or authorized to obtain payment or acceptance of the draft on behalf of a person entitled to enforce the draft;

(2) the draft has not been altered; and

(3) the warrantor has no knowledge that the signature of the drawer of the draft is unauthorized.

(b) A drawee making payment may recover from any warrantor damages for breach of warranty equal to the amount paid by the drawee less the amount the drawee received or is entitled to receive from the drawer because of the payment. In addition, the drawee is entitled to compensation for expenses and loss of interest resulting from the breach. The right of the drawee to recover damages under this subsection is not affected by any failure of the drawee to exercise ordinary care in making payment. If the drawee accepts the draft, breach of warranty is a defense to the obligation of the acceptor. If the acceptor makes payment with respect to the draft, the acceptor is entitled to recover from any warrantor for breach of warranty the amounts stated in this subsection.

(c) If a drawee asserts a claim for breach of warranty under subsection (a) based on an unauthorized indorsement of the draft or an alteration of the draft, the warrantor may defend by proving that the indorsement is effective under Section 3–404 or 3–405 or the drawer is precluded under Section 3–406 or 4–406 from asserting against the drawee the unauthorized indorsement or alteration.

(d) If (i) a dishonored draft is presented for payment to the drawer or an indorser or (ii) any other instrument is presented for payment to a party obliged to pay the instrument, and (iii) payment is received, the following rules apply:

(1) The person obtaining payment and a prior transferor of the instrument warrant to the person making payment in good faith that the warrantor is, or was, at the time the warrantor transferred the instrument, a person entitled to enforce the instrument or authorized to obtain payment on behalf of a person entitled to enforce the instrument.

(2) The person making payment may recover from any warrantor for breach of warranty an amount equal to the amount paid plus expenses and loss of interest resulting from the breach.

(e) The warranties stated in subsections (a) and (d) cannot be disclaimed with respect to checks. Unless notice of a claim for breach of warranty is given to the warrantor within 30 days after the claimant has reason to know of the breach and the identity of the warrantor, the liability of the warrantor under subsection (b) or (d) is discharged to the extent of any loss caused by the delay in giving notice of the claim.

(f) A [cause of action] for breach of warranty under this section accrues when the claimant has reason to know of the breach.

§ 3–418. Payment or Acceptance by Mistake.

(a) Except as provided in subsection (c), if the drawee of a draft pays or accepts the draft and the drawee acted on the mistaken belief that (i) payment of the draft had not been stopped pursuant to Section 4–403 or (ii) the signature of the drawer of the draft was authorized, the drawee may recover the amount of the draft from the person to whom or for whose benefit payment was made or, in the case of acceptance, may revoke the acceptance. Rights of the drawee under this subsection are not affected by failure of the drawee to exercise ordinary care in paying or accepting the draft.

(b) Except as provided in subsection (c), if an instrument has been paid or accepted by mistake and the case is not covered by subsection (a), the person paying or accepting may, to the extent permitted by the law governing mistake and restitution, (i) recover the payment from the person to whom or for whose benefit payment was made or (ii) in the case of acceptance, may revoke the acceptance.

(c) The remedies provided by subsection (a) or (b) may not be asserted against a person who took the instrument in good faith and for value or who in good faith changed position in reliance on the payment or acceptance. This subsection does not limit remedies provided by Section 3–417 or 4–407.

(d) Notwithstanding Section 4–215, if an instrument is paid or accepted by mistake and the payor or acceptor recovers payment or revokes acceptance under subsection (a) or (b), the instrument is deemed not to have been paid or accepted and is treated as dishonored, and the person from whom payment is recovered has rights as a person entitled to enforce the dishonored instrument.

§ 3–419. Instruments Signed for Accommodation.

(a) If an instrument is issued for value given for the benefit of a party to the instrument ("accommodated party") and another party to the instrument ("accommodation party") signs the instrument for the purpose of incurring liability on the instrument without being a direct beneficiary of the value given for the instrument, the instrument is signed by the accommodation party "for accommodation."

(b) An accommodation party may sign the instrument as maker, drawer, acceptor, or indorser and, subject to subsection (d), is obliged to pay the instrument in the capacity in which the accommodation party signs. The obligation of an accommodation party may be enforced notwithstanding any statute of frauds and whether or not the accommodation party receives consideration for the accommodation.

(c) A person signing an instrument is presumed to be an accommodation party and there is notice that the instrument is signed for accommodation if the signature is an anomalous indorsement or is accompanied by words indicating that the signer is acting as surety or guarantor with respect to the obligation of another party to the instrument. Except as provided in Section 3–605, the obligation of an accommodation party to pay the instrument is not affected by the fact that the person enforcing the obligation had notice when the instrument was taken by that person that the accommodation party signed the instrument for accommodation.

(d) If the signature of a party to an instrument is accompanied by words indicating unambiguously that the party is guaranteeing collection rather than payment of the obligation of another party to the instrument, the signer is obliged to pay the amount due on the instrument to a person entitled to enforce the instrument only if (i) execution of judgment against the other party has been returned unsatisfied, (ii) the other party is insolvent or in an insolvency proceeding, (iii) the other party cannot be served with process, or (iv) it is otherwise apparent that payment cannot be obtained from the other party.

(e) An accommodation party who pays the instrument is entitled to reimbursement from the accommodated party and is entitled to enforce the instrument against the accommodated party. An accommodated party who pays the instrument has no right of recourse against, and is not entitled to contribution from, an accommodation party.

§ 3–420. Conversion of Instrument.

(a) The law applicable to conversion of personal property applies to instruments. An instrument is also converted if it is taken by transfer, other than a negotiation, from a person not entitled to enforce the instrument or a bank makes or obtains payment with respect to the instrument for a person not entitled to enforce the instrument or receive payment. An action for conversion of an instrument may not be brought by (i) the issuer or acceptor of the instrument or (ii) a payee or indorsee who did not receive delivery of the instrument either directly or through delivery to an agent or a co-payee.

(b) In an action under subsection (a), the measure of liability is presumed to be the amount payable on the instrument, but recovery may not exceed the amount of the plaintiff's interest in the instrument.

(c) A representative, other than a depositary bank, who has in good faith dealt with an instrument or its proceeds on behalf of one who was not the person entitled to enforce the instrument is not liable in conversion to that person beyond the amount of any proceeds that it has not paid out.

Part 5 Dishonor

§ 3–501. Presentment.

(a) "Presentment" means a demand made by or on behalf of a person entitled to enforce an instrument (i) to pay the instrument made to the drawee or a party obliged to pay the instrument or, in the case of a note or accepted draft payable at a bank, to the bank, or (ii) to accept a draft made to the drawee.

(b) The following rules are subject to Article 4, agreement of the parties, and clearing-house rules and the like:

(1) Presentment may be made at the place of payment of the instrument and must be made at the place of payment if the instrument is payable at a bank in the United States; may be made by any commercially reasonable means, including an oral, written, or electronic communication; is effective when the demand for payment or acceptance is received by the person to whom presentment is made; and is effective if made to any one of two or more makers, acceptors, drawees, or other payors.

(2) Upon demand of the person to whom presentment is made, the person making presentment must (i) exhibit the instrument, (ii) give reasonable identi-

fication and, if presentment is made on behalf of another person, reasonable evidence of authority to do so, and (. . .) sign a receipt on the instrument for any payment made or surrender the instrument if full payment is made.

(3) Without dishonoring the instrument, the party to whom presentment is made may (i) return the instrument for lack of a necessary indorsement, or (ii) refuse payment or acceptance for failure of the presentment to comply with the terms of the instrument, an agreement of the parties, or other applicable law or rule.

(4) The party to whom presentment is made may treat presentment as occurring on the next business day after the day of presentment if the party to whom presentment is made has established a cut-off hour not earlier than 2 P.M. for the receipt and processing of instruments presented for payment or acceptance and presentment is made after the cut-off hour.

§ 3–502. Dishonor.

(a) Dishonor of a note is governed by the following rules:

(1) If the note is payable on demand, the note is dishonored if presentment is duly made to the maker and the note is not paid on the day of presentment.

(2) If the note is not payable on demand and is payable at or through a bank or the terms of the note require presentment, the note is dishonored if presentment is duly made and the note is not paid on the day it becomes payable or the day of presentment, whichever is later.

(3) If the note is not payable on demand and paragraph (2) does not apply, the note is dishonored if it is not paid on the day it becomes payable.

(b) Dishonor of an unaccepted draft other than a documentary draft is governed by the following rules:

(1) If a check is duly presented for payment to the payor bank otherwise than for immediate payment over the counter, the check is dishonored if the payor bank makes timely return of the check or sends timely notice of dishonor or nonpayment under Section 4–301 or 4–302, or becomes accountable for the amount of the check under Section 4–302.

(2) If a draft is payable on demand and paragraph (1) does not apply, the draft is dishonored if presentment for payment is duly made to the drawee and the draft is not paid on the day of presentment.

(3) If a draft is payable on a date stated in the draft, the draft is dishonored if (i) presentment for payment is duly made to the drawee and payment is not made on the day the draft becomes payable or the day of presentment, whichever is later, or (ii) presentment for acceptance is duly made before the day the draft becomes payable and the draft is not accepted on the day of presentment.

(4) If a draft is payable on elapse of a period of time after sight or acceptance, the draft is dishonored if presentment for acceptance is duly made and the draft is not accepted on the day of presentment.

(c) Dishonor of an unaccepted documentary draft occurs according to the rules stated in subsection (b)(2), (3), and (4), except that payment or acceptance may be delayed without dishonor until no later than the close of the third business day of the drawee following the day on which payment or acceptance is required by those paragraphs.

(d) Dishonor of an accepted draft is governed by the following rules:

(1) If the draft is payable on demand, the draft is dishonored if presentment for payment is duly made to the acceptor and the draft is not paid on the day of presentment.

(2) If the draft is not payable on demand, the draft is dishonored if presentment for payment is duly made to the acceptor and payment is not made on the day it becomes payable or the day of presentment, whichever is later.

(e) In any case in which presentment is otherwise required for dishonor under this section and presentment is excused under Section 3–504, dishonor occurs without presentment if the instrument is not duly accepted or paid.

(f) If a draft is dishonored because timely acceptance of the draft was not made and the person entitled to demand acceptance consents to a late acceptance, from the time of acceptance the draft is treated as never having been dishonored.

§ 3–503. Notice of Dishonor.

(a) The obligation of an indorser stated in Section 3–415(a) and the obligation of a drawer stated in Section 3–414(d) may not be enforced unless (i) the indorser or drawer is given notice of dishonor of the instrument complying with this section or (ii) notice of dishonor is excused under Section 3–504(b).

(b) Notice of dishonor may be given by any person; may be given by any commercially reasonable means, including an oral, written, or electronic communication; and is sufficient if it reasonably identifies the instrument and indicates that the instrument has been dishonored or has not been paid or accepted. Return of an instrument given to a bank for collection is sufficient notice of dishonor.

(c) Subject to Section 3–504(c), with respect to an instrument taken for collection by a collecting bank, notice of dishonor must be given (i) by the bank before midnight of the next banking day following the banking day on which the bank receives notice of dishonor of the instrument, or (ii) by any other person within 30 days following the day on which the person receives notice of dishonor. With respect to any other instrument, notice of dishonor must be given within 30 days following the day on which dishonor occurs.

§ 3–504. Excused Presentment and Notice of Dishonor.

(a) Presentment for payment or acceptance of an instrument is excused if (i) the person entitled to present the instrument cannot with reasonable diligence make presentment, (ii) the maker or acceptor has repudiated an obligation to pay the instrument or is dead or in insolvency proceedings, (iii) by the terms of the instrument presentment is not necessary to enforce the obligation of indorsers or the drawer, (iv) the drawer or indorser whose obligation is being enforced has waived presentment or otherwise has no reason to expect or right to require that the instrument be paid or accepted, or (v) the drawer instructed the drawee not to pay or accept the draft or the drawee was not obligated to the drawer to pay the draft.

(b) Notice of dishonor is excused if (i) by the terms of the instrument notice of dishonor is not necessary to enforce the obligation of a party to pay the instrument, or (ii) the party whose obligation is being enforced waived notice of dishonor. A waiver of presentment is also a waiver of notice of dishonor.

(c) Delay in giving notice of dishonor is excused if the delay was caused by circumstances beyond the control of the person giving the notice and the person giving the notice exercised reasonable diligence after the cause of the delay ceased to operate.

§ 3–505. Evidence of Dishonor.

(a) The following are admissible as evidence and create a presumption of dishonor and of any notice of dishonor stated:

(1) a document regular in form as provided in subsection (b) which purports to be a protest;

(2) a purported stamp or writing of the drawee, payor bank, or presenting bank on or accompanying the instrument stating that acceptance or payment has been refused unless reasons for the refusal are stated and the reasons are not consistent with dishonor;

(3) a book or record of the drawee, payor bank, or collecting bank, kept in the usual course of business which shows dishonor, even if there is no evidence of who made the entry.

(b) A protest is a certificate of dishonor made by a United States consul or vice consul, or a notary public or other person authorized to administer oaths by the law of the place where dishonor occurs. It may be made upon information satisfactory to that person. The protest must identify the instrument and certify either that presentment has been made or, if not made, the reason why it was not made, and that the instrument has been dishonored by nonacceptance or nonpayment. The protest may also certify that notice of dishonor has been given to some or all parties.

Part 6 Discharge and Payment

§ 3–601. Discharge and Effect of Discharge.

(a) The obligation of a party to pay the instrument is discharged as stated in this Article or by an act or agreement with the party which would discharge an obligation to pay money under a simple contract.

(b) Discharge of the obligation of a party is not effective against a person acquiring rights of a holder in due course of the instrument without notice of the discharge.

§ 3–602. Payment.

(a) Subject to subsection (b), an instrument is paid to the extent payment is made (i) by or on behalf of a party obliged to pay the instrument, and (ii) to a person entitled to enforce the instrument. To the extent of the payment, the obligation of the party obliged to pay the instrument is discharged even though payment is made with knowledge of a claim to the instrument under Section 3–306 by another person.

(b) The obligation of a party to pay the instrument is not discharged under subsection (a) if:

(1) a claim to the instrument under Section 3–306 is enforceable against the party receiving payment and (i) payment is made with knowledge by the payor that payment is prohibited by injunction or similar process of a court of competent jurisdiction, or (ii) in the case of an instrument other than a cashier's check, teller's check, or certified check, the party making payment accepted, from the person having a claim to the instrument, indemnity against loss resulting from refusal to pay the person entitled to enforce the instrument; or

(2) the person making payment knows that the instrument is a stolen instrument and pays a person it knows is in wrongful possession of the instrument.

§ 3–603. Tender of Payment.

(a) If tender of payment of an obligation to pay an instrument is made to a person entitled to enforce the instrument, the effect of tender is governed by principles of law applicable to tender of payment under a simple contract.

(b) If tender of payment of an obligation to pay an instrument is made to a person entitled to enforce the instrument and the tender is refused, there is discharge, to the extent of the amount of the tender, of the obligation of an indorser or accommodation party having a right of recourse with respect to the obligation to which the tender relates.

(c) If tender of payment of an amount due on an instrument is made to a person entitled to enforce the instrument, the obligation of the obligor to pay interest after the due date on the amount tendered is discharged. If presentment is required with respect to an instrument and the obligor is able and ready to pay on the due date at every place of payment stated in the instrument, the obligor is deemed to have made tender of payment on the due date to the person entitled to enforce the instrument.

§ 3–604. Discharge by Cancellation or Renunciation.

(a) A person entitled to enforce an instrument, with or without consideration, may discharge the obligation of a party to pay the instrument (i) by an intentional voluntary act, such as surrender of the instrument to the party, destruction, mutilation, or cancellation of the instrument, cancellation or striking out of the party's signature, or the addition of words to the instrument indicating discharge, or (ii) by agreeing not to sue or otherwise renouncing rights against the party by a signed writing.

(b) Cancellation or striking out of an indorsement pursuant to subsection (a) does not affect the status and rights of a party derived from the indorsement.

§ 3–605. Discharge of Indorsers and Accommodation Parties.

(a) In this section, the term "indorser" includes a drawer having the obligation described in Section 3–414(d).

(b) Discharge, under Section 3–604, of the obligation of a party to pay an instrument does not discharge the obligation of an indorser or accommodation party having a right of recourse against the discharged party.

(c) If a person entitled to enforce an instrument agrees, with or without consideration, to an extension of the due date of the obligation of a party to pay the instrument, the extension discharges an indorser or accommodation party having a right of recourse against the party whose obligation is extended to the extent the indorser or accommodation party proves that the extension caused loss to the indorser or accommodation party with respect to the right of recourse.

(d) If a person entitled to enforce an instrument agrees, with or without consideration, to a material modification of the obligation of a party other than an extension of the due date, the modification discharges the obligation of an indorser or accommodation party having a right of recourse against the person whose obligation is modified to the extent the modification causes loss to the indorser or accommodation party with respect to the right of recourse. The loss suffered by the indorser or accommodation party as a result of the modification is equal to the amount of the right of recourse unless the person enforcing the instrument proves that no loss was caused by the modification or that the loss caused by the modification was an amount less than the amount of the right of recourse.

(e) If the obligation of a party to pay an instrument is secured by an interest in collateral and a person entitled to enforce the instrument impairs the value of the interest in collateral, the obligation of an indorser or accommodation party having a right of recourse against the obligor is discharged to the extent of the impairment. The value of an interest in collateral is impaired to the extent (i) the value of the interest is reduced to an amount less than the amount of the right of recourse of the party asserting discharge, or (ii) the reduction in value of the interest causes an increase in the amount by which the amount of the right of recourse exceeds the value of the interest. The burden of proving impairment is on the party asserting discharge.

(f) If the obligation of a party is secured by an interest in collateral not provided by an accommodation party and a person entitled to enforce the instrument impairs the value of the interest in collateral, the obligation of any party who is jointly and severally liable with respect to the secured obligation is discharged to the extent the impairment causes the party asserting discharge to pay more than that party would have been obliged to pay, taking into account rights of contribution, if impairment had not occurred. If the party asserting discharge is an accommodation party not entitled to discharge under subsection (e), the party is deemed to have a right to contribution based on joint and several liability rather than a right to reimbursement. The burden of proving impairment is on the party asserting discharge.

(g) Under subsection (e) or (f), impairing value of an interest in collateral includes (i) failure to obtain or maintain perfection or recordation of the interest in collateral, (ii) release of collateral without substitution of collateral of equal value, (iii) failure to perform a duty to preserve the value of collateral owed, under Article 9 or other law, to a debtor or surety or other person secondarily liable, or (iv) failure to comply with applicable law in disposing of collateral.

(h) An accommodation party is not discharged under subsection (c), (d), or (e) unless the person entitled to enforce the instrument knows of the accommodation or has notice under Section 3–419(c) that the instrument was signed for accommodation.

(i) A party is not discharged under this section if (i) the party asserting discharge consents to the event or conduct that is the basis of the discharge, or (ii) the instrument or a separate agreement of the party provides for waiver of discharge under this section either specifically or by general language indicating that parties waive defenses based on suretyship or impairment of collateral.

ADDENDUM TO REVISED ARTICLE 3

Notes to Legislative Counsel

1. If revised Article 3 is adopted in your state, the reference in Section 2–511 to Section 3–802 should be changed to Section 3–310.

2. If revised Article 3 is adopted in your state and the Uniform Fiduciaries Act is also in effect in your state, you may want to consider amending Uniform Fiduciaries Act § 9 to conform to Section 3–307(b)(2)(iii) and (4)(iii). See Official Comment 3 to Section 3–307.

Revised Article 4
BANK DEPOSITS AND COLLECTIONS

Part 1 General Provisions and Definitions

§ 4–101. Short Title.

This Article may be cited as Uniform Commercial Code—Bank Deposits and Collections.

As amended in 1990.

§ 4–102. Applicability.

(a) To the extent that items within this Article are also within Articles 3 and 8, they are subject to those Articles.

If there is conflict, this Article governs Article 3, but Article 8 governs this Article.

(b) The liability of a bank for action or non-action with respect to an item handled by it for purposes of presentment, payment, or collection is governed by the law of the place where the bank is located. In the case of action or non-action by or at a branch or separate office of a bank, its liability is governed by the law of the place where the branch or separate office is located.

§ 4–103. Variation by Agreement; Measure of Damages; Action Constituting Ordinary Care.

(a) The effect of the provisions of this Article may be varied by agreement, but the parties to the agreement cannot disclaim a bank's responsibility for its lack of good faith or failure to exercise ordinary care or limit the measure of damages for the lack or failure. However, the parties may determine by agreement the standards by which the bank's responsibility is to be measured if those standards are not manifestly unreasonable.

(b) Federal Reserve regulations and operating circulars, clearing-house rules, and the like have the effect of agreements under subsection (a), whether or not specifically assented to by all parties interested in items handled.

(c) Action or non-action approved by this Article or pursuant to Federal Reserve regulations or operating circulars is the exercise of ordinary care and, in the absence of special instructions, action or non-action consistent with clearing-house rules and the like or with a general banking usage not disapproved by this Article, is prima facie the exercise of ordinary care.

(d) The specification or approval of certain procedures by this Article is not disapproval of other procedures that may be reasonable under the circumstances.

(e) The measure of damages for failure to exercise ordinary care in handling an item is the amount of the item reduced by an amount that could not have been realized by the exercise of ordinary care. If there is also bad faith it includes any other damages the party suffered as a proximate consequence.

As amended in 1990.

§ 4–104. Definitions and Index of Definitions.

(a) In this Article, unless the context otherwise requires:

(1) "Account" means any deposit or credit account with a bank, including a demand, time, savings, passbook, share draft, or like account, other than an account evidenced by a certificate of deposit;

(2) "Afternoon" means the period of a day between noon and midnight;

(3) "Banking day" means the part of a day on which a bank is open to the public for carrying on substantially all of its banking functions;

(4) "Clearing house" means an association of banks or other payors regularly clearing items;

(5) "Customer" means a person having an account with a bank or for whom a bank has agreed to collect items, including a bank that maintains an account at another bank;

(6) "Documentary draft" means a draft to be presented for acceptance or payment if specified documents, certificated securities (Section 8–102) or instructions for uncertificated securities (Section 8–102), or other certificates, statements, or the like are to be received by the drawee or other payor before acceptance or payment of the draft;

(7) "Draft" means a draft as defined in Section 3–104 or an item, other than an instrument, that is an order;

(8) "Drawee" means a person ordered in a draft to make payment;

(9) "Item" means an instrument or a promise or order to pay money handled by a bank for collection or payment. The term does not include a payment order governed by Article 4A or a credit or debit card slip;

(10) "Midnight deadline" with respect to a bank is midnight on its next banking day following the banking day on which it receives the relevant item or notice or from which the time for taking action commences to run, whichever is later;

(11) "Settle" means to pay in cash, by clearing-house settlement, in a charge or credit or by remittance, or otherwise as agreed. A settlement may be either provisional or final;

(12) "Suspends payments" with respect to a bank means that it has been closed by order of the supervisory authorities, that a public officer has been appointed to take it over, or that it ceases or refuses to make payments in the ordinary course of business.

(b) [Other definitions' section references deleted.]

(c) [Other definitions' section references deleted.]

(d) In addition, Article 1 contains general definitions and principles of construction and interpretation applicable throughout this Article.

§ 4–105. "Bank"; "Depositary Bank"; "Payor Bank"; "Intermediary Bank"; "Collecting Bank"; "Presenting Bank".

In this Article:

(1) "Bank" means a person engaged in the business of banking, including a savings bank, savings and loan association, credit union, or trust company;

(2) "Depositary bank" means the first bank to take an item even though it is also the payor bank, unless the item is presented for immediate payment over the counter;

(3) "Payor bank" means a bank that is the drawee of a draft;

(4) "Intermediary bank" means a bank to which an item is transferred in course of collection except the depositary or payor bank;

(5) "Collecting bank" means a bank handling an item for collection except the payor bank;

(6) "Presenting bank" means a bank presenting an item except a payor bank.

§ 4–106. Payable Through or Payable at Bank: Collecting Bank.

(a) If an item states that it is "payable through" a bank identified in the item, (i) the item designates the bank as a collecting bank and does not by itself authorize the bank to pay the item, and (ii) the item may be presented for payment only by or through the bank.

Alternative A

(b) If an item states that it is "payable at" a bank identified in the item, the item is equivalent to a draft drawn on the bank.

Alternative B

(b) If an item states that it is "payable at" a bank identified in the item, (i) the item designates the bank as a collecting bank and does not by itself authorize the bank to pay the item, and (ii) the item may be presented for payment only by or through the bank.

(c) If a draft names a nonbank drawee and it is unclear whether a bank named in the draft is a co-drawee or a collecting bank, the bank is a collecting bank.

As added in 1990.

§ 4–107. Separate Office of Bank.

A branch or separate office of a bank is a separate bank for the purpose of computing the time within which and determining the place at or to which action may be taken or notices or orders shall be given under this Article and under Article 3.

As amended in 1962 and 1990.

§ 4–108. Time of Receipt of Items.

(a) For the purpose of allowing time to process items, prove balances, and make the necessary entries on its books to determine its position for the day, a bank may fix an afternoon hour of 2 p.m. or later as a cutoff hour for the handling of money and items and the making of entries on its books.

(b) An item or deposit of money received on any day after a cutoff hour so fixed or after the close of the banking day may be treated as being received at the opening of the next banking day.

As amended in 1990.

§ 4–109. Delays.

(a) Unless otherwise instructed, a collecting bank in a good faith effort to secure payment of a specific item drawn on a payor other than a bank, and with or without the approval of any person involved, may waive, modify, or extend time limits imposed or permitted by this [act] for a period not exceeding two additional banking days without discharge of drawers or indorsers or liability to its transferor or a prior party.

(b) Delay by a collecting bank or payor bank beyond time limits prescribed or permitted by this [act] or by instructions is excused if (i) the delay is caused by interruption of communication or computer facilities, suspension of payments by another bank, war, emergency conditions, failure of equipment, or other circumstances beyond the control of the bank, and (ii) the bank exercises such diligence as the circumstances require.

§ 4–110. Electronic Presentment.

(a) "Agreement for electronic presentment" means an agreement, clearing-house rule, or Federal Reserve regulation or operating circular, providing that presentment of an item may be made by transmission of an image of an item or information describing the item ("presentment notice") rather than delivery of the item itself. The agreement may provide for procedures governing retention, presentment, payment, dishonor, and other matters concerning items subject to the agreement.

(b) Presentment of an item pursuant to an agreement for presentment is made when the presentment notice is received.

(c) If presentment is made by presentment notice, a reference to "item" or "check" in this Article means the presentment notice unless the context otherwise indicates.

As added in 1990.

§ 4–111. Statute of Limitations.

An action to enforce an obligation, duty, or right arising under this Article must be commenced within three years after the [cause of action] accrues.

As added in 1990.

Part 2 Collection of Items: Depositary and Collecting Banks

§ 4–201. Status of Collecting Bank as Agent and Provisional Status of Credits; Applicability of Article; Item Indorsed "Pay Any Bank".

(a) Unless a contrary intent clearly appears and before the time that a settlement given by a collecting bank for an item is or becomes final, the bank, with respect to an item, is an agent or sub-agent of the owner of the item and any settlement given for the item is provisional. This provision applies regardless of the form of indorsement or lack of indorsement and even though credit given for the item is subject to immediate withdrawal as of right or is in fact withdrawn; but the continuance of ownership of an item by its owner and any rights of the owner to proceeds of the item are subject to rights of a collecting bank, such as those resulting from outstanding advances on the item and rights of recoupment or setoff. If an item is handled by banks for purposes of presentment, payment, collection, or return, the relevant provisions of this Article apply even though action of the parties clearly establishes that a particular bank has purchased the item and is the owner of it.

(b) After an item has been indorsed with the words "pay any bank" or the like, only a bank may acquire the rights of a holder until the item has been:

(1) returned to the customer initiating collection; or

(2) specially indorsed by a bank to a person who is not a bank.

As amended in 1990.

§ 4–202. Responsibility for Collection or Return; When Action Timely.

(a) A collecting bank must exercise ordinary care in:

(1) presenting an item or sending it for presentment;

(2) sending notice of dishonor or nonpayment or returning an item other than a documentary draft to the bank's transferor after learning that the item has not been paid or accepted, as the case may be;

(3) settling for an item when the bank receives final settlement; and

(4) notifying its transferor of any loss or delay in transit within a reasonable time after discovery thereof.

(b) A collecting bank exercises ordinary care under subsection (a) by taking proper action before its midnight deadline following receipt of an item, notice, or settlement. Taking proper action within a reasonably longer time may constitute the exercise of ordinary care, but the bank has the burden of establishing timeliness.

(c) Subject to subsection (a)(1), a bank is not liable for the insolvency, neglect, misconduct, mistake, or default of another bank or person or for loss or destruction of an item in the possession of others or in transit.

As amended in 1990.

§ 4–203. Effect of Instructions.

Subject to Article 3 concerning conversion of instruments (Section 3–420) and restrictive indorsements (Section 3–206), only a collecting bank's transferor can give instructions that affect the bank or constitute notice to it, and a collecting bank is not liable to prior parties for any action taken pursuant to the instructions or in accordance with any agreement with its transferor.

§ 4–204. Methods of Sending and Presenting; Sending Directly to Payor Bank.

(a) A collecting bank shall send items by a reasonably prompt method, taking into consideration relevant instructions, the nature of the item, the number of those items on hand, the cost of collection involved, and the method generally used by it or others to present those items.

(b) A collecting bank may send:

(1) an item directly to the payor bank;

(2) an item to a nonbank payor if authorized by its transferor; and

(3) an item other than documentary drafts to a nonbank payor, if authorized by Federal Reserve regulation or operating circular, clearing-house rule, or the like.

(c) Presentment may be made by a presenting bank at a place where the payor bank or other payor has requested that presentment be made.

As amended in 1990.

§ 4–205. Depositary Bank Holder of Unindorsed Item.

If a customer delivers an item to a depositary bank for collection:

(1) the depositary bank becomes a holder of the item at the time it receives the item for collection if the customer at the time of delivery was a holder of the item, whether or not the customer indorses the item, and, if the bank satisfies the other requirements of Section 3–302, it is a holder in due course; and

(2) the depositary bank warrants to collecting banks, the payor bank or other payor, and the drawer that the amount of the item was paid to the customer or deposited to the customer's account.

As amended in 1990.

§ 4–206. Transfer Between Banks.

Any agreed method that identifies the transferor bank is sufficient for the item's further transfer to another bank.

As amended in 1990.

§ 4–207. Transfer Warranties.

(a) A customer or collecting bank that transfers an item and receives a settlement or other consideration warrants to the transferee and to any subsequent collecting bank that:

(1) the warrantor is a person entitled to enforce the item;

(2) all signatures on the item are authentic and authorized;

(3) the item has not been altered;

(4) the item is not subject to a defense or claim in recoupment (Section 3–305(a)) of any party that can be asserted against the warrantor; and

(5) the warrantor has no knowledge of any insolvency proceeding commenced with respect to the maker or acceptor or, in the case of an unaccepted draft, the drawer.

(b) If an item is dishonored, a customer or collecting bank transferring the item and receiving settlement or other consideration is obliged to pay the amount due on the item (i) according to the terms of the item at the time it was transferred, or (ii) if the transfer was of an incomplete item, according to its terms when completed as stated in Sections 3–115 and 3–407. The obligation of a transferor is owed to the transferee and to any subsequent collecting bank that takes the item in good faith. A transferor cannot disclaim its obligation under this subsection by an indorsement stating that it is made "without recourse" or otherwise disclaiming liability.

(c) A person to whom the warranties under subsection (a) are made and who took the item in good faith may recover from the warrantor as damages for breach of warranty an amount equal to the loss suffered as a result of the breach, but not more than the amount of the item plus expenses and loss of interest incurred as a result of the breach.

(d) The warranties stated in subsection (a) cannot be disclaimed with respect to checks. Unless notice of a claim for breach of warranty is given to the warrantor within 30 days after the claimant has reason to know of the breach and the identity of the warrantor, the warrantor is discharged to the extent of any loss caused by the delay in giving notice of the claim.

(e) A cause of action for breach of warranty under this section accrues when the claimant has reason to know of the breach.

As amended in 1990.

§ 4–208. Presentment Warranties.

(a) If an unaccepted draft is presented to the drawee for payment or acceptance and the drawee pays or accepts the draft, (i) the person obtaining payment or acceptance, at the time of presentment, and (ii) a previous transferor of the draft, at the time of transfer, warrant to the drawee that pays or accepts the draft in good faith that:

(1) the warrantor is, or was, at the time the warrantor transferred the draft, a person entitled to enforce the draft or authorized to obtain payment or acceptance of the draft on behalf of a person entitled to enforce the draft;

(2) the draft has not been altered; and

(3) the warrantor has no knowledge that the signature of the purported drawer of the draft is unauthorized.

(b) A drawee making payment may recover from a warrantor damages for breach of warranty equal to the amount paid by the drawee less the amount the drawee received or is entitled to receive from the drawer because of the payment. In addition, the drawee is entitled to compensation for expenses and loss of interest resulting from the breach. The right of the drawee to recover damages under this subsection is not affected by any failure of the drawee to exercise ordinary care in making payment. If the drawee accepts the draft (i) breach of warranty is a defense to the obligation of the acceptor, and (ii) if the acceptor makes payment with respect to the draft, the acceptor is entitled to recover from a warrantor for breach of warranty the amounts stated in this subsection.

(c) If a drawee asserts a claim for breach of warranty under subsection (a) based on an unauthorized indorsement of the draft or an alteration of the draft, the warrantor may defend by proving that the indorsement is effective under Section 3–404 or 3–405 or the drawer is precluded under Section 3–406 or 4–406 from asserting against the drawee the unauthorized indorsement or alteration.

(d) If (i) a dishonored draft is presented for payment to the drawer or an indorser or (ii) any other item is presented for payment to a party obliged to pay the item, and the item is paid, the person obtaining payment and a prior transferor of the item warrant to the person making payment in good faith that the warrantor is, or was, at the time the warrantor transferred the item, a person entitled to enforce the item or authorized to obtain payment on behalf of a person entitled to enforce the item. The person making payment may recover from any warrantor for breach of warranty an amount equal to the amount paid plus expenses and loss of interest resulting from the breach.

(e) The warranties stated in subsections (a) and (d) cannot be disclaimed with respect to checks. Unless notice of a claim for breach of warranty is given to the warrantor within 30 days after the claimant has reason to know of the breach and the identity of the warrantor, the warrantor is discharged to the extent of any loss caused by the delay in giving notice of the claim.

(f) A cause of action for breach of warranty under this section accrues when the claimant has reason to know of the breach.

As amended in 1990.

§ 4–209. Encoding and Retention Warranties.

(a) A person who encodes information on or with respect to an item after issue warrants to any subsequent collecting bank and to the payor bank or other payor that the information is correctly encoded. If the customer of a depositary bank encodes, that bank also makes the warranty.

(b) A person who undertakes to retain an item pursuant to an agreement for electronic presentment warrants to any subsequent collecting bank and to the payor bank or other payor that retention and presentment of the item comply with the agreement. If a customer of a depositary bank undertakes to retain an item, that bank also makes this warranty.

(c) A person to whom warranties are made under this section and who took the item in good faith may recover from the warrantor as damages for breach of warranty an amount equal to the loss suffered as a result of the breach, plus expenses and loss of interest incurred as a result of the breach.

As added in 1990.

§ 4–210. Security Interest of Collecting Bank in Items, Accompanying Documents and Proceeds.

(a) A collecting bank has a security interest in an item and any accompanying documents or the proceeds of either:

(1) in case of an item deposited in an account, to the extent to which credit given for the item has been withdrawn or applied;

(2) in case of an item for which it has given credit available for withdrawal as of right, to the extent of the credit given, whether or not the credit is drawn upon or there is a right of charge-back; or

(3) if it makes an advance on or against the item.

(b) If credit given for several items received at one time or pursuant to a single agreement is withdrawn or applied in part, the security interest remains upon all the items, any accompanying documents or the proceeds of either. For the purpose of this section, credits first given are first withdrawn.

(c) Receipt by a collecting bank of a final settlement for an item is a realization on its security interest in the item, accompanying documents, and proceeds. So long as the bank does not receive final settlement for the item or give up possession of the item or accompanying documents for purposes other than collection, the security interest continues to that extent and is subject to Article 9, but:

(1) no security agreement is necessary to make the security interest enforceable (Section 9–203(1)(a));

(2) no filing is required to perfect the security interest; and

(3) the security interest has priority over conflicting perfected security interests in the item, accompanying documents, or proceeds.

As amended in 1990 and 1999.

§ 4–211. When Bank Gives Value for Purposes of Holder in Due Course.

For purposes of determining its status as a holder in due course, a bank has given value to the extent it has a security interest in an item, if the bank otherwise complies with the requirements of Section 3–302 on what constitutes a holder in due course.

As amended in 1990.

§ 4–212. Presentment by Notice of Item Not Payable by, Through, or at Bank; Liability of Drawer or Indorser.

(a) Unless otherwise instructed, a collecting bank may present an item not payable by, through, or at a bank by sending to the party to accept or pay a written notice that the bank holds the item for acceptance or payment. The notice must be sent in time to be received on or before the day when presentment is due and the bank must meet any requirement of the party to accept or pay under Section 3–501 by the close of the bank's next banking day after it knows of the requirement.

(b) If presentment is made by notice and payment, acceptance, or request for compliance with a requirement under Section 3–501 is not received by the close of business on the day after maturity or, in the case of demand items, by the close of business on the third banking day after notice was sent, the presenting bank may treat the item as dishonored and charge any drawer or indorser by sending it notice of the facts.

As amended in 1990.

§ 4–213. Medium and Time of Settlement by Bank.

(a) With respect to settlement by a bank, the medium and time of settlement may be prescribed by Federal Reserve regulations or circulars, clearing-house rules, and the like, or agreement. In the absence of such prescription:

(1) the medium of settlement is cash or credit to an account in a Federal Reserve bank of or specified by the person to receive settlement; and

(2) the time of settlement is:

(i) with respect to tender of settlement by cash, a cashier's check, or teller's check, when the cash or check is sent or delivered;

(ii) with respect to tender of settlement by credit in an account in a Federal Reserve Bank, when the credit is made;

(iii) with respect to tender of settlement by a credit or debit to an account in a bank, when the credit or debit is made or, in the case of tender of settlement by authority to charge an account, when the authority is sent or delivered; or

(iv) with respect to tender of settlement by a funds transfer, when payment is made pursuant to Section 4A–406(a) to the person receiving settlement.

(b) If the tender of settlement is not by a medium authorized by subsection (a) or the time of settlement is not fixed by subsection (a), no settlement occurs until the tender of settlement is accepted by the person receiving settlement.

(c) If settlement for an item is made by cashier's check or teller's check and the person receiving settlement, before its midnight deadline:

(1) presents or forwards the check for collection, settlement is final when the check is finally paid; or

(2) fails to present or forward the check for collection, settlement is final at the midnight deadline of the person receiving settlement.

(d) If settlement for an item is made by giving authority to charge the account of the bank giving settlement in the bank receiving settlement, settlement is final when the charge is made by the bank receiving settlement if there are funds available in the account for the amount of the item.

As amended in 1990.

§ 4–214. Right of Charge-Back or Refund; Liability of Collecting Bank: Return of Item.

(a) If a collecting bank has made provisional settlement with its customer for an item and fails by reason of dishonor, suspension of payments by a bank, or otherwise to receive settlement for the item which is or becomes final, the bank may revoke the settlement given by it, charge back the amount of any credit given for the item to its customer's account, or obtain refund from its customer, whether or not it is able to return the item, if by its midnight deadline or within a longer reasonable time after it learns the facts it returns the item or sends notification of the facts. If the return or notice is delayed beyond the bank's midnight deadline or a longer reasonable time after it learns the facts, the bank may revoke the settlement, charge back the credit, or obtain refund from its customer, but it is liable for any loss resulting from the delay. These rights to revoke, charge back, and obtain refund terminate if and when a settlement for the item received by the bank is or becomes final.

(b) A collecting bank returns an item when it is sent or delivered to the bank's customer or transferor or pursuant to its instructions.

(c) A depositary bank that is also the payor may charge back the amount of an item to its customer's account or obtain refund in accordance with the section governing return of an item received by a payor bank for credit on its books (Section 4–301).

(d) The right to charge back is not affected by:

(1) previous use of a credit given for the item; or

(2) failure by any bank to exercise ordinary care with respect to the item, but a bank so failing remains liable.

(e) A failure to charge back or claim refund does not affect other rights of the bank against the customer or any other party.

(f) If credit is given in dollars as the equivalent of the value of an item payable in foreign money, the dollar amount of any charge-back or refund must be calculated on the basis of the bank-offered spot rate for the foreign money prevailing on the day when the person entitled to the charge-back or refund learns that it will not receive payment in ordinary course.

As amended in 1990.

§ 4–215. Final Payment of Item by Payor Bank; When Provisional Debits and Credits Become Final; When Certain Credits Become Available for Withdrawal.

(a) An item is finally paid by a payor bank when the bank has first done any of the following:

(1) paid the item in cash;

(2) settled for the item without having a right to revoke the settlement under statute, clearing-house rule, or agreement; or

(3) made a provisional settlement for the item and failed to revoke the settlement in the time and manner permitted by statute, clearing-house rule, or agreement.

(b) If provisional settlement for an item does not become final, the item is not finally paid.

(c) If provisional settlement for an item between the presenting and payor banks is made through a clearing house or by debits or credits in an account between them, then to the extent that provisional debits or credits for the item are entered in accounts between the presenting and payor banks or between the presenting and successive prior collecting banks seriatim, they become final upon final payment of the item by the payor bank.

(d) If a collecting bank receives a settlement for an item which is or becomes final, the bank is accountable to its customer for the amount of the item and any provisional credit given for the item in an account with its customer becomes final.

(e) Subject to (i) applicable law stating a time for availability of funds and (ii) any right of the bank to apply the credit to an obligation of the customer, credit given by a bank for an item in a customer's account becomes available for withdrawal as of right:

(1) if the bank has received a provisional settlement for the item, when the settlement becomes final and the bank has had a reasonable time to receive return of the item and the item has not been received within that time;

(2) if the bank is both the depositary bank and the payor bank, and the item is finally paid, at the opening of the bank's second banking day following receipt of the item.

(f) Subject to applicable law stating a time for availability of funds and any right of a bank to apply a deposit to an obligation of the depositor, a deposit of money becomes available for withdrawal as of right at the opening of the bank's next banking day after receipt of the deposit.

As amended in 1990.

§ 4– 216. Insolvency and Preference.

(a) If an item is in or comes into the possession of a payor or collecting bank that suspends payment and the item has not been finally paid, the item must be returned by the receiver, trustee, or agent in charge of the closed bank to the presenting bank or the closed bank's customer.

(b) If a payor bank finally pays an item and suspends payments without making a settlement for the item with its customer or the presenting bank which settlement is or becomes final, the owner of the item has a preferred claim against the payor bank.

(c) If a payor bank gives or a collecting bank gives or receives a provisional settlement for an item and thereafter suspends payments, the suspension does not prevent or interfere with the settlement's becoming final if the finality occurs automatically upon the lapse of certain time or the happening of certain events.

(d) If a collecting bank receives from subsequent parties settlement for an item, which settlement is or becomes final and the bank suspends payments without making a settlement for the item with its customer which settlement is or becomes final, the owner of the item has a preferred claim against the collecting bank.

As amended in 1990.

Part 3 Collection of Items: Payor Banks

§ 4–301. Deferred Posting; Recovery of Payment by Return of Items; Time of Dishonor; Return of Items by Payor Bank.

(a) If a payor bank settles for a demand item other than a documentary draft presented otherwise than for immediate payment over the counter before midnight of the banking day of receipt, the payor bank may revoke the settlement and recover the settlement if, before it has made final payment and before its midnight deadline, it

(1) returns the item; or

(2) sends written notice of dishonor or nonpayment if the item is unavailable for return.

(b) If a demand item is received by a payor bank for credit on its books, it may return the item or send notice of dishonor and may revoke any credit given or recover the amount thereof withdrawn by its customer, if it acts within the time limit and in the manner specified in subsection (a).

(c) Unless previous notice of dishonor has been sent, an item is dishonored at the time when for purposes of dishonor it is returned or notice sent in accordance with this section.

(d) An item is returned:

(1) as to an item presented through a clearing house, when it is delivered to the presenting or last collecting bank or to the clearing house or is sent or delivered in accordance with clearing-house rules; or

(2) in all other cases, when it is sent or delivered to the bank's customer or transferor or pursuant to instructions.

As amended in 1990.

§ 4–302. Payor Bank's Responsibility for Late Return of Item.

(a) If an item is presented to and received by a payor bank, the bank is accountable for the amount of:

(1) a demand item, other than a documentary draft, whether properly payable or not, if the bank, in any case in which it is not also the depositary bank, retains the item beyond midnight of the banking day of receipt without settling for it or, whether or not it is also the depositary bank, does not pay or return the item or send notice of dishonor until after its midnight deadline; or

(2) any other properly payable item unless, within the time allowed for acceptance or payment of that item, the bank either accepts or pays the item or returns it and accompanying documents.

(b) The liability of a payor bank to pay an item pursuant to subsection (a) is subject to defenses based on breach of a presentment warranty (Section 4–208) or proof that the person seeking enforcement of the liability presented or transferred the item for the purpose of defrauding the payor bank.

As amended in 1990.

§ 4–303. When Items Subject to Notice, Stop-Payment Order, Legal Process, or Setoff; Order in Which Items May Be Charged or Certified.

(a) Any knowledge, notice, or stop-payment order received by, legal process served upon, or setoff exercised by a payor bank comes too late to terminate, suspend, or modify the bank's right or duty to pay an item or to charge its customer's account for the item if the knowledge, notice, stop-payment order, or legal process is received or served and a reasonable time for the bank to act thereon expires or the setoff is exercised after the earliest of the following:

(1) the bank accepts or certifies the item;

(2) the bank pays the item in cash;

(3) the bank settles for the item without having a right to revoke the settlement under statute, clearing-house rule, or agreement;

(4) the bank becomes accountable for the amount of the item under Section 4–302 dealing with the payor bank's responsibility for late return of items; or

(5) with respect to checks, a cutoff hour no earlier than one hour after the opening of the next banking day after the banking day on which the bank received the check and no later than the close of that next banking day or, if no cutoff hour is fixed, the close of the next banking day after the banking day on which the bank received the check.

(b) Subject to subsection (a), items may be accepted, paid, certified, or charged to the indicated account of its customer in any order.

As amended in 1990.

Part 4 Relationship Between Payor Bank and Its Customer

§ 4–401. When Bank May Charge Customer's Account.

(a) A bank may charge against the account of a customer an item that is properly payable from the account even though the charge creates an overdraft. An item is properly payable if it is authorized by the customer and is in accordance with any agreement between the customer and bank.

(b) A customer is not liable for the amount of an overdraft if the customer neither signed the item nor benefited from the proceeds of the item.

(c) A bank may charge against the account of a customer a check that is otherwise properly payable from the account, even though payment was made before the date of the check, unless the customer has given notice to the bank of the postdating describing the check with reasonable certainty. The notice is effective for the period stated in Section 4–403(b) for stop-payment orders, and must be received at such time and in such manner as to afford the bank a reasonable opportunity to act on it before the bank takes any action with respect to the check described in Section 4–303. If a bank charges against the account of a customer a check before the date stated in the notice of postdating, the bank is liable for damages for the loss resulting from its act. The loss may include damages for dishonor of subsequent items under Section 4–402.

(d) A bank that in good faith makes payment to a holder may charge the indicated account of its customer according to:

(1) the original terms of the altered item; or

(2) the terms of the completed item, even though the bank knows the item has been completed unless the bank has notice that the completion was improper.

As amended in 1990.

§ 4–402. Bank's Liability to Customer for Wrongful Dishonor; Time of Determining Insufficiency of Account.

(a) Except as otherwise provided in this Article, a payor bank wrongfully dishonors an item if it dishonors an item that is properly payable, but a bank may dishonor an item that would create an overdraft unless it has agreed to pay the overdraft.

(b) A payor bank is liable to its customer for damages proximately caused by the wrongful dishonor of an item. Liability is limited to actual damages proved and may include damages for an arrest or prosecution of the customer or other consequential damages. Whether any consequential damages are proximately caused by the wrongful dishonor is a question of fact to be determined in each case.

(c) A payor bank's determination of the customer's account balance on which a decision to dishonor for insufficiency of available funds is based may be made at any time between the time the item is received by the payor bank and the time that the payor bank returns the item or gives notice in lieu of return, and no more than one determination need be made. If, at the election of the payor bank, a subsequent balance determination is made for the purpose of reevaluating the bank's decision to dishonor the item, the account balance at that time is determinative of whether a dishonor for insufficiency of available funds is wrongful.

As amended in 1990.

§ 4–403. Customer's Right to Stop Payment; Burden of Proof of Loss.

(a) A customer or any person authorized to draw on the account if there is more than one person may stop payment of any item drawn on the customer's account or close the account by an order to the bank describing the item or account with reasonable certainty received at a time and in a manner that affords the bank a reasonable opportunity to act on it before any action by the bank with respect to the item described in Section 4–303. If the signature of more than one person is required to draw on an account, any of these persons may stop payment or close the account.

(b) A stop-payment order is effective for six months, but it lapses after 14 calendar days if the original order was oral and was not confirmed in writing within that period. A stop-payment order may be renewed for additional six-month periods by a writing given to the bank within a period during which the stop-payment order is effective.

(c) The burden of establishing the fact and amount of loss resulting from the payment of an item contrary to a stop-payment order or order to close an account is on the customer. The loss from payment of an item contrary to a stop-payment order may include damages for dishonor of subsequent items under Section 4–402.

As amended in 1990.

§ 4–404. Bank Not Obliged to Pay Check More Than Six Months Old.

A bank is under no obligation to a customer having a checking account to pay a check, other than a certified check, which is presented more than six months after its date, but it may charge its customer's account for a payment made thereafter in good faith.

§ 4–405. Death or Incompetence of Customer.

(a) A payor or collecting bank's authority to accept, pay, or collect an item or to account for proceeds of its collection, if otherwise effective, is not rendered ineffective by incompetence of a customer of either bank existing at the time the item is issued or its collection is undertaken if the bank does not know of an adjudication of incompetence. Neither death nor incompetence of a customer revokes the authority to accept, pay, collect, or account until the bank knows of the fact of death or of an adjudication of incompetence and has reasonable opportunity to act on it.

(b) Even with knowledge, a bank may for 10 days after the date of death pay or certify checks drawn on or before the date unless ordered to stop payment by a person claiming an interest in the account.

As amended in 1990.

§ 4–406. Customer's Duty to Discover and Report Unauthorized Signature or Alteration.

(a) A bank that sends or makes available to a customer a statement of account showing payment of items for the account shall either return or make available to the customer the items paid or provide information in the statement of account sufficient to allow the customer reasonably to identify the items paid. The statement of account provides sufficient information if the item is described by item number, amount, and date of payment.

(b) If the items are not returned to the customer, the person retaining the items shall either retain the items or, if the items are destroyed, maintain the capacity to furnish legible copies of the items until the expiration of seven years after receipt of the items. A customer may request an item from the bank that paid the item, and that bank must provide in a reasonable time either the item or, if the item has been destroyed or is not otherwise obtainable, a legible copy of the item.

(c) If a bank sends or makes available a statement of account or items pursuant to subsection (a), the customer must exercise reasonable promptness in examining the statement or the items to determine whether any payment was not authorized because of an alteration of an item or because a purported signature by or on behalf of the customer was not authorized. If, based on the statement or items provided, the customer should reasonably have discovered the unauthorized payment, the customer must promptly notify the bank of the relevant facts.

(d) If the bank proves that the customer failed, with respect to an item, to comply with the duties imposed on the customer by subsection (c), the customer is precluded from asserting against the bank:

(1) the customer's unauthorized signature or any alteration on the item, if the bank also proves that it suffered a loss by reason of the failure; and

(2) the customer's unauthorized signature or alteration by the same wrongdoer on any other item paid in good faith by the bank if the payment was made before the bank received notice from the customer of the unauthorized signature or alteration and after the customer had been afforded a reasonable period of time, not exceeding 30 days, in which to examine the item or statement of account and notify the bank.

(e) If subsection (d) applies and the customer proves that the bank failed to exercise ordinary care in paying the item and that the failure substantially contributed to loss, the loss is allocated between the customer precluded and the bank asserting the preclusion according to the extent to which the failure of the customer to comply with subsection (c) and the failure of the bank to exercise ordinary care contributed to the loss. If the customer proves that the bank did not pay the item in good faith, the preclusion under subsection (d) does not apply.

(f) Without regard to care or lack of care of either the customer or the bank, a customer who does not within one year after the statement or items are made available to the customer (subsection (a)) discover and report the customer's unauthorized signature on or any alteration on the item is precluded from asserting against the bank the unauthorized signature or alteration. If there is a preclusion under this subsection, the payor bank may not recover for breach or warranty under Section 4–208 with respect to the unauthorized signature or alteration to which the preclusion applies.

As amended in 1990.

§ 4–407. Payor Bank's Right to Subrogation on Improper Payment.

If a payor has paid an item over the order of the drawer or maker to stop payment, or after an account has been closed, or otherwise under circumstances giving a basis for objection by the drawer or maker, to prevent unjust enrichment and only to the extent necessary to prevent loss to the bank by reason of its payment of the item, the payor bank is subrogated to the rights

(1) of any holder in due course on the item against the drawer or maker;

(2) of the payee or any other holder of the item against the drawer or maker either on the item or under the transaction out of which the item arose; and

(3) of the drawer or maker against the payee or any other holder of the item with respect to the transaction out of which the item arose.

As amended in 1990.

Part 5 Collection of Documentary Drafts

§ 4–501. Handling of Documentary Drafts; Duty to Send for Presentment and to Notify Customer of Dishonor.

A bank that takes a documentary draft for collection shall present or send the draft and accompanying documents for presentment and, upon learning that the draft has not been paid or accepted in due course, shall seasonably notify its customer of the fact even though it may have discounted or bought the draft or extended credit available for withdrawal as of right.

As amended in 1990.

§ 4–502. Presentment of "On Arrival" Drafts.

If a draft or the relevant instructions require presentment "on arrival", "when goods arrive" or the like, the collecting bank need not present until in its judgment a reasonable time for arrival of the goods has expired. Refusal to pay or accept because the goods have not arrived is not dishonor; the bank must notify its transferor of the refusal but need not present the draft again until it is instructed to do so or learns of the arrival of the goods.

§ 4–503. Responsibility of Presenting Bank for Documents and Goods; Report of Reasons for Dishonor; Referee in Case of Need.

Unless otherwise instructed and except as provided in Article 5, a bank presenting a documentary draft:

(1) must deliver the documents to the drawee on acceptance of the draft if it is payable more than three days after presentment, otherwise, only on payment; and

(2) upon dishonor, either in the case of presentment for acceptance or presentment for payment, may seek and follow instructions from any referee in case of need designated in the draft or, if the presenting bank does not choose to utilize the referee's services, it must use diligence and good faith to ascertain the reason for dishonor, must notify its transferor of the dishonor and of the results of its effort to ascertain the reasons therefor, and must request instructions.

However, the presenting bank is under no obligation with respect to goods represented by the documents except to follow any reasonable instructions seasonably received; it has a right to reimbursement for any expense incurred in following instructions and to prepayment of or indemnity for those expenses.

As amended in 1990.

§ 4–504. Privilege of Presenting Bank to Deal With Goods; Security Interest for Expenses.

(a) A presenting bank that, following the dishonor of a documentary draft, has seasonably requested instructions but does not receive them within a reasonable time may store, sell, or otherwise deal with the goods in any reasonable manner.

(b) For its reasonable expenses incurred by action under subsection (a) the presenting bank has a lien upon the goods or their proceeds, which may be foreclosed in the same manner as an unpaid seller's lien.

As amended in 1990.

Article 4A FUNDS TRANSFERS

Part 1 Subject Matter and Definitions

§ 4A–101. Short Title.

This Article may be cited as Uniform Commercial Code—Funds Transfers.

§ 4A–102. Subject Matter.

Except as otherwise provided in Section 4A–108, this Article applies to funds transfers defined in Section 4A–104.

§ 4A–103. Payment Order–Definitions.

(a) In this Article:

(1) "Payment order" means an instruction of a sender to a receiving bank, transmitted orally, electronically, or in writing, to pay, or to cause another bank to pay, a fixed or determinable amount of money to a beneficiary if:

(i) the instruction does not state a condition to payment to the beneficiary other than time of payment,

(ii) the receiving bank is to be reimbursed by debiting an account of, or otherwise receiving payment from, the sender, and

(iii) the instruction is transmitted by the sender directly to the receiving bank or to an agent, funds-transfer system, or communication system for transmittal to the receiving bank.

(2) "Beneficiary" means the person to be paid by the beneficiary's bank.

(3) "Beneficiary's bank" means the bank identified in a payment order in which an account of the beneficiary is to be credited pursuant to the order or which otherwise is to make payment to the beneficiary if the order does not provide for payment to an account.

(4) "Receiving bank" means the bank to which the sender's instruction is addressed.

(5) "Sender" means the person giving the instruction to the receiving bank.

(b) If an instruction complying with subsection (a)(1) is to make more than one payment to a beneficiary, the instruction is a separate payment order with respect to each payment.

(c) A payment order is issued when it is sent to the receiving bank.

§ 4A–104. Funds Transfer–Definitions.

In this Article:

(a) "Funds transfer" means the series of transactions, beginning with the originator's payment order, made for the purpose of making payment to the beneficiary of the order. The term includes any payment order issued by the originator's bank or an intermediary bank intended to carry out the originator's payment order. A funds transfer is completed by acceptance by the beneficiary's bank of a payment order for the benefit of the beneficiary of the originator's payment order.

(b) "Intermediary bank" means a receiving bank other than the originator's bank or the beneficiary's bank.

(c) "Originator" means the sender of the first payment order in a funds transfer.

(d) "Originator's bank" means (i) the receiving bank to which the payment order of the originator is issued if the originator is not a bank, or (ii) the originator if the originator is a bank.

§ 4A–105. Other Definitions.

(a) In this Article:

(1) "Authorized account" means a deposit account of a customer in a bank designated by the customer as a source of payment of payment orders issued by the customer to the bank. If a customer does not so designate an account, any account of the customer is an authorized account if payment of a payment order from that account is not inconsistent with a restriction on the use of that account.

(2) "Bank" means a person engaged in the business of banking and includes a savings bank, savings and loan association, credit union, and trust company. A branch or separate office of a bank is a separate bank for purposes of this Article.

(3) "Customer" means a person, including a bank, having an account with a bank or from whom a bank has agreed to receive payment orders.

(4) "Funds-transfer business day" of a receiving bank means the part of a day during which the receiving bank is open for the receipt, processing, and transmittal of payment orders and cancellations and amendments of payment orders.

(5) "Funds-transfer system" means a wire transfer network, automated clearing house, or other communication system of a clearing house or other association of banks through which a payment order by a bank may be transmitted to the bank to which the order is addressed.

(6) "Good faith" means honesty in fact and the observance of reasonable commercial standards of fair dealing.

(7) "Prove" with respect to a fact means to meet the burden of establishing the fact (Section 1–201(8)).

(b) Other definitions applying to this Article and the sections in which they appear are:

"Acceptance"	Section 4A–209
"Beneficiary"	Section 4A–103

"Beneficiary's bank"	Section 4A–103
"Executed"	Section 4A–301
"Execution date"	Section 4A–301
"Funds transfer"	Section 4A–104
"Funds-transfer system rule"	Section 4A–501
"Intermediary bank"	Section 4A–104
"Originator"	Section 4A–104
"Originator's bank"	Section 4A–104
"Payment by beneficiary's bank to beneficiary"	Section 4A–405
"Payment by originator to beneficiary"	Section 4A–406
"Payment by sender to receiving bank"	Section 4A–403
"Payment date"	Section 4A–401
"Payment order"	Section 4A–103
"Receiving bank"	Section 4A–103
"Security procedure"	Section 4A–201
"Sender"	Section 4A–103

(c) The following definitions in Article 4 apply to this Article:

"Clearing house"	Section 4–104
"Item"	Section 4–104
"Suspends payments"	Section 4–104

(d) In addition, Article 1 contains general definitions and principles of construction and interpretation applicable throughout this Article.

§ 4A–106. Time Payment Order Is Received.

(a) The time of receipt of a payment order or communication cancelling or amending a payment order is determined by the rules applicable to receipt of a notice stated in Section 1–201(27). A receiving bank may fix a cut-off time or times on a funds-transfer business day for the receipt and processing of payment orders and communications cancelling or amending payment orders. Different cut-off times may apply to payment orders, cancellations, or amendments, or to different categories of payment orders, cancellations, or amendments. A cut-off time may apply to senders generally or different cut-off times may apply to different senders or categories of payment orders. If a payment order or communication cancelling or amending a payment order is received after the close of a funds-transfer business day or after the appropriate cut-off time on a funds-transfer business day, the receiving bank may treat the payment order or communication as received at the opening of the next funds-transfer business day.

(b) If this Article refers to an execution date or payment date or states a day on which a receiving bank is required to take action, and the date or day does not fall on a funds-transfer business day, the next day that is a funds-transfer business day is treated as the date or day stated, unless the contrary is stated in this Article.

§ 4A–107. Federal Reserve Regulations and Operating Circulars.

Regulations of the Board of Governors of the Federal Reserve System and operating circulars of the Federal Reserve Banks supersede any inconsistent provision of this Article to the extent of the inconsistency.

§ 4A–108. Exclusion of Consumer Transactions Governed by Federal Law.

This Article does not apply to a funds transfer any part of which is governed by the Electronic Fund Transfer Act of 1978 (Title XX, Public Law 95–630, 92 Stat. 3728, 15 U.S.C. § 1693 et seq.) as amended from time to time.

Part 2 Issue and Acceptance of Payment Order

§ 4A–201. Security Procedure.

"Security procedure" means a procedure established by agreement of a customer and a receiving bank for the purpose of (i) verifying that a payment order or communication amending or cancelling a payment order is that of the customer, or (ii) detecting error in the transmission or the content of the payment order or communication. A security procedure may require the use of algorithms or other codes, identifying words or numbers, encryption, callback procedures, or similar security devices. Comparison of a signature on a payment order or communication with an authorized specimen signature of the customer is not by itself a security procedure.

§ 4A–202. Authorized and Verified Payment Orders.

(a) A payment order received by the receiving bank is the authorized order of the person identified as sender if that person authorized the order or is otherwise bound by it under the law of agency.

(b) If a bank and its customer have agreed that the authenticity of payment orders issued to the bank in the name of the customer as sender will be verified pursuant to a security procedure, a payment order received by the receiving bank is effective as the order of the customer, whether or not authorized, if (i) the security procedure is a commercially reasonable method of providing security against unauthorized payment orders, and (ii) the bank proves that it accepted the payment order in good faith and in compliance with the security procedure and any written agreement or instruction of the customer restricting acceptance of payment orders issued in the name of the customer. The bank is not required to follow an instruction that violates a written agreement with the customer or notice of which is not received at a time and in a manner affording the bank a reasonable opportunity to act on it before the payment order is accepted.

(c) Commercial reasonableness of a security procedure is a question of law to be determined by considering the wishes of the customer expressed to the bank, the circumstances of the customer known to the bank, including the size, type, and frequency of payment orders normally issued by the customer to the bank, alternative security procedures offered to the customer, and security procedures in general use by customers and receiving banks similarly situated. A security procedure is deemed to be commercially reasonable if (i) the security procedure was chosen by the customer after the bank offered, and the customer refused, a security procedure that was commercially reasonable for that customer, and (ii) the customer expressly agreed in writing to be bound by any payment order, whether or not authorized, issued in its name and accepted by the bank in compliance with the security procedure chosen by the customer.

(d) The term "sender" in this Article includes the customer in whose name a payment order is issued if the order is the authorized order of the customer under subsection (a), or it is effective as the order of the customer under subsection (b).

(e) This section applies to amendments and cancellations of payment orders to the same extent it applies to payment orders.

(f) Except as provided in this section and in Section 4A–203(a)(1), rights and obligations arising under this section or Section 4A–203 may not be varied by agreement.

§ 4A–203. Unenforceability of Certain Verified Payment Orders.

(a) If an accepted payment order is not, under Section 4A–202(a), an authorized order of a customer identified as sender, but is effective as an order of the customer pursuant to Section 4A–202(b), the following rules apply:

(1) By express written agreement, the receiving bank may limit the extent to which it is entitled to enforce or retain payment of the payment order.

(2) The receiving bank is not entitled to enforce or retain payment of the payment order if the customer proves that the order was not caused, directly or indirectly, by a person (i) entrusted at any time with duties to act for the customer with respect to payment orders or the security procedure, or (ii) who obtained access to transmitting facilities of the customer or who obtained, from a source controlled by the customer and without authority of the receiving bank, information facilitating breach of the security procedure, regardless of how the information was obtained or whether the customer was at fault. Information includes any access device, computer software, or the like.

(b) This section applies to amendments of payment orders to the same extent it applies to payment orders.

§ 4A–204. Refund of Payment and Duty of Customer to Report with Respect to Unauthorized Payment Order.

(a) If a receiving bank accepts a payment order issued in the name of its customer as sender which is (i) not authorized and not effective as the order of the customer under Section 4A–202, or (ii) not enforceable, in whole or in part, against the customer under Section 4A–203, the bank shall refund any payment of the payment order received from the customer to the extent the bank is not entitled to enforce payment and shall pay interest on the refundable amount calculated from the date the bank received payment to the date of the refund. However, the customer is not entitled to interest from the bank on the amount to be refunded if the customer fails to exercise ordinary care to determine that the order was not authorized by the customer and to notify the bank of the relevant facts within a reasonable time not exceeding 90 days after the date the customer received notification from the bank that the order was accepted or that the customer's account was debited with respect to the order. The bank is not entitled to any recovery from the customer on account of a failure by the customer to give notification as stated in this section.

(b) Reasonable time under subsection (a) may be fixed by agreement as stated in Section 1–204(1), but the obligation of a receiving bank to refund payment as stated in subsection (a) may not otherwise be varied by agreement.

§ 4A–205. Erroneous Payment Orders.

(a) If an accepted payment order was transmitted pursuant to a security procedure for the detection of error and the payment order (i) erroneously instructed payment to a beneficiary not intended by the sender, (ii) erroneously instructed payment in an amount greater than the amount intended by the sender, or (iii) was an erroneously transmitted duplicate of a payment order previously sent by the sender, the following rules apply:

(1) If the sender proves that the sender or a person acting on behalf of the sender pursuant to Section 4A–206 complied with the security procedure and that the error would have been detected if the receiving bank had also complied, the sender is not obliged to pay the order to the extent stated in paragraphs (2) and (3).

(2) If the funds transfer is completed on the basis of an erroneous payment order described in clause (i) or (iii) of subsection (a), the sender is not obliged to pay the order and the receiving bank is entitled to recover from the beneficiary any amount paid to the beneficiary to the extent allowed by the law governing mistake and restitution.

(3) If the funds transfer is completed on the basis of a payment order described in clause (ii) of subsection (a), the sender is not obliged to pay the order to the extent the amount received by the beneficiary is greater than the amount intended by the sender. In that case, the receiving bank is entitled to recover from the beneficiary the excess amount received to the extent allowed by the law governing mistake and restitution.

(b) If (i) the sender of an erroneous payment order described in subsection (a) is not obliged to pay all or part of the order, and (ii) the sender receives notification from the receiving bank that the order was accepted by the bank or that the sender's account was debited with respect to the order, the sender has a duty to exercise ordinary care, on the basis of information available to the sender, to discover the error with respect to the order and to advise the bank of the relevant facts within a reasonable time, not exceeding 90 days, after the bank's notification was received by the sender. If the bank proves that the sender failed to perform that duty, the sender is liable to the bank for the loss the bank proves it incurred as a result of the failure, but the liability of the sender may not exceed the amount of the sender's order.

(c) This section applies to amendments to payment orders to the same extent it applies to payment orders.

§ 4A–206. Transmission of Payment Order through Funds-Transfer or Other Communication System.

(a) If a payment order addressed to a receiving bank is transmitted to a funds-transfer system or other third party communication system for transmittal to the bank, the system is deemed to be an agent of the sender for the purpose of transmitting the payment order to the bank. If there is a discrepancy between the terms of the payment order transmitted to the system and the terms of the payment order transmitted by the system to the bank, the terms of the payment order of the sender are those transmitted by the system. This section does not apply to a funds-transfer system of the Federal Reserve Banks.

(b) This section applies to cancellations and amendments to payment orders to the same extent it applies to payment orders.

§ 4A–207. Misdescription of Beneficiary.

(a) Subject to subsection (b), if, in a payment order received by the beneficiary's bank, the name, bank account number, or other identification of the beneficiary refers to a nonexistent or unidentifiable person or account, no person has rights as a beneficiary of the order and acceptance of the order cannot occur.

(b) If a payment order received by the beneficiary's bank identifies the beneficiary both by name and by an identifying or bank account number and the name and number identify different persons, the following rules apply:

(1) Except as otherwise provided in subsection (c), if the beneficiary's bank does not know that the name and number refer to different persons, it may rely on the number as the proper identification of the beneficiary of the order. The beneficiary's bank need not determine whether the name and number refer to the same person.

(2) If the beneficiary's bank pays the person identified by name or knows that the name and number identify different persons, no person has rights as beneficiary except the person paid by the beneficiary's bank if that person was entitled to receive payment from the originator of the funds transfer. If no person has rights as beneficiary, acceptance of the order cannot occur.

(c) If (i) a payment order described in subsection (b) is accepted, (ii) the originator's payment order described the beneficiary inconsistently by name and number, and (iii) the beneficiary's bank pays the person identified by number as permitted by subsection (b)(1), the following rules apply:

(1) If the originator is a bank, the originator is obliged to pay its order.

(2) If the originator is not a bank and proves that the person identified by number was not entitled to receive payment from the originator, the originator is not obliged to pay its order unless the originator's bank proves that the originator, before acceptance of the originator's order, had notice that payment of a payment order issued by the originator might be made by the beneficiary's bank on the basis of an identifying or bank account number even if it identifies a person different from the named beneficiary. Proof of notice may be made by any admissible evidence. The originator's bank satisfies the burden of proof if it proves that the originator, before the payment order was accepted, signed a writing stating the information to which the notice relates.

(d) In a case governed by subsection (b)(1), if the beneficiary's bank rightfully pays the person identified by number and that person was not entitled to receive payment from the originator, the amount paid may be recovered from that person to the extent allowed by the law governing mistake and restitution as follows:

(1) If the originator is obliged to pay its payment order as stated in subsection (c), the originator has the right to recover.

(2) If the originator is not a bank and is not obliged to pay its payment order, the originator's bank has the right to recover.

§ 4A–208. Misdescription of Intermediary Bank or Beneficiary's Bank.

(a) This subsection applies to a payment order identifying an intermediary bank or the beneficiary's bank only by an identifying number.

(1) The receiving bank may rely on the number as the proper identification of the intermediary or beneficiary's bank and need not determine whether the number identifies a bank.

(2) The sender is obliged to compensate the receiving bank for any loss and expenses incurred by the receiving bank as a result of its reliance on the number in executing or attempting to execute the order.

(b) This subsection applies to a payment order identifying an intermediary bank or the beneficiary's bank both by name and an identifying number if the name and number identify different persons.

(1) If the sender is a bank, the receiving bank may rely on the number as the proper identification of the intermediary or beneficiary's bank if the receiving bank, when it executes the sender's order, does not

know that the name and number identify different persons. The receiving bank need not determine whether the name and number refer to the same person or whether the number refers to a bank. The sender is obliged to compensate the receiving bank for any loss and expenses incurred by the receiving bank as a result of its reliance on the number in executing or attempting to execute the order.

(2) If the sender is not a bank and the receiving bank proves that the sender, before the payment order was accepted, had notice that the receiving bank might rely on the number as the proper identification of the intermediary or beneficiary's bank even if it identifies a person different from the bank identified by name, the rights and obligations of the sender and the receiving bank are governed by subsection (b)(1), as though the sender were a bank. Proof of notice may be made by any admissible evidence. The receiving bank satisfies the burden of proof if it proves that the sender, before the payment order was accepted, signed a writing stating the information to which the notice relates.

(3) Regardless of whether the sender is a bank, the receiving bank may rely on the name as the proper identification of the intermediary or beneficiary's bank if the receiving bank, at the time it executes the sender's order, does not know that the name and number identify different persons. The receiving bank need not determine whether the name and number refer to the same person.

(4) If the receiving bank knows that the name and number identify different persons, reliance on either the name or the number in executing the sender's payment order is a breach of the obligation stated in Section 4A–302(a)(1).

§ 4A–209. Acceptance of Payment Order.

(a) Subject to subsection (d), a receiving bank other than the beneficiary's bank accepts a payment order when it executes the order.

(b) Subject to subsections (c) and (d), a beneficiary's bank accepts a payment order at the earliest of the following times:

(1) When the bank (i) pays the beneficiary as stated in Section 4A–405(a) or 4A–405(b), or (ii) notifies the beneficiary of receipt of the order or that the account of the beneficiary has been credited with respect to the order unless the notice indicates that the bank is rejecting the order or that funds with respect to the order may not be withdrawn or used until receipt of payment from the sender of the order;

(2) When the bank receives payment of the entire amount of the sender's order pursuant to Section 4A–403(a)(1) or 4A–403(a)(2); or

(3) The opening of the next funds-transfer business day of the bank following the payment date of the order if, at that time, the amount of the sender's order is fully covered by a withdrawable credit balance in an authorized account of the sender or the bank has otherwise received full payment from the sender, unless the order was rejected before that time or is rejected within (i) one hour after that time, or (ii) one hour after the opening of the next business day of the sender following the payment date if that time is later. If notice of rejection is received by the sender after the payment date and the authorized account of the sender does not bear interest, the bank is obliged to pay interest to the sender on the amount of the order for the number of days elapsing after the payment date to the day the sender receives notice or learns that the order was not accepted, counting that day as an elapsed day. If the withdrawable credit balance during that period falls below the amount of the order, the amount of interest payable is reduced accordingly.

(c) Acceptance of a payment order cannot occur before the order is received by the receiving bank. Acceptance does not occur under subsection (b)(2) or (b)(3) if the beneficiary of the payment order does not have an account with the receiving bank, the account has been closed, or the receiving bank is not permitted by law to receive credits for the beneficiary's account.

(d) A payment order issued to the originator's bank cannot be accepted until the payment date if the bank is the beneficiary's bank, or the execution date if the bank is not the beneficiary's bank. If the originator's bank executes the originator's payment order before the execution date or pays the beneficiary of the originator's payment order before the payment date and the payment order is subsequently cancelled pursuant to Section 4A–211(b), the bank may recover from the beneficiary any payment received to the extent allowed by the law governing mistake and restitution.

§ 4A–210. Rejection of Payment Order.

(a) A payment order is rejected by the receiving bank by a notice of rejection transmitted to the sender orally, electronically, or in writing. A notice of rejection need not use any particular words and is sufficient if it indicates that the receiving bank is rejecting the order or will not execute or pay the order. Rejection is effective when the notice is given if transmission is by a means that is reasonable in the circumstances. If notice of rejection is given by a means that is not reasonable, rejection is effective when the notice is received. If an agreement of the sender and receiving bank establishes the means to be used to reject a payment order, (i) any means complying with the agreement is reasonable and (ii) any means not complying is not reasonable unless no significant delay in receipt of the notice resulted from the use of the noncomplying means.

(b) This subsection applies if a receiving bank other than the beneficiary's bank fails to execute a payment order despite the existence on the execution date of a withdrawable credit balance in an authorized account of the sender sufficient to cover the order. If the sender does not receive notice of rejection of the order on the execution date and the authorized account of the sender does not bear interest, the bank is obliged to pay interest to the sender on the amount of the order for the number of days elapsing after the execution date to the earlier of the day the order is cancelled pursuant to Section 4A–211(d) or the day the sender receives notice or learns that the order was not executed, counting the final day of the period as an elapsed day. If the withdrawable credit balance during that period falls below the amount of the order, the amount of interest is reduced accordingly.

(c) If a receiving bank suspends payments, all unaccepted payment orders issued to it are are deemed rejected at the time the bank suspends payments.

(d) Acceptance of a payment order precludes a later rejection of the order. Rejection of a payment order precludes a later acceptance of the order.

§ 4A–211. Cancellation and Amendment of Payment Order.

(a) A communication of the sender of a payment order cancelling or amending the order may be transmitted to the receiving bank orally, electronically, or in writing. If a security procedure is in effect between the sender and the receiving bank, the communication is not effective to cancel or amend the order unless the communication is verified pursuant to the security procedure or the bank agrees to the cancellation or amendment.

(b) Subject to subsection (a), a communication by the sender cancelling or amending a payment order is effective to cancel or amend the order if notice of the communication is received at a time and in a manner affording the receiving bank a reasonable opportunity to act on the communication before the bank accepts the payment order.

(c) After a payment order has been accepted, cancellation or amendment of the order is not effective unless the receiving bank agrees or a funds-transfer system rule allows cancellation or amendment without agreement of the bank.

(1) With respect to a payment order accepted by a receiving bank other than the beneficiary's bank, cancellation or amendment is not effective unless a conforming cancellation or amendment of the payment order issued by the receiving bank is also made.

(2) With respect to a payment order accepted by the beneficiary's bank, cancellation or amendment is not effective unless the order was issued in execution of an unauthorized payment order, or because of a mistake by a sender in the funds transfer which resulted in the issuance of a payment order (i) that is a duplicate of a payment order previously issued by the sender, (ii) that orders payment to a beneficiary not entitled to receive payment from the originator, or (iii) that orders payment in an amount greater than the amount the beneficiary was entitled to receive from the originator. If the payment order is cancelled or amended, the beneficiary's bank is entitled to recover from the beneficiary any amount paid to the beneficiary to the extent allowed by the law governing mistake and restitution.

(d) An unaccepted payment order is cancelled by operation of law at the close of the fifth funds-transfer business day of the receiving bank after the execution date or payment date of the order.

(e) A cancelled payment order cannot be accepted. If an accepted payment order is cancelled, the acceptance is nullified and no person has any right or obligation based on the acceptance. Amendment of a payment order is deemed to be cancellation of the original order at the time of amendment and issue of a new payment order in the amended form at the same time.

(f) Unless otherwise provided in an agreement of the parties or in a funds-transfer system rule, if the receiving bank, after accepting a payment order, agrees to cancellation or amendment of the order by the sender or is bound by a funds-transfer system rule allowing cancellation or amendment without the bank's agreement, the sender, whether or not cancellation or amendment is effective, is liable to the bank for any loss and expenses, including reasonable attorney's fees, incurred by the bank as a result of the cancellation or amendment or attempted cancellation or amendment.

(g) A payment order is not revoked by the death or legal incapacity of the sender unless the receiving bank knows of the death or of an adjudication of incapacity by a court of competent jurisdiction and has reasonable opportunity to act before acceptance of the order.

(h) A funds-transfer system rule is not effective to the extent it conflicts with subsection (c)(2).

§ 4A–212. Liability and Duty of Receiving Bank Regarding Unaccepted Payment Order.

If a receiving bank fails to accept a payment order that it is obliged by express agreement to accept, the bank is liable for breach of the agreement to the extent provided in the agreement or in this Article, but does not otherwise have any duty to accept a payment order or, before acceptance, to take any action, or refrain from taking action, with respect to the order except as provided in this Article or by express agreement. Liability based on acceptance arises only when acceptance occurs as stated in Section 4A–209, and liability is limited to that provided in this Article. A receiving bank is not the agent of the sender or beneficiary of the payment order it accepts, or of any other party to the funds transfer, and the bank owes no duty to any party to the funds transfer except as provided in this Article or by express agreement.

Part 3 Execution of Sender's Payment Order by Receiving Bank

§ 4A–301. Execution and Execution Date.

(a) A payment order is "executed" by the receiving bank when it issues a payment order intended to carry out the payment order received by the bank. A payment order received by the beneficiary's bank can be accepted but cannot be executed.

(b) "Execution date" of a payment order means the day on which the receiving bank may properly issue a payment order in execution of the sender's order. The execution date may be determined by instruction of the sender but cannot be earlier than the day the order is received and, unless otherwise determined, is the day the order is received. If the sender's instruction states a payment date, the execution date is the payment date or an earlier date on which execution is reasonably necessary to allow payment to the beneficiary on the payment date.

§ 4A–302. Obligations of Receiving Bank in Execution of Payment Order.

(a) Except as provided in subsections (b) through (d), if the receiving bank accepts a payment order pursuant to Section 4A–209(a), the bank has the following obligations in executing the order:

(1) The receiving bank is obliged to issue, on the execution date, a payment order complying with the sender's order and to follow the sender's instructions concerning (i) any intermediary bank or funds-transfer system to be used in carrying out the funds transfer, or (ii) the means by which payment orders are to be transmitted in the funds transfer. If the originator's bank issues a payment order to an intermediary bank, the originator's bank is obliged to instruct the intermediary bank according to the instruction of the originator. An intermediary bank in the funds transfer is similarly bound by an instruction given to it by the sender of the payment order it accepts.

(2) If the sender's instruction states that the funds transfer is to be carried out telephonically or by wire transfer or otherwise indicates that the funds transfer is to be carried out by the most expeditious means, the receiving bank is obliged to transmit its payment order by the most expeditious available means, and to instruct any intermediary bank accordingly. If a sender's instruction states a payment date, the receiving bank is obliged to transmit its payment order at a time and by means reasonably necessary to allow payment to the beneficiary on the payment date or as soon thereafter as is feasible.

(b) Unless otherwise instructed, a receiving bank executing a payment order may (i) use any funds-transfer system if use of that system is reasonable in the circumstances, and (ii) issue a payment order to the beneficiary's bank or to an intermediary bank through which a payment order conforming to the sender's order can expeditiously be issued to the beneficiary's bank if the receiving bank exercises ordinary care in the selection of the intermediary bank. A receiving bank is not required to follow an instruction of the sender designating a funds-transfer system to be used in carrying out the funds transfer if the receiving bank, in good faith, determines that it is not feasible to follow the instruction or that following the instruction would unduly delay completion of the funds transfer.

(c) Unless subsection (a)(2) applies or the receiving bank is otherwise instructed, the bank may execute a payment order by transmitting its payment order by first class mail or by any means reasonable in the circumstances. If the receiving bank is instructed to execute the sender's order by transmitting its payment order by a particular means, the receiving bank may issue its payment order by the means stated or by any means as expeditious as the means stated.

(d) Unless instructed by the sender, (i) the receiving bank may not obtain payment of its charges for services and expenses in connection with the execution of the sender's order by issuing a payment order in an amount equal to the amount of the sender's order less the amount of the charges, and (ii) may not instruct a subsequent receiving bank to obtain payment of its charges in the same manner.

§ 4A–303. Erroneous Execution of Payment Order.

(a) A receiving bank that (i) executes the payment order of the sender by issuing a payment order in an amount greater than the amount of the sender's order, or (ii) issues a payment order in execution of the sender's order and then issues a duplicate order, is entitled to payment of the amount of the sender's order under Section 4A–402(c) if that subsection is otherwise satisfied. The bank is entitled to recover from the beneficiary of the erroneous order the excess payment received to the extent allowed by the law governing mistake and restitution.

(b) A receiving bank that executes the payment order of the sender by issuing a payment order in an amount less than the amount of the sender's order is entitled to payment of the amount of the sender's order under Section 4A–402(c) if (i) that subsection is otherwise satisfied and (ii) the bank corrects its mistake by issuing an additional payment order for the benefit of the beneficiary of the sender's order. If the error is not corrected, the issuer of the erroneous order is entitled to receive or retain payment from the sender of the order it accepted only to the extent of the amount of the erroneous order. This subsection does not apply if the receiving bank executes the sender's payment order by issuing a payment order in an amount less than the amount of the sender's order for the purpose of obtaining payment of its charges for services and expenses pursuant to instruction of the sender.

(c) If a receiving bank executes the payment order of the sender by issuing a payment order to a beneficiary different from the beneficiary of the sender's order and the funds transfer is completed on the basis of that error, the sender of the payment order that was erroneously executed and all previous senders in the funds transfer are not obliged to pay the payment orders they issued. The issuer of the erroneous order is entitled to recover from the beneficiary of the order the payment received to the extent allowed by the law governing mistake and restitution.

§ 4A–304. Duty of Sender to Report Erroneously Executed Payment Order.

If the sender of a payment order that is erroneously executed as stated in Section 4A–303 receives notification from the receiving bank that the order was executed or that the sender's account was debited with respect to the order, the sender has a duty to exercise ordinary care to determine, on the basis of information available to the sender, that the order was erroneously executed and to notify the bank of the relevant facts within a reasonable time not exceeding 90 days after the notification from the bank was received by the sender. If the sender fails to perform that duty, the bank is not obliged to pay interest on any amount refundable to the sender under Section 4A–402(d) for the period before the bank learns of the execution error. The bank is not entitled to any recovery from the sender on account of a failure by the sender to perform the duty stated in this section.

§ 4A–305. Liability for Late or Improper Execution or Failure to Execute Payment Order.

(a) If a funds transfer is completed but execution of a payment order by the receiving bank in breach of Section 4A–302 results in delay in payment to the beneficiary, the bank is obliged to pay interest to either the originator or the beneficiary of the funds transfer for the period of delay caused by the improper execution. Except as provided in subsection (c), additional damages are not recoverable.

(b) If execution of a payment order by a receiving bank in breach of Section 4A–302 results in (i) noncompletion of the funds transfer, (ii) failure to use an intermediary bank designated by the originator, or (iii) issuance of a payment order that does not comply with the terms of the payment order of the originator, the bank is liable to the originator for its expenses in the funds transfer and for incidental expenses and interest losses, to the extent not covered by subsection (a), resulting from the improper execution. Except as provided in subsection (c), additional damages are not recoverable.

(c) In addition to the amounts payable under subsections (a) and (b), damages, including consequential damages, are recoverable to the extent provided in an express written agreement of the receiving bank.

(d) If a receiving bank fails to execute a payment order it was obliged by express agreement to execute, the receiving bank is liable to the sender for its expenses in the transaction and for incidental expenses and interest losses resulting from the failure to execute. Additional damages, including consequential damages, are recoverable to the extent provided in an express written agreement of the receiving bank, but are not otherwise recoverable.

(e) Reasonable attorney's fees are recoverable if demand for compensation under subsection (a) or (b) is made and refused before an action is brought on the claim. If a claim is made for breach of an agreement under subsection (d) and the agreement does not provide for damages, reasonable attorney's fees are recoverable if demand for compensation under subsection (d) is made and refused before an action is brought on the claim.

(f) Except as stated in this section, the liability of a receiving bank under subsections (a) and (b) may not be varied by agreement.

Part 4 Payment

§ 4A–401. Payment Date.

"Payment date" of a payment order means the day on which the amount of the order is payable to the beneficiary by the beneficiary's bank. The payment date may be determined by instruction of the sender but cannot be earlier than the day the order is received by the beneficiary's bank and, unless otherwise determined, is the day the order is received by the beneficiary's bank.

§ 4A–402. Obligation of Sender to Pay Receiving Bank.

(a) This section is subject to Sections 4A–205 and 4A–207.

(b) With respect to a payment order issued to the beneficiary's bank, acceptance of the order by the bank obliges the sender to pay the bank the amount of the order, but payment is not due until the payment date of the order.

(c) This subsection is subject to subsection (e) and to Section 4A–303. With respect to a payment order issued to a receiving bank other than the beneficiary's bank, acceptance of the order by the receiving bank obliges the sender to pay the bank the amount of the sender's order. Payment by the sender is not due until the execution date of the sender's order. The obligation of that sender to pay its payment order is excused if the funds transfer is not completed by acceptance by the beneficiary's bank of a payment order instructing payment to the beneficiary of that sender's payment order.

(d) If the sender of a payment order pays the order and was not obliged to pay all or part of the amount paid, the bank receiving payment is obliged to refund payment to the extent the sender was not obliged to pay. Except as provided in Sections 4A–204 and 4A–304, interest is payable on the refundable amount from the date of payment.

(e) If a funds transfer is not completed as stated in subsection (c) and an intermediary bank is obliged to refund payment as stated in subsection (d) but is unable to do so because not permitted by applicable law or because the bank suspends payments, a sender in the funds transfer that executed a payment order in compliance with an instruction, as stated in Section 4A–302(a)(1), to route the funds transfer through that intermediary bank is entitled to receive or retain payment from the sender of the payment order that it accepted. The first sender in the funds transfer that issued an instruction requiring routing through that intermediary bank is subrogated to the right of the bank that paid the intermediary bank to refund as stated in subsection (d).

(f) The right of the sender of a payment order to be excused from the obligation to pay the order as stated in subsection (c) or to receive refund under subsection (d) may not be varied by agreement.

§ 4A–403. Payment by Sender to Receiving Bank.

(a) Payment of the sender's obligation under Section 4A–402 to pay the receiving bank occurs as follows:

(1) If the sender is a bank, payment occurs when the receiving bank receives final settlement of the obligation through a Federal Reserve Bank or through a funds-transfer system.

(2) If the sender is a bank and the sender (i) credited an account of the receiving bank with the sender, or (ii) caused an account of the receiving bank in another bank to be credited, payment occurs when the credit is withdrawn or, if not withdrawn, at midnight of the day on which the credit is withdrawable and the receiving bank learns of that fact.

(3) If the receiving bank debits an account of the sender with the receiving bank, payment occurs when the debit is made to the extent the debit is covered by a withdrawable credit balance in the account.

(b) If the sender and receiving bank are members of a funds-transfer system that nets obligations multilaterally among participants, the receiving bank receives final settlement when settlement is complete in accordance with the rules of the system. The obligation of the sender to pay the amount of a payment order transmitted through the funds-transfer system may be satisfied, to the extent permitted by the rules of the system, by setting off and applying against the sender's obligation the right of the sender to receive payment from the receiving bank of the amount of any other payment order transmitted to the sender by the receiving bank through the funds-transfer system. The aggregate balance of obligations owed by each sender to each receiving bank in the funds-transfer system may be satisfied, to the extent permitted by the rules of the system, by setting off and applying against that balance the aggregate balance of obligations owed to the sender by other members of the system. The aggregate balance is determined after the right of setoff stated in the second sentence of this subsection has been exercised.

(c) If two banks transmit payment orders to each other under an agreement that settlement of the obligations of each bank to the other under Section 4A–402 will be made at the end of the day or other period, the total amount owed with respect to all orders transmitted by one bank shall be set off against the total amount owed with respect to all orders transmitted by the other bank. To the extent of the setoff, each bank has made payment to the other.

(d) In a case not covered by subsection (a), the time when payment of the sender's obligation under Section 4A–402(b) or 4A–402(c) occurs is governed by applicable principles of law that determine when an obligation is satisfied.

§ 4A–404. Obligation of Beneficiary's Bank to Pay and Give Notice to Beneficiary.

(a) Subject to Sections 4A–211(e), 4A–405(d), and 4A–405(e), if a beneficiary's bank accepts a payment order, the bank is obliged to pay the amount of the order to the beneficiary of the order. Payment is due on the payment date of the order, but if acceptance occurs on the payment date after the close of the funds-transfer business day of the bank, payment is due on the next funds-transfer business day. If the bank refuses to pay after demand by the beneficiary and receipt of notice of particular circumstances that will give rise to consequential damages as a result of nonpayment, the beneficiary may recover damages resulting from the refusal to pay to the extent the bank had notice of the damages, unless the bank proves that it did not pay because of a reasonable doubt concerning the right of the beneficiary to payment.

(b) If a payment order accepted by the beneficiary's bank instructs payment to an account of the beneficiary, the bank is obliged to notify the beneficiary of receipt of the order before midnight of the next funds-transfer business day following the payment date. If the payment order does not instruct payment to an account of the beneficiary, the bank is required to notify the beneficiary only if notice is required by the order. Notice may be given by first class mail or any other means reasonable in the circumstances. If the bank fails to give the required notice, the bank is obliged to pay interest to the beneficiary on the amount of the payment order from the day notice should have been given until the day the beneficiary learned of receipt of the payment order by the bank. No other damages are recoverable. Reasonable attorney's fees are also recoverable if demand for interest is made and refused before an action is brought on the claim.

(c) The right of a beneficiary to receive payment and damages as stated in subsection (a) may not be varied by agreement or a funds-transfer system rule. The right of a beneficiary to be notified as stated in subsection (b) may be varied by agreement of the beneficiary or by a funds-transfer system rule if the beneficiary is notified of the rule before initiation of the funds transfer.

§ 4A–405. Payment by Beneficiary's Bank to Beneficiary.

(a) If the beneficiary's bank credits an account of the beneficiary of a payment order, payment of the bank's obligation under Section 4A–404(a) occurs when and to the extent (i) the beneficiary is notified of the right to withdraw the credit, (ii) the bank lawfully applies the credit to a debt of the beneficiary, or (iii) funds with respect to the order are otherwise made available to the beneficiary by the bank.

(b) If the beneficiary's bank does not credit an account of the beneficiary of a payment order, the time when payment of the bank's obligation under Section 4A–404(a) occurs is governed by principles of law that determine when an obligation is satisfied.

(c) Except as stated in subsections (d) and (e), if the beneficiary's bank pays the beneficiary of a payment order under a condition to payment or agreement of the beneficiary giving the bank the right to recover payment from the beneficiary if the bank does not receive payment of the order, the condition to payment or agreement is not enforceable.

(d) A funds-transfer system rule may provide that payments made to beneficiaries of funds transfers made through the system are provisional until receipt of payment by the beneficiary's bank of the payment order it accepted. A beneficiary's bank that makes a payment that is provisional under the rule is entitled to refund from the beneficiary if (i) the rule requires that both the beneficiary and the originator be given notice of the provisional nature of the payment before the funds transfer is initiated, (ii) the beneficiary, the beneficiary's bank, and the originator's bank agreed to be bound by the rule, and (iii) the beneficiary's bank did not receive payment of the payment order that it accepted. If the beneficiary is obliged to refund payment to the beneficiary's bank, acceptance of the payment order by the beneficiary's bank is nullified and no payment by the originator of the funds transfer to the beneficiary occurs under Section 4A–406.

(e) This subsection applies to a funds transfer that includes a payment order transmitted over a funds-transfer system that (i) nets obligations multilaterally among participants, and (ii) has in effect a loss-sharing agreement among participants for the purpose of providing funds necessary to complete settlement of the obligations of one or more participants that do not meet their settlement obligations. If the beneficiary's bank in the funds transfer accepts a payment order and the system fails to complete settlement pursuant to its rules with respect to any payment order in the funds transfer, (i) the acceptance by the beneficiary's bank is nullified and no person has any right or obligation based on the acceptance, (ii) the beneficiary's bank is entitled to recover payment from the beneficiary, (iii) no payment by the originator to the beneficiary occurs under Section 4A–406, and (iv) subject to Section 4A–402(e), each sender in the funds transfer is excused from its obligation to pay its payment order under Section 4A–402(c) because the funds transfer has not been completed.

§ 4A–406. Payment by Originator to Beneficiary; Discharge of Underlying Obligation.

(a) Subject to Sections 4A–211(e), 4A–405(d), and 4A–405(e), the originator of a funds transfer pays the beneficiary of the originator's payment order (i) at the time a payment order for the benefit of the beneficiary is accepted by the beneficiary's bank in the funds transfer and (ii) in an amount equal to the amount of the order accepted by the beneficiary's bank, but not more than the amount of the originator's order.

(b) If payment under subsection (a) is made to satisfy an obligation, the obligation is discharged to the same extent discharge would result from payment to the beneficiary of the same amount in money, unless (i) the payment under subsection (a) was made by a means prohibited by the contract of the beneficiary with respect to the obligation, (ii) the beneficiary, within a reasonable time after receiving notice of receipt of the order by the beneficiary's bank, notified the originator of the beneficiary's refusal of the payment, (iii) funds with respect to the order were not withdrawn by the beneficiary or applied to a debt of the beneficiary, and (iv) the beneficiary would suffer a loss that could reasonably have been avoided if payment had been made by a means complying with the contract. If payment by the originator does not result in discharge under this section, the originator is subrogated to the rights of the beneficiary to receive payment from the beneficiary's bank under Section 4A–404(a).

(c) For the purpose of determining whether discharge of an obligation occurs under subsection (b), if the beneficiary's bank accepts a payment order in an amount equal to the amount of the originator's payment order less charges of one or more receiving banks in the funds transfer, payment to the beneficiary is deemed to be in the amount of the originator's order unless upon demand by the beneficiary the originator does not pay the beneficiary the amount of the deducted charges.

(d) Rights of the originator or of the beneficiary of a funds transfer under this section may be varied only by agreement of the originator and the beneficiary.

Part 5 Miscellaneous Provisions

§ 4A–501. Variation by Agreement and Effect of Funds-Transfer System Rule.

(a) Except as otherwise provided in this Article, the rights and obligations of a party to a funds transfer may be varied by agreement of the affected party.

(b) "Funds-transfer system rule" means a rule of an association of banks (i) governing transmission of payment orders by means of a funds-transfer system of the association or rights and obligations with respect to those orders, or (ii) to the extent the rule governs rights and obligations between banks that are parties to a funds transfer in which a Federal Reserve Bank, acting as an intermediary bank, sends a payment order to the beneficiary's bank. Except as otherwise provided in this Article, a funds-transfer system rule governing rights and obligations between participating banks using the system may be effective even if the rule conflicts with this Article and indirectly affects another party to the funds transfer who does not consent to the rule. A funds-transfer system rule may also govern rights and obligations of parties other than participating banks using the system to the extent stated in Sections 4A–404(c), 4A–405(d), and 4A–507(c).

§ 4A–502. Creditor Process Served on Receiving Bank; Setoff by Beneficiary's Bank.

(a) As used in this section, "creditor process" means levy, attachment, garnishment, notice of lien, sequestration, or similar process issued by or on behalf of a creditor or other claimant with respect to an account.

(b) This subsection applies to creditor process with respect to an authorized account of the sender of a payment order if the creditor process is served on the receiving bank. For the purpose of determining rights with respect to the creditor process, if the receiving bank accepts the payment order the balance in the authorized account is deemed to be reduced by the amount of the payment order to the extent the bank did not otherwise receive payment of the order, unless the creditor process is served at a time and in a manner affording the bank a reasonable opportunity to act on it before the bank accepts the payment order.

(c) If a beneficiary's bank has received a payment order for payment to the beneficiary's account in the bank, the following rules apply:

(1) The bank may credit the beneficiary's account. The amount credited may be set off against an obligation owed by the beneficiary to the bank or may be applied to satisfy creditor process served on the bank with respect to the account.

(2) The bank may credit the beneficiary's account and allow withdrawal of the amount credited unless creditor process with respect to the account is served at a time and in a manner affording the bank a reasonable opportunity to act to prevent withdrawal.

(3) If creditor process with respect to the beneficiary's account has been served and the bank has had a reasonable opportunity to act on it, the bank may not reject the payment order except for a reason unrelated to the service of process.

(d) Creditor process with respect to a payment by the originator to the beneficiary pursuant to a funds transfer may be served only on the beneficiary's bank with respect to the debt owed by that bank to the beneficiary. Any other bank served with the creditor process is not obliged to act with respect to the process.

§ 4A–503. Injunction or Restraining Order with Respect to Funds Transfer.

For proper cause and in compliance with applicable law, a court may restrain (i) a person from issuing a payment order to initiate a funds transfer, (ii) an originator's bank from executing the payment order of the originator, or (iii) the beneficiary's bank from releasing funds to the beneficiary or the beneficiary from withdrawing the funds. A court may not otherwise restrain a person from issuing a payment order, paying or receiving payment of a payment order, or otherwise acting with respect to a funds transfer.

§ 4A–504. Order in Which Items and Payment Orders May Be Charged to Account; Order of Withdrawals from Account.

(a) If a receiving bank has received more than one payment order of the sender or one or more payment orders and other items that are payable from the sender's account, the bank may charge the sender's account with respect to the various orders and items in any sequence.

(b) In determining whether a credit to an account has been withdrawn by the holder of the account or applied to a debt of the holder of the account, credits first made to the account are first withdrawn or applied.

§ 4A–505. Preclusion of Objection to Debit of Customer's Account.

If a receiving bank has received payment from its customer with respect to a payment order issued in the name of the customer as sender and accepted by the bank, and the customer received notification reasonably identifying the order, the customer is precluded from asserting that the bank is not entitled to retain the payment unless the customer notifies the bank of the customer's objection to the payment within one year after the notification was received by the customer.

§ 4A–506. Rate of Interest.

(a) If, under this Article, a receiving bank is obliged to pay interest with respect to a payment order issued to the bank, the amount payable may be determined (i) by agreement of the sender and receiving bank, or (ii) by a funds-transfer system rule if the payment order is transmitted through a funds-transfer system.

(b) If the amount of interest is not determined by an agreement or rule as stated in subsection (a), the amount is calculated by multiplying the applicable Federal Funds rate by the amount on which interest is payable, and then multiplying the product by the number of days for which interest is payable. The applicable Federal Funds rate is the average of the Federal Funds rates published by the Federal Reserve Bank of New York for each of the days for which interest is payable divided by 360. The Federal Funds rate for any day on which a published rate is not available is the same as the published rate for the next preceding day for which there is a published rate. If a receiving bank that accepted a payment order is required to refund payment to the sender of the order because the funds transfer was not completed, but the failure to complete was not due to any fault by the bank, the interest payable is reduced by a percentage equal to the reserve requirement on deposits of the receiving bank.

§ 4A–507. Choice of Law.

(a) The following rules apply unless the affected parties otherwise agree or subsection (c) applies:

(1) The rights and obligations between the sender of a payment order and the receiving bank are governed by the law of the jurisdiction in which the receiving bank is located.

(2) The rights and obligations between the beneficiary's bank and the beneficiary are governed by the law of the jurisdiction in which the beneficiary's bank is located.

(3) The issue of when payment is made pursuant to a funds transfer by the originator to the beneficiary is governed by the law of the jurisdiction in which the beneficiary's bank is located.

(b) If the parties described in each paragraph of subsection (a) have made an agreement selecting the law of a particular jurisdiction to govern rights and obligations between each other, the law of that jurisdiction governs those rights and obligations, whether or not the payment order or the funds transfer bears a reasonable relation to that jurisdiction.

(c) A funds-transfer system rule may select the law of a particular jurisdiction to govern (i) rights and obligations between participating banks with respect to payment orders transmitted or processed through the system, or (ii) the rights and obligations of some or all parties to a funds transfer any part of which is carried out by means of the system. A choice of law made pursuant to clause (i) is binding on participating banks. A choice of law made pursuant to clause (ii) is binding on the originator, other sender, or a receiving bank having notice that the funds-transfer system might be used in the funds transfer and of the choice of law by the system when the originator, other sender, or receiving bank issued or accepted a payment order. The beneficiary of a funds transfer is bound by the choice of law if, when the funds transfer is initiated, the beneficiary has notice that the funds-transfer system might be used in the funds transfer and of the choice of law by the system. The law of a jurisdiction selected pursuant to this subsection may govern, whether or not that law bears a reasonable relation to the matter in issue.

(d) In the event of inconsistency between an agreement under subsection (b) and a choice-of-law rule under subsection (c), the agreement under subsection (b) prevails.

(e) If a funds transfer is made by use of more than one funds-transfer system and there is inconsistency between choice-of-law rules of the systems, the matter in issue is governed by the law of the selected jurisdiction that has the most significant relationship to the matter in issue.

Revised Article 5
LETTERS OF CREDIT

§ 5–101. Short Title.

This article may be cited as Uniform Commercial Code—Letters of Credit.

§ 5–102. Definitions.

(a) In this article:

(1) "Adviser" means a person who, at the request of the issuer, a confirmer, or another adviser, notifies or requests another adviser to notify the beneficiary that a letter of credit has been issued, confirmed, or amended.

(2) "Applicant" means a person at whose request or for whose account a letter of credit is issued. The term includes a person who requests an issuer to issue a letter of credit on behalf of another if the person making the request undertakes an obligation to reimburse the issuer.

(3) "Beneficiary" means a person who under the terms of a letter of credit is entitled to have its complying presentation honored. The term includes a person to whom drawing rights have been transferred under a transferable letter of credit.

(4) "Confirmer" means a nominated person who undertakes, at the request or with the consent of the issuer, to honor a presentation under a letter of credit issued by another.

(5) "Dishonor" of a letter of credit means failure timely to honor or to take an interim action, such as acceptance of a draft, that may be required by the letter of credit.

(6) "Document" means a draft or other demand, document of title, investment security, certificate, invoice, or other record, statement, or representation of fact, law, right, or opinion (i) which is presented in a written or other medium permitted by the letter of credit or, unless prohibited by the letter of credit, by the standard practice referred to in Section 5–108(e) and (ii) which is capable of being examined for compliance with the terms and conditions of the letter of credit. A document may not be oral.

(7) "Good faith" means honesty in fact in the conduct or transaction concerned.

(8) "Honor" of a letter of credit means performance of the issuer's undertaking in the letter of credit to pay or deliver an item of value. Unless the letter of credit otherwise provides, "honor" occurs

(i) upon payment,

(ii) if the letter of credit provides for acceptance, upon acceptance of a draft and, at maturity, its payment, or

(iii) if the letter of credit provides for incurring a deferred obligation, upon incurring the obligation and, at maturity, its performance.

(9) "Issuer" means a bank or other person that issues a letter of credit, but does not include an individual who makes an engagement for personal, family, or household purposes.

(10) "Letter of credit" means a definite undertaking that satisfies the requirements of Section 5–104 by an issuer to a beneficiary at the request or for the account of an applicant or, in the case of a financial institution, to itself or for its own account, to honor a documentary presentation by payment or delivery of an item of value.

(11) "Nominated person" means a person whom the issuer (i) designates or authorizes to pay, accept, negotiate, or otherwise give value under a letter of

credit and (ii) undertakes by agreement or custom and practice to reimburse.

(12) "Presentation" means delivery of a document to an issuer or nominated person for honor or giving of value under a letter of credit.

(13) "Presenter" means a person making a presentation as or on behalf of a beneficiary or nominated person.

(14) "Record" means information that is inscribed on a tangible medium, or that is stored in an electronic or other medium and is retrievable in perceivable form.

(15) "Successor of a beneficiary" means a person who succeeds to substantially all of the rights of a beneficiary by operation of law, including a corporation with or into which the beneficiary has been merged or consolidated, an administrator, executor, personal representative, trustee in bankruptcy, debtor in possession, liquidator, and receiver.

(b) Definitions in other Articles applying to this article and the sections in which they appear are:

"Accept" or "Acceptance" Section 3–409

"Value" Sections 3–303, 4–211

(c) Article 1 contains certain additional general definitions and principles of construction and interpretation applicable throughout this article.

§ 5–103. Scope.

(a) This article applies to letters of credit and to certain rights and obligations arising out of transactions involving letters of credit.

(b) The statement of a rule in this article does not by itself require, imply, or negate application of the same or a different rule to a situation not provided for, or to a person not specified, in this article.

(c) With the exception of this subsection, subsections (a) and (d), Sections 5–102(a)(9) and (10), 5–106(d), and 5–114(d), and except to the extent prohibited in Sections 1–102(3) and 5–117(d), the effect of this article may be varied by agreement or by a provision stated or incorporated by reference in an undertaking. A term in an agreement or undertaking generally excusing liability or generally limiting remedies for failure to perform obligations is not sufficient to vary obligations prescribed by this article.

(d) Rights and obligations of an issuer to a beneficiary or a nominated person under a letter of credit are independent of the existence, performance, or nonperformance of a contract or arrangement out of which the letter of credit arises or which underlies it, including contracts or arrangements between the issuer and the applicant and between the applicant and the beneficiary.

§ 5–104. Formal Requirements.

A letter of credit, confirmation, advice, transfer, amendment, or cancellation may be issued in any form that is a record and is authenticated (i) by a signature or (ii) in accordance with the agreement of the parties or the standard practice referred to in Section 5–108(e).

§ 5–105. Consideration.

Consideration is not required to issue, amend, transfer, or cancel a letter of credit, advice, or confirmation.

§ 5–106. Issuance, Amendment, Cancellation, and Duration.

(a) A letter of credit is issued and becomes enforceable according to its terms against the issuer when the issuer sends or otherwise transmits it to the person requested to advise or to the beneficiary. A letter of credit is revocable only if it so provides.

(b) After a letter of credit is issued, rights and obligations of a beneficiary, applicant, confirmer, and issuer are not affected by an amendment or cancellation to which that person has not consented except to the extent the letter of credit provides that it is revocable or that the issuer may amend or cancel the letter of credit without that consent.

(c) If there is no stated expiration date or other provision that determines its duration, a letter of credit expires one year after its stated date of issuance or, if none is stated, after the date on which it is issued.

(d) A letter of credit that states that it is perpetual expires five years after its stated date of issuance, or if none is stated, after the date on which it is issued.

§ 5–107. Confirmer, Nominated Person, and Adviser.

(a) A confirmer is directly obligated on a letter of credit and has the rights and obligations of an issuer to the extent of its confirmation. The confirmer also has rights against and obligations to the issuer as if the issuer were an applicant and the confirmer had issued the letter of credit at the request and for the account of the issuer.

(b) A nominated person who is not a confirmer is not obligated to honor or otherwise give value for a presentation.

(c) A person requested to advise may decline to act as an adviser. An adviser that is not a confirmer is not obligated to honor or give value for a presentation. An adviser undertakes to the issuer and to the beneficiary accurately to advise the terms of the letter of credit, confirmation, amendment, or advice received by that person and undertakes to the beneficiary to check the apparent authenticity of the request to advise. Even if the advice is inaccurate, the letter of credit, confirmation, or amendment is enforceable as issued.

(d) A person who notifies a transferee beneficiary of the terms of a letter of credit, confirmation, amendment, or advice has the rights and obligations of an adviser under subsection (c). The terms in the notice to the transferee beneficiary may differ from the terms in any notice to the transferor beneficiary to the extent permitted by the letter of credit, confirmation, amendment, or advice received by the person who so notifies.

§ 5–108. Issuer's Rights and Obligations.

(a) Except as otherwise provided in Section 5–109, an issuer shall honor a presentation that, as determined by the standard practice referred to in subsection (e), appears on its face strictly to comply with the terms and conditions of the letter of credit. Except as otherwise provided in Section 5–113 and unless otherwise agreed with the applicant, an issuer shall dishonor a presentation that does not appear so to comply.

(b) An issuer has a reasonable time after presentation, but not beyond the end of the seventh business day of the issuer after the day of its receipt of documents:

(1) to honor,

(2) if the letter of credit provides for honor to be completed more than seven business days after presentation, to accept a draft or incur a deferred obligation, or

(3) to give notice to the presenter of discrepancies in the presentation.

(c) Except as otherwise provided in subsection (d), an issuer is precluded from asserting as a basis for dishonor any discrepancy if timely notice is not given, or any discrepancy not stated in the notice if timely notice is given.

(d) Failure to give the notice specified in subsection (b) or to mention fraud, forgery, or expiration in the notice does not preclude the issuer from asserting as a basis for dishonor fraud or forgery as described in Section 5–109(a) or expiration of the letter of credit before presentation.

(e) An issuer shall observe standard practice of financial institutions that regularly issue letters of credit. Determination of the issuer's observance of the standard practice is a matter of interpretation for the court. The court shall offer the parties a reasonable opportunity to present evidence of the standard practice.

(f) An issuer is not responsible for:

(1) the performance or nonperformance of the underlying contract, arrangement, or transaction,

(2) an act or omission of others, or

(3) observance or knowledge of the usage of a particular trade other than the standard practice referred to in subsection (e).

(g) If an undertaking constituting a letter of credit under Section 5–102(a)(10) contains nondocumentary conditions, an issuer shall disregard the nondocumentary conditions and treat them as if they were not stated.

(h) An issuer that has dishonored a presentation shall return the documents or hold them at the disposal of, and send advice to that effect to, the presenter.

(i) An issuer that has honored a presentation as permitted or required by this article:

(1) is entitled to be reimbursed by the applicant in immediately available funds not later than the date of its payment of funds;

(2) takes the documents free of claims of the beneficiary or presenter;

(3) is precluded from asserting a right of recourse on a draft under Sections 3–414 and 3–415;

(4) except as otherwise provided in Sections 5–110 and 5–117, is precluded from restitution of money paid or other value given by mistake to the extent the mistake concerns discrepancies in the documents or tender which are apparent on the face of the presentation; and

(5) is discharged to the extent of its performance under the letter of credit unless the issuer honored a presentation in which a required signature of a beneficiary was forged.

§ 5–109. Fraud and Forgery.

(a) If a presentation is made that appears on its face strictly to comply with the terms and conditions of the letter of credit, but a required document is forged or materially fraudulent, or honor of the presentation would facilitate a material fraud by the beneficiary on the issuer or applicant:

(1) the issuer shall honor the presentation, if honor is demanded by (i) a nominated person who has given value in good faith and without notice of forgery or material fraud, (ii) a confirmer who has honored its confirmation in good faith, (iii) a holder in due course of a draft drawn under the letter of credit which was taken after acceptance by the issuer or nominated person, or (iv) an assignee of the issuer's or nominated person's deferred obligation that was taken for value and without notice of forgery or material fraud after the obligation was incurred by the issuer or nominated person; and

(2) the issuer, acting in good faith, may honor or dishonor the presentation in any other case.

(b) If an applicant claims that a required document is forged or materially fraudulent or that honor of the presentation would facilitate a material fraud by the beneficiary on the issuer or applicant, a court of competent jurisdiction may temporarily or permanently enjoin the issuer from honoring a presentation or grant similar relief against the issuer or other persons only if the court finds that:

(1) the relief is not prohibited under the law applicable to an accepted draft or deferred obligation incurred by the issuer;

(2) a beneficiary, issuer, or nominated person who may be adversely affected is adequately protected against loss that it may suffer because the relief is granted;

(3) all of the conditions to entitle a person to the relief under the law of this State have been met; and

(4) on the basis of the information submitted to the court, the applicant is more likely than not to succeed under its claim of forgery or material fraud and the person demanding honor does not qualify for protection under subsection (a)(1).

§ 5–110. Warranties.

(a) If its presentation is honored, the beneficiary warrants:

(1) to the issuer, any other person to whom presentation is made, and the applicant that there is no fraud or forgery of the kind described in Section 5–109(a); and

(2) to the applicant that the drawing does not violate any agreement between the applicant and beneficiary or any other agreement intended by them to be augmented by the letter of credit.

(b) The warranties in subsection (a) are in addition to warranties arising under Article 3, 4, 7, and 8 because of the presentation or transfer of documents covered by any of those articles.

§ 5–111. Remedies.

(a) If an issuer wrongfully dishonors or repudiates its obligation to pay money under a letter of credit before presentation, the beneficiary, successor, or nominated person presenting on its own behalf may recover from the issuer the amount that is the subject of the dishonor or repudiation. If the issuer's obligation under the letter of credit is not for the payment of money, the claimant may obtain specific performance or, at the claimant's election, recover an amount equal to the value of performance from the issuer. In either case, the claimant may also recover incidental but not consequential damages. The claimant is not obligated to take action to avoid damages that might be due from the issuer under this subsection. If, although not obligated to do so, the claimant avoids damages, the claimant's recovery from the issuer must be reduced by the amount of damages avoided. The issuer has the burden of proving the amount of damages avoided. In the case of repudiation the claimant need not present any document.

(b) If an issuer wrongfully dishonors a draft or demand presented under a letter of credit or honors a draft or demand in breach of its obligation to the applicant, the applicant may recover damages resulting from the breach, including incidental but not consequential damages, less any amount saved as a result of the breach.

(c) If an adviser or nominated person other than a confirmer breaches an obligation under this article or an issuer breaches an obligation not covered in subsection (a) or (b), a person to whom the obligation is owed may recover damages resulting from the breach, including incidental but not consequential damages, less any amount saved as a result of the breach. To the extent of the confirmation, a confirmer has the liability of an issuer specified in this subsection and subsections (a) and (b).

(d) An issuer, nominated person, or adviser who is found liable under subsection (a), (b), or (c) shall pay interest on the amount owed thereunder from the date of wrongful dishonor or other appropriate date.

(e) Reasonable attorney's fees and other expenses of litigation must be awarded to the prevailing party in an action in which a remedy is sought under this article.

(f) Damages that would otherwise be payable by a party for breach of an obligation under this article may be liquidated by agreement or undertaking, but only in an amount or by a formula that is reasonable in light of the harm anticipated.

§ 5–112. Transfer of Letter of Credit.

(a) Except as otherwise provided in Section 5–113, unless a letter of credit provides that it is transferable, the right of a beneficiary to draw or otherwise demand performance under a letter of credit may not be transferred.

(b) Even if a letter of credit provides that it is transferable, the issuer may refuse to recognize or carry out a transfer if:

(1) the transfer would violate applicable law; or

(2) the transferor or transferee has failed to comply with any requirement stated in the letter of credit or any other requirement relating to transfer imposed by the issuer which is within the standard practice referred to in Section 5–108(e) or is otherwise reasonable under the circumstances.

§ 5–113. Transfer by Operation of Law.

(a) A successor of a beneficiary may consent to amendments, sign and present documents, and receive payment or other items of value in the name of the beneficiary without disclosing its status as a successor.

(b) A successor of a beneficiary may consent to amendments, sign and present documents, and receive payment or other items of value in its own name as the disclosed successor of the beneficiary. Except as otherwise provided in subsection (e), an issuer shall recognize a disclosed successor of a beneficiary as beneficiary in full substitution for its predecessor upon compliance with the requirements for recognition by the issuer of a transfer of drawing rights by operation of law under the standard practice referred to in Section 5–108(e) or, in the absence of such a practice, compliance with other reasonable procedures sufficient to protect the issuer.

(c) An issuer is not obliged to determine whether a purported successor is a successor of a beneficiary or whether the signature of a purported successor is genuine or authorized.

(d) Honor of a purported successor's apparently complying presentation under subsection (a) or (b) has the consequences specified in Section 5–108(i) even if the purported successor is not the successor of a beneficiary. Documents signed in the name of the beneficiary or of a disclosed successor by a person who is neither the beneficiary nor the successor of the beneficiary are forged documents for the purposes of Section 5–109.

(e) An issuer whose rights of reimbursement are not covered by subsection (d) or substantially similar law and any confirmer or nominated person may decline to recognize a presentation under subsection (b).

(f) A beneficiary whose name is changed after the issuance of a letter of credit has the same rights and obligations as a successor of a beneficiary under this section.

§ 5–114. Assignment of Proceeds.

(a) In this section,"proceeds of a letter of credit" means the cash,check,accepted draft,or other item of value paid or delivered upon honor or giving of value by the issuer or any nominated person under the letter of credit. The term does not include a beneficiary's drawing rights or documents presented by the beneficiary.

(b) A beneficiary may assign its right to part or all of the proceeds of a letter of credit. The beneficiary may do so before presentation as a present assignment of its right to receive proceeds contingent upon its compliance with the terms and conditions of the letter of credit.

(c) An issuer or nominated person need not recognize an assignment of proceeds of a letter of credit until it consents to the assignment.

(d) An issuer or nominated person has no obligation to give or withhold its consent to an assignment of proceeds of a letter of credit, but consent may not be unreasonably withheld if the assignee possesses and exhibits the letter of credit and presentation of the letter of credit is a condition to honor.

(e) Rights of a transferee beneficiary or nominated person are independent of the beneficiary's assignment of the proceeds of a letter of credit and are superior to the assignee's right to the proceeds.

(f) Neither the rights recognized by this section between an assignee and an issuer, transferee beneficiary, or nominated person nor the issuer's or nominated person's payment of proceeds to an assignee or a third person affect the rights between the assignee and any person other than the issuer, transferee beneficiary, or nominated person. The mode of creating and perfecting a security interest in or granting an assignment of a beneficiary's rights to proceeds is governed by Article 9 or other law. Against persons other than the issuer, transferee beneficiary, or nominated person, the rights and obligations arising upon the creation of a security interest or other assignment of a beneficiary's right to proceeds and its perfection are governed by Article 9 or other law.

§ 5–115. Statute of Limitations.

An action to enforce a right or obligation arising under this article must be commenced within one year after the expiration date of the relevant letter of credit or one year after the [claim for relief] [cause of action] accrues, whichever occurs later. A [claim for relief] [cause of action] accrues when the breach occurs, regardless of the aggrieved party's lack of knowledge of the breach.

§ 5–116. Choice of Law and Forum.

(a) The liability of an issuer, nominated person, or adviser for action or omission is governed by the law of the jurisdiction chosen by an agreement in the form of a record signed or otherwise authenticated by the affected parties in the manner provided in Section 5–104 or by a provision in the person's letter of credit, confirmation, or other undertaking. The jurisdiction whose law is chosen need not bear any relation to the transaction.

(b) Unless subsection (a) applies, the liability of an issuer, nominated person, or adviser for action or omission is governed by the law of the jurisdiction in which the person is located. The person is considered to be located at the address indicated in the person's undertaking. If more than one address is indicated, the person is considered to be located at the address from which the person's undertaking was issued. For the purpose of jurisdiction, choice of law, and recognition of interbranch letters of credit, but not enforcement of a judgment, all branches of a bank are considered separate juridical entities and a bank is considered to be located at the place where its relevant branch is considered to be located under this subsection.

(c) Except as otherwise provided in this subsection, the liability of an issuer, nominated person, or adviser is governed by any rules of custom or practice, such as the Uniform Customs and Practice for Documentary Credits, to which the letter of credit, confirmation, or other undertaking is expressly made subject. If (i) this article would govern the liability of an issuer, nominated person, or adviser under subsection (a) or (b), (ii) the relevant undertaking incorporates rules of custom or practice, and (iii) there is conflict between this article and those rules as applied to that undertaking, those rules govern except to the extent of any conflict with the nonvariable provisions specified in Section 5–103(c).

(d) If there is conflict between this article and Article 3, 4, 4A, or 9, this article governs.

(e) The forum for settling disputes arising out of an undertaking within this article may be chosen in the manner and with the binding effect that governing law may be chosen in accordance with subsection (a).

§ 5–117. Subrogation of Issuer, Applicant, and Nominated Person.

(a) An issuer that honors a beneficiary's presentation is subrogated to the rights of the beneficiary to the same extent as if the issuer were a secondary obligor of the underlying obligation owed to the beneficiary and of the applicant to the same extent as if the issuer were the secondary obligor of the underlying obligation owed to the applicant.

(b) An applicant that reimburses an issuer is subrogated to the rights of the issuer against any beneficiary, presenter, or nominated person to the same extent as if the applicant were the secondary obligor of the obligations owed to the issuer and has the rights of subrogation of the issuer to the rights of the beneficiary stated in subsection (a).

(c) A nominated person who pays or gives value against a draft or demand presented under a letter of credit is subrogated to the rights of:

(1) the issuer against the applicant to the same extent as if the nominated person were a secondary obligor of the obligation owed to the issuer by the applicant;

(2) the beneficiary to the same extent as if the nominated person were a secondary obligor of the underlying obligation owed to the beneficiary; and

(3) the applicant to same extent as if the nominated person were a secondary obligor of the underlying obligation owed to the applicant.

(d) Notwithstanding any agreement or term to the contrary, the rights of subrogation stated in subsections (a) and (b) do not arise until the issuer honors the letter of credit or otherwise pays and the rights in subsection (c) do not arise until the nominated person pays or otherwise gives value. Until then, the issuer, nominated person, and the applicant do not derive under this section present or prospective rights forming the basis of a claim, defense, or excuse.

§ 5–118. Security Interest of Issuer or Nominated Person.

(a) An issuer or nominated person has a security interest in a document presented under a letter of credit to the extent that the issuer or nominated person honors or gives value for the presentation.

(b) So long as and to the extent that an issuer or nominated person has not been reimbursed or has not otherwise recovered the value given with respect to a security interest in a document under subsection (a), the security interest continues and is subject to Article 9, but:

(1) a security agreement is not necessary to make the security interest enforceable under Section 9–203(b)(3);

(2) if the document is presented in a medium other than a written or other tangible medium, the security interest is perfected; and

(3) if the document is presented in a written or other tangible medium and is not a certificated security, chattel paper, a document of title, an instrument, or a letter of credit, the security interest is perfected and has priority over a conflicting security interest in the document so long as the debtor does not have possession of the document.

As added in 1999.

Transition Provisions

§ [ ]. Effective Date.

This [Act] shall become effective on _______, 20__.

§ [ ]. Repeal.

This [Act] [repeals] [amends] [insert citation to existing Article 5].

§ [ ]. Applicability.

This [Act] applies to a letter of credit that is issued on or after the effective date of this [Act]. This [Act] does not apply to a transaction, event, obligation, or duty arising out of or associated with a letter of credit that was issued before the effective date of this [Act].

§ [ ]. Savings Clause.

A transaction arising out of or associated with a letter of credit that was issued before the effective date of this [Act] and the rights, obligations, and interests flowing from that transaction are governed by any statute or other law amended or repealed by this [Act] as if repeal or amendment had not occurred and may be terminated, completed, consummated, or enforced under that statute or other law.

Repealer of Article 6 BULK TRANSFERS and [Revised] ARTICLE 6 BULK SALES (States to Select One Alternative)

Alternative A

[§ 1. Repeal

Article 6 and Section 9–111 of the Uniform Commercial Code are hereby repealed, effective ________.

§ 2. Amendment

Section 1–105(2) of the Uniform Commercial Code is hereby amended to read as follows:

(2) Where one of the following provisions of this Act specifies the applicable law, that provision governs and a contrary agreement is effective only to the extent permitted by the law (including the conflict of laws rules) so specified:

Rights of creditors against sold goods. Section 2–402.

Applicability of the Article on Leases. Section 2A–105 and 2A-106.

Applicability of the Article on Bank Deposits and Collections. Section 4–102.

Applicability of the Article on Investment Securities. Section 8–106.

Perfection provisions of the Article on Secured Transactions. Section 9–103.

§ 3. Amendment.

Section 2–403(4) of the Uniform Commercial Code is hereby amended to read as follows:

(4) The rights of other purchasers of goods and of lien creditors are governed by the Articles on Secured Transactions (Article 9) and Documents of Title (Article 7).

§ 4. Savings Clause.

Rights and obligations that arose under Article 6 and Section 9–111 of the Uniform Commercial Code before their repeal remain valid and may be enforced as though those statutes had not been repealed.]

§ 6–101. Short Title.

This Article shall be known and may be cited as Uniform Commercial Code—Bulk Sales.

§ 6–102. Definitions and Index of Definitions.

(1) In this Article, unless the context otherwise requires:

(a) "Assets" means the inventory that is the subject of a bulk sale and any tangible and intangible personal property used or held for use primarily in, or arising from, the seller's business and sold in connection with that inventory, but the term does not include:

(i) fixtures (Section 9–102(a)(41)) other than readily removable factory and office machines;

(ii) the lessee's interest in a lease of real property; or

(iii) property to the extent it is generally exempt from creditor process under nonbankruptcy law.

(b) "Auctioneer" means a person whom the seller engages to direct, conduct, control, or be responsible for a sale by auction.

(c) "Bulk sale" means:

(i) in the case of a sale by auction or a sale or series of sales conducted by a liquidator on the seller's behalf, a sale or series of sales not in the ordinary course of the seller's business of more than half of the seller's inventory, as measured by value on the date of the bulk-sale agreement, if on that date the auctioneer or liquidator has notice, or after reasonable inquiry would have had notice, that the seller will not continue to operate the same or a similar kind of business after the sale or series of sales; and

(ii) in all other cases, a sale not in the ordinary course of the seller's business of more than half the seller's inventory, as measured by value on the date of the bulk-sale agreement, if on that date the buyer has notice, or after reasonable inquiry would have had notice, that the seller will not continue to operate the same or a similar kind of business after the sale.

(d) "Claim" means a right to payment from the seller, whether or not the right is reduced to judgment, liquidated, fixed, matured, disputed, secured, legal, or equitable. The term includes costs of collection and attorney's fees only to the extent that the laws of this state permit the holder of the claim to recover them in an action against the obligor.

(e) "Claimant" means a person holding a claim incurred in the seller's business other than:

(i) an unsecured and unmatured claim for employment compensation and benefits, including commissions and vacation, severance, and sick-leave pay;

(ii) a claim for injury to an individual or to property, or for breach of warranty, unless:

(A) a right of action for the claim has accrued;

(B) the claim has been asserted against the seller; and

(C) the seller knows the identity of the person asserting the claim and the basis upon which the person has asserted it; and

(States to Select One Alternative)

Alternative A

[(iii) a claim for taxes owing to a governmental unit.]

Alternative B

[(iii) a claim for taxes owing to a governmental unit, if:

(A) a statute governing the enforcement of the claim permits or requires notice of the bulk sale to be given to the governmental unit in a manner other than by compliance with the requirements of this Article; and

(B) notice is given in accordance with the statute.]

(f) "Creditor" means a claimant or other person holding a claim.

(g)(i) "Date of the bulk sale" means:

(A) if the sale is by auction or is conducted by a liquidator on the seller's behalf, the date on which more than ten percent of the net proceeds is paid to or for the benefit of the seller; and

(B) in all other cases, the later of the date on which:

(I) more than ten percent of the net contract price is paid to or for the benefit of the seller; or

(II) more than ten percent of the assets, as measured by value, are transferred to the buyer.

(ii) For purposes of this subsection:

(A) delivery of a negotiable instrument (Section 3–104(1)) to or for the benefit of the seller in exchange for assets constitutes payment of the contract price pro tanto;

(B) to the extent that the contract price is deposited in an escrow, the contract price is paid to or for the benefit of the seller when the seller acquires the unconditional right to receive the deposit or when the deposit is delivered to the seller or for the benefit of the seller, whichever is earlier; and

(C) an asset is transferred when a person holding an unsecured claim can no longer obtain through judicial proceedings rights to the asset that are superior to those of the buyer arising as a result of the bulk sale. A person holding an unsecured claim can obtain those superior rights to a tangible asset at least until the buyer has an unconditional right, under the bulk-sale agreement, to possess the asset, and a person holding an unsecured claim can obtain those superior rights to an intangible asset at least until the buyer has an unconditional right, under the bulk-sale agreement, to use the asset.

(h) "Date of the bulk-sale agreement" means:

(i) in the case of a sale by auction or conducted by a liquidator (subsection (c)(i)), the date on which the seller engages the auctioneer or liquidator; and

(ii) in all other cases, the date on which a bulk-sale agreement becomes enforceable between the buyer and the seller.

(i) "Debt" means liability on a claim.

(j) "Liquidator" means a person who is regularly engaged in the business of disposing of assets for businesses contemplating liquidation or dissolution.

(k) "Net contract price" means the new consideration the buyer is obligated to pay for the assets less:

(i) the amount of any proceeds of the sale of an asset, to the extent the proceeds are applied in partial or total satisfaction of a debt secured by the asset; and

(ii) the amount of any debt to the extent it is secured by a security interest or lien that is enforceable against the asset before and after it has been sold to a buyer. If a debt is secured by an asset and other property of the seller, the amount of the debt secured by a security interest or lien that is enforceable against the asset is determined by multiplying the debt by a fraction, the numerator of which is the value of the new consideration for the asset on the date of the bulk sale and the denominator of which is the value of all property securing the debt on the date of the bulk sale.

(l) "Net proceeds" means the new consideration received for assets sold at a sale by auction or a sale conducted by a liquidator on the seller's behalf less:

(i) commissions and reasonable expenses of the sale;

(ii) the amount of any proceeds of the sale of an asset, to the extent the proceeds are applied in partial or total satisfaction of a debt secured by the asset; and

(iii) the amount of any debt to the extent it is secured by a security interest or lien that is enforceable against the asset before and after it has been sold to a buyer. If a debt is secured by an asset and other property of the seller, the amount of the debt secured by a security interest or lien that is enforceable against the asset is determined by multiplying the debt by a fraction, the numerator of which is the value of the new consideration for the asset on the date of the bulk sale and the denominator of which is the value of all property securing the debt on the date of the bulk sale.

(m) A sale is "in the ordinary course of the seller's business" if the sale comports with usual or customary practices in the kind of business in which the seller is engaged or with the seller's own usual or customary practices.

(n) "United States" includes its territories and possessions and the Commonwealth of Puerto Rico.

(o) "Value" means fair market value.

(p) "Verified" means signed and sworn to or affirmed.

(2) The following definitions in other Articles apply to this Article:

(a) "Buyer."	Section 2–103(1)(a).
(b) "Equipment."	Section 9–102(a)(33).
(c) "Inventory."	Section 9–102(a)(48).
(d) "Sale."	Section 2–106(1).
(e) "Seller."	Section 2–103(1)(d).

(3) In addition, Article 1 contains general definitions and principles of construction and interpretation applicable throughout this Article.

As amended in 1999.

§ 6–103. Applicability of Article.

(1) Except as otherwise provided in subsection (3), this Article applies to a bulk sale if:

(a) the seller's principal business is the sale of inventory from stock; and

(b) on the date of the bulk-sale agreement the seller is located in this state or, if the seller is located in a jurisdiction that is not a part of the United States, the seller's major executive office in the United States is in this state.

(2) A seller is deemed to be located at his [or her] place of business. If a seller has more than one place of business, the seller is deemed located at his [or her] chief executive office.

(3) This Article does not apply to:

(a) a transfer made to secure payment or performance of an obligation;

(b) a transfer of collateral to a secured party pursuant to Section 9–503;

(c) a disposition of collateral pursuant to Section 9–610;

(d) retention of collateral pursuant to Section 9–620;

(e) a sale of an asset encumbered by a security interest or lien if (i) all the proceeds of the sale are applied in partial or total satisfaction of the debt secured by the security interest or lien or (ii) the security interest or lien is enforceable against the asset after it has been sold to the buyer and the net contract price is zero;

(f) a general assignment for the benefit of creditors or to a subsequent transfer by the assignee;

(g) a sale by an executor, administrator, receiver, trustee in bankruptcy, or any public officer under judicial process;

(h) a sale made in the course of judicial or administrative proceedings for the dissolution or reorganization of an organization;

(i) a sale to a buyer whose principal place of business is in the United States and who:

(i) not earlier than 21 days before the date of the bulk sale, (A) obtains from the seller a verified and dated list of claimants of whom the seller has notice three days before the seller sends or delivers the list to the buyer or (B) conducts a reasonable inquiry to discover the claimants;

(ii) assumes in full the debts owed to claimants of whom the buyer has knowledge on the date the buyer receives the list of claimants from the seller or on the date the buyer completes the reasonable inquiry, as the case may be;

(iii) is not insolvent after the assumption; and

(iv) gives written notice of the assumption not later than 30 days after the date of the bulk sale by sending or delivering a notice to the claimants identified in subparagraph (ii) or by filing a notice in the office of the [Secretary of State];

(j) a sale to a buyer whose principal place of business is in the United States and who:

(i) assumes in full the debts that were incurred in the seller's business before the date of the bulk sale;

(ii) is not insolvent after the assumption; and

(iii) gives written notice of the assumption not later than 30 days after the date of the bulk sale by sending or delivering a notice to each creditor whose debt is assumed or by filing a notice in the office of the [Secretary of State];

(k) a sale to a new organization that is organized to take over and continue the business of the seller and that has its principal place of business in the United States if:

(i) the buyer assumes in full the debts that were incurred in the seller's business before the date of the bulk sale;

(ii) the seller receives nothing from the sale except an interest in the new organization that is subordinate to the claims against the organization arising from the assumption; and

(iii) the buyer gives written notice of the assumption not later than 30 days after the date of the bulk sale by sending or delivering a notice to each creditor whose debt is assumed or by filing a notice in the office of the [Secretary of State];

(l) a sale of assets having:

(i) a value, net of liens and security interests, of less than $10,000. If a debt is secured by assets and other property of the seller, the net value of the assets is determined by subtracting from their value an amount equal to the product of the debt multiplied by a fraction, the numerator of which is the value of the assets on the date of the bulk sale and the denominator of which is the value of all property securing the debt on the date of the bulk sale; or

(ii) a value of more than $25,000,000 on the date of the bulk-sale agreement; or

(m) a sale required by, and made pursuant to, statute.

(4) The notice under subsection (3)(i)(iv) must state: (i) that a sale that may constitute a bulk sale has been or will be made; (ii) the date or prospective date of the bulk sale; (iii) the individual, partnership, or corporate names and the addresses of the seller and buyer; (iv) the address to which inquiries about the sale may be made, if different from the seller's address; and (v) that the buyer has assumed or will assume in full the debts owed to claimants of whom the buyer has knowledge on the date the buyer receives the list of claimants from the seller or completes a reasonable inquiry to discover the claimants.

(5) The notice under subsections (3)(j)(iii) and (3)(k)(iii) must state: (i) that a sale that may constitute a bulk sale has been or will be made; (ii) the date or prospective date of the bulk sale; (iii) the individual, partnership, or corporate names and the addresses of the seller and buyer; (iv) the address to which inquiries about the sale may be made, if different from the seller's address; and (v) that the buyer has assumed or will assume the debts that were incurred in the seller's business before the date of the bulk sale.

(6) For purposes of subsection (3)(l), the value of assets is presumed to be equal to the price the buyer agrees to pay for the assets. However, in a sale by auction or a sale conducted by a liquidator on the seller's behalf, the value of assets is presumed to be the amount the auctioneer or liquidator reasonably estimates the assets will bring at auction or upon liquidation.

As amended in 1999.

§ 6–104. Obligations of Buyer.

(1) In a bulk sale as defined in Section 6–102(1)(c)(ii) the buyer shall:

(a) obtain from the seller a list of all business names and addresses used by the seller within three years before the date the list is sent or delivered to the buyer;

(b) unless excused under subsection (2), obtain from the seller a verified and dated list of claimants of whom the seller has notice three days before the seller sends or delivers the list to the buyer and including, to the extent known by the seller, the address of and the amount claimed by each claimant;

(c) obtain from the seller or prepare a schedule of distribution (Section 6–106(1));

(d) give notice of the bulk sale in accordance with Section 6–105;

(e) unless excused under Section 6–106(4), distribute the net contract price in accordance with the undertakings of the buyer in the schedule of distribution; and

(f) unless excused under subsection (2), make available the list of claimants (subsection (1)(b)) by:

(i) promptly sending or delivering a copy of the list without charge to any claimant whose written request is received by the buyer no later than six months after the date of the bulk sale;

(ii) permitting any claimant to inspect and copy the list at any reasonable hour upon request received by the buyer no later than six months after the date of the bulk sale; or

(iii) filing a copy of the list in the office of the [Secretary of State] no later than the time for giving a notice of the bulk sale (Section 6–105(5)). A list filed in accordance with this subparagraph must state the individual, partnership, or corporate name and a mailing address of the seller.

(2) A buyer who gives notice in accordance with Section 6–105(2) is excused from complying with the requirements of subsections (1)(b) and (1)(f).

§ 6–105. Notice to Claimants.

(1) Except as otherwise provided in subsection (2), to comply with Section 6–104(1)(d) the buyer shall send or deliver a written notice of the bulk sale to each claimant on the list of claimants (Section 6–104(1)(b)) and to any other claimant of which the buyer has knowledge at the time the notice of the bulk sale is sent or delivered.

(2) A buyer may comply with Section 6–104(1)(d) by filing a written notice of the bulk sale in the office of the [Secretary of State] if:

(a) on the date of the bulk-sale agreement the seller has 200 or more claimants, exclusive of claimants holding secured or matured claims for employment compensation and benefits, including commissions and vacation, severance, and sick-leave pay; or

(b) the buyer has received a verified statement from the seller stating that, as of the date of the bulk-sale agreement, the number of claimants, exclusive of claimants holding secured or matured claims for employment compensation and benefits, including commissions and vacation, severance, and sick-leave pay, is 200 or more.

(3) The written notice of the bulk sale must be accompanied by a copy of the schedule of distribution (Section 6–106(1)) and state at least:

(a) that the seller and buyer have entered into an agreement for a sale that may constitute a bulk sale under the laws of the State of ________;

(b) the date of the agreement;

(c) the date on or after which more than ten percent of the assets were or will be transferred;

(d) the date on or after which more than ten percent of the net contract price was or will be paid, if the date is not stated in the schedule of distribution;

(e) the name and a mailing address of the seller;

(f) any other business name and address listed by the seller pursuant to Section 6–104(1)(a);

(g) the name of the buyer and an address of the buyer from which information concerning the sale can be obtained;

(h) a statement indicating the type of assets or describing the assets item by item;

(i) the manner in which the buyer will make available the list of claimants (Section 6–104(1)(f)), if applicable; and

(j) if the sale is in total or partial satisfaction of an antecedent debt owed by the seller, the amount of the debt to be satisfied and the name of the person to whom it is owed.

(4) For purposes of subsections (3)(e) and (3)(g), the name of a person is the person's individual, partnership, or corporate name.

(5) The buyer shall give notice of the bulk sale not less than 45 days before the date of the bulk sale and, if the buyer gives notice in accordance with subsection (1), not more than 30 days after obtaining the list of claimants.

(6) A written notice substantially complying with the requirements of subsection (3) is effective even though it contains minor errors that are not seriously misleading.

(7) A form substantially as follows is sufficient to comply with subsection (3):

Notice of Sale

(1) ________, whose address is ________, is described in this notice as the "seller."

(2) ________, whose address is ________, is described in this notice as the "buyer."

(3) The seller has disclosed to the buyer that within the past three years the seller has used other business names, operated at other addresses, or both, as follows: ________________.

(4) The seller and the buyer have entered into an agreement dated ________, for a sale that may constitute a bulk sale under the laws of the state of ________________.

(5) The date on or after which more than ten percent of the assets that are the subject of the sale were or will be transferred is ________, and [if not stated in the schedule of distribution] the date on or after which more than ten percent of the net contract price was or will be paid is ________.

(6) The following assets are the subject of the sale: ________________.

(7) [If applicable] The buyer will make available to claimants of the seller a list of the seller's claimants in the following manner: ________________.

(8) [If applicable] The sale is to satisfy $ ________ of an antecedent debt owed by the seller to ________.

(9) A copy of the schedule of distribution of the net contract price accompanies this notice.

[End of Notice]

§ 6–106. Schedule of Distribution.

(1) The seller and buyer shall agree on how the net contract price is to be distributed and set forth their agreement in a written schedule of distribution.

(2) The schedule of distribution may provide for distribution to any person at any time, including distribution of the entire net contract price to the seller.

(3) The buyer's undertakings in the schedule of distribution run only to the seller. However, a buyer who fails to distribute the net contract price in accordance with the buyer's undertakings in the schedule of distribution is liable to a creditor only as provided in Section 6–107(1).

(4) If the buyer undertakes in the schedule of distribution to distribute any part of the net contract price to a person other than the seller, and, after the buyer has given notice in accordance with Section 6–105, some or all of the anticipated net contract price is or becomes unavailable for distribution as a consequence of the buyer's or seller's having complied with an order of court, legal process, statute, or rule of law, the buyer is excused from any obligation arising under this Article or under any contract with the seller to distribute the net contract price in accordance with the buyer's undertakings in the schedule if the buyer:

(a) distributes the net contract price remaining available in accordance with any priorities for payment stated in the schedule of distribution and, to the extent that the price is insufficient to pay all the debts having a given priority, distributes the price pro rata among those debts shown in the schedule as having the same priority;

(b) distributes the net contract price remaining available in accordance with an order of court;

(c) commences a proceeding for interpleader in a court of competent jurisdiction and is discharged from the proceeding; or

(d) reaches a new agreement with the seller for the distribution of the net contract price remaining available, sets forth the new agreement in an amended schedule of distribution, gives notice of the amended schedule, and distributes the net contract price remaining available in accordance with the buyer's undertakings in the amended schedule.

(5) The notice under subsection (4)(d) must identify the buyer and the seller, state the filing number, if any, of the original notice, set forth the amended schedule, and be given in accordance with subsection (1) or (2) of Section 6–105, whichever is applicable, at least 14 days before the buyer distributes any part of the net contract price remaining available.

(6) If the seller undertakes in the schedule of distribution to distribute any part of the net contract price, and, after the buyer has given notice in accordance with Section 6–105, some or all of the anticipated net contract price is or becomes unavailable for distribution as a consequence of the buyer's or seller's having complied with an order of court, legal process, statute, or rule of law, the seller and any person in control of the seller are excused from any obligation arising under this Article or under any agreement with the buyer to distribute the net contract price in accordance with the seller's undertakings in the schedule if the seller:

(a) distributes the net contract price remaining available in accordance with any priorities for payment stated in the schedule of distribution and, to the extent that the price is insufficient to pay all the debts having a given priority, distributes the price pro rata among those debts shown in the schedule as having the same priority;

(b) distributes the net contract price remaining available in accordance with an order of court;

(c) commences a proceeding for interpleader in a court of competent jurisdiction and is discharged from the proceeding; or

(d) prepares a written amended schedule of distribution of the net contract price remaining available for distribution, gives notice of the amended schedule, and distributes the net contract price remaining available in accordance with the amended schedule.

(7) The notice under subsection (6)(d) must identify the buyer and the seller, state the filing number, if any, of the original notice, set forth the amended schedule, and be given in accordance with subsection (1) or (2) of Section 6–105, whichever is applicable, at least 14 days before the seller distributes any part of the net contract price remaining available.

§ 6–107. Liability for Noncompliance.

(1) Except as provided in subsection (3), and subject to the limitation in subsection (4):

(a) a buyer who fails to comply with the requirements of Section 6–104(1)(e) with respect to a creditor is liable to the creditor for damages in the amount of the claim, reduced by any amount that the creditor would not have realized if the buyer had complied; and

(b) a buyer who fails to comply with the requirements of any other subsection of Section 6–104 with respect to a claimant is liable to the claimant for damages in the amount of the claim, reduced by any amount that the claimant would not have realized if the buyer had complied.

(2) In an action under subsection (1), the creditor has the burden of establishing the validity and amount of the claim, and the buyer has the burden of establishing the amount that the creditor would not have realized if the buyer had complied.

(3) A buyer who:

(a) made a good faith and commercially reasonable effort to comply with the requirements of Section 6–104(1) or to exclude the sale from the application of this Article under Section 6–103(3); or

(b) on or after the date of the bulk-sale agreement, but before the date of the bulk sale, held a good faith and commercially reasonable belief that this Article does not apply to the particular sale is not liable to creditors for failure to comply with the requirements of Section 6–104. The buyer has the burden of establishing the good faith and commercial reasonableness of the effort or belief.

(4) In a single bulk sale the cumulative liability of the buyer for failure to comply with the requirements of Section 6–104(1) may not exceed an amount equal to:

(a) if the assets consist only of inventory and equipment, twice the net contract price, less the amount of any part of the net contract price paid to or applied for the benefit of the seller or a creditor; or

(b) if the assets include property other than inventory and equipment, twice the net value of the inventory and equipment less the amount of the portion of any part of the net contract price paid to or applied for the benefit of the seller or a creditor which is allocable to the inventory and equipment.

(5) For the purposes of subsection (4)(b), the "net value" of an asset is the value of the asset less (i) the amount of any proceeds of the sale of an asset, to the extent the proceeds are applied in partial or total satisfaction of a debt secured by the asset and (ii) the amount of any debt to the extent it is secured by a security interest or lien that is enforceable against the asset before and after it has been sold to a buyer. If a debt is secured by an asset and other property of the seller, the amount of the debt secured by a security interest or lien that is enforceable against the asset is determined by multiplying the debt by a fraction, the numerator of which is the value of the asset on the date of the bulk sale and the denominator of which is the value of all property securing the debt on the date of the bulk sale. The portion of a part of the net contract price paid to or applied for the benefit of the seller or a creditor that is "allocable to the inventory and equipment" is the portion that bears the same ratio to that part of the net contract price as the net value of the inventory and equipment bears to the net value of all of the assets.

(6) A payment made by the buyer to a person to whom the buyer is, or believes he [or she] is, liable under subsection (1) reduces pro tanto the buyer's cumulative liability under subsection (4).

(7) No action may be brought under subsection (1)(b) by or on behalf of a claimant whose claim is unliquidated or contingent.

(8) A buyer's failure to comply with the requirements of Section 6–104(1) does not (i) impair the buyer's rights in or title to the assets, (ii) render the sale ineffective, void, or voidable, (iii) entitle a creditor to more than a single satisfaction of his [or her] claim, or (iv) create liability other than as provided in this Article.

(9) Payment of the buyer's liability under subsection (1) discharges pro tanto the seller's debt to the creditor.

(10) Unless otherwise agreed, a buyer has an immediate right of reimbursement from the seller for any amount paid to a creditor in partial or total satisfaction of the buyer's liability under subsection (1).

(11) If the seller is an organization, a person who is in direct or indirect control of the seller, and who knowingly, intentionally, and without legal justification fails, or causes the seller to fail, to distribute the net contract price in accordance with the schedule of distribution is liable to any creditor to whom the seller undertook to make payment under the schedule for damages caused by the failure.

§ 6–108. Bulk Sales by Auction; Bulk Sales Conducted by Liquidator.

(1) Sections 6–104, 6–105, 6–106, and 6–107 apply to a bulk sale by auction and a bulk sale conducted by a liquidator on the seller's behalf with the following modifications:

(a) "buyer" refers to auctioneer or liquidator, as the case may be;

(b) "net contract price" refers to net proceeds of the auction or net proceeds of the sale, as the case may be;

(c) the written notice required under Section 6–105(3) must be accompanied by a copy of the schedule of distribution (Section 6–106(1)) and state at least:

(i) that the seller and the auctioneer or liquidator have entered into an agreement for auction or liquidation services that may constitute an agreement to make a bulk sale under the laws of the State of ________;

(ii) the date of the agreement;

(iii) the date on or after which the auction began or will begin or the date on or after which the liquidator began or will begin to sell assets on the seller's behalf;

(iv) the date on or after which more than ten percent of the net proceeds of the sale were or will be paid, if the date is not stated in the schedule of distribution;

(v) the name and a mailing address of the seller;

(vi) any other business name and address listed by the seller pursuant to Section 6–104(1)(a);

(vii) the name of the auctioneer or liquidator and an address of the auctioneer or liquidator from which information concerning the sale can be obtained;

(viii) a statement indicating the type of assets or describing the assets item by item;

(ix) the manner in which the auctioneer or liquidator will make available the list of claimants (Section 6–104(1)(f)), if applicable; and

(x) if the sale is in total or partial satisfaction of an antecedent debt owed by the seller, the amount of the debt to be satisfied and the name of the person to whom it is owed; and

(d) in a single bulk sale the cumulative liability of the auctioneer or liquidator for failure to comply with the requirements of this section may not exceed the amount of the net proceeds of the sale allocable to inventory and equipment sold less the amount of the portion of any part of the net proceeds paid to or applied for the benefit of a creditor which is allocable to the inventory and equipment.

(2) A payment made by the auctioneer or liquidator to a person to whom the auctioneer or liquidator is, or believes he [or she] is, liable under this section reduces pro tanto the auctioneer's or liquidator's cumulative liability under subsection (1)(d).

(3) A form substantially as follows is sufficient to comply with subsection (1)(c):

Notice of Sale

(1) ________, whose address is ________, is described in this notice as the "seller."

(2) ________ ,whose address is ________ ,is described in this notice as the "auctioneer" or "liquidator."

(3) The seller has disclosed to the auctioneer or liquidator that within the past three years the seller has used other business names, operated at other addresses, or both, as follows: ________________ .

(4) The seller and the auctioneer or liquidator have entered into an agreement dated ________ for auction or liquidation services that may constitute an agreement to make a bulk sale under the laws of the State of ________ .

(5) The date on or after which the auction began or will begin or the date on or after which the liquidator began or will begin to sell assets on the seller's behalf is ________,and [if not stated in the schedule of distribution] the date on or after which more than ten percent of the net proceeds of the sale were or will be paid is ________ .

(6) The following assets are the subject of the sale: ________________________________ .

(7) [If applicable] The auctioneer or liquidator will make available to claimants of the seller a list of the seller's claimants in the following manner: ________ .

(8) [If applicable] The sale is to satisfy $ ________ of an antecedent debt owed by the seller to ________ .

(9) A copy of the schedule of distribution of the net proceeds accompanies this notice.

[End of Notice]

(4) A person who buys at a bulk sale by auction or conducted by a liquidator need not comply with the requirements of Section 6–104(1) and is not liable for the failure of an auctioneer or liquidator to comply with the requirements of this section.

§ 6–109. What Constitutes Filing; Duties of Filing Officer; Information from Filing Officer.

(1) Presentation of a notice or list of claimants for filing and tender of the filing fee or acceptance of the notice or list by the filing officer constitutes filing under this Article.

(2) The filing officer shall:

(a) mark each notice or list with a file number and with the date and hour of filing;

(b) hold the notice or list or a copy for public inspection;

(c) index the notice or list according to each name given for the seller and for the buyer; and

(d) note in the index the file number and the addresses of the seller and buyer given in the notice or list.

(3) If the person filing a notice or list furnishes the filing officer with a copy, the filing officer upon request shall note upon the copy the file number and date and hour of the filing of the original and send or deliver the copy to the person.

(4) The fee for filing and indexing and for stamping a copy furnished by the person filing to show the date and place of filing is $ ________ for the first page and $ ________ for each additional page. The fee for indexing each name beyond the first two is $ ________ .

(5) Upon request of any person, the filing officer shall issue a certificate showing whether any notice or list with respect to a particular seller or buyer is on file on the date and hour stated in the certificate. If a notice or list is on file, the certificate must give the date and hour of filing of each notice or list and the name and address of each seller, buyer, auctioneer, or liquidator. The fee for the certificate is $ ________ if the request for the certificate is in the standard form prescribed by the [Secretary of State] and otherwise is $ ________ . Upon request of any person, the filing officer shall furnish a copy of any filed notice or list for a fee of $ ________ .

(6) The filing officer shall keep each notice or list for two years after it is filed.

§ 6–110. Limitation of Actions.

(1) Except as provided in subsection (2), an action under this Article against a buyer, auctioneer, or liquidator must be commenced within one year after the date of the bulk sale.

(2) If the buyer, auctioneer, or liquidator conceals the fact that the sale has occurred, the limitation is tolled and an action under this Article may be commenced within the earlier of (i) one year after the person bringing the action discovers that the sale has occurred or (ii) one year after the person bringing the action should have discovered that the sale has occurred, but no later than two years after the date of the bulk sale. Complete noncompliance with the requirements of this Article does not of itself constitute concealment.

(3) An action under Section 6–107(11) must be commenced within one year after the alleged violation occurs.

Conforming Amendment to Section 2–403

States adopting Alternative B should amend Section 2–403(4) of the Uniform Commercial Code to read as follows:

(4) The rights of other purchasers of goods and of lien creditors are governed by the Articles on Secured Transactions (Article 9), Bulk Sales (Article 6) and Documents of Title (Article 7).

Article 7
Warehouse Receipts, Bills of Lading and Other Documents of Title

Part 1 General

§ 7–101. Short Title.

This Article shall be known and may be cited as Uniform Commercial Code–Documents of Title.

§ 7–102. Definitions and Index of Definitions.

(1) In this Article, unless the context otherwise requires:

(a) "Bailee" means the person who by a warehouse receipt, bill of lading or other document of title acknowledges possession of goods and contracts to deliver them.

(b) "Consignee" means the person named in a bill to whom or to whose order the bill promises delivery.

(c) "Consignor" means the person named in a bill as the person from whom the goods have been received for shipment.

(d) "Delivery order" means a written order to deliver goods directed to a warehouseman, carrier or other person who in the ordinary course of business issues warehouse receipts or bills of lading.

(e) "Document" means document of title as defined in the general definitions in Article 1 (Section 1–201).

(f) "Goods" means all things which are treated as movable for the purposes of a contract of storage or transportation.

(g) "Issuer" means a bailee who issues a document except that in relation to an unaccepted delivery order it means the person who orders the possessor of goods to deliver. Issuer includes any person for whom an agent or employee purports to act in issuing a document if the agent or employee has real or apparent authority to issue documents, notwithstanding that the issuer received no goods or that the goods were misdescribed or that in any other respect the agent or employee violated his instructions.

(h) "Warehouseman" is a person engaged in the business of storing goods for hire.

(2) Other definitions applying to this Article or to specified Parts thereof, and the sections in which they appear are:

"Duly negotiate". Section 7–501.

"Person entitled under the document". Section 7–403(4).

(3) Definitions in other Articles applying to this Article and the sections in which they appear are:

"Contract for sale". Section 2–106.

"Overseas". Section 2–323.

"Receipt" of goods. Section 2–103.

(4) In addition Article 1 contains general definitions and principles of construction and interpretation applicable throughout this Article.

§ 7–103. Relation of Article to Treaty, Statute, Tariff, Classification or Regulation.

To the extent that any treaty or statute of the United States, regulatory statute of this State or tariff, classification or regulation filed or issued pursuant thereto is applicable, the provisions of this Article are subject thereto.

§ 7–104. Negotiable and Non-Negotiable Warehouse Receipt, Bill of Lading or Other Document of Title.

(1) A warehouse receipt, bill of lading or other document of title is negotiable

(a) if by its terms the goods are to be delivered to bearer or to the order of a named person; or

(b) where recognized in overseas trade, if it runs to a named person or assigns.

(2) Any other document is nonnegotiable. A bill of lading in which it is stated that the goods are consigned to a named person is not made negotiable by a provision that the goods are to be delivered only against a written order signed by the same or another named person.

§ 7–105. Construction Against Negative Implication.

The omission from either Part 2 or Part 3 of this Article of a provision corresponding to a provision made in the other Part does not imply that a corresponding rule of law is not applicable.

Part 2 Warehouse Receipts: Special Provisions

§ 7–201. Who May Issue a Warehouse Receipt; Storage Under Government Bond.

(1) A warehouse receipt may be issued by any warehouseman.

(2) Where goods including distilled spirits and agricultural commodities are stored under a statute requiring a bond against withdrawal or a license for the issuance of receipts in the nature of warehouse receipts, a receipt issued for the goods has like effect as a warehouse receipt even though issued by a person who is the owner of the goods and is not a warehouseman.

§ 7–202. Form of Warehouse Receipt; Essential Terms; Optional Terms.

(1) A warehouse receipt need not be in any particular form.

(2) Unless a warehouse receipt embodies within its written or printed terms each of the following, the warehouseman is liable for damages caused by the omission to a person injured thereby:

(a) the location of the warehouse where the goods are stored;

(b) the date of issue of the receipt;

(c) the consecutive number of the receipt;

(d) a statement whether the goods received will be delivered to the bearer, to a specified person, or to a specified person or his order;

(e) the rate of storage and handling charges, except that where goods are stored under a field warehousing arrangement a statement of that fact is sufficient on a non-negotiable receipt;

(f) a description of the goods or of the packages containing them;

(g) the signature of the warehouseman, which may be made by his authorized agent;

(h) if the receipt is issued for goods of which the warehouseman is owner, either solely or jointly or in common with others, the fact of such ownership; and

(i) a statement of the amount of advances made and of liabilities incurred for which the warehouseman claims a lien or security interest (Section 7–209). If the precise amount of such advances made or of such liabilities incurred is, at the time of the issue of the receipt, unknown to the warehouseman or to his agent who issues it, a statement of the fact that advances have been made or liabilities incurred and the purpose thereof is sufficient.

(3) A warehouseman may insert in his receipt any other terms which are not contrary to the provisions of this Act and do not impair his obligation of delivery (Section 7–403) or his duty of care (Section 7–204). Any contrary provisions shall be ineffective.

§ 7–203. Liability for Non-Receipt or Misdescription.

A party to or purchaser for value in good faith of a document of title other than a bill of lading relying in either case upon the description therein of the goods may recover from the issuer damages caused by the nonreceipt or misdescription of the goods, except to the extent that the document conspicuously indicates that the issuer does not know whether any part or all of the goods in fact were received or conform to the description, as where the description is in terms of marks or labels or kind, quantity or condition, or the receipt or description is qualified by "contents, condition and quality unknown", "said to contain" or the like, if such indication be true, or the party or purchaser otherwise has notice.

§ 7–204. Duty of Care; Contractual Limitation of Warehouseman's Liability.

(1) A warehouseman is liable for damages for loss of or injury to the goods caused by his failure to exercise such care in regard to them as a reasonably careful man would exercise under like circumstances but unless otherwise agreed he is not liable for damages which could not have been avoided by the exercise of such care.

(2) Damages may be limited by a term in the warehouse receipt or storage agreement limiting the amount of liability in case of loss or damage, and setting forth a specific liability per article or item, or value per unit of weight, beyond which the warehouseman shall not be liable; provided, however, that such liability may on written request of the bailor at the time of signing such storage agreement or within a reasonable time after receipt of the warehouse receipt be increased on part or all of the goods thereunder, in which event increased rates may be charged based on such increased valuation, but that no such increase shall be permitted contrary to a lawful limitation of liability contained in the warehouseman's tariff, if any. No such limitation is effective with respect to the warehouseman's liability for conversion to his own use.

(3) Reasonable provisions as to the time and manner of presenting claims and instituting actions based on the bailment may be included in the warehouse receipt or tariff.

(4) This section does not impair or repeal . . .

Note: *Insert in subsection (4) a reference to any statute which imposes a higher responsibility upon the warehouseman or invalidates contractual limitations which would be permissible under this Article.*

§ 7–205. Title Under Warehouse Receipt Defeated in Certain Cases.

A buyer in the ordinary course of business of fungible goods sold and delivered by a warehouseman who is also in the business of buying and selling such goods takes free of any claim under a warehouse receipt even though it has been duly negotiated.

§ 7–206. Termination of Storage at Warehouseman's Option.

(1) A warehouseman may on notifying the person on whose account the goods are held and any other person known to claim an interest in the goods require payment of any charges and removal of the goods from the warehouse at the termination of the period of storage fixed by the document, or, if no period is fixed, within a stated period not less than thirty days after the notification. If the goods are not removed before the date specified in the notification, the warehouseman may sell them in accordance with the provisions of the section on enforcement of a warehouseman's lien (Section 7–210).

(2) If a warehouseman in good faith believes that the goods are about to deteriorate or decline in value to less than the amount of his lien within the time prescribed in subsection (1) for notification, advertisement and sale, the warehouseman may specify in the notification any reasonable shorter time for removal of the goods and in case the goods are not removed, may sell them at public sale held not less than one week after a single advertisement or posting.

(3) If as a result of a quality or condition of the goods of which the warehouseman had no notice at the time of deposit the goods are a hazard to other property or to the warehouse or to persons, the warehouseman may sell the goods at public or private sale without advertisement on reasonable notification to all persons known to claim an interest in the goods. If the warehouseman after a reasonable effort is unable to sell the goods he may dispose of them in any lawful manner and shall incur no liability by reason of such disposition.

(4) The warehouseman must deliver the goods to any person entitled to them under this Article upon due

demand made at any time prior to sale or other disposition under this section.

(5) The warehouseman may satisfy his lien from the proceeds of any sale or disposition under this section but must hold the balance for delivery on the demand of any person to whom he would have been bound to deliver the goods.

§ 7-207. Goods Must Be Kept Separate; Fungible Goods.

(1) Unless the warehouse receipt otherwise provides, a warehouseman must keep separate the goods covered by each receipt so as to permit at all times identification and delivery of those goods except that different lots of fungible goods may be commingled.

(2) Fungible goods so commingled are owned in common by the persons entitled thereto and the warehouseman is severally liable to each owner for that owner's share. Where because of overissue a mass of fungible goods is insufficient to meet all the receipts which the warehouseman has issued against it, the persons entitled include all holders to whom overissued receipts have been duly negotiated.

§ 7-208. Altered Warehouse Receipts.

Where a blank in a negotiable warehouse receipt has been filled in without authority, a purchaser for value and without notice of the want of authority may treat the insertion as authorized. Any other unauthorized alteration leaves any receipt enforceable against the issuer according to its original tenor.

§ 7-209. Lien of Warehouseman.

(1) A warehouseman has a lien against the bailor on the goods covered by a warehouse receipt or on the proceeds thereof in his possession for charges for storage or transportation (including demurrage and terminal charges), insurance, labor, or charges present or future in relation to the goods, and for expenses necessary for preservation of the goods or reasonably incurred in their sale pursuant to law. If the person on whose account the goods are held is liable for like charges or expenses in relation to other goods whenever deposited and it is stated in the receipt that a lien is claimed for charges and expenses in relation to other goods, the warehouseman also has a lien against him for such charges and expenses whether or not the other goods have been delivered by the warehouseman. But against a person to whom a negotiable warehouse receipt is duly negotiated a warehouseman's lien is limited to charges in an amount or at a rate specified on the receipt or if no charges are so specified then to a reasonable charge for storage of the goods covered by the receipt subsequent to the date of the receipt.

(2) The warehouseman may also reserve a security interest against the bailor for a maximum amount specified on the receipt for charges other than those specified in subsection (1), such as for money advanced and interest. Such a security interest is governed by the Article on Secured Transactions (Article 9).

(3)(a) A warehouseman's lien for charges and expenses under subsection (1) or a security interest under subsection (2) is also effective against any person who so entrusted the bailor with possession of the goods that a pledge of them by him to a good faith purchaser for value would have been valid but is not effective against a person as to whom the document confers no right in the goods covered by it under Section 7-503.

(b) A warehouseman's lien on household goods for charges and expenses in relation to the goods under subsection (1) is also effective against all persons if the depositor was the legal possessor of the goods at the time of deposit. "Household goods" means furniture, furnishings and personal effects used by the depositor in a dwelling.

(4) A warehouseman loses his lien on any goods which he voluntarily delivers or which he unjustifiably refuses to deliver.

§ 7-210. Enforcement of Warehouseman's Lien.

(1) Except as provided in subsection (2), a warehouseman's lien may be enforced by public or private sale of the goods in bloc or in parcels, at any time or place and on any terms which are commercially reasonable, after notifying all persons known to claim an interest in the goods. Such notification must include a statement of the amount due, the nature of the proposed sale and the time and place of any public sale. The fact that a better price could have been obtained by a sale at a different time or in a different method from that selected by the warehouseman is not of itself sufficient to establish that the sale was not made in a commercially reasonable manner. If the warehouseman either sells the goods in the usual manner in any recognized market therefor, or if he sells at the price current in such market at the time of his sale, or if he has otherwise sold in conformity with commercially reasonable practices among dealers in the type of goods sold, he has sold in a commercially reasonable manner. A sale of more goods than apparently necessary to be offered to ensure satisfaction of the obligation is not commercially reasonable except in cases covered by the preceding sentence.

(2) A warehouseman's lien on goods other than goods stored by a merchant in the course of his business may be enforced only as follows:

(a) All persons known to claim an interest in the goods must be notified.

(b) The notification must be delivered in person or sent by registered or certified letter to the last known address of any person to be notified.

(c) The notification must include an itemized statement of the claim, a description of the goods subject to the lien, a demand for payment within a specified time not less than ten days after receipt of the notification, and a conspicuous statement that unless the claim is paid within the time the goods will be advertised for sale and sold by auction at a specified time and place.

(d) The sale must conform to the terms of the notification.

(e) The sale must be held at the nearest suitable place to that where the goods are held or stored.

(f) After the expiration of the time given in the notification, an advertisement of the sale must be published once a week for two weeks consecutively in a newspaper of general circulation where the sale is to be held. The advertisement must include a description of the goods, the name of the person on whose account they are being held, and the time and place of the sale. The sale must take place at least fifteen days after the first publication. If there is no newspaper of general circulation where the sale is to be held, the advertisement must be posted at least ten days before the sale in not less than six conspicuous places in the neighborhood of the proposed sale.

(3) Before any sale pursuant to this section any person claiming a right in the goods may pay the amount necessary to satisfy the lien and the reasonable expenses incurred under this section. In that event the goods must not be sold, but must be retained by the warehouseman subject to the terms of the receipt and this Article.

(4) The warehouseman may buy at any public sale pursuant to this section.

(5) A purchaser in good faith of goods sold to enforce a warehouseman's lien takes the goods free of any rights of persons against whom the lien was valid, despite noncompliance by the warehouseman with the requirements of this section.

(6) The warehouseman may satisfy his lien from the proceeds of any sale pursuant to this section but must hold the balance, if any, for delivery on demand to any person to whom he would have been bound to deliver the goods.

(7) The rights provided by this section shall be in addition to all other rights allowed by law to a creditor against his debtor.

(8) Where a lien is on goods stored by a merchant in the course of his business the lien may be enforced in accordance with either subsection (1) or (2).

(9) The warehouseman is liable for damages caused by failure to comply with the requirements for sale under this section and in case of willful violation is liable for conversion.

As amended in 1962.

Part 3 Bills of Lading: Special Provisions

§ 7–301. Liability for Non-Receipt or Misdescription; "Said to Contain"; "Shipper's Load and Count"; Improper Handling.

(1) A consignee of a non-negotiable bill who has given value in good faith or a holder to whom a negotiable bill has been duly negotiated relying in either case upon the description therein of the goods, or upon the date therein shown, may recover from the issuer damages caused by the misdating of the bill or the nonreceipt or misdescription of the goods, except to the extent that the document indicates that the issuer does not know whether any part of all of the goods in fact were received or conform to the description, as where the description is in terms of marks or labels or kind, quantity, or condition or the receipt or description is qualified by "contents or condition of contents of packages unknown", "said to contain", "shipper's weight, load and count" or the like, if such indication be true.

(2) When goods are loaded by an issuer who is a common carrier, the issuer must count the packages of goods if package freight and ascertain the kind and quantity if bulk freight. In such cases "shipper's weight, load and count" or other words indicating that the description was made by the shipper are ineffective except as to freight concealed by packages.

(3) When bulk freight is loaded by a shipper who makes available to the issuer adequate facilities for weighing such freight, an issuer who is a common carrier must ascertain the kind and quantity within a reasonable time after receiving the written request of the shipper to do so. In such cases "shipper's weight" or other words of like purport are ineffective.

(4) The issuer may by inserting in the bill the words "shipper's weight, load and count" or other words of like purport indicate that the goods were loaded by the shipper; and if such statement be true the issuer shall not be liable for damages caused by the improper loading. But their omission does not imply liability for such damages.

(5) The shipper shall be deemed to have guaranteed to the issuer the accuracy at the time of shipment of the description, marks, labels, number, kind, quantity, condition and weight, as furnished by him; and the shipper shall indemnify the issuer against damage caused by inaccuracies in such particulars. The right of the issuer to such indemnity shall in no way limit his responsibility and liability under the contract of carriage to any person other than the shipper.

§ 7–302. Through Bills of Lading and Similar Documents.

(1) The issuer of a through bill of lading or other document embodying an undertaking to be performed in part by persons acting as its agents or by connecting carriers is liable to anyone entitled to recover on the document for any breach by such other persons or by a connecting carrier of its obligation under the document but to the extent that the bill covers an undertaking to be performed overseas or in territory not contiguous to the continental United States or an undertaking including matters other than transportation this liability may be varied by agreement of the parties.

(2) Where goods covered by a through bill of lading or other document embodying an undertaking to be performed in part by persons other than the issuer are received by any such person, he is subject with respect to his own performance while the goods are in his possession to the obligation of the issuer. His obligation is

discharged by delivery of the goods to another such person pursuant to the document, and does not include liability for breach by any other such persons or by the issuer.

(3) The issuer of such through bill of lading or other document shall be entitled to recover from the connecting carrier or such other person in possession of the goods when the breach of the obligation under the document occurred, the amount it may be required to pay to anyone entitled to recover on the document therefor, as may be evidenced by any receipt, judgment, or transcript thereof, and the amount of any expense reasonably incurred by it in defending any action brought by anyone entitled to recover on the document therefor.

§ 7–303. Diversion; Reconsignment; Change of Instructions.

(1) Unless the bill of lading otherwise provides, the carrier may deliver the goods to a person or destination other than that stated in the bill or may otherwise dispose of the goods on instructions from

(a) the holder of a negotiable bill; or

(b) the consignor on a non-negotiable bill notwithstanding contrary instructions from the consignee; or

(c) the consignee on a non-negotiable bill in the absence of contrary instructions from the consignor, if the goods have arrived at the billed destination or if the consignee is in possession of the bill; or

(d) the consignee on a non-negotiable bill if he is entitled as against the consignor to dispose of them.

(2) Unless such instructions are noted on a negotiable bill of lading, a person to whom the bill is duly negotiated can hold the bailee according to the original terms.

§ 7–304. Bills of Lading in a Set.

(1) Except where customary in overseas transportation, a bill of lading must not be issued in a set of parts. The issuer is liable for damages caused by violation of this subsection.

(2) Where a bill of lading is lawfully drawn in a set of parts, each of which is numbered and expressed to be valid only if the goods have not been delivered against any other part, the whole of the parts constitute one bill.

(3) Where a bill of lading is lawfully issued in a set of parts and different parts are negotiated to different persons, the title of the holder to whom the first due negotiation is made prevails as to both the document and the goods even though any later holder may have received the goods from the carrier in good faith and discharged the carrier's obligation by surrender of his part.

(4) Any person who negotiates or transfers a single part of a bill of lading drawn in a set is liable to holders of that part as if it were the whole set.

(5) The bailee is obliged to deliver in accordance with Part 4 of this Article against the first presented part of a bill of lading lawfully drawn in a set. Such delivery discharges the bailee's obligation on the whole bill.

§ 7–305. Destination Bills.

(1) Instead of issuing a bill of lading to the consignor at the place of shipment a carrier may at the request of the consignor procure the bill to be issued at destination or at any other place designated in the request.

(2) Upon request of anyone entitled as against the carrier to control the goods while in transit and on surrender of any outstanding bill of lading or other receipt covering such goods, the issuer may procure a substitute bill to be issued at any place designated in the request.

§ 7–306. Altered Bills of Lading.

An unauthorized alteration or filling in of a blank in a bill of lading leaves the bill enforceable according to its original tenor.

§ 7–307. Lien of Carrier.

(1) A carrier has a lien on the goods covered by a bill of lading for charges subsequent to the date of its receipt of the goods for storage or transportation (including demurrage and terminal charges) and for expenses necessary for preservation of the goods incident to their transportation or reasonably incurred in their sale pursuant to law. But against a purchaser for value of a negotiable bill of lading a carrier's lien is limited to charges stated in the bill or the applicable tariffs, or if no charges are stated then to a reasonable charge.

(2) A lien for charges and expenses under subsection (1) on goods which the carrier was required by law to receive for transportation is effective against the consignor or any person entitled to the goods unless the carrier had notice that the consignor lacked authority to subject the goods to such charges and expenses. Any other lien under subsection (1) is effective against the consignor and any person who permitted the bailor to have control or possession of the goods unless the carrier had notice that the bailor lacked such authority.

(3) A carrier loses his lien on any goods which he voluntarily delivers or which he unjustifiably refuses to deliver.

§ 7–308. Enforcement of Carrier's Lien.

(1) A carrier's lien may be enforced by public or private sale of the goods, in bloc or in parcels, at any time or place and on any terms which are commercially reasonable, after notifying all persons known to claim an interest in the goods. Such notification must include a statement of the amount due, the nature of the proposed sale and the time and place of any public sale. The fact that a better price could have been obtained by a sale at a different time or in a different method from that selected by the carrier is not of itself sufficient to establish that the sale was not made in a commercially reasonable manner. If the carrier either sells the goods in the usual manner in any recognized market therefor or if he sells at the price current in such market at the time of his sale or if he has otherwise sold in conformity with commercially reasonable practices among dealers in the type of goods sold he has sold in a commercially reasonable manner. A sale of more

goods than apparently necessary to be offered to ensure satisfaction of the obligation is not commercially reasonable except in cases covered by the preceding sentence.

(2) Before any sale pursuant to this section any person claiming a right in the goods may pay the amount necessary to satisfy the lien and the reasonable expenses incurred under this section. In that event the goods must not be sold, but must be retained by the carrier subject to the terms of the bill and this Article.

(3) The carrier may buy at any public sale pursuant to this section.

(4) A purchaser in good faith of goods sold to enforce a carrier's lien takes the goods free of any rights of persons against whom the lien was valid, despite noncompliance by the carrier with the requirements of this section.

(5) The carrier may satisfy his lien from the proceeds of any sale pursuant to this section but must hold the balance, if any, for delivery on demand to any person to whom he would have been bound to deliver the goods.

(6) The rights provided by this section shall be in addition to all other rights allowed by law to a creditor against his debtor.

(7) A carrier's lien may be enforced in accordance with either subsection (1) or the procedure set forth in subsection (2) of Section 7–210.

(8) The carrier is liable for damages caused by failure to comply with the requirements for sale under this section and in case of willful violation is liable for conversion.

§ 7–309. Duty of Care; Contractual Limitation of Carrier's Liability.

(1) A carrier who issues a bill of lading whether negotiable or nonnegotiable must exercise the degree of care in relation to the goods which a reasonably careful man would exercise under like circumstances. This subsection does not repeal or change any law or rule of law which imposes liability upon a common carrier for damages not caused by its negligence.

(2) Damages may be limited by a provision that the carrier's liability shall not exceed a value stated in the document if the carrier's rates are dependent upon value and the consignor by the carrier's tariff is afforded an opportunity to declare a higher value or a value as lawfully provided in the tariff, or where no tariff is filed he is otherwise advised of such opportunity; but no such limitation is effective with respect to the carrier's liability for conversion to its own use.

(3) Reasonable provisions as to the time and manner of presenting claims and instituting actions based on the shipment may be included in a bill of lading or tariff.

Part 4 Warehouse Receipts and Bills of Lading: General Obligations

§ 7–401. Irregularities in Issue of Receipt or Bill or Conduct of Issuer.

The obligations imposed by this Article on an issuer apply to a document of title regardless of the fact that

(a) the document may not comply with the requirements of this Article or of any other law or regulation regarding its issue, form or content; or

(b) the issuer may have violated laws regulating the conduct of his business; or

(c) the goods covered by the document were owned by the bailee at the time the document was issued; or

(d) the person issuing the document does not come within the definition of warehouseman if it purports to be a warehouse receipt.

§ 7–402. Duplicate Receipt or Bill; Overissue.

Neither a duplicate nor any other document of title purporting to cover goods already represented by an outstanding document of the same issuer confers any right in the goods, except as provided in the case of bills in a set, overissue of documents for fungible goods and substitutes for lost, stolen or destroyed documents. But the issuer is liable for damages caused by his overissue or failure to identify a duplicate document as such by conspicuous notation on its face.

§ 7–403. Obligation of Warehouseman or Carrier to Deliver; Excuse.

(1) The bailee must deliver the goods to a person entitled under the document who complies with subsections (2) and (3), unless and to the extent that the bailee establishes any of the following:

(a) delivery of the goods to a person whose receipt was rightful as against the claimant;

(b) damage to or delay, loss or destruction of the goods for which the bailee is not liable [, but the burden of establishing negligence in such cases is on the person entitled under the document];

Note: *The brackets in (1)(b) indicate that State enactments may differ on this point without serious damage to the principle of uniformity.*

(c) previous sale or other disposition of the goods in lawful enforcement of a lien or on warehouseman's lawful termination of storage;

(d) the exercise by a seller of his right to stop delivery pursuant to the provisions of the Article on Sales (Section 2–705);

(e) a diversion, reconsignment or other disposition pursuant to the provisions of this Article (Section 7–303) or tariff regulating such right;

(f) release, satisfaction or any other fact affording a personal defense against the claimant;

(g) any other lawful excuse.

(2) A person claiming goods covered by a document of title must satisfy the bailee's lien where the bailee so requests or where the bailee is prohibited by law from delivering the goods until the charges are paid.

(3) Unless the person claiming is one against whom the document confers no right under Sec. 7–503(1), he must surrender for cancellation or notation of partial deliveries any outstanding negotiable document covering the

goods, and the bailee must cancel the document or conspicuously note the partial delivery thereon or be liable to any person to whom the document is duly negotiated.

(4) "Person entitled under the document" means holder in the case of a negotiable document, or the person to whom delivery is to be made by the terms of or pursuant to written instructions under a non-negotiable document.

§ 7–404. No Liability for Good Faith Delivery Pursuant to Receipt or Bill.

A bailee who in good faith including observance of reasonable commercial standards has received goods and delivered or otherwise disposed of them according to the terms of the document of title or pursuant to this Article is not liable therefor. This rule applies even though the person from whom he received the goods had no authority to procure the document or to dispose of the goods and even though the person to whom he delivered the goods had no authority to receive them.

Part 5 Warehouse Receipts and Bills of Lading: Negotiation and Transfer

§ 7–501. Form of Negotiation and Requirements of "Due Negotiation".

(1) A negotiable document of title running to the order of a named person is negotiated by his indorsement and delivery. After his indorsement in blank or to bearer any person can negotiate it by delivery alone.

(2)(a) A negotiable document of title is also negotiated by delivery alone when by its original terms it runs to bearer.

(b) When a document running to the order of a named person is delivered to him the effect is the same as if the document had been negotiated.

(3) Negotiation of a negotiable document of title after it has been indorsed to a specified person requires indorsement by the special indorsee as well as delivery.

(4) A negotiable document of title is "duly negotiated" when it is negotiated in the manner stated in this section to a holder who purchases it in good faith without notice of any defense against or claim to it on the part of any person and for value, unless it is established that the negotiation is not in the regular course of business or financing or involves receiving the document in settlement or payment of a money obligation.

(5) Indorsement of a nonnegotiable document neither makes it negotiable nor adds to the transferee's rights.

(6) The naming in a negotiable bill of a person to be notified of the arrival of the goods does not limit the negotiability of the bill nor constitute notice to a purchaser thereof of any interest of such person in the goods.

§ 7–502. Rights Acquired by Due Negotiation.

(1) Subject to the following section and to the provisions of Section 7–205 on fungible goods, a holder to whom a negotiable document of title has been duly negotiated acquires thereby:

(a) title to the document;

(b) title to the goods;

(c) all rights accruing under the law of agency or estoppel, including rights to goods delivered to the bailee after the document was issued; and

(d) the direct obligation of the issuer to hold or deliver the goods according to the terms of the document free of any defense or claim by him except those arising under the terms of the document or under this Article. In the case of a delivery order the bailee's obligation accrues only upon acceptance and the obligation acquired by the holder is that the issuer and any indorser will procure the acceptance of the bailee.

(2) Subject to the following section, title and rights so acquired are not defeated by any stoppage of the goods represented by the document or by surrender of such goods by the bailee, and are not impaired even though the negotiation or any prior negotiation constituted a breach of duty or even though any person has been deprived of possession of the document by misrepresentation, fraud, accident, mistake, duress, loss, theft or conversion, or even though a previous sale or other transfer of the goods or document has been made to a third person.

§ 7–503. Document of Title to Goods Defeated in Certain Cases.

(1) A document of title confers no right in goods against a person who before issuance of the document had a legal interest or a perfected security interest in them and who neither

(a) delivered or entrusted them or any document of title covering them to the bailor or his nominee with actual or apparent authority to ship, store or sell or with power to obtain delivery under this Article (Section 7–403) or with power of disposition under this Act (Sections 2–403 and 9–307) or other statute or rule of law; nor

(b) acquiesced in the procurement by the bailor or his nominee of any document of title.

(2) Title to goods based upon an unaccepted delivery order is subject to the rights of anyone to whom a negotiable warehouse receipt or bill of lading covering the goods has been duly negotiated. Such a title may be defeated under the next section to the same extent as the rights of the issuer or a transferee from the issuer.

(3) Title to goods based upon a bill of lading issued to a freight forwarder is subject to the rights of anyone to whom a bill issued by the freight forwarder is duly negotiated; but delivery by the carrier in accordance with Part 4 of this Article pursuant to its own bill of lading discharges the carrier's obligation to deliver.

As amended in 1999.

§ 7–504. Rights Acquired in the Absence of Due Negotiation; Effect of Diversion; Seller's Stoppage of Delivery.

(1) A transferee of a document, whether negotiable or nonnegotiable, to whom the document has been

delivered but not duly negotiated, acquires the title and rights which his transferor had or had actual authority to convey.

(2) In the case of a nonnegotiable document, until but not after the bailee receives notification of the transfer, the rights of the transferee may be defeated

(a) by those creditors of the transferor who could treat the sale as void under Section 2–402; or

(b) by a buyer from the transferor in ordinary course of business if the bailee has delivered the goods to the buyer or received notification of his rights; or

(c) as against the bailee by good faith dealings of the bailee with the transferor.

(3) A diversion or other change of shipping instructions by the consignor in a nonnegotiable bill of lading which causes the bailee not to deliver to the consignee defeats the consignee's title to the goods if they have been delivered to a buyer in ordinary course of business and in any event defeats the consignee's rights against the bailee.

(4) Delivery pursuant to a nonnegotiable document may be stopped by a seller under Section 2–705, and subject to the requirement of due notification there provided. A bailee honoring the seller's instructions is entitled to be indemnified by the seller against any resulting loss or expense.

§ 7–505. Indorser Not a Guarantor for Other Parties.

The indorsement of a document of title issued by a bailee does not make the indorser liable for any default by the bailee or by previous indorsers.

§ 7–506. Delivery Without Indorsement: Right to Compel Indorsement.

The transferee of a negotiable document of title has a specifically enforceable right to have his transferor supply any necessary indorsement but the transfer becomes a negotiation only as of the time the indorsement is supplied.

§ 7–507. Warranties on Negotiation or Transfer of Receipt or Bill.

Where a person negotiates or transfers a document of title for value otherwise than as a mere intermediary under the next following section, then unless otherwise agreed he warrants to his immediate purchaser only in addition to any warranty made in selling the goods

(a) that the document is genuine; and

(b) that he has no knowledge of any fact which would impair its validity or worth; and

(c) that his negotiation or transfer is rightful and fully effective with respect to the title to the document and the goods it represents.

§ 7–508. Warranties of Collecting Bank as to Documents.

A collecting bank or other intermediary known to be entrusted with documents on behalf of another or with collection of a draft or other claim against delivery of documents warrants by such delivery of the documents only its own good faith and authority. This rule applies even though the intermediary has purchased or made advances against the claim or draft to be collected.

§ 7–509. Receipt or Bill: When Adequate Compliance With Commercial Contract.

The question whether a document is adequate to fulfill the obligations of a contract for sale or the conditions of a credit is governed by the Articles on Sales (Article 2) and on Letters of Credit (Article 5).

Part 6 Warehouse Receipts and Bills of Lading: Miscellaneous Provisions

§ 7–601. Lost and Missing Documents.

(1) If a document has been lost, stolen or destroyed, a court may order delivery of the goods or issuance of a substitute document and the bailee may without liability to any person comply with such order. If the document was negotiable the claimant must post security approved by the court to indemnify any person who may suffer loss as a result of non-surrender of the document. If the document was not negotiable, such security may be required at the discretion of the court. The court may also in its discretion order payment of the bailee's reasonable costs and counsel fees.

(2) A bailee who without court order delivers goods to a person claiming under a missing negotiable document is liable to any person injured thereby, and if the delivery is not in good faith becomes liable for conversion. Delivery in good faith is not conversion if made in accordance with a filed classification or tariff or, where no classification or tariff is filed, if the claimant posts security with the bailee in an amount at least double the value of the goods at the time of posting to indemnify any person injured by the delivery who files a notice of claim within one year after the delivery.

§ 7–602. Attachment of Goods Covered by a Negotiable Document.

Except where the document was originally issued upon delivery of the goods by a person who had no power to dispose of them, no lien attaches by virtue of any judicial process to goods in the possession of a bailee for which a negotiable document of title is outstanding unless the document be first surrendered to the bailee or its negotiation enjoined, and the bailee shall not be compelled to deliver the goods pursuant to process until the document is surrendered to him or impounded by the court. One who purchases the document for value without notice of the process or injunction takes free of the lien imposed by judicial process.

§ 7–603. Conflicting Claims; Interpleader.

If more than one person claims title or possession of the goods, the bailee is excused from delivery until he has had a reasonable time to ascertain the validity of the adverse claims or to bring an action to compel all claimants to interplead and may compel such interpleader, either in defending an action for nondelivery of the goods, or by original action, whichever is appropriate.

Revised (1994) Article 8
INVESTMENT SECURITIES

Part 1 Short Title and General Matters

§ 8–101. Short Title.

This Article may be cited as Uniform Commercial Code—Investment Securities.

§ 8–102. Definitions.

(a) In this Article:

(1) "Adverse claim" means a claim that a claimant has a property interest in a financial asset and that it is a violation of the rights of the claimant for another person to hold, transfer, or deal with the financial asset.

(2) "Bearer form," as applied to a certificated security, means a form in which the security is payable to the bearer of the security certificate according to its terms but not by reason of an indorsement.

(3) "Broker" means a person defined as a broker or dealer under the federal securities laws, but without excluding a bank acting in that capacity.

(4) "Certificated security" means a security that is represented by a certificate.

(5) "Clearing corporation" means:

(i) a person that is registered as a "clearing agency" under the federal securities laws;

(ii) a federal reserve bank; or

(iii) any other person that provides clearance or settlement services with respect to financial assets that would require it to register as a clearing agency under the federal securities laws but for an exclusion or exemption from the registration requirement, if its activities as a clearing corporation, including promulgation of rules, are subject to regulation by a federal or state governmental authority.

(6) "Communicate" means to:

(i) send a signed writing; or

(ii) transmit information by any mechanism agreed upon by the persons transmitting and receiving the information.

(7) "Entitlement holder" means a person identified in the records of a securities intermediary as the person having a security entitlement against the securities intermediary. If a person acquires a security entitlement by virtue of Section 8–501(b)(2) or (3), that person is the entitlement holder.

(8) "Entitlement order" means a notification communicated to a securities intermediary directing transfer or redemption of a financial asset to which the entitlement holder has a security entitlement.

(9) "Financial asset," except as otherwise provided in Section 8–103, means:

(i) a security;

(ii) an obligation of a person or a share, participation, or other interest in a person or in property or an enterprise of a person, which is, or is of a type, dealt in or traded on financial markets, or which is recognized in any area in which it is issued or dealt in as a medium for investment; or

(iii) any property that is held by a securities intermediary for another person in a securities account if the securities intermediary has expressly agreed with the other person that the property is to be treated as a financial asset under this Article.

As context requires, the term means either the interest itself or the means by which a person's claim to it is evidenced, including a certificated or uncertificated security, a security certificate, or a security entitlement.

(10) "Good faith," for purposes of the obligation of good faith in the performance or enforcement of contracts or duties within this Article, means honesty in fact and the observance of reasonable commercial standards of fair dealing.

(11) "Indorsement" means a signature that alone or accompanied by other words is made on a security certificate in registered form or on a separate document for the purpose of assigning, transferring, or redeeming the security or granting a power to assign, transfer, or redeem it.

(12) "Instruction" means a notification communicated to the issuer of an uncertificated security which directs that the transfer of the security be registered or that the security be redeemed.

(13) "Registered form," as applied to a certificated security, means a form in which:

(i) the security certificate specifies a person entitled to the security; and

(ii) a transfer of the security may be registered upon books maintained for that purpose by or on behalf of the issuer, or the security certificate so states.

(14) "Securities intermediary" means:

(i) a clearing corporation; or

(ii) a person, including a bank or broker, that in the ordinary course of its business maintains securities accounts for others and is acting in that capacity.

(15) "Security," except as otherwise provided in Section 8–103, means an obligation of an issuer or a share, participation, or other interest in an issuer or in property or an enterprise of an issuer:

(i) which is represented by a security certificate in bearer or registered form, or the transfer of which may be registered upon books maintained for that purpose by or on behalf of the issuer;

(ii) which is one of a class or series or by its terms is divisible into a class or series of shares, participations, interests, or obligations; and

(iii) which:

(A) is, or is of a type, dealt in or traded on securities exchanges or securities markets; or

(B) is a medium for investment and by its terms expressly provides that it is a security governed by this Article.

(16) "Security certificate" means a certificate representing a security.

(17) "Security entitlement" means the rights and property interest of an entitlement holder with respect to a financial asset specified in Part 5.

(18) "Uncertificated security" means a security that is not represented by a certificate.

(b) Other definitions applying to this Article and the sections in which they appear are:

Appropriate person	Section 8–107
Control	Section 8–106
Delivery	Section 8–301
Investment company security	Section 8–103
Issuer	Section 8–201
Overissue	Section 8–210
Protected purchaser	Section 8–303
Securities account	Section 8–501

(c) In addition, Article 1 contains general definitions and principles of construction and interpretation applicable throughout this Article.

(d) The characterization of a person, business, or transaction for purposes of this Article does not determine the characterization of the person, business, or transaction for purposes of any other law, regulation, or rule.

§ 8–103. Rules for Determining Whether Certain Obligations and Interests Are Securities or Financial Assets.

(a) A share or similar equity interest issued by a corporation, business trust, joint stock company, or similar entity is a security.

(b) An "investment company security" is a security. "Investment company security" means a share or similar equity interest issued by an entity that is registered as an investment company under the federal investment company laws, an interest in a unit investment trust that is so registered, or a face-amount certificate issued by a face-amount certificate company that is so registered. Investment company security does not include an insurance policy or endowment policy or annuity contract issued by an insurance company.

(c) An interest in a partnership or limited liability company is not a security unless it is dealt in or traded on securities exchanges or in securities markets, its terms expressly provide that it is a security governed by this Article, or it is an investment company security. However, an interest in a partnership or limited liability company is a financial asset if it is held in a securities account.

(d) A writing that is a security certificate is governed by this Article and not by Article 3, even though it also meets the requirements of that Article. However, a negotiable instrument governed by Article 3 is a financial asset if it is held in a securities account.

(e) An option or similar obligation issued by a clearing corporation to its participants is not a security, but is a financial asset.

(f) A commodity contract, as defined in Section 9–102(a)(15), is not a security or a financial asset.

As amended in 1999.

§ 8–104. Acquisition of Security or Financial Asset or Interest Therein.

(a) A person acquires a security or an interest therein, under this Article, if:

(1) the person is a purchaser to whom a security is delivered pursuant to Section 8–301; or

(2) the person acquires a security entitlement to the security pursuant to Section 8–501.

(b) A person acquires a financial asset, other than a security, or an interest therein, under this Article, if the person acquires a security entitlement to the financial asset.

(c) A person who acquires a security entitlement to a security or other financial asset has the rights specified in Part 5, but is a purchaser of any security, security entitlement, or other financial asset held by the securities intermediary only to the extent provided in Section 8–503.

(d) Unless the context shows that a different meaning is intended, a person who is required by other law, regulation, rule, or agreement to transfer, deliver, present, surrender, exchange, or otherwise put in the possession of another person a security or financial asset satisfies that requirement by causing the other person to acquire an interest in the security or financial asset pursuant to subsection (a) or (b).

§ 8–105. Notice of Adverse Claim.

(a) A person has notice of an adverse claim if:

(1) the person knows of the adverse claim;

(2) the person is aware of facts sufficient to indicate that there is a significant probability that the adverse claim exists and deliberately avoids information that would establish the existence of the adverse claim; or

(3) the person has a duty, imposed by statute or regulation, to investigate whether an adverse claim exists, and the investigation so required would establish the existence of the adverse claim.

(b) Having knowledge that a financial asset or interest therein is or has been transferred by a representative imposes no duty of inquiry into the rightfulness of a transaction and is not notice of an adverse claim. However, a person who knows that a representative has transferred a financial asset or interest therein in a transaction that is, or whose proceeds are being used, for the individual benefit of the representative or otherwise in breach of duty has notice of an adverse claim.

(c) An act or event that creates a right to immediate performance of the principal obligation represented by a security certificate or sets a date on or after which the certificate is to be presented or surrendered for redemption or exchange does not itself constitute notice of an adverse claim except in the case of a transfer more than:

(1) one year after a date set for presentment or surrender for redemption or exchange; or

(2) six months after a date set for payment of money against presentation or surrender of the certificate, if money was available for payment on that date.

(d) A purchaser of a certificated security has notice of an adverse claim if the security certificate:

(1) whether in bearer or registered form, has been indorsed "for collection" or "for surrender" or for some other purpose not involving transfer; or

(2) is in bearer form and has on it an unambiguous statement that it is the property of a person other than the transferor, but the mere writing of a name on the certificate is not such a statement.

(e) Filing of a financing statement under Article 9 is not notice of an adverse claim to a financial asset.

§ 8–106. Control.

(a) A purchaser has "control" of a certificated security in bearer form if the certificated security is delivered to the purchaser.

(b) A purchaser has "control" of a certificated security in registered form if the certificated security is delivered to the purchaser, and:

(1) the certificate is indorsed to the purchaser or in blank by an effective indorsement; or

(2) the certificate is registered in the name of the purchaser, upon original issue or registration of transfer by the issuer.

(c) A purchaser has "control" of an uncertificated security if:

(1) the uncertificated security is delivered to the purchaser; or

(2) the issuer has agreed that it will comply with instructions originated by the purchaser without further consent by the registered owner.

(d) A purchaser has "control" of a security entitlement if:

(1) the purchaser becomes the entitlement holder;

(2) the securities intermediary has agreed that it will comply with entitlement orders originated by the purchaser without further consent by the entitlement holder; or

(3) another person has control of the security entitlement on behalf of the purchaser or, having previously acquired control of the security entitlement, acknowledges that it has control on behalf of the purchaser.

(e) If an interest in a security entitlement is granted by the entitlement holder to the entitlement holder's own securities intermediary, the securities intermediary has control.

(f) A purchaser who has satisfied the requirements of subsection (c) or (d) has control, even if the registered owner in the case of subsection (c) or the entitlement holder in the case of subsection (d) retains the right to make substitutions for the uncertificated security or security entitlement, to originate instructions or entitlement orders to the issuer or securities intermediary, or otherwise to deal with the uncertificated security or security entitlement.

(g) An issuer or a securities intermediary may not enter into an agreement of the kind described in subsection (c)(2) or (d)(2) without the consent of the registered owner or entitlement holder, but an issuer or a securities intermediary is not required to enter into such an agreement even though the registered owner or entitlement holder so directs. An issuer or securities intermediary that has entered into such an agreement is not required to confirm the existence of the agreement to another party unless requested to do so by the registered owner or entitlement holder.

As amended in 1999.

§ 8–107. Whether Indorsement, Instruction, or Entitlement Order Is Effective.

(a) "Appropriate person" means:

(1) with respect to an indorsement, the person specified by a security certificate or by an effective special indorsement to be entitled to the security;

(2) with respect to an instruction, the registered owner of an uncertificated security;

(3) with respect to an entitlement order, the entitlement holder;

(4) if the person designated in paragraph (1), (2), or (3) is deceased, the designated person's successor taking under other law or the designated person's personal representative acting for the estate of the decedent; or

(5) if the person designated in paragraph (1), (2), or (3) lacks capacity, the designated person's guardian, conservator, or other similar representative who has power under other law to transfer the security or financial asset.

(b) An indorsement, instruction, or entitlement order is effective if:

(1) it is made by the appropriate person;

(2) it is made by a person who has power under the law of agency to transfer the security or financial asset on behalf of the appropriate person, including, in the case of an instruction or entitlement order, a person who has control under Section 8–106(c)(2) or (d)(2); or

(3) the appropriate person has ratified it or is otherwise precluded from asserting its ineffectiveness.

(c) An indorsement, instruction, or entitlement order made by a representative is effective even if:

(1) the representative has failed to comply with a controlling instrument or with the law of the State having jurisdiction of the representative relationship, including any law requiring the representative to obtain court approval of the transaction; or

(2) the representative's action in making the indorsement, instruction, or entitlement order or using the proceeds of the transaction is otherwise a breach of duty.

(d) If a security is registered in the name of or specially indorsed to a person described as a representative, or if a securities account is maintained in the name of a person described as a representative, an indorsement, instruction, or entitlement order made by the person is effective even though the person is no longer serving in the described capacity.

(e) Effectiveness of an indorsement, instruction, or entitlement order is determined as of the date the indorsement, instruction, or entitlement order is made, and an indorsement, instruction, or entitlement order does not become ineffective by reason of any later change of circumstances.

§ 8–108. Warranties in Direct Holding.

(a) A person who transfers a certificated security to a purchaser for value warrants to the purchaser, and an indorser, if the transfer is by indorsement, warrants to any subsequent purchaser, that:

(1) the certificate is genuine and has not been materially altered;

(2) the transferor or indorser does not know of any fact that might impair the validity of the security;

(3) there is no adverse claim to the security;

(4) the transfer does not violate any restriction on transfer;

(5) if the transfer is by indorsement, the indorsement is made by an appropriate person, or if the indorsement is by an agent, the agent has actual authority to act on behalf of the appropriate person; and

(6) the transfer is otherwise effective and rightful.

(b) A person who originates an instruction for registration of transfer of an uncertificated security to a purchaser for value warrants to the purchaser that:

(1) the instruction is made by an appropriate person, or if the instruction is by an agent, the agent has actual authority to act on behalf of the appropriate person;

(2) the security is valid;

(3) there is no adverse claim to the security; and

(4) at the time the instruction is presented to the issuer:

(i) the purchaser will be entitled to the registration of transfer;

(ii) the transfer will be registered by the issuer free from all liens, security interests, restrictions, and claims other than those specified in the instruction;

(iii) the transfer will not violate any restriction on transfer; and

(iv) the requested transfer will otherwise be effective and rightful.

(c) A person who transfers an uncertificated security to a purchaser for value and does not originate an instruction in connection with the transfer warrants that:

(1) the uncertificated security is valid;

(2) there is no adverse claim to the security;

(3) the transfer does not violate any restriction on transfer; and

(4) the transfer is otherwise effective and rightful.

(d) A person who indorses a security certificate warrants to the issuer that:

(1) there is no adverse claim to the security; and

(2) the indorsement is effective.

(e) A person who originates an instruction for registration of transfer of an uncertificated security warrants to the issuer that:

(1) the instruction is effective; and

(2) at the time the instruction is presented to the issuer the purchaser will be entitled to the registration of transfer.

(f) A person who presents a certificated security for registration of transfer or for payment or exchange warrants to the issuer that the person is entitled to the registration, payment, or exchange, but a purchaser for value and without notice of adverse claims to whom transfer is registered warrants only that the person has no knowledge of any unauthorized signature in a necessary indorsement.

(g) If a person acts as agent of another in delivering a certificated security to a purchaser, the identity of the principal was known to the person to whom the certificate was delivered, and the certificate delivered by the agent was received by the agent from the principal or received by the agent from another person at the direction of the principal, the person delivering the security certificate warrants only that the delivering person has authority to act for the principal and does not know of any adverse claim to the certificated security.

(h) A secured party who redelivers a security certificate received, or after payment and on order of the debtor delivers the security certificate to another person, makes only the warranties of an agent under subsection (g).

(i) Except as otherwise provided in subsection (g), a broker acting for a customer makes to the issuer and a purchaser the warranties provided in subsections (a) through (f). A broker that delivers a security certificate to its customer, or causes its customer to be registered as the owner of an uncertificated security, makes to the customer the warranties provided in subsection (a) or (b), and has the rights and privileges of a purchaser under this section. The warranties of and in favor of the broker acting as an agent are in addition to applicable warranties given by and in favor of the customer.

§ 8–109. Warranties in Indirect Holding.

(a) A person who originates an entitlement order to a securities intermediary warrants to the securities intermediary that:

(1) the entitlement order is made by an appropriate person, or if the entitlement order is by an agent, the agent has actual authority to act on behalf of the appropriate person; and

(2) there is no adverse claim to the security entitlement.

(b) A person who delivers a security certificate to a securities intermediary for credit to a securities account or originates an instruction with respect to an uncertificated security directing that the uncertificated security be credited to a securities account makes to the securities intermediary the warranties specified in Section 8–108(a) or (b).

(c) If a securities intermediary delivers a security certificate to its entitlement holder or causes its entitlement holder to be registered as the owner of an uncertificated security, the securities intermediary makes to the entitlement holder the warranties specified in Section 8–108(a) or (b).

§ 8–110. Applicability; Choice of Law.

(a) The local law of the issuer's jurisdiction, as specified in subsection (d), governs:

(1) the validity of a security;

(2) the rights and duties of the issuer with respect to registration of transfer;

(3) the effectiveness of registration of transfer by the issuer;

(4) whether the issuer owes any duties to an adverse claimant to a security; and

(5) whether an adverse claim can be asserted against a person to whom transfer of a certificated or uncertificated security is registered or a person who obtains control of an uncertificated security.

(b) The local law of the securities intermediary's jurisdiction, as specified in subsection (e), governs:

(1) acquisition of a security entitlement from the securities intermediary;

(2) the rights and duties of the securities intermediary and entitlement holder arising out of a security entitlement;

(3) whether the securities intermediary owes any duties to an adverse claimant to a security entitlement; and

(4) whether an adverse claim can be asserted against a person who acquires a security entitlement from the securities intermediary or a person who purchases a security entitlement or interest therein from an entitlement holder.

(c) The local law of the jurisdiction in which a security certificate is located at the time of delivery governs whether an adverse claim can be asserted against a person to whom the security certificate is delivered.

(d) "Issuer's jurisdiction" means the jurisdiction under which the issuer of the security is organized or, if permitted by the law of that jurisdiction, the law of another jurisdiction specified by the issuer. An issuer organized under the law of this State may specify the law of another jurisdiction as the law governing the matters specified in subsection (a)(2) through (5).

(e) The following rules determine a "securities intermediary's jurisdiction" for purposes of this section:

(1) If an agreement between the securities intermediary and its entitlement holder specifies that it is governed by the law of a particular jurisdiction, that jurisdiction is the securities intermediary's jurisdiction.

(2) If an agreement between the securities intermediary and its entitlement holder does not specify the governing law as provided in paragraph (1), but expressly specifies that the securities account is maintained at an office in a particular jurisdiction, that jurisdiction is the securities intermediary's jurisdiction.

(3) If neither paragraph (1) nor paragraph (2) applies and an agreement between the securities intermediary and its entitlement holder governing the securities account expressly provides that the securities account is maintained at an office in a particular jurisdiction, that jurisdiction is the securities intermediary's jurisdiction.

(4) If none of the preceding paragraph applies, the securities intermediary's jurisdiction is the jurisdiction in which the office identified in an account statement as the office serving the entitlement holder's account is located.

(5) If none of the preceding paragraphs applies, the securities intermediary's jurisdiction is the jurisdiction in which the chief executive office of the securities intermediary is located.

(f) A securities intermediary's jurisdiction is not determined by the physical location of certificates representing financial assets, or by the jurisdiction in which is organized the issuer of the financial asset with respect to which an entitlement holder has a security entitlement, or by the location of facilities for data processing or other record keeping concerning the account.

As amended in 1999.

§ 8–111. Clearing Corporation Rules.

A rule adopted by a clearing corporation governing rights and obligations among the clearing corporation and its participants in the clearing corporation is effective even if the rule conflicts with this [Act] and affects another party who does not consent to the rule.

§ 8–112. Creditor's Legal Process.

(a) The interest of a debtor in a certificated security may be reached by a creditor only by actual seizure of the security certificate by the officer making the attachment or levy, except as otherwise provided in subsection (d). However, a certificated security for which the certificate has been surrendered to the issuer may be reached by a creditor by legal process upon the issuer.

(b) The interest of a debtor in an uncertificated security may be reached by a creditor only by legal process upon the issuer at its chief executive office in the United States, except as otherwise provided in subsection (d).

(c) The interest of a debtor in a security entitlement may be reached by a creditor only by legal process upon the securities intermediary with whom the debtor's securities account is maintained, except as otherwise provided in subsection (d).

(d) The interest of a debtor in a certificated security for which the certificate is in the possession of a secured party, or in an uncertificated security registered in the name of a secured party, or a security entitlement maintained in the name of a secured party, may be reached by a creditor by legal process upon the secured party.

(e) A creditor whose debtor is the owner of a certificated security, uncertificated security, or security entitlement is entitled to aid from a court of competent jurisdiction, by injunction or otherwise, in reaching the certificated security, uncertificated security, or security entitlement or in satisfying the claim by means allowed at law or in equity in regard to property that cannot readily be reached by other legal process.

§ 8–113. Statute of Frauds Inapplicable.

A contract or modification of a contract for the sale or purchase of a security is enforceable whether or not there is a writing signed or record authenticated by a party against whom enforcement is sought, even if the contract or modification is not capable of performance within one year of its making.

§ 8–114. Evidentiary Rules Concerning Certificated Securities.

The following rules apply in an action on a certificated security against the issuer:

(1) Unless specifically denied in the pleadings, each signature on a security certificate or in a necessary indorsement is admitted.

(2) If the effectiveness of a signature is put in issue, the burden of establishing effectiveness is on the party claiming under the signature, but the signature is presumed to be genuine or authorized.

(3) If signatures on a security certificate are admitted or established, production of the certificate entitles a holder to recover on it unless the defendant establishes a defense or a defect going to the validity of the security.

(4) If it is shown that a defense or defect exists, the plaintiff has the burden of establishing that the plaintiff or some person under whom the plaintiff claims is a person against whom the defense or defect cannot be asserted.

§ 8–115. Securities Intermediary and Others Not Liable to Adverse Claimant.

A securities intermediary that has transferred a financial asset pursuant to an effective entitlement order, or a broker or other agent or bailee that has dealt with a financial asset at the direction of its customer or principal, is not liable to a person having an adverse claim to the financial asset, unless the securities intermediary, or broker or other agent or bailee:

(1) took the action after it had been served with an injunction, restraining order, or other legal process enjoining it from doing so, issued by a court of competent jurisdiction, and had a reasonable opportunity to act on the injunction, restraining order, or other legal process; or

(2) acted in collusion with the wrongdoer in violating the rights of the adverse claimant; or

(3) in the case of a security certificate that has been stolen, acted with notice of the adverse claim.

§ 8–116. Securities Intermediary as Purchaser for Value.

A securities intermediary that receives a financial asset and establishes a security entitlement to the financial asset in favor of an entitlement holder is a purchaser for value of the financial asset. A securities intermediary that acquires a security entitlement to a financial asset from another securities intermediary acquires the security entitlement for value if the securities intermediary acquiring the security entitlement establishes a security entitlement to the financial asset in favor of an entitlement holder.

Part 2 Issue and Issuer

§ 8–201. Issuer.

(a) With respect to an obligation on or a defense to a security, an "issuer" includes a person that:

(1) places or authorizes the placing of its name on a security certificate, other than as authenticating trustee, registrar, transfer agent, or the like, to evidence a share, participation, or other interest in its property or in an enterprise, or to evidence its duty to perform an obligation represented by the certificate;

(2) creates a share, participation, or other interest in its property or in an enterprise, or undertakes an obligation, that is an uncertificated security;

(3) directly or indirectly creates a fractional interest in its rights or property, if the fractional interest is represented by a security certificate; or

(4) becomes responsible for, or in place of, another person described as an issuer in this section.

(b) With respect to an obligation on or defense to a security, a guarantor is an issuer to the extent of its guaranty, whether or not its obligation is noted on a security certificate.

(c) With respect to a registration of a transfer, issuer means a person on whose behalf transfer books are maintained.

§ 8–202. Issuer's Responsibility and Defenses; Notice of Defect or Defense.

(a) Even against a purchaser for value and without notice, the terms of a certificated security include terms stated on the certificate and terms made part of the security by reference on the certificate to another instrument, indenture, or document or to a constitution, statute, ordinance, rule, regulation, order, or the like, to the extent the terms referred to do not conflict with terms stated on the certificate. A reference under this subsection does not of itself charge a purchaser for value with notice of a defect going to the validity of the security, even if the certificate expressly states that a person accepting it admits notice. The terms of an uncertificated security include those stated in any instrument, indenture, or document or in a constitution, statute, ordinance, rule, regulation, order, or the like, pursuant to which the security is issued.

(b) The following rules apply if an issuer asserts that a security is not valid:

(1) A security other than one issued by a government or governmental subdivision, agency, or instrumentality, even though issued with a defect going to its validity, is valid in the hands of a purchaser for value and without notice of the particular defect unless the defect involves a violation of a constitutional provision. In that case, the security is valid in the hands of a purchaser for value and without notice of the defect, other than one who takes by original issue.

(2) Paragraph (1) applies to an issuer that is a government or governmental subdivision, agency, or instrumentality only if there has been substantial compliance with the legal requirements governing the issue or the issuer has received a substantial consideration for the issue as a whole or for the particular security and a stated purpose of the issue is one for which the issuer has power to borrow money or issue the security.

(c) Except as otherwise provided in Section 8–205, lack of genuineness of a certificated security is a complete defense, even against a purchaser for value and without notice.

(d) All other defenses of the issuer of a security, including nondelivery and conditional delivery of a certificated security, are ineffective against a purchaser for value who has taken the certificated security without notice of the particular defense.

(e) This section does not affect the right of a party to cancel a contract for a security "when, as and if issued" or "when distributed" in the event of a material change in the character of the security that is the subject of the contract or in the plan or arrangement pursuant to which the security is to be issued or distributed.

(f) If a security is held by a securities intermediary against whom an entitlement holder has a security entitlement with respect to the security, the issuer may not assert any defense that the issuer could not assert if the entitlement holder held the security directly.

§ 8–203. Staleness as Notice of Defect or Defense.

After an act or event, other than a call that has been revoked, creating a right to immediate performance of the principal obligation represented by a certificated security or setting a date on or after which the security is to be presented or surrendered for redemption or exchange, a purchaser is charged with notice of any defect in its issue or defense of the issuer, if the act or event:

(1) requires the payment of money, the delivery of a certificated security, the registration of transfer of an uncertificated security, or any of them on presentation or surrender of the security certificate, the money or security is available on the date set for payment or exchange, and the purchaser takes the security more than one year after that date; or

(2) is not covered by paragraph (1) and the purchaser takes the security more than two years after the date set for surrender or presentation or the date on which performance became due.

§ 8–204. Effect of Issuer's Restriction on Transfer.

A restriction on transfer of a security imposed by the issuer, even if otherwise lawful, is ineffective against a person without knowledge of the restriction unless:

(1) the security is certificated and the restriction is noted conspicuously on the security certificate; or

(2) the security is uncertificated and the registered owner has been notified of the restriction.

§ 8–205. Effect of Unauthorized Signature on Security Certificate.

An unauthorized signature placed on a security certificate before or in the course of issue is ineffective, but the signature is effective in favor of a purchaser for value of the certificated security if the purchaser is without notice of the lack of authority and the signing has been done by:

(1) an authenticating trustee, registrar, transfer agent, or other person entrusted by the issuer with the signing of the security certificate or of similar security certificates, or the immediate preparation for signing of any of them; or

(2) an employee of the issuer, or of any of the persons listed in paragraph (1), entrusted with responsible handling of the security certificate.

§ 8–206. Completion of Alteration of Security Certificate.

(a) If a security certificate contains the signatures necessary to its issue or transfer but is incomplete in any other respect:

(1) any person may complete it by filling in the blanks as authorized; and

(2) even if the blanks are incorrectly filled in, the security certificate as completed is enforceable by a purchaser who took it for value and without notice of the incorrectness.

(b) A complete security certificate that has been improperly altered, even if fraudulently, remains enforceable, but only according to its original terms.

§ 8–207. Rights and Duties of Issuer with Respect to Registered Owners.

(a) Before due presentment for registration of transfer of a certificated security in registered form or of an instruction requesting registration of transfer of an uncertificated security, the issuer or indenture trustee may treat the registered owner as the person exclusively entitled to vote, receive notifications, and otherwise exercise all the rights and powers of an owner.

(b) This Article does not affect the liability of the registered owner of a security for a call, assessment, or the like.

§ 8–208. Effect of Signature of Authenticating Trustee, Registrar, or Transfer Agent.

(a) A person signing a security certificate as authenticating trustee, registrar, transfer agent, or the like, warrants to a purchaser for value of the certificated security, if the purchaser is without notice of a particular defect, that:

(1) the certificate is genuine;

(2) the person's own participation in the issue of the security is within the person's capacity and within the scope of the authority received by the person from the issuer; and

(3) the person has reasonable grounds to believe that the certificated security is in the form and within the amount the issuer is authorized to issue.

(b) Unless otherwise agreed, a person signing under subsection (a) does not assume responsibility for the validity of the security in other respects.

§ 8–209. Issuer's Lien.

A lien in favor of an issuer upon a certificated security is valid against a purchaser only if the right of the issuer to the lien is noted conspicuously on the security certificate.

§ 8–210. Overissue.

(a) In this section, "overissue" means the issue of securities in excess of the amount the issuer has corporate power to issue, but an overissue does not occur if appropriate action has cured the overissue.

(b) Except as otherwise provided in subsections (c) and (d), the provisions of this Article which validate a security or compel its issue or reissue do not apply to the extent that validation, issue, or reissue would result in overissue.

(c) If an identical security not constituting an overissue is reasonably available for purchase, a person entitled to issue or validation may compel the issuer to purchase the security and deliver it if certificated or register its transfer if uncertificated, against surrender of any security certificate the person holds.

(d) If a security is not reasonably available for purchase, a person entitled to issue or validation may recover from the issuer the price the person or the last purchaser for value paid for it with interest from the date of the person's demand.

Part 3 Transfer of Certificated and Uncertificated Securities

§ 8–301. Delivery.

(a) Delivery of a certificated security to a purchaser occurs when:

(1) the purchaser acquires possession of the security certificate;

(2) another person, other than a securities intermediary, either acquires possession of the security certificate on behalf of the purchaser or, having previously acquired possession of the certificate, acknowledges that it holds for the purchaser; or

(3) a securities intermediary acting on behalf of the purchaser acquires possession of the security certificate, only if the certificate is in registered form and is (i) registered in the name of the purchaser, (ii) payable to the order of the purchaser, or (iii) specially indorsed to the purchaser by an effective indorsement and has not been indorsed to the securities intermediary or in blank.

(b) Delivery of an uncertificated security to a purchaser occurs when:

(1) the issuer registers the purchaser as the registered owner, upon original issue or registration of transfer; or

(2) another person, other than a securities intermediary, either becomes the registered owner of the uncertificated security on behalf of the purchaser or, having previously become the registered owner, acknowledges that it holds for the purchaser.

As amended in 1999.

§ 8–302. Rights of Purchaser.

(a) Except as otherwise provided in subsections (b) and (c), upon delivery of a certificated or uncertificated security to a purchaser, the purchaser acquires all rights in the security that the transferor had or had power to transfer.

(b) A purchaser of a limited interest acquires rights only to the extent of the interest purchased.

(c) A purchaser of a certificated security who as a previous holder had notice of an adverse claim does not improve its position by taking from a protected purchaser.

As amended in 1999.

§ 8–303. Protected Purchaser.

(a) "Protected purchaser" means a purchaser of a certificated or uncertificated security, or of an interest therein, who:

(1) gives value;

(2) does not have notice of any adverse claim to the security; and

(3) obtains control of the certificated or uncertificated security.

(b) In addition to acquiring the rights of a purchaser, a protected purchaser also acquires its interest in the security free of any adverse claim.

§ 8–304. Indorsement.

(a) An indorsement may be in blank or special. An indorsement in blank includes an indorsement to bearer. A special indorsement specifies to whom a security is to be transferred or who has power to transfer it. A holder may convert a blank indorsement to a special indorsement.

(b) An indorsement purporting to be only of part of a security certificate representing units intended by the issuer to be separately transferable is effective to the extent of the indorsement.

(c) An indorsement, whether special or in blank, does not constitute a transfer until delivery of the certificate on which it appears or, if the indorsement is on a separate document, until delivery of both the document and the certificate.

(d) If a security certificate in registered form has been delivered to a purchaser without a necessary indorsement, the purchaser may become a protected purchaser only when the indorsement is supplied. However, against a transferor, a transfer is complete upon delivery and the purchaser has a specifically enforceable right to have any necessary indorsement supplied.

(e) An indorsement of a security certificate in bearer form may give notice of an adverse claim to the certificate, but it does not otherwise affect a right to registration that the holder possesses.

(f) Unless otherwise agreed, a person making an indorsement assumes only the obligations provided in Section 8–108 and not an obligation that the security will be honored by the issuer.

§ 8–305. Instruction.

(a) If an instruction has been originated by an appropriate person but is incomplete in any other respect, any person may complete it as authorized and the issuer may rely on it as completed, even though it has been completed incorrectly.

(b) Unless otherwise agreed, a person initiating an instruction assumes only the obligations imposed by Section 8–108 and not an obligation that the security will be honored by the issuer.

§ 8–306. Effect of Guaranteeing Signature, Indorsement, or Instruction.

(a) A person who guarantees a signature of an indorser of a security certificate warrants that at the time of signing:

(1) the signature was genuine;

(2) the signer was an appropriate person to indorse, or if the signature is by an agent, the agent had actual authority to act on behalf of the appropriate person; and

(3) the signer had legal capacity to sign.

(b) A person who guarantees a signature of the originator of an instruction warrants that at the time of signing:

(1) the signature was genuine;

(2) the signer was an appropriate person to originate the instruction, or if the signature is by an agent, the agent had actual authority to act on behalf of the appropriate person, if the person specified in the instruction as the registered owner was, in fact, the registered owner, as to which fact the signature guarantor does not make a warranty; and

(3) the signer had legal capacity to sign.

(c) A person who specially guarantees the signature of an originator of an instruction makes the warranties of a signature guarantor under subsection (b) and also warrants that at the time the instruction is presented to the issuer:

(1) the person specified in the instruction as the registered owner of the uncertificated security will be the registered owner; and

(2) the transfer of the uncertificated security requested in the instruction will be registered by the issuer free from all liens, security interests, restrictions, and claims other than those specified in the instruction.

(d) A guarantor under subsections (a) and (b) or a special guarantor under subsection (c) does not otherwise warrant the rightfulness of the transfer.

(e) A person who guarantees an indorsement of a security certificate makes the warranties of a signature guarantor under subsection (a) and also warrants the rightfulness of the transfer in all respects.

(f) A person who guarantees an instruction requesting the transfer of an uncertificated security makes the warranties of a special signature guarantor under subsection (c) and also warrants the rightfulness of the transfer in all respects.

(g) An issuer may not require a special guaranty of signature, a guaranty of indorsement, or a guaranty of instruction as a condition to registration of transfer.

(h) The warranties under this section are made to a person taking or dealing with the security in reliance on the guaranty, and the guarantor is liable to the person for loss resulting from their breach. An indorser or originator of an instruction whose signature, indorsement, or instruction has been guaranteed is liable to a guarantor for any loss suffered by the guarantor as a result of breach of the warranties of the guarantor.

§ 8–307. Purchaser's Right to Requisites for Registration of Transfer.

Unless otherwise agreed, the transferor of a security on due demand shall supply the purchaser with proof of authority to transfer or with any other requisite necessary to obtain registration of the transfer of the security, but if the transfer is not for value, a transferor need not comply unless the purchaser pays the necessary expenses. If the transferor fails within a reasonable time to comply with the demand, the purchaser may reject or rescind the transfer.

Part 4 Registration

§ 8–401. Duty of Issuer to Register Transfer.

(a) If a certificated security in registered form is presented to an issuer with a request to register transfer or an instruction is presented to an issuer with a request to register transfer of an uncertificated security, the issuer shall register the transfer as requested if:

(1) under the terms of the security the person seeking registration of transfer is eligible to have the security registered in its name;

(2) the indorsement or instruction is made by the appropriate person or by an agent who has actual authority to act on behalf of the appropriate person;

(3) reasonable assurance is given that the indorsement or instruction is genuine and authorized (Section 8–402);

(4) any applicable law relating to the collection of taxes has been complied with;

(5) the transfer does not violate any restriction on transfer imposed by the issuer in accordance with Section 8–204;

(6) a demand that the issuer not register transfer has not become effective under Section 8–403, or the issuer has complied with Section 8–403(b) but no legal process or indemnity bond is obtained as provided in Section 8–403(d); and

(7) the transfer is in fact rightful or is to a protected purchaser.

(b) If an issuer is under a duty to register a transfer of a security, the issuer is liable to a person presenting a certificated security or an instruction for registration or to the person's principal for loss resulting from unreasonable delay in registration or failure or refusal to register the transfer.

§ 8–402. Assurance That Indorsement or Instruction Is Effective.

(a) An issuer may require the following assurance that each necessary indorsement or each instruction is genuine and authorized:

(1) in all cases, a guaranty of the signature of the person making an indorsement or originating an instruction including, in the case of an instruction, reasonable assurance of identity;

(2) if the indorsement is made or the instruction is originated by an agent, appropriate assurance of actual authority to sign;

(3) if the indorsement is made or the instruction is originated by a fiduciary pursuant to Section 8–107(a)(4) or (a)(5), appropriate evidence of appointment or incumbency;

(4) if there is more than one fiduciary, reasonable assurance that all who are required to sign have done so; and

(5) if the indorsement is made or the instruction is originated by a person not covered by another provision of this subsection, assurance appropriate to the case corresponding as nearly as may be to the provisions of this subsection.

(b) An issuer may elect to require reasonable assurance beyond that specified in this section.

(c) In this section:

(1) "Guaranty of the signature" means a guaranty signed by or on behalf of a person reasonably believed by the issuer to be responsible. An issuer may adopt standards with respect to responsibility if they are not manifestly unreasonable.

(2) "Appropriate evidence of appointment or incumbency" means:

(i) in the case of a fiduciary appointed or qualified by a court, a certificate issued by or under the direction or supervision of the court or an officer thereof and dated within 60 days before the date of presentation for transfer; or

(ii) in any other case, a copy of a document showing the appointment or a certificate issued by or on behalf of a person reasonably believed by an issuer to be responsible or, in the absence of that document or certificate, other evidence the issuer reasonably considers appropriate.

§ 8–403. Demand That Issuer Not Register Transfer.

(a) A person who is an appropriate person to make an indorsement or originate an instruction may demand that the issuer not register transfer of a security by communicating to the issuer a notification that identifies the registered owner and the issue of which the security is a part and provides an address for communications directed to the person making the demand. The demand is effective only if it is received by the issuer at a time and in a manner affording the issuer reasonable opportunity to act on it.

(b) If a certificated security in registered form is presented to an issuer with a request to register transfer or an instruction is presented to an issuer with a request to register transfer of an uncertificated security after a demand that the issuer not register transfer has become effective, the issuer shall promptly communicate to (i) the person who initiated the demand at the address provided in the demand and (ii) the person who presented the security for registration of transfer or initiated the instruction requesting registration of transfer a notification stating that:

(1) the certificated security has been presented for registration of transfer or the instruction for registra-

tion of transfer of the uncertificated security has been received;

(2) a demand that the issuer not register transfer had previously been received; and

(3) the issuer will withhold registration of transfer for a period of time stated in the notification in order to provide the person who initiated the demand an opportunity to obtain legal process or an indemnity bond.

(c) The period described in subsection (b)(3) may not exceed 30 days after the date of communication of the notification. A shorter period may be specified by the issuer if it is not manifestly unreasonable.

(d) An issuer is not liable to a person who initiated a demand that the issuer not register transfer for any loss the person suffers as a result of registration of a transfer pursuant to an effective indorsement or instruction if the person who initiated the demand does not, within the time stated in the issuer's communication, either:

(1) obtain an appropriate restraining order, injunction, or other process from a court of competent jurisdiction enjoining the issuer from registering the transfer; or

(2) file with the issuer an indemnity bond, sufficient in the issuer's judgment to protect the issuer and any transfer agent, registrar, or other agent of the issuer involved from any loss it or they may suffer by refusing to register the transfer.

(e) This section does not relieve an issuer from liability for registering transfer pursuant to an indorsement or instruction that was not effective.

§ 8–404. Wrongful Registration.

(a) Except as otherwise provided in Section 8–406, an issuer is liable for wrongful registration of transfer if the issuer has registered a transfer of a security to a person not entitled to it, and the transfer was registered:

(1) pursuant to an ineffective indorsement or instruction;

(2) after a demand that the issuer not register transfer became effective under Section 8–403(a) and the issuer did not comply with Section 8–403(b);

(3) after the issuer had been served with an injunction, restraining order, or other legal process enjoining it from registering the transfer, issued by a court of competent jurisdiction, and the issuer had a reasonable opportunity to act on the injunction, restraining order, or other legal process; or

(4) by an issuer acting in collusion with the wrongdoer.

(b) An issuer that is liable for wrongful registration of transfer under subsection (a) on demand shall provide the person entitled to the security with a like certificated or uncertificated security, and any payments or distributions that the person did not receive as a result of the wrongful registration. If an overissue would result, the issuer's liability to provide the person with a like security is governed by Section 8–210.

(c) Except as otherwise provided in subsection (a) or in a law relating to the collection of taxes, an issuer is not liable to an owner or other person suffering loss as a result of the registration of a transfer of a security if registration was made pursuant to an effective indorsement or instruction.

§ 8–405. Replacement of Lost, Destroyed, or Wrongfully Taken Security Certificate.

(a) If an owner of a certificated security, whether in registered or bearer form, claims that the certificate has been lost, destroyed, or wrongfully taken, the issuer shall issue a new certificate if the owner:

(1) so requests before the issuer has notice that the certificate has been acquired by a protected purchaser;

(2) files with the issuer a sufficient indemnity bond; and

(3) satisfies other reasonable requirements imposed by the issuer.

(b) If, after the issue of a new security certificate, a protected purchaser of the original certificate presents it for registration of transfer, the issuer shall register the transfer unless an overissue would result. In that case, the issuer's liability is governed by Section 8–210. In addition to any rights on the indemnity bond, an issuer may recover the new certificate from a person to whom it was issued or any person taking under that person, except a protected purchaser.

§ 8–406. Obligation to Notify Issuer of Lost, Destroyed, or Wrongfully Taken Security Certificate.

If a security certificate has been lost, apparently destroyed, or wrongfully taken, and the owner fails to notify the issuer of that fact within a reasonable time after the owner has notice of it and the issuer registers a transfer of the security before receiving notification, the owner may not assert against the issuer a claim for registering the transfer under Section 8–404 or a claim to a new security certificate under Section 8–405.

§ 8–407. Authenticating Trustee, Transfer Agent, and Registrar.

A person acting as authenticating trustee, transfer agent, registrar, or other agent for an issuer in the registration of a transfer of its securities, in the issue of new security certificates or uncertificated securities, or in the cancellation of surrendered security certificates has the same obligation to the holder or owner of a certificated or uncertificated security with regard to the particular functions performed as the issuer has in regard to those functions.

Part 5 Security Entitlements

§ 8–501. Securities Account; Acquisition of Security Entitlement from Securities Intermediary.

(a) "Securities account" means an account to which a financial asset is or may be credited in accordance with an agreement under which the person maintaining the account undertakes to treat the person for whom the account is maintained as entitled to exercise the rights that comprise the financial asset.

(b) Except as otherwise provided in subsections (d) and (e), a person acquires a security entitlement if a securities intermediary:

(1) indicates by book entry that a financial asset has been credited to the person's securities account;

(2) receives a financial asset from the person or acquires a financial asset for the person and, in either case, accepts it for credit to the person's securities account; or

(3) becomes obligated under other law, regulation, or rule to credit a financial asset to the person's securities account.

(c) If a condition of subsection (b) has been met, a person has a security entitlement even though the securities intermediary does not itself hold the financial asset.

(d) If a securities intermediary holds a financial asset for another person, and the financial asset is registered in the name of, payable to the order of, or specially indorsed to the other person, and has not been indorsed to the securities intermediary or in blank, the other person is treated as holding the financial asset directly rather than as having a security entitlement with respect to the financial asset.

(e) Issuance of a security is not establishment of a security entitlement.

§ 8–502. Assertion of Adverse Claim against Entitlement Holder.

An action based on an adverse claim to a financial asset, whether framed in conversion, replevin, constructive trust, equitable lien, or other theory, may not be asserted against a person who acquires a security entitlement under Section 8–501 for value and without notice of the adverse claim.

§ 8–503. Property Interest of Entitlement Holder in Financial Asset Held by Securities Intermediary.

(a) To the extent necessary for a securities intermediary to satisfy all security entitlements with respect to a particular financial asset, all interests in that financial asset held by the securities intermediary are held by the securities intermediary for the entitlement holders, are not property of the securities intermediary, and are not subject to claims of creditors of the securities intermediary, except as otherwise provided in Section 8–511.

(b) An entitlement holder's property interest with respect to a particular financial asset under subsection (a) is a pro rata property interest in all interests in that financial asset held by the securities intermediary, without regard to the time the entitlement holder acquired the security entitlement or the time the securities intermediary acquired the interest in that financial asset.

(c) An entitlement holder's property interest with respect to a particular financial asset under subsection (a) may be enforced against the securities intermediary only by exercise of the entitlement holder's rights under Sections 8–505 through 8–508.

(d) An entitlement holder's property interest with respect to a particular financial asset under subsection (a) may be enforced against a purchaser of the financial asset or interest therein only if:

(1) insolvency proceedings have been initiated by or against the securities intermediary;

(2) the securities intermediary does not have sufficient interests in the financial asset to satisfy the security entitlements of all of its entitlement holders to that financial asset;

(3) the securities intermediary violated its obligations under Section 8–504 by transferring the financial asset or interest therein to the purchaser; and

(4) the purchaser is not protected under subsection (e).

The trustee or other liquidator, acting on behalf of all entitlement holders having security entitlements with respect to a particular financial asset, may recover the financial asset, or interest therein, from the purchaser. If the trustee or other liquidator elects not to pursue that right, an entitlement holder whose security entitlement remains unsatisfied has the right to recover its interest in the financial asset from the purchaser.

(e) An action based on the entitlement holder's property interest with respect to a particular financial asset under subsection (a), whether framed in conversion, replevin, constructive trust, equitable lien, or other theory, may not be asserted against any purchaser of a financial asset or interest therein who gives value, obtains control, and does not act in collusion with the securities intermediary in violating the securities intermediary's obligations under Section 8–504.

§ 8–504. Duty of Securities Intermediary to Maintain Financial Asset.

(a) A securities intermediary shall promptly obtain and thereafter maintain a financial asset in a quantity corresponding to the aggregate of all security entitlements it has established in favor of its entitlement holders with respect to that financial asset. The securities intermediary may maintain those financial assets directly or through one or more other securities intermediaries.

(b) Except to the extent otherwise agreed by its entitlement holder, a securities intermediary may not grant any security interests in a financial asset it is obligated to maintain pursuant to subsection (a).

(c) A securities intermediary satisfies the duty in subsection (a) if:

(1) the securities intermediary acts with respect to the duty as agreed upon by the entitlement holder and the securities intermediary; or

(2) in the absence of agreement, the securities intermediary exercises due care in accordance with rea-

sonable commercial standards to obtain and maintain the financial asset.

(d) This section does not apply to a clearing corporation that is itself the obligor of an option or similar obligation to which its entitlement holders have security entitlements.

§ 8–505. Duty of Securities Intermediary with Respect to Payments and Distributions.

(a) A securities intermediary shall take action to obtain a payment or distribution made by the issuer of a financial asset. A securities intermediary satisfies the duty if:

(1) the securities intermediary acts with respect to the duty as agreed upon by the entitlement holder and the securities intermediary; or

(2) in the absence of agreement, the securities intermediary exercises due care in accordance with reasonable commercial standards to attempt to obtain the payment or distribution.

(b) A securities intermediary is obligated to its entitlement holder for a payment or distribution made by the issuer of a financial asset if the payment or distribution is received by the securities intermediary.

§ 8–506. Duty of Securities Intermediary to Exercise Rights as Directed by Entitlement Holder.

A securities intermediary shall exercise rights with respect to a financial asset if directed to do so by an entitlement holder. A securities intermediary satisfies the duty if:

(1) the securities intermediary acts with respect to the duty as agreed upon by the entitlement holder and the securities intermediary; or

(2) in the absence of agreement, the securities intermediary either places the entitlement holder in a position to exercise the rights directly or exercises due care in accordance with reasonable commercial standards to follow the direction of the entitlement holder.

§ 8–507. Duty of Securities Intermediary to Comply with Entitlement Order.

(a) A securities intermediary shall comply with an entitlement order if the entitlement order is originated by the appropriate person, the securities intermediary has had reasonable opportunity to assure itself that the entitlement order is genuine and authorized, and the securities intermediary has had reasonable opportunity to comply with the entitlement order. A securities intermediary satisfies the duty if:

(1) the securities intermediary acts with respect to the duty as agreed upon by the entitlement holder and the securities intermediary; or

(2) in the absence of agreement, the securities intermediary exercises due care in accordance with reasonable commercial standards to comply with the entitlement order.

(b) If a securities intermediary transfers a financial asset pursuant to an ineffective entitlement order, the securities intermediary shall reestablish a security entitlement in favor of the person entitled to it, and pay or credit any payments or distributions that the person did not receive as a result of the wrongful transfer. If the securities intermediary does not reestablish a security entitlement, the securities intermediary is liable to the entitlement holder for damages.

§ 8–508. Duty of Securities Intermediary to Change Entitlement Holder's Position to Other Form of Security Holding.

A securities intermediary shall act at the direction of an entitlement holder to change a security entitlement into another available form of holding for which the entitlement holder is eligible, or to cause the financial asset to be transferred to a securities account of the entitlement holder with another securities intermediary. A securities intermediary satisfies the duty if:

(1) the securities intermediary acts as agreed upon by the entitlement holder and the securities intermediary; or

(2) in the absence of agreement, the securities intermediary exercises due care in accordance with reasonable commercial standards to follow the direction of the entitlement holder.

§ 8–509. Specification of Duties of Securities Intermediary by Other Statute or Regulation; Manner of Performance of Duties of Securities Intermediary and Exercise of Rights of Entitlement Holder.

(a) If the substance of a duty imposed upon a securities intermediary by Sections 8–504 through 8–508 is the subject of other statute, regulation, or rule, compliance with that statute, regulation, or rule satisfies the duty.

(b) To the extent that specific standards for the performance of the duties of a securities intermediary or the exercise of the rights of an entitlement holder are not specified by other statute, regulation, or rule or by agreement between the securities intermediary and entitlement holder, the securities intermediary shall perform its duties and the entitlement holder shall exercise its rights in a commercially reasonable manner.

(c) The obligation of a securities intermediary to perform the duties imposed by Sections 8–504 through 8–508 is subject to:

(1) rights of the securities intermediary arising out of a security interest under a security agreement with the entitlement holder or otherwise; and

(2) rights of the securities intermediary under other law, regulation, rule, or agreement to withhold performance of its duties as a result of unfulfilled obligations of the entitlement holder to the securities intermediary.

(d) Sections 8–504 through 8–508 do not require a securities intermediary to take any action that is prohibited by other statute, regulation, or rule.

§ 8–510. Rights of Purchaser of Security Entitlement from Entitlement Holder.

(a) An action based on an adverse claim to a financial asset or security entitlement, whether framed in conversion, replevin, constructive trust, equitable lien, or other theory, may not be asserted against a person who purchases a security entitlement, or an interest therein, from an entitlement holder if the purchaser gives value, does not have notice of the adverse claim, and obtains control.

(b) If an adverse claim could not have been asserted against an entitlement holder under Section 8–502, the adverse claim cannot be asserted against a person who purchases a security entitlement, or an interest therein, from the entitlement holder.

(c) In a case not covered by the priority rules in Article 9, a purchaser for value of a security entitlement, or an interest therein, who obtains control has priority over a purchaser of a security entitlement, or an interest therein, who does not obtain control. Except as otherwise provided in subsection (d), purchasers who have control rank according to priority in time of:

(1) the purchaser's becoming the person for whom the securities account, in which the security entitlement is carried, is maintained, if the purchaser obtained control under Section 8–106(d)(1);

(2) the securities intermediary's agreement to comply with the purchaser's entitlement orders with respect to security entitlements carried or to be carried in the securities account in which the security entitlement is carried, if the purchaser obtained control under Section 8–106(d)(2); or

(3) if the purchaser obtained control through another person under Section 8–106(d)(3), the time on which priority would be based under this subsection if the other person were the secured party.

(d) A securities intermediary as purchaser has priority over a conflicting purchaser who has control unless otherwise agreed by the securities intermediary.

As amended in 1999.

§ 8–511. Priority among Security Interests and Entitlement Holders.

(a) Except as otherwise provided in subsections (b) and (c), if a securities intermediary does not have sufficient interests in a particular financial asset to satisfy both its obligations to entitlement holders who have security entitlements to that financial asset and its obligation to a creditor of the securities intermediary who has a security interest in that financial asset, the claims of entitlement holders, other than the creditor, have priority over the claim of the creditor.

(b) A claim of a creditor of a securities intermediary who has a security interest in a financial asset held by a securities intermediary has priority over claims of the securities intermediary's entitlement holders who have security entitlements with respect to that financial asset if the creditor has control over the financial asset.

(c) If a clearing corporation does not have sufficient financial assets to satisfy both its obligations to entitlement holders who have security entitlements with respect to a financial asset and its obligation to a creditor of the clearing corporation who has a security interest in that financial asset, the claim of the creditor has priority over the claims of entitlement holders.

Part 6 Transition Provisions for Revised Article 8

§ 8–601. Effective Date.

This [Act] takes effect . . . .

§ 8–602. Repeals.

This [Act] repeals . . . .

§ 8–603. Savings Clause.

(a) This [Act] does not affect an action or proceeding commenced before this [Act] takes effect.

(b) If a security interest in a security is perfected at the date this [Act] takes effect, and the action by which the security interest was perfected would suffice to perfect a security interest under this [Act], no further action is required to continue perfection. If a security interest in a security is perfected at the date this [Act] takes effect but the action by which the security interest was perfected would not suffice to perfect a security interest under this [Act], the security interest remains perfected for a period of four months after the effective date and continues perfected thereafter if appropriate action to perfect under this [Act] is taken within that period. If a security interest is perfected at the date this [Act] takes effect and the security interest can be perfected by filing under this [Act], a financing statement signed by the secured party instead of the debtor may be filed within that period to continue perfection or thereafter to perfect.

Revised Article 9
SECURED TRANSACTIONS

Part 1 General Provisions

[Subpart 1. Short Title, Definitions, and General Concepts]

§ 9–101. Short Title.

This article may be cited as Uniform Commercial Code—Secured Transactions.

§ 9–102. Definitions and Index of Definitions.

(a) In this article:

(1) "Accession" means goods that are physically united with other goods in such a manner that the identity of the original goods is not lost.

(2) "Account", except as used in "account for", means a right to payment of a monetary obligation, whether or not earned by performance, (i) for property that has been or is to be sold, leased, licensed, assigned, or

otherwise disposed of, (ii) for services rendered or to be rendered, (iii) for a policy of insurance issued or to be issued, (iv) for a secondary obligation incurred or to be incurred, (v) for energy provided or to be provided, (vi) for the use or hire of a vessel under a charter or other contract, (vii) arising out of the use of a credit or charge card or information contained on or for use with the card, or (viii) as winnings in a lottery or other game of chance operated or sponsored by a State, governmental unit of a State, or person licensed or authorized to operate the game by a State or governmental unit of a State. The term includes health-care insurance receivables. The term does not include (i) rights to payment evidenced by chattel paper or an instrument, (ii) commercial tort claims, (iii) deposit accounts, (iv) investment property, (v) letter-of-credit rights or letters of credit, or (vi) rights to payment for money or funds advanced or sold, other than rights arising out of the use of a credit or charge card or information contained on or for use with the card.

(3) "Account debtor" means a person obligated on an account, chattel paper, or general intangible. The term does not include persons obligated to pay a negotiable instrument, even if the instrument constitutes part of chattel paper.

(4) "Accounting", except as used in "accounting for", means a record:

(A) authenticated by a secured party;

(B) indicating the aggregate unpaid secured obligations as of a date not more than 35 days earlier or 35 days later than the date of the record; and

(C) identifying the components of the obligations in reasonable detail.

(5) "Agricultural lien" means an interest, other than a security interest, in farm products:

(A) which secures payment or performance of an obligation for:

(i) goods or services furnished in connection with a debtor's farming operation; or

(ii) rent on real property leased by a debtor in connection with its farming operation;

(B) which is created by statute in favor of a person that:

(i) in the ordinary course of its business furnished goods or services to a debtor in connection with a debtor's farming operation; or

(ii) leased real property to a debtor in connection with the debtor's farming operation; and

(C) whose effectiveness does not depend on the person's possession of the personal property.

(6) "As-extracted collateral" means:

(A) oil, gas, or other minerals that are subject to a security interest that:

(i) is created by a debtor having an interest in the minerals before extraction; and

(ii) attaches to the minerals as extracted; or

(B) accounts arising out of the sale at the wellhead or minehead of oil, gas, or other minerals in which the debtor had an interest before extraction.

(7) "Authenticate" means:

(A) to sign; or

(B) to execute or otherwise adopt a symbol, or encrypt or similarly process a record in whole or in part, with the present intent of the authenticating person to identify the person and adopt or accept a record.

(8) "Bank" means an organization that is engaged in the business of banking. The term includes savings banks, savings and loan associations, credit unions, and trust companies.

(9) "Cash proceeds" means proceeds that are money, checks, deposit accounts, or the like.

(10) "Certificate of title" means a certificate of title with respect to which a statute provides for the security interest in question to be indicated on the certificate as a condition or result of the security interest's obtaining priority over the rights of a lien creditor with respect to the collateral.

(11) "Chattel paper" means a record or records that evidence both a monetary obligation and a security interest in specific goods, a security interest in specific goods and software used in the goods, a security interest in specific goods and license of software used in the goods, a lease of specific goods, or a lease of specific goods and license of software used in the goods. In this paragraph, "monetary obligation" means a monetary obligation secured by the goods or owed under a lease of the goods and includes a monetary obligation with respect to software used in the goods. The term does not include (i) charters or other contracts involving the use or hire of a vessel or (ii) records that evidence a right to payment arising out of the use of a credit or charge card or information contained on or for use with the card. If a transaction is evidenced by records that include an instrument or series of instruments, the group of records taken together constitutes chattel paper.

(12) "Collateral" means the property subject to a security interest or agricultural lien. The term includes:

(A) proceeds to which a security interest attaches;

(B) accounts, chattel paper, payment intangibles, and promissory notes that have been sold; and

(C) goods that are the subject of a consignment.

(13) "Commercial tort claim" means a claim arising in tort with respect to which:

(A) the claimant is an organization; or

(B) the claimant is an individual and the claim:

(i) arose in the course of the claimant's business or profession; and

(ii) does not include damages arising out of personal injury to or the death of an individual.

(14) "Commodity account" means an account maintained by a commodity intermediary in which a commodity contract is carried for a commodity customer.

(15) "Commodity contract" means a commodity futures contract, an option on a commodity futures contract, a commodity option, or another contract if the contract or option is:

(A) traded on or subject to the rules of a board of trade that has been designated as a contract market for such a contract pursuant to federal commodities laws; or

(B) traded on a foreign commodity board of trade, exchange, or market, and is carried on the books of a commodity intermediary for a commodity customer.

(16) "Commodity customer" means a person for which a commodity intermediary carries a commodity contract on its books.

(17) "Commodity intermediary" means a person that:

(A) is registered as a futures commission merchant under federal commodities law; or

(B) in the ordinary course of its business provides clearance or settlement services for a board of trade that has been designated as a contract market pursuant to federal commodities law.

(18) "Communicate" means:

(A) to send a written or other tangible record;

(B) to transmit a record by any means agreed upon by the persons sending and receiving the record; or

(C) in the case of transmission of a record to or by a filing office, to transmit a record by any means prescribed by filing-office rule.

(19) "Consignee" means a merchant to which goods are delivered in a consignment.

(20) "Consignment" means a transaction, regardless of its form, in which a person delivers goods to a merchant for the purpose of sale and:

(A) the merchant:

(i) deals in goods of that kind under a name other than the name of the person making delivery;

(ii) is not an auctioneer; and

(iii) is not generally known by its creditors to be substantially engaged in selling the goods of others;

(B) with respect to each delivery, the aggregate value of the goods is $1,000 or more at the time of delivery;

(C) the goods are not consumer goods immediately before delivery; and

(D) the transaction does not create a security interest that secures an obligation.

(21) "Consignor" means a person that delivers goods to a consignee in a consignment.

(22) "Consumer debtor" means a debtor in a consumer transaction.

(23) "Consumer goods" means goods that are used or bought for use primarily for personal, family, or household purposes.

(24) "Consumer-goods transaction" means a consumer transaction in which:

(A) an individual incurs an obligation primarily for personal, family, or household purposes; and

(B) a security interest in consumer goods secures the obligation.

(25) "Consumer obligor" means an obligor who is an individual and who incurred the obligation as part of a transaction entered into primarily for personal, family, or household purposes.

(26) "Consumer transaction" means a transaction in which (i) an individual incurs an obligation primarily for personal, family, or household purposes, (ii) a security interest secures the obligation, and (iii) the collateral is held or acquired primarily for personal, family, or household purposes. The term includes consumer-goods transactions.

(27) "Continuation statement" means an amendment of a financing statement which:

(A) identifies, by its file number, the initial financing statement to which it relates; and

(B) indicates that it is a continuation statement for, or that it is filed to continue the effectiveness of, the identified financing statement.

(28) "Debtor" means:

(A) a person having an interest, other than a security interest or other lien, in the collateral, whether or not the person is an obligor;

(B) a seller of accounts, chattel paper, payment intangibles, or promissory notes; or

(C) a consignee.

(29) "Deposit account" means a demand, time, savings, passbook, or similar account maintained with a bank. The term does not include investment property or accounts evidenced by an instrument.

(30) "Document" means a document of title or a receipt of the type described in Section 7–201(2).

(31) "Electronic chattel paper" means chattel paper evidenced by a record or records consisting of information stored in an electronic medium.

(32) "Encumbrance" means a right, other than an ownership interest, in real property. The term includes mortgages and other liens on real property.

(33) "Equipment" means goods other than inventory, farm products, or consumer goods.

(34) "Farm products" means goods, other than standing timber, with respect to which the debtor is engaged in a farming operation and which are:

(A) crops grown, growing, or to be grown, including:

(i) crops produced on trees, vines, and bushes; and

(ii) aquatic goods produced in aquacultural operations;

(B) livestock, born or unborn, including aquatic goods produced in aquacultural operations;

(C) supplies used or produced in a farming operation; or

(D) products of crops or livestock in their unmanufactured states.

(35) "Farming operation" means raising, cultivating, propagating, fattening, grazing, or any other farming, livestock, or aquacultural operation.

(36) "File number" means the number assigned to an initial financing statement pursuant to Section 9–519(a).

(37) "Filing office" means an office designated in Section 9–501 as the place to file a financing statement.

(38) "Filing-office rule" means a rule adopted pursuant to Section 9–526.

(39) "Financing statement" means a record or records composed of an initial financing statement and any filed record relating to the initial financing statement.

(40) "Fixture filing" means the filing of a financing statement covering goods that are or are to become fixtures and satisfying Section 9–502(a) and (b). The term includes the filing of a financing statement covering goods of a transmitting utility which are or are to become fixtures.

(41) "Fixtures" means goods that have become so related to particular real property that an interest in them arises under real property law.

(42) "General intangible" means any personal property, including things in action, other than accounts, chattel paper, commercial tort claims, deposit accounts, documents, goods, instruments, investment property, letter-of-credit rights, letters of credit, money, and oil, gas, or other minerals before extraction. The term includes payment intangibles and software.

(43) "Good faith" means honesty in fact and the observance of reasonable commercial standards of fair dealing.

(44) "Goods" means all things that are movable when a security interest attaches. The term includes (i) fixtures, (ii) standing timber that is to be cut and removed under a conveyance or contract for sale, (iii) the unborn young of animals, (iv) crops grown, growing, or to be grown, even if the crops are produced on trees, vines, or bushes, and (v) manufactured homes. The term also includes a computer program embedded in goods and any supporting information provided in connection with a transaction relating to the program if (i) the program is associated with the goods in such a manner that it customarily is considered part of the goods, or (ii) by becoming the owner of the goods, a person acquires a right to use the program in connection with the goods. The term does not include a computer program embedded in goods that consist solely of the medium in which the program is embedded. The term also does not include accounts, chattel paper, commercial tort claims, deposit accounts, documents, general intangibles, instruments, investment property, letter-of-credit rights, letters of credit, money, or oil, gas, or other minerals before extraction.

(45) "Governmental unit" means a subdivision, agency, department, county, parish, municipality, or other unit of the government of the United States, a State, or a foreign country. The term includes an organization having a separate corporate existence if the organization is eligible to issue debt on which interest is exempt from income taxation under the laws of the United States.

(46) "Health-care-insurance receivable" means an interest in or claim under a policy of insurance which is a right to payment of a monetary obligation for health-care goods or services provided.

(47) "Instrument" means a negotiable instrument or any other writing that evidences a right to the payment of a monetary obligation, is not itself a security agreement or lease, and is of a type that in ordinary course of business is transferred by delivery with any necessary indorsement or assignment. The term does not include (i) investment property, (ii) letters of credit, or (iii) writings that evidence a right to payment arising out of the use of a credit or charge card or information contained on or for use with the card.

(48) "Inventory" means goods, other than farm products, which:

(A) are leased by a person as lessor;

(B) are held by a person for sale or lease or to be furnished under a contract of service;

(C) are furnished by a person under a contract of service; or

(D) consist of raw materials, work in process, or materials used or consumed in a business.

(49) "Investment property" means a security, whether certificated or uncertificated, security entitlement, securities account, commodity contract, or commodity account.

(50) "Jurisdiction of organization", with respect to a registered organization, means the jurisdiction under whose law the organization is organized.

(51) "Letter-of-credit right" means a right to payment or performance under a letter of credit, whether or not the beneficiary has demanded or is at the time entitled to demand payment or performance. The term does not include the right of a beneficiary to demand payment or performance under a letter of credit.

(52) "Lien creditor" means:

(A) a creditor that has acquired a lien on the property involved by attachment, levy, or the like;

(B) an assignee for benefit of creditors from the time of assignment;

(C) a trustee in bankruptcy from the date of the filing of the petition; or

(D) a receiver in equity from the time of appointment.

(53) "Manufactured home" means a structure, transportable in one or more sections, which, in the traveling mode, is eight body feet or more in width or 40 body feet or more in length, or, when erected on site, is 320 or more square feet, and which is built on a permanent chassis and designed to be used as a dwelling with or without a permanent foundation when connected to the required utilities, and includes the plumbing, heating, air-conditioning, and electrical systems contained therein. The term includes any structure that meets all of the requirements of this paragraph except the size requirements and with respect to which the manufacturer voluntarily files a certification required by the United States Secretary of Housing and Urban Development and complies with the standards established under Title 42 of the United States Code.

(54) "Manufactured-home transaction" means a secured transaction:

(A) that creates a purchase-money security interest in a manufactured home, other than a manufactured home held as inventory; or

(B) in which a manufactured home, other than a manufactured home held as inventory, is the primary collateral.

(55) "Mortgage" means a consensual interest in real property, including fixtures, which secures payment or performance of an obligation.

(56) "New debtor" means a person that becomes bound as debtor under Section 9–203(d) by a security agreement previously entered into by another person.

(57) "New value" means (i) money, (ii) money's worth in property, services, or new credit, or (iii) release by a transferee of an interest in property previously transferred to the transferee. The term does not include an obligation substituted for another obligation.

(58) "Noncash proceeds" means proceeds other than cash proceeds.

(59) "Obligor" means a person that, with respect to an obligation secured by a security interest in or an agricultural lien on the collateral, (i) owes payment or other performance of the obligation, (ii) has provided property other than the collateral to secure payment or other performance of the obligation, or (iii) is otherwise accountable in whole or in part for payment or other performance of the obligation. The term does not include issuers or nominated persons under a letter of credit.

(60) "Original debtor", except as used in Section 9–310(c), means a person that, as debtor, entered into a security agreement to which a new debtor has become bound under Section 9–203(d).

(61) "Payment intangible" means a general intangible under which the account debtor's principal obligation is a monetary obligation.

(62) "Person related to", with respect to an individual, means:

(A) the spouse of the individual;

(B) a brother, brother-in-law, sister, or sister-in-law of the individual;

(C) an ancestor or lineal descendant of the individual or the individual's spouse; or

(D) any other relative, by blood or marriage, of the individual or the individual's spouse who shares the same home with the individual.

(63) "Person related to", with respect to an organization, means:

(A) a person directly or indirectly controlling, controlled by, or under common control with the organization;

(B) an officer or director of, or a person performing similar functions with respect to, the organization;

(C) an officer or director of, or a person performing similar functions with respect to, a person described in subparagraph (A);

(D) the spouse of an individual described in subparagraph (A), (B), or (C); or

(E) an individual who is related by blood or marriage to an individual described in subparagraph (A), (B), (C), or (D) and shares the same home with the individual.

(64) "Proceeds", except as used in Section 9–609(b), means the following property:

(A) whatever is acquired upon the sale, lease, license, exchange, or other disposition of collateral;

(B) whatever is collected on, or distributed on account of, collateral;

(C) rights arising out of collateral;

(D) to the extent of the value of collateral, claims arising out of the loss, nonconformity, or interference with the use of, defects or infringement of rights in, or damage to, the collateral; or

(E) to the extent of the value of collateral and to the extent payable to the debtor or the secured party, insurance payable by reason of the loss or nonconformity of, defects or infringement of rights in, or damage to, the collateral.

(65) "Promissory note" means an instrument that evidences a promise to pay a monetary obligation, does not evidence an order to pay, and does not contain an acknowledgment by a bank that the bank has received for deposit a sum of money or funds.

(66) "Proposal" means a record authenticated by a secured party which includes the terms on which the secured party is willing to accept collateral in full or partial satisfaction of the obligation it secures pursuant to Sections 9–620, 9–621, and 9–622.

(67) "Public-finance transaction" means a secured transaction in connection with which:

(A) debt securities are issued;

(B) all or a portion of the securities issued have an initial stated maturity of at least 20 years; and

(C) the debtor, obligor, secured party, account debtor or other person obligated on collateral, assignor or assignee of a secured obligation, or assignor or assignee of a security interest is a State or a governmental unit of a State.

(68) "Pursuant to commitment", with respect to an advance made or other value given by a secured party, means pursuant to the secured party's obligation, whether or not a subsequent event of default or other event not within the secured party's control has relieved or may relieve the secured party from its obligation.

(69) "Record", except as used in "for record", "of record", "record or legal title", and "record owner", means information that is inscribed on a tangible medium or which is stored in an electronic or other medium and is retrievable in perceivable form.

(70) "Registered organization" means an organization organized solely under the law of a single State or the United States and as to which the State or the United States must maintain a public record showing the organization to have been organized.

(71) "Secondary obligor" means an obligor to the extent that:

(A) the obligor's obligation is secondary; or

(B) the obligor has a right of recourse with respect to an obligation secured by collateral against the debtor, another obligor, or property of either.

(72) "Secured party" means:

(A) a person in whose favor a security interest is created or provided for under a security agreement, whether or not any obligation to be secured is outstanding;

(B) a person that holds an agricultural lien;

(C) a consignor;

(D) a person to which accounts, chattel paper, payment intangibles, or promissory notes have been sold;

(E) a trustee, indenture trustee, agent, collateral agent, or other representative in whose favor a security interest or agricultural lien is created or provided for; or

(F) a person that holds a security interest arising under Section 2–401, 2–505, 2–711(3), 2A–508(5), 4–210, or 5–118.

(73) "Security agreement" means an agreement that creates or provides for a security interest.

(74) "Send", in connection with a record or notification, means:

(A) to deposit in the mail, deliver for transmission, or transmit by any other usual means of communication, with postage or cost of transmission provided for, addressed to any address reasonable under the circumstances; or

(B) to cause the record or notification to be received within the time that it would have been received if properly sent under subparagraph (A).

(75) "Software" means a computer program and any supporting information provided in connection with a transaction relating to the program. The term does not include a computer program that is included in the definition of goods.

(76) "State" means a State of the United States, the District of Columbia, Puerto Rico, the United States Virgin Islands, or any territory or insular possession subject to the jurisdiction of the United States.

(77) "Supporting obligation" means a letter-of-credit right or secondary obligation that supports the payment or performance of an account, chattel paper, a document, a general intangible, an instrument, or investment property.

(78) "Tangible chattel paper" means chattel paper evidenced by a record or records consisting of information that is inscribed on a tangible medium.

(79) "Termination statement" means an amendment of a financing statement which:

(A) identifies, by its file number, the initial financing statement to which it relates; and

(B) indicates either that it is a termination statement or that the identified financing statement is no longer effective.

(80) "Transmitting utility" means a person primarily engaged in the business of:

(A) operating a railroad, subway, street railway, or trolley bus;

(B) transmitting communications electrically, electromagnetically, or by light;

(C) transmitting goods by pipeline or sewer; or

(D) transmitting or producing and transmitting electricity, steam, gas, or water.

(b) The following definitions in other articles apply to this article:

"Applicant."	Section 5–102
"Beneficiary."	Section 5–102
"Broker."	Section 8–102
"Certificated security."	Section 8–102
"Check."	Section 3–104
"Clearing corporation."	Section 8–102
"Contract for sale."	Section 2–106
"Customer."	Section 4–104
"Entitlement holder."	Section 8–102
"Financial asset."	Section 8–102
"Holder in due course."	Section 3–302
"Issuer" (with respect to a letter of credit or letter-of-credit right).	Section 5–102
"Issuer" (with respect to a security).	Section 8–201
"Lease."	Section 2A–103
"Lease agreement."	Section 2A–103
"Lease contract."	Section 2A–103
"Leasehold interest."	Section 2A–103
"Lessee."	Section 2A–103
"Lessee in ordinary course of business."	Section 2A–103
"Lessor."	Section 2A–103
"Lessor's residual interest."	Section 2A–103
"Letter of credit."	Section 5–102
"Merchant."	Section 2–104
"Negotiable instrument."	Section 3–104
"Nominated person."	Section 5–102
"Note."	Section 3–104
"Proceeds of a letter of credit."	Section 5–114
"Prove."	Section 3–103
"Sale."	Section 2–106
"Securities account."	Section 8–501
"Securities intermediary."	Section 8–102
"Security."	Section 8–102
"Security certificate."	Section 8–102
"Security entitlement."	Section 8–102
"Uncertificated security."	Section 8–102

(c) Article 1 contains general definitions and principles of construction and interpretation applicable throughout this article.

Amended in 1999 and 2000.

§ 9–103. Purchase-Money Security Interest; Application of Payments; Burden of Establishing.

(a) In this section:

(1) "purchase-money collateral" means goods or software that secures a purchase-money obligation incurred with respect to that collateral; and

(2) "purchase-money obligation" means an obligation of an obligor incurred as all or part of the price of the collateral or for value given to enable the debtor to acquire rights in or the use of the collateral if the value is in fact so used.

(b) A security interest in goods is a purchase-money security interest:

(1) to the extent that the goods are purchase-money collateral with respect to that security interest;

(2) if the security interest is in inventory that is or was purchase-money collateral, also to the extent that the security interest secures a purchase-money obligation incurred with respect to other inventory in which the secured party holds or held a purchase-money security interest; and

(3) also to the extent that the security interest secures a purchase-money obligation incurred with respect to software in which the secured party holds or held a purchase-money security interest.

(c) A security interest in software is a purchase-money security interest to the extent that the security interest also secures a purchase-money obligation incurred with respect to goods in which the secured party holds or held a purchase-money security interest if:

(1) the debtor acquired its interest in the software in an integrated transaction in which it acquired an interest in the goods; and

(2) the debtor acquired its interest in the software for the principal purpose of using the software in the goods.

(d) The security interest of a consignor in goods that are the subject of a consignment is a purchase-money security interest in inventory.

(e) In a transaction other than a consumer-goods transaction, if the extent to which a security interest is a purchase-money security interest depends on the application of a payment to a particular obligation, the payment must be applied:

(1) in accordance with any reasonable method of application to which the parties agree;

(2) in the absence of the parties' agreement to a reasonable method, in accordance with any intention of the obligor manifested at or before the time of payment; or

(3) in the absence of an agreement to a reasonable method and a timely manifestation of the obligor's intention, in the following order:

(A) to obligations that are not secured; and

(B) if more than one obligation is secured, to obligations secured by purchase-money security interests in the order in which those obligations were incurred.

(f) In a transaction other than a consumer-goods transaction, a purchase-money security interest does not lose its status as such, even if:

(1) the purchase-money collateral also secures an obligation that is not a purchase-money obligation;

(2) collateral that is not purchase-money collateral also secures the purchase-money obligation; or

(3) the purchase-money obligation has been renewed, refinanced, consolidated, or restructured.

(g) In a transaction other than a consumer-goods transaction, a secured party claiming a purchase-money security interest has the burden of establishing the extent to which the security interest is a purchase-money security interest.

(h) The limitation of the rules in subsections (e), (f), and (g) to transactions other than consumer-goods transactions is intended to leave to the court the determination of the proper rules in consumer-goods transactions. The court may not infer from that limitation the nature of the proper rule in consumer-goods transactions and may continue to apply established approaches.

§ 9–104. Control of Deposit Account.

(a) A secured party has control of a deposit account if:

(1) the secured party is the bank with which the deposit account is maintained;

(2) the debtor, secured party, and bank have agreed in an authenticated record that the bank will comply with instructions originated by the secured party directing disposition of the funds in the deposit account without further consent by the debtor; or

(3) the secured party becomes the bank's customer with respect to the deposit account.

(b) A secured party that has satisfied subsection (a) has control, even if the debtor retains the right to direct the disposition of funds from the deposit account.

§ 9–105. Control of Electronic Chattel Paper.

A secured party has control of electronic chattel paper if the record or records comprising the chattel paper are created, stored, and assigned in such a manner that:

(1) a single authoritative copy of the record or records exists which is unique, identifiable and, except as otherwise provided in paragraphs (4), (5), and (6), unalterable;

(2) the authoritative copy identifies the secured party as the assignee of the record or records;

(3) the authoritative copy is communicated to and maintained by the secured party or its designated custodian;

(4) copies or revisions that add or change an identified assignee of the authoritative copy can be made only with the participation of the secured party;

(5) each copy of the authoritative copy and any copy of a copy is readily identifiable as a copy that is not the authoritative copy; and

(6) any revision of the authoritative copy is readily identifiable as an authorized or unauthorized revision.

§ 9–106. Control of Investment Property.

(a) A person has control of a certificated security, uncertificated security, or security entitlement as provided in Section 8–106.

(b) A secured party has control of a commodity contract if:

(1) the secured party is the commodity intermediary with which the commodity contract is carried; or

(2) the commodity customer, secured party, and commodity intermediary have agreed that the commodity intermediary will apply any value distributed on account of the commodity contract as directed by the secured party without further consent by the commodity customer.

(c) A secured party having control of all security entitlements or commodity contracts carried in a securities account or commodity account has control over the securities account or commodity account.

§ 9–107. Control of Letter-of-Credit Right.

A secured party has control of a letter-of-credit right to the extent of any right to payment or performance by the issuer or any nominated person if the issuer or nominated person has consented to an assignment of proceeds of the letter of credit under Section 5–114(c) or otherwise applicable law or practice.

§ 9–108. Sufficiency of Description.

(a) Except as otherwise provided in subsections (c), (d), and (e), a description of personal or real property is sufficient, whether or not it is specific, if it reasonably identifies what is described.

(b) Except as otherwise provided in subsection (d), a description of collateral reasonably identifies the collateral if it identifies the collateral by:

(1) specific listing;

(2) category;

(3) except as otherwise provided in subsection (e), a type of collateral defined in [the Uniform Commercial Code];

(4) quantity;

(5) computational or allocational formula or procedure; or

(6) except as otherwise provided in subsection (c), any other method, if the identity of the collateral is objectively determinable.

(c) A description of collateral as "all the debtor's assets" or "all the debtor's personal property" or using words of similar import does not reasonably identify the collateral.

(d) Except as otherwise provided in subsection (e), a description of a security entitlement, securities account, or commodity account is sufficient if it describes:

(1) the collateral by those terms or as investment property; or

(2) the underlying financial asset or commodity contract.

(e) A description only by type of collateral defined in [the Uniform Commercial Code] is an insufficient description of:

(1) a commercial tort claim; or

(2) in a consumer transaction, consumer goods, a security entitlement, a securities account, or a commodity account.

[Subpart 2. Applicability of Article]

§ 9–109. Scope.

(a) Except as otherwise provided in subsections (c) and (d), this article applies to:

(1) a transaction, regardless of its form, that creates a security interest in personal property or fixtures by contract;

(2) an agricultural lien;

(3) a sale of accounts, chattel paper, payment intangibles, or promissory notes;

(4) a consignment;

(5) a security interest arising under Section 2–401, 2–505, 2–711(3), or 2A–508(5), as provided in Section 9–110; and

(6) a security interest arising under Section 4–210 or 5–118.

(b) The application of this article to a security interest in a secured obligation is not affected by the fact that the obligation is itself secured by a transaction or interest to which this article does not apply.

(c) This article does not apply to the extent that:

(1) a statute, regulation, or treaty of the United States preempts this article;

(2) another statute of this State expressly governs the creation, perfection, priority, or enforcement of a security interest created by this State or a governmental unit of this State;

(3) a statute of another State, a foreign country, or a governmental unit of another State or a foreign country, other than a statute generally applicable to security interests, expressly governs creation, perfection, priority, or enforcement of a security interest created by the State, country, or governmental unit; or

(4) the rights of a transferee beneficiary or nominated person under a letter of credit are independent and superior under Section 5–114.

(d) This article does not apply to:

(1) a landlord's lien, other than an agricultural lien;

(2) a lien, other than an agricultural lien, given by statute or other rule of law for services or materials, but Section 9–333 applies with respect to priority of the lien;

(3) an assignment of a claim for wages, salary, or other compensation of an employee;

(4) a sale of accounts, chattel paper, payment intangibles, or promissory notes as part of a sale of the business out of which they arose;

(5) an assignment of accounts, chattel paper, payment intangibles, or promissory notes which is for the purpose of collection only;

(6) an assignment of a right to payment under a contract to an assignee that is also obligated to perform under the contract;

(7) an assignment of a single account, payment intangible, or promissory note to an assignee in full or partial satisfaction of a preexisting indebtedness;

(8) a transfer of an interest in or an assignment of a claim under a policy of insurance, other than an assignment by or to a health-care provider of a health-care-insurance receivable and any subsequent assignment of the right to payment, but Sections 9–315 and 9–322 apply with respect to proceeds and priorities in proceeds;

(9) an assignment of a right represented by a judgment, other than a judgment taken on a right to payment that was collateral;

(10) a right of recoupment or set-off, but:

(A) Section 9–340 applies with respect to the effectiveness of rights of recoupment or set-off against deposit accounts; and

(B) Section 9–404 applies with respect to defenses or claims of an account debtor;

(11) the creation or transfer of an interest in or lien on real property, including a lease or rents thereunder, except to the extent that provision is made for:

(A) liens on real property in Sections 9–203 and 9–308;

(B) fixtures in Section 9–334;

(C) fixture filings in Sections 9–501, 9–502, 9–512, 9–516, and 9–519; and

(D) security agreements covering personal and real property in Section 9–604;

(12) an assignment of a claim arising in tort, other than a commercial tort claim, but Sections 9–315 and 9–322 apply with respect to proceeds and priorities in proceeds; or

(13) an assignment of a deposit account in a consumer transaction, but Sections 9–315 and 9–322 apply with respect to proceeds and priorities in proceeds.

§ 9–110. Security Interests Arising under Article 2 or 2A.

A security interest arising under Section 2–401, 2–505, 2–711(3), or 2A–508(5) is subject to this article. However, until the debtor obtains possession of the goods:

(1) the security interest is enforceable, even if Section 9–203(b)(3) has not been satisfied;

(2) filing is not required to perfect the security interest;

(3) the rights of the secured party after default by the debtor are governed by Article 2 or 2A; and

(4) the security interest has priority over a conflicting security interest created by the debtor.

Part 2 Effectiveness of Security Agreement; Attachment of Security Interest; Rights of Parties to Security Agreement

[Subpart 1. Effectiveness and Attachment]

§ 9–201. General Effectiveness of Security Agreement.

(a) Except as otherwise provided in [the Uniform Commercial Code], a security agreement is effective according to its terms between the parties, against purchasers of the collateral, and against creditors.

(b) A transaction subject to this article is subject to any applicable rule of law which establishes a different rule for consumers and [insert reference to (i) any other statute or regulation that regulates the rates, charges, agreements, and practices for loans, credit sales, or other extensions of credit and (ii) any consumer-protection statute or regulation].

(c) In case of conflict between this article and a rule of law, statute, or regulation described in subsection (b), the rule of law, statute, or regulation controls. Failure to comply with a statute or regulation described in subsection (b) has only the effect the statute or regulation specifies.

(d) This article does not:

(1) validate any rate, charge, agreement, or practice that violates a rule of law, statute, or regulation described in subsection (b); or

(2) extend the application of the rule of law, statute, or regulation to a transaction not otherwise subject to it.

§ 9–202. Title to Collateral Immaterial.

Except as otherwise provided with respect to consignments or sales of accounts, chattel paper, payment intangibles, or promissory notes, the provisions of this article with regard to rights and obligations apply whether title to collateral is in the secured party or the debtor.

§ 9–203. Attachment and Enforceability of Security Interest; Proceeds; Supporting Obligations; Formal Requisites.

(a) A security interest attaches to collateral when it becomes enforceable against the debtor with respect to the collateral, unless an agreement expressly postpones the time of attachment.

(b) Except as otherwise provided in subsections (c) through (i), a security interest is enforceable against the debtor and third parties with respect to the collateral only if:

(1) value has been given;

(2) the debtor has rights in the collateral or the power to transfer rights in the collateral to a secured party; and

(3) one of the following conditions is met:

(A) the debtor has authenticated a security agreement that provides a description of the collateral and, if the security interest covers timber to be cut, a description of the land concerned;

(B) the collateral is not a certificated security and is in the possession of the secured party under Section 9–313 pursuant to the debtor's security agreement;

(C) the collateral is a certificated security in registered form and the security certificate has been delivered to the secured party under Section 8–301 pursuant to the debtor's security agreement; or

(D) the collateral is deposit accounts, electronic chattel paper, investment property, or letter-of-credit rights, and the secured party has control under Section 9–104, 9–105, 9–106, or 9–107 pursuant to the debtor's security agreement.

(c) Subsection (b) is subject to Section 4–210 on the security interest of a collecting bank, Section 5–118 on the security interest of a letter-of-credit issuer or nominated person, Section 9–110 on a security interest arising under Article 2 or 2A, and Section 9–206 on security interests in investment property.

(d) A person becomes bound as debtor by a security agreement entered into by another person if, by operation of law other than this article or by contract:

(1) the security agreement becomes effective to create a security interest in the person's property; or

(2) the person becomes generally obligated for the obligations of the other person, including the obligation secured under the security agreement, and acquires or succeeds to all or substantially all of the assets of the other person.

(e) If a new debtor becomes bound as debtor by a security agreement entered into by another person:

(1) the agreement satisfies subsection (b)(3) with respect to existing or after-acquired property of the new debtor to the extent the property is described in the agreement; and

(2) another agreement is not necessary to make a security interest in the property enforceable.

(f) The attachment of a security interest in collateral gives the secured party the rights to proceeds provided by Section 9–315 and is also attachment of a security interest in a supporting obligation for the collateral.

(g) The attachment of a security interest in a right to payment or performance secured by a security interest or other lien on personal or real property is also attachment of a security interest in the security interest, mortgage, or other lien.

(h) The attachment of a security interest in a securities account is also attachment of a security interest in the security entitlements carried in the securities account.

(i) The attachment of a security interest in a commodity account is also attachment of a security interest in the commodity contracts carried in the commodity account.

§ 9–204. After-Acquired Property; Future Advances.

(a) Except as otherwise provided in subsection (b), a security agreement may create or provide for a security interest in after-acquired collateral.

(b) A security interest does not attach under a term constituting an after-acquired property clause to:

(1) consumer goods, other than an accession when given as additional security, unless the debtor acquires rights in them within 10 days after the secured party gives value; or

(2) a commercial tort claim.

(c) A security agreement may provide that collateral secures, or that accounts, chattel paper, payment intangibles, or promissory notes are sold in connection with, future advances or other value, whether or not the advances or value are given pursuant to commitment.

§ 9–205. Use or Disposition of Collateral Permissible.

(a) A security interest is not invalid or fraudulent against creditors solely because:

(1) the debtor has the right or ability to:

(A) use, commingle, or dispose of all or part of the collateral, including returned or repossessed goods;

(B) collect, compromise, enforce, or otherwise deal with collateral;

(C) accept the return of collateral or make repossessions; or

(D) use, commingle, or dispose of proceeds; or

(2) the secured party fails to require the debtor to account for proceeds or replace collateral.

(b) This section does not relax the requirements of possession if attachment, perfection, or enforcement of a security interest depends upon possession of the collateral by the secured party.

§ 9–206. Security Interest Arising in Purchase or Delivery of Financial Asset.

(a) A security interest in favor of a securities intermediary attaches to a person's security entitlement if:

(1) the person buys a financial asset through the securities intermediary in a transaction in which the person is obligated to pay the purchase price to the securities intermediary at the time of the purchase; and

(2) the securities intermediary credits the financial asset to the buyer's securities account before the buyer pays the securities intermediary.

(b) The security interest described in subsection (a) secures the person's obligation to pay for the financial asset.

(c) A security interest in favor of a person that delivers a certificated security or other financial asset represented by a writing attaches to the security or other financial asset if:

(1) the security or other financial asset:

(A) in the ordinary course of business is transferred by delivery with any necessary indorsement or assignment; and

(B) is delivered under an agreement between persons in the business of dealing with such securities or financial assets; and

(2) the agreement calls for delivery against payment.

(d) The security interest described in subsection (c) secures the obligation to make payment for the delivery.

[Subpart 2. Rights and Duties]

§ 9–207. Rights and Duties of Secured Party Having Possession or Control of Collateral.

(a) Except as otherwise provided in subsection (d), a secured party shall use reasonable care in the custody and preservation of collateral in the secured party's possession. In the case of chattel paper or an instrument, reasonable care includes taking necessary steps to preserve rights against prior parties unless otherwise agreed.

(b) Except as otherwise provided in subsection (d), if a secured party has possession of collateral:

(1) reasonable expenses, including the cost of insurance and payment of taxes or other charges, incurred in the custody, preservation, use, or operation of the collateral are chargeable to the debtor and are secured by the collateral;

(2) the risk of accidental loss or damage is on the debtor to the extent of a deficiency in any effective insurance coverage;

(3) the secured party shall keep the collateral identifiable, but fungible collateral may be commingled; and

(4) the secured party may use or operate the collateral:

(A) for the purpose of preserving the collateral or its value;

(B) as permitted by an order of a court having competent jurisdiction; or

(C) except in the case of consumer goods, in the manner and to the extent agreed by the debtor.

(c) Except as otherwise provided in subsection (d), a secured party having possession of collateral or control of collateral under Section 9–104, 9–105, 9–106, or 9–107:

(1) may hold as additional security any proceeds, except money or funds, received from the collateral;

(2) shall apply money or funds received from the collateral to reduce the secured obligation, unless remitted to the debtor; and

(3) may create a security interest in the collateral.

(d) If the secured party is a buyer of accounts, chattel paper, payment intangibles, or promissory notes or a consignor:

(1) subsection (a) does not apply unless the secured party is entitled under an agreement:

(A) to charge back uncollected collateral; or

(B) otherwise to full or limited recourse against the debtor or a secondary obligor based on the nonpayment or other default of an account debtor or other obligor on the collateral; and

(2) subsections (b) and (c) do not apply.

§ 9–208. Additional Duties of Secured Party Having Control of Collateral.

(a) This section applies to cases in which there is no outstanding secured obligation and the secured party is not committed to make advances, incur obligations, or otherwise give value.

(b) Within 10 days after receiving an authenticated demand by the debtor:

(1) a secured party having control of a deposit account under Section 9–104(a)(2) shall send to the bank with which the deposit account is maintained an authenticated statement that releases the bank from any further obligation to comply with instructions originated by the secured party;

(2) a secured party having control of a deposit account under Section 9–104(a)(3) shall:

(A) pay the debtor the balance on deposit in the deposit account; or

(B) transfer the balance on deposit into a deposit account in the debtor's name;

(3) a secured party, other than a buyer, having control of electronic chattel paper under Section 9–105 shall:

(A) communicate the authoritative copy of the electronic chattel paper to the debtor or its designated custodian;

(B) if the debtor designates a custodian that is the designated custodian with which the authoritative copy of the electronic chattel paper is maintained for the secured party, communicate to the custodian an authenticated record releasing the designated custodian from any further obligation to comply with instructions originated by the secured party and instructing the custodian to comply with instructions originated by the debtor; and

(C) take appropriate action to enable the debtor or its designated custodian to make copies of or revisions to the authoritative copy which add or change an identified assignee of the authoritative copy without the consent of the secured party;

(4) a secured party having control of investment property under Section 8–106(d)(2) or 9–106(b) shall send to the securities intermediary or commodity intermediary with which the security entitlement or commodity contract is maintained an authenticated record that releases the securities intermediary or commodity intermediary from any further obligation to comply with entitlement orders or directions originated by the secured party; and

(5) a secured party having control of a letter-of-credit right under Section 9–107 shall send to each person having an unfulfilled obligation to pay or deliver proceeds of the letter of credit to the secured party an authenticated release from any further obligation to pay or deliver proceeds of the letter of credit to the secured party.

§ 9–209. Duties of Secured Party If Account Debtor Has Been Notified of Assignment.

(a) Except as otherwise provided in subsection (c), this section applies if:

(1) there is no outstanding secured obligation; and

(2) the secured party is not committed to make advances, incur obligations, or otherwise give value.

(b) Within 10 days after receiving an authenticated demand by the debtor, a secured party shall send to an account debtor that has received notification of an assignment to the secured party as assignee under Section 9–406(a) an authenticated record that releases the account debtor from any further obligation to the secured party.

(c) This section does not apply to an assignment constituting the sale of an account, chattel paper, or payment intangible.

§ 9–210. Request for Accounting; Request Regarding List of Collateral or Statement of Account.

(a) In this section:

(1) "Request" means a record of a type described in paragraph (2), (3), or (4).

(2) "Request for an accounting" means a record authenticated by a debtor requesting that the recipient provide an accounting of the unpaid obligations secured by collateral and reasonably identifying the transaction or relationship that is the subject of the request.

(3) "Request regarding a list of collateral" means a record authenticated by a debtor requesting that the recipient approve or correct a list of what the debtor believes to be the collateral securing an obligation and reasonably identifying the transaction or relationship that is the subject of the request.

(4) "Request regarding a statement of account" means a record authenticated by a debtor requesting that the

recipient approve or correct a statement indicating what the debtor believes to be the aggregate amount of unpaid obligations secured by collateral as of a specified date and reasonably identifying the transaction or relationship that is the subject of the request.

(b) Subject to subsections (c), (d), (e), and (f), a secured party, other than a buyer of accounts, chattel paper, payment intangibles, or promissory notes or a consignor, shall comply with a request within 14 days after receipt:

(1) in the case of a request for an accounting, by authenticating and sending to the debtor an accounting; and

(2) in the case of a request regarding a list of collateral or a request regarding a statement of account, by authenticating and sending to the debtor an approval or correction.

(c) A secured party that claims a security interest in all of a particular type of collateral owned by the debtor may comply with a request regarding a list of collateral by sending to the debtor an authenticated record including a statement to that effect within 14 days after receipt.

(d) A person that receives a request regarding a list of collateral, claims no interest in the collateral when it receives the request, and claimed an interest in the collateral at an earlier time shall comply with the request within 14 days after receipt by sending to the debtor an authenticated record:

(1) disclaiming any interest in the collateral; and

(2) if known to the recipient, providing the name and mailing address of any assignee of or successor to the recipient's interest in the collateral.

(e) A person that receives a request for an accounting or a request regarding a statement of account, claims no interest in the obligations when it receives the request, and claimed an interest in the obligations at an earlier time shall comply with the request within 14 days after receipt by sending to the debtor an authenticated record:

(1) disclaiming any interest in the obligations; and

(2) if known to the recipient, providing the name and mailing address of any assignee of or successor to the recipient's interest in the obligations.

(f) A debtor is entitled without charge to one response to a request under this section during any six-month period. The secured party may require payment of a charge not exceeding $25 for each additional response.

As amended in 1999.

Part 3 Perfection and Priority

[Subpart 1. Law Governing Perfection and Priority]

§ 9–301. Law Governing Perfection and Priority of Security Interests.

Except as otherwise provided in Sections 9–303 through 9–306, the following rules determine the law governing perfection, the effect of perfection or nonperfection, and the priority of a security interest in collateral:

(1) Except as otherwise provided in this section, while a debtor is located in a jurisdiction, the local law of that jurisdiction governs perfection, the effect of perfection or nonperfection, and the priority of a security interest in collateral.

(2) While collateral is located in a jurisdiction, the local law of that jurisdiction governs perfection, the effect of perfection or nonperfection, and the priority of a possessory security interest in that collateral.

(3) Except as otherwise provided in paragraph (4), while negotiable documents, goods, instruments, money, or tangible chattel paper is located in a jurisdiction, the local law of that jurisdiction governs:

(A) perfection of a security interest in the goods by filing a fixture filing;

(B) perfection of a security interest in timber to be cut; and

(C) the effect of perfection or nonperfection and the priority of a nonpossessory security interest in the collateral.

(4) The local law of the jurisdiction in which the wellhead or minehead is located governs perfection, the effect of perfection or nonperfection, and the priority of a security interest in as-extracted collateral.

§ 9–302. Law Governing Perfection and Priority of Agricultural Liens.

While farm products are located in a jurisdiction, the local law of that jurisdiction governs perfection, the effect of perfection or nonperfection, and the priority of an agricultural lien on the farm products.

§ 9–303. Law Governing Perfection and Priority of Security Interests in Goods Covered by a Certificate of Title.

(a) This section applies to goods covered by a certificate of title, even if there is no other relationship between the jurisdiction under whose certificate of title the goods are covered and the goods or the debtor.

(b) Goods become covered by a certificate of title when a valid application for the certificate of title and the applicable fee are delivered to the appropriate authority. Goods cease to be covered by a certificate of title at the earlier of the time the certificate of title ceases to be effective under the law of the issuing jurisdiction or the time the goods become covered subsequently by a certificate of title issued by another jurisdiction.

(c) The local law of the jurisdiction under whose certificate of title the goods are covered governs perfection, the effect of perfection or nonperfection, and the priority of a security interest in goods covered by a certificate of title from the time the goods become covered by the certificate of title until the goods cease to be covered by the certificate of title.

§ 9–304. Law Governing Perfection and Priority of Security Interests in Deposit Accounts.

(a) The local law of a bank's jurisdiction governs perfection, the effect of perfection or nonperfection, and the priority of a security interest in a deposit account maintained with that bank.

(b) The following rules determine a bank's jurisdiction for purposes of this part:

(1) If an agreement between the bank and the debtor governing the deposit account expressly provides that a particular jurisdiction is the bank's jurisdiction for purposes of this part, this article, or [the Uniform Commercial Code], that jurisdiction is the bank's jurisdiction.

(2) If paragraph (1) does not apply and an agreement between the bank and its customer governing the deposit account expressly provides that the agreement is governed by the law of a particular jurisdiction, that jurisdiction is the bank's jurisdiction.

(3) If neither paragraph (1) nor paragraph (2) applies and an agreement between the bank and its customer governing the deposit account expressly provides that the deposit account is maintained at an office in a particular jurisdiction, that jurisdiction is the bank's jurisdiction.

(4) If none of the preceding paragraphs applies, the bank's jurisdiction is the jurisdiction in which the office identified in an account statement as the office serving the customer's account is located.

(5) If none of the preceding paragraphs applies, the bank's jurisdiction is the jurisdiction in which the chief executive office of the bank is located.

§ 9–305. Law Governing Perfection and Priority of Security Interests in Investment Property.

(a) Except as otherwise provided in subsection (c), the following rules apply:

(1) While a security certificate is located in a jurisdiction, the local law of that jurisdiction governs perfection, the effect of perfection or nonperfection, and the priority of a security interest in the certificated security represented thereby.

(2) The local law of the issuer's jurisdiction as specified in Section 8–110(d) governs perfection, the effect of perfection or nonperfection, and the priority of a security interest in an uncertificated security.

(3) The local law of the securities intermediary's jurisdiction as specified in Section 8–110(e) governs perfection, the effect of perfection or nonperfection, and the priority of a security interest in a security entitlement or securities account.

(4) The local law of the commodity intermediary's jurisdiction governs perfection, the effect of perfection or nonperfection, and the priority of a security interest in a commodity contract or commodity account.

(b) The following rules determine a commodity intermediary's jurisdiction for purposes of this part:

(1) If an agreement between the commodity intermediary and commodity customer governing the commodity account expressly provides that a particular jurisdiction is the commodity intermediary's jurisdiction for purposes of this part, this article, or [the Uniform Commercial Code], that jurisdiction is the commodity intermediary's jurisdiction.

(2) If paragraph (1) does not apply and an agreement between the commodity intermediary and commodity customer governing the commodity account expressly provides that the agreement is governed by the law of a particular jurisdiction, that jurisdiction is the commodity intermediary's jurisdiction.

(3) If neither paragraph (1) nor paragraph (2) applies and an agreement between the commodity intermediary and commodity customer governing the commodity account expressly provides that the commodity account is maintained at an office in a particular jurisdiction, that jurisdiction is the commodity intermediary's jurisdiction.

(4) If none of the preceding paragraphs applies, the commodity intermediary's jurisdiction is the jurisdiction in which the office identified in an account statement as the office serving the commodity customer's account is located.

(5) If none of the preceding paragraphs applies, the commodity intermediary's jurisdiction is the jurisdiction in which the chief executive office of the commodity intermediary is located.

(c) The local law of the jurisdiction in which the debtor is located governs:

(1) perfection of a security interest in investment property by filing;

(2) automatic perfection of a security interest in investment property created by a broker or securities intermediary; and

(3) automatic perfection of a security interest in a commodity contract or commodity account created by a commodity intermediary.

§ 9–306. Law Governing Perfection and Priority of Security Interests in Letter-of-Credit Rights.

(a) Subject to subsection (c), the local law of the issuer's jurisdiction or a nominated person's jurisdiction governs perfection, the effect of perfection or nonperfection, and the priority of a security interest in a letter-of-credit right if the issuer's jurisdiction or nominated person's jurisdiction is a State.

(b) For purposes of this part, an issuer's jurisdiction or nominated person's jurisdiction is the jurisdiction whose law governs the liability of the issuer or nominated person with respect to the letter-of-credit right as provided in Section 5–116.

(c) This section does not apply to a security interest that is perfected only under Section 9–308(d).

§ 9–307. Location of Debtor.

(a) In this section, "place of business" means a place where a debtor conducts its affairs.

(b) Except as otherwise provided in this section, the following rules determine a debtor's location:

(1) A debtor who is an individual is located at the individual's principal residence.

(2) A debtor that is an organization and has only one place of business is located at its place of business.

(3) A debtor that is an organization and has more than one place of business is located at its chief executive office.

(c) Subsection (b) applies only if a debtor's residence, place of business, or chief executive office, as applicable, is located in a jurisdiction whose law generally requires information concerning the existence of a nonpossessory security interest to be made generally available in a filing, recording, or registration system as a condition or result of the security interest's obtaining priority over the rights of a lien creditor with respect to the collateral. If subsection (b) does not apply, the debtor is located in the District of Columbia.

(d) A person that ceases to exist, have a residence, or have a place of business continues to be located in the jurisdiction specified by subsections (b) and (c).

(e) A registered organization that is organized under the law of a State is located in that State.

(f) Except as otherwise provided in subsection (i), a registered organization that is organized under the law of the United States and a branch or agency of a bank that is not organized under the law of the United States or a State are located:

(1) in the State that the law of the United States designates, if the law designates a State of location;

(2) in the State that the registered organization, branch, or agency designates, if the law of the United States authorizes the registered organization, branch, or agency to designate its State of location; or

(3) in the District of Columbia, if neither paragraph (1) nor paragraph (2) applies.

(g) A registered organization continues to be located in the jurisdiction specified by subsection (e) or (f) notwithstanding:

(1) the suspension, revocation, forfeiture, or lapse of the registered organization's status as such in its jurisdiction of organization; or

(2) the dissolution, winding up, or cancellation of the existence of the registered organization.

(h) The United States is located in the District of Columbia.

(i) A branch or agency of a bank that is not organized under the law of the United States or a State is located in the State in which the branch or agency is licensed, if all branches and agencies of the bank are licensed in only one State.

(j) A foreign air carrier under the Federal Aviation Act of 1958, as amended, is located at the designated office of the agent upon which service of process may be made on behalf of the carrier.

(k) This section applies only for purposes of this part.

[Subpart 2. Perfection]

§ 9–308. When Security Interest or Agricultural Lien Is Perfected; Continuity of Perfection.

(a) Except as otherwise provided in this section and Section 9–309, a security interest is perfected if it has attached and all of the applicable requirements for perfection in Sections 9–310 through 9–316 have been satisfied. A security interest is perfected when it attaches if the applicable requirements are satisfied before the security interest attaches.

(b) An agricultural lien is perfected if it has become effective and all of the applicable requirements for perfection in Section 9–310 have been satisfied. An agricultural lien is perfected when it becomes effective if the applicable requirements are satisfied before the agricultural lien becomes effective.

(c) A security interest or agricultural lien is perfected continuously if it is originally perfected by one method under this article and is later perfected by another method under this article, without an intermediate period when it was unperfected.

(d) Perfection of a security interest in collateral also perfects a security interest in a supporting obligation for the collateral.

(e) Perfection of a security interest in a right to payment or performance also perfects a security interest in a security interest, mortgage, or other lien on personal or real property securing the right.

(f) Perfection of a security interest in a securities account also perfects a security interest in the security entitlements carried in the securities account.

(g) Perfection of a security interest in a commodity account also perfects a security interest in the commodity contracts carried in the commodity account.

Legislative Note: Any statute conflicting with subsection (e) must be made expressly subject to that subsection.

§ 9–309. Security Interest Perfected upon Attachment.

The following security interests are perfected when they attach:

(1) a purchase-money security interest in consumer goods, except as otherwise provided in Section 9–311(b) with respect to consumer goods that are subject to a statute or treaty described in Section 9–311(a);

(2) an assignment of accounts or payment intangibles which does not by itself or in conjunction with other assignments to the same assignee transfer a significant part of the assignor's outstanding accounts or payment intangibles;

(3) a sale of a payment intangible;

(4) a sale of a promissory note;

(5) a security interest created by the assignment of a health-care-insurance receivable to the provider of the health-care goods or services;

(6) a security interest arising under Section 2–401, 2–505, 2–711(3), or 2A–508(5), until the debtor obtains possession of the collateral;

(7) a security interest of a collecting bank arising under Section 4–210;

(8) a security interest of an issuer or nominated person arising under Section 5–118;

(9) a security interest arising in the delivery of a financial asset under Section 9–206(c);

(10) a security interest in investment property created by a broker or securities intermediary;

(11) a security interest in a commodity contract or a commodity account created by a commodity intermediary;

(12) an assignment for the benefit of all creditors of the transferor and subsequent transfers by the assignee thereunder; and

(13) a security interest created by an assignment of a beneficial interest in a decedent's estate; and

(14) a sale by an individual of an account that is a right to payment of winnings in a lottery or other game of chance.

§ 9–310. When Filing Required to Perfect Security Interest or Agricultural Lien; Security Interests and Agricultural Liens to Which Filing Provisions Do Not Apply.

(a) Except as otherwise provided in subsection (b) and Section 9–312(b), a financing statement must be filed to perfect all security interests and agricultural liens.

(b) The filing of a financing statement is not necessary to perfect a security interest:

(1) that is perfected under Section 9–308(d), (e), (f), or (g);

(2) that is perfected under Section 9–309 when it attaches;

(3) in property subject to a statute, regulation, or treaty described in Section 9–311(a);

(4) in goods in possession of a bailee which is perfected under Section 9–312(d)(1) or (2);

(5) in certificated securities, documents, goods, or instruments which is perfected without filing or possession under Section 9–312(e), (f), or (g);

(6) in collateral in the secured party's possession under Section 9–313;

(7) in a certificated security which is perfected by delivery of the security certificate to the secured party under Section 9–313;

(8) in deposit accounts, electronic chattel paper, investment property, or letter-of-credit rights which is perfected by control under Section 9–314;

(9) in proceeds which is perfected under Section 9–315; or

(10) that is perfected under Section 9–316.

(c) If a secured party assigns a perfected security interest or agricultural lien, a filing under this article is not required to continue the perfected status of the security interest against creditors of and transferees from the original debtor.

§ 9–311. Perfection of Security Interests in Property Subject to Certain Statutes, Regulations, and Treaties.

(a) Except as otherwise provided in subsection (d), the filing of a financing statement is not necessary or effective to perfect a security interest in property subject to:

(1) a statute, regulation, or treaty of the United States whose requirements for a security interest's obtaining priority over the rights of a lien creditor with respect to the property preempt Section 9–310(a);

(2) [list any certificate-of-title statute covering automobiles, trailers, mobile homes, boats, farm tractors, or the like, which provides for a security interest to be indicated on the certificate as a condition or result of perfection, and any non-Uniform Commercial Code central filing statute]; or

(3) a certificate-of-title statute of another jurisdiction which provides for a security interest to be indicated on the certificate as a condition or result of the security interest's obtaining priority over the rights of a lien creditor with respect to the property.

(b) Compliance with the requirements of a statute, regulation, or treaty described in subsection (a) for obtaining priority over the rights of a lien creditor is equivalent to the filing of a financing statement under this article. Except as otherwise provided in subsection (d) and Sections 9–313 and 9–316(d) and (e) for goods covered by a certificate of title, a security interest in property subject to a statute, regulation, or treaty described in subsection (a) may be perfected only by compliance with those requirements, and a security interest so perfected remains perfected notwithstanding a change in the use or transfer of possession of the collateral.

(c) Except as otherwise provided in subsection (d) and Section 9–316(d) and (e), duration and renewal of perfection of a security interest perfected by compliance with the requirements prescribed by a statute, regulation, or treaty described in subsection (a) are governed by the statute, regulation, or treaty. In other respects, the security interest is subject to this article.

(d) During any period in which collateral subject to a statute specified in subsection (a)(2) is inventory held for sale or lease by a person or leased by that person as lessor and that person is in the business of selling goods of that kind, this section does not apply to a security interest in that collateral created by that person.

Legislative Note: This Article contemplates that perfection of a security interest in goods covered by a certificate of title occurs upon receipt by appropriate State officials of a properly tendered application for a certificate of title on which the security interest is to be indicated, without a relation back to an earlier time. States whose certificate-of-title statutes provide for perfection at a different time or contain a relation-back provision should amend the statutes accordingly.

§ 9–312. Perfection of Security Interests in Chattel Paper, Deposit Accounts, Documents, Goods Covered by Documents, Instruments, Investment Property, Letter-of-Credit Rights, and Money; Perfection by Permissive Filing; Temporary Perfection without Filing or Transfer of Possession.

(a) A security interest in chattel paper, negotiable documents, instruments, or investment property may be perfected by filing.

(b) Except as otherwise provided in Section 9–315(c) and (d) for proceeds:

(1) a security interest in a deposit account may be perfected only by control under Section 9–314;

(2) and except as otherwise provided in Section 9–308(d), a security interest in a letter-of-credit right may be perfected only by control under Section 9–314; and

(3) a security interest in money may be perfected only by the secured party's taking possession under Section 9–313.

(c) While goods are in the possession of a bailee that has issued a negotiable document covering the goods:

(1) a security interest in the goods may be perfected by perfecting a security interest in the document; and

(2) a security interest perfected in the document has priority over any security interest that becomes perfected in the goods by another method during that time.

(d) While goods are in the possession of a bailee that has issued a nonnegotiable document covering the goods, a security interest in the goods may be perfected by:

(1) issuance of a document in the name of the secured party;

(2) the bailee's receipt of notification of the secured party's interest; or

(3) filing as to the goods.

(e) A security interest in certificated securities, negotiable documents, or instruments is perfected without filing or the taking of possession for a period of 20 days from the time it attaches to the extent that it arises for new value given under an authenticated security agreement.

(f) A perfected security interest in a negotiable document or goods in possession of a bailee, other than one that has issued a negotiable document for the goods, remains perfected for 20 days without filing if the secured party makes available to the debtor the goods or documents representing the goods for the purpose of:

(1) ultimate sale or exchange; or

(2) loading, unloading, storing, shipping, transshipping, manufacturing, processing, or otherwise dealing with them in a manner preliminary to their sale or exchange.

(g) A perfected security interest in a certificated security or instrument remains perfected for 20 days without filing if the secured party delivers the security certificate or instrument to the debtor for the purpose of:

(1) ultimate sale or exchange; or

(2) presentation, collection, enforcement, renewal, or registration of transfer.

(h) After the 20-day period specified in subsection (e), (f), or (g) expires, perfection depends upon compliance with this article.

§ 9–313. When Possession by or Delivery to Secured Party Perfects Security Interest without Filing.

(a) Except as otherwise provided in subsection (b), a secured party may perfect a security interest in negotiable documents, goods, instruments, money, or tangible chattel paper by taking possession of the collateral. A secured party may perfect a security interest in certificated securities by taking delivery of the certificated securities under Section 8–301.

(b) With respect to goods covered by a certificate of title issued by this State, a secured party may perfect a security interest in the goods by taking possession of the goods only in the circumstances described in Section 9–316(d).

(c) With respect to collateral other than certificated securities and goods covered by a document, a secured party takes possession of collateral in the possession of a person other than the debtor, the secured party, or a lessee of the collateral from the debtor in the ordinary course of the debtor's business, when:

(1) the person in possession authenticates a record acknowledging that it holds possession of the collateral for the secured party's benefit; or

(2) the person takes possession of the collateral after having authenticated a record acknowledging that it will hold possession of collateral for the secured party's benefit.

(d) If perfection of a security interest depends upon possession of the collateral by a secured party, perfection occurs no earlier than the time the secured party takes possession and continues only while the secured party retains possession.

(e) A security interest in a certificated security in registered form is perfected by delivery when delivery of the certificated security occurs under Section 8–301 and remains perfected by delivery until the debtor obtains possession of the security certificate.

(f) A person in possession of collateral is not required to acknowledge that it holds possession for a secured party's benefit.

(g) If a person acknowledges that it holds possession for the secured party's benefit:

(1) the acknowledgment is effective under subsection (c) or Section 8–301(a), even if the acknowledgment violates the rights of a debtor; and

(2) unless the person otherwise agrees or law other than this article otherwise provides, the person does not owe any duty to the secured party and is not required to confirm the acknowledgment to another person.

(h) A secured party having possession of collateral does not relinquish possession by delivering the collateral to a person other than the debtor or a lessee of the collateral from the debtor in the ordinary course of the debtor's business if the person was instructed before the delivery or is instructed contemporaneously with the delivery:

(1) to hold possession of the collateral for the secured party's benefit; or

(2) to redeliver the collateral to the secured party.

(i) A secured party does not relinquish possession, even if a delivery under subsection (h) violates the rights of a debtor. A person to which collateral is delivered under subsection (h) does not owe any duty to the secured party and is not required to confirm the delivery to another person unless the person otherwise agrees or law other than this article otherwise provides.

§ 9–314. Perfection by Control.

(a) A security interest in investment property, deposit accounts, letter-of-credit rights, or electronic chattel paper may be perfected by control of the collateral under Section 9–104, 9–105, 9–106, or 9–107.

(b) A security interest in deposit accounts, electronic chattel paper, or letter-of-credit rights is perfected by control under Section 9–104, 9–105, or 9–107 when the secured party obtains control and remains perfected by control only while the secured party retains control.

(c) A security interest in investment property is perfected by control under Section 9–106 from the time the secured party obtains control and remains perfected by control until:

(1) the secured party does not have control; and

(2) one of the following occurs:

(A) if the collateral is a certificated security, the debtor has or acquires possession of the security certificate;

(B) if the collateral is an uncertificated security, the issuer has registered or registers the debtor as the registered owner; or

(C) if the collateral is a security entitlement, the debtor is or becomes the entitlement holder.

§ 9–315. Secured Party's Rights on Disposition of Collateral and in Proceeds.

(a) Except as otherwise provided in this article and in Section 2–403(2):

(1) a security interest or agricultural lien continues in collateral notwithstanding sale, lease, license, exchange, or other disposition thereof unless the secured party authorized the disposition free of the security interest or agricultural lien; and

(2) a security interest attaches to any identifiable proceeds of collateral.

(b) Proceeds that are commingled with other property are identifiable proceeds:

(1) if the proceeds are goods, to the extent provided by Section 9–336; and

(2) if the proceeds are not goods, to the extent that the secured party identifies the proceeds by a method of tracing, including application of equitable principles, that is permitted under law other than this article with respect to commingled property of the type involved.

(c) A security interest in proceeds is a perfected security interest if the security interest in the original collateral was perfected.

(d) A perfected security interest in proceeds becomes unperfected on the 21st day after the security interest attaches to the proceeds unless:

(1) the following conditions are satisfied:

(A) a filed financing statement covers the original collateral;

(B) the proceeds are collateral in which a security interest may be perfected by filing in the office in which the financing statement has been filed; and

(C) the proceeds are not acquired with cash proceeds;

(2) the proceeds are identifiable cash proceeds; or

(3) the security interest in the proceeds is perfected other than under subsection (c) when the security interest attaches to the proceeds or within 20 days thereafter.

(e) If a filed financing statement covers the original collateral, a security interest in proceeds which remains perfected under subsection (d)(1) becomes unperfected at the later of:

(1) when the effectiveness of the filed financing statement lapses under Section 9–515 or is terminated under Section 9–513; or

(2) the 21st day after the security interest attaches to the proceeds.

§ 9–316. Continued Perfection of Security Interest Following Change in Governing Law.

(a) A security interest perfected pursuant to the law of the jurisdiction designated in Section 9–301(1) or 9–305(c) remains perfected until the earliest of:

(1) the time perfection would have ceased under the law of that jurisdiction;

(2) the expiration of four months after a change of the debtor's location to another jurisdiction; or

(3) the expiration of one year after a transfer of collateral to a person that thereby becomes a debtor and is located in another jurisdiction.

(b) If a security interest described in subsection (a) becomes perfected under the law of the other jurisdiction before the earliest time or event described in that subsection, it remains perfected thereafter. If the security interest does not become perfected under the law of the other jurisdiction before the earliest time or event, it becomes unperfected and is deemed never to have been perfected as against a purchaser of the collateral for value.

(c) A possessory security interest in collateral, other than goods covered by a certificate of title and as-extracted collateral consisting of goods, remains continuously perfected if:

(1) the collateral is located in one jurisdiction and subject to a security interest perfected under the law of that jurisdiction;

(2) thereafter the collateral is brought into another jurisdiction; and

(3) upon entry into the other jurisdiction, the security interest is perfected under the law of the other jurisdiction.

(d) Except as otherwise provided in subsection (e), a security interest in goods covered by a certificate of title which is perfected by any method under the law of another jurisdiction when the goods become covered by a certificate of title from this State remains perfected until the security interest would have become unperfected under the law of the other jurisdiction had the goods not become so covered.

(e) A security interest described in subsection (d) becomes unperfected as against a purchaser of the goods for value and is deemed never to have been perfected as against a purchaser of the goods for value if the applicable requirements for perfection under Section 9–311(b) or 9–313 are not satisfied before the earlier of:

(1) the time the security interest would have become unperfected under the law of the other jurisdiction had the goods not become covered by a certificate of title from this State; or

(2) the expiration of four months after the goods had become so covered.

(f) A security interest in deposit accounts, letter-of-credit rights, or investment property which is perfected under the law of the bank's jurisdiction, the issuer's jurisdiction, a nominated person's jurisdiction, the securities intermediary's jurisdiction, or the commodity intermediary's jurisdiction, as applicable, remains perfected until the earlier of:

(1) the time the security interest would have become unperfected under the law of that jurisdiction; or

(2) the expiration of four months after a change of the applicable jurisdiction to another jurisdiction.

(g) If a security interest described in subsection (f) becomes perfected under the law of the other jurisdiction before the earlier of the time or the end of the period described in that subsection, it remains perfected thereafter. If the security interest does not become perfected under the law of the other jurisdiction before the earlier of that time or the end of that period, it becomes unperfected and is deemed never to have been perfected as against a purchaser of the collateral for value.

[Subpart 3. Priority]

§ 9–317. Interests That Take Priority over or Take Free of Security Interest or Agricultural Lien.

(a) A security interest or agricultural lien is subordinate to the rights of:

(1) a person entitled to priority under Section 9–322; and

(2) except as otherwise provided in subsection (e), a person that becomes a lien creditor before the earlier of the time:

(A) the security interest or agricultural lien is perfected; or

(B) one of the conditions specified in Section 9–203(b)(3) is met and a financing statement covering the collateral is filed.

(b) Except as otherwise provided in subsection (e), a buyer, other than a secured party, of tangible chattel paper, documents, goods, instruments, or a security certificate takes free of a security interest or agricultural lien if the buyer gives value and receives delivery of the collateral without knowledge of the security interest or agricultural lien and before it is perfected.

(c) Except as otherwise provided in subsection (e), a lessee of goods takes free of a security interest or agricultural lien if the lessee gives value and receives delivery of the collateral without knowledge of the security interest or agricultural lien and before it is perfected.

(d) A licensee of a general intangible or a buyer, other than a secured party, of accounts, electronic chattel paper, general intangibles, or investment property other than a certificated security takes free of a security interest if the licensee or buyer gives value without knowledge of the security interest and before it is perfected.

(e) Except as otherwise provided in Sections 9–320 and 9–321, if a person files a financing statement with respect to a purchase-money security interest before or within 20 days after the debtor receives delivery of the collateral, the security interest takes priority over the rights of a buyer, lessee, or lien creditor which arise between the time the security interest attaches and the time of filing.

As amended in 2000.

§ 9–318. No Interest Retained in Right to Payment That Is Sold; Rights and Title of Seller of Account or Chattel Paper with Respect to Creditors and Purchasers.

(a) A debtor that has sold an account, chattel paper, payment intangible, or promissory note does not retain a legal or equitable interest in the collateral sold.

(b) For purposes of determining the rights of creditors of, and purchasers for value of an account or chattel paper from, a debtor that has sold an account or chattel paper, while the buyer's security interest is unperfected, the debtor is deemed to have rights and title to the account or chattel paper identical to those the debtor sold.

§ 9–319. Rights and Title of Consignee with Respect to Creditors and Purchasers.

(a) Except as otherwise provided in subsection (b), for purposes of determining the rights of creditors of, and purchasers for value of goods from, a consignee, while the goods are in the possession of the consignee, the consignee is deemed to have rights and title to the goods identical to those the consignor had or had power to transfer.

(b) For purposes of determining the rights of a creditor of a consignee, law other than this article determines the rights and title of a consignee while goods are in the consignee's possession if, under this part, a perfected security interest held by the consignor would have priority over the rights of the creditor.

§ 9–320. Buyer of Goods.

(a) Except as otherwise provided in subsection (e), a buyer in ordinary course of business, other than a person buying farm products from a person engaged in farming operations, takes free of a security interest created by the buyer's seller, even if the security interest is perfected and the buyer knows of its existence.

(b) Except as otherwise provided in subsection (e), a buyer of goods from a person who used or bought the goods for use primarily for personal, family, or household purposes takes free of a security interest, even if perfected, if the buyer buys:

(1) without knowledge of the security interest;

(2) for value;

(3) primarily for the buyer's personal, family, or household purposes; and

(4) before the filing of a financing statement covering the goods.

(c) To the extent that it affects the priority of a security interest over a buyer of goods under subsection (b), the period of effectiveness of a filing made in the jurisdiction in which the seller is located is governed by Section 9–316(a) and (b).

(d) A buyer in ordinary course of business buying oil, gas, or other minerals at the wellhead or minehead or after extraction takes free of an interest arising out of an encumbrance.

(e) Subsections (a) and (b) do not affect a security interest in goods in the possession of the secured party under Section 9–313.

§ 9–321. Licensee of General Intangible and Lessee of Goods in Ordinary Course of Business.

(a) In this section, "licensee in ordinary course of business" means a person that becomes a licensee of a general intangible in good faith, without knowledge that the license violates the rights of another person in the general intangible, and in the ordinary course from a person in the business of licensing general intangibles of that kind. A person becomes a licensee in the ordinary course if the license to the person comports with the usual or customary practices in the kind of business in which the licensor is engaged or with the licensor's own usual or customary practices.

(b) A licensee in ordinary course of business takes its rights under a nonexclusive license free of a security interest in the general intangible created by the licensor, even if the security interest is perfected and the licensee knows of its existence.

(c) A lessee in ordinary course of business takes its leasehold interest free of a security interest in the goods created by the lessor, even if the security interest is perfected and the lessee knows of its existence.

§ 9–322. Priorities among Conflicting Security Interests in and Agricultural Liens on Same Collateral.

(a) Except as otherwise provided in this section, priority among conflicting security interests and agricultural liens in the same collateral is determined according to the following rules:

(1) Conflicting perfected security interests and agricultural liens rank according to priority in time of filing or perfection. Priority dates from the earlier of the time a filing covering the collateral is first made or the security interest or agricultural lien is first perfected, if there is no period thereafter when there is neither filing nor perfection.

(2) A perfected security interest or agricultural lien has priority over a conflicting unperfected security interest or agricultural lien.

(3) The first security interest or agricultural lien to attach or become effective has priority if conflicting security interests and agricultural liens are unperfected.

(b) For the purposes of subsection (a)(1):

(1) the time of filing or perfection as to a security interest in collateral is also the time of filing or perfection as to a security interest in proceeds; and

(2) the time of filing or perfection as to a security interest in collateral supported by a supporting obligation is also the time of filing or perfection as to a security interest in the supporting obligation.

(c) Except as otherwise provided in subsection (f), a security interest in collateral which qualifies for priority over a conflicting security interest under Section 9–327, 9–328, 9–329, 9–330, or 9–331 also has priority over a conflicting security interest in:

(1) any supporting obligation for the collateral; and

(2) proceeds of the collateral if:

(A) the security interest in proceeds is perfected;

(B) the proceeds are cash proceeds or of the same type as the collateral; and

(C) in the case of proceeds that are proceeds of proceeds, all intervening proceeds are cash proceeds, proceeds of the same type as the collateral, or an account relating to the collateral.

(d) Subject to subsection (e) and except as otherwise provided in subsection (f), if a security interest in chattel paper, deposit accounts, negotiable documents, instruments, investment property, or letter-of-credit rights is perfected by a method other than filing, conflicting perfected security interests in proceeds of the collateral rank according to priority in time of filing.

(e) Subsection (d) applies only if the proceeds of the collateral are not cash proceeds, chattel paper, negotiable documents, instruments, investment property, or letter-of-credit rights.

(f) Subsections (a) through (e) are subject to:

(1) subsection (g) and the other provisions of this part;

(2) Section 4–210 with respect to a security interest of a collecting bank;

(3) Section 5–118 with respect to a security interest of an issuer or nominated person; and

(4) Section 9–110 with respect to a security interest arising under Article 2 or 2A.

(g) A perfected agricultural lien on collateral has priority over a conflicting security interest in or agricultural lien on the same collateral if the statute creating the agricultural lien so provides.

§ 9–323. Future Advances.

(a) Except as otherwise provided in subsection (c), for purposes of determining the priority of a perfected security interest under Section 9–322(a)(1), perfection of the security interest dates from the time an advance is made to the extent that the security interest secures an advance that:

(1) is made while the security interest is perfected only:

(A) under Section 9–309 when it attaches; or

(B) temporarily under Section 9–312(e), (f), or (g); and

(2) is not made pursuant to a commitment entered into before or while the security interest is perfected by a method other than under Section 9–309 or 9–312(e), (f), or (g).

(b) Except as otherwise provided in subsection (c), a security interest is subordinate to the rights of a person that becomes a lien creditor to the extent that the security interest secures an advance made more than 45 days after the person becomes a lien creditor unless the advance is made:

(1) without knowledge of the lien; or

(2) pursuant to a commitment entered into without knowledge of the lien.

(c) Subsections (a) and (b) do not apply to a security interest held by a secured party that is a buyer of accounts, chattel paper, payment intangibles, or promissory notes or a consignor.

(d) Except as otherwise provided in subsection (e), a buyer of goods other than a buyer in ordinary course of business takes free of a security interest to the extent that it secures advances made after the earlier of:

(1) the time the secured party acquires knowledge of the buyer's purchase; or

(2) 45 days after the purchase.

(e) Subsection (d) does not apply if the advance is made pursuant to a commitment entered into without knowledge of the buyer's purchase and before the expiration of the 45-day period.

(f) Except as otherwise provided in subsection (g), a lessee of goods, other than a lessee in ordinary course of business, takes the leasehold interest free of a security interest to the extent that it secures advances made after the earlier of:

(1) the time the secured party acquires knowledge of the lease; or

(2) 45 days after the lease contract becomes enforceable.

(g) Subsection (f) does not apply if the advance is made pursuant to a commitment entered into without knowledge of the lease and before the expiration of the 45-day period.

As amended in 1999.

§ 9–324. Priority of Purchase-Money Security Interests.

(a) Except as otherwise provided in subsection (g), a perfected purchase-money security interest in goods other than inventory or livestock has priority over a conflicting security interest in the same goods, and, except as otherwise provided in Section 9–327, a perfected security interest in its identifiable proceeds also has priority, if the purchase-money security interest is perfected when the debtor receives possession of the collateral or within 20 days thereafter.

(b) Subject to subsection (c) and except as otherwise provided in subsection (g), a perfected purchase-money security interest in inventory has priority over a conflicting security interest in the same inventory, has priority over a conflicting security interest in chattel paper or an instrument constituting proceeds of the inventory and in proceeds of the chattel paper, if so provided in Section 9–330, and, except as otherwise provided in Section 9–327, also has priority in identifiable cash proceeds of the inventory to the extent the identifiable cash proceeds are received on or before the delivery of the inventory to a buyer, if:

(1) the purchase-money security interest is perfected when the debtor receives possession of the inventory;

(2) the purchase-money secured party sends an authenticated notification to the holder of the conflicting security interest;

(3) the holder of the conflicting security interest receives the notification within five years before the debtor receives possession of the inventory; and

(4) the notification states that the person sending the notification has or expects to acquire a purchase-money security interest in inventory of the debtor and describes the inventory.

(c) Subsections (b)(2) through (4) apply only if the holder of the conflicting security interest had filed a financing statement covering the same types of inventory:

(1) if the purchase-money security interest is perfected by filing, before the date of the filing; or

(2) if the purchase-money security interest is temporarily perfected without filing or possession under Section 9–312(f), before the beginning of the 20-day period thereunder.

(d) Subject to subsection (e) and except as otherwise provided in subsection (g), a perfected purchase-money security interest in livestock that are farm products has priority over a conflicting security interest in the same livestock, and, except as otherwise provided in Section 9–327, a perfected security interest in their identifiable proceeds and identifiable products in their unmanufactured states also has priority, if:

(1) the purchase-money security interest is perfected when the debtor receives possession of the livestock;

(2) the purchase-money secured party sends an authenticated notification to the holder of the conflicting security interest;

(3) the holder of the conflicting security interest receives the notification within six months before the debtor receives possession of the livestock; and

(4) the notification states that the person sending the notification has or expects to acquire a purchase-money security interest in livestock of the debtor and describes the livestock.

(e) Subsections (d)(2) through (4) apply only if the holder of the conflicting security interest had filed a financing statement covering the same types of livestock:

(1) if the purchase-money security interest is perfected by filing, before the date of the filing; or

(2) if the purchase-money security interest is temporarily perfected without filing or possession under Section 9–312(f), before the beginning of the 20-day period thereunder.

(f) Except as otherwise provided in subsection (g), a perfected purchase-money security interest in software has priority over a conflicting security interest in the same collateral, and, except as otherwise provided in Section 9–327, a perfected security interest in its identifiable proceeds also has priority, to the extent that the purchase-money security interest in the goods in which the software was acquired for use has priority in the goods and proceeds of the goods under this section.

(g) If more than one security interest qualifies for priority in the same collateral under subsection (a), (b), (d), or (f):

(1) a security interest securing an obligation incurred as all or part of the price of the collateral has priority over a security interest securing an obligation incurred for value given to enable the debtor to acquire rights in or the use of collateral; and

(2) in all other cases, Section 9–322(a) applies to the qualifying security interests.

§ 9-325. Priority of Security Interests in Transferred Collateral.

(a) Except as otherwise provided in subsection (b), a security interest created by a debtor is subordinate to a security interest in the same collateral created by another person if:

(1) the debtor acquired the collateral subject to the security interest created by the other person;

(2) the security interest created by the other person was perfected when the debtor acquired the collateral; and

(3) there is no period thereafter when the security interest is unperfected.

(b) Subsection (a) subordinates a security interest only if the security interest:

(1) otherwise would have priority solely under Section 9–322(a) or 9–324; or

(2) arose solely under Section 2–711(3) or 2A–508(5).

§ 9-326. Priority of Security Interests Created by New Debtor.

(a) Subject to subsection (b), a security interest created by a new debtor which is perfected by a filed financing statement that is effective solely under Section 9–508 in collateral in which a new debtor has or acquires rights is subordinate to a security interest in the same collateral which is perfected other than by a filed financing statement that is effective solely under Section 9–508.

(b) The other provisions of this part determine the priority among conflicting security interests in the same collateral perfected by filed financing statements that are effective solely under Section 9–508. However, if the security agreements to which a new debtor became bound as debtor were not entered into by the same original debtor, the conflicting security interests rank according to priority in time of the new debtor's having become bound.

§ 9-327. Priority of Security Interests in Deposit Account.

The following rules govern priority among conflicting security interests in the same deposit account:

(1) A security interest held by a secured party having control of the deposit account under Section 9–104 has priority over a conflicting security interest held by a secured party that does not have control.

(2) Except as otherwise provided in paragraphs (3) and (4), security interests perfected by control under Section 9–314 rank according to priority in time of obtaining control.

(3) Except as otherwise provided in paragraph (4), a security interest held by the bank with which the deposit account is maintained has priority over a conflicting security interest held by another secured party.

(4) A security interest perfected by control under Section 9–104(a)(3) has priority over a security interest held by the bank with which the deposit account is maintained.

§ 9–328. Priority of Security Interests in Investment Property.

The following rules govern priority among conflicting security interests in the same investment property:

(1) A security interest held by a secured party having control of investment property under Section 9–106 has priority over a security interest held by a secured party that does not have control of the investment property.

(2) Except as otherwise provided in paragraphs (3) and (4), conflicting security interests held by secured parties each of which has control under Section 9–106 rank according to priority in time of:

(A) if the collateral is a security, obtaining control;

(B) if the collateral is a security entitlement carried in a securities account and:

(i) if the secured party obtained control under Section 8–106(d)(1), the secured party's becoming the person for which the securities account is maintained;

(ii) if the secured party obtained control under Section 8–106(d)(2), the securities intermediary's agreement to comply with the secured party's entitlement orders with respect to security entitlements carried or to be carried in the securities account; or

(iii) if the secured party obtained control through another person under Section 8–106(d)(3), the time on which priority would be based under this paragraph if the other person were the secured party; or

(C) if the collateral is a commodity contract carried with a commodity intermediary, the satisfaction of the requirement for control specified in Section 9–106(b)(2) with respect to commodity contracts carried or to be carried with the commodity intermediary.

(3) A security interest held by a securities intermediary in a security entitlement or a securities account maintained with the securities intermediary has priority over a conflicting security interest held by another secured party.

(4) A security interest held by a commodity intermediary in a commodity contract or a commodity account maintained with the commodity intermediary has priority over a conflicting security interest held by another secured party.

(5) A security interest in a certificated security in registered form which is perfected by taking delivery under Section 9–313(a) and not by control under Section 9–314 has priority over a conflicting security interest perfected by a method other than control.

(6) Conflicting security interests created by a broker, securities intermediary, or commodity intermediary which are perfected without control under Section 9–106 rank equally.

(7) In all other cases, priority among conflicting security interests in investment property is governed by Sections 9–322 and 9–323.

§ 9–329. Priority of Security Interests in Letter-of-Credit Right.

The following rules govern priority among conflicting security interests in the same letter-of-credit right:

(1) A security interest held by a secured party having control of the letter-of-credit right under Section 9–107 has priority to the extent of its control over a conflicting security interest held by a secured party that does not have control.

(2) Security interests perfected by control under Section 9–314 rank according to priority in time of obtaining control.

§ 9–330. Priority of Purchaser of Chattel Paper or Instrument.

(a) A purchaser of chattel paper has priority over a security interest in the chattel paper which is claimed merely as proceeds of inventory subject to a security interest if:

(1) in good faith and in the ordinary course of the purchaser's business, the purchaser gives new value and takes possession of the chattel paper or obtains control of the chattel paper under Section 9–105; and

(2) the chattel paper does not indicate that it has been assigned to an identified assignee other than the purchaser.

(b) A purchaser of chattel paper has priority over a security interest in the chattel paper which is claimed other than merely as proceeds of inventory subject to a security interest if the purchaser gives new value and takes possession of the chattel paper or obtains control of the chattel paper under Section 9–105 in good faith, in the ordinary course of the purchaser's business, and without knowledge that the purchase violates the rights of the secured party.

(c) Except as otherwise provided in Section 9–327, a purchaser having priority in chattel paper under subsection (a) or (b) also has priority in proceeds of the chattel paper to the extent that:

(1) Section 9–322 provides for priority in the proceeds; or

(2) the proceeds consist of the specific goods covered by the chattel paper or cash proceeds of the specific goods, even if the purchaser's security interest in the proceeds is unperfected.

(d) Except as otherwise provided in Section 9–331(a), a purchaser of an instrument has priority over a security interest in the instrument perfected by a method other than possession if the purchaser gives value and takes possession of the instrument in good faith and without knowledge that the purchase violates the rights of the secured party.

(e) For purposes of subsections (a) and (b), the holder of a purchase-money security interest in inventory gives new value for chattel paper constituting proceeds of the inventory.

(f) For purposes of subsections (b) and (d), if chattel paper or an instrument indicates that it has been assigned to an identified secured party other than the purchaser, a purchaser of the chattel paper or instrument has knowledge that the purchase violates the rights of the secured party.

§ 9–331. Priority of Rights of Purchasers of Instruments, Documents, and Securities under Other Articles; Priority of Interests in Financial Assets and Security Entitlements under Article 8.

(a) This article does not limit the rights of a holder in due course of a negotiable instrument, a holder to which a negotiable document of title has been duly negotiated, or a protected purchaser of a security. These holders or purchasers take priority over an earlier security interest, even if perfected, to the extent provided in Articles 3, 7, and 8.

(b) This article does not limit the rights of or impose liability on a person to the extent that the person is protected against the assertion of a claim under Article 8.

(c) Filing under this article does not constitute notice of a claim or defense to the holders, or purchasers, or persons described in subsections (a) and (b).

§ 9–332. Transfer of Money; Transfer of Funds from Deposit Account.

(a) A transferee of money takes the money free of a security interest unless the transferee acts in collusion with the debtor in violating the rights of the secured party.

(b) A transferee of funds from a deposit account takes the funds free of a security interest in the deposit account unless the transferee acts in collusion with the debtor in violating the rights of the secured party.

§ 9–333. Priority of Certain Liens Arising by Operation of Law.

(a) In this section, "possessory lien" means an interest, other than a security interest or an agricultural lien:

(1) which secures payment or performance of an obligation for services or materials furnished with respect to goods by a person in the ordinary course of the person's business;

(2) which is created by statute or rule of law in favor of the person; and

(3) whose effectiveness depends on the person's possession of the goods.

(b) A possessory lien on goods has priority over a security interest in the goods unless the lien is created by a statute that expressly provides otherwise.

§ 9–334. Priority of Security Interests in Fixtures and Crops.

(a) A security interest under this article may be created in goods that are fixtures or may continue in goods that become fixtures. A security interest does not exist under this article in ordinary building materials incorporated into an improvement on land.

(b) This article does not prevent creation of an encumbrance upon fixtures under real property law.

(c) In cases not governed by subsections (d) through (h), a security interest in fixtures is subordinate to a conflicting interest of an encumbrancer or owner of the related real property other than the debtor.

(d) Except as otherwise provided in subsection (h), a perfected security interest in fixtures has priority over a conflicting interest of an encumbrancer or owner of the real property if the debtor has an interest of record in or is in possession of the real property and:

(1) the security interest is a purchase-money security interest;

(2) the interest of the encumbrancer or owner arises before the goods become fixtures; and

(3) the security interest is perfected by a fixture filing before the goods become fixtures or within 20 days thereafter.

(e) A perfected security interest in fixtures has priority over a conflicting interest of an encumbrancer or owner of the real property if:

(1) the debtor has an interest of record in the real property or is in possession of the real property and the security interest:

(A) is perfected by a fixture filing before the interest of the encumbrancer or owner is of record; and

(B) has priority over any conflicting interest of a predecessor in title of the encumbrancer or owner;

(2) before the goods become fixtures, the security interest is perfected by any method permitted by this article and the fixtures are readily removable:

(A) factory or office machines;

(B) equipment that is not primarily used or leased for use in the operation of the real property; or

(C) replacements of domestic appliances that are consumer goods;

(3) the conflicting interest is a lien on the real property obtained by legal or equitable proceedings after the security interest was perfected by any method permitted by this article; or

(4) the security interest is:

(A) created in a manufactured home in a manufactured-home transaction; and

(B) perfected pursuant to a statute described in Section 9–311(a)(2).

(f) A security interest in fixtures, whether or not perfected, has priority over a conflicting interest of an encumbrancer or owner of the real property if:

(1) the encumbrancer or owner has, in an authenticated record, consented to the security interest or disclaimed an interest in the goods as fixtures; or

(2) the debtor has a right to remove the goods as against the encumbrancer or owner.

(g) The priority of the security interest under paragraph (f)(2) continues for a reasonable time if the debtor's right to remove the goods as against the encumbrancer or owner terminates.

(h) A mortgage is a construction mortgage to the extent that it secures an obligation incurred for the construction of an improvement on land, including the acquisition cost of the land, if a recorded record of the mortgage so indicates. Except as otherwise provided in subsections (e) and (f), a security interest in fixtures is subordinate to a construction mortgage if a record of the mortgage is recorded before the goods become fixtures and the goods become fixtures before the completion of the construction. A mortgage has this priority to the same extent as a construction mortgage to the extent that it is given to refinance a construction mortgage.

(i) A perfected security interest in crops growing on real property has priority over a conflicting interest of an encumbrancer or owner of the real property if the debtor has an interest of record in or is in possession of the real property.

(j) Subsection (i) prevails over any inconsistent provisions of the following statutes:

[List here any statutes containing provisions inconsistent with subsection (i).]

Legislative Note: States that amend statutes to remove provisions inconsistent with subsection (i) need not enact subsection (j).

§ 9–335. Accessions.

(a) A security interest may be created in an accession and continues in collateral that becomes an accession.

(b) If a security interest is perfected when the collateral becomes an accession, the security interest remains perfected in the collateral.

(c) Except as otherwise provided in subsection (d), the other provisions of this part determine the priority of a security interest in an accession.

(d) A security interest in an accession is subordinate to a security interest in the whole which is perfected by compliance with the requirements of a certificate-of-title statute under Section 9–311(b).

(e) After default, subject to Part 6, a secured party may remove an accession from other goods if the security interest in the accession has priority over the claims of every person having an interest in the whole.

(f) A secured party that removes an accession from other goods under subsection (e) shall promptly reimburse any holder of a security interest or other lien on, or owner of, the whole or of the other goods, other than the debtor, for the cost of repair of any physical injury to the whole or the other goods. The secured party need not reimburse the holder or owner for any diminution in value of the whole or the other goods caused by the absence of the accession removed or by any necessity for replacing it. A person entitled to reimbursement may refuse permission to remove until the secured party gives adequate assurance for the performance of the obligation to reimburse.

§ 9–336. Commingled Goods.

(a) In this section, "commingled goods" means goods that are physically united with other goods in such a manner that their identity is lost in a product or mass.

(b) A security interest does not exist in commingled goods as such. However, a security interest may attach to a product or mass that results when goods become commingled goods.

(c) If collateral becomes commingled goods, a security interest attaches to the product or mass.

(d) If a security interest in collateral is perfected before the collateral becomes commingled goods, the security interest that attaches to the product or mass under subsection (c) is perfected.

(e) Except as otherwise provided in subsection (f), the other provisions of this part determine the priority of a security interest that attaches to the product or mass under subsection (c).

(f) If more than one security interest attaches to the product or mass under subsection (c), the following rules determine priority:

(1) A security interest that is perfected under subsection (d) has priority over a security interest that is unperfected at the time the collateral becomes commingled goods.

(2) If more than one security interest is perfected under subsection (d), the security interests rank equally in proportion to the value of the collateral at the time it became commingled goods.

§ 9–337. Priority of Security Interests in Goods Covered by Certificate of Title.

If, while a security interest in goods is perfected by any method under the law of another jurisdiction, this State issues a certificate of title that does not show that the goods are subject to the security interest or contain a statement that they may be subject to security interests not shown on the certificate:

(1) a buyer of the goods, other than a person in the business of selling goods of that kind, takes free of the security interest if the buyer gives value and

receives delivery of the goods after issuance of the certificate and without knowledge of the security interest; and

(2) the security interest is subordinate to a conflicting security interest in the goods that attaches, and is perfected under Section 9–311(b), after issuance of the certificate and without the conflicting secured party's knowledge of the security interest.

§ 9–338. Priority of Security Interest or Agricultural Lien Perfected by Filed Financing Statement Providing Certain Incorrect Information.

If a security interest or agricultural lien is perfected by a filed financing statement providing information described in Section 9–516(b)(5) which is incorrect at the time the financing statement is filed:

(1) the security interest or agricultural lien is subordinate to a conflicting perfected security interest in the collateral to the extent that the holder of the conflicting security interest gives value in reasonable reliance upon the incorrect information; and

(2) a purchaser, other than a secured party, of the collateral takes free of the security interest or agricultural lien to the extent that, in reasonable reliance upon the incorrect information, the purchaser gives value and, in the case of chattel paper, documents, goods, instruments, or a security certificate, receives delivery of the collateral.

§ 9–339. Priority Subject to Subordination.

This article does not preclude subordination by agreement by a person entitled to priority.

[Subpart 4. Rights of Bank]

§ 9–340. Effectiveness of Right of Recoupment or Set-Off against Deposit Account.

(a) Except as otherwise provided in subsection (c), a bank with which a deposit account is maintained may exercise any right of recoupment or set-off against a secured party that holds a security interest in the deposit account.

(b) Except as otherwise provided in subsection (c), the application of this article to a security interest in a deposit account does not affect a right of recoupment or set-off of the secured party as to a deposit account maintained with the secured party.

(c) The exercise by a bank of a set-off against a deposit account is ineffective against a secured party that holds a security interest in the deposit account which is perfected by control under Section 9–104(a)(3), if the set-off is based on a claim against the debtor.

§ 9–341. Bank's Rights and Duties with Respect to Deposit Account.

Except as otherwise provided in Section 9–340(c), and unless the bank otherwise agrees in an authenticated record, a bank's rights and duties with respect to a deposit account maintained with the bank are not terminated, suspended, or modified by:

(1) the creation, attachment, or perfection of a security interest in the deposit account;

(2) the bank's knowledge of the security interest; or

(3) the bank's receipt of instructions from the secured party.

§ 9–342. Bank's Right to Refuse to Enter into or Disclose Existence of Control Agreement.

This article does not require a bank to enter into an agreement of the kind described in Section 9–104(a)(2), even if its customer so requests or directs. A bank that has entered into such an agreement is not required to confirm the existence of the agreement to another person unless requested to do so by its customer.

Part 4 Rights of Third Parties

§ 9–401. Alienability of Debtor's Rights.

(a) Except as otherwise provided in subsection (b) and Sections 9–406, 9–407, 9–408, and 9–409, whether a debtor's rights in collateral may be voluntarily or involuntarily transferred is governed by law other than this article.

(b) An agreement between the debtor and secured party which prohibits a transfer of the debtor's rights in collateral or makes the transfer a default does not prevent the transfer from taking effect.

§ 9–402. Secured Party Not Obligated on Contract of Debtor or in Tort.

The existence of a security interest, agricultural lien, or authority given to a debtor to dispose of or use collateral, without more, does not subject a secured party to liability in contract or tort for the debtor's acts or omissions.

§ 9–403. Agreement Not to Assert Defenses against Assignee.

(a) In this section, "value" has the meaning provided in Section 3–303(a).

(b) Except as otherwise provided in this section, an agreement between an account debtor and an assignor not to assert against an assignee any claim or defense that the account debtor may have against the assignor is enforceable by an assignee that takes an assignment:

(1) for value;

(2) in good faith;

(3) without notice of a claim of a property or possessory right to the property assigned; and

(4) without notice of a defense or claim in recoupment of the type that may be asserted against a person entitled to enforce a negotiable instrument under Section 3–305(a).

(c) Subsection (b) does not apply to defenses of a type that may be asserted against a holder in due course of a negotiable instrument under Section 3–305(b).

(d) In a consumer transaction, if a record evidences the account debtor's obligation, law other than this article requires that the record include a statement to the effect that the rights of an assignee are subject to claims or defenses that the account debtor could assert against the original obligee, and the record does not include such a statement:

(1) the record has the same effect as if the record included such a statement; and

(2) the account debtor may assert against an assignee those claims and defenses that would have been available if the record included such a statement.

(e) This section is subject to law other than this article which establishes a different rule for an account debtor who is an individual and who incurred the obligation primarily for personal, family, or household purposes.

(f) Except as otherwise provided in subsection (d), this section does not displace law other than this article which gives effect to an agreement by an account debtor not to assert a claim or defense against an assignee.

§ 9–404. Rights Acquired by Assignee; Claims and Defenses against Assignee.

(a) Unless an account debtor has made an enforceable agreement not to assert defenses or claims, and subject to subsections (b) through (e), the rights of an assignee are subject to:

(1) all terms of the agreement between the account debtor and assignor and any defense or claim in recoupment arising from the transaction that gave rise to the contract; and

(2) any other defense or claim of the account debtor against the assignor which accrues before the account debtor receives a notification of the assignment authenticated by the assignor or the assignee.

(b) Subject to subsection (c) and except as otherwise provided in subsection (d), the claim of an account debtor against an assignor may be asserted against an assignee under subsection (a) only to reduce the amount the account debtor owes.

(c) This section is subject to law other than this article which establishes a different rule for an account debtor who is an individual and who incurred the obligation primarily for personal, family, or household purposes.

(d) In a consumer transaction, if a record evidences the account debtor's obligation, law other than this article requires that the record include a statement to the effect that the account debtor's recovery against an assignee with respect to claims and defenses against the assignor may not exceed amounts paid by the account debtor under the record, and the record does not include such a statement, the extent to which a claim of an account debtor against the assignor may be asserted against an assignee is determined as if the record included such a statement.

(e) This section does not apply to an assignment of a health-care-insurance receivable.

§ 9–405. Modification of Assigned Contract.

(a) A modification of or substitution for an assigned contract is effective against an assignee if made in good faith. The assignee acquires corresponding rights under the modified or substituted contract. The assignment may provide that the modification or substitution is a breach of contract by the assignor. This subsection is subject to subsections (b) through (d).

(b) Subsection (a) applies to the extent that:

(1) the right to payment or a part thereof under an assigned contract has not been fully earned by performance; or

(2) the right to payment or a part thereof has been fully earned by performance and the account debtor has not received notification of the assignment under Section 9–406(a).

(c) This section is subject to law other than this article which establishes a different rule for an account debtor who is an individual and who incurred the obligation primarily for personal, family, or household purposes.

(d) This section does not apply to an assignment of a health-care-insurance receivable.

§ 9–406. Discharge of Account Debtor; Notification of Assignment; Identification and Proof of Assignment; Restrictions on Assignment of Accounts, Chattel Paper, Payment Intangibles, and Promissory Notes Ineffective.

(a) Subject to subsections (b) through (i), an account debtor on an account, chattel paper, or a payment intangible may discharge its obligation by paying the assignor until, but not after, the account debtor receives a notification, authenticated by the assignor or the assignee, that the amount due or to become due has been assigned and that payment is to be made to the assignee. After receipt of the notification, the account debtor may discharge its obligation by paying the assignee and may not discharge the obligation by paying the assignor.

(b) Subject to subsection (h), notification is ineffective under subsection (a):

(1) if it does not reasonably identify the rights assigned;

(2) to the extent that an agreement between an account debtor and a seller of a payment intangible limits the account debtor's duty to pay a person other than the seller and the limitation is effective under law other than this article; or

(3) at the option of an account debtor, if the notification notifies the account debtor to make less than the full amount of any installment or other periodic payment to the assignee, even if:

(A) only a portion of the account, chattel paper, or payment intangible has been assigned to that assignee;

(B) a portion has been assigned to another assignee; or

(C) the account debtor knows that the assignment to that assignee is limited.

(c) Subject to subsection (h), if requested by the account debtor, an assignee shall seasonably furnish reasonable proof that the assignment has been made. Unless the assignee complies, the account debtor may discharge its obligation by paying the assignor, even if the account debtor has received a notification under subsection (a).

(d) Except as otherwise provided in subsection (e) and Sections 2A–303 and 9–407, and subject to subsection (h), a term in an agreement between an account debtor and an assignor or in a promissory note is ineffective to the extent that it:

(1) prohibits, restricts, or requires the consent of the account debtor or person obligated on the promissory note to the assignment or transfer of, or the creation, attachment, perfection, or enforcement of a security interest in, the account, chattel paper, payment intangible, or promissory note; or

(2) provides that the assignment or transfer or the creation, attachment, perfection, or enforcement of the security interest may give rise to a default, breach, right of recoupment, claim, defense, termination, right of termination, or remedy under the account, chattel paper, payment intangible, or promissory note.

(e) Subsection (d) does not apply to the sale of a payment intangible or promissory note.

(f) Except as otherwise provided in Sections 2A–303 and 9–407 and subject to subsections (h) and (i), a rule of law, statute, or regulation that prohibits, restricts, or requires the consent of a government, governmental body or official, or account debtor to the assignment or transfer of, or creation of a security interest in, an account or chattel paper is ineffective to the extent that the rule of law, statute, or regulation:

(1) prohibits, restricts, or requires the consent of the government, governmental body or official, or account debtor to the assignment or transfer of, or the creation, attachment, perfection, or enforcement of a security interest in the account or chattel paper; or

(2) provides that the assignment or transfer or the creation, attachment, perfection, or enforcement of the security interest may give rise to a default, breach, right of recoupment, claim, defense, termination, right of termination, or remedy under the account or chattel paper.

(g) Subject to subsection (h), an account debtor may not waive or vary its option under subsection (b)(3).

(h) This section is subject to law other than this article which establishes a different rule for an account debtor who is an individual and who incurred the obligation primarily for personal, family, or household purposes.

(i) This section does not apply to an assignment of a health-care-insurance receivable.

(j) This section prevails over any inconsistent provisions of the following statutes, rules, and regulations:

[List here any statutes, rules, and regulations containing provisions inconsistent with this section.]

Legislative Note: States that amend statutes, rules, and regulations to remove provisions inconsistent with this section need not enact subsection (j).

As amended in 1999 and 2000.

§ 9–407. Restrictions on Creation or Enforcement of Security Interest in Leasehold Interest or in Lessor's Residual Interest.

(a) Except as otherwise provided in subsection (b), a term in a lease agreement is ineffective to the extent that it:

(1) prohibits, restricts, or requires the consent of a party to the lease to the assignment or transfer of, or the creation, attachment, perfection, or enforcement of a security interest in an interest of a party under the lease contract or in the lessor's residual interest in the goods; or

(2) provides that the assignment or transfer or the creation, attachment, perfection, or enforcement of the security interest may give rise to a default, breach, right of recoupment, claim, defense, termination, right of termination, or remedy under the lease.

(b) Except as otherwise provided in Section 2A–303(7), a term described in subsection (a)(2) is effective to the extent that there is:

(1) a transfer by the lessee of the lessee's right of possession or use of the goods in violation of the term; or

(2) a delegation of a material performance of either party to the lease contract in violation of the term.

(c) The creation, attachment, perfection, or enforcement of a security interest in the lessor's interest under the lease contract or the lessor's residual interest in the goods is not a transfer that materially impairs the lessee's prospect of obtaining return performance or materially changes the duty of or materially increases the burden or risk imposed on the lessee within the purview of Section 2A–303(4) unless, and then only to the extent that, enforcement actually results in a delegation of material performance of the lessor.

As amended in 1999.

§ 9–408. Restrictions on Assignment of Promissory Notes, Health-Care-Insurance Receivables, and Certain General Intangibles Ineffective.

(a) Except as otherwise provided in subsection (b), a term in a promissory note or in an agreement between an account debtor and a debtor which relates to a health-care-insurance receivable or a general intangible, including a contract, permit, license, or franchise, and which term prohibits, restricts, or requires the consent of the person obligated on the promissory note or the account debtor to, the assignment or transfer of, or creation, attachment, or perfection of a security interest in, the promissory note, health-care-insurance receivable, or general intangible, is ineffective to the extent that the term:

(1) would impair the creation, attachment, or perfection of a security interest; or

(2) provides that the assignment or transfer or the creation, attachment, or perfection of the security interest may give rise to a default, breach, right of recoupment, claim, defense, termination, right of termination, or remedy under the promissory note, health-care-insurance receivable, or general intangible.

(b) Subsection (a) applies to a security interest in a payment intangible or promissory note only if the security interest arises out of a sale of the payment intangible or promissory note.

(c) A rule of law, statute, or regulation that prohibits, restricts, or requires the consent of a government, governmental body or official, person obligated on a promissory note, or account debtor to the assignment or transfer of, or creation of a security interest in, a promissory note, health-care-insurance receivable, or general intangible, including a contract, permit, license, or franchise between an account debtor and a debtor, is ineffective to the extent that the rule of law, statute, or regulation:

(1) would impair the creation, attachment, or perfection of a security interest; or

(2) provides that the assignment or transfer or the creation, attachment, or perfection of the security interest may give rise to a default, breach, right of recoupment, claim, defense, termination, right of termination, or remedy under the promissory note, health-care-insurance receivable, or general intangible.

(d) To the extent that a term in a promissory note or in an agreement between an account debtor and a debtor which relates to a health-care-insurance receivable or general intangible or a rule of law, statute, or regulation described in subsection (c) would be effective under law other than this article but is ineffective under subsection (a) or (c), the creation, attachment, or perfection of a security interest in the promissory note, health-care-insurance receivable, or general intangible:

(1) is not enforceable against the person obligated on the promissory note or the account debtor;

(2) does not impose a duty or obligation on the person obligated on the promissory note or the account debtor;

(3) does not require the person obligated on the promissory note or the account debtor to recognize the security interest, pay or render performance to the secured party, or accept payment or performance from the secured party;

(4) does not entitle the secured party to use or assign the debtor's rights under the promissory note, health-care-insurance receivable, or general intangible, including any related information or materials furnished to the debtor in the transaction giving rise to the promissory note, health-care-insurance receivable, or general intangible;

(5) does not entitle the secured party to use, assign, possess, or have access to any trade secrets or confidential information of the person obligated on the promissory note or the account debtor; and

(6) does not entitle the secured party to enforce the security interest in the promissory note, health-care-insurance receivable, or general intangible.

(e) This section prevails over any inconsistent provisions of the following statutes, rules, and regulations:

[List here any statutes, rules, and regulations containing provisions inconsistent with this section.]

Legislative Note: States that amend statutes, rules, and regulations to remove provisions inconsistent with this section need not enact subsection (e).

As amended in 1999.

§ 9–409. Restrictions on Assignment of Letter-of-Credit Rights Ineffective.

(a) A term in a letter of credit or a rule of law, statute, regulation, custom, or practice applicable to the letter of credit which prohibits, restricts, or requires the consent of an applicant, issuer, or nominated person to a beneficiary's assignment of or creation of a security interest in a letter-of-credit right is ineffective to the extent that the term or rule of law, statute, regulation, custom, or practice:

(1) would impair the creation, attachment, or perfection of a security interest in the letter-of-credit right; or

(2) provides that the assignment or the creation, attachment, or perfection of the security interest may give rise to a default, breach, right of recoupment, claim, defense, termination, right of termination, or remedy under the letter-of-credit right.

(b) To the extent that a term in a letter of credit is ineffective under subsection (a) but would be effective under law other than this article or a custom or practice applicable to the letter of credit, to the transfer of a right to draw or otherwise demand performance under the letter of credit, or to the assignment of a right to proceeds of the letter of credit, the creation, attachment, or perfection of a security interest in the letter-of-credit right:

(1) is not enforceable against the applicant, issuer, nominated person, or transferee beneficiary;

(2) imposes no duties or obligations on the applicant, issuer, nominated person, or transferee beneficiary; and

(3) does not require the applicant, issuer, nominated person, or transferee beneficiary to recognize the security interest, pay or render performance to the secured party, or accept payment or other performance from the secured party.

As amended in 1999.

Part 5 Filing

[Subpart 1. Filing Office; Contents and Effectiveness of Financing Statement]

§ 9–501. Filing Office.

(a) Except as otherwise provided in subsection (b), if the local law of this State governs perfection of a security interest or agricultural lien, the office in which to file a financing statement to perfect the security interest or agricultural lien is:

(1) the office designated for the filing or recording of a record of a mortgage on the related real property, if:

(A) the collateral is as-extracted collateral or timber to be cut; or

(B) the financing statement is filed as a fixture filing and the collateral is goods that are or are to become fixtures; or

(2) the office of [ ] [or any office duly authorized by [ ]], in all other cases, including a case in which the collateral is goods that are or are to become fixtures and the financing statement is not filed as a fixture filing.

(b) The office in which to file a financing statement to perfect a security interest in collateral, including fixtures, of a transmitting utility is the office of [ ]. The financing statement also constitutes a fixture filing as to the collateral indicated in the financing statement which is or is to become fixtures.

Legislative Note: The State should designate the filing office where the brackets appear. The filing office may be that of a governmental official (e.g., the Secretary of State) or a private party that maintains the State's filing system.

§ 9–502. Contents of Financing Statement; Record of Mortgage as Financing Statement; Time of Filing Financing Statement.

(a) Subject to subsection (b), a financing statement is sufficient only if it:

(1) provides the name of the debtor;

(2) provides the name of the secured party or a representative of the secured party; and

(3) indicates the collateral covered by the financing statement.

(b) Except as otherwise provided in Section 9–501(b), to be sufficient, a financing statement that covers as-extracted collateral or timber to be cut, or which is filed as a fixture filing and covers goods that are or are to become fixtures, must satisfy subsection (a) and also:

(1) indicate that it covers this type of collateral;

(2) indicate that it is to be filed [for record] in the real property records;

(3) provide a description of the real property to which the collateral is related [sufficient to give constructive notice of a mortgage under the law of this State if the description were contained in a record of the mortgage of the real property]; and

(4) if the debtor does not have an interest of record in the real property, provide the name of a record owner.

(c) A record of a mortgage is effective, from the date of recording, as a financing statement filed as a fixture filing or as a financing statement covering as-extracted collateral or timber to be cut only if:

(1) the record indicates the goods or accounts that it covers;

(2) the goods are or are to become fixtures related to the real property described in the record or the collateral is related to the real property described in the record and is as-extracted collateral or timber to be cut;

(3) the record satisfies the requirements for a financing statement in this section other than an indication that it is to be filed in the real property records; and

(4) the record is [duly] recorded.

(d) A financing statement may be filed before a security agreement is made or a security interest otherwise attaches.

Legislative Note: Language in brackets is optional. Where the State has any special recording system for real property other than the usual grantor-grantee index (as, for instance, a tract system or a title registration or Torrens system) local adaptations of subsection (b) and Section 9–519(d) and (e) may be necessary. See, e.g., Mass. Gen. Laws Chapter 106, Section 9–410.

§ 9–503. Name of Debtor and Secured Party.

(a) A financing statement sufficiently provides the name of the debtor:

(1) if the debtor is a registered organization, only if the financing statement provides the name of the debtor indicated on the public record of the debtor's jurisdiction of organization which shows the debtor to have been organized;

(2) if the debtor is a decedent's estate, only if the financing statement provides the name of the decedent and indicates that the debtor is an estate;

(3) if the debtor is a trust or a trustee acting with respect to property held in trust, only if the financing statement:

(A) provides the name specified for the trust in its organic documents or, if no name is specified, provides the name of the settlor and additional information sufficient to distinguish the debtor from other trusts having one or more of the same settlors; and

(B) indicates, in the debtor's name or otherwise, that the debtor is a trust or is a trustee acting with respect to property held in trust; and

(4) in other cases:

(A) if the debtor has a name, only if it provides the individual or organizational name of the debtor; and

(B) if the debtor does not have a name, only if it provides the names of the partners, members, associates, or other persons comprising the debtor.

(b) A financing statement that provides the name of the debtor in accordance with subsection (a) is not rendered ineffective by the absence of:

(1) a trade name or other name of the debtor; or

(2) unless required under subsection (a)(4)(B), names of partners, members, associates, or other persons comprising the debtor.

(c) A financing statement that provides only the debtor's trade name does not sufficiently provide the name of the debtor.

(d) Failure to indicate the representative capacity of a secured party or representative of a secured party does not affect the sufficiency of a financing statement.

(e) A financing statement may provide the name of more than one debtor and the name of more than one secured party.

§ 9–504. Indication of Collateral.

A financing statement sufficiently indicates the collateral that it covers if the financing statement provides:

(1) a description of the collateral pursuant to Section 9–108; or

(2) an indication that the financing statement covers all assets or all personal property.

As amended in 1999.

§ 9–505. Filing and Compliance with Other Statutes and Treaties for Consignments, Leases, Other Bailments, and Other Transactions.

(a) A consignor, lessor, or other bailor of goods, a licensor, or a buyer of a payment intangible or promissory note may file a financing statement, or may comply with a statute or treaty described in Section 9–311(a), using the terms "consignor", "consignee", "lessor", "lessee", "bailor", "bailee", "licensor", "licensee", "owner", "registered owner", "buyer", "seller", or words of similar import, instead of the terms "secured party" and "debtor".

(b) This part applies to the filing of a financing statement under subsection (a) and, as appropriate, to compliance that is equivalent to filing a financing statement under Section 9–311(b), but the filing or compliance is not of itself a factor in determining whether the collateral secures an obligation. If it is determined for another reason that the collateral secures an obligation, a security interest held by the consignor, lessor, bailor, licensor, owner, or buyer which attaches to the collateral is perfected by the filing or compliance.

§ 9–506. Effect of Errors or Omissions.

(a) A financing statement substantially satisfying the requirements of this part is effective, even if it has minor errors or omissions, unless the errors or omissions make the financing statement seriously misleading.

(b) Except as otherwise provided in subsection (c), a financing statement that fails sufficiently to provide the name of the debtor in accordance with Section 9–503(a) is seriously misleading.

(c) If a search of the records of the filing office under the debtor's correct name, using the filing office's standard search logic, if any, would disclose a financing statement that fails sufficiently to provide the name of the debtor in accordance with Section 9–503(a), the name provided does not make the financing statement seriously misleading.

(d) For purposes of Section 9–508(b), the "debtor's correct name" in subsection (c) means the correct name of the new debtor.

§ 9–507. Effect of Certain Events on Effectiveness of Financing Statement.

(a) A filed financing statement remains effective with respect to collateral that is sold, exchanged, leased, licensed, or otherwise disposed of and in which a security interest or agricultural lien continues, even if the secured party knows of or consents to the disposition.

(b) Except as otherwise provided in subsection (c) and Section 9–508, a financing statement is not rendered ineffective if, after the financing statement is filed, the information provided in the financing statement becomes seriously misleading under Section 9–506.

(c) If a debtor so changes its name that a filed financing statement becomes seriously misleading under Section 9–506:

(1) the financing statement is effective to perfect a security interest in collateral acquired by the debtor before, or within four months after, the change; and

(2) the financing statement is not effective to perfect a security interest in collateral acquired by the debtor more than four months after the change, unless an amendment to the financing statement which renders the financing statement not seriously misleading is filed within four months after the change.

§ 9–508. Effectiveness of Financing Statement If New Debtor Becomes Bound by Security Agreement.

(a) Except as otherwise provided in this section, a filed financing statement naming an original debtor is effective to perfect a security interest in collateral in which a new debtor has or acquires rights to the extent that the financing statement would have been effective had the original debtor acquired rights in the collateral.

(b) If the difference between the name of the original debtor and that of the new debtor causes a filed financing statement that is effective under subsection (a) to be seriously misleading under Section 9–506:

(1) the financing statement is effective to perfect a security interest in collateral acquired by the new debtor before, and within four months after, the new debtor becomes bound under Section 9B–203(d); and

(2) the financing statement is not effective to perfect a security interest in collateral acquired by the new debtor more than four months after the new debtor becomes bound under Section 9–203(d) unless an initial financing statement providing the name of the new debtor is filed before the expiration of that time.

(c) This section does not apply to collateral as to which a filed financing statement remains effective against the new debtor under Section 9–507(a).

§ 9–509. Persons Entitled to File a Record.

(a) A person may file an initial financing statement, amendment that adds collateral covered by a financing statement, or amendment that adds a debtor to a financing statement only if:

(1) the debtor authorizes the filing in an authenticated record or pursuant to subsection (b) or (c); or

(2) the person holds an agricultural lien that has become effective at the time of filing and the financing statement covers only collateral in which the person holds an agricultural lien.

(b) By authenticating or becoming bound as debtor by a security agreement, a debtor or new debtor authorizes the filing of an initial financing statement, and an amendment, covering:

(1) the collateral described in the security agreement; and

(2) property that becomes collateral under Section 9–315(a)(2), whether or not the security agreement expressly covers proceeds.

(c) By acquiring collateral in which a security interest or agricultural lien continues under Section 9–315(a)(1), a debtor authorizes the filing of an initial financing statement, and an amendment, covering the collateral and property that becomes collateral under Section 9–315(a)(2).

(d) A person may file an amendment other than an amendment that adds collateral covered by a financing statement or an amendment that adds a debtor to a financing statement only if:

(1) the secured party of record authorizes the filing; or

(2) the amendment is a termination statement for a financing statement as to which the secured party of record has failed to file or send a termination statement as required by Section 9–513(a) or (c), the debtor authorizes the filing, and the termination statement indicates that the debtor authorized it to be filed.

(e) If there is more than one secured party of record for a financing statement, each secured party of record may authorize the filing of an amendment under subsection (d).

As amended in 2000.

§ 9–510. Effectiveness of Filed Record.

(a) A filed record is effective only to the extent that it was filed by a person that may file it under Section 9–509.

(b) A record authorized by one secured party of record does not affect the financing statement with respect to another secured party of record.

(c) A continuation statement that is not filed within the six-month period prescribed by Section 9–515(d) is ineffective.

§ 9–511. Secured Party of Record.

(a) A secured party of record with respect to a financing statement is a person whose name is provided as the name of the secured party or a representative of the secured party in an initial financing statement that has been filed. If an initial financing statement is filed under Section 9–514(a), the assignee named in the initial financing statement is the secured party of record with respect to the financing statement.

(b) If an amendment of a financing statement which provides the name of a person as a secured party or a representative of a secured party is filed, the person named in the amendment is a secured party of record. If an amendment is filed under Section 9–514(b), the assignee named in the amendment is a secured party of record.

(c) A person remains a secured party of record until the filing of an amendment of the financing statement which deletes the person.

§ 9–512. Amendment of Financing Statement.

[Alternative A]

(a) Subject to Section 9–509, a person may add or delete collateral covered by, continue or terminate the effectiveness of, or, subject to subsection (e), otherwise amend the information provided in, a financing statement by filing an amendment that:

(1) identifies, by its file number, the initial financing statement to which the amendment relates; and

(2) if the amendment relates to an initial financing statement filed [or recorded] in a filing office described in Section 9–501(a)(1), provides the information specified in Section 9–502(b).

[Alternative B]

(a) Subject to Section 9–509, a person may add or delete collateral covered by, continue or terminate the effectiveness of, or, subject to subsection (e), otherwise amend the information provided in, a financing statement by filing an amendment that:

(1) identifies, by its file number, the initial financing statement to which the amendment relates; and

(2) if the amendment relates to an initial financing statement filed [or recorded] in a filing office described in Section 9–501(a)(1), provides the date [and time] that the initial financing statement was filed [or recorded] and the information specified in Section 9–502(b).

[End of Alternatives]

(b) Except as otherwise provided in Section 9–515, the filing of an amendment does not extend the period of effectiveness of the financing statement.

(c) A financing statement that is amended by an amendment that adds collateral is effective as to the added collateral only from the date of the filing of the amendment.

(d) A financing statement that is amended by an amendment that adds a debtor is effective as to the added debtor only from the date of the filing of the amendment.

(e) An amendment is ineffective to the extent it:

(1) purports to delete all debtors and fails to provide the name of a debtor to be covered by the financing statement; or

(2) purports to delete all secured parties of record and fails to provide the name of a new secured party of record.

Legislative Note: States whose real-estate filing offices require additional information in amendments and cannot search their records by both the name of the debtor and the file number should enact Alternative B to Sections 9–512(a), 9–518(b), 9–519(f), and 9–522(a).

§ 9–513. Termination Statement.

(a) A secured party shall cause the secured party of record for a financing statement to file a termination statement for the financing statement if the financing statement covers consumer goods and:

(1) there is no obligation secured by the collateral covered by the financing statement and no commitment to make an advance, incur an obligation, or otherwise give value; or

(2) the debtor did not authorize the filing of the initial financing statement.

(b) To comply with subsection (a), a secured party shall cause the secured party of record to file the termination statement:

(1) within one month after there is no obligation secured by the collateral covered by the financing statement and no commitment to make an advance, incur an obligation, or otherwise give value; or

(2) if earlier, within 20 days after the secured party receives an authenticated demand from a debtor.

(c) In cases not governed by subsection (a), within 20 days after a secured party receives an authenticated demand from a debtor, the secured party shall cause the secured party of record for a financing statement to send to the debtor a termination statement for the financing statement or file the termination statement in the filing office if:

(1) except in the case of a financing statement covering accounts or chattel paper that has been sold or goods that are the subject of a consignment, there is no obligation secured by the collateral covered by the financing statement and no commitment to make an advance, incur an obligation, or otherwise give value;

(2) the financing statement covers accounts or chattel paper that has been sold but as to which the account debtor or other person obligated has discharged its obligation;

(3) the financing statement covers goods that were the subject of a consignment to the debtor but are not in the debtor's possession; or

(4) the debtor did not authorize the filing of the initial financing statement.

(d) Except as otherwise provided in Section 9–510, upon the filing of a termination statement with the filing office, the financing statement to which the termination statement relates ceases to be effective. Except as otherwise provided in Section 9–510, for purposes of Sections 9–519(g), 9–522(a), and 9–523(c), the filing with the filing office of a termination statement relating to a financing statement that indicates that the debtor is a transmitting utility also causes the effectiveness of the financing statement to lapse.

As amended in 2000.

§ 9–514. Assignment of Powers of Secured Party of Record.

(a) Except as otherwise provided in subsection (c), an initial financing statement may reflect an assignment of all of the secured party's power to authorize an amendment to the financing statement by providing the name and mailing address of the assignee as the name and address of the secured party.

(b) Except as otherwise provided in subsection (c), a secured party of record may assign of record all or part of its power to authorize an amendment to a financing statement by filing in the filing office an amendment of the financing statement which:

(1) identifies, by its file number, the initial financing statement to which it relates;

(2) provides the name of the assignor; and

(3) provides the name and mailing address of the assignee.

(c) An assignment of record of a security interest in a fixture covered by a record of a mortgage which is effective as a financing statement filed as a fixture filing under Section 9–502(c) may be made only by an assignment of record of the mortgage in the manner provided by law of this State other than [the Uniform Commercial Code].

§ 9–515. Duration and Effectiveness of Financing Statement; Effect of Lapsed Financing Statement.

(a) Except as otherwise provided in subsections (b), (e), (f), and (g), a filed financing statement is effective for a period of five years after the date of filing.

(b) Except as otherwise provided in subsections (e), (f), and (g), an initial financing statement filed in connection with a public-finance transaction or manufactured-home transaction is effective for a period of 30 years after the date of filing if it indicates that it is filed in connection with a public-finance transaction or manufactured-home transaction.

(c) The effectiveness of a filed financing statement lapses on the expiration of the period of its effectiveness unless before the lapse a continuation statement is filed pursuant to subsection (d). Upon lapse, a financing statement ceases to be effective and any security interest or agricultural lien that was perfected by the financing statement becomes unperfected, unless the security interest is perfected otherwise. If the security interest or agricultural lien becomes unperfected upon lapse, it is deemed never to have been perfected as against a purchaser of the collateral for value.

(d) A continuation statement may be filed only within six months before the expiration of the five-year period specified in subsection (a) or the 30-year period specified in subsection (b), whichever is applicable.

(e) Except as otherwise provided in Section 9–510, upon timely filing of a continuation statement, the effectiveness of the initial financing statement continues for a period of five years commencing on the day on which the financing statement would have become ineffective in the absence of the filing. Upon the expiration of the five-year period, the financing statement lapses in the same manner as provided in subsection (c), unless, before the lapse, another continuation statement is filed pursuant to subsection (d). Succeeding continuation statements may be filed in the same manner to continue the effectiveness of the initial financing statement.

(f) If a debtor is a transmitting utility and a filed financing statement so indicates, the financing statement is effective until a termination statement is filed.

(g) A record of a mortgage that is effective as a financing statement filed as a fixture filing under Section 9–502(c) remains effective as a financing statement filed as a fixture filing until the mortgage is released or satisfied of record or its effectiveness otherwise terminates as to the real property.

§ 9–516. What Constitutes Filing; Effectiveness of Filing.

(a) Except as otherwise provided in subsection (b), communication of a record to a filing office and tender of the filing fee or acceptance of the record by the filing office constitutes filing.

(b) Filing does not occur with respect to a record that a filing office refuses to accept because:

(1) the record is not communicated by a method or medium of communication authorized by the filing office;

(2) an amount equal to or greater than the applicable filing fee is not tendered;

(3) the filing office is unable to index the record because:

(A) in the case of an initial financing statement, the record does not provide a name for the debtor;

(B) in the case of an amendment or correction statement, the record:

(i) does not identify the initial financing statement as required by Section 9–512 or 9–518, as applicable; or

(ii) identifies an initial financing statement whose effectiveness has lapsed under Section 9–515;

(C) in the case of an initial financing statement that provides the name of a debtor identified as an individual or an amendment that provides a name of a debtor identified as an individual which was not previously provided in the financing statement to which the record relates, the record does not identify the debtor's last name; or

(D) in the case of a record filed [or recorded] in the filing office described in Section 9–501(a)(1), the record does not provide a sufficient description of the real property to which it relates;

(4) in the case of an initial financing statement or an amendment that adds a secured party of record, the record does not provide a name and mailing address for the secured party of record;

(5) in the case of an initial financing statement or an amendment that provides a name of a debtor which was not previously provided in the financing statement to which the amendment relates, the record does not:

(A) provide a mailing address for the debtor;

(B) indicate whether the debtor is an individual or an organization; or

(C) if the financing statement indicates that the debtor is an organization, provide:

(i) a type of organization for the debtor;

(ii) a jurisdiction of organization for the debtor; or

(iii) an organizational identification number for the debtor or indicate that the debtor has none;

(6) in the case of an assignment reflected in an initial financing statement under Section 9–514(a) or an amendment filed under Section 9–514(b), the record does not provide a name and mailing address for the assignee; or

(7) in the case of a continuation statement, the record is not filed within the six-month period prescribed by Section 9–515(d).

(c) For purposes of subsection (b):

(1) a record does not provide information if the filing office is unable to read or decipher the information; and

(2) a record that does not indicate that it is an amendment or identify an initial financing statement to which it relates, as required by Section 9–512, 9–514, or 9–518, is an initial financing statement.

(d) A record that is communicated to the filing office with tender of the filing fee, but which the filing office refuses to accept for a reason other than one set forth in subsection (b), is effective as a filed record except as against a purchaser of the collateral which gives value in reasonable reliance upon the absence of the record from the files.

§ 9–517. Effect of Indexing Errors.

The failure of the filing office to index a record correctly does not affect the effectiveness of the filed record.

§ 9–518. Claim Concerning Inaccurate or Wrongfully Filed Record.

(a) A person may file in the filing office a correction statement with respect to a record indexed there under the person's name if the person believes that the record is inaccurate or was wrongfully filed.

[Alternative A]

(b) A correction statement must:

(1) identify the record to which it relates by the file number assigned to the initial financing statement to which the record relates;

(2) indicate that it is a correction statement; and

(3) provide the basis for the person's belief that the record is inaccurate and indicate the manner in which the person believes the record should be amended to cure any inaccuracy or provide the basis for the person's belief that the record was wrongfully filed.

[Alternative B]

(b) A correction statement must:

(1) identify the record to which it relates by:

(A) the file number assigned to the initial financing statement to which the record relates; and

(B) if the correction statement relates to a record filed [or recorded] in a filing office described in Section 9–501(a)(1), the date [and time] that the initial financing statement was filed [or recorded] and the information specified in Section 9–502(b);

(2) indicate that it is a correction statement; and

(3) provide the basis for the person's belief that the record is inaccurate and indicate the manner in which the person believes the record should be amended to cure any inaccuracy or provide the basis for the person's belief that the record was wrongfully filed.

[End of Alternatives]

(c) The filing of a correction statement does not affect the effectiveness of an initial financing statement or other filed record.

Legislative Note: States whose real-estate filing offices require additional information in amendments and cannot search their records by both the name of the debtor and the file number should enact Alternative B to Sections 9–512(a), 9–518(b), 9–519(f), and 9–522(a).

[Subpart 2. Duties and Operation of Filing Office]

§ 9–519. Numbering, Maintaining, and Indexing Records; Communicating Information Provided in Records.

(a) For each record filed in a filing office, the filing office shall:

(1) assign a unique number to the filed record;

(2) create a record that bears the number assigned to the filed record and the date and time of filing;

(3) maintain the filed record for public inspection; and

(4) index the filed record in accordance with subsections (c), (d), and (e).

(b) A file number [assigned after January 1, 2002,] must include a digit that:

(1) is mathematically derived from or related to the other digits of the file number; and

(2) aids the filing office in determining whether a number communicated as the file number includes a single-digit or transpositional error.

(c) Except as otherwise provided in subsections (d) and (e), the filing office shall:

(1) index an initial financing statement according to the name of the debtor and index all filed records relating to the initial financing statement in a manner that associates with one another an initial financing statement and all filed records relating to the initial financing statement; and

(2) index a record that provides a name of a debtor which was not previously provided in the financing statement to which the record relates also according to the name that was not previously provided.

(d) If a financing statement is filed as a fixture filing or covers as-extracted collateral or timber to be cut, [it must be filed for record and] the filing office shall index it:

(1) under the names of the debtor and of each owner of record shown on the financing statement as if they were the mortgagors under a mortgage of the real property described; and

(2) to the extent that the law of this State provides for indexing of records of mortgages under the name of the mortgagee, under the name of the secured party as if the secured party were the mortgagee thereunder, or, if indexing is by description, as if the financing statement were a record of a mortgage of the real property described.

(e) If a financing statement is filed as a fixture filing or covers as-extracted collateral or timber to be cut, the filing office shall index an assignment filed under Section 9–514(a) or an amendment filed under Section 9–514(b):

(1) under the name of the assignor as grantor; and

(2) to the extent that the law of this State provides for indexing a record of the assignment of a mortgage under the name of the assignee, under the name of the assignee.

[Alternative A]

(f) The filing office shall maintain a capability:

(1) to retrieve a record by the name of the debtor and by the file number assigned to the initial financing statement to which the record relates; and

(2) to associate and retrieve with one another an initial financing statement and each filed record relating to the initial financing statement.

[Alternative B]

(f) The filing office shall maintain a capability:

(1) to retrieve a record by the name of the debtor and:

(A) if the filing office is described in Section 9–501(a)(1), by the file number assigned to the initial financing statement to which the record relates and the date [and time] that the record was filed [or recorded]; or

(B) if the filing office is described in Section 9–501(a)(2), by the file number assigned to the initial financing statement to which the record relates; and

(2) to associate and retrieve with one another an initial financing statement and each filed record relating to the initial financing statement.

[End of Alternatives]

(g) The filing office may not remove a debtor's name from the index until one year after the effectiveness of a financing statement naming the debtor lapses under Section 9–515 with respect to all secured parties of record.

(h) The filing office shall perform the acts required by subsections (a) through (e) at the time and in the manner prescribed by filing-office rule, but not later than two business days after the filing office receives the record in question.

[(i) Subsection[s] [(b)] [and] [(h)] do[es] not apply to a filing office described in Section 9–501(a)(1).]

Legislative Notes:

1. States whose filing offices currently assign file numbers that include a verification number, commonly known as a "check digit," or can implement this requirement before the effective date of this Article should omit the bracketed language in subsection (b).

2. In States in which writings will not appear in the real property records and indices unless actually recorded the bracketed language in subsection (d) should be used.

3. States whose real-estate filing offices require additional information in amendments and cannot search their records by both the name of the debtor and the file number should enact Alternative B to Sections 9–512(a), 9–518(b), 9–519(f), and 9–522(a).

4. A State that elects not to require real-estate filing offices to comply with either or both of subsections (b) and (h) may adopt an applicable variation of subsection (i) and add "Except as otherwise provided in subsection (i)," to the appropriate subsection or subsections.

§ 9–520. Acceptance and Refusal to Accept Record.

(a) A filing office shall refuse to accept a record for filing for a reason set forth in Section 9–516(b) and may refuse to accept a record for filing only for a reason set forth in Section 9–516(b).

(b) If a filing office refuses to accept a record for filing, it shall communicate to the person that presented the record the fact of and reason for the refusal and the date and time the record would have been filed had the filing office accepted it. The communication must be made at the time and in the manner prescribed by filing-office rule but [, in the case of a filing office described in Section 9–501(a)(2),] in no event more than two business days after the filing office receives the record.

(c) A filed financing statement satisfying Section 9–502(a) and (b) is effective, even if the filing office is required to refuse to accept it for filing under subsection (a). However, Section 9–338 applies to a filed financing statement providing information described in Section 9–516(b)(5) which is incorrect at the time the financing statement is filed.

(d) If a record communicated to a filing office provides information that relates to more than one debtor, this part applies as to each debtor separately.

Legislative Note: A State that elects not to require real-property filing offices to comply with subsection (b) should include the bracketed language.

§ 9–521. Uniform Form of Written Financing Statement and Amendment.

(a) A filing office that accepts written records may not refuse to accept a written initial financing statement in the following form and format except for a reason set forth in Section 9–516(b):

[NATIONAL UCC FINANCING STATEMENT (FORM UCC1)(REV. 7/29/98)]

[NATIONAL UCC FINANCING STATEMENT ADDENDUM (FORM UCC1Ad)(REV. 07/29/98)]

(b) A filing office that accepts written records may not refuse to accept a written record in the following form and format except for a reason set forth in Section 9–516(b):

[NATIONAL UCC FINANCING STATEMENT AMENDMENT (FORM UCC3)(REV. 07/29/98)]

[NATIONAL UCC FINANCING STATEMENT AMENDMENT ADDENDUM (FORM UCC3Ad)(REV. 07/29/98)]

§ 9–522. Maintenance and Destruction of Records.

[Alternative A]

(a) The filing office shall maintain a record of the information provided in a filed financing statement for at least one year after the effectiveness of the financing statement has lapsed under Section 9–515 with respect to all secured parties of record. The record must be retrievable by using the name of the debtor and by using the file number assigned to the initial financing statement to which the record relates.

[Alternative B]

(a) The filing office shall maintain a record of the information provided in a filed financing statement for at least one year after the effectiveness of the financing statement has lapsed under Section 9–515 with respect to all secured parties of record. The record must be retrievable by using the name of the debtor and:

(1) if the record was filed [or recorded] in the filing office described in Section 9–501(a)(1), by using the file number assigned to the initial financing statement to which the record relates and the date [and time] that the record was filed [or recorded]; or

(2) if the record was filed in the filing office described in Section 9–501(a)(2), by using the file number assigned to the initial financing statement to which the record relates.

[End of Alternatives]

(b) Except to the extent that a statute governing disposition of public records provides otherwise, the filing office immediately may destroy any written record evidencing a financing statement. However, if the filing office destroys a written record, it shall maintain another record of the financing statement which complies with subsection (a).

Legislative Note: States whose real-estate filing offices require additional information in amendments and cannot search their records by both the name of the debtor and the file number should enact Alternative B to Sections 9–512(a), 9–518(b), 9–519(f), and 9–522(a).

§ 9–523. Information from Filing Office; Sale or License of Records.

(a) If a person that files a written record requests an acknowledgment of the filing, the filing office shall send to the person an image of the record showing the number assigned to the record pursuant to Section 9–519(a)(1) and the date and time of the filing of the record. However, if the person furnishes a copy of the record to the filing office, the filing office may instead:

(1) note upon the copy the number assigned to the record pursuant to Section 9–519(a)(1) and the date and time of the filing of the record; and

(2) send the copy to the person.

(b) If a person files a record other than a written record, the filing office shall communicate to the person an acknowledgment that provides:

(1) the information in the record;

(2) the number assigned to the record pursuant to Section 9–519(a)(1); and

(3) the date and time of the filing of the record.

(c) The filing office shall communicate or otherwise make available in a record the following information to any person that requests it:

(1) whether there is on file on a date and time specified by the filing office, but not a date earlier than three business days before the filing office receives the request, any financing statement that:

(A) designates a particular debtor [or, if the request so states, designates a particular debtor at the address specified in the request];

(B) has not lapsed under Section 9–515 with respect to all secured parties of record; and

(C) if the request so states, has lapsed under Section 9–515 and a record of which is maintained by the filing office under Section 9–522(a);

(2) the date and time of filing of each financing statement; and

(3) the information provided in each financing statement.

(d) In complying with its duty under subsection (c), the filing office may communicate information in any medium. However, if requested, the filing office shall communicate information by issuing [its written certificate] [a record that can be admitted into evidence in the courts of this State without extrinsic evidence of its authenticity].

(e) The filing office shall perform the acts required by subsections (a) through (d) at the time and in the manner prescribed by filing-office rule, but not later than two business days after the filing office receives the request.

(f) At least weekly, the [insert appropriate official or governmental agency] [filing office] shall offer to sell or license to the public on a nonexclusive basis, in bulk, copies of all records filed in it under this part, in every medium from time to time available to the filing office.

Legislative Notes:

1. States whose filing office does not offer the additional service of responding to search requests limited to a particular address should omit the bracketed language in subsection (c)(1)(A).

2. A State that elects not to require real-estate filing offices to comply with either or both of subsections (e) and (f) should specify in the appropriate subsection(s) only the filing office described in Section 9–501(a)(2).

§ 9–524. Delay by Filing Office.

Delay by the filing office beyond a time limit prescribed by this part is excused if:

(1) the delay is caused by interruption of communication or computer facilities, war, emergency conditions, failure of equipment, or other circumstances beyond control of the filing office; and

(2) the filing office exercises reasonable diligence under the circumstances.

§ 9–525. Fees.

(a) Except as otherwise provided in subsection (e), the fee for filing and indexing a record under this part, other than an initial financing statement of the kind described in subsection (b), is [the amount specified in subsection (c), if applicable, plus]:

(1) $[X] if the record is communicated in writing and consists of one or two pages;

(2) $[2X] if the record is communicated in writing and consists of more than two pages; and

(3) $[1/2X] if the record is communicated by another medium authorized by filing-office rule.

(b) Except as otherwise provided in subsection (e), the fee for filing and indexing an initial financing statement of the following kind is [the amount specified in subsection (c), if applicable, plus]:

(1) $_______ if the financing statement indicates that it is filed in connection with a public-finance transaction;

(2) $_______ if the financing statement indicates that it is filed in connection with a manufactured-home transaction.

[Alternative A]

(c) The number of names required to be indexed does not affect the amount of the fee in subsections (a) and (b).

[Alternative B]

(c) Except as otherwise provided in subsection (e), if a record is communicated in writing, the fee for each name more than two required to be indexed is $_______.

[End of Alternatives]

(d) The fee for responding to a request for information from the filing office, including for [issuing a certificate showing] [communicating] whether there is on file any financing statement naming a particular debtor, is:

(1) $_______ if the request is communicated in writing; and

(2) $_______ if the request is communicated by another medium authorized by filing-office rule.

(e) This section does not require a fee with respect to a record of a mortgage which is effective as a financing statement filed as a fixture filing or as a financing statement covering as-extracted collateral or timber to be cut under Section 9–502(c). However, the recording and satisfaction fees that otherwise would be applicable to the record of the mortgage apply.

Legislative Notes:

1. To preserve uniformity, a State that places the provisions of this section together with statutes setting fees for other services should do so without modification.

2. A State should enact subsection (c), Alternative A, and omit the bracketed language in subsections (a) and (b) unless its indexing system entails a substantial additional cost when indexing additional names.

As amended in 2000.

§ 9–526. Filing-Office Rules.

(a) The [insert appropriate governmental official or agency] shall adopt and publish rules to implement this article. The filing-office rules must be[:

(1)] consistent with this article[; and

(2) adopted and published in accordance with the [insert any applicable state administrative procedure act]].

(b) To keep the filing-office rules and practices of the filing office in harmony with the rules and practices of filing offices in other jurisdictions that enact substantially this part, and to keep the technology used by the filing office compatible with the technology used by filing offices in other jurisdictions that enact substantially this part, the [insert appropriate governmental official or agency], so far as is consistent with the purposes, policies, and provisions of this article, in adopting, amending, and repealing filing-office rules, shall:

(1) consult with filing offices in other jurisdictions that enact substantially this part; and

(2) consult the most recent version of the Model Rules promulgated by the International Association of Corporate Administrators or any successor organization; and

(3) take into consideration the rules and practices of, and the technology used by, filing offices in other jurisdictions that enact substantially this part.

§ 9–527. Duty to Report.

The [insert appropriate governmental official or agency] shall report [annually on or before _______] to the [Governor and Legislature] on the operation of the filing office. The report must contain a statement of the extent to which:

(1) the filing-office rules are not in harmony with the rules of filing offices in other jurisdictions that enact substantially this part and the reasons for these variations; and

(2) the filing-office rules are not in harmony with the most recent version of the Model Rules promulgated by the International Association of Corporate Administrators, or any successor organization, and the reasons for these variations.

Part 6 Default

[Subpart 1. Default and Enforcement of Security Interest]

§ 9–601. Rights after Default; Judicial Enforcement; Consignor or Buyer of Accounts, Chattel Paper, Payment Intangibles, or Promissory Notes.

(a) After default, a secured party has the rights provided in this part and, except as otherwise provided in Section 9–602, those provided by agreement of the parties. A secured party:

(1) may reduce a claim to judgment, foreclose, or otherwise enforce the claim, security interest, or agricultural lien by any available judicial procedure; and

(2) if the collateral is documents, may proceed either as to the documents or as to the goods they cover.

(b) A secured party in possession of collateral or control of collateral under Section 9–104, 9–105, 9–106, or 9–107 has the rights and duties provided in Section 9–207.

(c) The rights under subsections (a) and (b) are cumulative and may be exercised simultaneously.

(d) Except as otherwise provided in subsection (g) and Section 9–605, after default, a debtor and an obligor have the rights provided in this part and by agreement of the parties.

(e) If a secured party has reduced its claim to judgment, the lien of any levy that may be made upon the collateral by virtue of an execution based upon the judgment relates back to the earliest of:

(1) the date of perfection of the security interest or agricultural lien in the collateral;

(2) the date of filing a financing statement covering the collateral; or

(3) any date specified in a statute under which the agricultural lien was created.

(f) A sale pursuant to an execution is a foreclosure of the security interest or agricultural lien by judicial procedure within the meaning of this section. A secured party may purchase at the sale and thereafter hold the collateral free of any other requirements of this article.

(g) Except as otherwise provided in Section 9–607(c), this part imposes no duties upon a secured party that is a consignor or is a buyer of accounts, chattel paper, payment intangibles, or promissory notes.

§ 9–602. Waiver and Variance of Rights and Duties.

Except as otherwise provided in Section 9–624, to the extent that they give rights to a debtor or obligor and impose duties on a secured party, the debtor or obligor may not waive or vary the rules stated in the following listed sections:

(1) Section 9–207(b)(4)(C), which deals with use and operation of the collateral by the secured party;

(2) Section 9–210, which deals with requests for an accounting and requests concerning a list of collateral and statement of account;

(3) Section 9–607(c), which deals with collection and enforcement of collateral;

(4) Sections 9–608(a) and 9–615(c) to the extent that they deal with application or payment of noncash proceeds of collection, enforcement, or disposition;

(5) Sections 9–608(a) and 9–615(d) to the extent that they require accounting for or payment of surplus proceeds of collateral;

(6) Section 9–609 to the extent that it imposes upon a secured party that takes possession of collateral without judicial process the duty to do so without breach of the peace;

(7) Sections 9–610(b), 9–611, 9–613, and 9–614, which deal with disposition of collateral;

(8) Section 9–615(f), which deals with calculation of a deficiency or surplus when a disposition is made to the secured party, a person related to the secured party, or a secondary obligor;

(9) Section 9–616, which deals with explanation of the calculation of a surplus or deficiency;

(10) Sections 9–620, 9–621, and 9–622, which deal with acceptance of collateral in satisfaction of obligation;

(11) Section 9–623, which deals with redemption of collateral;

(12) Section 9–624, which deals with permissible waivers; and

(13) Sections 9–625 and 9–626, which deal with the secured party's liability for failure to comply with this article.

§ 9–603. Agreement on Standards Concerning Rights and Duties.

(a) The parties may determine by agreement the standards measuring the fulfillment of the rights of a debtor or obligor and the duties of a secured party under a rule stated in Section 9–602 if the standards are not manifestly unreasonable.

(b) Subsection (a) does not apply to the duty under Section 9–609 to refrain from breaching the peace.

§ 9–604. Procedure If Security Agreement Covers Real Property or Fixtures.

(a) If a security agreement covers both personal and real property, a secured party may proceed:

(1) under this part as to the personal property without prejudicing any rights with respect to the real property; or

(2) as to both the personal property and the real property in accordance with the rights with respect to the real property, in which case the other provisions of this part do not apply.

(b) Subject to subsection (c), if a security agreement covers goods that are or become fixtures, a secured party may proceed:

(1) under this part; or

(2) in accordance with the rights with respect to real property, in which case the other provisions of this part do not apply.

(c) Subject to the other provisions of this part, if a secured party holding a security interest in fixtures has priority over all owners and encumbrancers of the real property, the secured party, after default, may remove the collateral from the real property.

(d) A secured party that removes collateral shall promptly reimburse any encumbrancer or owner of the real property, other than the debtor, for the cost of repair of any physical injury caused by the removal. The secured party need not reimburse the encumbrancer or owner for any diminution in value of the real property caused by the absence of the goods removed or by any necessity of replacing them. A person entitled to reimbursement may refuse permission to remove until the secured party gives adequate assurance for the performance of the obligation to reimburse.

§ 9–605. Unknown Debtor or Secondary Obligor.
A secured party does not owe a duty based on its status as secured party:

(1) to a person that is a debtor or obligor, unless the secured party knows:

(A) that the person is a debtor or obligor;

(B) the identity of the person; and

(C) how to communicate with the person; or

(2) to a secured party or lienholder that has filed a financing statement against a person, unless the secured party knows:

(A) that the person is a debtor; and

(B) the identity of the person.

§ 9–606. Time of Default for Agricultural Lien.
For purposes of this part, a default occurs in connection with an agricultural lien at the time the secured party becomes entitled to enforce the lien in accordance with the statute under which it was created.

§ 9–607. Collection and Enforcement by Secured Party.
(a) If so agreed, and in any event after default, a secured party:

(1) may notify an account debtor or other person obligated on collateral to make payment or otherwise render performance to or for the benefit of the secured party;

(2) may take any proceeds to which the secured party is entitled under Section 9–315;

(3) may enforce the obligations of an account debtor or other person obligated on collateral and exercise the rights of the debtor with respect to the obligation of the account debtor or other person obligated on collateral to make payment or otherwise render performance to the debtor, and with respect to any property that secures the obligations of the account debtor or other person obligated on the collateral;

(4) if it holds a security interest in a deposit account perfected by control under Section 9–104(a)(1), may apply the balance of the deposit account to the obligation secured by the deposit account; and

(5) if it holds a security interest in a deposit account perfected by control under Section 9–104(a)(2) or (3), may instruct the bank to pay the balance of the deposit account to or for the benefit of the secured party.

(b) If necessary to enable a secured party to exercise under subsection (a)(3) the right of a debtor to enforce a mortgage nonjudicially, the secured party may record in the office in which a record of the mortgage is recorded:

(1) a copy of the security agreement that creates or provides for a security interest in the obligation secured by the mortgage; and

(2) the secured party's sworn affidavit in recordable form stating that:

(A) a default has occurred; and

(B) the secured party is entitled to enforce the mortgage nonjudicially.

(c) A secured party shall proceed in a commercially reasonable manner if the secured party:

(1) undertakes to collect from or enforce an obligation of an account debtor or other person obligated on collateral; and

(2) is entitled to charge back uncollected collateral or otherwise to full or limited recourse against the debtor or a secondary obligor.

(d) A secured party may deduct from the collections made pursuant to subsection (c) reasonable expenses of collection and enforcement, including reasonable attorney's fees and legal expenses incurred by the secured party.

(e) This section does not determine whether an account debtor, bank, or other person obligated on collateral owes a duty to a secured party.

As amended in 2000.

§ 9–608. Application of Proceeds of Collection or Enforcement; Liability for Deficiency and Right to Surplus.
(a) If a security interest or agricultural lien secures payment or performance of an obligation, the following rules apply:

(1) A secured party shall apply or pay over for application the cash proceeds of collection or enforcement under Section 9–607 in the following order to:

(A) the reasonable expenses of collection and enforcement and, to the extent provided for by agreement and not prohibited by law, reasonable attorney's fees and legal expenses incurred by the secured party;

(B) the satisfaction of obligations secured by the security interest or agricultural lien under which the collection or enforcement is made; and

(C) the satisfaction of obligations secured by any subordinate security interest in or other lien on the collateral subject to the security interest or agricultural lien under which the collection or enforcement is made if the secured party receives an authenticated demand for proceeds before distribution of the proceeds is completed.

(2) If requested by a secured party, a holder of a subordinate security interest or other lien shall furnish reasonable proof of the interest or lien within a reasonable time. Unless the holder complies, the secured party need not comply with the holder's demand under paragraph (1)(C).

(3) A secured party need not apply or pay over for application noncash proceeds of collection and enforcement under Section 9–607 unless the failure to do so would be commercially unreasonable. A secured party that applies or pays over for application

(3) ... noncash proceeds shall do so in a commercially reasonable manner.

(4) A secured party shall account to and pay a debtor for any surplus, and the obligor is liable for any deficiency.

(b) If the underlying transaction is a sale of accounts, chattel paper, payment intangibles, or promissory notes, the debtor is not entitled to any surplus, and the obligor is not liable for any deficiency.

As amended in 2000.

§ 9–609. Secured Party's Right to Take Possession after Default.

(a) After default, a secured party:

(1) may take possession of the collateral; and

(2) without removal, may render equipment unusable and dispose of collateral on a debtor's premises under Section 9–610.

(b) A secured party may proceed under subsection (a):

(1) pursuant to judicial process; or

(2) without judicial process, if it proceeds without breach of the peace.

(c) If so agreed, and in any event after default, a secured party may require the debtor to assemble the collateral and make it available to the secured party at a place to be designated by the secured party which is reasonably convenient to both parties.

§ 9–610. Disposition of Collateral after Default.

(a) After default, a secured party may sell, lease, license, or otherwise dispose of any or all of the collateral in its present condition or following any commercially reasonable preparation or processing.

(b) Every aspect of a disposition of collateral, including the method, manner, time, place, and other terms, must be commercially reasonable. If commercially reasonable, a secured party may dispose of collateral by public or private proceedings, by one or more contracts, as a unit or in parcels, and at any time and place and on any terms.

(c) A secured party may purchase collateral:

(1) at a public disposition; or

(2) at a private disposition only if the collateral is of a kind that is customarily sold on a recognized market or the subject of widely distributed standard price quotations.

(d) A contract for sale, lease, license, or other disposition includes the warranties relating to title, possession, quiet enjoyment, and the like which by operation of law accompany a voluntary disposition of property of the kind subject to the contract.

(e) A secured party may disclaim or modify warranties under subsection (d):

(1) in a manner that would be effective to disclaim or modify the warranties in a voluntary disposition of property of the kind subject to the contract of disposition; or

(2) by communicating to the purchaser a record evidencing the contract for disposition and including an express disclaimer or modification of the warranties.

(f) A record is sufficient to disclaim warranties under subsection (e) if it indicates "There is no warranty relating to title, possession, quiet enjoyment, or the like in this disposition" or uses words of similar import.

§ 9–611. Notification before Disposition of Collateral.

(a) In this section, "notification date" means the earlier of the date on which:

(1) a secured party sends to the debtor and any secondary obligor an authenticated notification of disposition; or

(2) the debtor and any secondary obligor waive the right to notification.

(b) Except as otherwise provided in subsection (d), a secured party that disposes of collateral under Section 9–610 shall send to the persons specified in subsection (c) a reasonable authenticated notification of disposition.

(c) To comply with subsection (b), the secured party shall send an authenticated notification of disposition to:

(1) the debtor;

(2) any secondary obligor; and

(3) if the collateral is other than consumer goods:

(A) any other person from which the secured party has received, before the notification date, an authenticated notification of a claim of an interest in the collateral;

(B) any other secured party or lienholder that, 10 days before the notification date, held a security interest in or other lien on the collateral perfected by the filing of a financing statement that:

(i) identified the collateral;

(ii) was indexed under the debtor's name as of that date; and

(iii) was filed in the office in which to file a financing statement against the debtor covering the collateral as of that date; and

(C) any other secured party that, 10 days before the notification date, held a security interest in the collateral perfected by compliance with a statute, regulation, or treaty described in Section 9–311(a).

(d) Subsection (b) does not apply if the collateral is perishable or threatens to decline speedily in value or is of a type customarily sold on a recognized market.

(e) A secured party complies with the requirement for notification prescribed by subsection (c)(3)(B) if:

(1) not later than 20 days or earlier than 30 days before the notification date, the secured party requests, in a commercially reasonable manner, information concerning financing statements indexed

under the debtor's name in the office indicated in subsection (c)(3)(B); and

(2) before the notification date, the secured party:

(A) did not receive a response to the request for information; or

(B) received a response to the request for information and sent an authenticated notification of disposition to each secured party or other lienholder named in that response whose financing statement covered the collateral.

§ 9–612. Timeliness of Notification before Disposition of Collateral.

(a) Except as otherwise provided in subsection (b), whether a notification is sent within a reasonable time is a question of fact.

(b) In a transaction other than a consumer transaction, a notification of disposition sent after default and 10 days or more before the earliest time of disposition set forth in the notification is sent within a reasonable time before the disposition.

§ 9–613. Contents and Form of Notification before Disposition of Collateral: General.

Except in a consumer-goods transaction, the following rules apply:

(1) The contents of a notification of disposition are sufficient if the notification:

(A) describes the debtor and the secured party;

(B) describes the collateral that is the subject of the intended disposition;

(C) states the method of intended disposition;

(D) states that the debtor is entitled to an accounting of the unpaid indebtedness and states the charge, if any, for an accounting; and

(E) states the time and place of a public disposition or the time after which any other disposition is to be made.

(2) Whether the contents of a notification that lacks any of the information specified in paragraph (1) are nevertheless sufficient is a question of fact.

(3) The contents of a notification providing substantially the information specified in paragraph (1) are sufficient, even if the notification includes:

(A) information not specified by that paragraph; or

(B) minor errors that are not seriously misleading.

(4) A particular phrasing of the notification is not required.

(5) The following form of notification and the form appearing in Section 9–614(3), when completed, each provides sufficient information:

NOTIFICATION OF DISPOSITION OF COLLATERAL

To: *[Name of debtor, obligor, or other person to which the notification is sent]*

From: *[Name, address, and telephone number of secured party]*

Name of Debtor(s): *[Include only if debtor(s) are not an addressee]*

[For a public disposition:]

We will sell [or lease or license, as applicable] the [describe collateral] [to the highest qualified bidder] in public as follows:

Day and Date: ______

Time: ______

Place: ______

[For a private disposition:]

We will sell [or lease or license, *as applicable*] the [*describe collateral*] privately sometime after [*day and date*].

You are entitled to an accounting of the unpaid indebtedness secured by the property that we intend to sell [or lease or license, *as applicable*] [for a charge of $_____]. You may request an accounting by calling us at [telephone number].

[End of Form]

As amended in 2000.

§ 9–614. Contents and Form of Notification before Disposition of Collateral: Consumer-Goods Transaction.

In a consumer-goods transaction, the following rules apply:

(1) A notification of disposition must provide the following information:

(A) the information specified in Section 9–613(1);

(B) a description of any liability for a deficiency of the person to which the notification is sent;

(C) a telephone number from which the amount that must be paid to the secured party to redeem the collateral under Section 9–623 is available; and

(D) a telephone number or mailing address from which additional information concerning the disposition and the obligation secured is available.

(2) A particular phrasing of the notification is not required.

(3) The following form of notification, when completed, provides sufficient information:

[Name and address of secured party]

[Date]

NOTICE OF OUR PLAN TO SELL PROPERTY

[Name and address of any obligor who is also a debtor]

Subject: [*Identification of Transaction*]

We have your [*describe collateral*], because you broke promises in our agreement.

[For a public disposition:]

We will sell [*describe collateral*] at public sale. A sale could include a lease or license. The sale will be held as follows:

Date: ______

Time: ______

Place: ______

You may attend the sale and bring bidders if you want.

[*For a private disposition:*]

We will sell [*describe collateral*] at private sale sometime after [*date*]. A sale could include a lease or license.

The money that we get from the sale (after paying our costs) will reduce the amount you owe. If we get less money than you owe, you [*will or will not, as applicable*] still owe us the difference. If we get more money than you owe, you will get the extra money, unless we must pay it to someone else.

You can get the property back at any time before we sell it by paying us the full amount you owe (not just the past due payments), including our expenses. To learn the exact amount you must pay, call us at [*telephone number*].

If you want us to explain to you in writing how we have figured the amount that you owe us, you may call us at [*telephone number*] [or write us at [*secured party's address*]] and request a written explanation. [We will charge you $______ for the explanation if we sent you another written explanation of the amount you owe us within the last six months.]

If you need more information about the sale call us at [*telephone number*] [or write us at [*secured party's address*]].

We are sending this notice to the following other people who have an interest in [*describe collateral*] or who owe money under your agreement:

[*Names of all other debtors and obligors, if any*]

[End of Form]

(4) A notification in the form of paragraph (3) is sufficient, even if additional information appears at the end of the form.

(5) A notification in the form of paragraph (3) is sufficient, even if it includes errors in information not required by paragraph (1), unless the error is misleading with respect to rights arising under this article.

(6) If a notification under this section is not in the form of paragraph (3), law other than this article determines the effect of including information not required by paragraph (1).

§ 9–615. Application of Proceeds of Disposition; Liability for Deficiency and Right to Surplus.

(a) A secured party shall apply or pay over for application the cash proceeds of disposition under Section 9–610 in the following order to:

(1) the reasonable expenses of retaking, holding, preparing for disposition, processing, and disposing, and, to the extent provided for by agreement and not prohibited by law, reasonable attorney's fees and legal expenses incurred by the secured party;

(2) the satisfaction of obligations secured by the security interest or agricultural lien under which the disposition is made;

(3) the satisfaction of obligations secured by any subordinate security interest in or other subordinate lien on the collateral if:

(A) the secured party receives from the holder of the subordinate security interest or other lien an authenticated demand for proceeds before distribution of the proceeds is completed; and

(B) in a case in which a consignor has an interest in the collateral, the subordinate security interest or other lien is senior to the interest of the consignor; and

(4) a secured party that is a consignor of the collateral if the secured party receives from the consignor an authenticated demand for proceeds before distribution of the proceeds is completed.

(b) If requested by a secured party, a holder of a subordinate security interest or other lien shall furnish reasonable proof of the interest or lien within a reasonable time. Unless the holder does so, the secured party need not comply with the holder's demand under subsection (a)(3).

(c) A secured party need not apply or pay over for application noncash proceeds of disposition under Section 9–610 unless the failure to do so would be commercially unreasonable. A secured party that applies or pays over for application noncash proceeds shall do so in a commercially reasonable manner.

(d) If the security interest under which a disposition is made secures payment or performance of an obligation, after making the payments and applications required by subsection (a) and permitted by subsection (c):

(1) unless subsection (a)(4) requires the secured party to apply or pay over cash proceeds to a consignor, the secured party shall account to and pay a debtor for any surplus; and

(2) the obligor is liable for any deficiency.

(e) If the underlying transaction is a sale of accounts, chattel paper, payment intangibles, or promissory notes:

(1) the debtor is not entitled to any surplus; and

(2) the obligor is not liable for any deficiency.

(f) The surplus or deficiency following a disposition is calculated based on the amount of proceeds that would have been realized in a disposition complying with this part to a transferee other than the secured party, a person related to the secured party, or a secondary obligor if:

(1) the transferee in the disposition is the secured party, a person related to the secured party, or a secondary obligor; and

(2) the amount of proceeds of the disposition is significantly below the range of proceeds that a complying disposition to a person other than the secured party, a person related to the secured party, or a secondary obligor would have brought.

(g) A secured party that receives cash proceeds of a disposition in good faith and without knowledge that the receipt violates the rights of the holder of a security interest or other lien that is not subordinate to the security interest or agricultural lien under which the disposition is made:

(1) takes the cash proceeds free of the security interest or other lien;

(2) is not obligated to apply the proceeds of the disposition to the satisfaction of obligations secured by the security interest or other lien; and

(3) is not obligated to account to or pay the holder of the security interest or other lien for any surplus.

As amended in 2000.

§ 9–616. Explanation of Calculation of Surplus or Deficiency.

(a) In this section:

(1) "Explanation" means a writing that:

(A) states the amount of the surplus or deficiency;

(B) provides an explanation in accordance with subsection (c) of how the secured party calculated the surplus or deficiency;

(C) states, if applicable, that future debits, credits, charges, including additional credit service charges or interest, rebates, and expenses may affect the amount of the surplus or deficiency; and

(D) provides a telephone number or mailing address from which additional information concerning the transaction is available.

(2) "Request" means a record:

(A) authenticated by a debtor or consumer obligor;

(B) requesting that the recipient provide an explanation; and

(C) sent after disposition of the collateral under Section 9–610.

(b) In a consumer-goods transaction in which the debtor is entitled to a surplus or a consumer obligor is liable for a deficiency under Section 9–615, the secured party shall:

(1) send an explanation to the debtor or consumer obligor, as applicable, after the disposition and:

(A) before or when the secured party accounts to the debtor and pays any surplus or first makes written demand on the consumer obligor after the disposition for payment of the deficiency; and

(B) within 14 days after receipt of a request; or

(2) in the case of a consumer obligor who is liable for a deficiency, within 14 days after receipt of a request, send to the consumer obligor a record waiving the secured party's right to a deficiency.

(c) To comply with subsection (a)(1)(B), a writing must provide the following information in the following order:

(1) the aggregate amount of obligations secured by the security interest under which the disposition was made, and, if the amount reflects a rebate of unearned interest or credit service charge, an indication of that fact, calculated as of a specified date:

(A) if the secured party takes or receives possession of the collateral after default, not more than 35 days before the secured party takes or receives possession; or

(B) if the secured party takes or receives possession of the collateral before default or does not take possession of the collateral, not more than 35 days before the disposition;

(2) the amount of proceeds of the disposition;

(3) the aggregate amount of the obligations after deducting the amount of proceeds;

(4) the amount, in the aggregate or by type, and types of expenses, including expenses of retaking, holding, preparing for disposition, processing, and disposing of the collateral, and attorney's fees secured by the collateral which are known to the secured party and relate to the current disposition;

(5) the amount, in the aggregate or by type, and types of credits, including rebates of interest or credit service charges, to which the obligor is known to be entitled and which are not reflected in the amount in paragraph (1); and

(6) the amount of the surplus or deficiency.

(d) A particular phrasing of the explanation is not required. An explanation complying substantially with the requirements of subsection (a) is sufficient, even if it includes minor errors that are not seriously misleading.

(e) A debtor or consumer obligor is entitled without charge to one response to a request under this section during any six-month period in which the secured party did not send to the debtor or consumer obligor an explanation pursuant to subsection (b)(1). The secured party may require payment of a charge not exceeding $25 for each additional response.

§ 9–617. Rights of Transferee of Collateral.

(a) A secured party's disposition of collateral after default:

(1) transfers to a transferee for value all of the debtor's rights in the collateral;

(2) discharges the security interest under which the disposition is made; and

(3) discharges any subordinate security interest or other subordinate lien [other than liens created under [cite acts or statutes providing for liens, if any, that are not to be discharged]].

(b) A transferee that acts in good faith takes free of the rights and interests described in subsection (a), even if the secured party fails to comply with this article or the requirements of any judicial proceeding.

(c) If a transferee does not take free of the rights and interests described in subsection (a), the transferee takes the collateral subject to:

(1) the debtor's rights in the collateral;

(2) the security interest or agricultural lien under which the disposition is made; and

(3) any other security interest or other lien.

§ 9–618. Rights and Duties of Certain Secondary Obligors.

(a) A secondary obligor acquires the rights and becomes obligated to perform the duties of the secured party after the secondary obligor:

(1) receives an assignment of a secured obligation from the secured party;

(2) receives a transfer of collateral from the secured party and agrees to accept the rights and assume the duties of the secured party; or

(3) is subrogated to the rights of a secured party with respect to collateral.

(b) An assignment, transfer, or subrogation described in subsection (a):

(1) is not a disposition of collateral under Section 9–610; and

(2) relieves the secured party of further duties under this article.

§ 9–619. Transfer of Record or Legal Title.

(a) In this section, "transfer statement" means a record authenticated by a secured party stating:

(1) that the debtor has defaulted in connection with an obligation secured by specified collateral;

(2) that the secured party has exercised its post-default remedies with respect to the collateral;

(3) that, by reason of the exercise, a transferee has acquired the rights of the debtor in the collateral; and

(4) the name and mailing address of the secured party, debtor, and transferee.

(b) A transfer statement entitles the transferee to the transfer of record of all rights of the debtor in the collateral specified in the statement in any official filing, recording, registration, or certificate-of-title system covering the collateral. If a transfer statement is presented with the applicable fee and request form to the official or office responsible for maintaining the system, the official or office shall:

(1) accept the transfer statement;

(2) promptly amend its records to reflect the transfer; and

(3) if applicable, issue a new appropriate certificate of title in the name of the transferee.

(c) A transfer of the record or legal title to collateral to a secured party under subsection (b) or otherwise is not of itself a disposition of collateral under this article and does not of itself relieve the secured party of its duties under this article.

§ 9–620. Acceptance of Collateral in Full or Partial Satisfaction of Obligation; Compulsory Disposition of Collateral.

(a) Except as otherwise provided in subsection (g), a secured party may accept collateral in full or partial satisfaction of the obligation it secures only if:

(1) the debtor consents to the acceptance under subsection (c);

(2) the secured party does not receive, within the time set forth in subsection (d), a notification of objection to the proposal authenticated by:

(A) a person to which the secured party was required to send a proposal under Section 9–621; or

(B) any other person, other than the debtor, holding an interest in the collateral subordinate to the security interest that is the subject of the proposal;

(3) if the collateral is consumer goods, the collateral is not in the possession of the debtor when the debtor consents to the acceptance; and

(4) subsection (e) does not require the secured party to dispose of the collateral or the debtor waives the requirement pursuant to Section 9–624.

(b) A purported or apparent acceptance of collateral under this section is ineffective unless:

(1) the secured party consents to the acceptance in an authenticated record or sends a proposal to the debtor; and

(2) the conditions of subsection (a) are met.

(c) For purposes of this section:

(1) a debtor consents to an acceptance of collateral in partial satisfaction of the obligation it secures only if the debtor agrees to the terms of the acceptance in a record authenticated after default; and

(2) a debtor consents to an acceptance of collateral in full satisfaction of the obligation it secures only if the debtor agrees to the terms of the acceptance in a record authenticated after default or the secured party:

(A) sends to the debtor after default a proposal that is unconditional or subject only to a condition that collateral not in the possession of the secured party be preserved or maintained;

(B) in the proposal, proposes to accept collateral in full satisfaction of the obligation it secures; and

(C) does not receive a notification of objection authenticated by the debtor within 20 days after the proposal is sent.

(d) To be effective under subsection (a)(2), a notification of objection must be received by the secured party:

(1) in the case of a person to which the proposal was sent pursuant to Section 9–621, within 20 days after notification was sent to that person; and

(2) in other cases:

(A) within 20 days after the last notification was sent pursuant to Section 9–621; or

(B) if a notification was not sent, before the debtor consents to the acceptance under subsection (c).

(e) A secured party that has taken possession of collateral shall dispose of the collateral pursuant to Section 9–610 within the time specified in subsection (f) if:

(1) 60 percent of the cash price has been paid in the case of a purchase-money security interest in consumer goods; or

(2) 60 percent of the principal amount of the obligation secured has been paid in the case of a non-purchase-money security interest in consumer goods.

(f) To comply with subsection (e), the secured party shall dispose of the collateral:

(1) within 90 days after taking possession; or

(2) within any longer period to which the debtor and all secondary obligors have agreed in an agreement to that effect entered into and authenticated after default.

(g) In a consumer transaction, a secured party may not accept collateral in partial satisfaction of the obligation it secures.

§ 9–621. Notification of Proposal to Accept Collateral.

(a) A secured party that desires to accept collateral in full or partial satisfaction of the obligation it secures shall send its proposal to:

(1) any person from which the secured party has received, before the debtor consented to the acceptance, an authenticated notification of a claim of an interest in the collateral;

(2) any other secured party or lienholder that, 10 days before the debtor consented to the acceptance, held a security interest in or other lien on the collateral perfected by the filing of a financing statement that:

(A) identified the collateral;

(B) was indexed under the debtor's name as of that date; and

(C) was filed in the office or offices in which to file a financing statement against the debtor covering the collateral as of that date; and

(3) any other secured party that, 10 days before the debtor consented to the acceptance, held a security interest in the collateral perfected by compliance with a statute, regulation, or treaty described in Section 9–311(a).

(b) A secured party that desires to accept collateral in partial satisfaction of the obligation it secures shall send its proposal to any secondary obligor in addition to the persons described in subsection (a).

§ 9–622. Effect of Acceptance of Collateral.

(a) A secured party's acceptance of collateral in full or partial satisfaction of the obligation it secures:

(1) discharges the obligation to the extent consented to by the debtor;

(2) transfers to the secured party all of a debtor's rights in the collateral;

(3) discharges the security interest or agricultural lien that is the subject of the debtor's consent and any subordinate security interest or other subordinate lien; and

(4) terminates any other subordinate interest.

(b) A subordinate interest is discharged or terminated under subsection (a), even if the secured party fails to comply with this article.

§ 9–623. Right to Redeem Collateral.

(a) A debtor, any secondary obligor, or any other secured party or lienholder may redeem collateral.

(b) To redeem collateral, a person shall tender:

(1) fulfillment of all obligations secured by the collateral; and

(2) the reasonable expenses and attorney's fees described in Section 9–615(a)(1).

(c) A redemption may occur at any time before a secured party:

(1) has collected collateral under Section 9–607;

(2) has disposed of collateral or entered into a contract for its disposition under Section 9–610; or

(3) has accepted collateral in full or partial satisfaction of the obligation it secures under Section 9–622.

§ 9–624. Waiver.

(a) A debtor or secondary obligor may waive the right to notification of disposition of collateral under Section 9–611 only by an agreement to that effect entered into and authenticated after default.

(b) A debtor may waive the right to require disposition of collateral under Section 9–620(e) only by an agreement to that effect entered into and authenticated after default.

(c) Except in a consumer-goods transaction, a debtor or secondary obligor may waive the right to redeem collateral under Section 9–623 only by an agreement to that effect entered into and authenticated after default.

[Subpart 2. Noncompliance with Article]

§ 9–625. Remedies for Secured Party's Failure to Comply with Article.

(a) If it is established that a secured party is not proceeding in accordance with this article, a court may order or restrain collection, enforcement, or disposition of collateral on appropriate terms and conditions.

(b) Subject to subsections (c), (d), and (f), a person is liable for damages in the amount of any loss caused by a failure to comply with this article. Loss caused by a failure to comply may include loss resulting from the debtor's inability to obtain, or increased costs of, alternative financing.

(c) Except as otherwise provided in Section 9–628:

(1) a person that, at the time of the failure, was a debtor, was an obligor, or held a security interest in or other lien on the collateral may recover damages under subsection (b) for its loss; and

(2) if the collateral is consumer goods, a person that was a debtor or a secondary obligor at the time a secured party failed to comply with this part may recover for that failure in any event an amount not less than the credit service charge plus 10 percent of the principal amount of the obligation or the time-price differential plus 10 percent of the cash price.

(d) A debtor whose deficiency is eliminated under Section 9–626 may recover damages for the loss of any surplus. However, a debtor or secondary obligor whose deficiency is eliminated or reduced under Section 9–626 may not otherwise recover under subsection (b) for noncompliance with the provisions of this part relating to collection, enforcement, disposition, or acceptance.

(e) In addition to any damages recoverable under subsection (b), the debtor, consumer obligor, or person named as a debtor in a filed record, as applicable, may recover $500 in each case from a person that:

(1) fails to comply with Section 9–208;

(2) fails to comply with Section 9–209;

(3) files a record that the person is not entitled to file under Section 9–509(a);

(4) fails to cause the secured party of record to file or send a termination statement as required by Section 9–513(a) or (c);

(5) fails to comply with Section 9–616(b)(1) and whose failure is part of a pattern, or consistent with a practice, of noncompliance; or

(6) fails to comply with Section 9–616(b)(2).

(f) A debtor or consumer obligor may recover damages under subsection (b) and, in addition, $500 in each case from a person that, without reasonable cause, fails to comply with a request under Section 9–210. A recipient of a request under Section 9–210 which never claimed an interest in the collateral or obligations that are the subject of a request under that section has a reasonable excuse for failure to comply with the request within the meaning of this subsection.

(g) If a secured party fails to comply with a request regarding a list of collateral or a statement of account under Section 9–210, the secured party may claim a security interest only as shown in the list or statement included in the request as against a person that is reasonably misled by the failure.

As amended in 2000.

§ 9–626. Action in Which Deficiency or Surplus Is in Issue.

(a) In an action arising from a transaction, other than a consumer transaction, in which the amount of a deficiency or surplus is in issue, the following rules apply:

(1) A secured party need not prove compliance with the provisions of this part relating to collection, enforcement, disposition, or acceptance unless the debtor or a secondary obligor places the secured party's compliance in issue.

(2) If the secured party's compliance is placed in issue, the secured party has the burden of establishing that the collection, enforcement, disposition, or acceptance was conducted in accordance with this part.

(3) Except as otherwise provided in Section 9–628, if a secured party fails to prove that the collection, enforcement, disposition, or acceptance was conducted in accordance with the provisions of this part relating to collection, enforcement, disposition, or acceptance, the liability of a debtor or a secondary obligor for a deficiency is limited to an amount by which the sum of the secured obligation, expenses, and attorney's fees exceeds the greater of:

(A) the proceeds of the collection, enforcement, disposition, or acceptance; or

(B) the amount of proceeds that would have been realized had the noncomplying secured party proceeded in accordance with the provisions of this part relating to collection, enforcement, disposition, or acceptance.

(4) For purposes of paragraph (3)(B), the amount of proceeds that would have been realized is equal to the sum of the secured obligation, expenses, and attorney's fees unless the secured party proves that the amount is less than that sum.

(5) If a deficiency or surplus is calculated under Section 9–615(f), the debtor or obligor has the burden of establishing that the amount of proceeds of the disposition is significantly below the range of prices that a complying disposition to a person other than the secured party, a person related to the secured party, or a secondary obligor would have brought.

(b) The limitation of the rules in subsection (a) to transactions other than consumer transactions is intended to leave to the court the determination of the proper rules in consumer transactions. The court may not infer from that limitation the nature of the proper rule in consumer transactions and may continue to apply established approaches.

§ 9–627. Determination of Whether Conduct Was Commercially Reasonable.

(a) The fact that a greater amount could have been obtained by a collection, enforcement, disposition, or acceptance at a different time or in a different method from that selected by the secured party is not of itself sufficient to preclude the secured party from establishing that the collection, enforcement, disposition, or acceptance was made in a commercially reasonable manner.

(b) A disposition of collateral is made in a commercially reasonable manner if the disposition is made:

(1) in the usual manner on any recognized market;

(2) at the price current in any recognized market at the time of the disposition; or

(3) otherwise in conformity with reasonable commercial practices among dealers in the type of property that was the subject of the disposition.

(c) A collection, enforcement, disposition, or acceptance is commercially reasonable if it has been approved:

(1) in a judicial proceeding;

(2) by a bona fide creditors' committee;

(3) by a representative of creditors; or

(4) by an assignee for the benefit of creditors.

(d) Approval under subsection (c) need not be obtained, and lack of approval does not mean that the collection, enforcement, disposition, or acceptance is not commercially reasonable.

§ 9–628. Nonliability and Limitation on Liability of Secured Party; Liability of Secondary Obligor.

(a) Unless a secured party knows that a person is a debtor or obligor, knows the identity of the person, and knows how to communicate with the person:

(1) the secured party is not liable to the person, or to a secured party or lienholder that has filed a financing statement against the person, for failure to comply with this article; and

(2) the secured party's failure to comply with this article does not affect the liability of the person for a deficiency.

(b) A secured party is not liable because of its status as secured party:

(1) to a person that is a debtor or obligor, unless the secured party knows:

(A) that the person is a debtor or obligor;

(B) the identity of the person; and

(C) how to communicate with the person; or

(2) to a secured party or lienholder that has filed a financing statement against a person, unless the secured party knows:

(A) that the person is a debtor; and

(B) the identity of the person.

(c) A secured party is not liable to any person, and a person's liability for a deficiency is not affected, because of any act or omission arising out of the secured party's reasonable belief that a transaction is not a consumer-goods transaction or a consumer transaction or that goods are not consumer goods, if the secured party's belief is based on its reasonable reliance on:

(1) a debtor's representation concerning the purpose for which collateral was to be used, acquired, or held; or

(2) an obligor's representation concerning the purpose for which a secured obligation was incurred.

(d) A secured party is not liable to any person under Section 9–625(c)(2) for its failure to comply with Section 9–616.

(e) A secured party is not liable under Section 9–625(c)(2) more than once with respect to any one secured obligation.

Part 7 Transition

§ 9–701. Effective Date.

This [Act] takes effect on July 1, 2001.

§ 9–702. Savings Clause.

(a) Except as otherwise provided in this part, this [Act] applies to a transaction or lien within its scope, even if the transaction or lien was entered into or created before this [Act] takes effect.

(b) Except as otherwise provided in subsection (c) and Sections 9–703 through 9–709:

(1) transactions and liens that were not governed by [former Article 9], were validly entered into or created before this [Act] takes effect, and would be subject to this [Act] if they had been entered into or created after this [Act] takes effect, and the rights, duties, and interests flowing from those transactions and liens remain valid after this [Act] takes effect; and

(2) the transactions and liens may be terminated, completed, consummated, and enforced as required or permitted by this [Act] or by the law that otherwise would apply if this [Act] had not taken effect.

(c) This [Act] does not affect an action, case, or proceeding commenced before this [Act] takes effect.

As amended in 2000.

§ 9–703. Security Interest Perfected before Effective Date.

(a) A security interest that is enforceable immediately before this [Act] takes effect and would have priority over the rights of a person that becomes a lien creditor at that time is a perfected security interest under this [Act] if, when this [Act] takes effect, the applicable requirements for enforceability and perfection under this [Act] are satisfied without further action.

(b) Except as otherwise provided in Section 9–705, if, immediately before this [Act] takes effect, a security interest is enforceable and would have priority over the rights of a person that becomes a lien creditor at that time, but the applicable requirements for enforceability or perfection under this [Act] are not satisfied when this [Act] takes effect, the security interest:

(1) is a perfected security interest for one year after this [Act] takes effect;

(2) remains enforceable thereafter only if the security interest becomes enforceable under Section 9–203 before the year expires; and

(3) remains perfected thereafter only if the applicable requirements for perfection under this [Act] are satisfied before the year expires.

§ 9–704. Security Interest Unperfected before Effective Date.

A security interest that is enforceable immediately before this [Act] takes effect but which would be subordinate to the rights of a person that becomes a lien creditor at that time:

(1) remains an enforceable security interest for one year after this [Act] takes effect;

(2) remains enforceable thereafter if the security interest becomes enforceable under Section 9–203 when this [Act] takes effect or within one year thereafter; and

(3) becomes perfected:

(A) without further action, when this [Act] takes effect if the applicable requirements for perfection under this [Act] are satisfied before or at that time; or

(B) when the applicable requirements for perfection are satisfied if the requirements are satisfied after that time.

§ 9–705. Effectiveness of Action Taken before Effective Date.

(a) If action, other than the filing of a financing statement, is taken before this [Act] takes effect and the action would have resulted in priority of a security interest over the rights of a person that becomes a lien creditor had the security interest become enforceable before this [Act] takes effect, the action is effective to perfect a security interest that attaches under this [Act] within one year after this [Act] takes effect. An attached security interest becomes unperfected one year after this [Act] takes effect unless the security interest becomes a perfected security interest under this [Act] before the expiration of that period.

(b) The filing of a financing statement before this [Act] takes effect is effective to perfect a security interest to the extent the filing would satisfy the applicable requirements for perfection under this [Act].

(c) This [Act] does not render ineffective an effective financing statement that, before this [Act] takes effect, is filed and satisfies the applicable requirements for perfection under the law of the jurisdiction governing perfection as provided in [former Section 9–103]. However, except as otherwise provided in subsections (d) and (e) and Section 9–706, the financing statement ceases to be effective at the earlier of:

(1) the time the financing statement would have ceased to be effective under the law of the jurisdiction in which it is filed; or

(2) June 30, 2006.

(d) The filing of a continuation statement after this [Act] takes effect does not continue the effectiveness of the financing statement filed before this [Act] takes effect. However, upon the timely filing of a continuation statement after this [Act] takes effect and in accordance with the law of the jurisdiction governing perfection as provided in Part 3, the effectiveness of a financing statement filed in the same office in that jurisdiction before this [Act] takes effect continues for the period provided by the law of that jurisdiction.

(e) Subsection (c)(2) applies to a financing statement that, before this [Act] takes effect, is filed against a transmitting utility and satisfies the applicable requirements for perfection under the law of the jurisdiction governing perfection as provided in [former Section 9–103] only to the extent that Part 3 provides that the law of a jurisdiction other than the jurisdiction in which the financing statement is filed governs perfection of a security interest in collateral covered by the financing statement.

(f) A financing statement that includes a financing statement filed before this [Act] takes effect and a continuation statement filed after this [Act] takes effect is effective only to the extent that it satisfies the requirements of Part 5 for an initial financing statement.

§ 9–706. When Initial Financing Statement Suffices to Continue Effectiveness of Financing Statement.

(a) The filing of an initial financing statement in the office specified in Section 9–501 continues the effectiveness of a financing statement filed before this [Act] takes effect if:

(1) the filing of an initial financing statement in that office would be effective to perfect a security interest under this [Act];

(2) the pre-effective-date financing statement was filed in an office in another State or another office in this State; and

(3) the initial financing statement satisfies subsection (c).

(b) The filing of an initial financing statement under subsection (a) continues the effectiveness of the pre-effective-date financing statement:

(1) if the initial financing statement is filed before this [Act] takes effect, for the period provided in [former Section 9–403] with respect to a financing statement; and

(2) if the initial financing statement is filed after this [Act] takes effect, for the period provided in Section 9–515 with respect to an initial financing statement.

(c) To be effective for purposes of subsection (a), an initial financing statement must:

(1) satisfy the requirements of Part 5 for an initial financing statement;

(2) identify the pre-effective-date financing statement by indicating the office in which the financing statement was filed and providing the dates of filing and file numbers, if any, of the financing statement

and of the most recent continuation statement filed with respect to the financing statement; and

(3) indicate that the pre-effective-date financing statement remains effective.

§ 9–707. Amendment of Pre-Effective-Date Financing Statement.

(a) In this section, "Pre-effective-date financing statement" means a financing statement filed before this [Act] takes effect.

(b) After this [Act] takes effect, a person may add or delete collateral covered by, continue or terminate the effectiveness of, or otherwise amend the information provided in, a pre-effective-date financing statement only in accordance with the law of the jurisdiction governing perfection as provided in Part 3. However, the effectiveness of a pre-effective-date financing statement also may be terminated in accordance with the law of the jurisdiction in which the financing statement is filed.

(c) Except as otherwise provided in subsection (d), if the law of this State governs perfection of a security interest, the information in a pre-effective-date financing statement may be amended after this [Act] takes effect only if:

(1) the pre-effective-date financing statement and an amendment are filed in the office specified in Section 9-501;

(2) an amendment is filed in the office specified in Section 9–501 concurrently with, or after the filing in that office of, an initial financing statement that satisfies Section 9–706(c); or

(3) an initial financing statement that provides the information as amended and satisfies Section 9–706(c) is filed in the office specified in Section 9–501.

(d) If the law of this State governs perfection of a security interest, the effectiveness of a pre-effective-date financing statement may be continued only under Section 9–705(d) and (f) or 9–706.

(e) Whether or not the law of this State governs perfection of a security interest, the effectiveness of a pre-effective-date financing statement filed in this State may be terminated after this [Act] takes effect by filing a termination statement in the office in which the pre-effective-date financing statement is filed, unless an initial financing statement that satisfies Section 9–706(c) has been filed in the office specified by the law of the jurisdiction governing perfection as provided in Part 3 as the office in which to file a financing statement.

As amended in 2000.

§ 9–708. Persons Entitled to File Initial Financing Statement or Continuation Statement.

A person may file an initial financing statement or a continuation statement under this part if:

(1) the secured party of record authorizes the filing; and

(2) the filing is necessary under this part:

(A) to continue the effectiveness of a financing statement filed before this [Act] takes effect; or

(B) to perfect or continue the perfection of a security interest.

As amended in 2000.

§ 9–709. Priority.

(a) This [Act] determines the priority of conflicting claims to collateral. However, if the relative priorities of the claims were established before this [Act] takes effect, [former Article 9] determines priority.

(b) For purposes of Section 9–322(a), the priority of a security interest that becomes enforceable under Section 9–203 of this [Act] dates from the time this [Act] takes effect if the security interest is perfected under this [Act] by the filing of a financing statement before this [Act] takes effect which would not have been effective to perfect the security interest under [former Article 9]. This subsection does not apply to conflicting security interests each of which is perfected by the filing of such a financing statement.

As amended in 2000.

APPENDIX D

The United Nations Convention on Contracts for the International Sale of Goods (Excerpts)

Part I. SPHERE OF APPLICATION AND GENERAL PROVISIONS

* * * *

Chapter II—General Provisions

* * * *

Article 8

(1) For the purposes of this Convention statements made by and other conduct of a party are to be interpreted according to his intent where the other party knew or could not have been unaware what that intent was.

(2) If the preceding paragraph is not applicable, statements made by and other conduct of a party are to be interpreted according to the understanding that a reasonable person of the same kind as the other party would have had in the same circumstances.

(3) In determining the intent of a party or the understanding a reasonable person would have had, due consideration is to be given to all relevant circumstances of the case including the negotiations, any practices which the parties have established between themselves, usages and any subsequent conduct of the parties.

Article 9

(1) The parties are bound by any usage to which they have agreed and by any practices which they have established between themselves.

(2) The parties are considered, unless otherwise agreed, to have impliedly made applicable to their contract or its formation a usage of which the parties knew or ought to have known and which in international trade is widely known to, and regularly observed by, parties to contracts of the type involved in the particular trade concerned.

* * * *

Article 11

A contract of sale need not be concluded in or evidenced by writing and is not subject to any other requirement as to form. It may be proved by any means, including witnesses.

* * * *

Part II. FORMATION OF THE CONTRACT

Article 14

(1) A proposal for concluding a contract addressed to one or more specific persons constitutes an offer if it is sufficiently definite and indicates the intention of the offeror to be bound in case of acceptance. A proposal is sufficiently definite if it indicates the goods and expressly or implicitly fixes or makes provision for determining the quantity and the price.

(2) A proposal other than one addressed to one or more specific persons is to be considered merely as an invitation to make offers, unless the contrary is clearly indicated by the person making the proposal.

Article 15

(1) An offer becomes effective when it reaches the offeree.

(2) An offer, even if it is irrevocable, may be withdrawn if the withdrawal reaches the offeree before or at the same time as the offer.

Article 16

(1) Until a contract is concluded an offer may be revoked if the revocation reaches the offeree before he has dispatched an acceptance.

(2) However, an offer cannot be revoked:

(a) If it indicates, whether by stating a fixed time for acceptance or otherwise, that it is irrevocable; or

(b) If it was reasonable for the offeree to rely on the offer as being irrevocable and the offeree has acted in reliance on the offer.

Article 17

An offer, even if it is irrevocable, is terminated when a rejection reaches the offeror.

Article 18

(1) A statement made by or other conduct of the offeree indicating assent to an offer is an acceptance. Silence or inactivity does not in itself amount to acceptance.

(2) An acceptance of an offer becomes effective at the moment the indication of assent reaches the offeror. An acceptance is not effective if the indication of assent does not reach the offeror within the time he has fixed or, if no time is fixed, within a reasonable time, due account being taken of the circumstances of the transaction, including the rapidity of the means of communication employed by the offeror. An oral offer must be accepted immediately unless the circumstances indicate otherwise.

(3) However, if, by virtue of the offer or as a result of practices which the parties have established between themselves or of usage, the offeree may indicate assent by performing an act, such as one relating to the dispatch of the goods or payment of the price, without notice to the offeror, the acceptance is effective at the moment the act is performed, provided that the act is performed within the period of time laid down in the preceding paragraph.

Article 19

(1) A reply to an offer which purports to be an acceptance but contains additions, limitations or other modifications is a rejection of the offer and constitutes a counter-offer.

(2) However, a reply to an offer which purports to be an acceptance but contains additional or different terms which do not materially alter the terms of the offer constitutes an acceptance, unless the offeror, without undue delay, objects orally to the discrepancy or dispatches a notice to that effect. If he does not so object, the terms of the contract are the terms of the offer with the modifications contained in the acceptance.

(3) Additional or different terms relating, among other things, to the price, payment, quality and quantity of the goods, place and time of delivery, extent of one party's liability to the other or the settlement of disputes are considered to alter the terms of the offer materially.

* * * *

Article 22

An acceptance may be withdrawn if the withdrawal reaches the offeror before or at the same time as the acceptance would have become effective.

* * * *

Part III. SALE OF GOODS

Chapter I—General Provisions

Article 25

A breach of contract committed by one of the parties is fundamental if it results in such detriment to the other party as substantially to deprive him of what he is entitled to expect under the contract, unless the party in breach did not foresee and a reasonable person of the same kind in the same circumstances would not have foreseen such a result.

* * * *

Article 28

If, in accordance with the provisions of this Convention, one party is entitled to require performance of any obligation by the other party, a court is not bound to enter a judgment for specific performance unless the court would do so under its own law in respect of similar contracts of sale not governed by this Convention.

Article 29

(1) A contract may be modified or terminated by the mere agreement of the parties.

(2) A contract in writing which contains a provision requiring any modification or termination by agreement to be in writing may not be otherwise modified or terminated by agreement. However, a party may be precluded by his conduct from asserting such a provision to the extent that the other party has relied on that conduct.

* * * *

Chapter II—Obligations of the Seller

* * * *

Section II. Conformity of the Goods and Third Party Claims

Article 35

(1) The seller must deliver goods which are of the quantity, quality and description required by the contract and which are contained or packaged in the manner required by the contract.

(2) Except where the parties have agreed otherwise, the goods do not conform with the contract unless they:

(a) Are fit for the purposes for which goods of the same description would ordinarily be used;

(b) Are fit for any particular purpose expressly or impliedly made known to the seller at the time of the conclusion of the contract, except where the circumstances show that the buyer did not rely, or that it was unreasonable for him to rely, on the seller's skill and judgment;

(c) Possess the qualities of goods which the seller has held out to the buyer as a sample or model;

(d) Are contained or packaged in the manner usual for such goods or, where there is no such manner, in a manner adequate to preserve and protect the goods.

(3) The seller is not liable under subparagraphs (a) to (d) of the preceding paragraph for any lack of conformity of the goods if at the time of the conclusion of the contract the buyer knew or could not have been unaware of such lack of conformity.

* * * *

Article 64

(1) The seller may declare the contract avoided:

(a) If the failure by the buyer to perform any of his obligations under the contract or this Convention amounts to a fundamental breach of contract; or

(b) If the buyer does not, within the additional period of time fixed by the seller in accordance with paragraph (1) of article 63, perform his obligation to pay the price or take delivery of the goods, or if he declares that he will not do so within the period so fixed.

(2) However, in cases where the buyer has paid the price, the seller loses the right to declare the contract avoided unless he does so:

(a) In respect of late performance by the buyer, before the seller has become aware that performance has been rendered; or

(b) In respect of any breach other than late performance by the buyer, within a reasonable time:

(i) After the seller knew or ought to have known of the breach; or

(ii) After the expiration of any additional period of time fixed by the seller in accordance with paragraph (1) of article 63, or after the buyer has declared that he will not perform his obligations within such an additional period.

* * * *

Chapter IV—Passing of Risk

* * * *

Article 67

(1) If the contract of sale involves carriage of the goods and the seller is not bound to hand them over at a particular place, the risk passes to the buyer when the goods are handed over to the first carrier for transmission to the buyer in accordance with the contract of sale. If the seller is bound to hand the goods over to a carrier at a particular place, the risk does not pass to the buyer until the goods are handed over to the carrier at that place. The fact that the seller is authorized to retain documents controlling the disposition of the goods does not affect the passage of the risk.

(2) Nevertheless, the risk does not pass to the buyer until the goods are clearly identified to the contract, whether by markings on the goods, by shipping documents, by notice given to the buyer or otherwise.

* * * *

Chapter V—Provisions Common to the Obligations of the Seller and of the Buyer

Section I. Anticipatory Breach and Instalment Contracts

Article 71

(1) A party may suspend the performance of his obligations if, after the conclusion of the contract, it becomes apparent that the other party will not perform a substantial part of his obligations as a result of:

(a) A serious deficiency in his ability to perform or in his creditworthiness; or

(b) His conduct in preparing to perform or in performing the contract.

(2) If the seller has already dispatched the goods before the grounds described in the preceding paragraph become evident, he may prevent the handing over of the goods to the buyer even though the buyer holds a document which entitles him to obtain them. The present paragraph relates only to the rights in the goods as between the buyer and the seller.

(3) A party suspending performance, whether before or after dispatch of the goods, must immediately give notice of the suspension to the other party and must continue with performance if the other party provides adequate assurance of his performance.

Article 72

(1) If prior to the date for performance of the contract it is clear that one of the parties will commit a fundamental breach of contract, the other party may declare the contract avoided.

(2) If time allows, the party intending to declare the contract avoided must give reasonable notice to the other party in order to permit him to provide adequate assurance of his performance.

(3) The requirements of the preceding paragraph do not apply if the other party has declared that he will not perform his obligations.

Article 73

(1) In the case of a contract for delivery of goods by instalments, if the failure of one party to perform any of his obligations in respect of any instalment constitutes a fundamental breach of contract with respect to that instalment, the other party may declare the contract avoided with respect to that instalment.

(2) If one party's failure to perform any of his obligations in respect of any instalment gives the other party good grounds to conclude that a fundamental breach of contract will occur with respect to future instalments, he may declare the contract avoided for the future, provided that he does so within a reasonable time.

(3) A buyer who declares the contract avoided in respect of any delivery may, at the same time, declare it avoided in respect of deliveries already made or of future deliveries if, by reason of their interdependence, those deliveries could not be used for the purpose contemplated by the parties at the time of the conclusion of the contract.

Section II. Damages

Article 74

Damages for breach of contract by one party consist of a sum equal to the loss, including loss of profit, suffered by the other party as a consequence of the breach. Such damages may not exceed the loss which the party in breach foresaw or ought to have foreseen at the time of the conclusion of the contract, in the light of the facts and matters of which he then knew or ought to have known, as a possible consequence of the breach of contract.

Article 75

If the contract is avoided and if, in a reasonable manner and within a reasonable time after avoidance, the buyer has bought goods in replacement or the seller has resold the goods, the party claiming damages may recover the difference between the contract price and the price in the substitute transaction as well as any further damages recoverable under article 74.

Article 76

(1) If the contract is avoided and there is a current price for the goods, the party claiming damages may, if he has not made a purchase or resale under article 75, recover the difference between the price fixed by the contract and the current price at the time of avoidance as well as any further damages recoverable under article 74. If, however, the party claiming damages has avoided the contract after taking over the goods, the current price at the time of such taking over shall be applied instead of the current price at the time of avoidance.

(2) For the purposes of the preceding paragraph, the current price is the price prevailing at the place where delivery of the goods should have been made or, if there is no current price at that place, the price at such other place as serves as a reasonable substitute, making due allowance for differences in the cost of transporting the goods.

Article 77

A party who relies on a breach of contract must take such measures as are reasonable in the circumstances to mitigate the loss, including loss of profit, resulting from the breach. If he fails to take such measures, the party in breach may claim a reduction in the damages in the amount by which the loss should have been mitigated.

APPENDIX E

The Uniform Partnership Act (Excerpts)

(The Uniform Partnership Act was amended in 1997 to provide limited liability for partners in a limited liability partnership. Over half the states, including District of Columbia, Puerto Rico, and the U.S. Virgin Islands, have adopted this latest version of the UPA.)

Article 1
GENERAL PROVISIONS

SECTION 101. Definitions In this [Act]:

* * * *

(6) "Partnership" means an association of two or more persons to carry on as co-owners a business for profit formed under Section 202, predecessor law, or comparable law of another jurisdiction.

(7) "Partnership agreement" means the agreement, whether written, oral, or implied, among the partners concerning the partnership, including amendments to the partnership agreement.

(8) "Partnership at will" means a partnership in which the partners have not agreed to remain partners until the expiration of a definite term or the completion of a particular undertaking.

(9) "Partnership interest" or "partner's interest in the partnership" means all of a partner's interests in the partnership, including the partner's transferable interest and all management and other rights.

(10) "Person" means an individual, corporation, business trust, estate, trust, partnership, association, joint venture, government, governmental subdivision, agency, or instrumentality, or any other legal or commercial entity.

* * * *

SECTION 103. Effect of Partnership Agreement; Nonwaivable Provisions.

(a) Except as otherwise provided in subsection (b), relations among the partners and between the partners and the partnership are governed by the partnership agreement. To the extent the partnership agreement does not otherwise provide, this [Act] governs relations among the partners and between the partners and the partnership.

(b) The partnership agreement may not:

(1) vary the rights and duties under Section 105 except to eliminate the duty to provide copies of statements to all of the partners;

(2) unreasonably restrict the right of access to books and records under Section 403(b);

(3) eliminate the duty of loyalty under Section 404(b) or 603(b)(3), but:

(i) the partnership agreement may identify specific types or categories of activities that do not violate the duty of loyalty, if not manifestly unreasonable; or

(ii) all of the partners or a number or percentage specified in the partnership agreement may authorize or ratify, after full disclosure of all material facts, a specific act or transaction that otherwise would violate the duty of loyalty;

(4) unreasonably reduce the duty of care under Section 404(c) or 603(b)(3);

(5) eliminate the obligation of good faith and fair dealing under Section 404(d), but the partnership agreement may prescribe the standards by which the performance of the obligation is to be measured, if the standards are not manifestly unreasonable;

(6) vary the power to dissociate as a partner under Section 602(a), except to require the notice under Section 601(1) to be in writing;

(7) vary the right of a court to expel a partner in the events specified in Section 601(5);

* * * *

SECTION 105. Execution, Filing, and Recording of Statements.

(a) A statement may be filed in the office of [the Secretary of State]. A certified copy of a statement that is filed in an office in another State may be filed in the office of [the Secretary of State]. Either filing has the effect provided in this [Act] with respect to partnership property located in or transactions that occur in this State.

(b) A certified copy of a statement that has been filed in the office of the [Secretary of State] and recorded in the office for recording transfers of real property has the effect provided for recorded statements in this [Act]. A recorded statement that is not a certified copy of a statement filed in the office of the [Secretary of State] does not have the effect provided for recorded statements in this [Act].

* * * *

SECTION 106. Governing Law.

(a) Except as otherwise provided in subsection (b), the law of the jurisdiction in which a partnership has its chief executive office governs relations among the partners and between the partners and the partnership.

(b) The law of this State governs relations among the partners and between the partners and the partnership and the liability of partners for an obligation of a limited liability partnership.

* * * *

Article 2
NATURE OF PARTNERSHIP

SECTION 201. Partnership as Entity.

(a) A partnership is an entity distinct from its partners.

(b) A limited liability partnership continues to be the same entity that existed before the filing of a statement of qualification under Section 1001.

SECTION 202. Formation of Partnership.

* * * *

(c) In determining whether a partnership is formed, the following rules apply:

(1) Joint tenancy, tenancy in common, tenancy by the entireties, joint property, common property, or part ownership does not by itself establish a partnership, even if the co-owners share profits made by the use of the property.

(2) The sharing of gross returns does not by itself establish a partnership, even if the persons sharing them have a joint or common right or interest in property from which the returns are derived.

(3) A person who receives a share of the profits of a business is presumed to be a partner in the business, unless the profits were received in payment:

(i) of a debt by installments or otherwise;

(ii) for services as an independent contractor or of wages or other compensation to an employee;

(iii) of rent;

(iv) of an annuity or other retirement or health benefit to a beneficiary, representative, or designee of a deceased or retired partner;

(v) of interest or other charge on a loan, even if the amount of payment varies with the profits of the business, including a direct or indirect present or future ownership of the collateral, or rights to income, proceeds, or increase in value derived from the collateral; or

(vi) for the sale of the goodwill of a business or other property by installments or otherwise.

SECTION 203. Partnership Property.

Property acquired by a partnership is property of the partnership and not of the partners individually.

SECTION 204. When Property is Partnership Property.

* * * *

(d) Property acquired in the name of one or more of the partners, without an indication in the instrument transferring title to the property of the person's capacity as a partner or of the existence of a partnership and without use of partnership assets, is presumed to be separate property, even if used for partnership purposes.

Article 3
RELATIONS OF PARTNERS TO PERSONS DEALING WITH PARTNERSHIP

SECTION 301. Partner Agent of Partnership.

Subject to the effect of a statement of partnership authority under Section 303:

(1) Each partner is an agent of the partnership for the purpose of its business. An act of a partner, including the execution of an instrument in the partnership name, for apparently carrying on in the ordinary course the partnership business or business of the kind carried on by the partnership binds the partnership, unless the partner had no authority to act for the partnership in the particular matter and the person with whom the partner was dealing knew or had received a notification that the partner lacked authority.

(2) An act of a partner which is not apparently for carrying on in the ordinary course the partnership business or business of the kind carried on by the partnership binds the partnership only if the act was authorized by the other partners.

* * * *

SECTION 303. Statement of Partnership Authority.

(a) A partnership may file a statement of partnership authority, which:

(1) must include:

(i) the name of the partnership;

(ii) the street address of its chief executive office and of one office in this State, if there is one;

(iii) the names and mailing addresses of all of the partners or of an agent appointed and maintained by the partnership for the purpose of subsection (b); and

(iv) the names of the partners authorized to execute an instrument transferring real property held in the name of the partnership; and

(2) may state the authority, or limitations on the authority, of some or all of the partners to enter into other transactions on behalf of the partnership and any other matter.

* * * *

(d) Except as otherwise provided in subsection (g), a filed statement of partnership authority supplements the authority of a partner to enter into transactions on behalf of the partnership as follows:

(1) Except for transfers of real property, a grant of authority contained in a filed statement of partnership authority is conclusive in favor of a person who gives value without knowledge to the contrary, so long as and to the extent that a limitation on that authority is not then contained in another filed statement. A filed cancellation of a limitation on authority revives the previous grant of authority.

(2) A grant of authority to transfer real property held in the name of the partnership contained in a certified copy of a filed statement of partnership authority recorded in the office for recording transfers of that real property is conclusive in favor of a person who gives value without knowledge to the contrary, so long as and to the extent that a certified copy of a filed statement containing a limitation on that authority is not then of record in the office for recording transfers of that real property. The recording in the office for recording transfers of that real property of a certified copy of a filed cancellation of a limitation on authority revives the previous grant of authority.

(e) A person not a partner is deemed to know of a limitation on the authority of a partner to transfer real property held in the name of the partnership if a certified copy of the filed statement containing the limitation on authority is of record in the office for recording transfers of that real property.

(f) Except as otherwise provided in subsections (d) and (e) and Sections 704 and 805, a person not a partner is not deemed to know of a limitation on the authority of a partner merely because the limitation is contained in a filed statement.

* * * *

SECTION 305. Partnership Liable for Partner's Actionable Conduct.

(a) A partnership is liable for loss or injury caused to a person, or for a penalty incurred, as a result of a wrongful act or omission, or other actionable conduct, of a partner acting in the ordinary course of business of the partnership or with authority of the partnership.

(b) If, in the course of the partnership's business or while acting with authority of the partnership, a partner receives or causes the partnership to receive money or property of a person not a partner, and the money or property is misapplied by a partner, the partnership is liable for the loss.

SECTION 306. Partner's Liability.

(a) Except as otherwise provided in subsections (b) and (c), all partners are liable jointly and severally for all obligations of the partnership unless otherwise agreed by the claimant or provided by law.

(b) A person admitted as a partner into an existing partnership is not personally liable for any partnership obligation incurred before the person's admission as a partner.

(c) An obligation of a partnership incurred while the partnership is a limited liability partnership, whether arising in contract, tort, or otherwise, is solely the obligation of the partnership. A partner is not personally liable, directly or indirectly, by way of contribution or otherwise, for such an obligation solely by reason of being or so acting as a partner. This subsection applies notwithstanding anything inconsistent in the partnership agreement that existed immediately before the vote required to become a limited liability partnership under Section 1001(b).

SECTION 307. Actions by and Against Partnership and Partners.

(a) A partnership may sue and be sued in the name of the partnership.

* * * *

(d) A judgment creditor of a partner may not levy execution against the assets of the partner to satisfy a judgment based on a claim against the partnership unless the partner is personally liable for the claim under Section 306 and:

(1) a judgment based on the same claim has been obtained against the partnership and a writ of execution on the judgment has been returned unsatisfied in whole or in part;

(2) the partnership is a debtor in bankruptcy;

(3) the partner has agreed that the creditor need not exhaust partnership assets;

(4) a court grants permission to the judgment creditor to levy execution against the assets of a partner based on a finding that partnership assets subject to

execution are clearly insufficient to satisfy the judgment, that exhaustion of partnership assets is excessively burdensome, or that the grant of permission is an appropriate exercise of the court's equitable powers; or

(5) liability is imposed on the partner by law or contract independent of the existence of the partnership.

(e) This section applies to any partnership liability or obligation resulting from a representation by a partner or purported partner under Section 308.

SECTION 308. Liability of Purported Partner.

(a) If a person, by words or conduct, purports to be a partner, or consents to being represented by another as a partner, in a partnership or with one or more persons not partners, the purported partner is liable to a person to whom the representation is made, if that person, relying on the representation, enters into a transaction with the actual or purported partnership. If the representation, either by the purported partner or by a person with the purported partner's consent, is made in a public manner, the purported partner is liable to a person who relies upon the purported partnership even if the purported partner is not aware of being held out as a partner to the claimant. If partnership liability results, the purported partner is liable with respect to that liability as if the purported partner were a partner. If no partnership liability results, the purported partner is liable with respect to that liability jointly and severally with any other person consenting to the representation.

(b) If a person is thus represented to be a partner in an existing partnership, or with one or more persons not partners, the purported partner is an agent of persons consenting to the representation to bind them to the same extent and in the same manner as if the purported partner were a partner, with respect to persons who enter into transactions in reliance upon the representation. If all of the partners of the existing partnership consent to the representation, a partnership act or obligation results. If fewer than all of the partners of the existing partnership consent to the representation, the person acting and the partners consenting to the representation are jointly and severally liable.

* * * *

Article 4
RELATIONS OF PARTNERS TO EACH OTHER AND TO PARTNERSHIP

SECTION 401. Partner's Rights and Duties.

* * * *

(b) Each partner is entitled to an equal share of the partnership profits and is chargeable with a share of the partnership losses in proportion to the partner's share of the profits.

* * * *

(f) Each partner has equal rights in the management and conduct of the partnership business.

(g) A partner may use or possess partnership property only on behalf of the partnership.

(h) A partner is not entitled to remuneration for services performed for the partnership, except for reasonable compensation for services rendered in winding up the business of the partnership.

(i) A person may become a partner only with the consent of all of the partners.

(j) A difference arising as to a matter in the ordinary course of business of a partnership may be decided by a majority of the partners. An act outside the ordinary course of business of a partnership and an amendment to the partnership agreement may be undertaken only with the consent of all of the partners.

* * * *

SECTION 403. Partner's Rights and Duties with Respect to Information.

(a) A partnership shall keep its books and records, if any, at its chief executive office.

(b) A partnership shall provide partners and their agents and attorneys access to its books and records. It shall provide former partners and their agents and attorneys access to books and records pertaining to the period during which they were partners. The right of access provides the opportunity to inspect and copy books and records during ordinary business hours. A partnership may impose a reasonable charge, covering the costs of labor and material, for copies of documents furnished.

* * * *

SECTION 404. General Standards of Partner's Conduct.

(a) The only fiduciary duties a partner owes to the partnership and the other partners are the duty of loyalty and the duty of care set forth in subsections (b) and (c).

(b) A partner's duty of loyalty to the partnership and the other partners is limited to the following:

(1) to account to the partnership and hold as trustee for it any property, profit, or benefit derived by the partner in the conduct and winding up of the partnership business or derived from a use by the partner of partnership property, including the appropriation of a partnership opportunity;

(2) to refrain from dealing with the partnership in the conduct or winding up of the partnership business as or on behalf of a party having an interest adverse to the partnership; and

(3) to refrain from competing with the partnership in the conduct of the partnership business before the dissolution of the partnership.

(c) A partner's duty of care to the partnership and the other partners in the conduct and winding up of the partnership business is limited to refraining from engaging in grossly negligent or reckless conduct, intentional misconduct, or a knowing violation of law.

(d) A partner shall discharge the duties to the partnership and the other partners under this [Act] or under the partnership agreement and exercise any rights consistently with the obligation of good faith and fair dealing.

(e) A partner does not violate a duty or obligation under this [Act] or under the partnership agreement merely because the partner's conduct furthers the partner's own interest.

* * * *

SECTION 405. Actions by Partnership and Partners.

(a) A partnership may maintain an action against a partner for a breach of the partnership agreement, or for the violation of a duty to the partnership, causing harm to the partnership.

(b) A partner may maintain an action against the partnership or another partner for legal or equitable relief, with or without an accounting as to partnership business, to:

(1) enforce the partner's rights under the partnership agreement;

(2) enforce the partner's rights under this [Act], including:

(i) the partner's rights under Sections 401, 403, or 404;

(ii) the partner's right on dissociation to have the partner's interest in the partnership purchased pursuant to Section 701 or enforce any other right under [Article] 6 or 7; or

(iii) the partner's right to compel a dissolution and winding up of the partnership business under or enforce any other right under [Article] 8; or

(3) enforce the rights and otherwise protect the interests of the partner, including rights and interests arising independently of the partnership relationship.

* * * *

Article 5
TRANSFEREES AND CREDITORS OF PARTNER

SECTION 501. Partner Not Co-Owner of Partnership Property.

A partner is not a co-owner of partnership property and has no interest in partnership property which can be transferred, either voluntarily or involuntarily.

SECTION 502. Partner's Transferable Interest in Partnership.

The only transferable interest of a partner in the partnership is the partner's share of the profits and losses of the partnership and the partner's right to receive distributions. The interest is personal property.

SECTION 503. Transfer of Partner's Transferable Interest.

(a) A transfer, in whole or in part, of a partner's transferable interest in the partnership:

(1) is permissible;

(2) does not by itself cause the partner's dissociation or a dissolution and winding up of the partnership business; and

(3) does not, as against the other partners or the partnership, entitle the transferee, during the continuance of the partnership, to participate in the management or conduct of the partnership business, to require access to information concerning partnership transactions, or to inspect or copy the partnership books or records.

* * * *

SECTION 504. Partner's Transferable Interest Subject to Charging Order.

(a) On application by a judgment creditor of a partner or of a partner's transferee, a court having jurisdiction may charge the transferable interest of the judgment debtor to satisfy the judgment. The court may appoint a receiver of the share of the distributions due or to become due to the judgment debtor in respect of the partnership and make all other orders, directions, accounts, and inquiries the judgment debtor might have made or which the circumstances of the case may require.

* * * *

Article 6
PARTNER'S DISSOCIATION

SECTION 601. Events Causing Partner's Dissociation.

A partner is dissociated from a partnership upon the occurrence of any of the following events:

(1) the partnership's having notice of the partner's express will to withdraw as a partner or on a later date specified by the partner;

(2) an event agreed to in the partnership agreement as causing the partner's dissociation;

(3) the partner's expulsion pursuant to the partnership agreement;

(4) the partner's expulsion by the unanimous vote of the other partners if:

(i) it is unlawful to carry on the partnership business with that partner;

(ii) there has been a transfer of all or substantially all of that partner's transferable interest in the partnership, other than a transfer for security purposes, or a court order charging the partner's interest, which has not been foreclosed;

(iii) within 90 days after the partnership notifies a corporate partner that it will be expelled because it has filed a certificate of dissolution or the equivalent, its charter has been revoked, or its right to conduct business has been suspended by the jurisdiction of its incorporation, there is no revocation of the certificate of dissolution or no reinstatement of its charter or its right to conduct business; or

(iv) a partnership that is a partner has been dissolved and its business is being wound up;

(5) on application by the partnership or another partner, the partner's expulsion by judicial determination because:

(i) the partner engaged in wrongful conduct that adversely and materially affected the partnership business;

(ii) the partner willfully or persistently committed a material breach of the partnership agreement or of a duty owed to the partnership or the other partners under Section 404; or

(iii) the partner engaged in conduct relating to the partnership business which makes it not reasonably practicable to carry on the business in partnership with the partner;

(6) the partner's:

(i) becoming a debtor in bankruptcy;

(ii) executing an assignment for the benefit of creditors;

(iii) seeking, consenting to, or acquiescing in the appointment of a trustee, receiver, or liquidator of that partner or of all or substantially all of that partner's property; or

(iv) failing, within 90 days after the appointment, to have vacated or stayed the appointment of a trustee, receiver, or liquidator of the partner or of all or substantially all of the partner's property obtained without the partner's consent or acquiescence, or failing within 90 days after the expiration of a stay to have the appointment vacated;

(7) in the case of a partner who is an individual:

(i) the partner's death;

(ii) the appointment of a guardian or general conservator for the partner; or

(iii) a judicial determination that the partner has otherwise become incapable of performing the partner's duties under the partnership agreement;

* * * *

SECTION 602. Partner's Power to Dissociate; Wrongful Dissociation.

(a) A partner has the power to dissociate at any time, rightfully or wrongfully, by express will pursuant to Section 601(1).

(b) A partner's dissociation is wrongful only if:

(1) it is in breach of an express provision of the partnership agreement; or

(2) in the case of a partnership for a definite term or particular undertaking, before the expiration of the term or the completion of the undertaking:

(i) the partner withdraws by express will, unless the withdrawal follows within 90 days after another partner's dissociation by death or otherwise under Section 601(6) through (10) or wrongful dissociation under this subsection;

(ii) the partner is expelled by judicial determination under Section 601(5);

(iii) the partner is dissociated by becoming a debtor in bankruptcy; or

(iv) in the case of a partner who is not an individual, trust other than a business trust, or estate, the partner is expelled or otherwise dissociated because it willfully dissolved or terminated.

(c) A partner who wrongfully dissociates is liable to the partnership and to the other partners for damages caused by the dissociation. The liability is in addition to any other obligation of the partner to the partnership or to the other partners.

SECTION 603. Effect of Partner's Dissociation.

(a) If a partner's dissociation results in a dissolution and winding up of the partnership business, [Article] 8 applies; otherwise, [Article] 7 applies.

(b) Upon a partner's dissociation:

(1) the partner's right to participate in the management and conduct of the partnership business terminates, except as otherwise provided in Section 803;

(2) the partner's duty of loyalty under Section 404(b)(3) terminates; and

(3) the partner's duty of loyalty under Section 404(b)(1) and (2) and duty of care under Section 404(c) continue only with regard to matters arising and events occurring before the partner's dissociation, unless the partner participates in winding up the partnership's business pursuant to Section 803.

Article 7

PARTNER'S DISSOCIATION WHEN BUSINESS NOT WOUND UP

SECTION 701. Purchase of Dissociated Partner's Interest.

(a) If a partner is dissociated from a partnership without resulting in a dissolution and winding up of the partnership business under Section 801, the partnership shall cause the dissociated partner's interest in the partnership to be purchased for a buyout price determined pursuant to subsection (b).

(b) The buyout price of a dissociated partner's interest is the amount that would have been distributable to the dissociating partner under Section 807(b) if, on the date of dissociation, the assets of the partnership were sold at a price equal to the greater of the liquidation value or the value based on a sale of the entire business as a going concern without the dissociated partner and the partnership were wound up as of that date. Interest must be paid from the date of dissociation to the date of payment.

(c) Damages for wrongful dissociation under Section 602(b), and all other amounts owing, whether or not presently due, from the dissociated partner to the partnership, must be offset against the buyout price. Interest must be paid from the date the amount owed becomes due to the date of payment.

* * * *

SECTION 702. Dissociated Partner's Power to Bind and Liability to Partnership.

(a) For two years after a partner dissociates without resulting in a dissolution and winding up of the partnership business, the partnership, including a surviving partnership under [Article] 9, is bound by an act of the dissociated partner which would have bound the partnership under Section 301 before dissociation only if at the time of entering into the transaction the other party:

(1) reasonably believed that the dissociated partner was then a partner;

(2) did not have notice of the partner's dissociation; and

(3) is not deemed to have had knowledge under Section 303(e) or notice under Section 704(c).

(b) A dissociated partner is liable to the partnership for any damage caused to the partnership arising from an obligation incurred by the dissociated partner after dissociation for which the partnership is liable under subsection (a).

SECTION 703. Dissociated Partner's Liability to Other Persons.

(a) A partner's dissociation does not of itself discharge the partner's liability for a partnership obligation incurred before dissociation. A dissociated partner is not liable for a partnership obligation incurred after dissociation, except as otherwise provided in subsection (b).

(b) A partner who dissociates without resulting in a dissolution and winding up of the partnership business is liable as a partner to the other party in a transaction entered into by the partnership, or a surviving partnership under [Article] 9, within two years after the partner's dissociation, only if the partner is liable for the obligation under Section 306 and at the time of entering into the transaction the other party:

(1) reasonably believed that the dissociated partner was then a partner;

(2) did not have notice of the partner's dissociation; and

(3) is not deemed to have had knowledge under Section 303(e) or notice under Section 704(c).

* * * *

SECTION 704. Statement of Dissociation.

(a) A dissociated partner or the partnership may file a statement of dissociation stating the name of the partnership and that the partner is dissociated from the partnership.

(b) A statement of dissociation is a limitation on the authority of a dissociated partner for the purposes of Section 303(d) and (e).

(c) For the purposes of Sections 702(a)(3) and 703(b)(3), a person not a partner is deemed to have notice of the dissociation 90 days after the statement of dissociation is filed.

* * * *

Article 8

WINDING UP PARTNERSHIP BUSINESS

SECTION 801. Events Causing Dissolution and Winding Up of Partnership Business.

A partnership is dissolved, and its business must be wound up, only upon the occurrence of any of the following events:

(1) in a partnership at will, the partnership's having notice from a partner, other than a partner who is dissociated under Section 601(2) through (10), of that partner's express will to withdraw as a partner, or on a later date specified by the partner;

(2) in a partnership for a definite term or particular undertaking:

(i) within 90 days after a partner's dissociation by death or otherwise under Section 601(6) through (10) or wrongful dissociation under Section 602(b), the express will of at least half of the remaining partners to wind up the partnership business, for which purpose a partner's rightful dissociation pursuant to Section 602(b)(2)(i) constitutes the expression of that partner's will to wind up the partnership business;

(ii) the express will of all of the partners to wind up the partnership business; or

(iii) the expiration of the term or the completion of the undertaking;

(3) an event agreed to in the partnership agreement resulting in the winding up of the partnership business;

(4) an event that makes it unlawful for all or substantially all of the business of the partnership to be continued, but a cure of illegality within 90 days after notice to the partnership of the event is effective retroactively to the date of the event for purposes of this section;

(5) on application by a partner, a judicial determination that:

(i) the economic purpose of the partnership is likely to be unreasonably frustrated;

(ii) another partner has engaged in conduct relating to the partnership business which makes it not reasonably practicable to carry on the business in partnership with that partner; or

(iii) it is not otherwise reasonably practicable to carry on the partnership business in conformity with the partnership agreement; or

* * * *

SECTION 802. Partnership Continues after Dissolution.

(a) Subject to subsection (b), a partnership continues after dissolution only for the purpose of winding up its business. The partnership is terminated when the winding up of its business is completed.

(b) At any time after the dissolution of a partnership and before the winding up of its business is completed, all of the partners, including any dissociating partner other than a wrongfully dissociating partner, may waive the right to have the partnership's business wound up and the partnership terminated. In that event:

(1) the partnership resumes carrying on its business as if dissolution had never occurred, and any liability incurred by the partnership or a partner after the dissolution and before the waiver is determined as if dissolution had never occurred; and

(2) the rights of a third party accruing under Section 804(1) or arising out of conduct in reliance on the dissolution before the third party knew or received a notification of the waiver may not be adversely affected.

SECTION 803. Right to Wind Up Partnership.

(a) After dissolution, a partner who has not wrongfully dissociated may participate in winding up the partnership's business, but on application of any partner, partner's legal representative, or transferee, the [designate the appropriate court], for good cause shown, may order judicial supervision of the winding up.

(b) The legal representative of the last surviving partner may wind up a partnership's business.

(c) A person winding up a partnership's business may preserve the partnership business or property as a going concern for a reasonable time, prosecute and defend actions and proceedings, whether civil, criminal, or administrative, settle and close the partnership's business, dispose of and transfer the partnership's property, discharge the partnership's liabilities, distribute the assets of the partnership pursuant to Section 807, settle disputes by mediation or arbitration, and perform other necessary acts.

SECTION 804. Partner's Power to Bind Partnership After Dissolution.

Subject to Section 805, a partnership is bound by a partner's act after dissolution that:

(1) is appropriate for winding up the partnership business; or

(2) would have bound the partnership under Section 301 before dissolution, if the other party to the transaction did not have notice of the dissolution.

SECTION 805. Statement of Dissolution.

(a) After dissolution, a partner who has not wrongfully dissociated may file a statement of dissolution stating the name of the partnership and that the partnership has dissolved and is winding up its business.

(b) A statement of dissolution cancels a filed statement of partnership authority for the purposes of Section 303(d) and is a limitation on authority for the purposes of Section 303(e).

(c) For the purposes of Sections 301 and 804, a person not a partner is deemed to have notice of the dissolution and the limitation on the partners' authority as a result of the statement of dissolution 90 days after it is filed.

* * * *

SECTION 807. Settlement of Accounts and Contributions among Partners.

(a) In winding up a partnership's business, the assets of the partnership, including the contributions of the partners required by this section, must be applied to discharge its obligations to creditors, including, to the extent permitted by law, partners who are creditors. Any surplus must be applied to pay in cash the net amount distributable to partners in accordance with their right to distributions under subsection (b).

(b) Each partner is entitled to a settlement of all partnership accounts upon winding up the partnership business. In settling accounts among the partners, profits and losses that result from the liquidation of the partnership assets must be credited and charged to the partners' accounts. The partnership shall make a distribution to a partner in an amount equal to any excess of the credits over the charges in the partner's account. A partner shall contribute to the partnership an amount equal to any excess of the charges over the credits in the partner's account but excluding from the calculation charges attributable to an obligation for which the partner is not personally liable under Section 306.

* * * *

(d) After the settlement of accounts, each partner shall contribute, in the proportion in which the partner shares partnership losses, the amount necessary to satisfy partnership obligations that were not known at the time of the settlement and for which the partner is personally liable under Section 306.

* * * *

Article 10

LIMITED LIABILITY PARTNERSHIP

SECTION 1001. Statement of Qualification.

(a) A partnership may become a limited liability partnership pursuant to this section.

(b) The terms and conditions on which a partnership becomes a limited liability partnership must be approved by the vote necessary to amend the partnership agreement except, in the case of a partnership agreement that expressly considers obligations to contribute to the partnership, the vote necessary to amend those provisions.

(c) After the approval required by subsection (b), a partnership may become a limited liability partnership by filing a statement of qualification. The statement must contain:

(1) the name of the partnership;

(2) the street address of the partnership's chief executive office and, if different, the street address of an office in this State, if any;

(3) if the partnership does not have an office in this State, the name and street address of the partnership's agent for service of process;

(4) a statement that the partnership elects to be a limited liability partnership; and

(5) a deferred effective date, if any.

* * * *

SECTION 1002. Name.

The name of a limited liability partnership must end with "Registered Limited Liability Partnership", "Limited Liability Partnership", "R.L.L.P.", "L.L.P.", "RLLP," or "LLP".

SECTION 1003. Annual Report.

(a) A limited liability partnership, and a foreign limited liability partnership authorized to transact business in this State, shall file an annual report in the office of the [Secretary of State] which contains:

(1) the name of the limited liability partnership and the State or other jurisdiction under whose laws the foreign limited liability partnership is formed;

(2) the street address of the partnership's chief executive office and, if different, the street address of an office of the partnership in this State, if any; and

(3) if the partnership does not have an office in this State, the name and street address of the partnership's current agent for service of process.

(b) An annual report must be filed between [January 1 and April 1] of each year following the calendar year in which a partnership files a statement of qualification or a foreign partnership becomes authorized to transact business in this State.

* * * *

Article 11

FOREIGN LIMITED LIABILITY PARTNERSHIP

SECTION 1101. Law Governing Foreign Limited Liability Partnership.

(a) The law under which a foreign limited liability partnership is formed governs relations among the partners and between the partners and the partnership and the liability of partners for obligations of the partnership.

* * * *

SECTION 1102. Statement of Foreign Qualification.

(a) Before transacting business in this State, a foreign limited liability partnership must file a statement of foreign qualification. The statement must contain:

(1) the name of the foreign limited liability partnership which satisfies the requirements of the State or other jurisdiction under whose law it is formed and ends with "Registered Limited Liability Partnership", "Limited Liability Partnership", "R.L.L.P.", "L.L.P.", "RLLP," or "LLP";

(2) the street address of the partnership's chief executive office and, if different, the street address of an office of the partnership in this State, if any;

(3) if there is no office of the partnership in this State, the name and street address of the partnership's agent for service of process; and

(4) a deferred effective date, if any.

* * * *

SECTION 1104. Activities Not Constituting Transacting Business.

(a) Activities of a foreign limited liability partnership which do not constitute transacting business for the purpose of this [article] include:

(1) maintaining, defending, or settling an action or proceeding;

(2) holding meetings of its partners or carrying on any other activity concerning its internal affairs;

(3) maintaining bank accounts;

(4) maintaining offices or agencies for the transfer, exchange, and registration of the partnership's own securities or maintaining trustees or depositories with respect to those securities;

(5) selling through independent contractors;

(6) soliciting or obtaining orders, whether by mail or through employees or agents or otherwise, if the orders require acceptance outside this State before they become contracts;

(7) creating or acquiring indebtedness, with or without a mortgage, or other security interest in property;

(8) collecting debts or foreclosing mortgages or other security interests in property securing the debts, and holding, protecting, and maintaining property so acquired;

(9) conducting an isolated transaction that is completed within 30 days and is not one in the course of similar transactions; and

(10) transacting business in interstate commerce.

(b) For purposes of this [article], the ownership in this State of income-producing real property or tangible personal property, other than property excluded under subsection (a), constitutes transacting business in this State.

* * * *

APPENDIX F

The Revised Uniform Limited Partnership Act (Excerpts)

Article 1
GENERAL PROVISIONS

Section 101. Definitions.

As used in this [Act], unless the context otherwise requires:

(1) "Certificate of limited partnership" means the certificate referred to in Section 201, and the certificate as amended or restated.

(2) "Contribution" means any cash, property, services rendered, or a promissory note or other binding obligation to contribute cash or property or to perform services, which a partner contributes to a limited partnership in his capacity as a partner.

(3) "Event of withdrawal of a general partner" means an event that causes a person to cease to be a general partner as provided in Section 402.

(4) "Foreign limited partnership" means a partnership formed under the laws of any state other than this State and having as partners one or more general partners and one or more limited partners.

(5) "General partner" means a person who has been admitted to a limited partnership as a general partner in accordance with the partnership agreement and named in the certificate of limited partnership as a general partner.

(6) "Limited partner" means a person who has been admitted to a limited partnership as a limited partner in accordance with the partnership agreement.

(7) "Limited partnership" and "domestic limited partnership" mean a partnership formed by two or more persons under the laws of this State and having one or more general partners and one or more limited partners.

(8) "Partner" means a limited or general partner.

(9) "Partnership agreement" means any valid agreement, written or oral, of the partners as to the affairs of a limited partnership and the conduct of its business.

(10) "Partnership interest" means a partner's share of the profits and losses of a limited partnership and the right to receive distributions of partnership assets.

(11) "Person" means a natural person, partnership, limited partnership (domestic or foreign), trust, estate, association, or corporation.

(12) "State" means a state, territory, or possession of the United States, the District of Columbia, or the Commonwealth of Puerto Rico.

Section 102. Name.

The name of each limited partnership as set forth in its certificate of limited partnership:

(1) shall contain without abbreviation the words "limited partnership";

(2) may not contain the name of a limited partner unless (i) it is also the name of a general partner or the corporate name of a corporate general partner, or (ii) the business of the limited partnership had been carried on under that name before the admission of that limited partner;

(3) may not be the same as, or deceptively similar to, the name of any corporation or limited partnership organized under the laws of this State or licensed or registered as a foreign corporation or limited partnership in this State; and

(4) may not contain the following words [here insert prohibited words].

Section 103. Reservation of Name.

(a) The exclusive right to the use of a name may be reserved by:

(1) any person intending to organize a limited partnership under this [Act] and to adopt that name;

(2) any domestic limited partnership or any foreign limited partnership registered in this State which, in either case, intends to adopt that name;

(3) any foreign limited partnership intending to register in this State and adopt that name; and

(4) any person intending to organize a foreign limited partnership and intending to have it register in this State and adopt that name.

(b) The reservation shall be made by filing with the Secretary of State an application, executed by the applicant, to reserve a specified name. If the Secretary of State finds that the name is available for use by a domestic or foreign limited partnership, he [or she] shall reserve the name for the exclusive use of the applicant for a period of 120 days. Once having so reserved a name, the same applicant may not again reserve the same name until more than 60 days after the expiration of the last 120-day period for which that applicant reserved that name. The right to the exclusive use of a reserved name may be transferred to any other person by filing in the office of the Secretary of State a notice of the transfer, executed by the applicant for whom the name was reserved and specifying the name and address of the transferee.

Section 104. Specified Office and Agent.

Each limited partnership shall continuously maintain in this State:

(1) an office, which may but need not be a place of its business in this State, at which shall be kept the records required by Section 105 to be maintained; and

(2) an agent for service of process on the limited partnership, which agent must be an individual resident of this State, a domestic corporation, or a foreign corporation authorized to do business in this State.

Section 105. Records to Be Kept.

(a) Each limited partnership shall keep at the office referred to in Section 104(1) the following:

(1) a current list of the full name and last known business address of each partner, separately identifying the general partners (in alphabetical order) and the limited partners (in alphabetical order);

(2) a copy of the certificate of limited partnership and all certificates of amendment thereto, together with executed copies of any powers of attorney pursuant to which any certificate has been executed;

(3) copies of the limited partnership's federal, state and local income tax returns and reports, if any, for the three most recent years;

(4) copies of any then effective written partnership agreements and of any financial statements of the limited partnership for the three most recent years; and

(5) unless contained in a written partnership agreement, a writing setting out:

(i) the amount of cash and a description and statement of the agreed value of the other property or services contributed by each partner and which each partner has agreed to contribute;

(ii) the times at which or events on the happening of which any additional contributions agreed to be made by each partner are to be made;

(iii) any right of a partner to receive, or of a general partner to make, distributions to a partner which include a return of all or any part of the partner's contribution; and

(iv) any events upon the happening of which the limited partnership is to be dissolved and its affairs wound up.

(b) Records kept under this section are subject to inspection and copying at the reasonable request and at the expense of any partner during ordinary business hours.

Section 106. Nature of Business.

A limited partnership may carry on any business that a partnership without limited partners may carry on except [here designate prohibited activities].

Section 107. Business Transactions of Partners with Partnership.

Except as provided in the partnership agreement, a partner may lend money to and transact other business with the limited partnership and, subject to other applicable law, has the same rights and obligations with respect thereto as a person who is not a partner.

Article 2
FORMATION; CERTIFICATE OF LIMITED PARTNERSHIP

Section 201. Certificate of Limited Partnership.

(a) In order to form a limited partnership, a certificate of limited partnership must be executed and filed in the office of the Secretary of State. The certificate shall set forth:

(1) the name of the limited partnership;

(2) the address of the office and the name and address of the agent for service of process required to be maintained by Section 104;

(3) the name and the business address of each general partner;

(4) the latest date upon which the limited partnership is to dissolve; and

(5) any other matters the general partners determine to include therein.

(b) A limited partnership is formed at the time of the filing of the certificate of limited partnership in the office of the Secretary of State or at any later time specified in the certificate of limited partnership if, in either case, there has been substantial compliance with the requirements of this section.

Section 202. Amendment to Certificate.

(a) A certificate of limited partnership is amended by filing a certificate of amendment thereto in the office of the Secretary of State. The certificate shall set forth:

(1) the name of the limited partnership;

(2) the date of filing the certificate; and

(3) the amendment to the certificate.

(b) Within 30 days after the happening of any of the following events, an amendment to a certificate of limited partnership reflecting the occurrence of the event or events shall be filed:

(1) the admission of a new general partner;

(2) the withdrawal of a general partner; or

(3) the continuation of the business under Section 801 after an event of withdrawal of a general partner.

(c) A general partner who becomes aware that any statement in a certificate of limited partnership was false when made or that any arrangements or other facts described have changed, making the certificate inaccurate in any respect, shall promptly amend the certificate.

(d) A certificate of limited partnership may be amended at any time for any other proper purpose the general partners determine.

(e) No person has any liability because an amendment to a certificate of limited partnership has not been filed to reflect the occurrence of any event referred to in subsection (b) of this section if the amendment is filed within the 30-day period specified in subsection (b).

(f) A restated certificate of limited partnership may be executed and filed in the same manner as a certificate of amendment.

Section 203. Cancellation of Certificate.

A certificate of limited partnership shall be cancelled upon the dissolution and the commencement of winding up of the partnership or at any other time there are no limited partners. A certificate of cancellation shall be filed in the office of the Secretary of State and set forth:

(1) the name of the limited partnership;

(2) the date of filing of its certificate of limited partnership;

(3) the reason for filing the certificate of cancellation;

(4) the effective date (which shall be a date certain) of cancellation if it is not to be effective upon the filing of the certificate; and

(5) any other information the general partners filing the certificate determine.

Section 204. Execution of Certificates.

(a) Each certificate required by this Article to be filed in the office of the Secretary of State shall be executed in the following manner:

(1) an original certificate of limited partnership must be signed by all general partners;

(2) a certificate of amendment must be signed by at least one general partner and by each other general partner designated in the certificate as a new general partner; and

(3) a certificate of cancellation must be signed by all general partners.

(b) Any person may sign a certificate by an attorney-in-fact, but a power of attorney to sign a certificate relating to the admission of a general partner must specifically describe the admission.

(c) The execution of a certificate by a general partner constitutes an affirmation under the penalties of perjury that the facts stated therein are true.

Section 205. Execution by Judicial Act.

If a person required by Section 204 to execute any certificate fails or refuses to do so, any other person who is adversely affected by the failure or refusal may petition the [designate the appropriate court] to direct the execution of the certificate. If the court finds that it is proper for the certificate to be executed and that any person so designated has failed or refused to execute the certificate, it shall order the Secretary of State to record an appropriate certificate.

Section 206. Filing in Office of Secretary of State.

(a) Two signed copies of the certificate of limited partnership and of any certificates of amendment or cancellation (or of any judicial decree of amendment or cancellation) shall be delivered to the Secretary of State. A person who executes a certificate as an agent or fiduciary need not exhibit evidence of his [or her] authority as a prerequisite to filing. Unless the Secretary of State finds that any certificate does not conform to law, upon receipt of all filing fees required by law he [or she] shall:

(1) endorse on each duplicate original the word "Filed" and the day, month, and year of the filing thereof;

(2) file one duplicate original in his [or her] office; and

(3) return the other duplicate original to the person who filed it or his [or her] representative.

(b) Upon the filing of a certificate of amendment (or judicial decree of amendment) in the office of the Secretary of State, the certificate of limited partnership shall be amended as set forth therein, and upon the effective date of a certificate of cancellation (or a judicial decree thereof), the certificate of limited partnership is cancelled.

Section 207. Liability for False Statement in Certificate.

If any certificate of limited partnership or certificate of amendment or cancellation contains a false statement, one who suffers loss by reliance on the statement may recover damages for the loss from:

(1) any person who executes the certificate, or causes another to execute it on his behalf, and knew, and any general partner who knew or should have known, the statement to be false at the time the certificate was executed; and

(2) any general partner who thereafter knows or should have known that any arrangement or other fact described in the certificate has changed, making the statement inaccurate in any respect within a sufficient

time before the statement was relied upon reasonably to have enabled that general partner to cancel or amend the certificate, or to file a petition for its cancellation or amendment under Section 205.

Section 208. Scope of Notice.

The fact that a certificate of limited partnership is on file in the office of the Secretary of State is notice that the partnership is a limited partnership and the persons designated therein as general partners are general partners, but it is not notice of any other fact.

Section 209. Delivery of Certificates to Limited Partners.

Upon the return by the Secretary of State pursuant to Section 206 of a certificate marked "Filed," the general partners shall promptly deliver or mail a copy of the certificate of limited partnership and each certificate of amendment or cancellation to each limited partner unless the partnership agreement provides otherwise.

Article 3
LIMITED PARTNERS

Section 301. Admission of Additional Limited Partners.

(a) A person becomes a limited partner on the later of:

(1) the date the original certificate of limited partnership is filed; or

(2) the date stated in the records of the limited partnership as the date that person becomes a limited partner.

(b) After the filing of a limited partnership's original certificate of limited partnership, a person may be admitted as an additional limited partner:

(1) in the case of a person acquiring a partnership interest directly from the limited partnership, upon compliance with the partnership agreement or, if the partnership agreement does not so provide, upon the written consent of all partners; and

(2) in the case of an assignee of a partnership interest of a partner who has the power, as provided in Section 704, to grant the assignee the right to become a limited partner, upon the exercise of that power and compliance with any conditions limiting the grant or exercise of the power.

Section 302. Voting.

Subject to Section 303, the partnership agreement may grant to all or a specified group of the limited partners the right to vote (on a per capita or other basis) upon any matter.

Section 303. Liability to Third Parties.

(a) Except as provided in subsection (d), a limited partner is not liable for the obligations of a limited partnership unless he [or she] is also a general partner or, in addition to the exercise of his [or her] rights and powers as a limited partner, he [or she] participates in the control of the business. However, if the limited partner participates in the control of the business, he [or she] is liable only to persons who transact business with the limited partnership reasonably believing, based upon the limited partner's conduct, that the limited partner is a general partner.

(b) A limited partner does not participate in the control of the business within the meaning of subsection (a) solely by doing one or more of the following:

(1) being a contractor for or an agent or employee of the limited partnership or of a general partner or being an officer, director, or shareholder of a general partner that is a corporation;

(2) consulting with and advising a general partner with respect to the business of the limited partnership;

(3) acting as surety for the limited partnership or guaranteeing or assuming one or more specific obligations of the limited partnership;

(4) taking any action required or permitted by law to bring or pursue a derivative action in the right of the limited partnership;

(5) requesting or attending a meeting of partners;

(6) proposing, approving, or disapproving, by voting or otherwise, one or more of the following matters:

(i) the dissolution and winding up of the limited partnership;

(ii) the sale, exchange, lease, mortgage, pledge, or other transfer of all or substantially all of the assets of the limited partnership;

(iii) the incurrence of indebtedness by the limited partnership other than in the ordinary course of its business;

(iv) a change in the nature of the business;

(v) the admission or removal of a general partner;

(vi) the admission or removal of a limited partner;

(vii) a transaction involving an actual or potential conflict of interest between a general partner and the limited partnership or the limited partners;

(viii) an amendment to the partnership agreement or certificate of limited partnership; or

(ix) matters related to the business of the limited partnership not otherwise enumerated in this subsection (b), which the partnership agreement states in writing may be subject to the approval or disapproval of limited partners;

(7) winding up the limited partnership pursuant to Section 803; or

(8) exercising any right or power permitted to limited partners under this [Act] and not specifically enumerated in this subsection (b).

(c) The enumeration in subsection (b) does not mean that the possession or exercise of any other powers by a limited partner constitutes participation by him [or her] in the business of the limited partnership.

(d) A limited partner who knowingly permits his [or her] name to be used in the name of the limited partnership, except under circumstances permitted by Section 102(2), is liable to creditors who extend credit to the limited partnership without actual knowledge that the limited partner is not a general partner.

Section 304. Person Erroneously Believing Himself [or Herself] Limited Partner.

(a) Except as provided in subsection (b), a person who makes a contribution to a business enterprise and erroneously but in good faith believes that he [or she] has become a limited partner in the enterprise is not a general partner in the enterprise and is not bound by its obligations by reason of making the contribution, receiving distributions from the enterprise, or exercising any rights of a limited partner, if, on ascertaining the mistake, he [or she]:

(1) causes an appropriate certificate of limited partnership or a certificate of amendment to be executed and filed; or

(2) withdraws from future equity participation in the enterprise by executing and filing in the office of the Secretary of State a certificate declaring withdrawal under this section.

(b) A person who makes a contribution of the kind described in subsection (a) is liable as a general partner to any third party who transacts business with the enterprise (i) before the person withdraws and an appropriate certificate is filed to show withdrawal, or (ii) before an appropriate certificate is filed to show that he [or she] is not a general partner, but in either case only if the third party actually believed in good faith that the person was a general partner at the time of the transaction.

Section 305. Information.

Each limited partner has the right to:

(1) inspect and copy any of the partnership records required to be maintained by Section 105; and

(2) obtain from the general partners from time to time upon reasonable demand (i) true and full information regarding the state of the business and financial condition of the limited partnership, (ii) promptly after becoming available, a copy of the limited partnership's federal, state, and local income tax returns for each year, and (iii) other information regarding the affairs of the limited partnership as is just and reasonable.

Article 4
GENERAL PARTNERS

Section 401. Admission of Additional General Partners.

After the filing of a limited partnership's original certificate of limited partnership, additional general partners may be admitted as provided in writing in the partnership agreement or, if the partnership agreement does not provide in writing for the admission of additional general partners, with the written consent of all partners.

Section 402. Events of Withdrawal.

Except as approved by the specific written consent of all partners at the time, a person ceases to be a general partner of a limited partnership upon the happening of any of the following events:

(1) the general partner withdraws from the limited partnership as provided in Section 602;

(2) the general partner ceases to be a member of the limited partnership as provided in Section 702;

(3) the general partner is removed as a general partner in accordance with the partnership agreement;

(4) unless otherwise provided in writing in the partnership agreement, the general partner: (i) makes an assignment for the benefit of creditors; (ii) files a voluntary petition in bankruptcy; (iii) is adjudicated a bankrupt or insolvent; (iv) files a petition or answer seeking for himself [or herself] any reorganization, arrangement, composition, readjustment, liquidation, dissolution, or similar relief under any statute, law, or regulation; (v) files an answer or other pleading admitting or failing to contest the material allegations of a petition filed against him [or her] in any proceeding of this nature; or (vi) seeks, consents to, or acquiesces in the appointment of a trustee, receiver, or liquidator of the general partner or of all or any substantial part of his [or her] properties;

(5) unless otherwise provided in writing in the partnership agreement, [120] days after the commencement of any proceeding against the general partner seeking reorganization, arrangement, composition, readjustment, liquidation, dissolution, or similar relief under any statute, law, or regulation, the proceeding has not been dismissed, or if within [90] days after the appointment without his [or her] consent or acquiescence of a trustee, receiver, or liquidator of the general partner or of all or any substantial part of his [or her] properties, the appointment is not vacated or stayed or within [90] days after the expiration of any such stay, the appointment is not vacated;

(6) in the case of a general partner who is a natural person,

(i) his [or her] death; or

(ii) the entry of an order by a court of competent jurisdiction adjudicating him [or her] incompetent to manage his [or her] person or his [or her] estate;

(7) in the case of a general partner who is acting as a general partner by virtue of being a trustee of a trust, the termination of the trust (but not merely the substitution of a new trustee);

(8) in the case of a general partner that is a separate partnership, the dissolution and commencement of winding up of the separate partnership;

(9) in the case of a general partner that is a corporation, the filing of a certificate of dissolution, or its equivalent, for the corporation or the revocation of its charter; or

(10) in the case of an estate, the distribution by the fiduciary of the estate's entire interest in the partnership.

Section 403. General Powers and Liabilities.

(a) Except as provided in this [Act] or in the partnership agreement, a general partner of a limited partnership has the rights and powers and is subject to the restrictions of a partner in a partnership without limited partners.

(b) Except as provided in this [Act], a general partner of a limited partnership has the liabilities of a partner in a partnership without limited partners to persons other than the partnership and the other partners. Except as provided in this [Act] or in the partnership agreement, a general partner of a limited partnership has the liabilities of a partner in a partnership without limited partners to the partnership and to the other partners.

Section 404. Contributions by General Partner.

A general partner of a limited partnership may make contributions to the partnership and share in the profits and losses of, and in distributions from, the limited partnership as a general partner. A general partner also may make contributions to and share in profits, losses, and distributions as a limited partner. A person who is both a general partner and a limited partner has the rights and powers, and is subject to the restrictions and liabilities, of a general partner and, except as provided in the partnership agreement, also has the powers, and is subject to the restrictions, of a limited partner to the extent of his [or her] participation in the partnership as a limited partner.

Section 405. Voting.

The partnership agreement may grant to all or certain identified general partners the right to vote (on a per capita or any other basis), separately or with all or any class of the limited partners, on any matter.

Article 5
FINANCE

Section 501. Form of Contribution.

The contribution of a partner may be in cash, property, or services rendered, or a promissory note or other obligation to contribute cash or property or to perform services.

Section 502. Liability for Contribution.

(a) A promise by a limited partner to contribute to the limited partnership is not enforceable unless set out in a writing signed by the limited partner.

(b) Except as provided in the partnership agreement, a partner is obligated to the limited partnership to perform any enforceable promise to contribute cash or property or to perform services, even if he [or she] is unable to perform because of death, disability, or any other reason. If a partner does not make the required contribution of property or services, he [or she] is obligated at the option of the limited partnership to contribute cash equal to that portion of the value, as stated in the partnership records required to be kept pursuant to Section 105, of the stated contribution which has not been made.

(c) Unless otherwise provided in the partnership agreement, the obligation of a partner to make a contribution or return money or other property paid or distributed in violation of this [Act] may be compromised only by consent of all partners. Notwithstanding the compromise, a creditor of a limited partnership who extends credit, or, otherwise acts in reliance on that obligation after the partner signs a writing which reflects the obligation and before the amendment or cancellation thereof to reflect the compromise may enforce the original obligation.

Section 503. Sharing of Profits and Losses.

The profits and losses of a limited partnership shall be allocated among the partners, and among classes of partners, in the manner provided in writing in the partnership agreement. If the partnership agreement does not so provide in writing, profits and losses shall be allocated on the basis of the value, as stated in the partnership records required to be kept pursuant to Section 105, of the contributions made by each partner to the extent they have been received by the partnership and have not been returned.

Section 504. Sharing of Distributions.

Distributions of cash or other assets of a limited partnership shall be allocated among the partners and among classes of partners in the manner provided in writing in the partnership agreement. If the partnership agreement does not so provide in writing, distributions shall be made on the basis of the value, as stated in the partnership records required to be kept pursuant to Section 105, of the contributions made by each partner to the extent they have been received by the partnership and have not been returned.

Article 6
DISTRIBUTIONS AND WITHDRAWAL

Section 601. Interim Distributions.

Except as provided in this Article, a partner is entitled to receive distributions from a limited partnership before his [or her] withdrawal from the limited partnership and before the dissolution and winding up thereof to the extent and at the times or upon the happening of the events specified in the partnership agreement.

Section 602. Withdrawal of General Partner.

A general partner may withdraw from a limited partnership at any time by giving written notice to the other partners, but if the withdrawal violates the partnership agreement, the limited partnership may recover from the withdrawing general partner damages for breach of the partnership agreement and offset the damages against the amount otherwise distributable to him [or her].

Section 603. Withdrawal of Limited Partner.

A limited partner may withdraw from a limited partnership at the time or upon the happening of events specified in writing in the partnership agreement. If the agreement does not specify in writing the time or the events upon the happening of which a limited partner may withdraw or a definite time for the dissolution and winding up of the limited partnership, a limited partner may withdraw upon not less than six months' prior written notice to each general partner at his [or her] address on the books of the limited partnership at its office in this State.

Section 604. Distribution Upon Withdrawal.

Except as provided in this Article, upon withdrawal any withdrawing partner is entitled to receive any distribution to which he [or she] is entitled under the partnership agreement and, if not otherwise provided in the agreement, he [or she] is entitled to receive, within a reasonable time after withdrawal, the fair value of his [or her] interest in the limited partnership as of the date of withdrawal based upon his [or her] right to share in distributions from the limited partnership.

Section 605. Distribution in Kind.

Except as provided in writing in the partnership agreement, a partner, regardless of the nature of his [or her] contribution, has no right to demand and receive any distribution from a limited partnership in any form other than cash. Except as provided in writing in the partnership agreement, a partner may not be compelled to accept a distribution of any asset in kind from a limited partnership to the extent that the percentage of the asset distributed to him [or her] exceeds a percentage of that asset which is equal to the percentage in which he [or she] shares in distributions from the limited partnership.

Section 606. Right to Distribution.

At the time a partner becomes entitled to receive a distribution, he [or she] has the status of, and is entitled to all remedies available to, a creditor of the limited partnership with respect to the distribution.

Section 607. Limitations on Distribution.

A partner may not receive a distribution from a limited partnership to the extent that, after giving effect to the distribution, all liabilities of the limited partnership, other than liabilities to partners on account of their partnership interests, exceed the fair value of the partnership assets.

Section 608. Liability Upon Return of Contribution.

(a) If a partner has received the return of any part of his [or her] contribution without violation of the partnership agreement or this [Act], he [or she] is liable to the limited partnership for a period of one year thereafter for the amount of the returned contribution, but only to the extent necessary to discharge the limited partnership's liabilities to creditors who extended credit to the limited partnership during the period the contribution was held by the partnership.

(b) If a partner has received the return of any part of his [or her] contribution in violation of the partnership agreement or this [Act], he [or she] is liable to the limited partnership for a period of six years thereafter for the amount of the contribution wrongfully returned.

(c) A partner receives a return of his [or her] contribution to the extent that a distribution to him [or her] reduces his [or her] share of the fair value of the net assets of the limited partnership below the value, as set forth in the partnership records required to be kept pursuant to Section 105, of his [or her] contribution which has not been distributed to him [or her].

Article 7
ASSIGNMENT OF PARTNERSHIP INTERESTS

Section 701. Nature of Partnership Interest.

A partnership interest is personal property.

Section 702. Assignment of Partnership Interest.

Except as provided in the partnership agreement, a partnership interest is assignable in whole or in part. An assignment of a partnership interest does not dissolve a limited partnership or entitle the assignee to become or to exercise any rights of a partner. An assignment entitles the assignee to receive, to the extent assigned, only the distribution to which the assignor would be entitled. Except as provided in the partnership agreement, a partner ceases to be a partner upon assignment of all his [or her] partnership interest.

Section 703. Rights of Creditor.

On application to a court of competent jurisdiction by any judgment creditor of a partner, the court may charge the partnership interest of the partner with payment of the unsatisfied amount of the judgment with interest. To the extent so charged, the judgment creditor has only the rights of an assignee of the partnership interest. This [Act] does not deprive any partner of the benefit of any exemption laws applicable to his [or her] partnership interest.

Section 704. Right of Assignee to Become Limited Partner.

(a) An assignee of a partnership interest, including an assignee of a general partner, may become a limited partner if and to the extent that (i) the assignor gives the assignee that right in accordance with authority described in the partnership agreement, or (ii) all other partners consent.

(b) An assignee who has become a limited partner has, to the extent assigned, the rights and powers, and is subject to the restrictions and liabilities, of a limited partner under the partnership agreement and this [Act]. An assignee who becomes a limited partner also is liable for the obligations of his [or her] assignor to make and return contributions as provided in Articles 5 and 6. However, the assignee is not obligated for liabilities unknown to the assignee at the time he [or she] became a limited partner.

(c) If an assignee of a partnership interest becomes a limited partner, the assignor is not released from his [or her] liability to the limited partnership under Sections 207 and 502.

Section 705. Power of Estate of Deceased or Incompetent Partner.

If a partner who is an individual dies or a court of competent jurisdiction adjudges him [or her] to be incompetent to manage his [or her] person or his [or her] property, the partner's executor, administrator, guardian, conservator, or other legal representative may exercise all of the partner's rights for the purpose of settling his [or her] estate or administering his [or her] property, including any power the partner had to give an assignee the right to become a limited partner. If a partner is a corporation, trust, or other entity and is dissolved or terminated, the powers of that partner may be exercised by its legal representative or successor.

Article 8
DISSOLUTION

Section 801. Nonjudicial Dissolution.

A limited partnership is dissolved and its affairs shall be wound up upon the happening of the first to occur of the following:

(1) at the time specified in the certificate of limited partnership;

(2) upon the happening of events specified in writing in the partnership agreement;

(3) written consent of all partners;

(4) an event of withdrawal of a general partner unless at the time there is at least one other general partner and the written provisions of the partnership agreement permit the business of the limited partnership to be carried on by the remaining general partner and that partner does so, but the limited partnership is not dissolved and is not required to be wound up by reason of any event of withdrawal if, within 90 days after the withdrawal, all partners agree in writing to continue the business of the limited partnership and to the appointment of one or more additional general partners if necessary or desired; or

(5) entry of a decree of judicial dissolution under Section 802.

Section 802. Judicial Dissolution.

On application by or for a partner the [designate the appropriate court] court may decree dissolution of a limited partnership whenever it is not reasonably practicable to carry on the business in conformity with the partnership agreement.

Section 803. Winding Up.

Except as provided in the partnership agreement, the general partners who have not wrongfully dissolved a limited partnership or, if none, the limited partners, may wind up the limited partnership's affairs; but the [designate the appropriate court] court may wind up the limited partnership's affairs upon application of any partner, his [or her] legal representative, or assignee.

Section 804. Distribution of Assets.

Upon the winding up of a limited partnership, the assets shall be distributed as follows:

(1) to creditors, including partners who are creditors, to the extent permitted by law, in satisfaction of liabilities of the limited partnership other than liabilities for distributions to partners under Section 601 or 604;

(2) except as provided in the partnership agreement, to partners and former partners in satisfaction of liabilities for distributions under Section 601 or 604; and

(3) except as provided in the partnership agreement, to partners first for the return of their contributions and secondly respecting their partnership interests, in the proportions in which the partners share in distributions.

Article 9
FOREIGN LIMITED PARTNERSHIPS

Section 901. Law Governing.

Subject to the Constitution of this State, (i) the laws of the state under which a foreign limited partnership is organized govern its organization and internal affairs and the liability of its limited partners, and (ii) a foreign limited partnership may not be denied registration by reason of any difference between those laws and the laws of this State.

Section 902. Registration.

Before transacting business in this State, a foreign limited partnership shall register with the Secretary of State. In order to register, a foreign limited partnership shall submit to the Secretary of State, in duplicate, an application for registration as a foreign limited partnership, signed and sworn to by a general partner and setting forth:

(1) the name of the foreign limited partnership and, if different, the name under which it proposes to register and transact business in this State;

(2) the State and date of its formation;

(3) the name and address of any agent for service of process on the foreign limited partnership whom the foreign limited partnership elects to appoint; the agent must be an individual resident of this State, a domestic corporation, or a foreign corporation having a place of business in, and authorized to do business in, this State;

(4) a statement that the Secretary of State is appointed the agent of the foreign limited partnership for service of process if no agent has been appointed under paragraph (3) or, if appointed, the agent's authority has been revoked or if the agent cannot be found or served with the exercise of reasonable diligence;

(5) the address of the office required to be maintained in the state of its organization by the laws of that state or, if not so required, of the principal office of the foreign limited partnership;

(6) the name and business address of each general partner; and

(7) the address of the office at which is kept a list of the names and addresses of the limited partners and their capital contributions, together with an undertaking by the foreign limited partnership to keep those records until the foreign limited partnership's registration in this State is cancelled or withdrawn.

Section 903. Issuance of Registration.

(a) If the Secretary of State finds that an application for registration conforms to law and all requisite fees have been paid, he [or she] shall:

(1) endorse on the application the word "Filed", and the month, day, and year of the filing thereof;

(2) file in his [or her] office a duplicate original of the application; and

(3) issue a certificate of registration to transact business in this State.

(b) The certificate of registration, together with a duplicate original of the application, shall be returned to the person who filed the application or his [or her] representative.

Section 904. Name.

A foreign limited partnership may register with the Secretary of State under any name, whether or not it is the name under which it is registered in its state of organization, that includes without abbreviation the words "limited partnership" and that could be registered by a domestic limited partnership.

Section 905. Changes and Amendments.

If any statement in the application for registration of a foreign limited partnership was false when made or any arrangements or other facts described have changed, making the application inaccurate in any respect, the foreign limited partnership shall promptly file in the office of the Secretary of State a certificate, signed and sworn to by a general partner, correcting such statement.

Section 906. Cancellation of Registration.

A foreign limited partnership may cancel its registration by filing with the Secretary of State a certificate of cancellation signed and sworn to by a general partner. A cancellation does not terminate the authority of the Secretary of State to accept service of process on the foreign limited partnership with respect to [claims for relief] [causes of action] arising out of the transactions of business in this State.

Section 907. Transaction of Business Without Registration.

(a) A foreign limited partnership transacting business in this State may not maintain any action, suit, or proceeding in any court of this State until it has registered in this State.

(b) The failure of a foreign limited partnership to register in this State does not impair the validity of any contract or act of the foreign limited partnership or prevent the foreign limited partnership from defending any action, suit, or proceeding in any court of this State.

(c) A limited partner of a foreign limited partnership is not liable as a general partner of the foreign limited partnership solely by reason of having transacted business in this State without registration.

(d) A foreign limited partnership, by transacting business in this State without registration, appoints the Secretary of State as its agent for service of process with respect to [claims for relief] [causes of action] arising out of the transaction of business in this State.

Section 908. Action by [Appropriate Official].

The [designate the appropriate official] may bring an action to restrain a foreign limited partnership from transacting business in this State in violation of this Article.

Article 10

DERIVATIVE ACTIONS

Section 1001. Right of Action.

A limited partner may bring an action in the right of a limited partnership to recover a judgment in its favor if general partners with authority to do so have refused to bring the action or if an effort to cause those general partners to bring the action is not likely to succeed.

Section 1002. Proper Plaintiff.

In a derivative action, the plaintiff must be a partner at the time of bringing the action and (i) must have been a partner at the time of the transaction of which he [or she] complains or (ii) his [or her] status as a partner must have devolved upon him by operation of law or pursuant to the terms of the partnership agreement from a person who was a partner at the time of the transaction.

Section 1003. Pleading.

In a derivative action, the complaint shall set forth with particularity the effort of the plaintiff to secure initiation of the action by a general partner or the reasons for not making the effort.

Section 1004. Expenses.

If a derivative action is successful, in whole or in part, or if anything is received by the plaintiff as a result of a judgment, compromise, or settlement of an action or claim, the court may award the plaintiff reasonable expenses, including reasonable attorney's fees, and shall direct him [or her] to remit to the limited partnership the remainder of those proceeds received by him [or her].

Article 11

MISCELLANEOUS

Section 1101. Construction and Application.

This [Act] shall be so applied and construed to effectuate its general purpose to make uniform the law with respect to the subject of this [Act] among states enacting it.

Section 1102. Short Title.

This [Act] may be cited as the Uniform Limited Partnership Act.

Section 1103. Severability.

If any provision of this [Act] or its application to any person or circumstance is held invalid, the invalidity does not affect other provisions or applications of the [Act] which can be given effect without the invalid provision or application, and to this end the provisions of this [Act] are severable.

Section 1104. Effective Date, Extended Effective Date, and Repeal.

Except as set forth below, the effective date of this [Act] is ______ and the following acts [list existing limited partnership acts] are hereby repealed:

(1) The existing provisions for execution and filing of certificates of limited partnerships and amendments thereunder and cancellations thereof continue in effect until [specify time required to create central filing system], the extended effective date, and Sections 102, 103, 104, 105, 201, 202, 203, 204 and 206 are not effective until the extended effective date.

(2) Section 402, specifying the conditions under which a general partner ceases to be a member of a limited partnership, is not effective until the extended effective date, and the applicable provisions of existing law continue to govern until the extended effective date.

(3) Sections 501, 502 and 608 apply only to contributions and distributions made after the effective date of this [Act].

(4) Section 704 applies only to assignments made after the effective date of this [Act].

(5) Article 9, dealing with registration of foreign limited partnerships, is not effective until the extended effective date.

(6) Unless otherwise agreed by the partners, the applicable provisions of existing law governing allocation of profits and losses (rather than the provisions of Section 503), distributions to a withdrawing partner (rather than the provisions of Section 604), and distributions of assets upon the winding up of a limited partnership (rather than the provisions of Section 804) govern limited partnerships formed before the effective date of this [Act].

Section 1105. Rules for Cases Not Provided For in This [Act].

In any case not provided for in this [Act] the provisions of the Uniform Partnership Act govern.

Section 1106. Savings Clause.

The repeal of any statutory provision by this [Act] does not impair, or otherwise affect, the organization or the continued existence of a limited partnership existing at the effective date of this [Act], nor does the repeal of any existing statutory provision by this [Act] impair any contract or affect any right accrued before the effective date of this [Act].

APPENDIX G

The Revised Model Business Corporation Act (Excerpts)

Chapter 2. INCORPORATION

§ 2.01 Incorporators

One or more persons may act as the incorporator or incorporators of a corporation by delivering articles of incorporation to the secretary of state for filing.

§ 2.02 Articles of Incorporation

(a) The articles of incorporation must set forth:

(1) a corporate name * * * ;

(2) the number of shares the corporation is authorized to issue;

(3) the street address of the corporation's initial registered office and the name of its initial registered agent at that office; and

(4) the name and address of each incorporator.

(b) The articles of incorporation may set forth:

(1) the names and addresses of the individuals who are to serve as the initial directors;

(2) provisions not inconsistent with law regarding:

(i) the purpose or purposes for which the corporation is organized;

(ii) managing the business and regulating the affairs of the corporation;

(iii) defining, limiting, and regulating the powers of the corporation, its board of directors, and shareholders;

(iv) a par value for authorized shares or classes of shares;

(v) the imposition of personal liability on shareholders for the debts of the corporation to a specified extent and upon specified conditions;

(3) any provision that under this Act is required or permitted to be set forth in the bylaws; and

(4) a provision eliminating or limiting the liability of a director to the corporation or its shareholders for money damages for any action taken, or any failure to take any action, as a director, except liability for (A) the amount of a financial benefit received by a director to which he is not entitled; (B) an intentional infliction of harm on the corporation or the shareholders; (C) [unlawful distributions]; or (D) an intentional violation of criminal law.

(c) The articles of incorporation need not set forth any of the corporate powers enumerated in this Act.

§ 2.03 Incorporation

(a) Unless a delayed effective date is specified, the corporate existence begins when the articles of incorporation are filed.

(b) The secretary of state's filing of the articles of incorporation is conclusive proof that the incorporators satisfied all conditions precedent to incorporation except in a proceeding by the state to cancel or revoke the incorporation or involuntarily dissolve the corporation.

§ 2.04 Liability for Preincorporation Transactions

All persons purporting to act as or on behalf of a corporation, knowing there was no incorporation under this Act, are jointly and severally liable for all liabilities created while so acting.

§ 2.05 Organization of Corporation

(a) After incorporation:

(1) if initial directors are named in the articles of incorporation, the initial directors shall hold an organizational meeting, at the call of a majority of the directors, to complete the organization of the corporation by appointing officers, adopting bylaws, and carrying on any other business brought before the meeting;

(2) if initial directors are not named in the articles, the incorporator or incorporators shall hold an organizational meeting at the call of a majority of the incorporators:

(i) to elect directors and complete the organization of the corporation; or

(ii) to elect a board of directors who shall complete the organization of the corporation.

(b) Action required or permitted by this Act to be taken by incorporators at an organizational meeting may be taken without a meeting if the action taken is evidenced by one or more written consents describing the action taken and signed by each incorporator.

(c) An organizational meeting may be held in or out of this state.

* * * *

Chapter 3. PURPOSES AND POWERS

§ 3.01 Purposes

(a) Every corporation incorporated under this Act has the purpose of engaging in any lawful business unless a more limited purpose is set forth in the articles of incorporation.

(b) A corporation engaging in a business that is subject to regulation under another statute of this state may incorporate under this Act only if permitted by, and subject to all limitations of, the other statute.

§ 3.02 General Powers

Unless its articles of incorporation provide otherwise, every corporation has perpetual duration and succession in its corporate name and has the same powers as an individual to do all things necessary or convenient to carry out its business and affairs, including without limitation power:

(1) to sue and be sued, complain and defend in its corporate name;

(2) to have a corporate seal, which may be altered at will, and to use it, or a facsimile of it, by impressing or affixing it or in any other manner reproducing it;

(3) to make and amend bylaws, not inconsistent with its articles of incorporation or with the laws of this state, for managing the business and regulating the affairs of the corporation;

(4) to purchase, receive, lease, or otherwise acquire, and own, hold, improve, use, and otherwise deal with, real or personal property, or any legal or equitable interest in property, wherever located;

(5) to sell, convey, mortgage, pledge, lease, exchange, and otherwise dispose of all or any part of its property;

(6) to purchase, receive, subscribe for, or otherwise acquire; own, hold, vote, use, sell, mortgage, lend, pledge, or otherwise dispose of; and deal in and with shares or other interests in, or obligations of, any other entity;

(7) to make contracts and guarantees, incur liabilities, borrow money, issue its notes, bonds, and other obligations (which may be convertible into or include the option to purchase other securities of the corporation), and secure any of its obligations by mortgage or pledge of any of its property, franchises, or income;

(8) to lend money, invest and reinvest its funds, and receive and hold real and personal property as security for repayment;

(9) to be a promoter, partner, member, associate, or manager of any partnership, joint venture, trust, or other entity;

(10) to conduct its business, locate offices, and exercise the powers granted by this Act within or without this state;

(11) to elect directors and appoint officers, employees, and agents of the corporation, define their duties, fix their compensation, and lend them money and credit;

(12) to pay pensions and establish pension plans, pension trusts, profit sharing plans, share bonus plans, share option plans, and benefit or incentive plans for any or all of its current or former directors, officers, employees, and agents;

(13) to make donations for the public welfare or for charitable, scientific, or educational purposes;

(14) to transact any lawful business that will aid governmental policy;

(15) to make payments or donations, or do any other act, not inconsistent with law, that furthers the business and affairs of the corporation.

* * * *

Chapter 5. OFFICE AND AGENT

§ 5.01 Registered Office and Registered Agent

Each corporation must continuously maintain in this state:

(1) a registered office that may be the same as any of its places of business; and

(2) a registered agent, who may be:

(i) an individual who resides in this state and whose business office is identical with the registered office;

(ii) a domestic corporation or not-for-profit domestic corporation whose business office is identical with the registered office; or

(iii) a foreign corporation or not-for-profit foreign corporation authorized to transact business in this state whose business office is identical with the registered office.

* * * *

§ 5.04 Service on Corporation

(a) A corporation's registered agent is the corporation's agent for service of process, notice, or demand required or permitted by law to be served on the corporation.

(b) If a corporation has no registered agent, or the agent cannot with reasonable diligence be served, the corporation may be served by registered or certified mail, return receipt requested, addressed to the secretary of the corporation at its principal office. Service is perfected under this subsection at the earliest of:

(1) the date the corporation receives the mail;

(2) the date shown on the return receipt, if signed on behalf of the corporation; or

(3) five days after its deposit in the United States Mail, if mailed postpaid and correctly addressed.

(c) This section does not prescribe the only means, or necessarily the required means, of serving a corporation.

Chapter 6. SHARES AND DISTRIBUTIONS

* * * *

Subchapter B. Issuance of Shares

* * * *

§ 6.21 Issuance of Shares

(a) The powers granted in this section to the board of directors may be reserved to the shareholders by the articles of incorporation.

(b) The board of directors may authorize shares to be issued for consideration consisting of any tangible or intangible property or benefit to the corporation, including cash, promissory notes, services performed, contracts for services to be performed, or other securities of the corporation.

(c) Before the corporation issues shares, the board of directors must determine that the consideration received or to be received for shares to be issued is adequate. That determination by the board of directors is conclusive insofar as the adequacy of consideration for the issuance of shares relates to whether the shares are validly issued, fully paid, and nonassessable.

(d) When the corporation receives the consideration for which the board of directors authorized the issuance of shares, the shares issued therefor are fully paid and nonassessable.

(e) The corporation may place in escrow shares issued for a contract for future services or benefits or a promissory note, or make other arrangements to restrict the transfer of the shares, and may credit distributions in respect of the shares against their purchase price, until the services are performed, the note is paid, or the benefits received. If the services are not performed, the note is not paid, or the benefits are not received, the shares escrowed or restricted and the distributions credited may be cancelled in whole or part.

* * * *

§ 6.27 Restriction on Transfer or Registration of Shares and Other Securities

(a) The articles of incorporation, bylaws, an agreement among shareholders, or an agreement between shareholders and the corporation may impose restrictions on the transfer or registration of transfer of shares of the corporation. A restriction does not affect shares issued before the restriction was adopted unless the holders of the shares are parties to the restriction agreement or voted in favor of the restriction.

(b) A restriction on the transfer or registration of transfer of shares is valid and enforceable against the holder or a transferee of the holder if the restriction is authorized by this section and its existence is noted conspicuously on the front or back of the certificate or is contained in the information statement [sent to the shareholder]. Unless so noted, a restriction is not enforceable against a person without knowledge of the restriction.

(c) A restriction on the transfer or registration of transfer of shares is authorized:

(1) to maintain the corporation's status when it is dependent on the number or identity of its shareholders;

(2) to preserve exemptions under federal or state securities law;

(3) for any other reasonable purpose.

(d) A restriction on the transfer or registration of transfer of shares may:

(1) obligate the shareholder first to offer the corporation or other persons (separately, consecutively, or simultaneously) an opportunity to acquire the restricted shares;

(2) obligate the corporate or other persons (separately, consecutively, or simultaneously) to acquire the restricted shares;

(3) require the corporation, the holders of any class of its shares, or another person to approve the transfer of the restricted shares, if the requirement is not manifestly unreasonable;

(4) prohibit the transfer of the restricted shares to designated persons or classes of persons, if the prohibition is not manifestly unreasonable.

(e) For purposes of this section, "shares" includes a security convertible into or carrying a right to subscribe for or acquire shares.

* * * *

Chapter 7. SHAREHOLDERS

Subchapter A. Meetings

§ 7.01 Annual Meeting

(a) A corporation shall hold annually at a time stated in or fixed in accordance with the bylaws a meeting of shareholders.

(b) Annual shareholders' meetings may be held in or out of this state at the place stated in or fixed in accordance with the bylaws. If no place is stated in or fixed in accordance with the bylaws, annual meetings shall be held at the corporation's principal office.

(c) The failure to hold an annual meeting at the time stated in or fixed in accordance with a corporation's bylaws does not affect the validity of any corporate action.

* * * *

§ 7.05 Notice of Meeting

(a) A corporation shall notify shareholders of the date, time, and place of each annual and special shareholders' meeting no fewer than 10 nor more than 60 days before the meeting date. Unless this Act or the articles of incorporation require otherwise, the corporation is required to give notice only to shareholders entitled to vote at the meeting.

(b) Unless this Act or the articles of incorporation require otherwise, notice of an annual meeting need not include a description of the purpose or purposes for which the meeting is called.

(c) Notice of a special meeting must include a description of the purpose or purposes for which the meeting is called.

(d) If not otherwise fixed * * *, the record date for determining shareholders entitled to notice of and to vote at an annual or special shareholders' meeting is the day before the first notice is delivered to shareholders.

(e) Unless the bylaws require otherwise, if an annual or special shareholders' meeting is adjourned to a different date, time, or place, notice need not be given of the new date, time, or place if the new date, time, or place is announced at the meeting before adjournment. * * *

* * * *

§ 7.07 Record Date

(a) The bylaws may fix or provide the manner of fixing the record date for one or more voting groups in order to determine the shareholders entitled to notice of a shareholders' meeting, to demand a special meeting, to vote, or to take any other action. If the bylaws do not fix or provide for fixing a record date, the board of directors of the corporation may fix a future date as the record date.

(b) A record date fixed under this section may not be more than 70 days before the meeting or action requiring a determination of shareholders.

(c) A determination of shareholders entitled to notice of or to vote at a shareholders' meeting is effective for any adjournment of the meeting unless the board of directors fixes a new record date, which it must do if the meeting is adjourned to a date more than 120 days after the date fixed for the original meeting.

(d) If a court orders a meeting adjourned to a date more than 120 days after the date fixed for the original meeting, it may provide that the original record date continues in effect or it may fix a new record date.

Subchapter B. Voting

§ 7.20 Shareholders' List for Meeting

(a) After fixing a record date for a meeting, a corporation shall prepare an alphabetical list of the names of all its shareholders who are entitled to notice of a shareholders' meeting. The list must be arranged by voting group (and within each voting group by class or series of shares) and show the address of and number of shares held by each shareholder.

(b) The shareholders' list must be available for inspection by any shareholder, beginning two business days after notice of the meeting is given for which the list was prepared and continuing through the meeting, at the corporation's principal office or at a place identified in the meeting notice in the city where the meeting will be held. A shareholder, his agent, or attorney is entitled on written demand to inspect and, subject to the requirements of section 16.02(c), to copy the list, during regular business hours and at his expense, during the period it is available for inspection.

(c) The corporation shall make the shareholders' list available at the meeting, and any shareholder, his agent, or attorney is entitled to inspect the list at any time during the meeting or any adjournment.

(d) If the corporation refuses to allow a shareholder, his agent, or attorney to inspect the shareholders' list before or at the meeting (or copy the list as permitted by subsection (b)), the [name or describe] court of the county where a corporation's principal office (or, if none in this state, its registered office) is located, on application of the shareholder, may summarily order the inspection or copying at the corporation's expense and may postpone the meeting for which the list was prepared until the inspection or copying is complete.

(e) Refusal or failure to prepare or make available the shareholders' list does not affect the validity of action taken at the meeting.

* * * *

§ 7.22 Proxies

(a) A shareholder may vote his shares in person or by proxy.

(b) A shareholder may appoint a proxy to vote or otherwise act for him by signing an appointment form, either personally or by his attorney-in-fact.

(c) An appointment of a proxy is effective when received by the secretary or other officer or agent authorized to tabulate votes. An appointment is valid for 11 months unless a longer period is expressly provided in the appointment form.

* * * *

§ 7.28 Voting for Directors; Cumulative Voting

(a) Unless otherwise provided in the articles of incorporation, directors are elected by a plurality of the votes cast by the shares entitled to vote in the election at a meeting at which a quorum is present.

(b) Shareholders do not have a right to cumulate their votes for directors unless the articles of incorporation so provide.

(c) A statement included in the articles of incorporation that "[all] [a designated voting group of] shareholders are entitled to cumulate their votes for directors" (or words of similar import) means that the shareholders designated are entitled to multiply the number of votes they are entitled to cast by the number of directors for whom they are entitled to vote and cast the product for a single candidate or distribute the product among two or more candidates.

(d) Shares otherwise entitled to vote cumulatively may not be voted cumulatively at a particular meeting unless:

(1) the meeting notice or proxy statement accompanying the notice states conspicuously that cumulative voting is authorized; or

(2) a shareholder who has the right to cumulate his votes gives notice to the corporation not less than 48 hours before the time set for the meeting of his intent to cumulate his votes during the meeting, and if one shareholder gives this notice all other shareholders in the same voting group participating in the election are entitled to cumulate their votes without giving further notice.

* * * *

Subchapter D. Derivative Proceedings

* * * *

§ 7.41 Standing

A shareholder may not commence or maintain a derivative proceeding unless the shareholder:

(1) was a shareholder of the corporation at the time of the act or omission complained of or became a shareholder through transfer by operation of law from one who was a shareholder at that time; and

(2) fairly and adequately represents the interests of the corporation in enforcing the right of the corporation.

§ 7.42 Demand

No shareholder may commence a derivative proceeding until:

(1) a written demand has been made upon the corporation to take suitable action; and

(2) 90 days have expired from the date the demand was made unless the shareholder has earlier been notified that the demand has been rejected by the corporation or unless irreparable injury to the corporation would result by waiting for the expiration of the 90 day period.

* * * *

Chapter 8. DIRECTORS AND OFFICERS

Subchapter A. Board of Directors

* * * *

§ 8.02 Qualifications of Directors

The articles of incorporation or bylaws may prescribe qualifications for directors. A director need not be a resident of this state or a shareholder of the corporation unless the articles of incorporation or bylaws so prescribe.

§ 8.03 Number and Election of Directors

(a) A board of directors must consist of one or more individuals, with the number specified in or fixed in accordance with the articles of incorporation or bylaws.

(b) If a board of directors has power to fix or change the number of directors, the board may increase or decrease by 30 percent or less the number of directors last approved by the shareholders, but only the shareholders may increase or decrease by more than 30 percent the number of directors last approved by the shareholders.

(c) The articles of incorporation or bylaws may establish a variable range for the size of the board of directors by fixing a minimum and maximum number of directors. If a variable range is established, the number of directors may be fixed or changed from time to time, within the minimum and maximum, by the shareholders or the board of directors. After shares are issued, only the shareholders may change the range for the size of the board or change from a fixed to a variable-range size board or vice versa.

(d) Directors are elected at the first annual shareholders' meeting and at each annual meeting thereafter unless their terms are staggered under section 8.06.

* * * *

§ 8.08 Removal of Directors by Shareholders

(a) The shareholders may remove one or more directors with or without cause unless the articles of incorporation provide that directors may be removed only for cause.

(b) If a director is elected by a voting group of shareholders, only the shareholders of that voting group may participate in the vote to remove him.

(c) If cumulative voting is authorized, a director may not be removed if the number of votes sufficient to elect him under cumulative voting is voted against his removal. If cumulative voting is not authorized, a director may be removed only if the number of votes cast to remove him exceeds the number of votes cast not to remove him.

(d) A director may be removed by the shareholders only at a meeting called for the purpose of removing him and the meeting notice must state that the purpose, or one of the purposes, of the meeting is removal of the director.

* * * *

Subchapter B. Meetings and Action of the Board

§ 8.20 Meetings

(a) The board of directors may hold regular or special meetings in or out of this state.

(b) Unless the articles of incorporation or bylaws provide otherwise, the board of directors may permit any or all directors to participate in a regular or special meeting by, or conduct the meeting through the use of, any means of communication by which all directors participating may simultaneously hear each other during the meeting. A director participating in a meeting by this means is deemed to be present in person at the meeting.

* * * *

§ 8.22 Notice of Meeting

(a) Unless the articles of incorporation or bylaws provide otherwise, regular meetings of the board of directors may be held without notice of the date, time, place, or purpose of the meeting.

(b) Unless the articles of incorporation or bylaws provide for a longer or shorter period, special meetings of the board of directors must be preceded by at least two days' notice of the date, time, and place of the meeting. The notice need not describe the purpose of the special meeting unless required by the articles of incorporation or bylaws.

* * * *

§ 8.24 Quorum and Voting

(a) Unless the articles of incorporation or bylaws require a greater number, a quorum of a board of directors consists of:

(1) a majority of the fixed number of directors if the corporation has a fixed board size; or

(2) a majority of the number of directors prescribed, or if no number is prescribed the number in office immediately before the meeting begins, if the corporation has a variable-range size board.

(b) The articles of incorporation or bylaws may authorize a quorum of a board of directors to consist of no fewer than one-third of the fixed or prescribed number of directors determined under subsection (a).

(c) If a quorum is present when a vote is taken, the affirmative vote of a majority of directors present is the act of the board of directors unless the articles of incorporation or bylaws require the vote of a greater number of directors.

(d) A director who is present at a meeting of the board of directors or a committee of the board of directors when corporate action is taken is deemed to have assented to the action taken unless: (1) he objects at the beginning of the meeting (or promptly upon his arrival) to holding it or transacting business at the meeting; (2) his dissent or abstention from the action taken is entered in the minutes of the meeting; or (3) he delivers written notice of his dissent or abstention to the presiding officer of the meeting before its adjournment or to the corporation immediately after adjournment of the meeting. The right of dissent or abstention is not available to a director who votes in favor of the action taken.

* * * *

Subchapter C. Standards of Conduct

§ 8.30 General Standards for Directors

(a) A director shall discharge his duties as a director, including his duties as a member of a committee:

(1) in good faith;

(2) with the care an ordinarily prudent person in a like position would exercise under similar circumstances; and

(3) in a manner he reasonably believes to be in the best interests of the corporation.

(b) In discharging his duties a director is entitled to rely on information, opinions, reports, or statements, including financial statements and other financial data, if prepared or presented by:

(1) one or more officers or employees of the corporation whom the director reasonably believes to be reliable and competent in the matters presented;

(2) legal counsel, public accountants, or other persons as to matters the director reasonably believes are within the person's professional or expert competence; or

(3) a committee of the board of directors of which he is not a member if the director reasonably believes the committee merits confidence.

(c) A director is not acting in good faith if he has knowledge concerning the matter in question that makes reliance otherwise permitted by subsection (b) unwarranted.

(d) A director is not liable for any action taken as a director, or any failure to take any action, if he performed the duties of his office in compliance with this section.

* * * *

Subchapter D. Officers

* * * *

§ 8.41 Duties of Officers

Each officer has the authority and shall perform the duties set forth in the bylaws or, to the extent consistent with the bylaws, the duties prescribed by the board of directors or by direction of an officer authorized by the board of directors to prescribe the duties of other officers.

§ 8.42 Standards of Conduct for Officers

(a) An officer with discretionary authority shall discharge his duties under that authority:

(1) in good faith;

(2) with the care an ordinarily prudent person in a like position would exercise under similar circumstances; and

(3) in a manner he reasonably believes to be in the best interests of the corporation.

(b) In discharging his duties an officer is entitled to rely on information, opinions, reports, or statements, including financial statements and other financial data, if prepared or presented by:

(1) one or more officers or employees of the corporation whom the officer reasonably believes to be reliable and competent in the matters presented; or

(2) legal counsel, public accountants, or other persons as to matters the officer reasonably believes are within the person's professional or expert competence.

(c) An officer is not acting in good faith if he has knowledge concerning the matter in question that makes reliance otherwise permitted by subsection (b) unwarranted.

(d) An officer is not liable for any action taken as an officer, or any failure to take any action, if he performed the duties of his office in compliance with this section.

* * * *

Chapter 11. MERGER AND SHARE EXCHANGE

§ 11.01 Merger

(a) One or more corporations may merge into another corporation if the board of directors of each corporation adopts and its shareholders (if required * * *) approve a plan of merger.

(b) The plan of merger must set forth:

(1) the name of each corporation planning to merge and the name of the surviving corporation into which each other corporation plans to merge;

(2) the terms and conditions of the merger; and

(3) the manner and basis of converting the shares of each corporation into shares, obligations, or other securities of the surviving or any other corporation or into cash or other property in whole or part.

(c) The plan of merger may set forth:

(1) amendments to the articles of incorporation of the surviving corporation; and

(2) other provisions relating to the merger.

* * * *

§ 11.04 Merger of Subsidiary

(a) A parent corporation owning at least 90 percent of the outstanding shares of each class of a subsidiary corporation may merge the subsidiary into itself without approval of the shareholders of the parent or subsidiary.

(b) The board of directors of the parent shall adopt a plan of merger that sets forth:

(1) the names of the parent and subsidiary; and

(2) the manner and basis of converting the shares of the subsidiary into shares, obligations, or other securities of the parent or any other corporation or into cash or other property in whole or part.

(c) The parent shall mail a copy or summary of the plan of merger to each shareholder of the subsidiary who does not waive the mailing requirement in writing.

(d) The parent may not deliver articles of merger to the secretary of state for filing until at least 30 days after the date it mailed a copy of the plan of merger to each shareholder of the subsidiary who did not waive the mailing requirement.

(e) Articles of merger under this section may not contain amendments to the articles of incorporation of the parent corporation (except for amendments enumerated in section 10.02).

* * * *

§ 11.06 Effect of Merger or Share Exchange

(a) When a merger takes effect:

(1) every other corporation party to the merger merges into the surviving corporation and the separate existence of every corporation except the surviving corporation ceases;

(2) the title to all real estate and other property owned by each corporation party to the merger is vested in the surviving corporation without reversion or impairment;

(3) the surviving corporation has all liabilities of each corporation party to the merger;

(4) a proceeding pending against any corporation party to the merger may be continued as if the merger did not occur or the surviving corporation may be substituted in the proceeding for the corporation whose existence ceased;

(5) the articles of incorporation of the surviving corporation are amended to the extent provided in the plan of merger; and

(6) the shares of each corporation party to the merger that are to be converted into shares, obligations, or other securities of the surviving or any other corporation or into cash or other property are converted and the former holders of the shares are entitled only to the rights provided in the articles of merger or to their rights under chapter 13.

(b) When a share exchange takes effect, the shares of each acquired corporation are exchanged as provided in the plan, and the former holders of the shares are entitled only to the exchange rights provided in the articles of share exchange or to their rights under chapter 13.

* * * *

Chapter 13. DISSENTERS' RIGHTS

Subchapter A. Right to Dissent and Obtain Payment for Shares

* * * *

§ 13.02 Right to Dissent

(a) A shareholder is entitled to dissent from, and obtain payment of the fair value of his shares in the event of, any of the following corporate actions:

(1) consummation of a plan of merger to which the corporation is a party (i) if shareholder approval is required for the merger by [statute] or the articles of incorporation and the shareholder is entitled to vote on the merger or (ii) if the corporation is a subsidiary that is merged with its parent under section 11.04;

(2) consummation of a plan of share exchange to which the corporation is a party as the corporation whose shares will be acquired, if the shareholder is entitled to vote on the plan;

(3) consummation of a sale or exchange of all, or substantially all, of the property of the corporation other than in the usual and regular course of business, if the shareholder is entitled to vote on the sale or exchange, including a sale in dissolution, but not including a sale pursuant to court order or a sale for cash pursuant to a plan by which all or substantially all of the net proceeds of the sale will be distributed to the shareholders within one year after the date of sale;

(4) an amendment of the articles of incorporation that materially and adversely affects rights in respect of a dissenter's shares because it:

(i) alters or abolishes a preferential right of the shares;

(ii) creates, alters, or abolishes a right in respect of redemption, including a provision respecting a sinking fund for the redemption or repurchase, of the shares;

(iii) alters or abolishes a preemptive right of the holder of the shares to acquire shares or other securities;

(iv) excludes or limits the right of the shares to vote on any matter, or to cumulate votes, other than a limitation by dilution through issuance of shares or other securities with similar voting rights; or

(v) reduces the number of shares owned by the shareholder to a fraction of a share if the fractional share so created is to be acquired for cash * * *; or

(5) any corporate action taken pursuant to a shareholder vote to the extent the articles of incorporation, bylaws, or a resolution of the board of directors provides that voting or nonvoting shareholders are entitled to dissent and obtain payment for their shares.

(b) A shareholder entitled to dissent and obtain payment for his shares under this chapter may not challenge the corporate action creating his entitlement unless the action is unlawful or fraudulent with respect to the shareholder or the corporation.

* * * *

Subchapter B. Procedure for Exercise of Dissenters' Rights

* * * *

§ 13.21 Notice of Intent to Demand Payment

(a) If proposed corporate action creating dissenters' rights under section 13.02 is submitted to a vote at a shareholders' meeting, a shareholder who wishes to assert dissenters' rights (1) must deliver to the corporation before the vote is taken written notice of his intent to demand payment for his shares if the proposed action is effectuated and (2) must not vote his shares in favor of the proposed action.

(b) A shareholder who does not satisfy the requirements of subsection (a) is not entitled to payment for his shares under this chapter.

* * * *

§ 13.25 Payment

(a) * * * [A]s soon as the proposed corporate action is taken, or upon receipt of a payment demand, the corporation shall pay each dissenter * * * the amount the corporation estimates to be the fair value of his shares, plus accrued interest.

* * * *

§ 13.28 Procedure If Shareholder Dissatisfied with Payment or Offer

(a) A dissenter may notify the corporation in writing of his own estimate of the fair value of his shares and amount of interest due, and demand payment of his estimate (less any payment under section 13.25) * * * if:

(1) the dissenter believes that the amount paid under section 13.25 * * * is less than the fair value of his shares or that the interest due is incorrectly calculated;

(2) the corporation fails to make payment under section 13.25 within 60 days after the date set for demanding payment; or

(3) the corporation, having failed to take the proposed action, does not return the deposited certificates or release the transfer restrictions imposed on uncertificated shares within 60 days after the date set for demanding payment.

(b) A dissenter waives his right to demand payment under this section unless he notifies the corporation of his demand in writing under subsection (a) within 30 days after the corporation made or offered payment for his shares.

* * * *

Chapter 14. DISSOLUTION

Subchapter A. Voluntary Dissolution

* * * *

§ 14.02 Dissolution by Board of Directors and Shareholders

(a) A corporation's board of directors may propose dissolution for submission to the shareholders.

(b) For a proposal to dissolve to be adopted:

(1) the board of directors must recommend dissolution to the shareholders unless the board of directors determines that because of conflict of interest or other special circumstances it should make no recommendation and communicates the basis for its determination to the shareholders; and

(2) the shareholders entitled to vote must approve the proposal to dissolve as provided in subsection (e).

(c) The board of directors may condition its submission of the proposal for dissolution on any basis.

(d) The corporation shall notify each shareholder, whether or not entitled to vote, of the proposed shareholders' meeting in accordance with section 7.05. The notice must also state that the purpose, or one of the purposes, of the meeting is to consider dissolving the corporation.

(e) Unless the articles of incorporation or the board of directors (acting pursuant to subsection (c)) require a greater vote or a vote by voting groups, the proposal to dissolve to be adopted must be approved by a majority of all the votes entitled to be cast on that proposal.

* * * *

§ 14.05 Effect of Dissolution

(a) A dissolved corporation continues its corporate existence but may not carry on any business except that appropriate to wind up and liquidate its business and affairs, including:

(1) collecting its assets;

(2) disposing of its properties that will not be distributed in kind to its shareholders;

(3) discharging or making provision for discharging its liabilities;

(4) distributing its remaining property among its shareholders according to their interests; and

(5) doing every other act necessary to wind up and liquidate its business and affairs.

(b) Dissolution of a corporation does not:

(1) transfer title to the corporation's property;

(2) prevent transfer of its shares or securities, although the authorization to dissolve may provide for closing the corporation's share transfer records;

(3) subject its directors or officers to standards of conduct different from those prescribed in chapter 8;

(4) change quorum or voting requirements for its board of directors or shareholders; change provisions for selection, resignation, or removal of its directors or officers or both; or change provisions for amending its bylaws;

(5) prevent commencement of a proceeding by or against the corporation in its corporate name;

(6) abate or suspend a proceeding pending by or against the corporation on the effective date of dissolution; or

(7) terminate the authority of the registered agent of the corporation.

* * * *

Subchapter C. Judicial Dissolution

§ 14.30 Grounds for Judicial Dissolution

The [name or describe court or courts] may dissolve a corporation:

(1) in a proceeding by the attorney general if it is established that:

(i) the corporation obtained its articles of incorporation through fraud; or

(ii) the corporation has continued to exceed or abuse the authority conferred upon it by law;

(2) in a proceeding by a shareholder if it is established that:

(i) the directors are deadlocked in the management of the corporate affairs, the shareholders are unable to break the deadlock, and irreparable injury to the corporation is threatened or being suffered, or the business and affairs of the corporation can no longer be conducted to the advantage of the shareholders generally, because of the deadlock;

(ii) the directors or those in control of the corporation have acted, are acting, or will act in a manner that is illegal, oppressive, or fraudulent;

(iii) the shareholders are deadlocked in voting power and have failed, for a period that includes at least two consecutive annual meeting dates, to elect successors to directors whose terms have expired; or

(iv) the corporate assets are being misapplied or wasted;

(3) in a proceeding by a creditor if it is established that:

(i) the creditor's claim has been reduced to judgment, the execution on the judgment returned unsatisfied, and the corporation is insolvent; or

(ii) the corporation has admitted in writing that the creditor's claim is due and owing and the corporation is insolvent; or

(4) in a proceeding by the corporation to have its voluntary dissolution continued under court supervision.

* * * *

Chapter 16. RECORDS AND REPORTS

Subchapter A. Records

§ 16.01 Corporate Records

(a) A corporation shall keep as permanent records minutes of all meetings of its shareholders and board of directors, a record of all actions taken by the shareholders or board of directors without a meeting, and a record of all actions taken by a committee of the board of directors in place of the board of directors on behalf of the corporation.

(b) A corporation shall maintain appropriate accounting records.

(c) A corporation or its agent shall maintain a record of its shareholders, in a form that permits preparation of a list of the names and addresses of all shareholders, in alphabetical order by class of shares showing the number and class of shares held by each.

(d) A corporation shall maintain its records in written form or in another form capable of conversion into written form within a reasonable time.

(e) A corporation shall keep a copy of the following records at its principal office:

(1) its articles or restated articles of incorporation and all amendments to them currently in effect;

(2) its bylaws or restated bylaws and all amendments to them currently in effect;

(3) resolutions adopted by its board of directors creating one or more classes or series of shares, and fixing their relative rights, preferences, and limitations, if shares issued pursuant to those resolutions are outstanding;

(4) the minutes of all shareholders' meetings, and records of all action taken by shareholders without a meeting, for the past three years;

(5) all written communications to shareholders generally within the past three years, including the financial statements furnished for the past three years * * *;

(6) a list of the names and business addresses of its current directors and officers; and

(7) its most recent annual report delivered to the secretary of state * * *.

§ 16.02 Inspection of Records by Shareholders

(a) Subject to section 16.03(c), a shareholder of a corporation is entitled to inspect and copy, during regular business hours at the corporation's principal office, any of the records of the corporation described in section 16.01(e) if he gives the corporation written notice of his demand at least five business days before the date on which he wishes to inspect and copy.

(b) A shareholder of a corporation is entitled to inspect and copy, during regular business hours at a reasonable location specified by the corporation, any of the following records of the corporation if the shareholder meets the requirements of subsection (c) and gives the corporation written notice of his demand at least five business days before the date on which he wishes to inspect and copy:

(1) excerpts from minutes of any meeting of the board of directors, records of any action of a committee of the board of directors while acting in place of the board of directors on behalf of the corporation, minutes of any meeting of the shareholders, and records of action taken by the shareholders or board of directors without a meeting, to the extent not subject to inspection under section 16.02(a);

(2) accounting records of the corporation; and

(3) the record of shareholders.

(c) A shareholder may inspect and copy the records identified in subsection (b) only if:

(1) his demand is made in good faith and for a proper purpose;

(2) he describes with reasonable particularity his purpose and the records he desires to inspect; and

(3) the records are directly connected with his purpose.

(d) The right of inspection granted by this section may not be abolished or limited by a corporation's articles of incorporation or bylaws.

(e) This section does not affect:

(1) the right of a shareholder to inspect records under section 7.20 or, if the shareholder is in litigation with the corporation, to the same extent as any other litigant;

(2) the power of a court, independently of this Act, to compel the production of corporate records for examination.

(f) For purposes of this section, "shareholder" includes a beneficial owner whose shares are held in a voting trust or by a nominee on his behalf.

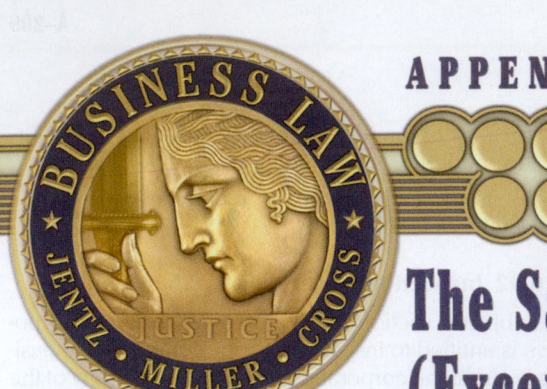

APPENDIX H

The Sarbanes-Oxley Act of 2002 (Excerpts and Explanatory Comments)

Note: The author's explanatory comments appear in italics following the excerpt from each section.

SECTION 302

Corporate responsibility for financial reports[1]

(a) Regulations required

The Commission shall, by rule, require, for each company filing periodic reports under section 13(a) or 15(d) of the Securities Exchange Act of 1934 (15 U.S.C. 78m, 78o(d)), that the principal executive officer or officers and the principal financial officer or officers, or persons performing similar functions, certify in each annual or quarterly report filed or submitted under either such section of such Act that—

(1) the signing officer has reviewed the report;

(2) based on the officer's knowledge, the report does not contain any untrue statement of a material fact or omit to state a material fact necessary in order to make the statements made, in light of the circumstances under which such statements were made, not misleading;

(3) based on such officer's knowledge, the financial statements, and other financial information included in the report, fairly present in all material respects the financial condition and results of operations of the issuer as of, and for, the periods presented in the report;

(4) the signing officers—

(A) are responsible for establishing and maintaining internal controls;

(B) have designed such internal controls to ensure that material information relating to the issuer and its consolidated subsidiaries is made known to such officers by others within those entities, particularly during the period in which the periodic reports are being prepared;

(C) have evaluated the effectiveness of the issuer's internal controls as of a date within 90 days prior to the report; and

(D) have presented in the report their conclusions about the effectiveness of their internal controls based on their evaluation as of that date;

(5) the signing officers have disclosed to the issuer's auditors and the audit committee of the board of directors (or persons fulfilling the equivalent function)—

(A) all significant deficiencies in the design or operation of internal controls which could adversely affect the issuer's ability to record, process, summarize, and report financial data and have identified for the issuer's auditors any material weaknesses in internal controls; and

(B) any fraud, whether or not material, that involves management or other employees who have a significant role in the issuer's internal controls; and

(6) the signing officers have indicated in the report whether or not there were significant changes in internal controls or in other factors that could significantly affect internal controls subsequent to the date of their evaluation, including any corrective actions with regard to significant deficiencies and material weaknesses.

(b) Foreign reincorporations have no effect

Nothing in this section shall be interpreted or applied in any way to allow any issuer to lessen the legal force of the statement required under this section, by an issuer having reincorporated or having engaged in any other transaction that resulted in the transfer of the corporate domicile or offices of the issuer from inside the United States to outside of the United States.

(c) Deadline

The rules required by subsection (a) of this section shall be effective not later than 30 days after July 30, 2002.

EXPLANATORY COMMENTS: *Section 302 requires the chief executive officer (CEO) and chief financial officer (CFO) of each public company to certify that they have reviewed the company's quarterly and annual reports to be filed with the Securities and Exchange Commission (SEC). The CEO and CFO must certify that, based on their knowledge, the reports do not contain any untrue statement of a material fact or any half-truth that would make the report*

1. This section of the Sarbanes-Oxley Act is codified at 15 U.S.C. Section 7241.

misleading, and that the information contained in the reports fairly presents the company's financial condition.

In addition, this section also requires the CEO and CFO to certify that they have created and designed an internal control system for their company and have recently evaluated that system to ensure that it is effectively providing them with relevant and accurate financial information. If the signing officers have found any significant deficiencies or weaknesses in the company's system or have discovered any evidence of fraud, they must have reported the situation, and any corrective actions they have taken, to the auditors and the audit committee.

SECTION 306

Insider trades during pension fund blackout periods[2]

(a) Prohibition of insider trading during pension fund blackout periods

(1) In general

Except to the extent otherwise provided by rule of the Commission pursuant to paragraph (3), it shall be unlawful for any director or executive officer of an issuer of any equity security (other than an exempted security), directly or indirectly, to purchase, sell, or otherwise acquire or transfer any equity security of the issuer (other than an exempted security) during any blackout period with respect to such equity security if such director or officer acquires such equity security in connection with his or her service or employment as a director or executive officer.

(2) Remedy

(A) In general

Any profit realized by a director or executive officer referred to in paragraph (1) from any purchase, sale, or other acquisition or transfer in violation of this subsection shall inure to and be recoverable by the issuer, irrespective of any intention on the part of such director or executive officer in entering into the transaction.

(B) Actions to recover profits

An action to recover profits in accordance with this subsection may be instituted at law or in equity in any court of competent jurisdiction by the issuer, or by the owner of any security of the issuer in the name and in behalf of the issuer if the issuer fails or refuses to bring such action within 60 days after the date of request, or fails diligently to prosecute the action thereafter, except that no such suit shall be brought more than 2 years after the date on which such profit was realized.

(3) Rulemaking authorized

The Commission shall, in consultation with the Secretary of Labor, issue rules to clarify the application of this subsection and to prevent evasion thereof. Such rules shall provide for the application of the requirements of paragraph (1) with respect to entities treated as a single employer with respect to an issuer under section 414(b), (c), (m), or (o) of Title 26 to the extent necessary to clarify the application of such requirements and to prevent evasion thereof. Such rules may also provide for appropriate exceptions from the requirements of this subsection, including exceptions for purchases pursuant to an automatic dividend reinvestment program or purchases or sales made pursuant to an advance election.

(4) Blackout period

For purposes of this subsection, the term "blackout period", with respect to the equity securities of any issuer—

(A) means any period of more than 3 consecutive business days during which the ability of not fewer than 50 percent of the participants or beneficiaries under all individual account plans maintained by the issuer to purchase, sell, or otherwise acquire or transfer an interest in any equity of such issuer held in such an individual account plan is temporarily suspended by the issuer or by a fiduciary of the plan; and

(B) does not include, under regulations which shall be prescribed by the Commission—

(i) a regularly scheduled period in which the participants and beneficiaries may not purchase, sell, or otherwise acquire or transfer an interest in any equity of such issuer, if such period is—

(I) incorporated into the individual account plan; and

(II) timely disclosed to employees before becoming participants under the individual account plan or as a subsequent amendment to the plan; or

(ii) any suspension described in subparagraph (A) that is imposed solely in connection with persons becoming participants or beneficiaries, or ceasing to be participants or beneficiaries, in an individual account plan by reason of a corporate merger, acquisition, divestiture, or similar transaction involving the plan or plan sponsor.

(5) Individual account plan

For purposes of this subsection, the term "individual account plan" has the meaning provided in section 1002(34) of Title 29, except that such term shall not include a one-participant retirement plan (within the meaning of section 1021(i)(8)(B) of Title 29).

(6) Notice to directors, executive officers, and the Commission

2. Codified at 15 U.S.C. Section 7244.

In any case in which a director or executive officer is subject to the requirements of this subsection in connection with a blackout period (as defined in paragraph (4)) with respect to any equity securities, the issuer of such equity securities shall timely notify such director or officer and the Securities and Exchange Commission of such blackout period.

* * * *

EXPLANATORY COMMENTS: *Corporate pension funds typically prohibit employees from trading shares of the corporation during periods when the pension fund is undergoing significant change. Prior to 2002, however, these blackout periods did not affect the corporation's executives, who frequently received shares of the corporate stock as part of their compensation. During the collapse of Enron, for example, its pension plan was scheduled to change administrators at a time when Enron's stock price was falling. Enron's employees therefore could not sell their shares while the price was dropping, but its executives could and did sell their stock, consequently avoiding some of the losses. Section 306 was Congress's solution to the basic unfairness of this situation. This section of the act required the SEC to issue rules that prohibit any director or executive officer from trading during pension fund blackout periods. (The SEC later issued these rules, entitled Regulation Blackout Trading Restriction, or Reg BTR.) Section 306 also provided shareholders with a right to file a shareholder's derivative suit against officers and directors who have profited from trading during these blackout periods (provided that the corporation has failed to bring a suit). The officer or director can be forced to return to the corporation any profits received, regardless of whether the director or officer acted with bad intent.*

SECTION 402

Periodical and other reports[3]

* * * *

(i) Accuracy of financial reports

Each financial report that contains financial statements, and that is required to be prepared in accordance with (or reconciled to) generally accepted accounting principles under this chapter and filed with the Commission shall reflect all material correcting adjustments that have been identified by a registered public accounting firm in accordance with generally accepted accounting principles and the rules and regulations of the Commission.

(j) Off-balance sheet transactions

Not later than 180 days after July 30, 2002, the Commission shall issue final rules providing that each annual and quarterly financial report required to be filed with the Commission shall disclose all material off-balance sheet transactions, arrangements, obligations (including contingent obligations), and other relationships of the issuer with unconsolidated entities or other persons, that may have a material current or future effect on financial condition, changes in financial condition, results of operations, liquidity, capital expenditures, capital resources, or significant components of revenues or expenses.

(k) Prohibition on personal loans to executives

(1) In general

It shall be unlawful for any issuer (as defined in section 7201 of this title), directly or indirectly, including through any subsidiary, to extend or maintain credit, to arrange for the extension of credit, or to renew an extension of credit, in the form of a personal loan to or for any director or executive officer (or equivalent thereof) of that issuer. An extension of credit maintained by the issuer on July 30, 2002, shall not be subject to the provisions of this subsection, provided that there is no material modification to any term of any such extension of credit or any renewal of any such extension of credit on or after July 30, 2002.

(2) Limitation

Paragraph (1) does not preclude any home improvement and manufactured home loans (as that term is defined in section 1464 of Title 12), consumer credit (as defined in section 1602 of this title), or any extension of credit under an open end credit plan (as defined in section 1602 of this title), or a charge card (as defined in section 1637(c)(4)(e) of this title), or any extension of credit by a broker or dealer registered under section 78o of this title to an employee of that broker or dealer to buy, trade, or carry securities, that is permitted under rules or regulations of the Board of Governors of the Federal Reserve System pursuant to section 78g of this title (other than an extension of credit that would be used to purchase the stock of that issuer), that is—

(A) made or provided in the ordinary course of the consumer credit business of such issuer;

(B) of a type that is generally made available by such issuer to the public; and

(C) made by such issuer on market terms, or terms that are no more favorable than those offered by the issuer to the general public for such extensions of credit.

(3) Rule of construction for certain loans

Paragraph (1) does not apply to any loan made or maintained by an insured depository institution (as defined in section 1813 of Title 12), if the loan is subject to the insider lending restrictions of section 375b of Title 12.

(l) Real time issuer disclosures

Each issuer reporting under subsection (a) of this section or section 78o(d) of this title shall disclose to the public on a rapid and current basis such additional information concerning material changes in the financial condition or operations of the issuer, in plain English, which may

3. This section of the Sarbanes-Oxley Act amended some of the provisions of the 1934 Securities Exchange Act and added the paragraphs reproduced here at 15 U.S.C. Section 78m.

include trend and qualitative information and graphic presentations, as the Commission determines, by rule, is necessary or useful for the protection of investors and in the public interest.

EXPLANATORY COMMENTS: *Corporate executives during the Enron era typically received extremely large salaries, significant bonuses, and abundant stock options, even when the companies for which they worked were suffering. Executives were also routinely given personal loans from corporate funds, many of which were never paid back. The average large company during that period loaned almost $1 million a year to top executives, and some companies, including Tyco International and Adelphia Communications Corporation, loaned hundreds of millions of dollars to their executives every year. Section 402 amended the 1934 Securities Exchange Act to prohibit public companies from making personal loans to executive officers and directors. There are a few exceptions to this prohibition, such as home-improvement loans made in the ordinary course of business. Note also that while loans are forbidden, outright gifts are not. A corporation is free to give gifts to its executives, including cash, provided that these gifts are disclosed on its financial reports. The idea is that corporate directors will be deterred from making substantial gifts to their executives by the disclosure requirement—particularly if the corporation's financial condition is questionable—because making such gifts could be perceived as abusing their authority.*

SECTION 403

Directors, officers, and principal stockholders[4]

(a) Disclosures required

(1) Directors, officers, and principal stockholders required to file

Every person who is directly or indirectly the beneficial owner of more than 10 percent of any class of any equity security (other than an exempted security) which is registered pursuant to section 78l of this title, or who is a director or an officer of the issuer of such security, shall file the statements required by this subsection with the Commission (and, if such security is registered on a national securities exchange, also with the exchange).

(2) Time of filing

The statements required by this subsection shall be filed—

(A) at the time of the registration of such security on a national securities exchange or by the effective date of a registration statement filed pursuant to section 78l(g) of this title;

(B) within 10 days after he or she becomes such beneficial owner, director, or officer;

(C) if there has been a change in such ownership, or if such person shall have purchased or sold a security-based swap agreement (as defined in section 206(b) of the Gramm-Leach-Bliley Act (15 U.S.C. 78c note)) involving such equity security, before the end of the second business day following the day on which the subject transaction has been executed, or at such other time as the Commission shall establish, by rule, in any case in which the Commission determines that such 2-day period is not feasible.

(3) Contents of statements

A statement filed—

(A) under subparagraph (A) or (B) of paragraph (2) shall contain a statement of the amount of all equity securities of such issuer of which the filing person is the beneficial owner; and

(B) under subparagraph (C) of such paragraph shall indicate ownership by the filing person at the date of filing, any such changes in such ownership, and such purchases and sales of the security-based swap agreements as have occurred since the most recent such filing under such subparagraph.

(4) Electronic filing and availability

Beginning not later than 1 year after July 30, 2002—

(A) a statement filed under subparagraph (C) of paragraph (2) shall be filed electronically;

(B) the Commission shall provide each such statement on a publicly accessible Internet site not later than the end of the business day following that filing; and

(C) the issuer (if the issuer maintains a corporate website) shall provide that statement on that corporate website, not later than the end of the business day following that filing.

* * * *

EXPLANATORY COMMENTS: *This section dramatically shortens the time period provided in the Securities Exchange Act of 1934 for disclosing transactions by insiders. The prior law stated that most transactions had to be reported within ten days of the beginning of the following month, although certain transactions did not have to be reported until the following fiscal year (within the first forty-five days). Because some of the insider trading that occurred during the Enron fiasco did not have to be disclosed (and was therefore not discovered) until long after the transactions, Congress added this section to reduce the time period for making disclosures. Under Section 403, most transactions by insiders must be electronically filed with the SEC within two business days. Also, any company that maintains a Web site must post these SEC filings on its site by the end of the next business day. Congress enacted this section in the belief that if insiders are required to file reports of their transactions promptly with the SEC, companies will do more to police themselves and prevent insider trading.*

4. This section of the Sarbanes-Oxley Act amended the disclosure provisions of the 1934 Securities Exchange Act, at 15 U.S.C. Section 78p.

SECTION 404

Management assessment of internal controls[5]

(a) Rules required

The Commission shall prescribe rules requiring each annual report required by section 78m(a) or 78o(d) of this title to contain an internal control report, which shall—

(1) state the responsibility of management for establishing and maintaining an adequate internal control structure and procedures for financial reporting; and

(2) contain an assessment, as of the end of the most recent fiscal year of the issuer, of the effectiveness of the internal control structure and procedures of the issuer for financial reporting.

(b) Internal control evaluation and reporting

With respect to the internal control assessment required by subsection (a) of this section, each registered public accounting firm that prepares or issues the audit report for the issuer shall attest to, and report on, the assessment made by the management of the issuer. An attestation made under this subsection shall be made in accordance with standards for attestation engagements issued or adopted by the Board. Any such attestation shall not be the subject of a separate engagement.

EXPLANATORY COMMENTS: *This section was enacted to prevent corporate executives from claiming they were ignorant of significant errors in their companies' financial reports. For instance, several CEOs testified before Congress that they simply had no idea that the corporations' financial statements were off by billions of dollars. Congress therefore passed Section 404, which requires each annual report to contain a description and assessment of the company's internal control structure and financial reporting procedures. The section also requires that an audit be conducted of the internal control assessment, as well as the financial statements contained in the report. This section goes hand in hand with Section 302 (which, as discussed previously, requires various certifications attesting to the accuracy of the information in financial reports).*

Section 404 has been one of the more controversial and expensive provisions in the Sarbanes-Oxley Act because it requires companies to assess their own internal financial controls to make sure that their financial statements are reliable and accurate. A corporation might need to set up a disclosure committee and a coordinator, establish codes of conduct for accounting and financial personnel, create documentation procedures, provide training, and outline the individuals who are responsible for performing each of the procedures. Companies that were already well managed have not experienced substantial difficulty complying with this section. Other companies, however, have spent millions of dollars setting up, documenting, and evaluating their internal financial control systems. Although initially creating the internal financial control system is a one-time-only expense, the costs of maintaining and evaluating it are ongoing. Some corporations that spent considerable sums complying with Section 404 have been able to offset these costs by discovering and correcting inefficiencies or frauds within their systems. Nevertheless, it is unlikely that any corporation will find compliance with this section to be inexpensive.

5. Codified at 15 U.S.C. Section 7262.

SECTION 802 (A)

Destruction, alteration, or falsification of records in Federal investigations and bankruptcy[6]

Whoever knowingly alters, destroys, mutilates, conceals, covers up, falsifies, or makes a false entry in any record, document, or tangible object with the intent to impede, obstruct, or influence the investigation or proper administration of any matter within the jurisdiction of any department or agency of the United States or any case filed under title 11, or in relation to or contemplation of any such matter or case, shall be fined under this title, imprisoned not more than 20 years, or both.

Destruction of corporate audit records[7]

(a)(1) Any accountant who conducts an audit of an issuer of securities to which section 10A(a) of the Securities Exchange Act of 1934 (15 U.S.C. 78j-1(a)) applies, shall maintain all audit or review workpapers for a period of 5 years from the end of the fiscal period in which the audit or review was concluded.

(2) The Securities and Exchange Commission shall promulgate, within 180 days, after adequate notice and an opportunity for comment, such rules and regulations, as are reasonably necessary, relating to the retention of relevant records such as workpapers, documents that form the basis of an audit or review, memoranda, correspondence, communications, other documents, and records (including electronic records) which are created, sent, or received in connection with an audit or review and contain conclusions, opinions, analyses, or financial data relating to such an audit or review, which is conducted by any accountant who conducts an audit of an issuer of securities to which section 10A(a) of the Securities Exchange Act of 1934 (15 U.S.C. 78j-1(a)) applies. The Commission may, from time to time, amend or supplement the rules and regulations that it is required to promulgate under this section, after adequate notice and an opportunity for comment, in order to ensure that such rules and regulations adequately comport with the purposes of this section.

(b) Whoever knowingly and willfully violates subsection (a)(1), or any rule or regulation promulgated by the Securities and Exchange Commission under subsection (a)(2), shall be fined under this title, imprisoned not more than 10 years, or both.

(c) Nothing in this section shall be deemed to diminish or relieve any person of any other duty or obligation

6. Codified at 15 U.S.C. Section 1519.
7. Codified at 15 U.S.C. Section 1520.

imposed by Federal or State law or regulation to maintain, or refrain from destroying, any document.

EXPLANATORY COMMENTS: *Section 802(a) enacted two new statutes that punish those who alter or destroy documents. The first statute is not specifically limited to securities fraud cases. It provides that anyone who alters, destroys, or falsifies records in federal investigations or bankruptcy may be criminally prosecuted and sentenced to a fine or to up to twenty years in prison, or both. The second statute requires auditors of public companies to keep all audit or review working papers for five years but expressly allows the SEC to amend or supplement these requirements as it sees fit. The SEC has, in fact, amended this section by issuing a rule that requires auditors who audit reporting companies to retain working papers for seven years from the conclusion of the review. Section 802(a) further provides that anyone who knowingly and willfully violates this statute is subject to criminal prosecution and can be sentenced to a fine, imprisoned for up to ten years, or both if convicted.*

This portion of the Sarbanes-Oxley Act implicitly recognizes that persons who are under investigation often are tempted to respond by destroying or falsifying documents that might prove their complicity in wrongdoing. The severity of the punishment should provide a strong incentive for these individuals to resist the temptation.

SECTION 804

Time limitations on the commencement of civil actions arising under Acts of Congress[8]

(a) Except as otherwise provided by law, a civil action arising under an Act of Congress enacted after the date of the enactment of this section may not be commenced later than 4 years after the cause of action accrues.

(b) Notwithstanding subsection (a), a private right of action that involves a claim of fraud, deceit, manipulation, or contrivance in contravention of a regulatory requirement concerning the securities laws, as defined in section 3(a)(47) of the Securities Exchange Act of 1934 (15 U.S.C. 78c(a)(47)), may be brought not later than the earlier of—

(1) 2 years after the discovery of the facts constituting the violation; or

(2) 5 years after such violation.

EXPLANATORY COMMENTS: *Prior to the enactment of this section, Section 10(b) of the Securities Exchange Act of 1934 had no express statute of limitations. The courts generally required plaintiffs to have filed suit within one year from the date that they should (using due diligence) have discovered that a fraud had been committed but no later than three years after the fraud occurred. Section 804 extends this period by specifying that plaintiffs must file a lawsuit within two years after they discover (or should have discovered) a fraud but no later than five years after the fraud's occurrence. This provision has prevented the courts from dismissing numerous securities fraud lawsuits.*

SECTION 806

Civil action to protect against retaliation in fraud cases[9]

(a) Whistleblower protection for employees of publicly traded companies.—

No company with a class of securities registered under section 12 of the Securities Exchange Act of 1934 (15 U.S.C. 78l), or that is required to file reports under section 15(d) of the Securities Exchange Act of 1934 (15 U.S.C. 78o(d)), or any officer, employee, contractor, subcontractor, or agent of such company, may discharge, demote, suspend, threaten, harass, or in any other manner discriminate against an employee in the terms and conditions of employment because of any lawful act done by the employee—

(1) to provide information, cause information to be provided, or otherwise assist in an investigation regarding any conduct which the employee reasonably believes constitutes a violation of section 1341, 1343, 1344, or 1348, any rule or regulation of the Securities and Exchange Commission, or any provision of Federal law relating to fraud against shareholders, when the information or assistance is provided to or the investigation is conducted by—.

(A) a Federal regulatory or law enforcement agency;

(B) any Member of Congress or any committee of Congress; or

(C) a person with supervisory authority over the employee (or such other person working for the employer who has the authority to investigate, discover, or terminate misconduct); or

(2) to file, cause to be filed, testify, participate in, or otherwise assist in a proceeding filed or about to be filed (with any knowledge of the employer) relating to an alleged violation of section 1341, 1343, 1344, or 1348, any rule or regulation of the Securities and Exchange Commission, or any provision of Federal law relating to fraud against shareholders.

(b) Enforcement action.—

(1) In general.—A person who alleges discharge or other discrimination by any person in violation of subsection (a) may seek relief under subsection (c), by—

(A) filing a complaint with the Secretary of Labor; or

(B) if the Secretary has not issued a final decision within 180 days of the filing of the complaint and there is no showing that such delay is due to the

8. Codified at 28 U.S.C. Section 1658.

9. Codified at 18 U.S.C. Section 1514A.

bad faith of the claimant, bringing an action at law or equity for de novo review in the appropriate district court of the United States, which shall have jurisdiction over such an action without regard to the amount in controversy.

(2) Procedure.—

(A) In general.—An action under paragraph (1)(A) shall be governed under the rules and procedures set forth in section 42121(b) of title 49, United States Code.

(B) Exception.—Notification made under section 42121(b)(1) of title 49, United States Code, shall be made to the person named in the complaint and to the employer.

(C) Burdens of proof.—An action brought under paragraph (1)(B) shall be governed by the legal burdens of proof set forth in section 42121(b) of title 49, United States Code.

(D) Statute of limitations.—An action under paragraph (1) shall be commenced not later than 90 days after the date on which the violation occurs.

(c) Remedies.—

(1) In general.—An employee prevailing in any action under subsection (b)(1) shall be entitled to all relief necessary to make the employee whole.

(2) Compensatory damages.—Relief for any action under paragraph (1) shall include—

(A) reinstatement with the same seniority status that the employee would have had, but for the discrimination;

(B) the amount of back pay, with interest; and

(C) compensation for any special damages sustained as a result of the discrimination, including litigation costs, expert witness fees, and reasonable attorney fees.

(d) Rights retained by employee.—Nothing in this section shall be deemed to diminish the rights, privileges, or remedies of any employee under any Federal or State law, or under any collective bargaining agreement.

EXPLANATORY COMMENTS: *Section 806 is one of several provisions that were included in the Sarbanes-Oxley Act to encourage and protect whistleblowers—that is, employees who report their employer's alleged violations of securities law to the authorities. This section applies to employees, agents, and independent contractors who work for publicly traded companies or testify about such a company during an investigation. It sets up an administrative procedure at the Department of Labor for individuals who claim that their employer retaliated against them (fired or demoted them, for example) for blowing the whistle on the employer's wrongful conduct. It also allows the award of civil damages—including back pay, reinstatement, special damages, attorneys' fees, and court costs—to employees who prove that they suffered retaliation. Since this provision was enacted, whistleblowers have filed numerous complaints with the Department of Labor under this section.*

SECTION 807

Securities fraud[10]

Whoever knowingly executes, or attempts to execute, a scheme or artifice—

(1) to defraud any person in connection with any security of an issuer with a class of securities registered under section 12 of the Securities Exchange Act of 1934 (15 U.S.C. 78l) or that is required to file reports under section 15(d) of the Securities Exchange Act of 1934 (15 U.S.C. 78o(d)); or

(2) to obtain, by means of false or fraudulent pretenses, representations, or promises, any money or property in connection with the purchase or sale of any security of an issuer with a class of securities registered under section 12 of the Securities Exchange Act of 1934 (15 U.S.C. 78l) or that is required to file reports under section 15(d) of the Securities Exchange Act of 1934 (15 U.S.C. 78o(d)); shall be fined under this title, or imprisoned not more than 25 years, or both.

EXPLANATORY COMMENTS: *Section 807 adds a new provision to the federal criminal code that addresses securities fraud. Prior to 2002, federal securities law had already made it a crime—under Section 10(b) of the Securities Exchange Act of 1934 and SEC Rule 10b-5, both of which are discussed in Chapter 41—to intentionally defraud someone in connection with a purchase or sale of securities, but the offense was not listed in the federal criminal code. Also, paragraph 2 of Section 807 goes beyond what is prohibited under securities law by making it a crime to obtain by means of false or fraudulent pretenses any money or property from the purchase or sale of securities. This new provision allows violators to be punished by up to twenty-five years in prison, a fine, or both.*

SECTION 906

Failure of corporate officers to certify financial reports[11]

(a) Certification of periodic financial reports.—Each periodic report containing financial statements filed by an issuer with the Securities Exchange Commission pursuant to section 13(a) or 15(d) of the Securities Exchange Act of 1934 (15 U.S.C. 78m(a) or 78o(d)) shall be accompanied by a written statement by the chief executive officer and chief financial officer (or equivalent thereof) of the issuer.

10. Codified at 18 U.S.C. Section 1348.

11. Codified at 18 U.S.C. Section 1350.

(b) Content.—The statement required under subsection (a) shall certify that the periodic report containing the financial statements fully complies with the requirements of section 13(a) or 15(d) of the Securities Exchange Act of 1934 (15 U.S.C. 78m or 78o(d)) and that information contained in the periodic report fairly presents, in all material respects, the financial condition and results of operations of the issuer.

(c) Criminal penalties.—Whoever—

(1) certifies any statement as set forth in subsections (a) and (b) of this section knowing that the periodic report accompanying the statement does not comport with all the requirements set forth in this section shall be fined not more than $1,000,000 or imprisoned not more than 10 years, or both; or

(2) willfully certifies any statement as set forth in subsections (a) and (b) of this section knowing that the periodic report accompanying the statement does not comport with all the requirements set forth in this section shall be fined not more than $5,000,000, or imprisoned not more than 20 years, or both.

EXPLANATORY COMMENTS: *As previously discussed, under Section 302 a corporation's CEO and CFO are required to certify that they believe the quarterly and annual reports their company files with the SEC are accurate and fairly present the company's financial condition. Section 906 adds "teeth" to these requirements by authorizing criminal penalties for those officers who intentionally certify inaccurate SEC filings. Knowing violations of the requirements are punishable by a fine of up to $1 million, ten years in prison, or both. Willful violators may be fined up to $5 million, sentenced to up to twenty years in prison, or both. Although the difference between a knowing and a willful violation is not entirely clear, the section is obviously intended to remind corporate officers of the serious consequences of certifying inaccurate reports to the SEC.*

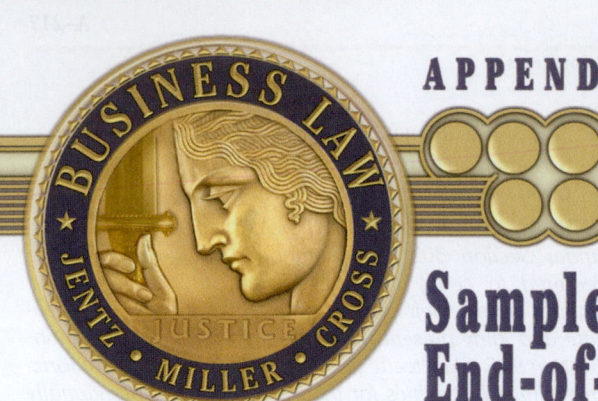

APPENDIX I

Sample Answers for End-of-Chapter Questions with Sample Answer

1–2A. QUESTION WITH SAMPLE ANSWER

At the time of the Nuremberg trials, "crimes against humanity" were new international crimes. The laws criminalized such acts as murder, extermination, enslavement, deportation, and other inhumane acts committed against any civilian population. These international laws derived their legitimacy from "natural law." Natural law, which is the oldest and one of the most significant schools of jurisprudence, holds that governments and legal systems should reflect the moral and ethical ideals that are inherent in human nature. Because natural law is universal and discoverable by reason, its adherents believe that all other law is derived from natural law. Natural law therefore supersedes laws created by humans (national, or "positive," law), and in a conflict between the two, national or positive law loses its legitimacy. The Nuremberg defendants asserted that they had been acting in accordance with German law. The judges dismissed these claims, reasoning that the defendants' acts were commonly regarded as crimes and that the accused must have known that the acts would be considered criminal. The judges clearly believed the tenets of natural law and expected that the defendants, too, should have been able to realize that their acts ran afoul of it. The fact that the "positivist law" of Germany at the time required them to commit these acts is irrelevant. Under natural law theory, the international court was justified in finding the defendants guilty of crimes against humanity.

2–2A. QUESTION WITH SAMPLE ANSWER

Trial courts, as explained in the text, are responsible for settling "questions of fact." Often, when parties bring a case to court there is a dispute as to what actually happened. Different witnesses have different versions of what they saw or heard, and there may be only indirect evidence of certain issues in dispute. During the trial, the judge and the jury (if it is a jury trial) listen to the witnesses and view the evidence firsthand. Thus, the trial court is in the best position to assess the credibility (truthfulness) of the witnesses and determine the weight that should be given to various items of evidence. At the end of the trial, the judge and the jury (if it is a jury trial) decide what will be considered facts for the purposes of the case. Trial courts are best suited to this job, as they have the opportunity to observe the witnesses and evidence, and they regularly determine the reliability of certain evidence. Appellate courts, in contrast, see only the written record of the trial court proceedings and cannot evaluate the credibility of witnesses and the persuasiveness of evidence. For these reasons, appellate courts nearly always defer to trial courts' findings of fact. An appellate court can reverse a lower court's findings of fact, however, when so little evidence was presented at trial that no reasonable person could have reached the conclusion that the judge or jury reached.

3–2A. QUESTION WITH SAMPLE ANSWER

(a) After all of the pleadings (the complaint, answer, and any counterclaim and reply) have been filed, either party can file a motion for judgment on the pleadings. This may happen because it is clear from just the pleadings that the plaintiff has failed to state a cause of action. This motion is also appropriate when all the parties agree on the facts, and the only question remaining is how the law applies to those facts. The court may consider only those facts pleaded in the documents and stipulated (agreed to) by the parties. This is the difference between a motion for judgment on the pleadings and a motion for summary judgment (discussed below). In a motion for summary judgment, there may be some facts in dispute and the parties may supplement the pleadings with sworn statements and other materials.

(b) During the trial, at the conclusion of the plaintiff's case, the defendant may move for a directed verdict. If the defendant does this, he or she will argue to the court that the plaintiff presented inadequate evidence that he or she is entitled to the remedy being sought. In considering a motion for a directed verdict (federal courts use the term "motion for a judgment as a matter of law"), the judge looks at the evidence in the light most favorable to the plaintiff and grants the motion only if there is insufficient evidence to raise an issue of fact. These motions are rarely granted at this stage of a trial. At the end of the defendant's case, the parties have another opportunity to move for a directed verdict. This time, either party can seek the motion. The motion will be granted only if there is no reasonable way to find for the party against whom the motion is made. In other words, if, after the defense's case is concluded, the plaintiff asks the court to direct a verdict against the defendant, the court will do so if no reasonable interpretation of the evidence would allow the defendant to win the case.

(c) As noted in part (a) of this answer, a motion for summary judgment is similar to a motion for a judgment on the pleadings in that it asks the court to grant a judgment without a trial. Either party can file a summary judgment motion when the only question is how the law applies to the facts in a case. When a court considers a motion for summary judgment, it can take into account evidence outside the pleadings. The evidence may consist of sworn statements by parties or witnesses as well as documents. The use of this additional evidence distinguishes the motion for summary judgment from the motion for judgment on the pleadings. Summary judgment motions will be granted only when there are no questions of fact that need to be decided and the only question is a question of law, which requires a judge's ruling. These motions can be made before or during a trial.

(d) If a losing party has previously moved for a directed verdict, that party can make a motion for a judgment *n.o.v.* (notwithstanding the verdict) after the jury issues its verdict. The standards for granting a judgment *n.o.v.* are the same as those for granting a motion to dismiss a case or a motion for a directed verdict. Essentially, the losing party argues that even if the evidence is viewed in the light most favorable to the other party, a reasonable jury could not have found in that party's favor. If the judge finds this contention to be correct or decides that the law requires the opposite result, the motion will be granted.

4–2A. Question with Sample Answer

As the text points out, Thomas has a constitutionally protected right to his religion and the free exercise of it. In denying his unemployment benefits, the state violated these rights. Employers are obligated to make reasonable accommodations for their employees' beliefs, right or wrong, that are openly and sincerely held. Thomas's beliefs were openly and sincerely held. By placing him in a department that made military goods, his employer effectively put him in a position of having to choose between his job and his religious principles. This unilateral decision on the part of the employer was the reason Thomas left his job and why the company was required to compensate Thomas for his resulting unemployment.

5–2A. Question with Sample Answer

This question essentially asks whether good behavior can ever be unethical. The answer to this question depends on which approach to ethical reasoning you are using. Under the outcome-based approach of utilitarianism, it is simply not possible for selfish motives to be unethical if they result in good conduct. A good outcome is moral regardless of the nature of the action itself or the reason for the action. Under a duty-based approach, motive would be more relevant in assessing whether a firm's conduct was ethical. You would need to analyze the firm's conduct in terms of religious truths or to determine whether human beings were being treated with the inherent dignity that they deserve. Although a good motive would not justify a bad act to a religious ethicist, in this situation the actions were good and the motive was questionable (because the firm was simply seeking to increase its profit). Nevertheless, unless one's religion prohibited making a profit, the firm's actions would likely not be considered unethical. Applying Kantian ethics would require you to evaluate the firm's actions in light of what would happen if everyone in society acted that way (categorical imperative). Here, because the conduct was good, it would be positive for society if every firm acted that way. Hence, the profit-seeking motive would be irrelevant in a Kantian analysis. In a debate between motive and conduct, then, conduct is almost always given greater weight in evaluating ethics.

6–2A. Question with Sample Answer

To answer this question, you must first decide if there is a legal theory under which Harley may be able to recover. You may recall from your reading the intentional tort of "wrongful interference with a contractual relationship." To recover damages under this theory, Harley would need to show that he and Martha had a valid contract, that Lothar knew of this contractual relationship between Martha and Harley, and that Lothar intentionally convinced Martha to break her contract with Harley. Even though Lothar hoped that his advertisments would persuade Martha to break her contract with Harley, the question states that Martha's decision to change bakers was based solely on the advertising and not on anything else that Lothar did. Lothar's advertisements did not constitute a tort. Note, though, that while Harley cannot collect from Lothar for Martha's actions, he does have a cause of action against Martha for her breach of their contract.

7–2A. Question with Sample Answer

This is a causation question. You will recall from the chapter that four elements must be proved for a plaintiff to recover in a claim for negligence: that the defendant owed a duty of care, the defendant breached this duty, the plaintiff suffered a legally recognizable injury, and the defendant's breach of the duty of care caused the injury. Ruth did breach the duty of care that she owed Jim (and others in society) when she parked carelessly on the hill. Jim also clearly suffered an injury. The only remaining question, then, has to do with causation. Causation is broken down into two parts, causation in fact and proximate cause. In order for Jim to recover, he must prove that both kinds of causation existed in this case. Causation in fact is answered by the "but for" test and readily answered here.

Ruth's car set into motion a chain of events without which the barn would not have fallen down. Meeting the proximate cause test will be more difficult for Jim. Recall that proximate cause exists only when the connection between an act and an injury is strong enough to justify imposing liability. Careless parking on a hill creates a risk that a reasonable person can foresee could result in harm. The question here is whether the electric spark, the grass fire, the barn full of dynamite, and the roof falling in are *foreseeable* risks stemming from a poor parking job. In this case, it would be a question of fact for a jury to determine whether there were enough intervening events between Ruth's parking and Jim's injury to defeat Jim's claim.

8–2A. Question with Sample Answer

(a) Ursula will not be held liable for copyright infringement in this case because her photocopying pages for use in scholarly research falls squarely under the "fair use" exception to the Copyright Act.

(b) While Ursula's actions are improper, they could constitute trademark infringement, not copyright infringement. Copyrights are granted for literary and artistic productions; trademarks are distinctive marks created and used by manufacturers to differentiate their goods from those of their competitors. Trademark infringement occurs when a mark is copied to a substantial degree, intentionally or unintentionally.

(c) As with the answer to (a) above, Ursula's actions fall within the "fair use" doctrine of copyright law. Her use of the taped television shows for teaching is the exact type of use the exception is designed to cover.

9–3A. Question with Sample Answer

As you read in the text, some torts, including assault and battery, provide a basis for criminal prosecution as well as civil liability. This question aptly demonstrates this principle. Double jeopardy is a criminal law concept and does not constitute a defense against a civil lawsuit. The Fifth Amendment prohibition against double jeopardy means that once Armington has been tried and found guilty or not guilty for this assault, he may not be tried for it again. Nevertheless, Jennings may seek damages for his injuries in a civil lawsuit because Armington's prison sentence will do nothing to reimburse him for his medical bills and disability. Armington's guilty verdict has no bearing on the civil lawsuit. The criminal conviction, however, having been proved beyond a reasonable doubt, will likely improve Jennings's chances of recovering damages from Armington in a civil case. As you will recall, in a civil suit the plaintiff merely has to prove his or her case by a preponderance of the evidence. For Jennings, this burden of proof will probably be much easier to meet, given Armington's conviction.

10–2A. Question with Sample Answer

According to the question, Janine was apparently unconscious or otherwise unable to agree to a contract for the nursing services she received while she was in the hospital. As you read in the chapter, however, sometimes the law will create a fictional contract in order to prevent one party from unjustly receiving a benefit at the expense of another. This is known as a *quasi contract* and provides a basis for Nursing Services to recover the value of the services it provided while Janine was in the hospital. As for the at-home services that were provided to Janine, because Janine was aware that those services were being provided for her, Nursing Services can recover for those services under an implied-in-fact contract. Under this type of contract, the conduct of the parties creates and defines the terms. Janine's acceptance of the services constitutes her agreement to form a contract, and she will probably be required to pay Nursing Services in full.

11–2A. Question with Sample Answer

(a) Death of either the offeror or the offeree prior to acceptance automatically terminates a revocable offer. The basic legal reason is that the offer is personal to the parties and cannot be passed on to others, not even to the estate of the deceased. This rule applies even if the other party is unaware of the death. Thus, Schmidt's offer terminates on Schmidt's death, and Barry's later acceptance does not constitute a contract.

(b) An offer is automatically terminated by the destruction of the specific subject matter of the offer prior to acceptance. Thus, Barry's acceptance after the fire does not constitute a contract.

(c) When the offer is irrevocable, under an option contract, death of the offeror does not terminate the option contract, and the offeree can accept the offer to sell the equipment, binding the offeror's estate to performance. Performance is not personal to Schmidt, as the estate can transfer title to the equipment. Knowledge of the death is immaterial to the offeree's right of acceptance. Thus, Barry can hold Schmidt's estate to a contract for the purchase of the equipment.

(d) When the offer is irrevocable, under an option contract, death of the offeree also does not terminate the offer. Because the option is a separate contract, the contract survives and passes to the offeree's estate, which can exercise the option by acceptance within the option period. Thus, acceptance by Barry's estate binds Schmidt to a contract for the sale of the equipment.

12–2A. Question with Sample Answer

The legal issue deals with the preexisting duty rule, which basically states that a promise to do what one already has a legal or contractual duty to do does not constitute consideration, and thus the return promise is unenforceable. In this case, Shade was required contractually to build a house according to a specific set of plans for $53,000, and Bernstein's later agreement to pay an additional $3,000 for exactly what Shade was required to do for $53,000 is without consideration and unenforceable. One of the purposes of this general rule is to prevent commercial blackmail. There are four basic exceptions to this rule:

(a) If the duties of Shade are modified, for example, by changes made by Bernstein in the specifications, these changes can constitute consideration and bind Bernstein to pay the additional $3,000.

(b) Rescission and new contract theory could be applied, by which the old contract of $53,000 would mutually be canceled and a new contract for $56,000 would be made. Most courts would not apply this theory unless there was a clear intent to cancel the original contract. It appears here that the intent to cancel the $53,000 contract is lacking (there is merely an intent to modify), so this exception would not apply.

(c) A few states have statutes that allow any modification to be enforceable if it is in writing. The facts stated give no evidence that Bernstein's agreement to the additional $3,000 is in writing, but, if it is, Bernstein is bound in those states.

(d) The unforeseen difficulty or hardship rule could be argued. This rule, however, applies only to unknown risks not ordinarily assumed in business transactions. Because inflation and price rises are risks ordinarily assumed in business, this exception cannot be used by Shade.

13–2A. Question with Sample Answer

Contracts in restraint of trade are usually illegal and unenforceable. An exception to this rule applies to a covenant not to compete that is ancillary to certain types of business contracts in which some fair protection is deemed appropriate (such as in the sale of a business). The covenant, however, must be reasonable in terms of time and area to be legally enforceable. If either term is excessive, the court can declare that the restraint goes beyond what is necessary for reasonable protection. In this event, the court can either declare the covenant illegal or it can reform the covenant to make the terms of time and area reasonable and then enforce it. Suppose the court declares the covenant illegal and unenforceable. Because the covenant is ancillary and severable from the primary contract, the primary contract is not affected by such a ruling. In the case of Hotel Lux, the primary contract concerns employment; the covenant is ancillary and desirable for the protection of the hotel. The time period of one year may be considered reasonable for a chef with an international reputation. The reasonableness of the three-state area restriction may be questioned, however. If it is found to be reasonable, the covenant probably will be enforced. If it is not found to be reasonable, the court could declare the entire covenant illegal, allowing Perlee to be employed by any restaurant or hotel, including one in direct competition with Hotel Lux. Alternatively, the court could reform the covenant, making its terms reasonable for protecting Hotel Lux's normal customer market area.

14–2A. Question with Sample Answer

Four basic elements are necessary to prove fraud, thus rendering a contract voidable: (1) an intent to deceive, usually with knowledge of the falsity; (2) a misrepresentation of material facts; (3) a reliance by the innocent party on the misrepresentation; and (4) usually damage or injury caused by the misrepresentation. Statements of events to take place in the future or statements of opinions are generally not treated as representations of fact. Therefore, even though the prediction or opinion may turn out to be incorrect, a contract based on this type of statement would remain enforceable. Grano's statement that the motel would make at least $45,000 next year would probably be treated as a prediction or opinion; thus, one of the elements necessary to prove fraud—misrepresentation of facts—would be missing. The statement that the motel netted $30,000 last year is a deliberate falsehood (with intent and knowledge). Grano's defense will be that the books in Tanner's possession clearly indicated that the figure stated was untrue, and therefore Tanner cannot be said to have purchased the motel in reliance on the falsehood. If the innocent party, Tanner, knew the true facts, or should have known the true facts because they were available to him, Grano's argument will prevail.

Finally, the issue centers on Grano's duty to tell Tanner of the bypass. Ordinarily, neither party in a nonfiduciary relationship has a duty to disclose facts, even when the information might bear materially on the other's decision to enter into the contract. Exceptions are made, however, when the buyer cannot reasonably be expected to discover the information known by the seller, in which case fairness imposes a duty to speak on the seller. Here, the court can go either way. If the court decides there was no duty to disclose, deems the prediction of future profits to be opinion rather than a statement of fact, and also decides there was no justifiable reliance by Tanner because the books available to Tanner clearly indicated Grano's profit statement for the last year to be false, then Tanner cannot get his money back on the basis of fraud.

15–2A. Question with Sample Answer

In this situation, Mallory becomes what is known as a *guarantor* on the loan; that is, she guarantees to the hardware store that she will pay for the mower if her brother fails to do so. This kind of collateral promise, in which the guarantor states that he or she will become responsible *only* if the primary party does not perform, must be in writing to be enforceable. There is an exception, however. If the main purpose in accepting secondary liability is to secure a personal benefit—for example, if Mallory's brother bought the mower for her—the contract need not be in writing. The assumption is that a court can infer from the circumstances of the case whether the main purpose was to secure a personal benefit and thus, in effect, to answer for the guarantor's own debt.

16–2A. Question with Sample Answer

Thrift is a creditor beneficiary. To be a creditor beneficiary one must be the creditor in a previously established debtor-creditor relationship, and then the debtor's subsequent contract terms with a third party must confer a benefit on the creditor. The contract made between the debtor and third party is not made expressly for the benefit of the creditor (as is required for a donee beneficiary). Rather, it is made for the benefit of the contracting parties. In this case, the original mortgage contract created a debtor-creditor relationship between Hensley and Thrift. Hensley's contract of sale in which Sylvia agreed to assume the mortgage payments conferred a benefit on Thrift as to payment of the debt. The primary purpose of the contract was strictly to benefit the contracting parties. Hensley was to receive money for the sale of the house, and Sylvia was to receive the low mortgage interest rate. Thrift still has the house and lot as security for the loan, can hold Hensley personally liable for the mortgage note, and as a creditor beneficiary can hold Sylvia personally liable on the basis of her contract with Hensley to assume the mortgage.

17–2A. Question with Sample Answer

A novation exists when a new, valid contract expressly or impliedly discharges a prior contract by the substitution of a party. Accord and satisfaction exists when the parties agree that the original obligation can be discharged by a substituted performance. In this case, Fred's agreement with Iba to pay off Junior's debt for $1,100 (as compared to the $1,000 owed) is definitely a valid contract. The terms of the contract substitute Fred as the debtor for Junior, and Junior is definitely discharged from further liability. This agreement is a *novation*.

18–2A. Question with Sample Answer

Generally, the equitable remedy of specific performance will be granted only if two criteria are met: monetary damages (under the situation) must be inadequate as a remedy, and the subject matter of the contract must be unique.

(a) In the sale of land, the buyer's contract is for a specific piece of real property. The land under contract is unique, because no two pieces of real property have the same legal description. In addition, money damages would not compensate a buyer adequately, as the same land cannot be purchased elsewhere. Specific performance is an appropriate remedy.

(b) The basic criteria for specific performance do not apply well to personal-service contracts. If the identical service contracted for is readily available from others, the service is not unique, and monetary damages for nonperformance are adequate. If, however, the services are so personal that only the contract party can perform them, the contract meets the test of uniqueness; but the courts will refuse to decree specific performance if (1) the enforcement of specific performance requires involuntary servitude (prohibited by the Thirteenth Amendment to the U.S. Constitution), or (2) it is impractical to attempt to force meaningful performance by someone against his or her will. In the case of Amy and Fred, specific performance is not an appropriate remedy.

(c) A rare coin is unique, and monetary damages for breach are inadequate, as Hoffman cannot obtain a substantially identical substitute in the market. This is a typical case in which specific performance is an appropriate remedy.

(d) The key issue here is that this is a closely held corporation. Therefore, the stock is not available in the market, and the shares become unique. The uniqueness of these shares is enhanced by the fact that if Ryan sells her 4 percent of the shares to Chang, Chang will control the corporation. Because of this, monetary damages for Chang are totally inadequate as a remedy. Specific performance is an appropriate remedy.

19–2A. Question with Sample Answer

Anne has entered into an enforceable contract to subscribe to *E-Commerce Weekly*. In this problem, the offer to deliver, via e-mail, the newsletter was presented by the offeror with a statement of how to accept—by clicking on the "SUBSCRIBE" button. Consideration was in the promise to deliver the newsletter and in the price that the subscriber agreed to pay. The offeree had an opportunity to read the terms of the subscription agreement before making the contract. Whether she actually read those terms does not matter.

20–2A. Question with Sample Answer

The entire answer falls under UCC 2–206(1)(b), because the situation deals with a buyer's order to buy goods for prompt shipment. The law is that such an order or offer invites acceptance by a prompt promise to ship conforming goods. If the promise (acceptance) is sent by a medium reasonable under the circumstances, the acceptance is effective when sent. Therefore, a contract was formed on October 8, and it required Martin to ship 100 model Color-X television sets. Martin's shipment is nonconforming, and Flint is correct in claiming that Martin is in breach. Martin's claim would be valid if Martin had not sent its promise of shipment. The UCC provides that shipment of nonconforming goods constitutes an acceptance *unless* the seller seasonably notifies the buyer that such shipment is sent only as an accommodation. Thus, had a contract not been formed on October 8, the nonconforming shipment on the 28th would not be treated as an acceptance, and no contract would be in existence to breach.

21–2A. Question with Sample Answer

There is no question that the suit is in existence and identified to the contract. Nor do the facts indicate that there was an agreement as to when title or risk of loss would pass. Therefore, these situations deal with passage of title and risk of loss to goods that are "to be delivered" without physical movement of the goods by the seller and not represented by a document of title. The rules of law are that title passes to the buyer on the making of the contract, and risk of loss passes from a *merchant* seller to the buyer when the buyer *receives* the goods.

(a) In the case of the major creditor, title is with Sikora, and the major creditor cannot levy on the suit.

(b) The risk of loss on the suit destroyed by fire falls on Carson. Carson is a merchant, and because Sikora has not taken possession, Carson retains the risk of loss. This problem illustrates that title and risk of loss do not always pass from seller to buyer at the same time.

22–2A. Question with Sample Answer

Topken basically has the following remedies.

(a) Topken can identify the 500 washing machines to the contract and resell the goods [UCC 2–704].

(b) Topken can withhold delivery and proceed with other remedies [UCC 2–703].

(c) Topken can cancel the contract and proceed with other remedies [UCC 2–703 and 2–106(4)].

(d) Topken can resell the goods in a commercially reasonable manner (public or private sale with notice to Lorwin, holding Lorwin liable for any loss and retaining any profits) [UCC 2–706]. If Topken cannot resell after making a reasonable effort, Topken can sue for the purchase price [UCC 2–709 (1)(b)].

(e) Topken can sue Lorwin for breach of contract, recovering as damages the difference between the market price (at the time and place of tender) and the contract price, plus incidental damages [UCC 2–708].

The student should note the combination of remedies that would be most beneficial for Topken under the circumstances.

23–2A. Question with Sample Answer

If Colt can prove that all due care was exercised in the manufacture of the pistol, Colt cannot be held in an action based on negligence. Under the theory of strict liability in tort, however, Colt can be held liable regardless of the degree of care exercised. The doctrine of strict liability states that a merchant seller who sells a defective product that is unreasonably dangerous is liable for injuries caused by that product (even if all possible care in preparation and sale is exercised), provided that the product has not been substantially changed after the time of sale. Therefore, if Wayne can prove the pistol is defective, unreasonably dangerous, and caused him injury, Colt as a merchant is strictly liable, because there is no evidence that the pistol has been altered since the date of its manufacture.

24–2A. Question with Sample Answer

For an instrument to be negotiable, it must meet the following requirements:

(a) Be in writing.
(b) Be signed by the maker or drawer.
(c) Be an unconditional promise or order.
(d) State a fixed amount of money.
(e) Be payable on demand or at a definite time.
(f) Be payable to bearer or order (unless it is a check).

The instrument in this case meets the writing requirement in that it is handwritten and on something with a degree of permanence that is transferable. The instrument meets the requirement of being signed by the maker, as Juan Sanchez's signature (his name in his handwriting) appears in the body of the instrument. The instrument's payment is not conditional and contains Juan Sanchez's definite promise to pay. In addition, the sum of $100 is both a fixed amount and payable in money (U.S. currency). Because the instrument is payable on demand and to bearer (Kathy Martin or any holder), it is negotiable.

25–2A. Question with Sample Answer

(a) The bank does qualify as a holder in due course (HDC) for the amount of $5,000. To qualify as an HDC under UCC 3–302, one must take the instrument for value, in good faith, and without being put on notice that a defense exists against it, that it has been dishonored, or that it is overdue. In this situation the bank has given full value for the instrument—$4,850 ($5,000 – $150 discount). Therefore, the bank is entitled to be an HDC for the face value of the instrument ($5,000). In addition, the bank took the instrument in good faith and without notice of the original incompleteness of the instrument (completed when purchased by the bank) or the lack of authority of Hayden to complete the instrument in an amount over $2,000. The instrument was also taken before overdue (before the maturity date). Thus, First National Bank is an HDC.

(b) The sale to a stranger in a bar for $500 creates an entirely different situation. One of the requirements for the status of an HDC is that a holder take the instrument in good faith. *Good faith* is defined in the UCC as "honesty in fact in the conduct or transaction concerned" [UCC 1–201(19)]. Although the UCC does not provide clear guidelines to determine what is or is not good faith, both the amount paid (as compared to the face value of the instrument) and the circumstances under which the instrument is taken (as interpreted by a reasonable person) dictate whether the holder honestly believed the instrument was not defective when taken. In this case, taking a $5,000 note for $500 in a bar would raise a serious question of the stranger's good faith. Thus, the stranger would not qualify as a holder in due course.

26–3A. Question with Sample Answer

Frazier can recover the $1,500 from Kennedy if he is a holder in due course (HDC). He will be an HDC only if he, as a holder, took the check (a) for value, (b) in good faith, and (c) without notice that the check was overdue or dishonored or that a claim or defense against it exists. In this instance, Frazier qualifies for HDC status. First, he is a holder as the check was properly negotiated to him (by indorsement). Second, the facts indicate that he gave value. Third, there is nothing to indicate that he took the instrument in bad faith. Fourth, he was unaware of Niles's fraud (claim or defense), and he took the check before it was overdue (within thirty days of issue). Thus, Frazier is a holder in due course and can hold Kennedy liable.

27–2A. Question with Sample Answer

Citizens Bank will not have to recredit Gary's account for the $1,000 check and probably will not have to recredit his account for the first forged check for $100. Generally, a drawee bank is responsible for determining whether the signature of its customer is genuine, and when it pays on a forged customer's signature, the bank must recredit the customer's account [UCC 3–401, 4–406]. There are, however, exceptions to this general rule. First, when a customer's negligence substantially contributes to the making of an unauthorized signature (including a forgery), the drawee bank that pays the instrument in good faith will not be obligated to recredit the customer's account for the full amount of the check [UCC 3–406]. In addition, when a drawee bank sends to its customer a statement of account and canceled checks, the customer has a duty to exercise reasonable care and promptness in examining the statement to discover any forgeries and report them to the drawee bank. Failure of the customer to do so relieves the drawee from liability to the customer to the extent that the drawee bank suffers a loss [UCC 4–406(c)]. Therefore, Gary's negligence in allowing his checkbook to be stolen and his failure to report the theft or examine his May statement will preclude his recovery on the $100 check from the Citizens Bank. Under UCC 3–406(b) and 4–406(e), however, the bank could be liable to the extent that its negligence substantially contributes to the loss. Second, when a series of forgeries is committed by the same wrongdoer, the customer must discover and report the initial forgery within fourteen calendar days from the date that the statement of account and canceled checks (containing the initial forged check) are made available to the customer [UCC 4–406(d)(2)]. Failure to discover and report a forged check releases the drawee bank from liability for all additional forged checks in the series written after the thirty-day period. Therefore, Gary's failure to discover the May forged check by June 30 relieves the bank from liability for the June 20 check of $1,000.

28–2A. Question with Sample Answer

Three basic actions are available to Holiday:

(a) Attachment—a court-ordered seizure of nonexempt property prior to Holiday's reducing the debt to judgment. The grounds for granting the writ of attachment are limited, but in most states (when submitted), the writ is granted on introduction of evidence that a debtor intends to remove the property from the jurisdiction in which a judgment would be rendered. Holiday would have to post a bond and reduce its claim to judgment; then it could sell the attached property to satisfy the debt, returning any surplus to Kanahara.

(b) Writ of execution, on reducing the debt to judgment. The writ is an order issued by the clerk directing the sheriff or other officer of the court to seize (levy) nonexempt property of the debtor located within the court's jurisdiction. The property is then sold, and the proceeds are used to pay for the judgment and cost of sale, with any surplus going to the debtor (in this case, Kanahara).

(c) Garnishment of the wages owed to Kanahara by the Cross-Bar Packing Corp. Whenever a third person, the garnishee, owes a debt, such as wages, to the debtor, the creditor can proceed to have the court order the employer garnishee to turn over a percentage of the take-home pay (usually no more than 25 percent) to pay the debt. Garnishment actions are continuous in some states; in others, the action must be taken for each pay period.

Holiday can proceed with any one or a combination of these three actions. Because the property may be removed from the jurisdiction, and perhaps Kanahara himself may leave the jurisdiction (he may quit his job), prompt action is important.

29–3A. Question with Sample Answer

Generally, under Article 9, a secured party, on repossession of the collateral, has the right to keep it in full satisfaction of the debt (on proper notice and if no objection is received within twenty-one days) or to sell it or dispose of it, using the proceeds to cancel the debt. If the debtor has paid 60 percent of the cash price of a purchase-money security interest in consumer goods and has not after default signed a waiver of rights, the secured party cannot keep the collateral in full satisfaction of the debt. The secured party is forced to dispose of the collateral within ninety days [UCC 9–620(f)]. *Consumer goods* are defined as those used or bought primarily for personal, family, or household purposes [UCC 9–102(a)(23)]. In this case, Cummings has paid $400 ($100 down plus six $50 payments) of the $600 purchase price. Because the security interest is purchase money in consumer goods and the amount paid exceeds 60 percent of the price, Delgado cannot keep the repossessed set in full satisfaction of the debt. Therefore, Delgado has a duty to sell, lease, or otherwise dispose of the collateral and to apply the proceeds as prescribed in UCC 9–610.

30–3A. Question with Sample Answer

A trustee is given avoidance powers by the Bankruptcy Code. One situation in which the trustee can avoid transfers of property or payments by a debtor to a creditor is when such transfer constitutes a *preference*. A preference is a transfer of property or payment that favors one creditor over another. For a preference to exist, the debtor must be insolvent and must have made payment for a preexisting debt within ninety days of the filing of the petition in bankruptcy. The Code provides that the debtor is *presumed* to be insolvent during this ninety-day period. If the payment is made to an insider (and in this case payment was made to a close relative), the preference period is extended to one year, but the presumption of insolvency still applies only to the ninety-day period. In this case, the trustee has an excellent chance of having both payments declared preferences. The payment to Cool Springs was within ninety days of the filing of the petition, and it is doubtful that Cool Springs could overcome the presumption that Peaslee was insolvent at the time the payment was made. The $5,000 payment was made to an insider, Peaslee's father, and any payment made to an insider within one year of the petition of bankruptcy is a preference—as long as the debtor was insolvent at the time of payment. The facts indicate that Peaslee probably was insolvent at the time he paid his father. If he was not, the payment is not a preference, and the trustee's avoidance of the transfer would be improper.

31–2A. Question with Sample Answer

On creation of an agency, the agent owes certain fiduciary duties to the principal. Two such duties are the duty of loyalty and the duty to inform or notify. The duty of loyalty is a fundamental concept of the fiduciary relationship. The agent must act solely for the benefit of the principal, not in the agent's own interest or in the interest of another person. One of the principles invoked by this duty is that an agent employed to sell cannot become a purchaser without the principal's consent. When the agent is a partner, contracting to sell to another partner is equivalent to selling to oneself and is therefore a breach of the agent's duty. In addition, the agent has a duty to disclose to the principal any facts pertinent to the subject matter of the agency. Failure to disclose to Peter the knowledge of the shopping mall and the increased market value of the property also was a breach of Alice's fiduciary duties. When an agent breaches fiduciary duties owed to the principal by becoming a recipient of a contract, the contract is voidable at the election of the principal. Neither Carl nor Alice can hold Peter to the contract, and Alice's breach of fiduciary duties also allows Peter to terminate the agency relationship.

32–2A. Question with Sample Answer

As a general rule, a principal and third party are bound only to a contract made by the principal's agent within the scope of the agent's authority. An agent's authority to act can come from actual authority given to the agent (express or implied), apparent authority, or authority derived from an emergency. Express authority is directly given by the principal to the agent. Implied authority is deemed customary or inferred from the agent's position. Apparent authority is created when a principal gives a third person reason to believe the agent possesses authority not truly possessed. In this case, no express authority was given, and certainly no implied authority exists for a purchasing agent of goods to acquire realty. Moreover, A & B did nothing to lead Wilson to believe that Adams had authority to purchase land on its behalf. In addition, there was no emergency creating a need for Adams to purchase the land. Therefore, although Adams indicated in the contract that she was an agent, she acted outside the scope of her authority. Because of this, the contract between Adams and Wilson is treated merely as an unaccepted offer. As such, neither Wilson nor A & B is bound unless A & B ratifies (accepts) the contract before Wilson withdraws (revokes) the offer. Ratification can take place only when the principal is aware of all material facts and makes some act of affirmation. If A & B affirms the contract before Wilson withdraws, A & B can enforce Adams's contract. If Wilson withdraws first, Adams's contract cannot be enforced by A & B.

33–2A. Question with Sample Answer

The Occupational Health and Safety Act (OSHA) requires employers to provide safe working conditions for employees. The act prohibits employers from discharging or discriminating against any employee who refuses to work when the employee believes in good faith that he or she will risk death or great bodily harm by undertaking the employment activity. Denton and Carlo had sufficient reason to believe that the maintenance job required of them by their employer involved great risk, and therefore, under OSHA, their discharge was wrongful. Denton and Carlo can turn to the Occupational Safety and Health Administration, which is part of the Department of Labor, for assistance.

34–2A. Question with Sample Answer

An employer can legally impose an educational requirement if the requirement is directly related to, and necessary for, performance of the job. In this situation, the employer is requiring a high school diploma as a condition of employment for its cleaning crew. A high school diploma is not related to, or necessary for, the competent performance of a job on a cleaning crew. Chinawa obviously comes under Title VII of the 1964 Civil Rights Act, as amended. Therefore, if someone were to challenge Chinawa's practices, a court would be likely to consider the disparate impact that the educational requirement had on Chinawa's hiring of minorities. Chinawa's educational requirement resulted in its hiring an all-white cleaning crew in an area in which 75 percent of the pool of qualified applicants were minorities. Therefore, Chinawa's educational requirement would likely be considered unintentional (disparate-impact) discrimination against minorities.

35–2A. Question with Sample Answer

The court would likely conclude that National Foods was responsible for the acts of harassment by the manager at the franchised restaurant, on the ground that the employees were the agents of National Foods. An agency relationship can be implied from the circumstances and conduct of the parties. The important question is the degree of control that a franchisor has over its franchisees. Whether it exercises that control is beside the point. Here, National Foods retained considerable control over the new hires and the franchisee's policies, as well as the right to terminate the franchise for violations. That its supervisors routinely approved the policies would not undercut National Foods' liability.

36–2A. Question with Sample Answer

(a) A limited partner's interest is assignable. In fact, assignment allows the assignee to become a substituted limited partner with the consent of the remaining partners. The assignment, however, does not dissolve the limited partnership.

(b) Bankruptcy of the limited partnership itself causes dissolution, but bankruptcy of one of the limited partners does not dissolve the partnership unless it causes the bankruptcy of the firm.

(c) The retirement, death, or insanity of a general partner dissolves the partnership unless the business can be continued by the remaining general partners. Because Dorinda was the only general partner, her death dissolves the limited partnership.

37–2A. Question with Sample Answer

Although a joint stock company has characteristics of a corporation, it is usually treated as a partnership. Therefore, although the joint stock company issues transferable shares of stock and is managed by directors and officers, the shareholders have personal liability. Unless the shareholders transfer their stock and ownership to a third party, not only are the joint stock company's assets available for damages caused by a breach, but the individual shareholders' estates are also subject to such liability. The business trust resembles and is treated like a corporation in many respects. One similarity is the limited liability of the beneficiaries. Unless by state law beneficiaries are treated as partners, making them liable to business trust creditors, Bateson Corp. can look to only business trust assets in the event of breach.

38–2A. Question with Sample Answer

(a) As a general rule, a promoter is personally liable for all preincorporation contracts made by the promoter. The basic theory behind such liability is that the promoter cannot be an agent for a nonexistent principal (a corporation not yet formed). It is immaterial whether the contracting party knows of the prospective existence of the corporation, and the general rule of promoter liability continues even after the corporation is formed. Three basic exceptions to promoter liability are:

(1) The promoter's contract with a third party can stipulate that the third party will look only to the new corporation, not to the promoter, for performance and liability.

(2) The third party can release the promoter from liability.

(3) After formation, the corporation can assume the contractual obligations and liability by *novation*. (If it is by *adoption*, most courts hold that the promoter is still personally liable.)

Peterson is therefore personally liable on both contracts, because (1) neither Owens nor Babcock has released him from liability, (2) the corporation has not assumed contractual responsibility by novation, and (3) Peterson's contract with Babcock did not limit Babcock to holding only the corporation liable. (Peterson's liability was conditioned only on the corporation's formation, which did occur.)

(b) Incorporation in and of itself does not make the newly formed corporation liable for preincorporation contracts. Until the newly formed corporation assumes Peterson's contracts by novation (releasing Peterson from personal liability) or by adoption (undertaking to perform Peterson's contracts, which makes both the corporation and Peterson liable), Babcock cannot enforce Peterson's contract against the corporation.

39–2A. Question with Sample Answer

Directors are personally answerable to the corporation and the shareholders for breach of their duty to exercise reasonable care in conducting the affairs of the corporation. Reasonable care is defined as being the degree of care that a reasonably prudent person would use in the conduct of personal business affairs. When directors delegate the running of the corporate affairs to officers, the directors are expected to use reasonable care in the selection and supervision of such officers. Failure to do so will make the directors liable for negligence or mismanagement. A director who dissents to an action by the board is not personally liable for losses resulting from that action. Unless the dissent is entered into the board meeting minutes, however, the director is presumed to have assented. Therefore, the first issue in the case of AstroStar, Inc., is whether the board members failed to use reasonable care in the selection of the president. If so, and particularly if the board failed to provide a reasonable amount of supervision (and openly embezzled funds indicate that failure), the directors will be personally liable. This liability will include Eckhart unless she can prove that she dissented and that she tried to reasonably supervise the new president. Considering the facts in this case, it is questionable that Eckhart could prove this.

40–2A. Question with Sample Answer

Ajax apparently has given shareholder Alir notice of the meeting for approval of the merger. In addition, however, Ajax should have notified Alir of her right to dissent and of her right, should the merger be approved, to be paid a fair value for her shares. The law recognizes that a dissenting shareholder should not be forced to become an unwilling shareholder in a new corporation. If Alir adheres strictly to statutory procedures, she has appraisal rights for the Ajax shares she holds after approval of the merger. Alir's appraisal rights entitle her to be paid by Zeta the "fair value" of her shares. Fair value is the value of the shares on the day prior to the date on which the vote for merger is taken. This value must not reflect appreciation or depreciation of the stock in anticipation of the approval. If $20 is a true value (the market value on the day before the vote), Alir will receive $200,000 for her 10,000 Ajax shares.

41–2A. Question with Sample Answer

No. Under federal securities law, a stock split is exempt from registration requirements. This is because no *sale* of stock is involved. The existing shares are merely being split, and no consideration is received by the corporation for the additional shares created.

42–2A. Question with Sample Answer

A court might initially consider whether a member of a limited liability company (LLC) who has a material conflict of interest should be prohibited from dealing with matters of the LLC. Most likely, a court would conclude that a member—even a member with a conflict of interest—can vote to transfer LLC property, but must do so fairly. In this problem, the transfer of BP's sole asset by two of BP's members to themselves, disguised as Excel (a newly created LLC), represented a material conflict of interest. Not only did Amy and Carl engage in self-dealing, but in doing so, they increased their interests in Excel. This conflict did not prohibit Amy and Carl from voting to transfer BP's sole asset to Excel, however, so long as they dealt fairly with Dave. To judge the fairness, a court might consider the members' conduct, the end result, the purpose of the LLC, and the parties' expectations. Here, the transfer was arguably unfair in two respects. First, it was not an "arm's length transaction" because it did not occur on the open market. Second, the sale undercut BP's capacity to carry on its intended business (to own the property as a long-term investment). The court might still rule in favor of Amy and Carl if they could argue successfully that the transaction did not need to be, or could not be, at "arm's length" and that BP's investment capacity was not undercut.

43–2A. Question with Sample Answer

The court will consider first whether the agency followed the procedures prescribed in the Administrative Procedure Act (APA). Ordinarily, courts will not require agencies to use procedures beyond those of the APA. Courts will, however, compel agencies to follow their own rules. If an agency has adopted a rule granting extra procedures, the agency must provide those extra procedures, at least until the rule is formally rescinded. Ultimately, in this case, the court will most likely rule for the food producers.

44–3A. Question with Sample Answer

Yes. A regulation of the Federal Trade Commission (FTC) under Section 5 of the Federal Trade Commission Act makes it a violation for door-to-door sellers to fail to give consumers three days to cancel any sale. In addition, a number of state statutes require this three-day "cooling off" period to protect consumers from unscrupulous door-to-door sellers. Because the Gonchars sought to rescind the contract within the three-day period, Renowned Books was obligated to agree to cancel the contract. Its failure to allow rescission was in violation of the FTC regulation and of most state statutes.

45–2A. Question with Sample Answer

Fruitade has violated a number of federal environmental laws if such actions are being taken without a permit. First, because the dumping is in a navigable waterway, the River and Harbor Act of 1886, as amended, has been violated. Second, the Clean Water Act of 1972, as amended, has been violated. This act is designed to make the waters safe for swimming, to protect fish and wildlife, and to eliminate discharge of pollutants into the water. Both the crushed glass and the acid violate this act. Third, the Toxic Substances Control Act of 1976 was passed to regulate chemicals that are known to be toxic and could have an effect on human health and the environment. The acid in the cleaning fluid or compound could come under this act.

46–2A. Question with Sample Answer

Instant Foto has created a tying arrangement. To get Instant Foto's film, the purchaser is virtually required to also have the film developed by Instant Foto. The legality of a tying agreement depends on many factors, such as the purpose of the agreement and its likely effect on competition in the relevant markets (the market for the tying product and the market for the tied product). When the effect of the tying agreement is to substantially lessen competition, the agreement violates either the Sherman Act, Section 1, or the Clayton Act, Section 3. In this scenario, the fact that Instant Foto holds 50 percent of the film-sale market enables it to have a substantial effect on the film-processing market (the tied product). The combination substantially restricts the buyer's freedom of choice in processing the film and thus is illegal. Although Instant Foto might claim that the tie is required as a quality control, it is highly unlikely that only Instant Foto can provide such quality processing. Therefore, the business purpose is suspect, and the tie is a definite anticompetitive device.

47–2A. Question with Sample Answer

For Curtis to recover against the hotel, he must first prove that a bailment relationship was created between himself and the hotel as to the car or the fur coat, or both. For a bailment to exist, there must be a delivery of the personal property that gives the bailee exclusive possession of the property, and the bailee must knowingly accept the bailed property. If either element is lacking, there is no bailment relationship and no liability on the part of the bailee hotel. The facts clearly indicate that the bailee hotel took exclusive possession and control of Curtis's car, and it knowingly accepted the car when the attendant took the car from Curtis and parked it in the underground guarded garage, retaining the keys. Thus, a bailment was created as to the car, and, because a mutual benefit bailment was created, the hotel owes Curtis the duty to exercise reasonable care over the property to and to return the bailed car at the end of the bailment. Failure to return the car creates a presumption of negligence (lack of reasonable care), and unless the hotel can rebut this presumption, the hotel is liable to Curtis for the loss of the car. As to the fur coat, the hotel neither knew nor expected that the trunk contained an expensive fur coat. Thus, although the hotel knowingly took exclusive possession of the car, the hotel did not do so with the fur coat. (But for a regular coat and other items likely to be in the car, the hotel would be liable.) Because no bailment of the expensive fur coat was created, the hotel has no liability for its loss.

48–3A. Question with Sample Answer

Wilfredo understandably wants a general warranty deed, as this type of deed will give him the most extensive protection against any defects of title claimed against the property transferred. The general warranty would have Patricia warranting the following covenants:

(a) Covenant of seisin and right to convey—a warranty that the seller has good title and power to convey.

(b) Covenant against encumbrances—a guaranty by the seller that, unless stated, there are no outstanding encumbrances or liens against the property conveyed.

(c) Covenant of quiet possession—a warranty that the grantee's possession will not be disturbed by others claiming a prior legal right. Patricia, however, is conveying only ten feet along a property line that may not even be accurately surveyed. Patricia therefore does not wish to make these warranties. Consequently, she is offering a quitclaim deed, which does not convey any warranties but conveys only whatever interest, if any, the grantor owns. Although title is passed by the quitclaim deed, the quality of the title is not warranted.

Because Wilfredo really needs the property, it appears that he has three choices: he can accept the quitclaim deed; he can increase his offer price to obtain the general warranty deed he wants; or he can offer to have a title search made, which should satisfy both parties.

49–2A. Question with Sample Answer

Ajax will probably not be able to void the policy. Most life insurance policies contain what is called an incontestability clause. Such a clause provides that a policy cannot be contested for misstatements by the insured after the policy has been in effect for a given period, usually two years. Even though the application is part of the policy (attached to the policy), Patrick's innocent error in answering the question dealing with heart problems or ailments can no longer be contested by the insurer, as the incontestability clause is now in effect (three years have passed since the issuance of the policy). In addition, a misstatement about age is not grounds in and of itself for Ajax to avoid the policy. Ajax does, however, have the right to adjust premium payments to reflect the correct age or to reduce the amount of the insurance coverage accordingly. Thus, Ajax cannot escape liability on Patrick's death, but it can reduce the $50,000 coverage to account for the premiums that should have been paid for a person who is thirty-three years old, not thirty-two years old.

50–3A. Question with Sample Answer

(a) State laws vary on whether a will written and executed before marriage is revoked by the marriage. Some states declare that the will is revoked by a subsequent marriage only if a child is born out of that marriage. Under the Uniform Probate Code, a subsequent marriage does not revoke a will; however, the new spouse is entitled to share the estate as if the deceased has died intestate, and the balance passes under the will. In this case, if the will is revoked by marriage, Lisa will receive the entire estate, and Carol, as James's mother, will receive nothing. If the marriage does not revoke the will, Lisa will probably receive one-half the estate under the laws of intestacy, and the balance will go to Carol.

(b) At common law and under the Uniform Probate Code, divorce does not in and of itself revoke a will made and executed during a previous marriage. If the divorce is accompanied by a property settlement, most states revoke that portion of the will that disposed property to the former spouse. Although this matter is frequently controlled by statute, in the absence of such a statute, if Lisa received a property settlement on divorce, the will of James would be revoked and Mandis would recover the entire estate by the laws of intestacy.

(c) If a child is born after a will has been executed and the child is not provided for in the will, the law will allow the child to inherit as if the testator had died intestate. The philosophy is that unless the child is specifically excluded by the will, the child was intended to inherit and was omitted in error. Therefore, Claire would receive one-half of the estate in most states.

51–2A. Question with Sample Answer

Assuming that the court has abandoned the *Ultramares* rule, it is likely that the accounting firm of Goldman, Walters, Johnson & Co. will be held liable to Happydays State Bank for negligent preparation of financial statements. There are various policy reasons for holding accountants liable to third parties even in the absence of privity. The potential liability would make accountants more careful in the preparation of financial statements. Moreover, in some situations the accountants may be the only solvent defendants, and hence, unless liability is imposed on accountants, third parties who reasonably rely on financial statements may go unprotected. Accountants, rather than third parties, are in better positions to spread the risks. If third parties such as banks have to absorb the costs of bad loans made as a result of negligently prepared financial statements, then the cost of credit to the public in general will increase. In contrast, accountants are in a better position to spread the risk by purchasing liability insurance.

52–2A. Question with Sample Answer

Each system has its advantages and its disadvantages. In a common law system, the courts independently develop the rules governing certain areas of law, such as torts and contracts. This judge-made law exists in addition to the laws passed by a legislature. Judges must follow precedential decisions in their jurisdictions, but courts may modify or even overturn precedents when deemed necessary. Also, if there is no case law to guide a court, the court may create a new rule of law. In a civil law system, the only official source of law is a statutory code. Courts are required to interpret the code and apply the rules to individual cases, but courts may not depart from the code and develop their own laws. In theory, the law code will set forth all the principles needed for the legal system. Common law and civil law systems are not wholly distinct. For example, the United States has a common law system, but crimes are defined by statute as in civil law systems. Civil law systems may allow considerable room for judges to develop law: law codes cannot be so precise as to address every contested issue, so the judiciary must interpret the codes. There are also significant differences among common law countries. The judges of different common law nations have produced differing common law principles. The roles of judges and lawyers under the different systems should be taken into account. Among other factors that should be considered in establishing a business law system and in deciding what regulations to impose are the goals that the system and its regulations are intended to achieve and the expectations of those to whom both will apply, including foreign and domestic investors.

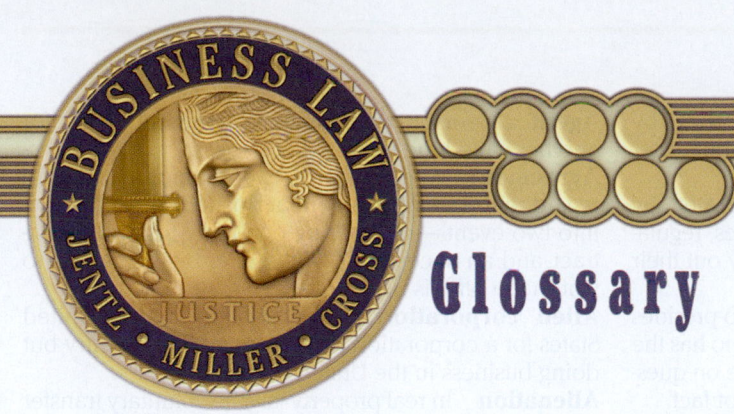

Glossary

A

Abandoned property Property with which the owner has voluntarily parted, with no intention of recovering it.

Abandonment In landlord-tenant law, a tenant's departure from leased premises completely, with no intention of returning before the end of the lease term.

Abatement A process by which legatees receive reduced benefits if the assets of an estate are insufficient to pay in full all general bequests provided for in the will.

Acceleration clause A clause in an installment contract that provides for all future payments to become due immediately on the failure to tender timely payments or on the occurrence of a specified event.

Acceptance (1) In contract law, the offeree's notification to the offeror that the offeree agrees to be bound by the terms of the offeror's proposal. Although historically the terms of acceptance had to be the mirror image of the terms of the offer, the Uniform Commercial Code provides that even modified terms of the offer in a definite expression of acceptance constitute a contract. (2) In negotiable instruments law, the drawee's signed agreement to pay a draft when presented.

Acceptor The person (the drawee) who accepts a draft and who agrees to be primarily responsible for its payment.

Accession Occurs when an individual adds value to personal property by either labor or materials. In some situations, a person may acquire ownership rights in another's property through accession.

Accommodation party A person who signs an instrument for the purpose of lending his or her name as credit to another party on the instrument.

Accord and satisfaction An agreement for payment (or other performance) between two parties, one of whom has a right of action against the other. After the payment has been accepted or other performance has been made, the "accord and satisfaction" is complete and the obligation is discharged.

Accredited investors In the context of securities offerings, "sophisticated" investors, such as banks, insurance companies, investment companies, the issuer's executive officers and directors, and persons whose income or net worth exceeds certain limits.

Acquittal A certification or declaration following a trial that the individual accused of a crime is innocent, or free from guilt, and is thus absolved of the charges.

Act of state doctrine A doctrine that provides that the judicial branch of one country will not examine the validity of public acts committed by a recognized foreign government within its own territory.

Actionable Capable of serving as the basis of a lawsuit.

Actual authority Authority of an agent that is express or implied.

Actual malice A condition that exists when a person makes a statement with either knowledge of its falsity or a reckless disregard for the truth. In a defamation suit, a statement made about a public figure normally must be made with actual malice for liability to be incurred.

Actus reus (pronounced *ak*-tus *ray*-uhs) A guilty (prohibited) act. The commission of a prohibited act is one of the two essential elements required for criminal liability, the other element being the intent to commit a crime.

Adequate protection doctrine In bankruptcy law, a doctrine that protects secured creditors from losing their security as a result of an automatic stay on legal proceedings by creditors against the debtor once the debtor petitions for bankruptcy relief. In certain circumstances, the bankruptcy court may provide adequate protection by requiring the debtor or trustee to pay the creditor or provide additional guaranties to protect the creditor against the losses suffered by the creditor as a result of the stay.

Adhesion contract A "standard-form" contract, such as that between a large retailer and a consumer, in which the stronger party dictates the terms.

Adjudication The process of resolving a dispute by presenting evidence and arguments before a neutral third party decision maker in a court or an administrative law proceeding.

Administrative agency A federal, state, or local government agency established to perform a specific function. Administrative agencies are authorized by legislative acts to make and enforce rules to administer and enforce the acts.

Administrative law The body of law created by administrative agencies (in the form of rules, regulations, orders, and decisions) in order to carry out their duties and responsibilities.

Administrative law judge (ALJ) One who presides over an administrative agency hearing and who has the power to administer oaths, take testimony, rule on questions of evidence, and make determinations of fact.

Administrative process The procedure used by administrative agencies in the administration of law.

Administrator One who is appointed by a court to handle the probate (disposition) of a person's estate if that person dies intestate (without a valid will) or if the executor named in the will cannot serve.

Adverse possession The acquisition of title to real property by occupying it openly, without the consent of the owner, for a period of time specified by a state statute. The occupation must be actual, open, notorious, exclusive, and in opposition to all others, including the owner.

Affidavit A written or printed voluntary statement of facts, confirmed by the oath or affirmation of the party making it and made before a person having the authority to administer the oath or affirmation.

Affirm To validate; to give legal force to. *See also* Ratification

Affirmative action Job-hiring policies that give special consideration to members of protected classes in an effort to overcome present effects of past discrimination.

Affirmative defense A response to a plaintiff's claim that does not deny the plaintiff's facts but attacks the plaintiff's legal right to bring an action. An example is the running of the statute of limitations.

After-acquired evidence A type of evidence submitted in support of an affirmative defense in employment discrimination cases. Evidence that, prior to the employer's discriminatory act, the employee engaged in misconduct sufficient to warrant dismissal had the employer known of it earlier.

After-acquired property Property of the debtor that is acquired after the execution of a security agreement.

Age of majority The age at which an individual is considered legally capable of conducting himself or herself responsibly. A person of this age is entitled to the full rights of citizenship, including the right to vote in elections. In contract law, one who is no longer an infant and can no longer disaffirm a contract.

Agency A relationship between two parties in which one party (the agent) agrees to represent or act for the other (the principal).

Agency by estoppel An agency that arises when a principal negligently allows an agent to exercise powers not granted to the agent, thus justifying others in believing that the agent possesses the requisite agency authority.

Agent A person who agrees to represent or act for another, called the principal.

Agreement A meeting of two or more minds in regard to the terms of a contract; usually broken down into two events—an offer by one party to form a contract, and an acceptance of the offer by the person to whom the offer is made.

Alien corporation A designation in the United States for a corporation formed in another country but doing business in the United States.

Alienation In real property law, the voluntary transfer of property from one person to another (as opposed to a transfer by operation of law).

Allegation A statement, claim, or assertion.

Allege To state, recite, assert, or charge.

Allonge (pronounced uh-*lohnj*) A piece of paper firmly attached to a negotiable instrument, on which transferees can make indorsements if there is no room left on the instrument itself.

Alternative dispute resolution (ADR) The resolution of disputes in ways other than those involved in the traditional judicial process. Negotiation, mediation, and arbitration are forms of ADR.

Amend To change through a formal procedure.

American Arbitration Association (AAA) The major organization offering arbitration services in the United States.

Analogy In logical reasoning, an assumption that if two things are similar in some respects, they will be similar in other respects also. Often used in legal reasoning to infer the appropriate application of legal principles in a case being decided by referring to previous cases involving different facts but considered to come within the policy underlying the rule.

Annuity An insurance policy that pays the insured fixed, periodic payments for life or for a term of years, as stipulated in the policy, after the insured reaches a specified age.

Annul To cancel; to make void.

Answer Procedurally, a defendant's response to the plaintiff's complaint.

Antecedent claim A preexisting claim. In negotiable instruments law, taking an instrument in satisfaction of an antecedent claim is taking the instrument for value—that is, for valid consideration.

Anticipatory repudiation An assertion or action by a party indicating that he or she will not perform an obligation that the party is contractually obligated to perform at a future time.

Antitrust law The body of federal and state laws and statutes protecting trade and commerce from unlawful restraints, price discrimination, price fixing, and monopolies. The principal federal antitrust statues are the Sherman Act of 1890, the Clayton Act of 1914, and the Federal Trade Commission Act of 1914.

Apparent authority Authority that is only apparent, not real. In agency law, a person may be deemed to have had the power to act as an agent for another party if the other party's manifestations to a third party led the third party to believe that an agency existed when, in fact, it did not.

Appeal Resort to a superior court, such as an appellate court, to review the decision of an inferior court, such as a trial court or an administrative agency.

Appellant The party who takes an appeal from one court to another.

Appellate court A court having appellate jurisdiction.

Appellate jurisdiction Jurisdiction that is exercised by reviewing courts, or appellate courts. Generally, cases can be brought before appellate courts only on appeal from an order or a judgment of a trial court or other lower court.

Appellee The party against whom an appeal is taken—that is, the party who opposes setting aside or reversing the judgment.

Appraisal right The right of a dissenting shareholder, if he or she objects to an extraordinary transaction of the corporation (such as a merger or consolidation), to have his or her shares appraised and to be paid the fair value of his or her shares by the corporation.

Appropriation In tort law, the use by one person of another person's name, likeness, or other identifying characteristic without permission and for the benefit of the user.

Arbitrary and capricious test A court reviewing an informal administrative agency action applies this test to determine whether or not that action was in clear error. The court gives wide discretion to the expertise of the agency and decides if the agency had sufficient factual information on which to base its action. If no clear error was made, then the agency's action stands.

Arbitration The settling of a dispute by submitting it to a disinterested third party (other than a court), who renders a decision. The decision may or may not be legally binding.

Arbitration clause A clause in a contract that provides that, in the event of a dispute, the parties will submit the dispute to arbitration rather than litigate the dispute in court.

Arraignment A procedure in which an accused person is brought before the court to answer the criminal charges. The charge is read to the person, and he or she is asked to enter a plea—such as "guilty" or "not guilty."

Arson The malicious burning of another's dwelling. Some statutes have expanded this to include any real property regardless of ownership and the destruction of property by other means—for example, by explosion.

Articles of incorporation The document filed with the appropriate governmental agency, usually the secretary of state, when a business is incorporated; state statutes usually prescribe what kind of information must be contained in the articles of incorporation.

Articles of organization The document filed with a designated state official by which a limited liability company is formed.

Articles of partnership A written agreement that sets forth each partner's rights and obligations with respect to the partnership.

Artisan's lien A possessory lien given to a person who has made improvements and added value to another person's personal property as security for payment for services performed.

Assault Any word or action intended to make another person fearful of immediate physical harm; a reasonably believable threat.

Assignee The person to whom contract rights are assigned.

Assignment The act of transferring to another all or part of one's rights arising under a contract.

Assignor The person who assigns contract rights.

Assumption of risk A defense against negligence that can be used when the plaintiff is aware of a danger and voluntarily assumes the risk of injury from that danger.

Attachment (1) In the context of secured transactions, the process by which a security interest in the property of another becomes enforceable. (2) In the context of judicial liens, a court-ordered seizure and taking into custody of property prior to the securing of a judgment for a past-due debt.

Attempted monopolization Any actions by a firm to eliminate competition and gain monopoly power.

Authenticate To sign a record, or with the intent to sign a record, to execute or to adopt an electronic sound, symbol, or the like to link with the record. A *record* is retrievable information inscribed on a tangible medium or stored in an electronic or other medium.

Authority In agency law, the agent's permission to act on behalf of the principal. An agent's authority may be actual (express or implied) or apparent. *See also* Actual authority; Apparent authority.

Authorization card A card signed by an employee that gives a union permission to act on his or her behalf in negotiations with management. Unions typically use authorization cards as evidence of employee support during union organization.

Authorized means In contract law, the means of acceptance authorized by the offeror.

Automatic stay In bankruptcy proceedings, the suspension of virtually all litigation and other action by creditors against the debtor or the debtor's property; the stay is effective the moment the debtor files a petition in bankruptcy.

Award In the context of litigation, the amount of money awarded to a plaintiff in a civil lawsuit as damages. In the context of arbitration, the arbitrator's decision.

B

Bailee One to whom goods are entrusted by a bailor. Under the Uniform Commercial Code, a party who, by a bill of lading, warehouse receipt, or other document of title, acknowledges possession of goods and contracts.

Bailee's lien A possessory lien, or claim, that a bailee entitled to compensation can place on the bailed property to ensure that he or she will be paid for the services provided. The lien is effective as long as the bailee retains possession of the bailed goods and has not agreed to extend credit to the bailor. Sometimes referred to as an artisan's lien.

Bailment A situation in which the personal property of one person (a bailor) is entrusted to another (a bailee), who is obligated to return the bailed property to the bailor or dispose of it as directed.

Bailor One who entrusts goods to a bailee.

Bait-and-switch advertising Advertising a product at a very attractive price (the "bait") and then informing the consumer, once he or she is in the store, that the advertised product is either not available or is of poor quality; the customer is then urged to purchase ("switched" to) a more expensive item.

Banker's acceptance A negotiable instrument that is commonly used in international trade. A banker's acceptance is drawn by a creditor against the debtor, who pays the draft at maturity. The drawer creates a draft without designating a payee. The draft can pass through many parties' hands before a bank (drawee) accepts it, transforming the draft into a banker's acceptance. Acceptances can be purchased and sold in a way similar to securities.

Bankruptcy court A federal court of limited jurisdiction that handles only bankruptcy proceedings. Bankruptcy proceedings are governed by federal bankruptcy law.

Bargain A mutual undertaking, contract, or agreement between two parties; to negotiate over the terms of a purchase or contract.

Basis of the bargain In contract law, the affirmation of fact or promise on which the sale of goods is predicated, creating an express warranty.

Battery The unprivileged, intentional touching of another.

Bearer A person in the possession of an instrument payable to bearer or indorsed in blank.

Bearer instrument Any instrument that is not payable to a specific person, including instruments payable to the bearer or to "cash."

Beneficiary One to whom life insurance proceeds are payable or for whose benefit a trust has been established or property under a will has been transferred.

Bequest A gift by will of personal property (from the verb—to bequeath).

Beyond a reasonable doubt The standard used to determine the guilt or innocence of a person criminally charged. To be guilty of a crime, one must be proved guilty "beyond and to the exclusion of every reasonable doubt." A reasonable doubt is one that would cause a prudent person to hesitate before acting in matters important to him or her.

Bilateral contract A type of contract that arises when a promise is given in exchange for a return promise.

Bill of lading A document that serves both as evidence of the receipt of goods for shipment and as documentary evidence of title to the goods.

Bill of Rights The first ten amendments to the U.S. Constitution.

Binder A written, temporary insurance policy.

Binding authority Any source of law that a court must follow when deciding a case. Binding authorities include constitutions, statutes, and regulations that govern the issue being decided, as well as court decisions that are controlling precedents within the jurisdiction.

Blank indorsement An indorsement that specifies no particular indorsee and can consist of a mere signature. An order instrument that is indorsed in blank becomes a bearer instrument.

Blue laws State or local laws that prohibit the performance of certain types of commercial activities on Sunday.

Blue sky laws State laws that regulate the offer and sale of securities.

Bona fide Good faith. A bona fide obligation is one made in good faith—that is, sincerely and honestly.

Bona fide occupational qualification (BFOQ) Identifiable characteristics reasonably necessary to the normal operation of a particular business. These characteristics can include gender, national origin, and religion, but not race.

Bond A certificate that evidences a corporate (or government) debt. It is a security that involves no ownership interest in the issuing entity.

Bounty payment A reward (payment) given to a person or persons who perform a certain service—such as informing legal authorities of illegal actions.

Boycott A concerted refusal to do business with a particular person or entity in order to obtain concessions or to express displeasure with certain acts or practices of that person or business. *See also* Secondary boycott

Breach To violate a law, by an act or an omission, or to break a legal obligation that one owes to another person or to society.

Breach of contract The failure, without legal excuse, of a promisor to perform the obligations of a contract.

Bribery The offering, giving, receiving, or soliciting of anything of value with the aim of influencing an official action or an official's discharge of a legal or public duty or (with respect to commercial bribery) a business decision.

Brief A formal legal document submitted by the attorney for the appellant—or the appellee (in answer to the appellant's brief)—to an appellate court when a case is appealed. The appellant's brief outlines the facts and issues of the case, the judge's rulings or jury's findings that should be reversed or modified, the applicable law, and the arguments on the client's behalf.

Browse-wrap terms Terms and conditions of use that are presented to an Internet user at the time certain products, such as software, are being downloaded but that need not be agreed to (by clicking "I agree," for example) before being able to install or use the product.

Bureaucracy A large organization that is structured hierarchically to carry out specific functions.

Burglary The unlawful entry into a building with the intent to commit a felony. (Some state statutes expand this to include the intent to commit any crime.)

Business ethics Ethics in a business context; a consensus of what constitutes right or wrong behavior in the world of business and the application of moral principles to situations that arise in a business setting.

Business invitees Those people, such as customers or clients, who are invited onto business premises by the owner of those premises for business purposes.

Business judgment rule A rule that immunizes corporate management from liability for actions that result in corporate losses or damages if the actions are undertaken in good faith and are within both the power of the corporation and the authority of management to make.

Business necessity A defense to allegations of employment discrimination in which the employer demonstrates that an employment practice that discriminates against members of a protected class is related to job performance.

Business plan A document describing a company, its products, and its anticipated future performance. Creating a business plan is normally the first step in obtaining loans or venture-capital funds for a new business enterprise.

Business tort The wrongful interference with the business rights of another.

Business trust A voluntary form of business organization in which investors (trust beneficiaries) transfer cash or property to trustees in exchange for trust certificates that represent their investment shares. Management of the business and trust property is handled by the trustees for the use and benefit of the investors. The certificate holders have limited liability (are not responsible for the debts and obligations incurred by the trust) and share in the trust's profits.

Buyer in the ordinary course of business A buyer who, in good faith and without knowledge that the sale to him or her is in violation of the ownership rights or security interest of a third party in the goods, purchases goods in the ordinary course of business from a person in the business of selling goods of that kind.

Buyout price The amount payable to a partner on his or her dissociation from a partnership, based on the amount distributable to that partner if the firm were wound up on that date, and offset by any damages for wrongful dissociation.

Buy-sell agreement In the context of partnerships, an express agreement made at the time of partnership formation for one or more of the partners to buy out the other or others should the situation warrant—and thus provide for the smooth dissolution of the partnership.

Bylaws A set of governing rules adopted by a corporation or other association.

Bystander A spectator, witness, or person standing nearby when an event occurred and who did not engage in the business or act leading to the event.

C

C.I.F. or C.&F. Cost, insurance, and freight—or just cost and freight. A pricing term in a contract for the sale of goods requiring, among other things, that the seller place the goods in the possession of a carrier before risk passes to the buyer.

C.O.D. Cash on delivery. In sales transactions, a term meaning that the buyer will pay for the goods on delivery and before inspecting the goods.

Callable bond A bond that may be called in and the principal repaid at specified times or under conditions specified in the bond when it is issued.

Cancellation The act of nullifying, or making void. *See also* Rescission

Capital Accumulated goods, possessions, and assets used for the production of profits and wealth; the equity of owners in a business.

Carrier An individual or organization engaged in transporting passengers or goods for hire. *See also* Common carrier

Case law The rules of law announced in court decisions. Case law includes the aggregate of reported cases that interpret judicial precedents, statutes, regulations, and constitutional provisions.

Case on point A previous case involving factual circumstances and issues that are similar to the case before the court.

Cash surrender value The amount that the insurer has agreed to pay to the insured if a life insurance policy is canceled before the insured's death.

Cashier's check A check drawn by a bank on itself.

Categorical imperative A concept developed by the philosopher Immanuel Kant as an ethical guideline for behavior. In deciding whether an action is right or wrong, or desirable or undesirable, a person should evaluate the action in terms of what would happen if everybody else in the same situation, or category, acted the same way.

Causation in fact An act or omission without ("but for") which an event would not have occurred.

Cause of action A situation or set of facts sufficient to justify a right to sue.

Cease-and-desist order An administrative or judicial order prohibiting a person or business firm from conducting activities that an agency or court has deemed illegal.

Certificate of deposit (CD) A note of a bank in which a bank acknowledges a receipt of money from a party and promises to repay the money, with interest, to the party on a certain date.

Certificate of limited partnership The basic document filed with a designated state official by which a limited partnership is formed.

Certification mark A mark used by one or more persons, other than the owner, to certify the region, materials, mode of manufacture, quality, or accuracy of the owner's goods or services. When used by members of a cooperative, association, or other organization, such a mark is referred to as a collective mark. Examples of certification marks include the "Good Housekeeping Seal of Approval" and "UL Tested."

Certified check A check that has been accepted by the bank on which it is drawn. Essentially, the bank, by certifying (accepting) the check, promises to pay the check at the time the check is presented.

Certiorari *See* Writ of *certiorari*

Chain-style business franchise A franchise that operates under a franchisor's trade name and that is identified as a member of a select group of dealers that engage in the franchisor's business. The franchisee is generally required to follow standardized or prescribed methods of operation. Examples of this type of franchise are McDonald's and most other fast-food chains.

Chancellor An adviser to the king at the time of the early king's courts of England. Individuals petitioned the king for relief when they could not obtain an adequate remedy in a court of law, and these petitions were decided by the chancellor.

Charging order In partnership law, an order granted by a court to a judgment creditor that entitles the creditor to attach profits or assets of a partner on dissolution of the partnership.

Charitable trust A trust in which the property held by a trustee must be used for a charitable purpose, such as the advancement of health, education, or religion.

Chattel All forms of personal property.

Chattel paper Any writing or writings that show both a debt and the fact that the debt is secured by personal property. In many instances, chattel paper consists of a negotiable instrument coupled with a security agreement.

Check A draft drawn by a drawer ordering the drawee bank or financial institution to pay a certain amount of money to the holder on demand.

Checks and balances The national government is composed of three separate branches: the executive, the legislative, and the judicial branches. Each branch of the government exercises a check on the actions of the others.

Choice-of-language clause A clause in a contract designating the official language by which the contract will be interpreted in the event of a future disagreement over the contract's terms.

Choice-of-law clause A clause in a contract designating the law (such as the law of a particular state or nation) that will govern the contract.

Citation A reference to a publication in which a legal authority—such as a statute or a court decision—or other source can be found.

Civil law The branch of law dealing with the definition and enforcement of all private or public rights, as opposed to criminal matters.

Civil law system A system of law derived from that of the Roman Empire and based on a code rather than case law; the predominant system of law in the nations of continental Europe and the nations that were once their colonies. In the United States, Louisiana is the only state that has a civil law system.

Claim As a verb, to assert or demand. As a noun, a right to payment.

Clearinghouse A system or place where banks exchange checks and drafts drawn on each other and settle daily balances.

Click-on agreement An agreement that arises when a buyer, engaging in a transaction on a computer, indicates his or her assent to be bound by the terms of an offer by clicking on a button that says, for example, "I agree"; sometimes referred to as a *click-on license* or a *click-wrap agreement.*

Close corporation A corporation whose shareholders are limited to a small group of persons, often including only family members. The rights of shareholders of a close corporation usually are restricted regarding the transfer of shares to others.

Closed shop A firm that requires union membership by its workers as a condition of employment. The closed shop was made illegal by the Labor-Management Relations Act of 1947.

Closing The final step in the sale of real estate—also called settlement or closing escrow. The escrow agent coordinates the closing with the recording of deeds, the obtaining of title insurance, and other concurrent closing activities. A number of costs must be paid, in cash, at the time of closing, and they can range from several hundred to several thousand dollars, depending on the amount of the mortgage loan and other conditions of the sale.

Closing argument An argument made after the plaintiff and defendant have rested their cases. Closing arguments are made prior to the jury charges.

Codicil A written supplement or modification to a will. A codicil must be executed with the same formalities as a will.

Collateral Under Article 9 of the Uniform Commercial Code, the property subject to a security interest.

Collateral promise A secondary promise that is ancillary (subsidiary) to a principal transaction or primary contractual relationship, such as a promise made by one person to pay the debts of another if the latter fails to perform. A collateral promise normally must be in writing to be enforceable.

Collecting bank Any bank handling an item for collection, except the payor bank.

Collective bargaining The process by which labor and management negotiate the terms and conditions of employment, including working hours and workplace conditions.

Collective mark A mark used by members of a cooperative, association, or other organization to certify the region, materials, mode of manufacture, quality, or accuracy of the specific goods or services. Examples of collective marks include the labor union marks found on tags of certain products and the credits of movies, which indicate the various associations and organizations that participated in the making of the movies.

Comity A deference by which one nation gives effect to the laws and judicial decrees of another nation. This recognition is based primarily on respect.

Comment period A period of time following an administrative agency's publication or a notice of a proposed rule during which private parties may comment in writing on the agency proposal in an effort to influence agency policy. The agency takes any comments received into consideration when drafting the final version of the regulation.

Commerce clause The provision in Article I, Section 8, of the U.S. Constitution that gives Congress the power to regulate interstate commerce.

Commercial impracticability A doctrine under which a seller may be excused from performing a contract when (1) a contingency occurs, (2) the contingency's occurrence makes performance impracticable, and (3) the nonoccurrence of the contingency was a basic assumption on which the contract was made. Despite the fact that UCC 2–615 expressly frees only sellers under this doctrine, courts have not distinguished between buyers and sellers in applying it.

Commercial paper *See* Negotiable instrument

Commingle To mix together. To put funds or goods together into one mass so that the funds or goods are so mixed that they no longer have separate identities. In corporate law, if personal and corporate interests are commingled to the extent that the corporation has no separate identity, a court may "pierce the corporate veil" and expose the shareholders to personal liability.

Common area In landlord-tenant law, a portion of the premises over which the landlord retains control and maintenance responsibilities. Common areas may include stairs, lobbies, garages, hallways, and other areas in common use.

Common carrier A carrier that holds itself out or undertakes to carry persons or goods of all persons indifferently, or of all who choose to employ it.

Common law That body of law developed from custom or judicial decisions in English and U.S. courts, not attributable to a legislature.

Common stock Shares of ownership in a corporation that give the owner of the stock a proportionate interest in the corporation with regard to control, earnings, and net assets; shares of common stock are lowest in priority with respect to payment of dividends and distribution of the corporation's assets on dissolution.

Community property A form of concurrent ownership of property in which each spouse technically owns an undivided one-half interest in property acquired during the marriage. This form of joint ownership occurs in only a minority of states and Puerto Rico.

Comparative negligence A theory in tort law under which the liability for injuries resulting from negligent acts is shared by all parties who were negligent (including the injured party), on the basis of each person's proportionate negligence.

Compensatory damages A money award equivalent to the actual value of injuries or damages sustained by the aggrieved party.

Complaint The pleading made by a plaintiff alleging wrongdoing on the part of the defendant; the document that, when filed with a court, initiates a lawsuit.

Complete performance Performance of a contract strictly in accordance with the contract's terms.

Composition agreement *See* Creditors' composition agreement

Computer crime Any wrongful act that is directed against computers and computer parties, or wrongful use or abuse of computers or software.

Concentrated industry An industry in which a large percentage of market sales is controlled by either a single firm or a small number of firms.

Concurrent conditions Conditions in a contract that must occur or be performed at the same time; they are mutually dependent. No obligations arise until these conditions are simultaneously performed.

Concurrent jurisdiction Jurisdiction that exists when two different courts have the power to hear a case. For example, some cases can be heard in either a federal or a state court.

Concurrent ownership Joint ownership.

Concurring opinion A written opinion outlining the views of a judge or justice to make or emphasize a point that was not made or emphasized in the majority opinion.

Condemnation The process of taking private property for public use through the government's power of eminent domain.

Condition A possible future event, the occurrence or nonoccurrence of which will trigger the performance of a legal obligation or terminate an existing obligation under a contract.

Condition precedent A condition in a contract that must be met before a party's promise becomes absolute.

Condition subsequent A condition in a contract that operates to terminate a party's absolute promise to perform.

Confession of judgment The act of a debtor in permitting a judgment to be entered against him or her by a creditor, for an agreed sum, without the institution of legal proceedings.

Confiscation A government's taking of privately owned business or personal property without a proper public purpose or an award of just compensation.

Conforming goods Goods that conform to contract specifications.

Confusion The mixing together of goods belonging to two or more owners so that the separately owned goods cannot be identified.

Conglomerate merger A merger between firms that do not compete with each other because they are in different markets (as opposed to horizontal and vertical mergers).

Consent Voluntary agreement to a proposition or an act of another. A concurrence of wills.

Consequential damages Special damages that compensate for a loss that is not direct or immediate (for example, lost profits). The special damages must have been reasonably foreseeable at the time the breach or injury occurred in order for the plaintiff to collect them.

Consideration Generally, the value given in return for a promise or a performance. The consideration, which must be present to make the contract legally binding, must be something of legally sufficient value and bargained for.

Consignment A transaction in which an owner of goods (the consignor) delivers the goods to another (the consignee) for the consignee to sell. The consignee pays the consignor for the goods when they are sold by the consignee.

Consolidation A contractual and statutory process in which two or more corporations join to become a completely new corporation. The original corporations cease to exist, and the new corporation acquires all their assets and liabilities.

Constitutional law Law that is based on the U.S. Constitution and the constitutions of the various states.

Constructive condition A condition in a contract that is neither expressed nor implied by the contract but rather is imposed by law for reasons of justice.

Constructive delivery An act equivalent to the actual, physical delivery of property that cannot be physically delivered because of difficulty or impossibility; for example, the transfer of a key to a safe constructively delivers the contents of the safe.

Constructive discharge A termination of employment brought about by making an employee's working conditions so intolerable that the employee reasonably feels compelled to leave.

Constructive eviction A form of eviction that occurs when a landlord fails to perform adequately any of the undertakings (such as providing heat in the winter) required by the lease, thereby making the tenant's further use and enjoyment of the property exceedingly difficult or impossible.

Constructive trust An equitable trust that is imposed in the interests of fairness and justice when someone wrongfully holds legal title to property. A court may require the owner to hold the property in trust for the person or persons who rightfully should own the property.

Consumer credit Credit extended primarily for personal or household use.

Consumer-debtor An individual whose debts are primarily consumer debts (debts for purchases made primarily for personal or household use).

Consumer goods Goods that are primarily for personal or household use.

Consumer law The body of statutes, agency rules, and judicial decisions protecting consumers of goods and services from dangerous manufacturing techniques, mislabeling, unfair credit practices, deceptive advertising, and the like. Consumer laws provide remedies and protections that are not ordinarily available to merchants or to businesses.

Contingency fee An attorney's fee that is based on a percentage of the final award received by his or her client as a result of litigation.

Continuation statement A statement that, if filed within six months prior to the expiration date of the original financing statement, continues the perfection of the original security interest for another five years. The perfection of a security interest can be continued in the same manner indefinitely.

Contract An agreement that can be enforced in court; formed by two or more parties, each of whom agrees to perform or to refrain from performing some act now or in the future.

Contract implied in law *See* Quasi contract

Contract under seal A formal agreement in which the seal is a substitute for consideration. A court will not invalidate a contract under seal for lack of consideration.

Contractual capacity The threshold mental capacity required by the law for a party who enters into a contract to be bound by that contract.

Contribution *See* Right of contribution

Contributory negligence A theory in tort law under which a complaining party's own negligence contributed to or caused his or her injuries. Contributory negligence is an absolute bar to recovery in a minority of jurisdictions.

Conversion The wrongful taking, using, or retaining possession of personal property that belongs to another.

Convertible bond A bond that can be exchanged for a specified number of shares of common stock under certain conditions.

Conveyance The transfer of a title to land from one person to another by deed; a document (such as a deed) by which an interest in land is transferred from one person to another.

Conviction The outcome of a criminal trial in which the defendant has been found guilty of the crime.

Cooperative An association that is organized to provide an economic service to its members (or shareholders). An incorporated cooperative is a nonprofit corporation. It will make distributions of dividends, or profits, to its owners on the basis of their transactions with the cooperative rather than on the basis of the amount of capital they contributed. Examples of cooperatives are consumer purchasing cooperatives, credit cooperatives, and farmers' cooperatives.

Co-ownership Joint ownership.

Copyright The exclusive right of authors to publish, print, or sell an intellectual production for a statutory period of time. A copyright has the same monopolistic nature as a patent or trademark, but it differs in that it applies exclusively to works of art, literature, and other works of authorship, including computer programs.

Corporate governance The relationship between a corporation and its shareholders—specifically, a system that details the distribution of rights and responsibilities of those within the corporation and spells out the rules and procedures for making corporate decisions.

Corporate social responsibility The concept that corporations can and should act ethically and be accountable to society for their actions.

Corporation A legal entity formed in compliance with statutory requirements. The entity is distinct from its shareholders-owners.

Cosign The act of signing a document (such as a note promising to pay another in return for a loan or other benefit) jointly with another person and thereby assuming liability for performing what was promised in the document.

Cost-benefit analysis A decision-making technique that involves weighing the costs of a given action against the benefits of the action.

Co-surety A joint surety. One who assumes liability jointly with another surety for the payment of an obligation.

Counteradvertising New advertising that is undertaken pursuant to a Federal Trade Commission order for the purpose of correcting earlier false claims that were made about a product.

Counterclaim A claim made by a defendant in a civil lawsuit that in effect sues the plaintiff.

Counteroffer An offeree's response to an offer in which the offeree rejects the original offer and at the same time makes a new offer.

Course of dealing Prior conduct between parties to a contract that establishes a common basis for their understanding.

Course of performance The conduct that occurs under the terms of a particular agreement; such conduct indicates what the parties to an agreement intended it to mean.

Court of equity A court that decides controversies and administers justice according to the rules, principles, and precedents of equity.

Court of law A court in which the only remedies that could be granted were things of value, such as money damages. In the early English king's courts, courts of law were distinct from courts of equity.

Covenant against encumbrances A grantor's assurance that on land conveyed there are no encumbrances—that is, that no third parties have rights to or interests in the land that would diminish its value to the grantee.

Covenant not to compete A contractual promise to refrain from competing with another party for a certain period of time (not excessive in duration) and within a reasonable geographic area. Although covenants not to compete restrain trade, they are commonly found in partnership agreements, business sale agreements, and employment contracts. If they are ancillary to such agreements, covenants not to compete will normally be enforced by the courts unless the time period or geographic area is deemed unreasonable.

Covenant not to sue An agreement to substitute a contractual obligation for some other type of legal action based on a valid claim.

Covenant of quiet enjoyment A promise by a grantor (or landlord) that the grantee (or tenant) will not be evicted or disturbed by the grantor or a person having a lien or superior title.

Covenant of the right to convey A grantor's assurance that he or she has sufficient capacity and title to convey the estate that he or she undertakes to convey by deed.

Covenant running with the land An executory promise made between a grantor and a grantee to which they and subsequent owners of the land are bound.

Cover A buyer or lessee's purchase on the open market of goods to substitute for those promised but never delivered by the seller. Under the Uniform Commercial Code, if the cost of cover exceeds the cost of the contract goods, the buyer or lessee can recover the difference, plus incidental and consequential damages.

Cram-down provision A provision of the Bankruptcy Code that allows a court to confirm a debtor's Chapter 11 reorganization plan even though only one class of creditors has accepted it. To exercise the court's right under this provision, the court must demonstrate that the plan does not discriminate unfairly against any creditors and is fair and equitable.

Creditor A person to whom a debt is owed by another person (the debtor).

Creditor beneficiary A third party beneficiary who has rights in a contract made by the debtor and a third person. The terms of the contract obligate the third person to pay the debt owed to the creditor. The creditor beneficiary can enforce the debt against either party.

Creditors' composition agreement An agreement formed between a debtor and his or her creditors in which the creditors agree to accept a lesser sum than that owed by the debtor in full satisfaction of the debt.

Crime A wrong against society proclaimed in a statute and, if committed, punishable by society through fines and/or imprisonment—and, in some cases, death.

Criminal act *See Actus reus*

Criminal intent *See Mens rea*

Criminal law Law that defines and governs actions that constitute crimes. Generally, criminal law has to do

with wrongful actions committed against society for which society demands redress.
Cross-border pollution Pollution across national boundaries; air and water degradation in one nation resulting from pollution-causing activities in a neighboring country.
Cross-collateralization The use of an asset that is not the subject of a loan to collateralize that loan.
Cross-examination The questioning of an opposing witness during the trial.
Cumulative voting A method of shareholder voting designed to allow minority shareholders to be represented on the board of directors. With cumulative voting, the number of members of the board to be elected is multiplied by the total number of voting shares held. The result equals the number of votes a shareholder has, and this total can be cast for one or more nominees for director.
Cure Under the Uniform Commercial Code, the right of a party who tenders nonconforming performance to correct his or her performance within the contract period.
Cyber crime A crime that occurs online, in the virtual community of the Internet, as opposed to the physical world.
Cyber mark A trademark in cyberspace.
Cyber tort A tort committed via the Internet.
Cyberlaw An informal term used to refer to all laws governing electronic communications and transactions, particularly those conducted via the Internet.
Cybernotary A legally recognized authority that can certify the validity of digital signatures.
Cybersquatting The act of registering a domain name that is the same as, or confusingly similar to, the trademark of another and then offering to sell that domain name back to the trademark owner.
Cyberterrorist A hacker whose purpose is to exploit a target computer for a serious impact, such as the corruption of a program to sabotage a business.

D

Damages Money sought as a remedy for a breach of contract or for a tortious act.
Debenture bond A bond for which no specific assets of the corporation are pledged as backing; rather, the bond is backed by the general credit rating of the corporation, plus any assets that can be seized if the corporation allows the debentures to go into default.
Debit card A plastic card issued by a financial institution that allows the user to access his or her accounts online via automated teller machines.
Debtor Under Article 9 of the Uniform Commercial Code, a debtor is any party who owes payment or performance of a secured obligation, whether or not the party actually owns or has rights in the collateral.
Debtor in possession (DIP) In Chapter 11 bankruptcy proceedings, a debtor who is allowed to continue in possession of the estate in property (the business) and to continue business operations.
Deceptive advertising Advertising that misleads consumers, either by making unjustified claims concerning a product's performance or by omitting a material fact concerning the product's composition or performance.
Declaratory judgment A court's judgment on a justiciable controversy when the plaintiff is in doubt as to his or her legal rights; a binding adjudication of the rights and status of litigants even though no consequential relief is awarded.
Decree The judgment of a court of equity.
Deed A document by which title to property (usually real property) is passed.
Defalcation The misuse of funds.
Defamation Any published or publicly spoken false statement that causes injury to another's good name, reputation, or character.
Default The failure to observe a promise or discharge an obligation. The term is commonly used to mean the failure to pay a debt when it is due.
Default judgment A judgment entered by a court against a defendant who has failed to appear in court to answer or defend against the plaintiff's claim.
Defendant One against whom a lawsuit is brought; the accused person in a criminal proceeding.
Defense Reasons that a defendant offers in an action or suit as to why the plaintiff should not obtain what he or she is seeking.
Deficiency judgment A judgment against a debtor for the amount of a debt remaining unpaid after collateral has been repossessed and sold.
Delegatee One to whom contract duties are delegated by another, called the delegator.
Delegation The transfer of a contractual duty to a third party. The party delegating the duty (the delegator) to the third party (the delegatee) is still obliged to perform on the contract should the delegatee fail to perform.
Delegation doctrine A doctrine based on Article I, Section 8, of the U.S. Constitution, which has been construed to allow Congress to delegate some of its power to make and implement laws to administrative agencies. The delegation is considered to be proper as long as Congress sets standards outlining the scope of the agency's authority.
Delegator One who delegates his or her duties under a contract to another, called the delegatee.
Delivery In contract law, one party's act of placing the subject matter of the contract within the other party's possession or control.
Delivery order A written order to deliver goods directed to a warehouser, carrier, or other person who, in the ordinary course of business, issues warehouse receipts or bills of lading [UCC 7–102(1)(d)].
Demand deposit Funds (accepted by a bank) subject to immediate withdrawal, in contrast to a time

deposit, which requires that a depositor wait a specific time before withdrawing or pay a penalty for early withdrawal.

De novo Anew; afresh; a second time. In a hearing *de novo*, an appellate court hears the case as a court of original jurisdiction—that is, as if the case had not previously been tried and a decision rendered.

Depositary bank The first bank to receive a check for payment.

Deposition The testimony of a party to a lawsuit or a witness taken under oath before a trial.

Destination contract A contract in which the seller is required to ship the goods by carrier and deliver them at a particular destination. The seller assumes liability for any losses or damage to the goods until they are tendered at the destination specified in the contract.

Devise To make a gift of real property by will.

Digital cash Funds contained on computer software, in the form of secure programs stored on microchips and other computer devices.

Dilution With respect to trademarks, a doctrine under which distinctive or famous trademarks are protected from certain unauthorized uses of the marks regardless of a showing of competition or a likelihood of confusion. Congress created a federal cause of action for dilution in 1995 with the passage of the Federal Trademark Dilution Act.

Direct examination The examination of a witness by the attorney who calls the witness to the stand to testify on behalf of the attorney's client.

Directed verdict *See* Motion for a directed verdict

Disaffirmance The legal avoidance, or setting aside, of a contractual obligation.

Discharge The termination of an obligation. (1) In contract law, discharge occurs when the parties have fully performed their contractual obligations or when events, conduct of the parties, or operation of the law releases the parties from performance. (2) In bankruptcy proceedings, the extinction of the debtor's dischargeable debts.

Discharge in bankruptcy The release of a debtor from all debts that are provable, except those specifically excepted from discharge by statute.

Disclosed principal A principal whose identity is known to a third party at the time the agent makes a contract with the third party.

Discovery A phase in the litigation process during which the opposing parties may obtain information from each other and from third parties prior to trial.

Dishonor To refuse to accept or pay a draft or a promissory note when it is properly presented. An instrument is dishonored when presentment is properly made and acceptance or payment is refused or cannot be obtained within the prescribed time.

Disparagement of property An economically injurious false statement made about another's product or property. A general term for torts that are more specifically referred to as slander of quality or slander of title.

Disparate-impact discrimination A form of employment discrimination that results from certain employer practices or procedures that, although not discriminatory on their face, have a discriminatory effect.

Disparate-treatment discrimination A form of employment discrimination that results when an employer intentionally discriminates against employees who are members of protected classes.

Dissenting opinion A written opinion by a judge or justice who disagrees with the majority opinion.

Dissociation The severance of the relationship between a partner and a partnership when the partner ceases to be associated with the carrying on of the partnership business.

Dissolution The formal disbanding of a partnership or a corporation. It can take place by (1) acts of the partners or, in a corporation, of the shareholders and board of directors; (2) the death of a partner; (3) the expiration of a time period stated in a partnership agreement or a certificate of incorporation; or (4) judicial decree.

Distributed network A network that can be used by persons located (distributed) around the country or the globe to share computer files.

Distribution agreement A contract between a seller and a distributor of the seller's products setting out the terms and conditions of the distributorship.

Distributorship A business arrangement that is established when a manufacturer licenses a dealer to sell its product. An example of a distributorship is an automobile dealership.

Diversity of citizenship Under Article III, Section 2, of the Constitution, a basis for federal court jurisdiction over a lawsuit between (1) citizens of different states, (2) a foreign country and citizens of a state or of different states, or (3) citizens of a state and citizens or subjects of a foreign country. The amount in controversy must be more than $75,000 before a federal court can take jurisdiction in such cases.

Divestiture The act of selling one or more of a company's parts, such as a subsidiary or plant; often mandated by the courts in merger or monopolization cases.

Dividend A distribution to corporate shareholders of corporate profits or income, disbursed in proportion to the number of shares held.

Docket The list of cases entered on a court's calendar and thus scheduled to be heard by the court.

Document of title Paper exchanged in the regular course of business that evidences the right to possession of goods (for example, a bill of lading or a warehouse receipt).

Domain name The series of letters and symbols used to identify site operators on the Internet; Internet "addresses."

Domestic corporation In a given state, a corporation that does business in, and is organized under the laws of, that state.

Domestic relations court A court that deals with domestic (household) relationships, such as adoption, divorce, support payments, child custody, and the like.

Donee beneficiary A third party beneficiary who has rights under a contract as a direct result of the intention of the contract parties to make a gift to the third party.

Double jeopardy A situation occurring when a person is tried twice for the same criminal offense; prohibited by the Fifth Amendment to the U.S. Constitution.

Double taxation A feature (and disadvantage) of the corporate form of business. Because a corporation is a separate legal entity, corporate profits are taxed by state and federal governments. Dividends are again taxable as ordinary income to the shareholders receiving them.

Draft Any instrument (such as a check) drawn on a drawee (such as a bank) that orders the drawee to pay a certain sum of money, usually to a third party (the payee), on demand or at a definite future time.

Dram shop act A state statute that imposes liability on the owners of bars and taverns, as well as those who serve alcoholic drinks to the public, for injuries resulting from accidents caused by intoxicated persons when the sellers or servers of alcoholic drinks contributed to the intoxication.

Drawee The party that is ordered to pay a draft or check. With a check, a financial institution is always the drawee.

Drawer The party that initiates a draft (writes a check, for example), thereby ordering the drawee to pay.

Due diligence A required standard of care that certain professionals, such as accountants, must meet to avoid liability for securities violations. Under securities law, an accountant will be deemed to have exercised due diligence if he or she followed generally accepted accounting principles and generally accepted auditing standards and had, "after reasonable investigation, reasonable grounds to believe and did believe, at the time such part of the registration statement became effective, that the statements therein were true and that there was no omission of a material fact required to be stated therein or necessary to make the statements therein not misleading."

Due process clause The provisions of the Fifth and Fourteenth Amendments to the Constitution that guarantee that no person shall be deprived of life, liberty, or property without due process of law. Similar clauses are found in most state constitutions.

Dumping The selling of goods in a foreign country at a price below the price charged for the same goods in the domestic market.

Durable power of attorney A document that authorizes a person to act on behalf of a person—write checks, collect insurance proceeds, and otherwise manage the person's affairs, including health care—when he or she becomes incapacitated. Spouses often give each other durable power of attorney and, if they are advanced in age, may give a second such power of attorney to an older child.

Duress Unlawful pressure brought to bear on a person, causing the person to perform an act that he or she would not otherwise perform.

Duty of care The duty of all persons, as established by tort law, to exercise a reasonable amount of care in their dealings with others. Failure to exercise due care, which is normally determined by the "reasonable person standard," constitutes the tort of negligence.

E

E-agent A computer program, electronic, or other automated means used to perform specific tasks without review by an individual.

E-commerce Business transacted in cyberspace.

E-contract A contract that is entered into in cyberspace and is evidenced only by electronic impulses (such as those that make up a computer's memory), rather than, for example, a typewritten form.

E-evidence A type of evidence that consists of computer-generated or electronically recorded information, including e-mail, voice mail, spreadsheets, word-processing documents, and other data.

E-money Prepaid funds recorded on a computer or a card (such as a *smart card*).

E-signature As defined by the Uniform Electronic Transactions Act, "an electronic sound, symbol, or process attached to or logically associated with a record and executed or adopted by a person with the intent to sign the record."

Early neutral case evaluation A form of alternative dispute resolution in which a neutral third party evaluates the strengths and weakness of the disputing parties' positions; the evaluator's opinion forms the basis for negotiating a settlement.

Easement A nonpossessory right to use another's property in a manner established by either express or implied agreement.

Electronic fund transfer (EFT) A transfer of funds with the use of an electronic terminal, a telephone, a computer, or magnetic tape.

Emancipation In regard to minors, the act of being freed from parental control; occurs when a child's parent or legal guardian relinquishes the legal right to exercise control over the child. Normally, a minor who leaves home to support himself or herself is considered emancipated.

Embezzlement The fraudulent appropriation of money or other property by a person to whom the money or property has been entrusted.

Eminent domain The power of a government to take land for public use from private citizens for just compensation.

Employee A person who works for an employer for a salary or for wages.

Employer An individual or business entity that hires employees, pays them salaries or wages, and exercises control over their work.

Employment at will A common law doctrine under which either party may terminate an employment relationship at any time for any reason, unless a contract specifies otherwise.
Employment discrimination Treating employees or job applicants unequally on the basis of race, color, national origin, religion, gender, age, or disability; prohibited by federal statutes.
Enabling legislation A statute enacted by Congress that authorizes the creation of an administrative agency and specifies the name, composition, purpose, and powers of the agency being created.
Encryption The process by which a message (plaintext) is transformed into something (ciphertext) that the sender and receiver intend third parties not to understand.
Endowment insurance A type of insurance that combines life insurance with an investment so that if the insured outlives the policy, the face value is paid to him or her; if the insured does not outlive the policy, the face value is paid to his or her beneficiary.
Entrapment In criminal law, a defense in which the defendant claims that he or she was induced by a public official—usually an undercover agent or police officer—to commit a crime that he or she would otherwise not have committed.
Entrepreneur One who initiates and assumes the financial risks of a new enterprise and who undertakes to provide or control its management.
Entrustment rule The transfer of goods to a merchant who deals in goods of that kind and who may transfer those goods and all rights to them to a buyer in the ordinary course of business [UCC 2–403(2)].
Environmental impact statement (EIS) A statement required by the National Environmental Policy Act for any major federal action that will significantly affect the quality of the environment. The statement must analyze the action's impact on the environment and explore alternative actions that might be taken.
Environmental law The body of statutory, regulatory, and common law relating to the protection of the environment.
Equal dignity rule In most states, a rule stating that express authority given to an agent must be in writing if the contract to be made on behalf of the principal is required to be in writing.
Equal protection clause The provision in the Fourteenth Amendment to the Constitution that guarantees that no state will "deny to any person within its jurisdiction the equal protection of the laws." This clause mandates that state governments treat similarly situated individuals in a similar manner.
Equitable maxims General propositions or principles of law that have to do with fairness (equity).
Equity of redemption The right of a mortgagor who has breached the mortgage agreement to redeem or purchase the property prior to foreclosure proceedings.
Escheat The transfer of property to the state when the owner of the property dies without heirs.
Escrow account An account that is generally held in the name of the depositor and escrow agent; the funds in the account are paid to a third person only on fulfillment of the escrow condition.
Establishment clause The provision in the First Amendment to the U.S. Constitution that prohibits Congress from creating any law "respecting an establishment of religion."
Estate The interest that a person has in real and personal property.
Estate planning Planning in advance how one's property and obligations should be transferred on one's death. Wills and trusts are two basic devices used in the process of estate planning.
Estop To bar, impede, or preclude.
Estoppel The principle that a party's own acts prevent him or her from claiming a right to the detriment of another who was entitled to and did rely on those acts. *See also* Agency by estoppel; Promissory estoppel
Estray statute A statute defining finders' rights in property when the true owners are unknown.
Ethical reasoning A reasoning process in which an individual links his or her moral convictions or ethical standards to the particular situation at hand.
Ethics Moral principles and values applied to social behavior.
Evidence Proof offered at trial—in the form of testimony, documents, records, exhibits, objects, and the like—for the purpose of convincing the court or jury of the truth of a contention.
Eviction A landlord's act of depriving a tenant of possession of the leased premises.
Exclusionary rule In criminal procedure, a rule under which any evidence that is obtained in violation of the accused's constitutional rights guaranteed by the Fourth, Fifth, and Sixth Amendments, as well as any evidence derived from illegally obtained evidence, will not be admissible in court.
Exclusive distributorship A distributorship in which the seller and the distributor of the seller's products agree that the distributor has the exclusive right to distribute the seller's products in a certain geographic area.
Exclusive jurisdiction Jurisdiction that exists when a case can be heard only in a particular court or type of court, such as a federal court or a state court.
Exclusive-dealing contract An agreement under which a seller forbids a buyer to purchase products from the seller's competitors.
Exculpatory clause A clause that releases a contractual party from liability in the event of monetary or physical injury, no matter who is at fault.
Executed contract A contract that has been completely performed by both parties.
Execution An action to carry into effect the directions in a court decree or judgment.
Executive agency An administrative agency within the executive branch of government. At the federal

level, executive agencies are those within the cabinet departments.

Executor A person appointed by a testator to see that his or her will is administered appropriately.

Executory contract A contract that has not as yet been fully performed.

Export To sell products to buyers located in other countries.

Express authority Authority expressly given by one party to another. In agency law, an agent has express authority to act for a principal if both parties agree, orally or in writing, that an agency relationship exists in which the agent had the power (authority) to act in the place of, and on behalf of, the principal.

Express contract A contract in which the terms of the agreement are fully and explicitly stated in words, oral or written.

Express warranty A seller's or lessor's oral or written promise, ancillary to an underlying sales or lease agreement, as to the quality, description, or performance of the goods being sold or leased.

Expropriation The seizure by a government of privately owned business or personal property for a proper public purpose and with just compensation.

Extension clause A clause in a time instrument that allows the instrument's date of maturity to be extended into the future.

F

F.A.S. Free alongside. A contract term that requires the seller, at his or her own expense and risk, to deliver the goods alongside the ship before risk passes to the buyer.

F.O.B. Free on board. A contract term that indicates that the selling price of the goods includes transportation costs (and that the seller carries the risk of loss) to the specific F.O.B. place named in the contract. The place can be either the place of initial shipment (for example, the seller's city or place of business) or the place of destination (for example, the buyer's city or place of business).

Family limited liability partnership (FLLP) A limited liability partnership (LLP) in which the majority of the partners are persons related to each other, essentially as spouses, parents, grandparents, siblings, cousins, nephews, or nieces. A person acting in a fiduciary capacity for persons so related could also be a partner. All of the partners must be natural persons or persons acting in a fiduciary capacity for the benefit of natural persons.

Federal form of government A system of government in which the states form a union and the sovereign power is divided between a central government and the member states.

Federal question A question that pertains to the U.S. Constitution, acts of Congress, or treaties. A federal question provides a basis for federal jurisdiction.

Federal Reserve System A network of twelve district banks, located around the country and headed by the Federal Reserve Board of Governors. Most banks in the United States have Federal Reserve accounts.

Federal Rules of Civil Procedure (FRCP) The rules controlling procedural matters in civil trials brought before the federal district courts.

Fee simple An absolute form of property ownership entitling the property owner to use, possess, or dispose of the property as he or she chooses during his or her lifetime. On death, the interest in the property passes to the owner's heirs; a fee simple absolute.

Fee simple absolute An ownership interest in land in which the owner has the greatest possible aggregation of rights, privileges, and power. Ownership in fee simple absolute is limited absolutely to a person and his or her heirs.

Felony A crime—such as arson, murder, rape, or robbery—that carries the most severe sanctions, usually ranging from one year in a state or federal prison to the forfeiture of one's life.

Fictitious payee A payee on a negotiable instrument whom the maker or drawer does not intend to have an interest in the instrument. Indorsements by fictitious payees are not treated as unauthorized under Article 3 of the Uniform Commercial Code.

Fiduciary As a noun, a person having a duty created by his or her undertaking to act primarily for another's benefit in matters connected with the undertaking. As an adjective, a relationship founded on trust and confidence.

Fiduciary duty The duty, imposed on a fiduciary by virtue of his or her position, to act primarily for another's benefit.

Filtering software A computer program that includes a pattern through which data are passed. When designed to block access to certain Web sites, the pattern blocks the retrieval of a site whose URL or key words are on a list within the program.

Final order The final decision of an administrative agency on an issue. If no appeal is taken, or if the case is not reviewed or considered anew by the agency commission, the administrative law judge's initial order becomes the final order of the agency.

Financial institution An organization authorized to do business under state or federal laws relating to financial institutions. Financial institutions may include banks, savings and loan associations, credit unions, and other business entities that directly or indirectly hold accounts belonging to consumers.

Financing statement A document prepared by a secured creditor and filed with the appropriate government official to give notice to the public that the creditor claims an interest in collateral belonging to the debtor named in the statement. The financing statement must contain the names and addresses of both the debtor and the creditor, and describe the collateral by type or item.

Firm offer An offer (by a merchant) that is irrevocable without consideration for a period of time (not longer than three months). A firm offer by a merchant must be in writing and must be signed by the offeror.

Fitness for a particular purpose *See* Implied warranty of fitness for a particular purpose

Fixed-term tenancy A type of tenancy under which property is leased for a specified period of time, such as a month, a year, or a period of years; also called a *tenancy for years.*

Fixture A thing that was once personal property but that has become attached to real property in such a way that it takes on the characteristics of real property and becomes part of that real property.

Floating lien A security interest in proceeds, after-acquired property, or property purchased under a line of credit (or all three); a security interest in collateral that is retained even when the collateral changes in character, classification, or location.

Forbearance The act of refraining from an action that one has a legal right to undertake.

Force majeure (pronounced mah-*zhure*) **clause** A provision in a contract stipulating that certain unforeseen events—such as war, political upheavals, acts of God, or other events—will excuse a party from liability for nonperformance of contractual obligations.

Foreclosure A proceeding in which a mortgagee either takes title to or forces the sale of the mortgagor's property in satisfaction of a debt.

Foreign corporation In a given state, a corporation that does business in the state without being incorporated therein.

Foreseeable risk In negligence law, the risk of harm or injury to another that a person of ordinary intelligence and prudence should have reasonably anticipated or foreseen when undertaking an action or refraining from undertaking an action.

Forfeiture The termination of a lease, according to its terms or the terms of a statute, when one of the parties fails to fulfill a condition under the lease and thereby breaches it.

Forgery The fraudulent making or altering of any writing in a way that changes the legal rights and liabilities of another.

Formal contract A contract that by law requires a specific form, such as being executed under seal, to be valid.

Forum A jurisdiction, court, or place in which disputes are litigated and legal remedies are sought.

Forum-selection clause A provision in a contract designating the court, jurisdiction, or tribunal that will decide any disputes arising under the contract.

Franchise Any arrangement in which the owner of a trademark, trade name, or copyright licenses another to use that trademark, trade name, or copyright, under specified conditions or limitations, in the selling of goods and services.

Franchise tax A state or local government tax on the right and privilege of carrying on a business in the form of a corporation.

Franchisee One receiving a license to use another's (the franchisor's) trademark, trade name, or copyright in the sale of goods and services.

Franchisor One licensing another (the franchisee) to use his or her trademark, trade name, or copyright in the sale of goods or services.

Fraud Any misrepresentation, either by misstatement or omission of a material fact, knowingly made with the intention of deceiving another and on which a reasonable person would and does rely to his or her detriment.

Fraud in the execution In the law of negotiable instruments, a type of fraud that occurs when a person is deceived into signing a negotiable instrument, believing that he or she is signing something else (such as a receipt); also called fraud in the inception. Fraud in the execution is a universal defense to payment on a negotiable instrument.

Fraud in the inducement Ordinary fraud. In the law of negotiable instruments, fraud in the inducement occurs when a person issues a negotiable instrument based on false statements by the other party. The issuing party will be able to avoid payment on that instrument unless the holder is a holder in due course; in other words, fraud in the inducement is a personal defense to payment on a negotiable instrument.

Fraudulent misrepresentation (fraud) Any misrepresentation, either by misstatement or omission of a material fact, knowingly made with the intention of deceiving another and on which a reasonable person would and does rely to his or her detriment.

Free exercise clause The provision in the First Amendment to the U.S. Constitution that prohibits Congress from making any law "prohibiting the free exercise" of religion.

Free writing prospectus A free writing prospectus is any type of written, electronic, or graphic offer that describes the issuing corporation or its securities and includes a legend indicating that the investor may obtain the prospectus at the SEC's Web site.

Frustration of purpose A court-created doctrine under which a party to a contract will be relieved of his or her duty to perform when the objective purpose for performance no longer exists (due to reasons beyond that party's control).

Full faith and credit clause A clause in Article IV, Section 1, of the Constitution that provides that "Full Faith and Credit shall be given in each State to the public Acts, Records, and Judicial Proceedings of every other State." The clause ensures that rights established under deeds, wills, contracts, and the like in one state will be honored by the other states and that any judicial decision with respect to such property rights will be honored and enforced in all states.

Full warranty A warranty as to full performance covering generally both labor and materials.

Fungible goods Goods that are alike by physical nature, by agreement, or by trade usage. Examples of fungible goods are wheat, oil, and wine that are identical in type and quality.

G

Garnishment A legal process used by a creditor to collect a debt by seizing property of the debtor (such as wages) that is being held by a third party (such as the debtor's employer).

General jurisdiction Exists when a court's subject-matter jurisdiction is not restricted. A court of general jurisdiction normally can hear any type of case.

General partner In a limited partnership, a partner who assumes responsibility for the management of the partnership and liability for all partnership debts.

General partnership *See* Partnership

Generally accepted accounting principles (GAAP) The conventions, rules, and procedures that define accepted accounting practices at a particular time. The source of the principles is the Financial Accounting Standards Board.

Generally accepted auditing standards (GAAS) Standards concerning an auditor's professional qualities and the judgment exercised by him or her in the performance of an examination and report. The source of the standards is the American Institute of Certified Public Accountants.

Genuineness of assent Knowing and voluntary assent to the terms of a contract. If a contract is formed as a result of a mistake, misrepresentation, undue influence, or duress, genuineness of assent is lacking, and the contract will be voidable.

Gift Any voluntary transfer of property made without consideration, past or present.

Gift *causa mortis* A gift made in contemplation of death. If the donor does not die of that ailment, the gift is revoked.

Gift *inter vivos* A gift made during one's lifetime and not in contemplation of imminent death, in contrast to a gift *causa mortis*.

Good faith Under the Uniform Commercial Code, good faith means honesty in fact; with regard to merchants, good faith means honesty in fact *and* the observance of reasonable commercial standards of fair dealing in the trade.

Good faith purchaser A purchaser who buys without notice of any circumstance that would put a person of ordinary prudence on inquiry as to whether the seller has valid title to the goods being sold.

Good Samaritan statute A state statute that provides that persons who rescue or provide emergency services to others in peril—unless they do so recklessly, thus causing further harm—cannot be sued for negligence.

Grand jury A group of citizens called to decide, after hearing the state's evidence, whether a reasonable basis (probable cause) exists for believing that a crime has been committed and whether a trial ought to be held.

Grant deed A deed that simply recites words of consideration and conveyance. Under statute, a grant deed may impliedly warrant that at least the grantor has not conveyed the property's title to someone else.

Grantee One to whom a grant (of land or property, for example) is made.

Grantor A person who makes a grant, such as a transferor of property or the creator of a trust.

Group boycott The refusal to deal with a particular person or firm by a group of competitors; prohibited by the Sherman Act.

Guarantor A person who agrees to satisfy the debt of another (the debtor) only after the principal debtor defaults; a guarantor's liability is thus secondary.

H

Habitability *See* Implied warranty of habitability

Hacker A person who uses one computer to break into another. Professional computer programmers refer to such persons as "crackers."

Health-care power of attorney A document that designates a person who will have the power to choose what type of and how much medical treatment a person who is unable to make such a choice will receive.

Hearsay An oral or written statement made out of court that is later offered in court by a witness (not the person who made the statement) to prove the truth of the matter asserted in the statement. Hearsay is generally inadmissible as evidence.

Hirfindahl-Hirschman Index (HHI) An index of market power used to calculate whether a merger of two businesses will result in sufficient monopoly power to violate antitrust laws.

Historical school A school of legal thought that emphasizes the evolutionary process of law and that looks to the past to discover what the principles of contemporary law should be.

Holder Any person in the possession of an instrument drawn, issued, or indorsed to him or her, to his or her order, to bearer, or in blank.

Holder in due course (HDC) A holder who acquires a negotiable instrument for value; in good faith; and without notice that the instrument is overdue, that it has been dishonored, that any person has a defense against it or a claim to it, or that the instrument contains unauthorized signatures, alterations, or is so irregular or incomplete as to call into question its authenticity.

Holding company A company whose business activity is holding shares in another company.

Holographic will A will written entirely in the signer's handwriting and usually not witnessed.

Homestead exemption A law permitting a debtor to retain the family home, either in its entirety or up to a specified dollar amount, free from the claims of unsecured creditors or trustees in bankruptcy.

Horizontal merger A merger between two firms that are competing in the same market.

Horizontal restraint Any agreement that in some way restrains competition between rival firms competing in the same market.

Hot-cargo agreement An agreement in which employers voluntarily agree with unions not to handle, use, or deal in nonunion-produced goods of other employers; a type of secondary boycott explicitly prohibited by the Labor-Management Reporting and Disclosure Act of 1959.

I

I-9 verification All employers must verify the employment eligibility and identity of any worker hired in the United States. To comply with the law, employers must complete an I-9 Employment Eligibility Verification Form for all new hires within three business days.

I-551 Alien Registration Receipt Commonly referred to as a "green card," the I-551 Alien Registration Receipt is proof that a foreign-born individual is Lawfully Admitted for Permanent Residence in the United States. Persons seeking employment can prove to prospective employers that they are legally within the U.S. by showing this receipt.

Identification In a sale of goods, the express designation of the specific goods provided for in the contract.

Identity theft The act of stealing another's identifying information—such as a name, date of birth, or Social Security number—and using that information to access the victim's financial resources.

Illusory promise A promise made without consideration, which renders the promise unenforceable.

Immunity A status of being exempt, or free, from certain duties or requirements. In criminal law, the state may grant an accused person immunity from prosecution—or agree to prosecute for a lesser offense—if the accused person agrees to give the state information that would assist the state in prosecuting other individuals for crimes. In tort law, freedom from liability for defamatory speech. *See also* Privilege

Implied authority Authority that is created not by an explicit oral or written agreement but by implication. In agency law, implied authority (of the agent) can be conferred by custom, inferred from the position the agent occupies, or implied by virtue of being reasonably necessary to carry out express authority.

Implied warranty A warranty that the law derives by implication or inference from the nature of the transaction or the relative situation or circumstances of the parties.

Implied warranty of fitness for a particular purpose A warranty that goods sold or leased are fit for a particular purpose. The warranty arises when any seller or lessor knows the particular purpose for which a buyer or lessee will use the goods and knows that the buyer or lessee is relying on the skill and judgment of the seller or lessor to select suitable goods.

Implied warranty of habitability An implied promise by a landlord that rented residential premises are fit for human habitation—that is, in a condition that is safe and suitable for people to live in.

Implied warranty of merchantability A warranty that goods being sold or leased are reasonably fit for the ordinary purpose for which they are sold or leased, are properly packaged and labeled, and are of fair quality. The warranty automatically arises in every sale or lease of goods made by a merchant who deals in goods of the kind sold or leased.

Implied-in-fact contract A contract formed in whole or in part from the conduct of the parties (as opposed to an express contract).

Impossibility of performance A doctrine under which a party to a contract is relieved of his or her duty to perform when performance becomes impossible or totally impracticable (through no fault of either party).

Imposter One who, by use of the mail, telephone, or personal appearance, induces a maker or drawer to issue an instrument in the name of an impersonated payee. Indorsements by imposters are not treated as unauthorized under Article 3 of the Uniform Commercial Code.

In pari delicto At equal fault.

***In personam* jurisdiction** Court jurisdiction over the "person" involved in a legal action; personal jurisdiction.

***In rem* jurisdiction** Court jurisdiction over a defendant's property.

Incidental beneficiary A third party who incidentally benefits from a contract but whose benefit was not the reason the contract was formed; an incidental beneficiary has no rights in a contract and cannot sue to have the contract enforced.

Incidental damages Losses reasonably associated with, or related to, actual damages resulting from a breach of contract.

Incontestability clause A clause within a life or health insurance policy that states after the policy has been in force for a specified length of time—most often two or three years—the insurer cannot contest statements made in the policyholder's application.

Indemnify To compensate or reimburse another for losses or expenses incurred.

Independent contractor One who works for, and receives payment from, an employer but whose working conditions and methods are not controlled by the employer. An independent contractor is not an employee but may be an agent.

Independent regulatory agency An administrative agency that is not considered part of the government's executive branch and is not subject to the authority of the president. Independent agency officials cannot be removed without cause.

Indictment (pronounced in-*dyte*-ment) A charge by a grand jury that a reasonable basis (probable cause)

exists for believing that a crime has been committed and that a trial should be held.

Indorsee The person to whom a negotiable instrument is transferred by indorsement.

Indorsement A signature placed on an instrument for the purpose of transferring one's ownership rights in the instrument.

Indorser A person who transfers an instrument by signing (indorsing) it and delivering it to another person.

Informal contract A contract that does not require a specified form or formality in order to be valid.

Information A formal accusation or complaint (without an indictment) issued in certain types of actions (usually criminal actions involving lesser crimes) by a law officer, such as a magistrate.

Information return A tax return submitted by a partnership that only reports the income earned by the business. The partnership as an entity does not pay taxes on the income received by the partnership. A partner's profit from the partnership (whether distributed or not) is taxed as individual income to the individual partner.

Infringement A violation of another's legally recognized right. The term is commonly used with reference to the invasion by one party of another party's rights in a patent, trademark, or copyright.

Initial order In the context of administrative law, an agency's disposition in a matter other than a rulemaking. An administrative law judge's initial order becomes final unless it is appealed.

Injunction A court decree ordering a person to do or refrain from doing a certain act or activity.

Innkeeper An owner of an inn, hotel, motel, or other lodgings.

Innkeeper's lien A possessory or statutory lien allowing the innkeeper to take the personal property of a guest, brought into the hotel, as security for nonpayment of the guest's bill (debt).

Innocent misrepresentation A false statement of fact or an act made in good faith that deceives and causes harm or injury to another.

Inside director A person on the board of directors who is also an officer of the corporation.

Insider A corporate director or officer, or other employee or agent, with access to confidential information and a duty not to disclose that information in violation of insider-trading laws.

Insider trading The purchase or sale of securities on the basis of "inside information" (information that has not been made available to the public) in violation of a duty owed to the company whose stock is being traded.

Insolvent Under the Uniform Commercial Code, a term describing a person who ceases to pay "his [or her] debts in the ordinary course of business or cannot pay his debts as they become due or is insolvent within the meaning of federal bankruptcy law" [UCC 1–201(23)].

Installment contract Under the Uniform Commercial Code, a contract that requires or authorizes delivery in two or more separate lots to be accepted and paid for separately.

Instrument *See* Negotiable instrument

Insurable interest An interest either in a person's life or well-being or in property that is sufficiently substantial that insuring against injury to (or the death of) the person or against damage to the property does not amount to a mere wagering (betting) contract.

Insurance A contract in which, for a stipulated consideration, one party agrees to compensate the other for loss on a specific subject by a specified peril.

Intangible property Property that is incapable of being apprehended by the senses (such as by sight or touch). Intellectual property is an example of intangible property.

Integrated contract A written contract that constitutes the final expression of the parties' agreement. If a contract is integrated, evidence extraneous to the contract that contradicts or alters the meaning of the contract in any way is inadmissible.

Intellectual property Property resulting from intellectual, creative processes. Patents, trademarks, and copyrights are examples of intellectual property.

Intended beneficiary A third party for whose benefit a contract is formed; an intended beneficiary can sue the promisor if such a contract is breached.

Intentional tort A wrongful act knowingly committed.

***Inter vivos* gift** *See* Gift *inter vivos*

***Inter vivos* trust** A trust created by the grantor (settlor) and effective during the grantor's lifetime (that is, a trust not established by a will).

Intermediary bank Any bank to which an item is transferred in the course of collection, except the depositary or payor bank.

International law The law that governs relations among nations. International customs and treaties are generally considered to be two of the most important sources of international law.

International organization In international law, a term that generally refers to an organization composed mainly of nations and usually established by treaty. The United States is a member of more than one hundred multilateral and bilateral organizations, including at least twenty through the United Nations.

Interpretive rule An administrative agency rule that is simply a statement or opinion issued by the agency explaining how it interprets and intends to apply the statutes it enforces. Such rules are not automatically binding on private individuals or organizations.

Interrogatories A series of written questions for which written answers are prepared and then signed under oath by a party to a lawsuit, usually with the assistance of the party's attorney.

Intestacy laws State statutes that specify how property will be distributed when a person dies intestate (without a valid will); statutes of descent and distribution.

Intestate As a noun, one who has died without having created a valid will; as an adjective, the state of having died without a will.

Investment company A company that acts on behalf of many smaller shareholder-owners by buying a large portfolio of securities and professionally managing that portfolio.

Investment contract In securities law, a transaction in which a person invests in a common enterprise reasonably expecting profits that are derived primarily from the efforts of others.

Invitee A person who, either expressly or impliedly, is privileged to enter onto another's land. The inviter owes the invitee (for example, a customer in a store) the duty to exercise reasonable care to protect the invitee from harm.

Irrevocable offer An offer that cannot be revoked or recalled by the offeror without liability. A merchant's firm offer is an example of an irrevocable offer.

Issue The first transfer, or delivery, of an instrument to a holder.

J

Joint and several liability In partnership law, a doctrine under which a plaintiff may sue, and collect a judgment from, one or more of the partners separately (severally, or individually) or all of the partners together (jointly). This is true even if one of the partners sued did not participate in, ratify, or know about whatever it was that gave rise to the cause of action.

Joint liability Shared liability. In partnership law, partners incur joint liability for partnership obligations and debts. For example, if a third party sues a partner on a partnership debt, the partner has the right to insist that the other partners be sued with him or her.

Joint stock company A hybrid form of business organization that combines characteristics of a corporation (shareholder-owners, management by directors and officers of the company, and perpetual existence) and a partnership (it is formed by agreement, not statute; property is usually held in the names of the members; and the shareholders have personal liability for business debts). Usually, the joint stock company is regarded as a partnership for tax and other legally related purposes.

Joint tenancy The joint ownership of property by two or more co-owners in which each co-owner owns an undivided portion of the property. On the death of one of the joint tenants, his or her interest automatically passes to the surviving joint tenants.

Joint venture A joint undertaking of a specific commercial enterprise by an association of persons. A joint venture is normally not a legal entity and is treated like a partnership for federal income tax purposes.

Judgment The final order or decision resulting from a legal action.

Judgment *n.o.v.* *See* Motion for judgment *n.o.v.*

Judgment rate of interest A rate of interest fixed by statute that is applied to a monetary judgment from the moment the judgment is awarded by a court until the judgment is paid or terminated.

Judicial lien A lien on property created by a court order.

Judicial process The procedures relating to, or connected with, the administration of justice through the judicial system.

Judicial review The process by which courts decide on the constitutionality of legislative enactments and actions of the executive branch.

Junior lienholder A person or business who holds a lien that is subordinate to one or more other liens on the same property.

Jurisdiction The authority of a court to hear and decide a specific action.

Jurisprudence The science or philosophy of law.

Justiciable (pronounced jus-*tish*-a-bul) **controversy** A controversy that is not hypothetical or academic but real and substantial; a requirement that must be satisfied before a court will hear a case.

K

King's court A medieval English court. The king's courts, or *curiae regis*, were established by the Norman conquerors of England. The body of law that developed in these courts was common to the entire English realm and thus became known as the common law.

L

Laches The equitable doctrine that bars a party's right to legal action if the party has neglected for an unreasonable length of time to act on his or her rights.

Landlord An owner of land or rental property who leases it to another person, called the tenant.

Larceny The wrongful taking and carrying away of another person's personal property with the intent to permanently deprive the owner of the property. Some states classify larceny as either grand or petit, depending on the property's value.

Last clear chance A doctrine under which a plaintiff may recover from a defendant for injuries or damages suffered, notwithstanding the plaintiff's own negligence, when the defendant had the opportunity—a last clear chance—to avoid harming the plaintiff through the exercise of reasonable care but failed to do so.

Law A body of enforceable rules governing relationships among individuals and between individuals and their society.

Lawsuit The litigation process. *See* Litigation

Lease In real property law, a contract by which the owner of real property (the landlord, or lessor) grants to a person (the tenant, or lessee) an exclusive right to use and possess the property, usually for a specified period of time, in return for rent or some other form of payment.

Lease agreement In regard to the lease of goods, an agreement in which one person (the lessor) agrees to transfer the right to the possession and use of property to another person (the lessee) in exchange for rental payments.

Leasehold estate An estate in realty held by a tenant under a lease. In every leasehold estate, the tenant has a qualified right to possess and/or use the land.

Legacy A gift of personal property under a will.

Legal positivists Adherents to the positivist school of legal thought. This school holds that there can be no higher law than a nation's positive law—law created by a particular society at a particular point in time. In contrast to the natural law school, the positivist school maintains that there are no "natural" rights; rights come into existence only when there is a sovereign power (government) to confer and enforce those rights.

Legal rate of interest A rate of interest fixed by statute as either the maximum rate of interest allowed by law or a rate of interest applied when the parties to a contract intend, but do not fix, an interest rate in the contract. In the latter case, the rate is frequently the same as the statutory maximum rate permitted.

Legal realism A school of legal thought that was popular in the 1920s and 1930s and that challenged many existing jurisprudential assumptions, particularly the assumption that subjective elements play no part in judicial reasoning. Legal realists generally advocated a less abstract and more pragmatic approach to the law, an approach that would take into account customary practices and the circumstances in which transactions take place. The school left a lasting imprint on American jurisprudence.

Legal reasoning The process of reasoning by which a judge harmonizes his or her decision with the judicial decisions of previous cases.

Legatee One designated in a will to receive a gift of personal property.

Legislative rule An administrative agency rule that carries the same weight as a congressionally enacted statute.

Lessee A person who acquires the right to the possession and use of another's property in exchange for rental payments.

Lessor A person who sells the right to the possession and use of property to another in exchange for rental payments.

Letter of credit A written instrument, usually issued by a bank on behalf of a customer or other person, in which the issuer promises to honor drafts or other demands for payment by third persons in accordance with the terms of the instrument.

Leveraged buyout (LBO) A corporate takeover financed by loans secured by the acquired corporation's assets or by the issuance of corporate bonds, resulting in a high debt load for the corporation.

Levy The obtaining of money by legal process through the seizure and sale of property, usually done after a writ of execution has been issued.

Liability Any actual or potential legal obligation, duty, debt, or responsibility.

Libel Defamation in writing or other form (such as in a videotape) having the quality of permanence.

License A revocable right or privilege of a person to come on another person's land.

Licensee One who receives a license to use, or enter onto, another's property.

Lien (pronounced *leen*) A claim against specific property to satisfy a debt.

Lien creditor One whose claim is secured by a lien on particular property, as distinguished from a general creditor, who has no such security.

Life estate An interest in land that exists only for the duration of the life of some person, usually the holder of the estate.

Limited jurisdiction Exists when a court's subject-matter jurisdiction is limited. Bankruptcy courts and probate courts are examples of courts with limited jurisdiction.

Limited liability Exists when the liability of the owners of a business is limited to the amount of their investments in the firm.

Limited liability company (LLC) A hybrid form of business enterprise that offers the limited liability of the corporation but the tax advantages of a partnership.

Limited liability limited partnership (LLLP) A type of limited partnership. The difference between a limited partnership and an LLLP is that the liability of the general partner in an LLLP is the same as the liability of the limited partner. That is, the liability of all partners is limited to the amount of their investments in the firm.

Limited liability partnership (LLP) A form of partnership that allows professionals to enjoy the tax benefits of a partnership while limiting their personal liability for the malpractice of other partners.

Limited partner In a limited partnership, a partner who contributes capital to the partnership but has no right to participate in the management and operation of the business. The limited partner assumes no liability for partnership debts beyond the capital contributed.

Limited partnership A partnership consisting of one or more general partners (who manage the business and are liable to the full extent of their personal assets for debts of the partnership) and one or more limited partners (who contribute only assets and are liable only to the extent of their contributions).

Limited-payment life A type of life insurance for which premiums are payable for a definite period, after which the policy is fully paid.

Limited warranty A written warranty that fails to meet one or more of the minimum standards for a full warranty.

Liquidated damages An amount, stipulated in the contract, that the parties to a contract believe to be a reasonable estimation of the damages that will occur in the event of a breach.
Liquidated debt A debt that is due and certain in amount.
Liquidation (1) In regard to bankruptcy, the sale of all of the nonexempt assets of a debtor and the distribution of the proceeds to the debtor's creditors. Chapter 7 of the Bankruptcy Code provides for liquidation bankruptcy proceedings. (2) In regard to corporations, the process by which corporate assets are converted into cash and distributed among creditors and shareholders according to specific rules of preference.
Litigant A party to a lawsuit.
Litigation The process of resolving a dispute through the court system.
Living will A document that allows a person to control the methods of medical treatment that may be used after a serious accident or illness.
Long arm statute A state statute that permits a state to obtain personal jurisdiction over nonresident defendants. A defendant must have "minimum contacts" with that state for the statute to apply.
Lost property Property with which the owner has involuntarily parted and then cannot find or recover.

M

Magistrate's court A court of limited jurisdiction that is presided over by a public official (magistrate) with certain judicial authority, such as the power to set bail.
Mailbox rule A rule providing that an acceptance of an offer becomes effective on dispatch (on being placed in a mailbox), if mail is, expressly or impliedly, an authorized means of communication of acceptance to the offeror.
Main purpose rule A rule of contract law under which an exception to the Statute of Frauds is made if the main purpose in accepting secondary liability under a contract is to secure a personal benefit. If this situation exists, the contract need not be in writing to be enforceable.
Majority *See* Age of majority
Majority opinion A court's written opinion, outlining the views of the majority of the judges or justices deciding the case.
Maker One who promises to pay a certain sum to the holder of a promissory note or certificate of deposit (CD).
Malpractice Professional misconduct or the failure to exercise the requisite degree of skill as a professional. Negligence—the failure to exercise due care—on the part of a professional, such as a physician or an attorney, is commonly referred to as malpractice.
Manufacturing or processing-plant franchise A franchise that is created when the franchisor transmits to the franchisee the essential ingredients or formula to make a particular product. The franchisee then markets the product either at wholesale or at retail in accordance with the franchisor's standards. Examples of this type of franchise are Coca-Cola and other soft-drink bottling companies.
Marine insurance Insurance protecting shippers and vessel owners from losses or damages sustained by a vessel or its cargo during the transport of goods by water.
Mark *See* Trademark
Market concentration A situation that exists when a small number of firms share the market for a particular good or service. For example, if the four largest grocery stores in Chicago accounted for 80 percent of all retail food sales, the market clearly would be concentrated in those four firms.
Market power The power of a firm to control the market price of its product. A monopoly has the greatest degree of market power.
Marketable title Title to real estate that is reasonably free from encumbrances, defects in the chain of title, and other events that affect title, such as adverse possession.
Market-share liability A method of sharing liability among several firms that manufactured or marketed a particular product that may have caused a plaintiff's injury. This form of liability sharing is used when the true source of the product is unidentifiable. Each firm's liability is proportionate to its respective share of the relevant market for the product. Market-share liability applies only if the injuring product is fungible, the true manufacturer is unidentifiable, and the unknown character of the manufacturer is not the plaintiff's fault.
Market-share test The primary measure of monopoly power. A firm's market share is the percentage of a market that the firm controls.
Marshalling assets The arrangement or ranking of assets in a certain order toward the payment of debts. In equity, when two creditors have recourse to the same property of the debtor, but one has recourse to other property of the debtor, that creditor must resort first to those assets of the debtor that are not available to the other creditor.
Material fact A fact to which a reasonable person would attach importance in determining his or her course of action. In regard to tender offers, for example, a fact is material if there is a substantial likelihood that a reasonable shareholder would consider it important in deciding how to vote.
Mechanic's lien A statutory lien on the real property of another, created to ensure payment for work performed and materials furnished in the repair or improvement of real property, such as a building.
Mediation A method of settling disputes outside of court by using the services of a neutral third party, called a mediator. The mediator acts as a

communicating agent between the parties and suggests ways in which the parties can resolve their dispute.

Member The term used to designate a person who has an ownership interest in a limited liability company.

Mens rea (pronounced *mehns ray*-uh) Mental state, or intent. A wrongful mental state is as necessary as a wrongful act to establish criminal liability. What constitutes a mental state varies according to the wrongful action. Thus, for murder, the *mens rea* is the intent to take a life; for theft, the *mens rea* must involve both the knowledge that the property belongs to another and the intent to deprive the owner of it.

Merchant A person who is engaged in the purchase and sale of goods. Under the Uniform Commercial Code, a person who deals in goods of the kind involved in the sales contract; for further definitions, see UCC 2–104.

Merger A contractual and statutory process in which one corporation (the surviving corporation) acquires all of the assets and liabilities of another corporation (the merged corporation). The shareholders of the merged corporation receive either payment for their shares or shares in the surviving corporation.

Meta tags Words inserted into a Web site's key-words field to increase the site's appearance in search engine results.

Metes and bounds A system of measuring boundary lines by the distance between two points, often using physical features of the local geography, such as roads, intersections, rivers, or bridges. The legal descriptions of real property contained in deeds often are phrased in terms of metes and bounds.

Minimum-contacts requirement The requirement that before a state court can exercise jurisdiction over a foreign corporation, the foreign corporation must have sufficient contacts with the state. A foreign corporation that has its home office in the state or that has manufacturing plants in the state meets this requirement.

Minimum wage The lowest wage, either by government regulation or union contract, that an employer may pay an hourly worker.

Mini-trial A private proceeding in which each party to a dispute argues its position before the other side and vice versa. A neutral third party may be present and act as an adviser if the parties fail to reach an agreement.

Mirror image rule A common law rule that requires, for a valid contractual agreement, that the terms of the offeree's acceptance adhere exactly to the terms of the offeror's offer.

Misdemeanor A lesser crime than a felony, punishable by a fine or imprisonment for up to one year in other than a state or federal penitentiary.

Mislaid property Property with which the owner has voluntarily parted and then cannot find or recover.

Misrepresentation A false statement of fact or an action that deceives and causes harm or injury to another. *See also* Fraudulent misrepresentation (fraud); Innocent misrepresentation

Mitigation of damages A rule requiring a plaintiff to have done whatever was reasonable to minimize the damages caused by the defendant.

Money laundering Falsely reporting income that has been obtained through criminal activity as income obtained through a legitimate business enterprise—in effect, "laundering" the "dirty money."

Monopolization The possession of monopoly power in the relevant market and the willful acquisition or maintenance of that power, as distinguished from growth or development as a consequence of a superior product, business acumen, or historic accident.

Monopoly A term generally used to describe a market in which there is a single seller or a limited number of sellers.

Monopoly power The ability of a monopoly to dictate what takes place in a given market.

Moral minimum The minimum degree of ethical behavior expected of a business firm, which is usually defined as compliance with the law.

Mortgage A written instrument giving a creditor (the mortgagee) an interest in (a lien on) the debtor's (mortgagor's) property as security for a debt.

Mortgage bond A bond that pledges specific property. If the corporation defaults on the bond, the bondholder can take the property.

Mortgagee Under a mortgage agreement, the creditor who takes a security interest in the debtor's property.

Mortgagor Under a mortgage agreement, the debtor who gives the creditor a security interest in the debtor's property in return for a mortgage loan.

Motion A procedural request or application presented by an attorney to the court on behalf of a client.

Motion for a directed verdict In a state court, a party's request that the judge enter a judgment in her or his favor before the case is submitted to a jury because the other party has not presented sufficient evidence to support the claim. The federal courts refer to this request as a *motion for judgment as a matter of law.*

Motion for a new trial A motion asserting that the trial was so fundamentally flawed (because of error, newly discovered evidence, prejudice, or other reason) that a new trial is necessary to prevent a miscarriage of justice.

Motion for judgment as a matter of law In a federal court, a party's request that the judge enter a judgment in her or his favor before the case is submitted to a jury because the other party has not presented sufficient evidence to support the claim. The state courts refer to this request as a *motion for a directed verdict.*

Motion for judgment *n.o.v.* A motion requesting the court to grant judgment in favor of the party making the motion on the ground that the jury verdict against him or her was unreasonable and erroneous.

Motion for judgment on the pleadings A motion by either party to a lawsuit at the close of the pleadings requesting the court to decide the issue solely on the pleadings without proceeding to trial. The motion will be granted only if no facts are in dispute.

Motion for summary judgment A motion requesting the court to enter a judgment without proceeding to trial. The motion can be based on evidence outside the pleadings and will be granted only if no facts are in dispute.

Motion to dismiss A pleading in which a defendant asserts that the plaintiff's claim fails to state a cause of action (that is, has no basis in law) or that there are other grounds on which a suit should be dismissed.

Multiple product order An order issued by the Federal Trade Commission to a firm that has engaged in deceptive advertising by which the firm is required to cease and desist from false advertising not only in regard to the product that was the subject of the action but also in regard to all the firm's other products.

Municipal court A city or community court with criminal jurisdiction over traffic violations and, less frequently, with civil jurisdiction over other minor matters.

Mutual assent The element of agreement in the formation of a contract. The manifestation of contract parties' mutual assent to the same bargain is required to establish a contract.

Mutual fund A specific type of investment company that continually buys or sells to investors shares of ownership in a portfolio.

Mutual rescission An agreement between the parties to cancel their contract, releasing the parties from further obligations under the contract. The object of the agreement is to restore the parties to the positions they would have occupied had no contract ever been formed. *See also* Rescission

N

National law Law that pertains to a particular nation (as opposed to international law).

Natural law The belief that government and the legal system should reflect universal moral and ethical principles that are inherent in human nature. The natural law school is the oldest and one of the most significant schools of legal thought.

Necessaries Necessities required for life, such as food, shelter, clothing, and medical attention; may include whatever is believed to be necessary to maintain a person's standard of living or financial and social status.

Necessity In criminal law, a defense against liability; under Section 3.02 of the Model Penal Code, this defense is justifiable if "the harm or evil sought to be avoided" by a given action "is greater than that sought to be prevented by the law defining the offense charged."

Negligence The failure to exercise the standard of care that a reasonable person would exercise in similar circumstances.

Negligence *per se* An act (or failure to act) in violation of a statutory requirement.

Negligent misrepresentation Any manifestation through words or conduct that amounts to an untrue statement of fact made in circumstances in which a reasonable and prudent person would not have done (or failed to do) that which led to the misrepresentation. A representation made with an honest belief in its truth may still be negligent due to (1) a lack of reasonable care in ascertaining the facts, (2) the manner of expression, or (3) the absence of the skill or competence required by a particular business or profession.

Negotiable instrument A signed writing that contains an unconditional promise or order to pay an exact sum of money, on demand or at an exact future time, to a specific person or order, or to bearer.

Negotiation (1) In regard to dispute settlement, a process in which parties attempt to settle their dispute without going to court, with or without attorneys to represent them. (2) In regard to instruments, the transfer of an instrument in such a way that the transferee (the person to whom the instrument is transferred) becomes a holder.

Nominal damages A small monetary award (often one dollar) granted to a plaintiff when no actual damage was suffered or when the plaintiff is unable to show such loss with sufficient certainty.

Nonconforming goods Goods that do not conform to contract specifications.

Nonpossessory interest An interest in land, such as a right-of-way, that does not include any right to possess the land, but only confers the right to use the real property of another for a specified purpose. Nonpossessory interests include easements, profits, and licenses.

No-par shares Corporate shares that have no face value—that is, no specific dollar amount is printed on their face.

Normal trade relations (NTR) status A status granted through an international treaty by which each member nation must treat other members at least as well as it treats the country that receives its most favorable treatment. This status was formerly known as most-favored-nation status.

Notary public A public official authorized to attest to the authenticity of signatures.

Note A written instrument signed by a maker unconditionally promising to pay a fixed amount of money to a payee or a holder on demand or on a specific date.

Notice-and-comment rulemaking An administrative rulemaking procedure that involves the publication of a notice of a proposed rulemaking in the *Federal Register*, a comment period for interested parties to express their views on the proposed rule, and the publication of the agency's final rule in the *Federal Register*.

Notice of Proposed Rulemaking A notice published (in the *Federal Register*) by an administrative agency describing a proposed rule. The notice must give the time and place for which agency proceedings on the proposed rule will be held, a description of the nature of the proceedings, the legal authority for the proceedings (which is usually the agency's enabling legislation), and the terms of the proposed rule or the subject matter of the proposed rule.

Novation The substitution, by agreement, of a new contract for an old one, with the rights under the old one being terminated. Typically, there is a substitution of a new person who is responsible for the contract and the removal of an original party's rights and duties under the contract.

Nuisance A common law doctrine under which persons may be held liable for using their property in a manner that unreasonably interferes with others' rights to use or enjoy their own property.

Nuncupative will An oral will (often called a deathbed will) made before witnesses; usually limited to transfers of personal property.

O

Objective theory of contracts A theory under which the intent to form a contract will be judged by outward, objective facts (what the party said when entering into the contract, how the party acted or appeared, and the circumstances surrounding the transaction) as interpreted by a reasonable person, rather than by the party's own secret, subjective intentions.

Obligee One to whom an obligation is owed.

Obligor One that owes an obligation to another.

Offer A promise or commitment to perform or refrain from performing some specified act in the future.

Offeree A person to whom an offer is made.

Offeror A person who makes an offer.

Omnibus clause A provision in an automobile insurance policy that protects the vehicle owner who has taken out the insurance policy and anyone who drives the vehicle with the owner's permission.

Online Dispute Resolution (ODR) The resolution of disputes with the assistance of organizations that offer dispute-resolution services via the Internet.

Opening statement A statement made to the jury at the beginning of a trial by a party's attorney, prior to the presentation of evidence. The attorney briefly outlines the evidence that will be offered and the legal theory that will be pursued.

Operating agreement In a limited liability company, an agreement in which the members set forth the details of how the business will be managed and operated.

Opinion A statement by the court expressing the reasons for its decision in a case.

Option contract A contract under which the offeror cannot revoke his or her offer for a stipulated time period and the offeree can accept or reject the offer during this period without fear that the offer will be made to another person. The offeree must give consideration for the option (the irrevocable offer) to be enforceable.

Order for relief A court's grant of assistance to a complainant. In bankruptcy proceedings, the order relieves the debtor of the immediate obligation to pay the debts listed in the bankruptcy petition.

Order instrument A negotiable instrument that is payable "to the order of an identified person" or "to an identified person or order."

Ordinance A law passed by a local governing unit, such as a municipality or a county.

Original jurisdiction Jurisdiction that is exercised by courts of the first instance, or trial courts—that is, courts in which lawsuits begin, trials take place, and evidence is presented.

Output contract An agreement in which a seller agrees to sell and a buyer agrees to buy all or up to a stated amount of what the seller produces.

Outside director A person on the board of directors who does not hold a management position at the corporation.

Overdraft A check written on a checking account in which there are insufficient funds to cover the amount of the check.

P

Parent-subsidiary merger A merger of companies in which one company (the parent corporation) owns most of the stock of the other (the subsidiary corporation). A parent-subsidiary merger (short-form merger) can use a simplified procedure when the parent corporation owns at least 90 percent of the outstanding shares of each class of stock of the subsidiary corporation.

Parol evidence A term that originally meant "oral evidence," but which has come to refer to any negotiations or agreements made prior to a contract or any contemporaneous oral agreements made by the parties.

Parol evidence rule A substantive rule of contracts under which a court will not receive into evidence the parties' prior negotiations, prior agreements, or contemporaneous oral agreements if that evidence contradicts or varies the terms of the parties' written contract.

Partially disclosed principal A principal whose identity is unknown by a third person, but the third person knows that the agent is or may be acting for a principal at the time the agent and the third person form a contract.

Partner A co-owner of a partnership.

Partnering agreement An agreement between a seller and a buyer who frequently do business with each other on the terms and conditions that will apply to all subsequently formed electronic contracts.

Partnership An agreement by two or more persons to carry on, as co-owners, a business for profit.

Partnership by estoppel A judicially created partnership that may, at the court's discretion, be imposed for purposes of fairness. The court can prevent those who present themselves as partners (but who are not) from escaping liability if a third person relies on an alleged partnership in good faith and is harmed as a result.

Par-value shares Corporate shares that have a specific face value, or formal cash-in value, written on them, such as one dollar.

Past consideration An act done before the contract is made, which ordinarily, by itself, cannot be consideration for a later promise to pay for the act.

Patent A government grant that gives an inventor the exclusive right or privilege to make, use, or sell his or her invention for a limited time period. The word *patent* usually refers to some invention and designates either the instrument by which patent rights are evidenced or the patent itself.

Payee A person to whom an instrument is made payable.

Payor bank The bank on which a check is drawn (the drawee bank).

Peer-to-peer (P2P) networking The sharing of resources (such as files, hard drives, and processing styles) among multiple computers without necessarily requiring a central network server.

Penalty A sum inserted into a contract, not as a measure of compensation for its breach but rather as punishment for a default. The agreement as to the amount will not be enforced, and recovery will be limited to actual damages.

Per capita A Latin term meaning "per person." In the law governing estate distribution, a method of distributing the property of an intestate's estate in which each heir in a certain class (such as grandchildren) receives an equal share.

Per curiam By the whole court; a court opinion written by the court as a whole instead of being authored by a judge or justice.

Per se A Latin term meaning "in itself" or "by itself."

***Per se* violation** A type of anticompetitive agreement—such as a horizontal price-fixing agreement—that is considered to be so injurious to the public that there is no need to determine whether it actually injures market competition; rather, it is in itself (*per se*) a violation of the Sherman Act.

Per stirpes A Latin term meaning "by the roots." In the law governing estate distribution, a method of distributing an intestate's estate in which each heir in a certain class (such as grandchildren) takes the share to which his or her deceased ancestor (such as a mother or father) would have been entitled.

Perfect tender rule A common law rule under which a seller was required to deliver to the buyer goods that conformed perfectly to the requirements stipulated in the sales contract. A tender of nonconforming goods would automatically constitute a breach of contract. Under the Uniform Commercial Code, the rule has been greatly modified.

Perfection The legal process by which secured parties protect themselves against the claims of third parties who may wish to have their debts satisfied out of the same collateral; usually accomplished by the filing of a financing statement with the appropriate government official.

Performance In contract law, the fulfillment of one's duties arising under a contract with another; the normal way of discharging one's contractual obligations.

Periodic tenancy A lease interest in land for an indefinite period involving payment of rent at fixed intervals, such as week to week, month to month, or year to year.

Personal defense A defense that can be used to avoid payment to an ordinary holder of a negotiable instrument but not a holder in due course (HDC) or a holder with the rights of an HDC.

Personal identification number (PIN) A number given to the holder of an access card (debit card, credit card, ATM card, or the like) that is used to conduct financial transactions electronically. Typically, the card will not provide access to a system without the number, which is meant to be kept secret to inhibit unauthorized use of the card.

Personal jurisdiction *See In personam* jurisdiction

Personal property Property that is movable; any property that is not real property.

Personalty Personal property.

Petition in bankruptcy The document that is filed with a bankruptcy court to initiate bankruptcy proceedings. The official forms required for a petition in bankruptcy must be completed accurately, sworn to under oath, and signed by the debtor.

Petitioner In equity practice, a party that initiates a lawsuit.

Petty offense In criminal law, the least serious kind of criminal offense, such as a traffic or building-code violation.

Pierce the corporate veil To disregard the corporate entity, which limits the liability of shareholders, and hold the shareholders personally liable for a corporate obligation.

Plaintiff One who initiates a lawsuit.

Plea In criminal law, a defendant's allegation, in response to the charges brought against him or her, of guilt or innocence.

Plea bargaining The process by which a criminal defendant and the prosecutor in a criminal case work out a mutually satisfactory disposition of the case, subject to court approval; usually involves the defendant's pleading guilty to a lesser offense in return for a lighter sentence.

Pleadings Statements made by the plaintiff and the defendant in a lawsuit that detail the facts, charges, and defenses involved in the litigation; the complaint and answer are part of the pleadings.

Pledge A common law security device (retained in Article 9 of the Uniform Commercial Code) in which personal property is turned over to the creditor as security for the payment of a debt and retained by the creditor until the debt is paid.

Police powers Powers possessed by states as part of their inherent sovereignty. These powers may be exercised to protect or promote the public order, health, safety, morals, and general welfare.

Policy In insurance law, a contract between the insurer and the insured in which, for a stipulated consideration, the insurer agrees to compensate the insured for loss on a specific subject by a specified peril.

Positive law The body of conventional, or written, law of a particular society at a particular point in time.

Positivist school A school of legal thought whose adherents believe that there can be no higher law than a nation's positive law—the body of conventional, or written, law of a particular society at a particular time.

Possessory lien A lien that allows one person to retain possession of another's property as security for a debt or obligation owed by the owner of the property to the lienholder. An example of a possessory lien is an artisan's lien.

Potentially responsible party (PRP) A potentially liable party under the Comprehensive Environmental Response, Compensation and Liability Act (CERCLA). Any person who generated the hazardous waste, transported the hazardous waste, owned or operated a waste site at the time of disposal, or currently owns or operates a site may be responsible for some or all of the clean-up costs involved in removing the hazardous chemicals.

Power of attorney A written document, which is usually notarized, authorizing another to act as one's agent; can be special (permitting the agent to do specified acts only) or general (permitting the agent to transact all business for the principal).

Preauthorized transfer A transaction authorized in advance to recur at substantially regular intervals. The terms and procedures for preauthorized electronic fund transfers through certain financial institutions are subject to the Electronic Fund Transfer Act.

Precedent A court decision that furnishes an example or authority for deciding subsequent cases involving identical or similar facts.

Predatory pricing The pricing of a product below cost with the intent to drive competitors out of the market.

Predominant-factor test A test courts use to determine whether a contract is primarily for the sale of goods or for the sale of services.

Preemption A doctrine under which certain federal laws preempt, or take precedence over, conflicting state or local laws.

Preemptive rights Rights held by shareholders that entitle them to purchase newly issued shares of a corporation's stock, equal in percentage to shares already held, before the stock is offered to any outside buyers. Preemptive rights enable shareholders to maintain their proportionate ownership and voice in the corporation.

Preference In bankruptcy proceedings, property transfers or payments made by the debtor that favor (give preference to) one creditor over others. The bankruptcy trustee is allowed to recover payments made both voluntarily and involuntarily to one creditor in preference over another.

Preferred creditor One who has received a preferential transfer from a debtor.

Preferred stock Classes of stock that have priority over common stock both as to payment of dividends and distribution of assets on the corporation's dissolution.

Prejudgment interest Interest that accrues on the amount of a court judgment from the time of the filing of a lawsuit to the court's issuance of a judgment.

Preliminary hearing An initial hearing used in many felony cases to establish whether it is proper to detain the defendant. A magistrate reviews the evidence and decides if there is probable cause to believe that the defendant committed the crime with which he or she has been charged.

Premium In insurance law, the price paid by the insured for insurance protection for a specified period of time.

Prenuptial agreement An agreement made before marriage that defines each partner's ownership rights in the other partner's property. Prenuptial agreements must be in writing to be enforceable.

Preponderance of the evidence A standard in civil law cases under which the plaintiff must convince the court that, based on the evidence presented by both parties, it is more likely than not that the plaintiff's allegation is true.

Presentment The act of presenting an instrument to the party liable on the instrument to collect payment; presentment also occurs when a person presents an instrument to a drawee for acceptance.

Presentment warranties Any person who presents an instrument for payment or acceptance impliedly warrants that (1) he or she is entitled to enforce the instrument or authorized to obtain payment or acceptance on behalf of a person who is entitled, (2) the instrument has not been altered, and (3) he or she has no knowledge that the signature of the drawer is unauthorized.

Pretrial conference A conference, scheduled before the trial begins, between the judge and the attorneys litigating the suit. The parties may settle the dispute, clarify the issues, schedule discovery, and the like during the conference.

Pretrial motion A written or oral application to a court for a ruling or order, made before trial.

Price discrimination Setting prices in such a way that two competing buyers pay two different prices for an identical product or service.

Price-fixing agreement An agreement between

competitors in which the competitors agree to fix the prices of products or services at a certain level; prohibited by the Sherman Act.

***Prima facie* case** A case in which the plaintiff has produced sufficient evidence of his or her conclusion that the case can go to to a jury; a case in which the evidence compels the plaintiff's conclusion if the defendant produces no evidence to disprove it.

Primary liability In negotiable instruments law, absolute responsibility for paying a negotiable instrument. Makers and acceptors are primarily liable.

Principal In agency law, a person who agrees to have another, called the agent, act on his or her behalf.

Principle of rights The principle that human beings have certain fundamental rights (to life, freedom, and the pursuit of happiness, for example). Those who adhere to this "rights theory" believe that a key factor in determining whether a business decision is ethical is how that decision affects the rights of others. These others include the firm's owners, its employees, the consumers of its products or services, its suppliers, the community in which it does business, and society as a whole.

Private equity capital A financing method by which a company sells equity in an existing business to a private or institutional investor.

Privatization The replacement of government-provided products and services by private firms.

Privilege In tort law, the ability to act contrary to another person's right without that person's having legal redress for such acts. Privilege may be raised as a defense to defamation.

Privileges and immunities clause Special rights and exceptions provided by law. Article IV, Section 2, of the Constitution requires states not to discriminate against one another's citizens. A resident of one state cannot be treated as an alien when in another state; he or she may not be denied such privileges and immunities as legal protection, access to courts, travel rights, or property rights.

Privity of contract The relationship that exists between the promisor and the promisee of a contract.

Pro rata Proportionately; in proportion.

Probable cause Reasonable grounds to believe the existence of facts warranting certain actions, such as the search or arrest of a person.

Probate The process of proving and validating a will and the settling of all matters pertaining to administration, guardianship, and the like.

Probate court A state court of limited jurisdiction that conducts proceedings relating to the settlement of a deceased person's estate.

Procedural due process The requirement that any government decision to take life, liberty, or property be made fairly. For example, fair procedures must be used in determining whether a person will be subjected to punishment or have some burden imposed on him or her.

Procedural law Rules that define the manner in which the rights and duties of individuals may be enforced.

Procedural unconscionability Occurs when, due to one contractual party's vastly superior bargaining power, the other party lacks knowledge or understanding of the contract terms due to inconspicuous print or the lack of an opportunity to read the contract or to ask questions about its meaning. Procedural unconscionability often involves an *adhesion contract*, which is a contract drafted by the dominant party and then presented to the other—the adhering party—on a take-it-or-leave-it basis.

Proceeds Under Article 9 of the Uniform Commercial Code, whatever is received when the collateral is sold or otherwise disposed of, such as by exchange.

Product liability The legal liability of manufacturers, sellers, and lessors of goods to consumers, users, and bystanders for injuries or damages that are caused by the goods.

Product misuse A defense against product liability that may be raised when the plaintiff used a product in a manner not intended by the manufacturer. If the misuse is reasonably foreseeable, the seller will not escape liability unless measures were taken to guard against the harm that could result from the misuse.

Professional corporation A corporation formed by professional persons, such as physicians, lawyers, dentists, and accountants, to gain tax benefits. Subject to certain exceptions (when a court may treat a professional corporation as a partnership for liability purposes), the shareholders of a professional corporation have the limited liability characteristic of the corporate form of business.

Profit In real property law, the right to enter onto and remove things from the property of another (for example, the right to enter onto a person's land and remove sand and gravel therefrom).

Promise A person's assurance that he or she will or will not do something.

Promisee A person to whom a promise is made.

Promisor A person who makes a promise.

Promissory estoppel A doctrine that applies when a promisor makes a clear and definite promise on which the promisee justifiably relies; such a promise is binding if justice will be better served by the enforcement of the promise. *See also* Estoppel

Promissory note A written promise made by one person (the maker) to pay a fixed sum of money to another person (the payee or a subsequent holder) on demand or on a specified date.

Promoter A person who takes the preliminary steps in organizing a corporation, including (usually) issuing a prospectus, procuring stock subscriptions, making contract purchases, securing a corporate charter, and the like.

Property Legally protected rights and interests in

anything with an ascertainable value that is subject to ownership.

Prospectus A document required by federal or state securities laws that describes the financial operations of the corporation, thus allowing investors to make informed decisions.

Protected class A class of persons with identifiable characteristics who historically have been victimized by discriminatory treatment for certain purposes. Depending on the context, these characteristics include age, color, gender, national origin, race, and religion.

Proximate cause Legal cause; exists when the connection between an act and an injury is strong enough to justify imposing liability.

Proxy In corporation law, a written agreement between a stockholder and another under which the stockholder authorizes the other to vote the stockholder's shares in a certain manner.

Proxy fight A conflict between an individual, group, or firm attempting to take control of a corporation and the corporation's management for the votes of the shareholders.

Public figures Individuals who are thrust into the public limelight. Public figures include government officials and politicians, movie stars, well-known businesspersons, and generally anybody who becomes known to the public because of his or her position or activities.

Public policy A government policy based on widely held societal values and (usually) expressed or implied in laws or regulations.

Public prosecutor An individual, acting as a trial lawyer, who initiates and conducts criminal cases in the government's name and on behalf of the people.

Puffery A salesperson's exaggerated claims concerning the quality of property offered for sale. Such claims involve opinions rather than facts and are not considered to be legally binding promises or warranties.

Punitive damages Money damages that may be awarded to a plaintiff to punish the defendant and deter future similar conduct.

Purchase-money security interest (PMSI) A security interest that arises when a seller or lender extends credit for part or all of the purchase price of goods purchased by a buyer.

Q

Qualified indorsement An indorsement on a negotiable instrument in which the indorser disclaims any contract liability on the instrument; the notation "without recourse" is commonly used to create a qualified indorsement.

Quantum meruit (pronounced *kwahn*-tuhm *mehr*-oo-wuht) Literally, "as much as he deserves"—an expression describing the extent of liability on a contract implied in law (quasi contract). An equitable doctrine based on the concept that one who benefits from another's labor and materials should not be unjustly enriched thereby but should be required to pay a reasonable amount for the benefits received, even absent a contract.

Quasi contract A fictional contract imposed on parties by a court in the interests of fairness and justice; usually, quasi contracts are imposed to avoid the unjust enrichment of one party at the expense of another.

Question of fact In a lawsuit, an issue involving a factual dispute that can be decided only by a judge (or, in a jury trial, a jury).

Question of law In a lawsuit, an issue involving the application or interpretation of a law; therefore, the judge, and not the jury, decides the issue.

Quiet enjoyment *See* Covenant of quiet enjoyment

Quitclaim deed A deed intended to pass any title, interest, or claim that the grantor may have in the property but not warranting that such title is valid. A quitclaim deed offers the least amount of protection against defects in the title.

Quorum The number of members of a decision-making body that must be present before business may be transacted.

Quota An assigned import limit on goods.

R

Ratification The act of accepting and giving legal force to an obligation that previously was not enforceable.

Reaffirmation agreement An agreement between a debtor and a creditor in which the debtor reaffirms, or promises to pay, a debt dischargeable in bankruptcy. To be enforceable, the agreement must be made prior to the discharge of the debt by the bankruptcy court.

Real property Land and everything attached to it, such as foliage and buildings.

Reasonable care The degree of care that a person of ordinary prudence would exercise in the same or similar circumstances.

Reasonable doubt *See* Beyond a reasonable doubt

Reasonable person standard The standard of behavior expected of a hypothetical "reasonable person." The standard against which negligence is measured and that must be observed to avoid liability for negligence.

Rebuttal The refutation of evidence introduced by an adverse party's attorney.

Receiver In a corporate dissolution, a court-appointed person who winds up corporate affairs and liquidates corporate assets.

Record According to the Uniform Electronic Transactions Act, information that is either inscribed on a tangible medium or stored in an electronic or other medium and that is retrievable. The Uniform Computer Information Transactions Act uses the term *record* instead of *writing*.

Recording statutes Statutes that allow deeds, mortgages, and other real property transactions to be recorded so as to provide notice to future purchasers or creditors of an existing claim on the property.

Red herring prospectus A preliminary prospectus that can be distributed to potential investors after the registration statement (for a securities offering) has been filed with the Securities and Exchange Commission. The name derives from the red legend printed across the prospectus stating that the registration has been filed but has not become effective.

Redemption A repurchase, or buying back. In secured transactions law, a debtor's repurchase of collateral securing a debt after a creditor has taken title to the collateral due to the debtor's default but before the secured party disposes of the collateral.

Reformation A court-ordered correction of a written contract so that it reflects the true intentions of the parties.

Regulation E A set of rules issued by the Federal Reserve System's Board of Governors under the authority of the Electronic Fund Transfer Act to protect users of electronic fund transfer systems.

Regulation Z A set of rules promulgated by the Federal Reserve Board to implement the provisions of the Truth-in-Lending Act.

Rejection In contract law, an offeree's express or implied manifestation not to accept an offer. In the law governing contracts for the sale of goods, a buyer's manifest refusal to accept goods on the ground that they do not conform to contract specifications.

Rejoinder The defendant's answer to the plaintiff's rebuttal.

Release A contract in which one party forfeits the right to pursue a legal claim against the other party.

Relevant evidence Evidence tending to make a fact at issue in the case more or less probable than it would be without the evidence. Only relevant evidence is admissible in court.

Remainder A future interest in property held by a person other than the original owner.

Remanded Sent back. If an appellate court disagrees with a lower court's judgment, the case may be remanded to the lower court for further proceedings in which the lower court's decision should be consistent with the appellate court's opinion on the matter.

Remedy The relief given to an innocent party to enforce a right or compensate for the violation of a right.

Remedy at law A remedy available in a court of law. Money damages are awarded as a remedy at law.

Remedy in equity A remedy allowed by courts in situations where remedies at law are not appropriate. Remedies in equity are based on settled rules of fairness, justice, and honesty, and include injunction, specific performance, rescission and restitution, and reformation.

Remitter A person who sends money, or remits payment.

Rent The consideration paid for the use or enjoyment of another's property. In landlord-tenant relationships, the payment made by the tenant to the landlord for the right to possess the premises.

Rent escalation clause A clause providing for an increase in rent during a lease term.

Repair-and-deduct statutes Statutes providing that a tenant may pay for repairs and deduct the cost of the repairs from the rent, as a remedy for a landlord's failure to maintain leased premises.

Replevin (pronounced ruh-*pleh*-vin) An action to recover specific goods in the hands of a party who is wrongfully withholding them from the other party.

Reply Procedurally, a plaintiff's response to a defendant's answer.

Reporter A publication in which court cases are published, or reported.

Repudiation The renunciation of a right or duty; the act of a buyer or seller in rejecting a contract either partially or totally. *See also* Anticipatory repudiation

Requirements contract An agreement in which a buyer agrees to purchase and the seller agrees to sell all or up to a stated amount of what the buyer needs or requires.

Res ipsa loquitur (pronounced *rehs ehp*-suh *low*-quuh-duhr) A doctrine under which negligence may be inferred simply because an event occurred, if it is the type of event that would not occur in the absence of negligence. Literally, the term means "the facts speak for themselves."

Resale price maintenance agreement An agreement between a manufacturer and a retailer in which the manufacturer specifies the minimum retail price of its products.

Rescind (pronounced reh-*sihnd*) To cancel. *See also* Rescission

Rescission (pronounced reh-*sih*-zhen) A remedy whereby a contract is canceled and the parties are returned to the positions they occupied before the contract was made; may be effected through the mutual consent of the parties, by their conduct, or by court decree.

Residuary The surplus of a testator's estate remaining after all of the debts and particular legacies have been discharged.

Respondeat superior (pronounced ree-*spahn*-dee-uht soo-*peer*-ee-your) In Latin, "Let the master respond." A doctrine under which a principal or an employer is held liable for the wrongful acts committed by agents or employees while acting within the course and scope of their agency or employment.

Respondent In equity practice, the party who answers a bill or other proceeding.

Restitution An equitable remedy under which a person is restored to his or her original position prior to loss or injury, or placed in the position he or she would have been in had the breach not occurred.

Restraint of trade Any contract or combination that tends to eliminate or reduce competition, effect a monopoly, artificially maintain prices, or otherwise hamper the course of trade and commerce as it would be carried on if left to the control of natural economic forces.

Restrictive covenant A private restriction on the use of land that is binding on the party that purchases the property originally as well as on subsequent purchasers. If its benefit or obligation passes with the land's ownership, it is said to "run with the land."

Restrictive indorsement Any indorsement on a negotiable instrument that requires the indorsee to comply with certain instructions regarding the funds involved. A restrictive indorsement does not prohibit the further negotiation of the instrument.

Resulting trust An implied trust arising from the conduct of the parties. A trust in which a party holds the actual legal title to another's property but only for that person's benefit.

Retained earnings The portion of a corporation's profits that has not been paid out as dividends to shareholders.

Retainer An advance payment made by a client to a law firm to cover part of the legal fees and/or costs that will need to be incurred on that client's behalf.

Retaliatory eviction The eviction of a tenant because of the tenant's complaints, participation in a tenant's union, or similar activity with which the landlord does not agree.

Reverse To reject or overrule a court's judgment. An appellate court, for example, might reverse a lower court's judgment on an issue if it feels that the lower court committed an error during the trial or that the jury was improperly instructed.

Reverse discrimination Discrimination against majority groups, such as white males, that results from affirmative action programs, in which preferences are given to minority members and women.

Reversible error An error by a lower court that is sufficiently substantial to justify an appellate court's reversal of the lower court's decision.

Revocation In contract law, the withdrawal of an offer by an offeror. Unless an offer is irrevocable, it can be revoked at any time prior to acceptance without liability.

Right of contribution The right of a co-surety who pays more than his or her proportionate share on a debtor's default to recover the excess paid from other co-sureties.

Right of entry The right to peaceably take or resume possession of real property.

Right of first refusal The right to purchase personal or real property—such as corporate shares or real estate—before the property is offered for sale to others.

Right of redemption *See* Equity of redemption; Redemption

Right of reimbursement The legal right of a person to be restored, repaid, or indemnified for costs, expenses, or losses incurred or expended on behalf of another.

Right of subrogation The right of a person to stand in the place of (be substituted for) another, giving the substituted party the same legal rights that the original party had.

Right-to-work law A state law providing that employees are not to be required to join a union as a condition of obtaining or retaining employment.

Risk A prediction concerning potential loss based on known and unknown factors.

Risk management Planning that is undertaken to protect one's interest should some event threaten to undermine its security. In the context of insurance, risk management involves transferring certain risks from the insured to the insurance company.

Robbery The act of forcefully and unlawfully taking personal property of any value from another; force or intimidation is usually necessary for an act of theft to be considered a robbery.

Rule of four A rule of the United States Supreme Court under which the Court will not issue a writ of *certiorari* unless at least four justices approve of the decision to issue the writ.

Rule of reason A test by which a court balances the positive effects (such as economic efficiency) of an agreement against its potentially anticompetitive effects. In antitrust litigation, many practices are analyzed under the rule of reason.

Rule 10b-5 *See* SEC Rule 10b-5

Rulemaking The process undertaken by an administrative agency when formally adopting a new regulation or amending an old one. Rulemaking involves notifying the public of a proposed rule or change and receiving and considering the public's comments.

Rules of evidence Rules governing the admissibility of evidence in trial courts.

S

S corporation A close business corporation that has met certain requirements as set out by the Internal Revenue Code and thus qualifies for special income tax treatment. Essentially, an S corporation is taxed the same as a partnership, but its owners enjoy the privilege of limited liability.

Sale The passing of title (evidence of ownership rights) from the seller to the buyer for a price.

Sale on approval A type of conditional sale in which the buyer may take the goods on a trial basis. The sale becomes absolute only when the buyer approves of (or is satisfied with) the goods being sold.

Sale or return A type of conditional sale in which title and possession pass from the seller to the buyer; however, the buyer retains the option to return the goods during a specified period even though the goods conform to the contract.

Sales contract A contract for the sale of goods under which the ownership of goods is transferred from a seller to a buyer for a price.

Satisfaction *See* Accord and satisfaction

Scienter (pronounced *sy-en*-ter) Knowledge by the misrepresenting party that material facts have been falsely represented or omitted with an intent to deceive.

Search warrant An order granted by a public authority, such as a judge, that authorizes law enforcement personnel to search particular premises or property.

Seasonably Within a specified time period, or, if no period is specified, within a reasonable time.

SEC Rule 10b-5 A rule of the Securities and Exchange Commission that makes it unlawful, in connection with the purchase or sale of any security, to make any untrue statement of a material fact or to omit a material fact if such omission causes the statement to be misleading.

Secondary boycott A union's refusal to work for, purchase from, or handle the products of a secondary employer, with whom the union has no dispute, for the purpose of forcing that employer to stop doing business with the primary employer, with whom the union has a labor dispute.

Secondary liability In negotiable instruments law, the contingent liability of drawers and indorsers. A secondarily liable party becomes liable on an instrument only if the party that is primarily liable on the instrument dishonors it or, in regard to drafts and checks, the drawee fails to pay or to accept the instrument, whichever is required.

Secured party A lender, seller, or any other person in whose favor there is a security interest, including a person to whom accounts or chattel paper has been sold.

Secured transaction Any transaction in which the payment of a debt is guaranteed, or secured, by personal property owned by the debtor or in which the debtor has a legal interest.

Securities Generally, corporate stocks and bonds. A security may also be a note, debenture, stock warrant, or any document given as evidence of an ownership interest in a corporation or as a promise of repayment by a corporation.

Security agreement An agreement that creates or provides for a security interest between the debtor and a secured party.

Security interest Any interest "in personal property or fixtures which secures payment or performance of an obligation" [UCC 1–201(37)].

Self-defense The legally recognized privilege to protect one's self or property against injury by another. The privilege of self-defense protects only acts that are reasonably necessary to protect one's self or property.

Seniority system In regard to employment relationships, a system in which those who have worked longest for the company are first in line for promotions, salary increases, and other benefits; they are also the last to be laid off if the workforce must be reduced.

Service mark A mark used in the sale or the advertising of services, such as to distinguish the services of one person from the services of others. Titles, character names, and other distinctive features of radio and television programs may be registered as service marks.

Service of process The delivery of the complaint and summons to a defendant.

Settlor One creating a trust; also called a *grantor.*

Severance pay A payment by an employer to an employee that exceeds the employee's wages due on termination.

Sexual harassment In the employment context, the granting of job promotions or other benefits in return for sexual favors or language or conduct that is so sexually offensive that it creates a hostile working environment.

Share A unit of stock. *See also* Stock

Share exchange In a share exchange, some or all of the shares of one corporation are exchanged for some or all of the shares of another corporation, but both corporations continue to exist. Share exchanges are often used to create *holding companies* (companies that own part or all of other companies' stock).

Shareholder One who purchases shares of a corporation's stock, thus acquiring an equity interest in the corporation.

Shareholder's derivative suit A suit brought by a shareholder to enforce a corporate cause of action against a third person.

Sharia Civil law principles of some Middle Eastern countries that are based on the Islamic directives that follow the teachings of the prophet Muhammad.

Shelter principle The principle that the holder of a negotiable instrument who cannot qualify as a holder in due course (HDC), but who derives his or her title through an HDC, acquires the rights of an HDC.

Sheriff's deed The deed given to the purchaser of property at a sheriff's sale as part of the foreclosure process against the owner of the property.

Shipment contract A contract in which the seller is required to ship the goods by carrier. The buyer assumes liability for any losses or damage to the goods after they are delivered to the carrier. Generally, all contracts are assumed to be shipment contracts if nothing to the contrary is stated in the contract.

Short-form merger A merger between a subsidiary corporation and a parent corporation that owns at least 90 percent of the outstanding shares of each class of stock issued by the subsidiary corporation. Short-form mergers can be accomplished without the approval of the shareholders of either corporation.

Short-swing profits Profits made by officers, directors, and certain large stockholders resulting from the use of nonpublic (inside) information about their companies; prohibited by Section 12 of the 1934 Securities Exchange Act.

Shrink-wrap agreement An agreement whose terms are expressed in a document located inside a box in which goods (usually software) are packaged; sometimes called a *shrink-wrap license.*

Sight draft In negotiable instruments law, a draft payable on sight—that is, when it is presented for payment.

Signature Under the Uniform Commercial Code, "any symbol executed or adopted by a party with a present intention to authenticate a writing."

Slander Defamation in oral form.

Slander of quality (trade libel) The publication of false information about another's product, alleging that it is not what its seller claims.

Slander of title The publication of a statement that denies or casts doubt on another's legal ownership of any property, causing financial loss to that property's owner.

Small claims courts Special courts in which parties may litigate small claims (usually, claims involving $2,500 or less). Attorneys are not required in small claims courts, and in many states attorneys are not allowed to represent the parties.

Smart card Prepaid funds recorded on a microprocessor chip embedded on a card. One type of *e-money.*

Sociological school A school of legal thought that views the law as a tool for promoting justice in society.

Sole proprietorship The simplest form of business, in which the owner is the business; the owner reports business income on his or her personal income tax return and is legally responsible for all debts and obligations incurred by the business.

Sovereign immunity A doctrine that immunizes foreign nations from the jurisdiction of U.S. courts when certain conditions are satisfied.

Spam Bulk, unsolicited ("junk") e-mail.

Special indorsement An indorsement on an instrument that indicates the specific person to whom the indorser intends to make the instrument payable; that is, it names the indorsee.

Special warranty deed A deed in which the grantor only covenants to warrant and defend the title against claims and demands of the grantor and all persons claiming by, through, and under the grantor.

Specific performance An equitable remedy requiring the breaching party to perform as promised under the contract; usually granted only when money damages would be an inadequate remedy and the subject matter of the contract is unique (for example, real property).

Spendthrift trust A trust created to prevent the beneficiary from spending all the money to which he or she is entitled. Only a certain portion of the total amount is given to the beneficiary at any one time, and most states prohibit creditors from attaching assets of the trust.

Spot zoning Granting a zoning classification to a parcel of land that is different from the classification given to other land in the immediate area.

Stale check A check, other than a certified check, that is presented for payment more than six months after its date.

Standing to sue The requirement that an individual must have a sufficient stake in a controversy before he or she can bring a lawsuit. The plaintiff must demonstrate that he or she either has been injured or threatened with injury.

Stare decisis (pronounced *ster*-ay dih-*si*-ses) A common law doctrine under which judges are obligated to follow the precedents established in prior decisions.

Statute of Frauds A state statute under which certain types of contracts must be in writing to be enforceable.

Statute of limitations A federal or state statute setting the maximum time period during which a certain action can be brought or certain rights enforced.

Statute of repose Basically, a statute of limitations that is not dependent on the happening of a cause of action. Statutes of repose generally begin to run at an earlier date and run for a longer period of time than statutes of limitations.

Statutory law The body of law enacted by legislative bodies (as opposed to constitutional law, administrative law, or case law).

Statutory lien A lien created by statute.

Statutory period of redemption A time period (usually set by state statute) during which the property subject to a defaulted mortgage, land contract, or other contract can be redeemed by the debtor after foreclosure or judicial sale.

Stock An equity (ownership) interest in a corporation, measured in units of shares.

Stock certificate A certificate issued by a corporation evidencing the ownership of a specified number of shares in the corporation.

Stock option *See* Stock warrant

Stock warrant A certificate that grants the owner the option to buy a given number of shares of stock, usually within a set time period.

Stockholder *See* Shareholder

Stop-payment order An order by a bank customer to his or her bank not to pay or certify a certain check.

Strict liability Liability regardless of fault. In tort law, strict liability may be imposed on defendants in cases involving abnormally dangerous activities, dangerous animals, or defective products.

Strike An extreme action undertaken by unionized workers when collective bargaining fails; the workers leave their jobs, refuse to work, and (typically) picket the employer's workplace.

Subject-matter jurisdiction Jurisdiction over the subject matter of a lawsuit.

Sublease A lease executed by the lessee of real estate to a third person, conveying the same interest that the lessee enjoys but for a shorter term than that held by the lessee.

Subpoena A document commanding a person to appear at a certain time and place or give testimony concerning a certain matter.

Subrogation *See* Right of subrogation

Subscriber An investor who agrees, in a subscription agreement, to purchase capital stock in a corporation.

Substantial performance Performance that does not vary greatly from the performance promised in a contract; the performance must create substantially the same benefits as those promised in the contract.

Substantive due process A requirement that focuses on the content, or substance, of legislation. If a law or other governmental action limits a fundamental right, such as the right to travel or to vote, it will be held to violate substantive due process unless it promotes a compelling or overriding state interest.

Substantive law Law that defines the rights and duties of individuals with respect to each other, as opposed to procedural law, which defines the manner in which these rights and duties may be enforced.

Substantive unconscionability Results from contracts, or portions of contracts, that are oppressive or overly harsh. Courts generally focus on provisions that deprive one party of the benefits of the agreement or leave that party without remedy for nonperformance by the other. An example of substantive unconscionability is the agreement by a welfare recipient with a fourth-grade education to purchase a refrigerator for $2,000 under an installment contract.

Suit *See* Lawsuit; Litigation

Summary judgment *See* Motion for summary judgment

Summary jury trial (SJT) A method of settling disputes in which a trial is held, but the jury's verdict is not binding. The verdict acts only as a guide to both sides in reaching an agreement during the mandatory negotiations that immediately follow the summary jury trial.

Summons A document informing a defendant that a legal action has been commenced against him or her and that the defendant must appear in court on a certain date to answer the plaintiff's complaint. The document is delivered by a sheriff or any other person so authorized.

Superseding cause An intervening force or event that breaks the connection between a wrongful act and an injury to another; in negligence law, a defense to liability.

Supremacy clause The provision in Article VI of the Constitution that provides that the Constitution, laws, and treaties of the United States are "the supreme Law of the Land." Under this clause, state and local laws that directly conflict with federal law will be rendered invalid.

Surety A person, such as a cosigner on a note, who agrees to be primarily responsible for the debt of another.

Suretyship An express contract in which a third party to a debtor-creditor relationship (the surety) promises to be primarily responsible for the debtor's obligation.

Surviving corporation The remaining, or continuing, corporation following a merger. The surviving corporation is vested with the merged corporation's legal rights and obligations.

Syllogism A form of deductive reasoning consisting of a major premise, a minor premise, and a conclusion.

Symbolic speech Nonverbal conduct that expresses opinions or thoughts about a subject. Symbolic speech is protected under the First Amendment's guarantee of freedom of speech.

Syndicate An investment group of persons orfirms brought together for the purpose of financinga project that they would not or could not undertake independently.

T

Tag In the context of the World Wide Web, a code in an HTML document. *See* Meta tags.

Takeover The acquisition of control over a corporation through the purchase of a substantial number of the voting shares of the corporation.

Taking The taking of private property by the government for public use. Under the Fifth Amendment to the Constitution, the government may not take private property for public use without "just compensation."

Tangible employment action A significant change in employment status, such as firing or failing to promote an employee, reassigning the employee to a position with significantly different responsibilities, or effecting a significant change in employment benefits.

Tangible property Property that has physical existence and can be distinguished by the senses of touch, sight, and so on. A car is tangible property; a patent right is intangible property.

Target corporation The corporation to be acquired in a corporate takeover; a corporation to whose shareholders a tender offer is submitted.

Tariff A tax on imported goods.

Technology licensing Allowing another to use and profit from intellectual property (patents, copyrights, trademarks, innovative products or processes, and so on) for consideration. In the context of international business transactions, technology licensing is sometimes an attractive alternative to the establishment of foreign production facilities.

Teller's check A negotiable instrument drawn by a bank on another bank or drawn by a bank and payable at or payable through a bank.

Tenancy at sufferance A type of tenancy under

which one who, after rightfully being in possession of leased premises, continues (wrongfully) to occupy the property after the lease has been terminated. The tenant has no rights to possess the property and occupies it only because the person entitled to evict the tenant has not done so.

Tenancy at will A type of tenancy under which either party can terminate the tenancy without notice; usually arises when a tenant who has been under a tenancy for years retains possession, with the landlord's consent, after the tenancy for years has terminated.

Tenancy by the entirety The joint ownership of property by a husband and wife. Neither party can transfer his or her interest in the property without the consent of the other.

Tenancy for years *See* Fixed-term tenancy.

Tenancy in common Co-ownership of property in which each party owns an undivided interest that passes to his or her heirs at death.

Tenant One who has the temporary use and occupation of real property owned by another person, called the landlord; the duration and terms of the tenancy are usually established by a lease.

Tender An unconditional offer to perform an obligation by a person who is ready, willing, and able to do so.

Tender of delivery Under the Uniform Commercial Code, a seller's or lessor's act of placing conforming goods at the disposal of the buyer or lessee and giving the buyer or lessee whatever notification is reasonably necessary to enable the buyer or lessee to take delivery.

Tender offer An offer to purchase made by one company directly to the shareholders of another (target) company; often referred to as a "takeover bid."

Term insurance A type of life insurance policy for which premiums are paid for a specified term. Payment on the policy is due only if death occurs within the term period. Premiums are less expensive than for whole life or limited-payment life, and there is usually no cash surrender value.

Testamentary trust A trust that is created by will and therefore does not take effect until the death of the testator.

Testate The condition of having died with a valid will.

Testator One who makes and executes a will.

Third party beneficiary One for whose benefit a promise is made in a contract but who is not a party to the contract.

Time draft A draft that is payable at a definite future time.

Tippee A person who receives inside information.

Title insurance Insurance commonly purchased by a purchaser of real property to protect against loss in the event that the title to the property is not free from liens or superior ownership claims.

Tombstone ad An advertisement, historically in a format resembling a tombstone, of a securities offering. The ad informs potential investors of where and how they may obtain a prospectus.

Tort A civil wrong not arising from a breach of contract. A breach of a legal duty that proximately causes harm or injury to another.

Tortfeasor One who commits a tort.

Totten trust A trust created by the deposit of a person's own money in his or her own name as a trustee for another. It is a tentative trust, revocable at will until the depositor dies or completes the gift in his or her lifetime by some unequivocal act or declaration.

Toxic tort Failure to use or to clean up properly toxic chemicals that cause harm to a person or society.

Trade acceptance A draft that is drawn by a seller of goods ordering the buyer to pay a specified sum of money to the seller, usually at a stated time in the future. The buyer accepts the draft by signing the face of the draft, thus creating an enforceable obligation to pay the draft when it comes due. On a trade acceptance, the seller is both the drawer and the payee.

Trade dress The image and overall appearance of a product—for example, the distinctive decor, menu, layout, and style of service of a particular restaurant. Basically, trade dress is subject to the same protection as trademarks.

Trade fixture The personal property of a commercial tenant that has been installed or affixed to real property for a business purpose. When the lease ends, the tenant can remove the fixture but must repair any damage to the real property caused by the fixture's removal.

Trade libel The publication of false information about another's product, alleging it is not what its seller claims; also referred to as slander of quality.

Trade name A term that is used to indicate part or all of a business's name and that is directly related to the business's reputation and goodwill. Trade names are protected under the common law (and under trademark law, if the name is the same as the firm's trademarked property).

Trade secret Information or a process that gives a business an advantage over competitors who do not know the information or process.

Trademark A distinctive mark, motto, device, or implement that a manufacturer stamps, prints, or otherwise affixes to the goods it produces so that they may be identified on the market and their origins made known. Once a trademark is established (under the common law or through registration), the owner is entitled to its exclusive use.

Transfer warranties Implied warranties, made by any person who transfers an instrument for consideration to subsequent transferees and holders who take the instrument in good faith, that (1) the transferor is entitled to enforce the instrument; (2) all signatures are authentic and authorized; (3) the instrument has not been altered; (4) the instrument is not subject to a defense or claim of any party that can be asserted against the transferor; and (5) the transferor has no knowledge of any insolvency proceedings against the maker, the acceptor, or the drawer of the instrument.

Transferee In negotiable instruments law, one to whom a negotiable instrument is transferred (delivered).

Transferor In negotiable instruments law, one who transfers (delivers) a negotiable instrument to another.

Traveler's check A check that is payable on demand, drawn on or payable through a bank, and designated as a traveler's check.

Treasure trove Cash or coin, gold, silver, or bullion found hidden in the earth or other private place, the owner of which is unknown; literally, treasure found.

Treasury shares Corporate shares that are authorized by the corporation but that have not been issued.

Treaty An agreement formed between two or more independent nations.

Treble damages Damages consisting of three times the amount of damages determined by a jury in certain cases as required by statute.

Trespass to land The entry onto, above, or below the surface of land owned by another without the owner's permission or legal authorization.

Trespass to personal property The unlawful taking or harming of another's personal property; interference with another's right to the exclusive possession of his or her personal property.

Trespasser One who commits the tort of trespass in one of its forms.

Trial court A court in which trials are held and testimony taken.

Trust An arrangement in which title to property is held by one person (a trustee) for the benefit of another (a beneficiary).

Trust indorsement An indorsement for the benefit of the indorser or a third person; also known as an agency indorsement. The indorsement results in legal title vesting in the original indorsee.

Trustee One who holds title to property for the use or benefit of another (the beneficiary).

Tying arrangement An agreement between a buyer and a seller in which the buyer of a specific product or service becomes obligated to purchase additional products or services from the seller.

U

U.S. trustee A government official who performs certain administrative tasks that a bankruptcy judge would otherwise have to perform.

Ultra vires (pronounced *uhl*-trah *vye*-reez) A Latin term meaning "beyond the powers"; in corporate law, acts of a corporation that are beyond its express and implied powers to undertake.

Unanimous opinion A court opinion in which all of the judges or justices of the court agree to the court's decision.

Unconscionable (pronounced un-*kon*-shun-uh-bul) **contract or clause** A contract or clause that is void on the basis of public policy because one party, as a result of his or her disproportionate bargaining power, is forced to accept terms that are unfairly burdensome and that unfairly benefit the dominating party. *See also* Procedural unconscionability; Substantive unconscionability

Underwriter In insurance law, the insurer, or the one assuming a risk in return for the payment of a premium.

Undisclosed principal A principal whose identity is unknown by a third person, and the third person has no knowledge that the agent is acting for a principal at the time the agent and the third person form a contract.

Unenforceable contract A valid contract rendered unenforceable by some statute or law.

Uniform law A model law created by the National Conference of Commissioners on Uniform State Laws and/or the American Law Institute for the states to consider adopting. If the state adopts the law, it becomes statutory law in that state. Each state has the option of adopting or rejecting all or part of a uniform law.

Unilateral contract A contract that results when an offer can only be accepted by the offeree's performance.

Union shop A place of employment in which all workers, once employed, must become union members within a specified period of time as a condition of their continued employment.

Universal defense A defense that is valid against all holders of a negotiable instrument, including holders in due course (HDCs) and holders with the rights of HDCs. Universal defenses are also called real defenses.

Universal life A type of insurance that combines some aspects of term insurance with some aspects of whole life insurance.

Unlawful detainer The unjustifiable retention of the possession of real property by one whose right to possession has terminated—as when a tenant holds over after the end of the lease term in spite of the landlord's demand for possession.

Unliquidated debt A debt that is uncertain in amount.

Unreasonably dangerous product In product liability, a product that is defective to the point of threatening a consumer's health and safety. A product will be considered unreasonably dangerous if it is dangerous beyond the expectation of the ordinary consumer or if a less dangerous alternative was economically feasible for the manufacturer, but the manufacturer failed to produce it.

Usage of trade Any practice or method of dealing having such regularity of observance in a place, vocation, or trade as to justify an expectation that it will be observed with respect to the transaction in question.

Usurpation In corporation law, the taking advantage of a corporate opportunity by a corporate officer or director for his or her personal gain and in violation of his or her fiduciary duties.

Usury Charging an illegal rate of interest.

Utilitarianism An approach to ethical reasoning in which ethically correct behavior is not related to any absolute ethical or moral values but to an evaluation of the consequences of a given action on those who will be affected by it. In utilitarian reasoning, a "good" decision is one that results in the greatest good for the greatest number of people affected by the decision.

V

Valid contract A contract that results when elements necessary for contract formation (agreement, consideration, legal purpose, and contractual capacity) are present.

Validation notice An initial notice to a debtor from a collection agency informing the debtor that he or she has thirty days to challenge the debt and request verification.

Vendee One who purchases property from another, called the vendor.

Vendor One who sells property to another, called the vendee.

Venture capital Capital (funds and other assets) provided by professional, outside investors (*venture capitalists,* usually groups of wealthy investors and investment banks) to start new business ventures.

Venture capitalist A person or entity that seeks out promising entrepreneurial ventures and funds them in exchange for equity stakes.

Venue (pronounced *ven*-yoo) The geographical district in which an action is tried and from which the jury is selected.

Verdict A formal decision made by a jury.

Vertical merger The acquisition by a company at one stage of production of a company at a higher or lower stage of production (such as its supplier or retailer).

Vertical restraint Any restraint on trade created by agreements between firms at different levels in the manufacturing and distribution process.

Vertically integrated firm A firm that carries out two or more functional phases—such as manufacture, distribution, retailing—of a product.

Vesting Under the Employee Retirement Income Security Act of 1974, a pension plan becomes vested when an employee has a legal right to the benefits purchased with the employer's contributions, even if the employee is no longer working for this employer.

Vicarious liability Legal responsibility placed on one person for the acts of another.

Virtual courtroom A courtroom that is conceptual and not physical. In the context of cyberspace, a virtual courtroom could be a location on the Internet at which judicial proceedings take place.

Virtual property Property that, in the context of cyberspace, is conceptual, as opposed to physical. Intellectual property that exists on the Internet is virtual property.

Void contract A contract having no legal force or binding effect.

Voidable contract A contract that may be legally avoided (canceled, or annulled) at the option of one of the parties.

Voidable preference In bankruptcy law, a preference that may be avoided, or set aside, by the trustee.

Voir dire (pronounced *vwahr deehr*) A French phrase meaning, literally, "to see, to speak." In jury trials, the phrase refers to the process in which the attorneys question prospective jurors to determine whether they are biased or have any connection with a party to the action or with a prospective witness.

Voting trust An agreement (trust contract) under which legal title to shares of corporate stock is transferred to a trustee who is authorized by the shareholders to vote the shares on their behalf.

W

Waiver An intentional, knowing relinquishment of a legal right.

Warehouse receipt A document of title issued by a bailee-warehouser to cover the goods stored in the warehouse.

Warehouser One in the business of operating a warehouse.

Warranty A promise that certain facts are truly as they are represented to be.

Warranty deed A deed in which the grantor guarantees to the grantee that the grantor has title to the property conveyed in the deed, that there are no encumbrances on the property other than what the grantor has represented, and that the grantee will enjoy quiet possession of the property; a deed that provides the greatest amount of protection for the grantee.

Warranty disclaimer A seller's or lessor's negation or qualification of a warranty.

Warranty of fitness *See* Implied warranty of fitness for a particular purpose.

Warranty of merchantability *See* Implied warranty of merchantability.

Warranty of title An implied warranty made by a seller that the seller has good and valid title to the goods sold and that the transfer of the title is rightful.

Waste The abuse or destructive use of real property by one who is in rightful possession of the property but who does not have title to it. Waste does not include ordinary depreciation due to age and normal use.

Watered stock Shares of stock issued by a corporation for which the corporation receives, as payment, less than the fair market value of the shares.

Wetlands Areas of land designated by government agencies (such as the Army Corps of Engineers or the Environmental Protection Agency) as protected areas that support wildlife and that therefore cannot be filled in or dredged by private contractors or parties.

Whistleblowing An employee's disclosure to government, the press, or upper-management authorities that the employer is engaged in unsafe or illegal activities.

White-collar crime Nonviolent crime committed by individuals or corporations to obtain a personal or business advantage.

Whole life A life insurance policy in which the insured pays a level premium for his or her entire life and in which there is a constantly accumulating cash value that can be withdrawn or borrowed against by the borrower. Sometimes referred to as straight life insurance.

Will An instrument directing what is to be done with the testator's property on his or her death, made by the testator and revocable during his or her lifetime. No interests in the testator's property pass until the testator dies.

Willful Intentional.

Winding up The second of two stages involved in the termination of a partnership or corporation. Once the firm is dissolved, it continues to exist legally until the process of winding up all business affairs (collecting and distributing the firm's assets) is complete.

Workers' compensation laws State statutes establishing an administrative procedure for compensating workers' injuries that arise out of—or in the course of—their employment, regardless of fault.

Working papers The various documents used and developed by an accountant during an audit. Working papers include notes, computations, memoranda, copies, and other papers that make up the work product of an accountant's services to a client.

Workout An out-of-court agreement between a debtor and his or her creditors in which the parties work out a payment plan or schedule under which the debtor's debts can be discharged.

Writ of attachment A court's order, prior to a trial to collect a debt, directing the sheriff or other officer to seize nonexempt property of the debtor; if the creditor prevails at trial, the seized property can be sold to satisfy the judgment.

Writ of *certiorari* (pronounced sur-shee-uh-*rah*-ree) A writ from a higher court asking the lower court for the record of a case.

Writ of execution A court's order, after a judgment has been entered against the debtor, directing the sheriff to seize (levy) and sell any of the debtor's nonexempt real or personal property. The proceeds of the sale are used to pay off the judgment, accrued interest, and costs of the sale; any surplus is paid to the debtor.

Wrongful discharge An employer's termination of an employee's employment in violation of an employment contract or laws that protect employees.

Z

Zoning The division of a city by legislative regulation into districts and the application in each district of regulations having to do with structural and architectural designs of buildings and prescribing the use to which buildings within designated districts may be put.

Table of Cases

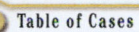

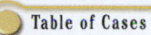

T

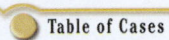

Index

A

B

E

F

G

H

I

N

Q

R

U

Helpful Internet Uniform Resource Locators (URLs)

General Legal Resources

www.findlaw.com FindLaw, which is a part of West Group, is one of the most comprehensive sources of free legal information. You can access all federal and state cases, codes, and agency regulations, as well as journal articles, newsletters, and links to other useful sites and discussion groups.

www.law.cornell.edu The Legal Information Institute (LII) at Cornell Law School also is a great site for legal research and includes federal, state, and international law. You can access materials by topic or by jurisdiction, or you can browse through one of its topical libraries.

www.lectlaw.com/bus.html The 'Lectric Law Library has general legal resources.

www.lawguru.com/ilawlib The Internet Law Library provides many legal resources relating to American and foreign law.

www.law.com/index.shtml This site provides up-to-date legal news articles and information, and has links to other legal news publications, including the *National Law Journal.*

Helpful Government Sites

www.usa.gov The U.S. government's official Web site provides links to every branch of the federal government, including federal agencies.

www.loc.gov The Library of Congress has links to state and federal government resources, and the THOMAS system allows you to search through several legislative databases.

www.sec.gov/edgar.shtml The Web site of the Securities and Exchange Commission offers a searchable electronic database (called EDGAR) of information about public companies.

www.gpoaccess.gov/index.html The U.S. Government Printing Office posts official information from each of the three branches of the federal government, including publications such as the *Code of Federal Regulations* and the *Federal Register.*

www.uspto.gov The U.S. Patent and Trademark Office has a searchable database of patents and trademarks. This site also provides general information and a way to check the status of pending applications.

www.copyright.gov The U.S. Copyright Office provides information on copyrights and a searchable database of copyright records.

www.eeoc.gov/index.html The Equal Employment Opportunity Commission (EEOC) posts information on employment discrimination, EEOC regulations, compliance, and enforcement.

www.epa.gov The Environmental Protection Agency offers information on environmental laws, regulations, and compliance assistance.

www.sbaonline.sba.gov The U.S. Small Business Administration assists in forming, financing, and operating small businesses.

www.usdoj.gov The U.S. Department of Justice provides information on many areas of law, including civil rights, employment, crime, and immigration.

www.csg.org The Council of State Governments offers state news, information, legislation, and links to state home pages.

www.nccusl.org The National Conference of Commissioners on Uniform State Laws posts the text of uniform laws (such as the Uniform Commercial Code) and information on state adoptions and pending state legislation.

Federal and State Courts

www.supremecourtus.gov This official site of the United States Supreme Court provides case opinions, orders, and other information about the Court, including its history, procedures, schedule, and transcripts of oral arguments.

www.oyez.org This site offers in addition to United States Supreme Court opinions, a multimedia guide to the Court, including a virtual tour of the building and digital audio of selected oral arguments and Court decisions.

www.uscourts.gov/index.html The federal judiciary provides access to every federal court (including district courts, appellate courts, and bankruptcy courts).

www.ncsconline.org The National Center for State Courts offers links to the Web pages of all state courts.

www.abiworld.org The American Bankruptcy Institute is a good resource for bankruptcy court opinions, news, and other information.